THE AUTHOR

A professional writer for fifteen years, Mark Lewisohn is acknowledged as a leading TV and radio historian. He has contributed to *Radio Times* every week since 1990 and, with an emphasis on comedy, compiled audio- and video-tapes for commercial release. As a researcher, consultant, archivist, broadcaster and writer, he has contributed to scores of newspapers, magazines and radio and TV series and has himself been the subject of features in the *New York Times, Los Angeles Times, Daily Telegraph, Sunday Express* and other publications. He is referred to, internationally, as the foremost authority on the Beatles, a subject about which he has written two bestsellers: *The Complete Beatles Recording Sessions* (1988) and *The Complete Beatles Chronicle* (1992). These books are recognised as the definitive works of reference. He has also been involved in dozens of projects for Paul McCartney, EMI and the Beatles' company Apple Corps.

Born in Kingsbury, north London, in 1958, Mark Lewisohn attended the nearby Glebe Primary School and Pinner Grammar School before working for the BBC, *Music Week* and then turning freelance. He is married, has two children and lives in Hertfordshire.

RadioTimes
GUIDE TO
TV COMEDY

Mark Lewisohn

BBC

to Gordon Ottershaw

Published by BBC Worldwide Ltd, Woodlands, 80 Wood Lane, London W12 0TT

First published 1998

© Mark Lewisohn 1998

The moral right of the author has been asserted

ISBN 0 563 36977 9

Commissioning Editor: Nicky Copeland
Project Editor: Anna Ottewill
Copy Editors: Christine King and Nick Griffiths
Art Editor: Ellen Wheeler
Design: Ben Cracknell Studios

Set in Century Old Style and Franklin Gothic

Printed and bound in Great Britain by Butler and Tanner, Frome and London
Cover printed by Belmont Press, Northampton

The opinions expressed in this book are those of the author, not *Radio Times*

Contents

Introduction

As an infant, I clearly remember hearing the names Bilko, Bootsie, Snudge and Hancock being bandied around the kitchen table at meal times. I was, at that age, considered too young to be watching such programmes, and had to be content with children's TV. But soon I was catching all of the comedy shows that I could, usually doing so in the company of my parents. As often as not, judgement would be made about the quality of the fare after the final credits had passed – either a brusque word of dismissal or a longer assimilation in praise. At the end of *Monty Python* shows we would talk, often at length, about the astonishing scope of the ideas, the possible deeper meanings beneath the humour (intended or not by the Pythons themselves) and the bravura with which the team put across their work. We could also be very cutting: certain programmes and performers routinely came in for a blasting. In essence, I was fortunate to grow up in a family where good comedy was truly appreciated, and where certain names – Peter Jones, Thora Hird, Eric Sykes, Ronnie Barker, Irene Handl, Patricia Hayes spring instantly to mind, and there were many others – were uttered with respect. We felt that, although we hadn't met them, we knew these people well enough to trust them to appear in programmes worthy of their talents … and our time. They rarely disappointed.

My love of comedy has not wavered since, and although one has to wade through a good deal of rubbish to find the quality, a great sitcom remains a joy to behold: a perfect *Seinfeld* (and there are many such episodes), a sumptuous *Frasier*, a joyful *Dad's Army*, a hysterical *Fawlty Towers*, these are all masterpieces in miniature, half-hour gems that ought to rank with other great pieces of art.

I came up with the idea for this book about 10 years ago, and took it to BBC Worldwide in 1992. Although I consider myself a researcher, I really ought to have looked harder at what I was committing myself to: in finding information and writing about *every* comedy programme ever aired on British TV, I was set for an almighty stretch. Now that it's finished, though, I know that all the effort was worthwhile; and as for Bilko, Bootsie, Snudge, Hancock, *Monty Python*, Jones, Hird, Sykes, Barker, Handl, Hayes, *Seinfeld, Frasier, Dad's Army* and *Fawlty Towers*, they're all in here … along with the programmes I loathe. All told, there are some 2600 different productions detailed.

Apart from soaps, comedy remains the most discussed and loved strand of TV programming. We watch old comedy because we want to laugh again with tried and trusted characters and lines, and to remember an earlier age. We watch new comedy in the hope (usually forlorn, but, thankfully, not always) to be in at the start of a great new show or a great new career. While this book (to quote the title of Granada's old archive series) is 'all our yesterdays', then, it is also 'all our todays'.

Mark Lewisohn

Mark Lewisohn

Information in this book has been researched as carefully as possible, but the author apologises for any errors or misrepresentations that may have occurred and will be happy to make amendments in the second edition. To this end, he would be pleased to hear from anyone – especially TV contributors whose work is reflected in the text – who has additional information or comments about the content of this book. Please write to Mark Lewisohn c/o BBC Worldwide, Room A3144, Woodlands, 80 Wood Lane, London W12 0TT.

Foreword
·················

Firstly, let me express my enormous delight in the publication of this wonderful book. It contains everything worth knowing about the thousands of comedy shows that have graced (or sometimes sullied) our TV screens since those black and white evenings in the days before the War. I hasten to add that I refer to the 1939 War, not the ratings war. Those early days now seem distant, smudgy, blurred in my memory, as indeed did the images flickering on those primitive eight-inch screens at the time.

I remember standing in front of this enormous box with its tiny wobbly picture in the summer of 1937. Its proud owner beamed at us children, happy in the knowledge that he was the only man in the road who could afford one. As I stared goggle-eyed at the electric marvel, I little realised that one day I would make it my career. It's 42 years since my first appearance on television. Before that I had been a stage actor, and had worked with a great man called Glenn Melvyn, who I always maintain taught me almost everything I know about comedy. He was starring in his own television show *I'm Not Bothered* (q.v.) and he asked me to play a small part. I was terrified, mainly because I'd been told by some actor that it was a very precise medium – if you moved an inch to the left or right of the shot you would not be seen by the camera or heard by the microphones. Imagine my relief to find that I was playing a patient in a hospital bed, and had no moves at all!

Television comedy has changed a lot since then. It has been my life, and that of countless other performers, directors and writers. That is why I'm so glad that this book recognises and lists those people who are indispensable to the success of any comedy. Writers, especially, deserve a separate accolade because if a show is badly directed not many viewers will actually notice, but if it is badly written it will never work. The script spells success or failure. So many of the shows which have stood the test of time – *Bilko, Hancock, Steptoe, Lucille Ball* – have survived because they are funny. If a joke is funny, it stays funny. Which brings me back again to the book. How many thousands of funny lines have been produced by the writers referred to within its pages? It's an overwhelming thought.

This book is a monumental work. Now, at last, we can find out every little detail we always wondered about (such as, was there ever a science–fiction show called *They Came From Somewhere Else* or was it a Mel Brooks gag?). We will be able to play *Telly Addicts* amongst ourselves, without suffering Noel Edmonds' boyish charm. We will win all the pub quizzes. In short, this work, meticulously assembled, is of inestimable value and will prove a source of great pleasure to viewers everywhere. I welcome it with open arms.

Ronnie Barker

Acknowledgements

This book has been a labour of love, and my foremost thanks go to the three closest loves of my life: my children Oliver and Tom, fine boys both, and my wife Anita Epstein who has been a fantastic rock of support – endlessly encouraging, enthusiastic, understanding and calming. Like me, she has lived, breathed and lost sleep over this project for a very long time.

Everyone at BBC Worldwide has been wonderfully understanding and accommodating. In particular, I owe a deep debt of gratitude to Nicky Copeland and Anna Ottewill at BBC Books; and Nick Brett, Sue Robinson and Liz Vercoe at *Radio Times*. Thanks also go to two BBC Books stalwarts who left during the book's six-year journey from genesis to realisation: Doug Young and, most especially, Heather Holden-Brown, without whose vision, sympathy and nurturing this book would not have happened. I am fortunate too to have had the services of three talented freelance editors: Nick Griffiths, Christine King and Charlotte Lochhead, and the proofreading skills of Bill Games. My literary agent, Bill Hamilton of A M Heath & Co, has also been involved in the project since the outset. I am deeply indebted, too, to Ben Cracknell, who designed the book with sympathy and understanding, effecting what I believe to be an easy-to-read layout that belies the density of information, and to Jon Schotten, who painstakingly avoided working on the layout of this book by chatting about the Beatles and quoting *Monty Python*.

For providing invaluable computer assistance, my sincerest thanks go to Richard Lucas and Andy Finney, who never seemed to tire of my questions and gave liberally of their time, energy and interest.

Special thanks to Barry McCann for loaning essential source materials, to Shirley Sankey and Anita Epstein for entering records into the database, and, for a variety of reasons, to Stafford Gordon, Simon Bates, Richard Buskin, Gwyniver Jones (for the Welsh translations), Dave Lee, Sydney E Lewis, Alastair Scott and the late Derek Taylor. For providing information, thanks to Mark Cousins, Allan Kozinn, Piet Schreuders, Adam Smith, Christopher Perry and Richard Down at Kaleidoscope, Adam Lee in BBC Information & Archives, Sarah Morrell in BBC Radio Light Entertainment, Julie Pearce and Veronica Taylor at the BFI and, for answering hole-plugging last-minute questions, Raymond Kingsbury at Aarkamint, Nikki Chaplin in BBC Children's Acquisition, April Chamberlain and Amanda Moran at the Comedy Unit in Glasgow, Peter Tatchell (of *Laugh* magazine) and Paul Balsillie in Australia, Analisa Barbosa at Showtime Networks, Nancy S Dillon at PBS, Julia Lewis at LWT, Sylvia Cowling at Granada, Bill Parker at Pearson, Tim Ritchie in the BBC Sound Archive and, for extensive help *well* beyond the call of reasonable duty, Jeff Walden at the BBC's Written Archives Centre.

I am especially indebted to Dick Fiddy, who came on board the project when I was behind schedule, and joined me for two/three days a week of writing sessions. His knowledge of and enthusiasm for TV comedy are fantastic, and his sense of humour, sensibilities, viewpoints, opinions, advice and encouragement made him marvellous company during two years of serious industry.

A TV consultant to the BFI, Dick Fiddy writes about TV for *The Daily Telegraph*, was a co-founder of *Primetime* magazine, edited *The Television Yearbook* (published 1985), contributed scripts to several TV comedies (check the index of writers) and was closely involved in three archive celebrations screened by C4. He is as decent, honest and friendly an individual as one could wish to meet, a handsome, witty, urbane and ... (*sorry, Dick, can't read your writing here*) ...

What is in this book?

An entry for every made-for-TV comedy programme aired on British television (see qualifying remarks about regional screenings below) from its launch on 2 November 1936 up to 31 December 1997. This includes sitcoms, sketch shows, satires and standup, whether presented as series, specials or one-offs and of any length, from five minute shorts to telethons, made in Britain or bought-in from overseas, live, filmed or taped, made in colour or black and white.

Except for the Second World War 'interlude', television has been beamed to the British public since 1936, but this book covers 146 'years' of TV programming … just over 54 years of BBC1 (November 1936 to August 1939; June 1946 to December 1997), almost 34 of BBC2 (on air since April 1964), more than 42 of ITV (from September 1955), more than 15 of C4 (from November 1982) and a little under one year of C5 (since March 1997).

What is a TV comedy?

In this book, a comedy programme is one made with the express intention of making people laugh, smile or smirk. (Whether or not certain shows succeeded is entirely another matter …, and there are exclusions – see below.) The lengths vary, but typically they're half-hours. They usually (but not always) employ a studio audience or 'canned' laugh-track. They're usually (but not always) pre-scripted. For British-made shows, they're mostly made by the broadcaster's Comedy (or Light Entertainment Comedy) department, rather than its Drama or Light Entertainment Variety departments. (Although children's comedies are usually made by the Children's department.)

Here are the genres excluded from the book:

'Variety' shows. While *Seaside Special*, *Val Parnell's Sunday Night At The London Palladium* and others of that ilk feature comedy acts, they are not comedy programmes *per se*, the comics taking their turn along with jugglers, dancers, magicians, spoon-benders, and so on.

Shows that combine comedy with chat (for example, Clive Anderson, Noel Edmonds, Des O'Connor, Frank Skinner). Even though they use a studio audience and make people laugh, these are talk-shows rather than comedies.

'People-shows' – everything from *Candid Camera* to Jeremy Beadle's series, *That's Life*, etc.

Shows with a quiz or points-scoring element. *Whose Line Is It Anyway?*, *Have I Got News For You*, *Shooting Stars*, *They Think It's All Over*, *Never Mind The Buzzcocks*, *Call My Bluff* and many others like them employ a studio audience and make people laugh but still they are not 'comedy programmes'. *What's My Line?* used to have a studio audience, and much laughter was generated, but it was hardly a comedy show.

Shows with magic. Like David Nixon before him, Paul Daniels makes people laugh, but he is not a comedian or comic-actor, and his shows are 'light entertainment', not comedy.

Puppetry. Pinky and Perky, Sooty, Basil Brush, *Hector's House*, *The Magic Roundabout* and Emu provided entertainment but, again, they fall outside the definition of 'comedy shows'. *The Muppet Show* is an exception – this was a bona fide sketch-show, albeit with the principal human contributors out of shot.

Animations. Cartoons have been the staple of children's TV programming for decades, but although *The Adventures Of Yogi Bear*, *Wacky Races*, *The Flintstones* and the like are designed to make people laugh, they are beyond the parameters of this *Comedy Guide*, details of such entertainments belonging in a dedicated animations book. *The Simpsons* and *King Of The Hill* are exceptions. These are at the forefront of the new breed of half-hour adult-themed sitcoms that happen to be drawn rather than acted. Hence they appear in this book.

Ventriloquism. Tich and Quackers, Lord Charles and Lamb Chops all left their mark on a generation of children, but these were not comedy shows as such.

Comedy-dramas and light-dramas. The single biggest 'grey area'. Performers and programme-makers have always been keen to blur the lines between one TV genre and another but, especially in the 1980s–90s, there have been dozens of dramas labelled as comedies but which, more accurately, are 'dramas with a light touch'. While productions like *A Very Peculiar Practice, Minder, Auf Wiedersehen, Pet* and *All Quiet On The Preston Front* undeniably feature moments of humour, they are not comedy productions *per se* and so are absent from this book. (Other productions, however, such as *A Bit Of A Do*, *Blott On The Landscape* and *Charters And Caldicott*, are comedy-dedicated, albeit within a dramatic framework and with dramatic moments, and so are included.) At the time of writing (1997), children's TV producers are attaching the 'comedy' label to all manner of dramas, perhaps in the hope of reaching a wider audience. Every such 'borderline' programme has been watched and the choice as to which category a programme falls into made with care.

In essence, the rule-of-thumb was, 'If there was a book like this dedicated solely to, say, TV drama, would programme *x* be more appropriate here in this *Comedy Guide* or there, in that other book?' If the answer was 'there', it was usually omitted from 'here'.

How to use this book/guidance notes

Essentially, the book comprises an **A-Z listing of programmes** and thus is **title-led**. So *Ben Elton – The Man From Auntie* appears under 'Ben' and *Paul Merton – The Series* under 'Paul'. And while Dick Van Dyke was the name of its star, *The Dick Van Dyke Show* was the title of his sitcom, thus this show appears under 'Dick'.

The exceptions to this are those sections with a grey tint – 'combined entries' – where, for the sake of convenience and clarity, and also to plot the course of a TV career, certain performer's shows have been grouped together, under his or her surname. So all of Joyce Grenfell's television work, irrespective of programme title, can be found under 'Grenfell', Bob Monkhouse's under 'Monkhouse' and Victoria Wood's under 'Wood'. A few programmes have been given this 'combined' treatment too: the many Alf Garnett shows, for example, follow the entry for parent programme *Till Death Us Do Part*. Also, certain sequels have been grouped with their founding show, thus *Whatever Happened To The Likely Lads* follows the entry for *The Likely Lads*, under 'L', and *The Legacy Of Reggie Perrin* appears after *The Fall And Rise Of Reginald Perrin*, under 'F'. **In all instances where the A-Z rule has been deviated from, cross-references will guide the reader to the entries**.

Programmes where the titles begin with 'A', 'An' or 'The' are listed under the first letter of the next word. Thus, *A Bit Of Fry And Laurie*, *An Evening With Lee Evans* and *The Two Ronnies* appear under 'B', 'E' and 'T' respectively.

In keeping with the style of British listings magazines, a TV day is interpreted as being 6am-6am. So, for example, a programme reported as '24 May 1997, Saturday 1am' was actually screened an hour into Sunday morning.

A programme's stated duration is that of its transmission slot – for example, a show beginning at 8.30 and ending at 9.00 is 'a 30 minute programme', even if it did not last that long. Typically, a half-hour programme made/screened by the BBC runs 28–29 minutes. A half-hour programme on ITV is actually, leaving time for commercials, 24 minutes. A programme made for an American TV half-hour is only 21–23 minutes (which explains why, when such shows are imported by the BBC, they fit comfortably into a 25-minute transmission slot).

This same rule applies, *pro rata*, up and down the time scale. Programmes made to fill an ITV hour do not exceed 50 minutes; an American TV 'hour' is usually no more than 48 minutes, and so on.

Although too many aspects of British life are London-centred – to the great annoyance of those living elsewhere – the screening information in this book necessarily reflects TV broadcasting in the capital and the Home Counties, which is the biggest single area in terms of British viewing. ITV is the problem here: until the advent of the Network Centre in the 1990s, which dictates primetime schedules to all the regional companies, a great many ITV programmes were shown at different times, and even on different days, from one region to another. (Indeed, imported programmes are still scheduled in this way.)

So, to simplify matters, the ITV programme details in this book reflect London-area screenings unless otherwise indicated. Every comedy programme shown by any of the London ITV companies – Associated-Rediffusion (then Rediffusion), ATV, Thames, LWT and Carlton – is listed, ditto the programmes imported by them from overseas. In the very few instances where a comedy programme was made by an ITV company but not shown in London, there will not usually be a dedicated entry but information will be found as a postscript to another, appropriate entry.

With a few exceptions, mostly local news programmes, the output of BBC1 is 'fully networked', so most of its comedy shows are seen by people all over Britain at the same time. BBC2, C4 and the new C5 are fully networked channels.

Episode-counts for imported programmes on ITV reflect the London screenings, and for *all* broadcasts, irrespective of channel, they reflect *the initial-run*. For example, while 143 episodes were made of *The Phil Silvers Show,* only 130 were screened by the BBC at the time. Numerous repeat runs, as far as the 1990s, have resulted in all but one of the 143 trickling on to the screen, but the figure given in the entry remains 130, reflecting the 1957–60 transmissions.

Sample entry

Programme title —

Bless This House UK

— Qualifying remark, if relevant (there is also a US series with this title)

Country of origin —
Broadcaster —
UK · ITV (THAMES) · SITCOM

— Type of comedy
— Production company

Total number of episodes —
Length of programme —
65 × 30 mins (58 × colour · 7 × b/w)

— Format

Series One (7 × b/w · 5 × colour) 2 Feb–20 Apr 1971 · Tue around 7pm

— Programmes shown on Tuesdays, at varying times circa 7pm

Series Two (12) 21 Feb–15 May 1972 · Mon 8.30pm

— Number of episodes in this series

Transmission information —

Series Three (12) 22 Jan–12 Mar 1973 (7) · Mon 8.30pm; 30 Apr–28 May 1973 (5) · Mon 8pm

— Series split into two blocks

Series Four (6) 20 Feb–10 Apr 1974 · Wed 8pm

— All programmes shown on this day/time throughout the series

Series Five (10) 14 Oct–16 Dec 1974 · Mon 8pm

Series Six (13) 29 Jan–22 Apr 1976 · Thu mostly 8pm

MAIN CAST

Character names —

Sid Abbott	Sidney James
Jean Abbott	Diana Coupland
Mike Abbott	Robin Stewart
Sally Abbott	Sally Geeson
Trevor	Anthony Jackson
Betty	Patsy Rowlands

— Actor names

CREDITS

Principal behind-the-scenes personnel —

creators Vince Powell/Harry Driver · *writers* Carla Lane/Myra Taylor (15), Carla Lane (10), Vince Powell/Harry Driver (12), Dave Freeman (12), Jon Watkins (8), Bernie Sharp (4), David Cumming/Derek Collyer (1), Adele Rose (1), Mike Sharland/B C Cummins (1), Lawrie Wyman/George Evans (1) · *director/producer* William G Stewart

— Number of episodes written by those named

Synopsis/critique —

Perhaps the most typical and therefore best loved of ITV's many 1970s studio-based ...ostic' sitcoms. with

creat.... ...buted a dozen scrip.. Carla Lane, while penning *The Liver Birds* for the BBC, wrote 25, including 22 out of the first 42 episodes. And as usual for 1970s hit sitcoms, there was a weak spin-off cinema-movie too, made in 1972 by the *Carry On* producer Gerald Thomas, scripted by Dave Freeman and featuring all of the Abbott family except Robin Stewart.

— Cross-reference

Footnote/cross-reference —
See also *Home Sweet Home*.

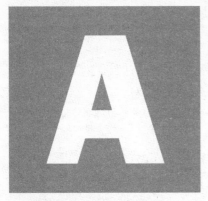

A J Wentworth, BA

UK · ITV (THAMES) · SITCOM

6 × 30 mins · colour

12 July–23 Aug 1982 · Mon 8pm

MAIN CAST

A J Wentworth · · · · · · · · · · · · · Arthur Lowe
The Rev R Gregory Saunders (Headmaster) ·
· Harry Andrews
Matron · · · · · · · · · · · · · · · · Marion Mathie
Miss Coombes · · · · · · · · · · · Deddie Davies
Rawlinson · · · · · · · · · · · · · Ronnie Stevens
Gilbert · · · · · · · · · · · · · · · Michael Bevis

THE BOYS:

Mason · · · · · · · · · · · · · · · · Marcus Evans
Anderson · · · · · · · · · · · · Alistair Callender
Atkins · · · · · · · · · · · · · · · Stephen Rooney
Etheridge · · · · · · · · · · · Andrew McDonnell
Hillman · · · · · · · · · · · Michael Underwood
Hopgood II · · · · · · · · · · · · · Paul Hawkins
Otterway · · · · · · · · · · · · · · · Simon Curry
Sapoulos · · · · · · · · · · · · · · · · Halil Halil
Trench · · · · · · · · · · · · · · Benjamin Taylor

CREDITS

creator H F Ellis · adapter/writer Basil Boothroyd ·
director/producer Michael Mills

This was Arthur Lowe's last sitcom, made shortly before his death on 16 April 1982 and screened posthumously. The role was just right for him, combining a gentle humour with the subtle blend of bumble, pleasant foolishness, earnestness and pomposity that Lowe had so perfected in **Dad's Army** and **Bless Me, Father**.

His role was that of a magnanimous mortar-boarded mathematics master at Burgrove, a boys' preparatory school in rural Wilminster, in the 1940s. A J (Arthur James) Wentworth is keen on school pride but poor at disciplining his boys, and both his kindliness and accident-prone nature are taken advantage of by the boys. Just as bad, his ways are not entirely understood by his fellow teachers and the snobbish headmaster (nicknamed 'Squid' by the boys), nor by matron, Wentworth's sworn enemy.

The episodes were adapted by Basil Boothroyd from the finely crafted pieces written by his contemporary, H F Ellis, which first appeared in the magazine *Punch* and

were subsequently compiled into two books, *The Papers Of A J Wentworth, BA* (published 1949) and *The Papers Of A J Wentworth, BA (Ret'd)* (1962); the pair were combined into a single edition in 1980. Arthur Lowe had read selections from the books in the daily literary slot in the BBC radio programme *Woman's Hour*, and, entirely appropriately, one of the *A J Wentworth* pieces was read by Harry Andrews – the veteran stage and screen actor who played the headmaster in this sitcom – at Lowe's memorial service.

Aah Sean

UK · C4 (INDIGO PRODUCTIONS) · STANDUP

1 × 45 mins · colour

10 Jan 1992 · Fri 10.30pm

MAIN CAST

Sean Hughes

CREDITS

writer Sean Hughes · producer Kim Turberville

In 1989, aged 24, Sean Hughes became the youngest-ever winner of the annual Perrier Award as Best Comedy Newcomer, with his Edinburgh Festival Fringe show *A One Night Stand With Sean Hughes*, a surreal mix of standup and sitcom staged within a purpose-built living-room set. The Irish comedian utilised the same format in his later C4 series **Sean's Show**, but before that he appeared in this one-off special, looking around Dublin (European City of Culture at the time), reminiscing about his boyhood there and commenting upon its contemporary nature. This humorous travelogue was interspersed with clips from Hughes' current live act, recorded at the Town And Country Club in London.

See also **Sean Hughes Is Thirty Somehow.**

Russ Abbot

Born Russell Roberts, in Chester on 16 September 1947, Abbot was a drummer and comic turn with the humorous pop cabaret group **The Black Abbots** for 15 years before leaving music to concentrate full-time on comedy. Occasional supporting status in **Who Do You Do?** in 1973, followed six years later by a regular role in the 1979 series **Freddie Starr's Variety Madhouse** led to Abbot taking over this latter series when Starr quit. He immediately made the show his own, winning awards and swiftly securing a place at the top of his profession with his knowingly corny jokes and routines delivered under the guise of a phalanx of created characters.

Russ Abbot's Madhouse

UK · ITV (LWT) · SKETCH

45 editions (39 × 30 mins · 3 × 45 mins · 3 × 60 mins) · colour

Series One (8 × 30 mins) *Russ Abbot's Madhouse* 12 Apr–31 May 1980 · Sat 6pm

Special (45 mins) *Russ Abbot And A Show Of His Very Own* 2 Jan 1981 · Fri 7.45pm

Series Two (8 × 30 mins) *Russ Abbot's Saturday Madhouse* 13 June–1 Aug 1981 · Sat mostly 7.45pm

Special (45 mins) *Russ Abbot's Christmas Madhouse* 26 Dec 1981 · Sat 6.30pm

Series Three (6 × 30 mins) *Russ Abbot's Saturday Madhouse* 17 July–21 Aug 1982 · Sat 7.15pm

Special (60 mins) *Russ Abbot's Madhouse Annual* 7 Nov 1982 · Sun 7.15pm

Special (45 mins) *Russ Abbot's Hogmanay Madhouse* (repeated as *Russ Abbot's Scottish Madhouse*) 31 Dec 1982 · Fri 8pm

Series Four (6 × 30 mins) *Russ Abbot's Saturday Madhouse* 23 Apr–28 May 1983 · Sat mostly 7pm

Series Five (5 × 30 mins) *Russ Abbot's Saturday Madhouse* 22 Oct–19 Nov 1983 · Sat 7pm

Special (60 mins) *Russ Abbot's Christmas Madhouse* 22 Dec 1984 · Sat 6.50pm

Special (60 mins) *Russ Abbot's Summer Madhouse* 29 June 1985 · Sat 7.30pm

Series Six (6 × 30 mins) *Russ Abbot's Saturday Madhouse* 31 Aug–5 Oct 1985 · Sat 7pm

MAIN CAST

Russ Abbot

REGULAR SUPPORTING CAST

Michael Barrymore
Susie Blake
Les Dennis
Bella Emberg
Dustin Gee
Sherrie Hewson
Jeffrey Holland

CREDITS

writers Colin Bostock-Smith, Garry Chambers, Maureen Darbyshire, Barry Faulkner, David Hansen, Tony Hare, Lennie Hart, Howard Imber, Russel Lane, Paul Minett/Brian Leveson, Andrew Marshall/David Renwick, Eric Merriman, Bill Naylor, Paul Owen, Geoff Rowley, Brian Wade, Bernard Wilkie and others · directors John Kaye Cooper, Ken O'Neill, Alan Boyd, David Bell, Alasdair Macmillan · producers John Kaye Cooper, Ken O'Neill, David Bell

In *Madhouse*, Russ Abbot carved a particular niche with an array of catchy comedy characters – among them Cooper-man, a bungling Superman; Secret Agent X; Geronimo, the stupid aviator Boggles; wide-boy Sid the Spiv; German madman Fritz Crackers; quaffed rocker Vince Prince; Wilf Bumworthy; Barratt Holmes the detective with Dr Wimpey; Miss Marbles; the orange-haired Scot Jimmy McJimmy; and the Harley Street heart-throb Dr Profile – which he seemed able to dream up with relative ease. All the while, Abbot received sterling support from a regular back-up team, two of whom – Les Dennis and Michael Barrymore – found *Madhouse* the perfect springboard to individual successes.

After six years with the *Madhouse* on ITV, five of them as headliner, Russ Abbot jumped across to the BBC in 1986.

The Russ Abbot Show BBC

UK · BBC · SKETCH

66 editions (60 × 30 mins · 2 × 35 mins · 3 × 40 mins · 1 × 45 mins) · colour

Special (35 mins) 26 May 1986 · BBC1 Mon 8.55pm

Series One (8 × 30 mins) 13 Sep–25 Oct 1986 · BBC1 Sat around 7.30pm

Special (35 mins) *The Russ Abbot Christmas Show* 25 Dec 1986 · BBC1 Thu 5.25pm

Series Two (8 × 30 mins) 12 Sep–31 Oct 1987 · BBC1 Sat 7.25pm

Special (40 mins) *The Russ Abbot Christmas Show* 25 Dec 1987 · BBC1 Fri 5.45pm

Series Three (8 × 30 mins) 3 Sep–22 Oct 1988 · BBC1 Sat 8.45pm

Special (45 mins) *The Russ Abbot Christmas Show* 25 Dec 1988 · BBC1 Sun 8.30pm

Series Four (12 × 30 mins) 2 Sep–18 Nov 1989 · BBC1 Sat mostly 7.30pm

Special (40 mins) *The Russ Abbot Christmas Show* 25 Dec 1989 · BBC1 Mon 5.35pm

Series Five (12 × 30 mins) 1 Sep–17 Nov 1990 · BBC1 Sat 7.20pm

Special (40 mins) *The Russ Abbot Christmas Show* 26 Dec 1990 · BBC1 Wed 5.25pm

Series Six (12 × 30 mins) 6 Sep–29 Nov 1991 · BBC1 Fri 8pm

MAIN CAST
Russ Abbot
Les Dennis
Bella Emberg
Tom Bright (series 1–5)
Maggie Moone (series 1–4)
Suzy Aitchison (series 1–4)
Gordon Kennedy (series 1)
Paul Shearer (series 2–4)
Sherrie Hewson (series 5 & 6)

CREDITS
writers Colin Bostock-Smith, Mark Burton, Gary Clapperton, Barry Cryer, Craig Ferguson, James Hendrie, David Hurst, Richard Kates, Paul Minett/Brian Leveson, Bill Naylor, Peter Robinson/Peter Vincent, Neil Shand, Dick Vosburgh and others · *producers/directors* John Bishop (all except series 6), Tudor Davies (series 6)

Abbot came to the BBC with a bigger budget and some new characters, but he also kept many of the old favourites and the zany mania continued much as before. Memorable characters included: C U Jimmy (a variation on Jimmy McJimmy), a tartan-clad lout with an impenetrable accent, whose catchphrase, 'See you Jimmy', was the only coherent part of his speech; suave but stupid secret agent Basildon Bond; Spanish heart-throb singer Julio Doubleglazias; portly opera singer Fatman; RAF doubletalk speaker and flying ace Dirk

Handlebar-Moustache; and manic composer Wolfgang Amadeus Mozart. Each show overflowed with quickfire gags and elaborate slapstick, and Abbot was supported in his efforts by his regular troupe of players and some newcomers. These BBC series, sometimes titled simply *Russ Abbot*, ensured his continuing popularity – until, that is, the BBC failed to renew his contract, considering him too corny.

Abbot wasn't content to remain a 'one-trick pony', however, and was determined to explore new fields, including straight stage-plays, musicals and the ITV drama series *September Song* (Granada, 1993–95). Later in 1994 he returned to the madcap sketch format, once again on ITV, for a Granada version of *The Russ Abbot Show* …

The Russ Abbot Show ITV

UK · ITV (GRANADA) · SKETCH

15 editions (14 × 30 mins · 1 × 45 mins) · colour

Series One (7 × 30 mins) 5 Sep–17 Oct 1994 · Mon 7pm

Series Two (7 × 30 mins) 10 July–21 Aug 1995 · Mon 7pm

Special (45 mins) 26 Dec 1996 · Thu 6.45pm

MAIN CAST
Russ Abbot
Bella Emberg
Les Dennis (series 2 & special)

CREDITS
writers Hugh Smith, Art Lamb, David Kind, Jim Pullin, Mike Lepine, Mark Leigh, Mike Haskins and others · *additional material* Neil Curry, Patrick Morgan, Robert Mills, Matthew King, Jamie Richards and others · *script editor* Laurie Rowley · *directors* Jonathan Glazier (series 1), John O'Regan/Tony Prescott/Chris Power (series 2), Tony Prescott (special) · *executive producer* Brian Park · *producers* Mark Wells (series 1), Mark Gorton (series 2 & special)

Between the second and third series of the ITV drama *September Song* Russ Abbot took the opportunity to remind viewers of his comic prowess, launching a whole new gamut of characters in a seven-week ITV run of *The Russ Abbot Show*. Accompanied by long-serving assistant Bella Emberg, Abbot unveiled, among many others, the Noisy Family; the Clueless Cleric; and the inhabitants of Pimple Town, a mock children's TV series laden with sexual innuendo, characters including Mrs Verruca, her next-door neighbour Percy Pervert, PC Bunion and Mr Hernia. In the process, Abbot dropped Cooperman, Basildon Bond and other former favourites.

A second series followed in 1995, in which Abbot was additionally assisted by Les Dennis and unveiled more new characters including the police psychologist

Fatz, a spin on the acclaimed ITV drama *Cracker* and its lead character Fitz (portrayed by Robbie Coltrane).

In 1996 Abbot starred in the ITV sitcom **Married For Life**, the British version of the American series **Married … With Children**.

In 1997 *The Russ Abbot Show* was brought to radio for the first time as Abbot, with Les Dennis, Bella Emberg, Jeffrey Holland and Susie Blake, re-recorded winning TV sketches featuring Vince Prince, Basildon Bond, Barratt Holmes, Julio Doubleglazias and other characters of old. The eight-part series was broadcast on BBC Radio 2 from 13 November 1997 to 15 January 1998.

The Abbott And Costello Show

USA · SYNDICATION (MCA/REVUE) · SITCOM

52 × 30 mins · b/w

US dates: late 1952–1954

*UK dates: 14 Sep 1957–4 Jan 1958 (16 episodes) ITV Sat 6pm

MAIN CAST
Bud Abbott · himself
Lou Costello · · · · · · · · · · · · · · · · · himself
Sid Fields · · · · · · · · · · · · · · · · · · · himself
Hillary Brooke · · · · · · · · · · · · · · · · herself
Stinky Jones · · · · · · · · · · · · · · · Joe Besser
various roles · · · · · · · · · · · · · Joan Shawlee

CREDITS
writers Eddie Foreman, Sid Fields, Clyde Bruckman, Felix Adler, Jack Townley · *director* Jean Yarbrough · *producers* Pat Costello, Alex Gottlieb

Bud Abbott (born William Abbott in Asbury Park, New Jersey, on 2 October 1895) and Lou Costello (Louis Francis Cristillo, Paterson, New Jersey, 6 March 1906), achieved long-lasting fame as a double-act through 38 movies, conveyor-belt-produced in the 1940s, some being very funny, others woefully poor. The basis of their act, not dissimilar to Laurel and Hardy's, Dud and Pete's or any other of the classic double-act routines, was the idiot and the complete idiot, the manipulator and the manipulated, one using his supposed intellectual advantage to lord it over the other. Bud was the tall, thin, knowing one, with the gravel voice and mean mind; Lou was the dumpy, accident-prone, easily led, foolish one.

Come 1951, Lou Costello wanted the pair to own outright, for the first time, performances of all the best routines and skits they had made famous in their burlesque shows, radio appearances and movies. The result was *The Abbott And Costello Show*, one of the earliest US TV sitcoms, massacred by the critics and, mostly, loved by audiences. (Those viewing at home, that is; the episodes themselves were marked by a clumsily added 'canned' laugh-track.) In order to maintain creative control, the series became something of a family affair: Lou Costello's brother, Pat, produced and his brother-in-law, Joe Kirk, played minor roles.

Filmed at the Hal Roach lot in Hollywood where Laurel and Hardy had created their masterpieces 20 years earlier, the series depicted Abbott and Costello as out-of-work and down-at-heel actors living together in a Los Angeles apartment house run by a cigar-chewing landlord, Sid Fields (who also played other roles as and when necessary). Also in the house was a mischief-maker nicknamed Stinky, and Hillary Brooke, who acted as Costello's girlfriend. Outside the house, always short of money and late with the rent, A&C tried out a number of different jobs and got into every scrape imaginable. Essentially, albeit in keeping with Lou Costello's original wish, the plots were little more than an excuse for the comics to indulge in the violent slapstick or wordplay skits made famous in their movies, including the legendary 'Who's On First?' routine (to be remembered in the 1989 Dustin Hoffman and Tom Cruise movie *Rain Man*) and the one about the Susquehanna Hat Company.

After the first 26 episodes Abbott and Costello had cribbed pretty much every worthwhile routine from their movies and so, for the next 26, a more consistent storyline was attempted. Sadly, by this time, the pair were also suffering from declining health. After the best part of 25 years together, the partnership broke up in 1956, reputedly on amicable terms. Two years later, however, Abbott sued Costello, alleging that he was being denied his share of the money ($222,666) made from the TV series. This was the ultimate irony: the conman was accusing his patsy of having conned him. Whatever the truth, Costello died soon afterwards, on 3 March 1959, and Abbott followed 15 years later, on 24 April 1974. In between times, short of cash, Abbott had voiced his own character in a series of five-minute TV cartoon films, *Abbott And Costello*, made by Hanna-Barbera in 1967. (Stan Irwin voiced Costello's part.) These were screened in Britain by BBC1 from 23 November 1969.

Approaching 50 years of age, episodes of *The Abbott And Costello Show* continue to show up on American TV, the occasional slow pace of the comedy being artificially speeded up by a film-to-tape transfer process.

*Note. Thirty-eight of these same pro-grammes were screened in Britain by C4 from 29 December 1982 to 29 January 1985, followed by some 70 repeats until 24 July 1989. C4 also showed (on 3 November 1985) *Hey Abbott!*, a specially compiled US TV tribute to the comedy duo, screened there by HBO on 30 January 1980.

ABC Of Britain

UK · BBC · SATIRE/MUSICAL HUMOUR

1 × 50 mins · b/w

8 Sep 1964 · BBC1 Tue 8pm

MAIN CAST
Millicent Martin
David Kernan
Gordon Jackson
Peter Jeffrey

CREDITS
writers Gerald Kaufman (sketches), Herbert Kretzmer/Dave Lee (songs) · *director/producer* Ned Sherrin

A whimsical, alphabetical whizz through British life in songs and sketches. There was a strong connection with *That Was The Week That Was* courtesy of director/producer Sherrin, actor/singers Martin and Kernan, and writer Kaufman (later to become a prominent Labour politician).

Abigail And Roger

UK · BBC · SITCOM

9 × 20 mins · b/w

4 July–29 Aug 1956 · Wed 7.30pm

MAIN CAST
Abigail · · · · · · · · · · · · · · · · · · · Julie Webb
Roger · · · · · · · · · · · · · · · David Drummond
Shirl · · · · · · · · · · · · · · · · · Rosina Enright
Clive · John Stone
Mrs Moloch · · · · · · · Grace Denbeigh-Russell

CREDITS
writer/producer Kevin Sheldon

The comedy adventures of an engaged couple living separately (this *was* the 1950s) in London's bedsitter land. The cornerstone of the series was the couple's interest in the wide diversity of attractions on offer in the capital, and much of the humour, such as it was, arose from their differing attitudes to life: Abigail – a shorthand typist by profession – was an outspoken and capable individual who could cook, drive a car, mend a fuse and so on, and whose boundless enthusiasm meant that she took up good causes at the drop of a hat; Roger was a more stolid type who worked in the City, had fixed views on the economy and was into keeping fit and planning for their future.

The series was originally intended to run for 13 weeks, as a summer replacement for the BBC's popular soap opera *The Grove Family*, but it aired for only nine.

About Face

UK · ITV (CENTRAL FILMS FOR CENTRAL) · SITCOMS

12 × 30 mins · colour

Series One (6) 6 Nov–11 Dec 1989 · Mon 8pm
Series Two (6) 7 Jan–11 Feb 1991 · Mon 9.30pm

Owing to nothing more than coincidence, Maureen Lipman launched a series of six individual comedy playlets on ITV just ten days before Victoria Wood did likewise on BBC1, late in 1989. The premises were similar: the star appeared each week in a different part, exploring a variety of comedic roles. If anything, Lipman's series, *About Face*, was received better, and drew the more favourable reviews. Although written by different authors, the six Lipman playlets shared a common theme: that of women with what the star described as 'a certain emptiness in their lives'.

Despite the success of the first batch of six, Central TV were reluctant to commission a second series. Perhaps they feared diminution of audience share, recognising that television viewers prefer to see familiar faces in familiar, not ever-changing, roles, but they did eventually comply late in 1990. This, however, much to Lipman's disappointment, was as far as the brave and ever interesting *About Face* idea was taken.

Searching For Señor Duende   6 NOV 1989

MAIN CAST
Carol · · · · · · · · · · · · · · · Maureen Lipman
Trevor · · · · · · · · · · · · · · · Michael Gambon
Manolette · · · · · · · · · · · · · Trader Faulkner
Deirdre · · · · · · · · · · · · · · · · Penny Morrell
Fiona · · · · · · · · · · · · · · Amanda Dickinson

CREDITS
writer Richard Harris · *executive producer* Tony Wolfe · *director/producer* John Henderson

Carol, a dowdy south London telephonist, becomes obsessed by the glamour of flamenco dancing, giving her an 'olé new sense of life but bringing to an end her relationship with humdrum boyfriend Trevor.

Stand By Your Man   13 NOV 1989

MAIN CAST
Helen · · · · · · · · · · · · · · · Maureen Lipman
Michael · · · · · · · · · · · · · · Michael Jayston
Jim · Terry Taplin
Andrew · · · · · · · · · · · · · · · · John Tordoff

CREDITS
writer Geoffrey Perkins · *executive producer* Tony Wolfe · *director/producer* John Henderson

A wife exacts revenge on her domineering and probably philandering MP husband when the Press come to the house for an interview.

Gracie   20 NOV 1989

MAIN CAST
Gracie · · · · · · · · · · · · · · · Maureen Lipman
Jessica · · · · · · · · · · · · · · · · Diana Weston
Lady Ann · · · · · · · · · · · · · · · Phyllida Law
Ruth · · · · · · · · · · · · · · · · · · · Tacy Kneale

CREDITS

writers Chips Hardy/John Henderson · *executive producer* Tony Wolfe · *director/producer* John Henderson

A Cypriot immigrant, Gracie has been the Ladies-cloakroom attendant at a swish London night-club for 25 years, and confidante to many a secret. But celebrations to mark the special anniversary are altered by the arrival of Jessica, an American film star.

Mrs Worthington's Daughter   27 NOV 1989

MAIN CAST

Patience	Maureen Lipman
Jamie	Neil Duncan
Maxwell	Basil Henson

CREDITS

writer Astrid Ronning · *executive producer* Tony Wolfe · *director/producer* John Henderson

Patience, an American theatrical stage-manager working with a lowly rep company, attends a first-night party that unexpectedly revives her flagging morale. (The title, of course, was a twist on Noël Coward's famous piece of musical wit 'Don't Put Your Daughter On The Stage, Mrs Worthington'.)

Send Her Victorious   4 DEC 1989

MAIN CAST

Margaret Thatcher	Maureen Lipman
Denis Thatcher	John Wells
Maurice Picarda	John Cater
Bingham	Richard Vernon
Howell	Paul Brooke
Police Chief	Nick Stringer
Duc De Herm	Tony Slattery
Terrorist 1	Brian Croucher
Terrorist 2	Jonathan Kydd

CREDITS

writer John Wells · *executive producer* Tony Wolfe · *director/producer* John Henderson

Margaret and Denis Thatcher are kidnapped while on holiday abroad. Virtually a sequel to *Anyone For Denis?*, also written by Denis actor John Wells.

Bag Lady   11 DEC 1989

MAIN CAST

Wendy (The Bag Lady)	Maureen Lipman

CREDITS

writer Jack Rosenthal · *executive producer* Tony Wolfe · *director/producer* John Henderson

A vagrant tramps the streets of London, rifling through litter bins in search of papers, and hoping to retrieve the furniture she believes she lost to the Prime Minister 30 years ago. (Writer Jack Rosenthal is Lipman's real-life husband.)

Tourist Attraction   7 JAN 1991

MAIN CAST

Louise	Maureen Lipman
Ken	Keith Barron
Mrs Maldini	Libby Morris
Mrs Rodgers	Carol Cleveland

CREDITS

writers Paul Smith/Terry Kyan · *director* John Henderson · *producer* Johnny Goodman

Louise, a guide for foreign tourists, tries to speed up her day's work in order to meet her German boyfriend for the evening. He's only in town for the one night, but can she persuade coach driver Ken to make more haste?

This For The Half Darling   14 JAN 1991

MAIN CAST

Peggy	Maureen Lipman
Guy	Mark Kingston
Jasper	Declan Traynor
Lucy	Michelle Wesson

CREDITS

writer Richard Harris · *director* John Henderson · *producer* Johnny Goodman

Peggy is a golf widow – her husband Guy prioritises his sport above his marriage. But then matters take a different course when Peggy has golfing lessons and becomes obsessed too.

Requiem   21 JAN 1991

MAIN CAST

Anne	Maureen Lipman
Sheila	Stephanie Cole
Christine	Flip Webster
Geoffrey	Stanley Lebor
Keith	Brian McDermott

CREDITS

writer Carol Bunyan · *director* John Henderson · *producer* Johnny Goodman

Anne, a suburban clothes-shop saleswoman cum local amateur opera diva, is keen for her husband Keith to be in the audience when she stands solo in the spotlight, but he seems to care more for his Rotary Club function.

Briefcase Encounter   28 JAN 1991

MAIN CAST

Deirdre	Maureen Lipman
Graham	Simon Cadell
Dave	Robert Bathurst
Chris	Owen Brenman
Simon	Philip Bird

CREDITS

writers Ian Hislop/Nick Newman · *director* John Henderson · *producer* Johnny Goodman

A sharply written satire on office politics and corporate life, focusing on a romance between Deirdre in the Reading office and Graham, the area manager from the Swindon office.

Monkey Business   4 FEB 1991

MAIN CAST

Helen Firebrace	Maureen Lipman
Bryce	Bernard Hill
Interpreter	Rory McGrath

CREDITS

writers Paul Smith/Terry Kyan · *director* John Henderson · *producer* Johnny Goodman

Going through customs, Helen Firebrace, an animal-rights campaigner, is found in possession of cocaine. It's all the result of a mix-up, but the customs officer has lost his sense of humour. When he finally allows Helen to pass he does so without noticing the smuggled chimpanzee.

Sleeping Sickness   11 FEB 1991

MAIN CAST

Dr MacBride	Maureen Lipman
Mr Sheridan	William Gaunt
Dr Powell	Martin Clunes
Mr Morley	James Grout
Mr Roebuck	Roger Sloman

CREDITS

writer Jack Rosenthal · *director* John Henderson · *producer* Johnny Goodman

Doctor MacBride is an over-worked and perpetually exhausted NHS hospital registrar, ambitious for a job as a consultant.

Abracadigance

see DIGANCE, Richard

Absolutely

UK · C4 (ABSOLUTELY PRODUCTIONS) · SKETCH

28 editions (14 × 45 mins · 14 × 35 mins) · colour

Series One (6 × 45 mins) 23 May–27 June 1989 · Tue 11pm

Series Two (8 × 45 mins) 22 Aug–10 Oct 1990 · Wed mostly 10pm

Series Three (8 × 35 mins) 17 May–5 July 1991 · Fri 10.30pm

Series Four (6 × 35 mins) 22 Jan–26 Feb 1993 · Fri 10.30pm

MAIN CAST

Pete Baikie
Morwenna Banks
Moray Hunter
Jack Docherty
Gordon Kennedy
John Sparkes

CREDITS

writers cast · *directors* Phil Chilvers (series 1), Alan Nixon (2 editions in series 2), Alistair Clark (6 editions in series 2, series 3), Graham C Williams (series 4) · *producers* Alan Nixon (series 1–3), David Tyler (series 4)

Sketch humour with a pronounced Scots accent and bias from comics who, though they began as relative unknowns, have certainly made an impact since. Morwenna Banks – to become an established actress, writer and director – was often featured here as a whining St Trinian's-like brash schoolgirl. Jack Docherty – elevated to nightly chat-show stardom with the launch of C5 in 1997 – appeared as the rabid Scots nationalist ('all English are pooves') McGlashan, a version of which graduated to a sitcom pilot *Mac*; he also appeared with Moray Hunter as Don and George McDiarmid, perplexed Scots step-cousins later given their own spin-off sitcom by C4, *Mr Don And Mr George*. Hunter also played the part of the dull 'anorak' Calum Gilhooley. John Sparkes (Welsh, not Scottish) developed various characters including a grumpy old man called Bert, complete with Zimmer frame, the Welsh do-it-yourself maestro Denzil, and dirty Frank Hovis. Gordon Kennedy – later to co-host the initial National Lottery presentations for BBC1 – played a number of roles, often as straight-man/foil, and was most often seen as the loopy leader of the dense villagers in Stoneybridge.

The combination of all these characters, and more, blending songs and sketches but never satire, made for 28 programmes, always worth watching but not always on the mark.

Absolutely Fabulous

UK · *BBC, BBC (SAUNDERS AND FRENCH PRODUCTIONS) · SITCOM

20 episodes (18 × 30 mins · 2 × 45 mins)

*Series One (6 × 30 mins) 12 Nov–17 Dec 1992 · BBC2 Thu 9pm

Series Two (6 × 30 mins) 27 Jan–10 Mar 1994 · BBC1 Thu 9.30pm

Series Three (6 × 30 mins) 30 Mar–11 May 1995 · BBC1 Thu 9.30pm

Special (45 mins) *The Last Shout: Part 1* 6 Nov 1996 · BBC1 Wed 9.30pm

Special (45 mins) *The Last Shout: Part 2* 7 Nov 1996 · BBC1 Thu 9.30pm

MAIN CAST

Edina Monsoon	Jennifer Saunders
Patsy Stone	Joanna Lumley
Saffron Monsoon	Julia Sawalha
Mother	June Whitfield
Bubble	Jane Horrocks (series 1 & 3)
Catriona	Helen Lederer (series 2 & 3)

OTHER APPEARANCES

Justin	Christopher Malcolm
Marshall	Christopher Ryan
Bo	Mo Gaffney
Magda	Kathy Burke
Fleur	Harriet Thorpe

CREDITS

creators Jennifer Saunders/Dawn French · *writer* Jennifer Saunders · *script editor* Ruby Wax · *director* Bob Spiers · *producers* Jon Plowman, Jon Plowman/Janice Thomas (specials)

An absolutely sizzling sitcom that caused waves on both sides of the Atlantic and could easily have been subtitled 'Women Behaving Badly'.

In their *French And Saunders* series, Dawn French and Jennifer Saunders performed a sketch with the former as a level-headed, health-conscious teenager and the latter as her tearaway mother. This role-reversal situation inspired Saunders to expand the theme into *Absolutely Fabulous* (colloquially abbreviated to *AbFab*), in which Saunders played the jet-setting, bad-living PR agent and single mother Edina (Eddy) Monsoon, and Julia Sawalha played her strait-laced and disapproving daughter Saffron (Saffy). Added to this mix were veteran comedy star June Whitfield as Edina's mother, and Joanna Lumley as Patsy Stone, a chain-smoking, hard-drinking, drug-imbibing, near-nymphomaniac chum of Eddy's since schooldays.

Eddy and Patsy had been young firebrands in the heady atmosphere of the late 1960s/ early 1970s and here they were 20 or so years later still with the same sensibilities, philosophies and outlook of that period. They had also done remarkably well for themselves in the money-motivated 1980s, Patsy as a fashion magazine editor, Edina with her PR/fashion company. Both women seemed to have virtually unlimited amounts of cash yet rarely found themselves engaged in real work, although Edina often went to her office where she barked orders at her inefficient and mentally bizarre secretary Bubble. At the start of the series Edina was supplementing her income with alimony from her two ex-husbands but this cashflow ceased when they tumbled to the fact that they had both been paying her. The inverted generation gap theme between mother and daughter was central to the idea, with Saffy cast in the role of the responsible one to her errant mother. Edina's own, faintly senile, mother had much in common with Saffy in outlook, so mostly the two were united in their abhorrence of Edina and Patsy's hedonistic lifestyle.

So much for the premise. It was the *style* of the show that elevated *Absolutely Fabulous* out of the mainstream, however, and made it arguably the most groundbreaking British sitcom of the 1990s. As a backlash against rampant 'political correctness', Saunders unashamedly delivered a jet-black, rollicking, rude, crude sitcom that took the public by storm. Patsy and Edina were monstrous creations: selfish, shallow poseurs hell-bent on living life to the excess. They enthusiastically imbibed hard liquor, hashish, cigarettes and cocaine, and generally acted like irresponsible 20-year-olds. Their behaviour was outrageous, their rudeness devastating and their callous and acidic attitude towards good causes and traditional values absolutely shocking. In one

stroke Saunders dealt a telling blow against the rarefied PC atmosphere that, arguably and certainly unintentionally, she and her ilk had helped to start.

The fact that people responded to this brash humour was amply demonstrated by the enormous ratings that *Absolutely Fabulous* generated almost from the start. Critical acclaim followed too in the shape of Bafta and Emmy awards. Central to the series' success was the fact that it didn't under-estimate its audience, and what some programme-makers might have considered obscure references to designers, fashion gurus, trendy shops and new fads was the norm in *AbFab*. Likewise, much of the humour revolved around untypical subjects: sensory-deprivation tanks, colonic irrigation, liposuction and other concerns to certain modern-day people. But British viewers took it all in their stride, as did the Americans when the show became a cult hit there on cable. What is more, almost unique was the fact that many of the situations, references and themes were tailored for female viewers – with particularly feminine jokes leaving most males baffled.

After three series, in a move typical of her generation of comedy writers, Saunders decided to call it a day and wrapped the series up with a pair of special episodes in which Eddy and Patsy went their separate ways, only to be reunited at the end, realising that they were two sides of the same flawed coin. (A coda to the episode showed them 25 years in the future: infirm, aged hideously – with, in Patsy's case, a colostomy bag – yet still guzzling vodka and visiting trendy nite-spots.) But the public wasn't willing to let them go so easily and Saunders contemplated sating them with an *Absolutely Fabulous* feature film until ditching the idea. Roseanne (Barr/Arnold) picked up the US-format rights to the series but, as of late 1997, it was deemed dead in the water (but see footnote); however the 29 October 1996 episode of *Roseanne* (screened in the UK on 21 February 1997) featured Saunders and Lumley as Edina and Patsy in a special Hallowe'en episode. Rumours suggest that the *AbFab* cast may reunite for a new millennium special but Saunders has stated quite clearly that she wants to move on and that there will be no more episodes.

Absolutely Fabulous was a triumph for its writer and star Jennifer Saunders, but the entire cast and crew deserve credit for the verve of the production, and script editor and sometime collaborator Ruby Wax merits a special mention. Julia Sawalha was consistently good in the most thankless role, that of a dull antidote to her mother's and Patsy's excesses, and the casting of comedy stalwart June Whitfield as Edina's mother was a masterstroke that neatly gave a nod to traditional sitcom and yet at the same time undermined it by the shocking surroundings in which she was placed. As for Joanna Lumley, theatregoers may have been used to seeing her play comedy effectively, but to the majority of TV viewers – who hitherto knew her best as Purdey in *The New Avengers* – her comedy expertise came as a revelation. And despite the ultra-trendy references, garish outfits and savagely witty lines, some of the series' best moments were classically physical, with Saunders and Lumley demonstrating that they were absolutely fabulous at that most ancient and tricky of comedic arts: the sozzled pratfall.

Note. Although not a direct adaptation of *AbFab*, the US sitcom *High Society* (which ran on CBS for 13 episodes, from 30 October 1995 to 26 February 1996, before being cancelled) seemed to be based upon a similar premise. The series depicted the Manhattan-based lives of a novelist, Ellie Walker (played by Jean Smart), and her best friend, publisher Dott Emerson (Mary McDonnell), and the expanded cast of other characters included Dott's mother (Jayne Meadows) and 17-year-old Republican son Brendan (Dan O'Donoghue). But while the two leading women had more clothes than their wardrobes could handle, and liked to drink and swagger about, drugs were not a part of their (that is, CBS's) scene.

According To Dora

UK · BBC · SKETCH

15 editions (14 × 25 mins · 1 × 30 mins) · b/w

Series One (7 × 25 mins) 23 July–3 Sep 1968 · BBC1 Tue 9.05pm

Special (30 mins) 31 Dec 1968 · BBC1 Tue 7.30pm

Series Two (7 × 25 mins) 2 May–13 June 1969 · BBC1 Fri 7.55pm

MAIN CAST
Dora Bryan

CREDITS
writers David Cumming (7), Lew Schwarz (7), Peter Robinson (5), Keith Waterhouse/Willis Hall (4), Tony Hare (3), Alan Melville (3), David Climie (3), Ronald Wolfe/Ronald Chesney (3), Arthur Macrae (3), John Junkin (2), Chic Jacob (2), Barry Knowles (2), Les Lilley (2), John Waterhouse (2), Bob Block (1), Robert Buckland (1), Jan Butlin (1), John Law (1), David Morton (1), William Lynn (1), Roderick Robertson (1), Norman Tucker (1), Richard Cumming (1), Bernard Cranwell (1), Sid Green/Dick Hills (1), Eric Idle (1), Marty Feldman (1), Ray Dunbobbin (1), Myles Rudge (1), John Hudson (1), Tony Fletcher (1), John Muir/Eric Geen (1), Jeremy Kingston/Peter Knight (1), Harold Pinter (1), Neville Phillips (1), Johnny Whyte (1) · *producer* Robin Nash

A themed-sketch show for funny-lady Dora Bryan who was a dab hand at this sort of revue-style comedy. She was born Dora Broadbent in Southport on 7 February 1924 and worked as a dancer before discovering her gift for humour and making a name for herself on stage (from 1947) and TV, both as a guest star and in her own series. In *According To Dora* (subtitled 'A Bryan's-Eye View On The World'), a different subject was broached each week and various writers submitted material on such topics as entertainment, home and beauty, travel and transportation, creature comforts, and the future. Helping her out in the sketches were a slew of well-known British comedy faces, including Joan Sims, John Junkin, Clive Dunn, Patricia Hayes, Richard Wattis, Tony Selby, Kenneth Connor, Graham Stark, Wilfrid Brambell and Deryck Guyler.

Notes. Some years earlier, on 22 August 1964, BBC2 presented *Dora Bryan*, a single show in which the talented star had performed songs and sketches from many of the stage-shows and revues in which she had appeared.

Writer Alan Melville worked often with Bryan, sometimes appearing as her straight-man, and their names are linked through many of her TV appearances. She starred in the first episode of *The Brighton Belle* (BBC1, 6 January–20 January 1972), a three-part comedy-drama written by Melville to mark the demise of the famous train that had long shuttled commuting theatricals to London from the south coast. (Bryan lived in Brighton.)

For Dora Bryan's principal comedy series, see *Both Ends Meet*, *Happily Ever After*, *Mother's Ruin* and *My Wife's Sister*.

Ace Crawford, Private Eye

USA · CBS (CONWAY ENTERPRISES) · SITCOM

5 × 30 mins · colour

US dates: 15 Mar–12 Apr 1983
UK dates: 9 Nov 1985–7 Dec 1985 (5 episodes) ITV Sat around 1.45am

MAIN CAST

Ace Crawford	Tim Conway
Toomey	Joe Regalbuto
Inch	Billy Barty
Luana	Shera Danese
Mello	Bill Henderson
Lt Fanning	Dick Christie

CREDITS
writers Ron Clark, Tim Conway, Rudy Deluca, Ron Friedman, Arnold H Kogen, Mickey Rose · *directors* not known · *producers* Philip Weltman, Ron Clark

A flop US sitcom that ought to have worked. Ace Crawford is a private eye *par flatulence* – although dressed in the obligatory crumpled trench-coat and hat, he farts around without a clue about how to find a clue. By pure luck, however, and much to the amazement of police 'tec Lieutenant Fanning, he regularly stumbles upon the solutions to the most difficult of crime cases, and has at least two women lusting after him: his accountant-cum-assistant Toomey, and sexy singer Luana. The latter works at a tacky wharfside bar, the Shanty, where Ace drinks and hangs out with its owner/barman, a midget named Inch, and Mello, the blind black pianist (played by the real-life jazz star Bill Henderson).

Actor Tim Conway, who played Ace Crawford, had none of his character's luck, however. The series was cancelled after just five episodes, adding to a career list of flops that included cowboy series *Rango* (1967), *The Tim Conway Comedy Hour* (1970), *The Tim Conway Show* (1970) and tasteless sketch show *Turn-On* (1979).

An Actor's Life For Me

UK · BBC · SITCOM

6 × 30 mins · colour

14 Nov–19 Dec 1991 · BBC1 Thu 8.30pm

MAIN CAST

Robert Neilson	John Gordon-Sinclair
Sue Bishop	Gina McKee
Desmond Shaw	Victor Spinetti
Sebastian Groom	Benedict Taylor

CREDITS
writer Paul Mayhew-Archer · *director/producer* Bryan Izzard

A fresh and lively theatrical series depicting Robert Neilson, a struggling actor convinced that he is on the verge of the big time. Although events tend to conspire against him in his quest for fame, Robert remains optimistic that success is just an audition away. His agent Desmond Shaw and his girlfriend Sue do their best to keep his feet on the ground but Robert maintains his head in the clouds.

Paul Mayhew-Archer's thespian comedy started out on BBC Radio 2 with John Gordon-Sinclair in the role of Robert Wilson (not Neilson), Caroline Quentin as Sue and Gary Waldhorn as Desmond. After the 1991 TV run it returned to radio once more, this time with the TV Sue, Gina McKee, in the cast. The series worked well in both media and Gordon-Sinclair made for a likeable lead. One TV episode ('May The Farce Be With You') stood out from the bunch, wherein Robert obtained a job in a theatrical farce; the account of his participation was itself written as a farce.

Note. There were three BBC Radio 2 series of *An Actor's Life For Me*: seven episodes broadcast from 20 January to 3 March 1989, six from 11 February to 18 March 1990 and a final run of six from 5 January to 9 February 1993.

See also *Nelson's Column*.

The Adam And Joe Show

UK · C4 (WORLD OF WONDER) · SKETCH

8 × 30 mins · colour

Series One (4) 6 Dec–31 Dec 1996 · mostly
Fri 12.10am

Series Two (4) 22 Nov–13 Dec 1997 · Sat 11pm

MAIN CAST

Adam Buxton
Joe Cornish

CREDITS

writers/directors Adam Buxton/Joe Cornish ·
executive producers Fenton Bailey, Randy
Barbato · *producer* Debbie Searle

An irreverent, late-night exercise in studentish
humour. Not only written and presented by
two so-called 'popular culture junkies', Adam
Buxton and Joe Cornish, but also, ostensibly,
shot and edited from their bedsit in Brixton,
south London, this DIY comedy show
deconstructed various facets of 1990s
lifestyle. A popular weekly feature was the
re-creation of popular movies and TV series
such as *Showgirls*, *Trainspotting*, *The English
Patient*, *Crash*, *Shine*, *ER*, *This Life* and
Friends, utilising their collection of soft toys.
Movie mogul 'Ken Korda' (Buxton) showed
how to make it in the movies – not. And
Adam's father, nicknamed BaadDad, who
knew zilch about pop music or pop culture,
reviewed the latest singles and, in the 1997
series, the summer's rock festivals, smoking
his first joint and discovering their other
various pleasures. Adam and Joe themselves
went out and about to investigate pressing
consumer issues and, dressed as policemen,
exposed the most embarrassing records
in someone's collection in the weekly spot
Vinyl Justice.

Note. On 31 December 1997 – as part of C4's
ongoing 15th birthday celebrations *Growing
Up With 4* – the youthful twosome fronted
Adam And Joe's Fourmative Years, bringing
their brand of humour to bear on a collection
of clips, highlighting odd, esoteric or just
plain bad moments from the channel's
archives.

Adam's Family Tree

UK · ITV (YORKSHIRE) · CHILDREN'S SITCOM

6 × 25 mins · colour

6 Jan–10 Feb 1997 · Mon 4.20pm

MAIN CAST

Adam · · · · · · · · · · · · · · · · · · Anthony Lewis
Jane · · · · · · · · · · · · · · · · · · Samia Ghadie

CREDITS

writers Brian Walsh/Neil Armstrong · *directors*
Richard Callanan (4), Colin Nobbs (2) · *executive
producer* Patrick Titley · *producer* Richard Callanan

A fantasy-comedy for children, charting the
adventures of a 12-year-old boy, Adam, who
can call upon the services of his ancestors
through a CD-Rom in his home computer.

The disc contains records of his entire family
tree, extending back (implausibly) thousands
of years, and all Adam needs to do is find the
appropriate ancestor, hit the 'return' key and
said relative will materialise in the present
through a hole in the space-time continuum,
ready and willing to help the schoolboy
Adam out of his latest sticky situation.

With his best friend Jane sharing his secret,
Adam calls upon everyone from cavemen
and medieval knights to a Victorian detective
and a romantic silent movie heroine, such
figures being portrayed by guest stars,
one per episode, who included Bill Oddie
(*The Goodies*), Brenda Gilhooly (*Gayle's
World*), Tiffany Chapman (Rachel Jordache
in *Brookside*), Jean Alexander (Hilda Ogden
in *Coronation Street*) and John Altman (Nick
Cotton in *EastEnders*).

A second series was set for screening in
early 1998.

Adam's Rib

USA · ABC (MGM/PETER HUNT) · SITCOM

**13 episodes (12 × 30 mins · 1 × 60 mins) ·
colour**

US dates: 14 Sep–28 Dec 1973

UK dates: 8 Jan 1974–14 Jan 1975 (11 × 30
mins) ITV mostly Tue 11.30pm

MAIN CAST

Adam Bonner · · · · · · · · · · · · · · Ken Howard
Amanda Bonner · · · · · · · · · · · Blythe Danner
Grace Peterson · · · · · · · · · · · Dena Dietrich
Asst DA Roy Mendelsohn · · · · · · · Ron Rifkin
Kip Kipple · · · · · · · · · · · · · · Edward Winter
DA Donahue · · · · · · · · · · · · Norman Bartold

CREDITS

creators Ruth Gordon/Garson Kanin ·
director/producer Peter Hunt

An attempt to generate a weekly sitcom
based upon the 1949 Oscar-nominated hit
comedy movie of the same name, in which
Spencer Tracy and Katharine Hepburn
played husband and wife attorneys Adam
and Amanda Bonner, their opposite positions
in a court case unleashing a witty battle of the
sexes. The TV series lacked both the
sophistication of the George Cukor-directed
movie and the big names to carry off the
script, and lasted only 13 episodes.

The Addams Family

USA · ABC (FILMWAYS) · SITCOM

64 × 30 mins · b/w

US dates: 18 Sep 1964–8 Apr 1966

*UK dates: 1 Oct 1965–27 Dec 1966 (27
episodes) ITV various days and times

MAIN CAST

Gomez Addams · · · · · · · · · · · · · John Astin
Morticia Addams · · · · · · · · · · Carolyn Jones
Lurch · · · · · · · · · · · · · · · · · Ted Cassidy
Uncle Fester · · · · · · · · · · · · Jackie Coogan
Grandmama Addams · · · · · · · Blossom Rock
Wednesday Addams · · · · · · · · · Lisa Loring
Pugsley Addams · · · · · · · · · Ken Weatherwax
Cousin Itt · · · Felix Silla (voice by Tony Magro)
Thing · · · · · · · · · · · the hands of Ted Cassidy/
· Jack Voglin

CREDITS

creator Charles Addams · *writers* Hannibal
Coons/Harry Winkler (25 episodes) and others ·
directors Sidney Lanfield (48), Jerry Hopper (4),
Sidney Salkow (4), Jean Yarbrough (3), Arthur
Hiller (1), Arthur Lubin (1), Nat Perrin (1), Sidney
Miller (1), Stanley Z Cherry (1) · *executive producer*
David Levy · *producer* Nat Perrin

No one is certain about what made two
rival US networks launch 'gruesome' sitcoms
in the same week, but, back in 1964, six
days before CBS unveiled *The Munsters*,
ABC premiered *The Addams Family*. The
unfortunate thing is that, because of this
coincidence of chronology, the shows have
always been, and will forever be, compared.
Actually, the two were radically different.
The Munsters, while undoubtedly a good
series with excellent casting and fine
moments, played for easy laughs. *The
Addams Family*, conversely, was rich, dark
and delicious. Though some episodes have
not worn well – indeed, they may not have
been very good at the time – others remain
extremely funny. And even in the weaker
ones there is always something in which to
delight: a line, a character trait, a perverse
comedic idea.

The series was based on the work of
Charles Addams, whose macabre cartoon
creations about this ghoulish family appeared
regularly in the American magazine *New
Yorker* from circa 1937. The characters never
had names – Morticia, Gomez, Lurch, Fester
et al were coined expressly for the TV
series; indeed, the clan was not even known
as the Addams Family. All the same, among
aficionados Charles Addams' work was
celebrated for its black humour and delightful
morbidity. It seemed inevitable that someone
would turn these magazine cartoons into a
TV series and, in 1964, NBC executive David
Levy did just that. Addams was paid $1000
per show and the series was named after him
in homage.

While intellectuals grumbled about the
transfer of the cult *New Yorker* cartoons into
a mass-market sitcom, few could deny that
Levy did a wonderful job, and that his casting
was first class. Though leaner and taller than
the cartoon 'Gomez Addams', John Astin was
brought in to play the leading man about the
house, a dashing, life-loving lawyer (wealthy
enough not to have to do much work), full of
joie-de-vivre and unfettered enthusiasm.
Carolyn Jones was wonderful as his darkly
mysterious and sexy wife Morticia, slinking
around in her figure-hugging, full-length
black dress. Former child-star Jackie
Coogan – he had been in films since the age of
two and had starred in Chaplin's *The Kid* in

1921 – was cast as the repulsive Uncle Fester, and giant Ted Cassidy – standing 6ft 9in – played the hulking, sulking house-servant Lurch, whose 'You rang?', said with a voice that seemed to resonate from the bowels of the earth, became an international catchphrase. The other characters were inessential – except, perhaps, for Thing, a living, dismembered hand that resided inside a box but would pop up to lend itself (ie, a helping hand) when the phone needed answering, the mail arrived or someone was playing bridge and was a hand short. (The hand was that of Ted Cassidy on all but the nine occasions when Thing and Lurch appeared together in the same scene. On these occasions, assistant director Jack Voglin lent a hand to the proceedings.)

Most of the action took place inside the Addams' creepy mansion but, as mentioned earlier, it was all done with a playful eye. These were *happy* people who simply couldn't understand how others did not see life as they did. The hub of the series, and the principal element that has maintained its longevity, was the torrid love affair between Gomez and Morticia. No seven-year itch for these two: each was deeply bound up in the other, and although there were no bedroom scenes (this was the 1960s, remember) it didn't take much imagination to work out that this pair enjoyed married life to the full. Gomez's affection for his 'Tish' was unbridled, and she only had to utter a French word or phrase, even unwittingly, for him to launch at her, grab her arm and plant a thousand kisses in an ascending direction until propriety or circumstance stopped him. (No such revelry was present in Charles Addams' *New Yorker* cartoons, it was the invention of the TV writers.)

Rounded off by Vic Mizzy's inventive finger-clicking theme song (he also wrote the similarly inspired music for **Green Acres**), *The Addams Family* was a treasure of a sitcom. As such, it did not remain buried for long when the 64-episode series came to an end. First, Hanna-Barbera created a 37-episode animated version for NBC (screened in the USA in 1973–74 and first aired in the UK when ITV screened 16 episodes from 6 April to 20 July 1975). Of the original cast, only Jackie Coogan and Ted Cassidy voiced their roles, while the voice of Gomez and Morticia's pug-ugly son Pugsley was rendered by an eight-year-old child-actress, Jodie Foster. Then the TV cast (all except for an unwell Blossom Rock) reunited for a dreadful 90-minute TV movie, *Halloween With The Addams Family*, which aired in the USA on 30 October 1977 and was notable only for one thing: it showed the family in colour for the first time.

The next revival was the most successful, though: in 1991 Orion/Paramount produced a feature film, *The Addams Family*, based

directly on the 1960s TV version (that is, it employed all the names and traits invented for that series). Barry Sonnenfeld directed, Raul Julia played Gomez and Anjelica Huston was Morticia. Such was the acclaim, and so great the box-office takings, that a follow-up, the not-so-good *Addams Family Values*, was released in 1993 (same director and cast). To tie in with these revivals, Hanna-Barbera created another run of TV cartoons from September 1992 (screened by BBC1 in 1994), John Astin returning to voice the part of Gomez, with Ruth Buzzi and Broadway star Carol Channing also lending their talents. With all these successes came a welcome re-appreciation of the 1960s TV series – and, inevitably, another comparison with *The Munsters*: the relentless mining of old TV ideas had latterly given rise to an appalling small-screen revival called **The Munsters Today**, whereas *The Addams Family* had been treated with much more class.

*Note. Although London-area ITV screened only 27 episodes in the 1960s, C4 screened the entire run of 64 from 4 January 1983 to 29 March 1985, and BBC2 did likewise from 24 February 1992 to 13 December 1993, with further screenings in 1994 and 1996.

The Adventures Of Aggie

UK · ME FILMS · SITCOM

26 × 30 mins · b/w

*17 Sep 1956–18 Mar 1957 · ITV Mon mostly 7.05pm

MAIN CAST
Aasgard Agnette Anderson · · · Joan Shawlee

CREDITS
writers Martin Stern, Ernest Borneman · directors John Guillermin (15), Henry Kaplan (7), John Gilling (2), Desmond Davis (1), Wolf Rilla (1) · producer Michael Sadleir

An independently-made British series that aired on ITV but was aimed too at the American TV market (as simply *Aggie*, it was screened there in syndication from December 1957). Joan Shawlee, the 27-year-old US actress best known at this time for her roles in **The Abbott And Costello Show**, was the undoubted star, cast as one Aasgard Agnette Anderson, an American fashion buyer working in London for an internationally renowned fashion house. Aggie's job required a good deal of global travelling (hence there was no regular supporting cast) but our heroine had a tendency to cause incidents and accidents, and become caught up in dangerous – but humorous – situations with the likes of spies, smugglers and murderers.

The series provided useful opportunities for talent-spotting: among those passing through the episodes, mostly when completely unknown, were Christopher Lee, Patrick McGoohan (twice), Gordon Jackson, Patrick

Allen, Dick Emery, Anthony Valentine and the future film director John Schlesinger. Other contributors included Rupert Davies, Wilfrid Brambell and Richard Wattis.

*Note. These dates reflect screenings in the Midlands area. At first, only 12 of the 26 episodes were shown by London-ITV, from 23 March to 1 June 1957; more followed later.

The Adventures Of Brigadier Wellington-Bull

UK · BBC · SITCOM

5 × 30 mins · b/w

12 June–17 July 1959 · Fri 7.30pm

MAIN CAST
Brigadier Garnet Wellington-Bull · · · · · · · · · ·
· Alexander Gauge
Jane Wellington-Bull · · · · · · Valerie Singleton
Capt 'Sooty' Pilkington · · · · · Donald Hewlett

CREDITS
writer Austin Melford · producer Ronald Marsh

A sitcom following the barnstorming antics of Brigadier Wellington-Bull, a career soldier, now retired from the service, who has to come to terms with civilian life and gets into all sorts of injudicious situations.

Donald Hewlett played 'Sooty' Pilkington, a young officer who had served under the Brigadier, and Valerie Singleton, described by *Radio Times* as a 'bright-eyed television newcomer', was the Brigadier's daughter. (She later found fame as a *Blue Peter* presenter.)

The Adventures Of Charlie Quick

UK · BBC · CHILDREN'S SITCOM

6 × approx 10 mins · b/w

11 Nov–16 Dec 1957 · Mon around 5.15pm

MAIN CAST
Charlie Quick · · · · · · · · · · · · · · · · Clive Dunn

CREDITS
writer Peter Newington · producer John Hunter Blair

Clive Dunn presented within the BBC's Monday magazine slot for children, *Studio E*.

The Adventures Of Hiram Holliday

USA · NBC (CALIFORNIA NATIONAL PRODUCTIONS) · SITCOM

26 × 30 mins · b/w

US dates: 3 Oct 1956–27 Feb 1957

UK dates: 2 Aug 1960–21 June 1961 (26 episodes) BBC weekdays around 7pm

MAIN CAST
Hiram Holliday · · · · · · · · · · · · · · · Wally Cox
Joel Smith · · · · · · · · · · · · · · · · Ainslie Pryor

CREDITS
creator Paul Gallico · writers Philip Rapp, Richard Powell and others · directors George Cahan, William J Hole and others · producer Philip Rapp

A charming sitcom based on the short stories by Paul Gallico (published in 1939) about a bespectacled, meek, mild-mannered newspaperman with amazing powers. No, not Superman but plain old Hiram Holliday who, while working as a proof-reader for a New York newspaper, has accrued amazing skills in a huge variety of areas, from sword-fencing to scuba-diving. When Hiram corrects a potentially damaging error in his newspaper, the relieved proprietor rewards him with an around-the-world trip to indulge all of his startling technical powers. Holliday is accompanied by a reporter, Joel Smith, to record the resulting adventures. Our self-effacing hero, who lives only to help others, saves the day for many of those that cross his path.

The part of Hiram Holliday was played by night-club comedian Wally Cox, who had already scored a notable TV success with his portrayal of a bespectacled, meek, mild-mannered science teacher in *Mr Peepers* (NBC, 1952–55), not screened in Britain.

Note. *The Adventures Of Hiram Holliday* was the first sitcom to be 'stripped' on British television – a TV term meaning that it was screened in the same slot on consecutive days, the BBC showing it Mondays through Fridays around 7pm when its current affairs programme *Tonight* was taking seasonal breaks. BBC1 repeated 13 episodes from 22 February to 24 May 1966 under the abbreviated title *Hiram Holliday*.

The Adventures Of Mr Pastry

see Mr Pastry

The Adventures Of Tugboat Annie

CANADA/USA · SYNDICATION (NORMANDIE PRODUCTIONS) · SITCOM

39 × 30 mins · b/w

Canadian dates: autumn 1957–summer 1958

UK dates: 31 Dec 1957–9 Dec 1958 (39 episodes) ITV Tue 7pm then Wed 7pm then Mon mostly 6.30pm

MAIN CAST

Annie Brennan	Minerva Urecal
Horatio Bullwinkle	Walter Sande
Whitey	Don Baker
Pinto	Don Orlando
Jake	James Barron

CREDITS

creator Norman Reilly Raine · *writers* various · *director* Leslie Goodwins · *executive producers* Leon Fromkess, Anthony Veiller

Norman Reilly Raine's stories of the salty tugboat captain Annie Brennan first appeared in prose form in the weekly US journal *Saturday Evening Post* in the late 1920s. She was soon developed into a movie character,

being depicted in three films (*Tugboat Annie*, 1933; *Tugboat Annie Sails Again*, 1940; and *Captain Tugboat Annie*, 1945), each time portrayed by a different actress. Finally, in 1954, a TV series was commissioned by the independent US production company TPA. It was far from plain sailing: the pilot took two whole years to complete and cost a then-record $129,000. (Elsa Lanchester, Jay C Flippen and Chill Wills were all in line for major roles at one point or another at this early stage.) When the series finally followed it was filmed and first shown in Canada, attracting ratings good enough to interest US television stations. Sadly, what had gone down well in Canada proved something of a disappointment south of the border, where, perhaps, the viewing audiences had become used to greater sophistication than this series' simplistic humour could provide.

Former opera singer Minerva Urecal and Walter Sande were the main stars, she as the widowed captain of the tugboat *Narcissus*, he as the captain of the *Salamander*. Both were veteran actors with appropriately weather-beaten faces, and their characters 'enjoyed' a rivalry that could only be described as arch. Trading insults and trying to queer each other's pitch, they battled their way through 39 episodes, all of which then crossed the Atlantic for consumption by ITV viewers.

Affairs Of The Heart

UK · ITV (GRANADA) · SITCOM

7 × 30 mins · colour

Pilot · 23 Aug 1983 · Tue 8.30pm

One series (6) 22 July–26 Aug 1985 · Mon mostly 8pm

MAIN CAST

Peter Bonamy	Derek Fowlds
Jane Bonamy	Sarah Badel
Rosemary Bonamy	Elizabeth Anson (pilot); Holly Aird (series)

CREDITS

writer Paul Daneman · *directors* Richard Holthouse (pilot), Charles Kitchen (series) · *producer* Brian Armstrong

A series written by the TV, stage and film actor Paul Daneman who, bizarrely, suffered a heart attack during a West End play in which he was portraying a man suffering from a heart attack. During his convalescence, when he was advised to delay his return to acting, Daneman was prompted to try writing and *Affairs Of The Heart* was the result.

Peter Bonamy is the main character. In the 1983 pilot, essentially re-made as the opening episode of the 1985 series, he has a heart attack, goes into hospital and then leaves to resume life with a greater degree of care. 'Maybe it was overwork,' Bonamy considers, so he decides to allow others to look after him for a while. His wife Jane and 13-year-old daughter Rosemary tend towards molly-

coddling, and his heart-attack survivors' group is populated by a strange lot. Unable yet to return to driving his Porsche, or to resume working for his own building company, Bonamy twiddles his thumbs and watches his finances dwindle away – albeit from the splendour of a very comfortable house in south London.

Affairs Of The Heart was a strange combination of sitcom and light-drama, but while the writing was clearly tailored for audience laughter Granada did not engage one, and the funny lines were left in limbo-land, reducing the effect of the humour. Combined with a lack of pace, the net result was hollow.

After Henry

UK · ITV (THAMES, *COMPULSIVE VIEWING FOR THAMES) · SITCOM

38 × 30 mins · colour

Series One (6) 4 Jan–8 Feb 1988 · Mon 8pm

Special · 26 Dec 1988 · Mon 9.30pm

Series Two (12) 10 Jan–11 Apr 1989 · Tue 8.30pm

Special · 25 Dec 1989 · Mon 8.30pm

Series Three (12) 23 Jan–17 Apr 1990 · Tue 8.30pm

*Series Four (6) 20 July–24 Aug 1992 · Mon 8pm

MAIN CAST

Sarah France	Prunella Scales
Eleanor Prescott	Joan Sanderson
Clare France	Janine Wood
Russell Bryant	Jonathan Newth

OTHER APPEARANCES

Vera Poling	Peggy Ann Wood
Mary	Anne Priestley (series 2)
Sam Greenland	Edward de Souza (series 2 & 3)

CREDITS

writer Simon Brett · *directors* Peter Frazer-Jones (series 1–3 & specials), Liddy Oldroyd (series 4) · *executive producer* John Howard Davies (series 4) · *producers* Peter Frazer-Jones (series 1–3 & specials), Bill Shepherd (series 4)

Sarah France is 42 and a widow of two years, her GP husband, Henry, having been killed in a car crash. Dr France has left Sarah well provided for, with a large Edwardian detached house in a leafy town about 70 miles out of London, which she shares with their 18-year-old daughter Clare and her seventy-something mother Eleanor. 'Mother' is a manipulative sort, but Henry had assured Sarah that, between the two of them, and with Clare's help, they would cope with her presence without undue trouble. Now he's gone and all three women have to cope After Henry.

Of the three generations in the one household, Sarah is most definitely piggy in the middle, not only by her age but also by simple geography – mother Eleanor resides in the upstairs flat and daughter

Clare moves into the basement; Sarah is in between. Both women bring her grief. Mother is the ultimate in cunning, forever sapping Sarah's confidence and undermining her principles. She is also a terrible gossip (Sarah calls Eleanor and her friends 'The Geriatric Mafia'), prone to making pronouncements about what she's heard from 'Valerie Brown on the pension counter's sister Mary's gentleman friend Maurice' or from her friend Vera Poling who lives at the Sycamores, a residential home for the elderly. Clare, meanwhile, is at that precocious age, keen to assert her independence when it suits her but equally quick to go running back to mother when it doesn't. Life being what it is, Eleanor and Clare frequently gang up on Sarah, whose only source of refuge is Russell, the owner of Bygone Books, the second-hand bookshop where she works. Russell is Sarah's counsel, and, because he's homosexual, they can exchange frank confidences without threat of romantic entanglement.

A gentle and sensitive comedy, *After Henry* was a special creation, exploring parallel mother/daughter relationships within an intelligent framework. The episodes were scripted superbly, with all loose ends neatly tied up inside every story. Originally created for BBC radio, *After Henry* shone within that medium and quickly became a favourite among listeners. 'These are scripts of rare economy and distinction,' Prunella Scales, who starred as Sarah, told *Radio Times* in 1986, before the start of the second radio series. Mystifyingly, the BBC is reported to have turned down the TV adaptation, however, so it went instead to Thames, an inexplicable error of judgement. Although unlike ITV's normal sitcom fare, *After Henry* was given the perfect treatment by Thames, which omitted any fancy graphics or visuals to present the series for what it was: a radio sitcom with reams of literate dialogue and little action, beautifully played by a fine cast – and by Prunella Scales and Joan Sanderson in particular, their combined chemistry being a most potent force.

After Henry was a triumph for its writer Simon Brett, a BBC radio producer for ten years (he worked on *Week Ending*, *The News Huddlines*, *The Burkiss Way* and initial episodes of *The Hitch-Hiker's Guide To The Galaxy*) before becoming a producer at LWT (*The Glums*, *End Of Part One*, *Poppy And Her*) and then turning to full-time writing (he created the amateur sleuth Charles Paris who went about his detection in a series of crime novels). Observing that the situation in *After Henry* could never work with an all-male cast, since few men talk candidly about their emotions, Brett seemed never less than comfortable writing about and for women. Soon after it began, the *Daily Telegraph* was calling *After Henry* 'The best ever domestic

comedy radio series'. And if not the *very* best in its sphere, the visual version ought at least to be hailed as *one* of the best TV sitcoms produced in this country.

Note. There were four BBC Radio 4 series of eight episodes apiece (17 April–5 June 1985, 16 August–4 October 1986, 22 September–10 November 1987, and 17 January–7 March 1989) and two Christmas specials (22 December 1985 and 25 December 1987). Scales and Sanderson played the same roles in the radio and TV versions, but Benjamin Whitrow was Russell and Gerry Cowper was Clare in the radio run. Most of the 34 radio scripts transferred directly to television, 18 with episode titles intact. Joan Sanderson's death on 24 May 1992, between the recording and transmission of the fifth TV series, ensured that the story ended there, however.

After Hours

see BENTINE, Michael

After That, This

UK · BBC · SKETCH
....
6 × 30 mins · colour
....
2 Jan–6 Feb 1975 · BBC2 Thu 9pm

MAIN CAST
Eleanor Bron
John Bird
Derek Fowlds

CREDITS
writers Eleanor Bron/John Fortune · *additional material* John Bird (1) · *director* Gareth Gwenlan · *producer* Robert Chetwyn

Another classy series of whimsy and satire starring Eleanor Bron, this time co-starring with Derek Fowlds and another of her Cambridge contemporaries, John Bird.

After The Boom Was Over

UK · ITV (ATV) · SITCOM
....
1 × 30 mins · colour
....
25 Aug 1977 · Thu 7pm

MAIN CAST
Jack Tatham · · · · · · · · · · · · · · · Tim Wylton
Sally Ashcroft · · · · · · · · · · · · Gabrielle Lloyd
Mr Airedale · · · · · · · · · · · · Martin C Thurley
Mr Ambrose · · · · · · · · · · · · · Jonathan Pryce

CREDITS
writer Connor Fraser · *director/producer* Les Chatfield

A single comedy within the season *The Sound Of Laughter* that followed the disastrous course of house-hunting endured by a young couple, fishing in the shark-infested waters of estate agencies. No series developed.

Agent Z And The Penguin From Mars

UK · BBC · CHILDREN'S SITCOM
....
6 × 30 mins · colour
....
3 Jan–7 Feb 1996 · BBC1 Wed 4.35pm

MAIN CAST
Ben Simpson · · · · · · · · · · · · Duncan Barton
Barney · · · · · · · · · · · · · · · Andrew McKay
Jenks · · · · · · · · · · · · · · · · Reggie Yates
Mrs Simpson · · · · · · · · · Catherine Shipton
Trevor Simpson · · · · · · · · · · · · Ian Sharrock
Tod Sidebottom · · · · · · · · · Andrew Wheeler
Samantha Sidebottom · · · · · · Nicola Mycroft
Dennis Sidebottom · · · · · · · · Rod Culbertson
Patricia Sidebottom · · · · · · · · Pamela Power
Finlay · · · · · · · · · · · · · · · Stephen Churchett

CREDITS
creator Mark Haddon · *writer* Jeremy Front · *director* John Smith · *producer* Angela Beeching

Ben Simpson and his pals Barney and Jenks form the Crane Grove Gang, a secret society dedicated to playing ingenious practical jokes in an initiative called Agent Z. The gang are named after the street where they live (Ben at number 36), which they feel is the dullest place in the United Kingdom. The arrival of a boring new neighbour, supposed lottery-winner Dennis Sidebottom and his family, inspires the gang to plot their biggest ever practical joke: they set up an elaborate plan involving a penguin, an alien from Mars, a spaceship and a 'message for mankind' carved on a meteorite. These disparate objects are delivered in the middle of the night to Dennis Sidebottom's garden while he innocently studies the heavens from his own personal observatory.

Based on Mark Haddon's book of the same title, this was a likeable children's series with various subplots adding texture to the whole piece. These included the light-fingered activities of the disturbing Sidebottom son Tod, and Ben's infatuation with Tod's sister Samantha. Extra style was added by Ben's fevered imagination, which led to extravagant dream sequences (especially a recurring image featuring him as a millionaire complete with Finlay, a man-servant), and the device of using material they have seen on television to introduce comic scenes.

Agony

UK · ITV (LWT) · SITCOM
....
20 × 30 mins · colour
....
Series One (6) 11 Mar–29 Apr 1979 · Sun 9.15pm
Series Two (7) 13 Apr–25 May 1980 · Sun 10pm
Series Three (7) 18 Jan–1 Mar 1981 · Sun 10pm

MAIN CAST
Jane Lucas · · · · · · · · · · · · Maureen Lipman
Laurence Lucas · · · · · · · · · Simon Williams
Bea · · · · · · · · · · · · · · · · Maria Charles
Andy Evol · · · · · · · · · · · · · · · Peter Blake
Rob · · · · · · · · · · · · · · · · Jeremy Bulloch

Michael	Peter Denyer
Val Dunn	Diana Weston
Diana	Jan Holden
Vincent Fish	Bill Nighy (series 2)
Junior Truscombe	Robert Austin
	(series 2 & 3)

CREDITS

creators Len Richmond/Anna Raeburn · *writers* Len Richmond/Anna Raeburn (series 1), Stan Hey/Andrew Nickolds (series 2 & 3) · *director/producer* John Reardon

Real-life press and radio 'agony aunt' Anna Raeburn advised and (for the first series) co-wrote this sometimes daring and always entertaining sitcom about her own work, casting Maureen Lipman as a cosmopolitan Jewish wife and mother, Jane Lucas, radio broadcaster and author of the problem page in the (fictitious) magazine *Person*.

The main premise was that Jane spent so much time sorting out other people's problems that she was unable to handle her own – and they were many: she had a psychiatrist husband, Laurence, a philandering ex-public schoolboy and a Christian too; a needy and manipulative archetypal Jewish widowed mother, Bea; a magazine boss, Diana, who was impossible to work for; a gung-ho office secretary, Val; and, at Happening Radio 242, a DJ colleague, Andy, who was shallow and narcissistic. The only people to offer Jane real comfort and support were Rob and Michael, her gay neighbours. The portrayal of this homosexual couple as non-camp, sensitive, intelligent, witty and generally happy was a notable first in the British sitcom genre, and *Agony* efficiently tackled many other taboos along the way. The series' media setting and Jewish background meant that the lead character could be legitimately witty, delivering wisecracks and sharp one-liners in a style more usually associated with American sitcoms. Indeed, deviser and co-writer Len Richmond was a Californian who had worked on US TV, notably on ***Three's Company***, the Americanised version of ***Man About The House***.

Agony was carefully supervised by LWT's Head of Comedy, Humphrey Barclay, and by all accounts it was a volatile production, with much friction and many off-screen arguments. However, the finished programme certainly looked good and managed to maintain a high quality throughout its run.

Agony ended after three series but enjoyed two further leases of life: the first was a US translation, *The Lucie Arnaz Show* (with scripts from Richmond), not screened in Britain, which starred the daughter of Lucille Ball and Desi Arnaz and ran for six episodes on CBS in 1985. The second was a 1995 British sequel (made by the BBC, not ITV this time), ***Agony Again***, with Lipman still starring.

Note. An ITV episode of *Agony* was screened by BBC2 on 18 October 1997 following a tribute deservedly paid to Maureen Lipman in the series *Funny Women*.

Agony Again

UK · BBC (HUMPHREY BARCLAY PRODUCTIONS) · SITCOM

7 × 30 mins · colour

31 Aug–12 Oct 1995 · BBC1 Thu 8.30pm

MAIN CAST

Jane Lucas	Maureen Lipman
Bea	Maria Charles
Daniel	David Harewood
Debra	Doon Mackichan
Michael	Sacha Grunpeter
Richard	Niall Buggy
Catherine	Valerie Edmond

OTHER APPEARANCES

Laurence Lucas	Simon Williams

CREDITS

writers Carl Gorham/Michael Hatt/Amanda Swift · *script consultant* Len Richmond · *director* Bob Spiers · *executive producer* Al Mitchell · *producers* Humphrey Barclay, Christopher Skala

Following the American lead, the 1990s saw a trend towards resurrecting vintage TV sitcoms, with some, if not all, of the original cast members re-employed. The ***Doctor*** series, ***The Liver Birds*** and ***Reginald Perrin*** were all renewed by the BBC, as was the cute and clever ***Agony***, now titled *Agony Again*. Maureen Lipman returned as the sharp-tongued 'agony aunt', Jane Lucas, who no longer works for *Person* magazine but hosts her own afternoon TV show, *Lucas Live*, which presents contemporary debates in front of a studio audience (in the style of *Oprah* et al). As before, Jane spends most of her hours trying to sort out other people's problems rather than her own. This time her cases include Richard, a homeless ex-company director whom she was sheltering; her fledgling inter-racial romance with social worker Daniel; the damaging aspirations of her producer Debra; the revelation that her son Michael is gay; and the still-suffocating presence of her mother Bea, whose sole purpose in life is to get Jane remarried.

Like its antecedent, *Agony Again* was fast-paced and its Jewish dialogue and media setting gave an American feel to the production. It may not have been as groundbreaking this time around, but in the more enlightened era of the 1990s this was only to be expected. However, it did seem to suffer from a clash of styles, with Doon Mackichan's Debra seeming to exist on a different plain of reality to the rest of the group: her attempts to sensationalise and trivialise Jane's TV programmes led to some good comedy but perhaps were too extreme. So *Agony Again* was not perfect, but it was a decent enough revival and one that may have found its feet had it been given a further series in which to develop.

Ain't Misbehavin'

UK · BBC · SITCOM

12 × 30 mins · colour

Series One (6) 20 Mar–24 Apr 1994 · BBC1 Sun 8.20pm

Series Two (6) 10 Jan–14 Feb 1995 · BBC1 Tue 8.30pm

MAIN CAST

Clive Quigley	Peter Davison
Sonia Drysdale	Nicola Pagett
Melissa Quigley	Lesley Manville (series 1);
	Karen Drury (series 2)
Dave Drysdale	John Duttine
Ramona Whales	Polly Hemingway
Lester Whales	Barry Stanton (series 2)
Chuck Purvis	Ian McNeice (series 1);
	Paul Brooke (series 2)

CREDITS

writer Roy Clarke · *directors* Tony Dow (6), John Kilby (6) · *executive producer* James Gilbert · *producer* Tony Dow

A complicated Roy Clarke comedy about adultery. Clive Quigley thinks he is happily married to Melissa but a visit from Sonia Drysdale shows how wrong he is. Sonia informs him that her husband Dave is engaged in an affair with his wife Melissa. At first Clive refuses to believe Sonia but he is convinced when they follow the straying couple to a secret rendezvous. Clive is devastated, and even contemplates suicide, but the more sanguine Sonia talks him into joining her in a campaign to split up the affair. It transpires that actual adultery hasn't taken place yet, mostly owing to the procrastination of the faintly frigid Melissa, but by the end of the first series the act is committed and, surprisingly, Melissa turns into a rampant sex kitten. Other characters in this passion play are Chuck Purvis, the private detective Clive and Sonia hire, and Lester and Ramona Whales – Ramona is Clive's secretary, and her jealous husband Lester, an exterminator, is convinced that his wife is having an affair with Clive, and takes to following him around.

This was a somewhat stilted effort from the usually sure-footed Clarke, although he did manage to stretch the thin premise into two series. The first was not well received but did enjoy some notoriety when one of the scenes, showing Clive attempting to hang himself from a light fitting, was condemned for being irresponsible. It was probably Clarke's track record that persuaded the BBC to go for a second run, but *Ain't Misbehavin'* failed to live up to his high standards.

The series was unrelated to a three-part comedy-drama of the same title, screened by ITV from 28 July 1997, starring Robson Green and Jerome Flynn.

The Airbase

UK · BBC · SITCOM

6 × 25 mins · b/w

24 Mar–28 Apr 1965 · BBC2 Wed 8pm

MAIN CAST

Sqdn-Ldr Terence Elgin Heatherton · · · · · · ·
· David Kelsey
Staff Sgt George Tillman Miller · · · David Healy
Airman Randy Ricks · · · · · · · Eddie Matthews
Col Hoggart · · · · · · · · · · · · · · · Alan Gifford

CREDITS

writer John Briley · producer Douglas Moodie

A service sitcom written by the British-based American John Briley, drawn from his own experiences as a serviceman stationed in England. The series followed the would-be high-flying Squadron-Leader Heatherton who, although the commanding officer at RAF Wittlethorpe, more often than not found his time taken up by acting as liaison between his US charges and the local community.

David Kelsey was the 'typically British' actor chosen to play Heatherton: he and Briley had previously worked together in a stage revue, *Seven Bob A Buck*, which was televised as *See America First, Or How To Survive As An American Tourist In London* (BBC2, 28 November 1964). This explored similar cross-cultural themes to those in *The Airbase* and also featured David Healy and Eddie Matthews in the cast.

Al Read Says What A Life!

UK · BBC · STANDUP

6 × 30 mins · b/w

6 April–11 May 1966 · BBC1 Wed 7.30pm

MAIN CAST

Al Read
Len Lowe

CREDITS

director William G Stewart · producer Albert Stevenson

Popular on BBC radio since 1951, Al Read – Salford's comic chronicler of working-class Lancashire life – returned his famous 'right monkey' catchphrase to TV in this 1966 series, following an ITV run in 1963 with *Life And Al Read*. The surrounding publicity pointed out that there was no script to speak of, with Al being left to his own devices in six shows that were rounded off by weekly MOR pop acts such as Anita Harris, the Seekers and Herman's Hermits.

See also *It's All In Life*.

The Alan King Show   BBC

UK · BBC · STANDUP

1 × 45 mins · b/w

13 Sep 1959 · Sun 7.30pm

MAIN CAST

Alan King

CREDITS

writer Alan King · producer Ernest Maxin

The cigar-smoking US comedian Alan King (born in Brooklyn on 26 December 1927) headlined this one-off show for the BBC. King was a master of that typical American comedy style: topical observational monologue. His world-weary and caustic wit differed vastly from the music-hall patter dominated British TV standup comedy of the time, and it gave him great, if temporary, popularity in the UK.

See also the following entry.

The Alan King Show   ITV

UK · ITV (ATV) · STANDUP

3 editions (2 × 60 mins · 1 × 50 mins) · b/w

6 June 1959 · Sat 7.55pm (60 mins)
8 Apr 1961 · Sat 7.40pm (50 mins)
4 Aug 1963 · Sun 8.25pm (60 mins)

MAIN CAST

Alan King

CREDITS

writer Alan King · producers Alan Tarrant (show 1), Josephine Douglas (show 2), Albert Locke (show 3)

Three single shows spotlighting the US comedian, with guests.

See previous entry for further information.

Alan Young

UK · ITV (JACK HYLTON TV PRODUCTIONS FOR ASSOCIATED-REDIFFUSION) · STANDUP

6 editions (3 × 60 mins · 2 × 45 mins · 1 × 30 mins) · b/w

28 Aug–6 Nov 1958 · fortnightly Thu 9pm

MAIN CAST

Alan Young
Eleanor Drew

CREDITS

directors Michael Westmore (4), Douglas Hurn (2)

Following his exposure in Granada's *Personal Appearance* series, the British-born Canadian light-comedy actor Alan Young was showcased by impresario Jack Hylton in six fortnightly programmes of humour and music. Young, who had been born Angus Young in Northumberland in 1919, would later become famous as the straight-man to talking horse *Mister Ed*, and by the 1950s he was already a major comedy star of American radio, cast as a shy grocery store employee in *The Alan Young Show*, on air 1944–49.

In these British TV appearances Young was supported by the British comedian Eleanor Drew.

Alas Smith And Jones

see Smith and Jones

Albert!

see *Dear Mother ... Love Albert*

Albert And Victoria

UK · ITV (YORKSHIRE) · SITCOM

13 episodes (12 × 30 mins · 1 × short special) · colour

Series One (6 × 30 mins) 13 June–18 July 1970 · Sat 6.45pm

Short special · part of *All-Star Comedy Carnival* 25 Dec 1970 · Fri 6pm

Series Two (6 × 30 mins) 14 Aug–17 Sep 1971 · mostly Sat 5.40pm

MAIN CAST

Albert Hackett · · · · · · · · · · · · · Alfred Marks
Victoria Hackett · · · · Zena Walker (series 1);
· · · · Barbara Murray (first 2 eps of series 2);
· · · Frances Bennett (last 4 eps of series 2)
Emma Hackett · · · Kika Markham (series 1);
· · · · · · · · · · · · · · · · Gay Hamilton (series 2)
Lydia Hackett · · · · · · · · · · · Petra Markham
George Hackett · · · · · · · · · · · · · · John Alkin
Maud · · · · · · · · · · Helen Cotterill (series 1);
· · · · · · · · · · · · · · · · · · Julia Sutton (series 2)

CREDITS

writer Reuben Ship · directors/producers Quentin Lawrence (7), John Nelson Burton (4), David Mallet (2)

The names Albert and Victoria give the clue: this series was set in the late 19th-century, when men were men, women knew their place and children were supposed to be seen but not heard. It starred the venerable Alfred Marks as Albert Hackett, a man with nine children and a wife (Victoria) to support, espousing middle-class views as bold as his moustache and used to getting the last word.

There was real-life drama during the shooting of the second series when Barbara Murray (familiar to viewers of the 1965–69 ITV drama *The Power Game*), who had taken over the role of Victoria from Zena Walker, miscarried a baby. Frances Bennett (best known as Gussie in the 1962–65 BBC soap *Compact*) was drafted in to complete the remaining episodes.

The Alberts' Channel Too

UK · BBC · SKETCH

1 × 30 mins · b/w

21 Apr 1964 · BBC2 Tue 7.30pm

MAIN CAST

The Alberts
Ivor Cutler

CREDITS

writers Denis Gifford, Tom Parkinson · producer Dennis Main Wilson

The anarchic musical-comedy conglomerate known as the Alberts (brothers Tony and Dougie Grey and the novelty robot inventor 'Professor' Bruce Lacey) were set to launch BBC2 in their own inimitable style on

20 April 1964 when a power blackout of that entire opening night caused a postponement until the next evening, the 21st. That fine eccentric Ivor Cutler, the Scots poet/painter/comic/songwriter, was on hand to provide support.

Alcock And Gander

UK · ITV (THAMES) · SITCOM

6 × 30 mins · colour

5 June–10 July 1972 · Mon 8.30pm

MAIN CAST

Marigold Alcock	Beryl Reid
Richard Gander	Richard O'Sullivan
Ernest	John Cater

CREDITS

writers Johnnie Mortimer/Brian Cooke · *director/producer* Alan Tarrant

A short-lived Mortimer and Cooke creation starring Beryl Reid, ably supported by the fast-rising comedy-actor Richard O'Sullivan. Reid played Mrs Alcock, who, assisted by Gander and old retainer Ernest, runs a number of highly dubious organisations – the Alcock Group of Companies – from a seedy two-room office in the Soho district of London.

Alexander The Greatest

UK · ITV (ATV) · SITCOM

13 × 30 mins · colour

Series One (6) 15 July–19 Aug 1971 · Thu 9pm
Series Two (7) 3 Mar–21 Apr 1972 · Fri 10.30pm

MAIN CAST

Alexander Green	Gary Warren
Joe Green	Sydney Tafler
Fay Green	Libby Morris (series 1);
	Stella Moray (series 2)
Renata Green	Adrienne Posta

OTHER APPEARANCES

Murray	Peter Birrel (series 1)
Barney	Cyril Shaps (series 1)
Archie	Vic Wise (series 1)
Sam	David Lodge (series 2)

CREDITS

creator/writer Bernard Kops · *script editor* Philip Hinchcliffe · *director/producer* Shaun O'Riordan

Sitcom about a 16-year-old self-styled rebel (played by Gary Warren, the young boy in Lionel Jeffries' 1970 movie *The Railway Children*), desperate to ditch schooling and his comfortable Jewish middle-class home life in Golders Green (London's most Jewish area), despite the remarkable efforts of his parents Joe and Fay to understand their son's delinquent desires. The writer Bernard Kops, himself Jewish, based the central character on his own son, Adam, then 14. Adrienne Posta played Alexander's sister Renata and she bagged a similar role five years later in Jack Rosenthal's marvellous TV play *Bar Mitzvah Boy* (BBC1, 14 September 1976) where she

again found herself coping with a bothersome brother rebelling against traditional Judaism.

Alexei Sayle's Stuff

UK · BBC · SKETCH/STANDUP

18 × 30 mins · colour

Series One (6) 13 Oct–17 Nov 1988 · BBC2 Thu 9pm
Series Two (6) 19 Oct–23 Nov 1989 · BBC2 Thu 9pm
Series Three (6) 3 Oct–7 Nov 1991 · BBC2 Thu 9pm

MAIN CAST

Alexei Sayle
Angus Deayton
Tony Millan
Jan Ravens (series 2 & 3)
Owen Brenman (series 2 & 3)

CREDITS

writers Alexei Sayle, Andrew Marshall/David Renwick · *director/producer* Marcus Mortimer

Alexei Sayle was born in Liverpool on 7 August 1952 to parents who were members of the Communist Party, a fact that, if it didn't exactly define his comedy, certainly gave him some unlikely material and a fascinating viewpoint. After various jobs and a spell as a freelance illustrator, Sayle joined friends touring in a Brechtian cabaret troupe. From here, in the late 1970s, he graduated to standup comedy, developing an edgy act in which, combining aggression with a surreal imagination, he produced a foul-mouthed stream-of-consciousness rant embracing bizarre topics. The act baffled his early audiences since this type of full-frontal comedy attack, while common in the USA, was virtually unheard of in Britain at the time.

Sayle's big break came when his wife saw an advertisement requesting new comedy talent for a London club that was shortly to open, and urged him to go along. At the audition he impressed the club owner, Peter Rosengard, who immediately offered him the role of compere at the new venue, to be called the Comedy Store. Sayle excelled at the job, a big sweaty man in a suit several sizes too small, verbally duffing up the crowd and coming across as the worst imaginable person to meet in a pub. Above all, Sayle was consistently funny, his brand of manic vitriol peculiarly suited to being spat out in small chunks between other acts. If anything, Sayle's problem was that he was too good, so that many of the acts he was introducing suffered by comparison. His stage impact assured him of TV exposure, although many were concerned that his cutting-edge observational material might be too extreme for the medium. But Sayle was no fool: he tailored his act accordingly, and although dispensing with some of the more colourful and graphic ideas, it worked well, and his

noisy, machine-gun-like delivery meant that his humour lost little of its raw power.

Like a new-wave comic mercenary, Sayle freelanced around the world of 'alternative' comedy, guesting in a handful of *The Comic Strip Presents …* films, co-writing and appearing in *The Young Ones* and taking a number of other acting roles, both straight and comic. He appeared in *Whoops Apocalypse* and then teamed up with that series' writers to work on his own starring show, *Alexei Sayle's Stuff*. The result was a winning combination of Pythonesque surrealism and 'alternative' comedy philosophy, honed with a satirical edge. As with all cutting-edge comedy, it occasionally fell into the realms of sheer weirdness, but this was a small price to pay for the enjoyment meted out by this fast-paced sketch show crammed with so many ideas that, like Alexei's suit, it seemed fit to burst at the seams.

Alexei Sayle's Stuff proved conclusively that Sayle's material could work on TV and that the comedian was a big enough talent to front other such series.

See also *The All New Alexei Sayle Show*.

ALF

USA · NBC (ALIEN PRODUCTIONS) · SITCOM

102 episodes (101 × 30 mins · 1 × 60 mins) · colour

US dates: 22 Sep 1986–24 Mar 1990

UK dates: 25 Apr 1987–30 Dec 1989 (39 × 30 mins · 1 × 60 mins) ITV Sat various times

MAIN CAST

Willie Tanner	Max Wright
Kate Tanner	Anne Schedeen
Lynn Tanner	Andrea Elson
Brian Tanner	Benji Gregory
The voice of ALF	Paul Fusco
Neal Tanner	J M J Bullock (1989–90)
Trevor Ochmonek	John La Motta
Raquel Ochmonek	Liz Sheridan
Jake Ochmonek	Josh Blake

CREDITS

creators Paul Fusco/Tom Patchett · *writers* various · *directors* Nick Havinga (28), Burt Brinckerhoff (15), Gary Shimokawa (12), Peter Bonerz (9), Paul Miller (8), Tom Patchett (7), Paul Fusco (6), Nancy Heydorn (5), Tony Csiki (3), Peter Baldwin (2), Rick Gough (1), Howard Storm (1), not known (5) · *executive producers* Tom Patchett, Bernie Brillstein · *producer* Paul Fusco

The Tanner family, parents and two children, are enjoying a quiet middle-class Californian life when a 229-year-old – but young with it – furry creature from outer space crash-lands its spaceship through the roof of their garage, drawn there by some equally wayward frequencies emitted from Willie Tanner's short-wave radio set. The alien's craft is too damaged to work again, and, besides, home – the planet Melmac – has blown up since his departure, so there's no point in leaving anyway. The Tanners are quickly won over by the alien's charms: they nickname him ALF (an acronym of Alien Life Form) and decide not to turn him in to the authorities. Rather, they keep him as a family pet (as you do, in sitcoms).

ALF gets on famously with all the Tanner family, especially children Lynn and Brian. The only creature not to welcome ALF's arrival is Lucky, the family cat: in common with all Melmacians, ALF likes to eat cats. To keep his presence a secret, ALF is instructed to dive under the kitchen table whenever the front-door bell sounds – the visitors usually being the Ochmonek family who live next door but remain unaware of ALF's presence. ALF loves food – 'everything with everything on it' – and one of his most-used phrases is 'Are you going to finish that sandwich?'. Standing 38 inches tall and looking like a cross between Miss Piggy and an aardvark, ALF is always watching television and regurgitating the information he gleans. (This isn't all he regurgitates: he has the manners of … well, an animal.) He has four fingers and, having learned the lingo from TV, likes to hold out his hand and demand, 'Gimme four'. Personality-wise, he's something of a cross between ET and Jackie Mason, exercising a sharp sense of humour and speaking with a gravel voice that actually belonged to the show's co-creator, occasional writer, director and puppeteer Paul Fusco. (When ALF was immobile a puppet was used; when he moved an actor was working inside a furry costume.) The final episode of *ALF* was a real tantaliser: as Alien Task Force US government agents zeroed in on him, ALF was offered a chance to escape to another planet by a pair of fellow Melmac refugees; he accepted and bade a fond farewell to the Tanners, but then all three aliens were captured by the Feds.

Networked in America in an adult time-slot, 8pm, *ALF* (sometimes written as *A.L.F.*) was a phenomenally successful sitcom, a fact not quite as daft as it would appear, for as well as entertaining children at its most simplistic level, the scripts gently satirised American culture and politics and employed a morality theme familiar to so many US series. Additional adult credence was given to *ALF* by way of the episode titles (almost every one was named after a hit rock song or lyric) and by personal furry appearances that the creature made in everything from sports programmes to quiz-shows, and trailers for his own series that featured, for example, Bea Arthur and Betty White from *The Golden Girls*, in character.

ALF character merchandising took off in a big way in the late 1980s, grossing more than $200m a year at its peak, and the sitcom spawned a Saturday-morning cartoon series,

ALF, which was a form of 'prequel', looking at the alien's life on Melmac before he ended up on Earth, screened in the USA from 12 September 1987. This in turn led to a further animated production, *ALF Tales*, aired from 16 September 1989. Paul Fusco voiced the character in both series.

Apart from re-runs, the story went quiet in the 1990s, but a new production, in the shape of a 92-minute movie (*Project: ALF*), a joint venture between German and US producers, was released theatrically in Germany in 1996 (screened on TV in the USA and UK), written by Paul Fusco and Tom Patchett and directed by Dick Lowry. Miguel Ferrer, Martin Sheen and Jensen Daggett starred, and Fusco once more supplied the voice of ALF.

Alfred Marks Time

UK · ITV (ASSOCIATED-REDIFFUSION, *JACK HYLTON PRODUCTIONS FOR ASSOCIATED-REDIFFUSION) · SKETCH

37 editions (17×60 mins · 12×30 mins · 5×55 mins · 3×45 mins) · b/w

Series One (7×60 mins) 16 Feb–2 Aug 1956 · Thu every four weeks · mostly 8pm

*Series Two (7×60 mins · 1×45 mins · 1×30 mins) 11 Oct 1956–20 June 1957 · Thu every four weeks · mostly 9pm

*Series Three (3×60 mins · 2×45 mins · 5×30 mins) 12 Sep 1957–22 May 1958 · Thu every four weeks · around 9pm

*Series Four (6×30 mins) 2 Feb–27 Apr 1959 · Mon mostly fortnightly · mostly 9.30pm

Special (55 mins) 29 June 1960 · Wed 8.30pm

Special (55 mins) 10 Aug 1960 · Wed 8.30pm

Special (55 mins) 14 Dec 1960 · Wed 8.30pm

Special (55 mins) 15 Feb 1961 · Wed 8.30pm

Special (55 mins) 10 May 1961 · Wed 8pm

MAIN CAST
Alfred Marks
Paddie O'Neil
Ronald Brittain

CREDITS
writers Dick Vosburgh, Brad Ashton, Barry Pevan · *directors* Douglas Hurn (1956–59), Michael Westmore, Peter Croft, James Sutherland (1960–61)

The former resident comic at the ('we never close') Windmill Theatre in London, Alfred Marks was given his own series soon after ITV started up – typically for the time, it ran with regular irregularity.

Some music was included in *Alfred Marks Time* but the shows chiefly comprised sketches, including send-ups of popular movies and TV programmes. These were effected within the framework of a fictitious TV station, Channel 24, perhaps the most memorable parody being of the ITV courtroom drama *Boyd QC* in which Dulcie Gray (the actress wife of Michael Denison, who played Boyd) came along to help out. Marks' own wife, Paddie O'Neil, appeared alongside her husband, and each programme

(until the later editions) was introduced, in best barking fashion, by the uniformed former Regimental Sergeant-Major Ronald Brittain.

Three of the series were produced for ITV by the impresario Jack Hylton, and some of these were tele-recorded on Marks' home patch: the East End of London, on stage at the Hackney Empire. Hylton's involvement also saw writers Dick Vosburgh and Brad Ashton adapting sketches originally used in the USA by Sid Caesar, to which he had bought the UK rights. The 37 programmes also featured occasional guest appearances, by the likes of Spike Milligan, Sydney Tafler, Max Wall, Irene Handl and other leading comic contemporaries.

See also *Don't Look Now*.

Alfresco

UK · ITV (GRANADA) · SKETCH

13×30 mins · colour

Series One (7) 1 May–12 June 1983 · Sun around 10pm

Series Two (6) 28 Apr–2 June 1984 · Sat mostly 11pm

MAIN CAST
Robbie Coltrane
Ben Elton
Stephen Fry
Hugh Laurie
Siobhan Redmond
Emma Thompson

CREDITS
main writer Ben Elton · *additional material* Stephen Fry/Hugh Laurie, Paul Shearer, Nick Symons, Emma Thompson · *director* Stuart Orme · *executive producer* Steve Morrison · *producers* Sandy Ross (series 1), John G Temple (series 2)

Hoping to mount ITV's answer to *Monty Python* and, latterly, *Not The Nine O'Clock News*, Granada assembled some of the best, fresh young talent around and built two series which, despite the soon-to-be-stellar names, failed to amount to a great deal.

Alfresco came about after Granada approached Rik Mayall – shortly to be starring in *The Young Ones* – to front a series. Having agreed, on the proviso that Granada engage Ben Elton to write the scripts, Mayall then withdrew. In the meantime, looking to make a comedy team comprising four men and two women, Granada producer Sandy Ross went talent-spotting at the Edinburgh Festival Fringe, returning with Siobhan Redmond and four members of the 1981 Cambridge Footlights revue: Stephen Fry, Hugh Laurie, Paul Shearer and Emma Thompson. With Ben Elton making up the sextet, a mini-series of three resulting programmes, made under the title *There's Nothing To Worry About!*, was screened locally by Granada, in the North-West only, beginning on 4 June 1982. A full series, *Alfresco*, followed a year later, with Robbie Coltrane replacing Paul Shearer.

Much of *Alfresco*, as the title suggests, was shot outside the confines of the TV studio, and it was the first British comedy series to be taped using the lightweight ENG (Electronic News Gathering) equipment utilised for news bulletins. The programmes were largely hit-and-miss but everyone seems to have profited from the experience, not least Ben Elton who, to use his own words, learned 'not to be cocksure and young and think I was always right'.

See also *The Crystal Cube*.

Alice

USA · CBS (WARNER BROS) · SITCOM

202 × 30 mins · colour

US dates: 31 Aug 1976–19 Mar 1985

UK dates: 27 Aug 1984–8 Oct 1986 (188 episodes) C4 weekdays mostly 5pm

MAIN CAST

Alice Hyatt · · · · · · · · · · · · · · · · · Linda Lavin
Mel Sharples · · · · · · · · · · · · · · Vic Tayback
Vera Louise Gorman · · · · · · · · Beth Howland
Flo (Florence Jean) Castleberry · · · · · · · · · · ·
· · · · · · · · · · · · · · · · Polly Holliday (1976–80)
Tommy Hyatt · · · · · · · · · · Alfred Lutter (pilot);
· · · · · · · · · · · · · · · · · Phillip McKeon (series)
Jolene Hunnicutt · · Celia Weston (1981–85)
Belle DuPree · · · · · · · Diane Ladd (1980–81)
Carrie Sharples · · · · Martha Raye (1982–84)
Elliot Novak · · · · · · Charles Levin (1983–85)
Henry Beesmyer · · Marvin Kaplan (1977–85)
Nicholas Stone · · Michael Durrell (1984–85)
Andy · · · · · · · · · · · Pat Cranshaw (1976–78)

CREDITS

creator Robert Getchell · writers various · directors various · executive producers David Susskind, William D'Angelo, Ray S Allen, Harvey Bullock, Thomas Kuhn, Chris Hayward · producers Bruce Johnson, Madelyn Davis, Bob Carroll Jr, Noam Pitlik

Alice was a successful US sitcom about a 35-year-old widow, Alice Hyatt, who, following the death of her lorry-driver husband, moves out west from New Jersey to California but breaks down en route, just outside Phoenix, Arizona. Here she takes a 'temporary' (but seemingly permanent) job as a pink-uniformed waitress at a roadside restaurant, Mel's Diner. Alice is an aspiring singer, working to keep the wolf from the door, raise her son Tommy (a precocious 12-year-old who scarcely develops much of a personality in the series) and save enough dough to shoot for stardom. Along the way, her character became a role model for millions of blue-collar American women workers, much as Mary Richards (in **The Mary Tyler Moore Show**) had for American white-collar women.

As with so many fine US sitcoms, much of the comedy spawned from the immediate ensemble, in particular Alice's two waitress-

ing colleagues, Flo – the feisty veteran whose expression 'well kiss mah grits!' became a catchphrase throughout America, and yet hid a warm heart – and Vera, who was meek but also scatterbrained. Also worth his salt was Mel Sharples himself, the crusty character who owned the joint, gave it his name, cooked the mostly inadequate food and barked at his waitresses but who, when push came to shove, was also their protector. The diner too was a major player in that customers came and went and brought with them a never ending supply of new angles. There was a cast of regular eaters, most notably Henry Beesmyer, a telephone-line repair man who was always complaining.

The series was loosely based on the 1974 movie *Alice Doesn't Live Here Anymore*, directed by Martin Scorsese, in which the widow woman set out for Monterey and stopped to work at a diner. (It was far from being a comedy film.) Initially at least, the only actor to reprise his movie role in the TV series was Vic Tayback (Mel); in 1980, though, Diane Ladd (who had appeared in the film as Flo) joined the cast as Belle. As it turned out, the Flo character had already left the series, spun-off into a CBS sitcom all her own (*Flo*, 1980–81, never screened on British TV) in which she ran a café in Houston.

In pushing beyond 200 episodes, *Alice* undoubtedly grew weaker as the years passed. Belle, who had replaced Flo, also left and was replaced by Jolene, while another new cast member was Mel's mother, Carrie, whose awesome personality soon came to dominate the diner. As the production wound to a close, Vera got married, Alice gained a boyfriend and, in the final episode, Mel sold the diner and awarded each of his waitresses a $5000 bonus – Alice used hers to get to Nashville and trail the rocky road to stardom.

Surprisingly, considering it was such a hit Stateside, *Alice* did not show in Britain until 1984, some eight years after it had been launched, at which time C4 'stripped' the show – that is, it screened episodes daily – on weekday afternoons, airing 188 episodes in a little over two years.

All-American Girl

USA · ABC (SANDOLLAR TELEVISION/HEARTFELT PRODUCTIONS/TOUCHSTONE TELEVISION) · SITCOM

19 × 30 mins · colour

US dates: 14 Sep 1994–15 Mar 1995

UK dates: 22 Feb–28 June 1995 (19 episodes) C4 Wed 6pm

MAIN CAST

Margaret Kim · · · · · · · · · · · · · Margaret Cho
Katherine Kim · · · · · · · · · · · · · · · · Jodi Long
Benny Kim · · · · · · · · · · · · · · Clyde Kusatsu
Grandma · · · · · · · · · · · · · · · · · · · Amy Hill
Ruthie · · · · · · · · · · · · · · · · Maddie Corman
Gloria · Judy Gold
Eric Kim · J B Quon
Stuart Kim · · · · · · · · · · · · · · · · · · B D Wong

CREDITS

creator/main writer Gary Jacobs · other writers various · directors various · executive producers Gary Jacobs, Sandy Gallin, Gail Berman, Stuart Sheslow · producer Bruce Johnson

Asian-American standup star Margaret Cho made her mark with an act that comedically detailed the conflict of being both Korean and American. The young comedian proved particularly popular with college audiences and with other Asian-Americans who could identify with her frustrations and 'foot-in-each-camp' dilemmas. She often sniped about the lack of Asians on US TV, quipping that there were 'more extra-terrestrials than Asians' on the box. So it was fitting justice that she should be given her own show, *All-American Girl*, based on the standup act and featuring more Asians than Caucasians in its cast.

Cho was cast as Margaret Kim, a westernised Korean constantly at odds with a traditionalist mother, Katherine, who is determined that her daughter should respect the ways and customs of the old country. Margaret is equally determined to live her own life and seems to prefer being around her American friends. The bitterest bone of contention is Margaret's attraction to white American boys, which drives Katherine to distraction. Desperately, she tries to matchmake Margaret with suitable Korean boys, but to no avail. At least her brother Stuart has grown up to be a model son, a reverent young man studying to be a cardiologist. Margaret's father refuses to be drawn either way on the argument, although the matriarch of the family, Grandma, comes down firmly on her grand-daughter's side, encouraging her to follow her instincts. This sanctioning of Margaret's activities is diminished somewhat, however, by the fact that Grandma is barking mad.

All-American Girl was quietly groundbreaking in its theme but oddly relied on hackneyed Asian stereotypes for most of its jokes. Although patently not as funny as Cho's standup act, it was at least a commendable attempt to say something pertinent within the genre. Cho handled the acting chores well enough and other cast members provided decent support, but they could not rescue the show from its central weaknesses: it was trying too hard to be liked and so suffered from a lack of edge; the aforementioned stereotyping for easy laughs; and the trouble it had in spinning enough entertaining variations from its main theme to warrant a second season. One episode was a real talking point, however: 'Pulp Sitcom', which featured a guest appearance by Quentin Tarantino.

Note. The final episode of *All-American Girl*, shot on film rather than tape, was a pilot for a proposed but unrealised follow-up series, *The Young Americans*. In this story Margaret moved away from home and into an apartment shared with three men (Phil, Jimmy and Spencer).

All At No 20

UK · ITV (THAMES) · SITCOM

12 × 30 mins · colour

Series One (6) 10 Feb–17 Mar 1986 · Mon 8pm

Series Two (6) 27 Oct–1 Dec 1987 · Tue 8pm

MAIN CAST

Sheila Haddon	Maureen Lipman
Monica Haddon	Lisa Jacobs
Henry	Martin Clunes
Richard Beamish	Gary Waldhorn (series 1)
Carol	Gabrielle Glaister (series 1)
Chris	Gregory Doran (series 1)
Hamish	David Bannerman (series 1)
Candy	Carol Hawkins (series 2)
Frankie	Desmond McNamara (series 2)

CREDITS

creator Richard Ommanney · *writers* Richard Ommanney (series 1), Ian Davidson/Peter Vincent (4 episodes in series 2), Alex Shearer (2 episodes in series 2) · *directors/producers* Peter Frazer-Jones (series 1), Mark Stuart (series 2)

Old Chinese sitcom proverb say 'stick plenty wacky characters in room and sparks fly'. This was probably the intention here, but the sparks failed to light any great fires, despite the starring presence of Maureen Lipman in her first comedy series since *Agony*.

Lipman played Sheila Haddon, whose husband – as the first series begins – has died 18 months earlier without insurance cover of any kind. Left not only to grieve but to pay off the whacking mortgage on their house (situated, to explain the title, at number 20), she decides to take in lodgers, preferably younger ones because the house's limited facilities do not provide for separated dwelling. She would rather do this than doff the cap and go asking for help, or sell up, because, aged in her early forties, Sheila is fiercely independent. Her daughter Monica, a 20-year-old art college student, is charged with the job of finding likely lodgers, and she brings in all manner of people, like her art-student friend Carol, Hamish the Scotsman, Henry the doctor, vain Chris, who has just arrived in London and is looking for a place to stay, Candy, Frankie and others. Soon Sheila has a full house, but the odds, inevitably, are now stacked against her enjoying a quiet life. To ward off the bank manager Sheila also tries to get part-time jobs, with limited success, working as a PA and then typing book manuscripts. Plus, she is troubled by the increasing attentions of a blazer-and-cravat man, Richard Beamish, an old friend of her and her late husband's, who fancies his

chances with the widow to the point where he proposes marriage. Sheila declines, exit Beamish, few laugh.

All Change

UK · ITV (CHILDSPLAY PRODUCTIONS FOR YORKSHIRE) · CHILDREN'S SITCOM

12 × 30 mins · colour

Series One (6) 15 Nov–20 Dec 1989 · Wed 4.40pm

Series Two (6) 5 Feb–12 Mar 1991 · Tue mostly 4.30pm

MAIN CAST

Uncle Bob	Frankie Howerd
Henry Herewith	Roger Milner
Fabia London	Maggie Steed
Julian London	William McGillivray
Charles London	David Quilter
Polly London	Lisa Butler
Brian Oldfield	Tony Haygarth (series 1);
	Bobby Knutt (series 2)
Maggie Oldfield	Pam Ferris
Vicky Oldfield	Donna Durkin
Nathan Oldfield	Robert Ellis
Hornbeam	Andrew Normington
Aunt Fanny	Peggy Mount (series 2)

CREDITS

writers John Stevenson (6), Tony McHale (3), Morwenna Banks/Chris England (1), Chris England (1), Chris England/Paul Simpkin (1) · *directors* Graham Dixon (series 1), Garth Tucker (series 2) · *producers* Peter Tabern/Greg Brenman (series 1), Greg Brenman (series 2)

A children's sitcom starring Frankie Howerd – cast here, in ghostly presence, as rich Uncle Bob, who has died and offered a million-pound inheritance to two ghastly families – with conditions attached. To the dual sets of relatives Uncle Bob had been a virtually forgotten figure, but their greed is such that they rise to the bait and accept the challenge he has set for them: that they swap places. Hitherto, the swanky, wealthy Londons have lived the life of Riley, appropriately enough, in England's capital city, while the downtrodden Oldfields have been forced to muck in and operate a greasy-spoon café oop north. Exercising a lust for money, and a mutual loathing, the families duly exchange lifestyles and the fun begins.

In addition to Frankie Howerd – appearing here in his last scripted TV series – *All Change* delivered a fine cast, including Roger Milner, Maggie Steed, Liz Smith, Tony Haygarth, Pam Ferris, and, appearing in the second series as Uncle Bob's sister, Peggy Mount.

Note. Morwenna Banks and Chris England, who contributed to the writing of *All Change*, had previously scripted a pair of humorous children's story series for ITV, *Revolting Animals* (from 26 February 1988) and *Jellyneck* (from 14 June 1989).

All Cricket And Wellies

see *And There's More*

All Gas And Gaiters

UK · BBC · SITCOM

34 episodes (33 × 30 mins · 1 × short special) · 14 × b/w · 20 × colour

Pilot (b/w) *The Bishop Rides Again* 17 May 1966 · BBC1 Tue 7.30pm

Series One (6 × b/w) 31 Jan–7 Mar 1967 · BBC1 Tue 7.30pm

Series Two (6 × b/w) 24 Nov–29 Dec 1967 · BBC1 Fri 8.20pm

Short special (b/w) *Oh Brother!* and *All Gas And Gaiters* combination as part of *Christmas Night With The Stars* 25 Dec 1968 · BBC1 Wed 6.40pm

*Series Three (7 × colour) 8 Jan–19 Feb 1969 · BBC1 Wed 7.30pm

Series Four (7 × colour) 15 Apr–27 May 1970 · BBC1 Wed 7.30pm

Series Five (6 × colour) 13 May–17 June 1971 · BBC1 Thu mostly 7.45pm

MAIN CAST

The Archdeacon	Robertson Hare
The Bishop	William Mervyn
Rev Mervyn Noote	Derek Nimmo
The Dean	John Barron (pilot, series 1 & 4);
	Ernest Clark (special, series 2 & 3)

OTHER APPEARANCES

Mrs Pugh-Critchley	Joan Sanderson

CREDITS

writers Pauline Devaney/Edwin Apps, David Climie/Austin Steele (co-writers of the special) · *producers* Stuart Allen (pilot, series 1 & 2), John Howard Davies (special, series 3–5), Robin Nash (1 episode)

Drawing gentle fun from the church, *All Gas And Gaiters* is a fondly remembered sitcom centred on the ecclesiastical rivalries at St Oggs, a 13th-century cathedral. The series was one of many to spring from the BBC's *Comedy Playhouse* initiative, which gave new writers a peak-time slot in which to try out. This idea, which began life under the title *The Bishop Rides Again*, proved particularly durable, with 33 half-hours exploring its simple theme. Husband-and-wife writing team Devaney and Apps were handsomely served by a fine cast and the show elevated Derek Nimmo to the top rank of British comic character actors, at the same time giving him a religious connection in the public's mind that he cheerfully explored for many years. He was cast here as Reverend Mervyn Noote, a pleasing but accident-prone naïf who causes all manner of problems for the Bishop, the ageing Archdeacon and the somewhat severe Dean.

During the run of *All Gas And Gaiters*, Nimmo moonlighted as novice monk Brother Dominic in *Oh Brother!* and the two shows combined for a segment of the BBC's 1968 *Christmas Night With The Stars*. A radio version of *All Gas And Gaiters* aired for 33 episodes (5 January 1971–4 December 1972, BBC Radio 4) featuring the main TV cast but with Derek Nimmo leaving after the first series of 13 to be replaced by Jonathan Cecil.

Notes. Writers Devaney and Apps used the pseudonym John Wraith for the *Comedy Playhouse* pilot.

*Although made in colour, and repeated so, the third series originally aired in monochrome on the pre-colour BBC1.

See also *Oh Brother!* and *Oh Father!*

All In Good Faith

UK · ITV (THAMES) · SITCOM

19 episodes (18 × 30 mins · 1 × short special) · colour

Series One (6) 30 Dec 1985–3 Feb 1986 · Mon 8pm

Series Two (6) 26 Feb–2 Apr 1987 · Thu 8.30pm

Series Three (6) 11 Apr–23 May 1988 · Mon 8pm

Short special · part of *ITV Telethon '88* 30 May 1988 · Mon afternoon

MAIN CAST

Rev Philip Lambe · · · · · · · · · · Richard Briers
Emma Lambe · · · · · · · · · · · · Barbara Ferris
· (series 1 & 2);
· · · · · · · · · · · · · · · Susan Jameson (series 3)
Miranda Lambe · · · Lydia Smith (series 1 & 2)
Peter Lambe · · · · · · · · · · · James Campbell
· (series 1 & 2)
Alec Dugdale · · · · · · · · · · Nigel Humphreys
· (series 1 & 2)
Major Andrews · · · James Cossins (series 1)
Wilf · · · · · · · · · · · Robert Bridges (series 1)
Desmond Frank · · · · · · · · Frank Middlemass
· (series 2 & 3)
Oscar Randolph · · · · T P McKenna (series 2);
· · · · · · · · · · · · · · John Woodvine (series 3)

CREDITS

writer John Kane · directors/producers John Howard Davies (series 1 & 2), Peter Frazer-Jones (series 3)

Philip Lambe, a vicar's son who has himself taken up the cloth, reaches middle-age and goes through a sort of male menopause, losing confidence to such an extent that he feels a change of horizon is necessary. Leaving behind his wealthy parishioners in rural Oxfordshire, and listening to his bishop's recommendation, Lambe opts for a move to a challenging urban area: the bustling, tough (fictitious) Midlands city of Edendale. With a naïve drive to 'get things done', Lambe tackles his new flock's problems with determination, though they're often unfamiliar to him: having to exorcise spirits and finding homeless people on his doorstep looking for a place to stay. The move also comes as quite a shock to Philip's wife Emma and their two children, Miranda (16 when the series began) and Peter (12).

A disappointing first ITV sitcom for Richard Briers, following a number of successes with the BBC. Writer John Kane,

who created the series especially for the star, appeared in a couple of the episodes.

All In The Family

USA · CBS (TANDEM PRODUCTIONS) · SITCOM

202 episodes (196 × 30 mins · 5 × 60 mins · 1 × 90 mins) · colour

US dates: 12 Jan 1971–8 Apr 1979

UK dates: 8 July 1971–13 June 1975 (41 × 30 mins) BBC2 Thu 8.50pm then Sat around 11.30pm then Thu 9pm

MAIN CAST

Archie Bunker · · · · · · · · · · Carroll O'Connor
Edith Bunker · · · · · · · · · · · Jean Stapleton
Michael Stivic · · · · · · · · · · · · · Rob Reiner
Gloria Bunker Stivic · · · · · · · Sally Struthers
Louise Jefferson · · · · · · · · · Isabel Sanford
· (1971–75)
Lionel Jefferson · · · · Mike Evans (1971–75)
Henry Jefferson · · · · Mel Stewart (1971–73)
George Jefferson · · · · · · · Sherman Hemsley
· (1973–75)
Stephanie Mills · · · · · · · · Danielle Brisebois
· (1978–79)
Barney Hefner · · · · · Allan Melvin (1973–79)

CREDITS

creator Johnny Speight · writers Norman Lear, Michael Ross/Bernie West, Don Nicholl, Burt Styler, Susan Harris, Philip Mishkin, Lee Kalcheim, Rob Reiner, Austin Kalish/Irma Kalish, Lou Derman, Milt Josefsberg, Mel Tolkin, Larry Rhine, William Davenport, Douglas Arango, Bob Weiskopf, Phil Sharp, Bob Schiller, Patt Shea/Harriet Weiss and others · directors Paul Bogart, John Rich, Bob LaHendro, H Wesley Kenney and others · executive producers Norman Lear, Bud Yorkin, Mort Lachman · producer Milt Josefsberg

A landmark US sitcom based on the equally groundbreaking British series *Till Death Us Do Part*. For Americans, *All In The Family* re-invented the family-style sitcom of the 1950s, imbuing it with the hitherto unacknowledged vein of bigotry that still festered inside many middle-aged, patriotic family men. It also seemingly single-handedly rescued the sitcom genre from the 1960s excesses of inanity (*Gilligan's Island*), ruralism (*Green Acres*) and fantasy (*I Dream Of Jeannie*), to pioneer a new age of social realism for US television comedy.

The series' producer, Norman Lear, first became aware of *Till Death Us Do Part* early in 1968, while he was re-editing the feature film *The Night They Raided Minskys*. The short reports he read about the British series alerted him that something very interesting was happening across the Atlantic and he instantly started weighing up the possibilities of creating an American version. Lear obtained the rights and began creating his version which was initially titled *Those Were The Days*. Lear was already way down the line, creatively, when he finally got to see an episode of *Till Death Us Do Part*, and he found it even more abrasive than he had envisaged. To make the series work in

the USA, he realised, he would have to soften the tone and move away from the blueprint of the Garnetts, building a new family that he based loosely on his own.

Lear's initial choice for the lead role was Mickey Rooney, but Rooney had reservations about the character and declined. Figuring that ABC, as the smallest of the three major networks, would be more willing to take a risk on such a difficult show, Lear approached them and raised the money to make a pilot. Early in 1969 they shot an experimental episode of *Those Were The Days*, with Carroll O'Connor and Jean Stapleton as Archie and Edith Justice, and their children played by Tim McIntire and Kelly Jean Peters. It didn't air: ABC were unhappy and asked for a re-think. A second *Those Were The Days* pilot was shot a few months later, with the family name changed to Bunker and the kids played by Chip Oliver and Candy Azzara. Again, it was not screened, and with ABC experiencing mixed feelings about the merits of the show they decided to release their option, possibly sensing that the subject matter was too volatile. Enter CBS.

Unbeknown to Lear, CBS had already tried to option an adaptation of *Till Death Us Do Part*, having also sensed the potential for such a groundbreaking series and with an eye towards the sort of audience to which their rural comedies just weren't appealing. They had envisaged the sitcom as a showcase for Jackie Gleason, who had previously portrayed the nearest character American TV had ever got to an Alf Garnett: Ralph Kramden in **The Honeymooners**. So CBS expressed an interest in Lear's project and invited him to make a third pilot, this time titled *All In The Family*. Carroll O'Connor and Jean Stapleton were retained but their daughter and son-in-law were now played by Rob Reiner (son of Carl Reiner, creator of **The Dick Van Dyke Show**) and Sally Struthers. This time the show was deemed a runner and 13 episodes were ordered. When the show went out CBS executives and Lear held their breaths, waiting for the storms of protest – but scarcely any came through. It transpired that few people had been watching and it wasn't until months later, following a sketch that the cast performed at the annual Emmy Awards, that the storm began.

Archie was a bigoted loudmouth. His squeaky-voiced wife Edith was (initially at least) cowered by her loutish hubby though she loved him nonetheless. Their daughter Sally was bright and personable but her liberal husband, Michael, represented all that Archie hated, and the scabrous arguments between the two formed the central conflict from which the comedy flowed. It was noisy, harsh, rude, crude and unlike anything aired before on a US TV network. Once it gained an audience, the howls of protest echoed those visited on its British antecedent. Brilliant writing and first-class performances meant that the show had as many supporters as detractors and, if the ratings were anything to go by, both camps were watching it in numbers – by its second season *All In The Family* was established in the number-one slot in the Nielsen ratings. It remained there for five years, but it was never an easy success for Lear because he not only had to respond constantly to his critics, but also to deal with creative conflicts within the production crew, most especially in clashes with star Carroll O'Connor.

Despite the differences between the Bunkers and the Garnetts, many of *Till Death*'s plot lines suited the US show, and creator Johnny Speight made a considerable sum of money from the show's American-isation. But the US version, perhaps because of the sheer number of its team-written episodes, 202, extended its parameters far beyond the UK model to explore all kinds of taboo areas with varying degrees of success. Perhaps the most ambitious and difficult show was 'Edith's 50th Birthday', in which Edith became the victim of an attempted rape, while next door her family and friends awaited her at a surprise party. The episode was unsettling and not altogether successful, but it shows how committed the creative team were to stretching the sitcom genre to the very edge.

In the UK, *All In The Family* was perceived, somewhat snootily, as a watered-down version of a British original, partly because it was viewed in the more liberal surroundings of UK television, a liberty which programmes like *That Was The Week That Was*, *Steptoe And Son* and *Till Death Us Do Part* itself had helped create years earlier. But in the USA the series, and others that followed its line, forced a relaxation of the very strict, censorial broadcast regulations.

During its run *All In The Family* gave birth to two long-lasting spin-off series. The first was *Maude* (CBS, 1972–78), which followed the adventures of Archie's cousin Maude (played by Bea Arthur, later to become one of *The Golden Girls*). Although as outspoken as Archie, Maude was a determined liberal and proved more than a match for her corpulent cousin. The second spin-off was *The Jeffersons* (CBS, 1975–85), which related the lives of the black family who had been the Bunkers' neighbours, and thus the target of much of Archie's venom, before they settled into an uneasy peace, moving out to Manhattan and their own series. After it finished, *All In The Family* itself transmuted into *Archie Bunker's Place* and also spawned a third spin-off, *Gloria*, which depicted Archie and Edith's daughter. *Maude* then generated a British adaptation,

Nobody's Perfect, and a spin-off US series *Good Times* (CBS, 1974–79) which, along with *The Jeffersons*, inspired the British series *The Fosters*. A US children's cartoon series, *Wait Till Your Father Gets Home* (Hanna-Barbera, 1972–74, screened in Britain by ITV), was heavily inspired by the antics and relationships of the Bunkers. Finally, in 1994, even the Bunkers' house got its own show with *704 Hauser* (the Bunkers' address), in which a black family move into Archie and Edith's former residence.

The success of *All In The Family* resulted in producers Lear and Yorkin creating a comedy dynasty within US TV, and also kicked off a feeding frenzy with many other producers optioning British sitcom formats with a view to Americanising them into enormous hits.

Notes. On 16 February 1991 CBS aired *All In The Family 20th Anniversary Special* which reunited the cast for a nostalgic look back at the series.

Carroll O'Connor starred in a 90 minute TV version of George and Ira Gershwin's 1931 Broadway musical *Of Thee I Sing*, made by David L Wolper Productions for CBS (screened in the UK by BBC2 on 31 August 1972). Described as a comedy-musical, with a new script from established TV writers, it became the first musical show to win a Pulitzer Prize. A solid comedy cast filled the supporting roles, including Cloris Leachman and Ted Knight from *The Mary Tyler Moore Show*, the latter in his familiar guise as a news commentator.

The All New Alexei Sayle Show

UK · BBC · SKETCH/STANDUP

13 editions (12 × 30 mins · 1 × short special) · colour

Series One (6) 6 Jan–17 Feb 1994 · BBC2 Thu 9pm

Short special · part of Fry And Laurie Host A Christmas Night With The Stars 27 Dec 1994 · BBC2 Tue 9pm

Series Two (6) *The All New Alexei Sayle Show 2* 16 June–28 July 1995 · BBC2 Fri 9.30pm

MAIN CAST
Alexei Sayle
John Sparkes
Jean Marsh (series 1)
Peter O'Brien (series 1)
Peter Capaldi (series 2)
Jenny Agutter (series 2)
Alfred Marks (series 2)
Arabella Weir (series 2)
Stephen Lewis (series 2)

CREDITS
writers Alexei Sayle, Graham Linehan, Arthur Mathews · *additional material* David Stafford, Arabella Weir, Dennis Berson · *director* Metin Hüseyin · *producer* Alan Nixon

'It's completely different from my last series except for the bits that are exactly the same,' the star announced at the start of this new series – and he was right. *The All New Alexei Sayle Show* featured the same high-quality gags and oddly effective, free-ranging, somewhat ramshackle style of his previous series, *Alexei Sayle's Stuff*.

Kitted out in his trademark tight suit, sketches were linked by Sayle in different locations, from the picturesque (woods, riverbanks, valleys, beaches) to the non-descript (B-roads, trains, shopping centres), where he would deliver rambling but well-crafted monologues. Often these items, filmed in one take, were quite long and served as a testament to the comedian's ability to remember and reproduce complex comedy pieces while on the hoof. This was a device Sayle had toyed with in his previous TV work but one that he perfected here. He also showcased a few recurring characters, most notably: the sad warm-up man Bobby Chariot, who would appear on screen to fill in when the show 'broke down' for supposed technical reasons; a caricature of the then Labour leader John Smith; performance artists Egbert and Bill (a lampoon of real-life artists Gilbert and George); and Hackney lesbian cycle-shop owners Nancy and Spike. There was also a serialised sketch in series one: 'Psycho Ward 11', a spoof Australian hospital soap featuring Jean Marsh and Peter O'Brien, while, in the second series, 'Drunk In Time' satirised 1960s cult sci-fi TV series *The Time Tunnel* and featured Peter Capaldi as Sayle's fellow drunk time-travelling companion, with Jenny Agutter and Alfred Marks as the scientists back at base. Special mention must also be made of the brilliant credit sequence, which featured Sayle as an innocent, newly arrived man in London, in a series of humorous vignettes around town, shot in a stereotypical sitcom style most obviously reminiscent of *The Mary Tyler Moore Show*.

Recognition of the show's quality came with the award of the Bronze Rose at the 1994 Montreux Festival.

All Night Long

UK · BBC · SITCOM

6 × 30 mins · colour

11 July–22 Aug 1994 · BBC1 Mon 8.30pm

MAIN CAST

Bill Chivers	Keith Barron
Vanda	Maureen Beattie
Clare	Dinah Sheridan
Tom	Angus Lennie
WPC Hannah Jackson	Jan Winters
PC Digby	John Phythian
Terry	Jacqueline Reddin
Courtney	Robert McKewley
Wally	Paul Grunert

CREDITS
writers Dick Fiddy/Mark Wallington ·
director/producer Harold Snoad

A sitcom set in a London bakery, the action taking place through the night as the employees prepare the daily bread for local hotels and cafés amid frequent interruptions from visitors.

The owner of the business, Bill Chivers, is an ex-con who learned baking while doing a spell in prison for armed robbery. Determined to turn over a new leaf, he is trying his utmost to keep away from crime and toil at an honest living, despite the temptations that London's night urchins occasionally put his way. Helping Chivers at the bakery is a motley crew consisting of Vanda, an illegally employed Romanian who is a better baker than her boss; Tom, a confused Scot prone to boasting that he 'was once the shortest man ever to work for British Rail'; and Courtney, given the chance to prove himself by Chivers after he is caught breaking into the bakery in the first episode. Others populating the kitchens are Clare (a surprising sitcom role for film actress Dinah Sheridan), a wheelchair-bound crime writer who needs the night-bakery life to inspire her; Wally, a shady mini-cab driver; Terry, a striptease and stripagram act; and the community-beat police pairing of PC Digby and WPC Jackson. Digby is prone to jump to conclusions, wanting to arrest Chivers for anything and everything going; Jackson leans the other way, not least because she fancies the ex-criminal.

Sadly, *All Night Long* raised few laughs, coming across as an oil-and-water blend of dark comedy and straight-quip humour. Not surprisingly, the writers ended up as dissatisfied with the mix as the viewers, their original intention (proven by an untransmitted pilot, *In The Dark*, with Jim Carter as Bill Chivers, and only Angus Lennie cast in both pilot and series) being to dwell mostly on the black side, depicting the lot of a once-violent criminal being given a second chance, only to dally with his freedom as opportunities for crime present themselves.

All Our Saturdays

UK · ITV (YORKSHIRE) · SITCOM
6 × 30 mins · colour
14 Feb–21 Mar 1973 · Wed 8.30pm
MAIN CAST
Di Dorkins · · · · · · · · · · · · · · · · Diana Dors
Ken Hicks · · · · · · · · · · · · · · · · Tony Caunter
Stan Maycock · · · · · · · · · · · · · Norman Jones
Frank Bosomworth · · · · · · · Anthony Jackson
Wilf · John Comer
Ronnie Rendell · · · · · · · · · · · · Doug Fisher
CREDITS
writers Stuart Harris (2), Oliver Free (1), Eric Geen (1), Anthony Couch (1), Peter Robinson/David

Rutherford (1) · *directors* Roger Cheveley (4), Ian Davidson (2) · *producer* Ian Davidson

Following the end of **Queenie's Castle**, Yorkshire TV came up with a new sitcom for Diana Dors, also not without easy laughs but equally lacking in subtlety. In *All Our Saturdays* she played the no-nonsense Di Dorkins – known as 'Big D' – who runs a large textile company, Garsley Garments, and manages the firm's amateur rugby league team which regularly sits at the bottom of the local league. Tougher than her players, but determined to make men of them, she renames the team the Frilly Things and sets about the job of winning matches at any cost. Tony Caunter, also from *Queenie's Castle*, supported.

All Square

see BENTINE, Michael

All-Star Comedy Carnival

UK · ITV · COMEDY SPECIALS
5 editions · colour

ITV's response to the BBC's annual Christmas night comedy/variety special. Each edition featured custom-written Christmas scenes from some of ITV's most popular programmes – mostly sitcoms and sketch shows but also other genres.

The following indicates the comedy artists appearing – **see each programme's own entry for more details**.

1969; 250 mins · Thu 6pm

Doctor In The House (see entry under The Doctor Series …); *On The Buses*; *Please, Sir!*; *Mr Digby, Darling*; *The Dustbinmen*; *Cribbins*; *Father, Dear Father*; *Never Mind The Quality, Feel The Width*; *Dear Mother … Love Albert*; *Two In Clover*; Mike Yarwood

1970; 250 mins · Fri 6pm

Girls About Town; *The Worker*; *The Lovers*; *Hark At Barker*; *Doctor In The House*; *Dear Mother … Love Albert*; *Albert And Victoria*; *For The Love Of Ada*; *Cribbins*; *Father, Dear Father*; *The Des O'Connor Show*

1971; 245 mins · Sat 6.05pm

Mike And Bernie Winters' All-Star Christmas Comedy Carnival

Doctor At Large; *The Lovers*; *… And Mother Makes Three*; *His And Hers*; *Please, Sir!*; *The Fenn Street Gang*; *Girls About Town*; *Dear Mother … Love Albert*; *Sez Les*; *Lollipop Loves Mr Mole*; *Father, Dear Father*

1972; 105 mins · Mon 5.45pm

Love Thy Neighbour; *On The Buses*; *Nearest And Dearest*; *Thirty Minutes Worth*; *Sez Les*; *The Fenn Street Gang*; *Father, Dear Father*

1973; 90 mins · Tue 6.30pm

Man About The House; *My Good Woman*; *Sez Les*; *Billy Liar*; *Spring And Autumn*; *Doctor In Charge*

An All-Star Toast To The Improv

USA · HBO · STANDUP
1 × 65 mins · colour
US date: 30 Jan 1988
UK date: 3 Jan 1992 · C4 Fri 12.10am
MAIN CAST
host · Robert Klein
Robin Williams
Billy Crystal
CREDITS
writers cast · *director* Walter C Miller

A one-off show in which all-star guests paid tribute to the Improv Theatre in Los Angeles, where many US standup comics have made their name.

All This And Corbett Too

see The Ronnie Corbett Specials

Allan In Wonderland

UK · BBC · STANDUP
1 × 40 mins · b/w
29 Aug 1964 · BBC2 Sat 8.50pm
MAIN CAST
Allan Sherman
CREDITS
writer Allan Sherman · *producer* Dennis Main Wilson

Born in 1924, Allan Sherman worked steadily for 18 years in the business of writing comedy material for others to perform before going behind the microphone himself and becoming an astonishing success thanks to a record release. Sherman had often performed comic versions of famous songs, as well as making up new ditties, and was persuaded to put them out as an album, *My Son The Folk Singer*. The result was staggering: the record became one of the fastest- and biggest-selling comedy discs of all time in the USA, and its spin-off single sold over a million copies and established his fame in the UK and other English-speaking territories. This was 'Hello Muddah, Hello Faddah', taking the form of a child's letter home from summer camp, sung to the strains of Ponchielli's *Dance Of The Hours*. Thus, Sherman found himself catapulted, quite unexpectedly, into the spotlight and becoming a frequently seen face on TV. He made regular trips to the UK, appearing in variety shows and occasionally fronting his own TV programmes such as this one, *Allan In Wonderland*, and **Allan Sherman – Folk Singer?** (see next entry).

Allan Sherman died in 1973, aged 49.

Allan Sherman – Folk Singer?

UK · BBC · STANDUP

2×30 mins · b/w

18 Sep & 25 Sep 1965 · BBC1 Sat 9.05pm

MAIN CAST
Allan Sherman

CREDITS
writer Allan Sherman · *producer* Stewart Morris

Two further programmes featuring the popular American comedian Allan Sherman, made especially for the BBC in its London studios.

See previous entry for further details.

The Allan Stewart Show

UK · ITV (THAMES) · SKETCH

1×30 mins · colour

29 Dec 1980 · Mon 8.30pm

MAIN CAST
Allan Stewart
Terence Alexander
Anna Dawson
Bob Todd

CREDITS
writers John Junkin, Alex Shearer · *director/producer* Stuart Hall

A one-off primetime special for the Scottish comic and impressionist, made in London by Thames.

See following entry for further details.

The Allan Stewart Tapes

UK · ITV (SCOTTISH) · STANDUP/SKETCH

5×30 mins · colour

*29 Apr–27 May 1980 · Tue 3.45pm

MAIN CAST
Allan Stewart
Jack Douglas

CREDITS
executive producer Bryan Izzard · *producer* David Macmahon

Scottish-born impressionist Allan Stewart, aged 29 but already with 20 years' stage experience under his belt (his career began in the 1960s when he performed as a cabaret pop singer and musician), made strides beyond his native country when five programmes from his 1979 STV series were picked up by Thames and screened in the London area. The skits were set in a penthouse flat with a view of Edinburgh Castle, and *Carry On* film comic Jack Douglas was cast as Stewart's upright, Sassenach butler.

*Note. These dates refer to London-ITV transmissions.

See also the previous entry and *Hello, Good Afternoon And Welcome*.

Dave Allen

Dave Allen was born David Tynan O'Mahony in Tallaght, County Dublin, on 6 July 1936, and began his adult life as a newspaper journalist for the *Drogheda Argus*. He came to Britain in 1955, entering show business by way of a lengthy stint as a Butlin's Redcoat at Skegness (a not uncommon route to stardom at the time). Allen's quintessential standup routine, honed over years of stage performances, had him perched on a stool, holding a lighted cigarette in a hand that lacks the tip of one finger (he lost it in a car accident in his youth), taking the occasional tipple of whiskey and weaving lyrical stories and observations about life in general and religion in particular, especially Catholicism, his own brand. Allen became a firm favourite on TV, which suited his style perfectly; ambitious and so reluctant to continue for very long in the same vein, Allen tried his hand at chat-shows, quirky documentaries, straight acting and whimsical travelogues (*Dave Allen In The Melting Pot*, *Dave Allen And Friends* and others) along the way. Standup remained his forte, however, and his views, along with his lavishly filmed sketch sequences, ensured lasting – and sometimes controversial – popularity.

Allen's back catalogue of masterly sketches and standup routines was exploited to good effect in the six-part series *The Unique Dave Allen* (BBC1, 31 December 1997 to 1 February 1998). In between the artfully compiled collections of old footage, Allen reminisced on his life and comedy career, and recalled the creation and, in a few cases, adverse public reaction to some of the items. It was a salient reminder of the quality of work which he had maintained over four decades.

Tonight With Dave Allen

UK · ITV (ATV) · STANDUP/SKETCH

31 editions (17×45 mins · 14×40 mins) · b/w

Series One (13×40 mins) 9 July–1 Oct 1967 · Sun mostly 11.05pm

Special (40 mins) 23 Dec 1967 · Sat 11.05pm

Series Two (17×45 mins) 29 Sep 1968–19 Jan 1969 · Sun mostly 11.20pm

MAIN CAST
Dave Allen

CREDITS
writer Dave Allen · *additional material* Eric Merriman (series 1 & special), George Martin (series 2) · *directors* Gordon Reece (series 1), Colin Clews/Anthony Flanagan (special), Colin Clews (8 eds in series 2), David Foster (9 eds in series 2) · *producers* Gordon Reece (series 1), Colin Clews (special & series 2)

This was Dave Allen's first series on British TV, in which he combined compelling monologues and sometimes bizarre sketches with turns by amateur eccentrics from the general public who were invited on to the studio floor. The first of the two series was good enough to land Allen the Variety Club's ITV Personality Of 1967 award, and from here on the Irishman's success was established.

Although this was Allen's first *own* UK series, he already was well known by the time of its launch through his comedy spots in BBC1's *The Val Doonican Show*, which starred the Emerald Isle crooner in his rocking chair. Allen appeared in every one of the 11 editions in Doonican's 1965 series, from 7 October to 16 December, and occasionally in the following run, from 22 October 1966 to 14 January 1967. Following this, he was the central figure in *Around With Allen*, a pilot edition for a sketch series to have been titled *The Dave Allen Show* but which failed to be developed that far. The pilot was screened on 5 March 1967 in the Midlands and the North – but not in London – by the ITV company ABC, as part of its season *The Sound Of Laughter*. Allen's contribution to the pilot comprised a number of solo spots (written for him by Eric Merriman), while other players (Patrick Cargill, Ronnie Stevens, Victor Maddern, Arthur Mullard, Penny Ann France and Bob Todd) performed sketches written by Alistair Foot and Tony Marriott. Produced by Malcolm Morris, the show was taped in September 1966 but ABC declined to take up its option on a long-term agreement and let Allen go elsewhere.

Also worthy of note is the fact that, before attaining fame in Britain, Allen had become established as a star of Australian TV. Following his discovery by a local producer in a Sydney nightclub, Allen made some 84 *Tonight* shows there in the mid-1960s. He later returned Down Under, taping four 50 minute shows for the 7 Network in 1975 and six 90-minute shows for 9 Network in 1977, and was at the hub of a controversial live 90-minute special for the 9 Network (*The Dave Allen Show*, 18 September 1971) in which he appeared with Peter Cook and Dudley Moore. One of the subjects they discussed was masturbation, and this, together with a few mild swear words, so horrified viewers that, for a while, all three were banned for life from Australian screens, although this was soon rescinded.

The Dave Allen Show

UK · BBC · STANDUP/SKETCH

5 editions (3×b/w · 2×colour)

Special (60 mins · colour) 23 June 1968 · BBC2 Sun 8.15pm

Special (50 mins · colour) 8 June 1969 · BBC2 Sun 10.35pm

One series (3 × 45 mins · b/w) 11 Oct–1 Nov 1969 · BBC1 Sat 7.30pm

MAIN CAST
Dave Allen

CREDITS
writers Dave Allen (5), Eric Davidson (4), Bill Stark/Bernie Sharp (3), David Cumming (1), Brad Ashton (1), Eric Merriman (1), Michael Bentine (1) · *producer* Ernest Maxin

After two successful programmes under BBC2's *Show Of The Week* banner, the first made in between his ITV seasons, Dave Allen was given a three-week BBC1 series that concentrated on comedy sketches and standup routines and also featured comic and musical guest stars.

Inside The Mind Of Dave Allen

UK · ITV (THAMES) · STANDUP/SKETCH

1 × 60 mins · colour
8 July 1970 · Wed 8pm

MAIN CAST
Dave Allen
Bob Todd

CREDITS
writers Dave Allen, Bill Stark, Chris Hughes · *director/producer* John Robins

A one-hour programme featuring the sit-down Irish standup in a barrage of short sketches and jokes.

Dave Allen At Large

UK · BBC · STANDUP/SKETCH

33 editions (26 × 45 mins · 6 × 50 mins · 1 × 35 mins) · colour
Series One (6 × 45 mins) 21 Jan–1 Apr 1971 · BBC2 fortnightly Thu 9.20pm
Series Two (6 × 45 mins) 27 Jan–6 Apr 1972 · BBC2 fortnightly Thu 9.20pm
Series Three (6 × 45 mins) 15 Jan–26 Mar 1973 · BBC2 fortnightly Mon 9.25pm
Special (45 mins) *Dave Allen Once Again* 24 Jan 1974 · BBC2 Thu 9pm
Series Four (6 × 45 mins) 27 Feb–3 Apr 1975 · BBC2 Thu 9pm
Series Five (6 × 50 mins) 18 Oct–20 Dec 1976 · BBC2 fortnightly mostly Mon 8.10pm
Special (35 mins) *Montreux 78* 24 Apr 1978 · BBC2 Mon 8.15pm
Special (45 mins) 26 Dec 1979 · BBC1 Wed 9.40pm

MAIN CAST
Dave Allen
Ronnie Brody
Michael Sharvell-Martin
Jacqueline Clarke (series 1–3 & 5)
Ian Burford (series 1)
Chris Serle (series 1)
Peter Hawkins (series 2–4)
Simon Barnes (series 2)
Robert East (series 3 & 4)
Doran Goodwin (series 4)
Susie Baker (series 5)
Paul McDowell (series 5)
Ralph Watson (series 5)

CREDITS
writers Dave Allen/Peter Vincent/Austin Steele (31), Dave Allen/Peter Vincent (1), Dave Allen/Peter Vincent/Ian Davidson (1) · *producer* Peter Whitmore

Dave Allen At Large consolidated Allen's standing as a top-flight TV comic and further confirmed the format for which he was most closely associated: an introductory standup routine leading to handsomely mounted sketches that continued on the themes touched on in the opening monologue. The comedian's trademark debunking of religious, especially Catholic, ritual throughout each episode made for minor controversy which, coupled with some quite frank material, earned the series a somewhat undeserved risqué reputation.

Note. The 1974 special was a compilation of material from the first three seasons of *Dave Allen At Large* linked by Allen with some new material. Ditto the 1978 special, which was made as a British entry for the annual Montreux Festival.

Dave Allen   BBC

UK · BBC · STANDUP/SKETCH

11 editions (6 × 30 mins · 4 × 50 mins · 1 × 55 mins) · colour
Special (50 mins) 20 Apr 1981 · BBC1 Mon 10pm
Special (55 mins) 29 May 1981 · BBC2 Fri 9.30pm
Special (50 mins) 26 Dec 1984 · BBC1 Wed 9.55pm
Special (50 mins) 8 Apr 1985 · BBC1 Mon 10pm
Special (50 mins) 31 Dec 1986 · BBC1 Wed 9pm
One series (6 × 30 mins) 6 Jan–10 Feb 1990 · BBC1 Sat 10pm

MAIN CAST
Dave Allen
Jacqueline Clarke (specials)
Michael Sharvell-Martin (specials)
Paul McDowell (specials)
Susan Jameson (specials)

CREDITS
writers Dave Allen/Peter Vincent (11), Ian Davidson (6), Penny Hallowes (6), Dick Vosburgh (1), Andrew Marshall/David Renwick (1), Andy Hamilton (1), Dick Fiddy/Mark Wallington (1) · *director* Bill Wilson · *producers* Bill Wilson (6), Bill Wilson/Peter Whitmore (3), James Moir (2)

The specials were virtually a continuation of *Dave Allen At Large*, mostly scheduled for Christmas or Easter when Allen's irreverent religious material was even more pertinent. The 1990 series saw a new departure for the comedian: six programmes of solo standup with no supporting guests or sketches. These enabled Allen to explore different themes linked by his routine, and allowed him to feature more adult material than was usual – leading to questions in the House of Commons over his 'strong language'. It was a style Allen would continue to use, just as controversially, in a London stage-show, *An Evening With Dave Allen*, which ran at the Strand Theatre from February to May 1991, and back on TV with Carlton in 1993.

Dave Allen   ITV

UK · ITV (NOEL GAY TELEVISION FOR CARLTON) · STANDUP

7 editions (6 × 30 mins · 1 × 45 mins) · colour
One Series (6 × 30 mins) 7 Jan–18 Feb 1993 · Thu 9.30pm
Special (45 mins) 26 Dec 1994 · Mon 10.30pm

MAIN CAST
Dave Allen

CREDITS
writers Dave Allen, Ian Davidson, Peter Vincent · *additional material* Kevin Day, Chips Hardy, Parrot, Nick Revell, Penny Hallowes · *script editors* Ian Davidson, Peter Vincent · *director* Tom Poole · *executive producer* Bill Cotton Jr (special) · *producer* Nick Symons

Carlton, the new ITV franchise in London, utilised Dave Allen to launch its comedy output, touting not only his return to TV after a three-year absence but the claim that he would be uncensored. The resulting series was both mildly controversial and, it has to be said, slightly disappointing, even though it won Allen the Best Comedy Performer honour at the British Comedy Awards. Recorded before a receptive audience at the Mermaid Theatre in London, the programmes featured Allen in typical repose, seated in or standing close by his leather chair, a tumbler within easy reach (no cigarettes this time, though: Allen had recently quit smoking and indeed had become vehement in his opposition to the practice). Through six programmes, and a later special, Allen proceeded to deliver his customary sidelong observations on everyday life, but the flair of old was replaced, it seems, by a swagger and crankiness not previously present. As such, the comedy essays came across a little more than a succession of tirades – enlivened, as promised, by undeleted expletives (although still no f-word) – which did Allen few favours.

Allitälli

see The Montreux Festival

'Allo 'Allo!

UK · BBC · SITCOM

85 episodes (55 × 30 mins · 26 × 25 mins · 3 × 45 mins · 1 × 35 mins) · colour

Pilot (35 mins) 30 Dec 1982 · BBC1 Thu 8.25pm

Series One (7 × 30 mins) 7 Sep–26 Oct 1984 · BBC1 Fri 7.35pm

Series Two (6 × 30 mins) 21 Oct–25 Nov 1985 · BBC1 Mon 8.25pm

Special (45 mins) 26 Dec 1985 · BBC1 Thu 7.40pm

Series Three (5 × 30 mins · 1 × 45 mins) 5 Dec 1986–9 Jan 1987 · BBC1 Fri 7.35pm

Series Four (6 × 30 mins) 7 Nov–12 Dec 1987 · BBC1 Sat 7.20pm

Series Five (26 × 25 mins) 3 Sep 1988–25 Feb 1989 · BBC1 Sat 6.45pm

Series Six (8 × 30 mins) 2 Sep–21 Oct 1989 · BBC1 Sat 7pm

Series Seven (10 × 30 mins) 5 Jan–16 Mar 1991 · BBC1 Sat 6.55pm then 6.25pm

Special (45 mins) 24 Dec 1991 · BBC1 Tue 8.20pm

Series Eight (7 × 30 mins) 12 Jan–1 Mar 1992 · BBC1 Sun 7.15pm

Series Nine (6 × 30 mins) 9 Nov–14 Dec 1992 · BBC1 Mon 8pm

MAIN CAST

René Artois	Gorden Kaye
Edith Artois	Carmen Silvera
Yvette	Vicki Michelle
Michelle	Kirsten Cooke
M Leclerc (1)	Jack Haig (series 1–5)
M Leclerc (2)	Derek Royle (series 6);
	Robin Parkinson (series 7)
Flying Officer Fairfax	John D Collins
Flying Officer Adamson	Nicholas Frankau
Otto Flick	Richard Gibson (series 1–8);
	David Janson (series 9)
Helga	Kim Hartman
Col Von Strohm	Richard Marner
Lieutenant Gruber	Guy Siner
Mother (Fanny 'Fifi' Lafanne)	Rose Hill
Crabtree	Arthur Bostrom
M Alfonse	Kenneth Connor
	(series 2 onwards)
Maria	Francesca Gonshaw (series 1–3)
Capt Hans Geering	Sam Kelly
	(series 1 & 2)
General von Klinkerhoffen	Hilary Minster
	(series 3 onwards)
Von Smallhausen	John Louis Mansi
	(series 3 onwards)
Mimi La Bonque	Sue Hodge
	(series 5 onwards)
Capt Alberto Bertorelli	Gavin Richards
	(series 5 & 6);
	Roger Kitter (series 7)
'London Calling'	Philip Kendall
	(series 1 & 2);
	Paul Cooper (series 3 & 5);
	Peter Bradshaw (series 4)

CREDITS

writers Jeremy Lloyd/David Croft (59), Jeremy Lloyd/Paul Adam (24), John Chapman/Ian Davidson (1), Ronald Wolfe/Ronald Chesney (1) · *directors* David Croft, Mike Stephens, Susan Belbin, Martin Dennis, Richard Boden, Sue Longstaff, John B Hobbs · *producers* David Croft (61), John B Hobbs (14), Mike Stephens (10)

'Allo 'Allo! was a direct-hit domestic sitcom and huge international success that made a star out of its lead, the funny and talented

actor Gorden Kaye. At first sight, frolics in Nazi-occupied France may have seemed a dubious subject for humour, but the series' premise was not to make fun of the war but to spoof war-based film and TV dramas, and in particular a BBC1 drama series about the resistance movement, *Secret Army* (42 episodes, 7 September 1977 to 15 December 1979). A good deal of high farce and plenty of bawdy badinage also helped move *'Allo 'Allo!* away from reality and offence, and the fact that it was a huge hit on French TV (it was shown there on Canal Plus) indicates that writers Lloyd and Croft succeeded in getting the right balance. (What Germans may have thought of it is another matter …)

In *Secret Army*, Bernard Hepton had starred as Albert, a café owner involved in the resistance. In *'Allo 'Allo!* Kaye played René Artois, a café owner in the town of Nouvion who becomes unwittingly involved with the resistance when they use his establishment as a centre from which to hatch plans to smuggle two British airmen back to Blighty. This adds complications to René's life which is already convoluted enough: he is married to Edith, a formidable woman who entertains in the café by singing (badly), but like all good comedy Frenchman he is also enjoying a passionate affair. The object of his lust is the beautiful Yvette, a leggy waitress at the café. Much mirth is caused by their constant attempts to steal a few precious moments alone, which they rarely achieve without coming close to being rumbled. René himself is the target of the unwanted attentions of the fey Lieutenant Gruber, aide-de-camp to the Gestapo's Herr Flick. The patronage of Flick and other Germans causes René further problems when resistance agent Michelle embroils him in her (often ludicrous) secret plans.

The show had serial elements, and the sheer number of episodes, 85 in total, meant that similar themes often surfaced, including the continuing attempts to transport the airmen and Herr Flick's pursuit of a valuable painting (*The Fallen Madonna With The Big Boobies*, by Van Clomp). Early on in the series, to escape the wrath of the SS, René fakes his own death and continues through the remainder of the episodes as his own fictitious twin brother. This deception prompts aged lothario Monsieur Alfonse into pursuing René's 'widow', with a view to marriage. This prospect had its attractions because it would allow René to plight his troth with Yvette, but the drawbacks – losing the café and his savings – prove overwhelming and so he thwarts the courtship. Other characters in the series include the fat, thick German Von Strohm and his colleague Hans Geering; ice queen Helga, Herr Flick's right-hand-woman; diminutive waitress Mimi La Bonque; and Edith's mother

Fanny 'Fifi' Lafanne, who eventually marries Leclerc. The original Leclerc was played by Jack Haig but following the actor's death the writers invented Leclerc's twin brother who was played initially by Derek Royle and later by Robin Parkinson. David Janson appeared as Hitler in an episode of series eight and he returned to the cast for series nine, this time taking over the role of Herr Flick.

The series had a cunning method of dealing with language problems. French characters spoke their native tongue with pantomime-style exaggerated French accents, but when they spoke English they adopted equally exaggerated posh Oxford accents. The English characters spoke English normally, but when they spoke French it was with a poor, almost incomprehensible cod French accent. This was especially true of the Englishman named Crabtree, who survived in Nouvion disguised as a gendarme and whose strangulated English-French gave the show its most memorable catchphrase with his customary greeting 'Good Moaning'. The show's other principal catchphrase was resistance leader Michelle's, 'Leesen verrry carefully, I weel zay zis only once …'. Throughout the cast, the characterisations were uniformly broad and the series was an equal-opportunity offender when it came to stereotypes: it depicted the French as greedy and sex-obsessed, the Germans as inefficient bumblers and the British as upper-class twits.

Confounding its early critics, *'Allo 'Allo!* proved hugely popular almost from the start. Making the most of this, the fifth series extended to a massive 26 episodes, intended – unsuccessfully – to attract the US market. (The BBC boasted that this was the first time such a long haul had been attempted in the UK, overlooking the longer runs mounted by *The Army Game* and *Bootsie And Snudge*.) *'Allo 'Allo!* ended in 1992 as the war approached its end and the town was liberated.

The series gave rise to a massively successful, London and internationally touring stage-show from 1986, featuring most of the TV cast (see **Comic Relief**). In January 1990 Kaye's enormous popularity was demonstrated by the public's response following a horrific car accident that left the star with serious head injuries. The accident occurred just days after newspaper revelations of Kaye's homosexuality, but fears for his reputation proved groundless with thousands of cards and messages being sent to his hospital by well-wishers. During Kaye's convalescence the stage role of René in a London Palladium production was played by his understudy, John Larson, and by Australian comedian/impressionist Max Gilles when the show toured Down Under. Kaye made a remarkably quick recovery, and 24 weeks after the accident was back on stage and back in the role on TV too. He also played the starring role in a third London stage run, in 1992. Incidentally, the odd spelling of his first name, Gorden, owed to an Equity typing error, but the actor himself always joked that it was 'the sign of a misspelt youth'.

The Almost Complete History Of The 20th Century

UK · C4 (KUDOS) · SATIRE

11 × 15 mins · colour

6 Oct–15 Dec 1993 · Wed 9.45pm

MAIN CAST (VOICES ONLY)

narrator · · · · · · · · · · · · · · · · · Stephen Frost
Jon Glover
Steve Steen
Enn Reitel
Joanna Brookes

CREDITS

writers/directors/producers Geoff Atkinson/Kim Fuller · *executive producer* Stephen Garrett

Another series from the team behind *The Staggering Stories Of Ferdinand De Bargos* and *Pallas*, once again utilising the style of re-dubbing library footage to comic effect. But *The Almost Complete History Of The 20th Century* differed from those earlier efforts in that it had a serious edge to its humour. Using film material from Map TV and British Pathé News, the stories – while presented in an irreverent and scurrilous manner – were essentially true. The writing team of Atkinson and Fuller were aided in their task by history consultants Henry Hobhouse and Dr David Starkey and the result was a surprisingly acidic retelling of key moments from the century.

See also *Klinik!*

The Alphabet Soup Show

UK · BBC · SKETCH

1 × 30 mins · colour

17 Nov 1995 · BBC2 Fri 12.20am

MAIN CAST

Ali Briggs
Mandy Colleran
Mandy Redvers Higgins

CREDITS

writers cast · *producer* Elspeth Morrison

A one-off BBC2 comedy in which the Liverpool-based 'No Excuses' disability cabaret company presented an array of sketches designed to amuse and highlight issues of relevance to disabled people. The skits were introduced by looking at different letters of the alphabet (J was for jobs, E was for etiquette), although the items were not delivered in A–Z order. The three leads – one deaf, one blind, one in a wheelchair – introduced a number of characters and situations and used the opportunity to

campaign about aspects of community life in which the disabled remain poorly served – the continuing problem of access to buses and trains, for example.

Overall, there were some good ideas in a fast-paced and amusing half-hour, with pertinent points made along the way. The programme was made by the BBC's Disability Programmes Unit.

See also *In Stitches With Daphne Doesgood* and *Whose Diary Is It Anyway?*

The Alternative Christmas Message

see BREMNER, Rory

The Amazing Colossal Show

UK · BBC · SKETCH

1 × 30 mins · colour

8 Aug 1996 · BBC2 Thu 6.30pm

MAIN CAST

Neil Mullarkey
Greg Proops

CREDITS

writers Neil Mullarkey/Greg Proops · *producer* Nick Freand Jones

Comedians Mullarkey and Proops paying comedic salute to the worst excesses of 1950s Hollywood B-movies. The pair performed sketches and commented upon clips from the films, the themes of which encompassed hypnotism, monsters, teenage delinquency, rock and roll and sex.

Greg Proops, the gifted American standup comic who had risen to prominence in the UK as a regular on the ad-lib panel-game *Whose Line Is It Anyway?*, had also recently fronted *Potted History* (BBC2, 25 January to 8 February 1996), a series that took a humorous look at house plants.

Amen

USA · NBC (CARSON PRODUCTIONS/STEIN & ILLES PRODUCTIONS) · SITCOM

110 × 30 mins · colour

US dates: 27 Sep 1986–11 May 1991

UK dates: 30 Jan 1988–18 Aug 1988
(22 episodes) C4 Sat then Thu 8.30pm

MAIN CAST

Deacon Ernest J Frye · · · · Sherman Hemsley
Reverend Reuben Gregory · · · · · Clifton Davis
Thelma Frye/Gregory · · Anna Maria Horsford
Michelle · · · · · · · · · · · · · · · Maria McDonald
Casietta Hetebrink · · · · Barbara Montgomery
· (1986–90)
Amelia Hetebrink · · · · · · · · · · · · · Roz Ryan
Lorenzo Hollingsworth · · Little Richard (pilot);
· · · · · · · · · · · · · · Franklyn Seales (1986–87)
Rolly Forbes · · · · · · · · · · · · · Jester Hairston
Leola Forbes · · · Rosetta LeNoire (1987–89)

CREDITS

creator Ed Weinberger · *writers* various · *directors* John Sgueglia and others · *executive producers* Ed Weinberger, Arthur Julian, Lloyd David, James R Stein, Robert Illes · *producers* Ken Johnston, Bob Peete, Marilynn Loncar and others

Not only a black sitcom – still rare in 1986, although not so a decade on – but also the first religious sitcom on American TV. Sherman Hemsley, who had soared to fame in the States as the pushy George Jefferson in *The Jeffersons* (1975–85), starred here as Ernest Frye, part-time lawyer, part-time hip, egotistical, fast-talking deacon of the First Community Church of Philadelphia. Seeking to improve attendance at the inner-city church, the scheming Frye appoints a new minister, the Reverend Reuben Gregory, and meets his match because although both men want the church to succeed they have opposing views of how the turnaround can be achieved. (Clifton Davis, who played Gregory, was a minister in real life, and was assistant pastor in a Californian church while the series was being recorded.) Frye's unmarried 30-year-old daughter, Thelma, takes a shine to the Reverend Gregory and eventually (the US episode of 3 February 1990) they are married. Casietta and Amelia are spinster sisters who sit on the church's governing board; Rolly Forbes is Thelma's uncle and the church's elder statesman. In the final US series, Deacon Frye is elevated from lawyer to the position of court judge.

Little Richard played the part of Lorenzo Hollingsworth in the pilot episode of *Amen*, and there was a strong musical connection in the final episode some five years later, with James Brown and Lloyd Price making personal appearances as themselves: Brown sings 'I Feel Good' in a telethon to raise vital funds for the financially troubled church, and as he hits the top note the heavily pregnant Thelma gives birth to a baby boy, making Deacon Frye a grandfather.

American Carrott

see CARROTT, Jasper

The Amnesty Galas

On an irregular basis, the finest talent in British (and sometimes American) comedy has come together to put on shows in aid of Amnesty International, the organisation dedicated to campaigning on behalf of Prisoners Of Conscience worldwide, and challenging societies that deny people freedom of speech.

The earliest such benefit shows (the first was in 1976) featured the so-called 'Oxbridge Mafia' of players who formed the pantheon of the 1960s comedy boom: the *Beyond The Fringe* crowd, *Monty Python*, *The Goodies* and the Bron/Fortune/Bird axis. In recent years, however, the (again, so-called) 'alternative' crowd has taken over.

Since fund-raising is the prime objective, the shows have been variously released to TV, cinema and video, released on record and published in book form. *This entry details in full only those six shows shown first on British TV.* Others, filmed for the cinema or video, do not appear even though they may subsequently have been bought for TV screening. However, here is a quick check-list of *all* the productions to date:

1. *A Poke In The Eye (With A Sharp Stick).* (Issued on record with this title but screened on TV and later released theatrically as *Pleasure At Her Majesty's.*) Presented at Her Majesty's Theatre, London, 1–3 April 1976.

2. *An Evening Without Sir Bernard Miles.* (Issued on record and screened on TV as *The Mermaid Frolics.*) Presented at the Mermaid Theatre, London, 8 May 1977.

3. *The Secret Policeman's Ball.* Presented at Her Majesty's Theatre, London, 27–30 June 1979. Cross-media release; TV screening predated the theatrical release.

4. *The Secret Policeman's Other Ball.* Presented at the Theatre Royal, Drury Lane, London, 9–12 September 1981. Cross-media release; theatrical release first.

5. *The Secret Policeman's Third Ball.* Presented at the London Palladium, London, 26–29 March 1987. Cross-media release; theatrical release first.

6. *The Secret Policeman's Biggest Ball.* Presented at the Cambridge Theatre, London, 30 August–2 September 1989. Cross-media release; TV screening first.

7. *The Famous Compere's Police Dog Bites Back.* Presented at the Duke Of York's Theatre, London, 13, 20 and 27 January 1991. Video release first. Material also compiled into *Barf Bites Back*, a 60-minute programme screened by ITV on 24 August 1991.

8. *Amnesty International's Big 30.* Not a stage production; performed at Central TV's Nottingham studios, with pre-recorded inserts. Screened 28 December 1991.

9. *Amnesty International's Gala Of Irish Comedy.* Presented at the Gaiety Theatre, Dublin, 2 February 1997. (Screened on TV as *So You Think You're Irish.*)

Pleasure At Her Majesty's

UK · ESSENTIAL/AMNESTY INTERNATIONAL · STANDUP/SKETCH

1 × 100 mins · colour

29 Dec 1976 · BBC1 Wed 10.25pm

MAIN CAST
Alan Bennett, John Bird, Eleanor Bron, Tim Brooke-Taylor, Graham Chapman, John Cleese, Carol Cleveland, Peter Cook, John Fortune, Graeme Garden, Terry Gilliam, Barry Humphries, Neil Innes, Des Jones, Terry Jones, Jonathan Lynn, Jonathan Miller, Bill Oddie, Michael Palin

CREDITS
writers cast and others · *director/producer* Roger Graef

Presented on BBC1 under the *Omnibus* arts strand, this first Amnesty benefit, originally titled *A Poke In The Eye (With A Sharp Stick)* and directed by Jonathan Miller, set the tone for those that would follow, with many favourite comedy sketches being performed, their opening lines greeted with the same type of recognitive applause that greets familiar songs at a music concert. The film made for a valuable record of a whole style of satirical comedy, with not just the performances but backstage and rehearsal footage included, narrated by Dudley Moore.

Note. *Pleasure At Her Majesty's* was given a limited theatrical release after first being screened on TV.

The Mermaid Frolics

UK · AMNESTY INTERNATIONAL · STANDUP/SKETCH

1 × 60 mins · colour

10 Sep 1977 · ITV Sat 10.30pm

MAIN CAST
Pete Atkin, Connie Booth, John Cleese, Peter Cook, Des Jones, Terry Jones, Jonathan Miller, Peter Ustinov

CREDITS
writers cast and others · *director/producer* Roger Graef

The second Amnesty show, somewhat more low key than the first. Terry Jones directed the event, which was originally titled *An Evening Without Sir Bernard Miles.* (Miles then famously operated the Mermaid Theatre in London, where the event was held.) Various musical acts also played.

The Secret Policeman's Ball

UK · TIGON/FILMS OF RECORD/AMNESTY INTERNATIONAL · STANDUP/SKETCH

1 × 60 mins · colour

22 Dec 1979 · ITV Sat 11.15pm

MAIN CAST
Rowan Atkinson, Chris Beetles, Eleanor Bron, Rob Buckman, Ken Campbell, John Cleese, Billy Connolly, Peter Cook, Neil Innes, Clive James, Terry Jones, Sylvester McCoy, Michael Palin, David Rappaport

CREDITS
writers cast and others · *director* Roger Graef · *producers* Roger Graef, Thomas Schwalm

The first glimpse of a *Secret Policeman's Ball*, directed by John Cleese. Staged over four nights this was the most ambitious fund-raising event to date, with a huge cast of comics, supplemented by some top pop/rock musicians, all performing for free.

Again, after the TV screening the film was given a limited theatrical release, that version running to 94 minutes.

The Secret Policeman's Biggest Ball

UK · ITV (CENTRAL) · STANDUP/SKETCH

1 × 70 mins · colour

28 Oct 1989 · ITV Sat 10.20pm

MAIN CAST
John Bird, Rory Bremner, Kathy Burke, John Cleese, Robbie Coltrane, Peter Cook, Adrian Edmondson, Ben Elton, Dawn French, Lenny Henry, Chris Langham, Dudley Moore, Jimmy Mulville, National Theatre of Brent, Michael Palin, William Rushton, Jennifer Saunders, *Spitting Image*

CREDITS
writers cast and others · *director* Mike Holgate · *producer* Judith Holder

This Amnesty gala was stage directed by John Cleese and Jennifer Saunders. Among the highlights were Cleese and Michael Palin enacting the 'Parrot Shop' and 'Argument' sketches from *Monty Python*, Robbie Coltrane, Lenny Henry and Jimmy Mulville performing *Python*'s 'Whizzo Chocolate Assortment' sketch, and Peter Cook and Dudley Moore, back together on stage for the first time in years, performing the 'One-Legged Tarzan' sketch from *Beyond The Fringe* and 'The Frog And Peach', one of the Sir Arthur Streeb-Greebling (or was it Greeb-Streebling?) interviews from *Not Only … But Also.*

Amnesty International's Big 30

UK · ITV (WORKING TITLE TELEVISION FOR CENTRAL) · STANDUP/SKETCH

1 × 120 mins · colour

28 Dec 1991 · ITV Sat 10.40pm

MAIN CAST
hosts Alexei Sayle, Jonathan Ross, Cathy McGowan, Paula Yates · *stage cast* Keith Chegwin, Julian Clary, Steve Coogan, Phil Cornwell, Mark Little, Mike McShane, Emo Philips, Steve Punt, Hugh Dennis, Rowland Rivron, Frank Skinner, Spinal Tap (David St Hubbins and Derek Smalls), Trev and Simon · *pre-recorded links* Roseanne Barr, John Cleese, Angus Deayton, Gregor Fisher, Dawn French, Gareth Hale, Ian Hislop, Griff Rhys Jones, Paul Merton, Bob Mortimer, Norman Pace, Vic Reeves, Jennifer Saunders, Mel Smith, *Spitting Image*

CREDITS
writers cast and others · *director* David G Hillier · *producer* Dave Morley/Graham K Smith

Inside a TV studio for the first time, this 30th anniversary Amnesty show blended a number of musical acts with comics young and slightly older, some live in front of a studio audience, others pre-taped.

So You Think You're Irish

UK · ITV (AMNESTY INTERNATIONAL FOR GRANADA) · STANDUP/SKETCH

1 × 80 mins · colour

17 Mar 1997 · ITV Mon 11.35pm

MAIN CAST

host Barry Murphy · *stage cast* Kevin McAleer, Kevin Gildea, Brendan O'Carroll, Owen O'Neill, Pauline McLynn, Dermot Morgan

CREDITS

writers cast and others · *director* Gerry Stembridge · *executive producer* John Sutton

Recorded in Dublin during Amnesty International's Gala Of Irish Comedy, this broadcast featured some of the hottest Irish comedians in a blend of standup routines and stage sketches. Although some of the names may have been unfamiliar to non-Irish viewers, Pauline McLynn and Dermot Morgan were well known from their *Father Ted* TV series.

Amos 'n' Andy

USA · CBS (HAL ROACH) · SITCOM

78 × 30 mins · b/w

US dates: 28 June 1951–11 June 1953

UK dates: 22 Apr 1954–11 Sep 1957 (67 episodes) BBC fortnightly Thu 7.50pm then Sat 6.30pm then various days and times

MAIN CAST

Amos Jones · · · · · · · · · · · · · Alvin Childress
Andrew Hogg Brown ('Andy') · · · · · · · · · · · ·
· · · · · · · · · · · · · · · · · · · Spencer Williams
George Stevens ('The Kingfish') · · Tim Moore
Sapphire Stevens · · · · · · · · Ernestine Wade

CREDITS

writers Joe Connelly/Bob Mosher and others · *directors* Charles Barton and others · *producers* Freeman Gosden, Charles Correll

This infamous show was the first imported sitcom to air on British television, and it proved popular on both sides of the Atlantic. Much of the controversy that attended the series was rooted in its first incarnation as a long running (1929–60!), hugely successful radio show. The white producers of the television series, Gosden and Correll, had taken the lead roles in the radio version, adopting exaggerated Negro accents for the two working class friends Amos and Andy. When the show transferred to TV, Gosden and Correll wisely chose black actors for the roles and created a popular knockabout series with an all-black cast – a feat not repeated on US TV until *Sanford And Son* (the US version of **Steptoe And Son**) in the 1970s. Episodes centred around Amos and Andy's 'Fresh Air Taxi Company' based in Harlem, New York, and their silver-tongued friend, nicknamed 'Kingfish', a man with a thousand get-rich-quick ideas that never quite worked out.

However, *Amos 'n' Andy* attracted plenty of criticism in its afterlife in US syndication, its depiction of black stereotypes proving too distasteful in the more enlightened 1960s – such was the pressure, indeed, that the series was taken out of syndication in 1966. Since then it has remained virtually unseen anywhere, with TV historians remaining divided in their opinions of the show's merits and drawbacks. Supporters argue that the depiction of *any* blacks on TV was rare enough at the time, and see the show as some kind of landmark; they are also quick to point out that many of the show's black characters were hard-working and ran their own businesses. Detractors point to the highly dubious characterisations of the principal roles, their pantomime accents and eye-rolling antics suggesting the worse kind of stereo-typing, reminiscent of the shabby way that blacks were portrayed in Hollywood movies years earlier.

Principal writers Joe Connelly and Bob Mosher went on to create, write and produce the seminal middle-America middle-class sitcom *Leave It To Beaver* (CBS then ABC, 1957–1963) which, despite its huge cult status in the USA, has never been screened on British TV, and then proceeded to make *The Munsters*.

And Finally ... Rory Bremner

see BREMNER, Rory

And Here, All The Way From ...

UK · BBC · SITCOM

1 × 25 mins · b/w

8 Mar 1963 · Fri 8.50pm

MAIN CAST

Donald Lawrence · · · · · · · · · · · · Eric Barker
Pamela Lawrence · · · · · · · · · · · Erica Rogers
Robin Ampleforth · · · · · · · Terence Alexander

CREDITS

writers Ray Galton/Alan Simpson · *producer* Duncan Wood

A Galton and Simpson comedy, presented as a *Comedy Playhouse* one-off. It featured Eric Barker as District Commissioner Donald Lawrence, a man brought to Shepherd's Bush in west London all the way from his outpost in Borneo in order to greet his brother Rodney (not seen) who is being honoured on the TV show *This Is Your Life*. When he finally arrives, after overcoming many hurdles, Lawrence discovers that the programme has been called off because his brother got to hear about in advance and disapproved.

... And Mother Makes Three

UK · ITV (THAMES) · SITCOM

27 episodes (26 × 30 mins · 1 × short special) · colour

Series One (7) 27 Apr–8 June 1971 · Tue 7pm

Short special · part of Mike And Bernie Winters' All-Star Christmas Comedy Carnival 25 Dec 1971 · Sat 6.05pm

Series Two (6) 2 Dec 1971–6 Jan 1972 · Thu 9pm

Series Three (6) 14 Sep–19 Oct 1972 · Thu 7pm

Series Four (7) 16 May–27 June 1973 · Wed 8pm

MAIN CAST

Sally Harrison · · · · · · · · · · · · Wendy Craig
Simon Harrison · · · · · · · · · · · Robin Davies
Peter Harrison · · · · · · · · · · · · David Parfitt
Auntie Flo · · · · · · · · · · · · · · · Valerie Lush
Mr Campbell · · · · · · · · · · · George Selway
David Redway · · · · · · · · · Richard Coleman
· · · · · · · · · · · · · · · · · · · (series 3 & 4)
Jane Redway · · Miriam Mann (series 3 & 4)

CREDITS

creator Richard Waring · *writers* Peter Buchanan/Peter Robinson (series 1 & 2), Richard Waring (series 3 & 4) · *director/producer* Peter Frazer-Jones

An ITV version of the comedy premise that scored award-winning success in the BBC sitcom *Not In Front Of The Children*, with the much underrated actress Wendy Craig starring again as a somewhat scatter-brained, harassed mother in a series of domestic dilemmas written by Richard Waring. Here, indeed, the popularity was even greater.

Craig played the role of Sally Harrison, a widow faced with the everyday tribulations of raising two well-meaning but nonetheless troublesome children, a cat and a goldfish, 'helped' by her aunt (Valerie Lush), all while enjoying some occasional male interest and holding down a job as assistant to a vet (Mr Campbell). Phew.

Sally married father-of-one widower and antiquarian bookseller David Redway in the final series, leading to the sequel ... *And Mother Makes Five*.

... And Mother Makes Five

UK · ITV (THAMES) · SITCOM

26 × 30 mins · colour

Series One (7) 1 May–12 June 1974 · Wed 8pm

Series Two (6) 22 Oct–26 Nov 1974 · Tue 7.05pm

Series Three (7) 4 June–16 July 1975 · Wed 8pm

Series Four (6) 7 Jan–11 Feb 1976 · Wed 8pm

MAIN CAST

Sally Redway · · · · · · · · · · · · Wendy Craig
David Redway · · · · · · · · · Richard Coleman
Simon Redway · · · · · · · · · · · Robin Davies
Peter Redway · · · · · · · · · · · · David Parfitt

Jane Redway	Maxine Gordon
Auntie Flo	Valerie Lush

OTHER APPEARANCES

Monica Spencer	Charlotte Mitchell
Joss Spencer	Tony Britton
Mrs Fletcher	Patricia Routledge

CREDITS

creator Richard Waring · *writers* Richard Waring, Jonathan Marr (Wendy Craig), Brian Cooke, Johnnie Mortimer/Brian Cooke · *director/ producer* Peter Frazer-Jones

The sequel to *... And Mother Makes Three*, which ended with widow Sally Harrison marrying widower David Redway, and the two families becoming one. Mathematics apart, the domestic scope of the episodes was much the same, with Wendy Craig as harassed as before and the children growing older but remaining as wholesomely brattish as ever.

Craig wrote a number of the episodes under the pseudonym Jonathan Marr.

And Now The Good News

UK · BBC · STANDUP/SKETCH/SATIRE

9 × 25 mins · colour

30 Oct–26 Dec 1978 · BBC2 mostly Mon 6.50pm

MAIN CAST

Richard Stilgoe

CREDITS

writer Richard Stilgoe · *director* Tom Gutteridge · *producer* Ken Stephinson

Gentle satire for the early evenings, taking the week's news as a theme for jokes, sketches and songs. (The final show, on Boxing Day 1978, used the year's news for its inspiration.) The series was presented by Richard Stilgoe, who performed similar music and comedy acts on stage and who had become a well-known TV face thanks to regular appearances on BBC1's weekday magazine programme *Nationwide*, where he presented the 'Pigeonhole' section featuring viewers' letters. One of the most common comments he found in those letters was that the news scarcely featured any optimistic stories. This gave Stilgoe the idea of presenting a show full of good news, pointing out (with tongue slightly in cheek) that for 'every two or three people shot, a quarter of a million, or whatever, are alive'.

The series unashamedly wore rose-coloured spectacles when it gazed over the news stories, and although maybe lacking bite it did efficiently fulfil its brief. Guest artists appeared in each edition: most notably, from the world of comedy, Rowan Atkinson in the second show (6 November 1978). Stilgoe himself remained something of an acquired taste, often attracting criticism and falling into that category of celebrities that, in the words of the cliché, 'the public either love

or hate'. Perhaps, perversely, it was his very niceness that turned some people against him: a harder punch to his humour may have won him more admirers. However this isn't Stilgoe's style and, on TV at least, he always maintains an air of detachment. Off-air he never seems to seek the glare of publicity, is rumoured to donate substantial amounts of his earnings to charity, and is given to self-deprecating humour – at the time of *And Now The Good News* he described himself as 'a second-rate Tom Lehrer or Victor Borge' or, perhaps more accurately, 'a more masculine Joyce Grenfell'.

From 29 November 1979 a similar series, *Richard Stilgoe*, aired late evenings on BBC2. It likewise turned an optimistic eye to the week's news but emphasised musical content, rather than comedy.

See also *The Richard Stilgoe Show, A Class By Himself* and *Psst!*

And So To Bentley

UK · BBC · SKETCH

6 editions (5 × 30 mins · 1 × 45 mins) · b/w

1 Oct–10 Dec 1954 · fortnightly Fri around 9pm

MAIN CAST

Dick Bentley
Peter Sellers
Bill Fraser

CREDITS

writers Frank Muir/Denis Norden · *producers* Brian Tesler, Ernest Maxin

A TV showcase for the Australian comic actor Dick Bentley, who at this time was enjoying great success in Muir and Norden's BBC radio sketch show *Take It From Here*, especially in the character of gormless Ron Glum in the weekly sequence within that series, *The Glums*. Scripted by the same partnership, *And So To Bentley* featured comedy and music with various guests stars and regular support from Peter Sellers and Bill Fraser.

... And So To Ted

UK · BBC · STANDUP

6 × 30 mins · b/w

18 April–23 May 1965 · BBC1 Sun around 10.20pm

MAIN CAST

Ted Rogers

CREDITS

writers Dick Vosburgh, Ken Hoare, Mike Sharland · *producer* Michael Hurll

A late-night comedy showcase for the standup comic and former Butlin's Redcoat Ted Rogers (born in London, 20 July 1935), with supporting guests. This was his first own series and followed frequent TV variety

spots, notably in the BBC1 series *The Billy Cotton Band Show*.

See also *Ted On The Spot*.

And There's More

UK · ITV (CENTRAL) · STANDUP/SKETCH

25 editions (24 × 30 mins · 1 × 60 mins) · colour

Series One (6 × 30 mins) 28 June–2 Aug 1985 · Fri 7.30pm then 7pm

Special (60 mins) *All Cricket And Wellies* 5 July 1986 · Sat 7pm

Series Two (6 × 30 mins) *And There's More Cricket* 12 July–16 Aug 1986 · Sat 6.30pm

Series Three (6 × 30 mins) 3 July–7 Aug 1987 · Fri 7pm

Series Four (6 × 30 mins) 28 May–2 July 1988 · Sat 5.15pm

MAIN CAST

Jimmy Cricket

CREDITS

1985–86 writers Ray Alan, Charlie Adams, Trevor McCallum, Ray Martin, Tim Whitnall and others; *1987–88 writer* Eddie Braben · *script editor* Trevor McCallum (1985–86) · *directors/producers* Tony Wolfe (1985–86), Ken O'Neill (1987), Tom Poole (1988)

The cheerful Irish-born comic entertainer Jimmy Cricket (né James Mulgrew) graduated from Pontin's Bluecoat to Butlin's Redcoat and on to television by way of ITV's talent-spotting series *Search For A Star*. The network then gave him this starring vehicle, which promoted his talents for four years, Cricket indulging his likeable if unchallenging humour via such premises as his fictional Irish town of Ballygobackwards.

The initial series is notable for having given the first regular TV exposure to the impressionist supreme Rory Bremner, a year ahead of his premiere BBC show *Now – Something Else*. The second series gave early exposure to Brian Conley. In addition to these names, the following people appeared in *And There's More*: Jessica Martin, Adrian Walsh and Hi Ching (all in series 1); Bob Todd, Nicky Croydon, Fred Evans, Patti Gold, Paul Gyngell and Andrea Levine (all in series 2); Noreen Kershaw and Granville Saxton (in both series 3 & 4); Joan Sims, Nicholas Smith, Carla Mendonça, Les Meadows, Eddie Braben and Vic McGuire (all in series 3); Sherrie Hewson, Jon Glover, John Ringham and Kevin Lloyd (all in series 4).

See also *The Joke Machine*.

And Whose Side Are You On?

UK · BBC · SITCOM

1 × 30 mins · colour

21 Jan 1972 · BBC1 Fri 7.40pm

MAIN CAST

Major Sperling	Patrick Newell
Pomfret	Tim Barrett
Gaston	Freddie Earlle

Lt Dunkel	Terence Edmond
Muller	John Hollis

CREDITS
writers David Hardie/Di Hardie/Terence Edmond · *producer* Leon Thau

Pre-dating *'Allo 'Allo!* by ten years, this *Comedy Playhouse* pilot was set in occupied France during the Second World War. Patrick Newell (Mother in *The Avengers*) was cast as Major Sperling, a loveable German – in the style of Sgt Schultz in *Hogan's Heroes* – whose cheerful relationship with the villagers is put in jeopardy by the arrival of a far more ruthless Gestapo officer. Although perhaps ahead of its time, no series followed.

Andrew O'Connor's Joke Machine

see *The Joke Machine*

Andy Capp

UK · ITV (THAMES) · SITCOM
6 × 30 mins · colour
22 Feb–28 Mar 1988 · Mon 8pm

MAIN CAST

Andy Capp	James Bolam
Flo Capp	Paula Tilbrook
Bookie	Mike Savage
Chalkie	Keith Smith
Clifford	George Waring
Jack	John Arthur
Keith	Jeremy Gittins
Meredith	Andy Mulligan
Milkie	Ian Bleasdale
Mother-in-law	Shirley Dixon
Pawnbroker	Richard Tate
Percy	Keith Marsh
Ruby	Susan Brown
Shirley	Colette Stevenson
Vicar	Ian Thompson
Walter	Kevin Lloyd
Mr Watson	Philip Lowrie

CREDITS
creator Reg Smythe · *writer* Keith Waterhouse · *director/producer* John Howard Davies

That most slothful of characters, Andy Capp did a rare thing in the 1980s: he stretched his legs and got about a bit. The subject of a newspaper cartoon strip since 1957, when he first appeared in the northern edition of the *Daily Mirror*, Andy became the star of a British stage musical in 1982, written by Trevor Peacock and with music by Alan Price. Then, in 1988, he attracted his own ITV series, written by the redoubtable Keith Waterhouse.

Still being published, daily, as this book was being written (1997), Capp was created and drawn by Reg Smythe, a talented artist with no formal qualifications but a fine eye for character. Smythe has always seen Capp as someone from the north-east of England (he himself hails from Hartlepool), although

the Capp traits are certainly not confined to gentlemen of that area. In short, Andy Capp is the classic anti-hero, an idler never seen without his trademark cloth cap and fag-end hanging from his bottom lip, whose home life consists of endless cups of tea, TV and kipping on the sofa, and whose outdoor life comprises drinking endless ale at the pub, visits to the betting shop, dodging the debt collector and the odd game of football. Capp is also a terrible chauvinist, his wife Flo being perpetually frustrated by her negligent hubbie, although she does occasionally get the last laugh. Flo's trademarks are her slippers, rolling pin (used mostly as a weapon) and rollered-hair.

With the newspaper strip syndicated to more than 50 countries and translated into 14 languages (Andy Capp is known as Kasket Karl in Denmark, Willi Wakker in Germany, Angelo Capello in Italy and, best of all, André Chapeau in France), here was a situation ideal for TV exploitation. Surprisingly, it took 29 years (1957 to 1988) for the idea to be realised. Even more surprisingly, the series, when it did finally occur, was a pronounced flop. The ingredients for a success were there: the Waterhouse scripts and the ideal actor in the lead role – James Bolam's Terry in *The Likely Lads* and its *Whatever Happened To ...* sequel had often been likened to Andy Capp – but the series, shot entirely on film, without a studio audience, was unreal and much less funny than the scripts suggested, representing the only real disappointment in Bolam's glittering career as a comic actor.

Tch.

Animal Madness

UK · C5 (ACTION TIME) · SKETCH
1 × 30 mins · colour
7 Dec 1997 · Sun 8.30pm

MAIN CAST

host	Simon Bligh

Steve Nallon (voice only)
Enn Reitel (voice only)
Kate Robbins (voice only)

CREDITS
writers Simon Bligh, Mark Maier, Ted Robbins, Andre Vincent · *director* Paul Martingell · *executive producer* Stephen Leahy · *producer* Jacqui Wilson

In one of the quintessential British TV children's series *Animal Magic* (BBC1, 1962–83), presenter Johnny Morris used his talents as a vocal caricaturist to imbue the featured creatures with voices that suggested a whole personality. The same device was then used in reverse by Aardman Animations for its Oscar-winning short film *Creature Comforts* (1990), in which Plasticine animals were created to fit the voices of real people who had been interviewed. In 1995, animal footage was used for comic effect in

Squawkie Talkie, but *Animal Madness* returned to Johnny Morris's original premise – giving animals almost-human personalities.

Various source materials (wildlife documentaries, home-video footage, nature studies) were utilised and overdubbed vocally by *Spitting Image* impressionists Nallon, Reitel and Robbins. Although lacking the warmth of Morris's presentations they certainly succeeded in providing recognisable personalities for the animals (some celebrity impressions were used to good effect) and the resulting mini-sketches were hugely entertaining. Simon Bligh, on location at Chester Zoo, linked the clips and performed some comedy routines with the zoo's animals as foils. Any pre-supposed suspicion of animal exploitation was diffused by the end result, which was totally harmless and set out solely to amuse. It succeeded.

Anna And The King

USA · CBS (20TH CENTURY-FOX) · SITCOM
13 × 30 mins · colour
US dates: 11 Sep–21 Nov 1972
UK dates: 4 July–26 Sep 1973 (13 episodes) ITV Wed 7pm

MAIN CAST

King Mongkut	Yul Brynner
Anna Owens	Samantha Eggar
Louis Owens	Eric Shea
Prince Kralahome	Keye Luke
Crown Prince Chulalongkorn	Brian Tochi
Lady Thiang	Lisa Lu
Princess Serena	Rosalind Chao

CREDITS
writers Jerry Mayer (3), Jim Fritzell (2), William Idelson/Harvey Miller (2), Gene Thompson (2), Bud Freeman (1), Austin Kalish/Irma Kalish (1), Lester Pine/Tina Pine (1), Maurice Richlin (1) · *directors* various · *executive producer* Gene Reynolds · *producers* William Idelson (12), William Idelson/Harvey Miller (1)

The true story of how one Anna Leonowens, an English governess, went to Siam in 1862 to teach the king's 67 children, became first a personal biographical account (*The English Governess At The Siamese Court*), then a 1944 novel by Margaret Landon (*Anna And The King Of Siam*), then a film of the same name (1946) and then, most famously, a Rodgers and Hammerstein musical, *The King And I*, which opened on Broadway in 1951 and was adapted as a hugely successful second feature film in 1956. (Subsequent productions of the play have been mounted, as well as new recordings of the music.) What is often forgotten, however, is that the premise also spawned a sitcom.

Like *The King And I* before it, *Anna And The King* starred the shaven-headed Yul Brynner as the irascible king, prone to hasty pronouncements and prancing about his palace in loon pants, *et cetera et cetera et cetera*. Here, the governess had become Anna Owens, an American widow, arriving with a 12-year-old son in tow, Louis. Otherwise, it was much as before, without music – or very many laughs. The staging was well realised and the sets looked beautiful (some were those featured in *The King And I*) but CBS pulled the plug after 13 episodes.

Annie Doesn't Live Here Anymore

UK · ITV (ATV) · SITCOM

1 × 30 mins · b/w

11 Aug 1965 · Wed 9.10pm

MAIN CAST

Olive Taplow	Dora Bryan
Eddie	John Collin
Alf	John Alderton
Pop	Charles Carson

CREDITS

writer Ray Cooney · *director* Albert Locke · *producer* Alan Tarrant

One of ATV's *Comedy Playhouse*-style series *Six Of The Best*, this single-episode comedy starred Dora Bryan as a scatty piano teacher who takes up residency in a flat previously occupied by a prostitute named Annie, and assumes that the men who pay a call are coming for her lessons.

Ant And Dec Unzipped

UK · C4 (ANT N DEC PRODUCTIONS) · CHILDREN'S SKETCH

10 × 30 mins · colour

18 Feb–22 Apr 1997 · Tue 6.25pm

MAIN CAST

Anthony McPartlin

Declan Donnelly

CREDITS

writers Simon Heath/Marie Finlay, Gary Howe, James Payne, Richard Preddy, Dean Wilkinson, Emma Williams, Eddie Braben and others · *director* Steve Smith · *executive producer* Peter Murphy · *producer* Conor McAnally

Having found fame in their roles in the hard-hitting BBC1 children's drama serial *Byker Grove*, 'Ant' McPartlin and 'Dec' Donnelly went on to achieve music stardom, enjoying – under the name P J and Duncan – a string of Top 20 hits from 1994 to 1996. More came later under their Ant and Dec monikers, this name change following their TV success with a comedy/variety/miscellany series *The Ant And Dec Show* (BBC1, 17 editions over two series, 6 April 1995 to 30 May 1996). This was a controversial production, with much of the material deemed too adult for the show's youthful target audience, with one segment in particular, 'Beat The Barber', in which each losing contestant had his head shaved, attracting unprecedented levels of criticism. The two stars were unrepentant and found a

more suitable slot on C4 with their next series, *Ant And Dec Unzipped*.

This time the concentration was heavily on comedy, with the pranks and game-shows elements of the earlier series dropped. The slightly later airtime, and perhaps the fact that one can take greater liberties on the less closely scrutinised C4, permitted the duo further opportunities to stray into areas of dubious taste, but their laddish charm – especially appealing to their core juvenile audience – meant that the material caused less offence than before. Sharp, and full of confidence, the pair played heavily on their Geordie backgrounds in their sketches and routines, and a basic ongoing storyline allowed the duo to segue into sketches and introduce different characters, including Tony Blunt, who always spoke his mind, and Mr Swaps, who seemed to collect everything.

Adored by – and unquestionably on the same wavelength as – their fans, there nevertheless remained a suspicion that Ant and Dec tried just a tad too much to please and may have achieved more by straying into less obvious territories.

The Anthony Newley Show

UK · ITV (ATV) · SKETCH

3 editions (2 × 55 mins · 1 × 50 mins) · b/w

30 Jan 1960 · Sat 8pm (55 mins)

9 Apr 1960 · Sat 8pm (55 mins)

4 Mar 1961 · Sat 7.40pm (50 mins)

MAIN CAST

Anthony Newley

CREDITS

writers Sid Green/Dick Hills · *producers* Albert Locke (2), Francis Essex (1)

Some months before featuring Anthony Newley in the bizarre sitcom **The Strange World Of Gurney Slade**, ATV engaged the fast-rising actor, writer, composer, singer and comic for a pair of sketch-based *Saturday Spectacular* shows. A third followed in 1961, after *Gurney Slade* had finished. Green and Hills supplied the scripts and guest stars padded out the bills, with Peter Sellers appearing in the first of the three.

Anyone For Denis?

UK · ITV (THAMES) · COMEDY FILM

1 × 90 mins · colour

28 Dec 1982 · Tue 8.45pm

MAIN CAST

Denis	John Wells
Maggie	Angela Thorne
Maurice Picarda	John Cater
Vouvrey	Nicky Henson
Hamilton Thisp	Mark Kingston
Boris	Roy Kinnear
Eric	Alfred Molina
Jenkins	John Nettleton
Major	Terence Rigby
Rear-admiral	Joan Sanderson
Schubert	Robert Stephens

CREDITS

writer John Wells · *director* Dick Clement · *executive producers* Robert Fox/ Julian Seymour

A TV adaptation of the finely funny London stage-play based on the column in *Private Eye* magazine that ran during Margaret Thatcher's tenure as Prime Minister: fictional letters written by her husband Denis to his *Daily Telegraph* editor pal Bill Deedes. As in the stage version, Denis invites two of his drinking friends around to Chequers while the wife is away at a European conference; but then, taking everyone by surprise, she returns and assumes that Denis's guests are EEC commissioners.

John Wells also appeared in the persona of Denis Thatcher in an ITV Variety programme, *Make A Date*, made by Yorkshire TV and screened on New Year's Day 1988, and in *Send Her Victorious*, one of the comedy playlets in Maureen Lipman's *About Face* series, which he also wrote.

See also *Dunrulin'*, *Mrs Wilson's Diary*, *Grubstreet* and *Private Eye TV*.

Anyone For Pennis

see KAYE, Paul

An Apple A Day

UK · BBC · SITCOM

1 × 50 mins · colour

9 July 1971 · BBC1 Fri 10.35pm

MAIN CAST

Mr Elwood Sr	Peter Cook
Clive Elwood	Dudley Moore
Arnold Thrust	Spike Milligan
Dr Clerke	Kenneth Griffith
Muriel Thrust	Tracy Reed

CREDITS

writer John Antrobus · *producer* Michael Mills

An interesting one-off with a heavyweight comedy cast. Dudley Moore played Dr Clive Elwood, whose overwhelming desire to show his patients care and attention is liable to be misunderstood. Peter Cook played Elwood's father who, when he discovers his son's plans, sets out to destroy them.

The production reunited Cook, Moore, Spike Milligan and playwright John Antrobus, following their 1969 collaboration on the feature film *The Bed-Sitting Room* (directed by Richard Lester), which was itself based on the stage-play by Antrobus and Milligan.

The Appointments Of Dennis Jennings

UK/USA · BBC/HBO (NOEL GAY TELEVISION) · SATIRE

1 × 30 mins · colour

US date: 6 Mar 1989

UK date: 27 Mar 1989 · BBC2 Mon 9.40pm

MAIN CAST

Dennis Jennings · · · · · · · · · · Steven Wright
Dr Schooner · · · · · · · · · · · Rowan Atkinson
Emma · · · · · · · · · · · · · · · Laura Metcalfe

CREDITS

writers Steven Wright/Mike Armstrong · *director* Dean Parisot · *executive producers* David V Picker, Paul Jackson · *producer* Paula Mazur

A curious television comedy short made by the British company Noel Gay in association with the US cable channel HBO. Basically, the piece permitted the American standup star Steven Wright to repeat parts of his surreal stage material by casting him as a dysfunctional man visiting his psychiatrist. As Dr Schooner, Atkinson played the straight man, slowly being sent around the bend by his bizarre patient. The production was a great success, even winning an Oscar for 'best live action short film' at the 1989 Academy Awards.

See also *The Steven Wright Special.*

The April 8th Show (Seven Days Early)

UK · BBC · SKETCH

1 × 30 mins · b/w

1 Apr 1958 · Tue 7.30pm

MAIN CAST

Peter Sellers
Graham Stark
Patricia Hayes
David Lodge
Mario Fabrizi
Harry Fowler
Alec Bregonzi
Johnny Vyvyan
The Temperance Seven

CREDITS

writers Ray Galton/Alan Simpson, Johnny Speight, John Antrobus · *producer* Duncan Wood

Thirty minutes of mayhem presented by comedy's usual suspects for April Fool's Day.

April Fool's Day

see Mr Pastry

Archie Bunker's Place

USA · CBS (TANDEM/UGO PRODUCTIONS) · SITCOM

97 episodes (96 × 30 mins · 1 × 60 mins) · colour

US dates: 23 Sep 1979–21 Sep 1983

UK dates: 4 July 1983–22 July 1986 (20 × 30 mins) C4 Mon 8pm then Tue around 11.30pm

MAIN CAST

Archie Bunker · · · · · · · · · · Carroll O'Connor
Edith Bunker · · · · Jean Stapleton (1979–80)
Gloria Bunker Stivic · · Sally Struthers (1979)
Michael Stivic · · · · · · · · Rob Reiner (1979)
Stephanie Mills · · · · · · · Danielle Brisebois
Barbara Lee 'Billie' Bunker · · · · Denise Miller
· (1981–83)
Murray Klein · · · · · Martin Balsam (1979–81)
Barney Hefner · · · · · · · · · · · Allan Melvin
Gary Rabinowitz · · · Barry Gordon (1981–83)
Veronica Rooney · · · Anne Meara (1979–82)
José · · · · · · · · · · · · · · · Abraham Alvarez

CREDITS

writers various · *directors* various · *producers* Mort Lachman, Norman Lear/Bud Yorkin, Milt Josefsberg

Archie Bunker's Place began as not so much a sequel but a plain continuation of *All In The Family*. The October 1977 eighth-season opening episode of *AITF* had seen Archie trick his wife Edith into mortgaging their house so that he could buy half-ownership of his favourite watering hole, Kelsey's Bar, renaming it Archie Bunker's Place. This became the setting of the new series. Also, Archie and Edith were still the guardians of their abandoned niece, Stephanie Mills, as they had been in the final season of *All In The Family*, and they still lived in the same house (704 Hauser Street in the Queens district of New York). Archie Bunker's Place is turned into a bar-cum-short-order-restaurant, and Archie has a new partner, Murray Klein. As far as the ultra-bigoted Archie is concerned, it's a business marriage made in hell, for Murray is not only a Jew but a clearly intelligent man and, that worst of all types, a liberal.

Edith appeared only sporadically in the first US season, as Jean Stapleton did not wish to be typecast more than she already was. Then, in order for the writers to introduce new female interest for Archie if they so wished, it was decided that her part would be wholly 'killed off'. The stunning opening episode of the 1980–81 US season of *Archie Bunker's Place* duly revealed that, a month before, Edith had died of a stroke, in her sleep, and viewers witnessed Archie, solaced by Stephanie, grieving for his dead wife. Carroll O'Connor's performance in this episode alone, as a man unable to deal with his anguish, won him a prestigious Peabody Award. It was from this point on that *Archie Bunker's Place* really became distinct from its much-loved predecessor. To be truthful, though, a lot of the fizz had gone out of the character by this time. In 1981, Murray left to get married and Archie bought out his share. Archie was now taking care of a second pretty young girl, too: another niece (his brother's daughter), Billie Bunker, who got a job as a waitress at the bar/restaurant. Archie

also had to put up with Veronica, an Irish chef whose wit had more bite than her food, and José, a Puerto Rican boy assistant; but at least his old friend Barney Hefner (played by Allan Melvin, Corporal Henshaw in *The Phil Silvers Show*) remained one of his most loyal customers.

Note. The 28 February 1982 US episode of *Archie Bunker's Place*, an hour long, served as the pilot for a spin-off, *Gloria*.

Are Husbands Really Necessary?

UK · ITV (ASSOCIATED-REDIFFUSION) · SKETCH

6 × 5 mins · b/w

27 Sep–1 Nov 1955 · Tue 11.25am

MAIN CAST

John Blythe
Nan Blythe

CREDITS

writer John Blythe · *director* Joan Kemp-Welch

A revolutionary idea at the time, these five-minute domestic comedy sketches formed part of ITV's morning schedule when the channel first opened. They featured husband-and-wife team John and Nan Blythe; John claimed to have based the scripts on real-life matrimonial incidents.

Are There Any More At Home Like You?

UK · ITV (ATV) · SITCOM

1 × 30 mins · b/w

15 Sep 1965 · Wed 9.10pm

MAIN CAST

Ernest · · · · · · · · · · · · · · · · Graham Stark
Dorinda/Gertrude · · · · · · · Barbara Mitchell
Father/Uncle · · · · · · · · · · · · Robert Dorning

CREDITS

writer Tony Hawes · *director* Dicky Leeman · *producer* Alan Tarrant

The last single-episode comedy in ATV's *Comedy Playhouse*-style series *Six Of The Best* featured the talents of Barbara Mitchell and Robert Dorning – they each had two roles – and starred that familiar British character actor and comic foil, Graham Stark.

Are You Being Served?

UK · BBC · SITCOM

69 × 30 mins · colour

Pilot · 8 Sep 1972 · BBC1 Fri 9.30pm

Series One (5) 21 Mar–18 Apr 1973 · BBC1 Wed 7.30pm

Series Two (5) 14 Mar–11 Apr 1974 · BBC1 Thu 8pm

Series Three (8) 27 Feb–17 Apr 1975 · BBC1 Thu 8pm then 8.30pm

Special · 22 Dec 1975 · BBC1 Mon 8.45pm

Series Four (6) 8 Apr–13 May 1976 · BBC1 Thu 8pm

Special · 24 Dec 1976 · BBC1 Fri 7.30pm

Series Five (7) 25 Feb–8 Apr 1977 · BBC1
Fri 8pm

Series Six (5) 15 Nov–13 Dec 1978 · BBC1
Wed 6.45pm

Special · 26 Dec 1978 · BBC1 Tue 7pm

Series Seven (7) 19 Oct–30 Nov 1979 · BBC1
Fri 7.05pm

Special · 26 Dec 1979 · BBC1 Wed 6.40pm

Series Eight (7) 9 Apr–28 May 1981 · BBC1
Thu 8pm

Special · 24 Dec 1981 · BBC1 Thu 7.15pm

Series Nine (6) 22 Apr–27 May 1983 · BBC1
Fri 8.30pm

Series Ten (7) 18 Feb–1 Apr 1985 · BBC1
Mon 8.30pm

MAIN CAST

Mrs Slocombe · · · · · · · · · · · Mollie Sugden
Captain Stephen Peacock RASC (Ex) · · · · · ·
· Frank Thornton
Mr Humphries · · · · · · · · · · · · · John Inman
Miss Brahms · · · · · · · · · · · · Wendy Richard
Mr Cuthbert Rumbold · · · · · Nicholas Smith
Young Mr Grace · · · · · · · · · · Harold Bennett
· (series 1–8)
Mr Lucas · · · · · Trevor Bannister (series 1–7)
Mr Grainger · · · · · Arthur Brough (series 1–5)
Mr Harmen · · · · · · · · · · · · Arthur English
· · · · · · · · · · · · · · · · · · (series 4 onwards)
Mr Tebbs · · · · · · · · James Hayter (series 6)
Mr Goldberg · · · · · · · · · · Alfie Bass (series 7)
Mr Mash · · · · · · · · Larry Martyn (series 1–3)
Mr Spooner · · Mike Berry (series 8 onwards)
Mr Grossman · · · · · · Milo Sperber (series 8)
Mr Klein · · · · · · · · · · · Benny Lee (series 8)
Old Mr Grace · · · · · Kenneth Waller (series 8)
Secretary · · Stephanie Gathercole (series 1)
Secretary (Miss Bakewell) · · · · · Penny Irving
· (series 4–7)
Secretary · · · · · · · Debbie Linden (series 8)
Miss Thorpe · · · · · · · · · Moira Foot (series 3)
Nurse · · · · · · Vivienne Johnson (series 6–8)
Miss Belfridge · · · · · · · · · · · · · Candy Davis
· (series 9 onwards)
Mrs Peacock · · · · · · Diana King (occasional);
· · · · · · · · · · · · · Diane Lambert (series 10)

CREDITS

writers Jeremy Lloyd/David Croft (64), Jeremy
Lloyd/David Croft/Michael Knowles (4), Jeremy
Lloyd/John Chapman (1) · directors Ray Butt (16),
Bob Spiers (13), John Kilby (8), Gordon Elsbury (7),
Martin Shardlow (7), not known (18) · producers
David Croft (51), Martin Shardlow (7), Bob Spiers
(6), Harold Snoad (5)

'I'm free!,' shrieks Mr Humphries from
menswear as, tape measure in trembling
hand, he makes a beeline across the shop
floor towards an unsuspecting male inside
leg; meanwhile Mrs Slocombe, sporting an
outrageously dyed bouffant, wonders aloud
whether anyone has seen her pussy (she was,
of course, referring to her cat) – and the
British nation knew what it was in for: half an
hour of sub-Carry On innuendo, sauntering
alongside rather than attached to the
accompanying plot. Broad, rude, crude and
offensive were just a few of the criticisms
justifiably levelled at this scatological sitcom,

but the series had the perfect response to such
highbrow jibes: great ratings. It was loved by
the public and they watched it in huge
numbers, culminating in over 22 million
viewers for a 1979 episode. To date, it
remains phenomenally popular in re-runs
(the latest batch of repeats being broadcast
by BBC1 at tea-time on Saturdays from late
1997).

Are You Being Served? was the brainchild
of Jeremy Lloyd, who – upon his return to the
UK after a stint working in the USA on
Rowan And Martin's Laugh-In – was
having difficulty finding work. He dreamed
up this department-store idea and sent it off
to both the BBC and ITV. BBC producer
David Croft took an interest, suggested
himself as co-writer and producer and made a
pilot. This was quietly awaiting a broadcast
slot, almost certainly in the next series of
Comedy Playhouse, when tragedy struck at
the Munich Olympics with the murder of
Israeli athletes by Palestinian terrorists. This
resulted in major scheduling problems for the
BBC, which found itself with slots to fill and
no sport taking place. Thus they reached for
the shelf and rushed out a couple of Comedy
Playhouse pilots, Are You Being Served?
being one of them. Despite being unadvertised
the pilot was well received and the powers
that be ordered a series.

Are You Being Served? depicted the antics
of the staff of Grace Brothers, a somewhat
old-fashioned and past-its-prime department
store. The characters all sported affectations
designed to make recognition and acceptance
easier for an audience confronted by such a
large cast. Captain Peacock was the floor
walker, a dapper, silky-voiced officious sort
determined to keep the staff on their toes. Mrs
Slocombe, head of ladies fashion, had ideas
above her station and an unerring ability to
say the wrong thing at the wrong time and in
the loudest voice. Her assistant Miss Brahms
was the target of leering sexist remarks,
usually from junior shop assistant Mr Lucas.
Mr Rumbold was the fussing manager and
direct link to the board of directors and its
chairman 'young Mr Grace' – who was
actually fantastically old and, in common
with the other members of senior
management, lived in the past, still treating
staff with a feudal arrogance and blissfully
unaware of the rapidly fading status of the
store. Most memorable of the main characters
was Mr Humphries, senior sales assistant in
the menswear department, a camp and effete
man, sharp-tongued and as light as a fairy on
his feet. John Inman's portrayal of the limp-
wristed, pouting Humphries drew as much
criticism as it did plaudits. In 1976 he was
voted 'Funniest Man On Television' by
TVTimes readers and was declared BBC
TV's Personality Of The Year, but at
the same time he was under attack from

gay groups offended by his stereotypical
portrayal of a theatrical homosexual. (Rather
limply, Inman always denied that the
character was homosexual.) In hindsight,
some of Humphries' detractors, revisiting the
character, grudgingly admit that they find
him funny, but others still see the portrayal
as indefensible, especially because, in its
time, there were so few positive images
of homosexuals to redress the balance.
Strangely, the portrayal drew hardly any
controversy when the series suddenly became
a cult hit in the USA in the late 1980s Britcom
boom – the American audiences saw the
character as so over-the-top as to be
beyond offence.

The success of Are You Being Served?
spawned a feature film spin-off of the same
title (1977, directed by Bob Kellett) that took
the cast to the fictional Spanish resort of
Costa Plonka. They also appeared in a
popular stage version. A US adaptation was
attempted, Beane's Of Boston, with a script
adapted by Lloyd and Croft – it aired on CBS
on 5 May 1979 but wasn't picked up for a
series. A more successful transference was
made in Australia, however, where a local
version of Are You Being Served? (again, with
the same title) ran for 16 episodes on the
10 Network in 1980–81 during a break in the
British run. John Inman reprised his role as
Mr Humphries, Lloyd and Croft wrote the
scripts (recycling some previous ideas but
adding local references) and Bob Spiers
oversaw the production and direction. Again,
it failed to duplicate the success of the British
original.

In 1985, after many minor cast changes,
and umpteen variations on the plots, Grace
Brothers finally closed for business. But still
the story hadn't ended – in 1992 many of the
cast were reunited for a revamped version of
the show, **Grace And Favour**.

Note. The cast also performed in character for
a stage sketch in the BBC1 variety series
Seaside Special on 19 June 1976.

Arkady Raikin

UK · BBC · SKETCH

2×45 mins · b/w

21 Apr 1964 · BBC2 Tue 9.35pm

19 June 1965 · BBC2 Sat 9.50pm

MAIN CAST

Arkady Raikin
William Campbell

CREDITS

writer Arkady Raikin (translated by William
Campbell) · producers Joe McGrath (show 1),
Ernest Maxin (show 2)

Two BBC shows for the leading comedian in
the Soviet Union. The first, produced by Joe
McGrath, who had met Raikin in Leningrad,
was originally scheduled for BBC2's opening

night, 20 April 1964, but a power failure caused a hasty rearranging of the schedules; it aired the following evening instead. Raikin presented a series of sketches including a quick-change routine for which he was justly famous. The first show was performed mostly in Russian but the second was presented almost entirely in English, a testament to Raikin's speed in mastering the language.

See also Xa! Xa!

The Armistice Party Bucket

see *The Saturday Night Armistice*

Armstrong And Miller   1

UK · PARAMOUNT COMEDY CHANNEL
(ABSOLUTELY PRODUCTIONS) · SKETCH

1 × 45 mins · colour

7 Apr 1997 · C4 Mon 11pm

MAIN CAST
Alexander Armstrong
Ben Miller

OTHER APPEARANCES
Sarah Alexander
Charlie Condou
Tony Gardner
Simon Greenall
Jessica Stevenson

CREDITS
writers Alexander Armstrong/Ben Miller ·
additional material Tony Gardner · *script editor*
David Spicer · *director/producer* Matt Lipsey ·
executive producers Miles Bullough/Myfanwy
Moore

Quirky double-act Armstrong and Miller had been performing together since 1992 when they met at the Gate Theatre in London. Their two Edinburgh Festival Fringe shows, *Bare Naked Fighting* in 1994 and *The Quality Shag* in 1996, brought them into the public eye and they broke into TV with appearances in the Carlton pilot **Sardines**, on LWT's **Comedy Club** and **Saturday Live**, MTV's **So 90's** and their own series for the Paramount Comedy Channel. The success of this latter venture encouraged C4 to offer the duo a terrestrial slot and the channel went into co-production with Paramount for an Armstrong and Miller series.

First, to whet viewers' appetites, C4 aired this 45-minute compilation comprising the best sketches from the original Paramount series, aired on the cable/satellite channel from 5 February 1997. Among the many characters on view were Armstrong and Miller's most famous creation, the Norwegian heavy-metal band Strijka, which comprised 'Eurorock sexgods' Matthau Tijorkildsen and Mick Gjootemuunden. Another fine sketch was *Nude Practice*, a parody of the ITV drama series *Peak Practice*, in which the three stars were all naked.

Armstrong And Miller   2

UK · C4/PARAMOUNT COMEDY CHANNEL
(ABSOLUTELY PRODUCTIONS) · SKETCH

7 × 30 mins · colour

10 Nov 1997–5 Jan 1998 · Mon mostly 11.05pm

MAIN CAST
Alexander Armstrong
Ben Miller

OTHER APPEARANCES
Charlie Condou
Tony Gardner
Melissa Lloyd
Dave Lamb
Jessica Stevenson
Simon Greenall

CREDITS
writers Alexander Armstrong/Ben Miller ·
additional material David Spicer, Tony Gardner ·
director/producer Matt Lipsey · *executive producer*
Miles Bullough

A fully-fledged C4 series (jointly produced with the Paramount Comedy Channel, which aired the programmes from 7 January 1998) saw the young comedians consolidate their position as TV's brightest twosome. In the seven shows the pair presented spoof costume drama *Brunswicke Park*; Hollywood octogenarians Kip and Tam; lame detectives Parsons and Lampkin – and Lampkin's friend Steve; Flavia and Venetia, the frightening owners of the Tiny Vegetarian Restaurant; the dodgy Fairground Assistants; and old favourites Strijka.

A delightful surrealistic edge ran through the shows, becoming more evident in certain sketches, like the recurring 'Japanese kids' segment where Armstrong and Miller and their supporting cast spoke in cod-Japanese while subtitles allowed viewers to follow the often bafflingly banal conversations. The support cast were uniformly good but special mention should go to Tony Gardner (Parsons in the 'Parsons and Lampkin' skits) who was particularly good value.

This was a high-quality production graced with consistently strong material and endearing performances. It would be no surprise to find Armstrong and Miller in the primetime comedy vanguard as the new millenium dawns.

The Army Game

UK · ITV (GRANADA) · SITCOM

*154 × 30 mins · b/w

Series One (13) 19 June–4 Dec 1957 · fortnightly
Wed 8.30pm then 10pm

Series Two (26) 20 Dec 1957–13 June 1958 ·
Fri 8.30pm

Series Three (39) 19 Sep 1958–12 June 1959 ·
Fri 8.30pm

*Series Four (37) 9 Oct 1959–17 June 1960 ·
Fri mostly 8.25pm

Series Five (39) 27 Sep 1960–20 June 1961 ·
Tue 8pm then 8.55pm

MAIN CAST
Maj Upshot-Bagley · · · · · · · Geoffrey Sumner
· (series 1, 2 & 5);
· · · · · · · · · Jack Allen (some eps in series 2)
Sgt Maj Percy Bullimore · · · · William Hartnell
· (series 1, 2 & 5)
Cpl Springer · · · Michael Medwin (series 1–3)
Pvt Montague 'Excused Boots' Bisley · · · · · ·
· · · · · · · · · · · · · · · Alfie Bass (series 1–4)
Pvt 'Cupcake' Cook · · · · Norman Rossington
· (series 1–3);
· · · · · · · Keith Banks (some eps in series 2)
Pvt 'Professor' Hatchett · · · Charles Hawtrey
· (series 1 & 2);
· · · · · · · Keith Smith (some eps in series 2)
Pvt 'Popeye' Popplewell · · Bernard Bresslaw
· (series 1 & 2)
Sgt Maj Claude Snudge · · · · · · · · · Bill Fraser
· (series 2–4)
Capt Pilsworthy · · · Bernard Hunter (series 2)
Pvt Leonard Bone · · · · Ted Lune (series 3–5)
Cpl 'Flogger' Hoskins · · · · · · · · Harry Fowler
· (series 3–5)
Capt T R Pocket · · · · · · · · · · Frank Williams
· (series 3–5)
Maj Geoffrey Gervaise Duckworth · · · · · · · ·
· · · · · · · · · · · · · · · · · C B Poultney (series 3)
L/Cpl Ernest 'Moosh' Merryweather · · · · · · ·
· · · · · · · · · · · · · · Mario Fabrizi (series 4 & 5)
Pvt Dooley · · · · · · · · · · Harry Towb (series 4)
Pvt Billy Baker · · · Robert Desmond (series 4)
Pvt 'Chubby' Catchpole · · · · · · · · Dick Emery
· (series 5)

CREDITS
creator Sid Colin

Series One · *writers* Sid Colin (5), Larry
Stephens/Maurice Wiltshire (5), Lew Schwarz (1),
John Jowett (1), not credited (1) ·
director/producer Milo Lewis

Series Two · *writers* Larry Stephens/Maurice
Wiltshire (9), Sid Colin (7), Lew Schwarz (6), John
Antrobus (2), John Foley (1), not credited (1) ·
director/producer Milo Lewis

Series Three · *writers* Sid Colin, Larry
Stephens/Maurice Wiltshire, Lew Schwarz and
probably others but no specific details available ·
directors/producers Milo Lewis (21), Max Morgan-
Witts (18)

Series Four · *writers* Sid Colin (11), Lew Schwarz
(10), Maurice Wiltshire (10), Marty Feldman/Barry
Took (4), David Climie (2), not credited (1) ·
directors Max Morgan-Witts (18), Gordon Flemyng
(17), not credited (2) · *producers* Peter Eton (22),
Max Morgan-Witts (13), not credited (2)

Series Five · *writers* David Cumming/Derek Collyer
(15), Maurice Wiltshire (14), Sid Colin/Maurice
Wiltshire (1), John Junkin/Maurice Wiltshire (1),
Brad Ashton/Maurice Wiltshire (1), John Antrobus
(1), Talbot Rothwell (1), Sidney Nelson/Maurice
Harrison (1), Marty Feldman/Barry Took (1),
Stan Mars (1), Bob Perkins (1), Alan MacKinnon
(1) · *directors* Graeme McDonald (15), Max
Morgan-Witts (14), Eric Fawcett (9), Gordon
Flemyng (15) · *producers* Eric Fawcett (24), Peter
Eton (15)

A giant of a sitcom in its time, *The Army Game* dominated ITV comedy output of the late 1950s and was one of those shows that everyone talked about and everyone knew. Like the best ideas, the concept was simple: a group of men serving out time as conscripts in the army are determined to dodge duty and derive maximum fun out of a situation they'd rather not be in. The fact that National Service was still compulsory in Britain when the series began, and also that the Second World War had only been over for 12 years, meant that audiences could readily identify with the situation, and sympathise with the plight of the conscript.

Because the characters – and *what* characters! – were so accurately drawn, viewers took to them immediately. At the height of the series' fame, the gormless, lanky Private 'Popeye' Popplewell, whose dim-witted 'I only arsked' was one of many of the show's catchphrases to enter the national consciousness, was receiving 200 letters a week from adoring women. And he wasn't the only one: instant popularity was visited upon some of the series' other leading lights, among them Private Bisley, nicknamed 'Excused Boots', abbreviated to 'Bootsie', because of a condition that permitted him to wear plimsolls instead of army issue footwear; Private Cook, nicknamed 'Cupcake' because he was always eating and received food parcels from his family in Liverpool; and Private Hatchett, who was into knitting and was dubbed 'The Professor'. It is easily forgotten now but these and a number of other cast members enjoyed pop-star-style fame in late 1950s Britain.

The series arrived on ITV two months after the BBC began screening **The Phil Silvers Show**, but *The Army Game* creator/writer Sid Colin's inspiration came not from this US series but a British feature film, *Private's Progress*, made in 1956 and starring Ian Carmichael. William Hartnell, cast in *The Army Game* as the bullying (appropriately-named) Sgt Major Bullimore, had appeared in that movie, and would later leave the TV series for another film, *Carry On Sergeant*, shot in 1958. This was the first *Carry On* and it is not be unrealistic to consider that the popularity of *The Army Game* (to say nothing of its motif) influenced its making. Indeed, one might further observe that Charles Hawtrey and Norman Rossington also appeared in both the TV series and the *Carry On* film.

Cinemagoers in 1958, in fact, could see not only *Carry On Sergeant* but also *I Only Arsked!*, a movie that, undeniably, was based on *The Army Game*. Bernard Bresslaw, Michael Medwin (as the Bilko-like Cockney conniver Corporal Springer), Alfie Bass, Geoffrey Sumner, Charles Hawtrey and Norman Rossington all appeared in this Hammer production directed by Montgomery Tully. And such was the fame of *The Army Game* that the TV signature tune, sung by

Michael Medwin, Bernard Bresslaw, Alfie Bass and Leslie Fyson, reached number five in the pop singles chart in June 1958, with Bresslaw then scoring another smash of his own, singing 'Mad Passionate Love' in the style of 'Popeye' Popplewell.

The cast of *The Army Game* changed a great deal over the years (remarkably, for a short while, three of the characters were played by different actors before their principals returned to the roles), with most of the original members leaving after the second series. In their places came another remarkable bunch, led by the new Sergeant-Major – a brusque, evil-minded snob of a man who went under the wonderful name Snudge and whose mission was to get 'the shower' – his and his predecessor's word for the conscripts – into shape. (Snudge's main catchphrase was "ave no fear, Snudge is 'ere'. Bisley's was 'Still, ne'er mind, eh?') Snudge forged a violently hostile relationship with 'Excused Boots' Bisley, and it wasn't long before Granada executives realised that these two could live in a TV series of their own and **Bootsie And Snudge** was born. Other new arrivals who felt honour-bound to devise skiving stratagems included the cowardly Private Bone, Corporal 'Flogger' Hoskins (another Cockney sharpster, to replace the departed Springer) and Private 'Chubby' Catchpole, played by Dick Emery. Emphasising its position in the national consciousness, a short performance of *The Army Game* was given before the Queen Mother by Michael Medwin (Springer), Alfie Bass (Bisley), Bill Fraser (Snudge), the skinny Lancashire 'face' comedian Ted Lune (Bone) and Norman Rossington ('Cupcake') in the 1959 *Royal Variety Show*; it was the last such event *not* to be televised, although highlights were broadcast by BBC radio six days later, on 29 June.

Based in Hut 29 at the Surplus Ordnance Department at Nether Hopping, somewhere in deepest Staffordshire, most episodes of *The Army Game* utilised only a few simple sets; furthermore, certainly in its early days, the programmes were screened live, usually from Granada's London studio, situated in Chelsea. Remarkably for a British series, an American-style production schedule was employed, with a team of writers turning out episodes for 39-week seasons that stretched from September through to the following June. Fortunately, most of the writers, and indeed the actors, had recently performed service in the army or RAF and so were able to draw upon their own experiences.

The episodes of *The Army Game* that have survived the passing years do not seem anywhere near as funny now as they once were, probably because the era of National Service has since long passed into the memory. One further peacetime army sitcom

was tried in the 1970s (**Get Some In!**) but, otherwise, subsequent service productions have harked back further, to the war years, the most notable example being the BBC's **Dad's Army**. (Frank Williams – the effete vicar in *Dad's Army* – was the dithering Captain Pocket in *The Army Game*, while Colin Bean, who played Private Sponge in the BBC series, appeared in one episode of Granada's.)

*Note. Granada programme records indicate that two further episodes were taped for the fourth series but not transmitted; these would bring the total number of programmes to 156. Also, only 36 of the 37 episodes in the fourth series were screened in London and elsewhere. The other was shown only in the North – Granada's patch – on 6 July 1960, during a run that otherwise comprised repeats.

Arnie

USA · CBS (20TH CENTURY-FOX) · SITCOM

48 × 30 mins · colour

US dates: 19 Sep 1970–9 Sep 1972

UK dates: 26 Jan 1971–6 Dec 1973 (48 episodes) ITV Tue around 6.30pm then various days and times

MAIN CAST

Arnie Nuvo	Herschel Bernardi
Lillian Nuvo	Sue Ane Langdon
Andrea Nuvo	Stephanie Steele
Richard Nuvo	Del Russell
Hamilton Majors Jr	Roger Bowen
Neil Ogilvie	Herb Voland
Julius	Tom Pedi

CREDITS

producers E Duke Vincent, Bruce Johnson, David Swift

Burly Arnie Nuvo works as a blue-collar dock foreman at the Continental Flange Company, but, to his surprise, is suddenly appointed as the firm's Director of Product Improvement, a white-collar executive position. This American sitcom, which ran for only two seasons there and was screened in its entirety in Britain by some ITV companies, depicted Arnie's attempts to master his new position and come to terms with his change of status, supported by his wife Lillian and two teenage children.

CBS had high hopes for this series, figuring that the background of its principal characters, and its unusual setting in a workplace featuring physical labour, had something relevant to say to 1970s America. It arrived on screen amid much publicity because of this perceived groundbreaking situation but *Arnie* distinctly failed to make the grade, and it was a less heralded show that followed it in its time slot which made its mark in sitcom history: **The Mary Tyler Moore Show**.

Around The Town

UK · BBC · STANDUP/SKETCH

1×60 mins · b/w

1 Oct 1955 · BBC1 Sat 8.30pm

MAIN CAST
Terry-Thomas
Max Miller

CREDITS
producer John Warrington

In the week that the BBC first experienced rivalry, in the shape of ITV, the Corporation proved it was no slouch where big-name comedy entertainment was concerned, presenting this special that featured two of the biggest names of the day: irreplaceable standup star Max Miller and the gap-toothed cad Terry-Thomas.

Note. Both these stars have been the subject of C4's excellent *Heroes Of Comedy* documentaries, screened on 27 October and 17 November 1995 respectively.

See also **You'd Never Believe It.**

L'Arroseur Arrosé

see **The Montreux Festival**

The Arte Johnson Show

see **Ver-r-r-ry Interesting**

The Artful Dodger

UK · BBC · SITCOM

6×25 mins · b/w

28 Sep–2 Nov 1959 · Mon 6.20pm

MAIN CAST
Dave Morris · · · · · · · · · · · · · · · · · himself
Cedric Butterworth · · · · · · · · · · Joe Gladwin
Sylvia Morris · · · · · · · · · · Gretchen Franklin
Mr Grimshaw · · · · · · · · · · · · · · · John Barrie

CREDITS
writers Frank Roscoe/Dave Morris · *producer* John Ammonds

A return to TV for the swaggering, work-shy, know-all character that the comedian Dave Morris had developed on radio and television in the series **Club Night**. In *The Artful Dodger*, Morris renewed his acquaintance with Joe Gladwin, and the dodger's wife, Sylvia, was played by comedy actress Gretchen Franklin.

Arthur And Phil Go Off …

UK · C4 (VULGAR PRODUCTIONS) · SITCOM

5 editions (4×45 mins · 1×90 mins) · colour

To Boulogne 16 Dec 1985 · Mon 9.25pm (45 mins)

*Around Channel 4 etc 18 Jan 1986 · Sat 8.30pm (90 mins)

To Loch Ness 18 July 1987 · Sat 11pm (45 mins)

Up The M1 25 July 1987 · Sat 11pm (45 mins)

To Marbella 1 Aug 1987 · Sat 11pm (45 mins)

MAIN CAST
Phil Nice
Arthur Smith

CREDITS
writers Phil Nice/Arthur Smith · *additional material* Ian Brown/James Hendrie (eds 3–5) · *directors* Geoff Wonfor (ed 1), David Macmahon (ed 2), Niall Leonard (eds 3–5) · *producer* Sue Hayes

An occasional series of comedy playlets written and performed by Phil Nice and Arthur Smith – alias the comedy double-act Fiasco Job Job – in which the pair turned intrepid reporters, setting off to various places to do on-the-spot investigations.

*Note. The full title of the second programme was actually *Arthur And Phil Go Off Around Channel 4 And Look At The Good Bits From The Channel 4 Archives, Fail To Find A Short Title, But Try To Redeem Themselves By Getting Into* The Guinness Book Of Records *For The World's Longest Title For A Television Programme*. Unless any reader can prove otherwise, this author believes that Phil and Arthur succeeded.

Arthur Askey … [various shows]

see **ASKEY, Arthur**

Arthur Askey In The Old Boy Network

see **The Old Boy Network**

Arthur Haynes Entertains

UK · ITV (ATV) · STANDUP

1×10 mins · b/w

18 Feb 1961, Sat 11pm

MAIN CAST
Arthur Haynes

CREDITS
not known

A staple of ITV's comedy output for ten years, **The Arthur Haynes Show** (see following entry) ran from 1957 to 1966. This show, *Arthur Haynes Entertains*, was a single ten-minute programme from the same maker, ATV, used as 'filler' late one Saturday night.

The Arthur Haynes Show

UK · ITV (ATV) · SKETCH

158 editions (95×30 mins · 62×35 mins · 1×50 mins) · b/w

Series One (12×30 mins) 2 Jan–5 June 1957 · fortnightly Wed 9.30pm

Series Two (7×30 mins) 18 Sep–11 Dec 1957 · fortnightly Wed 10pm

Series Three (2×30 mins) 12 Dec & 19 Dec 1958 · Fri 10.15pm

Series Four (16×30 mins) 6 Mar–19 June 1959 · mostly Fri 10.15pm

Series Five (6×30 mins) 14 Sep–19 Oct 1959 · Mon 8pm then 7pm

Series Six (8×30 mins) 21 Mar–25 Apr 1960; 13 June & 20 June 1960 · Mon 8pm

Series Seven (16×30 mins) 15 Sep–29 Dec 1960 · Thu 8pm

Special (50 mins) 18 Mar 1961 · Sat 7.40pm

Series Eight (6×30 mins) 30 Mar–4 May 1961 · Thu 8pm

Series Nine (6×30 mins) 16 Sep–25 Nov 1961 · fortnightly Sat 9.30pm

Series Ten (16×30 mins) 3 Feb–19 May 1962 · Sat 7.40pm then 7.25pm

Series Eleven (21×35 mins) 8 Dec 1962–27 Apr 1963 · Sat 8.25pm

Series Twelve (13×35 mins) 4 Jan–28 Mar 1964 · Sat 8.25pm

Series Thirteen (13×35 mins) 10 Oct 1964–2 Jan 1965 · Sat mostly 8.25pm

Series Fourteen (9×35 mins) 20 Nov 1965–15 Jan 1966 · Sat 8.25pm

Series Fifteen (6×35 mins) 26 Mar–30 Apr 1966 · Sat mostly 8.35pm

MAIN CAST
Arthur Haynes
Nicholas Parsons (series 1–9, 11–13 & special)
Ken Morris (series 1–3, 6 & 7, 9 & 10)
Joan Savage (series 1 & 2, 9 & 10)
Malcolm Goddard (series 1)
Lucille Map (series 2)
Aileen Cochrane (series 4–7)
Freddie Frinton (series 4 & 5)
Joe 'Mr Piano' Henderson (series 4, 5 & 11)
Leslie Noyes (series 6–15 & special)
Dorothy Dampier (series 7)
Teddy Johnson & Pearl Carr (special & series 8)
Tony Fayne (series 10, 14 & 15)
Dermot Kelly (series 11–15)
Patricia Hayes (series 13–15)
Michael Henry (series 13–15)
Rita Webb (series 13 & 14)
Audrey Nicholson (series 13)

CREDITS
writers Johnny Speight (140), Johnny Speight/Johnny Johnson/Michael Keen (6), John Law/Bill Craig (12) · *directors* Dicky Leeman (58), Peter Glover (28), Francis Essex (21), Colin Clews (20), Bill Stewart (16), Stephen Wade (6), Josephine Douglas (3), Dinah Thetford (3), Bill Lyon-Shaw (1), Albert Locke (1), Jon Scoffield (1) · *producers* Dicky Leeman (53), Colin Clews (35), Peter Glover (28), Alan Tarrant (16), Josephine Douglas (6), Stephen Wade (6), Albert Locke (5), Bill Stewart (4), Dinah Thetford (3), Bill Lyon-Shaw (1), Jon Scoffield (1)

A forgotten king of British TV comedy, Arthur Haynes enjoyed ten years topping the bill on the commercial channel. With his natural ability to mimic actions and mannerisms and thus portray *character* so well, and with cracking scripts from Johnny Speight, *The Arthur Haynes Show* made for compelling viewing.

Born on 19 May 1914, the only child of a baker, Haynes was not a Cockney in the true sense of the word (he hailed from the west part of London), but his speech and mannerisms were what one *thinks* of as Cockney. Before the Second World War he had scratched around for work (he later said that he was everybody's mate – plumber's mate, carpenter's mate and painter's mate – which made him particularly convincing when, in his TV shows, he portrayed the working man) and trod the variety stages with little success. Then came the war, during which Haynes entertained the forces with Charlie Chester. The relationship continued in peacetime when he was a member of Chester's own Crazy Gang in the hit BBC radio series *Stand Easy* (1946–49). A period of quiet then followed until impresarios George and Alfred Black put Haynes on the bill in the first edition of their ATV variety series *Strike A New Note* on 21 February 1956. In both this and his first solo spot the following week Haynes showed such promise that he was soon employed in both this run and another variety series, *Get Happy* (written by Dick Barry, Johnny Speight and John Antrobus), and then given a show of his own.

What particularly impressed the viewers was a Haynes character by the name of Oscar Pennyfeather, invented for him by comedy writers Sid Colin and Ronnie Wolfe and first seen in that opening *Strike A New Note*. Oscar was a mischievous little devil, well versed in the art of dishonesty and deceit – and, remarkably, entirely silent. His 'conscience', as it were, would be spoken for him by Haynes' comedy foil (usually Nicholas Parsons). Oscar didn't become famous so much as notorious, and was such a hard act to follow that Haynes, fearing his other work was becoming overlooked, ditched the character by 1960. He was also tired of being accosted by strangers in the street, one woman shouting out to him, 'You're Oscar, you horrible little man. I've seen you on the telly!'

Other characters soon developed, though: most famously an aggressive, argumentative, know-all tramp who, with a row of medals on his chest, got under everyone's skin. Sometimes the tramp would merely sit on a park-bench, philosophising with another vagrant (played by the Irish actor Dermot Kelly). Perhaps the most remarkable aspect of Haynes' TV work is that his humour often edged into the black. This tramp character – Hobo Haynes – was invented by Johnny Speight and the dialogue would crackle with belligerence and either implied or explicit physical threats. While this did not always make for comfortable viewing, such excellent writing in the hands of such a skilled comedy actor – Haynes was never less than utterly natural and convincing – was a real eye-opener. Haynes Hobo displayed more than a nod towards Speight's other great creation Alf Garnett (first seen in 1965), and, as

Speight himself has since observed, Hobo was so hard-left and Garnett so hard-right that there was very little difference between them.

Throughout his ten-year reign as ITV's leading comic – a position for which he was generously compensated by ATV – Haynes was well supported by a number of regular comics, all of whom he promoted as much as he could, rightly realising that their work and happiness would make for better shows. Easily Haynes' most frequent companion was Nicholas Parsons, today best known for chairing the BBC Radio 4 panel-game *Just A Minute* (1967 to date) and Anglia TV's game-show *Sale Of The Century* (1971–83). Back in the 1950s and early 60s, however, Parsons was an actor comfortable with both straight and comedic work, and his sparring roles, often as the voice of officialdom, were the perfect foil for Haynes' acerbity.

Although, on screen, he was very combative, Arthur Haynes was by all accounts a very likeable and unassuming man off stage. He received the Variety Club Award as ITV Personality of 1961 and never worked out of primetime on British TV. Along with other UK comics Dave King and Terry-Thomas, Haynes appeared in the 1965 Rock Hudson and Gina Lollobrigida movie *Strange Bedfellows*, but shortly after contributing to a second film, *Doctor In Clover*, he died, aged a mere 52. He left behind, preserved on tele-film, a rich legacy of work that thoroughly deserves reappraisal. (A welcome appreciation was shown in the series *Heroes Of Comedy*, screened by C4 on 3 November 1995.)

Note. *The Arthur Haynes Show* was also a success on the radio, recorded anew before audiences in BBC studios. Four series were broadcast, beginning 22 October 1962, 23 June 1963, 28 April 1964 and 15 July 1965, and there were other, similar radio programmes, such as *Arthur Again*. Johnny Speight wrote the scripts, with the tramp character featuring prominently, and Nicholas Parsons reprised his TV role as the foil. Tony Fayne, Patricia Hayes, Leslie Noyes and, in the final series, Warren Mitchell – confirming the link with Speight that had lead to **Till Death Us Do Part**, first screened just the week before the final Haynes radio series began – also appeared.

Arthur's Treasured Volumes

see ASKEY, Arthur

As Good Cooks Go

UK · BBC · SITCOM

6 × 30 mins · b/w

Pilot · 5 May 1969 · BBC1 Mon 7.30pm

One series (5) 28 Jan–25 Feb 1970 · BBC1 Wed 7.30pm

MAIN CAST

Blodwen O'Reilly · · · · · · · · · Tessie O'Shea
Mr Bullock · · · · · · · · · Robert Dorning (pilot);
· · · · · · · · · · · · · · · · · Frank Williams (series)

CREDITS

writers John Warren/John Singer · *producer* John Howard Davies

First shown as a *Comedy Playhouse* pilot, this sitcom was a vehicle for Tessie O'Shea, who played Blodwen O'Reilly, a jobbing cook who, variously, turns a transport café into a high-class restaurant, works in an army canteen and prepares meals in an old people's home. Although the premise promised to serve up a plateful of laughs, viewers found it hard to swallow and the series was curtailed early – it had originally been planned to run for six episodes but the episode scheduled for 4 March 1970 was cancelled. Thus, as good cooks go … she went.

As Time Goes By

UK · BBC (THEATRE OF COMEDY/D L TAFFNER) · SITCOM

47 × 30 mins · colour

Series One (6) 12 Jan–16 Feb 1992 · BBC1 Sun 8.35pm

Series Two (7) 10 Jan–21 Feb 1993 · BBC1 Sun 7pm

Series Three (10) 2 Jan–6 Mar 1994 · BBC1 Sun 7pm

Series Four (10) 5 Mar–7 May 1995 · BBC1 Sun 7pm

Series Five (7) 7 Jan–25 Feb 1996 · BBC1 Sun 8.20pm

Series Six (7) 18 May–29 June 1997 · BBC1 Sun mostly 8pm

MAIN CAST

Jean Pargetter · · · · · · · · · · · · · Judi Dench
Lionel Hardcastle · · · · · · · · · Geoffrey Palmer
Judith Pargetter · · · · · · · · · · · Moira Brookner
Sandy · · · · · · · · · · · · · · · · · Jenny Funnell
Alistair · · · · · · · · · · · · · · · · · Philip Bretherton

OTHER APPEARANCES

Rocky Hardcastle · · · · · · · Frank Middlemass
Madge · · · · · · · · · · · · · · · · · · · Joan Sims
Penny · · · · · · · · · · · · · · · · Moyra Fraser
Stephen · · · · · · · · · · · · · · · Paul Chapman
Daisy · · · · · · · · · · · · · · · · · · · Zoe Hilson

CREDITS

creator Colin Bostock-Smith · *writer* Bob Larbey · *executive producer* Philip Jones · *director/producer* Sydney Lotterby

An unexpectedly long-lasting romantic sitcom in which two masters of the genre, Geoffrey Palmer and Dame Judi Dench, made the art of comedy look easy. Palmer played Lionel, an ex-army officer and Kenyan coffee planter who returns to England to write his memoirs, entitled *My Life In Kenya*. Seeking the help of a temporary secretary to take care of the typing, an agency offers him the services of Judith Pargetter. Attracted by her youthful vigour, Lionel invites her out to dinner but chances to meet too with her mother Jean. Long, long ago she and Lionel had been very close, intent on marriage, but the war had dashed their relationship when letters went astray and each thought the other had given up. The point now was, could the old fires be stoked after a 38-year parting? And what about Judith, who was rather keen on Lionel herself? Such was the situation and the dilemmas at the start of the first series. As time went by *As Time Goes By* changed tack somewhat and in the middle period concentrated on getting Jean and Lionel back together. Eventually they cohabited and married but things were never that simple for the prickly couple who were both too independent to settle easily into married life.

As Lionel progressed in the literary world complications arose. First there was Alistair, his smarmy agent who soon started dating Judith and whom, to Lionel, represented all that was wrong with the modern generation. Then there was Lionel's eccentric father Rocky and his pursuit of his dream woman Madge. But the biggest diversion of all, outside of the central relationship, was the fact that Lionel had sold the story of his and Jean's romance to an American TV company, who were going to turn it into a glossy mini-series. Numerous episodes followed the progress of the production before they all got to see the finished article.

Throughout its run, *As Time Goes By* was a smooth-running vehicle, expertly driven by its lead actors and fine-tuned to perfection by writer Bob Larbey. (He had previously explored a similar entanglement-of-the-not-so-young scenario in **A Fine Romance**, also co-starring Judi Dench.) The series was not suited to all tastes, being perhaps best appreciated by middle-class middle-agers, but it certainly was not as twee as it might have seemed on the surface, with some genuinely sharp and edgy moments puncturing its cosy image. Larbey himself must have enjoyed lampooning the US treatment of scripts and storylines and possibly attained some of his ammunition from his own experiences in such situations.

So successful was the BBC1 series that *As Time Goes By* transferred to radio, with seven episodes adapted and re-recorded by the main cast for the sound medium, broadcast by BBC Radio 2 from 18 March to 30 April 1997 and more promised for 1998. The opening week included a flashback sequence to Jean and Lionel's original relationship, 38 years earlier, not seen by TV viewers.

Ask Mr Pastry

see Mr Pastry

Arthur Askey

Arthur Bowden Askey was born in Liverpool on 6 June 1900 and first made his mark as an entertainer in the First World War, when he performed at army shows. Following the war he worked for 14 years on the concert-party circuit before achieving 'overnight' success on the BBC radio series *Band Waggon* (1938–39). This show was an important one in radio history for it was the first weekly comedy/variety programme to appear at a fixed time on a fixed day and was the first to feature a 'resident comedian' (Askey). With his radio cross-talk partner Richard Murdoch, Askey took the 'resident comedian' angle literally and, with writer Vernon Harris, conjured up the idea that the pair lived in a flat on the top of Broadcasting House, which, although only erected a few years earlier, was a renowned London landmark. The listening audience loved *Band Waggon*, and 'Big-Hearted Arthur' and 'Stinker Murdoch' became huge stars. *Band Waggon* inspired a successful stage-show and feature film (1939) and Askey went on to star in a number of British comedy movies. A short (5ft 3in), energetic man, prone to forming an 'O' with his thumb and fore-finger and skipping nimbly around the stage, Askey's performance persona was that of a mischievous, hyperactive schoolboy in an adult's body, and he maintained this alter ego throughout his professional life. He also introduced many catchphrases that caught the public's imagination, the most famous of which were 'Hello playmates!', 'Ay-thank-yew' (meaning 'I thank you'), 'Doesn't it make you want to spit?' and 'Before your very eyes'.

Askey continued working until into his eighties – he appeared in the 1980 *Royal Variety Show* – but then suffered circulatory problems in his legs that necessitated amputation. He died on 16 November 1982.

Aside from the shows listed below, Askey made hundreds of TV variety appearances and turned up as a panellist in various game-shows. On 8 March 1967 he appeared in an edition of BBC2's *Suddenly It's …* series, *Suddenly It's Arthur Askey*, subtitled 'Before Your Very Eyes', in which he looked back over his career.

See also *Peter Cavanagh, Raise Your Glasses, The Old Boy Network* and *The Green Tie On The Little Yellow Dog.*

Arthur Askey   1

UK · BBC · STANDUP

2 × 15 mins · b/w

10 Aug 1951 · Fri 9.30pm

7 Sep 1951 · Fri 9pm

MAIN CAST
Arthur Askey
Sydney Jerome
Jerry Desmonde (show 2)

CREDITS
producer Graeme Muir

Two shows presented under the *Starlight* banner, both featuring Sydney Jerome at the piano. The second, featuring Jerry Desmonde as the straight-man, was broadcast from the annual Radio Show at Earls Court in London. From this same event, Askey also starred in *Holiday Camp*, a live 75-minute closing-night gala screened the following evening.

Before Your Very Eyes   BBC

UK · BBC · SKETCH/STANDUP

14 editions (11 × 30 mins · 3 × 15 mins) · b/w

Series One (3 × 15 mins) 6 Apr–4 May 1952 · Sun mostly 8.15pm

Series Two (6 × 30 mins) 18 Feb–9 Apr 1953 · Wed around 9pm

Series Three (5 × 30 mins) 18 Feb–15 Apr 1955 · Fri around 8.30pm

MAIN CAST
Arthur Askey
Diana Decker (series 2)
Dickie Henderson (series 2)
Sabrina (series 3)
Wallas Eaton (series 3)

CREDITS
writers Sid Colin/Talbot Rothwell (series 1–3), David Climie (series 2) · *producers* Kenneth Carter (series 1), Bill Ward (series 2 & 3)

A fondly remembered programme, named after Askey's best-known catchphrase. The third series introduced viewers to the voluptuous Sabrina (née Norma Sykes), whose big-busted figure and penchant for tight dresses made her one of British TV's first sex symbols. Following the third series Askey transferred the show to the ITV network where his friend Jack Hylton had the lucrative task of advising on, and producing, light-entertainment shows for the new service.

Note. The first BBC series was written with an exclamation mark, *Before Your Very Eyes!*

Arthur Askey   2

UK · BBC · SKETCH

1 × 15 mins · b/w

17 Mar 1955 · Thu 9pm

MAIN CAST
Arthur Askey

CREDITS
not known

A 15-minute visit with Askey and his company, 'in rehearsal' for *Before Your Very Eyes* (see previous entry).

Before Your Very Eyes   ITV

UK · ITV (JACK HYLTON TV PRODUCTIONS FOR
ASSOCIATED-REDIFFUSION) · SKETCH

14 × 30 mins · b/w

Series One (6) 10 Feb–20 Apr 1956 · fortnightly
Fri 8.30pm

Series Two (4) 26 Oct–7 Dec 1956 · fortnightly
Fri 8.30pm

Series Three (3) 18 Nov–16 Dec 1957 ·
fortnightly Mon mostly 9.30pm

*Series Four (1) 21 Apr 1958 · Mon 9.30pm

MAIN CAST
Arthur Askey
Anthea Askey
Sabrina
June Whitfield

CREDITS
writers Kavanagh Productions (series 1 & 2), Sid
Colin/Talbot Rothwell (series 3 & 4) ·
producers/directors Kenneth Carter (series 1–3),
Bill Hitchcock (series 4)

More of the same for Askey, following his
successful shows for the BBC. These ITV
programmes were unashamedly 'live' and
the various prop failures and forgotten lines
just added to the fun. Askey's style was to
acknowledge the audience through the
'fourth wall' whenever possible, often
keeping up a running commentary with the
audience about how appalling the show was.
(He was often right.) The highlight of every
edition was an extended final sketch, usually
spoofing a film or theatre genre.

*Notes. The final series, which was to have
run for only two programmes, was reduced
to a single edition when Askey suffered ill-
health.

In between the second and third series,
Askey celebrated 30 years in show business
with a special ITV programme, *Arthur's
Anniversary*, which was produced by Jack
Hylton and screened on 15 March 1957. Sid
Colin wrote the scripted material.

Love And Kisses

UK · ITV (JACK HYLTON TV PRODUCTIONS FOR
ASSOCIATED-REDIFFUSION) · SITCOM

5 × 30 mins · b/w

4 Nov–2 Dec 1955 · Fri 9pm

MAIN CAST
Bill Brown · · · · · · · · · · · · · · · Arthur Askey
Sal Brown · · · · · · · · · · · · · · · Lally Bowers
Rose Brown · · · · · · · · · · · · · Anthea Askey
Percy Brown · · · · · · · · · · · · · Ian Gardiner
Wally Binns · · · · · · · · · · · · · Glenn Melvyn
Emma Binns · · · · · · · · · · · · Barbara Miller
Alf Hall · · · · · · · · · · · · · · · · Danny Ross
Terence Steel · · · · · · · · · Bernard Graham
Mr Seymour · · · · · · · · · · Leonard Williams
Pam · · · · · · · · · · · · · · · Margaret Anderson

CREDITS
writer Glenn Melvyn · *directors* Richard Bird,
Maclean Rogers · *producers* Bill Luckwell, Derek
E A Winn

This summer 1955 Blackpool stage-show –
especially filmed for TV in London by
impresario Jack Hylton – starred Askey as
Bill Brown, once an engine driver and now
the skiving landlord of a pub. The comedy
revolved around Bill's relationships with his
family – wife Sal, daughter Rose (actually
Askey's real-life daughter Anthea) and son
Percy, and his drinking customers –
milkman Alf and the witless, stuttering
W-W-W-Wally. To remind viewers what
had gone before, and to implore them to tune
in again, Askey appeared on screen at the
beginning and end of each episode.

Note. A composite edition of the entire
production was screened in the North by
ABC on 23 December 1956.

**See also *I'm Not Bothered* and *Beside The
Seaside*.**

Living It Up

UK · ITV (JACK HYLTON TV PRODUCTIONS FOR
ASSOCIATED-REDIFFUSION) · SITCOM

9 × 30 mins · b/w

Series One (3) 12 Apr–10 May 1957 · fortnightly
Fri 8.30pm

Series Two (6) 27 Oct–1 Dec 1958 ·
Mon 9.30pm

MAIN CAST
Arthur Askey
Richard Murdoch
Anthea Askey
Danny Ross
Billy Percy
Hugh Morton

CREDITS
writers Sid Colin/Talbot Rothwell ·
directors/producers Eric Fawcett (series 1), Bill
Hitchcock (series 2)

Taking advantage of his production
arrangement with Associated-Rediffusion,
impresario Jack Hylton reunited, after an
18-year interval, the two stars of the BBC
radio comedy *Band Waggon* for a TV
version, *Living It Up*. That wireless version
and later feature film (in which Hylton had
appeared) had the two characters living in a
flat on top of the BBC's Broadcasting House
HQ. Now, predictably, they were ensconced
in a similar arrangement on top of A-R's
Television House, overlooking the Aldwych.
The humour was somewhat thin, and the
two leading players would often directly
address the studio audience.

Of the supporting cast, Anthea Askey
appeared as herself, Danny Ross played a
silly props boy and Billy Percy delivered
the post and the milk. There were guest
appearances too, by the likes of Sabrina
(Arthur's famously busty sidekick),
Valentine Dyall and Leila Williams (the
first presenter of *Blue Peter*).

The Arthur Askey Show   1

UK · ITV (ATV) · SKETCH/STANDUP

6 editions (3 × 60 mins · 3 × 55 mins) · b/w

28 Feb 1959 · Sat 7.55pm (60 mins)

12 Sep 1959 · Sat 8pm (55 mins)

24 Oct 1959 · Sat 8pm (55 mins)

5 Dec 1959 · Sat 8pm (55 mins)

23 July 1960 · Sat 7.55pm (60 mins)

3 Sep 1960 · Sat 7.55pm (60 mins)

MAIN CAST
Arthur Askey

CREDITS
writers Sid Green/Dick Hills/Jimmy Grafton (ed
1), Sid Green/Dick Hills (eds 2 & 3, 5 & 6), Dave
Freeman (ed 4) · *producers* Brian Tesler (eds
1–4), Francis Essex (eds 5 & 6)

Six single ITV programmes featuring the
little Liverpool comic, all screened in the
Saturday Spectacular strand. Guests varied
but all were aggregated under the 'Company
Of Talented Players' moniker. (Indeed, the
fourth show was actually titled *The Arthur
Askey And His Company Of Talented
Players Show*.)

Arthur's Treasured Volumes

UK · ITV (ATV) · SITCOMS

6 × 30 mins

2 May–6 June 1960 · Mon 8pm

MAIN CAST
Arthur Askey
Anthea Askey
Sam Kydd
Arthur Mullard

CREDITS
writer Dave Freeman · *producer* Bill Ward

An unusual vehicle for Arthur Askey, who
was more usually associated with standup
and sketch material. Each of the six
programmes in this series took the form of
a comedy dramatisation of a book, every
episode beginning with Arthur's grown-up
daughter Anthea (herself very much a TV
regular at this time) pulling down a volume
from the shelf and launching into the plot.
Each week, therefore, Arthur assumed a
different character, and the casts changed
too, with the exception of Sam Kydd and
Arthur Mullard who appeared throughout.
Guest appearances were made by, among
others, Wilfrid Brambell, Barbara Mitchell,
Patrick Newell, June Whitfield and Geoffrey
Palmer.

The six stories (none was actually a
book – they were all scripts written
especially for TV by Dave Freeman) were
A Blow In Anger, *The History Of Mr Lacey*,
The Command Performer, *Pilbeam Of
Twickenham*, *A Slight Case Of Deception*
and *The Curse Of The Bellfoots*.

The Arthur Askey Show 2

UK · ITV (ATV) · SITCOM

6 × 30 mins · b/w

11 Mar–22 Apr 1961 · Sat 9.30pm

MAIN CAST

Arthur Pilbeam · · · · · · · · · · · Arthur Askey
Emily Pilbeam · · · · · · · · · · · June Whitfield
Mr Rossiter · · · · · · · · · · · · Arthur Mullard
Mrs Rossiter · · · · · · · · · · · Patricia Hayes

CREDITS

writer Dave Freeman · producer Josephine Douglas

One year after Arthur's Treasured Volumes, ATV networked a further sitcom with which Arthur Askey could entertain his 'playmates' (that is, the viewing audience). He was again joined by another Arthur, the thick-eared cockney Mullard, and by June Whitfield. She, incongruously, portrayed Askey's wife, although he was 60 at the time and she 35. The series was set in the year 1910, and the Rossiters were the Pilbeams' neighbours. Among the guest stars who turned up were Sydney Tafler (twice), Sam Kydd and the long-established film actor Guy Middleton.

Note. Askey made another bid for sitcom stardom when he appeared in No Strings, a pilot screened (but not in London) by ABC on 29 January 1967, written by Fred Robinson and produced by Milo Lewis. He was cast as Arthur Anders, a piano tuner who was happy to be a bachelor; in typical Askey style, he addressed the camera – that is, the audience – directly. The supporting cast included Ann Lancaster, Jack Haig, Muriel Zillah, Arthur Hewlett, Norman Mitchell, Bob Todd and Shirley Stelfox; no series developed.

Assaulted Nuts

UK · C4 (PRIMETIME TV PRODUCTIONS/WILDWOOD PRODUCTIONS) · SKETCH

7 × 30 mins · colour

17 Jan–28 Feb 1985 · Thu mostly 11.15pm

MAIN CAST

Tim Brooke-Taylor
David Peacock
Cleo Rocos
Barry Cryer
Wayne Knight
Bill Sadler
Elaine Hausman
Marcelle Rosenblatt

CREDITS

writers Ray Cameron,.Barry Cryer, Andrew Marshall/David Renwick, Terry Ravenscroft, Peter Vincent · director/producer Ray Cameron

Assaulted Nuts delivered forth a barrage of rapid-fire jokes, many of which exceeded the borders of outrageousness – often it seemed, simply for the thrill of doing so. Any subject was up for grabs, not least sex, with Cleo Rocos mostly seen in her undies.

It's hard to resist the thought that this was **The Kenny Everett Television Show** without Everett. Not only was Rocos in that BBC series but the writers Ray Cameron, Barry Cryer and Andrew Marshall/David Renwick were all taking time out from working with the wacky DJ.

The Associates

USA · ABC (PARAMOUNT/JOHN CHARLES WALTERS PRODUCTIONS) · SITCOM

13 × 30 mins · colour

US dates: 23 Sep–28 Oct 1979 & 27 Mar–17 Apr 1980 (9 episodes)

UK dates: 15 July–14 Oct 1982 (13 episodes) BBC2 Thu around 10.15pm

MAIN CAST

Emerson Marshall · · · · · · Wilfrid Hyde White
Tucker Kerwin · · · · · · · · · · · · · Martin Short
Leslie Dunn · · · · · · · · · · · · · · · Alley Mills
Eliot Streeter · · · · · · · · · · · · · Joe Regalbuto
Sara James · · · · · · · · · · · · · Shelley Smith
Johnny Danko · · · · · · · · · · · Tim Thomerson

CREDITS

writers Charlie R Hauck, Earl Pomerantz, David Lloyd, Stan Daniels/Ed Weinberger, John Steven Owen · directors James Burrows, Tony Mordente, Charlotte Brown · executive producers James L Brooks, Stan Daniels, Ed Weinberger · producer Michael Leeson

A classy ensemble comedy set in the offices of Bass & Marshall, a prestigious Manhattan law firm, with episodes following the exploits of 'the associates' (apprentice lawyers) as they unravelled the complexities of the legal system. Martin Short (in an early role) played newcomer Tucker Kerwin, a bright and idealistic law school graduate whose freshness contrasted with the greedy opportunism of recently appointed partner Eliot Streeter. Tucker's girlfriend Leslie Dunn also found herself at odds with the system owing to her attempts to help the poor and oppressed, a class not usually considered by the firm to be worthy of their advice. The other associate, Sara James, had an easier time fitting into the style of the firm, being the product of an established Bostonian family. Overseeing them was the senior partner, Emerson Marshall, who ranged from paternalistic to domineering in his relation to his charges. Lastly there was the macho and lusty office boy, Johnny Danko (played by the capable Tim Thomerson who would go on to other TV projects and a successful career in B-movies).

The Associates had a formidable array of talent behind it, which resulted in fine, thoughtful scripts and plots based on subjects rarely tackled in sitcoms. One episode cheekily had the lawyers called in to sort out some censorship problems on a sitcom, and concluding that those censorship problems made it impossible to create a funny script. Critics loved The Associates – they applauded its thoughtfulness among the more simplistic fare on offer elsewhere, but the public disagreed. Their indifference sentenced the series to an early demise and it was taken off air in the USA after only nine episodes, with four unseen. All 13 aired in the UK, where the starring role for venerable British actor Wilfrid Hyde White was of particular appeal, and Americans finally got to catch up with the missing four when the cable A&E Network treated them to a full re-run, ensuring that justice was finally served.

Astronauts

UK · ITV (WITZEND PRODUCTIONS FOR ATV) · SITCOM

7 × 30 mins · colour

26 Oct–7 Dec 1981 · Mon 8pm

MAIN CAST

Commander Malcolm Mattocks · Christopher Godwin
Doctor Gentian Foster · · · Carmen Du Sautoy
Technical Officer David Ackroyd · Barrie Rutter
Beadle · · · · · · · · · · · · · · · · · · · Bruce Boa

CREDITS

writers Graeme Garden/Bill Oddie · script editors Dick Clement/Ian La Frenais · director Douglas Argent · executive producer Allan McKeown · producers Tony Charles/Douglas Argent

Britain's first three astronauts – two male, one female – blast off into outer space to occupy a 'sky lab' for six months, taking with them a dog and the usual cages of white mice and other insects. Beadle, an antipathetic American, is the astronauts' contact at Mission Control.

Written by Garden and Oddie, two of **The Goodies**, the comedy in Astronauts was rooted in the tensions that developed between the space travellers inside their claustrophobic two-room tin-can. As someone commented at the time, indeed, it seemed that only the dog was normal. (Said bitch, Bimbo, had hitherto appeared in The Goodies and so was comfortable with Garden and Oddie scripts.) While the writers had high hopes for their series, though, Astronauts made little impact – and not only in Britain either, but also in the USA, perhaps its more natural home. An American company, Elmar Productions, bought the adaptation rights to the series and persuaded CBS to network a pilot (on 11 August 1982), titled The Astronauts, but it failed to develop any further. Granville Van Dusen, Brianne Leary and Bruce Davison played the orbiting space explorers, McLean Stevenson (Henry Blake in M*A*S*H) was cast as the Mission Control contact.

At Home

UK · BBC · SITCOM

1 × 45 mins · b/w

3 June 1948 · Thu 8.45pm

MAIN CAST

Richard Murdoch
Kenneth Horne
Sam Costa

CREDITS

writers Richard Murdoch/Kenneth Horne · *producer* Walton Anderson

Starring on BBC radio in their much-loved sitcom *Much-Binding-In-The-Marsh* (on air from 2 January 1947 to 23 March 1954), Richard Murdoch and Kenneth Horne appeared in this one-off TV special that also featured another leading player from that radio series, Sam Costa, as the 'odd jobs man', and other special guests.

At Home With Dr Evadne Hinge And Dame Hilda Bracket

see Hinge and Bracket

At Home With Jimmy And Ben

see JEWEL, Jimmy and Ben Warriss

At Last … It's Mike Elliott

UK · C4 (TYNE TEES) · STANDUP

6 × 30 mins · colour

4 June–9 July 1983 · Sat mostly 11pm

MAIN CAST

Mike Elliott

CREDITS

writer Mike Elliott · *director* Tony Bulley · *producer* Heather Ging

A series for the outsize Geordie with a personality to match, whose humour was considered by the IBA too offensive and adult for mainstream ITV scheduling, even in a late-night slot – the six programmes were originally set for screening on ITV in autumn 1982 but the IBA forced their cancellation. The overseer relented less than a year later, however, permitting the series to be seen on the more daring C4 network.

Elliott, aged 37 at the time, was big news in the North-East, and accepted the inevitable comparisons with Billy Connolly suggested by their mutual affection for wringing humour out of bodily functions and other earthy subject matters.

At Last The 1948 Show

UK · ITV (REDIFFUSION) · SKETCH

13 × 30 mins · b/w

Series One (6) 15 Feb–22 Mar 1967 · Wed around 10pm

Series Two (7) 26 Sep–7 Nov 1967 · Tue around 8.30pm

MAIN CAST

Tim Brooke-Taylor
Graham Chapman
John Cleese
Marty Feldman
Aimi Macdonald

OTHER APPEARANCES

Eric Idle
Dick Vosburgh
Jo Kendall
Barry Cryer
Bill Oddie

CREDITS

writers Tim Brooke-Taylor, Graham Chapman, John Cleese, Marty Feldman · *executive producer* David Frost · *director* Ian Fordyce

In the family tree that plots the birth of ***Monty Python's Flying Circus*** in 1969, *At Last The 1948 Show*, from 1967, is the main supporting branch. It was here that Graham Chapman and John Cleese were first given the opportunity to write and perform the kind of unrelated skits that would change sketch comedy as we know it. (A third Python, Eric Idle, also appeared in some editions.) The series was also a platform for the major comic talents of Marty Feldman (hitherto a comic writer content to remain out of the spotlight, after *1948* he would become a major star) and the future ***Goodies*** member Tim Brooke-Taylor, who also wrote and performed their original material. The fifth member of the *1948* team, not a writer, was 'the lovely Aimi Macdonald', a dumb-blonde character who, by way of a long-running premise, thought that she was the star of the show. In the first series Macdonald would introduce her show and invite viewers to send in money to the 'Make the lovely Aimi Macdonald a rich lady fund'. For the second series new recurring hostesses were introduced each week alongside Aimi, each sharing her attributes of cuteness and dimness, so by the final show a small chorus line, all speaking at once, linked the items.

The series had great energy and the sketches exploded into all sorts of zany areas. It also offered opportunities for the male cast to dress up as women, a device that would be a hallmark of the later *Python* shows. The series' unusual title was, supposedly, a wry comment from Cleese relating to the length of time that it took programme controllers to green-light a show. David Frost, who had promoted John Cleese in his BBC series ***The Frost Report***, executive-produced *At Last The 1948 Show*.

Note. Despite its great success in the London area *1948* was not networked and some ITV regions did not screen it at all.

At The Drop Of A Hat

At The Drop Of Another Hat

see Flanders and Swann

At The Eleventh Hour

UK · BBC · SKETCH/SATIRE

10 × 35 mins · b/w

30 Dec 1967–2 Mar 1968 · BBC1 Sat around 11.15pm

MAIN CAST

Jeanie Lambe
Miriam Margolyes
Roger McGough
Richard Neville
Alan Shallcross
The Scaffold

CREDITS

director Peter Chafer · *producer* Anthony Smith

Subtitled 'An end-of-the-week look at the world or an end-of-the-world look at the week', this was a typical 1960s-format experiment combining comedy, comment, poetry and pop. Filling the slot vacated by the departing ***Twice A Fortnight***, the series was aimed squarely at the same post-pub or post-dinner-party Saturday night 'liberal' viewers.

Each show featured a topical song (*à la* Millicent Martin's ***That Was The Week That Was*** intro) sung by Jeanie Lambe and written by Ray Davies of the Kinks; Miriam Margolyes demonstrated her young comic talents; and Richard Neville, editor of the 'underground' paper *Oz*, brought a satirical edge to the proceedings by conducting weekly on-air experiments, some of a slightly risqué nature. In the first show he demonstrated just how illiberal 'Swinging London' really was, by representing an unmarried couple and trying to book for them a double berth on a ship, a double sleeper on a train, a double room at a hotel and a holiday camp chalet. Poetry was read by Roger McGough and music provided by his humorous combo the Scaffold and others.

At Your Service, Ltd

UK · BBC · CHILDREN'S SITCOM

7 × 30 mins · b/w

5 Sep–28 Nov 1951 · Wed around 5.30pm

MAIN CAST

Bob Sherwood · · · · · · · · · · · · Bruce Gordon
Alistair MacHine · · · · Peter Forbes-Robertson

CREDITS

writers Hazel Adair/Robert Tronson · *producer* Alan Bromly

A comedy-adventure series presented as part of the programming strand *For The Children*. In these years, a two-hour closedown, familiarly but informally known as the

Toddler's Truce, would follow *For The Children* to allow parents to put their children to bed.

Atletico Partick

UK · BBC · SITCOM

7 × 30 mins · colour

Pilot *Atletico Partick AFC* 28 Aug 1995 · BBC1 Mon 8.30pm
One series (6) 25 July–30 Aug 1996 · BBC1 Thu mostly 9.30pm then Fri around 10.50pm

MAIN CAST

Jack Roan	Gordon Kennedy
Karen Roan	Aline Mowat
Ally	Tom McGovern
Lachie	Steven McNicoll
Pettigrew	Iain McColl
Bonner	Clive Russell (series)
Marie	Anne Marie Timoney (series)
Gazza	Ronnie Letham (series)

CREDITS

writer Ian Pattison · *director/producer* Colin Gilbert

The difficulties in mounting authentic action and the degree of necessary location shooting has resulted in few sitcoms with a sporting theme. *Atletico Partick* managed to overcome both problems, first by having its protagonists play in a strictly amateur Sunday league – enabling overweight, lumbering actors with few football skills to accurately portray their real-life counterparts – and second by focusing the stories as much on pre-match preliminaries and after-match post-mortems as the actual games themselves. It also dealt at length with the players' relationships with their wives and girlfriends (and some players had both).

The central character was Jack Roan, an undemanding enough chap with a passion for football, a low sex-drive and a sensual but maritally unfulfilled wife, Karen. In the pilot we learn that she is having an affair with Ally, an Atletico Partick player renowned for his sexual philandering. Jack's closest friend is Pettigrew who has his own marital problems (his wife has taken up witchcraft), and most of the other major team members have similar problems. Typical of writer Ian Pattison (the creator of Rab C Nesbitt), there were dark undertones beneath the slapstick surface and some serious issues were tackled: the enduring theme was that the failings of the players' everyday lives could be counterbalanced by small victories on the pitch. The characters were endearing, and although the series may not always have delivered on the comedy front it was nevertheless amiable enough and highly watchable.

An Audience With Jasper Carrott

see CARROTT, Jasper

An Audience With ...

UK · ITV/*C4 (LWT) · STANDUP

23 editions (60 mins unless stated) · colour

1. 'Dame Edna Everage' · 26 Dec 1980 · Fri 10.15pm
2. Dudley Moore · 26 Dec 1981 · Sat 9.45pm
3. *Kenneth Williams · 23 Dec 1983 · Fri 10.25pm (90 mins)
4. *Mel Brooks (with Anne Bancroft) · 4 Feb 1984 · Sat 8.30pm
5. *Joan Rivers · 17 Mar 1984 · Sat 9.30pm
6. *'Dame Edna Everage' (*Another Audience With ...*) · 31 Dec 1984 · Mon 10.30pm
7. *Billy Connolly · 26 Oct 1985 · Sat 11pm
8. *Peter Ustinov · 3 Jan 1988 · Sun 9.15pm
9. Victoria Wood · 10 Dec 1988 · Sat 9.05pm
10. 'Dame Edna Everage' (*One More Audience With ...*) · 25 Dec 1988 · Sun 10.25pm
11. *Jackie Mason · 27 Dec 1990 · Thu 10pm
12. Bob Monkhouse · 21 May 1994 · Sat 9pm
13. Jimmy Tarbuck · 22 Oct 1994 · Sat 9pm
14. Ken Dodd · 3 Dec 1994 · Sat 8.05pm (75 mins)
15. Shirley Bassey · 21 Oct 1995 · Sat 9pm
16. Freddie Starr · 2 Mar 1996 · Sat 9.05pm
17. Sooty · 24 Oct 1996 · Thu 4.25pm (45 mins)
18. Bruce Forsyth · 1 Feb 1997 · Sat 9pm
19. 'Alf Garnett' (Warren Mitchell) · 5 Apr 1997 · Sat 9.05pm
20. Elton John · 27 Sep 1997 · Sat 9pm (90 mins)
21. Freddie Starr (*Another Audience With ...*) · 11 Oct 1997 · Sat 9pm
22. Ronnie Corbett · 25 Oct 1997 · Sat 9pm
23. The Spice Girls · 29 Nov 1997 · Sat 7.30pm

CREDITS (EDITION NUMBERS)

directors Alasdair Macmillan (1, 3–8, 11, 22), Ken O'Neill (2), David G Hillier (9 & 16), David Bell (10), Patricia Mordecai (12 & 14), Ian Hamilton (13 & 21), Nigel Lythgoe (15), Jonathan Glazier (17–20), Tony Gregory (23) · *executive producers* David Bell (1), Richard Drewett (4 & 7), Nicholas Barrett (9 & 10), Nigel Lythgoe (18, 21, 22), Nigel Lythgoe/Sydney Rose (19), Nigel Lythgoe/Derek Mackillop/John Reid (20), others not known · *producers* Richard Drewett (1–3, 6), Charles Brand (4), David Bell (5 & 10), Helen Fraser (7 & 8), David G Hillier (9), Nicholas Barrett/Claudia Rosencrantz (11), Lorna Dickinson (12, 14 & 20), Patricia McGowan (13), Graham Stuart (15), Mark Linsey (16), Elaine Gallagher (17), Paul Lewis (18 & 22), John Kaye Cooper (19), Ian Hamilton (21), Andi Peters (23)

A long-running series of occasional programmes, taped in London and usually screened at peak-time on weekend or holiday evenings. They star a top name typically presenting his or her stage routine or telling a life story, or a mixture of both, to an audience packed with celebrities, the camera spending most of the time on the star but plenty too on the audience. Although spontaneity is implied, questions to the star from members of the audience are worked out in advance and rehearsed. Much great material has been aired in these programmes and they can serve as an invaluable record of a performer's art – especially useful, as broadcasters who do these things would confirm, for preparing obituaries.

Notes. With effect from the Shirley Bassey programme, in 1995, *An Audience With ...* has no longer restricted itself solely to those whose trademark is humour, but for the sake of completeness non-comics have been included in the above details. *An Audience With ... Les Dawson* was to have been recorded in June 1993, but the comedian died a few days earlier. The Alf Garnett programme was written by Johnny Speight; Ronnie Corbett's by Ian Davidson and Peter Vincent with additional material by Spike Mullins, David Renwick, Dick Vosburgh and Georgia Pritchett. The Spice Girls' edition was anticipated by a half-hour documentary (*Zig-A-Zag-Ah: The Spice Of Life*, screened by children's ITV on 27 November 1997) which showed the production team putting the programme together. Shirley Bassey, who was accorded the *An Audience With ...* treatment in October 1995, also appeared in a similar-style special, *Happy Birthday Shirley*, screened on 11 January 1997.

References to relevant *An Audience With ...* programmes have also been made under these separate entries: Billy Connolly, Ken Dodd, Barry Humphries (for the three Dame Edna Everage shows), Bob Monkhouse, Freddie Starr, Jimmy Tarbuck and Victoria Wood.

See also *An Evening With ...*

Auntie's Bloomers

UK · BBC (CELADOR PRODUCTIONS*) · OUTTAKES COMEDY

10 editions (3 × 50 mins · 2 × 45 mins · 3 × 40 mins · 2 × 30 mins) · colour

*1. 29 Dec 1991 · BBC1 Sun 7.15pm (50 mins)
2. *More Auntie's Bloomers* 27 Dec 1992 · BBC1 Sun 7.15pm (50 mins)
3. *Auntie's New Bloomers* 26 Dec 1994 · BBC1 Mon 5.45pm (40 mins)
4. *Auntie's New Bloomers* 1 Jan 1995 · BBC1 Sun 8pm (45 mins)
5. *Auntie's Brand New Bloomers* 25 Dec 1995 · BBC1 Mon 6.45pm (45 mins)
6. *Auntie's All-New Christmas Bloomers* 25 Dec 1996 · BBC1 Wed 5.40pm (50 mins)
7. *Auntie's All-New Bloomers* 31 Mar 1997 · BBC1 Mon 6pm (40 mins)
8. *Auntie's Natural Bloomers* 14 July 1997 · BBC1 Mon 8.30pm (30 mins)
9. *Auntie's New Festive Bloomers* 25 Dec 1997 · BBC1 Thu 6pm (40 mins)
10. *Auntie's New Winter Bloomers* 29 Dec 1997 · BBC1 Mon 8.30pm (30 mins)

PRESENTER

Terry Wogan

CREDITS (PROGRAMME NUMBERS)

linking writers included Steve Knight/Mike Whitehill · *directors* Patricia Mordecai (1), Ian Hamilton (2), John L Spencer (3 & 4), not known (5), Richard Valentine (6), Jeremy Connor (7), Anne Gilchrist (8), Gareth Carrivick (9 & 10) · *producers* Paul Smith (1 & 2), Tom Webber (3–10)

In response to the success of ITV's long-running outtakes series *It'll Be Alright On The Night*, the BBC aired its own collection of boo-boos, mishaps, verbal indiscretions and general cock-ups. The ubiquitous Terry Wogan acted as link between the gallery of gaffes and the majority of the clips came from the BBC's own archive. By 1991 it was perhaps an unoriginal premise but there was a public appetite for such programmes and the fascination for unexpected slapstick and unplanned occurrences remained as strong as ever.

Note. The seventh programme, *Auntie's Natural Bloomers*, was a collection of gaffes captured during the filming of wildlife and animal programmes.

See also *Auntie's Sporting Bloomers*.

Auntie's Sporting Bloomers

UK · BBC · OUTTAKES COMEDY

10 × 30 mins · colour

Series One (5) 11 July–15 Aug 1995 · BBC1
Tue 8.30pm

Series Two (5) 20 June–18 July 1996 · BBC1
Thu 8.30pm

Series Three (6) 6 June–11 July 1997 · BBC1
Fri 8.30pm

MAIN CAST

host · Terry Wogan
Andy Parsons (series 3)
Henry Naylor (series 3)

CREDITS

directors John L Spencer (series 1), Richard Valentine (series 2), Anne Gilchrist (series 3) · *producer* Tom Webber

Sporting gaffes, miscues, pile-ups and own goals pulled from the archives and linked by Terry Wogan in this themed spin-off from *Auntie's Bloomers*. In series three, Wogan was joined each week by comedy duo Parsons and Naylor who took a specific look at one style of 'cock-up'.

A year before *Auntie's Sporting Bloomers* was first aired, ITV launched its own series of sporting outtakes and mistakes, *Oddballs* (made by Trans World International for Carlton). Presented by Eamonn Holmes, and taped before a studio audience, these erratically scheduled half-hour programmes typically featured guest celebrities from the sporting world, and mixed anecdotal-style interviews with the clips. Programmes screened to the end of the 1997 were: 13 July 1994, 19 October 1994, 6 September 1995 (guests included Steve Davis and Martin

Offiah, with sports personality impressionist Alistair McGowan), 27 September 1995 (Kriss Akabusi, Steven Redgrave and Alistair McGowan), 18 October 1995 (Andy Gray, Willie Carson and Alistair McGowan), 4 January 1996 (Oliver Skeete and Karren Brady), 4 April 1996 (William 'The Refrigerator' Perry, with comedian Kevin Day), 15 October 1996 (Barry McGuigan, Geoff Hurst, Kenneth Wolstenholme and comic actor Dermot Morgan), 19 March 1997 (Vinnie Jones, Allan Lamb and Alistair McGowan), 24 April 1997 (Frankie Dettori, Roger Black and Alistair McGowan) and 28 May 1997 (Colin Jackson, Ronnie O'Sullivan and Alistair McGowan). Trans World International's single programme *World Cup Bloopers*, spotlighting unintentionally funny moments from the soccer tournament held every four years, was made in 1994 and screened by London-area ITV on 16 May 1997.

ITV has also screened *Sports Bloopers*, American-made compilations of US outtakes. Of varying length – anything between five and 20 minutes long – these have been screened on different dates by different ITV regions, usually deep into the night. In London they were broadcast on 21 May 1989 and on nine dates from 10 May to 11 August 1991.

See also *Bad Sports*.

B-And-B

UK · BBC · SITCOM

7 × 30 mins · b/w

Pilot · 7 June 1968 · BBC1 Fri 8.20pm

One series (6) 13 Nov–18 Dec 1968 · BBC1 Wed 8.20pm

MAIN CAST

Bernie	Bernard Braden
Barbara	Barbara Kelly
Sally	Kim Braden
Johnny	Mark Griffith
Chantal	Pauline Collins (pilot)

CREDITS

writer Michael Pertwee · *producer* Michael Mills

Husband-and-wife partners Bernard Braden and Barbara Kelly starred in this domestic sitcom as a married couple each with a successful career in the entertainment world. (Their daughter Kim Braden also appeared.) The situation was obviously intended to represent realistic slices of their lives but the plots were purely fictitious, covering such relatively (for the time) sophisticated areas as, in the *Comedy Playhouse* pilot, Bernard falling for their French au-pair Chantal (played by Pauline Collins); Bernard thinking his wife is having an affair; the pair of them becoming convinced that their children are taking drugs; and, in the final episode, the pair seriously contemplating divorce.

See also *Barbara With Braden, Bath-Night With Braden, Early To Braden, An Evening At Home With Bernard Braden And Barbara Kelly* and *Kaleidoscope.*

Bachelor Father

UK · BBC · SITCOM

24 episodes (22 × 30 mins · 2 × short specials) · colour

Series One (13) 17 Sep–10 Dec 1970 · BBC1 Thu 7.45pm

Short special · part of *Christmas Night With The Stars* 25 Dec 1970 · BBC1 Fri 6.45pm

Series Two (9) 16 Sep–11 Nov 1971 · BBC1 Thu 8pm

Short special · part of *Christmas Night With The Stars* 25 Dec 1971 · BBC1 Sat 6.40pm

MAIN CAST

Peter Lamb	Ian Carmichael
Harry	Gerald Flood (series 1)
Mary	Rona Anderson (series 1)
Mr Gibson	Colin Gordon (series 1)
Mr Moore	Jack May (series 1)
Mrs Moore	Pauline Yates
	(series 1 & first special)
Mrs Rathbone	Sonia Graham
Norah	Diana King
Ben	Ian Johnson
Anna	Briony McRoberts
Donald	Roland Pickering
	(series 1 & first special)
	Andrew Bowen (series 2)
Mrs Pugsley	Joan Hickson
Freddie	Michael Douglas
Jane	Beverley Simons
Ginny	Jacqueline Cowper (series 2)
Jo	Gerry Cowper (series 2)
Christopher	Kevin Moran (series 2)

CREDITS

writer Richard Waring · *producer* Graeme Muir

A return to situation comedy for Ian Carmichael, following his top-hole role as upper-class ass Bertie Wooster in *The World Of Wooster*. *Bachelor Father* was a family comedy, loosely based on the life of Peter Lloyd Jeffcock, a bachelor foster-father to 12 children who had recounted his story in his autobiography *Only Uncle*.

The TV series was written by Carmichael's *Wodehouse* adapter Richard Waring, who based some of the plots upon incidents in *Only Uncle*. Waring admitted that he would have stuck closer to the original story but for the fact that it was so far-fetched that audiences would have had difficulty believing it – truth in this case clearly being stranger than fiction. In the series, Carmichael played well-to-do Peter Lamb, who had always wanted a family but failed to strike up a long-lasting romantic relationship. In the first episode he hit upon the idea of fostering and through the ensuing stories built up his surrogate family of diverse children.

Carmichael was something of a perfectionist and picked his projects carefully – he was not a jobbing actor and had to believe strongly in the worth of the material before accepting a role. Typically, he originated his own projects or became closely involved with the development of any productions in which he was involved. For this reason *Bachelor Father*, although ostensibly a middle-of-the-road family sitcom of no great ambition, came over as a polished and professional piece of work that pleased audiences over two extended series. Never one to outstay his welcome, Carmichael moved on to fresh challenges when he felt that the idea had been sufficiently explored.

Note. This BBC series is unrelated to an American sitcom of the same title, networked there by, in turn, CBS, NBC and ABC from 1957 to 1962, but not seen on British TV.

The Bachelor Girls

UK · BBC · SITCOM

1 × 25 mins · b/w

26 Oct 1963 · Sat 9.45pm

MAIN CAST

Sally	Tracy Reed
Joan	Anna Palk
Peter	Edward Fox

CREDITS

writer John Freeman · *producer* Douglas Moodie

A *Comedy Playhouse* pilot about two young ladies who share a flat in a fashionable area. Despite the fact that it was written by John Freeman, author of the very popular BBC sitcom *Hugh And I*, no series developed this time around.

Backs To The Land

UK · ITV (ANGLIA) · SITCOM

19 × 30 mins · colour

Series One (6) 15 Apr–20 May 1977 · Fri 7.30pm

Series Two (6) 2 Dec 1977–6 Jan 1978 · Fri 7.30pm

Series Three (7) 21 July–1 Sep 1978 · Fri 7.30pm

MAIN CAST

Shirley Bloom	Philippa Howell
Jenny Dabb	Terese Stevens
Daphne Finch-Beauchamp	
	Marilyn Galsworthy (first 7 episodes)
Bunny Burroughs	Pippa Page
	(from series 2)
Tom Whitlow	John Stratton
Ethel Whitlow	Della Paton
Roy Whitlow	David Troughton (series 1)
Eric Whitlow	Michael Troughton (series 1)
Captain Truscott	Jeremy Child (series 2)

OTHER APPEARANCES

Wally	Charles Lamb
Miss Rainbow	Geraldine Newman
Landlord	Peter Tuddenham

CREDITS

writer David Climie · *directors* David Askey (series 1 & 2), John Davies (series 3) · *executive producer* John Rosenberg

It is 1940, and three young women – Daphne (dizzy deb), Jenny (chirpy cockney) and Shirley (Jewish, level-headed and, appropriately, down to earth) – are in the Women's Land Army, replacing the male farmworkers who have gone off to fight in foreign fields. They land up in Clayfield, Norfolk, at Crabtree Farm, owned by stingy Farmer Tom, leading to three series of straw-biting, milk-churning comedy adventures from that lesser-spotted ITV sitcom provider, Anglia. Farmer's boys Roy and Eric (played by brothers David and Michael Troughton, sons of Patrick) provided a little love interest in the first series while the second saw Daphne leave to be replaced by a very theatrical actress – her character equally unbelievable – named Bunny.

Bad Boyes

UK · BBC · CHILDREN'S SITCOM

16 episodes (10 × 25 mins · 6 × 20 mins) · colour

Series One (6 × 20 mins) 15 Sep–20 Oct 1987 · BBC1 Tue 4.40pm

Series Two (10 × 25 mins) 20 Oct–22 Dec 1988 · BBC1 Thu 4.35pm

MAIN CAST

Bryan Arthur Derek Boyes · · · Steven Kember
Edward Slogg ('Slug') · · · · · · · Warren Brian
Mr Boyes · · · · · · · · · · · · · · · · Dean Harris
Mrs Boyes · · · · · · · · · · · · · Susan Jameson
Mr Wiggis · · · · · · · · · · · · · · · Gregory Cox
Headmaster · · · · · · · · · · · Christopher Owen
Bernetta Vincent · · · · · · · · Nicola Greenhill
Juggs · · · · · · · · · · · · · · · · · Nicholas Cox
Gran · Lila Kaye
Bonni · · · · · · · · · · · Anna Dawson (series 2)
Clyde · · · · · · · · · · · Berwick Kaler (series 2)
Herbert · · · · · · · · Michael Deeks (series 2)

CREDITS

writers Jim Eldridge/Duncan Eldridge · producer Jeremy Swan

The adventures of Bryan Boyes, an artful dodger who uses his keen brain to scheme rather than employ it for school work. Bryan's forte is pulling the wool over the eyes of his contemporaries and elders, so he is always one jump ahead of his teachers, the school bully 'Slug' and the other unsavoury characters who cross his path. An assortment of petty criminals are undone by his genius and a number of baffling mysteries are solved, but while Bryan's dad is completely taken in by his son's innocent façade, his mother isn't fooled so easily: she knows that behind his angelic features devilish plots are being hatched.

Writers Jim Eldridge and his son Duncan had created the character for the 'Diary Of X' sections of the best-selling children's books *How To Handle Grown-Ups*, *What Grown-Ups Say And What They Really Mean*, and *More Ways To Handle Grown-Ups*. When the BBC expressed an interest in making a TV series based around the diarist, the authors had to come up with a name for the character and so BAD (Bryan Arthur Derek) Boyes was born.

Jim Eldridge was also the author of a hit school-based series for BBC Radio 4 at this time, *King Street Junior* (51 episodes from 25 March 1985 to 28 May 1992), which was aimed at a more mature audience.

See also *The Uncle Jack Series*.

Bad Boys

UK · BBC · SITCOM

7 episodes (6 × 30 mins · 1 × 50 mins) · colour

Pilot (50 mins) 10 Jan 1995 · BBC1 Thu 9.30pm

One series (6 × 30 mins) 29 May–15 July 1996 · BBC1 Wed then Mon 10.10pm

MAIN CAST

Wayne Todd · · · · · · · · · · · · · Karl Howman
Fraser Hood · · · · · · · · · · · Freddie Broadley
Malky 'Tissue' Mulherron · · · · · Alex Norton
Betty Hood · · · · · · · Barbara Rafferty (pilot);
· · · · · · · · · · · · · · · · · · Aline Mowat (series)
Maureen · · · · · · · · · · · · · · · Sally Howitt
Morag Hood · · · · · · · · · · · Katy Hale (pilot);
· · · · · · · · · · · · · · · · Ashley Jensen (series)
Rumney · · · · · · · · · · · · · · Malcolm Shields

CREDITS

writers Ian Pattison (3) James MacInnes (1), Bernard McKenna (1), Patrick Harkins (1), Alan Whiting (1) · directors John Stroud (4), Ron Bain (2), Jim Shields (1) · producers Colin Gilbert, Tom Kinninmont

Camel-coated Glaswegian crook Fraser, with his shabby East End of London pal Wayne, first appeared in a series of TV commercials for McEwans beer. The pair struck a chord with the public, especially in Scotland, and *Rab C Nesbitt* writer Ian Pattison concocted a 50-minute comedy-drama for the pair as a prelude to a series. In the pilot, Wayne is driven out of London by a hardened villain and seeks refuge with his old cell mate Fraser. The series followed the exploits of the mismatched pair, the comedy arising from their rather volatile relationship.

Bad Sports

UK · BBC · OUTTAKES COMEDY

2 × 10 mins · colour

9 June & 16 June 1994 · BBC1 Thu 8.50pm

MAIN CAST
Jo Brand

CREDITS

director Alexis Giradet · producer Gerard Barry

Sporting foul-ups and blunders introduced and commented upon by the comedian Jo Brand.

See also *Auntie's Sporting Bloomers*.

Badger's Set

UK · ITV (YORKSHIRE) · SITCOM

1 × 30 mins · colour

23 Sep 1974 · Mon 8pm

MAIN CAST

Eric Badger/Dr Badger · · · · · · Julian Orchard
Natasha Karavanovna · · · · · · · · Gwen Taylor
Mrs Badger · · · · · · · · · · · · · · · Beryl Cooke
Mrs Robash · · · · · · · · · · · · · · Maggie Flint

CREDITS

writer Barry Took · producer Paddy Russell

An unsuccessful single comedy pilot produced by Yorkshire TV in 1974. (*Rising Damp* and *Oh No – It's Selwyn Froggitt* sprang from the same company.) This one was written by Barry Took and starred Julian Orchard – the supporting player in so many sitcoms – in not one but two roles: as a panel-game wit and camp ballet critic famous for

his devastating reviews, and as his non-comprehending father. (One wonders whether Kenneth Williams, with whom Took was associated for some years in the BBC radio series *Round The Horne*, was the writer's inspiration.)

Bagdad Cafe

USA · CBS (ZEV BRAUN PRODUCTIONS/NEW WORLD TELEVISION/PATCHETT KAUFMAN ENTERTAINMENT) · SITCOM

15 × 30 mins · colour

US dates: 30 Mar 1990–27 July 1991

*UK dates: 12 Sep–5 Dec 1991 (13 episodes) C4 Thu 8.30pm

MAIN CAST

Brenda · · · · · · · · · · · · · · Whoopi Goldberg
Jasmine Zweibel · · · · · · · · · Jean Stapleton
Rudy Cox · · · · · · · · · · · · · · James Gammon
Junie · · · · · · · · · · · · · · · · Scott Lawrence
Debbie · · · · · · · · · · · · · · · Monica Calhoun
Dewey Kunkle · · · · · · · · · · · · Sam Whipple
Sal · · · · · · · · · · · · · · · · · · Cleavon Little

CREDITS

creator Percy Adlon · writers various · director Paul Bogart · executive producers Sy Rosen, Mort Lachman, Tom Patchett, Kenneth Kaufman · producers Michael Mount, Vicki S Howits

German director Percy Adlon's delightful 1988 feature film *Bagdad Café* was a quirky comedy that made famous its big star Marianne Sägebrecht. In the movie Sägebrecht played a German tourist, Jasmine, abandoned by her husband in the Mojave desert in California, and finding a new life for herself among the eccentric characters working at and frequenting a rundown truck stop, the Bagdad Café. The TV series re-created this simple premise, but this time Jasmine was an American woman (Jean Stapleton from *All In The Family*) and the accented 'é' in café was dropped. Truck-stop owner Brenda (played in the movie by C C H Pounder) was played here by comedian Whoopi Goldberg, and the gravel-voiced regular Rudy (Jack Palance in the movie) was played by the gravel-voiced James Gammon. Brenda's boy-crazy daughter Debbie was played by Monica Calhoun who had played a similar role (Phyllis) in the original movie.

The central relationship in the piece was between Jasmine and Brenda, a true odd couple. Jasmine was white, neat, and thought well of everyone; Brenda was black, messy, with a deep sense of cynicism. The only thing they had in common was that they were both separated from their husbands. But despite their differences the women got along well and gradually came to rely on each other for companionship and sisterly solidarity.

Despite the fine leads, the TV series failed to match the off-centre appeal of the movie. It was a credible attempt, however, with an intentional low-key approach and soft tone that tried to capture some of the style of the original, though without Adlon's assured touch it lacked an edge. The whimsical charm of the movie was notably absent in the small-screen version, replaced instead by contrived attempts at 'cuteness' and sometimes heavy-handed sentimentality.

*Note. C4 screened 13 episodes of *Bagdad Cafe* in 1991. London-area ITV showed these and two additional episodes, for the full total of 15 programmes, late on Thursday evenings from 3 August to 16 November 1995.

The Bagthorpe Saga

UK · BBC · CHILDREN'S SITCOM

6 × 30 mins · colour
25 Mar–29 Apr 1981 · Wed 5.05pm

MAIN CAST
Henry Bagthorpe ······· Edward Hardwicke
Laura Bagthorpe ·········· Angela Thorne
Grandma ··············· Phillada Sewell
William Bagthorpe ············ Ceri Seel
Jack Bagthorpe ··········· Richard Orme
Tess Bagthorpe ·············· Ruth Potter
Mrs Fosdyke ············· Dandy Nichols
Uncle Parker ··············· Tim Preece
Daisy Parker ·········· Rebecca Lalonde
Aunt Celia ············· Madeline Smith

CREDITS
creator Helen Cresswell · *adapter/writer* James Andrew Hall · *director* Paul Stone · *executive producer* Anna Home

Comic adventures with a family of British eccentrics, the Bagthorpes. The series was based on the books by Helen Cresswell, creator of *Lizzie Dripping*, another character who had been successfully dramatised for BBC television. The Bagthorpes were a mad bunch: mother Laura wrote an agony column but her own life contained untold problems that she couldn't solve, father Henry was a neurotic TV comedy writer, and Gran was a Scrabble cheat always hiding the 'Q' in her handbag. The next generation were equally flawed, especially niece Daisy, a serial arsonist who left a trail of destruction in her wake. Only young Jack was normal – normal, that is, save for the fact that he had the power to see into the future. Adding to the fun was the family dog Zero (played by Lottie) an animal of stupendous denseness, too dumb even to fetch a stick. Despite this, Zero was still poised to become a celebrity when a TV company descended on the Bagthorpes in a three-part story that dominated the second half of the series.

Baker's Half-Dozen

UK · ITV (ATV) · SITCOMS

6 × 30 mins
*22 Sep–25 Oct 1967 · mostly Wed 9pm

Joe Baker, whose own series *The Joe Baker Show* (ITV, 1965) depicted the comic actor as the gormless short fat man, stepped out with a series of single comedy ideas, each week portraying a different role, ably supported by a resident team of actors (Toni Palmer, Brian Murphy, John Carlin, Charles Lloyd Pack and Mollie Peters).

*Note. Owing to scheduling problems only five episodes were originally screened. Bizarrely, the sixth and final programme went out (in London, at least) nine years later – in a post-midnight slot on 28 September 1976.

One Night With You   22 SEP 1967

MAIN CAST
Flying Officer Baker ··········· Joe Baker
Gladys Copthorne ··········· Toni Palmer
Taffy ···················· Brian Murphy
Roger ···················· John Carlin
Group Capt Foster ······ Charles Lloyd Pack
The Girl ················· Mollie Peters

CREDITS
writer David Cumming · *producer* Alan Tarrant

Crimewave 1967   27 SEP 1967

MAIN CAST
Joey ···················· Joe Baker
Freda Hopworthy ··········· Toni Palmer
Ernie Dexter ·············· Brian Murphy
PC Pendleton ·············· John Carlin
Rev Tankerton ········· Charles Lloyd Pack
The Girl ················· Mollie Peters

CREDITS
writer David Cumming · *producer* Alan Tarrant

Quarter Past One   4 OCT 1967

MAIN CAST
Jody Baker ················ Joe Baker
Katie ···················· Toni Palmer
Barman ··················· Brian Murphy
Lefter ···················· John Carlin
Andy ················· Charles Lloyd Pack
The Girl ················· Mollie Peters

CREDITS
writer David Cumming · *producer* Alan Tarrant

Love Thy Neighbour   18 OCT 1967

MAIN CAST
Joseph ··················· Joe Baker
Muriel Parker ············· Toni Palmer
Tom Parker ··············· Brian Murphy
Rev Brett ················· John Carlin
Mr Smedley ·········· Charles Lloyd Pack
Mrs Smedley ·············· Avis Bunnage
Evadne ··················· Mollie Peters

CREDITS
writer David Cumming · *producer* Alan Tarrant

The Guy Fawkes Night Massacre   25 OCT 1967

MAIN CAST
Joey ···················· Joe Baker
Legs Malone ·············· Toni Palmer
Captain Skelton ··········· Brian Murphy
Alex ···················· John Carlin
Commissioner Harvey ··· Charles Lloyd Pack
Al Capone ················ David Healy
The Girl ················· Mollie Peters

CREDITS
writer David Cumming · *producer* Alan Tarrant

'The Baker'   28 SEP 1976

MAIN CAST
The Baker ················ Joe Baker
Rest of cast: as above, character names not known

CREDITS
writer David Cumming · *producer* Alan Tarrant

A baker trying to sell a wedding cake becomes embroiled in the romantic problems of three couples.

Bakersfield PD

USA · FOX (ROCK ISLAND PRODUCTIONS/TOUCHSTONE TELEVISION) · SITCOM

17 × 30 mins · colour
US dates: 14 Sep 1993–25 Aug 1994
UK dates: 6 Oct 1994–14 Feb 1995 (17 episodes) C4 mostly Thu 10.30pm

MAIN CAST
Detective Wade Preston ········ Ron Eldard
Detective Paul Gigante ·· Ginacarlo Esposito
Officer Denny Boyer ········· Chris Mulkey
Officer Luke Ramirez ·········· Tony Plana
Captain Aldo Stiles ··········· Jack Hallett
Sergeant Phil Hampton ·· Brian Doyle-Murray

CREDITS
creator/main writer/executive producer Larry Levin · *director* Dean Parisot · *producer* Paula Mazur

A quirky, highly amusing cop comedy eschewing the normal trappings of sitcom and closer resembling the action series it sought to spoof.

The series, which aired without a laugh track, followed the misadventures of the hapless cops of Bakersfield PD, concentrating on Detective Paul Gigante. He had voluntarily transferred to Bakersfield (California) from Washington DC following revelations that an impotency expert he had consulted had used his own sperm in fertility operations, thereby ensuring that many of the local inhabitants, being fathered by the same man, would run the risk of inbreeding if they raised families in the same area. Arriving in Bakersfield, Gigante – half black and half Italian – is at first mistaken for a crook by his bigoted but essentially well-meaning colleagues. He is partnered with the ultra-keen Wade Preston, an overwhelming sort obsessed with TV trivia and woefully deficient in basic social skills. Preston is a good detective, however, a fact grudgingly acknowledged by Gigante who is himself a far more skilled operative than most of the locals. Ramirez and Boyer form another cop partnership, a long-term pairing devoted to each other (maybe too devoted in the case of Ramirez, who, despite being a happily married family man, makes no secret of his sexual attraction to the dense Boyer). The station captain is Aldo Stiles, a self-conscious nervy individual who seems totally incapable of making the simplest of decisions without an epic amount of soul searching. For this reason, the wily station sergeant Phil Hampton is the real power behind the throne, manipulating the captain to enable the station to operate smoothly.

Bakersfield PD was a cut above the norm, and was in style far removed from traditional sitcom, but its well-rounded characters, loose but effective plots and sharp dialogue guaranteed plenty of whimsical smiles as well as the odd belly laugh.

The Baldy Man

UK · ITV (*WORKING TITLE TELEVISION FOR CARLTON, **WORKING TITLE TELEVISION FOR YORKSHIRE) · SITCOMS

****13 × 30 mins · colour**

*Series One (5) 13 Apr–30 Aug 1995 · Thu 8.30pm then various days and times

**Series Two (7) 4 Sep–17 Dec 1997 · Thu then Wed 7pm

MAIN CAST
The Baldy Man · · · · · · · · · · · · Gregor Fisher

OTHER REGULAR APPEARANCES (VARIOUS ROLES)
Andy Gray
Iain Gouck
Graham McGregor
Louise Beattie
Sally Howitt

CREDITS
writers see below · *additional material* Iain Campbell, Niall Clark, Alan Hay, Neil MacVicar, Gordon McPherson, Ian Pattison, Louise Rennison, Jim Poulter, Graham Rose, John McGlade, Daniel Naylor, Malcolm Morrison, Dix/Gibson/Measures, Brendan McGeever · *script editors* Dod Pirbright, Johnny Cook · *executive producer* Simon Wright · *director/producer* Colin Gilbert

A series of dialogue-free, visual narratives – with two distinct stories per half-hour – that was strongly reminiscent of *Mr Bean*. Like Rowan Atkinson's more famous character, the Baldy Man is an intensely irritating chap whose other-worldly ideas and manners set him some distance apart from normality and cause intense resentment in others. He's a vain character, believing himself suave and smooth, a man of discernment indeed, someone who, inside or outside his stone-clad bungalow, cannot stop admiring himself in anything that gives off a reflection. What

the Baldy Man somehow doesn't notice is what the rest of us see: he's a rotund, sweaty, deeply unattractive man with but a few strands of hair greased across his pate, someone unable to fathom human relationships and who endures a succession of mishaps with inanimate objects.

The character of the Baldy Man was created by Gregor Fisher and Colin Gilbert for *Naked Video* but really caught the eye in a 1989 series of photo-booth TV commercials for Hamlet cigars, in which, vainly, he tried to obscure his shiny head before the flash popped. Fisher considered his alter ego as the archetypal little man who thinks highly of himself but who 'looks silly and does silly things'. Much effort went into making the TV series – for every day of its filming Fisher's head was painstakingly shaved around the straggly strands – and location shooting took place all over Britain. But this time around, the British public as a whole just didn't take to the character, and were impatient with the grunts and groans and humphs and harrhs that comprised the soundtrack. *The Baldy Man* sold very well internationally, however, much like *Mr Bean*, prompting its maker, Working Title Television, to produce further programmes principally for this market. A second series was screened by some ITV regions in 1997, but only one of the new episodes had aired in London before this book went to press. (The second series dates, above, are those of Scottish Television.)

***Note. Thirteen episodes have been made but only 12 screened.

13 Apr 1995 · Thu 8.30pm
New Look – Baldy Man tries to become a male supermodel. *Delegate* – Baldy Man attends a business conference.
writers Colin Gilbert; Philip Differ/Bob Black

27 Apr 1995 · Thu 8.30pm
Keep Fit – Baldy Man wages war with a fellow customer at a health centre. *Ill* – Baldy Man receives a medical encyclopedia and thinks he has every symptom in the book.
writers Colin Gilbert; Niall Clark

16 Aug 1995 · Wed 8pm
DIY – Baldy Man tries to decorate his best friend's spare room. *Reunion* – Baldy Man renews a rivalry when he attends an old-school gathering.
writers Brendan McGeever/Colin Gilbert; Bob Black/Francis McCrickard

25 Aug 1995 · Fri 8.30pm
Tearoom – Baldy Man displays his disgusting table manners at a café. *Pets* – Baldy Man seeks out the perfect domestic creature.
writers Colin Gilbert; Niall Clark/Bob Black

30 Aug 1995 · Wed 8pm
Bath – Baldy Man tries to take a soak but is interrupted by the doorbell. *Referee* – Baldy Man tries to adjudicate a football match.
writers Niall Clark; John McGlade

(not yet screened)
Hair – Baldy Man causes havoc in a trendy hair salon. *Crime* – Baldy Man is the prime suspect after a spate of neighbourhood burglaries.
writers Niall Clark/Colin Gilbert; Alan Hay/ Philip Differ

4 Sep 1997 · Thu 7pm (STV broadcast; not screened in London)
Goldrush – Baldy Man searches for treasure on the beach. *God* – Baldy Man is mistaken for the deity by a baldness-worshipping sect.
writers Stephen Arnott; Laurie Rowley

11 Sep 1997 · Thu 7pm (STV broadcast; screened in London 1 Jan 1998 · Thu 12.40pm)
Mother's Day – Baldy Man suffers sibling rivalry during the annual maternal celebration. *Smell* – Baldy Man tries to trace a strange odour in his bungalow.
writers Gary Brown; Moray Hunter/Jack Docherty

18 Sep 1997 · Thu 7pm (STV broadcast; not screened in London)
Casualty – Baldy Man causes problems at the local casualty department. *Babysitting* – Baldy Man loses a baby.
writers Colin Gilbert/Dave Burst; Laurie Rowley

22 Oct 1997 · Wed 7pm (STV broadcast; not screened in London)
Barbecue – Baldy Man remembers a long lost love. *China Doll* – Baldy Man tries to woo an attractive female.
writers Laurie Rowley; Moray Hunter/ Jack Docherty

26 Nov 1997 · Wed 7pm (STV broadcast; not screened in London)
Chauffeur Of The Bride – Baldy Man offers to drive a woman to her wedding. *Back Window* – Baldy Man thinks he has witnessed a murder.
writers Colin Gilbert/Dave Burst; Laurie Rowley

10 Dec 1997 · Wed 7pm (STV broadcast; not screened in London)
Litter Avenger – Baldy Man sets out to clean up the town. *Aliens* – Baldy Man is taken on board a UFO.
writers Brendan McGeever/John McGlade; Dave Burst/Donald McLeary

17 Dec 1997 · Wed 7pm (STV broadcast; not screened in London)
Jigsaw – Baldy Man hunts the missing piece. *Murder* – Baldy Man turns detective to solve some serial killings at a hotel.
writer Laurie Rowley (both)

Lucille Ball

Born in Bute, Montana, on 6 August 1911, Lucille Ball struggled determinedly for many years at various levels in the film industry before becoming the acknowledged queen of American television. Her features stopped just short of traditional Hollywood glamour but her dynamic do-anything approach, waspish figure, athleticism, comedic timing and rubber-faced expressions made her agreeable company in a number of romantic and musical comedies. Although standout performances in *Stage Door* (1937) and the Bob Hope vehicles *Sorrowful Jones* (1949) and *Fancy Pants* (1950) attracted attention, she still found the next step – from starlet to star – elusive.

In 1940 Ball had married a Cuban bandleader, Desi Arnaz, and the pair had taken to performing together in cross-country stage-shows. The on-stage relationship they developed for a sketch in one such tour, would, the couple thought, lend itself well to television situation comedy. They were right. The success of *I Love Lucy* (see below) established Lucille Ball as a bona-fide superstar and made she and Desi fabulously wealthy. So rich, indeed, that in an apposite turnaround, she eventually bought the old RKO studios, one of the Hollywood majors that had failed to recognise the starlet's potential. Desilu Productions, Lucy and Desi's company, then proceeded to become a giant player in the US TV industry.

Lucille Ball died on 27 April 1989 following open-heart surgery, but her flickering image lives on, endlessly re-run on television stations across the planet.

See also, within Jack Benny's combined entry, *Jack Benny's 20th Anniversary Show* and *A Love Letter To Jack Benny*.

I Love Lucy

USA · CBS (DESILU PRODUCTIONS) · SITCOM

180 × 30 mins · b/w

US dates: 15 Oct 1951–6 May 1957

*UK dates: 25 Sep 1955–26 Apr 1961 (173 episodes) ITV various days and times

MAIN CAST

Lucy Ricardo · · · · · · · · · · · · · · Lucille Ball
Ricky Ricardo · · · · · · · · · · · · · · Desi Arnaz
Ethel Mertz · · · · · · · · · · · · · · Vivian Vance
Fred Mertz · · · · · · · · · · · · · William Frawley
Little Ricky Ricardo · · · · · · · · Richard Keith
Betty Ramsey · · · · · · · · · Mary Jane Croft
Ralph Ramsey · · · · · · · · · · · Frank Nelson

CREDITS

creators Jess Oppenheimer/Madelyn Pugh/Bob Carroll Jr · *writers* Jess Oppenheimer/Madelyn Pugh/Bob Carroll Jr (127), Jess Oppenheimer/Madelyn Pugh/Bob Carroll Jr/Bob Schiller/Bob Weiskopf (26), Madelyn (Pugh)

Martin/Bob Carroll Jr/Bob Schiller/Bob Weiskopf (27) · *directors* William Asher (103), James V Kern (40), Marc Daniels (37) · *executive producer* Desi Arnaz · *producers* Jess Oppenheimer (153), Desi Arnaz (27)

TV comedies come and TV comedies go but, in America, *I Love Lucy* just runs and runs and runs. You can still see it there, daily, in every city across the continent. And here's why: despite the fact that it hasn't aged particularly well, *I Love Lucy* is a *giant* of a sitcom. It almost single-handedly defined the genre, and it made Lucille Ball, whether or not one likes her style of humour, the First Lady of TV Comedy. Where *I Love Lucy* led, virtually every other US sitcom followed. Its influence was big in Britain too, indeed it was the backbone of the new commercial network from the week that ITV went on air in September 1955.

I Love Lucy is all of this for a number of reasons, the primary one being the tight ensemble playing of the four leading players: red-haired, harebrained, scatter-brained, sometimes no-brained Lucy, her husband (real-life husband too) Ricky the Cuban bandleader, and their friends and next-door neighbours the Mertzes: frumpish Ethel and grumpish Fred. The scripts crackled with great one-liners, the situations – usually based on Lucy mishearing or misunderstanding something or other, or just being plain mischievous – were clever (if repetitive), and the guest stars were impressive: Bob Hope, Harpo Marx, Rock Hudson, Orson Welles, John Wayne and many other top names all appeared. But above all there was Ball herself, gloriously over the top as the incident-prone wife desperate to inveigle herself into the show-business world that her husband inhabited. Her gauche tactics and dynamic slapstick clowning combining to deliver a mélange of memorable sight gags.

Another notable breakthrough was that Lucille Ball and Desi Arnaz's own company, Desilu, which produced the series, made the very early decision to commit the episodes to film, even though most were performed live, and, moreover, did so with a revolutionary three-camera system. The move to film was a purely commercial one: the show's sponsors, tobacco giant Philip Morris, were concerned that the traditional way of broadcasting sitcoms – making a 'kinescope', a poor quality recording direct from the television screen – would mean that the show, taped in Los Angeles, would be sub-standard when screened in New York, where the majority of their smokers resided. Desi Arnaz decided that they could shoot on film, and although the cost of such an enterprise was huge he and Lucy cut $1000 from their own weekly salaries to pay for it.

In so doing, they tagged one vital rider to the contract: they would retain sole rights to the episodes. CBS agreed, cementing a deal that was worth many millions of dollars when Desilu sold the *I Love Lucy* syndication rights some years later. As a result of such foresight and happenstance, there are no lost *I Love Lucy* shows and they've been seen around the world in almost perpetual re-run for nearly half a century.

Notes. The original pilot episode of *I Love Lucy*, not screened at the time, and never shown in Britain, finally made it on to the air in America on 30 March 1990, after a print of the film was discovered among the possessions of a deceased actor who had appeared as a guest in the show. This has not been included in the 180-episode figure. Before the TV series, Lucille Ball had become a star through her appearances on US radio, and when *I Love Lucy* became a hit certain episodes were remade for the aural medium, broadcast over the CBS radio network. These were less successful and transmissions were cancelled after one season.

*C4 screened 141 episodes of *I Love Lucy* from 8 November 1982 to 14 April 1993, with repeats following this date.

See also *Happily Ever After*.

The Lucille Ball Show

USA · CBS (DESILU PRODUCTIONS) · SITCOM

13 × 60 mins · b/w

US dates: 6 Nov 1957–1 Apr 1960

UK dates: 23 July–12 Oct 1962 (12 episodes) ITV Mon then Fri 8pm

MAIN CAST

Lucy Ricardo · · · · · · · · · · · · · · · Lucille Ball
Ricky Ricardo · · · · · · · · · · · · · · Desi Arnaz
Ethel Mertz · · · · · · · · · · · · · Vivian Vance
Fred Mertz · · · · · · · · · · · · William Frawley
Little Ricky Ricardo · · · · · · · · Richard Keith

CREDITS

creators/writers Jess Oppenheimer/Madelyn Pugh/Bob Carroll Jr · *executive producer* Desi Arnaz · *producer* Bert Granet

Broadcast in the USA under the various titles *The Lucy-Desi Comedy Hour*, *The Lucille Ball-Desi Arnaz Show* and *The Desilu Playhouse*, these 13 hour-length programmes – all but one of which were shown in Britain by ITV – continued the theme of the staggeringly successful half-hour sitcom *I Love Lucy*, depicting more wacky adventures in the life of the Ricardos and their friends the Mertzes. Travel was a theme – single episodes were set in Mexico, Alaska, Havana and Japan – and another selection of top guest stars happily turned out, among them Betty Grable, Tallulah Bankhead, Fred MacMurray, Maurice Chevalier, Red Skelton,

Ida Lupino, Milton Berle, Bob Cummings and Ernie Kovacs.

The Desilu Playhouse, under whose banner the last eight of these programmes appeared in the USA, was a series of shows produced from 1958 to 1960 by Lucille Ball and Desi Arnaz's company and shot at their Hollywood studio. By no means were all the programmes comedic, indeed the accent was on single-episode dramas (some of which were also screened in Britain by ITV).

The Lucy Show

USA · CBS (DESILU PRODUCTIONS) · SITCOM

156 × 30 mins (30 b/w · 126 colour)

US dates: 1 Oct 1962–16 Sep 1968

*UK dates: 31 Dec 1962–28 Dec 1968 (130 episodes · b/w) BBC1 various days and times; 20 Oct 1964–1 June 1965 (26 episodes · b/w) ITV various days and times

MAIN CAST

Lucy Carmichael	Lucille Ball
Vivian Bagley	Vivian Vance (1962–65)
Theodore J Mooney	Gale Gordon
Mrs Barnsdahl	Charles Lane (1962–63)
Mary Jane Lewis	Mary Jane Croft (1965–68)
Harry Conners	Dick Martin (1962–64)
Chris Carmichael	Candy Moore (1962–65)
Jerry Carmichael	Jimmy Garrett (1962–66)
Sherman Bagley	Ralph Hart (1962–65)

CREDITS

writers various · *producers* Gary Morton, Lucille Ball, Desi Arnaz

Now divorced from Desi Arnaz, Lucille Ball returned to primetime TV with an inferior but nevertheless well-received follow-up sitcom. This time she played Lucy Carmichael, a working widow bringing up two children: daughter Chris and son Jerry. Her *I Love Lucy* neighbour Vivian Vance came along for the ride, too, cast as Vivian Bagley, Lucy's close friend and flatmate, also a widow.

Lucy Carmichael was slightly more sophisticated and less manic than Lucy Ricardo but they shared the same ability to find themselves in ridiculous and highly unlikely situations that made for winning visual comedy. Originally, Lucy worked for the First National Bank in Danfield, Connecticut, clashing often with her boss, the cantankerous Mr Barnsdahl. But when he was replaced by Theodore Mooney (played by Gale Gordon) the show really took off, creating one of television's most memorable friendly feuds, with Carmichael-created chaos causing Mr Mooney endless distress. The show's setting was later switched to San Francisco, with Mr Mooney taking up a position there and, most unwisely, still employing Lucy as his secretary, thus ensuring a continuation of their constant

battle of (half)wits. In San Francisco, Lucy's new 'best friend' was Mary Jane Lewis, although Vivian Bagley still made occasional visits. Throughout the series – also known as *The Lucille Ball Show* – 'name' guest stars appeared to give the show added allure, including Clint Walker, Jack Benny, Milton Berle, Mickey Rooney, Dean Martin, Carol Burnett and John Wayne.

*Note. Unusually, British screening of the series was divided between the two rival networks, with the BBC running 130 episodes from December 1962 to May 1964 and October 1965 to December 1968, and ITV filling in the additional 26 from October 1964 to June 1965.

See below for direct sequel, *Here's Lucy*.

The Lucille Ball Comedy Hour

USA · CBS (LUCILLE BALL PRODUCTIONS) · SITCOM

1 × 60 mins · colour

US date: 19 Apr 1964

UK date: 16 Apr 1965 · ITV Fri 9.40pm (in b/w)

MAIN CAST

Lucille Ball/Bonnie Barton	Lucille Ball
Bob Hope/Bill Barton	Bob Hope
Elliott Harvey	Gale Gordon
Cash	Jack Weston
Walter	Max Showalter
Henderson	John Dehner
Potter	Bill Lanteau

CREDITS

creator Sherwood Schwartz · *writer* Richard Powell · *director* Jack Donohue · *executive producers* Jess Oppenheimer, Edward H Feldman

A one-off special – screened in the UK as *Mr And Mrs* – in which Lucille Ball played the head of a TV studio, challenged by her board of directors to contract Bob Hope to do a major TV show about an ideal couple. The script was based on a play by Sherwood Schwartz.

Here's Lucy

USA · CBS (UNIVERSAL/LUCILLE BALL PRODUCTIONS) · SITCOM

144 × 30 mins · colour

US dates: 23 Sep 1968–2 Sep 1974

*UK dates: 4 Jan 1969–6 June 1971 (47 episodes; 24 b/w · 23 colour) BBC1 Sat around 6pm then Sun 5.40pm

MAIN CAST

Lucy Carter	Lucille Ball
Harrison Otis Carter	Gale Gordon
Kim Carter	Lucie Arnaz
Craig Carter	Desi Arnaz Jr (1968–71)
Mary Jane Lewis	Mary Jane Croft

CREDITS

writers various · *directors* various · *producers* Gary Morton, Cleo Smith

A direct follow-on from *The Lucy Show*, with the setting transferred to Los Angeles and a slightly different spin applied to the main characters. This time around Lucille Ball was Lucy Carter, a scatterbrained, over-zealous secretary to her boss and brother-in-law Harrison Otis Carter, played by Lucy's old sparring partner Gale Gordon. Lucy's real-life children portrayed her on-screen family and her friend and confidante was once again Mary Jane Croft using the same name she had in *The Lucy Show*, Mary Jane Lewis.

The change of format made little difference to the Lucille Ball style which by now was written in marble, and the series continued in much the same vein as those that had gone before, once again featuring occasional appearances from Vivian Vance and using celebrity guest stars to pep up the plots. This time they included Liberace, Jack Benny, Carol Burnett, Eva Gabor, Shelley Winters, Johnny Carson, Wally Cox and, in one memorable segment, Richard Burton and Elizabeth Taylor.

This still wasn't the end of Lucille Ball's remarkable television career, since she returned for one more series, *Life With Lucy*, which ran on the ABC network in the USA from 21 September to 15 November 1986, when she was 75 years old. It was a poor show, and while at least 13 episodes were made only eight aired; the series was not screened on British TV.

*Note. C4 screened 39 episodes of *Here's Lucy* from 8 August 1983 to 11 July 1984.

A Lucille Ball Special Starring Lucille Ball And Dean Martin

USA · CBS (LUCILLE BALL PRODUCTIONS) · SITCOM

1 × 60 mins · colour

US date: 1 Mar 1975

UK date: 31 May 1976 · ITV Mon 11.15pm

MAIN CAST

Lucy Collins	Lucille Ball
Dean Martin	himself
Gus Mitchell	Jackie Coogan
Max Vogel	Bruce Gordon

CREDITS

writer Bob O'Brien · *director* Jack Donohue · *executive producer* Lucille Ball · *producer* Gary Morton

A one-off Lucille Ball special – screened in the UK as *Lucy Gets Lucky* – in which she starred as an avid fan of Dean Martin, determined to see her idol perform in concert in Las Vegas. As usual, Lucy causes plenty of trouble along the way, and Martin has to step in and save her, and Las Vegas, from disaster.

A Lucille Ball Special Starring Lucille Ball And Jackie Gleason

USA · CBS (LUCILLE BALL PRODUCTIONS) · SITCOM

1 × 60 mins · colour

US date: 3 Dec 1975

UK date: 19 Aug 1976 · ITV Thu 10.30pm

MAIN CAST
Lucille Ball
Jackie Gleason

CREDITS
writers Renee Taylor, Joseph Bologna · *director* Charles Walters · *producers* Lucille Ball, Gary Morton

Lucille Ball and Jackie Gleason, two giants of American TV comedy, combined in this single special – screened in the UK as *Three For Two* – which broke down into three separate situations depicting marital crises. In the first, they discovered truths about one another after 24 years of marriage; the second took the theme of adultery; a Christmas family crisis formed the basis for the last.

The Ballad Of Snivelling And Grudge

see *The Two Ronnies*

Ballet 'How'

see GRENFELL, Joyce

Ballyskillen Opera House

UK · ITV (GRANADA) · SITCOM

6 × 30 mins · colour

6 Jan–10 Feb 1981 · Tue 7.30pm

MAIN CAST
Frank O'Grady · · · · · · · · · · · · · Frank Carson
Theresa Halligan · · · · · · · · · Anna Manahan
Seamus Maguire · · · · · · · · · Charlie Roberts
Kathleen McMorrow · · · · · Bernadette Shortt
Mary · · · · · · · · · · · · · · · · · Angela Catherall
Father Hennessey · · · · · · · · · · · Terry Iland

CREDITS
writer Linda Thornber · *director* David Liddiment · *executive producer* Johnny Hamp · *producer* Stephen Leahy

An unusual series, blending sitcom with variety, and showcasing Frank 'It's the way I tell 'em' Carson, the Irish standup who had found fame in *The Comedians* (also made by Granada and its producer Johnny Hamp). Here, Carson starred as the manager of Ballyskillen Opera House, a grand edifice crumbling through bad maintenance and his corrupt management but kept going by a dedicated staff that included Seamus, the electrician and general factotum; Theresa,

who cleans and runs the box-office; and barmaids Kathleen and Mary.

Different guest stars appeared each week, these being Peter Skellern in the first episode, Brendan Shine, Kelly Marie and Brendan Blake in the second, Tony Christie in the third, Lulu and Brendan Grace in the fourth, the Bachelors in the fifth and Sheila Bernette, St Winifred's School Choir, St Chad's Dancers and Beaudice in the last. The series was a first effort from former Liverpool RE primary-school teacher Linda Thornber.

Barbara

UK · ITV (CARLTON PRODUCTIONS FOR CENTRAL) · SITCOM

1 × 30 mins · colour

10 July 1995 · Mon 8pm

MAIN CAST
Barbara Liversage · · · · · · · · · · · Gwen Taylor
Ted Liversage · · · · · · · · · · · · · · · Sam Kelly
Jean · · · · · · · · · · · · · · · · · Shirley-Anne Field
Linda Benson · · · · · · · · · Caroline Milmoe
Martin Benson · · · · · · · · · · · · · Glen Davies
Doreen · · · · · · · · · · · · · · · · · Madge Hindle

CREDITS
writers Mark Bussell/Rob Clark/Ramsay Gilderdale/Graham Mark Walker · *director* Les Chatfield · *executive producer* Paul Spencer · *producer* Mark Bussell

The opening screening in ITV's 1995 *Comedy Firsts* season of pilots cast Gwen Taylor as Barbara, a 52-year-old heftily-opinionated, blunt-talking, advice-giving, ranting Yorkshirewoman. She despises her son-in-law Martin, a local chef, and when he applies for a job in Swansea she positively seethes, for while she can't wait to see the back of him she realises she'll lose the company of her daughter Linda and grandson George if Martin gets the posting. Her husband Ted, a mild-mannered cab driver, isn't much use – they've been married 35 years and, although he throws in the occasional spiked barb, he's obviously learned long ago to play second fiddle – nor is Barbara's nouveau-riche sister Jean much help, the victim of many a withering look and put-down. So Barbara decides to take matters into her own hands by calling Swansea and establishing – before even he learns the news – that Martin has not got the job.

Team-written in the manner of US sitcoms, *Barbara* showed some promise but, this brusque, the lead character was possibly too unremittingly harsh to warrant a full series.

Barbara With Braden

UK · BBC · SKETCH

1 × 40 mins · b/w

29 July 1953 · Wed 8.15pm

MAIN CAST
Barbara Kelly
Bernard Braden

CREDITS
writers Frank Muir/Denis Norden · *producer* Brian Tesler

Perceived as a humorous TV version of Braden and Kelly's BBC radio series *Bedtime With Braden*, this one-off was presumably intended to launch a series. It never materialised, but the easy-going and relaxed format was a worthwhile experiment, and this programme did at least provide the first TV credits for the top-notch radio-comedy writers Muir and Norden.

See also *B-And-B, Bath-Night With Braden, Early To Braden, An Evening At Home With Bernard Braden And Barbara Kelly* and *Kaleidoscope.*

Barf Bites Back

see The Amnesty Galas

Barnaby Spoot And The Exploding Whoopee Cushion

UK · BBC · SITCOM

1 × 25 mins · b/w

28 May 1965 · BBC1 Fri 8pm

MAIN CAST
Barnaby Spoot · · · · · · · · · · · · · · John Bird
Mr Bostock · · · · · · · · · · · · John Le Mesurier
Justin Fribble · · · · · · · · · · · · · Ronald Lacey
Narcissus Font · · · · · · · · · · · Sheila Steafel

CREDITS
writers Marty Feldman/Barry Took · *executive producer* Graeme Muir · *producer* Dick Clement

A *Comedy Playhouse* one-off featuring an outrageous plot typical of writers Feldman and Took. John Bird starred as Barnaby Spoot, an assistant in a joke shop where the proprietor (played by John Le Mesurier) consistently refuses to pay him for the jokes he invents. The rejection of his latest novelty item, a talking cheese called 'chatty cheddar', is the final straw for Spoot who decides to exact a fitting revenge by blowing up the board of directors with an exploding whoopee cushion.

They don't write them like that any more.

Barnet

UK · BBC · SITCOM

1 × 30 mins · colour

3 Apr 1985 · BBC2 Wed 9.45pm

MAIN CAST
Maurice Barnet · · · · · · · · · Donald Churchill
Clive Parmenter · · · · · · · · · · · Patrick Cargill
Phoebe · · · · · · · · · · · · · · · · · · Toni Palmer
Petal · · · · · · · · · · · · · · · · · · · Sarah Webb

CREDITS
writers Doris Richards/Allen Saddler · *director* Mandie Fletcher · *producer* Harold Snoad

Almost certainly a pilot for a never-made series, this single-episode sitcom told the tale of Maurice Barnet, once employed by the swanky Ponsonby's Hairdressing salon in the West End of London but now reduced to running a tatty establishment in the downmarket East End of the city. The constant carping of his disillusioned wife, Phoebe, and the demands of her shady relatives and her daughter by a previous marriage, Petal, all combine to give Maurice a constant headache. The big question is: will going unisex make any difference to his mundane life?

Barney Is My Darling

UK · BBC · SITCOM

6 × 30 mins · b/w

17 Dec 1965–21 Jan 1966 · BBC1 mostly Fri 7.30pm

MAIN CAST
Barney Pank · · · · · · · · · · · · · · · · · Bill Fraser
Ramona Pank · · · · · · · · · · · · · · Irene Handl
Cissie · · · · · · · · · · · · · · · · · · Angela Crow
Miss Hobbitt · · · · · · · · · · · · · · Pat Coombs

CREDITS
writers Marty Feldman/Barry Took · producer James Gilbert

Having written so successfully for Bill Fraser in **The Army Game** and its spin-off **Bootsie And Snudge**, Marty Feldman and Barry Took created this BBC series for the comic actor. He and Irene Handl were cast as a couple who, having spent much of their marriage apart – he being away in the merchant navy, she running a hairdressers in Willesden, north London – suddenly find themselves back together. The path of resurrected true love fails to run smoothly, however, because the intervening years have turned them into very different people. And, to make matters worse, Ramona is utterly devoted to her pet dog, a scruffy mongrel who viciously resents Barney's sudden presence in his mistress's life.

Barney Miller

USA · ABC (FOUR D PRODUCTIONS) · SITCOM

169 episodes (168 × 30 mins · 1 × 60 mins) · colour

US dates: 22 Aug 1974 (pilot); 23 Jan 1975–20 May 1982

*UK dates: 11 July 1979–7 Dec 1983 (76 × 30 mins · 1 × 60 mins) ITV various days and times

MAIN CAST
Capt Barney Miller · · · · · · · · · · · Hal Linden
Det Stan 'Wojo' Wojciehowicz · · Maxwell Gail
Det Sgt Phillip Fish · · Abe Vigoda (1975–77)
Det Sgt Chano Amenguale · · · Gregory Sierra
· (1975–76)
Det Sgt Nick Yemana · · Jack Soo (1975–78)
Det Sgt Ron Harris · · · · · · · · · · · Ron Glass
Insp Frank Luger · · · · · · · · · James Gregory
Det Sgt Arthur Dietrich · · · Steve Landesberg
· (1976–82)
Officer Carl Levitt · · · · Ron Carey (1976–82)

Det Janice Wentworth · · · · · · · · Linda Lavin
· (1975–76)
Elizabeth Miller · · · · · · · · Abby Dalton (pilot);
· · · · · · · · · · · · · · Barbara Barrie (1975–76)

CREDITS
creators Danny Arnold/Theodore J Flicker · writers Danny Arnold, Chris Hayward, Tony Sheehan, Thomas A Reeder, Reinhold Weege, Frank Dungan, Jeff Stein, Jordan Moffet and others · directors Noam Pitlik and others · executive producers Danny Arnold (all), Roland Kibbee (series 8) · producers Chris Hayward (series 1 & 2), Arne Sultan (series 2), Danny Arnold (series 3), Tony Sheehan (series 4–7), Reinhold Weege (series 5), Noam Pitlik (series 6 & 7), Frank Dungan (series 8), Jeff Stein (series 8)

One of the prime American ensemble sitcoms, *Barney Miller* remains scarcely known in Britain, and was dealt a poor hand by ITV: the series was not networked and those individual regions that screened episodes did so erratically – in the London area, they went out in midnight time slots and only began with the fourth US series.

Which is a great shame because *Barney Miller* deserves its placing in the sitcom hall of fame. Set in the New York Twelfth Precinct police station, in Greenwich Village, this was a cop series with a difference: it focused not on the atypical (but commonplace on TV) blazing guns, explosions and fast car-chases, nor, indeed, on lollipop-sucking or bumbling, dishevelled lieutenants, but on the people involved in *typical* police work: detectives who are not out for action, and do not necessarily abide to the strict letter of the law. Their idea of a good day's work might just as easily be the safe diffusion of a hot and sticky situation, allowing offenders time to cool off, and lending an ear to their troubles. Not surprisingly, the series was a major hit with police forces across the US, who felt that it more accurately depicted their day-to-day work than did *Starsky And Hutch*. The cast members were made honorary members of the NYPD.

The staff at the station were your typical New York ethnic mix: there was Barney Miller himself, Jewish; Ron Harris, a black jokester; Chano Amenguale, a verbose Puerto Rican; Nick Yemana, Oriental and a sucker for a bet; Stan 'Wojo' Wojciehowicz, a kindly, well-intentioned Pole; Arthur Dietrich, a WASP intellectual; and Phil Fish, not only Jewish but old, and never straying far away from the toilet, just in case. (Phil was so popular that he was spun-off into his own sitcom, *Fish*, which ABC aired in 1977–78 while, unusually, the character continued to appear in the parent series; there was also an attempt to float Wojo into a series of his own, but this stalled after the broadcast of a special one-hour episode of *Barney Miller* devoted to him.)

Early episodes, led by the pilot, split the action between the station-house and Barney's home life with his wife Elizabeth and a pair of children, but soon it focused solely on the relationships at work, and it was at this point that the series took off in a major way. Most of the action took place either in the detectives' room, complete with its own temporary cell, or in Barney's office. Miller was something of an elder statesmen for the other 'tecs, and many a visitor would lounge on his leather settee and share their angst about something or other to this compassionate man. Although a bizarre assortment of criminals and characters would weave in and out of the episodes – a decidedly clever way of introducing new faces and storylines – it was the cops themselves who brought the dramatic edge to the comedy. This, the crackling comic dialogue and the painstaking way in which each scene was lit inside the studio, re-creating the mood and gloom of a New York police station, were what made the series distinguishable. Most of the episodes were self-contained but strands of continuing storylines ran through the series: Fish, ever in need of a toilet but desperate to avoid the plight of retirement; Harris developing a novel, *Blood On The Badge* (or *B-O-B* as he called it), from his police-work observations.

Remarkably, considering the popularity and critical acclaim it would soon attract, *Barney Miller* very nearly failed get off the ground. Danny Arnold – the driving force behind the show – took years to persuade ABC to put it on screen, and the network did not seem to have been disappointed when the one-off pilot edition, *The Life And Times Of Barney Miller*, was declared a flop. It was only thanks to the intervention of top director John Rich that the series was revived. Rich had steered *All In The Family* to great heights and ABC were desperate to sign him to a contract for other work. Even though it was not his project, Rich virtually insisted that ABC develop the *Barney Miller* pilot into a full series if they wanted him to sign a deal.

Barney Miller also came to an unusual conclusion, after the producers and the network entered into an unresolveable dispute. The final story (which ran over three episodes) had an antique gun being discovered in the police station. This revealed that the building had been used by Roosevelt during his time as president of the New York Police Board in the 1890s. The building was made a historic landmark and the 12th were forced to disband and take different jobs around the city. While Barney was proud finally to get his long-awaited promotion from captain to deputy inspector he also knew that his team had reached the end of the line.

*Note. C4 screened 40 episodes of *Barney Miller*, from 9 January 1988 to 15 February

1989, mostly repeating those seen on London-area ITV from 1979 to 1983.

The Barnstormers

UK · BBC · STANDUP

1 × 30 mins · colour

10 Sep 1969 · BBC2 Wed 10pm

MAIN CAST
Stanley Holloway

CREDITS
writer Austin Steele · *monologues* G Marriot Edgar, Stanley Holloway · *director/producer* Barry Lupino

A one-off TV presentation that provided an opportunity for Stanley Holloway to re-create some of the marvellous monologues that had made him a big name in the 1930s, before he went on to star as Alfred P Dolittle in the musical *My Fair Lady*, the role for which he is perhaps best remembered today.

Holloway was born in east London in 1890, studied singing in Milan before the First World War and then launched his stage career in 'concert-party' performances, a rather more genteel form of music-hall. Later, Holloway created an act comprising a number of monologue short stories, some in rhyme. This form of entertainment was considered quite arcane by the time that Holloway started to perform it, but on the advice of Gracie Fields he continued to do so and undertook a tour of variety halls that was the start of his great success. His two most famous monologue characters were 'Old Sam', a sterling old trooper with rigid attitudes, depicted in such pieces as 'Pick Oop Tha' Musket, Sam', and the accident-prone lad Albert Ramsbottom ('Albert And The Lion' and other pieces), who featured in monologues written by G Marriot Edgar, brother of noted crime novelist Edgar Wallace. Both of these characters turned up in the TV show, which – through the device of Holloway reminiscing about his career – enabled him to deliver his most famous pieces.

See also Thingumybob.

The Barron Knights Show

UK · C4 (BARRON KNIGHTS) · SKETCH

1 × 60 mins · colour

28 Dec 1984 · Fri 8.30pm

MAIN CAST
The Barron Knights (Barron Anthony Osmond, Butch Baker, Dave Ballinger, Duke D'Mond, Peter 'Peanut' Langford)

CREDITS
director Tony Vanden-Ende · *executive producer* Tony Avern · *producer* Butch Baker

Another barren night of comedy on C4, following in the footfalls of *Twice Knightly* and *Get Knighted*.

Barry Humphries' Scandals
The Barry Humphries Show

see HUMPHRIES, Barry

Michael Barrymore

Born on 4 May 1952 in Bermondsey, south London, Michael Barrymore was a hairdresser and part-time failing standup comic when, in one last desperate measure, he and his wife Cheryl invested in a black dress-suit and he went into cabaret. He appeared in the last series of *Who Do You Do?* in 1976, became the studio audience warm-up man before recordings of the BBC sitcom *Are You Being Served?* and, eventually, was spotted and booked to appear as one of the assembled eccentrics in *Russ Abbot's Madhouse* through 1981 and 1982. These shows established Barrymore's identity for sometimes gentle, sometimes manic and unpredictable humour in the John Cleese mould, a similarity that also stretched to their physique and height. Soon Barrymore was being given his own starring vehicles, beginning with a sketch series for Thames in 1983.

Listed here are Michael Barrymore's two TV series that fall within the parameters of this book. Beyond its bounds are several others. *Michael Barrymore's Saturday Night Out* (BBC1, 12 editions, 23 July 1988 to 26 August 1989) was a variety show in which Barrymore developed his best-known style, interacting with guest stars in absurd comedy routines and involving the audience in the mayhem. In *Barrymore* (45 editions for LWT from 21 December 1991 to 9 April 1995, with 10 more from 19 April to 28 June 1997) the comic crystallised this style. But perhaps according him his greatest fame are the extraordinarily popular ITV quiz/game/people series Barrymore has hosted: *Strike It Lucky* (from 29 October 1986), *Strike It Rich* (from 12 December 1996) and *Michael Barrymore's My Kind Of People* (from 26 October 1995). This latter series appeared after several months of unrelenting tabloid-newspaper accounts about Barrymore's private life, focusing on his self-acknowledged homosexuality, drink problems and associated mental anguish. For a time the comic became rather better known for these factors than for his talent but he managed to weather the storm and has continued to appear on TV and enjoy huge popularity with viewers.

See also Mick And Mac.

Michael Barrymore

UK · ITV (THAMES) · SKETCH

6 × 30 mins · colour

28 Apr–13 June 1983 · mostly Thu 8pm

MAIN CAST
Michael Barrymore
Nicholas Lyndhurst

CREDITS
writers Eric Davidson, Spike Mullins, Sid Green · *director/producer* David Clark

In his first own series Barrymore was assisted in the comedy sketches by Nicholas Lyndhurst, already well established as Rodney in the BBC sitcom *Only Fools And Horses*. Barrymore indulged in his free-style comedy, including moments of unexpected audience participation. The series was not a great success, however, and the star-to-be had to wait until 1987 for his next major opportunity to shine beyond the boundary of game-shows.

The Michael Barrymore Special

UK · ITV (THAMES) · SKETCH

1 × 60 mins · colour

25 May 1987 · Mon 8pm

MAIN CAST
Michael Barrymore

CREDITS
writers Paul Minett/Brian Leveson, Cheryl St Clair, Geoff Atkinson, Barry Cryer, Sid Green, Jim Pullin, Andy Wakefield/Paul Sellars, Lars Mjoen, Trond Kirkvaag, Knut Lystad · *executive producer* Robert Louis · *director/producer* Brian Penders

A bank-holiday special for the *Strike It Lucky* host. Snooker champion Steve Davis was among the guest stars.

Bath H&C

UK · BBC · SKETCH

1 × 15 mins · b/w

28 Oct 1938 · Fri 3.45pm

MAIN CAST
Richard Hearne
Lily Palmer
George Nelson

CREDITS
producer Reginald Smith

Richard Hearne, before he invented **Mr Pastry**, in a slapstick sketch especially mounted for television.

See also Moving Furniture, S-s-s-h! The Wife! and Take Two Eggs.

Bath-Night With Braden

UK · BBC · SKETCH

6 × 30 mins · b/w

3 June–8 July 1955 · Fri 11pm

MAIN CAST
Bernard Braden

CREDITS
producer Brian Tesler

Following the experimental pilot ***Barbara With Braden***, TV producer Brian Tesler tried once more to duplicate the format of such Braden and Kelly BBC radio series as *Breakfast With Braden*, *Bedtime With Braden* and *Between Time With Braden*. Kelly did not participate this time – she had other TV commitments – but otherwise the mix was familiar. *Radio Times* described the production as 'the first weekly comedy show made for British television'. This was, presumably, because hitherto the convention had been to screen shows fortnightly, alternating them with other series.

See also **B-And-B, Early To Braden, Bath-Night With Braden, An Evening At Home With Bernard Braden And Barbara Kelly** and **Kaleidoscope.**

Battle Of The Sexes

UK · BBC · STANDUP/MUSICAL HUMOUR

6 × 30 mins · colour
19 Mar–23 Apr 1976 · BBC2 Fri 9.55pm

MAIN CAST
Judith Arthy
Jacqueline Clarke
Derek Griffiths
Julia McKenzie
James Smilie
Ralph Watson

CREDITS
script editor Austin Steele · *producer* Peter Whitmore

A combination of comedy and musical humour in a weekly look at different aspects of the relationship between men and women.

Stanley Baxter

The Scottish comedian, mimic and comic actor Stanley Baxter was born in Glasgow on 24 May 1926 and first showed his skills as an impressionist – impersonating, among others, Sir Harry Lauder and Mae West – in a 20-minute vaudeville routine that he put together with his mother. While still in his early teens Baxter performed in radio plays for children. Following the Second World War, when he was stationed with Kenneth Williams, Baxter appeared in a number of straight-acting roles before rediscovering his comedic potential. After making his TV debut in the BBC's *Shop Window* in 1952, and then securing a few guest roles in variety shows such as Granada TV's *Chelsea At Nine*, Baxter achieved his

breakthrough in the BBC revue series *On The Bright Side* (see below). He then remained a TV favourite for fully 25 years, enjoying a succession of starring shows on the BBC and ITV, distinguished by their ambition, budget and Baxter's startling talents. He also appeared in feature films.

Baxter's particular skill was in mixing his versatile vocal range with elaborate make-up and costume, creating richly detailed characters – more often than not female and usually based on real celebrities. This was similar to Benny Hill's early style but Baxter's creations had a more subtle edge, and when Hill moved to a broader comedy spectrum the field was clear for Baxter to dominate this niche. Those lavish 1970s shows established him as a British television superstar.

See also **Mr Majeika.**

On The Bright Side

UK · BBC · SKETCH

15 editions (14 × 45 mins · 1 × short special) · b/w

Series One (7 × 45 mins) 3 June–26 Aug 1959 · fortnightly Wed around 8.30pm

Series Two (7 × 45 mins) 14 June–6 Sep 1960 · fortnightly Tue around 8pm

Short special · part of *Christmas Night With The Stars* 25 Dec 1960 · Sun 6pm

MAIN CAST
Stanley Baxter
Betty Marsden
Pip Hinton
David Kernan
Richard Waring

CREDITS
writers Richard Waring, Ken Hoare · *script associate* Alec Grahame · *producer* James Gilbert

A fast-moving satirical sketch and music show fronted by Stanley Baxter with the popular BBC radio comedian Betty Marsden (appearing in *Beyond Our Ken* and later *Round The Horne*). Regular sketches spoofed other BBC productions, a compilation programme of such material airing on 14 February 1961 under the title *BBC Television*. The series' resident team of young dancers included Una Stubbs and Amanda Barrie among their number.

The series proved so popular that a stage revue, *On The Brighter Side*, opened in London on 12 April 1961, duplicating the TV format and featuring the original cast, augmented by Judy Carne, Bob Stevenson, Ronnie Barker, Una Stubbs, Greta Hamby, Victor Duret, Elizabeth Counsell, Allan Barnes and Amanda Barrie. A 40-minute extract from the show was screened by the BBC on 16 June 1961.

Lunch In The Park

UK · BBC · SITCOM

1 × 30 mins · b/w
22 Dec 1961 · Fri 8.45pm

MAIN CAST
Geoffrey Tupper · · · · · · · · · Stanley Baxter
Ethel Waring · · · · · · · · · Daphne Anderson

CREDITS
writers Ray Galton/Alan Simpson · *producer* James Gilbert

A change of pace for Baxter in this one-off *Comedy Playhouse* sitcom from Galton and Simpson. This told the tale of two middle-aged office workers, Geoffrey and Ethel, who for ten years have met for lunch every Tuesday on the same park bench but who, on this anniversary day, are in for a shock.

The script was re-used in 1997 in ***Paul Merton In Galton & Simpson's ....***

The Stanley Baxter Show

UK · BBC · SKETCH

22 editions (3 × 45 mins · b/w; 7 × 30 mins · colour; 10 × 25 mins · b/w; 1 × short special · b/w; 1 × short special · colour)

Series One (3 × 45 mins · b/w) 18 May–29 June 1963 · fortnightly Sat 7.45pm

Short special (b/w) · part of *Christmas Night With The Stars* 25 Dec 1963 · Wed 8.05pm

Series Two (4 × 25 mins · b/w) 3 Sep–24 Sep 1967 · BBC2 Sun mostly 10.35pm

Series Three (6 × 25 mins · b/w) 9 Sep–28 Oct 1968 · BBC1 Mon 9.55pm

Short special (colour) · part of *Christmas Night With The Stars* 25 Dec 1970 · Fri 6.45pm

Series Four (7 × 30 mins · colour) 8 Jan–19 Feb 1971 · BBC1 Fri 8pm

MAIN CAST
Stanley Baxter
Joan Sims (series 1)
Denise Coffey (occasional, series 3 & 4)

CREDITS
writers Ken Hoare (18), Kelso Robertson (17), Barry Cryer (7), J W Risley (7), Iain Macintyre (7), Jack Raymond (7), Denise Coffey (7), Dick Vosburgh (6), Hector Nicol (4), Stanley Baxter (3), Richard Waring (3) · *producers* David Bell (10), Roger Race (8), James Gilbert (4)

A traditional sketch show for Baxter. It concentrated on his powers of mimicry, with many sketches spoofing other TV shows and personalities. Although the series ran different lengths with different production credits, the content remained fairly consistent, except that the 1967 BBC2 series, made in Scotland, sported a distinctly Scots flavour. (Indeed, an extra edition was broadcast in Scotland only on 8 October 1968.)

Baxter On ...

UK · BBC · SKETCH

6 × 25 mins · b/w

11 Apr–20 June 1964 · BBC1 fortnightly Sat 8.50pm

MAIN CAST
Stanley Baxter
June Whitfield

CREDITS
writer Stanley Baxter · *producer* Michael Mills

This 1964 series, pairing Baxter with the dependable June Whitfield, differed from earlier Stanley Baxter shows by focusing on a specific subject each week: travel, television, law, theatre, class and films. It alternated on BBC1 with Jimmy Edwards' series *Bold As Brass*.

Time For Baxter

UK · BBC · SKETCH

1 × 45 mins · colour
1 Jan 1972 · BBC1 Sat 11.05pm

MAIN CAST
Stanley Baxter

CREDITS
writer Ken Hoare · *producer* David Bell

A New Year's Day special from BBC Scotland.

The Stanley Baxter Picture Show

UK · ITV (LWT) · SKETCH

7 editions (4 × 30 mins · 3 × 60 mins) · colour
One series (4 × 30 mins) 8–29 Oct 1972 · Sun 9.30pm
Special (60 mins) *The Stanley Baxter Big Picture Show* 21 Dec 1973 · Fri 9pm
Special (60 mins) *The Stanley Baxter Moving Picture Show* 7 Sep 1974 · Sat 8.45pm
Special (60 mins) *The Stanley Baxter Picture Show Part III* 19 Sep 1975 · Fri 9pm

MAIN CAST
Stanley Baxter

CREDITS
main writer Ken Hoare · *additional writers (series only)* Eric Merriman, Neville Phillips, Bill Solly, Paul Horner · *directors/producers* David Bell (6), Jon Scoffield (1)

Following the departure of his regular BBC producer, David Bell, to London Weekend Television, Stanley Baxter followed suit, making his first series for ITV in October 1972 and so beginning a relationship that would last for more than a decade. These first four programmes featured the classic Baxter set-up: brilliant impersonations of famous film and TV characters whom he named Malcolm Gibberidge, Alan Wicked, Glandy Jackson, Hicky Denderson, Dora Ryan, Benny Pill, Chic Gable, Koward Heel, Bette Davie, June Crawford and John Bitumen. Subsequent specials continued in much the same clever, big-budgeted vein.

Stanley Baxter's Christmas Box

UK · ITV (LWT) · SKETCH

1 × 60 mins · colour
26 Dec 1976 · Sun 7.25pm

MAIN CAST
Stanley Baxter

CREDITS
writer Ken Hoare · *additional material* Barry Cryer, Paul Horner, Iain Macintyre, Neil Shand, Stanley Baxter · *director* Bruce Gowers · *producer* Humphrey Barclay

A Christmas special featuring all the usual gaggle of 'guests', such as Bruce Fosdyke.

Stanley Baxter On Television

UK · ITV (LWT) · SKETCH

1 × 60 mins · colour
1 Apr 1979 · Sun 9.15pm

MAIN CAST
Stanley Baxter

CREDITS
writer Ken Hoare · *director/producer* John Kaye Cooper

His appearances becoming more and more sporadic, this was Baxter's first TV extravaganza in more than two years.

The Stanley Baxter Series

UK · ITV (LWT) · SKETCH

6 × 30 mins · colour
17 Oct–21 Nov 1981 · Sat 8.40pm

MAIN CAST
Stanley Baxter

CREDITS
writer Ken Hoare · *additional material* Russel Lane, David Cumming/Derek Collyer, Neville Phillips · *director* John Kaye Cooper · *producer* David Bell

A return to the weekly-series format not explored by Baxter since 1972.

The Stanley Baxter Hour

UK · ITV (LWT) · SKETCH

1 × 60 mins · colour
24 Dec 1982 · Fri 8.30pm

MAIN CAST
Stanley Baxter

CREDITS
writer Ken Hoare · *additional material* Alec Mitchell, Russel Lane, Paul Minett/Brian Leveson · *director* John Kaye Cooper · *producer* David Bell

A final ITV special, following which LWT – daunted by the huge production budget of his shows – failed to renew Baxter's contract.

Stanley Baxter's Christmas Hamper

UK · BBC · SKETCH

1 × 50 mins colour
27 Dec 1985 · BBC1 Fri 9.20pm

MAIN CAST
Stanley Baxter

CREDITS
writer Ken Hoare · *additional material* Stanley Baxter, Simon Brett, Denise Coffey, Peter Vincent, Brian Leveson · *producer* John Bishop

Stanley Baxter's return to the BBC after 13 years on the commercial network. The Corporation matched the expensive production values of Baxter's commercial network series, as well as providing the characteristically elaborate costumes. Sketches included spoofs of the perennial Christmas film favourite *The Wizard Of Oz*, and *A Raj Too Far*, a satirical dig at Granada's Indian epic *The Jewel In The Crown*.

Stanley Baxter's Picture Annual

UK · BBC · SKETCH

1 × 50 mins · colour
29 Dec 1986 · BBC1 Mon 9.30pm

MAIN CAST
Stanley Baxter
Lesley Collier

CREDITS
writers Ken Hoare, Paul Minett/Brian Leveson · *producer* John Bishop

More seasonal sketch tomfoolery from Baxter, cramming 37 different characters into 50 minutes' air time. Highlights included Baxter as Noël Coward appearing, incongruously, in a western, and a *Gone With The Wind* spoof featuring Mae West – an impersonation Baxter first flaunted nearly 50 years earlier.

Following this programme the BBC too cancelled Baxter's contract, citing the high expense of making his shows. Spurning their suggestion to wait around for a call inviting him back at some time in the future, Baxter decided to throw in the sketch-show towel, and accepted instead the opportunity to appear in a children's comedy programme, *Mr Majeika*. Running for three series over two years, that production came to an end in 1990.

Stanley Baxter Is Back

UK · C4 (LWT/MENTORN) · SKETCH

1 × 60 mins · colour
4 Jan 1996 · Thu 9pm

MAIN CAST
Stanley Baxter
Rory Bremner

CREDITS

writer Ken Hoare · *additional material* Russel Lane, Paul Minett/Brian Leveson, Jim Pullin · *executive producer* Tom Gutteridge · *director/producer* Alan Nixon

After a lengthy absence from the small-screen Baxter returned in a C4 special in which brand-new material was utilised to link a compilation of archival highlights from his BBC and LWT shows. The new skits showed that Baxter's style had changed a little: there was still plenty of dressing-up and make-up but less physical comedy and tomfoolery.

Stanley Baxter In Reel Terms

UK · C4 (LWT/MENTORN) · SKETCH

1 × 60 mins · colour

26 Dec 1996 · Thu 8pm

MAIN CAST

Stanley Baxter
Dawn French

CREDITS

writer Ken Hoare · *additional material* Russel Lane, Paul Minett/Brian Leveson, Jim Pullin · *director* Tom Gutteridge · *producer* Henry Eagles

A second show of classic clips linked by new material. Special guest this time around was Dawn French and many of the featured sketches were Baxter's famous and elaborate movie spoofs.

BBC-3

UK · BBC · SKETCH

24 × 60 mins · b/w

2 Oct 1965–16 Apr 1966 · BBC1 Sat around 10.30pm

MAIN CAST

John Bird
Robert Robinson
Patrick Campbell
Denis Norden
Harvey Orkin
Malcolm Muggeridge
Norman St John Stevas
Lynda Baron
David Battley
Alan Bennett
John Fortune
Bill Oddie
Roy Dotrice
Leonard Rossiter

CREDITS

writers Christopher Booker, Caryl Brahms, David Frost, Herbert Kretzmer, John Mortimer, Peter Lewis/Peter Dobereiner, David Nathan, Peter Shaffer, David Turner, Steven Vinaver, Dick Vosburgh, Keith Waterhouse/Willis Hall and others · *directors* Ned Sherrin, Darrol Blake · *producer* Ned Sherrin

The last major entry in the satire boom, following on from *That Was The Week*

That Was and *Not So Much A Programme, More A Way Of Life*, with many of the same luminaries involved.

BBC-3 (written thus because, stylistically, BBC-1 and BBC-2 were written with the dash at this time) combined filmed sketches, songs, standup routines and discussions. The programme obtained a degree of notoriety when, in the edition of 13 November 1965, during a discussion on censorship, the critic Kenneth Tynan casually used the f-word – the first time it had been uttered on British television. It took a long time for the storms of protest to subside.

See also *My Father Knew Lloyd George*.

Be Soon

UK · BBC · STANDUP/SKETCH

6 × 30 mins · b/w

25 Oct 1957–9 Jan 1958 · Fri various times

MAIN CAST

Hylda Baker
Cynthia · · · · · · · · · · · · · · · · · Guy Middleton

CREDITS

writers Jack Bradley/Ray Davies, Eddie Maguire · *producer* Barney Colehan

Having worked the stage since childhood, Hylda Baker – short in stature and with a rich Lancashire accent and famous line in malapropisms – rocketed to national stardom by way of an appearance in the BBC's music-hall celebration *The Good Old Days* on 11 March 1955. Two years on she starred in her own BBC series for that programme's producer, Barney Colehan.

Be Soon – also titled *Hylda Baker Says Be Soon* – gave Baker the opportunity to extend her standup stage routine, centring on the one-sided conversations she conducted with her improbably tall, gormless and entirely silent friend 'Cynthia' (a man in drag). The title of the series was one of Hylda Baker's catchphrases delivered to the stooge; another famous Baker catchphrase was, depending on the gender of the person to whom she was referring, 'She knows, you know' or 'He knows, you know'.

See also *Nearest And Dearest* and *Not On Your Nellie*.

Beat The Carrott

see CARROTT, Jasper

Beat Up The Town

UK · BBC · COMEDY/VARIETY

1 × 60 mins · b/w

22 Apr 1957 · Mon 8.15pm

MAIN CAST

Terry-Thomas
Bob Monkhouse
Cyril Fletcher
Jill Day

CREDITS

producer Francis Essex

A one-off Easter special with a comedic theme. Songs were especially written and composed by Paddy Roberts.

Bebe Daniels And Ben Lyon

UK · BBC · SKETCH

2 × 15 mins · b/w

14 Jan 1939 · Fri 9pm

2 Apr 1954 · Sat 11pm

CAST

Ben Lyon
Bebe Daniels
Barbara Lyon (show 2)
Richard Lyon (show 2)

CREDITS

producer Henry Caldwell (show 2)

The British-based American couple Bebe Daniels and Ben Lyon were a smash hit on BBC radio throughout the 1940s and 1950s and then made a successful transition to television (see *Life With The Lyons*). The content of their 1939 TV appearance is not known but the 1954 one, in which their children Barbara and Richard also appeared, was a contrived playlet detailing the Lyons' attempt to break into TV. Although it was scheduled to go out at 11pm cameras cut to the family throughout the evening, following their progress towards the big moment.

The Bed

see *Meet The Wife*

The Bed-Sit Girl

UK · BBC · SITCOM

12 × 25 mins · b/w

Series One (6) 13 Apr–18 May 1965 · BBC1 Mon 7.30pm

Series Two (6) 18 Apr–23 May 1966 · BBC1 Mon 7.30pm

MAIN CAST

Sheila · · · · · · · · · · · · · · · Sheila Hancock
Dilys · · · · · · · · · · · · · · Dilys Lane (series 1)
Liz · · · · · · · · · · · · · · · · · · Hy Hazell (series 2)
David · · · · · · · · · · · · Derek Nimmo (series 2)

CREDITS

writers Ronald Wolfe/Ronald Chesney · *producers* Duncan Wood (series 1), Graeme Muir (series 2)

Busy writers Wolfe and Chesney – they also had *Meet The Wife* running at this time – created this sitcom for Sheila Hancock, who had served them so handsomely in their famous earlier series *The Rag Trade*. Hancock was cast, helpfully, as Sheila, the bed-sit girl of the title, a dreamy typist who is slightly in awe of the 'glamorous' lifestyle of her bed-sitter neighbour, Dilys, an air hostess. In the second series Dilys was replaced by

Liz, Sheila's worldly-wise friend, and a new bed-sit neighbour, David (Derek Nimmo), who provided romantic interest.

Bedside Story

see The Montreux Festival

Before The Fringe

UK · BBC · SKETCH

14 × 30 mins · b/w

Series One (8) 30 Jan–20 Mar 1967 · BBC2 Mon 8.05pm

Series Two (6) More Before The Fringe 18 Sep–23 Oct 1967 · BBC2 Mon 8.05pm

MAIN CAST (NUMBER OF APPEARANCES)
Alan Melville (all)
Joan Sims (7)
Ronnie Barker (6)
Dora Bryan (5)
Beryl Reid (4)
Douglas Byng (4)
Hermione Baddeley (4)
Hugh Paddick (3)
Dilys Laye (3)
Hermione Gingold (2)
Cicely Courtneidge (2)
Betty Marsden (2)
Eunice Gayson (2)

CREDITS
main writers William Chappell, Noël Coward, Herbert Farjeon, Alan Melville, Douglas Byng, David Climie, Michael Flanders/Donald Swann, Charles Zwar, Arthur Macrae, Thorley Walters, Hermione Gingold, Peter Myers, Ray Galton/Alan Simpson · producer Robin Nash

Alan Melville was the guiding force behind this comedy-led series, which attempted to present humour from an era of revue 'before the fringe'. Melville's contention was that the undergraduate productions, the like of which had become especially popular since *Beyond The Fringe*, tended to overshadow the gentler, broader humour that had graced revues of the past. This series re-created the style and flavour of those earlier shows by, where possible, staging anew the original sketches and songs. Many of the guest artists who appeared were veterans of such shows. Apart from the recurring performers listed above, numerous others made one-off appearances, including Robert Dorning, Stanley Holloway, Thora Hird, Brenda Bruce, Wilfrid Brambell, Dame Edith Evans, Bud Flanagan, Peter Jones, Patrick Cargill and Barbara Windsor.

Before Your Very Eyes

see ASKEY, Arthur

Beggar My Neighbour

UK · BBC · SITCOM

24 episodes (23 × 30 mins · 1 × short special) · b/w

Pilot · 24 May 1966 · BBC1 Tue 7.30pm

Series One (7) 13 Mar–2 May 1967 · BBC1 Mon 7.30pm

Series Two (6) 2 July–6 Aug 1967 · BBC1 Sun 7.25pm

Short special · part of Christmas Night With The Stars 25 Dec 1967 · BBC1 Mon 6.40pm

Series Three (9) 30 Jan–26 Mar 1968 · BBC1 mostly Tue 7.30pm

MAIN CAST
Gerald Garvey · · · · · · · · · · · · · Peter Jones · · · · · · · · · · · · · · · · · · (pilot & series 1); · · · · · · · · · · · · · · · · · Desmond Walter-Ellis · · · · · · · · · · · · · (series 2 & 3 and special)
Rose Garvey · · · · · · · · · · · · · June Whitfield
Harry Butt · · · · · · · · · · · · · · Reg Varney
Lana Butt · · · · · · · · · · · · · · · Pat Coombs

OTHER APPEARANCES
Deirdre Garvey · · · · · · · · · · Rosemary Faith · (from series 2)

CREDITS
writers Ken Hoare/Mike Sharland · producers David Croft (pilot, series 1 & 2), Eric Fawcett (special & series 3)

A worthy keeping-up-with-the-Joneses sitcom, sprung from *Comedy Playhouse* and given added piquancy by the fact that the sparring neighbours were also related.

Married sisters Rose and Lana live next door to one another in Larkworthy Road, Muswell Hill, an area of north London, with their respective husbands Gerald and Harry. Gerald is an underpaid junior executive while Harry is a high-earning fitter, thus while the Garveys struggle to make ends meet the Butts enjoy the fat of the land. Gerald's upbringing has made him something of a snob and he coerces Rose into keeping up the pretence that they are doing quite well when the opposite is true. Lana puts on airs and graces perceiving their wealth to mean they have moved up a class, but her husband Harry remains a down-to-earth bloke and it's his sheer delight in the pleasures that his money brings (a large television, luxury car, foreign holidays and so on) that causes him to enthuse so. Needless to say, these inequities offend Gerald and often cause him to boast about something he and Rose have, often resulting in problems for them when they have to maintain a pretence.

The first series of *Beggar My Neighbour* reunited Peter Jones and Reg Varney in a kind of role-reversal to their boss/foreman positions in **The Rag Trade**. Jones then left (it was said that he was reluctant to become involved in another long-running show) and was replaced by Desmond Walter-Ellis, but the format remained the same.

Behind The Bike Sheds

UK · ITV (YORKSHIRE) · CHILDREN'S SKETCH

17 × 25 mins · colour

Series One (8) 19 Oct–7 Dec 1983 · Wed 4.20pm

Series Two (9) 8 Jan–5 Mar 1985 · Tue 4.20pm

MAIN CAST
Pericles Braithwaite · · · · · · · · Cal McCrystal · (series 1)
Poskitt the Caretaker · · · · · · · Kjartan Poskitt · (series 1)
Megapig · · · · · · · · · · · Val McLane (series 2)
Whistle Willie · · · · · · · · Ken Jones (series 2)
Trolly Molly · · · · Sara Mair-Thomas (series 2)
Joe · · · · · · · · · · · · Tony Slattery (series 2)

THE CHILDREN:
Paul Charles
Jenny Jay
Adam Sunderland
Marion Conroy (series 1)
Joanne Dukes (series 1)
Alix McAlister (series 1)
Nikki Stoter (series 1)
Lee Whitlock (series 1)
Andrew Jones (series 2)
Julie Macauley (series 2)
Martha Parsey (series 2)
Lee Sparke (series 2)
Linus Staples (series 2)

CREDITS
writers Rick Vanes/John Yeoman (series 1), Jan Needle/Tony Slattery (7 eps in series 2), Jan Needle/Tony Slattery/John Yeoman (2 eps in series 2) · directors/producers Alister Hallum (series 1), Peter Tabern (series 2)

Set in the worst kind of secondary school, Fulley Comprehensive (fictional), situated in the worst of areas, *Behind The Bike Sheds* was a witty look at school life by way of sketches, jokes, monologues, music and *Fame*-style dancing (first from the BTBS Dancers and then from members of the Harehills Youth Dance Theatre). The children got up to … well, all the things that teenage schoolchildren get up to, and have got up to, since time immemorial, their targets in the first series being the wily headmaster Pericles Braithwaite and his downtrodden caretaker Poskitt, and, in the second, the headmistress Miss Megan Bigge, alias Megapig, and her deputy, Whistle Willie. Clare Grogan appeared in one first-series episode while Tony Slattery, who co-wrote all of the second series, popped up a couple of times.

Behind The Fridge

UK · BBC · SKETCH

1 × 45 mins · colour

7 Mar 1974 · BBC2 Thu 9.25pm

MAIN CAST
Peter Cook
Dudley Moore

CREDITS
writers Peter Cook/Dudley Moore · producer Michael Hurll

A special BBC2 *Show Of The Week*, presenting extracts from Peter Cook and Dudley Moore's London stage revue *Behind The Fridge*, which, although an obvious play on the title of the **Beyond The Fringe** revue that had propelled them to stardom, was actually closer in style to their *Not Only ... But Also* TV series. The show was renamed *Good Evening* for its American tour.

Note. In November 1971, two 50-minute specials comprising highlights from the revue (which had debuted in Australia) were aired on the Nine Network, recorded in the company's Melbourne studios.

See also *Goodbye Again* and *An Apple A Day*.

Ben Elton – The Man From Auntie

UK · BBC · STANDUP/SKETCH

12 × 30 mins · colour

Series One (6) 15 Feb–22 Mar 1990 · BBC1 Thu 9.30pm

Series Two (6) 27 Jan–10 Mar 1994 · BBC1 Thu 10pm

MAIN CAST
Ben Elton

CREDITS
writer Ben Elton · *director* John Burrows · *producer* Geoffrey Perkins

A leading light of the comedy explosion of the late 1970s and early 1980s, Ben Elton rose to prominence through his prolific writing talent and quickfire standup delivery of topical observational humour, initially seen in *Saturday Live*.

Born in London in 1959, Elton first demonstrated his comic prowess while at Manchester University, where he wrote a number of comedy plays performed by students. Deciding upon a career as a writer, he returned to London in 1980 and checked out the talent appearing at the new comedy clubs in the capital. It was then that Elton first hit upon the idea of performing his own material, having delivered standup in his teens but using other people's work. After a few uninspiring appearances (with character-istic directness he described them as 'crap') Elton found his niche when he discovered a particular comedic style: declaring his outrage and disbelief over some modern lunacy in a funny, rambling rant that could veer wildly off the point but always, brilliantly, managed to get back on track at the end of the routine. This style earned Elton the nickname 'motormouth' and he added a visual accompaniment by appearing, mostly, in a dark suit flecked with sparkles – an outfit he dubbed his 'Sellafield suit'.

While Elton's stage act proved hugely successful with audiences, the anti-right-wing political views that ran through his act alienated a hefty percentage of the population, particularly tabloid newspaper readers who were regularly informed by their daily rags that Elton was a dangerous loony-leftie. All this 'helped' Elton earn the tag of a 'political

comedian' but, as with any such label, it obscured the truth, as well as the scope of his comedic political outbursts. Elton was creating routines based upon his actual feelings and concerns and, as a committed socialist and pragmatist, he naturally allowed these sensibilities to show in his act. But he was equally passionate about any subject that interested him, from the content of student fridges to nude sunbathing. Still, the 'political-comedian' label didn't seem to worry Elton very much and he eventually managed to win over many of his critics, who, while unable to condone his stance, had to admit that his act was very funny. Further, Elton's TV-writing credits – especially the *Blackadder* series – impressed many and proved that his talents ran deep. In 1989 he was deemed an appropriate replacement for Terry Wogan when the BBC1 chat-show host went on holiday, a measure of Elton's acceptability to a mainstream audience.

The following year he starred in his own series for the BBC, *Ben Elton – The Man From Auntie* (the name punning both the 1960s TV spy series *The Man From U.N.C.L.E.* and the BBC's nickname 'Auntie'). In this the comic combined some favourite items from his standup act with a great deal of new material in standup, short sketches and – an especially useful device for ranting – talking 'potato heads'. The series was of a very high quality and Elton's breathtaking pace ensured that it consumed comic material at a rate of knots. By the time that a second series appeared four years later (as simply *The Man From Auntie*) Elton had proved himself further, with stage-plays, massively successful eco-based novels and straight-acting roles. With less to prove, and perhaps less to be angry about, the Elton of the second series was noticeably more calm at the start of the shows. But once into his stride the pace picked up and much of the old fire was evident as the comic turned his sharp eye and even sharper tongue loose on more of the hypocrisies and inefficiencies of the modern world.

Ben Travers Farces

UK · BBC · SITCOMS

7 × 60 mins · colour

19 Sep–31 Oct 1970 · BBC1 Sat 9pm

MAIN CAST
Richard Briers
Arthur Lowe

CREDITS
writer Ben Travers · *producer* Eric Fawcett

BBC presentations of seven of Ben Travers' famous farces – *Rookery Nook*, *A Cuckoo In The Nest*, *Turkey Time*, *A Cup Of Kindness*, *Plunder*, *Dirty Work* and *She Follows Me About* – originally written for the Aldwych

Theatre (and so always referred to as the Aldwych Farces) and especially adapted for TV by Travers himself, at the age of 83.

Avoiding many of the pitfalls associated with trying to present farce on TV, Travers rewrote the plays to focus on the plot complications and verbal confusions rather than the frantic physical comedy and split-second timing that typifies the stage versions. Richard Briers and Arthur Lowe were the ever-dependable leads, Briers playing roles written for the famous Aldwych farceur Ralph Lynn, and Lowe in parts designed originally for Tom Walls and Robertson Hare. They were supported by a formidable troop of recurring guest stars, including Irene Handl, Megs Jenkins, Frank Thornton, Clive Dunn and Terence Alexander.

Beneath The News

UK · BBC · SATIRE/SKETCH

*4 × 30 mins · colour

*1 Aug–22 Aug 1975 · BBC1 Fri 9.25pm

MAIN CAST
John Bassett
Doug Fisher
Ian Davidson
Hilary Pritchard

CREDITS
writer John Hudson · *director* Ray Butt · *producer* John Duncan

A TV variation on the successful BBC Radio 4 series *Week Ending* with a resident team employing the week's news as the basis for satirical comedy. Producer/script-editor/comedy-writer Ian Davidson – a *Monty Python* collaborator – was in the team, as was Hilary Pritchard. The title referred to the series' positioning in *Radio Times*.

Beneath The News engendered a good deal of complaints for its racy language and perceived poor-quality mimicking of *Monty Python* and *Rutland Weekend Television*, but most of the outrage was aimed at an item that ridiculed the then-current teenybopper sensations the Bay City Rollers, renaming them the Bent City Danglers.

*Note. A fifth edition, scheduled for the 29 August 1975, was not screened.

Benny Hill ...   [various shows]

see HILL, Benny

Jack Benny

Born Benjamin Kubelsky in Illinois on 14 February 1894, Jack Benny became an American comic institution, triumphing on stage and in film, and – with long-running, hugely popular series – on US radio and television.

In addition to his crumpled, sympathy-arousing visage, Benny had two comedic gimmicks that he utilised throughout his career: his violin playing and his legendary meanness. He had taken violin lessons as a child and became extremely proficient, so when he started using comedy patter while fiddling, a style unique to Benny was born. Following limited success on stage and in film, he started working on American radio from 1932 and it was this medium that brought him superstar status. His writers discovered that they attracted big laughs whenever they suggested that Benny was stingy. Another running joke was Benny's age: he remained 39 for decades. Thus they concentrated on these aspects of his personality and the invented characteristics stuck.

By all accounts, Benny wasn't a naturally funny man and had to work extremely hard to make his scripts work, but this labour paid off handsomely, and through his graft he developed a brilliant sense of timing and awareness to audience response. His pauses were magical and, when allied to his perceived meanness, they brought audiences to hysterics.

Jack Benny remained at the top of his profession until his death on 26 December 1974.

The Jack Benny Show

UK · BBC · STANDUP

1 × 60 mins · b/w

3 June 1956 · Sun 9.30pm

MAIN CAST

Jack Benny

CREDITS

writers Sam Perrin, George Balzer · executive producer/director Ralph Levy · producer Ernest Maxin

The famous US comedian's British television debut, performing live from the stage of the King's Theatre in Hammersmith, west London. Radio Times described this as, 'the first in a new series of shows for the BBC' but no further editions materialised and viewers had to wait until the BBC started screening episodes from Benny's famous US series three months later before seeing him again.

Note. Benny next appeared 'exclusively' for the BBC on 28 August 1957 in The Birthday Show, a variety spectacular from the National Radio Show that celebrated the 21st anniversary of BBC Television. Benny introduced a host of stars and finished the programme with a 20-minute standup spot.

The Jack Benny Program

USA · CBS THEN NBC (J&M PRODUCTIONS) · SITCOM

343 × 30 mins · b/w

US dates: 28 Oct 1950–10 Sep 1965

UK dates: 30 Sep 1956–30 Dec 1965 (73 episodes) BBC1 then BBC2 various days and times

MAIN CAST

Jack Benny
Eddie 'Rochester' Anderson
Don Wilson
Dennis Day
Mary Livingstone
Professor LeBlanc · · · · · · · · · · · Mel Blanc

CREDITS

main writers Sam Perrin, George Balzer, Hal Goldman, Al Gordon, Milt Josefsberg, John Tackaberry · producer Fred DeCordova

The TV version of Benny's immensely popular US radio series (Blue/CBS/NBC, 1932–58), based solely on the personality of its star. Benny's radio regulars joined him for the TV series, notably his friend and announcer Don Wilson, black manservant Rochester and girlfriend Mary Livingstone (Benny's real-life wife). Also appearing were scatterbrained singer Dennis Day and Mel Blanc (the voice of Bugs Bunny, Tweety Pie, Woody Woodpecker et al), who, among other roles, provided the distinctive wheezy sounds of Benny's Maxwell car and Jack's violin teacher Professor LeBlanc.

Part sitcom, part variety – indeed, the only situational aspect was the putting on of the variety show – the series proved enormously popular. Eddie Anderson – whose part had grown from that of a Pullman porter heard only occasionally in the early radio shows to Benny's full-time, somewhat insolent butler – became the highest-paid black actor on US TV in the process. Like its radio antecedent, the TV series boasted a string of famous celebrity guest stars, including Phil Silvers, George Burns, Bob Hope, Carol Burnett, Edgar Bergen, Johnny Carson, Lucille Ball, the Smothers Brothers and, from Britain, Max Bygraves and Diana Dors. Although 343 episodes were made only 104 were recorded on film and available for repeat, syndication and overseas sale. In the UK, the series was known variously as The Jack Benny Programme, The Jack Benny Show and, in 1958, The Best Of Benny.

In 1989 BBC2 repeated some of the episodes in its Comedy Classics Double Bill (the second part being **The Honeymooners**), the first such screening being preceded by a tribute, Three Jacks And Two Kings (BBC2, 10 June 1989) in which US comedian Jackie Mason paid homage to those series' respective stars, Jack Benny and Jackie Gleason.

The Jack Benny Spectacular

USA · CBS (JACK BENNY PRODUCTIONS) · STANDUP

3 × 60 mins · b/w

US dates: 19 Mar · 23 May & 7 Nov 1959

UK dates: 28 July 1959 · 17 Sep 1959 & 22 Dec 1960 · BBC various days and times

MAIN CAST

Jack Benny
Bob Hope (show 1)
Gary Cooper (show 1)
Phil Silvers (show 2)
Julie Andrews (show 2)
Danny Thomas (show 3)
Raymond Burr (show 3)

CREDITS

writers Sam Perrin, George Balzer, Hal Goldman, Al Gordon · director/producer Bud Yorkin

British TV screenings for three of the five US Jack Benny Hour specials, combining music with Benny's distinctive brand of drollery. In the third edition Raymond Burr appeared in a Perry Mason skit, defending Benny who is up on a charge. (For British audiences some of the hilarity must have been muted owing to the fact that the Perry Mason series, featuring Burr, wouldn't be seen on British TV until 30 January 1961.)

Jack Benny

UK · BBC · STANDUP

1 × 50 mins · colour

1 Sep 1968 · BBC2 Sun 8.20pm

MAIN CAST

Jack Benny

CREDITS

producer Michael Hurll

A Show Of The Week special, tele-recorded at the Talk Of The Town nightclub in London.

An Evening With Jack Benny

UK · ITV (THAMES) · STANDUP

1 × 60 mins · b/w

26 May 1969 · Mon 10.30pm

MAIN CAST

Jack Benny
Ben Lyon

CREDITS

producer Peter Frazer-Jones

Thames TV taped a UK performance by the celebrated American comedian when he played his Stradivarius to the accompaniment of the London Philharmonic Orchestra and stood at the microphone to amuse with his usual deadpan panache. Benny had long been performing these black-tie charity-concert appearances – raising more than $4m between 1956 and 1967 – but this was the first he permitted to be televised.

Note. This programme was originally scheduled for broadcast on 20 August 1968, but the recording, due to take place two nights earlier at the Royal Albert Hall, was postponed owing to an ITV technicians dispute. The show was eventually taped at Teddington Studios.

Jack Benny's New Look

USA · NBC (JACK BENNY PRODUCTIONS) · COMEDY/VARIETY

1 × 60 mins · colour

US date: 7 Dec 1969

UK date: 3 June 1970 · BBC1 Wed 9.10pm

MAIN CAST
Jack Benny
Eddie 'Rochester' Anderson
George Burns
Gregory Peck
Nancy Sinatra

CREDITS
writers Sam Perrin, Hal Goldman, Al Gordon, Hillard Marks, Hugh Wedlock Jr · *director/producer* Norman Abbott

An American one-off special from the old master featuring a typical star-studded Hollywood guest cast.

Jack Benny's 20th Anniversary Show

USA · NBC (JACK BENNY PRODUCTIONS) · COMEDY/VARIETY

1 × 60 mins · colour

US date: 16 Nov 1970

UK date: 28 Dec 1970 · BBC1 Mon 9.15pm

MAIN CAST
Jack Benny
Eddie 'Rochester' Anderson
Lucille Ball
Mel Blanc
Dennis Day
Bob Hope
Mary Livingstone
Dean Martin
Dinah Shore
Frank Sinatra
Red Skelton
Don Wilson

CREDITS
writers Hal Goldman, Al Gordon, Hillard Marks, Hugh Wedlock Jr · *director* Stan Harris · *producers* Irving Fein, Stan Harris

A programme celebrating Benny's 20 years on TV, featuring an impressive array of stars and the regular cast from *The Jack Benny Program*.

A Love Letter To Jack Benny

USA · NBC (JACK BENNY PRODUCTIONS) · STANDUP/SKETCH

1 × 120 mins · b/w & colour

US date: 5 Jan 1981

UK date: 25 June 1981 · BBC1 Thu 9.25pm (60 mins)

MAIN CAST
George Burns
Johnny Carson
Bob Hope

CREDITS
writers Hal Goldman, Hugh Wedlock Jr · *director* Norman Abbott · *producers* Irving Fein, Fred DeCordova

A special tribute to Benny, hosted by George Burns, Johnny Carson and Bob Hope and featuring extracts from Benny's series and his last ten US television specials. The programme was edited for its UK broadcast.

Benson

USA · ABC (WITT/THOMAS/HARRIS PRODUCTIONS) · SITCOM

158 × 30 mins · colour

US dates: 13 Sep 1979–30 Aug 1986

UK dates: 5 Sep 1980–16 Apr 1989 (113 episodes) ITV various days and times

MAIN CAST
Benson DuBois · · · · · · · · Robert Guillaume
Governor Gene Gatling · · · · · · · James Noble
Gretchen Kraus · · · · · · · · · · · Inga Swenson
Katie Gatling · · · · · · · · · · · · · Missy Gold
John Taylor · · · · · Lewis J Stadlen (1979–80)
Marcie Hill · · Caroline McWilliams (1979–81)
Pete Downey · · · · · Ethan Phillips (1980–85)
Denise Stevens Downey · · · · · · · · Didi Conn
· (1981–85)
Clayton Endicott III · · · · · · Rene Auberjonois
· (1980–86)
Mrs Cassidy · · · · · · · · Billie Bird (1984–86)
Senator Diane Hartford · · · · · · Donna LaBrie
· (1985–86)

CREDITS
creator/main writer Susan Harris · *other writers* Thomas A Reeder, Robert Colleary, Paul Wayne, Paul J Raley/Robert Dolen-Smith, Russ Woody and others · *directors* Jay Sandrich, Peter Baldwin, John Bowab, Tony Mordente, Don Barnhart · *executive producers* Paul Junger Witt, Tony Thomas, John Rich · *producers* Susan Harris, Thomas A Reeder, Don Richetta, Tom Whedon

One episode of *Soap* had Benson, the dependable but bitingly sarcastic black butler, leaving the Tate family's employ and going off to work for Jessica's cousin Gene Gatling, a state Governor. The spin-off series *Benson* showed the man doing just that.

Even more so than in *Soap*, Benson's talents extended here to much more than carrying a silver salver. Although he's pleasant enough, the Governor, it turns out, is scarcely capable of doing his job and comes to rely more and more upon Benson's innate understanding of politics – in every sense of the word – and his general worldliness. In short, Benson becomes the hub around which every wheel turns, catching the Governor's fumbled political footballs and helping to raise his precocious daughter, Katie. (Gatling is a widower.) Being so indispensable, Benson comes up against two human obstacles, both of whom receive his trademark verbal short shrift: the Governor's ineffectual assistant John Taylor (later replaced by Clayton Endicott) and Gretchen Kraus, the house-keeper (portrayed by Inga Swenson, who for a while played a similar role, Ingrid Svenson, in *Soap*. Another *Soap* link was Caroline McWilliams, cast here as Marcie Hill; she was Sally in that earlier series.)

As *Benson* progressed, so the butler's political talents were increasingly recognised. In 1981 he was appointed budget director for the state, a position that allowed him a secretary, Denise Stevens Downey. In 1984 he was elected Lieutenant Governor. Finally, as the last series drew to a close, he ran against Gatling for the position of Governor. The final episode had the two men sitting together, awaiting the election results, but the victor was never revealed. What *was* revealed, at least, was the fate of lovely Jessica Tate from *Soap*. Although viewers did not see the grisly result, she faced a firing squad in the final episode of *Soap*, the camera taking its leave as the men pulled their triggers. They obviously completed the job, for Jessica's ghost visited Benson in one 1983 episode, passing through en route to a celestial home, to tell him how well he'd done with his life and career.

Michael Bentine

The archetypal crazy comic, whose flights of fancy knew absolutely no bounds, Michael Bentine (originally Bentin) was born on 26 January 1922. His father was an immigrant from Peru who had arrived in England at the turn of the century, and Bentine later claimed that he was the first Peruvian ever born in Watford. Although, as a child, he lost the ability to speak for 13 years, schooling took Bentine to Eton; he then launched a career as an entertainer in 1940, although it wasn't until he was serving Britain during the Second World War that he realised he wanted to become a comedian. After peace was declared – and temporarily calling himself Michael Forrest – Bentine formed a double-act with chum Tony Sherwood, and at a Windmill Theatre audition they met fellow ex-services entertainer Harry Secombe. This turned out to be fortuitous – Bentine and Secombe hit it off immediately, sharing a similarly zany sense of humour. Some time later, at the Grafton Arms pub in London, they met with Peter Sellers and Spike Milligan and developed the idea that would eventually become the BBC radio classic *The Goon Show*, aired from 28 May 1951. Along with his other Goon protagonists, Bentine gained his fame with this seminal programme, but he departed, amicably, after the second series (having been involved in the first 43 editions) to return to touring.

On a variety bill, Bentine met the practical-joking Crazy Gang member 'Monsewer' Eddie Gray who kidded to an unsuspecting acquaintance that Bentine was a foreign professor, expert on the subject of Pekinese dogs. The 'professor' soliloquy stuck and Bentine gained much mileage out of the character over the years, utilising it in his first TV-show success *The Bumblies*. His career from this point was full of highs, with only the occasional low, and he continued, too, to appear frequently on BBC radio – his series *The Best Of Bentine*, in which he provided all the voices, was a landmark. All the while, Bentine exercised a keen interest in the paranormal, which, some suggest, coloured his decidedly offbeat comedy. He was also an accredited scientist, a ballistics expert and a pilot.

Bentine's later life was beset with tragedy – his son was killed in a plane crash and two of his daughters died of cancer. Bentine himself, also a cancer sufferer, passed away on 26 November 1996.

For further Michael Bentine TV work see **Secombe And Friends**, **Summer's Here** and **Yes, It's The Cathode-Ray Tube Show!**

The Bumblies

UK · BBC · (RICHARD DENDY AND ASSOCIATES) · CHILDREN'S SKETCH

12 × 10 mins · b/w
Series One (6) 14 Feb–25 Apr 1954 · Sun 5pm
Series Two (6) 26 Sep–12 Dec 1954 · Sun 5pm

MAIN CAST
Michael Bentine (voice only)

CREDITS
writer Michael Bentine · *producer* Anthony de Lotbiniere

A comedy puppet series for children created and presented by 'professor' Michael Bentine. The Bumblies were three strange triangular-shaped aliens from the planet Bumble known simply as One, Two and Three. They were gravity-defying chaps who slept on the ceiling between shows. Whereas One and Two were reasonably smart, Three was humorously gormless and more than one contemporary observer drew parallels between Three and Eccles from *The Goon Show*. The puppetry was carried out by a process of remote control in a style that Bentine would return to later for his *Potty Time* series and in some of the

animated stunts in his zany masterpiece *It's A Square World*.

After Hours

UK · ITV (ABC) · SKETCH

28 × 25 mins · b/w
*Series One (15) 5 Oct 1958–18 Jan 1959 · Sun mostly 11.10pm
*Series Two (13) 12 Sep–19 Dec 1959 · Sat mostly 11pm

MAIN CAST
Michael Bentine
David Lodge (eds 1–6 of series 1)
Dick Emery (eds 7–15 of series 1 & series 2)
Benny Lee
Clive Dunn

CREDITS
writers Michael Bentine/Dick Lester · *director* Dick Lester

After Hours reunited both the co-star and director of **Yes, It's The Cathode-Ray Tube Show!** – Michael Bentine and the American-born TV (and later film) director Richard (Dick) Lester.

The humour here was drawn from musical and sporting guests and, in particular, film and news sketches, a formula that Bentine would later hone for his hit BBC TV series *It's A Square World* and was currently airing in his BBC radio series *Round The Bend*, which also featured Benny Lee and Clive Dunn. Bentine also invented three new animated characters seen each week: Sid, Ernie and George.

Guests in *After Hours* – which had the working title *Eleven-Plus* – included comics and actors (Frankie Howerd, Alan Young, Alfred Marks, Bernard Bresslaw, Tommy Cooper, Bernard Braden, Jayne Mansfield, William Bendix, Dave King, Shirley Eaton and others) and sportsmen (Brian London, Henry Cooper, Danny Blanchflower, Jimmy Greaves, Stirling Moss and John Surtees and others). Bentine and Lester wrote the scripts, Bentine was the host and appeared in many of the sketches, and Lester directed. The resident singer in the first six editions of the first series was the up-and-coming Shirley Bassey.

*Note. Only three first series editions (26 October–9 November 1958) were screened in the London area; the remaining 12, and the 13 programmes that comprised the second series, were seen only in the Midlands and the North.

It's A Square World

UK · BBC · SKETCH

58 editions (56 × 30 mins · 2 × short specials) · b/w
Special · 16 Sep 1960 · Fri 9pm

Series One (6) 26 Apr–31 May 1961 · Fri 8.30pm
Series Two (6) 5 Oct–9 Nov 1961 · Thu 8.45pm
Series Three (7) 19 Apr–31 May 1962 · Thu 8.45pm
Series Four (6) 4 Oct–8 Nov 1962 · Tue 8.45pm
Short special · part of *Christmas Night With The Stars* 25 Dec 1962 · Tue 7.15pm
Special · 19 Apr 1963 · Fri 8.20pm
Series Five (8) 3 May–21 June 1963 · Fri 8.50pm
Series Six (8) 14 Nov–31 Dec 1963 · Fri 8.50pm
Short special · part of *Christmas Night With The Stars* 25 Dec 1963 · Wed 8.05pm
Series Seven (13) 27 Sep–20 Dec 1964 · BBC1 Sun 7.25pm

MAIN CAST
Michael Bentine
Dick Emery
Frank Thornton
Clive Dunn
John Bluthal
Deryck Guyler

CREDITS
creators/writers Michael Bentine/John Law · *special effects* Jack Kine · *producers* Barry Lupino, James Gilbert, Joe McGrath, John Street

A groundbreaking, surreal sketch show from the madcap mind of Michael Bentine. This fast-moving production combined different comedic styles, from satire to straight slapstick with an 'anything-goes' sensibility. The series also had a unique visual style, created by an elaborate use of special effects and location filming. Following the pilot show, Bentine suffered a pulmonary embolism and was laid low for six months. While he was on the road to recovery the BBC commissioned a series of 12 editions, which were to form the first two series.

During its run the series featured many memorable skits, with three ideas in particular typifying its style: sinking the House of Commons with a Chinese Junk; discovering that the source of the Thames was a dripping tap; and sending BBC Television Centre into orbit with TV astronomer Patrick Moore (one of many routines using the Television Centre). The programmes were vastly entertaining and enormously popular; a special edition, screened by the BBC on 19 April 1963, won the Golden Rose of Montreux that year; in 1962 Bentine won the Bafta award for best comedy performance.

In 1977 a one-off BBC special revisited the *Square World* (see last entry).

All Square

UK · ITV (ATV) · SKETCH

14 × 30 mins

Series One (7) 1 Oct–12 Nov 1966 ·
Sat 8.40pm

Series Two (7) 1 Apr–13 May 1967 ·
Sat 8.55pm

MAIN CAST
Michael Bentine
Deryck Guyler
Benny Lee
Leon Thau
Joe Gibbons
Alfred Ravel

CREDITS
writers Michael Bentine/John Ennis · producer
Jon Scoffield

Unable to secure an increased production budget that would have permitted his ever more adventurous – but expensive – filming ideas, Michael Bentine reluctantly left the BBC and hauled his unique brand of surrealistic buffoonery over to 'the opposition' and launched *All Square*, completing two series for ATV that ran peak-time on Saturdays evenings. Although pleased to be asked to make these shows by the commercial channel, Bentine was unable to match the quality of his earlier BBC series, and although he brought with him many of his old team, he missed especially the special effects wizardry of Jack Kine.

Although a worthy effort and featuring moments of inspired lunacy, Bentine himself admitted that this series paled in comparison with its illustrious predecessor.

Mike, Phil And Albert

UK · ITV (THAMES) · MUSICAL HUMOUR

1 × 60 mins · colour

22 Aug 1971 · Tue 10.30pm

MAIN CAST
Michael Bentine
Jack Haig

CREDITS
writer Michael Bentine · director Christopher
Palmer

An anarchic concert at the Royal Albert Hall featuring the London Philharmonic Orchestra and devised by Bentine with special-effects expert Peter Roddis. The event owed as much to the heritage of Spike Jones as it did to Bentine's own brand of lunacy, with guns, a pram, a tea-trolley, ping-pong balls and a submarine used along with the more traditional orchestral elements to interpret the works of Mozart, Beethoven, Tchaikovsky and other composers. Along the way Bentine described how Prince Albert had designed the famous hall as the world's largest gasometer, and a fanciful centrepiece had Albert and Queen Victoria duetting on such well-known pieces as 'Tit Willow' and 'The Last Rose Of Summer'.

Although undoubtedly funny, the event was tinged with a bitter-sweet edge: Bentine conceived the show as a tribute to his son Stuart, who had been killed the previous year in a light aircraft crash.

By, With And From Bentine

UK · BBC · STANDUP

1 × 30 mins · colour

24 Sep 1971 · BBC2 Fri 10.35pm

MAIN CAST
Michael Bentine

CREDITS
writer Michael Bentine · producer Leon Thau

Half an hour of Bentine, who ran through a collection of anecdotes in an attempt to prove that some real events in his life had been funnier than those he had dreamed up for television.

Talk About London

UK · BBC · IMPROVISATIONAL

1 × 30 mins · colour

26 June 1972 · BBC1 Mon 7.30pm

MAIN CAST
Michael Bentine

CREDITS
writer Michael Bentine · director Leon Thau ·
producer Colin Morris

A one-off special in which Bentine led a comedy tour of London, creating humour with Billingsgate porters, Beefeaters, firemen and stockbrokers.

Michael BenTine Time

UK · BBC · CHILDREN'S SKETCH

13 × 30 mins · colour

15 Sep–8 Dec 1972 · BBC1 Fri 5.15pm

MAIN CAST
Michael Bentine

CREDITS
writer Michael Bentine · producer Johnny Downes

Bentine combined aspects of two previous shows, *The Bumblies* and *It's A Square World*, in this inventive entertainment for children. Regular features of *Michael BenTine Time* (sic) were the elaborate, special-effect laden mini-sets; *Yesterday's World*, a spoof of the BBC1 science-invention programme *Tomorrow's World*, in which Bentine looked back on (imaginary) inventions of the past; *Is This Your Life?*, looking at (fictitious) bizarre careers in a parody of *This Is Your Life*; and a 1970s variation of *The Bumblies* called *The Pottys*.

The Pottys proved particularly popular and the following year graduated to their own Thames TV series aimed at the very young.

Michael Bentine's Potty Time

UK · ITV (THAMES) · CHILDREN'S SKETCH

**78 editions (52 × 25 mins · 26 × 15 mins) ·
colour**

Series One (26 × 15 mins) 12 Nov 1973–6 May
1974 · Mon 12.25pm

Series Two (13 × 25 mins) 8 Jan–2 Apr 1975 ·
Wed 4.25pm

Series Three (13 × 25 mins) 4 Jan–5 Apr 1977 ·
Tue 4.20pm

Series Four (7 × 25 mins) 11 Jan–22 Feb 1978 ·
Wed 4.20pm

Series Five (6 × 25 mins) 31 May–12 July 1978 ·
Wed 4.20pm

Series Six (6 × 25 mins) 2 Jan–6 Feb 1979 ·
Tue 4.20pm

Series Seven (7 × 25 mins) 9 Apr–21 May
1980 · Wed 4.15pm

MAIN CAST
Michael Bentine

CREDITS
deviser/writer Michael Bentine · directors Leon
Thau (series 1 & 2, 5 eds in series 3, series 4, 5
& 7), Michael Custance (8 eds in series 3), Terry
Steel (series 6) · producers Leon Thau (series
1–5 & 7), Terry Steel (series 6)

Described by Bentine as 'Mark Two Bumblies', the Pottys embraced the surreal comic's fascination for and with puppets, resulting in 78 truly delightful programmes of entertainment aimed primarily at younger viewers but enjoyed by any adults who happened – whether by misfortune or design – to be around in the daytime. (The first series, indeed, was screened in a pre-school slot.)

The Pottys were short, stumpy characters whose legs, if they had any at all, were hidden by costumes. They were virtually faceless too, Bentine recognising that, without features, his characters would be free from prejudice since they could be any colour, any nationality, any religion and any age. Bentine set out to 'mock the accepted notions about history or science or courage' and the episodes (from the second series onwards each featured two self-contained stories) were wonderfully anarchic fun, enacting classic stories, real-life incidents and sending up popular TV series of the day (*On The Pirate Buses*, *Pottdark* and others), in Bentine's hallmark zany style. Along the way, viewers witnessed hundreds of different models – 285 were used in the first series alone – but some met with a sticky end: Pottys were often blown up and dis-membered, Bentine countering any accusa-tions of gratuitous violence by remarking that children's humour is naturally aggressive. One episode showed the Pottys playing 'drats', described by Bentine as one of Britain's ancient indoor sports, which, with humans in the roles, had been among the highlights of *It's A Square World*.

High tech it wasn't but great fun it certainly was, and credit should be paid to the series' designers who helped bring Bentine's flights of fancy to puppet form: John Plant, Colin Andrews, Frank Gillman, Bill Palmer, Mark Nerini, Anthony Cartledge, Frank Gillman and Jim Nicholson.

Note. Programmes in the first series, which filled 15-minute slots, were 11 minutes long; the remainder all lasted 22 to 23 minutes, even though the final series was aired in a half-hour slot.

Bentine

UK · ITV (THAMES) · SKETCH

1 × 45 mins · colour

22 Sep 1975 · Mon 6.45pm

MAIN CAST
Michael Bentine
Geoffrey Bayldon
James Berwick
Jack Haig
Jan Hunt
Nat Jackley

CREDITS
writer Michael Bentine · *additional material* John Ennis · *director* Leon Thau · *producer* David Clark

Having entertained children with his *Potty Time* programmes Michael Bentine had a slightly more mature audience in mind for this one-off Thames special in which he presented again the kind of surrealistic sketch comedy that had brought him such deserved plaudits with *It's A Square World*.

Michael Bentine's Square World

UK · BBC · SKETCH

1 × 30 mins · colour

19 Apr 1977 · BBC1 Tue 7.40pm

MAIN CAST
Michael Bentine
Jack Haig
Stuart Fell

CREDITS
writers Michael Bentine/John Ennis · *producer* Jim Franklin

A return trip to Bentine's *Square World* as part of the BBC's *Comedy Playhouse* successor, *Comedy Special*, which suggests that this may have been a pilot for a projected new series. Visual effects this time were handled by Dave Havard and puppets were made by Christopher Leith and operated by Theatre Of Puppets.

The Bernard Bresslaw Show

UK · ITV (ATV) · SKETCH/STANDUP

4 × 60 mins · b/w

24 Aug 1958 · Sun 8.30pm

22 Nov 1958 · Sat 7.55pm

18 Apr 1959 · Sat 7.55pm

18 July 1959 · Sat 8pm

MAIN CAST
Bernard Bresslaw

CREDITS
writers Sid Green/Dick Hills · *producers* Albert Locke (3), Kenneth Carter (1)

Four starring vehicles for the man who had shot to fame as the dimwit in Granada's tremendously popular sitcom *The Army Game*. The latter three were screened under the banner *Saturday Spectacular*.

Bresslaw also appeared in an untitled ITV variety show on 13 July 1958.

See also *Bresslaw And Friends*.

Bernard Manning

UK · ITV (GRANADA) · STANDUP

1 × 60 mins · colour

12 Mar 1980 · Wed 8pm

MAIN CAST
Bernard Manning

CREDITS
director Nicholas Ferguson · *producer* Johnny Hamp

A single hour-length special for the controversial comic who had found fame and fortune as one of *The Comedians*. The bulky, red-faced Manning was unquestionably a master joke-teller but his reliance upon dodgy material, much of it racist, drew considerable flak, especially when the emerging 'alternative comedians' of the 1980s aggressively rallied against such material. Manning, of course, was unrepentant.

Note. The comedian hosted an earlier ITV special, *Mr Nice Guy – Bernard Manning* (Granada, 18 May 1977), but this was a big-band spectacular rather than a comedy show. He also featured in *Bernard Manning In Las Vegas*, an hour-length ITV special on 8 February 1978. This Granada documentary programme followed Manning as he travelled from his Manchester club to Las Vegas, where, galvanised by advice from US comedians Joan Rivers, Pat Henry and others, he spent a week entertaining audiences at the MGM Grand Hotel.

The Bernard Show

see The Montreux Festival

Bernie

UK · ITV (THAMES) · SKETCH

13 × 30 mins · colour

Series One (7) 23 Oct–11 Dec 1978 · Mon 7pm

Series Two (6) 10 Jan–14 Feb 1980 · Thu 7.30pm

MAIN CAST
Bernie Winters

CREDITS
writers Johnnie Mortimer/Brian Cooke, David Renwick, Dave Freeman, Lawrie Kinsley, Ron McDonnell, Barry Cryer, Eric Merriman, John Warren/John Singer, George Evans, Bryan Blackburn, Howard Imber, Alex Shearer, Mark Hill, Peter Tilbury · *script editors* Johnnie Mortimer/Brian Cooke · *programme associate* Eric Merriman · *directors* Leon Thau (series 1), John Ammonds (4 eds), Stuart Hall (1 ed), Paul Stewart Laing (1 ed) · *producer* John Ammonds

Brothers for approaching 50 years, and on stage for all of 30, **Mike and Bernie Winters** split their act in 1978 amid a good deal of acrimony and went their separate ways, Mike heading for America and Bernie being offered a three-year contract by Thames TV. Although originally intended as a sitcom, this sketch series, *Bernie*, was the first fruit, scripted for him by an army of experienced writers and with guests to help move the comedy along – and not forgetting his massive St Bernard dog Schnorbitz, of course, who would sit with the star at the start and end of each show, listen to his stories and be fed sausages.

Bernie's later work embraced a circus-comedy series (*The Big Top Variety Show*, Thames from 15 August 1979) and various panel-game/quiz-shows including a couple that he hosted (*Make Me Laugh*, for Tyne Tees, and *Whose Baby?*, for Thames). He also co-starred with Leslie Crowther in ATV's *Bud 'n' Ches*, an affectionate tribute – presented as a play – to Bud Flanagan and Chesney Allen, screened by ITV on 16 June 1981. (See *Leslie Crowther's Scrapbook* for further details.)

Bernie Clifton On Stage

UK · ITV (ATV) · SKETCH/STANDUP

1 × 30 mins · colour

6 July 1980 · Sun 9.15pm

MAIN CAST
Bernie Clifton

CREDITS
writers Andrew Marshall/David Renwick, Max Sherrington · *director/producer* Royston Mayoh

A one-off special for the comedian usually seen in seaside shows and other people's programmes. *World Of Sport* anchorman Dickie Davies appeared in one of the sketches.

Beryl Reid   1

UK · BBC · STANDUP/SKETCH

2 editions (1 × 40 mins · 1 × short special) · b/w

Special (40 mins) 16 Sep 1967 · BBC2 Sat 7.10pm

Short special · part of *Christmas Night With The Stars* 25 Dec 1967 · BBC1 Mon 6.40pm

MAIN CAST
Beryl Reid

William Mervyn (long special)
Raymond Francis (long special)
Avril Angers (short special)

CREDITS
writers Beryl Reid, Arthur Macrae, Harold Pinter, Alan Melville, N F Simpson (long special); Alan Melville (short special) · *producers* Robin Nash (long special), Stewart Morris (short special)

A BBC2 *Show Of The Week* special, in which Beryl Reid was assisted in the sketches by two ITV detectives: William Mervyn (from Granada's *Mr Rose*) and Raymond Francis (Superintendent Lockhart from Rediffusion's *No Hiding Place*).

See **Beryl Reid Says Good Evening** for biographical info.

Beryl Reid   2
UK · BBC · SKETCH
3 editions (1 × 50 mins · 2 × 45 mins) · colour
12 Dec 1977 · BBC2 Mon 8.10pm (50 mins)
5 Feb 1979 · BBC2 Mon 8.15pm (45 mins)
18 Dec 1979 · BBC2 Tue 9.45pm (45 mins)

MAIN CAST
Beryl Reid
John Standing (show 1)
Avril Anger (show 1)
Derek Fowlds (show 1)
Malcolm McDowell (show 1)
Patricia Hayes (shows 2 & 3)
Derek Francis (show 2)
Norman Rossington (show 2)
Sheila Steafel (show 2)
David Lodge (show 3)
Avril Elgar (show 3)

CREDITS
show 1 writers Arthur Macrae, N F Simpson, John Mortimer, Joe Orton, Mike Craig/Lawrie Kinsley, Ron McDonnell/Paul Dehn, Neil Shand · *show 2 writers* Arthur Macrae, N F Simpson, Harold Pinter, William Congreve, Alan Melville, Peter Myers/Ronnie Cass · *show 3 writers* Noël Coward, Arthur Macrae, Alan Melville, Norman Newell, Harold Pinter, Richard Brinsley Sheridan, Eric Merriman · *producers* Robin Nash (shows 1 & 2), Brian Whitehouse (show 3)

Three presentations of Beryl Reid's favourite sketches and scenes, enacted anew. Some of these pieces suffered in comparison with their earlier TV versions but a scene from Joe Orton's *Entertaining Mr Sloane* (in the first show), in which Reid was supported by Malcolm McDowell, was wonderfully performed and presented.

Note. The second show was originally scheduled for 20 December 1978.

Beryl Reid Says Good Evening
UK · BBC · SKETCH
6 × 30 mins · b/w
4 Mar–8 Apr 1968 · BBC1 Mon 7.30pm

MAIN CAST
Beryl Reid

Hugh Paddick
Jake Thackray

CREDITS
main writer Alan Melville · *other writers* Arthur Macrae, Austin Steele, Harold Pinter, Paul Dehn, Robert Gould, John Mortimer, N F Simpson, Thorley Walters, P H Robinson · *producer* Robin Nash

An impressive revue for the brilliant Beryl Reid, whose mischievous demeanour and energetic performances in a variety of roles lifted the series above its contemporaries. The subject matter in many of the sketches (marital problems, tipsy stewardesses, love-starved spinsters and so on) imbued the series with a risqué atmosphere, quite bold for its early-evening BBC1 slot. Alan Melville wrote the lion's share of the material but he was ably supported by a heavyweight team of contributors including Harold Pinter, John Mortimer and surrealist N F Simpson. Witty, oddball folk singer Jake Thackray provided the music and acting support came from Hugh Paddick (a regular), Sheila Hancock and Joan Sims.

The series represents the high-point in Beryl Reid's television career. Born in Hereford on 17 June 1920, she proved herself adept in most areas of entertainment, appearing on stage from 1936, in films since 1954 (*The Belles Of St Trinian's*) as well as performing comedy on radio (most notably in *Educating Archie*, and her own series *Good Evening, Each*) and, from 1952, on television. She was a major attraction in *Educating Archie* and on stage in the character of Marlene, a Birmingham girl with an exaggerated Brummie twang. This laboured accent, in which Reid performed all sorts of verbal gymnastics, became a hallmark of her work, and an impression of that voice was used in *Spitting Image* as the voice of the Queen Mother.

Note. Beryl Reid died on 13 October 1996. A half-hour compilation of highlights from *Good Evening* was screened by BBC2 on 4 October 1997 following a tribute paid to her in the series *Funny Women*.

See also **The Most Likely Girl** and **Nanny Knows Best**.

Beryl's Lot
UK · ITV (YORKSHIRE) · SITCOM
52 episodes (26 × 60 mins · 26 × 30 mins) · colour
Series One (13 × 60 mins) 1 Nov 1973–31 Jan 1974 · Thu 8.30pm
Series Two (13 × 60 mins) 26 Sep–19 Dec 1975 · Fri 9pm
Series Three (26 × 30 mins) 31 Dec 1976–24 June 1977 · Fri 7pm

MAIN CAST
Beryl Humphries · · · · · · · · · Carmel McSharry

Tom Humphries · · · · · · · · · · · Mark Kingston
· (series 1 & 2);
· · · · · · · · · · · · · · George Selway (series 3)
Vi Tonks · · · · · · · · · · · · · · · Barbara Mitchell
Trev Tonks · · · · · · · · · · · · · · · · · Tony Caunter
Horace Harris · · · · · · · · · · · · · Robert Keegan
Wully Harris · · · · · · · · · · · · · · · · Annie Leake
Fred Pickering · · Robin Askwith (series 1 & 2)
Freda · · · · · · · · Queenie Watts (series 1 & 2)
Charlie Mills · · · · · · · · · · · Norman Mitchell
Rosie Humphries · · · · · · · · · · · Verna Harvey
Jack Humphries · · · · · · · · · · · Brian Capron
Babs Humphries · · · · · · · · · · · · Anita Carey

CREDITS
writers Kevin Laffan (39), Bill MacIlwraith (7), Charles Humphreys (6) · *directors* Derek Bennett (17), David Reynolds (9), John Frankau (7), Moira Armstrong (4), Gareth Davies (4), Roger Cheveley (4), Michael Ferguson (2), Brian Farnham (2), Matthew Robinson (1), Hugh David (1), Malcolm Taylor (1) · *executive producers* Peter Willes (series 1), David Cunliffe (series 2 & 3) · *producers* John Frankau (series 1), Jacky Stoller (series 2), Derek Bennett (series 3)

As her fortieth birthday approaches, Beryl Humphries realises that there must be more to life than running the family home, being a mother of three, milkman's wife, and a 'char' for others, and she decides to improve her 'lot', enrolling for philosophy evening classes and otherwise breaking her conventions.

Blending comedy with drama, the series was inspired by the life of Margaret Powell – who, in her sixties, was transformed, seemingly overnight, from household servant to best-selling author and explosively giggly celebrity – and she served as script consultant during the first series. The main writer, Kevin Laffan, created the rural soap *Emmerdale Farm* in 1972.

Beside The Seaside
UK · ITV (JACK HYLTON TV PRODUCTIONS FOR ASSOCIATED-REDIFFUSION) · SKETCH
6 × 30 mins · b/w
28 June–6 Sep 1957 · fortnightly Fri 9pm

MAIN CAST
Richard Murdoch
Glenn Melvyn
Danny Ross

CREDITS
director Bimbi Harris

Six shows of seaside humour from popular radio comic Richard 'Stinker' Murdoch, cast as the Entertainments Manager at a busy resort, with Glenn Melvyn and Danny Ross (stars of *Love And Kisses* – see Arthur Askey's entry for details – and *I'm Not Bothered*) as his laughter-providing attendants.

Notes. A similar theme to *Beside The Seaside* was explored at precisely the same time in the BBC series *Scott Free*.

Melvyn and Ross were later seen on television in an excerpt from Jack Hylton's theatrical farce *Friends And Neighbours,* mounted at the Victoria Palace in London. It was screened on ITV, by way of Hylton's production link with Associated-Rediffusion, on 8 December 1958. Valentine Dyall and Mollie Sugden were also among the cast.

The Best Of Enemies

UK · ITV (THAMES) · SITCOM

5 × 30 mins · b/w

6 Aug 1968 · Tue 8.45pm; 25 June–16 July 1969 · Wed mostly 10.30pm

MAIN CAST

Willie Gordon MP	Robert Coote
Geoffrey Broom MP	Tim Barrett
Wilkins	Deryck Guyler

CREDITS

writers Vince Powell/Harry Driver · *producers* Alan Tarrant (4), Malcolm Morris (1)

A Powell and Driver creation that set out to depict the humorous side of British politics. While no **Yes Minister**, it was the first sitcom to venture inside Parliament (an earlier BBC series, **The Whitehall Worrier**, was set mostly outside the chamber).

Episodes revolved around two rival MPs forced to share an office inside the inappropriately named House of Commons (these two men had *nothing* in common). Tim Barrett played the part of Geoffrey Broom, a newly elected Labour MP for Burnstone, Yorkshire, with Robert Coote appearing as William Sylvester Gordon, a canny old Conservative who represented the comfortable seat of Ryefield in Surrey.

The series was beset with problems: Powell and Driver wrote seven scripts but only five made it to the screen, and the original run, in 1968, ground to a halt after the premiere episode because of an ITV technicians dispute. The remaining four finally went out almost a year later.

Best Of Friends

UK · ITV (ABC) · SITCOM

13 × 30 mins · b/w

28 Apr–28 July 1963 · Sun mostly 5.10pm

MAIN CAST

Charles	Charles Hawtrey
Hylda	Hylda Baker
Sheena	Sheena Marshe
Uncle Sidney	Henry Longhurst

CREDITS

writers Brad Ashton, Bob Block, Gerry Maxin · *producer* Ernest Maxin

A rare sitcom outing for *Carry On* film star Charles Hawtrey, which pitched him alongside Hylda Baker. (Both had appeared in the 1960–61 ABC sitcom **Our House**, with essentially the same writers and production team.) Keeping the faith with his established lily-livered screen persona, *Best Of Friends* cast Hawtrey as a clerk in an insurance office situated next door to a café run by Baker. She accompanied him on insurance assignments and protected him when he was feeling put upon by his Uncle Sidney, who wished to – but could not – dismiss his nephew from the firm.

The Best Of Friends

UK · ITV (ATV) · SITCOM

1 × 30 mins · colour

1 Sep 1977 · Thu 7pm

MAIN CAST

Miss Vaughan	Jessie Evans
Nicholas Barry	Peter Blythe
Sally Morton	Catherine Chase
Olwyn Lloyd	Margaret Courtenay
Emily Lloyd	Megs Jenkins
Dr Hamer	Gerald James

CREDITS

writer Linette Purbi Perry · *director/producer* Shaun O'Riordan

A single comedy within ATV's season *The Sound Of Laughter,* starring Jessie Evans as an old woman whose nephew and girlfriend come to stay and expect the use of her double-bed – which proves especially embarrassing when the woman's oldest friends, the Lloyd sisters, take an interest.

The Best Of Show Of Shows

see *Your Show Of Shows*

Best Of The West

USA · ABC (PARAMOUNT/WEINBERGER-DANIELS PRODUCTIONS) · SITCOM

22 × 30 mins · colour

US dates: 10 Sep 1981–23 Aug 1982

UK dates: 23 July 1982–12 Aug 1983 (20 episodes) BBC1 Mon and Fri around 6.40pm then Tue 7.15pm

MAIN CAST

Sam Best	Joel Higgins
Elvira Best	Carlene Watkins
Daniel Best	Meeno Peluce
Parker Tillman	Leonard Frey
Doc Jerome Kullens	Tom Ewell
Laney Gibbs	Valri Bromfield
Frog	Tracey Walter
The Calico Kid	Christopher Lloyd

CREDITS

creator Earl Pomerantz · *writers* Earl Pomerantz, Michael Leeson, Mitch Markowitz, Chip Keyes/Doug Keyes, Sam Simon · *directors* James Burrows, Stan Daniels, Ed Weinberger, Will MacKenzie, Jeff Chambers, Doug Rogers, Tom Trbovich, Jeff Chambers · *producers* Earl Pomerantz, David Lloyd

A spoof cowboy series that plundered film and TV westerns for clichés and wove comedy around them. The series told the story of Sam Best, who moves to the town of Copper Creek with his Southern 'belle' wife Elvira and ten-year-old son Daniel, both of whom are unhappy with the relocation. Sam, who has bought the General Store, is immediately faced with the prospect of paying protection money to the town baddie, Parker Tillman, the double-dealing varmint who sold him the store in the first place. Sam refuses to pay and, despite his lack of prowess with a gun, accidentally scares off a notorious gunfighter (The Calico Kid), two acts that see him installed as the town marshal. Much mirth followed his attempts to perform the job despite a total lack of macho qualifications. He also had trouble at home, with his family yearning to return to civilisation. Others at large in the town included the permanently drunken doctor, Jerome Kullens; the formidable mountain woman Laney Gibbs; and a dense henchman, Frog.

Best Of The West was a well-mounted sitcom, from a good stable, which effortlessly fulfilled its own modest brief to be 'a kids programme for grown-ups' but only managed to remain in the saddle for one season.

The Best Things In Life

UK · ITV (ATV) · SITCOM

13 × 30 mins (6 × b/w · 7 × colour)

Series One (6 × b/w) 12 Aug–16 Sep 1969 · Tue 8.30pm

Series Two (7 × colour) 1 June–13 July 1970 · Mon 9.30pm

MAIN CAST

Alfred Wilcox	Harry H Corbett
Mabel Pollard	June Whitfield
Yvonne Armitage	Pat Heywood (series 1)
Vera	Samantha Birch (series 1)
Mr Davis	Kenneth Keeling (series 1)
Mr Pollard	Bob Todd (series 2)
Mrs Pollard	Pearl Hackney (series 2)
Pauline	Carmel McSharry (series 2)
Gloria	Diana Quick (series 2)

CREDITS

creator Bernard Botting · *writers* Bernard Botting (6), Adele Rose (2), Jack Trevor Story (2), Dave Freeman (2), Ted Willis (1) · *directors* Shaun O'Riordan (series 1), John Robins (series 2) · *producer* Shaun O'Riordan

Another series for Harry H Corbett who, much as he tried, found it hard to shake off the public's perception of him as Harold Steptoe. In *The Best Things In Life* he was cast as a cockney spiv, Alfred Wilcox, who works as a salesman for a plastics company and enjoys living by his wits. Alfred is always trying to keep two steps ahead of the game and short-cut his way to the top, but time and again his very ambition thwarts his progress. Much of Alfred's energy is spent avoiding marriage to his fiancée of 11 years, Mabel, who works in the office of the same company, because – as he sees it –

being 'hitched' will deny him his valued independence and, with it, the opportunity to continue grasping for that elusive success.

The first series of *The Best Things In Life* was written by Bernard Botting – his first TV job after scripting *Ray's A Laugh* for BBC radio from 1956 to 1960 – but other writers penned the second series, in which Mabel's parents (Bob Todd and Pearl Hackney) joined the cast, hoping to see their daughter finally married off. For June Whitfield, as the desperate, permanent fiancée, it must have felt like déjà vu: she had soared to fame on BBC radio in the 1950s as the ever-denied Eth in *The Glums*, part of *Take It From Here*.

Betsy Mae

UK · BBC · SITCOM

1 × 25 mins · b/w

19 Aug 1965 · BBC1 Thu 8.50pm

MAIN CAST
Betsy Mae Meadows · · · · · Hermione Gingold
Roger Kaye · · · · · · · · · · · · Nicholas Phipps

CREDITS
writers Ken Hoare/Mike Sharland · *executive producer* Graeme Muir · *producer* Douglas Moodie

A *Comedy Playhouse* production with the formidable Hermione Gingold cast as the equally formidable Betsy Mae Meadows, a successful children's novelist who shares W C Fields' decidedly non-PC views on the young.

Bette Midler's Mondo Beyondo Show

USA · HBO · SITCOM

1 × 60 mins · colour

US date: 19 Mar 1988

UK date: 5 Jan 1990 · BBC1 Fri 11.15pm

MAIN CAST
Mondo Beyondo · · · · · · · · · · · · Bette Midler
WITH
David Gale
Paul Zaloom
Bill Irwin

CREDITS
writers Jerry Blatt, Bette Midler · *director* Thomas Schlamme · *producers* Martin Von Hasleberg, Fred Berner

Bette Midler – 'The Divine Miss M' – made her name by way of her powerhouse vocal talent and storming stage-shows that combined straight pop songs with vamped-up versions of oldies, pastiche characters and impressions (especially of Sophie Tucker), with her gum-chewing, hip-grinding backing band, the Harlettes, accentuating the live shows' sleazy vaudeville flavour. Midler graduated through acting in musical pieces to straight acting with an emphasis on comedy roles. In this 1988 TV special she appeared as a statuesque Italian cable TV star, Mondo

Beyondo, linking sketches and musical items that highlighted the wacky, off-the-wall world of cable television.

Note. Katey Sagal, a member of the Harlettes, achieved stardom when she played Peg Bundy in the outrageous US sitcom *Married ... With Children*.

Better Not ...

UK · BBC · CHILDREN'S SKETCH

2 × 15 mins · b/w

23 Jan & 30 Jan 1952 · Wed 6pm

MAIN CAST
Desmond Tester

CREDITS
writer Desmond Tester · *producer* Alan Bromly

A comedy series presented as part of the *For The Children* strand, in which Desmond Tester took a humorous view of a different subject each week. He meant to look at ironing, cycling, cooking and spring cleaning but only the first two of these four programmes were made; the latter two – scheduled for 6 and 13 February 1952 – were cancelled owing to the sudden death of King George VI on 6 February and subsequent re-arrangement of all TV programming.

Better Than A Man

UK · BBC · SITCOM

1 × 30 mins · colour

18 Mar 1970 · BBC1 Wed 7.30pm

MAIN CAST
Wendy Hillbright · · · · · · · · · Sheila Hancock
George Hillbright · · · · · · · · · · · Leslie Sands
Llewellyn Chadwick · · · · · · Allan Cuthbertson
Sir Michael Binns · · · · · Willoughby Goddard
Arnold Pollock · · · · · · · · · · · · John Warner

CREDITS
writer Kenneth Eastaugh · *producer* Sydney Lotterby

Following her emergence as a comedian/actress of note, Sheila Hancock was ideal casting material for a hit sitcom; this *Comedy Playhouse* attempt failed to travel beyond a pilot episode, however. She played Wendy Hillbright, a self-made woman who overcomes sexist attitudes to become managing director of a steel company; her father, however, is a troublemaking foundryman at the works.

The Betty Driver Show

UK · BBC · STANDUP

6 × 30 mins · b/w

1 May–10 July 1952 · fortnightly mostly Thu around 9pm

MAIN CAST
Betty Driver
Geoffrey Sumner
Tom Macaulay

Harry Jacobson
Elizabeth Maude

CREDITS
creator Kenneth Milne-Buckley · *writers* John Jowett (shows 1 & 2), Chris Webb/Kenneth Milne-Buckley (shows 3–6) · *producer* Kenneth Milne-Buckley

Former child-star Betty Driver was already a stage and film veteran when she teamed up with bandleader Henry Hall during the Second World War to sing in the BBC radio programme *Henry Hall's Guest Night*. More radio work followed, including her own series *A Date With Betty*. On TV, in *The Betty Driver Show*, she displayed her comic talent in addition to her singing prowess. Music was provided each week by the Petersen Brothers, a South African close-harmony group, and Driver went on to marry singer Wally Petersen.

Later, following her premature retirement, *Coronation Street* producer Harry Kershaw approached Betty Driver to play the part of Betty Turpin in the long-running ITV soap, a role that once again made her a household name.

The Betty White Show

USA · CBS (MTM ENTERPRISES) · SITCOM

14 × 30 mins · colour

US dates: 12 Sep 1977–9 Jan 1978

UK dates: 14 Aug 1985–13 Nov 1985 (14 episodes) C4 Wed 6pm

MAIN CAST
Joyce Whitman · · · · · · · · · · · · · Betty White
John Elliot · · · · · · · · · · · · · · John Hillerman
Mitzi Maloney · · · · · · · · · · · · Georgia Engel
Hugo Muncy · · · · · · · · · · · · Charles Cyphers
Doug Porterfield · · · · · · · · · · Alex Henteloff
Tracy Garrett · · · · · · · · · · · · · · Caren Kaye
Fletcher Huff · · · · · · · · · · · · Barney Phillips

CREDITS
writers Sheldon Bull, Glen Charles/Les Charles, William Idelson, David Lloyd, Dale McRaven · *directors* Bill Persky, Doug Rogers, James Burrows, Noam Pitlik · *executive producers* Stan Daniels/Ed Weinberger (pilot), Bob Ellison · *producers* Charles Raymond/Dale McRaven

Another spin-off from *The Mary Tyler Moore Show*, although here the lead character had a new name. In that earlier series Betty White had played Sue Ann Nivens, host of the *Happy Homemaker Show* at WJM, the TV station where Mary worked. Manoeuvring and catty, Nivens was determined to climb the ladder of success any which way she could. Here, in her own series, White played Joyce Whitman, a witty and sharp-tongued film actress who, although not admitting so, has perhaps realised that she's a mite beyond her prime and so bows to the inevitable and consents to work on television. That she is cast in a typical mid-1970s downmarket all-action cop show, *Undercover Woman*, is only the start of her problems, however, for behind the scenes lies the real trouble (and humour): the director turns out to be her sarcastic ex-husband John Elliot; Tracy Garrett, her supporting actress, is ruthlessly ambitious and prepared to sleep her way to star billing; Fletcher Huff, who plays the police chief, is timid; her brawny stunt double Hugo Muncy is a pain in the proverbial; and Doug Porterfield, the series' network executive (like this sitcom, *Undercover Woman* was said to be a CBS show), is a feeble, interfering busybody.

Also appearing in *The Betty White Show* was another face familiar from *The Mary Tyler Moore Show*, that of Georgia Engel, who had been Ted Baxter's girlfriend, Georgette. There she had been a bit of a dumbelle (and so perfectly suited to Ted); here she was similarly cast, as Joyce Whitman's best pal and flat-sharer Mitzi.

In Britain, C4 screened the entire series of 14 episodes, beginning with the pilot. This particular episode had been screened once before, however, during the channel's *An Evening With MTM* on 10 December 1984, which celebrated MTM Enterprises' output.

Between The Lines

UK · BBC · STANDUP/SKETCH

6 × 25 mins · b/w

30 Apr–11 June 1964 · BBC1 Thu 6.35pm

MAIN CAST
Fulton Mackay
Tom Conti
Gay Hamilton
Una McLean
Alex McAvoy

CREDITS
writers Cliff Hanley (3), Jack Gerson (1), John Donaldson (1), Tom Wright (1) · *director* David Bell · *producer* Pharic Maclaren

Gently satirical observations on a different trivial subject each week. The show was presented by BBC Scotland, and singer Jeanie Lambe provided the musical interludes.

Note. Three years after this BBC series, Una McLean starred in a sitcom pilot, *Did You See Una?*, part-networked (but not shown in London) on 19 March 1967 by ITV company ABC, although made by Scottish TV. Subtitled 'Read Any Good Books Lately?', the programme was devised and written by Eric Merriman, and directed by Clarke Tait. The support cast included Margery Dalziel, Paul Kermack, Doris McLatchie, Glen Michael, Malcolm Ingram, Alex McAvoy (also in *Between The Lines*) and Glenys Marshall. No series developed.

The Beverly Hillbillies

USA · CBS (FILMWAYS) · SITCOM

274 × 30 mins (106 × b/w · 168 × colour)

US dates: 26 Sep 1962–7 Sep 1971

*UK dates: 29 Sep 1963–2 Jan 1971 (148 episodes; 95 × b/w · 27 × colour eps screened in b/w · 26 × colour) ITV Sun 10.35pm then various days and times

MAIN CAST

Jed Clampett	Buddy Ebsen
Granny	Irene Ryan
Elly May Clampett	Donna Douglas
Jethro Bodine	Max Baer Jr
Jane Hathaway	Nancy Kulp
Milburn Drysdale	Raymond Bailey
Margaret Drysdale	Harriet MacGibbon (1962–69)
Pearl Bodine	Bea Benaderet (1962–69)

CREDITS
creator/main writer/producer Paul Henning · *directors* various · *executive producer* Al Simon

Come and listen to this story about a man named Paul Henning. Back in the days when life seemed less perplexing, he decided to launch a simple comedy series, played by unassuming people, with easy laughs and uncomplicated, homespun philosophies. That series was *The Beverly Hillbillies* and it soared to the top of the ratings. But Henning had two more masterstrokes of a similar nature up his sleeve: *Petticoat Junction* and *Green Acres*. Both worked almost as well. As a consequence, just by playing it simple, and making light out of country hokum, Henning bestrode the American TV sitcom industry in the 1960s.

Critics, of course, hated all three shows, and, because it was the first, reserved their strongest vitriol for *The Beverly Hillbillies*. The public was having none of it: they loved the show and watched it in record numbers. Remarkably, the eight most-watched half-hours in the history of US television are all *Beverly Hillbillies* episodes. It was mighty popular in Britain too, with ITV screening 148 shows in the first run, and extensive repeats by C4 in the 1980s/1990s maintaining its high profile.

It's a deserved high profile too. *The Beverly Hillbillies* is a very funny series and draws upon a straightforward premise outlined at the start of every episode via the memorable theme music and title sequence: a poor Ozark hillbilly named Jed Clampett, who could barely keep his family fed, is out one day shooting for some food when his bullet strays into the swamp and up bubbles crude oil. Scarcely before recognising that his discovery is a life-changing one, a magnate from the OK Oil Company hands Jed $25m for his land and he is encouraged to move with his family from their one-room run-down mountain cabin to a 35-room mansion in Beverly Hills and live the life of the idle rich. That's the basic outline. From here on, through 274

sequential episodes, a wonderful vein of comedy was mined, in which the backwaters family tried to adapt their simple country ways to the LA lifestyle and millionaire's row.

Head of the house, and principal star of the series, is our friend Jed Clampett, a widower with a wise old head on his shoulders. Then there is Granny (Jed's late-wife's mother), a tough-minded battler who refuses to change her ways, hates the luxury life in Beverly Hills and longs to return to the cabin in the Ozarks. And there are two grown-up children: Elly May – Jed's daughter – a beautiful tomboy who fails to see why her love of animals and her oft-flexed muscles should deter male interest, and Jethro – Jed's nephew – a young hunk whose zest for the jet-set life, fast cars and beautiful women is hampered by his naïvety and lack of education. These four were the main players but there were three other major contributors. Milburn Drysdale runs the Commerce Bank where the Clampetts' $25m fortune is deposited, and where (because they continue to live their thrifty lifestyle of old) it remains largely untouched. Milburn is addicted to money and it governs his every waking moment. Anxious to ensure that the hillbillies come to no harm in the greedy real world, he installs them in the mansion neighbouring his, a fact that never ceases to upset his snob of a wife, Margaret. Also making a major impact was Miss Hathaway, whose job as Milburn's PA at the bank means that she has to help the hillbillies adapt to people and a lifestyle they cannot understand. Miss Hathaway is a bookish but occasionally outgoing spinster who chases but perpetually fails to catch the men, and whose interest in Jethro is never recognised by the dim-witted country boy.

With its excellent character portrayals, variety of rags-to-riches comedy ideas and fine acting performances, *The Beverly Hillbillies* always made for entertaining viewing, and many words and phrases from the hillbillies' vocabulary entered common usage at the time: 'ce-ment pond' for swimming pool, 'well, dog-ie' for goodness me, 'set a spell' for relax and sit down, 'younguns' for children, 'vittles' for food, 'critters' for animals and many more. Granny's meals (pickled hog jowls, gizzards in gristle, grits, southern-fried muskrat and other delectables) were also 'popular'.

But in 1970–71 CBS pulled the plug – and not just on this series but on *Petticoat Junction* and *Green Acres* too. All may have been past their prime but audience ratings remained high, and the network's only valid reason for cancelling was a commercial one: polls indicated that the series were attracting the wrong type of viewers for the advertisers. So that was that … until ten years later, when three of the original cast (Ebsen, Douglas and

Kulp) came together for a witless two-hour reunion special, *The Beverly Hillbillies Solve The Energy Crisis*, screened by CBS on 6 October 1981. Ray Young replaced Max Baer Jr to play Jethro while Irene Ryan (Granny) had died in 1973 and Raymond Bailey (Milburn Drysdale) in 1980. Harriet MacGibbon (Margaret Drysdale) was around 75 years old by this time and was not cast. Twelve years further on again, in 1993, 20th Century-Fox made a feature film of *The Beverly Hillbillies* (directed by Penelope Spheeris, with Jim Varney as Jed Clampett) that also failed to hit the mark, with only Lily Tomlin (cast as Miss Hathaway) outstanding. That same year (on 24 May 1993), CBS presented *The Legend Of The Beverly Hillbillies*, featuring surviving members of the original cast linking clips of the TV series and explaining what happened to the Clampetts and their acquaintances since it had ended.

*Note. C4 began a substantial screening of *The Beverly Hillbillies*, starting with the premiere episode, on 14 September 1987, ending on 15 August 1992, airing 106 shows in total.

Bewitched

USA · ABC (SCREEN GEMS) · SITCOM

254 × 30 mins · (74 × b/w · 180 × colour)

US dates: 17 Sep 1964–1 July 1972

*UK dates: 26 Oct 1964–28 Mar 1967 (91 episodes · b/w) BBC1 various days and times

MAIN CAST

Samantha Stephens/
Serena · · · · · · · · · · · Elizabeth Montgomery
Darrin Stephens · · · · · Dick York (1964–69);
· · · · · · · · · · · · · · Dick Sargent (1969–72)
Endora · · · · · · · · · · · · · Agnes Moorehead
Larry Tate · · · · · · · · · · · · · · · David White
Louise Tate · · · · · · Irene Vernon (1964–66);
· · · · · · · · · · · · · Kasey Rogers (1966–72)
Gladys Kravitz · · · · · Alice Pearce (1964–66);
· · · · · · · · · · · · · Sandra Gould (1966–72)
Abner Kravitz · · · · · · · · · · · George Tobias
Aunt Clara · · · · · · · Marion Lorne (1964–68)
Tabitha Stephens · · · Heidi and Laura Gentry
· (1966);
· · · · · · · · · · Tamar and Julie Young (1966);
· · · · · · · · Erin and Diane Murphy (1966–72)
Adam Stephens · · David and Greg Lawrence
· (1969–72)

OTHER APPEARANCES

Maurice · · · · · · · · · · · · · · · Maurice Evans
Uncle Arthur · · · · · · · · Paul Lynde (1965–72)
Esmerelda · · · · · · Alice Ghostley (1969–72)
Dr Bombay · · · · · · · · · · · · · · · Bernard Fox

CREDITS

creator Sol Saks · *writers* Ed Jurist, Michael Morris, Sol Saks, Danny Arnold and others · *directors* William Asher, Richard Michaels and others · *executive producer* Harry Ackerman · *producer* William Asher

A classic, long-running US sitcom depicting the adventures of an ordinary guy, Darrin,

and his wife, Samantha, who happens to be a witch. The comedy arose from the wife's attempts to refrain from using her magic powers and live life like a mortal to please her husband. In doing so, she perpetually disappointed her deeply embittered mother (Endora) who saw the marriage as a travesty, was forever trying to part the couple and never called Darrin by his true name, baiting him by referring to him as Darwin, Dobbin, Derwood, Dum-Dum and dozens of other corruptions.

Darrin Stephens worked for the New York advertising agency McMann and Tate, where his extraordinarily money-grabbing boss Larry Tate was oblivious to Samantha's background and just treated her as a normal, albeit somewhat eccentric, wife whose beauty made her a definite asset to her husband. Convinced that they presented a handsome front to the firm, Tate often insisted that the couple meet prospective clients, but Samantha's witchcraft – or, more often, her mother's – always made things very awkward. More complications arose through Gladys Kravitz, the Stephens' nosey neighbour from over the road, who often espied Samantha's supernatural prowess but was never able to convince her husband about the goings-on and often ended up even doubting the evidence of her own eyes.

Other members of Samantha's clan visited occasionally, including her father Maurice, her effete warlock Uncle Arthur and her wonderfully absent-minded eccentric Aunt Clara. They were a bizarre but harmless enough bunch, quite unlike Samantha's wacky identical cousin Serena (also played by Montgomery although she was credited in the cast as Pandora Sparks), a 1960s flower child who turned up occasionally to cause mayhem. The magical contingent were always funnier and more colourful than their human counterparts which must have made viewers wonder why Samantha would give up such a fantastic world for such a mundane one – especially as husband Darrin was somewhat dull.

Various cast changes occurred during the series' eight-year run, most of which were seamless, and even the major transition in the role of Darrin, from Dick York to Dick Sargent (necessary because York had a damaged spine) passed virtually unnoticed thanks to the similarity in looks and style between the two actors. Likewise, when Alice Pearce died in 1966, Sandra Gould stepped effortlessly into the shoes of Gladys Kravitz.

The series proved immensely popular and continued to deliver slick if innocuous entertainment during its long run. The glamorous Elizabeth Montgomery, daughter of veteran Hollywood actor Robert Montgomery and wife of the show's director/producer William

Asher, was a major factor in the success of *Bewitched* – her nose-twitching and mouth-wrinkling spell-casting enchanted viewers around the world, and her beauty delighted male viewers of all ages. **Tabitha**, a spin-off series, charted the adventures of the Stephens' magical daughter.

Although *Bewitched* was an original idea, it is worth noting two earlier feature films based on a similar premise that may have influenced its creation: *Bell, Book And Candle* (1958) and *I Married A Witch* (1942) – this latter movie was based on the novel *The Passionate Witch*, by Thorne Smith, who also wrote **Topper**. A *Bewitched* movie was due to go into production in 1998.

*Note. The BBC screened almost 100 episodes of *Bewitched* in the mid 1960s, and then ran repeat seasons. Seven episodes were shown by London-area ITV in the first half of 1972, and since then C4 has twice broadcast extensive runs, with 188 episodes shown from 28 July 1983 to 19 July 1988, and another extensive run in progress from 13 January 1997 (181 episodes by year's end).

Beyond A Joke

UK · BBC · STANDUP

6 × 30 mins · colour

21 Apr–26 May 1972 · BBC2 Fri mostly 10.10pm

MAIN CAST

Eleanor Bron
John Bird
Barrie Ingham

CREDITS

writers Eleanor Bron, Michael Frayn, John Bird · *director* Vernon Lawrence · *producer* Robert Chetwyn

A series built around the indefinable talents of actress and wit Eleanor Bron. She described herself as having an 'unfocused quality' that some of her collaborators found unsettling. Nonetheless, the finished product was always worth the effort, delivering humour with an ethereal edge that, if it was unfocused, still managed to find the target.

Beyond The Fringe

UK · BBC · SATIRE

1 × 60 mins · b/w

12 Dec 1964 · BBC2 Sat 9.10pm

MAIN CAST

Alan Bennett
Peter Cook
Jonathan Miller
Dudley Moore

CREDITS

writers Alan Bennett, Peter Cook, Jonathan Miller, Dudley Moore · *director* Duncan Wood · *producer* Don Silverman

One final performance of the famous stage revue by its original cast of Cook, Moore,

Bennett and Miller, especially recorded for TV and with some new items entwined with the original material. First mounted on the Edinburgh Festival Fringe on 22 August 1960 (and then in London from 10 May 1961 and New York from 27 October 1962) the success of *Beyond The Fringe* gave rise to a satire boom on both sides of the Atlantic and made international stars of the cast.

See also *Behind The Fridge*.

Big Boy Now!

see CROWTHER, Leslie

Big Deal At York City

UK · ITV (YORKSHIRE) · SITCOM

1 × 30 mins · colour

7 Apr 1977 · Thu 9pm

MAIN CAST
Albert · · · · · · · · · · · · · · · · · Warren Mitchell

CREDITS
writers/associate producers Ray Galton/Alan Simpson · *director* Len Lurcuck · *executive producer* Duncan Wood · *producer* Vernon Lawrence

The last of Yorkshire TV's *Galton & Simpson Playhouse* season, this comedy starred Warren Mitchell, far from his Alf Garnett character, as a long-haired gambler, returning home by train, somewhat intoxicated after a very successful day backing the horses, sharing a carriage with five passengers.

Big Girl's Blouse

AUSTRALIA · 7 NETWORK · SKETCH

9 editions (5 × 30 mins · 4 × 60 mins) · colour

Australian dates: 13 Oct 1994–8 Sep 1995

UK date: 6 Jan–24 Feb 1996 (8 × 30 mins) C4 Sat mostly 2.50am

MAIN CAST
Magda Szubanski
Jane Turner
Gina Riley

CREDITS
writers/producers cast · *director* Kevin Carlin · *executive producers* Ted Emery, Andrew Knight, Steve Vizard

Comedian/actress Magda Szubanski had been part of a Melbourne University revue team who had brought their talents to TV as *The D Generation* (ABC/7 Network, 1986–87). She then joined the *Fast Forward* troupe, which also included Jane Turner and Gina Riley. Here the three women combined their talents to present a collection of comedy sketches.

See also *Full Frontal*.

Big Jim And The Figaro Club

UK · BBC · SITCOM

6 × 30 mins · colour

Pilot · 24 June 1979 · BBC2 Sun 8.05pm

One series (5) 8 July–12 Aug 1981 · BBC2 Wed 8.30pm

MAIN CAST
narrator · · · · · · · · · · · · · · · · Bob Hoskins
Big Jim · · · · · · · · · · · · · Norman Rossington
Chick · · · · · · · · · · · · · · · · · David Beckett
Turps · · · · · · · · · · · · · · Sylvester McCoy
Old Ned · · · · · · · · · · · · · · Gordon Rollings
Harold Perkins · · · · · · · · · · · Roland Curram
Glad · · · · · · · · · · · · · · Helen Keating (pilot);
· · · · · · · · · · · · · · · Priscilla Morgan (series)
Nimrod · · · · · · · · · · · · · David John (series)
Titch · · · · · · · · · · · · · Tony Robinson (series)
College · · · · · · · · · · · · Patrick Murray (pilot)

CREDITS
writer Ted Walker · *director/producer* Colin Rose

Starting out as an edition of *Turning Year Tales*, a series of half-hour filmed plays, *Big Jim And The Figaro Club* impressed enough to earn itself a full comedy series. Set in a seaside town in the 1950s, the stories centred around the Figaro Club, a gang of lads involved in the building trade, led by the 'inscrutable but nimble-brained' Big Jim.

The club members relish in their private slang language and 'laddish' outlook, but beneath the surface there remains the suspicion that change is in the air. If not the father figure to the bunch, Big Jim is at least their big brother and he often has to curb the recklessness of Turps, the teddy boy wild-man of the bunch (played by Sylvester McCoy, who at the time was known as Sylveste McCoy). Conflict is provided by clerk of works Harold Perkins, a dictatorial social climber and all-round nasty. The series was shot on location in Exmouth.

In 1987 the scripts were adapted for a six-episode run on BBC Radio 4 (14 February to 21 March). All of the original TV cast reprised their roles except that Harold Goodwin replaced Gordon Rollings, who had died. The scene-setting narration for the radio series was undertaken by Bernard Cribbins.

The Big Job

see *Mr Big*

The Big Man

UK · BBC · SITCOM

1 × 30 mins · b/w

3 Sep 1954 · Fri 9pm

MAIN CAST
Fred Emney
Edwin Styles

CREDITS
writer Eric Sykes · *producer* Bill Ward

Scripted by Eric Sykes, this was a one-off Fred Emney special detailing 'a tiny incident in the life of a very large character'. The star's *Emney Enterprises* cohort Edwin Styles also appeared.

See also *The Fred Emney Show* and *Fred Emney Picks A Pop*.

The Big Noise

see MONKHOUSE, Bob

The Big One

UK · C4 (HAT TRICK PRODUCTIONS) · SITCOM

7 × 30 mins · colour

5 Mar–16 Apr 1992 · Thu 8.30pm

MAIN CAST
James Howard · · · · · · · · · · · Mike McShane
Deirdre 'Deddie' Tobert · · · · · · Sandi Toksvig

CREDITS
writers Elly Brewer/Sandi Toksvig · *director* John Henderson · *executive producer* Denise O'Donoghue · *producers* Mary Bell, Jimmy Mulville

Another series for players of *Whose Line Is It Anyway?* (see also *Paul Merton – The Series, S And M, Josie, John Sessions On The Spot*), this one featuring the American Mike McShane (here credited as Micheal – odd spelling intended – McShane) and the small but perfectly formed comedian Sandi Toksvig, the series' co-writer.

The premise of *The Big One* was surprisingly old-fashioned for a pairing perceived as being representative of TV's latest comedy revolution. McShane played romantic writer James Howard, a Bostonian with a rose-coloured view of England conjured up from period films and *Sherlock Holmes* novels. Toksvig was cast as 'Deddie' Tobert, a sharp-tongued British bulldog recovering from the latest in a series of failed relationships. Howard has come to England to research his latest novel – although his previous works have all been set here, this is his first visit – and he is in for a rude awakening. He is a neurotic type with a distrust of hotels, and for this reason his agent arranges, via a mutual friend, for Howard to stay with Deddie, a fellow writer but of smaller ambition: she's currently engaged in putting together a Barclaycard catalogue. Deddie's misgivings about the arrangement are allayed when she sees the dust-jacket of Howard's latest novel, sporting a photograph of the author as a ruggedly handsome, athletic type. This turns out to have been a marketing device and she is aghast when she actually meets the massively-built American. Clearly unsuited as flatmates, they nevertheless find themselves trapped into the arrangement and, gradually, an oddly romantic relationship develops.

The Big One had shades of *The Odd Couple* in its theme (Howard is tremendously fastidious and anally retentive in his attention to detail; Deddie is a slovenly type living on – and scattering remnants of – takeaways) and elements of *A Fine Romance* in its style (the two protagonists are uncomfortable and inarticulate with each other). Although the scripts sparkled with occasional gems, the mix just didn't gel, with both actors seeming self-conscious in their roles. The Howard character was clichéd to the point of caricature, contrasting sharply with Deddie who seemed to come from a more realistic and recognisable world. Strangely, they seemed hidebound by having to play to a script, and one longed for them to exercise some of the freedom of improv to lift the show into more interesting and surprising areas.

A Big Slice Of Jo Brand

see BRAND, Jo

The Big Snog

see *Hysteria*

Big Wave Dave's

USA · CBS (LEVINE & ISAACS PRODUCTIONS/ PARAMOUNT) · SITCOM

6 × 30 mins · colour

US dates: 9 Aug–13 Sep 1993

UK dates: 19 July–6 Sep 1994 (6 episodes) C4 Tue around 11.45pm

MAIN CAST

Dave Bell · · · · · · · · · · · · · · · · David Morse
Marshall Fisher · · · · · · · · · · · · · Adam Arkin
Karen Fisher · · · · · · · · · · · · Jane Kaczmarek
Richie Lamonica · · · · · · · · · · · Patrick Breen
Jack Lord · · · · · · · · · · · · · · Kurtwood Smith
Danny Kinimaka · · · · · · · · · · · · Ray Bumatai

CREDITS

creators Ken Levine/David Isaacs · *writers* Ken Levine/David Isaacs, Dan Staley/Rob Long, Larry Balmagia · *director* Andy Ackerman · *executive producers* Ken Levine/David Isaacs, Dan Staley/Rob Long · *producers* Larry Balmagia, Andy Ackerman, Lavinia Adamason

Despite the presence of a number of *Cheers* personnel within its production ranks, *Big Wave Dave's* was a disappointing sitcom that painstakingly set up its high-concept situation but was far more lax when it came to fleshing out its characters. The premise was that, following his divorce, Dave Bell (played by David Morse, best known at this time for playing Dr Jack Morrison in the US hospital drama *St Elsewhere*) had decided to give up his life as a stockbroker and relocate to Hawaii to pursue his dream of running a beach-front surfing store and spend most of his time surfing. He managed to persuade his two oldest friends, typing teacher Richie

(played by Patrick Breen) and lawyer Marshall (Adam Arkin, son of film star Alan Arkin), to accompany him, and Marshall brought his wife Karen (also a lawyer), who, it transpires, is pregnant with their first child. They sink their money into the store, called Big Wave Dave's, and with the help of local character Jack Lord (not to be confused with but doubtless inspired by the actor Jack Lord of *Hawaii Five-O* fame) attempt to carve out a new life.

The series was an oddly hollow affair, largely because the main characters so lacked charisma. Dave was woolly, Marshall tetchy and Richie wacky, Jack was a clichéd eccentric and Karen was the sensible, world-weary one. The 'politically correct' idea of making the only woman smarter and more together than the frankly childish men worked against the series, with Karen coming across as a dull, motherly spoil-sport. In time it may have improved, but in the choppy waters of American primetime TV only the fittest survive and the protagonists of *Big Wave Dave's* had little time to ride the tube before a tidal wave of audience indifference resulted in a wipe-out.

The Big Yin

see CONNOLLY, Billy

Bilko

see *The Phil Silvers Show*

Bill Cosby Does His Own Thing

USA · NBC (CAMPBELL-SILVER-COSBY CORPORATION) · STANDUP

1 × 60 mins · colour

US date: 9 Feb 1969

UK date: 12 June 1970 · BBC2 Fri 10.10pm

MAIN CAST

Bill Cosby

CREDITS

writers Frank Burton, Ed Weinberger · *director* Seymour Berns · *producers* Roy Silver, Bruce Campbell, Bill Cosby

A chance for Britons to see the standup comedian Bill Cosby in action, following his success as an actor in the 1965–68 adventure series *I Spy,* the first American TV show in which a black actor occupied a starring role alongside a white one. Cosby had explored a few opportunities for comedy in that unusually downbeat spy series but in this one-off, hour-length special he was given full rein to illustrate his sprawling comedic imagination.

Bill Cosby was born in Philadelphia on 12 July 1938 and in his early, poverty-stricken years met the characters (like Fat Albert) whom he would go on to re-create in his stage

routines. Although he was steadily developing a unique comedic style, in which he exaggerated his reminiscences into fantasy, Bill Cosby was still just a second-string club act in 1965 when he was spotted by NBC executives and given his big break in *I Spy*. But by the time of this special he was well on his way to becoming one of the highest-rated – and highest-earning – comedians in the USA.

See also *The Cosby Show*.

Bill Hicks – Relentless
Bill Hicks – Revelations

see HICKS, Bill

Billy

USA · ABC (EUSTIS ELIAS PRODUCTIONS/WARNER BROS) · SITCOM

13 × 30 mins · colour

US dates: 31 Jan–4 July 1992

UK dates: 30 Sep 1993–22 June 1994 (13 episodes) ITV Thu 11.15pm then Wed 1.55pm

MAIN CAST

Billy MacGregor · · · · · · · · · · · Billy Connolly
Mary Springer/MacGregor · · · Marie Marshall
Annie Springer · · · · · · · · · · · · · Clara Bryant
David Springer · · · · · · · · · · · Johnny Galecki
Laura Springer · · · · · · · · · · · · Natanya Ross

CREDITS

creators Rich Eustis/Michael Elias · *writers* Rich Eustis/Michael Elias, David Barlow, John Boni, Dick Clement/Ian La Frenais, Eva Duarte, David M Hurwitz, Raymond M Jessel, April Kelly, Ken Kuta, Bill Lawrence, Rebecca Parr, Ehrich Van Lowe, Diane E Wilk · *director* Sam Weisman · *executive producers* Rich Eustis/Michael Elias · *producer* Frank Pace

A vehicle for British comedian Billy Connolly during his spell in America. A spin-off from *Head Of The Class*, it found Billy MacGregor in Berkeley, California, teaching poetry in an evening class at the Community College. The only problem is that his work-permit, enabling the Scotsman to tender his services in the USA, has expired. In order that he may stay in the country, MacGregor enters into a marriage of convenience with Mary Springer, one of his students, and moves into her vacant basement apartment. Mary is a pretty divorcee – her husband has moved to Australia – and she has been left to bring up their three children, rebellious smart-aleck David (14), Laura (10) and Annie (5). Billy's basement presence brings in the rent – and, of course, helps with the parenting – and, inevitably, nature begins to take its course even though Billy and Mary try to keep their marital relationship platonic.

Connolly played his part well, and he had some good lines, but the series didn't amount to much and was soon cancelled. Hollywood-domiciled Britons Dick Clement and Ian La Frenais were among the writers.

Billy Bunter Of Greyfriars School

UK · BBC · CHILDREN'S SITCOM

51 × 30 mins · b/w

Series One (7) 19 Feb–25 Mar 1953 · Tue 5.40pm

Special · 7 July 1953 · Tue 5pm

Special · 1 July 1954. Thu 5.10pm

Series Two (6) 9 July–17 Sep 1955 · Sat 3.30pm then 5pm

Series Three (6) 9 Sep–14 Oct 1956 · Sun 5pm

Special · 12 Mar 1957 · Tue 5pm

Series Four (4) 20 July–17 Aug 1957 · Sat 5pm

Series Five (9) 13 June–29 Aug 1959 · Sat 5.30pm

Series Six (8) 16 July–24 Sep 1960 · Sat 5.30pm

Series Seven (8) 20 May–22 July 1961 · Sat 5.25pm

MAIN CAST

Billy Bunter · · · · · · · · · · · · Gerald Campion

CREDITS

writer Frank Richards (Charles Hamilton) · producers Joy Harington, Pharic Maclaren, Shaun Sutton, Clive Parkhurst

The overweight schoolboy oaf William George Bunter, known to one and all as the 'Fat Owl Of The Remove', was the invention of the writer Charles Hamilton, who worked under the pseudonym Frank Richards. The stories of Bunter's cowardly, greedy adventures first appeared in print in 1908, and he found especial fame through the pages of the popular children's paper *The Magnet* and in dozens of books.

Billy Bunter translated winningly to television in this well-remembered and consistently energetic sitcom, in which Gerald Campion was cast as the chubby, cake-loving, 'cripes'-uttering, work-shy, bespectacled boy in check-trousers. He played the role throughout the series but his fellow pupils and the masters of Greyfriars School were portrayed by different actors during the show's long run. (A young and then unknown Michael Crawford appeared as Frank Nugent in the 1959 series, and David Hemmings also found work in the programme at this time.) Although well into his eighties, the inexhaustible 'Richards' wrote all of the TV episodes, scripting the last series shortly before his death in 1961.

Notes. Five latter episodes – four in 1960 and one in 1961 – were new versions of scripts enacted between 1952 and 1955. The 12 March 1957 special was shot entirely on location at a sweet factory and was titled, punningly, *Billy Bunter At Large*. Each episode in the 1953 series was enacted twice, at 5.40pm for younger viewers and then again at 8pm for those of a more mature age.

See also *The Ken Dodd Show*.

Billy Connolly In Concert

see CONNOLLY, Billy

Billy Dainty, Esq

UK · ITV (THAMES) · STANDUP

7 editions (1 × 60 mins · 6 × 45 mins) · colour

Pilot (60 mins) 17 Sep 1975 · Wed 8pm

One series (6 × 45 mins) 17 May–21 June 1976 · Mon 6.45pm

MAIN CAST

Billy Dainty

CREDITS

writers Eric Davidson (6), Dick Hills (5), John Hudson (3), Brian Cooke (2), Johnnie Mortimer (1), Tony Bilbow (1), Vince Powell (1) · director/producer Dennis Kirkland

For years, William Hooper Frank John Dainty – abbreviated, thankfully, to Billy Dainty – had been an 'also-appearing' TV comic, the perennial guest artist on other stars' shows. But following a successful spot in the 1974 *Royal Variety Show* (reportedly the Queen Mother was wiping the tears away – presumably ones of laughter) this buck-toothed, singing, miming, dancing, musical gagster was given a single show of his own by Thames, with a full series following. The formula was familiar: accomplished script writers provided the funny lines; guests and a spot of music and dance were thrown in for good measure.

Note. Eight years before this Thames series, Dainty starred in a sitcom pilot, *That's Show Business*, screened (but not in London) by ABC on 12 February 1967, written for him by Vince Powell and Harry Driver and produced by John Paddy Carstairs. He was cast as Billy Cook, a comic cabaret performer working the northern clubs, and the support cast included Kenneth Connor, June Whitfield, Julian Holloway, Harold Berens and Joe Gladwin. No series developed.

Billy Liar

UK · ITV (LWT) · SITCOM

26 episodes (25 × 30 mins · 1 × short special) · colour

Series One (12) 2 Nov 1973–18 Jan 1974 · Fri 8.30pm

Short special · part of *All-Star Comedy Carnival* 25 Dec 1973 · Tue 6.30pm

Series Two (13) 14 Sep–6 Dec 1974 · Sat around 7pm then Fri 8.30pm

MAIN CAST

Billy Fisher · · · · · · · · · · · · · · · · · Jeff Rawle
Geoffrey Fisher · · · · · · · · · · George A Cooper
Alice Fisher · · · · · · · · · · · · · Pamela Vezey
Grandma · · · · · · · · · · · · · · · · May Warden
Mr Shadrack · · · · · · · · · · · · Colin Jeavons
Barbara · · · · · · · · · · · · · · · · · Sally Watts

CREDITS

creator Keith Waterhouse · writers Keith Waterhouse/Willis Hall · directors Stuart Allen (24), Alan Wallis (2) · producer Stuart Allen

Successful as a book (1959, by Keith Waterhouse), movie (1963, director John Schlesinger), stage-play, and soon to be a musical (*Billy*, which opened in London on 1 May 1974 with additional writing by Dick Clement and Ian La Frenais), *Billy Liar* was turned into two long series of sitcoms for ITV by its original author and his long-time associate Willis Hall. The premise was unchanged, with Jeff Rawle playing the young northerner who spends most of his life wrapped up in the fantastic fantasies of his runaway imagination. George A Cooper fulfilled his usual role – the blunt northerner – and got into mildly hot water with some scripted bad language; May Warden supported as the matriarchal Granny, dominating her family; Sally Watts was introduced in the first series for some love interest, becoming Billy's fiancee in the second; and Colin Jeavons appeared as Billy's boss at the funeral parlour.

The series was remade in the USA as *Billy* – running to just 13 CBS episodes, screened from 26 February to 28 April 1979 – starring Steve Guttenberg, who later scored success with the movies *Police Academy* and *Three Men And A Baby*.

Billy Maloney

UK · BBC · STANDUP

1 × 10 mins · b/w

26 Jan 1937 · Tue 3pm

MAIN CAST

Billy Maloney

CREDITS

producer Dallas Bower

A ten-minute spot for the debonair Australian comedy and music artist Billy Maloney, known as the 'man with a silver stick'.

The Bing Crosby Show

USA · ABC (BING CROSBY PRODUCTIONS) · SITCOM

28 × 30 mins · b/w

US dates: 14 Sep 1964–14 June 1965

UK dates: 7 July–29 Sep 1965 (13 episodes) BBC2 Wed mostly 8pm

MAIN CAST

Bing Collins · · · · · · · · · · · · · · · · Bing Crosby
Ellie Collins · · · · · · · · · · · · · Beverly Garland
Janice Collins · · · · · · · · · · · · · Carol Faylen
Joyce Collins · · · · · · · · · · · · · Diane Sherry

CREDITS

producer Steven Gethers

A typically formulaic domestic sitcom designed for a superstar. Bing Crosby played a recognisable variation of himself: Bing Collins, an ex-crooner who has given up a hectic show-business life in order to teach electrical engineering at a university. Stories revolved around his family life, with his wife, who craves a return to the glamorous showbiz world, and their two daughters: typical teenager Janice (15) and super-bright Joyce (10). The weekly plots invariably and implausibly made room for Bing to sing a song of wisdom.

Birds In The Bush

AUSTRALIA/UK · ABC/BBC (GEORGE ROCKNEY PRODUCTIONS) · SITCOM

13 × 30 mins · colour

Australian dates: 3 May–26 July 1972

UK dates : 10 July–21 Aug 1972 (7 episodes) BBC1 Mon 7.30pm

MAIN CAST

Hugh	Hugh Lloyd
Ron	Ron Fraser
Hoffnung	Alastair Duncan
Michelle	Kate Fitzpatrick
Abigail	Elli MacLure
Nanny	Ann Sidney
Lolita	Sue Lloyd
Friday	Kate Sheil
Tuesday	Briony Behets
Wednesday	Nicola Flamer-Caldera
Buster	Jenny Hayes

CREDITS

writer/director David Croft

An Australia/UK co-production comedy, written and directed by David Croft during a sabbatical from **Dad's Army**. Seven of the 12 episodes were screened by BBC1 as *The Virgin Fellas*. The series was also known as *Strike It Rich*.

This dreadful series, shot on film, had a fish-out-of-water premise: with his friend Ron (Ron Frazer), a hapless British water-diviner (Hugh Lloyd) arrives in Australia to take possession of his inheritance – which turns out to be a farm in the outback run by a bunch of beautiful women.

See also Which Way To The War.

Birds Of A Feather

UK · BBC (ALOMO PRODUCTIONS) · SITCOM

89 episodes (83 × 30 mins · 1 × 75 mins · 1 × 60 mins · 4 × 50 mins) · colour

Series One (6) 16 Oct–20 Nov 1989 · BBC1 Mon 8.30pm

Special (30 mins) 26 Dec 1989 · BBC1 Tue 9pm

Series Two (15) 6 Sep–13 Dec 1990 · BBC1 Thu 8.30pm

Special (75 mins) 25 Dec 1990 · BBC1 Tue 8.20pm

Series Three (12) 31 Aug–16 Nov 1991 · BBC1 Sat 8pm

Special (50 mins) 25 Dec 1991 · BBC1 Wed 8pm

Series Four (13) 6 Sep–29 Nov 1992 · BBC1 Sun 8.40pm

Special (50 mins) 25 Dec 1992 · BBC1 Fri 8pm

Series Five (13) 5 Sep–28 Nov 1993 · BBC1 Sun 8.20pm

Special (60 mins) 25 Dec 1993 · BBC1 Sat 8pm

Series Six (13) 18 Sep–18 Dec 1994 · BBC1 Sun 7.30pm

Special (50 mins) 24 Dec 1994 · BBC1 Sat 8.55pm

Series Seven (10) 26 May–28 July 1997 · BBC1 Mon 9.30pm

Special (50 mins) 27 Dec 1997 · BBC1 Sat 9.25pm

MAIN CAST

Sharon Theodopolopoudos	Pauline Quirke
Tracey Stubbs	Linda Robson
Dorien Green	Lesley Joseph

OTHER APPEARANCES

Chris Theodopolopoudos	David Cardy (series 1 & 7)
	Peter Polycarpou (series 2–6)
Darryl Stubbs	Alun Lewis (to 1994)
	Doug McFerran (series 7)
Garth Stubbs	Simon Nash (series 1);
	Matthew Savage (series 2 onwards)
Marcus Green	Nickolas Grace,
	Stephen Greif

CREDITS

creators Laurence Marks/Maurice Gran · *writers* Laurence Marks/Maurice Gran (21), Gary Lawson/John Phelps (15), Sue Teddern (12), Geoff Rowley (12), Peter Tilbury (9), Geoff Deane (7), Tony Millan/Mike Walling (3), Keith Lindsay/Martin Tomms (1), Steve Coombes/Dave Robinson (1), George Costigan/Julia North (1), John Ross (1), Frankie Bailey (1), Miles Tedinnick (1), Jenny Lecoat (1), Alun Lewis (1), Richard Preddy/Gary Howe (1), Damon Rochefort (1) · *directors* Terry Kinane (28), Charlie Hanson (26), Nic Phillips (15), Baz Taylor (10), Tony Dow (6), Sue Bysh (2), Geoffrey Sax (1), Hugh Thomas (1) · *executive producers* Allan McKeown, Claire Hinson · *producers* Nic Phillips (29), Charlie Hanson (28), Candida Julian-Jones (14), Tony Charles (11), Esta Charkham (7)

Sibling affection and rivalry formed the basis of this uncomplicated sitcom that became a smash hit almost overnight. Lead actresses Quirke and Robson had been friends since meeting at primary school when aged five and six respectively. Later, they both attended the Anna Scher Children's Theatre and made their professional debuts in the 1970 feature film *Junket 89*. When, as a teenager, Quirke appeared prominently in ITV children's series **You Must Be Joking!**, **Pauline's Quirkes**, *Pauline's People* and **You Can't Be Serious**, Robson often supported. They first met *Birds Of A Feather* creators Laurence Marks and Maurice Gran when appearing in **Shine On Harvey Moon**.

When the story begins, the two sisters are experiencing starkly different lifestyles: Sharon lives in a dilapidated tower block and is locked into a loveless marriage to the shiftless waster Chris; Tracey, on the other

hand, is happily wed to the successful Darryl and they have a son, Garth, whom they are putting through public school. The couple live in a huge house ('Dalentrace') in Chigwell, a real-life Essex millionaire's row populated by footballers, TV stars, pools winners, wide-boys made good and other worthies. Both sisters' lives are turned upside down, however, when their husbands are caught red-handed on a heist and sent to jail, convicted of armed robbery. Well conversant with Chris's shortcomings, Sharon is hardly surprised, but Tracey, innocent of Darryl's criminal activities, is 'totally gobsmacked'. Despite their differences, the sisters find themselves compatriots in adversity and for reasons of companionship and convenience Sharon moves in with the well-to-do Tracey.

Tracey's next door neighbour is the gossipy, sex-obsessed Dorien, a snobbish Jewess ostensibly happily married to accountant Marcus but actually indulging in a flurry of flings with muscular toy boys. She breezes in and out of the Stubbs' household and, despite her perennial rudeness and obvious disdain for the womens' social standing, gradually becomes good friends with them. Most early episodes centred around the difficulties of the prisoners' wives coming to terms with the separation and trying to get on with their own lives, but, inevitably, as the series progressed, it gathered a different momentum, latter episodes concentrating on the relationships and adventures of the three women, never exactly forgetting the original concept but occasionally ignoring it when the need arose.

The series achieved huge ratings almost from the off and managed to maintain good figures for most of its run. Undoubtedly, the friendship of Quirke and Robson helped here – the women played knowingly off one another and their mutual affection came through the characters, suggesting an air of reality to the sisterly relationship that might otherwise have been difficult to achieve. However, despite their strengths, and the earthy cockney humour of the Marks and Gran scripts, it was Lesley Joseph who managed to steal most of the honours, turning in a cracking performance as the man-eating Dorien. Joseph played up the stereotypical Jewishness and hard-heartedness of the characters and camped up her smouldering libido to create a cross between a dragon lady and a vamp. Her pert, selfish and yet sharp observations added welcome relief when Sharon and Tracey's problems started to pile up or when they were feeling morose.

Initially the sisters had no financial problems, as Darryl had fared rather well in his underworld enterprises, but eventually the tightened belt began to bite and Tracey opened a café to make ends meet. Against all odds, the enterprise thrived and gave the women new topics for argument. As the series developed so its scope widened and special seasonal episodes took the characters beyond their environment, most memorably the 25 December 1993 special in which the trio travelled to Hollywood and met real-life show-business stars including singer George Hamilton III and actor George Wendt (Norm in *Cheers*). In the 24 December 1994 special a dream sequence neatly reversed the situation of the series, with Sharon as the rich one of the family and her hubby Chris a successful pop star rather than a jailbird. Tracey lived in a council block with Darryl and Garth, and Dorien changed into Doreen, Sharon's dowdy char. The seventh series, in 1997, saw major changes: Chris and Darryl were released from prison but found themselves back inside within a couple of episodes, Tracey and Sharon were forced to move out of 'Dalentrace' and relocated in nearby but downmarket Hainault (in a house Dorien described as 'very *Brookside*'), while Dorien was appalled to discover that her husband Marcus – to whom she had been unfaithful on hundreds of occasions – had a second family, with wife and son. An eighth series was due to air in early 1998 in which the newly impoverished Birds were operating a cleaning agency, the Maids of Ongar.

Determined to explore the advantages of their American-style team-written series, Marks and Gran kept their eye on the US market and duly worked on an American version of their creation, *Stand By Your Man*, for the Fox network. Comedian Rosie O'Donnell was cast as Lorraine Popowski, the hard-up sister of Rochelle Dunphy, a rich New Jersey-ite played by Melissa Gilbert-Brinkman. Sam McMurray was Rochelle's husband Roger, Rick Hall was Lorraine's husband Artie, and Miriam Flynn played horny neighbour Adrienne Stone. But the series failed, being launched on 5 April 1992 and finishing after only eight episodes on 9 August.

Notes. The three *Birds* stars have appeared together, often in character, in a number of other miscellaneous TV ventures. One was *Trading Places*, a programme made to increase awareness of breast cancer, broadcast by ITV on 27 March 1992. On 26 November 1993 Quirke and Robson performed skits and musical routines for that year's *Children In Need* BBC1 charity event. They also appeared together in TV commercials, holiday programmes and the factual series *Jobs For The Girls* (BBC1 from 1995). Lesley Joseph has also appeared as a character identical to Dorien in TV commercials.

All ten episode titles in the 1997 series were named after other sitcoms, beginning,

ironically, with 'Stand By Your Man', followed by 'Nearest And Dearest', 'Cheers', 'Relative Strangers', 'Porridge', 'Rising Damp', 'Three Up, Two Down', 'Are You Being Served?', 'Never The Twain' and 'Three's Company'.

See also Comic Relief.

Birds On The Wing

UK · BBC · SITCOM

6 × 30 mins · colour

11 June–16 July 1971 · BBC2 Fri mostly 9.20pm

MAIN CAST

Charles Jackson · · · · · · · · · · · Richard Briers
Elizabeth · · · · · · · · · · · · · · Anne Rogers
Samantha · · · · · · · · · · · · · Julia Lockwood

CREDITS

writer Peter Yeldham · producer Graeme Muir

A slightly higher-brow BBC2 sitcom charting the comedic adventures of a one-man/two-women team of globetrotting confidence tricksters. Such was the depth of the double-dealing and cross-talking that the team members tried to swindle each other almost as much as they hoped to con their 'marks'.

Sitcom favourite Richard Briers starred, but he had to wait a few more years before *The Good Life* finally provided him with a character as popular with the public as his earlier role in *Marriage Lines*.

The Birthday

see *The Gordon Peters Show*

The Bishop Rides Again

see *All Gas And Gaiters*

A Bit Of A Do

UK · ITV (YORKSHIRE) · COMEDY SERIAL

13 × 60 mins · colour

Series One (6) 13 Jan–17 Feb 1989 · Fri 9pm
Series Two (7) 20 Oct–1 Dec 1989 · Fri 9pm

MAIN CAST

Ted Simcock · · · · · · · · · · · · · David Jason
Rita Simcock · · · · · · · · · · · · · Gwen Taylor
Liz Rodenhurst/Badger · · · · · · Nicola Pagett
Laurence Rodenhurst · · · · · · · Paul Chapman
· (series 1)
Neville Badger · · · · · · · · · · · Michael Jayston
Betty Sillitoe · · · · · · · · · · · · Stephanie Cole
Rodney Sillitoe · · · · · · · · · · · · Tim Wylton
Jenny Rodenhurst/ ·
Simcock · · · · · · · · · · · · · Sarah-Jane Holm
Paul Simcock · · · · · · David Thewlis (series 1)
Elvis Simcock · · · · · · · · · · · · Wayne Foskett
Simon Rodenhurst · · · · · · · · · Nigel Hastings
Carol Fordingbridge · · · · · · · · · · Karen Drury
Eric, the barman · · · · · · · · · Malcolm Hebden
Sandra · · · · · · · · · · · · · · · · Tracy Brabin
Percy Spragg · · · · · · · Keith Marsh (series 1)

Corinna Price-Rodgerson · · · · · Diana Weston
· (series 2)
Geoffrey Ellsworth-Smythe · · Malcolm Tierney
· (series 2)
Lucinda Snellmarsh · · · · · · · Amanda Wenban
· (series 2)

CREDITS

writer David Nobbs · directors David Reynolds (6), John Glenister (4), Ronnie Baxter (2), Les Chatfield (1) · executive producer Vernon Lawrence · producer David Reynolds

Thirteen episodes of rare delight, written by David Nobbs and starring David Jason, growing in stature with every succeeding TV appearance. (And, at this time, they were all succeeding.) Justly, *A Bit Of A Do* won numerous honours, including the TV and Radio Industries Club Award for the Best Situation Comedy of 1989.

Jason was cast as Ted Simcock, the self-professed 'blunt, no-nonsense Yorkshireman' owner of Jupiter Foundry, makers of toasting forks, coal scuttles, fire-irons, boot scrapers and door knockers. In the opening episode Ted's youngest and scruffiest son Paul married Jenny Rodenhurst, the already-pregnant only daughter of upper-crust dentist Laurence Rodenhurst. The union brought together two ill-fitting families – both obsessed with class, albeit from different ends of the spectrum – for some high old times of sordid love affairs, jealousy, hypocrisy, gossip and entanglements. Every one of the 13 episodes was set at a party, the two families in the small Yorkshire town, their members captivated by their own self-importance, enjoying a 'posh-nosh affair' or 'a bit of a do'. Whether it be the annual dentists' dinner dance, the angling club's bash, a race night to raise funds for the local theatre, Rodney Sillitoe's party on behalf of the battery-chicken industry to crown Miss Frozen Chicken (UK), a funeral, a christening, a fancy dress party or more weddings, there they could all be found.

Men did not dominate the series, however. They would have liked to, but the women made sure they got a decent look in. Rita Simcock, Ted's wife, was vulnerable at first, until she became fired up by her husband's infidelity and by her father Percy Spragg's encouragement for her to fight back (following which he died in her arms in episode two). Knowingly sexy, Liz Rodenhurst, Laurence's wife, satisfied her desire for a bit of a rough by encouraging Ted Simcock to enjoy sexual union in a private room following the marriage of his son and her daughter. Their moment of bliss had a resounding after-effect, however, when Liz fell pregnant, much to their – and especially Ted's – embarrassment.

Many other great characters populated *A Bit Of A Do*. Rodney Sillitoe was the repressed executive behind Cock-A-Doodle Chickens, and later – urged on by Jenny –

a vegetarian restaurant. His wife Betty always over-dressed for the occasion, and between them they took it in turns to get drunk at the parties. The smooth urbanity of Laurence's friend Neville Badger – a solicitor with the local practice of Badger, Badger, Fox and Badger – had been undone since his perfect wife Jane's sudden death, and he couldn't stop talking about her. Ensuring that the two families' loggerheads ran across all the generations, Elvis Simcock, Paul and Rita's other son, and Simon Rodenhurst, Jenny's estate-agent brother, liked to wind each other up at every opportunity. Ultimately, Ted and Rita's marriage broke up; Rita and Liz wouldn't talk; Jupiter Foundry went bankrupt; Ted started a relationship with a sophisticate calling herself Corinna Price-Rodgerson who turned out to be a con artist and bigamist, forcing Ted to scrap his plans to emigrate with her to Nairobi; Rita became a local Labour councillor and formed a relationship with Liz's brother, Geoffrey Ellsworth-Smythe; Laurence died; Liz married Neville Badger, who brought up Ted's baby as his own; and Jenny – having divorced the hapless Paul – promptly married a second Simcock, Elvis.

By having the stories of family strife played out at public functions, author David Nobbs ensured maximum laughs as the high drama of repressed and exposed feelings, snobbery and ambitions of social superiority came to light in the most claustrophobic of conditions. Each episode was full of awkward glances, pregnant pauses, forgotten lies, pointed barbs, mimed urgings, conspiratorial whispers, strangled expostulations and social gaffes, embracing the author's delicious observations about the British class structure, the goals of the working classes, the hypocrisy of the upper classes and the petty politics of small-town affairs.

The TV series was adapted by Nobbs from his 1986 novel *A Bit Of A Do*, subtitled 'A Story In Six Place Settings'. The second series prompted a 1990 sequel novel, *Fair Do's*.

David Nobbs is nothing if not prodigious. As well as the programmes listed in this book to which he was one of numerous contributors, he has been explicitly involved, either as sole or co-writer, in **Dogfood Dan And The Carmarthen Cowboy**, **Fairly Secret Army**, **The Fall And Rise Of Reginald Perrin** and **The Legacy Of Reggie Perrin** (see former *Perrin* entry for details), **The Glamour Girls**, **The Hello Goodbye Man**, **Keep It In The Family**, **Lance At Large**, **Love On A Branch Line**, **Rich Tea And Sympathy**, **Shine A Light** and **The Sun Trap**. Nobbs has also written a number of TV dramas, one-offs and series, that, while humorous to an extent, are more dramatic than funny in content, and so are beyond the parameters of this book – these

include three Yorkshire TV productions, *Cupid's Darts* (7 April 1981), *The Life And Times Of Henry Pratt* (four episodes, 9–30 November 1992) and the two-hour *Stalag Luft* (27 October 1993) that starred Stephen Fry, Nicholas Lyndhurst and Geoffrey Palmer.

A Bit Of Fry And Laurie

UK · BBC · SKETCH

26 editions (25 × 30 mins · 1 × 35 mins)

Special (35 mins) 26 Dec 1986 · BBC1 Sat 11.55pm

Series One (6 × 30 mins) 13 Jan–17 Feb 1989 · BBC2 Fri 9pm

Series Two (6 × 30 mins) 9 Mar–13 Apr 1990 · BBC2 Fri 9pm

Series Three (6 × 30 mins) 9 Jan–13 Feb 1992 · BBC2 Thu 9pm

Series Four (7 × 30 mins) 12 Feb–2 Apr 1995 · BBC1 Sun 10pm

MAIN CAST
Stephen Fry
Hugh Laurie
Deborah Norton (series 1)

CREDITS
writers Stephen Fry/Hugh Laurie · *directors* Roger Ordish (7), Bob Spiers (7), Nick Symons (6), Kevin Bishop (6) · *producers* Roger Ordish (13), Jon Plowman (7), Kevin Bishop (6)

Stephen Fry was born in 1957, Hugh Laurie in 1959; they met in the early 1980s when both at Cambridge. Fellow student Emma Thompson recommended Fry when Laurie was looking around for someone to help him write a pantomime. The two discovered a common sense of humour and have worked regularly together ever since. After guest appearances on various shows, and an instructive time as part of the **Alfresco** team, they graduated to their own series.

A Bit Of Fry And Laurie was a witty and sophisticated entertainment – quite the best humour to emanate from the toilets of Uttoxeter, one could say – that had an old-fashioned revue-type atmosphere and oddly 'British' sketches that rejoiced in literary turns of phrase and elaborate wordplay. The delicate innuendos, coupled with Fry's ability to suggest hidden meanings in everyday phrases, gave the impression that bubbling below the innocent surface were lewd undercurrents that threatened to burst through, although they never actually did. To add to this mix, Hugh Laurie demonstrated his keyboard talents with parodies of musical genres.

The pair have subsequently distinguished themselves as workaholic Renaissance Men with individual successes in many fields including the stage, feature films and literature, with both Fry and Laurie – the former with perhaps the most distinction – enjoying best-selling successes as novelists.

Note. Highlights from the TV series were compiled into a pair of half-hour audio programmes, broadcast by BBC Radio 4 on 11 and 18 August 1994.

See also Jeeves And Wooster and Christmas Night With The Stars.

Bizarre

USA · SHOWTIME/SYNDICATION (SHOWTIME) · SKETCH

125 × 30 mins · colour
US dates: 1980–1984
UK dates: 8 Jan 1982–29 June 1985 (45 editions) ITV Fri then Sat various late times

MAIN CAST
John Byner
Bob Einstein
Billy Barty

CREDITS
writers Allan Blye, Jack Handey, Mike Marmer and others · *producers* Allan Blye, Bob Einstein, Perry Rosemond

While American TV networks are well known for their prudence (certainly compared to British TV) and fear of alienating sponsors and advertisers, the advent of cable TV in the USA has permitted a much greater freedom. One early example of this was *Bizarre*, a show that seemed intent on shocking, not least by a liberal sprinkling of the f-word in its irreverent sketches and lampoons.

The series, made for Showtime pay-TV, was hosted by the comic impressionist John Byner (best known to British viewers as the buffoonish Detective Donahue in **Soap**) and the sketches also featured a repertory-style team of players. Material deemed particularly offensive was edited out when *Bizarre* was syndicated to terrestrial US stations and offered for export to, for example, London-area ITV, which began a sporadic showing of 45 of the 125 programmes in 1982.

The Black Abbots

UK · ITV (YORKSHIRE) · MUSICAL HUMOUR/SKETCH

2 × 30 mins · colour
3 Apr 1980 · Thu 8.30pm
19 Dec 1980 · Fri 7.30pm

MAIN CAST
Russ Abbot
Clive Jones
Lennie Reynolds
Bobby Turner

CREDITS
writers Mike Goddard/John Barlett · *director* Ian Bolt · *producers* Alan Tarrant (1), Ian Bolt (1)

On the verge of a tremendously successful solo career that would follow his stint in the 1979 series **Freddie Starr's Variety Madhouse**, Russ Abbot appeared here with the comedy-musical act he had played with for some 15 years, the Black Abbots. The cast of comic characters that Abbot would soon make famous were already well to the fore.

See also Russ Abbot's combined entry.

Blackadder

If *Fawlty Towers* demonstrated just how funny Pythonesque humour could be when visited upon the sitcom format, so the *Blackadder* series showed how well the style of the 'alternative comedians' could likewise enhance the genre. From humble beginnings, the *Blackadder* saga grew to be a work of greatness and one that, finally, even managed successfully to contain that most old-fashioned of ideas: A Message.

Arguably, Rowan Atkinson has never been funnier than when playing the many similar yet subtly different incarnations of Edmund Blackadder: an indolent rogue with a sharp tongue and an appealing ability to vacillate between naïve optimism and world-weary pessimism. The clever premise of the series was to visit the ancestors of this dastardly cad in subsequent generations of his family at key moments in history. This was a similar concept to that used by the *Carry On* film team, and meant that with each new manifestation, new sets, characters and situations could be explored while maintaining continuity by the recognisable characteristics of the lead players.

The Black Adder

UK · BBC · SITCOM

6 × 35 mins · colour

15 June–20 July 1983 · BBC1 Wed 9.25pm

MAIN CAST

Edmund Blackadder	Rowan Atkinson
Baldrick	Tony Robinson
Percy	Tim McInnerny
King Richard IV	Brian Blessed
The Queen	Elspet Gray
Prince Harry of Wales	Robert East

CREDITS

writers Richard Curtis/Rowan Atkinson · *director* Martin Shardlow · *producer* John Lloyd

This is the premise: Richard III didn't murder the princes in the tower and one of them grew up to be Richard, Duke of York, heir to the throne. Henry VII didn't win the battle of Bosworth Field in 1485, it was won by Richard who went on to become Richard IV. When Henry VII came to the throne 13 years later he changed to the Gregorian calendar, put the date back 13 years and destroyed all traces of the reign of Richard IV – all but one document, that is, recording the exploits of Richard IV's younger son,

Edmund, Duke of Edinburgh, who styled himself 'The Black Adder'. Edmund was decidedly hard-of-thinking but still much sharper than his two cohorts, Baldrick (dumb) and Percy (dumber). Together they schemed for an easier life, a better position and perhaps even a shot at the throne itself. But all of these ambitions were doomed to failure by the sheer incompetence of the three protagonists, who managed to combine their monumental stupidity with laziness and overwhelming cowardice.

Producer John Lloyd and actor Rowan Atkinson had conceived the notion of a period-piece sitcom when they were growing weary of working with contemporary sketch material in **Not The Nine O'Clock News**, but *The Black Adder*, although a fine idea, had more than its share of problems. It was an ambitious concept that turned out to be extremely costly – location shooting, locale dressing and set and costume design all pushed the budget up, and made the series difficult and timely to produce. Although the finished product had obvious potential, the mix wasn't quite right and, strangely, the extensive location work seemed to work against the whole. But, although flawed, the series struck a chord with many younger viewers and won an international Emmy in the popular arts category in 1983, enough (just) to convince the BBC to commission a second series.

Blackadder II

UK · BBC · SITCOM

6 × 30 mins · colour

9 Jan–20 Feb 1986 · BBC1 Thu 9.30pm

MAIN CAST

Lord Edmund Blackadder	Rowan Atkinson
Baldrick	Tony Robinson
Lord Percy	Tim McInnerny
Lord Melchett	Stephen Fry
Queen Elizabeth I	Miranda Richardson
Nursie	Patsy Byrne

CREDITS

writers Richard Curtis/Ben Elton · *director* Mandie Fletcher · *producer* John Lloyd

The premise: England 1560, and the flawed genes of the Blackadder family have resurfaced in the melting pot of history, giving us another Edmund, the bastard great, great grandson of the original Black Adder. Now with Blackadder as an established surname, this latest Edmund is markedly different from the first. As greedy, indolent and cowardly as his ancestor, this Blackadder has brains and cunning aplenty. Tudor England proved to be a dangerous time for the scheming Edmund, especially with a childlike and selfish Queen who could turn instantly from being enamoured with her subject to wanting him beheaded. Elsewhere, he had

an enemy in the court, Lord Melchett, a favourite with the Queen. Melchett regarded Edmund as a transparent yet still dangerous rival. By Blackadder's side was another Baldrick, whose family seemed compelled to produce sub-human specimens destined to serve the dastardly Blackadders.

Blackadder II nearly didn't happen, the cost of the first series deterring BBC executive Michael Grade from permitting a second. But major changes to the series were afoot: Atkinson realised that the location scenes got in the way of the comedy, and that by filming nearly everything in a studio, with an audience, they could cut costs and heighten the humour. Atkinson stepped down from writing duties and Ben Elton was brought in to work with Curtis on the scripts. He was an inspired choice, bringing to the production quickfire dialogue, rich verbal weaponry and a fitting dose of vulgarity. Atkinson was in his element as the sneering, superior Edmund, a cold and calculating man surrounded by fools. The new-style dialogue particularly suited him, his character revelling in wonderfully convoluted insults such as, 'Your brain is like the four-headed man-eating haddock-fish beast of Aberdeen. It doesn't exist'.

Blackadder The Third

UK · BBC · SITCOM

6 × 30 mins · colour

17 Sep–22 Oct 1987 · BBC1 Thu 9.30pm

MAIN CAST

Edmund Blackadder	Rowan Atkinson
Baldrick	Tony Robinson
The Prince Regent (George)	Hugh Laurie
Mrs Miggins	Helen Atkinson Wood

CREDITS

writers Richard Curtis/Ben Elton · *director* Mandie Fletcher · *producer* John Lloyd

The premise: England 1760–1815, and the latest Blackadder is butler to the Prince Regent, a man of severely limited intellect and foppish habits. Once again, this Blackadder has a stinging wit and a cowardly cunning, and once again he is aided, abetted and hindered by a virtually brain-dead member of the Baldrick family. Here we find a Blackadder no longer a member of the aristocracy but still ambitious to better himself by foul means. His demeaning position, in service to a man with a 'brain the size of a peanut', only strengthens his resolve to move up in the world. This time around, Blackadder also has to avoid a fate worse than death: he is the object of the affections of pie-shoppe proprietor Mrs Miggins, an awful cockney half-wit.

The series was now going from strength to strength and the character of Blackadder was pretty much the same as before, the creative team rightfully sensing that it was the type that most suited Atkinson's style. Writers Elton and Curtis delivered more marvellous verbal intricacies and the strongest plots yet. Notable guest stars in this series included Robbie Coltrane as Doctor Johnson, Nigel Planer as Lord Smedley and Hugh Paddick and Kenneth Connor as a couple of anarchists.

Blackadder: The Cavalier Years

UK · BBC · SITCOM

1 × 15 mins · colour

5 Feb 1988 · BBC1 Fri 9.45pm

MAIN CAST

Sir Edmund Blackadder · · · Rowan Atkinson
Baldrick · · · · · · · · · · · · · · · Tony Robinson
Charles the First · · · · · · · · · · · Stephen Fry
Oliver Cromwell · · · · · · · · · · Warren Clarke

CREDITS

writers Richard Curtis/Ben Elton

Part of the **Comic Relief** telethon evening of new and vintage comedy. This time dashing Sir Edmund Blackadder tries to save Charles I (Stephen Fry playing the character with the mannerisms of the current Prince Charles) from Oliver Cromwell and his Roundheads.

Blackadder's Christmas Carol

UK · BBC · SITCOM

1 × 45 mins · colour

23 Dec 1988 · BBC1 Fri 9.30pm

MAIN CAST

Ebenezer Blackadder · · · · · Rowan Atkinson
Baldrick · · · · · · · · · · · · · · · Tony Robinson
Spirit of Christmas · · · · · · · Robbie Coltrane
Lord Melchett · · · · · · · · · · · · Stephen Fry
The Prince Regent · · · · · · · · · · Hugh Laurie
Queen Elizabeth I · · · · Miranda Richardson
Queen Victoria · · · · · · · · Miriam Margolyes
Prince Albert · · · · · · · · · · · Jim Broadbent
King Bernard · · · · · · · · · · · · · Patsy Byrne
Mrs Scratchit · · · · · · · · · · Pauline Melville

CREDITS

writers Richard Curtis/Ben Elton · director Richard Boden · producer John Lloyd

The premise: Ebenezer is the white sheep of the awful Blackadder clan. Far from being mean, spiteful, greedy and cowardly, as his Dickensian name suggests, Ebenezer is a kindly, generous man. He is visited by the spirit of Christmas who, in the spirit of A Christmas Carol, takes him through time to witness the past, present and future. He encounters the Blackadders from Blackadder II and Blackadder The Third and travels to the future to spy on one of his descendants. All these Blackadders are loathsome creatures who seem to derive some pleasure out of their wickedness, thus Ebenezer returns to the present having learnt the moral that 'bad guys have more fun'. His personality changes accordingly, and he heaps insults upon Queen Victoria and Prince Albert who arrive to offer him a baronage and £50,000. Needless to say, he promptly loses both.

Blackadder Goes Forth

UK · BBC · SITCOM

6 × 30 mins · colour

28 Sep–2 Nov 1989 · BBC1 Thu 9.30pm

MAIN CAST

Captain Blackadder · · · · · · Rowan Atkinson
Private Baldrick · · · · · · · · · · Tony Robinson
General Hogmanay Melchett · · Stephen Fry
Lieutenant George Colthurst St Barleigh · Hugh Laurie
Captain Darling · · · · · · · · · · Tim McInnerny

CREDITS

writers Richard Curtis/Ben Elton · director Richard Boden · producer John Lloyd

The premise: Captain Blackadder is a career soldier who enlisted to escape the rigours of civilian life and who has enjoyed an action-free existence across three continents. He's a man of simple ambitions: an easy life, the occasional drink and promotion to an even safer, higher-paid position. Unfortunately, the Great War has interfered with his plans and he has found himself stuck in the trenches, uncomfortably close to the front. With him, as always, is a prize idiot from the Baldrick clan – this time a particularly unpleasant army private, serving as Blackadder's batman. Also entrenched, as it were, is Lieutenant George St Barleigh, a keen, vacuous type anxious to volunteer for all sorts of loony escapades and devoted to Captain Blackadder. Their very lives are in the hands of General Melchett, a direct conduit to General Haig, who delivers the plans and orders that dictate their movements. Melchett is quite mad – a gung-ho, bloodthirsty armchair warrior from a military family – and is assisted by an aide-de-camp, the sycophantic Captain Darling. Blackadder's main concern is how to dissuade Melchett from sending him and his men to certain death.

This was a marvellous finale to the Blackadder saga, bringing the tale to the 20th-century and the killing fields of the First World War. Despite sharing many of the despicable traits of his ancestors, this Blackadder character managed to elicit genuine affection from an audience in sympathy with his plight. The madness of war and of warmongers like Melchett were the real villains here and Blackadder's failed attempts to escape his inevitable fate seemed a realistic response rather than a cowardly one. More serious in approach than its predecessors, Blackadder Goes Forth still managed to mine many laughs out of the hopeless situation, with the sheer horror of their environment and the delicacy of their position adding to the blackness of the comedy. In the end, the creative team stuck to their guns and, instead of having Blackadder succeed in his quest, had him and his men forced to join the advance and fulfil their fears by going 'over the top' to their deaths. This grim image, the frame frozen and then dissolving into one depicting the same field full of poppies, memorably ended the series on a note of dark satire and was a fitting conclusion to a comedy premise that had always sported an underlying intelligence beneath its farcical surface.

Note. The 16 October 1989 edition of the BBC2 series Behind The Screen reported on the making of Blackadder Goes Forth.

Black And Blue

UK · BBC · SITCOMS

6 × 55 mins · colour

14 Aug–18 Sep 1973 · BBC2 Tue mostly 10.05pm

A series of six unrelated comedy playlets taking the theme of 'black comedy', Black And Blue was a commendable attempt to explore the boundaries of taste within the comedy format. Palin and Jones's Secrets was easily the best of the bunch.

Secrets   14 AUG

MAIN CAST

Rose · · · · · · · · · · · · · · · · · · Warren Mitchell
Robinson · · · · · · · · · · · · · · Julian Holloway
Atkinson · · · · · · · · · · · · · · · David Collings

CREDITS

writers Michael Palin/Terry Jones · director James Cellan Jones · producer Mark Shivas

A supremely bad-taste story relating what happens at a chocolate factory when three workers fall into a vat and become the special ingredient in a boxed assortment called Secrets. The management team find out too late to prevent the chocolates from going into distribution but their panic changes to something far more sinister when the chocolates became unfathomably popular. To keep up with demand and make huge profits, more 'special ingredients' are required. Warren Mitchell starred as Mr Rose, the management man with a moral dilemma.

In 1988 an expanded version of the script was made into a feature film, Consuming Passions (director Giles Foster), which was universally panned.

The Middle-Of-The-Road Roadshow For All The Family   21 AUG

MAIN CAST

N J · Bill Fraser
Jacki Darr · · · · · · · · · · · · · Adrienne Posta
Robin Bolt · · · · · · · · · · · · · Stephen Moore
Hi · · · · · · · · · · · · · · · · · · Anthony Hopkins
Peter Queech · · · · · · · · · · · · · · Ray Brooks

CREDITS

writer Philip Mackie · director Mark Cullingham ·
producer Mark Shivas

Set in the world of film-making, this edition featured Bill Fraser as a movie tycoon who accidentally pays the wrong writer £500,000.

High Kampf   28 AUG

MAIN CAST

Schultz · · · · · · · · · · · · · · · Kenneth Colley
Hartigan · · · · · · · · · · · · · Geoffrey Golden
Alacoque · · · · · · · · · · · · · Maureen Aherne
Haymes · · · · · · · · · · · · · · · · Philip Stone
Ellie · · · · · · · · · · · · · · · · · Brenda Fricker

CREDITS

writer Hugh Leonard · director Michael Apted ·
producer Mark Shivas

A view of a bunch of ill-assorted relatives gathering vulture-like around a dying wealthy man.

Rust   4 SEP

MAIN CAST

Sir Henry · · · · · · · · · · · · · John Le Mesurier
Eleanor · · · · · · · · · · · · · Elisabeth Spriggs
Philip Crane · · · · · · · · · · · Allan Cuthbertson
Thomas Richmond · · · · · · · · · · James Bree

CREDITS

writer Julian Mitchell · director Waris Hussein ·
producer Mark Shivas

A tale about a flu epidemic that threatens to wipe out the world's population and the British-made miracle-cure drug, which although effective, leaves its users impotent.

Soap Opera In Stockwell   11 SEP

MAIN CAST

Sylv · Alfie Bass
Bert · · · · · · · · · · · · · · · · · Michael Robbins
Carol · · · · · · · · · · · · · · · · · Cheryl Hall
May · · · · · · · · · · · · · · · · · George Tovey
Joan · · · · · · · · · · · · · · · · · Harry Landis
Mavis · · · · · · · · · · · · · · · · · · Tony Selby

CREDITS

writers Michael O'Neill/Jeremy Seabrook · director Tim Aspinall · producer Mark Shivas

The complex aftermath of a possibly accidental baby-snatching from a launderette.

Glorious Miles   18 SEP

MAIN CAST

Miles Miles · · · · · · · · · · · · · Peter Vaughan

Lord Grotton · · · · · · · · · · · Dinsdale Landen

CREDITS

writer Henry Livings · director Ian MacNaughton ·
producer Mark Shivas

A story of a misunderstanding. A millionaire employs a butler to impress his friends, but the butler believes he has been hired for a much more deadly job.

The Black Safari

UK · BBC · SATIRE

1 × 60 mins · colour

24 Nov 1972 · BBC2 Fri 9.55pm

MAIN CAST

Yemi Ajibade
Merdel Jordine
Bloke Modisane
Horace Ové
Douglas Botting

CREDITS

writer Douglas Botting · director Colin Luke

A role-reversal parody with a four-strong black expedition travelling the Liverpool-Leeds canal in search of the centre of Britain.

The writer, TV explorer Douglas Botting, got the idea after his balloon crashed in a Tanganyikan forest and he was rescued by Masai tribesman. He stayed with the tribesmen for a time and managed to experience from the inside what happens when a team of safari tourists come across tribesmen and treat them like a tourist attraction. Botting gave one of the tribesmen his camera and told him to take pictures of the tourists – which he did, much to the consternation of the interlopers.

Botting's idea for The Black Safari was to rig a safari that not only turned the tables but also revealed England as a truly foreign country. Acting as white safari guide, Botting led the team, which consisted of West Indian film director Horace Ové, Nigerian actor Yemi Ajibade, Jamaican painter Merdel Jordine and South African writer and refugee Bloke Modisane. The result was a quirky one-off, humorous yet with serious undertones.

Note. This programme followed a year after a previous expedition – more light-hearted than comedic – undertaken by explorer Sir Ranulph Twisleton-Wykeham-Fiennes with comic actress Liz Fraser and Douglas Botting (who also wrote the programme). The area of exploration this time was the capital's subterranean world of sewers, railway lines, shelters and vaults, screened as Under London Expedition in the BBC2 nature series The World About Us on 7 November 1971.

Blandings Castle

UK · BBC · SITCOM

6 × 30 mins · b/w

24 Feb–31 Mar 1967 · BBC1 Fri 7.30pm

MAIN CAST

Clarence, 9th Earl Of Emsworth · · · · · · · · ·
· · · · · · · · · · · · · · · · · · · Ralph Richardson
Beach · · · · · · · · · · · · · · · Stanley Holloway
Lady Constance · · · · · · · · · · · Meriel Forbes
McAllister · · · · · · · · · · · · · · Jack Radcliffe

CREDITS

creator P G Wodehouse · adapter/writer
John Chapman · producer Michael Mills

Presented under The World Of Wodehouse banner, the BBC cast finely for this TV adaptation of Wodehouse's wonderful stories about Clarence, the dreamy Ninth Earl of Emsworth, and his formidable sister Constance.

The Earl, a harmless chap obsessed with the well being of his prize pig, the Empress, is intent on a peaceful life but cannot bear to see injustice of any type – especially when it threatens to ruin the path of true love. This weakness often leads to his involvement with star-crossed young lovers and into complex plots of mistaken identity and misunderstanding, invariably bringing him into direct conflict with his daunting sister, Lady Constance. True to form for Wodehouse, the most fraught and frightful situations are retrieved at the eleventh hour by a stroke of whimsical genius on the part of the Earl or by the intervention of his ever-faithful butler, Beach. Jack Radcliffe appeared as McAllister, the Earl's gardener, and various guest stars popped up during the series, including Jimmy Edwards as Sir Geoffrey Parsloe-Parsloe, Fred Emney as Sir Eustace Chalfont and Derek Nimmo as the Hon Freddie Threepwood.

Note. In what was described as a 'short play for television', Emsworth had made an earlier BBC appearance in Lord Emsworth And The Little Friend, adapted by C E Webber and produced by Rex Tucker for the strand Children's Television, screened on 20 March 1956. Much later (24 December 1995) BBC1 aired a more lavish presentation, the feature-length TV movie P G Wodehouse's Heavy Weather, which featured Peter O'Toole as Clarence, Richard Briers as Threepwood, Roy Hudd as Beach and Judy Parfitt as Lady Constance. In between, Richard Vernon starred in the title role and Ian Carmichael played the part of the Threepwood in several BBC Radio 4 series of Blandings between 1985 and 1992.

See also **The World Of Wooster, Mr Wodehouse Speaking, The Reverent Wooing Of Archibald, Ukridge, Wodehouse Playhouse, Uncle Fred Flits By** and **Jeeves And Wooster.**

Bless Me, Father

UK · ITV (LWT) · SITCOM

21 × 30 mins · colour

Series One (7) 24 Sep–5 Nov 1978 · Sun 9.15pm

Series Two (7) 11 Nov 1979–6 Jan 1980 · Sun around 9pm

Series Three (7) 5 July–16 Aug 1981 · Sun 8.45pm

MAIN CAST

Father Duddleswell · · · · · · · · · · Arthur Lowe
Father Neil Boyd · · · · · · · · · Daniel Abineri
Mrs Pring · · · · · · · · · · · · · Gabrielle Daye

OTHER APPEARANCES

Bishop O'Reilly · · · · · · · · · · · Derek Francis
Mother Stephen · · · · · · · · · · · Sheila Keith

CREDITS

writer Peter De Rosa · director/producer David Askey

Within a year of **Dad's Army** coming to rest, Arthur Lowe donned another sitcom uniform, priestly robes, to star in ITV's *Bless Me, Father*. He was cast as Father Charles Duddleswell – a cheerfully mischievous and laconic Roman Catholic priest in the suburban London parish of St Jude's, Fairwater – and the stories were set in 1950.

All 21 episodes were written by Peter De Rosa, based upon his own experiences as a novice curate, which he had previously published in book form under the pseudonym Neil Boyd – no coincidence, therefore, that Father Neil Boyd, Father Duddleswell's young English charge, was the name of said novice curate in the series. Mrs Pring was their housekeeper, who had served Duddleswell for 20 years and was, to quote the priest himself, 'a perfect instance of the worst coming to the worst'. Actually, she had plenty to put up with, and did so with remarkable forbearance.

Bless Me, Father is one of the hidden gems in Britain's sitcom archives, made glorious by the cleverly subtle scripts and fine contributions by the three main players, with Arthur Lowe in particular never less than wholly convincing as the cunning priest with the gentle Irish brogue.

Peter De Rosa wrote four books about life at St Jude's: *Bless Me, Father*, *Father In A Fix*, *A Father Before Christmas* and *Father Under Fire*.

Bless My Soul

UK · C4 (ANTONINE PRODUCTIONS) · SKETCH

1 × 55 mins · colour

23 Apr 1984 · Mon 11.25pm

MAIN CAST

David Anderson
Arnold Brown
Peter Capaldi
David Hicks
David McNiven
Terry Neason
The Wildcat Theatre Company

CREDITS

writers David MacLennan/David Anderson · director/producer Sean Hardie · executive producer Paddy Higson

A collection of acts from the hip London comedy clubs and fringe venues came together for this single programme, screened, appropriately, on Easter Monday and presented in the form of a thanksgiving service from the Second Church of Christ Monetarist.

Bless This House   UK

UK · ITV (THAMES) · SITCOM

65 × 30 mins (58 × colour · 7 × b/w)

Series One (7 × b/w · 5 × colour) 2 Feb–20 Apr 1971 · Tue around 7pm

Series Two (12) 21 Feb–15 May 1972 · Mon 8.30pm

Series Three (12) 22 Jan–12 Mar 1973 (7) · Mon 8.30pm; 30 Apr–28 May 1973 (5) · Mon 8pm

Series Four (6) 20 Feb–10 Apr 1974 · Wed 8pm

Series Five (10) 14 Oct–16 Dec 1974 · Mon 8pm

Series Six (13) 29 Jan–22 Apr 1976 · Thu mostly 8pm

MAIN CAST

Sid Abbott · · · · · · · · · · · · · · Sidney James
Jean Abbott · · · · · · · · · · · · Diana Coupland
Mike Abbott · · · · · · · · · · · · · Robin Stewart
Sally Abbott · · · · · · · · · · · · · Sally Geeson
Trevor · · · · · · · · · · · · · · · Anthony Jackson
Betty · · · · · · · · · · · · · · · · Patsy Rowlands

CREDITS

creators Vince Powell/Harry Driver · writers Carla Lane/Myra Taylor (15), Carla Lane (10), Vince Powell/Harry Driver (12), Dave Freeman (12), Jon Watkins (8), Bernie Sharp (4), David Cumming/Derek Collyer (1), Adele Rose (1), Mike Sharland/B C Cummins (1), Lawrie Wyman/George Evans (1) · director/producer William G Stewart

Perhaps the most typical and therefore best loved of ITV's many 1970s studio-based 'domestic' sitcoms, with most of its humour rooted in generation-gap blues, *Bless This House* dominated the station's comedy output for half a decade. It starred Sid James in what, for him, was his first appearance on TV as a family man, although the obsessions for which he was previously known – his beer, his bird-fancying (the birds being young women, of course), his pipe and his football – remained a constant.

As the cheery but regularly frustrated Londoner (he must have said 'O' my gord' in every episode), a successful travelling stationery salesman by trade, Sid *thought* himself head of a household that also numbered his wife Jean (well played by Diana Coupland) and two young-adult children: Mike (Robin Stewart), aged 18 (at first), whose dress and philosophies reflected the late-hippy period and gave Sid cause to worry about his son's sexual preferences; and Sally (played by Sally Geeson, sister of film actress Judy), who, though just 16 at the start of the first series, embraced not only the principles of the free love generation but, it was suggested, partook of it too. Neighbours Trevor and Betty frequently popped in to stir

the troubled waters, the excessively laddish Trev seeing Sid's point of view (usually over a pint at the Hare and Hounds, on Clapham Common in south London) and Betty seeing Jean's. Plots incorporated all the standard sitcom situations: misunderstandings, small lies growing out of all proportion, conclusion jumping, fantastic coincidences and pride-fuelled fiascos – but it was all delivered with a rude energy and helped along by Sid James's and Diana Coupland's likeable screen personae. Snubbed by the critics perhaps, but the public watched it in droves and episodes regularly appeared in the national ratings top ten.

Bless This House was unusual in that its director/producer William G Stewart (the deviser/presenter of C4's daily quiz-show *Fifteen To One* from 1988 to date) fostered the American-style school of sitcom writing, commissioning episodes from a variety of authors. Vince Powell and Harry Driver, who created the series, contributed a dozen scripts but Carla Lane, while penning **The Liver Birds** for the BBC, wrote 25, including 22 out of the first 42 episodes. And as usual for 1970s hit sitcoms, there was a weak spin-off cinema-movie too, made in 1972 by the *Carry On* producer Gerald Thomas, scripted by Dave Freeman and featuring all of the Abbott family except Robin Stewart.

See also Home Sweet Home.

Bless This House   USA

USA · CBS (MOHAWK PRODUCTIONS/WARNER BROS) · SITCOM

16 × 30 mins · colour

US dates: 11 Sep 1995–17 Jan 1996

UK dates: 16 Sep–24 Dec 1996 (16 episodes) C4 weekdays mostly 9am

MAIN CAST

Alice Clayton · · · · · · · · · · · · · Cathy Moriarty
Burt Clayton · · · · · · · · · · · · · · Andrew Clay
Phyllis · · · · · · · · · · · · · · · · · · Molly Price
Lenny · · · · · · · · · · · · · · · · · · · Don Stark
Danny Clayton · · · · · · · · · · · · · Raegan Kotz
Sean Clayton · · · · · · · · · · · · · · Sam Gifaldi
Cuba · · · · · · · · · · · · · · · · · Wren T Brown
Vicki Shetski · · · · · · · · · · · · · Patricia Healy
Jane Shetski · · · · · · · · · · · · Kimberly Cullum

CREDITS

creator Bruce Helford · writers Diane Burroughs/Joey Gutierrez (3), Matt Ember (2), Bruce Helford (2), Bill Masters (2), Susan Cridland Wick (2), Janice Jordan (1), Jeff Lowell (1), Bruce R Rasmussen (1), Lona Williams (1), Billy Van Zandt/Jane Milmore (1) · directors Barnet Kellman (11), Pamela Fryman (3), Shelley Jensen (2) · executive producers Bruce Helford, Billy Van Zandt, Jane Milmore · producer Frank Pace

Andrew 'Dice' Clay became renowned as the bad boy of US comedy with a volatile, racist and sexist standup act that shocked the liberal media establishment. For his part, Clay always claimed that his bully-boy stage persona was just that: an alter ego he invented for his act; nevertheless, the comic found himself tainted by the stigma of the character for many years. Thus it was a surprise to find him in the lead role in *Bless This House*, a family sitcom the production team unashamedly described as a 1990s version of **The Honeymooners**. The premise certainly did employ aspects of that classic 1950s series – Clay starred as Burt Clayton, a Ralph Kramden-like belligerent mailman with set blue-collar views and a deep belief in the American system. His wife Alice (a definite nod to Ralph's wife Alice) was more than a match for him, and the two were constantly engaged in noisy but good-natured spats in their cramped New York apartment. Their neighbours were Burt's fellow worker, the gormless Lenny (a modern day Ed Norton) and his wife Phyllis, a close friend of Alice's (much like Trixie had been). Adding to the mix (and finally deviating from *The Honeymooners*, for the Kramdens had no offspring) were Burt and Alice's children – a smart-aleck and precocious daughter named Danny and her younger brother Sean – and their near neighbour Vicki, a voluptuous single mother whose daughter Jane spent much time at the Claytons. Stories revolved around the interplay between these characters but concentrated particularly on the battle of wills between Burt and Alice.

While it was no *Honeymooners*, the series had good moments and Clay was surprisingly effective in the lead. His relationship with his wife was highly volatile but, as with *The Honeymooners*, the couple remained deeply in love and even seemed to thrive on the constant bickering. There was also a touch of **Roseanne** and **Married ... With Children** in the show's determination to candidly discuss sex between the married couple.

All in all, *Bless This House* was an unambitious show with an honest desire to raise laughs without grinding any axes. Lacking that certain something extra that ensures longevity, it was cancelled after one short season.

Blind Men

UK · ITV (LWT) · SITCOM

6 × 30 mins · colour

21 Nov 1997–2 Jan 1998 · Fri 8.30pm

MAIN CAST

Graham Holdcroft	Jeremy Swift
Phil Carver	Jesse Birdsall
Caroline Holdcroft	Sophie Thompson
Valerie Carver	Tamsin Greig
Tony Preston	Andy Taylor
Ian Stapleton	Danny Swanson
Neil	Raji James
Bob	Roger Blake

CREDITS

creator Chris England · *writers* Chris England/Nick Hancock · *directors* Tony Dow, David Askey · *executive producer* Humphrey Barclay · *producer* Mark Robson

Graham Holdcroft is a hard-working but not always successful salesman for Luxus Interiors, whose principal product is window blinds. At work, a keen rivalry is encouraged among the sales team (Graham, Tony, Neil and Bob) by their young and verbally aggressive boss Ian Stapleton. Graham, Neil and Bob do well, although the obsequious Tony can be annoying, but when wonder-salesman Phil Carver is transferred from the company's Midlands branch, the ball-game suddenly changes and an intense, bitter rivalry breaks out between Graham and the newcomer, a battle that is both professional and personal. To make matters worse, Phil and his artistic wife Valerie (played by Tamsin Greig, Debbie Aldridge in *The Archers*) move into a house opposite Graham and his wife Caroline, and Phil seems to be making a play for Caroline. All of this allows the two men to continue their competitive carping outside of work hours – dirty tricks, practical jokes and an escalating animosity threatening the well-being of both protagonists.

For quite a few years in the 1990s ITV struggled to find a successful sitcom, while the BBC – although not without problems in this area – still managed to notch up a few winners (**Keeping Up Appearances, The Vicar Of Dibley, Men Behaving Badly, Goodnight Sweetheart** and others) and even C4 produced its own home-grown hits (**Drop The Dead Donkey, Father Ted**). *Blind Men* joined ITV's roster of under-achieving 1997 sitcoms, and a marked clue as to the public's lack of faith in the channel's comedy offerings was the fact that only 5.7 million people tuned in for the first episode, at least three million fewer than the norm. Obviously this was no fault of the series, but, traditionally, debut sitcom episodes attract good figures, viewers being keen to find new comedies. Those who did watch the opening of *Blind Men* saw a middle-of-the-road, middle-class sitcom with a couple of sharp lines and a few neat scenes that delivered the goods. The rivalry between the two lead characters was a good device for creating comic moments and the cast tried hard, but the tendency to use the old sitcom clichés of unlikely coincidences and misunderstandings, plus the very subject matter (a favourite topic of old jokes) gave the piece an old-fashioned feel. It just didn't seem like an idea for the 1990s. Indeed, its theme was similar to one explored in Barry Levinson's fine 1987 film comedy *Tin Men*, in which two competing aluminium-siding

salesman became embroiled in a bitter rivalry that nearly destroys their marriages, careers and health. Tellingly, *Tin Men* was a period piece (set in the early 1960s); *Blind Men* might have benefited from similar treatment.

Note. Granada managed to persuade the American TV network NBC into considering a US adaptation of *Blind Men*, putting a pilot episode into production as this book was being written.

Bloomers

UK · BBC · SITCOM

5 × 30 mins · colour

27 Sep–25 Oct 1979 · BBC2 Thu 9.30pm

MAIN CAST

Stan	Richard Beckinsale
Lena	Anna Calder-Marshall
George	Paul Curran
Dingley	David Swift
Pub Landlord	Pat Gorman

CREDITS

writer James Saunders · *producer* Roger Race

A well-written comedy series that was totally overshadowed by the tragic death of its young star Richard Beckinsale during its production. Beckinsale played Stan, an actor more out of work than in, who decides to make ends meet by taking a part-time job in a local florist. Writer James Saunders was a well-known playwright and brought a more thoughtful style than was normal to the genre, in this, his first sitcom. It also featured some adult themes (such as sexual liaisons), hence its BBC2 slotting.

But the series' potential was never to be fully realised. Beckinsale died suddenly of a heart attack on 19 March 1979, on a day scheduled for a rehearsal of the final *Bloomers* episode. The public was deeply grieved by the news, not just because of the suddenness (Beckinsale had no knowledge of a heart condition), nor his youth (he was only 31), but because the actor was much loved in Britain for his roles in **The Lovers**, **Rising Damp** and **Porridge**, playing characters that displayed a vulnerable young man with an underlying decency, warmth and genuineness that Beckinsale himself clearly possessed.

Bloomin' Marvellous

UK · BBC (DLT ENTERTAINMENT UK/THEATRE OF COMEDY) · SITCOM

8 × 30 mins · colour

8 Sep–27 Oct 1997 · BBC1 Mon 9.30pm

MAIN CAST

Jack Deakin	Clive Mantle
Liz Deakin	Sarah Lancashire
Dad	David Hargreaves
Mam	Judith Barker
Shaz	Kathryn Hunt
Jeff	Iain Rogerson

Ron · Bill Dean

CREDITS

creators John Godber/Jane Thornton · *writers* John Godber (5), Jane Thornton (3) · *director* Dewi Humphreys · *executive producers* John Reynolds, Geoffrey Perkins · *producer* Sydney Lotterby

Described in pre-publicity as 'a bittersweet comedy', *Bloomin' Marvellous* was top heavy on the bitter, with only a dash of the sweet. The series was written and conceived by the husband and wife pairing of playwright John Godber and actress Jane Thornton – loosely based upon their own experiences of conceiving a child rather late in life.

In *Bloomin' Marvellous*, Jack and Liz Deakin, two successful, late-thirty-somethings – she's a radio producer, he's a writer and occasional lecturer – decide to try for a child. Friends warn that it won't be easy and could take years, but the Deakins conceive at the first attempt. The rest of the series detailed their experiences during Liz's pregnancy: breaking the news to their parents, attending maternity classes, hearing their friends' parenting horror stories, and more.

Jack was also in the process of recuperating from a serious illness (clots in the lung), a recovery not helped by stress, but he is a nervous man, prone to panic attacks, and his constant worrying leads to many arguments with Liz. Their bickering remains good-natured however, unlike the spiteful spats of their best friends Shaz and Jeff, whose marriage is slowly crumbling. There was some real venom in these exchanges, at a level rarely associated with sitcoms. Jack's parents are another flawed couple: she ('Mam') is a constantly moaning misanthrope who sees the bad side of everything, while he keeps his head down and hopes for a quieter life. It is only when Mam learns that she is to become a grandmother that she shows any warmth. At the end of the series' eight-week run the Deakins finally produced their baby – a girl they name Rosie.

Bloomin' Marvellous was an adult comedy with two competent lead actors working well together, but the series suffered several major flaws, not least the fact that it featured some truly disagreeable characters (the ever-shouting know-all Jeff, and Jack's harridan of a mother) and seemed driven solely by arguments, to the extent where they became annoying to the viewer. It had some good moments – especially in its realistic depiction of the relationship between the four Deakins, and its uncompromising look at the pitfalls of parenting – but, on reflection, the series' uncomfortable mix of serious themes and witty lines might have been better suited to a light-drama production.

Blossom

USA · NBC (IMPACT ZONE PRODUCTIONS/WITT-THOMAS PRODUCTIONS/TOUCHSTONE TELEVISION) · SITCOM

111 episodes (110 × 30 mins · 1 × 120 mins) · colour

US dates: 5 July 1990 (pilot); 3 Jan 1991–27 Feb 1995

UK dates: 24 Apr 1992–18 Aug 1995 (107 × 30 mins · 1 × 120 mins) C4 Fri mostly 6pm

MAIN CAST

Blossom Russo · · · · · · · · · · · · Mayim Bialik
Joey Russo · · · · · · · · · · · · · · Joey Lawrence
Anthony Russo · · · · · · · · Michael Stoyanov
Nick Russo · · · · · · · · · · · · · · · · · Ted Wass
Six LeMuere · · · · · · · · · · · · · Jenna Von Oy
Buzz Richman · · · · · · · · · · Barnard Hughes
Vinnie Bonitardi · · David Lascher (1992–94)
Shelly (later Shelly Russo) · · · · · · · · · · · · · ·
· · · · · · · · · · · · · Samaria Graham (1993–95)
Carol · · · · · · · · · · Finola Hughes (1994–95)

CREDITS

creator Don Reo · *writers* various · *directors* Zane Buzby, Bill Bixby and others · *executive producers* Gene Reynolds, Paul Junger Witt, Tony Thomas, Don Reo · *producers* John Ziffren, Josh Goldstein, Jonathan Prince, Roxie Wenk Evans, Glen Merzer

A 1990s teen comedy featuring an unashamedly imperfect family striving to remain a close unit in contemporary Los Angeles. Centre of attention was Blossom, a smart and mature-beyond-her-years teenage girl (13 at the series' start) who was acutely aware that she wasn't cheerleader or prom-queen material but who was determined to make the most of life all the same. Her best friend at school was the smart Six LeMuere (so called because she was the sixth child) and many of the stories revolved around the exploits of the two. At home, Blossom's father, a musician named Nick, was divorced and her eldest brother Anthony was recovering from drug dependency and substance abuse. Lighter comedy relief came with Blossom's other brother Joey, a thick lad who was obsessed with cars and girls.

In the first few seasons much was made of fantasy sequences in which special guest stars appeared in Blossom's dreams to offer her advice or empathy, but this trend was downplayed in latter episodes. Another recurring theme was to have Blossom present the stories in the form of a video diary, another nod at modernity. Later, Anthony began dating a black girl, Shelly, and the two finally married and had a baby. Nick also attracted a new love interest – a British girl, Carol – and they too were wed. For a while Blossom had a steady boyfriend, Vinnie, a streetwise Italian kid, but the writers found more mileage when she was on the lookout for romance.

Blossom may seem contrived in retrospect, a calculated attempt to create a show that touched all the bases, but it undoubtedly succeeded in striking a chord with teen viewers. But its tendency to moralise, albeit with a light touch, was still probably too mawkish for British audiences. Whatever the show's flaws may have been, though, its principal strength was its star, the delightful Mayim Bialik, who turned in a consistent and highly credible performance as Blossom.

Blott On The Landscape

UK · BBC · COMEDY SERIAL

6 episodes (1 × 50 mins · 5 × 55 mins) · colour

6 Feb–13 Mar 1985 · BBC2 Wed 9pm

MAIN CAST

Sir Giles Lynchwood MP · · · · · · · George Cole
Lady Maud Lynchwood · · · · Geraldine James
Blott · · · · · · · · · · · · · · · · David Suchet
Mrs Forthby · · · · · · · · · · · · Julia McKenzie
Dundridge · · · · · · · · · · · · · · Simon Cadell
Ganglion · · · · · · · · · · · · · Geoffrey Bayldon
Minister · · · · · · · · · · · · · · Geoffrey Chater
Mr Bullett-Finch · · · · · · · · · · · Patrick Godfrey
Mrs Bullett-Finch · · · · · · · Georgine Anderson

CREDITS

creator Tom Sharpe · *adapter/writer* Malcolm Bradbury · *director* Roger Bamford · *producer* Evgeny Gridneff

A hilarious adaptation of Tom Sharpe's farce novel (first published in 1975) about the controversial proposed building of a motorway. George Cole added yet another memorable comic character to his CV with his portrayal of the awful Sir Charles Lynchwood MP, a man driven by his lust for power, money and strange sexual practices. Reacting against his wife Maud's insistence that they should have children, Sir Giles sets in motion a series of events intended to result in a motorway being built across Lady Maud's ancestral home, Handyman Hall. The six episodes followed the increasingly desperate plans of Maud and her fellow protesters to thwart the road planners, represented in person by the Ministry of Environment's bumbling troubleshooter, Dundridge. In her campaign, Maud attracts unlikely assistance from her handyman Blott, a mysterious former Italian PoW who is gradually revealed as a bomb-making anarchist and who dedicates himself to the cause.

But there was more to the piece than the central plot. Manic characters and farcical situations abounded and the whole production seemed blessed with a colourful and vulgar *joie de vivre* never better demonstrated than by Julia McKenzie's portrayal of the homely dominatrix who pandered to Sir Giles' more devious sexual desires.

For a second TV adaptation of Tom Sharpe, see *Porterhouse Blue*. Another of his novels, *Wilt*, was made into a feature film in 1989, starring Griff Rhys Jones, Mel Smith and Alison Steadman.

Blouse And Skirt

UK · C4 (FULL FORCE FILMS) · STANDUP

1 × 60 mins · colour
26 Feb 1992 · Wed 11.30pm

MAIN CAST
Oliver Samuels
Dennis Hall
Errol Fabien
Winston Bell
Owen Ellis
Charles Tomlin
Blacka and Bello
Devon Morgan
Lovena Brown

CREDITS
writers various · *director* Brian Puig · *producer* Malcolm Frederick

An hour of Caribbean comic talent presented by host Oliver Samuel from the Montego Bay beach bar.

Note. The title was later used for a comedy segment in the black entertainment wrap-around strand *The A Force* (BBC2, 18 October to 20 December 1996).

See also *Tall, Dark And Handsome*.

Blue Heaven

UK · C4 (FINE TIME FILM AND TELEVISION PRODUCTIONS) · SITCOM

7 episodes (6 × 35 mins · 1 × 30 mins) · colour
Pilot (30 mins) 10 June 1992 · Wed 10.30pm
One series (6 × 35 mins) 30 July–3 Sep 1994 · Sat around 10pm

MAIN CAST
Frank Sandford · · · · · · · · · · · Frank Skinner
Roache · · · · · · · · · · · · · · · · · Conleth Hill
Ivy Sandford · · · · · · · · · · · · · · Paula Wilcox
Jim Sandford · · · · · · · · · · · · John Forgeham

CREDITS
writer Frank Skinner · *directors* Tony Dow (pilot), Carol Wiseman (series) · *executive producer* Jon Blair · *producer* Jo Sargent

Frank Skinner is actually Chris Collins but as that name was already in use in the entertainment field when, at the age of 30, he decided to try his hand at being a comedian, he changed it, oddly honouring the name of a member of his dad's pub dominoes team. As Skinner, he made his stage debut in 1987, the same year that he gave up a considerable alcohol intake, and he soon found a niche as MC at a Birmingham comedy club. In 1991 he won the coveted Perrier Award at the Edinburgh Festival Fringe, beating a powerful shortlist comprising Jack Dee, Eddie Izzard and Bruce Morton with a winning stage mixture of fine jokes, good-natured laddishness and friendly patter blended with extreme

lewdness – when Skinner made his TV debut on a regional ITV show, *Oo-er*, his act received 131 complaints.

After appearing on C4 in 1991–92 in *Packet Of Three* and *Packing Them In*, Skinner scripted a sitcom pilot for C4's *Bunch Of Five*, aired on 10 June 1992, which was then developed into the series *Blue Heaven*. Semi-autobiographical, episodes depicted the struggles of Frank (vocals) and Roache (keyboards) as they tried to make a success with their musical duo, Blue Heaven. Set in Birmingham to a background of working-class pubs and West Bromwich Albion football matches – Skinner is probably WBA's best-known dedicated fan – each episode saw the two heroes battle to crack the big time against enormous public apathy and parental hostility. Singularly failing to set the world on fire, *Blue Heaven*'s most crowd-pleasing song was 'Please Stop Booing Us, We're Going Soon'.

The series was well written with plenty of sharp lines and hilarious observations. The lack of a studio audience gave the production a low-key feel and meant that some of the sparkling one-liners were greeted by an odd and undeserved silence. The support acting was fine, with a welcome return to sitcom for Paula Wilcox, who relished using a broad Brummie accent as Frank's screen mum. All in all, *Blue Heaven* was quality, likeable entertainment that arguably suffered from the decision not to use a studio audience.

Note. Around this time Skinner was enjoying a good deal of TV exposure, firstly as co-host, with his then flatmate David Baddiel, of the humorous game/chat-show *Fantasy Football League* (BBC2, three series, starting 14 January 1994, ending 10 May 1996) and then by fronting his own BBC1 chat-show *Frank Skinner* (six editions, 3 September–8 October 1995) and *The Frank Skinner Show* (nine editions, 29 December 1996–20 February 1997) in which, prior to conversations with his guests, Skinner performed a few minutes of standup.

The Bob Cummings Show

USA · NBC THEN CBS THEN NBC (LOURMAC PRODUCTIONS) · SITCOM

173 × 30 mins · b/w
US dates: 2 Jan 1955–15 Sep 1959
UK dates: 18 Sep 1956–15 Dec 1958 (77 episodes) ITV mostly Tue various times

MAIN CAST
Bob Collins · · · · · · · · · · · · · Bob Cummings
Margaret MacDonald · · · Rosemary DeCamp
Charmaine 'Schultzy' Schultz · · · Ann B Davis
Chuck MacDonald · · · · · · · Dwayne Hickman
Pamela Livingston · · · · · · · · · · · Nancy Kulp
Paul Fonda · · · · · · · · · · · · · · · · Lyle Talbot

CREDITS
writers various · *directors* various · *producers* Bob Cummings, Al Simon, Bob Mosher, Paul Henning

The comic adventures of dashing, skirt-chasing Hollywood fashion photographer Bob Collins (without coincidence, the same initials as the star), who resists the overtures of his many curvaceous conquests to tie the knot, fighting every inch to maintain his footloose bachelor status. Life was quieter at home, just, where Bob lived with Margaret, his widowed sister, and her teenage crew-cut son Chuck who, as he grew older, clearly aspired to emulate his uncle's lifestyle. (Dwayne Hickman, who played Chuck, went on to star in a hugely successful US sitcom, *The Many Loves Of Dobie Gillis*.) At work, life was hectic, and the dizzying parade of shapely lovelies left quite an impression upon Bob. Although not especially good looking – he would be certainly no match for the 'hunks' of the 1990s – Collins was smooth and sophisticated in the Dean Martin style, and women simply flocked to his feet. Collins had a female assistant, nicknamed Schultzy, who idolised her boss and dreamed of a romantic connection, but her plain-Jane looks meant that Bob was always looking elsewhere.

The Bob Cummings Show was a typical product of a now outdated era when the love-'em-and-leave-'em macho lifestyle was considered fair play, before popular culture swung back to something approaching equality and social diseases became more prominent. (The best British example of the genre might be Galton and Simpson's *Casanova '73*, a short-lived vehicle for Leslie Phillips in his best amorous guise.) *The Bob Cummings Show* was also known in the USA as *Love That Bob*, usefully distinguishing it from a second series entitled *The Bob Cummings Show* (1961–62, not screened in Britain) in which our sophisticated hero, this time named Bob Carson, was a rich playboy with three aeroplanes and, yes, that same penchant for the girls. Later still, Cummings hit the mother and father of all macho fantasies in *My Living Doll* (CBS, 1964–65, again, not screened in Britain), in which he played Dr Robert McDonald, a psychiatrist in charge of a stunningly attractive female robot (played by the statuesque Julie Newmar) programmed to obey his every whim. Being 1960s US television, McDonald never takes advantage of this 'Stepford' woman in the obvious way, but for the avid male viewers the thought of a malleable Julie Newmar was titillation enough.

The Bob Downe Show

UK · ITV (WATCHMAKER PRODUCTIONS FOR YORKSHIRE) · SKETCH/STANDUP

1×60 mins · colour

31 Dec 1996 · Tue 10.15pm

MAIN CAST
Bob Downe

CREDITS
writer Bob Downe · *director* Brian Klein · *executive producer* Elaine Bedell · *producer* Martin Cunning

A British TV special, aired primetime on New Year's Eve, in which the gay Australian comic, self-styled daytime TV host and 'Beige Sensation' – resplendent in his trademark glitzy, if ill-fitting, polyester and crimplene safari suits – presided over a wacky blend of surreal sketches and songs, with humorous and musical guests (including Ant and Dec and Anthony Newley). The programme also included extracts from Downe's Australian TV series.

Four years before this one-off, the comic hosted the series *Bob Downe Under* (screened late-night on London-area ITV by LWT from 30 October 1992) in which he cast the spotlight on current life in Australia with news about the arts, sport, politics and comedy.

Bob Hope ...   [various shows]

see HOPE, Bob

Bob Monkhouse ...   [various shows]

see MONKHOUSE, Bob

Bobby Davro ... [various shows]

see DAVRO, Bobby

Bobby Thompson – The Little Waster

UK · C4 (TYNE TEES) · STANDUP

1×60 mins · colour

18 Dec 1982 · Sat 8.15pm

MAIN CAST
Bobby Thompson

CREDITS
writer Bobby Thompson · *director* Malcolm Dickinson · *executive producer* Heather Ging · *producer* Brian Holland

A rare opportunity for TV viewers to see in action Bobby Thompson – the man who has been acclaimed, with justification, as the North-East's finest comic. By the time of this programme Thompson was 72 (he was born in 1910 into a poor mining family) and had been treading the boards in local working men's clubs for some 20 years, but he had

rarely ventured outside of the region or appeared on TV. Much of Thompson's comic material drew upon the circumstances of his beloved north-east region – unemployment, debt, aggression and the working classes – making him a particular favourite for those there who identified with such issues.

Six days before this programme, C4 screened a half-hour documentary (*Bobby Thompson ... The Little Waster*, directed by Jim Goldby for Tyne Tees) that painted a portrait of this remarkable man.

Bodger And Badger

UK · BBC · CHILDREN'S SITCOM

110×15 mins · colour

Series One (8) 13 Sep–1 Nov 1989 · BBC1 Wed 4.05pm

Series Two (12) 9 Jan–27 Mar 1991 · BBC1 Wed 3.50pm

Series Three (12) 1 Oct–17 Dec 1991 · BBC1 Tue 3.55pm

Series Four (9) 13 Sep–8 Nov 1993 · BBC1 Mon 3.55pm

Series Five (13) 9 Jan–3 Apr 1995 · BBC1 Mon 3.45pm

Series Six (12) 15 Jan–27 Mar 1996 · BBC1 mostly Mon 3.55pm

Series Seven (29) 9 Sep 1996–24 Mar 1997 · BBC1 mostly Mon 3.55pm

Series Eight (15) 15 Dec 1997– 30 Mar 1998 · BBC1 Mon 4pm

MAIN CAST
Simon Bodger · · · · · · · · · Andy Cunningham
Mavis · · · · · · · · · Joanne Campbell (series 1)
Mr Troff · · · · · · · · · · Roger Walker (series 1)
Mrs Trout · · · · · · · · Lila Kaye (series 2 & 3)
Miss Moon · · · · · Selina Cadell (series 2 & 3)
Brains · · · · · · · · Andrew Fraser (series 2 & 3)
Danny · · · · · · · Neil Kattenhorn (series 2 & 3)
Millie/ ·
Mousey · · · · · Jane Bassett (from series 5)
Mrs Dribelle · · Carol Macready (series 6 & 7)
Alec Smart · · · · · · · Ricky Diamond (series 8)
Miss Peake · · · · · · · Valerie Minifie (series 8)
Mrs Bobbins · · · · · · · · · · Jo Warne (series 8)
Mr Tucknott · · · · · · · · Bill Thomas (series 8)

CREDITS
creator/main writer Andy Cunningham · *other writers* Wayne Jackman, Jane Bassett, Pierre Hollins · *director* Claire Winyard (series 2 & 3) · *executive producer* Judy Whitfield · *producers* Judy Whitfield (series 1), Greg Childs (series 2), Christine Hewitt (series 6 onwards) [other credits not known]

A sitcom aimed at young children that originally followed the adventures of an odd-job man, Simon Bodger, and his pet badger (a puppet). In the first series Bodger worked at Troff's Nosherama where he tried to keep the existence of his badger a secret. The second and third series had the pair at Letsby Avenue Junior School, where once again Simon tried to hide Badger from prying eyes. The fourth series found Bodger looking for new jobs and the fifth and sixth saw the

emphasis move away from Bodger's involvement towards a straight puppet series that followed the escapades of Badger and his friend Mousey. The format changed slightly in the eighth series, when the three main characters and Millie ran a seaside hotel, Seagull's Rest.

Note. Bodger And Badger made a guest appearance in *The Red Nose Zone*, the Children's BBC contribution to **Comic Relief**, screened by BBC1 on 14 March 1997.

Bold As Brass

UK · BBC · SITCOM

7 episodes (6×25 mins · 1×60 mins) · b/w

Special (60 mins) *Man O' Brass* 28 Nov 1963 · Thu 9.35pm

One series (6×25 mins) 4 Apr–13 June 1964 · BBC1 fortnightly Sat mostly 8.05pm

MAIN CAST
Ernie Briggs · · · · · · · · · · · · Jimmy Edwards
Bessie Briggs · · · · · · · · · · · · · · · Beryl Reid
Peggy Briggs · · · · · · · Diane Aubrey (special);
· Jill Hyem (series)
Dennis Blaney · · · · · · David Kernan (special)
Mr Longbottom · · · · · · · Wallas Eaton (special)
Mr Oakroyd · · · · · · · · Ronnie Barker (series)
Jack · · · · · · · · · · · · · · Ronnie Brody (series)
Mr Thursby · · · · · · · · · · Ernest Arnley (series)
Harry Parker · · · · · · · · · Bill Treacher (series)

CREDITS
creator Ron Watson · *writers* Ron Watson (special), Ron Watson/David Climie (series) · *producers* Douglas Moodie (special), Philip Barker (series)

A single hour-length comedy in 1963, *Man O' Brass*, introduced viewers to brass-band enthusiast Ernie Briggs and his wife Bessie who failed to see the attraction of music or musicians. The episode was set in the North, with Edwards (an accomplished musician in real life) playing the double B flat bass brass in the local band.

The partnership of Jimmy Edwards and Beryl Reid proved successful enough to launch a series about the couple, *Bold As Brass*, the following year. Described as 'a sort of Paunch and Judy Show', the series was a variation of the traditional sitcom format, permitting musical guest stars to appear, among them the great violinist Stephane Grappelli. Rising comedy actor Ronnie Barker was one of the minor players.

Bombardier Secombe Back Among The Boys

see SECOMBE, Harry

Bonehead

UK · BBC · CHILDREN'S SITCOM

15×25 mins · b/w

Series One (6) 1 Oct–29 Oct 1960 · Sat 5.25pm

Series Two (5) 29 July–26 Aug 1961 · Sat 5.25pm
Series Three (4) 14 July–11 Aug 1962 · Sat 5.25pm

MAIN CAST
Bonehead · · · · · · · · · · · · · · Colin Douglas
Boss · · · · · · · · · · · · Paul Whitsun-Jones
Happy · · · · · · · · · · · · · · Douglas Blackwell
PC Pilchard · · · · · · · · · · · · · Bruce Gordon

CREDITS
writer/producer Shaun Sutton

Described by its creator Shaun Sutton as 'A weekly reminder that crime doesn't pay', *Bonehead* depicted the misfortunes of the most inept bunch of crooks ever known to television viewers. Bonehead himself was the gang's muscle but his inability to hold more than a single thought in his head at any one time was usually behind the failure of the gang's plans.

Bonjour La Classe

UK · BBC (TALKBACK PRODUCTIONS) · SITCOM
6 × 30 mins · colour
15 Feb–22 Mar 1993 · BBC1 Mon 8.30pm

MAIN CAST
STAFF:
Laurence Didcott · · · · · · · · · · · Nigel Planer
Leslie Piper · · · · · · · · · Nicholas Woodeson
Jean Halifax · · · · · · · · · · · · · Polly Adams
Mr Wigley · · · · · · · · · · · · · Timothy Bateson
Harriet Humphrey · · · · · · · · Victoria Carling
Gilbert Herring · · · · · · · · · Robert Gillespie
Eric Sweety · · · · · · · · · · · David Troughton
PUPILS:
Adam Huntley · · · · · · · · · · · · · Bryan Dick
Lucy Cornwall · · · · · · · · · · Rebecca Callard
Hugo Botney · · · · · · · · · · · Daniel Newman
Anthony Zalacosta · · · · · · · · Simeon Pearl

CREDITS
writers Paul Smith/Terry Kyan · director John Henderson · producer Jamie Rix

Schools have been a fertile ground for sitcoms, viz *Whack-O!*, *Please, Sir!*, the infamous *Hardwicke House*, *Chalk*, *Head Of The Class* and *Welcome Back, Kotter*. Observing the chaos visited upon a fee-paying independent school by its new French teacher Laurence Didcott, *Bonjour La Classe*, like its predecessors, divided its time between the classroom and the staff room, most of the humour arising from the interplay between the masters and Didcott, a naïve, desperately keen and uncompromisingly honest man who was a stickler for the rules. Didcott's honesty proved especially damaging because his forthright views and unintentionally callous candour often caused outrage and the airing of embarrassing facts best kept concealed. But he remained oblivious to the effects of his personality and the angst he caused, and thick-skinned in regard to the withering criticisms levelled at him by his colleagues.

Didcott's pupils were a bright and well-spoken lot, not averse to using their master's idiosyncrasies to suit their own ends, and at least they looked like schoolchildren, unlike the members of Class 5C in *Please, Sir!* who looked like a group of late-twenty-something delinquents. But after one series *Bonjour La Classe* was not recommissioned – it suffered from a distinct lack of edge and may have benefited from a (small) dose of the sort of bad taste that had *Hardwicke House* prematurely forced off the screen.

Bonkers!

see MONKHOUSE, Bob

Bonny!

UK · BBC · CHILDREN'S SITCOM
10 × 30 mins · colour
Series One (4) 4 Mar–25 Mar 1974 · BBC1 Mon 5.15pm
Series Two (6) 20 Aug–24 Sep 1974 · BBC1 Tue mostly 5.15pm

MAIN CAST
Flora Havers/Capt Bonny · · · · · Una McLean
Mr Knott/Grannyknott · · · · · · · · Walter Carr
Auld Jock/Toothy · · · · · · · · · · · Alex McAvoy
Mr Black/Blackbeard · · · · · · · · · Ian Collier
Rev Swash/ ·
Swashbuckle · · · · · · · · · · Jon Yule (series 1)
Billy/Billy Bones · · · Gordon Belbin (series 1)

CREDITS
writers John Morley (8), Philip Griffin/Paul Ciani/John Morley (1), Philip Griffin/Paul Ciani (1) · producer Paul Ciani

A Scottish fantasy sitcom for younger viewers featuring Una McLean as Flora Havers: by day, the meek, mild-mannered postmistress in the Highlands village of Ballikillern, but by night the writer of exciting adventure stories. Her secret writings come to life and Flora, in her alter ego as Captain Bonny, becomes locked in a battle with the evil Mr Black. By the second series, Flora's writings were no longer secret and had been turned into a successful TV show, earning her money and fame. She then found herself able to live out real-life adventures in the style of her Bonny creation.

A later, similar series, *Supergran*, also followed the far-fetched exploits of a feisty heroine battling against evil-doers.

Book 'Em An' Risk It

UK · C4 (BRIGHT THOUGHTS) · STANDUP
1 × 60 mins · colour
11 Aug 1983 · Thu 10.30pm

MAIN CAST
Jim Barclay
Arnold Brown
Jock McLog and McNikki
The Oblivion Boys (Mark Arden/Stephen Frost)

Adrian Hedley
Trimmer and Jenkins
The Chip Shop Show
Cathy La Creme
The Joeys
Steve Dixon

CREDITS
writers cast · director Bryan Izzard · producers Neil Anthony, Bryan Izzard

An honest title for a show that was perhaps more hit than miss but worth the effort all the same. Rather like the pop groups left behind in the Cavern Club in 1963 after the original batch had found fame, the acts here were those who were working the stage at the Comedy Store and Comic Strip clubs in London after the first generation (Mayall, Edmondson, Planer, French, Saunders, Coltrane, Sayle, Elton, etc) had attained stardom. Some of these second-wave acts achieved a moderate degree of success and most were assured at least of a long career on the standup circuit.

Oddly, the entire show was performed in the foyer of the Royal Festival Hall, London, in front of a motley audience of fans, a few bystanders, some wearied commissionaires and people outside, looking in through the window.

Boom Boom … Out Go The Lights

UK · BBC · SKETCH/STANDUP
2 × 30 mins · colour
14 Oct 1980 · BBC2 Tue 10.20pm
5 May 1981 · BBC2 Tue 9.45pm

MAIN CAST
Rik Mayall
Nigel Planer
Alexei Sayle
Tony Allen
Keith Allen (show 1)
Adrian Edmondson (show 2)
Peter Richardson (show 2)
Andy de la Tour (show 2)
Pauline Melville (show 2)

CREDITS
writers cast · producer Paul Jackson

At the end of the 1970s a slew of new comedy talent began working in Britain. By 1980, this influx of fresh faces was large enough in number to prompt the opening of new comedy venues. (Usually these were rooms hired on a once-a-week basis, though there were a few dedicated clubs.) the Comedy Store in London, which opened on 19 May 1979 and was based on The Comedy Store in Los Angeles, quickly became established as the pre-eminent venue on the circuit and inevitably attracted interest from TV producers keen to spot new talent. BBC producer Paul Jackson was the first to succeed in presenting that new talent on the small-screen in *Boom Boom … Out Go The Lights*, a modest cabaret-style half-hour that, retrospectively, can be considered of seminal importance.

Peter Rosengard, an insurance salesman and major comedy fan, had launched the Comedy Store after being impressed by the original US club during a trip to Los Angeles. There was currently a huge following for live comedy in America, where a new generation of feisty standup acts had appeared, giving rise to the subsequently oft-used saying that 'comedy was the new rock and roll'. Now, a few years later, a similar phenomenon was occurring in Britain, with many of the emerging acts rebelling against their predecessors' style, material and presentation. They were also united in their disrespect for TV and its reliance upon cosy, innocuous family sitcoms and standup acts who were either staid or sexually and racially offensive. These were possibly the only unifying factors that the many diverse acts had in common, although the majority were left-wing. They all seemed to share a philosophy that ensured their humour savaged middle-class morality, political hypocrisy, religious inadequacy and business duplicity, rallying equally against sexism, racism and homophobia. It was not all diatribe, however: there was also obscene language, some very funny lines and, occasionally, worryingly violent slapstick.

Jackson gathered together some ringleaders of this 'new wave' and obtained one day of BBC studio time to tape them. Although Rik Mayall and Adrian Edmondson, and Nigel Planer and Peter Richardson, were performing on the circuit as double-acts, Jackson opted to present Mayall solo, performing his mock poetry, and Nigel Planer in his hippy-character guise, Neil (later reprised as 'neil' in *The Young Ones*).Thus Edmondson and Richardson didn't appear in the first show. Ruby Wax also performed but her part was cut from the transmitted version. The other contributors performed material from their existing acts, with Alexei Sayle's aggressive style and use of bad language causing some problems, and Keith Allen and Tony Allen unable to resist adding some caustic lines pertaining to the TV experience. A second show went out in 1981 which displayed the growing confidence and professionalism of the acts. Neither show attracted a sizeable audience or much critical interest but they introduced to television a good deal of the talent that would change the face of TV comedy in the 1980s.

Note. The show's title came from the fact that Jackson's budget didn't permit him to commission a signature tune, so instead he chose 'Boom Boom … Out Go The Lights', one of the songs on the playlist of musical guests Paul Jones and the Blues Band. (Playing in the second show were Dexy's Midnight Runners.)

The Boot Street Band

UK · BBC · CHILDREN'S SITCOM

12 × 25 mins · colour

Series One (6) 11 Nov–16 Dec 1993 · BBC1 Thu 4.35pm

Series Two (6) 10 Nov–15 Dec 1994 · BBC1 Thu 4.20pm

MAIN CAST

STAFF:

Mr K Lear	Roland MacLeod
Mrs Springit	Linda Polan
Dai Cramp	Richard Davies (series 1); Peter Woodthorpe (series 2)
Mr Prince	Gerald Home
Clarissa Trump	Janie Dee (series 2)

PUPILS:

Mikala	Nadia Williams
Ruth	Suzy Weitz
Joe	Alexander Ward
Dobbsy	James Hunt
Egbert	Jonathan Cordell
Linda	Lisa O'Connell
Rampur	Sanjay Shelat
Curly McCabe	Joe Gazzano
Spike	Idreas Elba
Blocknose	Adam Beard

CREDITS

writers Andrew Davies/Steve Attridge (series 1), Steve Attridge (series 2) · *director* John Smith · *producer* Angela Beeching

Many children's programmes are labelled comedy-drama to explain their light style but *The Boot Street Band* was genuinely funny; had it been recorded in front of a studio audience it would have garnered many laughs.

On the surface, Boot Street School was an ordinary enough establishment, but underneath was a different story. The everyday running of the school was carried out by a team of pupils from Class 4D who called themselves 'The Management'. They sorted out all of the problems and glitches that occurred, which was just as well because the headmaster, Mr Lear, was a *bona fide* fruitcake. And this wasn't the full extent of The Management's activities either, for they also ran a highly successful business using the school's equipment (such as computers) and, by way of a massive recycling plant that they had constructed as a science project, they were turning waste produce into saleable items which they then distributed to chains of shops. Opposition to their schemes came from Deputy Headmistress Mrs Springit, and the caretaker, Dai Cramp, who fawned over her. A more serious threat came in the second series from efficient school secretary Clarissa Trump, who could be as devious as members of The Management.

Basically, the set up was a school *Bilko*, and it was a well-made piece with uniformly good acting and an occasional streak of weirdness – as in the case of Mr Prince, who was still teaching at the school despite dressing

entirely in a dog costume and being unable to utter anything except 'woof'.

Bootle Saddles

UK · BBC · SITCOM

6 × 30 mins · colour

10 Sep–15 Oct 1984 · BBC2 Mon 8.30pm

MAIN CAST

Percy James	Kenneth Cope
Isobel James	Anne Carroll
Betty James	Debbie Arnold
Tom Henderson	John Normington
Rita Henderson	Shirley Stelfox
The Kid	Gordon Rollings
Cyril	Robert Owen
Bert	Mike Walling

CREDITS

writers Ray Mansell/Paul Benn · *director/producer* David Askey

Six humorous meditations on the nature of obsessions, depicting a bunch of cowboy fanatics whose hobby is re-creating the Wild West, complete with full costume, horses and all the incumbent clichés of the genre. For the protagonists this is no ordinary pastime: the western scenario brings out their most fervent passions, and often threatens to take over their real lives.

The comedy arose from the British northerners' earnest yet often ham-fisted attempts to emulate the gun-slinging, baccy-chewing, spittoon-pinging, rye-drinking anti-heroes of the American West.

Bootsie And Snudge

UK · ITV (GRANADA) · SITCOM

104 × 30 mins (98 × b/w · 6 × colour)

Series One (40 × b/w) 23 Sep 1960–23 June 1961 · Fri 8.55pm

Series Two (29 × b/w) 27 Oct 1961–10 May 1962 · Fri 8.55pm then Thu 8.30pm

Series Three (29 × b/w) 8 Nov 1962–30 May 1963 · Thu 7.30pm

Series Four (6 × colour) 16 Oct–20 Nov 1974 · Wed 8.30pm

MAIN CAST

Montague 'Bootsie' Bisley	Alfie Bass
Claude Snudge	Bill Fraser
Henry Beerbohm Johnson	Clive Dunn (series 1–3)
Rt Hon Sec Hesketh Pendleton	Robert Dorning (series 1–3)

CREDITS 1960–63

writers Marty Feldman/Barry Took (32), Marty Feldman/Barry Took/John Antrobus (10), Marty Feldman/Barry Took/Ray Rigby (1), Marty Feldman (10), Marty Feldman/David Cumming/Derek Collyer (1), Barry Took (13), Barry Took/Peter Miller/James Kelly (1), Barry Took/Hugh Woodhouse (1), John Antrobus (2), Ray Whyberd (Ray Alan, 11), Peter Miller/James Kelly (8), David Cumming/Derek Collyer (3), Peter Lambda (1), Stanley Myers/Tom Espie (1), Jack Rosenthal/Harry Driver (1), Patrick Ryan (1), John Smith/Doug Eden (1) · *producers* Peter Eton (82), Eric Fawcett

(8), Milo Lewis (8) · *directors* Milo Lewis (78), Eric Fawcett (18), Derek Bennett (2)

CREDITS 1974
writers David Climie/Ronnie Cass, Lew Schwarz · *director/producer* Bill Podmore

Two of the most popular personalities in the very successful Granada sitcom **The Army Game** were Private 'Excused Boots' Bisley (played by Alfie Bass) and Sergeant-Major Claude Snudge (Bill Fraser). Not only were both characters rich in terms of comic exploitation but there was a special interplay between the two – Snudge revelled in his position of superiority over Bootsie, while Bootsie felt comfortable in his inferior role because it allowed him to mock, and indeed hate, Snudge and, in so doing, jeer at authority in general. So while the parent series continued, the pair were 'demobbed' and given a series of their own, *Bootsie And Snudge*. (The first six episodes were actually titled *Bootsie And Snudge In Civvy Life*.)

Continuing their hostile relationship as idle dreamer and bully, respectively, Bootsie and Snudge remained a 'partnership' and were employed as handyman and hall porter at the Imperial, a Pall Mall (Central London) gentlemen's club run by a hot-headed secretary, the Rt Hon Sec Hesketh Pendleton, and wherein worked an employee of some 40 years, Henry Beebohm Johnson. This was yet another 'old man' TV role for comedian Clive Dunn (he was 38 when the series started in 1960 and was playing an 83-year-old), and almost all of the bumbling, befuddled traits that he would later bring to the part of Corporal Jones in *Dad's Army* were evident – Old Johnson's addled mind convinced him to believe, at first, that Snudge was Lord Kitchener returned to life, and he was prone to prattling on about the 'fuzzy-wuzzies'. Snudge assumed a position of superiority over Johnson too, but Bootsie recognised a kindred spirit in the old man and proved to be a sympathetic ally.

Storylines centred nominally around complications caused by the Imperial's members and guests but mostly around the inter-relationships between the four staff and, in particular, Bootsie and Snudge. Ahead of its time in some ways – **Steptoe And Son** and **Porridge** would later pick up the two-men-trapped-together mantle – the dialogue between the pair was tetchy at best, although both had defeat etched into their voices no matter what position they were assuming in the verbal battle. Extending to 98 episodes, some of the half-hours, inevitably, were weak, but others were outstanding, and brave ideas were tried, one episode pastiching Hitchcock's classic movie *Rear Window*, for example. Marty Feldman and Barry Took (together, alone and with others) wrote the majority of

the episodes, and were also script editors for part of the time, but had moved on to pastures new by the third and last original series in 1962–63. (Ray Whyberd, another of the writers, was a pseudonym for Ray Alan, better known as the Lord Charles/Tich and Quackers ventriloquist.) A number of future TV stars – among them Geoffrey Palmer, Dudley Foster, Honor Blackman, Warren Mitchell and Mollie Sugden – passed through the series in minor roles when relatively or completely unknown, and it remained popular from start to finish.

In 1964 Bootsie and Snudge moved into the diplomatic service in **Foreign Affairs** and then the names were laid to rest until an unsuccessful one-series revival in 1974 when, in a reversal of positions and following a period of separation, Bootsie wins a million pounds and 27 pence on the football pools and has to suffer Snudge, hitherto an employee of Permapools, in a subservient role as his self-appointed financial adviser.

Victor Borge

Born as Borg Rosenbaum in Copenhagen on 3 January 1909, Victor Borge studied music from the age of four and went on to become the most famous entertainer in Denmark when he combined his musical prowess with comedy patter, embracing a superb sense of timing in both spheres. In the 1930s he was his country's most popular performer, but in 1940, when the Nazis took over his home country, Borge fled to America fearing retribution for the savage ridicule he had hitherto heaped upon Hitler and his cohorts. After a long period as support on US radio in *The Bing Crosby Show*, and then his own series *The Victor Borge Show* (1943–51, NBC then ABC), Borge took his one-man show on the road and, after a slow start, eventually won audiences over in a big way. Such was his reputation that *Radio Times* gave Borge the front cover to announce his British television debut on 31 July 1956.

Borge subsequently performed on British TV with some regularity, including a definitive 1974 BBC2 series, and he has continued to appear in concert all over the world, delighting audiences with his bone-dry, intelligent wit. (Although credited as the author of his shows, Borge is reputed to have employed scriptwriters, however.)

Victor Borge Presents … Comedy In Music

UK · BBC · MUSICAL HUMOUR
4 × various lengths · b/w
31 July 1956 · Tue 8.30pm (45 mins)

16 June 1958 · Mon 8.20pm (55 mins)
30 Aug 1959 · Sun 7.30pm (60 mins)
29 Sep 1964 · BBC1 Tue 8pm (50 mins)
MAIN CAST
Victor Borge
CREDITS
writer Victor Borge · *producers* Barry Lupino (shows 1 & 2), Bryan Sears (show 3), Ernest Maxin (show 4)

Specially presented versions of Borge's long-running Broadway show.

Borge Presents Borge / Borge Encore

UK · ITV (THAMES) · MUSICAL HUMOUR
2 editions (1 × 60 mins · 1 × 45 mins) · b/w
Borge Presents Borge 24 Dec 1968 · Tue 10.30pm
Borge Encore 18 Mar 1969 · Tue 10.30pm
MAIN CAST
Victor Borge
CREDITS
writer Victor Borge · *producer* Peter Frazer-Jones

Two programmes of material written especially by the Danish musical comedian for ITV, presenting more of his unique blend of classical piano and wry, dry humour.

The LP Show With Victor Borge

UK · ITV (LWT) · MUSICAL HUMOUR
1 × 60 mins · colour
24 Dec 1972 · Sun 10pm
MAIN CAST
Victor Borge
Sahan Arzruni
Maina Gielgud
CREDITS
writer Victor Borge · *script associate* Eric Merriman · *director* Bruce Gowers

A Christmas special. The LP in the title referred to the London Philharmonic Orchestra.

The Complete Victor Borge

UK · BBC · MUSICAL HUMOUR
6 × 30 mins · colour
31 Oct–5 Dec 1974 · BBC2 Thu 9.30pm
MAIN CAST
Victor Borge
OCCASIONAL APPEARANCES
Marilyn Mulvey
CREDITS
writer Victor Borge · *director* Alan Boyd · *producer* James Moir

Six weekly programmes in BBC2's *Show Of The Week* slot. The aim was an ambitious one, but joyously fulfilled: Borge performed *all* of his preferred stage routines. The shows were recorded in front of an audience, taped over six successive nights, and were an outstanding success – probably the pinnacle of Borge's worldwide TV endeavours and certainly his best exposure on British screens.

Victor Borge In Concert

UK · ITV (THAMES) · MUSICAL HUMOUR

1 × 60 mins · colour

27 June 1979 · Wed 8pm

MAIN CAST

Victor Borge

CREDITS

writer Victor Borge · *director/producer* Robert Reed

A TV taping of Borge's *Tinkling The Ivories, Tickling The Ribs* concert at Wembley Conference Centre, edited down from the full three hours.

Borge's next major appearance on British TV was in an ITV screening of the charity concert *A Gala Evening* on 12 September 1982.

Born And Bred

UK · ITV (THAMES) · SITCOM/DRAMA

12 × 60 mins · colour

Series One (6) 13 Sep–18 Oct 1978 · Wed 9pm

Series Two (6) 2 Sep–7 Oct 1980 · Tue 9pm

MAIN CAST

Frank Benge	James Grout
Daphne Benge	Gillian Raine
Stephen Benge	Richard O'Callaghan
Ray Benge	Gorden Kaye
Marge Benge	Kate Williams
Annie Benge	Rose Hill
Iris Tonsley	Susan Tracy
Tommy Tonsley	Max Wall
Rose Tonsley	Constance Chapman
Dennis Tonsley	Trevor Peacock
Shirley Tonsley	Helen Cotterill
Molly Peglar	Joan Sims
Arthur Peglar	Ivor Roberts
Pam Redstone	Susie Blake
Paul Redstone	Ian Redford

CREDITS

writer Douglas Livingstone · *producers* Peter Duguid (series 1), Tim Aspinall (series 2) · *directors* Derek Bennett (3), Robert Tronson (3), Baz Taylor (2), Gareth Davies (2), Peter Duguid (2)

The Tonsleys and the Benges – two large inter-related south London families – reunite when the oldest member of the family is awarded a British Empire medal, but they remain far from convinced that blood is thicker than water.

Through two series of hour-long Thames black-comedy-dramas, with such veteran names as Max Wall and Joan Sims among the cast, the clans were ever at loggerheads, but all came good at the end.

See also *Cockles*.

Born Every Minute

UK · BBC · SITCOM

1 × 30 mins · colour

28 Jan 1972 · BBC1 Fri 7.30pm

MAIN CAST

Harry	Ronald Fraser
Johnny	James Beck
Girl	Juliet Harmer
Sir Rufus	Campbell Singer
Lady Wright	Mollie Sugden

CREDITS

writer Jack Popplewell · *producer* David Croft

Moonlighting from *Dad's Army*, James Beck co-starred with Ronald Fraser in this *Comedy Playhouse* pilot set in the world of con men. Harry and Johnny are partners in a scheme to swindle rich Sir Rufus, but deadly rivals for the attentions of a pretty girl.

Bosom Buddies

USA · ABC (MILLER-MILKIS-BOYETT PRODUCTIONS/PARAMOUNT) · SITCOM

37 × 30 mins · colour

US dates: 26 Nov 1980–26 May 1982

UK dates: 17 July 1982–13 Apr 1984 (18 episodes) ITV mostly Fri 11pm

MAIN CAST

Kip/Buffy Wilson	Tom Hanks
Henry/Hildegarde Desmond	Peter Scolari
Amy Cassidy	Wendie Jo Sperber
Sonny Lumet	Donna Dixon
Ruth Dunbar	Holland Taylor
Isabelle Hammond	Telma Hopkins
Lilly Sinclair	Lucille Benson (1980–81)

CREDITS

creators Robert L Boyett, Thomas L Miller, Chris Thompson · *writers* Chris Thompson (7), Lenny Ripps (7), Jack Carrerow/David Chambers (5), David Chambers (2), Terry Hart (2), David Lerner/Bruce Ferber (2), Gary H Miller (2), Chris Thompson/Howard Gewirtz/Ian Pariser (1), Gary H Miller/Jack Carrerow (1), Ian Pariser/Howard Gewirtz (1), Terry Hart/Lenny Ripps (1), Terry Hart/Jeff Franklin (1), Jack Carrerow (1), Jeff Franklin (1), Roger Garrett (1), Stu Silver (1), Will MacKenzie (1) · *directors* Joel Zwick (19), Will MacKenzie (7), Chris Thompson/Don Van Atta (4), John Bowab (3), John Tracy (2), Herb Kenwith (1), Tom Trbovich (1) · *executive producers* Chris Thompson, Thomas L Miller, Edward K Milkis, Robert L Boyett · *producers* Don Van Atta and others

It is almost forgotten now that screen giant and heart-throb Tom Hanks started off his career in a TV sitcom. And a fairly good one at that, blessed with some witty scripts that never took the job in hand too seriously. The plot clearly borrowed from the Jack Lemmon/ Tony Curtis/Marilyn Monroe movie *Some Like It Hot*, for in *Bosom Buddies* two good-looking young men and very close friends, Kip Wilson and Henry Desmond, dressed up as women.

This is why: without a place to stay in Manhattan after their old apartment block is demolished (almost with them still inside), the two men's advertising-agency colleague Amy informs them about a vacancy where she lives, the rent stable at only $150 a month. The trouble is, it's the Susan B Anthony Hotel, open only to women. Although it seems preposterous, the men are desperate for shelter (and fancy the idea of seeing women walking freely around in states of undress), so, with Amy's assistance, they drag themselves up as their fictional sisters and, remarkably, pass muster. Spikily, each gives the other a ghastly name: Kip introduces Henry as Hildegarde, while Henry retaliates by introducing his friend as Buffy; they hate the names but are stuck with them, and each continues to make life hard for the other by weaving them into fabricated, complicated stories. From this point on, we see the two lead actors in both male and female roles for most of the series. Men find them attractive and want dates. Kip and Henry, however, still want women: Kip is more than interested in Amy's sexy room-mate Sonny while Amy herself desires Henry.

Towards the end of the two-year run, the two men reveal their true selves (bringing an end to the cross-dressing) and also switch jobs, taking over an independent commercial production company formerly run by Henry's uncle. Here they again work alongside Amy, who has also made the switch, and are baled out, financially, by their former boss Ruth, who becomes a sleeping majority shareholder in the firm.

Both Ends Meet

UK · ITV (LWT) · SITCOM

13 × 30 mins · colour

Series One (7) 19 Feb–1 Apr 1972 · Sat mostly 5.10pm

Series Two (6) *Dora* 29 Sep–10 Nov 1972 · Fri 8.30pm

MAIN CAST

Dora Page	Dora Bryan
Ronnie Page	David Howe (series 1);
	Peter Vaughan Clarke (series 2)
Julius Cannon	Ivor Dean
Maudie	Wendy Richard
Glad	Pat Ashton
Flo	Deddie Davies
George Rogers	Timothy Bateson
Hilda Rogers	Fanny Carby
Mrs Templeton-Smythe	Joan Benham (series 1)
Mr Page	Meadows White (series 1)

BOTH ENDS MEET CREDITS

writers Brian Chasser/Len Downs/Mike Firman/ Patrick Radcliffe · *script editor* Lew Schwarz · *producers* Philip Casson (4), Mark Stuart (3)

DORA CREDITS

writers Tom Boyd/Stanley Segal/Jessica Taylor · *director* George Evans · *producer* Mark Stuart

Veteran film, TV and stage comic actress Dora Bryan starred in this LWT sitcom, cast as Dora Page, a cash-strapped widow who has to raise her son Ronnie while working at the factory of Cannon's Family Sausages, run by Julius Cannon. The first series of seven episodes went out as *Both Ends Meet* but the second was titled simply *Dora*. The filling was much the same, however.

Bottle Boys

UK · ITV (LWT) · SITCOM

13 × 30 mins · colour

Series One (6) 1 Sep–6 Oct 1984 · Sat 7.30pm
Series Two (7) 13 July–24 Aug 1985 · Sat mostly 7.15pm

MAIN CAST

Dave Deacon · · · · · · · · · · · · · Robin Askwith
Billy Watson · · · · · · · · · · · · · · David Auker
Joe Phillips · · · · · · · · · · · · · · · Oscar James
Jock Collins · · · · · · · · · · · · · · Phil McCall
Stan Evans · · · · · · · · · · · · · Richard Davies
Sharon Armstrong · · · · · · · · · · · · Eve Ferret
Mr Dawson · · · · · · · Patrick Newell (series 1)
Wilf Foley · · · · · · · · · · · · · · · · Leo Dolan

OTHER APPEARANCES

Harry · Alan Gear

CREDITS

writer Vince Powell · directors Stuart Allen (12), Nic Phillips (1) · producer Stuart Allen

Star of the oh-so-British series of saucy *Confessions* movies, Robin Askwith was the leading man in *Bottle Boys*, portraying an accident-prone football-mad milkman doing the rounds for Dawson Diaries, based in south London. His fellow milkmen were blokish and berkish – among them Jock the boozy Scotsman, teddy-boy Billy Watson and Joe the obligatory black, while Stan was the Welsh-born depot manager and Sharon his big-boobed, unable-to-type secretary.

The series was predictably high on low-brow humour and slapstick, but, while his impish grin was much in evidence, viewers were at least spared the famed Askwith derriere that had loomed so large and so often on British cinema screens in the 1970s. They were, however, treated to the sight of the actor sporting chicken and cow costumes (don't ask) and performing such dangerous stunts as clinging from a sixth-floor parapet and meeting Mrs Thatcher (not the real one, of course). It is with a certain degree of relief that one notes that, reputedly, *Bottle Boys* was despised within ITV circles and its lack of political correctness was the last straw for certain of its comedy executives. ITV sitcoms had often plumbed the depths, but this was the limit.

Bottom

UK · BBC · SITCOM

18 × 30 mins · colour

Series One (6) 17 Sep–29 Oct 1991 · BBC2 Tue 9pm

*Series Two (5) 1 Oct–29 Oct 1992 · BBC2 Thu 9pm
Series Three (6) 6 Jan–10 Feb 1995 · BBC2 Fri 9pm
*Special · 10 Apr 1995 · BBC2 Mon 10pm

MAIN CAST

Richie Richard · · · · · · · · · · · · · · · Rik Mayall
Eddie Hitler · · · · · · · · · · Adrian Edmondson

CREDITS

writers Rik Mayall/Adrian Edmondson · directors Ed Bye (12), Bob Spiers (6) · producers Ed Bye (12), Jon Plowman (6)

Adventures in the sordid life of two of the world's most repellent bachelors. Double-act Rik Mayall and Ade Edmondson, who have both enjoyed individual successes, wrote and performed this series which tapped the anarchic, sick, violent slapstick style of their earlier stage act.

As Richie Richard and Eddie Hitler, they portrayed a pair of nasty, unhygienic, vicious, self-centred, arrogant slobs who share a squalid flat and spend as much time ridiculing, irritating and maiming each other as they do terrifying any poor misfortunates who stray into their lives. Hopelessly inadequate at the nitty-gritty of everyday life, the pair pour all their energies into drinking, gluttony, masturbating and gambling. Episodes often explode into violence with the pair clouting each other with heavy industrial equipment, or causing eye-watering pain to each others genitalia with pliers or similar instruments. Explosions and fires were also commonplace.

Bottom was intentionally and unashamedly juvenile, with even its title pointing to the schoolboy nature of its humour. Mayall and Edmondson had originally named the show *Your Bottom* and delighted in the double entendres that it might present (eg, 'I saw *Your Bottom* on television last night'), but, eventually, they settled on the more succinct *Bottom* and instead derived pleasure from the suffixed episode titles (eg, *Bottom*: Smells, and *Bottom*: 's Up). Its gross bad taste alienated some viewers but, like a pile of mildewing Y-fronts, *Bottom* wasn't short of support, as proven by its successes on stage in 1993, 1995 and 1997 when the pair took 'stronger' versions of the show on tour around British theatres. Rude, crude and of dubious social value, *Bottom* was nevertheless a lively and funny attempt at producing something that only existed to make people laugh and had no moral standpoint or base in reality. Part of its grotesque allure was the strange fascination of the sleazy lifestyle it portrayed, which caused viewers to squirm but kept them hooked, much as the squeamish may be drawn to watch a televised operation.

*Note. The sixth and final episode of Series Two was pulled from transmission as its subject matter – Eddie and Richie living rough on Wimbledon Common – coincided with a horrific real-life murder at the same location. It was also missed out from repeat runs but finally surfaced a few weeks after the end of the third series in 1995.

The Bounder

UK · ITV (YORKSHIRE) · SITCOM

14 × 30 mins · colour

Series One (7) 16 Apr–28 May 1982 · Fri 8.30pm
Series Two (7) 16 Sep–28 Oct 1983 · Fri 8.30pm

MAIN CAST

Howard Booth · · · · · · · · · · · · · Peter Bowles
Trevor Mountjoy · · · · · · · · · · · · George Cole
Mary Mountjoy · · · · · · · · · · · Rosalind Ayres
Laura Miles · · · · · · · · · · · · · · · · Isla Blair

CREDITS

writer Eric Chappell · director/producer Vernon Lawrence

Howard Booth is a Raffles-like cultured cad, newly released from open prison after serving two years for fraud. Sadly, jail has not altered him one jot, a fact that does not go unnoticed by his much put-upon brother-in-law Trevor Mountjoy, local estate agent and dour pillar of the business community. And there's no avoiding him: Howard moves in as the Mountjoys' lodger, a stay encouraged by his sister Mary (Trevor's wife), whom he manages to wrap around his finger.

As the title suggests, Howard is a bounder through and through, pathologically compelled to lie, cheat and deceive, suckering men and women alike, all of whom fall for his suave manner and Savile Row suits. One person not so easily conquered, however, is Laura, an attractive widow who lives next door to the Mountjoys and whom Howard pursues because she's wealthy.

The Bounder began while its star, Peter Bowles, was still appearing in another Eric Chappell creation, **Only When I Laugh** (indeed, Bowles told Yorkshire TV he'd only commit to another run of *OWIL* if he was also given his own series), and it returned George Cole to sitcoms, otherwise best known at this time for his wonderful portrayal of Arthur Daley in Thames' light-drama series *Minder*.

An American adaptation of *The Bounder* was made and screened, but failed to develop into a full series. CBS aired the pilot – also called *The Bounder* – on 7 July 1984, with Michael McKeown as Howard, Jeannette Arnette as his sister Bonnie, Richard Masur as her husband Charles and Francine Tacker as Laura, the next-door lovely.

Bowler

UK · ITV (LWT) · SITCOM

13 × 30 mins · colour

29 July–19 Oct 1973 · Sun 7.25pm then Fri 7.30pm

MAIN CAST

Stanley Bowler · · · · · · · · · · · George Baker
Reg · · · · · · · · · · · · · · · · · Fred Beauman
Doreen Bowler · · · · · · · · · · · · Renny Lister
Mum · · · · · · · · · · · · · · · Gretchen Franklin

CREDITS

writers John Esmonde/Bob Larbey · _directors/producers_ Philip Casson (9), Derrick Goodwin (4)

Written subsequently but as a 'prequel' to **The Fenn Street Gang** (itself spun-off from **Please, Sir!**), this sitcom harked back to the earlier life of Bowler, the wealthy wide-boy villain who can swagger his way into any situation but cannot grasp the things to which he truly aspires: urbanity and social class. Renny Lister appeared as his estranged wife Doreen, Gretchen Franklin as his cockney mum and Fred Beauman as his valet, Reg.

Boy Meets World

USA · ABC (MICHAEL JACOBS PRODUCTIONS/ TOUCHSTONE TELEVISION) · SITCOM

99 episodes (98 × 30 mins · 1 × 60 mins to 31/12/97 · continuing into 1998) · colour

US dates: 24 Sep 1993 to date

UK dates: 22 June 1994 to date (88 episodes to 31/12/97) C4 mostly Wed 6.30pm then Thurs 6pm

MAIN CAST

Cory Matthews · · · · · · · · · · · · Ben Savage
George Feeny · · · · · · · · · · · William Daniels
Amy Matthews · · · · · · · · · · · Betsy Randle
Eric Matthews · · · · · · · · · · · · Will Friedle
Shawn Hunter · · · · · · · · · · · · Rider Strong
Morgan Matthews · · Lily Nicksay (1993–96);
· · · · · · · · · · · · · · · · Lindsay Ridgeway (from 1997)
Topanga Lawrence · · · · · · · · Danielle Fishel
Alan Matthews · · · · · · William 'Rusty' Russ
Stuart Lempke/Minkus · · · · · · · · Lee Norris
· (1993–94)
Jonathan Turner · · · · · · · Anthony Tyler Quinn
· (from 1994)
Harley · · · · · · · · Danny McNulty (from 1994)
Frankie · · · · · · · · · Ethan Suplee (from 1994)
Joey · · · · · · · · · · · Blake Soper (from 1994)
Jack Newman · · · · · · · · Matthew Lawrence
· (from 1997)

CREDITS

creators Michael Jacobs/April Kelly · _writers_ various · _directors_ Jeff McCracken and others · _executive producers_ Michael Jacobs, Bob Young · _producers_ Arlene Grayson, Jeffrey C Sherman, Karen MacKain

Pitched as a contemporary version of **The Wonder Years**, _Boy Meets World_ starred Ben Savage (younger brother of that previous series' lead, Fred Savage) as Cory Matthews, a level-headed kid treading that difficult path between childhood and adulthood. The series followed Cory's journey, with stories revolving around the normal 'rites of passage' undergone by US TV teens. On hand to help or hinder Cory were his liberal parents Amy

and Alan, his cool elder brother Eric, his smart and cute kid sister Morgan, his best buddy Shawn and his girlfriend Topanga. Rounding out the principal cast was George Feeny, Cory's neighbour and elementary-school teacher who later became Cory's high-school teacher too. Feeny subscribed to the firm-but-fair method of teaching and was always willing to belie his gruff demeanour by offering some surprisingly streetwise snippets of advice when the occasion required.

Boy Meets World sported customary American TV moralistic undercurrents, with Cory learning valuable character-building lessons en route, but the series was knowing enough not to overplay this card and sufficiently canny to allow Cory to learn from each experience. Rarely has a series dealt so honestly with the ageing of its juvenile leads, with Cory, Morgan, Shawn and Topanga seeming to grow up quicker on screen than they were in real life. Instead of attempting artificially to hold them at a specific age, the producers embraced their maturation and efficiently exploited it.

Although not as classy as _The Wonder Years_, _Boy Meets World_ still had its moments. But its contemporary setting proved problematic, with the series seeming old-fashioned despite its overt attempts to cover modern-day issues. The hindsight factor of _The Wonder Years_ allowed the series to lovingly re-create a period of recent history, whereas TV tends to be a couple of years behind in its depiction of modern-day life. Another flaw was that _Boy Meets World_ tried hard to make all of its characters likeable and thereby eschewed the edge that would have provided some sorely needed bite.

Max Boyce

Born on 27 September 1943 in Glynneath, a small South Wales village which has remained his home, Max Boyce – who worked as a coal miner for a time – attained fame as a comedian from his performances on the folk club circuit. Much as Mike Harding, Billy Connolly and Jasper Carrott had, Boyce gradually added comedy and performed fewer songs as his act became more and more humorous, although his numerous albums continue to promote both talents.

Boyce's comic style draws upon the warmth, humour, sadness and passion of Welsh communities, and often centres upon Welsh fanaticism for rugby union. He has a phalanx of loyal fans in Wales and plenty more besides, as far afield as Australia and the Far East. Most of his British TV appearances originated with BBC Wales.

See also _How Green Was My Father._

Max Boyce Entertains

UK · BBC · STANDUP

1 × 50 mins · colour

28 Feb 1976 · BBC1 Sat 11.05pm

MAIN CAST

Max Boyce

CREDITS

writer Max Boyce · _producer_ Jack Williams

A starring show for the Welsh folk singer who was by this time featuring large doses of comedy within and between his songs. This one-off led to the following TV shows ...

Max Boyce

UK · BBC · STANDUP

14 editions (7 × 40 mins · 5 × 30 mins · 2 × 35 mins) · colour

Series One (4 × 40 mins) 25 Feb–18 Mar 1977 · BBC1 Fri 10.45pm

Special (40 mins) 21 Dec 1977 · BBC1 Wed 9.25pm

Series Two (4 × 30 mins) 27 Jan–17 Feb 1978 · BBC1 Fri 10.50pm

Special (40 mins) 27 Dec 1978 · BBC1 Wed 10.45pm

Special (40 mins) 15 Nov 1979 · BBC1 Thu 10.30pm

Special (35 mins) 15 May 1980 · BBC1 Thu 8.25pm

Special (30 mins) 2 Jan 1981 · BBC1 Fri 9.15pm

Special (35 mins) 21 Dec 1981 · BBC1 Mon 9.25pm

MAIN CAST

Max Boyce

CREDITS

writer Max Boyce · _producers_ Jack Williams (13), David Richards (1)

Sometimes called _Max Boyce In Concert_, these short series and sporadic specials presented Boyce's customary mix of musical musings and humorous between-song chat. The shows were recorded at various theatres around Britain. Some additional programmes aired only on BBC Wales.

The Road And The Miles Of Max Boyce

UK · BBC · STANDUP

1 × 30 mins · colour

26 Dec 1979 · BBC1 Wed 4.35pm

MAIN CAST

Max Boyce

CREDITS

writer Max Boyce · _producer_ Jack Williams

A Boxing Day special, filmed on tour.

Max Boyce And Friends

UK · BBC · STANDUP

3 × 40 mins · colour

4 May–18 May 1983 · BBC1 Wed around 9.25pm

MAIN CAST
Max Boyce
Ruth Madoc
Aiden J Harvey

CREDITS
writer Max Boyce · *producer* Jack Williams

Three shows depicting Boyce and his regular guests performing in different theatres in Wales.

Boyce Goes West

UK · BBC (OPIX FILMS) · COMEDY FILM

4 × 30 mins · colour

21 June–12 July 1984 · BBC1 Thu 8.30pm

MAIN CAST
Max Boyce

CREDITS
director Terry Ryan · *producer* Ray Marshall

A four-part comic documentary following Boyce to the Wild West, where he attempts to learn how to be a cowboy.

Without so much accent on humour, Boyce had previously undertaken a similar expedition into American Football (what with him being a famous rugby fan and all). A TV programme resulted – *Max Boyce Meets The Dallas Cowboys* – made by Opix Films and screened by C4 on 4 November 1982. The BBC later screened another Opix Films production, showing Boyce taking part in the 1985 World Elephant Polo Championships in Nepal.

It's Max Boyce

UK · BBC · SKETCH/STANDUP

4 × 30 mins · colour

3 Dec–30 Dec 1984 · BBC1 mostly Mon 7.40pm

MAIN CAST
Max Boyce
Richard Davies
Jane Freeman
Dorothea Phillips
Sue Roderick
Geoff Morgan

CREDITS
writer Max Boyce · *director/producer* Gareth Rowlands

Boyce described this as his 'first proper TV series' because it was taped in a studio and wasn't simply a recording of his stage act. The comedian appeared in sketches, sang and performed some of the monologues that made him famous.

Note. *Choice Boyce*, a made-for-video recording of the comedian in concert at the Alhambra Theatre, Bradford, was subsequently sold to TV. (It was screened by London-area ITV on 11 October 1991.)

The Boys And Mrs B

UK · BBC · SITCOM

1 × 30 mins · colour

26 Apr 1977 · BBC1 Tue 7.40pm

MAIN CAST
Mrs B · Thora Hird
Councillor Cooper · · · · · · · Richard Caldicot
Joe Bates · · · · · · · · · · · · · · · John Tordoff
Mr Hobkirk · · · · · · · · · · · · · · · Gorden Kaye
The Stripper · · · · · · · · · · · · · · Luan Peters
Lenny · · · · · · · · · · · · · · · · · · Peter Cleall
THE BOYS:
Dodger · · · · · · · · · · · · · · · · Michael Deeks
Pete · · · · · · · · · · · · · · · · · · · Sean Clarke
Billy · · · · · · · · · · · · · · · · Simon Henderson
Nick · · · · · · · · · · · · · · · · · Herbert Norville
Mark · · · · · · · · · · · · · · · · · Tony Robinson
Tiny · · · · · · · · · · · · · · · · · · Jeff Stevenson
THE GIRLS:
Hilda · · · · · · · · · · · · · Lynette McMorrough
Jackie · · · · · · · · · · · · · · · · · · · Sue Upton

CREDITS
writers Ronald Wolfe/Ronald Chesney · *producer* Dennis Main Wilson

Thora Hird reunited with her *Meet The Wife* writers Wolfe and Chesney for this one-off *Comedy Special* pilot. She played Mrs B, a local councillor charged with maintaining the physical, spiritual and moral well-being of a bunch of tearaways at a youth club. The weight of her task was highlighted when the boys hired a stripper for a club party.

The chief troublemaker was Dodger, played by Michael Deeks. He would later become a pre-teen pin-up as Swiftnick in *Dick Turpin* (ITV, 1979–82).

The Boys From The Bush

UK · BBC (ENTERTAINMENT MEDIA/CINEMA VERITY) · SITCOM

20 × 50 mins · colour

Series One (10) 25 Jan–5 Apr 1991 · BBC1 Fri 9.30pm

Series Two (10) 12 May–14 July 1992 · BBC1 Tue 9.30pm

MAIN CAST
Reg Toomer · · · · · · · · · · · · · · · · · Tim Healy
Dennis · · · · · · · · · · · · · · · Chris Haywood
Leslie · · · · · · · · · · · · · · Mark Haddigan
Arlene · · · · · · · · · · · · · · Nadine Garner
Doris · · · · · · · · · · · · · · · · Pat Thomson
Delilah · · · · · · · · · · · · · · Kris McQuade
Corrie · · · · · · · · · · · · · · · · · Kirsty Child

CREDITS
writer Douglas Livingstone · *directors* Robert Marchand (10), Shirley Barrett (10) · *producers* Verity Lambert (10), Verity Lambert/David Shanks (10)

A comedy-drama series shot mostly on location in Australia and a little in the UK, depicting the misadventures of 'pom' Reg and 'strine' Dennis, a mismatched couple who are partners in Melbourne Confidential, a business that is part-marriage-bureau, part-private-detective-agency, but which actually takes almost any work with a fee attached. It is Reg and Dennis's desire to make money that keeps them together, despite their wildly different outlooks on life. Although Reg has been in Australia for a long time, he still insists that Britain is best, pining for proper food, decent beer and his beloved QPR football team. Dennis's obsessions also include a love of his country but are dominated by his love of women. Suddenly, Reg's innocent nephew Les arrives from the UK and becomes embroiled in the complex lifestyles and cases of the Melbourne Confidential agents.

Brace Yourself Sydney

see CLARY, Julian

Bradley

UK · ITV (GRANADA) · CHILDREN'S SITCOM

6 × 30 mins · colour

21 Mar–25 Apr 1989 · Tue 4.20pm

MAIN CAST
Bradley · · · · · · · · · · · · · · · · · · Paul Bradley

CREDITS
writers Bernard Kelly (3), Paul Bradley/Michael Fenton Stevens (2), David Till (1) · *director* James Wynn · *executive producer* Nick Wilson · *producer* Richard Morss

A children's sitcom starring Paul Bradley, fresh from Granada's sketch series *Stop That Laughing At The Back* (and also *The Kate Robbins Show*). He played a pleasant, accommodating chap forever finding himself wrapped up in difficulties caused by his badly behaved mirror-reflection.

The Brady Bunch

USA · ABC (PARAMOUNT) · SITCOM

117 × 30 mins · colour

US dates: 26 Sep 1969–8 Mar 1974

UK dates: 21 May 1975–8 Sep 1982 (114 episodes) ITV various days mostly 5.15pm

MAIN CAST
Mike Brady · · · · · · · · · · · · · · · Robert Reed
Carol Brady · · · · · · · · · · Florence Henderson
Marcia Brady · · · · · · · · Maureen McCormick
Jan Brady · · · · · · · · · · · · · · · · Eve Plumb
Cindy Brady · · · · · · · · · · · · · Susan Olsen
Greg Brady · · · · · · · · · · · · · Barry Williams
Peter Brady · · · · · · · · · · Christopher Knight
Bobby Brady · · · · · · · · · · · Mike Lookinland
Alice Nelson · · · · · · · · · · · · · Ann B Davis
Sam Franklin · · · · · · · · · · · · · Allan Melvin

CREDITS
creator Sherwood Schwartz · *writers* various · *directors* Oscar Rudolph (28), Jack Arnold (15), Hal Cooper (8), Peter Baldwin (7), John Rich (7), Russ Mayberry (6), Richard Michaels (6), Leslie H Martinson (6), Robert Reed (4), Jerry London (4), Bruce Bilson (4), Jack Donohue (3), George Tyne (3), George Cahan (3) and others (13) · *executive*

producer Sherwood Schwartz · *producers* Howard Leeds, Lloyd J Schwartz

Perhaps the last of the nicey-nice American sitcoms of the period, *The Brady Bunch* would be anathema to today's more sophisticated TV viewers. (At least, one might think it so – but persistent re-runs on US TV are indicative of its tremendous cult following.) In 1969, however, the mass audience still thought kindly of twinkling eyes, neat hairstyles, homely looks and rows of flashing white straight teeth, and laughed merrily at the type of innocent middle-class problems that only these US sitcom families got into. In short, *The Brady Bunch* is the most typical example of the 'happy-families' US comedy genre – in it, a widowed man with three brats … sorry, children, and a widowed woman with three little darlings of her own, marry and settle down as parents of their six-pack. (Clearly, divorce was still too sensitive an issue for mainstream America to handle in 1969, whereas to be widowed was kinda *respectable*.)

The widower was Mike, an architect, dad to three boys (Gregg, Peter and Bobby) and once voted Father of the Year by a newspaper. Carol Martin, the widow whom he meets and marries, is mom to three girls (Marcia, Jan and Cindy). Together, they set up home in a four-bedroom house in suburban Los Angeles, employing ageing (but wacky) housekeeper Alice Nelson and keeping a cat and shaggy dog. Stories abounded of clubhouses, camping trips, high phone bills, illnesses, school proms, and, as the children grew older, lovesickness. All good clean fluff.

Spin-offs from *The Brady Bunch* are *many*, so unceasing is the Americans' interest in seeing how the Brady kids turned out as adults. (They also prove how creator/executive producer Sherwood Schwartz had a knack for exploiting ideas – remembering how he was also responsible for the all-pervading **Gilligan's Island**.) First came the cartoon version *The Brady Kids* (22 episodes, 1972–74), then *The Brady Bunch Variety Hour/The Brady Bunch Hour* (nine editions, 1977), *The Brady Brides* (ten episodes, 1981, some re-edited from a two-hour TV movie titled *The Brady Girls Get Married*), *A Very Brady Christmas* (a one-off TV movie, 1988), *The Bradys* (six episodes, 1990) and a stage production, *The Real Live Brady Bunch*, which ran in Chicago in 1990–91. Then, in 1995, Paramount Pictures released *The Brady Bunch Movie* (director Betty Thomas) which, thankfully, sent-up the whole premise somewhat, in that the Brady family were still living in the 1970s while all around them time had moved on a couple of decades. Good reviews meant that a second movie (*A Very Brady Sequel*, director Arlene Sanford) was released in 1996.

See also *Step By Step*, which utilised a similar premise.

Jo Brand

Born in 1957 in Clapham, south London, former psychiatric nurse Jo Brand has often cited this previous occupation as ideal preparation for her new career as a standup comic. She came to comedy at the age of 29 (in 1987, performing in a Greenpeace benefit at a disco in Wardour Street, London) and after less than two years on the circuit was successful enough to give up her day job. In these early performances, Brand styled herself as 'the Sea Monster' and her act mostly comprised self-deprecating one-liners that made fun of her penchant for booze and cakes, her out-sized physique and what she considers to be her unglamorous looks. She interspersed these personal put-downs with some wickedly witty and venomous attacks on specific sections of the male species, and marginally less vicious assaults on men in general. Later, she developed a more rounded and versatile routine – although men remain the principal butt of her humour – a progression that led to a Perrier Award nomination at the Edinburgh Festival Fringe in 1992. Her stage success and regular TV guest appearances resulted in her first starring TV series, which arrived on C4 in 1993.

But Brand's ride to the top has not been an easy one. Although her material has been consistently funny and she permits a genuine warmth to undercut her most acerbic attacks, she has suffered more than her fair share of verbal abuse during live performances. Comedians accept heckling as part of the experience, but Brand seems to attract a particularly nasty and personal backbite from sections of her audience – usually male-orientated. She has developed a number of stinging rebukes, and for all the world seems not to care; clearly, though, Brand has exposed the fact that plenty of men are threatened by powerful, witty, savvy women who do not conform to their physical ideals.

See also Comic Relief and *One On Two*.

Jo Brand Through The Cakehole

UK · C4 (CHANNEL X) · STANDUP/SKETCH

14 editions (13 × 35 mins · 1 × 45 mins) · colour

Special · 30 Dec 1993 · Thu 10.40pm

Series One (6) 8 Apr–13 May 1994 · Fri 10.30pm

Special (45 mins) *Jo Brand Through The Christmas Cakehole* 23 Dec 1994 · Fri 9.30pm

Series Two (6) 12 Jan–16 Feb 1996 · Fri 10.30pm

MAIN CAST
Jo Brand

OTHER APPEARANCES
Maria McErlane
Jim Sweeney
Chris Lang
Morwenna Banks

CREDITS
writers Jo Brand/Jim Miller · *additional material* Jeff Green, Georgia Pritchett and others · *directors* Mike Adams (7), Declan Lowney (6), Marcus Mortimer (1) · *executive producer* Katie Lander · *producers* Geoff Atkinson (13), Marcus Mortimer (1)

A starring show for Brand who, while toning down her live act, still incorporated many of her favourite topics (periods, gluttony, smoking, boozing, male inadequacy and male immaturity) into the routines and sketches. Although comfortable delivering standup material, Brand initially seemed uneasy in the sketches, coming across as self-conscious. But she improved quickly and by the second series was adept in both areas. In the first series, a recurring film sketch, 'Drudge Squad', followed the exploits of a special police unit run by dowdy housewives wearing scarves over their curlers and carrying shopping bags. Each week their police work would be interrupted by a domestic crisis of their own.

Top-name guest stars appeared throughout – including Steve Coogan, Alan Davies and Imelda Staunton – but special mention must be made of the very funny Maria McErlane, an underrated but always marvellous support. The series was jointly written by Brand and her boyfriend/partner Jim Miller. The 26 January 1996 edition, which took health as its theme, and which drew on some of Brand's own experiences in the field, was repeated as *Jo Brand – Rude Health* on 3 January 1997 in C4's *Doctors And Nurses* strand.

Note. Brand wrote and fronted BBC2's *Jo Brand Goes Back To Bedlam* (3 May 1995), a piece debunking many of the myths surrounding mental illness, presented as part of the channel's *States Of Mind* strand.

A Big Slice Of Jo Brand

UK · C4 (CHANNEL X/STONE RANGER PRODUCTIONS) · STANDUP

1 × 50 mins · colour

10 Oct 1996 · Thu 10.45pm

MAIN CAST
Jo Brand

CREDITS
writers Jo Brand/Jim Miller · *producer* Katie Lander · *executive producer* Vivienne Clore

A one-off in which Brand delivered her characteristic mixture of withering observation and biting wit. Subjects under scrutiny included her thoughts about an indecent proposal from Robert Redford and the problems the Queen may have encountered on a visit to Australia.

Jo Brand – All The Way To Worcester

UK · C4 (VERA) · STANDUP

1 × 60 mins · colour

27 Dec 1996 · Fri 10pm

MAIN CAST
Jo Brand

CREDITS
director Geraldine Dowd · *producers* Geoff Atkinson, Elaine Morris

An on-stage and behind-stage look at Jo Brand's new touring show. A film crew recorded 24 hours in the life of the comedian as she arrived in Worcester to mount the twenty-eighth show of her tour. The resulting programme featured extracts of Brand performing all-new material in front of a packed house and then followed her back to a hotel where she had a drink, unwound and became involved in a fracas.

Jo Brand: Like It Or Lump It

UK · C4 (VERA) · STANDUP/SKETCH

6 × 35 mins · colour

12 Sep–17 Oct 1997 · Fri 10.30pm

MAIN CAST
Jo Brand
Ricky, the tour manager · · · · · Ricky Grover
John, the sound man · · · · · · · John Sparkes
Janet, the make-up girl · · · · Mandy Knight
Malcolm, the driver · · · · · Malcolm Hardee
Policewoman ('Drudge' sketches) · · · · · · ·
· · · · · · · · · · · · · · · · · · Maria McErlane

CREDITS
writer Jo Brand · *additional material* Kevin Day, Ricky Grover, Mandy Knight, John Sparkes · *director* Geraldine Dowd · *producer* Geoff Atkinson

Maintaining the basic idea of *Jo Brand – All The Way To Worcester*, this series took the premise one step further by presenting a fictionalised account of life on the road with Brand, built around her British tour. Film of her live act was interspersed with short sketches purporting to be a fly-on-the-wall-style documentary of the behind-the-scenes story of the tour. The actors (from the world of standup comedy) used a naturalistic style and bad behaviour and strong language was to the fore. Ricky Grover was particularly impressive as the gauche, hapless tour manager, endlessly inventing lies in order to get his own way. All the usual revelations associated with such documentaries (arguments, tantrums, pranks, blazing rows, scuffles) were expertly spoofed and the whole enterprise fitted together pleasingly well. The series also featured a recurring bona fide sketch, 'Drudge', revisiting the

Drudge Squad officers introduced in *Jo Brand Through The Cakehole*.

On 23 December 1997 Jo Brand and her team were featured in the C4 documentary *Jo Brand Burns Rubber*, which followed them through the gruelling qualifying rounds for the RAC Rally and reported on their participation in the subsequent three-day race.

Note. Ricky Grover participated in *It's Later Than You Think* (30 November 1997–25 January 1998), a late-night BBC1 series in which a number of personalities sat around a table discussing items from the week's news. Other regulars from the world of comedy were Annabel Giles and Dexter Fletcher. Although the shows sometimes featured short sketches, this was not a comedy series as such.

Brass

UK · ITV, *C4 (GRANADA) · SITCOM

32 × 30 mins · colour

Series One (13) 21 Feb–23 May 1983 · Mon 8pm
Series Two (13) 21 May–20 Aug 1984 · Mon mostly 8pm
*Series Three (6) 23 Apr–28 May 1990 · Mon 8.30pm

MAIN CAST
Bradley Hardacre · · · · · · · · · Timothy West
Lady Patience Hardacre · · Caroline Blakiston
Agnes Fairchild · · · · · · · · · · · Barbara Ewing
George Fairchild · · · · · · · · · Geoffrey Hinsliff
· (series 1 & 2);
· · · · · · · · · · · Geoffrey Hutchings (series 3)
Dr (later Inspector) MacDuff · · · David Ashton
Austin Hardacre · · · · · · · · Robert Reynolds
· (series 1 & 2);
· · · · · · · · · · · · · Patrick Pearson (series 3)
Morris Hardacre · · · · · · · · · · · James Saxon
Isobel Hardacre · · · · · · · · · · Gail Harrison
Charlotte Hardacre · · · · · · · · · Emily Morgan
Jack Fairchild · · · · · · · · · · · · · Shaun Scott
Matthew Fairchild · · · · · · · · · · · Gary Cady
Job Lott · · · · · · · · Bill Monks (series 1 & 2)
Hattersley · · · · · · · · · John Pickles (series 3)
Paxo · · Thomas Hannay Matthews (series 3)
Henri Lecoq · · · · · · · · · Philip Bird (series 3)

OTHER APPEARANCES
Guy Baggers · · · · · · · · · · · · · Anthony Smee
Lord Mountfast · · · · John Nettleton (series 2)
Prudence Makepeace · · · · · · Joanna David
· (series 2)
Talbot · · · · · · · · · · · John de Frates (series 2)
Marshall Snelgrove QC · · · · · Ian Richardson
· (series 2)

CREDITS
writers John Stevenson/Julian Roach · *directors* Gareth Jones (series 1 & 2), Les Chatfield (series 3) · *executive producers* Bill Podmore (series 2), David Liddiment (series 3) · *producers* Bill Podmore (series 1), Gareth Jones (series 2), Mark Robson (series 3)

Produced at no little expense by Granada, *Brass* (meaning, of course, money) was a

splendidly over-the-top pastiche of the gritty northern mill dramas that have proliferated on British TV (and radio, stage and screen) for aeons. Like a cross between *Soap* and *When The Boat Comes In*, the series was set in the fictional Lancashire town of Utterley (location shooting was done in Ramsbottom, near Manchester) in the 1930s, when men were men and ferrets something you stuffed down t'trousers.

Brass depicts the lives of two families at opposite ends of the social spectrum. One is the Hardacres: wealthy, living in the big house at the top of the hill. The other is the Fairchilds: employed by the Hardacres, they live in a tiny back-to-back terraced house away down at the bottom of the hill. Despite the differences in class and wealth, however, plenty of sexual intermingling takes place. The series was not played for laughs as such, but by its very deadpan straightness it drew rich humour out of the situations. Another source of fun was in the names given to certain characters: the two Hardacre sons were Austin and Morris, other people were named Job Lott, Lords Mountfast and Sodbury, Schickelgruber (Hitler's birth name), Von Beckenbauer, Sgt Pepper, Young Scargill, Hattersley and (ironically, considering what he did for the miners in 1993) Heseltine.

But these people were the small fry. The big fish in the pond was undoubtedly Bradley Hardacre, owner of the coal mine, the cotton mill, shipyard, aircraft factory and much else – even the munitions factory. Timothy West was in fine form as the (all adjectives apply) gruff, cigar-puffing, ruthless, greedy, wily, blunt, brusque northern work baron, lusting after power, money and women alike. He has scrapped his way out of the workhouse and into the Rolls-Royce league, but he hates his old background – the working classes – with a vengeance and forces them to work for him in appalling, risky conditions. Hardacre didn't only get to t'top by graft, nay lad – he won 'social standing' by seducing a baronet's daughter into marrying him. (She, in turn, was hungry for a share of his self-made lucre.) Now Lady Patience Hardacre is self-pitying and gin-dependent. Their marital relationship is a disastrous sham; indeed, to ward off any unlikely attempt by her husband at pursuance of his marital rights she has convinced him that she must remain confined to a wheelchair, whereas, in reality, she is a walking, if loopy, cauldron of desire.

Before her denial of the conjugals, Lady Patience delivered to Bradley two daughters and two sons. Red-headed Isobel is promiscuous to the extent of nymphomaniacal. (She eventually marries an ageing lecher, Lord Mountfast.) Mousey-haired Charlotte is an idealist who has a social conscience and likes to help the local hospital doctor (MacDuff), sometimes ripping off her blouse to patch up the injuries inflicted upon her father's workers in the course of their employment. Austin is ambitious but constantly thwarted by his father while Morris has a zest for life, lights and teddy bears, and, horror of all horrors, is homosexual, attending Cambridge with his chums Kim, Guy and Morris.

Turning to the Fairchilds, George – nominal head of the house – is a flat-capped working-class fool. Immensely grateful to Hardacre for providing gainful employment, he won't hear a bad word said about his boss. His wife Agnes is a sexual object for Hardacre, but she also fires up her two sons to revolt against their downtrodden working-class existence and leads a strike against Hardacre's working practices. A bold feminist, Agnes exudes a magnetic, if earthy, sexual attraction, helped no end by her ever-revealing cleavage. George and Agnes have had two sons. Jack, the elder, works at the coal mine and is admired by his pals for his defiant attitude. Matthew, more reflective – he writes poetry in secret, which attracts him to Morris – is a clerk at Hardacre's mill but yearns for a different life. (After he's murdered Hardacre, that is.)

The third series of *Brass*, after a six-year gap, kicked off on 1 September 1939, at the dawn of the Second World War. Austin is an MP, working with Neville Chamberlain; Morris has become a Russian spy under the guise of a vicar in Mayfair; Isobel has been widowed and continues to feed her gluttonous diet for men; Agnes is a socialist MP; Charlotte has married Matthew – she is a pacifist working for PAP (Peace at Any Price) while he has joined the RAF – and tough-as-boots Bradley Hardacre, mindful of the aircraft and munitions he can supply the British government, is desperate for the war to start – 'I've worked for it and I want it!'

Brass Eye

UK · C4 (TALKBACK PRODUCTIONS) · SATIRE

6 × 30 mins · colour

29 Jan–5 Mar 1997 · Wed 9.30pm

MAIN CAST
Chris Morris

OTHER APPEARANCES
Peter Baynham
Bill Cashmore
Hugh Dennis
Doon Mackichan
Claire Skinner

CREDITS
writers Chris Morris/Peter Baynham · *additional material* Graham Linehan/Arthur Mathews · *director* Michael Cumming · *executive producer* Peter Fincham · *producers* Chris Morris, Caroline Leddy

Chris Morris is no stranger to controversy. His outrageous stunts (like releasing helium around a radio newsreader, causing him to read solemn news items in a squeaky, high-pitched voice), bad-taste routines (he knowingly reported on-air the death of the very-much-alive British politician Michael Heseltine) and off-colour gimmicks (enticing children and old people to read out arcane and obscure obscenities) have often led to his being censured and dismissed from previous programmes. Morris's BBC radio show was similarly dogged with legal problems. But, as proven by his appearances in *The Day Today*, Morris is well worth studying, despite the hassles he causes, for he is a savage satirist with seemingly no scruples or moralistic inhibitions, who can produce, without a moment's notice, comedy of a most exquisite and devastatingly funny, or plain over-the-top, nature. His forte is lampooning the presentation of modern-day news and current affairs programming, and he is cruelly brilliant at his art.

In some ways, *Brass Eye* was a hybrid of *The Day Today* and *The Saturday Night Armistice*, combining the spoof, overcooked pretentious style and graphics of the former with the satirical vox-pop approach of the latter. Editions of *Brass Eye* involved on-camera appearances from a wide sweep of celebrities and politicians, brought on to comment upon ludicrous news items – often, one suspected, unaware that the material was spurious, a technique that blurred the line between truth and fantasy and increased the controversial nature of the show. Originally scheduled to launch on 19 November 1996, *Brass Eye* was postponed at the last minute owing to fears over its taste and fairness, especially concerning one item in which an unsuspecting Tory politician was goaded into commenting on the government's policy towards a (totally fabricated) new youth drug, 'cake'. Although accused of cowardice in their eleventh-hour withdrawal of *Brass Eye*, C4 insisted that the series as a whole needed tweaking and that it would reappear – true to their word, it surfaced two months later. Even if it had been toned down, it was still powerful stuff. Each of the six editions pursued a theme ('Science: Good or Bad?', 'The Sex Issue' and so on) and exploited the topic to ridiculous extremes, using the 'in-your-face' approach of tabloid-TV news programmes and 'infotainment' shows (particularly prevalent on cable and satellite channels) to hammer home their point.

A press release for *Brass Eye* promised that it would 'take media terrorism to a level never seen on British TV before' which, when the six programmes had been aired, seemed nothing less than fair comment. The series was fascinating from first edition to last, if more shocking in scope than funny, and its mix of outrageous ideas and spot-on satirical observation ensured that viewers' mouths, as well as their eyes, remained wide open.

Bread

UK · BBC · SITCOM

74 episodes (71 × 30 mins · 2 × 50 mins · 1 × 70 mins) · colour

Series One (6) 1 May–5 June 1986 · BBC1
Thu 9.30pm

Series Two (6) 8 Jan–19 Feb 1987 · BBC1
Thu 9.30pm

Series Three (13) 6 Sep–29 Nov 1987 · BBC1
Sun 8.35pm

Series Four (13) 18 Sep–11 Dec 1988 · BBC1
Sun 8.35pm

Special (70 mins) 25 Dec 1988 · BBC1
Sun 7.15pm

Series Five (13) 10 Sep–3 Dec 1989 · BBC1
Sun 8.35pm

Special (50 mins) 25 Dec 1989 · BBC1
Mon 3.15pm

Series Six (10) 9 Sep–4 Nov 1990 · BBC1
Sun 8.35pm

Special (50 mins) 25 Dec 1990 · BBC1
Tue 7.30pm

Series Seven (10) 1 Sep–3 Nov 1991 · BBC1
Sun 7.45pm

MAIN CAST

Nellie Boswell	Jean Boht
Adrian Boswell	Jonathon Morris
Freddie Boswell	Ronald Forfar (series 1–6)
Joey Boswell	Peter Howitt (series 1–4);
	Graham Bickley (series 5 onwards)
Aveline Boswell	Gilly Coman (series 1–4);
	Melanie Hill (series 5 onwards)
Jack Boswell	Victor McGuire
	(series 1–3 and 5 onwards)
Billy Boswell	Nick Conway
Grandad	Kenneth Waller
Martina	Pamela Power
Oswald	Giles Watling
Julie	Caroline Milmoe (series 1 & 2);
	Hilary Crowson (series 3 onwards)
Shifty	Bryan Murray (series 4 onwards)
Celia Higgins	Rita Tushingham (series 4)

OTHER APPEARANCES

Lilo Lil	Eileen Pollock
Roxy	Joanna Phillips-Lane
Derek	Peter Byrne
Fr Dooley	J G Devlin
Yizzel	Charles Lawson
Yizzel's mate	Simon Rouse
Leonora Campbell	Deborah Grant
Irenee	Sharon Byatt
Carmen	Jenny Jay

CREDITS

writer Carla Lane · *directors* Robin Nash (35), John B Hobbs (20), Susan Belbin (18), Robin Nash/John B Hobbs (1) · *producers* Robin Nash (51), John B Hobbs (22), Robin Nash/John B Hobbs (1)

Carla Lane seemed to be set inexorably upon a path taking her deeper and deeper into the realms of tragi-comedy when she confounded her critics and spellbound viewers with *Bread*, a colourful, multi-layered slice of Liverpool life. Following closely on from

I Woke Up One Morning, her sobering look at alcoholism, *Bread* found her firmly back in the mainstream waters into which she had first waded with **The Liver Birds**. The Boswells (a familiar name to followers of that earlier series) were a sprawling, larger-than-life Catholic family, ducking and diving through life, often exploiting the system to survive. At the centre of the storm stood matriarch Nellie Boswell, a robust and capable woman using her sheer force of personality to keep the family on her version of the straight and narrow. Nellie's husband was the unfaithful Freddie, an unreliable but likeable sort, and they had five grown-up children: boys Adrian, Joey, Jack and Billy, and their sister Aveline. Completing the immediate family was Grandad, who lived next door. Then there were various wives and girlfriends of the lads (Julie for Billy, Carmen for Jack, Irenee for Adrian) and Aveline's beau (later husband) Oswald. To round off the set was Lilo Lil, Freddie's 'bit on the side', a sharp-tongued DHSS official named Martina, Shifty (who was, by name and nature), his ex-girlfriend Celia and a whole gang of memorable irregulars. (Celia, played by Rita Tushingham, was a successful writer who returned to Liverpool following a period living and hobnobbing in London. Some of the inspiration for the Boswells derived from Carla Lane's own family and her recollections of Liverpool and it is plausible that this character was based on Lane herself.)

Initially, response to the series was poor. Critics, who had often attacked Lane's shows, took a predictable stance, labelling it 'stale' and 'crummy' and utilising other bread-pun insults. More damning was the response from Lane's beloved Liverpool, where local reviewers accused her of enforcing the clichéd stereotype of the Scouse scrounger. This controversy abated, however, when the show fell into its stride and the audience figures picked up.

The series had respectable ratings right from the start but by the fourth series its popularity was gigantic: one episode (Oswald and Aveline's wedding on 11 December 1988) attracted more than 21 million viewers. This size of British TV audience is more common for soap operas than for sitcoms, and herein lies a possible clue to the series' success. *Bread* featured many soap elements: a dominating female central character; constantly changing states of relationships; earthy, recognisably realistic dialogue; prevailing accent and speech patterns; a strong sense of location; and a large number of regular and occasional identifiable characters. With all these elements and Lane's pungently funny dialogue, *Bread* couldn't lose.

The struggles of this family to 'make bread out of nothing at all' gave rise to many notable moments. The 30 October 1988 episode had cameo appearances from Lane's friends Paul and Linda McCartney; a scripted mini-episode in the 1988 *Royal Variety Show* (televised on 26 November by BBC1); and a 1991 stage production based on the series, performed at Dominion Theatre in London. Linda McCartney made a second appearance with Jean Boht in *The Last Waltz*, a specially scripted production featuring characters from Carla Lane's *Bread*, **Butterflies**, **Solo** and *The Liver Birds*, aired by BBC1 on 10 March 1989 as part of **Comic Relief**.

A Break Of Wind

UK · S4C/C4 (HTV WALES) · SKETCH

1 × 30 mins · colour

28 Feb 1985 · Thu 6.30pm

MAIN CAST
Dewi Morris

CREDITS
producer Ronw Protheroe

A rare outing on English-language TV for the Welsh comedian Dewi 'Pws' Morris, performing songs and sketches and appearing in such guises as William McTell, 'the Welsh Billy Connolly-lookalike crossbow champion'. This single half-hour was a compilation of highlights, re-worked in English, from Morris's Welsh-language series on S4C (Channel 4 Wales).

Rory Bremner

The richly talented impressionist Rory Bremner was born in Edinburgh on 6 April 1961. His home city proved an ideal place to see his comic heroes, being invaded, *en masse*, by comedy talent each summer for the Fringe festival, and it was from attending many gigs that he too decided to become a performer. Bremner started to work the stage while studying at King's College in London, eschewing the revue trail to go out instead as a solo standup act. He was soon 'noticed' and invited to perform at the Edinburgh Festival Fringe, where his reputation blossomed further. Presentational duties on BBC Radio 4's *The Fringe* show led to appearances on the same network's topical comedy series *Week Ending*, where Bremner first teamed up with writer John Langdon, later his permanent script collaborator. A somewhat dodgy but nonetheless valuable engagement in Jimmy Cricket's ITV series **And There's More** followed but so meteoric was Bremner's rise that he was only 24 when he was given his first starring TV series by the BBC.

By his thirties, Bremner was recognised as the foremost impressionist in Britain, able not only to imitate the complete spectrum of public figures but also to perform impressions of famous people as if *other* famous people were doing them. His talent, and his cutting edge, puts him in a class of his own.

Now – Something Else

UK · BBC · IMPRESSIONISM

12 × 30 mins · colour

Series One (6) 3 Mar–14 Apr 1986 · BBC2 Mon 9pm

Series Two (6) 27 Mar–8 May 1987 · BBC2 Fri 9pm

MAIN CAST
Rory Bremner
Sara Crowe
John Dowie
Jeremy Hardy
Steve Steen
Jim Sweeney
Ann Bryson (series 1)

CREDITS
writers Rory Bremner/John Langdon (12), Pete Sinclair (12), John Dowie (8), Ian Brown (6), Dick Vosburgh (6), Barry Cryer (6), Steve Punt (6), Steve Steen/Jim Sweeney (6), Nick Revell (5), Terry Ravenscroft (5), Jeremy Hardy (5), James Hendrie (5), Guy Jenkin (5), Paul B Davies (4), Jeremy Pascall (4), Andrea Solomons (4), Chris Stagg (4), Clare Taylor (4), Dick Hills (1), Michael Barfield (1), Mark Brisenden (1) · *director* Marcus Mortimer · *producer* Bill Wilson

Following a successful appearance on the premiere edition of the weekday *Wogan* chat-show on 18 February 1985, and the ITV series *And There's More* that summer, Rory Bremner launched his first starring series *Now – Something Else*, which contained an element of sharp satire not usually found in the work of his contemporaries. This gave the series a definite edge, as did Bremner's gatling-gun delivery which enabled him to switch character at lightning speed. Bremner took his victims from a wide sphere: politicians, radio commentators, sportsmen, interviewers and newsreaders but, unusually, he tended to avoid impersonating other entertainers and comedians. A class act in a classy show, Bremner was proving the most likely candidate to inherit the mantle of 'Britain's best impressionist' from Mike Yarwood.

The Rory Bremner Show

UK · BBC · IMPRESSIONISM

6 × 30 mins · colour

5 May–9 June 1988 · BBC2 Thu 9pm

MAIN CAST
Rory Bremner
Sara Crowe

Steve Steen
Jim Sweeney

CREDITS
writers Rory Bremner/John Langdon (6), Barry Cryer (6), Steve Steen/Jim Sweeney (6), Dick Vosburgh (6), Pete Sinclair (4), Geoff Atkinson (3), Dave Cohen (2), Angus Deayton (2), Steve Punt (2) · *director/producer* Marcus Mortimer

A name change for the series (Bremner claimed that some people thought *Now – Something Else* was a documentary and failed to tune in) but the same brand of quick-fire impressions and satire-laced scripts as before. Bremner gave the writers a list of 105 characters that he would be willing to attempt, although he admitted to only having about half of them in his repertoire at the start of the series.

Rory Bremner

UK · BBC · IMPRESSIONISM
24 × 30 mins · colour
Series One (6) 31 Mar–5 May 1989 · BBC2 Fri 9pm
Series Two (6) 20 Apr–25 May 1990 · BBC2 Fri 9pm
Series Three (6) 15 Mar–19 Apr 1991 · BBC2 Fri 9pm
Series Four (6) 8 May–12 June 1992 · BBC2 Fri 9pm

MAIN CAST
Rory Bremner
John Bird
John Fortune (series 3 & 4)
Enn Reitel (series 1 & 2)
Steve Nallon (series 1 & 2)

CREDITS
main writers Rory Bremner/John Langdon, John Bird, Kim Fuller, Geoff Atkinson, Patrick Marber, David Baddiel · *other writers* Steve Punt, Michael Barfield, Ged Parsons, Steve Nallon, Angus Deayton, Graeme Garden, Hattie Hayridge and others · *directors* Marcus Mortimer (6), Kevin Bishop (6), Simon Spencer (6), Sean Hardie (6) · *producers* Geoff Atkinson (12), Marcus Mortimer (6), Kevin Bishop (6)

Bremner's huge roster of impressions grew exponentially in these four series. They also saw the start of his professional relationship with ace satirists John Bird and John Fortune, who would go on to become a permanent fixture in the impressionist's programmes, creating a renewed double act for the 1990s.

Rory Bremner … And The Morning After The Year Before

UK · C4 (KUDOS) · IMPRESSIONISM
1 × 65 mins · colour
1 Jan 1993 · Fri 10pm

MAIN CAST
Rory Bremner

CREDITS
writers Rory Bremner/John Langdon · *directors* Phil Chilvers, David G Hillier · *producer* Geoff Atkinson

A New Year's Day special for Bremner that launched his C4 output. The premise of this one-off had Prime Minister John Major waking on 1 January 1993 to find he has no memory of the events of 1992. Luckily, he has taped the previous evening's *Rory Bremner Show* and watching it brings his memories flooding back.

Rory Bremner … Who Else?

UK · C4 (*KUDOS, VERA) · IMPRESSIONISM
53 × 40 mins · colour
*Series One (9) 9 Oct–4 Dec 1993 · Sat 10.05pm
Series Two (10) 8 Oct–10 Dec 1994 · Sat 10.05pm
Series Three (8) 7 Oct–25 Nov 1995 · Sat around 10.30pm
Series Four (8) 5 Apr–24 May 1996 · Fri 10.30pm
Series Five (10) 27 Sep–29 Nov 1996 · Fri 10.30pm
Series Six (8) 24 Oct–12 Dec 1997 · Fri 10.30pm

MAIN CAST
Rory Bremner
John Bird
John Fortune

CREDITS
main writers Geoff Atkinson, Rory Bremner, John Langdon, John Fortune/John Bird, Jon Magnusson · *other writers* Sean Hardie, Stewart Currie and many others · *directors* Steve Connelly/Tom Poole (series 1), Steve Connelly/Sean Hardie (series 2), Steve Connelly/David Crean (series 3), Steve Connelly/Steve Smith (series 4), Steve Smith (series 5), Geraldine Dowd/Henry Murray (series 6) · *producers* Geoff Atkinson, Elaine Morris, Jon Magnusson

Recorded on the eve of transmissions, this was Bremner's most ambitious attempt yet at performing truly topical satire. The show had a simple format: Bremner would deliver long routines on a simple stage set, in which he would rapidly segue from one impression to the next. The material would all be based around recent events and news stories. There were a few filmed sketches using the minimum of props – perhaps a desk or a sofa.

In a separate weekly sequence, John Fortune and John Bird, now firmly established as the Two Johns, delivered a scathing attack on an aspect of government policy or public life in the form of a TV interview. (The roles of interviewer and interviewee alternated weekly but the latter was almost always named George Parr.) These sections, in which the victim tended to

condemn himself out of his own mouth yet be totally oblivious to the fact, had the air of being totally improvised and, indeed, were performed with little more than a sketched outline of how the conversation might proceed. Edited for broadcast in *Rory Bremner … Who Else?*, extended versions of the interviews were screened as a stand-alone series **The Long Johns**.

Another regular slot in the early series, was a savage but poignant monologue about an aspect of life in Britain in the 1990s, delivered each week by a (usually female) guest star. (One such piece, *Stuart*, written by Geoff Atkinson and delivered by Annette Crosbie, was extended into a stand-alone half-hour, screened by C4 on 15 September 1996.). Following Labour's landslide victory in the 1997 General Election, Bremner was able to add impressions of new Prime Minister Tony Blair and the new Tory leader of whom nobody was taking much notice ('I'm William bloody Hague!'), and voice a succession of devastating lampoons of Blair's 'spin doctor' Peter Mandelson, who appeared in the form of a three-dimensional computer-generated figure.

These Bafta Award-winning series saw Bremner consolidate his deserved reputation as Britain's greatest-ever impressionist. At a time when *Spitting Image* had ended and new sketch comedies were concerned more with surrealism and music-hall pastiche than biting contemporary commentary, Bremner was standing virtually alone in the field.

Rory Bremner: The Man And His Music

UK · C4 (KUDOS) · IMPRESSIONISM
1 × 65 mins · colour
1 Jan 1994 · Sat 10pm

MAIN CAST
Rory Bremner

CREDITS
writers Rory Bremner/John Langdon · *director* Steve Connelly · *producers* Geoff Atkinson, Elaine Morris

Another New Year's Day special from the *Rory Bremner … Who Else?* creative team. Bremner looked back at the events of the previous year – as he had done the previous year and would continue to do for the ensuing years.

Note. On 1 May 1994, Bremner appeared in C4's *The Charter 88 Bad Government Awards*, a spoof awards ceremony highlighting the individuals and offices that have done the most to restrict the flow of information to the general public.

Rory Bremner's Christmas Turkey

UK · C4 (VERA) · IMPRESSIONISM

1 × 65 mins · colour

30 Dec 1994 · Fri 10pm

MAIN CAST
Rory Bremner
John Fortune
John Bird

CREDITS
writers Rory Bremner/John Langdon, John Fortune/John Bird · *directors* Steve Connelly/Juliet May · *producers* Geoff Atkinson, Elaine Morris

Another annual résumé.

Bremner's Bulletins

UK · C4 (VERA) · IMPRESSIONISM

5 × 5 mins · colour

20 Mar–24 Mar 1995 · Mon–Fri 7.55pm

MAIN CAST
Rory Bremner

CREDITS
writers Rory Bremner/John Langdon · *director* Geoff Atkinson · *producer* Elaine Morris

Brief, satirical news bulletins from Bremner as part of C4's themed *Whose News?* strand. A 15-minute compilation of the five short items was screened on 9 April 1995.

Rory Bremner, Apparently

UK · C4 (VERA) · IMPRESSIONISM

1 × 60 mins · colour

29 Dec 1995 · Fri 9.30pm

MAIN CAST
Rory Bremner
John Fortune
John Bird

CREDITS
writers Rory Bremner/John Langdon, John Fortune/John Bird · *director* Steve Connelly · *producers* Elaine Morris

A further annual résumé.

The Alternative Christmas Message

UK · C4 (VERA) · IMPRESSIONISM

1 × 15 mins · colour

25 Dec 1996 · Wed 3pm

MAIN CAST
Rory Bremner

CREDITS
writers Rory Bremner/John Langdon · *director* Steve Smith · *producers* Geoff Atkinson, Elaine Morris

At precisely the same time as the Queen was appearing on BBC1 and ITV delivering her annual Christmas message, Rory Bremner popped up on C4 in the guise of Diana, Princess of Wales, sending a variation of the festive greetings.

Two Fat Rorys

UK · C4 (VERA) · IMPRESSIONISM

1 × 30 mins · colour

29 Dec 1996 · Sun 6.30pm

MAIN CAST
Rory Bremner

CREDITS
writers Rory Bremner/John Langdon · *director* Steve Smith · *producers* Geoff Atkinson, Elaine Morris

To celebrate this, his fiftieth show for C4, Bremner allowed two of his favourite TV characterisations to take centre stage, leaving an entire half-hour in the hands of his weatherman Ian McCaskill and the smooth BBC sports anchorman Desmond Lynam. Both impersonations were affectionately presented, in contrast to Bremner's other work which could be cutting. The McCaskill impressions in particular had moved into an almost surreal area, with Bremner spinning out ever more outlandish variations on the theme, and stretching the performance until the trick of mimicry could be accomplished with mere sounds, gestures and expressions rather than words. Bremner perpetuated a joke at this time that his McCaskill impression was impossible to kill off, although ghastly fates befell the character week by week. At its most extreme, this invention rivalled the bizarre creations of abstract impressionist Phil Cool (*Cool It*).

The title, *Two Fat Rorys*, was a play on the raucous *Two Fat Ladies* (Jennifer Paterson and Clarissa Dickson Wright), a pair of 'colossal chefs' who rose to fame on BBC2 in 1996.

Bremner, Bird And Fortune: Three Men And A Vote

UK · C4 (VERA) · IMPRESSIONISM

2 × 50 mins · colour

26 April & 3 May 1997 · Sat 9.45pm

MAIN CAST
Rory Bremner
John Bird
John Fortune

CREDITS
writers Rory Bremner/John Langdon · *director* Steve Smith · *producers* Geoff Atkinson, Elaine Morris

Pre- and post-General Election specials in which Bremner was once again joined by the Two Johns. The team avoided the British TV tendency to steer clear of satirical shows around election time by being equally savage to all parties.

Note. A lifelong cricket fan, Bremner hosted two special half-hour programmes, *It's Just Not Cricket With Rory Bremner* (BBC2, 25 August and 7 September 1997), in which he chatted informally to cricketing personalities and fans. The shows took a light-hearted anecdotal approach and allowed Bremner plenty of room for pertinent impressions (Richie Benaud, Ray Illingworth, Fred Trueman, Geoffrey Boycott, David Lloyd) as well as featuring some filmed spoof segments on the nature of the game.

And Finally … Rory Bremner

UK · C4 (VERA) · IMPRESSIONISM

1 × 60 mins · colour

30 Dec 1997 · Tue 10.30pm

CAST
Rory Bremner

CREDITS
writers Geoff Atkinson, David Tyler, Debbie Barham, Rory Bremner, Sean Hardie, John Fortune, John Langdon · *director* John Birkin · *executive producer* Geoff Atkinson · *producers* David Tyler, Sean Hardie

The traditional seasonal special, this time featuring several sequences with the computer-generated Peter Mandelson image (see *Rory Bremner … Who Else?* above) and extended impressions of newsreader Trevor McDonald, whom Bremner was now portraying as the hip, egocentric TV superstar at the hub of an ever more glitzy ITN. Unusually, there was no appearance for the Two Johns in this edition.

Bresslaw And Friends

UK · ITV (ASSOCIATED-REDIFFUSION) · SKETCH

1 × 50 mins · b/w

29 Mar 1961 · Wed 8pm

MAIN CAST
Bernard Bresslaw
Dickie Valentine
Graham Stark
Eunice Gayson
Warren Mitchell
Libby Morris
Ronnie Stevens

CREDITS
writers Dick Vosburgh, Brad Ashton · *director* J Murray Ashford

Featuring Bernard Bresslaw, the fast-rising former star of *The Army Game* and sundry British comedy movies, this was touted as a new series but only one edition was screened.

See also *The Bernard Bresslaw Show*.

Brett Butler: The Child Ain't Right

USA · SHOWTIME (THE CARSEY-WERNER COMPANY) · STANDUP

1 × 35 mins · colour

US date: 9 Aug 1993

UK date: 13 Jan 1995 · C4 Fri 10.30pm

MAIN CAST
Brett Butler

CREDITS
writer Brett Butler · *director* Gary Halvorson · *producer* Rob Miller

A one-off special starring the US comedian and actress Brett Butler, the star of the sitcom *Grace Under Fire* (see that entry for biographical information). In *The Child Ain't Right*, a standup performance recorded live in San Francisco, she exercised her dry wit in recalling the objectionable people she has met (and she has met more than her fair share).

Brian Conley … [various shows]

see CONLEY, Brian

Brian Rix Farces

From the 1950s, Brian Rix presented on BBC television many of his Whitehall and Garrick Theatre farces. Rix became an actor-manager while in his twenties and he had the foresight to equip his theatre permanently for TV recordings (a first). He tele-recorded stage performances for screening on bank holidays or at other festive occasions.

Because these farces, although performed for television, were played on the theatre stage with the cast that one could see there nightly, they are considered theatrical productions rather than TV-conceptions, and so fall beyond the parameters of this book.

For reference, such farces were either titled as they were in the theatre (eg, *Not Now Comrade* and *Reluctant Heroes*) or went under generic series titles such as *Brian Rix Presents*, *Brian Rix Farces*, *Six Of Rix*, *Laughter From Whitehall* and *The Brian Rix Theatre Of Laughter*.

See also *Dial RIX*.

Bricks Without Straw

UK · ITV (ATV) · SITCOM

1 × 30 mins · colour
11 Aug 1977 · Thu 7pm

MAIN CAST
Ernie Randle · · · · · · · · · · · · Michael Elphick
Phoebe · · · · · · · · · · · · · · · · Amanda Reiss

CREDITS
writers Andrew McCuloch/John Flanagan · *director/producer* Les Chatfield

A single pilot from the ITV series *The Sound Of Laughter*, this starred Michael Elphick as a builder, given the job of erecting a family home with all possible speed. It was not developed into a series.

Bridget Loves Bernie

USA · CBS (SCREEN GEMS/DOUGLAS S CRAMER CO/THORNHILL PRODUCTIONS) · SITCOM

24 × 30 mins · colour
US dates: 16 Sep 1972–8 Sep 1973
UK dates: 4 Apr–19 Dec 1974 (24 episodes) ITV Thu 7pm

MAIN CAST
Bridget Fitzgerald · · · · · · · · Meredith Baxter
Bernie Steinberg · · · · · · · · · · · David Birney
Walt Fitzgerald · · · · · · · · · · · · David Doyle
Amy Fitzgerald · · · · · · · · · · · · Audra Lindley
Michael Fitzgerald · · · · · · · Robert Sampson
Sam Steinberg · · · · · · · · · · · Harold J Stone
Sophie Steinberg · · · · · · · · · Bibi Osterwald
Moe Plotnic · · · · · · · · · · · · · · Ned Glass

CREDITS
creator Anne Nichols · *writers* various · *directors* various · *executive producer* Douglas S Cramer · *producers* William Frye, Arthur Alsberg, Don Nelson

Cultural and ethnic divisions between two families served as the basis for this US sitcom, in which Bridget Theresa Mary Colleen Fitzgerald – with a wealthy Irish-American Republican background and a brother for a priest – meets, falls in love with and marries Bernard 'Bernie' Steinberg, a Jewish taxi driver and struggling writer whose unsophisticated parents live over the top of their Steinberg's Delicatessen, in which they work all the hours that God sends them. The series scored highly in the ratings at first but was cancelled after one season, either because the writers were running out of ideas or because of the controversy it caused, focusing as it did on the religious divide. So evidently convincing was the pairing, however, that Bridget and Bernie fell in love in real life too, Meredith Baxter and David Birney marrying in 1973. The series had been the first on US television to show a married couple canoodling in bed – obviously it was a particularly nice feeling. As Meredith Baxter-Birney, the star went on to headline in *Family Ties*.

If the *Bridget Loves Bernie* premise sounds vaguely familiar, that's because it was a TV adaptation of *Abie's Irish Rose*, a comedy play that ran for more than 2300 Broadway performances from 1922 (in London from 1927), became a novel in 1927, a silent movie in 1928, a US radio series in 1942–44 (taken off the air following protests about the religious/ethnic stereotyping) and a talking movie in 1946, directed by Edward A Sutherland and produced by (but not starring) Bing Crosby. The premise became even more familiar in 1989 when American TV viewers had to suffer yet another variation on the theme, *Chicken Soup*, a very short-lived debacle for ABC, which, despite featuring British-born Lynn Redgrave in the cast, has never been screened in the UK.

The Bright Side

UK · C4 (REGENT PRODUCTIONS) · SITCOM

6 × 30 mins · colour
9 May–13 June 1985 · Thu 9pm

MAIN CAST
Cynthia Bright · · · · · · · · · · · · · Paula Wilcox
Lionel Bright · · · · · · · · · · · · · · · Paul Copley
Mr Lithgow · · · · · · · · · · · · · Geoffrey Hughes
Mrs Pickles · · · · · · · · · · · · · · · Annie Leake
Mrs Bright · · · · · · · · · · · · · · · · Hilda Braid
Mrs Beasley · · · · · · · · · · · · · · Stella Tanner
Mrs Chadwick · · · · · · · · · · · · Madge Hindle
Mr Royal · · · · · · · · · · · · · · · · · Derek Martin
Chadwick · · · · · · · · · · · · · · · · Bill Treacher
Humphries · · · · · · · · · · · · · · Johnny Shannon

CREDITS
writer Willis Hall · *director/producer* William G Stewart

Having played a sexually elusive single woman in *The Lovers*, a single-but-married-at-the-last woman in *Man About The House*, and a single mum in *Miss Jones And Son*, Paula Wilcox returned to the sitcom stage as Cynthia Bright, a young wife whose husband is ensconced in an open prison. Cynthia endeavours as best she can to manage on her own – which is not very well, because she's somewhat scatty – learning how to cope with the absence of her man and the acute financial position in which she's been landed. Along the way she gets herself a job, she drives the mild-mannered prison warder, Mr Lithgow (played by Geoffrey Hughes, Eddie Yeats in *Coronation Street*), to distraction, and she makes friends with Mrs Chadwick, wife of one of the two men with whom her Lionel is sharing a dorm (the other being Humphries).

Bright's Boffins

UK · ITV (SOUTHERN) · CHILDREN'S SITCOM

39 episodes (13 × 25 mins · 26 × 30 mins) · colour
Series One (13 × 25 mins) 4 Aug–27 Oct 1970 · Tue 4.55pm
Series Two (13 × 30 mins) 21 Apr–14 July 1971 · Wed 5.20pm
Series Three (13 × 30 mins) 7 Jan–31 Mar 1972 · Fri 5.20pm

MAIN CAST
Bertram Bright · · · · · · · · · · · Alexander Doré
Molly McCrandle · · · · · · · · · · · Avril Angers
Sergeant Thumper · · · · · · · · · · Denis Shaw
Berk · · · · · · · · · · · · · · · · · · George Moon
Dogsears Dawson · · · · · · · Gordon Rollings
Marmaduke · · · · · · · · · · · · · Eddie Reindeer

OTHER APPEARANCES
Catseyes Kavanagh and other roles · Dominic Roche
Tippy The Tipster · · · · · · · · · · · Johnny Briggs

CREDITS
writers Dominic Roche (25), Dominic Roche/Denis Goodwin (3), Denis Goodwin (1), Denis

Goodwin/Keith Miles (6), Keith Miles (4) ·
producer Peter Croft

A delightful, bizarre children's comedy starring Alexander Doré as a bumbling, old-fashioned (and, quite frankly, mad) scientist-inventor, leader of a team of similarly minded boffins working for an under-funded and irrelevant Whitehall ministry. The loopy group based themselves, in the first series at least, in the appropriately named Halfwitt House, although when this burned down they moved into a disused railway station, Larst Halt, from where they would set out on their missions, trying their best to be inconspicuous.

Johnny Briggs (Mike Baldwin in *Coronation Street*) appeared in a number of episodes as Tippy the Tipster, and some notable screen actors popped up in the series, among them Valentine Dyall (twice), Jack Watling and Wee Georgie Wood, who was cast as the seldom-seen Sir Desmond Dark, the man from the ministry.

Brighton Belles

UK · ITV (HUMPHREY BARCLAY PRODUCTIONS FOR CARLTON) · SITCOM

11 × 30 mins · colour

Pilot · 9 Mar 1993 · Tue 8.30pm

One series (10) 7 Sep–12 Oct 1993 · Tue 8.30pm · and 7 Dec–28 Dec 1994 · Wed mostly 7pm

MAIN CAST

Frances	Sheila Hancock
Annie	Wendy Craig
Bridget	Sheila Gish
Josephine	Jean Boht

CREDITS

creator Susan Harris · *writers* Susan Harris and others · *scripts adapter* Christopher Skala · *director* James Cellan Jones · *executive producer* Al Mitchell · *producer* Humphrey Barclay

A month before **The Golden Girls** ended on C4, a British adaptation – *Brighton Belles* – premiered on ITV, as perhaps the flagship pilot in the network's *Comedy Playhouse* season, with a full first series of ten further episodes already in the pipeline. The laugh-packed US scripts were being reused, a fine cast was in place, working under the wing of an experienced British sitcom producer, and everything pointed towards not only a success but a long-running one. What no one anticipated was that *Brighton Belles* would be a massive ratings flop – indeed, so poor were the viewing figures that the ten-part series was axed by ITV Network Centre after just six weeks. (The four remaining episodes went out quietly more than a year later.) Why did it fail? Several explanations apply, but the simplest has to be that *The Golden Girls* itself was already familiar to most British TV watchers (although the C4 ratings were never very high, millions had seen at least a few

episodes), and people felt no reason to tune into a UK adaptation delivering the same lines. When an original piece is already nigh-on perfect, and has sated its public, why try to sell a replica? Most transatlantic sitcom adaptations air without the original series having been seen in that territory. To pitch to viewers a carbon copy of an already successful series seems pointless – in hindsight, at least.

With local changes, the *Comedy Playhouse* pilot of *Brighton Belles* used the same script as the premiere episode of *The Golden Girls*, swiftly introducing us to the four principal women. For *Golden*'s Dorothy there was Frances, a sardonic, divorced former school headmistress. For Dorothy's mother Sophia there was Frances's mother Josephine, a tactless 80-year-old stroke victim once married to a Glasgow mobster. For Blanche there was Bridget, a busty, man-mad museum curator of Irish stock. For Rose there was Annie, a widowed farmer's daughter from Wiltshire, a bereavement counsellor light on brain cells. For the luxurious home on Miami Beach owned by Blanche there was the luxurious Regency house in Brighton owned by Bridget.

Brighton Belles was advertised as being about 'frank and funny women'. Frankly, too few people tuned in to find it funny, and a youthful Carlton was left with egg on its face.

The Brittas Empire

UK · BBC · SITCOM

53 episodes (51 × 30 mins · 2 × short specials) · colour

Series One (6) 3 Jan–14 Feb 1991 · BBC1 Thu 8.30pm

Series Two (7) 2 Jan–20 Feb 1992 · BBC1 Thu 8.30pm

Series Three (6) 7 Jan–11 Feb 1993 · BBC1 Thu 8.30pm

Series Four (8) 10 Jan–7 Mar 1994 · BBC1 Mon 8.30pm

Series Five (8) 31 Oct–19 Dec 1994 · BBC1 Mon 8.30pm

Special · 27 Dec 1994 · BBC1 Tue 6.20pm

Short special · part of *Children In Need* 24 Nov 1995 · BBC1 Fri approx 10.30pm

Series Six (6) 27 Feb–23 Apr 1996 · BBC1 Tue 8.30pm

Short special · part of *Children In Need* 22 Nov 1996 · BBC1 Fri around 10pm

Special · 24 Dec 1996 · BBC1 Tue 6.30pm

Series Seven (8) 6 Jan–24 Feb 1997 · BBC1 Mon 8.30pm

MAIN CAST

Gordon Brittas	Chris Barrie
Helen Brittas	Pippa Haywood
Laura Lancing	Julia St John
Colin Wetherby	Mike Burns
Tim Whistler	Russell Porter
Gavin Featherly	Tim Marriott
Carole	Harriet Thorpe
Julie	Judy Flynn
Linda	Jill Greenacre

OTHER APPEARANCES

Councillor Jack Drugget	Stephen Churchett
Michael T Farrell III	David Crean

CREDITS

creators Richard Fegen/Andrew Norriss · *writers* Richard Fegen/Andrew Norriss (36), Tony Millan/Mike Walling (5), Terry Kyan (3), Paul Smith (3), Ian Davidson/Peter Vincent (3), Ian Davidson (1), not known (2) · *directors* Mike Stephens (48), Christine Gernon (5) · *producer* Mike Stephens

It was a sign of the 1990s that a leisure centre should be the setting for a sitcom, such establishments having become popular in a health-conscious age. But it was not so much the proliferation of these places that attracted writers Fegen and Norriss, as the fact that leisure centres are usually dull and lifeless buildings – a least likely setting for belly laughs. Their intention, perversely, was to create bizarre and outrageous events in such tedious surroundings, and to this end they staffed their fictional leisure centre with a bunch of generally well-meaning but ultimately ineffectual characters. While this may have been sufficient for a traditional ensemble comedy, they also added to the mix a true television *enfant terrible*, the dreaded Gordon Brittas. TV grotesques come in all shapes and sizes: Alf Garnett was a ranting bigot, Basil Fawlty a maniacal snob and Victor Meldrew an angry curmudgeon. Gordon Brittas was an annoying, anal-retentive twerp.

Brittas was installed as manager of the newly built Whitbury Leisure Centre in the first episode, and the lives of his staff were never the same again. Whatever Brittas did ended in disaster, yet somehow he would emerge unscathed, refusing to acknowledge any responsibility and blithely planning what, inevitably, would become his next debacle. Brittas's wife Helen held the least enviable position: constant exposure to Gordon left her dazed, confused and mentally unstable (although she must have been crazy even to consider marriage to such an insufferable dolt). The staff of the leisure centre were soon suffering much the same symptoms as Gordon bombarded them with new rules and initiatives – most of them unworkable – and drove them to distraction with his nauseating, nasal drone of a voice. His level-headed, efficient assistant Laura did better than most at holding things together but the others were less successful. Homeless receptionist Carole (who kept her baby in a drawer behind the desk) was fraught enough as it was, and sports coaches Tim and Gavin were so eager to please that they fell in with most of Brittas's extreme notions and usually suffered into the bargain.

In fact, Brittas was so unbearable in the sitcom's first series that the writers toned him down thereafter, emphasising that he carried out most of his schemes to better mankind, not for personal gain. This altruism softened the character enough to make him watchable, but he remained someone you would never wish to meet.

The Brittas Empire operated almost on a cartoon level, with plots embracing many death-defying moments and, on more than one occasion, screen fatalities. Brittas himself was the victim of attempted murder when the brakes of his car were tampered with, but his wife was driving when they failed and she ended up in traction. As blasé as ever, her husband ascribed the fault to pesky squirrels. On two other occasions Brittas was presumed to have been killed, much to the joy of his staff (except for his only supporter, the gormless handyman Colin), but he returned both times, fighting fit and raring to go. Over the seven series, Carole had another child, Helen gave birth to twins and Brittas's career ambitions led him to a job in Brussels. It was generally assumed *The Brittas Empire* had ended after the fifth series, when Brittas was appointed European Minister for Sport, indeed the following Christmas special (27 December 1994) was set in 2019 and had the main characters looking back at the life of the man who had become Sir Gordon Brittas. But, like the earlier statements declaring Brittas's demise, this was false and the character returned for two more series (although Fegen and Norriss absented themselves as writers).

The Brittas Empire had some fine moments, especially with its surreal plot twists and unusual obsession with death and danger, but perhaps relied upon plain repetition of a single theme – Brittas's tremendously irritating character – with too little variation. Having seemingly cornered the market in enervating and annoying characters, Chris Barrie was also starring in *Red Dwarf* during the life of *The Brittas Empire*, and the workings of the Brittas brain were equal to anything his sci-fi alter ego Rimmer encountered.

Note. Appearing in character, Chris Barrie was the main contributor to *Get Fit With Brittas*, a BBC1 series of six ten-minute programmes offering advice about fitness and good health, screened from 18 July to 22 August 1997.

Broad And Narrow

UK · ITV (ATV) · SATIRE

6 × 30 mins · b/w

21 Aug–25 Sep 1965 · Sat 11.05pm

MAIN CAST
Ralph Bates
Terence Brady
Roger Ordish
Chris Serle
Joanna Van Gyseghem
Bill Wallis

CREDITS
writers Terence Brady, Michael Bogdanov · *director* Albert Locke · *producer* Anthony Firth

With *That Was The Week That Was*, the BBC established late Saturday night as a proven slot for satire, revue and other 'intellectual' comedy ideas – to the extent, indeed, that some were labelling it 'Satireday'. ITV dipped into the market with this six week series featuring a group of bright young things and their views of life in Britain in 1965. Of the half-dozen players, Ralph Bates went on to the stage and also married Joanna Van Gyseghem, who remained on stage and screen (*Duty Free*), Roger Ordish went on to a successful career as a BBC comedy director/producer, Chris Serle became a regular radio broadcaster as well as one of the team on *That's Life*, Bill Wallis was a bastion of Radio 4's biting satirical review *Week Ending*, and Terence Brady, who already had some credentials – he had replaced Peter Cook in a stage run of *Beyond The Fringe* – went into stage and TV writing.

Broaden Your Mind

UK · BBC · SKETCH

13 × 30 mins · colour

Series One (6) 28 Oct–2 Dec 1968 · BBC2 Mon 9.35pm

Series Two (7) 17 Nov–29 Dec 1969 · BBC2 Mon 9.10pm

MAIN CAST
Tim Brooke-Taylor
Graeme Garden
Jo Kendall
Nick McArdle
Bill Oddie (series 2)
Roland MacLeod (series 2)

CREDITS
creators/writers Graeme Garden/Tim Brooke-Taylor · *additional material* Bill Oddie, Barry Cryer, Marty Feldman/Barry Took, John Law, David McKellar, John Cleese/Graham Chapman, Bob Block, Simon Brett, C Stuart-Clark, Terry Jones/Michael Palin, Eric Idle, Derek Collyer/George Evans, Roland MacLeod, Jim Franklin · *director (film)* Jim Franklin · *producer* Sydney Lotterby

Misleadingly described as a part-quiz, part-educational programme, *Broaden Your Mind* was in fact a fast-paced themed-sketch show, albeit with those two ingredients worked into the mix. Tim Brooke-Taylor conceived the idea, which was subtitled 'An Encyclopaedia Of The Air', inspired by the proliferation of weekly part-work magazines that built eventually into an all-encompassing tome. He realised that a spoof of the format would enable the players to fit any number of sketches around each week's chosen theme. One of most popular recurring sketches featured two old men, Teddy and Freddy (Graeme Garden and Brooke-Taylor)

lecturing on a given topic but finding it hard to stick to the subject.

Michael Palin, Terry Jones and Bill Oddie appeared as guest artists during the first series and Oddie joined the cast as a regular for the second series, meaning that the trio who would make *The Goodies* was assembled. As it was, adding Jo Kendall's involvement, *Broaden Your Mind* featured four of the six troopers from the smash-hit BBC radio comedy series *I'm Sorry, I'll Read That Again*, excepting John Cleese and David Hatch.

Brotherly Love

UK · ITV (YORKSHIRE) · SITCOM

1 × 30 mins · colour

16 Sep 1974 · Mon 8pm

MAIN CAST
Mike Hanson · · · · · · · · · · · · · · Keith Barron
Eddie Hanson · · · · · · · · · · · · · · David Swift
Sarah · · · · · · · · · · · · · · · · Bridget Armstrong

CREDITS
writers Roy Bottomley/Tom Brennand · *director/producer* Derrick Goodwin

A pilot for a comedy that failed to take off, this was one of a series of single sitcoms produced by Yorkshire TV for consideration by ITV audiences. Future successes *Rising Damp* and *Oh No – It's Selwyn Froggitt* gave the series a laudable 33-per-cent strike rate but *Brotherly Love* did not make the grade, and Keith Barron's character – a miner turned flash property-speculator with a fancy apartment and fancy bird – was not seen again.

Brothers

USA · SHOWTIME (PARAMOUNT/GARY NARDINO PRODUCTIONS) · SITCOM

115 × 30 mins · colour

US dates: 13 July 1984–25 July 1989

UK dates: 29 Nov 1985–14 Mar 1986 (13 episodes) C4 Fri 9pm

MAIN CAST
Cliff Waters · · · · · · · · · · · · · · · · Paul Regina
Joe Waters · · · · · · · · · · · · · · Robert Walden
Lou Waters · · · · · · · · · · · · Brandon Maggart
Donald Maltby · · · · Philip Charles MacKenzie
Penny Waters · · · · · · · · · · · · · · · Hallie Todd
Kelly · Robin Riker
Samantha 'Sam' Waters · · · Mary Ann Pascal

CREDITS
creator David Lloyd · *writers* various · *directors* various · *producers* Greg Antonacci, Gary Nardino, Stu Silver

A groundbreaking US sitcom, imported to the UK by C4 in a limited number of episodes, which dealt in a *real* way with homosexuality, a million miles from John Inman's mincing TV personas in Britain. Dealing as it did with such areas as Aids, gay-bashing and male kissing, *Brothers* was way too hot a topic for the major US networks to handle – ABC and NBC turned it down flat – so the series went out in the States on the Showtime cable channel, fast becoming one of the prime places to see material that stepped out of the mainstream. Indeed, *Brothers* was the first sitcom made specifically for cable.

Set in New York (although filmed in Hollywood), the series focused on the three Waters brothers – Lou (eldest), Joe (middle) and Cliff (youngest). Lou is a construction worker and something of a father figure to his siblings; Joe (played by Robert Walden, the likeable but pushy newspaper reporter Paul Rossi in *Lou Grant*) is a former professional (American) football hero who has retired and opened his own restaurant; and Cliff … Cliff is gay. This was revealed in dramatic fashion in the series' opening episode, when he 'came out' on the eve of his planned wedding.

Because Cliff looks and acts 'straight' this makes the news particularly hard for his brothers to accept. Indeed, this inability of Lou and Joe to come to terms with the fact that their baby brother was not one of them, but, rather, 'one of them', formed the basis for much of the comedy. (And yes, apart from the 'issues' the series was also funny.) Acceptance was an especially tough proposition for Lou, the very macho, very hetero ex-sportsman, and he also had trouble coming to terms with Cliff's visiting effeminate friend Donald.

Other regularly featured characters were Sam, who married Joe midway through the series, Penny Waters, Joe's daughter (from his first marriage); and Kelly, a waitress at Joe's restaurant.

Brothers In Law

UK · BBC · SITCOM

13 × 30 mins · b/w

17 Apr–10 July 1962 · Tue 7.55pm then 8.45pm

MAIN CAST

Roger Thursby · · · · · · · · · · · · Richard Briers
Henry Blagrove · · · · · · · · · · · Richard Waring
Kendall Grimes · · · · · · · · · · John Glyn-Jones
Sally Mannering · · · · · · · · · · · · · June Barry

CREDITS

creator Henry Cecil · *writers* Frank Muir/Denis Norden (6), Richard Waring (5), Myles Rudge (1), David Climie (1) · *additional material* Henry Cecil · *script editors* Frank Muir/Denis Norden · *producer* Graeme Muir

Henry Cecil's 1955 book *Brothers In Law*, set in the legal profession in London, had already been made into a successful film (starring Ian Carmichael and Terry-Thomas) in 1957 before this adaptation for television. The series gave 27-year-old actor Richard Briers his first starring role, cast as the innocent barrister Roger Thursby in his first year in chambers, with actor/writer Richard Waring co-starring as Henry Blagrove, Thursby's senior. (While playing on stage a couple of

years earlier, Briers had been spotted as a likely talent by Frank Muir.) Henry Cecil still practised as a County Court judge at this time (as His Honour Judge Henry Cecil Leon) and his writings on the subject, like the man himself, were urbane, witty and clever.

The TV series had some far-reaching effects. The following year, Waring scripted Briers' next starring vehicle, **Marriage Lines**, also produced by Graeme Muir; and in 1970 Waring resurrected *Brothers In Law* for BBC Radio 4, in which he and Briers, and also John Glyn-Jones, reprised their TV roles. (It ran for 39 episodes, from 9 June 1970 to 17 July 1972.) One episode of *Brothers In Law* marked the TV debut of Yootha Joyce, hitherto only a stage performer, and the final episode led to a spin-off series, **Mr Justice Duncannon**, featuring Andrew Cruickshank in the title role.

The Brothers McGregor

UK · ITV (GRANADA) · SITCOM

26 × 30 mins · colour

Series One (7) 4 Sep–16 Oct 1985 · Wed 8.30pm
Series Two (6) 3 Apr–8 May 1986 · Thu 8.30pm
Series Three (6) 16 Feb–23 Mar 1987 · Mon 8pm
Series Four (7) 13 July–24 Aug 1988 · Wed 10.35pm

MAIN CAST

Wesley McGregor · · · · · · · · · · · · Paul Barber
Cyril McGregor · · · · · · · · · Philip Whitchurch
Dolly McGregor · · · · · · · · · · · Jean Heywood
Glenys Pike · · · · · · · · · · · · · Jackie Downey
Colwyn Stanley · · · · · · · · · · · Allan Surtees
Nigel · · · · · · · · · · · · · · · · Terry Cundall

OTHER APPEARANCES

Mr Cox · · · · · · · · · Robert Vahey (series 1–3)
Dodgy Dennis · · · · Robert Booth (series 1–3)

CREDITS

creators Julian Roach/John Stevenson · *writers* Julian Roach (10), John Stevenson (10), Julian Roach/John Stevenson (6) · *director/producer* Bernard Thompson · *executive producer* Bill Podmore

Pre-dating and then running contemporaneously with Carla Lane's better-known BBC creation **Bread**, *The Brothers McGregor* was a deservedly popular ITV sitcom set in Liverpool and among Scousers, embracing the sharp-tongued laconic wit for which its people are famous.

As the title suggests, the series focused on a pair of siblings – two Catholic half-brothers – the older one (Cyril) white-skinned, the younger (Wesley) black, being the son of a missionary from West Africa who went in for a spot of altar-jilting before returning to his own continent. The half-brothers are in partnership together, running a *very* dodgy second-hand car dealership called Rathbone Motors from one of Liverpool's many bomb sites, and they have fingers in other pies too. Cyril works as a co-bouncer (with the

humourless Nigel) and occasional singer in a seedy niterie, the Blue Cockatoo Club, owned by the cigar-puffing Colwyn Stanley, a former bed-mate of Cyril's mother. Wesley, who thinks of himself as the brains behind the duo, reads the *Financial Times* and, with tycoonery in mind, has appointed himself president (and sole member) of the CBI – the Confederation of Black Industrialists. Though they scarcely agree on anything – Cyril is a socialist, Wesley a Tory – the brothers cannot operate without each other, and each shares a fascination for money. When he's not busy writing letters to every important person he can think of, Wesley acts as unofficial agent/representative for Cyril, who hopes to become England's answer to Frank Sinatra but stands no chance.

Both the brothers adore their mum, Dolly McGregor, who works in a café and, at home, knits constantly. Jilted by Wesley's father and widowed when Cyril's father was knocked down by a tram while trying to prise a half-crown from the tramline in Scotland Road, she is the rock upon which their lives are built, and they all live together in a high-rise council block. Here they are often visited by Glenys, Cyril's dozy fiancee. They've been engaged for six years (at the series' start) but Cyril is in no hurry to tie the knot because, he says, his estranged first wife Rita is paying him maintenance.

Throughout the 26 episodes the high level of Scouse humour was maintained, even if the ratings did slip after the first series. All the episodes were written (together and individually) by Roach and Stevenson, the team that created the excellent **Brass** and contributed scripts to *Coronation Street*. Indeed, one forgotten but interesting point of trivia is that the brothers McGregor first appeared on television in *Coronation Street*, as a couple of rowdies who enlivened the Rovers' Return at Eddie Yeats' engagement bash, an episode screened on 12 May 1982. The actors then were Tony Osoba (Wesley) and Carl Chase (Cyril).

The Brown Man

UK · BBC · SITCOM

1 × 30 mins · colour

7 Sep 1993 · BBC2 Tue 9pm

MAIN CAST

Arnold Brown
Gemma Craven

CREDITS

writer Jonathan Bernstein · *director* David Blair · *producer* Colin Gilbert

An offbeat one-off with the wry, dry Arnold Brown playing a private detective investigating murder on the talent-night circuit.

Brown had made many appearances on TV but had never graduated to star status and this piece may have been intended as a pilot to showcase his talents.

Bruce And Ronnie

UK · BBC · SKETCH

1 × 45 mins · colour

26 Dec 1988 · BBC1 Mon 10.55pm

MAIN CAST
Bruce Forsyth
Ronnie Corbett
Fiona Fullerton

CREDITS
writers Barry Cryer, Ian Davidson, Spike Mullins, Laurie Rowley, Peter Vincent, Dick Vosburgh · *script editors* Barry Cryer/Peter Vincent · *director/producer* Marcus Mortimer

Following their successful teaming-up for the 1988 *Royal Variety Show* (screened by BBC1 on 26 November) Bruce Forsyth and Ronnie Corbett presented this Christmas special with guest star Fiona Fullerton. The highlight of the show was a *Gone With The Wind* spoof with Fullerton appearing as Scarlett O'Hara. With his usual partner, Ronnie Barker, announcing his retirement at this time, Corbett and the BBC must have hoped that this new double-act would strike the same chord with the public, but the pairing remained a seasonal oddity.

The Bruce Forsyth Show

UK · ITV (ATV, *ABC, **YORKSHIRE, ***THAMES), BBC · SKETCH

36 editions (16 × 60 mins · 10 × 35 mins · 8 × 30 mins · 1 × 65 mins. 1 × 45 mins) · 33 × b/w · 3 × colour

Special (60 mins · b/w) 29 Mar 1959 · Sun 8pm

Series One (10 × 35 mins · b/w) 29 Sep–1 Dec 1962 · Sat 8.25pm

*Special (65 mins · b/w) 25 Dec 1965 · Sat 10.05pm

*Series Two (6 × 60 mins · b/w) 14 Aug–18 Sep 1966 · Sun 10.05pm

*Series Three (6 × 60 mins · b/w) 20 Aug–24 Sep 1967 · Sun 10.05pm

Special (60 mins · b/w) *A Night In The Life Of …* 7 Sep 1968 · Sat 9.30pm

**Series Four (8 × 30 mins · b/w) 31 May–19 July 1969 · Sat mostly 7.30pm

Special (60 mins · colour) 28 Apr 1973 · Sat 8pm

***Special (60 mins · colour) *Nice To See You!* 21 Dec 1981 · Mon 8pm

Special (45 mins · colour) 27 Dec 1989 · BBC1 Wed 8.15pm

MAIN CAST
Bruce Forsyth

CREDITS
1959 special *writer* not known · *producer* Albert Locke

1962 series *writers* Sid Green/Dick Hills (and one show with Richard Waring) · *producer* Francis Essex

1965 special *writers* Sid Green/Dick Hills · *producer* Philip Jones

1966 series *writers* Sid Green/Dick Hills · *producer* Philip Jones

1967 series *writers* Sid Green/Dick Hills · *producer* Keith Beckett

1968 special *writers* Sid Green/Dick Hills · *producer* Jon Scoffield

1969 series *writers* Spike Mullins, Joe Steeples · *director/producer* Gordon Reece

1973 special *writers* Bryan Blackburn, Tony Hawes, Eric Merriman · *director/producer* Alan Tarrant

1981 special *writers* Dick Hills, Barry Cryer, Bruce Forsyth, Garry Chambers, Eric Merriman, Andrew Marshall/David Renwick · *director/producer* Keith Beckett

1989 special *writers* Dick Hills, Barry Cryer, Peter Vincent, Paul Minett/Brian Leveson · *director/producer* Nigel Lythgoe

Although known today primarily for hosting TV game-shows, a genre that has dominated since first fronting *The Generation Game* in 1971, Bruce Forsyth (born in north London on 22 February 1928) has always specialised in an all-round entertainment, with the accent firmly on comedy. This was especially true in his early years on TV, for after making his name as the gifted MC of *Val Parnell's Sunday Night At The London Palladium* (from September 1958), Forsyth starred in several sketch-show series of his own, mostly scripted by the ultra-prolific team of Sid Green and Dick Hills. All the programmes featured guest stars, with whom Bruce would perform, and many top names thus appeared, including Tommy Cooper, Dudley Moore (twice), Harry Secombe (twice) and Frankie Howerd (this particular union led to three joint programmes, *Frankie And Bruce*). The first full series, in 1959, had a particularly interesting diversion in that Forsyth regularly appeared in sketches with sports stars, among them boxer Henry Cooper, jockey Scobie Breasley, swimmer Anita Lonsborough, former tennis champion Fred Perry and snooker player Joe Davis.

Forsyth still gains plenty of laughs from his patter in game-shows but has not performed a dedicated sketch comedy show *per se* for some years. Among his music-dancing-comedy variety-led specials are *Whatever Happened To Christmas* (ATV, 24 December 1968), *Bring On The Girls* (Thames, 28 July 1976), *Bruce And More Girls* (Thames, 13 April 1977), *The Entertainers* (29 August 1977), *Bruce And Sammy* (LWT, 21 September 1980), *Bruce Meets The Girls* (Thames, 2 December 1981), *Forsyth's Follies*

(Thames, 23 February 1982) and *Forsyth's Show* (BBC1, 1 April 1991). *Bruce Forsyth's Big Night* (LWT, 7 October–24 December 1978 and 4 April 1980) was a wraparound entertainment series in which the host introduced pre-recorded elements featuring, among others, *The Glums* and *Cannon And Ball*, and *Bruce's Guest Night* (two series for BBC1, 10 April–15 May 1992, and 19 April–21 June 1993) was a variety show that often featured comedy guest stars.

See also *Bruce And Ronnie*, *New Look* and *Slinger's Day*.

Brush Strokes

UK · BBC · SITCOM

40 × 30 mins · colour

Series One (13) 1 Sep–24 Nov 1986 · BBC1 Mon 8.30pm

Series Two (7) 12 Oct–23 Nov 1987 · BBC1 Mon 8pm

Series Three (6) 28 Nov 1988–16 Jan 1989 · BBC1 Mon 8pm

Series Four (6) 22 Feb–29 Mar 1990 · BBC1 Thu 8pm

Series Five (8) 17 Feb–7 Apr 1991 · BBC1 Sun 7.15pm

MAIN CAST

Jacko	Karl Howman
Lionel	Gary Waldhorn (series 1–3)
Veronica	Elizabeth Counsell
Lesley	Kim Thompson (series 1);
	Erika Hoffman (series 2–5)
Eric	Mike Walling
Sandra	Jackie Lye
Jean	Nicky Croydon
Elmo	Howard Lew Lewis

CREDITS
writers John Esmonde/Bob Larbey · *directors* Mandie Fletcher (20), John B Hobbs (14), Harold Snoad (6) · *producers* John B Hobbs (14), Sydney Lotterby (13), Mandie Fletcher (7), Harold Snoad (6)

An Esmonde and Larbey sitcom set in south London and depicting the (mostly) amorous adventures of a good-looking, wisecracking house painter, Jacko. He was a sort of Alfie-type on the surface: a seemingly happy-go-lucky, uncomplicated womaniser, but part of Jacko's charm was his sincerity and tendency genuinely to fall for the women he pursued. He appeared to love most women, and not simply in the sexual sense. At work, his boss was the hard-to-please Lionel, who was thankfully ignorant of the fact that his daughter Lesley was one of Jacko's conquests. When Lionel died, his wife Veronica took over the business and our hero found his working life more pleasant. Jacko's prime romance was with the firm's secretary Sandra, to whom he became engaged. *Brush Strokes* was a serial comedy and at the end of the second series the writers introduced a real soap-like cliffhanger when Jacko, about to be married to Sandra, turned to his best man Eric, as the bride walked down the aisle, and whispered 'I think I've made a terrible mistake …'. (They didn't marry, but went on honeymoon regardless.)

The main action in *Brush Strokes* was split between the decorating agency where Jacko worked, the house he shared with his sister Jean and her husband, Jacko's friend and work colleague Eric, and (in later episodes) Elmo's Wine Bar, a garish, gaudy, tasteless establishment run by the equally garish, gaudy and tasteless Elmo. As the series progressed viewers saw less of the flippant devil-may-care side of Jacko and more of his melancholic quality as he found himself becoming a lone single guy, his friends and acquaintances all gradually pairing off. Never fully losing his emotional naïvety, Jacko nevertheless matured through his experiences. The character proved very popular, especially with women viewers, and provided a breakthrough for the actor Karl Howman.

Note. Karl Howman and Howard Lew Lewis also appeared as Jacko and Elmo in a sketch in a **Comic Relief** production, screened by BBC1 on 10 March 1989.

The Bubblegum Brigade

UK · ITV (HTV WEST) · CHILDREN'S SITCOM

6 × 30 mins · colour

2 May–6 June 1989 · Tue 4.20pm

MAIN CAST

William · Bill Oddie
Alph · Ian Kirkby
Auntie Doodah · · · · · · · · · Veronica Clifford
Bunny · · · · · · · · · · · · · · · · · Michelle Moore
Fuddle · · · · · · · · · · · · · · · · · James Hyden
Jinx · Flora Fenton

CREDITS

creator/executive producer Peter Murphy · *writers* Bill Oddie/Laura Beaumont · *directors* Pennant Roberts (3), Alistair Clark (3) · *producer* Pennant Roberts

Written by Bill Oddie and his wife Laura Beaumont (they also scripted *From The Top*), this children's comedy starred the former Goodie as a do-gooder, joining forces with four children – Alph, Bunny, Fuddle and Jinx – and dear old Auntie Doodah, to form the Bubblegum Brigade, whose motto was 'Broken hearts mended while you wait' and whose efforts, often unsolicited, usually resulted in comic confusion. Just one series was made.

Bud

UK · ITV (ATV) · SITCOM

6 × 30 mins · b/w

26 July–30 Aug 1963 · Fri 10.15pm

MAIN CAST

Bud Flanagan
Charlie Naughton
Jerry Desmonde

OTHER APPEARANCES

Chesney Allen
Jack Hylton
'Monsewer' Eddie Gray

CREDITS

writer Kevin Laffan · *producer* Philip Barker

That much-loved member of the Crazy Gang, Bud Flanagan, made his first ever TV series – claiming, too, to be playing his first acting roles of *any* kind – in this fascinating ATV sitcom. The theme was simple: the Crazy Gang had disbanded and Bud needed a new job, so each week would find him scouting around in new directions: as a bookmaker (appropriately, for in real life Flanagan co-owned three turf accountant shops in the East End of London); as a night security guard; as a male nurse, and so on. Fellow Gang members Chesney Allen, Charlie Naughton and 'Monsewer' Eddie Gray appeared here and there, as did perennial straight-man Jerry Desmonde and showman/band leader Jack Hylton. Down among the small print, Nigel Hawthorne had a minor role in the final episode.

See also *The Crazy Gang, Friday Night With …* and *Together Again.*

Buffalo Bill

USA · NBC (STAMPEDE PRODUCTIONS) · SITCOM

26 × 30 mins · colour

US dates: 1 June 1983–5 Apr 1984
UK dates: 19 May–11 Aug 1984 (13 episodes)
C4 Sat 4.35pm

MAIN CAST

Bill Bittinger · · · · · · · · · · · · Dabney Coleman
Jo-Jo White · · · · · · · · · · · · · Joanna Cassidy
Karl Shub · · · · · · · · · · · · · · · · · Max Wright
Woody · · · · · · · · · · · · · · · · · · · John Fielder
Wendy Killian · · · · · · · · · · · · · Geena Davis
Newdell Spriggs · · · · · · · · Charles Robinson

CREDITS

creators Jay Tarses/Tom Patchett · *writers* Jay Tarses/Tom Patchett, Geena Davis, Carol D Gary, Dennis B Klein, Merrill Markoe, Gary Markowitz, Mitch Markowitz · *directors* various · *producers* Jay Tarses/Tom Patchett

Far from the cowboy association the name suggests, *Buffalo Bill* was an unusual sitcom, especially so in America, in that the lead character was not at all a nice chap. As the host of *The Buffalo Bill Show* – a chat-show at WBFL-TV, a local TV station in Buffalo, upstate New York – Bill Bittinger is conceited, rude, obdurate, self-obsessed, narcissistic and displays a pronounced mean streak. He's plain horrible *off* the air, using and abusing his staff – his director and sometime girlfriend Jo Jo, station manager Karl Shub, meek floor manager Woody, programme researcher Wendy Killian and the no-nonsense make-up man Newdell Spriggs – and scarcely better *on* it, asking

rude questions and putting down his guests to the point where the next writ is never far away. Good always wins out, however, which means that Bill always ends up the loser.

The series was created, written and produced by Jay Tarses and Tom Patchett, two veterans of that wonderful US sitcom – yet to be screened in the UK – *The Bob Newhart Show*. This new creation of theirs was also among the best.

See also *The 'Slap' Maxwell Story.*

Bulldog Breed

UK · ITV (GRANADA) · SITCOM

7 × 30 mins · b/w

19 Sep–31 Oct 1962 · Wed 9.15pm

MAIN CAST

Tom Bowler · · · · · · · · · · · · · · Donald Churchill
Sandra Prentiss · · · · · · · · · · · Amanda Barrie
Henry Broadbent · · · · · · · · Peter Butterworth
Lillian Broadbent · · · · · · Betty Huntley-Wright
Billy Broadbent · · · · · · · · Geoffrey Whitehead
Mr Meadows · · · · · · · · · · · · Geoffrey Palmer

CREDITS

creator Derek Granger · *storylines* Harry Driver · *writers* Jack Rosenthal (6), Peter Eckersley (1) · *directors* Graeme McDonald (6), Howard Baker (1) · *producer* Derek Granger

A single-series sitcom with Donald Churchill in the part of Tom Bowler, a perennial optimist who refuses to take life seriously – despite the persuasions of those who risk life and limb getting close to him, like his parents Henry and Lilian, best friend Billy and remarkably persistent girlfriend Sandra. Tom simply goes through life wreaking havoc upon everyone and everything around him.

The series was created and produced by the former *Coronation Street* producer Derek Granger; one further link with the *Street* was that *Bulldog Breed* gave young actress Amanda Barrie – to become famous as Alma Sedgewick/Baldwin – her first major TV role.

Bullpen

see *Hardball*

The Bullshitters

UK · C4 (MICHAEL WHITE/DINKY DOO PRODUCTIONS) · COMEDY FILM

1 × 50 mins · colour

3 Nov 1984 · Sat 11pm

MAIN CAST

Bonehead · · · · · · · · · · · · · · · · · Keith Allen
Foyle · · · · · · · · · · · · · · · · · Peter Richardson
Commander Jackson · · · · · · Robbie Coltrane
Alana Pellay · · · · · · · · · · · · · · · · · herself
Jimmy Fagg · · · · · · · · · · · · · · · · · himself
Janie · · · · · · · · · · · · · · · · · Fiona Hendley
Admiral · · · · · · · · · · · · · · · · · Al Matthews
Thompson · · · · · · · · · · · · · · George Khan
Stone Deaf A&R Man · · · · · · · Elvis Costello

CREDITS
writers Keith Allen/Peter Richardson · *director*
Stephen Frears · *executive producer*
Michael White · *producer* Elaine Taylor

Virtually a **Comic Strip Presents ...** film
but not quite because co-writer and co-star
Keith Allen did not want it to be associated
with that series, *The Bullshitters* was a fine
one-off parody of the cop/adventure shows
that proliferated on British and US TV in the
1970s – in particular *The Professionals*.
That particular ITV series had featured two
characters, Bodie and Doyle; here, Allen and
co-star Peter Richardson were Bonehead and
Foyle, employed by the ruthless Commander
Jackson (in *The Professionals* the commanding
officer was played by Gordon Jackson) to
rescue his kidnapped daughter. As theirs is an
undercover operation, though, Bonehead and
Foyle have to make do with bus passes and
public telephones, but they still dash around
shouting, 'Let's go!'. One choice scene was
a shtick routine in which Jackson (Robbie
Coltrane) showed his two young charges how
TV tough guys get into their car.

The Bumblies

see BENTINE, Michael

Bunch Of Five

UK · C4 (VARIOUS) · SITCOMS

5 × 30 mins · colour

A C4 variation of the BBC's *Comedy Playhouse*-
style pilot series, designed to try out new
sitcom ideas.

These are the five pilot titles with first
broadcast dates. Only *Blue Heaven*, marked
below with an asterisk, graduated to a full
series. See individual entries for further
details.

One series

3 June 1992	Dead At Thirty
10 June 1992	*Blue Heaven
17 June 1992	The Weekenders
24 June 1992	Shall We Gather At The River?
1 July 1992	Miles Better

Carol Burnett

Born in San Antonio, Texas, on 26 April
1934, comic, actress and singer Carol
Burnett worked her way to the big time after
being the subject of a $1000 wager by a
wealthy businessman who was impressed
by her performance at a society party. She
used the money to go to New York,
struggled initially but finally came good,
paying back the money and carving out a

Broadway career. She first came to TV
prominence as a regular on *The Garry
Moore Show* (1959–62) before leaving to go
solo and appearing often in variety shows.
In common with most of the all-time-great
comedy sketch artists, whose ranks she
certainly joins, she was adept at acting, and
in her trademark series, *The Carol Burnett
Show*, she created a number of memorable
comic characters including the awful
secretary Mrs Wiggins, ex-movie queen
Nora Desmond, and – Burnett's most
famous invention – the Cleaning Lady,
whom she always played with a touch of
pathos.

Despite her major status in the USA,
Carol Burnett remains relatively unknown in
the UK. Their gain is Britain's loss.

See also *Fresno*.

The Carol Burnett Show   UK

UK · ITV (GRANADA) · STANDUP/SKETCH

1 × 30 mins · b/w

16 Sep 1960 · Fri 8.55pm

MAIN CAST
Carol Burnett
Milt Kamen

CREDITS
director Eric Fawcett

Burnett visited Britain in 1960 and made
this single half-hour special in Granada's
Manchester studios. The actor/comedian
Milt Kamen also made the journey across
the Atlantic as her guest star.

An Evening With Carol Burnett

USA · CBS · SKETCH

1 × 60 mins · colour

US date: 24 Feb 1963

UK date: 18 Apr 1965 · BBC2 Sun 7.25pm
(b/w)

MAIN CAST
Carol Burnett
Robert Preston

CREDITS
writer Igor Peshkowsky · *director* Ernest
Chambers · *producer* Bob Banner

Screened in Britain as *Carol And Company*,
Burnett was joined in this US special
by Robert Preston for a US TV hour
(50 minutes on the commercial-free BBC2)
of slick humour.

The Carol Burnett Show In London

UK · BBC · SKETCH

1 × 50 mins · colour

28 June 1970 · BBC2 Sun 7.25pm

MAIN CAST
Carol Burnett
Harvey Korman
Lyle Waggoner

Vicki Lawrence
Juliet Prowse

CREDITS
writer Arnie Rosen · *director* Dave Powers ·
executive producer Arnie Rosen · *producer* John
Street

Taped in London by and for the BBC, this
one-off special featured the cast of *The
Carol Burnett Show*, and was screened as a
prelude to the BBC2 transmissions of that
famous US series which began the following
week.

The Carol Burnett Show   USA

USA · CBS (WHACKO PRODUCTIONS) · SKETCH

244 × 60 mins · colour

US dates: 11 Sep 1967–8 Sep 1979

UK dates: 5 July–27 Sep 1970 (13 editions)
BBC2 Sun mostly 8.15pm

MAIN CAST
Carol Burnett
Harvey Korman
Lyle Waggoner
Vicki Lawrence

CREDITS
writers Ed Simmons and others · *director* Dave
Powers · *executive producer* Joe Hamilton ·
producer Ed Simmons

The Carol Burnett Show was America's
favourite TV sketch series of the 1960s–70s,
held there in similar esteem to that of **The
Morecambe And Wise Show** in Britain,
and likewise featured big-name celebrity
guests. At a time when this type of comedy-
variety show was all but disappearing from
US TV, Burnett kept the genre alive, mainly
through the brilliantly funny extended
sketches played with panache by her regular
acting group.

Her support crew was first rate and later
in the run was supplemented by comedy
actor Tim Conway, with whom Burnett did
some of her best work. Harvey Korman
matched Burnett in the humour stakes and
Lyle Waggoner, mostly cast in the role
of straight-man, was a dependable and
generous foil. Vicki Lawrence, the other
female member of the regular cast, bore a
uncanny resemblance to Burnett and would
often portray her younger sister.

The series failed to click with British
audiences but remains a first-rate example
of American sketch comedy at its best.

Carol & Company

USA · NBC (KALOLA PRODUCTIONS/WIND
DANCER PRODUCTIONS/TOUCHSTONE
TELEVISION) · COMEDY ANTHOLOGY

37 × 30 mins · colour

US dates: 31 Mar 1990–20 July 1991

UK dates: 1 June 1993–15 Dec 1994 (26
editions) BBC1 then BBC2 mostly Tue 11.05am

MAIN CAST
Carol Burnett
Anita Barone
Meagen Fay
Richard Kind
Terry Kiser
Jeremy Piven
Peter Krause

CREDITS
writers various · *directors* Andrew D Weyman and others · *executive producers* Matt Williams, David McFadzean · *producer* Gayle S Maffeo

Having proved herself the mistress of sketch comedy over many years, Carol Burnett extended her repertoire with this series of comedy playlets, which gave her the opportunity to show her skill at creating vastly different characters. Filmed in front of a studio audience, Burnett opened each show as herself, introducing her special guest stars and the regular troupe of supporting players. The pieces were really extended sketches rather than fully rounded stories, but the longish running time meant that darker, more serious themes than usual could be explored. There was an obvious parallel here with *The Tracey Ullman Show*, running concurrently on American TV, but Burnett had plenty of track history to disprove any suggestions of plagiarism.

George Burns

George Burns was born Nathan Birnbaum in New York on 20 January 1896. He left school at 13 to support his fatherless family and tried his hand at a number of jobs on the fringes of show business before becoming a fully fledged vaudevillian with a succession of song and dance acts. Then, a chance meeting with Gracie Allen changed his life, and her's too. She was born in San Francisco on 26 July 1906 to a vaudeville family and had an act with her sisters at an early age. When she met Burns in 1923, Allen had all but given up entertainment, having enrolled in secretarial college. Meeting backstage after one of his shows, Burns immediately took a shine to Allen and they formed a double-act; at first, they took the traditional route, with Gracie as the feed and George the funny-man. But Burns noticed that, despite the fact they he had all the witty lines, Allen was attracting all the laughs. Cannily, he switched the roles and success followed. Burns and Allen married in real life in 1926 but didn't acknowledge the union professionally until the 1940s as they felt they could accrue more comedy mileage from routines that cast them as a courting couple. They began making movies and became quite well known, but it was when

Eddie Cantor brought them to CBS radio in 1932 that they attained superstardom. *The George Burns And Gracie Allen Show* was a national phenomenon and consolidated the pairing's reputation as the outstanding male/female comedy duo of the day. The series ended in 1950 and transferred to television with no apparent loss of quality.

Burns continued to work for the next 40 years. This longevity became something of a gimmick in itself and in his later years he put his grand age to good use, appearing as God in the feature films *Oh God!* (1977, directed by Carl Reiner), *Oh God! Book 2* (1980, Gilbert Gates) and *Oh God! You Devil* (1984, Paul Bogart), and, most memorably, as half of a veteran vaudeville double-act in Neil Simon's *The Sunshine Boys* (1975, Herbert Ross) the film that revitalised his career. Burns died on 8 March 1996, having fulfilled the wishes of his millions of fans by reaching 100 years of age. (On 24 March 1996 BBC1 screened *A Tribute To George Burns*, repeating an appearance made by Burns in 1991 on the chat-show *Wogan*.)

The Burns And Allen Show

USA · SYNDICATED (MCCADDEN PRODUCTIONS/SCREEN GEMS) · SITCOM

291 × 30 mins · b/w

US dates 12 Oct 1950–22 Sep 1958

UK dates: 16 Sep 1955–9 Sep 1961 (132 episodes) BBC various days and times

MAIN CAST
George Burns · · · · · · · · · · · · · · · himself
Gracie Allen · · · · · · · · · · · · · · · · herself
Ronnie Burns · · · · · · · · · · · · · · · himself
Harry Von Zell · · · · · · · · · · · · · · himself
Blanche Morton · · · · · · · · · Bea Benaderet
Harry Morton · · · · Larry Keating (1953–58)

CREDITS
writers Harvey Helm, Keith Fowler, Norman Paul, William Burns · *producer* Fred DeCordova

The UK airing of selected episodes from the 239 filmed editions of *The Burns And Allen Show* (an earlier 52 episodes had gone out live in the USA) proved that top-quality comedy could find a willing audience on both sides of the Atlantic. *The Burns And Allen Show* – also titled *The George Burns And Gracie Allen Show* – was only the second sitcom imported to Britain, following *Amos 'n' Andy* and just pipping *I Love Lucy*.

Having honed their double-act on stage, in films and in their long-running radio show, Burns and Allen were master exponents of their particular comedy style, with George cast in the role of husband to the staggeringly obtuse Gracie. She was not so much stupid as surreal, an original thinker whose thought patterns could turn the world upside down, reverse it and then replace it as a square, aptly demonstrated by

their famous sign-off gag where Burns would say, 'Say Goodnight Gracie' to which Allen would respond, in all innocence, 'Goodnight Gracie'. Despite the domestic setting, and the sitcom trappings and plots involving neighbours and family, the couple still seemed to be playing a sophisticated stage routine, occasionally talking to the audience, and the show benefited immensely for it.

The George Burns Show

USA · NBC (ROD AMATEAU PRODUCTIONS) · SITCOM

25 × 30 mins · b/w

US dates: 21 Oct 1958–14 Apr 1959

UK dates: 4 Jan–5 Apr 1959 (13 episodes) BBC Sun mostly 7.30pm

MAIN CAST
George Burns · · · · · · · · · · · · · · · · himself
Blanche Morton · · · · · · · · · Bea Benaderet
Harry Morton · · · · · · · · · · · · · Larry Keating

CREDITS
writers various · *producer* Rod Amateau

Gracie Allen retired in 1958 (and died on 28 August 1964) so George Burns continued solo in this sitcom that featured many of the regulars from *The Burns And Allen Show*. This time George was cast as a comedian turned theatrical producer. The series was not a success and was quickly revamped, moving away from the sitcom format and employing guest stars to become more of a variety show, but still it lasted just one season.

In the UK, the BBC screened episodes of this series in parallel with *The Burns And Allen Show*.

The George Burns One-Man Show

USA · CBS (GBF PRODUCTIONS) · STANDUP

1 × 60 mins · colour

US date: 23 Nov 1977

UK date: 28 Mar 1978 · BBC1 Tue 8.10pm

MAIN CAST
George Burns
Bob Hope

CREDITS
writers Elon Packard, Fred S Fox, Seaman Jacobs · *director* Stan Harris · *producer* Stan Harris

Despite the title, veteran vaudevillian George Burns appeared here with guests: Bob Hope, Gladys Knight and the Pips and John Denver. Aged 81 at the time, Burns was still the consummate comedian, master of the one-liner, singer and soft-shoe-shuffle man. As a solo act he had reverted to delivering quick gags, using his ever-present cigar as a prop and an aid to his always immaculate timing.

George Burns In Nashville???

USA · NBC (GBF PRODUCTIONS) · STANDUP

1 × 60 mins · colour

US date: 13 Apr 1981

UK date: 5 Apr 1981 · BBC1 Sun 11.20pm

MAIN CAST
George Burns

CREDITS
writers Fred S Fox, Seaman Jacobs, Hal Goldman · *director* Walter C Miller · *producer* Irving Fein

The octogenarian jokester (then 84) celebrated 77 years in show business with this TV special filmed in the country-music capital Nashville. (The improbability of city-slicker Burns performing in such surroundings gave rise to the question marks in the title.) Burns' trademark style of drily delivered one-liners continued to stand him in good stead.

Note. The BBC transmission was originally scheduled for 25 March. All the same, it went out ahead of the US screening.

George Burns' Early, Early, Early Christmas Show

USA · NBC (GBF PRODUCTIONS) · STANDUP

1 × 60 mins · colour

US date: 16 Nov 1981

UK date: 26 Nov 1982 · BBC1 Fri 9.30pm

MAIN CAST
George Burns
Bob Hope
Ann-Margret

CREDITS
writers Fred S Fox, Seaman Jacobs, Hal Goldman · *director* Walter C Miller · *producer* Irving Fein

Another special for the music-hall Methuselah, here celebrating Christmas early on the off-chance that he might not be around for the real date. Burns needn't have worried: merely 85 at this time, he lived for another 15 years.

George Burns Celebrates 80 Years In Show Business

USA · NBC (GBF PRODUCTIONS) · STANDUP

1 × 90 mins · colour

US date: 19 Sep 1983

UK date: 23 Sep 1984 · BBC1 Sun 9.30pm (60 mins)

MAIN CAST
host · · · · · · · · · · · · · · · · · · John Forsythe
Milton Berle
Bob Hope
Carol Channing
Johnny Carson
Danny Thomas
Buddy Hackett
Phyllis Diller
Red Buttons
Don Rickles

CREDITS
writers Seaman Jacobs, Fred S Fox · *director* Walter C Miller · *producer* Irving Fein

A back-slapping session for the Jurassic jester, celebrating his 80th year as an audience pleaser.

George Burns And Other Sex Symbols

USA · NBC (GBF PRODUCTIONS) · STANDUP

1 × 60 mins · colour

US date: 8 Nov 1982

UK date: 4 Sep 1985 · BBC1 Wed 10.55pm

MAIN CAST
George Burns
Bernadette Peters
John Schneider
Linda Evans

CREDITS
writers Fred S Fox, Seaman Jacobs, Hal Goldman · *director* Walter C Miller · *producer* Irving Fein

With the help of his guests, the enduring entertainer cast his eye over the subject of sex and what makes a sex symbol.

George Burns' 90th Birthday Party – A Very Special Special

USA · NBC (GBF PRODUCTIONS) · STANDUP

1 × 60 mins · colour

US date: 17 Jan 1986

UK date: 4 May 1987 · BBC1 Mon 11.20pm

MAIN CAST
George Burns
Steve Allen
Milton Berle
Red Buttons
Chevy Chase
Bill Cosby
Billy Crystal
Bob Hope
Don Rickles
Joan Rivers
Danny Thomas

CREDITS
writer Hal Goldman · *director* Walter C Miller · *producers* Irving Fein, Walter C Miller

A star-studded tribute to the timeless trooper, featuring a host of comedy superstars.

George Burns: An Hour Of Jokes And Songs

USA · HBO (BRIGHTSIDE PRODUCTIONS) · STANDUP

1 × 60 mins · colour

US date: 22 Jan 1984

UK date: 29 May 1989 · C4 Mon 7pm

MAIN CAST
George Burns

CREDITS
writer George Burns · *director* Jerome Shaw · *producer* Riff Markowitz

An independently made film of Burns in concert, screened in America to mark his 88th birthday but not shown in Britain until the comedian was 93. (It was screened by C4 under the title *George Burns In Concert*.)

But Seriously – It's Sheila Hancock

UK · BBC · SKETCH

6 × 30 mins · colour

3 Dec 1972–14 Jan 1973 · BBC2 Sun around 9.10pm

MAIN CAST
Sheila Hancock

CREDITS
writers N F Simpson (6), Paul McDowell (5), John Dalby (3), Geoff Rowley/Andy Baker (3), Peter Jones (2), John Bird (2), John Betjeman (2), Denise Hurst (1), Germaine Greer (1), Ivor Treby (1), Ogden Nash (1), Michael Frayn (1), Christopher Marlowe (1), Harold Pinter (1), Roger McGough (1) · *director* Vernon Lawrence · *producer* Barry Took

A topic-themed sketch/chat-show hybrid with the odd song thrown in for good measure. Tired of playing dizzy blondes in sitcoms, Sheila Hancock had scored a hit with her 1968 TV show **Simply Sheila** and was intent on consolidating that success, showing the sharper, more satirical side of her nature in this ambitious series.

Combating the usual TV-industry reservations about funny women, Hancock found a sympathetic producer in Barry Took (his first BBC production role) and together they set about honing a biting satirical show with a feminist edge. Despite this rare opportunity to front a series, Hancock was somewhat depressed at the time, following the recent deaths of her mother and husband, and this made her determined to perform a show with an edge that was not only comedic. Her choice of guest stars was eclectic (Dudley Moore, Anthony Hopkins, Peter Jones, Peter Hall, Alfie Bass, Kenneth Allsop, John Mortimer and John Bird) and the first show, subtitled 'The Woman's Place', featured Germaine Greer. This hard-edged edition set the tone for the remainder, polarising audience reaction. In retrospect, the series was probably ahead of its time, being received uneasily by an industry and viewership still years away from the excesses of **French And Saunders**, Ruby Wax and **Absolutely Fabulous**.

Butterflies

UK · BBC · SITCOM

29 episodes (28 × 30 mins · 1 × short special) · colour

Series One (6) 10 Nov–15 Dec 1978 · BBC2 Fri 9pm

Series Two (7) 29 Oct–10 Dec 1979 · BBC2 Mon 9pm

Special · 22 Dec 1979 · BBC1 Sat 7.25pm

Series Three (7) 9 Sep–21 Oct 1980 · BBC2 Tue 9pm

Short special (10 mins) part of *The Funny Side Of Christmas* 27 Dec 1982 · BBC1 Mon 8.05pm

Series Four (7) 7 Sep–19 Oct 1983 · BBC2 Wed 9pm

MAIN CAST

Ria Parkinson · · · · · · · · · · · · · Wendy Craig
Ben Parkinson · · · · · · · · · · · Geoffrey Palmer
Russell Parkinson · · · · · · · · · · · Andrew Hall
Adam Parkinson · · · · · · · Nicholas Lyndhurst
Leonard · · · · · · · · · · · · · · · Bruce Montague
Thomas · · · · · · · · · · · · · · · Michael Ripper
Ruby · · · · · · · · · · · · · · · · · · Joyce Windsor

CREDITS

writer Carla Lane · *directors* John B Hobbs, Sydney Lotterby, Mandie Fletcher · *producers* Sydney Lotterby (15), Gareth Gwenlan (14)

Though neither attracting the huge audiences of **Bread** nor defining an era like **The Liver Birds**, *Butterflies* is arguably the most successful of Carla Lane's sitcoms in terms of its style, oblique yet revolutionary theme and the affection in which it remains held. The story depicts Ria Parkinson, an attractive middle-class woman approaching middle-age and worrying that she has not made the most of her life. Her husband Ben, a dentist and collector of butterflies, is a stable yet essentially dull man; their children Russell and Adam are typical teenagers, with a typical teenage rivalry.

On the surface, Ria seemed an extension of other Wendy Craig TV characters (**Not In Front Of The Children, ... And Mother Makes Three/Five**) but whereas they wondered aloud at their lot, Ria became obsessed with it in her every waking moment, her thoughts being dominated by the notion that time was slipping through her fingers. The series' bitter-sweet nature and sometimes downbeat atmosphere set it apart from other sitcoms, and dramatic undertones allowed it to deal with subjects (like teenage pregnancy and suicidal feelings) that many others series would have avoided. The central theme in *Butterflies*, indeed, was the temptation of adultery, with Ria being wooed by a wealthy businessman, Leonard, who represented the sort of adventure missing from her life. But Ria's upbringing and natural timidity made it impossible for her to consummate the relationship, so instead she daydreamed about it and, in this way, actually seemed to achieve some solace.

The series was very well cast. Wendy Craig brought believability and vulnerability to the part of Ria, Geoffrey Palmer proved that 'less is more' with his fine, understated performance as Ben, and Andrew Hall and Nicholas Lyndhurst were excellent as Russell and Adam. Bruce Montague as Leonard, Michael Ripper as his enigmatic chauffeur and Joyce Windsor as the Parkinsons' cleaning lady Ruby, all supported well. But they couldn't have made it work without Carla Lane's finely judged script, which had just enough traditional sitcom elements (the family's reaction to Ria's gruesome attempts at cookery, the adolescent bickering of the boys) to keep the mood light before exploring the darker areas of her frustration, her marital boredom and ageing.

In 1979 the format of *Butterflies* was sold to the USA and Carla Lane flew to Los Angeles to work on the script (also to be titled *Butterflies*) with the producer Milt Josefsberg. A pilot episode was screened by NBC on 1 August 1979 with Jennifer Warren as Rea (*sic*) Parkinson, John McMartin as Ben, Craig Wasson as Russell, Robert Doran as Adam and Jim Hutton as Leonard. Lane was hugely disappointed with the US version, lamenting the loss of most of the idea's subtlety, and it failed to graduate to a full series.

The title *Butterflies* seems to suggest many things, among them the idea that Ria and her family were pinned down (like the butterflies in Ben's collection) for us to study each week. Publicity for the US version suggested that the title came from the saying 'We are like kids chasing butterflies – we see it, we want it'. But introducing the series in an article in *Radio Times*, Carla Lane remarked that the title could refer to lost opportunities and the sudden realisation that time is running out, leaving people fluttering around, 'like butterflies with so much to do and so little time to do it'.

Note. Wendy Craig reprised her *Butterflies* role in *The Last Waltz*, a specially scripted production featuring characters from four Carla Lane series (*Bread*, *Solo* and *The Liver Birds* were the others) aired by BBC1 on 10 March 1989 as part of **Comic Relief**.

Peter Butterworth

Peter Butterworth was a well-loved British comedy character-actor whose most popular persona was that of an amiable oaf bumbling through life in a bewildered state. He portrayed variations on this character throughout his career, most notably as a regular member of the *Carry On* film team. He was also a regular on radio and TV.

Born in Cheshire in February 1919, Butterworth launched his show-business career during the Second World War by producing variety shows for fellow prisoners-of-war in Germany. He then appeared in a number of post-war BBC radio shows, most notably *One For The Boys* with comedian Michael Howard, before scoring his biggest TV success as a regular on the BBC's comedy flagship *How Do You View?*. Butterworth's biggest body of work was as a children's entertainer, though, and he appeared in a number of shows for the young, most famously as the skipper of *The SS Saturday Special*, a boat-based variety entertainment in which he appeared alongside a number of popular puppets, including Porterhouse the Parrot and the perennial favourite Sooty. Most of Butterworth's other TV appearances were in the BBC's *For The Children* strand, usually comprising short comedy slapstick sketches. Some such pieces went under individual titles but they tended to be called *Peter's Troubles*.

Peter Butterworth was married to the impressionist Janet Brown, and he died in January 1979, aged 59, shortly after a pantomime performance in Coventry.

See also *Bulldog Breed, Carry On ..., A Class By Himself, Friends And Neighbours, Kindly Leave The Kerb, Odd Man Out, Porterhouse – Private Eye* and *Those Kids*.

Peter's Troubles

UK · BBC · CHILDREN'S SKETCH

40 × 10 mins · b/w

Special · 27 Mar 1953 · Fri 5pm

Series One (3) 16 Sep–11 Nov 1953 · monthly Wed 5pm

Series Two (6) 11 Jan–22 Mar 1954 · fortnightly Mon 5pm

Special · 27 Aug 1954 · Fri 5pm

Special · 30 Nov 1954 · Tue 5pm

Series Three (5) 26 Jan–23 Mar 1955 · fortnightly Mon 5pm

Series Four (6) 27 Apr–6 July 1955 · fortnightly Wed 5pm

Series Five (3) 3 Oct–28 Nov 1955 · fortnightly Mon 5pm

Series Six (5) 7 Mar–3 May 1956 · fortnightly Thu 5pm

Series Seven (5) 30 Aug–1 Nov 1956 · fortnightly Thu 5pm

Series Eight (3) 14 Oct–11 Nov 1957 · fortnightly Mon 5pm

Special · 20 Jan 1958 · Mon 5pm

MAIN CAST

Peter Butterworth

CREDITS

writer Peter Butterworth · *producers* David Boisseau (9), Johnny Downes (8), Desmond O'Donovan (7), Peter Graham Scott (4), John Hunter Blair (4), Douglas Mair (2), Peter Newington

(2), David Goddard (1), Cliff Michelmore (1), not known (2)

A popular recurring slot within the *For The Children* strand.

Kept In

UK · ITV (ASSOCIATED-REDIFFUSION) · CHILDREN'S SKETCH

7 × 15 mins · b/w

28 Sep–21 Dec 1955 · fortnightly Wed 5.15pm

MAIN CAST
Peter Butterworth

CREDITS
writer Tom Twigge

Peter Butterworth maintained his busy schedule in the realm of children's television with this very early ITV series, in which he aided and abetted the adventures of a small cartoon bird, Buddy Budgerigar, drawn and animated by Reginald Jeffryes.

Butterworth Time

UK · BBC · CHILDREN'S STANDUP/SKETCH

3 × 30 mins · b/w

4 Aug–18 Aug 1956 · Sat around 5pm

MAIN CAST
Peter Butterworth
Janet Brown
Peter Claughton

CREDITS
writer Sheila Hodgson · *producer* Vere Lorrimer

Part of the BBC's *For Older Children* strand. Butterworth appeared here with his wife Janet Brown. As a couple, they regularly appeared together on television throughout the 1950s.

By Request

see Mr Pastry

By The Sea

see *The Two Ronnies*

By, With And From Bentine

see BENTINE, Michael

Max Bygraves

Comedian and singer Max Bygraves enjoyed spectacular success throughout the 1950s and 1960s, proof of his durability and popularity being that he holds the record for the most appearances (19) in the *Royal Variety Show*. Born Walter William

Bygraves on 16 October 1922, in Rotherhithe, in the East End of London, Max (as he came to call himself, in honour of the comedian Max Miller) demonstrated an early interest in entertainment, winning a talent contest when he was 12. He first broadcast on BBC radio in *A C Smith Entertains* in 1943 and followed this with many guest spots in variety shows (on both sides of the Atlantic) before becoming a major player in the star-making BBC radio series *Educating Archie*. Bygraves made his BBC TV debut on 30 October 1947, described in *Radio Times* as an 'impressionist', and then guested before getting his first starring role in 1953 with *A Good Idea – Son!*, this being one of his catchphrases from *Educating Archie*. (He also had, 'I've arrived, and to prove it I'm 'ere' and, 'Ooh blimey!') Bygraves was also making a name for himself as an actor at this time and later in his career he split his time between acting, comedy and, in particular, ballad singing (he wrote his own songs as well as performing standards). In the latter sphere, by combining music and episodes from his life, Bygraves developed his best known catchphrase of all, 'I wanna tell you a story'.

The following lists only those TV shows or series that have included a definite comedic element; programmes that featured Bygraves singing or telling stories, with only a little or no scripted humour, are *not* included (eg, *Singalongamax, Lingalongamax* and *Max In The Roaring Twenties*).

A Good Idea – Son!

UK · BBC · STANDUP

1 × 60 mins · b/w

9 May 1953 · Sat 9.30pm

MAIN CAST
Max Bygraves

CREDITS
writer Eric Sykes · *producer* Bill Lyon-Shaw

Max Bygraves' first headlining TV appearance. The script was by Eric Sykes, with whom he had worked on BBC radio's *Educating Archie*.

Note. The title was used again for an ATV special, screened on 12 February 1964, in which Bygraves co-starred with his son Ant. This followed three months after a previous ATV special, *Side By Side* (6 November 1963), which featured the same combination. (These programmes were more musical than comedic.)

Max Bygraves

UK · BBC · STANDUP

4 × 30 mins · b/w

8 Sep 1955 · Thu 8.15pm

8 Jan 1956 · Sun 7.45pm
28 Sep 1956 · Fri 7.45pm
27 Dec 1956 · Thu 7.45pm

MAIN CAST
Max Bygraves

CREDITS
writer Eric Sykes · *producers* Ernest Maxin (shows 1–3), Graeme Muir (show 4)

Four early BBC comedy shows from one of the very few stars to be popular on stage, radio, television, film and record.

The Max Bygraves Show 1

UK · ITV (ITP PRODUCTIONS FOR ATV/ABC) · SKETCH/STANDUP

2 × 45 mins · b/w

24 Nov 1956 · Sat 9pm
9 Mar 1957 · Sat 8.30pm

MAIN CAST
Max Bygraves

CREDITS
writer Eric Sykes · *directors/producers* Bill Ward (show 1), Brian Tesler (show 2)

Two starring shows on ITV, screened as part of the weekly series *Val Parnell's Saturday Spectacular*.

Roamin' Holiday

UK · ITV (BLOSSOM TV PRODUCTIONS FOR ATV) · SITCOM

6 × 30 mins · b/w

28 Jan–4 Mar 1961 · Sat 9.30pm

MAIN CAST
Max Bygraves
Tony Sandler
Tim Dorman

CREDITS
writers Max Bygraves, Eric Sykes, Peter Dulay · *director* Dicky Leeman · *producer* Bill Ward

Early in 1961, as Britons weathered another cold winter, they could tune into ITV and watch – doubtless with envy – Max Bygraves rompin' his way through *Roamin' Holiday*, a blend of situation comedy and songs filmed in the town of Alassio, on the Italian Riviera. The Bygraves family happened to venture to this part of the Med every year for their vacation, indeed here they all were on screen: 13-year-old son Anthony – called Ant by his father – sang and danced in four of the episodes, while Max's wife Blossom and their two daughters Christine (17) and Maxine (9) appeared in crowd scenes. The series was independently produced for ATV by the Bygraves' own company, Blossom Productions, and some viewers found it difficult not to conclude that this was a family holiday turned into a TV series. Max helped Eric Sykes and Peter Dulay write the scripts.

Max Bygraves Entertains

UK · BBC · STANDUP

2 × 45 mins · b/w

4 Nov 1965 · BBC2 Thu 9.25pm

2 Apr 1966 · BBC1 Sat 8.30pm

MAIN CAST
Max Bygraves

CREDITS
writers Eric Merriman, Spike Mullins (show 1), John Law, Spike Mullins (show 2) · *producers* George Inns (show 1), Michael Hurll (show 2)

Two programmes. In the first, screened within BBC2's *Show Of The Week* strand, Max performed solo, singing and telling stories (some scripted) about his travels around the world. In the second, shown by BBC1, he was joined by his singing son Anthony and by guests Deryck Guyler and pop-picking DJ Alan Freeman for sketches and music.

Max   1

UK · ITV (THAMES) · SKETCH/STANDUP

15 editions (7 × 30 mins · b/w; 6 × 30 mins · colour; 2 × 60 mins · b/w)

Special (60 mins · b/w) 31 July 1968 · Wed 8pm

Series One (7 × 30 mins · b/w) 2 Jan–13 Feb 1969 · Thu 9pm

Special (60 mins · b/w) 9 Apr 1969 · Wed 8pm

Series Two (6 × 30 mins · colour) 29 Jan–5 Mar 1970 · Thu 9pm

MAIN CAST
Max Bygraves

CREDITS
writers Barry Cryer (15), Dick Vosburgh (15), Spike Mullins (15), Joe Steeples (7), Bernie Sharp (6), Bill Solly (6), Bill Stark (4), Eric Davidson (1), Neil Shand (1) · *script associate* Spike Mullins (series 2) · *director/producer* William G Stewart

A special one-man programme on 31 July 1968, networked by Thames Television in its second day as London's new ITV franchise, led to two full series and a further special – some shows being performed solo, others with guests – with the accent on comedy and song. Later Thames shows bearing this title switched the emphasis heavily on to music and so are not listed here.

The Max Bygraves Hour

UK · ITV (THAMES) · SKETCH/STANDUP

1 × 60 mins · colour

7 Jan 1970 · Wed 8pm

MAIN CAST
Max Bygraves
George Burns
Jim Backus

CREDITS
writers Barry Cryer, Dick Vosburgh, Joe Steeples, Bill Solly · *script associate* Spike Mullins · *director/producer* William G Stewart

Max with two star American guests. A later show (17 April 1974) bearing the same title concentrated on music and thus is not listed here.

The Max Bygraves Show   2

UK · ITV (THAMES) · SKETCH/STANDUP

2 × 60 mins · colour

27 Oct 1971 · Wed 8pm

17 May 1972 · Wed 8pm

MAIN CAST
Max Bygraves

CREDITS
writers Spike Mullins (shows 1 & 2), Eric Davidson (show 1), Joe Steeples (show 2) · *script editor* Peter Dulay (show 2) · *directors/producers* William G Stewart (show 1), Alan Tarrant (show 2)

Following the one-man-show format of *Max*, Bygraves reverted to a more traditional show style. The first edition saw him paired with sitcom stalwarts Rodney Bewes *(The Likely Lads, Dear Mother … Love Albert)* and Stephen Lewis *(On The Buses)*. The second show had an animal theme and alongside Rod Hull (with his lethal Emu) were Zsa Zsa the elephant and Beryl Hall and her dog Ben. Max sang with the dog and also found himself serenading a chimpanzee, dancing with a penguin and dining with a gourmet goat.

Max Bygraves At The Royalty

UK · ITV (THAMES) · SKETCH/STANDUP

6 × 30 mins · colour

3 Aug–7 Sep 1972 · Thu 8.45pm then 9pm

MAIN CAST
Max Bygraves
Anthony Bygraves

CREDITS
writer Eric Davidson · *script editor* Peter Dulay · *director/producer* Terry Henebery

Six programmes recorded at the Royalty Theatre in London, with weekly guests that included Hattie Jacques (from *Sykes*), Diana Coupland *(Bless This House)*, Jack Smethurst *(Love Thy Neighbour)* and, from *On The Buses*, first Anna Karen and then Michael Robbins.

Max   2

UK · ITV (ATV) · SKETCH/STANDUP

4 × 30 mins · colour

20 Mar–10 Apr 1974 · Wed 8.30pm

MAIN CAST
Max Bygraves

CREDITS
writer Eric Davidson · *director/producer* Dicky Leeman

After delivering *Singalongamax*, an eight-part music series for ATV in 1973, Bygraves returned to comedy with a revival of *Max* for the same company. A later edition of the series (24 June 1974) switched the emphasis on to music.

Max Bygraves Says 'I Wanna Tell You A Story'

UK · BBC · STANDUP

1 × 75 mins · colour

31 Dec 1975 · BBC1 Wed 10.30pm

MAIN CAST
Max Bygraves

CREDITS
writer Eric Davidson · *producers* Yvonne Littlewood, John Ammonds

A humorous look back at 75 years of comedy and music using reminiscences, impersonations and film clips. The same title was later used for a 1977 BBC musical series in which Bygraves looked back at the history of popular songs.

Max's Holiday Hour

UK · ITV (THAMES) · SKETCH/STANDUP

1 × 60 mins · colour

27 Dec 1977 · Tue 7.30pm

MAIN CAST
Max Bygraves
Jim Davidson
Charlie Cairoli
Margaret Powell

CREDITS
writer Eric Davidson · *director/producer* Mark Stuart

A Christmas special combining music and laughter.

Max Bygraves – Side By Side

UK · ITV (THAMES) · SKETCH/STANDUP

6 × 30 mins · colour

23 Feb–30 Mar 1982 · Tue 7.30pm

MAIN CAST
Max Bygraves

CREDITS
writers Eric Davidson, Spike Mullins, Max Bygraves · *director/producer* Peter Frazer-Jones

More comedy than song, with guests including Jimmy Tarbuck and Eric Sykes.

Byng-Ho!

UK · BBC · SKETCH

2 editions (1 × 20 mins · 1 × 35 mins) · b/w

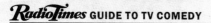
17 Mar 1938 · Thu 3pm (second performance at
9pm) (20 mins)

24 Apr 1939 · Mon 9.05pm (second performance
27 Apr at 3pm) (35 mins)

MAIN CAST
Douglas Byng

CREDITS
producer Reginald Smith

Two shows for female impersonator Douglas
Byng, who, unlike most of his contemporaries,
had a roster of different characters rather
than just one alter ego. Byng's exaggerated
menagerie included all manner of larger-than-
life female characters such as 'Minnie the
messy old mermaid' and historical characters
such as Nell Gwynne and Boadicea; although
his work was risqué it was never went beyond
the bounds of acceptability. An acknowledged
influence on the later drag-star Danny La Rue,
Douglas Byng holds the distinction of being
the first comedy drag act to have his own
starring show on British television, the
forerunner of a host of popular acts including
Norman Evans, Rex Jameson (Mrs
Shufflewick), the aforementioned La Rue,
George Logan and Patrick Fyffe (Hinge And
Bracket), Barry Humphries (Dame Edna
Everage) and Paul O'Grady (Lily Savage).
Born in Nottinghamshire on 17 March 1893,
Byng was a top-ranking star of the London
cabaret and revue scene in the 1930s and
appeared in 26 Christmas pantomimes before
retiring. He died in 1988, aged 94.

Guest acts appeared with Byng in these
two BBC shows: Doris Hare, Richard
Murdoch and Cyril Fletcher in the first show,
Edward Cooper, Patricia Burke and Nugent
Marshall in the second.

Cabaret

UK · BBC · STANDUP/SATIRE

4 × 45 mins · colour

23 Jan–20 Feb 1985 · BBC2 Wed 9.55pm

MAIN CAST

Desmond 'Olivier' Dingle · · · · Patrick Barlow
Bertice Reading
Robyn Archer

CREDITS

director/producer Phil Chilvers

A spoof cabaret series set in a fictitious night-club 'somewhere in the heart of a bustling metropolis' and hosted by Patrick Barlow's hapless alter ego Desmond 'Olivier' Dingle (*The National Theatre Of Brent Presents ...*). Resident entertainers – singer Bertice Reading and famed torch singer/drag act Robyn Archer – provided songs and satire, and each of the four editions featured different guest acts from the world of comedy – respectively John Dowie; Rory Bremner; Amanda Swift and Margo Random; and Simon Fanshawe and Rory Bremner.

Cabaret At The Jongleurs

UK · BBC (REAL TO REEL TELEVISION) · STANDUP

7 × 30 mins · colour

25 Feb–7 Apr 1988 · BBC2 Thu 10.10pm

MAIN CAST

see below

CREDITS

writers cast and others · *director* Christian Clegg · *producer* Brian Marshall

A showcase for the leading lights of the blossoming comedy cabaret circuit, this series was filmed at the 300-seat Jongleurs club in south London. A different host each week introduced his fellow comics and musical guests also featured. Mark Steel appeared in five of the series' seven programmes, Jeremy Hardy and John Sparkes three times, Andy Greenhalgh, Arthur Smith and Will Durst twice apiece and there were single spots for Simon Fanshawe, Kit Hollerbach, Neil Mullarkey, Nick Hancock, Bob Mills, Nick

Revell, the Joan Collins Fan Club (Julian Clary), Phil Cornwell and Felix Dexter.

See also *Live At Jongleurs*.

The Cabbage Patch

UK · ITV (CENTRAL) · SITCOM

7 × 30 mins · colour

29 July–9 Sep 1983 · Fri 8.30pm

MAIN CAST

Janet	Julia Foster
Lillian	Betty Marsden
Tony	Emlyn Price
Kate	Natasha Byrne
Elizabeth	Amelia Lowdell
Ruth	Jill Benedict
Amanda	Jeni Barnett
Susie	Belinda Lang
John	Graham McGrath
Craig	Martin Connor

CREDITS

writer Joan Greening · *directors* Shaun O'Riordan (4), Paul Harrison (3) · *producer* Shaun O'Riordan

A view of family life from one key perspective – the mother's/wife's – *The Cabbage Patch* focused on Janet, a suburban housewife who, at the age of 36, has allowed herself to go to seed and is maniacal in the easily distracted, bad-tempered way that she deals with her domestic strife. Young daughters Kate and Elizabeth, while not uniquely problematic, cause her plenty of turmoil, and husband Tony's work in computers affords him the right, he thinks, to loll about at the house in a 'notice-me!' kind of way. Janet also has to endure her friends Ruth and Susie, who consider themselves superior, and her meddlesome mother, Lillian, whose idea of encouragement is to suggest that her daughter quits the scene and marries somebody else.

While not necessarily autobiographical, the series was written with a definite understanding and knowledge of the housewife's plight: author Joan Greening was herself 36 at the time of writing, the mother of two and the wife of a man working as a computer consultant.

Cabbages And Kings

UK · BBC · CHILDREN'S SKETCH

8 × 25 mins · colour

Series One (3) 30 June–14 July 1972 · BBC1 Fri 5.20pm
Series Two (5) 19 Apr–17 May 1974 · BBC1 Fri 5.15pm

MAIN CAST

Johnny Ball
Julie Stevens
Derek Griffiths

CREDITS

writer Johnny Ball · *producer* Peter Ridsdale Scott

Children's entertainment that, like *The Complete And Utter History Of Britain*, presented historical sketches, each programme covering a particular period. Johnny Ball was the writer and star. After dallying on the fringes of the Liverpool beat boom in the late 1950s, Ball entered show business as a Butlin's Redcoat and then became a popular figure on BBC children's television as one of the *Play School* presenters. Joining him here from that series were Julie Stevens and Derek Griffiths.

Marti Caine

Born Lynne Shepherd, in Sheffield on 26 January 1945, former model Marti Caine entered show business when aged 19. She performed as a singer/compere and toured northern clubs as a comedy act for 11 years before achieving 'overnight' success as a comedian when she won the annual grand final of the ITV talent-search series *New Faces* in July 1975. (Later, 1986–89, she returned to host the show.) Originally, Caine's TV persona was that of a gawky 'housewife from Sheffield' but her image altered dramatically by the time of her second starring series, *Marti*, after she had plastic surgery to make her nose smaller ('the old one,' she joked, 'kept knocking people off bicycles') and appeared in glamorous, sexy gowns in the realisation that slipping on a banana skin is funnier if you are dressed elegantly.

Caine admitted that she was a bundle of nervous energy who only performed well when scared, buzzing on the adrenaline released by fear. It was this vulnerability and her disarming honesty that endeared her to the viewing public. She twice (in 1978 and 1979) appeared in the *Royal Variety Show* and made numerous other theatre appearances, including her one-woman show *An Evening With Marti*.

Marti Caine died on 4 November 1995 following a well-publicised seven-year battle with cancer. ITV celebrated her career on the 26th of that month with *A Tribute To Marti*, and BBC1 did likewise on 13 March 1996 with *Funny Girl ... A Tribute To Marti Caine*.

Nobody Does It Like Marti

UK · ITV (ATV) · STANDUP/SKETCH

9 × 30 mins · colour

3 July–28 Aug 1976 · Sat 5.15pm

MAIN CAST

Marti Caine

CREDITS
writer Jon Watkins · *director/producer* Colin Clews

Following her success on *New Faces*, and a five-week August 1975 ATV series *The Summer Show* with other *New Faces* winners (including Lenny Henry and Victoria Wood), Marti Caine was given her own series to display her talents. Guest stars from the world of comedy appeared each week to act in sketches and perform humorous songs with the star, including Arthur Lowe, Leslie Crowther, Michael Robbins, Nina Baden-Semper, Yootha Joyce, Patrick Cargill, Barbara Windsor and Pat Coombs.

Marti

UK · ITV (ATV) · STANDUP/SKETCH

8 editions (1 × 60 mins · 7 × 30 mins)

Special (60 mins) 4 May 1977 · Wed 8pm

One series (7 × 30 mins) 23 July–3 Sep 1977 · Sat 9.45pm

MAIN CAST
Marti Caine
Bobbie Knutt

CREDITS
writers Wally Malston (8), Barry Cryer (1) · *situation sketches* Sid Green/Dick Hills (special), Terence Brady/Charlotte Bingham, Dick Hills, Patricia Newman, John Kane, Marti Caine, Bob Monkhouse (series) · *director/producer* John Pullen

As a result of cosmetic and wardrobe changes, there was a new-look Marti Caine in these ATV programmes. Tall and thin, with a trademark mane of flame-red hair, she was now a glamorous, stunningly dressed star.

Each edition of *Marti* featured an extended sketch (usually of a domestic nature) which indicated that Caine was already toying with the notion of moving into sitcom acting.

The Marti Caine Show

UK · BBC · STANDUP/SKETCH

29 editions · (22 × 45 mins · 7 × 50 mins) · colour

Special (50 mins) 3 Oct 1977 · BBC2 Mon 8.10pm

Series One (4 × 45 mins) 8 Jan–29 Jan 1979 · BBC2 Mon 8.15pm

Series Two (6 × 45 mins) 3 Mar–14 Apr 1980 · BBC2 Mon 8.15pm

Series Three (6 × 45 mins) 9 Mar–13 Apr 1981 · BBC2 Mon 8.15pm

Series Four (6 × 45 mins) 22 Feb–5 Apr 1982 · BBC2 Mon 8.15pm

Special (50 mins) 27 Dec 1982 · BBC2 Mon 9.35pm

Series Five (5 × 50 mins) 13 Mar–10 Apr 1984 · BBC2 Tue 9pm

MAIN CAST
Marti Caine

CREDITS
writers Spike Mullins (16), Neil Shand (13), Terry Ravenscroft (8), Joe Steeples (6), Laurence Marks/Maurice Gran (5), David McKellar (4), Boris Day (3), Peter Spence (2), Andy Hamilton (2), Wally Malston (1), Peter Robinson (1), Jon Watkins (1) · *directors* Stanley Appel, Brian Waterhouse · *producers* Stanley Appel (18), Stewart Morris (5), Terry Hughes (4), John Ammonds (1), Brian Waterhouse (1)

After a 1977 special, Marti Caine graduated to her own BBC series. Her style, moving towards a less broad and more sophisticated comedy, was reflected by the fact that the series appeared on BBC2. Comedy guests included Mike Harding, Spike Milligan, Alfred Marks, Barry Took, Barry Cryer and Tom O'Connor.

Hilary

UK · BBC · SITCOM

12 × 30 mins · colour

Pilot · 10 Dec 1984 · BBC2 Mon 9pm

Series One (5) 14 Jan–11 Feb 1985 · BBC2 Mon 9pm

Series Two (6) 7 July–25 Aug 1986 · BBC2 Mon 9pm

MAIN CAST
Hilary Myers · · · · · · · · · · · · · · · Marti Caine
Lyn · Carolyn Moody
George · · · · · · · · · · · · · · · Philip Madoc
Kimberley · · · · · · · · · · · · · Jack Smethurst
Wesley · · · · · · · · · · · · · Philip Fox (series 1)
'Arthur' · · · · · · · · Percy Edwards (series 1)

CREDITS
writers Peter Robinson/Peter Vincent · *directors* Harold Snoad (6), Ray Butt (5), Martin Shardlow (1) · *producers* Harold Snoad (6), Ray Butt (6)

Intentionally moving away from her glamorous cabaret image, Marti Caine decided to re-create herself as a comedy actress with this series about the scatterbrained Hilary Myers, a TV researcher for Eagle Television. Hilary was a divorcee with a 19-year-old son, and sitcom chaos was assured because of her absent-mindedness and habit of saying the wrong thing at the wrong time. Initially, Hilary had a mynah bird called Arthur for company, the bird's voice provided by veteran animal impersonator Percy Edwards.

Typically candid in self criticism, Caine admitted that she wasn't very good in the first series, and ascribed her overacting to being used to making grand gestures on stage so that the people at the back could see. Determining to do better, she improved noticeably in the second series.

Marti Caine

UK · ITV (CENTRAL) · STANDUP/SKETCH

1 × 60 mins · colour

18 Dec 1989 · Mon 8pm

MAIN CAST
Marti Caine
Joan Rivers

CREDITS
script editor John Langdon · *director* David G Hillier · *producer* Richard Holloway

A seasonal one-off for Caine, co-starring Joan Rivers, that embraced her talents as a comedian and, with other guests, as a singer and dancer. Caine was well into her battle with cancer by this point.

In 1992 Marti Caine presented *Joker In The Pack* (12 editions, BBC1, 22 May to 4 September) in which she travelled the countryside urging 'real folk' to tell jokes, while in the studio two teams competed in a comedy contest called a 'jokathon'. This was her final TV series.

California Dreams

USA · NBC (PETER ENGEL PRODUCTIONS) · CHILDREN'S SITCOM

78 × 30 mins · colour

US dates: 12 Sep 1992–14 Dec 1996

UK dates: 25 Apr 1993–23 Mar 1997 (76 episodes) C4 weekdays around 9.30am then Sundays 9.50am

MAIN CAST
Tiffani Smith · · · · · · · · · · · · · · Kelly Packard
Sylvester 'Sly' Winkle · · · · · · · Michael Cade
Tony Wicks · · · · · · · · · William James Jones
Matt Garrison · · · · · · · Brent Gore (1992–93)
Jennifer Garrison · · · · · · Heidi Noelle Lenhart
· (1992–93)
Dennis Garrison · · · · Ryan O'Neill (1992–93)
Richard Garrison · · · Michael Cutt (1992–93)
Melody Garrison · · · Gail Ramsey (1992–93)
Jake Sommers · · · · · · · · Jay Anthony Franke
· (1993–96)
Samantha Woo · · · · Jennie Kwan (1993–96)
Lorena Costa · · · · · · Diana Uribe (1994–96)
Mark Winkle · · · · · Aaron Jackson (1994–96)

CREDITS
creators Ronald B Solomon/Brett Dewey · *writers* various · *directors* various · *executive producer* Peter Engel · *producer* Franco E Bario

These were 'Surf dudes with attitude', explained the theme song's lyrics, but it was hard to see what attitude this bunch of anodyne adolescents employed beyond fawning obsequiousness to good old-fashioned morality. Indeed, for all its attempts at 'hip' storylines and modern situations, *California Dreams* remained resolutely old-fashioned.

The series revolved around a crew of West Coast high-school students who had formed a soft-rock band, the California Dreams, and attempted to succeed musically as well as academically while dealing with romances, friendships, feuds and all of the other manifestations of youth. Although the band's membership changed, all its personnel shared certain attributes: physical perfection, flawless skin, more teeth than was strictly necessary, and nauseating cuteness. The band's manager, Sly Winkle, was supposedly the black sheep of the group, with his selfishness and greed, but in the moralising lessons underpinning every episode he would regularly be shown to be a decent sort underneath – more of an off-white sheep than a truly black one. This ethnically balanced, politically correct collection of real life Barbies and Kens was supported by background characters from the same mould who seemed to delight in the Dream's dreary, middle-of-the-road pop. One longed for a glimpse of a tattooed, pierced, spotty, angst-ridden extra to add even the thinnest veneer of realism to the fantasy version of California presented to viewers.

The cast availed themselves well enough but, in truth, had little to do. Despite the fact that its moralising tone, safe storylines and irony-free style recalled family sitcoms of the 1950s, the series proved consistently popular in the 1990s. *California Dreams* may have meant well but it was a perfect example of the old adage 'the road to hell is paved with good intentions'.

F-minus. Must try harder.

Call Earnshaw

UK · C4 (YORKSHIRE) · SITCOM

1 × 30 mins · colour
17 Dec 1984 · Mon 8.30pm

MAIN CAST
Earnshaw · · · · · · · · · · · · · Trevor Bannister
Mavis · · · · · · · · · · · · · · · · Diana Rayworth
Higgins · · · · · · · · · · · · · · · Derek Royale

CREDITS
writer Graham White · *director/producer* Alan Tarrant

The third of a trio of single-episode sitcoms (the others were *It's Never Too Late* and *It's Going To Be Alright*) produced by Yorkshire TV and screened by C4 in December 1984. *Call Earnshaw* starred Trevor Bannister (Mr Lucas in *Are You Being Served?*) as a former policeman who has become a less-than-successful private eye, sharing office accommodation with a typing bureau.

Call It What You Like

UK · BBC · SKETCH

6 × 25 mins · b/w
5 May–9 June 1965 · BBC2 Wed 8pm

MAIN CAST
Eric Merriman

June Whitfield
Gwendolyn Watts
Tony Tanner
Joe Melia

CREDITS
writer Eric Merriman · *producer* John Street

A further experiment by the BBC's new, second channel in its search for its own style of comedy. This six-part series was described as 'A sort of television show!' in *Radio Times*, and the title indicates a similar uncertainty over the genre.

Call Me Sam

UK · BBC · SITCOM

6 × 30 mins · b/w
26 Aug–30 Sep 1959 · Wed 7.30pm

MAIN CAST
Sam Callahan · · · · · · · · · · · · · · Eddie Byrne
Hetty Callahan · · · · · · · · · · Betty McDowall

CREDITS
writer Lee Loeb · *producer* Harry Carlisle

An early BBC sitcom in which Irish actor Eddie Byrne starred as Sam Callahan, and Betty McDowall as his wife Hetty. The Callahans run a restaurant 'somewhere off the Strand' in central London, where Sam's easy-going nature and willingness to do a good turn for his customers makes him easy to take advantage of. It is up to the more level-headed Hetty to keep things on track.

The series was scripted by Lee Loeb, who had extensive experience of US television writing.

The Cambridge Footlights

Founded in 1883, the Cambridge University Footlights Club is renowned as a breeding ground for sharp young comedians, and its annual revue, these days mostly satirical in nature, has been a highlight of the comedy year for more than a century. Early shows took the form of musical comedies, where, because of the club's men-only membership, many of the cast had to perform in drag. In 1932 women were permitted to perform for the first time but it was perceived to be so horrendous an experience – for the men, that is – that the following year's show was titled *No More Women* and, indeed, female membership of the Footlights was banned until the 1960s. Television presentations of the Footlights performances have been irregular but, in recent years at least, important in giving exposure to young artists who have gone on to become stalwarts of the British TV comedy scene.

In addition to presentations of revues as dedicated programmes, set out below, extracts from Footlight productions have been screened within coverage of the annual Edinburgh Festival Fringe, where the shows have long been presented.

A special programme commemorating the centenary of the Cambridge Footlights aired on BBC1 on 4 June 1983. Called *Footlights: 100 Years Of Comedy*, it featured reminiscences and observations from Peter Cook, John Cleese, David Frost, Jonathan Miller, Graeme Garden, Bill Oddie, Tim Brooke-Taylor, Richard Murdoch, Lord Killanin, Jimmy Edwards, Richard Baker, Miriam Margolyes, Germaine Greer, Richard Stilgoe, Frederick Raphael and Griff Rhys Jones.

See also *Oxford Accents*.

La Vie Cambridgienne

UK · BBC · SKETCH

1 × 45 mins · b/w
28 July 1948 · Wed 8.30pm

MAIN CAST
host · · · · · · · · · · · · · · · · · · Claude Hulbert
Michael Westmore, Kenneth Poolman, John Morley, Ian Lang, Michael O'Donnell, John Silverlight, Charles Parker, Adrian Vale, Stephen Lucas, Christopher Pike, Maurice Price, Michael Wilson, John Shearme, Ronald Shephard, David Eady, John Marriott, D'Arcy Orders, Harold Perkin, Cyril Hartley, Elster Kay

CREDITS
writers Michael Westmore, Kenneth Poolman, John Morley, Charles Parker, Adrian Vale, David Eady, Richard Armitage, Geoffrey Beaumont, Peter Tranchell, Ted Cranshaw, Richard Baker, Stephen Joseph, Ian Clements, Simon Phipps, Ben Gradwell · *stage director* Stephen Joseph · *producer* John Glyn-Jones

Light-comedy stage and film stars Claude and Jack Hulbert began their careers in the Footlights before achieving fame in the 1930s. Here 'silly ass' Claude was on hand to introduce some fresh faces from the class of '48. The Cambridge monopoly of the production was broken by producer John Glyn-Jones, an Oxford man. The title was a play on Offenbach's comic opera *La Vie Parisienne*.

Footlights '64

UK · ITV (ATV) · SKETCH

1 × 30 mins · b/w
27 Sep 1964 · Sun 11.10pm

MAIN CAST
Eric Idle, Graeme Garden, David Gooderson, Susan Hanson, Miriam Margolyes, John Cameron

CREDITS
writers cast and Flick Hough, Mark Lushington, Andrew Mayer, Jim Beach, Brian Gascoigne, Jeremy Heal, Anthony Buffery, Robert Cushman, Sue Heber-Percy, Jonathan Lynn, Richard Eyre · *director* Albert Locke

The wild success of *Beyond The Fringe* caused TV, and the media in general, to pay close attention to the Footlights productions. This single half-hour featured the young Turks of 1964 – and it was quite a cast. Jonathan Lynn, Guy Slater, Mark Lushington, Flick Hough and Sue Heber-Percy also performed in the full-length production, which was titled *Stuff What Dreams Are Made Of*.

Cambridge Footlights Dramatic Club

UK · BBC · SKETCH

1 × 45 mins · colour

3 Sep 1968 · BBC2 Tue 8.45pm

MAIN CAST
Pete Atkin, Al Sizer, Julie Covington, Maggie Scott, Clive James, Jonathan James-Moore, Russell Davies, Rob Buckman

CREDITS
writers cast and Barry Brown · *directors* Clive James/Jonathan James-Moore · *producer* Philip Lewis

Traditionally, the Footlights brigade presented a performance at the Robin Hood Theatre, Averham, where they tested out material from which to select sketches and skits for the Edinburgh Festival Fringe shows. This 1968 production, *'Turn It On' Or Is It Up?*, was recorded and presented by the BBC. One of the leading lights was Pete Atkin who would go on to have a successful career as a contemporary folk singer – his lyrics written here by Clive James – and would later enjoy even more success as a BBC radio producer – as, indeed, would Jonathan James-Moore.

Cambridge Footlights Revue 1

UK · BBC · SKETCH

1 × 35 mins · colour

20 Sep 1969 · BBC2 Sat 9pm

MAIN CAST
Rob Buckman, Russell Davies, Adrian Edwards, Bill Gutteridge, Robert Orledge, Maggie Scott, Ian Taylor

CREDITS
writers cast and Clive James, David Turner · *footlights director* Clive James · *producer* Philip Lewis

A BBC presentation of the latest Cambridge revue material (the 1969 production was titled *Fools Rush In*) which they hoped would afford a sneak preview of future TV comedy talent.

Cambridge Footlights Revue 2

UK · BBC · STANDUP

1 × 50 mins · colour

26 Aug 1974 · BBC2 Mon 9.55pm

MAIN CAST
Sue Aldred, Clive Anderson, Jon Canter, Jane Ellison, Geoffrey McGivern, Griff Rhys Jones, Martin Smith, Crispin Thomas

CREDITS
writers cast and Will Adams, Martin Smith, Douglas Adams, Robert Benton, Simon Levene, Nigel Hess, Simon Joly, John Lloyd, Jim Seigelman · *producer* Dennis Main Wilson

The Footlights had proved such a rich breeding ground for new TV talent that producers scanned each new year carefully, trying to spot the stars of tomorrow. From this class of '74 – the production was titled *Chox* – Griff Rhys Jones (billed in these days as Griffith Rhys Jones), Clive Anderson and Douglas Adams went on to achieve fame.

The 1977 Cambridge Footlights Revue

UK · BBC · STANDUP/SKETCH/SATIRE

1 × 40 mins · colour

16 Dec 1977 · BBC2 Fri 9pm

MAIN CAST
Robert Bathurst, Martin Bergman, Paul Hudson, Nicholas Hytner, Rory McGrath, Jimmy Mulville, Carrie Simcocks

CREDITS
writers Martin Bergman, Rory McGrath, Nicholas Hytner, Jimmy Mulville, Griff Rhys Jones · *additional material* Charles Bott, Paul Hudson, Pete Smith · *director* Griff Rhys Jones · *producer* Bernard Thompson

Extracts from the 1977 revue, titled *Tag!* Mulville and McGrath would make the most impact both on and behind the screen in the years to come.

Cambridge Footlights Revue 3

UK · BBC · STANDUP/SKETCH

1 × 50 mins · colour

20 May 1982 · BBC2 Thu 9.30pm

MAIN CAST
Stephen Fry, Hugh Laurie, Emma Thompson, Tony Slattery, Paul Shearer, Penny Dwyer

CREDITS
writers cast · *director* John Kilby · *producer* Dennis Main Wilson

Extracts from the 1981 production, *The Cellar Tapes*. There were particularly rich pickings here, with Tony Slattery, Emma Thompson, Stephen Fry and Hugh Laurie all moving on to TV success and beyond, the latter three quite quickly in *Alfresco*. The stage production was by Jan Ravens, the first woman president of the Footlights.

Three years earlier, members of the Footlights appeared in BBC2's late-night miscellany programme *Friday Night … Saturday Morning* (16 November 1979). Those appearing were Emma Thompson, Hugh Laurie, Martin Bergman, Robert Bathurst, Simon McBurney, with Footlights old-boy Peter Cook.

Camp Runamuck

USA · NBC (SCREEN GEMS) · SITCOM

26 × 30 mins · colour

US dates: 17 Sep 1965–2 Sep 1966

UK dates: 29 Mar–1 Nov 1975 (26 episodes) BBC1 Sat 10am

MAIN CAST
Commander Wivenhoe · · · · · · · Arch Johnson
Senior Counselor Spiffy · · · · · Dave Ketchum
Counselor Pruett · · · · · · · · · · · David Madden
Counselor Malden · · · · · · · · · · Mike Wagner
Doc Joslyn · · · · · Frank DeVol (first episode);
· · · · · · · · · · · · · · Leonard Stone (remainder)
Mahala May Gruenecker · · · · · · · · Alice Nunn
Counselor Nadine Smith · · · · Beverly Adams
Counselor Ivy · · · · · · · · · · · · Carol Anderson
Caprice Yeudleman · · · · · · · · · · Nina Wayne
Eulalia Divine · · · · · · · · · Hermione Baddeley
The Sheriff · · · · · · · · · · · · · · · George Dunn

CREDITS
writers Sid Mandel/Bob Rodgers (13), David Swift (10), William Freedman/Ben Gershman (2), Ann Marcus (1) · *directors* David Swift (7), Robert Rosenbaum (7), Howard Duff (7), Hal March (2), Charles Barton (1), David Butler (1), Bruce Bilson (1) · *producer* David Swift

The slapstick adventures had in two adjacent US summer camps for children: the haphazard Camp Runamuck for boys and its big rival across the lake, the efficient Camp Divine for girls. The competitiveness of the two camps and the incidents and accidents typical of such holidays – missing kids, people falling in the lake, food poisoning, and so on – formed the basis of the plots.

It all added up to innocent, wholesome fun, suitable for showing by the BBC on Saturday mornings ten years after it aired in the States. (Although this was the first network UK screening of *Camp Runamuck*, the series was aired by some ITV regional stations in 1969.)

The bandleader Frank DeVol played the part of Doc Joslyn in the opening episode but illness forced him to quit the role.

Camp Wilder

USA · ABC (VANITY LOGO PRODUCTIONS) · SITCOM

18 × 30 mins · colour

US dates: 18 Sep 1992–26 Feb 1993

UK dates: 24 July–18 Aug 1995 (18 episodes) BBC2 weekdays 10.05am

MAIN CAST
Ricky Wilder · · · · · · · · · · · Mary Page Keller

Brody Wilder	Jerry O'Connell
Melissa Wilder	Meghann Haldeman
Sophie Wilder	Tina Majorino
Dorfman	Jay Mohr
Daniella	Hilary Swank
Beth	Margaret Langrick

CREDITS

creator/main writer Matthew Carlson · *director* Arlene Stafford · *executive producer* Matthew Carlson

When her parents die suddenly, 28-year-old divorcee Ricky Wilder returns to the family home and, as their eldest child, takes on the responsibility of looking after her teenage brother (Brody) and sister (Melissa), in addition to her own daughter, six-year-old Sophie. With a guardian not much older than her charges, the Wilders are perceived as being more liberal and 'cooler' than most households in the area and so become an inspiration for Brody's close friends Beth and Daniella and the gormless Dorfman. Ricky's job as a registered nurse means she can't be at home all the time and her absences, at which time Brody is left in charge, add to the general laid-back atmosphere of the family home, a situation that concerns some of their neighbours.

Camp Wilder was a saccharine-sweet sitcom, with the sort of sledgehammer moralising that ought to have disappeared in the 1960s. All the characters were uniformly nice, meaning that conflict was virtually non-existent, dilemmas were solved with sound, albeit liberal, reasoning, and the teenagers behaved (eventually) in a moral and adult way. Granted, there were some sharp one-liners, and the cast was appealing enough, but the general feelgood factor of the show worked against memorable comedy. Laughs were wrought occasionally from Dorfman's crush on Ricky, and his clumsy attempts to seduce her, but this was the sole abrasive idea in an otherwise too-smooth product. *Camp Milder* would have been a more accurate title.

Camping

see Mr Pastry

Campus Cops

USA · USA NETWORK (CHELSEA AVENUE/ST CLARE ENTERTAINMENT/MTE) · SITCOM

13 × 30 mins · colour

US dates: 6 Jan–30 Mar 1996

UK dates: 26 Sep 1997 to date (1 episode to 31/12/97) ITV Fri 12 midnight

MAIN CAST

Andy	Ron Bodé
Wayne Simko	Ryan Hurst
Royce	Jerry Kernion
Meg	LaRita Shelby
Raskin	J D Cullum
Hingle	David Sage
Dean Pilkington	Monte Markham

CREDITS

creators Michael Baser/Frank Dungan · *writers* Chris Henchy and others · *directors* John Landis, Carl Gottlieb, Iain Paterson, Frank Bonner, Scott White · *executive producers* Andrew Nicholls, Darrell Vickers, John Landis, Leslie Belzberg

An American cable-TV sitcom centred on the campus police squad at Canfield University. Andy and Wayne are long-term buddies, currently employed as campus cops, who regularly abuse their positions in order to meet, date, or simply spy on the university's more beautiful female students. Wayne is usually the instigator of such shenanigans, with the hapless Andy pulled along for the ride. In support were fellow cops Meg, a competent Afro-American; Raskin, a weird weapon-obsessed nutcase; Royce, an overweight sycophant; and their boss Hingle, a dedicated career policeman. The other regular character was Dean Pilkington, a manic and slightly crazed individual worryingly prone to bouts of extreme verbal or physical violence.

The presence of John Landis's name in the credits goes some way towards explaining the thrust of the piece, which, in parts, recalled the director's earlier university comedy movie *Animal House* (1978). Like his 1990s sitcom **Dream On**, *Campus Cops* also had more than its fair share of scantily clad women and sexual situations, but what had seemed comical in the late 1970s, and sophisticated in the HBO series, came across as old-hat and sexist here.

Can We Get On Now, Please?

UK · ITV (GRANADA) · SITCOM

6 × 30 mins · colour

2 June–7 July 1980 · Mon 8pm

MAIN CAST

Mrs Prior JP	Sheila Steafel
Mr Pettigrew	Hugh Paddick
Mr Butterfield JP	Robert Dorning
Mr Skinner JP	Michael Barrington
Mr Bailey	Charles Lamb
Miss Teasdale	Valerie Phillips

CREDITS

writer Dennis Woolf · *directors* Eric Prytherch (5), Richard Holthouse (1) · *producer* Brian Armstrong

Based upon his experiences and research as an occasional writer and producer of Granada TV's daily *Crown Court* drama, Dennis Woolf scripted this six-part sitcom about life in the lower courts, with Hugh Paddick cast as the efficient Clerk to the Justices Mr. Pettigrew, and Sheila Steafel as Justice of the Peace Mrs Prior. In truth, the cast was strong throughout, and each week saw them dealing with the lighter side of everyday problems: neighbourly squabbles, football-fan rowdiness and such.

Canada Goose

UK · BBC · SKETCH

1 × 30 mins · colour

10 Nov 1969 · BBC2 Mon 9.10pm

MAIN CAST

Don Cullen
David Healy
David Jason
Paul McDowell
Diana Quick

CREDITS

writers John Morgan/Martin Bronstein · *additional material* The Second City · *producer* Ian Davidson

A one-off show in which Canadian comedy material was performed by a multinational team of Canadians, Americans and Britons, produced by the BBC's Ian Davidson. Some of the material was provided by members of Chicago's famous improvisational comedy ensemble the Second City, a famous breeding ground for new talent that boasts among its alumni Alan Arkin, Mike Nichols and Elaine May, Valerie Harper, Shelley Berman, John Candy, John Belushi, Dan Aykroyd, Gilda Radner, Shelley Long and George Wendt.

Five years earlier, members of the Second City troupe combined with actors from Peter Cook's Establishment Club to present *The Tale Of Two Cities* (BBC1, 23 April 1964), a film produced and directed by William Friedkin in which the two ensembles exchanged views and comments on Chicago and London.

Canned Carrott

see CARROTT, Jasper

Cannon And Ball

UK · ITV (LWT, *YORKSHIRE) · SKETCH/STANDUP/**SITCOM

75 editions (43 × 30 mins · 22 × 45 mins · 6 × 60 mins · 4 × approx 15 mins) · colour

Series One (4 × approx 15 mins) 4 Nov–18 Nov 1978 · part of *Bruce Forsyth's Big Night* · Sat from 7.25pm; 24 Dec 1978 · part of *Bruce Forsyth's Christmas Eve* · Sun from 7.15pm

Series Two (first own series) (6 × 30 mins) 28 July & 4 Aug 1979 · Sat 8pm; 26 Oct–16 Nov 1979 · Sat 8.30pm

Series Three (7 × 30 mins) 11 Apr–23 May 1980 · Fri 7.30pm

Special (45 mins) *Cannon And Ball For Christmas* 20 December 1980 · Sat 6pm

Series Four (6 × 30 mins) 25 Apr–30 May 1981 · Sat 7.35pm

Special (60 mins) *Cannon And Ball At Drury Lane* 2 Jan 1982 · Sat 7pm

Series Five (6 × 30 mins) *The Cannon And Ball Show* 8 May–12 June 1982 · Sat 7.15pm

Special (60 mins) *The Cannon And Ball Easter Show* 2 Apr 1983 · Sat 8.15pm

Series Six (6 × 45 mins) 3 Dec 1983–21 Jan 1984 · Sat 7pm

Series Seven (6 × 45 mins) 13 Oct–17 Nov 1984 · Sat 7pm

Special (60 mins) *Christmas Cannon And Ball* 21 Dec 1985 · Sat 7.45pm

**Series Eight (6 × 30 mins) 26 Apr–31 May 1986 · Sat 7pm

Special (60 mins) *The Cannon And Ball Special* 27 Dec 1986 · Sat 6.30pm

**Series Nine (6 × 30 mins) 10 Jan–14 Feb 1987 · Sat 6.45pm

Special (60 mins) *The Cannon And Ball Special* 2 Jan 1988 · Sat 7.40pm

Series Ten (6 × 30 mins) 28 May–2 July 1988 · Sat 7pm

*Special (60 mins) *The Cannon And Ball Show* 24 Dec 1988 · Sat 5.15pm

*Series Eleven (9 × 45 mins) *Casino* 19 May–25 Aug 1990 · Sat 6.10pm

MAIN CAST
Tommy Cannon
Bobby Ball

CREDITS
writers various · *directors* Geoffrey Sax, David Crossman, David Bell, Alasdair Macmillan, Paul Jackson, Terry Kinane, Marcus Plantin, Ian Hamilton, Michael Hurll, Graham Wetherell · *producers* Humphrey Barclay, David Bell, Sid Green, Paul Jackson, Marcus Plantin, Ian Hamilton, Michael Hurll, Graham Wetherell

After years on the northern cabaret circuit, comedians Tommy Cannon (the lighter-haired one, real name Thomas Derbyshire) and Bobby Ball (the darker-haired, moustachioed and smaller one, real name Robert Harper) broke into TV as part of *Bruce Forsyth's Big Night*, a weekly compendium of stand-alone items presented by Brucie on Saturday nights in late 1978. The former welders from Oldham, who had previously worked under the name the Harper Brothers, became major stars very quickly, soon winning their first own series, which, unfortunately for them, was interrupted by the ITV network strike of 1979. Nonetheless, with their Abbott And Costello-like antics and catchphrases such as 'Rock on, Tommy' they retained a strong presence on ITV through the 1980s, and moved into the cinema in 1983 with their one-off movie *The Boys In Blue* (director Val Guest).

Three of their 11 series were distinct from the others: in the six programmes beginning 26 April 1986 and also the six beginning 10 January 1987 (the second set all written by Bryan Blackburn) a sitcom premise was explored, in which Tommy and Bobby stayed in a well-appointed London flat when they were down south, away from their Rochdale homes. *Casino*, from 19 May 1990, was part comedy-show, part game-show (with Cannon and Ball as question-masters). Clearly, the comics were eager to try something new, and a year later they appeared in the ITV sitcom *Plaza Patrol*.

Capstick Capers

UK · C4 (SECKER WALKER/NCA-TV) · STANDUP/SKETCH

8 × 30 mins · colour
15 Apr–3 June 1983 · Fri 9.30pm

MAIN CAST
Tony Capstick

CREDITS
writers Tony Capstick, Dave Secker, Stan Walker · *director* Dave Secker · *producer* Stan Walker

Jokes and stories from the Yorkshire comic/guitarist whose double-A-sided single 'Sheffield Grinder'/'Capstick Comes Home', the latter set to the tune of the Hovis TV commercial, had accorded him fame in the spring of 1981 when it reached number three in the charts. Weekly musical guests included Earl Okin (four times) and Peter Skellern (twice), while Capstick himself also appeared as Our Kid (northern-speak for his brother).

Captain Butler

UK · C4 (ESSENTIAL FILM AND TELEVISION PRODUCTIONS) · SITCOM

6 × 30 mins · colour
3 Jan–7 Feb 1997 · Fri mostly 10.30pm

MAIN CAST
Captain Butler · · · · · · · · · · · · Craig Charles
Bosun · · · · · · · · · · · · · · · · · · Shaun Curry
Cliff · · · · · · · · · · · · · · · · · Roger Griffiths
Lord Roger · · · · · · · · · · · · · · · Lewis Rae
Adeel · · · · · · · · · · · · · · · Sanjeev Bhaskar

CREDITS
writers John Smith/Rob Sprackling · *director* Iain McLean · *executive producer* Al Mitchell · *producer* Christopher Skala

Avast ye swabs, shiver me timbers, splice the mainbrace and other such nautical clichés were awash in this high-seas sitcom, which displayed a broad and bawdy style of humour with precious little subtlety. Craig Charles was the clear focal point, cast as Butler, the cowardly captain of a motley bunch of pirates who sail the seven seas desperately trying to avoid involvement in skirmishes. His crew was pleasingly multi-ethnic and multi-cultural but the jokes were decidedly monochrome, music-hall and sub-*Carry On*, with an over-reliance upon contemporary swear words to curry cheap (but loud) laughs. Much of the comedy revolved around such anachronisms, with the 18th-century protagonists often using 20th-century references and visited by modern-day concerns. To be fair, the gaudy and gauche nature of the piece was intentional and the production made a virtue of the fact that everything was played out in an obvious studio set.

Contemporaneously with *Captain Butler*, Charles could also be seen in *Red Dwarf*, and there was a distinct similarity between the two series: both featured wacky crews in ramshackle vessels traversing wide gulfs and encountering all sorts of bizarre irritants and foes. In a further link, Robert Llewellyn – Kryten in *Red Dwarf* – turned up in *Captain Butler* as Admiral Nelson.

Captain Moonlight – Man Of Mystery

UK · BBC · CHILDREN'S SITCOM

6 × 30 mins · b/w
22 Mar–26 Apr 1958 · Sat mostly 5.10pm

MAIN CAST
Captain Moonlight (Tony) · · · · · Jeremy White
Alice · · · · · · · · · · · · · · · · · Lorraine Peters

CREDITS
writer/producer Kevin Sheldon

An intriguing children's comedy serial. Captain Moonlight is a radio action hero battling fearlessly against international spies and other nefarious villains. He is played by Tony, a mild, bespectacled man to whom the idea of physical violence is abhorrent. But when Tony becomes unwittingly involved in a dangerous escapade he has to call upon the assistance of his Captain Moonlight alter ego.

A second series of *Captain Moonlight – Man Of Mystery* (BBC, 12 March–16 April 1960) was less comedic in approach and more of a straight adventure. In this, the name of the action hero was Stephen Sycamore and he was played by Bernard Horsfall.

Captive Audience

UK · BBC · SITCOM

1 × 30 mins · colour
2 July 1975 · BBC1 Wed 9.25pm

MAIN CAST
Leonard · · · · · · · · · · · · · · · · Derek Fowlds
Mum · · · · · · · · · · · · · · · · · · Daphne Heard
Uncle Jeffrey · · · · · · · · · · · · · Leslie Dwyer
Avril · · · · · · · · · · · · · · · · · · · Cheryl Hall
Eric · Léon Vitali

CREDITS
writers Dick Clement/Ian La Frenais · *producer* Roger Race

The fourth in a series of unrelated single sitcoms screened by BBC1 in the summer of 1975. Following *Thick As Thieves* and *Porridge*, writers Clement and La Frenais once again depicted a likeable criminal, in this case it was Leonard, who has reached 40 but still harbours get-rich-quick schemes, most of which are illegal. In this script he hit upon the idea of kidnapping a pop star and holding him to ransom. No series developed.

Car Along The Pass

UK · ITV (YORKSHIRE) · SITCOM

1 × 30 mins · colour

17 Feb 1977 · Thu 9pm

MAIN CAST

Harry Duckworth · · · · · · · · · · · · Arthur Lowe
Harry's wife · · · · · · · · · · · Mona Washbourne

OTHER APPEARANCES

Anton Diffring
André Maranne

CREDITS

writers/associate producers Ray Galton/Alan
Simpson · *executive producer* Duncan Wood ·
director/producer Vernon Lawrence

Eight years after their previous series of
individual sitcoms for ITV (LWT's *The
Galton & Simpson Comedy* in 1969) the pair
with the golden pens turned in seven new
programmes for Yorkshire Television – under
the title *The Galton & Simpson Playhouse* –
each starring a major comic actor. This
episode, the first, featured Arthur Lowe as
Harry Duckworth, a stoical, flag-flying Brit
from Twickenham, away with his wife on a
camping holiday in the Alps, determined to
show everyone how things are done The
British Way and maintaining that stiff upper
lip despite every embarrassing catastrophe he
invoked.

Car 54, Where Are You?

USA · NBC (EUPOLIS PRODUCTIONS) · SITCOM

60 × 30 mins · b/w

US dates: 17 Sep 1961–14 Apr 1963

*UK dates: 21 July 1964–28 Dec 1965 (38
episodes) ITV mostly Tue 8pm

MAIN CAST

Officer Gunther Toody · · · · · · · · Joe E Ross
Officer Francis Muldoon · · · · · Fred Gwynne
Capt Martin Block · · · · · · · · · · · Paul Reed
Lucille Toody · · · · · · · · · · · · Beatrice Pons
Officer Leo Schnauser · · · · · · · · · · Al Lewis
Sylvia Schnauser · · · · · · · · · Charlotte Rae
Officer O'Hara · · · · · · · · · Albert Henderson
Officer Anderson · · · · · · · · · Nipsey Russell
· (1961–62)
Officer Kissel · · · · · · · · · · · · · · Bruce Kirby

CREDITS

creator/producer Nat Hiken · *writers* Nat Hiken and
others · *director* Al De Caprio

A gem of a sitcom, and a relatively
undiscovered one at that, *Car 54, Where
Are You?* depicts the escapades of a pair of
entirely different but equally inept police
officers, Toody and Muldoon – their patrol
vehicle is Car 54 – working at the 53rd
Precinct in the Bronx area of New York.
(Much of the series was shot on location; to
avoid confusion, their car was a different
colour to regular police vehicles though this
did not show in the black and white film.)

The series was the creation and labour of
Nat Hiken, whose genius had given birth to
The Phil Silvers Show – *Sergeant Bilko* –
at CBS in 1955. Indeed, *Car 54* was an
especial joy for *Bilko* fans, for not only did it
benefit from more of Hiken's inventive comic

touches but also the cast and crew included a
number of *Bilko* alumni, most notably Joe E
Ross, who maintained the 'ooh-ooh' hallmark
of stupidity that had delighted previously in
the guise of chef Rupert Ritzik. Rupert's wife
in *Bilko*, the hectoring Beatrice Pons, even
transferred to *Car 54* as his hectoring wife in
this series. The Colonel Hall character in *Bilko*
– the man who knows that his weak grip
on command is becoming ever looser – was
represented in *Car 54* by Captain Block.
Other *Bilko* faces – where they had appeared
as guest stars – were familiar to viewers of
Car 54, including Charlotte Rae and Fred
Gwynne. The latter was elevated to co-star
status in *Car 54*, and both he and Al Lewis –
wonderful as Officer Schnauser – would
later move on together into **The Munsters**.

Clearly, then, *Car 54* is manna to TV
historians – more than that, though, and quite
independent of all the *Bilko* links, it is also
funny in its own right, with the sublime
characterisation and comedic traits that were
the hallmarks of Nat Hiken. The idea that
such a pulsating, crime-ridden city as New
York could employ, and welcome, two such
dolts as Toody and the quietly shy Muldoon
as a policing partnership was ridiculous,
of course, but the pair clicked together in a
reversal of the Laurel and Hardy mould: the
tall thin one had the brains, the dumpy one
employed the moronic and illogical line in
thought. Their colleagues at the 53rd were
not much better, though, especially the
excitable Schnauser – indeed, one can but
wonder how this lot managed to capture
any criminals at all.

As the 1990s dawned, and Hollywood
movie producers began to look back fondly
and with covetous eyes at their childhood TV
favourites, so *Car 54* was updated for the big
screen. It could have worked, had it been done
well, but it was not. The *Car 54, Where Are
You?* movie (directed by Bill Fishman) was a
crass, insulting shambles, made without
regard to the light-fingered qualities of the
original and an ill-judged wholesale embrace
of the 'rap' culture that heaps embarrassment
upon the production. David Johansen starred
as the gravel-voiced Toody, John C McGinley
was cast as Muldoon and Rosie O'Donnell as
Lucille. One nice touch was that two veterans
of the TV series were employed: Al Lewis as
the about-to-retire Leo Schnauzer (clearly, no
regard was paid to spelling either) and Nipsey
Russell appeared again as Anderson, now
promoted to the rank of station captain. When
completed, the best possible thing happened
to this travesty of a movie: Orion Pictures, the
production company, went into bankruptcy
and the film never came out. It has, however,
been shown on cable/satellite-TV film
channels.

*Note. All 60 episodes of *Car 54, Where Are
You?* were screened by C4 between 19 May
1983 and 13 March 1987.

Carmichael's Night Out

UK · BBC · SKETCH

1 × 30 mins · b/w

14 Mar 1957 · Thu 8pm

MAIN CAST

Ian Carmichael

CREDITS

writers Sid Colin, Peter Jones, Ian Carmichael ·
producer Francis Essex

BBC producer and performer Ian Carmichael
had been a familiar TV face for some years
but by this time was becoming better known
as a comedy film actor. Indeed, he was under
contract to the Boulting Brothers, the film
producers, when this TV special was made.
In it, Carmichael appeared as 'The man
taking the mike' and the programme as a
whole 'took the mickey' out of a famous BBC
show of 1956, *Saturday Night Out*, in which
BBC cameras travelled to various places to
film live events, ranging from circuses to, on
one remarkable occasion, a specially staged
train crash.

Carol Burnett ... [various shows]

see BURNETT, Carol

Caroline In The City

USA · NBC (BARRON PENNETTE
PRODUCTIONS/SISTER ENTERTAINMENT/NBC
ENTERTAINMENT PRODUCTIONS) · SITCOM

**60 episodes (59 × 30 mins · 1 × 60 mins to
31/12/97 · continuing into 1998) · colour**

US dates: 21 Sep 1995 to date

UK dates: 20 Sep 1996 to date (24 × 30 mins to
31/12/97) C4 Fri 9pm

MAIN CAST

Caroline Duffy · · · · · · · · · · · · Lea Thompson
Del Cassidy · · · · · · · · · · · · · · · · · Eric Lutes
Richard Karinsky · · · · · · · · · · Malcolm Gets
Annie Spadaro · · · · · · · · · · · · · · · Amy Pietz
Charlie · · · · · · · · · · · · · · · · · · · Andy Lauer
Remo · · · · · · · · · · · · · · · · · · · Tom La Grua
Julia · · · · · · · · · Sofia Milos (1997 onwards)

OTHER APPEARANCES

Angie Spadaro · · · · Candy Azzara (1995–97)
Shelly · · · · · · · · Lauren Graham (1995–96)
Joe DeStefano · · Mark Feuerstein (1996–97)

CREDITS

creators Fred Barron, Marco Pennette, Dottie
Dartland · *writers* Fred Barron/Marco Pennette and
others · *directors* James Burrows, Tom Cherones,
Rod Daniel, Gordon Hunt, Will MacKenzie and
others · *executive producers* Fred Barron, Marco
Pennette · *producers* Faye Oshima Belyeu, Bill
Prady, Bill Masters

Displaying a winning combination of
glamour and comedy, Lea Thompson made a

splash as the girlfriend/mother of Michael J Fox's character in the three *Back To The Future* movies. Largely as a result, she was given this surprisingly durable – and deceptively simple – TV sitcom in which to star.

Thompson was cast as Caroline Duffy, a cartoonist whose life experiences form the background to her nationally syndicated *Caroline In The City* comic strip. (For some reason, though, Caroline never seems as financially well-off as she should be, considering the success of her product – with its lucrative spin-off merchandising of greetings cards, calendars and more.) Her friend and neighbour is Annie, a confident realist and sharp, sexually promiscuous New Yorker who sings in the chorus line of the long-running Broadway musical *Cats*. An obvious, somewhat exaggerated version of Annie appears in the comic strip as the 'slutty neighbour', but this dubious portrayal never bothers her, indeed she seems quite proud of the caricature.

At the beginning of the series Caroline has just split up with Del, a macho hunk who runs the greeting card firm that licenses the strip. Despite the ending of their sexual relationship, Caroline and Del are determined to remain friends, although Del regularly confesses that he still lusts after her. Del's madcap assistant, Charlie, is also frequently on hand to provide laughs. Then there's Richard, whom Caroline employs as her strip's colourist, engaged in the first episode after her previous employee leaves to get married. Richard is a struggling artist who makes no bones of the fact that he considers himself too good for the comic-strip job. He is an intense, neurotic, broody sort who initially views the comings and goings in Caroline's life with the detachment of an anthropologist studying a strange species. Gradually, however, he becomes drawn into her world, and, inevitably, a smouldering sexual frisson develops between them. As the series progresses, further romances complicate matters (Caroline reunites with Del and then gets it together with Joe; Richard has a fling with Shelly and then resuscitates an old relationship with Julia) but these are mainly red herrings, prolonging the foreplay element of Richard and Caroline's inevitable coupling.

This was *Caroline In The City* in a nutshell – an easy-going, middle-of-the-road sitcom. The nearest it got to being innovative was its use of between-scenes comic strip panels and occasional animations of the strip to illustrate events in the plot (cartoonist Bonnie Timmons actually drew these). Yet despite its unambitious stance, *Caroline In The City* was a fine series that understood its limitations and realised its full potential. The ensemble cast interacted well and the whole thing was held together by Thompson's

funny and endearing portrayal of an essentially naïve girl in the big city. Her on-off romance with Del was spun cleverly throughout the series, with the underlying sexual tension between Caroline and Richard also handled masterfully, creating the sort of intriguing friction so successfully mined in *Cheers* with Sam and Diane. The dialogue was crisp and witty throughout and the performers pulled off the tricky job of making the comedy seem effortless. All in all, then, *Caroline In The City* was a prime example of a well-crafted, hugely amusing yet essentially 'ordinary' sitcom.

Jasper Carrott

Born Bob Davies on 4 March 1945 in Birmingham, the comic re-created himself as Jasper Carrott in his teens when, on a whim, he added the vegetal surname to the nickname Jasper that was stuck on him at school. Carrott's first foray into show business was entrepreneurial: he opened a folk club, the Boggery, in Solihull. Although intending to become a booking agent, Carrott soon started performing at his venue, and elsewhere, to support the agency. Citing Tom Lehrer as an influence, his act at this time combined folk songs with short comic monologues, but gradually, as his confidence grew, the comedy sections became longer and the musical ones shorter.

Carrott's breakthrough came in 1975 when his comedy single 'Funky Moped' became a huge hit, mostly because of the publicity it attained when the BBC banned its flip-side, a risqué send up of the children's TV puppet programme *The Magic Roundabout*. Carrott capitalised on this success with a series of tours around the country and TV guest spots. These led to a starring series for LWT, *An Audience With Jasper Carrott*, and, once on the small-screen, Carrott was established. Never one to rest on his laurels, he has frequently changed the format of his shows, but his personal style remains the same: he comes across as a likeable Brummie with an intimate delivery that endears him to audiences, performing material that ranges from autobiographical reminiscences to observations on bureaucracy and other modern-day lunacies.

An Audience With Jasper Carrott

UK · ITV (LWT) · STANDUP

6 × 30 mins · colour

20 Jan–3 Mar 1978 · Fri 10.40pm

MAIN CAST
Jasper Carrott

CREDITS
writer Jasper Carrott · *director/producer* Paul Smith

Although he had appeared in a one-off special, *A Half Hour Mislaid With Jasper Carrott*, screened on 17 September 1976 by the BBC's Midlands transmitters, the Brummie comedian's first series, ironically, was for London Weekend Television. Michael Grade, director of programmes for LWT, caught Carrott's act at the Shakespeare Memorial Theatre in Stratford-upon-Avon and invited him to record a pilot for the company. That led to this series of half-hour standup shows in which Carrott appeared in his trademark denim and with a rarely used acoustic guitar. His material, honed on stage, was adapted for TV, and mostly revolved around stories of his life, especially a trip to America where he had discovered his favourite word, 'zit' (meaning facial spot). Carrott claimed that nine years' worth of touring material was used up during these six shows but it proved worthwhile, the comedian winning a Pye Award as Outstanding New Personality, and establishing himself as a reliable TV entertainer.

The Unrecorded Jasper Carrott

UK · ITV (LWT) · STANDUP

1 × 60 mins · colour

18 Feb 1979 · Sun 9.15pm

MAIN CAST
Jasper Carrott

CREDITS
writer Jasper Carrott · *director/producer* Paul Smith

A live broadcast from the Theatre Royal, Drury Lane, London, starring the standup act of the man still being referred to as a 'folk' comic. To illustrate that the show was really 'live' Carrott took a television on to the stage and showed the audience and viewers at home what was on the other channels.

A tape of the programme was repeated on 30 December 1979 but the title remained *Unrecorded*. Later, Carrott made another regional appearance in the BBC Midlands region, starring in the *Tell Me …* series on 20 July 1979.

Carrott Gets Rowdie

UK · ITV (OPIX FILMS FOR LWT) · STANDUP

1 × 60 mins · colour

2 Nov 1979 · Fri 9pm

MAIN CAST
Jasper Carrott

CREDITS
writer Jasper Carrott · *director* Terry Ryan · *producer* Ray Marshall

A single programme showing the Brummie comic in Florida, where he followed the fortunes of the Tampa Rowdies soccer team and met some of their supporters. Carrott's fascination with the US would provide him with a good deal more material and programmes in the ensuing years.

Carrott Del Sol

UK · ITV (OPIX FILMS FOR LWT) · SITCOM

1 × 60 mins · colour

2 Jan 1981 · Fri 10.15pm

MAIN CAST

Sago	Jasper Carrott
Wayne	Bernard Latham
Kevin	Terry Molloy

CREDITS

writer Jasper Carrott · director Terry Ryan · producer Ray Marshall

A one-off situation comedy, starring Carrott as Sago, a likely lad who flies off to Spain with his two mates Wayne and Kevin (the latter played by the man who voices Mike Tucker in *The Archers*) for a knotted-hankie-on-heads-style package holiday. While there they encounter German tourists and other hazards.

Beat The Carrott

UK · ITV (LWT) · STANDUP

1 × 60 mins · colour

18 Sep 1981 · Fri 10.15pm

MAIN CAST

Jasper Carrott

CREDITS

writer Jasper Carrott · director/producer Paul Smith

A special performance, filmed at the London Palladium.

Carrott's Lib

UK · BBC · STANDUP/SKETCH

17 editions (8 × 45 mins · 9 × 40 mins) · colour

Series One (7 × 45 mins) 9 Oct–13 Nov 1982 · BBC1 Sat around 10.40pm

Special (40 mins) *Election Special* 9 June 1983 · BBC1 Thu 10pm

Series Two (8 × 40 mins) 22 Oct–30 Dec 1983 · BBC1 Sat mostly 11pm

Special (45 mins) 30 Dec 1983 · BBC1 Fri 10.40pm

MAIN CAST

Jasper Carrott
Nick Wilton
Mark Arden (series 1)
Steve Frost (series 1)
Kay Stoneham (series 1)
Emma Thompson (election special)
Chris Barrie (election special & series 2)
Jan Ravens (series 2)
Nick Maloney (series 2)

CREDITS

writers Jasper Carrott (17), Kim Fuller (17), Rob Grant/Doug Naylor (17), Tony Sarchet/ Bob Sinfield (17), James Hendrie (9), Amanda Solomons (9), Ian Hislop (1) · script associate Neil Shand · directors Geoff Posner (16), Paul Jackson (1) · producers Paul Jackson (8), John Bishop (8), Geoff Posner (1)

Carrott moved to the BBC and carried on much as before. These shows were screened live, and thus carried a certain 'edge'. Carrott was proving himself adept at handling live shows, delighting in the adrenaline rush that accompanies such performances. On this series he started to refine his material, his act becoming less autobiographical and more expansive. He settled on certain recurring targets for his humour, such as *The Sun* newspaper, turning traditional Irish jokes into *Sun*-reader jibes. Relaxed on stage and working with a strong writing team, Carrott found his niche with *Carrott's Lib* and, confident in his style, he ventured once again to the USA for his next TV project.

American Carrott

UK/USA · C4 (OPIX FILMS/HBO) · STANDUP/SKETCH

1 × 65 mins · colour

19 Jan 1985 · Sat 11pm

MAIN CAST

Jasper Carrott	himself
Evangelist	Bob Shields
Ellie	Ellyn Stern
Gus	Pat O'Brien
Bev	Richard Taylor
Dave	Daniel Radell

CREDITS

writers Jasper Carrott, Guy Jenkin, Jon Stephen Fink, Tony Sarchet, Mieke van der Linden · director Terry Ryan · producer Ray Marshall

A fascinating and funny one-off programme that blended standup footage of Carrott, filmed in concert in Santa Monica, California, with a series of sketches depicting his view of American life. The two were combined by way of a plot whereby Carrott, in Los Angeles, was trying desperately to gain access to a TV set so that he could see his own show. Along the way he became involved with a preacher who declares that the devil is English, a violent church congregation, a rock band staying in the same hotel ('Hey, you're English! We used to be English!') and an actress who operates a telephone sex-line: she and Carrott combine to produce sound effects to satisfy her client, utilising not only moans and groans but also mayonnaise, a whisk and a bicycle pump.

Unrelated to this programme, but closely preceding it, ITV screened a single 15-minute animated film of one of Carrott's most famous routines, *Jasper Carrott Got*

This Mole (also known as *I've Got This Mole*), written and narrated by the comic, which related an account of one man's obsession to rid his garden of said pesky insectivorous animal. It was shown in the London area on 23 December 1984.

Carrott Confidential

UK · BBC · STANDUP/SKETCH

25 editions (24 × 35 mins · 1 × 30 mins) · colour

Series One (8) 3 Jan–21 Feb 1987 · BBC1 Sat 9.05pm

Special (30 mins) *Jasper Carrott's Election Confidential* 11 June 1987 · BBC2 Thu 10pm

Series Two (8) 16 Jan–5 Mar 1988 · BBC1 Sat 9.55pm

Series Three (8) 4 Feb–25 Mar 1989 · BBC1 Sat around 10pm

MAIN CAST

Jasper Carrott
Steve Punt
Hugh Dennis
Vicky Ogden

CREDITS

writers Jasper Carrott (25), Steve Punt (25), Neil Shand (25), Dick Hills (25), Paul Alexander (16), Christian Howgill (14), Geoff Atkinson (9), Barry Cryer (9), John Langdon (9), Kim Fuller (9), Paul B Davies (8), Pete Sinclair/Nick Yapp (8), Jon Stephen Fink (6), Simon Fanshawe (5), Spike Mullins (3), Ian Davidson (2), Nick Revell (1), Laurie Rowley (1), Johnny Speight (1) · director Geoff Miles · producer Bill Wilson

In the three years since *Carrott's Lib*, Carrott had appeared in America, toured in the comedy play *The Nerd*, released an album, published a book and worked with Phil Cool on *Cool It*. When he returned to the Saturday-night live-TV arena it was with a fresh series that demonstrated his growing maturity as a comedian. The format differed slightly from *Carrott's Lib* in that there were fewer topical sketches and more filmed inserts, but the central thrust of the show remained the same, with Carrott coming across as an amiable, average sort who wonders aloud at the absurdities of modern life. His cunning and seemingly instinctive use of emphasis on certain words or phrases enabled Carrott to wring comedy out of the flattest of lines and highlight the inanity of the most humdrum of occurrences. Guest stars appeared throughout, with double-act Punt and Dennis appearing as regulars, usually in a topical and satirical sketch or crosstalk routine.

Later in 1989 Carrott presented *Carrott's Commercial Breakdown* (BBC1, 29 December) in which he commented comically on TV commercials from around the world. This programme proved hugely popular and won the Independent Producers award at the Golden Rose competition and the gold medal for comedy/satire at New

York's Film and Television Festival. Three more programmes (27 December 1991, 28 December 1993 and 5 March 1996, all BBC1) continued in the same vein. Later comedian Rory McGrath took over the reins hosting 7 editions of *Rory McGrath's Commercial Breakdown* (BBC1, 2 September–18 November 1997)

Jasper Carrott – Stand Up America

UK · BBC · STANDUP

6 × 35 mins · colour

7 July–11 Aug 1987 · BBC1 Tue 10.35pm

MAIN CAST

host · · · · · · · · · · · · · · · · · · · Jasper Carrott

CREDITS

writers cast and others · *director* Jasper Carrott · *producers* John Starkey, Les Ward

Jasper Carrott conceived and directed this series, introducing acts recorded at the Comic Strip in New York and the Improv in Los Angeles. Jerry Seinfeld, Joe Bolster and Glenn Hirsch appeared three times apiece, Gilbert Gottfried, Rita Rudner, Kip Adotta, John Mendoza, Emo Philips, Marsha Warfield, Bill Kirchinbauer and Dennis Wolfberg twice each, and there were single spots for Fred Stoller, Kevin Pollack, Mike McDonald, Rondell Sheridan, Carol Leifer and Bobby Slayton.

Canned Carrott

UK · BBC (CELADOR PRODUCTIONS) · STANDUP/SKETCH

12 × 30 mins · colour

Series One (6) 3 Oct–7 Nov 1990 · BBC1 Wed 9.30pm

Series Two (6) 21 Nov 1991–2 Jan 1992 · BBC1 Thu 9.30pm

MAIN CAST

Jasper Carrott
Robert Powell
Steve Punt
Hugh Dennis

CREDITS

writers Jasper Carrott, Steve Knight/Mike Whitehill, Paul Alexander, Steve Punt/Hugh Dennis, David Smith, David Treloar and others · *director/producer* Ed Bye · *executive producer* Paul Smith

A pre-recorded series, hence the title. There were two recurring strands: 'Wiggy' featured the adventures of a man with a bad wig as he went through silent escapades accompanied by an explanatory voice-over. (These slapstick sketches employed a style somewhere between *The Benny Hill Show* and *Mr Bean*.) The other was 'The Detectives', the filmed misadventures of a pair of dim police officers (Carrott and Robert Powell) who have watched too many TV cop shows and spend their working lives

trying, unsuccessfully, to emulate their small-screen heroes. This segment proved so popular that it was spun off into a separate series, *The Detectives*.

24 Carrott Gold

UK · BBC (CELADOR PRODUCTIONS) · STANDUP

1 × 50 mins · colour

28 Dec 1990 · BBC1 Fri 9.30pm

MAIN CAST

Jasper Carrott

CREDITS

writer Jasper Carrott · *director/producer* Paul Smith

A standup concert filmed at the Royal Shakespeare Theatre in Stratford-upon-Avon, in which Carrott blended classic material with new routines. Among the targets of his withering gaze were Birmingham City Football Club, Chinese restaurants and Space Invader machines.

One Jasper Carrott

UK · BBC (CELADOR PRODUCTIONS) · STANDUP

1 × 50 mins · colour

28 Dec 1992 · BBC1 Mon 9.05pm

MAIN CAST

Jasper Carrott

CREDITS

writer Jasper Carrott · *director/producer* Paul Smith

Recorded at the Theatre Royal in London this concert depicted Carrott in a more acidic frame of mind. He explained that this edge was caused by the many things about modern life that made him angry.

Carrott-U-Like

UK · BBC (CELADOR PRODUCTIONS) · STANDUP/SKETCH

1 × 50 mins · colour

27 Dec 1994 · BBC1 Tue 10pm

MAIN CAST

Jasper Carrott
Sara Crowe
Ann Bryson

CREDITS

writer Jasper Carrott · *director/producer* Ed Bye

Two years after his previous Christmas special for the BBC, Carrott was back with two actresses to provide sketch support. Crowe and Bryson were becoming recognised as a double-act as a result of their appearances in a series of comical TV commercials for Philadelphia Cheese. (See also *Sometime, Never.*) Otherwise the mix was as before, with Carrott's fuming monologues on the lunacy of life interspersed with short sketches, many of them spoofing TV commercials.

The Jasper Carrott Trial

UK · BBC (CELADOR PRODUCTIONS) · STANDUP/SKETCH

6 × 30 mins · colour

20 May–26 June 1997 · BBC1 Tue then Thu 9.30pm

MAIN CAST

Jasper Carrott · · · · · · · · · · · · · · · · ·	himself
The Judge · · · · · · · · · · · · · · ·	Robert Lang
QC · · · · · · · · · · · · · · · · ·	Richard Cordery
James Morgan · · · · · · · ·	Geoffrey Whitehead
The reporter · · · · · · · · · ·	Caroline Webster
The stenographer · · · · · · ·	Corinna Richards
The security guard · · · · · · ·	Jason Griffiths

CREDITS

creator Dirk Maggs · *writers (new material)* Steve Knight/Mike Whitehill · *director/producer* Nic Phillips

A neat way of gaining extra mileage from old material – Carrott stood trial on a number of offences relating to his career, accusations illustrated by clips of previous programmes (from BBC and LWT). The first three shows represented the prosecution's case, with examples of 'verbal violence', 'unprovoked attacks on astrologers, diets, pigeons, Reliant Robins and so on', 'animal cruelty' and other so-called criminal acts. The second batch of three presented the defence's case, with supportive selections recounting Carrott's lifelong campaign against cant, hypocrisy, bureaucracy and mint humbugs.

The idea originally aired on BBC Radio 2, in seven editions from 6 June to 18 July 1996 followed by six more from 24 July to 28 August 1997.

Carry On …

The *Carry On* film comedy team, cast and crew alike, effected a transition from big-screen to small in 17 made-for-TV programmes, comprising four 60-minute Christmas specials and two series (13 programmes) of half-hour shows. For the sake of convenience and clarity they are outlined here together.

Not included in the following listing is *What A Carry On!* – a visit that ATV paid to the Victoria Palace Theatre in London on 4 October 1973, to see the opening night of the first *Carry On* stage revue, *Carry On London!* This hour-long programme screened highlights of the show, sequences from some of the *Carry On* movies and interviews with cast members.

Also not detailed here are the many compilations of clips from the *Carry On* cinema films, made into half-hours for TV broadcast and screened by ITV and BBC1.

See also *Our House*.

Carry On Christmas

UK · ITV (THAMES) · SITCOM

4 × 60 mins · colour

1. *Carry On Christmas* 24 Dec 1969 · Wed 9.15pm
2. *Carry On Again Christmas: Carry On Long John* 24 Dec 1970 · Thu 9.10pm
3. *Carry On Christmas: Carry On Stuffing* 20 Dec 1972 · Wed 8pm
4. *Carry On Christmas* 24 Dec 1973 · Mon 9pm

MAIN CAST (NUMBERS REFER TO SHOWS)
Barbara Windsor (1–4)
Sidney James (1, 2, 4)
Bernard Bresslaw (1, 2, 4)
Peter Butterworth (1, 3, 4)
Kenneth Connor (2–4)
Terry Scott (1, 2)
Charles Hawtrey (1, 2)
Hattie Jacques (1, 3)
Frankie Howerd (1)
Bob Todd (2)
Joan Sims (3, 4)
Jack Douglas (3, 4)
Wendy Richard (2)
Norman Rossington (3)
Brian Oulton (3)
Julian Holloway (4)

CREDITS
writers Talbot Rothwell (1, 3, 4), Sid Colin (2), Dave Freeman (2, 3) · *directors* Ronnie Baxter (1, 3), Alan Tarrant (2), Ronald Fouracre (4) · *executive producers* Peter Eton (2), Peter Rogers (3, 4) · *producers* Peter Eton (1), Alan Tarrant (2), Gerald Thomas (3, 4)

Thames was the first TV company to persuade the *Carry On* camp to bring their art to the small-screen, presenting four one-hour romps along festive themes. The first was a loose spin on Dickens' *A Christmas Carol*, the second a parody of *Treasure Island* (with Barbara Windsor cast in the unlikely role of cabin boy Jim Hawkins), the third was a collection of Christmas tales, the last was a final, *Carry On*-style rewriting of history.

Carry On Laughing

UK · ITV (ATV) · SITCOM

13 × 30 mins · colour

Series One (6) 4 Jan–8 Feb 1975 · Sat 6.20pm
Series Two (7) 26 Oct–7 Dec 1975 · Sun 7.25pm

MAIN CAST (NUMBERS REFER TO SHOWS)
Kenneth Connor (1, 2, 4–13)
Jack Douglas (1, 3–13)
Joan Sims (1–3, 5–12)
Peter Butterworth (1–3, 7–11, 13)
Barbara Windsor (1–4, 6, 11–13)
David Lodge (1–3, 5–8)
Bernard Bresslaw (9–13)
Sidney James (1–4)
Hattie Jacques (4)

SOME OTHER REGULAR APPEARANCES
Brian Osborne (2–5, 8–10, 12)
Norman Chappell (4, 5, 7–10, 13)
John Carlin (2, 4–7, 13)
Sherrie Hewson (7, 8, 11, 12)
Vivienne Johnson (8, 11, 12)
Diane Langton (1, 2, 5)
Victor Maddern (4, 6, 9)
Billy Cornelius (5, 9, 10)
Ronnie Brody (1, 9)
Linda Hooks (2, 5)
Michael Nightingale (7, 13)
Desmond McNamara (9, 10)
Brian Capron (9, 10)
Oscar James (9, 13)
Carol Hawkins (11, 12)
Andrew Ray (11, 12)
McDonald Hobley (4)
Nosher Powell (5)
Patsy Rowlands (6)
Melvyn Hayes (7)
Johnny Briggs (8)

CREDITS
writers Dave Freeman (1–3, 6–8), Lew Schwarz (5, 9–13), Barry Cryer/Dick Vosburgh (4) · *director* Alan Tarrant · *executive producer* Peter Rogers · *producer* Gerald Thomas

Following the four Christmas specials made by Thames, ATV commissioned two series of half-hour comedies, both screened in 1975. Most episodes parodied a famous book, film or historical period. Of the regular *Carry On* team, Sid James only appeared in the first series, Charles Hawtrey did not appear at all and Kenneth Williams was also absent – indeed, he had not taken part in the Thames programmes either.

Briefly, these were the 13 *Carry On Laughing* TV productions.

1. *The Prisoner Of Spenda*. Foreign historical romp.
2. *The Baron Outlook*. British historical romp.
3. *The Sobbing Cavalier*. Oliver Cromwell and the Roundheads romp.
4. *Orgy And Bess*. The court of Elizabeth I romp.
5. *One In The Eye For Harold*. Battle Of Hastings romp.
6. *The Nine Old Cobblers*. A detective romp.
7. *The Case Of The Screaming Winkles*. Another detective romp.
8. *The Case Of The Coughing Parrot*. Yet a third detective romp.
9. *Under The Round Table*. An Arthurian romp.
10. *Short Knight, Long Daze*. Another Arthurian romp.
11. *And In My Lady's Chamber*. A romping parody of *Upstairs, Downstairs*.
12. *Who Needs Kitchener?* Another romping parody of *Upstairs, Downstairs*.
13. *Lamp-Posts Of The Empire*. An exploration romp.

Casanova '73

UK · BBC · SITCOM

7 × 30 mins · colour

13 Sep–29 Oct 1973 · BBC1 Thu 8pm then Mon 9.25pm

MAIN CAST
Henry Newhouse · · · · · · · · · · Leslie Phillips
Carol Newhouse · · · · · · · · · · · Jan Holden

CREDITS
writers Ray Galton/Alan Simpson · *producer* Harold Snoad

Leslie Phillips had developed the persona of a super-smooth, lusting womaniser in a number of films (particularly the *Doctor* comedies) and stage farces (*Boeing-Boeing* and *The Man Most Likely To …*) before appearing, precisely within that type, in this Galton and Simpson sitcom, subtitled 'The Adventures Of A 20th-Century Libertine'.

Phillips played Henry Stonehouse, who works in PR and is happily married to Carol. Henry's problem is that he cannot keep his hands off other women, and has to lead a double-life in order to maintain peace at home. This philandering often lands him in farcical situations, one example being when he spends three days in a wardrobe after his latest conquest's husband returns home unexpectedly.

The title capitalised on Dennis Potter's notoriously successful TV dramatisation of the original *Casanova* book, depicting the life of the 18th-century *bon vivant*, screened by BBC2 from 16 November to 21 December 1971.

The Case

UK/SWEDEN/NORWAY/FINLAND · BBC/SR/NRK/YLE · MUSICAL COMEDY

1 × 60 mins · colour

2 Sep 1972 · BBC1 Sat 8.15pm

MAIN CAST
Cliff Richard
Tim Brooke-Taylor
Olivia Newton-John
Matti Ranin
Pekka Laiho

CREDITS
writer Eric Davidson · *producer* Michael Hurll

An unusual comedy/thriller with music, shot on location in the summer of 1971. The premise was somewhat ludicrous: Cliff Richard and Tim Brooke-Taylor have embarked upon a tour of Scandinavia; at a busy railway station Tim disguises himself in character and Cliff accidentally picks up someone else's suitcase. It contains the loot from a bank robbery and the two perpetrators of that crime (Ranin and Laiho) pursue them in a frantic chase across Sweden, Norway and Finland.

Casino

see Cannon and Ball

Casting Off

UK · ITV (THAMES) · SITCOM

4 × 30 mins · colour

7 Oct–28 Oct 1988 · Fri 1.30pm

MAIN CAST

Bernard	Jim McManus
Gary	Ashley Gunstock
Sheena	Jacqueline de Peza
Helen	Pamela Merrick
Tim	John Forgeham
Gillian	Siobhan Redmond
other roles	John Sloman

CREDITS

writer David Stafford · *director/producer* Alan Afriat · *executive producer* Simon Buxton

Labelled an 'informative comedy', *Casting Off* was screened in order to enlighten viewers about the world of business, with Thames TV publishing a free accompanying booklet.

Bernard is sacked from his job and becomes interested in a knitwear machine belonging to friends Gary and Sheena. Joined by married couple Tim and Helen, the five decide to set up business together, forming a co-operative to manufacture jumpers. But they each bring their different personalities to bear and the resulting strain of being in business together is such that Tim and Helen break up, Tim branching out on his own and forming a rival knitwear company. They soon reunite, however, receive outside funding and win an award.

The series' first transmission slot was Friday lunchtime, with a C4 repeat run in January 1989 going out on Monday evenings. *Casting Off* was the second time that Thames had produced a series with the dual intentions of amusing and educating – see also *The Setbacks*.

Caught Napping

UK · BBC · CHILDREN'S SITCOM

5 × 15 mins · b/w

24 Oct–19 Dec 1951 · Wed 5.30pm

MAIN CAST

Claude Hulbert

CREDITS

writer Godfrey Harrison · *producer* John Warrington

Star of stage and screen, Claude Hulbert played an overgrown, dim schoolboy in this fortnightly series of programmes within the strand *For The Children*.

Caxton's Tales

UK · BBC · SITCOM

4 × 30 mins · b/w

21 Feb–18 Apr 1958 · fortnightly Fri mostly 7.30pm

MAIN CAST

*David Caxton	Wilfred Pickles
*Mary Caxton	Mabel Pickles
Sally Caxton	Mary Webster
Willie	Peter Hodgson
Miss Brearley	Evelyn Lund
Charlie Haskell	Richard Curnstock
Sam Widgeon	Allan Bracewell

CREDITS

writers Sidney Nelson/Maurice Harrison · *producer* Barry Lupino

The first sitcom for long-time radio and TV favourite Wilfred Pickles cast him as a jobbing printer who owns his own small business, aided by a young assistant, Willie, and by Miss Brearley, who writes verses for the greetings cards that Caxton prints. Caxton's wife Mary – mother to their 19-year-old daughter Sally – was played by Pickles' real-life wife Mabel. Joining in the fun was cockney next-door neighbour Charlie.

The series had a bumpy start. The first episode, scheduled for 27 December 1957, did not go out, and the re-announced launch, set for 7 February 1958, was postponed owing to the previous night's Munich air crash that killed many Manchester United footballers. Since that particular *Caxton's Tales* episode was titled 'Match Abandoned' its screening was deemed inappropriate. (It was recorded instead and shown as the last in the series, on 18 April)

*Note. Wilfred Pickles' character, which started off as David Caxton, was renamed Wilfred Caxton as the series progressed. Similarly, Mabel Pickles' character switched from Mary Caxton to Mabel Caxton.

Chalk

UK · BBC (POLA JONES FILM PRODUCTIONS) · SITCOM

12 × 30 mins · colour

Series One (6) 20 Feb–27 Mar 1997 · BBC1 Thu mostly 9.35pm

Series Two (6) 17 Sep–22 Oct 1997 · BBC1 Wed mostly 10.15pm

MAIN CAST

Eric Slatt	David Bamber
Suzy Travis	Nicola Walker
Janet Slatt	Geraldine Fitzgerald
Dan McGill	Martin Ball
Amanda Trippley	Amanda Boxer
Mr Carkdale	John Grillo
Mr Humboldt	Andrew Livingstone
Richard Nixon	John Wells (series 1)
Mr Kennedy	Duncan Preston (series 2)
Jason Cockfoster	Damien Matthews (series 2)

CREDITS

writer Steven Moffat · *director* Juliet May · *executive producer* Kevin Lygo · *producer* Andre Ptaszynski

Chalk crashed on to television on a wave of expectation. With the domestic audience crying out for a great new British sitcom, advance word hinted that this really was one of the most exciting productions in quite a while. Indeed, the BBC even let it be known that a second series had been commissioned before the first one had aired. The hype was such that *Chalk* nearly drowned in the stuff; yes, it was funny, and dark, and wild, but few series could have lived up to such trumpet-blowing.

Chalk was a school sitcom for the 1990s, set in Galfast High, a characterless, concrete comprehensive populated by unruly pupils and staffed by weary, jaundiced teachers ranging from the mildly eccentric to the completely barmy. Into this situation arrives a young woman, Suzy Travis, straight out of teaching college and keen to get to grips with her charges and do her bit for the world of education. She then realises that she is the only sane member of the staff and her eagerness and vitality are eroded by the sheer madness of her environment. The headmaster, Richard Nixon, seems to exist in a world far removed from reality; gormless teacher Dan McGill is harmless enough but becomes a liability after he falls hopelessly in love with Suzy at first glance; Head of English Mr Carkdale is only ever heard to mutter obscenities, especially his favourite phrase 'Bastards!'; Amanda Trippley (music and guidance) is a whimpering and simpering stack of neuroses; and school secretary Janet, who, on the surface, seems certifiably insane, is married to Eric Slatt, the deputy headmaster. Slatt is the whirling dervish at the centre of *Chalk*. In comparison, the other members of staff appear totally reasonable. A volatile mix of self-obsession, anger, hatred and fear, and with an ego the size of Jupiter, Eric Slatt is a true TV monster – hyperactive, homophobic and ruinously paranoid, his flaws are the catalytic to the school's problems, setting in motion a chain of outrageous events that results in his and its weekly downfall.

Critics were divided on *Chalk*, its detractors pointing out that Eric Slatt was a carbon copy of John Cleese's Basil Fawlty, its supporters praising its non-PC, off-the-wall approach and the breathlessly paced plots that delivered moments of high farce. Although it featured some of the elements of *Please, Sir!* (an idealistic new teacher, jaundiced staff, out-of-touch headmaster), *Chalk* more closely resembled the ill-fated *Hardwicke House*, with its concentration on the teachers rather than the pupils, dark themes and overall depiction of the teachers as, well, nuts. The early-promised second series saw some changes: Suzy had become as hardened and world-weary as the rest of the staff, and headmaster Nixon had been replaced by the apparently sane but actually loopy Mr Kennedy. Slatt remained his old manic self, his character perhaps still toiling in the shadow of Basil Fawlty but showing enough original sparks to suggest scope for greater development.

Chalk And Cheese

UK · ITV (THAMES) · SITCOM

7 × 30 mins · colour

Pilot *Spasms* 9 Nov 1977 · Wed 8pm

One series (6) 2 Apr–14 May 1979 · Mon mostly 8pm

MAIN CAST

Dave Finn	Jonathan Pryce (pilot); Michael Crawford (series)
Roger Scott	Robin Hawdon
Rose Finn	Miriam Margolyes (pilot); Gillian Martell (series)
Amanda Scott	Jenny Cox (pilot); Julia Goodman (series)

CREDITS

writer Alex Shearer · *director/producer* Michael Mills

Riding the crest of a wave following massive successes with the BBC sitcom **Some Mothers Do 'Ave 'Em** and the London stage-show *Billy*, Michael Crawford starred in this short-lived Thames series. He found no such favour here.

Chalk And Cheese cast him as an unrestrained proletarian, the pig-headed, sexist, bearded Dave Finn, truculently living out his cockney adages and lifestyle in a gentrified street, a tin bath hanging on the front of his house like a badge of honour. Robin Hawdon was cast as Finn's adjoining neighbour, Roger Scott, a Sloane-style marketing director. Scott was the very antithesis of Finn and the series explored these differences, which, under the mere superficialities of outlook, attitudes, values, dress and prospects, were, perhaps, not too dissimilar after all.

In *Spasms*, the single-episode pilot screened 15 months before the series (which had Jonathan Pryce in the Michael Crawford role), Finn and Scott were at the hospital, waiting for their wives to give birth to their first children. This was re-enacted as the opening episode of *Chalk And Cheese*.

The Chamber

UK · BBC · SITCOM

1 × 30 mins · colour

11 Sep 1995 · BBC1 Mon 8.30pm

MAIN CAST

Percy Lygoe	John Bird
Graham Tombs	John Wells
Evelyn Tombs	Diane Fletcher
Beebie Singleton	Lesley Vickerage
Melanie Singleton	Karen Salt
Neville Transom	John Barron
Les Driffield	Owen Brenman
Noel Washburn	Michael Bertenshaw
Fletcher Mills	Geoffrey McGivern
Slaney	Phil Nice

CREDITS

writer John Bird · *director/producer* Richard Boden

The fifth in a series of unrelated comedies that appeared on consecutive Monday evenings without a generic title. Veteran satirist John Bird wrote and starred in this sharp piece of politicising, which echoed the comedic interplay of **Yes Minister**.

Dunsall is a medium-sized metropolitan borough with the Conservatives in control of the local council. Their main opponent is the wily, long-serving Labourite, Percy Lygoe, a dedicated politico who has learned the devious mechanisms of the murky world he inhabits. The death of Neville Transom, head of the council, sparks off a battle between members of his party over who will get his job, and Lygoe calculates that if he can manipulate the weak Graham Tombs into the position, Labour councillors will be able to exert more influence. Lygoe's scheme pays off, although with different ramifications to those he expected, for he reckoned without Tombs' titled wife, Evelyn, a formidable woman who proves to be an expert manipulator determined to guide her husband to the political heights. The scene is set for an ongoing battle of wills and subterfuge between Lygoe and Evelyn.

The Chamber constituted the usual premium-quality work from Bird, with his old associate John Wells providing fine support. There was a good performance too by Diane Fletcher, who, as Evelyn, was playing a role remarkably similar to her portrayal of Elizabeth Urquhart in the trilogy of satirical political dramas *House Of Cards*, *To Play The King* and *The Final Cut*.

Chance In A Million

UK · C4 (THAMES) · SITCOM

18 × 30 mins · colour

Series One (6) 10 Sep–15 Oct 1984 · Mon 8.30pm

Series Two (6) 6 Jan–10 Feb 1986 · Mon mostly 9.25pm

Series Three (6) 27 Oct–1 Dec 1986 · Mon 8.30pm

MAIN CAST

Tom Chance	Simon Callow
Alison Little	Brenda Blethyn

OTHER APPEARANCES

Mr Little	Hugh Walters
Mrs Little	Deddie Davies
Mr Wingent	Angus Mackay
Sgt Gough	Bill Pertwee (series 2 & 3)
Barbara	Geraldine Gardner (series 2 & 3)
Janet	Rosemary Smith (series 3)

CREDITS

writers Richard Fegen/Andrew Norriss · *director/producer* Michael Mills

Tom Chance is trouble in human form, someone for whom life is one long uninterrupted litany of misfortunes. He must have run over a dozen black cats and smashed as many mirrors, so dogged is he by coincidental bad luck. As a result of one of his confusions, Tom meets Alison Little, a shy and retiring librarian, and right from the start she too becomes embroiled in his catalogue of disasters, returning home from their first meeting dressed only in her underwear. (This turns out to be portentous, for under her timid, mannered surface she is a simmering cauldron of desire.) The pair become engaged (in the second series), much to the despair of Alison's parents, and married (in the last), in Tom's usual disastrous circumstances: the wedding day begins with the bride and groom in jail, no best man, bridesmaids or guests, and the in-laws and the cake trapped in a sewer.

If this all sounds a little extreme it was meant to be, for *Chance In A Million* was a sitcom that set out to send up the sitcom genre. Writers Norriss and Fegen's intention was to take to their most ludicrous extremes the plethora of unlikely coincidences that litter comedy scripts. The 'hero' here – with his strange staccato way of talking and odd vocabulary; beginning each sentence with a verb and omitting all definite articles – suffered ridiculous flukes, such as when a paratrooper descended right into his house on a quest for bizarre objects and Tom discovered – to his own surprise – that he had them, including a nude photograph of Shirley Williams and a cricket bat signed by Alec Bedser. Or when – just as Alison's parents were about to visit for the first time – his bedroom was invaded by young women undressing in rehearsal for their attempt on the greatest-number-of-girls-in-their-underwear-in-one-telephone-box world record.

Brenda Blethyn, who co-starred as Alison, went on to appear in another Fegen and Norriss sitcom, **The Labours Of Erica**, but the writers' best-known creation to date is **The Brittas Empire**. *Chance In A Million* was certainly a distinguished debut – and it was wrought in unusual circumstances: Norriss lived in England and Fegen in Ireland, and they collaborated by telephone for a time before organising script meetings that took place in hotels adjacent to Shannon and Heathrow airports on alternate weekends. Having proven the partnership, the pair next went on to create the sitcom **Ffizz** and write ITV's long-running children's drama *Woof!* (18 February 1989 to date), which was occasionally humorous and played with a light touch. Norriss alone also wrote *Matt's Millions*, an ITV children's light-drama series (20 November–11 December 1996).

A Chance To Meet ...

see *The Old Boy Network*

Channel Izzard

see *Lust For Glorious*

The Channel Swimmer

UK · BBC · SITCOM

1 × 30 mins · b/w

16 Feb 1962 · Fri 8.45pm

MAIN CAST

Lionel	Sydney Tafler
Austin	Warren Mitchell
Clive	Michael Brennan
Official	Frank Thornton
Boat pilot	Bob Todd
Other swimmer's manager	Joe Gibbons

CREDITS

writers Ray Galton/Alan Simpson · producer Barry Lupino

The last offering in the first series of *Comedy Playhouse*, which was scripted exclusively by Galton and Simpson. This single comedy followed the fortunes of a channel swimmer (played by Michael Brennan) and those who exploit him.

Charge!

UK · BBC · SITCOM

5 × 30 mins · b/w

28 Feb–28 Mar 1969 · BBC1 Fri 8.20pm

MAIN CAST

Herbert Todhunter	Robert Morley
Partridge	Robert Raglan
Mrs Midden	Jumoke Debayo

CREDITS

writers Robert Morley/Jeremy Paul · producer Graeme Muir

Described as 'a sort of upper-class Alf Garnett', the awful Todhunter was the co-creation of actor and wit Robert Morley who cheerfully admitted that the overbearing, snobbish, bigoted, ignorant, distrustful character was, in part, based on himself. For five weeks Morley squeezed his larger-than-life stature on to the TV to rant and rave at the inequities of life and lament the passing of the British Empire. Todhunter lived on a River Thames houseboat near Hampton Court with seemingly his only chum, his brother-in-law Partridge, the secretary of the local golf club. Each week they sallied forth from their floating castle to do battle with life in the 20th-century, with Partridge acting as Sancho Panza to Herbert Todhunter's portly Don Quixote.

See also *An Evening With Robert Morley* and *If The Crown Fits ...*

Charles Heslop

UK · BBC · STANDUP

3 editions (1 × 15 mins · 1 × 10 mins · 1 × 30 mins) · b/w

1 June 1937 · Tue 3pm (15 mins)

6 July 1937 · Tue 3pm (10 mins)

25 Dec 1937 · Sat 3pm (30 mins)

MAIN CAST

Charles Heslop

CREDITS

producer Reginald Smith

Adaptable stage and film character-comic Charles Heslop made his starring TV debut in these three comedy sketch shows (the first of which was presented under the *Starlight* banner). The third, a Christmas special, also featured Viennese singer Irene Prador.

Heslop went on to become a regular pre-war TV fixture, turning up in a number of revues and variety shows, including *Fun And Games* (1 December 1938), *Moonlight 'n' Everything* (28 June 1939) and *Bits And Pieces* (28 August 1939). He was also the star of what, were it not for the intervention of war and consequent closing down of the television service, may well have become British TV's first hit comedy character, **Percy Ponsonby**.

Charles In Charge

USA · CBS/SYNDICATION (UNIVERSAL TELEVISION/SCHOLASTIC PRODUCTIONS/AL BURTON PRODUCTIONS) · SITCOM

126 × 30 mins · colour

US dates: 30 Oct 1984–24 July 1985 (CBS); 3 Jan 1987–12 Nov 1990 (syndication)

UK dates: 3 Sep 1985–21 Apr 1986 (21 CBS episodes) BBC1 Tue then Mon 5.35pm

MAIN CAST

Charles	Scott Baio
Buddy Lembeck	Willie Aames
Jill Pembroke	Julie Cobb (1984–85)
Stan Pembroke	James Widdoes (1984–85)
Lila Pembroke	April Lerman (1984–85)
Douglas Pembroke	Jonathan Ward (1984–85)
Jason Pembroke	Michael Pearlman (1984–85)
Gwendolyn Pierce	Jennifer Runyon (1984–85)
Ellen Powell	Sandra Kerns (1987–90)
Jamie Powell	Nicole Eggert (1987–90)
Sara Powell	Josie Davis (1987–90)
Adam Powell	Alexander Polinsky (1987–90)
Walter Powell	James Callahan (1987–90)
Lillian	Ellen Travolta (1987–90)

CREDITS

writers Michael Jacobs and others · director Alan Rifkin and others · producers Michael Jacobs, Al Burton, Jane Startz

Scott Baio had made a name for himself playing Fonzie's younger cousin in **Happy Days** and its spin-off **Joanie Loves Chachi**. Following the demise of those series American TV bosses still considered the actor a 'hot' item, and his 'hunk' status led to this purpose-built series. Baio played Charles (no last name), a young college student who secures a job as live-in house-boy to Stan and Jill Pembroke. The comedy arose from Charles' attempts at raising the Pembroke's three mischievous children, Lila (14), Douglas (12) and Jason (10). Charles has a girlfriend, fellow college student Gwendolyn, and a best buddy named, appropriately, Buddy.

CBS dropped the show after just one season but new episodes, utilising a slightly different format, were made for first-run syndication. In these, Charles returned from vacation to find that the Pembrokes had moved to Seattle and sub-let their house to the Powell family. Luckily, they too needed a house-boy and Charles moved back in, carrying on much as before. John Travolta's sister Ellen joined the new cast as Charles' mother Lillian, an on-screen relationship they had previously explored in *Joanie Loves Chachi*.

See also *Who's The Boss?*

Charley's Grants

UK · BBC · SITCOM

6 × 25 mins · colour

22 Mar–26 Apr 1970 · BBC2 Sun around 10.15pm

MAIN CAST

Lord Charley	Willoughby Goddard
Miss Manger	Hattie Jacques
Angus Black	Aubrey Morris
Waterbrain	Howard Goorney

OTHER APPEARANCES

Keith Smith

Diana King

CREDITS

writers John Fortune/John Wells/N F Simpson · producer Ian MacNaughton

A surreal sitcom from Johns Wells and Fortune and the playwright N F Simpson. Willoughby Goddard starred as the monstrous Lord Charley, who sought artistic grants from Miss Manger (Hattie Jacques) of the Heritage Trust. Various grotesque characters flitted in and out of the plots which doggedly attempted to ridicule the 'arts-grants' system.

Charlie Chester On Laughter Service

UK · BBC · STANDUP

13 × 45 mins · b/w

1 July–23 Sep 1961 · Sat 7.45pm

MAIN CAST

Charlie Chester

Eric 'Jeeves' Grier

CREDITS

writers Charlie Chester, Bernard Botting/Charlie Hart · producer Albert Stevenson

For 13 weeks in the summer of 1961 Charlie Chester invited viewers to 'switch on to the Laughter Service', a touring music and comedy show visiting forces bases throughout Britain. Sixty different variety acts were shown during the course of the series and the crew travelled a total of 21,000 miles.

See also the following entry.

The Charlie Chester Show

UK · BBC · STANDUP/SKETCH

46 editions (17 × 60 mins · 13 × 45 mins · 12 × 30 mins · 1 × 40 mins · 1 × 35 mins · 1 × 25 mins · 1 × short special) · b/w

Special (45 mins) 12 Jan 1949 · Sat 8.30pm

Series One (5 × 60 mins) 17 Mar–14 July 1951 · monthly Sat 8.30pm

Series Two (4 × 60 mins) 24 Sep–17 Dec 1955 · monthly Sat 8.30pm

Series Three (7 × 60 mins) 7 Apr–22 Sep 1956 · monthly Sat 9pm

Series Four (9 × 30 mins) 4 Apr–30 May 1957 · Sat 8pm

Special (60 mins) 22 Mar–22 Mar 1958 · Mon 7.30pm

Series Five (3 × 30 mins) 12 Sep–26 Sep 1958 · Fri 7.30pm

Short special · part of Christmas Night With The Stars 25 Dec 1958 · Thu 6.25pm

Series Six (5 × 45 mins) 16 Oct–11 Dec 1958 · Thu 7.30pm

Series Seven (7 × 45 mins · 1 × 35 mins · 1 × 40 mins · 1 × 25 mins) 4 Apr–6 June 1960 · Mon 7.30pm

MAIN CAST
Charlie Chester

OTHER APPEARANCES
Eric 'Jeeves' Grier
Edwina Carroll (special 1 & series 1)
Arthur Haynes (special 1)
Ken Morris
Fred Ferrari
Len Marten
Edna Fryer
Deryck Guyler
Len Lowe

CREDITS
writers Charlie Chester (46), Bernard Botting/Charlie Hart (29), Harold Parsons (5) · producers Henry Caldwell (5 eds), Walton Anderson (3 eds), Bill Ward (2 eds), Albert Stevenson (remainder of series 2–7)

The first programme in this long-running series brought standup comedian 'Cheeky' Charlie Chester's radio show *Stand Easy* to TV, with many of his radio 'crazy gang' (including Arthur Haynes) among the cast. During the show's subsequent 11 years on screen it underwent several cast and format alterations, often reflecting changes in Chester's radio programmes. Eric 'Jeeves' Grier and Len Lowe were the most featured regulars, surviving the show's many developments. Born in Eastbourne on 26 April 1914, Chester was a boy singer who turned to comedy in his early teens and scored great success in all media for most of

the 20th-century, broadcasting virtually up to his death on 26 June 1996.

Botting and Hart, the writers of Chester's radio series *A Proper Charlie* and *That Man Chester*, provided many of these TV scripts. Later editions incorporated a quiz-show element, *Pot Luck*, which was awarded its own series in 1957. Following the final TV series of *The Charlie Chester Show*, the production hit the road, visiting services bases in the series **Charlie Chester On Laughter Service** (see previous entry).

A one-time King Rat of the show-business charity fraternity Water Rats, Chester also appeared in *The Water Rat Rag* (BBC, 15 September 1957), an all-star variety show that launched a series of Water Rats programmes (see *Ray's A Rat*).

See also **Christmas Box, I Object** and **The Two Charleys.**

Charlie Drake ... [various shows]

see DRAKE, Charlie

The Charlie Farnsbarns Show

UK · ITV (ASSOCIATED-REDIFFUSION) · SKETCH

7 × 30 mins · b/w

30 July–10 Sep 1956 · Mon 9.30pm

MAIN CAST
Sam Costa
Kenneth Connor
Avril Angers
Sandra Dorne

CREDITS
writers George Wadmore/Ronnie Hanbury · directors Richard Carrickford (3), Michael Westmore (2), Kenneth Carter (2)

A light-hearted sketch series built around Sam Costa, the singer-cum-wisecracking Londoner who had risen to fame in the wartime BBC radio programmes *ITMA* and *Merry-Go-Round* and the post-war *Much-Binding-In-The-Marsh.*

As explained by Costa, the curious title was coined because old Charlie Farnsbarns – a fictitious character Costa often referred to, but who was never heard, in *Merry-Go-Round* and *Much-Binding* – never had a show of his own. Indeed, Costa dedicated the series to all Charlies everywhere.

The Charlie Williams Show

UK · BBC · STANDUP

1 × 45 mins · colour

30 July 1973 · BBC2 Mon 9.25pm

MAIN CAST
Charlie Williams

CREDITS
writers Wally Malston/Garry Chambers · producer Michael Hurll

A BBC2 *Show Of The Week* special for Charlie Williams, the Yorkshire-born standup comic, of Jamaican descent, who had shot to fame as one of the regular jokesters in Granada's **The Comedians**, becoming the first British black comic to enjoy mainstream TV success.

In his TV material Williams often poked fun at his colour and racial issues, and so was essentially non-confrontational in style; conversely, his routines often concluded with him getting the better of those who maligned him.

Williams had been a professional footballer (with Doncaster Rovers) before entering show business as a singer. When his between-songs comic patter proved more popular with the punters than his music he decided to focus entirely on a standup routine.

See also **It's Charlie Williams.**

Charlie's Place

UK · ITV (ATV) · SITCOM

1 × 30 mins · b/w

25 Aug 1965 · Wed 9.10pm

MAIN CAST
Charlie · · · · · · · · · · · · · · · · · · Ray Brooks
Doris · · · · · · · · · · · · · · · · · · Yootha Joyce
Sid · John Junkin
Vanessa · · · · · · · · · · · · · · · · Helen Fraser

CREDITS
writer Alan Plater · director Dicky Leeman · producer Alan Tarrant

More than a year before establishing his name in the controversial BBC play *Cathy Come Home*, Ray Brooks starred in this single-episode comedy written by Alan Plater and screened as part of ATV's *Six Of The Best* season. Yootha Joyce (later to hit pay-dirt in **Man About The House** and **George And Mildred**) was the principal support.

The Charmings

USA · ABC (STERNIN & FRASER INK PRODUCTIONS/COLUMBIA-EMBASSY TV) · SITCOM

28 × 30 mins · colour

US dates: 20 Mar 1987–11 Feb 1988

UK dates: 17 Apr–28 Dec 1992 (10 episodes) ITV mostly Sat 9am

MAIN CAST
Snow White Charming · · · · · Caitlin O'Heaney
· (early episodes);
· · · · · · · · · · · · · · Carol Huston (thereafter)
Prince Eric Charming · · · · · Christopher Rich
Queen Lillian White · · · · · · · · · · · Judy Parfitt
Thomas Charming · · · · · · · · · Brandon Call
Cory Charming · · · · · · · · · · · Garette Ratliffe
Luther · · · · · · · · · · · · · · · · · · · Cork Hubbert
voice of the mirror · · · · · · · · · · Paul Winfield

CREDITS
writers Christopher Ames/Carolyn Shelby, Douglas Bernstein, Mark Fink, Robert Sternin/Prudence

Fraser, Jeff Greenstein, Ellen Guylas, Carrie Honigblum/Renee Phillips, Danny Kallis, Denis Markell, Bob Meyer/Bob Young, Lan O'Kun, Richard J Reinhart, Jeff Strauss · *directors* various · *producers* Robert Sternin, Prudence Fraser

Charmless – indeed Grimm – comedy in this fairy-tale-to-now transformation comedy that pitched Snow White and Prince Charming a thousand years into the future, into the 1980s and Van Oaks, California, to see how they coped.

As it happened, Snow and Eric, as they renamed themselves, did well, being youthful, clean and wholesome just like everyone else in their neighbourhood, and raising a couple of sons, Thomas and Cory, who also were much like everyone else. Snow's hag of a wicked stepmother, Lillian, did not fare so well, however, and spent much of the time confiding in her magic mirror, a looking glass that cracked sarcastic jibes. The family dwarf Luther also found the transformation tricky, although he began attending college and was a dab hand with the housework.

The Chars

UK · BBC · SITCOM

1 × 30 mins · b/w

23 Nov 1963 · Sat 9.35pm

MAIN CAST

Cissy · Doris Waters
Flo · Elsie Waters
Amanda · · · · · · · · · · · · · · · · Ann Lancaster
Cyril · · · · · · · · · · · · · · · · · · Michael Balfour
Sydney · · · · · · · · · · · · · · · · · · James Beck
Frank · · · · · · · · · · · · · · · · Arthur Lovegrove
Mr Thornton · · · · · · · · · · · · · · Derek Nimmo

CREDITS

writers Harry Driver/Jack Rosenthal · *producer* Douglas Moodie

Famous double-act sisters Elsie and Doris Waters made a rare return to TV following their 1959 ITV series *Gert And Daisy*. In this *Comedy Playhouse* episode they were cast as charwomen at the Ministry of Agriculture and Fisheries. Cissy (Doris) was the leader, boasting that she'd 'done' every stately home in Britain; with her were the genteel Flo (Elsie) and the younger Amanda, who was convinced that all men were lusting after her. Despite the classy writing team and famous cast, no series followed.

Charters And Caldicott

UK · BBC · COMEDY SERIAL

6 × 50 mins · colour

10 Jan–14 Feb 1985 · BBC1 Thu 9.25pm

MAIN CAST

Charters · · · · · · · · · · · · · · · · · Robin Bailey
Caldicott · · · · · · · · · · · · · · Michael Aldridge
Gregory · · · · · · · · · · · · · · Granville Saxton
Margaret Mottram · · · · · · Caroline Blakiston
Grimes · · · · · · · · · · · · · · · · Patrick Carter

Jenny · · · · · · · · · · · · · · Tessa Peake-Jones

CREDITS

writer Keith Waterhouse · *director* Julian Amyes · *producer* Ron Craddock

Bumbling but brave cricket-mad duffers Charters and Caldicott, a pair who frequently become entangled in crime-solving adventures, first appeared on screen as comic relief in Alfred Hitchcock's light-hearted thriller film *The Lady Vanishes* in 1938. The inspired casting of Basil Radford as Charters and Naunton Wayne as Caldicott created a memorable double-act, and such was their impact that scriptwriters Frank Launder and Sidney Gilliat resurrected the pair for another comedy thriller, *Night Train To Munich* (1940, director Carol Reed). Once again the duo fared well, graduating to their own BBC radio serials *Crooks Tour* (1941) and *Secret Mission 609* (1942).

Crooks Tour was in turn made into a feature film (1941, John Baxter) and the pair made another big-screen foray with a cameo role in the wartime propaganda movie *Millions Like Us* (1943, Launder and Gilliat). They were intended to reappear in *I See A Dark Stranger* (1945, Launder) but the actors considered the roles too small now that their characters enjoyed such a high profile. Writers Launder and Gilliat disagreed and Radford and Wayne opted out of the project. (Two similar but differently named characters appeared in their stead.) Following this falling out, Radford and Wayne, whose careers had blossomed thanks to Charters and Caldicott, found themselves contractually unable to portray the characters. BBC radio was anxious to broadcast more of the popular comedy thriller serials, however, so Radford and Wayne resurrected their successful partnership with the character names Woolcot and Spencer, starring thus in *Double Bedlam* (1946) and *Traveller's Joy* (1947). Subsequent name changes cast them as Berkeley and Bulstrode in *Crime Gentleman, Please* (1948), Hargreaves and Hunter in *Having A Wonderful Crime* (1949) and Fanshaw and Fothergill in *That's My Baby* (1950), before they returned as Woolcot and Spencer for *May I Have The Treasure* (1951) and *Rogue's Gallery* (1952). Basil Radford died suddenly of a heart attack at 55, halfway through the *Rogue's Gallery* story, and Naunton Wayne, indicative of the indomitable spirit that had so endeared the characters to the nation, finished off the adventure on his own.

The pair had also continued to appear together, usually playing variations on the Charters and Caldicott characters in films *The Next Of Kin* (1942, director Thorald Dickinson), *Dead Of Night* (1946, sequence directed by Charles Crichton), *A Girl In A Million* (1946, Francis Searle) and *Quartet* (1948, sequence directed by Ralph Smart).

They were also cast as the Charters and Caldicott clones Bright and Early in *It's Not Cricket* (1948, Alfred Roome), *Helter Skelter* (1949, Ralph Thomas) and *Stop Press Girl* (1949, Michael Barry).

Skipping on 30 years, Charters and Caldicott were played by Arthur Lowe and Ian Carmichael in the 1979 movie remake of *The Lady Vanishes* (director Anthony Page) before the pair made their TV debut in this six-part comedy thriller. Now older and retired, Charters is a widower living in a country cottage near Reigate, travelling up to his Pall Mall club in a Green Line bus which he hails on the street as if it were a taxi; Caldicott is a city dweller residing in the splendid Viceroy Court in Kensington. When a young girl is found murdered there, Charters and Caldicott forsake their regular Friday lunch and cinema visit once again to involve themselves in a spot of derring-do. Sympathetically adapted by Keith Waterhouse, and delightfully overplayed by Bailey and Aldridge, the result was a handsome series that added another sterling innings to the Charters and Caldicott legend.

See also *Naunton Wayne*.

Chateaux Du Dracula

see The Montreux Festival

Cheap At Half The Price

UK · ITV (THAMES) · SITCOM

1 × 30 mins · colour

22 May 1972 · Mon 8.30pm

MAIN CAST

Jimmy Wilcox · · · · · · · · · · · · · · Roy Kinnear
Charlie · · · · · · · · · · · · · · · · · · Doug Fisher
Madge · · · · · · · · · · · · · · · Marjie Lawrence

CREDITS

writers Vince Powell/Harry Driver · *director/producer* Les Chatfield

Plugging a gap in the schedules, this single-episode sitcom, not developed into a full series, starred Roy Kinnear as Jimmy Wilcox, the owner of the Treasure House, an antique shop in the Chelsea district of London. But Wilcox's fanciful dreams of becoming an expert are held back by his wife Madge, clottish assistant Charlie and his own inadequacy.

Checkpoint Chiswick

UK · C4 (REGENT PRODUCTIONS) · SITCOM

1 × 60 mins · colour

18 Mar 1987 · Wed 10pm

MAIN CAST

Brian Stebbings · · · · · · · · · · · Hywel Bennett
Sally Stebbings · · · · · · · · · · · · Gil Brailey
Sean Stebbings · · · · · · · · · · · Simon Nash
Mrs Atkins · · · · · · · · · · · · Charlotte Mitchell

Donna · · · · · · · · · · · · · · · Laura Calland
Clive · · · · · · · · · · · · · · · · · Justin Pickett

CREDITS
writer Andy Hamilton · *director* Cyril Coke ·
producer William G Stewart

The third of six single comedies screened under the banner *Tickets For The Titanic*. Brian Stebbings believes that anarchy is just around the corner and may, indeed, be knocking on his door at any moment. He and his family besiege themselves in an attempt to keep it at bay … only inviting trouble for themselves in the process.

Cheers   UK

UK · ITV (YORKSHIRE) · SITCOM

1 × 30 mins · colour
3 Mar 1977 · Thu 9pm

MAIN CAST
Charles · · · · · · · · · · · · · · · · Charles Gray
Peter · · · · · · · · · · · · · · · · · Freddie Jones

CREDITS
writers/associate producers Ray Galton/Alan Simpson · *director/producer* Vernon Lawrence · *executive producer* Duncan Wood

Esteemed actors Charles Gray and Freddie Jones co-starred in this single-episode sitcom, a production in *The Galton & Simpson Playhouse* series for Yorkshire TV. The pair have been inseparable friends since school-days, brothers in battles, joint leaseholders of a maisonette, two very urbane English and gentlemen – until their relationship is put under unexpected strain.

Cheers   USA

USA · NBC (CHARLES-BURROW-CHARLES PRODUCTIONS/PARAMOUNT) · SITCOM

270 episodes (267 × 30 mins · 2 × 60 mins · 1 × 90 mins) · colour
US dates: 30 Sep 1982–20 May 1993
UK dates: 4 Feb 1983–13 June 1993 (270 episodes · as above) C4 Sat then Fri mostly 10pm

MAIN CAST
Sam Malone · · · · · · · · · · · · · · · Ted Danson
Diane Chambers · · · · · · · · · · · Shelley Long
· (1982–86, 1993)
Rebecca Howe · · · · · Kirstie Alley (1986–93)
'Coach' Ernie Pantusso · · · · · · · · · · · · · ·
· · · · · · · · · · Nicholas Colasanto (1982–85)
Woody Boyd · · Woody Harrelson (1985–93)
Carla Lupozone Tortelli LeBec · · · · · · · · · · ·
· Rhea Perlman
Norm Peterson · · · · · · · · · · · George Wendt
Cliff Clavin · · · · · · · · · · · John Ratzenberger
Dr Frasier Crane · · · · · · · · Kelsey Grammer
· (1984–93)
Dr Lilith Sternin-Crane · · · · · · Bebe Neuwirth
· (1986–93)
Robin Colcord · · · · · · Roger Rees (1989–91)
OTHER APPEARANCES
Nick Tortelli · · · · · · · Dan Hedeya (1983–86)
Al · · · · · · · · · · · · · · · · Al Rosen (1984–89)

Paul Creypens · · · · · Paul Willson (1985–93)
Esther Clavin · · · · · · · · Frances Sternhagen
· (1986–93)
Kelly Gaines · · · · Jackie Swanson (1989–93)
Evan Drake · · · · · · · Tom Skerritt (1987–88)
Eddie LeBec · · · · · · · Jay Thomas (1987–89)
John Allen Hill · · · · · Keene Curtis (1990–93)
Henri · · · · · · · · · Anthony Cistaro (1990–92)
Harry The Hat · · · · · · · · · · · Harry Anderson

CREDITS
creators Glen Charles, Les Charles, James Burrows · *writers* Glen Charles/Les Charles, Heide Perlman, David Lloyd, Earl Pomerantz, Dan Staley/Rob Long, Ken Estin, Ken Levine/David Isaacs, Sam Simon, Cheri L Eichen/Bill Steinkellner, David Angell, Phoef Sutton and others · *directors* James Burrows and others · *executive producers* Glen Charles/James Burrows/Les Charles, Tom Anderson, Dan Staley/Rob Long and others · *producers* Glen Charles/James Burrows/Les Charles, Ken Levine/David Isaacs, Tim Berry

Created by *Taxi* alumni Charles, Burrows and Charles, *Cheers* was a US ensemble comedy extraordinaire, a consistent and reliable provider of laughs. A giant sitcom on all levels (number of characters, popularity, longevity, and, above all, comedic quality), the premise – the comings and goings at a Boston bar – was deceptively simple, but the finely drawn characters populating the bar, coupled with the razor-sharp dialogue and succinct plotting, made *Cheers* anything but simple.

The Cheers bar is owned by Sam Malone, a shameless Lothario whose claim to fame is his former career as a relief pitcher for the Boston Red Sox baseball team. Sam is a recovering alcoholic and so never touches the brews he sells, preferring instead to swig soft drinks from a bottle. Initially, Sam's staff consists of his ex-sporting-coach Ernie Pantusso, a well-meaning but obtuse sort whose odd logic has become even more baffling with age; and barmaid Carla, a no-nonsense spitfire with a feisty attitude and savage tongue. They are joined in the first episode by a neurotic academic, Diane Chambers, who begins working in the bar after being jilted by her snobbish suitor. The main regular customers are the omnipresent beer-swilling Norm Peterson and the trivia-spouting postman Cliff Claven, a strong believer in conspiracy theories and urban myths. Later they are joined by psychiatrist Dr Frasier Crane, introduced as Diane's new boyfriend, whose initial superior attitude to the rest of the gang is gradually undercut by their unconditional acceptance of him as 'one of the boys'. Following the death of actor Nicholas Colasanto, a new barman, the equally intellectually askew Woody, joins the staff. Later, when Diane Chambers leaves, the beautiful but jinxed Rebecca Howe is installed behind the bar. The last major regular to arrive is the brilliant but daunting Lilith, a professional colleague of Dr Crane's who

eventually becomes his lover and, later still, his wife.

From this basic set of characters a master-piece of comedy was created. But the series had another star: the set itself. Once the producers had chosen the Bull and Finch pub in Boston as the external setting for *Cheers* the task was on to re-create in a studio the inside of such an establishment. Because the bar area itself was to constitute practically the only set the series would use – Sam's adjacent office was also seen – the producers spent lavishly on it and art director Richard Sylbert and set director George Gaines were given licence to create a classic TV setting. The bar not only looked real but was extremely practical: the long counter meant that characters at opposite ends could be isolated in shots almost as if in separate sets. Likewise with the customer booths. However, when the plot called for it, a long shot could take in the entire set and once again place all the characters together. Simple but brilliant.

The main drive for the early *Cheers* episodes was the 'square-peg-in-a-round-hole' theme of having the snobbish Diane work in the bar, among those she considered of lesser intelligence and lower class. The ensuing conflict set up much of the humour, especially the clash between Diane and the less academic but verbally sharper Carla. Adding to this dynamic, Sam found himself irrationally attracted to Diane and after a season of smouldering love-hate foreplay they finally united, enjoying a hugely passionate but understandably volatile affair. Their on-off relationship provided the axis to the first three years of the series. When the couple finally split, Sam sold the bar, bought a boat and set off to sail around the world as therapy. His ketch sunk, however, and he soon found himself back at the bar, no longer as the owner but as barman under new manager Rebecca Howe. Rebecca tried desperately, and nearly succeeded, to run an efficient operation but ultimately her self-consciousness and constant bad luck conspired against her and, following an ill-fated fling with fraudulent tycoon Robin Colcord, she lost her position and Sam regained control of Cheers, turning the tables by employing Rebecca as the help. The pair occasionally found themselves attracted to one another and experienced a hot-and-cold relationship, even trying to have a baby together. As with the earlier Sam/Diane situation, the Sam/Rebecca relationship operated as a continuing pivot around which the show revolved.

Although the Sam Malone character was undeniably the linchpin of *Cheers*, it was the brilliant layering of the other characters that gave the series its depth. Unusually for a sitcom, Diane, Rebecca and Frasier all profited from their experiences to develop:

Diane eventually succeeded as a writer, Rebecca shirked her money-motivated ambitions to marry a plumber, Frasier found friends for the first time in his life, got married and became a father. The other bar staff and customers, however, remained constant: Woody may have stretched his wings as an actor and later as a husband but he never changed his illogical thought processes; Norm remained the most-regular regular, losing his job, changing careers, but never altering his views on life or allowing us sight of his stop-at-home wife Vera; Cliff finally had an affair but neither cut himself loose from his mother's apron-strings nor ceased to ramble on about bizarre and dubious facts or unlikely stories; and Carla seemed doomed to repeat her history of falling for, and becoming impregnated by, unreliable characters – and every once in a while wondering what might have been had she and Sam had ever got together.

Unusually for such ensemble pieces there was no villain in the cast. Sure, Sam Malone was sexist and sex-obsessed (he even went to therapy for it), and, yes, Carla's verbal cruelty was merciless; but essentially they were both likeable characters with recognisable vulnerability and flaws. Despite the characters' warmth, *Cheers* pointedly remained unsentimental, with would-be 'slushy' moments confounded by a witty line or a sudden plot reversal. The series simply had no need to fall back on sentimentality, often the first recourse in a US sitcom: it was enough that Cliff, Norm and Frasier vicariously lived their sex lives through Sam's exploits; that Rebecca tried to put on a brave face as her world collapsed; that Sam tried to come to terms with the ageing process, as epitomised by his thinning hair and subsequent use of a toupee; that Carla coped with her out-of-control children and a problematic life which she believed was supernaturally pre-determined.

Although amassing good ratings for the minority channel C4, *Cheers* never achieved mainstream popularity in the UK. Critics, TV executives and its devoted audience raved about the show, making it seem more influential in Britain than perhaps it really was. But the majority of British TV viewers remained immune to the series' charms, preferring instead the broader appeal of home-grown sitcoms such as *Bread* and *'Allo 'Allo!* In the USA, the series was a phenomenal success, rising through the ratings to become a smash-hit by its fourth season and remaining in the top ten thereafter. The extended last episode, screened there on 20 May 1993, was watched by 150 million people, then the highest rating ever for a TV broadcast. In this finale, Diane Chambers returned and Sam found that the old flame still flickered; however – in

keeping with the nature of the series – their relationship foundered once more, leaving Sam to contemplate life forever in the bar. After such sterling work, the writers/ producers could be forgiven the rare touches of sentimentality that tinged this finale. For all of them, and for many of us, it was an emotional moment.

Cheers spawned two spin-off series: *The Tortellis* (NBC, 22 January to 12 May 1987, 13 episodes) starring Dan Hedaya as Carla's ex-husband Nick with his new wife Loretta (Jean Kasem); and *Frasier*.

Notes. The cast of *Cheers* turned up, in character, in *Mickey's 60th Birthday*, an hour-length Walt Disney TV tribute to its famous mouse, which combined animation with specially shot live action sequences. Screened in the USA by NBC on 3 November 1988, the programme was first shown in Britain by ITV some eight weeks later, on Christmas Day morning, under the title *Mickey Mouse At 60*.

Voiced by the original actors, certain *Cheers* characters also appeared fleetingly in an episode of the ace cartoon sitcom *The Simpsons*.

Chef!

UK · BBC (*CRUCIAL-APC, CRUCIAL) · SITCOM
20 × 30 mins · colour

*Series One (6) 28 Jan–11 Mar 1993 · BBC1 Thu 9.30pm
Special · 24 Dec 1993 · BBC1 Fri 10.10pm
Series Two (7) 8 Sep–27 Oct 1994 · BBC1 Thu 9.30pm
Series Three (6) 25 Nov–30 Dec 1996 · BBC1 Mon 8.30pm

MAIN CAST

Gareth Blackstock	Lenny Henry
Janice	Caroline Lee Johnson
Everton	Roger Griffiths
Piers	Gary Parker (series 1)
Lucinda	Claire Skinner (series 1)
Otto	Erkan Mustapha (series 1)
Gustave	Ian McNeice (series 2);
	Jeff Nuttall (series 3)
Alice	Hilary Lyon (series 2)
Debra	Pui Fan Lee (series 2)
Donald	Gary Bakewell (series 2)
Alphonse	Jean Luc Rebaliati (series 2)
Savannah	Lorelei King (series 3)
Cyril	Dave Hill (series 3)
Renee	Sophie Walker (series 3)

OTHER APPEARANCES

Restaurant manager	Peter Tilbury
	(series 1)
Quentin Blackstock	Oliver Samuels

CREDITS

writers Peter Tilbury (14), Paul Makin (3), Geoff Deane (2), Geoff Deane/Paul Makin (1) · directors John Birkin (14), Dewi Humphreys (6) · executive producer Polly McDonald (series 2) · producer Charlie Hanson

It had long been a cliché that comedy was the new rock and roll, but in the mid 1990s there was a stronger argument that cookery was the new rock and roll. The cult of the super-chefs, with their infamous huge prices, small portions and short tempers, had caught the public imagination, and millions of Britons who could never afford to eat in these establishments were suddenly conversant with the names, cooking styles and flamboyant nature of these new culinary megastars. In 1993 the sitcom *Chef!* arrived on TV, neatly tapping into this super-cook fashion.

Lenny Henry was cast in the lead role of Gareth Blackstock, an *enfant terrible* of culinary art, impossibly difficult to work for, anally fastidious about his creations and possessing a volcanic temper and savage tongue. In short, Blackstock was an amalgam of all the super-chef clichés, the very acceptance of the character proving how much the culture had been absorbed by the general public. Shot entirely on location, the series was set at the fictitious La Château Anglais, a country restaurant in Oxfordshire that was fast becoming an essential stop-off point on gourmet tours. Blackstock's expertise was beyond question, and the humour of the series arose from his failings in every other walk of life: his disregard for customers, his tyrannical abuse of kitchen staff and, above all, his neglect of his beautiful wife Janice. Quite simply, Blackstock was dedicated to cookery and everything else took second place.

But what seemed like an unbearable character on paper proved to be quite sympathetic in the skilled hands of Lenny Henry, who cleverly hinted at the humanity beneath Blackstock's hostile surface. He played the chef as a victim, cursed by his obsession with the preparation of food and suffering in his private life because of it. Blackstock found it difficult to nurture friendships and impossible to make small-talk, and was unable to treat his wife with the same respect that he treated food. As the series progressed, Blackstock's tender side surfaced more, and it became obvious that underneath the bluster was a decent guy trying to get out. He even managed an uneasy but enduring friendship with the kitchen hand, Everton, although Janice grew increasingly fed up with her position on the backburner of her husband's life and they separated at the end of the second series. She continued to appear, however, as the couple attempted to conduct their divorce arrangements in a civilised way, and Gareth was desperate to instigate a reconciliation. But Janice was certain that despite his insistence that he would give up cooking for her, the lure of the kitchen was too strong.

Blackstock's staff changed from series to series and began to play a greater role in the third season with the new boss – wide-boy Cyril – and his haughty daughter Renee (who had a fling with Everton) giving the harassed chef a new crop of problems. Also on hand was an American, Savannah, who had a crush on Blackstock, and the misogynist Gustave who wanted to crush Savannah.

All in all, the show was a fine concoction, with first-class ingredients and impeccable presentation. The producers experimented with a US sitcom style and the first two series were shot on film. This device delivered a slick product but proved too time consuming and so the third series reverted to videotape, albeit retaining much of the earlier visual quality. Lenny Henry was excellent in the lead role and the series intentionally made no truck of the fact that he was black; a deliberate ploy that made its point in a much more subtle manner than many 'issue-related' series have done.

Note. In the guise of Gareth Blackstock, Lenny Henry assisted Delia Smith, probably Britain's most famous cook, to prepare one of the recipes she concocted for **Comic Relief** 1997. This short, five-minute taster for the full blown Comic Relief feast was screened by BBC2 on 11 March 1997 as *Delia's Red Nose Collection*.

See also combined Lenny Henry entry.

Chelmsford 123

UK · C4 (HAT TRICK PRODUCTIONS) · SITCOM

13 × 30 mins · colour

Series One (6) 9 Mar–13 Apr 1988 · Wed mostly 10pm

Series Two (7) 9 Jan–20 Feb 1990 · Tue 10pm

MAIN CAST

Aulus Paulinus	Jimmy Mulville
Badvoc	Rory McGrath
Grasientus	Philip Pope
Mungo	Neil Pearson
Blag	Howard Lew Lewis
Functio	Robert Austin (series 1)
Gargamadua	Erika Hoffman (series 1)

OTHER APPEARANCES

Wolfbane	Geoffrey McGivern
Viatorus	Geoffrey Whitehead

CREDITS

writers Rory McGrath/Jimmy Mulville · *directors* John Stroud (series 1), Vic Finch (series 2) · *producers* Denise O'Donoghue (series 1), Adrian Bate/Denise O'Donoghue (series 2)

The story of life in Roman Britain – with a twist. The series was set in AD 123, in Chelmsford. Britain was still cold and wet, and the town had few redeeming features, except for Thursday's late-night shopping. Aulus Paulinus was despatched from Rome to be the new Governor of Britain, his punishment for accidentally insulting the Holy Roman Emperor's girlfriend. Aulus (played by Jimmy Mulville) was a puny and somewhat delicate Roman, usually outwitted by the bearded Badvoc (Rory McGrath), a scheming, ill-natured and revolting Celt who ruled over the disgusting local tribe, in particular his ugly cohorts Mungo and Blag. Aulus also had a Roman assistant/brother-in-law, the unctuous Grasientus.

Chelmsford 123 was the first series from Hat Trick Productions, set to become the most successful independent company making comedy and comedy-quiz-shows for British TV in the 1990s. Here, the humour was laid on thick, with many good lines and some corny but worthwhile laughs coming from abuse of vernacular English in a style that was part *I'm Sorry, I'll Read That Again* and part cheapo **Blackadder**.

The Chicago Teddy Bears

USA · CBS (WARNER BROS) · SITCOM

13 × 30 mins · colour

US dates: 17 Sep–17 Dec 1971

UK dates: 24 Sep–17 Dec 1983 (12 episodes) C4 Sat mostly 4.35pm

MAIN CAST

Linc McCray	Dean Jones
Uncle Latzi	John Banner
Big Nick Marr	Art Metrano
Marvin	Marvin Kaplan
Lefty	Jamie Farr
Dutch	Huntz Hall
Julius	Mike Mazurki
Duke	Mickey Shaughnessy

CREDITS

writers various · *director* Norman Tokar · *producer* Jerry Thorpe

A somewhat flimsy sitcom that sent up the notoriously crime-ridden Chicago of the 1920s, when violent evasion of the prohibition laws was rampant. Production company Warner Bros had previously (1960–62) made *The Roaring Twenties*, a drama series set in the same period.

Together with his Uncle Latzi, Linc McCray is the laid-back co-owner of a speakeasy – a surprisingly legal one – called the Paradise Club. His cousin, the appropriately nicknamed Big Nick, is the leader of a gang of hoodlums (personnel: Duke, Dutch, Lefty and Julius), most inappropriately nicknamed the Chicago Teddy Bears. The gang try to take over the Paradise and add it to the cache of illegal joints, and Linc has to spend much of his time (and most of the episodes) thwarting them in order to retain control. For while everyone else in the neighbourhood is terrified of Big Nick, Linc and their mutual uncle, Latzi, know his background – in particular, Latzi finds it impossible to believe that young Nicholas, his own nephew, is not a pleasant young man underneath that gruff exterior.

What the series lacked in terms of comedy content – ie, laughs – it made up for with viewer familiarity. Perseverance in front of the screen permitted sight of, among others, Huntz Hall (one of the legendary Dead End Kids/Bowery Boys) in his only regular TV role, Jamie Farr, who went on to become cross-dresser Klinger in *M*A*S*H* and Marvin Kaplan, the voice of Choo-Choo in the children's cartoon series *Top Cat*, who appeared here as Linc and Latzi's meek, bespectacled accountant.

Note. A few ITV regions, but not London, screened *The Chicago Teddy Bears* in 1972, but C4 gave the series its first UK network airing in 1983.

Las Chicas de Hoy en Día

SPAIN · RTVE · SITCOM

30 mins · colour

Spanish dates: 1990–91

UK date: 1 Oct 1990 (1 episode) BBC2 Mon 6pm

MAIN CAST

Nathalie Seseña and others

CREDITS

director Fernando Colomo

Despite the fact that the sitcom genre thrives domestically in many countries, very few series from outside the UK and North America enjoy wide-ranging international sales. So this episode of a Spanish sitcom, imported to the UK as part of BBC2's youth TV strand *DEF II*, was a rare and exotic beast indeed; not only that, BBC2 claimed to be showing it ahead of the Spanish transmission, set for 1991.

This pilot episode from *Las Chicas de Hoy en Día* – which translates to *Today's Girls* – showed how two young Spanish women, job hunting in Madrid, come to share a flat together. This episode took the story one step further: Nuri, the local equivalent of a London 'Sloane Ranger', misses an audition for an acting job and ends up on a cookery course; Charo loses her job as a baby-sitter.

Chico And The Man

USA · NBC (KOMACK/DAVID WOLPER PRODUCTIONS) · SITCOM

88 × 30 mins · colour

US dates: 13 Sep 1974–21 July 1978

UK dates: 12 Sep 1974–15 Nov 1975 (21 episodes) BBC1 Thu 7.30pm

MAIN CAST

Ed Brown (The Man)	Jack Albertson
Chico Rodriguez	Freddie Prinze (1974–77)
Raul Garcia	Gabriel Melgar (1977–78)
Mabel	Bonnie Boland (1974–75)
Louie Wilson	Scatman Crothers
Mando	Isaac Ruiz (1974–77)
Della Rogers	Della Reese (1976–78)

CREDITS

writers Gary Jacobs, Ann L Gibbs/Joel Kimmel, Jay Moriarty, Mike Milligan · *producer* James Komack

Launched on British TV one day before its US debut, *Chico And The Man* was a worthy sitcom-with-a-message, unfortunately mostly remembered today for the 'suicide' [see first footnote] of its young leading-man Freddie Prinze during the run of the show. Prinze's rise to fame had been truly meteoric: graduating in 1973 from the New York High School for Performing Arts (the real-life inspiration for the film and TV series *Fame*), he was hotly pursued by TV executives after a brilliant standup performance on NBC's *The Tonight Show* in December 1973. Now here he was at 20, less than a year later, starring in the first US sitcom to feature a Chicano (Mexican-American) character in a leading role [see second footnote].

Chico And The Man depicted a surrogate father-son relationship between a cantankerous, irascible, sarcastic garage owner, Ed Brown, and the young, keen Chicano, Chico, who comes to work for him. At first the couple clash on everything, but gradually Ed warms to the tireless enthusiasm of the youth who is determined to turn the run-down garage on the Mexican-American border into a success. The series' underlying theme was tolerance: it demonstrated that people from different ethnic and racial backgrounds might disagree on many things but essentially have the same emotions, feelings and problems, and can, with a little effort, co-exist in perfect harmony. In fact, the series indicated, they may even become friends. But the sharp humour, and the realistic, streetwise plots, prevented the sitcom from becoming mawkish or overwhelmed by its message. At its best, the crisp dialogue between the two was reminiscent of *Steptoe And Son*, itself adapted for American consumption as *Sanford And Son*.

Chico And The Man was an instant hit and Prinze's inexorable rise to fame and fortune accelerated accordingly. As a standup comedian, his act, with its plentiful racial references, was in great demand, and he was likened to America's most notorious standup comedian Lenny Bruce. (Indeed, at one time, he was engaged to Lenny's daughter Kitty Bruce.) Prinze was also in demand for TV specials, starring in an NBC TV movie, *The Million Dollar Rip-Off*, in 1976. But when his marriage to a Las Vegas travel agent ended, and she took custody of their baby son, Prinze was devastated; already feeling the pressure of a long-running lawsuit with a former agent, he became dependent on drugs, especially Quaaludes, and developed a gun fixation, often mimicking the act of shooting himself. One night in January 1977 the mime led to disaster when Prinze picked up a gun and

shot himself in the head. He died 33 hours later following intensive brain surgery, having lived just 22 years. The story of Prinze's tragic life was told in the TV movie *Can You Hear The Laughter?* (CBS, 11 September 1979, directed by Burt Brinckerhoff), with lookalike Ira Angustain in the lead role. (The film was screened in the UK by BBC1 28 June 1985.)

Prinze's death was a crushing blow to his Hollywood friends and colleagues, but with *Chico And The Man* riding high in the ratings NBC were reluctant to pull the plug. Their decision was to continue with a new Chico, a 12-year-old Hispanic boy, Raul, who, returning from a fishing trip, finds himself smuggled across the US border in the boot of Ed's car. Inevitably, Raul's age altered the emphasis of the show, which became far more family orientated, but it remained eminently watchable, not least because of Jack Albertson's performance as The Man. But Prinze's likeable charm was sorely missed and his death cast a shadow over the series from which, arguably, it never recovered.

Notes. Prinze's mother mounted a vigorous campaign to prove that her son's death was an accident. She claimed that Prinze was showing off as usual, and was unaware that his gun was loaded. The courts eventually agreed and the original suicide verdict was changed.

Prinze himself wasn't a Chicano. His mother was Puerto Rican and his father Hungarian, which Prinze claimed made him a 'Hungarican'.

A Child's Guide To Screenwriting

UK · ITV (REDIFFUSION) · SKETCH

1 × 30 mins · b/w

28 April 1964 · Tue 10.50pm

MAIN CAST
Frank Muir
Denis Norden
Roy Kinnear
Lance Percival
June Whitfield (voice only)
John Bluthal (voice only)

CREDITS

writers Frank Muir/Denis Norden, Keith Waterhouse/Willis Hall, Aaron Ruben/Carl Reiner · *director* John P Hamilton · *producer* Sid Colin

A one-off programme in which top comedy authors – members of the Screenwriters Guild – sent up the job of TV and movie scriptwriting.

Chintz

UK · ITV (GRANADA) · SITCOM

7 × 30 mins · colour

27 Apr–8 June 1981 · Mon mostly 8pm

MAIN CAST

Kate Carter	Michele Dotrice
Richard Carter	Richard Easton
Dottie Nelson	Dilys Laye
Fred Nelson	Christopher Benjamin
Grace Hills	Claire Nielson

CREDITS

creator/writer Peg Lynch · *adapters/writers* Dilys Laye/Alex Adams · *director* Eric Prytherch · *producer* Brian Armstrong

A middle-class, middle-of-the-road, middle-England, middle-aged, mediocre sitcom, starring Michele Dotrice – forever locked in viewers' minds as Betty, wife of the hapless Frank Spencer in *Some Mothers Do 'Ave 'Em* – as harebrained Kate Carpenter. Full of good intentions but invariably finding life a bit of a muddle, Kate lives in domestic 'bliss' with her hubbie Richard in leafy Cheshire and is forever getting into scrapes with their neighbours, Dottie and Fred Nelson.

The *Chintz* situation and scripts were based on the very early US sitcom *Ethel And Albert*, which – also titled *The Private Lives Of Ethel And Albert* – began life on American ABC radio (1944–1950), then transferred to TV (1953–56, first for NBC then CBS and finally ABC) before returning to radio as *The Couple Next Door*. The TV version starred Peg Lynch (also the series' author) and Alan Bunce as the Arbuckles, who lived in Sandy Harbor. Before finding fame as a film actor, Richard Widmark played Albert when the series first aired on radio. One of the earliest forces for women in American radio and TV, Lynch, born in 1917, continues to perform *Ethel And Albert* scripts at US universities.

Chopsticks

UK · BBC · CHILDREN'S SKETCH/STANDUP

6 × 25 mins · colour

23 Feb–29 Mar 1980 · BBC2 Sat 4.45pm

MAIN CAST
Justin Case
Peter Wear

CREDITS

writers Justin Case/Peter Wear · *producer* Judy Whitfield

A miscellany of comedy and music for younger viewers from double-act Case and Wear. Case was a mime artist, with a flexible frame and an equally malleable face; Wear was taller, with a distinguished air and a pseudo-classical delivery. They were the hosts, clowning about and extemporising comedy while filming on location, and each week they featured eclectic guest artists such as tap dancers and jazz musicians.

Wear went on to appear in the late-night C4 series *Little Armadillos*.

Chris Cross

UK · ITV (CARLTON UK PRODUCTIONS/CINAR PRODUCTIONS FOR CENTRAL) · CHILDREN'S SITCOM

13 × 30 mins · colour

Series One (6) 18 Mar–29 Apr 1994 · Fri 4.40pm

Series Two (7) 14 Feb–28 Mar 1995 · Tue 4.40pm

MAIN CAST

Chris Hilton	Simon Fenton
Oliver Cross	Eugene Byrd
Dinah McGee	Rachel Blanchard
Mr Rogers	Alan David
X	Timothy Douek
Mookie	Tom Brodie
Charles Barkley	Oliver Gilbody
Casey Down	Nicola Stewart

CREDITS

creator D J McHale · *writers* D J McHale (series 1), D J McHale, Gary Cohen, Ned Kandel (series 2) · *directors* Ron Oliver (series 1, 3 eps of series 2), Dennis Abey (4 eps of series 2) · *executive producers* Gary Cohen, Lewis Rudd

An internationally produced children's sitcom – made by Central TV in England and the Canadian independent company Cinar, in association with the US cable station Showtime – set in an international boarding school in England, Stansfield Academy. Oliver Cross, a teenager, is the established school king cool when, at the start of a new term, two things occur to change the situation: Stansfield becomes mixed-sex (or co-ed, as the Americans have it) and a new teenage male pupil, Chris Hilton, joins the fray, immediately becoming popular with the girls and a clear challenge to Cross's established authority. Neither Chris nor Cross like school very much so they decide to join forces to liven up the hitherto stuffy establishment, playing practical jokes galore. They represent a formidable team: Cross is black and has built his status on the back of his wisecracking and his abilities as a DJ; Chris is white, the all-American athlete, a perfect student. Bossy fellow pupil Rachel is the headmaster's grand-daughter.

Mixing comedy with spirited drama, *Chris Cross* episodes were also laden with rock music by the likes of U2, Sinead O'Connor and Annie Lennox – at least, the British screenings were. Episodes broadcast in America carried different soundtracks as well as alternate accents in the mouths of the actors, synced in post-production, and differently edited scripts.

English actor Simon Fenton (who played the American Chris Hilton) was something of a heart-throb at this time, and was appearing as Luke Bouverie in the C4 dramatisation of Joanne Trollope's *The Rector's Wife* when the first series of *Chris Cross* began. The remarkable popularity of *Chris Cross* on American TV – it won an award there – led Fenton to pursue a career in the States, gaining him a principal role in the movie *Matinee*.

The Christmas Armistice

see *The Saturday Night Armistice*

Christmas Box

UK · BBC · STANDUP

1 × 45 mins · b/w

25 Dec 1955 · Sun 9pm

MAIN CAST

Charlie Chester
Jimmy James
Bill Maynard
Bob Monkhouse

CREDITS

producers Ronnie Taylor, Nicholas Crocker, Douglas Fleming, Bryan Sears

A departure from other Christmas comedy specials of the period: instead of gathering artists together at the BBC studios in Lime Grove, west London, the programme went out and about to visit parties. The stars in question were appearing in seasonal productions – Bob Monkhouse presented his section from the Ice Rink at Bournemouth, and Charlie Chester from the Empire Theatre, Sheffield.

Christmas Cracker

UK · BBC · STANDUP

1 × 60 mins · b/w

22 Dec 1956 · Sat 8.30pm

MAIN CAST

Tessie O'Shea
Spike Milligan
Alfred Marks
Charlie Drake
George Martin

CREDITS

deviser/producer George Inns

A seasonal special from some of the cast and the production crew of *Tess And Jim*. By this edition (which would have been the last in that series), Jimmy Wheeler had been released to appear in pantomime so Tessie O'Shea hosted, with guests, and the show was retitled *Christmas Cracker*.

Christmas Is Coming …

UK · ITV (YORKSHIRE) · SKETCH

1 × 60 mins · colour

23 Dec 1987 · Wed 9pm

MAIN CAST

Miriam Stoppard
Gwen Taylor
Alun Armstrong
Liz Smith
Kenneth Waller
Richard Digance

CREDITS

writers Barry Took, Raymond Briggs, Alan Coren, Ken Hoare, Angela Marshall · *executive producer* Vernon Lawrence · *director* Graham Wetherell · *producer* Simon Welfare

A humorous look at all things Christmas, subtitled 'This Is A Government Health Warning!', scripted by established wits (Took and Coren among them) and delivered by a strongly comedic cast.

Christmas Night With The Stars

UK · BBC · COMEDY SPECIALS

13 editions · 1958–94 · b/w and colour

The BBC's annual entertainment beanfeast, screened peak-time on Christmas night, in which many of its top stars appeared in especially made short (five- to ten-minute) versions of their popular shows. It followed an earlier, similar idea, *Television's Christmas Party* (1951–54)

The following indicates the comedy artists appearing – **see each programme's own entry for more details**.

1958; 75 mins, b/w, Thu 6.25pm
The Charlie Chester Show; Tony Hancock, Charlie Drake In …; The Ted Ray Show; Whack-O!

1959; 75 mins, b/w, Fri 6.20pm
The Jimmy Logan Show; Charlie Drake In …; Whack-O!

1960; 75 mins, b/w, Sun 6pm
Citizen James; Harry Worth; On The Bright Side; Jimmy Edwards (see *Whack-O!*)

1962; 95 mins, b/w, Tue 7.15pm
The Rag Trade; Raise Your Glasses; It's A Square World; Faces Of Jim; Steptoe And Son

1963; 80 mins, b/w, Wed 8.05pm
Hugh And I; It's A Square World; Marriage Lines; The Stanley Baxter Show; The Dick Emery Show

1964; 90 mins, b/w, BBC1 Fri 7.15pm
Hugh And I; The Likely Lads; Marriage Lines; Meet The Wife; The Dick Emery Show; The Benny Hill Show

1967; 120 mins, b/w, BBC1 Mon 6.40pm
Till Death Us Do Part; Beggar My Neighbour; The Illustrated Weekly Hudd; Harry Worth; Steptoe And Son; Kenneth Williams (see *The Kenneth Williams Show*); *Beryl Reid*

1968; 125 mins, b/w, BBC1 Wed 6.40pm
Not In Front Of The Children; Dad's Army; Oh Brother! and *All Gas And Gaiters; It's Marty; Harry Worth* (a repeat of the 1967 segment); hosted by Morecambe and Wise (their script written by Sid Green/Dick Hills)

1969; 90 mins, colour, BBC1 Thu 6.45pm
Extracts from (not new material) *The Dick Emery Show; It's Marty; Not In Front Of The Children; Monty Python's Flying Circus; Dad's Army*

1970; 90 mins, colour, BBC1 Fri 6.45pm
Dad's Army; Bachelor Father; Scott On ...; The Stanley Baxter Show; The Dick Emery Show

1971; 80 mins, colour, BBC1 Sat 6.40pm
The Two Ronnies; Till Death Us Do Part; Bachelor Father; Look – Mike Yarwood; A Policeman's Lot; The Dick Emery Show

1972; 80 mins, colour, BBC1 Mon 6.55pm
Dad's Army; Look – Mike Yarwood; The Goodies; The Liver Birds; The Two Ronnies

1994; 75 mins, colour, BBC2 Tue 9pm
Stephen Fry and Hugh Laurie; Felix Dexter; Ronnie Corbett; *The Fast Show; Knowing Me, Knowing You ... With Alan Partridge; Rab C Nesbitt; The Real McCoy; The All New Alexei Sayle Show; The Smell Of Reeves And Mortimer*

This last programme was an attempt to resurrect and modernise the BBC's all-star Christmas comedy blockbuster. New material from various contemporary shows (see cast) was supplemented by archive footage from previous specials. Fry and Laurie hosted (indeed, the programme's full title was *Fry And Laurie Host A Christmas Night With The Stars*).

Note. ITV networked a programme titled *Christmas Night With The Stars* in 1996, hosted by Des O'Connor, but this was much more variety-centred, the only comedians to appear being Joe Pasquale and Lily Savage.

Christmas Oneupmanship

see *One-upmanship*

Christmas Robbins

see *Kate And Ted's Show*

Christmas With Mike Harding And The Fivepenny Piece

see HARDING, Mike

Chucklevision

UK · BBC · CHILDREN'S SKETCH
138 editions (127 × 20 mins · 11 × 15 mins) · colour
Series One (12) 26 Sep–19 Dec 1987 · BBC1 Sat 8.40am
Series Two (13) 19 Nov 1988–18 Feb 1989 · BBC1 Sat 8.40am
Series Three (11 × 15 mins) 2 Dec 1989–24 Feb 1990 · BBC1 Sat 8.20am
Series Four (12) 28 Sep–28 Dec 1991 · BBC1 Sat 8.15am
Series Five (15) 26 Sep 1992–2 Jan 1993 · BBC1 Sat 8.15am
Series Six (15) 8 Jan–16 Apr 1994 · BBC1 Sat 8.15am

Series Seven (15) 7 Jan–15 Apr 1995 · BBC1 Sat 8.15am
Series Eight (15) 20 Dec 1995–29 Mar 1996 · BBC1 mostly Tue 3.55pm
Series Nine (15) 4 Dec 1996–26 Mar 1997 · BBC1 Wed 3.50pm
Series Ten (15) 17 Dec 1997–2 Apr 1998 · BBC1 mostly Wed 3.50pm
MAIN CAST
The Chuckle Brothers ·· Paul and Barry Elliot
Billy Butler (series 1 & 2)
Simon Lovell (series 1)
OTHER APPEARANCES
No Slacking · · · · · · · · · · · · · Jimmy Patton

CREDITS
main writer John Sayle · *other writers* Terry Randall, Nick McIvor, Ramsay Gilderdale/Philip Hazelby, Rory Clark/Robert Taylor, Paul Elliot/Barry Elliot, Jo Boyle, Isabelle Amyes/Peter Symonds, Ian Cooke/Adrian Baldwin, John Lester Hall, Dominic MacDonald, Richard Preddy/Gary Howe, Alan Hyland, Gail Renard · *directors* John Northover, Celia Thomson, Martin Hughes · *producer* Martin Hughes

Fast-paced comic fun, with a strong whiff of circus slapstick, for the discerning younger viewer. Paul and Barry Elliot, from Rotherham, were a comedy double-act for about 25 years before this long-running series began in 1987, but they had only started to call themselves the Chuckle Brothers some eight years previously. Their first TV hit was a toddler's series entitled *Chucklehounds*, in which the pair dressed up as huge fluffy dogs, but with *Chucklevision* (sometimes *Chuckle Vision*) they aimed their humour at the 8–12 age group. Typically, episodes found the brothers embarking on a quest or mounting a presentation (such as a celebration of the Australian bi-centenary-and-a-bit, or a spoof investigation into UFOs), and the first two series also featured Billy Butler's 'Armchair Theatre' in which the Liverpool radio DJ travelled to strange places and recounted weird stories from his lounge. Later editions showed the brothers trying their hands at different jobs or exploring new places. Their boss was No Slacking, who stuck with the lads despite their chequered record. A conjuror, Simon Lovell, provided magical entertainment in the first series but by the second he had disappeared.

Note. The brothers also presented a children's game-show named after their catchphrase, a mantra they frequently repeated when moving heavy objects, *To Me To You* (BBC1, from 21 June 1996).

Cilla's Comedy Six

UK · ITV (ATV) · SITCOMS
6 × 30 mins · colour
15 Jan–19 Feb 1975 · Wed 8pm
MAIN CAST
Cilla Black (six different roles)

CREDITS
writer Ronnie Taylor · *executive producers* Vic Lewis, Bobby Willis · *director/producer* Les Chatfield

En route to switching from successful singer to TV celebrity, Cilla Black was still studying the map when she made two series of sitcoms with ATV (the other was *Cilla's World Of Comedy* – see following entry).

Following the earlier BBC experiment *The World Of Cilla*, *Cilla's Comedy Six* saw the Liverpudlian step inside six different roles, one each week. Brief details of each episode follow:

No Harem For Henry   15 JAN

MAIN CAST
Linda Pearson · · · · · · · · · · · · · · Cilla Black
Henry Pearson · · · · · · · · · · · · · Keith Barron
Kathleen Micklehurst · · · · · · · Anna Sharkey

Linda starts to wonder whether her husband really is working late at the office.

See also *She'll Have To Go* in the following entry.

Every Husband Has One!   22 JAN

MAIN CAST
Doris Livesey · · · · · · · · · · · · · · Cilla Black
Jack Livesey · · · · · · · · · · · · · · · Tony Selby
Russell Stanhope · · · · · · · · · · Henry McGee

Doris is the archetypal average housewife, so is chosen as a guinea pig by a consumer-research organisation.

Sea View   29 JAN

MAIN CAST
Thelma Fosset · · · · · · · · · · · · · Cilla Black
Barry Fosset · · · · · · · · · · · · · Alan Rothwell
Mrs Pomfrey · · · · · · · · · · · · Maggie Jones

Accompanying two small children to the seaside is tough enough, but when it's time for them to leave Thelma and Barry face even greater problems.

Father's Doing Fine   5 FEB

MAIN CAST
Christine Bradshaw · · · · · · · · · · Cilla Black
Charlie Bradshaw · · · · · · · · · · Leslie Sands
Gloria · · · · · · · · · · · · · · · · · Helen Fraser

Christine has dedicated her life to looking after her widowed father, but when he meets Gloria things are set to change.

See also *Get Me To The Church!* in the following entry.

Who's Rocking The Boat?   12 FEB

MAIN CAST
Vera Clayton · · · · · · · · · · · · · · Cilla Black
Donald · · · · · · · · · · · · Norman Rossington
Roger Patterson · · · · · · · · · · Dudley Sutton

It takes nerve to sail around the world, especially as Vera is sharing the boat with two single men.

Dictation Speed   19 FEB

MAIN CAST
Sally Norton · · · · · · · · · · · · · · · Cilla Black
Philip Speed · · · · · · · · · · · Dinsdale Landen
Pamela Short · · · · · · · Nicolette MacKenzie

Temporary secretary Sally can usually cope with the needs of business executives, but can she deal with the amorous advances of Philip Speed, the Lothario of Corinthia Chemicals?

Cilla's World Of Comedy

UK · ITV (ATV) · SITCOMS
6 × 30 mins · colour
31 Aug–4 Oct 1976 · mostly Tue 8pm
MAIN CAST
Cilla Black (six different roles)

CREDITS
writer Ronnie Taylor · director/producer Les Chatfield

Eighteen months after *Cilla's Comedy Six*, ATV engaged Cilla Black for another season of six individual sitcoms:

She'll Have To Go   31 AUG

Linda Pearson · · · · · · · · · · · · · · · Cilla Black
Henry Pearson · · · · · · · · · · · Keith Barron
Elaine Pearson · · · · · · · · Dorothy Reynolds

Henry has his hands full keeping the peace between two warring females, his wife Linda and his mother Elaine.
A sequel to *No Harem For Henry*, the opening episode of *Cilla's Comedy Six*.

Home And Away   7 SEP

Barbara Norton · · · · · · · · · · · · · · Cilla Black
Frank Gallagher · · · · · · · · · · · Neil McCarthy
Jim Lockhead · · · · · · · · · Patrick McAlinney
Kenny Norton · · · · · · · · · · · Paul Greenwood

Kenny Norton may be a hot-shot footballer but it's his wife Barbara who wears the shorts in their family.

Desirable Property   14 SEP

Helen Parker · · · · · · · · · · · · · · · Cilla Black
Edwin Dawkins · · · · · · · · · · · Richard Wilson
Derek Parker · · · · · · · · · · · James Hazeldine

Helen wants to make a fresh start and feels that buying a new home will help. But Helen's past catches up with her when she looks over an empty house.

Sisters   21 SEP

Carole Coombs · · · · · · · · · · · · · · Cilla Black
Elizabeth Dorning · · · · · · · · Cheryl Kennedy
Roger Fulwood · · · · · · · · · Geoffrey Hughes

Biology teacher Carole questions the meaning of her own life.

Get Me To The Church!   28 SEP

Christine Bradshaw · · · · · · · · · · Cilla Black
Charlie Bradshaw · · · · · · · · · · Leslie Sands
Kevin Talbot · · · · · · · · · · · · · · David Wood

Christine is just a short drive away from the church where she will marry Lawrence, but with her father in the bridal car the journey starts to seem awfully long.
A sequel to *Father's Doing Fine*, the fourth episode of *Cilla's Comedy Six*.

Who's Your Friend?   4 OCT

Vera Wilkinson · · · · · · · · · · · · · Cilla Black
Morton Gillard · · · · · · · · Frank Middlemass
Philip Travers · · · · · · · · · · · · Philip Lowrie

Philip Travers plans to marry the boss's daughter but office typist Vera has her own ideas on the subject.

Citizen James

UK · BBC · SITCOM
33 episodes (32 × 25 mins · 1 × short special) · b/w
Series One (6) 24 Nov–29 Dec 1960 · Thu 7.30pm
Short special · part of *Christmas Night With The Stars* 25 Dec 1960 · Sun 6pm
Series Two (13) 2 Oct–25 Dec 1961 · Mon 7.30pm
Series Three (13) 31 Aug–23 Nov 1962 · Fri 8.50pm
MAIN CAST
Sidney Balmoral James · · · · · · Sidney James
Bill · · · · · · · · · · · · · · · · · · Bill Kerr (series 1)
Liz · · · · · · · · · · · · · · · · · Liz Fraser (series 1)
Charlie Davenport · · · · · · · · · Sydney Tafler

CREDITS
writers Ray Galton/Alan Simpson (series 1), Sid Green/Dick Hills (series 2 & 3) · producers Duncan Wood, Ronald Marsh

When Tony Hancock famously decided that he no longer required the services of a regular supporting cast, and so dispensed with his long-time sparring partner Sid James, the BBC offered the actor a series of his own, to be written for him by Hancock's writers Galton and Simpson. Initially, James was supported in his new venture by another former member of the Hancock rep, Bill Kerr, cast as his keen henchman, and by Liz Fraser as James's marriage-craving, long-term fiancé, the owner of a drinking club.
The Sidney Balmoral James in *Citizen James* was a variation on the *Hancock's Half Hour* character: a fast-talking, quick-thinking gambler with an eye for a buck and a tendency to become involved in dubious schemes. But as the series progressed the crafty cockney developed a sense of social

justice and, in the later episodes scripted by Sid Green and Dick Hills, he became something of a people's champion, taking up causes. With this character development came changes in the cast, and Kerr and Fraser were phased out.
Citizen James certainly wasn't a classic, but it was an entertaining vehicle for the popular James, whose trademark kyah-kyah-kyah cackle brightened up many a cold, dark winter's evening at the start of the 1960s.
Note. Sid James's next major TV venture, also for the BBC, was a drama series, *Taxi!*, in which he was cast as a London cabbie, Sid Stone. Although some of the stories were lightly humorous this was certainly no comedy, and thus it was a real departure for the *Carry On* and Hancock star. There were two series of 13 episodes apiece, screened from 10 July to 28 September 1963 and 4 April to 27 June 1964 (BBC1).

Citizen Smith

UK · BBC · SITCOM
30 × 30 mins · colour
Pilot · 12 Apr 1977 · BBC1 Tue 7.40pm
Series One (7) 3 Nov–15 Dec 1977 · BBC1 Thu 7.40pm
Special · 22 Dec 1977 · BBC1 Thu 8pm
Series Two (6) 1 Dec 1978–5 Jan 1979 · BBC1 Fri 8pm & 16 Aug 1979 · BBC1 Thu 8pm
Series Three (7) 20 Sep–1 Nov 1979 · BBC1 Thu 8.30pm
Series Four (7) 23 May–4 July 1980 · BBC1 Fri 7.50pm
Special · 31 Dec 1980 · BBC1 Wed 7.35pm
MAIN CAST
Wolfie Smith · · · · · · · · · · · · Robert Lindsay
Shirley · · · · · · · · · · · · · · · · · · · Cheryl Hall
Ken · · · · · · · · · · · · · · · · · · · Mike Grady
Tucker · · · · · · · · · · · · · · · Anthony Millan
Dad (Charles Johnson) · · Artro Morris (pilot);
· · · · · · · · · · · Peter Vaughan (series 1 & 2);
· · · · · · · · · · Tony Steedman (from series 3)
Mum (Mrs Johnson) · · · · · · · · · · · Hilda Braid
Speed · · · · · · · · · · · · · · · · John Sweeney
Harry Fenning · · · · · · · · · · · · Stephen Greif
Desiree · · · · · · · · · · · · · · · · · · Anna Nygh

CREDITS
writer John Sullivan · director Ray Butt · producers Peter Whitmore (pilot), Dennis Main Wilson (21), Ray Butt (8)

A fondly remembered – if not classic – sitcom, most notable now for having propelled the actor Robert Lindsay into the big-time and marking the debut of the comedy writer John Sullivan, who went on to become one of Britain's most successful.
Sullivan's entrée was an unusual one: a scenery shifter at the BBC, he was so disillusioned by the standards of its comedy programmes that he believed he could do better himself and, after completing a script, pestered Dennis Main Wilson to read it.

The veteran BBC producer did so – not expecting very much because non-commissioned scripts are usually found to be below acceptable quality – and was surprised at its energy and wit. Wilson recommended that it be knocked into shape and screened in *Comedy Special*, a successor to *Comedy Playhouse* in which one-off ideas were tried out. The pilot proved a winner, and after some cast and character tinkering, the resulting series caught the public's imagination.

Citizen Smith followed the activities of the Tooting Popular Front, a feeble but ambitious agitprop organisation masterminded by a would-be revolutionary Marxist, Wolfie Smith. Sullivan based Smith's character on a brash, loud-mouthed, drunken lad he had encountered in 1968 in a pub with the unlikely name of the Nelson Arms. Sullivan described the lad as 'a Master Dreamer in an age of fantasy' and built his sitcom around such a character. Wolfie Smith had all the jargon of a revolutionary, and the requisite passion. He also had a committed (well, semi-committed) trio of followers: his best friend Ken, the randomly violent Sweeney and the drained family man Tucker. But Smith was constantly thwarted by the minutiae of everyday life: problems with his girlfriend Shirley (played by Robert Lindsay's then wife Cheryl Hall) and her parents, financial insecurity, the ups and downs (mostly downs) of his favourite football team, Fulham, and people's general indifference to his cause. Smith was also somewhat work-shy, a factor absent in most successful revolutionaries. Nonetheless, he did make some progress with his schemes, changing from the harmless and hapless hippy of the first series into a slightly lunatic anarchist as it progressed. He even went to jail for his crimes at the end of the third series. In the end, though, Smith was beginning to realise the futility of trying to liberate a proletariat that seemed quite content to remain unliberated, and found it hard to take such a flawed activist seriously. (After all, even Che Guevara would have difficulty maintaining his respect if he had to ride around on a decrepit motor scooter.) A final, special episode screened on New Year's Eve 1980 heard Wolfie's last cry of 'Power To The People!'

Note. One of the episodes (27 September 1979) was titled 'Only Fools And Horses'. Writer John Sullivan reused this as the name of his next TV series, which began eight months after *Citizen Smith* ended.

City Lights

UK · BBC · SITCOM

30 × 30 mins · colour

Series One (6) 24 July–28 Aug 1987 · BBC2 Fri 9pm

Series Two (6) 5 Jan–9 Feb 1988 · BBC2 Tue 8pm

Series Three (6) 2 Mar–13 Apr 1989 · BBC2 Thu 9pm

Series Four (6) 14 June–19 July 1990 · BBC2 Thu 8pm

Series Five (6) 28 Feb–4 Apr 1991 · BBC2 Thu 8pm

MAIN CAST

Willie Melvin · · · · · · · · · · · · · · Gerard Kelly
Chancer · Andy Gray
Mum · Jan Wilson
Brian · · · · · · · · · · · · · · · · · Jonathan Watson
Mr McLelland · · · · · · · · · · · · Dave Anderson
Tam · Iain McColl
Irene · · · · · · · · · · · · · · · · · Elaine C Smith
Vicki · · · · · · · · · · · · Louise Beattie (series 1)
Janice McLachlan · · · · · · · · · · Elaine Collins
· (series 2 & 3)
Fiona · · · · · · · · · · · Ann Bryson (series 4 & 5)

CREDITS

writer Bob Black · *directors* Ron Bain (18), Colin Gilbert (12) · *producers* Colin Gilbert (24), Ron Bain (6)

Bank-teller Willie Melvin's grandiose dreams of becoming a successful novelist run riot after he wins a short-story competition, causing him no end of problems. His acquaintances also suffer, with friend Brian, boss Mr McLelland, and Chancer, a dodgy sort who spends some time in jail (between series one and two). Willie also has a couple of romances during the series, most notably with Janice, whom he almost marries. By the end of the run, however, he is courting Fiona.

Writer Bob Black had served his apprenticeship on BBC Scotland sketch shows *A Kick Up The Eighties* and *Naked Video* before creating this successful and durable Scottish sitcom; Willie's home in the series was Black's own flat.

Note. The broadcast dates at the head of this entry refer to network BBC2 transmissions. All of the episodes had already been screened via local transmitters by BBC Scotland.

The Clairvoyant

UK · BBC · SITCOM

6 × 30 mins · colour

Pilot · 27 Nov 1984 · BBC2 Tue 9pm

One series (5) 15 May–19 June 1986 · BBC2 Thu 9pm

MAIN CAST

Arnold Bristow · · · · · · · · · · · · · Roy Kinnear
Lily · · · · · · · · · · · · · · · · · Sandra Dickinson
Burma · · · · · · · · · · · · · · · · · · · Hugh Lloyd
Newton · · · · · · · · · · · · · · · · · Shaun Curry
Dawn · · · · · · · · · · · · · · · · · Glynis Brooks
Carmen · · · · · · · · · · · · · · · · Carmel Cryan

CREDITS

writer Roy Clarke · *director/producer* Alan J W Bell

Arnold Bristow is a used-car salesman with an impressive line in patter and shameless lack of principles. When he is knocked down in a hit-and-run accident, he regains consciousness to find he has developed amazing psychic powers. At least that's what he thinks – to the casual observer, it appears only that Arnold is deluding himself, and that his flashes of clairvoyance are so abstract that almost any incident can be accommodated within them. Nevertheless, to Arnold, the change seems real and he alters his lifestyle accordingly, becoming more moral and honest in his business dealings – which, of course, results in near financial ruin.

A fairly odd idea, this, and not one that ran as smoothly as most of Roy Clarke's work. Kinnear was faultless as the confused Arnold and the support cast fared well enough, but the idea seemed flawed and the supposed psychic phenomenon too vague to hold much interest.

Note. The introductory episode of *The Clairvoyant* aired as the first in a four week run of BBC2 pilots with no generic title. Amazingly, all four developed into series, the others being *The New Statesman* [BBC], *Hilary* and *Comrade Dad*.

Clapham And Dwyer

UK · BBC · STANDUP

1 × 10 mins · b/w

13 May 1937 · Thu 9pm

MAIN CAST

Charlie Clapham
Bill Dwyer

CREDITS

producer Reginald Smith

A *Starlight* pre-war showcase appearance for the stage and radio stars Clapham and Dwyer, double-act masters of nonsensical crosstalk. Dwyer played straight-man to Clapham's tall, dapper, top-hatted, monocle-wearing clown.

Clarence

UK · BBC · SITCOM

6 × 30 mins · colour

4 Jan–8 Feb 1988 · BBC1 Mon 9pm

MAIN CAST

Clarence Sale · · · · · · · · · · · · Ronnie Barker
Jane Travers · · · · · · · · · Josephine Tewson

CREDITS

writer Bob Ferris (Ronnie Barker) · *director/producer* Mike Stephens

Finding that he was no longer deriving as much enjoyment from performing as he once had, and worrying that his work might suffer as a result, Ronnie Barker announced his retirement in 1987. Rumours suggested that he was suffering from poor health – high blood pressure in particular – but Barker rejected this: he had lived with this condition for many years and was controlling it with medication. The truth was that he genuinely thought it was time to retire, to bow out at the top, and had the rare courage to do so. Before bidding farewell, however, there was time for one last series, *Clarence*. Even still, Barker only agreed to it because, as its writer (he used the pseudonym Bob Ferris), he could set it in Oxfordshire, near to his home.

Barker had faced criticism from some quarters over his employment of a stammer to attract laughs in **Open All Hours**. Here, mischievously, he showed that he had no remorse by having the character of Clarence the removal man suffer severe myopia. The slapstick possibilities of a short-sighted furniture shifter must have seemed irresistible. Set in 1937, the series was mostly concerned with Clarence's courtship of a ladies' maid, Jane Travers. When he proposes marriage, Jane decides, with a modernity years ahead of its time, that they should have a trial period of living together – respectably: a bolster was placed between them in the bed to preserve her chasteness – to see if they are compatible. Clarence agrees but as the nights grow longer so his resolve grows weaker …

Clarence was a reworking of *The Removals Person*, an episode of the 1971 ITV series **Six Dates With Barker**. That comedy playlet, written by Hugh Leonard, had also featured Tewson in the Travers role, but the main character's name was Fred. However all the 'Clarence' characteristics and mannerisms were in place, including the short-sightedness that led to his clumsy attempts at romance. The BBC series that emerged 17 years later was an efficient enough sitcom, and pleasingly beyond the mainstream, but Barker had been in better. For the public, he had a high-quality back catalogue with which it had to compete, and *Clarence* offered nothing to suggest, in retrospect at least, that Barker's decision to retire gracefully while still at the peak of his profession was the wrong one.

As good as his word, Barker was rarely tempted back into the limelight following his retirement (although he has been seen occasionally accepting or giving awards) and settled into a new life running an antique shop in Chipping Norton, Oxfordshire. In BBC1's special 50-minute interview/tribute *Ronnie Barker – A Life In Comedy* (1 January 1997), and two half-hour programmes of an identical title from the same channel (24 and 28 August 1997), he enthused about his pleasurable retirement. TV seemed smaller without him, a comedy character actor/ writer of exquisite talent, who brilliantly entertained the public for more than 35 years. Fortunately, so many of his finest moments exist complete in the archives and enjoy regular exposure on terrestrial television, cable and satellite.

Clarissa Explains It All

USA · NICKELODEON (THUNDER PICTURES) · CHILDREN'S SITCOM

65 × 30 mins · colour

US dates: 23 Mar 1991–1 Oct 1994

UK dates: 31 Dec 1994–19 Apr 1997 (65 episodes) BBC1 Sat mornings then Thu 4.35pm

MAIN CAST

Clarissa Darling · · · · · · · Melissa Joan Hart
Ferguson W Darling · · · · · · · · Jason Zimbler
Mum (Janet Darling) · · · · · · · Elizabeth Hess
Dad (Marshall Darling) · · · · · · Joe O'Connor
Sam Anders · · · · · · · · · · · · · · Sean O'Neal

CREDITS

creator Mitchell Kriegman · writers Neena Beber and others · directors Liz Plonka and others · producers Chris Gifford and others

An American children's sitcom centred around a precocious 14-year-old, Clarissa Darling (played by 18-year-old Melissa Joan Hart), who has definite opinions upon most things. Each episode begins with Melissa addressing the camera, holding forth on such topics as rock and roll, boys, school, her parents, her brother and so on, and these monologues lead into the stories. Bright and breezy, the series painted a rosy picture of life and proved hugely popular in the USA with its target audience of 6–11-year-olds. It also struck something of a chord in the UK, graduating from screenings within the BBC1 Saturday-morning children's magazine show *Live & Kicking* to a slot in its own right.

Melissa Joan Hart went on to star in **Sabrina The Teenage Witch**.

Julian Clary

A purveyor of outrageously delightful double entendres and sexually orientated one-liners, Julian Clary emerged from the 'alternative comedy' chorus line to become a mainstream comedy star. Fey, precise and uncommonly handsome, the comedian mixed gay witticisms with an exaggerated vaudevillian style to become a comic icon for the 1990s.

Born in Teddington, south-west London, on 25 June 1959, Clary's upbringing was far from alternative: his father was a policeman, his mother a social worker. He studied drama at Goldsmith's College, earning extra money by delivering singing telegrams and later, at the height of themed 'grams' craze, working as a 'Gay Tarzan-O-Gram'. Taking to the stage, Clary was originally billed as Gillian Pieface before making his big breakthrough as the Joan Collins Fan Club, an act in which he played second fiddle to a marvellously morose pooch named Fanny The Wonder Dog. After some years, and many TV appearances, Joan Collins' lawyers reputedly threatened Clary with legal action, so Fanny was retired and Clary began to perform under his own name, attaining even greater fame, with numerous TV shows, BBC radio series and theatrical tours.

Openly homosexual, Clary's OTT campness is a far cry from the pantomime antics of Mr Humphries in **Are You Being Served?** Rather, his matter-of-fact delivery and genuinely clever verbal contrivances are closer to the music-hall wit of Max Miller or the *Carry On* style of Kenneth Williams. Few others, when offering a plate of biscuits, could imbue such a seemingly innocent line as, 'would you like a fudge finger?' with so much hidden meaning. Clary's early 1990s ad-lib joke about having sex with the then Chancellor of the Exchequer Norman Lamont landed him in hot water, leading to a temporary reduction in his British TV work, but he survived to regain his old standing.

Desperately Seeking Roger

UK · C4 (WONDERDOG PRODUCTIONS) · STANDUP

1 × 60 mins · colour

17 Apr 1992 · Fri 11pm

MAIN CAST

Julian Clary

CREDITS

writer Julian Clary · director John Henderson · producer Toni Yardley

An Easter special in which Clary tramped the mean streets of New York. The show interspersed clips of the comic's American shows with his search for Roger Whittaker, the middle-of-the-road folk singer renowned for his whistling prowess, who had a few hits in the late 1960s and early 1970s. During his quest Clary was aided/hindered by Eartha Kitt, Quentin Crisp, Brooke Shields and the rapper L L Cool J, before finally linking up with Roger.

Note. Clary's first starring TV series was the comedy game-show *Sticky Moments With Julian Clary* (C4, 11 editions, 17 October–31 December 1989), written and conceived by Clary and Paul Merton. The show later went on the road, airing on C4 as *Sticky Moments On Tour With Julian Clary* (C4, 9 editions, 17 October–19 December 1990).

Terry And Julian

UK · C4 (WONDERDOG PRODUCTIONS) · SITCOM

6 × 30 mins · colour

11 Sep–16 Oct 1992 · Fri 10.30pm

MAIN CAST

Julian	Julian Clary
Terry	Lee Simpson
Rene	Kate Lonergan

CREDITS

writers Julian Clary/Paul Merton/John Henderson · director Liddy Oldroyd · executive producer John Henderson · producer Toni Yardley

Another attempt at a post-modern sitcom that ignores 'the fourth wall' and acknowledges the presence of the studio audience and the viewers at home. The fantasy premise is that 'normal' (ie, straight) chap Terry advertises for a lodger and is responded to by 'homeless C4 celebrity' Julian, a 'flamboyant' (ie, gay) personality. Julian immediately disrupts Terry's mundane existence, transforming his Streatham flat into something reminiscent of an 18th-century Turkish boudoir (with the unusual addition of a portrait of Roger Whittaker – see Desperately Seeking Roger, above). Julian also attempts to disrupt Terry's relationship with girlfriend Rene, a manic policewoman.

In Terry And Julian – the title clearly spoofing the BBC's long-running cosy sitcom Terry And June – the Julian character is allowed to stroll among the audience, interacting with them or even choosing one of them to play a character in the ongoing show. The basic plots are really just excuses for Clary to strut his stuff and shock with his outrageous innuendoes and double entendres. And he doesn't disappoint, sprinkling his sex-related one-liners throughout each episode.

Although this wasn't a wholly successful meld of different TV genres – few such hybrids are – Terry And Julian was an intriguing route for Clary to explore. If nothing else, he deserves plaudits for attempting to fit his talents into such a difficult premise.

Brace Yourself Sydney

UK · C4 (WONDERDOG PRODUCTIONS) · STANDUP

1 × 45 mins · colour

28 Dec 1993 · Tue 11.30pm

MAIN CAST

Julian Clary
Warren Mitchell
Danny La Rue

CREDITS

writer Julian Clary · director John Henderson · producer Elaine Morris

Another on-the-road special. This one found Clary in Australia, seeking helpful career advice from a number of celebrities including Warren Mitchell and one of TV's most famous drag artists, Danny La Rue.

Notes. On 1 May 1994, Clary appeared in C4's The Charter 88 Bad Government Awards, a satirical ceremony highlighting the individuals and offices that have done the most to restrict the flow of information to the general public.

Clary's next series, All Rise For Julian Clary, was screened by BBC2, in seven parts from 27 September to 8 November 1996. In this, another hybrid of TV formats, Clary was cast as a judge, with Frank Thornton as his clerk, presiding over the trial of public grievances and domestic disputes, with visiting celebrity guests. A second, six-part series ran on BBC2 from 15 November to 21 December 1997, with a Christmas special screened on 22 December, in which Thornton was replaced by June Whitfield.

Clary also starred in an ITV game-show, In The Dark With Julian Clary, screened on 23 December 1996, in which he invited three couples to compete for a star prize by undertaking challenges in total darkness. The format of this show has been sold to the USA, and at the time of writing Clary was expected to star in the American version too.

A Class By Himself

UK · ITV (HTV) · SITCOM

6 × 30 mins · colour

13 Sep–18 Oct 1972 · Wed 11pm

MAIN CAST

Lord Bleasham	John Le Mesurier
Clutton	Peter Butterworth
Barnaby Locke	Richard Stilgoe

CREDITS

writer Richard Stilgoe · director/producer David Boisseau

On the crest of a wave with his **Dad's Army** role, John Le Mesurier starred in this rare networked sitcom from HTV, the Wales and West of England ITV franchise. He was cast as Lord Bleasham (pronounced Blessem), an eccentric peer living in the family seat (yes … pronounced Blessem 'all) in Somerset, short of money but reluctant to let go of what little he has. Peter Butterworth played the part of his chauffeur Clutton while the author of the series, the former Cambridge Footlighter Richard Stilgoe, very much a rising star at this time, appeared as a young student, Barnaby Locke, full of ideas about how Bleasham could make money. Stilgoe had created the Locke character for a 1971 HTV series (not fully networked) entitled The Thumb Of Barnaby Locke.

Claude Dampier

UK · BBC · STANDUP

3 editions (1 × 10 mins · 1 × 15 mins · 1 × 35 mins) · b/w

21 Nov 1936 · Sat 3.35pm (15 mins)
3 Sep 1937 · Fri 4.25pm (35 mins; re-staged at 9.20pm)
19 July 1939 · Wed 9.30pm (10 mins; re-staged 22 July at 3.50pm)

MAIN CAST

Claude Dampier
Billie Carlyle

CREDITS

producers Harry Pringle (1936), George More O'Farrell (1937), not known (1939)

Billed as 'The Professional Idiot', Claude Dampier was a popular stage and radio comedian whose comedy persona was that of a slow-witted, provincial type. His gimmick, said to have been developed by accident, was to address a fictitious member of the audience whom he called Mrs Gibson.

Dampier was assisted in all of these pre-war television sketches by his wife Billie Carlyle, who performed as his 'straight-woman'.

A Clerical Error

UK · BBC · SITCOM

1 × 25 mins · b/w

5 Apr 1963 · Fri 8.50pm

MAIN CAST

Caleb Bullrush	John Le Mesurier
Police Inspector	Russell Napier
Rita	Yootha Joyce

CREDITS

writers Ray Galton/Alan Simpson · producer Graeme Muir

A Comedy Playhouse one-off from Galton and Simpson, with John Le Mesurier starring as a con-man, recently released from Wormwood Scrubs prison, who dresses up as a clergyman and turns up in a pub collecting for a highly dubious charity.

The script is unrelated to the similarly titled The Clerical Error, televised in the series Dawson's Weekly in 1975 and Paul Merton In Galton & Simpson's … in 1997.

Clicquot Et Fils

UK · BBC · SITCOM

1 × 30 mins · b/w

15 Dec 1961 · Fri 8.45pm

MAIN CAST

Pierre Clicquot	Eric Sykes
Alphonse Lagillarde	Warren Mitchell

CREDITS

writers Ray Galton/Alan Simpson · producer Duncan Wood

The first edition in the BBC's highly successful series of unrelated sitcom half-hours, Comedy Playhouse. Because of Ray Galton and Alan Simpson's success in the field, notably with their work for Tony Hancock, the BBC's then Head of Light

Entertainment, Tom Sloan, invited the pair to write the first two series. Later in the run of *Comedy Playhouse*, when other writers submitted scripts, the format was utilised as a testing ground for pilot episodes of proposed new series, but Galton and Simpson wrote their scripts as one-offs, with possible future development not an issue. As it happened, though, the fourth programme, *The Offer*, became **Steptoe And Son**.

In this opener, set in France in 1926, Eric Sykes played an undertaker, Pierre Clicquot, who, during a quiet period for the profession, hits upon a novel idea to drum up business.

The Climber

UK · BBC · SITCOM

6 × 30 mins · colour

20 Jan–24 Feb 1983 · BBC1 Thu 8.30pm

MAIN CAST

Harry Lumsdon	Robin Nedwell
Ted	David Battley
Shirley	Jacqueline Tong
Reg	David Williams
Mr Thomas	Jack Watson

CREDITS

writer Alex Shearer · *director/producer* Alan J W Bell

Star of the various **Doctor** series, Robin Nedwell took the lead here as a baker, Harry Lumsdon, whose life changes when he takes an IQ test and discovers that he has a 'genius' rating of 165. Aware for the first time that he is a good deal brighter, though perhaps not as practical, as his colleagues, Lumsdon sets about utilising his newly discovered brain power to better himself. Unfortunately, things do not go as smoothly as planned, and although Harry manages to improve his position, becoming a salesman for the company, he finds it difficult to maximise his cerebral potential.

The series, with its obvious message about the nature of intelligence, failed to attract ratings to match Harry's high IQ, and stalled after six episodes.

Clive Dunn

UK · BBC · CHILDREN'S SKETCH

2 × 10 mins · b/w

28 Jan 1954 · Thu 5pm

25 Oct 1957 · Fri 5.35pm

MAIN CAST

Clive Dunn

CREDITS

producers Peter Graham Scott (1954), Peter Newington (1957)

Two short comedy sketches for Clive Dunn. In the first, he introduced younger viewers to a character called Cousin Crumpet, who was having a birthday; the second was billed simply as 'Clive Dunn causes a bit of excitement'.

See also Friday Funny Man.

Clochemerle

UK/WEST GERMANY · BBC/BAVARIA ATELIER · SITCOM

9 × 30 mins · colour

18 Feb–14 Apr 1972 · BBC2 Fri mostly 10.05pm

MAIN CAST

narrator	Peter Ustinov (voice only)
Mayor Barthelemy Piechut	Cyril Cusack
Curé Ponosse	Roy Dotrice
Justine Putet	Wendy Hiller
Schoolmaster Ernest Tafardel	Kenneth Griffith
François Toumignon	Freddie Earlle
Judith Toumignon	Catherine Rouvel
Innkeeper Arthur Torbayon	Barry Linehan
Adèle Torbayon	Cyd Hayman
Nicholas The Beadle	Bernard Bresslaw
Lawyer Hyacinthe Girodot	Wolfe Morris
Madame Girodot	Elspeth MacNaughton
Hortense Girodot	Madeline Smith

CREDITS

creator Gabriel Chevallier · *adapters/writers* Ray Galton/Alan Simpson · *producer* Michael Mills

An audacious and ambitious comedy series co-produced by the BBC and Bavaria Atelier of Munich and shot on location in the rolling hills of Beaujolais country in France. Galton and Simpson adapted the novel by Chevallier, written 40 years earlier, which dealt with the farcical repercussions that followed the erection of a *pissoir*, a gentleman's public convenience, in the very centre of the village of Clochemerle.

Chevallier drew upon a number of different local villages for his inspiration but for the purpose of the TV production a near-ideal location, the village of Marchmampt, was made the centre of proceedings and set-dressed to become the between-the-wars Clochemerle. The location shooting and large international cast playing the colourful inhabitants added to the Gallic atmosphere and the resulting production was a beautifully crafted, high-class slice of sophisticated farce that enjoyed further success when it was repeated by BBC2 in 1991.

Clock On

UK · BBC · CHILDREN'S SKETCH

5 × 20 mins · colour

1 Nov–29 Nov 1982 · BBC1 Mon 4.40pm

MAIN CAST

Su Pollard

Christopher Lillicrap

Tony Maiden

CREDITS

director Sue Lochead · *executive producer* David Brown · *producer* Cyril Gates

A children's comedy series in which viewers were urged to 'Clock on at the Laughter Factory for a jaunty jamboree of jokes and jingles'. The trio of presenters freely admitted that no joke was too corny and no sketch too silly for them to perform. Skits parodied other TV programmes and personalities, and each week a totally unknown person was chosen as guest star.

A Close Shave

see Wallace & Gromit

Close To Home

UK · ITV (LWT) · SITCOM

19 × 30 mins · colour

Series One (9) 1 Oct–26 Nov 1989 · Sun 7.15pm

Series Two (10) 16 Sep–18 Nov 1990 · Sun 7.15pm

MAIN CAST

James Shepherd	Paul Nicholas
Helen DeAngelo	Angharad Rees
Rose	Jane Briers
Kate Shepherd	Lucy Benjamin
Robbie Shepherd	Andrew Read
Frank DeAngelo	Stephen Frost (series 1)
Tom	John Arthur (series 2)
Vicky	Pippa Guard (series 2)
Jenny	Angela Curran (series 2)

CREDITS

creator Brian Cooke · *writers* Brian Cooke (8), Brian Cooke/Ken Steele (1), Paul Minett/Brian Leveson (6), Lucy Flannery (2), Alex Shearer (1), Jack Huffham (1) · *directors* Ian Hamilton (10), Nic Phillips (5), Alistair Clark (4) · *executive producers* Marcus Plantin (series 1), Robin Carr (series 2) · *producers* Nic Phillips (series 1), Ian Hamilton (series 2)

A mediocre ITV sitcom starring Paul Nicholas as James Shepherd, a man juggling with life's responsibilities: he's a vet with his own practice, he's divorced but his remarried ex-wife Helen remains a millstone around his neck – indeed he probably sees more of her now than when they were married – and he also looks after their children Kate (19) and Robbie (14) and runs the family home. As if he doesn't have enough strife, Shepherd's veterinary assistant, Rose (played by Jane Briers, sister of Richard), is a former showgirl who claims to dislike animals. Shepherd cannot even distance himself from his problems because the vet's surgery is attached to the house.

Close To Home was the British adaptation of a dire American sitcom, **Starting From Scratch**, which ran there for 24 episodes in 1988–89 and has also aired in the UK. While hardly a rarity – it ranks among tens of transatlantic sitcom crossovers – this one was unique in that it was created by the British writer Brian Cooke while he was living in the States. Adaptation rights to many of Cooke's previous British creations had been sold to the USA – *Man About The House*, *George And Mildred*, *Robin's Nest*, *Keep It In The Family*, *Tom, Dick And Harriet*, *Tripper's Day*/*Slinger's Day* and *Full House* – but here was one coming back the other way. Cooke duly returned to England from the US to oversee the production of *Close To Home*.

Closing Night

see SYKES, Eric

Club Class

UK · C5/PARAMOUNT COMEDY CHANNEL (INITIAL FILM AND TELEVISION) · STANDUP

13 × 30 mins · colour

4 Apr–27 June 1997 · Fri mostly 11.40pm

MAIN CAST
Richard Blackwood (host)
Jo Martin (sketches)
Yvette Rochester-Duncan (sketches)

CREDITS
writers Michael Buffong, Roger Griffiths, Dave Lawrence, Jo Martin, Josephine Melville and others · *script editor* Paul McKenzie · *director* Phil Chilvers · *executive producer* Malcolm Gerrie · *producer* Beverley Randall

A black-orientated standup show introduced by the comedian Richard Blackwood and featuring weekly guests from both sides of the Atlantic, but mostly British. The standup routines were punctuated with short sketches performed by regulars Jo Martin and Yvette Rochester-Duncan.

All of the resident performers were black but with a commendable spirit of equality some of the guest artists were white. Although unexceptional, the series (made in association with the Paramount Comedy Channel) was as good as any other of its type and gave welcome exposure to a considerable array of new comic talent.

Club Night

UK · BBC · SITCOM

14 × 30 mins · b/w

Series One (8) 9 July–27 Sep 1957 · Wed 7.30pm
Series Two (6) 23 Oct–27 Nov 1957 · Wed 7.30pm

MAIN CAST
Dave Morris · · · · · · · · · · · · · · · · · · · himself
Cedric · · · · · · · · · · · · · · · · · · · Joe Gladwin
The Wacker · · · · · · · · · · · · · · · · · Fred Ferris
'Pongo' Bleasdale · · · · · · · Leonard Williams
'Snuffy' Hargreaves · · · · · · · · · · Frank Bass

CREDITS
writers Dave Morris/Frank Roscoe · *producer* Ronnie Taylor

The TV version of a long-running BBC radio series, set in a fictitious working-men's club 'oop north'. With his trademark cigar, straw hat and glasses, Dave Morris was the somewhat loud-mouthed 'know-all' club treasurer, ably assisted by comedy character actor Joe Gladwin as Cedric, and by Liverpool comedian Fred Ferris as 'The Wacker', whose primary ambition seemed to be to scrounge a drink. But Morris was the star – the quintessential Blackpool comedian, he was a veteran of northern clubs and pubs. Born in Middlesbrough in 1896, he died in 1960.

Notes. On 13 June 1958 the cast returned to TV in a 30-minute extract from a *Club Night* stage-show at the Palace Theatre, Blackpool.

The radio series of the same title was launched in the BBC Home Service's north region on 7 November 1950, where it ran for 52 editions until 6 June 1955. At this point the series attracted a networked Light Programme slot, with a further five editions broadcast nationally from 1 September to 29 September 1955, with ten more from 5 July to 6 September 1956, making 67 radio *Club Night* shows in total.

See also *The Artful Dodger*.

Clueless

USA · ABC THEN UPN (COCKAMAMIE/PARAMOUNT) · SITCOM

28 × 30 mins (to 31/12/97 · continuing into 1998) · colour

US dates: 20 Sep 1996–14 Feb 1997 (ABC); 23 Sep 1997 to date (UPN)
UK dates: 4 Jan–26 Apr 1997 (12 episodes) ITV Sat 5.20pm

MAIN CAST
Cher Horowitz · · · · · · · · · Rachel Blanchard
Dionne ('Dee') · · · · · · · · · · · · · Stacey Dash
Murray · · · · · · · · · · · Donald Adeosun Faison
Sean · · · · · · · · · · · · · · · · · · · Sean Holland
Amber · · · · · · · · · · · · · · · · Elisa Donovan
Mel Horowitz · · · · · · · · · · · · Michael Lerner
Josh · · · · · · · · · · · David Lascher (1996–97)
Miss Geist · · · · · · · Twink Caplan (1996–97)
Mr Hall · · · · · · · · Wallace Shawn (1996–97)

CREDITS
creator Amy Heckerling · *writers* Amy Heckerling, Julie Brown and others · *directors* John Fortenberry, Amy Heckerling and others · *executive producers* Amy Heckerling, Pamela Pettley, Twink Caplan · *producers* Scott Rudin, Adam Schroeder, Robert Lawrence

Based on the 1995 movie of the same name (directed by Amy Heckerling), *Clueless* continued the adventures of the ultra-rich teen brat Cher and her classmates. The feature film – loosely based on Jane Austen's *Emma* – was a cynical satire on the mores and lifestyles of the Beverly Hills pack, and its gusto and freshness earned it numerous awards and unexpectedly good box-office reward. Rising star Alicia Silverstone played the chirpy but vacuous Cher, at the centre of a bunch of fashion-obsessed, micro-skirted, high-heeled, Barbie-perfect teens.

For the TV series – conceived before the movie, but appearing after – Rachel Blanchard (quite a Silverstone lookalike) nabbed the lead role and more than adequately filled Cher's fancy shoes, and her in-thought monologues (often rambling) commented on the plots and provided linking information between scenes. The young supporting cast all acquitted themselves well, giving the veteran members of the cast (Michael Lerner as Cher's father, Mel, and Wallace Shawn as teacher Mr Hall) a run for their money. But despite these good points, the TV series – although emanating from the same stable as the original feature – suffered from a lack of bite. Worse, this edge was replaced by a sweet and sickly sentimentality that, coupled with the often heavy-handed moralising, meant that the series soon began to resemble the very thing the movie had sought to spoof.

Coach

USA · ABC (BUNGALOW 78/UNIVERSAL TELEVISION) · SITCOM

211 episodes (208 × 30 mins · 3 × 60 mins) · colour

US dates: 28 Feb 1989–14 May 1997
UK dates: 23 Sep 1989 to date (109 × 30 mins · 2 × 60 mins to 31/12/97) ITV various days and times · mostly late night

MAIN CAST
Hayden Fox · · · · · · · · · · · · · · Craig T Nelson
Luther Van Dam · · · · · · · · · · · Jerry Van Dyke
Christine Armstrong · · · · · · · Shelley Fabares
Kelly Fox Rosebrock · · · · · · · · · · Clare Carey
· (1989–95)
Michael 'Dauber' Dybinski · · Bill Fagerbakke
Stuart Rosebrock · · · · Kris Kamm (1989–92)
Howard Burleigh · · · · · Kenneth Kimmins
Judy Watkins · · · · · · · · · · · · · · Pam Stone
Doris Sherman · · · · · · · · Katherine Helmond
· (1995–97)
Shirley Burleigh · · · Georgia Engel (1991–97)

CREDITS
creator Barry Kemp · *writers* Kathryn Baker, Warren Bell, Bill Bryan, Sheldon Bull, Sean Clark, Pat Dougherty, Mark Ganzel, Eric Horsted, Barry Kemp, Thad Mumford, Lyla Oliver-Noah, Tom Palmer, John Peaslee, Judd Pillot, Don Rhymer, Jordan Rush, Nell Scovell, Elliot Stern, Miriam Trogdon, Seth A Weisbord and others · *directors* Alan Rafkin, Craig T Nelson and others · *executive producers* Barry Kemp, Sheldon Bull, John Peaslee, Judd Pillot, Craig T Nelson · *producers* Warren Bell, Mark Ganzel, Jay Kleckner, Tom Palmer, Nell Scovell, Craig Wyrick, Joseph Staretski, Oliver Goldstick, Phil Rosenthal, Jeremy Stevens and others

Episodes in the life of Hayden Fox, head coach for the (American) football team at a small midwestern college, the Minnesota State University Screaming Eagles. He's very much a man's man, living in a cabin in the woods and driving around in a truck, but is plagued by life getting in the way of his job. As the first series begins, Fox has scarcely seen his daughter Kelly since becoming divorced 16 years ago, but then she enrols at the same university and he has to polish up his rusty fathering skills. Fox's football team rarely puts together a winning streak, not surprising considering that Luther and Dauber, his coaching assistants, form a duo not dissimilar to Laurel and Hardy in terms of intelligence and guile. Luther (played by Dick Van Dyke's brother, Jerry) has assisted Fox for 22 years; Dauber was once Fox's star player. Looking on the bright side, Fox begins a relationship with Christine Armstrong, not only a beautiful woman but sports commentator for a local TV station.

Despite its somewhat fragile foundation, *Coach* refused to take its leave of American TV for fully eight years. Inevitably, it underwent changes along the way – after dating for six years, and falling out of love as often as they were falling into it, Hayden and Christine were finally married in a November 1992 episode. Kelly also married, to fellow student Stuart Rosebrock – thoroughly disliked by Coach – but then they divorced and she left the series. Fox was eventually granted his own coaching programme on a local TV station. Then, seeking a complete change of scenery, the 1995–96 US TV season saw Hayden, Christine, Luther and Dauber switch location from Minnesota to Florida, where Hayden became the coach of a pro football team, the Orlando Breakers. At this point, Katherine Helmond (Jessica Tate in *Soap*) joined the regular cast as Doris, the team's owner.

Barry Kemp, the executive script consultant on *Taxi* and creator of *Newhart*, was the driving force behind *Coach*, and it was he who, casting against type, placed Craig T Nelson in the starring role of his new sitcom. Previously known for his parts in heavily dramatic movies such as *Poltergeist I* and *II* and *The Killing Fields*, Nelson proved surprisingly adept at comedy, not only starring in excess of 200 *Coach* episodes but also becoming co-executive producer and, occasionally, its director.

Picked up for British TV by ITV, *Coach* remains the subject of an erratic screening schedule in the UK. Some regions have never shown it; LWT, in London, had aired (to the end of 1997) 111 episodes and 36 repeats – but, still, few Londoners will have seen it since it tends to be broadcast deep into the night, sometimes not starting until 5am.

The Coal Hole Club

UK · BBC · CHILDREN'S SKETCH/STANDUP

13 × 25 mins · colour

Series One (7) 27 Apr–8 June 1973 · BBC1 Fri 4.50pm

Series Two (6) *Grumbleweeds* 20 Feb–27 Mar 1974 · BBC1 Wed 5.15pm

MAIN CAST
The Grumbleweeds (Robin Colville, Maurice Lee, Albert Sutcliffe, Carl Sutcliffe, Graham Walker)

CREDITS
writer Garry Chambers · *producer* Tony Harrison

Fun for younger viewers, with comedy/ impressionist group the Grumbleweeds inviting them to the Coal Hole Club for a 'fast moving party with songs, jokes and impressions'. Different guests appeared each week, including Freddie 'Parrot Face' Davies, Stan Stennett, Stanley Unwin and Ken Goodwin (twice). The second series was called simply *Grumbleweeds* but the format was identical and the Coal Hole Club still thrived.

See also *The Grumbleweeds Radio Show*.

The Cobblers Of Umbridge

UK · BBC · SITCOM

1 × 25 mins · colour

17 May 1983 · BBC2 Tue 7.30pm

MAIN CAST
John Fortune
John Wells
Roy Kinnear
Lance Percival
William Rushton
Joan Sims
Derek Griffiths

CREDITS
writers John Fortune/John Wells · *directors* Ned Sherrin, Ian Wilson · *producers* Ned Sherrin, Terry Glinwood

The BBC's daily radio drama serial *The Archers* (1951 to date) has long been an easy target for pastiche, the best example being 'The Bowmans', an episode of *Hancock*, screened by the BBC on 2 June 1961.

In this 1983 BBC2 spoof – its title lampooning Ambridge, the fictional 'Borsetshire' village where the radio serial is set – various luminaries from *That Was The Week That Was*, including producer Ned Sherrin, joined forces with other comedic talent to poke gentle fun.

Cockles

UK · BBC · SITCOM/DRAMA

6 × 55 mins · colour

4 Jan–8 Feb 1984 · BBC1 Wed 8.05pm

MAIN CAST
Arthur Dumpton · · · · · · · · · · · · James Grout
Jacques du Bois · · · · · · · · · Norman Rodway
Gloria du Bois · · · · · · · · · · · · · · Joan Sims
Emma · · · · · · · · · · · · · · Elizabeth Edmonds
Madame Rosa · · · · · · · · · · · · · Fanny Carby
Mabel Gutteridge · · · · · · · · · · · · Jane Lowe

CREDITS
writer Douglas Livingstone · *director* Barry Davis · *producer* Ruth Boswell

Seaside shenanigans set in the fictional coastal resort of Cocklesea, a faded holiday destination of yesteryear. As a child, Arthur Dumpton spent many happy holidays there. Now, years later, he returns, fat with redundancy money, to restore the resort to what he remembers as its former glory. Dumpton seeks out his old friend Jacques du Bois, now an unsuccessful landscape painter married to Gloria, Arthur's boyhood sweet-heart, the landlady of the Sunnysides Guest House. He tries to enlist their support for his grandiose schemes but, although fond of him, they – in common with most of the residents of Cocklesea – are greedy and duplicitous. The result is that amiable but gullible Arthur finds himself fleeced by friends and strangers alike.

Cockles was a neat idea graced with strong acting talent, especially the underrated James Grout, who seems incapable of a poor performance. Writer Douglas Livingstone developed the characters of Arthur and Gloria from *Born And Bred*, which had featured Grout as a similarly good-natured salesman and Sims as a similarly strident pub owner.

The Cold Old Days

see The Montreux Festival

Colin's Sandwich

UK · BBC · SITCOM

12 × 30 mins · colour

Series One (6) 18 Oct–22 Nov 1988 · BBC2 Tue 9pm

Series Two (6) 12 Jan–16 Feb 1990 · BBC2 Fri 9pm

MAIN CAST
Colin Watkins · · · · · · · · · · · · · · Mel Smith
Jenny · Louise Rix
Des · Mike Grady

CREDITS
writers Paul Smith/Terry Kyan · *director* John Kilby · *producers* John Kilby/Jamie Rix

Paul Smith and Terry Kyan, part of the *Alias Smith And Jones* writing team, created this series as a vehicle for Mel Smith. He was cast as Colin Watkins, a British Rail office worker with ambitions to become a professional writer. Colin's chosen literary field was horror, and he dreamed of becoming the next Stephen King. His smart and together girlfriend Jenny tried to humour him in his quest, as did his sympathetic friend Des, but bad luck seemed to conspire to ensure that Colin never quite grabbed his slice of fame. However, unusually for a sitcom with aspirant dreams at its core, Colin did make some headway, having a short story published and being commissioned to write a film treatment.

Colin's Sandwich was a wordy, thoughtful piece, with Smith – very much at the centre – often delivering rambling monologues as, while trying to write, Colin talked to himself. Watkins' overall glumness, all-thumbs clumsiness and shortage of social skills was reminiscent of Tony Hancock's stage persona; indeed, Smith likened the writing to Galton and Simpson's work for **Hancock's Half Hour**. This statement worked against the series, tempting critics to compare it with that 1950s TV classic, against which very few shows could possibly look good. Nevertheless, *Colin's Sandwich* developed well enough and extended to a second set of episodes, of equal quality.

Collages '65

see The Montreux Festival

Colonel Trumper's Private War

UK · ITV (GRANADA) · SITCOM

6 × 30 mins
15 Sep–20 Oct 1961 · Fri 8.55pm

MAIN CAST

Col Basil Trumper	Dennis Price
Prof Pan Malcov	Warren Mitchell
Hicks	George Tovey
Lt Hasting	William Gaunt

CREDITS

writers Barry Took/Hugh Woodhouse/Bill Craig/Dick Vosburgh · *script editors* Barry Took/Bill Craig · *directors* Stuart Latham (5), Graeme McDonald (1) · *producer* Peter Eton

It is June 1940 and Colonel Trumper of British counter-intelligence – described as a man 'with the mind of a criminal and the morals of a Borgia' – is ordered to go undercover and venture out to rescue a Polish professor, Pan Malcov, with whom he and his secret army will win the war for Britain.

This was a single-series sitcom made by Granada and broadcast in the Friday evening slot vacated by **Bootsie And Snudge**. Producer Peter Eton and writer Barry Took worked on both series.

Come Back Mrs Noah

UK · BBC · SITCOM

6 × 30 mins · colour
Pilot · 13 Dec 1977 · BBC1 Tue 8pm
One series (5) 17 July–14 Aug 1978 · BBC1 Mon around 6.50pm

MAIN CAST

Gertrude Noah	Mollie Sugden
Clive Cunliffe	Ian Lavender
Carstairs	Donald Hewlett
Fanshaw	Michael Knowles
TV presenter	Gorden Kaye
Garfield Hawk	Tim Barrett
Scarth Dare	Ann Michelle
Technician	Jennifer Lonsdale

CREDITS

writers Jeremy Lloyd/David Croft · *director* Bob Spiers · *producer* David Croft

A sci-fi sitcom featuring many of the actors who had appeared, or would later appear, in other productions from the Jeremy Lloyd/Jimmy Perry/David Croft theatre of comedy, including Mollie Sugden (**Are You Being Served?**), Ian Lavender (**Dad's Army**), Donald Hewlett and Michael Knowles (whose characters were based on their **It Ain't Half Hot Mum** personae) and Gorden Kaye ('**Allo 'Allo!**).

Like *Dad's Army* and *It Ain't Half Hot Mum*, *Come Back Mrs Noah* was another period piece, but this time that period was the future: the year 2050. Mollie Sugden played a housewife, Mrs Noah, whose prize, as the winner of a cookery competition, is to be shown around Britain's new Space Exploration Vehicle, the space station Britannia Seven. In the pilot episode, a series of mishaps result in the craft accidentally blasting off, with Mrs Noah and the station's skeleton crew catapulted into outer space. The full series followed the attempts to bring Mrs Noah and the errant craft back down to Earth.

Not without good reason, *Come Back Mrs Noah* has been cited in some quarters as one of the worst British sitcoms of all time, but there were some funny lines, especially in the Earth news bulletins (read by Gorden Kaye) which reported on a future where Britain's North Sea oil revenues had re-established it as the most prosperous and successful nation on the planet, with once powerful economies like Germany and the USA struggling to survive and turning to the UK for assistance. But, overall, the series fared pretty badly, failing to take off with an audience who found the quantum leap of fantasy required to accept Mollie Sugden as an astronaut light-years beyond their capabilities.

Come Dancing With Jools Holland

UK · C4 (TYNE TEES) · STANDUP/SKETCH

1 × 105 mins · colour
31 Dec 1986 · Wed 10.45pm

MAIN CAST
Rik Mayall
Nigel Planer
Adrian Edmondson
Peter Richardson
Ruby Wax
Raw Sex (Rowland Rivron and Simon Brint)
Rory McGrath
Jimmy Mulville
Philip Pope
Tony Robinson
Julia Hills

CREDITS

writers cast · *producer* Peter McHugh · *director/executive producer* Royston Mayoh

A year-straddling C4 show well populated by comedy stars, including three of **The Young Ones** and the entire **Who Dares, Wins** combo.

The Comedians

UK · ITV (GRANADA) · STANDUP

81 editions (78 × 30 mins · 1 × 45 mins · 2 × 60 mins) · colour

Series One (7 × 30 mins) 12 June–24 July 1971 · Sat mostly 7pm

Series Two (7 × 30 mins) 18 Sep–30 Oct 1971 · Sat 6pm

Special (45 mins) *The Comedians Christmas Party* 24 Dec 1971 · Fri 7pm

*Series Three (7 × 30 mins) 18 Feb–1 Apr 1972 · mostly Sat 6.05pm

*Series Four (7 × 30 mins) 14 July–2 Sep 1972 · mostly Fri 7pm

*Series Five (7 × 30 mins) 17 Nov–29 Dec 1972 · mostly Fri 8.30pm

*Series Six (8 × 30 mins) 7 Apr–2 June 1973 · Sat mostly 8.25pm

Special (60 mins) *Christmas Comedians Music Hall* 22 Dec 1973 · Sat 9pm

Series Seven (7 × 30 mins) 26 Jan–16 Mar 1974 · Sat mostly around 7.50pm

Series Eight (13 × 30 mins) 22 July–5 Aug 1979; 23 Nov 1979–15 Feb 1980 · mostly Fri 9.30pm

Series Nine (3 × 30 mins) 2 June –16 June 1984 · Sat 7pm

Series Ten (7 × 30 mins) 1 June–13 July 1985 · Sat mostly 7pm

Series Eleven (5 × 30 mins) 9 July–23 July 1992 · mostly Tue 8.30pm

Special (60 mins) *The Comedians Christmas Cracker* 28 Dec 1993 · Tue 10.45pm

MAIN CAST

1972–74 EDITIONS
Russ Abbot, Lennie Bennett, Jim Bowen, Alan Brady, Duggie Brown, Mike Burton, Dave Butler, Kenny Cantor, Jackie Carlton, Frank Carson, Paddy Cassidy, Mike Coyne, Colin Crompton, Steve Faye, Ray Fell, Eddie Flanagan, Stu Francis, Syd Francis, Alan Fox, Mike Goddard, Ken Goodwin, Jackie Hamilton, Jerry Harris, Dennis Jones, Bobby Knoxall, Bernard Manning, Jimmy Marshall, Paul Melba, Pat Mooney, Johnny More, Hector Nicol, Tom O'Connor, Bryn Phillips, Colin Price, Mike Reid, George Roper, Tony Stewart, Sammy Thomas, Johnny 'Goon' Tweed, Johnny Wager, Jos White, Charlie Williams, Stu Williams

1979–80 EDITIONS
Stan Boardman, Jim Bowen, Johnny Carroll, Frank Carson, Bob Curtiss, Ivor Davies, Charlie Daze, Vince Earl, Ken Goodwin, Bobby Kaye, Mike Kelly, George King, Bernard Manning, Mick Miller, Hal Nolan, Mike Reid, George Roper, Harry Scott, Paul Shane, Kenny Smiles, Paul Squire, Pat Tansey, Roy Walker, Lee Wilson, Lenny Windsor

1984–85 EDITIONS
Harry Black, Pauline Daniels, Tony Jo, Greg Rogers, Ollie Spencer

1992–93 EDITIONS
Jimmy Bright, Johnnie Casson, Eddie Colinton, Les Dennis, Pauline Daniels, Tom Pepper, Don Reid

CREDITS
writers various · *directors* Wally Butler (series 1–5), Baz Taylor (special 1), Peter Walker (series 6), David Warwick (special 2 & series 7–10), Ian Hamilton (series 11), Jonathan Glazier (special 3) · *producers* Johnny Hamp (series 1–10, specials 1 & 2), Ian Hamilton (series 11), Jane Macnaught (special 3)

Remarkably popular during its earlier series, *The Comedians* was standup humour plain and simple. Recruited from the hard-drinking northern night-clubs that were their staple environment, Granada put the North's best 'unknown' comics into the studio – even though some had been working for 20 years many were appearing on TV for the first time – taped their (expletives-deleted) acts and edited the material into non-stop barrages of cracks and quips to slay the audiences at home, packing up to 50 jokes into each half-hour show. True, many of the lines were so old that they creaked, and there was a fair dose of racist, sexist and physical-defect material that was only just acceptable then and would not be so today, but mostly the jokes were of the three-men-in-a-bar, Irishman and mother-in-law variety. Viewers took to the series with enthusiasm and from those first few golden series many stars were born, among them Frank Carson (a bluff Irishman), Colin Crompton (a weedy northerner), Ken Goodwin (a stutterer), Charlie Williams (a black Yorkshireman), Bernard Manning (a portly clubman), Tom O'Connor (the boy next door), Jim Bowen (a stone-faced ex-deputy headmaster), Lennie Bennett (a giggler) and Mike Reid (a cockney), all of whom found their nightly fees skyrocketing from around £50 to £1000 or more. So popular was the series at this time that in the summer of 1972 *The Comedians* became a stage-show, mounted in Blackpool, Great Yarmouth and London, and a record album made the lower reaches of the chart.

The series was created by Granada's light entertainment producer Johnny Hamp, whose father had been a magician playing music-halls as the Great Hamp, and it was directed by Wally Butler, whose parents had both worked the stage. Being steeped in the tradition of old-fashioned stage entertainment, both knew exactly where to find the best local talent, and had the stamina not only to last the exhausting three-hour recording sessions, where each comedian would perform a standup spot of around 15 to 20 minutes, but also to edit the resulting tape into finished programmes, the only relief from humour

coming courtesy of musical interludes provided by the plucky Shep's Banjo Boys. In 1974, on the back of its major success with *The Comedians*, Granada launched a northern club variety show, *The Wheeltappers And Shunters Social Club* (46 editions, 13 April 1974 to 2 July 1977), which featured many of the same comics.

Although *The Comedians* was still turning up fresh TV talent (Russ Abbot was among the cast in 1974), audiences at home grew tired of the formula after three years and the series appeared to come to an end after some 50 editions. Three separate revivals then followed and although none matched the success of the earlier shows some new stars were unearthed, among them Stan Boardman and Roy Walker – indeed, perhaps the best epitaph for *The Comedians* is that it spawned more TV game-show hosts than any other series before or since.

*Notes. These dates reflect London-area screenings. In Granada's own North-West region series three began on 19 February 1972, series four spanned 7 July to 18 August 1972, series five began on 10 November and series six ran from 6 April to 25 May 1973.

Having gained much mileage from showing 1970s editions of *The Comedians*, the cable/satellite channel Granada Sky Broadcasting commissioned a revival of the format, with a raft of new shows titled *The New Comedians* being screened from December 1997, independently made by Andrew McLaughlin Associates. As before, the performers were drawn from the northern club circuit, and were unfamiliar to TV viewers.

Comedians Do It On Stage

UK · C4 (CELADOR PRODUCTIONS) · STANDUP/SKETCH

1 × 85 mins · colour

23 Dec 1986 · Tue 11.15pm

MAIN CAST
Dawn French
Jennifer Saunders
Gareth Hale
Norman Pace
Neil Innes
Terry Jones
Rory McGrath
Jimmy Mulville
Michael Palin
Mel Smith
Griff Rhys Jones
Richard Stilgoe
Victoria Wood
Rob Buckman
Chris Langham

CREDITS
writers cast · *director* David Macmahon · *producer* Paul Smith

The TV recording of a charity concert in aid of doctor/TV presenter/comic Rob Buckman's Oncology Club Fund, raising money to train cancer treatment specialists.

Comedy Bandbox

UK · ITV (ABC) · STANDUP/SKETCH

55 editions (24 × 55 mins · 16 × 50 mins · 14 × 40 mins · 1 × 35 mins) · b/w

Series One (10 × 55 mins) 1 Dec 1962–9 Feb 1963 · Sat 6.30pm

Series Two (13 × 40 mins · 2 × 50 mins · 1 × 35 mins) 28 Sep 1963–11 Jan 1964 · Sat 6.35pm

Special (40 mins) *Holiday Bandbox* 16 May 1964 · Sat 6.35pm

Special (50 mins) *Holiday Bandbox* 27 June 1964 · Sat 6.35pm

Series Three (14 × 55 mins) 10 Oct 1964–16 Jan 1965 · Sat 6.35pm Series Four (13 × 50 mins) *David Nixon's Comedy Bandbox* 1 Jan–27 Mar 1966 · Sat 6.35pm then Sun 4.40pm

MAIN CAST
hosts · · · Mike Hope/Albie Keen (special 1);
· · · · · · David Nixon (special 2, series 3 & 4)

and see below

CREDITS
linking writers Gerry Maxin (1 ed of series 2), John Warren/John Singer (special 1), Austin Steele (special 2 & series 3) · *directors* Ronnie Baxter (24 & special 1), David Main (7 eds of series 1), Ronnie Taylor (3 eds of series 1), Pat Johns (special 2 & 3 eds of series 3), Milo Lewis (3 eds of series 4) · *producers* Peter Dulay (series 1, 11 eds of series 2, specials, series 4), Ernest Maxin (2 eds of series 2), Mark Stuart (11 eds of series 3)

An important series in its day, *Comedy Bandbox* gave a platform to aspiring humorists, and scores of successfully established ones, working in Britain in the early 1960s. In so doing, it gave primary TV exposure to several major artists of the future. (Because of its northern bias it was never screened in London, not even after its proven successes. But although this puts *Comedy Bandbox* beyond this book's stated parameters, the series is simply too significant in British TV comedy history to be omitted.)

As pop music had its *Thank Your Lucky Stars*, so humour had its *Comedy Bandbox*. Both were cut of the same cloth: ABC series, screened early on Saturday evenings, featuring around a half-dozen acts each week, with a clear hierarchy from top-of-the-bill downwards. The Beatles made their national TV debut on *Lucky Stars*; Les Dawson (on the same date, 19 January 1963), Dave Allen (9 February 1963), Jimmy Tarbuck (19 October 1963) and Mike Yarwood (21 December 1963) all did so on *Bandbox*. The fast and boisterous series also gave good exposure to up-and-coming acts such as, in the 1962–63 series, Mike and Bernie Winters and Dick Emery, while other performers and bill-toppers over the full run included Jewel and Warriss, Jimmy Clitheroe, Stubby Kaye, Ted Ray, Arthur Askey, Terry Scott and Hugh Lloyd, Frankie Howerd, Max Wall, Alfred Marks, Hylda Baker, Tommy Trinder, Jimmy James, Des O'Connor, Bob Monkhouse, Charlie Chester, Sid James, Sandy Powell, Richard Hearne and Norman Vaughan. Such impressive roll calls were not enough to ensure the programmes' preservation, however: it is thought that no editions of *Comedy Bandbox* survive today.

From the second of the two 1964 holiday specials onwards, *Comedy Bandbox* was hosted by David Nixon, the likeable and witty magician much seen on British TV in the 1960s and 1970s, and indeed the final series, in 1966, was retitled *David Nixon's Comedy Bandbox*.

Comedy Cabaret

UK · BBC · STANDUP

4 × 30 mins · b/w

18 Jan 1938 · Tue 9.30pm
22 Jan 1938 · Sat 3.30pm
28 Feb 1938 · Mon 9pm
5 Mar 1938 · Sat 3pm

MAIN CAST
Arthur Prince (shows 1 & 2)
Molly Fisher (shows 1 & 2)
Charles Heslop (shows 3 & 4)
George Robey (shows 3 & 4)

CREDITS
producer Harry Pringle

An irregular slot affording short presentations of a number of comedy acts. The second show was a re-staging of the first with a slightly different cast; the fourth was a re-staging of the third with an identical line-up.

Comedy Capers

UK · BBC · STANDUP/SKETCH

1 × 30 mins · b/w

8 Mar 1948 · Mon 3pm

MAIN CAST
George Gee
Tommy Cooper
Georgie Wood

CREDITS
producer Richard Afton

An early TV appearance for Tommy Cooper in this half-hour comedy show that blended standup material with a domestic sketch featuring Georgie Wood. The show was re-staged later the same week, on 10 March.

Comedy Central – Special Delivery

USA · COMEDY CENTRAL (COMEDY PARTNERS) · SKETCH/STANDUP

60 mins · colour

US dates: (see below)
UK dates: 5 July–20 Dec 1996 (26 editions) ITV Fri mostly 12.40am

MAIN CAST
various (see below)

PACKAGE CREDITS
executive producer Nick Symons · *producer* Josh Lebowitz

A US series that, as such, has never aired in its native country, although its constituent parts have. To Americans, Comedy Central is a TV channel, not a programme. Priding itself 'The laughing stock of cable', CC launched in April 1991 upon the merger of two existing stations, HA! and The Comedy Channel. A good deal of Comedy Central's programming is non-original – it screens sitcoms in re-run and imports series from abroad. (In 1996, for example, it was showing the BBC's *Absolutely Fabulous* and *Keeping Up Appearances*.) In terms of original programming, Comedy Central's output is distinctly contemporary, and in 1996 the channel packaged together hour-length programmes featuring such material, in all its diversity, and sold it to British ITV.

Thus, viewers of *Comedy Central – Special Delivery* never quite knew what they were in for. There might be some extended sketches from the series written and performed by the comedy team Exit 57 (comprising Stephen Colbert, Paul Dinello, Jodi Lennon, Mitch Rouse and Amy Sedaris). This might be followed by Jonathan Katz's adult *Simpsons*-style animation *Dr Katz: Professional Therapist*, in which the doctor – who has plenty of problems himself – offers analysis to visiting (animated) real-life standup comedians. (These programmes, standing alone, have also been visible in the UK on the cable/satellite Paramount Comedy Channel.) There might be extended extracts from *The A-List*, hosted by Richard Lewis, and *Politically Incorrect*, a humorous political/topical TV debate, in which the host – the American standup comic Bill Maher (pronounced Marr) – leads conversations with four real guests from the worlds of entertainment, education or politics, before an enthusiastic studio audience. Or there might be a few minutes from Comedy Central's *2 Drink Minimum*, a comedy-club standup show with several performers in each edition.

The packaged shows even include between-programmes spots and other miscellaneous Comedy Central trailers of the kind that one would probably 'mute' if watching the station in the USA. But these and a good deal of the other American-centred material on offer lose much of their meaning as they journey across the Atlantic, much in the way that, for example, the British-slanted *Have I Got News For You* would leave American viewers nonplussed.

Comedy Club

UK · ITV (LWT) · STANDUP

10 × 30 mins · colour

5 Feb–9 Apr 1994 · Sat around midnight

MAIN CAST
various (see below)

CREDITS
writers cast · *directors* Ian Hamilton/Steven Wood · *producer* Rosemary McGowan

Late-night blasts of standup humour from the West End of London, showcasing the latest talent on the comedy-club circuit. The host each week was Jeff Green and among those seen in the series were Caroline Aherne, Alexander Armstrong and Ben Miller, Simon Bligh, Alan Davies, Felix Dexter, Tony Hawks, Hattie Hayridge, Mark Hurst, Mickey Hutton, Phill Jupitus, Phil Kay, Matt Lucas, Fred MacAulay, Alistair McGowan, Donna McPhail, Sean Meo, Bob Mills, John Moloney, Richard Morton, Andy Parsons and Henry Naylor, Parrot, the Rubber Bishops, Linda Smith, Mark Steel, Tim Vine and David Wolstencroft.

Comedy Corner

UK · BBC · CHILDREN'S STANDUP

2 editions (1 × 10 mins · 1 × 15 mins) · b/w

16 Mar 1952 · Sun 5.15pm
14 Aug 1952 · Thu 5.25pm

MAIN CAST
Harry Locke

CREDITS
producer Walton Anderson

A pair of comedy shorts, screened in the BBC's *Children's Television* slot, with film actor Harry Locke in the starring role.

The Comedy Crowd

UK · ITV (THAMES) · IMPRESSIONISM/SKETCH

1 × 30 mins · colour

5 Apr 1988 · Tue 6.30pm

MAIN CAST
Allan Stewart
Aiden J Harvey
Tony Slattery
Martin Connor
Sherrie Hewson

CREDITS
writers Bryan Blackburn, Peter Corey, Richard Eadie, Phil Haynes, Russel Lane, Gerald Mahlowe, Trevor McCallum, Paul Minett/Brian Leveson, Peter Vincent · *script consultant* Ian Davidson · *script editor* Bryan Blackburn · *director/producer* David Bell

A one-off barrage of skits, send-ups and impersonations for Easter, led by Allan Stewart and Aiden J Harvey from the LWT series *Copy Cats*.

Comedy Firsts

UK · ITV (VARIOUS) · SITCOMS (5), SKETCH (1)

6 × 30 mins · colour

Two years after its *Comedy Playhouse* series of eight one-off sitcom pilots ITV launched *Comedy Firsts* – different title, same idea – throwing half a dozen new comedies at viewers to see which might stick. One of the six, *Now What*, was a sketch show, the others, in line with tradition, were sitcoms.

These are the pilot titles with first broadcast dates. The title preceded by an asterisk graduated to its own series. See individual entries for further details.

10 July 1995	Barbara
17 July 1995	*Sometime, Never
24 July 1995	Sardines
31 July 1995	Waiting
7 Aug 1995	The Smiths
14 Aug 1995	Now What

Comedy Four

UK · ITV (GRANADA) · SITCOMS

4 × 30 mins · b/w

Four individual comedy playlets linked by the wide-ranging theme of 'the struggle of some people to keep up with the Sixties' (and this was only 1963 …).

For details see entries for:

6 June 1963	Tea At The Ritz
13 June 1963	Fit For Heroes
20 June 1963	Scoop
27 June 1963	Home From Home

Note. Originally planned for the series, *Tin Pan Alice* was postponed and aired independently some months later.

The Comedy Network

UK · C5 (AVALON TELEVISION) · STANDUP

8 × 30 mins · colour

3 Nov–22 Dec 1997 · Mon 10pm

MAIN CAST

host · · · · · · · · · · · · · · · · · Boothby Graffoe
Jenny Eclair
Jim Tavaré
Stewart Lee

CREDITS

writers various · *director* Peter Orton · *executive producers* Jon Thoday, Richard Allen-Turner · *producer* James Bobin

Yet another in the long line of late-1990s standup shows. This one was hosted by Boothby Graffoe and featured regular performances from Eclair, Tavaré and Lee, with weekly guests. The host started off proceedings with a short routine and then, in various locations on film, linked the other acts who performed in the studio.

The guest performers were Sean Lock (4 appearances), Ed Byrne (3), Julian Barratt (3), Jason Freeman (3), Adam Bloom (3), Junior Simpson (2), Dave Gorman (2), Neil Bromley (1) and Chris Addison (1).

Comedy Playhouse
BBC

UK · BBC · SITCOMS

120 × circa 30 mins (77 × b/w, 43 × colour)

A famous, long-running strand in which the BBC aired half-hour comedy sitcoms, many of which were pilot try-outs for projected series. (A remarkable 28 series were spawned in this way.) The first two batches of *Comedy Playhouse* were written solely by top comedy writing team Ray Galton and Alan Simpson, but subsequent series were penned by a variety of writers.

The following details the individual programme titles and broadcast dates. The first three series aired on the BBC's only TV channel at that time; subsequently, they were screened by BBC1. Titles preceded by an asterisk graduated to their own series. In *all* instances see separate entries for further details.

Series One (b/w)

15 Dec 1961	Clicquot Et Fils
22 Dec 1961	Lunch In The Park
29 Dec 1961	The Private Lives Of Edward Whiteley
5 Jan 1962	*The Offer (see *Steptoe And Son*)
12 Jan 1962	The Reunion
19 Jan 1962	The Telephone Call
26 Jan 1962	The Status Symbol
2 Feb 1962	Visiting Day
9 Feb 1962	Sealed With A Loving Kiss
16 Feb 1962	The Channel Swimmer

Series Two (b/w)

1 Mar 1963	Our Man In Moscow
8 Mar 1963	And Here, All The Way From …
15 Mar 1963	Impasse
29 Mar 1963	Have You Read This Notice?
5 Apr 1963	A Clerical Error
12 Apr 1963	The Handyman

Series Three (b/w)

28 Sep 1963	On The Knocker
5 Oct 1963	Underworld Knights
12 Oct 1963	Fools Rush In
19 Oct 1963	Shamrot
26 Oct 1963	The Bachelor Girls
2 Nov 1963	The Plan
9 Nov 1963	A Picture Of Innocence
16 Nov 1963	Nicked At The Bottle
23 Nov 1963	The Chars
30 Nov 1963	Comrades In Arms
14 Dec 1963	*The Walrus And The Carpenter
28 Dec 1963	*The Bed (see *Meet The Wife*)
3 Jan 1964	The Mate Market
10 Jan 1964	The Hen House
17 Jan 1964	The Siege Of Sydney's Street
24 Jan 1964	The Mascot
31 Jan 1964	Good Luck Sir, You've Got A Lucky Face

Series Four (b/w)

28 May 1965	Barnaby Spoot And The Exploding Whoopee Cushion
4 June 1965	Mother Came Too
11 June 1965	Here I Come Whoever I Am
18 June 1965	Happy Family
2 July 1965	Memoirs Of A Chaise Longue
8 July 1965	Murray And Me
15 July 1965	*Hudd
22 July 1965	*Till Death Us Do Part
29 July 1965	The Time And Motion Man
5 Aug 1965	Sam The Samaritan
12 Aug 1965	*The Vital Spark (see *Para Handy*)
19 Aug 1965	Betsy Mae

Series Five (b/w)

17 May 1966	*The Bishop Rides Again (see *All Gas And Gaiters*)
24 May 1966	*Beggar My Neighbour
31 May 1966	A Little Learning
7 June 1966	Judgement Day For Elijah Jones
14 June 1966	*Room At The Bottom · [BBC]
21 June 1966	The End Of The Tunnel
28 June 1966	Seven Year Hitch
5 July 1966	*The Mallard Imaginaire (see *The Whitehall Worrier*)
2 Aug 1966	*The Reluctant Romeo

Series Six (b/w)

19 May 1967	Hughie
26 May 1967	*House In A Tree (see *Not In Front Of The Children*)
2 June 1967	Spanner In The Works
9 June 1967	Heirs On A Shoestring
16 June 1967	Uncle Fred Flits By
23 June 1967	Loitering With Intent
29 June 1967	To Lucifer – A Son
30 June 1967	*The Old Campaigner

Series Seven (b/w)

26 Apr 1968	State Of The Union
3 May 1968	*View By Appointment (see *Wink To Me Only*)
10 May 1968	The Family Of Fred
17 May 1968	Stiff Upper Lip
24 May 1968	*Wild, Wild Women
31 May 1968	Thank You Sir, Thank You Madam (see footnote)
7 June 1968	*B-And-B
14 June 1968	*Me Mammy
28 June 1968	The Gold Watch Club

Series Eight (b/w)

14 Apr 1969	*The Liver Birds
21 Apr 1969	The Valley Express
28 Apr 1969	Tooth And Claw
5 May 1969	*As Good Cooks Go
12 May 1969	The Loves Of Larch Hill
19 May 1969	The Making Of Peregrine

Series Nine (colour)

18 Dec 1969	Joint Account
1 Jan 1970	The Jugg Brothers

8 Jan 1970	An Officer And A Gentleman
15 Jan 1970	Who's Your Friend?

Series Ten (colour)

11 Mar 1970	Keep 'Em Rolling
18 Mar 1970	Better Than A Man
25 Mar 1970	*Last Tribute (see *That's Your Funeral*)
1 Apr 1970	Haven Of Rest

Series Eleven (colour)

8 July 1970	Mind Your Own Business
15 July 1970	The Old Contemptible
29 July 1970	Don't Ring Us … We'll Ring You
5 Aug 1970	Meter Maids

Special (colour)

8 Jan 1971	*Under And Over

Series Twelve (colour)

1 Apr 1971	*Just Harry And Me (see *Now Take My Wife*)
8 Apr 1971	Uncle Tulip
15 Apr 1971	*It's Awfully Bad For Your Eyes, Darling …
22 Apr 1971	The Rough With The Smooth
29 Apr 1971	Equal Partners
6 May 1971	The Importance Of Being Hairy

Series Thirteen (colour)

14 Jan 1972	Idle At Work
21 Jan 1972	And Whose Side Are You On?
28 Jan 1972	Born Every Minute

Special (colour)

27 Mar 1972	The Dirtiest Soldier In The World

Specials (colour)

7 Sep 1972	Weren't You Marcia Honeywell?
8 Sep 1972	*Are You Being Served?

Series Fourteen (colour)

4 Jan 1973	*Last Of The Summer Wine
11 Jan 1973	The Rescue
18 Jan 1973	Elementary, My Dear Watson
25 Jan 1973	The Birthday (see *The Gordon Peters Show*)
1 Feb 1973	Marry The Girls
8 Feb 1973	Home From Home

Series Fifteen (colour)

16 Apr 1974	*No Strings [BBC]
23 Apr 1974	Franklyn And Johnnie
30 Apr 1974	Howerd's History Of England
7 May 1974	*Happy Ever After
14 May 1974	The Dobson Doughnut
21 May 1974	*The Big Job (see *Mr Big*)
28 May 1974	It's Only Me Whoever I Am
4 June 1974	The Last Man On Earth
11 June 1974	Sitting Pretty
25 June 1974	Pygmalion Smith
3 July 1974	A Girl's Best Friend
9 July 1974	The Reverent Wooing Of Archibald

Notes. *Thank You Sir, Thank You Madam* (31 May 1968) replaced the advertised episode, *Current Affairs*, which was purportedly about the staff at an electrical power station. Written by George Wadmore and Pat Dunlop, and set to feature Harold Goodwin and Arthur White, *Current Affairs* never aired.

Individual pilot episodes for *Up Pompeii!* (17 September 1969) and *It Ain't Half Hot Mum* (3 January 1974) aired during the above time-frame but *not* under the *Comedy Playhouse* banner.

An individual comedy playlet, *No Peace On The Western Front* (30 August 1972), was presented under the *Comedy Special* banner, not *Comedy Playhouse*.

Weren't You Marcia Honeywell? (7 September 1972) and *Are You Being Served?* (8 September 1972) were unscheduled broadcasts, transmitted in BBC1 slots originally intended for Olympic Games coverage but vacated following the Games' suspension after the terrorist massacre of Israeli athletes.

In 1970 BBC1 aired six comedy episodes in Scotland only, under the title *Scottish Comedy Playhouse*. Although beyond the parameters of this book, these are brief details, for the record: 22 September: *Stand In For A Hearse* by Jack Gerson from a short story by James Wood. 29 September: *The Siege Of Castle Drumlie* by James Scotland. 20 October: *The Dinner Party* by John Lawson. 28 October: *To Grace A Son* by Pat Flynn. 3 November: *Stobo Takes The Chair* by Tom Wright. 10 November: *Take Your Partners* by John Lawson. The series was produced by Eddie Fraser. During this run viewers in the rest of Britain had the opportunity to watch *Monty Python's Flying Circus*.

The final *Comedy Playhouse* episode, scheduled for 16 July 1974, was intended to be *French Relish*, a pilot reuniting *All Gas And Gaiters* writers Devaney and Apps with its star Derek Nimmo. He was to play Simon Pollack, the dynamic and ambitious managing director of a family firm producing the old and established condiment 'Major Pollack's Relish'. The episode never aired, however, and a repeat of the *Seven Of One* episode *Open All Hours* was screened in its place.

On 12 December 1974 BBC1 aired a one-off comedy half-hour, *Too Much Monkey Business*, which may have been intended as a *Comedy Playhouse*.

A year after the demise of *Comedy Playhouse* BBC1 screened a five-week series of unrelated sitcom one-offs, without a generic title. For details see separate entries for:

11 June 1975	The Melting Pot
18 June 1975	Only On Sunday
25 June 1975	For Richer … For Poorer
2 July 1975	Captive Audience
9 July 1975	Going, Going, Gone … Free?

Twenty years after this, BBC1 screened a six-week series of unrelated sitcom one-offs, again without a generic title. Those with an asterisk graduated to full series. For details see separate entries for:

14 Aug 1995	*Oh, Doctor Beeching!
21 Aug 1995	Where The Buffalo Roam
28 Aug 1995	*Atletico Partick AFC
4 Sep 1995	*The Peter Principle
11 Sep 1995	The Chamber
18 Sep 1995	Under The Moon

See also *Comedy Special*.

Comedy Playhouse   ITV

UK · ITV (VARIOUS) · SITCOMS
8 × 30 mins · colour

Shortly after its launch in January 1993, London's new ITV franchise, Carlton, networked a series of eight one-off sitcom pilots under the same generic name, *Comedy Playhouse*, that the BBC had put to such successful use in earlier decades. Carlton's aim, it was said, was to float off three (or more) full-fledged series from the eight, and it already knew that *Brighton Belles* would be one of them. (It was, but it was a ratings disaster.) As it transpired, only one other pilot, *The 10%ers*, was developed further and the project, although worthwhile, was deemed unsuccessful.

These are the eight pilot titles with first broadcast dates. Those preceded by an asterisk graduated to their own series. See individual entries for further details.

23 Feb 1993	*The 10%ers
2 Mar 1993	Wild Oats
9 Mar 1993	*Brighton Belles
16 Mar 1993	Stuck On You
23 Mar 1993	Once In A Lifetime
30 Mar 1993	Cut And Run
13 Apr 1993	The Complete Guide To Relationships
20 Apr 1993	Sailortown

Comedy Premiere

UK · ITV (ATV) · SITCOMS
6 × 30 mins · colour

An ITV (ATV) comedy try-out series, in a similar vein to the BBC's *Comedy Playhouse*. The fifth title in the series (31 August 1975) was actually billed as *Children's Comedy Premiere*, although, oddly, it was the concluding episode of an already popular series, *The Kids From 47A*.

These are the six pilot titles with first broadcast dates. See individual entries for further details.

7 Aug 1975	What A Turn Up
14 Aug 1975	For Richer For Poorer
21 Aug 1975	Honey
28 Aug 1975	The Truth About Verity

31 Aug 1975	Home Sweet Home (see *The Kids From 47A*)	
26 Nov 1975	Milk-O	

Note. One year before the ATV series, Yorkshire TV underwent a similar exercise. This six-part series of unrelated sitcoms was broadcast without an overall title but, for completeness, details are shown below. Titles preceded by an asterisk graduated to their own series. Once again, full information will be found under the separate entries:

2 Sep 1974	*Rising Damp
9 Sep 1974	You'll Never Walk Alone
16 Sep 1974	Brotherly Love
23 Sep 1974	Badger's Set
30 Sep 1974	*Oh No – It's Selwyn Froggitt
3 Dec 1974	Slater's Day

Earlier in 1974, two other ITV comedy pilots were aired: *Sprout* (Thames, 1 July) and *The Squirrels* (ATV, 8 July) – see entries for details.

Comedy Showcase

UK · ITV (LWT) · SITCOMS (2), IMPRESSIONISM (1)

3 × 30 mins · colour

An ITV title-of-convenience embracing three separate comedy half-hours.

The first title, preceded by an asterisk, graduated to its own series. The second programme was a special edition of the long-running *Who Do You Do?* See individual entries for further details.

13 Aug 1976	*Poppy And Her (see *Maggie And Her*)
20 Aug 1976	Now Who Do You Do?
27 Aug 1976	Just Like Mum

The Comedy Slot

UK · C4 (URPH PRODUCTIONS/CHANNEL X) · SKETCH

4 editions (3 × 10 mins · 1 × 5 mins) · colour

26 Aug–29 Aug 1997 · Tue–Fri mostly 7.50pm

MAIN CAST
Lee Mack (show 1)
Johnny Vegas (show 2)
Owen O'Neill (show 3)
Tommy Tiernan (show 4)

CREDITS
writers cast · *director* Jim Reid · *producer* Jo Sargent

Four short shows in which standup comics performed straight-to-camera routines while on location at the Edinburgh Festival Fringe. In the first, Lee Mack played a hopeless dullard continually thwarting a TV interviewer who was trying to elicit his views on the Festival; the second show had Johnny Vegas as a 'comedy counsellor'; the third featured Owen O'Neill portraying an ex-footballer; and the final edition had Tommy Tiernan, not in character, reminiscing comically upon his first kiss. Cheap and cheering stuff.

Comedy Special

UK · BBC · SITCOMS (5), SKETCH (1)

6 × 30 mins · colour

The title used was for one individual comedy playlet during the run of *Comedy Playhouse*, then, five years later, for a follow-up series in the same style.

These are the six programme titles with first broadcast dates. Those preceded by an asterisk graduated to their own series. See individual entries for further details.

30 Aug 1972	No Peace On The Western Front
5 Apr 1977	*A Roof Over My Head
12 Apr 1977	*Citizen Smith
19 Apr 1977	Michael Bentine's Square World
26 Apr 1977	The Boys And Mrs B
3 May 1977	Maggie – It's Me!

The Comedy Store   1

UK · ITV (MIKE MANSFIELD ENTERPRISES) · STANDUP

11 editions (1 × 55 mins · 10 × 10 mins) · colour

Special (55 mins) 23 Dec 1989 · Sat 2.15am

One series (10 × 10 mins) 24 Dec 1989–21 May 1990 · irregular days and times · all post-midnight

MAIN CAST
see below

CREDITS
director/producer Mike Mansfield

Eleven programmes, linked by Chris Tarrant and screened in the early hours by London-area ITV, which ventured inside the Comedy Store in the West End of London to feature some of the best standup acts of the period. All 11 were recorded in a single sponsored event-week at the famous Leicester Square venue, the tapes being edited into an hour-length special, for which guest comics were flown in from the USA, and ten short 'filler' programmes.

Among those seen in performance during the series were Will Durst, Arthur Smith, Kit And The Widow (Kit Hesketh-Harvey and Richard Sissons), Bobby Slayton, Chris Overton, Michael Redmond, Jack Dee, Chris Lynam, Andrew Bailey, Jenny Eclair, Steve Punt and Hugh Dennis.

The Comedy Store   2

UK · C5 (OPEN MIKE PRODUCTIONS) · STANDUP

15 × 30 mins · colour

30 Mar–24 Jun 1997 · mostly Tue 11.40pm

MAIN CAST
see below

CREDITS
directors Jon Blow, Steve Bendelack · *executive producer* Addison Cresswell · *producers* Dave Morley, Pete Ward

Another looksee behind the doors at the Comedy Store, with 15 shows screened by the new C5 in association with the cable/satellite Paramount Channel (later the Paramount Comedy Channel). Some editions featured a single act, in others five or six performers appeared, their routines intercut. Richard Morton was the MC, and the comics included Sean Meo, Ed Byrne, Bill Bailey, Eddie Brill, Mark Hurst, Fred MacAulay and Dylan Moran.

A regular sidebar feature was a snappy, soundbite interview with an established comic and/or celebrity once associated with the famed London venue (including its former compere Clive Anderson, Alexei Sayle, Ben Elton, Jenny Eclair, Jonathan Ross, Bob Mills, Frank Skinner and David Baddiel). The comics recalled their earlier days at the Comedy Store and answered some innocuous questions put to them by fellow comic Arthur Smith ('What is your favourite all-time sitcom?', 'Who do you rate most as a standup performer?', 'Have you ever been heckled?').

Comedy Tonight   1

see HUDD, Roy

Comedy Tonight   2

UK · ITV (THAMES) · SKETCH/MUSICAL HUMOUR

1 × 60 mins · colour

2 Apr 1980 · Wed 8pm

MAIN CAST
Richard Briers
Ian Carmichael
Harry H Corbett
Sheila Hancock
Patricia Hayes
Frankie Howerd
Arthur Lowe
Frank Muir
Ian Ogilvy
Lance Percival
Beryl Reid
Dennis Waterman

CREDITS
writers H F Ellis, Reginald Purdell, Ray Galton/Alan Simpson, Douglas Furber, John Mortimer, Cole Porter, Michael Brown · *director/producer* Michael Mills

A single hour-length programme, hosted by Frank Muir, in which top names of British TV comedy re-created some vintage sketch and humorous-song material stretching back, in some cases, 50 years.

Note. Thirteen years earlier, in 1967, *Comedy Tonight* was used as the generic title for a short series of individual comedies made by

ITV company ABC and screened in the Midlands and the North but not in London. Information on these programmes can be found within the entries for **Room At The Bottom** [BBC], **The Hen House** and **Wild, Wild Women**.

Comedy Wavelength

UK · C4 (CHAPTER ONE) · SKETCH/STANDUP

10 × 25 mins · colour

17 Feb–28 Apr 1987 · Tue mostly 11.20pm

MAIN CAST

host · Paul Merton

CREDITS

writers cast and others · directors Tony Keene (8), David Macmahon (2) · producers Bob Clarke, David Macmahon

A ten-week attempt at launching new comedy talent – not only performers but writers too. Editions were taped in front of an audience at the Town And Country Club in London. As its weekly host, the series gave standup comic Paul Merton his first regular television exposure.

Comic Asides

UK · BBC · VARIOUS

15 × 30 mins · colour

A BBC2 series of individual comedies, some of which, serving as pilot episodes, were developed into series.

The following details the individual programme titles and broadcast dates. The six titles preceded by an asterisk graduated to their own series. In all instances see separate entries for further details.

Series One

12 May 1989	*KYTV
19 May 1989	*Tygo Road
26 May 1989	Dowie
2 June 1989	The Stone Age
9 June 1989	*I, Lovett
16 June 1989	*Mornin' Sarge

Special

25 May 1993	It's A Mad World, World, World, World

Series Two

9 Jan 1994	*The High Life
16 Jan 1994	Woodcock
23 Jan 1994	The Last Word
30 Jan 1994	The Honeymoon's Over

Series Three

18 Aug 1995	*Pulp Video
25 Aug 1995	N7
1 Sep 1995	Mac
8 Sep 1995	Felix Dexter On TV

Comic Relief

Following Bob Geldof's globe-spanning charity rock-music event Live Aid (13 July 1985), the horror of famine was at the forefront of the public's awareness as never before. The Band Aid charity, organisers of Live Aid, proved that entertainers could raise vast amounts of money by offering their talents for free and using the stage as a soapbox from which not only to entertain but also to entreat the public to donate cash. On a much smaller scale the concept was nothing new – the Royal Variety Show had raised funds for the Variety Artistes' Benevolent Fund (later the Entertainment Artistes' Benevolent Fund) since 1913, and entertainers have often given one-off performances for charity – but on this scale it was unparalleled. The notion of using TV as the primary medium, rather than the theatre, was first explored in the USA, where the annual Telethon events, chiefly associated with the efforts of the comic Jerry Lewis, raise enormous sums for a variety of worthy causes.

In 1976, the combined talents of the **Beyond The Fringe/Monty Python** teams put on the first event to raise money for Amnesty International (see **The Amnesty Galas**) and spin-off merchandising in the form of records, books, videos and films raised a good deal more revenue than mere box-office takings. Then, taking the lead from Band Aid and Live Aid, the first Comic Relief event took place, in 1986. At first, it was intended to raise money to aid famine relief but then its scope enlarged to encompass all manner of needy causes at home and abroad. The British version of Comic Relief (there is an American counterpart) has been a massive success story, with the cream of the UK's comedy talent pitching in their ideas and skills for free, to generate substantial proceeds (many millions of pounds per biannual event). Along the way, of course, TV viewers have been treated to some spectacular and downright unusual comedy moments.

Comic Relief   1986

UK · BBC (BBC/COMIC RELIEF) SKETCH/STANDUP

1 × 90 mins · colour

25 Apr 1986 · BBC1 Fri 10.15pm

MAIN COMEDY CAST

Rowan Atkinson, Pamela Stephenson, Rik Mayall, Ben Elton, Dawn French, Jennifer Saunders, Lenny Henry, Billy Connolly, Stephen Fry, Rory Bremner, Ronnie Corbett, Paul Eddington, Cliff Richard and The Young Ones, Spitting Image

CREDITS

writers cast and others · stage director Rowan Atkinson · TV directors Phil Chilvers, Paul Jackson, Geoff Posner · producer Roger Graef

Charity worker Jane Tewson left Mencap in 1985 to set up Charity Projects, an organisation designed to bring charities together to share expertise and resources. A collaboration between Charity Projects and Band Aid in 1986 resulted in the decision, for this event, to support the less emotive side of famine relief: rather than buying grain and other foodstuffs, the charity opted to pay the running costs of a famine-relief camp in Umbala in the west of Sudan, including the wages of its doctors and nurses. To raise those funds, an array of comedy and music talent was assembled under the command of 'ringmaster' Rowan Atkinson, and three two-hour shows were staged at the Shaftesbury Theatre in London. All three sold out on the basis of a mention on BBC Radio One, and despite the fact that tickets were priced as high as £50. This TV presentation was distilled from the three performances; screened in the BBC1 Omnibus arts strand, it featured most of the good routines, including a performance of the Comic Relief charity single 'Living Doll' by Cliff Richard and **The Young Ones** (Mayall, Edmondson, Planer, Ryan) that had recently shot to number one; Lenny Henry and boxer Frank Bruno as Romeo (Henry) and Juliet (Bruno); and Rowan Atkinson, as a Las Vegas crooner, duetting with Kate Bush. Live Aid leading lights Midge Ure and Bob Geldof appeared as singing guests and in a comedy sketch with Stephen Fry. The TV screening was preceded by a specially taped sequence featuring Paul Eddington as Jim Hacker (**Yes, Prime Minister**) explaining why his government enthusiastically supported the worthy Comic Relief cause yet couldn't actually give it any money. Comedy stars who had appeared in the stage-shows but failed to make the television edit included Terry Jones, Graham Chapman, Michael Palin and Hugh Laurie.

Comic Relief   1988

UK · BBC · SKETCH/STANDUP

1 × 450 mins · colour

5 Feb 1988 · BBC1 Fri 7.35pm

MAIN COMEDY CAST

Lenny Henry, Griff Rhys Jones, Jim Davidson, Rod Hull and Emu, Harry Enfield, Syd Little, Eddie Large, Rory Bremner, Victoria Wood, Julie Walters, Stephen Fry, Hugh Laurie, Ernie Wise, Ronnie Corbett, Warren Mitchell, Michael Palin, Phil Cool, Barry Humphries, Dawn French, Jennifer Saunders, Ben Elton, Gareth Hale, Norman

Pace, Tommy Cannon, Bobby Ball, Pamela Stephenson, Max Headroom (Matt Frewer)

CREDITS
various

An extended evening of TV humour, combining new material with old favourites. The entire BBC1 Friday evening schedule was given over to the marathon programme, and the whole population was encouraged to wear red noses and become involved in money-raising stunts, many of which were co-ordinated via the television presentation. Comedy highlights of the long programme included *A Question Of Sport Meets Spitting Image*, in which sportsmen Mike Gatting, Barry McGuigan, Daley Thompson and presenter/commentator David Coleman met their rubber-caricature counterparts; *73 Of A Kind*, where 73 different celebrities appeared in short sketches peppered through the evening, in the style of *Three Of A Kind*; special mini-editions of *Blackadder* and *The New Statesman*, and *Select A Sketch*, an airing of Radio One listeners' favourite classic TV comedy sketches.

Hosts Lenny Henry and Griff Rhys Jones popped up throughout the evening, liaising with Harry Enfield (in his Stavros persona) who was keeping an eye on the totals raised. Vintage sitcom episodes (*Dad's Army*, *Steptoe And Son*) and filmed reports from the famine troublespots were also slotted in during the event. The evening was rounded off with a screening of the anarchic comedy film *The Bed Sitting Room*. Highlights from the programme were repeated in *Comic Relief's Nose At Ten*, screened by BBC1 on 31 December 1988.

A Night Of Comic Relief 2 1989

UK · BBC · SKETCH/STANDUP

1 × 390 mins · colour

10 Mar 1989 · BBC1 Fri 7.30pm

MAIN COMEDY CAST
Lenny Henry, Griff Rhys Jones, Jonathan Ross, Gareth Hale, Norman Pace, Syd Little, Eddie Large, Billy Connolly, Ken Dodd, Harry Enfield, Dave Allen, Dawn French, Jennifer Saunders, Phil Cool, Frank Carson, Julian Clary, Rory Bremner, Stephen Fry, Hugh Laurie, John Sessions

CREDITS
various

Highlights this time included *The Last Waltz*, a special Carla Lane creation featuring characters from *Bread*, *Butterflies*, *Solo* and *The Liver Birds* (Nerys Hughes, Jean Boht, Wendy Craig, Felicity Kendal and Polly James, with Caroline Blakiston, Linda McCartney and Kim Wilde); a scene from the stage-show version of *'Allo 'Allo!* from the London

Palladium; *The Night Of The Comic Dead*, a horror film spoof starring Phil Cool and Frank Carson; mini-editions of *Hot Metal* and C4's improvisational panel-game *Whose Line Is It Anyway?*; Lenny Henry performing as his sex-symbol soul singer Theophilus P Wildebeeste; the on-screen death by road accident of Harry Enfield's character Loadsamoney; and a plethora of other celebrities featuring in the familiar cornucopia of sketches.

Comic Relief's Nose Trek II: The Search For Cash, a report on the money raised, was screened by BBC1 on 1 May 1989.

Comic Relief 1991

UK · BBC · SKETCH/STANDUP

1 × 395 mins · colour

15 Mar 1991 · BBC1 Fri 7.25pm

MAIN COMEDY CAST
Lenny Henry, Griff Rhys Jones, Jonathan Ross, Tony Robinson, Chris Tarrant, Julian Clary, Dawn French, Jennifer Saunders, Pauline Quirke, Linda Robson, Rowan Atkinson, Ben Elton, Victoria Wood, Paul Whitehouse, Harry Enfield, Hale and Pace, Mel Smith, Vic Reeves, Steve Wright, Nicholas Lyndhurst, Rory Bremner, Peter Cook

CREDITS
various

Highlights included *Four Birds Of A Feather* (which combined **French And Saunders** with **Birds Of A Feather**); *Viz* comic's ghastly cartoon TV presenter Roger Mellie (voiced by Peter Cook) in *Mellie At Midnight*; Paul Whitehouse and Harry Enfield as Smashie and Nicey; a performance by the *Comic Strip*'s spoof heavy-metal band Bad News; and the usual celebrity-led glut of mini-sketches generically called *Star Crazy*. Other talking points were *Blind Snog*, where blindfolded victims were kissed by celebrities of both sexes; *Battle Of The Sex Gods*, where Lenny Henry's Theophilus P Wildebeeste went head to head against Tom Jones to see who was the sexiest; and *Late 'N' Hot 'N' Live*, a compilation of clips from standup acts.

Comic Relief 1992 – Behind The Nose, a two-hour programme screened by BBC1 on 17 April 1992, reported on the money raised and looked back at the comedy highlights of all the TV marathons to date.

Total Relief 1993

UK · BBC · SKETCH/STANDUP

1 × 425 mins · colour

12 Mar 1993 · BBC1 Fri 7pm

MAIN COMEDY CAST
Lenny Henry, Rowan Atkinson, Paul Whitehouse, Harry Enfield, Joanna Lumley, Jonathan Ross, Frank Carson, Griff Rhys Jones, Angus Deayton, Ian Hislop, Paul Merton, Dawn French, Jennifer Saunders,

Richard Wilson, Ben Elton, Jo Brand, Rob Newman, David Baddiel

CREDITS
various

Highlights included *Mr Bean On Blind Date*; *Have I Got Sports News For You*, a special combination of comedy news quiz *Have I Got News For You* with *A Question Of Sport*; a monster duet between Prince and Barry White, both imitated by Lenny Henry; a mini-edition of **One Foot In The Grave** with Victor Meldrew delivering a rambling rant from his bath; and **Friday Night Live** *– Lives Again!*, a mini-revival of C4's 1988 comedy smash. The evening finished off with a showing of the mock 'rockumentary' movie *This Is Spinal Tap*.

The Night Of Comic Relief 1995

UK · BBC · SKETCH/STANDUP

1 × 425 mins · colour

17 Mar 1995 · BBC1 Fri 7pm

MAIN COMEDY CAST
Chris Evans, Richard Wilson, Pauline Collins, Timothy Spall, Angus Deayton, Ron Moody, Michael Palin, Stephen Fry, Kathy Burke, Richard Briers, Harry Enfield, Rowan Atkinson, Dawn French, Jennifer Saunders, Ruby Wax, Vic Reeves, Bob Mortimer, Lenny Henry, Jonathan Ross, Mel Smith, Griff Rhys Jones, Victoria Wood, Steve Coogan, Jo Brand, Julian Clary, Ben Elton

CREDITS
various

Highlights included *Torvill And Bean*, in which **Mr Bean** took to the ice with skating star Jayne Torvill; *Oliver 2: Let's Twist Again*, a star-studded Dickens spoof in three segments, replacing the usual collection of mini-sketches; *Dawn*, a parody of *Oprah*-style chat-shows featuring Dawn French and Victoria Wood; and *Belfast Live*, standup comedy from Belfast in celebration of St Patrick's Day featuring Lenny Henry, Jo Brand, Julian Clary and Ben Elton. Also featured were skits featuring Reeves and Mortimer, French and Saunders, Smith and Jones with Victoria Wood, Steve Coogan as Alan Partridge, and Harry Enfield with Kathy Burke in a variety of characters from **Harry Enfield And Chums**. The evening finished with a screening of the movie *Blazing Saddles*.

Comic Relief 1997

UK · BBC · SKETCH/STANDUP

1 × 370 mins · colour

14 Mar 1997 · BBC1 Fri 7pm

MAIN COMEDY CAST
Lenny Henry, Dame Edna Everage (Barry Humphries), Stephen Tompkinson, Dawn French, Jennifer Saunders, Jonathan Ross, Griff Rhys Jones, Harry Enfield, Kathy Burke,

Steve Coogan, Robbie Coltrane, Paul Whitehouse, Jo Brand, Rowan Atkinson, Angus Deayton, Ben Elton and the casts of *Only Fools And Horses*, *Father Ted*, *The Vicar Of Dibley* and *Men Behaving Badly*

CREDITS
various

The biannual charitable buffoonathon returned with a whole host of new, weird and wonderful comic moments. Highlights were plentiful and included *The Great Big Stupid Celebrity Sketch Show* – a series of star-studded short sketches that ran at intervals throughout the evening; a special **Only Fools And Horses** segment; *Prime Cracker*, a comedic blending of the UK's two top 'tec shows *Cracker* and *Prime Suspect*, in which stars Robbie Coltrane and Helen Mirren delightfully satirised their screen characters; *BallykissDibley*, in which Father Peter Clifford (Stephen Tompkinson) from the successful BBC1 drama *Ballykissangel* met up with Geraldine Granger (Dawn French) and her friends from **The Vicar Of Dibley**, Dermot Morgan and Ardal O'Hanlon hosting a sequence in their **Father Ted** characters; Steve Coogan in his Tony Ferrino guise, duetting with the singer Björk; Jonathan Ross and Griff Rhys Jones 'snogging' the Spice Girls; Martin Clunes and Neil Morrissey in their **Men Behaving Badly** characters, behaving very badly indeed with guest star Kylie Minogue; and a specially edited sequence of outtakes and bloopers from **Blackadder**, **Bottom**, **Harry Enfield And Chums**, **French And Saunders** and **Red Dwarf**.

From 11.50pm, the marathon presented *The Empire Strikes Back*, a live hour of comedy and music from the Shepherd's Bush Empire, just along the road from BBC Television Centre. Highlights from this section included Rowan Atkinson performing his excruciatingly funny Indian Waiter sketch, in which a resigned waiter in a British curry house has to put up with the abuse and pathetic behaviour of nine lager-swilling drunks out on a bender (Atkinson himself coped manfully with a rowdy, noisy, rock-concert type crowd while performing it); Steve Coogan as Pauline Calf offering to (and eventually doing a) streak for money; and the Sugar Lumps (French and Saunders, Lulu, Llewella Gideon and Kathy Burke), a comedy send-up of the Spice Girls, who performed as a quintet before linking up with the real Spice Girls to perform the latter's Comic Relief charity hit 'Who Do You Think You Are'.

At the end of the evening Ben Elton announced the massive sum raised on the night (£11,688,316) and introduced a repeat of the *Omnibus* special covering the very first Comic Relief initiative back in 1986.

Comic Strip

UK · BBC · SKETCH
4 × 20 mins · b/w
11 Oct 1937 · Mon 9.10pm
23 Nov 1937 · Tue 3.40pm
20 Jan 1938 · Thu 9.40pm
7 May 1938 · Sat 11pm

MAIN CAST
Joan Miller

CREDITS
producer Eric Crozier

Four programmes of American literary humour. As was a normal practice at this time, each was re-staged within seven days of its original transmission.

The Comic Strip Presents ...

UK · C4 THEN BBC (SEE BELOW FOR PRODUCTION COMPANIES) · COMEDY FILMS
35 films (all colour except #3) · various durations
1 & 3: Filmworks/Comic Strip
2, 4–14: Michael White/Comic Strip
15–35: Comic Strip

1. *Five Go Mad In Dorset* 2 Nov 1982 · C4 Tue 10.15pm (30 mins)
2. *War* 3 Jan 1983 · C4 Mon 9pm (30 mins)
3. *The Beat Generation* 17 Jan 1983 · C4 Mon 9pm (30 mins)
4. *Bad News Tour* 24 Jan 1983 · C4 Mon 9pm (30 mins)
5. *Summer School* 31 Jan 1983 · C4 Mon 9pm (30 mins)
6. *Five Go Mad On Mescalin* 2 Nov 1983 · C4 Wed 10pm (40 mins)
7. *Dirty Movie* 7 Jan 1984 · C4 Sat 10.25pm (40 mins)
8. *Susie* 14 Jan 1984 · C4 Sat 10.30pm (40 mins)
9. *Fistful Of Travellers Cheques* 21 Jan 1984 · C4 Sat 10.30pm (45 mins)
10. *Gino – Full Story And Pics* 28 Jan 1984 · C4 Sat 10.30pm (40 mins)
11. *Eddie Monsoon – A Life?* 4 Feb 1984 · C4 Sat 10.30pm (35 mins)
12. *Slags* 11 Feb 1984 · C4 Sat 10.35pm (40 mins)
13. *Consuela* 1 Jan 1986 · C4 Wed 11pm (45 mins)
14. *Private Enterprise* 2 Jan 1986 · C4 Thu 11pm (40 mins)
15. *The Strike* 20 Feb 1988 · C4 Sat 10.50pm (75 mins)
16. *More Bad News* 27 Feb 1988 · C4 Sat 10.50pm (60 mins)
17. *Mr Jolly Lives Next Door* 5 Mar 1988 · C4 Sat 10.50pm (60 mins)
18. *The Yob* 12 Mar 1988 · C4 Sat 10.50pm (65 mins)
19. *Didn't You Kill My Brother?* 19 Mar 1988 · C4 Sat 10.50pm (65 mins)
20. *Funseekers* 26 Mar 1988 · C4 Sat 10.50pm (60 mins)
21. *South Atlantic Raiders – Part 1* 1 Feb 1990 · BBC2 Thu 9pm (30 mins)
22. *South Atlantic Raiders – Part 2* 8 Feb 1990 · BBC2 Thu 9pm (35 mins)
23. *GLC* 15 Feb 1990 · BBC2 Thu 9pm (30 mins)
24. *Oxford* 22 Feb 1990 · BBC2 Thu 9pm (30 mins)
25. *Spaghetti Hoops* 1 Mar 1990 · BBC2 Thu 9pm (30 mins)
26. *Les Dogs* 8 Mar 1990 · BBC2 Thu 9pm (30 mins)
27. *Red Nose Of Courage* 9 Apr 1992 · BBC2 Thu 10.30pm (50 mins)
28. *The Crying Game* 5 May 1992 · BBC2 Tue 10pm (30 mins)
29. *Wild Turkey* 24 Dec 1992 · BBC2 Thu 10pm (30 mins)
30. *Detectives On The Edge Of A Nervous Breakdown* 22 Apr 1993 · BBC2 Thu 9pm (35 mins)
31. *Space Virgins From Planet Sex* 29 Apr 1993 · BBC2 Thu 9pm (35 mins)
32. *Queen Of The Wild Frontier* 6 May 1993 · BBC2 Thu 9pm (35 mins)
33. *Gregory – Diary Of A Nut Case* 13 May 1993 · BBC2 Thu 9pm (40 mins)
34. *Demonella* 20 May 1993 · BBC2 Thu 9pm (30 mins)
35. *Jealousy* 27 May 1993 · BBC2 Thu 9pm (30 mins)

MAIN CAST (NUMBERS REFER TO FILMS)
Adrian Edmondson (1–18, 21–24, 26, 27, 30, 31, 33, 34)
Dawn French (1–17, 21–25, 27, 30, 31)
Peter Richardson (1–31, 34, 35)
Jennifer Saunders (1–17, 21–25, 27, 29–31, 34, 35)
Robbie Coltrane (1–3, 5–8, 10, 15, 21–23, 27, 30, 31, 34, 35)
Rik Mayall (2–5, 7, 9, 10, 13–17, 23, 27)
Nigel Planer (2–5, 7–9, 12, 14–16, 20–25, 27, 28, 30, 33–35)
SOME OTHER REGULAR APPEARANCES
Daniel Peacock (1–3, 6, 9, 10, 15, 26)
Ronald Allen (1, 6, 15, 22, 24)
Keith Allen (3, 9, 10, 15, 18–20, 22, 23, 25–28, 30, 31, 33, 34)
Serena Evans (4, 10, 13, 14)
Alexei Sayle (15, 19, 25–27, 30)
Lenny Henry (21, 24)
Kathy Burke (21, 22, 35)
Pete Richens (15, 22, 24)
Miranda Richardson (26, 30, 31, 34)
Phil Cornwell (28–30, 33)
SOME SPECIAL APPEARANCES
Fiona Richmond (1, 6)
Michael White (3, 11)
Tony Bilbow (11)
Peter Cook (17)
Nicholas Parsons (17)
Gary Olsen (18)
Peter Wyngarde (18)
Beryl Reid (19)
Jeff Beck (22)
Leslie Phillips (24)
Tim McInnerny (25, 26)
Kate Bush (26)
Julie T Wallace (26, 30, 32)
Ruby Wax (29)
Mike McShane (29)
Jim Broadbent (30)

Miriam Margolyes (30)
Josie Lawrence (32)
Ernest Clark (32)

CREDITS

writers Peter Richardson/Pete Richens (1–3, 6, 8, 10, 15, 21–29, 31–33), Peter Richardson/Pete Richens/Rik Mayall (9), Peter Richardson/Keith Allen (30), Adrian Edmondson/Rik Mayall (7), Adrian Edmondson/Rik Mayall/Rowland Rivron (17), Adrian Edmondson (4, 11, 14, 16), Dawn French (5), Dawn French/Jennifer Saunders (13), Jennifer Saunders (12), Keith Allen/Daniel Peacock (18), Alexei Sayle/Pauline Melville/David Stafford (19), Nigel Planer/Doug Lucie (20), Paul Bartrell/Barry Dennen (34), Morag Fullarton/Robbie Coltrane (35) · *directors* Bob Spiers (1–3, 6, 8–10, 19), Sandy Johnson (4, 5, 7, 11, 12), Stephen Frears (13, 17), Adrian Edmondson (14, 16), Peter Richardson (15, 21–27, 29, 33), Ian Emes (18), Baz Taylor (20), Peter Richardson/Keith Allen (28, 30–32), Paul Bartrell (34), Robbie Coltrane (35) · *executive producers* Michael White (1–26), Michael White/Peter Richardson (27–35) · *producers* Andrew St John (1, 2, 4, 5), Michael Hall/Victoria Poushkine-Relf (3), Sarah Radclyffe (6–12), Elaine Taylor (13, 14, 17), Chris Brown (15), Simon Wright (16), Chris Brown/Peter Richardson (18), Peter Richardson/Simon Wright (19), Simon Wright (20), Lolli Kimpton (21–35)

'I think we're halfway between a *Carry On* film and a Joe Orton play,' Robbie Coltrane told *Radio Times* in 1990. While many thousands of words have been written about the *Comic Strip Presents* ... TV films – mostly in praise but some vitriolic in their scorn – it is likely that no better description exists of these unique contributions to British TV.

All 35 films are distinct productions, self-contained from the others, their dialogue stuffed with dangerous lines, their action containing hefty quantities of seemingly gratuitous physical violence. By the same token, all the programmes contain some wonderfully funny dialogue, creative ideas and perhaps the most astute film pastiches ever attempted on TV. Whether the results were good or bad, to have missed a *Comic Strip* production meant that you missed *something* of note.

Financed by theatrical impresario Michael White – who presented the 1963 revue *Cambridge Circus* in the West End, which led, eventually, to **Monty Python** and **The Goodies** by way of radio gem *I'm Sorry, I'll Read That Again* – the Comic Strip club had opened in October 1980 at the Boulevard Theatre in London. Like the Comedy Store before it, this was located within a Soho strip joint, but, unlike that other and more famous venue, what was staged at the Comic Strip was more like a show, with the same personnel repeating nightly – and honing, all the while – the same act. The eight-strong core team at the venue comprised Alexei Sayle, Arnold Brown and three double-acts: Mayall and Edmondson, Planer and

Richardson and French and Saunders. Peter Richardson was keen to get the team on to TV, and was especially interested in using film as the medium. After some ideas had been thrashed around, Richardson took a list to Jeremy Isaacs, head of Britain's fourth TV channel, due to open in November 1982, whereupon six films were commissioned. With the exceptions of Arnold Brown (whom *Comic Strip* TV viewers never saw) and Alexei Sayle (who showed up in only six of the 35 films), the six other protagonists appeared in most of the productions. Added to round off the eight were Pete Richens (who co-scripted a good many of them and had tiny roles in two latter productions) and Robbie Coltrane, who had not played the Comic Strip club but was brought in as a friend by Rik Mayall. These eight formed their own production company, Comic Strip Productions, with Peter Richardson the linchpin and driving force of the collective.

The first film, the fabulous Enid Blyton parody *Five Go Mad In Dorset*, went out on the opening night of C4, and four of the other films were screened soon after. This opening batch contained all the hallmarks of the *Comic Strip Presents* productions that would remain true to the end: shot on film, they were high on production values, pacy and stylish. The humour, too, more often than not, was spot on – despite the dreaded sobriquet, one aspect in which this new comedy was truly 'alternative' was in its choice of targets. Although capable of comedic savagery, these young comedians steered clear of the traditional areas of racism, sexism and religion to concentrate on more general, social and political themes, albeit with an anarchic edge. Their TV success did much to rid the small-screen of the outmoded and often downright offensive comedy that had followed the liberalisation of the medium in the 1960s, although this in turn coincided with (or possibly instigated) a wave of 'political correctness' that swept through British society. (The sixth original film for C4, *An Evening With Eddie Monsoon*, was pulled by the network and never screened. It was written as a co-operative by Edmondson, French, Planer, Richardson, Richens and Saunders, directed by Bob Spiers, and the script appears in the 1983 C4/Methuen book *The Comic Strip Presents* .... The Eddie Monsoon character did surface in *Eddie Monsoon – A Life?*, however, the eleventh *CS* production, screened on 4 February 1984, and also, eight years on, inspired the name of Jennifer Saunders' character in her sitcom **Absolutely Fabulous**: Edina 'Eddie' Monsoon.)

This, in a nutshell, is how the long story began. The films kept coming, at reasonably regular intervals, and switched in 1990 to BBC2. All the while, the various players were

enjoying glorious success with other TV productions (**The Young Ones** and **French And Saunders**, to name but two) and the 'alternative' comedians rapidly became primary stars of the medium. Plans for a new production in 1998, the first in five years, were in motion as this book was being written.

Note. While produced in association with C4, two *Comic Strip* films were made expressly for the cinema and so do not appear as part of this entry. *The Supergrass*, released in November 1985, and *Eat The Rich!*, October 1987, were written by Peter Richardson/Pete Richens and directed by Richardson. Five of the six 1988 TV productions (all but *Funseekers*) were also afforded a limited theatrical release in autumn 1987 but these were unquestionably made for television. The 1991 feature film *The Pope Must Die*, starring Robbie Coltrane, written by Peter Richardson/Pete Richens and directed by Richardson, was *not* made by Comic Strip Productions, however.

See also *The Bullshitters* and *The Glam Metal Detectives*.

What follows is a brief guide to the 35 *Comic Strip Presents* ... TV productions. Readers familiar with the films will know that they do not lend themselves to easy précis, however.

1. A send-up of Enid Blyton's *Famous Five* children's adventure yarns.
2. A couple on the run in foreign-army-occupied England.
3. A pastiche of the Beat Poets era, set in England in the summer of 1960.
4. A *Spinal Tap*-style send-up of a heavy-metal rock band, Bad News.
5. A group of students re-create life in the Iron Age for a project.
6. Another *Famous Five* pastiche.
7. A cinema manager is continually thwarted in his attempts to enjoy a private screening of an erotic film.
8. A horny Norfolk schoolteacher ditches her husband and runs off to live decadently with a pop star.
9. A pastiche of spaghetti westerns.
10. A gangster on the run sells his story to the media.
11. An alcoholic and violent South African TV personality has his programme banned by a British TV network.
12. A space-age gang, Slags, discuss evil tortures they can inflict on their enemy, the flower-proffering nice gang, Hawaiians.
13. A married man quickly loses interest in his wife and finds fascination with his dogs and Spanish housemaid. Virtually a parody of *Rebecca*.
14. A toilet-paper delivery man on prison parole pretends that he has made a rock demo tape which he has stolen.
15. An innocent writes a screenplay about the 1984 coal miners strike, but Goldie, a Hollywood mogul, wants to cast Al Pacino (Peter Richardson) and Meryl Streep (Jennifer Saunders) as Mr and Mrs Scargill.

(This film won the Golden Rose award at the Montreux Festival in 1988.)

16. Bad News reunite and make a new record and video. (Edmondson, Mayall, Richardson and Planer had latterly, in late 1987, been out on the road as Bad News; a later TV presentation of the band occurred in **Comic Relief**, screened by BBC1 on 15 March 1991.)

17. A hit-man (Peter Cook) becomes involved with two alcoholic proprietors of a squalid escort agency; his task: to kill Nicholas Parsons.

18. A parody of the recent horror-movie remake *The Fly*.

19. Wrongly imprisoned for crimes committed by his violent twin brother, Carl Moss is taken under the wing of his probation officer, who wants to marry him. Very Brechtian in style.

20. A bunch of 18–30s on holiday in Ibiza.

21/22. A Falkland Islands invasion – with a difference.

23. Hollywood stars play British political figures (echoing the theme of #15) – Robbie Coltrane as Charles Bronson as Ken Livingstone, Jennifer Saunders as Brigitte Neilson as the evil ice-maiden (Margaret Thatcher), Peter Richardson as Lee Van Cleef as Tony Benn.

24. Soap opera-style sexy characters get turned on by education and do anything for a degree.

25. An Italian businessman/freemason steals $200m and is shopped to the police. Hit men and kidnappings abound.

26. A Felliniesque film about a self-obsessed man who has a car crash, wanders into a wedding reception and falls in love with the bride.

27. The Labour leader, Miss Glenys Kinnock, falls in love with Coco the Clown, the night-time persona of John Major. (Screened on the eve of the 1992 General Election.)

28. A football star is too busy endorsing products to play the game, and the tabloid newspapers are prying into his private life.

29. A couple buy an unplucked turkey and find that it's not dead. The bird takes them hostage, demanding the release of all turkeys everywhere.

30. A spoof on 1970s TV detective shows.

31. A group of aliens travel to Earth to mate with its most brilliant inhabitants and so save their species.

32. Two escaped convicts seek refuge with a farmer and get more than they bargained for.

33. A serial killer makes his own video nasty.

34. A failing music producer accepts the demands of a mysterious beautiful woman in exchange for riches.

35. A man goes to extreme lengths to see if his wife is being unfaithful.

Coming Home

UK · BBC · SITCOM

6 × 30 mins · colour

27 Feb–3 Apr 1981 · BBC1 Fri mostly 7.30pm

MAIN CAST

Sheila Maddocks ·········· Sharon Duce
Donald Maddocks ········· Philip Jackson
Muriel Maddocks ········· Lynda Marchal
Ted Maddocks ············ Roger Sloman
Ruth ····················· Eva Griffith
Joey ··················· David Thackwray

CREDITS

writer David Fitzsimmons · director Martin Shardlow · producer Sydney Lotterby

A single-series sitcom from Bolton-based writer David Fitzsimmons, drawing upon situations and characterisations true to his own life. Fitzsimmons was a chemistry teacher, as was the lead character here, Donald Maddocks, and, acknowledged the author, both shared a certain indecisiveness that caused their wives to take the basic decisions in their marriages. Sharon Duce was cast as Donald's wife Sheila, a level-headed type coping as best she could with her bumbling husband. Sheila's sister Ruth, and Donald's parents Muriel and Ted, were the closest members of the extended Maddocks family but others cropped up in various episodes.

Coming Next ...

see **Pushing Up Daisies**

Coming Of Age

USA · CBS (BUNGALOW 78 PRODUCTIONS/ UNIVERSAL) · SITCOM

15 × 30 mins · colour

US dates: 15 Mar 1988–27 July 1989
UK dates: 11 May–21 Dec 1990 (15 episodes) ITV Fri mostly 1.20pm

MAIN CAST

Dick Hale ················· Paul Dooley
Ginny Hale ············· Phyllis Newman
Ed Pepper ················ Alan Young
Trudie Pepper ··········· Glynis Johns
Brian Binker ············· Kevin Pollak

CREDITS

writers Sheldon Bull, Jeffrey Duteil, Barry Kemp, Emily Prudum Marshall, Tom Palmer, Kevin Pollak, Earl Pomerantz · directors various · producers various

A weak comedy series set in the Dunes, an Arizona retirement village. It focused on two neighbouring couples and in particular the husbands, one of whom, Dick Hale, considered himself too young to be retired; the other, Ed Pepper, was completely immersed in activities and domestic duties. Hale had been an aeroplane pilot but was forced by the rules of his airline to retire at 60. Unable to live the lifestyle of his choice, Hale was perpetually grumpy: unhappy with being retired, unhappy with fellow Dunes residents, unhappy with the Arizona climate (he had moved from Pittsburgh with his wife Ginny), unhappy with life. Ed Pepper and his wife Trudie, conversely, loved the Dunes and were relentlessly enthusiastic about everything.

Coming Of Age 'enjoyed' a stop-start run on US TV, the episodes running in three blocks – March 1988, October–November 1988 and June–July 1989 – before CBS exercised voluntary euthanasia. In the absence of abundant laughs, the series' main attraction lay in its cast of ageing stars, including established movie character actor Paul Dooley, actress Phyllis Newman (she had appeared in the American version of **That Was The Week That Was**), British-born film/stage actress Glynis Johns (**Glynis**) and the British-born actor Alan Young, the star of **Mister Ed** (and **Alan Young, It's Young Again** and **Personal Appearance**).

Commander Badman

UK · ITV (THAMES) · CHILDREN'S SITCOM

1 × 30 mins · colour

24 May 1974 · Fri 4.50pm

MAIN CAST

Commander Badman ······· Aubrey Woods
Vince ···················· Henry Woolf
Boy Wonder ·············· David Battley
Anthea ················ Bridget Armstrong
Sgt Henderson ·········· Roland MacLeod

CREDITS

writer Eric Idle · director Darrol Blake · producer Ruth Boswell

The first of six half-hours in the ITV children's *Comedy Playhouse*-style series *Funny Ha Ha, Commander Badman* was written by Eric Idle between the third and fourth series of **Monty Python** and a year before he launched **Rutland Weekend Television** with Henry Woolf and David Battley, who appear here.

Badman fronts a gang of incapable crooks – Vince is an escapologist who's always tied up in knots, and Boy Wonder, 35, has been singularly unable to secure a criminal record – who decide to operate the great Library Book Caper: they plan, daringly, to keep a volume beyond its due return date.

The Common Lot

UK · ITV (ATV) · SITCOM

1 × 30 mins · colour

5 Apr 1977 · Tue 7pm

MAIN CAST

Gaffer ·················· Bernard Kay
Burridge ················ John Savident
Arthur ················· Leslie Dwyer

CREDITS

writer Caroline Graham · director/producer Alan Tarrant

A single-episode comedy that failed to develop into a full series. Bernard Kay – usually seen in supporting roles – starred as the leader of a team of council gardeners in a public park who plot to grow a new hybrid plant.

The Complete And Utter History Of Britain

UK · ITV (LWT) · SKETCH

*6×30 mins · b/w

12 Jan–16 Feb 1969 · Sun mostly 10.45pm

MAIN CAST

Michael Palin
Terry Jones
Wallas Eaton
Colin Gordon
Roddy Maude-Roxby
Melinda May
Ted Carson
Colin Cunningham
John Hughman
Johnny Vyvyan

CREDITS

writers Michael Palin/Terry Jones · *director* Maurice Murphy · *producer* Humphrey Barclay

Somehow finding the time in between writing and performing *Do Not Adjust Your Set*, writing sketches for Marty Feldman and *Frost On Saturday* and other work, Michael Palin and Terry Jones came up with scripts for a sketch series they modestly titled *The Complete And Utter History Of Britain*. Their idea (greatly expanded from a sketch in *Twice A Fortnight*) was to replay history as if television had been around at the time: interviewing the vital characters in the dressing-room after the Battle of Hastings; having Samuel Pepys present a TV chat-show; showing an estate agent trying to sell Stonehenge to a young couple looking for their first home ('It's got character, charm and a slab in the middle'); and replaying Caesar's home-movie footage of his British invasion. The scope of the series was 'The Dawn Of History' to Oliver Cromwell and each episode took the form of short (three- to four-minute) sketches within the given historical theme, combining film inserts shot on location with video-tape shot in the LWT studio. Remarkably, the series was not networked.

The sketches were well written but the series suffered slightly from the fact that, in this pre-*Monty Python* period, Jones and Palin were not yet able to dictate that they take on all the lead roles. As a consequence, a number of other actors joined them to form a historical repertory company – each person had several parts per show – and, while they were all capable, these outsiders perhaps did not fully sympathise with the material in the same way as the writers. Sadly, the shows were wiped after transmission and the only elements to survive are some filmed inserts that Terry Jones copied (he tries to archive all his own material). A better fate awaited Palin and Jones's next TV excursion into history, *Ripping Yarns*, shown by BBC2 in 1976 and 1979. Jones then made what he called another 'hectic jog through the passages of history' in the one-off humorous documentary

So This Is Progress …, screened by BBC2 on 6 December 1991.

*Note. Seven programmes were written and made but LWT amalgamated the highlights of the first two episodes into one, resulting in a six-part series.

The Complete Guide To Relationships

UK · ITV (KUDOS FOR CARLTON) · SITCOM

1×30 mins · colour

13 Apr 1993 · Tue 8.30pm

MAIN CAST

Mike	Michael Maloney
Julia	Anna Chancellor
Tony	Michael Simkins
Sarah	Maria Friedman
Val	Sophie Thompson
Chris	David Bamber
Donna	Diane Parish
Gary	Toby Whithouse
narrator (voice only)	Enn Reitel

CREDITS

writer/producer Kim Fuller · *director* Juliet May · *executive producer* Stephen Garrett

An unusual single-episode pilot, screened by Carlton as part of its *Comedy Playhouse* season in 1993, which charted the anything-but-smooth course of love for eight people. Mike and Julia have split up 14 times in their five years together, and now they make it 15. Sarah is wondering how to chuck Tony after being together for five years. (Tony is familiar with being chucked by his girl friends, and it's always for the same reason: he lives to make them happy and this drives them mad.) Val has been in scores of disastrous relationships, the latest fling being with a jerk named Trevor. Chris is a happily married man, faithful to his wife in body if not in his fantasies. Chris and Mike are joint owners of a restaurant wherein works Donna, a waitress always dumping men, and young Gary, a waiter who longs for some experiences of his own.

A computer voice (belonging to the comic Enn Reitel) dispassionately narrates the stories of the relationships, which heats up when Sarah, who is a writer, comes to interview Mike about his restaurant and they fall for one another.

The Complete Victor Borge

see BORGE, Victor

Comrade Dad

UK · BBC · SITCOM

8×30 mins · colour

Pilot · 17 Dec 1984 · BBC2 Mon 8pm

One series (7) 13 Jan–24 Feb 1986 · BBC2 Mon 9pm

MAIN CAST

Reg Dudgeon (Dad)	George Cole
Treen Dudgeon (Mum)	Colette O'Neill (pilot)
	Barbara Ewing (series)
Gran	Anna Wing (pilot);
	Doris Hare (series)
Zo Dudgeon	Claire Toeman
Bob Dudgeon	David Garlick

CREDITS

writers Ian Davidson/Peter Vincent · *director/producer* John Kilby

A smart satire set in 1999 in Londongrad, the capital of communist Britain. In the pilot episode we learn how the Russians have managed a remarkable bloodless coup – the revolution took place on 27 June 1989, when, upon learning that thousands of Russian missiles were approaching, the royal family, government and all the other 'important' members of British society took refuge in nuclear-fallout shelters. But the 'missiles' turned out to be aeroplanes full of soldiers who parachuted to land and calmly sealed off the entrances to the shelters, so removing all the powerful people from the picture at a single stroke and enabling the Russians to take control. (This explanatory pilot was remade as the opening episode of the series which began just over a year later, with slight changes in the cast and format).

The series was built around Reg Dudgeon, the 'Comrade Dad' of the title, a working-class man who thinks that the Russian takeover is wonderful, champions the work of his rulers and fervently toes the party line. But his beliefs are tested as the worst excesses of Russian life under the communists – food shortages, long queues, low wages – begin to take their toll. Nevertheless, Reg manages to keep the faith, despite even discovering, in one faintly surreal episode, that there exists another side of the communist British society where garden parties take place, enormous amounts of champagne are drunk and exotic food is eaten by a few elegantly dressed privileged party members.

Overall, *Comrade Dad* was a clever idea with more potential than could be realised in its one series run. George Cole was excellent as Reg and all of his family supported admirably, especially Barbara Ewing as his wife Treen and Claire Toeman as their daughter Zo.

Comrades In Arms

UK · BBC · SITCOM

1×30 mins · b/w

30 Nov 1963 · Sat 9.35pm

MAIN CAST

Ted	Graham Stark
Julie	Fenella Fielding
Bernard	Ian Bannen
Bernard's wife	Elvi Hale

CREDITS

writer Donald Churchill · *producer* Graeme Muir

The actor/writer Donald Churchill provided the script for this *Comedy Playhouse* entry. The hero is Ted, played by Graham Stark, a window-cleaner who gets more than he bargains for when, through an eighth-floor window, he witnesses an extramarital affair between the tenant of the flat, Julie, and a visiting military man, Bernard. Ted duly finds himself involved in some rapidly complicated events.

Cone Zone

UK · ITV (TETRA FILMS FOR CARLTON) · CHILDREN'S SITCOM

18 × 30 mins · colour

Series One (6) 15 Mar–19 Apr 1995 · Wed 4.40pm

Series Two (6) 6 Feb–12 Mar 1996 · Tue 4.30pm

Series Three (6) 26 Feb–2 Apr 1997 · Wed 4.40pm

MAIN CAST

Hayley	Natalie Morse (series 1 & 2)
Zandra	Victoria Hamilton (series 1 & 2)
Leo Summers	Mark Bagnall
Mr Bassett	Paul Shearer (series 1 & 2)
Rick Sullivan	Paul Reynolds
Nick	Ben Homewood (series 1 & 2)
Loretta Summers	Kacey Ainsworth (series 2 & 3)
Corrie Cunningham	Debra Stephenson (series 3)
Marnie	Susan Warren (series 1 & 3)

CREDITS

creators Lee Pressman/Grant Cathro · *writers* Lee Pressman/Grant Cathro (6), Lee Pressman (6), Lee Pressman/Ellen Fox (1), Rebecca Stevens (5) · *directors* Neville Green (series 1), Baz Taylor (series 2), Jo Johnson (series 3) · *executive producer* Michael Forte · *producer* Alan Horrox

A children's sitcom about two school-leaving teenage girls, Hayley and Zandra, who win over everyone from bank manager to franchise owner to open their own ice-cream parlour called Cone Zone. It becomes the hippest, coolest place in town, driven by Hayley's strong sense of logic and Zandra's enthusiasm. But both can be swept off their feet by good-looking young men entering their parlour, and some customers prove problematic – as do boyfriends, nights off, fashion, environmental health officers and other distractions. The girls are assisted in their work by the spotty, bespectacled, long-haired loveable nerd Leo, who serves in the parlour, and he helps them to fend off Hugh Bassett, the miserable manager of the shopping mall wherein Cone Zone is located.

By the third series of *Cone Zone* Hayley and Zandra had moved on and the parlour was under new ownership. Attractive, well-educated hippie Corrie Cunningham, prone to making decisions based upon horoscopes, is

appointed as the new manager but she continues to employ Leo, and also his brash Brummie sister Loretta, who becomes assistant manager. Now the bane of their life is the smarmy con artist Rick Sullivan. (Everyone, you'll gather, has their 'angle' – no one plays a straight role.)

From the same stock as *Mike & Angelo* and the several *T-Bag* light-drama series, *Cone Zone* was one of the better children's sitcoms of the 1990s. Viewers didn't see much ice cream, however: it was simulated using mashed potato because the frozen stuff melted under the hot studio lights.

Confidentially

UK · ITV (ASSOCIATED-REDIFFUSION) · SKETCH

13 × 30 mins · b/w

23 Sep 1955–9 Jan 1956 · Fri 9pm then Mon 9.30pm

MAIN CAST

Reg Dixon

The Wife · · · · · · · · · · · · · · · · · Lucia Guillon

OTHER APPEARANCES

Carl Bernard

Dorothy Blythe

Austin Melford

Dorothy Gordon

Victor Platt

Harold Casket

Stratford Johns

Deryck Guyler

Joan Hickson

Dorothy Blythe

CREDITS

writers Reg Dixon, Austin Melford, Len Astor · *director* Milo Lewis · *producer* Lloyd Williams

Well known through his BBC radio work, the comedian and composer Reg Dixon (not to be confused with the Blackpool organist Reginald Dixon) developed a sketch series for ITV that was titled after his signature tune and began the day after the service was launched. Produced by the London station Associated-Rediffusion, the half-hour shows mixed comedy and music and had an almost regular cast, with Lucia Guillon usually billed as The Wife. Deryck Guyler, Joan Hickson and Stratford Johns (who, more than six years ahead of *Z Cars*, appeared as here a policeman) were among the many players.

See also the follow-up series *Let's Stay Home* and a BBC programme, *Reg Dixon*.

Conjugal Rites

UK · ITV (HUMPHREY BARCLAY PRODUCTIONS FOR GRANADA) · SITCOM

13 × 30 mins · colour

Series One (6) 16 Apr–21 May 1993 · Fri 8pm

Series Two (7) 6 May–17 June 1994 · Fri 8.30pm

MAIN CAST

Gen Masefield	Gwen Taylor
Barry Masefield	Michael Williams
Gillian Masefield	Cordelia Bugeja
Philip Masefield	Stephen Moyer
Jack	Alan MacNaughtan
Toby (voice only)	Warren Clarke (series 1); Christopher Ellison (series 2)

CREDITS

writer Roger Hall · *directors* Mike Vardy (series 1), David Askey (series 2) · *executive producers* Andy Harries/Al Mitchell · *producers* Humphrey Barclay/Justin Greene

Two series depicting a mid-life marital crisis, of particular appeal to middle-class middle-agers – hence the higher-than-average audience ratings of some ten million – though justly deserving that success. Based on writer Roger Hall's own personal experiences, *Conjugal Rites* took all the ingredients for a good sitcom and used them to clever effect.

With experienced actors Gwen Taylor and Michael Williams in the leading roles, *Conjugal Rites* focused on a single couple, Gen and Barry Masefield, opening as they celebrate their 21st wedding anniversary and ponder whether they can keep the marriage going for another 21 years. Now that their children, Philip and Gillian, are grown-up late-teenagers, Gen takes up an all-consuming full-time job as a solicitor, ensuring that she moves in new and different circles. Barry, a dentist for more years than he cares to remember, feels alienated by Gen's work, is cross that he's no longer the breadwinner and that, with Gen working such long hours, many of the domestic chores suddenly fall to him. Going from strength to strength, and keen to make up for the 'lost' years of motherhood, Gen suddenly wants more than Barry can offer, looking to have separate bank accounts, separate holidays – they even consider separate beds, so that Barry can watch TV and she can work late on legal business and not be disturbed by his frequent night-time loo visits. Their long-diminishing sex life wanes with even greater speed not because the couple are disinterested but because they are no longer tuned to the same wavelength.

As the delicate balance of their union, which has kept equilibrium for 21 years, is suddenly altered, the couple are forced to re-assess their marriage. Their dog Toby (whose thoughts are voiced) feels the brunt of the marital discord, being taken for walks by one disgruntled party or the other (but usually Barry), although this does give him the opportunity to exercise his desire to urinate on specific models of cars. In the last episode of the first series Barry and Gen charge towards splitting up, with Gen sailing off into the sunset on a solo cruise, leaving recriminations, threats and uncertainty hanging in the air. Gen's father, Jack, an inveterate gambler, moves in during this time. When Gen returns it is touch and go whether the marriage will survive and there is hesitation and deviation in equal amounts as they both swing, confused, from the pull of the established to the lure of the new. They stick together in the end, though.

The TV series was adapted by Roger Hall from his own stage-play, also titled *Conjugal Rites*, which opened in Britain at the Palace Theatre, Watford, in January 1991. (Prior to this, it had played in New Zealand, to where the British-born Hall had emigrated in 1958.) Gwen Taylor appeared as Gen in the British production and the part of Barry was played by Nicky Henson. But although it developed into a TV series, in stage terms *Conjugal Rites* was not as successful as Hall's earlier *Middle Age Spread*, which ran in London for 18 months.

Brian Conley

Born on 7 August 1961 in Paddington, west London, and raised in nearby Wembley, Brian Conley trained as a child at the Barbara Speake Stage School and appeared in TV commercials at that time. He hit the road at 16, working first as a Pontin's Bluecoat in Devon and then appearing in a comedy cabaret act called Tomfoolery. Going solo a couple of years later, Conley earned his keep as an audience warm-up man for such ITV programmes as *Blockbusters* and *Catchphrase* before gaining occasional TV exposure in variety and regular appearances in *And There's More* and *Five Alive*. He was destined for greater things, however, eventually gaining his own starring shows to demonstrate his talents. In comedy terms, Conley is the quintessential likeable cockney – good-looking and sharp-minded but with an underlying warmth that endears him to viewers of all ages.

See also *The Krankies Klub*, *Laughs From The Palladium* and *The Main Attraction*.

Brian Conley – This Way Up

UK · ITV (LWT) · SKETCH/STANDUP

13 × 30 mins · colour

Series One (7) 20 May–1 July 1989 · Sat mostly 7.30pm

Series Two (6) 27 Apr–1 June 1990 · Fri mostly 8.30pm

MAIN CAST
Brian Conley
Andrew Secombe
Jonathan Kydd
Tony Mathews (series 1)

CREDITS
series 1 writers Mark Burton, Phil Hopkins, David Kind, John O'Farrell, Terry Ravenscroft, Keith Simmons and others · *series 2 writers* Mark Burton, Simon Greenall/Chris Lang, Phil Hopkins, Jonathan Kydd, Christopher Middleton, John O'Farrell, Terry Ravenscroft, Keith Simmons,

Clive Whichelow and others · *executive producer* Marcus Plantin · *director/producer* David G Hillier

Brian Conley was 27 when LWT gave him *This Way Up*, his first own series, and it was a great success. As a result, he rapidly climbed the ladder to become ITV's freshest comedy face of the period, honoured with the Most Promising Artiste title at the 1991 Variety Club awards and swiftly graduating to the West End stage in *Me And My Girl* and then *Jolson*, for which, justifiably, he won numerous awards.

The Brian Conley Show

UK · ITV (LWT) · STANDUP/SKETCH

27 editions (12 × 30 mins · 15 × 45 mins) · colour

Series One (6 × 30 mins) 22 Feb–28 Mar 1992 · Sat around 8pm

Series Two (6 × 30 mins) 15 May–26 June 1993 · Sat mostly 7.30pm

Series Three (7 × 45 mins) 7 May–18 June 1994 · Sat mostly 7.30pm

Series Four (8 × 45 mins) 3 June–22 July 1995 · Sat mostly 6.30pm

MAIN CAST
Brian Conley
John Sachs (series 2–4)
Fern Britton (series 2)

CREDITS
writers Colin Edmonds, Paul Minett/Brian Leveson, Terry Morrison, Keith Simmons, Dennis Berson, Bushell/Lee, Brian Conley, Alan Wightman and others · *additional material* Adrian Baldwin/Ian Cooke, Phil Davies, Jack Haley and others · *script associates* Paul Minett/Brian Leveson (series 1–3) · *directors* Nigel Lythgoe (series 1 & 2), Ian Hamilton (series 3 & 4) · *executive producer* John Kaye Cooper · *producer* Nigel Lythgoe

Populist Saturday-night ITV fare from the fast-rising cockney Conley, in the same sort of show and giving the same kind of performance that had elevated Russ Abbot some years earlier. Hoarse-voiced and slightly manic, but clearly able to sing, dance and make people laugh, Conley literally walked through each programme, switching from a sketch to a song to standup patter while changing costume en route – a neat way to maintain the show's pace. Regular Conley comic characters included children's TV presenter Nick Frisbee with glove-puppet sidekick Larry the Loafer, Dangerous Brian (a stuntman and mock *Gladiators* character interviewed by John Sachs, the announcer of that LWT series) and, in the fourth series, Septic Peg (a play on National Lottery soothsayer Mystic Meg). The humour was easy and laced with innuendo, Conley determining that members of the studio audience as well as those at home must 'enjoy yerself'.

With its weekly array of guest stars *The Brian Conley Show* bordered increasingly on variety, and the third series introduced a weekly game-show element, 'Conley's Car Boot Quiz', in which contestants stood to win upwards of £1000. Assisting Conley in this exercise was Jake, a multi-voiced and 'witty' silicon android from the year 3003. In the fourth series (specifically the edition of 15 July 1995) Conley portrayed Al Jolson for the first time on TV, three months ahead of what would become an award-winning performance in the role on the London stage.

Time After Time

UK · ITV (LWT) · SITCOM

14 × 30 mins · colour

Pilot *Brian Conley: Outside Chance* 3 July 1993 · Sat 7.30pm

Series One (7) 18 Mar–29 Apr 1994 · Fri 8.30pm

Series Two (7) 7 Apr–19 May 1995 · Fri 8.30pm

MAIN CAST
Kenny Conway · · · · · · · · · · · · Brian Conley
Gillian Walcott · · · · · · Kim Thomson (pilot); · · · · · · · · · · Samantha Beckinsale (series)
Jake Brewer · · · · · · · · · · · · Richard Graham
Ma Conway · · · · · · · · · · · · · Kate Williams
Donna Strachan · · · · · · · · · · · Georgia Allen
Michael Tredwell · · · · · · · · Neil McCaul
Robbie Conway · · · · · · · · · · · David Shane
Mr Eaton · · · · · · · · · · · · · Al Hunter-Ashton
· · · · · · · · · · · · · · · · · (pilot & series 1)
Auntie Dot · · · · · · · · · · · · · Deddie Davies

CREDITS
writers Paul Minett/Brian Leveson · *directors* John Kaye Cooper (8), Robin Carr (6), Mick Thomas (1) · *producer* John Kaye Cooper

A week after the conclusion of the second series of *The Brian Conley Show*, ITV networked, in the same Saturday transmission slot, *Brian Conley: Outside Chance*, a one-off half-hour that had a dramatic element but was the product of the LWT comedy department and sitcom writers Minett and Leveson. Conley was cast as Kenny Conway, a car thief given a nine-month prison sentence but paroled from Wormwood Scrubs and determined to 'go straight', a decision that alarms his family of hardened south London criminals, led by his ever-loving but brassy Ma. Kenny is soon embroiled in a tug of war – the Conways want him to continue the lifestyle that regularly leads them into jail (the writers surely must have been tempted to call their creation *Time And The Conways*), probation officers Gillian Walcott (pretty) and Mike Tredwell (austere) try their level best to ensure that Kenny doesn't break the law again, and girlfriend Donna wants to lead him to the altar.

The pilot was a distinct success (attracting a 43 per cent audience share) so, one year on, *Brian Conley: Outside Chance* became a series, renamed *Time After Time*. (The opening episode was a partial remake of the pilot, made necessary because Samantha Beckinsale, daughter of the late Richard Beckinsale, had taken over the key role of Gillian Walcott.) The series continued in much the same vein, with wisecracking Kenny trying to keep his hands clean while his family were forever trying to smear them with ill-gotten gains. In the meantime, despite drifting towards marriage, Kenny was becoming comfortable with the close attentions of probation officer Gillian Walcott, and Donna was attracted to Kenny's best pal, the dodgy car dealer Jake. The first series was voted Best ITV Sitcom in the 1994 British Comedy Awards.

Brian Conley – Alive And Dangerous

UK · ITV (TALENT TELEVISION FOR LWT) · STANDUP/SKETCH

1 × 60 mins · colour

28 Sep 1996 · Sat 9pm

MAIN CAST
Brian Conley

CREDITS
director/producer John Kaye Cooper

A one-off special, with guests, recorded at the Wimbledon Theatre in south London, showcasing Conley's comedic characters and songs from his starring role in the hit West End musical *Jolson*.

Brian Conley's Crazy Christmas

UK · ITV (TALENT TELEVISION FOR CARLTON) · STANDUP/SKETCH

1 × 60 mins · colour

23 Dec 1997 · Tue 8pm

MAIN CAST
Brian Conley
Suzy Aitchison
Ken Andrew
Gareth Marks

CREDITS
writers Paul Minett/Brian Leveson, Brian Conley, Mike Pugh · *additional material* Paul Tibby/Mark Simms, Adam Bostock-Smith · *director* Pati Marr · *executive producer* John Bishop · *producer* John Kaye Cooper

A Christmas special for ITV's resident funny-man, once again combining standup routines with sketches to good effect. Conley's standup act was interspersed with sketches that were introduced via the device of an elderly couple (Conley and Aitchison) watching the show at home and occasionally using the remote control to change channels.

Billy Connolly

Born in Anderston, Glasgow, on 24 November 1942, Connolly had been an apprentice welder in the Upper Clyde shipyards before he began to make waves as a folk singer and banjo player, playing in a group called the Humblebums. When he went solo, Connolly became something of a cult figure on the folk-club circuit, appealing particularly to audiences of CND supporters and anti-apartheid activists; he also wrote the music and lyrics for, and appeared in, a 1972 Edinburgh Festival Fringe and London stage production, *The Great Northern Welly-Boot Show*, a political satire based in the Upper Clyde shipyards, staged by a profit-sharing co-operative.

By this time, Connolly was mixing a good deal of comedy with his music, and developing a scatological, hard-hitting style that often caused offence, especially when he delved into religious areas: re-siting the story of Jesus to Glasgow was one of his most controversial but best-loved routines. The Big Yin, as he came to be known by his fans, was hugely popular in Scotland throughout the early 1970s but was virtually unknown in England until 1974–75 when a successful comedy album (*Cop Yer Whack For This*), a celebrated appearance on the BBC chat-show *Parkinson* and a sold-out national tour finally established him outside of his homeland.

In later years Connolly has moved away from standup comedy to concentrate on other areas, starring in two American sitcoms (**Head Of The Class** and **Billy**), in the BBC1 crime drama *Down Among The Big Boys* (19 September 1993) and playing a major role in the Oscar-nominated 1997 movie *Mrs Brown*. He also presented four BBC1 documentary/travelogue series: *The Bigger Picture* (1994), *Billy Connolly's World Tour Of Scotland* (1994), *A Scot In The Arctic* (1995) and *Billy Connolly's World Tour Of Australia* (1996).

Connolly was the subject of LWT's arts series for ITV, *The South Bank Show*, on 4 October 1992.

See also **Supergran**.

Connolly

UK · ITV (SCOTTISH) · STANDUP

1 × 45 mins · colour

31 Dec 1976 · Fri 10.45pm

MAIN CAST
Billy Connolly

CREDITS
writer Billy Connolly · *producer* David Bell

A rare TV appearance at this time for the Big Yin, beyond chat-shows and the like. Indeed, this was the first time one of his concert appearances had been televised, bringing viewers at home uncomfortably close to sketches about itchy bums.

Billy Connolly In Concert

UK · BBC · STANDUP

1 × 45 mins · colour

1 May 1978 · BBC2 Mon 10.25pm

MAIN CAST
Billy Connolly

CREDITS
writer Billy Connolly · *producer* Michael Hurll

Connolly's vociferous humour, while sometimes hysterically funny, was often considered too strong for mainstream television but as this performance proved, he could tone down his act a little for the TV without losing too much of its comic impact.

The Big Yin

UK · BBC · STANDUP

1 × 40 mins · colour

16 Feb 1985 · BBC2 Sat 10.55pm

MAIN CAST
Billy Connolly

CREDITS
producer David Ross

First shown in BBC Scotland, this programme showed Connolly ad-libbing answers to a friendly interrogation by 80 Scottish teenagers in the TV series *Out Of The Question*. Connolly humorously recalled tales about his schooldays, music lessons, parents, Glasgow bus passengers, gay nights at Partick discos, and he explored why rock drummers make rich husbands and the sources for good comedy.

An Audience With Billy Connolly

UK · C4 (LWT) · STANDUP

1 × 60 mins · colour

26 Oct 1985 · Sat 11pm

MAIN CAST
Billy Connolly

CREDITS
director Alasdair Macmillan · *executive producer* Richard Drewett · *producer* Helen Fraser

A standup performance in front of celebrities and friends. (See also separate listing for *An Audience With ...*)

Constant Hot Water

UK · ITV (CENTRAL) · SITCOM

6 × 30 mins · colour

10 Jan–14 Feb 1986 · Fri 8.30pm

MAIN CAST

Phyllis Nugent · · · · · · · · · · Patricia Phoenix
Miranda Thorpe · · · · · · · · · · · Prunella Gee
Frank Osborne · · · · · · · · · · · · · Steve Alder
Norman Nugent · · · · · · · · · · · · Roger Kemp
Trevor · · · · · · · · · · · · · · Mohammed Ashiq
Jeff · · · · · · · · · · · · · · · · · Kevin Lloyd
Paddy · · · · · · · · · · · · · · Joe McPartland
Brian · · · · · · · · · · · · · · · · · · Al Ashton

CREDITS

writer Colin Pearson · director Bernard Thompson · producer Paula Burdon

A starring sitcom role for Pat Phoenix, who played battling Bridlington guest-house landlady Phyllis Nugent, a woman who takes strong objection to the arrival next door of a widow, Miranda Thorpe, who has moved to the seaside and opens up her house as a rival B&B. Every man in the vicinity fancies Miranda but Phyllis, running a 'respectable residential private hotel' she has grandly named the Portofino, considers Miranda a 'loose woman' and fears for the area's refined quality. This, of course, does not stop her noseying around, interfering and gossiping to her heart's content, especially to her completely hen-pecked hubby Norman.

Forever associated in viewers' minds as *Coronation Street*'s scarlet woman Elsie Tanner, this was Pat Phoenix's first major TV role after she quit the Street in January 1984. It was also her penultimate job, for, after recording *Hidden Talents*, a Lynda La Plante TV play a few months later (screened posthumously), she died, on 18 September 1986. A pity she went out on such a low, for *Constant Hot Water* was rarely more than tepid stuff.

The Continental

see *The Ritz*

Steve Coogan

Born in Middleton, near Manchester, on 14 October 1965, Steve Coogan was introduced to comedy by his father, who used to encourage his family to experience together the delights of various comedy programmes from *Hancock* to *Fawlty Towers*. Coogan himself demonstrated a perverse comic streak from an early age, using make-up and household materials to paint convincing wounds about his person for shock/comedy effect. As a young adult his natural aptitude for mimicry found Coogan work as one of the vocal talents on *Spitting Image*. Then, for a season from 11 September 1989, he appeared weekly in Granada TV's mind-and-body challenge

competition *The Krypton Factor*, playing in a series of comedy-drama vignettes that tested the observational powers of the contestants. Once again, Coogan demonstrated his versatility by creating a number of different characters.

Steve Coogan's first standup performance was in 1986 at a Law Society revue at Manchester Polytechnic, and from here he developed a strong set of routines involving a number of characters he had created, including a dipsomaniac student-hater, Paul Calf, and an inept trainee comedian, Duncan Thickett. In 1992, Coogan achieved wider recognition when (with stage partner John Thomson) he won the coveted Perrier Award for comedy at the Edinburgh Festival Fringe. But it was on the radio that Coogan first made a national impact, initially in the news spoof *On The Hour* (leading to its TV version, *The Day Today*) and then in its spin-off *Knowing Me, Knowing You* (again, radio and then TV, see details below).

See also Comic Relief and Hysteria.

The Paul Calf Video Diary

UK · BBC (POZZITIVE PRODUCTIONS) · SITCOM

1 × 35 mins · colour

1 Jan 1994 · BBC2 Sat 9pm

MAIN CAST

Paul and Pauline Calf · · · · · · Steve Coogan
Fat Bob · · · · · · · · · · · · · · · John Thomson

CREDITS

writers Steve Coogan/Patrick Marber/Henry Normal · director Geoff Posner · producers Geoff Posner, David Tyler

Steve Coogan's ghastly but hilarious creations, the siblings Paul and Pauline Calf, had been established as characters-you-love-to-hate in a string of TV appearances on *Paramount City* (1990–91), *London Underground* (1992) and C4's variety series *Saturday Zoo* (1993). In this New Year's Day 1994 special for BBC2, Coogan satirised the currently popular *Video Diaries* series in which the 'person-in-the-street' was loaned professional video equipment to record some details of their life. Thus viewers were treated to a glimpse of the insulting, politically incorrect and perpetually drunk Paul and his sluttish sister Pauline.

The story centred around Paul's life, especially his pursuit of his occasional girlfriend Julie, and his ongoing crusade against students and all things cultural. Coogan's transformation into these characters was little short of miraculous: both were believable, fully-rounded creations, and he even managed to imbue in Pauline an earthy, feminine sexuality.

See also the sequel *Three Fights, Two Weddings And A Funeral*, below.

Knowing Me, Knowing You ... With Alan Partridge

UK · BBC (TALKBACK PRODUCTIONS) · SATIRE

9 editions (6 × 30 mins · 1 × 40 mins · 2 × short specials) · colour

One series (6) 16 Sep–21 Oct 1994 · BBC2 Fri 10pm

Short special · part of *Fry And Laurie Host A Christmas Night With The Stars* 27 Dec 1994 · BBC2 Tue 9pm

Short special · part of *The Night Of Comic Relief* 17 March 1995 · BBC1 Fri 10.30pm

Special (40 mins) *Knowing Me · Knowing Yule ... With Alan Partridge* 29 Dec 1995 · BBC2 Fri 9.40pm

MAIN CAST

Alan Partridge · · · · · · · · · · · Steve Coogan
Glenn Ponder · · · · · · · · · · · · · Steve Brown
other roles · · · · · · · · · · · · · Rebecca Front
other roles · · · · · · · · · · · · · Patrick Marber
other roles · · · · · · · · · · · Doon Mackichan

CREDITS

writers Steve Coogan, Armando Iannucci, Patrick Marber · additional material Rebecca Front · director Dominic Brigstocke · executive producer Peter Fincham · producer Armando Iannucci

The BBC Radio 4 series *Knowing Me, Knowing You* (six editions, 1 December 1992 to 5 January 1993, followed by a one-off 'behind-the-scenes' programme on 3 July 1993) showcased the talents of ace sports reporter Alan Partridge, who had appeared in the earlier *On The Hour* series. Likewise, after *On The Hour* was translated into the TV hit *The Day Today*, Alan Partridge was given his own starring TV chat-show.

Knowing Me, Knowing You ... With Alan Partridge followed closely along the lines of its radio predecessor, with an Abba theme running through the programmes: Partridge introduced his guests with the Abba refrain 'Knowing me, Alan Partridge, knowing you [name of guest]' and cajole the people to respond with the 'ah-hah' that follows the line in the song. Mostly these attempts fell on stony ground with the guests getting the timing or intonation wrong. Partridge, annoying and insensitive soul that he is, usually endeavoured to correct the person and have them try again.

The TV set was, in Alan's own words, 'modelled on the lobby of an internationally famous hotel', and even featured its own fountain. Each week, Partridge started the show with some forced chit-chat with his band leader Glenn Ponder (who fronted a different combo in every episode, each with a clichéd middle-of-the-road name such as Chalet, Debonair and Bangkok) before using a strangled metaphor to describe that night's show. In fact, Partridge's incredibly mangled, overdrawn metaphors were his trademark, alongside his crass questioning and nebulous grasp on his guest's careers. Partridge was totally unable to hide his true feelings and his hatred or jealousy of his guests could often be detected underneath a false, forced smile. In the final edition of *Knowing Me, Knowing You*, the 1995 Christmas special, Partridge fails in his attempt to ingratiate himself with the BBC's new Chief Commissioning Editor Tony Hayers (David Schneider) and hits him in the face with a dead fowl, an act that finally convinces Hayers to axe the show and banish Partridge from BBC TV. Thrown out into the hinterland of broadcasting, the next time viewers saw Partridge was in 1997, in *I'm Alan Partridge* (see below).

This was very funny stuff, much of it excruciatingly so – straight out of the theatre of embarrassment – making viewers squirm as well as laugh.

Three Fights, Two Weddings And A Funeral

UK · BBC (POZZITIVE PRODUCTIONS) · SITCOM

1 × 45 mins · colour

29 Dec 1994 · BBC2 Thu 9.50pm

MAIN CAST

Paul and Pauline Calf	Steve Coogan
Fat Bob	John Thomson
Mum	Sandra Gough
Julie	Sally Rogers
Spiros	Patrick Marber
Mark	John Hannah
Other Pauline	Jennifer Hennessey
Tony	Gary Olsen
Clive	Jason Yates
Darren	Henry Normal

CREDITS

writers Steve Coogan, Patrick Marber, Henry Normal · *director* Geoff Posner · *producer* David Tyler

A welcome return to the awful Calf siblings, this time with the emphasis on Pauline. The title (and some of the action) spoofed the recent smash-hit British film comedy *Four Weddings And A Funeral*; indeed the programme featured John Hannah satirising the character he had played in the movie.

In *Three Fights, Two Weddings And A Funeral* Pauline planned to marry the smarmy Spiros, but instead found romance nearer home with Paul's best mate, Fat Bob.

Tremendous stuff from a comedy team on top form.

Note. Coogan appeared as Pauline Calf in Comic Relief 1997.

Coogan's Run

UK · BBC (POZZITIVE PRODUCTIONS) · SITCOMS

6 × 30 mins · colour

17 Nov–22 Dec 1995 · BBC2 Fri 9.30pm

A fine series of six filmed comedy playlets permitting the versatile Coogan to appear in further character guises.

Get Calf
17 NOV 1995

MAIN CAST

Paul and Pauline Calf	Steve Coogan
Fat Bob	John Thomson
Mum	Sandra Gough
Grandma	Kathleen Worth
Julie	Sally Rogers
Barry Parry	George Costigan
Dean Parry	Andrew Livingstone
Ian Parry	Adam Fogerty

CREDITS

writers Steve Coogan/Henry Normal · *director* Geoff Posner · *producers* Geoff Posner/David Tyler

More fun with the flawed Calf family. Pauline is now married to Fat Bob and raising a daughter, Petula; Paul is the same as ever, unemployed and still mooning over his lost love Julie. But he soon has further problems when he becomes embroiled in an armed robbery and is pursued by three dangerous villains.

Dearth Of A Salesman
24 NOV 1995

MAIN CAST

Gareth Cheeseman	Steve Coogan
Douglas Crown	John Shrapnel
Alun	Richard Lumsden
Tony	Bernard Wrigley
Ruth Cole	Georgia Mitchell

CREDITS

writers Graham Linehan/Arthur Mathews · *director* Geoff Posner · *producers* Geoff Posner/David Tyler

Computer-software salesman Gareth Cheeseman is an insensitive, vacuous, success-obsessed, gauche sort whose superior, egotistical surface barely hides his insecurity and feelings of inadequacy. He spins a continuous web of lies and fantasy that fools nobody for very long and even fails to maintain his self-delusions of competence.

Another fine characterisation to add to the Coogan menagerie and one destined to re-appear – in 1997 it was announced that Cheeseman would feature in a new sitcom for Geoff Posner's Pozzitive TV.

Handyman For All Seasons
1 DEC 1995

MAIN CAST

Ernest Moss	Steve Coogan
Robin Moss	John Thomson
Florence Mullinger	Felicity Montagu
Francis Burgoyne	Jack Klaff
Valerie Thorne	Louis Delamere
Councillor Hillary Crabbe	
	Adrian Scarborough
PC Ted Cromwell	Philip Martin Brown
Reverend Dowd	Derek Howard
Post Office Barbara	Deddie Davies
Brian the landlord	Geoffrey Leesley
Harry Moss	Henry Normal

CREDITS

writers Steve Coogan/Henry Normal · *director* Geoff Posner · *producers* Geoff Posner/David Tyler

Set in 1960, this episode told the tale of stalwart handyman Ernest Moss, whose dedication and anally retentive attitude to 'doing a good job' may make him boring but also ensures he is a valued member of the community in the village of Ottle (later to become home to the Calfs too). Moss's intransigence and natural adversity to new-fangled short-cuts and modern methodology make him the only dissenting voice against a new development scheme. But his opposition proves heroic when the developers are finally unmasked as profiteers.

This was a lovingly shot piece, with most sequences in black and white to recall the style and tone of an Ealing comedy film. Embroidering the Calf mythology, a Peter Calf (Coogan again) appeared in a cameo role as Paul's father, a 1960s variation on the 1990s model.

Thursday Night Fever
8 DEC 1995

MAIN CAST

Mike Crystal	Steve Coogan
Debs	Theresa Banham
Clement Woods	Graham Fellows
Curtains	Sean McKenzie
Gerald	Stephen Marcus
Oliver Hardy	Peter Corey
Stan Laurel	Barry Wood
The Wurzels	themselves

CREDITS

writers Graham Linehan/Arthur Mathews, Geoffrey Perkins · *additional material* Steve Coogan/Henry Normal · *director* Geoff Posner · *producers* Geoff Posner/David Tyler

Half an hour in the company of some second-rate talents and past-their-sell-by-date acts inhabiting the lounge circuit. Coogan plays crooner and all-round talent Mike Crystal, an adequate interpreter of karaoke classics and disseminator of crass clichés and ill-judged alliterations. But Crystal's free falling career takes an unexpected upturn when he invents an abrasive, loud-mouthed agent.

Note. Graham Fellows, who appeared in this production, is better known as his comic alter ego John Shuttleworth (*500 Bus Stops*).

Natural Born Quizzers
15 DEC 1995

MAIN CAST

Guy Crump	Steve Coogan
Stuart Crump	Patrick Marber

Claire Briggs/	
WPC Cathy Briggs	Rebecca Front
Fraser	Jim Carter
Jeremy Monkhead	Duncan Preston
Dr Phillips	Oliver Ford Davies

CREDITS
writers Patrick Marber, David Tyler · *additional material* Steve Coogan/Henry Normal · *director* Geoff Posner · *producers* Geoff Posner/David Tyler

Meet the Crumps: trivia-obsessed, anorak-wearing adult brothers whose fanatical assimilation of facts, figures, obscure advertising jingles and media miscellany has trapped them, mentally, as juveniles. They also have a murderous past. Escaping from jail, the Crumps attempt to re-create the TV quiz-show they appeared on 20 years earlier.

A bristling black comedy with a devastatingly accurate poke at the ever-growing obsession with trivia.

The Curator   22 DEC 1995

MAIN CAST

Tim Fleck	Steve Coogan
Councillor Len Crabbe	
	Adrian Scarborough
Annette	Alison Steadman
Graham Lambert/	
Robin Moss	John Thomson
Alf	John Clegg
Maud	Debra Gillett

CREDITS
writer/director Patrick Marber · *additional material* Steve Coogan · *producers* Geoff Posner/David Tyler

More black comedy, this time centred on the Little Ottle Museum, the most tedious museum in the world. The fanatical curator Tim Fleck has little time for the outside world and expends most of his energy on rivalling the more professionally run Ottle Museum. But when plans are announced to demolish the Little Ottle Museum to make space for a Turp Inn Steakhouse, Fleck reacts with unexpected violence.

The Tony Ferrino Phenomenon

UK · BBC (POZZITIVE PRODUCTIONS) · SATIRE
1 × 45 mins · colour
1 Jan 1997 · BBC2 Wed 9.20pm

MAIN CAST
Tony Ferrino ·············· Steve Coogan

CREDITS
writer Steve Coogan · *director* Geoff Posner · *producers* Geoff Posner, David Tyler

Another grotesque Coogan character. Tony Ferrino is a smarmy, romantic Portuguese singing star with tight trousers, a loud shirt, big hair, deep tan, sexy moustache and an ego the size of Jupiter.

In this 45-minute special Ferrino arrived on TV with a fully developed history that depicted his early career, singing in a group with his brothers (who then mysteriously disappeared) before achieving international fame as the winner of the Eurovision Song Contest.

Guest stars Mick Hucknall, Kim Wilde and Gary Wilmot appeared as themselves to add authenticity to the Ferrino myth.

Introducing Tony Ferrino, Who And Why? A Quest

UK · BBC (POZZITIVE PRODUCTIONS) · SATIRE
1 × 30 mins · colour
3 Jan 1997 · BBC2 Fri 10pm

MAIN CAST
Tony Ferrino ·············· Steve Coogan

CREDITS
writer Steve Coogan · *director* Geoff Posner · *producers* Geoff Posner, David Tyler

A supposed in-depth interview with the Portuguese megastar, permitting further revelations into his chequered past.

This major launch of Ferrino (he also made TV guest appearances at this time) was a measure of how popular Steve Coogan and his characters had become, but Ferrino didn't have the same immediate impact as Alan Partridge and Paul/Pauline Calf.

Note. Coogan appeared as Tony Ferrino in Comic Relief 1997.

I'm Alan Partridge

UK · BBC (TALKBACK PRODUCTIONS) · SITCOM
6 × 30 mins · colour
3 Nov–8 Dec 1997 · BBC2 Mon 10pm

MAIN CAST

Alan Partridge	Steve Coogan
Lynn	Felicity Montagu
Susan	Barbara Durkin
Sophie	Sally Phillips
Michael	Simon Greenall
Dave Clifton	Phil Cornwell

CREDITS
writers Peter Baynham/Steve Coogan/Armando Iannucci · *director* Dominic Brigstocke · *producer* Armando Iannucci

Presenting the lowly *Up With The Partridge* at Radio Norwich, broadcast in the thankless 4.30–7am slot, Alan Partridge has slid a long way into obscurity since the ending of *Knowing Me, Knowing You* and his dismissal by BBC Television. Kicked out too by his wife Carol, we find him a permanent resident at the characterless Linton Travel Tavern, chosen by the presenter because it's equidistant between London and Norwich. The hotel manager, Susan, treats Alan with the respect he believes he deserves but the receptionist, Sophie, cannot stop laughing at him and often has to hurry away from the

counter when he talks to them. The hotel handyman, Michael, is a fan of Partridge's, but his Geordie accent is almost totally incomprehensible to Alan, often leading to weird misunderstandings. Alan's ego is shored up by his loyal PA, Lynn, who comes to see him on a daily basis and works hard at keeping him in the public eye and attracting sponsorship deals. A 50-year-old spinster, Lynn is devoted to her employer, praising him constantly, putting up with his incredibly insensitive comments and carrying a selection of medical supplies to alleviate Alan's various ailments (including flaking skin and fungal-infected feet).

The series looked at Alan's attempts to maintain the illusion that he is still a star, and propel himself back into the big time. His struggles might have evinced viewer sympathy were it not for the fact that, in Coogan's masterly hands, Partridge is a thoroughly unpleasant character with a bloated ego and an awesome disregard for those around him.

The previous radio and TV series featuring Partridge only skimmed the surface of the character; here viewers saw him in all his loathsome glory, and the result was a dazzling comedy tour de force that, even by Coogan's high standards, was a masterpiece.

Cool Head

UK · ITV (CENTRAL) · IMPRESSIONISM
6 × 30 mins · colour
17 Feb–24 Mar 1991 · Sun mostly 10pm

MAIN CAST
Phil Cool
Dillie Keane
Steven O'Donnell

CREDITS
writers Phil Cool, Ian Davidson, David Hansen, Paul Owen · *director* John Kilby · *producer* Judith Holder

A new series for the rubber-faced comic impressionist Phil Cool – see the following entry, *Cool It*, for further details.

Among those meted out the Cool treatment this time around were Rolf Harris, Prince Charles (Cool made him half-man/half-horse), Paul McCartney, Davids Attenborough and Frost, and Ben Elton, and there were frequent insights into the comic's brain.

See also *Phil Cool*.

Cool It

UK · BBC · IMPRESSIONISM
14 editions (11 × 30 mins · 3 × 25 mins) · colour
Series One (3 × 25 mins) 30 Aug–13 Sep 1985 · BBC2 Fri 10pm
Series Two (5 × 30 mins) 24 Nov–22 Dec 1986 · BBC2 Mon 9pm

Series Three (6 × 30 mins) 1 Sep–6 Oct 1988 · BBC2 Thu 9pm

MAIN CAST
Phil Cool

CREDITS
writers Phil Cool(14), Paul Alexander (6), Keith Donnelly (6), Barry Faulkner (6), Jasper Carrott (5) · director David Weir · producer Steve Weddle

Hard-working cabaret star Phil Cool had appeared in the new talent show **Rock With Laughter** in 1980 and as one of the regulars on **Saturday Stayback** in 1983, but he fully realised his potential in these series for BBC2. Cool had been championed by comedian Jasper Carrott, who was so impressed by the impressionist in cabaret that he took an active hand in furthering his career: Carrott acted as associate producer on the first series of *Cool It* and co-wrote the scripts for the second. His faith was justified: Cool was an amazing talent.

Whereas there were 'alternative comedians', Cool was an alternative impressionist. Sure, he did impersonations of the famous (Roy Hattersley, Mick Jagger etc) but he combined this with a far more eclectic mix of characters including Rolf Harris, Quasimodo, Rowan Atkinson, ET, the Pope and Rik Mayall. And these weren't just vocal impressions but fully fledged facial expressions, with Cool able to contort his features into a caricature semblance of the intended victim. Sometimes so uncanny was this facial transformation that he didn't need traditional sketch material to go with it and could rely solely upon the power of the transformation. The shows tipped into the realms of surrealism when Cool took his act even further, impersonating animals, cartoon characters and inanimate objects such as motor cars, inventing different personalities for Datsuns and Volkswagens.

See also **Cool Head** and **Phil Cool.**

Tommy Cooper

Tommy Cooper was born in Caerphilly, Glamorganshire, on 19 March 1922 and, like many of his contemporaries, first demonstrated his penchant for comedy while in uniform, as 'Trooper Cooper' of the Horse Guards. Upon demobilisation from the services in 1947 he embarked upon a career as entertainer, trying his hand at various acts including a stint as an impressionist. The story goes that while auditioning seriously as a magician Cooper fluffed the tricks so badly that his assessors assumed it was a deliberate and very funny routine. When he intentionally adopted such an act much success followed, including a long

spell at the Windmill Theatre in London, and an important London Palladium appearance in 1952. Cooper's first regular TV show *It's Magic* (see below) aired in 1952 and from then on he appeared on television with great regularity, and with good reason: his popularity was enormous, especially through the 1960s and 70s. A giant of comedy in every sense (he stood 6ft 4in), Cooper made a career out of badly performed magic and brilliantly told lame jokes, and his sense of timing was peerless. Simply by walking on stage, wearing his trademark fez hat, coughing or muttering catchphrases such as 'just like that!' Cooper had audiences in hysterics. His stage persona was that of a somewhat bewildered and unwieldy man, trying his 'best' to keep things on an even keel, despite numerous mishaps, and perspiring profusely while doing so.

Cooper made hundreds of TV appearances, especially as a guest on other shows, but he also enjoyed many series of his own, which are listed here.

See also **Comedy Capers.**

It's Magic

UK · BBC · STANDUP

8 × 45 mins · b/w

12 Mar–16 June 1952 · fortnightly Wed 9pm

MAIN CAST
Tommy Cooper

CREDITS
writer Miff Ferrie · producer Graeme Muir

Bearing the sobriquet 'nearly a magician', Tommy Cooper starred in this show which combined 'mischief, music and mystery'. His failure to pull off complex magic tricks was already becoming his recognised trademark and here he exploited that style under the writing supervision of impresario Miff Ferrie, who had previously booked Cooper into nightclubs and who recognised the huge potential of the giant funny man. Guest stars each week included fellow members of the Magic Circle.

Note. *It's Magic* continued with subsequent series hosted by David Nixon, when the emphasis switched from comedy to trickery.

Cooper (Or Life With Tommy)

UK · ITV (ASSOCIATED-REDIFFUSION) · SKETCH/STANDUP

12 × 30 mins · b/w

25 Mar–17 June 1957 · Mon 9.30pm

MAIN CAST
Tommy Cooper
Hugh Paddick
Richard Waring

CREDITS
writers Dave Freeman/Freddie Sadler (6), Richard Waring (4), Dave Freeman/Richard Waring (1), Richard Waring/Patrick Brawn (1) · director Peter Croft

Cooper was given his own series by the London ITV station Associated-Rediffusion early in 1957 – nine years after he had made his TV debut on the BBC's talent-spotting show *New To You* (8 March 1948). *Cooper (Or Life With Tommy)* – that was its actual title – invited viewers to witness the extraordinary things that happened to Cooper in everyday life.

The Tommy Cooper Hour   1

UK · ITV (ATV) · STANDUP/SKETCH

1 × 60 mins · b/w

23 Nov 1957 · Sat 8.30pm

MAIN CAST
Tommy Cooper
Aileen Cochrane

CREDITS
director/producer Albert Locke

A single show screened under the banner *Val Parnell's Saturday Spectacular*. Singer/dancer Aileen Cochrane provided some sketch support.

Cooper's Capers

UK · ITV (ATV) · SKETCH

6 × 30 mins · b/w

31 Oct–5 Dec 1958 · Fri 10.15pm

MAIN CAST
Tommy Cooper
Aileen Cochrane

CREDITS
writers Bill Craig/John Law · producers Hugh Rennie (3), Dicky Leeman (3)

Emphasising comedy sketches more than his magic, this short ATV series showed Cooper ambling through his daily routines with a vague manner and meeting troubles as a result.

Cooperama

UK · ITV (ABC) · SKETCH

7 × 35 mins · b/w

18 June–6 Aug 1966 · Sat 8.35pm

MAIN CAST
Tommy Cooper
Derek Bond
John Junkin

CREDITS
writers Brad Ashton, John Muir/Eric Geen, John Warren/John Singer, Austin Steele · director Mark Stuart

Another scripted sketch series in which, with a number of weekly guests, Cooper re-enacted some of the impossible situations he had fallen into over the years.

This same year, 1966, Cooper went to New York and made several appearances on the top-rated CBS variety series *The Ed Sullivan Show*.

Life With Cooper

UK · ITV (ABC, *THAMES) · SKETCH

20 × 30 mins · b/w

Series One (7) 31 Dec 1966–4 Feb 1967 · Sat 8.55pm

Series Two (7) 24 Feb–6 Apr 1968 · Sat 7pm

*Series Three (6) 8 Apr–20 May 1969 · Tue 8.30pm

MAIN CAST
Tommy Cooper

CREDITS
writers (in various permutations) John Muir/Eric Geen, John Warren/John Singer, Johnnie Mortimer/Brian Cooke, Brad Ashton, George Evans/Derek Collyer, Eric Merriman, Barry Cryer · *script editors* Barry Took (series 2), Eric Merriman (series 3) · *producers/directors* Mark Stuart (eds 1–11, 13, 14), Milo Lewis (eds 12, 15–20)

In the same vein as *Cooperama* (indeed, only the title was different), *Life With Cooper* once again saw our Tommy, with variable supporting casts, reliving fictional comic situations from his past.

Cooper King-Size

UK · ITV (THAMES) · STANDUP/SKETCH

***1 × 60 mins · b/w**

30 July 1968 · Tue 8.15pm

MAIN CAST
Tommy Cooper

CREDITS
writer Eric Merriman · *producer* Mark Stuart

Thames TV featured a Tommy Cooper special the day of its launch, in which the befezzed comedian ran though his classic routines from the unlikely location of his studio dressing room.

*Note. The show was meant to run for an hour but was on screen for only 20 minutes before being blacked out by industrial action.

Cooper At Large

UK · ITV (THAMES) · SKETCH

1 × 45 mins · b/w

6 Nov 1968 · Wed 9.15pm

MAIN CAST
Tommy Cooper

CREDITS
writers Eric Merriman, Mark Stuart · *producer* Mark Stuart

The second of Tommy Cooper's 'specials' for Thames, this one had him exploring comic fantasies in a dream world.

Tommy Cooper

UK · ITV (LWT) · STANDUP/SKETCH

13 × 30 mins · colour

Special · 26 Dec 1969 · Fri 7.30pm

One series (11) 7 Feb–18 Apr 1970 · Sat mostly 6.45pm

Special · 27 Mar 1971 · Sat 6.45pm

MAIN CAST
Tommy Cooper

CREDITS
writer Dick Vosburgh · *director* Bill Turner · *producer* Bill Hitchcock

More of the same mixture of bad jokes and bad magic, performed with the same irresistible charm and immaculately timed Cooper delivery.

The Tommy Cooper Hour

UK · ITV (THAMES) · STANDUP/SKETCH

9 × 60 mins, colour

31 Oct 1973 · Wed 8pm

Tommy Cooper's Christmas 25 Dec 1973 · Tue 8pm

2 Jan 1974 · Wed 8pm

24 Apr 1974 · Wed 8pm

11 Sep 1974 · Wed 8pm

2 Oct 1974 · Wed 9.10pm

27 Nov 1974 · Wed 8pm

25 Dec 1974 · Wed 6.15pm

26 Feb 1975 · Wed 8pm

MAIN CAST
Tommy Cooper

CREDITS
writers Johnnie Mortimer/Brian Cooke (shows 1–4), Dick Hills (5–9) · *directors/producers* Peter Frazer-Jones (shows 1 & 2), Terry Henebery (3 & 4), Royston Mayoh (5–9)

An irregular series of one-hour specials for Thames, with the larger-than-life Cooper demonstrating once again that he only had to walk on stage to cause hysterics.

Cooper

UK · ITV (THAMES) · STANDUP/SKETCH

6 × 30 mins · colour

15 Oct–19 Nov 1975 · Wed 8.30pm

MAIN CAST
Tommy Cooper
David Hamilton

CREDITS
writer Dick Hills · *director/producer* Royston Mayoh

A series with Cooper joined in each edition by actors for a pivotal sketch. These guests included Victor Spinetti (twice), Dandy Nichols, Norman Rossington, Michael

Robbins, Brian Pettifer and Ian Hendry. David Hamilton appeared each week as an interviewer grilling Cooper on a particular subject but constantly being confounded in his attempts to get 'sensible' replies to his questions.

Tommy Cooper's Guest Night

UK · ITV (THAMES) · STANDUP/SKETCH

1 × 60 mins · colour

28 Dec 1976 · Tue 7pm

MAIN CAST
Tommy Cooper
Arthur Askey
Lionel Blair

CREDITS
writers Dick Hills, Barry Cryer, Spike Mullins, Eddie Bayliss · *director/producer* William G Stewart

A Christmas special, taped at the Casino Theatre in London, which had Cooper join guest Arthur Askey for a song-and-dance act, take to the floor with Lionel Blair and, finally, sing the song 'What Now My Love'.

The Tommy Cooper Show

UK · ITV (THAMES) · STANDUP/SKETCH

1 × 60 mins · colour

28 Aug 1978 · Mon 8pm

MAIN CAST
Tommy Cooper

CREDITS
writer Dick Hills, Eddie Bayliss · *director/producer* Dennis Kirkland

Highlights from this programme were condensed by Thames into a half-hour show screened on 4 December 1978 under the title *Tommy Cooper's Magic Moments*.

Cooper – Just Like That

UK · ITV (THAMES) · STANDUP/SKETCH

6 × 30 mins · colour

11 Sep–16 Oct 1978 · Mon 7pm

MAIN CAST
Tommy Cooper

CREDITS
writers George Martin (6), Eddie Bayliss (6), Dick Hills (2) · *director* Stuart Hall · *producer* Peter Dulay

A series with Cooper helped out some weeks by guest comic actors, including Andrew Sachs, and, in two shows, Sheila Bernette.

Cooper's Half Hour

UK · ITV (THAMES) · STANDUP/SKETCH

6 × 30 mins · colour

2 Sep–7 Oct 1980 · Tue 8pm

MAIN CAST
Tommy Cooper

CREDITS
writers Eric Davidson, Eddie Bayliss, Laurie Rowley, Tommy Cooper · *director/producer* Keith Beckett

Suffering something of a decline on TV, this was Cooper's last own-series. He remained extremely popular, however, in entertainment specials and on stage: indeed he died, in front of millions of viewers, in the middle of his act on the LWT variety show *Live From Her Majesty's* on Sunday 15 April 1984.

Following Cooper's death there have been numerous tribute programmes and compilations of his archive material. The first was an hour-long production, introduced by Eric Sykes, networked on ITV by Thames on 13 June 1984. The second, also from Thames, was screened on 16 September 1986. C4 screened an independently made hour-long tribute, *Just Like That!*, on 28 December 1989, and ITV networked series of highlights from Cooper's Thames TV programmes as *The Best Of Tommy Cooper* from 23 July 1991 and 26 June 1993 and *Classic Cooper* from 27 May and 29 July 1996. Cooper was also the subject of an edition of C4's excellent *Heroes Of Comedy* series on 13 October 1995.

Coping With …

UK · C4 (CARLTON) · THEMED SKETCH

7 × 30 mins · colour

Special · *Coping With Grown-Ups* 26 Sep 1994 · Mon 8pm

Special · *Coping With Christmas* 25 Dec 1995 · Mon 5.45pm

One series (6) 29 Dec 1997–2 Jan 1998 · weekdays 12.05pm

MAIN CAST

Danny · · · · · · · · · · · · · · · · ·	Greg Chisholm
Sprog · · · · · · · · · · · · · · · · · · ·	Sara Cragg
Mel ·	Shauna Shim
other role · · · · ·	Emilie Oldknow (*Grown-Ups*)
other role · · · · · ·	Jeremy Colton (*Grown-Ups*)
Spider · · · · · · ·	Andrew Robinson (*Christmas*)
Kate · · · · · · · · · ·	Rosalie Sears (*Christmas*)
Samantha · · · · · · ·	Kerry Stacey (*Christmas*)
Nip · · · · · · · · · · · ·	Nicholas Harvey (series)
Rachel · · · · · · · · · · · · ·	Gail Kemp (series)
Div · · · · · · · · · · · ·	Darren Bastable (series)

CREDITS
writer Peter Corey · *directors* Brian Lighthill (*Grown-Ups*), Dan Zeff (*Christmas*), Dirk Campbell (series) · *executive producer* Lewis Rudd · *producer* Sue Nott

Coping With Grown-Ups was a Bafta Award-winning one-off (screened as part of C4's *Look Who's Talking* strand, which featured shows made for, by and about children) in which a group of youngsters from Central Television's Junior Television Workshop took a serio-comic, anthropological look at the habits,

attitudes and behaviour of adults. Its success led to *Coping With Christmas*, a more traditional sketch comedy that once again peered at the adult world through younger eyes. In 1997 the theme was extended to a six-part series, showing young actors, in fixed roles, looking at subjects of interest to pre-teens and teens ('Holidays', 'School', 'Cool', 'Relatives', 'Girls', 'Boys'); the team made mini-documentaries on the subjects using a hand-held video camera and then commented upon what they were watching. The ongoing inter-relationships between the characters meant that the series was as much sitcom as sketch show, with Danny's romantic pursuit of Mel the central plot strand.

An excellent, witty, well-acted production that deserved its many plaudits and proved that decent children's can be made without resorting to fantasy or slapstick.

The Copperfield Comedy Company

UK · BBC · SKETCH

1 × 30 mins · colour

14 July 1984 · BBC1 Sat 6.10pm

MAIN CAST

David Copperfield
Debbie Arnold
Joanne Campbell
Nick Maloney
Sonny Hayes & Co

CREDITS
writers Mike Craig/Ron McDonnell, Alan Walsh, David Copperfield, Malcolm Duffy/Howard Huntridge, Dave Brave/Lee Hurst, Susan Carter and others · *director/producer* Alan Walsh

Following his exposure in the successful *Three Of A Kind*, David Copperfield was given his own starring show by BBC Manchester. The result was this early-Saturday-evening mix of music and comedy featuring Copperfield in various roles but most notably as the 'medallion man' macho buffoon he had developed in *Three Of A Kind*.

Coppers And Co!

UK · BBC · CHILDREN'S SITCOM

9 × 25 mins · colour

5 May–30 June 1988 · BBC1 Thu 4.35pm

MAIN CAST

Coppers · · · · · · · · · · · · · ·	David Copperfield
Tony the janitor/ ·	
other roles · · · · · · · · · · · ·	Anthony Howes
Sally/Mrs Thingy/ ·	
other roles · · · · · · · · · · · · ·	Sally Dewhurst

CREDITS
writer Terry Ravenscroft · *producer* Judy Whitfield

A sort of sequel to *Lift Off! With Coppers And Co!* in which writer Terry Ravenscroft took elements from that sketch series and crafted them into a sitcom idea. The premise

now was that Copperfield was an entertainer who lived in a block of flats where everyone wanted to be in show business, from the janitor to ancient resident Mrs Thingy. With the support cast in multiple roles and flights of fancy added to the pot, the series enabled the cast to become involved in sketch-like scenes within the main body of the situations.

Coppers End

UK · ITV (ATV) · SITCOM

*13 × 30 mins (12 × colour, 1 × b/w)

*19 Feb–14 May 1971 · Fri 7.30pm then Sat 9.30pm

MAIN CAST

Sgt Sam Short · · · · · · · · · · · · · ·	Bill Owen
PC Eddie Edwards · · · · · · · · ·	Richard Wattis
WPS Penny Pringle · · · · · ·	Josephine Tewson
PC Chipper Collins · · · · · · · · · ·	George Moon
PC Dinkie Dinkworth · · · · · · · ·	Royce Mills
Chief Supt Ripper · · · · · · · · · ·	Kevin Brennan

CREDITS
creator Ted Willis · *writers* David Cumming/Derek Collyer (11), David Cumming/Derek Collyer/Paul Wheeler (1), David Cumming/Derek Collyer/Stuart Douglas (1) · *director* John Sichel · *producer* Shaun O'Riordan

Created by *Dixon Of Dock Green* mastermind/writer Ted Willis, *Coppers End* could, at a stretch, be considered a cross between *Dixon* and **The Phil Silvers Show**, wherein a bunch of policemen at a forgotten country station strive to do as little work as humanly possible while pursuing extramural endeavours such as hiring out the patrol car for weddings, funerals, driving lessons and stock-car racing. Their laziness is shaken, however, when WPS Penny Pringle joins the force and determines to put a stop to their antics.

*Note. The 13th episode was not screened by London ITV; the final screening in the capital was on 8 May 1971.

Copy Cats

UK · ITV (LWT) · IMPRESSIONISM

20 × 30 mins · colour

Series One (8) 30 Nov 1985–18 Jan 1986 · Sat mostly 7.15pm

Series Two (6) 30 Aug–4 Oct 1986 · Sat 7.15pm

Series Three (6) 31 Oct–5 Dec 1987 · Sat mostly 6.45pm

MAIN CAST

Bobby Davro (series 1 & 2)
Aiden J Harvey
Allan Stewart
Andrew O'Connor
Gary Wilmot (series 1)
Johnny More (series 1)
Dave Evans (series 1)
Jessica Martin (series 1)
Hilary O'Neil (series 2 & 3)
Mike Osman (series 2 & 3)

Cheryl Taylor (series 2)
Pauline Hannah (series 3)
Mark Walker (series 3)

CREDITS

series 1 writers Russel Lane, Andrew O'Connor ·
series 2 writers Charlie Adams, Geoff Atkinson,
Bryan Blackburn, Garry Chambers, Eric Davidson,
Richard Kates, Russel Lane, Tim Maloney, Andrew
O'Connor, Bob Phillips · *series 3 writers* Charlie
Adams, Geoff Atkinson, Jim Bell, Bryan Blackburn,
Lee Carroll, Gary Clapperton, Eric Davidson, Joe
Griffiths, Peter Hickey, Richard Kates, Gerald
Mahlowe, Tim Maloney, Bill Naylor, Andrew
O'Connor, John Palmer, Bob Phillips, Terry
Ravenscroft, Alan Wightman · *director* Vic Finch ·
executive producer John Ammonds (series 2 & 3) ·
producers David Bell (series 1), Vic Finch (series
2 & 3)

Typical cheap-and-cheerful ITV Saturday-
evening entertainment from LWT in the
mould of *Who Do You Do?* from the
previous decade, featuring an array of
talented but sub-Bremner impressionists
delivering a zap-bang-pow barrage of
impersonations in so-so-quality sketches
and standup material. Bobby Davro was the
leader of the gang, and viewers were treated
to impressions of, among *many* others,
Harry Secombe, Dave Allen, Prince, Michael
Jackson, Larry Grayson, Moira Anderson,
Moira Stuart, Shirley Bassey, Freddie
Mercury, Esther Rantzen, Gloria Hunniford,
Frank Bruno, Mike Reid, Tina Turner, David
Bellamy, Zola Budd, Harry Carpenter, Saint
and Greavsie, the Krankies, Prince Charles,
Alex Higgins, Rik Mayall as Kevin Turvey,
Russ Abbot's Jimmy McJimmy character and
various soap stars.

Note. Some of the *Copy Cats* team (Stewart,
Harvey, O'Connor, Osman, O'Neil and Taylor)
appeared together under the programme's
banner in a charity concert, *A Christmas
Night Of One Hundred Stars*, networked by
LWT on 26 December 1986.

See also *Go For It* and *The Comedy Crowd*.

The Corbett Follies

UK · ITV (LWT) · SKETCH/STANDUP
11 × 30 mins · b/w
11 Jan–26 Mar 1969 · Sat mostly 7pm

MAIN CAST
Ronnie Corbett

CREDITS
script editor Barry Cryer · *director/producer* Keith
Beckett

A comedy series with a difference for wee
Ronnie, presenting standup and sketch
material amid music and dancing acts in
which he also participated. Each show
featured a guest star, one of whom was his
wife, the actress Anne Hart. Another was
Ronnie Barker.

The Corner House

UK · C4 (RPM) · SITCOM
6 × 30 mins · colour
4 May–8 June 1987 · Mon 9.30pm

MAIN CAST
Gilbert · · · · · · · · · · · · · Christopher Eymard
Dave · · · · · · · · · · · · · · · · Robert Llewellyn
Pete · Aslie Pitter
Grace · · · · · · · · · · · · · · · · · · · Annie Hayes
Mr Cobham · · · · · · · · · · · Howard Lew Lewis
Sam · · · · · · · · · · · · · · · · · · · Martin Allan
Rosie · · · · · · · · · · · · · · · · · · Rosy Fordham
Annie · · · · · · · · · · · · · · · · · Arabella Weir

CREDITS
writers Christopher Eymard/Robert Llewellyn ·
director Don Coutts · *producer* David Jones

Writers Christopher Eymard and Robert
Llewellyn and producer David Jones were
three quarters of the comedy cabaret act the
Joeys (for a previous TV appearance see
Book 'Em An' Risk It), and during tours
they dreamed of finding a quiet cosy café,
operated by a *character* who served
gargantuan meals. This led to the creation of
a series in which Eymard and Llewellyn
played the two lead roles, Gilbert and Dave,
joint owners of just such an establishment. It
is in danger of being closed down by the fire
authorities – personalised in the form of Sam,
the regularly visiting fireman – for breaching
regulations, but life goes on merrily. This
café, of course, being a sitcom one, is
populated *entirely* by characters.

One series resulted, interesting only for the
fact that Gilbert and Dave were clearly a gay
couple – still a rare sight on British TV.
Robert Llewellyn went on to play Kryten in
Red Dwarf.

Corrigan Blake

UK · BBC · SITCOM
6 × 30 mins · b/w
1 May–5 June 1963 · Wed 9.45pm

MAIN CAST
Corrigan Blake · · · · · · · · · · · · · John Turner
Wallace St. John Smith · · · · · Paul Daneman

CREDITS
writer Alun Owen · *director* James MacTaggart ·
producer Elwyn Jones

Six comic 'adventures of a bird fancier' by
Alun Owen, starring John Turner as Cockney
roving layabout and womaniser Corrigan
Blake, with Paul Daneman as his aristocratic
sidekick Wallace St John Smith, nicknamed
Wally.

Blake had first surfaced in Owen's play
You Can't Win 'Em All (BBC, 7 February
1962), played then by Jack Hedley.

The Cosby Show

USA · NBC (THE CARSEY-WERNER COMPANY) ·
SITCOM
**197 episodes (193 × 30 mins · 4 × 60 mins) ·
colour**
US dates: 20 Sep 1984–30 Apr 1992
UK dates: 20 Jan 1985–2 Jan 1994 (197 × 30
mins · 2 × 60 mins) C4 mostly Sun 6.30pm

MAIN CAST
Dr Heathcliff 'Cliff' Huxtable · · · · · Bill Cosby
Clair Huxtable · · · · · · · · · · · Phylicia Rashad
Sondra Huxtable/ ·
Tibideaux · · · · · · · · · · · · · Sabrina Le Beauf
Denise Huxtable Kendall · · · · · · · Lisa Bonet
· (1984–91)
Theodore Huxtable · · Malcolm-Jamal Warner
Vanessa Huxtable · · · · · · Tempestt Bledsoe
Rudy Huxtable · · · · · · · Keshia Knight Pulliam
Elvin Tibideaux · · Geoffrey Owens (1986–92)
Anna Huxtable · · · · · · · · · · · · Clarice Taylor
Russell Huxtable · · · · · · · · · · · Earle Hyman
Peter Chiara · · · · · · · Peter Costa (1985–89)
Pam Turner · · · · · · · · · · · · · Erika Alexander

CREDITS
creators Bill Cosby, Ed Weinberger, Michael
Leeson · *writers* various · *directors* various ·
producers Terri Guarnieri, Steve Kline · *executive
producers* Marcy Carsey, Tom Werner, Bernie
Kukoff, John Markus, Earl Pomerantz

Virtually singlehandedly, *The Cosby Show*
revived sitcom domination on US TV,
overturning the mid-1980s prominence of
soaps such as *Dallas* and *Dynasty* and
crime/adventure dramas such as *Magnum PI*.
It was the top-rated sitcom in America for
four straight years, matching the feat of *I
Love Lucy* and bettered only by *All In The
Family*. In its second season, 13 episodes of
The Cosby Show were among the 15 most-
watched TV shows of the year, and it made
NBC the most successful network of the
decade. When the series was sold into
syndication for repeat airings it went for
record prices, earning around $1 million per
episode.

Bill Cosby is very much the self-made man,
having worked his way out of poverty and
into college, overcome colour prejudice and
established himself as a standup comedian on
the nightclub scene (*Bill Cosby Does His
Own Thing*) before breaking into films and
TV. Initially, he spread his humour via
albums – Cosby is reckoned to be the best-
selling comedian on record – discs which
indicated his special empathy for children and
deeply-held family values. These are subjects
that clearly fascinate the man: he even
returned to college in 1976, taking time off
from his career to emerge with a doctorate in
education. (Episodes of *The Cosby Show*
actually carried an executive consultant credit
for 'William H Cosby Jr, Ed D'.) One of Bill
Cosby's biggest successes was a US TV
children's cartoon show, *Fat Albert And
The Cosby Kids* (1972–80), which the comic

hosted, voiced and produced and wherein he again propounded his family and social viewpoints within an educational framework.

The Cosby Show was all of this in a sitcom. The star played Cliff Huxtable, an affluent obstetrician/gynaecologist with an office in his Brooklyn house. Although by no means a fuddy-duddy, being at least partially hip to his children's generation, Cliff's values are of very much of the old school: respect, care, caution are his bywords. Cliff's wife Clair is a corporate-attorney. Their children are cute and bright, and, as the series develops, so do they, gaining education, spouses and delivering grandchildren unto Cliff and Clair. The Huxtables are a family that plainly share, care and listen to one another; home is their refuge and mom and dad are reliable, dependable, witty and *around* for their children when they are in need of some sagely advice. Scripts for *The Cosby Show* contained no sex, swearing or ribaldry of any kind, and not every episode had a 'pay-off': quite simply, the many things that were going on within the house and the Huxtables' lives were resolved – usually happily – and the people moved on. If all this meant that the comedy was bland – well, it was. In Britain, where the best-rated sitcoms tend to carry an 'edge', the show rarely attracted an audience of more than 1.5 million and, although it was a staple of C4 for some nine years (13 including re-runs), it was never much of a talking point.

One reason that *The Cosby Show* seemed believable is that it closely mirrored the star's real life. Bill Cosby and his wife Camille had five children: daughters Erika, Erinn, Ensa and Evin, and son Ennis. In *The Cosby Show* Cliff Huxtable and his wife Clair had five children: daughters Sondra (20 at the start), Denise (16), Vanessa (8) and Rudy (5), and son Theo (14). The Huxtables' Brooklyn house, at 10 Stigwood Avenue, was even designed after the Cosby's family home in Massachusetts. The remarkable thing about *The Cosby Show* is that it *could* have featured a white cast – which means, in other words, that it underlined beautifully the point that colour should make no difference. But while it duly won 14 Image awards from the National Association for the Advancement of Colored Peoples (NAACP), it also upset the activists who wished Cosby to represent the black struggle. (Two American professors wrote a book claiming that the series was so middle-class that it immunised white Americans to the plight of the inner-city blacks. Remarkably, their research was part-funded by Cosby.) But black it *was*, and the guest stars who turned up during the series' run included Stevie Wonder, Sammy Davis Jr, B B King and Dizzy Gillespie.

At first, critics lined up to lambast *The Cosby Show* as safe and cutesy. What made

them change their view, and the series reap its huge audience share, was Cosby himself: he was never less than brilliant in the lead role, bringing to the part his impeccable sense of comic timing and facial mannerisms developed on stage. As star, joint creator, co-owner, script editor and executive consultant, and even co-author of the theme music, Cosby maintained tight control over his series, even insisting that the episodes were taped in New York, when almost every other US networked sitcom was (and still is) made in Hollywood.

The Cosby Show concluded on 30 April 1992 with a much-touted hour-length special in which Theo graduated from New York University and left the nest, prompting Cosby to dance for joy and break 'the fourth wall', walking off the studio set and out through the exit door. But events overshadowed the farewell, and also made for a pointed climax, for as the well-to-do Huxtables patted each other on the back one final time Los Angeles was in flames in the real-life aftermath of the acquittal of the white policemen who had beaten Rodney King. Local TV stations dumped all scheduled shows to carry live pictures of the burning and looting before the NBC affiliate cut to *The Cosby Show* for an hour. Even though it was topped and tailed by a couple of hastily taped messages from Cosby, requesting calm and 'a better tomorrow', the juxtaposition was uncomfortable.

Note. Four years later, Bill Cosby and Phylicia Rashad reunited in different roles, but again as husband and wife, in the American version of the British sitcom *One Foot In The Grave*, which took to the air in the USA in September 1996 as *Cosby. The Cosby Show* also led to a spin-off, *A Different World*, created by Bill Cosby and relating daughter Denise's college experiences. The pilot episode was couched as an episode of *The Cosby Show* (screened in the USA on 7 May 1987 and by C4 in the UK on 3 June 1988) and the series itself was scheduled in the USA immediately after its parent programme and so also enjoyed great ratings.

Cosmo And Thingy

UK · ITV (LWT) · SITCOM

1 × 30 mins · colour

29 Oct 1972 · Sun 12.30am

MAIN CAST

Cosmo	Graham Stark
Thingy	Ronnie Brody
Chattel	Stella Tanner
Chief	Neil McCarthy
Pune	Melvyn Hayes
Wiggle	Jill Kerman
Bag	May Warden

CREDITS

writers John Esmonde/Bob Larbey · *director* Mark Stuart

A single-episode comedy – possibly a pilot for a series that failed to materialise – this was a well-cast half-hour screened the wrong side of midnight and so seen by very few viewers.

Considering that it was written by John Esmonde and Bob Larbey, already the authors of *Please, Sir!* and *The Fenn Street Gang*, and later to create *The Good Life*, it must have been the wonky concept that put off the schedulers: *Cosmo And Thingy* was set in prehistoric times, with the entire cast playing humble cavespeople. In the story, Cosmo invents flying and finds one person, Thingy, who's prepared to try it out for him. Not really the stuff of a hit series.

Cowboys

UK · ITV (THAMES) · SITCOM

13 × 30 mins · colour

Series One (6) 3 Sep–8 Oct 1980 · Wed 8.30pm
Series Two (5) 20 Nov–18 Dec 1980 · Thu 8pm
Series Three (2) 8 & 15 Dec 1981 · Tue 8.30pm

MAIN CAST

Joe Jones	Roy Kinnear
Geyser	Colin Welland
Wobbly Ron	David Kelly
Eric	James Wardroper
Doreen	Debbie Linden (series 1)
Muriel Bailey	Janine Duvitski (series 2 & 3)

CREDITS

writer Peter Learmouth · *director/producer* Michael Mills

'If a job's worth doing, it's worth doing wrong,' went the words in the signature tune, pretty much summing up the premise of *Cowboys*, which depicted the 'working' lives of three hopelessly shoddy builders, Geyser, Wobbly Joe and Eric. They consider themselves 'skilled artisans' and, indeed, are not without brains, especially the plumber, Geyser, who has the capacity to reason out an argument. The terrible trio work for Joe Jones Ltd – someone has to, and nobody else seems keen – the proprietor being a dodgy character enamoured of his secretary Doreen (in the first series) and singularly unable to criticise his workmen, developing instead a habit of rolling his chin on his chest when unhappy or ill at ease.

Screened at the start of a decade when the reputation of desperately inadequate builders would become a sick national joke, *Cowboys* was a neat, well-written encapsulation of the world of botched jobs. It was the first work by Peter Learmouth – nine years later to create *Surgical Spirit*. He had once worked as a painter and decorator and knew the ways and thoughts of such men. Accordingly, the language, if not blue, was earthy and robust; the casting was excellent too, particularly Roy

Kinnear as Joe and Colin Welland (hitherto best known for his PC David Graham part in *Z Cars* and as a documentary maker for BBC2) who, as Geyser, delivered shrewd observations about life in the North. Welland went on to win an Oscar as the writer of the film *Chariots Of Fire*, released in 1981, the same year in which the final two *Cowboys* episodes were screened.

Cows

UK · C4 (ELLA COMMUNICATIONS) · SITCOM

1 × 60 mins · colour

1 Jan 1997 · Wed 10.25pm

MAIN CAST

Boo Johnson · · · · · · · · · · · · · · · · Pam Ferris
Thor Johnson · · · · · · · · · · · · · James Fleet
Great-Aunt Grace · · · · · · · · · Patrick Barlow
Rex Johnson · · · · · · · · · · · · · Jonathan Cake
Toby Johnson · · · · · · · · · · · · · Kevin Eldon
Shirley Johnson · · · · · · · · · · · Nicola Walker
Pinky · · · · · · · · · · · · · · · · · · Sally Phillips

CREDITS

writers Eddie Izzard/Nick Whitby · *director* Geoff Posner · *producers* David Tyler, Geoff Posner

The standup comic Eddie Izzard has strictly limited his TV appearances yet still achieved stardom with his surreal stage material, much of which centres on his anthropomorphism of animals, insects and even inanimate objects in a style similar to the Gary Larson cartoon strip *The Far Side*. Izzard and Larson were both intrigued by cows, finding troughs of humour in the humanisation of such creatures, and Izzard had long contemplated a sitcom based around a family of cows before this single hour-length comedy was screened, intended as a pilot for a series to follow. (None had, by the end of 1997.)

In the pilot we are introduced to the Johnsons, a typically wacky sitcom family who just happen to be cows. The cast wore elaborate, full-body cow suits yet skilfully managed to suggest the different personalities of the individual characters by body language and vocal talent. The cows walked on their hind legs and, although seeming to aspire to human status (or at least high-class bovines), still followed their basic herd instincts. This story centred on the consternation caused when cow son Rex introduced his new girlfriend Pinky (a human) to his family.

Cows included some sharp lines and bizarre and hilarious sight gags but the overall mix failed to gel – its blend of the surreal and mundane being perhaps just too unsettling. A rare disappointment for Izzard perhaps, but, undeniably, a fine attempt at subverting and re-inventing a traditional genre.

See also *Lust For Glorious* (which incorporates *Channel Izzard*).

The Craig Ferguson Show

UK · ITV (GRANADA) · STANDUP/SKETCH

1 × 30 mins · colour

4 Mar 1990 · Sun 10.05pm

MAIN CAST

Craig Ferguson
Paul Whitehouse
Charlie Higson
Helen Atkinson Wood

CREDITS

writers Craig Ferguson, Paul Whitehouse/Charlie Higson · *director* Les Chatfield · *producer* James Maw

An enterprising one-off show for the Scots comic Craig Ferguson, who had started his career under the stage pseudonym Bing Hitler. The show also represented the first credited TV appearance for Paul Whitehouse and his chum Charlie Higson, hitherto writers for Harry Enfield. Whitehouse's first BBC appearance followed eight months later, in ***Harry Enfield's Television Programme***; he and Higson would go on to form the backbone of ***The Fast Show***.

See also the following entry.

The Craig Ferguson Story

UK · C4 (TIGER TELEVISION) · SITCOM/STANDUP

1 × 60 mins · colour

12 Sep 1991 · Thu 11.50pm

MAIN CAST

Craig Ferguson · · · · · · · · · · · · · · · himself
Fergus Ferguson · · · · · · · · · · · Peter Cook
Mrs Ferguson · · · · · · · · · · · · June Whitfield
God of Comedy · · · · · · · · · · Frankie Howerd
Stage doorman · · · · · · · · · · · Gerald Harper
Beezie · · · · · · · · · · · · · · · · · · Jess Angus
Agnes · · · · · · · · · · · · · · · · · · Nan Forsythe

CREDITS

writers (sitcom section) Craig Ferguson, Jane Prowse · *additional material* Jon Canter · *writers (standup act)* Craig Ferguson, Paul Whitehouse/Charlie Higson · *director* Jane Prowse · *executive producer* Charles Brand · *producer* Sarah Williams

Sporting a similar premise to ***Packet Of Three***, this one-off C4 special combined a straightforward standup act with a backstage sitcom. The plot was that Ferguson, on a year-long tour, has come to give a show at the Glasgow Pavilion. In the audience is his father Fergus (Peter Cook), a dyed-in-the-wool vaudevillian who is fiercely overbearing in his attentions on his son. Craig is desperate to avoid his father and via a series of flashbacks we see his nightmarish home life in which Fergus practices magic acts on his wife (June Whitfield) and piles unwanted show-business advice on to his son while continually performing a ventriloquist act with a hideous dummy. Meanwhile, on stage, Craig delivers his standard standup act, the routine interrupted by these flashbacks and by a

dream sequence in which Craig is given some useless advice from the God of Comedy (Frankie Howerd).

Ferguson handled the rudimentary acting chores competently enough and smoothly trotted out his observational (and occasionally loud) standup act. Not entirely successful perhaps but a commendable attempt at something different and with some pleasingly black moments.

Craig Goes Mad In Melbourne

UK · C4 (NOEL GAY TELEVISION) · STANDUP/SKETCH

4 × 30 mins · colour

1 June–11 June 1988 · Wed/Sat mostly 11pm

MAIN CAST

Craig Charles

CREDITS

writers cast · *director/producer* Ed Bye · *executive producer* Paul Jackson

Four despatches from the British standup comic Craig Charles, visiting the second Melbourne International Comedy Festival (the first was not covered by British TV) earlier in 1988. Charles' behind-the-scenes exposés Down Under were interspersed with clips from such acts as Craig Ferguson, Americans Phyllis Diller and Rita Rudner and Aussie comics Rod Quantock and Mark Little.

For C4's coverage of the annual International Festival Of Comedy in Montreal, see ***Just For Laughs***.

The Crazy Gang

UK · ITV (JACK HYLTON TV PRODUCTIONS FOR ASSOCIATED-REDIFFUSION) · SKETCH

8 editions (5 × 60 mins · 1 × 40 mins · 2 × 30 mins) · b/w

24 Apr 1956 · Tue 7.20pm (40 mins)
24 May 1956 · Thu 8pm (60 mins)
19 July 1956 · Thu 9pm (60 mins)
26 July 1956 · Thu 9pm (60 mins)
6 Sep 1956 · Thu 9pm (60 mins)
13 Sep 1956 · Thu 9pm (60 mins)
21 Sep 1956 · Fri 8.30pm (30 mins)
The Crazy Gang's Party 23 Dec 1957 · Mon 9.30pm (30 mins)

MAIN CAST

Nervo and Knox
Bud Flanagan
Naughton and Gold
'Monsewer' Eddie Gray

CREDITS

director Michael Westmore

Theatrical impresario Jack Hylton brought the fondly remembered wartime comics the Crazy Gang to ITV under his production arrangement with Associated-Rediffusion, presenting them in a number of shows, not only these eight but also quizzes and variety programmes.

The Crazy Gang was a collection of zany comedians: three double acts – Jimmy Nervo and Teddy Knox, Bud Flanagan and Chesney Allen, and Charlie Naughton and Jimmy Gold – and, perhaps the most comical of them all, 'Monsewer' Eddie Gray, a slapstick maestro and comedy juggler of the first order. The acts had enjoyed individual successes but together they were a comedy phenomenon, packing theatres and appearing in a number of films, starting in 1938 with *Okay For Sound* (director Marcel Varney). 'Crazy' was the right word for them: their antics combined verbal gymnastics with farce and elaborate physical comedy, and it all seemed totally unstructured – lunatic stream-of-consciousness complemented by custard pies. Off stage too they developed an infamous reputation as practical jokers, and played many pranks on one another and fellow guest stars; hoaxes that ranged from the harmless to the cruel and, on some occasions, the downright dangerous. The team remained hugely popular for many years, Flanagan in particular being adored by the British public. It was an obvious idea to bring them to TV, and at least two of these first seven shows featured extracts from a Crazy Gang theatre production, *Jokers Wild*, which Jack Hylton had mounted at the Victoria Palace in London since the end of 1954.

Hylton screened one further Crazy Gang programme in 1957: a 45-minute excerpt from their latest Victoria Palace manoeuvre, *These Foolish Kings*, on 1 August. The following year the gang members were resident comics on the Hylton-produced *Make Me Laugh* (six editions, 15 September to 20 October 1958), a game-show based on an American format in which comedians attempted to make contestants laugh. Because the contestants' winnings mounted up for every second that they remained straight-faced, this was a difficult task. This show was an abject failure – horrendously misconceived, it is a legendary turkey in the annals of British television history and a black spot on the otherwise impeccable record of the irrepressible Crazy Gang.

See also *Friday Night With ...*, *Bud*, *Innocents Abroad* and *Together Again*.

Crazy House

see *Hope And Keen's Crazy House*

The Cream – As Seen By The Clot

UK · BBC · STANDUP
....
1 × 15 mins · b/w
....
16 Sep 1951 · Sun 8.15pm

MAIN CAST
Jimmy Edwards

CREDITS
producer Graeme Muir

Comic reminiscences from 'Professor' Jimmy Edwards, re-creating some of the routines he had performed at RAF concerts when he was Flight-Lieutenant Edwards. This one-off show was part of the year's RAF Sunday celebrations.

Credible Credits

UK · BBC · SATIRE
....
1 × 5 mins · colour
....
31 Aug 1992 · BBC2 Mon 10.45pm

MAIN CAST
Victor Lewis-Smith

CREDITS
writer Victor Lewis-Smith · *director* Richard Curson Smith

A short sequence within a themed night of BBC2 programming, *TV Hell*, which was a response to C4's admirable archive celebration, *TV Heaven*, screened over 13 weeks earlier the same year. Whereas C4's series resurrected classic TV from the past, albeit with a sense of irony, *TV Hell* set out to present the skeletons in television's cupboard: bad acting, awful premises, stilted dialogue, poor musical acts and more were all disinterred and mocked. Though most of the evening was taken up by old clips contextualised by the presenters, there was some original comedy programming, including two brief snippets from the team that had generated *Inside Victor Lewis-Smith*. *Credible Credits* was a smart idea in which Lewis-Smith commented on what TV title sequences would be like if they were truthful about the shows they prefixed.

See also *The Secret Life Of TV* and *TV Offal*.

Cribbins   BBC

UK · BBC · SKETCH
....
1 × 45 mins · b/w
....
27 Feb 1965 · BBC2 Sat 9.25pm

MAIN CAST
Bernard Cribbins
Peter Cushing
Hattie Jacques

CREDITS
writers Sid Green/Dick Hills · *producer* Dennis Main Wilson

A first starring vehicle for comedy actor Bernard Cribbins, best known at the time as a dependable support in British film comedies and TV shows, and for his hit records. The highlight of the show was a sketch featuring Cribbins and guest Peter Cushing as a pair of ornithologists, an interest they shared in real life.

Cribbins   ITV

UK · ITV (THAMES) · SKETCH
....
14 editions (12 × 30 mins · 2 × short specials) · colour
....
Series One (6) 18 Nov–23 Dec 1969 · Tue 8.30pm
....
Short special · part of *All-Star Comedy Carnival* 25 Dec 1969 · Thu 6pm
....
Series Two (6) 15 Sep–20 Oct 1970 · Tue 8.30pm
....
Short special · part of *All-Star Comedy Carnival* 25 Dec 1970 · Fri 6pm

MAIN CAST
Bernard Cribbins
Bob Todd
Carmel McSharry (series 1)
Terence Brady (series 2)
Sheila Steafel (series 2)
Tim Barrett (series 2)

CREDITS
writers Johnnie Mortimer/Brian Cooke · *director/producer* Alan Tarrant

After years of film, TV and recording work, this was Bernard Cribbins' first own TV series, comprising sketches galore (as many as 18 per show) scripted for him by the prolific Johnnie Mortimer and Brian Cooke, and launched in the week that ITV transmitted in colour for the first time. Additionally, each week the star sang a song written by Mortimer and Cooke with Ted Dicks, who had composed Cribbins' early hit singles 'Hole In The Ground' and 'Right, Said Fred'. Some programmes had themes, such as the army, or fishing.

Cribbins-Livings & Co

see *Get The Drift*

Leslie Crowther

Born in Nottingham on 6 February 1933, the son of a stage actor of the same name, the young Leslie Crowther's introduction to public entertainment was as a pianist. He studied the piano for many years and, while still at school, broadcast in BBC radio children's programmes, going on to become one of the so-called 'Ovaltineys' who appeared in shows on Radio Luxembourg to promote that particular bedtime beverage. The young Crowther was also beginning to prove an adept stage actor, appearing in rep at the Open Air Theatre in Regent's Park, and went on to enjoy a long and distinguished West End career. In the meantime, back on BBC radio, Crowther began to build his reputation as a comic, establishing a rapport with fellow comedy actor Ronnie Barker in the 1960 series of

Variety Playhouse. Barker was also on hand to give support when Crowther attained his own regular radio show, *Crowther's Crowd*, in 1963. This was earned on the back of his weekly residency in the BBC TV children's show *Crackerjack* ('Crackerjack!') in which Crowther appeared from 1960, forming a slapstick double-act with Peter Glaze. Children of the 1960s remember Crowther best in this guise, as the tall, thin man perpetually frustrating the little, rotund Glaze with his superior antics and verbal wit, until Glaze, exasperated, would throw up his hands and exclaim 'Oh, I don't know why I try …'.

By this point Crowther was a TV star for children and adults alike, his easy-going style winning him the job as host of BBC1's variety flagship *The Black And White Minstrel Show*. He appeared occasionally as a comedy character actor on television in the 1980s, usually in guest-star roles, but became better known at this time as an ITV game-show host, particularly *The Price Is Right* and *Stars In Their Eyes*. He was also deeply committed to charity work and fund-raising.

Leslie Crowther died on 28 September 1996, four years after a car crash that necessitated brain surgery. On 27 October 1996 BBC1 screened *Leslie Crowther – A Tribute*, an appreciation of this versatile show-business character.

See also *The Summer Show*.

Crowther Takes A Look

UK · BBC · SKETCH

2 × 45 mins · b/w

29 May 1965 · BBC2 Sat 9.30pm

12 June 1965 · BBC2 Sat 9.30pm

MAIN CAST
Leslie Crowther
Graham Stark
Sheila Bernette

CREDITS
writer Dave Freeman · *producer* George Inns

Two shows fronted by Crowther. The format was a typical one for a BBC2 comedy at this time, with all the sketches and routines built around a common theme: 'Love And Marriage' in the first show, 'People Of Britain' in the second.

The Reluctant Romeo

UK · BBC · SITCOM

8 × 30 mins · b/w

Pilot · 2 Aug 1966 · BBC1 Tue 7.30pm

One series (7) 15 May–3 July 1967 · BBC1 Mon 7.30pm

MAIN CAST

Thomas Jones · · · · · · · · · Leslie Crowther
Geraldine Woods · · · · · · · · Amanda Barrie

Sally Gardner · · · · · · · · · · · Margo Jenkins
Henry Copthorne · · · · · · · · Geoffrey Sumner
John Blazer · · · · · · · · · · · · · · · Keith Pyott

CREDITS
writers George Evans/Derek Collyer · *producer* Eric Fawcett

A first sitcom role for *Crackerjack*'s Crowther, authored by the writers of his hit BBC radio series *Crowther's Crowd*. In the *Comedy Playhouse* pilot and full series that followed, Crowther played Thomas 'Tom' Jones, who, like his 18th-century novel-hero namesake, is irresistibly alluring to women. This particular Tom Jones, though, would have been much happier without any such distractions, leaving him free to focus on his fiancée, Sally, and get on with his career as an advertising executive.

Crowther was a dab hand at this type of light comedy but his character's animal magnetism didn't click with viewers to any significant degree.

Crowther's In Town

UK · ITV (LWT) · STANDUP

7 × 45 mins · colour

26 Sep–31 Oct 1970 · Sat 7.15pm

MAIN CAST
Leslie Crowther

CREDITS
writers Spike Mullins (7), David A Yallop (7), Peter Dulay (1) · *producer* Gordon Hesketh

After earning a reputation as a reliable guest funny-man in other people's shows, LWT gave Leslie Crowther top-billing on ITV for the first time in this Saturday-evening series of sketches and music.

The Leslie Crowther Show

UK · ITV (LWT) · SKETCH

6 × 60 mins · colour

30 Jan–6 Mar 1971 · Sat mostly 7.15pm

MAIN CAST
Leslie Crowther
Arthur English
Chic Murray
Albert Modley

CREDITS
writers Peter Dulay, Spike Mullins, Dick Vosburgh · *director/producer* William G Stewart · *executive producer* Terry Henebery

Six programmes extemporising comedy from single themes (*Treasure Island*, King Arthur and others) starring Crowther with regulars Arthur English, Chic Murray and Albert Modley and various guests, among them Stubby Kaye, Larry Grayson (making his TV debut), Dickie Henderson, Aimi Macdonald, Don Maclean (who would follow Crowther as the wisecracking comic in *Crackerjack*), Jimmy Edwards and Dora Bryan.

My Good Woman

UK · ITV (ATV) · SITCOM

39 episodes (38 × 30 mins · 1 × short special) · colour

Series One (6) 24 Feb–30 Mar 1972 · Thu 9pm

Series Two (8) 12 Sep–24 Oct 1972 · Tue mostly 6.55pm

Series Three (5) 4 June–9 July 1973 · Mon 8pm

Series Four (6) 20 Nov 1973–1 Jan 1974 · Tue mostly 6.55pm

Short special · part of *All-Star Comedy Carnival* 25 Dec 1973 · Tue 6.30pm

Series Five (13) 21 July–15 Oct 1974 · Sun 7.25pm then Tue around 7pm

MAIN CAST
Clive Gibbons · · · · · · · · · · Leslie Crowther
Sylvia Gibbons · · · · · · · · · · · · Sylvia Syms
Rev Martin Hooper · · · · · · Richard Wilson
Philip Broadmore · · · · · · · · · · Keith Barron
· (series 1 & 2)
Carolyn Broadmore · · · · · · · · Marika Mann
· (series 1)
Bob Berris · · · · Glyn Houston (series 4 & 5)

CREDITS
writer Ronnie Taylor · *directors/producers* Les Chatfield (series 1–3), William G Stewart (series 4 & special), Ronnie Baxter (series 5)

A double-first: Leslie Crowther's first ITV sitcom and Sylvia Syms' first TV comedy of any kind. The pair first met when working for a charity organisation – both undertook much work in this area – and indeed charity was the focus of the humour.

Sylvia Gibbons is charitable to a fault: she's fanatical about giving things – and money – away, and is involved in all the local jumble sales and soup kitchens. The only thing she *collects* is clothes – to give away. Her harassed husband Clive wishes her to remember the adage about charity beginning at home, especially as he's in the antiques business and has trouble enough running his shop, but his pleas fall upon deaf ears. To relieve his exasperation Clive seeks solace in male company: first in next-door neighbour Philip Broadmore (whose thrift is the antithesis of Sylvia's compulsive generosity) and then skirt-chasing bachelor friend and darts player Bob Berris. Most of Sylvia's good deeds are channelled through the local vicar, the Reverend Hooper (played by Richard Wilson).

Love And Marriage

UK · ITV (ATV) · SKETCH

1 × 45 mins · colour

26 July 1975 · Sat 5.20pm

MAIN CAST
Leslie Crowther
Sylvia Sims

CREDITS
writers Bryan Blackburn, Dick Vosburgh, Tony Hawes · *director/producer* Colin Clews

A one-off programme in which Leslie Crowther and Sylvia Syms, who had appeared together in *My Good Woman*, explored the subject of matrimony in sketches depicting them as Adam and Eve, honeymooners, pensioners, and, curiously, as a sailor and mermaid. The topic 'Love And Marriage' had previously been explored in *Crowther Takes A Look*.

Big Boy Now!

UK · ITV (ATV) · SITCOM

14 × 30 mins · colour

Series One (7) 30 May–11 July 1976 · Sun 7.25pm
Series Two (7) 17 Feb–31 Mar 1977 · Thu 7pm

MAIN CAST

Tony Marchant · · · · · · · · · Leslie Crowther
Heather Marchant · · · · · · · · · Fabia Drake
Roy Marchant · · · · · Ronald Lewis (series 1)
Capt Edgar Bingham · · · · · · · · · Derek Farr

CREDITS

writer Ronnie Taylor · *director/producer* Les Chatfield

Crowther starred in this ATV sitcom as a middle-aged bachelor estate agent still living at home with his mother, Heather. She is a jealous, interfering widow who clings steadfastly to her 'little boy', so denying him his desperately sought-after freedom. Tony's only hope of liberation rests with Captain Bingham, Heather's boyfriend, whom he hopes will propose marriage.

The pairing of overbearing mother and henpecked son seems to strike a chord with British audiences, as witnessed by the success of a later, similar sitcom, *Sorry!*

Leslie Crowther's Scrapbook

UK · ITV (ATV) · SKETCH

2 × 60 mins · colour

27 May 1978 · Sat 7.30pm
18 Apr 1979 · Wed 8pm

MAIN CAST

Leslie Crowther
Francis Matthews
Johnny Vyvyan
Karen Kay (show 1)
Sheila Steafel (show 1)
Anna Dawson (show 2)

CREDITS

writers Bryan Blackburn, Garry Chambers, Leslie Crowther · *director/producer* Colin Clews

Two specials, in which Crowther flicked back through the pages of his scrapbook of funny memories. The programmes led to a full series, *The Crowther Collection*.

In the first show, comedy actress Sheila Steafel played a monstrous theatrical landlady, and impressionist Karen Kay appeared as Marlene Dietrich, Julie Andrews and Ingrid Bergman. In a second-show sketch, Crowther and Francis Matthews

teamed up for an affectionate tribute to the Crazy Gang founder-members Bud Flanagan and Chesney Allen. Crowther's love for the duo eventually led to a highly acclaimed single ATV play, *Bud 'n' Ches*, screened by ITV on 16 June 1981, in which he played Ches and Bernie Winters appeared as Bud. This in turn led to the pair touring the play around provincial theatres, performing a part of the act on *Starburst* (Central for ITV on 17 March 1982), game-show *3-2-1* (Yorkshire for ITV on 3 December 1983) and at the 1984 *Royal Variety Show* (screened by BBC1 that 25 November), and led to them taking over the London run of an existing alternative tribute to the duo, *Underneath The Arches*, created by another of Flanagan and Allen's great fans, Roy Hudd. See also *The Main Attraction*.

The Crowther Collection

UK · ITV (ATV) · SKETCH

7 × 30 mins · colour

One series (6) 26 July–30 Aug 1980 · Sat mostly 6.30pm
Special · 24 Aug 1981 · Mon 8pm

MAIN CAST

Leslie Crowther
Francis Matthews
Anna Dawson

CREDITS

writers John Junkin/Barry Cryer · *directors* Ron Francis (4), Colin Clews (3) · *producer* Colin Clews

Seven programmes of sketches, with Francis Matthews – at this time best known as the star of the BBC TV detective series *Paul Temple* – playing principal foil to comedian Crowther.

The Crystal Cube

UK · BBC · STANDUP/SKETCH

1 × 30 mins · colour

7 July 1983 · BBC2 Thu 10.10pm

MAIN CAST

Stephen Fry
Hugh Laurie
Emma Thompson
Robbie Coltrane
Fanny Carby

CREDITS

writers Stephen Fry/Hugh Laurie · *director/producer* John Kilby

A one-off show featuring more of the emerging talents of the 'alternative' comedy circuit. Sketches and routines were linked by having the leads look through the 'crystal cube'.

See also *Alfresco*.

Cuckoo College

UK · BBC · SITCOM

1 × 60 mins · b/w

13 May 1949 · Fri 8.45pm

MAIN CAST

Principal · · · · · · · · · · · · · · · Dennis Lawes
Janitor · · · · · · · · · · · · · · · Norman Wisdom
Matron · · · · · · · · · · · · · · · · Mai Bacon
Music master · · · · · · · · · · · · · · · Stanelli
Inspector · · · · · · · · · · · · · · Diana Morrison
English master · · · · · · · · · · · · · · Max Bacon
Intruder 1 · · · · · · · · · · · · · · Joe Linnane
Intruder 2 · · · · · · · · · · · · · Horace Percival
Pupil · · · · · · · · · · · · · · · · Graham Moffatt

CREDITS

writers Ted Kavanagh/Carey Edwards · *producer* Richard Afton

An educational farce centred around Cuckoo College, 'the co-ed college with the curious curriculum'. The plot concerned the principal's application for a government grant and consequent dealings with an officious schools inspector. Comedian Norman Wisdom, a recent television discovery hotly tipped for stardom, played the school's janitor and odd-job man, and Graham Moffatt, best known as Will Hay's film sidekick, was one of the dozen pupils.

Cuckoo Land

NEW ZEALAND · TVNZ (GIBSON GROUP) · CHILDREN'S SITCOM

6 × 30 mins · colour

New Zealand dates: 10 Aug–14 Sep 1986
UK dates: 8 Apr–20 May 1991 (6 episodes) BBC1 Mon 4.10pm

MAIN CAST

Petunia · · · · · · · · · · · · · · · Jennifer Ludlam
Branchy · · · · · · · · · · · · · · · · · Grant Tilly
narrator · · · · · · · · · · Paul Holmes (voice only)
Polly · · · · · · · · · · · · · · · · Eleanor Gibson
Patch · · · · · · · · · · · · · · · · Kendyl Robson

CREDITS

writer Margaret Mahy · *director* Yvonne Mackay · *producer* Dave Gibson

A fun, freewheeling children's series from New Zealand that blended wacky ideas with a zany premise set in and around a house (the director hinted at an influence of *The Young Ones*) and employed human actors, models and psychedelic special effects.

The heroes of the story were Petunia, an aspiring rock star, and her two children, Polly and Patch, who buy the house in question. They discover a neighbour, Branchy, who lives in a tree house and hammers all day long, and he and plenty of visiting characters populate the storylines. There were some nice ideas along the way: in one episode Inland Revenue inspectors arrived in triplicate complete with yards of red tape while a Library Task Force descends upon the scene with a mobile returns desk and 'due-date' stamp.

The Cuckoo Waltz

UK · ITV (GRANADA) · SITCOM

26 × 30 mins · colour

Series One (7) 27 Oct–8 Dec 1975 · Mon 8pm
Series Two (6) 8 July–12 Aug 1976 · Thu 8pm
Series Three (6) 10 Jan–14 Feb 1977 · Mon 8pm
Series Four (7) 26 June–7 Aug 1980 · Thu mostly 8pm

MAIN CAST

Chris Hawthorne · · · · · · · · · · David Roper
Fliss Hawthorne · · · · · · · · · · · Diane Keen
Gavin Rumsey · · · · · · · · · · · · · Lewis Collins
Connie Wagstaffe · · · · · · · · · · · Clare Kelly
Austen Tweedale · · · · · · · · · John McKelvey
Carol Rumsey · · Rachel Davies (series 1 & 2)
Adrian Lockett · · · · · · · Ian Saynor (series 4)

CREDITS

writer Geoffrey Lancashire · script associate John G Temple (series 1 & 2) · directors Bill Gilmour (series 1), Brian Mills (series 2 & 3), Douglas Argent (series 4) · directors/producers Bill Gilmour (series 1), Brian Armstrong (series 2), John G Temple (series 3 & 4)

If not quite three-in-a-bed, this Granada sitcom cast three-in-a-bedsit, with newly-weds Chris and 'Fliss' (Felicity) Hawthorne sharing their sparsely furnished Chorlton-cum-Hardy accommodation with a lodger, Gavin, who calls himself Chris's best friend. The trouble is, while Chris is a young northern newspaper reporter, typing his fingers to the bone to pay off the mortgage, and living with his pretty bride – who has delivered them twins – with little more than two pennies to rub together, Gavin is a wealthy young air-freight executive used to the luxury life and lavish spending sprees. Forced to leave his matrimonial home when he splits from his wife Carol, Gavin moves his fancy furniture, Scalextrix, hi-fi, abundantly stocked wardrobe, drinks cabinet and fast cars chez Hawthorne, at first only for a couple of days but then, it seems, indefinitely. All together, Gavin behaves like a cad, flaunting his wealth and suggesting romance with the disinterested Fliss – who, herself, is wondering what has happened to her life: three A-levels to her name and she's up to her hands in nappy-rash cream. Also closely involved in Chris and Fliss's lives are their neighbour Austen Tweedale and Fliss's prudish, interfering and materially-obsessed mother Connie.

Three such series were made, at which point Lewis Collins (who played Gavin) went off to become a star in ITV's dashing-and-daring cop series The Professionals, and The Cuckoo Waltz seemed to be at an end. Three years later, however, a final series was made – by this time the twins were of school age, Chris and Fliss had a little more money to spend and there was a new lodger to contend with, Adrian Lockett. Like his predecessor, Adrian was something of a scoundrel, and he made abundantly clear his appreciation for Fliss …

Cucumber Castle

UK · BBC · MUSICAL COMEDY

1 × 55 mins · colour

26 Dec 1970 · BBC2 Sat 1.30pm

MAIN CAST

The Bee Gees (Barry Gibb, Maurice Gibb, Robin Gibb)
Eleanor Bron
Pat Coombs
Julian Orchard
Frankie Howerd
Spike Milligan
Vincent Price

CREDITS

writers Barry Gibb/Maurice Gibb · director Hugh Gladwish · executive producer Robert Stigwood · producer Mike Mansfield

A strong comic cast combined for this medieval musical fantasy, written by Barry and Maurice Gibb of the Bee Gees. They, indeed, were the main stars, along with other musical guests Lulu and, bizarrely, the rock supergroup Blind Faith.

Cue Gary!

UK · ITV (CENTRAL) · SKETCH

13 editions (7 × 45 mins · 6 × 30 mins) · colour

Series One (6 × 45 mins) 4 July–8 Aug 1987 · Sat 6pm

Special (45 mins) Cue Gary's Christmas! 27 Dec 1987 · Sun 4.30pm

Series Two (6 × 30 mins) 23 July–27 Aug 1988 · Sat 5.40pm

MAIN CAST

Gary Wilmot
Martin Beaumont
Nikki Boughton

CREDITS

writers Gary Wilmot/Martin Beaumont, Peter Corey/Louise Gillis · additional material Barry Faulkner, Alan Simmons/Keith Simmons, Rog Johnson, Eddie Braben, Tim Maloney · directors Dennis Liddington (8), Tom Poole (2), Jon Scoffield (2), Mike Holgate (1) · executive producer Tony Wolfe (series 1) · producers Brian Wesley (series 1), Tony Wolfe (special), Rick Gardner (series 2)

A sketch series in which Gary Wilmot observed the funny side of life from the position of his flat, with help from companions Martin and Nikki. The Christmas special and all six editions in the second series also featured weekly guest stars. Wilmot was attracting increasingly better work at this time, having progressed from being a New Faces finalist to Copy Cats and now this starring vehicle.

Cuffy

UK · ITV (ELSTREE COMPANY/CENTRAL) · SITCOM

6 × 30 mins · colour

13 Mar–24 Apr 1983 · Sun 7.45pm

MAIN CAST

Cuffy · · · · · · · · · · · · · · · · · Bernard Cribbins
Jake · · · · · · · · · · · · · · · · · · · Jack Douglas
Rev Norris · · · · · · · · · · · · · · Nigel Lambert
Mandy · · · · · · · · · · · · · · · · · · Linda Hayden
Mrs Simkins · · · · · · · · · · · · · · · Diana King

CREDITS

writer Francis Essex · directors/producers Paul Harrison (5), Christopher Baker (1) · executive producer Greg Smith

Spun-off from Shillingbury Tales, Cuffy focused on the life of the rag-tag ragamuffin man who lived in discomfort in his tawdry caravan and moped around the village of Shillingbury wearing a grubby coat, flat cap and stubble. Underneath it all, though, the tinker had a heart of something approaching gold.

Others cast members from Shillingbury Tales reprised their roles, including Jack Douglas as farmer Jake, Linda Hayden as his daughter Mandy, Nigel Lambert as Reverend Norris, and (she appeared once in the original) Diana King as Mrs Simkins, the local spinster. Gareth Hunt and Beryl Reid appeared once apiece as guest stars.

The Culture Vultures

UK · BBC · SITCOM

5 × 30 mins · colour

24 Apr–22 May 1970 · BBC1 Fri 7.55pm

MAIN CAST

Dr Michael Cunningham · · · · · Leslie Phillips
Dr Ian Meredith · · · · · · · · · · · Jonathan Cecil
Prof George Hobbes · · · · · · · · · Peter Sallis
Vivienne · · · · · · · · · · · · · · · · Sally Faulkner

CREDITS

writers Colin Mares/Tim Brooke-Taylor (3), Colin Mares/David Climie (1), Colin Mares (1) · producer Graeme Muir

A campus comedy with super-smoothie Leslie Phillips cast as Dr Michael Cunningham, senior lecturer in anthropology at the 'swinging' University of Hampshire. Cunningham's craving for a life of ease, gambling and physical pleasures is invariably thwarted by problems at work, his colleagues and his friends, but although his casual attitude leads to clashes with his seniors he manages to survive intact.

Halfway through the production Phillips was rushed to hospital with an internal haemorrhage; while he managed to return he was far from fit and this probably accounts for the series lasting only five episodes.

The Curious Case Of Dr Hertz Van Rental

see *Dizzy Heights*

The Curious Case Of Santa Claus

UK · C4 (EDINBURGH FILM & VIDEO PRODUCTIONS) · COMEDY FILM

1 × 60 mins · colour

24 Dec 1982 · Fri 10pm

MAIN CAST

Santa Claus	James Coco
Dr Merryweather	Jon Pertwee
Barbara	Sabina Franklyn
Prof C C Moore	William Raymond

CREDITS

writer Bob Larbey · *director/producer* Robin Crichton

A seasonal single-comedy scripted by Bob Larbey and screened by C4 during its first Christmas on air. Jon Pertwee played a New York psychiatrist helping Santa to establish his own identity by reminding him – in humorous travelogue fashion – of the people and places in his past. The planned working title, *Is Santa Schizo?*, was deemed unsuitable.

Curry And Chips

see MILLIGAN, Spike

Curtains For Harry

UK · ITV (ASSOCIATED-REDIFFUSION) · SITCOM

1 × 60 mins · b/w

20 Oct 1955 · Thu 8pm

MAIN CAST

Harry Bates	Bobby Howes
other role	Joan Sims
other role	Sydney Tafler

CREDITS

writers Philip Saville, Jane Arden, Dick Lester · *director* Philip Saville

A single comedy, screened in the earliest days of ITV, starring Bobby Howes as Harry Bates, a bankrupt former music-hall idol, taken on by some racketeers as lookout for a jewel heist they have planned. Dick Lester, later to become a top film director, helped with the script and also composed music and lyrics for the programme.

Cut And Run

UK · ITV (ZENITH NORTH FOR CARLTON) · SITCOM

1 × 30 mins · colour

30 Mar 1993 · Tue 8.30pm

MAIN CAST

Stan	Tim Healy
Jerry Sprake	Wayne Foskett
Pete Bennett	Christopher Lang
Imo	Carla Mendonça
Steve Ditchfield	Paul Knyman
Derek Hogson	Gary Waldhorn
Genevieve Hogson	Steph Bramwell

CREDITS

writer Tim Firth · *script editor* Paul Mayhew-Archer · *executive producer* Ian Squires · *director/producer* Alan J W Bell

A fledgling independent video company, Reels On Wheels, is commissioned by a group of environmentalists to record the night-time wanderings of some badgers, proof that will ensure that an area of open countryside, the 80-acre Brackley Common, is protected under law and cannot be developed into an 18-hole golf course by dodgy businessman Derek Hogson. The trouble is, the badgers are camera-shy, the nights are long and the four staff of Reels On Wheels – accident-prone best-boy Stan, cameraman Jerry, assistant Imo and the company's unprincipled founder Pete – quickly lose what little patience they have. They do manage to get a £10,000 camera and a torch tied around the badger's neck but are then forced to pursue the animal as it runs amok, ransacking the bins of some fast-food takeaways and then heading for its outlier. Fortunately for all, the badger happens to film Mr and Mrs Hogson in the act of devil worshipping and sexual deviation, which wins the day.

A single-episode pilot screened by Carlton as part of its *Comedy Playhouse* season in 1993, *Cut And Run* showed some promise but was not developed into a series.

The Cut Price Comedy Show

UK · C4 (TSW) · SKETCH

10 × 30 mins · colour

3 Nov 1982–5 Jan 1983 · Wed 6pm

MAIN CAST

Lenny Windsor
Caroline Ellis
Royce Mills
Roger Ruskin Spear
Stefanie Marrian

CREDITS

writers cast · *director/producer* Stephen Wade

Promoted by its participants as 'the worst comedy show ever made' and claiming to utilise old Christmas-cracker jokes, *The Cut Price Comedy Show* – the first British-made sketch series screened by C4 – set out to be corny, and didn't fail.

Lenny Windsor was once the club comic Pete West and *Search For A Star* victor. Roger Ruskin Spear had been a member of the Bonzo Dog Doo-Dah Band.

Cybill

USA · CBS (JAY DANIEL PRODUCTIONS/CHUCK LORRE PRODUCTIONS/RIVER SIREN PRODUCTIONS/THE CARSEY-WERNER COMPANY/PARAMOUNT) · SITCOM

75 × 30 mins (to 31/12/97 · continuing into 1998) · colour

US dates: 2 Jan 1995 to date

UK dates: 5 Jan 1996 to date (63 episodes to 31/12/97) C4 Fri 9pm then 9.35pm

MAIN CAST

Cybill Sheridan	Cybill Shepherd
Maryann Thorpe	Christine Baranski
Ira Lowenstein	Alan Rosenberg
Zoey Lowenstein	Alicia Witt
Rachel Blanders	Dedee Pfeiffer
Jeff Robbins	Tom Wopat
Kevin	Peter Krause

CREDITS

creator Chuck Lorre · *writers* Mike Langworthy, Linda Wallem, Maria A Brown, Alan Ball, James L Freedman, Lee Aronsohn, Elaine Aronsohn, Howard M Gould, Chuck Lorre and others · *directors* Andrew D Weyman, Tom Moore, Robert Berlinger and others · *executive producers* Marcy Carsey, Tom Werner, Caryn Mandabach, Cybill Shepherd, Jay Daniel, Howard Gould, Chuck Lorre · *producers* Lee Aronsohn, Elaine Aronsohn, Dottie Darland

A sitcom that joyously carried a torch for the over-forties woman. It starred Cybill Shepherd as a struggling actress, Cybill Sheridan, a survivor of two marriages, and still close friends with both ex-husbands, and mother of two daughters, one from each partner.

Her first husband is the amiable but dumb Jeff, a stuntman who has ambitions to become a major action star, *à la* Stephen Segal. Her second ex is a neurotic writer, Ira, a talented but worried sort who still holds a candle for Cybill. The pretty and conventional Rachel is the product of the first marriage; she is married to the oddly distant Tom and they have a baby – making Cybill, much to her anguish, a grandmother. The younger daughter, from Cybill's marriage to Ira, is the fiercely bright, smart-talking, Zoey, an independent and often sullen girl with a revulsion to over-emotional scenes.

These four people define Cybill as the wife and mother, but she has a life beyond too: that of a jobbing actress with an eye on the big break. Early episodes invariably began on the set of a TV show, gaudy commercial or B-movie, in which Cybill was required to demean herself in some way. These pre-credit sketches were sometimes lavishly mounted and served as an ideal weekly reminder as to Cybill's low standing within the business. Eventually, Cybill gets her big break and for many weeks she enjoys success as the co-star of an *X-Files*-type fantasy series, *Lifeforms*, before bad luck and unfortunate scheduling causes its cancellation and deposits her once more in the 'struggling' section of the acting community. This, then, is Cybill the actress. But there is yet a fourth facet to her character: Cybill the mischievous funster, who refuses to grow up – and this proved the most endearing and enjoyable aspect of the series.

Central to this fun-loving side of Cybill is her best friend, confidante and neighbour Maryann, a sardonic, witty, feisty sex kitten with an enormous capacity for booze. The presence of Maryann allows Cybill to let down her hair and become involved in all manner of outrageous schemes and adventures. Maryann is hugely wealthy, living off the alimony of her ex-husband, a supremely successful doctor whose medical-school fees were paid by Maryann, who worked tirelessly in order for him to graduate. Then he leaves her for a younger woman and Maryann's bitterness soars to almost biblical proportions, inciting her to wage a covert war on him in order to make his life a misery. Whenever she mentions her ex it is with a contemptuous snarl that makes his title, 'Doctor Dick', sound like an unspeakable swearword. Maryann occasionally dallies with members of the opposite sex – including an extended fling with Ira – but more often than not she is unattached and a drinking/clubbing/bitching friend for Cybill.

The series had many other strengths, not least Cybill Shepherd's willingness to poke fun at her own image and show business. She goes to great lengths for a laugh, especially when having to dress wildly or behave stupidly for a role. Then there was the non-PC nature of the series, which, with its core depiction of two forty-something women refusing to grow up, and clashing with a more traditionalist younger generation, seemed to owe a debt to **Absolutely Fabulous**. Although not as extreme as *AbFab*, the sheer quantity of Maryann's drinking and the apparent lack of consequence that it brought (apart from a pre-series stay in the Betty Ford Clinic), added to the casual attitude of both women toward sex, was still bold by US mainstream standards.

Cyril Fletcher

UK · BBC · STANDUP

2 × 5 mins · b/w

2 Sep 1937 · Thu 9.05pm & 9.45pm

MAIN CAST
Cyril Fletcher

CREDITS
producer Reginald Smith

An early small-screen appearance for the silken-voiced Fletcher, reciting three humorous poems in a pair of five-minute slots from Alexandra Palace.

See also **Kaleidoscope**.

The Cyril Fletcher Show

UK · ITV (JACK HYLTON TV PRODUCTIONS FOR ASSOCIATED-REDIFFUSION) · SKETCH

6 × 30 mins · b/w

9 Apr–14 May 1959 · Thu 10.15pm

MAIN CAST
Cyril Fletcher
Betty Astell
Pat Coombs

CREDITS
writer Johnny Speight · *director* Milo Lewis

A star of BBC radio and the occasional TV variety show, Cyril Fletcher was given his own comedy sketch series by ITV impresario Jack Hylton as the 1950s drew to a close. Although scripted for him by Johnny Speight, there was still room for a few of those famous Fletcher 'odd odes', and the star's wife, Betty Astell, who was among the regular supporting cast.

Cyril's Saga

UK · BBC · SKETCH

1 × 30 mins · b/w

28 Mar 1957 · Thu 8pm

MAIN CAST
Cyril Fletcher
Betty Astell

CREDITS
writers Bob Monkhouse/Denis Goodwin · *producer* Francis Essex

Cyril Fletcher frequently appeared on TV but proved more popular on radio – until, that is, the early 1970s, when he appeared each week on BBC1, delivering his 'odd odes' in *That's Life*.

In this 1957 half-hour Fletcher was joined by his wife Betty Astell, who was returning to television for the first time after a serious illness.

DC Follies

USA · SYNDICATION (SID AND MARTY KROFFT PRODUCTIONS) · SATIRE

73 × 30 mins · colour

US dates: Sep 1987–1989
UK dates: 7 Feb–27 Mar 1988 (7 editions) ITV Sun mostly 11.30pm

MAIN CAST
Fred · Fred Willard
The Krofft Puppets

CREDITS
creators/executive producers Sid Krofft/Marty Krofft

Inspired, undoubtedly, by the British **Spitting Image**, American series *DC Follies* sent-up contemporary goings-on in the USA by way of puppet caricatures. While *Spitting Image* was savage in its humour, however, the American model was an altogether less hostile affair, coming across as comparatively toothless political cartoons rather than caustic satire. So shy of lawsuits was *DC Follies* that every edition ended with a disclaimer to the effect that it had all been done for fun, with no offence intended.

The premise was that the puppet characters – Reagan, Nixon, Bush, Sylvester Stallone, Michael Jackson, Woody Allen, Oprah Winfrey, Jack Nicholson et al – convened to drink in a Washington bar, DC Follies, where they were served by a real live person, its owner Fred Willard, and met a weekly guest.

The puppets were created by Sid and Marty Krofft, and the series ran for 72 editions and a special (*DC Follies Academy Award Special*). Some ITV regions imported *DC Follies* to British screens, LWT showing seven editions late on Sunday nights.

A Dabble With Digance

see DIGANCE, Richard

Dad

UK · BBC · SITCOM

6 × 30 mins · colour

25 Sep–30 Oct 1997 · BBC1 Thu 8.30pm

MAIN CAST
Brian Hook · · · · · · · · · · · · · · · George Cole
Alan Hook · · · · · · · · · · · · · Kevin McNally
Beryl Hook · · · · · · · · · · · · · · · · Julia Hills
Vincent Hook · · · · · · · · · · Toby Ross-Bryant

CREDITS
writer Andrew Marshall · *directors* Nick Wood (5), Marcus Mortimer (1) · *executive producer* Andrew Marshall · *producer* Marcus Mortimer

A generation-gap comedy that contrasted the relationship of Alan Hook and his father Brian, and Alan's relationship with his own son, Vincent.

Brian Hook (played by George Cole) is a well-meaning chap but his values, habits, likes and dislikes were developed in the 1950s and his outlook and personality clash badly with his son's. They had drifted apart for many years but Brian's recent illness has brought them close again, and Alan sees this as a second chance to really get to know his father, despite the fact that Dad tends to drives him mad. Vincent, meanwhile, is a bright enough typical teenager, who feels as distant from Alan as Alan does from Brian.

These mirror-image, cross-generation clashes formed the central basis of *Dad*. Cole was in fine form once more as the solid senior citizen set in his ways, and McNally ably suggested the mixed emotions confusing his character. Julia Hills (who had appeared in Marshall's *2 Point 4 Children*) had little to do as Alan's wife but turned in her usual winning performance all the same.

Dad was not wholly successful, but while the premise, in the hands of another writer, might have resulted in something altogether too twee, in Marshall's – a writer unafraid to explore the darker areas of an idea – it was imbued with a pleasingly quirky edge.

Dad's Army

UK · BBC · SITCOM

83 episodes (77 × 30 mins · 1 × 60 mins · 1 × 40 mins · 1 × 35 mins · 3 × short specials)
13 × b/w · 70 × colour

Series One (6 × 30 mins · b/w) 31 July–11 Sep 1968 · BBC1 Wed 8.20pm

Short special (b/w) · part of *Christmas Night With The Stars* 25 Dec 1968 · BBC1 Wed 6.40pm

Series Two (6 × 30 mins · b/w) 1 Mar–5 Apr 1969 · BBC1 Sat 7pm

Series Three (14 × 30 mins · colour) 11 Sep–11 Dec 1969 · BBC1 Thu 7.30pm

Series Four (13 × 30 mins · colour) 25 Sep–18 Dec 1970 · BBC1 Fri 8pm

Short special (colour) · part of *Christmas Night With The Stars* 25 Dec 1970 · BBC1 Fri 6.45pm

Special (60 mins · colour) 27 Dec 1971 · BBC1 Mon 7pm

Series Five (13 × 30 mins · colour) 6 Oct–29 Dec 1972 · BBC1 Fri 8.30pm

Short special (colour) · part of *Christmas Night With The Stars* 25 Dec 1972 · BBC1 Mon 6.55pm

Series Six (7 × 30 mins · colour) 31 Oct–12 Dec 1973 · BBC1 Wed 6.50pm

Series Seven (6 × 30 mins · colour) 15 Nov–23 Dec 1974 · BBC1 Fri 7.45pm

Series Eight (6 × 30 mins · colour) 5 Sep–10 Oct 1975 · BBC1 Fri 8pm

Special (40 mins · colour) 26 Dec 1975 · BBC1 Fri 6.05pm

Special (30 mins · colour) 26 Dec 1976 · BBC1 Sun 7.25pm

Series Nine (5 × 30 mins · 1 × 35 mins · colour) 2 Oct–13 Nov 1977 · BBC1 Sun 8.10pm

MAIN CAST
Capt George Mainwaring · · · · · · Arthur Lowe
Sgt Arthur Wilson · · · · · · · · John Le Mesurier
L-Cpl Jack Jones · · · · · · · · · · · · · Clive Dunn
Pvt James Frazer · · · · · · · · · · · · · John Laurie
Pvt Charles Godfrey · · · · · · · · Arnold Ridley
Pvt Joe Walker · · · · James Beck (series 1–6)
Pvt Frank Pike · · · · · · · · · · · · Ian Lavender
Air Raid Warden William Hodges · · · · · · · · · ·
· Bill Pertwee
The Vicar: The Reverend Timothy Farthing · · ·
· Frank Williams
The Verger: Maurice Yeatman · · · · · · · · · · · ·
· Edward Sinclair

OTHER APPEARANCES
Mrs Mavis Pike · · · · · · · · · · · · Janet Davies
Mrs Fox · · · · · · · · · · · · · Pamela Cundell
Mrs Edna Peters · · · · · · · · · Queenie Watts
Pvt Sponge · · · · · · · · · · · · · · · Colin Bean
Pvt Cheeseman · · · Talfryn Thomas (series 7)
Capt (Colonel) Pritchard · · · · · Robert Raglan
Capt Square · · · · · · · · · Geoffrey Lumsden
Mr Blewitt (Bluett) · · · · · · · · Harold Bennett
Gerald · · · · · · · · · · · · · · · · · Don Estelle

CREDITS
writers Jimmy Perry/David Croft · *directors* Harold Snoad (to series 8), Bob Spiers (series 9) · *producer* David Croft

The unmistakable voice of Bud Flanagan singing 'Who Do You Think You Are Kidding, Mr Hitler?', a cod-Second World War propaganda singalong written especially for the series (by Jimmy Perry), introduced *Dad's Army*, the zenith of the British broad-comedy ensemble sitcom. Consistently good writing and a wonderful cast of old timers and newer talents combined to produce a whimsical period-piece that continues, justifiably, to be savoured.

Walmington-on-Sea, an imaginary south-coast town not far from Eastbourne, was the setting for the Second World War adventures of a disparate group of men who, prevented by age or some other disability from enlisting in the services, enrolled as Local Defence Volunteers (LDV), forming part of Britain's 'last line of defence', a force which became known colloquially as 'Dad's Army'. Creator/writer Jimmy Perry had been in one such LDV group when he was 16 and based the idea upon his own experiences; it was his first sitcom. He and co-writer David Croft populated the show with a host of memorable characters, each with a recognisably different trait: the Captain, Mainwaring (pronounced Mannering), was pompous and suffered from delusions of grandeur that regularly led to his downfall; his Sergeant, Wilson, was vague and – to the perpetual annoyance of Mainwaring – cultured and public-school educated; Jones was dotty; Pike was precious; Walker was wily; Frazer was pessimistic; and Godfrey was frail. Often in opposition to them were the effete vicar, the oleaginous verger, the bullish ARP warden and the officious Colonel, Mainwaring's rival from a nearby town. All of the men had day jobs: Mainwaring was the local bank manager, Wilson his chief clerk and Pike the clerk; Jones was the local butcher; Frazer was the undertaker. The comedy arose from the bickering interplay between all these characters and the sometimes desperate attempts to solve the unlikely problems encountered by the accident-prone but determined and well-meaning platoon.

A huge cache of catchphrases from the show clicked with viewers, notably Mainwaring's 'Stupid boy', aimed, with a withering look, at Pike; Wilson's effete dispensing of military orders, such as 'Would you mind awfully falling into three lovely lines?'; Frazer's exaggeratedly Scots-accented 'We're doomed'; Hodges' heartfelt, 'Ruddy hooligans!'; Godfrey's 'Would you mind if I was excused?' as his ageing bladder necessitated yet another trip to the loo; and Jones's four gems, 'They don't like it up them', 'Handy-hock!' (German for 'Hands up!'), 'Permission to speak, sir!', and the perversely alarming 'Don't panic!'.

Dad's Army benefited from inspired casting, featuring many veterans of the business, some of whom had worked together in the past and formed professional friendships. Arthur Lowe (best known at the time as Leonard Swindley from *Coronation Street* and its sitcom spin-off **Pardon The Expression**) was originally invited to play the role of Wilson, with John Le Mesurier as Mainwaring, but they found themselves more comfortable in each other's roles. No spring chicken, Lowe was 52 when the series began and 62 when it finished, but he was a mere junior compared to some of the others – their ages at the beginning were: Le Mesurier 56, Laurie 71 and the daddy of them all, Arnold Ridley (the actor and playwright, best known beforehand as author of the stage and film favourite *The Ghost Train*), 72 at the start and 81 at the finish. Clive Dunn, who had carved a reputation by playing characters much older than himself, was merely a youthful 46 when the series began. Ironically, it was one of the youngest actors, James Beck

– only 35 when the first episode aired – who died during the run of the series, shockingly young, in 1973. The subsequent series without him failed to match the brilliance of the earlier episodes, perhaps indicating how integral his slightly dodgy spiv character was to the mix.

At its height, *Dad's Army* was a staggering success, spawning a feature film version in 1971 (director Norman Cohen) starring the main TV cast but with Liz Fraser in the role of Mrs Pike; and a musical stage-play in 1975 at the Shaftesbury Theatre, London, in which John Bardon took the Walker role and Hamish Roughead appeared as Frazer. (A musical number from the show was performed by the cast at the 1975 *Royal Variety Show*, televised on 16 November 1975 by ITV.) Six members of the cast (Lowe, Le Mesurier, Laurie, Beck, Ridley and Lavender) turned up as guests in the 22 April 1971 edition of **The Morecambe And Wise Show** on BBC2. A BBC Radio 4 version of *Dad's Army*, adapted from the TV scripts by Harold Snoad and Michael Knowles, ran for a total of 67 episodes (20 half-hours from 28 January to 10 June 1974, 20 more from 11 February to 24 June 1975 and 26 more from 16 March to 7 September 1976, with an hour-long special on Christmas Day 1974); and a Radio 2 sequel, *It Sticks Out A Mile* (six episodes, 20 November to 25 December 1983), again with new scripts from Snoad and Knowles, followed Wilson, Pike and Hodges' post-war pranks on a pier. (Years earlier, in 1971–72, Arthur Lowe and Ian Lavender – *not* in their *Dad's Army* characters – had teamed up in another Radio 2 sitcom, *Parsley Sidings*, written by Jim Eldridge.) *Rear Guard*, a US version of *Dad's Army* screened in America by ABC on 10 August 1976, failed to make it past the pilot stage, however; perhaps, as the United States was never seriously in danger of military invasion, a premise depicting the old codgers' last stand was never going to be appreciated. In Britain, few series have garnered such deeply entrenched and deserved love and affection.

La Dame Aux Gladiolas

Dame Edna Everage ... [various shows]

see HUMPHRIES, Barry

Danger – Marmalade At Work

see *Educating Marmalade*

Danger Theatre

USA · FOX (UNIVERSAL TELEVISION) · COMEDY ANTHOLOGY

7 × 30 mins · colour

US dates: 11 July–22 Aug 1993

UK dates: 13 May–24 June 1994 (7 episodes)
BBC2 Fri 12 midnight

MAIN CAST

host · · · · · · · · · · · · · · · · · · Robert Vaughn

The Searcher

The Searcher · · · · · · · · · · · Diedrich Bader

Tropical Punch

Captain Mike Morgan · · · · · · · · Adam West
Detective Tom McCormick · · Billy Morrissette
Detective Al Hamoki · · · · · · · · · · · · · · · · · ·
· · · · · · · · · · · · · · · Peter Navy Tuiasosopo

CREDITS

creators Robert Wolterstorff (*The Searcher*), Robert Wolterstorff/Penelope Spheeris (*Tropical Punch*) · writers Robert Wolterstorff, Mike Scott, Bruce Eric Kaplan · directors Penelope Spheeris, Greg Beeman, Mark Jean · executive producers Robert Wolterstorff, Penelope Spheeris · producers Mike Scott, Jack Bernstein, Marl Allen

A spoof comedy-anthology series introduced by Robert Vaughn, best known as Napoleon Solo in the 1960s spy series *The Man From U.N.C.L.E.* In keeping with the show's style, Vaughn deliberately lampooned his on-screen persona, caricaturing himself as a has-been actor reduced to hosting a cheap show, and he looked appropriately uncomfortable when introducing the stories, adding physical incompetence to the mix by missing his marks and wandering off camera.

The series chiefly comprised two recurring segments. The first was *The Searcher*, which depicted the adventures of a seemingly supernatural, black-clad biker, not unlike the lead figure in the adventure series *Knight Rider*, who rushes to the aid of people who express their need for help. The Searcher is an impossibly uptight, deep-voiced champion of the underdog who undermines his otherwise daunting presence by being massively clumsy and accident-prone. Luckily, he is near to indestructible – even when an aeroplane crashes on him in the credit sequence, he is left unscathed. The second segment was *Tropical Punch*, a *Hawaii Five-O* pastiche that featured Adam West in the same camp, stiff style he had employed in the 1960s TV light-adventure series *Batman*.

The spoofs were reasonably humorous and the actors, pleasingly, played their parts as straight as possible for the utmost comedic effect, but it was the phoney credits sequences (complete with pastiche themes from composer Leo Schifrin) that most impressed. Penelope Spheeris, the director of successful Hollywood comedy movies such as *Wayne's World*, was at work here and her contribution helped make the series a modest success.

The Danny Kaye Show

USA · CBS (DENA PICTURES) · SKETCH

124 × 60 mins · b/w and colour

US dates: 25 Sep 1963–12 Apr 1967

UK dates: 27 Apr 1964–26 Dec 1967 (115 × b/w · 1 × colour) BBC2 various days and times

MAIN CAST

Danny Kaye
Harvey Korman

CREDITS

producers Perry Lafferty, Robert Scheerer

A celebrated TV comedy-variety show for the brilliantly talented singer/actor/comedian/dancer Danny Kaye, born David Daniel Kominsky in Brooklyn, New York, on 18 January 1913. This long-running US television series featured weekly celebrity guest stars who joined Kaye in songs and/or sketches. The comedy sketches played a much greater part than was customary in such shows, with elaborate sets and staging, and Kaye's regular support Harvey Korman providing a touch of comic class. (Soon after the demise of *The Danny Kaye Show*, Korman continued his role as a comic foil with Carol Burnett, in her long-running smash hit US series *The Carol Burnett Show*.)

Danny Kaye died on 3 March 1987, aged 74. Tribute was paid to him in the 20 February 1994 edition of the LWT/ITV arts series *The South Bank Show*, which featured extracts from his many films.

Danny La Rue – The Ladies I Love

UK · ITV (LWT) · STANDUP

1 × 60 mins · colour

14 Sep 1974 · Sat 7.30pm

MAIN CAST

Danny La Rue

CREDITS

writer Bryan Blackburn · *director/producer* David Bell

Born Daniel Patrick Carroll, in Cork, Ireland, on 26 July 1928, Danny La Rue was the premier drag act in Britain for more than three decades. His first performance as a woman occurred in an Entertainments National Services Association (ENSA) production of *White Cargo* in the 1940s, a far cry from the lavish production numbers for which La Rue would become famous. His speciality was impersonating female celebrity icons, especially Hollywood superstars, which required him to don outrageously glamorous and elegant gowns, although part of La Rue's charm was that he never pretended to be female and emphasised the fact that he was in drag by uttering many asides to the audience. La Rue was influenced by, and took over the mantle from, Britain's first drag star Douglas Byng (see **Byng-Ho!**) and he, in turn,

inspired Barry Humphries' Dame Edna Everage creation, and Lily Savage.

A regular guest star on umpteen TV variety shows (especially the BBC's long-running music-hall series *The Good Old Days*), Danny La Rue also made telling TV appearances in *Charley's Aunt* (a BBC1 *Play Of The Month*, screened on 20 November 1969) and TV recordings of two of his long-running stage productions: *Danny La Rue At The Palace* (Thames, 22 June 1972) and *Come Spy With Me* (LWT, 11 September 1977). He also starred in a 1972 feature film built around his talents, *Our Miss Fred*.

In *Danny La Rue – The Ladies I Love*, the star appeared in the guise of the great ladies of stage and screen, including Shirley Temple and Old Mother Riley's daughter, Kitty.

The Darling Buds Of May

UK · ITV (YORKSHIRE/EXCELSIOR) · COMEDY SERIAL

20 × 60 mins · colour

Series One (6) 7 Apr–12 May 1991 · Sun 7.45pm
Special · 22 Dec 1991 · Sun 7.15pm
Series Two (6) 26 Jan–1 Mar 1992 · Sun 7.45pm
Special · 26 Dec 1992 · Sat 7.30pm
Series Three (6) 28 Feb–4 Apr 1993 · Sun 7.55pm

MAIN CAST

'Pop' Larkin	David Jason
'Ma' Larkin	Pam Ferris
Mariette Larkin/ Charlton	Catherine Zeta Jones
Cedric 'Charley' Charlton	Philip Franks
Edith Pilchester	Rachel Bell
Angela Snow	Kika Mirylees (not series 3)
Brigadier	Moray Watson (not series 3)
Primrose Larkin	Julie Davies (series 1); Abigail Rokison (after series 1)
Petunia Larkin	Christina Giles
Zinnia Larkin	Katherine Giles
Victoria Larkin	Stephanie Ralph
Montgomery Larkin	Ian Tucker (not series 3)

CREDITS

creator H E Bates · *adapters/writers* Bob Larbey (4 episodes in series 1), Robert Banks Stewart (2 eps in s1, 2 eps in s2), Richard Harris (1991 special, 2 eps in s2), Paul Wheeler (2 eps in s2, 4 eps in s3), Stephen Bill (1992 special), Barry Devlin (2 eps in s3) · *directors* Rodney Bennett (2 eps in s1, 2 eps in s3), Robert Tronson (2 eps in s1, 2 eps in s2, 2 eps in s3), David Giles (2 eps in s1, 1991 special, 2 eps in s2, 2 eps in s3), Steve Goldie (2 eps in s2), Gareth Davies (1992 special) · *executive producers* Vernon Lawrence, Richard Bates, Philip Burkey · *producers* Robert Banks Stewart (4 eps in s1), Richard Bates (2 eps in s1), Peter Norris (1991 special & all series 2), Simon Lewis (1992 special & all series 3)

One of the most popular British comedy series of them all, able, unlike virtually no other, to wrest the ratings crown away from the soap operas *Coronation Street* and *EastEnders* – indeed, the first series made

British TV history when all six episodes topped the ratings. A success on every level, *The Darling Buds Of May* promoted a feel-good factor all but forgotten by TV viewers, reassuring them that a good time could be derived from wholesome fun, with no guns, murders, explosions or sex in sight and no bad language within earshot. The series was in every sense family viewing.

The Darling Buds Of May was the creation of the prolific and successful British writer H E (Herbert Ernest) Bates. Born in 1905, he invented the Larkin family when he was 51, writing their uproarious stories into five novels, starting with *The Darling Buds Of May* in 1958 and following it over the next 12 years, to 1970, with *Breath Of Fresh Air*, *When The Green Woods Laugh*, *Oh! To Be In England* and *A Little Of What You Fancy*. Bates lived in Kent, near Ashford, and was inspired by the sight of a messy junk yard, situated three miles from his house, which he used to travel past several times a week. 'You never saw such a mess in your life,' Bates told *Radio Times* in 1969, 'bits and pieces of everything, ducks and geese and God knows what. A gorgeous mess. It just cried to be written about.' Around the same time, outside a village sweet shop the other side of Kent, Bates saw a home-painted van and a family tumbling out of the shop, all the kids sucking huge ice lollies. Putting together the two aspects, home and family, Bates invented the Larkins, a perpetually thirsty, hungry, lusty, happy and irrepressible bunch who lived life to the full.

Head of the family was Sidney Charles 'Pop' Larkin, a golden-hearted junk dealer and farmer of the family's 22-acre smallholding, with its pigs, turkeys, horses and cows. Pop exuded an unquenchable *joie de vivre*, if not an unquenchable thirst, and employed a rural wisdom that could never be out-argued. As far as Pop was concerned, life was 'perfick', his favourite word. His 'wife', whom everyone called 'Ma', was a plump, jolly Earth Mother, forever preparing grand banquets of honest fare, generously served and gratefully received in their comfortable farmhouse. Everyone loved Ma's food, and the fact that Pop tended to douse her servings – even her iced buns – in dollops of tomato ketchup was no insult, for he loved food in his own way and no slight was intended or taken. A true woman of the country, Ma just *gave* in every sense. Pop and Ma had never bothered to formalise their marriage – they were, in effect, common-law husband and wife (a point which momentarily scandalised in the 1950s but was soon overwhelmed by the public's appetite for more of Bates' books). The whole Larkins family oozed a zest for life, not just Pop and Ma but their six children too: Mariette (an abbreviation of Marie and Antoinette), Primrose (so named because she arrived in the spring), twins Zinnia and Petunia (named after Ma's favourite flowers), Victoria (she was born in the plum season) and Montgomery (named after the General). Relentlessly good-humoured, the Larkins loved life and loved each other from dawn chorus to midnight moon, birth to death.

Apart from Mariette falling in love with a visiting tax inspector, whom they nicknamed Charley, their marriage and her delivery of a grandson for Pop and Ma, not a lot happened in the TV stories. But they were so well written, played and enjoyed that it scarcely mattered – the episodes were simply swept along on a light-hearted air. Set in the 1950s, in the Kent countryside – the series did wonders for the tourist trade in the hitherto quiet Kent village of Pluckley, where it was filmed – the episodes were full of fresh food, bright yellow sunshine, balmy days under green trees and blue skies, golden ale, juicy red strawberries and rose-tinted lives. Viewers sensed that here was family life as they might wish themselves to live – carefree, oblivious to income tax or form-filling of any kind, paying no heed to class structure – and they warmed to the acting of David Jason as Pop (yet another brilliant performance) and Pam Ferris as Ma, a role for which she deliberately put on a couple of stones in weight. 'It's not original H E Bates,' Ferris said in 1991, 'but we hope it's very much in the right spirit.' As it happened, Richard Bates, son of the late H E (who had died in 1974), was on hand to ensure the correct translation. He had originally sold the TV rights in his father's Larkin stories to an American company, but these were rescinded when he felt progress towards the screen was too slow. And there was another Bates connection too: Daisy May Bates, great-grand-daughter of H E, played the occasionally seen part of John Blenheim, Mariette and Charley's son.

Notes. The 1991–93 TV series was not the first time the Larkin stories had been dramatised. The first book, *The Darling Buds Of May*, was adapted for the London stage in the late 1950s, with Peter Jones starring, and then was made by American company MGM into an uninspiring feature film, *The Mating Game*, in 1959. *Just Perfick*, a BBC radio adaptation that ran for two series, had starred Bernard Miles and Betty Marsden as Pop and Ma. The first run (12 episodes on Radio 2) aired from 4 November to 4 December 1969, the opening episode written by John Esmonde and Bob Larbey, the other 11 by Eddie Maguire. The second series (13 episodes on Radio 4) was broadcast from 14 April to 7 July 1971, written by Harry Ibbetson. The Bob Larbey association is an important one: 22 years on, when Yorkshire TV decided to invest heavily in bringing the H E Bates

creation to the small-screen, they brought in Larbey to adapt and write the first four episodes – and the transition from book to screen could not have been made better, the delightful two-episode opening story proving the ideal launching pad for a major success story. And in 1996, BBC Radio 4 dramatised the Bates stories once more, in a six-episode series called *A Little Of What You Fancy* – the last Larkin book, adapted/written by Eric Pringle and aired 15 February to 21 March. In this series David Jason and Pam Ferris reprised the TV roles they had made their own.

Although there were three six-week TV runs of *The Darling Buds Of May*, each series was broken down into three two-week stories. The initial two episodes, 7 and 14 April 1991, were titled simply *The Darling Buds Of May*, adapting H E Bates' original book of 1958; the next two, 21 and 28 April, were *When The Green Woods Laugh* (the third book, from 1960); the episodes of 5 and 12 May 1991 were *A Breath Of Fresh Air* (from the second H E Bates novel, published 1959). *Christmas Is Coming* was a single episode on 22 December 1991. The second series opened with *Oh! To Be In England* (published as a book in 1963), screened on 26 January and 2 February 1992, followed by *Stranger At The Gates* (9 and 16 February) and *A Season Of Heavenly Gifts* (23 February and 1 March). After another Christmas special on Boxing Day 1992 (*Le Grand Weekend*) came the final series: *The Happiest Days Of Your Life* (28 February and 7 March 1993), *Cast Not Your Pearls Before Swine* (14 and 21 March) and finally *Climb The Greasy Pole* (28 March and 4 April 1993).

In addition to the 20 hour-length episodes, the principal cast of *The Darling Buds Of May* appeared, in character, in a short sequence filmed especially for showing as part of ITV's *Telethon '92*, screened on 19 July 1992.

A Date With …

UK · C4 (KUDOS) · SATIRE

1 × 30 mins · colour

10 Aug 1997 · Sun 7.30pm

MAIN CAST

host · Tony Slattery
Karina Foxworth-Jones
Frederica Stabb
Danielle Tilley

CREDITS

writer Rob Colley · *director* Nick Bye · *executive producer* Stephen Garrett · *producer* Sally Woodward Gentle

Screened as part of C4's disability strand *Access! All Areas*, this half-hour hoax drew attention to the plight of the disabled by affecting a satirical send-up of a glitzy TV game-show. The host of the spoof show,

Tony Slattery, was deeply patronising to his three contestants, all women, each of whom had an impediment of one kind or another, and was oblivious to how hurtful these comments were. The quiz questions he put to them made important points about the poor facilities that disabled people were still having to contend with as the new millennium approached, and the harsh but subtle ways in which the disabled continued to be discriminated against.

Dave Allen …   [various shows]

see ALLEN, Dave

Dave King

The Dave King Show

see KING, Dave

The Dave Thomas Comedy Show

USA · CBS (REM PRODUCTIONS) · SKETCH/STANDUP

5 × 30 mins · colour

US dates: 28 May–25 June 1990
UK dates: 21 Feb–21 Mar 1993 (5 editions)
BBC2 Sun 11.30pm

MAIN CAST

Dave Thomas
Anson Downes
Teresa Ganzel
Don Lake
Fran Ryan
David Wiley
Julie Fulton

CREDITS

writers Mike Bayouth, Anson Downes, Mike Myers, Dave Thomas · *script editor* Michael Short · *director* Paul Miller · *producer* Kimber Rickabaugh

The Canadian-born Dave Thomas first came to prominence as one of the regulars on NBC's hit series *SCTV Network* (aka *SCTV Network 90* and later *SCTV Comedy Network*), which featured sketches themed around an imaginary TV station. The series was an extension of the earlier Second City Television and featured many performers from the Toronto-based Second City comedy ensemble. (See *Canada Goose*.) Thomas proved to be a sharp comedian and demonstrated a talent for accents and impressions (his Bob Hope was particularly lauded). This starring show allowed him full rein to plunder his comic armoury.

The set was a novel one, featuring a mock diner where Thomas sat with his guests, chatted a little and linked the filmed sketch inserts. The humour was intelligent and usually hit the mark, and the host's guest stars were mainly other members of Second City or refugees from *Saturday Night Live*. The five featured guest artists were

John Candy, Dan Aykroyd, Chevy Chase, Martin Short (who had been the other half of an occasional double-act with Thomas) and the Canadian comedian and actress Catherine O'Hara.

Dave's Kingdom

see KING, Dave

David Nixon's Comedy Bandbox

see *Comedy Bandbox*

Bobby Davro

A skilled impressionist, Bobby Davro was elevated to stardom via ITV series like *Go For It*, *The Krankies Klub* and *Copy Cats* and panel-games/quiz-shows such as *Punchlines*. Born on 13 September 1959 as Robert Nankeville – his father, Bill, was a runner who represented Britain in the 1948 and 1952 Olympic Games – Davro remains a small fish in a large comedic pond, but has brought pleasure to millions.

Detailed here are his specials and dedicated own series, but not his game-show and quiz-show work. In addition to the following programmes, Davro has starred in non-networked programmes, including a half-hour Christmas special for Central TV that aired in the Midlands on 22 December 1996.

Bobby Davro On The Box

UK · ITV (TVS) · STANDUP/SKETCH

7 editions (6 × 30 mins · 1 × 45 mins) · colour

Special (45 mins) 19 May 1985 · Sun 7.15pm

One series (6 × 30 mins) 15 Mar–19 Apr 1986 · Sat mostly 7pm

MAIN CAST
Bobby Davro
Jessica Martin (series)

CREDITS
writers (special) Geoff Atkinson, Paul Minett/Brian Leveson · *main writers (series)* Geoff Atkinson, Paul Minett/Brian Leveson, Charlie Adams · *other writers (series)* Moray Hunter/Jack Docherty, Maryanne Morgan, Bill Naylor, Paul B Davies, Phil Swern, David Hurst · *directors* John Kaye Cooper (special & 4 eds in series), Bob Collins (2 eds in series) · *producer* John Kaye Cooper

Previously seen in other shows and in variety, this was the comic impersonator's first full series, preceded in May 1985 by a water-testing special. Among those mimicked were Jim Davidson, Elton John, George Michael, Rod Stewart, Sting, Bob

Geldof, Freddie Starr (a case of one impressionist imitating another), Neil Sedaka and *The Tube* presenters Paula Yates and Jools Holland. Davro also teamed up with Jessica Martin, with whom he had worked in *Copy Cats*, to perform gravel-throated Rod Stewart and Bonnie Tyler duets, and the all-female pairing of Barbara Dickson and Elaine Paige.

Bobby Davro's TV Annual

UK · ITV (TVS) · STANDUP/SKETCH

2 editions (1 × 45 mins · 1 × 40 mins) · colour

27 Dec 1986 · Sat 5.15pm (45 mins)

26 Dec 1987 · Sat 6.50pm (40 mins)

MAIN CAST
Bobby Davro
Jessica Martin

CREDITS
writers Charlie Adams (both), Russel Lane (both), Paul Minett/Brian Leveson (both), Geoff Atkinson (1986), Eric Davidson (1986) · *director* Nigel Lythgoe · *executive producer* John Kaye Cooper (1987) · *producers* John Kaye Cooper (1986), Nigel Lythgoe (1987)

A pair of year-end round-ups for ITV's new star.

Bobby Davro's TV Weekly

UK · ITV (TVS) · STANDUP/SKETCH

14 × 30 mins · colour

Series One (7) 28 Feb–11 Apr 1987 · Sat 6.45pm

Series Two (7) 20 Feb–2 Apr 1988 · Sat mostly 6.35pm

MAIN CAST
Bobby Davro
Jessica Martin (series 1)
Ray Alan (series 2)

CREDITS
series 1 writers Charlie Adams, Geoff Atkinson, James Bibby, Eric Davidson, Joe Griffiths, Richard Kates, Russel Lane, Paul Minett/Brian Leveson, Bill Naylor · *series 2 writers* Charlie Adams, Barry Cryer, Russel Lane, Paul Minett/Brian Leveson, Dick Vosburgh · *director* Nigel Lythgoe · *producers* John Kaye Cooper (series 1), Nigel Lythgoe (series 2)

Two series for ITV's dazzling Davro, with viewers treated to impressions of all the usual lot plus others like Flowerpot Men Bill and Ben, Jim Davidson, the Bee Gees, Jonathan Ross, Mick Hucknall and Ben Elton. Jessica Martin supported only in the first series; in the second Davro played host to weekly guest stars and a new resident, the ventriloquist Ray Alan.

Bobby In Wonderland

UK · ITV (TVS) · STANDUP/SKETCH

1 × 50 mins · colour

24 Dec 1988 · Sat 6.15pm

MAIN CAST
eleven roles · · · · · · · · · · · · · · Bobby Davro
Mock Turtle · · · · · · · · · · · · · · · · Dave Lee
Duchess · · · · · · · · · · · · · · · Bernie Winters

CREDITS
writers Paul Minett/Brian Leveson · *executive producer* Gill Stribling-Wright · *director/producer* Nigel Lythgoe

A Christmas special, with impressionist Davro playing 11 roles in a comic spin on *Alice In Wonderland*.

Davro's Sketch Pad

UK · ITV (TVS) · STANDUP/SKETCH

6 × 30 mins · colour

8 Apr–13 May 1989 · Sat mostly 7.30pm

MAIN CAST
Bobby Davro
Joanna Brookes
Harry Fowler
Iain Rogerson

CREDITS
main writers Paul Minett/Brian Leveson · *other writers* Charlie Adams, Ronnie Barbour, Barry Cryer, Graham Deykin, Joe Griffiths, Sonny Hayes, Tim Maloney, Eric Merriman, Pete Mills, Bill Naylor, Dick Vosburgh · *script associate* Charlie Adams · *director/producer* Nigel Lythgoe

A new series introducing new regular characters: agony Auntie Claire, Small Daniels, Davros Stavros and others. Most editions featured a guest supporting act, and there was a rep company comprising Brookes, Rogerson and the versatile veteran Fowler.

Davro

UK · ITV (TVS) · STANDUP/SKETCH

14 × 30 mins · colour

Series One (7) 17 Mar–5 May 1990 · Sat 6.40pm

Series Two (7) 9 Mar–20 Apr 1991 · Sat mostly 6.40pm

MAIN CAST
Bobby Davro
Caroline Dennis
Ainsley Harriott
Phil Nice
Adam Wide (series 1)
Julie Kirk (series 2)

CREDITS
directors/producers Vic Finch/Danny Greenstone (series 1), Vic Finch (series 2) · *executive producer* John G Temple

More fun with the hard-working Davro, adding impressions of Alexei Sayle, Jeremy Beadle, Paul Gascoigne, the Pet Shop Boys and others to keep the portfolio current. Each programme in the first series included a soap opera send-up, *Flushing Meadows*. Ainsley Harriott, one of the regular supporting cast, went on to become a TV chef, combining his extrovert comedic personality with culinary skill.

Bobby Davro: Rock With Laughter

UK · BBC · STANDUP/SKETCH

6 × 30 mins · colour

6 July–10 Aug 1993 · BBC1 Tue 7pm

MAIN CAST
Bobby Davro

CREDITS
writers Alan Wightman, Bob Mills, Terry Morrison, David Kind, Jon Conway, Maddi Cryer, Clive Whichelow, Joe Griffiths, Joe Pasquale and others · *script associate* Terry Morrison · *director/producer* Tudor Davies

Davro switched to the BBC for a series based on his successful touring stage-shows, which blended comedy with variety acts. Each week he was joined by guest stars from the worlds of music and dance, and also introduced guest comedians including Shane Richie, Joe Pasquale, Bradley Walsh and the Grumbleweeds.

Les Dawson

Born in Manchester on 2 February 1933, Les Dawson soared to fame at the end of the 1960s, delivering – with tremendous deadpan panache – a succession of mother-in-law jokes and humorous observations on life. Dawson's jokes were greatly aided by his face – he himself described it as resembling 'a sack of spanners' – and he would use it to gurn in the manner of traditional British seasiders and effect wonderful female impressions, usually in the gossipy leaning-over-the-wall characters he evolved with Roy Barraclough, Cissie and Ada, which owed much (as Dawson openly admitted) to the Rochdale-born comic Norman Evans (see *Evans Abode* and *The Norman Evans Show*). In fact, Dawson invented a number of alter egos – another biggie was Cosmo Smallpiece – he was a first-rate pianist, an excellent pantomime artist (as was Evans) and delivered good value in sketches as well as standup. He also wrote books and had played in a jazz band. A protégé of Max Wall in the 1950s, Dawson's successes began to accumulate after TV appearances in *Comedy Bandbox* and the talent-spotting show *Opportunity Knocks* in 1963, which led to spots in variety shows and, eventually, in April 1969, his first own series, *Sez Les*, which propelled his name to the top. As well as his comedy shows – listed here in chronological order – Dawson presented the BBC1 game-show *Blankety*

Blank from 1984 to 1989 and *Opportunity Knocks* from 1990.

Les Dawson died on 10 June 1993, aged 60, while filming a cameo contribution to the ITV light-drama series *Demob* (15 October–19 November 1993), in which he played the variety legend Morton Stanley. On 5 July 1993 BBC1 screened *The Last Laugh – A Tribute To Les Dawson*, in which friends and admirers recalled the comedian's brilliance. Later that same year, on 26 December, ITV presented *A Tribute To Les Dawson*, the commercial company's salute to the funny man; on 2 October 1994, BBC1 presented *Les Dawson: The Entertainer*, the first of three specials looking at different aspects of the comedian's talents (the other two shows aired on 17 and 24 October); on 16 April 1997 Dawson was the subject of a *Heroes Of Comedy* documentary on C4, and in four programmes (17, 24 and 31 May and 20 June 1997) highlights from the comic's TV shows were compiled into *The Best Of Les Dawson*, screened by BBC1.

State Of The Union

UK · BBC · SITCOM

1 × 30 mins · b/w

26 Apr 1968 · BBC1 Fri 8.20pm

MAIN CAST

Les	Les Dawson
Gladys	Patsy Rowlands
Ernie	Michael Robbins
Russell	Melvyn Hayes

CREDITS
writer Ronnie Taylor · *producer* John Ammonds

In his first acting role, Les Dawson played Les, a trade union secretary, in this *Comedy Playhouse* tale of work relations. Patsy Rowlands was cast as his wife Gladys and Michael Robbins (later to score as Arthur in *On The Buses*) played shop-steward Ernie. No series developed.

Sez Les

UK · ITV (YORKSHIRE) · SKETCH/STANDUP

71 editions (49 × 30 mins [38 × colour · 11 × b/w]; 2 × 40 mins · colour; 12 × 45 mins · colour; 5 × 60 mins · colour; 3 × short specials · colour)

Series One (6 × 30 mins · b/w) 30 Apr–18 June 1969 · Wed mostly 10.30pm

Series Two (5 × 30 mins · b/w · 1 × 30 mins · colour) 10 Sep–19 Nov 1969 · Wed mostly 10.30pm

Series Three (4 × 30 mins · colour) 16 Aug–6 Sep 1971 · Mon mostly 8.30pm

Short special (colour) · part of *Mike And Bernie Winters' All-Star Christmas Comedy Carnival* 25 Dec 1971 · Sat 6.05pm

Series Four (6 × 30 mins · colour) 13 Jan–17 Feb 1972 · Thu mostly 9pm

Series Five (5 × 45 mins · 2 × 40 mins · colour) 29 July–9 Sep 1972 · Sat mostly 5.45pm

Series Six (6 × 30 mins · colour) *Les Sez* 30 Oct–4 Dec 1972 · Mon 8.30pm

Short special (colour) · part of *All-Star Comedy Carnival* 25 Dec 1972 · Mon 5.45pm

Series Seven (7 × 45 mins · colour) 28 July–8 Sep 1973 · Sat 6.35pm then 5.15pm

Short special (colour) · part of *All-Star Comedy Carnival* 25 Dec 1973 · Tue 6.30pm

Special (60 mins · colour) *That's Christmas Sez Les!* 26 Dec 1973 · Wed 3.30pm

Series Eight (7 × 30 mins · colour) 25 Jan–8 Mar 1974 · Fri 8.30pm

Series Nine (7 × 30 mins · colour) 28 June–9 Aug 1974 · Fri 8.30pm

Special (60 mins · colour) *Sez Les Special* 2 Jan 1976 · Fri 9pm

Series Ten (3 × 60 mins · colour) *Sez Les Special* 25 Feb–10 Mar 1976 · Wed mostly 9pm

Series Eleven (7 × 30 mins · colour) 19 Oct–6 Dec 1976 · mostly Mon 10.30pm

MAIN CAST
Les Dawson

OTHER APPEARANCES
Roy Barraclough (series 4 onwards)
Norman Chappell (series 11)
John Cleese (16 editions)
Brian Glover (series 5 & 6)
Brian Murphy (series 1 & 2)
Kathy Staff (series 11)

CREDITS
writers Les Dawson, Barry Cryer, John Hudson, Peter Vincent, Peter Dulay, Ron Weighell, David Nobbs, Alec Gerrard, Don Clayton · *script editors/associates* Peter Dulay, Brad Ashton, David Nobbs · *directors* David Mallet (series 1–5, 7–9 & specials to 1973), Bill Hitchcock (series 6), Vernon Lawrence (series 10 & 11 & 1976 specials) · *producers* John Duncan (series 1 & 2), David Mallet (series 3–5 & 9), Bill Hitchcock/Peter Dulay (series 6 & 1972 Xmas special), Bill Hitchcock (series 7 & 8 & both 1973 specials), Vernon Lawrence (series 10 & 11 & 1976 specials)

His definitive TV series, *Sez Les* established Dawson as one of Britain's best-loved comedians and extended to more than 70 editions over seven years. Roy Barraclough was his most regular sideman although, in two 1971 programmes and then two complete series in 1974, John Cleese – having quit the last *Monty Python* TV series – helped out.

Holiday With Strings

UK · ITV (YORKSHIRE) · SITCOM

1 × 35 mins · colour

26 Aug 1974 · Mon 8pm

MAIN CAST

Les	Les Dawson
Peregrine	Roy Barraclough
Air hostess	Patricia Hayes
Doris	Mollie Sugden
Travel agent	Frank Thornton

CREDITS

writers Ray Galton/Alan Simpson · *producer* Duncan Wood

A worthy single-episode comedy written for Dawson by the team behind *Hancock* and *Steptoe And Son* and screened on August Bank Holiday 1974. Les played 'Les', a traveller who has £22 burning a hole in his pocket and wishes to see the world with it. All he can afford, however, is a package holiday to Tossa del Mar with Kut-Price Holidays Ltd. The cheap price is reflected in the pared-to-the-bone travel arrangements – the check-in 'girl' (Mollie Sugden at her most brusque) makes Les leave his luggage behind because it weighs too much, the aeroplane tyres are covered in patches and its hull in graffiti ('Leeds for the cup'). On board, the air 'hostess' (the great Pat Hayes) distributes raffle tickets to determine who'll win the handful of lunches the company can afford to make. It is also announced that everyone must disembark upon reaching the Pyrenees, board a coach and reboard the plane on the other side. Dawson and fellow passengers – including Peregrine, a gay coal-miner in the adjacent seat with whom he strikes up conversation – even have to pool their loose change in order to pay for an unscheduled refuelling at Lyon.

Although the script was redolent of Tony Hancock's material – Dawson bristled in the face of authority, and he even uttered the Hancockian expostulation 'Nay!' at one point – this witty one-off was deemed successful enough to warrant a series of seven more single-episode Galton and Simpson scripts, screened a year later under the generic title *Dawson's Weekly*.

Sounds Like Les Dawson

UK · ITV (YORKSHIRE) · SKETCH/STANDUP

1 × 60 mins · colour

4 Dec 1974 · Wed 8pm

MAIN CAST

Les Dawson
Roy Barraclough

CREDITS

writers Barry Cryer, David Nobbs, Les Dawson, Dick Vosburgh · *director/producer* Vernon Lawrence

Another special for Dawson, with the comedian looking at Beethoven's private life and presenting *The Prisoner Of Zenda* as performed by the George and Thelma Grimsdike Formation Dance Team.

Les Dawson's Christmas Box

UK · ITV (YORKSHIRE) · SKETCH/STANDUP

2 × 60 mins · colour

21 Dec 1974 · Sat 8.30pm
26 Dec 1975 · Fri 10.15pm

MAIN CAST

Les Dawson
Roy Barraclough

CREDITS

writers Barry Cryer (2), David Nobbs (2), Les Dawson (2), Alec Gerrard (1), Eric Idle (1), Peter Robinson (1) · *director/producer* Vernon Lawrence

Two Christmas specials depicting Les with his usual cast of dubious characters – Cosmo Smallpiece, Cissie and Ada – perennial cohort Roy Barraclough, and guests.

Dawson's Electric Cinema

UK · ITV (YORKSHIRE) · SITCOM

1 × 60 mins · colour

3 April 1975 · Thu 9pm

MAIN CAST

Les Dawson
Roy Barraclough
Stuart Dawson

CREDITS

writers Barry Cryer, David Nobbs · *director/producer* Ronnie Baxter

A single Les Dawson special with an unusual sitcom premise: the Dawson family are running a flea-pit cinema in the mid 1920s.

Les played his own grandfather, kitted out in commissionaire's uniform, while his real-life son, seven-year-old Stuart, played Les as a child.

The Loner

UK · ITV (YORKSHIRE) · SITCOMS

3 × 30 mins · colour

7 May–21 May 1975 · Wed 9.30pm

Three single-comedy playlets, written by Alan Plater, in which Les acted out the life of an unassailable loner, simply named – *à la* Hancock – Dawson. Reginald Marsh appeared twice, as the publican Ted, but otherwise the supporting casts changed each week.

Note. To avoid repetition, the writer of the following three programmes was Alan Plater, the director was James Ormerod and the executive producer Peter Willes.

Dawson's Complaint   7 MAY

MAIN CAST

Dawson	Les Dawson
Jack	George Malpas
Hilda	Helen Rappaport
Harding	Brian Wilde
Lord Ross and Cromarty	Cyril Luckham

Dawson has an official complaint to make, and, doggedly, he takes it to the very top.

Dawson's Connection   14 MAY

MAIN CAST

Dawson	Les Dawson
Charlie	Fred Feast
Ted	Reginald Marsh
Sgt Hardaker	Roy Kinnear
Miss Douglas	Sharon Maughan
Sid	Ted Carroll
Ernie	Peter Ellis
Jack	Anthony Millan

Dawson ends up in a sticky situation after popping into the pub for a swift pint.

Dawson's Encounter   21 MAY

MAIN CAST

Dawson	Les Dawson
Mave	Anita Carey
The woman	Gillian Raine
Ted	Reginald Marsh

Dawson sets out to find a woman.

Dawson's Weekly

UK · ITV (YORKSHIRE) · SITCOMS

7 × 30 mins · colour

12 June–29 July 1975 · Thu 8pm then Tue 7.05pm

Seven single-comedy situations written for Dawson by the Galton and Simpson partnership. Named after the classified-advertisement newspaper *Dalton's Weekly*, the series followed the success of *Holiday With Strings*, the one-off ITV presentation in August 1974. Critics were definitely less than impressed this time around, however, and panned the series virtually from start to finish. Apart from Roy Barraclough's regular support, the remaining casts changed each week.

Note. To avoid repetition, the writers of all of the following were Ray Galton/Alan Simpson and the director/producer was Vernon Lawrence.

Les Miserables   12 JUNE

MAIN CAST

Les	Les Dawson
Roy	Roy Barraclough
Mrs Finch	Hilda Fenemore
Colonel	Campbell Singer
Psychiatrist	Jack May
Receptionist	Jenny McCracken

Les is suffering from a bad bout of melancholia and there's little chance of his spirits lifting.

Where There's A Will   19 JUNE

MAIN CAST

Les	Les Dawson
Roy	Roy Barraclough
Solicitor	Richard Vernon
Consultant	Terence Alexander

Freda	PeggyAnn Clifford
Minnie	Kathy Staff
George	John Sharp
Arthur	Bert Palmer
Receptionist	Lesley North

Uncle Enoch Dawson has died, and his surviving relatives gather for a reading of his will – and a good many surprises. To gain his inheritance, Les is required to marry within seven days.

This script was remade as 'Being Of Sound Mind', screened in *Paul Merton In Galton & Simpson's ...* in 1997.

Stage-Struck
26 JUNE

MAIN CAST

Les	Les Dawson
other role	Julian Orchard
Cleoberry	Josephine Tewson
Agent	Bernard Spear
Windthrift	Alan Curtis
Secretary	Pamela Manson
Councillor	Michael Gover
Call boy	Tony Sympson
Cynthia	Damaris Hayman
Gainford	John Harvey

Les becomes restless as a resting actor and aspires to set the stage alight once more with his prodigious talent.

Accident Prone
3 JULY

MAIN CAST

Les	Les Dawson
Roy	Roy Barraclough
Doctor	Richard Morant
Patient	Neil McCarthy
Stretcher-bearer	Gordon Rollings
Nurse	Georgina Moon

Les is an unbearably impatient patient.

All Pools Day
8 JULY

MAIN CAST

Les	Les Dawson
Roy	Roy Barraclough
First clerk	Patsy Rowlands
Second clerk	Avril Angers
Third clerk	Felix Bowness

Les finds it hard to wait for the 4.45pm football results to find out if he has won the football pools.

The Clerical Error
22 JULY

MAIN CAST

Les	Les Dawson
Rev Michael Ffoulkes	John Bird
Mrs Ffoulkes	Ann Beach
Sandra	Sharon Duce
Reporter	George A Cooper

Les becomes a child-minder when the Reverend and Mrs Ffoulkes are invited out to dinner with the Bishop.

This script was used again in *Paul Merton In Galton & Simpson's ...*, in 1997.

Strangers In The Night
29 JULY

MAIN CAST

Les	Les Dawson
Roy	Roy Barraclough
Girl	Sue Lloyd
Attendant	Kenny Lynch
Steward	Edward Sinclair

Les gets into scrapes on a British Rail sleeper train to Scotland.

The Les Dawson Show
1

UK · ITV (YORKSHIRE) · SKETCH/STANDUP

1 × 60 mins · colour

10 Sep 1975 · Wed 8pm

MAIN CAST

Les Dawson
Roy Barraclough
Cleo Laine
Joan Sanderson

CREDITS

writers Barry Cryer, David Nobbs · *director* Len Lurcuck · *producer* Vernon Lawrence

Dawson returned to better-known characters for this one-off, in which his lecherous creation Cosmo Smallpiece appeared in a sketch taking singing lessons from guest star Cleo Laine. There were also appearances for Cissie and Ada and another creation, Happy Harry Merrypepper.

Dawson And Friends

UK · ITV (YORKSHIRE) · SKETCH/STANDUP

4 × 60 mins · colour

20 Apr 1977 · Wed 8pm
25 May 1977 · Wed 8pm
15 June 1977 · Wed 8pm
29 June 1977 · Wed 8pm

MAIN CAST

Les Dawson
Julian Orchard
Roy Barraclough
William Rushton
Norman Chappell
Humphrey Lyttelton
Kathy Staff

CREDITS

writers Barry Cryer (4), David Nobbs (4), Les Dawson (4), Alec Gerrard (1), John Hudson (1), Bob Nicholson (1) · *directors* Len Lurcuck (3), Ivor Raymonde (1) · *producer* Vernon Lawrence

Four one-hour specials, with a team of regular players supporting the deadpan comic in sketch, standup and song material.

The Les Dawson Show
2

UK · BBC · SKETCH/STANDUP

33 editions (24 × 30 mins · 6 × 35 mins · 1 × 50 mins · 1 × 45 mins · 1 × 5 mins) · colour

Series One (6 × 30 mins) 21 Jan–1 Apr 1978 · BBC1 fortnightly Sat 8.35pm

Special (45 mins) 25 May 1981 · BBC1 Mon 9.35pm

Series Two (6 × 30 mins) 30 Jan–5 Mar 1982 · BBC1 Sat 8.05pm

Short special (5 mins) part of *The Funny Side Of Christmas* 27 Dec 1982 · BBC1 Mon 8.05pm

Series Three (6 × 35 mins) 15 Jan–19 Feb 1983 · BBC1 Sat 8.20pm

Series Four (6 × 30 mins) 21 Jan–25 Feb 1984 · BBC1 Sat 8.05pm

Special (50 mins) 28 Dec 1987 · BBC1 Mon 7.40pm

Series Five (6 × 30 mins) 19 Oct–23 Nov 1989 · BBC1 Thu 8pm

MAIN CAST

Les Dawson
Lulu (series 1)
Roy Barraclough (occasional)

CREDITS

writers Les Dawson (29), Terry Ravenscroft (19), Peter Robinson (12), Peter Vincent (7), Tony Hare (7), Charlie Adams (7), Paul Alexander/Gavin Osbon (7), Andy Walker (6), David Renwick (6), Eddie Braben (6), Ernest Maxin (2), Roy Barraclough (2), Barry Cryer (1), David Nobbs (1), Tom Magee-Englefield (1), Dennis Berson (1), Garry Chambers (1), Mick Loftus (1) · *producers* Ernest Maxin (13), Stewart Morris (7), John Ammonds (6), Robin Nash (6), John Bishop (1)

Dawson consolidated his fame with this popular BBC series featuring many of his trademark features: elaborate storyline jokes, cross-dressing and intentionally bad piano playing. The first series featured Lulu singing and acting in sketches.

Note. On 18 October 1981, the BBC presented *Mussolini With Knickers*, a programme discussing mother-in-law jokes, which featured Dawson performing some quips from his act and talking about the routines.

The Dawson Watch

UK · BBC · SKETCH/STANDUP

19 × 30 mins · colour

Series One (6) 23 Feb–6 Apr 1979 · BBC1 Fri 8.30pm

Series Two (6) 22 Nov–27 Dec 1979 · BBC1 Thu 8.30pm

Series Three (6) 17 Oct–28 Nov 1980 · BBC1 Fri 7.30pm

Special · 23 Dec 1980 · BBC1 Tue 8.30pm

MAIN CAST

Les Dawson
Roy Barraclough
Gordon Peters
Daphne Oxenford
April Walker

CREDITS

writers Les Dawson (19), Andy Hamilton (19), Terry Ravenscroft (19), Ian Davidson (6), Eric Geen (3), Tom Magee-Englefield (1), Colin Bostock-Smith (1) · *producer* Peter Whitmore

Themed sketch series have proved useful for concentrating writers' minds and providing a sense of continuity through a show. The *Scott On ...* series and *The Frost Report* enjoyed particular success with this format and here Les Dawson tried his hand at the formula. Each week sketches and Dawson's standup routines would be based around a single concept, the themes including estate agents, transport, crime, health, holidays, marriage, the environment and, in the final show, Christmas.

Note. On 19 October 1991, Dawson appeared as selfish grandmother Nona in a BBC2 adaptation of Argentinian dramatist Roberto Cossa's black farce *Nona*. The play has traditionally featured a male lead in the title role.

The Day I Shot My Dad

UK · BBC · CHILDREN'S SITCOM

1 × 25 mins · colour
2 Feb 1976 · BBC1 Mon 5.15pm

MAIN CAST
John Carveth · · · · · · · · · · · · · · · David Ford
Peter · Mark Case
Mr Carveth · · · · · · · · · · · Edward Hardwicke
Mrs Carveth · · · · · · · · · · Anne Cunningham

CREDITS
writer John Branfield · *director* Marilyn Fox · *producer* Anna Home

A one-off children's comedy about film-making. John wants to make a film about Cornwall but how can he stop his father from constantly interfering?

The Day Today

UK · BBC (TALKBACK PRODUCTIONS) · SATIRE

6 × 30 mins · colour
19 Jan–23 Feb 1994 · BBC2 Wed 9pm

MAIN CAST
Chris Morris
Steve Coogan
Rebecca Front
David Schneider
Doon Mackichan
Patrick Marber

CREDITS
devisers/main writers Chris Morris, Armando Iannucci · *other writers* Peter Baynham and cast · *additional material* Andrew Glover, Steven Wells/David Quantick, Graham Linehan/Arthur Mathews and others · *director* Andrew Gillman · *co-producer* Chris Morris · *producer* Armando Iannucci

A brilliant satire spoofing current affairs TV programmes and featuring a team relatively new to television. All the cast had been involved in a BBC radio series, *On The Hour* (13 editions from 9 August 1991 to 28 December 1992; 12 on Radio 4, the last on Radio 1), which had taken a similarly juicy swipe at radio current affairs programming.

Both the radio and TV series were produced by whiz kid Armando Iannucci and featured a number of recurring characters, most notably the sports correspondent Alan

Partridge, a creation of Steve Coogan later to be granted his own TV series, *Knowing Me ... Knowing You*. Other regulars included political cartoonist Brant (Schneider), 'enviromation' presenter Rosie May (Mackichan), business correspondent Collaterlie Sisters (Mackichan again), 'genutainment' presenter Remedy Malahide (Front) and the show's smarmy front-man played by Chris Morris. The entire team were deadly accurate in their impressions of personalities one sees in current affairs TV, but Morris was particularly impressive, perfectly catching the mannerisms, vocal inflections and visual style of such presenters. The show also scored with its choice of targets, moving away from the hackneyed areas of previous media-based sketch shows to concentrate on modern, virtually untouched strands of programming like the real-life emergency shows (*999*), reconstruction series (*Crimewatch UK*), home-video exploitation (*You've Been Framed*) and security-camera use (*Police Action Live*).

To make the spoof seem even more authentic, there was no studio laughter but liberal use of voice-over contemporary news stories, sports footage and library shots. There were also genuine 'vox pops' (random interviews) with the 'man in the street' about all manner of unlikely or fictitious subjects. To complete the parody, the series employed graphics and music that expertly caricatured the high-tech, dramatic style fast becoming commonplace in TV presentation.

See also *Brass Eye*.

The Days And Nights Of Molly Dodd

USA · NBC, LIFETIME (FINNEGAN COMPANY/ JUST YOU AND ME KID PRODUCTIONS) · SITCOM

65 × 30 mins · colour
US dates: 21 May 1987–29 June 1988 (NBC); 27 Feb 1989–8 Aug 1991 (Lifetime)

UK dates: 15 July 1990–17 Nov 1991 (39 episodes) BBC1 Sun around 11.05pm

MAIN CAST
Molly Dodd · · · · · · · · · · · · · · · · Blair Brown
Florence Bickford · · · · · · · · Allyn Ann McLerie
Davey McQuinn · · · · · · · · · · · James Greene
Mamie Grolnick · · · Sandy Faison (1987–88)
Dennis Widmer · · · · Victor Garber (1987–88)
Det Nathaniel Hawthorne · · · Richard Lawson
· (1989–91)
Fred Dodd · · · · · · · William Converse-Roberts

OTHER APPEARANCES
Moss Goodman · · · · · · · · · David Str.aithairn
· (1988–90)
Nick Donatello · · · · · · · · · · · · · · · Jay Tarses
Nina Shapiro · · · · · · · · Maureen Anderman

CREDITS
creator/main writer Jay Tarses · *other writers* Allan Burns/James L Brooks, Laurie S Gelman, Sheree Guitar, Wendy Kout and others · *producer* Jay Tarses

Jay Tarses had pioneered a new, more serious form of sitcom with the two Dabney Coleman shows *Buffalo Bill* and *The 'Slap' Maxwell Story*. It was a genre the Americans called 'dramadies', and Tarses' next 'dramady' was this bittersweet observation on the life of a New Yorker.

Blair Brown starred as Molly Dodd, a woman with an unsettled life who seems doomed to ride a merry-go-round of careers, friendships and unfulfilled relationships. Slightly scatty, she is perceived as neurotic, which seems par for the course in the New York she inhabits. Constantly nagged by her mother, Florence, Molly moves from job to job, starting off as an occasional singer with her ex-husband's group, The Fred Dodd Band, but then moving into real estate and working in a book store. A victim of habit, Molly invariably becomes romantically entangled with her bosses, but following her failed marriage to Fred she never finds a lasting relationship. Detective Nat Hawthorne becomes Molly's boyfriend and the father of her child, Emily, but Molly remains desperately unlucky as Nat dies, freakishly, as a result of severe food allergy, before their child is born.

As with most of Jay Tarses' output, critics loved the show; and, this time, even the public seemed content. But NBC were disappointed and cancelled it prematurely. Further episodes were then commissioned by the US cable channel Lifetime, which had attracted good viewing figures when airing repeats. Tarses himself appeared in the series, as Molly's occasionally seen garbage collector Nick Donatello, smitten with the thirty-something heroine. During the run, Donatello betters himself by becoming the mayoral chauffeur, but by the end of the series he has returned to emptying the trash cans.

Dead At Thirty

UK · C4 (TIGER TELEVISION) · SITCOM

1 × 30 mins · colour
3 June 1992 · Wed 10.30pm

MAIN CAST
Paterson Joseph
Lou Curram
Jesse Birdsall
Mark Williams

CREDITS
writers Paul Whitehouse/Charlie Higson · *director* John Stroud · *producer* David Tyler

This first edition in C4's comedy pilots series *Bunch Of Five* was penned by reliable writers Whitehouse and Higson and concerned four flat-sharers who become bitten by the video-game habit. Coming across as a sort of less frenzied version of *The Young Ones* for the 1990s, it failed to graduate to a full series.

Mark Williams would go on to join Whitehouse and Higson in *The Fast Show*.

Dead Ernest

UK · ITV (WITZEND PRODUCTIONS FOR CENTRAL) · SITCOM

7 × 30 mins · colour

15 Feb–29 Mar 1982 · Mon 8pm

MAIN CAST

Ernest Springer	Andrew Sachs
Archangel Derek	Ken Jones
Cherub Fred	Harry Fowler
Archangel Doreen	Janet Rawson
Edna Springer	Zena Walker
Arthur	Bill Waddington
Alice	Gretchen Franklin

CREDITS

writers John Stevenson/Julian Roach · *director* Alan Wallis · *executive producer* Allan McKeown · *producers* Alan Wallis/Tony Charles

It's the biggest day in Ernest Springer's life. Hitherto a fatigued schoolteacher, he has won a fortune on the football pools and receives the usual outsized cheque, posing for the photographers with a celebrity on one arm and a bathing beauty (Miss North Sea Oil) on the other. The champagne corks fly – and how: exploding at venomous speed, one hits him squarely between the eyes and Ernest Springer's biggest day, indeed his whole life, is over. When he awakes he is the last in the queue, behind the other new arrivals, in the British section of heaven.

But heaven, to paraphrase Dud and Pete, is not all it's cracked up to be. For a start, there's Cherub Fred, the 'Mr-Fixit' character of the British section, dashing about in his blue uniform. Then there's the supercilious 15-year-old Archangel Doreen, not to mention the bureaucracy and administration. A mistake in the paperwork, indeed, is the cause of Ernest's sudden calling in the first place – he was not meant to die for some time yet. He asks to be sent back, to wife Edna and friends Arthur and Alice, but is informed that his kidneys have already been transplanted into the body of a Dagenham bus-driver, so he's heaven-bound for eternity. He does, at least, get the chance to meet his mum and dad again, and Beethoven, Schubert, Mozart and the self-styled Head Of Plagues (played by John Le Mesurier), and gets to try his hand at being a heavenly radio DJ by the name of Otto.

Fresh from *Fawlty Towers*, Andrew Sachs was cast as Ernest, while the role of Cherub Fred was filled by that great Cockney character actor 'arry Fowler, reuniting on screen with Sachs 36 years after appearing together in the 1946 feature film *Hue And Cry*, when Sachs was 15 and Fowler 20.

Deadline Leeds

see The Leeds series

Dean Martin's Comedy Classic

USA · NBC (CLAUDE PRODUCTIONS/GREG GARRISON PRODUCTIONS) · STANDUP/SKETCH

1 × 60 mins · colour

US date: 12 May 1981
UK date: 2 July 1982 · BBC1 Fri 11.10pm

MAIN CAST

Dean Martin
Orson Welles
Dom DeLuise
Bob Newhart
Frank Sinatra
Goldie Hawn
Marty Feldman
Peter Falk

CREDITS

writer Bill Box · *director* Greg Garrison · *producers* Greg Garrison, Lee Hale

A look back at the best comedy moments from NBC's long-running *The Dean Martin Show* (1965–74), including the regular 'Man Of The Week Celebrity Roast' over which he had presided. Orson Welles introduced the show and numerous guests helped and hindered Martin in his reminiscences.

Dear Dotty

UK · BBC · SITCOM

6 × 30 mins · b/w

13 July–6 Oct 1954 · fortnightly Tue then Wed around 9pm

MAIN CAST

Dotty Binns	Avril Angers
Mr Tibbett	Jack Melford
Ian Prendergast	Cecil Brock/ Stephen Hancock
William	David Kinsey/Robert Dickens
Margo Fairfax	Naomi Chance

CREDITS

writers Sid Colin/Talbot Rothwell · *producer* Bill Ward

Best known at this time as Rosie Lea in Terry-Thomas's comedy series *How Do You View?*, Avril Angers starred in this early BBC sitcom that was set in the offices of a women's magazine, *Lady Fare*. Angers played Dotty Binns, a menial worker on the magazine's staff who aspires to be a journalist and so becomes involved in all manner of scrapes.

Writers Colin and Rothwell would go on to script numerous *Carry On* movies.

Dear Heart

UK · BBC · SKETCH

12 × 25 mins · colour

Series One (6) 26 Feb–2 Apr 1982 · BBC2 Fri 6.50pm

Series Two (6) 28 Apr–2 June 1983 · BBC2 Thu 6.20pm

MAIN CAST

Nicky Croydon
Billy Hartman
Colin Jeavons (series 1)
Toyah Willcox (series 1)
Mandy More (series 1)
Bob Goody (series 2)
Leni Harper (series 2)
Trevor Laird (series 2)

CREDITS

writers Helen Murry/Jamie Rix/Nick Wilton, Trevor McCallum, Kim Fuller/Vicky Pile, Roger Selves, John Dale, John Langdon, Kjartan Poskitt, Ian White and others · *script consultants* John Langdon/Nick Wilton (series 2) · *director* David Crichton (series 2) · *producer* Judy Whitfield

A sketch show based around the concept of a teen magazine, *Dear Heart*. Although an ensemble piece, media interest centred on Toyah Willcox who had made an impact on the 1980s pop scene with an outrageous (for the time) look and aggressive singing style. In the first series Willcox played the regular role of Super Advice Person (SAP), a confusing agony aunt, but she also took on other characters. Among her colleagues were the reliable Colin Jeavons and Nicky Croydon. Only Croydon and Hartman survived for the second series and they were joined by Leni Harper as the problem page woman, Trevor Laird as a frustrated writer and Bob Goody as a misguided medical correspondent.

Dear John ...   UK

UK · BBC · SITCOM

14 episodes (13 × 30 mins · 1 × 50 mins) · colour

Series One (7) 17 Feb–31 Mar 1986 · BBC1 Mon 8.30pm

Series Two (6) 7 Sep–12 Oct 1987 · BBC1 Mon 8.30pm

Special (50 mins) 21 Dec 1987 · BBC1 Mon 8.10pm

MAIN CAST

John	Ralph Bates
Kirk	Peter Blake
Kate	Belinda Lang
Ralph	Peter Denyer
Louise	Rachel Bell
Mrs Arnott	Jean Challis
Ken	Terence Edmond

OTHER APPEARANCES

Wendy	Wendy Allnut
Toby	William Bates
Rick	Kevin Lloyd (series 2)

CREDITS

writer John Sullivan · *directors* Ray Butt (7), Sue Bysh (7) · *producer* Ray Butt

John, a schoolteacher, is a recent divorcee whose wife Wendy has left him for his best friend. John is a mild-mannered chap but this event has left him shell-shocked, unable to speak without stumbling over his words and finding it difficult to face up to living alone. To aid the healing process, he joins a divorced and separated encounter group, 1-2-1, where others in a similar situation seek solace in each other's company. Unfortunately, on the surface at least, the group throws up more problems than it solves.

The 1-2-1 group is organised by Louise, a matronly woman determined to remain chirpy throughout, hoping to jollify the others by example. Prone to the odd insensitive remark – but oblivious to them – she sports an unhealthy interest in the sexual history of her charges, probing into the bedroom habits behind the failed marriages. This tendency embarrasses the rest of the group but Louise carries on regardless, seeming to derive a sensual thrill from the revelations. Apart from John, the group's regular members are Ralph, a timid, relentlessly ordinary chap beside whom John seems positively dynamic; Mrs Arnott, who mostly keeps herself to herself; the attractive and vulnerable but bitter Kate; and the 'black sheep' of the congregation, Kirk, a massively insecure soul who over-compensates by maintaining a braggardly front, boasting of a fabulously full life of wild parties and sexual adventures. Although the others see through him, and his lies, Kirk persists in keeping the pretence going. Despite all the hurdles, however, the group members slowly start to rebuild their lives.

A dysfunctional bunch of adults who rely upon one another for companionship and hope is not an obvious subject for comedy, but much humour was wrought from it thanks to John Sullivan's deft writing and well-observed characters. By his own high standards, the series was only a modest success, but Ralph Bates made a likeable lead – his real-life son William played his on-screen son, Toby, incidentally – and the series may have continued if a fatal illness hadn't claimed the actor's life prematurely in 1991.

Following its demise on the BBC, the series was sold to the USA where it was remade with the same title – see the next entry for details.

Dear John ...   USA

USA · NBC (ED WEINBERGER/PARAMOUNT) · SITCOM

90 × 30 mins · colour

US dates: 6 Jan 1988–15 Apr 1992

UK dates: 7 Jan 1990–31 May 1992 (37 episodes) BBC1 Sun around 10.45pm then various days around 11pm

MAIN CAST

John Lacey	Judd Hirsch
Kate McCarron	Isabella Hoffman
Kirk Morris	Jere Burns
Ralph Drang	Harry Groener (1988–91)
Louise Mercer	Jane Carr
Margie Philbert	Billie Bird

OTHER APPEARANCES

Wendy Lacey	Carlene Watkins (1988–1989);
	Deborah Harmon (1990–1992)
Matthew Lacey	Ben Savage (1988–1990);
	Billy Cohen (1990–1992)

CREDITS

creator John Sullivan · *writers* John Sullivan and others · *directors* James Burrows and others · *executive producers* Ed Weinberger, Hal Cooper, Rod Parker

Writer John Sullivan's attempts to sell the format of **Only Fools And Horses** to the USA had floundered, reputedly because Americans perceived the Trotter family as 'losers' and couldn't be persuaded that such characters were ideal fodder for primetime audiences. With *Dear John ...*, Sullivan recognised that he stood a better chance, encounter groups for divorcees being familiar to Americans. Sure enough, the series was bought and adapted by NBC.

Judd Hirsch – Alex in *Taxi* – was a good choice for the lead role, for, like Ralph Bates in the British *Dear John ...*, he easily suggested insecurity and inadequacy, and US audiences were used to seeing him play such flawed characters. The rest of the cast were virtually American clones of the British, except for Louise whose character was kept English.

At the start of the US adaptation, when an industrial dispute prevented NBC from employing writers, the network was forced to utilise Sullivan's BBC scripts, and so, unusually, the initial episodes were virtually word-for-word remakes of the originals. The show proved popular with American audiences and easily outstripped its progenitor in durability and numbers of episodes. Then, in a bizarre move, the BBC bought the US series for screening in Britain – it went out under the title *Dear John USA*.

Dear Ladies

see Hinge and Bracket

Dear Mother ... Love Albert

UK · ITV (*THAMES, YORKSHIRE) · SITCOM

29 episodes (6 × 30 mins · b/w; 20 × 30 mins · colour; 3 × short specials · colour)

*Series One (6 × b/w) 15 Sep–20 Oct 1969 · Mon 9.30pm

*Short special · part of *All-Star Comedy Carnival* 25 Dec 1969 · Thu 6pm

Series Two (7) 25 Apr–6 June 1970 · Sat 6.45pm

Short special · part of *All-Star Comedy Carnival* 25 Dec 1970 · Fri 6pm

Series Three (6) 1 Feb–8 Mar 1971 · Mon 8.30pm

Short special · part of *Mike And Bernie Winters' All-Star Christmas Comedy Carnival* 25 Dec 1971 · Sat 6.05pm

Series Four (7) *Albert!* 25 Apr–6 June 1972 · Tue 7pm

MAIN CAST

Albert Courtnay	Rodney Bewes
A C Strain	Garfield Morgan
Vivian McKewan	Sheila White (series 1 & 2)
Mrs McKewan	Geraldine Newman (series 1 & 2)
Doreen Bissel	Liz Gebhardt (series 3); Cheryl Hall (series 4)
Ada Bissel	Amelia Bayntun (series 3 & 4)

CREDITS

writers/producers Rodney Bewes/Derrick Goodwin (series 1–3, specials 1 & 2, 3 eps of series 4), Rodney Bewes (special 3 & 4 eps of series 4) · *directors* Derrick Goodwin (series 1–3 & special 1), David Mallet (specials 2 & 3), Bill Hitchcock (series 4) · *executive producer* John Duncan (series 2 & 3) · *producer* Rodney Bewes (series 4)

Three years after the end of **The Likely Lads**, a period in which his personal fortunes declined, Rodney Bewes again tasted sitcom success, this time with a series which he not merely starred in but also – with Derrick Goodwin – wrote and produced. (And he sang the theme song too, co-written with Mike Hugg.)

The concept came from Bewes' real-life letters home to his mother, reporting on recent events in his life. Correspondingly, the series cast him as Albert Courtnay, a 24-year-old innocent from the North, down in London to earn his fortune but finding reality very different. Always, however, and ever for the better, Albert romanticised and exaggerated his news out of all proportion. He found regular work with a confectionery company, at the end of the second series he moved into a flat with two 'dolly birds', and at the start of the third was in love and about to become engaged to Doreen Bissel.

Unusually, *Dear Mother ... Love Albert* switched production companies, from Thames to Yorkshire TV, during its run. It also spawned a sequel – titled simply *Albert!* – by the end of which Courtnay had been given the sack from the confectioner's and Doreen had severed their engagement.

The Debbie Reynolds Show

USA · NBC (HARMON PRODUCTIONS/FILMWAYS) · SITCOM

26 × 30 mins · colour

US dates: 16 Sep 1969–1 Sep 1970

UK dates: 3 Jan–15 Aug 1970 (26 episodes) BBC1 Sat 5.40pm

MAIN CAST

Debbie Thompson	Debbie Reynolds
Jim Thompson	Don Chastain
Charlotte Landers	Patricia Smith
Bob Landers	Tom Bosley

CREDITS

producer Jess Oppenheimer

Created by NBC following rival CBS's success with **The Doris Day Show**, this was a clear attempt to place another big-screen talent into a small-screen sitcom. Producer Jess Oppenheimer had also been integral to the success of *I Love Lucy*, and *The Debbie Reynolds Show* displayed some similar elements to that classic sitcom. Reynolds was cast as Debbie Thompson, who – like Lucy – was a dizzy housewife obsessed with interfering in her husband's job (in this case it was journalism). In her harebrained attempts to break into the newspaper world, Thompson was aided by her sister Charlotte – just as Lucy had her helpmate Ethel Mertz – and their schemes resulted in improbably comedic situations. Reynolds attacked the role with gusto but the sitcom lasted just one season.

Jack Dee

Born on 24 September 1962 in Petts Wood, near Orpington, south-east of London, the smartly dressed and stony-faced comic Jack Dee made an immediate impact with his debut performance in an open-mike slot at the Comedy Store in London. Encouraged to persist, he wrote much new material and soon made a name for himself on the comedy club circuit, proving particularly effective as a comedian/compere in addition to his straight standup act. Apart from his deadpan delivery and solemn face, Dee employed no gimmicks, but simply stood at the microphone and delivered a cleverly written stream of patter, most of it created from his apparent anger at certain aspects of society – this vitriol being all the more effective for its sneering but calm delivery. After Dee won the Best Stage Newcomer at the 1991 Comedy Awards, TV beckoned and he was soon given his own show by C4. His style worked well on the small-screen and he also impressed with a series of drily witty commercials for John Smiths beer, co-written by the comedian and drawing fun from his professionally miserable demeanour.

The Jack Dee Show 1

UK · C4 (OPEN MIKE PRODUCTIONS) · STANDUP

12 editions (12 × 30 mins · 1 × 60 mins) · colour

Series One (6) 26 Feb–1 Apr 1992 · Wed 10.30pm

Special (60 mins) 23 Dec 1992 · Wed 9pm

Series Two (6) 18 Feb–25 Mar 1994 · Fri 10.30pm

MAIN CAST
Jack Dee

CREDITS
writer Jack Dee · *directors* Juliet May (series 1 and special), David G Hillier (series 2) · *producer* Dave Morley

For his first starring TV series, Dee and his production team invented the fictitious Bohemia Club, a smoky, atmospheric version of an old supper club, the sort of place where, in Dee's own words, 'The Saint might take his best girl on a date, or where you might bump into John Steed'. The opening credits established the mood, with Dee in a 1960s sports car driving to the club through a neon-lit Soho. Dee then entered the stage to rapturous applause and delivered his clever, well-constructed routines via a 1940s-style microphone. (The old microphone became a Dee trademark, indeed it was the logo for his own company, Open Mike Productions.) Weekly musical guests provided a song or two but otherwise the shows were undiluted Dee, and went a long way to establishing the comic as a major TV figure.

Jack Dee Live At The Duke Of York Theatre

UK · C4 (OPEN MIKE PRODUCTIONS) · STANDUP

1 × 60 mins · colour

21 Apr 1995 · Fri 9.30pm

MAIN CAST
Jack Dee

CREDITS
writer Jack Dee · *director* Juliet May · *producer* Dave Morley

A standup show captured for the small-screen. TV being such a monstrous user of material, Dee's constant airing of new routines was indicative of his prolific writing.

Also in 1995, Dee showed his potential as a comic actor with a small but important role in the comedy feature film *The Steal*. Then, late in the year, he switched to ITV for the first time to front a six-part variety series, *Jack Dee's Saturday Night*, which, to quote its producer Dave Morley, was akin to 'a rock 'n' roll version of *The Good Old Days*'. Dee performed some standup material and introduced a bewildering array of guests – soap stars, rock bands, dance troupes, circus acts and other comics. Each show was rounded off with Dee taking an open question-and-answer session with the studio audience. The blend was not considered a success and it was abandoned after one series (9 December 1995 to 13 January 1996, made by Open Mike Productions for Granada). Its comedy highlights were compiled and aired with some new material in two 1997 specials – see *The Jack Dee Show* [2], below.

Jack And Jeremy's Police 4

UK · C4 (OPEN MIKE PRODUCTIONS) · SKETCH

1 × 30 mins · colour

28 Apr 1995 · Fri 10pm

MAIN CAST
Jack Dee
Jeremy Hardy

ALSO APPEARING
Rupert Bates
Sacha Baron Cohen
Lee Cornes
Stephen Frost
Norman Lovett
Maria McErlane
Ruby Milton
Richard Morton
Pat Roach
Meera Syal

CREDITS
writers Jack Dee/Jeremy Hardy · *additional material* Richard Morton · *director* Ed Bye · *producer* Dave Morley

A spoof of the real-life crime spotlight shows like *999* and *Crimewatch UK* proliferating on British TV at this time. Jack Dee and Jeremy Hardy took up the mantle for C4, portraying special constables ('We are trained to hit people properly') at Hedlow Police Station. Viewers were invited to view crime reconstructions, interactively swear themselves in as citizen police and take part in a 'Spared or Chaired' vote on the fate of a young offender – predictably, 250,000 phoned in to say that he should fry, and just three declared that it was an abomination. In one part Hardy played Jimmy Hard, a character based on Jimmy Nail in his *Spender* role.

Jack And Jeremy's Real Lives

UK · C4 (OPEN MIKE PRODUCTIONS) · SKETCH

6 × 35 mins · colour

31 May–5 July 1996 · Fri mostly 10.30pm

MAIN CAST
Jack Dee
Jeremy Hardy
Helen Lederer

CREDITS
writers Jack Dee/Jeremy Hardy · *additional material* Paul B Davies · *director* John Stroud · *producers* Ivan Douglass, Dave Morley

A series of 'mockumentaries' in the same style of *Jack And Jeremy's Police 4* – each programme included several linked sketches on a given theme, with Dee and Hardy portraying a number of characters (including Hardy's Jimmy Hard, from *Police 4*). Helen Lederer appeared in most of the editions and the changing supporting cast included Phil Nice, Stephen Frost, Mark Arden, Norman Lovett, Rowland Rivron, Willie Rushton, Lee Cornes, Felix Dexter, Carla Mendonça, Ben Keaton and Brenda Gilhooly – typically, each appeared in two or three programmes.

Shot on film, the programmes exuded a quality look, and the humour was wry and dry, with a hint of satire. There was no laughter track and despite the series' obvious merit, C4 (or its audience) failed to see the joke and after three editions it was relegated, unfairly, to a post-midnight slot.

Jack Dee's Christmas Show

UK · ITV (OPEN MIKE PRODUCTIONS FOR GRANADA) · STANDUP

1 × 45 mins · colour
21 Dec 1996 · Sat 10.45pm

MAIN CAST
Jack Dee

CREDITS
writer Jack Dee · *director* Julia Knowles · *producer* Dave Morley

A seasonal special, with Lily Savage among the guests.

The Jack Dee Show   2

UK · ITV (OPEN MIKE PRODUCTIONS FOR GRANADA) · STANDUP

2 × 45 mins · colour
12 July 1997 · Sat 10.50pm
19 July 1997 · Sat 10.45pm

MAIN CAST
Jack Dee

CREDITS
writers Jack Dee and others · *director* Julia Knowles · *producer* Dave Morley

Two shows combining comedy highlights from the variety series *Jack Dee's Saturday Night* (for details see above under *Jack Dee Live At The Duke Of York Theatre*) with some new material. Comedy guests featured were, in the first show, 'Gayle Tuesday' (Brenda Gilhooly) and Hale and Pace, with Lee Evans, Freddie Starr and Marty Putz in the second.

Jack Dee's Sunday Service

UK · ITV (OPEN MIKE PRODUCTIONS FOR GRANADA) · STANDUP

8 × 35 mins · colour
26 Oct–21 Dec 1997 · Sun 10pm

MAIN CAST
Jack Dee
Rich Hall

CREDITS
writers Jack Dee, Rich Hall · *additional material* Rob Colley, Richard Morton, Robert Saville, Mark Waites · *director* Steve Smith · *executive producers* Addison Cresswell, Andy Harries · *producer* Andy Davies

Another winning series, with a slightly revamped format but the same degree of high-quality material. In between liberal doses of his standup routine Dee appeared in filmed sketches, some with his regular guest, the American comedian Rich Hall, who was also given his own individual slot each week, 'Rich's Bit'. The series was fairly

topical, with much of the humour stemming from items in the week's news. The credit sequence showed Dee maliciously pricking an inflatable globe with a pin, which neatly summed up his intentions. Each edition of the series ended with Dee reacting to questions from members of the public via a travelling 'video box'. Those who posed the best, weirdest or funniest questions were invited to be among the studio audience, where Dee – in good-humoured fashion – humiliated them in person.

Deep And Crisp And Stolen

UK · ITV (REDIFFUSION) · SITCOM

1 × 90 mins · b/w
21 Dec 1964 · Mon 9.10pm

MAIN CAST
Det Chief-Supt Lockhart/
Percy · · · · · · · · · · · · · · · · · · Raymond Francis
William Carnville · · · · · · · · · · · Dennis Price
Leoni Broadway · · · · · · · · Maggie Fitzgibbon
Ted · George Moon
Bluey · · · · · · · · · · · · · · · · · · · Grant Taylor

CREDITS
writer Dave Freeman · *director* Ronald Marriott · *executive producer* Antony Kearey

A single programme, produced for the 1964 festive season, which was high on comedy (courtesy of writer Dave Freeman) and full of TV appearances, in character, by the stars of various ITV shows.

Three thieves plan to rob a prominent London store, Tarringes, of its Christmas Eve till takings, £100,000, but their plans do not gel until along comes a boozy petty thief named Percy who is the spitting image of Det Chief-Supt Lockhart (of the long-running ITV crime series *No Hiding Place*). Patrick Allen, Sam Kydd and Gerald Flood (all of *Crane*) also appeared, as did Michael Miles (the game-show *Take Your Pick*), Jimmy Hanley, Arthur Mullard, Muriel Young (various children's shows) and Keith Fordyce and Cathy McGowan (from *Ready, Steady, Go!*).

Dennis The Menace

USA · CBS (DIC ENTERPRISES) · SITCOM

146 × 30 mins · b/w
US dates: 4 Oct 1959–22 Sep 1963
UK dates: 14 Sep 1960–30 Mar 1966 (103 episodes) ITV various days · usually around 6.30pm

MAIN CAST
Dennis Mitchell · · · · · · · · · · · · · · · Jay North
Henry Mitchell · · · · · · · · · · Herbert Anderson
Alice Mitchell · · · · · · · · · · · · · Gloria Henry
George Wilson · · · Joseph Kearns (1959–62)
Martha Wilson · · · · · · · Sylvia Field (1959–62)
Esther Cathcart · · · · Mary Wickes (1959–61)
John Wilson · · · · · · · Gale Gordon (1962–63)

CREDITS
creator Hank Ketcham · *writers* various · *directors* various · *executive producer* Harry Ackerman

Hank Ketcham's cartoon *Dennis The Menace*, which first appeared in American newspapers in 1951, was brought to life in this long-running US sitcom that starred Jay North as the six-year-old imp. Permanently dressed in his stripy tee-shirt and dungarees, Dennis was the archetypal dynamo kid – and cute with it – seemingly intent on do-gooding but always ending up with trouble on his hands, usually having upset any one or all of the following: his parents Henry and Alice, his next-door neighbour Mr Wilson, or the local old maid Miss Cathcart.

The series ended in 1963, when Jay North was 11 (he was seven when the series began) but repeats kept it on US screens for many years afterwards. Since then there has been a one-off two-hour sequel in 1987, with Victor DiMattia as Dennis, a one-off animated special in 1981, a full animated series screened in the USA from 1986 to 1988 (screened by London and other ITV regions from 21 April 1987) and a 1993 feature film, *Dennis*, with Mason Gamble as Dennis and Walter Matthau as Mr Wilson.

Simultaneous with the birth of Hank Ketcham's US character, generally aimed at adults, the weekly British children's comic *Beano* launched an unrelated *Dennis The Menace* strip of its own. Because of this, the US TV series had to sport a different title for UK screening, so it aired as *Just Dennis*. A series based on the British *Dennis The Menace* creation was brought to BBC1 in animated form, courtesy of a British-led international co-production, from 2 April 1996.

The Denny Willis Show

UK · ITV (ATV) · SITCOM

2 × 30 mins · b/w
16 & 23 June 1962 · Sat 10.20pm

MAIN CAST
Denny Willis
Johnnie Mack
Janie Marden
Billy McComb

CREDITS
writers Jeremy Lloyd/Stan Mars · *producer* Colin Clews

A short-lived series for Denny Willis, who was a surprise hit in the 1960 *Royal Variety Show* when he performed as part of a singing quintet. In so doing, he was following in the footsteps of his father, Dave Willis, who worked the music-halls of the 1930s.

In this two-part series, Willis played the clumsy assistant stage manager of the Sedgewick Empire, spoiling all the acts. Johnnie Mack was the theatre manager.

Des O'Connor … [various shows]

see O'CONNOR, Des

The Desilu Playhouse

see BALL, Lucille

Desmond's

UK · C4 (HUMPHREY BARCLAY PRODUCTIONS) · SITCOM

71 episodes (70 × 30 mins · 1 × 60 mins) · colour

Series One (6 × 30 mins) 5 Jan–9 Feb 1989 · Thu 8.30pm

Series Two (13 × 30 mins) 22 Jan–16 Apr 1990 · Mon 8.30pm

Series Three (13 × 30 mins) 28 Oct 1991–3 Feb 1992 · Mon 8.30pm

Series Four (13 × 30 mins) 5 Oct–28 Dec 1992 · Mon 8.30pm

Series Five (13 × 30 mins) 27 Sep–20 Dec 1993 · Mon 8.30pm

Series Six (12 × 30 mins · 1 × 60 mins) 26 Sep–19 Dec 1994 · Mon 8.30pm

MAIN CAST

Desmond Ambrose	Norman Beaton
Shirley Ambrose	Carmen Munroe
Augustus 'Porkpie' Grant	Ram John Holder
Matthew	Gyearbuor Asante
Michael Ambrose	Geff Francis
Gloria Ambrose	Kim Walker
Sean Ambrose	Justin Pickett
Lee	Robbie Gee
Tony	Dominic Keating (series 1–5)
Louise	Lisa Geoghan (series 1–3)
Beverley	Joan Ann Maynard
Mandy Ambrose	Matilda Thorpe
Vince	Count Prince Miller
Ricky	Dean Gatiss (series 6)

CREDITS

creator Trix Worrell · writers Trix Worrell (39), Annie Bruce (7), Carol Williams (7), Paul McKenzie/Laurence Gouldbourne (4), Paul McKenzie (2), Laurence Gouldbourne (1), Joan Hooley (3), Alrick Riley (3), Panji Anoff (2), Paulette Randall (1), Patricia Elcock (1), Michael Ellis (1) · directors Charlie Hanson (17), Trix Worrell (10), David Askey (9), Iain McLean (9), Jan Sargent (8), Mandie Fletcher (6), Nic Phillips (5), Liddy Oldroyd (5), Lou Wakefield (2) · executive producers Al Mitchell, Humphrey Barclay · producers Humphrey Barclay/Charlie Hanson (series 1–3), Humphrey Barclay (series 4), Humphrey Barclay/Paulette Randall (series 5), Paulette Randall (series 6)

On a par with **Drop The Dead Donkey** as the most successful home-grown sitcom screened by C4, *Desmond's* finally established (hopefully, once and for all) the black British sitcom. It was not the first, but – to date – it has been the best.

Set in a barber shop – Desmond's – situated in the south London district of Peckham, its wry humour was wrung not only from the characters and situations but also from the generation gap and the attitudinal differences between West Indian immigrants and their British-born descendants. Desmond's salon was the Peckham equivalent of the *Cheers* bar in Boston, with family, friends and neighbours popping in to play out the latest episodes in their life. Little in the way of hairdressing seems to have been done, but as a local meeting place it was second to none. (In this, Desmond's typified many black-run barber shops which, like, say, Italian barber-shops, tend to be more welcoming and friendly, and more of a social centre, than their white-English counterparts.)

Desmond Ambrose himself was a grump, like a black Victor Meldrew, not beyond a laugh but easily exasperated by things; his wife Shirley had to put up with him throughout a long marriage, but she usually managed to trump his excesses and win in the end. After she and Desmond emigrated to Britain from the Caribbean in 1959, Shirley spent years in the service of her family, looking after her husband and their three children, now young adults, Michael, Sean and Gloria. She was also an experienced stylist with the scissors. As well as the Ambrose children we regularly saw Matthew, an African, and the permanent visitor Porkpie (so named because of his hat), a long-established friend of Desmond from the old country. Whites played their part too, principally by way of Gloria's friend Louise, and Tony, who worked in the salon.

The entire ensemble comprised very likeable characters, the type who, were *Desmond's* an American sitcom, would have attracted applause as they entered the stage; as it was, the British studio audiences were not discouraged from whistling, cheering or jeering at appropriate moments, adding to the air of conviviality of the piece. *Desmond's* was like an extended family, a series that somehow embraced the characters on screen, the audience in the studio and the viewers at home, and half an hour in its company would generate not only warm laughter but a sense of belonging.

The origin of *Desmond's* is an object lesson in simplicity. The writer Trix Worrell was en route to a meeting with TV comedy producer Humphrey Barclay when his bus stopped at a red light, enabling him to witness the three staff in a barber's shop ogling some passing schoolgirls. Raised in Peckham, and remembering a barber's shop there from his youth, Worrell promptly formulated the basis for a sitcom, which he pitched to Barclay at the meeting a few minutes later. Barclay agreed to provide development funds and Worrell went away to flesh out the characters. Had the traffic light been green, *Desmond's* wouldn't have happened. Once at the planning stage, Worrell – himself born in St Lucia – was keen to emphasise the fact that the West Indies comprises many islands, not just Jamaica, so he made his three main characters – Desmond, Shirley and Porkpie – of Guyanese origin. Then, having scripted the first two series, he started to pool the writing – instigating an all-too-rare pro-women writers policy – and began to direct some of the episodes.

By teaming Norman Beaton and Carmen Munroe as husband and wife, Worrell and Barclay united the two leading lights in British black acting in recent decades, a combination strong enough for the series to reap the Best Sitcom prize at the 1993 British Comedy Awards. Finely blending rascality and bravura, Beaton's Desmond was the linchpin character, everything flowing around him in the way that things centred on Bill Cosby in **The Cosby Show**. Indeed, the American star so enjoyed *Desmond's* (it was screened in the USA by the Black Entertainment Television cable network) that he invited Norman Beaton across to the USA to appear in *The Cosby Show*, where he played the part of a cricket-mad West Indian doctor (episode titled 'There's Still No Joy In Mudville', screened in Britain by C4 on 22 November 1992).

Norman Beaton died on 13 December 1994, aged 60, while visiting the island of his birth, Guyana. C4 screened *Beaton But Unbowed – A Tribute To An Artist* six days later, immediately after what was already announced as the last ever episode of *Desmond's*. (*Beaton But Unbowed* was also the title of the actor's 1986 autobiography.) The story wasn't quite over, however, as one of the *Desmond's* regulars was spun off into his own series – see **Porkpie**.

Desperately Seeking Roger

see CLARY, Julian

The Detectives

UK · BBC (CELADOR PRODUCTIONS) · SITCOM

30 episodes (29 × 30 mins · 1 × 50 mins) colour

Series One (6) 27 Jan–3 Mar 1993 · BBC1 Wed 8pm

Series Two (6) 2 Mar–6 Apr 1994 · BBC1 Wed 8pm

Series Three (6) 9 Jan–13 Feb 1995 · BBC1 Mon 8.30pm

Series Four (5) 15 Feb–14 Mar 1996 · BBC1 Thu 8.30pm

Series Five (6) 14 Jan–18 Feb 1997 · BBC1 Tue 8.30pm

Special (50 mins) 28 Dec 1997 · BBC1 Sun 8pm

MAIN CAST

Bob Louis	Jasper Carrott
Dave Briggs	Robert Powell
Superintendent Cottam	George Sewell

CREDITS

writers Steve Knight/Mike Whitehill · directors Ed Bye (18), Graeme Harper (9), Steve Knight (3) · producers Ed Bye (18), Nic Phillips (12)

The absurd adventures of two defective detectives, who – despite unbelievable incompetence – somehow manage to solve their cases (or be nearby when the cases are solved) and retain their jobs.

Developed from the series of five-minute sketches featured in *Canned Carrott*, *The Detectives* was shot on film and quite lavishly mounted. Basically, the characters of the cops were that one, Bob, was dumb and the other, Dave, was dumber. With their spectacular stupidity taken as read, the other difference between them was that Bob was more downbeat and tried (but failed) to be conscientious, whereas Dave fancied himself as a ladies' man and modelled his personality on TV and movie cops. The actor Robert Powell, cast as Dave, proved to be a dab hand at this type of comedy, recognising the importance of playing it straight, and the presence of George Sewell as their superintendent, Cottam, invited comparisons with his earlier smash-and-grab detective series *Special Branch* (Thames for ITV, 1969–74). But although it lampooned many of the clichés (and plots) of such series, *The Detectives* mostly resembled *The Sweeney* (Thames for ITV, 1975–78), Cottam being a deadpan spin on that series' Chief Inspector Haskins (Garfield Morgan).

Apart from its location filming, another distinctive feature of *The Detectives* was the special guest stars it showcased each week, some of whom appeared as the characters (or variations on the characters) they played in other series, notably John Nettles and Terence Alexander from *Bergerac* (BBC1, 1981–91) and Leslie Grantham as Danny Kane from *The Paradise Club* (BBC1, 1989–90). On the comedy front, Gareth Hunt and Louisa Rix (the volatile neighbours in *Side By Side*) turned up in one episode as married couple Mr and Mrs Sharp.

Devenish

UK · ITV (GRANADA) · SITCOM

13 × 30 mins · colour

Series One (7) 15 July–26 Aug 1977 · Fri 8.30pm then 10.30pm

Series Two (6) 3 Apr–14 May 1978 · Mon 8pm

MAIN CAST

Arthur Prufrock Devenish ·· Dinsdale Landen
Hugh Fitzjoy ·········· Terence Alexander
Angela Nuttall ·········· Veronica Roberts
Neville Liversedge ······· Geoffrey Bayldon
Admiral Wallow ········· Geoffrey Chater
George Craddock ······· Michael Robbins
Prudence Devenish ········ Polly Adams

CREDITS

writer Anthony Couch · *director* Brian Mills · *producer* John G Temple

An office-bound sitcom, revelling in the politics of desk life. Arthur P Devenish – played well by the acclaimed actor Dinsdale

Landen – is a brown-noser, an executive deviser of games for the manufacturing company Universal Pastimes Limited, not content with being good at his job, only in being *seen* to be good. With the company for ten years, Devenish believes that he has board-of-director potential, is jealous of those in his way and – full of big ideas about his own importance – endeavours to push himself as high as he can in the most irritating, ingratiating fashion. Like most people locked into middle-management positions, he also has to hustle to justify his job and ensure that no one edges ahead in the promotion stakes, passing off other people's good ideas as his own and fobbing off his own bad ideas on to others.

Dial RIX

UK · BBC · SITCOMS

9 × 50 mins · b/w

Series One (6) 12 Sep 1962–24 Jan 1963 · various days and times

Series Two (3) 23 June–15 Oct 1963 · various days and times

Topical farces written especially for TV and starring the acknowledged British master of the genre, Brian Rix. (Stylistically, the series was titled *Dial RIX*.) It employed a company of actors, one of whom was Rix's real-life wife Elspet Gray.

See also Brian Rix Farces.

Between The Balance Sheets   12 SEP 1962

MAIN CAST

Basil Rix ················ Brian Rix
Miss Logan ··············· Linda Dixon
Mr Hemingway ············· Terry Scott
Uncle Luke ·············· Leo Franklyn
Pamela Rix ·············· Elspet Gray
M Martell ··············· Patrick Cargill
Eloise ················· Helen Jessop

CREDITS

writer John Chapman · *director* Darcy Conyers

A delve into expense accounts leads to Paris and a good deal of running in and out of bedrooms.

What A Drag   5 OCT 1962

MAIN CAST

Bert Rix ················ Brian Rix
Dr Blinker ·············· Leo Franklyn
Sydney Keen ············· Terry Scott
George Frampton ········ John Le Mesurier
Cynthia ················ Elspet Gray
Ted ··················· John Chapman
Miss Nolan ·············· Helen Jessop
TV producer ············· Colin Douglas
Harry Daisy ············· Andrew Sachs

CREDITS

writer John Chapman · *director* Darcy Conyers

Bert Rix, a worker in a cigarette factory, is pressed into singing the product's praises in a TV commercial.

Round The Bend   26 OCT 1962

MAIN CAST

Barrington Rix ············ Brian Rix
Mrs Barrington Rix ········· Elspet Gray
Maple ················· Terry Scott
Sam ·················· Leo Franklyn
Mrs Birkett ············· Hazel Douglas
Bond ················· Patrick Cargill

CREDITS

writers Ray Cooney/Tony Hilton · *director* Darcy Conyers

Newly-weds Mr and Mrs Barrington Rix discover that their new house straddles both sides of a county boundary. Then one of the two councils wants the house demolished.

Nose To Wheel   13 DEC 1962

MAIN CAST

Barney Rix ·············· Brian Rix
Shirley Rix ·············· Joan Sims
Stan Waring ············· Leo Franklyn
Peter Dimmock ············· himself
Roger Pearson ··········· Patrick Cargill
Ted Ockley ·············· Larry Noble

CREDITS

writer John Chapman · *director* Wallace Douglas

The problems of being an amateur sportsman, as felt by keen cyclist Barney Rix.

No Plums In The Pudding   26 DEC 1962

MAIN CAST

Boy Rix ················ Brian Rix
Penelope Rix ············· Elspet Gray
Mr Jolliboy ·············· Larry Noble
Mrs Hathaway ··········· Joan Sanderson
Toby Murgatroyd ········· Terry Scott
Gunga Din ·············· Patrick Cargill
Jack Robinson ············ Leo Franklyn
Teddy Gibbons ··········· John Chapman
Fat furniture man ·········· Colin Douglas
Thin furniture man ········· Andrew Sachs
Norma Flatly ············· Helen Jessop

CREDITS

writer Christopher Bond · *director* Wallace Douglas

Boy Rix establishes his own one-man business but runs into financial trouble.

Come Prancing   24 JAN 1963

MAIN CAST

Bruce Rix ··············· Brian Rix
Mr Haythorne ············ Leo Franklyn
Mrs Haythorne ··········· Sheila Mercier
Rita Haythorne ············ Joan Sims
Reggie Brown-Dorset ······· John Chapman
Doreen Parsons ··········· Hazel Douglas
Ron Smith ·············· Peter Mercier
Miranda Marston ··········· Elspet Gray
Ambrose Moffat ··········· Patrick Cargill
Gloria ················· Helen Jessop

CREDITS
writer Christopher Bond · *director* Wallace Douglas

Bruce Rix is determined not to get caught up in the ballroom dancing boom.

Skin Deep   23 JUNE 1963

MAIN CAST
Bertram Rix	Brian Rix
Bertram's dad	Leo Franklyn
Mrs Ramsbotham	Marjorie Rhodes
Deirdre Chapman	Hazel Douglas
Councillor Bolton	Colin Douglas
Percival	Peter Mercier
Mr Ramsbotham	Larry Noble

CREDITS
writer Ray Cooney · *director* Wallace Douglas

Bertram Rix, a butcher and local councillor, is bribed and blackmailed when he is appointed the judge of bathing-beauty competition Miss Blackborough 1963.

Rolling Home   5 AUG 1963

MAIN CAST
Bunny Rix	Brian Rix
Angela Rix	Elspet Gray
Colin Enderby	Colin Douglas
Ted Barrett	John Crocker
PC Boot	Moray Watson
Sadie Enderby	Judith Furse
'Fruity' Frampton	Basil Lord
'Biffer' Bonce	Peter Mercier
'China' Bowles	Harold Goodwin
Mr Jennings	Larry Noble

CREDITS
writer Christopher Bond · *director* Wallace Douglas

Bunny Rix and his wife Angela quit the big city for a quiet life in the country with their caravan. But nothing goes to plan.

What A Chassis   15 OCT 1963

MAIN CAST
Bobby Rix	Brian Rix
Felicity Clarke	Dawn Beret
Sir William Pardon	John Barron
John Prentice	Arthur Barrett
Paul Stanford	John Cater
Jack Boyle	Peter Mercier
Jim Catlin	Larry Noble
Arthur Bates	Leo Franklyn
Velda	Sally Douglas
Raymond Baxter	himself

CREDITS
writer Christopher Bond · *director* Wallace Douglas

Bobby Rix, the new personnel officer at the Crispin Motor Company, has to keep the staff from striking in order to get the company's latest vehicle ready for the Motor Show.

Diana

USA · NBC (TALENT ASSOCIATES/NORTON SIMON) · SITCOM
15 × 30 mins · colour
US dates: 10 Sep 1973–7 Jan 1974
UK dates: 23 Oct 1973–5 Mar 1974 (15 episodes) BBC1 Tue 7.50pm then 3.30pm

MAIN CAST
Diana Smythe	Diana Rigg
Norman Brodnik	David Sheiner
Norma Brodnik	Barbara Barrie
Howard Tolbrook	Richard B Shull
Marshall Tyler	Robert Moore
Holly Green	Carol Androsky
Jeff Harmon	Richard Mulligan
Smitty	Liam Dunn

CREDITS
writers various · *director* Leonard Stern · *producers* Leonard Stern, Morris Barry

An attempt by NBC to capitalise on the American popularity of the British actress Diana Rigg, following her success in the cult fantasy-espionage series *The Avengers*. In the sitcom *Diana* – based on an unaired pilot, *The Diana Rigg Show* – she was cast as an English divorcee, Diana Smythe, who arrives in New York to launch a career as a fashion artist. She moves into her brother's apartment while he, an anthropologist, is away in South Africa, and soon discovers that many of his drinking buddies have keys to the place too, resulting in a stream of characters turning up without notice. Smythe works in a Manhattan department store, where her colleagues include its president Norman Brodnik; Norma, his wife and also the head of merchandising; Howard Tolbrook, an ill-tempered copywriter; and window dresser Marshall Tyler. Outside work, Diana's friends are neighbour Holly Green, a model, and mystery books writer Jeff Harmon.

Diana Rigg is said to have accepted this offer to move into situation comedy as a reaction to all the British scripts she was being sent at this time, which, she claimed, invariably instructed 'enter Diana, carrying a gun'. Unfortunately, then, *Diana* was too lightweight and 'normal' to force its viewers to see her as anything other 'Emma Peel in a sitcom'. And if she was indeed trying to escape the *Avengers* tag then she probably despaired when the writers/producers decided that one episode of the series ('You Can't Go Back', screened by BBC1 on 8 January 1974) reunited her with Patrick Macnee, who guested as a famous concert pianist visiting New York and trying to renew a former romance.

See also *Three Piece Suite*.

The Diana Dors Show

UK · ITV (ATV) · SKETCH
3 editions (2 × 60 mins · 1 × 50 mins) · b/w

9 May 1959 · Sat 7.55pm (60 mins)
1 Aug 1959 · Sat 8pm (60 mins)
29 Apr 1961 · Sat 7.40pm (50 mins)

MAIN CAST
Diana Dors

CREDITS
producer Albert Locke

Three starring shows for the versatile actress Diana Dors, showing off her talents as comedian, sketch artist, impersonator, singer and dancer. The first two, presented under the *Saturday Spectacular* banner, also featured her then husband Dickie Dawson, and (in the first show only) American guests Jack Cassidy and Shirley Jones – father and step-mother of David Cassidy, the latter eventually to star with him in **The Partridge Family**.

Note. *The Diana Dors Show* was also the title of a Southern Television (ITV) daytime chat-show, five programmes from 15 June 1981.

See also *All Our Saturdays, Of Mycenae And Men* and *Queenie's Castle*.

Dick And The Duchess

USA · CBS (SHELDON REYNOLDS PRODUCTIONS) · SITCOM
26 × 25 mins · b/w
US dates: 28 Sep 1957–16 May 1958
UK dates: 26 Sep 1958–2 Apr 1959 (26 episodes) ITV Fri 11.30pm then Thu 6.10pm

MAIN CAST
Dick Starrett	Patrick O'Neal
Jane Starrett	Hazel Court
Peter Jamison	Richard Wattis
Mathilda	Beatrice Varley
Rodney	Ronnie Stevens
Peabody	Roddy Hughes
Inspector Stark	Michael Shepley

CREDITS
writer Harry Kurnitz · *director/producer* Sheldon Reynolds

A US series that successfully blended comedy and adventure, starring Patrick O'Neal as Dick Starrett, an American insurance investigator based in London, whose upper-crust wife Jane – Dick called her 'The Duchess' – is an interfering blue-blooded Englishwoman.

The series had plenty of UK interest – set in London, it was filmed by CBS at MGM's studio in Elstree and featured a good many British actors, almost at the rate of one per episode. Richard Wattis appeared the most often (as Dick's business colleague Peter Jamison) and Irene Handl, Margaret Rutherford, Walter Fitzgerald, Lionel Jeffries, Alfie Bass, William Mervyn, Sydney Tafler, Michael Medwin, Leslie Dwyer, Joan Hickson, William Franklyn, Victor Maddern, Eric Barker, Peter Butterworth, Kenneth Williams (it was *very* unusual for him to appear in a sitcom), Warren Mitchell and a number of others all appeared too.

Not many TV series of the 1950s could boast that every episode ended with the married couple in bed – *Dick And The Duchess* did, although, in true American TV style, twin beds were used.

Dick Emery ...   [various shows]

see EMERY, Dick

Dick Gregory

UK · BBC · STANDUP
....
1 × 45 mins · b/w
10 June 1967 · BBC2 Sat 7.40pm
MAIN CAST
Dick Gregory

CREDITS
producer Dennis Main Wilson

A rare TV exposure for the black American comedian and civil rights campaigner Dick Gregory.

Gregory's style was far removed from the observational school of comedy, often tackling issues of racial discrimination head on. In this BBC2 *Show Of The Week* presentation he was joined by jazz singer Nina Simone.

The Dick Lester Show

UK · ITV (ASSOCIATED-REDIFFUSION) · SKETCH
....
1 × 30 mins · b/w
23 Dec 1955 · Fri 8.30pm
MAIN CAST
Dick Lester
Alun Owen

CREDITS
writers Dick Lester/Philip Saville · *director* Douglas Hurn

Before becoming a film director, the multi-talented American anglophile Richard Lester (only in England was his first name abbreviated to Dick) worked as a staff producer at Associated-Rediffusion. Soon enough a spot opened up in the schedule for this single half-hour show in which Lester could himself appear on screen, being funny, singing and playing piano, guitar and double-bass. It was not a success, however, and many of the moments that had shone in rehearsal failed in the live broadcast. Lester himself later considered the show 'puerile'.

In two other respects, however, the programme had far-reaching effects: in 1964, Lester, as director, employed Alun Owen (whom he first met here, when Owen was an actor) to write the Beatles' first feature film *A Hard Day's Night*; and Peter Sellers, who chanced to see *The Dick Lester Show*, called and suggested that he and the American have lunch, which resulted in three TV series in

1956 – *The Idiot Weekly, Price 2d*, *A Show Called Fred* and *Son Of Fred*. (These then led to the acclaimed 11 minute 'short', *The Running, Jumping And Standing Still Film*, made in 1959.)

The Dick Shawn Show

UK · ITV (ATV) · SKETCH/STANDUP
....
1 × 60 mins · b/w
26 Apr 1958 · Sat 8.30pm
MAIN CAST
Dick Shawn
Aileen Cochrane

CREDITS
producer Bill Lyon-Shaw

A rare British visit and even rarer British TV appearance (it was aired under the *Saturday Spectacular* strand) by the American comic actor who had not long risen to fame in his home country as a discovery on the talent-spotting programme *Arthur Godfrey's Talent Scouts*. Shawn later achieved big-screen immortality as a prancing Führer in the *Springtime For Hitler* play within Mel Brooks' movie *The Producers*.

Dick Van Dyke And The Other Woman

USA · CBS · SKETCH
....
1 × 60 mins · colour
US date: 13 Apr 1969
UK date: 4 Sep 1969 · BBC1 Fri 9.10pm (b/w)
MAIN CAST
Dick Van Dyke
Mary Tyler Moore

CREDITS
writers Bill Persky/Sam Denoff · *director* Dean Whitmore · *producers* Byron Paul, Sam Denoff, Bill Persky

A one-off music and comedy special that reunited, for the first time since 1966, the two stars of the classic TV sitcom *The Dick Van Dyke Show* (see following entry). As well as giving them an opportunity to reminisce about that series, on camera, the pair blossomed in a number of well-written comedy skits. Mary Tyler Moore's career had been in something of a decline in the previous three years, following a none too successful foray into the movies, but her performance in this programme prompted CBS executives to woo her back to television – *The Mary Tyler Moore Show*, another undoubted TV classic, being the result.

The Dick Van Dyke Show

USA · CBS (CALVADA PRODUCTIONS) · SITCOM
....
158 × 30 mins · b/w
US dates: 3 Oct 1961–1 June 1966

*UK dates: 4 July 1963–16 Sep 1967 (157 episodes) BBC1 Thu 8.50pm then various days and times
MAIN CAST
Rob Petrie · · · · · · · · · · · · · · · Dick Van Dyke
Laura Petrie · · · · · · · · · · · Mary Tyler Moore
Buddy Sorrell · · · · · · · · · Morey Amsterdam
Sally Rogers · · · · · · · · · · · · · · · Rose Marie
Mel Cooley · · · · · · · · · · · · · Richard Deacon
Alan Brady · · · · · · · · · · · · · · · · Carl Reiner
Ritchie Petrie · · · · · · · · · · · · Larry Matthews
Jerry Helper · · · · · · · · · · · · · · · Jerry Paris
Millie Helper · · · · · · · · · Ann Morgan Guilbert

CREDITS
creator Carl Reiner · *writers* Carl Reiner (48), Carl Reiner/Ronald Alexander (1), Carl Reiner/Howard Merrill (1), Carl Reiner/Bill Persky/Sam Denoff (5), Bill Persky/Sam Denoff (26), Garry Marshall/Jerry Belson (16), Dale McRaven/Carl Kleinschmitt (9), Sheldon Keller/Howard Merrill (7), John Whedon (7), Martin A Ragaway (5), others (33) · *directors* Jerry Paris (83), John Rich (40), Jerry Paris/John Rich (1), Howard Morris (5), Alan Rafkin (4), Lee Philips (4), Sheldon Leonard (4), others (17) · *executive producers* Sheldon Leonard, Ronald Jacobs · *producer* Carl Reiner

Inspired casting, tight writing, powerful performances and slick production values combined to make *The Dick Van Dyke Show* a bona-fide television classic. Pitching its middle-class comedy to a middle-class audience, rarely has a sitcom worked on so many levels. The American public lapped it up, British viewers did too, and the production team's decision to halt the series while it was still on a high ensured that it never lost its appeal. Quite simply, *The Dick Van Dyke Show* is one of the all-time greats.

Although Dick Van Dyke himself was the undoubted star, the guiding genius behind the series was its creator, principal writer and producer Carl Reiner, who had spent years as a writer and occasional performer working with Sid Caesar on such pioneering 1950s US comedy series as *Your Show Of Shows* and *Caesar's Hour*. Reiner realised that the life of a TV writer, sharing an office with other professional wagsters and then going home to his family, could be made into a sitcom. Finding his idea in favour, a pilot episode was made, titled *Head Of The Family*, in which Reiner himself played the lead character Rob Petrie, with Barbara Britton cast as his wife Laura, Gary Morgan as their young son Ritchie, and Sylvia Miles as Sally Rogers and Morty Gunty as Buddy Sorrell, Rob's co-writers. Although it made the air (it was networked in the USA by CBS under the *Comedy Spot* banner on 19 July 1960), no series developed at this time, and it wasn't until Reiner met TV producer Sheldon Leonard that the idea was resurrected. Leonard liked the show but felt that Reiner, despite his credentials, wasn't right as the lead, and suggested a total recasting. The list of possible Rob Petries was finally narrowed down to two names, Johnny Carson and Dick Van Dyke. Van Dyke got the role and the rest, as the cliché goes, although it's entirely true in this instance, is TV history.

The richly talented Dick Van Dyke was virtually a TV unknown when the series began – he had appeared in guest spots in variety shows and in a couple of episodes of *The Phil Silvers Show*, and hosted a cartoon series – but he became a global star in the role of Rob Petrie, bringing to the part his exemplary comedic timing, good looks and a marvellous athleticism born of his lithe frame. Right down the line, indeed, the series was impeccably cast. Stepping into the role of Rob's wife, Laura, was the similarly little-known Mary Tyler Moore, hitherto seen regularly only in a David Janssen TV series, *Richard Diamond, Private Detective*. *The Dick Van Dyke Show* made her a star too, and an apple-pie sex symbol, and, through her fame, she realised her own series, *The Mary Tyler Moore Show*, which made every bit as much an impact as its predecessor and, similarly, voluntarily bowed out in its prime. Rob and Laura made a great couple and rank right up there with Ralph and Alice Kramden (*The Honeymooners*) and Ricky and Lucy Ricardo (*I Love Lucy*) as the quintessential married couples of early US sitcoms. (Three decades on, Nick Hornby would use the names Rob and Laura for the lead characters in his novel *High Fidelity*, so, clearly, the influence is still felt.) About the only puzzling aspect of the Petries' marriage, indeed, was that, despite their clearly close relationship, husband and wife slept in twin beds, a point that jarred with viewers but says much about the conservative nature of US television in the early 1960s. Rob and Laura's son, Ritchie, grew up from a small infant to a blossoming child during the series' run, and their apartment neighbours, Jerry (a dentist) and Millie Helper, were often on hand to witness the latest crazy episode in the Petries' lives.

At work, Rob Petrie worked as head writer on *The Alan Brady Show*, crafting the gags for the star in a manner entirely in keeping with Carl Reiner's job for Sid Caesar and, indeed, in the same way that TV comedy writers have always written for a major star. Fittingly, Reiner himself was cast in the role of the egomaniacal Brady (although, until the 104th episode, his face was always obscured). Working with Rob were Buddy Sorrell and Sally Rogers (brilliantly played by the exceptionally talented actors and humorists Morey Amsterdam and former child starlet Rose Marie) who, as their profession dictated, were a laugh-a-minute pair, cracking jokes with their every utterance, some intended for their Alan Brady scripts, others simply for their own amusement. Sorrell, in particular, made constant and deliciously cutting

remarks about the producer of *The Alan Brady Show*, the balding Mel Cooley, both behind his back and very much to his face. Viewers were left with the definite impression that life in the office of a bunch of TV scriptwriters is both hilarious and intensely pressured, with a high standard to maintain and unbreakable deadlines to be met. One of the many reasons that *The Dick Van Dyke Show* works so well is that this situation was then, and remains, a real one: step, today, inside the creative hothouse that is the writers' room for any US comedy series, with ideas and insults thick in the air, and it'll be like a scene from *The Dick Van Dyke Show*.

More sophisticated than other sitcoms of the period, *The Dick Van Dyke Show* was shot in Hollywood, on the old *I Love Lucy* lot, but set on the East Coast (the office was in New York, the Petries' apartment in New Rochelle). The balance of Rob's home and office life, and the inter-relationship of the two, was finely judged and the fact that the characters worked in the world of comedy meant that they could genuinely be witty without spoiling the 'truth' of the show. And, of course, Van Dyke shone from first to last, catching the eye from the moment he appeared in the title sequence and one never knew whether he was going to trip over or side-step the ottoman in his lounge (mostly he side-stepped, but sometimes …). Very few episodes did not work out and the 158th and final screened episode was the perfect parting shot: all along, Rob Petrie has been writing a book and now it's finally finished. Laura reads it – it's Rob's autobiography, focusing primarily on his career as a writer for a TV comedy-variety show. Alan Brady (played by Carl Reiner, remember) considers that the story would make a great sitcom, and who could be better than he as its star and producer? Art imitating life, life imitating art – *The Dick Van Dyke Show* was both.

*Note. C4 screened 37 episodes of *The Dick Van Dyke Show* from 22 March 1983 to 16 January 1984.

See also *The New Dick Van Dyke Show*, *Dick Van Dyke And The Other Woman*, *The Mary Tyler Moore Show* and *Something Special*.

The Dickie Henderson Half-Hour
The Dickie Henderson Show

see HENDERSON, Dickie

Dickie Valentine

UK · ITV (ASSOCIATED-REDIFFUSION) · SKETCH

6 × 30 mins · b/w

24 June–29 July 1957 · Mon 9.30pm

MAIN CAST

Dickie Valentine

Shani Wallis
Kenneth Connor
Harry Worth
Eric Barker

CREDITS

writer Jimmy Grafton · *director/producer* Kenneth Carter

Six shows presented under the banner *Monday Date*, starring the singer-turned-light-comedian performing scripts, with his comic guests, written by Jimmy Grafton.

The Dickie Valentine Show

UK · ITV (ATV) · SKETCH/STANDUP

10 editions (6 × 45 mins · 4 × 60 mins) · b/w

One series (6 × 45 mins) 30 June–4 Aug 1956 · Sat 8.15pm

Special (60 mins) 26 Oct 1957 · Sat 8.30pm

Special (60 mins) 8 Mar 1958 · Sat 10.20pm

Special (60 mins) 10 May 1958 · Sat 8.30pm

Special (60 mins) 13 Dec 1958 · Sat 7.55pm

MAIN CAST

Dickie Valentine
Peter Sellers (series only)
Valentine Dyall (series only)
Susan Denny (series only)
Mario Fabrizi (series only)

CREDITS

writers Johnny Speight, Dick Barry · *directors/producers* Dicky Leeman (7), Albert Locke (3)

A star of stage, radio and disc, popular singer Dickie Valentine added comedy to his CV with these early ITV appearances, including a series in which Peter Sellers appeared throughout as his partner, performing material written by Johnny Speight. The later specials featured no such regular support but, rather, visiting guests, including Eric Sykes, Arthur Haynes, Dick Emery, Fenella Fielding, Clive Dunn, Irene Handl, Graham Stark and Pat Coombs.

Occasional one-off shows followed and then, in July 1966, some ten years after the last full series, ATV initiated a new nine-week revival of *The Dickie Valentine Show*, but all these shows were music and dance-led and so fall beyond the scope of this book.

See also *Dickie Valentine*, *Valentine's Night* and *Free And Easy*.

Diff'rent Strokes

USA · ABC THEN NBC (TANDEM PRODUCTIONS) · SITCOM

189 × 30 mins · colour

US dates: 3 Nov 1978–30 Aug 1986

UK dates: 24 Nov 1980–6 Aug 1987 (146 episodes) ITV various days · mostly 5.15pm

MAIN CAST

Arnold Jackson	Gary Coleman
Willis Jackson	Todd Bridges
Phillip Drummond	Conrad Bain

Kimberly Drummond	Dana Plato
	(1978–84)
Edna Garrett	Charlotte Rae (1978–79)
Adelaide Brubaker	Nedra Volz (1980–82)
Pearl Gallagher	Mary Jo Catlett (1982–86)
Aunt Sophia	Dody Goodman (1981–82)
Dudley Ramsey	Shavar Ross (1981–86)
Maggie McKinney	Dixie Carter (1984–85)
	Mary Ann Mobley (1985–86)

CREDITS

creators Jeff Harris, Bernie Kukoff · writers various · directors Herb Kenwith, Doug Rogers, Gerren Keith and others · executive producers Norman Lear, Budd Grossman, Howard Leeds · producers Budd Grossman, Howard Leeds, John Maxwell Anderson, Herb Kenwith

Arnold and Willis Jackson, aged eight and 13 respectively, are black brothers from Harlem (the wrong side of the tracks) adopted by Phillip Drummond, a millionaire white widower from Park Avenue (decidedly the right side of the tracks) after their mother, Lucy, who had been Drummond's housekeeper, suddenly dies. The kids become step-brothers to Drummond's pretty teenage daughter Kimberly and have to adjust to a white upper-class penthouse lifestyle, and a new housekeeper, the dotty Edna Garrett.

Diff'rent Strokes was very much a vehicle for 10-year-old Gary Coleman, a child prodigy who overcame a physical handicap – he was born with a defective kidney which stunted growth and made him appear younger than his real age – to become a real star, utilising his impeccable sense of comic timing. A star of TV commercials in Chicago, Coleman was spotted by producer Norman Lear, who enjoyed a Midas touch in 1970s TV, and had the sitcom built around him. Cast as Arnold Jackson, Coleman came across as a scamp, sometimes too 'lippy' for his own good but always, at the end of the day, likeable. Another key player, at least in the first two years, was Charlotte Rae, the much underestimated character actress who portrayed Edna Garrett here but, previously, had shone as Leo Schnauser's wife in *Car 54, Where Are You?* and had also appeared in a memorable episode, 'The Twitch', of *The Phil Silvers Show.* Garrett's character was spun-off into her own sitcom, *The Facts Of Life* (1979–88, not screened in Britain) at which point she was replaced in *Diff'rent Strokes* by Adelaide Brubaker, herself later succeeded by Pearl Gallagher.

As the years passed so the episodes mounted, reaching a whopping 189. Drummond finally fell in love and married a woman named Maggie McKinney who added another child, Sam, to the Park Avenue melting pot. There was plenty of fluff along the way, and lots of moralising, but some sensitive issues were addressed too, among them racial prejudice, child molestation and

drug abuse (the then First Lady, Nancy Reagan, appeared in this episode to promote her 'Just Say No!' campaign). Muhammad Ali was the guest star in another episode.

Oddly, all three starring children hit the headlines after the series ended. Gary Coleman had more major surgery in the 1980s and sued his parents and ex-manager for allegedly misappropriating his earnings; Todd Bridges was accused of murder, but later acquitted; and Dana Plato posed nude for *Playboy*.

A Different World

USA · NBC (THE CARSEY-WERNER COMPANY/ BILL COSBY) · SITCOM

143 episodes (142 × 30 mins · 1 × 60 mins) · colour

US dates: 24 Sep 1987–8 May 1993

UK dates: 22 Sep 1988–15 June 1994 (142 × 30 mins · 1 × 60 mins) C4 various days mostly 6.30pm

MAIN CAST

Denise Huxtable	Lisa Bonet (1987–88)
Whitley Gilbert	Jasmine Guy
Jaleesa Vinson	Dawnn Lewis (1987–92)
Dwayne Wayne	Kadeem Hardison
Ron Johnson	Darryl M Bell
Lettie Bostic	Mary Alice (1988–89)
Kim Reese	Charnele Brown (1988–93)
Winifred 'Freddie' Brooks	Cree Summer
	(1988–93)
Walter Oakes	Sinbad (David Atkins)
	(1987–91)
Colonel Clayton 'Dr War' Taylor	
	Glynn Turman (1988–93)
Maggie Lawton	Marisa Tomei (1987–88)
Millie	Marie-Alise Recasner (1987–88)
Stevie Rallen	Loretta Devine (1987–88)
Vernon Gaines	Lou Myers (1988–93)

CREDITS

creator Bill Cosby · writers Thad Mumford, Lissa A Levin, Jasmine Guy, Susan Fales and others · directors Debbie Allen, Ellen Falcon, Kadeem Hardison and others · executive producers Marcy Carsey, Tom Werner, Anne Beatts, Caryn Mandabach, Susan Fales · producers Debbie Allen, Thad Mumford, George Crosby, Lissa A Levin, Margie Peters, Joanne Curley Kerner, Cheryl Gard, Gary H Miller, Glenn Berenbeim, Jeanette Collins, Mimi Friedman, Brenda Hanes-Berg

A spin-off from *The Cosby Show*, featuring Denise, second eldest daughter of Cliff and Clair Huxtable, in her period as a freshman at the predominantly black Hillman College in Georgia, her parents' alma mater. Not the most obvious of the *Cosby Show* children to have been handed her own production – Sondra Huxtable and her partner Elvin were the most obvious candidates – Denise scarcely seemed comfortable in *A Different World*. Indeed, the series seemed distinctly unhappy with itself, going through several crew changes early on and drawing considerable critical flak – the American listings magazine *TV Guide* considered it

'the worst sitcom in recent memory to do so well in the ratings'. (The high figures were due to scheduling: NBC sandwiched the programme right between parent *The Cosby Show* and *Cheers*.)

Then, just when *A Different World* finally seemed to be settled into a pattern, Lisa Bonet (Denise) left the show to have a baby. (Her character, it was said, was unable to consistently make the grades required for her presence at college.) Rather than crumble without its star or its direct connection to *The Cosby Show*, the series immediately prospered, a fact not coincidental to the arrival – at Bill Cosby's suggestion – of Debbie Allen, the former star/dancer/choreographer of *Fame*, who took over as director/producer. *A Different World* turned overnight into a different sitcom, focusing attention on other students at the college – southern belle Whitley, Maggie and Jaleesa, among many others – and, occasionally, looking candidly, but always with humour, at aspects of student life. One special episode, guest-starring Whoopi Goldberg and personally introduced by Bill Cosby (he urged parents to watch it with their children), looked closely at Aids. For a long time NBC considered this too hot a potato to handle, and some advertisers withdrew, but Cosby et al forced it through and the audience rating remained as high as usual.

Bill Cosby served throughout as executive consultant to the series and co-wrote the music for the theme song, sung first by Phoebe Snow then Aretha Franklin and finally by Boyz II Men.

Dig This Rhubarb

UK · BBC · STANDUP/SATIRE

14 × 40 mins · b/w

6 Oct 1963–5 Apr 1964 · fortnightly Sun around 10pm

MAIN CAST

Tony Beckley
Terence Brady
John Gower
Anne Jameson
Robin Ray
Clive Swift
Bronwen Williams
John Fortune

CREDITS

writers Claud Cockburn, Cyril Connolly, Kenneth Tynan, Marghanita Laski, Peter Forster, Wynford Vaughan Thomas, Steven Watson and others · script editors Bamber Gascoigne, Nicholas Garland · director Nicholas Garland · producer Antony Jay

Late-night comedy with an unusual idea. Each week a topical subject was put under the microscope and debated by way of historical writings. For example, if the subject was 'smoking' the team enacted what James I had to say about it, or William Shakespeare, Lord Byron, George Bernard Shaw, Oscar Wilde and others of that ilk. Bamber Gascoigne – already famed as the question-master on *University Challenge* (Granada, from 21 September 1962) – was one of the script editors and the writers' work included as much research as original thinking.

At this time, Terence Brady and Robin Ray were starring in *Beyond The Fringe* at the Fortune Theatre in London, the original cast of Peter Cook (replaced by Brady), Dudley Moore (Ray), Alan Bennett and Jonathan Miller having moved on to New York to appear in a Broadway staging.

Richard Digance

Born in West Ham, east London, on 24 February 1949, the singer, composer and poet Richard Digance has exercised his adult, wry, deadpan wit in a number of ITV specials, casting a shrewd eye over life's everyday occurrences and turning them over to expose the humour underneath.

Having turned professional in 1973, Digance had long entertained in concert and in BBC Radio 2 series and specials before focusing on the small-screen, and he continues to work in these mediums in addition to his TV work, songwriting and book/play writing.

See also *Christmas Is Coming ...*

A Dabble With Digance

UK · ITV (THAMES) · STANDUP

1 × 30 mins · colour

13 Aug 1985 · Tue 11.30pm

MAIN CAST
Richard Digance

CREDITS
writer Richard Digance · *director/producer* Paul Jackson

Hitherto seen in variety, chat-shows and the like, this was the first solo TV show for the comic musician, performing songs and sketches, including a trip to the Isle Of Dogs (in London) where, Digance alleged, the *Mary Rose* met her watery grave with a shipment of Ford Cortina cars. Guests included the ITN news-reader Carol Barnes.

Digance At Work

UK · ITV (TVS) · STANDUP

6 × 30 mins · colour

8 Nov–13 Dec 1986 · Sat around 12 midnight

MAIN CAST
Richard Digance

CREDITS
writer Richard Digance · *script associate* Charlie Adams · *director* Bob Collins · *executive producer* John Kaye Cooper · *producer* Alan Nixon

Digance's first TV series, six half-hours in which he aired his non-PC observations on life. Ideal late-night viewing.

Abracadigance

UK · ITV (JOHN KAYE COOPER PRODUCTIONS FOR LWT) · STANDUP

4 editions (3 × 60 mins · 1 × 45 mins) · colour

27 Aug 1988 · Sat 10.45pm (45 mins)
7 Oct 1989 · Sat 10.20pm (60 mins)
20 Jan 1990 · Sat 10.45pm (60 mins)
7 Apr 1990 · Sat 10.30pm (60 mins)

MAIN CAST
Richard Digance
Doon Mackichan (1989)
The Fabulous Singlettes (1989)
Steve Rawlings (1990 ed 1)
Suzy Aitchison (1990 ed 1)
John Simonett (1990 ed 2)
Mike Osman (1990 ed 2)

CREDITS
writers Richard Digance (all eds), Paul Minett/Brian Leveson (not 1988), Alan Wightman (1990 ed 2) · *director/producer* John Kaye Cooper

Four special programmes for the witty musician who plucked his guitar while casting a shrewd eye over the British lifestyle.

Note. The second of the shows featured as a guest act the outrageous singing group the Fabulous Singlettes. Director/producer John Kaye Cooper went on to make a one-hour special featuring the band, screened by C4 on 26 December 1989.

Richard Digance

UK · ITV (MICHAEL HURLL TELEVISION FOR LWT) · STANDUP/SKETCH

8 editions (6 × 30 mins · 1 × 65 mins · 1 × 60 mins) · colour

One series (6 × 30 mins) 20 July–24 Aug 1991 · Sat mostly 10.20pm
Special (65 mins) 30 May 1992 · Sat 10pm
Special (60 mins) 12 Dec 1992 · Sat 10.25pm

MAIN CAST
Richard Digance

CREDITS
writer Richard Digance · *directors* Bob Wild (series), Michael Hurll (specials) · *executive producer* Michael Hurll

Following the four ITV specials that comprised *Abracadigance*, Richard Digance was awarded a six-part series to air more of his astutely irreverent observations on life, with two one-off specials following. The programmes also featured a mock TV quiz-show, *The Brain Game*, and guests – some conventional, others far beyond the norm – among them the farmyard impressionist Mike Osman, and Charlie Schmidt, The Singing Nose.

Richard Digance's Greatest Bits

UK · ITV (CELADOR PRODUCTIONS FOR LWT) · STANDUP

1 × 60 mins · colour

12 July 1992 · Sun 11.20pm

MAIN CAST
Richard Digance

CREDITS
writer Richard Digance · *director/producer* Paul Smith

A one-off special, showing the witty West Ham warbler in concert at the Brighton Dome.

Richard Digance Live

UK · ITV (LWT) · STANDUP

1 × 60 mins · colour

10 July 1994 · Sun 10.10pm

MAIN CAST
Richard Digance

CREDITS
writer Richard Digance · *director* David G Hillier · *producer* Mark Robson

Another special, taped at the Duke Of York's Theatre in London, with guests the Moody Blues.

Digance In Scotland

UK · ITV (LWT) · STANDUP

1 × 60 mins · colour

31 Dec 1994 · Sat 11.20pm

MAIN CAST
Richard Digance

CREDITS
writer Richard Digance · *director* Ian Hamilton · *producer* Mark Robson

Broadcast across midnight on New Year's Eve 1994–95, this special was recorded at Blair Athol Castle in the highlands of Scotland, with Scottish guests.

A Drop Of Digance

UK · ITV (LWT) · STANDUP

1 × 60 mins · colour

10 Aug 1996 · Sat 11pm

MAIN CAST
Richard Digance
Tim Vine

CREDITS
writer Richard Digance · *director* David G Hillier · *producer* Mark Robson

A popular performer in drinking venues, Digance was the ideal person to entertain a

200-strong audience in this show at the Bass Museum of Brewing in Burton-on-Trent.

Digance In A Field Of His Own

UK · ITV (LWT) · STANDUP

1 × 60 mins · colour

14 Dec 1996 · Sat 11pm

MAIN CAST

Richard Digance

CREDITS

writer Richard Digance · *director* Peter Orton · *executive producer* Nigel Lythgoe

Pursuing the unusual venues idea, this programme showed Digance performing before an audience of 800 in a marquee in a Cambridgeshire field. At least it made for a good title.

Note. In 1997, Digance made a series of four one-hour programmes for screening solely in ITV's West Country region, filmed in the locale. Titled *Richard Digance For One Night Only*, they were screened by Westcountry TV from 7 to 28 May.

Dinosaurs

USA · ABC (MICHAEL JACOBS PRODUCTIONS/ JIM HENSON PRODUCTIONS/WALT DISNEY TELEVISION & TOUCHSTONE TELEVISION) · SITCOM

58 × 30 mins · colour

US dates: 26 Apr 1991–20 July 1994

UK dates: 3 Nov 1991–19 Dec 1992 (26 episodes) ITV mostly Sun around 2.50pm

MAIN CAST (VOICES ONLY)

Earl Sinclair	Stuart Pankin
Fran Sinclair	Jessica Walter
Robbie Sinclair	Jason Willinger
Charlene Sinclair	Sally Struthers
Roy Hess	Sam McMurray
B P Richfield	Sherman Hemsley
Baby Sinclair	Kevin Clash
Grandma Ethyl	Florence Stanley

CREDITS

creators Michael Jacobs/Bob Young, based on an idea by Jim Henson · *writers* Michael Jacobs/Bob Young, Victor Fresco, Dava Savel, Rob Ulin, Andy Goodman and others · *directors* Tom Trbovich, Bruce Bilson and others · *executive producers* Michael Jacobs, Brian Henson · *producers* Dava Savel, David A Caplan/Brian LaPan, Mark Brull

An American sitcom about a family of blue-collar dinosaurs: not a cartoon, not a puppet series but a live-action comedy, with humans inside dinosaur costumes and actors' voices delivering the lines. A joint venture that merged the talents and resources of Michael Jacobs Productions with Jim Henson's company and Disney's Touchstone strand, *Dinosaurs* made use of a system known as animatronics to express and alter the dinosaurs' facial movements, a process developed by Jim Henson's son Brian at the

company's London studio, Jim Henson's Creature Shop.

An effective parody, in that the series showed dinosaurs behaving in much the same way as humans today, bringing about their own extinction, *Dinosaurs* was set in the year 60,000,003 BC, an era of sophistication for the reptiles. A million years earlier, the dinosaurs behaved … well, like animals, eating their offspring and living in swamps. Now they have evolved, raising families, living in houses, working and paying taxes. Dinosaur costumes apart, then, this was a sitcom of the conventional domestic kind, focusing on the lifestyle of a single family, the Sinclairs, who experience the kind of dilemmas familiar to us now. Earl Sinclair, a megalosaurus, works for the Wesayso Development Corporation, which, under the direction of the avaricious, fearsome boss B P Richfield, a triceratops, razes forests to make way for housing developments. His wife Fran, an allosaurus, runs the house and family. They have three children: 14-year-old son Robbie, who constantly questions the ethics of their way of life; materialistic 12-year-old daughter Charlene; and a precocious, demanding infant, named Baby, whose favourite TV programmes include *Mr Ugh* (a pastiche of *Mister Ed* but with a talking caveman instead of a horse) and the science series *Ask Mr Lizard*. The Sinclairs also have a house-pet: a human cavegirl, Sparky, whom they later set free.

All ways up, life is tough for the perpetually grumpy Earl: he tries but fails to leave his imprint on society; his work is no fun and family life less so; and Fran's wheelchair-bound mother, Grandma Ethyl, irritates him in much the same way that mothers-in-law would upset many a human sitcom character sixty million years on.

High on satire, *Dinosaurs* was full of delightful in-jokes – from the opening 'Honey, I'm home' titles down to the cast names: Sinclair, Richfield and Hess were former brands of petrol in the USA, and the same petroleum theme clearly suggested the name B P Richfield.

The Dirtiest Soldier In The World

UK · BBC · SITCOM

1 × 30 mins · colour

27 Mar 1972 · BBC1 Mon 7.30pm

MAIN CAST

Lt Macneill	John Standing
Pvt McAuslan	Freddie Earlle
RSM	Jack Watson
CSM	Moray Watson
Col Gordon	Allan Cuthbertson

CREDITS

creator George Macdonald Fraser · *writer* David Climie · *producer* Michael Mills

A *Comedy Playhouse* pilot for a proposed sitcom based on the book *The General Danced At Dawn* by George Macdonald Fraser, which described the adventures of a fictitious Highlands battalion, concentrating in particular on Private McAuslan, 'the dirtiest soldier in the world'. (Dirty in the sense of grubby clothes rather than mucky morals.) The robust escapades could have made for an entertaining series, but none followed.

George Macdonald Fraser is perhaps best known as the author of a series of books continuing the exploits of cowardly cad Harry Flashman, the school bully from Thomas Hughes' classic novel *Tom Brown's Schooldays*.

The Disorderly Room

UK · BBC · SKETCH

1 × 15 mins · b/w

17 Apr 1937 · Sat 3.45pm

MAIN CAST

Tommy Handley

CREDITS

writer Eric Blore

An early TV airing of Tommy Handley's famous skit in which army disciplinary proceedings were put to the music of popular songs.

Before his apotheosis with the BBC's hugely popular Second World War radio comedy *It's That Man Again* (known then to every Briton as *ITMA*), Handley was a moderately successful standup comic whose most acclaimed piece was this sketch, written by the actor Eric Blore who carved a career in Hollywood playing uppity British butlers.

In various lengths, *The Disorderly Room* was re-presented on TV five further times before the outbreak of war forced the fledgling medium off the air: twice on 30 August 1937 (35- and 30-minute versions), 23 December 1937 (15 minutes), 15 August 1939 (30 minutes) and 20 August 1939 (30 minutes).

Divided We Stand

UK · BBC · SITCOM

6 × 30 mins · colour

10 Nov 1987–5 Jan 1988 · BBC1 Tue 7pm

MAIN CAST

Maisie	Anna Keaveney
Bert	Shaun Curry
Rita	Maggie McCarthy
Jack	Peter Childs
Edna	Vivienne Martin
Susan	Michelle Holmes

CREDITS

writer Myra Taylor · *directors* Sue Bysh (studio), Harold Snoad (film)

After 17 years of marriage, Maisie, a housewife, has finally had enough of her inconsiderate lout of a husband, greengrocer Bert, so although they continue to share a house she creates dividing lines and strict chore rotas and attempts to live separately. Despite Maisie's determination, the thick-skinned Bert still thinks that his wife 'will snap out of it in the end' and tries to chisel every chink in her armour into a gaping hole. When their daughter Susan, whom they both love dearly, becomes pregnant and (in the final episode) leaves her Spanish husband, and Spain, and moves back home, Maisie is forced out of the spare room and back into the marital bed. Bert figures this will finally effect a full reconciliation, but his own failings continue to conspire against such an eventuality.

With *Divided We Stand*, Myra Taylor – the joint creator of **The Liver Birds** – displayed the same fondness as her former writing partner Carla Lane for eking humour out of a grim situation. Sadly, there was only one series, so viewers never discovered whether Maisie broke away.

Dizzy Heights

UK · BBC · CHILDREN'S SITCOM

27 × 25 mins · colour

Series One (6) 15 Feb–22 Mar 1990 · BBC1 Thu 4.30pm

Series Two (7) 14 Feb–28 Mar 1991 · BBC1 Thu 4.30pm

Series Three (7) 20 Feb–1 Apr 1992 · BBC1 Thu 4.30pm

Series Four (7) 18 Feb–1 Apr 1993 · BBC1 Thu 4.35pm

MAIN CAST

Alan Heap · · · · · · · · · · · · · · · · · · himself
Mick Wall · · · · · · · · · · · · · · · · · · himself
Victor Gristle · · Richard Robinson (voice only)
Vera Gristle · · · · · Marie Philips (voice only)
Eustace Gristle · · · · · · · William Todd-Jones
· (voice only)

CREDITS

writers Robin Kingsland (14), Andy Walker (13) · additional material Alan Heap/Mick Wall · director Claire Winyard (series 1 & 2) · producers Martin Fisher, Martin Hughes

A children's sitcom set in a seaside hotel, starring the entertaining double-act Heap and Wall, who united in 1983 through a shared talent for juggling, trapeze, tight-rope walking, unicycling and comedy. In *Dizzy Heights* they were cast as the hotel management, and indeed were the only humans to appear; the Gristle family, who also lived at the hotel, were life-size **Spitting Image**-style puppets. Chaos, predictably, was the order of the day, every day, usually as a by-product of the hotel's hopeless mismanagement.

The gruesome Gristles later graduated to their own all-puppet series, *House Of Gristle*, voiced by Richard Robinson, William Todd-Jones and Steve Nallon, which ran for nine episodes from 7 April to 2 June 1994. They also appeared in a one-off special, *The Curious Case Of Dr Hertz Van Rental* (BBC2, 31 December 1995), a comic gothic horror story.

Do Not Adjust Your Set

UK · ITV (REDIFFUSION, *THAMES) · CHILDREN'S SKETCH

29 editions (28 × 30 mins · 1 × 50 mins) · b/w

Series One (14 × 30 mins) 26 Dec 1967–28 Mar 1968 · Thu 5.25pm

Special (30 mins) 29 July 1968 · Mon 7pm

*Special (50 mins) *Do Not Adjust Your Stocking* 25 Dec 1968 · Wed 4.10pm

*Series Two (13 × 30 mins) 19 Feb–14 May 1969 · Wed 5.20pm

MAIN CAST

Denise Coffey
Eric Idle
David Jason
Terry Jones
Michael Palin
The Bonzo Dog Doo-Dah Band

CREDITS

writers Eric Idle, Terry Jones, Michael Palin · directors Daphne Shadwell (series 1, special 1 & all *Captain Fantastic* serials), Adrian Cooper (special 2 & series 2) · producers Humphrey Barclay (series 1 & special 1), Ian Davidson (series 2)

At Last The 1948 Show led directly to *Monty Python*, but so, in equal measure, did *Do Not Adjust Your Set*, a *children's* series of inspired sketches and skits that featured the combined, and then still largely unknown, talents of Eric Idle, Terry Jones and Michael Palin – and also propelled a decidedly unfamous young actor into television: David Jason, discovered by *DNAYS* producer Humphrey Barclay in an end-of-the-pier show in Bournemouth. The fifth and last member of the team, but by no means the least, was Denise Coffey, whom Barclay spotted in a play at the Edinburgh Festival.

As the producer of the brilliant BBC radio comedy *I'm Sorry, I'll Read That Again* (starring John Cleese and all three of what would become **The Goodies**), Barclay was invited by Rediffusion executive Jeremy Isaacs to produce, along similar lines, a witty TV series for children. He did so with great success (the show won the Prix Jeunesse, Munich, in 1968) and it soon amassed a cult following: a good many adults found excuses to leave work early and rush home for the 5.20pm transmissions. Just as the title *I'm Sorry, I'll Read That Again* came from the standard newsreaders' apology, so *Do Not Adjust Your Set* came from the standard fault card screened during TV breakdowns – still a

common sight in the late 1960s. And as *ISIRTA* had a weekly serial so did *DNAYS*, which featured David Jason as a bowler-hatted, old-raincoated and moustachioed Captain Fantastic in pursuit of, and trying to rid the world of, the evil Mrs Black (Coffey). Such was the popularity of *Captain Fantastic* that it lived on beyond *DNAYS* and new episodes were incorporated within Thames' children's magazine *Magpie*, from its debut edition on 30 July 1968. (Thames also took over *DNAYS* when it won the franchise from Rediffusion.)

Subtitled 'The Fairly Pointless Show', *DNAYS* also had two other trump cards: each edition featured an interlude from those wonderfully loopy musicians the Bonzo Dog Doo-Dah Band (likened by Denise Coffey to 'Spike Jones and his City Slickers on speed'), and, in the final few programmes, viewers were treated to the exciting work of a young American animator new to British TV, Terry Gilliam.

Five months after *DNAYS* finished BBC1 launched *Monty Python's Flying Circus*.

Do You Dig Dogs?

see The Montreux Festival

The Dobson Doughnut

UK · BBC · SITCOM

1 × 30 mins · colour

14 May 1974 · Tue 8.30pm

MAIN CAST

Henry Medway · · · · · · · · · · · · · Milo O'Shea
Dobson · · · · · · · · · · · · · · · · · Bernard Spear

CREDITS

writer Raymond Allen · producer Michael Mills

The writer Raymond Allen had struggled to find a hit before striking gold with **Some Mothers Do 'Ave 'Em**, and he attempted to mine the winning formula with this *Comedy Playhouse* vehicle for Milo O'Shea, but no series followed.

The Doctor Series ...

In 1952, using the pseudonym Richard Gordon, a doctor by the name of Gordon Ostlere wrote a humorous part-truth, part-fiction account of his experiences in the medical profession. Little could he have known the industry he was spawning. Titled *Doctor In The House*, the book soon became a best-seller and, the following year, was turned into a feature film starring Dirk Bogarde, Kenneth More, Donald Sinden, Kay Kendall and James Robertson Justice. This too was a great success. Fourteen more books and six more films followed, with radio and theatrical productions contributing to the fast-growing *Doctor* phenomenon.

All this time, just one *Doctor* production made it on to television, a single farce play of *Doctor In The House*, adapted by Ted Willis, which Brian Rix presented and starred in along with Dickie Henderson and Charles Cameron, screened by the BBC on 5 June 1960. Then, in 1969, 17 years after publication of the first book, came the first TV series. Again, it was the first of many – by 1991, 11 *Doctor* TV series, 161 episodes, had been screened, this figure not including an unrelated Richard Gordon series, ***Doctors' Daughters***.

Doctor In The House

UK · ITV (LWT) · SITCOM

28 episodes (26 × 30 mins · 2 × short specials) · colour*

Series One (13) 12 July–3 Oct 1969 · mostly Sat 7.35pm

Short special · part of *All-Star Comedy Carnival* 25 Dec 1969 · Thu 6pm

Series Two (13) 10 Apr–3 July 1970 · Fri 8.30pm

Short special · part of *All-Star Comedy Carnival* 25 Dec 1970 · Fri 6pm

MAIN CAST
Michael A Upton · · · · · · · · · · · Barry Evans
Duncan Waring · · · · · · · · · · Robin Nedwell
Dick Stuart-Clark · · · · · · · Geoffrey Davies
Paul Collier · · · · · · · · · · · · George Layton
Professor Geoffrey Loftus · · · · Ernest Clark
Dave Briddock · · · · · · · · · · · · · Simon Cuff
The Dean · · · · · · · · · · · · · Ralph Michael
Huw Evans · · · · · · · · Martin Shaw (series 1)
Danny Hooley · · · · Jonathan Lynn (series 2)

CREDITS
creator Richard Gordon · *writers* Graeme Garden/Bill Oddie (22 & special 1), Graham Chapman/Barry Cryer (3), John Cleese/Graham Chapman (1), Graham Chapman/Bernard McKenna (special 2) · *directors* David Askey (16), Maurice Murphy (8 & special 2), Bill Turner (2), Mark Stuart (special 1) · *producer* Humphrey Barclay

The TV *Doctor In The House* updated the cast of characters and the storylines of the original novel to reflect the 'swinging sixties' – in truth, these episodes, and all those that followed in the succeeding series, were based only loosely upon Gordon's original work, being authored for the small-screen by an array of young writing talent, with a decided *Monty Python* and *Goodies* bent. (Graham Chapman and Graeme Garden, who contributed to five and 22 of the scripts respectively, were both qualified medical doctors and so were especially appropriate writers.) As with the original Richard Gordon stories, all the action took place at a (fictional) teaching

hospital, St Swithin's, with a fair amount of nurse-chasing, nudge-nudge innuendo and bedpan humour thrown in, *Carry On* style. The cast was strong, though, and lesser-known parts were played by, among others, David Jason, James Beck and Susan George. The recurring theme of this series (and indeed most of the succeeding series) was the clash between the keen interns and their intimidating superior Professor Loftus, a fearsome variation on the formidable Sir Lancelot Spratt of the original books. Michael Upton was the lead character, an earnest type but easily led astray by his colleagues, the laddish Waring and Collier and the smooth wastrel Stuart-Clark.

The main force behind the TV series was Frank Muir who, as head of comedy at the new London ITV franchise LWT, was determined to get Richard Gordon's *Doctor* saga on to the small-screen for the first time. He was boosted in his efforts by a BBC Radio 4 adaptation of *Doctor In The House*, aired from 25 June 1968, with scripts written by Richard Waring. Richard Briers starred as Simon Sparrow, with Geoffrey Sumner (Major Upshot-Bagley in **The Army Game**) cast as Sir Lancelot Spratt.

*Notes. Although screened in b/w, the first series was made in colour, so when eight of the episodes were repeated early in 1970 they were seen in colour for the first time.

The original *Doctor In The House* movie was made in 1954 and six sequels followed: *Doctor At Sea, Doctor At Large, Doctor In Love, Doctor In Distress, Doctor In Clover* and *Doctor In Trouble*. TV series writer Graham Chapman appeared in the last of these, released in 1970.

Doctor At Large

UK · ITV (LWT) · SITCOM

30 episodes (29 × 30 mins · 1 × short special) · 6 × b/w & 24 × colour

One series (6 × b/w · 23 × colour) 28 Feb–12 Sep 1971 · Sun 7.25pm

Short special (colour) · part of *Mike And Bernie Winters' All-Star Christmas Comedy Carnival* 25 Dec 1971 · Sat 6.05pm

MAIN CAST
Michael A Upton · · · · · · · · · · · Barry Evans
Paul Collier · · · · · · · · · · · · · George Layton
Dick Stuart-Clark · · · · · · · Geoffrey Davies
Professor Geoffrey Loftus · · · · Ernest Clark
Lawrence Bingham · · · · · Richard O'Sullivan

OTHER APPEARANCES
Dr Maxwell · · · · · · · · · · · · · · Arthur Lowe

CREDITS
creator Richard Gordon · *writers* Graham Chapman/Bernard McKenna (9), Graeme Garden/Bill Oddie (8), Bernard McKenna (1), John Cleese (6), Geoff Rowley/Andy Baker (2), Oliver Fry/Jonathan Lynn (1 & special), Oliver Fry (1), David A Yallop (1) · *directors* Bill Turner (12),

Alan Wallis (10 & special), David Askey (7) · *producer/executive producer* Humphrey Barclay

LWT blocked out the Sunday evening comedy slot for whole of spring/summer 1971 to screen 29 consecutive episodes of the sequel to *Doctor In The House*. This saw the star of that series, Michael Upton, progress from being a school leaver of 18 to a newly qualified MB (Bachelor of Medicine) of 24, out and about in search of work. After an unsteady start, Upton suffers an unsteady middle, and ends, equally unsteadily, back at St Swithin's as a junior registrar. Along the way he works for, among others, Dr Maxwell, a GP and former major played by Arthur Lowe. (Lowe's **Dad's Army** co-star John Le Mesurier also popped up in this series, as did Maureen Lipman, Fulton Mackay, David Jason, Patricia Routledge and Hattie Jacques.) Adding to the general merriment was Richard O'Sullivan as Bingham, a wimpish sycophant and often the butt of other doctors' practical jokes.

The 29 episodes were scripted by a team of writers, among them John Cleese – he contributed six episodes, one of which, 'No Ill Feeling!' (30 May 1971), was a prototype **Fawlty Towers**, with Timothy Bateson appearing as a bizarre hotelier, George Clifford. Jonathan Lynn, who had appeared in *Doctor In The House*, now began contributing to the writing side.

Note. As with *Doctor In The House*, the TV version of *Doctor At Large* followed a BBC Radio 4 presentation, broadcast in 13 episodes from 10 June 1969. Richard Briers returned as Simon Sparrow, supported principally by Geoffrey Sumner as Sir Lancelot Spratt. The original Richard Gordon book was adapted for radio by Ray Cooney (who also appeared on microphone).

Doctor In Charge

UK · ITV (LWT) · SITCOM

44 episodes (43 × 30 mins · 1 × short special) · colour

Series One (27) 9 Apr–8 Oct 1972 · Sun 7.25pm

Series Two (16) 15 Sep–29 Dec 1973 · Sat mostly 6pm

Short special · part of *All-Star Comedy Carnival* 25 Dec 1973 · Tue 6.30pm

MAIN CAST
Duncan Waring · · · · · · · · · · Robin Nedwell
Paul Collier · · · · · · · · · · · · · George Layton
Dick Stuart-Clark · · · · · · · Geoffrey Davies
Lawrence Bingham · · · · · Richard O'Sullivan
Professor Geoffrey Loftus · · · · Ernest Clark

CREDITS
creator Richard Gordon · *writers* Graham Chapman/Bernard McKenna (12), Graham Chapman/David Sherlock (2), Bernard McKenna (4), George Layton/Jonathan Lynn (11 & special), Graeme Garden/Bill Oddie (9), Phil Redmond (3),

David Askey (1), Gail Renard (1) · *directors* Alan Wallis (21), David Askey (8), Bill Turner (7 & special), Maurice Murphy (5), David Boisseau (1), Bryan Izzard (1) · *producer/executive producer* Humphrey Barclay

The third in the *Doctor* series – it was fast becoming a saga, having been rarely off ITV screens since 1969. *Doctor In Charge* featured the usual mirth with the medics at St Swithin's and all the regular cast appeared bar Michael Upton, who, it was said, had fallen in love and gone away.

Jonathan Lynn co-wrote a dozen of the scripts (with George Layton, who again played Paul Collier in the series), writing himself back into the final episode as former medical student Danny Hooley, now Doctor Hooley. A young Tony Robinson also appeared in one episode, as an accident-prone student. Also notable among the writers was a young Liverpudlian, Phil Redmond, who turned in an unsolicited script, had it accepted and ended up as the author of three episodes. These launched his TV career, which would lead to his creation of *Grange Hill*, *Brookside*, *Hollyoaks* and other drama series.

With the departure of Evans, Robin Nedwell's character moved centre stage, forming with Collier and Stuart-Clark a sort of 'Three Musketeers' fraternity, the trio continuing to lust after the nurses, keep out of Loftus's way and be unpleasant to Bingham.

Doctor At Sea

UK · ITV (LWT) · SITCOM

13 × 30 mins · colour

21 Apr–14 July 1974 · Sun 7.25pm

MAIN CAST

Duncan Waring	Robin Nedwell
Dick Stuart-Clark	Geoffrey Davies
Captain Loftus	Ernest Clark
The Purser	John Grieve
Nurse Wynton	Elizabeth Counsell
Entertainments Officer	Bob Todd

CREDITS

creator Richard Gordon · *writers* Bernard McKenna/Richard Laing (6), George Layton/Jonathan Lynn (5), Gail Renard (1), Gail Renard/Phil Redmond (1) · *directors* David Askey (7), Alan Wallis (6) · *producer* Humphrey Barclay

Saucy goings-on on the old briny formed the fourth arm of the *Doctor* series, coming about after Dick Stuart-Clark was dismissed from St Swithin's and Duncan Waring registered his disapproval by quitting. Together they enlisted as ship's doctors on a cruise liner, the MS *Begonia*, but when they boarded they discovered that the captain was the twin brother of their old hospital adversary, Loftus. David Jason appeared in one episode as a young stowaway Spaniard, Manuel Sanchez.

Note. The original *Doctor At Sea* movie was made in 1955. Before this, Richard Gordon had adapted his original story for a BBC radio broadcast, aired on the Home Service on 27 August 1953, with David King-Wood, David Kossoff, Norman Shelley and John Laurie in the key roles.

Doctor On The Go

UK · ITV (LWT) · SITCOM

26 × 30 mins · colour

Series One (13) 27 Apr–20 July 1975 · Sun 7.25pm

Series Two (13) 16 Jan–10 Apr 1977 · Sun mostly 8pm

MAIN CAST

Duncan Waring	Robin Nedwell
Dick Stuart-Clark	Geoffrey Davies
Sir Geoffrey Loftus	Ernest Clark
Kate Wright	Jacquie-Ann Carr
Andrew MacKenzie	John Kane
James Gascoigne	Andrew Knox

CREDITS

creator Richard Gordon · *writers* Bernard McKenna/Richard Laing (6), Bernard McKenna (3), George Layton/Jonathan Lynn (5), Steve Thorn/Paul Wolfson (4), Rob Buckman/Chris Beetles (3), Gail Renard (1), Gail Renard/Brenda Crankmen [Bernard McKenna pseudonym] (1), David A Yallop (1), Selwyn Roberts (1), Graham Chapman/Douglas Adams (1) · *directors* Bryan Izzard (18), Gerry Mill (7), Alan Wallis (1) · *producer* Humphrey Barclay

Their sea-going adventures dispensed with, troublesome doctors Waring and Stuart-Clark returned to St Swithin's Hospital for more yarns of a nurse-chasing, adventuresome variety. Waring duly fell in love with a nurse, Kate, and they married in the 26th and final episode.

The producer, Humphrey Barclay, rounded up another fine collection of writers to script the two series, one especially notable credit being the 20 February 1977 episode, 'For Your Own Good', co-authored by Graham Chapman of *Monty Python* with Douglas Adams, a year before the latter's ***Hitch-Hiker's Guide To The Galaxy*** exploded on to the radio.

Doctor Down Under

AUSTRALIA · 7 NETWORK · SITCOM

13 × 30 mins · colour

Australian dates: 5 Feb 1979–10 May 1980

UK dates: 11 Jan–29 Mar 1981 (12 episodes) ITV Sun 3.30pm

MAIN CAST

Duncan Waring	Robin Nedwell
Dick Stuart-Clark	Geoffrey Davies
Norman Beaumont	Frank Wilson
Maurice Griffin	John Derum
Sister Cummings	Joan Bruce
Linda	Jennifer Mellet
Professor Wilkinson	Ken Wayne

CREDITS

creator Richard Gordon · *writers* Jon Watkins (6), Bernie Sharp (2), Bernard McKenna (2), Bernard McKenna/Jon Watkins (1), not known (2) · *directors* William G Stewart, John Eastway · *producer* William G Stewart

Imported from England, the *Doctor* TV series was fantastically successful Down Under and, like other British sitcoms before and after (***Father, Dear Father, Love Thy Neighbour, Are You Being Served?***), a number of episodes were then made in Australia for local screening. Robin Nedwell and Geoffrey Davies had toured there and in New Zealand in a stage version of *Doctor In The House* for seven months in 1974, the most successful stage-show mounted in Australasia for 25 years, affording the pair pop-star receptions wherever they travelled. This was then followed by another stage production, *Doctor In Love*. So, upon hearing that LWT had finally dropped the *Doctor* series, the two actors were invited to Australia to record two series of *Doctor Down Under*, based at St Barnabas Hospital. Of the 13 episodes made, 12 were imported on to British screens by ITV.

Doctor At The Top

UK · BBC · SITCOM

7 × 30 mins · colour

21 Feb–4 Apr 1991 · BBC1 Thu 8.30pm

MAIN CAST

Duncan Waring	Robin Nedwell
Dick Stuart-Clark	Geoffrey Davies
Paul Collier	George Layton
Sir Geoffrey Loftus	Ernest Clark
Emma Stuart-Clark	Jill Benedict
Rebecca Stuart-Clark	Chloë Annett
Dr Lionel Snell	Roger Sloman
Geraldine Waring	Georgina Melville

CREDITS

creator Richard Gordon · *writers* George Layton (4), Bill Oddie (3) · *directors* Susan Belbin (4), Sue Longstaff (3) · *producer* Susan Belbin

Fourteen years after the final ITV series, and ten after the Australian, Richard Gordon's *Doctor* stories returned to the small-screen – this time courtesy of the BBC. A lot had obviously happened in the interim: Waring had become a paediatrician at St Swithin's and was married with five daughters; Collier was a consultant at St Swithin's and also had a Harley Street practice; and Stuart-Clark was the hospital's Professor of Surgery. NHS under-funding and bed shortages were obviously issues to be tackled, and there was less emphasis on the female anatomy as the butt of all jokes. Indeed, despite the 'name' scriptwriters (including George Layton again in the dual role of author and actor) the jokes were not particularly appreciated and the comeback was not a great success. Only one series was made and that was the end of a sitcom that had been on and off screen for 22 years. (Until the *next* revival, that is …)

Doctors' Daughters

UK · ITV (ATV) · SITCOM

6 × 30 mins · colour
22 Feb–29 Mar 1981 · Sun 7.15pm

MAIN CAST
Dr Roland Carmichael · · · · · · · Jack Watling
Dr 'Biggin' Hill · · · · · · · · · Richard Murdoch
Dr Freddie Fellows-Smith · · · · · · · Bill Fraser
Dr Lucy Drake · · · · · · · · · · · · Lesley Duff
Dr Fay Liston · · · · · · · · · Victoria Burgoyne
Liz Arkdale · · · · · · · · · · Bridget Armstrong
Mr Windows · · · · · · · · · · Norman Chappell
Archdeacon Bellweather · · · · Patrick Newell

CREDITS
writers Richard Gordon/Ralph Thomas ·
director/producer Stuart Allen

Author of all the *Doctor* books that had become major successes for ITV in the 1970s (see previous entry), Richard Gordon wrote *Doctors' Daughters* not as a sequel – it was unrelated to all that had gone before – but as another angle on his favourite topic. The premise here was age: three seasoned family GPs at the Old Chapterhouse Surgery, situated in the cathedral city of Mitrebury with its cobbled streets and olde worlde appeal, are informed that, after 35 years' practice, they should consider giving way to a younger generation. Aware that two of their fellow medical students from aeons back – 'Loony' Liston and 'Rubberduck' Drake – have fathered young doctors themselves, they agree to a hand-over and are horrified when two women arrive on the scene. The three GPs – veterans of many a marriage, tweed jacket, appendectomies and Second World War campaigns – had automatically assumed that their friends' offspring were sons. Nothing could have been further from the truth: Doctors Fay Liston and Lucy Drake are pretty and sexy, the former being particularly forthright, only wearing a bra for exams and inquests. Together with Liz Arkdale, a gynaecologist and obstetrician, and Mr Windows, general factotum at the surgery, the new doctors begin to sweep away the cobwebs and bring the old town's ways up to date, not entirely without opposition.

Although no direct link is apparent, a sitcom pilot screened in the USA on 22 March 1971 pursued a similar theme. Titled *Is There A Doctor In The House?* the pilot focused on a woman doctor named Michael who is engaged, sight unseen, by a small-town practice on the assumption that she is a he.

Ken Dodd

Ken Dodd was born on 8 November 1927 in the Knotty Ash suburb of Liverpool, a city that had already produced its fair share of Britain's favourite comedians, including Tommy Handley, Robb Wilton, Arthur Askey and Ted Ray. Dodd started out as a ventriloquist but prospered without the dummy when he developed a style that combined zany surrealism with a seemingly endless stream of gags. Coupled with his eccentric looks – electric-shock hairstyle and (courtesy of a childhood bicycling accident) buck teeth – Dodd presented a distinctive image that would serve him well throughout his career. (Indeed, he famously claimed in 1960 that his teeth were insured for £10,000.) From 1954, Dodd built his reputation as a standup act with endless tours and stage performances, and then found a natural TV outlet in the BBC's long-running *The Good Old Days*, where his music-hall routines, crossed with his idiosyncratic world view, provided entertainment for a wide-ranging audience.

TV turned Ken Dodd into a national institution in the 1960s, and he appeared regularly in guest spots on variety shows and in many of his own series, wielding his infamous 'tickling stick' that was part feather-duster and part rib-tickler. Dodd also began to work extensively on BBC radio, with the series *The Ken Dodd Show* (irregularly 1963–79), *Doddy's Daft Half Hour* (1972), *Doddy's Comic Cuts* (1973), *Doddy's World Of Whimsy* (1975) and others. Dodd was fastidious in his work and assembled a log book that carried information on how certain routines had fared in certain areas, building up a database of jokes and spiel for different audiences. He studied the theory of comedy extensively but never let pure philosophy influence him unduly, stating famously his attitude to Freud's study of comedy: 'He might know his theory but Freud never went on second house at Glasgow Empire.' (Glasgow Empire was a notorious graveyard for visiting comics.) In 1977 Dodd was a guest at the International Humour Conference, an event that was analysed on BBC2 in *It's No Joke* on 31 March 1977.

On stage, Dodd's act, commonly lasting up to three hours, gradually grinds the audience down to helpless laughter with a barrage of one-liners, bizarrely drawn images and surreal patter, his language being peppered with Doddyisms that are 'tattifilarious' and 'plumpshious'. Embracing a *comparatively* muted style, a keenness for singing romantic ballads (he had three big hit singles in the 1960s, 'Love Is Like A

Violin', 'Tears' and 'Happiness') and his odd 'Diddymen' characters, Dodd has proved to be a huge favourite with TV viewers.

In the 1980s Ken Dodd was embroiled in tax evasion charges (of which he was eventually cleared), but rather than demoralising the comedian this seemed to spur him on, giving him a new lease of life and a new-found popularity on the standup circuit. A revealing interview with the comedian aired as part of BBC2's *Face To Face* series on 13 March 1995.

The Ken Dodd Show   1

UK · BBC · STANDUP

35 editions (25 × 45 mins · 5 × 60 mins · 5 × 50 mins) · b/w

Special (50 mins) 25 July 1959 · Sat 8.20pm
Series One (7 × 45 mins) 9 Jan–25 June 1960 · monthly Sat mostly 7.30pm
Series Two (2 × 45 mins) 12 Nov & 10 Dec 1960 · Sat 9.05pm and 8.35pm
Series Three (3 × 45 mins) 29 Apr–17 June 1961 · monthly Sat 7.45pm
Series Four (2 × 45 mins) 18 Nov & 9 Dec 1961 · Sat 7.15pm
Series Five (2 × 45 mins) 19 May & 2 June 1962 · Sat 7.30pm
Series Six (3 × 45 mins) 27 Oct–8 Dec 1962 · every three weeks Sat mostly 7.15pm
Special (45 mins) 8 June 1963 · Sat 8.15pm
Special (60 mins) 31 Oct 1965 · BBC2 Sun 7.30pm
Special (60 mins) 25 Dec 1965 · BBC1 Sat 9.30pm
Series Seven (4 × 45 mins · 4 × 50 mins) 24 July–11 Sep 1966 · BBC1 Sun 8.15pm
Special (45 mins) 25 Dec 1966 · BBC1 Sun 8pm
Special (60 mins) 25 Dec 1967 · BBC1 Mon 8.45pm
Special (60 mins) *Doddy For Christmas* 25 Dec 1968 · BBC1 Wed 8.45pm
Special (60 mins) 21 June 1969 · BBC1 Sat 7pm

MAIN CAST
Ken Dodd

CREDITS
writers Eddie Braben/Ken Dodd (25), Jimmy Casey (3), Frank Roscoe (2), Jimmy Casey/Arthur Laye (2), Bill Kelly (2), Brad Ashton (1) · producers Barney Colehan (16), Duncan Wood (8), Albert Stevenson (5), Michael Hurll (5), Bill Lyon-Shaw (1)

A long-running but irregular series, usually broadcast from a theatre stage, which established Dodd as one of the leading comedians of the day. Each edition featured guest stars from the worlds of music and comedy, and Patricia Hayes and Graham Stark appeared sporadically to provide support. In the 8 December 1962 edition Gerald Campion appeared as Billy Bunter, and in the edition of 24 July 1966 Wilfrid Brambell and Harry H Corbett appeared as in a *Steptoe And Son* sketch especially written by Galton and Simpson. The 31 October 1965 edition was especially screened by BBC2 to mark the expansion of the service to the north of England.

Dodd's odd creation the Diddymen – squeaky-voiced midget inhabitants of Knotty Ash – appeared in many editions, either as puppets operated by Roger Stevenson, or portrayed by children and midgets dressed in pantomime-style outfits and masks.

Doddy's Music Box

UK · ITV (ABC) · STANDUP
18 × 45 mins · b/w
Series One (10) 7 Jan–11 Mar 1967 · Sat 5.45pm
Series Two (8) 20 Jan–9 Mar 1968 · Sat 6.15pm

MAIN CAST
Ken Dodd
David Hamilton

CREDITS
writers Ken Dodd/Eddie Braben · *producer* Peter Frazer-Jones

A series of 'music and mirth', combining Ken Dodd's standup lunacy with the latest pop chart exponents. ABC TV announcer David Hamilton became Dodd's straight-man, and Dodd, taking in his sidekick's small stature, nicknamed him 'Diddy David', an epithet that stuck when Hamilton's career advanced him to being a BBC radio disc-jockey.

Ken Dodd And The Diddymen

UK · BBC · CHILDREN'S SITCOM (PUPPETS)
28 × 10 mins (8 × b/w · 20 × colour)
Series One (6 × b/w) 5 Jan–9 Feb 1969 · BBC1 Sun 5.55pm
Special (b/w) 6 Apr 1969 · BBC1 Sun 5.55pm
Special (b/w) 31 Aug 1969 · BBC1 Sun 5.55pm
Special (colour) 21 Dec 1969 · BBC1 Sun 5.55pm
Series Two (6 × colour) 1 Mar–12 Apr 1970 · BBC1 Sun 5.55pm
Series Three (7 × colour) 29 Nov 1970–10 Jan 1971 · BBC1 Sun mostly 3.20pm
Series Four (6 × colour) 9 Jan–27 Feb 1972 · BBC1 Sun mostly 2.55pm

MAIN CAST
Ken Dodd

CREDITS
writer Bob Block · *puppeteer* Roger Stevenson · *producer* Stan Parkinson

A children's series based on the popular Diddymen sequence from *The Ken Dodd Show*. The fictitious Diddyland, boasting the highest sunshine rate in the world, was situated in the centre of Knotty Ash in Liverpool. It was a thriving industrial community with world-famous jam-butty mines, snuff quarries, a moggie ranch where they bred police cats, a broken-biscuit repair works and the celebrated Knotty Ash gravy wells.

The principal Diddymen in these series were Dicky Mint, a jam-butty mine worker, and the Hon Nigel Ponsonby-Smallpiece, who was so rich that he owned a caviar allotment and possessed a pond full of 18-carat goldfish.

Roger Stevenson was the puppeteer who brought the characters to life and the scripts were written by Bob Block, inspired by the fertile Dodd imagination.

The Ken Dodd Show [2]

UK · ITV (LWT) · STANDUP
1 × 60 mins · colour
26 Dec 1969 · Fri 7.30pm

MAIN CAST
Ken Dodd
David Hamilton
Talfryn Thomas

CREDITS
script editor Barry Cryer · *director/producer* David Bell

A seasonal special for ITV, subtitled *Doddy's Christmas Bizarre*.

Note. The following year, Christmas Day 1970, Dodd was back on BBC1, starring in a 90-minute pantomime version of *Robinson Crusoe* along with his Diddymen, Peter Glaze, Arthur Mullard and Lyn Kennington.

Ken Dodd In 'Funny You Should Say That'

UK · ITV (ATV) · STANDUP/SKETCH
6 × 30 mins · colour
8 Apr–13 May 1972 · Sat mostly 5.45pm

MAIN CAST
Ken Dodd
David Hamilton
Talfryn Thomas

CREDITS
deviser Ken Dodd · *writers* Norman Beedle, David McKellar, Wally Malston, Malcolm Cameron, Stuart Campbell, Maurice Bird, Eddie McKay · *producer* Bill Hitchcock

Six ITV shows of 'discomknockerating' humour from new channel DDT – Doddy's Different Television.

Ken Dodd Says 'Stand By Your Beds!'

UK · BBC · STANDUP
1 × 60 mins · colour
24 Dec 1973 · BBC1 Mon 8.20pm

MAIN CAST
Ken Dodd
Neville King

CREDITS
writer Ken Dodd · *producer* Michael Hurll

An account of Dodd and his entourage entertaining British troops overseas, filmed on location in the Indian Ocean, Cyprus, Gibraltar and Ulster. It was also titled *Doddy's Christmas Forces Show*.

Note. On 26 December 1973, Dodd appeared in the first edition of ITV's *Look Who's Talking*, a long-running interview series made by Border TV. (The actual listed title was *It's Ken Dodd Saying Look Who's Talking*.) Dodd was always very funny in such interview situations and eight years later, on 4 June 1981, he paid a return visit to the show.

Ken Dodd's World Of Laughter

UK · BBC · STANDUP/SKETCH
19 × 45 mins · colour
Series One (6) 22 Nov 1974–3 Jan 1975 · BBC1 Fri 8.15pm
Series Two (6) 30 Oct–4 Dec 1975 · BBC1 Thu 7.45pm
Series Three (7) 29 Oct–10 Dec 1976 · BBC1 Fri 7.25pm

MAIN CAST
Ken Dodd
Bill Tidy (series 1)
Windsor Davies (series 1)
Miriam Margolyes (series 1)
Chris Emmett (series 2 & 3)
Hilda Fenemore (series 2 & 3)
Faith Brown (series 3)

CREDITS
creator Ken Dodd · *writers* Dave Dutton (13), Norman Beedle (13), Roy Dixon (7), Ken Wallis (7), Ken Dodd (6), David McKellar (6) · *producer* Michael Hurll (14), James Moir (5)

Another showcase for Ken Dodd's odd comedic talent, this time supported by the likes of cartoonist Bill Tidy, comedy actress Miriam Margolyes and impressionist Faith Brown.

The Ken Dodd New Year's Eve Special

UK · BBC · STANDUP
1 × 50 mins · colour
31 Dec 1975 · BBC1 Wed 7.50pm

MAIN CAST
Ken Dodd
Rolf Harris

CREDITS
writer Ken Dodd · *producer* Michael Hurll

A seasonal special filmed under the big top of Gerry Cottle's Circus.

The Ken Dodd Show [3]

UK · BBC · STANDUP
1 × 60 mins · colour

28 Dec 1978 · Thu 8pm

MAIN CAST
Ken Dodd
Graham Stark
Hilda Fenemore
Talfryn Thomas
Jo Manning Wilson
Michael McClain

CREDITS
writers Ken Dodd, Frank Hughes, Norman
Beedle · *director/producer* Dennis Kirkland

Another Christmas special.

The Ken Dodd Laughter Show

UK · ITV (THAMES) · STANDUP
6 × 30 mins · colour
8 Jan–12 Feb 1979 · Mon 7pm

MAIN CAST
Ken Dodd
Talfryn Thomas

CREDITS
writers Norman Beedle/Frank Hughes ·
director/producer Dennis Kirkland

A sketch series for ITV.

Dodd On His Todd

UK · BBC · STANDUP
6 × 30 mins · colour
14 Apr–19 May 1981 · BBC1 Tue 6.50pm

MAIN CAST
Ken Dodd

CREDITS
writers Ken Dodd, John Pye, Frank Hughes ·
executive producer Tony Broughton ·
producer/director Terry Wheeler

A series screened only by the BBC's north-west transmitters.

Note. Three seasonal specials (*Ken Dodd's Christmas Laughter Show*, 13 December 1977; *Ken Dodd's Christmas Feast* – aka *Squire Dodd's Christmas Special* – 19 December 1978; and *Ken Dodd's Christmas Show*, 18 December 1979) have similarly aired only in the north-west.

Doddy!

UK · BBC · STANDUP
1 × 40 mins · colour
1 Jan 1982 · BBC1 Fri 6.55pm

MAIN CAST
Ken Dodd
George Carl

CREDITS
writer Ken Dodd · *director* Geoff Posner ·
producer John Fisher

A New Year's Day one-off with, as the guest star, the American clown George Carl. This show led directly to Dodd's next BBC series, *Ken Dodd's Showbiz*.

Ken Dodd's Showbiz

UK · BBC · STANDUP
6 × 35 mins · colour
13 Mar–17 Apr 1982 · BBC1 Sat 7.05pm

MAIN CAST
Ken Dodd

CREDITS
writer Ken Dodd · *producer* John Fisher

A prestige series for Dodd, in which he introduced international guests from the world of variety, including French comedy magician Mac Ronay, the ventriloquist Neville King, Swiss musical comedian Alfredo, gobbledygook expert Stanley Unwin, Donald Duck voice Clarence Nash and French cabaret comedian Robert Dhéry. (This format – employing international guest stars, with an emphasis on magicians – is typical of the TV producer John Fisher, an authority on comedy and magic.)

Ken Dodd At The London Palladium

UK · ITV (THAMES) · STANDUP
1 × 75 mins · colour
25 Dec 1990 · Tue 6.15pm

MAIN CAST
Ken Dodd

CREDITS
director Paul Kirrage · *producer* John Fisher

A glorious post-tax-trauma return to primetime for the Knotty Ash man. Recorded at the London Palladium, where he had just completed a long season, this Christmas extravaganza saw Doddy joined on stage by his Diddymen, magicians and dancers.

An Audience With Ken Dodd

UK · ITV (LWT) · STANDUP
1 × 75 mins · colour
3 Dec 1994 · Sat 8.05pm

MAIN CAST
Ken Dodd

CREDITS
director Patricia Mordecai · *producer* Lorna Dickinson

Another of LWT's occasional *An Audience With …* series, showing Dodd tickling the fancies of a celebrity audience.

Does China Exist?

UK · BBC · SKETCH
1 × 30 mins · colour
15 Dec 1997 · BBC2 Mon 10pm

MAIN CAST
Paul Merton

WITH
Jim Sweeney

Lee Cornes
John Irwin

CREDITS
writers Paul Merton/John Irwin · *director* Martin Dennis · *producer* Phil Clarke

Week after week on the BBC2 comedy panel-game *Have I Got News For You* Paul Merton demonstrated his comic genius, ad-libbing with lightning speed and weaving surreal images from the slightest of openings. But away from the formula Merton struggled to find other TV vehicles suited to his talents. *Paul Merton – The Series* certainly had its moments, but *Paul Merton In Galton & Simpson's …*, his re-enactment of old-gold scripts, proved only that he was not much of an actor. A 1996 one-off, *The Paul Merton Show*, also failed to dazzle.

Sadly, he fared no better in this 'people show' spoof, *Does China Exist?*, a satire of the many US and UK TV shows in which a presenter – chatting with guests and interacting with a studio audience – probes a 'topic of the week'. As the host, Merton explored the paranormal, encompassing everything from Kennedy-conspiracy theories to supernatural sightings, but the result was an uneven hotch-potch of studio sketches that barely did justice to the comic's unquestionable abilities.

Dogfood Dan And The Carmarthen Cowboy

UK · ITV (YORKSHIRE), *BBC · SITCOM
7 episodes (1 × 60 mins · 6 × 30 mins) · colour
Special (60 mins) 24 July 1982 · Sat 9.45pm
*One series (6 × 30 mins) 4 Feb–10 Mar 1988 · BBC2 Thu 9pm

MAIN CAST
'Dogfood' Dan Milton · · · · · · · · · David Daker
· (premiere);
· · · · · · · · · · · · · · · · · Malcolm Storry (series)
Aubrey Owen (The Carmarthen Cowboy) · · · ·
· · · · · · · · · · · · · Gareth Thomas (premiere);
· · · · · · · · · · · · · · · · · · · Peter Blake (series)
Helen Milton · · · · · Diana Davies (premiere);
· · · · · · · · · · · · · · Elizabeth Mickery (series)
Gwyneth Owen · · · · · · · · Arbel Jones (series)
Myfanwy Owen · · · · Helen Cotterill (premiere)

CREDITS
writer David Nobbs · *directors/producers* Derek Bennett (premiere), Alan J W Bell (series)

Growing out of a single Yorkshire TV production in 1982 (screened in the series *ITV Playhouse*) and appearing as a one-series sitcom on the BBC six years later, *Dogfood Dan And The Carmarthen Cowboy* was a tale of two long-distance dogfood-carrying lorry drivers who, to the other's ignorance, are each having affairs with the other's wife. Although the men meet up on the road, exchange stories of their sexual escapades, and often talk to their wives about their travelling friend, the lies they spin and the false names they invent mean that neither the husbands nor the wives cotton on to the convoluted situation. Aubrey Owen likes to pass himself off as an MP, 'Aneurin', during his visits with Helen, while Dan claims he is carrying top secret 'abnormal' loads when pursuing the passionate Myfanwy (in the 1982 version.)

This was a complex, farcical idea from the ever-interesting David Nobbs, which employed sufficient detours and U-turns to make the extension from play to sitcom worthwhile.

Don't Ask Us – We're New Here

UK · BBC · SKETCH

18 editions (9 × 35 mins · b/w; 9 × 25 mins · colour)
Series One (9 × 35 mins · b/w) 11 July–5 Sep 1969 · BBC1 Fri 7.55pm
Series Two (9 × 25 mins · colour) *Don't Ask Us* 10 July–11 Sep 1970 · BBC1 Fri 7.55pm

MAIN CAST
Frank Abbott
Adrienne Posta
Peter Legge (series 1)
Mike Redway (series 1)
Toni Sinclair (series 1)
Maureen Lipman (series 2)
Richard Stilgoe (series 2)
Russell Davies (series 2)

CREDITS
script editors Dick Vosburgh (series 1), Austin Steele (series 2) · *producers* John Ammonds (series 1), David O'Clee/Roger Ordish (series 2)

Summarised as 'A new show with new faces', *Don't Ask Us – We're New Here* was a fast-paced revue-style show with the emphasis on comedy but also featuring musical numbers. The second series, re-described as 'a high-speed panorama of laughs, sketches and music', saw a partial change of cast (providing early TV exposure for Richard Stilgoe and Maureen Lipman) and a shortening of the title to simply *Don't Ask Us*.

Don't Blame Us!

UK · ITV (THAMES) · CHILDREN'S SKETCH

1 × 30 mins · colour
7 June 1974 · Fri 4.50pm

MAIN CAST
Anne Cunningham
Roddy Maude-Roxby
David Wood
Barry Stainton
Elaine Stritch
Nigel Pegram

CREDITS
director Darrol Blake · *producer* Ruth Boswell

The only non-sitcom among Thames' series of six *Funny Ha Ha* individual children's comedies, a studio audience of children suggested sketches and situations to the cast who improvised accordingly.

Don't Dilly Dally On The Way

UK · ITV (LWT) · SITCOM

1 × 30 mins · b/w
10 May 1969 · Sat 9.20pm

MAIN CAST
Mr Croucher · · · · · · · · · · · · Jimmy Edwards
Mrs Croucher · · · · · · · · · · · · · · Pat Coombs

CREDITS
writers Ray Galton/Alan Simpson · *director/producer* David Askey

The fourth of six single productions in the series *The Galton & Simpson Comedy*, this starred two great comics, Edwards and Coombs, in a fine domestic drama: he's ready to move from their tiny bungalow, which they've lived in for 23 years, but she isn't, locks herself in the toilet and won't come out.

The script was re-used in 1996 in *Paul Merton In Galton & Simpson's ...*

Don't Do It, Dempsey!

UK · BBC · SITCOM

6 × 30 mins · b/w
4 Apr–9 May 1960 · Mon 9pm

MAIN CAST
James Dempsey · · · · · · · · · · · · Brian Reece

CREDITS
writers Patrick Campbell/Vivienne Knight · *producer* John Harrison

Written by humorist Patrick Campbell and film publicist Vivienne Knight, this sitcom starred the likeable Brian Reece as an Irish womaniser, James Dempsey. Each episode found Dempsey involved in a comedy of errors, usually centring on a desirable woman. Guest stars included Adrienne Corri, Marla Landi and Vera Day.

Don't Drink The Water

UK · ITV (LWT) · SITCOM

13 × 30 mins · colour
Series One (7) 27 July–7 Sep 1974 · Sat 7.15pm
Series Two (6) 1 Nov–6 Dec 1975 · Sat 6.45pm

MAIN CAST
Cyril Blake · · · · · · · · · · · · · Stephen Lewis
Dorothy Blake · · · · · · · · · · · · · Pat Coombs
Carlos · · · · · · · · · · · · · · · · Derek Griffiths
Bill · · · · · · · · · · · · · · · Frank Coda (series 1)
Beryl · · · · · · · · · · Christine Shaw (series 1)

CREDITS
creators Ronald Wolfe/Ronald Chesney · *writers* Ronald Wolfe/Ronald Chesney (11), Jon Watkins (2) · *director/producer* Mark Stuart

Nothing more, or less, than one of the most excruciatingly poor ITV sitcoms of them all. In this sequel to *On The Buses* – created and largely written by the team behind that series, Ronalds Wolfe and Chesney – we learned that 'Blakey' had retired and moved to a flat in Spain, 25 Apartmentos El Paradiso, leaving behind the Britain of power cuts and the three-day week and affording him a view of the Mediterranean.

Unfortunately for our 'hero', he was encumbered by his spinster sister Dorothy, who didn't want to leave England and did nothing but moan, and by German neighbours, a layabout Spanish porter Carlos (played by Derek Griffiths) and some appalling expatriate Britons. Still, with a knotted handkerchief on his head, and his trouser legs rolled up, he was determined to make a splash of it.

Don't Forget To Write!

UK · BBC · SITCOM

12 × 50 mins · colour
Series One (6) 18 Apr–23 May 1977 · BBC2 Mon 9pm
Series Two (6) 18 Jan–22 Feb 1979 · BBC2 Thu 10pm

MAIN CAST
George Maple · · · · · · · · · · · · George Cole
Mabel Maple · · · · · · · · · · · · Gwen Watford
Tom Lawrence · · · · · · · · · Francis Matthews
Wilfred Maple · · · · · · · · · · · · · Ron Emslie
Mrs Field · · · · · · · · · · · · · · Daphne Heard
Jenny Lawrence · · · · · · · · · · · Renny Lister
Phillip Mounter · · · James Cossins (series 2)

CREDITS
writer Charles Wood · *directors* Christopher Baker (4), Alan Dossor (3), David Askey (3), John Bruce (2) · *producer* Joe Waters

A beautifully written comedy series graced with good performances from a well-chosen cast. George Cole played George Maple, a successful playwright who is nevertheless dogged by self-doubt and hidebound by his scruples. Gwen Watford was cast as his wife Mabel, who is a great support in his life: an efficient, loving woman who manages to remain serenely calm at the centre of any storm. The series' producer, Joe Waters, claimed that he fought to ensure it *wasn't* taped in front of a studio audience, figuring that the writing – long on laughter, short on jokes – wouldn't work in that arena; this suggests that *Don't Forget To Write!* may have been considered a half-hour sitcom at some stage. In retrospect, though, the 50-minute format certainly suited the piece.

In most of the episodes George is crippled by writer's block, a condition exacerbated by the fact that his near neighbour, Tom Lawrence, is a vastly more (financially) successful writer who seems to have no such constipation. In a *Radio Times* article previewing the series, the writer Sheridan Morley speculated that the genesis of the idea may have sprung from the fact that its author, Charles Wood, lived near the successful playwright Peter Nichols, and possibly had a similar relationship with him as George does with Tom. This might have been true, but Wood had used a similar theme eight years earlier in the Yorkshire TV drama anthology series *The Root Of All Evil* (episode titled 'A Bit Of A Holiday', ITV, 1 December 1969), which featured George Cole as Gordon (not George) Maple and Gwen Watford as his wife Mabel. This one-off comedy play depicted Gordon's misadventures in Rome, where he had been hired to rewrite a poor script. Eighteen months later the theme was explored again in Yorkshire TV's *The Ten Commandments*, the final episode of which, 'A Bit Of Family Feeling' (ITV, 1 June 1971), was written by Charles Wood and again featured George Cole, this time as Peter, a successful but embittered and sarcastic playwright – not a million miles away from the character of George Maple.

Don't Look Now

UK · BBC · SKETCH

6 × 30 mins · b/w

12 July–20 Sep 1950 · fortnightly Wed 9.15pm

MAIN CAST
Alfred Marks
Paddie O'Neil
Ian Carmichael

CREDITS
writer Sid Colin · *producer* Bill Ward

An Alfred Marks vehicle from the production team behind what, to date, was TV's most successful comedy, *How Do You View?* Its producer, Bill Ward, described *Don't Look Now* as 'another experiment, and an attempt to find the formula for comedy in television'. For viewers, it provided the opportunity to see what Marks' popular BBC radio invention Professor Schmendrick looked like in the flesh, and a chance to view the comedian's real-life wife Paddie O'Neil and the rising actor (and still a BBC TV producer) Ian Carmichael.

See also *Alfred Marks Time*.

Don't Ring Us ... We'll Ring You

UK · BBC · SITCOM

1 × 30 mins · colour

29 July 1970 · BBC1 Wed 7.30pm

MAIN CAST
Jimmy Duffy · · · · · · · · · Norman Rossington
Ernie Babcock · · · · · · · · · · · · · John Junkin
Dave Sullivan · · · · · · · · · · · · Colin Welland
Joe Ridsdale · · · · · · · · · · · · · Sandy Powell
Ethel · · · · · · · · · · · · · · · · Barbara Mullaney
Reg Aveyard · · · · · · · · · · · · · · Joe Gladwin

CREDITS
writers Mike Craig/Lawrie Kinsley · *producer* Dennis Main Wilson

A *Comedy Playhouse* pilot in which Norman Rossington and John Junkin co-starred as a pair of impoverished agents, the proprietors of Duffy and Babcock Theatrical Enterprises,

who supply third-rate acts to northern working men's clubs. A good supporting cast was on board, but not even the surprise presence of veteran music-hall comedian Sandy Powell ('Can you 'ear me, mother?') could elevate this to a full series.

Don't Rock The Boat

UK · ITV (THAMES) · SITCOM

12 × 30 mins · colour

Series One (6) 5 Jan–9 Feb 1982 · Tue 8pm

Series Two (6) 12 July–16 Aug 1983 · Tue 8.30pm

MAIN CAST
Jack · · · · · · · · · · · · · · · · · Nigel Davenport
Dixie · · · · · · · · · · · · · · · · · · Sheila White
Les · · · · · · · · · · · · · · · · · · · John Price
Billy · · · · · · · · · · · · · · · · · David Janson
OTHER APPEARANCES
Wally · · · · · · · · · · · · · · · · · John Horsley
Eric · · · · · · · · · · · · · · · · · · David Battley
Yvonne · · · · · · · · · · · · · · · · · · Judy Holt

CREDITS
writers John Esmonde/Bob Larbey · *director/producer* Mark Stuart

It ran for two series but this was not one of Esmonde and Larbey's better creations. Jack Hoxton is a young-at-heart middle-aged widower who operates a river boatyard. His children, Les and Billy, are pleased when he begins dating a woman but less than thrilled when they discover that she is half his age and something of a glamour-puss – indeed, she is an ex-magician's assistant and was once a chorus girl. Despite the opposition, they marry, and the hostility continues apace as she sets out to inject some zest into their lives.

Don't Spare The Horses

UK · BBC · SKETCH

3 × 60 mins · b/w

4 Oct–29 Nov 1952 · monthly Sat 9.20pm

MAIN CAST
Jimmy James

CREDITS
producer Bill Lyon-Shaw

Holding his omnipresent cigarette, the well-known gravel-voiced comedian Jimmy James hosted this live comedy-variety sketch show. Harry Secombe guested in the first and third editions, fellow Goons Peter Sellers and Spike Milligan appeared in the second.

Don't Tell Father 1

UK · ITV (ASSOCIATED-REDIFFUSION) · SITCOM

6 × 30 mins · b/w

1 June–6 July 1959 · Mon mostly 7.30pm

MAIN CAST
Julia Dean · · · · · · · · · · · · · · Julia Lockwood
Harry Dean · · · · · · · · · · · · · · · Colin Gordon

Helen Carter · · · · · · · · · · · · · · · Jill Booty
Elizabeth Carter · · · · · · · · · · · · · Noël Hood
Philip Lister · · · · · · · · · · · · · · Garry Marsh
OTHER APPEARANCES
Evelyn Wright · · · · · · · · · · · · · Joan Benham
Dave · · · · · · · · · · · · · · · · · Barry MacGregor
Diana · · · · · · · · · · · · · · · · · · Annika Wills
Hugh Collins · · · · · · · · · · · Robert Desmond
Peter King · · · · · · · · · · · · Kenneth Fortescue

CREDITS
writer Barry Baker · *director* Pat Baker

A light-comedy series co-starring Julia Lockwood, 17-year-old daughter of the venerable British film actress Margaret, and Colin Gordon, himself a film veteran, where he usually played bespectacled figures of authority with a slightly daffy air. Here he was cast in the role of Harry Dean, a slightly dotty writer of screenplays wont to be wrapped up in his latest storyline and so someone who has to be saved from himself by his daughter Julia (Lockhart).

Fizz was added by way of their location – they lived on a barge on the Thames – and by guest cameos by William Mervyn, Beryl Cooke (later to play Aunt Lucy in *Happy Ever After*) and veteran comic Charles Heslop, on TV since 1937.

Don't Tell Father 2

UK · BBC · SITCOM

6 × 30 mins · colour

26 Apr–31 May 1992 · BBC1 Sun 7.45pm

MAIN CAST
Vivian Bancroft · · · · · · · · · · · · Tony Britton
Natasha Bancroft · · · · · · · Susan Hampshire
Kate Bancroft · · · · · · · · · · Caroline Quentin
Garth Bancroft · · · · · · · · · · Richard Ashton
Marvin Whipple · · · · · · · · · · · · · Philip Fox

CREDITS
writer Roy Clarke · *director/producer* Harold Snoad

After creating the dreadful Hyacinth Bucket for *Keeping Up Appearances*, writer Roy Clarke turned his hand to inventing a male monster in *Don't Tell Father*: the vain, pompous, selfish, arrogant, eminent actor Vivian Bancroft, who swans about in an affected manner, the very epitome of the precious, egocentric characters of theatrical legend. Insensitive towards others, Vivian dominates his family and his fifth wife Natasha, 20 years his junior. Nevertheless, his powerful presence does contain some fascination for them and they find themselves falling under his spell. The main theme running through the episodes was Vivian's response to the arrival on the scene of Marvin Whipple, the new boyfriend of Vivian's daughter Kate.

Tony Britton hammed it up for all he was worth as the awful Vivian, and Caroline Quentin proved particularly adept at delivering Roy Clarke's witty dialogue, but the piece as a whole lacked that magic ingredient which made so many of the writer's ideas long-running series. *Don't Tell Father* lasted for just one.

Don't Wait Up

UK · BBC · SITCOM

39 × 30 mins · colour

Series One (7) 25 Oct–6 Dec 1983 · BBC1 Tue 7.40pm
Series Two (6) 18 Oct–22 Nov 1984 · BBC1 Thu 8pm
Series Three (7) 2 Dec 1985–27 Jan 1986 · BBC1 Mon 8.30pm
Series Four (6) 2 Mar–6 Apr 1987 · BBC1 Mon 8.30pm
Series Five (7) 6 June–18 July 1988 · BBC1 Mon 8pm
Series Six (6) 18 Feb–25 Mar 1990 · BBC1 Sun 7.15pm

MAIN CAST

Dr Toby Latimer · · · · · · · · · · · Tony Britton
Dr Tom Latimer · · · · · · · · · · · Nigel Havers
Angela Latimer · · · · · · · · · · Dinah Sheridan
Helen Latimer/Kramer · · · · · · · · · Jane How
Madeleine Forbes/Latimer · · Susan Skipper
Dr Charles Cartwright · · · · · · · Richard Heffer
· · · · · · · · · · · · (series 1 & 2);
· · · · · · · · · · · Simon Williams (series 3–6)
Susan Cartwright · · · · · · · · · Tricia George
Felicity Spicer-Gibbs · · · · · · · · Jane Booker
Mr Burton · · · Timothy Bateson (series 1 & 2)

CREDITS

writer George Layton · director/producer Harold Snoad

A surprisingly long-running sitcom depicting the exploits of father and son doctors, based on a somewhat thin premise that became richer as the series progressed.

In the beginning, Tom Latimer is in the throes of splitting up with his wife Helen, a situation fraught enough but further exacerbated by his father Toby's sudden announcement that he too is seeking a divorce after 30 years. Toby and Tom move in together, providing the perfect prescription for a character-clash comedy, with father (Harley Street smoothie) and son (hard-working National Health Service idealist) disagreeing about politics, morals, medicine and medical practices, while trying to deal with their respective divorces. Throughout the series, Tom attempts to reconcile his parents while he himself pursues Toby's receptionist Madeleine. Tom's mother, Angela, seems capable enough without Toby and discovers a different side to herself; nevertheless they spend much of the time on the verge of reconciliation. Likewise, Tom's romantic pursuit is beset with difficulties and he loses Madeleine for quite a time before she comes back into his life and they marry. The series ended with Toby and Angela back together and Tom and Madeleine producing a baby.

George Layton, best known as Dr Paul Collier in LWT's long-running *Doctor* sitcoms, returned to a medical theme as the writer of *Don't Wait Up*. Having been through a divorce, Layton had a keen ear for dialogue and wasn't afraid to allow moments of real anguish to show through the constant bickering of father and son. While most of the characters were somewhat underwritten, the production moved along smoothly thanks to the professionalism of its lead actors – veteran actress Dinah Sheridan and comedy old hand Tony Britton were more than adept at this sort of material and Nigel Havers made an encouraging sitcom debut.

Doogie Howser, MD

USA · ABC (STEVEN BOCHCO PRODUCTIONS/ 20TH CENTURY-FOX TELEVISION) · SITCOM

119 × 30 mins · colour

US dates: 19 Sep 1989–21 July 1993
UK dates: 5 Sep 1990–14 Feb 1993 (51 episodes) BBC1 Wed 7.35pm then Sun around 10.50pm

MAIN CAST

Dr Douglas 'Doogie' Howser · · · · · · · · · · · ·
· · · · · · · · · · · · · · · · · Neil Patrick Harris
Dr David Howser · · · · · · · · · James B Sikking
Katherine Howser · · · · · Belinda Montgomery
Vinnie Delpino · · · · · · · · · · · · · Max Casella
Dr Benjamin Canfield · · Lawrence Pressman
Nurse Curly Spaulding · · · · · · · Kathryn Layng
Dr Jack McGuire · · · · · · · · Mitchell Anderson
· (1989–91)
Janine Stewart · · · · · Lucy Boryer (1989–92)
Wanda Plenn · · · Lisa Dean Ryan (1989–92)
Nurse Michele Faber · · · · · · · · Robyn Lively
· (1991–93)

CREDITS

creator/writers Steven Bochco/David Kelley · writers Nat Bernstein, Nick Harding, Neil Landau, Linda Morris, Tara Ison, Tom Moore and others · directors various · producer Steven Bochco

Another offering of what Americans at the time were calling 'dramadies', this show came from TV wunderkind Steven Bochco, the creator of such groundbreaking series as *Hill Street Blues* and *LA Law*. Typically slick, it carried a serious theme beneath its sitcom-like exterior.

Doogie Howser, MD told the story of child prodigy Douglas Howser, who notched up perfect grades when he was six, breezed through high school in nine weeks and achieved a medical school degree when 14. Viewers first meet him at the age of 16, during his second year at Eastman Medical Centre in Los Angeles. Thus, the absurdly young 'Doogie' is experiencing a world where he has adult responsibilities and decisions to make, caught between the conflicting worlds of childhood and adulthood, and uncomfortable in both. In the adult world, the boy generates mistrust and jealousy, while children of his age are wary and treat him like

a freak. Only Doogie's closest friend, Vinnie, seems able to accept him at face value; through Vinnie, Doogie keeps up with many of the topics and trends affecting his contemporaries. At home Doogie's parents try their best to keep their son on the right path but his prestigious genius coupled with his adolescent thought processes baffles his mother Katherine and father Dr David Howser (played by James B Sikking, Lt Howard Hunter in *Hill Street Blues*).

Episodes juggled Doogie's professional and social lives and concentrated especially on the minefield of dating, which was made doubly difficult by Doogie's premature escalation into adulthood. Wanda was the first girl of his dreams but then he fell for Nurse Faber and moved on to operate as a free agent with the confidence that an extra couple of years had brought.

Dora

see *Both Ends Meet*

The Dora Bryan Show

see *Happily Ever After*

The Doris Day Show

USA · CBS (ARWIN HILLTOP COMPANY) SITCOM

128 × 30 mins · colour

US dates: 24 Sep 1968–10 Sep 1973
UK dates: 9 July 1973–12 Feb 1974 (26 episodes) ITV Mon 6.10pm then Tue 5.20pm

MAIN CAST

Doris Martin · · · · · · · · · · · · · · · · Doris Day
Billy Martin · · · · · · · Phillip Brown (1968–71)
Toby Martin · · · · · · · Todd Starke (1968–71)
Leroy B Simpson · · · · · · · · · James Hampton
· (1968–69)
Juanita · · · · · · · · Naomi Stevens (1968–69)
Buck Webb · · · · · · · · Denver Pyle (1968–70)
Aggie Thompson · · · · · · · · Fran Ryan (1968)
Michael Nicholson · · · · · McLean Stevenson
· (1969–71)
Myrna Gibbons · · · · · Rose Marie (1969–71)
Ron Harvey · · · · · · · · · Paul Smith (1969–71)
Angie Palucci · · · · · · Kaye Ballard (1970–71)
Louie Palucci · · · · · Bernie Kopell (1970–71)
Cy Bennett · · · · · · · · John Dehner (1971–73)
Jackie Parker · · · · Jackie Joseph (1971–73)
Dr Peter Lawrence · · · · · · · · · · Peter Lawford
· (1972–73)

CREDITS

creator Jim Fritzell · writers various · directors Bob Sweeney, Reza S Badiyi, William Wiard, Coby Ruskin, Denver Pyle, Marc Daniels, Paul Smith, Norman Tokar · executive producers Terry Melcher, Doris Day, Don Genson · producers Jack Elinson, Richard Dorso, Norman Paul, Bob Sweeney, Edward H Feldman, George Turpin

You could call it sickly sweet, and not be wrong, but *The Doris Day Show* was also a gentle, pleasing (and of course totally harmless)

sitcom. How the series came about, however, makes for a much more dramatic story.

The star of so many gooey soft-focus romantic feature films, and also a very successful singer, Doris Day had never appeared regularly on TV, and in fact was no great fan of the medium. But shortly after her beloved husband and manager Marty Melcher died, early in 1968, she learned that he had signed her up for this series, an arrangement of which she had no knowledge. Worse, Day then discovered that, together with a lawyer associate, Melcher had been siphoning off her prodigious income over some two decades and that she was, in effect, bankrupt. In dire need of money she reluctantly agreed to proceed.

Although she was in shock for some time, and this undoubtedly affected her performance, Doris Day made the right move, and by the time the series finished five years later she was financially stable once again and in the public eye for all the right reasons. All the same, *The Doris Day Show*, was, at best, a confusion, in that for four of the five years it was on the air, her character – Doris Martin – was cast in different situations and locations. First she was the widowed mother of two boys, living on a country farm with her father and their dog. Then she became 'a working mom', commuting daily to San Francisco where she was employed as a secretary on a magazine, *Today's World*. Then, after being promoted to reporter, she and the kids became city-dwellers. Finally (influenced, one suspects, by *The Mary Tyler Moore Show*), Doris was a single woman again (the children and dog disappeared from the storylines as if they had never existed), still reporting and, additionally, dating a dashing doctor. In Britain, ITV screened 26 episodes drawn from the latter two seasons, with Doris first as a part-time and then full-time journalist, romantically involved with the doc.

Some interesting names were involved along the way. McLean Stevenson, who played Day's first editor at *Today's World*, went on to star in *M*A*S*H*. Rose Marie, who was cast as the editor's secretary and Doris's friend, had shone in *The Dick Van Dyke Show*; Denver Pyle, Doris's farm-living father, was a star of TV westerns; Dr Lawrence, Doris's romantic interest, was played by the English-born Hollywood film star Peter Lawford; and Terry Melcher, executive producer of the series, was Doris's son, formerly the Byrds' record producer.

And, yes, the theme tune, sung every week by the star, was 'Que Sera Sera'. Whatever will be will be.

Dorus

see The Montreux Festival

Double Cross

see JEWEL, Jimmy and Ben Warriss

Double First

UK · BBC · SITCOM

7 episodes (6 × 30 mins · 1 × 60 mins) · colour

6 Sep–18 Oct 1988 · BBC1 Tue mostly 8.30pm

MAIN CAST

N V (Norman Vernon) Standish · Michael Williams
Mary Webster · · · · · · · · · · · · · · · · · · Ann Bell
Louise Hobson · · · · · · · · · · · · Jennifer Hilary
Ellen Hobson · · · · · · · · · · · · · · · · Holly Aird
Derek · · · · · · · · · · · · · · · · Clive Merrison
William · · · · · · · · · · · · · · Peter Tuddenham

CREDITS

writers John Esmonde/Bob Larbey · *director/producer* Gareth Gwenlan

Shot entirely on film, free of studio laughter and launched with a scene-setting one-hour special, *Double First* was a worthy attempt by all concerned to do something different in the world of TV comedy. Michael Williams, the co-star of co-writer Bob Larbey's *A Fine Romance*, was the hand-picked star, working with the writers and producer in the casting and development of the production.

Williams was cast as Norman Vernon Standish (known as N V), who had been a brilliant Oxford scholar, written a much praised book and left to embark on what promised to be a glittering career in the diplomatic service. But when he is rediscovered 20 years later by the Webster sisters (who had been at Oxford with him), Standish is making a living in the Home Counties by grilling hamburgers. The sisters, Mary and Louise, are appalled at what they perceive as a massive waste of his talent and take Standish under their wing, installing him in their house and attempting to persuade him to resume his writing career. But N V marches to his own drumbeat and what other people want from him is not necessarily what he wants for himself. He is content to stay, rent-free, with the ladies and seems none to keen to do anything much, which annoys next-door neighbour Derek who sees him as a scrounger and feels protective towards the sisters. Derek coerces N V into finding a variety of jobs, although none seem to last long. To complicate matters, Louise's daughter Ellen takes a shine to N V, seeing him as a cross between a father figure and an unlikely role model.

Double Six

see Morecambe and Wise

The Doug Anthony All-Stars

UK · BBC (POZZITIVE PRODUCTIONS) · STANDUP

1 × 30 mins · colour

31 Dec 1992 · BBC2 Thu 9.25pm

MAIN CAST

The Doug Anthony All-Stars (Tim Ferguson, Richard Fidler, Paul McDermott)
Flacco (Paul Livingston)

CREDITS

writers cast · *director/producer* Geoff Posner

One-off TV exposure for established Edinburgh Festival Fringe favourites the Doug Anthony All-Stars, a three-piece musical comedy outfit from Australia. The trio presented witty, rude, clever songs, mostly delivered at a ferocious pace. They also incorporated some standup material and physical comedy in their act but were probably best known for their tendency for audience involvement. Time and again they chose unsuspecting members of an audience and embroiled them in wacky games or ludicrous, sometimes cringingly embarrassing, situations. This could have been a recipe for disaster but the All-Stars had a genuine charm and warmth that prevented the act from developing into cruel spectacle, and kept it in the realm of hilarity rather than humiliation.

This TV show also featured a guest appearance by the comedian Flacco, a regular collaborator who had appeared with the trio in their Australian comedy sci-fi TV series *D*A*A*S Kapital* (ABC, 14 episodes, 15 July 1991–7 July 1992).

Dowie

UK · BBC · SKETCH/STANDUP

1 × 30 mins · colour

26 May 1989 · BBC2 Fri 9pm

MAIN CAST

John Dowie
Cathryn Harrison
Steve Steen
Jim Sweeney
Max Wall
Anna Wing

CREDITS

writer John Dowie · *director* John Kilby · *producers* John Kilby/Jamie Rix

Coming across as a drier, thinner, grimmer version of Jasper Carrott, John Dowie here fronted his own *Comic Asides* pilot show, which, despite reasonable reviews, failed to be developed into a series. The idea was for Dowie to take a different theme each week and subject it to his own particular brand of dark humour. In this pilot, the topic was death; following his own funeral Dowie encounters the living embodiment of Death (Jim Sweeney) and the Devil (Max Wall).

Down The 'Gate

see VARNEY, Reg

Down To Earth

UK · BBC · SITCOM

7 × 30 mins · colour

5 Jan–16 Feb 1995 · BBC1 Thu 8.30pm

MAIN CAST

Tony Fairfax · · · · · · · · · · · · · Richard Briers
Chris Fairfax · · · · · · · · · · · Christopher Blake
Molly Fairfax · · · · · · · · · · · · Kirsten Cooke
Jim · · · · · · · · · · · · · · · · · · · Steve Edwin
Oswald · · · · · · · · · · · · · · · · Stephen Bent
Ramon · · · · · · · · · · · · · · · · · Sandor Eles
Helen Thorpe · · · · · · · Joanna Van Gyseghem

CREDITS

writers John Esmonde/Bob Larbey ·
director/producer John B Hobbs

A strangely low-key project from Esmonde, Larbey and Briers, who had previously collaborated on **The Good Life**, **The Other One** and **Ever Decreasing Circles**.

In *Down To Earth*, Briers played a part written specifically for him – Tony Fairfax, an Oxford graduate who, upon leaving university, immediately went to work as a cultural adviser to fellow student Ramon, son of the president of a South American banana republic. Fairfax stays for 37 years, during which time Ramon succeeds his father, and Fairfax, his closest ally, finds himself involved in all manner of agreeable ventures: judging beauty contests, preparing the two-man Olympic team, escorting visiting dignitaries and so on. But his glorious existence is brought to a sudden end by a military coup and Fairfax is exiled, penniless, and forced to return to a Britain he barely recognises or understands. He turns up at the house of his younger brother Chris, who agrees, despite his wife Molly's objections, to put him up until he finds his feet. This proves harder than Fairfax has imagined and he is soon faced with the prospect of working as a labourer for Chris's struggling garden design business. From this point on, the sitcom takes on the traditional square-peg-in-a-round-hole theme, with Briers doing his best to squeeze every droplet of humour from a damp squib.

The arrival of a new client, Helen, enlivened the latter episodes but, overall, the series lacked flair – surprising, given its creators' pedigree. Fairfax's reminiscences of his previous life only served to emphasise that the tales of a snobbish cultural diplomat in a foreign country ought perhaps to have been the focus, not his crestfallen return home.

Downwardly Mobile

UK · ITV (PORTMAN PRODUCTIONS FOR YORKSHIRE) · SITCOM

7 × 30 mins · colour

21 July–1 Sep 1994 · Thu 8.30pm

MAIN CAST

Rosemary · · · · · · · · · · · · Frances de la Tour
Clem · · · · · · · · · · · · · · · · · Philip Jackson

Sophie · · · · · · · · · · · · · · · · Josie Lawrence
Mark · · · · · · · · · · · · · Stephen Tompkinson

CREDITS

writers Barry Pilton/Alistair Beaton · director Martin Dennis · executive producer David Reynolds · producer Philip Hinchcliffe

An agreeable but short-lived sitcom about two mismatched couples sharing the same house.

Clem is a craftsman of the old school, contentedly making a couple of medieval lutes each year from his cluttered workshop. Not married, he shares his tumbledown abode with Rosemary, a psychotherapist and Greenham Common veteran who is generous towards those who need help the most – her clients, the homeless and so on – · but doesn't always appeal to her loved ones. Mark is Clem's younger brother, a money-making high-flying yuppie who, upon suffering 'a bit of a glitch' in the City on Black Wednesday (he lost his company £438 million), receives a bumpy landing and, penniless, jobless and with the utmost reluctance, begs the use of Clem and Rosemary's spare bedroom. Mark brings along his spoilt wife Sophie, hitherto an habitué of Bond Street designer boutiques but now distraught over their reduced state (she has lost her design consultancy too) and making everyone else's life a misery because of it. The four-in-one arrangement is meant to be temporary but, if it is, they must have invented a new definition for the word. The four lifestyles clash horribly from the start, and there's not even the foundation of brotherhood upon which to build, since Clem and Mark remember only childhood squabbles and fail completely, still, to understand one another's point of view or chosen lifestyle.

Originally scheduled for broadcast in autumn 1992, *Downwardly Mobile* was delayed for almost a year upon the death of Simon Cadell, cast as Clem. When it finally made it on air the part was played by Philip Jackson.

Charlie Drake

Born Charles Springall in south London on 19 June 1925, the son of a newspaper vendor, round-faced Charlie Drake became one of the most famous personalities in Britain in a TV comedy career that stretched over more than 20 years. After entering show business as an amateur singer, he turned to comedy, making his radio debut in 1951 and TV bow two years later. The proverbial pint-sized comedy powerhouse – he jokingly claimed that his diminutive stature owed to 'being raised on condensed milk' – Drake delighted

audiences, firstly with straight slapstick and dangerous stunts and then via the invention of a number of mostly irritating characters at odds with authority or authority figures. His famous catchphrase 'Hello my darlings' came about when he was playing straight-man to Jimmy Wheeler and ad-libbed the line to 5ft 10in dancer Janet Ball, garnering plenty of laughs. Drake also enjoyed success as a singer of novelty songs, scoring four Top 30 hits from 1958 to 1961.

Over the years, Charlie Drake starred in many TV shows, and these are outlined below in chronological form. See also *The Plank*, *Rhubarb Rhubarb!* and *Mr H Is Late* (all within Eric Sykes' combined entry), **Tess And Jim** and **Christmas Cracker**.

Charlie Drake And Jack Edwardes

UK · BBC · CHILDREN'S SKETCH

16 × 10 mins · b/w

Series One (4) 29 Oct–12 Dec 1954 · fortnightly mostly Sat 5pm

Series Two (12) 15 Jan–18 June 1955 · fortnightly Sat 5pm

MAIN CAST

Mick · · · · · · · · · · · · · · · Jack Edwardes
Montmorency · · · · · · · · · · · · Charlie Drake

CREDITS

writers Charlie Drake/Jack Edwardes · director Robert Tronson

Charlie Drake (5ft 1in) and Jack Edwardes' (6ft 4½ in) famous knockabout double-act Mick and Montmorency made their TV bow as part of the BBC children's comedy magazine show *Jigsaw*. The comics had met while serving in the RAF, where an officer had icily suggested that they would make a good comedy double-act, but it wasn't until years later – when the two were rejected at the same Windmill Theatre audition – that they decided to try their hand as a duo. Soon afterwards, Edwardes was appointed entertainment producer at a holiday camp where, for 18 weeks, he and Drake presented a comedy show featuring themselves as Mick and Montmorency. *Jigsaw* producer Michael Westmore booked them on the strength of that show and also a 24 May 1954 spot in the new talent TV series *Showcase*.

Mick And Montmorency / Jobstoppers

UK · ITV (ASSOCIATED-REDIFFUSION) · CHILDREN'S SKETCH

91 editions (76 × 15 mins · 13 × 10 mins · 2 × 20 mins) · b/w

Series One (22) 30 Sep 1955–21 Feb 1956 · Fri mostly 5.30pm then Tue around 5.30pm

Series Two (17) 10 Apr–31 July 1956 · Tue around 5.30pm

Series Three (33) 21 Sep 1956–19 June 1957 ·
fortnightly then weekly Fri mostly 5.15pm · then
Wed around 5pm

Series Four (13) 13 Sep–5 Dec 1957 ·
Fri 5.15pm

Series Five (6) 14 Mar–22 May 1958 ·
fortnightly Fri 5pm

MAIN CAST
Mick · · · · · · · · · · · · · · · · · · Charlie Drake
Montmorency · · · · · · · · · · · Jack Edwardes

CREDITS
writers Charlie Drake/Jack Edwardes · directors
Jonathan Alwyn, Daphne Shadwell

Soon after finishing their series for the BBC,
Drake and Edwardes took clumsy chumps
Mick and Montmorency across to ITV for
three years of slapstick for the children.
(Latter editions ran within the strand *Jolly
Good Time*, introduced by Jimmy Hanley.)
Each short programme found the original
M&M working their cackhanded way
through every profession you could name
(they were chimney sweeps, window
cleaners, bakers, grocers, scientists,
plumbers, steeplejacks, potters, parcel
packers, carpenters, garage hands,
policemen, pot-holers, TV aerial fitters,
removal men, locksmiths, and *much* else),
always with the same disastrous results. By
the end of the run Drake was convinced that
they had taken the premise as far as it
would go and he and Edwardes went their
separate ways, although not before they
took the double-act out on a theatrical
variety package tour.

Note. The very first episode went out under
the title *Mick And Montmorency*, episodes 2
to 34 were titled *Jobstoppers* and then 35–91
reverted to *Mick And Montmorency*.

Laughter In Store

UK · BBC · SITCOM

1 × 30 mins · b/w
3 Jan 1957 · Thu 7.45pm

MAIN CAST
Charlie Drake
Charles Hawtrey
Irene Handl

CREDITS
writers George Wadmore, Charlie Drake ·
producer George Inns

After serving his apprenticeship in
Children's Television, Charlie Drake was
asked by the BBC's Head of Light
Entertainment, Ronnie Walden, to come up
with a half-hour comedy idea for a later
slot The single-episode production
Laughter In Store, with fellow funny folk
Charles Hawtrey and Irene Handl, was the
result.

Drake's Progress

UK · BBC · SKETCH

12 × 30 mins · b/w
Series One (6) 6 May–15 July 1957 · fortnightly
Mon 8pm

Series Two (6) 31 Mar–5 May 1958 · Mon 8pm

MAIN CAST
Charlie Drake

OTHER APPEARANCES
Irene Handl (series 1)
Warren Mitchell (series 1)
Willoughby Goddard (series 1)
Valentine Dyall (series 2)

CREDITS
writers George Wadmore, Charlie Drake, Maurice
Wiltshire, George Inns, Sid Green/Dick Hills ·
producer George Inns

A sign of TV success in the 1950s was to
have a show title that incorporated your
surname, usually in some awful pun: Ted
Ray had *Ray's A Laugh*, Norman Wisdom
had *Wit And Wisdom*, Norman Evans had
Evans Above. Charlie Drake achieved this
dubious distinction with *Drake's Progress*,
the first series of which reunited him with
his *Laughter In Store* co-star Irene Handl.
The success of that one-off led directly to
this series, and with it the diminutive comic
finally established himself as a comedy lead,
after sterling work as a straight-man to
Jimmy Wheeler, Benny Hill and Bob
Monkhouse.

The Charlie Drake Show   1

UK · ITV (ATV) · SKETCH/STANDUP

1 × 60 mins · b/w
31 Aug 1958 · Sun 8.30pm

MAIN CAST
Charlie Drake

CREDITS
producer Kenneth Carter

A single ITV special.

Charlie Drake In …

UK · BBC · SITCOM

**23 episodes (21 × 30 mins · 2 × short
specials) · b/w**
Series One (5) 11 Nov–9 Dec 1958 ·
Tue 7.30pm

Series Two (5) 7 Apr–5 May 1959 · Tue 7.30pm

Short special · part of *Christmas Night With The
Stars* 25 Dec 1958 · Thu 6.25pm

Series Three (7) 18 Nov–30 Dec 1959 ·
Wed 7.30pm

Short special · part of *Christmas Night With The
Stars* 25 Dec 1959 · Fri 6.20pm

Series Four (4) 7 July–4 Aug 1960 · Thu 8.30pm

MAIN CAST
Charlie Drake

CREDITS
writers Charlie Drake/Dave Freeman (series 1 &
2, special 1), Charlie Drake (special 2), Charlie

Drake/David Cumming/Derek Collyer (series 3 &
4) · producers Ernest Maxin (series 1–3,
specials), Barry Lupino (series 4)

Capitalising on his popularity, Drake
stretched himself (creatively) in this next
series, presenting a number of unrelated
comedy playlets that attracted seriously big
audiences. These comic adventures covered
many themes and Drake relished the
freedom of having separate ideas every
week. One of the characters from this series,
poet and film director Charles O'Casey
Drake, proved popular enough to reappear
sporadically.

Note. A 45-minute compilation of the best
moments from these series was screened
on 26 December 1960 as *Charlie Drake's
Christmas Show*.

The Charlie Drake Show   2

UK · BBC · SITCOM

12 × 30 mins · b/w
Series One (5) 25 Nov–30 Dec 1960 ·
Fri 7.30pm

Series Two (6) 23 Mar–27 Apr 1961 ·
Thu 7.30pm

Series Three (1) 24 Oct 1961 · Tue 8pm (then
abandoned)

MAIN CAST
Charlie Drake

CREDITS
writers Charlie Drake/Richard Waring · producer
Ronald Marsh

A new series and a new writing collaborator
for Drake: Richard Waring, who had
appeared as an actor in *Charlie Drake In …*
The first series of this new show differed
from its predecessor in that it had a single
unifying theme linking the different stories.
This was 'coping with the pressures of
modern day life in 1960' and episodes duly
dealt with financial worries, office life and
so on. In the second series there was a new
theme – 'adventure' – leading to spoofs
of TV drama programmes ('The World
Of Charlie Frazer' lampooned Francis
Durbridge's popular serial *The World
Of Tim Frazer*) and films ('Nine Little
White Men' parodying Agatha Christie's
Ten Little Indians).

The third series – supposed to last for six
programmes – was dramatically curtailed
part-way through the first transmission,
'Bingo Madness', when a stunt went horribly
wrong. The show was being transmitted
live, and a tricky slapstick sequence in
which Drake was pulled through a bookcase
and thrown through a window ended in
disaster: the comedian fractured his skull
and remained unconscious for three days.
The screen, like Drake himself, was blacked
out when the production crew finally
realised the seriousness of the situation.

(Ironically, producer Ronald Marsh had anticipated the dangerous elements of this very stunt in an article in that week's *Radio Times*.) A few months after the accident, Drake was at an awards dinner, receiving the honour of TV Comedian of the Year, when he announced his retirement. He took up painting, with some success, and remained off-screen for the best part of two years before returning in 1963.

The Charlie Drake Show · 3

UK · ITV (ATV) · SKETCH

6 × 35 mins · b/w

28 Sep–2 Nov 1963 · Sat mostly 8.25pm

MAIN CAST
Charlie Drake

CREDITS
writers Charlie Drake/Lew Schwarz · *producer* Colin Clews

In its time one of the most expensive comedy series put on screen, *The Charlie Drake Show* saw the little man break his self-imposed retirement in style. The series was all-action, with pre-filmed and carefully edited sketches: there were 33 in the first show and the other editions maintained a similar full-throttle pace. Drake was the linchpin but it wasn't all him: each show featured a number of other players, one of whom was the as yet unknown Olivia Hussey, soon to become a major film star.

The Worker · 1

UK · ITV (ATV) · SITCOM

13 × 35 mins · b/w

Series One (6) 27 Feb–3 Apr 1965 · Sat 8.25pm
Series Two (7) 2 Oct–13 Nov 1965 · Sat 8.25pm

MAIN CAST
Charlie · · · · · · · · · · · · · · · · · Charlie Drake
Mr Whittaker · · · · · Percy Herbert (series 1)
Mr Pugh · · · · · · · · · Henry McGee (series 2)

CREDITS
writers Charlie Drake/Lew Schwarz · *director* Shaun O'Riordan · *producer* Alan Tarrant

The premise of *Mick And Montmorency* had been that the pair wanted to work but were so clumsy that they made a mess of everything they touched. In *The Worker*, addressed to an adult audience and with Charlie Drake only, the idea was the same: he is willing to work but his appallingly bad luck guarantees that something always goes wrong. In fact, as the series begins, he has been frequenting his local Labour Exchange for some 20 years and been found 980 jobs, all ending in instant dismissal.

The cast of *The Worker* changed with every programme – it had to: Charlie was always working in a different place – and the only other regular player was the ever-

thwarted clerk at the Labour Exchange. In the first series this was the hot-headed Mr Whittaker (Percy Herbert), in the second (and in the 1970 and 1978 revivals) it was the easily infuriated Mr Pugh (played by Henry McGee, who had appeared in one episode in the first series as someone else).

Every incarnation of *The Worker* depicted the archetypal Charlie Drake situation: that of the little man up against life's big problems, and each provided plenty of opportunities for that famous Drake-style slapstick.

Who Is Sylvia?

UK · ITV (ATV) · SITCOM

7 × 30 mins · b/w

11 Feb–25 Mar 1967 · Sat 8.55pm

MAIN CAST
Charles Rameses Drake · · · · Charlie Drake
Mrs Proudpiece · · · · · · · · · Kathleen Byron

CREDITS
writers Charlie Drake/Donald Churchill · *director* Shaun O'Riordan · *executive producer* Alan Tarrant

The Worker had shown Drake as the little man looking for a job. *Who Is Sylvia?* cast him as Charles *Rameses* Drake, in top hat and tails, looking for a partner. Subtitled 'A Love Story In Seven Parts' it was, really, anything but this: Charlie is destined to be frustrated it seems, unable to find his Sylvia, the perfect little lady (with the emphasis on little, of course), despite the most earnest of endeavours. Aiding him in his search is Miss Proudpiece, secretary at a marriage bureau. A not yet famous Pauline Collins appeared in one of the episodes.

The Charlie Drake Show · 4

UK · BBC · SKETCH

11 editions (10 × 45 mins · 1 × 35 mins) · colour

10 Dec 1967–28 Apr 1968 · BBC2 fortnightly Sun 8.15pm

MAIN CAST
Charlie Drake
Henry McGee

CREDITS
writer Charlie Drake · *producer* Ernest Maxin

The Worker renewed Charlie Drake's huge popularity, bringing about a return to the BBC, this time for colour programmes. He was joined for these by his ITV co-star Henry McGee.

One edition, shortened to 35 minutes and screened on 14 April 1968 as *The World Of Charlie Drake*, was the BBC's entry in that year's Montreux Festival.

The Worker · 2

UK · ITV (ATV) · SITCOM

13 episodes (12 × 30 mins · 1 × short special) · colour

Series One (5) 29 Dec 1969–26 Jan 1970 · Mon 9.30pm
Series Two (7) 6 Aug–17 Sep 1970 · Thu 9pm
Short special · part of *All-Star Comedy Carnival* 25 Dec 1970 · Fri 6pm

MAIN CAST
Charlie · · · · · · · · · · · · · · · Charlie Drake
Mr Pugh · · · · · · · · · · · · · · · Henry McGee

CREDITS
writers Charlie Drake/Lew Schwarz · *directors* Paul Annett (series 1), John Scholz-Conway (series 2) · *producer* Shaun O'Riordan

The first revival of *The Worker* (see 1965 series for details).

Slapstick And Old Lace

UK · ITV (ATV) · SKETCH

7 × 30 mins · colour

4 Mar–15 Apr 1971 · Thu around 7pm

MAIN CAST
Charlie Drake
Henry McGee
Anna Dawson

CREDITS
writer Charlie Drake · *directors* John Scholz-Conway (6), Shaun O'Riordan (1) · *producer* Shaun O'Riordan

For some years Charlie Drake had the idea for a show in which he would singlehandedly revive vaudeville, and this was it: realised on screen in 1971, *Slapstick And Old Lace* was set in 'a new theatre', a TV studio in Borehamwood, just north of London, mocked up as the Imperial Vaudeville House, in which Drake was not only one of the acts but also the manager, handing out programmes and selling chocolate and popcorn to the audience. The mixture on stage comprised sketches, knockabout humour, dance and music, including eight songs written by Drake himself.

The Charlie Drake Comedy Hour

UK · ITV (THAMES) · SKETCH

1 × 60 mins · colour

20 Sep 1972 · Wed 8pm

MAIN CAST
Charlie Drake
Willoughby Goddard
Robert Dorning
Christopher Sandford

CREDITS
writers Charlie Drake/Lew Schwarz · *director/producer* Terry Henebery

Subtitled 'A Day In The Life Of Charles Drake', this single programme had Drake falling from a very high building in order to test out the old saying that, when you're falling to your death, your whole life flashes before you. In Drake's case, of course, it has all gone wrong, and he relives all the sorry experiences from birth through disastrous relationships, dismissals from all three armed services and more.

Apart from a brief, last fling with *The Worker* in 1978, this was Drake's last starring TV comedy show. In 1974 he made the difficult transition to straight acting, enjoying considerable success in his new career.

The Worker   3

UK · ITV (LWT) · SITCOM

10 × 15 mins · colour

Series One (8) part of *Bruce Forsyth's Big Night*
7 Oct–18 Nov; 16 Dec 1978 ·
Sat mostly 7.25pm
Special · 17 Dec 1978 · Sun 5pm
Short special · part of *Bruce Forsyth's Christmas Eve* 24 Dec 1978 · Sun 7.15pm

MAIN CAST
Charlie · · · · · · · · · · · · · · · Charlie Drake
Mr Pugh · · · · · · · · · · · · · · · Henry McGee

CREDITS
writer Charlie Drake · *director* Stuart Allen

One final return for *The Worker*, all but one of the episodes forming part of a Bruce Forsyth entertainment compendium programme.

Dream On

USA · HBO (KEVIN BRIGHT PRODUCTIONS/ST CLARE ENTERTAINMENT FOR MTE/MCA) · SITCOM

118 episodes (113 × 30 mins · 4 × 60 mins · 1 × 90 mins) · colour

US dates: 8 July 1990–27 Mar 1996
*UK dates: 9 Aug 1991–28 Feb 1992 (30 × 30 mins) C4 Fri 10pm

MAIN CAST
Martin Tupper · · · · · · · · · · · · Brian Benben
Judith Tupper/Stone · · · · · · · Wendie Malick
Jeremy Tupper · · · · · · · · · · · Chris Demetral
Toby Pedalbee · · · · · · · · · · · · Denny Dillon
Eddie Charles · · · · · · Jeff Joseph (1990–92);
· · · · · · · · · · · · · · Dorien Wilson (1992–96)

OTHER APPEARANCES
Gibby Fisk · · · · · · · · · · · · · Michael McKean
Mickey Tupper · · · · · · · · · · · · Paul Dooley
Doris · · · · · · · · · · · · · · · · · Renée Taylor
Harry · · · · · · · · · · · · · · · · · · Cliff Norton
Lu Fisk · · · · · · · Morwenna Banks (1995–96)

CREDITS
creators Marta Kauffman/David Crane · *writers* Stephen Engel and others · *directors* John Landis, Kevin S Bright and others · *executive producers* John Landis, Kevin S Bright, Leslie Belzberg, Robert K Weiss · *producers* Robb Idels, Ron Wolotzky, David Crane, Marta Kauffman, Jeff Greenstein, Jeff Strauss

A great 1990s sitcom, *Dream On* had a most unusual creation. MCA, the owner of literally thousands of hours of old monochrome TV footage, made a deal with HBO in which the US cable channel would create a comedy series to utilise archival clips. After deliberating on a variety of suggestions HBO decide to plump for writers Crane and Kauffman's idea of using the clips to highlight emotions, reactions, thoughts or moods in the life of a thirty-something New Yorker. The opening credit sequence to the series showed our hero as a child growing up watching 1950s and early 1960s shows, and in the episodes clips from these programmes flashed through his mind, seemingly unbidden, at relevant moments. Most of the extracts were very short – perhaps an aside comment, a cannon being fired to accompany the entrance of a pretty girl, a shot of someone being hit with a frying pan as a reaction to some *faux pas* – but they made their point. It was a gimmicky idea perhaps, but one that proved peculiarly effective. The editing of these clips into the shows was seamless, and indeed the existence of particularly unusual archive footage or dialogue – hundreds of hours of material was computed in infinitesimal detail by the producers – sometimes suggested subjects to the episode writers.

Martin Tupper is the dreamer in *Dream On*. A Jewish divorcee with one son (Jeremy, who mostly lives with the ex-wife, Judith), Martin works as editor for Whitestone, a Manhattan book publishing house. He is a pleasant enough guy, easy-going but with a neurotic streak and occasional feelings of insecurity. At work he is cowed by his feisty, fierce and unbelievably tetchy secretary Toby, a blonde bulldog of a woman who seems totally unacquainted with the traditional notion of a boss/secretary situation. Martin's best buddy is Eddie Charles, the black host of (at first) a tacky TV talk-show and (later) a tacky TV morning magazine show. Eddie is also a compulsive womaniser who seems in many ways (and often to Martin) to have the perfect, hitch-free, guilt-free life. Martin also has his fair share of sexual encounters (*more* than his fair share actually, *much* more some would say) but he still holds a torch for his ex, Judith, a beautiful and intelligent, if brittle, psychotherapist who counts Martin as a close friend and confidante. Martin's wish to win her return (rarely stated but nonetheless evident) is seriously dented when she marries renaissance man Dr Richard Stone, an internationally renowned genius who must rank as the World's Most Perfect Human Being. Although never seen in the series (rather like, say, Maris Crane in *Frasier*), Stone's presence is felt in every episode through newspaper headlines, TV reports or aside comments on his various mind-boggling

exploits, including miracle surgery, symphony-writing, mountain-climbing, life-saving, going into space and other fantastic achievements.

The series' other regular is Jeremy, who enters his teens and starts dating through the run of the series. He is a bright, confident kid who has inherited some of his father's bad habits (lustful thoughts, drinking, pot smoking). When confronting him about these things, Martin invariably finds himself cast in the role of his own father, despite his determination not to be. Martin's boss, occasionally seen, is Gibby, a loathsome, debased, avaricious Australian who treats people like dirt and has an unerring ability to sniff out salacious material to publish. To rub salt in the wound, Gibby even dates Judith following the tragic death of Richard Stone – the miracle-man passing away after the failure of a kidney donated to him by Martin. Eventually, though, Martin and Judith are reunited, Martin's only worry being that Stone, his body frozen until a cure is found, might soon be thawed and revived.

All the relationships in *Dream On* were artfully fleshed out, the direction was excellent (the highly successful comedy movie director John Landis was at the helm of many episodes) and the writing was sharp and, in the first 60 or so episodes especially, extremely funny. The clip flashes added a unique style, and with occasional big-name guests in cameo roles to add sparkle, the series would have worked well enough simply on that level. But there was still more to *Dream On*. Taking full advantage of its less regulated cable status, HBO went all out to make the series a truly adult sitcom. Many mature themes were covered: profanities (even the dreaded 'f' word) littered the scripts; there was lots of nudity (everything but genitalia, both male and female, but mostly female and straight out of the pages of *Penthouse* and *Playboy*); and oodles of vigorous simulated sex scenes in a variety of unlikely, complicated and downright dangerous positions. It could have all been gratuitous but it was deftly handled with a vitality and sureness of touch that kept the series funny rather than offensive. The appealing array of flawed but likeable characters (winningly portrayed) also helped to keep the fun factor high. Less salacious versions of the episodes were available for more traditional broadcasters, the Fox network screening many of the expurgated episodes in the USA from 1995.

*Note. In Britain, C4 screened the first two US seasons, comprising 30 episodes (the unexpurgated versions), in 1991–92, with a 1993 repeat run, after which the series continued to be screened on the cable/satellite channel Sky One (again, the uncut versions).

Dream Stuffing

UK · C4 (LIMEHOUSE PRODUCTIONS/
HUMPHREY BARCLAY PRODUCTIONS) · SITCOM

10 × 30 mins · colour
6 Jan–9 Mar 1984 · Fri mostly 9pm

MAIN CAST
Jude · · · · · · · · · · · · · · · · · Rachael Weaver
Mo · · · · · · · · · · · · · · · · Amanda Symonds
Richard · · · · · · · · · · · · · · · · · Ray Burdis
Bill · Frank Lee

OTHER APPEARANCES
May · · · · · · · · · · · · · · · · · Maria Charles
Brenda · · · · · · · · · · · · Caroline Quentin
Stella · · · · · · · · · · · · · · · · · Alison King
Mrs Tudge · · · · · · · · · · · · · Helen Brammer

CREDITS
writers Paul Hines/Su Wilkins · director John Kaye
Cooper · producer Humphrey Barclay

A Friday-night series on C4 – the first to be
made by the prominent sitcom producer
Humphrey Barclay under his own
independent aegis – depicting the lives of two
down-to-earth urchins, Mo and Jude, living in
a high-rise council tower block in the East
End of London. Others may think that there's
not much for them to laugh about in such
circumstances, but they manage well enough.
While Jude is permanently on the dole, Mo
has work, at a glass-eye factory, although a
strike to avert redundancy proves useless: she
is laid off part-way into the series, the two
friends becoming the scourge of their local
DHSS employment review officer Mrs Tudge.
Friends offer support and a joke, including
May (who runs the local launderette) and the
problematic Brenda (an early role for future
Men Behaving Badly star Caroline
Quentin), a colleague from the glass-eye
factory who has a baby as the series comes
to an end.

Dress Rehearsal

see SYKES, Eric

Dressing For Breakfast

UK · C4 (WARNER SISTERS) · SITCOM

13 × 30 mins · colour
Series One (6) 24 Nov–29 Dec 1995 · Fri 9pm
Series Two (7) 10 Jan–21 Feb 1997 · Fri 9pm

MAIN CAST
Louise · · · · · · · · · · · · · · · · · Beatie Edney
Carla · · · · · · · · · · · · · · · · · · · Holly Aird
Liz · · · · · · · · · · · · · · · · Charlotte Cornwall
Dave · · · · · · · · · · · · · · · · · Nigel Lindsay
Fabrizio ('Fab') · · · · · · Robert Langdon Lloyd
· (series 1)
Graham · · · · · · · · Richard Durdan (series 2)
Rose · · · · · · · · · · · · · · · · · Sophie Stanton

CREDITS
writer Stephanie Calman · directors Juliet May
(series 1), Jeremy Ancock (series 2) · producer
Jane Wellesley

A faintly feminist sitcom centring on the
friendship of two young women. Louise is a
bright, modern woman, fated, it seems, to be
unlucky in love. Her best friend Carla is a
similarly perky type, who has been in a
steady relationship with Dave for many
years. What Dave might lack in charisma
he more than compensates for with other
attributes, especially his reliability. Louise
longs for such a partner yet in the opening
episode she is let down yet again by her
current boyfriend, the faithless Tony, and
dumps him. Louise also endures a volatile
relationship with her mother, Liz, who is
obsessed with health food and good causes,
and who herself remarries in the first episode,
to a suave Italian, Fabrizio (known as Fab).
This especially irks Louise, who, lacking in
confidence, feels that everyone but her
is capable of making and sustaining a
relationship. By the start of the second series,
though, Fab has died and Liz is looking out
for new dates.

Developed from a 1988 book of the same
title, in which Stephanie Calman collected
together scores of short observations about
the female condition, *Dressing For Breakfast*
certainly had its moments, and the ability to
surprise with the candid and ribald nature
of some of the discussions between the two
women. Men came in for their fair share of
ribbing, but usually in a good-natured way.
The fulcrum friendship between the two lead
parts was refreshingly realistic, and their
lament – that it was impossible to have close
and supportive relationships with men – was
the underlying theme of the whole premise.

A third series was in production at the time
of writing, for screening in early 1998.

Drop Dead Gorgeous

USA · HBO (WORLD OF WONDER) · STANDUP

1 × 60 mins · colour
US date: 16 June 1997
UK date: 26 Nov 1997 · C4 Wed 11.50pm

MAIN CAST
Steve Moore

CREDITS
writer Steve Moore · directors Fenton Bailey,
Randy Barbato · executive producers Annie
Albrecht, Steve Kaplan, Bob Read, Sheila Nevins ·
producers Fenton Bailey, Randy Barbato, John
Hoffman

A recording of HIV-positive comedian Steve
Moore's live act, reflecting on his life and the
trauma of his exposure to the Aids virus.
Moore spoke candidly about his experiences,
and the monologue was punctuated by film
clips of his family (mother Wilma and father
Skeets) illustrating points in his story and at
other times talking directly to camera about
their feelings. Although structured like a
traditional standup act, the piece was

described as a 'tragicomedy', and occasionally
veered into more serious areas that were
moving to watch. Moore's honesty, sense
of humour and determination to carry
on regardless gave the programme an
inspirational aura, which, allied to the
unavoidable depth of the material, made
most other observational standup routines
seem slight by comparison.

A Drop Of Digance

see DIGANCE, Richard

Drop The Dead Donkey

UK · C4, *BBC (HAT TRICK PRODUCTIONS) ·
SITCOM

**60 episodes (58 × 30 mins · 2 × short specials) ·
colour**
Series One (10) 9 Aug–11 Oct 1990 ·
Thu 10.30pm
Series Two (13) 26 Sep–19 Dec 1991 ·
Thu 10pm
Series Three (11) 7 Jan–18 Mar 1993 ·
Thu 10pm
*Short special · part of *Children In Need*
26 Nov 1993 · BBC1 Fri around 12 midnight
Series Four (12) 29 Sep–15 Dec 1994 ·
Thu 10pm
*Short special · part of *Children In Need* 25 Nov
1994 · BBC1 Fri around 10pm
Series Five (12) 1 Oct–17 Dec 1996 · Tue 10pm

MAIN CAST
Gus Hedges · · · · · · · · · · · · · Robert Duncan
Alex Pates · · · · Haydn Gwynne (series 1 & 2)
Helen Cooper · · · · · · · · · · · · · Ingrid Lacey
· · · · · · · · · · · · · · · · · · · (series 3 onwards)
Dave Charnley · · · · · · · · · · · · · Neil Pearson
George Dent · · · · · · · · · · · · · · · Jeff Rawle
Henry Davenport · · · · · · · · · · · · David Swift
Damien Day · · · · · · · · Stephen Tompkinson
Sally Smedley · · · · · · · · · · · · Victoria Wicks
Joy Merryweather · · · · · · · · Susannah Doyle
· · · · · · · · · · · · · · · · · · · (series 2 onwards)

CREDITS
creators Andy Hamilton/Guy Jenkin · writers Andy
Hamilton/Guy Jenkin (50), Malcolm Williamson
(4), Nick Revell (3), Ian Brown (3) · director Liddy
Oldroyd · executive producer Denise O'Donoghue ·
producers Andy Hamilton/Guy Jenkin (50), Andy
Hamilton (10)

C4's second major home-made sitcom success
(following **Desmond's**) started out quietly
enough. Writers Hamilton and Jenkin were
both experienced in topical sketch writing
(**Not The Nine O'Clock News, A Kick
Up The Eighties, Who Dares, Wins …**),
sitcoms (**Shelley, Kit Curran**) and longer-
form comedy (three editions in **Tickets For
The Titanic**), and they decided to combine
these skills in a news-based sitcom that
was recorded very close to transmission,
permitting last-minute script tinkering to
incorporate maximum topicality. The writers
kicked around a number of titles for the series

but their personal favourite, *Dead Belgians Don't Count*, was deemed too offensive by C4, which feared – jokingly, perhaps – that it might harm sales to Belgian TV. So it became *Drop The Dead Donkey* instead, an all-purpose reference to a story bumped from the news agenda by a more important story or by time constraints. Hamilton and Jenkin were confident that they could make the topicality technique work and proved it by generating a fast-paced, witty, American-style production. However, while this topicality is a talking point, *Drop The Dead Donkey* became special for the same reasons that all fine sitcoms are special: the witty interplay between a richly observed bunch of diverse characters.

The action took place in the offices of Globelink News TV, a rival to CNN, ITN, Sky News and the like. In the opening episode the station is acquired by media tycoon Sir Royston Marchant, who, despite assurances to the contrary, sets in motion a 'dumbing down' process, making it sensationalist rather than controversial. Sir Royston is never seen to interfere (indeed, he is never seen) but his wishes are carried out by his yuppie 1980s-throwback lackey Gus Hedges, an immaculately groomed, vacuous man with all the warmth of a lizard. Gus communicates in an exaggerated 'media-speak', with most of his tortured utterances beginning with a reiteration of his 'unofficial' status as part of the news team – such as, 'As you know, I'm not here – I just wanted to watch the editorial unit synchromeshing with the production matrix …'. The head of the editorial unit, George Dent, is a perpetually harassed and nervous individual who means well but is too weak to stand up to Gus. Alex, George's second in command, has no such fears: she is a fiercely bright woman whose dedication to serious news gathering and reporting often brings her into confrontation with Hedges. Beneath Alex (literally, in one episode) is Dave Charnley, a compulsive womaniser who, despite his laddish tendencies, still cares about delivering a decent end-product. Then there's the field reporter Damien Day, an unprincipled, ambitious, glory-driven egotist quite happy with the enforced 'tabloidisation' of Globelink. Finally there's the anchor-team of newsreaders, Henry and Sally. Henry Davenport is a larger-than-life, old-fashioned newsman who embraces all the hard-living clichés of such characters – he drinks to excess, parties all night, dates women 20 years his junior and rants loudly about his many pet annoyances. Sally, recruited by Sir Royston, embodies all that Henry hates: she is a brainless bimbo, obsessed with her own career and completely unprofessional in her attitude to hard news stories. In the second series, the hugely misnamed Joy Merryweather was added to the cast. She is perpetually and dangerously angry, bluntly

refusing – although employed in a factotum capacity – to perform many of the chores she is given, often colouring her refusal with some venomous invective. In the third series Alex was replaced by the equally bright but softer Helen Cooper, who, it transpires, is a lesbian undecided about the wisdom of coming out.

With all these disparate characters, comic sparks were bound to fly, but as the concentration on topical gags lessened so the writers started opening out the characters. Although mere stereotypes at first sight, viewers gradually learned more about their flaws. Gus became increasingly out of step with the real world and started to doubt his sanity; George became a fatalist about his lot; Helen agonised over whether to tell her daughter that she was gay; Dave grew concerned over his inability to remain faithful to his lovers; Henry became anxious about growing old and living alone and unloved; Sally had a nervous breakdown and sought therapy to overcome her uncontrollable desires to bed rough tradesmen and lorry drivers. Damien remained unstable throughout and though Joy made positive efforts to control her anger when she realised it may have cost her any chance of bettering herself, she remained a frightening figure.

A *Drop The Dead Donkey* feature film was cancelled during production (it was shot between TV series four and five) but its spin-off novel *Drop The Dead Donkey 2000* (written by Guy Jenkin and Alistair Beaton) was published, telling how the Globelink staff measured up to the new millennium. The series itself grew from humble beginnings to become one of C4's most successful programmes and proved an important stepping stone in the careers of many of its cast, particularly Neil Pearson (who went on to appear in the BBC2 police drama *Between The Lines*) and Stephen Tompkinson (who scored with the BBC1 light-drama *Ballykissangel*). Hamilton and Jenkin also prospered, turning their hands to feature-length material: Hamilton with the football scandal satire *Eleven Men Against Eleven* (C4, 31 August 1995, which he also directed) and the six-part black comedy-drama series *Underworld* (C4, 4 November–9 December 1997, which he also co-produced); and Jenkin with the fast-written topical political satires *A Very Open Prison* (*Screen Two*, BBC2, 26 March 1995), *Lord Of Misrule* (*Screen One*, BBC1, 6 May 1996), *Crossing The Floor* (*Screen Two*, BBC2, 5 October 1996) and *Mr White Goes To Westminster* (C4, 30 December 1997).

Duet

USA · FOX (PARAMOUNT/UBU PRODUCTIONS) · SITCOM

78 × 30 mins · colour

US dates: 19 Apr 1987–20 Aug 1989
UK dates: 29 Jan–3 Sep 1991 (31 episodes) C4 Tue 6pm

MAIN CAST

Ben Coleman	Matthew Laurance
Laura Kelly	Mary Page Keller
Richard Phillips	Chris Lemmon
Linda Phillips	Alison LaPlaca
Geneva	Arleen Sorkin
Jane Kelly	Jodi Thelen

CREDITS

writers Charlene Seeger, Susan Seeger, Ruth Bennett, Russell Marcus and others · *directors* Arlene Sanford, David Steinberg and others · *producers* Susan Seeger, Ruth Bennett

A low-key romantic comedy charting the love paths of two couples: Ben and Laura, and Richard and Linda. The first meet in episode one and through the run of the series move from a casual relationship to a more intense affair and, ultimately, a bumpy marriage. Richard and Linda Phillips are stereotypical 1980s yuppies obsessed with material objects and financial success – they provide the light relief to Ben and Laura's more downbeat interludes. Stealing many moments was the Phillips' sexy and insolent maid Geneva, who possessed a fine line in withering put-downs.

As Ben and Laura's relationship developed so did the storylines. Ben realised his dream to become a published writer of mystery stories; Linda, fired from her executive position at World Wide Studios, joined Laura and her sister Jane in their catering business; and Richard and Linda had a baby, Amanda. The stories began to centre more on Richard and Linda, and indeed Linda became the focus of a spin-off series, *Open House* (Fox 1989–90, never screened in the UK), in which she and Laura (now divorced) worked for a real-estate company, selling expensive pads in Los Angeles.

Dunrulin'

UK · BBC (JON BLAIR FILM COMPANY) · SATIRE

1 × 30 mins · colour

23 Dec 1990 · BBC1 Sun 10.05pm

MAIN CAST

Margaret Thatcher	Angela Thorne
Denis Thatcher	John Wells
Mark Thatcher	Owen Brenman
Carol Thatcher	Hilary Gish
Kneecap	Kenneth Cranham
Mrs Trodd	Liz Smith
Vicar	John Cater

CREDITS

writers Alistair Beaton/John Wells · *director* Richard Boden · *producer* Jon Blair

A one-off satire set in Dulwich, south-east London, in the future, looking back at how Margaret Thatcher – recently deposed as Prime Minister – may have spent her twilight years. Thorne and Wells re-created their roles from Wells' play *Anyone For Denis* which had enjoyed a successful stage run during the Thatcher years.

See also *Mrs Wilson's Diary*, *Grubstreet*, *Private Eye TV* and the *Send Her Victorious* playlet in *About Face*.

The Dustbinmen

UK · ITV (GRANADA) · SITCOM

22 episodes (14×30 mins · colour; 6×30 mins · b/w; 1×90 mins · b/w; 1×short special · colour)

Pilot (90 mins · b/w) *There's A Hole In Your Dustbin, Delilah* 30 Sep 1968 · Mon 8.30pm

Series One (6×30 mins · b/w) 23 Sep–28 Oct 1969 · Tue 8.30pm

Short special (colour) · part of *All-Star Comedy Carnival* 25 Dec 1969 · Thu 6pm

Series Two (7×30 mins · colour) 24 Mar–5 May 1970 · Tue 8.30pm

Series Three (7×30 mins · colour) 20 July–31 Aug 1970 · Mon 9.30pm

MAIN CAST

Cheese and Egg ··· Jack MacGowran (pilot);
················· Bryan Pringle (series)
Smellie Ibbotson ··········· John Barrett
Winston Platt ········· Graham Haberfield
Heavy Breathing ···· Harold Innocent (pilot);
················· Trevor Bannister (series)
Eric ··············· Henry Livings (pilot);
················· Tim Wylton (series)
Bloody Delilah ······· Frank Windsor (pilot);
················· John Woodvine (series 1);
················· Brian Wilde (series 2 & 3)

CREDITS

writers Jack Rosenthal (pilot, special, series 1 & 2), Dave Freeman (2 episodes), Adele Rose (1), David Hodson (1), Jim Andrew (1), Kenneth Cope (1), John Antrobus (1) · *directors* Michael Apted (pilot), Les Chatfield (series 1–3), Dick Everitt (special) · *producers* John Finch (pilot), Jack Rosenthal (series 1), Dick Everitt (special, series 2 & 3)

In the battle to introduce a grittier, more realistic edge to sitcoms, *The Dustbinmen* was pitched right in there with the best of them: although not as controversial as *Till Death Us Do Part* – which mixed bad language with racism – Jack Rosenthal's series about refuse-collectors was certainly earthy, provoking the ire of the clean-up TV campaigners and, inevitably, proving very popular with viewers at home. It was so well liked, indeed, that every episode in the first series of six went to the top of the ratings – the first time this had happened – although the fact that there had been a refuse-collecting strike the same year was a help: clearly, the topic was on everyone's mind.

The Dustbinmen started out as a play, screened a year before the first series and written for a seven-week run of single dramas broadcast by Granada under the generic title *The System*. Jack Rosenthal drew his characters from real-life refuse-collectors he had met while out and about conducting research, and he set his play in the Lancashire

coastal town of Fylde, near Blackpool. The foul-mouthed, beret-wearing Cheese and Egg – so nicknamed because CE were his initials, and also, incongruously, those of the Church of England – was the foreman and acknowledged 'leader of the gang', respected by the others for his brains. Joining him *à la cart* were Heavy Breathing (so named because he believed he had a way with women), Eric (a dim-wit), Smellie (so named because he stank) and Winston (an ardent Manchester City supporter). They could barely stand the sight (or smell) of each other but their common enemy was the Corporation Cleansing Department, and in particular its new inspector, whom they nicknamed Bloody Delilah. (In the pilot this part was played by Frank Windsor; in the first series it was another *Z Cars* star, John Woodvine.) Driving around in their dustcart, which they named Thunderbird 3, the collectors flouted every rule, shirked work whenever possible, and discussed (usually disparagingly) local residents by their address or some other recognisable feature, hence 'Mrs 23 Valetta Street', 'Mrs 14b Kimberley Terrace', 'Mrs 24 The Alley' or 'Mrs Manchester United'.

Jack Rosenthal began to withdraw from *The Dustbinmen* part-way through its short life. Having written and produced the initial series he dropped first the production role and then the writing so that, by the final series, he no longer had any involvement in his creation, preferring, instead, to work on his next sitcom, *The Lovers* (which starred Paula Wilcox, who made two appearances in *The Dustbinmen* as Naomi, Winston's girlfriend). Julie Goodyear, of *Coronation Street* fame, also appeared in a pair of episodes. Years later, in 1985, Rosenthal wrote *The Chain*, a film about people moving house, which led to *Moving Story*, a fine ITV light-drama series on the same theme (six episodes – Rosenthal wrote the first three – from 26 May to 7 July 1994; seven more from 18 July to 29 August 1995). *Moving Story* displayed numerous similarities to *The Dustbinmen* – notably the idea of a group of men in a van, enjoying a strange brotherhood and mixing with strangers. Bryan Pringle even guest-starred in one episode. Unrelated is a BBC1 drama about refuse collectors, *Common As Muck* (series in 1994 and 1997).

Dusty's Trail

USA · SYNDICATION (METROMEDIA) · SITCOM

26×30 mins · colour

US dates: autumn 1973

UK dates: 23 July 1974–14 May 1975 (26 episodes) ITV Tue then Wed 5.20pm

MAIN CAST

Dusty ··················· Bob Denver
Mr Callahan ············· Forrest Tucker
Carter Brookhaven ·········· Ivor Francis
Daphne Brookhaven ·········· Lynn Wood
Lulu McQueen ··········· Jeannine Riley
Betsy ················· Lori Saunders
Andy ···················· Bill Cort

CREDITS

creator/executive producer Sherwood Schwartz · *producer* Elroy Schwartz

A US sitcom that, many Americans feel, was inflicted mercilessly upon them, and which, voting with their 'off' buttons, they quickly dismissed from their screens. Here in Britain, London-ITV opted to transmit the entire run of 26 episodes *and* screen some selected repeats – albeit in children's scheduling.

The series' premise was not complicated: creator Sherwood Schwartz had previously presented to Americans the sap sitcom ***Gilligan's Island***, reviled at first but, mysteriously, a cult in re-runs. In this, a group of people out on a pleasure cruise were shipwrecked on to a tiny isle. *Dusty's Trail* repeated the same formula but was set in the wild west of the 1880s, with a wagon train replacing the boat. The main star, Bob Denver, was back again, and his character, the dunce-headed Dusty, was a clone of his earlier Gilligan persona. Virtually all the other roles were mirror-images of *Gilligan* characters too.

But although American audiences were fooled once, they weren't going to fall for it again.

Duty Free

UK · ITV (YORKSHIRE) · SITCOM

22 episodes (21×30 mins · 1×60 mins) · colour

Series One (7×30 mins) 13 Feb–26 Mar 1984 · Mon 8pm

Series Two (7×30 mins) 6 Sep–18 Oct 1984 · Thu mostly 8pm

Series Three (7×30 mins) 8 Jan–19 Feb 1986 · Wed 8pm

Special (60 mins) *A Duty Free Christmas* 25 Dec 1986 · Thu 9pm

MAIN CAST

David Pearce ·············· Keith Barron
Amy Pearce ··············· Gwen Taylor
Linda Cochran ······ Joanna Van Gyseghem
Robert Cochran ············· Neil Stacy
Waiter ················ Carlos Douglas
Hotel manager ······· Bunny May (series 1);
·········· George Camiller (series 2 & 3)

OTHER APPEARANCES

George ··········· Ray Mort (series 1 & 2)
Zimmerman ········ Hugo Bower (series 1)

CREDITS

writers Eric Chappell/Jean Warr · *directors* Vernon Lawrence (series 1 & 2), Les Chatfield (series 3 & special) · *producer* Vernon Lawrence

Strangers beforehand, two couples meet in a Spanish hotel and a relationship instantly transpires between the husband of one marriage and the wife of the other. Episodes reflected their desire to get things together while the spouses tried their all to keep them apart.

One of the better ITV sitcoms – one episode even beat the soaps to top the ratings – *Duty Free* was a broad English comedy that combined witty lines with a strong sense of theatrical farce of the Brian Rix variety, and was yet another triumph for Eric Chappell (following **Rising Damp, Only When I Laugh, The Bounder** and other hits). In this instance, Chappell shared the writing credit with Jean Warr, his long-time assistant now extending herself into a more pro-active involvement, with his encouragement. (They wrote together again in 1988 – see **Singles**.) As *Rising Damp* had started life as the stage-play *The Banana Box*, so *Duty Free* too began in the theatre. Although unsuccessful in this mode, Yorkshire TV producer Vernon Lawrence saw enough promise in the writing and plot lines to suggest it be transferred into a seven-episode TV series, the rest following from there. Once established on the small-screen, *Duty Free* then returned to the theatre where it enjoyed greater fortunes.

Although all four leading parts in *Duty Free* had plenty of bite, Keith Barron was the main star. As David Pearce, he has just been laid off from his job as a draughtsman, and decides to blow some of his redundancy money on a holiday to the Costa del Sol. Never having vacationed abroad before, he has a romantic notion of foreign climes and a determination to enjoy it to the hilt. His wife, Amy, is mistrusting of her David – rightly, as it quickly turns out – and unimpressed by his glib tongue. Also ensconced at the San Remo Hotel in Marbella are the Cochrans: the staid Robert, a successful businessman whose jingoistic beliefs have formed in him a distinct dislike for all foreigners, and his more passionate, vivacious wife Linda, whose natural temperament has been blunted by years of an inadequate marriage. David and Linda immediately fall for one another, each representing to the other a welcome deviation from their dull married partners. Before long they're diving under beds, hiding in wardrobes, disguising themselves and meeting incognito in order to explore their feelings for one another, usually under the watchful gaze of the hotel waiter, whose natural inclination was to write off the whole lot of them – and everyone else dwelling in their home country – as 'crazee Engliishh'.

The first series of seven episodes of *Duty Free* reflected each day in the first week of the fortnight the couples had booked in the hotel. The second series took care, again in daily chunks, of the remaining seven days. The third series was set some 18 months later, wherein David and Linda's attempted private rendezvous, a flimsy fabric built upon David's lies to his wife, comes crashing down when Amy and also Robert arrive at the hotel, again denying the couple the intimacy they crave.

Chappell and Warr determined not to write any more episodes after the third series but Yorkshire tempted them into one final fling, offering an hour-length Christmas Day peak-time slot and bigger production budget as inducement. For the first time, the cast and crew actually went to Spain to film on location (except Gwen Taylor who, owing to a theatrical engagement, had to tape her contributions in London). Previously, everything had been taped in Yorkshire TV's Leeds studio, disappointing those viewers who, assuming it was made in Marbella, had requested details of the hotel. At last, then, if even they couldn't quite smell the Sangria, loyal viewers got to see the sea and sand.

Dweebs

USA · CBS (PETER NOAH PRODUCTIONS/ WARNER BROS) · SITCOM

10 × 30 mins · colour

US dates: 22 Sep–3 Nov 1995 (7 episodes)

UK dates: 29 June–31 Aug 1996 (10 episodes)
C4 Sat around 3.15am

MAIN CAST

Carey Garrett	Farrah Forke
Warren Mosby	Peter Scolari
Vic	Corey Feldman
Morley	David Kaufman
Todd	Adam Biesk
Noreen	Holly Folger
Karl	Stephen Tobolowsky

CREDITS

creator Peter Noah · *writers* various · *director* Pamela Fryman · *producers* Bill Barol, Pamela Grant

When beautiful Carey Garrett takes up the job of office manager at Cyberbyte Software she is determined to befriend her all-male staff of dysfunctional techno-nerds. Although they are all bona-fide geniuses (except for the office boy, Todd) they have no social skills, and experience great difficulty in forming friendships, especially with women. The series followed Carey's attempts to entice the men out of their shells and into the real world.

The simplistic stereotyping of *Dweebs* (all the men were like grown-up classroom swots) may have made for easy laughs but it seriously limited the scope of the show. There was no real depth of characterisation: all the men behaved like social losers, and although each had his own particular idiosyncrasies – Warren was inarticulate, Morley was strange, Vic was wild – collectively they were as one. The trendy settings – high-tech office, internet café – also somehow undermined the old-fashioned nature of the show, with its moral espousing that 'nerds are people too'. While it served up plenty of bytes, indeed, it sorely lacked bite. CBS deleted the show after just seven episodes.

The Eamonn Andrews Show

UK · BBC · SKETCH

5 × 60 mins · b/w

29 Dec 1956–20 Apr 1957 · Sat 8.30pm

MAIN CAST
Eamonn Andrews

CREDITS
writers Sid Green/Dick Hills · *producer* Ernest Maxin

Presented under the *Saturday Comedy Hour* banner, this was a comedy-variety series for the genial Andrews – the well-known sports broadcaster and panel-game chairman. He was aided each week by numerous guest stars, including Spike Milligan (who appeared in three of the shows) and Warren Mitchell (two).

Andrews' broadcasting career was extensive, spanning four decades, and the title *The Eamonn Andrews Show* was used again and again in later years, notably when he hosted his own late-night ITV chat-show in the 1960s. Although such programmes sometimes included a comedic element, this 1956–57 BBC series was Andrews' only comedy show – *per se.*

Early To Braden

UK · BBC · SKETCH

19 × 30 mins · b/w

Series One (12) 11 July–26 Sep 1957 · Thu 11pm

Series Two (7) 1 Jan–26 Mar 1958 · fortnightly Wed 11.15pm

MAIN CAST
Bernard Braden
Stanley Unwin

CREDITS
writers Bernard Braden, Frank Muir/Denis Norden, Ray Galton/Alan Simpson, Bob Monkhouse/Denis Goodwin, John Antrobus, Dave Freeman, Eric Merriman, Johnny Speight, Maurice Wiltshire and others · *producer* Philip Barker

Almost every major comedy-writer in the country worked on this sketch series, which was designed with that premise in mind. A

Canadian in Britain, Bernard Braden was very popular on BBC radio at this time, and a familiar TV face on both the BBC and ITV. Also appearing in these programmes was Stanley Unwin, the acknowledged master of gobbledygook-speak.

See also *B-And-B, Barbara With Braden, Bath-Night With Braden, An Evening At Home With Bernard Braden And Barbara Kelly* and *Kaleidoscope.*

East End – West End

UK · ITV (ASSOCIATED-REDIFFUSION) · SITCOM

6 × 30 mins · b/w

4 Feb–11 Mar 1958 · Tue mostly 8.30pm

MAIN CAST
Sidney James
Miriam Karlin

CREDITS
writer Wolf Mankowitz · *director* Peter Croft

Familiar to – and indeed loved by – radio listeners and TV viewers for his scamp roles in the *Hancock's Half-Hour* comedies, Sid James was cast in the lead role in this six-part sitcom. It was the first time he had starred, but at least the role was familiar: he played Sid, an honest (well, hones*tish*) Cockney trying to eke a living where he could, dealing, dodging, ducking and diving in and out of situations, any which way, in order to bring home 'the lolly'. Miriam Karlin provided some regular support and there were fleeting appearances by the likes of Sydney Tafler, Raymond Huntley, Bonar Colleano, Alfie Bass and others of that ilk.

East Of Howerd

see HOWERD, Frankie

East Of Sweden

see The Montreux Festival

Easy Street

USA · NBC (VIACOM PRODUCTIONS) · SITCOM

22 × 30 mins · colour

US dates: 13 Sep 1986–27 May 1987

UK dates: 15 Jan–27 Aug 1989 (17 episodes) ITV mostly Sun around 3.30am

MAIN CAST
L K McGuire · · · · · · · · · · · · · Loni Anderson
Alvin 'Bully' Stevenson · · · · · · · · Jack Elam
Ricardo Williams · · · · · · · · · · · · Lee Weaver
Eleanor Standard · · · · · · · · · · · · Dana Ivey
Quentin Standard · · · · · · · James Cromwell

CREDITS
creator Hugh Wilson · *writers* Andy Borowitz, Sheldon Bull, David Chambers, Janis E Hirsch, Bruce R Rasmussen, Mike Scott, Max D Tash, Hugh Wilson · *directors* various · *producer* Hugh Wilson

A late-night ITV schedule-filler starring Loni Anderson, who, as the blonde-bombshell receptionist Jennifer Marlowe, was one of the stars of *WKRP In Cincinnati.* Like that series, *Easy Street* was a Hugh Wilson creation, and again he cast Anderson as a deceptively wealthy character, L K McGuire, now a former Las Vegas showgirl who has married a rich casino-owning playboy named Ned. When, soon afterwards, Ned is killed in a plane crash she inherits both his fortune and Beverly Hills mansion, the point at which the first episode begins. To deliberately annoy both her late husband's snooty sister Eleanor and her hen pecked writer husband James – who live on, and share in, the estate – L K invites her old, scruffy, stony broke and hitherto suicidal Uncle Bully, and his black friend Ricardo, to quit their less then salubrious Los Angeles retirement home and move into the mansion, where they perpetually disgust snobbish Eleanor with their gross behaviour. (The modern-day British equivalent would pitch Harry Enfield's Old Gits into a house with Hyacinth Bucket.) When, after 22 episodes, every possible laugh had been wrung out of the situation, the series was cancelled.

Eddie In August

see HILL, Benny

Edinburgh Comedy

UK · BBC · STANDUP

1 × 45 mins · colour

16 Aug 1996 · BBC2 Fri 11.15pm

MAIN CAST
various

CREDITS
producer Archie Lauchlan

A look at the new comedy talent hoping to entertain and attain fame at the 1996 Edinburgh Festival Fringe. The show was hosted by Emma Freud and Jack Docherty.

Note. A previous programme with this title (BBC2, 28 August 1994) was a documentary that followed the judging and selection procedure of the 1994 Perrier Award, the coveted prize presented each year to the best comedy performer at the Fringe.

Edinburgh Comedy With Mark Lamarr

UK · BBC · STANDUP

3 × 40 mins · colour

15 Aug–29 Aug 1997 · BBC2 Fri 11.15pm

MAIN CAST
host · Mark Lamarr

CREDITS
writers various · *producer* Ron Bain

The 1997 look at the comedy talent on view at the Edinburgh Festival Fringe. Comedian Mark Lamarr introduced the acts – David Baddiel, Dylan Moran, Milton Jones and others.

Note. In addition to these three shows there were five others, *Edinburgh Nights With Mark Lamarr*, which looked at the broader range of entertainment mounted at the Festival. These were screened by BBC2 from 11 to 28 August 1997.

Edinburgh Live

UK · C4 (GRANADA) · STANDUP
2 editions (1 × 90 mins · 1 × 60 mins) · colour
24 Aug 1990 · Fri 11pm (90 mins)
23 Aug 1991 · Fri 11.20pm (60 mins)

MAIN CAST
see below

CREDITS
writers various · *director* Robert Khododad · *executive producer* David Liddiment (show 1) · *producers* Mark Robson (show 1), Brian Park (show 2)

ITV and the BBC have screened many programmes looking at the Edinburgh Festival and its Fringe, but such shows have rarely concentrated on comedy, offering instead an overview of *all* the various entertainments on offer at the annual arts event in the Scottish capital: dramas, musical performances, acrobatics, monologues and comedy. But in the 1990s the comedy side of the Fringe became increasingly important, especially to TV companies keen to spot fresh talent from the standup artists and Perrier Award nominees. Thus, these two C4 shows favoured a comedy bias (and for that reason are included here), featuring, among others, the nominees for the prized Perrier Award, which in 1990 included Sean Hughes (winner) and Dillie Keane; and in 1991 Frank Skinner (winner), Eddie Izzard, Bruce Morton and Jack Dee (who hosted the second of these shows).

Comedians Morwenna Banks and Kate Copstick also reported from the festival in 1990 (looking at all its aspects rather than concentrating on comedy) in their three-part series *Banks And Copstick At The Festival* (ITV, 21 August–4 September), and *The Best Of Edinburgh* (ITV, 30 August 1991) did likewise. In 1993, ITV did a similar job with *Julian Clary Presents The Best Of Edinburgh* (5 September).

BBC2's annual thrice-weekly festival reports *Edinburgh Nights* covered all the artistic activities on offer, but of particular comedy interest was the edition of 28 August 1992 which featured a performance by Louise Rennison of her marvellous comic monologue *Stevie Wonder Felt My Face.*

See also the previous entry.

Educated Evans

UK · BBC · SITCOM
23 × 30 mins · b/w
Series One (12) 2 Oct–18 Dec 1957 · Wed 8pm
Series Two (11) 8 Apr–24 June 1958 · Tue 7.30pm

MAIN CAST
'Educated' Evans · · ·· · · · · · · Charlie Chester
Det-Sgt Miller · · · · · · · · · · · · · Jack Melford
Emma Toggs · · · · · · · · · · · · · Patricia Hayes
Inspector Pine · · · · · · · · · · · · · Keith Pyott
Gertrude, the barmaid · · · · · · · Myrtle Reed
Man in pub · · · · · · · · · · · · Michael Balfour
Mrs Wilkes · · · · · · · · · · · · · · · Mai Bacon
Mrs Bolton · · · · · · · · · · · Dorothy Summers

CREDITS
creator Edgar Wallace · *writers* Sidney Nelson/ Maurice Harrison · *additional material* Bernard Botting/Charlie Hart · *producer* Eric Fawcett

Edgar Wallace's famous cockney horse-racing tipster 'Educated' Evans had been played on film by Max Miller in a 1936 feature film of that title. Here, another comedian, Charlie Chester (whose stage act and presentation was so similar that Miller had once taken legal action), brought the cheerful cove to TV for two series of comedic adventures in which he ducked and dived through the pubs, streets and law courts of London, pursued by Detective-Sergeant Miller, who himself was not averse to a wager on the nag's head.

Educating Archie

UK · ITV (ASSOCIATED-REDIFFUSION) · SITCOM
27 × 30 mins · b/w
Series One (13) 26 Sep 1958–20 Feb 1959 · fortnightly Fri 6.10pm
Series Two (14) 18 Sep–25 Dec 1959 · Fri 6.30pm

MAIN CAST
Peter Brough
Irene Handl
Dick Emery
Freddie Sales

OTHER APPEARANCES
Sheena Marshe
Ray Barrett
Peter Stanwick

CREDITS
writers Marty Feldman/Ronald Chesney (7), Marty Feldman/Barry Pevan (6), Marty Feldman/Ronald Wolfe (4), Marty Feldman/Ronald Wolfe/Ronald Chesney (8), Ronald Wolfe/Ronald Chesney (1), Ronald Chesney (1) · *directors* Christopher Hodson (21), Bill Turner (5), Pat Baker (1)

A BBC radio star since 1944, with his own series from 1948 to 1960, dummy Archie Andrews and his ventriloquist master Peter Brough first transferred to TV in 1956 with the live BBC programme **Here's Archie**. Two years later, ITV screened two full series of *Educating Archie* – the title of the many radio series – in which Archie was seen to

move not only his 'licks' but also, for the first time, his 'gody'. The technology which permitted this breakthrough was perfected in writer Ronald Chesney's workshop, at his house in Kingston upon Thames, and the programmes were filmed, each taking two weeks to produce. (Accordingly, the first series was screened fortnightly; but as the second went out weekly the production techniques must have been speeded up by then.)

Aiding the scamp schoolboy puppet in the series, in addition to Brough, were regulars Irene Handl (as the housekeeper Mrs Twissle), Dick Emery (doubling as the gardener and the versatile opportunist Mr Monty) and Freddie Sales (as the sponging lodger). The Jayne Mansfield lookalike Sheena Marshe also appeared, as did Ray Barrett and Peter Stanwick. Marty Feldman was involved in the writing of all but two of the episodes.

Archie was laid to rest in 1961 when, following the death of his father Arthur, also a ventriloquist, Peter Brough quit to take over his family's textile and menswear business. The dummy was still revived for occasional TV appearances, however.

Educating Marmalade

UK · ITV (THAMES) · CHILDREN'S SITCOM
21 episodes (10 × 20 mins · 10 × 15 mins · 1 × 30 mins) · colour
Pilot (30 mins) *Marmalade Atkins In Space* 2 Nov 1981 · Mon 4.45pm
Series One (10 × 20 mins) *Educating Marmalade* 25 Oct 1982–3 Jan 1983 · Mon 4.55pm
Series Two (10 × 15 mins) *Danger – Marmalade At Work* 20 Feb–30 Apr 1984 · Mon 4.45pm

MAIN CAST
Marmalade Atkins · · · · · · Charlotte Coleman
Mr Atkins · · · · · · · · · · · · · · · · · · · John Bird
Mrs Atkins · · · · · · · · · · · · · Lynda Marchal
· (pilot & series 1);
· · · · · · · · · · · · · · Carol Macready (series 2)
Mrs Allgood · · Gillian Raine (pilot & series 1)
Wendy Wooley · · · · · · · · Elizabeth Estensen
· (series 2)

OTHER APPEARANCES
Dr Glenfiddick · · · · · · John Fortune (series 1)

CREDITS
writer Andrew Davies · *directors* Colin Bucksey (pilot & 5 episodes in series 1), John Stroud (5 episodes in series 1), Peter Duguid (series 2) · *executive producer* Pamela Lonsdale · *producers* Sue Birtwistle (pilot & series 1), Marjorie Sigley (series 2)

Teenage actress Charlotte Coleman was the star of this enduring children's sitcom, and it was a good thing for her that the character did not stick, for Marmalade Atkins must rank as the most ghastly female ever born, labelled within the series, quite appropriately, 'the worst girl in the world'. Coming across as a feminine blend of Jennings and the Devil, the first programme (a pilot, in effect, especially commissioned by Thames TV for its *Theatre Box* season in late 1981) and initial series portrayed Marmalade as impossible to educate. She had already been expelled from as many as ten schools, and ten more soon passed by, the result of some wheezes ingeniously invented for her by the series creator/author Andrew Davies (later to write *A Very Peculiar Practice*), pranks like supergluing a head-girl to a chair. Marmalade's behaviour caused the utmost frustration both to her parents and, in series one, the education officer Mrs Allgood – in one episode they even conspired to send Marmalade to a new school nailed inside a crate.

In the sequel, *Danger – Marmalade At Work*, viewers followed the transformation of the horrid girl into a horrid young woman, falling foul of every job that her social worker, Wendy Wooley, can get her into, among them the army, police, navy, secret service and air stewarding.

A recurring theme in the Marmalade stories was that of parodying other TV shows, hence *Cringe Hill* and *The Kids From Shame*, and also casting guest actors within type: *Z Cars* and *Softly, Softly* tough 'tec Stratford Johns appeared as Chief-Superintendent Thumper and Windsor Davies, the barking officer in *It Ain't Half Hot Mum*, was cast as an army sergeant major.

The Eggheads

UK · BBC · SITCOM

7 × 25 mins · b/w

6 July–18 Aug 1961 · Thu 7.55pm then Fri around 10pm

MAIN CAST

Bryan · · · · · · · · · · · · · · · · · Bryan Blackburn
Peter · · · · · · · · · · · · · · · · · · Peter Reeves
Bob · · · · · · · · · · · · · · · · · · Robert Jackson
Vivien · · · · · · · · · · · · · · · · · · Vivien Grant

CREDITS

writers Richard Waring/David Croft (2), Richard Waring (2), David Croft (1), John Law (1), Brad Ashton (1) · director Vere Lorrimer · producer David Croft

Seven depictions of student life, set in a mixed-sex London flat-share and based on the premise that a student's life is one long round of parties and visits to coffee bars with only an occasional exam to spoil the festivities – a popular conception among non-students of the time … and probably still.

81 Take 2

UK · BBC · STANDUP/SKETCH

1 × 35 mins · colour

31 Dec 1981 · BBC1 Thu 11.20pm

MAIN CAST

John Bett
Ron Bain

Robbie Coltrane
Celia Imrie
Rik Mayall
Chic Murray
The Hee Bee Gee Bees

CREDITS

writers various · director Rod Natkiel · producer Sean Hardie

A New Year's Eve show from BBC Scotland (networked throughout the UK) featuring an irreverent collection of sketches, one-liners, songs and monologues that looked back at 1981. Most of the acts had Scottish connections.

The Hee Bee Gee Bees were a spoof music group who performed a devastatingly wicked pastiche of the Bee Gees, the trio comprising Angus Deayton, Phil Pope and Michael Fenton Stevens. They were first heard in the hit BBC Radio 4 comedy series *Radio Active* (which transferred to TV as *KYTV*).

Einfach Lächerlich

see The Montreux Festival

Eisenhower And Lutz

USA · CBS (MTM ENTERPRISES) · SITCOM

13 × 30 mins · colour

US dates: 14 Mar–20 June 1988

UK dates: 29 Sep–22 Dec 1989 (13 episodes) C4 Fri 5pm

MAIN CAST

Barnett 'Bud' Lutz Jr · · · · · · · · Scott Bakula
Kay Dunne · · · · · · · · · · Patricia Richardson
Barnett 'Big Bud' Lutz · · Henderson Forsythe
Megan O'Malley · · · · · · · DeLane Matthews
Millie Zamora · · · · · · · · · · · · · Rose Portillo
Dottie · · · · · · · · · · · · · · · · · Rebecca Schull
Dwayne Spitler · · · · · · · · · · · · · · Leo Geter

CREDITS

creator Allan Burns · writers James L Brooks/Allan Burns, Mark T Egan/Mark Solomon, Gina Fredrica Goldman, David Nichols, Burt Prelutsky, Dava Savel, Dan Wilcox, Shelley F Zellman · directors various · executive producers Allan Burns, Dan Wilcox · producers Mark T Egan/Mark Solomon, Gareth Davies

Enterprising young attorney Barnett 'Bud' Lutz Jr is the sole proprietor of Eisenhower And Lutz, a law firm based in Palm Springs, California. There is no Eisenhower – at his sign-artist father's suggestion, Lutz has merely added the name of the former US president because it sounds impressive and looks good on the stationery. Lutz, in all cases, is a man who chances his arm, indeed he only secured the capital for his business by winning $5000 in a Las Vegas casino while celebrating his graduation from that city's School of Law and Acupuncture. Now that he's in business, Lutz opens premises in a mini-mall adjacent to a famous accident black spot, hoping for plenty of walk-in clients. He

has a girlfriend, Megan O'Malley, but still hankers after an old flame from his schooldays, Kay Dunne, partner in the rival law firm of Griffith, McKendrick and Dunne. Keen to boost his business, Lutz is willing to shove O'Malley out of the way in favour of Dunne, but in attempting to do so he usually ends up the loser, and Megan, inexplicably, stays with her man.

Eisenhower And Lutz was made in the year that Mary Tyler Moore's company MTM was bought by the British ITV franchisee TVS, a move that ultimately resulted in dire consequences for the UK broadcaster. The series ought to have fared better – considering the involvement of James L Brooks and Allan Burns, whose joint CV includes such stellar TV series as *The Mary Tyler Moore Show*, *Rhoda*, *Lou Grant* and *Taxi* – but the prospect of growth that would make *Eisenhower And Lutz* into a long-running sitcom was not apparent and CBS cancelled the run after 13 episodes.

Elayne Boosler: Party Of One

USA · SHOWTIME (BROOKLYN PRODUCTIONS) · STANDUP

1 × 70 mins · colour

US date: 7 Oct 1986

UK date: 3 June 1989 · C4 Sat 10.55pm

MAIN CAST

Elayne Boosler
Bill Cosby
David Letterman

CREDITS

writer Elayne Boosler · director Steve Gerbson · producers Elayne Boosler, Steve Gerbson

A one-off special for the talented US comic, born on 18 August 1952 in Brooklyn, New York. Boosler graduated from being a hostess at the Improv in Manhattan to singing between the comedy acts and then becoming a standup star herself. She specialises in observational humour and the retelling of bizarre incidents from her life. Topics covered in this special – taped at the Bottom Line club in New York – included dating, unemployment, construction workers, and life as a single woman.

Elayne Boosler – Broadway Baby

USA · SHOWTIME (BROOKLYN PRODUCTIONS) · STANDUP

1 × 70 mins · colour

US date: 11 Sep 1987

UK date: 25 Jan 1992 · C4 Sat 10.30pm

MAIN CAST

Elayne Boosler

CREDITS

writer Elayne Boosler · director/producer Steve Gerbson

A second standup special for Boosler, recorded at the Ritz Theater on Broadway. Her subjects this time included pets, politicians, mothers, shopping and condoms.

The Election Night Armistice

see Saturday Night Armistice

Elementary, My Dear Watson

UK · BBC · SITCOM

1 × 30 mins · colour
18 Jan 1973 · BBC1 Thu 8pm

MAIN CAST
Sherlock Holmes · · · · · · · · · · · John Cleese
Dr Watson · · · · · · · · · · · · William Rushton
Lady Cynthia · · · · · · · · · · Josephine Tewson
Inspector Street · · · · · · · · · · · · Norman Bird
Constable · · · · · · · · · · · · · · · Chic Murray
Frank Potter · · · · · · · · · · · · · Bill Maynard
Fu Manchu · · · · · · · · · · · · · · · Larry Martyn

CREDITS
writer N F Simpson · *director* Harold Snoad · *producer* Barry Took

Aired as a one-off *Comedy Playhouse*, this surreal spin on Sherlock Holmes starred John Cleese as the great detective and Willie Rushton as his sidekick, Dr Watson. A fantastically involved plot featured the mystery of a roomful of dead solicitors, Fu Manchu's plans for world domination and a dodgy female impersonator, Frank Potter (played by Bill Maynard). Cleese delivered his customary hilarious performance but was merely a passenger on a runaway half-hour that not only went off the rails but ploughed headlong through various fields and genres. Weird event after weird event was thrown into the mix, like lumps of coal flung on to an already overheated boiler, propelling the vehicle ever faster and further off-course until it finally careered through the walls of television itself when one of the dead solicitors, slumped over his desk with a knife protruding from his back, turned up as 'Mystery Object Of The Week' on the BBC2 panel-game *Call My Bluff* (hence there were guest appearances by Robert Robinson, Frank Muir, Dawn Addams, Alan Coren, Patrick Campbell, Morag Hood and John Carson).

No series followed but Cleese returned to the role of Holmes in LWT's equally bizarre slant on the character, *The Strange Case Of The End Of Civilisation As We Know It*, a single hour-length TV movie made for the ITV company by Shearwater Productions, and screened on 18 September 1977. Written by Jack Hobbs, Joe McGrath and Cleese, produced by Humphrey Barclay and directed by Joe McGrath, the film also starred Arthur Lowe as Watson, and Connie Booth as both Mrs Hudson and a female Moriarty. Investigating the serial assassination of world

leaders, the story took place in contemporary times, the presence of a modern-day Holmes and Watson explained by making them the grandsons of the original pair.

Elephant's Eggs In A Rhubarb Tree

UK · ITV (THAMES) · CHILDREN'S SKETCH

6 × 30 mins (5 × b/w · 1 × colour)
2 Apr–7 May 1971 · Fri around 5.15pm

MAIN CAST
Richard Beckinsale
Paul Whitsun-Jones
David Rowlands
John Gould
Ann Beach

CREDITS
script editor Ian Davidson · *director* Robert Reed · *producer* Pamela Lonsdale

A weekly compilation of sketches, limericks and songs designed for 9–15-year-old viewers, and featuring a weekly cast headed by Richard Beckinsale, just beginning to achieve fame as Geoffrey in *The Lovers*. Each programme presented the works of a variety of authors, among them John Lennon, Hilaire Belloc, Ivor Cutler, Spike Milligan, Terry Jones and the *Beyond The Fringe* team.

Ellen

USA · ABC (BLACK-MARLENS COMPANY/ TOUCHSTONE TELEVISION) · SITCOM

97 episodes (96 × 30 mins · 1 × 60 mins to 31/12/97 · continuing into 1998) · colour
US dates: 29 Mar 1994 to date
UK dates: 28 Oct 1994 to date (67 × 30 mins to 31/12/97) C4 Fri then Wed 9pm, weekdays 1pm, Fridays 9.35pm

MAIN CAST
Ellen Morgan · · · · · · · · · · · Ellen DeGeneres
Holly · · · · · · · · · · · · · · · Holly Fulger (1994)
Anita · · · · · · · · · · · Maggie Wheeler (1994)
Adam Greene · · · · · · · Arye Gross (1994–95)
Joe Farrell · · · · · · · · · David Anthony Higgins
Paige Clark · · · · · · · · · · · Joely Fisher
Audrey Penney · · · · · Clea Lewis (from 1995)
Spence Kovak · · · · Jeremy Piven (from 1995)

CREDITS
creators Neal Marlens, Carol Black, David Rosenthal · *writers* various · *directors* various · *executive producers* Neal Marlens, Carol Black · *producers* David Rosenthal, Mark Grossan

This show's original title was *These Friends Of Mine* and that just about sums up the unambitious aspirations of the series. Standup comic Ellen DeGeneres had carved out a successful career with observational comedy which, unusually, *didn't* rely upon put-downs and assaults on political subjects. Hers was an essentially optimistic act, albeit quirky to the point of cute. The character she portrayed in this sitcom was very much a product of this comedy routine: an upbeat,

single career woman, with no axe to grind, but a trifle wacky.

Like *Seinfeld*, the thrust of the show was the interplay between the star and her offbeat friends. This was true character comedy – reliant not upon sharp one-liners but on the verbal meanderings of its cast. In *These Friends Of Mine*, Ellen worked in a Los Angeles book-store and literary café, Buy The Book; when the series reappeared the following season as *Ellen*, she was the owner of the establishment. (Anita and Holly were absent for the new series but Ellen's room-mate Adam remained.) Those earlier *These Friends Of Mine* episodes were repeated to introduce the new series, but this time they were screened under the *Ellen* banner, as they were when they aired in the UK. As the series developed, the principal support characters included Ellen's best friend Paige Clark, her cousin and new room-mate Spence Kovak, the so-called 'acerbic coffee count' Joe Farrell, and a friend, neighbour and employee Audrey Penney. At the end of the third US season, Buy The Book was all but destroyed in an earthquake, and in the fourth Ellen set about rebuilding her life.

Ellen proved highly popular and quickly settled down as one of a number of smart, urban-singles sitcoms (*Seinfeld*, *Friends*, *Dream On* and the like), providing plenty of laughs. But it was destined for a far greater notoriety – rumours circulated in mid-1996 that the show's producers were contemplating revealing Ellen as a lesbian, as, indeed, Ellen DeGeneres was in real life. This speculation caused a tidal-wave of interest and the issue became hotly debated. Opposition, predictably, arrived from church groups and from the moral majority, who attacked the idea as a further erosion of traditional family values. Advertisers, notoriously sensitive to such issues and easy victims for pressure groups, were also wary of the move, as was production company Touchstone Television, a subsidiary of Disney, an organisation already drawing flak from conservative groups for its new-found liberalism in the treatment of gays and other minorities. The problem was *Ellen*'s relatively high profile – while there had been recurring gay characters in previous sitcoms, here they were talking about the lead character in an 8pm series, one whom viewers had grown to love over a three-year period. Cynics declared that the move was a blatant ploy to reverse falling ratings. In reply, the producers pointed to a number of indicators about Ellen's sexuality in previous episodes, claiming that her lesbian nature had been on the agenda (albeit covertly) from the show's early days.

Amid such brouhaha, Ellen DeGeneres 'came out' in real life and then the fictional Ellen Morgan did likewise in an hour-length episode of the sitcom, screened in the USA on

30 April 1997, which topped the ratings with an audience or some 45 million Americans, and attracted huge coverage in the media. In the face of massive opposition from pressure groups, Touchstone and ABC bravely provided full support to the programme's creative team, and pro-gay groups expressed delight at finally having such a well-known TV icon to stand for them. From its humble beginnings, *Ellen* had emerged as a groundbreaking show, creating another milestone in the annals of US television.

Embassy

UK · BBC (TIGER ASPECT) · SITCOM

1 × 30 mins · colour

26 Mar 1997 · BBC2 Wed 10pm

MAIN CAST

Peter Nevin	Robert Daws
Belinda Thompson	Caroline Langrishe
Taylor Scott	Benjamin Whitrow
Señor Diace	Edward de Souza
Sarah Nevin	Candida Gubbins
Rupert Lightfoot	Robert Portal
Maria Escobar	Arancha De Juan
Señor Hernandez	Emil Wolk

CREDITS

writer Cris Cole · *director* Mark Chapman · *executive producer* Peter Bennett-Jones · *producer* Sophie Clarke-Jervoise

The pilot for a proposed series set in the British embassy in a fictitious Central American republic, Solandas. Peter Nevin is the new ambassador, whose past positions include four years in far less volatile Copenhagen. Such previous experiences have ill-prepared him for life in the powder-keg atmosphere of the sultry Solandas. At home, Peter's wife, the girlishly passionate but rather gullible Sarah, has to contend with the housekeeper Maria – a smart and devious wheeler-dealer. At work, Peter struggles to maintain the illusion of being in charge and knowing what he's doing, but it's all too obvious that he is a fish out of water, and the locals, especially Señor Diace, the Solandan government minister seemingly responsible for everything from agriculture to zoology, easily run rings around him. Chaos is prevented by the intervention of Peter's two assistants, both of whom have far greater experience of the country and its habits: Belinda Thompson, the sexy, ambitious second-in-command, and Taylor Scott, a diplomat who revels in his gayness. Rounding out the cast is the embassy dogsbody Rupert Lightfoot, a shy, nervous individual, and a shifty local handyman, Señor Hernandez (referred to by Peter as Señor Handymandez).

Embassy had only made one appearance by the end of 1997 but could be set to return for a full series, the pilot episode containing sufficiently intriguing characters and useful situations for comic exploitation. But the pilot also seemed somewhat too old-fashioned: its depiction of the Solandas as lazy, conniving and amoral people from peasant stock reeked of a 1950s British comedy film aiming for cheap laughs. With a tad more diplomacy, a decent series might ensue.

Dick Emery

Born Richard Gilbert Emery in London on 19 February 1917, Dick Emery was a 1960s and 1970s comedy giant beyond his small stature. He created a hugely successful BBC show and its gaggle of comic characters, most famously the doddery old man, Lampwick, and the peroxide blonde, Mandy, whose catchphrase 'Ooh, you are awful – but I like you' became a household expression. Although most of his characters were men, the five-times married Emery was certainly adept at portraying women.

Dick Emery was a show business natural, his parents having been the music-hall double-act Callan and Emery. During the Second World War he joined Ralph Reader's *Gang Show* and then, demobbed from the RAF, worked with the not yet famous Tony Hancock at the Windmill Theatre in London. Emery became established as a regular in the BBC radio run of *Educating Archie* from 1956 to 1958; his earliest advertised TV appearance was in *Kaleidoscope* in 1952 and then he popped up on the small-screen here, there and everywhere, most regularly in *Round The Bend* (1955–56), *Two's Company* (1956), the TV version of *Educating Archie* (1958–59) and *After Hours* (1959). But it was his posting to Granada's much-loved sitcom *The Army Game* that propelled Dick Emery several rungs up the stardom ladder, when he was added to the cast as 'Chubby' Catchpole in the programme's 1960–61 season. Soon afterwards, he was cast in *The Reunion*, a BBC *Comedy Playhouse* pilot, and it was only another year before Emery was granted his own series by the BBC. Neither he nor the Corporation could have imagined the success this would bring, nor its longevity – *The Dick Emery Show* lasted for 18 years and 166 editions and won the star countless awards and national fame. He also enjoyed a long run on BBC radio with *Emery At Large* (some editions of which were scripted by John Cleese).

Dogged by ill-health in his final years, Dick Emery died on 2 January 1983. His career was remembered in the BBC1 programme *Dick Emery – A Life On The Box*, screened on 20 August 1997.

See also *The Making Of Peregrine* and *Room At The Bottom* [1].

The Dick Emery Show

UK · BBC · SKETCH

166 editions (15 × 45 mins · 29 × 30 mins · 9 × 25 mins · 2 × short specials · b/w; 1 × 50 mins · 1 × 45 mins · 21 × 35 mins · 76 × 30 mins · 10 × 25 mins · 2 × short specials · colour)

Series One (4 × 45 mins · b/w) 13 July–24 Aug 1963 · fortnightly Sat 8.05pm

Series Two (10 × 45 mins · b/w) 6 Oct 1963–12 Apr 1964 · Mon 8.05pm

Short special (b/w) · part of *Christmas Night With The Stars* 25 Dec 1963 · Wed 8.05pm

Special (45 mins · b/w) 4 Dec 1964 · BBC1 Mon 8.05pm

Short special (b/w) · part of *Christmas Night With The Stars* 25 Dec 1964 · BBC1 Fri 7.15pm

Series Three (7 × 30 mins · b/w) 2 Oct–13 Nov 1965 · BBC2 Sat 8.45pm

Series Four (13 × 30 mins · b/w) 10 Aug–2 Nov 1966 · BBC2 Wed 8pm

Series Five (9 × 30 mins · b/w) 3 Apr–5 June 1967 · BBC2 Mon 8.05pm

Series Six (6 × 30 mins · colour) 4 Dec 1967–15 Jan 1968 · BBC2 Mon 8.05pm

Series Seven (9 × 25 mins · b/w) 7 Jan–7 Mar 1969 · BBC1 mostly Fri 7.55pm

Series Eight (10 × 25 mins · colour) 3 Apr–11 June 1970 · BBC1 Fri 8.25pm

Short special (colour) · part of *Christmas Night With The Stars* 25 Dec 1970 · BBC1 Fri 6.45pm

Series Nine (10 × 30 mins · colour) 5 Mar–7 May 1971 · BBC1 Fri 8.30pm

Short special (colour) · part of *Christmas Night With The Stars* 25 Dec 1971 · BBC1 Sat 6.40pm

Series Ten (13 × 30 mins · colour) 1 Jan–25 Mar 1972 · BBC1 Sat around 9pm

Series Eleven (11 × 30 mins · colour) 10 Mar–26 May 1973 · BBC1 Sat 8.30pm

Series Twelve (10 × 30 mins · colour) 5 Oct–14 Dec 1974 · BBC1 Sat around 8.10pm

Special (35 mins · colour) 24 Dec 1974 · BBC1 Tue 7.10pm

Series Thirteen (11 × 30 mins · colour) 30 Aug–15 Nov 1975 · BBC1 Sat around 8.35pm

Special (30 mins · colour) 24 Dec 1975 · BBC1 Tue 7.55pm

Series Fourteen (8 × 30 mins · colour) 7 Sep–26 Oct 1976 · BBC1 Tue 8pm

Series Fifteen (8 × 35 mins · colour) 3 Sep–22 Oct 1977 · BBC1 Sat 8.30pm

Special (45 mins · colour) *The Dick Emery Christmas Show: The Texan Connection* 24 Dec 1977 · BBC1 Sat 9.05pm

Series Sixteen (6 × 30 mins · colour) 17 Feb–24 Mar 1979 · BBC1 Sat 8.30pm

Series Seventeen (6 × 35 mins · colour) 5 Jan–9 Feb 1980 · BBC1 Sat 8.05pm

Special (50 mins · colour) *The Dick Emery Christmas Show: For Whom The Jingle Bells Toll* 27 Dec 1980 · BBC1 Sat 8.30pm

Series Eighteen (6 × 35 mins · colour) 3 Jan–7 Feb 1981 · BBC1 Sat 8.05pm

MAIN CAST

Dick Emery

Joan Sims (series 1 & 2)

Deryck Guyler (series 3)

Pat Coombs (series 10–12, then occasional)
Josephine Tewson (occasional)
Roy Kinnear (series 15–17 & special 6)

CREDITS
main writers David Cumming (series 1–5 & 1964 Xmas special), John Warren/John Singer (series 2–14 & 1964, 1974, 1975 specials), John Singer (series 15–17 & 1977 special), John Singer/Steven Singer (series 18 & 1980 special), Mel Brooks/Mel Tolkin (series 3), David Nobbs/Peter Tinniswood (series 3), Maurice Wiltshire (series 3 & 4), Peter Robinson/Eric Davidson (series 7 & 8) · *additional material* Dick Emery, Garry Chambers, Barry Cryer, Neville Phillips/John Jennings, Maurice Wiltshire, Dick Clement, John Esmonde/Bob Larbey, Selma Diamond, Lucille Kallen, Larry Gelbart, Lew Schwarz, Marty Feldman, Keith Waterhouse/ Willis Hall, Brad Ashton, Talbot Rothwell, Jimmy Grafton, Harold Pinter, Bryan Blackburn · *producers* David Croft (series 1, 1 edition in series 2, 1964 specials), James Gilbert (1 edition of series 2), John Street (1963 special, 8 editions of series 2), Dennis Main Wilson (series 3), Ernest Maxin (series 4–8), Colin Chapman (series 9–11), Harold Snoad (series 12–18 & 1974, 1975, 1977, 1980 specials)

A very long-running and perennially popular sketch show. Emery's flair with costume and make-up helped him put across a wealth of memorable TV characters – the man-hungry, sexually frustrated Hettie; the very forward blonde Mandy; the toothy vicar; the uncouth skin-head Bovver Boy; the excessively camp Clarence; the rocker Ton-Up Boy on his motor-bike; the ageing, breath-catching First World War veteran Lampwick, and numerous others – and these endeared him to the viewing audience and kept his show high in the ratings for nearly 20 years. The vox-pop street interviews conducted with Emery's bunch of eccentrics were developed by the writer David Cumming and they made Mandy a particular favourite, his confused but battling blonde who originally just gave stupefied looks in answer to questions but eventually, assuming a hidden double entendre, developed her own 'Ooh, you are awful' catchphrase, accompanied by an over-heavy push in the stomach – the first part of which gave Emery the title of his 1972 feature film that featured many of the TV characters.

The presence in early credits of American sketch writers (Mel Brooks, Mel Tolkin, Selma Diamond, Lucille Kallen and others) suggests that some sketch scripts were bought in from US shows, probably ones originally written for Sid Caesar. As *The Dick Emery Show* developed, however, the emphasis moved away from random sketch ideas to concentrate on Emery's cast of characters who would appear in their own segments each week. (A similar technique

was used later by Kenny Everett in his shows.) The programmes maintained a high standard throughout, thanks in no small part to Emery's surprisingly effective acting talent.

Note. Emery won his own starring series in July 1963 but he had been set to headline a very similar show a few months earlier, *A Touch Of The Sun*, announced as a fortnightly piece to run from 20 April 1963. In this, Emery's supporting cast was to have included Joan Sims, Patrick Cargill, singers Mary Millar and Gary Miller, and dancer Una Stubbs. But while listed in *Radio Times*, *A Touch Of The Sun* never materialised, although the entire cast (except Cargill) were on board for the first series of *The Dick Emery Show*.

Dick Emery's Grand Prix

UK · BBC · SITCOM/SKETCH

1 × 50 mins · colour
2 July 1970 · BBC1 Thu 9.10pm

MAIN CAST
Dick Emery
Graham Hill

CREDITS
writers Peter Buchanan, Peter Robinson, Ernest Maxin · *additional material* Dick Emery · *producer* Ernest Maxin

A one-off special set in the world of motor sport. The loose plot concerned the exploits of a wily veteran racer (Emery) as he took on modern-day drivers and machines in his vintage sports car.

The Dick Emery Comedy Hour

UK · ITV (THAMES) · SKETCH

1 × 60 mins · colour
6 June 1979 · Wed 8pm

MAIN CAST
Dick Emery
Beryl Reid
Tim Barrett

CREDITS
writers Eric Merriman, John Singer, Freddie Sales, Mike Winters · *director/producer* Keith Beckett

After 16 years on BBC this was Emery's first show for ITV, featuring all his usual characters.

The Dick Emery Special

UK · ITV (THAMES) · SKETCH

1 × 60 mins · colour
26 Dec 1979 · Wed 7.45pm

MAIN CAST
Dick Emery
Anna Dawson
Tim Barrett
Ronald Leigh-Hunt
Robert Dorning

David Rayner
John Rutland
Gemma Craven

CREDITS
writers Eric Merriman, John Singer, David Renwick · *director/producer* Keith Beckett

Emery's second hour-long special for Thames in 1979.

The Dick Emery Hour

UK · ITV (THAMES) · SKETCH

1 × 60 mins · colour
3 Dec 1980 · Wed 8pm

MAIN CAST
Dick Emery
Richard Todd
Lynda Carter
Anna Dawson
Tim Barrett
Bill Pertwee
Françoise Pascal
John Rutland

CREDITS
writers Eric Merriman, John Singer · *director/producer* Robert Reed

Another ITV special for the BBC regular. Hollywood-based British actor Richard Todd and Lynda Carter (*Wonder Woman*) guested.

Emery Presents

UK · BBC · SITCOM/SERIAL

12 episodes (6 × 35 mins · 6 × 30 mins) · colour
Series One (6 × 35 mins) *Legacy Of Murder*
16 Feb–23 Mar 1982 · BBC1 Tue 8pm
Series Two (6 × 30 mins) *Jack Of Diamonds*
3 June–15 July 1983 · BBC1 Fri 8.30pm

MAIN CAST
Bernie Weinstock · · · · · · · · · · · Dick Emery

OTHER RECURRING PARTS, SERIES ONE:
Lord Algrave/Joe Galleano/ · · · · · · · · · · · ·
Monica Danvers-Crichton/ · · · · · · · · · · · ·
Mrs Oldfield/Milkman/ · · · · · · · · · · · · · · ·
Bovver Boy/Toothy Vicar · · · · · · Dick Emery
Robin Bright · · · · · · · · · · · · · · Barry Evans
Roland Tolhurst · · · · · · · · · Richard Vernon
O'Toole · · · · · · · · · · · · · Thomas Baptiste
Marley · · · · · · · · · · · · · Michael Robbins
Thelma · · · · · · · · · · · · · Patsy Rowlands
Cousin Looby · · · · · · · · · · · · Irene Handl

OTHER RECURRING PARTS, SERIES TWO:
Caretaker/Vicar/ ·
Lady Holtye/Cyril Blackman/ · · · · · · · · · · · ·
Det Insp Dearlove/Northern · · · · · · · · · · · ·
Woman/Colonel Edgerton/ · · · · · · · · · · · · ·
Greta/General Von Klaus · · · · · Dick Emery
Norman Lugg · · · · · · · · · · · · · · Tony Selby
Reg · · · · · · · · · · · · · · · Glynn Edwards
George Billyard · · · · · · · · · James Villiers
Foxwell · · · · · · · · · · · · · · · · John Cater
Helen Carter · · · · · · · · · · · · · · Helen Gill
Sharon Finch · · · · · · · · · · · · Rosie Collins
Oliver Ottershaw · · · · Christopher Bramwell

CREDITS
writers John Singer/Steven Singer · *producers* Harold Snoad (series 1), Stuart Allen (series 2)

Comedy thrillers featuring Bernie Weinstock, the accident-prone and ultra-Jewish boss of a private detective agency, Crimebusters International. These serials, described as 'Francis Durbridge with laughs', were written by father and son team John and Steven Singer, and starred Dick Emery as Weinstock and as a bunch of other characters. Filmed on location – although studio applause was added later – the productions offered Emery a chance to stretch his talents, invent new characters and engage in less broad comedy than usual. Towards the end of its run, *The Dick Emery Show* had been featuring a good deal of location work and Emery considered it a natural step to move on to these shows, shot entirely on film. He was right, and his performances were impressive.

The first adventure, *Legacy Of Murder*, followed Weinstock and his assistant Bright's attempts to track down six people who had disappeared years earlier, with a reward of £5000 for each one found; the second series, *Jack Of Diamonds*, found Weinstock, with his new business partner Norman Lugg, on the trail of some diamonds hidden by a British soldier during the Second World War. This latter series had been scheduled to begin on 13 January 1983, but when Emery died on 2 January that year it was postponed to June as a mark of respect.

Emma Thompson: Up For Grabs

UK · C4 (LIMEHOUSE PRODUCTIONS) · SKETCH

1 × 45 mins · colour

28 Dec 1985 · Sat 12.15am

MAIN CAST
Emma Thompson
Daniel Massey
Mark Kingston
Phyllida Law
Stephen Moore

CREDITS
writer Emma Thompson · *director* John Kaye Cooper · *executive producer* Jeremy Wallington · *producer* Humphrey Barclay

A one-off C4 seasonal sketch show for the 'alternative' comedian Emma Thompson, who at this point was developing into a multi-faceted actress with her role in Stephen Fry's new version of the old comedy-musical *Me And My Girl* on the London stage.

See also *Thompson*.

Emney Enterprises

UK · BBC · SITCOM

22 × 30 mins · b/w

Special · 7 June 1954 · Mon 8.25pm
Series One (6) 20 Oct–29 Dec 1954 · fortnightly Wed 8.30pm
Special · 2 Sep 1955 · Fri 8pm
Series Two (12) 15 Sep 1955–16 Feb 1956 · fortnightly Thu mostly 7.30pm
Series Three (2) 10 & 24 Jan 1957 · fortnightly Thu 8pm

MAIN CAST
Fred Emney
Edwin Styles

CREDITS
writers Max Kester, Fred Emney · *producer* George Inns

The gruff, witty, monocle-wearing, cigar-smoking Churchill-lookalike Fred Emney appeared several times on pre-war TV, usually in sketches with Richard Hearne, but when the television service resumed after hostilities had ceased, commitments prevented him from returning to the medium until this mid-1950s series. Guest stars aiding Emney in his scripted enterprises included Deryck Guyler, Rita Webb and Kenneth Connor. Born in London on 12 February 1900, Emney made his first stage appearance at the age of 15 and became a regular both in the West End and in the USA during the succeeding decades. He died on Christmas Day 1980.

See also *The Fred Emney Show*, which continued immediately after *Emney Enterprises* closed its doors, *The Big Man* and *Fred Emney Picks A Pop*.

Emo Philips: Comedian And Mammal

UK · C4 (CONSOLIDATED PRODUCTION) · STANDUP

1 × 45 mins · colour

29 Dec 1990 · Sat 11pm

MAIN CAST
Emo Philips

CREDITS
writer Emo Philips · *producers* Juliet Blake, Trevor Hopkins

Forty-five minutes in the company of the hysterically weird American comedian Emo Philips. While his appearance and material could be unsettling, the fact that it was starched dry and laden with irony ensured plenty of laughs, and by 1990 he had acquired a considerable following in the UK. (This show was recorded at the Playhouse Theatre in London.)

Philips' stage persona was that of an awkward, dysfunctional man with a high-pitched, strangely intoned voice and a view of life reminiscent of a Charles Addams cartoon – his spiel embracing his nightmarish childhood and odd occurrences in his adult life.

Empire

USA · CBS (HUMBLE PRODUCTIONS/MGM-UA) · SITCOM

6 × 30 mins · colour

US dates: 4 Jan–1 Feb 1984

UK dates: 11 May–15 June 1984 (6 episodes) BBC2 Fri 9pm

MAIN CAST
Ben Christian · · · · · · · · · · · · Dennis Dugan
Calvin Cromwell · · · · · · · · · Patrick Macnee
Peg · · · · · · · · · · · · · · · · · · · Maureen Arthur
Jackie Willow · · · · · · · · · · · Christine Belford
Jack Willow · · · · · · · · · · · · · Richard Masur
Meredith Blake · · · · · · · · · · · · · Caren Kaye
Edward Roland · · · · · · · · · Michael McGuire
Arthur Broderick · · · · · · · · · · · Dick O'Neill
Roger Martinson · · · · · · · · · · · Howard Platt
T Howard Daniels · · · · · · · · · Edward Winter

CREDITS
writers Fred Freeman/Lawrence J Cohen, Dennis J Danziger/Ellen Sandler, George T Zateslo, Jim Geoghan · *director* Terry Hughes · *executive producers* Lawrence J Cohen, Fred Freeman · *producers* Terry Hughes, Milt Hoffman

A sophisticated six-part serialised sitcom centring on the financial wheeler-dealing of the enormous, New York-based conglomerate Empire Industries. Calvin Cromwell is the ruthless ruler of the multi-national corporation, a hard-nosed, heartless businessmen who keeps his employees in the grip of fear. Duplicity, oneupmanship and backstabbing are the order of the day among the company executives, and into this hotbed of cynicism arrives the aptly named Ben Christian, an honest, caring and moral man installed as vice-president of research and development. Christian's honesty throws the others into blind panic as they try to discover what fiendish motives he hides under his pleasant exterior. But Christian is all that he seems, a naïve among a nest of vipers.

This was a wild and extreme satire on the world of big business, spoofing the sort of boardroom battles seen in soaps like *Dallas* and *Dynasty*. Patrick Macnee was excellent as villainous Cromwell, and the cast followed his lead in gaining laughs by playing the wicked script dead straight. Financial fiddling and contractual irregularities may be par for the course in the quest for power, but in *Empire* there was even a casual murder to further a cause.

A short series perhaps, but one of some merit all the same.

The Empire Laughs Back

UK · BBC · STANDUP

1 × 40 mins · colour

11 Aug 1994 · BBC2 Thu 11.15pm

MAIN CAST
Patrick Kielty
The Hole In The Wall Gang
Jake Junior

Owen O'Neill
John Byrne
Kevin McAleer

CREDITS
writers cast · *director* Gerry Stembridge · *executive producer* Paul Evans

A one-off special – screened as part of BBC2's *25 Bloody Years* season to mark the anniversary of the 'troubles' in Northern Ireland – which reported on how standup comics in the province rise to the challenge of raising laughter in such a pressurised situation.

A club situated in the basement of an old Presbyterian church in the Botanic district of south Belfast was the venue, strategically situated a few hundred yards from the loyalist Sandy Row and nationalist Ormeau Road, both being scenes of recurring sectarian violence. For the comedians, performing the difficult-enough art of standup comedy has to be supplemented by the reading and handling of an audience whose political allegiances are uncertain. Usually the club plays host to touring comics but for this special performance the acts were all from the provinces – the programme being an important record of an intensely distressing and dangerous situation.

Note. The comedy troupe the Hole In The Wall Gang has appeared in a number of specials and series broadcast by BBC Northern Ireland, but not screened in mainland Britain. One has, however – see **Two Ceasefires And A Wedding**.

Empty Nest

USA · NBC (WITT-THOMAS-HARRIS PRODUCTIONS/TOUCHSTONE TELEVISION) · SITCOM

170 × 30 mins · colour
US dates: 8 Oct 1988–29 Apr 1995
UK dates: 18 Aug 1989–19 May 1992 (46 episodes) C4 Fri 9pm then Tue around 11.45pm

MAIN CAST
Dr Harry Weston · · · · · · · · Richard Mulligan
Barbara Weston · · · · · · · · · Kristy McNichol
· (1988–93)
Carol Weston · · · · · · · · · · · · Dinah Manoff
Nurse Laverne Todd · · · · · · · · · Park Overall
Charley Dietz · · · · · · · · · · · · · David Leisure
Patrick Arcola · · · · Paul Provenza (1992–93)
Emily Weston · · · · · · · · · Lisa Rieffel (1993)
Sophia Petrillo · · · · · Estelle Getty (1993–95)

CREDITS
creator Susan Harris · *writers* Susan Harris and others · *directors* Steve Zuckerman, Jay Sandrich and others · *executive producers* Paul Junger Witt, Tony Thomas, Susan Harris, Rod Parker, Hal Cooper, Gary Jacobs · *producers* Roger Garrett, Rob LaZebnick, David Sacks, Harold Kimmel, Gilbert Junger, Arnold H Kogen, Susan Beavers

A vehicle for **Soap** star Richard Mulligan, made for him by the creator of that series, Susan Harris, also the woman behind **The**

Golden Girls. *Empty Nest*, indeed, was closely related to this latter series – both were set in Miami Beach, and *Empty Nest* featured occasional guest appearances by the four *GG* women, in character.

Richard Mulligan's role in *Empty Nest* – that of paediatrician Harry Weston – was greatly removed from his Burt persona in *Soap*. As a widower of some 18 months at the series' start, still missing his late wife Libby, Harry found that his nest scarcely became his own before two of his three daughters moved back in after a spell living independently in the same city. His eldest child Carol (played by one of Burt's murdered step-daughters-in-law in *Soap*, Elaine) was a recent divorcee whose marital breakdown led to a nervous breakdown from which her recovery was slow and fragile. Barbara, his middle daughter, was an undercover law officer with the Miami Police Department. Both – but especially Carol – fussed around Harry when, it was clear, he wished they would leave him to get on with his life in his own way. Not that Harry wasn't a devoted father, or lacked love for his offspring, just that he had reached middle-age and wanted time to lead his busy life, socialising in the evening and working at the Community Medical Center in Miami during the daytime, where he was assisted by an acid-tongued Southern nurse, Laverne, whose awesome knowledge of medicine was text-book correct and invariably better than his own.

Various people in the series tried to get Harry hitched, and there was no shortage of women seeking to align themselves with one of the area's most eligible unmarried men. Much of the time, however, Harry was left to pour out his emotions to his only regular companion, a lazy doe-eyed giant of a dog called Dreyfuss. One person whom Harry wanted to see less of, although there was little chance of this, was Charley Dietz, his scrounging, womanising next-door neighbour, who was always letting himself into Harry's house with his key and making loose with the contents of the fridge.

A genuinely funny sitcom, *Empty Nest* ran for seven years in the USA, first scheduled on the coat-tails of *The Golden Girls* but then moving to a new slot and, ultimately, garnering the better audience ratings of the two. The cast changed little over the years, but Harry's third daughter Emily, hitherto only referred to, was brought into the series after Kristy McNichol (who played Barbara) became ill. The plots required that Harry have two daughters on the scene, not just one, so Emily was the obvious replacement. She didn't hang around long, though, and Sophia Petrillo from *The Golden Girls* became a regular in the final seasons. Harry became a grandfather in 1993 after Carol gave birth to a baby boy conceived with her boyfriend

Patrick. She then married in the final episode, Laverne also wed and Harry left Florida for a new job in Vermont.

Seventeen months before the series' premiere in the USA, NBC, following a traditional US custom, aired a pilot of *Empty Nest* as if it was an episode of *The Golden Girls*. (Screened in the UK by C4 on 5 February 1988.) In this, Paul Dooley and Rita Moreno were cast as George and Renee Corliss, the Golden Girls' next-door neighbours, a middle-aged couple who have to repair their marriage after their daughter Jenny (played by Jane Harnick) goes off to university. Of the principal cast, only David Leisure appeared in both the pilot and the full series, albeit as different characters. Beatrice Arthur, Betty White, Rue McClanahan and Estelle Getty appeared in the pilot in their *Golden Girls* roles of Dorothy, Rose, Blanche and Sophia.

End Of Part One

UK · ITV (LWT) · SITCOM

14 × 30 mins · colour
Series One (7) 15 Apr–27 May 1979 · Sun 5.30pm
Series Two (7) 12 Oct–23 Nov 1980 · Sun 4pm

MAIN CAST
Vera Straightman · · · · · · · · · Denise Coffey
Norman Straightman · · · · · · · · · Tony Aitken
WITH
Fred Harris
Sue Holderness
Dudley Stevens
David Simeon

CREDITS
writers Andrew Marshall/David Renwick · *director* Geoffrey Sax · *producers* Simon Brett (series 1), Humphrey Barclay (series 2)

The first TV series from Andrew Marshall and David Renwick, who later helped write **Not The Nine O'Clock News** and other hit series and would, singly, develop **2 Point 4 Children** and **One Foot In The Grave**.

Fresh from their success on BBC Radio 4 with the comedy series *The Burkiss Way*, the writers here produced a novel idea in which husband and wife Norman and Vera Straightman persistently had their quiet life rudely interrupted by the Pythonesque intrusions of famous people from the world of television. (These were played by the other cast members, in various parody guises, one of whom, Fred Harris, was also in *The Burkiss Way*.)

The End Of The End Of The Pier Show

UK · ITV (SOUTHERN) · CHILDREN'S SITCOM

1 × 60 mins · colour
4 May 1981 · Mon 5.05pm

MAIN CAST

Alan Carter · · · · · · · · · · · · ·	Christopher Gable
Marilyn Jones · · · · · · · · · · ·	Cheryl Kennedy
Mr Pumphrey · · · · · · · · · · · ·	Jack Douglas
Mrs Pumphrey · · · · · · · · · · · ·	Peggy Mount
Mr Kirby · · · · · · · · · · · · ·	Norman Vaughan
Mr Banyard · · · · · · · · · · ·	Cardew Robinson

CREDITS

writers Sid Colin/Michael Marshall · *producer* Bryan Izzard

A bank holiday children's special, co-scripted by veteran comedy writer Sid Colin (*The Army Game* and much else), which celebrated the entertainments found on a typical seaside pier, and sadly pointed out the rusting, rotting decline of many such structures. The highly experienced cast fulfilled a variety of roles – Punch and Judy, pierrots, musicians, beauty queens and so on – and the action was set in the fictional town of Smallhaven.

The End Of The Pier Show

UK · BBC · SITCOM

6 editions (5 × 30 mins · 1 × 35 mins) · colour

One series (5) 17 Nov–15 Dec 1974 · BBC2 Sun around 11pm

Special (35 mins) 4 Jan 1975 · BBC2 Sat 6.45pm

MAIN CAST

John Wells
John Fortune
Carl Davis
Madeline Smith

CREDITS

director Andrew Gosling · *producer* Ian Keill

An odd BBC2 *divertissement* in which a regular 'End Of The Pier' company presented a series of six Victorian play parodies way out of season, way out to sea and way into the night.

The six individual titles were 'Intensive Care', 'Upstairs Downstairs', 'Rig O' Doom', 'A Kick In The Opera', 'Fanny By Starlight' (aka 'The 9.36 To Didcot') and, finally, 'Queen's Rhapsody' which was presented as an early-evening special for the normally late revellers. Guest stars appeared occasionally to help out the company, notably Rita Webb in 'Upstairs Downstairs', John Laurie and Ivor Cutler in 'Rig O' Doom', Peter Sellers in 'Fanny By Starlight' and John Bird in 'Queen's Rhapsody'. No writers' credits were given but it's safe to assume that the two Johns in the cast were responsible for the script, with composer Carl Davis providing the music.

The series followed an earlier musical collaboration between the main creative personnel (Fortune, Wells, Smith, Davis and Keill), *In The Looking Glass* (BBC2, 17 January–21 February 1978), a six-part musical miscellany of unconnected ideas, written by Wells and Fortune.

The End Of The Tunnel

UK · BBC · SITCOM

1 × 30 mins · b/w

21 June 1966 · BBC1 Tue 7.30pm

MAIN CAST

Charles · · · · · · · · · · · · · · ·	George Cole
Sheila · · · · · · · · · · · · · · ·	Lynn Redgrave
Harry · · · · · · · · · · · · · · · ·	Henry McGee
Bernard · · · · · · · · · · · · · ·	Tenniel Evans

CREDITS

writer Richard Waring · *producer* Graeme Muir

A *Comedy Playhouse* pilot for a projected series that was never realised. George Cole was cast as Charles, an affluent City businessman whose wife has left him and who now finds himself having to start all over again in the romance stakes. Lynn Redgrave was cast as Sheila, a woman he meets at a party.

The Entertainers

UK · C4 (LWT) · SKETCH/STANDUP

7 × 30 mins · colour

One series (6) 22 Sep–27 Oct 1983 · Thu mostly 8.30pm

Special · *Stomping On The Cat* 4 Jan 1984 · Wed 10.55pm

MAIN CAST

see below

CREDITS

writers various · *directors* Paul Jackson (6), Noel D Greene (1) · *producer* Paul Jackson

Seven entirely distinct programmes featuring the new talent taking up the vanguard of comedy in the 1980s. The essence of the series, indeed, was to spotlight performers or acts largely or wholly unknown to TV viewers. Along the way some soon-to-be-major names were on show: Hale and Pace (still performing at this time with Fundation, the resident weekend comics at the Tramshed club in Woolwich, south London), Ben Elton (with short hair and no spectacles), Helen Lederer, Paul Merton (appearing here as Paul Martin), Chris (or Christopher as he was still known) Barrie and, perhaps most notably of all, French and Saunders, whose programme was a virtual word-for-word TV studio recording of the stage-show they were touring around Britain's fringe theatres at the time. Interestingly, while the word penis had been allowed to stand (as it were) in a previous edition of *The Entertainers*, broadcast at 8.30pm, French and Saunders' inclusion of the word clitoris in their act resulted in a drastic rescheduling of their programme to 11.25pm, so hardly anyone saw it. Other performers included Joe Longthorne, Jim Barclay, Arnold Brown, Andy de la Tour, Jenny Lecoat, Mark Arden, Stephen Frost, Simon Fanshawe and John Hegley.

The series was produced and (mostly) directed by Paul Jackson. During his employment at the BBC, Jackson had been the first to put the so-called 'alternative' comics on TV via *Boom Boom ... Out Go The Lights*. As with those two programmes, Jackson here arranged for the acts to perform in front of people sitting at tables, similar to the cabaret settings with which they were most familiar.

Equal Partners

UK · BBC · SITCOM

1 × 30 mins · colour

29 Apr 1971 · BBC1 Thu 7.40pm

MAIN CAST

Nicky · · · · · · · · · · · · · · · · ·	Nicky Henson
Pauline · · · · · · · · · · · · · · ·	Angela Scoular
Mrs Jones · · · · · · · · · · · · · ·	Jessie Evans
Mary · · · · · · · · · · · · · · ·	Hilary Pritchard

CREDITS

writers John Lloyd/Graeme Garden · *producer* Graeme Muir

Yet another *Comedy Playhouse* pilot that failed to register sufficiently to ensure a follow-up series. Hilary Pritchard had a minor role but was enjoying better exposure as a comic turn in the BBC1 Saturday-night magazine series *Braden's Week*.

E/R

USA · CBS (EMBASSY TELEVISION) · SITCOM

22 × 30 mins · colour

US dates: 16 Sep 1984–27 Apr 1985

UK dates: 9 Jan–29 May 1987 (18 episodes) C4 Fri 9pm

MAIN CAST

Dr Howard Sheinfeld · · · · · · · ·	Elliott Gould
Dr Eve Sheridan · ·	Marcia Strassman (pilot);
· · · · · · · · · · · · · · ·	Mary McDonnell (series)
Nurse Joan Thor · · · · · · · ·	Conchata Ferrell
Nurse Julie Williams · · · · · · · ·	Lynne Moody
Maria Amardo · · · · · · · · · · · · ·	Shuko Akune
Fred Burdock · · · · · · · · · · ·	Bruce A Young
Nurse Cory Smith · · · · · · · · ·	Corinne Bohrer
Howard Stickley · · · · · · · ·	Jason Alexander

CREDITS

creators/executive producers Saul Turteltaub, Bernie Orenstein · *writers* various · *directors* Peter Bonerz and others · *producer* Eve Brandstein

Set in the bustling emergency room of a large inner-city hospital, Clark Street in Chicago, film star Elliott Gould was the pivot of this piece, cast as Dr Howard Sheinfeld, an ear-nose-and-throat specialist who has to rule-break and maintain 48-hour moonlight shifts in order to meet alimony payments to two former wives, look after his 15-year-old daughter and maintain his fanatical support for local sports teams. Despite his exhaustion, Sheinfeld is a sharpie, never short of a quip or poetry quotation, disconcerting Dr Eve Sheridan, to whom he reports.

The sitcom was developed from a play of the same title that was very successful at the Organic Theatre in Chicago, with Bruce A Young (one of its eight writers) and Shuko Akune reprising their stage roles in the TV version. The opening episode included a reference to the very successful black sitcom *The Jeffersons*, with George Jefferson (the actor Sherman Hemsley) coming to the hospital, in character, to visit his niece, Nurse Julie Williams.

Compared to *M*A*S*H*, as any American surgical sitcom must be, *E/R* was a distinct second best – although, to be fair, it worked the subject in a very different manner, shot on video tape and directed in an everything's-happening-at-once style typical of so many studio-bound US sitcoms. But *E/R* had its good moments, and a link with the forebear was made in the casting of Elliott Gould, who had played the part of Trapper John in the original *M*A*S*H* movie. Jason Alexander, later to be cast as George Costanza, a sidekick in *Seinfeld*, was cast here, with much more hair, as a sidekick to Sheinfeld, the funds-hungry hospital administrator.

Despite the title, this sitcom is unrelated to the medical drama *ER*, also set in the bustling emergency room of a Chicago hospital, networked in the USA by NBC from 19 September 1994 (and screened in Britain by C4 from 1 February 1995). The only connection between the two series, made a decade apart, was George Clooney. He was among the main cast in the 1990s *ER*, playing the womanising paediatrician Dr Douglas Ross, and he had an occasional, minor role in the 1980s *E/R*, playing Nurse Joan Thor's nephew Ace, a womanising hospital porter.

The Eric Barker Half-Hour

UK · BBC · SKETCH

21 × 30 mins · b/w

Series One (9) 10 Oct 1951–30 Jan 1952 · fortnightly Wed around 9pm

Series Two (6) 1 Oct–10 Dec 1952 · fortnightly Wed around 9pm

Series Three (6) 14 Oct–23 Dec 1953 · fortnightly Wed around 9pm

MAIN CAST
Eric Barker
Pearl Hackney
Nicholas Parsons
Deryck Guyler (series 3)

CREDITS
writer Eric Barker · *producer* Graeme Muir

Comedian and comic actor Eric Barker was enjoying huge success in *Merry-Go-Round* on BBC radio at the time of this TV series, in which he appeared (as usual) with his real-life wife Pearl Hackney. His 'Steady Barker' catchphrase and verbal stumbling over words beginning with the letter 'h' were well known

to audiences from the radio series, and they were expressed again here.

During the run of this TV show Barker was carefully expanding his radio range, moving away from the broad humour of his earlier shows to the more thoughtful, character comedy of *Just Fancy*, which ran on the wireless from 1951 to 1962.

See also *The Newcomer, Look At It This Way* and *Something In The City*.

Eric Sykes: One Of The Great Troupers

see *The Old Boy Network*

The Eric Sykes 1990 Show
Eric Sykes Presents Peter Sellers
The Eric Sykes Show

see SYKES, Eric

Ernie's Incredible Illucinations

UK · BBC · CHILDREN'S SITCOM

1 × 25 mins · colour

11 Nov 1987 · BBC1 Wed 5.10pm

MAIN CAST
Ernie · · · · · · · · · · · · · · · · · Anthony Flynn
Mum · · · · · · · · · · · · · · · · · Melanie Kilburn
Dad · Tim Barker
Doctor · · · · · · · · · · · · · · · · · · John Landry

CREDITS
writer Alan Ayckbourn · *adapter/writer* Chris Barlas · *executive producer* Paul Stone · *director* Colin Cant

Alan Ayckbourn wrote *Ernie's Incredible Illucinations* in 1967 as a stage-play specifically designed to be performed by 11–15-year-olds. The story centres around Ernie, whose extraordinary 'illucinations' can also be seen by those around him, resulting in all sorts of mayhem and chaos. This one-off TV adaptation may have been a pilot try-out for a series that never materialised.

Ev

see EVERETT, Kenny

Evans Abode

UK · BBC · SITCOM

4 × 60 mins · b/w

Evans Above 10 Nov 1956 · Sat 9.45pm

8 Dec 1956 · Sat 8.30pm

18 May 1957 · Sat 8.30pm

15 June 1957 · Sat 8.30pm

MAIN CAST
Norman Evans
Jon Pertwee

CREDITS
writers Barry Pevan, Johnny Speight, Dick Barry, Richard Afton · *producer* Richard Afton

Following on the heels of *The Norman Evans Show*, the BBC screened four more programmes starring the Rochdale comedian. *Evans Above* was the punning title of the first, the remainder were titled *Evans Abode*. All were broadcast under the *Saturday Comedy Hour* banner. In these shows Evans was cast as a boarding-house landlady, taking in an odd assortment of guests; some of them were variety acts who, naturally, performed for her and the cameras.

Evans returned to TV in 1958, hosting the variety series *Make Yourself At Home* (three shows, monthly from 11 October to 8 December), in which he introduced the acts, one of whom was his daughter, the singer Norma Evans. All three programmes included an extended 'domestic sketch', written by Frank Roscoe and featuring Evans with Patricia Burke and the future *Coronation Street* star Violet Carson.

An Evening At Home With Bernard Braden And Barbara Kelly

UK · BBC · SITCOM

6 × 30 mins · b/w

24 Jan–4 Apr 1951 · fortnightly Wed 8.15pm

MAIN CAST
Bernard Braden
Barbara Kelly
George Benson
Hester Paton-Brown

CREDITS
writers Bernard Braden/Barbara Kelly · *producer* Leslie Jackson

The Canadian husband and wife team Bernard Braden and Barbara Kelly were familiar faces on British TV throughout the 1950s and 1960s. In this sitcom oddity, viewers were supposedly invited to spend informal evenings with them and their regularly visiting neighbours (played by George Benson and Hester Paton-Brown) and occasional guest stars.

Although they appeared regularly on screen for another quarter-century, the only other TV sitcom to have featured Braden and Kelly was postponed and never shown, despite being announced in the published listings. Produced by ABC, it was to have been titled *The Rolling Stones* (and this was well before the rock group) and broadcast on ITV from 23 January 1960. Although vaguely autobiographical, in that Bernard was a film producer, Barbara was his wife, and they travelled places with their three children, the scripts were written by Tom Espie and Stanley Myers. On the night the first programme was due, an article in the *Manchester Evening News* reported that 'the

Bradens felt scripts and general standard were not good enough'.

See also *B-And-B, Barbara With Braden, Bath-Night With Braden, Early To Braden* and *Kaleidoscope.*

An Evening For Nicaragua

UK · C4 (IBT PRODUCTIONS) · STANDUP

1 × 60 mins · colour

1 Sep 1983 · Thu 10.30pm

MAIN CAST
Andy de la Tour
Maggie Steed
Ben Elton
Dawn French
Jennifer Saunders
Emma Thompson
Rik Mayall

CREDITS
writers cast · *director* John Longley · *executive producer* David Tereshchuk

A TV recording of a benefit concert given at the Shaftesbury Theatre in London, compered by Andy de la Tour and inspired by a visit to the African country he made in 1982 with the comic actress Maggie Steed. A number of his contemporary comics contributed, as well as (not listed above) actors and singers.

Evening Shade

USA · CBS (BLOODWORTH-THOMASON/MOZARK PRODUCTIONS/MTM ENTERPRISES) · SITCOM

99 episodes (97 × 30 mins · 2 × 60 mins) · colour

US dates: 21 Sep 1990–23 May 1994

*UK dates: 10 Feb 1992–8 Dec 1994 (71 × 30 mins · 2 × 60 mins) C4 Mon 8.30pm then weekdays 9.30am

MAIN CAST
Wood Newton · · · · · · · · · · · · Burt Reynolds
Ava Evans Newton · · · · · · · · · Marilu Henner
Taylor Newton · · · · · · · · · · · Jay R Ferguson
Molly Newton · · · Melissa Martin (1990–91);
· · · · · · · · · · · · · · · · Candace Hutson (1991–94)
Will Newton · · · · · · · · · · · · · Jacob Parker
Evan Evans · · · · · · · · · · · · · Hal Holbrook
Herman Stiles · · · · · · · · · · · Michael Jeter
Dr Harlan Elldridge · · · · · · · · Charles Durning
Merleen Elldridge · · · · · · · · Ann Wedgeworth
Fontana Beausoleil · · · · · · · Linda Gehringer
Ponder Blue · · · · · · · · · · · · · Ossie Davis
Nub Oliver · · · · · · · · · · · · · Charlie Dell
Emily Newton · · · · · · · Alexa Vega (1993–94)

CREDITS
creator Linda Bloodworth-Thomason · *writers* various · *directors* Burt Reynolds (36), James Hampton (16), Harry Thomason (16), Robby Benson (8), David Steinberg (7), Charles Frank (4), Charles Nelson Reilly (4), Frank Bonner (1), Sheldon Epps (1), Dennis Erdman (1), Robert Ginty (1), Michael Jeter (1), Richard T Kline (1), John Ratzenberger (1), Don Rhymer (1) · *executive producers* Linda Bloodworth-Thomason/Harry Thomason, Burt Reynolds · *producers* Tommy Thompson, Douglas Jackson, David Nichols

Hollywood heart-throb Burt Reynolds graduated to movie stardom after more than a decade of laudable TV work that embraced regular appearances in cowboy series *Riverboat* (NBC, 1959–60) and *Gunsmoke* (CBS, 1962–65); and starring roles in contemporary crime series *Hawk* (ABC, 1966) and *Dan August* (ABC, 1970–71). After this came many years as a major cinema attraction, where, in a number of light-hearted action/adventure movies, he was usually cast as a shady but likeable hero. During his TV appearances at this time, on chat-shows and as a guest star, Reynolds tended to undermine this tough guy screen image, displaying a line in self-deprecating humour and demonstrating some skill as a comedy performer. He enjoyed moderate success in a number of unassuming movie comedies – *The End* (1977), *Paternity* (1981), *The Best Little Whorehouse In Texas* (1982) and *The Man Who Loved Women* (1983) – before inexplicably finding himself out of favour, both as an action hero and a light-comedy star. With suggestions that his marriage (to Loni Anderson of *WKRP In Cincinnati*) was not going well, and amid rumours of health problems (which included unfounded speculation that he had the Aids virus), it seemed that Reynolds was on the ropes. But, courtesy of TV, he bounced back: in 1989 he began to resurrect his career with the short-lived crime series *B L Stryker* (ABC), and in 1990 he shot back into the limelight with *Evening Shade*, a popular sitcom that reunited him on screen with former *Taxi* star Marilu Henner. (They had worked together in *The Man Who Loved Women*.)

In *Evening Shade*, Reynolds played Wood Newton, an ex-pro (American) football star now back in his Arkansas home town of Evening Shade, coaching the high school football team, the Mules. Henner was cast as his wife of many years, Ava, a civil-minded woman who, during the first season, while pregnant with the couple's fourth child, is elected the town's prosecuting attorney. Their eldest son Taylor is quarterback for the Evening Shade Mules but he has inherited little of his father's sporting prowess. Indeed the whole team is a bit of a shambles, not having won a game in two years. Assisting Wood Newton with the coaching is Herman Stiles, a fragile mathematics teacher uncommonly unsuited to the task. The other regulars included the wonderful Charles Durning as the cantankerous Dr Elldridge, and Hal Holbrook as Ava's father Evan, who disapproves of Wood's laid-back lifestyle and who has never forgiven him for stealing his daughter away at such a young age. (Ava was 18 when she got hitched to the 30-year-old Wood.) The series was narrated by Ossie Davis as Ponder Blue, the laconic and philosophical proprietor of Ponder Blue's

Barbecue Villa, around which much of the action takes place.

Although, on the surface, the premise seemed to have a good deal in common with *Coach*, an ABC sitcom launched the previous year (and for which, incidentally, Reynolds had also been considered), *Evening Shade* was quite a different beast – marked by its measured and almost leisurely pacing, a style dictated by Reynolds with his deliberately understated performance as Newton. *Evening Shade* was a thoughtful piece, nearer in mood to *Frank's Place* than anything else, and Reynolds was the fulcrum of the series (he also produced, wrote and directed episodes). The sharp writing also helped to flesh out the relationships, so that the usual sitcom clichés of misunderstandings and misconstructions could be jettisoned in favour of strong, albeit basic, plots based on recognisable situations. Especially pleasing was the sexually charged central relationship between Wood and Ava, a couple who, if they had any problems, talked about them candidly rather than (like lesser sitcom marriages) circumnavigating the issues and convoluting them out of all proportion.

*Note. In Britain, C4 screened the first three US seasons of *Evening Shade* – with every episode also repeated – but omitted to show the fourth and final season of 26 episodes.

An Evening With ...

UK · ITV (WATCHMAKER PRODUCTIONS FOR CARLTON) · STANDUP

2 × 60 mins · colour

1. Spike Milligan · 24 Feb 1996 · Sat 9pm
2. 'Lily Savage' · 6 Nov 1996 · Wed 9pm

CREDITS (PROGRAMME NUMBERS)
writers cast · *director* Brian Klein (2) · *executive producer* Elaine Bedell (1 & 2) · *producers* Carolyn Longton (1), Martin Cunning (2)

To outward appearances – especially to viewers at home – there is no difference between Carlton's *An Evening With ...* series, launched in 1996, and LWT's long-running *An Audience With ...*, launched in 1980, not least since they are made in the same studio on London's South Bank. Once more, top comedy names stand before an audience packed with celebrities and give of their best, the resulting TV hours including frequent (too frequent, some might say) cutaways to catch celebrities in the act of laughing.

Note. Reference to these *An Evening With ...* programmes has also been made within the separate entries for Spike Milligan and Lily Savage.

An Evening With Carol Burnett

see BURNETT, Carol

An Evening With Dave Evans

UK · ITV (YORKSHIRE) · IMPRESSIONISM

1 × 60 mins · colour

29 Apr 1978 · Sat 7.30pm

MAIN CAST
Dave Evans

CREDITS
writers Spike Mullins, Mike Goddard ·
director/producer Vernon Lawrence

Another special for the comedy impressionist Dave Evans, who had appeared in such TV series as *Who Do You Do?* and earned his first starring special the previous year, *A Show Of My Own*. Evans's speciality was music spoofs and in this programme he imitated punk rockers, Tom Jones and his own musical guest Acker Bilk.

An Evening With Francis Howerd

see HOWERD, Frankie

An Evening With Jack Benny

see BENNY, Jack

An Evening With Lee Evans

UK · C4 (OPEN MIKE PRODUCTIONS) · STANDUP

1 × 30 mins · colour

30 Dec 1993 · Thu 10.10pm

MAIN CAST
Lee Evans

CREDITS
writer Lee Evans · *director* David G Hillier ·
executive producer Pete Ward · *producer* Dave Morley

Lee Evans is a truly impressive, hard-working physical comedian who exploded into view following his Perrier Award-winning performance at the 1993 Edinburgh Festival Fringe. Although many of the 'new wave' comedians who rose to prominence in the 1980s included violent slapstick as part of their act, it had been many years since a comedian so efficiently combined physical mime with sharp dialogue – Rowan Atkinson had perhaps been the last to emerge. But whereas Atkinson's stage characterisations tended to be paced slowly for full comedic effect, Evans came over like a whirling dervish – a tightly coiled spring bouncing on to the stage and zapping about in all directions. Sweating profusely in a suit that seemed a couple of sizes too small, the diminutive comic inevitably attracted comparisons with Norman Wisdom, and there were certainly parallels in their energetic approach, use of pathos and loose limbs.

In this show, recorded at Duke of York's Theatre in London, TV viewers were given their first chance to see Evans in a long set rather than the guest spots he had made in a number of standup and variety shows. Evans then eschewed the common routes by striking immediately at the big time, starring in a feature film, *Funny Bones*, in 1994, and snagging the starring role in *MouseHunt*, a major Hollywood movie from Steven Spielberg's company DreamWorks, set for release in 1998.

See also *The Lee Evans Show* and *The World Of Lee Evans*.

An Evening With Max Wall

see WALL, Max

An Evening With Robert Morley

USA · SCREEN GEMS · STANDUP

1 × 60 mins · b/w

US date: not known

UK date: 17 Oct 1964 · BBC2 Sat 9.30pm

MAIN CAST
Robert Morley

CREDITS
writer Robert Morley

The British writer, humorist, actor, bon vivant and all-round entertainer Robert Morley was a familiar face on stage, screen and television, and because the characters he portrayed were mostly exaggerated variations of his own self, his style and demeanour were well known to viewers on both sides of the Atlantic. In this American TV special, imported to British screens by BBC2, Morley held forth on a number of subjects, presented under the generic title 'The Creative Urge', in a self-penned script liberally laced with the eccentric comical observations for which he was renowned.

See also *Charge!* and *If The Crown Fits ...*

Ever Decreasing Circles

UK · BBC · SITCOM

27 episodes (26 × 30 mins · 1 × 80 mins) · colour

Series One (5 × 30 mins) 29 Jan–26 Feb 1984 · BBC1 Sun 8.35pm

Series Two (8 × 30 mins) 21 Oct–23 Dec 1984 · BBC1 Sun 7.15pm

Series Three (6 × 30 mins) 31 Aug–5 Oct 1986 · BBC1 Sun 7.15pm

Series Four (7 × 30 mins) 25 Oct–6 Dec 1987 · BBC1 Sun 7.15pm

Special (80 mins) 24 Dec 1989 · BBC1 Sun 7.45pm

MAIN CAST

Martin Bryce	Richard Briers
Ann Bryce	Penelope Wilton
Paul Ryman	Peter Egan
Howard	Stanley Lebor
Hilda	Geraldine Newman

CREDITS
writers John Esmonde/Bob Larbey ·
directors/producers Sydney Lotterby (series 1 & 2), Harold Snoad (series 3 onwards)

This series reunited actor Richard Briers with the writers of his huge hit *The Good Life*, but here, instead of playing an amiable idealist, he was cast as the awful Martin Bryce, an anally retentive, interfering know-all and ceaseless, do-gooding, tradition-loving organiser who tried the patience of all his neighbours and acquaintances but especially tested his wife Ann's endurance. In time-honoured but inexplicable sitcom fashion, she suffered without ever throttling him, emigrating or trying to have him committed.

Tenacious in his never-say-die attitudes, a compulsive arranger of committees and relentless volunteer and supporter of every cause going, Martin undoubtedly meant well, but he was the type of insufferable bore who has 'four different kinds of spade in his garage' and who 'changes the water in his car battery every three days'. Pitiful the lead character may have been, but viewing audiences somehow identified with him, and the series proved very popular. The nub of the show, beyond the fact that Martin was a crushing bore, was the threat he felt from his new next-door neighbour, Paul Ryman, a handsome and super-smooth bachelor who, just by doing nothing, made Martin look and feel inferior – and, of course, Martin never did nothing, digging himself deeper and deeper into holes from which he refused to emerge. They all lived in a cosy suburban close in Horsham, a little patch of greenery tucked away in a quiet corner of England, with Martin's well-meaning but a trifle sad friends Howard and his wife Hilda (they usually wore identical clothes) taking part in most of his endeavours.

It was obvious to all that a truer scenario would have pitched Paul and Ann as husband and wife, trying to put up with their obsessive neighbour Martin. But, despite an obvious closeness, Paul and Ann's friendship never quite ripened in this way, and while she should have run off with him, and been done with Bryce for ever, she remained the faithful wife.

Peter Egan, who played Paul, had previously appeared with Richard Briers on stage, in Shaw's *Arms And The Man* in 1982.

Kenny Everett

Born Maurice Cole in Liverpool on 25 December 1944, Kenny Everett was one of the all-time greats in British comedy. Although not a comedian as such, his incredible off-the-wall humour, unbridled enthusiasm and inventiveness, and free-spirited attitude – Everett was not one to obey conventions – made him a fascinating and endlessly entertaining figure.

Although he made a few forays into television, starting with *Nice Time* in 1968, Kenny Everett's talents were applied mostly to radio, his preferred medium, and one at which he was a true revolutionary. In the history of British pop radio (as yet unwritten) Everett's name must be writ the largest, so great were his contributions, first with pirate ship Radio London, then BBC Radio 1, Capital Radio in London, BBC Radio 2 and finally Capital Gold. No more inventive or daring disc-jockey has ever taken to the airwaves in the UK. Everett only really applied himself to the TV game from 1978 to 1988, when his series for ITV and the BBC, extending to 79 programmes largely similar in content and approach, won awards and performed very highly in the ratings.

In 1985, many of Everett's fans were surprised to learn from newspaper articles that, although living in a high-profile marriage, he was homosexual. But he made light of this revelation and, as his appeal was mainly to a young, liberal audience, it did little to dent his popularity. Genuine sadness greeted his later, brave public admission that he was HIV positive, and when he died on 4 April 1995 from Aids complications, British comedy lost a true original, who, although never *quite* managing to duplicate the genius of his radio programmes on television, nevertheless graced the small-screen with a posse of memorable characters and outrageous routines and sketches. On 26 May 1995 BBC1 screened *In The Best Possible Taste! – A Tribute To Kenny Everett* which looked back at his career with clips and reminiscences from friends and colleagues, and on 23 April 1997 he was the subject in C4's *Heroes Of Comedy* series.

See also *Up Sunday*.

The Kenny Everett Explosion

UK · ITV (LWT) · SKETCH

10 × 30 mins · colour

10 July–11 Sep 1970 · Fri 7pm

MAIN CAST
Kenny Everett
Crisp · · · · · · · · · · · · · · · · · · · Brian Colville

CREDITS
directors Gordon Hesketh (7), Bruce Gowers (3) · *executive producer* Terry Henebery

Following Everett's appearances in Granada's wacky *Nice Time*, and soon after the DJ was controversially dismissed by BBC radio, he was given his own series by LWT. This was, in fact, the first comedy series of any kind to be made at LWT after Barry Took was appointed Head of Entertainment there, replacing previous incumbents Frank Muir and Tito Burns.

Took booked Everett for not one but three series, to run successively, spanning 25 consecutive weeks, almost as if the ITV executives were eager to emphasise that they appreciated the wacky DJ even if the BBC did not. *The Kenny Everett Explosion* set the tone, mixing pop music with Everett's trademark style of presentation and every visual trick that TV studio equipment could produce at the time. There were occasional appearances too by the DJ's refined retainer, the Jeeves-like Crisp, who had also featured in the Radio 1 shows.

Making Whoopee

UK · ITV (LWT) · SKETCH

6 × 30 mins · colour

18 Sep–24 Oct 1970 · Fri 7pm then Sat 6.15pm

MAIN CAST
Kenny Everett
Bob Kerr's Whoopee Band

CREDITS
producer Bryan Izzard

Precisely seven days after concluding the ten-week season of *The Kenny Everett Explosion*, in the same Friday 7pm slot, the DJ appeared in this six-part series.

Making Whoopee also starred Bob Kerr's Whoopee Band, who served up the kind of surreal musical lunacy that had brought success to the Temperance Seven, the New Vaudeville Band and, more recently, the Bonzo Dog Doo-Dah Band. Each week, viewers were transported to a club in Putney to witness Everett introducing the band in a succession of loopy numbers.

Ev

UK · ITV (LWT) · SKETCH

9 × 30 mins · colour

31 Oct 1970–2 Jan 1971 · Sat 6.30pm then 5.40pm

MAIN CAST
Kenny Everett
Crisp · · · · · · · · · · · · · · · · · · Brian Colville

CREDITS
director Bruce Gowers · *producer* Bryan Izzard

A week after *Making Whoopee* came to a halt, again in virtually the same slot, Kenny Everett returned, combining chart music with linking films and comedy sketches, notably those featuring Crisp, his unflappable butler, and daffy Granny, ever ready to dispense silly advice. Both characters (the latter voiced by Everett) had graced Kenny's pre-dismissal BBC Radio 1 shows.

The Kenny Everett Video Show

UK · ITV (THAMES) · SKETCH

35 editions (25 × 30 mins · 9 × 45 mins · 1 × 60 mins) · colour

Series One (8 × 45 mins) 3 July–21 Aug 1978 · Mon 6.45pm

Special (45 mins) *The Didn't Quite Make It In Time For Christmas Video Show* 1 Jan 1979 · Mon 5.45pm

Series Two (10 × 30 mins) 19 Feb–30 Apr 1979 · Mon 7pm

Special (60 mins) *The 'Will Kenny Everett Make It To 1980?' Show* 31 Dec 1979 · Mon 11pm

Series Three (8 × 30 mins) 18 Feb–14 Apr 1980 · Mon 7pm

Special (30 mins) *The Kenny Everett New Year's Daze Show* 31 Dec 1980 · Wed 11.50pm

Series Four (6 × 30 mins) *The Kenny Everett Video Cassette* 16 Apr–21 May 1981 · Thu 7.30pm

MAIN CAST
Kenny Everett

OTHER APPEARANCES
Carla · · Anna Dawson (special 3 & series 5)

CREDITS
writers Barry Cryer (35), Ray Cameron (35), Kenny Everett (35), Dick Vosburgh (1) · *directors/producers* David Mallet (series 1–4, specials 1 & 2), Royston Mayoh (series 5 & special 3)

Although popular for more than a decade, the zany (truly, there was no better word to describe him) Everett was elevated to superstardom with this inspired Thames TV series. The radio DJ had tried his hand on TV before but he really found his niche with *The Kenny Everett Video Show*, which permitted the short-burst format ideal for his surreal sense of humour. Further, for a man who had pioneered truly creative *audio* entertainment in the pop field, visual technology had finally caught up with him by 1978, and Everett was able for the first time to be almost as inventive on TV as he was on the radio. The word 'video' in the title was all-important: the latest-available edit-suite trickery was used to full effect, and this, aided by computer technology that would seem primitive today but was innovative in 1978, combined for an eye-catching presentation. The shows were recorded in front of a minimal audience and the crew behind the cameras were encouraged to break their silence and laugh, call out or even be seen during the recordings, a technique new to almost all viewers but much copied since.

As with his radio shows, Kenny Everett presided over an array of characters and sketches that would appear each week, their very familiarity helping the comedy to work. As such, the audiences knew what they were in for, and would come away happy. Together with co-writers Barry Cryer and Ray Cameron, Everett invented an impressive roster of talent, among them Sid Snot (a greaser/biker who would end each skit by throwing a cigarette into the air and catching it in his mouth), Marcel Wave (an outrageously Gallic-accented Frenchman), the huge-handed gospel minister Brother Lee Love, Cupid Stunt (a huge-breasted, dangerously named woman who did everything 'in the best *possible* taste'), a Marceau-like mime artist, and Angry of Mayfair (a mouth-foaming City Gent who, it turned out, wore stockings and suspenders).

Each show would also feature the dancing act Arlene Phillips' Hot Gossip, who, dressed usually in leather, would 'bump and grind' their 'naughty bits' in a provocatively sexual manner designed to be the antithesis of the gently arousing but ultimately angelic Pan's People from the BBC's *Top Of The Pops*. Pop music played a large part in *The Kenny Everett Video Show*, and each edition featured a guest act or two, some of whom would happily join in the sketches. Another key element in each programme was an animated (courtesy of Cosgrove Hall Productions) serialisation of Captain Kremmen's adventures in space, familiar to all listeners of Everett's shows on Capital Radio. (It is perhaps worth noting here that, before this TV series, Everett had neither been seen nor heard nationally for some five years. He was, however, fantastically popular in the London area for his regular shows on Capital Radio. While Thames TV and Capital were unrelated there was a natural crossover at this time between London's commercial radio station and London's commercial TV station, not least because of their neighbouring HQs.) So popular were the Kremmen adventures that a half-hour Cosgrove Hall animated production, *Kremmen – The Movie*, was assembled for cinema distribution in 1980, with Everett, as ever, providing the voices of not only the Captain but also his dumb blonde and big-busted sidekick Carla and the brilliant scientist Gitfinger.

Although pursuing essentially the same format, the final series – retitled *The Kenny Everett Video Cassette* – presented the Captain Kremmen stories in real life (first done in the New Year's Eve 1980 special), with Anna Dawson appearing as Carla. This series also introduced another new element: Star Quiz, whereby a horrible fate would befall a guest celebrity if he or she failed to answer a usually impossible question.

A few months after that fifth and final series, Everett defected to the BBC where, arguably, he enjoyed even greater success with *The Kenny Everett Television Show*. But it was these ultra-slick and very funny Thames shows, with the star standing alone

in front of a bank of TV screens, which established the winning formula. And, of course, although much of the material was risqué, it was all done in the best *possible* taste.

The Kenny Everett Television Show

UK · BBC · SKETCH

44 × 30 mins · colour

Special · 24 Dec 1981 · BBC1 Thu 7.45pm

Series One (8) 25 Feb–15 Apr 1982 · BBC1 Thu 8pm

Special · 28 Dec 1982 · BBC1 Tue 8.45pm

Series Two (8) 24 Feb–14 Apr 1983 · BBC1 Thu 8pm

Special · 26 Dec 1983 · BBC1 Mon 7.15pm

Special · *The Kenny Everett Christmas Show* 27 Dec 1984 · BBC1 Thu 7.50pm

Series Three (8) 13 Apr–8 June 1985 · BBC1 Sat mostly 8.10pm

Special · *Kenny Everett's Christmas Carol* 24 Dec 1985 · BBC1 Tue 8pm

Series Four (8) 16 Oct–4 Dec 1986 · BBC1 Thu 8.30pm

Special · *Kenny's Christmas Cracker* 23 Dec 1986 · BBC1 Tue 8.30pm

Series Five (6) 30 Nov 1987–18 Jan 1988 · BBC1 Mon 8pm

MAIN CAST
Kenny Everett

OTHER APPEARANCES
Cleo Rocos

CREDITS
writers Barry Cryer (44), Kenny Everett (28), Ray Cameron (28), Andrew Marshall/David Renwick (14), Neil Shand (10), John Langdon (6), Paul Minett/Brian Leveson (6), Gary Clapperton (2) · *directors* Bill Wilson, John Bishop, Kevin Bishop · *producers* Bill Wilson (20), John Bishop (18), Paul Ciani (6)

Everett returned to the bosom of the BBC with both a Radio 2 series and this TV series, which continued in a virtually identical vein to *The Kenny Everett Video Show* and *The Kenny Everett Video Cassette*. New characters included Gizzard Puke, a sort of punk cousin to Sid Snot, and Reg Prescott, an incompetent DIY expert who invariably did himself some gory mischief during his instructional broadcasts.

After the final series, in 1988, Everett spent his remaining years solely in radio, broadcasting with the London station Capital Gold.

Every Silver Lining

UK · BBC · SITCOM

6 × 30 mins · colour

27 May–1 July 1993 · BBC1 Thu 8.30pm

MAIN CAST
Shirley Silver · · · · · · · · · Frances de la Tour
Nat Silver · · · · · · · · · · · · · · · Andrew Sachs

Lorraine Silver · · · · · · · · · · · · · Sarah Malin
Leonard · · · · · · · · · · · · · · · · · · David Yip
Willie · · · · · · · · · · · · · · · · · · Oscar Quitak
Dean · · · · · · · · · · · · · · · · Danny Swanson

CREDITS
writer Simon Block · *director* Nick Bye · *producer* Richard Boden

A remorselessly middle-of-the-road sitcom starring Andrew Sachs and Frances de la Tour as a bickering Jewish married couple running a café somewhere in the East End of London.

Aided by their daughter Lorraine, and two less than dynamic waiters (old Willie and young Dean), Nat and Shirley Silver struggle to make ends meet. Nat is small and timid, and just wants a quiet life; Shirley is tall and fiery and embodies many of the worst traits of the stereotypical Jewish mother: nagging, constantly airing the accusation that her loved ones are driving her to an early grave, dissatisfied with their standing in society, and burning with determination to have her daughter married off to the right man. Jewish references and themes were heavily spooned on, and, likewise, the phrasing and wording of the dialogue was stuffed with Jewish ethnicity. Enough, already!

Hanging discreetly on the wall of the Silver Diner was a photograph of Phil Silvers as Ernie Bilko, which only served to bring in sharp relief the difference between *The Phil Silvers Show*, a lovingly made salt-beef on rye, and *Every Silver Lining*, an undercooked potato latka.

Everyone A Winner

UK · C4 (REGENT PRODUCTIONS) · SITCOM

1 × 60 mins · colour

9 Mar 1988 · Wed 10.30pm

MAIN CAST
Rev Richard Hopkins · · · · · · · Jonathan Pryce
Sandra Hopkins · · · · · · · · · · · Anna Carteret
Mitch Gridgely · · · · · · · · · · · · Warren Clarke
Yvonne Gridgely · · · · · · Helen Atkinson Wood
Polly · · · · · · · · · · · · · · · · · · Emily Lloyd
Josh · · · · · · · · · · · · · · · Steven Mackintosh

CREDITS
writer Barry Pilton · *director* Paul Joyce · *producer* William G Stewart

The last of the six individual comedies in C4's *Tickets For The Titanic*, which took a wry look at Britain's 1980s decline, depicted a vicar and his wife struggling against the tide to make their community-caring cost-effective. Then their twin children, Josh and Polly, reach the school-leaving age, at which point they must go into employment (ironically, in *Everyone A Winner*, every family has 2.4 businesses), and come up with a startlingly different idea.

Exam Conditions

UK · ITV (CENTRAL) · CHILDREN'S SITCOM

1 × 30 mins · colour

3 July 1992 · Fri 4.30pm

MAIN CAST

Eric Shaffer · · · · · · · · · · · · · Paul Reynolds
Mr Carkdale · · · · · · · · · · · · · · Brian Blessed
Tracy · · · · · · · · · · · · · · · · Kate J Reynolds

CREDITS

writer Steven Moffat · executive producers Jos Tuerlinckx, Lewis Rudd · director/producer Jon Scoffield

A fine one-off comedy made by Central TV for the European Broadcasting Union's children's drama exchange programme. To aid foreign understanding, *Exam Conditions* was devoid of dialogue, placing the accent entirely on visual comedy, *à la Mr Bean*.

Paul Reynolds, familiar to younger viewers through his role as Colin Mathews in Central's long-running drama series *Press Gang*, starred as Eric Shaffer, a teenage schoolboy whose natural brilliance at life has given him a cocky confidence and a position of respect acknowledged even by the much-feared school bully. During an exam, Eric even finds the time to draw a picture of the stern invigilator Mr Carkdale (played by Brian Blessed), so easy has he found the questions. But, after handing in his paper early and leaving the room, he discovers, to his horror, that he has handed in the signed sketch instead of the exam answers. The bulk of the half-hour is given over to the drawn-out but comedically clever lengths that Shaffer invents to retrieve it, first from the exam hall and then from Carkdale's study. Eventually, by dint of a comedy of errors, hundreds of photocopies of the drawing are dispersed over the school playground, to the teachers and pupils gathered below.

Executive Stress

UK · ITV (THAMES) · SITCOM

19 × 30 mins · colour

Series One (7) 20 Oct–1 Dec 1986 · Mon 8pm
Series Two (6) 21 Sep–26 Oct 1987 · Mon 8pm
Series Three (6) 22 Nov–27 Dec 1988 · Tue 8.30pm

MAIN CAST

Caroline (Fielding) Fairchild · · Penelope Keith
Donald Fairchild · · · · · · · · · Geoffrey Palmer
· (series 1);
· · · · · · · · · · · · Peter Bowles (series 2 & 3)
Edgar Frankland Jr · · · · · · · · · · · Harry Ditson
Anthea Duxbury · · · · · · · · Elizabeth Counsell
Anthony · · · · · · · · · · · · · · · · · · Mark Caven
Nicky · Hilary Gish
Peter Stuart · · · · · Timothy Carlton (series 1);
· · · · · · · · · · · · · · · · David Neville (series 2)
Jackie · · · · · · · · Lorraine Doyle (series 1 & 2)
Stephen Cass · · · · · · · · · · · Ben Robertson
· (series 1 & 2)
Sylvia · · · · · · · · · Wanda Ventham (series 2)

Gordon · · · · · · · · Donald Pickering (series 2)
Tim Jackson · · · · · Vincent Brimble (series 3)
Peter Davenport · · · · · · · Geoffrey Whitehead
· (series 3)

CREDITS

writer George Layton · directors John Howard Davies (series 1 & 2), David Askey (series 3) · producers John Howard Davies (series 1 & 2), James Gilbert (series 3)

Married more than 25 years, Caroline and Donald have hatched and despatched five children. Donald commutes into London by train each day, from their home in leafy Buckinghamshire to his job at Ginsberg, a both-feet-in-the-past book publishing company. When Caroline decides to focus on work once more, after a gap of some three decades, Donald has in mind for his wife a part-time job in an Amersham florist's shop. She has in mind a return to her former career as a book editor and quickly lands a job with glitzy Oasis Publishing, owned by a US conglomerate called Frankland Corporation which is run by pushy American (the son of the ultimate boss) Edgar Frankland III. Here Caroline reunites with her former secretary Anthea Duxbury, now Oasis' export sales director.

The same day that Caroline starts her new job, Oasis takes over Ginsberg and, surprise, surprise, Caroline and Donald find themselves working for the same company, a situation that Donald, at first, finds incredible. Because Edgar Frankland refuses to allow his staff to fraternise, the new sales and marketing director (Donald) and editorial director (Caroline) must work closely together but keep their marriage secret, arriving and leaving separately, alluding to different-name spouses, having separate home phone lines installed and so on, this ruse taking up the weekly plot lines until, midway through the second series, Edgar finally discovers the truth. Surprisingly, he not only decides to keep both Caroline (who had been using her maiden surname Fielding) and Donald on the payroll, overlooking his own rule, but he makes them joint managing directors of the UK operation, from which point on *Executive Stress* becomes pretty much standard sitcom office fare.

Writer George Layton knows a thing or two about sitcoms, having starred in several (*For Richer For Poorer* and *It Ain't Half Hot Mum*), written others (*Don't Wait Up* and some episodes of *Robin's Nest* and *On The Buses*), and written/starred in (most memorably) the long *Doctor* series and also *My Brother's Keeper*. Choosing the publishing world as the location for his series was a smart move: it is perhaps unique among office situations in that the senior posts are populated mostly by women. This permitted Layton to legitimately place Caroline in a position that matched Donald's

seniority, and so introduce a feminist theme without being pushy in a *Spare Rib* way.

Cast changes were a problem, though. While Penelope Keith was still being wooed by Thames TV, who saw her as one of the guiding lights in their sitcom strategy (even though her first for them, *Moving*, had failed to take off), Geoffrey Palmer left after the first series. In his place came Peter Bowles, who had partnered Keith in *To The Manor Born*. Thames clearly hoped that they would gel as successfully as before. Lightning, however, being an awkward cuss, stubbornly refused to strike twice in the same place.

An Extra Bunch Of Daffodils

UK · ITV (LWT) · SITCOM

1 × 30 mins · b/w

24 May 1969 · Sat 7.30pm

MAIN CAST

Lawrence Warner · · · · · · · · Stratford Johns
Mrs Evans · · · · · · · · · · · · · Patsy Rowlands

CREDITS

writers Ray Galton/Alan Simpson · director/producer David Askey

The last in the series of individual comedies to be screened in the 1969 season *The Galton & Simpson Comedy*, this rewarding exercise in black humour bravely cast *Softly, Softly* heavyweight Stratford Johns in a Hancockesque role. He played a murderer who has killed his five wives in turn – Constance, Edith, Joyce, Mary and Beryl – each time reaping the rewards of their life insurance policies. When he tries to do the same to widower Mrs Evans (Patsy Rowlands), however, she turns the tables on him in an unexpected fashion – and turns out to be a mass-murderer herself.

F Troop

USA · ABC (WARNER BROS) · SITCOM

65 × 30 mins (34 × b/w · 31 × colour)

US dates: 14 Sep 1965–6 Apr 1967

UK dates: 29 Oct 1968–16 July 1974 (41 × b/w)
ITV Tue 6.30pm then Thu 6.05pm then
Fri 6.30pm

MAIN CAST

Capt Wilton Parmenter · · · · · · · · · Ken Berry
Sgt Morgan O'Rourke · · · · · · · Forrest Tucker
Cpl Randolph Agarn · · · · · · · · · Larry Storch
Wrangler Jane · · · · · · · · · Melody Patterson
Roaring Chicken · · · · · Edward Everett Horton
Chief Wild Eagle · · · · · · · · · · Frank DeKova
Crazy Cat · · · · · · · · · · · · · · · Don Diamond
Hannibal Dobbs · · · · · · · · · James Hampton
Trooper Duffy · · · · · · · · · · · · · Bob Steele
Trooper Vanderbilt · · · · · · · · · John Mitchum
Duddleson · · · · · · · · · · · · · · · · · Ivan Bell

CREDITS

creator Richard Bluel · writers Arthur Julian, Stan
Dreben, Seaman Jacobs, Howard Merrill, Ed
James · directors Charles Rondeau, Leslie
Goodwins · producers William T Orr, Hy Averback

A US sitcom that drew heavily upon
vaudeville-style humour to depict the
adventures of F Troop, a bunch of misfit
cavalrymen based at Fort Courage, an army
fortress in Kansas flanked on all sides by
Indian (that is, Native American) tribes. The
series was set in 1866, during the final days of
the Civil War, and the inept troop were led by
the ineffectual Captain Parmenter. Despite his
military ancestry, the captain was frequently
outsmarted by Sgt O'Rourke, who also
headed an illegal sideline dealing in Indian
souvenirs – the sergeant had negotiated a
clandestine peace treaty with the amenable
Hekawi Indians, a deal that benefited both
sides because it permitted the Indians to
trade and upgrade their living conditions,
and the troops to maintain the illusion that
they were involved in a deadly land war while
actually being in no danger. The only flaw in
this otherwise happy arrangement was the
troublesome Shugs, a genuine war-mongering
tribe who occasionally went into action.

F Troop was an entertaining enough
production which, in similar dubious taste to

Hogan's Heroes, made light of a deadly
serious period of history. The theme of
conniving military men pulling the wool over
the eyes of their superiors recalled the antics
of Sgt Bilko and his platoon, but *F Troop*
failed to hit the dizzy heights achieved by
The Phil Silvers Show.

Faces Of Jim

UK · BBC · SITCOMS

**20 editions (19 × 30 mins · 1 × short special) ·
b/w**

Series One (7) *The Seven Faces Of Jim* 16
Nov–28 Dec 1961 · Thu 8pm

Series Two (6) *Six More Faces Of Jim* 15 Nov–20
Dec 1962 · Thu 8.45pm

Short special *The Christmas Face Of Jim* 25 Dec
1962 · part of *Christmas Night With The Stars* ·
Tue 7.15pm

Series Three (6) *More Faces Of Jim* 28 June–9
Aug 1963 · Fri 8.45pm

MAIN CAST

Jimmy Edwards
June Whitfield
Ronnie Barker

CREDITS

writers Frank Muir/Denis Norden · producers
James Gilbert (series 1 & 2, special), Douglas
Moodie (series 3)

The star and writers of the BBC radio sketch-
comedy hit *Take It From Here* and the BBC
TV sitcom **Whack-O!** teamed again for these
three series of individual comedies, designed
to highlight Jimmy Edwards' versatility as a
comic actor rather than rely on the slightly
vulgar larger-than-life mannerisms with
which he had become most associated.
Edwards rose to the challenge, receiving fine
support from June Whitfield (another *Take It
From Here* hero) and Ronnie Barker, and the
programmes were a sizeable hit with viewers.

Note. All the stories in the first two series
were titled *The Face Of …*, whereas in the
third series they were *A Matter Of …*

The Face Of Devotion   16 NOV 1961

GUEST CAST
Victor Sylvester

Simple, honest and tender-hearted garage
owner Jim (Edwards) believes he might be
losing his beloved wife (Whitfield) to the lure
of professional ballroom dancing. (Ronnie
Barker was absent from this episode.)

The Face Of Genius   23 NOV 1961

GUEST CAST
Dick Emery
Paul Eddington
Prunella Scales

A sci-fi send up, with Edwards cast as a
brilliant scientist having to deal with a 'thing'
from 'outer somewhere-or-another'.

The Face Of Power   30 NOV 1961

GUEST CAST
Toke Townley

Ruthless Jimmy Micklethwaite (Edwards), a
maker of gas mantles, claws his way through
Victorian society to a position of luxury and
power despite a militant work force (led by
Ronnie Barker), only to have the rug pulled
from under him by the invention of electric
lighting.

The Face Of Dedication   7 DEC 1961

GUEST CAST
Richard Waring
Amanda Barrie

The village doctor (Edwards) may be saintly
now but his past holds a guilty secret that
could be exposed by the arrival of a
mysterious smiling stranger.

The Face Of Duty   14 DEC 1961

GUEST CAST
Richard Briers

A parody of the 1946 feature film *A Matter
Of Life And Death*, which told the story of a
Second World War fighter pilot. Here, retired
Wing Commander 'Iron Guts' Frobisher
(Edwards) and his plucky girl on the
microphone (Whitfield), who run a mini-cab
company, nervously guide back to base their
young 'flier' (Richard Briers) who is lost
somewhere on the foggy streets in the
company's one and only vehicle.

The Face Of Guilt   21 DEC 1961

GUEST CAST
Richard Briers

A ghost story set in a grim lighthouse off
the Cornish coast, where Caleb Tregarthen
(Edwards) is visited by the smouldering
Hannah Pengallon (Whitfield), the sister
of the previous lighthouse keeper who
mysteriously disappeared one year earlier.

The Face Of Enthusiasm   28 DEC 1961

GUEST CAST
Richard Briers
Amanda Barrie
Melvyn Hayes

A small-time theatrical agent (Edwards) has
a blinding flash of inspiration that enables
him to predict the next trends in popular
entertainment.

The Face Of Fatherhood   15 NOV 1962

GUEST CAST
Brian Oulton

A particularly notable edition, bringing to
vision for the first time the ghastly Glum

family, previously only heard in *Take It From Here*. Jimmy Edwards and June Whitfield reprised their wireless characters, with Ronnie Barker appearing as the hopeless Ron Glum (played on radio by Dick Bentley).

Sixteen years later the family resurfaced on ITV in **The Glums**. See also *The Christmas Face Of Jim*, below.

The Face Of Retribution   22 NOV 1962

GUEST CAST
Richard Waring
Donald Hewlett

Jim, the village grocer, suddenly discovers the ability to read minds. His appalled family want him to seek medical help, but then they start to appreciate the financial potential of the gift.

The Face Of Wisdom   29 NOV 1962

GUEST CAST
Jimmy Thompson

Although his younger colleague is sceptical, Doc Jamieson (Edwards) has lived in Java long enough not to underestimate the power of the local witch doctor (Barker).

The Face Of Perseverance   6 DEC 1962

GUEST CAST
Richard Waring
Patrick Newell
Eunice Black
Arthur Ridley

A Jane Austen spoof. James Bonnet determines to marry off his six unwed daughters by throwing a grand ball and tricking unsuspecting bachelors into compromising positions with them.

The Face Of Loyalty   13 DEC 1962

GUEST CAST
Patrick Newell
Pat Coombs
Vic Wise

Monger's Marauders were a crack commando unit during the war. Now, over 20 years later, the men, middle-aged, are brought together to aid their colonel with one more daring mission.

The Face Of Tradition   20 DEC 1962

GUEST CAST
Patrick Newell

Jim is deeply proud of the family tradition: a pantomime-horse act named the Withers Brothers and Dobbin. But his younger brother, Sid, has his heart set on the 'legit' theatre and walks out on the partnership. It is reconciled when Jim marries Sid's replacement, Gloria.

The Christmas Face Of Jim   25 DEC 1962

This short sketch for the BBC's traditional seasonal compilation *Christmas Night With The Stars* was another Glums performance (see *The Face Of Fatherhood*, above) – while a Christmas party is taking place around them, Ron and Eth try to complete a crossword puzzle and Pa is making amorous advances towards a neighbour.

A Matter Of Amnesia   28 JUNE 1963

Psychiatrist Dr Brunner (Barker) has his work cut out trying to unravel the puzzle of a patient suffering from severe amnesia (Edwards).

A Matter Of Growing Up   5 JULY 1963

GUEST CAST
Derek Nimmo

Mr Padgett (Edwards) finds fatherhood somewhat less than rewarding thanks to the attitude of his son Lennie (Barker). When Lennie performs a hormone operation on a potted plant, Mr Padgett finds the plant far more responsive than his son.

A Matter Of Spreadeagling   19 JULY 1963

GUEST CAST
Edwin Apps

With a nod towards *The Spread Of The Eagle*, the BBC's recent cycle of Shakespearean plays, this pre-*Up Pompeii!* farce featured Edwards as the wall-building Roman, Hadrian; Whitfield as the hostile Saxon leader, Rowena; and Barker as a lovelorn, blank-verse-spouting lieutenant, Lascivius.

A Matter Of Upbringing   26 JULY 1963

GUEST CAST
Amanda Barrie
Patrick Connor

Edwards starred as professional wrestler Big Jim Paxton, who has sacrificed the best years of his life in order to give his sons the advantages that he had been denied.

A Matter Of Espionage   2 AUG 1963

Retired secret agent Fleming (Edwards) makes a startling discovery about an incident in the last war and tries to use the information to return to active service, working for his old chief, Sanderson (Barker), whose code-name is 'M1'.

A Matter Of Empire   9 AUG 1963

The paradisiacal existence of Sir James Chubb (Edwards) as the Governor-General of the tropical island of Mandinao is threatened by the arrival of crusading politician Butters (Barker). But help is on hand from Madame Soo (Whitfield), the proprietor of 'The Teahouse Of A Thousand Delights', who has a plan to nullify the Butters effect.

The Fainthearted Feminist

UK · BBC · SITCOM

5 × 30 mins · colour

19 Mar–16 Apr 1984 · BBC2 Mon 9pm

MAIN CAST

Martha	Lynn Redgrave
Josh	Jonathan Newth
Mary	Sarah Neville
Mo	Helen Cotterill
Mother	Joan Sanderson
Irene	Polly Adams

CREDITS

writers Jill Tweedie/Christopher Bond · *director* Mandie Fletcher · *producer* Zanna Beswick

'Letters From A Fainthearted Feminist', Jill Tweedie's column in the newspaper *The Guardian*, was a great success – many readers could see aspects of their own life reflected in the dispatches from 'Martha' to 'Mary', in which the former bemoaned her mission of trying to maintain feminist principles in a chauvinist household, where her teenage male children believe that if their mother doesn't wash the dirty dishes then it must be their sister's turn. The column was so popular, indeed, that it was translated into this BBC2 sitcom, with Lynn Redgrave starring as the hapless Martha.

In the series, Martha, Mary and their friends at the Sebastapol Women's Centre are trying to do their bit for the feminist movement but are usually thwarted by the intransigence of conventional outlooks and hidebound attitudes to gender. At home, Martha's husband Josh is a decent enough chap but he suffers from the programming that dictates many of the infuriating responses of his sex. In his way, although not to any great extent, Josh tries to support Martha, but he is especially wary of the more militant Mary.

Although this is a subject largely ignored in British TV comedy, outside the work of Carla Lane, *The Fainthearted Feminist* failed to have the same sort of staying power on TV as the newspaper columns and its follow-up comic strip.

Fairly Secret Army

UK · C4 (VIDEO ARTS TELEVISION) · SITCOM

13 × 30 mins · colour

Series One (6) 22 Oct–26 Nov 1984 · Mon 8.30pm

Series Two (7) 1 Sep–13 Oct 1986 · Mon 8.30pm

MAIN CAST

Harry Truscott	Geoffrey Palmer
Beamish	Jeremy Child

Nancy · · · · · · · · · · · · · · · · ·	Diane Fletcher
Doris Entwhistle · · · · · · · · · · · · ·	Liz Fraser
Sgt Major Throttle · · · · · · · ·	Michael Robbins
Peg-Leg Pogson · · · · · · · · · · ·	Paul Chapman
Ron Boat · · · · · · · · · · · · ·	Richard Ridings
2nd Lt Bagnall · · · · · · · · · · ·	Jeremy Sinden
Crazy Colin Carstairs · · · · · · ·	James Cosmo
· ·	(series 1)
Stubby Collins · · · · ·	Ray Winstone (series 1)
Jill · · · · · · · · · · · · ·	Diana Weston (series 2)
Lennie · · · · · · · · · · · ·	Carl Chase (series 2)
Paul · · · · · · · · · · · · · · ·	Gary Cady (series 2)
Smith · · · · · · · · · · ·	John Nettleton (series 2)
The Cobra · · · · ·	Michael J Jackson (series 2)

CREDITS
writer David Nobbs · directors Robert Young (series 1), Roy Ward Baker (series 2) · producer Peter Robinson

Tricky wallahs, sitcoms. In *Fairly Secret Army*, writer David Nobbs took the basics of his Jimmy Anderson character from *The Fall And Rise Of Reginald Perrin*, extended the personality and landed a new series. But while the same actor, Geoffrey Palmer, played the part, viewers were no longer seeing Jimmy but Harry. Harry Kitchener Wellington Truscott.

True, there were many similarities between Harry and his role-model. Like Jimmy, Harry is a retired army johnnie, formerly a major with the Queen's Own West Mercian Lowlanders. Trouble is, although the services have retired him, Harry has not retired the service. He is singularly unqualified to do anything else, and still talks like a military machine ('cock-ups', 'nosh', 'caper', 'hush-hush', 'mum's the word', and so on).

One of the many highlights of *The Fall And Rise Of Reginald Perrin* was the episode in which Jimmy displayed to Reggie his secret cache of rifles, put aside 'in case the balloon goes up'. In *Fairly Secret Army* that inflatable object – Harry believes – is about to ascend. He supposes there's a battle to be fought, to 'rekindle the spirit of the British Lion' by forming a group dedicated to fighting the 'wet-leftie-feminist-loonies' taking over the country. He and his fraudulent and dangerous right-wing cronies set out to rescue the country from itself.

They're destined to fail, fighting among themselves much of the time. No surprise, really – Harry has been a failure all his life, not to mention two sandwiches short of a picnic. And naïve to the point of being ripped off at every turn, he doesn't have a clue how to relate to people, least of all the opposite sex, with one wrecked marriage behind him and more failings ahead, despite becoming engaged to Nancy. 'Treacherous chaps, women.' Indeed.

Shot on film and without an audience, *Fairly Secret Army* lasted two series but received little attention from viewers or critics. As Harry would have said, 'awkward blighters'.

The Faith Brown Chat Show

UK · ITV (LWT) · IMPRESSIONISM

6 × 30 mins · colour

26 Jan–1 Mar 1980 · Sat 8.15pm

MAIN CAST
Faith Brown

CREDITS
writers Dennis Berson, Garry Chambers, Ken Hoare · director/producer John Kaye Cooper · executive producer David Bell

Mimic and comedian Faith Brown found extra work after 1979 when, happily for her at least, there was sudden mileage to be gained from impersonating the country's new Prime Minister. Pam Ayres, Lene Lovich, Barbra Streisand, Eartha Kitt, Angela Rippon, Mae West, Diana Ross, Mary Whitehouse, Donna Summer, Zsa Zsa Gabor, Hylda Baker, Bette Midler, Lena Horne and others also came in for the Brown treatment.

Faith In The Future

UK · ITV (LWT) · SITCOM

15 × 30 mins · colour

Series One (7) 17 Nov–29 Dec 1995 · Fri 8.30pm
Series Two (8) 8 Nov–27 Dec 1996 · Fri 8.30pm

MAIN CAST

Faith Grayshot · · · · · · · · ·	Lynda Bellingham
Hannah · · · · · · · · · · · · · · ·	Julia Sawalha
Paul ·	Jeff Rawle
Jools · · · · · · · Charlie Creed-Miles (series 1);	
· · · · · · · · · · · · · · · · · ·	Simon Pegg (series 2)
Gareth · · · · · · · · · · · · · · · · ·	Robert Swann

CREDITS
writers Jan Etherington/Gavin Petrie · director Sylvie Boden · executive producer Mark Robson · producer Jamie Rix

The sequel to *Second Thoughts*. Faith has split up with Bill, her children have finally left home, and she's even off-loaded her loyal dog. The net result, much sought after, is that Faith is free and footloose for the first time since she was a teenager, with her own flat and a job as an adult education art teacher. The liberty is short-lived, though, because daughter Hannah returns from the around-the-world trip she started at the end of *Second Thoughts*, and moves back in, cramping Faith's new relationship with college colleague Paul, as if her menopausal mood swings were not already causing problems enough. As Faith battles with her weight, the change of life, her feelings for Paul and the return of her daughter, life takes on its customary chaotic turn. She and Paul eventually find their way into bed, only to discover that their conversations carry more spark than their carnal desires. Hannah, meanwhile, is being pursued by Jools, who stands little hope of capturing her heart but is relentless in the chase. Hannah says she wants to move out of Faith's flat but seems

destined to remain with Mum, carrying on their tempestuous relationship for ever.

Faith In The Future was very much a sitcom of the 1990s, with a clear borrowing of slick American production techniques, right down to the music in between scenes and, the first two series at least, 'filmised' video quality. Frantic and at times bewildering, it was something of a disappointment after the highs of *Second Thoughts*. Nonetheless, after taking a year out in 1997, a third series was scheduled to arrive on screens in early 1998, at the same time as a US adaptation of *Faith In The Future* was being piloted there by CBS (under the wing of American TV writer Pam Norris).

The Fall And Rise Of Reginald Perrin

UK · BBC · SITCOM

22 episodes (21 × 30 mins · 1 × 5 mins) · colour

Series One (7 × 30 mins) 8 Sep–20 Oct 1976 · BBC1 Wed 9.25pm
Series Two (7 × 30 mins) 21 Sep–2 Nov 1977 · BBC1 Wed 9.25pm
Series Three (7 × 30 mins) 29 Nov 1978–24 Jan 1979 · BBC1 Wed 9.35pm
Short special (5 mins) part of *The Funny Side Of Christmas* 27 Dec 1982 · BBC1 Mon 8.05pm

MAIN CAST

Reginald Perrin/ ·	
Martin Wellbourne · · · · · ·	Leonard Rossiter
Elizabeth Perrin · · · · · · · · · · ·	Pauline Yates
C J ·	John Barron
Joan Greengross/Webster · · ·	Sue Nicholls
'Doc' Morrisey · · · · · · · · · · · ·	John Horsley
Tony Webster · · · · · · · · · · · ·	Trevor Adams
David Harris-Jones · · · · · · · · ·	Bruce Bould
Prue Harris-Jones · · · · · · ·	Theresa Watson
Jimmy Anderson · · · · · · · ·	Geoffrey Palmer
Tom Patterson · · Tim Preece (series 1 & 2);	
· · · · · · · · · · · · · ·	Leslie Schofield (series 3)
Linda Patterson · · · · · · ·	Sally-Jane Spencer

OTHER APPEARANCES

Mark Perrin · · · · · ·	David Warwick (series 1)
Mr Pelham · · · · · ·	Glynn Edwards (series 2)
Miss Erith · · · · · ·	Joan Blackham (series 2)
Seamus Finnegan · ·	Derry Power (series 2)
McBlane · · · · · · · ·	Joseph Brady (series 3)

CREDITS
writer David Nobbs · producers Gareth Gwenlan (20), John Howard Davies (1), Robin Nash (special)

The Fall And Rise Of Reginald Perrin was quite unlike most other sitcoms: it employed a serial storyline and featured adult themes of disillusionment and loss, and a central character who was on the verge of a nervous breakdown. It was also fantastically funny. David Nobbs adapted his 1975 comic novel *The Death Of Reginald Perrin* as the first series of this quintessentially British sitcom (it was retitled *The Fall And Rise Of*

Reginald Perrin for paperback) and, originally, the author wanted Ronnie Barker to play the part of Perrin, a middle-aged sales executive combating a mid-life crises with flights of fantasy. Instead, he was blessed with Leonard Rossiter, who delivered an outstanding performance in the role.

The plot centres on Sunshine Desserts, a confectionary company where Perrin is a desk-bound sales executive. The business is run by C J, a powerful figure full of impressive-sounding aphorisms that, on analysis, prove meaningless, comprising a heap of mixed metaphors and clichés piled one on top of another. C J has a quality of elusiveness that makes dealing with him frustrating, for it is impossible to decipher what he actually thinks about any given subject. Most of his statements begin with the all-purpose introduction 'I didn't get where I am today by …' followed by a baffling example of what he did or didn't do to arrive at his present status. He also has a penchant for whoopee cushions, so that meetings begin with a definite air of farce.

Perrin's colleagues, Tony Webster and David Harris-Jones, are equally superficial and lacking in original thoughts, meeting any suggestion with a simple one-word platitude, 'Great!' (Tony) or 'Super!' (David), so that the only difference between them is chemical: Tony bluffs that he is one of life's great kidders, amazingly confident and about to go places, whereas David is an intensely nervous individual, with zero confidence and a perpetually sweaty disportment. The dithering company doctor is no use either: he knows nothing about medicine and lives in hope that a sick female employee might be 'feeling chesty' so that he can have an opportunity to examine the problem area.

Then there is Reggie Perrin's secretary Joan, a middle-aged bundle of simmering sexuality, fatally attracted to Reggie and liable at any moment to pounce on him. At home, Reggie's wife Elizabeth is pleasant and understanding, but it's her very tolerance and unchanging reliability that grates on Reggie and adds to his malaise. Then there is Reggie's exceedingly boring son-in-law Tom, who makes appalling home-made wine, and his wildly off-centre brother-in-law Jimmy, whose military background seems to have cast him adrift in civilian life where he appears hopelessly out of his depth, using militaristic forms of speech to explain his predicament ('No food. Bit of a cock-up on the catering front').

From episode one, Perrin's life is brain-numbingly predictable and repetitive – the train ride into London is always 11 minutes late, whatever the excuse – but there are already signs that he is going off the rails

with his lapses into surreal reverse logic and a bizarre habit of visualising a hippopotamus whenever thinking of his mother-in-law. In short, Perrin, at the age of 46, is questioning the meaning of life, and going through a real and quite terrifying mid-life crisis. Gradually his brain parts company with normality and madness becomes the order of the day. In a last-ditch attempt to preserve his sanity and escape the rat-race, he fakes his own suicide by leaving a pile of clothes on a beach and walking off into the sunset. (This plot was echoed in real life when prominent British politician John Stonehouse faked his own death in identical circumstances.) Wondering what it would be like to attend his own funeral, Reggie then wears a fake beard, calls himself Martin Wellbourne and falls in love anew with Elizabeth, who recognises his true identity but, for a while, pretends otherwise.

The Fall And Rise Of Reginald Perrin proved sufficiently popular for the BBC to recommission, and Nobbs once again wrote a novel, *The Return Of Reginald Perrin* (published 1977), which he then adapted for a second TV series. In this Reggie soon jettisons his Martin Wellbourne persona, reveals that he's not dead and reacquaints himself with his relatives and old work colleagues. After a brief spell working at a piggery for a Mr Pelham, and warding off the advances of a dowdy spinster Miss Erith, Perrin sports a new devil-may-care attitude and launches a shop, Grot, dedicated to selling useless things, and even he is amazed when it becomes a massive global success. Reggie remarries Elizabeth, who has become a Grot business executive, and when Sunshine Desserts collapses he relocates his former colleagues at the Grot HQ. But still Reggie is numbed by routine and eerily finds himself taking on the traits and mannerisms of C J. The second series ends with Perrin, his wife and C J *all* faking their suicides.

The third and final book, *The Better World Of Reginald Perrin* (1978, once again written in tandem with the TV scripts), formed the basis of the somewhat inferior final series. Here Reggie has his most ambitious project to date: he gathers the usual crew and launches Perrins, a self-contained commune for the middle-aged and middle-class, where its members can learn to live in harmony and then set out to spread the gospel. The dialogue was still sharp but the *Perrin* idea seemed to have run its course and there was a distinct lack of energy about this third series. In following the first two, however, which contained some of the sharpest and funniest comedy ever aired on TV, it did have a hard act to follow.

A poor US adaptation, called simply *Reggie*, was made by ABC in 1983, and a variation on the Jimmy character appeared in the C4 series *Fairly Secret Army* a year later. And then, fully 20 years after the original series, David Nobbs returned to the main theme, although this time his character (and the actor who portrayed him) had genuinely passed on …

The Legacy Of Reggie Perrin

UK · BBC · SITCOM

7 × 30 mins · colour

22 Sep–31 Oct 1996 · BBC1 mostly Sun around 8.30pm

MAIN CAST

Elizabeth Perrin	Pauline Yates
C J	John Barron
Joan Greengross	Sue Nicholls
'Doc' Morrisey	John Horsley
David Harris-Jones	Bruce Bould
Prue Harris-Jones	Theresa Watson
Jimmy Anderson	Geoffrey Palmer
Tom Patterson	Tim Preece
Linda Patterson	Sally-Jane Spencer
Geraldine Hackstraw	Patricia Hodge
Hank	Michael Fenton Stevens
Welton Ormsby	David Ryall
Morton Radstock	James Bannon

CREDITS

writer David Nobbs · *director/producer* Gareth Gwenlan

Oh dear. While it is easy to enter into retrospective criticism, David Nobbs would have done better than to succumb to temptation and revive the Reginald Perrin TV series. Not only did *The Legacy Of Reggie Perrin* badly miss its leading light – Leonard Rossiter, alas, having died in 1984 – but it lacked all the qualities that so distinguished the three 1976–79 series, and most especially the first two of these. True, every other actor returned to their posts (bar one, the Tony Webster character having been written out), all the old catchphrases were revived, and Gareth Gwenlan returned as producer, but scarcely a trace of the old sparkle remained.

The premise was thin, and might best have been suited to a single 60-minute production. Reggie has died (in 1995, according to his headstone) and left one million pounds to his wife, daughter, son-in-law, brother-in-law and former colleagues. To earn their share – and carry on where he himself had left off – each has to do something utterly ludicrous. After faffing about on their own for a while, the potential legatees unite to undertake one combined task, forming BROSCOR (the Bloodless Revolution of Senior Citizens and the Occupationally Rejected) to march on London and take over the running of the country. They fail, of course, and although they are applauded for their wacky idea, they are informed that this has not been quite absurd enough, the series ending without a pay-out.

One major new member was added to the cast for the revival, Patricia Hodge (she had previously appeared in David Nobbs' *Rich Tea And Sympathy*), cast as Geraldine Hackstraw, the seductive lawyer appointed by Reggie to reveal the content of his will and judge the merits of the ludicrous tasks the potential legatees must undertake. Along the way Miss Hackstraw is wined and dined by C J and the Doc, and even bedded by Jimmy, but, somehow, remains alluringly out of reach.

The final episode was left open-ended, so there may well be further explorations of the Reggie Perrin idea in the future. Without wishing to seem unkind, but with an immense reverence for the original books and 1975–79 TV series, perhaps it would be best if the whole thing is now left alone.

Family Affairs

UK · BBC · SITCOM

14 × 30 mins · b/w

29 Oct 1949–18 Feb 1950 · mostly Sat 9.30pm

MAIN CAST

Linda Connover · · · · · · · · Heather Thatcher
Henry Connover · · · · · · · · Michael Shepley
Tony Connover · · · · · · · · · · · Denis Gordon

CREDITS

creator Betty Farmer · *writer* Eric Maschwitz ·
producer Michael Mills

Broadcast live from Alexandra Palace most weekends in the winter of 1949–50, this series was an odd cross between sitcom and soap opera – with the emphasis on comedy – which detailed the domestic exploits of the Connovers, a middle-class family living in Northwood, prime 'Metroland' territory north of London. This was a period when much experimentation was being done within the TV medium to find winning formats and *Family Affairs* (initially billed as *Family Affair*) was one such experiment. Viewers were split over the programme's merits.

The Family Of Fred

UK · BBC · SITCOM

1 × 30 mins · b/w

10 May 1968 · BBC1 Fri 8.20pm

MAIN CAST

Fred Holmes · · · · · · · · · · · · Freddie Frinton
Aggie Plunkett · · · · · · · · · · · · Jean Kent
Carol Holmes · · · · · · · · · · · · Judi Bloom
Janet Holmes · · · · · · · · · · · Carolyn Moody
Vicki Holmes · · · · · · · · · · · · Roberta Rex

CREDITS

writer Peter Robinson · *producer* Douglas Argent

A *Comedy Playhouse* try-out that united comedian Freddie Frinton (who had enjoyed much success in *Meet The Wife*) with the 'bad girl of British films' Jean Kent. The premise was simple enough: a widower of 12 years, Fred Holmes' life is dominated by women – his three daughters and the husband-hunting Aggie Plunkett next door, who makes her quest, Fred, crystal clear.

No series ensued, this particular battle of the sexes lasting only one round.

Family Ties

USA · NBC (UBU PRODUCTIONS/PARAMOUNT) · SITCOM

*165 episodes (157 × 30 mins · 6 × 60 mins · 1 × 90 mins · 1 × 120 mins) · colour

US dates: 22 Sep 1982–14 May 1989

UK dates: 6 July 1985–20 Nov 1986 (50 × 30 mins) C4 Sat then Wed 6pm

MAIN CAST

Elyse Keaton · · · · · · · Meredith Baxter-Birney
Steven Keaton · · · · · · · · · · · Michael Gross
Alex P Keaton · · · · · · · · · · · · Michael J Fox
Mallory Keaton · · · · · · · · · · · Justine Bateson
Jennifer Keaton · · · · · · · · · · · Tina Yothers
Andrew Keaton · · · · Brian Bonsall (1986–89)
Skippy Handelman · · · · · · · · · · · Marc Price
Nick Moore · · · · · Scott Valentine (1985–89)
Ellen Reed · · · · · · · · Tracy Pollan (1985–86)
Lauren Miller · · · · Courteney Cox (1987–89)

CREDITS

creator/producer Gary David Goldberg · *writers* various · *directors* various

The premise of *Family Ties* is simple but neat: Elyse and Steven Keaton, who met and married in the hippy days of the late 1960s, continue to espouse liberal, counter-culture ideals. Their children, however, reflect the decade in which they are growing up: the 1980s, and their eldest son Alex (played by Michael J Fox), in particular, is firmly Republican (or, to put it into British terms, Conservative with a capital C). *Family Ties'* creator/producer Gary David Goldberg was a self-confessed former hippy, and the show was his statement about the Reagan (for UK, read Thatcher) era. President Reagan duly declared *Family Ties* his favourite TV show, and his administration team offered Fox the job of media spokesman for the committee to re-elect Ronnie for a second term. Fox rejected the approach, indicating that he was still a Canadian citizen and that, besides, his viewpoint was not the same as Alex's. (Perhaps just as well.)

The Keaton family live in suburban, well-to-do circles in Columbus, Ohio. Both parents are professionals: Elyse is an architect, Steven a journalist for a public TV station. Neither has forgotten the ideals of the late 1960s: they love one another, they are environmentalists and demanding of equality between races, religions and sexes, and they remember

Woodstock and Bob Dylan with affection and pride. So they are not best pleased to discover that their 17-year-old son Alex has developed into a Nixon- and Reagan-loving capitalist, out to enrich himself at the expense of others and unafraid to show his teeth in the dog-eat-dog world. He's bright, as sharp as the shirt and tie he always wears and sails through exams with an annoying degree of self-confidence.

Alex's siblings are not into politics but they're still children of the 1980s and so their values are anathema to their parents. Alex lords the intellectual superiority he assumes over his clothes-crazy dumb-brunette 15-year-old sister Mallory – and, later, over her Fonz-like boyfriend Nick. Jennifer (nine years old at the start of the series) initially comes under Alex's domination but, upon discovering her higher IQ level, keeps him pretty much at bay. Then (in the fourth US season of *Family Ties*, coinciding with Meredith Baxter-Birney's real-life pregnancy) a baby brother, Andy, comes along, over whom Alex can feel paternal. He gives Andy a model of Ronald and Nancy Reagan's ranch-house lovingly crafted out of lolly sticks, and does his best to instil greed in him – although his work is always undone by his parents' coaching.

The biggest problem faced by the *Family Ties* team was in ensuring that the radical and often rude Alex won over rather than alienated the viewers. Gary David Goldberg overcame this by maintaining an open-door policy on the set (which, of course, fitted perfectly with his ideals), embracing suggestions from the entire production crew. It was also customary for Alex to win his way through most of an episode but be defeated or deflated by show's end, and be depicted as someone who undoubtedly cherished his family, even if he did have an odd way of showing it. Love interest was provided for Alex when he began dating his first regular girlfriend, the art student Ellen, played by Tracy Pollan. As it happened, the attraction was genuine: Pollan married Michael J Fox in real life in 1988. She left the show soon after – Ellen, it was said, went to Paris – and a new entanglement was introduced for Alex, psychology student Lauren Miller, who encourages him to take part in a study of over-achievers, attend therapy sessions and reach inside to expose his repressed inner self. But it's all to no avail: the series concludes with a one-hour special in which Alex leaves home to take up a $75,000 a year position as an investment banker in New York, disagreeing with his parents to the last and – much to their distress – breaking the family ties.

It is one of life's ironies that baby-faced Michael J Fox, cast by Goldberg in the Alex role, was the only actor to whom NBC executives initially objected. (They wanted

Matthew Broderick to play the part.) But Goldberg held firm and within weeks of the show's premiere it was obvious that Alex, in Fox's hands, was the main attraction. Indeed, *Family Ties* turned the little-in-stature and hitherto little-known Canadian, just 21 at the time, into a major star, a position confirmed when he made a transition into the movies with Spielberg's *Back To The Future* in 1985.

Incidentally, Gary David Goldberg based the Alex character on the step-son of a friend with whom he had shared the 1960s experience, and, perhaps in an effort to alter that person's viewpoint, Goldberg employed him on *Family Ties*. The part of Jennifer was based upon Goldberg's own daughter, and Steven and Elyse were based on Goldberg and his partner Diana.

Goldberg and Fox reunited in 1996 for the US sitcom **Spin City**.

*Notes. Five further episodes, not screened in the first run, have turned up in repeat airings. Also, with the breaking down into 30-minute pieces of some of the extended episodes, 176 half-hours are now in regular syndication.

The cast of *Family Ties* turned up, in character, in *Mickey's 60th Birthday*, an hour-length Walt Disney TV tribute to its famous mouse that combined animation with specially shot live action sequences. Screened in the USA by NBC on 3 November 1988, the programme was first shown in Britain by ITV some eight weeks later, on Christmas Day morning, under the title *Mickey Mouse At 60*.

The Famous Teddy Z

USA · CBS (HUGH WILSON PRODUCTIONS/ COLUMBIA PICTURES TELEVISION) · SITCOM

20 × 30 mins · colour

US dates: 18 Sep 1989–12 Jan 1990 (17 episodes)

UK dates: 3 Oct 1989–11 Sep 1991 (20 episodes) BBC2 Tue 9pm then various days and times

MAIN CAST

Teddy Zakalokis	Jon Cryer
Grandma Deena Zakalokis	Erica Yohn
Al Floss	Alex Rocco
Laurie Parr	Jane Sibbett
Abe Werkfinder	Milton Selzer
Richie Herby	Tom La Grua
Aristotle Zakalokis	Josh Blake
Harland Keyvo	Dennis Lipscomb

CREDITS

creator Hugh Wilson · *writers* Hugh Wilson, Richard Dubin, Max D Tash, Craig Nelson, Wayne Lemon, Bob Wilcox and others · *directors* Hugh Wilson Jr, Richard Dubin, Max D Tash and others

Teddy Zakalokis was a humble mail-room employee at the Unlimited Talent Agency in Hollywood when an encounter with hot star Harland Keyvo changed his life. A 'difficult' talent, Keyvo was impressed by Teddy's straightforward manner and refusal to kow-

tow, and decided to make the youngster his agent – much to the amazement of Teddy's boss Richie and colleague Laurie, and much to the chagrin of Keyvo's current representative Al Floss. Teddy soon starts work and, although it is obvious that he knows nothing about the entertainment business, he manages to stumble along and baffles his Grandma Deena by earning vast amounts of money while seeming to do very little. His nephew Aristotle is hugely impressed however, and thinks the whole situation fabulous. As the work grows more complex, Teddy hires Laurie (on whom he has a crush) as an assistant, rightfully recognising that her obsession with the business makes her something of an expert in the field. Despite their collective inexperience, they manage to keep things ticking over well enough to placate the star and UTA boss Abe.

This show-business-based sitcom seemed tailor-made for Michael J Fox, but the star had already played a similar role in the 1987 movie *The Secret Of My Success*. Instead, Jon Cryer played the title role as a character destined to react to events rather than dictate them – trying to do his best while being carried along with the flow. Far-fetched though the premise might seem, it was actually inspired by a true story, that of Jay Kantor, who was working in the mailroom at MCA in 1947 when he crossed paths with rising star Marlon Brando. The actor admired Kantor's style and made him his agent, and Kantor turned out to be a natural, excelling as an agent and going on to become a successful film producer. Thus, in *The Famous Teddy Z*, the superstar's name Harland Keyvo has a similar ring.

Fancy Wanders

see KING, Dave

The Fanelli Boys

USA · NBC (KTMB/TOUCHSTONE TELEVISION) · SITCOM

20 × 30 mins · colour

US dates: 8 Sep 1990–16 Feb 1991

UK dates: 5 Sep–13 Oct 1995 (10 episodes) BBC1 Tue 2.40pm then daily 9.35am

MAIN CAST

Theresa Fanelli	Ann Morgan Guilbert
Dominic Fanelli	Joe Pantoliano
Anthony Fanelli	Ned Eisenberg
Frankie Fanelli	Chris Meloni
Ronnie Fanelli	Andy Hirsch
Father Angelo	Richard Libertini
Philamena	Vera Lockwood
Eddie DeTucci	Nick DeMauro

CREDITS

main writers/executive producers Barry Fanaro/Mort Nathan, Kathy Speer/Terry Grossman · *director* James Burrows

Through the work of directors Francis Ford Coppola and Martin Scorsese, US movie audiences have been fixated with Italian/American families and their involvement in organised crime. Their films were distinguished by the detailed interplay between the family members, a device which demonstrated that, although the protagonists were men of extortion and extreme violence, they were nevertheless good and loving family members. *The Fanelli Boys* concentrated on a Brooklyn-based Italian/American family that in many ways resembled those featured in such movies – employing the same rhythms and cadence in their Italian/American accents – but who, aside from one dubious member, were not involved in crime.

Widower Theresa Fanelli was the matriarch of a family of four boys: straitlaced Anthony, stupid Frankie, restless college kid Ronnie and the aforementioned dubious sort, wheeler-dealer Dominic (known as Dom). With the help, and sometimes hindrance, of her priest brother, Father Angelo, Theresa has always tried to keep the boys on the straight and narrow. Their problems were set out in the opening episode: Anthony, who has taken over the family's undertaking business, has allowed it to run down to near bankruptcy; Frankie has caught his fiancée *in flagrante delicto* and is in danger of returning to a life of womanising; Ronnie is contemplating dropping out of college after falling in love with a Jewish mother many years his senior; and Dom's nefarious schemes have backfired and now he too is destitute. With these factors in place, Theresa decides to cancel her proposed move to Florida to concentrate on getting her boys through their bad patches. Her solution is for Dom to work with Anthony in the family business (despite the friction that exists between them), for Frankie to only go out with women she has approved, and for Ronnie to continue his affair but only on the grounds that he lives at home and commutes to college. Adding a touch of colour to the proceedings was neighbour Philamena, a nutty spiritualist forever crashing in with bizarre predictions or feelings of dread.

The series was well acted, and played rather low key, allowing for moments of drama to develop between the laughs; it was also paced differently from most sitcoms and more resembled a stage-play. But despite its good points, the blood-is-thicker-than-water theme wore thin and after a few months US audiences bade the show *arrivederci*.

Farrington Of The FO

UK · ITV (YORKSHIRE) · SITCOM

14 × 30 mins · colour

Series One (7) *Farrington Of The FO* 13 Feb–27 Mar 1986 · Thu 8.30pm

Series Two (7) *Farrington* 3 June–15 July 1987 · Wed 8.30pm

MAIN CAST

Harriet Emily Farrington · · · · · Angela Thorne
Major Percy Willoughby-Gore · · · John Quayle
Fidel Sanchez · · · · · · · · · · · Tony Haygarth
Annie Begley · · · · · · · · · · · · · Joan Sims

OTHER APPEARANCES

P J Parker · · · · · · · · · · Tim Barrett (series 1)

CREDITS

writer Dick Sharples · *directors* Don Clayton (series 1), Ronnie Baxter (series 2) · *producer* Ronnie Baxter

Embassy comedies are almost as common as the cigarette coupons used to be – both ITV and the BBC had screened their **Foreign Affairs** before this Yorkshire TV venture. The twist here was that the diplomat in question was a woman.

Posted to a Latin American 'banana republic' as the new British Consul-General, Harriet Emily Farrington has to prove herself in a job that has been too hot to handle for her male predecessor, a task made even harder because her colleague, former Coldstream Guardsman Major Willoughby-Gore, wants her out. As he does his level best to take the shine off her brass plate, she has to deal with revolutions, budget cuts, corruption, defectors, lost tourists and the like. Fortunately, Farrington has plenty of experience, having worked all over the world and become known as 'the diplomatic bag', and so she succeeds.

Two series – 14 episodes – evolved, and the sitcom enjoyed moderate success. Sadly, it was blighted by two problems. The first was the incredible cheapness of the sets. While viewers would not have expected real location footage from South America, the scenery at Yorkshire TV's Leeds studio completely failed to convince. Secondly, the episodes were littered with characters with *the* most obvious Spanish names – Josef Alvarez, Lolita Fernandez, Josef Garcia, Luis Gomez, Jose Gonzales, Pedro Martinez, Carlos Ramos, Alberto Rodriguez and many others. Granted, Dick Sharples was writing a comedy about a South American country, but the names, and his series, seemed just too clichéd.

Fascinating Aïda

UK · BBC · STANDUP

1 × 40 mins · colour

28 Apr 1988 · BBC2 Thu 10.10pm

MAIN CAST

Dillie Keane
Adele Anderson
Denise Wharmby

CREDITS

writers Dillie Keane/Adele Anderson · *director* Keith Cheetham · *producer* Tony Staveacre

The fiendishly clever comedy cabaret trio Fascinating Aïda were already an established stage success and had appeared on TV in a number of guest spots before headlining in this show from BBC Bristol. Renowned for their witty songs, the group presented comedy and music with a feminine and feminist perspective, with a style that fell somewhere between Joyce Grenfell and Victoria Wood. The trio had formerly consisted of Dillie Keane, Adele Anderson and Marilyn Cutts, but by the time of this TV recording Cutts had left and been replaced by Denise Wharmby, a Tasmanian.

Note. In their book *The Jokes On Us*, about women in comedy, authors Morwenna Banks and Amanda Swift point out that, initially, Adele Anderson, who had undergone a sex-change, 'employed a more male aggressive stance within the group'. She later softened this attitude, feeling less vulnerable in front of audiences and gaining confidence from the all-female camaraderie of the group and from their director Nica Burns, of the Donmar Warehouse theatre in London.

Fast And Loose

see MONKHOUSE, Bob

Fast Forward   Australia

AUSTRALIA · 7 NETWORK (ARTIST SERVICE) · SKETCH

74 × 60 mins · colour

Australian dates: 12 Apr 1989–26 Nov 1992 (and specials on 30 Apr & 5 May 1993 · 13 Feb & 20 Feb 1994)

UK dates: 24 Sep 1994–9 Mar 1996 (13 × 25 mins) BBC2 Sat around 1.30am

MAIN CAST

Michael Veitch
Marg Downey
Magda Szubanski
Geoff Brooks
Steve Blackburn
Jane Turner
Gerry Connolly
Glen Robbins
Gina Riley
Steve Vizard
Alan Pentland
Brendan Luno
Peter Moon

CREDITS

writers cast and Andrew Knight, Tim Richards, Doug MacLeod, Tim Harris, Robert Adams, Gary McCaffrie, John Hercuvim, Ted Emery, Kevin Carlin, Max Dann, Paul McDonald, Jon Olb · *director* Ted Emery · *executive producers* Ted Emery, Andrew Knight, Steve Vizard · *producer* Mark Ruse

An earthy and funny sketch show, spoofing film and television and featuring, in its original version at least, some hilariously accurate impersonations of well-known Australian stars. Concentrating on these lampoons, the editions screened in the UK were especially re-edited 'international versions', slickly put together by Ray Cameron with the aid of consultant Barry Cryer. Well-designed sets, impressive look-alike make-up and commendable vocal impressions resulted in a barrage of high quality sketches, usually with scripts to match.

The same creative team went on to launch a similar sketch series, **Full Frontal**. See also **Big Girl's Blouse**.

Fast Forward   UK

UK · BBC · CHILDREN'S SKETCH

19 × 25 mins · colour

Series One (7) 7 Nov–19 Dec 1984 · BBC2 Wed 5.35pm

Series Two (6) 14 Jan–25 Feb 1986 · BBC2 Tue 5.35pm

Series Three (6) 25 Feb–1 Apr 1987 · BBC1 Wed 4.30pm

MAIN CAST

Floella Benjamin
Nick Wilton
Joanna Monro (series 1 & 2)
Andrew Secombe (series 1 & 2)
Robert Harley (series 2 & 3)
Sarah Mortimer (series 3)

CREDITS

writers various · *producers* Ann Reay, John Smith, David Crichton, Trevor McCallum

A zany, anything-goes quickfire comedy for kids with its title, taken from the VCR button, neatly defining its period. *Fast Forward* was a collection of loosely linked sketches and skits with a running joke concerning the show's pet, Tiny (a pastiche of the *Blue Peter* obsession with pets), who was never seen, although his enormous drinking bowl suggested that his name was ironic. In the final series recurring characters included Robert Harley as the wacky spaceman Milton Keenze from the planet Zymatron, and adventurer and explorer India Rubber Jones. Corny? Yes, but the children at whom it was aimed seemed to like it.

The Fast Show

UK · BBC · SKETCH

23 editions (21 × 30 mins · 1 × 45 mins · 1 × short special) · colour

Series One (6) 27 Sep–1 Nov 1994 · BBC2 Tue 10pm

Short special · part of *Fry And Laurie Host A Christmas Night With The Stars* 27 Dec 1994 · BBC2 Tue 9pm

Series Two (7) 10 Feb–29 Mar 1996 · BBC2 Fri 9pm

Special (45 mins) 27 Dec 1996 · BBC2 Fri 9.40pm

Series Three (8) 14 Nov–29 Dec 1997 · BBC2 mostly Fri 9.30pm

MAIN CAST
Paul Whitehouse
Charlie Higson
Mark Williams
John Thomson
Simon Day
Arabella Weir
Caroline Aherne (aka Caroline Hook)

OTHER APPEARANCES
Paul Shearer
Maria McErlane
Robin Driscoll
Felix Dexter
Colin McFarlane
Eryl Maynard

CREDITS
main writers Paul Whitehouse/Charlie Higson ·
other writers cast and Jane Bussman, Craig Cash,
Nathan Cockerill, David Cummings, Dave Gorman,
Richard Preddy/Gary Howe, Graham Linehan/
Arthur Mathews, Fiona Looney, Lise Mayer, Eryl
Maynard, Bob Mortimer, Henry Normal, Brendan
O'Casey, Jonathan Powell, Glen Power, David
Quantick, Paul Shearer, Rhys Thomas and others ·
directors Arch Dyson/John Birkin (series 1), Mark
Mylod/Sid Roberson (series 2), Mark Mylod
(special & series 3) · *executive producer* Geoffrey
Perkins · *producers* Paul Whitehouse/Charlie
Higson

A fast-paced sketch show assembled by Paul
Whitehouse and Charlie Higson. The pair
had put in sterling work for their friend
Harry Enfield, and Higson had contributed
considerably to Reeves and Mortimer's TV
successes, but here they demonstrated the full
range of their comic vision, coming up with
a galaxy of new comedy characters and
situations. In so doing, and in heading a
seven-strong team of creative talents, they
presented an ensemble sketch show to
challenge the very best in the genre.

The Fast Show had no narrative or abstract
link tying the sketches together; instead the
pieces tumbled out one after another. Most
were recurring ideas, appearing in successive
episodes or more than once in the same
programme – a device that had served
Harry Enfield well and one popularised by
Dick Emery. Here, the sketches were
short and quick, some of the material was
intentionally 'odd' rather than funny, and
several of the characters took a while to get
used to, although their reappearances soon
demonstrated their comic value.

Perhaps the show's most memorable
creation was the repressed homosexual
country squire Lord Ralph Mayhew (Higson)
and his deeply uncomfortable attempts at
forging an intimate relationship with Ted
(Whitehouse), his Irish estate worker ('Well,
I wouldn't know about that, sir'), but there
were dozens of other fine characters,
including – to name some of the more than
100 seen during the three series – the
nonsensical football pundit Ron Manager
(Whitehouse); the phlegm-ridden TV
presenter Bob Fleming (Higson); the accident-
prone northern pensioner Unlucky Alf
(Whitehouse) who greets his every accident
with a resigned 'Bugger'; the 'Competitive
Dad' Simon Johnstone (Day) always trying to
score over his children; the enthusiastic but
gullible young northern lad (Whitehouse)
who considers everything 'brilliant'; the
interfering pub know-all Billy Bleach (Day);
the rambling, brain-addled gentlemen's club
member Rowley Birkin QC (Whitehouse) who
is always 'very, very drunk'; the kindly man
Patrick Nice (Williams), usually found in his
kitchen or greenhouse, whose riposte for
every subject, irrespective of its import, is
'which was nice'; the ducking-and-diving
wide boy Chris Jackson, aka 'The Crafty
Cockney' (Whitehouse), who, being a 'geezer,
a little bit tasty, a little bit wooor and a
little bit waayyy', will 'nick anything'; Jesse
(Williams), the scruffy country bumpkin who,
in the first two series, emerged from a shed
to tell us about his diet and then, in the third,
particularly incongruously, about what
fashions he would be wearing this season;
Professor Denzil Dexter (Thomson), an
American university hippy science tutor;
Archie (Whitehouse), the sad old character
in a pub who, in order to strike up a
conversation, claims to have done the
stranger's occupation 'for 30 years, man and
boy', noting that 'it's the hardest job in the
world'; Louis Balfour (Thomson), the TV *Jazz
Club* presenter to whom everything is 'nice!'
or 'great!' or some such 'cool' adjective; the
13th Duke of Wymbourne (Whitehouse), an
old scoundrel who looks into the camera and
asks suggestively what he should be doing
semi-clad in a schoolgirls' changing room;
Janine Carr (Aherne), the gormless Rochdale
lass who tries to see the bright side of a glum
life; Simon Bush and Lyndsay Mottram
(Whitehouse and Higson), a pair of gung-ho
intrepids to whom everywhere is 'gripped'
and 'sorted'; Monkfish (Day), the TV cop; No
Offence (Weir), the South African department
store saleswoman who feels no remorse about
insulting the customers, theoretically in their
best interests; Chip Cobb, the Deaf Stuntman
(Thomson), who happily sends himself to
oblivion upon mishearing the TV director's
instructions; Carl Hooper (Day), the
Australian TV presenter of *That's Amazing*,
regularly angered by his inadequate studio
guests; the Tory MP Geoffrey Norman
(Higson) who says 'No' to everything; the vain
woman (Weir) who continually worries about
her figure, asking 'Does my bum look big in
this?'; Swiss Toni (Higson), the smoothie
used-car salesman who likens everything to
'making love to a beautiful woman'; the dim-
witted barmaid (Aherne) who states the
obvious yet cannot make sense of it; the
young man who agrees with whatever people
are saying, being swayed by every point of
view (Whitehouse); the squeamish zoo keeper
(Williams); Dave Angel (Day), a cockney who
presents a cheapo TV programme about
caring for the environment; Johnny (Higson),
the keen amateur painter whose brain flips
when he hears himself saying the word
'black'; Roger Nouveau (Thomson), a yuppie
of the 1980s who, in the 1990s, has jumped on
the suddenly upmarket football bandwagon;
and the nosey supermarket check-out girl
(Aherne) who makes deprecating observations,
oblivious to her rudeness, about the goods
people are buying.

Clever filming techniques enhanced the
appearances of music-hall comic Arthur
Atkinson (Whitehouse), who, until the third
series, was always seen in scratched black
and white footage accompanied by an
authentic-sounding audio track of audience
laughter. Atkinson's material, although
totally baffling and unfunny, was identical
in tone and style to the patter of a 1930s/
1940s comic (catchphrases: 'Where's me
washboard?' and 'How queer!') and was at all
times a stunningly accurate pastiche. By the
third series, time had moved on and we saw
Atkinson in a 1950s British TV sitcom and
playing a cameo role in a 1970s British
cinema *Confessions* sex romp – again,
lovingly crafted lampoons. These Atkinson
sequences were usually introduced by Simon
Day in the guise of his alter ego Tommy
Cockles.

Style also played a part in the sketches
featuring Chanel 9, a southern Europe (no
actual country given, but probably Spanish)
TV station, which parodied the simple
techniques, gaudy colours and sexist
presentations seen on certain Mediterranean
channels and was the source of the
catchphrase 'Scorchio!'. This was, perhaps, an
esoteric target for satire but the team rightly
figured that the majority of their viewers
would have seen such fare on overseas
holidays or on cable/satellite TV. The other
two major characters in *The Fast Show* were
the slimy, sex-obsessed menswear assistants
(Whitehouse and Williams) who delighted
in pumping customers for details of their
sex lives and littered their enquiries with
suggestions and blatant references to the sex
act – a sort of stream of single entendres –
while being alternately insulting and
ingratiating ('*Suits* you, sir!').

The combination was wonderful, and the
programmes were imbued with a way-above-
average share of pathos. There were more
ideas in one edition of *The Fast Show* than
many series have in their entirety. Such was
the show's influence that many of the
catchphrases entered the national
consciousness, and schools, offices, factories
and parties rang to the words long after each
series of *The Fast Show* had left the screen.
One of the characters knowingly anticipated
this: Colin Hunt, the archetypal office nerd

(played by Higson), who mindlessly repeats the catchphrases he's witnessed on TV the night before.

Perhaps this last point best sums up the ethos of *The Fast Show*: these people knew what they were doing. While not every scene was funny, the sheer in-your-face barrage of one-liners and catchphrases was overpowering. It was as if Whitehouse and Higson, keen students of TV comedy, recognised the old adage that Catchphrase Is King but wanted to subvert it to the point of insanity, with dozens of them assaulting viewers in every edition of the show. The fact that most of them hit the mark was nothing less than fantastic: many comedians are lucky if they can find one lasting, recognisable catchphrase in their entire career but *The Fast Show* luxuriated in them, even though one suspects that its participants – much like Harry Enfield with his posse of characters – will cheerfully ditch their inventions as their careers move on.

Notes. The cast of *The Fast Show* combined with the leading players in Vic Reeves and Bob Mortimer's anarchic game-show *Shooting Stars* for a long season of live performances in London at the beginning of 1998.

Caroline Aherne, aka Caroline Hook, one of *The Fast Show* team, enjoyed her own success with **The Mrs Merton Show**.

Father Charlie

UK · ITV (CENTRAL) · SITCOM

6 × 30 mins · colour

28 Feb–11 Apr 1982 · Sun mostly 8.15pm

MAIN CAST
Father Charlie · · · · · · · · · · · · · Lionel Jeffries
Reverend Mother Joseph · · · · · Anna Quayle
Sister Anna · · · · · · · · · · · · · · Annet Peters
Sister Bernadette · · · · · · · Denyse Alexander
Sister Clare · · · · · · · · · · · · Wendy Smith
Sister Frances · · · · · · · · · · · · Esther Byrd
Sister Lucy · · · · · · · · · · · · · Jamila Massey
Sister Mary · · · · · · · · · · · · Deddie Davies
Sister Mercedes · · · · · · · · · · Gillian Royale
Sister Theresa · · · · · · · Jean Buik Morton

OTHER APPEARANCES
Bishop Larkin · · · · · · · · · · · · John Savident
Father Costello · · · · · · · · Christopher Good

CREDITS
writers Vince Powell (4), Myles Rudge (2) ·
director/producer Stuart Allen

The eccentric and not altogether wholesome Father Charlie, converted to the cloth in his advancing years, is appointed chaplain to a convent, The Sisters of St Winifred's. His views are diametrically opposed to the Mother Superior's; worse, not that such things should matter, let alone within serious religion, he hails from a working-class background and she's clearly the product of a more refined stock. The six episodes drew

comedy from the differences, being basically a two-hander for those fine and experienced actors Lionel Jeffries and Anna Quayle.

Father, Dear Father

UK · ITV (THAMES) · SITCOM

49 episodes (13 × 30 mins · b/w; 32 × 30 mins · colour; 4 × short specials · colour)

Series One (7 × b/w) 5 Nov–17 Dec 1968 · Tue around 8.30pm
Series Two (6 × b/w) 27 May–1 July 1969 · Tue mostly 8.30pm
Short special (colour) · part of *All-Star Comedy Carnival* 25 Dec 1969 · Thu 6pm
Series Three (6 × colour) 12 May–16 June 1970 · Tue mostly 8.30pm
Short special (colour) · part of *All-Star Comedy Carnival* 25 Dec 1970 · Fri 6pm
Series Four (7 × colour) 15 June–27 July 1971 · Tue around 7pm
Series Five (6 × colour) 13 Sep–18 Oct 1971 · Mon 8.30pm
Short special (colour) · part of *Mike And Bernie Winters' All-Star Christmas Comedy Carnival* 25 Dec 1971 · Sat 6.05pm
Series Six (7 × colour) 13 June–25 July 1972 · Tue around 7pm
Short special (colour) · part of *All-Star Comedy Carnival* 25 Dec 1972 · Mon 5.45pm
Series Seven (6 × colour) 2 Jan–6 Feb 1973 · Tue around 7pm

MAIN CAST
Patrick Glover · · · · · · · · · · · Patrick Cargill
Anna Glover · · · · · · · · · · · · · Natasha Pyne
Karen Glover · · · · · · · · · · · · Ann Holloway
Matilda Harris ('Nanny') · · · · · · · Noël Dyson

OTHER APPEARANCES
Barbara Mossman · · · · · · · · Ursula Howells
Bill Mossman · · · · · · · · · · · · · Patrick Holt;
· Tony Britton
Georgie Thompson · · · · · · · · · Sally Bazely;
· Dawn Addams
Mrs Glover (Patrick's mother) · · · Joyce Carey
Timothy Tanner · · Jeremy Child (series 6 & 7)

CREDITS
writers Johnnie Mortimer/Brian Cooke ·
director/producer William G Stewart

A long-running sitcom that starred Patrick Cargill as the author of Bond-style adventure novels, left in charge of two nubile late-teen daughters, Anna and Karen, after his wife Barbara had gone off and married his best friend, Bill. In a permanent state of harassment, Patrick takes on 'Nanny' to look after the household and its three occupants, but she believes that the answer to every domestic dilemma (and there are *many*) is a cup of tea. Patrick's principal solace is his only male companion: a St Bernard dog called H G Wells, except that the dog prefers to sleep most of the time. The end of the sixth series saw eldest daughter Anna marry her boyfriend, Timothy Tanner, but the couple move in during the seventh and final series, preserving the domestic flavour of the comedy that was always more ho-hum than ho-ho.

In the fashion of US sitcoms, many episodes of *Father, Dear Father* featured a guest star, and among those who appeared (some more than once) were Eric Barker, Rodney Bewes, June Whitfield, Richard O'Sullivan, Bill Fraser, Donald Sinden, Dandy Nichols, Beryl Reid, Ian Carmichael, Hugh Paddick, Bill Pertwee, Peter Jones, Joan Sims, Richard Wattis, Leslie Phillips, Jack Hulbert, Hugh Paddick and Roy Kinnear. There was also a *Father, Dear Father* feature film (1972, same principal cast, writers and director) which, typically, failed to amount to very much, and then there was an Australian-made version of the TV series **Father, Dear Father In Australia** (next entry).

Note. In addition to the 49 episodes, Patrick Cargill, Ann Holloway and Natasha Pyne made a special appearance, in character, in the 1 March 1970 edition of the ATV game-show *The Golden Shot*. The three also turned up in Thames TV's *The Edward Woodward Hour* on 4 August 1971, in a sequence especially written by Mortimer and Cooke wherein the Glovers met Woodward's British secret agent Callan. Finally, Thames networked a one-hour Patrick Cargill special, *Patrick, Dear Patrick*, on 26 January 1972, part of which was set in the Glover household of *Father, Dear Father*.

Father, Dear Father In Australia

AUSTRALIA · 7 NETWORK (LYLE MCCABE PRODUCTIONS) · SITCOM

14 × 30 mins · colour

Australian dates: 25 June 1978–28 June 1980
*UK dates: 5 Sep 1978–17 Oct 1980 (10 episodes) ITV mostly Tue 7pm

MAIN CAST
Patrick Glover · · · · · · · · · · · Patrick Cargill
Matilda Harris ('Nanny') · · · · · · · Noël Dyson
Liz · · · · · · · · · · · · · · · · · · Sally Conabere
Sue · · · · · · · · · · · · · · · · · Sigrid Thornton

OTHER APPEARANCES
Jeffrey · · · · · · · · · · · · · · · · · · Ron Fraser

CREDITS
creators Johnnie Mortimer/Brian Cooke · writers Johnnie Mortimer/Brian Cooke, Richard Waring, Donald Churchill, Jon Watkins, Ken Sterling and others · director/producer William G Stewart

Five years after the last *Father, Dear Father* was made by Thames, Patrick Cargill and Noël Dyson went Down Under to star in a new version being made by the 7 Network, titled, appropriately enough, *Father, Dear Father In Australia*. One cannot but smile at the 'ingenuity' of the plot: finally shot of his two daughters, Patrick was in Australia for six months to research a new book, and had taken (why?) 'Nanny' with him. They intended to stay with Patrick's brother Jeffrey, but, upon their arrival, Jeffrey announced that he was being sent to London for six months. Could, said brother wondered, he leave his two nubile daughters, Liz and Sue, for Patrick and 'Nanny' to look after?

*Note. In first run, ten of the 14 episodes, which spanned two Australian series, were screened in the UK by London-area ITV under the title *Father, Dear Father*, dropping the Australian suffix. Ultimately, taking subsequent repeat runs into account, ending 28 September 1982, all 14 were screened.

Father Matthew's Daughter

UK · BBC · SITCOM

6 × 30 mins · colour

11 May–22 June 1987 · BBC2 Mon 9pm

MAIN CAST

Father Matthew · · · · · · · · · · · James Bolam
Sharon · · · · · · · · · · · · · · · · Gabrielle Lloyd
Father Charlie · · · · · · · · · · · · Ray Winstone
Holly · · · · · · · · · · · · · · · · Samantha Hurst

CREDITS

writers Terence Brady/Charlotte Bingham · *director/producer* David Askey

Married writing partners Brady and Bingham knew a Catholic priest whose sister had been killed in an accident and bequeathed her teenage daughter to his charge. The full story was that, when she had made the will, her brother was a soldier, a Protestant and something of a party animal. Years later, he had 'seen the light' and become a priest, but the will was never changed. Nearly 20 years after the accident, the writers took the situation as the theme for their new series, which they labelled with the American term 'dramady', a blend of drama and comedy.

James Bolam was cast as Father Matthew, the unlikely guardian of eight-year-old Holly. She seems a troubled child on the surface but Matthew is determined to get through to her and release the happy, normal girl he believes dwells within. To avoid any misunderstandings, the sister of Father Charlie, his curate, provides a bed for Holly.

Father Of The Bride

USA · CBS (MGM-TV) · SITCOM

34 × 25 mins · b/w

US dates: 29 Sep 1961–14 Sep 1962

UK dates: 20 Sep 1962–23 May 1963 (34 episodes) ITV mostly Tue 6.15pm

MAIN CAST

Stanley Banks · · · · · · · · · · · · · Leon Ames
Ellie Banks · · · · · · · · · · · · · · Ruth Warrick
Kay Banks/Dunston · · · · · · · · Myrna Fahey
Tommy Banks · · · · · · · · · · · Rickie Sorensen
Buckley Dunston · · · · · · · · · · Burt Metcalfe

CREDITS

creator Edward Streeter · *executive producer* Robert Maxwell

Although modelled on the Oscar-nominated 1950 film of the same name, which starred Spencer Tracy and Elizabeth Taylor, this US sitcom of suburbia never quite scaled the heights. Leon Ames starred as the lawyer Stanley Banks, decidedly uneasy about the plans of his 'princess' daughter Kay to marry Buckley Dunston. Ruth Warrick was cast as Ellie, Kay's mother, who held no such reservations. Indeed, the happy couple were engaged in the opening episode and married midway through the series, causing father plenty more worries.

Although the TV series was no great shakes, the original movie proved popular enough to result in a sequel, *Father's Little Dividend* (1951), and the durable premise resurfaced again in a 1991 remake, also called *Father Of The Bride*, which featured comedy actor Steve Martin in the Spencer Tracy role. This too spawned a sequel, *Father Of The Bride II*, released in 1995.

Father Ted

UK · C4 (HAT TRICK PRODUCTIONS) · SITCOM

17 episodes (16 × 30 mins · 1 × 70 mins) · colour

Series One (6) 21 Apr–26 May 1995 · Fri 9pm

Series Two (10) 8 Mar–10 May 1996 · Fri 9.30pm

Special (70 mins) 24 Dec 1996 · Tue 10pm

MAIN CAST

Father Ted Crilly · · · · · · · · · Dermot Morgan
Father Dougal McGuire · · · · · Ardal O'Hanlon
Father Jack Hackett · · · · · · · · · · Frank Kelly
Mrs Doyle · · · · · · · · · · · · · Pauline McLynn

CREDITS

writers Graham Linehan/Arthur Mathews · *director* Declan Lowney · *executive producer* Mary Bell · *producers* Geoffrey Perkins (series 1), Lissa Evans (series 2 & special)

Mostly successful in its choice of US comedy imports, C4 has proved less adept at developing home-grown sitcoms, relying instead upon standup acts and alternative variety shows to carry the British banner. The long-running and popular ***Desmond's*** and ***Drop The Dead Donkey*** have proved honourable exceptions to this rule and both have the credentials (ethnicity in the first, scathing satire in the second) one would expect from this constantly challenging channel. But C4's third major UK sitcom success, *Father Ted*, seemed, at first, an oddly old-fashioned product for such an adventurous outlet, being concerned as it was with religion. Such sitcoms in the past (***All Gas And Gaiters***, ***Oh Brother!***, ***Bless Me, Father*** and even Dawn French's ***The Vicar Of Dibley***) had all scored with the mainstream public with their gentle humour that lightly poked fun at the church. *Father Ted*'s premise – three priests living and working together on a bleak Irish isle – seemed to suggest similar fare, but nothing could have been further from the truth.

Father Ted was a rollicking success from day one, a marvellous, surreal, genuinely bizarre mix of whimsy, blarney, satire and violence packaged in outrageously funny plots. The action takes place in the priests' home on remote Craggy Island, where Father Ted Crilly struggles to control his two fellow priests, the young Dougal and the old Jack. Ted is a complex character, well-meaning on the surface but vain and greedy underneath, with a lust for fame and glory never far away. Dougal, his young protégé, is strangely obtuse and stupendously dense, with a habit of asking blindingly obvious questions (if Ted is reading a book, Dougal inevitably asks, 'Are you reading a book, Ted?') that seriously irritates Ted and leads to a torrent of un-priest-like language. But Ted is an amateur in the ways of curse words compared to the heinous, constantly-smashed Jack, a grizzled, nasty termagant whose brain has been addled by booze. Jack, the most extreme of the unholy trinity, is a scabby, foul-smelling wretch who sits in his chair either asleep or staring wildly into the distance, venomously cussing ('Feck!', 'Arse!', 'Knickers!' and so on). A hideous ratbag he may be, but a hysterically funny one nonetheless, and a monstrous comic creation blending all the hallmarks of Alf Garnett and Albert Steptoe.

Overseeing these three is the housekeeper, Mrs Doyle, another larger-than-life comic caricature. She seems normal enough at first but can easily slip into the weird zone, maddeningly repeating the same phrase over and over again ('go on, go on, go on, go on, go on, go on, go on, go on, go on') when attempting the simplest task like finding out if the priests want their tea. Another of Mrs Doyle's unnerving habits is her ability to hugely raise the decibel level of her voice from one end of a sentence to another. Sporting a permanent, prominent cold-sore on her lip, Mrs Doyle seems right at home in this bleak priest hole.

But in addition to the fine cast, the other stars of the piece were writers Graham Linehan and Arthur Mathews, who managed to create a refreshingly novel style that combined witty, oddball dialogue with mindbogglingly extreme situations, encompassing anything from the priests entering the Eurovision Song Contest, to Father Ted and a gang of his fellow priests being lost for hours in the women's lingerie section of a department store. And the writers weren't above indulging themselves by introducing silly names: Ted Crilly himself, but also characters like Father Dick Byrnes, Father Todd Unctious, and Sampras, Dougal's pet rabbit. (The character of Father Ted, incidentally, first appeared in Mathews' standup routine.)

All the priests in *Father Ted* came across as juvenile delinquents, arrested adults delighting in name-calling, point-scoring, taunting and flaunting their own personal successes. Although containing the odd salient swipe at the Catholic church and religion in general, such digs were softened by the series' overtly unreal nature and its surreal characterisation and plotting. It was, perhaps, an acquired taste, but one worth persevering with, for, as Mrs Doyle would say, even if you don't get it at first, eventually you will, you will, you will, you will, you will, you will, you will, you will …

Note. In their Father Ted and Father Dougal characters, Dermot Morgan and Ardal O'Hanlon hosted a section of BBC1's **Comic Relief** on 14 March 1997. Pauline McLynn (as Mrs Doyle) and Frank Kelly (as Father Jack) also had cameo parts in one of the routines. This was the only new appearance of *Father Ted* in 1997, although a third, and probably final, series was being readied for unveiling in March 1998.

Father's Day

UK · C4 (PICTURE PARTNERSHIP
PRODUCTIONS) · SITCOM

14 × 30 mins · colour

*Series One (6) 17 Apr–22 May 1983 ·
Sun 8.45pm

Special · 25 Dec 1983 · Sun 7.20pm

Series Two (7) 8 July–19 Aug 1984 · Sun 9.15pm

MAIN CAST

Lyall Jarvis · · · · · · · · · · · · · · · · John Alderton
Dee Jarvis · · · · · · · Rosalind Ayres (series 1);
· · · · · · · · · Karen Archer (special & series 2)
Gemma Jarvis · · · · · · · · · Dominique Barnes
Toby Jarvis · · · · · · · · · · · · · · Zac Nicholson
Tasha Jarvis · · · · · · · · · · · · · · Kate Alderton
Lyall's father · · · · · · · · · · · · · · Paul Angelis

CREDITS

creator Hunter Davies · writers Peter Spence (all except special), Stan Hey (special) · director Leszek Burzynski · producer Brian Eastman

A C4 series by Peter Spence (the writer of **To The Manor Born**) based on Hunter Davies' regular 'Father's Day' column in *Punch* magazine – collated into book form in 1981. The column was autobiographical to the extent that Davies related experiences with his own three children, albeit with a dash of journalistic licence. Played by John Alderton, the lead character in the TV series was named Lyall Jarvis and, like Davies, he was a northerner by birth, living in the south and working as a writer. Episodes related his struggle, as the father, to keep pace and keep in with his family, only to find that the children ran rings around him. Jarvis shouted and cajoled, but to little effect.

Kate Alderton, John's nine-year-old daughter, played his youngest daughter here, aged about seven, an example of the home-made, shoestring nature of *Father's Day*. John Alderton wore his own clothes – which also indicates how well he was cast – and took down paintings from his home to hang on the set, while the production crew supplied much of the furniture.

*Notes. Although produced for C4, one of the first series' six episodes (the fifth) was picked by ITV to premiere *Father's Day* during a special one-off evening, *ITV's Channel Four Showcase*, dedicated to the (relatively) new channel's programmes and screened on 7 April 1983. The episode was then given a second airing, by C4, at its rightful place in the first run, on 15 May 1983.

The American ABC network screened a pilot for a proposed new comedy series, also titled *Father's Day*, on 25 July 1986, in which a former 1960s radical, now an auditor for the IRS, tries to cope with his growing children. No series developed. It is not clear whether this was related to the British *Father's Day*.

Fawlty Towers

UK · BBC · SITCOM

12 × 30 mins · colour

Series One (6) 19 Sep–24 Oct 1975 · BBC2
Fri 9pm

Series Two (6) 19 Feb–26 Mar 1979 & 25 Oct 1979 · BBC2 mostly Mon 9pm

MAIN CAST

Basil Fawlty · · · · · · · · · · · · · · · John Cleese
Sybil Fawlty · · · · · · · · · · · · Prunella Scales
Manuel · · · · · · · · · · · · · · · · · Andrew Sachs
Polly · · · · · · · · · · · · · · · · · · · Connie Booth
Major Gowen · · · · · · · · · · · Ballard Berkeley
Terry · · · · · · · · · · · · · · · · Brian Hall (series 2)
Miss Tibbs · · · · · · · · · · · · · · · Gilly Flower
Miss Gatsby · · · · · · · · · · · · · Renée Roberts

CREDITS

writers John Cleese/Connie Booth · directors John Howard Davies (series 1), Bob Spiers (series 2) · producers John Howard Davies (series 1), Douglas Argent (series 2)

These 12 achingly funny visits to a Torquay hotel represent British situation comedy at its finest. On most people's top ten lists, it is a hot contender for the Best Sitcom Ever and would be an automatic choice for this honour had it managed to extend its outstandingly high level of quality for, say, another couple of series – consistency over a long run being perhaps the true measure of sitcom greatness. But John Cleese has never been one to outstay his welcome and he terminated *Fawlty Towers* precisely because he believed that he and his co-writer Connie Booth had extracted the best from the idea and further episodes would have resulted in ever-diminishing returns.

The genesis of the series began in 1971, when Cleese and some of the other *Monty Python* team stayed in a hotel in Torquay, Devon (reportedly the Gleneagles), managed by an incredibly ill-tempered man. Realising the comedic potential in such a situation, Cleese used the character in one of the episodes of **Doctor At Large** that he scripted, 'No Ill Feeling!' (the manager then was George Clifford, played by Timothy Bateson; his hectoring wife was played by Eunice Black), and that series' producer Humphrey Barclay suggested the character and the hotel could form a basis for a sitcom. Cleese wasn't so sure but kept the idea in the back of his mind.

Following his early departure from **Monty Python's Flying Circus**, Cleese was approached by the BBC's James (Jimmy) Gilbert and asked whether he would like to come up with a new series. Cleese said yes and stated that he wanted to write it in collaboration with his wife Connie Booth – they had already contributed a sketch, 'The Princess With The Wooden Teeth', for *Monty Python's Fliegende Zirkus*, and had adapted a Chekhov story for their 1974 short film *Romance With A Double Bass* (directed by Robert Young). The Torquay hotel setting was one of several ideas that they considered and Cleese realised that Barclay was right: there was a series in it.

Fawlty Towers made its first appearance on BBC2 on 19 September 1975. It had a simple but clever premise. Basil Fawlty, a frustrated, angry, short-tempered, super-snobbish misanthrope, is the very antithesis of the sort of person who should run a hotel, where a calm demeanour, winning smile, patience and a desire to make guests feel at home are the required attributes. But run a hotel Basil does, the quaint Fawlty Towers, or, rather, he runs it jointly with his formidable wife Sybil, a woman who has the ability to exude the required superficialities but is monstrously vitriolic towards her husband. Despite his anger and tendency to verbal violence, Basil is definitely under Sybil's thumb: she rules the roost, and rarely on TV have viewers witnessed such seething hatred, with no undercurrent of love, between a married couple. To help run the hotel the Fawltys employ Polly, a sensible, down-to-earth maid/waitress who is often embroiled in Basil's schemes and their inevitably disastrous consequences, being forced to lie on his behalf or extricate him from trouble (for which he rarely thanks her since she is merely an underling, the hired help). The Fawltys also employ a Spanish waiter/porter and general dogsbody, Manuel. A keen worker, Manuel is eager to please but possesses a poor command of the English language. In the position of the dog to be kicked following run-ins with his wife, Basil vents most of his frustrations on Manuel, screaming at the hapless soul, browbeating him and often physically assaulting him.

The varying hotel guests in each episode were, sometimes no more than nominally, plot catalysts, but it was the interplay between these four central characters that formed the series' engine. The episodes were paced like a stage farce, accelerating as the stew thickened, with Cleese playing Basil like a demented stick insect, employing an exaggerated style of physical comedy that viewers had only occasionally seen in *Monty Python*. Facially, Cleese can form the most intense expressions of anger or grief, but while witnessing Basil go through these routines was funny enough, Cleese realised that having other people catch Basil in the act was even funnier. Whatever absurd position or dilemma Basil found himself in, he exacerbated by lying with the most ridiculous explanations. Prunella Scales, meanwhile, who had shed her *Marriage Lines*-style vulnerability, portrayed Sybil as a hideous cross between a coiffeured sycophant and the Medusa. Even her voice was an instrument of terror, as she, so small in stature compared to his lumbering height, barked at Basil and made him literally shake with fear. His suffering at her hands would have been unbearable had he not so richly deserved it for his crass stupidity and snobbishness. Worse suffering was experienced by Manuel, whom Andrew Sachs portrayed as a frightened rabbit, often flinching in Basil's presence, expecting and usually receiving punishment for errors he was usually unaware he had committed. Manuel wasn't quite as stupid as Basil thought him, but the character was thought likely to offend Spaniards, so when the series aired in Spain he was made out to be Italian. Connie Booth rightly played Polly as the normal one of the bunch (Marilyn to the Fawlty Munsters, if you like), an innocent abroad trying to get by but being endlessly drawn in to Fawlty's farcical situations.

Cleese and Booth later admitted that they wrote the first series for their own pleasure as much as in the hope for a hit, but, despite being screened on the BBC's minority channel, reward came quickly in the shape of healthy viewing figures and rhapsodic reviews. After these first six episodes, the writers figured they had extracted all they could from the characters, but the BBC and the public were desperate for more. After much deliberation, the pair – whose marriage, by this time, was in steep decline – decided that if they *could* come up with six more scripts that satisfied their critical requirements they would continue. Sure enough, four years after the first series, a second set of six episodes were screened (the last of which was set adrift from the others by an industrial dispute). Once again, the standards were fantastically high, and although, initially, critics considered that the second series failed to capture the greatness of the sublime first run, the passing of time has allowed a reassessment which now places all dozen episodes on a plain.

Fawlty Towers scored on every level, being blessed with great performances, sensationally good lines, marvellous characters and, above all, beautifully crafted plots. Cleese and Booth laboured hard over the word-heavy scripts, rewriting many times to get them just *so*, and because they also starred in the show they were able to deliver the lines perfectly in tune with their intentions. Above all else, the time and dedication they invested in the writing is what made *Fawlty Towers* so good. Rarely for a British sitcom, it was a success in its original format in the US, and it elevated the already hallowed Cleese to even greater comic status.

Note. A US adaptation of *Fawlty Towers*, titled *Snavely* (aka *Chateau Snavely*), transferred the Torquay hotel setting to an off-highway hotel in middle America. Otherwise, the characters and situation mirrored the UK original, with Harvey Korman as the Basil-like Henry Snavely, Betty White as his domineering wife Gladys, Frank LaLoggia as the bellhop Petro who barely speaks English, and Deborah Zon as a college student Connie, working as a waitress. ABC screened the pilot episode on 24 June 1978 but it failed to be picked up for a series. ABC later reworked the concept as *Amanda's*, which aired from 10 February to 26 May 1983. The Basil character in this version was female – Bea Arthur (*Maude*, *The Golden Girls*) playing the formidable owner of Amanda's By The Sea, a hotel overlooking the Pacific. She had some of Basil's anger and frustration but the series had none of *Fawlty Towers'* class.

Feet First

UK · ITV (THAMES) · SITCOM
***7 × 30 mins · colour**
8 Jan–12 Feb 1979 · Mon 8pm

MAIN CAST

Terry Prince · · · · · · · · · · · · Jonathan Barlow
Viv Prince · · · · · · · · · · · · · · Jacquié Cassidy
Harry Turnbull · · · · · · · · · · · · Lee Montague
Hamilton Defries · · · · · · · · · · · Doug Fisher

CREDITS

writers John Esmonde/Bob Larbey · directors/ producers Michael Mills (4), Mark Stuart 2)

A soccer sitcom from Esmonde and Larbey in which young Midlands-based motor mechanic Terry Prince is playing football for his local team and is discovered by Harry Turnbull, the manager of a professional Division One club. He signs up and a whole new world beckons for him and his wife Viv.

The series was unrelated to the 1997 BBC sitcom *A Prince Among Men*, which charted the life of a former football star, Gary Prince, now retired from the game.

*Note. Seven episodes were made but only six were screened.

Marty Feldman

Born in East Ham, east London, in 1933, Marty Feldman ran away from home at 15 to join a wild west show, and then dallied with various musical stage acts before deciding on a career in comedy, establishing a humorous trio – Maurice, Marty And Mitch – who performed (not very well) in a Marx Brothers/Ole Olsen and Chick Johnson style. In 1954, when the struggling combo appeared at the Empire Theatre in York, Feldman met a fellow entertainer, Barry Took. After overcoming initial friction, they became friends, sharing an interest in comedy and the trumpet. Feldman assisted Took with his stage act and, coincidentally or otherwise, Took's career suddenly blossomed while the fortunes of Feldman's trio declined, the act folding soon after their only TV appearance, on *The Jimmy Wheeler Show*.

In 1956, with the encouragement of the writing partnership John Law and Bill Craig, Feldman and Took wrote and appeared in a number of comedy skits on various ATV afternoon programmes, and it was here that they learned the art of television production. Writing separately, they both found success on BBC radio – Feldman with *Educating Archie*, Took with *Beyond Our Ken* – but neither was completely happy with what he was doing. When Took split up with his then writing partner Eric Merriman, he and Feldman established themselves as a new and dynamic writing team, working on the BBC radio sketch series *Take It From Here* and, for Peter Jones, the sitcom *We're In Business*. Turning back to TV, their scripts for Granada's hit sitcom *The Army Game* led to *Bootsie And Snudge* and then many other programmes and series dotted throughout this book.

While scripting the classic *Round The Horne* series for BBC radio, Took and Feldman's relationship strained somewhat and, after writing for *On The Braden Beat*, Bernard Braden's witty weekly look at life (ATV), Feldman, alone, became the head writer on the seminal BBC TV series *The Frost Report*, bringing him into contact with the future members of the *Monty Python* team. Following this, David Frost was keen to capitalise on the comedic talents of his backroom boys and John Cleese suggested that Feldman go before the cameras in their next enterprise, to be *At Last The 1948 Show*. This was resisted at first because Feldman had rather disturbing, bulging eyes, the unhappy result of an operation he had undergone in the early 1960s for a severe hyperthyroid condition. But the powers-that-be were eventually convinced and Feldman was in, and those pop-eyes went on to become his trademark.

Feldman's TV appearances made an immediate impact with the public, and huge success followed when he was given his own series by the BBC, shows marked by Feldman's no-holds-barred, aggressive style of humour. He even found fame in the USA, firstly as a regular on *The Dean Martin Show* and then with his own show, *The Marty Feldman Comedy Machine*. The star eventually settled in Hollywood, appearing in a number of movies (notably those directed by Mel Brooks), although his career declined as the 1970s wound down. Feldman's lifestyle probably contributed to the heart attack he suffered while filming Graham Chapman's woeful star-packed movie *Yellowbeard* (released in 1983), and he died as a result, on 2 December 1982, aged just 49.

On 4 July 1995 BBC2 presented *It's Marty Resurrected: Some Of The Best Of Marty Feldman*, a welcome appreciation of the zany comic's television career.

It's Marty

UK · BBC · SKETCH

13 editions (12 × 30 mins · 1 × short special) · colour

Series One (6) 29 Apr–3 June 1968 · BBC2 Mon 8pm

Series Two (6) 9 Dec 1968–13 Jan 1969 · BBC2 Mon 8.50pm

Short special · part of *Christmas Night With The Stars* 25 Dec 1968 · BBC1 Wed 6.40pm

MAIN CAST
Marty Feldman
John Junkin
Tim Brooke-Taylor
Roland MacLeod
Mary Miller

CREDITS
main writers Marty Feldman/Barry Took · *other writers/additional material* John Cleese/Graham Chapman, Terry Jones/Michael Palin, John Law, John Junkin, Tim Brooke-Taylor, Michael Seddon, William Lynn, Roland MacLeod, Terry Gilliam, Dennis King, Donald Webster, Philip Jenkinson, Peter Dickinson, Tom Clarke · *director* Roger Race · *producer* Dennis Main Wilson

Marty Feldman's bug-eyed look may have grabbed the attention but it was his fine sense of comedy in *At Last The 1948 Show* that hastened his elevation to stardom. BBC executives wooed the star they had formerly known only as a writer and offered him this star vehicle, giving him the services of the richly experienced, risk-taking producer Dennis Main Wilson.

Many of the studio sketches in *It's Marty* – sometimes titled simply *Marty* – played on the aggressive, bureaucracy-destroying, weaselly characters Feldman had developed in *1948*, although perhaps the series' best-loved sketch, 'Funny He Never Married', performed with Tim Brooke-Taylor, was not one of them but, rather, a wickedly witty scene in which two ageing friends innocently ponder on why another chum, just dead, and obviously a queen among homosexuals, never married. Feldman and Brooke-Taylor also developed a neat line in dressing up as an old couple (the latter as the wife, Cynthia) who enjoy being incredibly aggressive, winding-up, in turn, a travel agent, a marriage counsellor and a Post Office counter-clerk (all played by John Junkin) until they have become quivering wrecks.

But it was the elaborate filmed sketches, sometimes embracing speeded-up footage, that were the hallmark of *It's Marty*. The most memorable of these were 'The Lightning Coach Tour', a hilarious day-long trip to the seaside accelerated to last three minutes; 'The Loneliness Of The Long Distance Golfer', with Feldman playing an intrepid golfer taking shots from ridiculous positions – the roof of a train, a woman's bath, a cliff-edge, and so on; two separate episodes of 'A Day In The Life Of A Stuntman', in which our hero leaves his home in semi-detached suburbia and enjoys, in both senses of the word, a truly action-packed day; and 'The Night Life Of A Chartered Accountant', in which a supposedly meek and henpecked chartered accountant enjoys a secret twilight existence of exotic trips and erotic encounters.

These virtually dialogue-free sketches are some of the best, most lavish and reportedly most expensive ever made by the BBC, but they were worth the cost: *It's Marty* duly won the Writers' Guild of Great Britain Award for the Best Light Entertainment Series and a Bafta Award for Best Script. A compilation episode (aired by BBC2 on 17 March 1969) narrowly failed to win the Golden Rose of Montreux and ended up with silver.

Feldman's impact on TV viewers was so fast that he was picked to star in the 1970 feature film *Every Home Should Have One*, which he co-wrote with Barry Took and Denis Norden, and which utilised the same aggressive style the comedian had developed for TV.

Note. On 26 November 1969 *The Wednesday Play* on BBC1 presented *Double Bill*, two half-hour straight-drama pieces – *Compartment* and *Playmates* – written by Johnny Speight, in which Feldman featured as Bill, an irritating man similar to the antagonistic character he often portrayed in sketches.

Marty Amok

1 × 45 mins · colour

30 Mar 1970 · BBC1 Mon 8pm

MAIN CAST
Marty Feldman
Robert Dhéry
John Junkin
Tim Brooke-Taylor
Vivian Stanshall
Mary Miller

CREDITS
writers Marty Feldman/Barry Took, Michael Palin/Terry Jones, Johnnie Mortimer/Brian Cooke · *director* Roger Race · *producer* Michael Mills

An Easter special for Feldman that also featured the French comic Robert Dhéry, whose cabaret material Feldman sometimes included in his own act.

Proof of Feldman's popularity was demonstrated by his appearance in the 1970 *Royal Variety Show* (screened by BBC1 on 15 November), in which he again performed with Tim Brooke-Taylor.

Marty Abroad

UK · BBC · SKETCH

1 × 40 mins · colour

1 Jan 1971 · BBC2 Fri 9.20pm

MAIN CAST
Marty Feldman
John Junkin

CREDITS
writers Johnnie Mortimer/Brian Cooke · *producer* Gordon Flemyng

A New Year's Day special set against the sunny backdrop of the Spanish Costa.

The Marty Feldman Comedy Machine

UK · ITV (ATV) · SKETCH

14 × 60 mins · colour

1 Oct 1971–14 Jan 1972 · Fri mostly 10.35pm

MAIN CAST
Marty Feldman
Spike Milligan
Bob Todd
Hugh Paddick
Clovissa Newcombe
Rudy de Luca
Barry Levinson

OTHER APPEARANCES
Frances de la Tour
Valentine Dyall

GUESTS
Barbara Feldon (5)
Godfrey Cambridge (2)
Orson Welles (2)
Art Carney (1)
Groucho Marx (1)
Roger Moore (1)
Beryl Reid (1)

CREDITS
writers Chris Allen, Rudy de Luca, Marty Feldman, Larry Gelbart, Barry Levinson, Spike Milligan, Sheldon Keller · *director* John Robins · *executive producer* Colin Clews · *producer* Larry Gelbart

The Marty Feldman Comedy Machine was the idea of Larry Gelbart, the brilliant American producer who was living in London at the time but would shortly return to the USA to develop the feature film *M*A*S*H* into a TV sitcom and then soar with it to unparalleled heights. Gelbart had seen Marty Feldman's hugely successful BBC TV series and wanted to produce some material geared especially for the American viewer. With his international track record and reputation, Sir Lew Grade was the obvious man with whom to do business, so *The Marty Feldman Comedy Machine* saw the comic switch to the commercial network – ITV – and work with the US audience in mind. Each weekly edition featured a prominent guest star – Orson Welles, Groucho Marx, Art Carney (*The Honeymooners*) and Barbara Feldon (*Get Smart*) among them – as well as internationally known singers like Thelma Houston and Randy Newman. To maintain British interest, Spike Milligan was engaged throughout the run and Terry Gilliam, scoring tremendous success with *Monty Python's Flying Circus*, provided animations, including the title sequence.

The result was an occasionally brilliant but ultimately patchy piece of work that went out in Britain late at night and, frankly, failed to amuse very much. Before long, Gelbart – like a number of Feldman's other collaborators – grew frustrated with the star's personality; indeed, he tried to withdraw from the series altogether. Grade persuaded him to stay and complete the 14 editions, but an option on a second series was never fulfilled. Some of the sketches were very good, though, indeed the best bits were worked into a half-hour compilation programme, screened in Britain on 15 February 1972 (repeated by C4 on 30 December 1987), which won the Top Comedy Award and also the Golden Rose at the 1972 Montreux Festival.

In America, where the series was networked by ABC, the 14 programmes were re-edited into half-hour shows, screened from 12 April to 23 August 1972. Although here too they were not an overwhelming success, the series served as Feldman's entrée into American popular culture. While he would work once more with the BBC in 1974, Feldman spent most of his remaining years in Hollywood, starring in US feature films that ranged from the excellent (notably Mel Brooks' *Young Frankenstein* and *Silent Movie*) to the dire (*In God We Trust*).

Marty Back Together Again

UK · BBC · SKETCH

4 × 30 mins · colour

20 Feb–27 Mar 1974 · BBC1 Wed around 9.30pm

MAIN CAST
Marty Feldman
James Villiers
Derek Griffiths
George Claydon

CREDITS
main writers Johnny Speight, Marty Feldman/Barry Took, Ken Hoare · *additional writers* Barry Cryer/Graham Chapman, Tom Lehrer · *producer* Dennis Main Wilson

The *Till Death Us Do Part* producer Dennis Main Wilson suggested to its writer Johnny Speight that, following the latest series of his sitcom, he might consider returning to the sort of sketch writing he had produced in the 1950s and early 1960s when working on, to name but one example, *The Arthur Haynes Show*. The result was this short-run series for Marty Feldman, the title of which pointed to the British public's concerns over the star's state of health and absence from the screen for more than two years.

Feldman was supported in the sketches by the midget comedian George Claydon, James Villiers (perfect as the sort of bureaucratic figure Feldman's characters delighted in ruffling) and black actor Derek Griffiths whose presence reflected Speight's input, with his customary controversial spin on racial discrimination. But *Marty Back Together Again* made for an uneasy mix, never reaching the giddy heights of *It's Marty*, and the star was not seen again on British TV.

Felix Dexter On TV

UK · BBC · STANDUP/SKETCH

1 × 30 mins · colour
8 Sep 1995 · BBC2 Fri 9.30pm

MAIN CAST
Felix Dexter
Phil Cornwell
Brian Bovell
Adrian Lester
Pip Torrens
Wilbert Johnson
Eileen Dunwoody

CREDITS
writer Felix Dexter · *script editors* Paul Whitehouse/Charlie Higson · *director* Chris Bould · *executive producer* Bill Wilson · *producer* Janice Thomas

Presented under the *Comic Asides* banner, this starring vehicle for Felix Dexter – familiar to viewers of *The Real McCoy* – took the format of a brief standup routine followed by several long sketches. (Too long in some cases.) Dexter turned in a classy performance and entertained with his caricatures of (mostly) black stereotypes, and

the audience treated each invention with whoops of delight, proving the accuracy of his observations and demonstrating that even in the mid-1990s black audiences were still mostly uncatered for in mainstream TV.

The show featured a number of strong characters who could have easily reappeared had the pilot been developed into a series, and it was no surprise to see the names of Paul Whitehouse and Charlie Higson among the creative team because the programme's feel and appearance were reminiscent of Harry Enfield's series and *The Fast Show*. The most memorable sequences featured Samuel, a militant London Underground ticket collector (a recurring character for Dexter); Nathaniel, an African mini-cab driver berating those around him in a library while he studies for exams; and a pair of East End of London wide boys (Dexter and Phil Cornwell), whose entire conversation consisted of muttered threats, growls, one-line clichés and meaningless stock phrases.

See also *Christmas Night With The Stars*.

The Fenn Street Gang

UK · ITV (LWT) · SITCOM

49 episodes (47 × 30 mins · 2 × short specials) · colour

*Series One (21) 24 Sep 1971–11 Feb 1972 · Fri mostly 8.30pm

Short special · part of *Mike And Bernie Winters' All-Star Christmas Comedy Carnival* 25 Dec 1971 · Sat 6.05pm

Series Two (18) 15 Oct 1972–18 Feb 1973 · Sun mostly 7.25pm

Short special · part of *All-Star Comedy Carnival* 25 Dec 1972 · Mon 5.45pm

Series Three (8) 27 May–15 July 1973 · Sun 7.25pm

MAIN CAST
Frankie Abbott	David Barry
Eric Duffy	Peter Cleall
Sharon Eversleigh	Carol Hawkins
Dennis Dunstable	Peter Denyer (series 1 & 2)
Maureen Bullock	Liz Gebhardt (series 1 & 2)
Peter Craven	Léon Vitali (series 1); Malcolm McFee (series 2 & 3)
Archie Drew	Neil Wilson (series 1)
Dolly	Sue Bond (series 1)
Mr Bowler	George Baker (series 2)

OTHER APPEARANCES
Mrs Abbott	Barbara Mitchell

CREDITS
creators John Esmonde/Bob Larbey · *writers* John Esmonde/Bob Larbey (36 & special 1), Geoff Rowley/Andy Baker (8), Tony Bilbow (2), David Barry (1), Lew Schwarz (special 2) · *directors* David Askey (12), Mark Stuart (9 & special 1), Philip Casson (8 & special 2), Alan Wallis (6), Bryan Izzard (5), Howard Ross (5), Graham Evans (2) · *executive producer* Mark Stuart

Such was the interest in the unruly mob that was Form 5C, *Please, Sir!* effectively split into two in the autumn of 1971, the original series carrying on and the bunch of delinquent pupils becoming school-leavers and gaining a series of their own, *The Fenn Street Gang*. Having so resolutely avoided any school work, the rowdy youths were now cast into the harsh world, forced to make ends meet. To maintain the ensemble, writers Esmonde and Larbey kept the former class-mates in close contact with one another throughout the new series, although, towards the end, episodes tended to focus on the exploits of each of them in turn.

So here they all were again, indulging in dole-signing, brushes with the law, birds, booze, strippers, shoplifting and, yes, some honest toil too. Sharon (now played by Carol Hawkins, who had also appeared in the role in the *Please, Sir!* movie) and Duffy continued the very bumpy relationship they had started in the third year at school, becoming engaged at the end of the second series and marrying in the third. Frankie Abbott – calling himself Hank Abbott – continued to live out his comic-book fantasies, fashioning himself as a clumsy, over-disguised amateur detective and having a relationship with Maureen, who trained as a nurse. And Craven became a wide-boy, working for a cockney crook named Bowler who had fingers in all manner of nefarious pies and was definitely the lord of the local manor. Without the constant presence of the teachers (they were seen occasionally, however), *The Fenn Street Gang* didn't amount to much, though: there were some good lines and ideas but the total was often crass, and the exaggerated, poorly acted cockney swagger of the 'kids' quickly palled.

George Baker was cast as Craven's boss and the role was so successful that it led to a spin-off series, **Bowler**. There were plans too for a spin-off for the deuce – far from ace, that is – detective Frankie 'Hank' Abbott and his mum (Barbara Mitchell) too, but this failed to materialise.

*Note. Of the first series' 21 episodes, only 20 were screened in the London area. All were repeated, however.

The Ferguson Theory

UK · BBC · STANDUP/SKETCH

5 × 30 mins · colour

21 Jan–25 Feb 1994 · BBC2 Fri 11.45pm

MAIN CAST

Craig Ferguson
Jonathan Watson
Louise Beattie
Grant Smeaton
Ross Stenhouse
Jonathan Kydd
Juliette Gilmour
Margaret Turner
Jonathan Parsons
Jennifer White
John Little

CREDITS

main writers Craig Ferguson, Neil Shand · *other writers* Rikki Brown, Iain Campbell, Rab Christie/Greg Hemphill, Alan Hay, Pamela Hughes, Brendan McGeever, Gordon McPherson, David Notman, Tex Winchester · *director* Caroline Roberts · *executive producer* Colin Gilbert · *producers* Caroline Roberts, Philip Differ

First screened by BBC Scotland in 1993, this was Scots comedian Craig Ferguson in his own show, blending his standup act with filmed sketches. Standing on a round stage, the comic delivered his rambling, somewhat manic monologues, usually themed on things that annoyed him. These formed the bulk of the shows, as the sketches were very short, most of them satirising advertisements or dramatising simple two-line gags. Ferguson's bonhomie and charm usually won over his audiences, permitting him to deliver scathing material that may have left a nasty taste if presented by a less likeable performer.

Note. Later the same year, Ferguson fronted *The Last Action Series*, shown on 27 August 1994 as part of BBC2's themed *ATV Night*. In the guise of a would-be producer, and using his Sean Connery vocal impersonation, the comic humorously linked clips from ITC's action/adventure TV series of the 1960s and 1970s.

Ffizz

UK · ITV (THAMES) · SITCOM

12 × 30 mins · colour

Series One (6) 9 Sep–14 Oct 1987 · Wed 8.30pm
Series Two (6) 25 July–29 Aug 1989 · Tue 8.30pm

MAIN CAST

Jack Mowbray	Richard Griffiths
Hugo Walker	Benjamin Whitrow
Griselda	Felicity Montagu
Alan	Robin Kermode
Samson	George Ballantine
Lady Boughton	Phyllida Law
Mrs Monaghan	Peggy Aitchison
Mrs Gosling	Gabrielle Drake (series 2)

CREDITS

writers Richard Fegen/Andrew Norriss · *director/producer* Derrick Goodwin

Having enjoyed a chance in a million success with *Chance In A Million*, writers Fegen and Norriss concocted this sitcom about a pair of partying chappies, Jack and Hugo, co-owners and co-directors of upmarket wine merchants Mowbray and Crofts. (Jack Mowbray has inherited the firm, and brought in his old university chum Hugo.) Unaccustomed as they are to hard work, the blazered and cravated pair find themselves strapped for cash and having to focus on business rather than their usual picnic 'n' party lifestyle that, until now, has seen them out and about in their Range Rover, huntin',

shootin' and fishin' at every opportunity. It's a change in lifestyle to which they scarcely adapt, however, and their bank is forced to send in its young troubleshooter, Alan, who becomes a director and slowly steers the ship out of troubled waters. In this he receives scarcely any help from Jack and Hugo or their associates: unreliable secretary-cum-tea-lady Mrs Monaghan and their god-daughter Griselda. In the second series, they are forced to work in a supermarket run by a Mrs Gosling.

Fiddlers Three

UK · ITV (YORKSHIRE) · SITCOM

14 × 30 mins · colour

19 Feb–28 May 1991 · Tue 8.30pm

MAIN CAST

Ralph West	Peter Davison
Ros West	Paula Wilcox
J J Morley	Charles Kay
Harvey	Peter Blake
Osborne	Tyler Butterworth

CREDITS

writer Eric Chappell · *executive producer* Vernon Lawrence · *director/producer* Graham Wetherell

Following a remarkably long line of sitcom successes – **The Bounder, Duty Free, Haggard, Home To Roost, Misfits, Only When I Laugh, Singles, The Squirrels** and, undoubtedly the best of them all, **Rising Damp** – *Fiddlers Three* was writer Eric Chappell's first damp squib. Although it marked a return to the subject of office politics explored in his first work, *The Squirrels* (on air 1974–77), this was a pretty limp affair, with laughs coming along in all the predictable places, as if stapled to the front of every scene.

The three 'fiddlers' were Ralph, Harvey and Osborne, a trio of middle-management accountants working in the finance department of a major business concern. While they were not the embezzlers suggested in the title, they appeared to do little if any work, being preoccupied with the fear of redundancy, conspiracies and other sundry paranoia, displaying dubious loyalties, grovelling, fibbing and scheming their way to promotion or, at best, justification and preservation of their existing job. Above all, they sought either the recognition of, or the replacement of, their immediate boss, J J Morley, a middle-ager tempted by the incompatible thoughts of early retirement or promotion to head office.

The central figure in *Fiddlers Three* was Ralph West (played by Peter Davison), ever trying to advance his career with a spot of office politicking that usually led him nowhere. His wife Ros (Paula Wilcox), the mother of their three children, was often seen, alternately soothing Ralph's battered brow or coming to his rescue. What really needed rescuing was the programme itself, though, and after 14 plodding episodes *Fiddlers Three* was laid off.

Filthy, Rich And Catflap

UK · BBC · SITCOM

6 × 30 mins · colour

7 Jan–11 Feb 1987 · BBC2 Wed 9.25pm

MAIN CAST

Filthy Ralph (aka Ralph Filthy) · · · Nigel Planer
Richie Rich · · · · · · · · · · · · · · · · · Rik Mayall
Eddie Catflap · · · · · · · · · · Adrian Edmondson

CREDITS

writer Ben Elton · *director/producer* Paul Jackson

A rare flop for the vanguards of new comedy, but then viewer expectations of the leading lights of *The Young Ones*, *Happy Families* and *The Comic Strip Presents* ... were understandably high by this time. Although rude and lively, *Filthy, Rich And Catflap* displayed signs of the strain and anguish that, reportedly, dogged the series' gestation. Mayall had originally planned to write the show in partnership with Elton, but the way it worked out meant that most of the input was Elton's, and Mayall – apparently without pique – withdrew his name from the author credits.

Critically, *Filthy, Rich And Catflap* suffered in comparison with *The Young Ones*, which must have been somewhat galling for the team considering that the earlier series had scarcely been welcomed with open arms by reviewers. By this period, however, it had come to be recognised as a classic of the new genre, and a yardstick against which to compare subsequent product. *Filthy, Rich And Catflap* just didn't measure up, but from this particular stable of talent, even a perceived failure was more interesting than many middle-of-the-road successes.

The series took a satirical swipe at the hypocrisy of show business. Mayall played Richie Rich, a minor celebrity with a major ego and negligible talent; Nigel Planer was his agent, Filthy Ralph, a feckless nonentity of colossal uselessness; and Adrian Edmondson was Richie's minder, Eddie Catflap, a devoted dipsomaniac who, despite his alcohol intake, still seemed more together than the other two, if perhaps less coherent. The characters inhabited a strange world, which, like *The Young Ones*, sported a weird reality completely at odds with the real one. This sort of fantastic setting was very distinctive of much of the 'alternative comedy' product but *Filthy, Rich And Catflap* had a particularly dark and vicious edge that imbued it with the sense of a cruel Victorian caricature. The six episodes found the three unfriendly low-lifes paddling about in the shallow end of show business, encountering parodies of media people in recognisable but exaggerated television settings, such as game-show sets and the TV-am studios.

Not a classic series certainly, but a commendable and risky attempt at generating something a little different.

A Fine Romance

UK · ITV (LWT) · SITCOM

26 × 30 mins · colour

Series One (7) 1 Nov–13 Dec 1981 · Sun mostly 10pm
Series Two (6) 17 Jan–21 Feb 1982 · Sun 8.15pm
Series Three (6) 4 Nov–9 Dec 1983 · Fri 8.30pm
Series Four (7) 6 Jan–17 Feb 1984 · Fri 8.30pm

MAIN CAST

Laura Dalton · · · · · · · · · · · · · · · Judi Dench
Mike Selway · · · · · · · · · · · Michael Williams
Helen · · · · · · · · · · · · · · · Susan Penhaligon
Phil · · · · · · · · · · · · · · · · · Richard Warwick

OTHER APPEARANCES

Harry · · · · · · · · · Geoffrey Rose (series 1 & 2)
Charlie · · · · · · · · George Tovey (series 1 & 2)
Terry · · · · · · · · · Karl Howman (series 3 & 4)
Elaine · · · · · · · · · · · Mary Maddox (series 4)
Mr Dalton · · · · · · Richard Pearson (series 4)
Mrs Dalton · · · · · · · Lally Bowers (series 4)
Mr Robinson · · · · · · Michael Lees (series 4)

CREDITS

writer Bob Larbey · *directors/producers* James Cellan Jones (series 1 & 2), Don Leaver (series 3 & 6 episodes in series 4), Graham Evans (1 episode in series 4) · *executive producer* Humphrey Barclay (series 3 & 4)

Laura is a translator by profession: brainy, content to accept that she's single, entering middle-age with dignity and her own agenda. Reluctantly, because she knows that her younger sister Helen and her husband Phil are incurable matchmakers, she goes to one of their parties and there, sure enough, is force-introduced to bachelor Mike, also in his forties, a landscape gardener who drives around in a van. Laura thinks Mike short, shy, nervous and boring but the pair agree to feign interest in one another in order to fool Laura and Phil and escape the party as soon as possible. As the first series develops so the couple are drawn to one another, as much through boredom as anything else, but soon they begin a real relationship that starts off plain strange, becomes estranged (at the end of the third series) but then clicks again, finally, with wedding bells in the air, at the last.

A Fine Romance was, indeed, a fine sitcom, made so by its two stars, real-life husband and wife Michael Williams and Judi Dench. This was Dench's first TV comedy series, her stage and film CV already so impressive that soon it would garner her a damehood. From first to last, too, Bob Larbey's scripts were well written, providing not only laughs but also an underlying intelligence. One got every impression that the players were enjoying themselves and certainly, with their great theatrical experience and real-life relationship, Dench and Williams were convincing as a couple.

The international television executive Don Taffner attempted to sell the format of *A Fine Romance* to American TV, partially succeeding in that CBS aired a one-off pilot there on 20 July 1983 (with the same title as the British version). Here, Laura was Laura Prescott and was played by Julie Kavner (best known as Brenda Morgenstern, sister of *Rhoda*, and the voice of Marge in *The Simpsons*), Mike Selway was played by Leo Burmester, Helen and Phil by Kristin Meadows and Kevin Conroy. No series developed.

Fire Crackers

UK · ITV (ATV) · SITCOM

13 × 30 mins · b/w

Series One (6) 29 Aug–3 Oct 1964 · Sat 9.35pm
Series Two (7) 9 Jan–20 Feb 1965 · Sat 8.25pm

MAIN CAST

Charlie · · · · · · · · · · · · · · · · · Alfred Marks
Hairpin · · · · · · · · Cardew Robinson (series 1)
Jumbo · Joe Baker
Weary Willie · · · · · · · · · · · Sidney Bromley
Loverboy · · · · · · · · · · · · · · · · Ronnie Brody
Tadpole · · · · · · · · · · · Clive Elliott (series 2)
Station Officer Blazer · · · · · · · · · John Arnatt
Leading Fireman Piggott · · Norman Chappell
George · · · · · · · · · · · · · · · · · Colin Douglas

CREDITS

writers Fred Robinson (10), Fred Robinson/John Warren/John Singer (1), John Warren/John Singer (2) · *director* Josephine Douglas · *producer* Alan Tarrant

A vintage British sitcom of the 1960s. The setting was the forgotten English village of Cropper's End (population: 70) where there was an even more forgotten fire service, manned by a bunch of characters who, when not at work, were playing poker, sleeping or quenching their thirst on the local brew down at the Cropper's Arms. When they *did* have to work (like when their fire station caught fire) they set to it with hatches, hoses and no little reluctance, 'speeding' to the blaze in their 60-year-old engine Bessie (made circa 1907, and borrowed for the series from the Montagu Motor Museum).

This ATV sitcom – the word 'zany' might almost have been invented for it – starred Alfred Marks as the fire chief and was reminiscent of Will Hay's finest. Indeed, it bore a close resemblance to Hay's film *Where's That Fire?*, made in the same Elstree studio 25 years earlier. Sidney Bromley – who played Weary Willie in the TV series – was even visibly similar to Moore Marriott.

First Aids

UK · ITV (NETWORK) · SKETCH/STANDUP

1 × 90 mins · colour

27 Feb 1987 · Fri 7.30pm

MAIN CAST

Spitting Image
Gareth Hale
Norman Pace
Stephen Fry
Hugh Laurie
Helen Lederer
Rik Mayall

CREDITS

writers cast · *director* Tony Orsten · *executive producer* David Cox · *producer* Michael Attwell

TV became besotted with the medical condition Aids in 1987 and among the first of a great many programmes was this special show aimed at making young people aware of the risks of unprotected sex. Numerous rock stars and comedians appeared (only the comics are named above), and in between the performances condoms were passed around the studio audience. Entering into the spirit of the event, Rik Mayall performed with one hanging from the fly of his trousers.

1st Exposure

UK · ITV (LWT) · STANDUP

16 editions (14 × 30 mins · 1 × 40 mins · 1 × 60 mins) · colour

Series One (6 × 30 mins · 1 × 40 mins · 1 × 60 mins) 8 July–26 Aug 1988 · Fri 11.35pm

Series Two (8 × 30 mins) 30 June–25 Aug 1989 · Fri mostly 11.05pm

MAIN CAST

Arthur Smith

CREDITS

writers cast · *directors* John Birkin (series 1), David G Croft (series 2) · *executive producer* Marcus Plantin · *producers* Juliet Blake/Trevor Hopkins (series 1), Juliet Blake (series 2)

Late-night comedy and music from new and unknown acts figuring on the fringe circuit, presented from east London by (south Londoner) Arthur Smith. The first series was recorded at the Theatre Royal, Stratford East, the second at the Hackney Empire.

Among the turns being seen on TV for the first or almost the first time were Jim Tavaré (show transmitted 15 July 1988), Eddie Izzard (5 August 1988), Jack Dee (12 August 1988), Steve Coogan (26 August 1988) and David Baddiel (11 August 1989).

See also *Pyjamarama* and *291 Club*.

First Impressions

USA · CBS (GRIEF-DORE COMPANY) · SITCOM

8 × 30 mins · colour

US dates: 27 Aug–1 Oct 1988

UK dates: 4 Sep–21 Sep 1989 (8 episodes)
BBC1 various days 11.35am

MAIN CAST

Frank Dutton	Brad Garrett
Lindsay Dutton	Brandy Gold
Dave Poole	Thom Sharp
Mrs Madison	Ruth Kobart
Donna Patterson	Sarah Abrell
Raymond Voss	James Noble

CREDITS

writers Dianne Dixon, Fred Freeman, Lawrence J Cohen, Susan Strauss · *director* Jack Shea

The tall (6ft 9in) comic impressionist Brad Garrett starred as Frank Dutton in this short-lived sitcom about a man trying to raise his daughter after his wife leaves for the West Coast to 'find herself'. Set, unusually, in Omaha, Nebraska, Dutton is an advertising writer for Media Of Omaha, a job where his skills as an impressionist can be utilised for both fun and profit. Brandy Gold was cast as Dutton's nine-year-old daughter Lindsay and Ruth Kobart played Mrs Madison, Dutton's interfering but well-meaning neighbour. At work were Dave, Frank's old school chum, the naïvely innocent receptionist Donna, and Raymond, the laid-back sound engineer. *First Impressions* made little impression on the viewing audience, however, and only eight episodes were made.

First Of The Summer Wine

UK · BBC · SITCOM

13 episodes (1 × 45 mins · 12 × 30 mins) · colour

Pilot (45 mins) 3 Jan 1988 · BBC1 Sun 7.15pm

Series One (6) 4 Sep–9 Oct 1988 · BBC1 Sun 7.15pm

Series Two (6) 3 Sep–8 Oct 1989 · BBC1 Sun 7.15pm

MAIN CAST

Mr Clegg	Peter Sallis
Norman Clegg	David Fenwick
Seymour	Paul McLain
Compo	Paul Wyett
Foggy Dewhurst	Richard Lumsden
Mrs Clegg	Maggie Ollerenshaw
Nora	Helen Patrick
Wally Batty	Gary Whitaker
Sherbert	Paul Oldham
Dilys	Joanne Heywood
Ivy	Sarah Dangerfield
Scrimshaw	Derek Benfield

CREDITS

writer Roy Clarke · *producers/directors* Gareth Gwenlan (pilot), Mike Stephens (series)

A clever but simple premise – a 'prequel' that looked at the characters in *Last Of The Summer Wine* when they were youths – in other words, in their first childhood as opposed to their second. Set in 1939, the series depicted the adventures of the lads as they sought jobs, chased girls and made plans for their future, all infused once more with their philosophical ramblings on the nature of life.

The shadow of the Grim Reaper again added an edge of blackness to an otherwise summer-filled existence, but this time it wasn't old age that was hanging over the trio but the Second World War gathering darkly on the horizon. Peter Sallis played Clegg Sr, the father of his character Norman Clegg in *Last Of The Summer Wine* (who was played here by David Fenwick) and the scene was set each week by readings from Norman's diary.

The young cast coped well with roles that were part straight-acting and part impersonation of the mannerisms and vocal phrasing of the actors already established as the elder versions. Roy Clarke's dialogue was as sharp as ever and he obviously relished inventing the youthful doppelgangers of the characters that he had already fully developed over a number of years, establishing the beginnings of relationships, romances and alliances that, in the earlier series, set at a later time, had already reached fruition.

Fish

USA · ABC (THE MIMIS CORPORATION) · SITCOM

35 × 30 mins · colour

US dates: 2 May 1977–6 Aug 1978

UK dates: 1 Apr–20 May 1978 (8 episodes) BBC1 Sat 5.50pm

MAIN CAST

Phil Fish	Abe Vigoda
Bernice Fish	Florence Stanley
Charlie Harrison	Barry Gordon
Mike	Lenny Bari
Loomis	Todd Bridges
Victor	John Cassisi
Jilly	Denise Miller
Diane	Sarah Natoli

CREDITS

writers Barbara Corday, Barbara H Avedon, Don Segall, Michael Loman, Richard Baer, Thomas A Reeder, William Idelson and others · *directors* Lee Bernhardi, Mike Warren, Dennis Steinmetz and others · *executive producer* Danny Arnold · *producers* Norman Barasch, Roy Kammerman, Steve Pretzker

Old, weary and perpetually miserable, Phil Fish was spun-off from ***Barney Miller*** into this rather contrived sitcom in which he and his wife Bernice became foster parents to five 'problem' Social Services children from mixed ethnic and racial origins. For the first few episodes, which ran concurrently with *Barney Miller*, poor Fish was still putting in time at the precinct house, but eventually he was allowed to retire and expend his energy trying to keep the young tearaways in order. The quarrelsome quintet put pressure on Phil and Bernice's marriage and by the end of the series they were contemplating separation. In real life, also being somewhat undisciplined, and with little of its parent show's class, the series was separating rapidly from its audience, and after 35 episodes *Fish* was finally reeled in.

ABC had attempted to float a Phil Fish spin-off two years before this series began, airing a pilot titled *Fish And Bernice* on 4 December 1975 which co-starred Doris Belack as his wife Bernice and Emily Levine as their daughter Beverley. This idea was not developed further.

Fist Of Fun

UK · BBC · SKETCH

12 × 30 mins · colour

Series One (6) 11 Apr–16 May 1995 · BBC2 Tue 9pm

Series Two (6) 16 Feb–22 Mar 1996 · BBC2 Fri 10pm

MAIN CAST
Stewart Lee
Richard Herring
Peter Baynham
Kevin Eldon (series 2)

CREDITS
writers Stewart Lee/Richard Herring · *directors* Nick Wood (6), Steve Bendelack/John L Spencer (4), Steve Bendelack/Guy Freeman (2) · *producer* Sarah Smith

Writer/performers Lee and Herring contributed to the seminal BBC Radio 4 comedy series *On The Hour* (see ***The Day Today***) before graduating to their own series. An off-the-wall double-act, the duo honed their style with stage performances that moved away from the traditional world of revue and into a more surreal area. Their comedy was based on a classic personality clash – the downbeat Lee being constantly at odds with the optimistic Herring – but their arguments and disagreements were mostly about curiously infantile things. Bringing their act to TV, the duo effortlessly – or so it seemed – combined the essence of their radio shows with the visual eccentricity of the live act. The watchword here was informality, with the pair linking skits and sketches in an amiable, easy-going manner. Their low-key set (described as a 'filthy den') was supposedly situated in a BBC basement, and subjects for their humour seemed to pop into their heads from nowhere, encompassing such diverse areas as 'starting a new religion', 'ridding the world of mice', 'eating some chocolate', and 'polluting a wall'. Peter Baynham appeared regularly as a Welsh Twiglet-masterchef from Balham in south London.

The second series brought a number of changes, the comics finally operating from 'a proper BBC studio' and introducing new recurring items, including pointless campaigns, and the news for Ians (read by Ian Lewis and Ian Ketterman). In common with their fellow youthful comic contemporaries Reeves and Mortimer, Newman and Baddiel and

Harry Enfield and Paul Whitehouse, Lee and Herring's style was decidedly post-modern, as was their show's minimalist credit sequence and sets. Another indication of their modernity was the fact that *Radio Times* invited contributions to the show via the series' e-mail address during the run of the first series.

Note. *Lionel Nimrod's Inexplicable World* was Lee and Herring's first own radio series, running in two batches of six editions on BBC Radio 4, from 8 October to 12 November 1992 and 15 July to 19 August 1993. Four series for Radio 1 followed, first *Lee And Herring's Fist Of Fun* (six editions, 12 October to 17 November 1993) and then *Lee And Herring* (seven editions, 18 July to 29 August 1994; six editions, 9 January to 13 February 1995; six editions, 15 November to 20 December 1995).

Fit For Heroes

UK · ITV (GRANADA) · SITCOM

1 × 30 mins · b/w

13 June 1963 · Thu 7.30pm

MAIN CAST
Major Hepplewhite · · · · · · · · · Deryck Guyler
Corporal Rust · · · · · · · · · · · Kenneth Connor

CREDITS
writers Barry Took/Peter Miller/James Kelly · *director* Graeme McDonald · *producer* Peter Eton

As part of Granada's *Comedy Four* season, writers Barry Took, Peter Miller and James Kelly scripted this single-episode sitcom in which a retired army major and his faithful batman decide to teach their local Post Office a lesson after their pensions are stopped, but swiftly come to regret their campaign.

Five Alive

UK · ITV (TVS) · SKETCH

15 editions (14 × 30 mins · 1 × 45 mins) · colour

Special (45 mins) 23 Aug 1986 · Sat 7.30pm

Series One (7 × 30 mins) 4 July–15 Aug 1987 · Sat mostly 7.15pm

Series Two (7 × 30 mins) 28 May–9 July 1988 · Sat mostly 5.45pm

MAIN CAST
Brian Conley
Peter Piper
Andrew Secombe (special & series 1)
Doon Mackichan (series 1 & 2)
Joanna Brookes (series 1 & 2)
Phil Nice (series 2)
Sharon Maiden (special)
Eve Ferret (special)

CREDITS
writers of special Charlie Adams, Geoff Atkinson, Paul Minett/Brian Leveson · *writers of series 1* Terry Ravenscroft, Phil Hopkins, Geoff Atkinson, Charlie Adams, James Bibby, Tim Maloney, Alan Simmons/Keith Simmons, Ray Martin, Stephen Sheridan, James Hendrie/Ian Brown · *writers of series 2* Terry Ravenscroft, Phil Hopkins, Alan

Simmons/Keith Simmons and others · *script associate* Paul Mayhew-Archer (series 1 & 2) · *directors* Bob Collins (special), David G Hillier (series 1 & 2) · *executive producer* John Kaye Cooper · *producer* Alan Nixon

A wham-bam sketch series – also known as *5 Alive* – built around new comic talents, among them Brian Conley (at this time best known for his work with child entertainers in the networked TVS variety series *Summertime Special*) and Harry Secombe's son Andrew. The opening special's high babe-count – it featured Sharon Maiden, and Eve Ferret, who had played Sharon Armstrong in the appalling sitcom ***Bottle Boys*** – was toned down for the two series that followed.

The Five Foot Nine Show

UK · BBC · SKETCH

1 × 50 mins · b/w

31 Jan 1964 · Fri 9.25pm

MAIN CAST
Roy Kinnear
Lance Percival
Tsai Chin
Gordon Peters

CREDITS
writer Dave Freeman · *producer* Barry Lupino

A one-off sketch comedy and music show reuniting ***That Was The Week That Was*** alumni Roy Kinnear and Lance Percival. The writer, Dave Freeman, was best known for his work with Benny Hill.

500 Bus Stops

UK · BBC · SITCOM

4 × 30 mins · colour

24 June–15 July 1997 · BBC2 Tue 11.15pm

MAIN CAST
John Shuttleworth/Ken Worthington (voice only)/ Mary Shuttleworth (voice only) · Graham Fellows

CREDITS
writer Graham Fellows · *additional material* Willy Smax, Martin Willis, Will Yapp · *director* Willy Smax · *executive producer* Peter Symes

Back in 1978, studying drama in Manchester, Graham Fellows invented an alter ego, Jilted John, and scored a number four hit on the British singles chart with a novelty 'new wave' song of the same title. Sadly, Fellows' second alter ego, the comic 'versatile singer-songwriter from Sheffield, South Yorkshire' John Shuttleworth, has enjoyed no such luck. In fact, he can't even get a recording contract.

Shuttleworth was invented in 1985 when Fellows made a deliberately awful demo tape to amuse a friend in the music business. Fleshing out the character, 'Shuttleworth' then performed regularly on stage at the Edinburgh Festival Fringe, being nominated for the prized Perrier Award, and was unleashed on the British nation at large in a succession of BBC Radio 4 and Radio 1 series and specials, attracting a cult (ie, relatively small but dedicated) following. Then, with life imitating art, the hopelessly inadequate musician got to play to 25,000 people when Blur invited him to be their support-act at a London stadium gig in 1996. With his own one-man show touring the smaller theatres in Britain around the same time, the moment had arrived for John Shuttleworth to break into big-time television.

Shuttleworth is a brilliant spoof comic creation – a persistently and hopelessly optimistic individual who leads a deeply mundane life and thinks deeply mundane thoughts. Although he recognises that's he's 'no spring-chicken' (he's probably approaching 50), he sincerely believes that he can become a rock star, tooting out tunes on his portable Casio keyboard about – though he doesn't have the nous to realise it – some complete irrelevancy or other that he has experienced in life. In fact, with his hopeless fashion sense and ugly looks (swept-back hair, black-framed glasses) he has as much chance of being a rock star as he does the Queen of England. When he's not playing music, life for John means trips to the garden centre and DIY superstores, where he obsesses over tiny details like discounted prices and the worthiness of the equipment. John's wife Mary, a dinner-lady at a local primary school, is generally fed up with her husband and his trivialities and gives him short-shrift. They have two children – Darren, 19, who works at Victoria Wine, and Karen, 15, who is still at school. (Detail, to Shuttleworth – and his fans – is everything, and those who follow the Shuttleworth radio shows and see the stage-show find out everything about this family, mostly of it deeply uninteresting.) The Shuttleworths'. next-door neighbour is Ken Worthington, John's 'sole agent', known (probably only to the two of them) as 'TV's clarinet man' thanks to an appearance he made on *New Faces* in 1973, when he came last and got a right slating from Tony Hatch. Ken and John are best friends, although they don't always see eye to eye, and Ken's idea of a good time is to get an Indian takeaway meal, complete with 'pompodums'. Both men think themselves smart and savvy without realising that they are a couple of berks.

The BBC radio programmes, typically only 15 minutes apiece, are fine encapsulations of Shuttleworth, his small world and his deluded notions of becoming a pop star. Fellows records them alone in his garden shed, supplying the voices of all three main characters (the children are never heard) and improvising over a roughly sketched script. Transferring John Shuttleworth to TV brought the same problems to Fellows as he

experienced on stage: he could only be one of the people. The solution was a clever one, with Mary being seen only fleetingly from the rear in the first episode and Ken becoming the cameraman who follows Shuttleworth around on his tour, shooting the 'rockumentary'. While Ken is heard often, adding his two penn'orth of useless opinion all over the place, he was never seen.

500 Bus Stops was an account of Shuttleworth's National Rock Tour, showing his performances at what he called 'significant venues throughout the UK'. The first stop was Bakewell Library. Unfortunately, of course, it all goes horribly wrong. John's beloved car (an Austin Ambassador Y-Reg) breaks down on the first day and he and Ken have to travel the remainder of the tour on public buses and coaches. None of the gigs occur as expected and Shuttleworth ends up performing in a freezer-centre, to camping boy scout cubs in the middle of a field, and in a Peak District cave, the latter being his attempt at a 'benefit gig for the environment'. Along the way John buys clothes from a charity shop, eats in a succession of unglamorous cafés and has plenty of spare time to share with the camera his unique, and wordy, perspective on life.

Where Shuttleworth goes from here is anyone's guess. The TV series was welcomed by his loyal fans and gained the character much publicity, but it was esoteric viewing at best. It seems that radio remains the best medium in which to appreciate this form of comedy, where one can conjure up mind-images of Ken and Mary and be swept away on Fellows' wonderful flights of comic fancy.

The 5 Mrs Buchanans

USA · CBS (WOOTEN & CHERRY PRODUCTIONS/ 20TH CENTURY-FOX) · SITCOM

17 × 30 mins · colour

US dates: 24 Sep 1994–18 Mar 1995

UK dates: 15 May–11 Sep 1995 (17 episodes) C4 Mon 5.30pm

MAIN CAST
Emma Buchanan · · · · · · · · · Eileen Heckart
Alex Buchanan · · · · · · · · · · · · · · Judith Ivey
Delilah Buchanan · · · · · · · · · · Beth Broderick
Vivian Buchanan · · · · Harriot Sansom Harris
Bree Buchanan · · · · · · · · · · · Charlotte Ross

CREDITS
writers Nancylee Myatt (3), David Flebotte (2), Tracy Gamble/Richard Vaczy (2), Jamie Wooten/Marc Cherry (2), Jenny Bicks (1), Linda Day (1), Lyn Greene/Richard Levine (1), Michael Patrick King (1), John Pardee (1), John Pardee/Joey Murphy (1), John Sgueglia (1), not known (1) · *directors* Linda Day (8), David Trainer (4), John Sgueglia (3), Philip Charles MacKenzie (1), not known (1) · *executive producers* Jamie Wooten/Marc Cherry

Emma Buchanan mothered four sons before her husband ran off with another woman,

leaving her to raise the boys on her own. Not only did she scrimp and save but, by taking on three jobs, she even managing to put them through college. She did all of this without once complaining of her lot, indeed she would have become a saint were it not for one deciding factor: Emma is an acid-tongued, scheming bitch. Now grown up, her four sons have all married, and the only way her four daughters-in-law can stand up to their monstrous mother-in-law is by forming a united front.

This was the premise of *The 5 Mrs Buchanans*, a neat device for bringing together four very different women to form an unlikely alliance in the face of a common enemy. Each, of course, was very different from the others – Alex was an intellectual New York Jew; Delilah was a tarty ex-cocktail waitress; Vivian was a snobbish local; and newcomer Bree was a winsome and innocent youngster full of the joys of life. They lived in Mercy, Indiana, pitting their wills against the gravel-voiced harridan Emma, whom they called Mother Buchanan. The four husbands (rarely seen in the series) were mere pawns in the battle, a struggle made harder by the powerful influence over her sons that Emma Buchanan asserted.

It seemed clear that those behind *The 5 Mrs Buchanans* were trying to mine the same vein of female friendship comedy that had proved fruitful for *Designing Women* (CBS, 1986–93) and *The Golden Girls*, but the series lacked the attraction and staying power of its antecedents and didn't last long.

The Fivepenny Piece Show

UK · BBC · STANDUP

4 × 30 mins · colour

4 May–25 May 1979 · BBC2 Fri 9pm

MAIN CAST
The Fivepenny Piece

CREDITS
producer Barry Bevins

Following an earlier series with Mike Harding, *MH & 5p*, the humorous folk group returned solo but with a different comedy guest star each week: first the cockney Derek Brimstone, then the comedy bomber Blaster Bates, Lancashire humorist Bernard Wrigley ('The Bolton Bullfrog') and finally the singer and standup comic Fred Wedlock.

Note. Three years before this series the Fivepenny Piece had featured in an edition of the BBC2 series *The Camera And The Song*, screened on 8 March 1976.

Fivepenny Piece And Mike Harding

see HARDING, Mike

Flanders And Swann

Michael Flanders (bearded, wheelchair-bound, the pianist and occasional singer) and Donald Swann (bespectacled, the singer) enjoyed a huge success on both sides of the Atlantic as a musical-comedy double-act performing their own witty, word-rich, jaunty songs, a style popularised from the 1920s to the 1940s on BBC radio by Flotsam and Jetsam (Malcolm McEachern and B C Hilliam).

Flanders was born in London on 1 March 1922, Swann in Llanelli on 30 September 1923, and the pair met at Westminster School, London, in 1940, collaborating in a revue. An informal double-act soon formed, and their performances at social gatherings were so well received that the pair decided to turn professional. Their revue *At The Drop Of A Hat* was the surprise hit of the London stage (and beyond) in 1957, followed by a second, *At The Drop Of Another Hat*, in 1963, ensuring the pair lasting international popularity. Both were recorded for disc and, eventually, adapted for TV screening.

Flanders died at the age of 53, on 15 April 1975, Swann aged 70 on 23 March 1994. On 27 December 1994, BBC2 screened an affectionate look back at the double-act that included recently discovered footage of performances they had given on Broadway.

At The Drop Of A Hat

UK · BBC (TALENT ASSOCIATES/PARAMOUNT/FESTIVAL OF PERFORMING ARTS) · MUSICAL HUMOUR
1 × 50 mins · b/w
21 June 1962 · Thu 7.55pm
MAIN CAST
Michael Flanders
Donald Swann
CREDITS
writers Michael Flanders/Donald Swann · *director* Harry Carlisle · *producers* David Susskind, James Fleming

Five years after it had opened on the London stage (Fortune Theatre, 24 January 1957), Flanders and Swann decided to perform their fabulously successful 'after dinner farrago' *At The Drop Of A Hat* for the BBC, with one eye on the domestic audience and the other on international sales. The songs performed included all the 'hits' – 'A Transport Of Delight', their ode about the double-decker bus; 'Madeira M'Dear'; the musical tongue-twister 'The Gnu Song'; and that other well-known animal observation piece, 'The Hippopotamus Song', the one that had inspired even the entire royal family, who saw the revue in the theatre, to join in with the 'mud, mud, glorious mud' chorus.

Note. A 15-minute extract from the stage-show, relayed from the Fortune Theatre in London, had been screened by the BBC in *Theatre Flash* five years before this dedicated TV production, on 3 June 1957.

At The Drop Of Another Hat   1

UK · ITV (REDIFFUSION) · MUSICAL HUMOUR
1 × 60 mins · b/w
30 Apr 1968 · Tue 8pm
MAIN CAST
Michael Flanders
Donald Swann
CREDITS
writers Michael Flanders/Donald Swann · *director* Ted Kotcheff · *executive producers* David Susskind, Alexander H Cohen

A made-for-TV recording, shot in New York, of Flanders and Swann's second revue, which had opened in London on 2 October 1963 at the Theatre Royal, Haymarket. Highlights this time included 'The Gas-Man Cometh', 'Sounding Brass' and 'A Song Of Patriotic Prejudice'. The programme was screened within the ITV strand *Star Performance*.

At The Drop Of Another Hat   2

UK · BBC (LINTE LISTER WELCH) · MUSICAL HUMOUR
1 × 45 mins · colour
27 Dec 1970 · BBC2 Sun 10.55pm
MAIN CAST
Michael Flanders
Donald Swann
CREDITS
writers Michael Flanders/Donald Swann · *producer* Ted Kotcheff

Another made-for-TV recording, again filmed in New York.

Flat Earth

UK · ITV (GRANADA) · SKETCH
1 × 40 mins · colour
14 Apr 1971 · Wed 10.30pm
MAIN CAST
Marty Cruickshank
Timothy Davies
Dave Hill
John Gorman
Paul McDowell
CREDITS
writers Fred Metcalf, Chris Miller, Pat O'Shea, Dave Hill, John Gorman, Paul McDowell · *director* John Birt · *producer* Andrew Mayer

A single programme – possibly a pilot – crammed with a 'non-stop series of sketches'. Its director, John Birt, went on to become director-general of the BBC.

A Flight Of Fancy

UK · BBC · SKETCH
1 × 30 mins · b/w
16 July 1952 · Wed 8.45pm
MAIN CAST
Jimmy Young
Jerry Desmonde
Victor Platt
CREDITS
deviser Alvin Rakoff · *producer* Dicky Leeman

The hit singer Jimmy Young – later to become even better known as a BBC radio disc-jockey – achieved fame through his successful records, but it was his comedy talents that were in demand on TV in the early 1950s. Young made his small-screen debut in Terry-Thomas' acclaimed sketch series *How Do You View?* (and then appeared in a BBC radio comedy series, *Treble Chance*, in 1953). In *A Flight Of Fancy*, a one-off TV sketch show, Young played alongside one of the great British comedy foils, Jerry Desmonde, soon to make his mark in a number of feature films with Norman Wisdom.

Flip

UK · BBC · CHILDREN'S SITCOM
13 × 20 mins · colour
25 Sep–18 Dec 1991 · BBC1 Wed 4.20pm
MAIN CAST
various
CREDITS
writers Nigel Douglas, Tim Firth/Tim De Jongh and others

A children's comedy series about the workings of FLIP (The Federation of Lost International Property), an organisation that links lost-property offices all over the world, and even beyond, to Venus. Each episode took place in an office in a different location: Manchester, India, Hollywood, Jamaica, and so on, and each office was manned by its own staff played by that week's guest stars, who were either comedians (like Nick Wilton and Neil Mullarkey) or personalities well known from other children's shows (Trev and Simon, to name but two).

The Flip Wilson Show

USA · NBC (CLEROW/BOB HENRY PRODUCTIONS) · STANDUP/SKETCH
52 × 60 mins · colour
US dates: 17 Sep 1970–27 June 1974
UK dates: 18 Apr–18 July 1971 (13 editions)
BBC2 Sun 7.25pm then around 11pm
MAIN CAST
Flip Wilson
CREDITS
director Tim Kiley · *producer* Bob Henry

Bill Cosby was the first black actor to be cast prominently in a major US TV series (*I Spy*), Diahann Carroll (*Julia*) was the first black actress and Flip Wilson became the first black TV comedy superstar. Unlike the other history-makers, who initially achieved success by (pressurised) playing down of their 'blackness', Wilson revelled in his skin colouring.

Born Clerow Wilson on 8 December 1933 in New Jersey, the comic spent his early years in poverty, in a series of foster homes, after his mother abandoned his drunken father and their 24 (*sic*) children. Wilson picked up his 'Flip' nickname while serving in the US Air Force, reputedly because his spontaneous comedy routines were said to 'flip out' his colleagues (well, it was the 1950s). Following his return to civvies he worked hard on developing a comedy routine and spent many years on the fringes of success before his breakthrough year, 1965, when he made an appearance on *The Tonight Show*. More TV bookings followed, with spots on variety series *The Ed Sullivan Show* and sketch show *Rowan And Martin's Laugh-In*, but it was a well-received 1969 NBC special with Jonathan Winters that convinced TV executives he could carry his own series; *The Flip Wilson Show* was launched in 1970.

The series was an instant smash, with Wilson discovering a sizeable crossover audience for his upfront and unashamedly black humour. Particular favourites were his characters Reverend Leroy, of the Church of What's Happening Now, a dishonest, somewhat lecherous gospel preacher; Freddie Johnson, a swinging bachelor; Danny Danger, Private Detective; and, most memorably, Geraldine Jones, a sassy, liberated lady who flirted teasingly before warning of her boyfriend 'Killer'. Wilson invented Geraldine in the 1960s and developed her into one of the funniest gender-bending acts ever seen on TV. Leroy later turned up in the Sidney Poitier-directed 1974 'blaxploitation' comedy movie *Uptown Saturday Night*.

A fine comedian in his own right, Flip Wilson always managed to slip a satirical message into his routines and had a high percentage of black guest stars on his show, including (in the 13 editions aired in the UK) Bill Cosby, Diahann Carroll, Stevie Wonder, Lena Horne, Louis Armstrong, the Supremes, Red Foxx, the Temptations and Nancy Wilson.

Flying Blind

USA · FOX (SWEETUM PRODUCTIONS/ PARAMOUNT) · SITCOM

22 × 30 mins · colour

US dates: 13 Sep 1992–2 May 1993

UK dates: 5 Jan 1994–22 Jun 1994 (22 episodes) C4 Wed around 12 midnight

MAIN CAST

Neil Barash	Corey Parker
Alicia	Téa Leoni
Jeremy Barash	Michael Tucci
Jordan	Robert Bauer
Megan Traynor	Clea Lewis
Ted Sharperson	Marcus Giamatti
Ellen Barash	Christine Rose

CREDITS

creator Richard Rosenstock · *writers* various · *directors* Michael Lembeck (5), Peter Bonerz (4), Ellen Falcon (4), Jeff Melman (3), Stan Daniels (2), James Burrows (1), Dennis Erdman (1), Joshua White (1), Jamie Widdoes (1) · *executive producers* Richard Rosenstock, Jay Kleckner · *producers* Terri Minsky, Michael Stanislavsky, Don Woodard, Tom Maxwell

An unexceptional marketing assistant, Neil Barash, has resigned himself to a dull existence now that he has left college, but at a party he meets the wild and uninhibited Alicia who turns his life around. She is a barnstorming free spirit with a colourful past and a pulsating sex drive. Neil finds himself inexorably pulled into her world of dangerous ex-boyfriends, revolutionaries, demented artists and government spies (Alicia's dad, occasionally seen in the series, played by Peter Boyle, is a spy). Life is anything but dull, but will it all prove to be too much for the hapless Neil? As it happens, yes: in the last episode the relationship breaks after he reads in her diary that she doesn't think it will last.

Flying Blind was a perky, adult sitcom from Fox with Téa Leoni proving to be a bewitching and sexy lead. This was one of a number of similar Fox sitcoms to featuring young singles enjoying sexual shenanigans, but despite its potential, the series found it hard to recover from one central dilemma: what on earth did the incandescent Alicia see in the dull Neil? Perhaps, then, she was the one who was flying blind.

See also *The Naked Truth*.

The Flying Nun

USA · ABC (SCREEN GEMS) · SITCOM

82 × 30 mins · colour

US dates: 17 Sep 1967–18 Sep 1970

UK dates: 6 Aug 1968–1 Jan 1970 (15 × b/w · 1 × colour) ITV various days and times

MAIN CAST

Elsie Ethrington/Sister Bertrille	Sally Field
Sister Jacqueline	Marge Redmond
Mother Superior	Madeline Sherwood
Sister Sixto	Shelley Morrison
Carlos Ramirez	Alejandro Rey
Marcello	Manuel Padilla Jr
Sister Ana	Linda Dangcil

CREDITS

creator Tere Rios · *writers* various · *directors* various · *producers* Harry Ackerman, William Sackheim

A very silly American sitcom – based on the book *The Fifteenth Pelican* by Tere Rios – that was screened by London-area ITV, albeit sketchily, when it ought not to have been touched with the proverbial bargepole.

The Flying Nun herself was Sister Bertrille, living and working at the Convent San Tanco, a hilltop order near San Juan in Puerto Rico. It's a windy place and, bizarrely, the nuns wear head-dresses with funny flappy bits on each side – lo and behold the wind gets caught up in the garment and the nuns, well, *fly*.

In her mission to help the unfortunate Hispanic kids, our heroine Sister – once plain Elsie Ethrington – is thwarted by the fact that she is unable to control her flying tendencies, not least because she weighs less than seven stone, and this leads her into all *sorts* of scrapes, as you can well imagine. The kids however, portrayed as 'noble savages', are perpetually grateful for the help of these brave, white, gravity-defying Americans ...

Fo A Fe

UK · BBC · SITCOM

15 × 30 mins · colour

Series One (8) 7 Mar–2 May 1972 · BBC1 Tue 12.55pm

Special · 27 Jan 1976 · BBC1 Tue 3.25pm

Series Two (6) 30 Nov 1976–18 Jan 1977 · BBC1 Tue 3.20pm

MAIN CAST

Twm Twm	Ryan Davies
Diana	Gaynor Morgan Rees
George	Clive Roberts
Ephraim	Guto Roberts
Sioni	Ieuan Rhys Williams
Mrs Cadwaladr	Dilys Davies

CREDITS

writers Gwenlyn Parry/Rhydderch Jones · *producer* Jack Williams

A Welsh-language sitcom originally transmitted only in Wales but then repeated in England for Welsh speakers (the dates, above, reflect the networked broadcasts). The series centred on two men, one a cheerful drunk, the other a God-fearing teetotaller, and the efforts of the drunk's daughter to keep the peace. The title *Fo A Fe* translates to *This One And That One*.

A Foggy Outlook

UK · ITV (LWT) · STANDUP

1 × 30 mins · colour

26 June 1982 · Sat 8.10pm

MAIN CAST

Fogwell Flax

CREDITS

writers Colin Bostock-Smith, Paul Minett/Brian Leveson, Christopher Blake · *director/producer* John Kaye Cooper

A one-off show for the Liverpool-born comedian-entertainer, who had won the *Search For A Star* talent-spotting TV series in December 1980 and become a regular on Central's anarchic children's series *Tiswas* once the first squad (Tarrant, Henry et al) had left for *O.T.T.*

Foley Square

USA · CBS (CBS ENTERTAINMENT) · SITCOM

14 × 30 mins · colour

US dates: 11 Dec 1985–23 July 1986

UK dates: 8 June–14 Sep 1986 (14 episodes)
BBC2 Sun 6.45pm

MAIN CAST

Alex Harrigan (Assistant DA) · Margaret Colin
Jesse Steinberg (DA) · · · · · · Hector Elizondo
Peter Newman · · · · · Michael Lembeck
Molly Dobbs (Assistant DA) · · · Cathy Silvers
Carter DeVries (Assistant DA) · Sanford Jensen
Denise Willums · · · · Vernee Watson-Johnson
Angel Gomez · · · · · · · · · · · · · · Israel Juarbe
Mole · Jon Lovitz

CREDITS

writers Diane English, Bernie Orenstein/Saul Turteltaub · director Peter Bonerz · producers Bernie Orenstein/Saul Turteltaub

A smart but short-lived series set in the Manhattan District Attorney's office, located in Foley Square. The central character was the bright and attractive Assistant DA Alex Harrigan, the series following her legal wrangles at work and personal situation at home.

The series is mostly remembered for featuring rising stars Hector Elizondo and Jon Lovitz, who was already taking his first steps to comedy fame by joining the regular cast of *Saturday Night Live* just as the first few episodes of *Foley Square* aired. Its cast also had a unique connection with *The Phil Silvers Show* – Cathy Silvers (Molly Dobbs) is Phil's daughter and Michael Lembeck (Peter Newman) is the son of Harvey Lembeck, who played Rocco Barbella, Ernie Bilko's sidekick, in that great 1950s sitcom.

Follies Of The Wise

see MILLIGAN, Spike

Follow That Dog

UK · ITV (SOUTHERN) · CHILDREN'S SITCOM

6 × 25 mins · colour

13 Nov–18 Dec 1974 · Wed 4.25pm

MAIN CAST

PC Fogg · · · · · · · · · · · · · Norman Rossington
Sgt Bryant · · · · · · · · · · · · Patsy Rowlands
Insp Bridges · · · · · · · · · · · Anthony Dawes
Peter · · · · · · · · · · · · · · · · · · Nigel Rhodes
Rosie · · · · · · · · · · · · · · · · · · Janet French

CREDITS

writer Michael Nelson · director Peter Croft

Police Constable Fogg is in danger of being drummed out of the force because he never solves any crimes. Then, when a mini-crimewave breaks out, he finds that he can – with the assistance of his dog, a mournful-faced Basset-hound named Parry, who, when they nap together, dreams the solutions and transfers them into Fogg's mind.

Norman Rossington starred, and Patsy Rowlands was cast as his tough sergeant.

Fools Rush In

UK · BBC · SITCOM

1 × 30 mins · b/w

12 Oct 1963 · Sat 9.30pm

MAIN CAST

Major Humphrey Carlton · · · · · Deryck Guyler
Wilfred · · · · · · · · · · · · · · · Gordon Rollings
Barney · · · · · · · · · · · · · · · · · Patrick Newell

CREDITS

writers Vince Powell/Frank Roscoe · producer John Ammonds

A *Comedy Playhouse* pilot from two of the writers of **Here's Harry**. The retired Major Carlton has been used to service life, where he was extremely well looked after by army batmen, but now he finds himself in civvy street employing a chauffeur-cum-gardener (Wilfred) and a cook-cum-valet (Barney). But private-sector servants are a completely different kettle of fish … The emphasis in this half-hour was on slapstick, but no series developed.

Football Crazy

UK · ITV (THAMES) · CHILDREN'S SITCOM

1 × 30 mins · colour

31 May 1974 · Fri 4.50pm

MAIN CAST

Arnold Smedley · · · · · · · · · · · · · · Bob Todd
Daphne · · · · · · · · · · · · · · · Madge Hindle
Carol · · · · · · · · · · · · · · · · · · Liz Gebhardt

CREDITS

writers John Esmonde/Bob Larbey · director Vic Hughes · producer Ruth Boswell

The second of Thames' series of *Funny Ha Ha* individual children's comedies. This one starred Bob Todd as Arnold Smedley, the football-mad manager of local side Wormwood Rovers, dismissed because of their poor record. Seeking to rouse him from his anguish, Arnold's daughter Carol pops a couple of pills into his cup of tea, only to find that he's invited back … as a player.

Footlights '64

see The Cambridge Footlights

For 4 Tonight

UK · C4 (LWT) · SATIRE

6 × 30 mins · colour

1 Oct–5 Nov 1983 · Sat mostly 11pm

MAIN CAST

Tony Royale · · · · · · · · · · · · · · George Irving
Avril Petrie · · · · · · · · · · · · · · · · · Rachel Bell

OTHER APPEARANCES

Norman Chappell

CREDITS

writer Ruby Wax · director/producer Michael Dolenz

Seemingly, albeit unofficially, a British version of the American show *Fernwood 2-Night* (see **Mary Hartman, Mary Hartman**) – a spoof TV chat-show with supposedly genuine hosts and guests. The six editions were broadcast direct from the (fictional) town of Newton Barnes, said to be located near Milton Keynes.

Although, on air, the series was said to be the creation of Avril Petrie, who co-hosted with the dashing Tony Royale, it was actually written by Ruby Wax, one of her earliest TV endeavours after moving to England from the USA. (Completing the American flavour, the director/producer was Michael Dolenz, once of **The Monkees** but, at this time, working behind the cameras for LWT.)

Being a send-up, and a *local* TV show, *For 4 Tonight* featured all manner of odd guests (played by actors, the only recurring contributor being Norman Chappell), including a pedicurist, a fishmonger, a stuntman and a mortuary superintendent. There was also a studio band.

For Richer ... For Poorer

UK · BBC · SITCOM

1 × 30 mins · colour

25 June 1975 · BBC1 Wed 9.25pm

MAIN CAST

Bert · Harry H Corbett
The boss · · · · · · · · · · · · · · · Eric Pohlmann
Nigel 'The Idle' · · · · · · · · · · · · David Battley
The mediator · · · · · · · · · · · Don Henderson

CREDITS

writer Johnny Speight · producer Dennis Main Wilson

The third in a series of unrelated sitcoms screened by BBC1 on consecutive Wednesdays, following the demise of its *Comedy Playhouse* strand.

Bert, a working man, was writer Johnny Speight's left-wing answer to his Alf Garnett creation, and the show's title mirrored that of **Till Death Us Do Part** (and the later **In Sickness And In Health**), being yet another line from the marriage vows. Played by Harry H Corbett, Bert was a barricade-manning union shop-steward who worshipped Stalin and dreamed of becoming a powerful left-wing leader.

For Richer For Poorer

UK · ITV (ATV) · SITCOM

1 × 30 mins · colour

14 Aug 1975 · Thu 7pm

MAIN CAST

Richard Bunting ·········· George Layton
Fiona Bunting ············· Susan Dury
Nigel Benson ············· Ian Ogilvy
Penelope Benson ··········· Jane How

CREDITS

writer Jon Watkins · director/producer John Scholz-Conway

Part of the *Comedy Premiere* season, this single-episode sitcom, featuring a particularly handsome cast, depicted the Buntings, a young married couple living in suburbia. Courtesy of another couple, the Bensons, they contrive to overcome their financial difficulties. No series developed.

For The Love Of Ada

UK · ITV (THAMES) · SITCOM

28 episodes (26 × 30 mins · 1 × 45 mins · 1 × short special) · colour

Series One (6 × 30 mins) 20 Apr–25 May 1970 · Mon mostly 9.30pm

Series Two (7 × 30 mins) 14 Sep–26 Oct 1970 · Mon 9.30pm

Short special · part of *All-Star Comedy Carnival* 25 Dec 1970 · Fri 6pm

Series Three (7 × 30 mins) 15 Mar–3 May 1971 · Mon 8.30pm

Series Four (6 × 30 mins) 26 Aug–30 Sep 1971 · Thu 9pm

Special (45 mins) 26 Dec 1971 · Sun 6.45pm

MAIN CAST

Ada Cresswell/Bingley ········ Irene Handl
Walter Bingley ············ Wilfred Pickles
Ruth Pollitt ············· Barbara Mitchell
Leslie Pollitt ············ Jack Smethurst

CREDITS

writers Vince Powell/Harry Driver · producer Ronnie Baxter

A fine, gentle comedy that sported all the ingredients for a success: scripts from Powell and Driver and starring roles for Wilfred Pickles, having a go at a TV sitcom for the first time in 12 years, and that wonderful comedy free-spirit Irene Handl. Rarely has ITV produced such a warm and enjoyable sitcom as this, and it ranks as one of the channel's very best.

The premise was that cockney Ada Cresswell (Handl), a pensioner widow of several years, and prone to speaking in malapropisms, begins having an affair with the grave-digger who buried her husband, Walter Bingley (Pickles), a stout Yorkshireman living at Cemetery Lodge. Ada lives with her thirty-something daughter Ruth, and her husband Leslie, and so this younger generation are on hand to witness the old 'uns' relationship develop. It doesn't progress

without the odd bump but the couple are engaged (at the end of the first series) and then married (at the end of the second). In the fourth and final series they become grandparents when Ruth gives birth to baby, Anthony. (Leslie, a Manchester United supporter – as was the actor who played him, Jack Smethurst – wanted to name the child Nobby, after Nobby Stiles, but Ruth refused.)

The series spawned a less-good feature film in 1972 and then a US TV spin-off, *A Touch Of Grace* (never screened in Britain), which ran for 22 episodes on ABC from January to June 1973 and starred Shirley Booth as Grace Sherwood, J Patrick O'Malley as grave-digger Herbert Morrison, and Marian Mercer and Warren Berlinger as Myra and Walter Bradley.

Foreign Affairs 1

UK · ITV (GRANADA) · SITCOM

8 × 30 mins · b/w

2 Jan–20 Feb 1964 · Thu 7.30pm

CAST

Montague 'Bootsie' Bisley ····· Alfie Bass
Claude Snudge ············· Bill Fraser
Ambassador ············ Nicholas Phipps
Third Secretary ··········· Arthur Barrett

CREDITS

writers Barry Took (5), Peter Jones (2), Richard Harris/Dennis Spooner (1) · script editor Peter Jones · director Milo Lewis · producers Peter Eton (6), Derek Granger (2)

After three very long series of *Bootsie And Snudge*, the not so dynamic duo from *The Army Game* were back on TV within seven months, Alfie Bass and Bill Fraser reprising their famous characters within the employ of the diplomatic service, at the British Embassy in 'Bosnik', somewhere in Europe. Snudge liked to think of himself as ambassador material while Bootsie, trendily sporting a Beatles haircut, was appointed security officer.

The characters were laid to rest after these eight episodes and not revived until *Bootsie And Snudge* was resurrected in 1974. But Bass and Fraser worked together again in 1967 in *Vacant Lot*, an ABC (British) sitcom screened in the Midlands and the North and other ITV regions – but not London – over seven Saturday nights (at 8.30pm) from 1 April to 13 May 1967. In their customary boss and underling roles, Fraser was cast as Bill Bendlove, the managing director of a building and decorating company called Bendlove And Bodium, and Bass played his brother-in-law, Alf Grimble, who was its wily works foreman. The other regular characters were Laurie Leigh as Sandra, and Jack Haig, Nicky Henson and Arthur Mullard as Stoker, Rock and Chippy. Dick Clement and Ian La Frenais wrote the pilot (actually screened as the final episode); Jeremy Lloyd and Jimmy

Grafton scripted four episodes, one of these with a third writer, David Climie, and Fred Robinson (author of *The Larkins*) wrote the remaining two, which were script edited by Jimmy Grafton. Apart from the pilot (made by Dick Clement) the series was produced by Milo Lewis, veteran of *The Army Game*, *Bootsie And Snudge* and *Foreign Affairs*.

Foreign Affairs 2

UK · BBC · SITCOM

6 × 30 mins · b/w

16 Sep–21 Oct 1966 · BBC1 Fri 7.30pm

MAIN CAST

Dennis Proudfoot ·········· Leslie Phillips
Taplow ··············· Richard O'Sullivan
Sir Hugh Marriot ··········· Austin Trevor
Miss Jessup ·············· Dorothy Frere
Grischa Petrovitch ········· Ronnie Barker
Serge Volchanivov ············ Joe Melia
Irinka ················· Sonia Graham

CREDITS

creator Leonard Samson · writers Johnnie Mortimer/Brian Cooke (5), Leonard Samson/Johnnie Mortimer/Brian Cooke (1) · producer John Street

A BBC sitcom depicting the lighter side of spying, set mainly in the Whitehall HQ of the Foreign Office, and starring Leslie Phillips as Dennis Proudfoot, personal assistant to the administrator of foreign relations, Sir Hugh Marriot. (Typical of Phillips' screen characters, he also found the time to woo a different young beauty in every episode.)

The series focused on the conflicts between British diplomats and their contemporaries at the Soviet embassy in London, with Ronnie Barker cast as the bumbling anglophile Grischa Petrovitch, PA to the Russkies' shrewd commissar for foreign relations, Serge Volchanivov.

Phillips and the fast-rising Barker had been working since 1959 in the BBC radio sitcom *The Navy Lark*, but this was their first TV appearance together. *Foreign Affairs* also played an important part in the career of another young actor, Richard O'Sullivan, cast here as a 20-year-old post-room boy at the Foreign Office. Through this introduction to writers Mortimer and Cooke he would go on to star in their ITV comedy hit *Man About The House*.

Foreign Bodies

UK · BBC · SITCOM

18 × 30 mins · colour

Series One (6) 5 Mar–9 Apr 1987 · BBC2 Thu 9pm

Series Two (6) 18 Sep–23 Oct 1987 · BBC2 Fri mostly 9pm

Series Three (6) 4 May–8 June 1989 · BBC2 Thu 9pm

MAIN CAST

Tom	Dan Gordon
Alex	Colum Convey
Roisin	Hilary Reynolds
Septa	Maeve Germaine
Soup	Louis Rolston
Madge	Trudy Kelly
Harry	John Hewitt
Elaine	Catherine Brennan
Mrs Fogarty	Eileen Colgan
Carol	Tracey Lynch
Dermot	Barry McGovern (series 1); Bosco Hogan (series 3)
Sammy	B J Hogg (series 2 & 3)
Bootlace	Walter McMonagle (series 2 & 3)
Mrs Parker	Margaret D'Arcy (series 2 & 3)

CREDITS

writers Bernard Farrell/Graham Reid · *directors* Sydney Lotterby (17), Sue Bysh (1) · *producer* Sydney Lotterby

Sitcoms set in Northern Ireland are few and far between – to 1997 there were just two: *Foreign Bodies* and **So You Think You've Got Troubles**. *Foreign Bodies* was the work of two playwrights, Graham Reid, from Ulster, and Bernard Farrell, from Dublin; neither had experienced the hatred they were led to believe would greet them when they mixed with people from across the border, and this was the basis for their series.

Although sporting a large cast of recurring characters, the episodes focused on four leading players, two young women and two young men. Roisin and Septa were the women, a pair of Catholic nurses from Dublin who crossed the great divide to work in a Belfast hospital. Roisin soon met and fell in love with Tom, a Protestant car mechanic. The youngsters, naturally, saw no problem in their relationship, but others did, and the question soon arose of whether they should be faithful to their faith or to each other. Their friends had differing opinions, and Tom's pal Alex caused strife for everyone.

The Fossett Saga

UK · ITV (LWT) · SITCOM

7 × 30 mins · b/w

10 Jan–21 Feb 1969 · Fri 8.30pm

MAIN CAST

James Fossett	Jimmy Edwards
Herbert Quince	Sam Kydd

CREDITS

writer Dave Freeman · *director/producer* David Askey

Set in the late-Victorian era, *The Fossett Saga* starred Jimmy Edwards as James Fossett, who writes 'penny-dreadfuls' but desires to earn his fortune by other means, fair or foul. He sets off on thrilling weekly adventures and is only prevented from making an complete ass of himself by his unpaid batman Herbert Quince. The series' title was an obvious send-up of *The Forsyte Saga*, the hugely popular

drama on BBC TV in 1967 and, in repeats, 1968–69.

The supporting cast changed each week, with Geraldine Newman, Graham Stark, Eric Barker, Erik Chitty and June Whitfield appearing once apiece. Whitfield and Edwards had appeared together many times, most famously in the BBC radio series *Take It From Here*.

The Fosters

UK · ITV (LWT) · SITCOM

27 × 30 mins · colour

Series One (13) 9 Apr–2 July 1976 · Fri 7.30pm then 8.30pm

Special *New Year With The Fosters* 1 Jan 1977 · Sat 10.30pm

Series Two (13) 16 Apr–9 July 1977 · Sat around 7.15pm

MAIN CAST

Samuel Foster	Norman Beaton
Pearl Foster	Isabelle Lucas
Sonny Foster	Lenny Henry
Shirley Foster	Sharon Rosita
Benjamin Foster	Lawrie Mark
Vilma	Carmen Munro

CREDITS

original US writers Jack Elinson, Norman Paul, Roland Wolpert, Lou Derman, William Davenport, John Donley, Kurt B Taylor, Michael Morris, Larry Siegel, Bob Shayne, Eric Cohen, Allan Manings, Bob Peete, Eric Monte and others · *US scripts adapter* Jon Watkins · *director/producer* Stuart Allen

Although best remembered today as a major stepping-stone to fame for a young Lenny Henry (he was 17 and had 'arrived' on TV in 1975 in the talent show *New Faces*), *The Fosters* holds a place in the annals of British television all its own: it was the first sitcom written for and starring blacks. Stories centred around the lives of one family: feisty Mum (Pearl), easy-going Dad (Samuel), both immigrants from Guyana, and their three British-born children, Sonny, Shirley and Benjamin. They are undeniably poor but Sam ekes the best living he can in a white man's country and they all live together high up in Flat 131 in a tower block on a south London housing estate. The other main character was Vilma, Pearl's friend and near neighbour from Flat 139.

The series was the British adaptation of an American sitcom, *Good Times* (133 episodes, CBS, 1974–79, set in Chicago and depicting the Evans family), which was itself spun-off from *Maude*, a spin-off from **All In The Family** which was the US version of **Till Death Us Do Part**. This is not to say that *The Fosters* was in any way controversial like its ancestors; in fact, it failed to make much of an impact even with black audiences and, once the 'colour' novelty had worn off, it came to an end. One reason for this could be that, under the contractual arrangement which

allowed the US-to-UK crossover, *The Fosters* was compelled to utilise the American *Good Times* scripts. Even allowing for some anglicising by Jon Watkins, to watch an episode of *The Fosters* was like looking at a US sitcom – and only an adequate one at that.

Lenny Henry, of course, put down his floppy hat and his easel (in *The Fosters* he was a budding artist) and went on to a glorious future. Norman Beaton went on to appear in the BBC's black soap *Empire Road* (which was vaguely comedic but more of a drama) and the C4 sitcom **Desmond's**, where he again appeared alongside Carmen Munro/Munroe. (She changed the spelling of her surname over the years.)

Four On The Floor

CANADA · SYNDICATION (PAINLESS PRODUCTIONS/PRODUCERS GROUP INTERNATIONAL) · SKETCH

13 × 30 mins · colour

Canadian dates: 1985–1986

UK dates: 10 June 1988–8 Sep 1989 (13 editions) C4 Fri 9pm then around 1.30am

MAIN CAST

Paul Chato
Rick Green
Dan Redican
Peter Wildman

CREDITS

director David Acomba · *producer* Morgan Earl

An at-times brilliant sketch series imported to C4 from Canada and featuring four men – Chato, Green, Redican and Wildman – who styled themselves the Frantics and concocted wild, inventive and very visual humour with such characters as Mr Canoehead.

The Four Seasons

USA · CBS (ALDA-BREGMAN/UNIVERSAL) · SITCOM

12 episodes (11 × 30 mins · 1 × 60 mins) · colour

US dates: 29 Jan–5 Aug 1984

UK dates: 30 Aug–15 Nov 1985 (11 × 30 mins · 1 × 60 mins) C4 Fri mostly 10pm

MAIN CAST

Danny Zimmer	Jack Weston
Claudia Zimmer	Marcia Rodd
Boris Elliott	Alan Arbus
Lorraine Elliott	Barbara Babcock
Ted Bolen	Tony Roberts
Pat Devon	Joanna Kerns
Beth Burroughs	Elizabeth Alda
Lisa Bolen	Beatrice Alda
Jack Burroughs	Alan Alda

CREDITS

creator Alan Alda · *writers* Alan Alda, Richard Baer, Marshall Goldberg, David M Hackel, Lindsay Harrison, John H Kostmayer, Philip F Margo, Gary W Ress, Don Segall, Rick Sultan · *directors* various · *executive producers* Alan Alda, Martin Bregman

A sitcom developed by Alan Alda out of the 1981 movie of the same title – which he wrote, directed and starred in. The film followed three young-middle-aged couples who holiday together on four occasions – in spring, summer, autumn and winter – and witness the crumbling of their own and the others' relationships, and their friendly companionship.

Alan Alda turned up in some episodes of the TV series, reprising his movie role of lawyer Jack Burroughs, but the main star was the neurotic dentist Danny Zimmer (Jack Weston, again from the film) who, with his wife Claudia, moves out from Manhattan to Los Angeles. Here Danny befriends Ted Bolen, who works in real estate and lives the Californian lifestyle to the hilt. Ted's girlfriend Pat is a stuntwoman.

The other characters included Boris (played by Alan Arbus, who had appeared in a few episodes of *M*A*S*H*, including the key role of Hawkeye's psychiatrist in the stunning final episode), a lawyer who has quit the legal business to open a bicycle shop; and his wife Lorraine, who teaches orthopaedic medicine at UCLA. Alan Alda's real-life daughters Elizabeth (as Beth Burroughs) and Beatrice (as Ted Bolen's daughter Lisa) also reprised their movie roles in the TV series.

Despite the solid cast and *thirtysomething*-played-for-laughs premise, *The Four Seasons* sitcom wasn't nearly as good as the movie and soon came off the air. The laughs it did get, sadly, were 'canned', and C4 viewers had to suffer the sound of this fake contrivance throughout the 12 episodes.

Four Tall Tinkles

see *Three Rousing Tinkles*

Foxy Lady

UK · ITV (GRANADA) · SITCOM

13 × 30 mins · colour

Series One (6) 25 Oct–29 Nov 1982 · Mon 8pm

Series Two (7) 18 Jan–29 Feb 1984 · Wed 8.30pm

MAIN CAST

Daisy Jackson	Diane Keen
Joe Prince	Geoffrey Burridge
J P Schofield	Patrick Troughton
Ben Marsh	Milton Johns
Tancred Taylour	Alan David
Hector Ross	Gregor Fisher
Acorn Henshaw	Tom Mennard
Owen Buckley	Steven Pinder

CREDITS

writer Geoffrey Lancashire · *directors* Richard Holthouse (series 1), Malcolm Taylor (series 2) · *producer* John G Temple

Previously cast as Fliss Hawthorne in *The Cuckoo Waltz*, also written by Geoffrey Lancashire, Diane Keen starred here as a

woman encroaching into a man's world and setting it abuzz. Her role was Daisy Jackson, appointed – despite having no previous experience – as the new editor at a failing northern weekly newspaper, *The Ramsden Reminder*. The previous incumbent had just died and, like his own, the paper's circulation had ceased to function. Worse, bankruptcy was only a whisker away. So along came the feisty Daisy with the metaphorical new broom.

With Daisy being a young and pretty woman, the men didn't know how to deal with or second-guess her as she set about reversing the paper's declining fortunes. She did so mostly against the wishes of its set-in-their-ways four reporting and two printing staff – among them the production manager J P Schofield, arts editor Tancred Taylour, sports editor Ben Marsh, and print-room apprentice Owen Buckley – and the friendly (he'd like to have been *more* friendly with Daisy) bank accountant Joe Prince.

While undoubtedly a sitcom, the period feel of *Foxy Lady* – the first series was set in 1959, the second 1960 – lent a whiff of light-drama to the atmosphere. The series is also notable for having given the first regular TV exposure to future comedy star Gregor Fisher (***Naked Video***, ***Rab C Nesbitt***, ***The Baldy Man***).

Frankie Howerd ...
[various shows]

see HOWERD, Frankie

Franklyn And Johnnie

UK · BBC · SITCOM

1 × 30 mins · colour

23 Apr 1974 · BBC1 Tue 8.30pm

MAIN CAST

Franklyn Sims	Geoffrey Bayldon
Johnnie Wetherby	Ronnie Barker
Mr Mawson	Richard Hurndall
Dora Phillips	Joyce Heron
Bernard Watson	Sydney Bromley

CREDITS

writer Richard Waring · *producer* Graeme Muir

A *Comedy Playhouse* one-off starring Ronnie Barker, depicting two life-long rivals who have a chance to bury the hatchet at the funeral of their one mutual friend.

Barker may have been relieved that this was not developed into a series, for his own bunch of comedy pilots, ***Seven Of One***, screened in 1973, was about to yield a bowlful of ***Porridge*** and then ***Open All Hours***.

Frank's Place

USA · CBS (VIACOM PRODUCTIONS) · SITCOM

22 × 30 mins · colour

US dates: 14 Sep 1987–1 Oct 1988

UK dates: 24 Aug 1990–25 Sep 1991 (22 episodes) C4 Fri 9pm then Wed around 11.45pm

MAIN CAST

Frank Parrish	Tim Reid
Hannah Griffin	Daphne Maxwell Reid
Sy 'Bubba' Weisburger	Robert Harper
Anna-May	Francesca P Roberts
Miss Marie Walker	Frances E Williams
Big Arthur	Tony Burton
Tiger Shepin	Charles Lampkin
Cool Charles	William Thomas Jr
Shorty La Roux	Don Yesso
Mrs Bertha Griffin-Lamour	Virginia Capers

CREDITS

creator Hugh Wilson · *writers* Hugh Wilson, Craig Nelson, David Chambers, Richard Dubin, Samm-Art Williams · *directors* various · *executive producers* Hugh Wilson, Tim Reid

An intelligent and literate sitcom starring Tim Reid as Frank Parrish, a Boston-based history professor who inherits a small New Orleans creole restaurant, Chez Louisiane, from an absentee father whom he hasn't seen since he was two years old. Frank travels to the restaurant with plans to sell it, being well aware that he isn't cut out to run such a place, but upon seeing the establishment he falls under its spell and is drawn to the eccentric bunch of people who work there or come to dine. These include the local mortician, Hannah Griffin (played by Reid's real-life wife), whom Frank immediately fancies. So he decides to stay, and try to manage the restaurant; the locals, who are initially wary of his intervention, are gradually won around.

Frank's Place was one of a number of serio-comedies that the Americans labelled as 'dramadies' owing to their low-key style, dramatic undertones and willingness to tackle serious subjects. The virtually all-black ensemble cast (Sy Weisburger was a rare white regular) played the piece like a drama; and the absence of a laughter track, and the director's decision not to employ quick cuts between multiple cameras, added to the classy feel of the series. (It was so real you could almost smell the food.) Critics and a loyal set of viewers responded to its thoughtful style but mass audiences were more resistant and the series was cancelled after one season.

Frasier

USA · NBC (GRUB STREET PRODUCTIONS/ PARAMOUNT) · SITCOM

105 × 30 mins (to 31/12/97 · continuing into 1998) · colour

US dates: 16 Sep 1993 to date

UK dates: 20 Apr 1994 to date (96 episodes to 31/12/97) C4 Wed 10pm then Fri mostly 10pm

MAIN CAST

Dr Frasier Crane	Kelsey Grammer
Dr Niles Crane	David Hyde Pierce
Martin 'Marty' Crane	John Mahoney

Daphne Moon	Jane Leeves
Roz Doyle	Peri Gilpin

OTHER APPEARANCES

Bob 'Bulldog' Briscoe	Dan Butler
Gil Chesterton	Edward Hibbert
Frederick	Luke Tarsitano
Sherry	Marsha Mason (from 1996)

CREDITS

creators David Angell, Peter Casey, David Lee · *writers* Chuck Ranberg/Anne Flett-Giordano, Christopher Lloyd, David Lloyd, Joe Keenan, Sy Dukane/Denise Moss, Linda Morris/Vic Rauseo, Ken Levine/David Isaacs, Steven Levitan and others · *directors* James Burrows, Andy Ackerman, David Lee, Philip Charles MacKenzie and others · *executive producers* David Angell, Peter Casey, David Lee, Christopher Lloyd · *producers* Elias Davis, David Pollock, Maggie Randell, Chuck Ranberg, Anne Flett-Giordano

When Boston bar Cheers closed its doors in 1993, the viewing public bade farewell to a bunch of sitcom characters who had become firm favourites. *Cheers* had consistently offered sharply written, brilliant comedy, and its final episode was watched by the largest US TV audience ever at that time. It was a hard act to follow – but, amazingly, a *Cheers* spin-off succeeded in being not just as good as its progenitor but, in most areas, better, for *Frasier* was a comedy masterpiece.

The character of Dr Frasier Crane had originally been introduced into *Cheers* to effect a break-up between the lovers Sam and Diane, and to provide a pompous foil to react with the bar gang. The absorption of the character into the regular team had added yet another spin to the complex comedic layers of that excellent series: the classically educated, uptight Dr Crane – and later his fiancée and eventual wife Lilith – were delightful additions to the popular clan. The Frasier character grew as the atmosphere of the bar began to humanise this initially frosty individual; indeed, by the end of the series, Frasier was almost a 'regular guy', albeit one with a lot of psychological baggage.

In *Frasier*, Dr Crane returns home to Seattle to start a new life following his divorce from Lilith, who has retained custody of their son Frederick. Feeling that his Boston practice had grown stagnant, he is keen to embark upon a career as a radio phone-in psychiatrist, and to enjoy the freedom of being a single man once more. However, these plans are immediately dashed when Frasier's brother Niles angles for Frasier to provide a home for their widowed father Martin, a career policeman who has been invalided out of the force with a gammy leg following a shooting incident. Despite the fact that father and children have never seen eye to eye – he is a beer and baseball buddy, they are anally retentive sophisticates – Frasier grudgingly accepts his responsibilities and Martin moves in, as does his psychic physical therapist and home-carer, Daphne, and his

unnervingly 'knowing' dog Eddie. The clash of personalities results in much tension but, gradually, Martin and Frasier achieve a bumpy though ultimately comfortable co-existence.

Frasier also settles quickly at work, being guided through the mechanical motions of radio by his producer, the man-hungry Roz Doyle. Frasier takes to the radio job at KACL with some enthusiasm and enjoys being a local celebrity, his biggest discontent being the station's super-exuberant and macho sports presenter, 'Bulldog', who perennially ribs Frasier, bombards him with practical jokes and takes every opportunity to air his opinion that Frasier is a wimp and that his profession is for the birds. Frasier's radio work is also treated with scorn by his brother Niles, a fellow psychiatrist (as was their late mother) who considers the phone-in a cheapening of the profession, a sort of fairground side-show version of real psychiatry. Niles is an extremely uptight individual, an undiluted version of Frasier who (at the start of the series) is married to the never seen but perpetually discussed Maris, a frail, pale, ghastly-sounding creature whose enormous wealth makes her a queen of Seattle society. Niles seems completely dominated by Maris but, as their relationship crumbles, he becomes more and more infatuated with Daphne, who – for a long time, at least – remains oblivious to Niles' attentions.

From this basic set-up, and from just three studio-bound locations – Frasier's fine apartment in Elliott Bay Towers, with its panoramic view of Seattle; the KACL studio; and the perfectly named Café Nervosa, where Frasier and Niles meet for coffee – truly great comedy was wrought.

The casting of *Frasier* was brilliant and the interplay between the cast was of the highest order. Particularly impressive was David Hyde Pierce as Niles, the younger version of an earlier Frasier, whose facial resemblance to Kelsey Grammer was remarkable. Pierce watched old episodes of *Cheers* to study Grammer's original interpretation of Frasier, to recapture the rigid pomposity that the character sported before his softening under the influence of the bar regulars. The resulting relationship between Niles and Frasier – a heady combination of closeness and intense fraternal rivalry – and was one of the most pleasing aspects of the show. Roz Doyle (named in honour of a colleague of the creators who had died of breast cancer) provided an excellent foil for Frasier at work, and John Mahoney, as Martin, was more than a match for him at home. Jane Leeves' character, the Mancunian Daphne Moon, brought a rich vein of eccentricity to the plots, and further surrealism was added by the wonderful playing of Eddie the dog (real

name Moose) who mentally tortured Frasier. Just as there was a talked-about-but-never-seen character in *Cheers* (Norm's wife Vera) so the creators repeated the trick in *Frasier* with Niles' wife Maris. Another idea, which faded as the series developed, was the celebrity call, whereby each episode would start with an anonymous problem call to Frasier's radio phone-in, voiced by a well-known US entertainment figure – recognising the voice before the acknowledgement in the closing credits became a weekly challenge.

On the odd occasion members of the *Cheers* cast (Lilith, Sam, Diane) visited the series but it was soon obvious that *Frasier* was its own animal and didn't need such fillips to court success. The producers remained determined throughout to keep *Frasier* adult and sophisticated – the scripts were literate, the plots tight and the one-liners extremely funny and incisive. The writers were never afraid to use classical references in the lines or make jokes about subjects that many of the viewers wouldn't have experienced. But this was a show about a psychiatrist and such topics came with the territory. Kelsey Grammer experienced widely publicised personal problems throughout the series' run but his performances rarely suffered, and when his part was downplayed to accommodate his absence the other members of this most excellent cast were more than capable of carrying the show.

All in all, *Frasier* was an 18-carat gem of a series, deserving of its place in the highest sitcom stratosphere.

Fred Emney Picks A Pop

UK · BBC · SITCOM

1 × 30 mins · b/w

1 July 1960 · Fri 7.30pm

MAIN CAST
Fred Emney
Avril Angers
Reginald Beckwith
Pat Coombs

CREDITS
writer Fred Emney · *producer* Ronald Marsh

A one-off spoof on the pop business, written by and starring the larger-than-life Emney.

See also *Emney Enterprises*, *The Big Man* and *The Fred Emney Show*.

The Fred Emney Show

UK · BBC · SKETCH

4 × 30 mins · b/w

7 Feb–21 Mar 1957 · fortnightly Thu 8pm

MAIN CAST
Fred Emney

CREDITS
writer Fred Emney · *producer* Barry Lupino

A sequel, of sorts, to *Emney Enterprises* with the 'Big Man' once again providing his own material in a series of sketches.

See also *The Big Man* and *Fred Emney Picks A Pop*.

Freddie And Max

UK · ITV (CLEMENT-LA FRENAIS/SELECTV FOR THAMES) · SITCOM

6 × 30 mins · colour

12 Nov–17 Dec 1990 · Mon 8pm

MAIN CAST

Maxine Chandler · · · · · · · · · · Anne Bancroft
Freddie Latham · · · · · · · Charlotte Coleman
Malcolm Parkes · · · · · · · · Richard Pearson
Gary · · · · · · · · · · · · · · · · Ian Congdon-Lee
Isabel · · · · · · · · · · · · · · · Flaminia Cinque

CREDITS

writers Dick Clement/Ian La Frenais · *executive producers* Tony Charles, Allan McKeown · *director/producer* John Stroud

Maxine 'Max' Chandler is a fading American screen actress who, with her pet poodle Ralphie, has taken up residence in a suite at the Savoy Hotel while she's appearing on the London stage and in BBC radio plays, and writing her autobiography. Although her best days are behind her, Max remains – in her ill-mannered comportment – every inch the tempestuous big shot, an egotistic, boorish, narcissistic, self-centred multi-divorcee.

As the series begins, Max bumps into a young cockney woman, Freddie Latham, an overworked but underpaid media researcher with a degree in communications from Birmingham Polytechnic, and on the rebound from a failed love affair. Although they are chalk and cheese, like the princess and the waif, Max employs Freddie as her assistant, and Freddie takes a room in the suite, where she also carries out her duties. Despite her status, however, Freddie, being a down-to-earth individual, takes it upon herself to tell her employer where she's going wrong in life, how her values suck and how obnoxious her Hollywood behaviour is – thoughts readily, if quietly, echoed by Max's London agent and social escort, Malcolm Parkes.

Although all the ingredients were in place for a long-running success, *Freddie And Max* represents a rare disappointment for writers Clement and La Frenais, and just one series of six episodes was screened. To date, it represents Anne Bancroft's only sitcom role.

Freddie Starr ... [various shows]

see STARR, Freddie

Free And Easy   1

UK · BBC · STANDUP

1 × 30 mins · b/w

9 Oct 1953 · Fri 8.45pm

MAIN CAST
Richard Murdoch
Kenneth Horne

CREDITS
writers Richard Murdoch/Kenneth Horne · *producer* Kenneth Carter

A one-off show in which Richard Murdoch and Kenneth Horne, who co-starred in the hit BBC radio comedy *Much-Binding-In-The-Marsh*, brought their particular brand of humour to the early days of television.

Free And Easy   2

UK · ITV (ASSOCIATED-REDIFFUSION) · SKETCH

2 × 30 mins · b/w

7 & 14 July 1958 · Mon 9.30pm

MAIN CAST
Dickie Valentine
John Hewer
Tony Bateman

CREDITS
writers Dick Sharples/Gerald Kelsey · *director* Joan Kemp-Welch

A pair of programmes featuring the singer/comedian Dickie Valentine.

See also *Dickie Valentine, The Dickie Valentine Show* and *Valentine's Night*.

French And Saunders

UK · BBC · SKETCH

34 editions (32 × 30 mins · 2 × 40 mins) · colour

Series One (6 × 30 mins) 9 Mar–13 Apr 1987 · BBC2 Mon 9pm

Series Two (6 × 30 mins) 4 Mar–15 Apr 1988 · BBC2 Fri 9pm

Special (40 mins) 28 Dec 1988 · BBC2 Wed 9pm

Series Three (7 × 30 mins) 15 Mar–26 Apr 1990 · BBC2 Thu 9pm

Series Four (7 × 30 mins) 18 Feb–1 Apr 1993 · BBC2 Thu 9pm

Special (40 mins) 30 Dec 1994 · BBC1 Fri 9.30pm

Series Five (6 × 30 mins) 4 Jan–8 Feb 1996 · BBC1 Thu 9.30pm

MAIN CAST
Dawn French
Jennifer Saunders
Raw Sex (Rowland Rivron and Simon Brint) (to 1993)

CREDITS
writers Dawn French/Jennifer Saunders · *additional material* Sue Perkins/Mel Giedroyc (series 5) · *directors* Bob Spiers (15), Geoff Posner (7), Kevin Bishop (6), John Birkin (6) · *producers* Jon Plowman (21), Geoff Posner (13)

Closer in stature to Little and Large but in talent to Morecambe and Wise, Dawn French and Jennifer Saunders (born 1957 and 1958 respectively) stepped out of the 'alternative comedy' ensemble to headline this marvellous series. Their double-act personae had been created and honed on stage, playing the London clubs and fringe cabaret venues in the late 1970s and early 1980s, but subsequent acting appearances as part of *The Comic Strip Presents ...* troupe and in the sitcom *Happy Families* had added further strings to their bows. The women had a firm idea on the type of series they wanted to make and wrote the sketches themselves, which resulted in a quirky mixture of satire, slapstick, sparky impressionism and other kinds of skits from a female perspective, the sum total successfully managing to bridge the gap between the new wave and the mainstream. For the first four series they were joined by the spoof middle-of-the-road comedy cabaret duo Raw Sex (Rivron and Brint), who also supported in the sketches.

Clever pastiches of famous movies (shot on film with the same dramatic qualities that had distinguished *The Comic Strip Presents ...* productions); schoolgirl and teenage skits; and song and dance parodies were memorable features of the shows, but arguably the sketches that made the biggest splash were those that featured the 'Two Fat Men'. These had French and Saunders in full body make-up and masses of padding, delivering a horrifyingly recognisable impression of a pair of grotesque, beer-swilling, sex-obsessed morons, constantly fiddling with their crotches while lewdly discussing the attributes of women, to the point where they become so excited that they obscenely simulate intercourse with inanimate objects, as if it was the person concerned. The men never for one moment considered that said women would find them the most disgusting creatures on Earth. One particularly memorable such skit showed these two original teletubbies mock-shagging their television set while it showed the Miss World 'lovelies' parading in their bathing suits. Men had often appeared in drag as monstrous parodies of females but rarely, if ever, had the tables been turned with such devastating effect. Later the 'Two Fat Men' were replaced by 'Two Fat Ladies', from the huntin', shootin' and fishin' class, but although these sketches featured gory scenes of self-mutilation by the gin-swilling twosome, they never quite managed to re-create the sheer side-splitting awfulness of the male version. Meanwhile, another highly effective swipe at the male species, equally merited, was the fine pastiche of two hole-in-the-road workmen – their trousers hanging so low, because of their prodigious beer-guts, that the tops of their buttocks were exposed – wolf-whistling at attractive women who passed by as if they would turn around and find the men remotely attractive.

Although not exactly a 'feminist' series, *French And Saunders* naturally promoted women, and unlikely personalities turned up as guest stars and gave great value, many from the more traditional side of TV entertainment – Betty Marsden, June Whitfield, Jane Asher, Stephanie Beecham, Lulu, Dusty Springfield and others, adding to the series' weird cross-cultural appeal. As the years passed and the show came under the guidance of producer Jon Plowman and *The Comic Strip Presents …* director Bob Spiers, it became more streamlined and the film parodies more lavish and esoteric, with quite brilliant spoofs of *The Silence Of The Lambs* and *Misery* alternating with pastiches of art-house superstars like Ingmar Bergman. (Such mock-ups were compiled into two special programmes, *French And Saunders Go To The Movies*, screened by BBC1 on 31 March and 7 June 1995.) In 1996, nearly three years after their previous series, the two comics returned, proving as sharp as ever with lampoons that included *Baywatch,* Fellini and Quentin Tarantino films, *Braveheart*, the singer Björk and *Batman* movies.

By the late 1980s, with the success of Dawn French, Jennifer Saunders, Ruby Wax and Victoria Wood, women had finally made powerful inroads into the hitherto male-dominated British TV comedy scene. While there had been female TV comedy stars before – Beryl Reid, Dora Bryan, Sheila Hancock, June Whitfield and others – the new stars were writing their own material and so maintaining greater control over their work. French and Saunders' distinctive style, which seemed to owe little to the heritage left by any male double-acts, came across to many as something new and fresh. By 1996 both had separately branched out into other successful areas too: French proving adept at traditional sitcom acting in **The Vicar Of Dibley** and the less traditional **Murder Most Horrid**; and Saunders creating a comedy classic as the writer/star of **Absolutely Fabulous**, an idea that was born in a *French And Saunders* sketch, 'Modern Mother And Daughter', which depicted the pair as a role-reversed mother and daughter.

Dawn French was the subject of the LWT/ITV arts series *The South Bank Show* on 17 April 1994.

See also **The Entertainers**, Comic Relief and **Girls On Top**.

Fresh Fields

UK · ITV (THAMES) · SITCOM

27 episodes (26 × 30 mins · 1 × 45 mins) · colour

Series One (6 × 30 mins) 7 Mar–11 Apr 1984 · Wed 8.30pm

Series Two (6 × 30 mins) 5 Sep–10 Oct 1984 · Wed 8.30pm

Series Three (6 × 30 mins) 4 Sep–9 Oct 1985 · Wed 8pm

Special (45 mins) 25 Dec 1985 · Wed 6.45pm

Series Four (8 × 30 mins) 4 Sep–23 Oct 1986 · Thu 7.30pm

MAIN CAST

Hester Fields	Julia McKenzie
William Fields	Anton Rodgers
Sonia Barratt	Ann Beach
Nancy Penrose	Fanny Rowe

OTHER APPEARANCES

Emma	Debby Cumming
Guy	Ballard Berkeley
Miss Denham	Daphne Oxenford

CREDITS

writer John Chapman · director/producer Peter Frazer-Jones

Married for 20 years, having bred two children who have flown the coop and made her a grandmother, Hester Fields is looking for a new start, a life of adventure in her middle years. She wants spice, she wants action, she wants to be endlessly interesting, but her husband William is an accountant in the City whose idea of excitement is to read the *Financial Times* over breakfast. Undaunted, Hester looks for activities to take her out of herself, and, living in Barnes (an upwardly mobile district in south-west London), the opportunities are endless – dieting, exercise, cycling, pottery classes, exercise classes, even fencing classes, and part-time jobs in catering, being an OAP meals-on-wheels deliverer, even at one point being William's office secretary. Life is complicated, however, by the Fields' daughter Emma, their noisy neighbour Sonia (who liked to turn up at meal times), and the lurking presence of Hester's mother (cue cupboard-full of mother-in-law jokes) who lives in a building at the end of the Fields' garden.

The author of *Fresh Fields* was John Chapman, and if one was looking for a comparison one might say that this was ITV's **Happy Ever After**, the BBC's suburban sitcom, also penned by Chapman, in which June Whitfield and Terry Scott had their domestic ups and downs in the trying presence of dear old Aunt Lucy. Both series, too, it has to be said, were very successful, running and running, without losing much puff, for years and years. For whatever the critics may say, there has always been, and will probably always be, a place in British TV schedules for easy, comfortable sitcoms that offend no one and raise an innocent chuckle. *Fresh Fields*, indeed, was held in such high regard that it won an International Emmy, and prompted a sequel …

French Fields

UK · ITV (THAMES) · SITCOM

19 episodes (18 × 30 mins · 1 × 45 mins) · colour

Series One (6 × 30 mins) 5 Sep–10 Oct 1989 · Tue 8.30pm

Series Two (6 × 30 mins) 24 Sep–29 Oct 1990 · Mon 8pm

Special (45 mins) 25 Dec 1990 · Tue 10pm

Series Three (6 × 30 mins) 3 Sep–8 Oct 1991 · Tue 8.30pm

MAIN CAST

Hester Fields	Julia McKenzie
William Fields	Anton Rodgers
Chantal Moriac	Pamela Salem
Jill Trendle	Liz Crowther (not series 3)
Hugh Trendle	Robin Kermode (not series 3)
Madame Remoleux	Valerie Lush
Emma	Sally Baxter (series 1); Karen Ascoe (after series 1)

OTHER APPEARANCES

Peter	Philip Bird
Henri Nadal	Brian de Salvo (series 1)
Marquis	Nicholas Courtney (series 1 & 2)
Monsieur Dax	Olivier Pierre (series 2 & special); Philip McGough (series 3)
Madame Dax	Bridget McConnel (not series 1)
Marie-Christine Dax	Victoria Baker (not series 1)

CREDITS

writers John Chapman/Ian Davidson · directors Mark Stuart (18), Derrick Goodwin (1) · producer James Gilbert

Hester wanted excitement and here she got it: offered double his salary, William accepts the offer of a posting in northern France and they're off *sur le continent* for a further 19 episodes of fun. On the plus side is the food and the wine, on the minus side the language and the culture, but they're willing to have bash, upping le sticks from Barnes to a rented house named Les Hirondelles in the village of St Martin (fictional), set in the verdant area south of Boulogne. Here they meet up with, among others, estate agent Chantal Moriac, English neighbours Hugh and Jill – a pair of swanky Londoners with a quite dreadful command of French – and the Fields' visiting daughter Emma with her husband Peter. Filmed in France, this sequel to *Fresh Fields* came about after writer John Chapman (who co-authored with Ian Davidson) bought a home in the Dordogne.

Incidental to these two series was an hour-length Thames TV special, *Julia & Company*, networked by ITV on 9 September 1986, which displayed the various talents of Ms McKenzie and in which Anton Rodgers made a guest appearance.

The Fresh Prince Of Bel Air

USA · NBC (STUFFED DOG/QUINCY JONES ENTERTAINMENT/NBC PRODUCTIONS) · SITCOM

145 episodes (142 × 30 mins · 3 × 60 mins) · colour

US dates: 10 Sep 1990–20 May 1996

UK dates: 21 Jan 1991–18 June 1996 (95 episodes) BBC2 Mon 6.30pm then Tue 6pm

MAIN CAST

Will Smith	Will Smith (The Fresh Prince)
Philip Banks	James Avery
Vivian Banks	Janet Hubert-Whitten (1990–93); Daphne Maxwell Reid (1993–96)
Hilary Banks	Karyn Parsons
Carlton Banks	Alfonso Ribeiro
Ashley Banks	Tatyana M Ali
Nicholas 'Nicky' Banks	Ross Bagley (1994–96)
Geoffrey	Joseph Marcell
Jackie Ames	Tyra Banks (1993–94)
Lisa	Nia Long (1994–96)
Jazz	Jeff Townes (DJ Jazzy Jeff) (1990–94)

CREDITS

creators Andy Borowitz/Susan Borowitz · *writers* various · *directors* Ellen Falcon and others · *executive producers* Quincy Jones, Kevin Wendle, Andy Borowitz, Susan Borowitz, Winifred Hervey Stallworth, Gary H Miller · *producers* Samm-Art Williams, Deborah Oppenheimer, Joanne Curley Kerner, Werner Walian, Lisa Rosenthal, Leslie Ray, David Steven Simon, Maiya Williams, Barry Gurstein, David Pitlik

A noisy sitcom that provided the means for Will Smith, rap star, to graduate to Will Smith, movie star. He and his partner Jeff Townes had already made the big time musically (as DJ Jazzy Jeff and the Fresh Prince) before Smith was given the opportunity to head up this youth-orientated, black-themed comedy. Townes came along for the ride, guesting occasionally as the Fresh Prince's long-time friend, Jazz.

The fish-out-of-water plot depicted the streetwise rapper Smith being sent away from his gritty Philadelphia neighbourhood to live with his fancy relatives in fashionable Bel Air, California. Obvious culture clashes came to the fore, providing comedic conflict, although, surprisingly, the series also displayed a softer edge with each side taking a reasonable attitude to the other's argument when pushed.

The shows were perhaps a little too preachy at times, hammering home morals, many of which commented on the lot of blacks living in a white society. But such typical US sitcom moralising was thankfully undercut by the look of the show. The film-making team of Reginald and Warrington Hudlin had created a fine visual style to complement black teen and rap culture in their unexpected smash-hit comedy movie *House Party* (1990, director Reginald Hudlin), and their mix of garish colours, tongue-in-cheek 'attitude' and cartoonish action was duplicated in *The Fresh Prince Of Bel Air*. As a result, the show looked different from anything else on TV, creating a truly revolutionary departure from the norm and giving its young black audience, rarely catered for by television, a recognisable style with which to identify. In its later years the series attracted many prominent guest stars, often portraying themselves.

In the UK, the series aired – initially, at least – as part of BBC2's *DEF II* strand, a trendy wraparound slot encompassing programmes designed to appeal to youth audiences into hip-hop and rap music and other aspects of black culture.

Fresno

USA · CBS (MTM ENTERPRISES) · COMEDY SERIAL

5 episodes (1 × 120 mins · 4 × 60 mins) · colour
US dates: 16 Nov–20 Nov 1986
UK dates: 1 Oct–29 Oct 1990 (1 × 120 mins · 4 × 60 mins) C4 Mon mostly 11pm

MAIN CAST

Charlotte Kensington	Carol Burnett
Tyler Cane	Dabney Coleman
Torch	Gregory Harrison
Talon Kensington	Teri Garr
Cane Kensington	Charles Grodin
Juan	Luis Avalos
Earl Duke	Pat Corley
Tiffany Kensington	Valerie Mahaffey
Kevin Kensington	Anthony Heald
Bobbi Jo Bobb	Teresa Ganzel
Billy Joe Bobb	Bill Paxton
Tucker Agajanian	Jerry Van Dyke
Charles	Charles Keating

CREDITS

creator/executive producer/producer Barry Kemp · *writers* Barry Kemp, Mark Ganzel, Michael Petryni · *director* Jeff Bleckner · *producer* R W Goodwin

Just as *Soap* parodied American daytime soap operas, so *Fresno* lampooned the primetime super-soaps *Dallas*, *Dynasty* and, in particular, *Falcon Crest*. This latter series focused on rival wine-making empires, whereas *Fresno* – a long-form comedy mini-series with a two-hour opening episode – depicted the power struggles between two rival raisin dynasties, the Kensingtons and the Canes.

Leading the clans were Charlotte Kensington, a bitch widow, and the hissable Tyler Cane, the pair played by top TV comic talents Carol Burnett and Dabney Coleman. Further down the cast were further heavyweight comedy exponents, Charles Grodin, Jerry Van Dyke and Teri Garr. But while they all performed with their usual expertise, the actors could not overcome the mini-series' main, if only, flaw: it was trying to parody something that had itself become a parody. Super-soaps had left reality so far behind, hunting ever more outrageous storylines and characterisations, that attempts at caricatures were bound to fail. Still, apart from the fine acting, *Fresno* boasted sharp writing, some exceptionally dry humour and spectacular location work (the production reputedly cost $12m). Although screened without a laugh track, one was added for a 1989 US repeat run, but it proved unnecessary and intrusive.

Friday Funny Man

UK · BBC · SKETCH

1 × 5 mins · b/w
22 Sep 1950 · Fri 5.25pm

MAIN CAST
Clive Dunn

CREDITS
producer Rex Tucker

Five minutes of fun with Clive Dunn, in which he sang 'The Galloping Major', to which he had rewritten the words, to the accompaniment of Steve Race. The comedy entertainer went on to become a firm favourite with younger viewers in the 1950s (see also *Clive Dunn*) before, conversely, becoming established with adult viewers by playing old men (*Bootsie And Snudge*, *Dad's Army*, *My Old Man*).

Friday Night Armistice

see *The Saturday Night Armistice*

Friday Night Live

UK · C4 (LWT)/*BBC · STANDUP/SKETCH

11 editions (10 × 75 mins · 1 × approx 60 mins) · colour
One series (10 × 75 mins) 19 Feb–29 Apr 1988 · Fri 10.30pm
*Special (approx 60 mins) part of *Total Relief* 12 Mar 1993 · BBC1 Fri 11pm

HOST
Ben Elton

APPEARING THROUGHOUT
Harry Enfield

MOST REGULAR GUEST APPEARANCES
Moray Hunter/Jack Docherty
Josie Lawrence

CREDITS

writers various, and certain cast members (notably Ben Elton, Harry Enfield) · *director* Ian Hamilton · *producers* Geoffrey Perkins/Geoff Posner

Replicating the comedy/music formula that had made the 1985–87 run of *Saturday Live* such a runaway success, and aimed primarily at the same youthful audience, *Friday Night Live* again proved to be a very worthwhile exercise for LWT/C4, with Ben Elton in sparkling form (and suit to match) as host and Harry Enfield appearing throughout.

Enfield it was stole the show, becoming a major comedy star during its run with his brilliant comic characters. Joining Stavros – a refugee from the earlier series – was Loadsamoney, a cockney plasterer of limited intelligence who was making a fortune in the boom part of Thatcher's boom-then-bust late 1980s property explosion. 'Loads' delighted in flashing his 'wad' of bank-notes at the audience/camera, and particularly at the unemployed, taunting them with his wealth and belittling their status in the process by shouting 'I got loadsamoney!!'. The catchphrase stuck fast with the public, to such an extent that the Eighties has since been described as 'the Loadsamoney decade'. To counteract his monster creation, Enfield (and friends) quickly invented an opposite character, a Geordie called Buggerallmoney.

Although Elton and Enfield were the only regulars, every edition of *Friday Night Live* was packed with guests, including Hunter and Docherty (***Absolutely***), Josie Lawrence (who appeared in monologues as well as sketches), Bob Mills, the American comic Emo Philips, Hugh Laurie, Julian Clary (still performing as the Joan Collins Fan Club), Lee Evans, Nick Revell, Jo Brand (her TV debut) and, in the last programme, Dame Edna Everage.

*Note. Some five years after Ben Elton stood at the *Friday Night Live* microphone and announced that there would be no more programmes, he and Harry Enfield united for a one-off edition as part of the BBC's 1993 **Comic Relief** telethon *Total Relief*. Jo Brand and Newman and Baddiel were among the guests in this special show.

Friday Night With ...

UK · ITV (JACK HYLTON TV PRODUCTIONS FOR ASSOCIATED-REDIFFUSION) · SKETCH

8 × 30 mins · b/w

Series One (3) *Terry-Thomas* 10 Aug–7 Sep 1956 · Fri 8.30pm

Series Two (3) *The Crazy Gang* 21 Sep–19 Oct 1956 · Fri 8.30pm

Specials (2) *Tommy Trinder* 2 Nov 1956 & 4 Jan 1957 · Fri 8.30pm

MAIN CAST
as above

CREDITS
directors John Phillips (Terry-Thomas series), Michael Westmore (Crazy Gang series), Eric Fawcett (Tommy Trinder specials)

A series of comedy programmes, screened fortnightly except for the final edition, featuring some of Britain's best-loved comics, presented for TV by the impresario Jack Hylton. 'Half an hour of fun and gaiety' was promised to viewers of the Terry-Thomas shows, while the Crazy Gang editions featured Nervo and Knox, Bud Flanagan, and Naughton and Gold.

Friday The 13th

see RAY, Ted

Friends

USA · NBC (BRIGHT-KAUFFMAN-CRANE PRODUCTIONS/WARNER BROS) · SITCOM

81 episodes (79 × 30 mins · 2 × 60 mins to 31/12/97 · continuing into 1998) · colour

US dates: 22 Sep 1994 to date

UK dates: 28 Apr 1995 to date (71 × 30 mins · 1 × 60 mins to 31/12/97) C4 Fri mostly 9.30pm then 9pm

MAIN CAST
Rachel Green · · · · · · · · · · · Jennifer Aniston
Monica Geller · · · · · · · · · · · Courteney Cox
Phoebe Buffay/Ursula Buffay · · Lisa Kudrow
Joey Tribbiani · · · · · · · · · · · Matt LeBlanc
Chandler Bing · · · · · · · · · · · Matthew Perry
Ross Geller · · · · · · · · · · · David Schwimmer

OTHER APPEARANCES
Carol Willick · · · · · · · · · · · · · Jane Sibbert
Susan Busch · · · · · · · · · · · · Jessica Hecht
Janice · · · · · · · · · Maggie Wheeler (1995–97)
Dr Richard Burke · · · Tom Selleck (1996–97)
Jack Geller · · · · · · · Elliott Gould (from 1995)
Judy Geller · · · Christine Pickles (from 1996)

CREDITS
creators Marta Kauffman/David Crane · *writers* various · *directors* various · *executive producers* Kevin S Bright/Marta Kauffman/David Crane · *producer* Todd Stevens

When *Friends* began, depicting the lives and loves of six twenty-something white Manhattanites, it was branded as mediocre by critics, who saw it as another in the long line of singles sitcoms that followed **Seinfeld** and **Ellen**. But viewers disagreed, taking to *Friends* immediately, and the critics were forced to review their opinions.

The series revolves around a sextet of good-looking young things, three men and three women, most of the action taking place in a local coffee-bar, the Central Perk, and Monica's penthouse apartment, where the six like to hang-out. Monica, a chef, has trouble making a lasting relationship, despite her stunning looks. Her most serious fling is with Dr Richard Burke, an older man and her parents' friend, but this too fails to work out. Her brother Ross is the serious one of the six, a divorced museum-worker whose pregnant wife (Carol) has left him for another woman (Susan). The lesbian couple are now raising his baby, and Ross – despite fits of pique and jealousy – tries to be a 'new man' about it and behave as if they were a normal heterosexual couple. His angst is tempered by a romance that he develops with Rachel, a sparky and sexy woman who works as a waitress at Central Perk. The smouldering build-up to this romance delighted viewers and helped propel the show towards the top of the ratings. The other young woman in the sextet is Phoebe, a trippy-hippy new-ager with an off-centre view on life. She is a part-time masseuse with a music bent, playing her own compositions on guitar, including the memorable 'Smelly Cat'. The other two men, Chandler and Joey, share an apartment across the way from Monica's. The former is bright, witty and manic, an office worker who, like Monica, has problems dating. He too has a serious fling, with the nasal Janice, but this peters out when she leaves him to return to

her estranged husband. Joey, of Italian stock, is an actor who experiences mixed career fortunes – at one time being gainfully employed in a daytime TV soap opera, at other times awaiting the big break and attending auditions. Joey is the least bright of the team – he's as witless as a box of hammers – and his denseness provides some of the show's easiest laughs.

While lacking in 'soul', and unambitiously centring on a bunch of essentially well-off WASPs, *Friends* certainly delivered on the laughter front, its scripts being littered with dynamite one-liners, precious put-downs and sizzling dialogue – at its best, the series matched the screwball Hollywood comedies of the 1940s for sparkling, quick-paced repartee. The success of *Friends* also owed a great deal to the wonderful ensemble cast, who dovetailed perfectly and whose real-life affection for one another made the on-screen friendships seem all the more believable. As the series prospered the principal cast put up a united front to demand more money, and, after a well-publicised scrap with NBC, they were eventually rewarded with wages reputed to be in the region of $100,000 per episode each. (As every episode of *Friends* was said to be worth about $4m in syndication rights, it could be argued that such a high wage bill was justified.)

In the UK, *Friends* became a huge hit for C4, attracting particularly strong audience figures for an imported comedy. The network gives the series a strong slot and airs plenty of repeats (which keeps it on screen virtually all year); the channel also invited LeBlanc, Perry and Schwimmer to appear together on *Friends With Gaby*, a special edition of Gaby Roslin's C4 chat-show, screened on 29 November 1996.

Note. Lisa Kudrow has also been cast in *Friends* as Phoebe's twin sister Ursula, an equally spaced-out character who originally appeared semi-regularly in the sitcom *Mad About You* (from 1992, see **Loved By You**), the show screened immediately before *Friends* in NBC's Thursday night line-up.

Friends And Neighbours

UK · BBC · SITCOM

6 × 30 mins · b/w

27 Jan–7 Apr 1954 · fortnightly Wed mostly 8.15pm

MAIN CAST
George Bird · · · · · · · · · · · Peter Butterworth
Constance Bird · · · · · · · · · · · · Janet Brown
Arthur Honeybee · · · · · · · · · · · · · Benny Lee
Maisie Honeybee · · · · · · · · · · · Avril Angers

CREDITS
writers Sid Colin/Talbot Rothwell · *producer* Bill Ward

An early BBC sitcom starring the four actors who had been a hit together in Terry-Thomas's *How Do You View?*, where they were cast as Lockit, the car-less chauffeur (Butterworth); the tea-obsessed canteen server Rosie Lee (Angers); the disorganised secretary Miss Happ (Brown); and the myopic tailor Mr Pegg (Lee). Two of the writers of that earlier series, Colin and Rothwell, created this sitcom (the worrying thought remains that they intended to call it *The Birds And The Bees*) which depicted two young married couples – George and Constance Bird (played by real-life husband and wife Brown and Butterworth) and Arthur and Maisie Honeybee – who live next door to one another in two-room flats converted inside a large Victorian house.

Friends In High Places

UK · ITV (LWT) · SITCOM

1 × 30 mins · b/w
26 Apr 1969 · Sat 7.30pm

MAIN CAST
George Gosling · · · · · · · · · · Bob Monkhouse
Joyce · · · · · · · · · · · · · · · · · · Patricia Hayes
First angel · · · · · · · · · · · · · · Frank Williams
Second angel · · · · · · · · · · · · Arthur English
Third angel · · · · · · · · · · · Richard O'Sullivan

CREDITS
writers Ray Galton/Alan Simpson · *director/producer* David Askey

The second of six single programmes presented by ITV under the banner *The Galton & Simpson Comedy*. In this edition Bob Monkhouse starred as George Gosling, fat, bald and unhappy at the age of 55, whose wish to be young again is granted.

From A Bird's Eye View

see MARTIN, Millicent

From The Top

UK · ITV (CENTRAL) · CHILDREN'S SITCOM

12 × 30 mins · colour

Series One (6) 23 Sep–28 Oct 1985 · Mon 4.45pm

Series Two (6) 10 Nov–15 Dec 1986 · Mon 4.45pm

MAIN CAST
William Worthington · · · · · · · · · · · Bill Oddie
Annie Jolly · · · · · · · · · · · · · · · Moyra Fraser
Dolly Jolly · · · · · · · · · · · · · Maggie Rennie
Leslie Finsberg · · · · · · · · · · · Gavin Forward
Janis Koplowitz · · · · · · · · Catherine Holman
Wayne Layne · · · · · · · · · · · · · Michael Quill
Joyce Torrington-Hawksby · · · · Erica Sheward
Humphrey Kulumbebwe · · · · · · Scott Sherrin
Polly Jolly · · · · · · · · · · · · · · Joiese Waller
Mr Spadley · · · · · · · · · · · · · · · Stan Holt

CREDITS
writers Bill Oddie/Laura Beaumont · *directors* Michael Dolenz (series 1), Paul Harrison (series

2) · *executive producer* Lewis Rudd · *producers* Michael Dolenz (series 1), Paul Harrison/Peter Murphy (series 2)

A children's series co-written by Bill Oddie and his wife Laura Beaumont, and starring the former *Goodies* man as William Worthington, a 43-year-old bearded bank manager who quits his job to realise his long-held ambition to become an actor, and so enrols at the full-time Jolly Theatre School. Worthington takes his place among his purple-uniformed young teenage classmates Humphrey, Janis, Joyce, Leslie, Polly and Wayne, and enjoys the second flush of youth while putting on shows and mixing in with the other pupils in the playground. Every episode provided an opportunity for Oddie to sing and play instruments; continuing the musical theme, Michael Dolenz (*The Monkees*) directed and produced the first series.

See also *The Bubblegum Brigade*.

The Front Line

UK · BBC · SITCOM

6 × 30 mins · colour
6 Dec 1984–17 Jan 1985 · BBC1 Thu 8pm

MAIN CAST
Malcolm · · · · · · · · · · · · · · · · · Paul Barber
Sheldon · · · · · · · · · · · · · · · · · · Alan Igbon

CREDITS
writer Alex Shearer · *director/producer* Roger Race

A black slant on writer Alex Shearer's earlier sitcom *Sink Or Swim*. The northerner brothers (actually half-brothers) this time were Malcolm, an unexceptional individual, and Sheldon, a dreadlocked Rastafarian with a deep distrust of the establishment. Their volatile sibling relationship was exacerbated when Malcolm joined the police force.

The Front Line was one of the first British sitcoms to portray black characters with depth and complexity. The two lead actors were encouraged to work out their own scenes together, in an attempt to secure a realistic edge to their conversations and arguments, and they duly succeeded in suggesting the ties that unite family members irrespective of individual characteristics. Despite this, the public did not express any great love for the series and it failed to return.

The Frost Report

UK · BBC · SKETCH

28 editions (26 × 25 mins · 1 × 35 mins · 1 × 40 mins) · b/w

Series One (13 × 25 mins) 10 Mar–9 June 1966 · BBC1 Thu mostly 9pm

Special (35 mins) *Frost Over England*
26 Mar 1967 · BBC1 Sun 7.25pm

Series Two (13 × 25 mins) 6 Apr–29 June 1967 · BBC1 Thu mostly 9.05pm

Special (40 mins) *Frost Over Christmas*
26 Dec 1967 · BBC1 Tue 7.30pm

MAIN CAST
David Frost
John Cleese
Ronnie Barker
Ronnie Corbett
Sheila Steafel
Nicky Henson

CREDITS
writers Marty Feldman, John Law, Antony Jay, John Cleese/Graham Chapman, Michael Palin/Terry Jones, Keith Waterhouse/Willis Hall, David Nobbs/Peter Tinniswood, Frank Muir/Denis Norden, Eric Idle and others · *producer* James Gilbert

A mixture of monologue, sketch and music, *The Frost Report* was one of the last such comedy shows to be broadcast live as a matter of course. Each edition of the show took on a different topic – authority, holidays, sin, elections, class, the news, education, love, law, leisure, medicine, food and drink, trends, money, women, the forces, Parliament, the countryside, industry, culture, crime, and others – and sketches were woven accordingly around those subjects. (This writing process began with Antony Jay writing David Frost's linking script, prompting others to provide skits to be performed by the regular cast.)

With some of the country's best TV comedy writers involved, many of the sketches were top-notch, and one recurring example forged a lasting place in viewers' affections: the 6ft 5in tall John Cleese, 5ft 8in Ronnie Barker and 5ft 1in Ronnie Corbett standing in a line, in that order, remarking upon life, and/or their place in society, with Cleese looking down on both the other men, Barker looking up to Cleese but down on Corbett and Corbett looking up to both of them. ('I know my place,' he declared, memorably, in Marty Feldman and John Law's brilliant sketch on the subject of class.) Music was provided by the acerbic Tom Lehrer and the folk singer Julie Felix.

The front man, David Frost, who had first crashed into the public consciousness with *That Was The Week That Was*, experienced great fortunes at this time, enjoying transatlantic success as a TV presenter/host, success that crystallised with his UK and US chat-shows later in the 1960s and succeeding decades. *The Frost Report* proved to be an important step too in the development of British TV comedy, bringing together for the first time the writing team (Palin, Jones, Cleese, Chapman and Idle) who would go on to create *Monty Python's Flying Circus*.

A special edition of the series, *Frost Over England*, which compiled highlights from the first 13 programmes with newly scripted material, won the Golden Rose at the Montreux Festival in 1967.

See also *Frost's Weekly*.

Frost's Weekly

UK · BBC · STANDUP/SKETCH

7 × 45 mins · colour

14 Dec 1973–25 Jan 1974 · BBC2 Fri 8.15pm

MAIN CAST

David Frost
Graham Stark
Julia McKenzie
Bill Pertwee
Roger Kitter
Henry Woolf
Alison Steadman
David Casey

CREDITS

writer Eddie Braben · *producer* Michael Hurll

David Frost returned to the BBC with this all-comedy series scripted by Eddie Braben, the regular writer at this time for Morecambe and Wise. Braben, a Liverpudlian who left school at 14 and worked on market stalls and as a refuse collector before becoming a professional writer, seemed an unusual choice to partner the Cambridge graduate and jet-setting Frost, but the two worked well together. *Frost's Weekly* – developed from Braben's own radio series *The Worst Show On The Wireless*, which aired on the BBC earlier in 1973 – utilised a magazine format to link the comedy items. These were performed by a regular troupe that included Bill Pertwee and Alison Steadman, who also appeared in the radio series.

Fry And Laurie Host A Christmas Night With The Stars

see *Christmas Night With The Stars*

Fudge

USA · ABC (AMBLIN TELEVISION/MCA) · CHILDREN'S SITCOM

24 × 30 mins · colour

US dates: 14 Jan–16 Dec 1995

UK dates: 1 Apr 1996–30 Sep 1997 (24 episodes) BBC1/BBC2 mostly Mon 4.10pm

MAIN CAST

Farley Drexel 'Fudge' Hatcher · Luke Tarsitano
Peter Hatcher · · · · · · · · · · Jake Richardson
Ann Hatcher (Mom) · · · · · · · · · · · · Eve Plumb
Warren Hatcher (Dad) · · · · · · · · Forrest Witt
Sheila · · · · · · · · · · · · · · · · · · Nassira Nicola
Jimmy · · · · · · · · · · · · · · · · · · · Alex Burrall
Henry · · · · · · · · · · · · · · · · · · · Rob Monroe

CREDITS

creator Judy Blume · *writers* various · *directors* Anson Williams and others · *executive producers* Carol Monroe, Steven Spielberg

Although its title utilised the nickname of his younger brother, the principal character in this US children's sitcom was nine-year-old Peter Hatcher, whose life was often complicated by his hyperactive, mischievous four-year-old sibling. Situated in a Manhattan apartment, the series – produced by Steven Spielberg's company, Amblin – was based on the enormously successful series of books by Judy Blume, and aimed unashamedly at a Saturday-morning family audience in need of gentle, unchallenging humour.

The characters were introduced in a feature-length US TV movie, *Fudge-A-Mania*, which aired there on 7 January 1995, just before the weekly episodes began. Confusingly, in the UK, *Fudge-A-Mania* was screened by BBC1 (on 6 May 1996) several weeks after the series had been launched.

Full Frontal

AUSTRALIA · 7 NETWORK (ARTIST SERVICES) · SKETCH

28 × 60 mins · colour

Australian dates: 13 May 1993–23 June 1994

UK dates: 29 June–23 Nov 1996 (13 × 30 mins) C4 Sat around 2.40am

MAIN CAST

Ross Williams
Glenn Butcher
Kitty Flanagan
Eric Bana
Shaun Micallef
Rima Te Wiata
Jennifer Ward-Lealand
Julia Morris
Francis Greenslade
Kim Gyngell
Gregg Fleet (1993)
Matt Parkinson (1993)
Matt Quartermaine (1993)
Michael Veitch
Denise Scott (1994)
John Walker (1994)

CREDITS

writers cast and others · *director* Ted Emery · *executive producers* Ted Emery, Andrew Knight, Steve Vizard · *producers* Andrew Knight, Doug MacLeod

A virtual continuation of **Fast Forward**, with a new team having picked up the comedy torch – although most of the leading players in that former series turned up here as guest stars. Spoof advertisements and pastiches of pop videos were among the series' most successful offerings, and it provided a high quality, fast-paced product throughout, with a pleasing tendency not to prolong sketches beyond their prime.

Although lacking the bite of some of the *Fast Forward* skits, *Full Frontal* was another good demonstration of the strengths of Australian sketch comedy.

See also **Big Girl's Blouse**.

Full House

UK · ITV (THAMES) · SITCOM

20 × 30 mins · colour

Series One (6) 7 Jan–11 Feb 1985 · Mon 8pm

Series Two (8) 16 Oct–4 Dec 1985 · Wed 8pm

Series Three (6) 15 Oct–19 Nov 1986 · Wed 8.30pm

MAIN CAST

Paul Hatfield · · · · · · · · · Christopher Strauli
Marsha Hatfield · · · · · · · · · · Sabina Franklyn
Diana McCoy · · · · · · · · · · · · · Natalie Forbes
Murray McCoy · · · · · · · · · · · · · Brian Capron

OTHER APPEARANCES

Paul's mother · · · · · · · Diana King (series 1); · · · · · · · · · · · · · · Joan Sanderson (series 3)

CREDITS

creators Johnnie Mortimer/Brian Cooke · *writers* Johnnie Mortimer (12), Johnnie Mortimer/Brian Cooke (3), Brian Cooke (1), Vince Powell (3), Richard Everett (1) · *directors* Peter Frazer-Jones (11), Anthony Parker (6), Douglas Argent (2), Mark Stuart (1) · *producers* Peter Frazer-Jones (13), Anthony Parker (6), Mark Stuart (1)

A four-in-a-house 'oops, sorry, whose drawers are these?'-type sitcom, stretched to three series.

Marsha and Paul Hatfield finally find their ideal home, having tied the knot three years ago. The only snag is, they cannot meet the mortgage repayments, so to pay the bill they share the burden with another couple, Diana and Murray, who aren't married.

Sitcom-wise, the *Full House* characters were absolutely formulaic. The marrieds were neat and prim – he was handsome in an M&S-type way, prone to prudishness, making lists and keeping order; she was pretty in a Freeman's catalogue-type way. The unmarrieds, of course, were altogether more raunchy: she was blonde and liberal, he was unkempt and anarchic, all denim jacket and rolled-up sleeves, MCP ideas and prone to the long-term unarranged borrowing of Paul's things. There was a role, too, for Marsha's mother-in-law, who had never quite become accustomed to the fact that her son Paul loved any woman but his mum. Diana and Murray were finally married at the end of the second series, with all the traditional sitcom-style complications on the big day, and Diana delivered a baby in the final episode of the last while Mr and Mrs Conventional remained *sans* offspring.

Like so many Thames sitcoms of the period, an attempt was made to sell the format of *Full House* to America. It got as far as a pilot episode, aired there by CBS on 6 September 1985 under the title *No Place Like Home*. Susan Hess and Jack Blessing played the married couple, Molly Cheek and Rick Lohman the unmarrieds. No series developed.

Fundamental Frolics

UK · BBC · STANDUP

1 × 75 mins · colour

31 July 1981 · BBC2 Fri 9pm

MAIN CAST
Rowan Atkinson
Griff Rhys Jones
Mel Smith
Pamela Stephenson
Chris Langham
Rik Mayall
Alexei Sayle
Neil Innes

CREDITS
writers cast · *producer* Rick Gardner

An all-star concert for the charity MENCAP, recorded at the Apollo Theatre in Victoria, London. The show reunited the current *Not The Nine O'Clock News* quartet with the series' original member Chris Langham. The presence on the bill of Rik Mayall and Alexei Sayle, two of the most prominent (on television, at least) 'alternative' comedians, demonstrates how the new generation was beginning to achieve wider recognition.

Funky Squad

AUSTRALIA · ABC (FRONTLINE TELEVISION PRODUCTIONS) · SITCOM

7 × 30 mins · colour

Australian dates: 24 Apr–5 Jun 1995

UK dates: 22 July–9 Dec 1995 (7 episodes) C4 Sat around 1.30am

MAIN CAST
Grant · · · · · · · · 'Blair Steele' (Tim Ferguson)
Cassie · · · · · · · · · · · · · 'Verity Svensön-Hart'
· (Jane Kennedy)
Stix · · · · · · · · · 'Joey Alvarez' (Santo Cilauro)
Poncho · · · 'Harvey Zdalka Jr' (Tom Gleisner)
The Chief · · · · · · · · · · · · · · · 'Baldwin Scott'
· (Barry Friedlander)

CREDITS
creators Scott Cilauro, Tom Gleisner, Jane Kennedy, Rob Sitch · *writers/directors* Scott Cilauro, Tom Gleisner, Jane Kennedy · *executive producer* Michael Hirsh · *producers* Scott Cilauro, Tom Gleisner, Jane Kennedy, Debra Choake

An entertaining crime-show spoof to add to a long list that includes *Police Squad*, *The Detectives*, *The Bullshitters*, *Lazarus And Dingwall* and *The Preventers*. *Funky Squad*, an Australian series, lampooned US police shows of the 1970s in general and the series *The Mod Squad* (ABC, 1968–73) in particular.

As with *The Mod Squad*, the heroes of *Funky Squad* were a team of young, 'hip' undercover cops, so cool and 'with-it' that they were able to pass undetected among kids on the street. Grant was the smooth leader, Cassie the brains, Stix the action man with the Afro haircut, and Poncho was the mute (his tongue had stopped a bullet) electronics

expert. They answered to the Chief, an intense, dramatic and extremely grim senior officer. Flares, tank-tops, paisley shirts, tasselled waistcoats, outrageous hairdos and all the other elements of early 1970s fashions were exploited to good comedic effect, and the camerawork and pastiche music neatly evoked the right mood and period atmosphere.

The credits at the beginning furthered the spoof by introducing the lead actors under false identities, satirising the sometimes peculiar names of US actors of the period. Cilauro, Gleisner and Kennedy were the creative forces behind the show, writing eccentric dialogue with just the right degree of seriousness. Along with co-creator Rob Sitch, the three had become well known Down Under for their work on the successful Australian TV sketch series *The Late Show* (ABC, 1992–93). Before *Funky Squad*, all but Gleisner had also worked on another spoof sitcom, *Frontline* (ABC, 1994), which lampooned Australian TV current affairs programmes.

The Funny Farm

UK · ITV (SCOTTISH) · STANDUP

36 × 30 mins · colour

Series One (6) 16 Mar–19 Apr 1990 · mostly Thu 11.10pm

Series Two (6) 1 Feb–15 Mar 1991 · Fri 11.10pm

Series Three (6) 24 Jan–6 Mar 1992 · Fri 11.10pm

Series Four (17) 6 Nov 1992–12 May 1993 · Fri then Wed mostly 11.10pm

Special · 31 Aug 1993 · Tue 11.30pm

MAIN CAST
Stu Who
Bruce Morton
Fred MacAulay

CREDITS
writers cast · *directors* Paul O'Dell (series 1 & 2), Haldane Duncan (series 3), Douglas Napier (series 4) · *producers* Paul O'Dell/Kim Kinnie (series 1 & 2), Kim Kinnie/Haldane Duncan (series 3), Kim Kinnie (series 4)

A Scottish TV series featuring new and established standup acts, mostly but not exclusively from north of the border. The programmes were anchored by the oddly named Stu Who – an acerbic but likeable standup comedian from Cumbernauld – who, in 1988, with Bruce Morton and Fred MacAulay, co-founded the Funny Farm, said to have been the only comedy collective in Scotland at that time. Guests acts included Harry Hill, Lee Hurst and Lee Evans.

Note. The dates above reflect the STV screenings. The first two series only (12 editions) travelled down to London-area ITV, where they were screened, respectively, 26 July–30 August 1990 (Thursdays at

3.30am) and 25 July–29 August 1991 (Thursdays at 4am).

See also *A Shoe Fetishist's Guide To Bruce Morton* and *Sin With Bruce Morton*.

Funny Ha Ha

UK · ITV (THAMES) · CHILDREN'S COMEDIES

6 × 30 mins · colour

In the style of the BBC's *Comedy Playhouse* series, Thames launched *Funny Ha Ha*, an innovative children's strand in 1974 which numbered six individual comedies (five of them sitcoms), written by different authors and featuring different casts.

These are the six pilot titles with first broadcast dates. The fifth, its title preceded by an asterisk, graduated to a full series. See individual entries for further details.

24 May 1974	Commander Badman
31 May 1974	Football Crazy
7 June 1974	Don't Blame Us!
14 June 1974	Who's Afraid Of The Big Bad Bear?
21 June 1974	*The Molly Wopsy (see *The Molly Wopsies*)
28 June 1974	Me 'n' Meep

The Funny Side

UK · ITV (THAMES) · SKETCH

6 × 30 mins · colour

10 July–14 Aug 1985 · Wed 8.30pm

MAIN CAST
Derek Waring
Derek Griffiths
Aiden J Harvey
Debbie Arnold
Tony Barton

OTHER APPEARANCES
Cherry Gillespie
Peter John
Alison Bell

CREDITS
writer Eddie Braben · *additional material* Dick Vosburgh (6), Sid Green/Dick Hills (3), Jackie Lynton (1), Laurie Rowley (1), Mick Shirley (1), John Palmer (1), Andrew Marshall/David Renwick (1), Bill Martin (1) · *director/producer* Mark Stuart

A weekly humour session, described as 'lively' and 'madcap' although 'dodgy' might have been better, which flung together a number of vaguely familiar faces (Derek Griffiths perhaps the best known, from his *Play School* days) performing sketches mostly written by Morecambe and Wise scribe Eddie Braben. Despite a weekly (incomplete) striptease act, *The Funny Side* was not a great success and only one series evolved.

Funny Thing This Wireless!

UK · BBC · SKETCH

1 × 60 mins · b/w

15 Nov 1947 · Sat 8.30pm

MAIN CAST
Claude Hulbert
Clive Dunn
Doris Hare
Vera Lynn
Frank Muir
Joan Mundy
Carroll Gibbons

CREDITS
writers Ronald Jeans, Henrik Ege, Ronnie Hill, Peter Dion Titheradge · *producer* Eric Fawcett

TV's light-hearted look back at 25 years of radio, one of many BBC silver anniversary shows broadcast at this time. The programme was re-performed on 13 December 1947.

Funnybone

UK · ITV (CENTRAL) · SITCOM
5 × 25 mins · colour
26 June–24 July 1982 · Sat 6.45pm

MAIN CAST
Barry Cheese and Mike Onion
Malc Stent
Sonny Hayes and Co (Sally)
Nina Finburgh

CREDITS
writers John Palmer and cast · *script editor* John Junkin · *director/producer* Colin Clews

Fast-paced, early-evening humour of the ITV kind: sometimes funny, sometimes not, from a gaggle of club comics. Malc Stent went on to appear in a single one-man BBC show, *Malc Up Market*.

Further Adventures Of Lucky Jim   1

UK · BBC · SITCOM
7 × 30 mins · b/w
2 May–13 June 1967 · BBC1 Tue 7.30pm

MAIN CAST
Jim Dixon · · · · · · · · · · · · · · · · · Keith Barron
Brian · · · · · · · · · · · · · · · · · · · Colin Jeavons

CREDITS
creator Kingsley Amis · *writers* Dick Clement/Ian La Frenais · *producer* Duncan Wood

Jim Dixon, the 'hero' of Kingsley Amis's notorious and extraordinarily successful first novel *Lucky Jim*, published in 1954, was portrayed on film by Ian Carmichael in the 1957 film of the same title, depicting the lifestyle of a hedonist who attends university not to acquire an education but to do as little work as possible and enjoy the good life and the company of women.

Ten years later, in this seven-part BBC sitcom scripted by Dick Clement and Ian La Frenais, the writers of *The Likely Lads*, Jim graduates from the war-torn 1950s to the Swinging Sixties. Newly arrived in London from Yorkshire, he finds himself at odds with the 'plastic jungle' of glossy journalism, boutiques and 'happenings', his only friend

being his much put-upon former college chum Brian, now an advertising executive.

Clement and La Frenais had a second stab at serialising Amis in a 1982 revival …

See also *The Importance Of Being Hairy*.

Further Adventures Of Lucky Jim   2

UK · BBC · SITCOM
7 × 30 mins · colour
1 Nov–13 Dec 1982 · BBC2 Mon 9pm

MAIN CAST
Jim Dixon · · · · · · · · · · · · · · · · · Enn Reitel
Lucy Simmons · · · · · · · · · · · · Glynis Barber
Philip Lassiter · · · · · · · · · · · · David Simeon
Joanna Lassiter · · · · · · · · · · · Barbara Flynn

CREDITS
creator Kingsley Amis · *writers* Dick Clement/Ian La Frenais · *producer* Harold Snoad

Fifteen years after their previous attempt, writers Clement and La Frenais returned to Kingsley Amis's *Lucky Jim* for a further seven episodes, this time with Enn Reitel in the lead role. The setting remained the 1960s: Jim has returned from a spell in Holland to try his luck in London, hoping to become part of the permissive society that he has heard so much about. To this end he acquires a job in publishing and then a position in the movie business. He also progresses from living in 'digs' to having his own flat, but despite his job and situation, he singularly fails to find the action. The 1960s, it seems, are happening around him but not *to* him.

This was a rather downbeat affair, albeit with all the trademark Clement and La Frenais verbal flair intact. Like its predecessor, it lasted only one series.

Further Up Pompeii

see *Up Pompeii!*

The Fuzz

UK · ITV (THAMES) · SITCOM
7 × 30 mins · colour
8 Sep–20 Oct 1977 · Thu 9pm

MAIN CAST
Det-Sgt Sidney Marble · · · · Michael Robbins
PC Stevie Cordwainer · · · · · · · Nigel Lambert
PC Jumbo Dickinson · · · · · · · · Mike Savage
WPC Pamela Purvis · · · · · · Lynda Bellingham
Supt Baldwyn Allardyce · · · · · · Colin Jeavons
Doris · Ena Cabayo

CREDITS
writer Willis Hall · *director/producer* Stuart Allen

A poor series depicting the work of a bunch of dozy cops stationed in a provincial police force. The cast was good but the plots were not, and the boys in blue spent their time in pursuance of knickers-nickers who hung

around garden washing-lines, a handbag-snatcher, husband-bashers, a fish and chip shop burglar and other such big-time crooks. Chips, indeed, were a regular source of attempted humour in the scripts, with Det-Sgt Sidney Marble (played by Michael Robbins – 'Arfur' in *On The Buses*) able to consume vast portions of them, particularly those served up by the police station canteen worker Doris, much to the disdain of PCs Cordwainer and Dickinson, who rarely had theirs. The PCs were also frustrated in their chase of the chaste WPC Pamela Purvis (an early TV role for Lynda Bellingham). The superintendent, meanwhile, was concerned only with the possibility that the Queen might soon bestow him with an MBE for services rendered to law enforcement, a prospect that his clumsy, skiving bobbies were making less and less likely.

The Gaffer

UK · ITV (YORKSHIRE) · SITCOM

20 × 30 mins · colour
Series One (6) 9 Jan–20 Feb 1981 · Fri 8.30pm
Series Two (7) 26 Feb–9 Apr 1982 · Fri 8.30pm
Series Three (7) 24 May–5 July 1983 ·
Tue mostly 8.30pm

MAIN CAST
Fred Moffat · · · · · · · · · · · · · Bill Maynard
Harry · · · · · · · · · · · · · · · · Russell Hunter
Betty · · · · · · · · · · · · · · · · · · Pat Ashton
Ginger · · · · · · · · · · · · · · · · David Gillies

OTHER APPEARANCES
Charlie · · · · · · · · · · · · · · · · · Don Crann
Wagstaff · · · · · · · · · · · Christopher Hancock
· · · · · · · · · · · · · · · · · · · (series 1 & 2)
Williams · · · · · · · · · Milton Johns (series 2)
Joe Gregory · · · · · Alan Hockey (series 2 & 3)
Henry Dodd · · · · · Keith Marsh (series 2 & 3)

CREDITS
writer Graham White · director/producer Alan
Tarrant

On the back of **Oh No – It's Selwyn
Froggitt** and its sequel, **Selwyn**, Yorkshire
TV was keen to build a new sitcom around
Bill Maynard. *The Gaffer* cast him as Fred
Moffat, the boss of his own north Midlands
light-engineering concern, Moffat
Engineering Company, always wearing a
beaten-up hat, exercising a wry wit and
driving around in a rusting white Rover.
Moffat's work book was rarely full and the
gaffer had to use all his wiles to fend off the
bank manager, the Inland Revenue, Customs
and Excise and the liquidator. Troubles also
resided closer at hand, in the shape of Betty,
his rarely supportive secretary, and a trade
union led by Harry, the Scottish shop-
steward. At the end of the second series
Moffat ran for a seat on the local council and
was elected, becoming a councillor in the
third series, which pitted him against fellow
councillor and business rival Joe Gregory. By
the final episode the gaffer had had enough:
he sold up and emigrated to Australia.
Writer Graham White intended *The Gaffer*
as a BBC radio sitcom and was, at the time of
writing it, himself the managing director of a

Derby-based engineering company. The
series was based upon his own experiences,
and Maynard, in turn, adopted his bearded
look from the author. It was White's first TV
series and there is no doubt that he turned
in a comedy brimming with clever lines.
Unfortunately, while they might have
looked great on paper, they were often too
complicated and wordy for TV.

A Gala Comedy Hour – Best Of The Prince's Trust

UK · ITV (DAVID PARADINE PRODUCTIONS FOR
CARLTON) · STANDUP

1 × 60 mins · colour
3 July 1996 · Wed 8pm

MAIN CAST
Russ Abbot
Rowan Atkinson
Michael Barrymore
Steve Coogan
Richard Digance
Dame Edna Everage · · · · · · Barry Humphries
Griff Rhys Jones
Rita Rudner
Mel Smith

CREDITS
writers cast · executive producers David Frost,
Richard Holloway

A compilation of the comedy performances
from three gala concerts, staged – in 1987,
1989 and 1995 – to raise money for the
Prince's Trust charity. The programme
was hosted and executive-produced by
Sir David Frost.

Gala Opening

see SYKES, Eric

Galloping Galaxies!

UK · BBC · CHILDREN'S SITCOM

10 × 25 mins · colour
Series One (5) 1 Oct–29 Oct 1985 · BBC1
Tue 4.35pm
Series Two (5) 20 Nov–18 Dec 1986 · BBC1
Thu 4.30pm

MAIN CAST
SID · · · · · · · · Kenneth Williams (voice only)
Capt Pettifer · · · · · · · · · · · · Robert Swales
First Officer Morton · · · · · · · · · · · Paul Wilce
Communications Officer Webster · · · · · · · ·
· · · · · · · · · · · · · · · · Nigel Cooke (series 1)
Miss Mabel Appleby · · · · · · Priscilla Morgan
Space Pirate Chief Mick Murphy · · · · · · · · ·
· · · · · · · · · · · · · · Sean Caffrey (series 1);
· · · · · · · · · · · · · · · · Niall Buggy (series 2)
Robot 7 · · · · · · · · · · · · · · Michael Deeks
Robot 20 · · · · · · · · · · · · · · Matthew Sim
Robot 35 · · · · · · · · · · · Julie Dawn Cole
Mr Elliot · · · · · · · · · · · · · James Mansfield

CREDITS
writer Bob Block · producer Jeremy Swan

A colourfully cosmic children's space comedy
from the creator of **Rentaghost**. Episodes
charted the exploits of the crew of a 25th-
century interplanetary merchant ship,
Voyager, as it ploughed a far from steady
furrow through the universe pursued by an
Irish space pirate, Murphy, and his band of
decomposing robots. *Voyager* was controlled
by a pompous and bossy computer, SID
(Space Investigation Detector) – voiced by
Kenneth Williams – and crewed by officers
Pettifer, Morton and Webster. With them
too was one Miss Appleby, a humble refugee
from the 20th-century accidentally beamed
on board by an errant time warp.

The Galton & Simpson Comedy

UK · ITV (LWT) · SITCOMS

6 × 30 mins · b/w

Writers Ray Galton and Alan Simpson –
authors of **Hancock's Half-Hour** and
Steptoe And Son and much else – were
wooed across to ITV by LWT's Head of
Entertainment Frank Muir, and charged with
providing six individual playlets in the style
they had utilised as sole writers for the first
two series of the BBC's *Comedy Playhouse*.
See individual entries for further details.

19 Apr 1969	The Suit
26 Apr 1969	Friends In High Places
3 May 1969	Never Talk To Strangers
10 May 1969	Don't Dilly Dally On The Way
17 May 1969	'Pity Poor Edie … Married To Him'
24 May 1969	An Extra Bunch Of Daffodils

The Galton & Simpson Playhouse

UK · ITV (YORKSHIRE) · SITCOMS

7 × 30 mins · colour

A further series of comedy playlets from
Galton and Simpson.
See individual entries for further details.

17 Feb 1977	Car Along The Pass
24 Feb 1977	Swap You One Of These For One Of Those
3 Mar 1977	Cheers
10 Mar 1977	Naught For Thy Comfort
17 Mar 1977	Variations On A Theme
31 Mar 1977	Big Deal At York City
7 Apr 1977	I Tell You It's Burt Reynolds

Galton & Speight's Tea Ladies

UK · BBC · SITCOM

1 × 30 mins · colour
4 Jan 1979 · BBC1 Thu 8.30pm

MAIN CAST
Lil · · · · · · · · · · · · · · · · · Mollie Sugden
Vi · · · · · · · · · · · · · · · · · · Dandy Nichols
Min · · · · · · · · · · · · · · · · Patricia Hayes
MP · · · · · · · · · · · · · · · · · · John Quayle

CREDITS
writers Ray Galton/Johnny Speight · *producer* Dennis Main Wilson

The writers' heavyweight credentials afforded them the rare accolade of seeing their names in the title of this one-off, which presumably was a try-out for a series. Everything seemed set for success – in Sugden, Nichols and Hayes the programme starred a dependable trio of comic actresses, and the action took place in the fruitful setting of the House of Commons. Also, not only was it scripted by two gilt-edged writers but it was produced by the BBC's top man. It was some surprise, then, that no series materialised.

Note. A similar, Australian sitcom titled *Tea Ladies*, screened Down Under in 1978, was more successful. Made by the British producer William G Stewart for the 10 Network, this series was written by Grahame Bond and Jim Burnett and featured Pat MacDonald and Sue Jones as two tea ladies working for members of the Federal Parliament. Eight episodes aired.

Game On

UK · BBC (HAT TRICK PRODUCTIONS) · SITCOM

12 × 30 mins · colour

Series One (6) 27 Feb–10 Apr 1995 · BBC2 Mon 9.30pm

Series Two (6) 16 Sep–21 Oct 1996 · BBC2 Mon 10pm

MAIN CAST
Matthew Malone · · · · Ben Chaplin (series 1); · · · · · · · · · · · · · · · · · Neil Stuke (series 2)
Martin Henderson · · · · · · · · Matthew Cottle
Mandy Wilkins · · · · · · · · · · Samantha Janus
Clare Monohan · · · · Tracy Keating (series 2)

CREDITS
writers Andrew Davies/Bernadette Davis · *director* John Stroud · *producers* Geoffrey Perkins (series 1), Geoffrey Perkins/Sioned Wiliam (series 2)

A 1990s flat-share sitcom which, in its tales of the sexual adventures and misadventures of three twenty-somethings living under the same roof, featured more than a dash of crudity. Ben Chaplin (in the first series) played Matthew, a wealthy, workshy landlord who, because of a strange phobia, never leaves the flat. Matthew Cottle was cast as the hapless, sexually innocent Martin, and Samantha Janus played the ambitious but confused and deeply insecure Mandy.

Martin and Matthew have been friends since schooldays and Mandy's connection is by way of her best friend Claudia, Martin's sister. Mandy is a bright young woman who wants to better herself and is tired of being treated as a sex object, yet she still tends to find herself jumping into bed with inappropriate men. Both Matthew and Martin

are obsessed with sex but neither is conspicuously successful in the field.

Deliberately and provocatively un-PC, some of the language in *Game On* was racy and the situations risqué, but the attendant vulgarity would have been easier to digest had the characters been more likeable. For this reason, while the script included undeniably funny lines, well delivered by the actors, the sum was bereft of the warmth that the similar series **Men Behaving Badly** possessed in depth.

For the second series, Ben Chaplin (who had struck gold in Hollywood with a starring role in Michael Lehmann's 1996 comedy *The Truth About Cats And Dogs*) was replaced by Neil Stuke, who had actually lost out to Chaplin in the original round of casting. And extra fizz was added with the introduction of Clare, a girlfriend for Martin.

At the time of writing, a third series of *Game On* was in production for screening in early 1998, and production company Hat Trick was attempting to sell a US adaptation.

The Gang Show Gala

UK · BBC · SKETCH/STANDUP

1 × 40 mins · colour

24 Dec 1970 · BBC1 Thu 8.20pm

MAIN CAST
Dick Emery
Cardew Robinson
Peter Sellers
David Lodge
Graham Stark
Reg Dixon

CREDITS
writers John Antrobus, Eddie Braben · *executive producer* Ralph Reader · *producer* Michael Hurll

Comedy was to the fore in this Christmas special that celebrated the 30th annual reunion of Ralph Reader's famous RAF *Gang Show*, featuring former Gang members who had gone on to stardom.

Y Garej

UK · BBC · SITCOM

6 × 30 mins · colour

19 Jan–23 Feb 1973 · BBC1 Fri 12.25pm

MAIN CAST
Yncl Defi · · · · · · · · · · · · · Charles Williams
Dafydd · · · · · · · · · · · · · · · · · Michael Povey
Metron · · · · · · · · · · · · · · · · · Beryl Williams
Plismon · · · · · · · · · · · · · · · · · Huw Ceredig

CREDITS
writers W S Jones/Guto Roberts · *producer* Rhydderch Jones

A Welsh-language sitcom originally transmitted only in Wales but then repeated in England for Welsh speakers (the dates, above, reflect the networked broadcasts). The title *Y Garej* literally translates to *The Garage*.

Gas

UK · C4 (SALT ISLAND PRODUCTIONS) · STANDUP

8 × 30 mins · colour

1 July–26 Aug 1997 · Tue mostly 11.30pm

MAIN CAST
host · Lee Mack

CREDITS
writers cast and various · *director* Stephen Stewart · *producer* Sandie Kirk

One of many standup shows on British TV in the late 1990s. *Gas* was presented by comedian Lee Mack and featured artists who were considered quirky or off the wall, including Noel Fielding, Will Smith, Peter Kay, Chris Addison, Julian Barratt, Steve Furst (as 'Lenny Beige'), Mike Gunn, Martin Bigpig, Brendan Burns, Andy Robinson and Jason Byrne.

The show looked more extravagant than many of its contemporaries and the highly coloured stage featured jets of vapour shooting upwards in celebration of the show's title. Recorded in the vast London Bridge Studios, it was another entertaining series that will be useful for looking back upon in future years.

At the time this book went to press, a second series was being planned for 1998 screening.

Gayle's World

UK · ITV (*TV21 FOR CARLTON · CARLTON) · STANDUP/SKETCH

7 × 30 mins · colour

*Pilot · 11 June 1996 · Tue 10.40pm

One series (6) 18 June–23 July 1997 · Wed mostly 10.40pm

MAIN CAST
Gayle Tuesday · · · · · · · · · · Brenda Gilhooly
OTHER APPEARANCES
Grant · · · · · · · · · · · · · · · · · · Ken Andrew
Lucinda Beanie-Toffingham · Charlotte Coleman

CREDITS
creator Brenda Gilhooly · *writers* Brenda Gilhooly/Nichola Hegarty · *directors* Tom Poole (pilot), Simon Spencer (series) · *executive producer* John Bishop (pilot), Nick Symons (series) · *producers* Pete Ward/Dave Morley (pilot), Pete Ward (series)

A fine comedic creation – along the lines of other counterfeit personalities Alan Partridge and Mrs Merton – Gayle Tuesday finally received her own show (with series to follow) in 1996. This was some four years after Brenda Gilhooly had first invented this giggly 'topless model and rising media star' at a Chelmsford student gig by putting on a blonde wig and transforming herself into a one-time 'stunna' from page three of *The Sun*, now branching out into other forms of showbiz. *Gayle's World* celebrated these extensions: Tuesday has an image consultancy business, she's an agony aunt ('You're suffering from clinical depression? Ooh, that's nice!'), she's a psychic, she has her House Of Tuesday fashion line, she releases records (the appalling charity single 'Save The Donkeys', followed by 'Big Up Top') and, on this TV show – mocked-up as a magazine programme – she chats with celebrity guests about 'key contemporary issues' like 'Can you beat chocolate addiction?' and 'What are your man's favourite hobbies?'

With her high, squealing south London voice and low-cut dresses – the only part of her that is long and flat are her vowels – Gayle Tuesday is a splendid spoof of the brainless bimbos that seem to populate the low end of the modelling business. ('I don't just do topless, there's a lot of bum work as well,' she remarks, proudly.) Her boyfriend/manager, Grant, also a second-hand car salesman, is a psychopathic monster. ('He's so lovely – very, very sensitive. Obviously there are the violent mood swings, but nobody's perfect!')

Despite the richness of the Gayle Tuesday character, and the expert manner in which she was conveyed, Gilhooly evidently guessed – rightly so – that viewers might tire of watching her, unadulterated, for six half-hours, so the 1997 series included other characters, like the newly crowned Miss Tannoy 1997, alias the stridently voiced Doreen who works for the appalling south London mini-cab company Common Cabs. Especially good were the exposés into the world of privileged 'babe' models – The 'It' Girls – Jemima Whore (her friends call her Jammy Whore), played by Gilhooly, and Lucinda Beanie-Toffingham (known as Liggy Bingy-Toffingham), played by Charlotte Coleman. These delightful vignettes placed a well-aimed and hefty boot into the Sloane Square set.

But with her winning grin, exposed cleavage and truly inane chatter, Gayle Tuesday stole the show, and there's every chance that she will soon become a much-loved 'household' comedy character. Reports that Samantha Fox was not amused by the series are without foundation; indeed, she turned up as a guest in the opening edition.

A Gentleman's Club

UK · BBC · SITCOM

6 × 30 mins · colour

23 Sep–28 Oct 1988 · BBC2 Fri 9pm

MAIN CAST

Aubrey	William Gaunt
George	Richard Vernon
Ann	Jill Meager
Willie	Christopher Benjamin
Quentin	Rupert Frazer

CREDITS

writer Richard Gordon · *director/producer* Sydney Lotterby

The staid, faded elegance of a gentleman's club was the setting for this sitcom from Richard Gordon, creator of the ***Doctor*** series of novels, films and TV series. The fictitious Albany club, situated off Pall Mall, 'up steps worn by five generations of gentlemanly leather', was based upon various actual clubs and shared some of the problems of the real-life establishments: lack of funds, grumbling members and a decaying building. A male preserve, the Albany deigned to doff its top-hat towards the fairer sex, with mixed 'dinner evenings' (albeit with the ladies segregated in their own dining chamber) and female employees. But this last, progressive move – brought in only after a woman was appointed Prime Minister – continued to raise the hackles of some of the older members, who hadn't absolutely forgiven womankind since Suffragettes smashed the club's windows in 1908.

George And Mildred

UK · ITV (THAMES) · SITCOM

38 × 30 mins · colour

Series One (10) 6 Sep–8 Nov 1976 · Mon 8pm

Series Two (7) 14 Nov–26 Dec 1977 · Mon 8pm

Series Three (6) 7 Sep–12 Oct 1978 · Thu mostly 8pm

Series Four (7) 16 Nov–27 Dec 1978 · mostly Thu 8pm

Series Five (8) 24 Oct–25 Dec 1979 · mostly Tue 8.30pm

MAIN CAST

George Roper	Brian Murphy
Mildred Roper	Yootha Joyce
Jeffrey Fourmile	Norman Eshley
Ann Fourmile	Sheila Fearn
Tristram Fourmile	Nicholas Bond-Owen

OTHER APPEARANCES

Ethel	Avril Elgar
Humphrey	Reginald Marsh
Jerry	Roy Kinnear
Mother	Gretchen Franklin

CREDITS

writers Johnnie Mortimer/Brian Cooke · *director/producer* Peter Frazer-Jones

Having just finished six series of ***Man About The House***, the ultra-prolific writers Mortimer and Cooke created two concurrent spin-offs: ***Robin's Nest*** (six more series) and ***George And Mildred*** (five). This latter one was the more acclaimed of the two, featuring the former landlord and landlady from *Man About The House* now moved upmarket into a new home at 46 Peacock Crescent, Hampton Wick, suburbia. For Mildred it is her long-awaited climb up the class structure – she calls it a 'town house'. For George – lazy, mostly unemployed (he does work for a short while as a traffic warden) and

aggressively determined to preserve his working-classness – it is a terraced house.

The comedy centred on three main issues: the couple's hopeless 25-year marriage in general, Mildred's sexual frustrations in particular – George has given up on sex completely and contrives any excuse to avoid it – and the class struggle. This last problem is exacerbated by the posh family next door, the Fourmiles – wife, husband and their brat child – who are befriended by Mildred but loathed by George.

Without question *George And Mildred* was, for the most part, a funny sitcom, but once again a spin-off feature film (1980, same stars and director, written by Dick Sharples) was an embarrassment. Mortimer and Cooke also wrote a *George And Mildred* stage production, which played at the Pier Theatre in Bournemouth in the 1977 summer season, with both Brian Murphy and Yootha Joyce appearing. There was also an American TV version of the series, *The Ropers* (spun-off from ***Three's Company***, itself the US adaptation of *Man About The House*), in which Norman Fell and Audra Lindley starred as Stanley and Helen, living at 46 Peacock Drive, Chevia Hills. This was produced by ABC and ran for 26 episodes in 1979–80.

George And The Dragon

UK · ITV (ATV) · SITCOM

26 × 30 mins · b/w

Series One (6) 19 Nov–24 Dec 1966 · Sat mostly 8.40pm

Series Two (7) 20 May–1 July 1967 · Sat mostly 8.30pm

Series Three (7) 6 Jan–17 Feb 1968 · Sat 7pm

Series Four (6) 26 Sep–31 Oct 1968 · Thu 8pm

MAIN CAST

George Russell	Sidney James
Gabrielle Dragon	Peggy Mount
Colonel Maynard	John Le Mesurier
Ralph	Keith Marsh

CREDITS

writers Vince Powell/Harry Driver · *director* Shaun O'Riordan · *producers* Alan Tarrant (series 1–3), Jack Williams (series 4)

George Russell is the chauffeur/handyman for rich retired Colonel Maynard, working at the latter's comfortable home. He is also an incorrigible lech, his sexual advances having prompted the resignations of 16 cook/house-keepers, all beautiful young foreigners, inside three months. Then an indomitable woman, a widow named Gabrielle Dragon, is appointed to the position. Considering her un-beautiful looks and personality, George has no wish whatsoever to interfere with Dragon (her maiden name: she reverted to it upon the death of her husband) but right away, in the opening episode, he perpetrates a mock-amorous advance in the hope that it will drive her away. Her retort – she threatens to punch his 'crinkly nose in' – sets the tone for the rest of the series: George has met his match and life *chez* Maynard is never going to be the same. When not at odds with each other, George and Gabrielle join forces to foil the Colonel's plans to bring order to the place, sometimes helped by Ralph, the compost-smelling gardener (Keith Marsh).

This was a fine sitcom that succeeded through good scripts and excellent casting, with its three principal stars in typical form: John Le Mesurier ambled, Peggy Mount bellowed, Sid James roistered and cackled. Mount was being typecast in battle-axe characters at this time, following her role in the stage-play and film *Sailor Beware!* and the TV series *The Larkins*. (Links between *George And The Dragon* and *The Larkins* went beyond Peggy Mount: Alan Tarrant produced that earlier series too and director Shaun O'Riordan, as an actor, had appeared in it as Peggy Mount's son.)

George Burns … [various shows]

see BURNS, George

The George Formby Show

UK · ITV (ATV) · SKETCH/STANDUP
1 × 60 mins · b/w
15 June 1957 · Sat 9.30pm
MAIN CAST
George Formby
CREDITS
director/producer Brian Tesler

A rare TV appearance for the Emperor Of Lancashire, starring in his own hour-long special presented under the banner *Val Parnell's Saturday Spectacular*. The musician Tito Gobbi and genial magician David Nixon helped out.

Formby was approaching the end of his career at this time – his last film was released in 1946 – but he still plucked his ukulele on stage and in rare broadcasts. He died on 6 March 1961, aged 56.

The George Gobel Show · USA

USA · NBC · SKETCH
36 × 60 mins · b/w
US dates: 4 Sep 1957–10 Mar 1959
UK dates: 12 Oct–12 Dec 1958 (3 × 45 mins)
BBC monthly Sun 8pm
MAIN CAST
George Gobel
Phyllis Avery
CREDITS
producers Fred DeCordova, Al Lewis, Hal Kanter

Three editions of a famous US comedy series, especially edited by the BBC (by Philip Barker) and screened in rotation with other imported American programmes *The Bob Hope Show*, *The Sid Caesar Show* and *The Steve Allen Show*. George Gobel (born George Goebel in Chicago on 20 May 1920) was a child singing star on the radio who became a major TV success in the USA in the 1950s with his easy-going comedy style. His method was to look at life from the point of view of a somewhat bewildered, henpecked little man, and his catchphrase 'Well I'll be a dirty bird' was famous all across the States. The most popular sketches on his show featured Gobel and his screen wife Alice (played by Phyllis Avery).

Note. There were three separate US incarnations of *The George Gobel Show* on US TV in the 1950s; the 1957–59 dates above refer to the version from which the BBC edited its programmes.

The George Gobel Show · UK

UK · ITV (ASSOCIATED-REDIFFUSION) · STANDUP
2 × 60 mins · b/w
17 June 1959 · Wed 9pm
8 July 1959 · Wed 9pm
MAIN CAST
George Gobel
CREDITS
director Bill Turner · *producer* Will Roland

Following the three BBC screenings of his US show, the American comic George Gobel came to London to star in a pair of networked specials for ITV. Guests in the first were the Peiro Brothers and the Nitwits; in the second Michael Bentine and Miriam Karlin.

The George Martin Show

UK · BBC · STANDUP
6 × 30 mins · b/w
25 June–17 Sep 1952 · fortnightly Wed around 8.30pm
MAIN CAST
George Martin
CREDITS
writer George Martin · *producer* Gordon Crier

The Aldershot-born standup comedian George Martin (not to be confused with the later famous record producer) graduated to TV after almost 2300 performances at the Windmill Theatre in London, a tough training-ground for many of Britain's best comics. This BBC series, produced by Gordon Crier (who had been behind the famous radio hit *Band Waggon*), featured Martin 'at large in the studio with a number of companions' and gave ample space for the comic to exercise his deft ability at creating gags and funny stories around contemporary events – indeed, his trademark was to wander on stage holding a newspaper, from which, while smoking a pipe, he extrapolated jokes from the day's stories.

In the late 1950s, after hosting his own ITV 'ad-mag' show *By George* until the practice of dressing up extended commercials as programmes was outlawed by the government, George Martin turned from performing to writing, contributing to TV series for Jimmy Tarbuck (*It's Tarbuck*), Dave Allen (*Tonight With Dave Allen*), Harry Worth (*Thirty Minutes Worth*) and Tommy Cooper (*Cooper – Just Like That*), as well as many variety programmes and David Nixon's magic shows. Through this latter connection he became the sole writer during the prime years of the children's series *The Basil Brush Show* (BBC1, from 14 June 1968).

See also *Christmas Cracker*.

Gert And Daisy

UK · ITV (JACK HYLTON TV PRODUCTIONS FOR ASSOCIATED-REDIFFUSION) · SITCOM
6 × 30 mins · b/w
10 Aug–16 Sep 1959 · mostly Mon 8.30pm
MAIN CAST

Gert	Elsie Waters
Daisy	Doris Waters
Boris	Hugh Paddick
Bonnie	Patsy Rowlands
Lulu	Jennifer Browne
Maureen	Dudy Nimmo
Harry	Julian d'Albie
Violet	Rosemary Scott

CREDITS
creator Ted Willis · *writers* Malcolm A Hulke/Eric Paice (3), Lew Schwarz (2), Ted Willis (1) · *director* Milo Lewis

Sisters and music-hall singers Elsie and Doris Waters had created their alter egos – the chatty, catty Gert and Daisy – · in 1930 and quickly scored success, especially on BBC radio. By 1959 their work was becoming thinner on the ground, until Ted Willis saw them in a TV commercial and decided to create a series for them. (At this time, Willis was writing the BBC police drama *Dixon Of Dock Green*, which starred Jack Warner, Elsie and Doris's real-life brother.)

The premise – Gert and Daisy were gossipy ex-show business proprietors of a boarding house for theatrical visitors – enabled the series to feature different guests each week. It was not a great success, though: having always prepared their own material, the sisters found it awkward to be funny with other writers' lines, and they were not acquainted with comedy borne out of situations rather than straight gags. Only one series was made.

See also *The Chars*.

Get Back

UK · BBC (ALOMO PRODUCTIONS/SELECTV) · SITCOM

15 × 30 mins · colour

Series One (7) 26 Oct–7 Dec 1992 · BBC1
Mon 8.30pm
Series Two (8) 27 Sep–15 Nov 1993 · BBC1
Mon 8.30pm

MAIN CAST

Martin Sweet	Ray Winstone
Loretta Sweet	Carol Harrison
Albert Sweet	Larry Lamb
Prudence Sweet	Jane Booker
Bernie Sweet	John Bardon
Eleanor Sweet	Kate Winslett
Joanna Sweet	Michelle Cattini
Bungalow Bill	Zoot Money
Lucy	Shirley Stelfox

CREDITS

creators Laurence Marks/Maurice Gran · *writers* Gary Lawson/John Phelps (7), Laurence Marks/Maurice Gran (6), Bernard McKenna (1), Paul Makin (1) · *directors* Graeme Harper (series 1), Terry Kinane (series 2) · *executive producers* Allan McKeown, Michael Pilsworth · *producers* Bernard McKenna, Rosie Bunting

A 'recession comedy' from Marks and Gran. Having successfully built a series around the lives of two sisters in different financial circumstances (**Birds Of A Feather**), they tried here to repeat the formula with two brothers.

Martin Sweet is the poor one; formerly the proprietor of Le Style Anglais – 'Hertfordshire's premier style boutique' – he has become destitute following the recession-caused collapse of his business. His brother Albert, however, has fared much better, reaping the rewards of the 'get rich quick' 1980s by selling jewellery and speculating on the stock market. An ardent believer in 'Thatcherism', Albert reckons that his brother's plight is of his own making and so is reluctant to offer much help, although – when he's not taunting him with his wealth – he often talks about doing so. Albert's wife Prudence genuinely sympathises with her brother-in-law's situation, but her concern is misconstrued by Martin's wife Loretta who is convinced that Prudence is 'rubbing it in'. While Albert and Prudence live in luxury, Martin, Loretta and their two daughters are forced to share the shabby council house of the brothers' skinflint father Bernie. Despite it all, Martin tries hard to rebuild his life, and his family – although worn down by their circumstances – do their best to support him. Each week Martin beavers away at improving their lot and the family survives on his occasional little victories.

Bernie, the father in *Get Back*, was based on Laurence Marks' own father, and his council flat in Finsbury Park, north London, served as the model for the flat in the series. The sobering topic made *Get Back* somewhat

downbeat, not as heavy as one of Carla Lane's serio-comedies perhaps but certainly a good distance away from *Birds Of A Feather*.

One intriguing sidebar to *Get Back* was its employment of Beatles songs as a source of inspiration. The series' very title was named after the band's 1969 hit, and the lead couple Loretta and Martin Sweet were named from a line in its lyric about 'sweet Loretta Martin'. Most of the regular cast were named after Beatles song characters (from 'Dear Prudence', 'The Continuing Story Of Bungalow Bill', 'Eleanor Rigby', 'Lucy In The Sky With Diamonds' and others) and all the individual episodes were named after other Beatles songtitles; most of them quite recognisable ('Help!', 'We Can Work It Out', 'She's Leaving Home' and so on) but one being the more obscure 'I Don't Want To See You Again', a song written by Paul McCartney (although credited to Lennon-McCartney) for Peter and Gordon.

Get Knighted

UK · C4 (BARRON KNIGHTS) · SKETCH

1 × 60 mins · colour

1 Jan 1983 · Sat 7.15pm

MAIN CAST

The Barron Knights (Barron Anthony Osmond, Butch Baker, Dave Ballinger, Duke D'Mond, Peter 'Peanut' Langford)

CREDITS

producers Butch Baker, Tony Avern

A rare 'own show' for the popular combo famous for sending up current chart hits. Hailing from Leighton Buzzard, the Barron Knights had been famous since the early 1960s and enjoyed several successes themselves. The band's manager, Tony Avern, was co-producer of the programme.

See also *Twice Knightly* and *The Barron Knights Show*.

Get Smart

USA · NBC THEN CBS (TALENT ARTISTS) · SITCOM

*138 × 30 mins (137 × colour · 1 × b/w)

US dates: 18 Sep 1965–13 Sep 1969 (NBC); 26 Sep 1969–11 Sep 1970 (CBS)

**UK dates: 16 Oct 1965–15 Feb 1967 (30 episodes · b/w) BBC1 Sat around 10pm then Wed around 6.20pm

MAIN CAST

Maxwell Smart, Agent 86	Don Adams
Agent 99	Barbara Feldon
Chief Thaddeus	Edward Platt

OTHER APPEARANCES

Agent 13	Dave Ketchum (1966–67)
Professor Carlson	Stacy Keach Sr
	(1966–67)
Conrad Siegfried	Bernie Kopell
Starker	King Moody
Hymie	Dick Gautier
Larabee	Robert Karvelas

CREDITS

creators Mel Brooks, Buck Henry, Dan Melnick · *writers* Mel Brooks, Buck Henry and others including Elroy Schwartz, Stan Burns/Mike Marmer, Gerald Gardner/Dee Caruso, Marvin Worth, Arne Sultan, Chris Hayward/Al Burns, Lloyd Turner, Don Adams, Gloria Burton, Leonard Stern · *executive producer* Leonard Stern · *producers* Arne Sultan, Mel Brooks

Mel Brooks and Buck Henry created this series as a spoof of James Bond and the many TV imitators that followed in 007's wake, in particular *The Man From U.N.C.L.E.* The Smart of the title was bumbling secret agent Maxwell Smart, an impossibly inept buffoon who nevertheless regarded himself as the very best in his profession. Max worked for CONTROL, where he was a constant source of irritation to his superior, The Chief. (Oddly, The Chief also seemed, at times, to think Max was the best in his field. At other times, he most certainly did not.) CONTROL waged a constant battle with the covert evil organisation KAOS, and Max was aided in his missions against KAOS by his beautiful partner Agent 99, whose level-headedness and clear-thinking usually saved the day. 86 and 99 eventually married as, despite insurmountable evidence to the contrary, she too regarded Max as the best agent in the business.

Get Smart was a timely pastiche that tickled the American funny-bone and soon made inroads into the British comic psyche. The series was especially popular among younger viewers and many of Smart's catchphrases entered teenage parlance, including 'Missed me by *that* much' – Smart's defensive response to his enemy's bungled shot; 'Would you believe …' – which prefixed Max's far-fetched attempts to lie his way out of tricky situations; and 'Ah, the old (insert appropriate phrase here) trick' – his way of feigning lack of surprise at outlandish events, as in 'Ah, the old gun-in-the-peg-leg trick' when a one-legged villain got the drop on him. Occasional players in the series included Hymie, CONTROL's humanoid robot with the oddly Jewish name; KAOS masterspy Siegfried; the Chief's assistant, Larabee, who was even dumber than Max; and Agent 13, whose forte was extremely long stake-outs (days at a time spent in such unlikely places as a mailbox).

The show was often very funny and Adams proved a dab hand at physical comedy, much of which stemmed from Max's run-ins with malevolent inanimate objects. Recurring jokes included Max's shoe-phone which always seemed to ring at inconvenient moments, and the wonderful 'cone of silence', an elaborate but hopelessly inefficient secrecy device comprising large plastic domes lowered over the heads of the Chief and Max – in order, theoretically, for them to have private conversations. (Of course, neither could hear a word the other said, even when they shouted.) Special honours should go to Barbara Feldon, who, as the shimmeringly sexy 99, proved a fine foil and was happy to play straight-woman to Smart's clod.

Truly, Smart was not an easy man to kill off, and the hapless agent was soon wooed back to the screen for *The Return Of Maxwell Smart*, originally intended to air on TV in the US and in cinemas elsewhere. Advance word on the project was so positive, however, that it was decided to turn it into a feature film everywhere and it appeared in cinemas in 1980 as *The Nude Bomb*. Only Adams and Karvelas returned from the original TV cast. Then, on 26 February 1989, ABC TV aired *Get Smart Again*, a feature-length TV movie that reunited most of the surviving original cast (but not Edward Platt, who had died in 1974). Here it was explained that CONTROL had been abolished, Max was now a state department officer and his wife 99 was writing her memoirs. But when KAOS re-emerged and threatened the world with a weather machine Max was drafted in to resurrect his old organisation. Even Hymie the robot returned, after spending the previous years as a crash test dummy. Finally, in 1995 the Fox network attempted a new version of *Get Smart* (under this title), with Don Adams returning to the role of Maxwell Smart but now as chief of CONTROL and Feldon back as 99, now a congresswoman. This time the stories revolved around the Smarts' son Zach (Andy Dick), a bumbling nerd who had recently become an agent. Repeating the pattern of the original set-up, Zach was partnered with the sexy and efficient Agent 66 (Elaine Hendrix) but the new series had none of the sparkle of its predecessor and vanished after only seven episodes.

Notes: Adams supplied the voice for a similarly inept lawman in the French-made 1980s children's cartoon series, *Inspector Gadget*. Gadget was bionic and had various contraptions built into his body, but his personality and some of his catchphrases were distinctly reminiscent of Maxwell Smart. The series has aired on British TV.

*This episode count refers to the original series of *Get Smart*, 1965–70, and does not include subsequent revivals.

**C4 screened 110 colour episodes of the 1960s *Get Smart* from 6 January 1983 to 10 October 1992.

Get Some In!

UK · ITV (THAMES) · SITCOM

34 × 30 mins · colour

Series One (7) 16 Oct–27 Nov 1975 · Thu 8.30pm

Special · 25 Dec 1975 · Thu 7.30pm
Series Two (7) 28 June–9 Aug 1976 · Mon 8pm
Series Three (6) 6 Jan–17 Feb 1977 · Thu mostly 7.05pm
Series Four (6) 16 June–21 July 1977 · Thu around 7pm
Series Five (7) 6 Apr–18 May 1978 · Thu 8pm

MAIN CAST

Cpl Percy Marsh	Tony Selby
Ken Richardson	David Janson
Matthew Lilley	Gerard Ryder
Jakey Smith	Robert Lindsay (series 1–4);
	Karl Howman (series 5)
Bruce Leckie	Brian Pettifer

OTHER APPEARANCES

Alice Marsh	Lori Wells
Sqdn-Ldr Baker	John D Collins

CREDITS

writers John Esmonde/Bob Larbey · *directors/producers* Michael Mills (all but special), Robert Reed (special)

Comedy of the short back 'n' sides variety, with writers Esmonde and Larbey harking back to 1955 and the era of compulsory national service, a situation so richly plundered in **The Army Game**. The title derived from the jeer that always greeted newcomers into the services, 'Get some in', meaning 'Get some time in' or 'Get some experience under your belt'.

The series revolved around four lads from contrasting backgrounds, each of whom had received his call-up papers – Jakey Smith (Robert Lindsay in his first major TV role) who was a reformed teddy boy; Bruce Leckie, a Scot without much brain power; Ken Richardson, a former grammar school pupil; and Matthew Lilley, the son of a vicar and so, in military mindset, appropriately, something of a lily-livered character.

Posted to 'C' Flight at RAF Skelton, but swiftly nicknamed the 'erks', the four swiftly come face to face with their permanent adversary, drill instructor Corporal Marsh, a nasty, mean, petty-minded and very vocal piece of work who loathed and despised the 'erks' much in the way that Sergeant Major Bullimore – oddly, his first name was also Percy – had done in *The Army Game*. Episodes centred around Marsh's ill-treatment of the privates and their attempts at gaining revenge.

During its run, *Get Some In!* featured single guest appearances by Alfred Marks, Roy Kinnear, Paul Eddington and Cheryl Hall (Robert Lindsay's real-life wife); the third series saw the cast move to RAF Midham, and the final one (with Karl Howman replacing Lindsay, who had demobbed to star in **Citizen Smith**) was set in the hospital at RAF Druidswater. Tony Selby, as Corporal Marsh, had previously appeared in a similar role in an episode of Esmonde and Larbey's **The Fenn Street Gang**.

Get The Drift

UK · BBC · STANDUP/SKETCH

13 × 30 mins · colour

Series One (6) 23 July–27 Aug 1971 · BBC2 Fri 9.20pm
Special *Cribbins-Livings & Co* 2 Jan 1976 · BBC2 Fri 10.55pm
Series Two (6) 9 Jan–13 Feb 1976 · BBC2 Fri 9.45pm

MAIN CAST

Henry Livings
Alex Glasgow
Bernard Cribbins (5)
Roy Kinnear (2)

CREDITS

writers Leonard Barras (7), Brian Thompson (3), Jim Andrew (2), Mike Haywood (2), John Norris (1), Alan Garner (1), Henry Livings (1), Norman Jackson (1) · *directors* Nick Hunter (series 1), Tony Harrison (special), Mike Toppin (series 2) · *producers* Alfred Bradley (series 1), Mike Healey (special & series 2)

Described as 'mild and bitter humour from the north of England', this showcase for new writing talent was a TV version of the touring stage-show *The Northern Drift* which likewise introduced northern talent. The regular performers, playwright/actor Henry Livings and Alex Glasgow, delivered the lion's share of the material, which chiefly comprised monologues, skits and comical songs.

Prior to the start of the second series, which appeared five years after the first, a New Year's special entitled *Cribbins-Livings & Co*, produced by the *Get The Drift* team, was aired, and the likeable Cribbins went on to become a fixture of the remaining shows.

Notes: Most of the *Get The Drift* team were involved in *Mother Nature's Bloomers*, a curious six-part series screened by BBC2 from 11 July to 15 August 1979. Described as an 'entertainment', it was recorded on stage at the Crucible Theatre in Sheffield and starred Roy Kinnear and Henry Livings, supported by Jean Boht, Colin Edwynn and Meg Johnson. The cast played a variety of weird roles – demented arch-moralists, a would-be nymphomaniac, a grit-blaster, genocidal lunatics and others. The piece was written by Leonard Barras, with music by Alex Glasgow, directed by Philip Hedley and produced by Tony Harrison. Kinnear also starred in *We Had Some Happy Hours*, a light-drama about a disastrous family cricket match and picnic, written by Livings and screened in the north-west by BBC1 on 25 May 1979 (shown nationally on 13 May 1981); Carmel Cryan also appeared, Mike Healey was the director and Ray Colley the producer.

The Northern Drift was also broadcast on BBC radio: Henry Livings and Alex Glasgow, with Pamela Craig and Julia Cooke, broadcast a half-hour selection of 'prose, poems and songs', compiled by Alan Plater, on Radio 3 on 5 December 1967. Livings and Glasgow did likewise nearly 14 years later, on 12 July 1981 (Radio 4). Both programmes were produced by Alfred Bradley.

Get Up, Stand Up

UK · C4 (BACHAKS) · SKETCH/STANDUP

14 × 30 mins · colour

Series One (3) 8 Dec–22 Dec 1994 · Thu 11.05pm

Series Two (5) 2 Nov–30 Nov 1995 · Thu mostly 11.35pm

Series Three (6) 8 Oct–12 Dec 1996 · Tue 11.05pm

MAIN CAST

Malcolm Frederick
Chris Tummings
Angie Le Mar

CREDITS

writers cast, Glen Cardno, Gail Renard, Nicholas Hyde, Gary Beadle, Pat Cumber, Joanne Campbell and others · *director* Glen Cardno · *producers* Malcolm Frederick, Keith Lakhan

Sketch and standup comedy from the all-black trio of Frederick, Tummings and Le Mar, providing an above-average share of laughs over 14 half-hours. Numerous styles of comedy were utilised, from old jokes to bad puns, from simple, studio-based sketches to more elaborate filmed material.

Short standup routines by Tummings and Le Mar punctuated the shows, and their personalities and willingness to play the fool for effect made for a consistently entertaining production. Many of the editions were themed to explore the experience of being black in Britain, but the series was never narrow and broader subjects were included if funny enough. Some of the longer sketches suffered from a strange slowness of pace but this is only a minor criticism of a show that, on the whole, succeeded in delivering a regular supply of good fun.

At the time this book went to press, a fourth series was being planned for 1998 screening.

Get Well Soon

UK · BBC · SITCOM

6 × 30 mins · colour

2 Nov–7 Dec 1997 · BBC1 Sun 6.40pm then 6.30pm

MAIN CAST

Roy Osborne · · · · · · · · · · · Matthew Cottle
Brian Clapton · · · · · · · · · · · · · Eddie Marsan
Ivy Osborne · · · · · · · · · · · · · Anita Dobson
Jilly Howell · · · · · · · · Samantha Beckinsale
Sqdn Ldr Harry 'Gribble' Fielding · · · · · · · · · ·
· Robert Bathurst
Mrs Clapton · · · · · · · · · · · Patsy Rowlands
Sister Shelley · · · · · · · · · · · · · Kate O'Toole
Jeffry · · · · · · · · · · · · · · · William Osborne
Padre Donald Peters · · · · Michael Troughton
Norman Tucker · · · · · · · · · Hugh Bonneville
Bernard Walpole · · · · · · · · · · · · · Neil Stacy

CREDITS

writers Ray Galton/John Antrobus · *director* Christine Gernon · *producer* Philip Kampff

After Galton and Simpson ended their brilliant comedy writing partnership, Ray Galton occasionally worked with another veteran of the art, John Antrobus. In *Get Well Soon* they came up with a series about life in a tuberculosis (TB) sanatorium in 1947. Galton and Simpson themselves first met in one such establishment and had used it as the setting for *Visiting Day*. Here the story turned full circle and Galton and Antrobus fleshed out an entire series based on the hospital experience. (It is an intriguing thought that had Galton and Simpson not been ill at the same time then the world would never have known *Hancock's Half-Hour* and *Steptoe And Son*.)

TB was rife in Britain after the Second World War and many men and women, young and old, had to spend extended periods in sanatoriums, where they tried – mostly by simply resting – to counteract the effects of the infection. In *Get Well Soon*, one such patient is Roy Osborne, deposited at Edgehill Sanatorium by his flighty mother, only to learn that what he imagines will be a stay of just a few weeks could turn into years. Roy is tucked up in the bed of a recently deceased patient, George Howell, and the late George's room-mate Brian Clapton is less than impressed with the new arrival. But after some initial friction, a bond of friendship is formed, and the streetwise Brian tries to educate the bright but naïve Roy in the ways of his new surroundings. Ruling the roost at Edgehill is the no-nonsense Sister Shelley, whose hands-on attitude to the patients is far removed from that of their spiritual guide, Padre Donald Peters, who has a pathological fear of catching their illness and wears a surgical mask whenever he is in a patient's vicinity. But TB was no respecter of class or distinction, and the other patients include a boorish snob, Norman Tucker, and the clinically insane Harry Fielding, who barks commands at an imaginary dog, Blackie, and believes that the war is still in progress, those around him being members of his squadron.

Visitors from the outside world include Brian's mother, the well-meaning Mrs Clapton; and George Howell's widow Jilly, who still visits Edgehill through habit and has taken a somewhat obsessive shine to Roy. Then there's Bernard Walpole, the manager of the Croydon Odeon, who, en route to visit his wife at the sanatorium, literally runs into Roy's mother. The gold-digging Ivy Osborne is entranced by Walpole's social standing and an affair materialises, much to Roy's chagrin: he fears that the liaison will be the subject of sanatorium gossip.

Get Well Soon was an interesting period-piece that sometimes bore a closer resemblance to a Perry/Croft/Lloyd creation than the richly verbal character comedies with which Galton was usually associated. As the series developed, however, it progressed to a more complex level and the writers were unafraid to flirt with melodrama – the first series ended on a cliffhanger when a poisoned chocolate looked destined to kill off one of the major cast members.

The Ghost And Mrs Muir

USA · NBC THEN ABC (20TH CENTURY-FOX) · SITCOM

50 × 30 mins · colour

US dates: 21 Sep 1968–18 Sep 1970

UK dates: 19 Nov 1969–19 Jan 1971 (49 episodes) ITV mostly Wed 6.30pm

MAIN CAST

Carolyn Muir · · · · · · · · · · · · · · Hope Lange
Capt Daniel Gregg · · · · · · · · Edward Mulhare
Candy Muir · · · · · · · · · · · · · Kellie Flanagan
Jonathan Muir · · · · · · · · · · · Harlen Carraher
Martha Grant · · · · · · · · · · · · · · · Reta Shaw
Claymore Gregg · · · · · · Charles Nelson Reilly

CREDITS

creator R A Dick · *writer* Jean Holloway · *directors* various · *executive producer* David Gerber · *producers* Howard Leeds, Stanley Rubin, Gene Reynolds

The ghost of Captain Gregg, a seafarer dead for more than 100 years, still haunts Gull Cottage, his former home in Schooner Bay, New England. He died here, still only middle-aged, in a fire. The phantom determinedly frightens away those people who, encouraged by the late Captain's sappy nephew Claymore, come to rent the place, but he is unable to discourage a widow, Mrs Muir, a freelance writer, who arrives with her two young children (Jonathan and Candy), their maid (Martha) and dog (Scruffy, appropriately named). Right away, the ghostly captain makes himself visible to Mrs Muir and, after a rocky start, soon enough they become friends. He even admits to having fallen in love with her but, of course, they don't stand even a ghostly chance of a fulfilling union.

This surprisingly good sitcom was based on a 1947 feature film of the same name, directed by Joseph L Mankiewicz and starring Gene Tierney as Mrs Muir (her first name was Lucy here) and Rex Harrison as the ghostly Captain. (In the film the couple do finally end up together.) Both the movie and the subsequent TV series were based on the original story by R A Dick.

The Ghosts Of Motley Hall

UK · ITV (GRANADA) · CHILDREN'S SITCOM

20 × 30 mins · colour

Series One (7) 25 Apr–6 June 1976 · Sun 4.35pm

Series Two (6) 26 Dec 1976–30 Jan 1977 · Sun mostly 5.05pm

Special · 26 Dec 1977 · Mon 5.45pm

Series Three (6) 29 Jan–5 Mar 1978 · Sun 5.45pm

MAIN CAST

Bodkin · · · · · · · · · · · · · · · · · · Arthur English
Sir George Uproar · · · · · · · · · Freddie Jones
Sir Francis ('Fanny') · · · · Nicholas Le Prevost
Matt · · · · · · · · · · · · · · · · · Sean Flanagan
The White Lady · · · · · · · · · · · Sheila Steafel
Mr Gudgin · · · · · · · · · · · · · · · · Peter Sallis

CREDITS

creator/writer Richard Carpenter · director/producer Quentin Lawrence

Richard Carpenter, who had written *Catweazle* (the popular light-drama series for children, 1970–71), conceived and wrote *The Ghosts Of Motley Hall*, lightly humorous stories that centred on a dilapidated empty mansion populated by five ghosts, four of whom had dwelled there during its better days. Although they were not beyond arguing among themselves, or spooking one another, the quintet were united in their determination to see off any potential building speculators and other sundry nosey-parkers who came sniffing around the for-sale Motley Hall, which they did by manoeuvring situations to their advantage while remaining invisible and inaudible to living humans.

As with so many children's series, the casting was exceptional: Freddie Jones played the irascible Victorian general Sir George Uproar, who had led his soldiers so ignominiously to their deaths; Nicholas Le Prevost played the gambler Sir Francis, nicknamed Fanny, an 18th-century fop who had died of drinking and duelling; Sheila Steafel was the vague but mysteriously moaning White Lady; teenage actor Sean Flanagan played Matt, a Regency-period stable boy who was not a part of Motley Hall's heritage but came to the ghosts' rescue in the first episode, stayed and became their nominal leader because he was the only spook who could roam beyond the house; and Arthur English appeared as Bodkin, jester to the original Uproar, Sir Richard, back in the 16th-century. Peter Sallis was cast as the local estate agent, proud of his links with the last Uproar (Sir Humphrey, killed by an elephant in 1976) and determined to see that Motley Hall did not fall into the hands of motley purchasers.

Gillie Potter

UK · BBC · STANDUP

14 editions (12×10 mins · 1×15 mins · 1×20 mins) · b/w

Special (20 mins) 5 Dec 1936 · Sat 3pm

Special (10 mins) 9 Jan 1937 · Sat 9.50pm

Special (10 mins) 19 Feb 1937 · Fri 3.50pm

Special (15 mins) *Punch And Judex: Mr Potter's Joyous Judicial Joke* · aka *Rex v Rattleribs* 29 May 1937 · Sat 9pm

One series (6×10 mins) *Mr Gillie Potter* 18 Nov 1937–5 Mar 1938 · irregular days and times

Special (10 mins) *Mr Gillie Potter* 24 May 1938 · Mon 9pm

Special (10 mins) *Mr Gillie Potter* 26 Aug 1938 · Mon 9pm

Special (10 mins) *Mr Gillie Potter* 12 Dec 1938 · Mon 9pm

Special (10 mins) *Mr Gillie Potter* 30 Aug 1939 · Mon 9pm

MAIN CAST

Gillie Potter

CREDITS

writer Gillie Potter · producers Stephen Thomas (specials 1 & 2), Dallas Bower (specials 3 & 8), Gordon Crier (special 4), J Royston Morley (3 editions of series), Moultrie R Kelsall (1 edition of series), Philip Bate (2 editions of series), Lanham Titchener (special 5), Stephen Harrison (special 6), Fred O'Donovan (special 7)

Early TV appearances by the celebrated comedian and BBC radio star Gillie Potter – but not his first: he was one of four entertainers who had taken part in experimental transmissions from Crystal Palace before the service was launched across London at another palace, Alexandra.

Born Hugh Peel in 1888, the plummy-voiced Potter's famous opening to his series of radio reports ('Good Evening, England. This is Gillie Potter speaking to you in English'), ostensibly broadcast from the fictitious hamlet of Hogsnorton, always heralded 15 minutes of mirth, with stories about the local squire Lord Marshmallow and his clan, or the career of his (Potter's) brother, who 'was educated at Borstal'. In the first of these three TV shows Potter, who described himself as 'outrageously the most handsome comedian of all time', delivered a spoof travel lecture, 'With Spaghetti To Italy', and presented a similar talk in the second show (which was re-staged later in the day). In the third show, subtitled 'Mr Justice Potter Sums Up', Potter appeared as a High Court judge.

See also *Kaleidoscope*.

Gilligan's Island

USA · CBS (GLADASYA PRODUCTIONS/UA-TV) · SITCOM

98×30 mins (36×b/w · 62×colour)

US dates: 26 Sep 1964–4 Sep 1967

UK dates: 8 June–26 Dec 1965 (13×b/w) ITV mostly Tue 8.30pm

MAIN CAST

Gilligan · · · · · · · · · · · · · · · · · · Bob Denver
Jonas Grumby ('The Skipper') · · · Alan Hale Jr
Thurston Howell III · · · · · · · · · · · Jim Backus
Lovey Howell · · · · · · · · · · · Natalie Schafer
Ginger Grant · · · · · · · · · · · · · · · Tina Louise
Roy Hinkley ('The Professor') · · · · · · · · · · ·
· · · · · · · · · · · · · · · · · · · Russell Johnson
Mary Ann Summers · · · · · · · · · · Dawn Wells

CREDITS

writers various · directors various · producer Sherwood Schwartz

A preposterously silly sitcom which stands up to no logical scrutiny whatever but has, inexplicably, become an icon of 1960s American TV and is fantastically popular in the perpetual re-runs it still enjoys there. Like all else about it, the premise of *Gilligan's Island* is simple: the passengers and crew aboard a small sightseeing vessel, the SS *Minnow*, set out from Hawaii on a pleasure cruise, are caught in the grip of a sudden storm and cast ashore on an uncharted isle somewhere in the South Pacific. Here they remain marooned for some 15 years, despite (and this formed the basis for each of the 98 episodes) some bizarre attempts to escape, plans that are usually scuppered, accidentally, by the bumbling first mate, Gilligan. There are many insoluble questions about *Gilligan's Island*, such as: why, if they're only a short distance from Hawaii, is the island uncharted and impossible to escape from? Why did the Howells have so many changes of clothes with them (even allowing for the fact that they're millionaires) for a half-day trip? And, most fantastically of all, how and why do so many additional people enter and leave the stories (American TV sitcoms traditionally featured weekly guest stars) without the *Minnow* castaways leaving with them? These visitors included a movie producer, a pair of Russian cosmonauts, a pop group, a wealthy hotel owner, a mad scientist, and many others equally fantastic.

Clearly, *Gilligan's Island* was made to be enjoyed and not analysed, and one can certainly see that the primary ingredient for a good sitcom was in place: a disparate bunch of people are stranded in one location together, allowing every opportunity for the expansion of and interplay between the characters. Only 13 episodes were screened by London ITV and the series has not been seen in Britain since; in America, *Gilligan's Island* has lived on not only in re-runs but in two animated versions for children – *The New Adventures Of Gilligan's Island*, 1974–77, and *Gilligan's Planet*, 1982–83 – and three one-off specials – *Rescue From Gilligan's Island*, 1978, *Castaways On Gilligan's Island*, 1979, and (this is getting ridiculous) *Harlem Globetrotters On Gilligan's Island*, 1981. *Roseanne*, meanwhile, tipped the hat to *Gilligan's Island* – sort of – with a special episode entitled 'Sherwood Schwartz – A Loving Tribute' (aired in the UK by C4 on 23 June 1995).

The Gingerbread Girl

UK · ITV (YORKSHIRE) · SITCOM

7 × 30 mins · colour

9 Apr–21 May 1993 · Fri 8.30pm

MAIN CAST

Linda · Janet Dibley
Matt · John Diedrich
Eddie · · · · · · · · · · · · · · · · Tyler Butterworth
Kerry · · · · · · · · · · · · · · · · · · Isabella Marsh
Stella · · · · · · · · · · · · · · · · · Tracie Bennett

CREDITS

writer Alex Shearer · executive producer David
Reynolds · director/producer Robin Carr

Following the end of **The Two Of Us**, that
series' co-star Janet Dibley expressed a wish
to its writer, Alex Shearer, that they work
together again, and suggested single-
parenting as the theme of a new series
Shearer might write. The Gingerbread Girl
was his response, with Dibley cast as Linda,
a divorced parent raising her eight-year-old
tomboyish daughter Kerry and trying to cope
with the perils of being a single mum: lack of
affection, shortage of cash, child behavioural
problems, continued but unsatisfactory
meetings with one's former spouse for the
sake of the child, the problems of dating, and
more. And Linda's struggle wasn't helped by
her Australian ex-husband Matt's unreliable
(indeed, non-existent) maintenance payments,
nor by his dishonest accounts of where he
took Kerry during their weekly outings
together.

In best sitcom style, other people were on
hand to assist or complicate matters: good
friend Stella, another single mum, with whom
Linda went out looking for men, and ardent
neighbour Eddie whose advances had to be
repeatedly spurned. While it had its moments,
and tried to blend punchlines with poignancy,
The Gingerbread Girl lacked bite and was not
renewed for a second series.

Girl Talk

UK · ITV (ATV) · SKETCH

3 × 30 mins · colour

12 Aug–26 Aug 1980 · Tue mostly 10.30pm

MAIN CAST

Frances Cuka
Carol Royle
Cheryl Branker
Michael Lees
Robert Austin
Robert Swales

CREDITS

writers Carol Bunyan, Judy Raines, Julie Welsh,
Frances Galleymore, Paula Milne, Jane Hollowood,
Ruth Carter, David A Yallop · director Hugh David ·
producer Susi Hush

In the era immediately before the rise of
Dawn French, Jennifer Saunders, Ruby Wax,
Tracey Ullman, Victoria Wood and others,
it was still novel to see women dominating

a comedy programme. Girl Talk, which
spanned just three editions in 1980, attempted
to arrest the situation with a volley of
sketches mostly written by and mostly
starring women, who made sure – and why
not? – that their sex came out on top.

A Girl's Best Friend

UK · BBC · SITCOM

1 × 30 mins · colour

3 July 1974 · BBC1 Wed 9.55pm

MAIN CAST

Audrey Dalton · · · · · · · · · · · · · Zena Walker
Lynn Dalton · · · · · · · · · · · · Carolyn Courage
Arnold · · · · · · · · · · · · · · · · · Reginald Marsh
Jack Shepherd · · · · · · · · · · · · · David Knight

CREDITS

writer Donald Churchill · producer John Howard
Davies

The actor/writer Donald Churchill wrote this
Comedy Playhouse pilot that looked at what
happens when an attractive divorcee, Audrey,
shares a flat with her grown-up daughter,
Lynn, and the fragile harmony of their
relationship is disturbed when they realise
that they are both dating the same man. It
was not developed into a series.

Girls About Town

UK · ITV (ATV · *THAMES) · SITCOM

**22 episodes (20 × 30 mins · 2 × short specials;
21 × colour · 1 × b/w)**

*Pilot (b/w) 2 Oct 1969 · Thu 9pm

Series One (6 × colour) 9 Mar–13 Apr 1970 ·
Mon mostly 9.30pm

Series Two (7 × colour) 2 Nov–14 Dec 1970 ·
Mon 9.30pm

Short special (colour) · part of All-Star Comedy
Carnival 25 Dec 1970 · Fri 6pm

Series Three (6 × colour) 2 Nov–7 Dec 1971 ·
Tue around 7pm

Short special (colour) · part of Mike And Bernie
Winters' All-Star Christmas Comedy Carnival
25 Dec 1971 · Sat 6.05pm

MAIN CAST

Rosemary Pilgrim · · · · · · Anna Quayle (pilot);
· · · · · · · · · · · · · · · · · · Julie Stevens (series)
Brenda Liversedge · · · Denise Coffey (series)
Sylvia · · · · · · · · · · · Barbara Mullaney (pilot)
George Pilgrim · · · · · · · · · · · Robin Parkinson
Harold Liversedge · · · · · · · · · Peter Baldwin

OTHER APPEARANCES

Mrs Pilgrim · · · · · · · · · · · Dorothy Reynolds

CREDITS

writer Adele Rose · directors Paul Annett (8), John
Scholz-Conway (7), Shaun O'Riordan (4), Ronnie
Baxter (pilot), Pembroke Duttson (1), Peter Duguid
(1) · producers Shaun O'Riordan (21), Ronnie
Baxter (pilot)

Mirroring its time, the subject of Girls About
Town was the emancipation of women. It
wasn't a strident voice for Women's Lib, and
that media obsession of the period, bra-

burning, did not feature; all the same, the
storylines did depict two female friends in
their early thirties, tired of slaving over their
kitchen sinks in Acacia Avenue and keen to
strike a blow for their sex. (If, at the same
time, this attracted the attention of their lesser
halves, so much the better.)

The stars of this ATV series were two
escapees from children's TV: Julie Stevens
(who had been in Play School) and Denise
Coffey (from the great Do Not Adjust Your
Set), although, in Thames' pilot episode,
Anna Quayle and Barbara Mullaney headed
the cast. Mullaney (under her married name,
Knox) went on to appear in Coronation Street
(as Rita Fairclough), as did Peter Baldwin
(who played Derek Wilton). Indeed, there was
a third Coronation Street connection in Girls
About Town in that Helen Worth (Gail
Tilsley) appeared in one episode.

Girls On Top

UK · ITV (WITZEND PRODUCTIONS FOR
CENTRAL) · SITCOM

13 × 30 mins · colour

Series One (7) 23 Oct–4 Dec 1985 · Wed 8.30pm

Series Two (6) 30 Oct–11 Dec 1986 ·
Thu mostly 9pm

MAIN CAST

Candice Valentine · · Tracey Ullman (series 1)
Amanda Ripley · · · · · · · · · · · · Dawn French
Jennifer Marsh · · · · · · · · Jennifer Saunders
Shelley Dupont · · · · · · · · · · · · · · · Ruby Wax
Lady Carlton · · · · · · · · · · · Joan Greenwood

CREDITS

writers Dawn French/Jennifer Saunders/Ruby
Wax · script editor Ben Elton · directors Paul
Jackson (series 1), Ed Bye (series 2) · executive
producer Allan McKeown · producer Paul Jackson

Although Girls On Top was akin to a
women's version of **The Young Ones**, it
went in for none of the extreme slapstick
or camera trickery that marked the earlier
male model. Here, the sheer strength of the
characters and the skill of the players carried
the comedy, depicting the hellish flat-share
scenario of four wildly different personalities
crammed into a couple of rooms in
Kensington, London, ruthlessly furthering
themselves at the expense of each other.

Dawn French and Jennifer Saunders first
met Ruby Wax at their literary agent's
Christmas party, and the basic outline of Girls
On Top resulted from a discussion between
the three of them. The fourth member of the
cast, Tracey Ullman, was suggested by
French's husband, Lenny Henry, who had
worked with her in **Three Of A Kind**.

In Girls On Top, the characters were
everything. Candice Valentine (Ullman) was
a bitchy, pathological liar and thief who used
a succession of feigned illnesses and every
other ploy under the sun to get her way,
and dressed in lurid clothes in the hope

of attracting new between-the-sheets acquaintances. Shelley Dupont (Wax) was the epitome of an avaricious, loud-mouthed, vulgar, catty, parent-sponsored rich American opportunist, going to any lengths to fulfil her desperate attempts at becoming a famous actress, an impossible dream since she was talentless. Amanda Ripley (French) was the archetypal feminist (she worked as sub-assistant editor at *Spare Cheeks* magazine), Greenham Common campaigner, cause-supporter and environmentalist who took life so seriously and claimed to hate men but would quickly have given it all up if one of them had showed any interest in her. Jennifer Marsh (Saunders) was an old Brownies friend of Amanda's who tagged along, not only to Amanda but in life generally, being a dopey dolt incapable of decision or developing the speed of her thought processes beyond that of a sloth. She needed Amanda to help her through life; Amanda clearly needed Jennifer in order to be able to boss about and lord it over someone. The quartet were supplemented in their zany lives by the landlady of the building, Lady Carlton, who lived downstairs. She was a gin-swilling crazy who adored her stuffed dachshund and somehow, despite being completely and utterly batty, managed to write romantic novels.

The parts worked because they were comfortable. Dawn French's insultingly bossy domination of Jennifer Saunders' easily trampled-upon witless soul would be exercised again and again in their *French And Saunders* TV sketches and stage material. Ruby Wax's portrayal of Shelley as the bitchy brash American was entirely in keeping with the persona she has used in pretty much all of her TV work, and veteran actress Joan Greenwood was superb as the landlady. Others seen in cameo roles in *Girls On Top* included Helen Lederer, Pauline Melville, Helen Atkinson Wood, Mark Arden, Stephen Frost, Robbie Coltrane, Harry Enfield, Hugh Laurie, Pauline Quirke, John Sessions and Arthur Smith plus the Beverley Sisters and visiting American *Soap* star Katherine Helmond who appeared once as Shelley's mother.

By the time the first series hit the screen Tracey Ullman was already making serious inroads into a career in America, beginning with her role in the Meryl Streep movie *Plenty*. Her husband, WitzEnd Productions' Allan McKeown, executive producer of *Girls On Top*, skilfully managed his wife's transatlantic move, and so successful was he in establishing her in *The Tracey Ullman Show*, on screen in the USA from April 1987, that she was unable to appear in the second series of *Girls On Top*; one of her many hypochondriacal complaints – a dodgy oesophagus – was borne out to be have been

true, and she had died, although there remained every possibility that she had been accidentally murdered by Shelley or Amanda. The 'killing off' of one of the lead characters was typical of the confidence that marked all the chief players in the so-called 'alternative comedy' boom. Like *The Young Ones* before it, the writers of *Girls On Top* had no intention of capitalising upon the success of their creation or characters by stretching them to umpteen series. They had explored the formula and wrought the best ideas from it, now they would move on. Hence, in the final episode, *all* the characters were killed off when Lady Carlton accidentally ignited a quantity of petrol she had accumulated (she was that type of person) and blew everything and everybody to pieces.

The strength of the comedy in *Girls On Top* – indeed, the series' sexually dominant title – emphasised the inescapable presence of women in British comedy at the time, proving once and for all that they were in no way inferior to men when it came to creating laughter. How ironic, then, that the second series had to skip a week mid-run in order for ITV to screen Miss World 1986. The old ways were enjoying one last gasp.

Note. WitzEnd Productions attempted to adapt *Girls On Top* for American TV, selling the idea to CBS. A pilot was produced but no series developed.

Glad Rags

AUSTRALIA/UK · NOMAD FILMS/SOUTHERN TELEVISION/NINE NETWORK/BBC · CHILDREN'S SITCOM

13 × 25 mins · colour

Australian dates: 3 July–21 July 1995

UK dates: 17 May–9 Aug 1995 · BBC1 Wed 4.35pm

MAIN CAST

Lizzie Forbes	Brooke 'Mikey' Adams
Patricia ('Trish') Forbes	Sarah Chadwick
Gino Ambino	John Munachen
Gilbert Ambino	Luciano Martucci
Brendan Punch	Brett Ferris
Fiorella Punch	Carmel Johnson
Graeme M Marsden	Jerome Ehlers

CREDITS

creator/writer Trevor Todd · *director* Robert Stewart · *executive producers* Kris Noble, Douglas Stanley · *producers* Kate Faulkner, Douglas Stanley

Fast-moving fun for younger viewers, centring on Lizzie Forbes, whose overworked imagination often embroils her in misunder-standings, muddles and miscellaneous mayhem. Lizzie lived with her mother Trish and together they ran a fancy-dress hire business, Glad Rags. Lizzie's father was divorced (amicably) from Trish but turned up occasionally to carry out his fatherly duties. Glad Rags was the middle property of

three businesses: on one side was Ambino Photography, run by a handsome Italian, Gilbert (a single parent rather attracted to Trish). On the other was Healthee Bodeez, a health shop owned by a widowed health-food enthusiast, Fiorella Punch. Gilbert's son Gino and Fiorella's son, the junk-food addicted Brendan, were Lizzie's good friends, although they were often exasperated by her tendency to jump to the wrong conclusions and act accordingly. Although each episode featured a self-contained story, there was a serial element concerning a smarmy property developer, Marsden, who owned the two adjoining buildings and was trying to force out Lizzie and Trish.

Glad Rags was an energetic series with well judged performances which, although broad, stopped short of caricature. On the down side, the scripts displayed a somewhat old-fashioned attitude towards health food and vegetarianism, harking back to a less enlightened age with its depiction of such fare as grey, tasteless goo suitable only for wimps and cranks.

The Glam Metal Detectives

UK · BBC (PETER RICHARDSON PRODUCTIONS) · SITCOM/SKETCH

6 × 30 mins · colour

23 Feb–6 Apr 1995 · BBC2 Thu 9pm

MAIN CAST

Gary	Gary Beadle
Phil	Phil Cornwell
Doon	Doon Mackichan
Sara	Sara Stockbridge
George	George Yiasoumi
Mark, the manager	Mark Craven

CREDITS

writers main cast and Peter Richardson, Lloyd Stanton · *director* Peter Richardson · *producer* Nira Park

Using as its linking device the technique of a random trawl through spoof cable/satellite TV channels, *The Glam Metal Detectives* was a lightning-paced sketch show which featured four recurring themes within its array of short visual jokes and soundbites. The main sketch each week was an adventure with the Glam Metal Detectives, a sort of secret-agent rock band pledged to take care of the world's ecological balance – led by their manager, the square-jawed Mark, they fight various nefarious threats to the balance of nature. This sketch ran throughout episodes, interrupted by the sudden zaps to other channels. Featuring regularly were 'Betty's Mad Dash', a satire of old TV (black and white) adventure serials, featuring Doon Mackichan as flapper Betty, a 1930s under-cover agent, and Sara Stockbridge as her sidekick, the man-hungry Maisie; 'The Big Me' a chat-show parody featuring Morag (Mackichan again) as an egomaniacal presenter; and 'Colin Corleone' (George Yiasoumi), a Londoner of supposed Italian extraction who behaved as if he was a mafia godfather.

This was a heady brew combining the cultish, the cliché-shattering and the contemporary kitsch, almost as if director Peter Richardson had taken all of his disparate **Comic Strip Presents ...** films and mixed them in a blender. The series had a distinct look, with high quality visuals and garish/gaudy colours aping the style of some of the 'in yer face' satellite channels. Vocal impressionist Phil Cornwell stood out, as did the wonderful Doon Mackichan who played a dizzying amount of different characters. And ex-Vivienne Westwood model Sara Stockbridge demonstrated a pleasing light-comedy touch and willingness to go to embarrassing lengths for a laugh. The show had enough quality to become a cult classic but for some reason failed to ignite the public imagination and lasted for only one series.

The Glamour Girls

UK · ITV (GRANADA) · SITCOM

13 × 30 mins · colour

Series One (6) 23 Oct–27 Nov 1980 ·
Thu 7.30pm

Series Two (7) 23 Feb–6 Apr 1982 · Tue 8pm

MAIN CAST

Veronica Haslett · · · · · · · · · · · Brigit Forsyth
Debbie Wilkinson · · · · · · · · · · · Sally Watts
Ernest Garstang · · · · · · · · · · · Duggie Brown
Brian Frodsham · · · · · · · · · · · · · Tom Price
Mr Meredith · · · · · · · · · · · · · James Warrior

CREDITS

writer David Nobbs · director Malcolm Taylor · producer John G Temple

Two attractive young women, Veronica (34, divorced, brunette) and Debbie (24, blonde), feel the need to jazz up their lives with glamour and adventure and give up their jobs in the Post Office and shoe shop respectively. Fortunately for them, a smooth-talking likely lad by the unlikely name of Ernest Garstang has just launched a new sales promotions agency, Glamgirl Ltd, and they become his first two charges. As it happens, the women have little in common and don't entirely get on, and they quickly discover that the exciting life leads them to places like ... Halifax, where they demonstrate non-stick pans at a trade fair, and a northern department store where dressing up as a mermaid in order to help sell fish is the order of the day. The slightly seedy Garstang also employs a keen and bright-eyed 'general dogsbody' assistant, Brian Frodsham.

Written by David Nobbs, whose brilliant creation **The Fall And Rise Of Reginald Perrin** ended in 1979, *The Glamour Girls* featured Brigit Forsyth (the crusty Thelma in **Whatever Happened To The Likely Lads**) and Duggie Brown (from **The Comedians** and the sitcom **Take My Wife**).

Glas Y Dorlan

UK · BBC · SITCOM

10 × 30 mins · colour

Series One (6) 1 Apr–13 May 1977 · BBC1
Fri mostly 3.20pm

Series Two (4) 1 Dec 1978–5 Jan 1979 · BBC1
Fri 3.20pm

MAIN CAST

Inspector Idris Vaughan · · · · · · Islwyn Morris
Sgt Ifan Puw · · · · · · · · · · · · · Stewart Jones
PC Gordon Hughes · · · · · · · · Geraint Jarman
Mrs Rosi Roberts · · · · · · · · · · Maureen Rhys
Idwal · · · · · · · · · · · · · · · · · Robin Griffith
PW Angela Evans · · · · · · · · Sharon Morgan

CREDITS

writers Michael Povey/John Pierce Jones · director Brydan Griffiths · producer Rhydderch Jones

A Welsh-language sitcom originally transmitted only in Wales but then repeated in England for Welsh speakers. (The dates above reflect the networked screenings.) The series depicted the misadventures of a country police force – *Glas Y Dorlan*, meaning kingfisher, literally translates to 'blue of the river'.

Glencannon

UK/USA · ITV/SYNDICATION (GROSSE-KRASNE-SILLEMAN/NTA) · SITCOM

39 × 30 mins · b/w

US dates: 1959

*UK dates: 14 Sep 1960–6 July 1961 (39 episodes) · Wed 7pm then Thu around 6.15pm

MAIN CAST

Glencannon · · · · · · · · · · · · Thomas Mitchell
Bosun Hughes · · · · · · · · · · · · Patrick Allen
Mr Montgomery · · · · · · · · · · · Barry Keegan
Cookie · · · · · · · · · · · · · · · Georgie Wood
Captain Ball · · · · · · · · · · · Charles Carson
Sparks · · · · · · · · · · · · · Peter Collingwood
Mr Macintosh · · · · · · · · · · · · Kerry Jordan
John Castle · · · · · · · · · · · · · · John Barron

CREDITS

creator Guy Gilpatrick · writers Basil Dawson, John Touron, Ian Dallas · director John Knight · executive producer Donald Hyde

A comedy adventure yarn which Americans seem to think was English-made and the British think was American. In truth, *Glencannon* was an international co-production, with the veteran Hollywood actor Thomas Mitchell – American of Irish parentage – starring as the mischievous chief engineer of a rusting, world-travelling tramp steam ship, *Inchcliffe Castle*, sailing from port and port and enjoying many a scrape therein. Except for pre-filmed exotic location shots, the series was made almost entirely in a studio in Elstree, and many British actors were among the casts, not only those detailed above but also, with one appearance apiece, Arthur Lowe, Jack Train, Jon Pertwee, Sydney Tafler, Irene Handl, Victor Maddern and Alfie Bass.

The British character actor Robert Newton had starred in a pilot version of *Glencannon*, screened in the USA by ABC on 19 April 1953 and not seen in the UK, but rights to the full series were vested in the widowed mother of Guy Gilpatrick, the author of the original *Glencannon* stories, who had died in 1949. In 1957, when aged 91, she finally permitted them to be turned into a TV series, but only on the condition that she see the episodes first.

*Note. These dates reflect screenings in the Midlands area, which screened the full complement of episodes. Only 18 of the 39 were shown by London-ITV, from 22 April to 6 September 1960.

Gloria

USA · CBS (EMBASSY TELEVISION) · SITCOM

21 × 30 mins · colour

US dates: 26 Sep 1982–21 Sep 1983

UK dates: 29 Oct 1984–17 July 1985 (21 episodes) BBC1 Mon then Wed 5.35pm

MAIN CAST

Gloria Stivic · · · · · · · · · · · · · Sally Struthers
Dr Willard Adams · · · · · · · · Burgess Meredith
Dr Maggie Lawrence · · · · · · · · · Jo de Winter
Clark Uhley · · · · · · · · · · · · · · Lou Richards
Joey Stivic · · · · · · · · · · · · · Christian Jacobs

CREDITS

writers Dan Guntzelman/Steve K Marshall, Frederick Hoffman, Fredric N Weiss/Harriet Weiss, Jeffrey Ferro, Joseph M Gannon, Jurgen M Wolff, Lew Levy, Lissa A Levin, Max D Tash, Melody A Rowland, Michael J Cassutt, Patt Shea, Richard Freiman, Richard J Reinhart, Tim O'Donnell · director Bob Claver · producers Dan Guntzelman, Steve K Marshall

The hour-length pilot of *Gloria* (aired in the USA on 28 February 1982) was actually an episode of **Archie Bunker's Place**. In this, it was explained that Gloria's husband Mike had left her to join a Californian commune and she was striking out on her own with her eight-year-old son Joey. The series opener, screened seven months later, duly found Gloria starting anew as an assistant to a veteran veterinarian, Dr Willard Adams, and subsequent episodes told of her new life and struggle to survive as a single working mother.

This final spin-off from **All In The Family** proved to be as pedestrian as its parent programme had been groundbreaking. Poor old Gloria: after years living under Archie Bunker's roof she now found herself working at a vet's practice, forever destined, it would seem, to be surrounded by dumb animals.

The Glums

UK · ITV (LWT) · SITCOM

17 editions (25 stories) · colour

Series One (9 × 10 mins) 7 Oct–24 Dec 1978 · mostly Sat 7.25pm

Series Two (8 × 30 mins; two stories each) 11 Nov–30 Dec 1979 · Sun 7.15pm

MAIN CAST

Pa Glum · · · · · · · · · · · · · · · Jimmy Edwards
Ron Glum · · · · · · · · · · · · · · · Ian Lavender
Eth · · · · · · · · · · · · · · · · · · Patricia Brake
Ted · · · · · · · · · · · · · · · · · Michael Stainton

CREDITS

writers Frank Muir/Denis Norden · directors John Kaye Cooper, John Reardon · producer Simon Brett

A most wonderful comedy creation, the Glums came to TV precisely 25 years after first being heard on the radio. Back in 1953, Frank Muir and Denis Norden, wireless humour writers par excellence, devised the Glums as an antidote to the nicey-nice BBC radio comedies that then proliferated, like *Meet The Huggetts* (with Jack Warner). Designed to run as a short weekly sketch within their series *Take It From Here*, Muir and Norden's Glums portrayed a much more true-to-life crowd. First there was Pa Glum, a roistering, cantankerous, boorish old soak. (Johnny Speight later admitted that his Alf Garnett invention was part-inspired by Pa Glum.) Then there was his ultra-thick son Ron, a man for whom the word gormless might have been invented. Completing the trio was Ron's fiancée Eth, a dowdy damsel whose horizons were set slightly higher than those of her 'beloved' but who clung to Ron because he represented her only chance of becoming a wife. Pa Glum was still married but Mrs Glum was never heard, except via off-set bumps and muffled shouts. In today's era of TV domination it's easy to forget that radio was *the* medium in the early 1950s and the Glums were its primary comedy outfit: everyone knew their names, discussed their goings-on and celebrated the talents of the three players: Jimmy Edwards, Dick Bentley and June Whitfield. Muir and Norden, for their part, wrote scripts that crackled with great lines and drew out the characters with a masterly touch.

Muir and Norden withdrew from *Take It From Here* in 1959, having completed 12 long series (306 editions); after Barry Took and Marty Feldman scripted 20 more Glums episodes for one final *TIFH* series, the characters were laid to rest in March 1960, re-emerging only briefly, in 1962, in two editions of the BBC TV series *Faces Of Jim*.

Cut to 16 years later: LWT was putting together *Bruce Forsyth's Big Night*, a compendium programme of fun and games to run each Saturday on ITV. Muir and Norden were invited to adapt some of their old Glums radio scripts for short (ten-minute) sketches.

They agreed; Jimmy Edwards was re-hired to play Pa, and Ian Lavender (Pike from *Dad's Army*) and Patricia Brake (Ronnie Barker's daughter in *Porridge* and *Going Straight*) were brought in to play Ron and Eth. A year later, LWT screened a further eight programmes, with two newly adapted old radio scripts enacted per half-hour broadcast, each story being depicted as a flashback, Pa Glum telling his publican/barman friend Ted the latest sorry episode.

Granted, the TV revival never recaptured the glory of the old radio episodes; but at the very least it brought the Glums to a fresh audience and caused new fans to seek out tapes of the earlier model.

Glynis

USA · CBS (DESILU PRODUCTIONS) · SITCOM

14 × 30 mins · b/w

US dates: 25 Sep–18 Dec 1963
UK dates: 1 June–25 Aug 1964 (13 episodes) BBC1 Mon mostly 8pm

MAIN CAST

Glynis Granville · · · · · · · · · · · Glynis Johns
Keith Granville · · · · · · · · · · · · Keith Andes
Chick Rogers · · · · · · · · · · George Matthews

CREDITS

producers Jess Oppenheimer, Edward H Feldman

An American sitcom for the Hollywood-based British film/stage actress Glynis Johns, in which she starred as Glynis Granville, a mystery writer and amateur sleuth. The device of having a wacky wife embroiling her down-to-earth husband (in this case an attorney) in a series of adventures had worked well enough before for producer Jess Oppenheimer with *I Love Lucy*, but despite this, and the resources of Lucille Ball and Desi Arnaz's studio Desilu, the formula didn't click this time around.

The Gnomes Of Dulwich

UK · BBC · SITCOM

6 × 30 mins · b/w

12 May–16 June 1969 · BBC1 Mon 8.50pm

MAIN CAST

Big · · · · · · · · · · · · · · · · · · Terry Scott
Small · · · · · · · · · · · · · · · · · Hugh Lloyd
Old · · · · · · · · · · · · · · · · · · · John Clive
Plastic · · · · · · · · · · · · · · · · · Leon Thau
Dolly · · · · · · · · · · · · · · · Anne de Vigeur
Rita · · · · · · · · · · · · · · · · · · Lynn Dalby

CREDITS

writer Jimmy Perry · producers Sydney Lotterby (5), Graeme Muir (1)

A sitcom with an insanely fascinating concept – like *The Flowerpot Men* for grown-ups, with garden gnomes living a clandestine existence alongside their oblivious human owners.

Storylines revolved around the clashes between the solid stone British gnomes of 25 Telegraph Road, led by Big, Small and Old, and their plastic European counterparts recently introduced to the neighbourhood. Passions ran high between the different factions, with racial and cultural differences at the centre of most of the arguments. These enabled the series to take satirical swipes at the Common Market controversies raging at the time. (The title itself was a play on Harold Wilson's famous 'gnomes of Zurich' description of Swiss bankers.) Elaborate make-up and costumes, along with the well-honed interplay between Scott and Lloyd (see *Hugh And I*), completed the bizarre equation.

Go For It

UK · ITV (LWT) · IMPRESSIONISM

6 × 30 mins · colour

27 May–1 July 1984 · Sun mostly 7.15pm

MAIN CAST

Les Dennis
Dustin Gee
Bobby Davro
Johnny More
Aiden J Harvey
Allan Stewart
Ann Byrne

CREDITS

writer Russel Lane · director Alasdair Macmillan · producer Russel Lane

Six shows in which new or nearly new impressionists performed off-the-peg impersonations stitched together in the usual rapid-fire fashion. All the subjects were current or past but nonetheless famous TV personalities, everyone from Ernie Bilko to Esther Rantzen.

See also *Copy Cats*.

Going, Going, Gone … Free?

UK · BBC · SITCOM

1 × 30 mins · colour

9 July 1975 · BBC1 Wed 9.25pm

MAIN CAST

Jen · · · · · · · · · · · · · · · · · · Pauline Yates
Molly · · · · · · · · · · · · · · · · · Beryl Cooke
Mark · · · · · · · · · · · · · · · · · Peter Duncan
Mrs Dean · · · · · · · · · · · · · · · Madge Ryan
Ralph · · · · · · · · · · · · · · · Geoffrey Palmer

CREDITS

writer Carla Lane · producer Gareth Gwenlan

The fifth in a series of unrelated sitcom pilots shown on consecutive Wednesdays but, following the recent demise of the *Comedy Playhouse* strand, without a generic title. Here, writer Carla Lane was attempting to find another long-running hit to match her massively successful *The Liver Birds*, and for the first time she tapped into the theme of a strong woman coming to terms with life after the breakdown of a relationship. Jen was the divorcee, looking forward to being single again, but feeling her new-found freedom thwarted by her ex-husband, her son, her home help and her mother. Lane explored similar themes later, especially in *Solo* and, to a lesser extent, *Luv* and *Screaming*.

Going My Way

USA · ABC (REVUE PRODUCTIONS/KERRY PRODUCTIONS) · SITCOM

39 × 60 mins · b/w

US dates: 3 Oct 1962–11 Sep 1963

UK dates: 31 Jan 1963–22 June 1963 (6 episodes) BBC Thu 8.25pm then Sat around 7pm

MAIN CAST

Father Chuck O'Malley · · · · · · · · Gene Kelly
Father Fitzgibbon · · · · · · · · · · · Leo G Carroll
Tom Colwell · · · · · · · · · · · · · · Dick York
Mrs Featherstone · · · · · · · · · Nydia Westman

CREDITS

creator Leo McCarey · *producers* Joe Connelly/Bob Mosher

Gene Kelly took the Bing Crosby role, and Leo G Carroll the Barry Fitzgerald part, in this TV adaptation of the famous multi-Oscar-winning 1944 movie of the same name (directed by Leo McCarey) which focused on the clashes between a fresh, progressive young priest (O'Malley) and an ageing, dyed-in-the-wool pastor (Fitzgibbon) at a church in New York. Dick York (shortly to become Darrin in *Bewitched*) was cast as Tom Colwell, a friend of O'Malley, and Nydia Westman played Mrs Featherstone, the beleaguered rectory housekeeper.

The original film led to a 1945 sequel, *The Bells Of St Mary's* – also directed by McCarey, starring Crosby as O'Malley and a multi-Oscar-winner – but the TV series petered out after one season.

Going Places

UK · BBC · SKETCH

4 × 40 mins · b/w

The Army · 13 May 1947 · Tue 8.30pm

Up Spirits – The Navy · 29 May 1947 · Thu 8.30pm

All Clear – The RAF · 18 June 1947 · Wed 8.30pm

Off Parade – The Army · 4 Aug 1947 · Mon 8.30pm

MAIN CAST

various

CREDITS

writers Dennis Castle (1 & 4), Ronnie Hill (2), Ralph Reader/Bill Sutton (3), Peter Dion Titheradge (4) · *producers* Stephen McCormack (1 & 4), Barrie Edgar (2), Douglas Mair/Kenneth Milne-Buckley (3)

A short post-war series featuring service entertainers performing for the TV cameras the revues they were staging for the forces.

Going Straight

UK · BBC · SITCOM

6 × 30 mins · colour

24 Feb–7 Apr 1978 · BBC1 Fri mostly 8.30pm

MAIN CAST

Norman Stanley Fletcher · · · · Ronnie Barker
Lennie Godber · · · · · · · · Richard Beckinsale
Ingrid Fletcher · · · · · · · · · · · Patricia Brake
Raymond Fletcher · · · · · · Nicholas Lyndhurst

OTHER APPEARANCES

Mrs Shirley Chapman · · · · · · Rowena Cooper

CREDITS

writers Dick Clement/Ian La Frenais · *producer* Sydney Lotterby

A sequel to *Porridge* and a slightly disappointing TV exit for Norman Stanley Fletcher. Released on parole from Slade Prison after what he ruefully calculates as being 'three years, eight months and four days' of wasted life, the loveable old lag is determined to 'go straight' – finally breaking his lifelong habit of crime. He's 45 now, and he's had enough of it. Sadly, life on the outside for Fletcher proves no bed of roses: he finds it hard to overcome the public's prejudices against ex-convicts, and this and soaring unemployment makes it doubly hard for him to secure a position of work. Eventually, to the relief of his probation officer Mrs Chapman, Fletcher lands a job as a hotel night-porter, but he has to fight hard to resist the lure of easy, money-making crimes.

Meanwhile, his former cell-mate, young Lennie Godber, has also been released from Slade and so is free to continue his relationship with Fletcher's 26-year-old daughter Ingrid (it had begun in 'Heartbreak Hotel', a quite brilliant second-series episode of *Porridge*). Now a long-distance lorry driver, Godber spends much of his week in the Fletcher household in Muswell Hill, north London, and he and Ingrid eagerly plan their wedding. (It takes place in the final episode.) Fletcher's wife Isobel has departed in the opposite direction, however: she has gone to live with another man, making Fletcher the nominal head of the household and in sole charge of his gauche 17-year-old teenage son Raymond (played by Nicholas Lyndhurst).

While Fletcher's mannerisms and sharp tongue were intact, and Ronnie Barker's performance a model of consistency, somehow the character didn't seem as complete as he had been behind bars, and one series of *Going Straight* was considered enough by the viewing public. The first episode was outstanding, however, showing Fletcher, just released from Slade, travelling by train back home to London in the company of his former nemesis Prison Officer MacKay, a situation in which the two discovered unforeseen similarities and a mutual respect while drinking the buffet-car all but dry.

The Gold Watch Club

UK · BBC · SITCOM

1 × 30 mins · b/w

28 June 1968 · BBC1 Fri 8.20pm

MAIN CAST

Edward Wilkins · · · · · · · · · · · · Dennis Price
Sarah Wilkins · · · · · · · · · · · · · Avice Landon
Brown · · · · · · · · · · · · · · · · · Peter Bayliss
Poulson · · · · · · · · · · · · · · · · Derek Waring
Cartwright · · · · · · · · · · · · · · · · · Bob Todd

CREDITS

writer Richard Waring · *producer* Graeme Muir

A single-episode *Comedy Playhouse* sitcom starring Dennis Price as Edward Wilkins, a man keenly looking forward to his imminent retirement after 40 years with the 'old firm'. He sees it as a time for lie-ins, afternoons at the cinema and general recreation, but – true to sitcom tradition – not everything goes as planned.

The Golden Girls

USA · NBC (WITT-THOMAS-HARRIS PRODUCTIONS/TOUCHSTONE TELEVISION) · SITCOM

178 episodes (176 × 30 mins · 2 × 60 mins) · colour

US dates: 14 Sep 1985–9 May 1992

UK dates: 1 Aug 1986–7 Apr 1993 (176 × 30 mins · 2 × 60 mins) C4 mostly Fri then Wed mostly 10pm

MAIN CAST

Dorothy Zbornak · · · · · · · · · · · · · Bea Arthur
Rose Nylund · · · · · · · · · · · · · · Betty White
Blanche Devereaux · · · · · · Rue McClanahan
Sophia Petrillo · · · · · · · · · · · · · Estelle Getty

OTHER APPEARANCES

Stan Zbornak · · · · · · · · · · · Herbert Edelman
Kate · · · · · · · · · · · · · · · · · Lisa Jane Persky
Miles Webber · · · · · · · · · · · · · Harold Green

CREDITS

creator Susan Harris · *writers* Susan Harris and others · *directors* Jay Sandrich, Matthew Diamond, Paul Bogart, Terry Hughes and others · *executive producers* Paul Junger Witt, Tony Thomas, Susan Harris, Marc Sotkin · *producers* various

A lively sitcom which, unprecedentedly, featured three middle-aged women and one particularly old woman, who supported one another, traded insults and talked about sex almost incessantly. Here, already, was *The Golden Girls* in a nutshell: 'old' people can have fun too, and sex is not the preserve of the young. By emphasising these points, and with its all-woman cast (a first), the series broke many barriers; with its pin-sharp scripts it also was very funny.

Best known for creating and writing the sensational *Soap*, Susan Harris created *The Golden Girls* with a mission in mind: to dispel the hoary old myth that, in her own words, 'when you grow older you are no longer vital, attractive, sexy and smart'. Good casting was critical: Bea Arthur and Rue McClanahan had appeared together in *Maude*, the former as the star; Betty White had enjoyed an important role in **The Mary Tyler Moore Show** before gaining her own starring vehicle **The Betty White Show**, and established stage actress Estelle Getty, much younger than the person she portrayed – a grey wig and an hour in make-up added the 20 years – was the vital fourth member of the team.

The series focused entirely on these four, this being the premise: a widowed Southern 'belle', Blanche, advertises for two new people to share her Miami Beach home, to provide company but, more importantly, to apportion the costs. She soon bumps into the first one, Rose, and says yes to an ad-respondent, Dorothy. Soon after, Dorothy's mother Sophia moves in too, after a fire at the retirement home where she was living. The characters were finely drawn. Blanche's initials spell out BED (her full name is Blanche Elizabeth Devereaux) and, truth is, she thinks of little else, with sex, not sleep, uppermost. She is fastidious about her appearance, fails to see why her advancing years should curb any of nature's appetites and is always, *always* on the look-out for men. (She even attempted to get a date at her husband's funeral.). Blanche works at a museum. Dorothy, a tall, elegant but earthy New Yorker, divorced her husband (Stan) of 38 years after he ran off with an air hostess. (Later, he wants to make amends, but she will have none of it.) They have a grown-up son and daughter (infrequently seen) and Dorothy works as a supply teacher. Of Scandinavian lineage, Rose is the illegitimate daughter of a monk, orphaned at birth and someone for whom the world remains a puzzle. A sweet person, but far from being the quickest, most alert on the planet, she muddles through life at a slower pace than the rest and manages to misunderstand more or less everything said in her presence – despite being, of all things, a grief counsellor. Rose married a man named Charlie Nylund but he died in the act of love-making and she remains widowed. Sophia, Dorothy's widowed mother, aged 80, is of Sicilian descent, and possesses a savagely sharp tongue (she has had a stroke and claims that it destroyed her brain's 'tact' cells) that cuts a swathe through any pretensions the others may harbour.

Witty, intelligent, wry and adult, much of the comedy was drawn from the perpetual verbal oneupwomanship played out between the four, even though they all clearly cared for one another. Sensitive issues were given a good airing too, including death, homosexuality and AIDS, and many episodes contained a 'kitchen-table scene' in which the four sat around and devoured cheesecake while discussing abortion or dodgy dentures or weak bladders or escaping wind or drooping breasts, always to hilarious, and often poignant, effect.

In its first five years *The Golden Girls* finished in the US top ten audience ratings every time. It also won ten Emmy Awards, including two as the Outstanding Comedy Series. After this, however, its success somewhat tailed off, and a poorly conceived NBC scheduling shift in 1991 caused it to lose viewers rapidly. At the end of that year Bea Arthur announced she was planning to quit the series, hence in the final episode Dorothy married Blanche's Uncle Lucas (guest-played by **Police Squad** and *Naked Gun* movie star Leslie Nielsen) and made her departure for Atlanta. At this point *The Golden Girls* came to an end, but its CBS sequel spin-off **The Golden Palace** started the following season. Other spin-offs were **Empty Nest** and the unsuccessful British adaptation **Brighton Belles**. So popular was the US series in Britain, due in no small part to consistent C4 scheduling, that the four Golden Girls were invited over to participate in a sketch, in character, in the 1988 *Royal Variety Show*. (This was screened by BBC1 on 26 November 1988.) They also appeared together in an edition of C4's late-night youth magazine show *The Word*, on 7 February 1992.

The Golden Palace

USA · CBS (WITT-THOMAS-HARRIS PRODUCTIONS/TOUCHSTONE TELEVISION) · SITCOM

25 × 30 mins · colour

US dates: 18 Sep 1992–6 Aug 1993

UK dates: 14 Apr–3 Nov 1993 (24 episodes) C4 Wed 10pm

MAIN CAST

Rose Nylund	Betty White
Blanche Devereaux	Rue McClanahan
Sophia Petrillo	Estelle Getty
Chuy Castillos	Cheech Marin
Roland Wilson	Don Cheadle
Oliver Webb	Billy L Sullivan

CREDITS

creator Susan Harris · *writers* Susan Harris and others · *directors* Terry Hughes and others · *executive producers* Paul Junger Witt, Tony Thomas, Susan Harris, Marc Sotkin · *producers* Jim Vallely, Nina Feinberg

A direct sequel to **The Golden Girls**, with three of the famous four pooling their savings and buying an art deco hotel, the Golden Palace, in Miami Beach. Following Dorothy's marriage and departure, Rose, Blanche and Sophia start their new life as hoteliers only to find that the commercial standing of their business has been greatly exaggerated and only a skeleton staff of three are on hand to run the premises. Unable to recover their investment, the three are forced to work flat out at the hotel to make it pay. Their co-workers are Chuy, a temperamental Mexican chef; young black manager/bellhop/receptionist/handyman/general dogsbody, Roland; and Roland's foster son Oliver, a white, mischievous youngster. What seems like a struggle for all concerned eventually settles into a surrogate family/partnership and the three 'golden girls' find that being thrown back into the work arena gives them a new lease of life.

With *The Golden Girls* stock still comparatively high a spin-off was inevitable, but it never managed to match its predecessor in wit or wisdom. Dorothy's absence was noticeable and the new regulars (including Cheech Marin of 1960s drug comedy duo Cheech And Chong fame) failed to fill the gap. The humour was broadened, ostensibly to play to the characters' comedic strength (Blanche's libido, Rose's lack of intelligence, Sophia's rudeness) but perhaps the formula had been around too long. There was still the odd funny line and cunning comic situation, indeed *The Golden Palace* was still as good as, if not better than, much other fare on offer from the US networks at this time, but it had to compete with its own ancestry as well as the opposition. The doors closed after one season and the 'girls' finally got the retirement they deserved.

Note. The British comedian Alexei Sayle had originally been in the cast, in a character similar to the one played by Cheech Marin, but there was a clear clash of styles between Sayle and the established stars (especially Rue McClanahan, it has been reported) and after just a couple of weeks on the set, before the first episode was taped, he departed the production.

The Golden Sea-Swallow Of Knokke 1976

see WISDOM, Norman

The Goldie Hawn Special

USA · CBS (GEORGE SCHLATTER/RUTLEDGE PRODUCTIONS) · STANDUP/SKETCH

1 × 60 mins · colour

US date: 1 Mar 1978

UK date: 23 Aug 1979 · BBC1 Thu 10.55pm

MAIN CAST

Goldie Hawn
George Burns
John Ritter

CREDITS

writer Digby Wolfe · *director* Don Mischer · *producer* George Schlatter

A comedy special for Goldie Hawn – screened in Britain under the title *Goldie* – who had made a big splash in **Rowan And Martin's Laugh-In** and had subsequently become a successful comedy film actress. Here she was joined by the veteran vaudevillian George Burns and *Three's Company* star John Ritter. The script was written by Digby Wolfe, a Londoner who had been one of the principal writers on *Laugh-In* and so was familiar with her style.

Note. A second special, *Goldie And Liza* (BBC1, 16 March 1980), teamed Hawn with Liza Minnelli and placed the emphasis on music and dance rather than comedy.

Good Advice

USA · CBS (IN FRONT PRODUCTIONS/ITZBINSO LONG PRODUCTIONS/TRISTAR TELEVISION) · SITCOM

19 × 30 mins · colour

US dates: 2 Apr 1993–7 May 1993; 23 May–10 Aug 1994

UK dates: 19 July 1994–17 Oct 1996 (19 episodes) ITV mostly Tue 1.55pm

MAIN CAST

Susan 'Susie' DeRuzza · · · · · · · Shelley Long
Jack Harold · · · · · · · · · · · · · · Treat Williams
Joey DeRuzza · · · · · · · · · · · · Chris McDonald
Michael DeRuzza · · · · · · · · · Ross Malinger
Artie Cohen · · · · · · · · · · · · · George Wyner
Lynn Casey · · · · · · · Kiersten Warren (1993)
Ronnie Cohen · · · · · · · Estelle Harris (1993)
Paige Turner · · · · · · · · · · · Teri Garr (1994)
Sean · · · · · · · · · · · · · · · · · Lightfield Lewis
Henriette Campbell · · · · · Henriette Mantel

CREDITS

creators Danny Jacobson/Norma Safford Vela · *writers* Danny Jacobson/Norma Safford Vela and others · *directors* Barnet Kellman and others · *executive producer* Danny Jacobson · *producers* Bruce Chevillat and others

A post-*Cheers* sitcom for Shelley Long. Kelsey Grammer would soon be relaunched in the wonderful *Frasier* but his one-time screen girlfriend had no such good fortune: *Good Advice* got off to a stumbling start, tripped half-way through and then fell over completely.

In a character she herself conceived, Long starred as Susan 'Susie' DeRuzza PhD, a successful marriage therapist and the author of a best-selling book on the subject, *Giving And Forgiving*. But – like Frasier Crane, the psychiatrist who could help others but needed help himself – the one person in *Good Advice* who needed marriage therapy was Susie herself: upon returning from a six-week author promotional tour she discovered her husband of 11 years, Joey, in the act of an adulterous affair and kicked him out, being left to take care of their nine-year-old son Michael.

Regularly seen in *Good Advice* were Jack Harold, a womanising, never-married divorce lawyer with whom Susie shared her Los Angeles office suite; Artie Cohen, a balding Jewish osteopath who also shared the suite (which he owned) and who tended to father Susie; office odd-job boy Sean (actually the

son of wealthy parents, who was seeking experience in 'the real world'); receptionist Lynn Casey (replaced in later episodes by Ronnie Cohen, Artie's mother, and then by Paige Turner, Susie's elder sister); and Henriette Campbell, Susie's housekeeper.

Good Advice suffered plenty of problems. Its launch was delayed from September 1992 to April 1993, first because Shelley Long was in poor health and then because the show's concept was changed. After just a handful of episodes it came off air to be altered again and relaunched in September 1993, but Long's health difficulties meant that it did not return for a full year, until May 1994. It then staggered through to August, with CBS giving it a new day and time slot, before it was cancelled.

Good Evening

see *Beryl Reid Says Good Evening*

Good Girl

UK · ITV (YORKSHIRE) · SITCOM

6 × 60 mins · colour

27 July–31 Aug 1974 · Sat 9.15pm

MAIN CAST

Angie Botley · · · · · · · · · · · · · · · Julia Foster
Eustace Morrow · · · · · · · · · Peter Barkworth
Mrs Morrow · · · · · · · · · · · · · Joan Hickson
Colin Peale · · · · · · · · · · · · · Peter Bowles
Henry Nutting · · · · · · · · · · · · Brian Deacon
Cyril Botley · · · · · · · · · · · · · Peter Hughes
Gwen Botley · · · · · · · · · · · · Brenda Cowling

CREDITS

writer Philip Mackie · *directors* David Cunliffe (4), Christopher Hodson (2) · *executive producer* Peter Willes

Six hour-length comedies starring Julia Foster as Angie Botley, a woman whose principal ambition in life is to please and make all those around her happy – do-gooding skills instilled in her by her parents, Cyril and the man-hating Gwen. The only trouble is, these traits tend to create chaos instead of happiness. In the first episode Angie is working as a masseuse in a (wholesome) sauna, where she meets the larger-than-life TV personality Eustace Morrow. Despite the protestations of *his* overbearing mother, Eustace takes a fancy to Angie, offers her a job as his secretary and establishes the premise for the remainder of the series, by the end of which marriage was in the air.

A Good Idea – Son!

see BYGRAVES, Max

The Good Life   USA

USA · NBC (SCREEN GEMS/HUMBLE/LORIMAR) · SITCOM

15 × 30 mins · colour

US dates: 23 Aug 1971–8 Jan 1972
UK dates: 5 Apr–16 Sep 1974 (15 episodes)
BBC1 Fri 2.20pm then Mon 1.50pm

MAIN CAST

Albert Miller · · · · · · · · · · · · · Larry Hagman
Jane Miller · · · · · · · · · · · · · · Donna Mills
Charles Dutton · · · · · · · · · · · David Wayne
Grace Dutton · · · · · · · · · · · Kate Reed (pilot);
· · · · · · · · · · · · Hermione Baddeley (series)
Nick Dutton · · · · · · · · · · · · Danny Goldman

CREDITS

director/producer Claudio Guzman · *executive producer* Lee Rich

Bored with their middle-class existence and keen to shrug off the expense of everyday living, Albert and Jane Miller decide to take on a whole new direction, passing themselves off to a millionaire industrialist, Charles Dutton, as an experienced butler/maid duo.

Another entry in the 'square pegs in round holes' sitcom formula, the humour here arose from the Millers' attempts to bluff their way around high society and their struggle to retain a servile attitude to their employer, as if they were born to be in service. Dutton's son Nick immediately saw through the charade but took a liking to the couple and was their saviour during tricky moments.

An unremarkable series, but executive producer Lee Rich went on to employ his two lead actors more prestigiously in later years, casting Hagman in his supersoap *Dallas* and Mills in its spin-off *Knots Landing*.

The Good Life   UK

UK · BBC · SITCOM

30 episodes (29 × 30 mins · 1 × 45 mins) · colour

Series One (7) 4 Apr–16 May 1975 · BBC1 Fri 8.30pm
Series Two (7) 5 Dec 1975–23 Jan 1976 · BBC1 Fri 8.30pm
Series Three (7) 10 Sep–22 Oct 1976 · BBC1 Fri 8.30pm
Series Four (7) 10 Apr–22 May 1977 · BBC1 Sun 8.05pm
Special (30 mins) 26 Dec 1977 · BBC1 Mon 7.35pm
Special (45 mins) 10 June 1978 · BBC1 Sat 7.40pm

MAIN CAST

Tom Good · · · · · · · · · · · · · · Richard Briers
Barbara Good · · · · · · · · · · · Felicity Kendal
Jerry Leadbetter · · · · · · · · · · Paul Eddington
Margo Leadbetter · · · · · · · · Penelope Keith

OTHER APPEARANCES

Sir · · · · · · · · · · · · · · · · · · · Reginald Marsh

CREDITS

writers John Esmonde/Bob Larbey · *producer* John Howard Davies

If *Till Death Us Do Part* and *Steptoe And Son* represent the finest examples of British working-class comedy, then *The Good Life* is the zenith of its middle-class humour.

A brilliant idea, clever scripts and first-rate acting from the four main players ensured the show high ratings and engendered deep affection in its viewers.

The series had an irresistible premise: a middle-class suburban couple, Tom and Barbara Good, decide to go back to the land and turn their Surbiton home into a self-sufficient farm-cum-allotment, growing their own food, keeping animals and making their own tools and equipment. This creates friction with their neighbours, especially the Leadbetters, located next door, prime examples of the gin-and-tonic set. In addition to a wealth of good storylines, it was the interplay between the two couples that really gave the show its appeal. It would have been easy for the writers to use Margo's snobbery and domination of her husband to simply set up the Leadbetters in the role of villains, constantly at odds with their idealistic neighbours, but the authors were more clever than this and instead drew a real affection between the couples.

Sitcom stalwart Richard Briers was cast as Tom Good, an irrepressibly chirpy man who, on his fortieth birthday, quits 'the rat race' to start afresh and invest in his back garden. Felicity Kendal played his wife Barbara, initially hesitant over the plan but who, when committed, mucks in with gusto. Tom and Barbara, it is abundantly clear, enjoy a great marriage, being fully attuned to one another's needs and desires. Paul Eddington was cast as Jerry Leadbetter, an executive at a company which designs plastic toys for cereal packets (Tom had been one of the designers of said items). Penelope Keith played his wife, Margo, a terrible snob on the surface but full of interesting aspects underneath. Margo and Jerry, whose marriage is apparently more conventional yet far less trusting and deep, have serious misgivings about the Goods' self-sufficiency venture, but as the series progresses they began to treat their neighbours with tolerance and warmth, and even a slight envy and a protectiveness bordering on the parental.

All the characters developed over the series but none more than Margo. In the initial episodes she was only a peripheral figure, but then, when one episode was running short, the writers added a filler scene showing her speaking on the telephone. Allowed more screen time than usual, Penelope Keith was able to expand the role and demonstrate the character's full potential to the writers. As the public became fascinated by Margo's intense snobbery, Esmonde and Larbey gave her bigger and bigger roles, effecting a transition from a two-dimensional snob to three-dimensional complex human being. Margo quickly established Penelope Keith as a top flight comedy actress – indeed, all four players enriched their worth in *The Good Life* and became the stars of subsequent sitcoms.

The producer of *The Good Life*, John Howard Davies, was quick to acknowledge the influence of playwright Alan Ayckbourn on the production. Davies had attended school with Ayckbourn and, being an admirer of his style, saw similarities in Esmond and Larbey's script which led him to cast in kind. All four leads were appearing in Alan Ayckbourn stage productions at the time: Kendal and Keith in *The Norman Conquests*, and Eddington in *Absurd Person Singular*, a production that Briers had only just left. (Briers and Keith later starred in Thames TV's version of *The Norman Conquests*, screened from 5 October to 19 October 1977.) The producer's hunch paid off and the cast's theatrical background stood them in good stead for the dialogue-heavy scripts, which they performed in a style classier than most sitcoms. After 28 regular episodes *The Good Life* bowed out with two specials: a 1977 Christmas offering and a prestigious royal performance on 10 June 1978. This latter screening also featured Richard Waring's warm-up for the show and shots of the audience, among whom was one of the show's most dedicated fans, the Queen.

Stylish and professional though the series was, its middle-class setting and somewhat benign plots did single it out for criticism, especially within the harsher 'alternative comedy' school that blazed on to TV in the early 1980s. In one episode of *The Young Ones* the psychopathic Vyvyan (Adrian Edmondson), in a rare moment of seriousness, reflected upon *The Good Life*, lamenting that such a neat idea, and one which in different hands could have produced a challenging comedy about ecological concerns, was handled in such an overbearingly twee way. This observation didn't prevent him from acknowledging the strong sex appeal of Felicity Kendal as Barbara Good, however. Most of the males in Britain were of a like mind on this one.

Note. When the series was syndicated in the USA its title was changed to *Good Neighbors* to avoid confusion with the earlier American sitcom *The Good Life* (see previous entry).

Good Luck Sir, You've Got A Lucky Face

UK · BBC · SITCOM

1 × 25 mins · b/w

31 Jan 1964 · Fri 7.35pm

MAIN CAST

Gomorrah Weevil · · · · · · · · · · Graham Stark
Harold Harbinger · · · · · · · · · · Derek Francis
Jessop · · · · · · · · · · · · · · · · Frank Thornton
Mrs Harbinger · · · · · · · · · · · · Thelma Ruby
Lord Fenwick · · · · · · · · · · · · Geoffrey Dunn

CREDITS

writer Marty Feldman · producer Dennis Main Wilson

A single-episode *Comedy Playhouse* pilot depicting one Gomorrah Weevil – another strange name from the bizarre imagination of writer Marty Feldman. Weevil is a shabby match-seller, a rogue, a liar and a cheat, who proves more than a match for extortionist slum landlord Harold Harbinger.

Good Night And God Bless

UK · ITV (CENTRAL) · SITCOM

6 × 30 mins · colour

12 Apr–17 May 1983 · Tue 8.30pm

MAIN CAST

Ronnie · · · · · · · · · · · · · · · Donald Churchill
Celia · Judy Loe
Geoffrey · · · · · · · · · · · · · · · James Cossins
Harry · · · · · · · · · · · · · · · · · Nick Stringer
Debbie · · · · · · · · · · · · · · · · Tracey Perry
Audrey · · · · · · · · · · · · · · · Rowena Cooper

CREDITS

writers Donald Churchill/Joe McGrath · director/producer Alan Dossor · executive producer Joe McGrath

The apparently jovial cove Ronnie Kemp used to be a standup comic. Now he's the *gagmeister* fronting a big-money TV quiz-show *Keeping Up With The Jones's*. Ronnie's very much a working-class hero, having made the big time from humble beginnings, and he's much loved by his audience for his loud clothes, wide smile, fulsome head of hair and the way he quips with his screen assistant, the lovely Debbie.

But while, on camera, his jokes are loved, off camera he's considered a bit of a joke himself. Ronnie's mean, worrisome, ill-tempered and wears a wig, and his private life is disordered: he is married to Celia, a beauty half his age which means that he is the same age as his new father-in-law, Geoffrey. Both Celia and Geoffrey loathe *Keeping Up With The Jones's*. Worse, by claiming alimony, his former wife Audrey still manages to drain him financially.

Good Night And God Bless was co-written by its star, the actor and playwright Donald Churchill, with its executive producer Joe McGrath, whose film and TV production credentials in the world of British comedy are probably second to none.

Good Stuff Comedy

UK · ITV (CARLTON/LONDON NEWS NETWORK) · STANDUP

4 × 30 mins · colour

29 May–19 June 1997 · Thu 11.10pm

HOSTS

Rowland Rivron
Davina McCall

CREDITS

writers various · *directors* Matthew Thompson, James Strong · *executive producer* Simon Port · *producer* Sandie Kirk

Good Stuff was an early-evening arts and entertainment preview show for the London region made for Carlton by the London News Network. This late-night comedy offshoot featured the series' presenters Rivron and McCall introducing live acts from the 'Good Stuff Comedy Club'. Each comic was given from five to ten minutes to present their material and many established and budding stars of the circuit were featured, including Tommy Tiernan, Ricky Grover, Matt Welcome, John Lenahan, Joe Enright, John Mann, Mark Hurst, Ian Stone, Junior Simpson, Norman Lovett, Matthew Hardy, Graham Norton, Rudy Lickwood and Keith Dover. The routines were interspersed with short interview extracts in which the comics discussed their work.

A simple premise, similar to and no better or worse than the many other 'live' standup presentations proliferating at this time. As with all such series, its worth, as well as vital exposure for new comics, was as an archive for the future.

Goodbye Again

UK · ITV (ATV/ITC) · SKETCH

4 × 60 mins · b/w

18 Aug 1968 · Sun 9pm

24 Aug 1968 · Sat 9.30pm

14 Sep 1968 · Sat 9.30pm

3 Aug 1969 · Sun 10.20pm

MAIN CAST

Peter Cook
Dudley Moore

CREDITS

writers Peter Cook/Dudley Moore · *director* Stan Harris (show 4) · *executive producer* Bill Ward · *producers* Shaun O'Riordan (shows 1–3), Gary Smith/Dwight Hemion (show 4)

The success of *Not Only ... But Also* had made Peter Cook and Dudley Moore national comic heroes, more even than *Beyond The Fringe* before it, although they were reluctant to make too many series lest the attraction wear thin. But while they refused the relatively generous offers made to them by the BBC, they could not shy away from the definitely lucrative sums being offered them by Lew Grade, the boss of ATV. More so than any other ITV franchise executive, Grade understood the US TV market and always had one eye on an American sale. His offer to Cook and Moore was not only financially attractive but it promised them network American exposure and a bigger production budget. They accepted, agreeing to make some specials under the title *Goodbye Again*,

screened in the USA in 1969 under the *Kraft Music Hall Presents ...* banner.

Four programmes were recorded, three in April/May 1968 and the fourth a year later. But as with so many such transferrals across the channel – be they by a single star, a double-act or even an entire show – the special chemistry of the BBC shows disappeared en route to ITV. *Goodbye Again* was no *NO ... BA*, and Cook and Moore quickly knew so: it is said that they were disappointed by what was offered by ATV, and the hour-length programmes (albeit with commercials) encouraged Cook, as the principal sketch writer, to relax the brilliant economy of his BBC work. On the positive side, the bigger budget and the US angle enabled Cook and Moore to attract musical guests of a more contemporary nature (Ike and Tina Turner, Donovan, Traffic and Julie Driscoll with the Brian Auger Trinity) while comedic support came from the likes of Rodney Bewes, John Wells, Brian Murphy, John Cleese and, in the fourth show (which had American producers and featured the American singer, Mel Tormé), Anne Bancroft.

Oddly, considering the money invested, and the televisual lure of Cook and Moore, the first two programmes were unannounced in the British TV listings of the time, the shows being dropped into the schedule with little notice during the ITV technicians dispute of the period. This scarcely helped to draw in the viewers, and further underlined the lack-lustre state of the entire *Goodbye Again* project.

Goodbye Mr Kent

UK · BBC · SITCOM

7 × 30 mins · colour

28 Jan–11 Mar 1982 · BBC1 Thu 8.30pm

MAIN CAST

Travis Kent · · · · · · · · · · · · · Richard Briers
Victoria Jones · · · · · · · · · · · Hannah Gordon
Lucy Jones · · · · · · · · · · · · · · · Talla Hayes

CREDITS

writer Peter Vincent/Peter Robinson · *producer* Gareth Gwenlan

With her husband having left her, hard-working divorcee Victoria Jones is forced to take in a lodger to help maintain herself and her daughter Lucy in the financial circumstances to which they are accustomed. But she gets more than she has bargained for in the shape of Travis Kent, a dishevelled journalist and hopeless but optimistic flounderer always convinced that his next break will be 'the big one'. Kent sees Victoria's place as an ideal base and tries to ingratiate himself by turning on what he believes to be his irresistible charm; Victoria finds it all too resistible, but does consider

his character oddly compelling. Thus the situation was set for a domestic comedy with an underlying suggestion of potential romance.

Writers Vincent and Robinson freely admitted that they based the character of Travis on the slobbish Oscar Madison from Neil Simon's *The Odd Couple*. They had reworked the script of that movie for a German screening (Robinson often adapted scripts and sketches for German TV) and were so taken by Oscar that they felt inspired to write about a similarly scruffy and optimistic yet constantly thwarted character. Briers found plenty to get his teeth into with the role and his co-star Hannah Gordon was popular in the genre, but, oddly, this couple survived for only one series.

The Goodies

UK · BBC · *ITV (LWT) · FARCE/SITCOM

77 episodes (73 × 30 mins · 1 × 50 mins · 1 × 45 mins · 1 × 25 mins · 1 × short special) · colour

Series One (7) 8 Nov–20 Dec 1970 · BBC2 Sun around 10pm

Series Two (13) 1 Oct 1971–14 Jan 1972 · BBC2 Fri mostly 10.10pm

Special (30 mins) *Montreux 72 – Kitten Kong*** 9 Apr 1972 · BBC2 Sun 10.05pm

Special (25 mins) *A Collection Of Goodies* 24 Sep 1972 · BBC2 Sun 8.15pm

Short special · part of *Christmas Night With The Stars* 25 Dec 1972 · BBC1 Mon 6.55pm

Series Three (6) 4 Feb–11 Mar 1973 · BBC2 Sun 8.15pm

Special (30 mins) *Superstar* 7 July 1973 · BBC2 Sat 9.50pm

Series Four (6) 1 Dec 1973–12 Jan 1974 · BBC2 Sat 8pm then 6.45pm

Special (45 mins) *The Goodies And The Beanstalk* 24 Dec 1973 · BBC2 Mon 5.15pm

Series Five (13) 10 Feb–5 May 1975 · BBC2 Mon 9pm

Special (50 mins) *Goodies Rule – OK?* 21 Dec 1975 · BBC2 Sun 7.25pm

Series Six (7) 21 Sep–2 Nov 1976 · BBC2 Tue 9pm

Series Seven (6) 1 Nov–22 Dec 1977 · BBC2 Tue 9pm

Series Eight (6) 14 Jan–18 Feb 1980 · BBC2 Mon 8.10pm

*Special (30 mins) *Snow White 2* 27 Dec 1981 · ITV Sun 7.15pm

*Series Nine (6) 9 Jan–13 Feb 1982 · ITV Sat 6.45pm

MAIN CAST

Tim Brooke-Taylor
Graeme Garden
Bill Oddie

CREDITS

writers Tim Brooke-Taylor/Graeme Garden/Bill Oddie** (64), Graeme Garden/Bill Oddie (13) · *film director* Jim Franklin (series 1 & 2 & special 1) · *director* Bob Spiers (series 7–9 & special 7) · *producers* John Howard Davies (series 1 & 2 &

special 1), Jim Franklin (series 3–8 & specials 2–6), Bob Spiers (special 7 & series 9)

By the second series of **Broaden Your Mind**, the Goodies trio of Brooke-Taylor, Garden and Oddie were assembled and determined to continue working together, focusing on the filmed visual comedy they had so enjoyed writing and performing in that earlier series. They approached the BBC's Head of TV Comedy, Michael Mills, with an idea based on 'an agency of three blokes, who do anything, any time' and Mills, despite receiving many similar outlines, had enough faith in the three comics to let them proceed. The resulting series, which had the working title *Narrow Your Mind* to follow its predecessor, was called *The Goodies* and it became a landmark in British comedy.

Put simply, *The Goodies* was a live-action version of a typical Warner Bros cartoon, replete with speeded-up footage, film trickery and violent slapstick. The characters bore the same names as the players and were caricature exaggerations of their real selves, hence Tim was the respectable establishment figure, an effete man who grew into a manic royalist; Graeme was the scatty, back-room boffin, the inventor of all manner of weird devices; and Bill was an aggressive, earthy, hairy individual who eventually tended towards environmentalism, socialism and feminism. Each week the three climbed aboard and promptly fell off their customised bicycle for three (the 'Trandem') before remounting to pedal off to their task.

Initially there was a traditional sitcom element to the shows, the characters starting off each episode in their huge all-encompassing office suite, where they would be employed by someone to undertake a difficult task. Later, though, the format became diffused and in the series' classic period, 1973–76, it was a joyous, unrestrained, lightly satirical festival of visual humour, with models, special effects, explosions, giant props and camera tricks combining to produce a variety of fast-paced wild antics rarely seen since the heyday of the slapstick silent movies. The plots always veered towards the surreal and very often storylines lurched off-course to explore unrelated areas, just to get laughs. And most of the time it worked. Most editions also included one or a few mock TV advertisements, which delightfully sent up the genre.

There was also a musical element to the shows, Bill Oddie providing songs or instrumental routines to fit in with the capers. This led to a long-lasting spin-off success for the team, with successful album releases and high-ranking chart entries for their singles 'The Inbetweenies', 'Funky Gibbon', 'Black Pudding Bertha', 'Nappy Love' and 'Make A Daft Noise For Christmas'. (Several such songs had first been performed by Oddie in

the BBC radio sketch comedy show *I'm Sorry, I'll Read That Again*, in which all three Goodies appeared.) Like the **Monty Python** team, the Goodies also published books that re-created their style of humour in print form. Successful though they were, however, critics never accorded the Goodies the same degree of cultural standing as the Pythons, probably considering their corny jokes and blatant slapstick less worthy than the Pythons' verbal artistry. If this snub bothered the Goodies they did not show it, and in one famous sequence they even featured John Cleese in a cameo role, as a genie taunting them with the jibe 'Kids' show!'. Such celebrity appearances were a feature of *The Goodies*, editions of which often spoofed other programmes and so were tailor-made for cameos, with all manner of unlikely TV personalities turning up, including presenters Michael Aspel, Sue Lawley, Michael Barrett, Raymond Baxter, McDonald Hobley, David Dimbleby, and Terry Wogan, DJs Tony Blackburn and John Peel, soccer commentator Kenneth Wolstenholme, quizmaster Magnus Magnusson, astronomer Patrick Moore and, perhaps most memorably of all, the rugby league commentator Eddie Waring.

In 1981 *The Goodies* switched from the BBC to ITV and presented a Christmas special, *Snow White 2* (which crossed the *Snow White* story with *Star Wars*), and the following month they launched a series on the commercial channel. Although it had some good moments – especially a clever parody of the paranormal investigation series *The Mysterious World Of Arthur C Clarke*, in which the Goodies searched for the mythical Arthur C Clarke – this was a disappointing venture, lacking the undisciplined anarchy that had characterised their finest BBC episodes. After this, the trio decided to call it a day.

During the BBC run, *The Goodies* twice won the Silver Rose of Montreux (*Kitten Kong*, the 1972 winner, was a partial remake of a second series episode which had first aired on 12 November 1971), and the Goodies also presented a programme about the festival, *The Golden Rose* (BBC1, 10 May 1975). The Goodies also appeared on *Top Of The Pops* (BBC1, various dates), *Crackerjack* (BBC1, 24 December 1974), *Seaside Special* (BBC1, 19 June 1976) and in the 1976 fund-raiser *A Poke In The Eye (With A Sharp Stick)* (**The Amnesty Galas**). They further performed a short, self-contained comedy segment in each programme of the 13-week BBC1 series *Engelbert With The Young Generation*, starring the singer Humperdinck (9 January–2 April 1972).

**Note. The credits for most editions read 'Written by Graeme Garden and Bill Oddie, with Tim Brooke-Taylor', but, owing to other

professional commitments, Brooke-Taylor was unable to contribute a great deal. Eventually, his name was dropped from the writing credits.

See also *The Twenty-First Century Show*.

Goodnight Sweetheart

UK · BBC (ALOMO PRODUCTIONS) · SITCOM

37 × 30 mins · colour

Series One (6) 18 Nov–23 Dec 1993 · BBC1 Thu 8.30pm

Series Two (10) 20 Feb–1 May 1995 · BBC1 Mon 8.30pm

Series Three (10) 1 Jan–4 Mar 1996 · BBC1 Mon 8.30pm

Series Four (11) 3 Mar–20 May 1997 · BBC1 Mon then Tue 8.30pm

MAIN CAST

Gary Sparrow	Nicholas Lyndhurst
Yvonne Sparrow	Michelle Holmes (series 1–3); Emma Amos (series 4)
Phoebe Bamford	Dervla Kirwan (series 1–3); Elizabeth Carling (series 4)
Ron Wheatcroft	Victor McGuire
PC Reg Deadman	Christopher Ettridge
Eric Bamford	David Ryall (series 1)
Mrs Bloss	Yvonne D'Alpra (series 2 & 3)

CREDITS

creators Laurence Marks/Maurice Gran · *writers* Laurence Marks/Maurice Gran (15), Gary Lawson/John Phelps (8), Paul Makin (7), Geoff Rowley (4), Sam Lawrence (3) · *directors* Robin Nash (26), Terry Kinane (11) · *executive producers* Allan McKeown, Claire Hinson · *producer* John Bartlett

When interviewed by *Radio Times* at the time of **Get Back**, writers Marks and Gran were asked about their next project. Gran replied, 'It's a love story between a guy of 30 and a woman of 80 who might be dead.' Although this seemed flippant it was a perfectly accurate answer. With *Goodnight Sweetheart*, the writers crossed the period-piece flavour of their **Shine On Harvey Moon** with the contemporary domestic setting of their drama *Love Hurts* (BBC1, 1992–94), a combination achieved by the simple expediency of introducing time-travel into the mix.

Nicholas Lyndhurst was cast as Gary Sparrow, a TV repairman whose marriage to Yvonne is in the doldrums. Out in London looking for a business address one day, Gary wanders down an alley, Duckett's Passage, and finds himself – though of course he does not immediately realise it – magically transported to the London of 1940. In a street-corner pub, which at first he mistakes for a 1940s themed hostelry, he meets Phoebe, the landlord's attractive daughter, and they are immediately smitten with one another. Returning through the same alley brings Gary back to the present, and he discovers that he can enter 1940s London the same way at any time. So begins his double life.

As the weeks pass, Gary begins a fiery 'past' romance with Phoebe (who, as her father Eric constantly reminds her, is engaged, albeit reluctantly, to a serviceman fighting overseas) while somehow managing to hold his 'present' marriage together. Yvonne knows nothing of her husband's time-traversing escapades but she is aware that his lame excuses to cover his absences mean that something 'funny' is going on. The only person in whom Gary confides his secret is his best friend Ron, who becomes increasingly embroiled in the expanding tissue of lies that Gary creates to allay his wife's fears. Ron, a printer by trade, spots the financial opportunities of Gary's time-travelling and gets him to acquire records and other items worth big money to collectors in the 1990s. In return for these favours, Ron forges 1940s papers so that Gary can move about in wartime London without suspicion. Back in the past, Gary weaves a similar web of lies to explain away the tell-tale idiosyncrasies and anachronisms that mark him out, to them, as an odd fish. Firstly he convinces Phoebe that he is working undercover for the government, a fib that neatly accounts for many anomalies, including his non-enrolment in the forces and his knowledge of forthcoming wartime events. Secondly, he claims to have spent a long time in the USA, so that whenever he accidentally produces modern-day gadgets and devices, years ahead of their time, he claims that they are American, using the country like a magical land where such advanced inventions are commonplace. Usually this explanation satisfies the somewhat naïve bar-drinkers but if a particular device, like a Walkman, is obviously revolutionary, Gary falls back on excuse one, claiming that it is a top-secret prototype. At the same time, Gary makes a great impression as an entertainer, playing and singing songs from the 1960s and beyond (especially those written by the Beatles) and claiming them as his own.

As the series progressed, Gary becomes increasingly obsessed with his life in the past and manages to cover his frequent absences by creating a successful 1940s memorabilia business, which purportedly sends him away on many trips. At home, Gary's marriage to Yvonne has survived despite all the problems. At various times Gary debates whether to give up one of his lifestyles and commit himself completely to the other, but the lure of living in both worlds is too strong. Eventually, to complicate matters still further, both the women in his life fall pregnant and Gary has to deal with fatherhood in two different time zones.

Yet another Marks and Gran creation named after a song title (following *Shine On Harvey Moon*, **Roll Over Beethoven**, *Love Hurts* and *Get Back*), *Goodnight Sweetheart* proved both durable and funny, providing the

writers with another monster hit, unusual not only for its fantasy premise but for the fact that its lead character was a practising adulterer. The casting of the likeable Nicholas Lyndhurst was an important factor in the public's acceptance of, and empathy with, such a philanderer. Dervla Kirwan made a bewitching 1940s beauty and Victor McGuire was consistently good as Gary's grumbling but loyal friend, Ron. But Michelle Holmes, as Gary's modern-day wife Yvonne, had the toughest and most thankless role – she had to be convincing as a character pleasant enough for a nice guy like Gary to marry and stay with, yet one who couldn't be too nice lest the audience be angry with Gary for being adulterous.

Michelle Holmes and Dervla Kirwan both left after the third series and were replaced by Emma Amos and Elizabeth Carling. The viewing figures did not suffer, however, and some nine million people tuned in to see Gary become a fully fledged bigamist in the fourth series, when he married Phoebe. At the time of writing, a fifth series was set to air in early 1998.

The Goon Show

Goonreel

see MILLIGAN, Spike

The Gordon Peters Show

UK · BBC · SITCOM

6 × 30 mins · colour

Pilot *The Birthday* 25 Jan 1973 · BBC1 Thu 8pm

One series (5) 25 Apr–23 May 1973 · BBC1 Wed 7.30pm

MAIN CAST

Gordon · · · · · · · · · · · · · · · · Gordon Peters
Mrs M · · · · · · · · · · Barbara Mitchell (series)

OTHER APPEARANCES (VARIOUS ROLES)
Bill Pertwee
Frank Thornton
Gorden Kaye
Mary Miller
Ritchie Stewart

CREDITS

writer Eric Davidson · *director* Brian Jones · *producer* Dennis Main Wilson

Gordon Peters, an actor who spent some time touring northern clubs as a standup comic, worked for many years before getting his break in this BBC sitcom about a bewildered, bespectacled loner at odds with the world. It sprang from a *Comedy Playhouse* pilot, titled *The Birthday*, which set the scene when Gordon threw a party and had to rent some young women when no one else turned up.

Actually, a number of familiar TV faces showed up during the series – those named above and, appearing once apiece, Derek Deadman, Henry McGee, John Junkin, Melvyn

Hayes, Robert Keegan, Tony Booth, Tony Selby and Victor Maddern.

The Governor And J J

USA · CBS (TALENT ASSOCIATES/NORTON SIMON) · SITCOM

39 × 30 mins · colour

US dates: 23 Sep 1969–30 Dec 1970

UK dates: 10 Apr 1973–19 June 1974 (26 episodes) BBC1 Tue 3.45pm then Wed 2.20pm

MAIN CAST

Governor William Drinkwater · · · · Dan Dailey
Jennifer Jo ('J J') Drinkwater · · · · · · · · · · · ·
· Julie Sommars
George Callison · · · · · · · · · · James Callahan
Maggie McLeod · · · · · · · · · · · Neva Patterson
Sara Andrews · · · · · · · · · · · · · Nora Marlowe

CREDITS

director Leonard Stern · *producer* Leonard Stern, Arne Sultan

Political shenanigans with experienced Hollywood actor Dan Dailey as US Governor William Drinkwater. He is a widower who meets resistance when he decides to make his 23-year-old daughter Jennifer Jo – nicknamed J J – his 'first lady', the director and organiser of his social-political events and trips. Some of the resistance comes from J J herself who, on the whole, would rather be pursuing her chosen career as a zoo worker. A mild satire, easily forgotten.

Grace And Favour

UK · BBC · SITCOM

12 × 30 mins · colour

Series One (6) 10 Jan–14 Feb 1992 · BBC1 Fri 8pm

Series Two (6) 4 Jan–8 Feb 1993 · BBC1 Mon 8pm

MAIN CAST

Mrs Slocombe · · · · · · · · · · · Mollie Sugden
Captain Stephen Peacock RASC (Ex) · · · · · ·
· Frank Thornton
Mr Humphries · · · · · · · · · · · · · · John Inman
Miss Brahms · · · · · · · · · · · Wendy Richard
Mr Cuthbert Rumbold · · · · · · Nicholas Smith
Jessica Lovelock · · · · · · · · · Joanne Heywood
Maurice Moulterd · · · · · · · · · · · Billy Burden
Mavis Moulterd · · · · · · · · · · · Fleur Bennett
Miss Prescott · · · · · · · · · · · Shirley Cheriton
Mr Thorpe · · · · · · · · · · · · · · Michael Bilton

CREDITS

writers Jeremy Lloyd/David Croft · *director/ producer* Mike Stephens

Seven years after the final episode of **Are You Being Served?** five of the characters returned in this follow-up series. In the opening episode, the staff of Grace Brothers department store are appalled to discover that, in his will, the late 'Young' Mr Grace bequeathed all of his money to a charity for fallen women, and invested the staff's pension fund by buying an old house, Millstone

Manor. The penniless quintet of Slocombe, Peacock, Humphries, Brahms and Rumbold decide to move in to the manor house and open it up as a hotel; thus they remain together but in a completely different environment.

The location aside, however, everything was much as before, with double entendres, mass confusions, broad slapstick and a good re-airing of old catchphrases being paramount: Mr Humphries gaily minced about hollering 'I'm free!' and Mrs Slocombe once again held forth on the condition of her pussy. The first series concentrated on the alteration of the manor house (actually Chavenage House in Gloucestershire) as a hotel, the second showed the staff dealing with guests. One of these, it turned out, was Cecil Slocombe (played by Donald Morley), Mrs Slocombe's husband whom she had not seen since he had 'popped out to the supermarket' 42 years earlier.

Writers Lloyd and Croft unashamedly kept the humour in the 1970s vein of high-jinks and low farce, which made *Grace And Favour* as different in style to the hotel-based classic *Fawlty Towers* as a London King's Cross B&B was to Singapore's Raffles. The term Grace and Favour traditionally applies to residences that the sovereign offers rent-free to those persons whom he or she wishes to repay for outstanding service.

Grace Under Fire

USA · ABC (THE CARSEY-WERNER COMPANY) · SITCOM

105 × 30 mins (to 31/12/97 · continuing into 1998) · colour

US dates: 29 Sep 1993 to date

UK dates: 27 Sep 1994–25 Sep 1996 (74 episodes) BBC2 Wed 9pm then daily 12 midnight

MAIN CAST

Grace Kelly	Brett Butler
Russell Norton	Dave Thomas
Wade Swobada	Casey Sander
Elizabeth 'Libby' Kelly	Kaitlin Cullum
Quentin Kelly	Jon Paul Steuer
Patrick Kelly	Dylan Sprouse/Cole Sprouse
Nadine Swobada	Julia White
Dougie	Walter Olkewicz
Vic	Dave Florek
Bill Davis	Charles Hallahan (1993–94)
John Shirley	Paul Dooley (1994–95)
Rick Bradshaw	Alan Autry (1995–96)
Faith Burdette	Valri Bromfield
Quentin Kelly	Sam Horrigan (from 1996)

CREDITS

creator Chuck Lorre · writers Chuck Lorre, Bill Masters, Paul J Raley/Robert Dolen-Smith, Ric Swartzlander, J J Wall and others · directors Michael Lessac and others · executive producers Chuck Lorre, Caryn Mandabach, Marcy Carsey/Tom Werner, Kevin Abbott, Jeff Abugov, Brett Butler · producers Joanne Curley Kerner, Dottie Dartland, J J Wall

The comedian Brett Butler was born in Montgomery, Alabama, and grew up in Marietta, Georgia. Her father walked out on the family when she was young and her mother remarried when Brett was six. As an adult, Brett also had a stormy and reportedly violent three-year marriage. After their divorce she obtained a job as a waitress and started performing standup routines – for which she had shown an aptitude when still a child – at local comedy clubs and at refuges for battered women. Her incisive, anti-male insults, delivered in a southern drawl, gave her a prominent reputation and within a few years she had started to appear in guest roles on TV. As her style developed she moved away from straight put-down one-liners to attacking wider targets, without losing her upfront, thrust-attack style, and in her sitcom *Grace Under Fire* she made an immediate impact, American viewers taking to this latest feisty female to compete in the same arena as Roseanne Arnold.

Butler was cast in a character role much like herself, a 'straight-shooting Southern woman who's both proletarian and literate'. Her character had a famous name, Grace Kelly, which belied her actual nature much in the way that the name Brett Butler mistakenly conjured up visions of Clark Gable's Rhett Butler in *Gone With The Wind*. This Grace Kelly was no actress turned princess: she was a divorcee who had endured abuse at the hands of her husband and emerged toughened and independent from the experience. She was also, with good reason, wary of making a similar mistake again. Like the real Brett Butler, Grace Kelly worked in a male-dominated world (an oil refinery) but, unlike the actress playing her, Kelly had three children from her marriage – a girl, Libby, who seemed to be coping well; a baby, Patrick, too young to appreciate the situation; and an older son, Quentin, who missed his redneck father and was quite troublesome. In true 1990s fashion, Grace juggled the working side of her life with the home side. She matched wisecracks and often out-smarted her rough but good-natured fellow workers at the oil refinery, and enjoyed a more rewarding relationship with her friend Nadine (currently with her fourth husband, Wade) and a caring chemist, Russell, recently divorced from his wife.

Like *Roseanne* and, later, *Cybill*, the show had well-publicised back-stage frictions, with Butler fighting tooth-and-nail to imprint her 'vision' on the show. These arguments resulted in the series' creator/executive producer Chuck Lorre being removed from production chores, although he continued as 'comedy consultant'. Typically, the trade press slant on the storm was of a woman being 'difficult', whereas a similar situation featuring a male star might have seen him labelled as 'resolute'. Despite the creative differences, *Grace Under Fire* thrived, and

although the show was sometimes guilty of not fully exploiting the potential of its premise or talents of its star, it deserves full marks for its depiction of another strong, witty, independent female on American television.

See also *Brett Butler: The Child Ain't Right*.

The Graham Stark Show

UK · BBC · SKETCH

7 × 25 mins · b/w

9 June–24 July 1964 · BBC1 various days mostly 8pm

MAIN CAST

Graham Stark

CREDITS

writer Johnny Speight · producer Sydney Lotterby

The film comedy character actor Graham Stark first came to prominence on BBC radio, making his debut in *Happy Go Lucky* and going on to *Ray's A Laugh*, *Educating Archie* and *The Goon Show*. Stark was a regular supporting player on TV – notably with his good friend Peter Sellers in *A Show Called Fred* and *Son Of Fred*, and with Benny Hill – before getting this, his own sketch series. All the editions were scripted by ace writer Johnny Speight and each one featured a different group of supporting actors, including Deryck Guyler, Arthur Mullard, Derek Nimmo, Patricia Hayes and Warren Mitchell.

Graham's Gang

UK · BBC · CHILDREN'S SITCOM

10 episodes (5 × 25 mins · 5 × 30 mins) · colour

Series One (5 × 25 mins) 21 Nov–19 Dec 1977 · BBC1 Mon 4.40pm

Series Two (5 × 30 mins) 14 Feb–14 Mar 1979 · BBC1 Wed 5.05pm

MAIN CAST

Graham	Mark Francis
Mildred	Melanie Gibson
William	Neill Lillywhite
Lux	Alan Corbett
Robert	Tommy Pender
Keith	Lloyd Mahoney
Denise	Katherine Hughes (series 2)

CREDITS

writer John Challen · director Marilyn Fox · executive producer Anna Home

Graham's gang consisted of five boys – Graham himself, William, Lux, Robert and Keith – and one girl, Mildred. The boys constantly rallied against Mildred's involvement but she was determined to take part in their escapades; if ever they were too beastly towards her she had powerful relations who would come to her aid, so the boys had no choice but to resign themselves to her membership. They were perhaps a bit of a motley bunch – Graham's leadership of the gang was threatened by William; Robert and Keith were always on the verge of fighting; and gormless Lux unwittingly provided comic relief because he was rather slow on the uptake – but they weren't a *bad* gang by any means; in fact, they looked quite smart and middle-class in their school uniforms.

The episodes involved dim-witted crooks, a camping trip, a go-kart race and other adolescent activities. A new regular female character, Denise, was introduced in the second series.

A Grand Day Out

see Wallace & Gromit

Grandad

UK · BBC · CHILDREN'S SITCOM

22 × 30 mins · colour

Series One (5) 3 Oct–31 Oct 1979 · BBC1
Wed 5.10pm

Series Two (6) 8 Oct–12 Nov 1980 · BBC1
Wed 5.10pm

Series Three (6) 17 Feb–24 Mar 1982 · BBC1
Wed 5.05pm

Series Four (5) 4 Jan–1 Feb 1984 · BBC1
Wed 4.40pm

MAIN CAST

Charlie Quick	Clive Dunn
Mr Watkins	Geoffrey Russell
Digby Rigby	Maurice Thorogood (series 1)
Mildred	Jane Waddell (series 1)
Bert Bamford	James Marcus (series 2–4)

CREDITS

writer Bob Block · *director/producer* Jeremy Swan

Another old-timer role for Clive Dunn, following his ITV series *My Old Man* (and, before that of course, *Bootsie And Snudge* and *Dad's Army*). Here Dunn played Charlie Quick, known to all and sundry as Grandad, the elderly but sprightly caretaker of the Parkview Rehearsal Hall. The eager OAP tried to help but he mostly hindered the acting and dancing students who hired the venue.

Dunn was quite happy to keep playing ancient men, and indeed he devised this particular character himself, inviting writer Bob Block to place him into storylines with the customary mix of verbal misunder-standings and frantic slapstick. The series' title recalled Dunn's slushily sentimental song that had somehow managed to reach number one in the British pop singles chart in 1971.

The Gravy Train

UK · C4 (PORTMAN PRODUCTIONS) · COMEDY SERIAL

4 × 60 mins · colour

27 June– 8 July 1990 · Wed 10pm

MAIN CAST

Hans-Joachim Dorfmann	Christoph Waltz

Michael Spearpoint	Ian Richardson
Gianna	Anita Zagaria
Villeneuve	Jacques Sereys
Hilda Spearpoint	Judy Parfitt
Nadine	Almanta Suska
Milcic	Alexei Sayle
Christa	Sabine Weber
Gustave	Geoffrey Hutchings

CREDITS

writer Malcolm Bradbury · *director* David Tucker · *executive producers* Tom Donald, Victor Glynn · *producers* Ian Warren, Philip Hinchcliffe

A satirical swipe at the swindles and financial frauds prevalent in the bureaucracy of the old European Economic Community. The author – black comedy supremo Malcolm Bradbury – delivered an account of Hans-Joachim Dorfmann, an earnest, honest but somewhat naïve young German who arrives to Brussels to work for the EEC's Directorate of Information and Culture and who, to his astonishment, finds himself involved with mysterious beautiful women, wholesale corruption and the European plum mountain. Dorfmann soon becomes an unwilling puppet in the hands of a number of string pullers, including the suave Spearpoint and the dubious chancer Milcic. Eventually, Dorfmann sees through the Machiavellian plotting and uncovers the true villains behind the biggest fraud in the Common Market's history.

This was a fast-moving, elegantly filmed production that pulled no punches in its revelations of inefficiency, corruption and incompetence within the EEC. Christoph Waltz made an appealing lead player, bringing the right amount of bewilderment to the role but cleverly extending his character as the plot progressed. All in all, *The Gravy Train* was a luxurious vehicle that took viewers on a first-class comedy excursion. A sequel reunited the main cast the following year – see next entry.

The Gravy Train Goes East

UK · C4 (PORTMAN PRODUCTIONS) · COMEDY SERIAL

4 × 65 mins · colour

28 Oct–18 Nov 1991 · Mon 10pm

MAIN CAST

Hans-Joachim Dorfmann	Christoph Waltz
Michael Spearpoint	Ian Richardson
Gianna	Anita Zagaria
Villeneuve	Jacques Sereys
Hilda Spearpoint	Judy Parfitt
Katya Princip	Francesca Annis
Steadiman	Jeremy Child
Tankic	Henry Goodman
Larson Parson	John Dicks

CREDITS

writer Malcolm Bradbury · *director* James Cellan-Jones · *producers* Ian Warren, Philip Hinchcliffe

For this follow-up to *The Gravy Train* writer Malcolm Bradbury recalled to life the fictitious Balkan state of Slaka that he had invented some years earlier, to great comic effect, for his spoof guide book *Why Come To Slaka?* The premise of this serial was that Slaka, recently liberated from communism, wants desperately to join the EEC but its entry is violently opposed by the British government (represented by spokesman Michael Spearpoint). Hans-Joachim Dorfmann is sent to Slaka to try and find out why this opposition exists, and once again finds himself at the centre of a labyrinthine plot.

Larry Grayson

Born William White, in Bolton on 31 August 1923, Larry Grayson had been working for some 30 years, wearily treading, without success, the cabaret and night-club circuit, when he was invited on to the premiere edition of ATV's *Saturday Variety* on 22 January 1972. (His TV debut was one year earlier, in *The Leslie Crowther Show*.) Proving once again how fickle fame can be, Grayson became an overnight star and within months was voted Show Business Personality Of The Year. Grayson liked to portray himself as 'the biggest hypochondriac in show-business' and, devoid of punchline-type jokes as such, his act usually amounted to a litany of bodily complaints, delivered confidentially, with pouted lips, hand on hip, a raised eyebrow or two and *heaps* of homosexual innuendo. Grayson epitomised high-camp British humour, was delighted to be able to sprinkle the word 'gay' into his patter as often as possible, and with his catchphrase 'Shut that door' and fictional characters Everard, the coalman's daughter Slack Alice, and Apricot Lil, a tart who worked in a jam factory, he remained successful through a number of ITV series, as outlined below. Grayson also made appearances in the ITV soap opera *Crossroads* and BBC1's music-hall series *The Good Old Days*, and quiz-shows/panel-games galore, notably hosting BBC1's *The Generation Game* (23 September 1978 to 25 December 1981) and Anglia's networked ITV series *Sweethearts* (from 31 March 1987). Grayson died on 7 January 1995, having returned to (relative) obscurity in his final years.

Shut That Door!!

UK · ITV (ATV) · STANDUP/SKETCH

13 × 30 mins · colour

Series One (7) 18 Aug–22 Sep 1972 · Fri 8.30pm

Series Two (6) 28 Mar–9 May 1973 · Wed 8pm

MAIN CAST
Larry Grayson

CREDITS
writers Peter Dulay (series 1& 2), Bernie Sharp (series 1 & 2), Bryan Blackburn (series 2) · *director/producer* Colin Clews

A few months after shooting to fame as a result of his appearances in *Saturday Variety*, Grayson was given his own series, named after his catchphrase. Perhaps unsure of its reception, ATV planned only four editions but this was immediately stretched to seven, with six more added the following spring. There were plenty of famous guests but all played second fiddle to Larry and his camp comedy act.

Larry's Christmas Party

UK · ITV (ATV) · STANDUP/SKETCH

1×60 mins · colour
22 Dec 1972 · Fri 7.30pm

MAIN CAST
Larry Grayson

CREDITS
writers Peter Dulay, Bernie Sharp, Bryan Blackburn · *director/producer* Colin Clews

A seasonal special, with more guests.

The Larry Grayson Hour Of Stars

UK · ITV (LWT) · STANDUP/SKETCH

1×60 mins · colour
13 Sep 1974 · Fri 9pm

MAIN CAST
Larry Grayson

CREDITS
directors/producers Philip Casson, William G Stewart

Larry Grayson here affected the role of movie star, leafing through his scrapbook of Hollywood success. He also met his guest, Dame Anna Neagle.

Larry Grayson

UK · ITV (LWT) · STANDUP/SKETCH

14 editions (13×30 mins · 1×60 mins) · colour
Series One (7) 19 Sep–31 Oct 1975 · Fri 8.30 then 7.30pm

Special (60 mins) 9 Jan 1977 · Sun 7.25pm

Series Two (6) 15 Jan–19 Feb 1977 · Sat mostly 6.30pm

MAIN CAST
Larry Grayson

OTHER APPEARANCES
Nigel Pegram
Bill Pertwee
David Lodge
Anna Dawson
Dennis Plowright

CREDITS
writers Neil Shand (series 1 & 2), Bernie Sharp (series 1 & 2), Derek Collyer (series 1) · *director* Bruce Gowers · *producer* Mark Stuart

With a format similar to *Shut That Door!!* these were Grayson's last own-series. In September 1978 he took over from Bruce Forsyth as host of BBC1's *The Generation Game*.

One further notable ITV appearance was a tribute paid to the comic on his 60th birthday by fellow stars, *At Home With Larry Grayson*, made by LWT and screened on 26 August 1983. The programme was also part autobiographical and part documentary.

The Great Detective

UK · BBC · CHILDREN'S SITCOM

6×30 mins · b/w
4 July–26 Sep 1953 · fortnightly Sat around 5.30pm

MAIN CAST
The Great Detective · · John Hewer (eps 1–4); · · · · · · · · · · · · · · · Graham Stark (eps 5 & 6)
Richard Rockhead · · · · · · · · · · · John Sinclair
Annabella Clutterbuck · · · · · Norah Gaussen
Soames, the butler · · · · · · · · · · Felix Felton
Gubbins, the gardener · · · · · · · · · Erik Chitty
Jasper Bloodstone · · · · · · · · · · · · Bill Shine

CREDITS
writer Philip Godfrey · *producers* Douglas Hurn (eps 1–4), Shaun Sutton (eps 5 & 6)

Described as a 'sinister comedy', this six-part detective serial for children contains a mystery of its own: why its star and producer changed four episodes into the run.

Great Scott – It's Maynard!

UK · BBC · SKETCH

17×30 mins · b/w
Series One (6) 4 Oct–13 Dec 1955 · fortnightly Tue mostly 8pm

Series Two (6) 10 Apr–15 May 1956 · Tue around 8.30pm

Series Three (5) 25 Oct–20 Dec 1956 · fortnightly Thu around 8pm

MAIN CAST
Bill Maynard
Terry Scott
Shirley Eaton
Hugh Lloyd
Pat Coombs (series 2 & 3)

CREDITS
writers Lew Schwarz/Eric Merriman (17), Johnny Speight (1), Dave Freeman (1) · *producer* Duncan Wood

Two of the biggest names in mid 1970s British sitcoms, Terry Scott and Bill Maynard, worked together as a double-act in the 1950s and enjoyed great success with

three early series for the BBC that, in its title, made typically punning use of their names: *Great Scott – It's Maynard!*

Bill Maynard made his stage debut as support to Scott in 1951 and they formed a touring partnership soon afterwards. The BBC series saw them lauded as the young blades of British comedy, delivering a fresh style of sketch-based humour from the nominal setting of their own flat.

Green Acres

USA · CBS (FILMWAYS) · SITCOM

170×30 mins · colour
US dates: 15 Sep 1965–2 Sep 1971
UK dates: 3 Apr 1966–13 Mar 1968 (46 episodes · b/w) BBC1 Sun 5.05pm then various days and times

MAIN CAST
Oliver Wendell Douglas · · · · · · · Eddie Albert
Lisa Douglas · · · · · · · · · · · · · · · · Eva Gabor
Eb Dawson · · · · · · · · · · · · · · · · Tom Lester
Mr Haney · · · · · · · · · · · · · · · · Pat Buttram
Fred Ziffel · · · · · · · · · · · · · Hank Patterson
Doris Ziffel · · · · · Barbara Pepper (1965–69); · · · · · · · · · · · · · · · · · · · Fran Ryan (1969–70)
Alf Monroe · · · · · · · · · Sid Melton (1966–69)
Ralph Monroe · · · · · · · Mary Grace Canfield · (1966–71)
Hank Kimball · · · · · · · · · · · · · · · Alvy Moore
Sam Drucker · · · · · · · · · · · · · · · Frank Cady

CREDITS
creator Jay Sommers · *writers* Jay Sommers/Dick Chevillat (131), Jay Sommers (3), Jay Sommers/ Dick Chevillat/Al Schwartz (1), Jay Sommers/John L Greene (3), Dick Chevillat/Al Schwartz (1), Dick Chevillat/Dan Beaumont (8), Dan Beaumont (7), Elroy Schwartz (2), Sam Locke/Joel Rapp (2), Scott Anderson (2), Joel Kane (1), David Braverman/Bob Marcus (1), Searle Kramer (1), Vince Packard (1), Bobby Bell/Bill Lee (1), Al Schwartz/Lou Huston (1), Arnold Horwitt (1), Elon Packard/Norman Hudis (1), Norman Hudis/ Howard Merrill/Stan Dreben (1), Phil Leslie (1) · *directors* Ralph Levy (pilot), Richard L Bare · *producers* Paul Henning, Jay Sommers, Dick Chevillat

TV producer Paul Henning had already struck gold with his rural sitcoms *The Beverly Hillbillies* and *Petticoat Junction* when he was approached by writer Jay Sommers, suggesting Henning make a TV version of his 13-episode 1950 CBS radio series *Granby's Green Acres* (itself based on S J Perelman's 1942 book *Acres And Pains*). Henning saw the potential in the idea, a mirror-image format to *The Beverly Hillbillies*, with powerful New York City lawyer Oliver Douglas (played by Eddie Albert) and his socialite wife Lisa (Eva Gabor, sister of Zsa Zsa) leaving Manhattan for 'the sticks' and having to come to terms with the rather primitive conditions of their new rural home. (Henning placed them just outside Hooterville, Illinois, fictional home of *Petticoat Junction*.) Lisa feared she'd be a fish-out-of-water in the country, missing her beloved Park Avenue shops, but hubby Oliver was hell-bent on enjoying the rural pleasures that Hooterville offered and persuaded his wife to move away from her beloved New York. The twist was that when they arrived in their new home it was Lisa who quickly adapted to the backwater, easily making friends and solving country problems with her big city solutions. Seriously scatty, it was almost as if she was oblivious to her surroundings and continued to live exactly as she had in Manhattan. Lawyer Oliver, on the other hand, despite his willingness to live as a son of the soil, never quite pulled it off, failing to master the country dwellers' insane logic, although Lisa grasped it easily.

While the lead characters were capable enough it was the fantastic collection of finely cast minor characters (a Henning speciality) that gave *Green Acres* most of its appeal – folks such as the quirkily-voiced conman Haney, county agent Hank Kimball, gormless handyman Eb, bumbling house builders Alf Monroe and his sister (*sic*) Ralph, pig farmer Fred Ziffel and his wife who treated their pet pig Arnold as if it were their son, and many others. Characters from the three Henning series often crossed into one another's shows, encouraging the notion that they all lived close by one another. But even by Henning's standards *Green Acres* was weird. Arnold the intelligent pig (his grunts were subtitled) actually behaved like a human, even avidly watching the archetypal US TV news anchorman Walter Cronkite. (In return for his stoicism, Arnold four times received the American Humane Association's Patsy Award, honouring animals outstanding on TV.)

All in all, *Green Acres* was closer to *Twin Peaks* and *Northern Exposure* than to traditional sitcoms, although it sported a high groan factor of terrible puns and malapropisms usually delivered by Lisa in her thick Hungarian accent, and a generous quota of in-jokes and running gags – Lisa's hotcakes, Oliver's speeches, the oddball electricity system, the bedroom wall building that was never finished, and plenty more. Incredibly popular during its initial run, after cancellation (CBS killed off all its rural shows with one swish of a scythe in 1971) *Green Acres* also proved an enduring success in syndication. And in common with Henning's other two hits, *Green Acres* featured an extremely catchy theme song (written by Vic Mizzy who also wrote the memorable theme for **The Addams Family**), this one sung by stars Albert and Gabor. A *Green Acres* movie was in production at the time of writing (1997).

Note. On 18 May 1990 CBS aired a two-hour TV movie, *Return To Green Acres*, with Eddie Albert, Eva Gabor and many of the remaining original cast re-creating their earlier roles. (The director was William Asher.) In this, Oliver and Lisa prevent a ruthless real-estate tycoon (played by Henry Gibson) from razing Hooterville in order to build a city of mini-malls, homes, parking lots and fast-food restaurants.

The Green Tie On The Little Yellow Dog

UK · C4 (BRIGHT THOUGHTS) · STANDUP

3 × 30 mins · colour

10 July–24 July 1983 · Sun 8.15pm

MAIN CAST
Arthur Askey
Cilla Black
Maureen Lipman
Alec McCowen
Leonard Rossiter
Julie Walters

OTHER APPEARANCES
Barry Cryer
Harold Innocent
Ronald Lacey
Diane Langton
Richard O'Callaghan

CREDITS
writers various · *director* Bryan Izzard · *producers* Neil Anthony, Bryan Izzard

An unusual foray into the realm of comic monologues, with latter-day stars reciting the works of Chesney Allen, Billy Bennett (the master of the art, who wrote the title piece), Albert Chevalier, Gracie Fields, Will Fyfe, Joyce Grenfell, Stanley Holloway, Jack Warner and the like, culled from music-hall days. The series – which, unlikely though it seems, was created by a Conservative MP, Michael Marshall, author of a book about the genre – was notable for including the last TV recording by Arthur Askey.

Joyce Grenfell

Joyce Grenfell, the niece of Nancy Astor, was born Joyce Phipps, to American parents, in London on 10 February 1910. She first publicly demonstrated her talent to amuse with humorous verses, published in *Punch* from 1935, but it was in 1938 that her career really started. At a dinner party, she so impressed the humorist Stephen Potter with a routine lampooning Woman's Institute lectures, that he introduced her to Herbert Farjeon, a theatrical impresario. Farjeon promptly put the young woman into his next show, *The Little Revue*, from April 1939, where she repeated the WI skit and began to make her name with the public – that name being Joyce Grenfell, for Miss Phipps had married Reggie Grenfell at the age of 19. She soon became popular on BBC radio, too, working with Potter, and after a long stint performing with the Entertainments National Services Association (ENSA), reunited with him to present a very popular series of humorous instructional talks, the *How* series. The style Grenfell developed for this series suited her so well that she utilised it for the rest of her performing career. She enjoyed huge success on both sides of the Atlantic with her stage revue *Joyce Grenfell Requests The Pleasure* (subsequently adapted for TV) and made a number of notable appearances in feature films, most memorably perhaps as policewoman Ruby Gates in the *St Trinian's* film series. Grenfell's trademark combination of humorous songs – she spoke or sang to a pianist's accompaniment – and funny or poignant monologues, in which she introduced a host of fascinating and memorable female characters ('Lumpy' Latimer, and the nursery-school teacher who said 'George … don't do that', to name but two), made her an international star and assured her of a lasting place in the pantheon of sophisticated British comedy talent. Grenfell made regular television appearances over the decades: her starring vehicles are listed below but she also appeared in hundreds of other shows, particularly gracing BBC2's genteel classical music light-quiz *Face The Music* in the 1970s.

Joyce Grenfell died on 30 November 1979 – 'Weep if you must/Parting is hell/But life goes on/So sing as well' she had written, anticipating her demise. All the same, more than 2000 attended her funeral at Westminster Abbey. On 1 January 1981, BBC2 presented a special one-hour tribute, featuring clips of her stage, TV and film work, and ten years later (see final paragraph of this entry) the same channel screened Maureen Lipman's superb tribute to the late star, *Re-Joyce*. Grenfell was also the subject of an excellent *Heroes Of Comedy* celebration, screened by C4 on 20 October 1995.

Ballet 'How'

UK · BBC · STANDUP

1 × 10 mins · b/w

18 Aug 1946 · Sun 8.30pm

MAIN CAST
Joyce Grenfell

CREDITS
writer Joyce Grenfell · *producer* D H Munro

A ten-minute comedy monologue that aired – within the *Starlight* strand – as a rather mischievous prelude to a BBC presentation of the New York Ballet

Theatre's performance of *Les Sylphides*. This was a TV version of Grenfell's famous radio *How* series, with Harry Jacobson accompanying her at the piano.

Joyce Grenfell   1

UK · BBC · STANDUP

3 editions (2 × 10 mins · 1 × 15 mins) · b/w

11 Sep 1946 · Wed 8.50pm (10 mins)

16 Jan 1947 · Thu 8.30pm (10 mins)

11 May 1949 · Wed 9pm (15 mins)

MAIN CAST

Joyce Grenfell

CREDITS

writer Joyce Grenfell · *producers* Robert Barr (show 1), Barrie Edgar (show 2), Michael Mills (show 3)

Three programmes presented under the long-running *Starlight* banner. The first was devoted solely to Grenfell's 'Local Library' sketch. Her accompanist was Harry Jacobson in the first two shows and Alan Paul in the third.

Another such programme, set for screening on 17 February 1947, was postponed because of a fuel crisis that temporarily curtailed TV broadcasting.

Joyce Grenfell   2

UK · BBC · STANDUP

3 editions (1 × 30 mins · 2 × 20 mins) · b/w

30 Aug 1950 · Wed 9.30pm (30 mins)

5 Jan 1951 · Fri 9pm (20 mins)

30 Jan 1953 · Fri 11.15pm (20 mins)

MAIN CAST

Joyce Grenfell

CREDITS

writer Joyce Grenfell · *producers* S E Reynolds (show 1), Ronnie Waldman (show 2), Brian Tesler (show 3)

A second batch of music and comedy shows, also screened under the title *Joyce Grenfell At Home*. By this time, improvements in TV production techniques and increased confidence in the medium had led to longer running times for shows like this, expanding from the 10- or 15-minute slots that previously had been the norm.

Joyce Grenfell Requests The Pleasure

UK · BBC · STANDUP/SKETCH

4 × 30 mins · b/w

13 July–24 Aug 1956 · fortnightly Fri 9.30pm

MAIN CAST

Joyce Grenfell

Daphne Oxenford

Elisabeth Welch

CREDITS

deviser Laurie Lister · *writer* Joyce Grenfell · *producer* John Street

In this series music was provided by the actress and singer Elisabeth Welch, and acting support came from Daphne Oxenford and an irregular team including Julian Orchard.

Joyce Grenfell   3

UK · BBC · STANDUP

4 × 50 mins · 3 × b/w · 1 × colour

8 Aug 1964 · BBC2 Sat 9pm (b/w)

26 Sep 1964 · BBC2 Sat 9.45pm (b/w)

15 Dec 1968 · BBC2 Sun 7.25pm (b/w)

18 May 1969 · BBC2 Sun 7.25pm (colour)

MAIN CAST

Joyce Grenfell

CREDITS

writer Joyce Grenfell · *producer* John Street

Characteristic comedy, often with a surprisingly dark undertone. All of Grenfell's favourite routines of the time were gathered together in the first two shows which, between them, form a marvellous record of the funny woman at the pinnacle of her profession. From her famous harassed school infants teacher to the well-spoken ladies hiding poignant secrets, these songs and monologues – honed after years of performance – stand the test of time admirably well.

The latter two shows, part of the *Show Of The Week* strand, found Grenfell repeating a few of the most requested routines but otherwise presenting material new to television audiences.

Joyce Grenfell   4

UK · BBC · STANDUP

4 × 30 mins · colour

21 Jan–11 Feb 1972 · BBC2 Fri 10.10pm

MAIN CAST

Joyce Grenfell

CREDITS

writer Joyce Grenfell · *producer* John Street

Further visits with the amusing monologist. She was once again teamed with her regular producer, John Street, and accompanied on piano by another old friend, William Blezard. Although perceived by this time as being slightly out of touch with modern sensibilities, Grenfell's talent remained bright and she delivered an elegant mixture of old favourites and new routines.

Note. In the 1980s, Maureen Lipman mounted a brilliant tribute to Joyce Grenfell on the London stage, in which, in the act of an affectionate impersonation, she performed one of the late comic's shows in its entirety, with added readings of some of Grenfell's published letters and monologues. Titled *Re-Joyce*, the show was a great success, but it took some years for any

British broadcaster to show much interest in a TV recording. Eventually, spurred on by Richard Price of independent producer Primetime, the BBC agreed to tape a presentation of the show, performed in front of an audience. Trimmed down to 105 minutes by Lipman, the programme was screened by BBC2 on 24 December 1991.

Grindl

USA · NBC (SCREEN GEMS/DAVID SWIFT PRODUCTIONS) · SITCOM

32 × 30 mins · b/w

US dates: 15 Sep 1963–13 Sep 1964

UK dates: 5 May–18 Aug 1964 (13 episodes) ITV Tue mostly 6.30pm

MAIN CAST

Grindl · · · · · · · · · · · · · · · · · Imogene Coca

Anson Foster · · · · · · · · · · · James Millhollin

CREDITS

creator David Swift · *writers* various · *directors* various · *executive producers* Harry Ackerman/Winston O'Keefe

A short-lived but interesting sitcom starring the diminutive and witty Imogene Coca, who shot to fame in the USA as co-star with Sid Caesar in the long-running US variety series *Your Show Of Shows*, screened from 1950 to 1954. Here she starred alone, as the oddly named Grindl, a dotty middle-aged maid employed by a domestic agency owned by one Mr Foster. Each episode saw Grindl engaged in a different household, allowing for the comedic exploitation of various situations – some of which were slightly eccentric; indeed, the stories veered, in places, towards black comedy.

The Groovy Fellers

UK · C4 (BORDER) · SITCOM

6 × 50 mins · colour

20 Jan–24 Feb 1989 · Fri 10.30pm

MAIN CAST

Jools Holland · · · · · · · · · · · · · · · · · himself

The Martian · · · · · · · · · · · · · Rowland Rivron

CREDITS

writers Rowland Rivron/Jools Holland · *director* Tim Pope · *executive producer* Paul Corley · *producer* John Gwyn

A curious and surreal series starring, as himself, Jools Holland, the pianist (with rock band Squeeze and his own jazzier outfits) and TV rock show presenter.

The series began with Holland, supposedly out of work, nursing a lonely pint in a Northumberland pub when in walked a Martian. (As they do.) Holland and the alien then set off around Britain on a series of bizarre adventures in an effort, probably, to unlock the meaning of life on Earth. Although dressed in 'human' clothes, the Martian – played by Rowland Rivron, half of the Raw Sex duo much seen with French and Saunders – was still obviously not of this planet because of the tiny three-pronged aerial sticking out of his skull.

More miss than hit, but with good moments.

The Growing Pains Of Adrian Mole

see *The Secret Diary Of Adrian Mole, Aged 13³⁄₄*

The Growing Pains Of PC Penrose

see *Rosie*

grown ups

UK · BBC (ALOMO PRODUCTIONS) · SITCOM

6 × 30 mins · colour

7 Jan–11 Feb 1997 · BBC2 Tue 10pm

MAIN CAST

Mel · Penny Bunton
Claire · · · · · · · · · · · · · · · · · · Pippa Haywood
Bob · Jason Watkins
Jim · · · · · · · · · · · · · · · · · · James Simmons
Murray · · · · · · · · · · · · · · · · · · Tony Gardner

OTHER APPEARANCES

Martin · · · · · · · · · · · · · · · · · Andrew Powell

CREDITS

writer Paul Makin · *director* Angela deChastelai Smith · *executive producers* Claire Hinson, Laurence Marks/Maurice Gran · *producer* Esta Charkham

The grown ups of *grown ups* (stylistically, the series was written thus) were five friends from university who were still close mates 15 years later. Bob, now a lecturer, is married to a social worker, Mel; womanising photographer Jim is married to philosophy teacher Claire (who works with Bob); and Murray, a doctor, is single and lives with his demanding mother. The underlying theme of the piece was the group's collective fear of growing old – seemingly, the years had passed and none of them had realised their potential or fulfilled ambitions. In short, then, the five had collectively embarked upon early mid-life crises, and each week they confronted the fact that they were not as young as they used to be, often indulging in activities designed to recapture their youth. Added to this was a complexity in the relationships: the unfaithful Jim had a crush on Mel, who, in turn, encouraged the flirtation because

it made her feel young and sexy. Claire, although seemingly oblivious to Jim's affairs, had also strayed from fidelity, sleeping with the dull Martin, a work colleague.

One hallmark of *grown ups* was its tendency to slip into fantasy or dream sequences to illustrate a point. Also, there was a definite US feel to the show – even the credit sequence was more typical of an American series than a British one – the subject matter (and all lower-case writing) recalling the US series *thirtysomething*. But *grown ups* lacked the kind of punchy dialogue and witty one-liners that graced such series as *Friends* or *Partners*. In fact, it seemed intentionally low-key, purposefully aiming for thoughtful exchanges rather than overt gags. The result was that, while the series remained watchable, there wasn't much laughter to be had.

Grubstreet

UK · BBC · STANDUP

8 × 30 mins · colour

Special · 26 Nov 1972 · BBC2 Sun 9.05pm
One series (7) 20 Oct–17 Nov 1973 · BBC2 Sat 8pm

MAIN CAST

Julian Orchard
Anna Quayle
William Rushton
John Bird
Michael Hordern (special)

CREDITS

deviser Barry Took · *writers* Alan Coren, Richard Ingrams/Barry Fantoni, Michael Green, J B Morton and others · *director* Vernon Lawrence · *producer* Barry Took

Subtitled 'a brisk stroll down the funnier side of Fleet Street', this series – devised and produced by Barry Took – gave life to some of the more colourful creations from the cartoons and columns of Britain's newspapers and magazines. Anna Quayle portrayed Richard Ingrams' and Barry Fantoni's hideous 'first lady of journalism', Glenda Slag, who was born in the pages of *Private Eye*; Willie Rushton played Michael Green's vile 18th-century diarist Squire Haggard from *The Daily Telegraph*; John Bird blacked-up as Alan Coren's General Amin Dada, a savage lampoon of Idi Amin, the president of Uganda, which was appearing in *Punch*; and Julian Orchard re-created characters from J B Morton's Beachcomber, including Roland Milk, the 'World's Worst Poet', published in the *Daily Express*.

See also *The World Of Beachcomber*, *Haggard* and *Private Eye TV*.

Gruey

UK · BBC · CHILDREN'S SITCOM

12 episodes (6 × 30 mins · 6 × 25 mins) · colour

Series One (6 × 30 mins) 24 Feb–30 Mar 1988 · BBC1 Wed 4.30pm
Series Two *Gruey Twoey* (6 × 25 mins) 5 Jan–9 Feb 1989 · BBC1 Thu 4.35pm

MAIN CAST

Stephen 'Gruey' Grucock · · · · Kieran O'Brien
Peter 'Wooly' Woolsmith · · · · · Danny Collier
Quidsia 'Quidsy' Rahim · · · · Ayesha Hussain
· (series 1)
Annie Mapin · · · · · · · · · Casey Lee (series 2)
Tricia ('Supermouse') · · · · · · Katisha Kenyon
· (series 2)
'Nidgey' Jackson · · · · · · · · · · · Scott Fletcher
Mr Grucock · · · · · · · · · · · · · · · · Paul Copley
Mrs Grucock · · · · · · · · · · · · · · · · Jane Lee
Mr Rahim · · · · · · · · · · · Marc Zuber (series 1)
Mrs Rahim · · · · · · · · · Indira Joshi (series 1)

CREDITS

writer Martin Riley · *director* Roger Singleton-Turner · *executive producer* Paul Stone

Stephen 'Gruey' Grucock was another in the long line of mischievous schoolboys – headed by *Jennings* and William Brown (*Just William*) – who was always involved in harebrained schemes and unlikely escapades. Mostly, Gruey's exploits resulted in direct confrontation with his arch-enemy, 'Nidgey' Jackson, a situation that usually caused problems for Gruey and his two pals – 'Wooly' and an Asian girl, 'Quidsy' – owing to Gruey's bad luck and sheer incompetence. A second series, bearing the punning *Gruey Twoey* title, aired in 1989, with Quidsy out of the picture and two new friends for Gruey – Annie and 'Supermouse'. Otherwise the hi-jinks were much the same as before.

Both series were written by former teacher Martin Riley, who took the name of Gruey from one of his former pupils but based the character on an amalgam of boisterous boys he had encountered.

The Grumbleweeds Radio Show

UK · ITV (GRANADA) · SKETCH/STANDUP

46 editions (44 × 30 mins · 1 × 60 mins · 1 × 45 mins) · colour

Special (30 mins) 29 Mar 1983 · Tue 5.15pm
Series One (7 × 30 mins) 5 May–16 June 1984 · Sat 6pm then 6.30pm
Special (30 mins) 22 Dec 1984 · Sat 5.40pm
Special (30 mins) 29 Dec 1984 · Sat 5.35pm
Series Two (7 × 30 mins) 13 Apr–25 May 1985 · Sat mostly 6.50pm
Special (30 mins) 27 Dec 1985 · Fri 6.30pm
Series Three (7 × 30 mins) *The Grumbleweeds Show* 25 Jan–8 Mar 1986 · Sat 6.30pm
Series Four (7 × 30 mins) *The Grumbleweeds Show* 12 July–23 Aug 1986 · Sat 5.05pm
Special (60 mins) *The Grumbleweeds Party Time* 7 Oct 1986 · Tue 8pm

Special (30 mins) *The Grumbleweeds Show*
28 Dec 1986 · Sun 5.30pm

Series Five (11 × 30 mins) *The Grumbleweeds Show* 18 Apr–27 June 1987 · Sat mostly 5.05pm

Special (45 mins) *The Grumbleweeds Show*
9 July 1988 · Sat 5.45pm

MAIN CAST
The Grumbleweeds (Robin Colville, Maurice Lee, Albert Sutcliffe, Carl Sutcliffe, Graham Walker)

CREDITS
writers cast · *directors* Ian Hamilton (1983 special), David Liddiment (series 1), Ian White (1984 specials), Ian White/David Warwick (series 2), David Warwick (1985 special & series 3), David Warwick/Noel D Greene (series 4), Noel D Greene (1986/88 specials & series 5) · *producer* Johnny Hamp

Combining sketches with comedy songs and impressions, this was a straight transferral to TV of the Grumbleweeds' long-running (1979–88) series on BBC Radio 2, first airing under this title and then as simply *The Grumbleweeds*. (Later still, also on R2, they had another series, *Someone And The Grumbleweeds*.)

Hailing from Leeds and particularly well followed in the north, the band – Robin, Maurice, Albert, Carl and Graham – have been in show business since 1963, their failure to stir more than a few claps on an *Opportunity Knocks* TV appearance leading them to ditch their career as a straight pop band in favour of humour, with gags, sketches and impressionism to the fore; another early TV spot was in a Granada one-off show, *Max Bygraves Introduces New Faces*, on 7 November 1967.

No famous person was spared, and no shortage of wacky characters were invented in their fast-cut, action-packed TV shows, with Carl Sutcliffe depicting his (relatively) famous alias Wilf 'Gasmask' Grimshaw, Albert Sutcliffe appearing as the 'Milky Bar Kid' and Robin Colville airing his celebrated impression of fellow Leeds man Jimmy Savile. (Note. Albert and Carl Sutcliffe left the group at the end of 1987, and were replaced by side-musicians who supplemented the remaining three. The new members were first seen in the July 1988 TV special.)

Interestingly, while *The Grumbleweeds Radio Show* was aimed at adults when it aired on BBC radio, the television version was usually scheduled for less mature viewing, and an even younger audience was addressed during the band's BBC TV series *The Coal Hole Club*.

Grundy

UK · ITV (THAMES) · SITCOM

6 × 30 mins · colour

14 July–18 Aug 1980 · Mon 8pm

MAIN CAST
Grundy · · · · · · · · · · · · · · · Harry H Corbett
Beryl · · · · · · · · · · · · · · · · · · Lynda Baron
Sharon · · · · · · · · · · · · · Julie Dawn Cole
Murray · · · · · · · · · · · · · · · David Janson

CREDITS
writer Ken Hoare · *directors* Robert Reed (5), Anthony Parker (1) · *producer* Robert Reed

The final starring sitcom role for Harry H Corbett, forever cast (in the minds of the viewers, at least) as Harold Steptoe. Here he played Grundy, a newsagent with a puritanical streak of *War Cry* proportions, a man who spends his life battling against the all-pervasive permissive society and railing against Britain's falling standards. Grundy's wife has defied his opinion that women who commit adultery should be stoned (with small rocks, that is, not drugs), and has run off with the local bookmaker. Now Grundy is divorced and trying to cope as a single man, and father to his teenage daughter Sharon. In the opening episode he meets a woman on a train, Beryl Loomis, who is the epitome of what he considers to be loose morals: she's a lusty, busty divorcee and sports a strong desire for … Grundy. The chase is on.

This series had been set for transmission in late 1979, but then the protracted ITV strike happened and, around the same time, Corbett suffered a heart attack. He had another, and died, on 21 March 1982, aged just 57 (three years before the death of his Steptoe father Wilfrid Brambell, who passed away on 18 January 1985, aged 72). Sadly, *Grundy* was not the most memorable way for Corbett to have made his final bow.

'Norman Gunston'

Born in Sydney on 30 October 1948, the talented comedian Garry McDonald enjoyed much success in his home country, and with his awful creation Norman Gunston ('the little Aussie bleeder') he achieved international cult status. Like his compatriot Barry Humphries with Dame Edna Everage, McDonald created a wholly believable character to inhabit. His thin hair slicked down over his forehead and his face festooned in trademark dabs of toilet paper where he had cut himself shaving (hence 'little bleeder'), Gunston was a spoof interviewer and entertainment journalist pre-dating similar 1990s icons like Steve Coogan's Alan Partridge, Caroline Aherne's Mrs Merton and Paul Kaye's Dennis Pennis. Like Pennis, the ill-informed Gunston shot rude, irreverent questions at his hapless guests and was often controversial when approaching unsuspecting stars who were unaware that they were victims of a send-up.

After only a brief gestation period, the Gunston character was delivered unto ABC TV in Australia on 18 May 1975 with the first of three series (24 half-hour programmes in total) of *The Norman Gunston Show* that swiftly elevated the character to widespread fame. McDonald wound down Gunston in the early 1980s, however, realising that his own act was being overlooked by his monster creation. Sadly, a 1993 revival series ended after just two editions.

The Norman Gunston Show UK

UK · BBC · STANDUP/SKETCH

1 × 45 mins · colour

19 Nov 1976 · BBC2 Fri 9.30pm

MAIN CAST
Norman Gunston · · · · · · · · Garry McDonald

CREDITS
writers Garry McDonald, John Sweetensen/Peter Thorburn · *producer* Robin Nash

British TV viewers' first sight of Norman Gunston was in this special programme, made in England by the BBC and screened six years ahead of C4's imported series. Here, Gunston's celebrity 'victims' were Michael Caine, Diana Dors, Glenda Jackson and Malcolm Muggeridge.

The Norman Gunston Show Australia

AUSTRALIA · 7 NETWORK · STANDUP/SKETCH

8 × 60 mins · colour

Australian dates: 19 Apr 1978–24 Oct 1979

UK dates: 27 Nov and 24 Dec 1982 (2 editions)
C4 Sat 8.15pm and Fri 11pm

MAIN CAST
Norman Gunston · · · · · · · · Garry McDonald

CREDITS
writer Garry McDonald · *producer* John Eastway

These shows were re-edited and repackaged for overseas sale by the Seven Network, utilising the best material from eight hour-length programmes broadcast on that network over an 18-month period in 1978–79. Among those seen being 'interrogated' by Gunston were the Bee Gees, Zsa Zsa Gabor, Elliott Gould, Charlton Heston, Mick Jagger, James Garner, Lee Marvin, Burt Reynolds, Phil Silvers and Elke Sommer.

Gunston's Australia

AUSTRALIA · 7 NETWORK · STANDUP/SKETCH

8 × 30 mins · colour

Australian dates: 19 Feb–26 Mar 1981 (6 editions)

UK dates: 7 Feb–28 Mar 1983 (8 editions) C4 Mon 9pm

MAIN CAST
Norman Gunston · · · · · · · · Garry McDonald

CREDITS
writer Garry McDonald · *producer* John Eastway

Eight programmes that showed the Gunston character approaching the end of his shelf-life. The aim was that he would travel around his home country, interfering and adventuring in high and low places in his usual cack-handed manner. However, poor audience ratings caused the final two editions to be dropped from the schedules in Melbourne, and – except for re-runs – this was the last Aussies saw of 'the little bleeder' for more than a decade, when he resurfaced for three shows in February and March 1993. As himself, however, Garry McDonald went on to star in two successful ABC sitcoms, *Mother And Son* and *Eggshells*.

Haddimassa

see The Montreux Festival

Haggard

UK · ITV (YORKSHIRE) · SITCOM

14 × 30 mins · colour

Series One (7) 27 Jan–10 Mar 1990 ·
Sat mostly 6.40pm

Series Two (7) 18 July–30 Aug 1992 · Sat
mostly 5.15pm then Sun 6pm

MAIN CAST

Squire Haggard · · · · · · · · · · · · Keith Barron
Roderick Haggard · · · · · · · · Reece Dinsdale
Grunge · Sam Kelly
Fanny Foulacre · · · · · · Sara Crowe (series 1)
Sir Joshua Foulacre · · · · · · · Michael Jayston
· (series 1)
Landlord · · · · · · · · · · · · · · · William Simons

CREDITS

creator Michael Green · writer Eric Chappell ·
directors Vernon Lawrence (11), Catherine
Morshead (3) · producer Vernon Lawrence

The adventures of three men – a deeply
indebted middle-aged country squire,
Haggard, his debauched 21-year-old son
Roderick and their cunning and intellectually
astute menial Grunge – as they drunkenly
swaggered their way around England
in 1777–78, enjoying wicked ways with
wenches, drinking, gambling, stealing and,
above all else, stooping to any ploy that might
restore the squire's ailing fortune.

A broad comedy, almost *Carry On*-like in
content and presentation, Haggard was
written by Eric Chappell (*Rising Damp,
Duty Free*, etc), based on Michael Green's
regular column in *The Daily Telegraph* and
subsequent comic novel *Squire Haggard's
Journal*, first published in 1975 (and then
reissued as *Haggard: The Squire's Journal* to
coincide with the TV series). The shows were
faithful to Green's diarised episodic account
of Haggard's eventful life, depicting an
eternal optimist whose schemes never quite
came to fruition, hampered as they were by
flawed ploys and immense quantities of
Madeira, port and wine. All three major

players – Keith Barron, Reece Dinsdale and
Sam Kelly – rose admirably to the task, with
Barron being especially convincing as the
womanising yet slightly effeminate Squire.

See also *Grubstreet*.

Hale And Pace

UK · ITV · *C4 (LWT) · SKETCH/STANDUP

62 editions (60 × 30 mins · 2 × 60 mins) · colour

*Special (60 mins) *Hale And Pace Christmas
Extravaganza* 20 Dec 1986 · Sat 9pm
Series One (7) 2 Oct–13 Nov 1988 ·
Sun mostly 10pm
Series Two (6) 1 Oct–5 Nov 1989 ·
Sun mostly 10.05pm
Series Three (6) 30 Sep–4 Nov 1990 ·
Sun 10.05pm
Series Four (6) 29 Sep–3 Nov 1991 ·
Sun mostly 10.05pm
Series Five (7) 24 Jan–7 Mar 1993 ·
Sun mostly 10.20pm
Series Six (7) 19 Sep–31 Oct 1993 ·
Sun mostly 10pm
Series Seven (7) 18 Sep–30 Oct 1994 ·
Sun 10pm
Series Eight (7) 8 Oct–19 Nov 1995 ·
Sun mostly 10pm
Special (60 mins) *Hale And Pace Down Under*
29 Dec 1996 · Sun 10.25pm
Series Nine (7) 5 Jan–16 Feb 1997 ·
Sun mostly 10pm

MAIN CAST

Gareth Hale
Norman Pace

CREDITS

main writers Gareth Hale/Norman Pace · other
writers Laurie Rowley (series 1–3), Richard Parker,
Sean Carson, David Tomlinson, Michael Henry,
Abi Grant, Geoff Lister, Jez Stephenson, Raymond
Dixon, David Kind, Geoff Cole/Clive Whichelow,
Ronnie Barbour, John Brown, Phil Hopkins, Terry
Morrison, Mike Lepine, Mark Leigh, Mike Haskins,
Eifion Jenkins, Gary Keating and others · script
associates/editors Laurie Rowley, Sean
Carson/David Tomlinson, Mike Lepine, Mark
Leigh · directors Vic Finch (1986 special & series
1), David G Hillier (series 2–6), Peter Orton (series
7–9), Nigel Lythgoe (1996 special) · executive
producers John Kaye Cooper, Humphrey Barclay ·
producers Marcus Plantin (1986 special), Alan
Nixon (series 1–3), David G Hillier (series 4–6),
Mark Robson (series 7–9 and 1996 special)

After regular exposure in BBC1's *The
Entertainers* (from April 1984), C4's
Pushing Up Daisies (from November 1984)
and its successor *Coming Next …* (from
September 1985), and LWT's *Saturday
Gang* (from October 1986), Hale and Pace
were granted their own special by LWT
for Christmas 1986. Although it was to be
another two years before they returned with a
full series, this was the start of a long run.

Born 27 days apart in early 1953, Gareth
Hale (the one with the black-turning-grey
moustache) and Norman Pace (the more
slightly built of the two) met at a teacher-

training college in Eltham, south London, in
1971. Rooming together, they discovered
much common ground, particularly humour,
and soon started playing together in Daffy,
a music-comedy group, supplementing the
income they derived as PE teachers in local
schools. By 1976 they had formed a double-
act, playing pubs and clubs in the area, and
this led to their regular engagements at the
Woolwich Tramshed as part of a troupe
called Fundation, and – inevitably – their
inclusion inside the 'alternative comedians'
bracket. It is a tag the pair have always
been keen to play down, although they also
acknowledge that they are a very long way
removed from Mike and Bernie Winters,
Morecambe and Wise or Little and Large,
what one might term 'seaside' comics.

While their work is varied, Hale and Pace
are known to be – perhaps, indeed, *best*
known to be – spoof-dangerous comedians,
whose humour has a definite, albeit tongue-in-
cheek, 'edge'. The Two Rons – also known as
The Management – is their most famous act,
the pair donning tuxedoes and black bow-ties
to assume the personas of a pair of unsmiling
East End of London 'heavies', with violent,
psychopathic thoughts that has seen them
likened to the Kray Twins. Among Hale and
Pace's other best-known personas are the
children's TV presenters Billy (Hale) and
Johnny (Pace), deadbeat cabbies Jed and
Dave, money-conscious evangelists Nathan
and Jeremiah, the brainless Curly and
Nige and, latterly, the Road Rage Milko. A
number of their TV sketches have aroused
controversy over the years, none more so than
when they pretended to have microwaved a
cat.

ITV networked *Hale And Pace – The
Business*, an hour-length compilation of
the best sketches (including the famous
Microwaved Moggy) on 26 December
1993, and there have been numerous other
compilations and repackaged repeats over
the years. An all-new 1996 programme, *Hale
And Pace Down Under* (reflected in the above
details), showed the pair out and about in
Australia during a concert tour. Hale and
Pace were also major participants in *Trading
Places*, a pair of TV programmes broadcast
to increase awareness of breast cancer –
theirs was shown by C4 on 27 March 1992.

Irritated by what they saw as poor
scheduling of their one-off comedy-drama
April Fool's Day (see next paragraph), Hale
and Pace decided to leave LWT in 1997, and
moved across to the BBC, their first venture
for the Corporation being to star in the three-
part series, *Jobs For The Boys*, a non-comedic
series in which they took on a variety of
challenges, screened from 16 November 1997.
In the meantime, LWT saluted their tenth
anniversary with the company by airing an
hour-length highlights compilation, *Hale And*

Pace – Ten Years Hard, on 22 November 1997. Their final series for LWT was set to air in early 1998.

Hale and Pace have also branched out into serious drama, playing the roles of Dalziel and Pascoe in the first TV realisation of Reginald Hill's detective characters, in the three-episode *A Pinch Of Snuff*, networked by ITV from 9 to 23 April 1994. (*Dalziel And Pascoe* – so titled – switched to BBC1 from 16 March 1996, with Warren Clarke and Colin Buchanan in the title roles.) They also starred in a comedy-drama, *April Fool's Day* (LWT, 29 March 1997), playing a pair of unlikeable neighbours trying to better each other with practical jokes. The hour-long film also featured Susie Blake and Roy Hudd.

See also **Comic Relief**, and *The Management*, the Two Rons' 1988 excursion into sitcom territory.

Halesapoppin!

UK · BBC · SKETCH

1 × 45 mins · b/w

29 May 1948 · Sat 8.30pm

MAIN CAST

Sonnie Hale
Doris Hare
Wallas Eaton

CREDITS

writers Loftus Wigram/Norman Hackforth · *producer* Henry Caldwell

A rare TV vehicle for the British comedian Sonnie Hale (born John Robert Hale-Munro in 1902, died 1959). A star of stage and screen, Hale made people laugh, did impressions, dance, sang, wrote and even directed much of his own material.

The title was a pun on Olsen and Johnson's famous zany Broadway revue and 1942 film *Hellzapoppin*.

Half-An-Hour

UK · BBC · STANDUP/SKETCH

1 × 30 mins · b/w

9 May 1938 · Mon 3pm

MAIN CAST

Charles Heslop
William Stephens
Irene North
Richard Hearne
Lily Palmer
George Nelson

CREDITS

writers various · *producer* Reginald Smith

The third edition in an irregular series that didn't always feature comedy. This one did, strongly, with Charles Heslop and William Stephens performing patter as That Uncertain Duo, and more fun provided by Richard Hearne in his pre-**Mr Pastry** days – the first TV performance of his sketch *Take*

Two Eggs, Lily Palmer and George Nelson assisted.

As usual, the programme was re-staged later in the week; unusually, it had a slightly different supporting cast on that second occasion (10 May at 9pm).

Halfway Across The Galaxy And Turn Left

AUSTRALIA · 7 NETWORK (CRAWFORD PRODUCTIONS/TAURUSFILM) · CHILDREN'S SITCOM

28 × 25 mins · colour

Australian dates: 19 June–18 Dec 1994

UK dates: 31 May–6 Sep 1994 (28 episodes) ITV Tue 4.15 and Thu 4.20pm

MAIN CAST

X (Charlotte)	Lauren Hewett
Qwrk (George)	Jeffrey Walker
Dovis (Astrella)	Silvia Seidel (body); Amanda Douge (voice)
Father (Mortimer)	Bruce Myles
Mother (Renee)	Jan Friedl
Mrs Roland	Colleen Hewett
Jenny Roland	Kellie Smythe
Colin Roland	Che Broadbent
Andrew Roland	Brandon McLean
Shane Roland	Michael Walsh
Mr Roland	Richard Neal
Michelle Froggat	Tenley Gillmore
Dallas Hohenhaus	Katrina Lambert
Sally	Celeste Lamenta
Lynne	Susan Ellis
Hecla	Sandy Gore
Lox	Paul Kelman

CREDITS

creator Robin Klein · *writers* John Reeves, Ray Boseley, Vince Moran and others · *directors* Rod Hardy, Paul Moloney, Brendan Maher and others · *executive producer* Terry Ohlsson · *producer* Jan Marnell

An Australian comedy-adventure series, based on the popular children's novel by Robin Klein, about a family from the planet Zyrgon who flee into outer space when the father is discovered to have fixed the national Klickscore lottery. Together with Lox, a space pilot, they make good their escape with only a single direction in mind: to speed halfway across the galaxy and turn left. This brings them to Earth, where they land and make good a transformation that enables them to pass without undue notice among its dwellers.

Like the US sitcom *3rd Rock From The Sun*, the humour came from the difficulties experienced by the aliens in adapting to the human way of life as inconspicuously as possible, and from age reversal: in *3rd Rock* the oldest alien appears in human form to be the youngest; here, the youngsters, led by the dour girl X, genuinely assume seniority over the elders, even if they do still have to attend school.

Hallelujah!

UK · ITV (YORKSHIRE) · SITCOM

15 × 30 mins · colour

Series One (7) 29 Apr–10 June 1983 · Fri mostly 7.30pm

Series Two (8) 2 Nov–21 Dec 1984 · Fri mostly 8.30pm

MAIN CAST

Captain Emily Ridley	Thora Hird
Sister Alice Meredith	Patsy Rowlands
Sister Dorothy Smith	Rosamund Greenwood (series 1)
Brother Benjamin	David Daker (series 2)

OTHER APPEARANCES

Brigadier Langton	Garfield Morgan (series 2)

CREDITS

writer Dick Sharples · *director/producer* Ronnie Baxter

Having written – indeed, he was still writing – a Thora Hird sitcom, *In Loving Memory*, Dick Sharples assembled another comedy role for this most wonderful actress and personality in which she portrayed a Salvation Army captain, doing her best (but usually failing) to transform darkened lives into oases of light. The part was entirely appropriate for Thora, being not only a devout Christian in real life (she went on to host the BBC1 hymn series *Praise Be!*) but also a fan and supporter of the so-called Sally Ann, reading the Bible at their meetings whenever she could. Dick Sharples knew this, and further guaranteed that vital ring of authenticity by enrolling himself as a temporary member of the Salvation Army, trooping around London streets with the brass band and around the pubs with the *War Cry* to conduct his research. It paid off: in May 1984 Sharples won an award for creating the best female comedy role of the previous year.

Thora was cast as the devout Captain Emily Ridley. She's been in the Salvation Army for 42 years and the top brass want her to retire. Rather than break this harsh news to her, however, they offer her a quiet posting in Brigthorpe. But where others see a nice enough Yorkshire town she sees sin lurking behind every net curtain, and determines to flush it out, much against the wishes of the 'sinners' concerned. Wearing her bonnet and rattling her tin, she zeroes in on moral transgressions, but her senses are almost always misguided and, to say the least, she's accident-prone.

Patsy Rowlands, as Emily's niece Alice Meredith, also in the Sally Ann, appeared in both series of *Hallelujah!* Rosamund Greenwood, as Sister Dorothy Smith, supported in the first while, following another relocation, David Daker as Brother Benjamin helped out in the second.

Tony Hancock

Widely considered the finest British comic actor of them all, Tony Hancock was born on 12 May 1924 in Birmingham. His parents moved to Bournemouth when he was three, running the Railway Hotel there. Touring music-hall acts who stayed at the hotel introduced the child to variety and he soon decided that he wanted to become a comic. As a young adult, after some not particularly useful amateur stage experience, he joined the RAF where he failed to get into ENSA but succeeded in joining Ralph Reader's *Gang Show* and gained his first real entertainment work. After the Second World War, Hancock toured in *Wings*, Reader's show for ex-forces talent, and in 1948 he formed a double-act with pianist Derek Scott, the pair appearing in residency at London's famous nude theatre, the Windmill. It was while performing here in *Revudeville* that they earned an audition for BBC TV that led to an appearance on the talent-spotting show *New To You* on 1 November 1948.

Two years passed before Hancock's next TV performance, in the musical revue show *Flotsam's Follies* (20 February 1950), wherein he appeared in a sketch as a conjuror. All the while he continued to appear on stage, and began also to forge a career on BBC radio before his next TV work came along – five appearances in **Kaleidoscope** in a series of extended sketches that carried the generic title *Fools Rush In*. Later in 1951, Hancock appeared in an edition of **The Lighter Side** but then radio work in *Happy Go Lucky* and *Educating Archie* kept him busy, building a reputation but preventing him from undertaking many TV appearances.

Tony Hancock first performed material written by Ray Galton and Alan Simpson in the BBC Light Programme radio series *All-Star Bill* (1952–54), and the pair went on to script all of Hancock's best-loved work from this point on, beginning with the radio series *Hancock's Half-Hour* (104 editions, 2 November 1954 to 29 December 1959), which established the doleful comedian as a master of his art and a bona-fide radio superstar. It was inevitable that TV, enjoying a huge explosion in popularity at this time, would beckon the comedian once more. The surprise was that, having conquered the audio medium, Hancock was destined for even greater honours on the small-screen.

The Tony Hancock Show

UK · ITV (JACK HYLTON TV PRODUCTIONS FOR ASSOCIATED-REDIFFUSION) · SKETCH

12 × 30 mins · b/w

Series One (6) 27 Apr–1 June 1956 · Fri 8.30pm
Series Two (6) 16 Nov 1956–25 Jan 1957 · fortnightly Fri 8.30pm

MAIN CAST
Tony Hancock
June Whitfield
John Vere
Clive Dunn

OTHER APPEARANCES
Dick Emery
Sam Kydd
Hattie Jacques
Eric Sykes

CREDITS
writers Eric Sykes (8), Eric Sykes/Larry Stephens (2), Ray Galton/Alan Simpson (2) · *directors/ producers* Kenneth Carter (series 1), Eric Fawcett (series 2) · *executive producer* Roland Gillett (series 1)

After three series (48 editions) of his brilliant BBC radio series *Hancock's Half-Hour*, Tony Hancock seriously entered the world of television for the first time in 1956. Surprisingly, however, this first considered TV endeavour was not with the BBC. Since June 1954 Hancock had been appearing on stage in the impresario Jack Hylton's revue *The Talk Of The Town*, until, tired of repeating the same lines night after night, he had unexpectedly quit. He agreed to do the TV series for Hylton (who at that time had an exclusive arrangement with London ITV station A-R to provide all the entertainment programmes) as a means of escaping his stage obligations.

As it transpired, the BBC were also keen to put Hancock on to the small-screen and launched the TV version of *Hancock's Half-Hour* just five weeks after the first A-R run came to an end. There was a major difference between the two productions: in the BBC series, Hancock's brilliant radio writers Galton and Simpson continued their depiction of the man as a sad buffoon via a weekly single story. Unable to persuade the BBC to have G&S script his series, however, Jack Hylton brought in Eric Sykes to write *The Tony Hancock Show*, and he opted for the sketch format. (Sykes had previously written for Hancock in the radio version of *Educating Archie*.) All 12 editions of the A-R series were broadcast live, which was an exacting task for the performers; Hancock pulled all the weight but he was very ably supported by the great young comedian June Whitfield, American straight-man John Vere and (often in his old man roles) Clive Dunn. Costume and scene changes were done on the run and the shows had a rough and ready approach that, although amateurish, somehow added to the charm. In the first series each week's show ended with a dance routine by resident hoofers the Teenagers that was then mimicked by Hancock and Whitfield for comedic effect.

The second series of A-R's *The Tony Hancock Show* was aired, fortnightly, in between the first and second series of BBC TV's *Hancock's Half-Hour*, and here the format changed: instead of a number of unrelated sketches, each programme was based on a single sketch theme. Eric Sykes continued to write the scripts until, with the final two programmes, the BBC finally permitted Galton and Simpson to contribute, albeit with the stipulation that they not receive a screen credit.

Although it would be accurate to say that *The Tony Hancock Show* failed to do Hancock much good, it also didn't harm his career. And while he will always be remembered for his BBC work, which, at times, achieved true greatness, he would later return to the commercial network for series in 1963 and 1967.

Hancock's Half-Hour

UK · BBC · SITCOM

58 episodes (56 × 30 mins · 1 × 43 mins · 1 × short special) · b/w

Series One (6) 6 July–14 Sep 1956 · fortnightly Fri mostly 9.30pm
Series Two (6) 1 Apr–10 June 1957 · fortnightly mostly Sun 8pm
Short special · part of *These Are The Shows* 28 Sep 1957 · Sat 8pm
Series Three (11) 30 Sep–16 Dec 1957 · Mon 8pm
Special (43 mins) *Hancock's Forty-Three Minutes* 23 Dec 1957 · Mon 8pm
Series Four (13) 26 Dec 1958–27 Mar 1959 · Fri 9.05pm then 7.30pm
Series Five (10) 25 Sep–27 Nov 1959 · Fri mostly 8.30pm
Series Six (10) 4 Mar–6 May 1960 · Fri 8.30pm then 7.30pm

MAIN CAST

Tony Hancock	· · · · · · · · · · · · · · · ·	himself
Sidney James	· · · · · · · · · · · · · · · ·	himself

OTHER REGULAR APPEARANCES (IN VARIOUS ROLES)
Alec Bregonzi
Mario Fabrizi
Irene Handl
Patricia Hayes
Hattie Jacques
Bill Kerr
Hugh Lloyd
John Vere
Johnny Vyvyan
Kenneth Williams

CREDITS
writers Ray Galton/Alan Simpson · *producers* Duncan Wood (56), Graeme Muir (1), Francis Essex (short special)

Hancock's Half-Hour is the yardstick against which all subsequent British sitcoms have been measured, the vast majority failing to size up to its extremely high standards. Based on his famous radio series of the same name, the TV run consolidated Tony Hancock's standing as Britain's leading comic of the day, the entertainer providing ample proof that his wonderfully flexible face could be as expressive as his dextrous radio voice.

Tony Hancock was at the height of his powers during the late 1950s, squeezing every comic ounce out of his lines, pulling off perfectly judged pauses and demonstrating a sense of timing to match the great Jack Benny's. His character – Anthony Aloysius St John Hancock – was invariably a loser, whose aspirations and plans were dashed by fate, circumstance, Sid James or, more often than not, his own pomposity or unfettered ambition. Hancock suffered the slings and arrows of outrageous fortune ruefully, occasionally lamenting his lot with the heartfelt phrase 'Stone me, what a life'. The screen Hancock's misery was the viewer's delight – the many millions who watched the shows saw something in the frustrated funster with which they could identify while consoling themselves that their lot wasn't as bad as his. Hancock's genius, coupled with Galton and Simpson's fabulously rich scripts, resulted in a very fine series indeed and a bunch of classic half-hours such as 'The Lawyer: The Crown v James S: Hancock QC Defending', 'The Set That Failed', 'The Economy Drive', 'Lord Byron Lived Here', 'Twelve Angry Men', 'The Big Night', 'The Cold', 'The Missing Page' and 'The Reunion Party'.

This was not a traditional sitcom, however: Hancock's character, position and profession changed from week to week, and the intentionally unreal feel of the production was compounded by the irregularly recurring support cast of actors appearing in different roles – affectionately named the East Cheam Repertory Company after the Surrey town in which the TV series, like the radio version, was ostensibly located (Hancock's abode, 23 Railway Cuttings, became the most famous address in British comedy). Sidney James, Hancock's friend and confidante, though also his nemesis, was the only constant player, but two of Hancock's radio regulars Hattie Jacques and Kenneth Williams appeared in the second TV series and stalwarts such as Johnny Vyvyan, Alec Bregonzi, John Vere, Mario Fabrizi, Irene Handl and Hugh Lloyd provided sterling support throughout.

Tony Hancock

UK · BBC · SKETCH

1 × short special · b/w

part of *Christmas Night With The Stars*
25 Dec 1958 · Thu 6.25pm

MAIN CAST
Tony Hancock

Totti Truman-Taylor
Alec Bregonzi
Percy Edwards.

CREDITS
writers Ray Galton/Alan Simpson · *producer* Graeme Muir

A performance of Hancock's well-known budgerigar sketch, in which, dressed in budgie costume, he contemplates life from within his cage. Screened within the BBC's Christmas-night extravaganza *Christmas Night With The Stars*.

Hancock   BBC

UK · BBC · SITCOM

6 × 25 mins · b/w

26 May–30 June 1961 · Fri 8pm

MAIN CAST
Tony Hancock · · · · · · · · · · · · · · · · himself

CREDITS
writers Ray Galton/Alan Simpson · *producer* Duncan Wood

It is well publicised that Tony Hancock, wishing to stretch his television character, decided to work without his sidekick Sid James and continue the series as solo lead. To accentuate the difference, and noting its reduced 25-minute time slot, the title was trimmed from *Hancock's Half-Hour* to plain *Hancock*.

The series was an unbridled triumph, with Galton and Simpson – in what turned out to be their final television collaboration with the comedian – coming up with six outstanding scripts that propelled the star's buffoonish character to new heights of hilarity and nudged the British sitcom into a new era. In the first episode, 'The Bedsitter', to emphasise that Hancock was now operating without James, he appeared solo, rambling around his flat while delivering a stream-of-consciousness monologue and desperately trying to find ways to pass the time. The other episodes were 'The Bowmans', a spoof on the BBC radio serial *The Archers*; 'The Radio Ham', where Hancock, at the controls of his amateur radio equipment, stumbles upon a mayday call; 'The Lift', in which Hancock tries to entertain but succeeds only in annoying a group of people trapped in a stalled lift at the BBC; 'The Succession – Son And Heir', where Hancock tries to find a suitable soul mate with whom to have children (this episode included a sparkling appearance by June Whitfield); and, most famously, 'The Blood Donor', where Hancock decides, altruistically, to give blood but finds there's more to the process than he realised. Immediately upon transmission 'The Blood Donor' became a part of British TV folklore

with lines from Galton and Simpson's script still in the public psyche three decades later.

On his way home from taping the fourth of the series' six shows, Tony Hancock was involved in a car accident, the result of which (as well as inflicting a couple of black eyes, which make-up had to conceal) was that he had no time to learn his lines for the fifth recording, 'The Blood Donor'. The producer, Duncan Wood, was keen to cancel the taping but Hancock was insistent that it should go ahead; Wood duly employed 'teleprompters' (modern versions of cue-cards or 'idiot boards' as they were unkindly called) from which Hancock could read his part during the taping. The result could have been disastrous – in fact, it was a triumph, but Hancock was so enamoured of this labour-saving device that he scarcely bothered to learn his lines again throughout the remainder of his TV career.

Hancock   ITV

UK · ITV (ATV) · SITCOM

13 × 30 mins · b/w

3 Jan–28 Mar 1963 · Thu mostly 8.30pm

MAIN CAST
Tony Hancock · · · · · · · · · · · · · · · · himself

CREDITS
writers Godfrey Harrison (6), Richard Harris/Dennis Spooner (3), Terry Nation (3), Ray Whyberd/Terry Nation (1) · *director* Alan Tarrant · *executive producer* Bernard Delfont · *producer* Tony Hancock

The sad decline of Tony Hancock has been well reported, and though much of it is known principally through the benefit of hindsight, viewers of this ATV series would have swiftly realised that something was going badly wrong with the brilliant and much adored comic's career. Screened just 18 months after the BBC's last *Hancock* run, it wasn't only the organisation that had changed; Tony Hancock had now, in a foolish move towards self-destruction that topped all previous foolish moves, arrogantly dispensed with the services of writers Galton and Simpson, considering that he was the star, with or without their input. Against their magnificent scripts his new series had to come off second best; as it happened, it was worse than that. The programmes were under-rehearsed and, because the series took to the air with half of the episodes still unwritten, obviously rushed. The latter episodes suffered additionally from Hancock's off-stage drinking, and his reliance once more upon 'teleprompters' to save him the bother of learning lines – which he hardly had the time to do because he had appointed himself as producer and so was saddled with additional, administrative burdens. There *were* some funny moments: with Hancock reprising his long-established role as a pompous buffoon, most of the episodes opened with him standing on a street corner, getting involved in the goings-on around him and allowing his strident thoughts to emerge loudly.

As Hancock no longer permitted the employment of a regular supporting cast the episodes featured a variety of name actors prepared to play second-fiddle to the great man. These included Martita Hunt, Patrick Cargill, Mario Fabrizi, Peter Vaughan, Allan Cuthbertson, Pauline Yates, Denholm Elliott, Dennis Price, Geoffrey Keen, John Bluthal, Edward Chapman, Gerald Harper, Shaw Taylor, Brian Wilde, Derek Nimmo, Donald Hewlett, John Le Mesurier, Francis Matthews, John Junkin, Pete Murray, Reginald Beckwith and Maggie Fitzgibbon.

Note. This same year, 1963, saw the release of Hancock's second and last starring feature film, *The Punch And Judy Man*. The first, *The Rebel*, had been issued in 1960.

Hancock At The Royal Festival Hall

UK · BBC · STANDUP

1 × 50 mins · colour

15 Oct 1966 · BBC2 Sat 9.05pm

MAIN CAST
Tony Hancock

CREDITS
writer Tony Hancock · *additional material* John Muir/Eric Geen, Ray Galton/Alan Simpson · *producer* Derek Burrell-Davis

Tony Hancock desperately wanted to deliver a knock-out live standup show featuring totally new material. Following the poor quality of his last TV series (which had nevertheless garnered good ratings) there was some trepidation towards his plans. By now Hancock had two new writers, John Muir and Eric Geen, who were providing material for the comedian in his role as compere of the eight-week variety series *The Blackpool Show* (ABC for ITV, 19 June–7 August 1966), and although they were encountering problems with the star they still came up with new routines for his live show.

The BBC decided to film the London performance at the Royal Festival Hall (given on 22 September 1966) but had contingency plans should the show have gone disastrously wrong or proved to be of insufficient quality. In the end, the Hancock segment of the show (the first, untelevised, sequence had featured singer Marion Montgomery) was, if not exactly a triumph, certainly better than many people had dared hope. Hancock threw himself into the act, using some new items but mainly relying on established material, with some old Galton

and Simpson routines especially rewritten by Muir and Geen. Hancock performed parodies of *Mutiny On The Bounty* (utilising his Robert Newton caricature), *The Hunchback Of Notre Dame* and *Richard III*, and also spoofed crooners and everlasting 'thank you' speeches. The huge round of applause he received at the end of the show demonstrated the respect and affection in which Hancock was held by the public. Buoyed with this success, he also turned in a memorable performance as a guest on ATV's *Secombe And Friends* on 13 November 1966.

Hancock's

UK · ITV (ABC) · SITCOM

6 × 30 mins · b/w

16 June–18 July 1967 · Fri 9.40pm then Tue 9.30pm

MAIN CAST
Tony Hancock · · · · · · · · · · · · · · · himself
Esmerelda Stavely-Smythe · · June Whitfield
Toulouse · · · · · · · · · · · · · · · · Joe Ritchie

CREDITS
writers John Muir/Eric Geen · *producer* Mark Stuart

By 1967, four years had elapsed since Tony Hancock last appeared in a British TV comedy series, a period that had marked an acceleration in his personal decline. Whereas others turned their faces away, the ITV franchise ABC was happy enough with Hancock's contribution to *The Blackpool Show* to support a new Hancock venture, although it ensured that the sitcom idea had a definite variety setting, so that other material could be brought to the fore in case the star failed to deliver.

The new situation landed Tony as the manager of a Swinging London night-club, Hancock's, permitting opportunities for him to mingle and enjoy routines with the customers and also for a weekly guest star to have a solo singing spot. (Vikki Carr appeared twice, Carmen MacRae, Dick Haymes, Marian Montgomery and Frankie Randall once apiece.) Joe Ritchie, who had worked with Hancock on stage, played the role of the club's head waiter, and June Whitfield appeared as a multi-functionary, from 'bunny girl' to hat-check girl. A similar set-up – Whitfield and Hancock (the latter in a variety of guises) running a rundown café called Chez Hancock's ('London's Britest Niterie') – had featured as the closing item in editions of his A-R series, *The Tony Hancock Show*, nine years earlier.

Sadly, Tony Hancock's spirits dropped as the ABC series progressed and his alcoholic spirit consumption increased. Once more he relied upon 'teleprompters' to save learning the scripts, causing him to remain rooted to

the spot instead of moving around. Off-set as well as on he was also perceived as problematic by ABC executives, and this, coupled with the disappointing viewing figures, caused them to dismiss any notion of a second series.

Despite his worsening condition, in 1968 Hancock was lined up for a 13-part Australian TV series, *The Tony Hancock Show*, being made by the 7 Network. The premise was that the Hancock character, with all his affected pomposity, emigrated Down Under, where, inevitably, he clashed with the Aussie way of life. Sadly, only three episodes were made (these were finally shown on Australian TV in a 90-minute presentation on 25 January 1972) before, on 25 June 1968, still in Australia, Tony Hancock took his own life, and the world of comedy, Britain in particular, lost a great, great figure. 'Things seemed to go wrong too many times,' he wrote in his suicide note. The great man was dead at just 44, and the world was robbed of a second half to what had already been an unforgettable career.

Notes: A prestige overview of Hancock and his career was presented in the BBC1 *Omnibus* arts strand on 26 April 1985. Entitled *From East Cheam To Earls Court*, the 75-minute special included many clips and key interviews with Galton and Simpson, producers Dennis Main Wilson and Duncan Wood and actors Bill Kerr, Patricia Hayes, Patrick Cargill, Hugh Lloyd and Eric Sykes. Another tribute, *Hancock's World*, was screened by BBC2 on 27 June 1995. Tony Hancock famously put his own life under the microscope in a compellingly frank interview with John Freeman in the BBC TV series *Face To Face*, screened on 7 February 1960.

On 1 September 1991 BBC1's *Screen One* presented *Hancock*, a dramatisation of the last eight years of the star's life, featuring Alfred Molina as Hancock, Jim Carter as Ray Galton and Clive Russell as Alan Simpson. The production attracted criticism over perceived inaccuracies yet nevertheless proved that there was still a fascination with the brilliant but tragic comedian many years after his premature death. Other TV depictions of Hancock have included Jim McManus portraying the man in *Super Troupers* (Tyne Tees for C4) on 24 March 1985.

Six scripts enacted by Tony Hancock on the BBC were re-performed in the ITV series **Paul Merton In Galton & Simpson's** … in 1996 and 1997 – 'Twelve Angry Men', 'The Missing Page' and 'The Wrong Man' from *Hancock's Half-Hour* and 'The Bedsitter', 'The Radio Ham' and 'The Lift' from *Hancock*.

The Handle Bar

UK · BBC · SITCOM

3 × 50 mins · b/w

24 Oct–21 Nov 1947 · Fri 8.50pm

MAIN CAST

Jimmy Edwards
Humphrey Lestocq
Richard Hearne

CREDITS

writers Josef Shellard (eds 1& 2), Josef Shellard/
Ted Willis (ed 3) · *producer* Michael Mills

Comedy and musical high jinks from the
Handle Bar Inn, a fictitious TV pub.

The Handy Gang

UK · ITV (ASSOCIATED-REDIFFUSION) ·
CHILDREN'S SITCOM

13 × 25 mins · b/w

3 May–26 July 1963 · Fri 5pm

MAIN CAST

Johnny · · · · · · · · · · · · · · · · Johnny Hutch
Dave · · · · · · · · · · · · · · · · · · Dave Jackley
Tiny · Bob Bryan
Mr Arkingshaw · · · · · · · · · · · · Freddie Foss
The Colonel · · · · · · · · · · · · Reginald Marsh

CREDITS

creators Johnny Hutch/Norman Murray · *writers*
David Edwards/Johnny Hutch · *directors* Harry
Sloan (6), J Murray Ashford (4), Pat Baker (3)

An entertaining children's series, produced
by A-R for the ITV network, in which every
episode contained strong doses of slapstick.
Dave and Johnny – the first considering
himself in charge, the second short and
excessively helpful – are odd-job men
working in a block of flats, Neverbin Court.
Tiny is their friend, a huge silly chap who
usually throws a spanner in the works, and
they work for the flats manager, first Mr
Arkingshaw then the Colonel (one of dozens
of officious-type roles for Reginald Marsh).

The Handyman

UK · BBC · SITCOM

1 × 25 mins · b/w

12 Apr 1963 · Fri 7.50pm

MAIN CAST

Lionel Hogg · · · · · · · · · · · · · · · Alfred Marks
Dr Dennison · · · · · · · · · · · · · Anthony Sharp
Matron · · · · · · · · · · · · · · Damaris Hayman
Labour Exchange clerk · · · · · · Frank Williams
First card player · · · · · · · · · · · · Edwin Apps
Second card player · · · · · · · · Julian Orchard

CREDITS

writers Ray Galton/Alan Simpson · *producer*
Duncan Wood

An episode of *Comedy Playhouse* from the
period when all the scripts were written by
Galton and Simpson. In this story Alfred
Marks starred as a highly qualified but out-
of-work machine minder given a temporary
job as handyman at an exclusive health clinic.

Hang Time

USA · NBC (PETER ENGEL PRODUCTIONS) ·
CHILDREN'S SITCOM

**52 × 30 mins (to 31/12/97 · continuing into
1998) · colour**

US dates: 9 Sep 1995 to date

UK dates: 26 Oct–29 Dec 1996 (13 episodes)
C4 mostly Sat 8.35am

MAIN CAST

Julie Connor · · · · · · · · · Daniella Deutscher
Coach Bill Fuller · · · · · · · · · · · Reggie Theus
Mary Beth Pepperton · · · · · · · · Megan Parlen
Danny Mellon · · · · · · · · · · · · · Chad Gabriel
Chris Atwater · · · · · David Hanson (1995–96)
Samantha Morgan · · Hillary Tuck (1995–96)
Michael Maxwell · · · · · · · Christian Belnavis
· (1995–96)
Earl Hatfield · · · · · · · · · Robert Michael Ryan
· (1995–96)
Amy Wright · · · · · Paige Patterson (1996–97)
Theodore 'Teddy' Brodis · · Anthony Anderson
· (from 1996)
Vince Demato · · · · · · · · · · · Michael Sullivan
· (from 1996)
Josh Sanders · · · · · · · Kevin Bell (from 1996)
Kristy Ford · · · · · Amber Barretto (from 1997)
Michael Manning · · · Adam Frost (from 1997)

CREDITS

creators Troy Shearer, Robert Tarlow, Mark Fink ·
writers various · *directors* various · *executive
producers* Peter Engel · *producer* Jon Spector

A standard sitcom that followed the exploits
of an Indiana high school basketball team,
the Deering Tornadoes. The school (and team)
paraded a multi-cultural, multi-ethnic bunch
and, in keeping with similar American
Saturday morning TV children's shows, there
was no trace of angst, xenophobia or racial
problems.

The one out-of-the-ordinary aspect about
the Tornadoes was that they featured a
female player, the athletic Julie, who looked
like a cheerleader but played like a pro. Julie's
best friend Sam (Danny's girlfriend) was the
team manager and Bill Fuller (competently
played by ex-NBA star Reggie Theus) was
the coach. Chris (Julie's boyfriend), Danny and
Michael were in the team, with rich kid Mary
Beth serving as the chief cheerleader. The
second US season saw the departure of Chris,
Michael and Earl, replaced by big-headed
Vince; the short, tubby but gifted Theodore;
and the brilliant Josh Sanders. Mary Beth
took over as team captain and Paige
Patterson joined the cast as Amy, the
new, staggeringly stupid cheerleader.

Hang Time was exactly what one expects
from such an undertaking: a moralistic, rites
of passage sitcom with – hey, guys – an
underlying message about the benefits of
working together as a team. The staged
matches were surprisingly effective, with the
cast members being genuinely adept at the
game, but this wasn't enough to lift the series
out of the sitcom doldrums.

Hangin' With Mr Cooper

USA · ABC (JEFF FRANKLIN PRODUCTIONS/
LORIMAR TELEVISION) · SITCOM

93 × 30 mins · colour

US dates: 22 Sep 1992–12 July 1997

UK dates: 16 July 1993–12 May 1997
(87 episodes) C4 various days · mostly 6pm

MAIN CAST

Mark Cooper · · · · · · · · · · · · · · · Mark Curry
Vanessa Russell · · · · · · · · · · Holly Robinson
Robin Dumars · · · · Dawnn Lewis (1992–93)
Geneva Lee · · · · · · · · · · Saundra Quaterman
· (1993–97)
Nicole Lee · · · · · · Raven-Symone (1993–97)
Earvin Rodman · · · · · · · · · · · Omar Gooding
Tyler Foster · · · · · · · · · · · · Marquise Wilson
Pamela Jane 'P J' Moore · · · · · · · Nell Carter
· (1993–95)

CREDITS

creator Jeff Franklin · *writers* Jeff Franklin and
others · *directors* various · *executive producer* Jeff
Franklin, William Bickley, Michael Warren ·
producers Kevin Abbott, Yvette Denise Lee, Bruce
Johnson, Suzy Friendly, Michael Morris, Leilani
Downer

A black 1990s variation on the 1977–84 US
hit series *Three's Company*, which was
itself a version of 1973–76 British series
Man About The House. Initially, *Hangin'
With Mr Cooper* had almost the same basic
premise: a single, horny guy shares an
apartment with two sexy women but despite
lusting after one of them never makes second
base. Despite these similarities, however,
Hangin' With Mr Cooper didn't have the
same risqué undercurrents and the humour
was not so broad.

The standup comic Mark Curry played the
title character, a former pro basketball player
now returned to his hometown of Oakland,
California, and working at his old high school
as a coach and substitute teacher. Mr Cooper
lives with his long-term friend Robin and a
vivacious career woman, Vanessa. Although
juvenile in many aspects of his life, Cooper
was honest enough about wanting sex and
didn't dress up his desires in innuendo. The
format later changed when Dawnn Lewis
left the series and was replaced by Saundra
Quaterman as Geneva Lee, Mark's cousin.
She in turn brought along her feisty daughter
Nicole, enabling the writers to exercise their
particular comedic fascination: the interplay
between Cooper and smart-mouthed
youngsters.

Safe, reliable and steadfastly middle-of-the-
road, *Hangin' With Mr Cooper* struck a chord
with viewers and attracted huge and loyal
audiences. Curry's comedic sensibilities
and standup style may have been the main
reason, but the many beautiful (and potent)
black women who shared the screen with him
also played their part.

The Hangover Show

UK · BBC · STANDUP

1 × 45 mins · colour
1 Jan 1991 · BBC2 Tue 10.55pm

MAIN CAST
Pete McCarthy

CREDITS
writers Pete McCarthy/John Dowie · *director/ producer* Caroline Roberts

Pete McCarthy's *Hangover Show* had been a hit at the 1990 Edinburgh Festival Fringe, leading to a successful nationwide tour. In this version, especially adapted for TV, the laconic comic mused on the pleasures and pains of the demon drink.

See also *I'm All Right Jacques.*

The Happening

UK · C4 (NOEL GAY TELEVISION) · STANDUP

6 × 60 mins · colour
6 Sep–11 Oct 1991 · Fri 11.50pm

MAIN CAST
host · · · · · · · · · · · · · · · · · · · Jools Holland

CREDITS
writers various · *producers* Dave Morley/Graham K Smith (4), Miles Ross/Rory Sheehan (2)

A music and comedy series with just enough standup content to warrant its inclusion here. Jack Dee made two appearances in the series while the comics who turned up once apiece were Vic Reeves, Bob Mills, Bill Hicks, Sean Hughes, Julian Clary, Craig Ferguson and Will Downing.

Happily Ever After

UK · ITV (NBC INTERNATIONAL FOR ABC) · SITCOM

*13 × 30 mins · b/w
*12 Feb–2 Apr 1961 · Sun 7.30pm (8); 10 May–31 May 1964 · Sun 3.35pm (4)

MAIN CAST
Dora Morgan · · · · · · · · · · · · · · Dora Bryan
Peter Morgan · · · · · · · · · · · · · · Pete Murray
Harry Watkins · · · · · · · · · · · · Bryan Coleman
Grace Watkins · · · · · · · · · · · · Audrey Noble

CREDITS
writers James Kelly/Peter Miller · *director* Philip Jones

Also screened (for contractual reasons) under the title *The Dora Bryan Show*, this was a purpose-bought vehicle for the Lancashire light-actress, revue performer and comedian. Cast – as she almost always was – under her own first name, this Dora was a scatter-brained blonde, getting herself and others into trouble and then getting out of it … just. In other words, she was the sort of woman so often seen in sitcoms: forgetful, prone to buying new dresses, someone who, when she can't find her wedding certificate, insists that

she and her husband get married all over again. The pop DJ and actor Pete Murray played the role of her hubby, a doctor whose medical expertise still doesn't qualify him to understand the ways of his wife. Harry and Grace Watkins were the Morgans' puzzled next-door neighbours.

Any resemblance between *Happily Ever After* and *I Love Lucy* is probably no coincidence, for the format was bought in from America. Oddly, however, while *Lucy* seems to be the obvious antecedent, the British ITV company ABC concluded its deal with NBC Productions whereas *I Love Lucy* was a CBS series made by Lucille Ball and Desi Arnaz's company Desilu. And while NBC itself piloted a US sitcom titled *Happily Ever After* at this time, the premise appears to be slightly different. Whatever its origin, though, the British *Happily Ever After* was no great shakes and poor ratings led to its cancellation.

*Note. These dates refer to ABC screenings in the Midlands and the North. Thirteen episodes were made; the pilot, directed by Philip Jones after the initial groundwork had been prepared by Francis Essex, was never aired. Eight episodes were then screened before the series was taken off, and the other four, which had originally been scheduled for the remaining Sundays in April 1961, were exhumed from the archive and shown (again, chiefly in the Midlands and the North) in 1964. Just eight episodes were shown by London-area ITV, 30 April–18 June 1961, in the 'buried' slot of 3.50 on Sunday afternoons.

The Happy Apple

UK · ITV (THAMES) · SITCOM

7 × 30 mins · colour
20 June–1 Aug 1983 · Mon 8pm

MAIN CAST
Nancy Gray · · · · · · · · · · · · · · · · Leslie Ash
Charles Murray · · · · · · · · · · · Nicky Henson
Freddie Maine · · · · · · · · · · · · Jeremy Child
Arthur Spender · · · · · · · · · · · John Nettleton
Bassington · · · · · · · · · · · · · · Derek Waring
Kenilworth · · · · · · · · · · · · Peter-Hugo Daly
Miss Wheeler · · · · · · · · · · · · · Judith Paris

CREDITS
creator Jack Pulman · *adapter/writer* Keith Waterhouse · *director/producer* Michael Mills

The Happy Apple was set in the offices of an advertising agency, Murray, Maine & Spender. The company's fortunes were in steep decline and they had just one client left, Bassington's Ice Cream, but all was saved for them by their loopy secretary Nancy Gray, who, singlehandedly – or singlemindedly, because she possessed great mental powers – was able to determine which products or advertising slogans the general public would find the most attractive. She could do this

because she was a true 'Miss Average'. From the point where Ms Gray's talent was discovered, success duly smiled upon MM&S.

The series was written by Keith Waterhouse, adapting a stage-play of the same title by Jack Pulman.

Happy Days

USA · ABC (MILLER-MILKIS PRODUCTIONS/ HENDERSON PRODUCTIONS) · SITCOM

256 × 30 mins · colour
US dates: 15 Jan 1974–12 July 1984
UK dates: 16 Oct 1976–27 Oct 1985 (187 episodes) ITV various days and times

MAIN CAST
Richie Cunningham · · · · · · · · · Ron Howard
· (1974–80)
Arthur 'Fonzie' Fonzarelli · · · · · Henry Winkler
Howard Cunningham · · · Harold Gould (pilot); · · · · · · · · · · · · · · · · · · Tom Bosley (series)
Marion Cunningham · · · · · · · · · Marion Ross
Warren 'Potsie' Webber · · · · Anson Williams
· (1974–83)
Ralph Malph · · · · · · · Donny Most (1974–80)
Joanie Cunningham · · · · · · · · · · · Erin Moran
Charles 'Chachi' Arcola · · · · · · · · Scott Baio
· (1977–84)
Arnold Takahashi · · · · · · · · · · · · Pat Morita
· · · · · · · · · · · · · · (1975–76 & 1982–83)
Al Delvecchio · · · · · · · Al Molinaro (1976–82)
Jenny Piccalo · · · · · Cathy Silvers (1980–83)

CREDITS
creator Garry Marshall · *writers* various · *directors* Jerry Paris and others · *executive producers* Garry Marshall, Thomas L Miller, Edward K Milkis · *producers* Jerry Paris, William Bickley, Tony Marshall, Bob Brunner

Few sitcoms in recent years have been anywhere near as successful as *Happy Days*. Even in a US market used to long-running, mega-episode series it is a giant: *Happy Days* spanned 10 years and 256 episodes (255 plus the original pilot); considering that British series usually extend to six episodes, this is the equivalent of 42 UK series. And it started out so quietly too, nostalgically reflecting the adventures of an honest-to-goodness-gracious-me Milwaukee family, the Cunninghams, in the late 1950s, and in particular the clean-cut teenage son in that family, Richie.

But *Happy Days*' impact grew exponentially when a lesser member of the cast, the delinquent, rebellious and altogether problematic motor-bike riding Arthur Fonzarelli, known to his friends as 'Fonzie' or 'the Fonz', suddenly scored big time with the viewing audiences at home. Soon, with the Fonz promoted to the major figure in the storylines, *Happy Days* was skyrocketing, and Fonz's stock catchphrase 'Heeeeeyyyy!' entered the popular vernacular. True, one got to see the softer side of the man as the years passed, but the essence of the tough 'cool' character remained, a tribute to the acting skills of

Henry Winkler. The other key members of the huge *Happy Days* ensemble – the above cast list reflects only the principal players – developed too, literally: the series saw the kids grow from teens into twenty-somethings. This was, in essence, a *happy* series, not too taxing on the brain but with real characters, in-jokes and plenty of wit – in essence, a good American sitcom. Most of the action took place in the various homes and at Arnold's Drive-In, a hamburger restaurant – owned first by Arnold Takahashi then by Al Delvecchio – where the gang liked to hang out and discuss the developments in their love, school and home lives while sipping a soda or two.

Love And The Happy Day, the single-episode pilot for *Happy Days*, which screened in the USA on 25 February 1972, starred Harold Gould as Howard Cunningham, Richie's father. Unsuccessful at the time, it was only turned into a full series after the success of the 1973 movie *American Graffiti* – which director George Lucas wanted to make after seeing *Love And The Happy Day*. Later, with its roaring success, *Happy Days* spawned a number of spin-off series of its own: first came **Mork And Mindy** (1978–82), starring Robin Williams, following the storyline of one February 1978 *Happy Days* episode, 'My Favorite Orkan'. Next was **Laverne And Shirley** (1981–82) followed by **Joanie Loves Chachi** (1982–83). Then there were the various cartoon series – *The Fonz And The Happy Days Gang* (1980–82), screened in Britain by BBC1 in 1985), *Laverne And Shirley In The Army* (1981–82), *Laverne And Shirley With The Fonz* (1982–83) and *Mork And Mindy* (1982–83). Back in the world of real people, a one-off 90-minute *Happy Days Reunion Special* aired on US TV on 3 March 1992 (first UK transmission on 24 December 1992, C4), which gathered together the prime members of the cast to look back fonzly – sorry, fondly – on the highlights of the 255 episodes. Finally, as this book was being written, plans were afoot for a *Happy Days* stage musical to open in London in late 1998, to be co-written and directed by Henry Winkler.

Note. C4 screened 252 episodes of *Happy Days* from 27 February 1989 to 19 August 1994 and then began showing them again from 26 August 1994, airing 113 by 31 December 1997.

Happy End

see The Montreux Festival

Happy Endings

UK · BBC · SITCOMS

5 × 30 mins · colour

5 Nov–3 Dec 1981 · BBC2 Thu 9pm

MAIN CAST
Peter Skellern

CREDITS
writer Peter Skellern · *producer* Simon Betts

Five unrelated musical playlets written and composed by the star of the series, Peter Skellern. Assisted by a different guest cast each week, Skellern used the songs and stories to make pertinent comments on different aspects of life. Only three of the five editions were overtly comic in composition; of the other two, one was a drama and the other a romance.

Happy Ever After

UK · BBC · SITCOM

42 × 30 mins · colour

Pilot · 7 May 1974 · BBC1 Tue 8.30pm

Series One (6) 17 July–21 Aug 1974 · BBC1 Wed 9.30pm

Series Two (10) 8 Jan–11 Mar 1976 · BBC1 Thu 7.40pm

Series Three (9) 9 Sep–4 Nov 1976 · BBC1 Thu 7.40pm

Special · 23 Dec 1976 · BBC1 Thu 8.30pm

Series Four (7) 8 Sep–20 Oct 1977 · BBC1 Thu 7.40pm

Special · 23 Dec 1977 · BBC1 Fri 7.55pm

Series (6) 5 Sep–10 Oct 1978 · BBC1 Tue 7.40pm

Special · 20 Dec 1978 · BBC1 Wed 6.45pm

MAIN CAST
Terry Fletcher · · · · · · · · · · · · · · Terry Scott
June Fletcher · · · · · · · · · · · · June Whitfield
Aunt Lucy · · · · · · · · · · · · · · · · Beryl Cooke
OTHER APPEARANCES
Susan Fletcher · · · · · · · Lena Clemo (pilot);
· · · · · · · · · · · · · · · · · · · Pippa Page (series)
Debbie Fletcher · · · · · · · · Caroline Whitaker

CREDITS
writers John Chapman/Eric Merriman (34), Eric Merriman/Christopher Bond (5), John Kane (2), Jon Watkins (1) · *producers* Peter Whitmore (38), Ray Butt (4)

Terry And June

UK · BBC · SITCOM

65 × 30 mins · colour

Series One (6) 24 Oct–28 Nov 1979 · BBC1 Wed 8.30pm

Series Two (6) 5 Sep–10 Oct 1980 · BBC1 Fri 8.20pm

Special · 23 Dec 1980 · BBC1 Tue 7.15pm

Series Three (6) 13 Nov–18 Dec 1981 · BBC1 Fri 7.30pm

Special · 28 Dec 1981 · BBC1 Mon 6.35pm

Series Four (6) 5 Jan–9 Feb 1982 · BBC1 Tue 8pm

Series Five (6) 19 Oct–23 Nov 1982 · BBC1 Tue 7.40pm

Special · 24 Dec 1982 · BBC1 Fri 8.40pm

Series Six (6) 15 Feb–22 Mar 1983 · BBC1 Tue 7.50pm

Series Seven (6) 31 Oct–12 Dec 1983 · BBC1 Mon 6.50pm

Series Eight (12) 7 Sep–23 Nov 1985 · BBC1 Sat 5.50pm

Special · 24 Dec 1985 · BBC1 Tue 9pm

Series Nine (7) 20 July–31 Aug 1987 · BBC1 Mon 8.30pm

MAIN CAST
Terry Medford · · · · · · · · · · · · · Terry Scott
June Medford · · · · · · · · · · · June Whitfield
OTHER APPEARANCES
Malcolm · Terence Alexander (series 1 & 2);
· · · · · · · · · · · · · · · Tim Barrett (series 3–8);
· · · · · · · · · · · · · · · · John Quayle (series 9)
Alan · · · · · · · · · · · · · · · · · · · Roger Martin
Sir Dennis Hodge · · · · · · · · Reginald Marsh
Beattie · · · · · · · · · · · · · Rosemary Frankau

CREDITS
writers John Kane (41), Terry Ravenscroft (9), Dave Freeman/Greg Freeman (5), Jon Watkins (4), Colin Bostock-Smith (2), Eric Merriman/John Chapman (2), Greg Freeman (1), David Grigson (1) · *directors* Peter Whitmore, Martin Shardlow · *producers* Peter Whitmore (39), Robin Nash (20), John B Hobbs (6)

Terry Scott and June Whitfield began their TV partnership in 1968 in **Scott On ...**, but it was this pair of closely-related sitcoms that branded them as a husband-and-wife team in the minds of millions of viewers, some of whom took the image so far as to believe that they were married in real life. They weren't, but such was their rapport in these 107 episodes that it was sometimes difficult to think of them as otherwise.

Although certain, small differences within the formats distinguish *Happy Ever After* from *Terry And June*, they share enough in common to be considered as a single entity. The former began as an episode of *Comedy Playhouse* and that pilot programme established the basic premise: Terry and June Fletcher are a middle-aged, middle-class, middle-England couple suddenly alone following the departure of their grown-up children. But their contemplation of this new-found freedom is short-lived when an aged relative – dotty Aunt Lucy – moves in, bringing along her chatty mynah bird. Although the daughters dropped in from time to time, the remaining 41 episodes focused on this ill-fitting trio. At all times, Terry was like a spoiled child – headstrong, foolhardy, incompetent and obsessive. When he hit upon an idea he followed it through to its illogical conclusion regardless of the consequences. As a result, June had to mother Terry as much as be his wife, keeping her feet on the ground and staying keen, patient and tolerant ... up to the point where he had to be stopped. Aunt Lucy, for her part, was never much more than a thorn in their sides, particularly Terry's.

After many farcical exploits, one of the original writers, John Chapman, declared that they had exhausted the idea and that *Happy Ever After* should end, but the BBC comedy department, loath to lose a hit series, persevered using other people to turn in the scripts. This led to legal complications over rights and so, eventually, the BBC decided to change the name and setting of the series to avoid further difficulties.

In *Terry And June*, the couple were the Medfords, just moved to Purley, south-east of London. Aunt Lucy and the mynah bird had disappeared, as had the occasionally visiting daughters. Terry and June now mixed with a friendly next-door neighbour, Beattie; Terry's chatty work colleague, Malcolm; and their gruff boss Sir Dennis Hodge. Otherwise, things were much as before, with Terry's pigheaded childishness causing no end of problems, usually thwarting June's attempts at leading a cosy life. Although Terry Scott suffered from a number of serious health problems during the run of the series he always managed to bring the same breathless energy to his character. For her part, June Whitfield, perhaps Britain's greatest comedy actress of the TV era, recognised that her role in the proceedings was to 'drift the laughter towards Terry's lines'.

Both *Happy Ever After* and *Terry And June* were much loved by viewers who sought simple, innocuous fare, and it regularly attracted audiences impressively in excess of ten million. But their very blandness singled the series out for some vituperative condemnation from those who prefer their comedy to be more cutting. The problem was that although they started after the era of such gritty sitcoms as **Till Death Us Do Part** and **Steptoe And Son**, the series lasted long enough to still be around during the 'alternative comedy' boom of the early 1980s, the exponents of which railed against safe middle-class comedies. Singling out *Terry And June* as a prime example, these critics were scathing in their accusations that its inane plots – eg, the domestic crises caused when the boss unexpectedly drops around for dinner – were old-fashioned, unreal, insulting and, most damnably, plain unfunny. But all those millions of *Happy Ever After/Terry And June* viewers – at least three times as many as those who watched anything 'alternative' – fundamentally disagreed. For sure, as much in TV comedy as anything else, life would be boring if everyone enjoyed the same things.

Notes. A feature-length episode, *Terry And June – The Movie*, was put into production by the BBC but remained uncompleted.

An episode of *Terry And June* was screened by BBC2 on 11 October 1997 following a tribute paid to June Whitfield in the series *Funny Women*.

Happy Families

UK · BBC · SITCOM

6 × 35 mins · colour

17 Oct–21 Nov 1985 · BBC1 Thu 8.25pm

MAIN CAST

Edith Fuddle/Cassie Fuddle/ · · · · · · · · · · · ·
Roxanne Fuddle/Joyce Fuddle/ · · · · · · · · · · · ·
Madeleine Fuddle · · · · · · · Jennifer Saunders
Guy Fuddle · · · · · · · · · · · Adrian Edmondson
Cook · · · · · · · · · · · · · · · · · · Dawn French
Dr De Quincy · · · · · · · · · · · · · · Stephen Fry
Flossie · · · · · · · · · · · · · · · Helen Lederer
Dalcroix · · · · · · · · · · · · · · · Jim Broadbent

CREDITS

writer Ben Elton · director/producer Paul Jackson

Ben Elton's spin on the brilliant 1949 Ealing film *Kind Hearts And Coronets* cast Jennifer Saunders in multiple roles: as all four daughters of the Fuddle family and also as their mad granny Edith. It was Edith who set the venture rolling when she charged her dopey grandson Guy with the task of tracking down and reuniting his four lost sisters, ostensibly so that, as her dying wish, she could see her family together one last time. So off went Guy to find his erstwhile siblings, with the middle four episodes dedicated to the hunt for each one: TV soap star Cassie, jailbird Roxanne, novice nun Joyce, and dumb beauty Madeleine. The final episode brought about the unlikely reunion and revealed Granny's real and sinister motive for bringing the grandchildren together – she required an organ transplant from each of them in order to save her life. The siblings agreed, provided that first she assign them her entire estate. At the last, however, it was discovered that Granny was not ill but, miraculously, pregnant, so she was left penniless but holding the baby.

Although typical off-the-wall stuff, Ben Elton and his players were once again trying something different, a self-contained comedy serial rather than a typical sitcom. The humour was robust, vulgar and semi-surreal – par for the course with these talents – while the production overflowed with cameos from a host of famous faces from both new-wave and traditional comedy, among them Mark Arden, Helen Atkinson Wood, Chris Barrie, Keith Chegwin, Andy de la Tour, Ben Elton, Stephen Frost, Gareth Hale, Carol Hawkins, Lenny Henry, Chris Langham, Hugh Laurie, Norman Lovett, Rik Mayall, Pauline Melville, Norman Pace, Lance Percival, Nigel Planer, Christopher Ryan, John Sessions, Arthur Smith, Steve Steen, Una Stubbs, Sandi Toksvig and Ruby Wax.

This was a particularly busy period for Jennifer Saunders, for just six days after BBC1 launched *Happy Families* ITV began screening **Girls On Top**, in which she appeared alongside Dawn French, Ruby Wax and Tracey Ullman, performing some sparkling scripts that she co-wrote with the first two of these, and which Ben Elton edited.

See also **Set Of Six**.

Happy Family

see RAY, Ted

Happy Go Crazy

UK · BBC · SKETCH

1 × 30 mins · b/w

13 Jan 1954 · Wed 8.15pm

MAIN CAST

Bonar Colleano

CREDITS

writers David Climie/Dick Vosburgh · script editor Sid Colin · producer Bill Ward

A half-hour special fronted by wisecracking comic actor Bonar Colleano. An American, Colleano came from a famous family of circus acrobats and was educated and spent much of his time in Britain. He died in 1958 at just 34.

Happy Holidays

UK · BBC · CHILDREN'S SITCOM

6 episodes (3 × 60 mins · 3 × 30 mins) · b/w

10 July–18 Sep 1954 · fortnightly Sat 5pm

MAIN CAST

Mrs Mulberry · · · · · · · · · · · · Hattie Jacques
Mr Mulberry · · · · · · · · · · · John Le Mesurier
Mr Grimble · · · · · · · · · · · · · · · · Clive Dunn

CREDITS

writer Peter Ling · director Robert Tronson · producer Michael Westmore

Husband and wife Hattie Jacques and John Le Mesurier played a married couple in this comedy serial produced to run throughout the school summer holidays, screened within the strand *Children's Television*.

All three players in *Happy Holidays* would go on to carve their niche in the upper echelons of British TV comedy.

Hard Time On Planet Earth

USA · CBS (DEMOS-BARD/SHANACHIE/ TOUCHSTONE-DISNEY) · SITCOM

13 × 60 mins · colour

US dates: 1 Mar–5 July 1989

UK dates: 9 Jan–1 May 1993 (10 episodes) ITV Sat 2.05pm

MAIN CAST

Jesse · · · · · · · · · · · · · · · · · · Martin Kove
Control (voice only) · · · · · · Charles Fleischer
· (pilot);
· · · · · · · · · · · · · · · · · · Danny Mann (series)

CREDITS

creators Jim Thomas/John Thomas · *writers* Richard Chapman/E Jack Kaplan (2), Michael Piller (2), Michael Piller/Ed Zuckerman (1), Bruce Cervi (1), Bruce Cervi/Nicholas Corea (1), Daniel Freudenberger (1), Van Gordon Sauter/David Percelay (1), Michael Eric Stein (1), Rob Swigart (1), Jim Thomas/John Thomas (1), Rob Ulin (1) · *directors* Roger Duchovny (3), James A Contner (2), Michael Lange (2), Timothy Bond (1), Bill Corcoran (1), Charles Correll (1), Robert Mandel (1), Ric Rondell (1), Al Waxman (1) · *executive producers* Richard Chapman, E Jack Kaplan, Jim Thomas/John Thomas · *producers* Ric Rondell, Michael Piller

A Disney sci-fi action-comedy about an all-fighting alien warrior found guilty of 'rebellion against the council' and condemned by an intergalactic tribunal not to 'termination', the customary practice, but to serve time on 'the primitive planet Earth' as a humanoid, where he can taste the milk of human kindness and reform his character. The alien, who takes the name Jesse from a pair of overalls he finds at the petrol station where he lands, is accompanied by his parole officer, a whiny, all-knowing hazelnut-shaped computer eye named Control, who advises Jesse about what kindly deeds to do next in order to amass do-gooding points, and reports back to the planet Andarius about his progress. When Jesse accumulates enough ticks he will be allowed home.

Control decides that Jesse should live in Los Angeles, so that he can blend in with the locals. Here Jesse gets a job and sets out to win his points, helping the oppressed and stymieing crooks with his fantastic strength and speed and, while doing so, joining the US Army, winning a TV quiz-show, becoming a wrestler, joining a rodeo and enjoying other such everyday human pursuits. (Well, this is LA.)

The result was scarcely amusing. CBS, which had been looking for a winning, light-hearted version of *The Incredible Hulk*, pulled the plug on Jesse after 13 episodes.

Hardball

USA · FOX (INTERBANG/MAGIC BEANS/TOUCHSTONE TELEVISION) · SITCOM

9 × 30 mins · colour

US dates: 4 Sep–23 Oct 1994

UK dates: 5 Jan–2 Mar 1995 (9 episodes) C4 Thu mostly 11.55pm

MAIN CAST

Dave Logan	Bruce Greenwood
Mike Widmer	Mike Starr
Ernest 'Happy' Talbot	Dann Florek
Frank Valente	Joe Rogan
Arnold Nixon	Phill Lewis
Brad Coolidge	Steve Hytner
Lloyd LaCombe	Chris Browning
Mitzi Balzer	Rose Marie
Lee Emory	Alexandra Wentworth

CREDITS

creators Kevin Curran · *writers* various · *directors* various · *executive producers* Jeff Martin, Kevin Curran, Bill Bryan · *producer* Peter Baldwin

The exploits of the Pioneers, a struggling American League (ie, minor league) baseball team, managed by the deadpan, ever grim Ernest Talbot, ironically nicknamed 'Happy' by his troops. Stories centred on 'nice guy' Dave Logan and his overweight colleague Mike Widmer, a one-time superstar now in the twilight of his career. The action took place mainly in the Pioneers' locker-room, the plots revolving around managerial struggles, financial problems, the team's consistent lack of form and the clashes between the players and the team owner, feisty widow Mitzi Balzer (played by Rose Marie of **The Dick Van Dyke Show**).

Apart from Mitzi, the only other regular female member of the cast was Lee Emory, the team's publicity agent. She seemed ill at ease in the all-male confines of the locker-room and the actress Alexandra Wentworth developed a weird but effective style of face-pulling to convey her character's nervy nature. And then there was Hardball, the team's mascot, a diminutive guy with a huge baseball for a head. The actor behind Hardball was not credited in the titles and he was never seen without the false head, leading to an unnerving suspicion that he really *was* half-man, half-baseball.

Hardball – curiously retitled *Bullpen* in the UK – was an unexceptional series which, while neatly editing shots of full baseball stadiums with close-ups of the actors on a field, never really overcame the difficulties of portraying sport in fictional TV. Pitched as an easy-going slice of basic comedy, *Hardball* failed to make much of an impact with a viewing audience who could tell that it was no diamond.

Mike Harding

The folk comic was born in Lower Crumpsall, near Manchester, in 1944 and achieved national fame with a hit single, 'The Rochdale Cowboy', in 1975. A favourite on the college circuit, Harding was an inveterate weaver of unlikely tales, and after he moved ever further away from his folk music roots, towards stand-up comedy, he attracted the attention of TV producers, appearing in guest roles and his own starring series.

MH & 5p

UK · BBC · STANDUP

8 editions (1 × 50 mins · 1 × 40 mins · 6 × 30 mins) · colour

Special (50 mins) *Fivepenny Piece And Mike Harding* 11 Apr 1977 · BBC2 Mon 10.35pm

One series (6 × 30 mins) 9 June–14 July 1978 · BBC2 Fri 9pm

Special (40 mins) *Christmas With Mike Harding And The Fivepenny Piece* 23 Dec 1978 · BBC2 Sat 9.10pm

MAIN CAST

Mike Harding
The Fivepenny Piece

CREDITS

writer Mike Harding · *producer* Barry Bevins

Described as 'a meeting of talents at the Poco-a-Poco Theatre Club, Stockport', the first of these shows combined the comedy of Mike Harding with the music of five-piece group the Fivepenny Piece. Harding made quite a splash with his quirky stories that tended to stray into surrealism, and the ensuing series had his initials up front: *MH & 5p*.

In 1979 the BBC gave Harding and the Fivepenny Piece their own series (see below and *The Fivepenny Piece*).

The Mike Harding Show

UK · BBC · STANDUP

20 × 30 mins · colour

Series One (6) 30 Oct–4 Dec 1979 · BBC2 Tue 10.15pm

Series Two (6) 5 Feb–12 Mar 1981 · BBC2 Thu 10.20pm

Series Three (2) 6 Nov & 13 Nov 1981 · BBC2 Fri 9pm

Series Four (6) 15 Mar–26 Apr 1982 · BBC2 Mon 9pm

MAIN CAST

Mike Harding

CREDITS

writer Mike Harding · *producer* Barry Bevins

All these programmes comprised recordings of Harding's one-man performances (although Stanley Unwin was a guest in one show), filmed at different theatres around the country. Harding made a justifiable claim for telling the longest joke ever told on TV when he dedicated one whole programme to a single budgerigar joke.

One Night In Lincoln

UK · BBC · STANDUP

6 × 30 mins · colour

6 Apr–11 May 1983 · BBC2 Wed 9pm

MAIN CAST

Mike Harding

CREDITS

writer Mike Harding · *director* Keith Mackenzie · *producer* Cyril Gates

A mammoth, three-hour Mike Harding performance at the Theatre Royal, Lincoln, was split into six bite-sized chunks for TV. Harding regaled the audience, presenting an ideal opportunity for gathering his best material in one place.

Mike Harding In Belfast

UK · BBC · STANDUP

6 × 30 mins · colour

29 Mar–3 May 1984 · BBC2 Thu 9pm

MAIN CAST
Mike Harding

CREDITS
writer Mike Harding · *director* John Rooney · *producer* Rod Taylor

Recorded at the newly restored Grand Opera House, these shows blended new material with some old favourites.

Following this series, the comedian got on his bike and appeared in a six-part travel series, *The Harding Trail* (BBC1, 16 July–20 August 1984), in which he was filmed on a cycling tour of America.

Hardwicke House

UK · ITV (CENTRAL) · SITCOM

7 episodes (1 × 60 mins · 6 × 30 mins) · colour

One series (1 × 60 mins · 1 × 30 mins · *5 × 30 mins cancelled*) 24 & 25 Feb 1987 · Tue 8pm then Wed 8.30pm

MAIN CAST

R G Wickham	Roy Kinnear
Paul Mackintosh	Roger Sloman
Cynthia Crabbe	Pam Ferris
Herbert Fowl	Granville Saxton
Dick Flashman	Gavin Richards
Erik 'Moose' Magnusson	Duncan Preston
Harry Savage	Tony Haygarth
Peter Philpott	Nick Wilton
Slasher Bates	Kevin Allen
Agnes	Liz Fraser
Ernie	Micky O'Donoughue
Spotty	Paul Spurrier

CREDITS
writers Richard Hall/Simon Wright · *director* John Stroud · *producer* Paula Burdon

Up to end of the 1980s four different school sitcoms had reflected their times. *Billy Bunter* in the 1950s depicted boyish pranks; *Whack-O!* in the 1960s was good clean fun, albeit with heavy use of the cane; *Please, Sir!* in the 1970s was more unruly and delinquent, but still light; and *Hardwicke House* in the 1980s offered no-holds-barred anarchy. The school's hapless headmaster, R G Wickham, was an alcoholic; deputy head (Mr Mackintosh) took a lewd pleasure in watching the sixth-form girls play hockey; French mistress Ms Crabbe was a fanatical cause supporter; PE teacher Mr Savage lived up to his name; Head of English Mr Fowl had twice murdered to climb his way up the pedagogic ladder; history teacher Dick Flashman was a spiv; maths teacher Mr Magnusson was a lunatic Icelandic prone

to eating raw fish; and geography master Mr Philpott liked to routinely electrocute selected pupils.

It was quite a brew – and one which ITV viewers did not enjoy one little bit. After the premiere hour-length episode, and the first of six more half-hours screened the following evening, they complained so loudly that network executives waved the white flag and promptly pulled the series off the air: the five remaining episodes (scheduled to have ended on 1 April 1987) were never shown, and work on a second series was immediately scrapped. Those whose cameo roles in series one were taped but not seen included John Fortune, Bryan Pringle and, in the roles of highly dangerous boys straight out of Borstal, Rik Mayall and Adrian Edmondson.

Perhaps, however, extending the analogy of school sitcoms reflecting their time, *Hardwicke House* was merely ahead of the game. *Chalk*, on BBC1 in 1997, was another uncompromising few-holds-barred comprehensive-school sitcom and it drew some rave reviews.

Hark At Barker

UK · ITV (LWT) · SITCOM

16 episodes (8 × 30 mins · b/w; 7 × 30 mins colour; 1 × short special · colour)

Series One (8 × b/w) 11 Apr–30 May 1969 · Fri mostly 10.30pm

Series Two (7 × colour) 10 July–21 Aug 1970 · Fri 8.30pm

Short special (colour) · part of *All-Star Comedy Carnival* 25 Dec 1970 · Fri 6pm

MAIN CAST

Lord Rustless	Ronnie Barker
Mildred Bates	Josephine Tewson
Badger	Frank Gatliff
Dithers	David Jason
Cook	Mary Baxter
Effie	Moira Foot (series 2)

CREDITS
creator Alun Owen · *principal writers of 1st series* Peter Caulfield (Alan Ayckbourn), John Brendan, Graeme Garden, Gerald Wiley (Ronnie Barker), Bill Oddie, John Junkin, Charles Kennedy, with contributions from Chris Miller, Philippe Le Bars, Mike Sharland, Tony Baird, Lew Schwarz; *writers of 2nd series* Peter Caulfield (Alan Ayckbourn, 7), Gerald Wiley (Ronnie Barker, 7), Bernard McKenna (6) · *writer of special* Gerald Wiley (Ronnie Barker) · *director* Maurice Murphy · *producer* Humphrey Barclay

Two series starring Ronnie Barker as the decrepit and somewhat lecherous peer Lord Rustless, pontificating on affairs of a worldly and local nature from the stately pile that is Chrome Hall.

Rustless is a rumbustious, cigar-smoking aristocrat with bushy white eyebrows and a moustache, and sex prominently on the brain, a man who grows mustard and cress for a living. The character was first seen in the

second edition of *The Ronnie Barker Playhouse*, screened on 10 April 1968, conceived by the playwright Alun Owen. But Barker's interpretation of Rustless was based on a similarly larger-than-life character he had played, under various names, in repertory in his pre-TV years.

The scripts for these 15 half-hours came from a team of writers, with Peter Caulfield (a pseudonym for Alan Ayckbourn, who was employed as a BBC radio drama producer at the time and was not supposed to work elsewhere), John Brendan, Bernard McKenna and Gerald Wiley (a pseudonym for Barker himself) involved in virtually all the episodes to a greater or lesser extent. Barker also played an extraordinary number of acting roles in the two series: he had several parts – as many as eight, in fact – in every episode, and multi-tasking was required of other actors too: David Jason was not only the heavily bearded, doddering gardener Dithers but had other parts to contend with, and Ronnie Corbett appeared in one episode in three different roles. Michael Palin made one appearance and there were occasional parts for David Jason's real-life brother, Arthur White.

The series earned Ronnie Barker the Variety Club's ITV Personality of the Year award for 1969, and led to a sequel, *His Lordship Entertains*, which ran on the BBC in 1972.

Harry And The Hendersons

USA · SYNDICATION (AMBLIN ENTERTAINMENT/ MCA/UNIVERSAL TELEVISION) · SITCOM

72 × 30 mins · colour

US dates: 1990–93

UK dates: 27 Sep 1991–29 Sep 1995 (69 episodes) BBC1 Fri 7.35pm then Sun 1.15pm then BBC2 daily 8.40am

MAIN CAST

Harry	Kevin Peter Hall (1990–91),
	Dawan Scott (1991–92),
	Brian Steele (1992–93)
George Henderson	Bruce Davison
Nancy Henderson	Molly Cheek
Ernie Henderson	Zachary Bostrom
Sara Henderson	Carol-Anne Plante
Walter Potter	David Coburn (1990–91)
Samantha Glick	Gig Rice (1990–91)
Tiffany Glick	Cassie Cole (1990–91)
Bret Douglas	Noah Blake (1991 onwards)
Darcy Payne/Farg	Courtney Peldon
	(1991–92)
Voice of Harry	Patrick Pinney

CREDITS
creators William Dear/William E Martin/Ezra D Rappaport · *writers* Laura Levine, Raymond De Laurentis, Susan Sebastian/Diane 'Jenny' Ayers and others · *directors* various · *executive producers* Lin Oliver, Alan Moskowitz · *producers* John H Ward, R J Colleary, Sheree Guitar, Alan Moskowitz

Legend has it that a huge, hairy beast stalks the backwoods of North America. This creature is sometimes referred to by the Native American name 'sasquatch' but is more commonly known as 'Bigfoot', thanks to the sizeable footprints that have been discovered and upon which the legend is largely built.

Given the characteristics of a powerful but sociable animal who looks a bit like Chewbacca from *Star Wars*, has the temperament of a Labrador puppy and the IQ of a young child, such a beast was the centrepiece of the 1987 family movie *Harry And The Hendersons* (aka *Bigfoot And The Hendersons*) directed by William Dear, which spawned this TV series. In both film and series, the creature is run down on the road by the Henderson family who take him home and nurse him back to health. The Hendersons name the hairy creature Harry, and when he recovers he decides that he wants to stay, the family considering him their giant pet. Episodes revolved around the Hendersons' attempts at looking after Harry and keeping his existence a secret from the authorities, while trying to lead a normal family life.

In their efforts to draw a veil over Harry's identity and whereabouts, keeping him out of harm's way, the Hendersons receive support from a local news reporter, Samantha Glick, and Bigfoot expert Walter Potter. They were then replaced by Nancy's brother Bret and new neighbour Darcy Payne (later called Darcy Farg). Towards the end of the series Harry's existence was uncovered and he became something of a celebrity in the Seattle area. In one emotional, if gooey, episode, Harry uttered his first English words, decided on a return to the forest and then, when taken there, was upset to find it razed by developers.

Both the film and the TV series benefited from special effects wizard Rick Baker's marvellous Bigfoot costume, and, initially, Kevin Peter Hall reprised his film role as Harry. But following Hall's death in 1991, Dawan Scott took over the role, later still given to Brian Steele, who had doubled as Harry throughout the run. The original big-screen Hendersons had been played by John Lithgow (George), Melinda Dillon (Nancy), Margaret Langrick (Sara) and Joshua Rudoy as Harry's special friend Ernie. None made the transfer to TV.

Harry Enfield's Television Programme

UK · BBC (HAT TRICK PRODUCTIONS) · SKETCH

13 editions (12 × 30 mins · 1 × 40 mins) · colour

Series One (6 × 30 mins) 8 Nov–13 Dec 1990 · BBC2 Thu 9pm

Series Two (6 × 30 mins) 2 Apr–7 May 1992 · BBC2 Thu 9pm

Special (40 mins) 24 Dec 1992 · BBC2 Thu 9.20pm

MAIN CAST
Harry Enfield

OTHER APPEARANCES
Paul Whitehouse
Kathy Burke
Gary Bleasdale
Charlie Higson
Joe McGann
Jon Glover

CREDITS
main writers Harry Enfield, Paul Whitehouse, Charlie Higson, Geoffrey Perkins · *additional material* Ian Hislop/Nick Newman and others · *film director* Geoffrey Perkins · *directors* John Birkin (series 1), Geoff Posner (from series 2), John Birkin/Metin Hüseyin (special) · *executive producer* Denise O'Donoghue · *producers* Mary Bell/Geoffrey Perkins (series 1), Geoff Posner (from series 2)

Harry Enfield was born in Sussex on 30 May 1961 and in the late 1970s attended York University, from where he graduated with a degree in politics. While at York he formed a double-act with his friend Brian Elsley and they wrote a piece entitled *Dusty And Dick's Lucky Escape From The Germans*, which was well received at the Edinburgh Festival Fringe. From this point, Enfield was determined to succeed as a performer, although it was as a voice artist for **Spitting Image** that he first made his name. He then became a real force in standup with a pair of characters he and some friends had invented, the cockney/Greek Stavros and the high-earning braggart Loadsamoney (see **Saturday Live** and **Friday Night Live** for more information). These gave Enfield a rock-star-like appeal, a fact underlined by his appearances on C4's trendy rock show *The Tube*. (And, very oddly, TVS's weekday daytime ITV women's fashion series *Frocks On The Box* in autumn 1987.) Finally, in 1990, Enfield was given his own starring series and was able to truly show the depths of his (and his team's) talents.

Enfield wanted *Harry Enfield's Television Programme* to be like the children's comics he had read, *The Topper* and *The Beezer*, a jamboree bag of different folk appearing every week in their own short segments. To this end he created a posse of brilliantly realised characters, each complete with their own distinctive voices, personalities and catchphrases. These included: the gibberish-spouting pop DJs Mike 'Smashie' Smash (played by Paul Whitehouse) and Dave 'Nicey' Nice (Harry Enfield); the positively awful and ultra-slovenly couple Wayne and Waynetta Slob (Enfield and Kathy Burke); Mr Don't Wanna Do It Like That (Enfield), an irritating know-all who announced his

unwanted presence with 'Only me!' and was forever counselling 'You don't want to do it like that ...'; the mean, moaning, cantankerous, foul and filthy OAPs known as the Old Gits (Enfield as Alf Git, Whitehouse as Fred Git); Kevin, the obnoxious Little Brother (Enfield); the mentally challenged and forever stunned Double Take Brothers (Enfield and Rupert Holliday Evans); 1930s spokesman Mr Chomondley-Warner (Jon Glover) and his assistant Mr Greyson (Enfield); Tim Nice-But-Dim, a toothy, pleasant but awesomely thick Hooray Henry-type (Enfield); and the battling Scousers (Enfield, Joe McGann, Gary Bleasdale) from the *Brookside* parody *Breadside*.

This diversity of recurring characters, coupled with the style of the shows, suggested comparisons with Dick Emery, but although valid to a point, such observations failed to take into account Enfield's ruthless desire to ditch his best-loved characters and invent new ones in their place. Whereas Emery stuck through two decades with characters like Mandy and the toothy vicar, Enfield quickly cast out the creations that others would all but kill to build a career around. By the time of *Harry Enfield's Television Programme*, indeed, Enfield had already done away with Loadsamoney (he killed him off after a British stage tour in October 1988), and by the second series he introduced a whole new selection of inventions, including the super-forgetful Leslie Norris (Enfield); the world's worst barman; and the nauseatingly twee lovebirds Mills and Boon. He even graduated one of the characters, changing Little Brother Kevin into a moping, whining teenager.

Harry Enfield's Television Programme was at all times a high-quality show, establishing Enfield as a television superstar of the 1990s. The series also promoted the talents of two sterling support players, Paul Whitehouse and Kathy Burke. The three combined again in 1994, with even greater success, for **Harry Enfield And Chums**.

Notes: Enfield provided all the voices for C4's adult cartoon series *Billy The Fish* (five episodes, 30 June–4 July 1990) and *The Further Adventures Of Billy The Fish* (four episodes, 25 December–28 December 1990), both based on the half-man, half-fish footballing character published in the adult comic *Viz*. He also contributed voices to another *Viz* TV spin-off, *It's Roger Mellie – The Man On The Telly* (see **A Life In Pieces** for details) and, along with Michael Palin, had appeared in *Viz – The Documentary* (C4, 4 May 1990), championing the comic's scabrous humour. From 4 March to 8 April 1993, also on C4, Enfield presented

Harry Enfield's Guide To Opera, a six-week series designed to take the mystique out of opera and make it more accessible to the masses. Although transmitting a serious message, the series had many funny moments and introduced new characters, the Opera Ponces and Dad and Son (two Covent Garden porters), with Paul Whitehouse supporting.

See also *Smashie And Nicey – The End Of An Era*, *Norbert Smith – A Life* and *The Fast Show*.

Harry Enfield And Chums

UK · BBC (TIGER ASPECT · *TIGER ASPECT/ POZZITIVE PRODUCTIONS) · SKETCH

14 editions (12 × 30 mins · 1 × 40 mins · 1 × short special) · colour

Series One (6) 4 Nov–16 Dec 1994 · BBC1 Fri 9.30pm

Short special · part of *The Night Of Comic Relief: Harry Enfield And His Charity Chums* 17 Mar 1995 · BBC1 Fri 8pm

Series Two (6) 7 Jan–11 Feb 1997 · BBC1 Tue mostly 9.30pm

*Special (40 mins) *Harry Enfield And Christmas Chums* 24 Dec 1997 · BBC1 Wed 10.15pm

MAIN CAST
Harry Enfield
Paul Whitehouse
Kathy Burke

CREDITS
main writers Harry Enfield, Paul Whitehouse · *other writers/additional material* Graham Linehan/Arthur Mathews, Richard Preddy/Gary Howe, David Cummings, Ian Hislop/Nick Newman, Geoffrey Perkins, Harry Thompson · *directors* John Stroud (series 1), Dominic Brigstocke (series 2), Geoff Posner (1997 special) · *executive producers* Peter Bennett-Jones/Maureen McMunn · *producers* Harry Thompson (series 1), Sophie Clarke-Jervoise (series 2), Geoff Posner (1997 special)

Now considered popular enough for BBC1, Enfield's new show was in many ways a continuation of *Harry Enfield's Television Programme* and had the same comic-cuts style of presentation. Old favourites Wayne and Waynetta Slob, Tim Nice-But-Dim, Kevin (the teenager with tons of adolescent attitude, exasperating his parents, played by Stephen Moore and Louisa Rix), the Old Gits and Mr Chomondley-Warner were joined by new characters including the two Lovely Wobbly Randy Old Ladies (Enfield and Burke) with their mock-shock cries of 'Young man!' when they ceaselessly invented the notion that a male with whom they were conversing had said something risqué; and the Self-Righteous Brothers (Enfield as Frank Doberman, Whitehouse as George), two vociferous and intensely angry individuals who put the world to rights from their pub armchairs while discussing celebrities by their surnames only.

Other recurring characters included: Stan and Pam Herbert (Enfield and Burke), the boastful, wealthy Brummies ('I could not help but notice that we are *considerably* richer than *yow*'); Lee (Enfield) and Lance (Whitehouse), thick and even thicker cockney wide-boys; Mister Dead (Whitehouse) the talking corpse (a macabre spoof of the talking horse sitcom *Mister Ed*); the apologetic German (Enfield), a youth backpacker who irritatingly vents his guilt over the war and Germany's subsequent industrial triumph; Tory Boy (Enfield) an obnoxious, spotty pubescent who, in the style of John Major, spouted Tory rhetoric (in the 1997 Christmas special, reflecting the recent change of government, Tory Boy metamorphosed into Labour Boy, a Tony Blair impression); De Dutch Coppersh – Ronald (Enfield) and Stefan (Whitehouse), dope-smoking, laid-back Amsterdam policemen who are also lovers; Julio Geordio (Whitehouse), a South American footballer now playing for Newcastle, whose dialogue and dialect, as heard in interviews with TV commentator Tony (Harry Enfield in a John Motson impression), blended Spanish with accent-perfect Geordie colloquialisms; the Toddlers, Lulu (Burke) and Harry (Enfield), where baby Lulu suffered constant physical abuse at the hands of her presumably jealous – or just plain vicious – toddler brother; the curtain-twitching nosey neighbour Michael Paine (a fine impersonation by Paul Whitehouse of the young Michael Caine); Steven (Enfield) and Jill (Julia St John), a constantly bickering couple whose arguments were laced with shocking insults and true venom, and who stayed together ostensibly For The Sake Of The Children; and the Camp Jockeys, a bizarre and hilarious feature in which jockeys indulged in gay banter during races.

A new trend in *Harry Enfield And Chums* seemed to be towards introducing longer and more elaborate sketches in which the characters could develop. Tim Nice-but Dim started a romance with Sophie Dim-but-Royal; Wayne and Waynetta Slob became National Lottery winners in the second series yet remained unchanged and unfazed by their new-found wealth; and Kevin the teenager gained a pal, Perry (a boy, brilliantly played by Kathy Burke), and eventually metamorphosed again when, after losing his virginity, he rejected adolescent affectations and turned into a model son. (In best *Dallas* style, this was turned around in the 1997 Christmas special, when the change was explained as having been a dream and Kevin was back to being ghastly again.) It all added up to an impressive roster of memorable grotesques, in a series that continued to demonstrate

Enfield's mastery of character comedy. The series also had strange but oddly effective title and credit sequences wherein Enfield, in a forced theatrical fashion, silently introduced his chums Whitehouse and Burke in front of a sterile, plain pink background and to an old-fashioned, nursery rhyme-like tune (actually an anglicised version of the soldiers' chorus from Verdi's *Il Trovatore*). Enfield explained that the opening sequence recalled Mike Yarwood's 1970s series, while the closing moments, in which he and his two chums accepted bouquets and applause, spoofed theatrical curtain calls.

Note. Harry Enfield and Kathy Burke appeared as Wayne and Waynetta in a sketch in **Comic Relief** 1997.

Harry Hill's Fruit Fancies

UK · BBC · COMEDY ANTHOLOGY

6 × 15 mins · b/w

19 Sep–24 Oct 1994 · BBC2 Mon 10.15pm

MAIN CAST
Harry Hill

CREDITS
writer Harry Hill · *director/producer* Jamie Rix

The eccentric Harry Hill – real name Matthew Hall – first made a splash in comedy at the Edinburgh Festival Fringe in 1992 when he won the Perrier Award as best newcomer. His strained delivery and quaint attire – large horn-rimmed spectacles, huge floppy shirt collars, suede shoes and drainpipe pin-striped suit with a pen-stuffed breast-pocket – complemented his offbeat style, which mixed surrealism with music-hall comedy and a modern-day edge. Hill seemed obsessed with everyday objects and waste products and managed to weave fantastic stories around these items. For instance, he told audiences that if they took a melon and scooped out the insides they could fit a whole shirt into it, while his favourite response to being heckled was to announce, 'You may heckle me now, but I'm safe in the knowledge that when I get home I've got a lovely chicken in the oven.'

It was a good bet that Hill's first TV series would be out of the norm and it certainly was: six 15-minute black and white films all shot silently and shown without dialogue but with some sound effects and full music tracks. The films tackled different subjects each week, but each had the Hill touch of surrealism and good visual jokes. It all added up to a welcome and successful attempt to deliver something new and surprising on the small-screen.

Note. By the time of this first regular TV exposure, Hill was well known to BBC Radio

4 listeners through his *Harry Hill's Fruit Corner* series, the first of which, broadcast in four editions, went out from 11 November to 2 December 1993. Three six-part series of the same title have followed, aired 17 November to 22 December 1994, 31 August to 5 October 1995 and 20 March to 24 April 1997. Hill first appeared on Radio 4 in a single comedy special, *When Harry Met Ally*, broadcast on 17 April 1992, in which he teamed up with Alistair McGowan.

Harry Hill

UK · C4 (AVALON TELEVISION) · STANDUP/
SKETCH

8 × 30 mins · colour

30 May–18 July 1997 · Fri 10.30pm

MAIN CAST
Harry Hill
Barrie Gosney
Al Murray
Matt Bradstock
Steve Bowditch
Evie Garratt
Burt Kwouk

CREDITS
writer Harry Hill · *director* Robin Nash · *executive producers* Richard Allen-Turner, Jon Thoday · *producer* Charlie Hanson

More comedy surrealism from a master of the art. Coming over like a cross between Eric Morecambe and Salvador Dali, Hill presented a rapid-paced mélange of absurdist nonsense full of mad ideas, baffling scenarios and unlikely characters. This series utilised much of the style and thrust of Hill's standup act and also harked back to the characters and ideas that had graced his award-winning Edinburgh shows *Flies* and *Eggs*.

Hill's long-term associate, the diminutive Matt Bradstock, was on hand mostly in the role of Harry's adopted son, Alan Hill; comedian Al Murray played Harry's 'Big Brother Alan'. Other regular characters included Nana Hill; the little orphan boy; wide-boy Finsbury Park; and glove puppet Stoofer the Cat. A recurring weekly theme was the imminent badger parade, which Harry panicked to get organised but was regularly thwarted by unpredictable events. The badger puppets that appeared recalled memories of Ken Dodd and his Diddy Men, but Hill's material was way beyond even Dodd's wild imaginings.

With Hill, opinions between critics and viewers alike were polarised: some just couldn't see the joke, but for others – those who could – the anarchic showman delivered a tidal wave of colourful and bizarre comedy situations which can be neatly summed up by Hill's low-key catchphrase, 'What are the chances of that happening, eh?'

The Harry Secombe Show

see SECOMBE, Harry

Harry Worth

see WORTH, Harry

Harry's Mad

UK · ITV (FILM & GENERAL PRODUCTIONS/
CARLTON PRODUCTIONS FOR CENTRAL) ·
CHILDREN'S SITCOM

36 × 30 mins · colour

Series One (6) 4 Jan–8 Feb 1993 · Mon 4.15pm
Series Two (10) 10 Jan–14 Mar 1994 ·
Mon 4.20pm
Series Three (10) 9 Jan–13 Mar 1995 ·
Mon 4.15pm
Series Four (10) 8 Jan–11 Mar 1996 ·
Mon 4.15pm

MAIN CAST
Madison Holdsworth · · · · · · · Anthony Asbury
· (voice only)
Harry Holdsworth · · · · · · · · Gareth Parrington
· (series 1, 2 & 4)
Mrs Angie Holdsworth · · · · · · · · · Jackie Lye
Mr John Holdsworth · · · · · · · · · Mike Walling
Jo · · · · · · · · · · Nadia Williams (series 1 & 2)
Terry Crumm · · · · · · · · · · · Mark Billingham
· (series 1, 2 & 4)
Marguerite · · · · · Andrea Waye (series 1 & 2)
Claude · · · · · · · James Warrior (series 1 & 2)
Hattie · · · · · · Amy Butterworth (series 3 & 4)
Jools · · · · · · · · · · Richard Castillo (series 3)
Mrs Turtle · · · · · · · · Shirley Stelfox (series 3)

CREDITS
creator Dick King-Smith · *writers* Dick King-Smith, Steve Attridge, Graham Alborough, Mark Billingham/David Lloyd, Paul Dornan, Jim Eldridge · *executive producers* Lewis Rudd, Clive Parsons, Davina Belling · *director/producer* Alex Kirby

An entertaining children's sitcom based on Dick King-Smith's best-selling book of the same title, published in 1984. The Harry in the title is a young boy, Harry Holdsworth, who inherits from his eccentric American great-uncle George his most cherished possession, a wisecracking, backchatting African Grey parrot named Madison – the 'Mad' in the title. The parrot considers himself a world expert on everything – he's a wag, an impersonator, he's able to throw his voice, he sings, and is a general all-round entertainer, or, as he himself has it, 'a parrot with a lot to say'. Needless to report, Madison soon transforms the lives of the Holdsworths – not only Harry's but his parents' too, getting them into, but also extricating them from, many a scrape.

Guest stars visiting *Harry's Mad* during the first two series included Dave Lee Travis, Michaela Strachan and snooker great Steve Davis, but the third series brought about major changes. Although he bequeathed the programme his name, Harry left the scene,

ostensibly to take his GCSE exams. In his place Madison entertained Hattie, a ten-year-old white girl who is the adopted daughter of Mrs Holdsworth's Aunt Agatha, and Jools, a 12-year-old black boy – and the two could scarcely believe their ears when they discovered that the parrot could talk. The children lived with Harry's parents, Angie and John Holdsworth, who took over the running of a rundown hotel (also inherited from Aunt Agatha), which they renamed the Madison Guest House. His studies complete, Harry returned in the fourth series, with Jools leaving the cast.

Hart Of The Yard

see *Nobody's Perfect* [USA]

Have A Harry Birthday

Have A Harry Christmas

see SECOMBE, Harry

Have I Got You ... Where You Want Me?

UK · ITV (GRANADA) · SITCOM

7 × 30 mins · colour

3 June–15 July 1981 · Wed 8.30pm

MAIN CAST
Tom · Ian Lavender
Valerie · Kim Braden
Monty · John Alkin
Jason · · · · · · · · · · · · · · · · · · · Jeremy Sinden
Vicky · · · · · · · · · · · · · · · · Susannah Fellows
Vera · Joanne Zorian

CREDITS
writers Philip Harland/Paul Harris · *director* Malcolm Taylor · *producer* Brian Armstrong

Tom is a dentist, Valerie is a teacher, living separately in the town of Eastwood. They have been partners for fully ten years and yet have never succumbed to formality and legalised their union in marriage. Not that Val is against the idea: she'd like nothing more than to stand at the altar, and hints as much every few minutes, but Tom finds himself pathologically incapable of marital commitment. *Have I Got You ... Where You Want Me?* charted the course of their relationship: full of frustration from Valerie, stubbornness from Tom, general sitcom misunderstandings and, ooh vicar, ups and downs. Friends Monty and Jason did their best to help in the muddle.

The series starred Ian Lavender, secure in the nation's heart as the 'stupid boy' Pike in *Dad's Army*, from which he went on to appear as the even more clueless clot, Ron, in *The Glums*. As Tom, he finally had a chance to appear as a 'normal' adult (whatever that is).

Have You Read This Notice?

UK · BBC · SITCOM

1 × 25 mins · b/w

29 Mar 1963 · Fri 8.20pm

MAIN CAST

Norman Fox	Frankie Howerd
First customs officer	Bill Kerr
Aeroplane passenger	Edwin Apps

CREDITS

writers Ray Galton/Alan Simpson · *producer* Graeme Muir

A one-off *Comedy Playhouse* with Frankie Howerd cast as Norman Fox, a man plagued by his conscience as he attempts to take through the 'nothing to declare' section of Customs a fine watch he has bought while on holiday in Switzerland.

See also Frankie Howerd's combined entry.

Haven Of Rest

UK · BBC · SITCOM

1 × 30 mins · colour

1 Apr 1970 · BBC1 Wed 7.30pm

MAIN CAST

Rupert Haliburton	Julian Orchard
Miss Barnett	Vivienne Bennett
Col Satchwell-Simpson	Ballard Berkeley
Bessie	Janie Booth
Daphne Delaney	Lally Bowers
Lady Henderson	Joyce Carey
Muriel Crump	Judith Furse
Arthur Plenderleith	Colin Gordon
Mr Benson	Deryck Guyler
Miss Batchelor	Patricia Hayes
Mr Prentice	John Le Mesurier
Thatcher	Tony Sympson

CREDITS

writer Alan Melville · *producer* Robin Nash

A one-off old folks' home sitcom, screened in the *Comedy Playhouse* season. Despite the strong cast of comedy character actors, and a script from the reliable veteran Alan Melville, no series developed.

Hazel

USA · NBC THEN CBS (SCREEN GEMS) · SITCOM

154 × 30 mins (34 × b/w · 120 × colour)

US dates: 28 Sep 1961–5 Sep 1966

UK dates: 23 Jan 1962–24 June 1963 (24 episodes · b/w) ITV Tue 8pm then various days and times

MAIN CAST

Hazel Burke	Shirley Booth
George Baxter	Don DeFore
Dorothy Baxter	Whitney Blake
Harold Baxter	Bobby Buntrock
Steve Baxter	Ray Fulmer
Barbara Baxter	Lynn Borden
Susie Baxter	Julia Benjamin
Rosie	Maudie Prickett
Harvey Griffin	Howard Smith

CREDITS

creator Ted Key · *writers* various · *producers* Harry Ackerman, James Fonda

Based on a long-running cartoon strip published in the USA in the *Saturday Evening Post*, *Hazel* became a TV series that spanned five years and two networks. London-area ITV viewers saw 24 of the 34 monochrome episodes that were made by NBC, with Shirley Booth starring as Hazel Burke, housemaid to the Baxter family, with a nose for getting involved in other people's business but always, it transpired, to everyone's benefit. Don DeFore appeared as George Baxter, a partner in the law firm Butterworth, Hatch, Noll and Baxter; Whitney Blake played the role of Dorothy, George's wife, who preferred shopping for lingerie to dirtying her hands with housework – hence the need for a maid; and Bobby Buntrock was cast as Harold, their young son. The subsequent CBS episodes showed Hazel working for George Baxter's younger brother Steve.

He & She

USA · CBS (TALENT ASSOCIATES) · SITCOM

26 × 30 mins · colour

US dates: 6 Sep 1967–18 Sep 1968

UK dates: 15 June 1968–2 Jan 1969 (26 episodes) BBC2 Sat 7.25pm

MAIN CAST

Paula Hollister	Paula Prentiss
Dick Hollister	Richard Benjamin
Oscar North	Jack Cassidy
Harry Zarakardos	Kenneth Mars
Andrew Hummel	Hamilton Camp
Norman Nugent	Harold Gould

CREDITS

creator Leonard Stern · *writers* Jay Sandrich, Allan Burns and others · *directors* various · *executive producers* Leonard Stern, Arnold Margolin, Arnie Rosen · *producer* Arne Sultan

A sophisticated and breezy white-collar sitcom that followed the exploits of cartoonist Dick Hollister and his dizzy, social-worker wife Paula, played by real-life husband and wife pairing Richard Benjamin and Paula Prentiss. The Hollisters were comfortably off rather than rich, despite the fact that Dick's super-hero comic strip *Jetman* had been made into a TV series starring an egocentric actor, Oscar North, who was prone to dropping in on the Hollisters in full *Jetman* costume to argue a point of interpretation. Other eccentric visitors included Harry, a fire-fighter from the next door fire station who entered the apartment through a window via a plank placed precariously between the buildings, and their janitor, the certifiable Andrew Hummel.

The series was obviously based on the blueprint of **The Dick Van Dyke Show** – cheekily, one episode about a painting was

entitled 'Dick's Van Dyke' – but it failed to duplicate that series' remarkable success. All the same, *He & She* had a slick, effortless professionalism about it which lifted it above the mainstream. Indeed, some of its creative staff went on to work on a series with similar attributes that enjoyed much greater success, **The Mary Tyler Moore Show**.

Head Of The Class

USA · ABC (EUSTIS ELIAS PRODUCTIONS/ WARNER BROS) · SITCOM

113 episodes (112 × 30 mins · 1 × 60 mins) · colour

US dates: 17 Sep 1986–25 June 1991

UK dates: 5 Mar 1987–27 Aug 1992 (92 × 30 mins) BBC1 mostly Mon around 7.35pm then Mon 3pm

MAIN CAST

Charlie Moore	Howard Hesseman (1986–90)
Dr Harold Samuels	William G Schilling
Billy MacGregor	Billy Connolly (1990–91)
Bernadette	Jeannetta Arnette
Alex	Michael DeLorenzo (1989–91)
Arvid	Dan Frischman
Darlene	Robin Givens
Simone Foster	Khrystyne Haje
Alan	Tony O'Dell
Viki	Lara Piper
Janice	Tannis Vallely (1986–89)
Jawaharlal	Jory Husain (1986–89)
Maria	Leslie Bega (1986–89)
T J	Rain Pryor (1988–91)
Eric	Brian Robbins
Sarah	Kimberly Russell
Dennis	Dan Schneider
Aristotle	De'voreaux White
Jasper	Jonathan Ke Quan (1990–91)

CREDITS

creators Rich Eustis/Michael Elias · *writers* Rich Eustis/Michael Elias, Jeffrey Duteil, Gary Gilbert, Brad Isaacs, Raymond M Jessel, Michael Reiss/ Al Jean, Alan Rosen, Ursula Zeigler and others · *directors* Peter Baldwin, John Tracy, Alan Rosen, Art Dielhenn, Frank Bonner, Kim Friedman, Lee Shallat and others · *executive producers* Rich Eustis/Michael Elias · *producer* Alan Rosen

Manhattan High School (later Fillmore High School) was the setting for this sitcom which featured the likeable Howard Hesseman as an idealistic teacher, Charlie Moore. The angle here was that his charges, unlike the typical sitcom school children, were all gifted students on the Honors Program. Pony-tailed Charlie found that while his multi-cultural, multi-ethnic class had immersed themselves in the sea of knowledge they had hardly dipped their fingers in the pool of life; hence he considered himself of greater use as a conduit to the 'real world' rather than as just another teacher. This neat reversal of the usual comic academia proved pleasingly durable, and Hesseman was his usual dependable self as the liberal, tolerant and empathetic Moore. The series hit its stride relatively quickly and soon became established as a consistent achiever, not the top of its year perhaps, but certainly above average. One notable coup for the show was that it became the first US sitcom to film on location in the Soviet Union, in a ground-breaking episode where the Manhattan students took on their equally gifted Soviet counterparts in an inter-school competition.

When Charlie (and Hesseman) departed for new challenges, Billy Connolly joined the cast as Billy MacGregor, a Glasgow-born, Oxford-educated teacher who continues the 'university of life' approach with the students, mixing liberal amounts of standup-style comedy in his lectures on life. Connolly's exotic accent and earthy style scored well with viewers and programme-makers and the character of MacGregor was spun-off into his own series, *Billy*.

Health And Efficiency

UK · BBC · SITCOM

12 × 30 mins · colour

Series One (6) 30 Dec 1993–3 Feb 1994 · BBC1 Thu 8.30pm
Series Two (6) 6 Jan 1995–10 Feb 1995 · BBC1 Fri 8.30pm

MAIN CAST

Dr Michael Jimson · · · · · · · · · · · Gary Olsen
Dr Kate Russell · · · · · · · · · Felicity Montagu
Dr Rex Regis · · · · · · · · · · · Roger Lloyd Pack
Diana Ewarts · · · · · · · · · · · Deborah Norton
Dr Phil Brooke · · · · · · · · · · · Victor McGuire
Sister Beth Williams · · · · · · · · Adjoa Andoh

CREDITS

writer Andrew Marshall · *director/producer* Richard Boden

Writer Andrew Marshall wrote the characters of *Health And Efficiency* with specific actors in mind and was lucky to get those choices for the roles. His *2 Point 4 Children* star Gary Olsen took the lead as Dr Michael Jimson, a hard-working senior registrar at St James's General Hospital who had been engaged to fellow doctor Kate Russell and was now involved in a love/hate relationship with her. Jimson's fellow ward workers were the scalpel-happy surgeon Rex Regis, the young houseman Phil Brooke (a role he had first played in a 1992 episode of *2 Point 4 Children*) and nurse Beth Williams.

The series took an up-to-date look at the problems facing the National Health Service and the then government's attempts to classify and reorganise it like a profit-making business. At St James's the executive in charge of restructuring hospital procedures was Diana Ewarts, a career businesswoman whose determination to make the place more efficient never took into consideration the health and welfare of the patients, or, as she referred to them, in the government's cold-

hearted but supposedly business-efficient manner, 'the units'. This constant clash between health and efficiency formed the centre of the series and was neatly reflected in the title, three words already well connected in Britain as the title of the innocent, but nonetheless slightly risqué, monthly magazine for naturists.

In attempting to accentuate the battle of service versus money, Marshall unashamedly polarised his characters into 'goodies' (the hard-working and compassionate doctors) and 'baddies' (the soulless bureaucrats, accountants and efficiency experts). Surgeon Rex Regis could have been in both camps but his callous disinterest in the patients and sexual pursuit of Diana Ewarts meant that he often fell in with the 'baddies'. The series had points to make, in spades, and the characters, although exaggerated, had a recognisable ring of truth about them. Deborah Norton impressed and there was more than a hint of Margaret Thatcher in her performance as the heartless Ewarts.

This series was enjoyable and witty, with a dash of *M*A*S*H* in its composition – pressurised doctors using humour to compensate for the grim nature of much of their work, while working for a lunatic master (the army in *M*A*S*H*, the government health trust in *Health And Efficiency*). As in the American series, our heroes weren't perfect, made mistakes and were often childish in their jokes, but they cared deeply for their patients.

The Heavy Mob

UK · ITV (THAMES) · SITCOM

1 × 30 mins · colour

24 Mar 1977 · Thu 7.30pm

MAIN CAST

George Fletcher · · · · · · · · · Windsor Davies
Bert Ramsden · · · · · · · · · · Michael Robbins
Sgt Ryan · · · · · · · · · · · · · · Robert Keegan
Alan Parker · · · · · · · · · · · · · John Flanagan
Lofty Harris · · · · · · · · · · · · · Ronnie Brody
Benny Bates · · · · · · · · · · · Norman Mitchell
Joe Higgins · · · · · · · · · · · · Bernard Stone
Sadie Higgins · · · · · · · · · · · · Toni Palmer

CREDITS

writer Terence Feely · *director/producer* Les Chatfield

A single-episode comedy from Thames that failed to make the grade into a full series. Windsor Davies – appearing at the time in the BBC's *It Ain't Half Hot Mum* – starred as an accident-prone man determined to do his bit to protect the vulnerable public. When he fails his police medical he sets up his own private security organisation, locates it next to the police station and recruits a rough, tough bunch of staff.

Heirs On A Shoestring

UK · BBC · SITCOM

1 × 30 mins · b/w

9 June 1967 · BBC1 Fri 7.30pm

MAIN CAST

James · · · · · · · · · · · · · · · Jimmy Edwards
Uncle Charles · · · · · · · · · · · · · Clive Dunn
Alfred · · · · · · · · · · · · · · · · · · · Sam Kydd
Winifred · · · · · · · · · · · · · Frances Bennett

CREDITS

writer Dave Freeman · *producer* John Street

Comedy writer Dave Freeman, whose first script was broadcast by Jimmy Edwards in 1952 in the BBC radio series *Workers' Playtime*, provided this *Comedy Playhouse* pilot for the star. Edwards was cast as James, who, with his wife Winifred, is eagerly anticipating an inheritance from an elderly uncle (played by Clive Dunn). But when a third heir, Alfred, appears on the scene, their legacy is jeopardised. No series developed.

Note. The programme was screened less than four months after Edwards, chiefly supported by Dunn, had starred in *Gentleman Jim*, an ITV sitcom pilot screened (but not in London) by ABC. Written by Jimmy Grafton and David Climie, and produced by Peter Dulay, it was shown in the Midlands and the North on 19 February 1967, virtually two years after its April 1965 recording. Edwards was cast as Squire Jim of Rookham Hall, Dunn as Jim Bules, his not-so-faithful butler, and the cast also included Alison Frazer, Marion Wilson, Eddie Malin, Bob Todd, Damaris Hayman, Will Stampe and Walter Sparrow, with special guest star Richard Wattis. Again, no series developed.

Hello Cheeky

UK · ITV (YORKSHIRE) · SKETCH

13 × 30 mins · colour

Series One (8) 19 Jan–22 Mar 1976 · Mon 8pm
Series Two (5) 26 May–23 June 1976 · Wed mostly 11pm

MAIN CAST

Barry Cryer
John Junkin
Tim Brooke-Taylor
Denis King

CREDITS

writers Barry Cryer, John Junkin, Tim Brooke-Taylor · *executive producer* Duncan Wood · *producer* Len Lurcuck

The TV version of an in-your-face skit-full comedy series – no frills, just fast-moving wit and appalling puns by the shovelful. *Hello Cheeky* had been delighting BBC radio audiences for more than three years when Yorkshire TV offered the resident team of wagsters, Tim Brooke-Taylor, Barry Cryer and John Junkin, with the musical accompanist Denis King, a chance to strike at a different happy medium: vision. Two series resulted.

The radio *Hello Cheeky* ran either side of the TV version. There were five series, all broadcast by BBC Radio 2: 7 April to 16 June 1973 (11 shows), 10 February to 18 May 1974 (15), 9 March to 1 June 1975 (13), 16 May to 29 August 1976 (16) and 7 October to 11 November 1979 (6), and three Christmas Day specials (1973, 1974 and 1976). Radio 2 also broadcast *The Least Worst Of Hello Cheeky*, a pair of shows that compiled highlights from previous editions, aired on 25 January and 1 February 1976.

Hello, Good Afternoon, Welcome

UK · ITV (SCOTTISH) · STANDUP/SKETCH

6 × 30 mins · colour

*4 Nov–9 Dec 1980 · Tue 3.45pm

MAIN CAST
Allan Stewart
Kristine
Phil Clarke

CREDITS
producer David Macmahon · *executive producer* Bryan Izzard

Comedy and music from Scotsman Allan Stewart (see *The Allan Stewart Tapes* for details) and a couple of cohorts. The series led to a Christmas special made by Thames and shown on 29 December 1980 (*The Allan Stewart Show*).

*Note. These dates reflect the London-area screenings.

The Hello Goodbye Man

UK · BBC · SITCOM

6 × 30 mins · colour

5 Jan–9 Feb 1984 · BBC2 Thu 9pm

MAIN CAST
Denis Ailing · · · · · · · · · · · · · · · Ian Lavender
Jennifer Reynoldston · · · · · · · · Mary Tamm
Ken Harrington · · · · · · · · · · · Paul Chapman
Glenn Harris · · · · · · · · · · · · Dominic Guard

CREDITS
writer David Nobbs · *director/producer* Alan J W Bell

The adventures of Denis Ailing, a 42-year-old peculiarly unsuited to be a salesman but who nevertheless obtains such a position with Cookham's Cures. These six episodes charted the appropriately named Ailing's attempts to make it in the competitive world of salesmanship. His chief rival was the smoothie Glenn Harris, who was not only successful in business but also managed to charm many attractive females with his gift of the gab. Denis managed to make a small splash when he finally overcame his psychological block against selling, only to find that he had another block about taking

the orders. *The Hello Goodbye Man* bade farewell after just one series, failing to sell itself to the public in the style of author Nobbs' earlier masterpiece – also set in the world of enterprise – **The Fall And Rise Of Reginald Perrin**.

Hello Mum

UK · BBC · SKETCH/STANDUP

6 × 30 mins · colour

23 Feb–30 Mar 1987 · BBC2 Mon 10.15pm

MAIN CAST
Helen Lederer
Clive Mantle
Nick Wilton
Arnold Brown

CREDITS
writers Jamie Rix/Nick Wilton (6), Simon Brint/Matthews/Rowland Rivron (6), Arnold Brown (6), Max Handley (6), Robin Driscoll (6), Paul B Davies (5), Roger Planer (5), Tony Allen (5), Abi Grant (4), John Dowie (4), Moray Hunter/Jack Docherty (4), Paul Smith/Terry Kyan (4), Jeremy Hardy (3), Morwenna Banks (3), Paul Durden (3), Steve Bell (3), Helen Lederer (2), Nigel Cooper (2), Paul Martin (2), Phil Nice/Arthur Smith (1), Bob Boulton/Barbara Boulton (1), Clive Mantle (1), John Irwin (1), Mary Hill (1) · *director* Robin Carr · *producer* Jamie Rix

A live, team-comedy show featuring a quartet of faces becoming increasingly familiar to TV viewers at this time. Lederer, Mantle and Wilton all graduated from *In One Ear* (BBC Radio 4, 1984–86), bringing with them some of the quirkiness of that series. The writing credits included a number of interesting names, satirical cartoonist Steve Bell, standup star Jeremy Hardy and aspiring comic Paul Merton (still working as Paul Martin) among them.

In common with many sketch shows, *Hello Mum* attracted a good deal of criticism, with particular condemnation of its perceived amateurishness and inconsistency. But the programme also had supporters – albeit not enough to bring about a second series.

Hell's Bells

UK · BBC · SITCOM

6 × 30 mins · colour

9 June–14 July 1986 · BBC1 Mon 8.30pm

MAIN CAST
Dean Selwyn Makepeace · · · · Derek Nimmo
Bishop Godfrey Hethercote · · · · · · · · · · · · ·
· Robert Stephens
Maudie Mountjoy · · · · · · · Penelope Horner
Emma Hethercote · · · · · · · · Susan Jameson
Edith Makepeace · · · · · · · · · · · Phyllida Law
Wilfred Hankey · · · · · · · · · · · · Milton Johns

CREDITS
writer Jan Butlin · *director/producer* Mike Stephens

By some miracle, Derek Nimmo found himself back in the church for yet another TV interpretation of his cloistered clergyman persona (*All Gas And Gaiters*, *Oh Brother!*, *Oh Father!*). This time he was the Dean of Norchester Cathedral, Selwyn Makepeace, engaged to be married to Maudie Mountjoy. Makepeace is a traditionalist whose cloistered views on spiritual life are tested by the arrival of a new, unconventional Bishop, the outspoken socialist Godfrey Hethercote, and his wife Emma. The new arrivals have radical ideas about how best to spread the word of the Lord and their first gesture is to forgo the comforts of their well-appointed quarters and set up home in a run-down council estate where they can be 'nearer to their erring flock'. Selwyn feared the worst from this shocking departure from the norm and the comedy arose from the clash of philosophies as convention and innovation met head on. Nimmo made such heaven-sent roles look easy, and his co-star was the fine stage actor Robert Stephens.

Writer Jan Butlin went on to author two further sitcoms starring Derek Nimmo, **Life Begins At Forty** and **Third Time Lucky**.

Help!

UK · BBC · SITCOM

12 × 30 mins · colour

Series One (6) 2 Sep–7 Oct 1986 · BBC1 Tue 8.30pm

Series Two (6) 9 Apr–14 May 1988 · BBC1 Sat around 5.45pm

MAIN CAST
Tex · · · · · · · · · · · · · · · · · Stephen McGann
Lenny · · · · · · · · · · · · · · · · · David Albany
Davva · · · · · · · · · · · · · · · Jake Abraham
Annie · · · · · · · · · · · · · · · · · · Sheila Fay

CREDITS
writer Joe Boyle · *directors* Mike Stephens (11), Tony Dow (1) · *producer* Mike Stephens

Another fictional series set in Liverpool and featuring characters struggling to survive on the dole. But unlike two of its more illustrious predecessors – the drama *Boys From The Blackstuff* and the sitcom **Bread** – *Help!* presented an unashamedly upbeat view of life, its three teenage heroes being constantly optimistic about their chances of finding success. Tex, the literary member of the group (he had passed Grade 4 CSE English), was played by Stephen McGann, one of the ubiquitous McGann acting clan. His constant companions were Lenny and Davva, and the three Merseysiders made a pact not to lie in their beds rotting, but to go out and meet life head on. Each episode concluded in the park shelter, where the trio convened to discuss their prospects. Two series were made, the first screened at 8.30pm, BBC1's favoured time-slot for sitcoms, the other, oddly, scheduled for younger viewers.

The Hen House

UK · BBC · SITCOM

1 × 25 mins · b/w
10 Jan 1964 · Fri 7.35pm

MAIN CAST
Teresa Fanwyn · · · · · · · · · · · · · · · Beryl Reid
Cynthia Spooner · · · · · · · · · Barbara Windsor
Edwin Russell · · · · · · · · · · · · · Dermot Kelly

CREDITS
writers George Evans/Derek Collyer · producer
Michael Mills

Screened as a pilot within the *Comedy Playhouse* strand, this single episode was set in the Khartoum House Girls' Hostel, run by the formidable Mrs Fanwyn (Beryl Reid), where her iron-clad rules forbidding male visitors met with disapproval from the female tenants. The ensuing conflicts would doubtless have formed the heart of a series, had one materialised.

Beryl Reid later appeared in another Evans and Collyer comedy pilot, also not developed further. Titled *Thicker Than Water*, it aired only in local areas by the Midlands/North ITV weekend franchise ABC, screened late-night on 9 December 1967 within a *Comedy Playhouse*-style strand titled *Comedy Tonight*. Reid and Sheila Hancock co-starred as two sisters, Rose and Charlotte, who own and run a wool shop but spend more time bickering with one another than selling yarn. Pat Johns was the producer.

Dickie Henderson

A genial and generous all-round entertainer, Dickie Henderson had show business in his blood. Born on 30 October 1922 as the son of Dickie Henderson (Senior), a Yorkshireman vaudeville entertainer of renown from the 1920s onwards, Henderson the younger appeared in a Hollywood film version of Noël Coward's *Cavalcade* when just ten years of age. At 16 he left school and became props boy for Jack Hylton's organisation, and then joined his sisters, Triss and Wyn, for a combined act they named the Henderson Twins and Dickie. The act broke up when the twins married, but Dickie Jr set out on his own as a humorous raconteur, singer, dancer and, no less, an acrobat.

After making his TV debut in the BBC's *Face The Music*, Dickie Henderson popped up in Arthur Askey's BBC series **Before Your Very Eyes**, made numerous variety appearances both in Britain and America (he appeared on *The Ed Sullivan Show* in March 1956) and then made his *Royal Variety Show* debut in 1956, precisely 30 years after his father had first appeared before royalty. From there Dickie Henderson was given his

own shows and series, became one of the regular *Val Parnell's Sunday Night At The London Palladium* comperes in 1958 and never looked back, appearing regularly on TV and, especially, on stage for more than 20 years.

Dickie Henderson died on 22 September 1985, one of his last jobs being to host Thames TV's game-show *Sounds Like London* (1982). His contemporaries paid tribute in a special two-hour show recorded at the Royalty Theatre in London and screened on ITV on 5 May 1986 as *The Stars Entertain: A Tribute To Dickie Henderson OBE*.

See also **Young And Foolish** and **I'm Bob, He's Dickie**.

The Dickie Henderson Show   1

UK · ITV (ATV) · SKETCH/STANDUP

5 editions (3 × 60 mins · 1 × 55 mins · 1 × 45 mins) · b/w

6 Apr 1957 · Sat 8.30pm (45 mins)
10 Aug 1957 · Sat 9.30pm (60 mins)
30 Nov 1957 · Sat 8.30pm (60 mins)
1 Mar 1958 · Sat 8.30pm (60 mins)
6 Sep 1959 · Sun 9.05pm (55 mins)

MAIN CAST
Dickie Henderson
Anthea Askey (eds 2–4)
Freddie Mills (eds 2–5)

CREDITS
writers Jimmy Grafton (2), Dickie Henderson/Jimmy Grafton (2), Alan Melville/Jimmy Grafton (1) · directors/producers Brian Tesler (4), Alan Tarrant (1)

These five shows were Henderson's first starring vehicles, mixed in and around the star's many appearances in TV variety programmes. The first four were aired in the *Val Parnell's Saturday Spectacular* strand, the last as *Bernard Delfont's Sunday Show*.

The success of the first four, in particular, paved the way for Henderson's first regular series with impresario Jack Hylton, with Anthea Askey and boxing champ turned TV performer Freddie Mills making the move with him.

The Dickie Henderson Half-Hour

UK · ITV (JACK HYLTON TV PRODUCTIONS FOR ASSOCIATED-REDIFFUSION) · SKETCH

19 × 30 mins · b/w
Series One (11) 4 July–12 Sep 1958 · Fri mostly 8.30pm
Series Two (8) 4 May–22 June 1959 · Mon 9.30pm

MAIN CAST
Dickie Henderson
Anthea Askey
Eve Lister
Bernard Hunter
Freddie Mills
June Cunningham (series 1)

Len Lowe (series 1)
Tom Payne (series 1)
Claire Gordon (series 1)
Clive Dunn (series 2)

CREDITS
writers see below · script associate Jimmy Grafton · director Bill Hitchcock

These two series cemented Henderson's popularity with TV audiences, and promoted the comedy element that would keep him at the top for years to come: his domestic bickering with his wife (here played by Anthea Askey, daughter of Arthur). The scripts were good: although not announced as such, Jack Hylton bought them from America, where they had been used by Sid Caesar in *Your Show Of Shows*.

The Dickie Henderson Show   2

UK · ITV (ATV) · STANDUP/SKETCH

1 × 55 mins · b/w
6 Sep 1959 · Sun 9.05pm

MAIN CAST
Dickie Henderson
Freddie Mills

CREDITS
producer Alan Tarrant

A single show, again with former boxer Freddie Mills.

The Dickie Henderson Show   3

UK · ITV (ASSOCIATED-REDIFFUSION/ *REDIFFUSION) · SITCOM

116 editions (115 × 30 mins · 1 × 60 mins) · b/w

Series One (26) 14 Nov 1960–8 May 1961 · Mon 8pm
Series Two (7) 13 Nov–26 Dec 1961 · mostly Mon 8pm
Series Three (7) 7 May–18 June 1962 · Mon 9.15pm
Series Four (18 × 30 mins · 1 × 60 mins) 21 Nov 1962–24 Apr 1963 · mostly Wed 9.15pm
Series Five (9) 14 June–8 Aug 1963 · mostly Fri 7pm
Series Six (15) 19 Sep–26 Dec 1963 · Thu 7.30pm
*Series Seven (12) 29 Apr–12 Aug 1964 · mostly Wed 9.10pm
*Series Eight (9) 20 May; 16 Aug–4 Oct 1965 · mostly Mon 9.10pm
*Series Nine (12) 3 Jan–20 Mar 1968 · Wed 8pm

MAIN CAST
Dickie · · · · · · · · · · · · · · Dickie Henderson
June · · · · · · · · · · June Laverick (series 1–8)
Jack · · · · · · · · · · · · · · · · Lionel Murton
John · · · · · · · · · · · John Parsons (series 1–5)
Richard Jr · · · · · · Danny Grover (series 6–8)
Maggie · · Eleanor Summerfield (series 7–9)
Jane · · · · · · · · · · · · · · · Isla Blair (series 9)
Mother-in-law · · · · · · Fabia Drake (series 9)

CREDITS
main writer Jimmy Grafton (115) · *co-writers* Jeremy Lloyd (87), Alan Fell (19), Stan Mars (19), Stanley Myers (19), Eric Newman (13), Robert Gray (6), Johnny Whyte (2), Teddy Peiro (1), Peter Griffiths (1), Maurice Wiltshire (1), David Climie (1), Peter Myers (1) · *executive producer* Ben Lyon (series 1–8) · *director* Bill Hitchcock

Exploring the same premise of *The Dickie Henderson Half-Hour* – man the entertainer, man the husband, man the father – this marathon series ran virtually the length of the 1960s and was extremely popular throughout that time. Dickie appeared as, well, himself, keeping busy on the stage, being offered film parts and, latterly, enjoying his own TV show. June Laverick played his somewhat dotty wife (and, as Dickie saw it, predictably, the cause of domestic trouble and strife), they had a young son, circa ten years old (first John Parsons then, when he had to concentrate on exams, Danny Grover), and Dickie had a musical manager, Jack, who, as often as not, was visiting the house.

In many ways, the series was similar to the American sitcoms of the period that were purposely built around a star name; to this end, each episode (until later in the 1960s) featured a prominent guest star playing roles within the sitcom scripts. These ranged from Spurs footballer Danny Blanchflower to Boris Karloff, some appearing in the TV parts for which they were familiar, like Raymond Francis appearing as Det-Chief Supt Lockhart of ITV crime series *No Hiding Place*. Further aping the American system, the series was always good clean fun, devoid of smut or bad language, drawing its humour from such domestic dilemmas as Dickie forgetting June's birthday, or Dickie failing to adhere to the life lectures he doled out to his son.

Dickie Henderson's real-life wife, Dixie, died young, in 1963, but the star determined that the *Show* must go on. The series appeared to end in 1965, but the best part of three years later it returned. June Laverick had retired from show business in the interim and so Dickie had a new wife (the mini-skirted Isla Blair as Jane) who was 23 to his 45. This series was the last and it marked the end of *The Dickie Henderson Show* as a sitcom, although the title was used again for his other TV outings and the sitcom premise was revived once last time in Thames' 1969–70 sequel *A Present For Dickie*.

The Dickie Henderson Show   4

UK · BBC · STANDUP

2 × 45 mins · b/w

1 Mar 1966 · BBC2 Tue 8.50pm
22 Apr 1967 · BBC2 Sat 7.40pm

MAIN CAST
Dickie Henderson

CREDITS
writers Jimmy Grafton (show 1), Robert Gray (show 2) · *producer* Michael Hurll

Two *Show Of The Week* specials that saw the comedian/singer/dancer in rare BBC appearances with guests Brian Rix, Roy Castle and Leslie A 'Hutch' Hutchinson.

A Present For Dickie

UK · ITV (THAMES) · SITCOM

6 × 30 mins · colour

30 Dec 1969–5 Feb 1970 · Thu 7pm

MAIN CAST
Dickie · · · · · · · · · · · · · Dickie Henderson
Mother-in-law · · · · · · · · · · · · · Fabia Drake
Parker · · · · · · · · · · · · · Dennis Ramsden
William · · · · · · · · · · · · · · · · Billy Burden

OTHER APPEARANCES
Jane · · · · · · · · June Laverick (final episode)

CREDITS
creator Jimmy Grafton · *writers* Jimmy Grafton/ Johnny Heyward (3), Jimmy Grafton/Johnny Heyward/Stan Mars (3) · *director/producer* Peter Frazer-Jones

In a clear sequel to the premise explored over eight years in *The Dickie Henderson Show*, new sitcom *A Present For Dickie* saw the star arrive home from a cabaret tour of the Far East to discover that Jane, his wife, was away, returning from Down Under on a slow boat. (She appeared only in the final episode, and turned out to be the back-from-retirement June Laverick.) But there remained Dickie's ever suspicious mother-in-law, and a gift in the bulky shape of a young female named Mini – an Indian elephant. 'Hilarious consequences' ensued, much as they had done when Henderson appeared on stage with an elephant in the variety series *The Blackpool Show* some years earlier.

The Dickie Henderson Show   5

UK · ITV (LWT) · SKETCH/STANDUP

7 × 60 mins · colour

13 Mar–23 Apr 1971 · mostly Sat 9pm

MAIN CAST
Dickie Henderson
Teddy Peiro
Lionel Blair

CREDITS
writers Jimmy Grafton/Jeremy Lloyd · *executive producer* Terry Henebery · *producer* Philip Casson

Comedy, singing and dancing from the all-round entertainer in seven one-hour shows. Teddy Peiro, who had co-written one of the A-R shows ten years earlier, appeared each week as a wit and juggler.

I'm Dickie – That's Showbusiness

UK · ITV (ATV) · SKETCH/STANDUP

2 × 60 mins · colour

20 May 1978 · Sat 7.30pm
4 Oct 1978 · Wed 8pm

MAIN CAST
Dickie Henderson

CREDITS
writers Garry Chambers, Dick Vosburgh · *director/producer* Paul Stewart Laing

Two 60-minute specials that emphasised Henderson's versatility as an entertainer. His old pantomime partner Arthur Askey was on hand to give comedy support in the first show (along with Michele Dotrice from *Some Mothers Do 'Ave 'Em*), and Prunella Scales (from *Fawlty Towers*) graced the second.

Lenny Henry

Born in Dudley on 29 August 1958, Lenny Henry burst on to TV at the age of 16, winning an edition of the talent-search show *New Faces* in 1975. Brimming with confidence, the black teenager impressed with quick-fire impressions of celebrities, particularly Muhammad Ali. Although his choice of targets was far from original, he overcame this by joking 'You may have seen some of these impressions before, but not in colour'. Overnight success persuaded Henry to quit technical college, where he was studying engineering, and enter show business full time, but the path to lasting fame wasn't always easy: he was short of material and experience and the novelty of his act soon wore off. However, a five-year stint touring with the Black And White Minstrels (perversely, he was the only member of the troupe who didn't have to apply swathes of black makeup) allowed him to hone his stage skills, and his regular appearances in the sitcom *The Fosters* in 1976–77 taught Henry the rudiments of comic acting.

But it was on ATV's (latterly Central's) anarchic Saturday-morning children's programme *Tiswas* that Henry made his first prolonged impact, proving at the same time how adept he was at live television. Instead of merely impersonating, Henry *created* characters for *Tiswas*, among them a Rastafarian he splendidly named Algernon Spencer Churchill Gladstone Disraeli Palmerston Pitt-The-Younger Razzamatazz, a noisy bundle of energy who loved condensed-milk sandwiches and whose catchphrase was a drawn-out 'Oooohhhhkaayyy!' He also perfected an exaggerated impression of naturalist David Bellamy and enjoyed a monopoly with his impersonation of ITN's black newsreader Trevor McDonald (whom Henry named Trevor McDoughnut). Henry experienced a rare flop with the adult *Tiswas* variation *O.T.T.* but re-established himself soon afterwards as a major player as part of the *Three Of A Kind* team. By 1984 Henry had matured to the point where he was rewarded with his own starring TV show (he also had one on BBC Radio 1), and subsequently he fully realised his potential, scoring as a wicked standup act, a fine dramatic and comedic actor, and an honorary member of the 'alternative' comedy wave which came to dominate TV in the 1980s. Henry has also made inroads into the US market, with stage performances and feature films, and been one of the guiding lights in the **Comic Relief** initiative.

Henry married Dawn French in 1984, and she has often been cited as a major influence on the direction and increasing sophistication of his comedy. Highlights from Henry's standup shows on BBC TV were compiled into three special editions, *The Beast Of Lenny Henry*, screened by BBC1 on 24 February, 10 March and 13 May 1997.

See also *Chef!, The Summer Show* and *Now What.*

The Lenny Henry Show   1

UK · BBC · SKETCH/STANDUP

13 editions (12 × 30 mins · 1 × 40 mins) · colour

Series One (6) 4 Sep–9 Oct 1984 · BBC1 Tue 7.30pm

Series Two (6) 12 Sep–10 Oct 1985 · BBC1 Thu 8.30pm

Special (40 mins) 24 Dec 1987 · BBC1 Thu 8pm

MAIN CAST

Lenny Henry

CREDITS

writers Lenny Henry (13), Kim Fuller (13), James Hendrie/Tony Sarchet (12), Andrea Solomons (10), Ian Brown (8), David Hansen/Paul Owen (7), Geoff Atkinson (7), James Bibby (6), Bob Sinfield (6), Garry Chambers (1), Moray Hunter/Jack Docherty (1) · *director/producer* Geoff Posner

Lenny Henry more than lived up to his early promise by excelling in this consistently high-quality sketch show that was distinguished by handsomely mounted filmed spoofs of films, other TV programmes and pop videos – with an especially memorable pastiche of Michael Jackson's 'Thriller' promo. The shows also featured a roster of recurring Henry characters, including the soul-singing sex-god Theophilus P Wildebeeste; PC Ganga;

dear old Deakus, one of the first batch of post-war Jamaican immigrants into England, now in his final years; and new creation Derek The Teacher, a lampoon of the sort of student-teachers torn to shreds by inner-city schoolkids. Geoff Posner's direction and production imbued the series with a touch of class and Henry turned in performances to match.

Lenny Henry Tonite

UK · BBC · SITCOMS

6 × 30 mins · colour

4 Sep–9 Oct 1986 · BBC1 Thu 8.30pm

As Henry's comedy style matured, he started to explore new vehicles for his talent. *Lenny Henry Tonite* was a sort of *Comedy Playhouse*, with Henry introducing a new character each week in episodes provided by different writers.

Pratt Outta Hell   4 SEP

MAIN CAST

Vince	Lenny Henry
Chain	Dicken Ashworth
Crow	David Ashworth
Boss	Chris Barrie
Norris	Ram John Holder
Lost Property Man	Norman Lovett

CREDITS

writer Ben Elton · *director/producer* Geoff Posner

The tale of a super-cool but demented motorcycle despatch rider.

Popsi   11 SEP

MAIN CAST

Popsi	Lenny Henry
Marvin	Chris Tummings
Pat	Cathy Tyson
Bugeye	Paul McKenzie
Albert	Cameron Miller
Lloydy	Rudolph Walker

CREDITS

writer Tunde Ikoli · *director/producer* Geoff Posner

Popsi, a Jamaican barber, finds it hard to come to terms with 1980s hair styles and accessories.

Gronk Zillman   18 SEP

MAIN CAST

Gronk Zillman	Lenny Henry
Stephanie	Harriet Thorpe
Controller	Connie Booth
Cabbie	Alan Talbot
Guard	Ronnie Brody
MP	George Baker
Busker	Midge Ure

CREDITS

writer Kim Fuller · *director/producer* Geoff Posner

Gronk Zillman, a time-travelling detective, is so far ahead of his time that he solves a crime that won't happen for another 49 years.

Neighbourhood Watch   25 SEP

MAIN CAST

Francis Disley	Lenny Henry
Julia Disley	Dawn French
Denny	Daniel Peacock
Roger	Lee Cornes
Neighbour	Jimmy Nail
Iranian	Harry Enfield

CREDITS

writers Dick Clement/Ian La Frenais · *director/producer* Geoff Posner

Living in suburbia, Francis Disley has mundane questions on his mind, and he seeks answers.

Mirroring real life, Lenny Henry and Dawn French played a married couple in this episode; it was written by Clement and la Frenais from an idea by Jimmy Nail (who also played a minor role).

What A Country   2 OCT

MAIN CAST

Desmond King	Lenny Henry
Pathé News interviewer	Chris Douglas
Commissionaire	Andy de la Tour
Mr Hodges	Victor Maddern
Vicar	John Fortune
Big Eddie Pilkington	Clive Mantle

CREDITS

writers Stan Hey/Andrew Nickolds · *director/producer* Geoff Posner

It is 1955 and Desmond King, newly arrived in England from Jamaica, cannot wait to sample the milk and honey land of unlimited job opportunities and civility. A qualified accountant, he manages to find work in a factory …

Heavenly Romance   9 OCT

MAIN CAST

Jupiter/Fielding Burchill	Lenny Henry
Juno/Carol	Debby Bishop
Trellick	Ellis Dale
Steve	Billy Hartman
Mercury	Chris Darwin

CREDITS

writers Kim Fuller/Simon Brint · *director/producer* Geoff Posner

The ultra-boring Fielding, and the other staff of a new video teen-magazine, tell their stories in words, pictures and music.

The Lenny Henry Show   2

UK · BBC · SITCOM

12 × 30 mins · colour

Series One (6) 27 Oct–1 Dec 1987 · BBC1
Tue 8.30pm

Series Two (6) 15 Sep–3 Nov 1988 · BBC1
Thu 9.30pm

MAIN CAST
Delbert Wilkins · · · · · · · · · · · Lenny Henry
Winston · · · · · · · · · · · · · · · Vas Blackwood
Rose · · · · · · · · · · · · · · · · · Ellen Thomas
Alex · · · · · · · · · · · · · · · · Michael Mears
Julie · · · · · · · · · · · · · · · · · Gina McKee
Wazim · · · · · · · · · · · · · · · · · Naim Kahn
Sgt Lillie · · · · · · · · · · · · Malcolm Rennie
PC Monkhouse · · · · · Pip Torrens (series 1)
Jake · · · · · · · · · · Louis Mahoney (series 1)
Claudette · · · · · · · Nimmy March (series 2)
Trevor · · · · · · · · · · · Trevor Laird (series 2)

CREDITS
writers Stan Hey/Andrew Nickolds · *director/ producer* Geoff Posner

When *The Lenny Henry Show* returned it was with an entirely new format, a sitcom based on the attempts of 'wicked' and 'crucial' south London pirate radio DJ Delbert Wilkins to break into the big time. Henry himself had created Wilkins, 'a dandy with a bit of chat and a reputation to live up to', for the late-night live series *O.T.T.*, basing the character on an amalgam of people he had met, including his big brother Seymour, his little brother Paul, and a friend, Kevin, who constantly said 'You know what I mean?' Scripts for the series were written by Hey and Nickolds who proved emphatically that you don't have to be black to create comedy of appeal to a black audience. Hey had first met the comedian when Henry starred in the writer's British road movie (for television) *Coast To Coast* (BBC2, 4 January 1987) and was quick to recognise his ability as a character actor.

The Lenny Henry Christmas Special

UK · BBC · STANDUP/SKETCH
1 × 40 mins · colour
24 Dec 1987 · BBC1 Thu 8pm

MAIN CAST
Lenny Henry
Robbie Coltrane

CREDITS
writers Kim Fuller, Geoff Atkinson, Lenny Henry · *director/producer* Geoff Posner

A return to the sketch format for this Christmas special, the highlight of which was an extended spoof of Michael Jackson's video for 'Bad'.

The Lenny Henry Special

UK · BBC · STANDUP/SKETCH
1 × 40 mins · colour
26 Dec 1988 · BBC1 Mon 10.05pm

MAIN CAST
Lenny Henry

Mark Burton
Dwaine Knight
Efua Taylor
Carla Mendonça
Tony Osoba
Nick Stringer

CREDITS
writers Kim Fuller, Geoff Atkinson, James Hendrie, Andrea Solomons, Garry Chambers, Anne Caulfield, Frankie Bailey · *director* Geoff Posner · *producers* Geoff Posner/Kim Fuller

Henry remained in standup and sketch mode for this Christmas special. Old favourites met new creations and new impersonations such as the comedian, in drag, spoofing Whitney Houston.

Following this special Henry demonstrated how much his stage act had progressed by issuing *Lenny Live And Unleashed* (1989, director Andy Harries), a feature film of his stage act. This sort of release was virtually unheard-of in Britain although Richard Pryor – whom Henry often cited as a key influence – and Eddie Murphy had succeeded with similar projects in the USA. (Shortly after its theatrical run, the film was released on video.) Another study of Henry's craft came in the LWT/ITV arts series *The South Bank Show* on 6 March 1988, which charted Henry's career from Dudley to New York. Guest appearances and **Comic Relief** duties kept him busy for the next few years. Henry's debut in a Hollywood feature film, *True Identity*, was unveiled in British cinemas in September 1991. To coincide with this, ITV screened a 30-minute behind-the-scenes look at its making, showing how the British comic fared in Los Angeles. Titled *Lenny In Hollywood*, it was broadcast on 11 September 1991. On 23 December 1991 Henry starred in the BBC1 comedy TV film *Bernard And The Genie*, written by Richard Curtis. It also featured Rowan Atkinson, Kevin Allen and Alan Cumming.

Lenny Go Home

UK · ITV (CENTRAL) · STANDUP
1 × 60 mins · colour
7 Dec 1991 · Sat 10.15pm

MAIN CAST
Lenny Henry

CREDITS
writer Lenny Henry · *additional material* Jon Canter, James Hendrie, Rick Siegel, Anne Caulfield · *script editor* Jon Canter · *executive producer* Kim Turberville · *director/producer* Tom Gutteridge

Blending Birmingham and Dudley location footage with studio standup performance taped at Central TV's Nottingham studios, this one-off Lenny Henry special (made in association with his Crucial Films) showed

the comic revisiting his West Midlands roots and looking back upon his early days – a brief clip of a 1975 *New Faces* appearance was included.

Lenny Henry: In Dreams

UK · BBC (APC) · SKETCH
1 × 60 mins · colour
23 Dec 1992 · BBC1 Wed 9.30pm

MAIN CAST
Lenny Henry
Dawn French
Bill Paterson

CREDITS
writer Jon Canter · *director* James Hendrie · *producer* Charlie Hanson

A one-off special taking the subject of dreams and their meaning for its theme. This was a deliberate attempt to get away from the suited standup observational routines for which Henry was best known. Bill Paterson played Henry's 'analyst', and his interpretation of the comic's dreams inspired the skits and comic ideas. Henry's wife Dawn French also guest-starred.

The Lenny Henry Christmas Show   1

UK · BBC · STANDUP/SKETCH
1 × 40 mins · colour
28 Dec 1994 · BBC1 Wed 9.15pm

MAIN CAST
Lenny Henry

CREDITS
writers Lenny Henry, Lenny Barker, Jane Bussman, Jon Canter, Carlton Dixon, Kim Fuller, Anne Caulfield, Paul Henry, David Quantick · *director* David G Hillier · *producer* Kevin Lygo

A seasonal special with a host of newly created characters, including the formidable Amazon model Deeva (Daring Explosive Electric Voluptuous Animal), the African Royal King Ade, and the militant Welsh rappers TWA (Taffies With Attitude). Sketches included a spoof of the film *Shaft*, and the show's guest actors included John Fortune and Peter Wyngarde.

The Lenny Henry Show   3

UK · BBC (CRUCIAL FILMS) · STANDUP/SKETCH
7 editions (6 × 30 mins · 1 × 45 mins) · colour
One series (6) 1 Apr–6 May 1995 · BBC1
Sat 10pm

Special (45 mins) 21 Jan 1996 · BBC1
Sun 10.40pm

MAIN CAST
Lenny Henry

CREDITS
writers Geoff Atkinson, Lenny Barker, Jane Bussman, Jon Canter, Anne Caulfield, Carlton Dixon, Kim Fuller, Lenny Henry, David Quantick · *script editor* Lenny Barker · *director* Juliet May ·

executive producers Kevin Lygo, Polly McDonald · *producer* Geoff Atkinson

This third incarnation of *The Lenny Henry Show* concentrated once again on standup and sketches and introduced some new characters alongside a few returning favourites. Recurring spots featured Squeako, a Liverpudlian with an exaggeratedly high voice; Las Vegas crooner Bunny Wyoming Jr, whose speciality was 'lounge' versions of Bob Marley songs; and formidable female Deeva (this time the acronym was said to stand for Dominant Erotic Enslaved Vibrating and All the way).

There was also a running 'blaxploitation' movie spoof *Nathan Gunn*, which featured Henry as a 1970s-style New York cop transferred to 1990s London (these segments were directed by David G Hillier); more fun with African King Ade, the world's richest man; and a filmed interview with 'legendary Hollywood director' Bud Chukowski, conducted by Barry Norman. Henry played the white Chukowski (with a great make-up job) like a cross between Sam Fuller and Sam Peckinpah. In another segment, 'The Henry Report', the comedian read jokey news items in a style similar to his old *Tiswas* routines, but this time without impersonating Trevor McDonald.

Various guest stars supported but particular input came from members of **The Real McCoy** team, with Felix Dexter appearing as Jeremy alongside Henry's Kenneth (two self-confessed intellectuals) in another recurring slot.

The Lenny Henry Christmas Show | 2

UK · BBC · STANDUP/SKETCH

1 × 30 mins · colour

28 Dec 1995 · BBC1 Thu 8.30pm

MAIN CAST
Lenny Henry

CREDITS
writers various · *directors* Steve Bendelack, Geoff Posner · *producer* Marcus Mortimer

A Christmas special in which Henry appeared as familiar favourites Theophilus P Wildebeeste and Deakus and also trod new ground with his own distinctive interpretation of the claymation megastars Wallace and Gromit.

Lenny Henry Gets Wild

UK · BBC · STANDUP/SKETCH

1 × 50 mins · colour

28 Dec 1996 · BBC1 Sat 7pm

MAIN CAST
Lenny Henry

CREDITS
writers Lenny Henry, Tony Sarchet, Jon Canter, Paul Henry, Andy Riley/Kevin Cecil, Andy Parsons/Henry Naylor, Lenny Barker, Karen McLachlan · *script associate* Tony Sarchet · *director* Tom Poole · *producer* Paul Jackson

A change of format for this Christmas special, which featured Henry on the road in Dublin and Exeter, as well as in front of a TV studio audience delivering standup and presenting sketches. These featured, among others, Deakus, Squeako and Radio Doncaster's agony-uncle, Iron Jack.

Her Majesty's Pleasure

UK · ITV (GRANADA) · SITCOM

13 × 30 mins · b/w

Series One (7) 25 Sep–20 Nov 1968 · Wed mostly 10.30pm

Series Two (6) 20 Feb–27 Mar 1969 · Thu 9pm

MAIN CAST
Prison Officer Leslie Mills · · · · · · · Ken Jones
Prison Officer Arnold Clissitt · · · · John Sharp
Mushy Williams · · · · · · · · · John Normington
Pongo Little · · · · · · · · · · · · John Nettleton
Sesame Ingram · · · · · · · · · · · Joe Gladwin
Freda Little · · · · · · · · · · · · · · Kate Brown
Grizzly Bear Ryan · · · · · · · · · · Tommy Mann
Governor · · · · · · · · Wensley Pithey (series 1);
· · · · · · · · · · · Michael Barrington (series 2)

CREDITS
creator Leslie Duxbury · *writers* Leslie Duxbury (9), John Stevenson (4) · *directors* June Howson (8), Cormac Newell (3), Michael Cox (1), Bill Podmore (1) · *producer* Peter Eckersley

Her Majesty's Pleasure was the first British TV sitcom series set inside a prison, predating **Porridge** by five years. There were links between the two: the fine character actor Ken Jones appeared in both, and they shared the two-prison-officers-with-contrasting-approaches idea: in *Her Majesty's Pleasure* Clissitt was the MacKay character, wanting all the men to serve hard labour, while Mills was like Barrowclough, a gentle soul who preferred the softer approach.

The original premise of *HMP* was to feature a prison football team and their endeavours to get fit, arrange fixtures and then win them. But as the series progressed so it stretched out to embrace other topics of a lock-up variety. Wensley Pithey (the bluff detective Charlesworth on BBC TV many years earlier) was the prison governor in the first series but Michael Barrington filled the role in the second.

Here And Now

UK · ITV (ASSOCIATED-REDIFFUSION) · SKETCH

9 × 30 mins · b/w

16 Dec 1955–17 Feb 1956 · Fri 10pm

MAIN CAST
Ian Carmichael
George Benson
Joan Sims
Nicholas Parsons
Nicolette Roeg
Denis Martin
Pamela Harrington
Malcolm Goddard
Hugh Paddick
Jimmy Thompson

CREDITS
director Peter Croft

Subtitled *A Laughter Revue*, this weekly compendium of sketches ran in the very early days of commercial television. Several of the stars – Carmichael, Sims, Parsons and Paddick in particular – continued to enjoy small- and big-screen success for many years after.

Here Come The Double Deckers

USA · ABC (20TH CENTURY-FOX) · CHILDREN'S SITCOM

17 × 30 mins · colour

US dates: 12 Sep 1970–3 Sep 1972

UK dates: 8 Jan–30 Apr 1971 (17 episodes) BBC1 Fri 4.55pm

MAIN CAST
Tiger · · · · · · · · · · · · · · · · · Debbie Russ
Brains · · · · · · · · · · · · · · Michael Audreson
Scooper · · · · · · · · · · · · · · · · Peter Firth
Sticks · · · · · · · · · · · · · · · · Bruce Clark
Doughnut · · · · · · · · · · · Douglas Simmonds
Billie · · · · · · · · · · · · · · · · Gillian Bailey
Spring · · · · · · · · · · · · · · · Brinsley Forde
Albert · · · · · · · · · · · · · · · · Melvyn Hayes

CREDITS
writers Peter Miller (4), Glyn Jones (3), Glyn Jones/Harry Booth (2), Glyn Jones/John Tully (1), Jan Butlin (1), Melvyn Hayes (1), Melvyn Hayes/Harry Booth (1), Michael Watson/Harry Booth (1), not known (3) · *directors* Harry Booth (14), Jeremy Summers (2), Charles Crichton (1) · *producer* Roy Simpson

Shot in England, where it was sometimes screened as simply *The Double Deckers*, this fondly remembered US comedy-adventure series for children proved popular on both sides of the Atlantic. The stories centred on a gang of children whose clubhouse was a double-decker bus situated in a junk yard. Each week the children became involved in some amusing escapade or other, assisted by their adult friend Albert (Melvyn Hayes). Although only 17 episodes were made, the series made a lasting impact on its generation, probably owing to the repeats that ran during subsequent school holidays. No lesser name than Charles Crichton, the esteemed director of many fine British comedy films, directed one of the episodes.

A big-screen appearance for the Double Deckers came courtesy of the 1972 Rank/20th Century-Fox feature film *Go For A Take* (produced and directed by Deckers Roy Simpson and Harry Booth), in which two waiters (Reg Varney and Norman Rossington) hide from gangsters at a film studio. On the lot, they encounter the set of *Here Come The Double Deckers* and some of the Deckers themselves, who aid them in their ride to freedom.

In keeping with the bus theme, no further episodes were made for 25 years but then a whole bunch came along at once when, in 1996, the Quintus Group announced it was making a new TV series of *The Double Deckers* for a new generation of children. (Not yet screened.)

Here Comes Charlie Callas

UK · ITV (LWT) · STANDUP

2 × 45 mins · b/w

27 Dec 1968 · Fri 7.30pm
3 Jan 1969 · Fri 7.30pm

MAIN CAST
Charlie Callas

CREDITS
script associate Eric Merriman · *director* Bill Turner · *producer* David Bell

The Greek-American Charlie Callas became a major figure in US comedy virtually overnight after an appearance there on *The Merv Griffin Show*, a chat-show, in 1966. Jerry Lewis happened to be watching, and delighted in promoting the new discovery in Hollywood. The American comic Joe Franklin wrote of Callas, 'He looks like an imperfectly dried prune on a 90-pound frame,' but despite (or because of) this, he attained stardom for a while, not least for his impressions of objects rather than people – he could, for example, physically and aurally suggest a bowl of cereal being heated.

Callas came to England in late 1968 and made impressive guest appearances in *Jones The Song* (a variety vehicle for the singer Tom Jones) and David Frost's chat-show *Frost On Sunday*, and so LWT quickly commissioned two special programmes, advertising their star (and this was many years ahead of Phil Cool) as 'the India-rubber man'. Up and coming US comedians Joan Rivers and Howard Storm also made the trip as Callas's guests.

Here I Come Whoever I Am

UK · BBC · SITCOM

1 × 30 mins · b/w

11 June 1965 · BBC1 Fri 8pm

MAIN CAST
Ambrose Twombly · · · · · · · Bernard Cribbins
Mousy Bird (Greta Spavin) · · · · · Helen Fraser

CREDITS
writer Marty Feldman · *executive producer* Graeme Muir · *producer* Dennis Main Wilson

A bold attempt by writer Marty Feldman to bring a touch of pathos to *Comedy Playhouse*. The single-episode *Here I Come Whoever I Am* was a bittersweet tale of a shy, lonely 32-year-old man looking for female company. There were shades of **The Strange World Of Gurney Slade** in the way that the character's feelings and thoughts were revealed in a voice-over.

Here We Go Again

USA · ABC (METROMEDIA/BOBKA PRODUCTIONS) · SITCOM

13 × 30 mins · colour

US dates: 20 Jan–23 June 1973
UK dates: 14 Aug–29 Oct 1973 (12 episodes) ITV various days around 11pm

MAIN CAST
Richard Evans · · · · · · · · · · · Larry Hagman
Susan Standish Evans · · · · · · · Diane Baker
Judy Evans · · · · · · · · · · · · · · Nita Talbot
Jerry Standish · · · · · · · · · · · Dick Gautier

CREDITS
writers various · *directors* various · *executive producer* Charles Fries · *producers* Stan Schwimmer, Robert Kaufman

Mining the 'divorce comedy' premise so successfully explored in a number of old Hollywood movies, this US sitcom – decidedly unsuccessful, it closed after just 13 episodes – drew few laughs from the inter-relationships of four adults.

Richard and Judy end their marriage after 17 years of incompatibility; Jerry and Susan end theirs after 10 (adultery). Richard and Susan meet, fall in love and wed, but their state of marital union is constantly interrupted by former spouses Jerry and Judy. Oh, and there were children involved too, and professional jobs. Five years later Larry Hagman (who played Richard) would find relationships even more trying in *Dallas*.

Here's Archie

UK · BBC · SITCOM

1 × 45 mins · b/w

30 May 1956 · Wed 9.15pm

MAIN CAST
Peter Brough
Irene Handl
Ronald Chesney

CREDITS
writers Ronald Wolfe/John Waterhouse · *producer* John Warrington

Unlikely though the concept is of ventriloquism on radio, Peter Brough's dummy Archie Andrews, of **Educating Archie** fame, was a phenomenon. Brough and Archie followed in the tradition of US ventriloquist Edgar Bergen and his insolent dummy Charlie McCarthy, who were hugely popular on film and radio both in the US

and UK. *Here's Archie* was the television debut of Britain's own cheeky young wooden lad.

The prolific sitcom writing partnership of the future, Ronald Wolfe and Ronald Chesney, were both involved in this one-off show, as writer and actor respectively. Irene Handl appeared as housekeeper Mrs Twissle.

Here's Harry

see WORTH, Harry

Here's Howard

UK · BBC · STANDUP

8 × 30 mins · b/w

14 Mar–20 June 1951 · Wed around 9.30pm

MAIN CAST
Michael Howard
Ossy Waller
John Blythe
Harry Lane

CREDITS
writer Michael Howard · *producer* Bryan Sears

The adage has it that every comedian secretly yearns to play Hamlet, but Michael Howard travelled in the opposite direction. He was once an Old Vic player and had been Horatio to Laurence Olivier's Hamlet, as well as appearing opposite luminaries Edith Evans and John Barrymore. Trained at the Royal Academy of Dramatic Art, Howard performed in straight plays on both sides of the Atlantic.

All the while, friends kept telling Howard that he was funny, and so, after some deliberation, he decided to try his hand at variety, bravely throwing himself into the deep end by touring music-halls and often being jeered in the process. He persevered and made good in 1941 when, like so many other funny men, he became a resident comic at the famous Windmill Theatre in London. BBC radio and TV success soon followed, with Howard headlining a number of shows on the wireless including *For The Love Of Mike*, *Leave It To The Boys*, *The Michael Howard Show* and *Here's Howard*. The latter transferred to television in 1951, with Howard bringing his particular brand of whimsical humour to the screen. His stage persona was that of a man who had wandered into the wrong place but was determined to carry on as if he had made no mistake, while his stage patter often had the air of a shaggy-dog story.

See also *Michael Howard*.

Here's Lucy

see BALL, Lucille

Here's Television

UK · BBC · SKETCH

1 × 60 mins · b/w

6 Jan 1951 · Sat 9pm

MAIN CAST

Sidney James
Ian Carmichael
Bill Fraser
Clive Moreton

CREDITS

writers Frank Muir/Denis Norden, Sid Colin ·
director/producer Michael Mills

An irreverent review of the previous year's TV, spoofing many of the medium's favourite shows. The production had a celebratory feel and, in addition to the artists mentioned above, a host of surprise stars also appeared.

This one-off marked the TV debut of writers Frank Muir and Denis Norden, who were becoming established on BBC radio as the authors of the sketch comedy series *Take It From Here*.

Herlock And Sholmes

UK · ITV (ASSOCIATED-REDIFFUSION) ·
CHILDREN'S SITCOM

13 × 15 mins · b/w

11 July–3 Oct 1958 · Fri mostly 5.15pm

MAIN CAST

Herlock · · · · · · · · · · · · · · · · Jack Edwardes
Sholmes · · · · · · · · · · · · · · · · Dickie Arnold

CREDITS

director Prudence Nesbitt

Immediately after his tall-and-small antics with Charlie Drake in **Mick And Montmorency** had come to an end, lanky Jack Edwardes started up a new series (in the same children's TV strand *Let's Get Together*), this time co-starring with diminutive Dickie Arnold as Herlock and Sholmes, a pair of defective detectives, of whom it was said 'they cook the books and book the crooks'. Dressed in deerstalkers and cloaks, and armed with nothing more than magnifying glasses, they ineptly, but no doubt boldly, went where no detectives had gone before.

Note. In 1959, Jack Edwardes resurrected the old *M&M* formula, taking on as a new partner Felix Bowness (later to become an audience warm-up entertainer at the BBC and have bit-parts in dozens of 1970s–80s sitcoms, and a regular role in **Hi-de-Hi!**). Mick And Marmaduke, so named, appeared in a few children's variety programmes on ITV but had no regular series of their own.

Herman's Head

USA · FOX (WITT-THOMAS PRODUCTIONS/
TOUCHSTONE TELEVISION) · SITCOM

72 × 30 mins · colour

US dates: 8 Sep 1991–21 Apr 1994
UK dates: 20 Nov 1993–3 Dec 1994 (50 episodes) C4 Sat various times after midnight

MAIN CAST

Herman Brooks · · · · · · · · · William Ragsdale
Jay Nichols · · · · · · · · · · · · · · · Hank Azaria
Heddy Thompson · · · · · · · · · · · Jane Sibbert
Louise Fitzer · · · · · · · · · · · · Yeardley Smith
Animal · · · · · · · · · · · · Ken Hudson Campbell
Angel · · · · · · · · · · · · · · · · · · Molly Hagan
Wimp · · · · · · · · · · · · · · · · · · · Rick Lawless
Genius · · · · · · · · · · · · · · Peter MacKenzie
Paul Bracken · · · · · · · · · · · · Jason Barnard

CREDITS

creators Andy Guerdat/Steve Kreinberg · *writers* Michael B Kaplan (12), Adam Markowitz/Bill Freiberger (11), Karl Fink/Roberto Benabib (7), David Landsberg (7), Douglas Tuber/Tim Maile (6), David Babcock (6) and others · *directors* J D Lobue, Greg Antonacci · *executive producers* Paul Junger Witt, Tony Thomas, David Landsberg, David Babcock · *producers* Karl Fink, Roberto Benabib, David Babcock, Nina Feinberg, Adam Markowitz, Bill Freiberger, Joel Madison

The British children's comic *The Beezer* featured a long-running strip, *The Numskulls*, that related the adventures of a group of little men who inhabited someone's head. These characters all had separate tasks to perform: the brain department did the thinking, the eye department looked, the ear department listened, and so on. Many years later the US sitcom *Herman's Head* utilised a remarkably similar idea, only this time the four characters inside the head were responsible for different emotional areas: thought, lust, sensitivity and anxiety.

The head belonged to Herman Brooks, an average guy who worked as a fact-checker for a publishing business, Waterton, in New York. He shared an office with the beautiful but heartless Heddy and the homely but sweet Louise, his boss was the firm but mostly fair Mr Bracken, and his best friend was Jay, a politically incorrect wide-boy. Herman encountered the everyday challenges of modern life: work problems, dating, financial worries and the like, but these typical sitcom plots were rescued from the mainstream by the regular visits that viewers made inside his head, in which his four driving forces bickered and argued before deciding upon an appropriate course of action. Inhabiting an unreal-looking front-room set festooned with odd objects, the individual personalities of the quartet meant that conflict was inevitable. Angel was a sweet girl who represented Herman's sensitivity, constantly thinking the best of everyone and encouraging Herman to be honest and open. The dapper, bespectacled Genius was his intellect – unconcerned with emotional influences, he wanted Herman to do the smart thing even if it meant lying or committing a wrongdoing. Wimp was Herman's anxiety, a nervous hypochondriac

who suffered from every known phobia and expected disaster at every turn – he usually counselled caution whenever Herman embarked upon a new or exciting course of action. Then there was Animal, a fat slob who embodied Herman's lust. Animal was the hedonistic one, who urged Herman to get laid, eat the wrong food, drink too much and indulge generally in base pastimes. A majority vote was usually required before Herman could make a decision, although, of course, he remained blissfully unaware of the dramas taking place in his head.

While Herman himself was too ordinary to incite much empathy, *Herman's Head* was a pleasant enough sitcom, probably unique in that one half of the cast (the head people) never appeared with the other (the human kind). Yeardley Smith, who played Louise, went on to sitcom immortality (or, rather, her voice did) as Lisa Simpson in *The Simpsons*.

He's Pasquale, I'm Walsh

UK · ITV (THAMES FOR CENTRAL) · STANDUP

1 × 30 mins · colour

5 July 1994 · Tue 8.30pm

MAIN CAST

Joe Pasquale
Bradley Walsh

CREDITS

director Paul Kirrage · *producer* John Fisher

A summer special for the two comics who worked together but not as a double-act – the squeaky-voiced bizarre magician and stunt comedian Pasquale (pronounced 'per-skwalee') and fast-talking standup Walsh. A hit in the recent *Royal Variety Show*, they had also gone down well on ITV's *Des O'Connor Tonight* on 9 February 1994.

See also *The Joe Pasquale Show*.

Hey Brian!

UK · ITV (YORKSHIRE) · STANDUP

7 × 30 mins · colour

Special *Our Brian* 29 Aug 1972 · Tue 10.45pm
One series (6) 15 May–19 June 1973 · Tue 7.05pm

MAIN CAST

Brian Marshall
Gemma Craven
Stu Francis (series only)

CREDITS

writers of special Peter Dulay, Brian Marshall · *writers of series* David Nobbs, Tony Hare, John Hudson, Peter Robinson, Peter Vincent, M F Cole · *directors* Keith Beckett (special), Roger Cheveley (series) · *executive producer* John Duncan (series) · *producer* Bill Hitchcock (series)

Following his role as 'Our Bunny', Diana Dors' son in the Yorkshire TV sitcom **Queenie's Castle**, 25-year-old Brian

Marshall was promoted to his own series, scripted for him by a number of top writers. Each show featured guests, although Stu Francis and Gemma Craven (then Marshall's real-life fiancée) appeared in every edition. To test the water a one-off programme (*Our Brian*) aired the previous year.

Hey, Jeannie!

USA · NBC (FOUR STAR/TARTAN PRODUCTIONS) · SITCOM
32 × 30 mins · b/w
US dates: 5 Sep 1956–4 May 1957
UK dates: 1 Dec 1956–26 May 1957
(27 episodes) BBC various days and times

MAIN CAST
Jeannie MacLennan · · · · · · · Jeannie Carson
Al Murray · · · · · · · · · · · · · Allen Jenkins
Liz Murray · · · · · · · · · · · · · · · · Jane Dulo

CREDITS
producer Charles Isaacs

The Scots actress Jeannie Carson (born Jean Shuff in Pudsey, Yorkshire, on 28 May 1929) was creating waves as a rising star – she was under contract to Rank and appeared in several British films – when she went to America to appear in this sitcom, created especially for her after she had made several appearances there on *The Ed Sullivan Show* and other programmes.

Carson was cast as a young and naïve Scots lass on her first visit to New York, who arrives with no job, no plans and no place to stay. She is befriended by Al Murray, the cab driver who picks her up (as a fare, that is) and soon finds herself living in the apartment of Al and his wife Liz and working in a donut shop.

Allen Jenkins, who played Al, later became known as the voice of Officer Dibble in the cartoon series *Top Cat*. British comic Dickie Henderson flew over to America to appear in one of the episodes.

See also **The Jeannie Carson Show.**

Hi There!

see HILL, Benny

Hi-de-Hi!

UK · BBC · SITCOM
58 episodes (53 × 30 mins · 3 × 45 mins · 1 × 60 mins · 1 × 40 mins) · colour
Pilot (40 mins) 1 Jan 1980 · BBC1 Tue 7.30pm
Series One (6) 26 Feb–2 Apr 1981 · BBC1 Thu 8pm
Series Two (6) 29 Nov 1981–3 Jan 1982 · BBC1 Sun 7.15pm
Series Three (12 × 30 mins · 1 × 45 mins) 31 Oct 1982–23 Jan 1983 · BBC1 Sun 7.15pm
Series Four (7) 27 Nov 1983–22 Jan 1984 · BBC1 Sun 7.15pm
Series Five (6) 3 Nov–25 Dec 1984 · BBC1 Sat 8pm
Series Six (6 × 30 mins · 1 × 60 mins) 25 Dec 1985–16 Feb 1986 · BBC1 mostly Sun 7.15pm
Series Seven (5 × 30 mins · 1 × 45 mins) 8 Nov–27 Dec 1986 · BBC1 Sat 7.40pm
Series Eight (5 × 30 mins · 1 × 45 mins) 26 Dec 1987–30 Jan 1988 · BBC1 mostly Sat 6.20pm

MAIN CAST
Jeffrey Fairbrother · · · · · · · · · Simon Cadell
· (series 1–4)
Sqdn Ldr Clive Dempster DFC · · David Griffin
· (series 5–8)
Ted Bovis · · · · · · · · · · · · · · · · · Paul Shane
Gladys Pugh · · · · · · · · · · · · · · Ruth Madoc
Spike Dixon · · · · · · · · · · · · Jeffrey Holland
Peggy · · · · · · · · · · · · · · · · · · · Su Pollard
Fred Quilly · · · · · · · · · · · · · Felix Bowness
Yvonne Stuart-Hargreaves · · · Diane Holland
Barry Stuart-Hargreaves · · · · · · Barry Howard
· (series 1–6)
Julian Dalrymple-Sykes · · · · · · · · · Ben Aris
· · · · · · · · · · · · · · · · · (series 6 onwards)
Mr Partridge · · · · · Leslie Dwyer (series 1–5)
Sylvia · Nikki Kelly
Betty · · · · · · · · · · · · · · · · · · · Rikki Howard
Yellowcoat Boys · · · · · · · · The Webb Twins,
· Chris Andrews
Mary · · · · · · · · · · · · · · Penny Irving (series 1)
April · · · · · · · · · · · · Linda Regan (series 5–8)
Dawn · · · · · · · · · Laura Jackson (series 5–8)
Babs · · · · · Julie-Christian Young (series 5–8)
Tracey · · · · · · Susan Beagley (series 3 & 4)
Charlie Dawson · · · · · Johnny Allan (series 4)
Sammy · · · · · Kenneth Connor (series 7 & 8)
Alec Foster · · · · · · · · Ewan Hooper (series 7)

CREDITS
writers Jimmy Perry/David Croft · *directors* John Kilby, David Croft, Robin Carr, Mike Stephens · *producers* David Croft (45), John Kilby (7), Mike Stephens (6)

Another period-piece sitcom culled from the real-life experiences of writers Jimmy Perry and David Croft. (The former had been a Butlin's Redcoat, the latter had worked as an actor/producer of summer shows for a holiday camp.) Building a series around the comical trials and tribulations suffered by an entertainment troupe at a typical British holiday camp at the end of the 1950s was a brilliant notion, and the fictional ideas – calling the camp Maplin's and the entertainers Yellowcoats – was an almost transparent veil behind which lay the truth: this series was all about the larks to be had, or not had, at Butlin's, and later Pontin's, holiday camps, in their kiss-me-quick 'golden' post-war heyday.

The pilot episode set the scene, with the entertainers returning for the 1959 holiday season only to find that the camp is now being run by a former college professor, the well-meaning but dreamy academic Jeffrey Fairbrother. He is a character in stark contrast to his team: the bluff, ale-guzzling working-class comic Ted Bovis, and his hapless understudy Spike; Gladys Pugh, the ambitious and passionate senior Yellowcoat from Wales; the dipsomaniacal, child-hating Punch And

Judy Man, Mr Partridge; the snobbish dance instructors Barry and Yvonne Stuart-Hargreaves; the diminutive, sour-faced jockey Fred Quilly; and the gormless, nervy Peggy, a lowly chalet maid with a burning ambition to become a Yellowcoat. After initial clashes, the team realise that they are on the same side and face far greater challenges from the holiday-makers and the never seen but ever-watchful head of Maplin's, the odious Joe Maplin. Personal relationships soon develop: Ted fails to be a father-figure to Spike; Gladys forms a smouldering but unrealised passion for Fairbrother; and Peggy increasingly exasperates the others with her nervous energy and Yellowcoat ambitions. But no seismic changes occurred in the series until Fairbrother left and was replaced by the wilier but still misplaced Clive Dempster. Two years later, Kenneth Connor joined the regular cast as the children's entertainer Uncle Sammy, who seemed to have a strange hold over Joe Maplin, but otherwise things continued much as before, with the 1959 holiday season eventually giving way to the 1960 holiday season. Plots became somewhat outlandish during the latter episodes – there was even a murder mystery when Mr Partridge was found dead in the camp – and by the time the BBC called it a day in 1988, it is arguable that the series had already outstayed its welcome by a good couple of years.

All in all, though, this was a good British sitcom, not aspiring to the heights and so not failing when it ascended to just above the half-way point. Its period setting had just the right degree of nostalgia and comedy potential, and the characters, as usual for Perry and Croft, were very well cast. Granted, the style was broad – *too* broad for some tastes – with a distinctly garish *Carry On* touch in places, and the female Yellowcoat uniform shorts were short by 1980s standards let alone those of the 1950s, but a fascinating era in 20th-century British social history was humorously explored, and – for those not around at the time – explained.

The title *Hi-de-Hi!* (changed from the unhyphenated and unexclaimed *Hi de Hi* of the early episodes) was the campers' rallying call, broadcast over Maplin's internal radio PA by Gladys Pugh. The campers' response was the at first enthusiastic but later weary 'Ho-de-Ho'.

Bill Hicks

Bill Hicks' premature death of pancreatic cancer at the age of 32 robbed the English-speaking world of a major comedic talent. Born on 16 September 1961, Hicks began performing while still in his early teens and worked hard to build a reputation, striking gold in 1991 with an astonishing standup show that took the 1991 Montreal Comedy Festival (*Just For Laughs*) by storm. Dressed in his trademark all-black outfit (suit and polo-neck sweater), Hicks – nicknamed 'The Prince Of Darkness' – stalked across the stage like a caged animal, never still and with an unsettling ability to switch from docility to danger within a single phrase. Although driven by anger, his routines were much more than mere rants, and, arguably, no comedian since Lenny Bruce has worn his heart so unashamedly on his sleeve. Like Bruce, Hicks had total conviction in what he was saying and there was no contrivance in his material – the ideas he presented were the things he believed in; as simple as that. Despite the blistering vitriol and bad language that, in some quarters, made him unpopular, most neutrals were won over by Hicks' naked honesty. But something in his eyes belied the surface hardness and pointed to a genuinely warm guy underneath. He was also painfully, hysterically, wonderfully funny.

Bill Hicks was popular in his native USA but perhaps even bigger in Britain, where C4 proffered him a TV base. Indeed, at the time of his death on 26 February 1994, he was about to record a pilot for C4, *The Counts Of The Netherworld*, a standup/sitcom hybrid that Hicks had developed. It remains one of TV comedy's unrealised potential gems.

Bill Hicks – Relentless

UK · C4 (TIGER TELEVISION) · STANDUP

1 × 60 mins · colour
2 Jan 1992 · C4 Thu 11.25pm

MAIN CAST
Bill Hicks

CREDITS
writer Bill Hicks · *director* Chris Bould · *executive producer* Charles Brand · *producer* Gillian Strachan

A recording of Hicks' famous one-man show at the 1991 Montreal *Just For Laughs* festival.

Bill Hicks – Revelations

UK · C4 (TIGER ASPECT) · STANDUP

1 × 60 mins · colour
27 May 1993 · C4 Thu 10.35pm

MAIN CAST
Bill Hicks

CREDITS
writer Bill Hicks · *director* Chris Bould · *producer* Gillian Strachan

Hicks' follow-up show to *Relentless*, recorded at the Dominion Theatre in London.

Notes. After his death, on 10 September 1994, C4 screened a documentary about the controversial comedian, *It's Just A Ride*, and then packaged together the documentary and *Bill Hicks – Revelations* as a video release.

Hicks was one of a number of comedians featured in the documentary *But … Seriously* (C4, 30 December 1994), looking at how comedy has shaped the American social conscience.

High & Dry

UK · ITV (YORKSHIRE) · SITCOM

7 × 30 mins · colour
7 Jan–18 Feb 1987 · Wed 8.30pm

MAIN CAST
Ron Archer · · · · · · · · · · · · Bernard Cribbins
Richard Talbot · · · · · · · · · · · Richard Wilson
Miss Baxter · · · · · · · · · · · · · Vivienne Martin
Trevor Archer · · · · · · · · · · · · Angus Barnett
Fred Whattle · · · · · · · · · · · · · Arthur English
Mrs Briggs · · · · · · · · · · · · · Diana Coupland

CREDITS
writers Alan Sherwood/Michael Knowles · *director/producer* Ronnie Baxter

After the BBC had aired a pilot episode to scarcely any reaction (*Walking The Planks*) and then passed up its option, Michael Knowles' co-creation ended up on network ITV courtesy of Yorkshire TV. The title changed, and instead of Michael Elphick the lead character Ron Archer was played here by Bernard Cribbins, with Richard Wilson and Vivienne Martin continuing their roles as bank manager and his secretary respectively; Angus Barnett came in to replace Gary Raynsford as Ron's gormless son Trevor.

The setting was as before: 1946, with the war just ended. Ron Archer buys a derelict seaside pier at Midbourne for a knock-down price, five shillings, on condition that he spend a considerable sum of money on its restoration. Archer has none, but his sister happens to be married to a Midbourne bank manager, Richard Talbot, and Ron bribes Talbot into advancing a loan, threatening to divulge an indiscretion if the money is not forthcoming.

Studio bound, and looking uncomfortably like it from first scene to last, *High & Dry* was pretty poor fare. Bernard Cribbins had been in much better series than this, and Richard (*One Foot In The Grave*) Wilson soon would be.

The High Life

UK · BBC · SITCOM

7 × 30 mins · colour
Pilot · 9 Jan 1994 · BBC2 Sun 9pm
One series (6) 6 Jan–10 Feb 1995 · BBC2 Fri 9.30pm

MAIN CAST
Sebastian Flight · · · · · · · · · · · Alan Cumming
Steve McCracken · · · · · · · · · Forbes Masson
Shona Spurtle · · · · · · · · Siobhan Redmond
Captain Duff · · · · · · · · · · · · Patrick Ryecart

CREDITS
writers Alan Cumming/Forbes Masson · *directors* Tony Dow (pilot), Angela deChastelai Smith (series) · *producer* Tony Dow

Writer/performers Cumming and Masson first met at the Royal Scottish Academy of Music and Dance, where they created Victor and Barry, a double-act they later performed in a number of stage revues and on TV in *Paramount City*. They also worked extensively as solo performers in both comedy and straight stage roles. Cumming won the British Comedy Award for Top TV Newcomer in 1992 (for his performance opposite Lenny Henry in Richard Curtis's TV film *Bernard And The Genie*, screened by BBC1 on 23 December 1991) and Masson had his own series on BBC Radio Scotland, *The Forbes Masson Half-Hour*.

Their sitcom, *The High Life*, depicted a cabin crew for Air Scotia, an airline flying out of Glasgow International Airport. The crew consisted of an effete steward, Sebastian; his sex-obsessed colleague Steve; the chief stewardess, Shona Spurtle; and the obtuse, semi-demented pilot Captain Duff. Sebastian and Steve longed to be promoted from the short-haul flights to landing the more exotic locales frequented on the long-haul routes, and they also wished to escape from the clutches of their hard-as-nails superior Shona, whom they described as 'Hitler in tights'. The seven episodes – a *Comic Asides* pilot and subsequent series of six – were frantically paced and the programme existed in an unreal, farcical world. Cumming and Masson's stage training was evident in the production of *The High Life*, which was more overtly theatrical than typical sitcoms, even down to the credits and closing sequences which were elaborate music and dance numbers.

Intermittently funny, its odd style made *The High Life* an acquired taste. Cumming and Masson threw themselves wholeheartedly into the project but Siobhan Redmond was such an appealing actress that it was hard to believe in her as the instinctively nasty and vindictive Shona.

High Street Blues

UK · ITV (LWT) · SITCOM

6 × 30 mins · colour
6 Jan–10 Feb 1989 · Fri 7pm

MAIN CAST
Charlie McFee · · · · · · · · · · · · · Phil McCall
Chesney Black · · · · · · · · · · · · Ron Pember
Mavis Drinkwater · · · · · · · · Elizabeth Stewart
Rita Franks · · · · · · · · · · · · · Valerie Walsh

Bob Farthing	Chris Pitt
Susan Drinkwater	Victoria Hasted
Sheila	Eve Bland
Paula Franks	Georgia Mitchell
Sharpe	Johnny Shannon
Valentine	Martin Turner
The Managing Director	Shirley Dixon
	(voice only)

CREDITS
writers Jimmy Perry/Robin Carr · executive producer Marcus Plantin · director/producer Robin Carr

Co-written by Jimmy Perry with the series' producer David Croft, *Dad's Army* was an all-time great. Co-written by Jimmy Perry with the series' producer Robin Carr, *High Street Blues* was pitiful. The laughs were woefully thin on the ground as the owners of four adjacent High Street shops in the town of Hatford fought to prevent their livelihoods and premises being demolished to make way for a hypermarket.

The potential doers of this dastardly deed were Waverley's Supermarkets, made flesh by the trio form of Sharpe, Valentine – the surnames-only approach marked them as out as obvious baddies – and the company's MD, whose evil was such that she was not only devoid of a name but also a face (she wasn't seen in the series, only heard). Fighting for tradition were your typical motley sitcom crew in your typical situations: the shoe repair shop, run by canny old Scotsman Charlie, assisted by school-leaver Bob Farthing; the flower shop, run by gossipy Jewess Rita Franks and her daughter Paula (played by Georgia Mitchell, the daughter of Warren); the wool shop, run by dowdy Mavis Drinkwater and her go-ahead niece Susan; and the junk shop, run by smug Chesney Black, who, alone among the shopkeepers, was prepared to sell up, provided that Waverley's met his inflated asking price; Chesney's girlfriend Sheila wished he was less interested in money, however, and more interested in intimate relations.

One series was made, one too many for most.

Highland Fling   1

UK · BBC · SKETCH/STANDUP
1 × 45 mins · b/w
10 Apr 1950 · Mon 8.30pm

MAIN CAST
Harry Gordon ('The Laird of Inversnecky')
Jack Holden

CREDITS
writer Harry Gordon · director/producer Henry Caldwell

A one-off exposure on TV in England for the Scottish funny-man Harry Gordon, who had first appeared on TV in a Baird experimental transmission in 1929. Gordon specialised in Scots character sketches and pantomime dame characterisations, offering viewers examples of both in this Easter special. As **Gillie Potter** had his Hogsnorton so Harry Gordon had his Inversnecky, and all the characters he impersonated were inhabitants of the fictitious village.

Highland Fling   2

see Mr Pastry

Hilary

see CAINE, Marti

Benny Hill

Born in Southampton on 25 January 1924 as Alfred Hawthorne Hill, Benny Hill attained fame not just in his home country but around the world as a purveyor of bawdy, nudge-nudge comedy – quintessentially British but, clearly, popular everywhere. A major star for more than 40 years – and there aren't many comics of whom that can be said – his work was, as a result, reviled by critics and loved by the masses. What is virtually forgotten now, however, is that, before focusing almost entirely on the seaside-postcard style of humour, Hill's early output was acclaimed for its cleverness. His TV work with the BBC in the 1950s was pioneering stuff: he wrote all his own material (he always composed and sang his own music, too, resulting in the 1971 number one cornball hit 'Ernie'), appeared in a fabulous array of guises and was a brilliant parodist of the medium in which he fast made his name and the other stars who populated it. Very fast, in fact: Hill was named Personality of the Year in the *Daily Mail* National Television Awards for 1954–55, a full 20 years before his long-running spell at Thames was at its height.

Demobilised from the army in 1947, Hill set out on the long road to stardom first under his real name, Alf Hill, then as Benny (in homage to Jack Benny), and along the way he formed an early, short-lived double-act with Reg Varney. Benny Hill made his TV debut in the BBC series *Music-Hall* on 23 March 1949 and then went into radio, appearing regularly in *Educating Archie*. Hill's TV fame amassed him a fortune well in excess of his needs and, in the 1970s, he spent most of his time globe-trotting, typically turning in just three programmes a year for Thames. His ambition to switch from TV to films was largely unrealised – *Who Done It?*, 1956, was designed to make him a big-screen star; *Light Up The Sky*, 1959, gave him a straight role; and he also made cameo appearances in *Chitty Chitty Bang Bang*, *The Italian Job* and a number of other movies – but it is Hill's TV work, delivered with that knowing, saucy twinkle in his eye, which will ensure that he is not forgotten.

The following documents Hill's principal TV work. He also appeared in dozens of variety shows in the 1950s and 1960s. See also *Kaleidoscope*.

Hi There!

UK · BBC · SKETCH
1 × 45 mins · b/w
20 Aug 1951 · Mon 8.15pm

MAIN CAST
Benny Hill
Ernest Maxin

CREDITS
writer Benny Hill · producer Bill Lyon-Shaw

The debut headlining show for the future comedy legend who hitherto had appeared only in supporting roles. The writer/comic's characteristic style was already in evidence: in this production he played a Frenchman bewildered by England, a man baffled by the moving-belt in a serve-yourself restaurant, and three foreign waiters. Hill often portrayed waiters later in his career and indeed in 1969 made a short cinema film, without dialogue, *The Waiters*.

The Benny Hill Show   1

UK · BBC · SKETCH
33 editions (16 × 60 mins · 16 × 45 mins · 1 × short special) · b/w
Series One (3 × 60 mins) 15 Jan–12 Mar 1955 · monthly Sat mostly 8.45pm
Series Two (6 × 60 mins) 5 Jan–1 June 1957 · monthly Sat around 8pm
Series Three (4 × 60 mins) 1 Feb–26 Apr 1958 · monthly Sat 8pm
Series Four (3 × 60 mins) 4 Feb–1 Apr 1961 · monthly Sat 7.45pm
Series Five (3 × 45 mins) 4 Nov–16 Dec 1961 · every three weeks Sat 7.15pm
Special (45 mins) 6 Nov 1964 · BBC1 Fri 8.25pm
Short special · part of *Christmas Night With The Stars* 25 Dec 1964 · BBC1 Fri 7.15pm
Series Six (4 × 45 mins) 10 Apr–22 May 1965 · BBC1 fortnightly Sat 7.30pm
Series Seven (4 × 45 mins) 6 Nov 1965–8 Jan 1966 · BBC1 every three weeks Sat 8.50pm
Special (45 mins) 20 Apr 1968 · BBC1 Sat 7.50pm
Series Eight (3 × 45 mins) 20 Nov–26 Dec 1968 · mostly Wed 7.30pm

MAIN CAST
Benny Hill

OTHER APPEARANCES
Patricia Hayes
June Whitfield
Henry McGee

CREDITS

writers Benny Hill (series 1, 4, 6–8, specials),
Dave Freeman/Benny Hill (series 2 & 3), Dave
Freeman (series 5) · *producers* Kenneth Carter
(series 1, 6–8, specials), Duncan Wood (3 eds of
series 2), John Street (3 eds of series 2, series 3
& 4), David Croft (series 5)

This was the series that made Benny Hill
into a major star. He had already scored
notable TV successes as the host of variety
series *Showtime* and *The Centre Show*, but it
was this sketch series – consistently funny
after the first few erratic editions – that
propelled Hill to the upper echelons of his
profession. The trademark of these BBC
shows was Hill's clever use of make-up
and voice mimicry to spoof other TV
personalities and programmes (famously,
wildlife experts Hans and Lotte Hass and the
current affairs show *Tonight*) – indeed he
was the first TV comedian to consistently
use the medium as a target, figuring that the
audience watching him (that is, owners of
television sets) would understand the jokes.
In one edition (10 April 1965) Hill portrayed
35 different characters. All the characteristics
that gave Hill his subsequent international
success are in these shows in embryo form:
the funny songs, the double entendres, the
clever use of mime, the elaborate costume
sketches, and more. Later editions became
irregular as Hill's celebrity meant that he
was in demand in other areas, and the final
shows featured recurring guest stars, most
notably June Whitfield, Patricia Hayes and
Henry McGee.

Note. Through much of 1955 and 1956
Benny Hill co-starred with Tommy Cooper
in a London stage production of the Folies
Bergère revue *Paris By Night*. An hour-long
TV adaptation, produced by ITP for ATV/
ABC, was screened by ITV on 9 September
1956. Some years later, on 24 June 1964, Hill
starred as Bottom in an all-star ITV
production of Shakespeare's *A Midsummer
Night's Dream*, made by Rediffusion. Alfie
Bass, Bernard Bresslaw, Peter Wyngarde,
Jill Bennett and Patrick Allen also appeared.

The Benny Hill Show · 2

UK · ITV (ATV) · SKETCH

8 editions (5 × 60 mins · 3 × 55 mins) · b/w

9 Nov 1957 · Sat 8.30pm (60 mins)
14 Dec 1957 · Sat 8.30pm (60 mins)
29 Nov 1958 · Sat 7.55pm (60 mins)
27 Dec 1958 · Sat 7.55pm (60 mins)
24 Jan 1959 · Sat 7.55pm (60 mins)
2 Apr 1960 · Sat 8pm (55 mins)
30 Apr 1960 · Sat 8pm (55 mins)
28 May 1960 · Sat 8pm (55 mins)

MAIN CAST
Benny Hill

PRINCIPAL SUPPORTING CAST
The Cuddlesome Cuties
The Handsome Herberts
The Layabouts

CREDITS

writers Dave Freeman/Benny Hill · *directors/
producers* Brian Tesler (show 1), Albert Locke
(show 2), Kenneth Carter (shows 3–8)

Capitalising on the high standing he had
gained through his work on BBC TV (and
also BBC radio, where he broadcast
throughout the 1950s and 1960s), Benny
Hill made a number of special occasional
appearances on the commercial channel,
treating viewers to his now familiar brand
of sketches, pastiches and self-composed
music.

Benny Hill

UK · BBC · SITCOM

19 × 25 mins · b/w

Series One (6) 23 Feb–30 Mar 1962 ·
Fri 8.45pm
Series Two (7) 30 Nov 1962–11 Jan 1963 ·
mostly Fri 8.50pm
Series Three (6) 3 Sep–8 Oct 1963 ·
Tue mostly 8pm

MAIN CAST
Benny Hill

OTHER APPEARANCES
Patricia Hayes
June Whitfield
Graham Stark
Ronnie Barker

CREDITS

writers Benny Hill/Dave Freeman (series 1), Dave
Freeman (series 2 & 3) · *producers* Duncan Wood
(series 1 & 2), John Street (series 2 & 3)

Three series of sitcoms, with Hill in a
different role every week. This was a
departure for the man who had made a
name for himself with guest appearances
on variety shows and in his own brilliant
sketch-shows of the 1950s, and he was ably
assisted by a range of dependable actors
including June Whitfield, Patricia Hayes,
Graham Stark and Ronnie Barker.

The Benny Hill Show · 3

UK · ITV (ATV) · SKETCH

1 × 60 mins · colour

26 Dec 1967 · Tue 7pm

MAIN CAST
Benny Hill
Nicholas Parsons
Rita Webb
Arthur Mullard
Dave Freeman

CREDITS

writer Benny Hill · *director* Philip Casson ·
producer Jon Scoffield

This ATV special was made in colour
(although necessarily screened in black and
white by the still monochrome ITV)
expressly for the American market, where it
was among a number of shows generated for
the CBS network by Lew Grade as summer
replacements for the comedy/variety series
The Red Skelton Show. Hill's desire to work
in colour was second only to his wish to
become a star in the USA, but fame on the
other side of the Atlantic eluded him for a
few years yet and certainly didn't spring
from this programme which, reportedly, left
the star feeling distinctly unhappy. What
this ATV special *did* do, however, was
greatly anger the BBC, which had enjoyed a
long and mutually beneficial working
relationship with Hill and always assumed
that the star would offer them first refusal
on his services.

The Benny Hill Show · 4

UK · ITV (THAMES) · SKETCH

58 × 60 mins (55 × colour · 3 × b/w)

*Unless otherwise stated: all shows colour and
shown Wed 8pm*

19 Nov 1969 · 25 Dec 1969 (Thu 8.30pm) ·
4 Feb 1970 · 11 Mar 1970 · 28 Oct 1970 ·
23 Dec 1970 (b/w) · 27 Jan 1971 (b/w) · 24
Feb 1971 (b/w) · 24 Mar 1971 · 24 Nov 1971 ·
22 Dec 1971 · 23 Feb 1972 · 22 Mar 1972 ·
25 Oct 1972 · 27 Dec 1972 · 22 Feb 1973
(Thu 9pm) · 29 Mar 1973 (Thu 9pm) · 5 Dec
1973 · 27 Dec 1973 (Thu 9pm) · 7 Feb 1974
(Thu 8.30pm) · 13 Mar 1974 · 8 Jan 1975 ·
12 Mar 1975 · 24 Sep 1975 · 17 Dec 1975 ·
18 Feb 1976 · 24 Mar 1976 (Wed 8.30pm) · 21
Apr 1976 · 26 Jan 1977 · 23 Feb 1977 · 23 Mar
1977 · 30 May 1978 (Tue 8pm) · 26 Dec 1978
(Tue 7.15pm) · 14 Mar 1979 · 25 Apr 1979 ·
6 Feb 1980 · 5 Mar 1980 · 16 Apr 1980 · 7 Jan
1981 · 11 Feb 1981 · 25 Mar 1981 · 6 Jan
1982 · 10 Feb 1982 · 5 Jan 1983 · 16 Mar
1983 · 16 Jan 1984 (Mon 8pm) · 25 Apr 1984 ·
2 Jan 1985 · 8 Apr 1985 (Mon 8pm) · 27 May
1985 (Mon 8pm) · 12 Mar 1986 · 31 Mar 1986
(Mon 8pm) · 16 Apr 1986 · 13 Jan 1988 ·
27 Apr 1988 · 8 Feb 1989 · 5 Apr 1989 · 1 May
1989 (Mon 8pm)

MAIN CAST
Benny Hill

PRINCIPAL SUPPORTING CAST
Jenny Lee-Wright
Henry McGee
Nicholas Parsons
Bob Todd
Rita Webb
Jack Wright

OTHER REGULAR APPEARANCES
Anna Dawson
Bella Emberg
Louise English
Lesley Goldie
Patricia Hayes
Eira Heath
Helen Horton
Jon Jon Keefe
Bettine Le Beau
Andree Melly
Sue Upton

CREDITS
writer Benny Hill · *directors/producers* John Robins (shows 1–9, 12 & 13, 18–20), David Bell (shows 10 & 11), Keith Beckett (shows 14–16, 32), Peter Frazer-Jones (shows 17), Mark Stuart (shows 21–24, 26–31), Ronald Fouracre (shows 25 & 33), Dennis Kirkland (shows 34–58)

In a move that further angered the BBC – the Corporation had commissioned and screened four new programmes with the comic in 1968, even after he had made a show for ATV the year before – Benny Hill upped sticks and moved to Thames in time for the week that ITV launched a regular colour service. (BBC1 went to colour at the same time; BBC2 had been screening programmes in colour since 1967.) Undoubtedly, even taking into account his achievements in the 1950s, it was these Thames programmes that gave Hill his greatest commercial success, leading to the big breakthrough in the USA for which the star had long hungered.

Quite simply, when most people today speak of Benny Hill they do so with these Thames shows in mind. He never made a series, as such, for the ITV company but did turn in a remarkable 58 hour-long productions in a 21-year run that, for the most part, featured very highly in the ratings. (Hill did little TV work except for these occasional specials and, being already wealthy beyond his modest needs, certainly didn't do them for the money.) It was here that most viewers came to know – maybe even love – the lisping, inept nitwit Fred Scuttle, the Chinaman Mr Chow Mein, the Milky Bar Kid and a host of other Hillesque characters in a village he named Little Dimpton. And, of course, there were the ever-present bevy of bikini-busting, boob-bouncing beauties who came to be dubbed (even by Benny himself) Hill's Angels. Hill's unusual twist on life was that rather than him chasing them, these girls chased *him*, and every programme ended with an extended, speeded-up sequence – set to corny but unforgettable music – in which the posse became longer and longer and longer. (The music was 'Yakety Sax', an instrumental composed by Randy Randolph and James Rich – Americans, but with highly appropriate names – and usually played by Ronnie Aldrich and his Orchestra.)

While it is largely thought now that these Thames shows comprised nothing but the scantily clad women and accompanying innuendo-laced 'toilet' humour, they also featured more of Hill's clever mime work and parodies of other entertainers and in-vogue TV shows. All the same, it was, more than anything else, the more simplistic, bawdy humour that continued to attract the viewers. Remarkably, a selection of the best Thames TV sketches from 1968 to 1974 was transferred from tape to film and released as a theatrically distributed movie, *The Best Of Benny Hill*, in 1974 (director/producer John Robins), and people paid in their droves to see it on the big screen.

It was around this time that Thames made an effort to kick-start Hill's career in the USA – with little effect. Five years later, however, in 1979, came the big breakthrough: his Thames material was re-compiled into a package of programmes by the American TV agent Don Taffner that were screened twice-nightly across the States, causing Hill to become arguably the biggest star on US television at that time and confounding those who had believed, wrongly, that like **Monty Python** the essential *Britishness* of the humour would not appeal to the Americans. That it did, and that they embraced Hill in such an all-encompassing fashion, owes much to his skill as a mime artist – many of Hill's best skits were silent – and the shock factor generated by the more risqué material at a time when, generally, US TV was somewhat more tame. And it wasn't just in the UK and USA that the shows became massively popular: Hill's work is cherished all over the world, regardless of how many times the same shows have been screened. Hill's visual comedy, much like that of **Mr Bean**, knows no boundaries.

Ironically, Hill's international triumphs coincided with a decline in his fortunes in his home country. His British TV ratings began to slip around 1984, not because he stopped being funny but because his humour had become 'politically incorrect' at home. Although Hill may have claimed a higher moral ground (or indeed may not have done), the fact remains that his trademark broad humour – lots of slap and tickle with sexy bimbettes, and treatment of women as brainless sexual objects – fast went out of fashion in the 1980s with the advent of the new wave of so-called 'alternative' young comics determined to do away with sexism and the ancient 'mother-in-law' style of jokes. One can also point to Hill's physical appearance in the latter Thames shows as a further reason for the decline – he did not age well and put on weight, so that the once cherubic features that had endeared him to viewers no longer evoked the same sympathies.

All the same, there was widespread shock when Thames terminated Hill's contract in 1989, leading to reports that he would make programmes expressly for screening in other countries. As it transpired, apart from the inexhaustible re-compiling of his Thames sketches for overseas sale (and, indeed, for frequent screening on British TV, usually as half-hour programmes), the only new material was featured in two half-hour shows aired in 1994, two years after his death.

Eddie In August

UK · ITV (THAMES) · SITCOM

1 × 30 mins · colour

3 June 1970 · Wed 7pm

MAIN CAST

Eddie	Benny Hill
Woman	Nicole Shelby

CREDITS
writer Benny Hill · *producers/directors* John Robins, Benny Hill

Benny Hill scripted, starred in, composed the music for and co-produced/directed this single silent half-hour comedy for Thames, in which he played Eddie, 28, baffled by life and in love with a woman who, patently, shares no feelings for him. He sets out, with wit, to woo, but the result was unsatisfying and Hill stayed away from such ventures after this.

Benny Hill In Australia

AUSTRALIA/UK · CHANNEL 10/THAMES · SKETCH

1 × 60 mins · colour

Australia date: 11 October 1977

UK date: 12 Apr 1978 · ITV Wed 8pm

MAIN CAST

Benny Hill
Ron Shand

CREDITS
writer Benny Hill

A one-off special – screened in Britain as *Benny Hill Down Under* – filmed with an Australian cast and crew in the Sydney area and featuring the usual cast of Hill character creations, with one new addition for local flavour: Ned Kelly Jr.

Benny Hill – Unseen

UK/USA · ITV (D L TAFFNER) · SKETCH

2 × 30 mins · colour

12 Apr 1994 · Tue 9.30pm

16 May 1994 · Mon 8pm

MAIN CAST

Benny Hill
Henry McGee
Johnny Hutch

CREDITS
writer Benny Hill · *executive producers* Philip Jones, Don Taffner

On 20 December 1991, a year before his death, the BBC arts documentary strand Omnibus presented Benny Hill: Clown Imperial, a high-profile salute to the comic that went some way towards restoring his latterly tarnished reputation in Britain.

Earlier the same year, Hill filmed some sketches in New York, which, together with further material to be shot in Australia and the Far East, he planned to turn into a series to be titled *Benny Hill's World Tour*. His death on 18 April 1992 ensured that the series remained unfinished, but the incomplete work was screened in these two half-hour specials.

Him And His Magic

UK · ITV (LWT) · SITCOM

1 × 30 mins · colour

1 June 1980 · Sun 8.45pm

MAIN CAST

Stanley · · · · · · · · · · · · · Philip Martin Brown
Mum · Joan Scott
Uncle Ernie · · · · · · · · · · · · · · · · Paul Luty

CREDITS

writer Geoff Rowley · *director* Geoffrey Sax · *producer* Humphrey Barclay

A single-episode comedy starring Philip Martin Brown as Stanley, on his way to London from Stockport with a suitcase in his hand and stiff lectures in his head, courtesy of his mum. It was the first solo comedy script by Geoff Rowley, following the end of his collaboration with Andy Baker (which had resulted in scripts for **Please, Sir!**, **The Fenn Street Gang**, **Doctor At Large** and other shows). No series resulted.

Hinge And Bracket

George Logan and Patrick Fyffe had appeared in drag as the sisterly spinsters Hinge and Bracket since 1972 but they came to prominence with a lauded appearance at the 1974 Edinburgh Festival Fringe that turned them into national cabaret stars virtually overnight. Their comic style was to portray a totally believable, refined pair of upper-middle-aged, music-loving women whose genteel banter sometimes, shockingly, slipped into areas of surprisingly bad taste.

Logan's alter ego was Dr Evadne Mona Hinge, the somewhat racier of the two, perhaps owing to her eccentric Scots upbringing. Fyffe was Dame Hilda Nemone Bracket, daughter of Sir Osbert Bracket, who bequeathed her the family estate in Stackton Tressel, Suffolk. The two supposedly met when they were both appearing in the Rosa Charles Opera Company, striking up a friendship after Dr Hinge fell into a box of chocolates that the Dame had open on her lap. Firm friends

and devoted to one another, Dr Hinge moved into the East Wing of Dame Hilda's stately pile.

As for Logan and Fyffe, both hailed from Scotland and met when they were on the same cabaret bill and Fyffe's tenor partner quit. Logan already had a drag act and the original concept was to feature Fyffe as the musical madam's male partner. In the end, however, they decided to perform as two ageing ladies, and a memorable double-act was born. They were, perhaps, unlikely television stars, and certainly an acquired taste, but their many dedicated fans found them to be a taste well worth acquiring.

See also *What's On Next?*

At Home With Dr Evadne Hinge And Dame Hilda Bracket

UK · ITV (SCOTTISH) · STANDUP

1 × 30 mins · colour

23 Sep 1977 · Fri 12.30pm

MAIN CAST

Dr Evadne Hinge · · · · · · · · · · George Logan
Dame Hilda Bracket · · · · · · · · Patrick Fyffe

CREDITS

writers George Logan/Patrick Fyffe · *producer* David Bell

Their popularity gaining strength at this time, Scottish Television accorded a special programme to the talents of Hinge and Bracket, those cross-dressed purveyors of high-class stage entertainment.

Hinge And Bracket

UK · BBC · STANDUP

7 editions (5 × 45 mins · 2 × 50 mins) · colour

31 Mar 1978 · BBC2 Fri 9.30pm (45 mins)
26 Dec 1978 · BBC2 Tue 9pm (45 mins)
29 Aug 1979 · BBC2 Wed 9.35pm (45 mins)
22 Dec 1979 · BBC2 Sat 9.50pm (45 mins)
24 Oct 1980 · BBC2 Fri 9pm (45 mins)
17 Apr 1981 · BBC2 Fri 8.40pm (50 mins)
Hinge And Bracket's New Year's Eve Party
31 Dec 1981 · BBC2 Thu 9.30pm (50 mins)

MAIN CAST

Dr Evadne Hinge · · · · · · · · · George Logan
Dame Hilda Bracket · · · · · · · · Patrick Fyffe
host · · · · · · · · · · Joseph Cooper (show 1),
· · · · · · · · · · Corbet Woodall (shows 2–4),
· · · · · · · · · · · · · · · · · Jon Curle (show 5)

CREDITS

writers George Logan/Patrick Fyffe · *directors* Hazel Lewthwaite (shows 1–6), Mike Stephens (show 7) · *producer* Peter Ridsdale Scott

Musical mayhem with the comical cabaret artists. These shows featured the Stackton Tressel Choir and Strings.

Dear Ladies

UK · BBC · SITCOM

21 episodes (20 × 30 mins · 1 × 40 mins) · colour

Series One (6) 15 Mar–19 Apr 1983 · BBC2 Tue 10.05pm

Special (40 mins) *Dear Ladies' Masterclass* 6 Jan 1984 · BBC2 Fri 9.25pm

Series Two (6) 16 Feb–22 Mar 1984 · BBC2 Thu 9pm

Series Three (8) 26 Sep–16 Dec 1984 · BBC2 Wed 9pm

MAIN CAST

Dr Evadne Hinge · · · · · · · · · George Logan
Dame Hilda Bracket · · · · · · · · Patrick Fyffe

CREDITS

writers George Logan/Patrick Fyffe with Gyles Brandreth · *director* Mike Stephens · *producers* Mike Stephens (9), Peter Ridsdale Scott (6), Mike Smith (6)

A weekly sitcom that afforded viewers 'a glimpse behind the scenes of Village Life in Stackton Tressel', where lived the delightful Doctor and Dame. This was very much a genteel confection on the surface but, with the usual undercurrent of satire and suggested vulgarity, it turned out to be anything but this. These televisual jaunts followed the ladies' similar escapades on BBC radio in the series *The Enchanted World Of Hinge And Bracket* (36 editions, 1 January 1977–19 September 1979) and *The Random Jottings Of Hinge And Bracket* (12 editions, 4 April 1982–8 May 1983).

Hip Hip Who Ray

see RAY, Ted

Hiram Holliday

see *The Adventures Of Hiram Holliday*

His And Hers

UK · ITV (YORKSHIRE) · SITCOM

20 episodes (19 × 30 mins · 1 × short special) · colour

Series One (6) 23 June–28 July 1970 · Tue 8.30pm

Short special · part of *Mike And Bernie Winters' All-Star Christmas Comedy Carnival* 25 Dec 1971 · Sat 6.05pm

*Series Two (13) 7 Apr–30 June 1972 · Fri 7.30pm then 8.30pm

MAIN CAST

Rupert Sherwin · · · · · · · · · · · · Ronald Lewis
Kay Sherwin · · · · · · · · Sue Lloyd (series 1);
· · · · · · · Barbara Murray (special & series 2)
Toby Burgess · · Tim Brooke-Taylor (series 1)
Janet Burgess · · · Madeline Smith (series 1)
Dorothy · · · · · · · · · · · · · · · · Janie Booth

CREDITS
writers Ken Hoare/Mike Sharland · directors/
producers David Mallet (2 eps in series 1),
Graham Evans (4 eps in series 1), Ian Davidson
(special & series 2) · executive producer John
Duncan (series 1)

Rupert Sherwin is an under-employed freelance magazine writer who stays at home, is contented with the cooking, satisfied with the shopping, does not wring his hands at the thought of the spin-drier and so is unconcerned at playing the role of house-husband to his wife. She, Kay, commutes by train to the City each day, bowler hat on head, where she works as an executive accountant and brings home the bread. The original idea for this Hoare and Sharland sitcom, then, was role-reversal, with next-door neighbours the Burgesses (Tim Brooke-Taylor and Madeline Smith) happy to ridicule the Sherwins' deviation from the norm.

But when His And Hers returned for a second series, virtually two years after the first, the role-reversal premise was largely overlooked in favour of the depiction of unlikely scrapes that one or other of the Sherwins (usually Rupert) got into – including such far-fetched stories as a defecting Russian ballet dancer taking refuge in their bathroom. Sue Lloyd did not return for this second run so Barbara Murray was cast as Kay, and the Burgesses were also gone, although, curiously, Tim Brooke-Taylor turned up in one later episode in a different role. Norman Rossington, Roy Kinnear, Peter Jones, Patricia Routledge and Freddie Jones appeared in guest roles in one episode apiece.

*Note. These dates represent the broadcasts in most ITV regions. In the London area the final three programmes in the second series – 16, 23, 30 June – were replaced by repeats of On The Buses. In a fate suffered by a few other desperately under-achieving series, they finally went out in the capital region in a post-midnight slot, on Sundays 26 November and 3 and 10 December 1972.

His Lordship Entertains

UK · BBC · SITCOM
....
7 × 30 mins · colour
5 June–17 July 1972 · BBC2 Mon 8.55pm

MAIN CAST
Lord Rustless · · · · · · · · · · · · Ronnie Barker
Mildred Bates · · · · · · · · · · Josephine Tewson
Dithers · · · · · · · · · · · · · · · · · David Jason
Cook · · · · · · · · · · · · · · · · · Mary Baxter
Effie · · · · · · · · · · · · · · · · · Moira Foot
Badger · · · · · · · · · · · · · · · · Frank Gatliff

CREDITS
writer Jonathan Cobbald (Ronnie Barker) ·
producer Harold Snoad

A change of channels for the crusty old peer Lord Rustless, who had earlier been seen in

two series of **Hark At Barker** on ITV. The remainder of the cast, and the setting, Chrome Hall, also made the switch.

In this series, Chrome Hall had been opened as a hotel, but various obstacles had to be overcome to make it a success. The ITV episodes had seen Barker cast in a bewildering number of additional roles; here he was just plain Rustless. He did write the seven episodes, however, hiding beneath the pseudonym Jonathan Cobbald.

Hit The Pitch

UK · ITV (THAMES) · SITCOM
....
1 × 30 mins · colour
11 Dec 1989 · Mon 10.35pm

MAIN CAST
V-Neck · · · · · · · · · · · · · · · · Sam Smart
Michael · · · · · · · · · · · · · Vincenzo Nicoli
Hector · · · · · · · · · · · · · · · Peter Benson
Becky · · · · · · · · · · · · · · Angela Catherall
Maria · · · · · · · · · · · · · · · · Ailsa Fairley
Karina · · · · · · · · · · · · · Suzannah Hitching
Andy · · · · · · · · · · · · · · Stephen Tompkinson

CREDITS
writer Alan Whiting · director/producer John Stroud

A single sitcom half-hour – potentially a pilot for a series that failed to develop – about the misfortunes that strike three members of a telephone sales team, V-Neck, Michael and Hector.

The Hitch-Hiker's Guide To The Galaxy

UK · BBC · SITCOM
....
6 × 30 mins · colour
5 Jan–9 Feb 1981 · BBC2 Mon 9pm

MAIN CAST
The Book · · · · · · · · Peter Jones (voice only)
Arthur Dent · · · · · · · · · · · · · · Simon Jones
Ford Prefect · · · · · · · · · · · · · · David Dixon
Zaphod Beeblebrox · · · · · · Mark Wing-Davey
Trillian · · · · · · · · · · · · Sandra Dickinson
Marvin · · · · · · · · · · · Stephen Moore (voice),
· · · · · · · · · · · · · · · · · David Learner (body)
Slartibartfast · · · · · · · · · · · · Richard Vernon

CREDITS
writer Douglas Adams · producer Alan J W Bell

The radio version of this series is quite possibly the favourite wireless show in the universe – and certainly every bit as good as a meal at Milliways. The Hitch-Hiker's Guide To The Galaxy was to listeners of the 1970s what ITMA had been in the 1940s, The Goon Show in the 1950s and I'm Sorry, I'll Read That Again in the 1960s – unmissable and excellent comic entertainment. Wildly inventive, harmless (well, mostly harmless) and with a groundbreaking use of special sound effects and voice techniques, the series' initial cult following soon attracted a mainstream audience.

The premise was complex and the show rich in wild ideas and eccentric characters. The story begins with the imminent destruction of Earth to make way for a hyperspace express route. The job is being handled by alien Vogons from the Galactic Hyperspace Planning Council who respond to human protests by pointing out that the plans had been on display on Alpha Centauri for many years and an objection could have been lodged at any time. Now it is too late. Earthling Arthur Dent is coerced by his pal Ford Prefect to escape the apocalypse by hitching a ride on the Vogon spacecraft. Prefect, it transpires, is an alien in human form, whose job was to research Earth for an updated edition of an electronic book, The Hitch-Hiker's Guide To The Galaxy. He and the stupefied Dent manage to board the ship, and their adventures begin as the Earth is destroyed with the minimum of fuss.

Apart from his remarkably weird characters, satirical ideas and delight in the imaginative use of language, Adams brought one more important factor to the project: a strong opinion of how the series should sound. The development in recording processes had recently resulted in rock albums becoming more lush, with a rich, textured sound, and Adams wanted his radio series to boast that same aural tapestry, to make it sound as seamless and luxuriant as a rock album. Adams was well served in this regard by his producer Geoffrey Perkins and a team that included John Lloyd, Simon Brett, Paddy Kirkland and many others.

The radio series gave birth to a veritable industry of Hitch-Hiker spin-offs: books, tapes, a stage production, computer games, people going around impersonating Marvin the paranoid android or the two-headed Zaphod Beeblebrox, T-shirts, towels (towels were an important part of the story) and, of course, this TV series. Simon Jones, Mark Wing-Davey, Stephen Moore and Richard Vernon all re-created their radio roles for the TV version and so, most importantly, did Peter Jones, whose mellifluous tones served as the voice of the Hitch-Hiker book, providing information and wonderfully dry comment. The importance of the voice cannot be overlooked, the book being both a survival pack and security blanket to the intergalactic drifter. (For a start, it had 'Don't Panic' written on the front … in friendly lettering.) In the TV series, the voice was complemented by screen graphics in an effort to place a visual image with the audio. Considering the awesome aural visions suggested by the radio, the TV equivalents were always bound to be second best, the production crew being unable to depict such grand ideas visually, no matter how big the budget. (It was, of course, painfully small.) Quite simply, the well-worn adage about radio pictures being better than those on TV was never more true than with *Hitch-Hiker*. A feature film version which might possibly do justice to the majestic radio series, has *long* been promised but only in late 1997 were announcements made to the effect that it is about to get off the ground, Adams having struck a deal with Disney.

For this and other reasons, the TV version of *The Hitch-Hiker's Guide To The Galaxy* is considered (by Adams especially) a poor cousin to the radio original, but actually it manages fairly well; certainly, had there been no preceding radio series, it would have fared much better. In the USA, where the radio version is not so well known, the TV series has attained a serious cult following. The TV series concludes where the first of the two radio series ends, with Dent and Prefect finding themselves back on Earth, but in Stone Age times, discovering, with horror, that the genesis of Man rests not with cave-dwelling grunters but with a bunch of useless middle-management types, hairdressers and telephone sanitisers cheerfully ejected from the planet of Golgafrincham.

Notes. The *Hitch-Hiker* radio series was broadcast in 12 episodes by BBC Radio 4. The brilliant first series, of six, went out from 8 March to 12 April 1978; there was a special on 24 December 1978, and a not quite so brilliant second series, of five episodes, aired daily from 21 to 25 January 1980. On radio, Geoffrey McGivern played Ford Prefect and Trillian was played by Susan Sheridan.

The 5 January 1992 edition of LWT's networked arts series *The South Bank Show* paid tribute to Douglas Adams and traced his career from *Doctor Who* scriptwriter to internationally renowned author and environmentalist. The hour-length programme included sections of the TV version of *The Hitch-Hiker's Guide To The Galaxy* as well as enacting, for the first time, Adams' subsequent creation, the detective Dirk Gently.

In 1993, BBC Video released *The Making Of The Hitch-Hiker's Guide To The Galaxy*, a behind-the-scenes look at the 1981 TV series, featuring amateur video tape recorded during the production and specially shot contemporary interviews.

HMS Paradise

UK · ITV (REDIFFUSION) · SITCOM
26 episodes (25 × 30 mins · 1 × 55 mins) · b/w
16 July 1964–7 Jan 1965 · Thu around 7pm
MAIN CAST
Captain Turvey · · · · · · · · · · Richard Caldicot
Commander Fairweather · · · · Frank Thornton
Lieutenant Pouter · · · · · · · · · · Robin Hunter
CPO Banyard · · · · · · · · · · · · · Ronald Radd
Able Seaman Murdoch · · · · · · · Angus Lennie
Amanda · · · · · · · · · · · · · · Priscilla Morgan

OTHER APPEARANCES
Commander Shaw · · · · · · · Graham Crowden
CREDITS
creator Lawrie Wyman · *writers* Maurice Wiltshire (12), Lawrie Wyman (8), Lew Schwarz (4), Maurice Wiltshire/David Climie (1), Maurice Wiltshire/Lew Schwarz (1) · *directors* Bill Hitchcock (20), Bill Turner (3), Ronald Marriott (2), John P Hamilton (1) · *producer* Sid Colin

One of the many similarly themed 'service' comedies that followed in the wake of **The Phil Silvers Show**, *HMS Paradise* was the creation of Lawrie Wyman, who had already mined the nautical deep for the long-running BBC radio sitcom *The Navy Lark*. It was between the sixth and seventh series of that wireless comedy that *HMS Paradise* hit the screens, relating the tales of a bunch of servicefolk posted to the island of Boonsey, a fictitious location supposedly situated a few miles off Portland, Dorset.

This is an easy posting, and although they are supposed to do *some* work most of the staff's time is spent in avoiding it and, instead, crafting shady deals. Commander Fairweather is in vague command of the post but he'd rather stick to his angling. Chief Petty Officer Banyard is a spiv, lovelorn Lieutenant Pouter is dozy, Able Seaman Murdoch is a dim Scotsman (in an appalling example of prejudice, most brainless people in English sitcoms at this time seemed to be Scottish) and Amanda, a perky Wren typist, is the lone woman on the post. The only thorn in their collective sides is Captain Turvey – nicknamed 'Old Thunderguts' – whose job it is to ensure that Queen's Regulations are adhered to, but who is singularly unable to prove they are being flouted on Boonsey.

A number of guest names appeared during the series, including Clive Dunn (the real-life husband of Priscilla Morgan, who played Amanda), Wendy Richard, Barbara Hicks, John Bluthal, Donald Hewlett, Patrick Troughton, Cardew Robinson and Stanley Unwin.

Note. The Christmas Eve 1964 edition was a 55-minute special titled *HMS Paradise Meets HMS Eagle*.

Hocus Focus

see The Montreux Festival

The Hogan Family

see *Valerie*

Hogan's Heroes

USA · CBS (BING CROSBY PRODUCTIONS) · SITCOM
168 × 30 mins (167 × colour · 1 × b/w)
US dates: 17 Sep 1965–4 July 1971

*UK dates: 6 Jan 1967–20 Feb 1971 (68 episodes · 60 in b/w) ITV various days and times
MAIN CAST
Col Robert Hogan · · · · · · · · · · · · · Bob Crane
Col Wilhelm Klink · · · · · · · Werner Klemperer
Sgt Hans Schultz · · · · · · · · · · · · John Banner
Cpl Louis LeBeau · · · · · · · · · · · Robert Clary
Cpl Peter Newkirk · · · · · · · · Richard Dawson
Sgt Andrew Carter · · · · · · · · · · · · Larry Hovis
Cpl James Kinchloe · · Ivan Dixon (1965–70)
Sgt Richard Baker · · · · Kenneth Washington
· (1970–71)
Gen Alfred Burkhalter · · · · · · · · · · Leon Askin
Helga · · · · · · · · · · · · Cynthia Lynn (1965–66)
Hilda · · · · · · · · · · · · Sigrid Valdis (1966–70)

CREDITS
creators Bernard Fein/Albert S Ruddy · *writers* Howard Marks and others · *directors* Gene Reynolds and others · *producer* Edward H Feldman

A long-running US series depicting Second World War antics inside Stalag 13, a German prisoner-of-war camp. In theory, the camp is run by the Germans; in reality, it is run by the POWs, who are so much in command that they have no wish to escape. Instead, the place becomes like a holiday camp – the prisoners have their own chef, sauna and hairdressing salon – they regularly nip into the local town for the evening, and they aid the Allies' war effort by feeding back valuable information gleaned from the inept Germans and committing acts of sabotage. The series appeared to be modelled on the 1953 movie *Stalag 17*, directed by Billy Wilder, although the emphasis there was more on drama than comedy. There were also touches of that ultimate in POW movies, *The Great Escape* (1962).

The leader of the prisoners was Colonel Hogan, an American sharpster with the homely touch, and his ethnic mix of inmates included Peter Newkirk, a spiv English RAF corporal with the cockney accent *de rigueur* for all British characters in US sitcoms of the day; and a French corporal, Louis LeBeau, who was (pfeu, but what else?) an expert cook. The bald, monocled German camp commander Colonel Klink may have looked the part of a screen Nazi but his massive insecurity, cowardice and fear of the Gestapo made him a far from menacing character. His incredibly dim sergeant Schultz was the main point of contact with the prisoners, but while the portly guard often caught Hogan and his cronies up to no good, his desire for a quiet life caused him to turn a blind eye and utter – in the best cod German accent – 'I zee nothink, I hear nothink, I know nothink'.

Hogan's Heroes has attracted a fair amount of criticism over the years for its flippant portrayal of a war that, for 99.9 per cent of people, was a terrible and deeply traumatic experience; and its two-dimensional presentation of the POW situation and portrayal of the Stalag Nazis as loveable goons (as opposed to the nasty Nazis of the

Gestapo) left a sour taste in the mouth for some. However, the series' cartoon-like innocence and mission to raise laughs make it hard to condemn it too harshly. In short, although the premise may seem dubious on paper, on screen it was just too lightweight and ludicrous to cause any serious offence.

*Note. In Britain, ITV screened an extended run of *Hogan's Heroes* between 1967 and 1971, and it was then shown again, 15 years later, by C4, which screened 39 episodes from 15 October 1986 to 24 August 1987.

Hogg's Back

UK · ITV (SOUTHERN) · CHILDREN'S SITCOM

19 × 30 mins · colour

Series One (13) 8 Sep–1 Dec 1975 · Mon mostly 4.55pm

Series Two (6) 16 June–21 July 1976 · Wed 4.50pm

MAIN CAST

Dr Hogg · · · · · · · · · · · · · · · · · Derek Royle
Pearl · · · · · · · Jacki Piper (series 1, eps 1–7);
· · · · · · Wendy Richard (series 1, eps 8–13)
Mrs Mac · · · · · · · · · · Pat Coombs (series 2)
General Balding · · · · · · · · · · Robert Dorning
Vicar · · · · · · · · · · · · · · · · · · · Eric Dodson
Mr Diehard · · · · · · · · · · · · Gordon Rollings

CREDITS

writer Michael Pertwee · *producer* Peter Croft

The veteran film and TV writer Michael Pertwee – author of only the second soap opera series on British TV, *The Grove Family*, from April 1954 (the first was *The Appleyards*, from October 1952) – wrote this children's series as a vehicle for Derek Royle, the athletic comic actor who performed all his own stunts (and there were many in *Hogg's Back*). A wacky and forgetful GP, with his own practice in the town of Belling-on-Sea, Hogg was aided in the first series by an assistant, Pearl (Jacki Piper and then, at the same time as she was attaining fame in *Are You Being Served?*, Wendy Richard), and in the second by housekeeper Mrs Mac (Pat Coombs). A number of once familiar TV faces were seen at times during the 19 episodes – among them Arnold Ridley, Alec Bregonzi, Hugh Lloyd and Valentine Dyall.

Hold The Front Page

UK · ITV (THAMES) · CHILDREN'S SITCOM

7 × 30 mins · colour

16 Jan–27 Feb 1974 · Wed 4.20pm

MAIN CAST

Gloria Glamorsox · · · · · · · · · · Denise Coffey
Gerry · · · · · · · · · · · · · · · · Gerry Marsden
Miss Harriet Heedless · · · · · · · · · Lois Lane
Harry Bracket · · · · · · · · · Andrew Robertson
The Judge · · · · · · · · · · · · · · Peter Dennis
R Hero/Ian Trepid · · · · · · · · · · · · Roy Hudd

CREDITS

creator Denise Coffey · *producer* Daphne Shadwell

It was hard to tell whether this was the most loopy British TV comedy of all time or an inspired and innovative piece of work. Created by Denise Coffey at the invitation of producer Daphne Shadwell (they had worked together on *Do Not Adjust Your Set* and the *Captain Fantastic* serials therein), the premise was that Coffey and her crazy gang of assistants worked for a newspaper where their job was to unmask a 'Mr Big' character who had instigated a Great Rug Scandal. The actors appeared on sets that were drawn in the style of comics (*The Dandy*, *Beano* and so on) and the characters had thought bubbles coming out of their heads. The series also made early use of Chroma Key technology, placing different background images behind people inside the studio.

Holding The Baby

UK · ITV (GRANADA) · SITCOM

7 × 30 mins · colour

24 Jan–7 Mar 1997 · Fri 8.30pm

MAIN CAST

Gordon Muir · · · · · · · · · · · · · Nick Hancock
Rob Muir · · · · · · · · · · · · · · · · Joe Duttine
Laura · · · · · · · · · · · · · · · · · Sally Phillips
Daniel Muir · · · · · · · · · · · Joshua Atherton/
· Jacob Atherton

CREDITS

writers Mark Wadlow (6), Dominic Minghella (1) · *directors* Paul Jackson (5), Beryl Richards (2) · *executive producer* Andy Harries · *producer* Justin Judd

A year before the timeframe in which the opening episode was set, Gordon Muir caught his wife Kate *in flagrante delicto* with another man (or, to put it in the crude terms of this series, 'shagging') on his front-room carpet. To make matters worse, the object of her desires was a 21-year-old and she immediately ran off with him, leaving Gordon to bring up their baby, Daniel, and contemplate the unfairness of life. As the series begins, Gordon's slobbish, womanising brother Rob moves in to assist with the chores, although he is more of a hindrance than a help. Also of questionable use is Gordon's friend Laura, who, while sympathising with his plight, feels that she has to remain neutral in the situation. So Gordon tries to get on with life as a single parent, and finds that it is far from easy.

Nick Hancock had scored with viewers as the host of the BBC1 comedy sports quiz *They Think It's All Over* and the BBC2 celebrity chat programme *Room 101* (both of which began on Radio 5), and on these shows he demonstrated a quick and sometimes savage wit. That kind of hard-edged humour would have helped his character in this series, for poor old Gordon was just too nice for his own

good. A permanent victim, it was hard to sympathise with someone who allowed himself to be so walked upon. The odd sharp line and funny situation failed to make up for the weakness of the central character, but ITV obviously hoped to wean their baby with care – a second series was in production at the time of writing, for screening in 1998, albeit with a new actor in the lead role: Hugh Bonneville replacing Nick Hancock. The idea has also been sold to American TV, where the Fox network is planning the production of a pilot episode.

Holding The Fort

UK · ITV (LWT) · SITCOM

20 × 30 mins · colour

Series One (7) 5 Sep–17 Oct 1980 · Fri 8.30pm

Series Two (6) 6 Mar–10 Apr 1981 · Fri 8.30pm

Series Three (7) 18 July–29 Aug 1982 · Sun 7.15pm

MAIN CAST

Russell Milburn · · · · · · · · · · · Peter Davison
Penny Milburn · · · · · · · · · · · · Patricia Hodge
Fitz · · · · · · · · · · · · · · · · · Matthew Kelly
Capt Hector Quilley · · · Christopher Godwin
Emma Milburn · · · · · Katie Louise Reynolds/
· · · · · · · · · · · · · · · · · · · Victoria Kendall

OTHER APPEARANCES

Jennifer Quilley · · · · · · · · · · Maev Alexander
Col Aubrey Sanderson · · · · · · · · · · · · · · · ·
· · · · · · · · · · · · · · · · · Christopher Benjamin
Annabel Chesterton · · · · · · · · · Brigit Forsyth
Terence Chesterton · · · · · · · · · Keith Barron
Dr Heather Wolstenholme · · · · · Arwen Holm

CREDITS

writers Laurence Marks/Maurice Gran · *directors* Derrick Goodwin (18), Les Chatfield (2) · *producer* Derrick Goodwin

Russell and Penny Milburn are a young couple with a baby daughter, Emma. In the opening episode, wisecracking Russell faces the choice of relocating his job (as a modestly paid brewery executive) away from London, to Workington, where he will gain promotion and a better salary, or staying put and being made redundant. He wants to move but Penny won't, and so – in a reversal of roles – Russell becomes a house-husband, staying at home with the baby, the nappies, the Hoover and some productive ale-barrels in the basement (he runs a home-brewing business, but it's only small beer), while Penny brings home the bacon by returning to her former post as a captain in the Women's Royal Army Corps. Russell is sometimes aided, and sometimes not, in his chores, and with the brewing side of things, by his free-spirited lorry-driving friend Fitzroy, known as 'Fitz'. Both share a penchant for pacifism – at odds with Penny's army career – beer and football.

Exploring the theme of role-reversal house-husbandry that was gaining in popularity at the time, *Holding The Fort* was the first sitcom to bear the writing credit of Marks and Gran, perhaps the most illustrious names in British situation comedy writing in the last 20 years of the 20th-century. They later floated off Fitz into a series of his own, *Relative Strangers*.

Holiday Bandbox

see *Comedy Bandbox*

Holiday With Strings

see DAWSON, Les

Holmes And Yoyo

USA · ABC (UNIVERSAL) · SITCOM

16 × 30 mins · colour

US dates: 25 Sep–11 Dec 1976 & 1 Aug 1977
UK dates: 29 Oct 1976–9 Feb 1977
(13 episodes) BBC1 Fri 7pm then Wed 6.45pm

MAIN CAST

Det Sgt Alexander Holmes	· · Richard B Shull
Det Sgt Gregory 'Yoyo' Yoyonovich	· · · · · · · ·
· ·	John Schuck
Captain Harry Sedford	· · · · · · · · Bruce Kirby
Officer Maxine Moon	· · · · · · · Andrea Howard

CREDITS

creators/writers Jack Sher/Lee Hewitt · *directors* Reza S Bidiyi, John Astin, Noam Pitlik, Richard Kinon, Leonard Stern · *executive producer* Leonard Stern · *producer* Arne Sultan

Alexander Holmes is a hapless cop whose partners tend to wind up in hospital while he remains unscathed. As an experiment, he is teamed with a top-secret new invention, an almost indestructible, human-looking, heavyweight android cop bearing the name of his scientist inventor Gregory Yoyonovich, 'Yoyo' for short. At first, Holmes believes that Yoyo is human, but when – succumbing to Holmes' apparent curse – the robot is shot on their very first case, he learns the truth and immediately sees the advantages of such a pairing. Holmes decides, wisely, to keep his partner's form a secret but this proves exceedingly difficult because, although impervious to the dangers of police work, Yoyo soon develops problems of his own: short-circuiting, malfunctioning and displaying a flawed understanding of the way humans work.

ABC had high hopes for this series and the actor John Schuck had previously scored as Sgt Enright, a comic foil in producer Leonard Stern's hit police drama *McMillan And Wife* on NBC. But, despite lively performances, *Holmes And Yoyo* failed to capture the public's imagination. A TV drama series, *Future Cop* (1977), utilised a similar basic premise and also failed to make the grade, but *RoboCop*, a more violent spin on the theme, became a movie hit in three different films (1987–91) before being adapted for a

moderately successful TV drama series (1994).

Some episodes of *Holmes And Yoyo* were directed by John Astin, best known as Gomez in *The Addams Family*.

Home From Home   1

UK · ITV (GRANADA) · SITCOM

1 × 30 mins · b/w

27 June 1963 · Thu 7.30pm

MAIN CAST

Paddy	· · · · · · · · · · · · · · · · Eddie Byrne
Max	· · · · · · · · · · · · · · · Harry Fowler
Nigel	· · · · · · · · · · · · · · Neil McCarthy
Governor	· · · · · · · · · · · · Richard Caldicot
Mr Rawson	· · · · · · · · · · · · · · Keith Pyott

CREDITS

writers Barry Took/Peter Miller/James Kelly · *director* Graeme McDonald · *producer* Peter Eton

Two convicts are embroiled in changes being made to the running of one of Her Majesty's prisons. This was a single-episode production in Granada's *Comedy Four* season, for which Dudley Foster and Bernard Bresslaw were originally cast in the Byrne and Fowler roles.

Home From Home   2

UK · BBC · SITCOM

1 × 30 mins · colour

8 Feb 1973 · BBC1 Thu 8pm

MAIN CAST

Pam Collins	· · · · · · · · · · · Carmel McSharry
Bill Collins	· · · · · · · · · · · · Michael Robbins
Ron Bates	· · · · · · · · · · · · · · · Tony Selby
Lil Wilson	· · · · · · · · · · · · · · Yootha Joyce

CREDITS

writer Eric Davidson · *producer* Harold Snoad

Domestic strife took centre stage here when Bill Collins' wife Pam, having for too long put up with his chauvinistic behaviour, suddenly snapped. She left him, moved into a bedsitter and took a job as a traffic warden, intent on making him her most frequent victim. A strong comedy cast filled the roles but no series developed from this *Comedy Playhouse* pilot.

The Home Front

UK · ITV (CENTRAL) · COMEDY SERIAL

6 × 60 mins · colour

2 Feb–9 Mar 1983 · Wed 9pm

MAIN CAST

Mrs Place	· · · · · · · · · · · · · · · Brenda Bruce
Hallam Place	· · · · Warren Clarke (3 eps)
Garfield Place	· · · · Malcolm Tierney (3 eps)
Hazel Place	· · · · · · · · Sue Robinson (2 eps)
Avril Hemingway	· · · · Cherith Mellor (2 eps)

OTHER APPEARANCES

Vernon Hemingway	· · · · · · · · · Karl Johnson
Mrs Mazarene	· · · · · · · · · · Rowena Cooper
Mr Garlick	· · · · · · · · · · · · Maurice Denham

CREDITS

writer Peter Tinniswood · *directors* Roy Battersby (4), Stuart Burge (2) · *producer* Nicholas Palmer

A northern black-comedy-drama series that focused on the dreadful antics of one Mrs Place, a nosey harridan who ruled mightily over her three disagreeable adult children: Avril (who, with her husband Vernon, has a precocious two-year-old son), Garfield and TV comedy scriptwriter Hallam, the latter 'contaminated by living in London'. Six weekly episodes showed Mrs Place in different situations, and she was the only regular member of the cast. Writer Peter Tinniswood had previously portrayed an awful northern family in *I Didn't Know You Cared*, and *The Home Front* was distinguished by that same fine Tinniswood touch and Mrs Place's arrogant catchphrase, 'Am I right? I am!'

Home Improvement

USA · ABC (WIND DANCER PRODUCTIONS/ TOUCHSTONE TELEVISION) · SITCOM

161 episodes (160 × 30 mins · 1 × 60 mins to 31/12/97 · continuing into 1998) · colour

US dates: 17 Sep 1991 to date
UK dates: 4 Feb 1994 to date (100 × 30 mins to 31/12/97) C4 various days mostly 6pm

MAIN CAST

Tim Taylor	· · · · · · · · · · · · · · · · · Tim Allen
Jill Taylor	· · · · · · · · · · · · Patricia Richardson
Wilson Wilson	· · · · · · · · · · · · Earl Hindman
Bradley ('Brad') Taylor	· · · · Zachery Ty Bryan
Randy Taylor	· · · · · · Jonathan Taylor Thomas
Mark Taylor	· · · · · · · · · · · Taran Noah Smith
Al Borland	· · · · · · · · · · · · · · Richard Karn
Lisa	· · · · · · · · · Pamela Anderson (1991–92)
Heidi	· · · · · · · · · Debbe Dunning (from 1993)
Jennifer	· · · · · · · Jessica Wesson (1991–93)

CREDITS

creators Carmen Finestra/David McFadzean/Matt Williams · *writers* various · *directors* Peter Bonerz, Peter Filsinger, Andy Cadiff, Geoffrey Nelson, Andrew Tsao and others · *executive producers* Carmen Finestra, David McFadzean, Matt Williams, Bob Bendetson, Andy Cadiff, Bruce Ferber, Gayle S Maffeo, Elliott Schoenman · *producers* Gayle S Maffeo, John Pasquin, Billy Riback, Maxine Lapiduss

In 1991, Tim Allen became the latest in a line of standup comedians to have situation comedies built around their stage persona. The ploy was proving successful, having already led to *Roseanne* and *Seinfeld*, and Allen's *Home Improvement* continued the trend, quickly becoming a huge hit in the US and eventually toppling *Roseanne* from the top of the ratings.

The show focused on Tim Taylor, a somewhat toned-down version of a power-tool-crazed, do-it-yourself fanatic that Allen had invented for his stage act. For the TV model, much of the character's bigotry and chauvinism was softened, although the essential comedic device of depicting a laughably inadequate, would-be macho 'man's man' remained intact. Taylor was a local celebrity through his role as the presenter of a cable TV series *Tool Time*, the 'show that tells you how to improve your home'. (It was probably a pastiche of *This Old House*, a long-running PBS information series about home repair and construction.) Taylor's love and knowledge of power-tools, especially those made by the show's sponsor Binfords, made him an ideal front man, although many of his suggestions on DIY were impractical and situations often had to be retrieved by his partner, the more adept Al Borland. Taylor's trouble was that his answer to every problem was 'more power!', a policy that rarely paid dividends. At home, where he was allowed free range to indulge his 'powering-up' prowess, he had suitably enhanced much of the domestic equipment, so that he had turbo-powered washing machines, blenders that could 'purée a brick' and hairdryers that could move yachts. Editions of *Tool Time* (until 1993) also featured a glamorous woman (played by Pamela Anderson) to attract male viewers.

Recognising that they had to flesh out Taylor's character, the creators made him a family man and provided him with a supportive yet individual wife, a trio of children, and a next-door neighbour, Wilson Wilson, whose face was always obscured by a wooden garden fence. This home interplay provided the biggest slice of the action, giving the series its heart. The sum total was a surprisingly gentle sitcom, given its aspirations as a satire of the modern urban American male, which won a large and loyal audience despite being one of those shows that is likely to be forgotten the moment it finishes.

See also *Tim Allen Rewires America.*

Home James

UK · BBC · STANDUP

3 × 60 mins · b/w

14 Jan–10 Mar 1956 · monthly Sat 8.30pm

MAIN CAST

Jimmy James
Joan Turner
Thora Hird (show 1)

CREDITS

writers Cass James, Frank Roscoe · *producer* Ronnie Taylor

A northern series, screened nationally, presided over by the wonderful stage-drunk Jimmy James, who delighted audiences with his inimitable style of story-telling that invariably included a string of ad-libbed and surreal rambling asides.

Born James Casey in 1892, this peerless music-hall and variety star didn't drink in real life but knew exactly how to imitate the inebriated state. Much loved and respected by his fellow comics – Roy Castle began his career as one of his stooges – James was selected to perform in the 1953 *Royal Variety Show*, the year of the coronation. He died on 4 August 1965, aged 71.

Home James!

UK · ITV (THAMES) · SITCOM

25 episodes (24 × 30 mins · 1 × 45 mins) · colour

Series One (6 × 30 mins) 1 July–5 Aug 1987 · Wed 8pm

Special (45 mins) *Home James For Christmas!* 21 Dec 1987 · Mon 8.30pm

Series Two (6 × 30 mins) 7 Sep–12 Oct 1988 · Wed 8pm

Series Three (6 × 30 mins) 25 Sep–30 Oct 1989 · Mon 8pm

Series Four (6 × 30 mins) 18 June–23 July 1990 · Mon 8pm

MAIN CAST

Jim London	Jim Davidson
Robert Palmer	George Sewell
Henry Compton	Harry Towb
Sarah Palmer	Vanessa Knox-Mawer
	(series 1 & 2 and special)
Paula	Sherrie Hewson
	(series 1 & 2 and special)
Terry	Owen Whittaker
	(series 1 & 2 and special)
Connie	Cecilia-Marie Carreon
	(series 1 & 2 and special)
Tony	Nigel Williams (series 1)
Eleanor Hayward	Juliette Grassby
	(series 4)

CREDITS

writers Geoff McQueen (14), Simon Moss (4), Chris Boucher (2), Christopher Russell (1), David Lloyd (1), David Firth (1), Spike Mullins (1), John Merryfield (1) · *script editor* John Junkin · *directors* Anthony Parker/Mark Stuart (pilot), Anthony Parker (series 1 & 2 and special), David Askey (series 3), Martin Shardlow (series 4) · *executive producer* Anthony Parker (series 3 & 4) · *producers* Anthony Parker (series 1 & 2 and special), David Askey (series 3), Martin Shardlow (series 4)

A sequel to *Up The Elephant And Round The Castle*. In the opening (pilot) episode Jim London witnesses the demolition of his old home at 17 Railway Terrace. With cocky cockneyness all too intact, he is also dismissed from his job as a delivery man. Luck comes Jim's way, however, when he is appointed chauffeur and general factotum to an electronics executive, Robert Palmer, whose industry has made him a millionaire. All problems solved – Jim has a place to live, in a scrubbed Edwardian house in Chelsea, no less, and a cushy job driving a 'Roller'. He has colleagues, too, among them the butler, Henry, who becomes an ally; the general assistant, Connie; and the upwardly mobile

Eleanor Hayward (Mr Palmer's PA in the final series). Jim also has to contend with Sarah, Palmer's beautiful daughter. Palmer's business empire collapses at the start of the third series, at which time Jim and Henry start their own enterprise, rent-a-butler, but the boss is soon bouncing back with a successful consultancy enterprise.

This was the last that viewers saw of standup comic Jim Davidson as an actor, a role in which he rarely seemed at ease. The scripts were leaden too – all that hackneyed 'guvnor' stuff and cockney rhyming slang palling very quickly – which is odd considering that chief writer Geoff McQueen created *The Bill* and other successful ITV series, such as the light-drama *Stay Lucky*.

Home Sweet Home   1

see *The Kids From 47A*

Home Sweet Home   2

AUSTRALIA · ABC (ABC/THAMES TELEVISION AUSTRALIA) · SITCOM

26 × 30 mins · colour

Australian dates: 31 July 1980–4 Sep 1982

UK dates: 6 Apr–14 Dec 1982 (20 episodes) ITV mostly Tue 3.45pm

MAIN CAST

Enzo Pacelli	John Bluthal
Maria Pacelli	Arianthe Galani
Tony Pacelli	Miles Buchanan
Bobby Pacelli	Christopher Bell
Anna Pacelli	Carmen Tanti

CREDITS

creator/main writer/script editor Vince Powell · *other writers* Charles Stamp, Ralph Petersen, Hugh Stuckey, David Dominic (Vince Powell pseudonym) · *producer* Michael Mills

Have you heard the one about the Polish/German/Russian/English/Italian/French/Hebrew/Yiddish-speaking Jewish Polish-born British/Australian comic actor starring in a TV series Down Under as a Catholic Italian émigré? No? Then you must have missed *Home Sweet Home*, starring John Bluthal.

It is 16 years since Enzo Pacelli (Bluthal) and his family have emigrated from Italy to Australia. Enzo has become a taxi driver but at their suburban home he and his wife Maria maintain the values and beliefs of their beloved old country and Catholic upbringing. Their children, however, have grown up in 'Oz' and so possess that country's values. The humour was drawn from the obligatory culture clashes.

Beyond John Bluthal's involvement, *Home Sweet Home* had other British links – some scripts borrowed from Thames TV's *Bless This House*, co-created by Vince Powell whose writing work was strongly in evidence here; and the series was produced by Michael Mills, the long-established director/producer at the London-ITV company. Thames, indeed, co-financed the entire project.

Four series of *Home Sweet Home* aired in Australia: six episodes from 31 July 1980, seven from 30 September 1980, seven from 18 May 1982 and six from 31 July 1982.

Home To Roost

UK · ITV (YORKSHIRE) · SITCOM

29 episodes (28 × 30 mins · 1 × 60 mins) · colour

Series One (7 × 30 mins) 19 Apr–31 May 1985 · Fri 8.30pm

Series Two (7 × 30 mins) 5 Sep–17 Oct 1986 · Fri 8.30pm

Series Three (7 × 30 mins) 24 Oct–5 Dec 1987 · Sat mostly 8pm

Special (60 mins) 27 Dec 1987 · Sun 7.15pm

Series Four (7 × 30 mins) 1 Dec 1989–19 Jan 1990 · Fri 8.30pm

MAIN CAST

Henry Willows · · · · · · · · · · · · · · John Thaw
Matthew Willows · · · · · · · · · Reece Dinsdale
Enid Thompson · · · · · · · · · Elizabeth Bennett
· (series 1 & 2)
Fiona Fennell · · · · · Joan Blackham (series 3)

CREDITS

writer Eric Chappell · *directors* David Reynolds (27), Graham Wetherell (2) · *executive producer* Vernon Lawrence (series 2, 3 & special) · *producers* Vernon Lawrence (series 1), David Reynolds (series 2–4 & special)

Henry Willows is a middle-aged man in middle-management, divorced from his wife and family for seven years and perfectly happy with the arrangement. Apart from his prudish and pernickety daily cleaner, Enid (later replaced by Fiona), he's alone, and revelling in his solitude. But Henry's peace is shattered when, out of the blue, his eldest child, Matthew, aged 18, arrives on his Grand Avenue doorstep announcing 'Hello, I'm your son'. Matthew is disenchanted with life at home because, he says, of his mum's new boyfriend. He wants to stay with his dad – for good. The truth of the matter is that he's been thrown out by his mum after she has realised that Willows Jr has the same annoying character traits as Willows Sr.

Through 29 episodes, *Home To Roost* charts the almost permanently virulent relationship that exists between father and his semi-delinquent son. Henry doesn't like Matthew because his privacy has been stolen from under him and because, he says, Matthew reminds him of his wife. The reality, however, is that father and son are completely alike, Matthew taking precisely the same high-spirited attitude to life that his father had in his youth. Rather than recognise each other's similarities, though, the two bicker constantly, red mist enveloping all their 'discussions'. Matthew also has a younger

brother Frank (seen only once) and sister Julie (seen three times, played by Rebecca Lacey).

Set in London (as, oddly, have been so many sitcoms made by Yorkshire TV), *Home To Roost* ranks as one of ITV's best comedies of the decade, distinguished by Eric Chappell's lively, word-heavy scripts that cleverly drew out the father–son enmities, and by some especially fine acting from John Thaw and Reece Dinsdale. Thaw's real-life wife Sheila Hancock also appeared in one episode, as Henry's ex-wife Sue, the only time this character was seen.

Home To Roost was adapted in the USA as *You Again?*, with Jack Klugman playing Henry Willows, John Stamos as Matthew Willows and Elizabeth Bennett reprising her role as Enid Tompkins (not Thompson) – the only known occasion that the same person has filled the same role in both British and American versions of the same sitcom. *You Again?* ran for 28 episodes on NBC between February 1986 and January 1987 but has not been screened in the UK.

The Home-Made Xmas Video

see Smith and Jones

Honey

UK · ITV (ATV) · SITCOM

1 × 30 mins · colour

21 Aug 1975 · Thu 7pm

MAIN CAST

Honey Jones · · · · · · · · · · Sandra Dickinson
Reg Forrester · · · · · · · · · · · · Michael Bates
Vera Forrester · · · · · · · · · · · Kathleen Byron
Peter Forrester · · · · · · · · · · · Bernard Holley

CREDITS

writers Mike Craig/Lawrie Kinsley/Ron McDonnell · *director/producer* John Scholz-Conway

A single sitcom produced under ATV's *Comedy Premiere* banner. Honey Jones decides to take the Forresters at their word after they airily invite her to 'Come and stay with us when you're around our way'.

Honey For Tea

UK · BBC · SITCOM

7 × 30 mins · colour

13 Mar–1 May 1994 · BBC1 Sun 7pm

MAIN CAST

Nancy Belasco · · · · · · · · · · · Felicity Kendal
Prof Simon Latimer · · · · · · · Nigel Le Vaillant
Sir Dickie Hobhouse · · · · · · · · Leslie Phillips
Jake Belasco · · · · · · · · · Patrick McCollough
Hon Lucy Courtney · · · · · · · Caroline Harker
Dr Basil Quinn · · · · · · · · · · · · · · Alan David

CREDITS

writer Michael Aitkens · *director/producer* Gareth Gwenlan

Upon the death of corporate crook Harry Belasco, his widow, Nancy, and their thick son Jake are insolvent. Much of Harry's money had been ploughed into a trust fund supporting a Cambridge college, St Maud's (pronounced Mud's), because Harry was crazy about Cambridge. (He only married Nancy because she was born there, the child of a GI bride.) In desperate straits, Nancy senses an opportunity to play on the gratitude of the college and so she and Jake travel to England to inveigle themselves into St Maud's. Soon she has landed a job as assistant bursar, displaying a winning way with investments, and manages to get Jake enrolled in the college by exaggerating his rowing prowess. Her guide down the unfamiliar byways of English academic life is the English professor Simon Latimer, while the Master of the college is the batty Sir Dickie Hobhouse.

Honey For Tea was a curiously old-fashioned sitcom that displayed a distinct 1920s feel with its stereotypical Americans (loud, forthright, money-obsessed) and English (uptight, introverted but well mannered). Despite the good credentials of its cast and crew, the result was soulless and suffered badly from the miscasting of English rose Felicity Kendal in the central role. Fine actress though she is, she failed to convince as the tough American Nancy Belasco, a part that seemed designed for a harsher style, someone more like Elaine Stritch or, indeed, anyone American.

The Honeymooners

USA · CBS (JACKIE GLEASON ENTERPRISES PRODUCTIONS) · SITCOM

39 × 30 mins · colour

US dates: 1 Oct 1955–22 Sep 1956

UK dates: 16 June 1989–11 Apr 1991 (38 episodes) BBC2 mostly Fri 11.45pm then various

MAIN CAST

Ralph Kramden · · · · · · · · · · · Jackie Gleason
Alice Kramden · · · · · · · · · Audrey Meadows
Edward 'Ed' Norton · · · · · · · · · · · Art Carney
Thelma 'Trixie' Norton · · · · · Joyce Randolph

CREDITS

writers Marvin Marx/Walter Stone (16), Leonard Stern/Sydney Zelinka (14), A J Russell/Herbert Finn (9) · *director* Frank Satenstein · *executive producer* Jack Philbin · *production supervisor* Jackie Gleason · *producer* Jack Hurdle

The American actor/comedian Jackie Gleason created a posse of memorable, larger-than-life characters in his career but none captured the imagination of the US public as much as bus driver Ralph Kramden, a pitiable loudmouth who had been making American audiences laugh ever since his first incarnation on the DuMont Network (the country's one-time fourth network which operated 1944–56) in the early 1950s.

In 1949, Gleason, already a popular figure with audiences, tried his hand at situation comedy, playing Chester A Riley in *The Life Of Riley*, but the series didn't suit his fast, aggressive style and it wasn't a major hit until he was replaced by William Bendix. But Gleason continued to get good TV offers and eventually, in July 1950, he took over as host of DuMont's *Cavalcade Of Stars*, a variety show that gave him free rein to invent and portray characters better suited to his talents. One of these was Ralph Kramden, created for a series of sketches in 1950 or 1951. (Sources differ and the precise date that Kramden first appeared seems not to have been pinpointed.)

Ralph Kramden was a hard-working but constantly complaining bus driver who entered into fiercely argumentative relationships with everyone he knew, most especially his wife Alice (played in those early appearances by Pert Kelton – one of the few people on McCarthy's infamous blacklist of supposed communists to find employment in the entertainment industry). A simmering cauldron of immense proportions – the jokes about his bulk, at least one per episode, were always brilliantly aimed and timed – Ralph could become so het up, so quickly, that he would often clench his fist, threatening to send Alice 'to the moon' with one mighty 'bang, zoom!' blow. While wife-beating is far beyond the bounds of humour, Ralph never did and never would have actually hit his Alice: 'Ralphie-boy' was 100 per cent bluster (and blubber too, as he was reminded on one memorable occasion) and loved his wife with a passionate intensity that, at least on camera, manifested itself via furious jealousy and, often, touching episode denouements where, realising that he'd made a fool of himself for the zillionth time, and feeling undeserving of her remarkable faithfulness, Ralph would grab Alice, exclaim, 'Baby, you're the greatest!' and kiss her.

Closely involved in Ralph's life was his best friend, upstairs neighbour, denizen of the deep (he worked in the sewers under New York City) and fellow Racoon Lodge member, Ed Norton (Art Carney), married to Alice's friend Trixie (played first by Elaine Stritch and later by Joyce Randolph). Norton was an endlessly enthusiastic but dense and wonderfully innocent individual with whom Kramden argued almost as much as he did Alice. Norton invariably became embroiled in Kramden's endless get-rich-quick schemes and was sometimes the cause of their failure – mostly, though, they failed because, through sheer swagger and hot-headed excitement, Ralph was destined to remain firmly in his place. The characters and situation struck a chord with audiences and these sketches became eagerly anticipated by the viewing audience.

DuMont was always the poor relation of the networks and, invariably, any major talent they nurtured would be lured away by the other broadcasters. Gleason was no exception – CBS signed the star for *The Jackie Gleason Show* (see footnote) and the entourage of players were sent out on a promotional tour, performing live at movie theatres across the country. The show – a mix of music and comedy – featured a *Honeymooners* segment, once again with Kelton as Alice, but when she became ill her place on the tour was taken by Gingr (*sic*) Jones. The tour was a marketing triumph and Gleason-awareness was increased nationally, ensuring a healthy viewing figure for the series that followed. Audrey Meadows was brought on board to play Alice in these CBS shows and the most famous *Honeymooners* line-up was now in place. *The Jackie Gleason Show*, for the period 1952–55, was a huge hit, with Gleason – nicknamed 'The Great One' – proving that the sobriquet described his talent as well as his physical stature.

In 1955, a historic decision was taken to spin-off *The Honeymooners* into a separate half-hour series, and thus was launched the famous run of episodes popularly referred to as 'The Classic 39'. Up to this time there existed the Kinescope, a primitive method of recording live TV pictures as they were transmitted (similar to the British tele-recordings), but DuMont had pioneered a new and much more efficient recording system called Electronicam. Gleason decided to use this system to film *The Honeymooners* so that they could be repeated. It was a far-sighted decision – to this day, these 39 episodes are constantly re-run in syndication, and the widespread love and regard for the series is such that it is recognised by all as a true American classic.

Of all the many incarnations of *The Honeymooners*, it is these 'Classic 39' episodes to which this entry is addressed, 38 of which (everything but 'The Sleepwalker') were aired by BBC2 from 1989, finally giving a national UK audience the opportunity to view a show that looms as large in US TV history as *Hancock's Half Hour* does in the UK. (The BBC claimed it was the series' first showing in Britain but some episodes turned up from 1958 to 1963 on ITV regions outside London; ABC screened it in the Midlands and the North from 6 July 1958.) The 1989–91 screenings were accompanied by a pair of tribute shows, *Three Jacks And Two Kings* (BBC2, 10 June 1989), in which the US comedian Jackie Mason paid homage to Gleason and also to Jack Benny, and *Gleason – The Great One* (BBC2, 25 March 1991).

What made *The Honeymooners* such a hit? For a start, it was an energetic and lively show with consistently funny scripts and good all-round performances – not just from Gleason (who, of course, was especially all-round) but from the whole cast. But there were three important factors that made it extra special. Firstly, *The Honeymooners* was a working-class comedy and its characters were ordinary, not witty sophisticates. The Kramdens (and the Nortons) were poor folk who believed in the modern-day American dream: that they could aspire to better things, perhaps through hard work but more likely through winning in a TV game-show or a competition. In the meantime, they lived in a crummy, sparsely furnished apartment in an unlovely section of New York, Bensonhurst. This was a recognisable landscape for millions of blue-collar Americans but quite unlike the comfortable, convenience-laden lifestyles portrayed elsewhere on US TV. Secondly, there were the central figures: both couples had realistic relationships and realistically tempestuous arguments. Sure, other TV couples bickered but none railed and shrieked at each other as Ralph and Alice did in *The Honeymooners*. Yet, despite their volatile exchanges, there was always the underlying affection and even a hint of sexuality, again unknown elsewhere on TV. Ralph's relationship with Ed was also believable, a typical comedic twosome of big dumb guy and small even dumber guy, with the especially dumb guy mostly getting the better of his larger companion, either by accident or by some idiot savant moment of genius. This is a classic combination, redolent of the brilliant, peerless partnership of Laurel and Hardy and almost as accomplished. Thirdly, there was the character of Kramden himself, a know-all with an all too obvious streak of vulnerability beneath his bluff exterior; a guy with the worst excesses of his personality on show yet who, beneath it all, still comes over as a decent human being. Gleason's own warmth made this possible but his acting talent, his ability to bawl, swagger and bug-out his eyes, made Kramden above all a recognisably realistic character, echoes of whom can be found in such later TV comedy bullterriers as Archie Bunker, Homer Simpson and Al Bundy.

Following 'The Classic 39', *The Honeymooners* was again produced as varying-length sketches on *The Jackie Gleason Show*, this section lasting 1956–57 and ending when Art Carney left to concentrate on other aspects of his career. Although not formally acknowledged, *The Honeymooners* unquestionably inspired the characters for Hanna-Barbera's *The Flintstones* cartoon series (from 1966), which not only repeated many of *The Honeymooners*' plot themes but also duplicated the main relationships and even their figures, faces and voices (such as Wilma's slightly oriental eyes, much like those of Audrey Meadows). The similarity of the two series was such that when *The Flintstones* was put into human form for the first time, in the 1994 movie starring John Goodman, it was like watching a prehistoric *Honeymooners*.

The *Honeymooners* characters were revived briefly in the 1960s for segments on *The Jackie Gleason Show: The American Scene Magazine* whenever Art Carney was available, this time with Sue Ann Langdon as Alice and Patricia Wilson as Trixie. In January 1966 a musical special was aired, *The Honeymooners: The Adoption*, with Audrey Meadows back as Alice. This led to the return of *The Honeymooners*, in colour for the first time, as part of the 1966–70 run of *The Jackie Gleason Show*, the premise this time having the foursome travel around Europe on a trip that Ralph had won in a competition. The emphasis in this period was on music with some of the skits lasting the full hour of the programme. The cast featured Sheila MacRae as Alice and Jane Kean as Trixie. (In the segment of 18 February 1967, the original Alice, Pert Kelton, guest-starred as Alice's mother, Mrs Gibson.) In 1970 CBS cancelled *The Jackie Gleason Show* and no new adventures of the Kramdens and Nortons were made until 1976 when ABC started transmitting reunion shows (*The Honeymooners Second Honeymoon*, 2 February 1976; *The Honeymooners Christmas*, 28 November 1977; *The Honeymooners Valentine Special*, 13 February 1978; and *The Honeymooners Christmas Special*, 10 December 1978.) In these shows, Audrey Meadows played Alice with Jane Kean cast as Trixie.

Since that time, the most significant *Honeymooners* activity occurred in the mid-1980s when Jackie Gleason made available his own collection of 'lost' *Honeymooners* material – most of the varying-length CBS sketches from the early 1950s. This significant 'rediscovery' (reportedly, Gleason always knew the whereabouts of the tapes and was just picking the right time to unveil them) caused major excitement among the legion of fans who had watched and studied 'The Classic 39' until they were word-perfect. Subsequently most of the 'lost' segments have re-emerged on US TV.

Note. As stated, *The Jackie Gleason Show* ran on CBS from 1952 to 1970. During this time it underwent several distinct changes of format, and for a couple of seasons from autumn 1962 it bore the suffixed title *The American Scene Magazine*, at which point the shows firmly accented variety, comprising guest acts, dancers, a resident orchestra and some comedy sketches. One edition from this period was screened in the UK by BBC1 (on 18 June 1964) as part of the Corporation's commitment to showing programmes that had performed well in the annual Golden Rose of Montreux competition. (It had come third, winning the bronze rose.) In this edition Gleason enacted

some of favourite characters from the series, including Joe the Barman, who – addressing the camera as if it were a customer named Mr Dunahay – spun topical tales of local life; and Reginald Van Gleason III, owner of the world's foremost troupe of performing fleas.

The Honeymoon's Over

UK · BBC · SITCOM

1 × 30 mins · colour

30 Jan 1994 · BBC2 Sun 9pm

MAIN CAST

Phil · Alex Lowe
Helen · · · · · · · · · · · · · · · · · · Angela Clarke
Norma · · · · · · · · · · · · · · · · · Georgina Hale
Billy 'Whiz' · · · · · · · · · · · · Paul Whitehouse
Skippy · · · · · · · · · · · · · · · · · Des McAleer
Martin · · · · · · · · · · · · · · · Mark Williams
Ginger · · · · · · · · · · · · Jim Moir (Vic Reeves)

CREDITS

writers Charlie Higson/Paul Whitehouse · *script editor* Sean Hardie · *director* John Birkin · *producers* Charlie Higson/Paul Whitehouse

There was a clash of styles in this *Comic Asides* pilot, with the central premise – the relationship of a constantly bickering couple – undermined by the appearance of a number of extreme minor characters who seemed to be refugees from a different reality.

Phil and Helen have married after living together for four years but this has done nothing to cut down their Olympian rate of arguments. As they contemplate splitting up, their lives are disrupted by a demented cycle messenger, Billy (Paul Whitehouse), who squats in the downstairs flat. Billy would have been more at home as a recurring character on writers Whitehouse and Higson's **The Fast Show** than in a sitcom, but even he wasn't as bizarrely out of place as Ginger, a hideously spotty customer at the bar where Helen works. Ginger was played in pantomime fashion by Vic Reeves (appearing under his real name, Jim Moir). Also on the scene was Skippy – a ranting wino who lives in a skip and constantly interrupts the arguing couple.

Phil and Helen disagreed vehemently about everything, even the lyrics of popular songs. In fact, they argued at such length that it was difficult to feel much sympathy for them, when, clearly, they would have been better off apart. However, it emerged finally that their arguing was exacerbated by their attempts to give up cigarettes, and when they started smoking again they began to agree with one another. With this in mind, perhaps, Whitehouse and Higson may have planned to develop a series showing the characters being less abrasive towards each other, but the relationship in the pilot was so annoying, and the mix of styles in the show so bizarre and unsettling, that there was no follow-up.

Honky Tonk Heroes

UK · ITV (ATV) · SITCOM

3 × 60 mins · colour

21 Jan– 4 Feb 1981 · Wed 9pm

MAIN CAST

Big Hal · · · · · · · · · · · · · · · · · · James Grout
Betty · · · · · · · · · · · · · · · · · Sheila Steafel
David · · · · · · · · · · · · · · · · · David Parfitt
George · · · · · · · · · · · · · · · · · Ken Wynne

CREDITS

writer Ray Connolly · *director* Bill Hays · *producer* David Reid

A three-part comedy series set in the 'Blue Moon Of Kentucky Club', a country and western venue in south London. The club caters for the sort of clients obsessed by the Wild West, and the place is owned by Big Hal, who lives out his whole life as a modern-day cowboy – much to the consternation of his wife Betty. Apart from Hal, Betty and their regulars, guest characters appeared each week and their stories formed the focus of individual episodes. The author, Ray Connolly, was a London *Evening Standard* columnist who had previously written the British movies *That'll Be The Day* and its sequel *Stardust*.

Hope & Gloria

USA · NBC (TEAM STEINKELLNER/WARNER BROS) · SITCOM

35 × 30 mins · colour

US dates: 9 Mar 1995–22 June 1996

UK dates: 8 July–23 Aug 1996 (35 episodes) ITV weekdays 9.50am

MAIN CAST

Hope Davidson · · · · · · · · Cynthia Stevenson
Gloria Utz · · · · · · · · · · · · · · · · Jessica Lundy
Louis Utz · · · · · · · · · · · · · Enrico Colantoni
'Dennis Dupree' · · · · · · · · · · · · · Alan Thicke
Sonny Utz · · · · · · · · · · · · · Robert Garrova

CREDITS

creators/executive producers Cheri Steinkellner/Bill Steinkellner · *writers* Cheri Steinkellner/Bill Steinkellner and others · *directors* Barnet Kellman and others · *producer* Stephen C Grossman

Two women – one a TV producer, the other a hairdresser – occupy neighbouring apartments in a Pittsburgh brownstone and form an unlikely but bonding friendship.

Hope Davidson, a soft-spoken TV producer with a positive, people-pleasing personality, is dumped by her philandering husband Jeffrey after years as high school sweethearts and a decade of marriage – unbeknownst to her, he had recently been 'putting it about'. Gloria Utz, a sassy scissors-snipper with her own salon, tends to look on the negative side of life, and though she continues to see her ex-husband Louis because of his visitation rights to their son (Sonny, age five), she gives him short shrift. For some reason they have married and divorced each other twice, and they endure – and almost seem to enjoy – a continually sparky relationship. Hope, meanwhile, produces *The Dennis Dupree Show*, a TV talk programme hosted by an insincere and extremely dense individual, and she gets Gloria an additional job, preparing Dupree's hair before he goes on air.

Hope & Gloria was a perky and enjoyable, if predictable, sitcom (unrelated to the British series **Land Of Hope And Gloria**). Similar to the premise in **Kate & Allie**, the two leads are not exactly compatible, indeed pretty much the only thing they have in common is the ill-treatment they consider has been meted out to them by their respective former male partners. Yet the two are able to provide support for one another in their times of need.

Hope And Keen

UK · ITV (ATV) · SKETCH

9 × 30 mins · b/w
22 Dec 1965–9 Mar 1966 · Wed 9.10pm

MAIN CAST
Mike Hope · himself
Albie Keen · himself

CREDITS
writers Sid Green/Dick Hills · *producer* Jon Scoffield

Nine programmes in which the humorous and physically dextrous Scottish double-act Mike Hope and Albie Keen – they were cousins – located themselves in curious foreign climes (Gold Nugget Creek, Old Pekin, Casablanca, Tropicsville, Zieto Tierra, Greece, Moonaboola, on board the SS *Bounty* and in Ballyduro) for comic effect. It was the pairing's first TV series, and Sid Green and Dick Hills – of *The Morecambe And Wise Show* fame – wrote the scripts.

The sons of comedians Syd and Max Harrison – Hope and Keen, hardly surprisingly, were stage names – Mike and Albie were stationed together in the RAF, where they so enjoyed its physical training that they became Olympic gymnastic coaches. After demobilisation they decided to remain together and tour an acrobatic act around provincial theatres, but when the premise wore thin they focused on comic routines and became a success, appearing on *Val Parnell's Sunday Night At The London Palladium* and in the 1965 *Royal Variety Show*.

The duo's other networked comedy series were aimed at children.

Hope And Keen's Crazy House

UK · BBC · CHILDREN'S SITCOM

13 episodes (12 × 25 mins · 1 × 30 mins) · colour
Special (30 mins) *Crazy House* 20 Aug 1970 · BBC1 Thu 5.15pm
Series One (6 × 25 mins) 7 July–11 Aug 1971 · BBC1 Wed 4.55pm

Series Two (6 × 25 mins) *Hope And Keen's Crazy Bus* 7 Apr–12 May 1972; 22 Aug 1973 · BBC1 Fri 5.20pm

MAIN CAST
Mike Hope · himself
Albie Keen · himself
Crumble the Butler · · · · · · · Peter Goodwright
Mrs Grapple the Cook · · · · · · Ruth Kettlewell
The Shadow · · · · · · · David Hatton (series 2)

CREDITS
writers Mike Craig/Lawrie Kinsley (9), John Morley (2), David A Yallop (2) · *additional material* Paul Ciani, Mike Hope/Albie Keen, Harry Jones · *producer* Paul Ciani

A fondly remembered children's romp. The cousins' crazy house encompassed zany goings-on in different rooms, one of which featured a performing musical guest. The regular cast featured Peter Goodwright as an ancient butler and Ruth Kettlewell as their larger-than-life cook. In the second series, the setting was changed to a bus and Hope and Keen set out on an adventure to find their Uncle Ebenezer's lost treasure – a quest that took them all over Britain. The butler and the cook came along for the ride and they even had a rival to deal with, the dastardly Shadow. (The third episode of this second series, originally scheduled for 21 April 1972, was cancelled owing to BBC1's Apollo 16 coverage. It aired for the first time 16 months later, during a repeat run.)

The Hope And Keen Scene

UK · BBC · CHILDREN'S SKETCH

6 × 25 mins · colour
24 Dec 1974–28 Jan 1975 · BBC1 Tue mostly 4.45pm

MAIN CAST
Mike Hope
Albie Keen
Jennifer Hill
Bob Kerr's Whoopee Band

CREDITS
writers John Morley (6), Harry Jones (6), Mike Hope/Albie Keen (2), Philip Griffin (2), Mitch Reveley (1), Jon Roman (1) · *producer* Paul Ciani

A sketch show in which the Scottish funsters wove comedy routines around a different theme each week (Christmas, summer holidays, etc).

Hope It Rains

UK · ITV (THAMES) · SITCOM

13 × 30 mins · colour
Series One (7) 3 June–15 July 1991 · Mon 8pm
Series Two (6) 24 June–29 July 1992 · Wed 8pm

MAIN CAST
Harry Nash · · · · · · · · · · · · · · · · · Tom Bell
Jace Elliott · · · · · · · · · · · · · · · · · Holly Aird
Dennis Portland · · · · · · · · · · Eamon Boland

CREDITS
writers John Esmonde/Bob Larbey · *director/producer* John Howard Davies

Taking a break from playing intimidatory tough guys in uncompromising dramas, Tom Bell starred in this promising but ultimately disappointing sitcom, written by Esmonde and Larbey but far from being among their best work.

Bell was cast as Harry Nash, perfectly content in his self-centred world until his 18-year-old god-daughter, Jace, burrows her way in upon the death of her parents. The victim of a tough childhood, but secretly keen on playing up to it, the abrasive Jace takes an instant dislike to Harry, a feeling that is most definitely reciprocated. Moody and selfish, and snug in his bachelor world, Harry runs the Empire Wax Museum in a rundown seaside resort, desirous of precipitation (hence the programme's title) because it brings in more customers. In life, Harry is no taker, so he doesn't expect to have to give either, but Jace's arrival as not only his lodger but also his legal ward means that he has to accommodate a second person. As far as Harry is concerned, Jace 'makes the Artful Dodger look like a choirboy', and her rudeness and poor temperament, matching Harry's, means that it's bitterness at seven paces. The personality clash is a situation that Dennis, Harry's kind-hearted friend and business neighbour (he's a holiday-snap photographer with his own company, Shutters), constantly tries to smooth. An idealist by nature, Dennis cares for Jace more than Harry does, but his attempts to pour oil on the waters of their stormy relationship are bound to fail.

Bob Hope

Born Leslie Townes Hope in Eltham, England, on 29 May 1903, Bob Hope is the quintessential wisecracking American comedian; a huge star on radio, on stage, in the movies and on TV. His stage and screen persona – that of a cowardly, quick-tongued, dame-obsessed braggart – is beloved of audiences, and his night-club-honed style of short gags woven into a running, humorous patter has served the artist well throughout his long career. Most famous for his double-act with the crooner/comedian Bing Crosby in the *Road* movies, Hope is also known as a tireless entertainer of troops, a service he provided during the Second World War, the Korean conflict and the Vietnam action. A brilliant deliverer of one-liners, he is equally at home with physical comedy, displaying a fine-tuned sense of timing. At his height, in such films as *The Cat And The Canary* (1939), *The Ghost Breakers* (1940), *My Favorite Blonde* (1942), *The Paleface* (1948), and the *Road* movies, he was unbeatable.

From 1950, Bob Hope became a regular face on television in a long-running series of specials, most of them featuring top-flight guest stars, and *The Bob Hope Show* became an American TV institution. By the 1970s, however, the American taste in humour had changed considerably and Hope's 'establishment' style was considered old-fashioned in the light of the 'hip' comedy revolution led by the Smothers Brothers and Rowan and Martin. Hope attracted criticism for his reliance upon a host of writers and for the almost mechanical way in which he presented the material (caused, it is said, by his reliance upon cue-cards). Nevertheless, he remained an immensely popular figure with huge swathes of the US TV audience, and this perceived complacency in the latter parts of his career should in no way undermine the huge contribution that the younger Hope made in the field of comedy.

The Bob Hope Show   UK

UK · ITV (ATV FOR ASSOCIATED-REDIFFUSION) · STANDUP/SKETCH

2 × 60 mins · b/w

2 Apr 1956 · Mon 9.45pm

31 July 1956 · Tue 8pm

MAIN CAST
Bob Hope

CREDITS
writers various · *director* Bill Ward · *producer* Jack Hope

Bob Hope returned to the country of his birth for a pair of ITV specials in 1956, representing, at that time, British commercial TV's biggest, best and most expensive variety shows yet, filmed at a cost of £70,000 each. To recoup the costs, the programmes were pre-sold to American TV, representing useful US exposure for the British and European guest stars/support players who mingled with the Americans. In the first show these included Diana Dors and Yana; in the second Douglas Fairbanks, Line Renaud, Cornel Wilde, Richard Wattis and Elsa Martinelli.

Note. The April 1956 broadcast was not the first occasion that Hope had performed a TV show in England – in November 1954, an edition of his NBC series *The Bob Hope Show* (see below) was recorded – with space left for commercials and all – at the BBC's Television Theatre in London for later broadcast back in the USA. (It was not shown in England owing to a Musicians' Union ban, in existence then, outlawing members from taking part in pre-recorded TV programmes.) The BBC loaned producer

Bill Ward (he then moved to ITV by 1956) to guide the show, which was introduced by McDonald Hobley and featured Maurice Chevalier, Moira Lister and Shirley Eaton among the guest cast.

The Bob Hope Show   USA

USA · NBC · STANDUP/SKETCH

269 × 60 mins · b/w and colour

US dates: 9 Apr 1950–14 May 1993

UK dates: 2 Nov 1958–10 Jan 1977 (21 editions) 19 × b/w BBC and ITV · 2 × colour BBC

2 Nov 1958 · BBC Tue 8pm (45 mins · b/w)

23 Dec 1958 · BBC Tue 7.30pm (45 mins · b/w)

6 Feb 1959 · BBC Fri 8pm (45 mins · b/w)

7 Apr 1959 · BBC Tue 8.30pm (45 mins · b/w)

9 May 1959 · BBC Sat 9.50pm (45 mins · b/w)

11 June 1959 · BBC Thu 8.15pm (45 mins · b/w)

30 June 1959 · BBC Tue 8pm (45 mins · b/w)

27 Oct 1959 · BBC Tue 8pm (45 mins · b/w)

5 Jan 1960 · BBC Tue 7.30pm (45 mins · b/w)

28 Jan 1960 · BBC Thu 9pm (45 mins · b/w)

3 July 1960 · BBC Sun 7.30pm (45 mins · b/w)

18 Aug 1961 · BBC Fri 8pm (35 mins · b/w)

30 July 1962 · BBC Mon 9.25pm (35 mins · b/w)

28 Aug 1962 · BBC Tue 8.15pm (30 mins · b/w)

7 Nov 1962 · ITV Wed 9.45pm (55 mins · b/w)

30 Jan 1963 · ITV Wed 9.45pm (45 mins · b/w)

22 May 1963 · ITV Wed 9.45pm (45 mins · b/w)

10 July 1963 · ITV Wed 9.45pm (40 mins · b/w)

14 Aug 1963 · ITV Wed 9.45pm (55 mins · b/w)

17 Mar 1976 · BBC2 Wed 9pm (70 mins · colour)

The Bob Hope World Of Comedy 10 Jan 1977 · BBC2 Mon 8.15pm (45 mins · colour)

MAIN CAST
Bob Hope

CREDITS
writers various · *directors* various · *producer* Jack Hope

These star-guest-studded shows were edited for British screening from the original NBC variety specials. The 1976 and 1977 programmes were compilations celebrating 25 years and 26 years of *The Bob Hope Show* respectively.

There's Always Hope

UK · ITV (ATV) · SKETCH/STANDUP

1 × 30 mins · b/w

28 Dec 1962 · Fri 8.30pm

MAIN CAST
Bob Hope

CREDITS
writers various · *producer* Bill Ward

A single special, made in Britain for ATV. Hope's guest was the British singer Yana.

The Bob Hope Special

USA · NBC (HOPE ENTERPRISES) · STANDUP

1 × 60 mins · colour

US date: 17 Feb 1969

UK date: 31 Dec 1969 · BBC1 Wed 7.10pm

MAIN CAST
Bob Hope
Bing Crosby
George Burns

CREDITS
writers various · *director* Dick McDonough · *producer* Mort Lachman

A US TV special presented in Britain as a seasonal treat and featuring, among the audience, stars from *Rowan And Martin's Laugh-In* (Rowan, Martin, Jo Anne Worley and Henry Gibson) and the comedy old guard of Hope, Crosby and Burns on stage.

The World Of Bob Hope

UK · BBC · STANDUP

1 × 50 mins · colour

8 Oct 1970 · BBC1 Thu 9.20pm

MAIN CAST
Bob Hope
Jack Benny
Cary Grant

CREDITS
writers various · *producer* Denis Pitts

An intriguing BBC record of Bob Hope's annual 100,000-mile concert tour of the USA. The tour was part entertainment extravaganza and part political rally, and Denis Pitts' programme covered the events surrounding the tour as well as those on the stages – including generous portions of Hope's act, one that was markedly different from the style of film humour for which he was perhaps better known (in the UK at least). Wisely, Pitts decided not to edit performance material that dealt with American references and characters unknown to British viewers, so this presented a remarkably true reflection of Hope's stage act of the time.

Bob Hope At The London Palladium

UK · ITV (ATV) · STANDUP

1 × 45 mins · colour

28 May 1979 · Mon 8pm

MAIN CAST
Bob Hope
Richard Burton
Raquel Welch

CREDITS
writers Dick Vosburgh, Garry Chambers, Gig Henry, Bob Mills · *executive producer* Syd Vinnedge

Hope, back in the UK, saluting London's famous Palladium theatre with a star-packed show, recorded a few weeks earlier and transmitted as a bank holiday special.

Unrelated to this, but worthy of passing note, are three further ITV specials. On 25 September 1982 LWT networked *The Bob Hope Classic Cabaret*, an 80-minute variety special filmed at the Grosvenor House Hotel in London in the presence of Princess Margaret. Another 80-minute star-studded special, *Bob Hope's Royal Birthday Party*, was filmed at the Lyric Theatre, London, and screened on 6 June 1985. And in the early hours of 10 April 1990, London-ITV broadcast *America's All-Star Tribute To Bob Hope* (aired in the USA by NBC on 5 March 1988), a one-hour special made in recognition of the opening of the Bob Hope Cultural Center in Palm Springs, California. On 12 October 1983, BBC1 presented the *Bob Hope Royal Gala Evening*, in which, as host, the comic introduced a number of acts, including comedians Dickie Henderson, Eric Sykes and Jonathan Winters. The performance was given in aid of the Stars' Organisation For Spastics.

Horne A'Plenty

UK · ITV (ABC · **THAMES) · SKETCH

11 × 30 mins · b/w

*Series One (5) 29 June–27 July 1968 · Sat mostly 10.15pm

**Series Two (6) 27 Nov 1968–1 Jan 1969 · Wed around 10pm

MAIN CAST

Kenneth Horne
Graham Stark
Sheila Steafel
Ken Parry
Alan Curtis
Donald Webster (series 2)

CREDITS

writers David Cumming, Michael Green, Johnnie Mortimer/Brian Cooke, Donald Webster, Geoff Rowley/Andy Baker and others · *script editor* Barry Took (series 1) · *director* Peter Frazer-Jones · *producers* Pat Johns (series 1), Barry Took (series 2)

A mere 20 days after the fourth (and what turned out to be final) series of the long-running BBC radio comedy *Round The Horne* had come to a close, *Horne A'Plenty* started up on ITV, presenting a similar jamboree-bag of sketches – although, this time, with a tad more up-to-the-minute satire and social comment thrown in. Barry Took, such an instrumental figure in *Round The Horne* and its radio predecessor *Beyond Our Ken*, was a key part of *Horne A'Plenty*, editing the scripts and, in the second TV run, turning producer for the first time. Other *Round The Horne* alumni were also in evidence: writers Johnnie

Mortimer and Brian Cooke and writer/ performer Donald Webster. The cast was different, though, with Graham Stark appearing in dozens of different character roles much in the way that Kenneth Williams had done on the radio. But one could not overlook Horne's own contribution, linking the material in his own inimitable, avuncular fashion, despite a deterioration in his health. There may have been more *Horne A'Plenty* series had not this great gentleman of comedy died, aged a mere 61, just six weeks after the Thames run finished, on 14 February 1969.

*Note. The first series, made by ABC principally for screening in the Midlands and the North, was not shown by London-area ITV.

Hospital!

UK · C5 (TIGER ASPECT) · SITCOM

1 × 60 mins · colour

30 Mar 1997 · Sun 8pm

MAIN CAST

Dr Jim Nightingale	Greg Wise
Dr Harley Benson	Bob Peck
Dickie Beaumont	Hywel Bennett
Dr Ralph Crosby	Mark Heap
Victoria Barking	Haydn Gwynne
Sister Muriel	Celia Imrie

OTHER APPEARANCES

Jock	Julian Clary
Claire Rayner	herself
X-ray operator	Alexei Sayle
Isolation patient	Martin Clunes
Cleaner	June Brown
Wheelchair man	Nicholas Parsons
Pianist	Philip Pope
U-Boat commander	Clive Anderson
Cheryl Chandler	Caprice Bourret

CREDITS

writer Laurie Rowley · *director* John Henderson · *executive producer* Charles Brand · *producer* Sue Vertue

A star-studded comedy extravaganza, one of the showpieces of Channel 5's opening night. Following C4's lead, C5 attempted to attract viewers to a new channel by mounting a specially commissioned comedy; C4's set piece (*Five Go Mad In Dorset*, the first edition of **Comic Strip Presents ...**) helped establish the channel's 'alternative' credentials; *Hospital!* marked C5's style and approach, being brash and exuberant.

Blending traditional British bawdiness with the **Police Squad** scatter-gun approach of visual and verbal jokes, *Hospital!* was a fizzy and fun-packed hour where anything and everything was thrown in to raise a laugh. The thin (*very* thin) plot centred on the threat of a ruthless property developer, Dickie Beaumont, to close down a hospital unless his son-in-law, currently in intensive care following an accident at his wedding, pulls

through. The only man who can save the hospital is the brilliant brain surgeon Dr Jim Nightingale, but fate complicates matters when a number of difficulties combine to make the doctor's work nigh-on impossible: power cuts, the homicidal tendencies of a past lover, a mad axeman on the loose, and his own illness, 'Saddam Hussein Syndrome'. But, really, the plot was incidental to the comic mayhem that drove the piece: patients exploded; the Elephant Man (and an Elephant Woman whom the credits jokingly claimed was played by Emma Thompson) staggered about the place; off-the-wall announcements ('Would Dr Johnson go to the library', 'Would Dr Livingstone go to Africa') were made over the PA system; Sister Muriel ran about wearing ever-sillier shaped nursing hats (ships, teapots, the Eiffel Tower); and, in one inspired moment, the hospital's corridor doors were smashed open by a speeding bobsleigh team.

The programme was a tongue-in-cheek spoof of popular hospital series such as *Casualty* and *ER*, and a number of famous faces appeared in cameo roles, which only slightly added to the fun. Lightweight it might have been, and even sprawling in some places; it was nevertheless difficult to find fault in a production that went at such full throttle simply to make viewers laugh.

Hot Metal

UK · ITV (HUMPHREY BARCLAY PRODUCTIONS FOR LWT) · *BBC · SITCOM

13 episodes (12 × 30 mins · 1 × short special) · colour

Series One (6) 16 Feb–23 Mar 1986 · Sun mostly 10pm

Series Two (6) 6 Mar–17 Apr 1988 · Sun mostly 10pm

*Short special *The Satellite Years* · part of *A Night Of Comic Relief* 10 Mar 1989 · BBC1 Fri after 7.30pm

MAIN CAST

Terence 'Twiggy' Rathbone/	
Russell Spam	Robert Hardy
Harry Stringer	Geoffrey Palmer
	(series 1 & special)
Richard Lipton	Richard Wilson (series 2)
Greg Kettle	Richard Kane
Max	Geoffrey Hutchings (series 1)
Bill Tytla	John Gordon-Sinclair (series 1)
Jack Thrush	David Barrass (series 2)
Maggie Troon	Caroline Milmoe (series 2)
Father Teasdale	John Horsley (series 1)
Keith	Geoffrey Greenhill (series 1)

OTHER APPEARANCES

Mrs Beatty	Doreen Keogh (series 1)
Sharon	Sarah Mortimer (series 1)
Prime Minister	Jack Watling (series 1)
Mrs Macnamara	Eliza Buckingham
	(series 1)
Kuznetsky	Michael Stainton (series 1)
Lt Scott Mackenzie	Nicolas Colicos
	(series 2)
Peter Snow	himself (special)

Mike Gatting · · · · · · · · · · himself (special)

CREDITS
writers Andrew Marshall/David Renwick · directors David Askey (series 1), Nic Phillips (series 2) · producer Humphrey Barclay · executive producer Marcus Plantin · [no production details available for special]

With its circulation and market-share steadily decreasing, the day-to-day running of the tabloid newspaper *The Daily Crucible* is suddenly taken over by its owner, 'Twiggy' Rathbone, the megalomaniacal press baron heading the global media concern Rathouse International. He pushes the paper drastically downmarket and relaunches it as tits 'n' sex scandal-sheet *The Crucible*. Former editor Harry Stringer is 'promoted' to the new position of managing editor – not so much a move 'upstairs' as a move outside: his new office is the building's lift – and is continually agog and ashamed at the treatment being meted out to his old rag. Rathbone brings in a new editor, Russell Spam, hitherto the editor of an obscure African newspaper. Spam is identical in appearance to Rathbone (Robert Hardy played both roles), leading Stringer to conclude, wrongly, that they are one and the same man. *The Crucible*'s new style of journalism is typified by reporter Greg Kettle, sacked by Stringer but re-instated by Spam, prone to introducing himself as one of 'Her Majesty's Press'. Kettle will stoop to any depth to get his crass stories, portraying an innocent priest, Father Teasdale, as a Marxist, and consulting a medium to obtain quotes from dead capital punishment victims when Rathbone dictates that his paper must argue for the restoration of hanging.

All the while (throughout the sitcom's first series) Stringer debates whether or not to jump ship. By the second series he's out, having gone missing in a 'mystery aeroplane accident'. His replacement Richard Lipton is a former TV presenter whose private mission to clean up the stinking paper soon amounts to naught when he realises that his job is to be a puppet figurehead.

As all of this suggests, *Hot Metal* was an over-the-top spoof on the gutter world of Fleet Street's tabloid journalism, played to the hilt by its actors, especially Robert Hardy – this was his first comedy series, following a succession of heavyweight roles in such dramas as *Winston Churchill: The Wilderness Years* and *Edward The Seventh*, and his performance as Siegfried in the lighter-hearted BBC1 drama *All Creatures Great And Small*. Hardy was wonderful as the outrageously ruthless and underhanded Rathbone, giving Marshall and Renwick's character the gravitas of both Murdoch and Maxwell wrapped up together, and then some. Rathbone sucks up to the governing Tory party in the first series but ditches his

old allegiances to fawn over the newly empowered Labour in the second. (*The Crucible* had singlehandedly brought down the Conservatives, having accused the Prime Minister of an affair with a Russian diplomat as part of its 'circulation at any price' drive.)

Topical, satirical, mad, much like Marshall and Renwick's previous **Whoops Apocalypse**, *Hot Metal* was broadcast in the Sunday-night spot usually occupied by **Spitting Image** and was aimed at a similar audience. In truth, not a lot of people watched it, but those who did were amply rewarded.

Hotel Imperial

UK · ITV (ASSOCIATED-REDIFFUSION) · SITCOM

24 × 30 mins · b/w

Series One (12) 18 Mar–3 June 1958 · Tue mostly 10.15pm
Series Two (12) 4 Jan–25 Mar 1960 · Mon 7pm then Fri around 11pm

MAIN CAST
Monsieur Victor · · · · · · · · · · · · · · Vic Oliver
Mr Hay · · · · · · · · · · · · · · · · · · Brian Oulton
Mr Pettigrew · · · · · · · · · · · · · · · · Tom Gill
Mr Griffiths · · · · · · · · · · · · · Leslie Heritage
Kate Brett · · · · · · · · Joan Benham (series 2)
Henry · · · · · · · · · · · Eddie Malin (series 2)

CREDITS
writer Alan Melville · directors John Phillips (series 1), Christopher Hodson (10 eps in series 2), John Frankau (2 eps in series 2) · executive producer Michael Westmore (series 2)

Presenter and playwright Alan Melville, whose TV work usually appeared on the BBC, wrote this early ITV comedy series about the goings-on in a plush, world-renowned London hotel, the Imperial, as seen through the eyes and recalled by the reminiscences of Monsieur Victor, the conductor of the hotel's Palm Court Orchestra. Each weekly episode began with Victor (played by the Viennese-born comedian/ musician Vic Oliver) drinking a glass of milk and settling down to tell his latest story to a journalist, so that it might be ghost-written into his autobiography. These accounts usually detailed the high-powered guests – film stars, prima donnas, foreign potentates, princes, diplomats and millionaires – who, space permitting, stayed at the Imperial when in town, and the parts were played by weekly guests, including leading drama figures drawn from the London stage, among them Mary Ellis, June Laverick, Elisabeth Welch, Richard Goolden, Bonar Colleano, Diana Decker, Evelyn Kaye, Donald Pleasence, Raymond Francis, Francis Matthews, John Barron, Bill Owen, Jean Kent and Betty Marsden. Among the characters who worked at the Imperial were the fussy manager Mr Hay, the boring but dedicated assistant manager Mr Griffiths, and the suave head receptionist Mr Pettigrew.

House Calls

USA · CBS (UNIVERSAL TELEVISION) · SITCOM

57 × 30 mins · colour

US dates: 17 Dec 1979–13 Sep 1982

UK dates: 27 June–31 Oct 1981 (13 episodes) BBC1 Sat 11.15pm and 18 Apr 1982–12 June 1983 (12 episodes) ITV mostly Sun 7.15pm

MAIN CAST
Dr Charley Michaels · · · · · · · · Wayne Rogers
Ann Anderson · · · · Lynn Redgrave (1979–81)
Jane Jeffries · · · · · · · · · Sharon Gless (1982)
Dr Amos Weatherby · · · · · · · · · David Wayne
Dr Norman Solomon · · · · · · · Ray Buktenica
Conrad Peckler · · · · · · · · · · · · Marc L Taylor
Mrs Phipps · · · · · · · · · · · · · · · Deedy Peters

CREDITS
writers Kathy Greer/Bill Greer, Lee Aronsohn, Max Shulman/Julius J Epstein, Mark T Egan/Mark Solomon and others · directors Mel Ferber, Nick Havinga, Bob Claver and others · producers Jerome Davis, Kathy Greer/Bill Greer, Sheldon Keller

Although ostensibly based on the 1978 movie of the same title (director Howard Zieff), actor Wayne Rogers' character here, Charley Michaels, seemed to have more in common with his *M*A*S*H* incarnation Trapper John than the movie role as portrayed by Walter Matthau. In the film, Glenda Jackson had played the English hospital administration assistant who alternately maddened and intoxicated the doctor (Matthau); in the series, the role of Ann Anderson was capably filled by another English actress, Lynn Redgrave.

The action takes place at Kensington General Hospital in San Francisco, where Charley has a reputation for being both a brilliant surgeon and a playboy. His *M*A*S*H*-style bending of the rules to eliminate red tape, and his general irreverence towards hospital bureaucracy, brings him into direct conflict with Ann, but beneath the friction there is obviously a smouldering passion. It was never allowed to burn freely, though, because Redgrave quit the series after a dispute with the producers. She was replaced by Sharon Gless as Jane Jeffries, who turned out to be a former lover of Charley's, thus prompting a similar love–hate relationship to the one he had experienced with Ann.

Only the early episodes featuring Lynn Redgrave were aired in the UK. Unusually, after the BBC had screened 13 of them, London-area ITV provider Thames broadcast 12 more.

House In A Tree

see *Not In Front Of The Children*

House Of Gristle

see *Dizzy Heights*

The House Of Windsor

UK · ITV (GRANADA) · SITCOM

6 × 30 mins · colour

15 May–26 June 1994 · Sun mostly 10.30pm

MAIN CAST

Lord Montague Bermondsey · · Leslie Phillips
Max Kelvin · · · · · · · · · · · · Warren Clarke
Giles Huntingdon · · · · · · · · · Jeremy Sinden
Caroline Finch · · · · · · · · · · Serena Gordon
Sir Nicholas Foulsham · · · · · · · · Neil Stacy
Danny Jackson · · · · · · · · · · · Barry Howard
Lady Sharpcott · · · · · · · Margaret Courtenay
Ray Barker · · · · · · · · · · · · Sean Gallagher
Kate Hargreaves · · · · · · · · Louise Germaine
Ambrose Stebbings · · · · · Preston Lockwood

CREDITS

writers Chris Fewtrell/Zeddy Lawrence (2), Mark Wadlow (1), Sally Wainwright (1), Russell T Davies (1), Luke Freeman (1) · *director* Graeme Harper · *executive producer* Andy Harries · *producer* Antony Wood

A true sign of the times: an irreverent sitcom purportedly set inside Buckingham Palace, proving that in the 1990s even the royals were fair game for a laugh.

No royal personage is seen in *The House Of Windsor*: all the action takes place behind the scenes at Buckingham Palace, where a new street-smart and street-talking PR man, Max Kelvin, has been appointed by a desperate royal family as the principal press officer. (He is a clear and horrifying amalgam of PR man Max Clifford and the former editor of *The Sun*, Kelvin MacKenzie.) Kelvin has retained all the instincts of a tabloid hack, whereby no story cannot be enlivened by the addition of 'a few tits'. He reckons the posting is a short-cut route to a knighthood – others say, and they're probably right, that he's 'a dirty little republicanist'. Kelvin's principal foe is Lord Montague Bermondsey who, as Lord Chamberlain, head of the household, is eager to keep the monarchy in high esteem. Joining in the battle against Kelvin are Caroline Finch, the Buckingham Palace press officer; Sir Nicholas Foulsham, the Private Secretary; Lady Sharpcott, the heavy-drinking lady-in-waiting with a keen line in sexual reminiscences; and, though he's usually unaware of the plot, Giles Huntingdon, the Lord Chamberlain's upper-class-twit nephew and assistant, a dab foot with a shooting rifle and so useless at his job that the other staff are continually forced to cover up his gaffes. Other Palace staff members include Danny, the oh-so-gay footman; Ray, his sharp junior; Kate, the chambermaid; and Ambrose Stebbings, winder of the royal clocks.

The House Of Windsor was a farce-sitcom with overtones of *Upstairs, Downstairs*, **Yes Minister**, *Are You Being Served?* and **Drop The Dead Donkey**. The scripts were written in advance but, in the manner of *Donkey*, late news items were inserted and the

programmes taped only two days before screening to ensure topicality. Some good ideas prevailed but there weren't many laughs to be had, and the subject ripe for comic exploitation in 1994 was not necessarily so in ensuing years, so only one series was made.

How Do You View?

UK · BBC · SKETCH

30 × 30 mins · b/w

Series One (4) 26 Oct–21 Dec 1949 · mostly fortnightly Wed 8.30pm
Series Two (4) 5 Apr–17 May 1950 · fortnightly Wed 8pm then 8.30pm
Series Three (9) 8 Nov 1950–28 Feb 1951 · fortnightly Wed 8pm then 8.45pm
Series Four (6) 19 Sep–28 Nov 1951 · fortnightly Wed around 9pm
Series Five (6) 2 Apr–11 June 1952 · fortnightly Wed 8.45pm then 9pm
Special · 9 Sep 1953 · Wed 8.45pm

MAIN CAST

Terry-Thomas
Adèle Dixon
Peter Butterworth
Janet Brown
Benny Lee
Avril Angers
H C Walton

CREDITS

writers Terry-Thomas (series 1), Terry-Thomas/Sid Colin (series 2), Terry-Thomas/Sid Colin/Talbot Rothwell (series 3–5), Sid Colin/Talbot Rothwell (special) · *producers* Bill Ward (27), Walton Anderson (3)

A number of BBC experiments to establish a comedy formula suited to the new TV medium finally paid off with this inventive Terry-Thomas series that was truly televisual and not just a radio programme in costume. The series coincided with the BBC's first experimentation in viewer research and in the 'appreciation index' *How Do You View?* picked up a very high score of 71 per cent. The TV screen was a good showcase for Terry-Thomas's gap-toothed smile and cigarette holder prop, and the series' main producer Bill Ward (his real name was Ivor William) created a visual style to match, with clever sets and a bold design. With *How Do You View?* British television finally had a workable sketch-show format that would become the blueprint for future series.

The shows consisted of skits, sketches and musical items, and featured visiting celebrity guest stars. The supporting cast often appeared as recurring characters – Peter Butterworth, for instance, was Lockit, Terry-Thomas's chauffeur, a plum job owing to the fact that Terry-Thomas had no car but wanted a chauffeur as a status symbol. H C Walton played the butler, Moulting, another allusion to a perceived high-class lifestyle. Avril Angers mostly appeared as Rosie Lee, Janet Brown as Miss Happ and Benny Lee as

Mr Pegg. Terry-Thomas invented a number of outlandish characters for the series and it was truly groundbreaking in its regular use of announcer Leslie Mitchell, who interviewed Terry-Thomas in his many guises. There has been a tradition ever since in newsreaders, announcers and other similarly authoritative TV faces appearing as foils in comedy shows (especially with Morecambe and Wise) and *How Do You View?* was the pioneer of the device.

See also *Friends And Neighbours*, *Terry-Thomas*, *The Terry-Thomas Show* and *Strictly T-T.*

How Green Was My Father

UK · BBC · SITCOM

1 × 50 mins · colour

1 Mar 1976 · BBC2 Mon 10.40pm

MAIN CAST

Jenkin Jenkins III Jr/
other roles · · · · · · · · · · · · · · · Ryan Davies
The Spirit Of The Valleys · · · · · · · Max Boyce

CREDITS

writer Harri Webb · *producer* Richard Lewis

Subtitled 'A Welsh Odyssey For 1976', this was a US Bicentennial special from BBC Wales starring Ryan (of **Ryan And Ronnie**) as Jenkin Jenkins III Jr, an American searching for his roots in Wales. He soon finds that he holds more than just a remarkable resemblance to the inhabitants of Jenkinstown, a village deep in the Valleys.

How To Be A Little S*d

UK · BBC · SITCOM

10 × 10 mins · colour

19 Sep–12 Dec 1995 · BBC1 Tue 8.50pm

MAIN CAST

Baby · · · · · · · · · · · · Rik Mayall (voice only)
Mum · · · · · · · · · · · · · · · · Harriet Thorpe
Dad · · · · · · · · · · · · · · · Steven O'Donnell

OTHER APPEARANCES

Maternal Grandmother · · · · · · Diane Langton
Paternal Grandmother · · · · Daphne Oxenford
Great Grandmother · · · · · · · · · · · Edna Doré

CREDITS

writer Simon Brett · *director* Daniel Kleinman · *executive producers* Judith Holder, Ed Bye · *producer* Jamie Rix

Ten short comedy vignettes showing the impact made by a baby on its parents. Rik Mayall provided a suitably grating voice for the angelic-looking but badly behaved infant – viewers without children might have considered it deliberately malevolent, those with would have recognised familiar traits – whose sole aim seemed to be to bring misery to its parents. Extreme, somewhat distorting close-ups represented the baby's point-of-view and links were provided by animation featuring a basic cartoon version of the 'little s*d'. Although all the situations were exaggerated for comic purposes there was a recognisable vein of truthful observation running throughout and many parents found the plight of the on-screen mother and father one with which they could all-too-easily identify. Simon Brett's scripts were based on his best-selling humour book of the same title.

How To Be An Alien

UK · ITV (ASSOCIATED-REDIFFUSION) · SKETCH
6 × 30 mins · b/w
12 Feb–1 Apr 1964 · Wed 9.10pm
MAIN CAST
Frank Muir
Denis Norden
VOICES ONLY:
June Whitfield (6 editions)
Ronnie Barker (4)
Gordon Rollings (3)
Kenneth Connor (2)
Peter Goodwright (2)
Gordon Rollings (2)
CREDITS
creator George Mikes · *writers* Frank Muir/Denis Norden, Edward J Mason, George Mikes · *director* Ian Fordyce · *producer* Sid Colin

Six half-hours that combined the wit and wisdom of Muir and Norden with the voices of at least two of Britain's finest comedy talents, June Whitfield and Ronnie Barker. Each edition took the shape of an old-style lantern lecture, with the hosts utilising slides, movie stills and held-up objects to put across the writers' contention that, in every area of our daily lives, the speech and behaviour patterns of the British were being influenced by Johnny Foreigners who had come to live in these isles.

All the images were given new voice-over comedy dialogue (utilising a style that would be reprised in the 1990s in *The Staggering Stories Of Ferdinand De Bargos* and other similar programmes) and the series was based on a 1946 book, also titled *How To Be An Alien*, written by the Hungarian-born humorist George Mikes (pronounced Mikesh), who had settled in London in 1938. Candidly, Denis Norden has since admitted that cribbing Mikes' title and idea was about as far as the adaptation went, however.

Although, at face value, this might appear to be one of the lost nuggets of British TV – none of the six programmes is believed to have survived on film or tape – the series went down like the proverbial lead balloon and was forgotten almost immediately.

How's Your Father

UK · ITV (GRANADA) · SITCOM
13 × 30 mins · colour
Series One (7) 24 July–4 Sep 1974 ·
Wed 9.30pm

Series Two (6) 24 Feb–7 Apr 1975 · Mon 8pm
MAIN CAST
Eddie Cropper · · · · · · · · · · Michael Robbins
Ted Cropper · · · · · · · · · · · · · · Arthur English
Doreen Cropper · · Barbara Young (series 1);
· · · · · · · · · · · · · Rosemary Martin (series 2)
Edward Cropper · · · · · · · · · · Nicholas Hoye
Christine Cropper · · · · · · · · Georgina Moon
Ivy Watkins · · · · · · · · · · · · · Sheila Steafel
Mr Winterbottom · · · · · · · · · Reginald Marsh
CREDITS
writer John Stevenson · *directors* Bill Podmore (8), Eric Prytherch (3), Bill Gilmour (2) · *producers* Bill Podmore (8), Brian Armstrong (5)

Focusing on the generation gap, this Granada sitcom featured three generations of Edwards – rascally grandfather Ted, father Eddie (Michael Robbins, the star of the series, 'fresh' from the recently ended *On The Buses*) and his drop-out son Edward. Eddie is caught in the middle, able to comprehend neither his father nor his son, although the two of them get along together perfectly well. And there's more trouble on the domestic front because Eddie also fails to understand his liberated wife Doreen and his flighty daughter Christine. There's little refuge at work, either: Eddie is employed by an insurance company – reporting to Reginald Marsh, the archetypal office boss in several sitcoms of the period – so, what with the goings-on in Laburnum Avenue and the troubles in the office, Eddie sure has his problems.

A decade after this, *After Henry* explored similar tri-generation gap themes but from the distaff side.

How's Your Father?

see WORTH, Harry

Frankie Howerd

Born Francis Alick Howard in York on 6 March 1917, Frankie Howerd enjoyed a roller-coaster career with many sharp turns, exhilarating highs and sudden dizzying drops. Suffering from a stammer, yet determined to break into show business, he rode many initial disappointments, being rejected by RADA and the Carroll Levis talent contest organisation, and had all but committed himself to working in an insurance office when the Second World War intervened. Like many of his contemporaries, the young man found that life in the services inspired him to develop an act and a comedy persona, and his confidence grew from this. After the war he tried his luck in troop shows, where he was noticed by an agent, and, in 1946, given a part in a travelling comedy show, *For The Fun Of It*, his first

professional engagement. It was around this time that Howard changed his surname to Howerd, figuring that it would distinguish him from the many other show business Howards. Very shortly afterwards, he auditioned for the BBC radio series *Variety Bandbox* and earned a regular place in the famous show. It was here that he joined forces with Eric Sykes, who went on to write much of Howerd's material in the next few years. When Howerd left *Variety Bandbox* in 1951 he immediately launched *Fine Goings On*, another Sykes-scripted show for BBC radio, which also featured Hattie Jacques in the cast, but he found greater success in *Frankie Howerd Goes East*, a series of BBC radio shows performed for British troops still serving abroad. After this, his next major venture was his TV debut, in 1952, in his own show *The Howerd Crowd*.

By this time Frankie Howerd had developed the act that would last him the remainder of his career: rolled eyes, asides to the audience, the sudden switch to a high-pitched voice and exaggerated 'ooohs' and 'aaahs' sprinkled liberally through his patter. A cosy but risqué rapport with the audience was another of his trademarks and Howerd would routinely titivate – eh? no, tit-*i-vate*, madam, it means to sprrrrruce up – stories with references to medical conditions ('Ooh missus, my back's killing me'), sartorial comments ('Yecch, these underpants keep riding up'), high-pitched expostulations ('I was amaaazed!') and archaic but fruity sounding – though actually innocuous – vocabulary ('Titter ye not'). Age improved the comic potential of Howerd's face, and he made full use of his expressive physiognomy and gossipy persona in his famous sitcom *Up Pompeii!* It came as some surprise, after Howerd's death, when some of his many scriptwriters revealed that the comic had always insisted that these trademark Howerdisms be written into his script at the appropriate places, and that, contrary to appearances, they were rarely ad-libbed.

Frankie Howerd obtained a reputation as a comeback king thanks to his habit of bouncing back into the limelight following periods when he had fallen out of popularity. One such hiatus took place in the late 1950s, until appearances on stage at Peter Cook's Establishment Club (performing a script by Johnny Speight, Ray Galton and Alan Simpson) and on *That Was The Week That Was* (script by Speight) returned him to favour. A similar situation occurred in the late 1980s when he again returned to popularity after a quiet period that followed the arrival of 'alternative comedy'.

During his career Frankie Howerd made literally hundreds of TV appearances, especially as a guest on other shows and in variety, but he also enjoyed several series and specials of his own. All of his major TV programmes appear here, together and chronologically, except for these sitcoms which appear under their respective titles – *All Change*, *Have You Read This Notice?*, *Then Churchill Said To Me*, *A Touch Of The Casanovas*, *Up Pompeii!* and *Whoops Baghdad*.

On 1 June 1990 the BBC2 arts series *Arena* presented *Oooh Er, Missus! – The Frankie Howerd Story*, a study of the comedian and his career for which he granted an exclusive interview. Howerd died on 19 April 1992, aged 75; tribute was paid to him in C4's *Heroes Of Comedy*, screened on 1 January 1995.

See also *The Bob Monkhouse Show*, *The Bruce Forsyth Show*, *Carry On …*, *Comedy Tonight*, *The Craig Ferguson Story*, *Cucumber Castle*, *The Plank*, *Saturday Live*, *Television's Christmas Party* and *Those Two Fellers*.

The Howerd Crowd · 1

UK · BBC · STANDUP

5 × 60 mins · b/w

Series One (3) 12 Jan–8 Mar 1952 · monthly Sat 8.45pm

Series Two (2) 11 June & 27 Aug 1955 · Sat 9.30pm

MAIN CAST
Frankie Howerd

CREDITS
writer Eric Sykes · *producers* Bill Lyon-Shaw (series 1), Ernest Maxin (series 2)

Frankie Howerd's TV debut. The comic was well aware of the difficulty that TV executives were experiencing at this time in trying to find a successful comedy format, and he insisted on trying out new ideas, including providing his own cameraman, who had instructions to keep track of Howerd alone throughout the complexities of the show. These demands were acceptable to the producer Bill Lyon-Shaw who was well acquainted with the often demanding Howerd, having produced the stage-show *For The Fun Of It* at the Empire Theatre, Sheffield – where, on 31 July 1946, the comedian had made his first professional post-war appearance in his native Yorkshire. The second series was produced by Ernest Maxin, who had worked as a choreographer and appeared in the first series.

Frankie Howerd's Korean Party

UK · BBC · STANDUP

1 × 45 mins · b/w

9 Dec 1952 · Tue 8.15pm

MAIN CAST
Frankie Howerd

Eve Boswell

CREDITS
writer Eric Sykes · *producer* Kenneth Carter

Back from Korea where he had been entertaining British troops, Frankie Howerd re-presented the same show at the Nuffield Centre before an audience of service-men and -women. This TV special broadcast excerpts from the performance.

Nuts In May

UK · BBC · SKETCH

1 × 40 mins · b/w

13 May 1953 · Wed 8.45pm

MAIN CAST
Frankie Howerd
Gilbert Harding
Carole Carr

CREDITS
writer Eric Sykes · *producer* Kenneth Carter

A 'spring frolic' scripted for Howerd by the ubiquitous Eric Sykes.

The Frankie Howerd Show · 1

UK · BBC · SKETCH

1 × 45 mins · b/w

10 Sep 1953 · Thu 9.05pm

MAIN CAST
Frankie Howerd
Joan Turner

CREDITS
writers Eric Sykes, Spike Milligan · *producer* Kenneth Carter

Forty-five fun-filled minutes with Frankie Howerd, broadcast live from the 1953 Radio Show at Earls Court in London, and scripted by Eric Sykes and *Goon Show* writer Spike Milligan.

Howerd was back on BBC TV a year later, playing the lead role in a farce play, *Tons Of Money*, aired on 27 December 1954.

Frankie Howerd · 1

UK · BBC · STANDUP

2 × 30 mins · b/w

11 Oct 1956 · Thu 9.50pm
3 Dec 1956 · Mon 9.45pm

MAIN CAST
Frankie Howerd

CREDITS
writers Johnny Speight, Dick Barry · *producer* George Inns

A pair of 30-minute specials. Singer Shani Wallis guested in the first show, comic actress Joan Sims did so in the second.

The Howerd Crowd · 2

UK · ITV (ATV) · SKETCH

1 × 45 mins · b/w

23 Feb 1957 · Sat 9pm

MAIN CAST
Frankie Howerd

CREDITS
writer Eric Sykes · *executive producer* Val Parnell · *director/producer* Brian Tesler

Howerd's first starring performance on ITV.

The Frankie Howerd Show · 2

UK · ITV (ATV) · STANDUP/SKETCH

1 × 60 mins · b/w

17 Aug 1958 · Sun 8.30pm

MAIN CAST
Frankie Howerd
Margaret Rutherford
Michael Denison
Sabrina
Joyce Shock

CREDITS
producer Kenneth Carter · *executive producer* Bernard Delfont

The great comic actress Margaret Rutherford made a rare television appearance as one of Howerd's guest stars.

Frankie Howerd In …

UK · BBC · SITCOM

2 × 30 mins · b/w

Pity Poor Francis 16 Dec 1958 · Tue 9.30pm
Shakespeare Without Tears 28 Jan 1959 · Wed 8.40pm

MAIN CAST
Frankie Howerd

CREDITS
writers Johnny Speight (ed 1), Reuben Ship/Phil Sharp (ed 2) · *producer* Eric Miller

Two separate episodes in the life of Frankie Howerd, described in the programme publicity as 'the laughing stock of television'. The second show was a particular success, its tale of a stage-struck shop assistant who yearns to act in Shakespeare being well suited to Howerd's style. (One of the writers, Phil Sharp, an American, was unaccredited owing to contractual complications. He also contributed to *The Phil Silvers Show*.)

Frankly Howerd

UK · BBC · SITCOM

6 × 30 mins · b/w

1 May–5 June 1959 · Fri 7.30pm

MAIN CAST

Frankie Howerd	himself
Fred Thompson	Sidney Vivian
Gladys Thompson	Helen Jessop
various roles	Sam Kydd

CREDITS
writer Reuben Ship (with Phil Sharp) · *producer* Harry Carlisle

With the success of *Hancock's Half-Hour* the BBC were keen to find another comedy star who could carry a successful sitcom. Howerd had proved a great success in *Shakespeare Without Tears*, an edition of *Frankie Howerd In … * scripted by the Canadian-born writer Reuben Ship with the unaccredited American Phil Sharp. BBC Light Entertainment executives thought the Ship/Sharp/Howerd team would result in a winner and commissioned a full series, with Helen Jessop cast as the star's girlfriend.

Despite the high expectations, *Frankly Howerd* was an unmitigated disaster, reputedly suffering from both a below-par script and a vacillating performance from the star, who around this time was building an undesirable reputation in the broadcasting business for being 'difficult'.

Ladies And Gentle-Men

UK · BBC · STANDUP/SKETCH

1 × 45 mins · b/w

24 Sep 1960 · Sat 8.50pm

MAIN CAST
Frankie Howerd
Richard Wattis
Dennis Price

CREDITS
writers Johnny Speight, Ray Galton/Alan Simpson, Barry Took · *producer* Richard Afton

Frankie Howerd, introduced by Richard Wattis, in what was described, perhaps all too knowingly by BBC executives, as '45 minutes of unpredictable entertainment'. Dennis Price guest-starred. The phrase 'Ladies And Gentle-Men' was one of Howerd's many comic catchphrases.

A Last Word On The Election

UK · BBC · STANDUP

1 × 25 mins b/w

18 Oct 1964 · BBC1 Sun 11.15pm

MAIN CAST
Frankie Howerd

CREDITS
writers Frankie Howerd, Ray Galton/Alan Simpson, Frank Muir/Denis Norden, David Nathan, Dennis Potter · *director/producer* Ned Sherrin

After almost three years in the wilderness, Frankie Howerd's TV career had been resurrected following a hugely successful guest appearance on *That Was The Week That Was* on 6 April 1963, in which the comedian had memorably lampooned the Chancellor of the Exchequer's Budget given three days earlier. That led to this one-off special in which he was let loose to cast a satirical eye over the previous Friday's General Election.

Frankie Howerd 2

UK · BBC · STANDUP/SITCOM

12 episodes (6 × 25 mins · 6 × 30 mins) · b/w

Series One (6 × 25 mins) 11 Dec 1964–15 Jan 1965 · BBC1 Fri 8pm

Series Two (6 × 30 mins) 22 Feb–29 Mar 1966 · BBC1 Tue 9.30pm

MAIN CAST
Frankie Howerd

CREDITS
writers Ray Galton/Alan Simpson · *producer* Duncan Wood

Galton and Simpson had first written for Frankie Howerd in the early 1950s when the comic appeared on BBC radio shows *Calling All Forces* and *All Star Bill*, so they understood his style well. In these two high quality series the comedian was on top form and obviously relished the material that the writers provided for him. The format of the show allowed for Howerd to come on stage, sit on a stool and start chatting to the audience, usually including a moan about how badly his BBC boss treated him. From this ramble the week's theme emerged and then the show cut to an extended sitcom-style sketch to illustrate the story he was telling. The dialogue and many of the situations recalled Galton and Simpson's work for Tony Hancock, but the scripts suited Howerd equally as well. Ably supported each week from the usual roster of comedy character actors, this was the comedian at his (apparently) effortless best.

East Of Howerd

UK · BBC (MITHRAS FILMS) · STANDUP

1 × 50 mins · b/w

1 Jan 1966 · BBC2 Sat 8.45pm

MAIN CAST
Frankie Howerd
Shirley Abicair
Al Koran

CREDITS
director John Irvin · *producer* Joe McGrath

When Frankie Howerd led a posse of entertainers to Malaysia, to perform for British forces, a crew filmed the event, going behind the scenes and observing how the troops were coping under the tensions of a long-drawn-out military engagement.

Frankie And Bruce

UK · ITV (ABC · *THAMES) · STANDUP/SKETCH

3 editions (2 × 90 mins · b/w; 1 × 60 mins · colour)

Frankie And Bruce's Christmas Show
24 Dec 1966 · Sat 9.40pm (90 mins · b/w)

Frankie And Bruce's Christmas Show
23 Dec 1967 · Sat 9.35pm (90 mins · b/w)

**Frankie And Bruce* 3 Sep 1975 · Wed 8pm (60 mins · colour)

MAIN CAST
Frankie Howerd
Bruce Forsyth

CREDITS
writers Sid Green/Dick Hills (shows 1–3), Barry Cryer (show 3) · *director* Peter Frazer-Jones (show 1) · *executive producer* Philip Jones · *producers* Peter Dulay (show 1), Peter Frazer-Jones (show 2), David Bell (show 3)

Three programmes uniting the twin entertainment forces of Frankie Howerd and Bruce Forsyth.

See also *The Bruce Forsyth Show*.

Howerd's Hour

UK · ITV (ABC) · SKETCH

1 × 60 mins · b/w

12 May 1968 · Sun 8.25pm

MAIN CAST
Frankie Howerd
Hattie Jacques
Patrick Wymark

CREDITS
writer Eric Sykes · *producer* Keith Beckett

A themed sketch-show in which Frankie recalled an episode in the life of that intrepid adventurer, his great-grandfather Howerd.

Frankie Howerd Meets The Bee Gees

UK · ITV (THAMES) · STANDUP/SKETCH

1 × 65 mins · b/w

20 Aug 1968 · Tue 8.55pm

MAIN CAST
Frankie Howerd
Arthur Mullard
Valentine Dyall
June Whitfield

CREDITS
writers Ray Galton/Alan Simpson · *producer* John Robins

A one-off special (unlisted in the schedules but screened following the postponement of *An Evening With Jack Benny*), with Howerd delivering the funny lines and the Bee Gees (Barry, Robin and Maurice Gibb, Colin Peterson and Vince Melouney) supplying the music and joining the comedian for three sketches. (Julie Driscoll with Brian Auger and the Trinity also contributed a musical interlude.)

Howerd and the Bee Gees (trimmed down to the three brothers Gibb) reunited ten years later for the ill-fated musical movie based on the Beatles' album *Sgt Pepper's Lonely Hearts Club Band*.

The Frankie Howerd Show 3

UK · ITV (THAMES) · STANDUP/SKETCH

1 × 50 mins · b/w

25 Sep 1968 · Wed 9.10pm

MAIN CAST
Frankie Howerd

CREDITS
writers Sid Green/Dick Hills · *producer* Peter Frazer-Jones

Another one-off ITV show.

Frankie Howerd At The Poco à Poco

UK · ITV (THAMES) · STANDUP

1 × 60 mins · b/w
7 May 1969 · Wed 8pm

MAIN CAST
Frankie Howerd
Patrick Wymark

CREDITS
writers Sid Green/Dick Hills · *director* William G Stewart

The master comic in concert at the Poco à Poco Club in Stockport, Cheshire.

The Frankie Howerd Show   4

UK · ITV (ATV) · STANDUP/SKETCH

6 × 45 mins · b/w
9 Aug–13 Sep 1969 · Sat mostly 6.15pm

MAIN CAST
Frankie Howerd

CREDITS
writers Sid Green/Dick Hills · *director* Milo Lewis · *producer* Sid Green

The usual star-with-guests combination. Two days before the last of these six ITV shows, Howerd starred in the first episode of *Up Pompeii!* over on the BBC.

Frankie Howerd: The Laughing Stock Of Television

UK · ITV (THAMES) · SKETCH

1 × 60 mins · colour
14 Apr 1971 · Wed 8pm

MAIN CAST
Frankie Howerd
Hattie Jacques
Peter Copley
Patricia Hayes

CREDITS
writers Marty Feldman/Barry Took, Ray Galton/Alan Simpson, Talbot Rothwell · *director/producer* John Robins

Frankie taking turns at parodying TV shows of the day, in sketches written for him by the top writers.

Frankie Howerd's Hour

UK · ITV (THAMES) · SKETCH

2 × 60 mins · colour
1 Sep 1971 · Wed 8pm
29 Sep 1971 · Wed 8pm

MAIN CAST
Frankie Howerd

CREDITS
writers Ray Galton/Alan Simpson · *director/producer* Peter Frazer-Jones

Two programmes, screened four weeks apart, in which Frankie performed material written for him by Galton and Simpson. The second (alternatively billed as *The Frankie Howerd Show*) included a sketch where Frankie met Adolf Hitler in 1944.

Frankie Howerd In Ulster

UK · BBC · STANDUP

1 × 45 mins · colour
14 Mar 1973 · BBC1 Wed 9.25pm

MAIN CAST
Frankie Howerd
June Whitfield
Wendy Richard
Allan Cuthbertson

CREDITS
writers Ray Galton/Alan Simpson, Chris Allen, Johnny Speight, Talbot Rothwell, Roy Tuvey/Maurice Sellar · *producer* Terry Hughes

A special TV recording of Howerd's concert tour of the military bases in Ulster.

An Evening With Francis Howerd

UK · BBC · STANDUP/SKETCH

3 × 45 mins · colour
30 Apr–14 May 1973 · BBC2 Mon mostly 9.25pm

MAIN CAST
Frankie Howerd
June Whitfield

CREDITS
writers Eric Merriman (3), Ray Galton/Alan Simpson (3), Roy Tuvey/Maurice Sellar (2), Tony Hare (1), Peter Robinson (1), David McKellar (1), David Nobbs (1), Mike Craig (1), Lawrie Kinsley/Ron McDonnell (1), Dave Freeman (1) · *producer* John Ammonds

Shedding the curly shoes and baggy pantaloons of *Whoops Baghdad*, Frankie Howerd returned to the world of standup, skits and sketches for this three-programme run presented under BBC2's *Show Of The Week* banner. June Whitfield guested in each edition.

Howerd's History Of England

UK · BBC · SKETCH

1 × 30 mins · colour
30 Apr 1974 · BBC1 Tue 8.30pm

MAIN CAST
Frankie Howerd
Patrick Newell
Patrick Holt
John Cazabon

CREDITS
writers Barry Took/Michael Mills · *producer* Michael Mills

Another period-comedy, riding on the coat-tails of Howerd's successful sitcom *Up Pompeii!* and the less good *Whoops Baghdad* – this time presented under the *Comedy Playhouse* banner.

Francis Howerd In Concert

UK · ITV (YORKSHIRE) · STANDUP/SKETCH

1 × 60 mins · colour
18 Sep 1974 · Wed 8pm

MAIN CAST
Frankie Howerd
John Le Mesurier
Kenny Lynch

CREDITS
writers Johnny Speight, Barry Cryer · *director* Vernon Lawrence · *producer* Duncan Wood

Co-writer Johnny Speight (*The Arthur Haynes Show*, *Till Death Us Do Part*, *Curry And Chips* and so on) had been given his first break in comedy writing by Howerd in the 1950s.

Frankie Howerd's Tittertime

UK · ITV (THAMES) · SKETCH

1 × 60 mins · colour
1 Oct 1975 · Wed 8pm

MAIN CAST
Frankie Howerd
Hughie Green

CREDITS
writers Barry Cryer, Ray Galton/Alan Simpson · *director/producer* Peter Frazer-Jones

Big titters, small titters, wobbly titters, all shapes and sizes of titters were most sincerely served up in this show.

The Howerd Confessions

UK · ITV (THAMES) · SKETCH

6 × 30 mins · colour
2 Sep–7 Oct 1976 · Thu 9.30pm

MAIN CAST
Frankie Howerd

OTHER APPEARANCES
Joan Sims (3)

CREDITS
writers Hugh Stuckey/Peter Robinson (3), Dave Freeman (2), Dick Hills (1) · *director/producer* Michael Mills

A series of sketches, each week focusing on a different theme.

Frankie Howerd Reveals All

UK · ITV (YORKSHIRE) · STANDUP/SKETCH

1 × 60 mins · colour
10 Dec 1980 · Wed 8pm

MAIN CAST
Frankie Howerd
Henry McGee
Sheila Steafel
Kenneth Connor

CREDITS
writers John Bartlett, Mike Goddard, Laurie Rowley · *director/producer* Alan Tarrant

Frankie investigates the class system.

Frankie Howerd Strikes Again

UK · ITV (YORKSHIRE) · STANDUP/SKETCH

6 × 30 mins · colour

1 Sep–6 Oct 1981 · Tue 9.30pm

MAIN CAST
Frankie Howerd
Henry McGee
Neil Innes

CREDITS
writers John Bartlett (6), Mike Goddard (2), Barry Cryer (2), Spike Mullins (2) · *executive producer* Alan Tarrant

Six more views of life as seen through the eyes of scriptwriters and the mouth of Francis. Neil Innes provided a humorously musical interlude each week.

The following year Howerd appeared in an edition of *The Other Side Of Me* (29 August 1982), a TVS programme that concentrated on the spiritual nature of celebrities and which recalled Howerd's earliest days in front of an audience, as a Sunday School teacher.

Superfrank!

UK · C4 (HTV) · STANDUP

1 × 60 mins · colour

12 Jan 1987 · Mon 10pm

MAIN CAST
Frankie Howerd

CREDITS
writers Vince Powell, Miles Tredinnick, Andrew Nickolds · *producers* Cecil Korer/Derek Clark

Frankie's one-man show, recorded live at the Playhouse Theatre in Weston-super-Mare. It marked Howerd's first headlining TV appearance after a five-year hiatus.

Frankie Howerd On Campus

UK · ITV (LWT) · STANDUP

1 × 60 mins · colour

24 Nov 1990 · Sat 10.10pm

MAIN CAST
Frankie Howerd

CREDITS
director Ian Hamilton · *producer* Paul Lewis

Frankie in performance at, of all places, Oxford University, reaping the rewards of a deserved renaissance in his career.

Note. A recording of Howerd in concert in 1991 at the Birmingham Hippodrome was independently produced by Sunset+Vine and issued on home-video as *Frankie Howerd At His Tittermost*. The 90-minute production was first screened on television by ITV on 17 December 1996.

Frankie's On …

UK · ITV (CENTRAL) · STANDUP

4 × 30 mins · colour

21 June–12 July 1992 · Sun 10pm

MAIN CAST
Frankie Howerd

CREDITS
director Dennis Liddington · *producer* Trevor McCallum

A series of shows featuring Frankie Howerd entertaining audiences from the stages of various locations (on board the aircraft carrier the *Ark Royal* in *Frankie's On … Board*, amid a Nottinghamshire mining community in *Frankie's On … The Coals*, at a Gloucestershire fire station in *Frankie's On … Fire* and at a medical centre in Nottingham in *Frankie's On … Call*). Six programmes were planned but only these four were made before Howerd's death.

Hububb

UK · BBC (NOEL GAY SCOTLAND) · CHILDREN'S SITCOM

13 × 15 mins · colour

7 Jan–1 Apr 1997 · BBC1 Tue 3.55pm

MAIN CAST
Les · Les Bubb
Rosa · · · · · · · · · · · · · · · · · Elaine C Smith
various roles · · · · · · · · · · · · Toby Sedgwick
various roles · · · · · · · · · Miltos Yerolemou

OTHER APPEARANCES
Mr Tight · · · · · · · · · · · · · · · · · · · Ben Keaton
Doreen · · · · · · · · · · · · · · · · Kate Donnelly

CREDITS
writers Les Bubb/Ben Keaton · *director* Tom Poole · *producer* Sarah Lawrence

An absurdist comedy series for children starring standup comic Les Bubb (hence the corrupted spelling of hubbub) as a pizza delivery man, Les, who – on his trusty mountain-bike – delivers his goods throughout the environs of Edinburgh. Les lives at the top of the Melville Monument in the heart of the city and earns a thin crust working for the pizza parlour owner Rosa.

The episodes embraced much surrealist slapstick, with poor Les involved in all sorts of precarious shenanigans, few of which were of his own making. An occasionally recurring storyline featured cast member Toby Sedgwick as rival pizza cyclist (*motor*-cyclist) the Dark Deliverer. The result was an

unusual, quirky but generally amenable series, if surprisingly violent in places.

A second series of *Hububb* was set for screening in early 1998.

Roy Hudd

Born on 16 May 1936 in Croydon, Roy Hudd's varied talents led to successes on stage, TV, film and radio, as both a comic – his foremost occupation – and, in the 1990s, a fine dramatic actor. As a comedian, Hudd is one of a dying breed: he made his stage bow in 1958 in the last days of theatrical variety, playing the last music-halls and provincial theatres as the tradition wound to a close – working with a partner as Hudd and Kay, he appeared in 1959 on the same Finsbury Park Empire bill as Max Miller, perhaps the greatest stage comic of the era. Hudd's love of and fascination for music-hall and variety remains undimmed – as the author of books, the president of the British Music Hall Society and the host of numerous radio, TV and stage-show revivals, he is Britain's best-known expert on the subject, and his own comedy routines strive to keep the old style alive.

Hudd made the transition from summer shows and pier productions to TV in 1964, when he appeared in the BBC's satirical series *Not So Much A Programme More A Way Of Life*. Straight away, there was a clear dichotomy: as a young blade of comedy, Hudd's elevation to stardom was much admired, but he was also not entirely at ease with the university graduates, and their more cerebral comedic style, that followed *Beyond The Fringe* and led, ultimately, to *Monty Python*. After exploring a number of different TV styles, Hudd opted for sketch-shows combined with opportunities to explore his saucier standup material. This formula has worked particularly well on radio, and his BBC Radio 2 series *The News Huddlines* became a national institution, first aired in 1975 and still active, in its 23rd year, as this book was in production. (Hudd is ably supported in the series by June Whitfield and Chris Emmett.) Hudd also continues to write, direct and perform in Christmas pantomimes, and has added a new paragraph to his CV with some fine performances in serious TV dramas, especially Dennis Potter's *Lipstick On Your Collar* (1993) and *Karaoke* (1996), and *Common As Muck* (1994).

See also ***Blandings Castle**, **Hale And Pace**, **Hold The Front Page**, **Inside George Webley**, **Leslie Crowther's Scrapbook** and **Our House**.*

Hudd

UK · BBC · SITCOM

7 episodes (1 × 25 mins · 6 × 30 mins) · b/w

Pilot (25 mins) 15 July 1965 · BBC1
Thu 8.50pm

One series (6 × 30 mins) 23 Nov–28 Dec 1965 ·
BBC1 Tue 7.30pm

MAIN CAST
Roy Hudd

CREDITS
writers George Evans/Derek Collyer · *executive
producer* Graeme Muir (pilot) · *producer* John
Paddy Carstairs

Piloted in *Comedy Playhouse*, this sitcom
vehicle for Roy Hudd had no other regular
characters and differing settings. The series
capitalised on Hudd's physical dexterity and
ability to conjure-up 'bits of business' with
various props, rather than on witty badinage.
John Paddy Carstairs (painter/writer/film
director and long-time Norman Wisdom
collaborator) was the producer.

The Maladjusted Busker

UK · BBC · SITCOM

1 × 30 mins · b/w

3 Mar 1966 · BBC1 Thu 9pm

MAIN CAST
Roy Hudd

CREDITS
deviser/writer John Law · *director* John Duncan ·
producer Dick Clement

This was a real oddity: a half-hour filmed
one-off special shot on the streets of London.
John Law's simple premise was to chart the
comic progress of one of a four-man team of
buskers who has been separated from his
colleagues and is attempting to find them
among the teeming capital streets. Roy
Hudd was Law's first choice to play the
wandering character.

Roy Hudd   1

UK · BBC · SKETCH

1 × 50 mins · b/w

17 May 1966 · BBC2 Tue 9pm

MAIN CAST
Roy Hudd
Barbara Young
Doug Fisher

CREDITS
writers Eric Davidson/Dick Vosburgh · *additional
material* Bill Solly, Marty Feldman/Barry Took ·
producer Michael Hurll

Comedy sketches on a single theme featuring
Hudd as the subject of a mock 'ruthless
documentary', using interviews with 'family
friends and colleagues' to uncover his true
character. The programme was presented
under the *Show Of The Week* banner.

The Illustrated Weekly Hudd

UK · BBC · SKETCH

**22 editions (14 × 30 mins · 7 × 25 mins · 1 ×
short special) · b/w**

Series One (7 × 25 mins) 17 Nov–29 Dec 1966 ·
BBC1 Thu 9.05pm

Series Two (6 × 30 mins) 7 Apr–12 May 1967 ·
BBC1 Fri 7.30pm

Series Three (8 × 30 mins) 2 Oct–20 Nov 1967 ·
BBC1 Mon 7.30pm

Short special · part of *Christmas Night With The
Stars* 25 Dec 1967 · BBC1 Mon 6.40pm

MAIN CAST
Roy Hudd
Doug Fisher
Sheila Steafel (series 1)
Patrick Newell (series 1)
Marcia Ashton (series 2 & 3 & special)

CREDITS
writers Eric Davidson (22), Dick Vosburgh (21),
Dave Freeman (14) · *producers* Michael Hurll
(15), James Gilbert (7)

An all-out comic assault, Hudd utilising
a number of comedic styles in an attempt
to appeal to the widest possible audience.
It proved to be a successful formula and
some editions crept into the top ten ratings.
The shows were crammed full of sketches,
some barely a minute long, and used
elaborate make-up and costume changes
along with location shooting to create its
visual style.

Roy Hudd   2

UK · BBC · STANDUP/SKETCH

1 × 50 mins · colour

26 May 1968 · BBC2 Sun 8.15pm

MAIN CAST
Roy Hudd
Freddie Jones
Joan Turner

CREDITS
writers John Antrobus, Michael Billington, Caryl
Brahms/Ned Sherrin, Ian Davidson, Keith
Waterhouse/Willis Hall, Roy Hudd, Peter Lewis/
Peter Dobereiner, David Nobbs/Peter
Tinniswood, David McKellar, Donald Webster ·
director Mel Cornish · *producer* John Duncan

Another *Show Of The Week* slot for Hudd,
who – despite his relative youth – was
gaining a reputation for keeping the classic
atmosphere of the British music-hall era
alive. This he demonstrated with a fine
impression of Max Miller and performances
of some long-forgotten music-hall comedy
songs that were combined with some
examples of the satirical style he had
developed in *Not So Much A Programme
More A Way Of Life*. The actor Freddie
Jones and the comedian Joan Turner helped
out in the sketches and music was provided
by the veteran rocker Bill Haley.

The Roy Hudd Show

UK · ITV (YORKSHIRE) · SKETCH

7 × 30 mins · b/w

17 Feb–31 Mar 1969 · Mon 9.30pm

MAIN CAST
Roy Hudd
Joan Turner
Freddie Jones
Frank Abbott

CREDITS
writers Keith Waterhouse/Willis Hall, David
Nobbs, Philip Purser, Peter Spence, Michael
Billington, John Duncan, Richard Ingrams, Don
Airey, John Antrobus and others · *director* Ronald
Fouracre · *producer* John Duncan

Hitherto known for his BBC work, Roy Hudd
hopped channels to present a fast-moving
sketch show on ITV, with sketches, songs,
cartoons (drawn by Hector Breeze) and more
loving impersonations of some of Hudd's
music-hall heroes: Max Miller, Billy Bennett
and the like.

Comedy Tonight

UK · BBC · STANDUP

7 × 45 mins · colour

7 Nov–19 Dec 1971 · BBC2 Sun around 10pm

MAIN CAST
Roy Hudd

CREDITS
director Roger Ordish · *producer* John Street

Presented from the stage of the Talk Of The
Town, in London, this series showed Hudd
performing routines – sometimes in the guise
of the great comics of yesteryear – and
introducing an array of comedy guests. These
included, most notably, Arthur Askey, Tessie
O'Shea, Billy Dainty, Henny Youngman, Clive
Dunn, Jimmy Edwards and Stan Stennett.

The Roy Hudd Family Show

UK · BBC · SKETCH

1 × 45 mins · colour

21 May 1972 · BBC2 Mon 9.25pm

MAIN CAST
Roy Hudd
Julia McKenzie
Richard Caldicot
Henry Woolf

CREDITS
writers Roy Hudd, Peter Vincent · *producer*
Michael Hurll

Another *Show Of The Week* special. In this,
the star presented sketches and routines
themed around the eccentric members of his
(fictional) family.

It's A Hudd Hudd World

UK · C4 (ANGLIA/GAMBIT ENTERPRISES) ·
SKETCH

1 × 25 mins · colour

31 Dec 1987 · Thu 7.05pm

MAIN CAST
Roy Hudd
June Whitfield
Chris Emmett
Suzy Aitchison
Robert Howie
Kalli Greenwood

CREDITS
writers cast · *director/producer* Ron Downing ·
executive producer Cecil Korer

A one-off C4 special. Principal among those
doing the aiding and abetting were his two
stalwarts from the long-running BBC Radio
2 series *The News Huddlines*, June Whitfield
and Chris Emmett.

Around this period (beginning 4
December 1984) Hudd also presented an
irregularly scheduled series on BBC1, *Halls
Of Fame*, in which he visited different
former variety theatres around the country
and turned the cameras on a range of local
performers, many of them survivors from
that golden age. Emphasising the meaning
of the term variety, by no means was every
performer a comedian, but the series was
notable for featuring one of the final TV
appearances by the great Scots comic
Chic Murray.

Hugh And I

UK · BBC · SITCOM

**79 episodes (40 × 25 mins · 37 × 30 mins ·
2 × short specials) · b/w**

Series One (9 × 30 mins) 17 July–11 Sep 1962 ·
Tue 8.45pm

Series Two (12 × 25 mins) 21 May–6 Aug 1963 ·
Tue 8pm

Short special · part of *Christmas Night With The
Stars* 25 Dec 1963 · Wed 8.05pm

Series Three (14 × 25 mins) 4 Jan–18 Jan;
22 Feb–15 May 1964 · BBC1 Sat around 9pm

Short special · part of *Christmas Night With The
Stars* 25 Dec 1964 · BBC1 Fri 7.15pm

Series Four (14 × 25 mins) 3 Jan–11 Apr 1965 ·
BBC1 Sun 7.25pm

Series Five (14 × 30 mins) 3 Jan–4 Apr 1966 ·
BBC1 Mon 7.30pm

Series Six (8 × 30 mins) 29 Nov 1966–17 Jan
1967 · BBC1 Tue 7.30pm

Series Seven (6 × 30 mins) *Hugh And I Spy*
22 Jan–26 Feb 1968 · BBC1 Mon 7.30pm

MAIN CAST
Terry Scott · himself
Hugh Lloyd · himself
Mrs Scott · · · · · · · · · Vi Stevens (series 1–5)
Mr Crispin · · · · · · · Wallas Eaton (series 1–5)
Mrs Crispin · · · · · Mollie Sugden (series 1–5)
Arthur Wormold · · · · · · Cyril Smith (series 1);
· · · · · · · · · · · · · · · · · · · Jack Haig (series 2–5)
Mrs Wormold · · · Patricia Hayes (series 1–5)

Hughie

UK · BBC · SITCOM

1 × 30 mins · b/w

19 May 1967 · BBC1 Fri 7.30pm

MAIN CAST
Hugh Lloyd · himself
Mr Gates · · · · · · · · · · · · · · · Patrick Cargill
Mrs Green · · · · · · · · · · · · · · Ann Lancaster
Padre · · · · · · · · · · · · · · · · · Robert Gillespie

CREDITS
writer John Chapman · *additional material* John
Junkin · *producers* David Croft (series 1–5,
specials, series 7), Duncan Wood (series 6)

A fondly remembered and long-running
sitcom that reunited Terry Scott and Hugh
Lloyd, who had worked together on stage
many years earlier. The episodes were built
around a simple but durable premise: at
his mother's house at 33 Lobelia Avenue,
Tooting, in south London (*Citizen Smith*,
a decade later, was also set in Tooting), Scott
is a rather hopeless youngish bachelor who
aspires to wealth, a situation he would prefer
to achieve without hard work, continually
dreaming up grandiose schemes that he then
seeks to explore. The more downbeat and
slight Lloyd, meanwhile, is the family's
lodger, who, while a trifle dozy, at least brings
some money into the house courtesy of his job
at a local factory. Although in no way a direct
parody of Laurel and Hardy, the relationship
– and physical characteristics – of the two
lead players was reminiscent of the great film
comics, and their friendship was often tested
to its limits when the gullible Lloyd was led
into one misadventure after another by Scott's
boisterous and usually blind enthusiasms.

By the end of the fifth series the principals
decided to bring it to an end, but when the
BBC asked for more they decided to continue
but with new settings, ending the suburban
domestic sagas and introducing different
backdrops. (At this point, Scott's screen mum,
and her Lobelia Avenue neighbours – the
Crispins and the Wormolds – left the cast.)
With Hugh having won £5000, a small fortune
in 1966, on the Premium Bonds, a sixth series
showed the pair undertaking a world cruise.
The seventh – its revised title punning the
US adventure series *I Spy*, then airing in the
UK on ITV – found the mismatched twosome
returned from their globetrotting but
embroiled in a variety of comedy adventures,
each episode ending in a cliffhanger.

Notes. A single-episode radio adaptation of
Hugh And I was broadcast by the BBC Light
Programme on 13 June 1963.

After *Hugh And I* Scott and Lloyd
continued to work together from time to time,
and they headlined a TV pantomime
performance of *Robin Hood* that was screened
by BBC1 on Christmas Day 1973.

CREDITS
creator Alexander Doré · *writers* Johnnie Mortimer/
Brian Cooke · *producer* Robin Nash

A single-episode *Comedy Playhouse* starring
Hugh Lloyd as a man who has served ten
years in prison and so likes the life there that
when he is allowed out he plots his return,
pleading 'take me back' to the Welfare
Officer, Mr Gates.

Hulbert Follies

UK · BBC · SKETCH

6 × 45 mins · b/w

8 July–29 Sep 1948 · fortnightly Wed/Thu 3pm

MAIN CAST
Jack Hulbert
Claude Hulbert
Adèle Dixon

CREDITS
creators/producers Jack Hulbert/Walton
Anderson · *writer* Max Kester

Described as 'a high-speed song-and-dance
entertainment interspersed with sketches',
Hulbert Follies was the first TV show to star
both the Hulbert brothers, Jack (1892–1978)
and Claude (1900–64), established comedy
stars of British radio and cinema. The series
was another in the long line of experiments to
find a successful format for such material on
television.

Note. Each of the six editions was represented, at around 8.30pm, within a few
days of their first broadcast.

Barry Humphries

The Australian comic/satirist/writer/
impersonator Barry Humphries was born in
Melbourne on 17 February 1934, entering
show business in revues and – despite
receiving no formal training – as a straight
actor. He had already invented his most
famous character, Edna Everage, by the
time he moved to England in 1959, where he
began by playing minor roles in London
theatre productions before landing a regular
part in Lionel Bart's stage musical *Oliver!*
(He later returned to it in triumph, taking
over from Ron Moody as Fagin.) But it was
his one-man show at Peter Cook's
Establishment Club that brought Humphries
to the attention of the main movers in the
1960s satire boom, leading directly to TV
appearances in *Not Only ... But Also* and
The Late Show and to his soon-famous
comic strip in *Private Eye* featuring the
disgustingly crass working-class Australian
Barry McKenzie, who knew limitless
numbers of ways to describe his most

regular habit: drink-induced vomiting – 'the Technicolor yawn', 'the liquid laugh', 'parking the tiger' and so on. Never featured in TV programmes, McKenzie was nonetheless Humphries' first major success, going on to star in a pair of movies, *The Adventures Of Barry McKenzie*, 1972, and *Barry McKenzie Holds His Own*, 1974 (both starring Barry Crocker and directed by Bruce Beresford).

Humphries rivalled Cook in his ability to improvise high comedy on any given theme, and it was as Edna Everage that he achieved immortality, developing the 'Melbourne suburban housewife with ideas above her station' into a gladiola-carrying television superstar. The dame became a Dame and grander with every appearance, being equally comfortable in the company of international film celebrities or the British royal family, and referring to commoners and aristocracy alike as 'possums'. In snatches of gossip, Edna revealed the convoluted aspects of her 'fictional' life, of her husband Norman Stoddart Everage (who eventually died) and their children, daughter Valmai and sons Bruce and Kenneth. Many such stories cast dubious reflections on the sexual interests and deviations of her family but Edna remained apparently oblivious throughout. In most of her later appearances the Dame had a constant companion, the stone-faced Madge Allsop (played by Emily Perry), a tiny, slight and almost always silent foil who fulfilled a similar role for Edna as had the gormless 'Cynthia' for music-hall star Hylda Baker (*Be Soon*) in the 1950s and 1960s. There was one further link too: 'Cynthia' was played by a tall man in drag, creating a visual clash with the diminutive Baker. So it was with Edna and Madge too, although this time the cross-dresser was dominant.

Dame Edna also appeared in the aforementioned Barry McKenzie films and many major stage-shows, including *Housewife Superstar*, *A Night With Dame Edna* and *Last Night Of The Poms*.

Barry Humphries' other principal alter ego was the monstrous, drunken philanderer Dr Sir Leslie Colin Patterson KBE, the sometime cultural attaché to Australia. Dame Edna and Sir Les's comedy-led appearances feature in the following list of Humphries' TV series.

Barry Humphries' Scandals

UK · BBC · STANDUP

6 editions (1×40 mins · 5×30 mins) · colour
Special (40 mins) *Strangers In The Night* 12 July 1969 · BBC2 Sat 9pm
One series (5×30 mins) 12 Jan–9 Feb 1970 · BBC2 Mon mostly 9.10pm

MAIN CAST
Barry Humphries

CREDITS
writers Barry Humphries/Ian Davidson · *director* David O'Clee · *producer* Dennis Main Wilson

Barry Humphries' Scandals began as a one-off, *Strangers In The Night*, introducing viewers to some of the many characters that the comic had created during his one-man-show tours in the previous years. This and the series that followed featured his most famous creation, Edna Everage – then merely Mrs Norm Everage and not yet the awesome superstar Dame – as well as a colourful bunch of other caricatures: the upper-class twit the Honourable Barrington Humphries, the stupefyingly boring Max Smallpiece, the clairvoyant Madame Barrie, the painter Clement Egg, the vicar Kevin Cock, the tramp Lawrence De'Ath and the affected, fey poet Stan Elroy Flecker.

Humphries' characters dominated the shows but guest stars also featured, among them Arthur Mullard, Dick Bentley, Diana Dors and Willie Rushton. As Humphries later admitted, he had a drink problem at this time which affected his judgement and consistency during the series. Later, when he had conquered alcohol, his shows became masterpieces of controlled chaos and lunatic humour.

The Barry Humphries Show

UK · BBC · STANDUP

3 editions (2×50 mins · 1×45 mins) · colour
3 Mar 1976 · BBC2 Wed 9.10pm (45 mins)
26 Sep 1977 · BBC2 Mon 8.10pm (50 mins)
5 Dec 1977 · BBC2 Mon 8.10pm (50 mins)

MAIN CAST
Dame Edna Everage · · · · · Barry Humphries
Betty Turner
Joan Bakewell

CREDITS
writers Barry Humphries/Ian Davidson · *producers* Terry Hughes (shows 1 & 3), Roger Race (show 2)

In show one, Edna Everage – now a Dame – made a pilgrimage to Shakespeare's birthplace, and – in an 'exclusive TV interview' – revealed the secrets of her life with her husband Norm. In the other two shows Humphries developed what was to become his regular TV format, with Edna, in characteristically outrageous form, joined by guest stars.

La Dame Aux Gladiolas

UK · BBC · STANDUP

1×55 mins · colour
19 Mar 1979 · BBC2 Mon 10.25pm

MAIN CAST
Dame Edna Everage · · · · · Barry Humphries

CREDITS
writer Barry Humphries · *director* Julian Jebb · *producer* Alan Yentob

Masquerading as 'an exclusive arts documentary about a living legend', this was another instalment in the Edna Everage saga, a creation by now considered real enough to warrant a full-blown spoof analysis in BBC2's *Arena* arts strand. The Dame was filmed in her 'fabulously appointed penthouse suite atop the Dorchester Hotel, London W1', at her home in the Melbourne suburb of Moonee Ponds, and on stage with her current hit show *A Night With Dame Edna*. Subtitled 'The Agony And Ecstasy Of Edna Everage', the programme purported to probe into the life of the enigmatic superstar through observations and in-depth interviews.

An Audience With Dame Edna Everage

UK · ITV (LWT) · STANDUP

1×60 mins · colour
26 Dec 1980 · Fri 10.15pm

MAIN CAST
Dame Edna Everage · · · · · Barry Humphries

CREDITS
writer Barry Humphries · *director* Alasdair Macmillan · *executive producer* David Bell · *producer* Richard Drewett

The first edition in LWT's long-running *An Audience With ...* series featured the Melbourne megastar, who proved so popular she/he returned in 1984 and 1988 for two more similar shows. The format for the entire series was in place for this first programme, the star answering prearranged questions from a celebrity studio audience that were designed to enable the funniest possible responses. Although contrived, the format actually was quite effective, especially in the delightfully manipulative hands of Dame Edna.

Last Night Of The Poms

UK · ITV (EVEN STEVEN PRODUCTIONS/LWT) · STANDUP

1×60 mins · colour
3 Jan 1982 · Sun 11.15pm

MAIN CAST
Dame Edna Everage · · · · · Barry Humphries

CREDITS
writer Barry Humphries · *director* Stanley Dorfman · *executive producers* Harvey Goldsmith/Allan McKeown

A TV recording of Dame Edna's stage-show at the Royal Albert Hall.

Dame Edna Everage – A Birthday Tribute

UK · BBC · STANDUP

1 × 50 mins · colour

17 Feb 1984 · BBC2 Fri 10.05pm

MAIN CAST

Sir Les Patterson/ ·
Dame Edna Everage · · · · · Barry Humphries

CREDITS

writer Barry Humphries · director Julian Jebb ·
producer Alan Yentob

A second *Arena* special focusing on Dame Edna. This spoof birthday celebration was introduced by another of Humphries' creations, the simply horrible Australian cultural attaché Sir Les Patterson. This man was awesome, an invention who exaggerated all the worst clichés of stereotypical Australian manhood, resulting in a scruffy, booze-swilling, vomit-stained, sex-obsessed, belching, farting, dribbling, genital-scratching party animal. Sir Les led the salute to the grand Dame on her birthday (*her* age wasn't revealed, but Humphries himself was celebrating his 50th) and clips from the earlier *La Dame Aux Gladiolas* were included.

Another Audience With Dame Edna Everage

UK · C4 (LWT) · STANDUP

1 × 60 mins · colour

31 Dec 1984 · Mon 10.30pm

MAIN CAST

Dame Edna Everage · · · · · Barry Humphries

CREDITS

writer Barry Humphries · director Alasdair Macmillan · producer Richard Drewett

Back by popular demand, Dame Edna returned to face questions from another audience of celebrities.

The Dame Edna Experience!

UK · ITV (LWT) · STANDUP

14 editions (12 × 50 mins · 1 × 65 mins · 1 × 60 mins) · colour

Series One (6 × 50 mins) 12 Sep–17 Oct 1987 · Sat 10.30pm

Special (65 mins) *The Dame Edna Christmas Experience!* 26 Dec 1987 · Sat 9.45pm

Series Two (6 × 50 mins) 4 Nov–16 Dec 1989 · Sat mostly 10.20pm

Special (60 mins) *The Dame Edna Satellite Experience* 22 Dec 1989 · Fri 10.20pm

MAIN CAST

Dame Edna Everage · · · · · Barry Humphries

CREDITS

writer Barry Humphries · directors Ian Hamilton (1987), Alasdair Macmillan (1989) · producers Judith Holder/Richard Drewett (1987), Claudia Rosencrantz/Nicholas Barrett (1989)

A long-running spoof chat-show for Dame Edna with top-line guests, all of whom had to be content to play second fiddle to the darling Aussie, visiting her 'luxury Mayfair penthouse'. (She herself arrived each week by helicopter, alighting on the roof.) Among the guests were Mary Whitehouse, Cliff Richard, Sean Connery, Zsa Zsa Gabor, Joan Rivers, Jane Seymour, Germaine Greer, Charlton Heston, John Mills, Rudolf Nureyev, Jane Fonda, Liza Minnelli, Edward Heath, Malcolm McDowell, Lauren Bacall and Tony Curtis. The last programme, the 1989 special, was a one-off extension of the usual premise that saw the esteemed lady transmitting twenty 24-hour TV stations around the globe via her own satellite, Ednasat. Celebrity guests included Sir Yehudi Menuhin and, problematically, Sir Les Patterson.

One More Audience With Dame Edna

UK · ITV (LWT) · STANDUP

1 × 65 mins · colour

25 Dec 1988 · Sun 10.25pm

MAIN CAST

Dame Edna Everage · · · · · Barry Humphries

CREDITS

writer Barry Humphries · executive producer Nicholas Barrett · director/producer David Bell

A testament to the Dame Edna's appeal was this, her third appearance on LWT's *An Audience With …* series, more than any other personality.

A Night On Mount Edna

UK · ITV (LWT) · STANDUP

1 × 60 mins · colour

15 Dec 1990 · Sat 10.05pm

MAIN CAST

Dame Edna Everage · · · · · Barry Humphries

CREDITS

writer Barry Humphries · director Alasdair Macmillan · producer Claudia Rosencrantz

A Christmas special in which Dame Edna invited a posse of her favourite show business possums to her exclusive Swiss chalet (actually LWT's studio on London's South Bank) to enjoy fondue and conversation and pay homage to the ultimate megastar. Among those who turned up were Mel Gibson, Charlton Heston, Julio Iglesias and Gina Lollobrigida. The programme won the 1991 Golden Rose of Montreux award.

Dame Edna's Hollywood

UK · ITV (DAME EDNA STUDIOS/TOGETHER AGAIN PRODUCTIONS FOR LWT) · STANDUP/ SKETCH

3 × 60 mins · colour

21 Dec 1991 · Sat 10.45pm

26 Dec 1993 · Sun 9pm

24 Dec 1994 · Sat 10.20pm

MAIN CAST

Dame Edna Everage · · · · · Barry Humphries

CREDITS

writers Barry Humphries/Ian Davidson · director Bruce Gowers · executive producer Barry Humphries · producer Claudia Rosencrantz

With Edna's fame spreading to the USA, LWT financed the making of three American TV specials, featuring Hollywood-based guest stars, all of whom had to pay a visit to the Dame's palatial home in Beverly Hills and play second fiddle to the Melbourne megastar in another spoof chat-show format. (Actually, all three programmes had a studio audience.) The first featured Cher, Mel Gibson, Bea Arthur, Larry Hagman and Jack Palance; the second (aired in the USA before being seen in Britain – NBC networked it there on 9 May 1992) included Ringo Starr, Burgess Meredith, Kim Basinger, George Hamilton IV, Chevy Chase, Rue McClanahan and Robin Williams; the third featured Burt Reynolds, Sean Young and Barry Manilow.

Back in Britain, in between the first two shows, Humphries introduced his great Dame to the game-show format for the first time, hosting two LWT/ITV series of *Dame Edna's Neighbourhood Watch*, in which the everyday Melbourne housewife teased domestic secrets out of her all-female audience. (Six editions from 19 September to 24 October 1992; six more from 18 September to 23 October 1993.) 'She' was also the subject of *J'accuse Dame Edna Everage*, screened on 16 February 1993 as part of C4's *Without Walls* arts documentary series, in which impressionist Rory Bremner argued that Dame Edna now personified the same suburban values she had set out to satirise.

Late Lunch With Sir Les

UK · C4 (LWT) · STANDUP

1 × 35 mins · colour

27 Dec 1991 · Fri 11.35pm

MAIN CAST

Sir Les Patterson · · · · · · · Barry Humphries

CREDITS

writer Barry Humphries · director Alasdair Macmillan · producer Claudia Rosencrantz

This time it was Australian cultural attaché Sir Les Patterson's turn to sit in the spoof chat-show chair, quizzing guests Marie Helvin and agony aunt Claire Rayner.

Dame Edna's Work Experience

UK · BBC (BBC/D L TAFFNER) · STANDUP/ SKETCH

1 × 45 mins · colour

3 Apr 1997 · BBC1 Thu 10pm

MAIN CAST

Dame Edna Everage · · · · · Barry Humphries

CREDITS
writers Barry Humphries/Ian Davidson · *director* Brian Klein · *executive producer* John Reynolds · *producer* Trevor McCallum

Australia's grand dame clattered back on to TV in this 1990s update of the old BBC radio favourite *Workers' Playtime*. Appearing in Wigan in front of an audience dressed in matching blue boiler-suits, Humphries delivered a virtuoso performance of especially written material. The show also contained elements of the series *An Audience With ...*, with (this time non-celebrity) audience members feeding Edna prearranged questions from which she could extemporise in her inimitable fashion. Along the way, Edna revealed that her daughter Valmai was now living in exile in Wigan (the two hadn't spoken for eight years following Valmai's publication of her tell-all book *Edna Dearest*) and told the audience that she, Edna, had herself lived in Wigan in a previous life when she had been George Formby's mother.

Dame Edna's previous TV appearance before this was as one of the hosts of **Comic Relief** 1997. The occasion was remarkable for her stoic friend Madge breaking years of silence by energetically performing a song and dance number. Perhaps chastened, in *Dame Edna's Work Experience* she returned to her old silent, unsmiling self.

Sir Les And The Great Chinese Takeaway

UK · BBC (TIGER ASPECT) · SATIRE

1 × 30 mins · colour

28 June 1997 · BBC2 Sat 8.30pm

MAIN CAST
Sir Les Patterson/ ·
Dame Edna Everage · · · · · Barry Humphries

CREDITS
writer Barry Humphries · *executive producer* Charles Brand · *director/producer* Clive Tulloh

A BBC2 documentary that showed Sir Les Patterson in Hong Kong, just prior to the British hand-over of the colony to China, giving, in his own words, 'an impartial, impersonal, unbiased overview' of the historic event. The result (from an idea by Ken Thomson) was a spoof travelogue featuring Sir Les, at his worst, in a number of contrived and genuine situations. Innocent onlookers were outraged, shocked but mostly genuinely amused by the booze-sodden, stain-suited behemoth blitzing through the colony. Dame Edna Everage appeared at one point, continuing her famous feud with the Australian superslob, but mainly this was Sir Les's baby. He lectured at the Australian Chamber of Commerce meeting in HK, broadcast on the forces' radio, tramped through the red-light district, was rickshawed around the city and sailed around the islands, visited

British troops and generally made a nuisance of himself. Vulgar, biting and very, very funny, Sir Les certainly succeeded in his quest to gauge the mood of the residents, both Chinese and others, acting, as he put it, 'as a rectal thermometer in the oriental orifice'.

Dame Edna Kisses It Better

UK · ITV (LWT) · STANDUP/SKETCH

1 × 60 mins · colour

26 Dec 1997 · Fri 9pm

MAIN CAST
Dame Edna Everage/ · · · · · · · · · · · · · · · ·
Sir Les Patterson · · · · · · · Barry Humphries
Dr James Dreyfus · · · · · · · · · James Dreyfus

CREDITS
writers Barry Humphries, Ian Davidson, Jez Stephenson · *director* John Birkin · *executive producer* Nigel Lythgoe · *producer* Patricia McGowan

The premise for this special was that the superstar had opened 'Saint Edna's Caring Clinic for the Stars' in Harley Street, London, boasting that she could cure most celebrity problems with a kiss. A number of famous guests (including Rolf Harris, Sir Cliff Richard, David Seaman, Melinda Messenger, Elle MacPherson) appeared in scripted or semi-scripted routines, all of them acting solely as a foil to Humphries' outrageous flights of fantasy. James Dreyfus played Edna's administrator and Kevin Lloyd and Seeta Indrani appeared briefly as hospital orderlies. Edna addressed her audience as 'outpatients' and involved a few of them in a game-show, 'Admission Impossible', in which the volunteers had to administer bed-baths to male strippers, the Dream Boys. Les Patterson turned up as a patient and was his usual repugnant self, leering and making passes at Melinda Messenger (they ended up in bed together), while Madge got to dance at the show's end with Sir Cliff Richard.

The usual paean to bad taste, immaculately carried out by a veteran performer whose comic sensibilities were still scalpel-sharp.

HurRah

see The Montreux Festival

Hysteria

All-star comedy concerts benefiting Aids charities, produced along the lines of **The Amnesty Galas**. The first *Hysteria* show, not televised, took place in 1987.

Hysteria 2

UK · C4 (TIGER TELEVISION) · STANDUP/SKETCH

1 × 120 mins · colour

1 Dec 1989 · Fri 10.30pm

MAIN CAST
Joss Ackland, Clive Anderson, Ed Asner, Rowan Atkinson, John Cleese, Robbie Coltrane, Paul Eddington, Adrian Edmondson, Harry Enfield, Fascinating Aïda, Craig Ferguson, Dawn French, Stephen Fry, Jeremy Hardy, Lenny Henry, Hugh Laurie, Jonathan Ross, Jennifer Saunders, Ruby Wax, *Who Dares, Wins* team

CREDITS
writers cast · *director* David Croft · *executive producer* Charles Brand · *producer* Trevor Hopkins

The film of a special Aids benefit concert directed by Stephen Fry and screened by C4 on World Aids Day. The show was packed with comics, and also musicians (Tina Turner, Dave Gilmour and others) and models (Jerry Hall, Marie Helvin). Additionally, Mel Smith, Griff Rhys Jones, Julian Clary and John Mortimer appeared in the TV programme, explaining how the proceeds would be spent.

Hysteria III

UK · C4 (NOEL GAY TELEVISION) · STANDUP/SKETCH

1 × 130 mins · colour

12 Oct 1991 · Sat 10.30pm

MAIN CAST
Stephen Fry, Lenny Henry, Mike McShane, Rowan Atkinson, Elton John, Dawn French, Julian Clary, Melvyn Bragg

CREDITS
writers cast · *director* Geoff Posner · *executive producer* Paul Jackson · *producer* Fiona Cotter Craig

The third of the biannual Aids benefits, all the stars giving their services free once more. The event took place on 30 June 1991 at the London Palladium.

The Big Snog

UK · C4 (POZZITIVE PRODUCTIONS) · STANDUP/SKETCH

1 × 90 mins · colour

25 Nov 1995 · Sat 10.45pm

MAIN CAST
Eddie Izzard, Steve Coogan (as Alan Partridge and Pauline Calf), Lenny Henry, Harry Enfield, Julian Clary, Dale Winton

CREDITS
writers cast and others · *director* Geoff Posner · *producers* Crispin Leyser, Geoff Posner

Another Hysteria Trust fund-raiser heralding World Aids Day on 1 December. Musical guests also featured and a quiz offered advice on safe sex.

I Didn't Know You Cared

UK · BBC · SITCOM

27 × 30 mins · colour

Series One (7) 27 Aug–15 Oct 1975 · BBC1
Wed 9.25pm

Series Two (6) 20 Apr–25 May 1976 · BBC1
Tue 9.25pm

Series Three (7) 11 Jan–22 Feb 1978 · BBC1
Wed 9.25pm

Series Four (7) 8 May–26 June 1979 · BBC1
Tue 9.25pm

MAIN CAST

Uncle Mort	Robin Bailey
Les Brandon	John Comer
Annie Brandon	Liz Smith
Carter Brandon	Stephen Rea (series 1 & 2);
	Keith Drinkel (series 3)
Pat Partington	Anita Carey (series 1 & 2);
	Liz Goulding (series 3)
Uncle Stavely	Bert Palmer (series 1–3);
	Leslie Sarony (series 4)
Linda Preston	Deirdre Costello

OTHER APPEARANCES

Auntie Lil	Gretchen Franklin (series 1 & 2)
Mrs Partington	Vanda Godsell

CREDITS

writer Peter Tinniswood · *producer* Bernard
Thompson

Peter Tinniswood's wonderful comic creation,
the Brandons – a truly awful, extended
northern family – was brought triumphantly
to TV in this artfully cast series. The
characters first appeared in a trilogy of books
written by Tinniswood in which, although
they were succinctly sketched by their
dialogue, the author avoided physical
descriptions. But he was more than satisfied
when the chosen BBC actors matched the
vision of the Brandons held in his mind.

Pivotal to the series is Uncle Mort, an
incredibly dour, awesomely pessimistic and
newly widowed pensioner – the type of man
who wears a flat-cap indoors – who positively
wallows in his misery. His dullard nephew,
Carter, has become reluctantly engaged to Pat
and is attempting to stall any wedding talk,
a ploy heartily endorsed by the other male
members of the clan, all of whom see marriage

as a gruesome crime against their gender.
The constant arguing of his parents, Les
and Annie (Mort's sister), is another factor in
Carter's hesitancy – but whatever his reasons,
his reservations are no match for Pat and her
mother's determination that a wedding must
take place, and at the end of the first series the
knot is tied. The marriage doesn't really alter
much in the scheme of things: even though his
wife aspires to an improved lifestyle and tries
to better her husband above his station, Carter
and the other men still go out on the ale and
'enjoy' one deeply gloomy night after another
– better yet than being with their women-folk
– while the wives sit at home and wait for
their beery husbands to return, stewing over
yet another dried-out dinner and more broken
promises. All the while, Carter tries too to
resist the temptations of a brassy admirer,
Linda Preston, persistently offering him
sensual delights behind the slag heap.

This battle-of-the-sexes was endless, with
even the powerful male characters Uncle Mort
and Les Brandon unable to come out on top
against the closed ranks of the formidable
family females. Only old Uncle Stavely
managed to stay unbeaten, due entirely to
his near-deafness and inability to mutter
anything beyond the incongruous 'I heard
that! Pardon?' or simply 'Pardon?'

Peter Tinniswood's acute observations of
the tough and stoic side of northern life, allied
to his wonderful ear for the humour inherent
in everyday dialogue, meant that *I Didn't
Know You Cared* was an excellent and highly
literate sitcom and a quiet triumph for all
concerned.

Notes. The three books depicting the
Brandons were *I Didn't Know You Cared*
(published 1973), *Except You're A Bird* (1974)
and *Stirk Of Stirk* (also 1974). On 1 August
1989 BBC1 presented *Tinniswood Country*,
which looked back at the places of the
writer's youth. He was aided in his quest by
the Brandon family, with Robin Bailey and
Liz Smith back in their roles of the previous
decade, joined by Peter Skellern as Carter
and Liz Goulding as Pat.

Tinniswood's Uncle Mort character has
become a firm favourite with BBC Radio 4
listeners in recent years, appearing in such
series as *Uncle Mort's North Country* and
Uncle Mort's South Country (both have also
been published in book form) and *Uncle
Mort's Celtic Fringe*.

I Dream Of Jeannie

USA · NBC (SIDNEY SHELDON PRODUCTIONS) ·
SITCOM

139 × 30 mins (30 × b/w · 109 × colour)

US dates: 18 Sep 1965–1 Sep 1970

*UK dates: 1 July 1970–20 Dec 1974
(100 episodes) ITV Tue then Fri 5.20pm

MAIN CAST

Jeannie	Barbara Eden
Captain (later Major) Anthony Nelson	Larry Hagman
Captain (later Major) Roger Healey	Bill Daily
Dr Alfred Bellows	Hayden Rorke
General Martin Peterson	Barton MacLane
Amanda Bellows	Emmaline Henry
	(1966–70)

CREDITS

creator/executive producer Sidney Sheldon ·
writers various · *directors* Claudio Guzman and
others · *producers* Claudio Guzman and others

A patently silly but enjoyable US sitcom
that sustained a strong sense of wit from
start almost to finish. During a test-flight,
astronaut Tony Nelson crash-lands on a
deserted island in the South Pacific and
stumbles upon an old bottle, releasing from
it a beautiful blonde genie. He names her,
appropriately enough, Jeannie, and she
returns with him to Florida where she falls
in love with him, calls him 'Master' and is
honoured to serve his every need. (He's a
single man, with a place of his own too, yet
he never seems to think of asking for the
one thing that all other men would want –
but then this *was* 1960s TV.) Not that Tony
doesn't care for Jeannie. He likes her, but
because she's a wilful genie whose attempts
to please her master land him in plenty of hot
water, this love remains strictly a one-way
affair, and it is only in the final series that
he accepts the inevitable and marries her.
(Actually, in the opening episode, Tony was
already engaged, to Melissa, the daughter of
a commanding officer.)

The real fun of *I Dream Of Jeannie* was in
the many scrapes that Jeannie got her master
into (and the few she genuinely rescued him
from), and the fact that, although Nelson's
best friend and co-pilot Roger Healey knew of
her existence, her trickery constantly amazed
the NASA psychiatrist, Dr Bellows, who did
not, and assumed Nelson to be responsible for
all the bizarre goings-on. Like Larry Tate in
Bewitched, which ran on ABC at the same
time, the senior man in *I Dream Of Jeannie*
never quite got to the bottom of all the
mysteries surrounding his underling.

I Dream Of Jeannie was the first starring
role for Larry Hagman, establishing him as a
comedy actor in the years preceding his role
in the soap opera *Dallas*. Indeed, it was his
Dallas commitments that prevented
Hagman from appearing in a single two-hour
TV movie revival (*I Dream Of Jeannie:
Fifteen Years Later*) screened in the USA
on 20 October 1985. Wayne Rogers (formerly
Trapper John in *M*A*S*H*) took his place.
In this TV movie viewers finally got to see
Jeannie's navel: sensitive producers had kept
it hidden by her harem slacks during the
original run – again, one thing that US TV

executives were not in the 1960s was daring. Six years on, on 20 October 1991, there was a second revival (*I Still Dream Of Jeannie*) but this time no one played the part of Nelson: conveniently, he was away, deep in space. Hanna-Barbera produced an animated spin-off, *Jeannie*, that aired in the US from 1973 to 1975 and was screened in the UK by the BBC from 6 September 1974, one of the characters being voiced by young actor and future *Star Wars* star Mark Hamill.

*Note. The series enjoyed a substantial re-run on C4 in the 1980s, which screened 65 episodes from 12 July 1985 to 8 June 1988.

I Feel Fine

UK · ITV (GRANADA) · STANDUP/SKETCH

2 × 60 mins · colour

12 July 1986 · Sat 7.30pm
22 Aug 1987 · Sat 6.30pm

MAIN CAST
Stan Boardman

CREDITS
directors Tim Sullivan/Noel D Greene (show 1), Noel D Greene (show 2) · *producer* Johnny Hamp

A couple of limp hours in the company of Stan Boardman and assorted Mersey guests (Ringo Starr, Gerry Marsden, Richard Stilgoe and others in the first programme; Richard Stilgoe, the Grumbleweeds, Gerry Marsden, Mick Miller, the Vernons Girls, Tommy Bruce, Dave Berry, Penny Page & Googie, and – oddly – Gloria Gaynor in the second). The first was aired to celebrate an event called the Liverpool Festival Of Comedy.

I Hate This House

UK · BBC · CHILDREN'S SITCOM

1 × 25 mins · colour

24 Mar 1996 · BBC2 Sun 10.05am

MAIN CAST
David · · · · · · · · · · · · · · · · · · · Peter England
Mum · · · · · · · · · · · · · · · · · · · Helen Lederer
Gran · · · · · · · · · · · · · · · · · · · Joan Turner
Tiger Girl/Susan · · · · · · Stephanie Bagshaw
Iron Mike Mason · · · · · · · · · · · Mike Harvey
Big Baby · · · · · · · · · · · · · · · · · Stan Nelson
Darren · · · · · · · · · · · · · · Matthew Kennard
Damon · · · · · · · · · · · · · · · Samuel Kennard

CREDITS
writers Daniel Peacock/Mickey Hutton · *producer* John Comerford

More madcap mayhem from writers Peacock and Hutton, who were making a habit of delivering boisterous, surreal entertainment in the fields of comedy and comedy-drama. *I Hate This House* began life as a short weekly feature within the BBC children's magazine strands *For Amusement Only* and *Highly Sprung*, where it focused on the exploits of David, a normal 12-year-old boy surrounded

by an extraordinary family – Mum, for example, is too busy to notice that David's twin brothers Darren and Damon are plotting to bring down the household, that Tiger Girl, his sister, thinks she is superhuman, that Gran constantly misunderstands everything, and that Big Baby is already the biggest person in the house. In this one-off stand-alone special, David is tricked by his family into boxing against Iron Mike Mason for the World Heavyweight Championship. To make matters worse, David's granny piles on the pressure by wagering all of the family's goods and savings on David to win.

Note. Danny Peacock starred in and wrote *Teenage Health Freak* (12 episodes on C4, 21 May–25 June 1991 and 22 February–29 March 1993), a boisterous and sometimes humorous drama for adolescents, depicting a modern teenager, his cowboy-obsessed dad, harassed mother and the object of his desire, Amanda, a rather selfish, aspiring model.

I Love Lucy

see BALL, Lucille

I, Lovett

UK · BBC · SITCOM

7 × 30 mins · colour

Pilot · 9 June 1989 · BBC2 Fri 9pm
One series (6) 24 Mar–28 Apr 1993 · BBC2 Wed mostly 10.05pm

MAIN CAST
Norman Lovett · · · · · · · · · · · · · · · himself
Darren · · · · · · · · · · · · · · · Dicken Ashworth
Darren's partner · · · · · · · · · · · · Sara Corper
Spider · · · · · · · · · Mary Riggans (voice only)
Horse · · · · · · · · · · Leon Sinden (voice only)
Dirk · · · · · · · · · · Geoffrey Hughes (voice only)

CREDITS
writers Norman Lovett/Ian Pattison (6), Norman Lovett (1) · *directors* Ron Bain (6), Colin Gilbert (1) · *producer* Colin Gilbert

Norman Lovett was born in 1946 and brought up in the Essex seaside town of Clacton. He didn't begin performing until he was 32, coming to prominence during the 'alternative' comedy boom in the early 1980s and featuring regularly in *Don't Miss Wax*, Ruby Wax's C4 series, in 1987–88. Lovett's delivery is slow, thoughtful and full of dangerously long pauses, and his material blends surrealism with a bizarre logic.

The sitcom *I, Lovett* had a similarly surreal edge, with the comic casting himself as an eccentric inventor who lives in a world created by his own imagination, where his constant companion is a talking dog, Dirk, and where inanimate objects – paintings, his letter-box and more – also speak to him. It took virtually four years after a pilot episode in *Comic Asides* before the appearance of the

series (co-written by *Rab C Nesbitt* author Ian Pattison) and only six episodes were made, but *I, Lovett* had a pleasing quirkiness and a peculiarly British eccentricity.

I Married Joan

USA · NBC (VOLCANO ENTERPRISES) · SITCOM

98 × 30 mins · b/w

US dates: 15 Oct 1952–6 Apr 1955

UK dates: 25 Sep 1955–22 Jan 1958 (83 episodes) BBC Sun mostly 4pm then various days and times

MAIN CAST
Joan Stevens · · · · · · · · · · · · · · · Joan Davis
Judge Bradley Stevens · · · · · · · · Jim Backus
Janet Tobin · · · · · Sheila Bromley (1954–55)
Kerwin Tobin · · · · · · · · Dan Tobin (1954–55)
Minerva Parker · · Hope Emerson (1952–53)
Beverly · · · · · · · · · · Beverly Wills (1953–55)
Mabel · · · · · · · · · Geraldine Carr (1953–54)
Charlie · · · · · · · · · · · · · · · · · · · Hal Smith

CREDITS
writers Phil Sharp, Frank Terloff · *producers* P J Wolfson, Dick Mack

Fade in: Judge Bradley Stevens sits in judgement in domestic court, the case he is trying reminding him of a recent incident involving his dizzy wife, Joan. Dissolve to: a 20-minute flashback of said incident. Cut to: Judge Stevens' summing-up, drawing upon the experiences of the flashback to make his point. Fade out.

This was *I Married Joan*, and so it continued, week after week for three years, one of many US sitcoms attempting to replicate the straitlaced-husband-with-wacky-wife formula of the phenomenally successful *I Love Lucy*. *I Married Joan* was reasonably well received and comedian Joan Davis proved adept enough at this sort of knockabout comedy. She enjoyed solid support from the likeable Jim Backus, whose voice was instantly recognisable as that of the myopic cartoon character *Mr Magoo*.

I Tell You It's Burt Reynolds

UK · ITV (YORKSHIRE) · SITCOM

1 × 30 mins · colour

31 Mar 1977 · Thu 9pm

MAIN CAST
Leonard Rossiter
Patricia Hayes
Gillian Raine
Ed Devereaux
Roy Barraclough
Kim Smith
Sally Watkins

CREDITS
writers/associate producers Ray Galton/Alan Simpson · *executive producer* Duncan Wood · *director/producer* Ronnie Baxter

This excellent single-episode comedy, within Yorkshire TV's season of *The Galton & Simpson Playhouse*, starred Leonard Rossiter as an annoying know-all determined to prove that the man he's just seen on television is Burt Reynolds. Not content with badgering everyone in the room, and dismissing their insistence that he's wrong, he goes so far as to call the great Burt himself on the phone, just to find out. Rossiter's real-life wife, actress Gillian Raine, appeared here with her husband.

The script was re-used in 1997 in *Paul Merton In Galton & Simpson's ...*

I Thought You'd Gone

UK · ITV (CENTRAL) · SITCOM

7 × 30 mins · colour

27 July–7 Sep 1984 · Fri 8.30pm

MAIN CAST

Gerald	Peter Jones
Alice	Pat Heywood
Ruby Pugh	Rosalind Knight
Justin	James Trelfa
Tony	Ian Gelder
Charlie	Norman Mitchell
Sue	Rowena Roberts
Virginia	Valerie Testa
Donald	Donald Delve
Lucy	Charlotte Walker
Mandy	Louisa Haigh

CREDITS

writers Peter Jones/Kevin Laffan · *director* Paul Harrison · *producer* Shaun O'Riordan

Co-written by and starring the fine humorist and actor Peter Jones, *I Thought You'd Gone* depicted the adventures of a middle-aged married couple, Gerald and Alice, who have worked hard as parents, waiting for the day when they would be alone together again, without children. Now that day has arrived, and to ensure they're not disturbed they move house, from Croydon out into the country, to a place without a spare room. But peace proves as easy to hold on to as a bar of wet soap, and what with the comings and goings of their daughter Sue, an unmarried mother, and their son Tony who is estranged from his wife Sandra, domestic strife rules once more.

I Thought You'd Gone lasted just one series; the BBC fared better with *No Place Like Home*, based on a similar concept and running contemporaneously.

I Woke Up One Morning

UK · BBC · SITCOM

12 × 30 mins · colour

Series One (6) 21 Mar–25 Apr 1985 · BBC1 Thu 9.35pm

Series Two (6) 6 Mar–17 Apr 1986 · BBC1 Thu 9.30pm

MAIN CAST

Derek	Frederick Jaeger
Max	Michael Angelis
Zero	Robert Gillespie
Danny	Peter Caffrey
Dolly Hamilton	Jean Boht

Rosa	Shirin Taylor
Sister May	Frances White
Doris	Marcia Warren
Irrelevant	Tim Potter (series 2)

CREDITS

writer Carla Lane · *directors* Roger Race (series 1), Gareth Rowlands (series 2) · *producer* Roger Race

A genre-stretching Carla Lane comedy series about four recovering alcoholics – Derek, Max, Zero and Danny – who meet while undergoing psychotherapy in hospital. The series dealt not with alcoholism so much as failure, with the men seemingly unable to cope with life alone and so drawing necessary strength from their companionship.

In screening the series on BBC1 – rather than BBC2, which had been home to Lane's two previous series, *Leaving* and *The Mistress* – the Corporation must have recognised the series' ambition. Some critics slated *I Woke Up One Morning* for having too much drama and not enough comedy, although this was obviously what the author was striving for. Regardless of any short-comings, however, few British comedy writers at this time were willing to propel the sitcom into such thoughtful and dark areas.

I'm Alan Partridge

see COOGAN, Steve

I'm All Right Jacques

UK · BBC · SATIRE

1 × 30 mins · colour

21 Dec 1992 · BBC2 Mon 9pm

MAIN CAST

Pete McCarthy

CREDITS

writer Pete McCarthy · *producer* Caroline Roberts

A one-off show – studio based with filmed inserts – in which writer/comedian McCarthy presented a wry look at the British, and the lifting, ten days from the broadcast, of all remaining trading obstacles between the member countries of the European Community. The programme was first shown by BBC Scotland (9 December 1992); the above date reflects the national (excluding Scotland) screening.

See also McCarthy's earlier BBC2 special *The Hangover Show*.

I'm Bland ... Yet All My Friends Are Krazy!

see Sitcom Weekend

I'm Bob, He's Dickie

see MONKHOUSE, Bob

I'm Dickens, He's Fenster

USA · ABC (HEYDEY PRODUCTIONS/LEONARD STERN) · SITCOM

32 × 30 mins · b/w

US dates: 28 Sep 1962–13 Sep 1963

UK dates: 9 Nov 1962–27 Jan 1964 (32 episodes) ITV Fri 8pm then Tue 7pm then Mon 6.15pm

MAIN CAST

Harry Dickens	John Astin
Arch Fenster	Marty Ingels
Kate Dickens	Emmaline Henry
Mel Warshaw	Dave Ketchum
Myron Bannister	Frank DeVol

CREDITS

writers various · *directors* various · *producer* Leonard Stern

The comedic yarns of two young blue-collar carpenters: the married (ie, henpecked) one Harry Dickens, and the worldly-wise bachelor one, Arch Fenster, the man with a 'little black book' of tempting phone numbers. Harry wants to lead a more exciting life – which means spending more time with Arch – but his beautiful wife Kate won't permit it. At work, often unable to agree solutions to their carpentry problems, they also find themselves at loggerheads with their boss at the Bannister Construction Company, Mr Bannister (when he's not checking the mirror over some concern about his appearance, that is).

This was a good US sitcom, and it allowed John Astin an outlet for his zany acting style which would later be put to even greater employment in *The Addams Family*.

I'm Dickie – That's Showbusiness

see HENDERSON, Dickie

I'm Not Bothered

UK · ITV (JACK HYLTON TV PRODUCTIONS FOR ASSOCIATED-REDIFFUSION) · SITCOM

26 × 30 mins · b/w

2 Mar–11 Sep 1956 · mostly Tue 7.30pm

MAIN CAST

Wally Binns	Glenn Melvyn
Alf Hall	Danny Ross
Dolly Binns	Betty Marsden
George Gallop	Arthur Rigby
Rose Binns	Eileen Mayers

CREDITS

creator Glenn Melvyn · *writers* Edward J Mason, Glenn Melvyn, Patrick Brawn, Max Kester, Cecilia Hale, Edward Dryhurst · *directors* Richard Carrickford, Robert Hartford-Davis, Milo Lewis · *producers* Richard Bird, Henry Kendall

Following on from *Love And Kisses*, screened on ITV in the autumn of 1955, writer/actor Glenn Melvyn dusted off his stuttering Wally Binns character, and that of his sidekick Alf Hall, for another turn. The result was *I'm Not Bothered*, a series of 26 episodes again produced by the impresario Jack Hylton. Among the writers was Edward J Mason, co-creator of radio serials *Dick Barton – Special Agent* and *The Archers*, while, in the episodes screened on 8 and 29 May, Ronnie Barker made his first two TV appearances. Despite the credentials, however, the result was disappointing, and after just one episode the series was switched from Fridays at 8.30pm to Tuesdays at 7.30pm in the hope that it would appeal to younger viewers.

See also *Beside The Seaside*.

The Idiot Weekly, Price 2d

UK · ITV (ASSOCIATED-REDIFFUSION) · SKETCH

5 × 30 mins · b/w

24 Feb–6 Apr 1956 · Fri 10pm

MAIN CAST
Peter Sellers
Spike Milligan
Eric Sykes
Valentine Dyall
Kenneth Connor
Graham Stark
June Whitfield
Patti Lewis
Max Geldray

CREDITS
writers Spike Milligan, Associated London Scripts · *script editor* Eric Sykes · *director/producer* Dick Lester

Screened only in the London area, *The Idiot Weekly, Price 2d* was the first of three Associated-Rediffusion series in 1956 that endeavoured to bring to TV the bizarre humour of the massively popular BBC radio series *The Goon Show*. (The other two were ***A Show Called Fred*** and ***Son Of Fred***.) Two of the three Goons – Peter Sellers and Spike Milligan – were involved in the venture and they were aided (and doubtless abetted) by a bunch of comic cronies rounded-up from elsewhere, including Eric Sykes, Kenneth Connor, Graham Stark and (making a name for herself in another BBC radio series, *Take It From Here*) June Whitfield. The premise of *The Idiot Weekly, Price 2d*, such as it was, saw Sellers cast as the editor of a tatty Victorian weekly magazine, its headlines and stories suggesting the skits and enabling the subject matter to change in quick fashion Less than a month after folding the magazine the team were back with *A Show Called Fred*.

Note. Associated London Scripts, given a writing credit on the series, was a co-operative based in London W12 that encompassed the writing talents of, at this time, John Antrobus, Brad Ashton, Dick Barry, Dave Freeman, Ray Galton, John

Junkin, Eric Merriman, Spike Milligan, Terry Nation, Lew Schwarz, Alan Simpson, Johnny Speight and Eric Sykes. Beryl Vertue, the office manager, also enjoyed a long and distinguished career in TV comedy, producing **Men Behaving Badly** fully 40 years after becoming involved with ALS.

Idle At Work

UK · BBC · SITCOM

1 × 30 mins · colour

14 Jan 1972 · BBC1 Fri 7.40pm

MAIN CAST
George Idle · · · · · · · · · · · · · Ronnie Barker
Mr Chesterton · · · · · · · · · · Graham Crowden
Restaurant Manager · · · · · · · · Derek Francis
Auntie · · · · · · · · · · · · · · · Mary Merrall
The 'General' · · · · · · · · · · William Kendall
The 'Bishop' · · · · · · · · · · · Roland MacLeod
Saunders · · · · · · · · · · · · Annabel Leventon
Naismith · · · · · · · · · · · · · Timothy Carlton

CREDITS
writers Graham Chapman/Bernard McKenna · *director* Harold Snoad · *producer* James Gilbert

Enjoying success at this time as part of *The Two Ronnies*, Ronnie Barker took time out to star in this Graham Chapman/Bernard McKenna *Comedy Playhouse* pilot, *Idle At Work*. Although bearing the name 'George' in the piece, the inspiration for the name probably came from Chapman's fellow Python Eric Idle. No series developed.

If It Moves, File It

UK · ITV (LWT) · SITCOM

6 × 30 mins · colour

28 Aug–2 Oct 1970 · Fri 8.30pm

MAIN CAST
Quick · · · · · · · · · · · · · · · · · · · John Bird
Foster · · · · · · · · · · · · · · · Dudley Foster
Froggett · · · · · · · · · · · · · · John Nettleton
Minister · · · · · · · · · · · · · · · John Barrard

CREDITS
writer Troy Kennedy Martin · *director/producer* Derek Bennett · *executive producer* Humphrey Barclay

Z Cars creator Troy Kennedy Martin conceived and wrote this series about the civil service, and in particular a pair of civil servants – Quick and Foster – for whom secrecy is everything and its veil something they can always hide behind, despite the attentions of Froggett, their boss. It was Kennedy Martin's first TV sitcom, although he also wrote the comedy-thriller movie *The Italian Job*. John Bird and Dudley Foster played the two *Men From The Ministry*-style 'experts' and John Nettleton (who would later play a civil servant in **Yes Minister**) was the boss at MI7.

If The Crown Fits ...

UK · ITV (ATV) · SITCOM

6 × 30 mins · b/w

29 Apr–3 June 1961 · Sat 9.30pm

MAIN CAST
King Rupert of Grabnia · · · · · · Robert Morley
Major Domos · · · · · · · · · · · · · · Peter Bull
Princess Amelia · · · · · · · · · · · · Tracy Reed
Prime Minister · · · · · · · · · · · Miles Malleson
Stevens the footman · · · · · · · · · · Erik Chitty
Horace the sentry · · · · · · · · · Richard Walter
George · · · · · · · · · · · · · · · · · David Cole
Chancellor · · · · · · · · · · Charles Lloyd Pack

OTHER APPEARANCES
(two roles) · · · · · · · · · · · · · Gladys Cooper
Fred Potter · · · · · · · · · · · · · · Robert Hardy
Paxton · · · · · · · · · · · · · · · Richard Caldicot

CREDITS
writer Robert Morley · *director* Alan Tarrant

A short-lived but eventful ATV sitcom that starred theatre giant Robert Morley as King Rupert, monarch of the small Mediterranean country of Grabnia. King Rupert has not fought his way to the crown, he has *bought* his way there, mostly for the fun of putting on the ceremonial robes and going to open some festivity or other. Tracy Reed played his daughter, Princess Amelia, the heir presumptive with a presumptive air: she prefers to follow a beatnik lifestyle, wearing jeans, going to college and riding around Grabnia on the back of a motor-scooter driven by her boyfriend George. The idea of tiny countries with grand plans was popular at this time thanks to the 1959 British comedy film *The Mouse That Roared* (director Jack Arnold), which led to a 1963 sequel *The Mouse On The Moon* (director Richard Lester).

Filmed on location in Spain, *If The Crown Fits ...* featured a number of guest players: Gladys Cooper (Robert Morley's real-life mother-in-law) played two roles, and Robert Hardy was in the opening edition as King Rupert's PR man. Future *Crackerjack* jokester Peter Glaze had a small part in one episode.

See also *Charge!* and *An Evening With Robert Morley*.

If You Can Get It

see *Nice Work*

If You Go Down In The Woods Today

see SYKES, Eric

If You See God, Tell Him

UK · BBC · SITCOM

4 × 45 mins · colour

11 Nov–2 Dec 1993 · BBC1 Thu around 9.35pm

MAIN CAST

Godfrey Spry · · · · · · · · · · · · · Richard Briers
Gordon Spry · · · · · · · · · · Adrian Edmondson
Muriel Spry · · · · · · · · · · · · Imelda Staunton

CREDITS

writers Andrew Marshall/David Renwick ·
director/producer Marcus Mortimer

A radical departure for the comic actor Richard Briers, who was cast as a totally passive character reacting to situations rather than instigating them. He played Godfrey Spry, who – having been struck on the head by a plummeting wheelbarrow full of rubble – is largely immobile and has an attention span of only 30 seconds. As a result, he obsesses over TV commercials because they represent one of the few things that he can follow from beginning to end, and starts to believe everything the advertisers claim. This causes an erratic twist in his behaviour, making life increasingly difficult for his son Gordon, and Gordon's wife Muriel.

A wry slice of black comedy, taking a swipe at the advertising industry, *If You See God, Tell Him* was dark even by Marshall and Renwick's standards, and at 45 minutes per each of the four episodes fell somewhere between a sitcom and a mini-series. Each episode featured well-known guest stars, some (like Gary Olsen and Angus Deayton) from the writers' other shows (*2 Point 4 Children* and *One Foot In The Grave*). The title – with Godfrey's name shortened to 'God' – was a reference to a recent, patronising advertising campaign in which a hapless character called Sid was the only person apparently unaware that one could apply for shares in the newly privatised British Gas.

Ignorants Abroad

UK · BBC · CHILDREN'S SITCOM

1 × 30 mins · b/w

21 May 1958 · Wed 5pm

MAIN CAST

Joe · Joe Baker
Jack · · · · · · · · · · · · · · · · · · · Jack Douglas
Lady Ghastly/Father · · · · · · · · Joe Baker Sr

CREDITS

writer Jimmy Grafton · producer Johnny Downes

A half-hour slot in the *Children's Television* strand for the comedy double-act Baker and Douglas, whose slapstick antics were popular with young viewers thanks to their many appearances in the BBC's entertainments jamboree-bag *Crackerjack* – they were the programme's first resident comedians, appearing in it from the premiere edition on 14 September 1955. Baker's father, Joe Baker Sr, also appeared in *Ignorants Abroad*.

See also *New Look.*

The Illustrated Wednesday Revue

UK · ITV (CENTRAL) · SKETCH

1 × 30 mins · colour

15 Feb 1984 · Wed 11.40pm

MAIN CAST

Glen Cardno

CREDITS

writer/producer Glen Cardno · director Shaun O'Riordan

A single comedy revue written and produced by Glen Cardno, the writer/producer of a number of TV comedies – mostly produced by Central TV – detailed elsewhere in this book. Viewers report that the programme had canned laughs but few genuine ones.

The Illustrated Weekly Hudd

see HUDD, Roy

The Imaginatively-Titled Punt & Dennis Show

UK · BBC · SKETCH/STANDUP

12 × 30 mins · colour

Series One (6) 7 July–11 Aug 1994 · BBC1 Thu 8.30pm

Series Two (6) *Punt And Dennis* 28 July–7 Sep 1995 · BBC1 mostly Fri 8pm

MAIN CAST

Steve Punt

Hugh Dennis

CREDITS

writers Steve Punt/Hugh Dennis · additional material Nick Hancock · director David G Hillier (series 1) · producers David Tyler (series 1), Caroline Leddy/Geoff Miles (series 2)

After going their separate ways, the two double-acts in *The Mary Whitehouse Experience* went on to star in, respectively, the BBC2 series *Newman And Baddiel In Pieces* and the BBC1 series *The Imaginatively-Titled Punt & Dennis Show*. Both blended studio routines with filmed sketches, but the latter series didn't come across anything like as trendy, sharp or off-the-wall as the former, perhaps because of its BBC1 status, its pre-watershed scheduling or the fact that Steve Punt and Hugh (real name Pete) Dennis both seemed like really decent, young, bright chaps, too nice for anything deeply cutting. Indeed, they and their comedy were reminiscent of Stephen Fry and Hugh Laurie, although not quite in the same league.

The humour was a bit hit and miss but, on balance, good fun and well presented, the filmed sketches being professional and effective but the studio items a little stilted and forced, with neither Punt nor Dennis appearing comfortable as 'traditional' comic and feed. Character inventions included the

Gullibles, who were 'always falling for scams'; Martin, the star of a TV adventure series; Kurt Wenker, a German tourist from hell; a scandal-riddled MP; and an ex-offender turned weatherman, and there were regular spoofs of TV drama series like *Bugs*, *ER*, *Heartbeat*, *The X-Files* and *Baywatch*. Each show in the second series – which was titled simply *Punt And Dennis* – had a musical interlude from some pretty hot acts, including the Beatles, the Rolling Stones, the Doors, Queen and T Rex – in the shape of lookalike/soundalike bands.

See also *Me, You And Him.*

Impasse

UK · BBC · SITCOM

1 × 25 mins · b/w

15 Mar 1963 · Fri 8pm

MAIN CAST

Mr Spooner · · · · · · · · · · · · Bernard Cribbins
Mr Ferris · · · · · · · · · · · · · · Leslie Phillips
AA man · · · · · · · · · · · · · · · · · Harry Locke
RAC man · · · · · · · · · · · · · · Duncan Macrae
Mrs Ferris · · · · · · · · · · · · Georgina Cookson
Mrs Spooner · · · · · · · · · · · · · · Yootha Joyce
Police Constable · · · · · · · · · Campbell Singer

CREDITS

writers Ray Galton/Alan Simpson · producer John Street

A *Comedy Playhouse* script from Galton and Simpson, never intended as a pilot for a future series but simply as a one-off idea. The story tells of an impasse between two drivers (one in a Bentley, the other in a small, rundown assembly-line car) who meet half-way along a narrow country lane and who both, belligerently, refuse to reverse and give way to the other. The class clash is exacerbated by the arrival of rival (AA, RAC) motoring organisation representatives. The drivers' respective wives, however, have to sit and watch the 'little boys' playing their power games.

The classic storyline proved durable: the script was used again for the 'pride' sequence in the 1971 feature film *The Magnificent Seven Deadly Sins* (directed by Graham Stark), with Ian Carmichael and Alfie Bass as the stubborn motorists, and the full, original TV script was re-performed in the 2 February 1996 edition of *Paul Merton In Galton & Simpson's ...*

The Importance Of Being Hairy

UK · BBC · SITCOM

1 × 30 mins · colour

6 May 1971 · BBC1 Thu 7.40pm

MAIN CAST

Peter Hastings · · · · · · · · · · · · · Gerald Flood
Tom Potts · · · · · · · · · · · · · · · · Doug Fisher
Dr Chatterjee · · · · · · · · · · · · · · John Cater
Jill Hastings · · · · · · · · · · · · · Louie Ramsey

Professor Shillito · · · · · · · · · · George Howe	
Dora Leach · · · · · · · · · · · · · Pearl Hackney	
Professor Macdonald · · · · · James Copeland	

CREDITS
writer Kingsley Amis · *producer* Graeme Muir

Kingsley Amis's second TV script (the first was an updating of the drama *The Duchess Of Malfi*) was this single *Comedy Playhouse* satire about student unrest at the progressive University of Wessex. The story followed an anxious group of lecturers at the new university, trying – amid slogans and sit-ins – to elect a Reader in the Popular Arts.

See also *Further Adventures Of Lucky Jim*.

In All Directions

UK · BBC · SATIRE

1 × 50 mins · b/w
26 Apr 1966 · BBC2 Tue 9pm

MAIN CAST
Peter Ustinov
Peter Jones

CREDITS
writer Peter Jones · *producer* Michael Mills

A TV special, presented as a *Show Of The Week*, that for one occasion only brought to TV a great BBC radio comedy of the 1950s, *In All Directions* (26 September 1952–4 March 1955), starring the two Peters, Ustinov and Jones. The series had borne out Ustinov's insistence that British people could enjoy satire, episodes centring on endless car journeys and the characters that the two men encountered along the way, the two most memorable inventions being the spivs Maurice and Dudley Grosvenor – Morry and Dud – who delighted audiences with their dodgy antics.

For the 1950s radio shows the two stars rambled their humorous meanderings into a tape recorder, which Frank Muir then edited into programmes. This single TV special, scripted by Jones, was commissioned by Muir in his executive capacity in BBC Television.

In Bed With Medinner

UK · ITV (LWT) · STANDUP/SKETCH

34 editions (28 × 30 mins · 6 × 60 mins) · colour
Special (30 mins) 20 Nov 1992 · Fri 11.10pm
Special (30 mins) 27 Nov 1992 · Fri 11.10pm
Series One (6 × 60 mins) 8 Apr–13 May 1994 · Fri around 12.30am
Series Two (26 × 30 mins) 11 Jan–22 Nov 1997 · mostly Sat around 12 midnight

MAIN CAST
Bob Mills

CREDITS
writer Bob Mills · *director* Mike Toppin (specials) · *executive producer* Jeff Pope · *producers* Brent Baker (series 1), Beverley Taylor (series 2)

Fun, mostly for 'blokes', broadcast in the late, back-from-the-pub slot at weekends. Standup comic Bob Mills specialised in a cynical view of life and its everyday objects, and in pastiches of popular culture icons – particularly evident in his work as a presenter on rock video channel VH-1. *In Bed With Medinner* – the title spoofing Madonna's movie *In Bed With Madonna* – thus began with a sequence parodying the ultimate cult TV adventure series, *The Prisoner*. The set was meant to be Mills' own flat – although there was also a studio audience – and he would walk around and cull humour from the objects and old TV extracts showing on his VCR.

Mills' wit has also been given free rein in ITV's weekday morning celebrity drawing game *Win, Lose Or Draw* (networked by Scottish TV), of which he is the host. (This series originated in the USA under the same title.) Mills has also presented *There's Only One Brian Moore*, ITV's late-night soccer archive series with a humorous twist.

Note. An hour-long compilation of the best moments from the programmes to date was aired by London-area ITV on 2 August 1996 as *Wot A Palaver – The Best Of In Bed With Medinner*. An all-new series was planned for early 1998.

In For A Penny

UK · ITV (LWT) · SITCOM

6 × 30 mins · colour
7 July–12 Aug 1972 · Fri 8.30pm then Sat mostly 5.15pm

MAIN CAST
Dan · Bob Todd	
The Sergeant · · · · · · · · · · · · · Jack Woolgar	
Ali · · · · · · · · · · · · · · · · · · Kevork Malikyan	
Councillor Bundy · · · · · · · · · · · · · Ivor Salter	

CREDITS
writers John Hawkesworth/John Whitney · *producers* Mark Stuart (3), Philip Casson (3)

Best known for his work with Benny Hill, *In For A Penny* was the first starring role for Bob Todd, one of TV comedy's most frequently seen sidemen. Sadly, it was one of the worst series ever made. The title says it all – Todd played the role of Dan (yes, as in 'Dan, Dan, the lavatory man') – and the series was flushed through with toilet humour and WC jokes. Worse, in common with a number of other early 1970s ITV comedies, there were plenty of off-colour jokes, with Ali, the Pakistani, being the butt of most.

For the record, the large Victorian-style public convenience in question was situated in the basement of the local Town Hall, and Dan had worked there for 25 years and was fastidious at his job: the toilets were spotless. But he enjoyed a love–hate relationship with the series' three regulars: Ali, a shifty character known as the Sergeant, and

Councillor Bundy. One way or another, this was real bog-standard fare.

In Loving Memory

UK · ITV (YORKSHIRE · *THAMES) · SITCOM

37 × 30 mins (1 × b/w, 36 × colour)
*Pilot (b/w) 4 Nov 1969 · Tue 8.30pm
Series One (7) 21 May–2 July 1979 · Mon mostly 8pm
Series Two (7) 27 Oct–8 Dec 1980 · Mon 8pm
Series Three (7) 12 Oct–23 Nov 1982 · Tue 8.30pm
Special · 24 Dec 1982 · Fri 8pm
Series Four (7) 28 Nov 1983–6 Feb 1984 · Mon 8pm
Series Five (7) 13 Feb–27 Mar 1986 · Thu 9pm

MAIN CAST
Ivy Unsworth · · · · · · Marjorie Rhodes (pilot);	
· · · · · · · · · · · · · · · · · · Thora Hird (series)	
Billy Henshaw · · · · · · · · · Christopher Beeny	
Harold Henshaw · · · · · Harold Goodwin (pilot)	
Ernie Hadfield · · · · · · · · · · · · · Colin Farrell	
Amy Jenkinson · · · Avis Bunnage (series 1–3)	
Mary Braithwaite/	
Henshaw · · · · · Sherrie Hewson (series 4–5)	

OTHER APPEARANCES
Jeremiah Unsworth · Edward Chapman (pilot); · · · · Freddie Jones (first 1979 episode only)
Flo Riley · · · · · · · · Rose Power (series 1 & 4)
Hilda Pardoe · · Liz Smith (series 3 & special)

CREDITS
writer Dick Sharples · *director/producer* Ronnie Baxter

Set, of all places, in an undertaker's business, *In Loving Memory* was a gentle comedy that proved popular over some 17 years. The original transmission was a single-episode pilot, produced by Thames in 1969. Ten years later, utilising the same writer/producer team of Dick Sharples and Ronnie Baxter, Yorkshire turned it into a full series, the first of five.

Unusually, the mainstay of the burial business in question, Jeremiah Unsworth, was killed off in the opening episode, meaning that neither Edward Chapman (who played this role in the pilot) nor Freddie Jones (the series) was seen again. Attention actually focused on the late Jeremiah's wife Ivy (the great Thora Hird in the series) and their gormless 28-year-old nephew Billy (Christopher Beeny), who carried on the 50-year-old funeral concern – which, being accident-prone, they undertook with monumental problems.

The series was set in the fictitious Lancashire mill town of Oldshaw (location shooting actually took place in Luddenden, Yorkshire), beginning in the year 1929 and moving into the 1930s, a period chosen by author Dick Sharples because this was when funeral parlours were on the cusp of switching from horse-drawn hearses to mechanisation. After experiencing girlfriend trouble throughout the run, Billy finally married at the start of the final series – although, in true sitcom style, the other main character, Ivy, insisted on going along on the honeymoon. (Billy's bride was played by Sherrie Hewson, who had filled the role of a different girlfriend in the first series.) Richard Wilson, then largely unknown, also popped up in two different episodes in two different guises.

Dick Sharples got the idea for his creation in a pub, upon hearing an undertaker's tale about a hearse that, after hitting a pothole, shed its coffin on to the street. Similar problems beset Ivy and Billy in most episodes.

In Sickness And In Health

see *Till Death Us Do Part*

In Stitches With Daphne Doesgood

UK · BBC · SKETCH

1 × 30 mins · colour
22 Oct 1997 · BBC2 Wed 11.15pm

MAIN CAST
Daphne Doesgood · · · · · · · · · · · · · Ali Briggs
Monica Smith · · · · · · · · · · · Mandy Colleran
WITH
Spike Breakwell
Stephen Caro
Alison Goldie
Pamela Mungroo
Liam O'Carroll
Caroline Parker
Mandy Redvers Higgins
Peter White

CREDITS
writers Spike Breakwell, Michael Hempstead, Mandy Redvers Higgins, Betty Morris, Maggie Woolley, Max Zadow · *director/producer* Elspeth Morrison

An entertaining sketch comedy programme made by the BBC's Disability Programmes Unit and linked by the character Daphne Doesgood (created by Mandy Redvers Higgins) who has no physical disabilities (although the actress who plays her, Ali Briggs, does). A spoof agony aunt, Doesgood is like every disabled persons' worst nightmare – she considers herself well-informed about disabled people and thinks that she knows best how to help them and give them what they want ('remember, whatever your emotional hurdle, I'll support you like the very best girdle,' she insists), whereas her attitudes towards what she calls 'unfortunates' are patronising and insensitive. Doesgood first appeared on TV in a number of short segments in the BBC2 series *From The Edge*, programmes made by and for the disabled.

In this one-off special, screened in the season *Over The Edge*, Daphne Doesgood

was joined by – and did her best to ignore – her disabled co-presenter Monica, who was more than capable of taking care of herself. The sketches they linked included a blind version of *The X-Files*, called *The Y-Files*; spoof news reports of a plan to move all wheelchair-users to the Netherlands, where they could enjoy the flat terrain; a doctor who advocated euthanasia for people with red hair; an agency that rented out disabled people to celebrities in order to help stars' public profiles; and a documentary that spoofed so many disabled TV programmes by focusing on a child who, tragically, was born 'perfectly normal'.

See also *The Alphabet Soup Show* and *Whose Diary Is It Anyway?*

In The Barber's Chair

see *Percy Ponsonby*

Incident On The Line

UK · C4 (REGENT PRODUCTIONS) · SITCOM

1 × 60 mins · colour
2 Mar 1988 · Wed 10.30pm

MAIN CAST
George · · · · · · · · · · · · · · · · Warren Mitchell
Zina · · · · · · · · · · · · · · · · · Alexandra Pigg
Miles · · · · · · · · · · · · · · · · · Trevor Laird
David · · · · · · · · · · · · · · · · Daniel Mitchell
Debbie · · · · · · · · · · · · · · · · Pamela Keevil

CREDITS
writer Alistair Beaton · *director/producer* William G Stewart

The fifth of six comedy playlets screened under the generic title *Tickets For The Titanic*. Warren Mitchell starred as George, a man for whom everything ought to be going right, but for whom it's actually all going wrong. Attempting suicide, he is interrupted by a bizarre woman, Zina (played by Alexandra Pigg, co-star of the movie *Letter To Brezhnev*), who introduces him to her life of crime and anti-authoritarianism, wherein George discovers latent aspects of his character. Warren Mitchell's real-life son, Daniel, was also among the cast.

The Incredible Adventures Of Professor Branestawm

UK · ITV (THAMES) · CHILDREN'S SITCOM

7 × 30 mins · b/w
10 July–28 Aug 1969 · Thu 5.20pm

MAIN CAST
Professor Branestawm · · · · · · · Jack Woolgar
Colonel Dedshott · · · · · Paul Whitsun-Jones
Mrs Flittersnoop · · · · · · · · · · · Freda Dowie

CREDITS
creator Norman Hunter · *adapter/writer* Trevor Preston · *director/producer* Pamela Lonsdale

To date, this Thames series represents the only British TV adaptation of Norman Hunter's remarkable Professor Branestawm character – and it was a good attempt too. *The Incredible Adventures Of Professor Branestawm*, first published in November 1933, is a wonderful work of invention by its author, with drawings to match by Heath Robinson. (Ironically, although the TV series was on the commercial channel, the original book was dedicated to a radio announcer at the BBC.) Hunter created surreal stories of crazy inventions, written in a marvellously bizarre vocabulary, with the Professor portrayed as a happy loony, creating odd contraptions to help the community of Pagwell, where he lives. They always go wrong, but he remains blissfully happy, working with his housekeeper Mrs Flittersnoop and his best friend – Colonel Dedshott, of the Catapult Cavaliers. Hunter went on to write several Branestawm sequels; indeed, this TV series was based on stories in both the original 1933 book and its successor, *Professor Branestawm's Treasure Hunt*, published in 1937.

The Incredible Mr Tanner

UK · ITV (THAMES) · SITCOM

6 × 30 mins · colour
19 Feb–26 Mar 1981 · Thu 8pm

MAIN CAST
Ernest Tanner · · · · · · · · · · · · Brian Murphy
Sidney Pratt · · · · · · · · · · · · · Roy Kinnear
Archie · · · · · · · · · · · · · · · · Tony Melody
Prudence · · · · · · · · · · · · · · Rosie Collins

CREDITS
writers Johnnie Mortimer/Brian Cooke · *director/producer* Peter Frazer-Jones

Ten years after LWT's **Kindly Leave The Kerb**, and 13 after first airing their idea in an episode of **The Ronnie Barker Playhouse**, writers Mortimer and Cooke revived the characters of hapless street-entertaining escapologist Ernest Tanner and his hat-passing assistant Sidney for another stroll along the pavements. Indeed, some of the shows re-worked the old scripts. Cast this time in the roles – following Ronnie Barker and Richard O'Sullivan, and Peter Butterworth and Peter Jones – were Brian Murphy and Roy Kinnear, who were long-standing friends in real life and had appeared together in the 1960 stage production *Every Man In His Humour* and the 1962 movie *Sparrows Can't Sing*. Murphy had previously appeared in Mortimer and Cooke sitcoms **Man About The House** and **George And Mildred** (as occasionally had Kinnear); indeed, it was in studio 'downtime' – following Yootha Joyce's sudden deterioration in health, leading to her death – that *The Incredible Mr Tanner* was made.

Inmates

UK · BBC · SITCOM

1 × 30 mins · colour

20 July 1992 · BBC2 Mon 7.25pm

MAIN CAST

The Director	Robert Gillespie
Mrs Prendergast	Janet Henfrey
Barney	Roger Bryan
Sparky	Nabil Shaban
Gobbo	Jag Plah
Nurse	Colum Convey
Wayne	Mik Scarlet
Irma	Joan Hooley
Mr Allan	Paddy Ward

CREDITS

writers Stuart Morris/Allan Sutherland · director Sue Longstaff · producer Sue Bysh

An unusual comedy pilot in which, according to the publicity blurb, 'the "inmates" try hard to "escape" from St Vitus, but are duly thwarted by the Director'. The words 'inmates' and 'escape' suggest that there was more to the premise than first apparent. But despite the plot convolutions, no series developed.

Innocents Abroad

UK · BBC · SKETCH

4 × 20 mins · b/w

22 July–2 Sep 1950 · fortnightly Sat 8pm

MAIN CAST

'Monsewer' Eddie Gray
Felix Felton
Geoffrey Wincott

CREDITS

writer Max Kester · producer Richard Afton

Comical observations on the subject of tourists, led by the irrepressible Eddie Gray. A brilliant juggler, and member of the famous **Crazy Gang**, Gray had once spent some time in Paris, where he invented a patter that combined cod-French with broad cockney and earned him the sobriquet 'Monsewer'. With his dotty sartorial sense, round spectacles and huge curly moustache, he created a strong visual impact on TV to go with his seemingly stream-of-conscious verbal delivery.

Inside George Webley

UK · ITV (YORKSHIRE) · SITCOM

12 × 30 mins (6 × b/w, 6 × colour)

Series One (6 × b/w) 24 Sep–29 Oct 1968 · Tue around 8.30pm

Series Two (6 × colour) 4 Feb–25 Mar 1970 · Wed mostly 10.30pm

MAIN CAST

George Meredith Webley	Roy Kinnear
Rosemary Webley	Patsy Rowlands

CREDITS

writers Keith Waterhouse/Willis Hall · directors Bill Hitchcock (series 1), David Mallet (series 2) · producers Bill Hitchcock (series 1), John Duncan (series 2)

The first of several TV sitcoms by Keith Waterhouse and Willis Hall, the partnership that turned Waterhouse's solo novel *Billy Liar* into a successful film and stage production (and, in 1973, the sitcom *Billy*).

The star of the series was that excellent British comedy actor Roy Kinnear, appearing as George Meredith Webley, a hypochondriac, crushing bore and (he thinks) man of action, the type of person everyone wants to avoid at parties, but cannot. George once bought and consumed the entire set of *Encyclopaedia Britannica* and is going to use it – he's a walking, talking expert on all matters, and he worries about *everything*. George works as a clerk at the Meanside and Beestley Savings Bank and lives in Leeds (at 23 Clement Attlee Drive on the Mahatma Gandhi Estate) with his wife Rosemary, who sometimes wonders why she didn't stay single. Viewers sympathised with her plight.

A number of guest stars appeared during the 12 episodes, among them Peter Butterworth, Julian Orchard, James Bolam, Clive Dunn, Graham Stark, Roy Hudd, Les Dawson, Hattie Jacques, Max Wall and Dandy Nichols.

Inside The Mind Of Dave Allen

see ALLEN, Dave

Inside Victor Lewis-Smith

UK · BBC · SITCOM/SKETCH

6 × 30 mins · colour

1 Nov–13 Dec 1993 · BBC2 Mon 10pm

MAIN CAST

narrator	Victor Lewis-Smith
Nurse	Annette Badland
Consultant	Nickolas Grace
Wife	Moya Brady
Taxi Driver	George Raistrick
Mr Lobley	Tim Barlow
Policeman	Roger Lloyd Pack

CREDITS

writers Victor Lewis-Smith/Paul Sparks · director/producer Richard Curson Smith

A blend of jet-black satire and close-to-the-edge comedy from the notorious Victor Lewis-Smith, a columnist and broadcaster renowned for dabbling in areas of dubious taste. *Inside Victor Lewis-Smith* was a riotous, free-wheeling trip through various genres and styles. The linking premise was that Lewis-Smith was in a coma and, bandaged head to foot, was being cared for in a sinister hospital by an overpowering nurse and a creepy consultant. To try and rouse him from the coma, a mixture of old TV programmes is pumped into his brain but, unexpectedly, Lewis-Smith has started to pump these programmes back out in a transmuted version. On the TV set beside his bed, Lewis-Smith's crazy, warped versions of TV shows spin out. This was one method to get into the sketches, which were often re-edited and re-voiced archival clips. Another linking device was a taxi which was literally *inside* Victor Lewis-Smith, driving through his organs and traversing the length and breadth of his body. The cab driver, a stereotypically verbose and opinionated individual, held an ongoing stream-of-consciousness conversation with Lewis-Smith, whom he viewed through his rear-view mirror as if Lewis-Smith was in the back seat. These strained conversations also acted as a springboard to sketches. One regular slot, *Kith And Kin*, wove stories around the supposed relationships of two people with a commonly pronounced surname – ie, Elisabeth Schwarzkopf and Norman Schwartzkopf, and Thora Hird and Douglas Hurd. This was heady stuff, often uncomfortable but undeniably watchable and refreshingly different.

Born in 1961, Lewis-Smith was a music graduate from York University who spent three years producing talk-shows on Radio 4. Even here his mischievous streak and talent for outrage was apparent: in one notable moment of inspired madness he hired the thick-eared cockney comic actor Arthur Mullard to stand in for an absent Libby Purves on the genteel discussion programme *Midweek*. After being fired from that position, Lewis-Smith contributed to Ned Sherrin's radio miscellany *Loose Ends* and began a practice of broadcasting dangerous prank telephone calls. In 1990 he got his own Radio 1 series, *Victor Lewis-Smith*, which featured his characteristic combination of spoofs, satire, sick humour and more infamous fake phone calls. Never far from controversy or censure, he was nevertheless admired for his potential and the BBC risked further complaints by giving him this TV series. His producer, Richard Curson Smith, had cut his teeth on celebratory archive programmes such as C4's *1001 Nights Of TV*, and this stood him in good stead for the archive segments of the show; he also seemed to share Lewis-Smith's love of the bizarre and sordid.

Note. Lewis-Smith often presented short TV segments looking at various aspects of the genre, often as strands within other shows. He presented a one-off BBC1 special, *Ads Infinitum*, on 19 December 1996, which took a satirical look at Christmas commercials from the past.

See also *Credible Credits*, *The Secret Life Of TV* and *TV Offal*.

Interference

UK · C4 (BRIGHT THOUGHTS) · STANDUP/SKETCH

6 × 30 mins · colour

12 Nov–17 Dec 1983 · Sat 11pm

MAIN CAST
Fiona Richmond
Jim Barclay
Martin and Nikki Beaumont
Arnold Brown
The Dialtones (Ronnie Golden, Terry MacDonald, Richie Robertson)

CREDITS
writers Arnold Brown/Jim Barclay, Ronnie Golden and other cast members · *script editor* Trevor McCallum · *director* Bryan Izzard · *producers* Neil Anthony, Bryan Izzard

Another vehicle for some of the so-labelled 'alternative' humorists who were treading the stages of the comedy clubs and fringe theatres in the early 1980s. The odd woman out in the cast was the nude model Fiona Richmond who, far from being a comic, alternative or otherwise, appeared at the start of each of these six shows attempting to present a programme entitled *A Friend On Four*. As soon as she began speaking, however, the vision suffered the interference referred to in the series' title and the viewers were hijacked by a pirate TV service, Station S (for subversive), beaming from somewhere in the Home Counties. The comics then made play of the fact that they had 23 minutes or thereabouts to do their stuff before quitting the airwaves, lest the police catch up with them. (Illegal broadcasting was a popular subject at this time: in his Radio 1 shows and TV series, Lenny Henry's DJ character Delbert Wilkins was also a pirate.)

Introducing Tony Ferrino, Who And Why? A Quest

see COOGAN, Steve

Is It Legal?

UK · ITV (HARTSWOOD FILMS FOR CARLTON) · SITCOM
14 × 30 mins · colour
Series One (7) 12 Sep–24 Oct 1995 · Tue 8.30pm
Series Two (7) 24 Oct–5 Dec 1996 · Thu 8.30pm

MAIN CAST
Bob · · · · · · · · · · · · · · · · · · · Patrick Barlow
Stella Phelps · · · · · · · · · · · Imelda Staunton
Colin Lotus · · · · · · · · · · · Richard Lumsden
Dick Spackman · · · · · · · · · · · · · Jeremy Clyde
Alison · Kate Isitt
Darren · · · · · · · · · · · · · Matthew Ashforde
Sarah · · · · · · · · · · · · · · · · Nicole Arumugam

CREDITS
writer Simon Nye · *director* Martin Dennis · *producer* Beryl Vertue

From the same writer/director/producer and company as **Men Behaving Badly**, the sitcom *Is It Legal?* won an award as Best ITV Comedy in its first year. For others, the jury deliberating Is It Really That Good? is still out. Granted, the 14 episodes screened to the

end of 1996 made for entertaining viewing, but the series was perhaps too light on laughs and too obviously laboured to be branded a great sitcom. (ITV Network Centre seemed to agree with this when, in December 1997, it rejected a third series of *Is It Legal?*, Hartswood selling it instead to C4 for screening in late 1998. The decision is identical to that made, disastrously, in 1994, when ITV rejected the third series of *Men Behaving Badly* only to see it transfer to the BBC and enjoy spectacular success. Only time will tell whether ITV has cause to regret a second time, but it seems less likely.)

Is It Legal? was set in a chaotic solicitors' office, Lotus, Spackman & Phelps, based on the High Street in Hounslow, west of London. The company is staffed by half a dozen people, whose degree of ineptitude bears no relation to their qualifications, or lack of them. The senior partners are Dick Spackman and Stella Phelps – he's a sherry-quaffing smoothie, in love with sailing but not much good at legal practice, she's thrice-married with temperamental mood swings and unpalatable personal habits (a role played by Imelda Staunton much as she played Izzy Comyn in **Up The Garden Path**). Their junior partner Colin Lotus – who consistently failed his law exams but got the position because his father transferred his partnership to him – is hopeless but doesn't let his inabilities stymie his enthusiasm or pride. Most of the action is centred on the senior clerk Bob, however, a man endowed with oh-so-British repressed emotions, who moans pathetically over his marital problems and moons pathetically over Sarah, the attractive delivery girl from the Mr Bappy sandwich company located on the ground floor of the building. The other staff are the scruffy and dense office factotum Darren, and the secretary Alison who is bored out of her wits and indolent beyond belief.

There really aren't many laughs to be had in a solicitors' office, of course, so, conveniently, little work seems to be done. Instead, the characters play out their latest problems and wind each other up by cheerfully treading on one another's sensitivities. A photocopy of Alison's bare bottom ends up in the mail of a prudish, important client; the police catch Stella drink-driving; Colin accidentally kills an aged benefactor with a paper-knife, and is tempted when a prostitute offers to pay her legal bill in kind; Bob breaks into his own house after his wife has changed the locks – these and other such situations made the comedy in the initial series, setting the tone for the second. The humour in *Is It Legal?* really came down to the interplay between the ensemble, which was the proverbial curate's egg: good – very good, even – but only in parts.

It Ain't Half Hot Mum

UK · BBC · SITCOM
56 × 30 mins · colour
Series One (8) 3 Jan–21 Feb 1974 · BBC1 Thu 8pm
Series Two (8) 2 Jan–20 Feb 1975 · BBC1 Thu 8pm
Series Three (6) 2 Jan–6 Feb 1976 · BBC1 Fri 8pm
Series Four (8) 2 Nov–28 Dec 1976 · BBC1 Tue mostly 8pm
Series Five (6) 25 Oct–29 Nov 1977 · BBC1 Tue 8pm
Series Six (7) 23 Oct–18 Dec 1978 · BBC1 Mon 6.50pm
Series Seven (6) 17 Oct–21 Nov 1980 · BBC1 Fri 7pm
Series Eight (7) 23 July–3 Sep 1981 · BBC1 Thu 8.30pm

MAIN CAST
Rangi Ram · · · · · Michael Bates (series 1–5)
Bombardier 'Solly' Solomons · · · · · · · · · · · ·
· · · · · · · · · · · · George Layton (series 1 & 2)
Battery Sergeant Major Williams · · · · · · · · · ·
· Windsor Davies
Gunner/Bombardier 'Gloria' Beaumont · · · ·
· Melvyn Hayes
Colonel Reynolds · · · · · · · · Donald Hewlett
Captain Ashwood · · · · · · · Michael Knowles
Captain/Gunner Graham · · · · · · · John Clegg
Gunner 'Lofty' Sugden · · · · · Don Estelle
Gunner Parkins · · · · · · · Christopher Mitchell
Gunner Evans · · · · · · · · · · · · · Mike Kinsey
Gunner Clark · · · · · · · · Kenneth MacDonald
Gunner Mackintosh · · · · · · · Stuart McGugan
Punka-Wallah Rumzan · · · · · · · · Babar Bhatti
· (series 1–6)
Char-Wallah Muhammed · · · · · Dino Shafeek
Ah Syn, the cook · · · · Andy Ho (series 7 & 8)

CREDITS
writers Jimmy Perry/David Croft · *directors* Bob Spiers, Ray Butt, Paul Bishop, John Kilby · *producers* David Croft (50), Graeme Muir (6)

The exploits of a Royal Artillery Concert Party – a theatrical troupe – based in India during the Second World War. Following the success of **Dad's Army**, co-creator Jimmy Perry adapted some more of his memories into another winning period-sitcom – he had been part of a Royal Artillery Concert Party in Deolali, India (the setting used in the sitcom), in 1945, and so based the episodes upon his own experiences. The characters reflected Perry's former colleagues – although, the writer indicated, the bulldog-natured Battery Sergeant Major Williams was actually less harsh than the man upon whom he was based.

Although Michael Bates, blacked-up as Rangi Ram, the anglophile Indian servant, was at the centre of most of the proceedings, the focus in most of the episodes was the antagonistic relationship between Williams and his charges. A fanatic for military procedure, fitness and *manly* men, the barking BSM positively hated his underlings, whom he considered 'a bunch of pooftahs'. They were indeed, by anyone's measure, a motley crew, a hapless bunch of lily-livered gunners (the Royal Artillery term for privates) that included Beaumont, a temperamental and somewhat feminine man who appeared on stage in drag as a sexy Hollywood-style starlet, 'Gloria'; the dense Gunner Parkins, whose use of the phrase 'It ain't half hot mum' in letters home gave the series its title; the intellectual pianist Graham; the diminutive lead singer 'Lofty' Sugden; and – in the first two series – Bombardier (the Royal Artillery version of corporal) Solomons. Williams wasn't only frustrated by his airy-fairy underlings, however: he was also far more militarily minded than his two superior officers: the vague Colonel Reynolds and his second-in-command, the chinless wonder Ashwood. Assisting Rangi Ram and the British 'soldiers' were a couple of Wallahs (chargehands), Muhammed and Rumzan.

The high-camp hi-jinks allowed for a broad music-hall-style humour to emerge, and the production had a manic energy about it, creating a wholly different atmosphere to the rather measured pace of *Dad's Army*. All the same, there were some similarities, principally the writers' dogged attempts to give most of the characters their own catchphrases. (Unlike their earlier series, however, few of them stuck this time around.) Some viewers considered that there was a racial element to the humour, with critics singling out Michael Bates in the black-face make-up as the most obvious example. Detractors claimed that, at the very least, a real Indian actor could have been cast in the part rather than a white-skinned man. Bates had a tongue-in-cheek response: he pointed out that he was born in Janshi, India, spoke Hindustani before he learned English, and, as the two genuinely brown faces in the cast actually belonged to a Pakistani and a Bangladeshi, he was in fact the only real Indian in the production! Following Bates' death in 1978, the part of Char-Wallah Muhammed was increased to maintain the balance.

By this time the vengeful, petty-minded BSM Williams was the dominant force in the show, constantly boiling over with anger at the inefficiency of his gunners. Only Parkins escaped his wrath – indeed, he was referred to by the BSM as 'lovely boy' because Williams suspected him of being his illegitimate son. But the physical contrast in size and volume between Williams (Windsor Davies) and 'Lofty' (Don Estelle) drew the biggest rewards and the two created an unlikely double-act that resulted, incredibly, in a number one hit single in 1975 with their rendition of 'Whispering Grass'.

The last episode of the series showed the team 'demobbed' and on their way home.

It Happened Next Year

UK · BBC · SKETCH

1 × 25 mins · colour

4 Oct 1996 · BBC2 Fri 12.05am

MAIN CAST

Roger Blake
Melanie Hudson
Pauline McLynn
Sally Phillips
Kim Wall
Brian Perkins (voice only)

CREDITS

writers Mark Burton/John O'Farrell, Pete Sinclair · *directors* Dominic Brigstocke, Simon Delaney · *producer* Phil Clarke

A one-off sketch show that – with its contrived interviews, mock advertisements, re-voiced footage and political satire – purported to be a news bulletin from one year in the future, October 1997. Although the team rightly predicted an incoming Labour government, most of the skits and one-liners were aimed squarely at the then current government's policies of 'Care In The Community', youth training schemes and privatisation. The recognisable voice of BBC Radio 4 newsreader Brian Perkins introduced many of the items and the on-screen anchorwoman was Pauline McLynn (the maddening housekeeper in *Father Ted*).

A neat idea, although somewhat derivative – it wasn't as funny as *Not The Nine O'Clock News* or as clever as *The Day Today*. But the cast, especially Sally Phillips, worked hard enough to convince of their comedy potential.

It Pays To Be Ignorant

UK · BBC · STANDUP/SKETCH

2 × 30 mins · b/w

3 June 1957 · Mon 7.30pm
17 June 1957 · Mon 7.30pm

MAIN CAST

Murray Kash
Michael Bentine
Kitty Bluett
Harold Berens
Corinne Grey

CREDITS

writer Talbot Rothwell · *producer* Kenneth Milne-Buckley

The British-based Canadian actor Murray Kash led an ensemble cast in these two comedy specials. Among those featured were Michael Bentine and the Australian comic actress Kitty Bluett, Ted Ray's wife in his BBC radio series *Ray's A Laugh*, running at this time.

It Takes A Worried Man

UK · ITV · *C4 (THAMES) · SITCOM

19 × 30 mins · colour

Series One (6) 27 Oct–1 Dec 1981 · Tue 8.30pm
Series Two (7) 13 Jan–24 Feb 1983 · Thu 8pm
*Series Three (6) 16 Oct–20 Nov 1983 · C4 Sun 8.45pm

MAIN CAST

Philip Roath	Peter Tilbury
Liz	Sue Holderness (series 2 & 3)
Ruth	Diana Payan
Napley	Andrew Tourell
Simon	Nicholas Le Prevost
The Old Man	Christopher Benjamin
Lillian	Angela Down (series 1)

CREDITS

creator Peter Tilbury · *writers* Peter Tilbury (14), Peter Tilbury/Colin Bostock-Smith (1), Colin Bostock-Smith (2), Barry Pilton (2), Bernard McKenna (1) · *directors/producers* Anthony Parker (series 1 & 2), Douglas Argent (series 3)

Written by and starring **Shelley** creator/author Peter Tilbury, *It Takes A Worried Man* revealed the life of Philip Roath, an indecisive 35-year-old insurance salesman whose wife Ellen has walked out, leaving him confused and saddled with a plethora of self-debilitating thoughts. He worries that his hair and gums are receding, and his office colleagues – among them the neurotic Old Man and Napley – do not help one little bit. The depressive Roath is going through life with a perpetually low morale, seeing the worst in every situation. To help, he talks to himself and also, perhaps (or perhaps not) of greater value, to Simon, his nervous psychiatrist. (Many of the episodes, indeed, were told by way of Roach recounting his recent experiences to the analyst.) Not even the arrival in his life of Liz (in series two) helps matters much, their relationship producing as many anxieties as it calms.

It'll All Be Over In Half An Hour

UK · C4 (TELEKATION INTERNATIONAL) · SKETCH

3 × 30 mins · colour

24 May–26 May 1983 · Tue–Thu around 11pm

MAIN CAST

Sue Jones-Davis
James Grout
David Hayman
Nicholas Lyndhurst
Andrew Sachs
Jonathan Dimbleby

CREDITS

writers Alistair Beaton/Jonathan Dimbleby · *director/producer* Barbara Derkow

Three sketch programmes, screened on consecutive nights, that embraced comedy and music within a broadly educational framework, and a rare excursion away from current affairs for Jonathan Dimbleby.

It'll Be Alright On The Night

UK · ITV · *C4 (LWT) · OUTTAKES COMEDY

13 editions (12 × 60 mins · 1 × 45 mins) · colour

1. 18 Sep 1977 · Sun 7.45pm
2. *It'll Be Alright On The Night 2*
   28 Oct 1979 · Sun 7.15pm
3. *It'll Be Alright On The Night 3*
   25 Dec 1981 · Fri 8.30pm
4. *It'll Be Alright On The Night 4*
   11 Mar 1984 · Sun 7.15pm
*5. *It'll Be Alright Late At Night*
   11 July 1985 · Thu 11.10pm (45 mins)
6. *The Second Worst Of Alright On The Night*
   24 Nov 1985 · Sun 7.45pm
7. *It'll Be Alright On Christmas Night;*
   aka *It'll Be Alright On The Night 5*
   25 Dec 1987 · Fri 8pm
8. *It'll Be Alright On The Night 6*
   2 Dec 1990 · Sun 7.50pm
9. *It'll Be Alright On The Night 7*
   2 Jan 1993 · Sat 8.05pm
10. *The Kids From Alright On The Night*
    26 Nov 1994 · Sat 8.15pm
11. *It'll Be Alright On The Night 8*
    10 Dec 1994 · Sat 8.05pm
12. *Alright On The Night's Cockup Trip*
    12 Oct 1996 · Sat 9pm
13. *It'll Be Alright On The Night 10*
    15 Nov 1997 · Sat 9pm

PRESENTER
Denis Norden

CREDITS (PROGRAMME NUMBERS)
linking writer Denis Norden (all) · *directors* Paul Smith (1–4), Terry Kinane (5–7, 13), Keith Haley (8), Pati Marr (9), Alasdair Macmillan (10 & 11), Ian Hamilton (12) · *executive producer* Richard Drewett · *producers* Paul Smith (1–3), Paul Lewis (4–13)

A long-running series collecting together outtakes from the floor of TV cutting rooms, mostly but not exclusively British. Presented by the witty and affable Denis Norden – with his standard prop, the clipboard, as if he's just arrived in the studio from the edit suite – the programmes are phenomenally popular, regularly attracting audiences in excess of 12 million.

The public's appetite and fascination for seeing others take accidental pratfalls, or fluff their scripted lines, is ceaseless, and the result is usually a good laugh no matter the physical or mental anguish inflicted on the hapless subject – and the more famous the person made foolish, the funnier it seems. Astutely linked by Norden, *It'll Be Alright On The Night*'s collection of gaffes, most originating from ITV programming, is thus always good for a giggle. Editing-room staff at TV organisations, particularly the BBC, have long compiled tapes of the latest and biggest boo-boos for private circulation, usually at Christmas, but LWT took the step to presenting some on-screen following the success in America of series like *Bloopers* and *TV Censored Bloopers* (see footnote),

and some gatherings of wireless gaffes aired by BBC radio.

It'll Be Alright On The Night almost stopped after the second programme because Norden felt that viewers would not take to watching any more. It continued because the wishes of LWT director of programmes Michael Grade prevailed, and because the second programme won the Silver Rose at Montreux in 1980. Still, only 12 programmes had been made to the end of 1996 – each has been repeated on numerous occasions, however, giving the illusion that many more have been originated.

Some information further to the above details: *It'll Be Alright Late At Night*, featuring more adult outtakes, is the only one of the programmes to have been screened first on C4 (although it has been subsequently repeated on ITV). Rory Bremner was a studio guest in *The Second Worst Of Alright On The Night*. In *ITV Telethon '88* (30 May 1988) Denis Norden hosted a brief selection of bloopers from previous telethons, in the style of *It'll Be Alright On The Night*. ITV networked *10 Years Of Alright On The Night* on Christmas Day 1988, an hour-length compilation of the best clips from previous shows and adding a few new ones to the pile, and another compilation, *The Utterly Worst Of Alright On The Night*, shown on 10 April 1994, did likewise. *Alright On The Night's Cockup Trip*, in 1996, was the first to be presented from a location – the trio of Lake District peaks called Cockup, Little Cockup and Great Cockup. At the time of going to press, LWT was planning to celebrate the programme's 21st anniversary in 1998.

It'll Be Alright On The Night inspired the BBC to compile **Auntie's Bloomers**, and, together with the American series *Sports Bloopers*, inspired two British-made series of sports-action outtakes: the BBC's *Auntie's Sporting Bloomers* and ITV's *Oddballs*. For details of these, and *Sports Bloopers*, see **Auntie's Sporting Bloomers**.

ITV stations have also screened *Bloopers* and *TV Censored Bloopers*, the American programmes – just under an hour long and generally hosted by Dick Clark and Ed McMahon – that started the whole thing. These have been shown in Britain on different dates in different regions but usually deep into the night – in London on 4 January 1985, 24 October 1987, weekly from 15 November to 13 December 1987, 3 April 1988 and 19 June 1988.

Again, prompted by the success of *It'll Be Alright On The Night*, Norden has hosted several other LWT 'clipboard' programmes. *Denis Norden's World Of Television* (28 December 1980) presented a collection of TV oddities from around the globe; *In On The Act* (four shows, 7 April–28 April 1988) picked over the highlights of 1960s TV

variety programmes; *21 Years Of Laughter* (29 July 1989) cobbled together the choice cuts from LWT's comedy shows since 1968; *Pick Of The Pilots* (six shows, 21 July–25 August 1990) saw Norden sift through mountains of failed US TV experimental programmes; *Denis Norden's Laughter File* (22 September 1991) and *Denis Norden's 2nd Laughter File* (4 October 1997) comprised 'a collection of the hilarious pranks and stunts TV personalities play on each other'; *Laughter By Royal Command* (13 November 1993) compiled highlights from the comic acts at the televised *Royal Variety Shows*, as did *A Right Royal Song And Dance* (21 September 1996); and *40 Years Of ITV Laughter* (23 September, 4 November and 18 November 1995) gathered together humorous highlights from the vaults of commercial TV. For Thames, Norden compiled … *With Hilarious Consequences*, a celebration of the company's sitcom output, screened by ITV on 27 December 1988.

It's A Hudd Hudd World

see HUDD, Roy

It's A Living

see JEWEL, Jimmy and Ben Warriss

It's A Mad World, World, World, World

UK · BBC (POZZITIVE PRODUCTIONS) · SKETCH

1 × 30 mins · colour

25 May 1993 · BBC2 Tue 9pm

MAIN CAST
Caroline Aherne
Tim De Jongh
Alistair McGowan
William Vandyck
Flip Webster

CREDITS
writers cast · *director* Geoff Posner · *producer* David Tyler

A one-off sketch-show loosely based on the 1990–91 BBC Radio 4 series *And Now, In Colour* … that starred the Throbbs, a four-piece Cambridge revue group (comprising Tim Firth, Tim De Jongh, Michael Rutger and William Vandyck). Subjects included the weirdest snooker match ever played, and the real story of the invention of earthquakes. Screened under the *Comic Asides* banner, the programme obviously derived its title from the famously epic 1963 US comedy movie *It's A Mad, Mad, Mad, Mad World*.

It's A Square World

see BENTINE, Michael

It's All In Life

UK · ITV (ATV) · STANDUP

8 × 30 mins · colour

Pilot · 8 Aug 1972 · Tue 10.30pm

*One Series (7) 5 Jan–16 Feb 1973 · Fri 7.30pm

MAIN CAST
Al Read

CREDITS
writer Ronnie Taylor · *producer* Les Chatfield

Almost ten years after his previous ITV series (*Life And Al Read*), northern comic Al Read made a return with much the same recipe as before: philosophising about the British way of life – the pub, foreign holidays, 'teaching the wife to drive' and so on. Long-time associate Ronnie Taylor wrote the programmes.

*Note. These dates represent the broadcast dates in *most* ITV regions. In the London area the final two programmes – 9 and 16 February 1973 – did not go out until 1 and 8 July of that year.

See also *Al Read Says What A Life!*

It's Awfully Bad For Your Eyes, Darling …

UK · BBC · SITCOM

7 × 30 mins · colour

Pilot · 15 Apr 1971 · BBC1 Thu 7.45pm

One series (6) 18 Nov–30 Dec 1971 · BBC1 Thu 8pm

MAIN CAST
Gillian Page-Wood ('Pudding') · · · · Jane Carr
Virginia Walker · · · · · · · · · · Anna Palk (pilot);
· · · · · · · · · · · · · · · · Jennifer Croxton (series)
Samantha Ryder-Ross · · · · · · Joanna Lumley
Clover Mason · · · · · · · · · · · Elizabeth Knight
· (series only)
Bobby Dutton · · · · · · · · · · · · · Jeremy Lloyd

CREDITS
creator Jilly Cooper · *writers* Jilly Cooper/ Christopher Bond · *producers* John Howard Davies (pilot), Leon Thau (series)

A flat-share sitcom that aired as a pilot in *Comedy Playhouse* and then graduated to a full series. The original idea and first script drafts were Jilly Cooper's – representing her first TV work – and she then collaborated with Christopher Bond to knock the words into sitcom shape.

In the pilot episode there were just the three trendy young women sharing the London apartment but this was expanded to four for the series. Its premise differed greatly from *The Liver Birds*, principally because the women here were from wealthy backgrounds and had accents and desires to match – 'Pudding' was the sensible one, Clover the scatty one, Virginia the posh one and Samantha the sexy one. Although from well-to-do backgrounds, the quartet shared similar

problems to all sitcom singles – lack of rent money, a dearth of suitable dates, interference from parents and conflict among themselves. A spicy edge was added by Samantha's habit of unselfconsciously wandering around the flat semi-clothed or just in underwear – actress Joanna Lumley picking up some of the useful comedy experience that, 20 years later, she brought to *Absolutely Fabulous*.

It's Charlie Williams

UK · ITV (GRANADA) · STANDUP

2 × 45 mins · colour

22 July 1972 · Sat 6.15pm

22 Dec 1972 · Fri 10.30pm

MAIN CAST
Charlie Williams

CREDITS
director Peter Walker · *producer* Johnny Hamp

One of the leading lights of *The Comedians*, the likeable black Yorkshireman had a big year in 1972: he was the subject of *This Is Your Life*, made a royal gala appearance, performed a six-month season at the London Palladium and had these two TV shows of his own.

See also *The Charlie Williams Show*.

It's Garry Shandling's Show

USA · SHOWTIME · SITCOM

72 × 30 mins · colour

US dates: 10 Sep 1986–8 June 1990

UK dates: 5 July 1987–15 Apr 1990 (29 episodes) BBC2 Sun 6.45pm then Thu 10.10pm then Tue 10.25pm

MAIN CAST
Garry Shandling · · · · · · · · · · · · · · · himself
Ruth Shandling · · · · · · · · · · · Barbara Cason
Nancy Bancroft · · · · · · · · · · · · · Molly Cheek
Pete Schumaker · · · · · · · · · · · Michael Tucci
Jackie Schumaker · · · · · · Bernadette Birkett
Grant Schumaker · · · · · · · · · · · Scott Nemes
Leonard Smith · · · · · · · · · · · · · Paul Willson
Phoebe Bass · · · Jessica Harper (from 1989)
Ian · · · · · · · · · · · · Ian Buchanan (from 1989)

CREDITS
creators Garry Shandling/Alan Zweibel · *writers* Garry Shandling/Alan Zweibel and others · *director* Alan Rafkin and others · *producers* Bernie Brillstein, Brad Grey, Vic Kaplan, Alan Zweibel

In the early 1980s the landscape of US broadcasting changed dramatically, with the growth in popularity of cable channels such as Home Box Office (HBO). (Later, an even bigger change occurred when Rupert Murdoch's Fox 'network' – a powerful amalgam of one-time independent UHF stations – began to challenge the hitherto omnipotent triumvirate of CBS, ABC and NBC.) HBO was in the vanguard of the new picture but Viacom's Showtime, which began broadcasting in 1976, was also a major player

and it aired two new comedy series that attracted much attention. One was *Brothers*, the other *It's Garry Shandling's Show*.

Garry Shandling was a popular standup comedian whose stage persona was that of a nervy, angst-ridden, constantly baffled individual. He had often guested on network TV shows but it was with two specials for the less regulated Showtime (*Garry Shandling: Alone In Vegas* in 1984 and *The Garry Shandling Show: 25th Anniversary Show Special*) that he was able to display his true TV potential. On 7 March 1985 Shandling was a guest on NBC's *Michael Nesmith In Television Parts*, and a sketch in this programme inspired the creation of *It's Garry Shandling's Show*. Shandling and his co-writer – *Saturday Night Live* scribe Alan Zweibel – fleshed out a concept that allowed the comedian to break the conventions of sitcom by going through 'the fourth wall', to involve viewers and his studio audience in the fictional antics.

Such deconstruction had occurred before: back in the 1950s George Burns had regularly started his shows by talking to the studio audience and often made comments while following the action himself on a TV set. In the late 1970s, the BBC series *Kelly Monteith* had also toyed with this warping of the genre. But no other programme stretched the elasticity of TV formatting as far as *It's Garry Shandling's Show*. The star played a version of himself, roughly based on his stage persona, and he was supported by actors playing his mother and friends, including a close female platonic pal (Nancy) and neighbours Pete and Jackie Schumaker and their ultra-bright son, Grant. The nub of the series was that all these characters were aware they were in a sitcom and often discussed plots and occurrences, sometimes with themselves and sometimes aloud to the viewers. Shandling too regularly confided in the audience, yet somehow all the players managed to contain the sum within a fairly disciplined structure – even with the departures from conventional disciplines, and the often extreme plots, the show still worked and the viewers managed to take this new TV reality in its stride.

Perhaps the series' great strength was that it didn't underestimate its audience, and treated them as equals, introducing storylines that relied on prior knowledge of other TV shows (such as *The Fugitive*) and never stopping to explain why the characters continued as if they were real, despite the fact that they knew they were in a sitcom.

The series gained major exposure when the new Fox network picked it up in 1988 and started to screen episodes to a wider audience. Such was its success that by 1990 the Fox broadcasts were airing just a month after the original Showtime transmissions. Fox abruptly cancelled the series in March 1990 and the last few episodes aired solely on Showtime. In the UK the BBC, showing great initiative, picked up the series while it was still showing only on US cable, screening it to a national audience in Britain a year before its Fox exposure in the US.

Not content with creating and starring in one landmark sitcom, Garry Shandling went on to even greater success and acclaim with another, *The Larry Sanders Show*.

See also *Sean's Show*.

It's George

UK · C4 (GRAMPIAN) · STANDUP

1 × 60 mins · colour

1 Jan 1983 · Sat 9pm

MAIN CAST

George Duffus

CREDITS

writer George Duffus · *producer* Alan Franchi

A single special for a rising star on the Scottish scene, performing standup as himself and in local character, and music.

It's Going To Be Alright

UK · C4 (YORKSHIRE) · SITCOM

1 × 30 mins · colour

10 Dec 1984 · Mon 8.30pm

MAIN CAST

Margie Hansen · · · · · · · · · · · June Whitfield
Renata Dwyer · · · · · · · · · · · Anna Dawson
Cyril · · · · · · · · · · · · · · · Ronnie Stevens
Sarah Hansen · · · · · · · Vanessa Knox-Mawer

CREDITS

writer Peter Uney · *director/producer* Graeme Muir

A single-episode comedy depicting what happens to a woman, Margie Hansen – played by June Whitfield – after her husband has walked out on her.

It's Magic

see COOPER, Tommy

It's Marty

see FELDMAN, Marty

It's Max Boyce

see BOYCE, Max

It's Mike Reid

UK · ITV (GRANADA) · STANDUP

1 × 45 mins · colour

9 Aug 1973 · Thu 9.15pm

MAIN CAST

Mike Reid
Arthur English

Bob Todd
Nicola Pagett

CREDITS

script associate Spike Mullins · *director* Peter Walker · *producer* Johnny Hamp

A special show for the chirpy cockney from *The Comedians* (and much later the car dealer Frank Butcher in *EastEnders*). Musical guests included George Melly and the vintage British rock and roller Wee Willie Harris.

It's Mike Yarwood

see YARWOOD, Mike

It's Murder. But Is It Art?

UK · BBC · COMEDY SERIAL

6 × 30 mins · colour

23 Mar–27 Apr 1972 · BBC1 Thu 8pm

MAIN CAST

Phineas Drake · · · · · · · · · · · · · Arthur Lowe
Inspector Hook · · · · · · · · · · · Dudley Foster
Sillitoe · · · · · · · · · · · · · · Arthur Howard
Brigadier Austin Binghop · · · Richard Hurndall
Lady Skerrington-Mallett · · · · · · · · · · · · · · ·
· · · · · · · · · · · · · · · · · Ambrosine Phillpotts
Det-Sgt Watson · · · · · · · · · · Anthony Sagar
Mrs MacPherson · · · · · · · · · · · Sheila Keith

CREDITS

writers David Pursall/Jack Seddon · *producer* Graeme Muir

A comedy-thriller starring Arthur Lowe as an eccentric amateur detective, Phineas Drake, investigating the murder of a pretty blonde, Tina Kent. The police are convinced that they have their man, Brigadier Binghop, but Drake is not so sure and sets out to prove the Brigadier's innocence and bring the real killer to justice – a quest that lands him in great personal danger.

A neat idea this, with the always reliable Lowe taking a furlough from his *Dad's Army* duties to create yet another perfectly developed TV character.

It's Never Too Late

UK · C4 (YORKSHIRE) · SITCOM

1 × 30 mins · colour

3 Dec 1984 · Mon 8.30pm

MAIN CAST

Winifred Walker · · · · · · · · · · · Peggy Mount
May Priggs · · · · · · · · · · · · · · Pat Coombs
Geoffrey Wicks · · · · · · · · · · · · Hugh Lloyd
Jimmy Jackson · · · · · · · · · · · Harold Goodwin

CREDITS

writer Ian Masters · *director/producer* Graeme Muir

A one-off comedy half-hour from Yorkshire TV that reunited the stars of its series *You're Only Young Twice*. Here, Peggy Mount and Pat Coombs were pensioner sisters and members of a local bowls club.

At an event in the social club, they meet Geoffrey and Jimmy, two other players, and romance potentially enters the frame.

It's Norman

see WISDOM, Norman

It's Not Me – It's Them!

UK · BBC · SITCOM

6 × 25 mins · b/w

28 July–1 Sep 1965 · BBC2 Wed around 8.30pm

MAIN CAST

Albert Curfew · · · · · · · · · · · Donald Churchill
Mr Partridge · · · · · · · · · · · · · · Norman Bird
Lavinia · · · · · · · · · · · · · · · · · Dilys Laye

CREDITS

writer Donald Churchill · *producer* Graeme Muir

Albert Curfew's lament – which gave this series its title – referred to his inability to hold down a job for any length of time; although a conscientious worker, he was inexplicably prone to easy dismissal.

The series was created by the actor/writer Donald Churchill, who based the character on a friend; he also played the lead role. Liz Fraser, Bill Kerr and young actress Kate O'Mara appeared in one episode apiece.

It's Only Me – Whoever I Am

UK · BBC · SITCOM

1 × 30 mins · colour

28 May 1974 · BBC1 Tue 8.30pm

MAIN CAST

Quentin · · · · · · · · · · · · · · · · David Jason
Blanche · · · · · · · · · · · · · · · Patricia Hayes
Auntie Vee · · · · · · · · · · · · · · Daphne Heard
Maurice · · · · · · · · · · · · · · Paul Greenwood
Brenda · · · · · · · · · · · · · · Christine Ozanne

CREDITS

writer Roy Clarke · *producer* Sydney Lotterby

Yet another script from the prolific Roy Clarke. This *Comedy Playhouse* pilot cast David Jason as Quentin, a Rochdale lad not a million miles away in personality from his Granville character in *Open All Hours* (also written by Clarke). Quentin is an impressionable young man who is swamped by his well-meaning mother (played by Patricia Hayes) and finds it difficult to be his own man. No series developed.

It's Saturday Night

see RAY, Ted

It's Tarbuck

see TARBUCK, Jimmy

It's Ulrika!

UK · BBC (CHANNEL X) · SKETCH

1 × 30 mins · colour

25 Aug 1997 · BBC2 Mon 10.15pm

MAIN CAST
Ulrika Jonsson

WITH
Laura Brattan
Steve Burge
Charlie Higson
Matt Lucas
Jim Moir (Vic Reeves)
Bob Mortimer
Steve Brody
Rhys Thomas
David Walliams

CREDITS
writers/producers Vic Reeves/Bob Mortimer ·
additional material Steve Burge, Rhys Thomas ·
director John Birkin · *executive producer* Alan
Marke

When she first appeared on television, the TV-am weather-presenter Ulrika Jonsson seemed destined to follow the path taken by many pretty, telegenic personalities who had enjoyed a short career in TV without seeming to possess much in the way of talent (or meteorological qualifications). Her following TV engagement, as one of the hosts of *The Gladiators*, also seemed to be only another temporary halt on the inevitable road back from whence she had arrived. But the Swedish-born Jonsson confounded her critics – and showed she was willing to take risks and poke fun at her own image – when she appeared in a segment of *At Home With Vic And Bob* (see **Reeves And Mortimer**) as a contestant in a surreal game-show. When that idea was expanded to become a fully fledged and highly successful series (*Shooting Stars*, BBC2 from 22 September 1995), Jonsson was installed as a regular team captain, cheerfully enduring many weeks of slapstick humiliation, displaying a dark sense of humour and happy to go to extraordinary lengths for a laugh. The series sometimes featured short sketch-like sequences and Jonsson held her own in this area too. So pleased were they with their comedy protégée, that Reeves and Mortimer decided to write a show for her, offering Jonsson the chance to show even more of her unexpected talents.

It's Ulrika! showed Jonsson impersonating celebrities (Cher, Dusty Springfield, Phil Collins, Anne Robinson, Anthea Turner and others) and appearing in a number of sketches, helped by a strong supporting cast – Reeves and Mortimer figuring that, although game, she would be hard pushed to carry a show without such help. Although in true trooper fashion, she threw herself into the parts, she was not entirely successful, and the whole production would have been unexceptional and forgettable were it not for the unmistakable imprint of producers/

writers Reeves and Mortimer turning what started out as traditional sketches into something altogether more weird. Their surreal vision hung over the show so strongly that at times it seemed that she was merely a front for their ideas, rather than a star in her own right. Perhaps this was understandable, however: Jonsson had come a long way in a hort time and much of her new-found success was down to their patronage. To the delight of the studio audience, she also demonstrated a particular skill for which she had gained something of a reputation: her ability to sink a pint of beer in under four seconds, a feat that seemed all the more impressive considering her svelte model-like build.

It's Young Again

UK · ITV (GRANADA) · STANDUP

5 × 30 mins · b/w

4 July–1 Aug 1963 · Thu 7.30pm

MAIN CAST
Alan Young

CREDITS
directors Milo Lewis (4), Eric Fawcett (1)

After his Associated-Rediffusion series in 1958 (*Alan Young*), the North Shields-born comedian returned to North America – to where his family had emigrated when he was 13 – and continued to build his career on US TV. Granada then tempted him back to England in 1963 with the offer of seven new programmes to be made at the company's studio in Chelsea, London. Only five were screened, however.

It's Your Move   1

see SYKES, Eric

It's Your Move   2

USA · NBC (EMBASSY TELEVISION) · SITCOM

18 × 30 mins · colour

US dates: 26 Sep 1984–10 Aug 1985
UK dates: 14 Feb–26 Dec 1986 (18 episodes)
BBC1 mostly Mon 7.35pm

MAIN CAST

Matthew Burton	Jason Bateman
Eileen Burton	Caren Kaye
Julie Burton	Tricia Cast
Norman Lamb	David Garrison
Lou Donatelli	Ernie Sabella
Eli	Adam Sadowsky

CREDITS
writers Ron Leavitt/Michael G Moye, Fred Fox Jr, Herb Kenwith, Katherine D Green, Marcy Vosburgh, Michael J Ahnemann, Pamela R Norris, Sandy Sprung · *directors* Peter Bonerz and others · *producers* Ron Leavitt/Michael G Moye

A bland US sitcom starring Jason Bateman (brother of *Family Ties* actress Justine Bateman) as Matthew Burton, a 14-year-old

fast-talking con artist, who meets his match when Norman Lamb, a thirty-something fast-talking con artist, moves into the apartment opposite and starts to make a play for Matthew's widowed mother, Eileen. Bluff and double-bluff was the name of the game, but the slick plotting couldn't compensate for the shallow characterisation of the leads, which meant, as far as British viewers were concerned, that when confronted by *It's Your Move*, the smartest move was to flip channels.

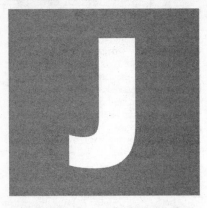

Jack And Jeremy's Police 4

Jack And Jeremy's Real Lives

see DEE, Jack

Jack Benny ...   [various shows]

see BENNY, Jack

Jack Dee ...   [various shows]

see DEE, Jack

Jack Of Diamonds

see EMERY, Dick

The Jackie Gleason Show

see *The Honeymooners* and The Montreux Festival

Jackie Mason At The London Palladium

UK · BBC · STANDUP

1 × 60 mins · colour

27 Dec 1996 · BBC1 Fri 12 midnight

MAIN CAST

Jackie Mason

CREDITS

writer Jackie Mason · *director* Paul Jackson

The quintessential Jewish night-club comedian Jackie Mason was born Yacov Moshe Maza, of Russian ancestry, in Wisconsin on 9 June 1930. His father was an Orthodox rabbi and Yacov, after gaining a BA from City College in New York, also studied for the rabbinate. When he was 25 he was given a congregation but found reaching the people difficult until he broke the ice by telling a few jokes. Such was the success of his quips that an agent tried to get him interested in performing at clubs, something he could not accept while his father was alive. Following his father's

death in 1957, he started performing under the name Jacob Masler, soon attracting TV offers (his first appearance was on *The Steve Allen Show*) and becoming famous under a newly assumed stage name, Jackie Mason. His act incorporated all manner of Jewish jokes and his linking patter covered all aspects of the Jewish experience. Working hard and sticking rigidly to his style, Mason – for whom the term 'gravel-voiced' could have been invented – gradually built up a huge following.

Although highly regarded among the British Jewish community – not that his routines are without criticism of Judaica or its people – Mason's humour reached a wider audience following a show-stopping performance in the 1989 *Royal Variety Show*. The following year he was the subject of LWT's *An Audience With ...* and in both 1991 and 1996 repeated his *Royal Variety* success. In this BBC show, taped at the London Palladium, Mason presented mostly new material, although the subject matter, his effortless patter and delivery style were as recognisable and fine as ever.

Jackson Pace: The Great Years

UK · ITV (GRANADA) · CHILDREN'S SITCOM

6 × 30 mins · colour

11 Oct–15 Nov 1990 · Thu 4.40pm

MAIN CAST

Jackson Pace · · · · · · · · · · · · · · · Keith Allen
Roger Whibley · · · · · · · · · · · Daniel Peacock
Ryveeta Tusk · · · · · · · · · · · · Josie Lawrence
Lord Taggon · · · · · · · · · · · · · Hugh Paddick
Princess Layme · · · · · · · · · · · Cory Pulman
Lord Layta · · · · · · · · · · · · · Paul B Davies
Filo · · · · · · · · · · · · · · · · · Gian Sammarco
Daken · · · · · · · · · · · · · · · · Nic D'Avirro

CREDITS

writer Daniel Peacock · *director* Alistair Clark · *producer* Mark Robson

A children's comedy series with a vague 'alternative' air (writer/co-star Peacock and star Allen had **Comic Strip Presents ...** stripes) about a Great British explorer. In fact, Peacock wrote the series for adult consumption, and had to delete the rude bits so that it could be presented to younger viewers.

The series was an *Indiana Jones*-style comedy. Jackson Pace and his hardy assistant Roger Whibley discover an ancient casket close to the Earth's core, inside which is a parchment detailing the location of the treasure of Kinard and of the three Keystones that unlock the gates of a mysterious temple deep in the jungle of Ja Ja Bar, where the treasure lies. The six episodes depicted their stirring deeds of global derring-do as they raced to grab the booty and keep one step ahead of the evil Daken.

Jane

UK · BBC · SITCOM

10 × 10 mins · colour

Series One (5) 2 Aug–6 Aug 1982 · BBC2 daily Mon–Fri 9pm

Series Two (5) *Jane In The Desert* 3 Sep–7 Sep 1984 · BBC2 daily Mon–Fri 9pm

MAIN CAST

Jane · · · · · · · · · · · · · · · · · · · Glynis Barber
Tombs · · · · · · · · · · · · · · · · · · · Max Wall
The Colonel · · · · · · · · Robin Bailey (series 1)
Lola · · · · · · · · Suzanne Danielle (series 1)
Commander L · · · · Frank Thornton (series 2)
Casper Cutler · · · · · · · · John Bird (series 2)
Professor Crankshaft · · · · · · · · · · Bob Todd
Bob Danvers-Walker (voice only)

CREDITS

creator Norman Pett · *writer* Mervyn Haisman · *director* Andrew Gosling · *producer* Ian Keill

Jane, the comic-strip heroine with the habit of losing most of her clothes most of the time, was created in 1932 by the artist Norman Pett for a *Daily Mirror* comic-strip originally entitled *Jane's Journal – Or The Diary Of A Bright Young Thing*. Enormously popular as a morale-boosting fillip during the Second World War, the strip gave rise to a successful, fairly risqué stage-play in the 1940s that starred Pett's life-model for Jane, Christabel Leighton-Porter. She also reprised the role for a film version, *The Adventures Of Jane* (1949, director Edward G Whiting).

The *Daily Mirror* strip finished in 1959 and things went quiet for Jane until the 1970s when Lesley Duff portrayed the pin-up in the musical stage-play *Happy As A Sandbag*. Then, a few years later, came this intriguing 1980s TV revival, which starred Glynis Barber as the skirt-shedding adventuress, mixed up with sinister spies and nasty Nazis, and giving her all for the British war effort. The director Andrew Gosling had conceived the idea of reviving Jane after he picked up a copy of a book containing the reprinted strips, and he tried to do something truly groundbreaking with the series – using Chroma Key technology and other state-of-the-art visual effects, he made the series semi-animated with the real actors appearing in front of comic-strip backgrounds.

Of the remaining cast, Robin Bailey was suitably stiff-upper-lipped as the Colonel, Max Wall grotesquely amusing as the funereal butler at Ghastly Grange, and Glynis Barber alluring as Jane, although it was difficult to be anything other than two-dimensional given the limitations of the technique. The series' music was provided by Neil Innes (who had worked with producer Ian Keill on **Rutland Weekend Television** and his own series, *The Innes Book Of Records*).

The promised glimpses of stockings and suspenders, and the silk undergarments that

Jane always seemed to wear despite wartime rationing, may have been an attraction for some viewers but the novelty of the technique and the brevity of the episodes prevented *Jane* from being little more than an interesting curio. However, this revival did prompt another movie based on the character, *Jane And The Lost City Of Gold* (1987, director Terry Marcel), which also featured Robin Bailey, and cast Kirsten Hughes in the lead role.

Note. The first series was compiled into a single programme for a repeat on 1 January 1983.

Janet And Company

UK · ITV (THAMES) · SKETCH/STANDUP
12 × 30 mins · colour
Special · 25 Dec 1980 · Tue 10pm
Series One (5) 17 Feb–17 Mar 1981 · Tue 8.30pm
*Series Two (6) 8 Apr–13 May 1982 · Thu 9pm ; 30 June & 7 July 1982 · Wed 10.30pm then 10.35pm

MAIN CAST
Janet Brown

CREDITS
writers Eric Davidson (12), Laurie Rowley (12), David Renwick (5), Chris Miller (5), Andy Hamilton (2), Clifford Henry (1) · *director/producer* Keith Beckett

Following her single special *Meet Janet Brown*, the comic was given a Christmas gift of a slot in which to exercise her impressionist routines, one highlight being a Margaret Thatcher Pantomime. This in turn led to two full series of impersonations, covering everyone from Kate Bush to Zsa Zsa Gabor. Different guest stars featured with her in sketches each week.

*Note. Two editions in the second series were postponed because of emergency TV programming about the Falkland Islands conflict. Despite the loss of their topicality, the programmes were rescheduled a few weeks later.

Janet Brown

UK · BBC · STANDUP
3 × 15 mins · b/w
10 July 1953 · Fri 8.50pm
25 Sep 1953 · Fri 9.20pm
21 Oct 1955 · Fri 9pm

MAIN CAST
Janet Brown

CREDITS
producers Duncan Wood (show 1), Ronnie Taylor (show 2), Richard Gilbert (show 3)

Three short shows starring the talented comedian and impressionist Janet Brown,

presented as part of the long-running *Starlight* entertainment strand. She performed humorous songs in each programme, accompanied in the first and third by the Steve Race Trio and in the second by the Jack Martin Trio.

Jasper Carrott ...
[various shows]

see CARROTT, Jasper

Jeanne de Casalis

see *Mrs Feather*

The Jeannie Carson Show

UK · ITV (ATV) · SKETCH
1 × 60 mins · b/w
23 May 1959 · Sat 7.55pm

MAIN CAST
Jeannie Carson

CREDITS
producer Alan Tarrant

Making a brief return visit to Britain from America, where she had settled and become a star (*Hey, Jeannie!*), Scots comedian Jeannie Carson appeared in this single hour-long special screened under the *Saturday Spectacular* banner.

Jeeves And Wooster

UK · ITV (PICTURE PARTNERSHIP FOR GRANADA) · SITCOM
23 × 60 mins · colour
Series One (5) 22 Apr–20 May 1990 · Sun 8.45pm
Series Two (6) 14 Apr–19 May 1991 · Sun mostly 9.05pm
Series Three (6) 29 Mar–3 May 1992 · Sun mostly 9.05pm
Series Four (6) 16 May–20 June 1993 · Sun 9pm

MAIN CAST
Jeeves · · · · · · · · · · · · · · · · · · Stephen Fry
Bertie Wooster · · · · · · · · · · · · · Hugh Laurie
Hildebrand 'Tuppy' Glossop · · · Robert Daws
Cyril 'Barmy' Fotheringay-Phipps · · · · · · · · · ·
· · · · · · · · · · · · Adam Blackwood (series 1);
· · · · · · · · · · · · · · · Martin Clunes (series 2)
Alexander 'Oofy' Prosser · · · · · Richard Dixon
· · · · · · · · · · · · · · · · · · · (series 1, 2 & 4)
Aunt Agatha · · · Mary Wimbush (series 1–3);
· · · · · · · · · · · · · · Elizabeth Spriggs (series 4)
Aunt Dahlia · · · · · · · Brenda Bruce (series 1);
· · · · · · · · · · · · · · Vivian Pickles (series 2);
· · · · · · · · · · · Patricia Lawrence (series 3);
· · · · · · · · · · · · · Jean Heywood (series 4)
Augustus 'Gussie' Fink-Nottle · · · · · · · · · · ·
· · · · · · · · · · · Richard Garnett (series 1 & 2);
· · · · · · · · · · · · · Richard Braine (series 3 & 4)
Madeline Bassett · · · · · · · · Francesca Folan
· (series 1);

· · · · · · · · · · · · Diana Blackburn (series 2);
· · · · · · · · · · Elizabeth Morton (series 3 & 4)
Roderick Spode · · · John Turner (series 2–4)
Sir Watkyn Bassett · · · · · · · · John Woodnutt

CREDITS
creator P G Wodehouse · *adapter/writer* Clive Exton · *directors* Robert Young (series 1), Simon Langton (series 2), Ferdinand Fairfax (series 3 & 4) · *executive producer* Sally Head (series 4) · *producer* Brian Eastman

Twenty-three years after the BBC laid *The World Of Wooster* to rest, Granada TV revived P G Wodehouse's comic stories with spectacular success, casting, in a stroke of genius, comedy double-act Hugh Laurie and Stephen Fry in the roles, respectively, of gentleman and gentleman's gentleman. (For a fuller explanation of Wodehouse's characters and stories see that chronologically earlier BBC series, which had starred Ian Carmichael and Dennis Price.)

Although there was some doubt among members of the Wodehouse Society about their appropriateness for the parts, Fry and Laurie were simply perfect in the roles of unsurpassable valet Jeeves and bally ass Wooster, living in a 1920s–30s world of Hooray Henries and splendidly indomitable aunts. Both were major fans of the original books, and Fry had even written Wodehouse a letter, before the master's death in 1975, which elicited a signed photograph that remains much treasured.

Shot on film, production values were high throughout the 23 episodes and all of them were very funny. The scripts were dramatised from the Wodehouse originals by Clive Exton (who also adapted Agatha Christie's *Poirot* books for ITV), six of them being set in New York City.

See also *Blandings Castle, The Reverent Wooing Of Archibald, Ukridge, Uncle Fred Flits By, Wodehouse Playhouse* and *Mr Wodehouse Speaking*.

The Jeff Green Show

UK · ITV (LITTLE MO FILMS FOR YORKSHIRE) · STANDUP
1 × 45 mins · colour
30 Dec 1996 · Mon 11.25pm

MAIN CAST
Jeff Green

CREDITS
writer Jeff Green · *director* Tom Poole · *producers* Miles Ross/Alan Marke

A rare but welcome TV special for the good-looking and affable but sharp comedian who has remained huge in the London clubs without (yet) attaining fame beyond. Recorded at Her Majesty's Theatre in London, the programme displayed Green's characteristically shrewd eye for the absurdities of everyday life.

Jennings

UK · BBC · CHILDREN'S SITCOM

6 × 25 mins · b/w

5 Sep–10 Oct 1966 · BBC1 Mon 5.25pm

MAIN CAST

Jennings	David Schulten
Darbishire	Robert Bartlett
Atkinson	Edward McMurray
Temple	William Burleigh
Venables	Iain Burton
Mr Carter	Ian Gardiner
Mr Wilkins	John Moore

CREDITS

writer Anthony Buckeridge · *producer* Johnny Downes

A second series of *Jennings* TV episodes, produced in the BBC's Manchester studios by Johnny Downes (the creator of *Crackerjack*). David Schulten was cast in the lead role. See the following entry for further information.

Jennings At School

UK · BBC · CHILDREN'S SITCOM

10 × 30 mins · b/w

6 Sep–8 Nov 1958 · Sat mostly 5.10pm

MAIN CAST

Jennings	John Mitchell
Darbishire	Derek Needs
Atkinson	Jeremy Ward
Temple	Peter Wood
Venables	Colin Spaull
Mr Carter	Geoffrey Wincott
Mr Wilkins	Wilfred Babbage

CREDITS

writer Anthony Buckeridge · *producer* Kevin Sheldon

The lively 12-year-old schoolboy John Christopher Timothy Jennings made his first appearance on BBC radio in 1948, when Anthony Buckeridge, an established radio playwright (for adults), and former prep school master, sent in a script to be dramatised in *Children's Hour*. The reaction to the broadcast was so positive that Buckeridge was invited to write more stories about the rascally boy, leading not only to whole radio series but a veritable Jennings industry: 23 books published from 1959 to 1991 (selling more than five million copies worldwide), a stage-play and even a stage musical. And in 1958 he became a TV star. Here, as ever, the stories were set in Linbury Court, a boarding school where Jennings, his bespectacled friend Darbishire and other pupils perpetually got under the skin of the masters, in particular Mr Wilkins.

In the radio version the lead roles changed often as the child actors grew older, but the masters – Geoffrey Wincott and Wilfred Babbage – were constant throughout, and they reprised their parts for this first television production.

Jewel And Warriss

Born in Sheffield on 4 December 1909, Jimmy Jewel (real name James Marsh) was the son of a Yorkshire comedian who adopted the same stage name. The younger Jewel made his first professional appearance in show business in Huddersfield in 1919 and his London debut six years later. In 1934 he teamed with his cousin Ben Warriss – born 29 May 1909 in the same bed; on stage from age ten – to form a double-act that went on to achieve great popularity, becoming arguably the foremost comedy partnership in Britain after Chesney Allen's (first) retirement from his act with Bud Flanagan. After appearing in the 1946 *Royal Variety Show*, the pair scored big-time with their long-running BBC radio series *Up The Pole*, on air from 1947 to 1952, which – although initially set at a trading post in the Arctic circle – found the pair in hot water week after week. That series, as with the majority of their work in the numerous radio series that followed, featured them as variations of their stage personae: Jewel as the rather gormless funnier half, Warriss as the smarter straight-man who invariably came out on top.

Their act was rooted in the traditions of northern music-hall, and this served them well until the sharper, new style of comics emerged in the 1960s, at which time Jewel and Warriss began to encounter problems. It took a brave man to break the act after some 30 years, but Warriss did so in 1967, intending to run a hotel. Reasonably wealthy from his career, Jewel prepared to get pursue business interests for the rest of his working life but, soon after the split, was offered (by BBC comedy executive Frank Muir) a part in a one-off BBC sitcom (*Spanner In The Works*) and then a prestigious TV play (*Lucky For Some*, Rediffusion/ITV, 8 January 1968), and these led to the sitcoms *Nearest And Dearest*, *Thicker Than Water*, *Spring And Autumn*, Thames' acclaimed drama series *Funny Man* (23 April to 23 July 1981) and more, the comic arguably enjoying greater success in the second half of his professional life than the first, which was no mean feat. Ben Warriss, cut of a different cloth from his more outgoing cousin, went into standup comedy and hotel-entertainment compering, without great success, before heading into self-imposed retirement at Brinsworth, the home for old theatricals, and – apart from panel-game bookings and an appearance in the 1980 *Royal Variety Show*, televised by BBC1 on 23 November – made no further substantial TV appearances before his death

on 14 January 1993. Jimmy Jewel died on 3 December 1995.

Note. In *Suddenly It's Jimmy Jewel* (BBC2, 11 September 1967) the comic looked back at his career to date.

Turn It Up!

UK · BBC · STANDUP/SKETCH

4 × 60 mins · b/w

29 Sep–15 Dec 1951 · monthly Sat mostly 8.30pm

MAIN CAST

Jimmy Jewel
Ben Warriss

CREDITS

writers Jimmy Jewel, Ronnie Hanbury · *producer* Michael Mills

Having made their TV debut in variety in 1948, this was the first TV series for the *Up The Pole* stars. It drew record ratings for a TV light entertainment show at this time, further cementing the success of the Jewel and Warriss double-act.

Re-Turn It Up!

UK · BBC · STANDUP/SKETCH

8 × 60 mins · b/w

Series One (4) 21 Mar–13 June 1953 · monthly Sat mostly 9.20pm

Series Two (4) 7 Sep–5 Dec 1953 · monthly mostly Sat 9pm

MAIN CAST

Jimmy Jewel
Ben Warriss

CREDITS

creator Jimmy Jewel · *writer* Ronnie Hanbury · *producer* Michael Mills

Eight more shows of 'express entertainment', from – variously – three London venues: the Stoll Theatre, the King's Theatre in Hammersmith and the BBC's new Television Theatre. Sequels to the 1951 series.

Double Cross

UK · BBC · SITCOM

6 × 30 mins · b/w

5 Apr–10 May 1956 · Thu around 8pm

MAIN CAST

Jimmy Seymour/	
Smithers MI5	Jimmy Jewel
Ben Wait/Carstairs MI5	Ben Warriss
Betty Patterson	Jill Day

CREDITS

creator Jimmy Jewel · *writers* Sid Green/Dick Hills · *producer* Ernest Maxin

A comedy thriller starring Jewel and Warriss in dual roles: as variety artists Seymour and Wait and as MI5 officials Smithers and Carstairs. Actress and singer Jill Day, at the time under exclusive contract to the BBC, provided the glamour. Jewel and Warriss were clearly into 'comedy thrillers' for they had already broadcast one on the radio, *Jimmy And Ben*, in 1950–51.

The Jewel And Warriss Show   1

UK · BBC · STANDUP/SKETCH

1 × 60 mins · b/w

15 Sep 1956 · Sat 8pm

MAIN CAST
Jimmy Jewel
Ben Warriss

CREDITS
writer Ronnie Hanbury · *producer* Ernest Maxin

A one-off special.

The Jewel And Warriss Show   2

UK · ITV (ATV) · STANDUP/SKETCH

9 editions (5 × 60 mins · 4 × 55 mins) · b/w

30 Mar 1957 · Sat 8.30pm (60 mins)
18 Sep 1958 · Thu 9pm (60 mins)
2 Oct 1958 · Thu 9pm (60 mins)
16 Oct 1958 · Thu 9pm (60 mins)
30 Oct 1958 · Thu 9pm (60 mins)
31 Oct 1959 · Sat 8pm (55 mins)
28 Nov 1959 · Sat 8pm (55 mins)
9 Nov 1960 · Wed 8.30pm (55 mins)
30 Nov 1960 · Wed 8.30pm (55 mins)

MAIN CAST
Jimmy Jewel
Ben Warriss

CREDITS
writers not known (show 1), Sid Green/Dick Hills (shows 2–9) · *directors/producers* Bill Lyon-Shaw (show 1), Dicky Leeman (shows 2–5), Albert Locke (shows 6 & 7), Colin Clews (shows 8 & 9)

Nine starring shows on ITV for the comic duo, all with the usual quota of guests – including Peter Butterworth in four of the shows, Glenn Melvyn and Mike and Bernie Winters once apiece. (The first show was screened within the strand *Val Parnell's Saturday Spectacular*; shows 2–5 and 8–9 under *Val Parnell's Startime*; shows 6–7 as *Saturday Spectacular*.)

Note. Jewel and Warriss were the resident hosts, introducing the star variety turns, in ten editions of *Val Parnell's Startime*, screened from 31 October 1957 to 15 May 1958.

The Jewel And Warriss Scrapbook

UK · ITV (ATV) · STANDUP/SKETCH

4 × 60 mins · b/w

26 June–7 Aug 1958 · fortnightly Thu mostly 9pm

MAIN CAST
Jimmy Jewel
Ben Warriss
Aileen Cochrane

CREDITS
writers Sid Green/Dick Hills · *producer* Dicky Leeman

Jimmy and Ben with their guests and resident dancers (one of whom was future *Rowan And Martin's Laugh-In* star Judy Carne).

At Home With Jimmy And Ben

UK · ITV (ASSOCIATED-REDIFFUSION) · SITCOM

1 × 15 mins · b/w

24 Jan 1962 · Wed 9.15pm

MAIN CAST
Jimmy Jewel
Ben Warriss

CREDITS
writers Sid Green/Dick Hills · *director* Peter Croft

A one-off programme. The length was short (15 minutes) and the premise simple: having eaten and guzzled themselves through the festive season just elapsed, Jimmy and Ben had only the company of each other and of their TV set to keep them going through 1962.

It's A Living

UK · ITV (ASSOCIATED-REDIFFUSION) · SITCOM

4 × 30 mins · b/w

11 Oct–1 Nov 1962 · Thu 7.30pm

MAIN CAST
Jimmy Jewel
Ben Warriss
Lance Percival
Fanny Carby
Adrienne Poster

CREDITS
writer Fred Robinson · *director* Peter Croft

A short-run sitcom (just four episodes) that cast Jewel and Warriss as the new owners of a small general shop, believing it to be 'a little gold mine' but swiftly coming to realise that they'll have to be careful with the pennies, industrious and, yes, lawful if they want to turn in a decent living. Fanny Carby and 13-year-old Adrienne Poster (later Posta) played the roles of Warriss's wife and daughter, with Jewel as the family's lodger. Lance Percival appeared as the dodgy-dealing 'Foxy' Flint and there were cameos by, among others, Wallas Eaton, Hugh Paddick, Johnny Briggs and Arthur Brough.

The Jill Day Show

UK · BBC · SKETCH

6 × 30 mins · b/w

7 Mar–11 Apr 1957 · Thu 7.30pm then 6.45pm

MAIN CAST
Jill Day
Robert Ayres

CREDITS
writer Jill Day · *producers* Russell Turner (5), Barry Lupino (1)

A music and comedy sketch-show with a backstage setting, written by and starring Jill Day. She was popular at this time on radio and as a cabaret artist and was under exclusive contract to BBC TV, a common practice for the Corporation following the arrival of its rival broadcaster ITV.

Although adept in many areas of the business – she could sing and dance as well as act – Day admitted to *Radio Times* that she found writing this show the hardest job of all, but the most fulfilling.

Jim And The Night And The Music

UK · BBC · STANDUP

1 × 45 mins · b/w

18 Jan 1966 · BBC2 Tue 8.50pm

MAIN CAST
Jimmy Edwards
Clive Dunn

CREDITS
writers Dick Vosburgh, John Law · *producer* Graeme Muir

A *Show Of The Week* presentation highlighting the considerable musical comedy talents of the ubiquitous Jimmy Edwards.

The Jim Backus Show

USA · SYNDICATION (CNP) · SITCOM

39 × 30 mins · b/w

US dates: Sep 1960–June 1961

UK dates: 19 July 1961–9 Jan 1962 (26 episodes) ITV mostly Wed 6.15pm

MAIN CAST
John Michael 'Mike' O'Toole · · · · Jim Backus
Dora · Nita Talbot
Sidney · · · · · · · · · · · · · · · · · Bobs Watson
'Fingers' Larkin · · · · · · · · · · · Lewis Charles

CREDITS
writers various · *directors* various · *producers* Ray Singer, Dick Chevillat

Famous since 1949 as the voice of cartoon character *Mr Magoo*, and later to become a star in the flesh with his portrayal of Thurston Howell III in *Gilligan's Island*, Jim Backus starred here in his own sitcom, syndicated around the United States in 1960–61 and screened in Britain only a few months later. He was cast as Mike O'Toole, the fast-talking owner of a New York-based news-reporting company, the Headline Press Service, trying to keep his business out of financial trouble and ahead of competitors. As such, he often resorted to his former days as a journalist, going out to get the stories himself, being aided by his attractive secretary Dora, office boy Sidney and his 'supergrass' in the criminal fraternity,

'Fingers' Larkin. The series attempted to balance comedy and dramatic storylines, but rarely succeeded. In America it was also known as *Press Time* and *Hot Off The Wire*.

See also *I Married Joan.*

The Jim Davidson Show

UK · ITV (THAMES) · STANDUP/SKETCH

38 editions (26 × 30 mins · 11 × 60 mins · 1 × 45 mins) · colour

Series One (5 × 30 mins) 11 Jan–15 Feb 1979 · Thu 7.30pm

Special (30 mins) *The Jim Davidson Special* 31 Dec 1979 · Mon 7pm

Series Two (6 × 30 mins) 21 Feb–27 Mar 1980 · Thu 7.30pm

Special (30 mins) 23 Dec 1980 · Tue 8pm

Series Three (5 × 30 mins) 8 Jan–12 Feb 1981 · Thu 7.30pm

Special (30 mins) 22 Dec 1981 · Tue 7.30pm

Series Four (6 × 30 mins) 5 Jan–9 Feb 1982 · Tue 7.30pm

Special (60 mins) 29 Dec 1982 · Wed 8pm

Special (60 mins) *Jim Davidson's Special* 8 June 1983 · Wed 8pm

Special (60 mins) *Jim Davidson's Special* 28 Dec 1983 · Wed 8pm

Special (60 mins) *Jim Davidson's Special* 6 June 1984 · Wed 8pm

Special (60 mins) *Jim Davidson's Special* 6 Sep 1984 · Thu 9pm

Special (60 mins) *Jim Davidson's Falklands Special* 24 Dec 1984 · Mon 8pm

Special (60 mins) *Jim Davidson's Special* 5 June 1985 · Wed 8pm

Special (45 mins) *Jim Davidson's Special* 26 Aug 1985 · Mon 8pm

Special (60 mins) 16 July 1986 · Wed 8pm

Special (60 mins) 2 Sep 1986 · Tue 8pm

Special (60 mins) *Jim Davidson In Germany – Special* 24 Dec 1986 · Wed 8pm

Special (60 mins) *Jim Davidson Comedy Package* 8 Dec 1987 · Tue 8pm

MAIN CAST
Jim Davidson

OTHER REGULAR APPEARANCES
Tim Barrett
Bob Todd

CREDITS
writers Eric Davidson, Jackie Lynton, Johnny Hammond, Alex Shearer, Eddie Braben, Jim Davidson, Russel Lane, Wally Malston, Andrew Marshall/David Renwick, Bill Martin, Bernie Sharp, Hugh Stuckey, Ian Brown, Barry Cryer, Graham Deykin, Dave Freeman, Gareth Hale/Norman Pace, James Hendrie, Jack Higgins, Douglas Hilton, John Junkin, Trevor McCallum, Chris Miller, Johnnie Mortimer/Brian Cooke, John Muir, Terry Ravenscroft, John Revell, Andrea Solomons, Bob Young · *directors* Mark Stuart (series 1 & 3 & 1980 & 1982 specials), Stuart Hall (1979 special, series 2 & June 1985 special), Neville Green (1981 special & series 4), Dennis Kirkland (1983 & June/Sep 1984 specials), Stuart Hall (Dec 1984, Aug 1985 & Dec 1986 specials), David Bell (June & Sep 1986 specials), Royston Mayoh (1987 special) · *producers* Mark Stuart (series 1,

3 & 4 & 1980–82 specials), John Ammonds (1979 special & series 2), Dennis Kirkland (1983 & June/Sep 1984 specials), Stuart Hall (Dec 1984, Aug 1985 & Dec 1986 specials), Robert Louis (June 1985 special), David Bell (June & Sep 1986 specials), Royston Mayoh (1987 special)

Born in Blackheath, south London, on 13 December 1953, Jim Davidson broke into TV in 1976 by winning an edition of the talent-spotting show *New Faces* (ironically, he had previously flopped badly at an audition for *Opportunity Knocks*). The public soon warmed to Davidson's TV performances which, although toned down from his 'blue' stage act, hinted at the danger lurking underneath. After appearing in the ITV sketch series *What's On Next?*, Davidson took his police-mocking catchphrase 'nick-nick' and characters like his friend 'Chalky' into his first starring vehicle, launched by Thames in January 1979. Three more series and various specials were screened by ITV over the next few years, with Davidson cementing his image as a tabloid newspaper favourite by visiting 'our boys' in the Falklands and on the Rhine. *The Sun*, in particular, long felt that Davidson summed up their ethos perfectly, entertaining the troops, cracking right-wing jokes, rallying for the Conservative Party and going through a succession of tempestuous marriages ridden with drugs, drink and violence. In short, he has always been good for a story.

Jim Davidson's later TV work took him into sitcoms (*Up The Elephant And Round The Castle* and *Home James!*), variety (he hosted Thames' *Wednesday At Eight* in 1988) and highly popular game-shows – most notably the BBC1 series *Big Break* and *The Generation Game*. Additionally, on Christmas Day 1987, he hosted a compilation of TV comedy clips, *Comedy Christmas Box*, screened by ITV. (The linking script was written by Neil Shand.)

See also *Stand Up Jim Davidson.*

Jim Tavaré Pictures Presents …

UK · BBC · SITCOM

6 × 10 mins · colour

10 Jan–13 Feb 1995 · BBC2 Tue 10.20pm

MAIN CAST
Jim Tavaré

CREDITS
writers Jim Tavaré/David Dowse/Al Murray · *director* Ian Emes · *producer* Sarah Smith

It must have been an interesting moment when comedian Jim Tavaré pitched this entertaining but off-centred idea to the BBC's light entertainment department:

Jim: 'It's six dialogue-free films about a man whose girlfriend is a double-bass.'

Commissioning producer: 'Oh, not that old chestnut again …'

Nevertheless, Tavaré sold the series, and the result was a delightful oddity, beautifully filmed with a classy, big-screen look. The soundtrack comprised music and sound effects in the same style as Eric Sykes' *The Plank* and *Rhubarb Rhubarb!*, but Tavaré's comedy was more subtle and less broad than those predecessors. The comic had risen through the standup ranks, working hard at developing an act after his initial performances drew derision. He sometimes fronted a spoof kosher rock band, Guns 'n' Moses, but it was the introduction of the double-bass as a stooge in his standup act that proved to be a decisive move. Tavaré expanded his stage relationship with the instrument for the TV series, which took place in a world where such human/double-bass romances were commonplace.

Jimmy Cricket's Joke Machine

see *The Joke Machine*

Jimmy Logan

UK · ITV (ATV) · SKETCH/STANDUP

6 × 45 mins · b/w

10 Mar–14 Apr 1956 · Sat 8.15pm

MAIN CAST
Jimmy Logan

CREDITS
writer Eric Sykes · *director/producer* Bill Lyon-Shaw

Born in Glasgow on 4 April 1927, Jimmy Logan came from a famous theatrical family and was one of the few Scottish comics to make the tricky transition to stardom throughout Britain via 1950s TV. He also worked extensively on stage, building an impressive repertoire of routines, and was virtually resident during the summer season at the Alhambra Theatre in his home city. Logan's stage act included character-based sketches that came across well on TV, and his Scots accent – although broad – was not as indecipherable to English ears as many of his homeland contemporaries. Later in his career, the comedian filled out considerably, this extra bulk seeming to add an aggressive edge to his humour.

These six shows – Logan's first major TV exposure, following some six years of radio appearances in Scotland in the series *It's All Yours!* – were written for the comic by Eric Sykes and screened within ITV's *Saturday Showtime* strand.

The Jimmy Logan Show

UK · BBC · STANDUP

16 editions (13 × 45 mins · 1 × 60 mins · 1 × 50 mins · 1 × short special) · b/w

Special (50 mins) 30 Nov 1957 · Sat 8pm

Special (60 mins) 24 May 1958 · Sat 8pm

One series (12 × 45 mins) 21 Nov 1959–23 Apr 1960 · fortnightly Sat mostly 7.50pm

Short special · part of *Christmas Night With The Stars* 25 Dec 1959 · Fri 6.20pm

Special (45 mins) 14 Oct 1961 · Sat 7.15pm

MAIN CAST
Jimmy Logan

CREDITS
writers Stan Mars, Jimmy Logan (special 1), Dave Freeman, Jimmy Logan (special 2), Terry Nation/John Junkin, Stan Daniels (series eds 1–6), Terry Nation/John Junkin (series eds 7 & 8, special 3), Dick Vosburgh, Brad Ashton (series eds 9–12) · *producers* George Inns, Eddie Fraser (specials 1 & 2), Bryan Sears (series), Richard Francis (special 3), Eddie Fraser (special 4)

A long run of BBC programmes for 'Scotland's favourite comedian'. Burt Kwouk was a guest in the first special, Deryck Guyler appeared in the first two, and the third was broadcast from the Alhambra Theatre in Glasgow.

Notes. On 1 January 1963 a special edition of *The Jimmy Logan Show* aired on TV exclusively in BBC Scotland. A later series of *The Jimmy Logan Show* (BBC2, fortnightly, six editions, 26 January–20 April 1969) had a strong musical emphasis with only a few comedy sketches between numbers and so is not listed separately here.

Logan has also made many TV appearances in variety, and in documentaries such as *One Man's Lauder*, a tribute he paid to perhaps the premier Scots entertainer, Sir Harry Lauder, produced by ATV and screened on ITV on 31 December 1980.

The Jimmy Stewart Show

USA · NBC (WARNER BROS) · SITCOM

24 × 30 mins · colour

US dates: 19 Sep 1971–27 Aug 1972
UK dates: 14 Apr–2 Sep 1973 (14 episodes) ITV Sat mostly 12.15am then Sun 12.05am

MAIN CAST
Professor James K Howard · · Jimmy Stewart
Martha Howard · · · · · · · · · · · · Julie Adams
Peter Howard · · · · · · · · · · · · Jonathan Daly
Wendy Howard · · · · · · · · · · · · · Ellen Geer
Jake Howard · · · · · · · · · · · · · Kirby Furlong
Teddy Howard · · · · · · · · · · · · Dennis Larson
Dr Luther Quince · · · · · · · · · · John McGiver

CREDITS
writers various · *director/producer* Hal Kanter

Movie superstar James (Jimmy) Stewart, a major Hollywood figure since his film debut in 1935, found TV much harder going, appearing regularly in only two series – this sitcom and the drama *Hawkins*. Both were unsuccessful, particularly *The Jimmy Stewart Show*, which was launched with an understandably prolonged fanfare by NBC but soon fell in the ratings and was dropped after a single season. The star was cast as an

amiable California-based anthropology college professor, James Howard, who allows his 29-year-old son Peter – with his wife Wendy and child Jake – to move back home, *pro tempore*, after their house had been destroyed in a fire. As James and his new, young wife Martha themselves had a young child, the same age (eight) as his grandson, this caused plenty of conflict and taught the Prof plenty more than he wanted to know about the facts of life.

Fourteen episodes were screened by London-area ITV in 1973, in a post-midnight slot.

The Jimmy Tarbuck Show

see TARBUCK, Jimmy

The Jimmy Wheeler Show

UK · BBC · STANDUP

13 × 60 mins · b/w

Series One (6) 14 Apr–1 Sep 1956 · monthly Sat mostly 9pm

Series Two (7) 4 May–12 Oct 1957 · monthly Sat 8pm

MAIN CAST
Jimmy Wheeler
Thora Hird (series 1)

CREDITS
writers Talbot Rothwell/Sid Colin (series 1), John Antrobus, Alec Pleon, Ronald Tate (series 2) · *producers* Harry Carlisle (5 eds in series 1), George Inns (1 ed in series 1), Barry Lupino (series 2)

Jimmy Wheeler was born Ernest Remnant in Battersea, south London, on 16 September 1910, and chose his stage name by a combination of fate and history. The 'Jim' part he picked up from entertainer George Formby Sr, who – when summoning him for a curtain-call – nicknamed the comedian 'lucky Jim'; the 'Wheeler' came from his father's old double-act 'Wheeler and Wilson'. (Eventually, the youngster played his part in the team, playing Wheeler to his father's Wilson.)

The moustachioed Jimmy Wheeler was a dedicated comedian, working hard to get laughs, and a regular performer on stage since the age of five, in films since he was of school age, on radio since 1928 and experimental TV from 1932. The comic was a student of television who, like so many of his contemporaries, went to some lengths to formulate a style for what was proving a difficult area for comedians to crack. Wheeler decided that the answer was to keep his TV performances as close as possible to his stage act, and this seemed to work well enough, earning him two starring series and another – *Tess And Jim*, with Tessie O'Shea – in between.

Jo Brand ...   [various shows]

see BRAND, Jo

Joan And Leslie / Leslie Randall Entertains

UK · ITV (ATV · *INCORPORATED TELEVISION PROGRAMME PRODUCTIONS FOR ATV) · SITCOM

71 episodes (19 × 15 mins · 52 × 30 mins) · b/w

**Series One (19 × 15 mins) *Leslie Randall Entertains* then *Joan And Leslie* 2 Oct 1955–3 June 1956 · fortnightly Sun mostly 4.30pm then 6pm

*Series Two (38 × 30 mins) *Joan And Leslie* 17 Sep 1956–10 June 1957 · Mon 8.30pm

Series Three (14 × 30 mins) *Joan And Leslie* 16 Sep 1957–19 Mar 1958 · mostly Mon 8.30pm

MAIN CAST
Leslie Randall · · · · · · · · · · · · · · · · himself
Joan Reynolds · · · · · · · · · · · · · · · · herself
Mike Kelly · · · · · · · Harry Towb (series 2 & 3)
Mrs Henshawe · · · Noël Dyson (series 2 & 3)

CREDITS
writers Gerald Kelsey/Dick Sharples (27), John Law/Bill Craig (25), Leslie Randall (all 19 eps in series 1) · *director* Dicky Leeman (series 1) · *producers* Bill Ward (series 1), Hugh Rennie (series 1–3)

Although described at the time as 'an intimate comedy series', the stars of these programmes – real-life husband and wife partners Leslie Randall and Joan Reynolds – did not get up to anything risqué. The original premise was merely that they would introduce viewers to some of the interesting and unusual people they had met, and replay the many amusing crises that obviously occurred in their own domestic lives, like Leslie trying in vain to make breakfast in bed for Joan. (He was a man, after all. How was he expected to know his way around his own kitchen?)

Leslie was the freelance writer of a column under the name Dorothy Goodheart, while – a bit rich this, after the aforementioned kitchen episode – Joan was cast as the 'dumb belle'. That was the first series, anyway, which ran fortnightly for 15 minutes a time. (See footnote below for a further, titular complication.) The second and third series were different kettles of tepid tap water, however: these were half-hours, weekly at first and then fortnightly, with a regular supporting cast (Harry Towb and Noël Dyson as friend and charlady respectively) and new writers. The first batch of these programmes was independently produced for Lew Grade's ATV by Lew Grade's ITP, and some of them were filmed on stage at the Hackney Empire, in the East End of London. This restricted the scenario to the domestic dwelling but does not appear to have hampered its success, nor indeed the fame of the Joan and Leslie who, on the strength of the series, were signed to star in a series of one-minute washing-powder commercials titled *The Randalls And Fairy Snow* that ran on ITV for almost ten years, through the 1960s.

Notes. The first series, which began on ITV's second Sunday and ran through to the following summer, started out as *Leslie Randall Entertains* but changed its name on 8 April 1956 to *Joan And Leslie*. This new title then continued through to mid-1958 at which time, after a three-month pause, Leslie Randall and Joan Reynolds returned with a distinctly new series, ***The Randall Touch*.

From 3 October to 19 December 1969, more than ten years after *Joan And Leslie* ended on ITV, the couple made a new 12-episode series for the Seven Network in Australia, the storylines depicting Leslie's journalistic endeavours in Melbourne. Leila Blake, Neville Thurgood and Stan Penrose supported. These programmes, also titled *Joan And Leslie*, were never screened in Britain.

Joan Rivers And Friends Salute Heidi Abromowitz

USA · HBO (SHOWTIME/RIVERS-ROSENBERG PRODUCTIONS) · STANDUP

1 × 65 mins · colour

US date: 1985
UK date: 27 May 1989 · C4 Sat 10.35pm

MAIN CAST
Joan Rivers
Lynn Redgrave
Anthony Perkins
Dr Ruth Westheimer

CREDITS
writers Joan Rivers, Kenny Solms/Martha A Williamson · *director* Bruce Gowers · *executive producers* Edgar Rosenberg, Bill Sammeth · *producer* Kenny Solms

A one-off special, taped at Caesar's Palace in Las Vegas, with Rivers and some show business friends paying affectionate tribute to Heidi Abromowitz, Rivers' 'tramp' (meaning promiscuous) alter ego.

In Britain, or for those who watched it at least, the programme went some way to reaffirming Rivers' deserved place in the pantheon of female standup acts of the 20th-century, a position she had endangered here by way of an appalling six-week chat-show series on BBC2 in 1986 (10 March to 14 April), *Joan Rivers: Can We Talk?* Not that she was the only culprit: the entire production was ill-conceived, and Peter Cook's role as her witty sideman (like Ed McMahon's job as support to Johnny Carson on *The Tonight Show* in America, or indeed Rivers' role as support to Carson, only nowhere near as effective) was perhaps the worst job the great British wit ever had.

In America, Rivers' reputation remains no more unsullied than she herself would wish.

Born Joan Molinsky on 8 June 1933 in Brooklyn, New York, she made a career out of being wickedly funny, delightfully vulgar and refreshingly – brutally – frank, conduct that has redefined the role of the female comic and arguably inspired more followers than anyone else in the field.

Joanie Loves Chachi

USA · ABC (MILLER-MILKIS-BOYETT PRODUCTIONS/HENDERSON PRODUCTIONS) · SITCOM

17 × 30 mins · colour

US dates: 23 Mar–23 Dec 1982
UK dates: 21 Aug 1983–16 Feb 1986 (14 episodes) ITV Sun mostly 1.30pm

MAIN CAST
Joanie Cunningham · · · · · · · · · · Erin Moran
Charles 'Chachi' Arcola · · · · · · · · Scott Baio
Al Delvecchio · · · · · · · · · · · · · Al Molinaro
Louisa Delvecchio · · · · · · · · · Ellen Travolta
Uncle Rico · · · · · · · · · · · · · · Art Metrano
Bingo · · · · · · · · · · · · · · Robert Pierce
Mario · · · · · · · · · · · · · · · Derrel Maury
Annette · · · · · · · · · · · · Winifred Freedman

CREDITS
creator Garry Marshall · *writers* various · *producers* Garry Marshall, Thomas L Miller, Lowell Ganz, Ronny Hallin

A poor spin-off from ***Happy Days***. In that series, Joanie – the youngest of the Cunninghams – was in love with the Fonz's cousin Charles, nicknamed Chachi; ABC TV executives spotted the potential for the pair to develop within a series of their own and duly launched *Joanie Loves Chachi*.

This was the ruse. Chachi's widowed mother Louisa (played by the sister of John Travolta) gets married to the co-owner of the *Happy Days* hamburger joint Arnold's Drive-In, Al Delvecchio. They move to Chicago, where Al opens an Italian restaurant and hires a rock group to supply the live music. They're awful, so – in an effort to improve them – Chachi joins the band as a singer and summons Joanie to come from Milwaukee to do likewise. (The other members of the band are Chachi's cousins Mario and Annette and a wacky drummer named Bingo.)

The result was a confused series that seemed unable to make up its mind whether it was a lame comedy or, with Joanie and Chachi singing songs in every episode, a musical vehicle for Hollywood to produce new teenybop stars, *à la **The Monkees***. After just 17 episodes – with, remarkably, at least 27 writers contributing to the scripts – the series was cancelled. Together with Al, Joanie and Chachi returned to *Happy Days* and were married in the final episode.

Jobstoppers

see DRAKE, Charlie

The Joe Baker Show

UK · ITV (ATV) · STANDUP/SKETCH

6 × 35 mins · b/w

29 May–3 July 1965 · Sat mostly 8.25pm

MAIN CAST
Joe Baker
Shona Leslie
Gerald Harper
Geoffrey Palmer

CREDITS
writers John Warren/John Singer · *producer* Jon Scoffield

Having separated from his comedy sparring partner Jack Douglas, Joe Baker went first into the sitcom ***Fire Crackers*** and then into this sketch series, the first under his own name. Much emphasis was placed on Baker's stature as an amiable plump man – publicity material, lacking in any subtlety, called him 'a short, fat comedian' – and sketches pitted him as a chap looked down upon by all the world. The tall, leggy starlet Shona Leslie (*much taller than Baker*) appeared in every edition, and at the start of each show sensually stretched out an arm to light his cigarette. Only one series was made but Baker starred in two sitcoms in 1967, ***My Man Joe*** and ***Baker's Half-Dozen***.

Joe Longthorne Entertains

UK · ITV (THAMES) · STANDUP

1 × 30 mins · colour

26 Aug 1987 · Wed 8pm

MAIN CAST
Joe Longthorne
Kate Robbins

CREDITS
writer Roy Tuvey · *additional material* Colin Edmonds · *director/producer* Keith Beckett

The first starring show on British TV for the rising impressionist/singer Longthorne, hailing from Hull and very popular in Blackpool clubs. He made his first TV appearance in 1969, on Yorkshire TV's *Junior Showtime*, when aged 14, going on to host the series for two years before graduating some time later as a winner on the adult talent-spotting programme *Search For A Star*.

See also the following entry.

The Joe Longthorne Show

UK · ITV (CENTRAL) · STANDUP

19 editions (18 × 30 mins · 1 × 60 mins) · colour

Series One (6 × 30 mins) 7 Sep–12 Oct 1988 · Wed 8.30pm

Series Two (6 × 30 mins) 26 July–30 Aug 1989 · Wed 7pm

Special (60 mins) 25 Apr 1990 · Wed 8pm

Series Three (6 × 30 mins) 3 June–8 July 1991 · Mon 7pm

MAIN CAST
Joe Longthorne
Wayne Dobson (series 1 & 2 & special)
Lisa Maxwell (series 1)
Darryl Sivad (series 2)
Kelly Monteith (series 3)

CREDITS
writer Joe Longthorne · *directors* Nigel Lythgoe (series 1 & 2 & special), Jon Scoffield/Nigel Lythgoe (series 3) · *executive producer* Tony Wolfe · *producer* Nigel Lythgoe

Following Thames' one-off *Joe Longthorne Entertains*, and a succession of appearances in TV variety shows, Central awarded the musical comedy impressionist his own series, giving the star the chance to shine with his impersonations of, among others, Nat 'King' Cole, Luciano Pavarotti, the Pet Shop Boys, John Lennon, Frank Sinatra and, swapping sexes, Shirley Bassey, Eartha Kitt, Judy Garland and Tina Turner. Helping out were comic magician Wayne Dobson, British comedian Lisa Maxwell (series 1) and American comedians Darryl Sivad (2) and Kelly Monteith (3).

The Joe Pasquale Show

UK · ITV (LWT) · STANDUP/SKETCH

1 × 50 mins · colour
28 Dec 1996 · Sat 8pm

MAIN CAST
Joe Pasquale

CREDITS
director Paul Kirrage · *executive producer* Nigel Lythgoe · *producer* John Bartlett

A Christmas special for the squeaky-voiced 'madcap' comic; guests included Eric Sykes.

See also *He's Pasquale, I'm Walsh*.

John Browne's Body

UK · ITV (ATV) · SITCOM

7 × 30 mins · b/w
3 Apr–15 May 1969 · Thu 9pm

MAIN CAST
Virginia Browne · · · · · · · · · · · Peggy Mount
Fitzroy · · · · · · · · · · · · · · · · Naunton Wayne
French · · · · · · · · · · · · · · · · · Philip Stone
Kiki · · · · · · · · · · · · · · · · · Trisha Mortimer
Spiro · Eric Kent

CREDITS
writer Rene Basilico · *director/producer* Shaun O'Riordan

A sitcom with dramatic overtones. Virginia Browne (Peggy Mount) is a respectable and important member of staff at an insurance company when she learns that her brother John has died, leaving her his half ownership of the Fitzroy Browne detective agency. She forms an unlikely alliance with Fitzroy (played by the veteran actor Naunton Wayne) and together they carry on the business.

John Sessions ... [various shows]

see SESSIONS, John

John Wells And The Three Wise Men

UK · C4 (OPEN MEDIA PRODUCTIONS) · SATIRE

1 × 40 mins · colour
25 Dec 1988 · Sun 4.40pm

MAIN CAST
John Wells

CREDITS
writer John Wells · *director* Simon Holder · *producers* Justin Scroggie, Kathy Ceaton

A wry spin on the birth of Jesus, delivered on Christmas Day by ace satirist John Wells.

See also *Just What I Always Wanted*.

Join Jim Dale

UK · ITV (ATV) · STANDUP

6 × 30 mins · b/w
3 July–14 Aug 1969 · Thu 9pm

MAIN CAST
Jim Dale

CREDITS
writers Jim Dale/Barry Cryer · *director/producer* Dennis Vance

Born in Rothwell, Northamptonshire, on 15 August 1935, Jim Dale decided to become an entertainer at an early age. He took dancing lessons, launched a 'comedy tumbling' act and was trying to carve out a career as a standup comedian when he achieved his big break: while performing as a studio warm-up man for the BBC pop show *Six-Five Special* his looks so impressed the producers that they offered him an on-screen try-out as a singer. Thus Dale drifted into pop music, scoring four hits on the British chart in 1957–58 – including the number two single 'Be My Girl' that, for a short time, made him a teen idol – and becoming a full-time host on *Six-Five Special*. During the late 1950s and early 1960s Dale was a familiar face on TV as a singer, comedian, host and actor. In 1969 he was given his own show, *Join Jim Dale*, joined each week by a guest – Beryl Reid, Kenneth Williams, Anna Quayle, Hattie Jacques, Dame Sybil Thorndike and Roy Kinnear – to assist him with the comedy routines.

Dale went on to huge success, as compere of *Val Parnell's Sunday Night At The London Palladium*, as a National Theatre player, as the star of top-flight London and Broadway musicals and in regular film appearances, including a stint as one of the *Carry On* team.

Note. Two years before this ATV series, Dale starred in a sitcom pilot, *Mister Misfit*, screened in the Midlands and the North (but not in London) by ABC on 5 February 1967, written by George Evans and Derek Collyer and produced by Peter Frazer-Jones. He was cast as Jim Didsbury (the ABC studios were based in Didsbury, Manchester), a social outcast, the sort of man whom people want as a friend but is so unfortunate that he leaves chaos trailing in his wake. The support cast included Hugh Morton, Ken Parry, Damaris Hayman, Deborah Watling, Amy Dalby, Joanna Wake and a very young Warren Clarke. No series developed.

See also *Pet Pals*.

Joint Account · 1

UK · BBC · SITCOM

1 × 30 mins · colour
18 Dec 1969 · BBC1 Thu 7.30pm

MAIN CAST
Rodney · · · · · · · · · · · · · · · · Keith Barron
Celia · · · · · · · · · · · · · · · · Sarah Atkinson
George · · · · · · · · · · · · · Geoffrey Whitehead

CREDITS
writer Michael Seddon · *producer* Michael Mills

A *Comedy Playhouse* pilot starring the ubiquitous Keith Barron, cast here as newly wed Rodney, happily hitched to the beautiful Celia. Life should be blissful but there's a problem (sitcom cliché number 471) – Celia is a hopeless cook. How will Rodney survive? Who cares? Certainly not the viewers, as this particular half-baked concoction failed to be developed into a series.

Joint Account · 2

UK · BBC · SITCOM

16 × 30 mins · colour
Series One (6) 26 Jan–2 Mar 1989 · BBC1 Thu 8.30pm
Series Two (10) 19 Mar–21 May 1990 · BBC1 Mon 8.30pm

MAIN CAST
Belinda Braithwaite · · · · · · · Hannah Gordon
David Braithwaite · · · · · · · · · · · · Peter Egan
Ned Race · · · · · · · · · · · · · · · · · John Bird
Louise · · · · · · · · · · · · · · · · Lill Roughley
Jessica · · · · · · · · · · · · · · · · Ruth Mitchell
Charles Ruby · · · · · · · · · · · · Richard Aylen

CREDITS
writer Don Webb · *director/producer* Mike Stephens

A middle-of-the-road role-reversal series featuring dependable sitcom stalwarts Hannah Gordon and Peter Egan. Gordon was cast as Belinda, a successful bank manager, Egan as her spouse David, who has become a house-husband and charity worker. Belinda is the efficient, soft-spoken but authoritative half of their relationship, David the more innocent and gullible one.

With the increasing rise in unemployment, and the elevation of women to more high-powered jobs, such role-reversals were becoming more common and formed the basis for a number of feature films and TV programmes around this time, the first of which was the ITV sitcom *Holding The Fort*.

The Joke Machine

UK · ITV (BORDER) · CHILDREN'S STANDUP/ SKETCH

43 editions (1 × 25 mins · 9 × 20 mins · 13 × 15 mins · 19 × 10 mins · 1 × short special) · colour

Series One (9 × 20 mins) 12 July–6 Sep 1985 · Fri 4.55pm

Series Two (12 × 15 mins · 7 × 10 mins · 1 × 25 mins) *Andrew O'Connor's Joke Machine* 19 June–27 Oct 1987 · Fri 4.20pm then Tue 4.25pm

Special (15 mins) *Andrew O'Connor's Joke Machine* 30 Dec 1987 · Wed 10.10am

Short special · part of *ITV Telethon '88* 30 May 1988 · Mon early-am

Series Three (12 × 10 mins) *Jimmy Cricket's Joke Machine* 14 Apr–30 June 1989 · Fri 4.20pm

MAIN CAST
The Krankies (Ian and Janette Tough)
(series 1)
Andrew O'Connor (series 2 & specials)
Jimmy Cricket (series 3)

CREDITS
executive producers Paul Corley (series 1 & 3 & 1987 special), Ken Stephinson (series 2 & 1988 special) · *director/producer* Harry King

Three batches of children's humour starring a mechanical joke teller, called Fearless Fred in the first series and Charles in the second. The first permitted more 'fandabidozi' fun with the Krankies (see *The Krankies Klub*, *The Krankies Elektronik Komik* and *Krankies Television* for further details on the Scots dynamic duo); the second was fronted by Andrew O'Connor, the third by Jimmy Cricket (with occasional assistance from Pat Coombs and Jim Bowen).

Joking Apart

UK · BBC (POLA JONES FILMS) · SITCOM

13 × 30 mins · colour

Pilot · 12 July 1991 · BBC2 Fri 9pm

Series One (6) 7 Jan–11 Feb 1993 · BBC2 Thu 9pm

Series Two (6) 3 Jan–7 Feb 1995 · BBC2 Tue 9pm

MAIN CAST
Mark Taylor · · · · · · · · · · · · · Robert Bathurst
Becky Johnson · · · · · · · · · · · · · Fiona Gillies
Robert · · · · · · · · · · · · · · · · · Paul Raffield
Tracy · · · · · · · · · · · · · · · · · · Tracie Bennett
Trevor · · · · · · · · · · · · · · · · Paul Mark Elliott

CREDITS
writer Steven Moffat · *directors* John Kilby (pilot), Bob Spiers (series) · *producer* Andre Ptaszynski

A refreshingly adult sitcom from the writer of *Press Gang*, the hit children's drama, *Joking*

Apart looked at divorce from the viewpoint of would-be standup comedian Mark Taylor, who was still obsessed about – and maybe even loved – his ex-wife, Becky Johnson.

In the pilot – extensively revised when it was aired as the premiere episode of the first full series – viewers learned how Mark and Becky had met at a funeral, enjoyed a whirlwind romance and then married. The series then took place in two time frames: the present, with Mark trying to come to terms with life without Becky; and the past, viewed by Mark's reminiscences of their time together. These memories were usually sparked by a routine in his standup act, and caused his pain at her absence to grow even stronger. Becky, meanwhile, seemed quite capable of building herself a new life, and had a new partner, Trevor. Sympathising with Mark's plight but remaining on friendly, neutral terms with both him and Becky were couple Robert and Tracy, whose own relationship was rocky at times.

Robert Bathurst gave a good performance as the flawed but likeable Mark, and Fiona Gillies softened the hard edges of Becky's character with an appealing charm that made Mark's angst all the more understandable. The humour was often bitter or based on embarrassment, and was all the better for it. The first series won a Bafta Award but the show's slow gestation period (two years from pilot to first series and another two years from there to the second series) meant it experienced some difficulty attracting viewers' loyalty – a pity, because *Joking Apart* deserved better.

Jon, Brian, Kirsti And Jon

UK/NORWAY · BBC/NRK · SKETCH

1 × 55 mins · colour

7 Apr 1980 · BBC2 Mon 4.35pm

MAIN CAST
Brian Cant
Jonathan Cohen
Kirsti Sparboe
Jon Skolmen

CREDITS
writers Jon Skolmen, Brian Cant · *directors* John Andreassen, Leslie Pitt · *executive producer* Cynthia Felgate · *producer* Ann Reay

An Easter Monday one-off comedy and musical collaboration between Norwegian Television and two of the stars of the BBC's children's series *Play Away*, filmed in Norwegian studios and masterminded by Jon Skolmen, who had featured in his country's Montreux entry for 1976, *The Nor-Way To Broadcasting* (see **Montreux Festival**). Oddly, one of the skits involved an appearance by the stars of Ipswich Town football club.

Josie

UK · C4 (POZZITIVE PRODUCTIONS) · STANDUP/ SKETCH/IMPROVISATIONAL

6 × 30 mins · colour

1 May–5 June 1991 · Wed 10.30pm

MAIN CAST
Josie Lawrence
Richard Vranch

CREDITS
writers Josie Lawrence, Paul Merton, Arthur Smith and others · *director/producer* Geoff Posner

The actress Josie Lawrence first made waves in comedy circles as a pioneering member of a constantly changing group of players who appeared in a twice-weekly residency at the Comedy Store in London. The improvisational skills of these players delighted audiences, especially the musical items conjured up – seemingly without effort – by Richard Vranch, the resident wizard at the keyboards. BBC radio producer Dan Patterson and Mark Leveson captured the spirit of these moments in a Radio 4 parlour-game series *Whose Line Is It Anyway?* (six editions, 2 January–6 February 1988) which worked exceedingly well and tipped off C4 to the television potential of such a panel show. C4 poached Patterson and presented a TV version of the series with the same title (made by Hat Trick Productions, 23 September 1988 to the present) that was an even greater success and became the centre of a mini 'improv' boom in the UK, emulating a similar movement that had occurred a few years earlier in the USA. The C4 show involved many of the Comedy Store regulars, including Vranch, Paul Merton and Josie Lawrence. Another player, John Sessions, made the most immediate impact with viewers, but Lawrence also impressed, especially with her ability to ad-lib lyrics from suggested subjects. The show raised her profile considerably and audiences, pigeon-holing her as a comedian, were surprised when she turned up in a number of straight acting roles soon afterwards – many being unaware of her background in this sphere.

The success of French and Saunders, and Victoria Wood, had done much to erode the traditional TV bias against women and comedy, so it was no surprise when Lawrence was given her own series, *Josie*. This time she appeared in scripted routines and long-form sketches (almost playlets) with the emphasis on a number of different characters whom she created, such as the East End of London gangster Rita Tuffnell; budding night-club singer Shirley; country and western singer Mary Lou Bochnick; spiritualist Madame Faitour; and pop singer turned soap star Trudi Kellogg. Playing to her improvisational strengths, however, Richard Vranch was on hand to provide musical accompaniment to the ad-libbed song that closed each show.

Jossy's Giants

UK · BBC · CHILDREN'S SITCOM

10 × 30 mins · colour

Series One (5) 23 Apr–21 May 1986 · BBC1
Wed 5.05pm

Series Two (5) 11 Mar–8 Apr 1987 · BBC1
Wed 5.05pm

MAIN CAST

Joswell 'Jossy' Blair · · · · · · · · · Jim Barclay
Councillor Glenda Fletcher · · · · · · · · · · · · ·
· · · · · · · · · · · · · · · · · · · Jenny McCracken
Albert Hanson · · · · · · · Christopher Burgess
Tracey Gaunt · · · · · · · · · · · · · · · · Julie Foy
Bob Nelson · · · · · · · · · · · · · · · · John Judd
Ross Nelson · · · · · · · · · · · · · Mark Gillard
Ricky Sweet · · · · · · · · · · · · Paul Kirkbright
Harvey McGuinn · · · · · · · · · · · Julian Walsh
Glenn Rix · · · · · · · · · · Stuart McGuinness
Wayne Chapman · · · · · · · · · · · · · Oliver Orr
Ian 'Selly' Selleck · · · · · · · · · · Ian Sheppard
Opal · · · · · · · · · · · · Suzanne Hall (series 2)
Shaz · · · · · · · · · · Jenny Luckraft (series 2)
Noleen · · · · · · · · · · Jo-Anne Green (series 2)
Lisa · · · · · · · · · Angela Freear (series 2)
Melanie · · · · · · · · Lucy Keightley (series 2)
Daz · · · · · · · · · · · · · · · · · · · Lee Quarmby

CREDITS

writer Sid Waddell · director Edward Pugh ·
producer Paul Stone

The BBC's Geordie-accented darts commentator Sid Waddell turned his hand to comedy writing with this boisterous children's sitcom that followed the adventures of a boys' football team. The idea for the series came to Waddell when his son Daniel joined one such local team based in West Leeds, the Churwell Lions, who – despite their nickname – 'didn't exactly roar'. The father saw the comedic potential in the son's situation and created a fictional side called the Glipton Grasshoppers, a motley assortment of misfits who are unable to win a match. Then they are taken under the wing of a new coach, Joswell 'Jossy' Blair, a brilliant child footballer, famed in the north-east, whose professional career with Newcastle United was curtailed by injury in his debut first-team match. Blair starts to knock the Grasshoppers into shape and they are transformed into the Jossy's Giants of the title.

The young actors who portrayed the Grasshoppers weren't professionals but were picked from local pitches and schools around Manchester by the programme-makers, who considered it easier to teach football-skilled youngsters to act rather than acting-skilled lads to play football. Those chosen then received further training from the series' consultant, the former Manchester United star Paddy Crerand. In a game in the opening episode, the Grasshoppers' opposition was the actual Churwell Lions (complete with Daniel Waddell). The second series (novelised as *Glipton Romeos*) found the boys slightly older and beginning to get more interested in girls

than football, while Jossy himself was also getting deeper involved with Councillor Glenda Fletcher.

Sid Waddell returned to a sporting theme with *Sloggers* (BBC1, six episodes, 6 January–10 February 1994; and six more, 5 January–9 February 1995), a light-drama about the youngsters who play for Slogthwaite Cricket Club.

Joyce Grenfell … [various shows]

see GRENFELL, Joyce

Judgement Day For Elijah Jones

UK · BBC · SITCOM

1 × 30 mins · b/w

7 June 1966 · BBC1 Tue 7.30pm

MAIN CAST

Elijah Jones · · · · · · · · · · · · · · · Clive Dunn
Arnold · · · · · · · · · · · · · · · Bernard Cribbins
Elijah's wife · · · · · · · · · · · · Priscilla Morgan

CREDITS

writer Marty Feldman · director John Street ·
producer Dennis Main Wilson

Another characteristically odd one-off *Comedy Playhouse* sitcom from the manic mind of Marty Feldman. Clive Dunn (*not* this time in an old-man role) was cast as Elijah Jones, and Bernard Cribbins as his pal, 'Brother' Arnold, a pair of sandwich-board-men who walk the streets displaying their warnings that the world is about to end. To avoid the apocalypse, Elijah plans to build an ark and emulate Noah, and so he embarks upon a plan to steal selected animals from a zoo (sequences were filmed at Chessington). Elijah's wife was played by Dunn's real-life wife Priscilla Morgan.

The Jugg Brothers

UK · BBC · SITCOM

1 × 30 mins · colour

1 Jan 1970 · BBC1 Thu 7.30pm

MAIN CAST

Stephen Jugg · · · · · · · · · · · Stephen Lewis
Robert Jugg · · · · · · · · · · · · · · · · Bob Grant
Lilly Dolly · · · · · · · · · · · · · · · Fanny Carby
Annie Bundle · · · · · · · · · · · · Queenie Watts

CREDITS

writers Bob Grant/Stephen Lewis · producer
Dennis Main Wilson

On The Buses was already well established on ITV when two of its stars, Bob Grant (Jack) and Stephen Lewis (Inspector Blake), collaborated on this *Comedy Playhouse* one-off sitcom for the BBC, in which they also starred as the Jugg Brothers. A future series failed to materialise but some years later Grant and Lewis realised their writing potential by scripting a dozen episodes of *On The Buses*.

Julia

USA · NBC (20TH CENTURY-FOX TV) · SITCOM

86 × 30 mins · colour

US dates: 17 Sep 1968–25 May 1971

UK dates: 11 Apr 1969–11 July 1971
(26 episodes) ITV mostly Fri 7pm

MAIN CAST

Julia Baker · · · · · · · · · · · · Diahann Carroll
Corey Baker · · · · · · · · · · · · · Marc Copage
Dr Morton Chegley · · · · · · · · · · · Lloyd Nolan
Hannah Yarby · · · · · · · · · · · · Lurene Tuttle
Earl J Waggedorn · · · · · · · · · · Michael Link
Marie Waggedorn · · · · · · · · · · Betty Beaird
Len Waggedorn · · · · · · · · · · · · Hank Brandt
Sol Cooper · · · · · · · · · · · · · · · Ned Glass

CREDITS

creator/producer Hal Kanter · writers various ·
directors Hal Kanter, Bernard Wiesen, Barry Shear,
Coby Ruskin

Following the comedy antics of *Beulah* and *Amos 'n' Andy* – early 1950s series which many deemed patronising – black people scarcely featured in starring roles on US television until this NBC sitcom, *Julia*, came along in 1968. True, Bill Cosby had been prominent in the adventure series *I Spy*, but he was not the main star. *Julia*, with Diahann Carroll starring and an integrated supporting cast underneath, was therefore something of a breakthrough – even though it was criticised by some black people as being unrepresentative of their lifestyle: she lived in a swanky apartment and appeared unaffected by any of the racial troubles that marked the period.

The premise had Julia as the beautiful widow of an air force captain, killed in the line of duty in Vietnam, endeavouring to raise Corey, their son (aged six when the series began). She worked as a nurse at the Inner Aero-Space Center, an industrial health complex in Los Angeles, and the comedy revolved around her friendships and relationships at work and play.

Julia Jekyll And Harriet Hyde

UK · BBC · CHILDREN'S SITCOM

39 × 15 mins · colour

Series One (24) 29 Sep 1995–15 Mar 1996 ·
BBC1 Fri 4.20pm

Series Two (15) 12 Sep–19 Dec 1996 · BBC1
Thu 4.20pm

MAIN CAST

Julia Jekyll · · · · · · · · · · · · · Olivia Hallinan
Harriet Hyde · · · · · · · · · · · · · John Asquith
Moira Jekyll · · · · · · · · · · · Victoria Williams
Jerry Jekyll · · · · · · · · · · · · · · · Bill Fellows
Sharon Blister · · · · · · · · · · · · · · Karen Salt
Nicola Blister · · · · · · · · · · · · Tiffany Griffiths
Lester Blister · · · · · · Robert Portal (series 1);
· · · · · · · · · · · · · · · · · · · Dale Rapley (series 2)
Memphis Rocket · · · · · · · · · · · Simon Green
Mrs Rocket · · · · · · · · · · · · · · · · Ann Emery
Mrs Smith · · · · · · · · · · · · · · Christine Lohr
Mr Slime · · · · · · · · · · · · · · · Philip Philmar
Roger · · · · · · · · · · · · · · · · Anthony Tobias

Edward Knickers	Guy Edwards
Sarah Slocombe	Emma Barnett

CREDITS

creator/producer Jeremy Swan · *writers* Jim Eldridge (28), Jeremy Swan (11) · *directors* Jeremy Swan, Albert Barber · *executive producer* Anna Home

Julia Jekyll is the star pupil at the eccentric Rocket Academy, a school run by a 1960s hippie throwback, Memphis Rocket, and his 76-year-old mother. Julia is good at everything, much to the disgust of the school bullies, a pair of extortionists named Sharon and Nicola Blister. One day – in the science class taken by the Blisters' uncle, Lester Blister – the evil sisters doctor a potion that Julia is concocting, with the result that, upon drinking the draught, she is transformed into the monstrous Harriet Hyde: a huge, hairy, menacing-looking but mostly harmless beast. No one knows that Julia and Harriet are the same person and Julia has her hands full in keeping this a secret – a task made especially difficult by the fact that she alters from one state to another without warning.

A noisy, energetic but somewhat vacuous children's offering that was low on charm and high on the piercing-scream count. It probably held some appeal for its target audience of very small children, though – enough, anyway, for a third series to be commissioned for 1998.

Julie

USA · ABC (BLAKE EDWARDS TELEVISION PRODUCTIONS/ VIACOM) · SITCOM

6 × 30 mins · colour

US dates: 30 May–4 July 1992

UK dates: 21 Dec–31 Dec 1993 (6 episodes) C4 weekdays 1.30pm

MAIN CAST

Julie Carlyle/McGuire	Julie Andrews
Sam McGuire	James Farentino
I F 'Wooly' Woolstein	Eugene Roche
Allie McGuire	Hayley Tyrie
Adam McGuire	Rider Strong
Joy Foy	Alicia Brandt
Bernie Farrell	Laurel Cronin
Dickie Duncan	Kevin Scannell

CREDITS

writers various · *director/producer* Blake Edwards

A curiously old-fashioned family sitcom starring actress/singer Julie Andrews and produced by her husband Blake Edwards. Andrews was cast as Julie Carlyle, a successful TV variety star who throws over her glamorous lifestyle to play housewife to new husband Sam and mother to his children, Allie and Adam. In doing so, she moves from New York City to Sioux City, Iowa, and tries to readjust to her new life despite a past that cannot be shrugged off so easily.

In a period when shows like *Seinfeld*, *Married ... With Children* and *The Simpsons* were redefining the sitcom genre, *Julie* came across as hopelessly lame and limped off into the sunset after just six episodes.

Julie And Carol: Together Again

USA · ABC · SITCOM

1 × 60 mins · colour

US date: 7 Dec 1971

UK date: 9 Apr 1972 · BBC1 Sun 7.25pm

MAIN CAST

Julie Andrews
Carol Burnett

CREDITS

writers Bob Ellison, Marty Farrell · *director* Dave Powers · *producer* Joe Hamilton

A US TV special (aired by BBC1 as *Julie And Carol*) that reunited the American comic Carol Burnett with the British singer/actress Julie Andrews. The couple had first teamed up for a similar special in 1962 and would combine again in the 1980s.

Julie Walters And Friends

UK · ITV (LWT) · SKETCH

1 × 60 mins · colour

29 Dec 1991 · Sun 10.05pm

MAIN CAST

Julie Walters
Victoria Wood
Alan Bennett
Willy Russell
Alan Bleasdale

CREDITS

writers Victoria Wood, Alan Bennett, Willy Russell, Alan Bleasdale · *director* Alasdair Macmillan · *producer* Nicholas Barrett

A classy seasonal special for the fine actress so adept at comic roles. Walters was joined here by four eminent writers who had helped shape her career to this point and who now wrote new character sketches especially for the programme. (Walters was synonymous with Wood's TV work, appeared in one of Bennett's stunningly good *Talking Heads* monologues, received wonderful notices in Russell's movie *Educating Rita* and starred in Bleasdale's C4 drama series *GBH*.)

For some of Julie Walters' other TV appearances, see Victoria Wood's combined entry.

Just A Gigolo

UK · ITV (CENTRAL) · SITCOM

7 × 30 mins · colour

8 Apr–20 May 1993 · Thu 8.30pm

MAIN CAST

Nick Brim	Tony Slattery
Simon Brim	Paul Bigley
Natalie	Rowena King
Marge Payne	Wanda Ventham

CREDITS

writers Carl Gorham/Michael Hatt/Amanda Swift · *director* Martin Dennis · *producer* Paul Spencer

Nick Brim resigns from his job as a comprehensive-school teacher and falls, accidentally, into a new career when a middle-aged woman, Marge Payne, mistakes him for her paid escort and gives him £100 for his troubles. Nick becomes a reluctant and most definitely virginal but nonetheless successful gigolo, donning the dinner-jacket, black bow tie, shiny shoes and cuff-links to step out on the town with those who require his services. It certainly brings in the money, and he needs it, having to pay the rent on the flat he shares with his brother Simon, who has been made redundant from his job. Simon duly encourages his sibling's new career – until, eventually, Nick joins an agency – but all this proves problematic to Nick who lusts after a beautiful woman, Natalie, and has to prevent her from finding out how he earns his income.

A funny sitcom – with the dependable Tony Slattery graduating to his own vehicle after appearing in *That's Love* – *Just A Gigolo* entertained for seven witty episodes but the premise would stretch no further.

Just Dennis

see *Dennis The Menace*

Just For Fun!

UK · BBC · SKETCH

1 × 20 mins · b/w

15 Sep 1937 · Wed 3pm (re-staged 9pm)

MAIN CAST

Aldrich and Aspinall
Richard Murdoch

CREDITS

producer Reginald Smith

A very early TV comedy show co-starring Richard Murdoch. A year later he was catapulted to stardom (and saddled with the unenviable nickname 'Stinker') when the BBC launched its massively successful radio series *Band Waggon*.

Just For Fun 1

see *Mr Pastry*

Just For Fun 2

UK · BBC · CHILDREN'S SKETCH

1 × 15 mins · b/w

2 Apr 1952 · Wed 5.40pm

MAIN CAST

Harry Tate Jr

CREDITS

writers Wal Pink/Harry Tate (Sr) · *producer* Michael Westmore

A hugely popular star of 1920s music-hall, Harry Tate devised a number of well-loved sketches on themes like golfing and fishing, the most famous of them all being one about motoring. Following his death in 1940, Harry's son Ronnie Tate, who had performed with his father, took over the act – and Harry's name – and continued to be successful. In this *Children's Television* slot, Harry Tate Jr presented a variation of the famous motoring sketch, 'On The Road'.

Just For Laughs

UK · C4 (VARIOUS) · STANDUP

48 editions (38 × 30 mins · 2 × 35 mins · 2 × 40 mins · 1 × 45 mins · 3 × 60 mins · 1 × 90 mins · 1 × 120 mins) · colour

Series One (6 × 30 mins) 17 Mar–21 Apr 1987 · Tue mostly 10.50pm

Series Two (6 × 30 mins) 27 Oct–1 Dec 1987 · Tue 11.15pm

Series Three (6 × 30 mins) 11 Apr–16 May 1989 · Tue 11pm

Series Four (6 × 30 mins) 10 Apr–15 May 1990 · Tue 10pm

Series Five (6 × 30 mins) 26 June–31 July 1991 · Wed mostly 11pm

Series Six (6 × 30 mins) 23 Jan–27 Feb 1992 · Thu 11.05pm

Special (120 mins) 4 Sep 1992 · Fri 10.30pm

Special (90 mins) 4 Sep 1993 · Sat 9pm

Series Seven (3 × 60 mins) 9 Sep–23 Sep 1994 · Fri mostly 11.10pm

Series Eight (2 × 30 mins · 2 × 35 mins · 2 × 40 mins · 1 × 45 mins) 23 Sep 1995–14 July 1996 · various days and times

MAIN CAST
see below

CREDITS
see below

As Cannes has its film festival and Edinburgh its arts festival so Montreal has an annual celebration of comedy, *Just For Laughs*, which began in 1983 as a two-day event with 16 performers and by the late 1990s had turned into a two-week extravaganza at dozens of the city's clubs and theatres and to which hundreds of standup acts arrived from all over the world. They performed in front of not just Quebecois but fun fans who made pilgrimages to the city for the July fortnight, and plenty of TV talent scouts too – it is reported that some 30 development deals were inked at the 1995 and 1996 events.

The first week of the festival is mostly given over to French-speaking acts (the French Canadians call the festival *Juste Pour Rire*) but the second is an English-speaking affair, with plenty of British interest. For this reason, C4 screened 48 programmes of highlights between 1987 and 1996, covering ten consecutive festivals. (In 1997, for the fifteenth annual event, the British TV rights went to the cable/satellite station Paramount Comedy Channel, which screened 13 programmes as *Festival Of Fun* from 7 October, in partnership with the newly formed Channel 5, which intended to show them in 1998.)

What follows is a year-by-year guide to C4's screenings.

Series 1 was recorded at the fourth festival, in 1986. TV production by Paul Jackson Productions/Les Films Rozon (directors Ed Bye, Laurent Larouche; producer Paul Jackson). Comics included Helen Lederer, Howard Busgang, Wayne Fleming, Jay Leno, Paul Reiser, David Tyree, Phil Cool, Pep Bou, Chris Elliot, Gilbert Gottfried, Jean-Jacques Vanier, Marsha Warfield, Gareth Hale and Norman Pace, Louie Anderson, Anthony Gatto, Maurice Lamarche, Jerry Lewis (the famous film comic), Lenny Henry, Joe Bolster, Rick Ducommon, Andrea Martin, Steve Mittleman, Otto Wessely, Jeremy Hardy, Norm MacDonald, Paula Poundstone, Marty Putz, Yakov Smirnoff (America's only Russian émigré comic), Stephen Fry, the Frantics, Mike MacDonald, Gord Paynter, Emo Philips and Carrie Snow.

Series 2 was recorded at the fifth festival, in 1987. TV production by Noel Gay Television/Les Films Rozon (directors Ed Bye, Laurent Larouche; producer Paul Jackson). Comics included Rowan Atkinson, Stevie Ray Fromstein, Wendy Harmer, Roland Magdane, Mark McCollum, the Frantics, Craig Ferguson (appearing as Bing Hitler), Don Gavin, David Strassman and Chuck Wood, Steven Wright, Henny Youngman, Harry Enfield, Rich Jeni, Carol Leifer, Mat Plendl, David Steinberg, Richard Belzer, Crusher Comic, Les Foubrac, Norman Lovett, Rita Rudner, A Whitney Brown, Chas Elstner, Jake Johannsen, MacLean and MacLean, John Mendoza, Ruby Wax, Brighton Bottle Orchestra, Graham Chapman, Karen Haber, Mike MacDonald and Phil Nee.

Series 3 was recorded at the sixth festival, in 1988. TV production by Noel Gay Television/Les Films Rozon (director Graham Hutchings; executive producers Paul Jackson, Gilbert Rozon; producer Keith Stewart). Comics included Louie Anderson, Emo Philips, Bowser and Blue, Les Foubrac, Jo Brand, Dan Redican, Michel Courtemanche, Jeff Altman, Dom Irrera, Kit Hollerbach, Brett Butler, Doug Anthony All-Stars, Eno, Allan Havey, Mike MacDonald, Nick Revell, Blake Clark, Gilbert Gottfried, Institut de Jonglage, Margaret Smith, John Sparkes, Craig Charles, Christopher, Gladwyn and Kearney, Robert Schimmel, Bobby Slayton, John Candy, Rich Hall, Hattie Hayridge, Denis Lacombe, Kevin Meaney and Barry Sobel.

Series 4 was recorded at the seventh festival, in 1989. TV production by Tiger Television/Les Films Rozon (director Jane Prowse; producer Sarah Williams). Each programme was a self-contained special. The first in the series, *Joy Of Canada* (scripted by Jon Canter and Lise Mayer), starred Rowan Atkinson as Casey Rogers, a Canadian entertainer looking at aspects of Canada and its culture. With Jack Docherty as Finlay MacIntyre, the Scottish Alan Whicker, and Vic Reeves as a trainee heckler. The second show, *Great Scots!*, starred Jack Docherty (again as Finlay MacIntyre) with Moray Hunter, Craig Ferguson, Franklyn Ajaye and Anita Wise. The third show, *Hyperbowl*, featured Mick Luckhurst as TV sports commentators John Bonson and Bob Johnson, with Kenny Robinson, Fred Stoller, Mike MacDonald and Michael Lauziere. Other programmes in this series featured Charlie Higson, Phyllis Diller, Michael Redmond, Rick Overton, Rowan Atkinson, Ted Dillon, Jenny Lecoat, Mark Camacho, Michael Winslow, Jimmy Tingle, Vic Reeves, Pam Matteson, Rick Ducommon and Kevin Meaney.

Series 5 was recorded at the eighth festival, in 1990. TV production by Tiger Television/Les Films Rozon. Every programme hosted by Jimmy Mulville and Muriel Gray. Comics included Stephanie Hodge, Thea Vidal, Larry Miller, Julian Clary and Mike MacDonald.

Series 6 was recorded at the ninth festival, in 1991. TV production by Tiger Television/Les Films Rozon (director Chris Bould; producer Gillian Strachan). Every programme hosted by Clive Anderson. Comics included Roseanne Barr, Bill Hicks, Denis Leary, Jane Curtin, Milton Berle (the veteran US TV comedy hero), Sean Hughes, Frank Skinner, Jerry Hotz, Richard Belzer and Alistair MacAlistair.

The 1992 special was recorded at the tenth festival, in 1992. TV production by Tiger Aspect/Les Films Rozon (director Geoff Posner). Comics included Ben Elton, Jack Dee, Harry Enfield, Eddie Izzard, Penn And Teller, Vic Reeves and Bob Mortimer, Eddie Griffin, Stomp, Mark Thomas, Lily Tomlin, Paul Whitehouse and Steven Wright.

The 1993 special was recorded at the eleventh festival, in 1993. TV production by Tiger Aspect/Les Films Rozon (director Geoff Posner; producers Charles Brand, Alan Nixon). Comics included Paul Merton, Owen O'Neill, Jeremy Hardy, Steve Punt and Hugh Dennis, Caroline Aherne (her Sister Mary Immaculate act) and Lee Evans.

Series 7 was recorded at the twelfth festival, in 1994. TV production by Tiger Aspect/Les Films Rozon (director Geoff Posner; producers Geoff Posner, Alan Nixon). Every programme hosted by Chris Evans. Comics included Emo Philips, Nick Revell, Mark Thomas, Donna McPhail, Harry Hill, Mr Methane (Britain's only performing Petomane), Steady Eddy (Australian cerebral palsy act), Dom Irrera and Anthony Clark. One of the three programmes was a tape of the all-gay show *Queer Comics*, linked by Julian Clary and featuring Bob Downe, Mark Davis, Bob Smith, Suzanne Westenhoefer, Elvira Kurt and Steve Moore.

Series 8 was recorded at the thirteenth festival, in 1995. TV production by Tiger Aspect/Les Films Rozon (director Mark Chapman; executive producers Charles Brand/Sue Vertue, Andy Nulman/Gilbert Rozon/Francois Rozon; producers John Tiffney, Bruce Hills). Every programme hosted by Frank Skinner. Comics included Eddie Izzard, Richard Jeni, Boothby Graffoe, Margaret Smitral, Ardal O'Hanlon (Father Dougal McGuire in *Father Ted*), Tom Rhodes, Phil Kay, Mark Roberts, Jimeoin, Rich Hall, Alan Davies and Chris Bliss.

See also *Craig Goes Mad In Melbourne*.

Just Good Friends

UK · BBC · SITCOM

22 episodes (20 × 30 mins · 1 × 35 mins · 1 × 90 mins) · colour

Series One (7 × 30 mins) 22 Sep–3 Nov 1983 · BBC1 Thu 9.25pm

Series Two (7 × 30 mins) 7 Oct–18 Nov 1984 · BBC1 Sun 8.45pm

Special (90 mins) 25 Dec 1984 · BBC1 Tue 7.25pm

Series Three (6 × 30 mins) 13 Nov–18 Dec 1986 · BBC1 Thu 9.30pm

Special (35 mins) 25 Dec 1986 · BBC1 Thu 6pm

MAIN CAST
Vince Pinner · · · · · · · · · · · · · · · Paul Nicholas
Penny Warrender · · · · · · · · · · · · · Jan Francis

OTHER APPEARANCES
Daphne Warrender · · · · · · · · · · · · Sylvia Kay
Norman Warrender · · · · · · · · · John Ringham
Rita Pinner · · · · · · · · · · · · · · · · Ann Lynn
Les Pinner · · · · · · · · · · · · · · · Shaun Curry
Clifford Pinner · · · · · · · · · · · · Adam French

CREDITS
writer John Sullivan · directors Ray Butt (15), Sue Bysh (7) · producer Ray Butt

A deservedly popular and witty John Sullivan sitcom about a rocky relationship that has to overcome not only the different philosophies of the two players but also the class differences that divide them.

In the summer of 1976 Penny Warrender and Vince Pinner meet at a Rolling Stones concert in Hyde Park, London. After a stormy two-year courtship they finally plan to get married but, just two days before the event, Vince gets a severe case of cold feet, hops on his motorbike and rides off into the sunset, leaving Penny broken-hearted. Five years later they meet again, by chance, and Penny – to her own horror – finds that the old attraction is still there. Although they insist on remaining 'just good friends' the old feelings quickly resurface and for the run

of the series they conduct a love–hate, on-again-and-off-again affair. Neither is helped in this venture by their respective parents, Penny's snobbish mother and unemployed father, and Vince's embarrassingly raucous mum and dad.

John Sullivan was well aware that his TV writings thus far had featured very few women, his current smash hit being the (then) male-dominated *Only Fools And Horses*. Deciding, therefore, to base a comedy around a woman – but anxious not to create one of the unreal, stereotypical females evident in most sitcoms – he was intrigued by a problem page letter in a magazine being read by his wife, written by a woman who had been jilted at the altar. In Penny Warrender, Sullivan developed a sensitive, believable character with real wit and intelligence, and no more or less vulnerability than one might expect to find in real life, suffering bouts of self-doubt and an appealing handicap in her inexplicable addiction to Vince. He was less well drawn, a typical wide-boy who wanted to have his cake and eat it. Vince's one saving grace was that, underneath it all, he did genuinely care for his 'Pen', although, because of his tendency to follow the dictates of his 'laddish' programming, this wasn't always evident. The class differences between the two were succinctly illustrated in their names: prim and proper Penny compared to the faintly vulgar Vince, and those of their parents, Daphne and Norman versus Les and Rita.

The series certainly had plenty of charm and many of the scripts sparkled with delightful situations and terrific rejoinders, but it suffered somewhat by the over-stretching of its 'will-they-won't-they?' theme. This may not have been Sullivan's fault. It is possible that he intended to end the series with the 1984 Christmas special, in which Penny split with Vince for what she said was the final time and flew off to Paris, leaving Vince with the half-intended pact that should meet again on the Eiffel Tower three years later. (This was a crib from the classic 1957 Cary Grant weepy *An Affair To Remember*, which in turn inspired sequences in the 1995 comedy movie *Sleepless In Seattle*.) But viewers like a happy ending and two years later Sullivan brought the couple back for one final shot. Now we met a different Penny: gone were the pangs of self-doubt, the young woman going nowhere, having been replaced by a successful careerist, working in Paris. Only one aspect of her old character remained – the incurable, destructive yet indestructible attraction to Vince. So they satisfied their public and married at last, destined to always be more than 'just good friends'.

Just Harry And Me

see *Now Take My Wife*

Just Jimmy

UK · ITV (ABC) · CHILDREN'S SITCOM

49 × 30 mins · b/w

*Series One (6) 29 Nov 1964–3 Jan 1965 · Sun 5.10pm

*Series Two (11) 30 Oct 1965–29 Jan 1966 · Sat 5.15pm

*Series Three (12) 1 Oct–24 Dec 1966 · Sat 5.15pm

*Series Four (14) 7 Oct 1967–27 Jan 1968 · Sat mostly 5.15pm

*Series Five (6) 20 Apr–25 May 1968 · Sat 5.50pm

MAIN CAST
Jimmy Clitheroe · · · · · · · · · · · · · · · himself
Mrs Clitheroe · · · · · · · · · · · · Mollie Sugden
Danny · · · · · · · · · · · · · · · · · · Danny Ross

CREDITS
writers Jan Butlin, Alick Hayes, Keith Lancaster, Ron McDonnell, Fred Robinson, Frank Roscoe, Bernie Sharp, Harry Stansfield, Bill Stark, Ronnie Taylor and others · director/producer Ronnie Baxter

He's all but forgotten now, but little Jimmy Clitheroe was once a massively successful comic. At its height (no pun intended), his marathon BBC radio show, spanning 16 series from 1958 to 1972, attracted as many as ten million listeners. But transferring *The Clitheroe Kid* to television was never as successful.

In the modern vernacular, Clitheroe was vertically challenged – using the non-PC word, he was a midget – standing 4ft 3in 'tall' in his socks. He also had a high flutey voice, and these elements, combined with short trousers, enabled him to play the perpetual schoolboy, a role he carried through until his death in 1973, aged 51. The TV series *Just Jimmy* was based on the same domestic situation as the radio version, with Clitheroe cast as the naughty laddie from Lancashire, Mollie Sugden appearing as his mother (although Patricia Burke was the radio mother, Sugden used to play the role in live stage-shows) and Danny Ross as his girl-mad, motor bike-mad cousin.

*Notes. The TV series never achieved fully networked status, and these dates refer to transmissions in the Midlands and the North, where the shows were produced by ABC. It wasn't until 12 March 1968, when the ABC run had finally ended, that London-area viewers got to see *Just Jimmy*. In total, London ITV screened 23 of the ABC episodes, the last on 20 September 1968. Plans for Thames to make more – ABC had lost its franchise by this time – did not materialise.

Clitheroe also appeared in a 1963 sitcom for ABC not screened by London-area ITV. This was *That's My Boy* (not to be confused with the identically titled Mollie Sugden series of the 1980s) and it ran in the Midlands and the North over seven weeks, 10 November to

22 December, screened at 4.05pm on Sundays. Deryck Guyler, June Monkhouse, Vicky Harrington and Gordon Rollings supported the mischievous schoolboy Clitheroe, who was usually in trouble in his family and looking out for more. The series was written by Bob Block; four episodes were directed by David Main and three by Mark Stuart.

Earlier, Clitheroe had appeared in *Call Boy*, a BBC music-hall variety series which ran monthly from 16 January to 8 May 1957. Clitheroe was the young man of the title, a stage-hand assisting stage manager Eddie Leslie, introducing the guest artists and getting them on to the stage in time.

Alick Hayes, one of the *Just Jimmy* writers, had previously scripted and produced *My Sister And I* (ABC, 19 May–21 July 1956), the first ITV sitcom made in and for the North. Dinah Lee and Jane Taylor co-starred as Sally and Jo, the series depicting 'the daily lives of two endearing sisters'. James George and then Stuart Latham directed, and Jack Howarth (later to be cast as Albert Tatlock in *Coronation Street*) and Ray Cooney were among the regular supporting cast. The series was not screened in London.

Just Like Mum

UK · ITV (LWT) · SITCOM

1 × 30 mins · colour

27 Aug 1976 · Fri 7pm

MAIN CAST

Mrs Jordan ·············· Peggy Mount
Edward Unsworth ········ Leonard Preston
Alwyn Williams ·············· Mike Grady
Billy Norris ·············· Roderick Smith
Mrs Fairfax ············· Frances Bennett

CREDITS

writer John Stevenson · *director/producer* Stuart Allen

One of three single comedies screened by LWT under the *Comedy Showcase* banner, *Just Like Mum* starred Peggy Mount as know-all landlady Mrs Parker, whose nosey-parker instincts cramped the style of her student lodgers.

Just Liz

UK · ITV (THAMES) · SITCOM

6 × 30 mins · colour

1 Sep–6 Oct 1980 · Mon 8.30pm

MAIN CAST

Liz Parker ················ Sandra Payne
Reg Last ················ Rodney Bewes
Jessie Worth ··············· Avril Angers

OTHER APPEARANCES

Mr Dalzell ············ Terence Alexander
Trevor ················· Mike Walling
Mr Chatto ················ Gorden Kaye

CREDITS

writers John Esmonde/Bob Larbey · *director/producer* Robert Reed

Although on the crest of a wave following the tremendous success of *The Good Life*, Thames' *Just Liz* was a far from successful venture for writers Esmonde and Larbey, lasting only one series. Sandra Payne starred as Liz Parker, whose fiancé Nigel has gone to invest his talents in Bahrain for a year and a half, in order to make plenty of tax-free money to invest in their marriage. This leaves Liz free to look after herself … and look after her interests. Fortunately – or not, as the case may be – she has her travel agency colleague Reg Last to fuss around and protect her.

Just Our Luck

USA · ABC (LAWRENCE GORDON PRODUCTIONS/ LORIMAR) · SITCOM

13 × 30 mins · colour

US dates: 20 Sep–27 Dec 1983

UK dates: 6 Jan–30 Mar 1984 (13 episodes) ITV Fri 2pm

MAIN CAST

Shabu ····················· T K Carter
Keith Barrow ··········· Richard Gilliland
Meagan Huxley ············· Ellen Maxted
Nelson Marriott ············· Rod McCary
Chuck ················· Richard Schaal
Professor Bob ··········· Hamilton Camp

CREDITS

creators Larry Gordon/Charles A Gordon · *writers* James Berg, Tony Colvin, Robert J Comfort, Scott S Gorden, Charles A Gordon, Larry Gordon, Danny Jacobs, Rick Kellard, Linda Morris, Ria Nepus, Vic Rauseo, Fred Rubin, Michael A Russnow, Barry Vigon, Stan Zimmerman · *directors* various · *producer* Ronald Frazier

A short-lived US sitcom about Keith Barrow, a mild TV weatherman-cum-reporter, who – out jogging one day in Venice, California – accidentally cracks and so is forced to buy an old bottle … wherein resides a genie, Shabu. The 3000-year-old magic one, hip to palaces and former employers like Napoleon and Cleopatra, is less than impressed with the status of his new master and proceeds to get him into all sorts of trouble. He especially causes problems at Barrow's station, KPOX-TV, where the weatherman is already out of favour with the management (especially the programme director Meagan Huxley and her fiancé, the station manager Nelson Marriott) and where his post has been taken over by one Professor Bob (a move, surely, that Barrow ought to have forecast).

There was more than a shade of *I Dream Of Jeannie* about *Just Our Luck* but Shabu was much more streetwise than his feminine counterpart. Black, jive-talking, disloyal and altogether more mischievous though he was, however, the portrayal of a black man as slave to a white caused problems with civil rights organisations, and the National Association for the Advancement of Colored People (NAACP) pressed hard to win subtle changes to the characters – Shabu stopped calling Keith Barrow 'master' – and a black presence among the script-writing team.

A number of famous names passed through the episodes in cameo roles, including Wink Martindale (the 'Deck Of Cards' warbler) and Roy Orbison.

Just Polly And Me

USA · CBS · SKETCH

1 × 60 mins · b/w

US date: 8 Oct 1960

UK date: 24 Jan 1962 · ITV Wed 8pm

MAIN CAST

Phil Silvers
Polly Bergen

CREDITS

writer Nat Hiken · *director* Coby Ruskin · *producer* Nick Vanoff

Following *The Slowest Gun In The West*, writer Nat Hiken got together once again with his star from *The Phil Silvers Show* to make a second TV special. In this one Silvers co-starred with Tennessee singer and actress Polly Bergen.

Just Sally

UK · BBC · STANDUP/SKETCH

2 × 15 mins · b/w

20 Jan 1954 · Wed 8.15pm

24 Mar 1954 · Wed 8.15pm

MAIN CAST

Sally Barnes

CREDITS

writer Eddie Maguire · *producer* Graeme Muir

On her TV debut as one of the guests in Henry Hall's BBC variety series *Face The Music*, Sally Barnes stormed her way into viewers' hearts, making an immediate impact with a waif-like comedy character imbued with more than a hint of pathos. The BBC quickly gave her these two starring shows in which she could introduce more characters and cement her stardom.

Barnes' great strength was her seemingly unflagging energy, throwing herself into strenuous and hilarious dance routines with the appearance of a double-jointed contortionist, but these two shows failed to emulate her impressive debut, nor her successes on stage. The impresario Jack Hylton then tried to concoct a lasting TV career for Barnes by teaming her with the comedian Reg Dixon in *People Like Us*, but this too failed to shine and so her undeniable potential was never realised.

Just What I Always Wanted

UK · BBC · SATIRE

1 × 5 mins · colour

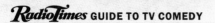

25 Dec 1991 · BBC1 Wed 11.50pm

MAIN CAST

John Wells · · · · · · · · · · · · · · · · · · · himself
Auntie Flo · · · · · · · · · · · · · · · · Margot Boht

CREDITS

writer John Wells · *producer* Chris Loughlin

A five-minute satirical monologue in which
John Wells commented on the festive season
and pondered whether the 'joys' of Christmas
are all they are cracked up to be. The programme was the product of the BBC's
religious department.

See also *John Wells And The Three Wise Men*.

Just William   ITV

UK · ITV (LWT) · CHILDREN'S SITCOM

**27 episodes (26 × 30 mins · 1 × 60 mins) ·
colour**

Series One (13 × 30 mins) 6 Feb–1 May 1977 ·
Sun mostly 4.35pm

Series Two (13 × 30 mins · 1 × 60 mins) 23 Oct
1977–22 Jan 1978 · Sun mostly 5.45pm

MAIN CAST

William Brown · · · · · · · · · · · · Adrian Dannatt
Ginger · · · · · · · · · · · · · · · · Michael McVey
Henry · · · · · · · · · · · · · · · · Colin McFarlane
Douglas · · · · · · · · · · · · · · · · · · · Tim Rose
Violet Elizabeth Bott · · · · · · Bonnie Langford
Mrs Brown · · · · · · · · · · · · · · Diana Fairfax
Mr Brown · · · · · · · · · · · · · · · · Hugh Cross
Ethel Brown · · · · · · · · · · · · · · Stacy Dorning

OTHER APPEARANCES

Mrs Bott · · · · · · · · · · · · · · · · · · Diana Dors

CREDITS

creator Richmal Crompton · *adapter/writer* Keith
Dewhurst · *executive producer* Stella Richman ·
director/producer John Davies

A further small-screen outing for William
Brown, who had featured on the BBC in the
William series in 1962–63 (see that entry
for background information). This LWT
series, adapted by Keith Dewhurst, cast
Westminster School pupil Adrian Dannatt as
the grubby but endearing 11-year-old urchin,
leader of the all-boy gang the Outlaws (other
members: Ginger, Henry and Douglas) and
victim of the attentions of the dreadfully
spoilt, lisping Violet ('I'll thkweam and I'll
thkweam until I'm thick'). Mrs Bott, Violet's
mother, was seen from time to time, played
by guest star Diana Dors. Other occasional
guests included David Langton, Freddie
Jones, Wilfrid Brambell, Ronald Lacey and
Nigel Hawthorne.

See also the following entry.

Just William   BBC

UK · BBC (TALISMAN) · CHILDREN'S SITCOM

12 × 30 mins · colour

Series One (6) 13 Nov–18 Dec 1994 · BBC1
Sun 5.35pm

Series Two (6) 12 Nov–17 Dec 1995 · BBC1
Sun 7pm

MAIN CAST

William Brown · · · · · · · · · · · · Oliver Rokison
Violet Elizabeth Bott · · · · · · · Tiffany Griffiths
Mrs Brown · · · · · · · · · · · · · · · Polly Adams
Mr Brown · · · · · · · · · · · · · David Horovitch
Ethel Brown · · · · · · · · · · · · Rebecca Johnson
Robert Brown · · · · · · · · · · · Benjamin Pullen

OTHER APPEARANCES

Mrs Bott · · · · · · · · · · · · · · · · Lill Roughley
Mr Bott · · · · · · · · · · · · · · · · Robert Austin

CREDITS

creator Richmal Crompton · *adapters/writers*
Simon Booker (9), Allan Baker (3) · *director* David
Giles · *producer* Alan Wright

A dozen further outings for the mischief-
making schoolboy, this time portrayed by the
suitably rebellious-looking Oliver Rokison.
Not wishing to tamper with a proven classic,
the production team remained faithful to the
original spirit of the stories, unconcerned that
some of William's antics and his attitudes
towards girls were likely to attract criticism
in the politically correct 1990s.

Kaleidoscope

UK · BBC · SKETCH/STANDUP

Seven series × **60 mins** · **b/w**

22 Nov 1946–26 June 1953 · fortnightly
mostly Fri 8.30pm

MAIN CAST
see below

CREDITS
producers John Irwin, Stephen McCormack,
Bill Ward, Ronnie Waldman, Graeme Muir,
Bryan Sears, Leslie Jackson, Douglas Moodie

A long-running light entertainment magazine
programme – the staple of immediate post-
war British TV viewing on Friday nights –
that included a number of separate items
within its hour-long running time. Comedy
sketches and standup routines were regularly
featured. The following list represents the
most notable comedic items.

Hogsnorton Calling! with Gillie Potter as the
Station Director. 20 February 1948.

Sir! I Have An Idea! with Richard Murdoch and
Kenneth Horne. 5 March, 19 March, 2 April,
16 April, 30 April, 14 May 1948.

Madam, I Have No Idea! with Richard Hearne.
28 May, 11 June, 25 June 1948.

Every Man His Own ... with Richard Hearne,
written by Max Kester. 20 September, 4 October,
18 October, 13 December 1948, 11 March,
25 March 1949.

Better–Or Worse!! with Cliff Gordon and Diana
Decker. 1 November 1948.

Peeps Into Pottle's Past with Nan Kenway and
Douglas Young. 15 November, 29 November
1948.

The Lodger with Cyril Fletcher and Betty Astell.
14 January, 28 January, 11 February 1949.

Football with Cyril Fletcher and Betty Astell.
25 February 1949.

Mr Pastry Gets A Job with Richard Hearne.
14 April, 28 April, 12 May, 26 May, 9 June,
23 June, 7 July, 21 July 1950. (See **Mr Pastry**.)

First Date with Bernard Braden and Barbara Kelly
(their first TV series together), written by Eric
Nicol. 3 November, 17 November, 1 December,
15 December, 29 December 1950.

These Are The Days with Desmond Walter-Ellis,
written by Godfrey Harrison. 12 January,
26 January, 9 February, 23 February, 9 March,
6 April, 20 April 1951. (See **Reggie Little**.)

Fools Rush In with Tony Hancock (his first TV
series), written by Godfrey Harrison. 4 May,
18 May, 1 June, 15 June, 29 June 1951.

Come Along With Us! with Anthony Oliver and
Mary Mackenzie, written by Godfrey Harrison.
26 October, 9 November, 23 November,
7 December, 21 December 1951, 4 January,
18 January, 1 February 1952.

Our Neighbours with Reginald Purdell and Mai
Bacon, written by Henrik Ege. 26 October,
9 November, 23 November, 7 December 1951.

The Lives Of Colonel Chinstrap (the famous
character created by Ted Kavanagh for the BBC
radio series *It's That Man Again*) with Jack Train
as the ineffable Colonel, written by Michael
Bishop. 4 January, 18 January, 1 February 1952.

After The Show with Benny Hill. 29 February 1952.

Look Here! with George Moon, written by Ronnie
Hanbury. 14 March, 28 March, 18 April, 2 May,
16 May 1952.

Dick Emery (the first TV appearance for the
comic/mimic). 13 June 1952.

Deputies Inc with Jerry Desmonde. 27 June 1952.

Kappatoo

UK · ITV (WORLDWIDE INTERNATIONAL TV FOR
TYNE TEES) · CHILDREN'S SITCOM

14 × **30 mins** · **colour**

Series One (7) 23 May–4 July 1990 ·
Wed 4.40pm

Series Two (7) *Kappatoo II*
9 Apr–21 May 1992 · Thu 4.05pm

MAIN CAST

Kappatoo/Simon Cashmere · · · Simon Nash
Computer · · · · · · · · · · · · · · Andrew O'Connor
Carol Cashmere · · · · · · · · · · · Gillian Eaton
Derek Cashmere · · · · · · · · · · · · John Abbott
Lucy Cashmere · · · · · · · · · Nina Muschallik
Steve Williams · · · · · · · · · · · Graeme Hawley
Sigmasix · · · · · · · · · · · · · · · Felipe Izquierdo
Donut · Lou Hirsch
Tracey Cotton · · · · · Denise Outen (series 1)
Belinda Blunt · · · Tika Viker-Bloss (series 1)
Martin Midgeley · · · · David Dexter (series 1)
Mufour · · · · · · · Vanessa Hadaway (series 1)
Zeta · · · · · · · · · · · · · · Rula Lenska (series 2)
Hazel · · · · · · · · · · · · Janet Dale (series 2)
Brian · · · · · · · · · · · · Nicholas Day (series 2)
Sharon · · · · · · · · · · · · Joanna Hall (series 2)
Melanie · · · · · · · · Sarah Alexander (series 2)
Psycho · · · · · · · · · · · · · Peter Kelly (series 2)

CREDITS
creator Ben Steed · *writers* Ben Steed (series 1),
Ray Marshall/Andrew O'Connor (series 2) ·
directors Tony Kysh (series 1), Alistair Clark
(series 2) · *executive producer* Michael Chapman
(series 1) · *producer* Ray Marshall

A children's sci-fi comedy series, not noticeably high on laughs, that combined the
time-travel element of *Doctor Who* with the
gadgetry of *Star Trek*, the futuristic speak of
Luna and the role-switching of *The Prince
And The Pauper*.

Kappatoo is a 16-year-old boy from the
year 2270 – his real name is Kappa 29643 –
who lands, out of the blue, on top of a
wardrobe belonging to Simon Cashmere,
a 16-year-old boy in present day (1990)

England. Kappatoo needs a favour, someone
to represent him and beat the evil Sigmasix in
a Droid Elimination Contest, and Kappatoo's
smartly dressed humanoid personal computer
(played by Andrew O'Connor) has informed
him of the past existence of a twin. Simon
agrees to help, so they exchange lives. Living
three centuries before his time, Kappatoo is
rescued from predicaments by his futuristic
wrist-band – forced to play in Simon's
football team, for instance, he scores 17 goals
even though he's never seen the game before.
Puzzled by life in 1990, and in particular by
Simon's family, the futureman longs to go
home, back to where words like 'swotmaster'
(meaning school) and 'braindrift' (hangover)
are in use, but Simon Cashmere is enjoying
himself in the 23rd century and doesn't want
to return. But in the second series, Simon,
still resident in the future, has to do battle
with Kappatoo's villainous Aunt Zeta, who
traverses the centuries stealing works of art,
and only just manages to keep one matter-
transference step ahead of the Time Police.

Based on a pair of children's books by
Ben Steed (*Kappatoo* and *Kappatoo 2*), the
TV stories were episodic. Simon Nash –
unconvincing as a 16-year-old for he looked
well into his twenties – played the dual roles
of Kappatoo and Simon Cashmere, Rula
Lenska was Zeta and Nicholas Parsons
guested in three second-series episodes as the
quizmaster on *Ultramatch*, a 23rd-century
'vidi-screen' (TV) game-show.

Karen Kay

UK · BBC · IMPRESSIONISM/STANDUP

16 × **30 mins** · **colour**

Series One (4) 2 Nov–30 Nov 1983 · BBC2
Wed 9.30pm

Series Two (6) 8 Nov–13 Dec 1984 · BBC2
Thu 10.10pm

Series Three (6) 6 Mar–10 Apr 1986 · BBC2
Thu 9pm

MAIN CAST
Karen Kay
Jim Sweeney (series 3)
Steve Steen (series 3)

CREDITS
writers Vicky Pile (8), Bryan Blackburn (5), Karen
Kay (5), Alex Brown/Pat Murray (3), Roger Planer
(3), Angus Deayton (1), Geoffrey Perkins (1) ·
script associates John Junkin (series 1 & 2),
Colin Edmonds (series 3) · *director/producer*
Dave Perrotet

Singer/impressionist Karen Kay had been
working hard in the business for 20 years
when she achieved these starring series.
Initially, the emphasis was on the musical
side of her talents, and her guest stars
reflected this, but by the final series,
encouraged by the acceptability of Marti
Caine and Joan Rivers, Kay switched the
emphasis strongly on to comedy and her

mimicry talents. Popular among her impressions were Dame Edna Everage, Shirley Bassey, Cilla Black, Barbra Streisand, Sybil Fawlty, Peggy from *Hi-de-Hi!*, Julie Walters, Cleo Laine, Edith Piaf, Zola Budd and the rather more difficult Max Boyce, Jimmy Cricket and, intriguingly, E L Wisty. (The last was a famously tedious character invented by Peter Cook, made famous during his weekly stint on ATV's part-networked satirical commentary/magazine show *On The Braden Beat* in the autumn of 1964.)

Kate & Allie

USA · CBS (LACHMAN PRODUCTIONS/REEVES ENTERTAINMENT) · SITCOM
122 × 30 mins · colour
US dates: 19 Mar 1984–11 Sep 1989
UK dates: 17 Feb 1986–1 Jan 1993
(121 episodes) C4 Mon 9.25pm then various days and times

MAIN CAST
Kate McArdle	Susan Saint James
Allison 'Allie' Lowell	Jane Curtin
Emma McArdle	Ari Meyers (1984–88)
Jennie Lowell	Allison Smith
Chip Lowell	Frederick Koehler
Bob Barsky	Sam Freed (1987–89)
Lou Carello	Peter Onorati (1988–89)
Ted Bartelo	Gregory Salata (1984–88)
Dr Charles Lowell	Paul Hecht (1984–86)

CREDITS
creator Sherry Coben · *writers* Bob Randall and others · *director* Bill Persky · *executive producers* Mort Lachman, Merrill Grant, Bill Persky, Saul Turteltaub, Bernie Orenstein · *producers* Bob Randall, Anne Flett, Chuck Ranberg

High-school friends in the 1960s, married in the 1970s and divorced in the 1980s, Kate McArdle, with one child, and Allie Lowell, with two, decide to pool their revenue and expenses by sharing a Greenwich Village flat. The arrangement also allows for each to be a rock of support for the other during a time of emotional need.

Blessed with a level of humour which, while not hard to understand, was far from plebeian, *Kate & Allie* worked within adult parameters: it dealt with the divorcee situation sensibly, without making the two women addle-brained or helpless. And while the overall impression was one of two women surviving perfectly well without men, these were not quite *Spare Rib* readers – they had experienced men the hard way and were certainly going to be more careful in the future, but they knew that, in time, providing the right men came along, they would remarry. (Meanwhile, to avoid allegations of encouraging lesbianism, CBS made certain that the women were often filmed heading upstairs for their separate bedrooms and single beds.)

Although they were friends, Kate and Allie were very different. Kate (the dark-haired one)

was the experienced, modern girl, once a bra-burning, march-participating activist. Allie (the blondeish one), less worldly in her experiences, was governed by an older set of values. The two set about rebuilding their lives and raising the three children (who, in the time-honoured fashion of American sitcoms, enjoyed razor-sharp wit) while trying to survive as single parents. Ex-husbands were seen from time to time, usually to be the butt of some cutting remarks; Kate had a job as a travel agent while Allie ran the household and tried out several part-time jobs – until, in 1987, they decided to work together, launching their own food concern, Kate & Allie Caterers. That same year, having grown through most of their teenage years, Emma McArdle and Jennie Lowell became students at Columbia University. Dates came and went, and the occasional romance blossomed: Kate was briefly engaged to Italian-American plumber Ted Bartelo while Allie began to see former (American) football star turned TV sports commentator Bob Barsky. After he proposed to her on-air, they married, which of course removed her from her daily live-in partnership with Kate that was everything to the series' continuation. This was resolved by having Bob take a job in Washington DC from which he only returned at weekends; Kate moved in with Allie and Chip to provide company.

Sherry Coben was inspired to create *Kate & Allie* while attending a high-school reunion and discovering that many of her former classmates were now divorced single parents. A big fan of *The Mary Tyler Moore Show*, she set out to assemble a new female–female friendship for TV that echoed all that was good in Mary's relationship with Rhoda. It worked: building upon the great chemistry between the two lead actresses, and employing fine writing, *Kate & Allie* was a major success story of 1980s American television.

Susan Saint James had come to small-screen fame via drama series *The Name Of The Game* (NBC, 1968–71) and the comedy/mystery *McMillan And Wife* (NBC, 1971–77). Jane Curtin had made her mark as one of the regular *Saturday Night Live* team, and following *Kate & Allie* she struck sitcom gold anew as one of the few Earthlings in sci-fi comedy *3rd Rock From The Sun*.

Kate And Ted's Show

UK · ITV (GRANADA) · SKETCH/STANDUP
7 editions (6 × 30 mins · 1 × 45 mins) · colour
One series (6 × 30 mins) 4 July–8 Aug 1987 · Sat 6.45pm
Special (45 mins) *Christmas Robbins* 26 Dec 1987 · Sat 5.05pm

MAIN CAST
Kate Robbins
Ted Robbins

Ainslie Foster
Michael Fenton Stevens

CREDITS
script editor Geoff Atkinson · *director* Mike Adams · *executive producers* Stephen Leahy (series), David Liddiment (special) · *producer* Trish Kinane

Following Granada's single special *Robbins*, siblings Kate and Ted were given their own series, easy comic entertainment for summer Saturday evenings. Both worked well but Kate, in particular, shone, impressing with her imitations of Cilla Black and Sarah Ferguson.

The Kate Robbins Show

UK · ITV (GRANADA) · SKETCH/STANDUP
6 × 30 mins · colour
23 July–27 Aug 1988 · Sat 7pm

MAIN CAST
Kate Robbins
Ted Robbins
Michael Fenton Stevens
Paul Bradley

CREDITS
script editor Michael Fenton Stevens · *director* Keith Beckett · *executive producer* David Liddiment · *producer* James Maw

A starring vehicle for the exciting impressionist, promoted through the ranks from her all-siblings show *Robbins* to the series shared with her brother (*Kate And Ted's Show*). She shone once again, startling audiences with her convincing impersonations of, among others, Cilla Black, Anneka Rice, Princesses Anne, Diana and Sarah, Cagney and Lacey, Tina Turner, Julie Andrews, Margaret Thatcher, Raisa Gorbachev, Debbie Greenwood and cast members from soaps *Emmerdale Farm* and *Neighbours*.

Paul Kaye

A talented satirist, Paul Kaye is a fearless purveyor of confrontational comedy, one of a new breed of 'in your face' comedians who dares to go into the darker, edgier corners of the genre. He has appeared in a number of guises, but his most famous creation so far has been Dennis Pennis, the gormless, gauche, feckless, guerrilla interviewer – a sort of **Norman Gunston** for the 1990s. The dangerously-named Pennis had many of the 'qualities' of his Australian antecedent: impervious to embarrassment or the sensitivities of his victims, he approached celebrities and bombarded them with the most ridiculous, insulting and hurtful questions. His unsuspecting victims initially tried to maintain their practised urbane detachment but usually lost their cool a few seconds later. Pennis's BBC status enabled him to get close to his interviewees and this must have contributed to the wrong-footing of his targets, especially the American ones – the image of the BBC there is of a rather stuffy and responsible institution, a point that left them unprepared for such a cutting onslaught. As in all cases where such duplicity is employed, the situation was totally unfair but, with Pennis's dogged determination, and his quick wit, the result was often a hilarious confrontation.

In late 1997 Paul Kaye announced that he was preparing to ditch his Dennis Pennis persona in order to explore other character ideas. The first of these, it seems, was Seamus Webb, unveiled in a C4 programme soon afterwards.

Anyone For Pennis

UK · BBC · SATIRE

1 × 30 mins · colour

15 Sep 1995 · BBC2 Fri 9.30pm

MAIN CAST
Dennis Pennis · · · · · · · · · · · · · Paul Kaye

CREDITS
writers Paul Kaye/Anthony Hines · producer Lucy Robinson

Pennis had been contributing his trademark celebrity 'hits' for segments of *The Sunday Show*, a late-night BBC2 miscellany screened earlier in 1995, and *Anyone For Pennis* was a one-off compilation of titbits filmed for that series. Those brutally interrogated by the microphone-thrusting Pennis included Hugh Grant, Liz Hurley, Madonna, Clive Anderson, Angus Deayton, Michael Heseltine, Edwina Currie and Ian Botham.

Note. Immediately before BBC2 screened this one-off, the star launched his own live music series, *Pennis Pops Out*, screened late nights by ITV over six weeks from 18 August to 22 September 1995.

Very Important Pennis

UK · BBC · SATIRE

3 × 30 mins · colour

9 Aug 1996 · BBC2 Fri 10pm
16 Aug 1996 · BBC2 Fri 10pm
6 June 1997 · BBC2 Fri 9.30pm

MAIN CAST
Dennis Pennis · · · · · · · · · · · · · Paul Kaye

CREDITS
writers Paul Kaye/Anthony Hines · producer Lucy Robinson

More segments from *The Sunday Show*, compiled with brand-new verbal attacks on unsuspecting celebrities. Included in the firing line this time were: Steve Martin, Kevin Costner, Pierce Brosnan, Chris Eubank and Andrew Lloyd Webber (all

show 1), Richard Gere, Dudley Moore and Sandra Bullock (show 2) and Demi Moore, Tony Curtis, Barry Manilow and Jeffrey Archer (show 3).

Kaye also hosted *The Enormous Election With Dennis Pennis* (BBC2, 26 April 1997) in which Pennis linked various items looking into politics, the forthcoming General Election and issues of particular interest to a youth audience. Kaye also appeared in other guises. The programme was repeated the next day in a slightly revised form.

Wrath

UK · C4 (PIRATE) · SATIRE

1 × 30 mins · b/w

3 Nov 1997 · Mon 10.55pm

MAIN CAST
Seamus Declan Webb · · · · · · · · Paul Kaye
Gavin · · · · · · · · · · · · · · · · · David Walliams
Brian · · · · · · · · · · · · · · · · · · Virgil Tracy
Sophie · · · · · · · · · · · · · · Vicky Pepperdine
Mrs Webb · · · · · · · · · · · · · Elaine C Smith
Natalie · · · · · · · · · · · · Candida Scott-Knight
Fan · · · · · · · · · · · · · · · · · · Sam James
Annie Griffin · · · · · · · · · · · · · · · herself
David Arnold · · · · · · · · · · · · · · · himself
Sheryl Garratt · · · · · · · · · · · · · · herself
Johnny Cigarettes · · · · · · · · · · · · himself

CREDITS
writer/director/producer Annie Griffin

Paul Kaye offered up a new creation, Seamus Webb – the lead singer for 'indie' band Spunk – in *Wrath*, the final edition of C4's *Seven Sins* series (15 September– 3 November 1997) in which, each week, someone took an idiosyncratic, 1990s look at one of the seven deadly sins.

Wrath presented a spoof look at Webb, nicknamed 'Britain's angriest man'. In the manner of *This Is Spinal Tap*, the satire took the form of a fly-on-the-wall documentary spending a few days in the company of a mega-hit band. Film-maker Annie Griffin appeared as herself, questioning Seamus Webb and organising events that she hoped would shed light on the enigmatic star. Webb himself, a foul-mouthed, perpetually boozing, angst-ridden rock star, was a recognisable parody of a number of modern-day superstar personalities, with a fair dose of Johnny Rotten about his demeanour, body language and aggression. The other two members of Spunk (the band name, it was explained, *could* stand for s'punk – ie, it's punk) were less the focus of Griffin's gaze, much to the displeasure of the guitarist Gavin, who, fed up with being ignored, claimed that he too was angry although, unlike Webb, he didn't make a noise about it or throw things around. Poor Gavin seemed to bear the brunt of Seamus's wrath, frequently getting objects hurled in his direction, being punched and, on one

occasion, seriously injured by having a glass smashed over his head.

This was a clever, beautifully crafted satire of the sort of arty, hand-held camera documentaries that make a virtue of capturing bad behaviour on film. Shooting in black and white, writer/director/producer Griffin managed to squeeze some sharp new wrinkles out of a hackneyed theme.

Keep 'Em Rolling

UK · BBC · SITCOM

1 × 30 mins · colour

11 Mar 1970 · BBC1 Wed 7.30pm

MAIN CAST
Reggie Turpin · · · · · · · · · · · · · Derek Nimmo
C D Birtwistle · · · · · · · · · · · · · Peter Bayliss
Gladys Smith · · · · · · · · · · · · · · Sheila White
Brownie Brown · · · · · · · · · · Timothy Bateson
Duchess of Haverstock · · · · · · · Fabia Drake
Major Fitzwarren · · · · · · · · · · · Jonathan Cecil

CREDITS
writers David Climie/John Law · film director Jim Franklin · producer Michael Mills

A period-piece comedy set in the early days of photography (utilising authentic vintage equipment supplied by the Kodak Museum). Derek Nimmo was enjoying great popularity at the time but not even he could help this *Comedy Playhouse* pilot develop into a series.

Keep In Step

see *The Phil Silvers Show*

Keep It In The Family   1

UK · ITV (YORKSHIRE) · SITCOM

6 × 30 mins · colour

21 Sep–26 Oct 1971 · Tue mostly 6.55pm

MAIN CAST
James · · · · · · · · · · · · · · · · · · Tim Barrett
Yvonne · · · · · · · · · · · · · · · Vivienne Martin
Val · · · · · · · · · · · · · · · · · · · Tony Maiden
Norah · · · · · · · · · · · · · · · · · · Joyce Grant
Des · · · · · · · · · · · · · · · · · · · Jack Haig

CREDITS
writers David Nobbs/Peter Vincent · director/producer Ian Davidson · executive producer John Duncan

James and Yvonne Bannister have two big problems on their hands: his mother Norah and her war-veteran father Des. Invited to stay the weekend, the grandparents have managed to stretch this to two years, and the word incompatible might well have been invented for them.

Written by the well-established team of Nobbs and Vincent, this series was the first starring role for Tim Barrett, for so long a sideman to the likes of Bernard Cribbins, Brian Rix, Norman Wisdom and others.

Keep It In The Family · 2

UK · ITV (THAMES) · SITCOM

31 × 30 mins · colour

Series One (6) 7 Jan–11 Feb 1980 · Mon 8pm
Series Two (7) 1 Sep–13 Oct 1980 · Mon 8pm
Series Three (6) 1 Sep–6 Oct 1981 · Tue 7.30pm
Series Four (6) 19 Oct–23 Nov 1982 · Tue 8pm
Series Five (6) 7 Sep–19 Oct 1983 · Wed 8.30pm

MAIN CAST

Dudley Rush · · · · · · · · · · · Robert Gillespie
Muriel Rush · · · · · · · · · · · · · Pauline Yates
Susan Rush · · · · · · · · · · · · · Stacy Dorning
Jacqui Rush · · · Jenny Quayle (series 1 & 2);
· · · · · · · · · · · · Sabina Franklyn (series 3–5)
Duncan Thomas · · · · · · · · · · · Glyn Houston

CREDITS

creator Brian Cooke · writers Brian Cooke (16),
Dave Freeman/Greg Freeman (9), David Barry (3),
Peter Learmouth (2), Alex Shearer (1) · directors/
producers Mark Stuart (24), Robert Reed (6),
Michael Mills (1)

The domestic dilemmas of the Rush family:
Dudley and his wife Muriel, who live in the
upstairs section of their Highgate (north
London) home, and their sexy daughters
Susan and Jacqui, who live in the downstairs
flat. Dudley works from home, drawing his
newspaper cartoon-strip Barney – Adventures
Of A Bionic Bulldog. Most of the action centres
on Dudley's over-protective relationship
with his gorgeous and libidinous daughters,
whom the conservative Dudley invites to
live downstairs in order that he can keep a
proprietorial eye over their activities; instead,
he becomes alarmed at the steady stream of
male arrivals and departures. Dudley's boss
Duncan Thomas was worked into most of the
episodes; indeed, when Muriel fails to show in
the final series – she was said to have gone to
Australia to visit her mother – he too moved
into the house. A then unknown Robbie
Coltrane had a minor role in one episode.

Like several other Thames sitcoms of the
period, the format was sold to the USA by Don
Taffner, where it was remade as *Too Close
For Comfort* (and latterly *The Ted Knight
Show*), enjoying a success that endured for 151
episodes between 1980 and 1986, and which
ended only when Knight died of cancer.

Keeping Mum

UK · BBC · SITCOM

8 × 30 mins · colour

17 Apr–5 June 1997 · BBC1 Thu 8.30pm

MAIN CAST

Peggy Beare · · · · · · · · · · · · Stephanie Cole
Andrew Beare · · · · · · · · · · · · · Martin Ball
Richard Beare · · · · · · · · · · · · · David Haig
Tina Beare · · · · · · · · · · · · · · Meera Syal

CREDITS

writer Geoffrey Atherden · director Sylvie Boden ·
executive producer Geoffrey Perkins · producer
Stephen McCrum

A British adaptation of Australian hit sitcom
Mother And Son, featuring the 55-year-old
Stephanie Cole once again (as in *Waiting
For God*) playing a much older woman. The
BBC's version, adapted by the original writer
Geoffrey Atherden, was very similar to its
progenitor but failed to click with the British
public in the same way that the original had
scored with Australian audiences. All the same,
the series boasted some notable firsts: it was
the first BBC adaptation of an Australian
comedy; the UK's (and perhaps the world's)
first all-digital, widescreen studio comedy;
and the first series in the UK to utilise the
same sort of sophisticated sound equipment
used on US shows like *Cheers*.

The cast were effective but there was no
doubt that *Keeping Mum* lacked spark. It
did, however, cause quite a controversy: its
premise – a dotty mother unable to cope for
herself, forcing her youngest son to stay at
home to look after her – was considered in
some quarters to be in poor taste. The
Alzheimer's Disease Society made an official
complaint to the Broadcasting Standards
Commission, and other groups and individuals expressed concern over what they
considered to be the depiction of senile
dementia as a topic of fun. None of these
issues stopped the BBC from commissioning
a second series, set to air in early 1998.

Keeping Score

UK · C4 (REGENT PRODUCTIONS) · SITCOM

1 × 60 mins · colour

4 Mar 1987 · Wed 10pm

MAIN CAST

Banks · · · · · · · · · · · · · · · · Martyn Hesford
Penelope · · · · · · · · · · · · Tessa Peake-Jones
The Earl of Albany · · · · · · · · · · Charles Gray
Prime Minister · · · · · · · · · · · · Gaye Brown

CREDITS

writer Guy Jenkin · director/producer William G
Stewart

The first of six hour-length comedies made
by William G Stewart and aired by C4 under
the collective banner *Tickets For The Titanic*,
all sharing the theme of Britain's 1980s slide.
Keeping Score was written by Guy Jenkin;
two of the others were by his writing partner
Andy Hamilton – the pair consciously trying
to stretch themselves beyond the half-hour
format.

In this edition, Martyn Hesford played a
punk rocker – all tattoos, chains and Mohican
hairstyle – whose appearance and poor
background appeal to the daughter of the
Earl of Albany, played by Tessa Peake-Jones.
(They met when he was signing on for the
dole; she's a DHSS clerk.) Nicknaming
themselves the Dread Brigade, the pair keep
a note of the insults hurled at them and,
ultimately, present this to the Thatcher-like

Prime Minister, who happens to be keeping a
list of her own.

Keeping Up Appearances

UK · BBC · SITCOM

**45 episodes (42 × 30 mins · 1 × 60 mins · 1 × 50
mins · 1 × short special) · colour**

Series One (6) 29 Oct–3 Dec 1990 · BBC1
Mon 8.30pm
Series Two (10) 1 Sep–3 Nov 1991 · BBC1
Sun 7.15pm
Special · 25 Dec 1991 · BBC1 Wed 8.50pm
Series Three (7) 6 Sep–18 Oct 1992 · BBC1
Sun 7.15pm
Series Four (7) 5 Sep–17 Oct 1993 · BBC1
Sun 7pm
Special (60 mins) 26 Dec 1993 · BBC1 Sun 7pm
Special (50 mins) 25 Dec 1994 · BBC1
Sun 5.25pm
Series Five (10) 3 Sep–5 Nov 1995 · BBC1
Sun 8.30pm
Short special · part of Children In Need 24 Nov
1995 · BBC1 Fri around 8pm
Special · 25 Dec 1995 · BBC1 Mon 8pm

MAIN CAST

Hyacinth Bucket · · · · · · · · Patricia Routledge
Richard Bucket · · · · · · · · · · · · · Clive Swift
Liz · · · · · · · · · · · · · · · · · Josephine Tewson
Emmet · · · · · David Griffin (series 2 onwards)
Daisy · · · · · · · · · · · · · · · · · Judy Cornwell
Onslow · · · · · · · · · · · · · · · Geoffrey Hughes
Rose · · · · · · · · · · · Shirley Stelfox (series 1);
· · · · · · · · · · · Mary Millar (series 2 onwards)

OTHER APPEARANCES

Vicar · · · · · · · · · · · · · · · · · Jeremy Gittins
Vicar's wife · · · · · · · · · · · · · Marion Barron

CREDITS

writer Roy Clarke · director/producer Harold Snoad

Snobs have long been sitcom anti-heroes –
Hancock was a snob, as were Basil Fawlty,
Rupert Rigsby and even, in his rallies against
'inferior' racial minorities, Alf Garnett – but
Hyacinth Bucket, which she insisted was
pronounced 'bouquet', was the mother of all
snobs. She was a barnstorming, interfering,
thick-skinned monster, who compulsively
organised other people's lives and existed
totally in a self-obsessed world, completely
oblivious to the thoughts and feelings of
others. In the front line of her social assaults
was her husband Richard, a meek, hen-pecked
individual who yearned for a quiet life but
instead found himself steamrollered into
falling in with his wife's plans. Neighbours
Liz and Emmet also bore the brunt of her
schemes, while Hyacinth's sisters Rose and
Daisy – both major disappointments to her –
who lived with their dotty father on a nearby
council estate, were also too close for comfort,
Daisy particularly so: she mooned about most
of the time, complaining about the paucity of
sexual activity given her by her beery slob of
a husband, Onslow.

The prolific Roy Clarke was still writing
Last Of The Summer Wine when he

brought *Keeping Up Appearances* to TV, but he managed to maintain a high quality product – in the dialogue, at least – and the excellent Patricia Routledge did full justice to his lines, delivering them with venom and relish. But the plotting and characterisations were less polished, and it stretched belief to consider that anyone would put up with Hyacinth for as long as they did. Sure, she suffered occasional setbacks, and was put in her place from time to time, but only momentarily, and then she was bouncing back, ploughing another path through the lives of her friends, relatives and acquaintants, never once truly learning from her numerous mistakes.

But while Hyacinth Bucket was a ghastly creation, she attracted huge audiences and was beloved by a large proportion of the population, proof positive of the British viewer's inexhaustible appetite for comic snobbery. The series was also an unexpected hit in the USA, achieving relatively high ratings when screened there by a number of Public Broadcasting Service (PBS) stations. This US popularity led to the making of a special programme, *The Memoirs Of Hyacinth Bucket*, screened by PBS stations in March 1997 but not seen in Britain; the show featured highlights from previous episodes with a newly taped linking narration, in character, by Onslow and Daisy. Hyacinth was considered by Americans to be a character worthy of further TV exploitation too, and network producers were contemplating a US adaptation of the series as this book was being written, their intention being to set the show in Boston, perceived as the heartland of American social snobbery.

Kelly Monteith

UK · BBC · SITCOM/STANDUP/SKETCH

36 × 30 mins · colour

Series One (6) 15 Nov–20 Dec 1979 · BBC2 Thu 9pm

Series Two (6) 28 Oct–2 Dec 1980 · BBC2 Tue 9pm

Series Three (6) 2 Nov–7 Dec 1981 · BBC2 Mon 9pm

Series Four (6) 23 Sep–28 Oct 1982 · BBC2 Thu 9pm

Series Five (6) 1 Nov–6 Dec 1983 · BBC2 Tue 9pm

Series Six (6) 10 Sep–15 Oct 1984 · BBC2 Mon 9pm

MAIN CAST
Kelly Monteith
Gabrielle Drake (series 1 & 2)

CREDITS
writers Kelly Monteith/Neil Shand · *director* Stanley Appel (series 1) · *producers* James Moir (series 1–3), Bill Wilson (series 4), Geoff Posner (series 5), John Kilby (series 6)

A sharply funny series for the American standup comic Kelly Monteith that pre-dated the show-within-a-show spoofs *It's Garry Shandling's Show* and *Sean's Show*. Born in 1943, Monteith grew up in St Louis and left for California when he was 16 to break into show business, which he achieved by selling one-liner jokes to Phyllis Diller. After gaining much work experience on the strip-club circuit in Florida, Monteith was noticed by TV producers and started appearing on late-night chat-shows, particularly NBC's flagship *Tonight*. In 1976, he landed his own four-week CBS comedy/variety series *The Kelly Monteith Show* and the following year won over a British audience when he appeared on *Des O'Connor Tonight* (BBC2, 21 November 1977); after he returned for a second appearance on the show (18 September 1978) the BBC decided to offer Monteith his own series. The comic had already been hawking one particular idea around the US networks, without success, and he concluded that while the censorious nature of American TV was working against him, he would be given more creative freedom by the BBC.

Monteith paired up with the British writer Neil Shand, a long-time writer of jokes for David Frost and the resident script-man on *Des O'Connor Tonight*, and the resulting series had a simple but slick premise: it depicted the humorous events in the life of a standup comic. Monteith played a character who shared his name, career and many of his own characteristics, but who had a different life-situation and a screen wife, played by Gabrielle Drake. (Such was the blurred relationship between fact and fiction that many viewers believed that Monteith and Drake *were* a married couple.) What made the series different from previous show-business-based scenarios (like, say, *The Burns And Allen Show*) was the fact that it often dispensed with an overall plot in favour of a series of sketches showing aspects of Monteith's life. It also broke new ground by showing the character preparing for a scene, performing it and then dissecting it afterwards in the dressing-room or at home, such self-referential devices being perfectly acceptable within the format.

Kelly Monteith was sophisticated and featured adult themes, albeit spicy rather than shocking. By the third series his screen wife was no longer part of the plot and subsequent editions showed the comic as a divorcee, trying to get back into the routine of dating. This was a direct, but unintentional, reflection on Monteith's own life: he divorced from his real-life wife about the same time that he was deserted by his on-screen wife. Monteith remained throughout a likeable guy, riddled with insecurities and endlessly philosophical, able to comedically reflect aloud on life in a

manner not seen again on TV until *Seinfeld*. For British TV audiences, the sight of an American standup comedian appearing regularly on 'our television', in shows made in BBC studios and with a sexy English female co-star, was an appealing diversion from the norm, and Monteith – considered less brash and more personable than most of his compatriots – gained a good deal of personal popularity in the UK as a result.

Note. Throughout the run of the BBC series Monteith continued to work on US television, commuting back and forth between the countries, and in 1980 he fronted a comedy/music/news series on CBS, *No Holds Barred*. He also made special films, such as *Kelly Monteith's Swinging London*, screened in the UK by C4 on 23 June 1983.

Kelly Monteith In One

UK · BBC · STANDUP

1 × 40 mins · colour

13 May 1985 · BBC2 Mon 9.35pm

MAIN CAST
Kelly Monteith

CREDITS
writer Kelly Monteith · *producer* Geoff Posner

Monteith in standup mode, in a performance recorded at the Ambassador's Theatre in London. The comedian's stage act covered many of the topics touched upon in his earlier BBC2 series.

Kelly's Eye

UK · ITV (TVS) · SKETCH

6 × 45 mins · colour

20 July–24 Aug 1985 · Sat 6.30pm

MAIN CAST
Matthew Kelly
Helen Atkinson Wood
Felicity Montagu
David Simeon
Jim Sweeney

CREDITS
writers Colin Bostock-Smith (6), Geoff Atkinson (6), Paul Minett/Brian Leveson (6), James Hendrie (3), Jim Pullin (3) · *script editor* Colin Bostock-Smith · *director* David G Hillier · *producer* John Kaye Cooper

A hit-and-miss sketch show fronted by Matthew Kelly, known to ITV sitcom watchers thanks to *Room Service*, *Holding The Fort* and *Relative Strangers*, but still thought of as the *Game For A Laugh* prankster. *Kelly's Eye* was broadcast in the same Saturday evening slot, presumably in the hope of attracting the same audience.

Ken Dodd … [various shows]

see DODD, Ken

Kenan And Kel

USA · NICKELODEON (TOLLINS-ROBBINS PRODUCTIONS) · CHILDREN'S SITCOM

26 × 30 mins (to 31/12/97 · continuing into 1998) · colour

US dates: 12 Oct 1996 to date

UK dates: 27 Sep 1997 to date (11 episodes to 31/12/97) BBC1 Sat around 11am

MAIN CAST

Kenan Rockmore · · · · · · · · Kenan Thompson
Kel Kimble · · · · · · · · · · · · · · Kel Mitchell
Kyra Rockmore · · · · · · · · · · Vanessa Baden
Roger Rockmore · · · · · · · · · · · · · Ken Foree
Chris Rigby · · · · · · · · · · · · · Dan Frischman

CREDITS

creator Kim Bass · *writers* various · *directors* Brian Robbins, Alan Rosen, Malcolm-Jamal Warner · *executive producers* Dan Schneider, Brian Robbins, Mike Tollin · *producers* Kevin Kopelow, Heath Seifert, Nick Donatelli

Like a young and black Abbott and Costello, Kenan and Kel are a comedy double-act in which one is dumb (Kenan) and the other (Kel) dumber. Kenan Thompson is the plumper of the pair, but (unlike Abbott and Costello) it is the wirier one, Kel Mitchell, who is involved in most of the physical comedy.

Episodes of their sitcom began with the duo, as themselves, standing on stage and introducing the week's story – the curtains then parted to depict a typical sitcom set and the pair entered the story in character. Much of the action took place at Kenan's house, where Kel was a constant and disruptive visitor. The plots were lightweight – typically, for a US teen comedy – but the studio audiences and those at home lapped it up. Despite the hip references and street slang, *Kenan And Kel* was, in many ways, an old-fashioned show, its principal strengths being the two energetic and keen leads, their only real failing being that, occasionally, they tried just too hard to please.

At the same time as starring in this sitcom, Thompson and Mitchell were appearing too in a sketch comedy series, *All That*, also screened by the US cable company Nickelodeon. The success of both series led to starring roles for Thompson and Mitchell in the 1997 movie *Good Burger* (directed by Brian Robbins).

Note. BBC1 screened *Kenan And Kel* within the Saturday-morning children's magazine show *Live & Kicking*.

The Kenneth Williams Show

UK · BBC · SKETCH

7 editions (6 × 30 mins · 1 × 45 mins) · colour

One series (6) 9 Feb–16 Mar 1970 · BBC1 Mon 9.10pm

Special (45 mins) 21 Jan 1976 · BBC2 Wed 9pm

MAIN CAST

Kenneth Williams
Joan Sims (series)

Lance Percival (special)
Anna Karen (special)

CREDITS

writers of series John Law/Kenneth Williams (5), John Law/Kenneth Williams/Austin Steele (1) · *writers of special* David Nobbs/Peter Vincent, Derek Collyer, Ian Davidson, Eric Geen, Howard Imber, Spike Mullins · *producers* Roger Ordish (series), Terry Hughes (special)

Kenneth Williams was a somewhat difficult talent for television, never seeming as comfortable as he was on radio – where his vocal dexterity was allowed full rein – or in feature films, where his wide and outlandish range of acting abilities was unhindered. Until this 1970 BBC1 sketch series, in which he was paired with his *Carry On* stablemate Joan Sims, Williams' only regular TV exposure was as the host of a long-running (1966–68) BBC2 series, *International Cabaret*, in which he introduced some fairly dodgy continental variety stars, and of which, according to his published diaries, he tired rapidly.

Sadly, Williams' writing collaborator John Law was taken ill during rehearsals for the first show of the BBC1 series and died (in his early forties) during the taping of the second. Most of the series was already written, but his passing cast a pall over the proceedings.

The 1976 special paired Williams with Lance Percival. A week later they launched a combined BBC radio series, *Oh, Get On With It!*, which also featured Miriam Margolyes.

Note. Three years before the series, Williams starred in a short vignette screened within the 1967 version of BBC1's annual comedy jamboree *Christmas Night With The Stars*. The piece was co-written with John Law and produced by Stewart Morris.

Kenny Everett ... [various shows]

see EVERETT, Kenny

Kept In

see BUTTERWORTH, Peter

Kevin Turvey – The Man Behind The Green Door

UK · BBC · SITCOM/SKETCH

1 × 40 mins · colour

13 Sep 1982 · BBC2 Mon 9pm

MAIN CAST

Kevin Turvey · · · · · · · · · · · · · · · Rik Mayall

OTHER APPEARANCES

Robbie Coltrane
Adrian Edmondson
Gwyneth Guthrie
Roger Sloman

CREDITS

writers Rik Mayall/Colin Gilbert · *executive producer* Sean Hardie · *producer* Colin Gilbert

Rik Mayall's bizarre alter ego Kevin Turvey earned this one-off spoof documentary after his successful cameo appearances in *A Kick Up The Eighties*. A self-appointed investigative journalist, Turvey was a wide-eyed berk from Redditch with a disjointed outlook on life that was mostly a cover for his pathetic existence. In this show, a BBC documentary crew spent a week with Turvey, capturing the flavour of his lifestyle and deeply flawed, off-beam philosophies. The programme's other performers appeared in sketches within the sitcom format.

A Kick Up The Eighties

UK · BBC · SKETCH

10 × 30 mins · colour

Series One (6) 21 Sep–26 Oct 1981 · BBC2 Mon 9pm

Series Two (4) 3 Jan–24 Jan 1984 · BBC2 Tue 9pm

MAIN CAST

Ron Bain
Miriam Margolyes
Roger Sloman
Tracey Ullman
Kevin Turvey · · · · · · · · · · · · · · · Rik Mayall
Richard Stilgoe (series 1)
Robbie Coltrane (series 2)

CREDITS

writers Rik Mayall, Kim Fuller, Lawrence Wormald, Bob Black, Mick Deasey, Andrew Smith, Terry Treloar, Ian Pattison, Pete Sargeant, Bill Smith, Ed McHenry, Bob Sinfield, Tex Winchester, Dennis McHale, Niall Clark, Robbie Coltrane, Paul Eldergill, Guy Jenkin, Donnie Kerr, Rona Munro, Barry Faulkner, Simon Holder, Dudley Rogers, Jim Pollock, Laurie Ventre, John Speer, Alec Adcock, Tim Douglas, Tim Hilton, Derek Harris, John Williams, Gerald Mahlowe, Glyn Rees, David Slade, Frank Walsh, Andrew Smith, Roger David Lewis · *script editor* Laurie Rowley · *director* Brian Jobson (series 2) · *producers* Tom Gutteridge (series 1), Colin Gilbert (series 2)

A finely judged contemporary sketch show of the *Not The Nine O'Clock News* ilk but with a nod to the emerging wave of 'alternative' comedy, in which a strong team combined well to perform short sketches and musical parodies. Tracey Ullman and Miriam Margolyes demonstrated their versatility once more, as indeed did all of the cast, effortlessly slipping into and out of different characters in a variety of well-written and genuinely funny sketches. Rik Mayall appeared only in self-contained sequences as 'investigative journalist' Kevin Turvey, a boorish, dysfunctional time-waster with a wide-eyed stare. To maintain the illusion that his invention was real, Mayall's name did not appear in the closing credits whereas Kevin

Turvey's did. (For more on Turvey, see previous entry.)

For the second series, Colin Gilbert was brought in as producer, his debut TV production with the newly formed BBC Scotland Comedy Unit. Richard Stilgoe had left and Robbie Coltrane took his place. This second series was more slick and competent than the first, and Coltrane was particularly impressive with his vocal range, powerful delivery and natural acting technique.

Overall, *A Kick Up The Eighties* successfully blended straight comedy sketches with satire and remained consistently amusing. It compared well with *Not The Nine O'Clock News*, yet for some reason never loomed as large in the public's affection. Later, with a slight change of personnel, the production returned under with *Laugh??? I Nearly Paid My Licence Fee*.

The Kids From 47A

UK · ITV (ATV) · CHILDREN'S SITCOM

42 × 30 mins · colour

Series One (15) 30 May–5 Sep 1973 · Wed 4.50pm

Series Two (13) 23 Jan–17 Apr 1974 · Wed 4.50pm

Series Three (13) 7 Aug–30 Oct 1974 · Wed 4.50pm

Special *Home Sweet Home* 31 Aug 1975 · Sun 5.35pm

MAIN CAST

Jess Gathercole	Christine McKenna
Willy Gathercole	Nigel Greaves
Binny Gathercole	Gaynor Hodgson
George Gathercole	Russell Lewis

OTHER APPEARANCES

Miss East	Joan Newell
Mr Stephens	Lloyd Lamble
Mrs Batty	Maryann Turner (series 1)
Mrs Grubb	PeggyAnn Clifford (series 1 & 2)
Mr Grubb	Reg Lye (series 1 & 2)

CREDITS

creator Charlotte Mitchell · *writers* John Kane (9), Lynda Marchal (8), Chris Allen (4), Philip Neil (4), Gail Renard (3), Phil Redmond (3), Charlotte Mitchell (2), Aubrey Cash (2), Gerald Frow (1), Michael G Jackson (1), not known (5) · *script editor* Gail Renard · *directors* Richard Bramall (23), Alan Coleman (14), Jonathan Wright Miller (4), John Scholz-Conway (special) · *producer* Alan Coleman (series 1 & 2), Richard Bramall (series 3), John Scholz-Conway (special)

An innovative children's sitcom that managed to wring comedy out of what was anything but a funny situation. Four children – Jess, 16, Willy, 14, Binny, 12, and George, 8 – live with their widowed mother. Suddenly, mum is rushed into hospital, leaving the children without a guardian, at least until their Aunt Olive arrives. But Auntie never does come and mum (in the programmes, at least) is never seen again, so the children have to fend for themselves. Without adult supervision they get into plenty of scrapes, trying to cope with the shopping, cooking, washing, bills, and keeping sweet with the neighbours. The title came from the children's address: they live at number 47A.

By the start of the second series mum had died and the children were fully-fledged orphans. Jess, the only one in work, becomes a mother-figure, her wages supporting the family. Willy (who wants to play football full-time when he grows up), Binny (who likes the Arts and wants to be a writer) and George (the villain of the piece) are all still at school.

The Kids In The Hall

CANADA · CBC (BROADWAY VIDEO INTERNATIONAL) · SKETCH

110 (approx) editions × mostly 30 mins · colour

Canadian dates: 1989–95

UK dates: 20 Apr–13 July 1994 (12 × 30 mins · 1 × 50 mins) C4 Wed mostly 10.30pm

MAIN CAST

David Foley
Bruce McCulloch
Kevin McDonald
Mark McKinney
Scott Thompson

CREDITS

creators cast · *writers* cast and Paul Bellini, Brian Hartt, Norm Hiscock · *directors* John Blanchard, Stephen Surjik, Michael Kennedy · *executive producers* Lorne Michaels, Jeff Ross · *producers* Joe Forristal, Jeffrey Berman, Cindy Park

Although many shows are labelled 'cult' few deserve the epithet as much as *The Kids In The Hall*. The Canadian comedy troupe of this name formed in Toronto in 1984; subsequently, two of its members, McCulloch and McKinney, went on to write for *Saturday Night Live*, the creator/producer of which, Lorne Michaels (also a Canadian), having decided that they were ripe for TV stardom. Then, in 1988, Michaels produced a *Kids In The Hall* special for HBO, and a regular series, co-financed by the Canadian Broadcasting Corporation, followed soon afterwards. The series aired on CBC in Canada and on HBO in America; a bowdlerised version appeared later on CBS, and 13 uncut editions found their way across the Atlantic to C4. In all places, the series quickly found an enthusiastic young audience who were captivated by its risqué and irreverent nature.

A straightforward sketch show on the surface, *The Kids In The Hall* had enough idiosyncrasies to lift it out of the mainstream. The five-man team took most of the roles, appearing in drag – *à la Monty Python* – to portray any female parts. They were also responsible for most of the writing, and developed a characteristic style in which strange things happened in normal places and oddly intense people held forth on a number of subjects. There were several recurring characters and themes, notably 'the half-human chicken lady', 'the weight-obsessed ladies that lunch', 'office idiot boy', 'the overly aggressive police interrogators' and the 'head crusher', a bizarrely angry individual who squinted at people from a distance and imagined crushing their heads between his fingers.

The series was voluntarily ended by the troupe in 1995 but they released a feature film spin-off, *The Kids In The Hall: Brain Candy*, in 1996, directed by Kelly Makin.

Kin Of The Castle

UK · BBC · CHILDREN'S SITCOM

1 × 30 mins · colour

30 Sep 1987 · BBC1 Wed 5.05pm

MAIN CAST

Sackville	James Aidan
Crypes	Aubrey Woods
Phenomena	Anna Quayle
Cecil	Simeon Pearl
Pamela	Joely Richardson

CREDITS

writers Nick Symons/Sandi Toksvig · *producer* Jeremy Swan

An odd one-off for younger viewers, possible a pilot try-out for a series, co-written by standup comic Sandi Toksvig. The programme was a bizarre fantasy featuring a family many hundreds of years old.

A Kind Of Living

UK · ITV (CENTRAL) · SITCOM

26 × 30 mins · colour

Series One (6) 19 Feb–25 Mar 1988 · Fri 8pm

Series Two (7) 11 Nov–23 Dec 1988 · Fri mostly 7.30pm

*Series Three (13) 25 Mar–19 Aug 1990 · Sun mostly 7.15pm then 5.30pm

MAIN CAST

Trevor Beasley	Richard Griffiths
Carol Beasley	Frances de la Tour (series 1 & 2)
Brian Thompson	Tim Healy
Ken Dixon	C J Allen
Og	Christopher Rothwell
Tedstill	Alec Christie (series 1 & 2)
Linda	Anita Carey (series 3)
Baby Joe	Luke Freeman (series 3)

CREDITS

writers Paul Makin (25), Geoff Rowley (1) · *script consultants* Laurence Marks/Maurice Gran · *director* Paul Harrison · *producer* Glen Cardno

Established actors Richard Griffiths and Frances de la Tour headed the line-up in this ITV sitcom that seemed to delight in the unexpected and combined witty verbiage with occasional slapstick.

As Trevor and Carol Beasley, the two are married, and newly moved down to London from Bolton because Trevor, a teacher – often referred to by surname only – has a new job as Head of English in a local school. Carol, to her deep chagrin, has no job, yet, and proves like a bear with a sore head until she finds one. She does, however, have a baby to look after, six months old but not yet named and so referred to as Og. Brian Thompson, Trevor's blunt friend from Bolton, happens to live just down the road from them, and the two renew their friendship, not having seen one another for five years. Brian still runs a chip shop and remains keen on removing beer-bottle caps with his teeth. All Trevor's relationships – with wife, with friend, with jolly next-door neighbour Ken Dixon, and with others – are stormy, because he's a man full of pent-up frustration, cynicism and regret.

By the final series Carol has finally left Trevor and gone off to seek a career in pastures new. Trevor and Brian return to Bolton where the former embarks upon a relationship with the latter's sister Linda, whom he has known since their childhood. Linda too is the single parent of a baby son, Joe, and the two decide to marry.

*Note. LWT temporarily ceased carrying *A Kind Of Living* on 13 May 1990, eight episodes into the final series of 13. Although, in other regions, the series carried on until 24 June, the remaining five episodes were screened in the London area from 22 July to 19 August 1990, relegated to an earlier, off-peak time slot.

Kindly Leave The Kerb

UK · ITV (LWT) · SITCOM

6 × 30 mins · colour
22 May–26 June 1971 · Sat 9.30pm

MAIN CAST
Ernest Tanner ·········· Peter Butterworth
Sidney Rochester ··········· Peter Jones
Archie ··············· Meredith Edwards

CREDITS
writers Johnnie Mortimer/Brian Cooke · producer Derek Bennett

Prolific partners Mortimer and Cooke had long wished to write about what they saw as 'the chancier side of the entertainment business'. Their first effort was *The Incredible Mister Tanner*, a 1968 episode of *The Ronnie Barker Playhouse*, in which Barker starred as a hopeless Houdini act, Cyril Tanner, busking the streets of London with his younger partner Arthur (played by Richard O'Sullivan). Three years later the writers developed this into a full series, making the ages of the two characters the same and casting Peter Butterworth and the ever-excellent Peter Jones as the two street entertainers, now renamed Ernest and Sidney. As before, their stage is the London streets, and Tanner is a second-rate (at absolute best) escapologist while earnest Ernest goes

around with the brimmed hat and glib spiel. The pair live in a basement flat, earning just enough to keep themselves going, and frequent a run-down café run by the equally run-down Archie.

Kindly Leave The Kerb ran for only one series but, still not finished with the idea, Mortimer and Cooke revived it again ten years later with a Thames series that reverted to the original title – **The Incredible Mr Tanner**.

Kindly Leave The Stage

UK · BBC · STANDUP

7 × 25 mins · b/w
17 Aug–12 Oct 1968 · BBC1 Sat mostly 11.15pm

MAIN CAST
Billy Dainty
Don Smoothey
Len Lowe
Dorothy Wayne
Ken Roberts

CREDITS
writers Edwin Hicks/Philip Hindin (5), Len Lowe (4), Bob Block (3), Bert Platt/Harry Bright (1), Gerry Maxin (1), Don Ross (1), J B Boothroyd (1), Con West (1) · script editor Bob Block · producer Sydney Lotterby

The brief of *Kindly Leave The Stage* was to unashamedly plunder the most groan-inducing jokes from the British music-hall era and unleash them on a late-Saturday-night audience more used to savage satire than gags about nose-less dogs and slack knicker elastic. Each week a (somewhat obscure) music-hall act joined the regular troupe in the necro-comedy. Although Hicks, Hindin, Lowe and Block took the main 'writers' credits, 'archaeologists' might have been a more apt description.

Dave King

Born in Twickenham on 23 June 1929, Dave King was among Britain's most popular comics in the late 1950s, his BBC and ITV programmes in that period living up to the cliché of 'emptying the pubs on a Saturday night'. King left school at the age of 12 and, at 15, after dallying with several occupations, toured the music-halls as a member of Morton Fraser's Harmonica Gang, a humorous combo of musicians fronted by a midget who tended to steal the show. After a spell of National Service with the RAF, King went solo and followed in the footsteps of Norman Wisdom and Benny Hill as the compere of the BBC TV series *Show Case* before being given his own series in late

1955, followed soon after by an appearance in the *Royal Variety Show*. Television made King a national star and such was his talent that he was spotted by American TV executives and given a series of his own there in 1959. King also enjoyed great success as a singer in the late 1950s, scoring a British top ten single with 'Memories Are Made Of This'. But being a star in the States captured King's fancy, and he made a further, later attempt to crack Hollywood, albeit without particular success. Wishing to move into straight acting, King appeared in several movies, including *Pirates Of Tortuga* (USA, 1961), *Go To Blazes* (UK, 1962), *The Road To Hong Kong* (USA, 1962), *Strange Bedfellows* (USA, 1965), *Cuba* (USA, 1979), *The Long Good Friday* (UK, 1979) and *Reds* (USA, 1981) as well as TV plays *Arsenic And Old Lace* and *The Machine Calls It Murder*. From just before and subsequent to his last TV comedy series in 1980, King concentrated solely on drama, appearing in *The Sweeney*, *Coronation Street*, *Pennies From Heaven*, *Target*, *Minder*, *Bleak House*, *Rumpole Of The Bailey*, *Perfect Scoundrels*, *Heartbeat* and other programmes.

See also *The Robert Horton Show* and *Round And Round*.

The Dave King Show   1

UK · BBC · SKETCH

11 × 60 mins · b/w
Series One (6) 15 Oct 1955–3 Mar 1956 · monthly Sat 8.30pm
*Series Two (5) 15 Dec 1956–6 Apr 1957 · monthly Sat 8.30pm

MAIN CAST
Dave King

CREDITS
writers Sid Green/Dick Hills · producer Ernest Maxin

Comedy writers Sid Green and Dick Hills, who later found fame not only scripting for Morecambe and Wise but appearing on screen with them too, made their break-through with Dave King, whom they discovered playing third fiddle on a theatrical bill when he was a member of Morton Fraser's Harmonica Gang. The writers determined to make their name by turning King into a star, and achieved both aims with some ease. King was bright and sharp and put across their material with brilliant timing.

*Note. Like the first, this second series was intended to run to six editions, but the opening show (17 November 1956) was cancelled after King was rushed into hospital with appendicitis. A month later he was back, however, with the remaining five programmes.

The Dave King Show   2

UK · ITV (ATV) · SKETCH

11 editions (7 × 60 mins · 3 × 55 mins · 1 × 45 mins) · b/w

12 Apr 1958 · Sat 8.30pm (60 mins)
24 May 1958 · Sat 8.30pm (60 mins)
5 July 1958 · Sat 8pm (60 mins)
27 Sep 1958 · Sat 8pm (55 mins)
8 Nov 1958 · Sat 7.55pm (60 mins)
20 Dec 1958 · Sat 7.55pm (60 mins)
7 Feb 1959 · Sat 7.55pm (60 mins)
21 Mar 1959 · Sat 7.55pm (60 mins)
2 May 1959 · Sat 8pm (45 mins)
10 Oct 1959 · Sat 8pm (55 mins)
21 Nov 1959 · Sat 8pm (55 mins)

MAIN CAST
Dave King

CREDITS
writers Sid Green/Dick Hills · *producer* Brian Tesler

Eleven programmes screened within the commercial network's *Saturday Spectacular* strand. The first nine caught the attention of American TV executives, who took the three-man team of King, Green and Hills across to the USA for 19 live programmes, screened by NBC as *Kraft Music Hall Presents: The Dave King Show* from 20 May to 23 September 1959. Sid and Dick appeared in these shows too, and were aided in their writing by a then unknown young American, Mel Brooks.

All three Englishmen then returned home for two further ITV specials later in the year.

The Dave King Show   3

UK · ITV (ATV) · SKETCH

7 × 30 mins · b/w

9 Nov–21 Dec 1962 · Fri 8.30pm

MAIN CAST
Dave King
Lisa Daniely

CREDITS
writers Sid Green/Dick Hills · *producer* Albert Locke

A weekly series of seven programmes, in which Lisa Daniely appeared throughout as King's wife.

The Dave King Show   4

UK · ITV (ABC) · SKETCH

6 × 30 mins · b/w

4 May–8 June 1963 · Sat 8.30pm

MAIN CAST
Dave King

CREDITS
writers Brad Ashton/Bob Block/Gerry Maxin · *producer* Ernest Maxin

With a new writing/production team behind him, King starred in a six-week series for

ABC, performing sketch material with his special guests, including Dennis Price, Bernard Bresslaw and Patrick Macnee.

Dave's Kingdom

UK · ITV (ATV) · SITCOM

6 × 30 mins · b/w

21 Oct–9 Dec 1964 · Wed 9.10pm

MAIN CAST
Dave King
Victor Maddern
Pat Goh
Jack Douglas
Billy Cornelius
John Hewer
Nicholas Brent

CREDITS
writers John Warren/John Singer (5), Mike Pratt/Jay Webb (1) · *producer* Francis Essex

Now 35, and back from his latest spell in America, King was quickly offered a weekly half-hour series by ATV that involved him in a variety of fantasy situations, Walter Mitty-style, occurring in and around his apartment, or – to utilise the title – his kingdom. Victor Maddern offered the main support, appearing as Dave's landlord and henchman.

Sixteen years later, King turned up in another sitcom utilising a whimsical fantasy style, *Fancy Wanders* (see final entry, below).

Dave King

UK · BBC · STANDUP

1 × 40 mins · colour

20 Feb 1969 · BBC2 · Fri 8.25pm

MAIN CAST
Dave King

CREDITS
writers Sid Green/Dick Hills · *producer* John Ammonds

A one-off recording of King's standup show at the popular London night-spot, the Talk Of The Town.

Note. Also in 1969, King starred in a short (28-minute) cinema film, *It's The Only Way To Go*, a black comedy, in mime, about a man who dies from excitement while watching a striptease act. It was written by Sid Green and Dick Hills.

The Dave King Show   5

UK · ITV (ATV) · SKETCH

9 × 30 mins · colour

20 Nov 1969–22 Jan 1970 · Thu 9pm

MAIN CAST
Dave King

CREDITS
writers Sid Green/Dick Hills · *director* Pat Johns · *producer* Dick Hills

King reunited with Sid Green and Dick Hills, and with ATV, for this nine-week series that attempted to recapture his glory days. It was only partially successful, and King never again returned to the sketch-show genre, turning instead to sitcom (the single-episode *Tell It To The Judge* and the seven-week series *Fancy Wanders*, both written by Sid Green) and then straight acting.

Tell It To The Judge

UK · ITV (LWT) · SITCOM

1 × 30 mins · colour

23 Mar 1980 · Sun 8.45pm

MAIN CAST
Det-Insp Vic Saggers · · · · · · · · · · Dave King
Det-Insp Jock Stuart · · · · · · · · John Grieve
Det-Con Ossie Sullivan · · · · · · · · Linal Haft
Det-Con Martin Walters · · · · · Karl Howman
Det-Con Dennis Baxter · · · · · · · Paul Barber

CREDITS
writer Sid Green · *director/producer* Derrick Goodwin

A single-episode script, broadcast in LWT's *Comedy Tonight* strand, that cast King as a senior police detective, Vic Saggers. Stationed at the fictitious Catley CID, his patience was worn thin by the erratic actions of his juniors, and the fact that it was also a Friday – and Saggers hated Fridays – made everything worse.

Notes. King had recently taken a straight acting role in a BBC one-off, a 35-minute oddity called *The Big 'H'* (BBC2, 23 September 1978), written by Shaun Usher and produced by Anne Head, in which he played the compere of a television game-show. King also starred in *Rat Trap*, a stage-play by Bob Baker and Dave Martin that was recorded in performance at the Northcott Theatre in Exeter by HTV and networked by ITV on 3 November 1979. The other main performers in the 75-minute production were Garfield Morgan, George Sewell, Ram John Holder and Barry Stanton.

Fancy Wanders

UK · ITV (LWT) · SITCOM

7 × 30 mins · colour

24 Oct–5 Dec 1980 · Fri 7.30pm

MAIN CAST
Fancy · Dave King
Alastair · · · · · · · · · · · · · · · Joseph Marcell
Landlady · · · · · · · · · · · · · · Hilda Fenemore

CREDITS
writer Sid Green · *directors* David Crossman (4), David Crossman/Les Chatfield (2), Les Chatfield/Derrick Goodwin (1) · *producers* Tony Cornford (5), Tony Cornford/Derrick Goodwin (2)

Twenty years after the thought-provoking (but downright peculiar) *The Strange World Of Gurney Slade*, which had starred Anthony Newley, that series' co-author Sid Green turned in a new idea plotted along distinctly similar lines, now starring Dave King. *Fancy Wanders*, the series' title, was also the name of the lead character, an unemployed working-class white man who went around London with his dole-drawing black pal Alastair, expostulating long and fancifully about life as they saw it, flitting from topic to topic and philosophising about how the world would be if they had an influential role.

Like *Gurney Slade*, the characters enjoyed what Sid Green called 'illustrated thought comedy', and viewers spent much of the time inside the characters' minds, witnessing them holding conversations with inanimate objects, like statues and – bringing the concept up to date – Space Invader machines.

King Of The Hill

USA · FOX (DEEDLE-DEE PRODUCTIONS/JUDGEMENTAL FILMS/3 ARTS ENTERTAINMENT/20TH CENTURY-FOX/FILM ROMAN PRODUCTIONS) · ANIMATED SITCOM

21 × 30 mins (to 31/12/97 · continuing into 1998) · colour

US dates: 12 Jan 1997 to date
UK dates: 1 Aug 1997 to date (13 episodes to 31/12/97) C4 Fri 10.30pm then mostly 11.05pm

MAIN CAST (VOICES)

Hank Hill/Boomhauer/Dooley	Mike Judge
Peggy Hill	Kathy Najimy
Bobby Hill	Pamela Segall
Luanne Platter/	
Joseph Gribble	Brittany Murphy
Dale Gribble	Johnny Hardwick

CREDITS

creators/main writers Mike Judge/Greg Daniels · *other writers* various · *directors* Wes Archer and others · *executive producers* Mike Judge, Greg Daniels, Michael Rotenberg, Dave Stern, Howard Klein, Phil Roman · *producers* Joe Boucher, Richard Raynis

Once **The Simpsons** had demonstrated the potential of adult-orientated animations, the floodgates opened and the US airwaves were awash with new and interesting series of the same ilk: *The Critic*, *Dr Katz: Professional Therapist* (see **Comedy Central – Special Delivery**), *Ren And Stimpy* (BBC2, from 24 January 1994) and others, although arguably the series that made the most impact was MTV's *Beavis And Butt-head* (C4, 8 April 1994–12 April 1996), about a couple of anti-social teenagers obsessed by music and sex, who communicate in barely intelligible grunts and half-sentences liberally peppered with their trademark laugh ('heh-heh-heh'), the verbal equivalent of a lustful leer. The characters took off big time and the usual merchandising and character exploitation

followed, including a 1997 feature film, *Beavis And Butt-head Do America*. The series' creator was the animator Mike Judge, whose next creation, the comedy series *King Of The Hill*, also became an overnight smash. Along with co-creator Greg Daniels (who had written outstanding episodes of **The Simpsons** and **Seinfeld**), Judge conjured up a complex and realistic set of characters based loosely on real people whom he knew in Texas.

The Hill family comprise Hank Hill, a propane salesman and proud American; his wife Peggy, a smart and rational substitute teacher; their only son, 12-year-old Bobby, a chubby and unconfident child; and Peggy's niece, the naïve and provocative Luanne, who spends most of her time with the Hills owing to the adverse nature of her own dysfunctional parents' household. The other regular characters in the series were Hank's three neighbourhood friends – Bill, his friend since high school, a US army sergeant who believes in actively exercising his military training, even at weekends; the incomprehensible Boomhauer; and Dale, a conspiracy theorist and all-round redneck who is blissfully unaware that his wife has been conducting a long-term affair, and that his son Johnny is almost certainly not his biological child. As with *The Simpsons*, it was the three-dimensional depth and complexity of these characters that made *King Of The Hill* work so well.

Most episodes began with Hank pontificating to his friends about a contemporary subject and the others chipping in their own peculiarly 'southern' views on the state of present-day America; plots revolved around Hank's attempts to come to terms with the modern world, be a reasonable husband and father, understand the feelings of others and yet remain true to his heritage as a southerner, with all the baggage that carries. Politically right-wing (like all the characters), Hank nevertheless tries manfully to 'see the other person's point of view' and he is never ashamed to bow to his wife's superior commonsense when his own methods let him down.

Rarely in the metro-centric world of American TV had such ordinary southern characters been allowed the space to breathe and display themselves in all their glory. Although sometimes sentimental, the series took great pains to avoid obvious manipulation and odious caricature. The vocal talents of the cast added immeasurably to the overall package, with Judge himself (who had been the voice of both Beavis and Butt-head) particularly effective as Hank. And, again like *The Simpsons*, the show attracted a long list of celebrities – including Willie Nelson, Burt Reynolds, Dennis Hopper, Chuck Mangione, Stockard Channing, Laurie Metcalf, M Emmet

Walsh – playing themselves or providing voices for guest characters.

Kinvig

UK · ITV (LWT) · SITCOM

7 × 30 mins · colour

4 Sep–16 Oct 1981 · Fri mostly 8.30pm

MAIN CAST

Des Kinvig	Tony Haygarth
Netta Kinvig	Patsy Rowlands
Jim Piper	Colin Jeavons
Miss Griffin	Prunella Gee
Mrs Snell	Betty Hardy
Loon	Stephen Bent
Bat	Alan Bodenham
Sagga	Danny Schiller
Mr Horsley	Patrick Newell
Buddo	Simon Williams
Howard	Don McKillop

CREDITS

writer Nigel Kneale · *directors* Les Chatfield (6), Les Chatfield/Brian Simmons (1) · *producer* Les Chatfield

Douglas Adams' **Hitch-Hiker's Guide To The Galaxy** proved, were it not already recognised, that the worlds of humour and science-fiction could mix and match. *Kinvig*, while not in the same league as Adams' creation, was nonetheless the work of a true great in the sci-fi field: Nigel Kneale, a major contributor to the TV genre, not least via his ground-breaking BBC *Quatermass* series in the 1950s.

Kinvig was so titled because of the central character, a dreamy electrical repair man of that name whose existence, we see, revolves around wiring, sockets, the customers who call into his run-down street-corner repair shop in Bingleton, and home life with his attentive if scatty wife Netta and Cuddly, their loving pooch. One night, out walking the dog, Kinvig meets Miss Griffin, a beautiful woman dressed (but only just) in clothes that leave little to the imagination. Miss Griffin – nicknamed 'Quatermiss' by one Fleet Street wag – is more than just sexy, however, she hails from Mercury and is a swift interplanetary traveller. Suddenly, Des's life consists not just of corner-shop banality but being zoomed off to other planets. This is the cause of great frustration to his friend Jim Piper who has long been fascinated by the idea of UFOs and so cannot understand why someone so unresponsive to the notion of extraterrestrial life should have all the luck. Des would not exactly call it 'luck' though – together with Miss Griffin and Buddo, who also comes from Mercury and is 500-years-old, their job, no less, is to save the planet Earth from the dreaded ant-like Xux tribe.

What was made never clear to viewers, however, is whether all these things really happened to Kinvig or whether they were just the product of a fertile imagination.

Kit And The Widow

UK · C4 (FILM AND GENERAL PRODUCTIONS) · MUSICAL HUMOUR

2 editions (1 × 60 mins · 1 × 40 mins) · colour

Lavishly Mounted 1 Jan 1992 · Wed 10.15pm (60 mins)

9 Apr 1992 · Thu 12.10am (40 mins)

MAIN CAST

Kit	Kit Hesketh-Harvey
'The Widow'	Richard Sissons

CREDITS

writers Kit Hesketh-Harvey/Richard Sissons · *executive producer* Judy Cramer · *producer* Jon Plowman

Calling themselves Kit And The Widow, the satirical musical double-act comprising Kit Hesketh-Harvey and his pianist partner, a male mysteriously named the Widow, have been described as 'a Flanders And Swann for the 1990s' although some of the modern duo's more risqué material would have shocked the earlier, genteel partnership whose 'mud, mud, glorious mud' chorus in 'The Hippopotamus Song' was the closest they got to filth. In *Lavishly Mounted*, the first of these two intimate revues (previously produced on the London stage, at the Vaudeville and Ambassador's theatres), they wittily spoofed a number of musical formats and styles with the help of special guests Julia McKenzie, Leslie Crowther, Geoffrey Palmer and Mary Archer. The second show was a General Election-night special which also featured comedian Sandi Toksvig.

Note. The pair fronted a BBC Radio 2 special on 24 September 1994, recorded at the Edinburgh Festival Fringe, and went on the road for their next series, *Kit And The Widow's Grand Tour* (Radio 4, six editions, 5 July–9 August 1997).

The Kit Curran Radio Show

UK · ITV · *C4 (THAMES) · SITCOM

12 × 30 mins · colour

Series One (6) 2 Apr–14 May 1984 · Mon 8pm

*Series Two (6) *Kit Curran* 21 July–25 Aug 1986 · Mon 8.30pm

MAIN CAST

Kit Curran	Denis Lawson
Roland Simpson	Brian Wilde (series 1)
Les Toms	Paul Brooke
Damien Appleby	Clive Merrison
Sally Beamish	Debbi Blythe (series 1)
Constantine	Joseph Marcell (series 1);
	Pamela Scott (series 2)

CREDITS

writers Andy Hamilton (series 1), Andy Hamilton/Guy Jenkin (series 2) · *directors/producers* Derrick Goodwin (series 1), Anthony Parker (series 2)

Kit Curran is a pop DJ at – hey! – local commercial station Radio Newtown. Unfortunately, he's also blighted by certain unfortunate character defects: he's a liar, a rogue, a con-merchant, greedy, self-obsessed and apathetic towards the listeners and radio station staff alike. Unfortunately for Kit, the station gets a new boss, Roland Simpson, with whom he clashes big time, and towards whom he is more than cavalier. In talking himself up so big, the self-professed 'world's best DJ' ends up talking himself out of a job …

… so by the second series (C4, two years later) Kit is no longer in radio. He wants to be – he talks of owning his own station – but instead he's flexing his inventive and wildly egocentric mind within the grandly named Curran Associates Incorporated, situated in Brentford (west London) and in the business of house conversions and double-glazing, anything, indeed, to make money, even down to launching his own NHS.

While Kit Curran was only a mild success, writers Andy Hamilton and Guy Jenkin later returned to the media theme with spectacular results with *Drop The Dead Donkey*.

Klinik!

UK · C4 (VERA) · SATIRE

5 × 10 mins · colour

1 Jan–5 Jan 1997 · Wed–Sun mostly 10.15pm

MAIN CAST (VOICES ONLY)

Dr Werther	Alistair McGowan
other roles	Steve Steen
other roles	Ronnie Ancona
other roles	Joanna Brookes

CREDITS

writers Geoff Atkinson/Kim Fuller · *director* Robert Katz · *producer* Geoff Atkinson

In the style of *The Staggering Stories Of Ferdinand De Bargos*, *Pallas* and *The Almost Complete History Of The 20th Century*, *Klinik!* added English comic dialogue to a medical soap opera from Netherlands TV to satirical effect, the 'new' plot focusing on the attempts of Dr Werther to attract money-making NHS Trust patients to his Dutch clinic (klinik). The five short programmes were screened within a themed C4 season, *Doctors And Nurses*.

Knees-Up

UK · ITV (LWT) · STANDUP

6 × 30 mins · colour

15 Apr–20 May 1984 · Sun 7.15pm

MAIN CAST

host	Jeff Stevenson

CREDITS

writers cast · *director* Alasdair Macmillan · *producer* Bruce McClure

Luv-a-duck-style 'lively' humour and singalong music from a bunch of mostly cockney comics positioned 'arand the old joanna dann the local'. The presenter was Jeff Stevenson; Brian Conley appeared twice in the series, and these comics once: Lee Clark, Malcolm J White, Tom Pepper, Dave & Amos, Dave Evans, J J Stewart, Dudley Dolittle, Lenny Windsor, Tom Pepper, Dave Wolfe, Terri Rogers, Adrian Walsh, Al Dean and Stan Boardman. Music was supplied by Lonnie Donegan, Anita Harris and fave raves Renee and Renato and Showaddywaddy.

Knight And Daye

USA · NBC (IMAGINE ENTERTAINMENT) · SITCOM

7 × 30 mins · colour

US dates: 8 July–14 Aug 1989

UK dates: 7 June–3 Oct 1992 (7 episodes) BBC1/BBC2 mostly Sun around 11pm

MAIN CAST

Hank Knight	Jack Warden
Everett Daye	Mason Adams
Gloria Daye	Hope Lange
Janet Glickman	Julia Campbell
Eleanor 'Ellie' Escobar	Lela Ivey
Cito Escobar	Joe Lala

CREDITS

writers various · *directors* Bill Persky and others · *producer* Jeffrey Ganz · *executive producers* Lowell Ganz, Babaloo Mandel

A somewhat disappointing short-run summer-replacement US sitcom about two American radio personalities – Hank Knight and Everett Daye – who had been the presenters of *Knight And Daye*, a New York morning radio talk-show back in the 1940s, until the partnership dissolved amid their love for the same woman. Forty years later, in 1989, Janet Glickman – the manager at KLOP, a radio station in San Diego, California – invites the two to patch up their differences and reunite in the hope that they will increase the station's lowly listenership ratings. Straight away, on their new morning show, they continue where they had left off, arguing, even though the subject of their 1940s verbal tussles, Gloria, has long been married to Everett (their daughter Ellie, with her husband Cito, having made them grandparents three times over).

Knight School

UK · ITV (GRANADA) · CHILDREN'S SITCOM

6 × 30 mins · colour

2 Sep–7 Oct 1997 · Tue 4.40pm

MAIN CAST

Sir Hubert Grindcobbe	Peter Jeffrey
Sir Baldwin De'Ath	Roger Lloyd Pack
Wally Scrope	Stuart Rooker
Sir Arthur Melton-Mowbray	Anthony Hamblin
Scrubbe	Mark Billingham
Grockle	Peter Cocks
Sir Roger de Courcey	Blake Ritson
Sir Roland of Poland	Charlie Watts
Lady Elizabeth de Gossard	Amy Phillips
Eunice Spongge-Bagley	Susie Williams

CREDITS

writers Mark Billingham/Peter Cocks · *script consultant* Tony Robinson · *director* Andrew Morgan · *executive producer* Danielle Lux · *producer* Kieran Roberts

A quality, filmed children's sitcom set in the 13th-century at St Cuthbert's Academe (*sic*) for Young Knights. Grindcobbe is the forward-thinking headmaster who wishes to allow 'scholarship boys' (local lads without refined breeding) to attend the fee-paying and somewhat snobbish knight school. Its governors are opposed to the idea but agree to admit one such boy as a test case. They make it clear, though, that should the boy fail the idea will be dispensed with – ditto the headmaster. The sinister deputy-head, Sir Baldwin De'Ath, sees this as a perfect opportunity to be rid of his superior and thus inherit the job, so – appearing to help the Head with his plans – he volunteers to find the new pupil, quietly determined to pick the worst possible subject. This turns out to be Wally Scrope, from Sludgecombe, a girl-chasing, dirty, indolent peasant of limited education. To doubly ensure the success of his dastardly deed, De'Ath also enlists the aid of the high-class head-boy, Sir Roger de Courcey, charging him with the task of baiting Wally and making his life at the school unbearable. But he has underestimated Wally's determination, wiliness and fiery spirit and the new recruit manages to constantly better his enemies. At the same time, Wally attempts to woo Lady Elizabeth de Gossard, head-girl of the nearby St Catherine's finishing school, and a prize catch also sought by Sir Roger.

Knight School was a spirited romp with a neat central premise that was cleverly exploited. Much of the comedy arose from using 1990s vernacular and concerns anachronistically utilised in the historic period. (For instance, Wally complains that the crowing cock doesn't come with a snooze button.) The adult actors pitched their performances at just the right level to draw out the farcical nature of the zany situations, and more spice was added by occasional guest stars like Shane Richie, Matthew Kelly and Tony Robinson (script consultant on the series, and well versed in such period sitcoms thanks to *Blackadder* and his own *Maid Marian And Her Merry Men*). There was also a single appearance by Geoffrey Bayldon as school alchemist Dr Spencer Depenser, a character not a million miles away from his fondly remembered title role in the 1970s light-drama for children, *Catweazle*.

Knowing Me, Knowing You ... With Alan Partridge

see COOGAN, Steve

Kopykats

UK · ITV (ATV/ITC) · IMPRESSIONISM

7 × 60 mins · colour

6 May 1972 · Sat 8pm

27 May 1972 · Sat 8pm

17 June 1972 · Sat 8pm

23 Sep 1972 · Sat 9.30pm

14 Oct 1972 · Sat 9.30pm

MAIN CAST (NUMBER OF SHOWS)

Joe Baker (5)

Frank Gorshin (5)

Rich Little (5)

Marilyn Michaels (5)

George Kirby (4)

Fred Travalena (4)

Charlie Callas (3)

Peter Goodwright (1)

OTHER APPEARANCES (SOME AS HOSTS)

Debbie Reynolds (2)

Orson Welles (2)

Raymond Burr (2)

Robert Young (2)

Ron Moody (2)

Tony Curtis (2)

Steve Lawrence (1)

CREDITS

writers Jack Burns, Bryan Blackburn, Tony Hawes, Jay Burton · *script editors* Frank Peppiatt, John Aylesworth · *director* Dwight Hemion · *producers* Gary Smith, Dwight Hemion

Seven hour-length specials made in England by ATV, five of which were screened occasionally within its ITV *Saturday Variety* strand in 1972. The series was clearly intended not only for domestic consumption but also an American TV sale – indeed, all seven shows were broadcast first in the USA, under the banner of a Wednesday-night series, *The ABC Comedy Hour*, from 12 January to 5 April 1972. (The programmes were also repeated/syndicated there as *The Kopykats*.)

British comic Joe Baker was an ever-present (Peter Lorre was among his impressions), and he was joined by the Americans Frank Gorshin (best known to British TV viewers as the Riddler in *Batman*), Rich Little (who impersonated the then president Nixon), Marilyn Michaels (Lena Horne), George Kirby (who changed sex to imitate Ella Fitzgerald and Pearl Bailey), Fred Travalena (Glen Campbell was among his impressions), Charlie Callas and the British comic Peter Goodwright.

Guest celebrities and star hosts, all of whom were happy to try out their own talents as impressionists, included the British entertainer Ron Moody, Orson Welles, Debbie Reynolds, Raymond Burr (he imitated Ray Charles), Robert Young, Tony Curtis and, not seen in the ITV screenings, Ed Sullivan.

The Krankies Elektronik Komik

UK · BBC · CHILDREN'S SKETCH

12 editions (6 × 35 mins · 6 × 25 mins) · colour

Series One (6 × 25 mins) 30 Nov 1985–4 Jan 1986 · BBC1 Sat 5.20pm

Series Two (6 × 35 mins) 25 July–29 Aug 1987 · BBC1 Sat 5.20pm

MAIN CAST

The Krankies (Ian and Janette Tough)

The Great Soprendo

CREDITS

writers Brian Marshall (9), Sid Green (6), Jim Cammel (6), Ron Ottoway (6), Bryan Blackburn (6), Russel Lane (6), Graham Deykin (1) · *director/producer* Paul Ciani

Husband and wife in real life but man and shrill-voiced naughty schoolboy on stage, noisy Scottish double-act the Krankies proved popular with younger viewers who identified with wee Jimmy's (that is, Janette's) anti-establishment childish behaviour, oblivious to the fact that she was a vertically challenged (4ft 5½in) woman in her late thirties.

This BBC series – following two seasons of *The Krankies Klub* on ITV – took the features of a typical children's comic as its format, with regular items including a spoof Agatha Christie-style mystery serial, *Mayhem On The Overland Express*, Jimmy's attempts to teach Ian a new skill, comedy magic from the Great Soprendo and a musical guest slot. Another feature was a weekly visit to Café Macaroni, home of further frantic goings-on. In the second series the regular serial was *The Adventures Of Jimmy Burgermac* which featured the entire Krankie family. The series was great fun for kids, admittedly, but older viewers probably found *The Krankies Elektronik Komik* completely unwatchable.

See also the following two entries and *The Joke Machine*.

The Krankies Klub

UK · ITV (LWT) · CHILDREN'S SKETCH

14 editions (12 × 30 mins · 2 × 45 mins) · colour

Special (45 mins) *The Krankies Christmas Club* 26 Dec 1982 · Sun 3.30pm

Series One (6 × 30 mins) 10 Sep–15 Oct 1983 · Sat 5.05pm

Special (45 mins) *The Krankies At Christmas* 24 Dec 1983 · Sat 4.30pm

Series Two (6 × 30 mins) 1 Sep–6 Oct 1984 · Sat 5.05pm

MAIN CAST

The Krankies (Ian and Janette Tough)

Jimmy Cricket (not special 1)

Bobby Davro (series 2)

CREDITS

writer/script associate Russel Lane (1982–83), Russel Lane/Howard Imber (1984) · *directors* Alasdair Macmillan (special 1), Noel D Greene (series 1 & special 2), Vic Finch (series 2) · *producers* David Bell (special 1), Noel D Greene (series 1 & 2 and special 2)

Established as regulars on the BBC1 children's series *Crackerjack*, the Krankies' first own series kame kourtesy of LWT, where they heaped skool-dinner size (and just about as palatable) helpings of 'fandabidozi' fun at younger viewers. Like a kross between Jimmy Clitheroe and Andy Stewart, wee Jimmy's short-trousered and skool-kapped kwips provided many a merry mirthful moment, and they were aided by regular supporting acts and special guests (including the then unknown Lisa Stansfield and Brian Conley).

Krankies Television

UK · ITV (BORDER) · CHILDREN'S SKETCH

21 editions (14×25 mins · 7×30 mins) · colour

Series One (7×25 mins) *K.T.V.* 18 July–29 Aug 1989 · Tue 4.45pm

Series Two (7×30 mins) *Krankies Television* 11 July–29 Aug 1990 · Wed 4.40pm

Series Three (7×25 mins) *Krankies Television* 18 Mar–13 May 1991 · Mon mostly 4.20pm

MAIN CAST

The Krankies (Ian and Janette Tough)
Jack Jobsworth · · · · · Russel Lane (series 2)

CREDITS

writers Russel Lane/Brian Marshall · *executive producer* Paul Corley · *director/producer* Harry King

Three series in which the Krankies supposedly opened up their own satellite TV station, Krankie Television, broadcasting their usual merry madness via such programmes as a fund-raising Krankathon and the blockbuster movies *Indiana Jimmy And The Temple Of Dougal* and *Jim Tracy*. Other regular characters seen lending a 'helping' hand were Aunt Maud, Grannie, Jessie, Bernard Birdbrain and Dougal McDougal. Somewhat surprisingly, the usually deadpan Magnus Magnusson made two appearances as himself.

KYTV

UK · BBC · SKETCH

19×30 mins · colour

Pilot · 12 May 1989 · BBC2 Fri 9pm

Series One (6) 3 May–7 June 1990 · BBC2 Thu 9pm

Series Two (6) 17 Mar–21 Apr 1992 · BBC2 Tue 8.30pm

Series Three (6) 17 Sep–22 Oct 1993 · BBC2 Fri 9pm

MAIN CAST

Anna Daptor · · · · · · · Helen Atkinson Wood
Mike Channel · · · · · · · · · · · Angus Deayton
Mike Flex · · · · · · · · · · · · · Geoffrey Perkins
Martin Brown · · · · · · Michael Fenton Stevens
Mark Mountjoy/David Arke/ · · · · · · · · · · · ·
Colonel Bartlett/Ken Nash/ · · · · · · · · · · · ·
Mr Hartford and other characters Philip Pope
Mary · · · · · · · · · · · · · · Caroline Leddy (pilot)
Mrs Thatcher · · · · · · · · · Steve Nallon (pilot)

CREDITS

writers Angus Deayton/Geoffrey Perkins · *music* Philip Pope · *directors* John Kilby (13), John Stroud (6) · *producer* Jamie Rix

First came *Radio Active* (52 editions on BBC Radio 4, 8 September 1981 to 2 January 1988), an anarchic and hilarious sketch series that spoofed the relentlessly colloquial nature of local radio. This then begat *KYTV* – an idea seen in the pilots strand *Comic Asides* – which brought those same characters to television and changed the target of the satire to satellite TV.

In each edition of *KYTV* an aspect of cheapo satellite broadcasting was lampooned, with all the hazards of 'live' television exploited for laughs: malfunctioning equipment, corny links, unprepared announcers, correspondents being surprised by the camera cutting to them too early, and so on. A central report – a royal wedding, the opening of the Channel Tunnel, the making of a costume drama – also featured in every edition, and, rather like **Rutland Weekend Television** (only with a bigger budget), the premise allowed for different segments of the show to be played out as sketches allied to the week's main theme. Although satellite television was a relative newcomer to the UK, with few viewers at this time, the general public had a reasonable perception of the service having seen enough cheap daytime or late-night terrestrial TV to understand the concepts that were being spoofed.

While not as accomplished as its radio predecessor, *KYTV* nevertheless delivered well on the comedy front, with consistently sharp scripts from Deayton and Perkins. Both went on to greater things, Deayton becoming a major TV personality through his hosting of the comedy panel-game *Have I Got News For You* (from 28 September 1990) and as an actor in **One Foot In The Grave**; Perkins, more active behind-the-scenes, became an executive for successful independent company Hat Trick Productions and then Head of Comedy at the BBC. The *KYTV* producer Jamie Rix (son of the farceur Brian Rix) had also produced *Radio Active*.

Note. On 26 November 1993 the team reunited for a special segment of that year's *Children In Need* charity telethon on BBC1.

See also *81 Take 2*.

L For Lester

UK · BBC · SITCOM

6 × 30 mins · colour

8 Oct–12 Nov 1982 · BBC2 Fri 9pm

MAIN CAST

Lester Small	Brian Murphy
Mrs Davies	Hilda Braid
Chief Insp Rodgers	James Cossins
Sally Small	Amanda Barrie
Bert	Colin Spaull
Mrs Davies	Richard Vernon
PC Bright	Dudley Long
Jenny	Linda Robson

CREDITS

writer Dudley Long · *director* John B Hobbs · *producer* Dennis Main Wilson

Shrugging off the henpecked-husband persona of George Roper in **George And Mildred**, Brian Murphy bounced back on to TV as Lester Small, owner of his own motoring school in a West Country town. Small's life was never easy but his one main headache was the banker's wife, Mrs Davies, his most frequent customer, whose attempts to master the controls of a motor vehicle only succeeded in driving Lester (metaphorically – just) up the wall. Lester also had more than his fair share of clashes with the local constabulary, especially Chief Inspector Rodgers, with whom he had a long-lasting feud. Described as an action-comedy, this series was far less broad than most examples of the genre, hence its scheduling on BBC2. The series' writer, Dudley Long, appeared occasionally as PC Bright, and Linda Robson cropped up too, seven years before **Birds Of A Feather**. Despite the interesting array of characters and the potential for laughs in the complexities of small-town social politics, the series failed to make an impression and failed to return.

The Labours Of Erica

UK · ITV (THAMES) · SITCOM

12 × 30 mins · colour

Series One (6) 13 Mar–24 Apr 1989 · Mon 8pm

Series Two (6) 5 Mar–9 Apr 1990 · Mon 9pm

MAIN CAST

Erica Parsons	Brenda Blethyn
Clive Bannister	Clive Merrison
Dexter Rook	Geoffrey Davies
Jeremy Parsons	Paul Spurrier
Robert Beresford	Simeon Pearl
Myrna Burton	Rona Anderson

CREDITS

writers Richard Fegen/Andrew Norriss · *directors* John Stroud (11), John Howard Davies (1) · *producers* James Gilbert (11), John Howard Davies (1)

A series created expressly for Brenda Blethyn by writers Fegen and Norriss after she had impressed as the slow-witted librarian in their **Chance In A Million**. Here she was cast as Erica Parsons, a single mother who, as her fortieth birthday approaches, realises that life is passing her by. After a long entanglement with her boss, Dexter Rook, comes to an end, Erica rediscovers a diary kept when she was aged 14 – which happens to be the age of her son Jeremy – containing a list of the ambitions she hoped to realise in her life. Determined to make changes, and an impact, she sets out to fulfil these unrequited teenage dreams via a succession of quests and adventures that seem distinctly odd to those around her. Son, friends and colleagues never get to see the list and so can only guess at what long-lost ambition she might next be pursuing.

Note. A year after the demise of *The Labours Of Erica* Blethyn starred in *All Good Things* (BBC1, 14 May–18 June 1991), a series focusing on a 39-year-old woman who decides to become a do-gooder following the birth of her third child. Described in publicity as a comedy, the series was more of a drama (and so does not receive its own entry in this book).

Ladies And Gentle-Men

see HOWERD, Frankie

Ladies' Man

USA · CBS (HERBERT B LEONARD PRODUCTIONS/20TH CENTURY-FOX) · SITCOM

15 × 30 mins · colour

US dates: 27 Oct 1980–21 Feb 1981

UK dates: 29 Apr 1982–1 July 1983 (15 episodes) ITV Thu 11.35pm then various days and times

MAIN CAST

Alan Thackeray	Lawrence Pressman
Elaine Holstein	Louise Sorel
Betty Brill	Karen Morrow
Amy Thackeray	Natasha Ryan
Reggie	Herb Edelman
Betty Brill	Karen Morrow
Gretchen	Simone Griffith
Susan	Allison Argo
Andrea	Betty Kennedy

CREDITS

writers various · *producers* Herbert B Leonard, Lee Miller, Michael Loman

Alan Thackeray is the only male staff member contributing to the US monthly magazine *Women's Life*. He is also – like so many sitcom figures – a single parent (by divorce), looking after his precocious eight-year-old daughter Amy. In child-rearing, at least, Alan is aided by advice from his Manhattan apartment neighbour, Betty Brill. At work, his managing editor is the tough-talking Elaine Holstein and his colleagues (predictably) are beautiful creatures: typically, one is romantic (a writer, Andrea), one is a feminist (another writer, Susan) and one is earnest (a researcher, Gretchen). Alan's assignments are fruity: he has to research and write articles on such topics as sexual harassment and women who pose nude for men's magazines, and interview the visiting Margaret Thatcher. As a result, he often has to seek solace from the only other man in the office, the accountant Reggie.

The Lady Is A Tramp

UK · C4 (REGENT PRODUCTIONS) · SITCOM

13 × 30 mins · colour

Series One (6) 8 Jan–12 Feb 1983 · Sat 9.30pm

Series Two (7) 17 Feb–30 Mar 1984 · Fri 9.30pm

MAIN CAST

Old Pat	Patricia Hayes
Lanky Pat	Pat Coombs

CREDITS

writer Johnny Speight · *directors* Douglas Argent (series 1 & 1 ep in series 2), Dennis Main Wilson (6 eps in series 2) · *producer* William G Stewart

It may not have gelled into a sitcom of the unforgettable kind, but *The Lady Is A Tramp* – hallmarked by its top-brass cast/crew – was still eminently worthy of air time. The writer Johnny Speight happily renewed his long-time professional acquaintance with Patricia Hayes, a relationship that stretched back to her appearances in **The Arthur Haynes Show** 19 years earlier and also embraced *Till Death Us Do Part* and *Spooner's Patch*. Surprisingly perhaps, *The Lady Is A Tramp* was Hayes' first starring sitcom.

Previously, Hayes had won awards, and justifiably so, for her portrayal of a vagrant in *Edna, The Inebriate Woman* (*Play For Today*, BBC1, 21 October 1971). Now once again she was cast (or, more appropriately, outcast) as a tramp, shuffling around London with her steady companion (played by the great Pat Coombs). Having lived for years on park benches, they now reside inside a disused wheel-less van in a yard; neither drunkards nor pitiable, the common enemy of these bag ladies is authority, a fight taken up principally by Old Pat (Hayes), a battling character, and followed by Lanky Pat (Coombs).

As ever, Johnny Speight's scripts were worthy of viewer's close attention, and they were timely too, Britain's so-called 'boom' economy of the 1980s producing an echoed explosion in the number of vagrants and homeless people sleeping rough in its cities. Douglas Argent (*Fawlty Towers* etc) and Dennis Main Wilson (Eric Sykes, Tony Hancock, *Till Death Us Do Part* etc) were the directors and some prime guests appeared in various guises in odd episodes, even – to further the *Till Death* connection – Warren Mitchell, who showed up as a tramp.

See also *Them*.

Lame Ducks

UK · BBC · SITCOM

12 × 30 mins · colour

Series One (6) 22 Oct–26 Nov 1984 · BBC2 Mon 8.30pm

Series Two (6) 17 Sep–22 Oct 1985 · BBC2 Tue 9pm

MAIN CAST

Brian Drake · · · · · · · · · · · · · · John Duttine
Angie · · · · · · · · · · · · · · · · · Lorraine Chase
Ansell · · · · · · · · · · · · · · · · · Brian Murphy
Maurice · · · · · · · · · · · · · · · · Tony Millan
Tommy · · · · · · · · · · · · · · · · · Patric Turner
Mrs Drake · · · · · · Primi Townsend (series 1)

CREDITS

writer Peter J Hammond · *director/producer* John B Hobbs

Brian Drake's life changes dramatically when he is hit by a lorry on the way to work, for not only is he badly injured but also, while recovering in hospital, his glamorous wife tells him that she wants a divorce. Upon his recovery, Brian decides to opt out of the rat race and use his share of the proceeds from selling their house to go away and start over anew as a hermit. But things don't go according to plan. He is joined in his quest for a new life by Tommy, a reformed pyromaniac whom he met in the hospital, and on their way to their country cottage they pick up a hitch-hiker, Angie, a young woman who has drifted from relationship to relationship and seems to have no purpose in life. They in turn are joined by Maurice, another drifter whose peculiar ambition it is to 'ball-walk' (that is, walk on a ball) around the world, and who has left his job with the Post Office because they would not let him go to work on his ball.

This disparate bunch of lame ducks become Brian Drake's (oh dear, it's the old ducks-and-drakes pun again) surrogate family and join him in his new existence. Meanwhile, Brian's awkward wife hires a private detective, Ansell, to track down her errant husband. He pursues them to the country cottage but, also being a loser despised by his wife, he joins the others in the mini-community building up.

This was comedy with a serious edge from Peter J Hammond, who was best known as a writer of drama. Straight actor John Duttine proved his expertise at such low-key comedy, tingeing his performance with the necessary pathos. Lorraine Chase demonstrated that there was more to her than make-up and cockney catchphrases, and Brian Murphy and the underrated Tony Millan were as reliable as usual.

Lance At Large

UK · BBC · SITCOM

6 × 25 mins · b/w

13 Aug–17 Sep 1964 · BBC1 Thu mostly 8.50pm

MAIN CAST

Alan Day · · · · · · · · · · · · · · · · Lance Percival

CREDITS

writers David Nobbs/Peter Tinniswood · *producer* Dennis Main Wilson

The first television series from writers Nobbs and Tinniswood, who had previously scripted for *That Was The Week That Was*, including material for Lance Percival with whom they were reunited here. The early 1960s proved to be a golden period for British TV, with much experimentation and innovation: *Lance At Large* was an attempt to explore new ground in the sitcom genre, the premise being that Percival's character, Alan Day, became involved with different people and situations in each episode. The series made extensive use of location filming and featured heavyweight comedy guest stars each week, including Eric Barker, Fred Emney, Bernard Bresslaw and fellow former *TW3* star Millicent Martin.

Note. Four months before *Lance At Large*, Percival was one of three regular participants in an improvisational parlour-game show, *Impromptu*, (BBC2, eight editions, 27 April–15 June 1964). He and other regulars Victor Spinetti and Betty Impey had to improvise comic characters and situations presented to them from a set of cards by the 'boss man' (Jeremy Hawk). Una Stubbs also appeared each week, improvising a dance routine.

The Lance Percival Show

UK · BBC · SKETCH

12 editions (6 × 30 mins, 6 × 25 mins), b/w

Series One (6 × 25 mins) 6 July–10 Aug 1965 · BBC1 Tue 8pm

Series Two (6 × 30 mins) 11 Mar–15 Apr 1966 · BBC1 Fri 7.30pm

MAIN CAST

Lance Percival

CREDITS

writers Sid Green/Dick Hills (series 1), Lew Schwarz/Maurice Wiltshire (series 2) · *producer* Kenneth Carter

Another starring series for Percival, the *That Was The Week That Was* calypso crooner, a tall thin man with a malleable and expressive face and a pleasing Kenneth Williams-ish line in funny voices, who had entered TV after appearances in cabaret in the late 1950s. In this show he was joined by *TW3* alumni Kenneth Cope (in the first series) and Roy Kinnear and Millicent Martin (in separate editions of the second series).

The Lance Percival Show combined 'quickies' with more elaborate sketches and music from resident singer Anita Harris (series 1). It also occasionally featured a calypso from Percival himself, but scripted this time, not improvised as his *TW3* songs had been. Regular items included comic interviews with people in the street and a mock documentary slot. Guest stars in the second series included Dick Emery, Jon Pertwee, Hugh Lloyd and Hattie Jacques.

Note. Thirty years later, on 25 August 1995, Percival presented *The Friday Calypso*, a five-minute topical calypso, looking forward to the summer of 1996, screened by C4.

Land Of Hope And Gloria

UK · ITV (THAMES) · SITCOM

6 × 30 mins · colour

24 June–29 July 1992 · Wed 8.30pm

MAIN CAST

Gloria Hepburn · · · · · · · · · · · Sheila Ferguson
Gerald Hope-Beaumont · · · · Andrew Bicknell
Nanny Princeton · · · · · · · · · Joan Sanderson
Evelyn Spurling · · · · · · · · · Daphne Oxenford
Crompton · · · · · · · · · · · · · · · · John Rapley
Vanessa · · · · · · · · · · · · · · · · Vivien Darke

CREDITS

writer Simon Brett · *director/producer* Peter Frazer-Jones

An unimpressive series from the usually watchable writer Simon Brett, not screened by Thames until some time after its making, which dwelled upon the working relationship between an upfront, brash, liberated American woman and an upper-class Englishman and his retainers.

Upon the death of its incumbent administrator – the old-school-tie Brigadier Transom – Gloria Hepburn, a Philadelphian with a proven track record in 'leisure management', is appointed by the trustees as the new estate business manager at Gerald Hope-Beaumont's stately pile, Beaumont House, set in the English country village of Hope Maltravers. Her job is to oversee the marketing of the house which will be its financial salvation. The appointment is broadly welcomed by Gerald Hope-Beaumont, the 16th Viscount Debleigh, but less than unanimously so by his staff: young secretary/PA Vanessa and the ageing general factotum Crompton are in favour, but the venerable

Evelyn, hitherto the tour guide, and Gerald's indomitable old Nanny Princeton, who takes the money at the door, are firmly against Gloria Hepburn's intrusion into their cosy world – she's a woman, she's in her prime, she's a foreigner and, although no prejudice is clearly expressed, she's black. (None of the people at Beaumont House, not even Gerald, know this last detail until she arrives.)

At 38 years of age, Gerald Hope-Beaumont is not only a widower – his wife died in a hunting accident – but the last surviving member of an aristocratic dynasty, burdened by nine centuries of tradition and expectation, and slowly reconciling himself to the fact that he will fail to match up. Fortunately, he reconciles himself more quickly to Gloria, welcoming the initiatives she brings and finding a place in his affections for her direct personality. Her profound changes to the everyday running of Beaumont House meet with stiff resistance from other quarters, however, as proven when she requests that everyone at the house urge tourists to 'have a nice day'.

Like *After Henry*, an infinitely better Simon Brett sitcom, *Land Of Hope And Gloria* was graced by the presence of Joan Sanderson, who died between the series' recording and transmission. Brett wrote the series especially for Sheila Ferguson, however, after the former member of the singing trio the Three Degrees told a Thames executive that there were too few starring roles for black women in British TV comedy. The Three Degrees were ridiculously blown up by the media as Prince Charles' favourite singing group, but there's no saying whether *Land Of Hope And Gloria* was his favourite sitcom. One would suspect not.

Langley Bottom

UK · ITV (YORKSHIRE) · SITCOM

6 × 30 mins · colour

14 July–18 Aug 1986 · Mon 8pm

MAIN CAST

Seth Raven · · · · · · · · · · · · Bernard Cribbins
Rev Dennis Claybourne · · · · · · · Tim Barrett
Vernon Nobbs · · · · · · · · · · · · · Don Crann
Mrs Wentworth · · · · · · · · · · · · · Elvi Hale
Mr Patel · · · · · · · · · · · · · · Kaleem Janjua
Mrs Patel · · · · · · · · · · · · · Jamila Massey
Miss Madge Howarth · · · · · · · Barbara Hicks
Miss Hilda Howarth · · · · · · · · · Rhoda Lewis
Brenda · · · · · · · · · · · · · · · · · Lisa David
Oswald · · · · · · · · · · · · · · · · John Rutland
Herbert · · · · · · · · · · · · · Christopher Clarke

CREDITS

writers Barry Cryer/John Junkin · *director/producer* Alan Tarrant

Seth Raven resides in the beautiful Yorkshire Dales village of Langley Bottom (actually filmed in the delightfully named Kirkby Overblow, near Harrogate). His occupation is

the local odd-job man but in reality he's the local interfering, fingers-in-every-pie merchant, with his allies and (like the local school headmaster Vernon Nobbs) his enemies. Life for Seth means getting *embroiled*, usually down at the village inn, the Old Dun Cow, with a variety of Langley Bottom misfits: the two spinster sisters, the vicar, the bobby, the publican and Mr and Mrs Patel, who run the village greengrocery.

The first sitcom venture for sketch/standup gagmeisters Cryer and Junkin, *Langley Bottom* created a starring role for Bernard Cribbins that was not dissimilar to a previous one, in *Cuffy* and its predecessor **Shillingbury Tales**. Despite the decent credentials, though, *Langley Bottom* wasn't very good.

The Larkins

UK · ITV (ATV) · SITCOM

40 episodes (24 × 30 mins · 14 × 35 mins · 2 × 45 mins) · b/w

Series One (5 × 30 mins · 1 × 45 mins) 19 Sep–24 Oct 1958 · Fri 10.15pm

Special (30 mins) 26 Dec 1958 · Fri 10.15pm

Series Two (6 × 30 mins) 2 Feb–9 Mar 1959 · Mon 8pm

Series Three (6 × 30 mins) 8 Feb–14 Mar 1960 · Mon mostly 8pm

Series Four (6 × 30 mins) 10 Sep–15 Oct 1960 · Sat 8.35pm

Series Five (7 × 35 mins · 1 × 45 mins) 9 Nov–28 Dec 1963 · Sat 8.25pm

Series Six (7 × 35 mins) 4 July–22 Aug 1964 · Sat mostly 9.45pm

MAIN CAST

Ada Larkins · · · · · · · · · · · · · Peggy Mount
Alf Larkins · · · · · · · · · · · · · David Kossoff
Jeff Rogers · · · · Ronan O'Casey (series 1–4)
Joyce Rogers · · · · Ruth Trouncer (series 1–4)
Eddie Larkins · · · · · · · · · · Shaun O'Riordan
· (series 1–4)
Hetty Prout · · · · · · · · · · · Barbara Mitchell
Myrtle Prout · · · Hilary Bamberger (series 1–4)
Sam Prout · · · · George Roderick (series 1–3)

OTHER APPEARANCES

Rev Spoonforth · · · · · · · Charles Lloyd Pack
Osbert Rigby Soames · · · · · · · Hugh Paddick
· (series 5 & 6)
Vic · · · · · · · · · · · · · Victor Maddern (series 5)
Lofty · · · · · · · · David Jackson (series 5 & 6)
Henry · · · · · · · · Willie Payne (series 5 & 6)
Mrs Gannett · · · Hazel Coppen (series 5 & 6)
Sid Gannett · · · · Norman Chappell (series 5)
Fred Gannett · · · Robin Wentworth (series 6)
Georgie · · · · · · · · · Hugh Walters (series 5)
Paddy · · · · · · · · · · · · Derry Power (series 6)

CREDITS

writer Fred Robinson · *director* Dicky Leeman (series 5 & 6) · *producers* Alan Tarrant (27), Bill Ward (9), Antony Kearey (4)

Acclaimed at the time, with justification, as the funniest sitcom British TV had produced, *The Larkins* was a joyful celebration of a cockney lifestyle unchanged for decades and seemingly unaffected by the poverty of the

area. The Larkins were a family: parents with adult children. The head of the family was undoubtedly the wife and mother, Ada, who stormed through every episode, bellowing and bawling, the toughest of tough cookies, purveying a canny woman's wisdom and meting out her own unique style of justice – yet, still holding in her ample bosom that vital soft spot for a hard-luck story. Her hubbie, Alf – employed in the works canteen of a plastics factory – fought and fought and fought and may not have been as put-upon as he appeared, but, ultimately, he knew he could never win any battle with his Ada. (And there were many.)

The cast of *The Larkins* was particularly strong. The part of Ada was played – to the hilt – by Peggy Mount, a no-nonsense woman off-stage who had appeared as the ranting battleaxe mother-in-law Emma Hornett in the long-running stage-show *Sailor Beware!* (from 1955), also made into a feature film (1956), following which she was more or less typecast in the role. It was Mount who recommended David Kossoff for the part of Alf, after playing opposite him in a TV presentation of the play *Arsenic And Old Lace*. Kossoff had usually played foreign parts in films and TV but was, in reality, a cockney, which helped authenticity.

Shaun O'Riordan (who would later become a successful TV producer, with many credits in this book) appeared as Ada and Alf's dim-witted but enthusiastic, freckle-faced son Eddie, in and out of jobs and only really useful as an assistant scout master. Canadian actor Ronan O'Casey was Ada and Alf's ex-GI American son-in-law Jeff Rogers, married to their daughter, Joyce (Ruth Trouncer). Jeff wrote cowboy stories for a comic, *The Bullet*, until being fired from the job. Barbara Mitchell played the typical nosey next-door neighbour Hetty Prout, her hair tied up in a cloth, borrowing and interfering in equal measure, and ever coo-eeing for a conversation over the garden fence. (Mitchell had played Emma Hornett in an out-of-town stage production of *Sailor Beware!* and had been seen in the part by Mount, who recommended her for *The Larkins*.) Hilary Bamberger (daughter of the music-hall comics Freddie and Pam Bamberger) played the girl-next-door Myrtle Prout, daughter of Hetty and, potentially, a girlfriend for gormless Eddie. These characters formed the basis of every episode, with action usually taking place in the pub and at the Larkins' slum-like home, at 66 Sycamore Street, somewhere in the East End of London. (Actually, the programmes were made at the former Wood Green Empire, utilised as a studio by ATV.)

The writer, Fred Robinson, was a cockney through and through, and the story behind his creation of *The Larkins* is a particularly novel one. Employed as a builders' clerk, he used to write plays in his spare time for a boy scout group in Harringay, north London, which could not afford to pay royalties to perform existing works. Robinson also earned a crust by playing piano in a pub in Clapton, and one night observed an argumentative couple, pouring back the ale in rapid fashion, who formed the basis for the Ada and Alf Larkins characters. In 1948, ten years before it arrived on TV, Robinson first wrote *The Larkins* especially for a scout-troop production, appearing himself as Alf. (In the TV series Robinson appeared occasionally as Fred, the pub barman.)

Even with the success of *The Larkins* TV series Robinson continued to live in Hackney, in a street later demolished under a Compulsory Service Order, and it was this 1960s East End slum-clearance programme that led to a revival of the series in 1963, after three years off air. In this, the family home at 66 Sycamore Street had been demolished, Eddie had left home, Joyce and Jeff had gone to America (although Jeff returned to appear in one episode) and Alf had been laid off by the plastics factory. With his redundancy money he and Ada had bought and were running a 'greasy-spoon' café, with a couple of upstairs bedrooms for overnight B&B accommodation, one resident guest being the down-on-his-heels toff Osbert Rigby Soames. The café idea allowed plenty of scope for Ada to yell long and loud at her customers and swing a frying pan or two in the vicinity of Alf.

The Larkins also generated a spin-off feature film, made after only 13 episode of the TV series and released in 1960 as *Inn For Trouble* (director C M Pennington-Richards). In this, Ada and Alf took over the running of a country pub.

Larry Grayson … [various shows]

see GRAYSON, Larry

The Larry Sanders Show

USA · HBO (BRILLSTEIN-GREY ENTERTAINMENT) · SITCOM

77 episodes (76 × 30 mins · 1 × 60 mins to 31/12/97 · continuing into 1998) · colour

US dates: 15 Aug 1992 to date

UK dates: 22 Oct 1993 to date (61 × 30 mins at 31/12/97) BBC2 various days after 11.15pm

MAIN CAST

Larry Sanders	Garry Shandling
Arthur ('Artie')	Rip Torn
Hank Kingsley	Jeffrey Tambor
Phil	Wallace Langham
Paula	Janeane Garofalo
Beverly	Penny Johnson
Jeannie Sanders	Megan Gallagher
	(1992–93)
Darlene	Linda Doucet (1992–95)
Jerry	Jeremy Piven (1992–94)
Francine	Kathryn Harrold (1993–94)
Brian	Scott Thompson (from 1995)

CREDITS

creators Garry Shandling/Dennis B Klein · *writers* various · *directors* Todd Holland and others · *executive producers* Garry Shandling/Brad Grey · *producer* John Ziffren

Garry Shandling had already toyed with the boundaries of the sitcom genre with *It's Garry Shandling's Show*, but with *The Larry Sanders Show* – a true 24-carat gem of a series – he pushed back the barriers even further, blurring fact and fiction in a style rarely seen before. Shandling played the part of Larry Sanders, a successful late-night US TV chat-show host, based on an amalgam of real-life hosts. Shandling himself, who had often guest-hosted *The Tonight Show* in the absence of Jay Leno, and who had been considered the natural successor to David Letterman on *Late Night*, was clearly familiar with the territory he was spoofing and was adept enough at the craft to make the pastiche a very accurate one indeed. His Larry Sanders was a complex character: egocentric yet lacking in confidence; single-minded but often swayed by advice from the strangest corners; fearful of being fired by the network yet constantly complaining that he was treated badly and that the punishing schedule left him little time to himself. On the set, Sanders was the perfect self-effacing host, happy to play straight-man to his guests or to enliven a dull show with pertinent ad-libs and stupid sketches. Backstage, he vacillated between being a whiny, complaining individual who needed constant attention, to being 'one of the boys' with the production team. Whatever his failings, the rest of the production team was well aware that Sanders was the captain of their ship and trod carefully around him.

All, that is, except for his producer Artie – a bluff, gruff, hard-nosed TV professional who knew that it was in the show's interests to keep Larry sweet but was not averse to stooping to devious means to ensure so. Artie was the closest thing to a true friend that Sanders had, but he had to be all things to him: father, mother, manager, sounding board, complaints department, go-between, drinking buddy and three-o'clock-in-the-morning-telephone-nursemaid. Then there was Larry's on-screen sidekick Hank Kingsley (late-night US TV chat-shows typically feature such a 'stooge' figure), a none-too-intelligent crawler who could be self-obsessed and vain. Hank was shameless in his sycophancy and usually unaware of the embarrassment caused by his actions; he was also money-motivated, pursuing various cash-making schemes beyond his TV work. Larry, Artie and Hank were the triumvirate at the centre of the show but the other characters were uniformly well drawn and

portrayed. Sanders' scriptwriters, especially Phil, were paranoid and felt that their best work was being wasted, and the support staff were much put upon and rarely appreciated, especially Hank's assistant, Darlene and later Brian. Two notable members of the second string were Beverly, Larry's PA, whose duties were manifold, and the show's harassed talent booker Paula (played by Janeane Garofalo, who continued a successful career as a fine comedy actress).

As Sanders' guests each week, real-life celebrities appeared under their own names but often playing parodies of themselves and allowing themselves to be seen in a poor but perhaps more truthful light. (Such guests included a very diverse range of personalities, from William Shatner to Sting by way of Carol Burnett, Sally Field and Billy Crystal, with multiple appearances by Roseanne, David Duchovny and Elvis Costello, and, splendidly, David Letterman and Jay Leno.) The presence of such stars, allied to Shandling's devastatingly accurate portrayal of a chat-show host, and the excellent production techniques – the series was shot on film but the actual on-air chat-show elements were video-taped to engender the appropriate garish realism – imbued the episodes with both an uncanny authenticity and edge-of-seat tension. All ingredients considered, *The Larry Sanders Show* probably has to rank as the best adult sitcom there has been to date, taking a bitterly sarcastic look at the TV industry, and the sourness and phenomenal cynicism that lies behind the sweet, smiling faces and apparent sincerity. Because it aired on the less regulated cable channel HBO, the series was able to be uncompromising in its subject matter and use of bad language. Profanities didn't actually *litter* the production but the episodes did feature some of the most colourful language ever heard on TV. But while Shandling was suitably oily as the smarmy Sanders, and Rip Torn completely believable as the growling Artie, the top acting honour must go to Jeffrey Tambor, who was willing and able to step with his Hank Kingsley character into unbelievably dark, unpleasant and excruciatingly embarrassing situations. His debasement was above and beyond the call of duty.

The Last Goon Show Of All
The Last Laugh Before TV-am

see MILLIGAN, Spike

The Last Man On Earth

UK · BBC · SITCOM

1 × 30 mins · colour

4 June 1974 · BBC1 Tue 8.30pm

MAIN CAST

Mother · · · · · · · · · · · · · · · · · Dandy Nichols
Henry · · · · · · · · · · · · · · · · · · Ronald Fraser

CREDITS

writer Ray Galton/Alan Simpson · producer Graeme Muir

A whimsical, post-apocalyptic *Comedy Playhouse* segment from Galton and Simpson about a pair who return from painting their caravan in Frinton to find that everyone else in the world has vanished.

A similar idea was explored years later in the UK sitcom *Not With A Bang* and the US series *Woops!*

Last Night Of The Poms

see HUMPHRIES, Barry

The Last Of The Baskets

UK · ITV (GRANADA) · SITCOM

13 × 30 mins · colour

Series One (6) 10 May–21 June 1971 · Mon 8.30pm

Series Two (7) 3 Jan–14 Feb 1972 · Mon 8.30pm

MAIN CAST

Redvers Bodkin · · · · · · · · · · · Arthur Lowe
Clifford Basket · · · · · · · · · · · · Ken Jones
Mrs Basket · · · · · · · · · · · · · Patricia Hayes

OTHER APPEARANCES

Earl of Clogborough · · · · · · · Richard Hurndall
· (first episode)

CREDITS

creator John Stevenson · writers John Stevenson (12), Andy Maher (1) · director/producer Bill Podmore

The Last Of The Baskets was a cut above the period's ITV sitcom output. The opening episode set the scene: the 12th Earl of Clogborough is dying, at the end of a misspent 93 years, and the time has come to pass on his title and stately mansion, Clogborough Hall, to its rightful heir. After a search, this turns out to be Clifford Basket, an uncouth and unmarried factory boiler tender. Moving in to the crumbling mock-medieval-style pile with his 'mam', Clifford inherits a sheaf of bills printed in red ink and, worse, the Earl's sniffy (though markedly loyal) butler, Redvers Bodkin. For a while the Baskets enjoy living the good life, having Bodkin serve them their bottles of brown ale on a silver platter, but soon enough they have to concern themselves with loftier matters, like keeping the proverbial wolf from the door and preventing the soot-stained mansion from collapsing into the Pennines.

This was a tightly written, amusing and well-cast series. Arthur Lowe was excellent as Bodkin (strangely, he later played another Redvers, in *Potter*), Patricia Hayes was her usual marvellous self as 'mam' and Ken Jones played the last Basket with the characteristic

wheezy laugh and elbow-in-the-ribs style that he reproduced so splendidly in *Porridge*.

The Last Of The Best Men

UK · ITV (THAMES) · SITCOM

1 × 30 mins · colour

19 May 1975 · Mon 8.30pm

MAIN CAST

Henry · · · · · · · · · · · · · · · · · Derek Fowlds
Annette · · · · · · · · · · · · · · · Prunella Gee
Geoff · · · · · · · · · · · · · Geoffrey Whitehead
Pamela · · · · · · · · · · · · · · Jacqueline Clarke

CREDITS

writer Richard Waring · director/producer Michael Mills

Once there were seven young men, all lads together, putting it about a bit. Now five have 'settled down', leaving only Geoff and Henry to maintain the old ways. Then Geoff announces his impending 'hitch' and Henry becomes the last bastion of bachelordom. This single-episode sitcom did not lead to a full series but it did provide Derek Fowlds with a welcome opportunity to regain control of his acting career after gaining fame as the straight-man to the feisty fox puppet Basil Brush.

Last Of The Summer Wine

UK · BBC · SITCOM

162 episodes (149 × 30 mins · 1 × 90 mins · 2 × 85 mins · 4 × 60 mins · 1 × 50 mins · 1 × 45 mins · 3 × 35 mins · 1 × short special) · colour

Pilot · 4 Jan 1973 · BBC1 Thu 8pm

Series One (6) 12 Nov–17 Dec 1973 · BBC1 Mon 9.25pm

Series Two (7) 5 Mar–16 Apr 1975 · BBC1 Wed 9.25pm

Series Three (7) 27 Oct–8 Dec 1976 · BBC1 Wed 9.25pm

Series Four (8) 9 Nov 1977–4 Jan 1978 · BBC1 Wed 9.25pm

Special · 26 Dec 1978 · BBC1 Tue 10.40pm

Series Five (7) 18 Sep–30 Oct 1979 · BBC1 Tue 8.30pm

Special · 27 Dec 1979 · BBC1 Thu 8.30pm

Special · 25 Dec 1981 · BBC1 Fri 7.15pm

Series Six (7) 4 Jan–15 Feb 1982 · BBC1 Mon 9.25pm

Special (35 mins) 25 Dec 1982 · BBC1 Sat 6.55pm

Short special · part of *The Funny Side Of Christmas* 27 Dec 1982 · BBC1 Mon 8.05pm

Series Seven (6) 30 Jan–6 Mar 1983 · BBC1 Sun 7.15pm

Special (90 mins) 27 Dec 1983 · BBC1 Tue 8.50pm

Special · 30 Dec 1984 · BBC1 Sun 7.15pm

Series Eight (6) 10 Feb–17 Mar 1985 · BBC1 Sun 8.10pm

Special (85 mins) 1 Jan 1986 · BBC1 Wed 8.15pm

Special (35 mins) 28 Dec 1986 · BBC1 Sun 7.15pm

Series Nine (11 × 30 mins · 1 × 35 mins) 4 Jan–22 Mar 1987 · BBC1 Sun 7.15pm

Special (85 mins) 27 Dec 1987 · BBC1 Sun 7.15pm

Series Ten (6) 16 Oct–20 Nov 1988 · BBC1 Sun 7.15pm

Special (60 mins) 24 Dec 1988 · BBC1 Sat 8pm

Series Eleven (7) 15 Oct–26 Nov 1989 · BBC1 Sun 7.15pm

Special (50 mins) 23 Dec 1989 · BBC1 Sat 8.30pm

Series Twelve (10) 2 Sep–4 Nov 1990 · BBC1 Sun 7.15pm

Special · 27 Dec 1990 · BBC1 Thu 8pm

Series Thirteen (6) 18 Oct–29 Nov 1991 · BBC1 Fri 8pm

Special · 22 Dec 1991 · BBC1 Sun 7.15pm

Series Fourteen (10) 25 Oct–26 Dec 1992 · BBC1 Sun 7.15pm

Series Fifteen (9) 24 Oct–19 Dec 1993 · BBC1 Sun 7pm

Special · 27 Dec 1993 · BBC1 Mon 8.35pm

Special (60 mins) 1 Jan 1995 · BBC1 Sun 7pm

Series Sixteen (8) 8 Jan–26 Feb 1995 · BBC1 Sun 7pm

Series Seventeen (10) 3 Sep–5 Nov 1995 · BBC1 Sun 7pm

Special (60 mins) 24 Dec 1995 · BBC1 Sun 7.15pm

Special (45 mins) 29 Dec 1996 · BBC1 Sun 6.30pm

Series Eighteen (10) 20 Apr–22 June 1997 · BBC1 Sun mostly 6.45pm

Special (60 mins) 28 Dec 1997 · BBC1 Sun 7pm

MAIN CAST

Compo · · · · · · · · · · · · · · · · · Bill Owen
Norman Clegg · · · · · · · · · · · · Peter Sallis
Blamire · · · · · · · · · · · · · · · Michael Bates
· · · · · · · · · · · · · · · · · · · (series 1 & 2)
Foggy Dewhurst · · · · · · · · · · · Brian Wilde
· · · · · · · · · · · · · · (series 3–8, 12 onwards)
Seymour Utterthwaite · · · · · Michael Aldridge
· · · · · · · · · · · · · · · · · · · (series 9–11)
Nora Batty · · · · · · · · · · · · · Kathy Staff
Wally Batty · · · · · · · · · · · · · · Joe Gladwin
Wesley Pegden · · · · · · · · · Gordon Wharmby
· · · · · · · · · · · · · · · · · (series 8 onwards)
Edie Pegden · · · · · · · · · · · · · Thora Hird
· · · · · · · · · · · · · · · · · (series 9 onwards)
Crusher (Milburn) · · · · · · · · Jonathan Linsey
· · · · · · · · · · · · · · · · · · · (series 8–12)
Sid · · · · · · · · · · · · · · · · · · John Comer
Ivy · · · · · · · · · · · · · · · · · · Jane Freeman
Barry · · · · · · · Mike Grady (series 9 onwards)
Glenda · · · Sarah Thomas (series 9 onwards)
Howard · · · · · · · · · · · · · · · · Robert Fyfe
Pearl · · · · · · · · · · · · · · · · Juliette Kaplan
Marina · · · · · · · · · · · · · · · Jean Fergusson
Pub Landlord · · · · · · · · · · · James Duggan
Eli · · · · · · · Danny O'Dea (series 11 onwards)
Smiler · · Stephen Lewis (series 12 onwards)
Auntie Wainwright · · · · · · · · Jean Alexander
· · · · · · · · · · · · · · · · · (series 8 onwards)
Truly · · · Frank Thornton (from 1997 special)

CREDITS

writer Roy Clarke · directors Alan J W Bell, Sydney Lotterby, Ray Butt, Martin Shardlow · producers Alan J W Bell (115), Sydney Lotterby (32), James Gilbert (7), Bernard Thompson (7), Robin Nash (1)

Last Of The Summer Wine: the very *Cider With Rosie*-like title of the longest-running British TV sitcom of all time suggests an atmosphere of golden nostalgia, of hazy summer days and the slow but inexorable passing of an era. The series certainly evoked all of these images, but the episodes depicted not childhood romps or teenage affairs in swaying, golden fields of wheat but the twilight years of a trio of oddly philosophising, whimsical old duffers in the Yorkshire Pennines who return to a carefree second childhood. They get up to all sorts of mischief and are determined to fulfil ambitions for which younger men would have already considered themselves too old.

That (when this book was being written) the series was still active after 25 years is remarkable enough; more so, perhaps, is the fact that every episode has been scripted by just one writer, Roy Clarke, a man who, over the same period, has also created and written other successful series for the BBC, notably *Rosie*, *Open All Hours* and *Keeping Up Appearances*. Before *Last Of The Summer Wine*, Clarke had contributed scripts to a number of TV drama series, including *The Troubleshooters*, *The Power Game* and a series he also created, *The Misfit*. But the former schoolteacher found his true niche with this sitcom, which demonstrated that he had a flair for dialogue and an ear for the patterns of everyday northern speech to match those of the master TV playwrights Alun Owen, Alan Bennett and Alan Plater.

Last Of The Summer Wine originated as a *Comedy Playhouse* pilot (at which point it was titled *The Last Of The Summer Wine*, but the first definite article was dropped after this) and at this point – and for the first two series – the trio comprised Blamire, the unofficial ringleader and chief instigator of their misadventures; Clegg, the unobtrusive, wary one; and Compo, the small, rough, mucky, fearless, perennial adolescent, easily goaded into risky ventures. *Dad's Army* had demonstrated that veteran actors could bring out the best in a comedy script, and the three (slightly younger) stars of *Last Of The Summer Wine* provided further proof. Michael Bates was forced to quit after the second series on health grounds (he died shortly afterwards) and his character was replaced by Foggy Dewhurst (Brian Wilde), a determined ex-army man who planned their subsequent adventures with military precision and a painstaking eye for detail. Invariably, these plans proved flawed and usually resulted in the hapless Compo coming down to earth with a thud or being up to his neck in water. With Foggy on board the series scaled new heights, and this trio came to be regarded as the classic combination. Later, Brian Wilde, tiring of the series and the reputed friction off the set, left for pastures

new and was replaced by the classy Seymour Utterthwaite, an amateur inventor whose contraptions were often the springboard for their continuing adventures. His actor, Michael Aldridge, then left and Brian Wilde returned to the fold, reprising the series' strongest line-up for the subsequent episodes.

But whichever trio was operating, there was always a fourth star: the Yorkshire town of Holmfirth and its surroundings, which were used as the location for the series. Holmfirth possesses a timeless, stark quality that contrasts with the surrounding sweeping countryside and made it a favourite place for film and TV directors long before *Last Of The Summer Wine* came along. However, the success of the series (after a slow start, it became a ratings smash) really put Holmfirth into the public consciousness and since the 1980s it has become a regular and popular stop on the tourist map. In a case of life imitating art, certain aspects of the village eventually took on their TV roles: Ivy's café, for instance, was actually a paint shop dressed for effect but eventually it was turned into a real café to cash in on tourist interest.

Complementing the central trio and the superb location were a bevy of minor characters drawn from Yorkshire folklore and Clarke's distorted comedic imagination: formidable wives, henpecked husbands, sexually-charged mistresses, inventors, pigeon fanciers, balding Lotharios and more. The largest of these larger-than-life caricatures was Nora Batty, the daunting, uncompromising, wrinkled-stocking housewife who, in Compo's lustful eye, was a veritable sex-bomb. Poor Nora had to use a broom to beat off the tiny, sex-starved smelly one who launched himself at her in a frenzy of groping hands, like an octogenarian octopus. Other recurring characters included Nora's husband Wally, who was unconcerned over Compo's advances, half-hoping that he would succeed; and the *ménage à trois* comprising Howard, his wife Pearl and his floozy Marina. As the series progressed some of these lesser characters enjoyed ever greater roles, and when Thora Hird joined the cast the lads finally found a permanent and serious threat to their shenanigans. Guest/cameo appearances have also been made by, among others, Ron Moody, Norman Wisdom and John Cleese (who used the pseudonym Kim Bread).

Note. Compo, Clegg and Foggy performed in the 1984 *Royal Variety Show* (televised by BBC1 on 25 November) and there was also a *Last Of The Summer Wine* stage production, which ran in British theatres in 1983. On 30 March 1997, BBC1 presented *25 Years Of Last Of The Summer Wine*, an affectionate look back at the show, which included amusing outtakes and highlights, interviews

with the cast and crew and comments from the series' legions of dedicated fans.

See also *First Of The Summer Wine*.

The Last Song

UK · BBC · SITCOM

13 × 30 mins · colour

Series One (6) 3 Nov–8 Dec 1981 · BBC2 Tue 9pm

Series Two (7) 18 Feb–1 Apr 1983 · BBC2 Fri 9pm

MAIN CAST

Leo Bannister · · · · · · · · · · · Geoffrey Palmer
Liz · · · · · · · · · · · · · · Nina Thomas (series 1)
Alice Bannister · · · · · · · · Caroline Blakiston
Jane · · · · · · · · · · · · · · · · · · Hetty Baynes
Alison · · · · · · · · · · · · · · · · · · Gay Wilde
Shirley · · · · · · · · · · · Barbara Flynn (series 1)

CREDITS

writer Carla Lane · producer Sydney Lotterby

Concerned about being typecast as a woman who wrote only for women, Carla Lane centred this sitcom on the problems of a man, Leo Bannister (played by Geoffrey Palmer who had also appeared in her series *Butterflies*). At the start of *The Last Song*, Leo, 50, is separated from his wife Alice and awaiting a divorce; the last thing on his mind is another relationship, but he has reckoned without the 24-year-old Liz, who slips under his defences and into his heart. This 'spring and autumn' relationship causes more than its fair share of problems, especially when the petulant Alice begins back-pedalling on the divorce proceedings. By the second series Liz had disappeared and the emphasis switched to Leo's interaction with his daughters Jane and Alison, and his attempts to enjoy an amicable relationship with his estranged wife.

Last Tribute

see *That's Your Funeral*

The Last Turkey In The Shop Show

see MILLIGAN, Spike

The Last Word

UK · BBC · SITCOM

1 × 30 mins · colour

23 Jan 1994 · BBC2 Sun 9pm

MAIN CAST

Michael Dimmock · · · · · · · · · Mark McGann
Andy · · · · · · · · · · · · · Michael N Harbour
Donald · · · · · · · · · · · · · · · · Paul Shelley
Gill · · · · · · · · · · · · · · · · · · Hazel Ellerby
Paul · · · · · · · · · · · · · · · · · · · Philip Fox

CREDITS

writer Tony Bagley · director Roy Gould · producer Justin Sbresni

In the world of situation comedy there are many examples of synchronicity, with different writers coming up with similar ideas at the same time. In 1994 the theme was newspapers, with a sudden glut of scripts about journalists. One was *The Last Word* (it was to have been titled *Obit*), a black comedy about an arrogant and vicious newspaperman, Michael Dimmock, who has finally gone too far and, as punishment, is demoted to writing the obituaries column. It then becomes apparent that, with his caustic view of the world, this is not such a brilliant idea.

Mark McGann played the despicable Dimmock well enough, but – with *Nelson's Column* and the BBC1 light-drama series *Harry*, which starred Michael Elphick as the head of a news agency – there may have been too many such programmes around at this time for the show to shine, and the first appearance of *The Last Word*, presented as a *Comic Asides* pilot, was also its swansong.

A Last Word On The Election

see HOWERD, Frankie

Late Expectations

UK · BBC · SITCOM

6 × 30 mins · colour

7 Apr–12 May 1987 · BBC1 Tue 8.30pm

MAIN CAST

Ted Jackson	Keith Barron
Liz Jackson	Nanette Newman
Suzie Jackson	Caroline Mander
Polly Jackson	Sara Griffiths
George Jackson	Paul McCarthy
Harry	Norman Ashley
Joyce	Sally Hughes

CREDITS

writer John Gleeson · *directors* John B Hobbs (3), Sue Bysh (3) · *producer* John B Hobbs

Returning from a 'holiday of a lifetime' second honeymoon, a couple in their forties, Ted and Liz Jackson, discover that the trip has re-created the early days of their marriage all too accurately and that, at age 43, Liz has fallen pregnant. This news arrives as a huge shock to the Jacksons, their three grown-up children and their close friends, and just when everyone is getting used to the idea, a second shockwave reverberates through their world when it turns out that Liz is expecting twins.

In true sitcom fashion, husband Ted is the hopeless male aghast at the prospect of the 'late arrivals' while wife Liz holds the fort together and attempts to take it all in her stride. Further episodes, which might have seen their attempts at parenting the twins, were never made because the series failed to return.

For a similar series see *Life Begins At Forty*.

Late Lunch With Sir Les

see HUMPHRIES, Barry

The Late Show

UK · BBC · SKETCH

23 editions (8 × 45 mins · 8 × 35 mins · 4 × 40 mins · 1 × 50 mins · 1 × 25 mins · 1 × 20 mins) · b/w

15 Oct 1966–1 Apr 1967 · BBC1 Sat mostly 10.55pm

MAIN CAST

John Bird
Eleanor Bron
John Fortune
John Wells
Barry Humphries
Andrew Duncan
Anthony Holland

OTHER APPEARANCES

Malcolm Muggeridge
Sandra Caron

CREDITS

writers John Bird, John Fortune, Eleanor Bron, Barry Humphries, Michael Palin/Terry Jones · *producers* Jack Gold (13), Hugh Burnett (10)

The last of the principal entries in the 1960s satire boom (and one of the few such series not to have creative input from Ned Sherrin) *The Late Show* was notable for two main reasons: the occasional appearances of Barry Humphries as the Australian housewife Edna Everage (in her formative years, long before Damehood and superstardom), and a number of filmed sketches written by Michael Palin and Terry Jones that were similar in style to the material they later contributed to *Monty Python's Flying Circus*. Otherwise, the series did not have a particularly great deal to commend, although the improvised sketches performed by John Bird, John Fortune and Eleanor Bron sometimes struck a chord. (Bird and Fortune continued to explore their rare talent in this area three decades later, in *Rory Bremner ... Who Else?* and *The Long Johns*.) The singer Sandra Caron appeared occasionally in latter editions and the other, less familiar, names from the cast, Andrew Duncan and Anthony Holland were humorists from Chicago.

Laugh Attack

UK · BBC · IMPRESSIONISM/STANDUP

1 × 30 mins · colour

23 Aug 1986 · BBC1 Sat 9.35pm

MAIN CAST

David Copperfield
Jeff Stevenson
Roy Walker
Duncan Norvelle
Rory Bremner

CREDITS

writers cast and Barry Cryer, Terry Ravenscroft, Michael Barfield, Mark Brisenden, Duncan

Norvelle, Mark Walker · *additional material* Steve Brown · *script editor* Barry Cryer · *director* Marcus Mortimer · *producer* John Bishop

An attempt to take a quartet of comedy entertainers and create a permanent team to perform standup routines and impressions. Rory Bremner was the guest star in this one-off that failed to develop into a full series.

Laugh??? I Nearly Paid My Licence Fee

UK · BBC · SKETCH

6 × 30 mins · colour

29 Oct–3 Dec 1984 · BBC2 Mon 9pm

MAIN CAST

Robbie Coltrane
Ron Bain
Lisa Gold
John Sessions

CREDITS

writers Philip Differ (6), Laurie Rowley (6), Neil MacVicar (4), Bob Black (4), Niall Clark (3), Ian Pattison (3), Donnie Kerr (2), Paul Smith/Terry Kyan (1), Robbie Coltrane (1), Robbie Coltrane/John Sessions (1), David McNiven (songs) · *director/producer* Colin Gilbert

More mirth from BBC Scotland, in a similar vein to the series' predecessor *A Kick Up The Eighties*, apart from some cast changes it was business as usual, with plenty of costume sketches and winning skits. Robbie Coltrane enjoyed a recurring role in parodies of the film narrator Edgar Lustgarten (see also *The Robbie Coltrane Special*).

Laugh-In

see *Rowan And Martin's Laugh-In*

Laughs From Her Majesty's

UK · ITV (LWT) · STANDUP

1 × 60 mins · colour

20 Dec 1986 · Sat 8pm

MAIN CAST

Jimmy Tarbuck
Russ Abbot
Michael Barrymore
Max Bygraves
Jimmy Cricket
Bobby Davro
Les Dennis
Phyllis Diller
Dustin Gee
Joe Longthorne
Kenny Lynch
Jessica Martin
Des O'Connor
Allan Stewart
Frankie Vaughan
Gary Wilmot

CREDITS

writers cast and Dennis Berson, Garry Chambers, Colin Edmonds, Wally Malston, Alan Wightman · *director* Alasdair Macmillan · *producer* David Bell

A best-of compendium of humour from three series (totalling 19 editions) of LWT's Sunday-evening variety series *Live From Her Majesty's*, which had featured the blend of music, mirth and the odd spot of magic customary for this type of show, hosted by Jimmy Tarbuck. (The first series was 16 January to 27 February 1983; the second was 11 March to 22 April 1984; the third was 6 October to 10 November 1985.) The cast list, above, gives an idea of the degree of wit that the producers were looking for. Sadly, the series will only be remembered for the night (15 April 1984) that Tommy Cooper suffered a fatal heart attack on stage in the middle of act, in front of the theatre audience and millions watching at home.

Laughs From The Palladium

UK · ITV (LWT) · STANDUP

1 × 60 mins · colour

6 Dec 1987 · Sat 8pm

MAIN CAST
Jimmy Tarbuck
Russ Abbot
Tommy Cannon
Bobby Ball
Bob Carolgees
Frank Carson
Brian Conley
Richard Digance
Bella Emberg
Gareth Hale
Norman Pace
Dr Evadne Hinge · · · · · · · · · · George Logan
Dame Hilda Bracket · · · · · · · · · Patrick Fyffe
Dave Lee

CREDITS
writers cast and Charlie Adams, Bryan Blackburn, Garry Chambers, Russel Lane, Gerald Mahlowe, Wally Malston, Alan Wightman · *director* Ian Hamilton · *producer* Alasdair Macmillan

A best-of compendium of humour from the first two series – 12 editions – of LWT's Sunday-evening variety series *Live From The Palladium* (see previous entry, **Laughs From Her Majesty's**, for description), hosted by Jimmy Tarbuck. (The first series was 5 April to 10 May 1987; the second was 11 October to 15 November 1987.)

Laughter In Store

see DRAKE, Charlie

The Laughter Show

UK · BBC · IMPRESSIONISM/STANDUP

17 × 35 mins · colour

Series One (4) 7 Apr–28 Apr 1984 · BBC1
Sat 6.30pm

Series Two (6) 16 Feb–23 Mar 1985 · BBC1
Sat 6.40pm

Series Three (7) *Les And Dustin's Laughter Show*
28 Dec 1985–22 Feb 1986 · BBC1
Sat mostly 6.45pm

MAIN CAST
Les Dennis
Dustin Gee
Roy Jay (series 1)
Gareth Hale (series 1)
Norman Pace (series 1)

CREDITS
writers Neil Shand (16), Neil Shand/Barry Cryer (7), Paul Minett/Brian Leveson (15), Helen Murry/Jamie Rix/Nick Wilton (13), Dennis Berson (8), David Hansen/Paul Owen (5), Rick Freeman (4), Tony Hare (4), James Hendrie (4), Peter Hickey (4), Fred Metcalf (4), Mike Radford (4), Bryan Blackburn (3), Graham Deykin (3), David Hurst (3), Ian Phillipson (3) and others · *script associate* Neil Shand · *director/producer* John Bishop

Comedy impressionists Les Dennis and Dustin Gee first met while working on **Who Do You Do?** and first performed together successfully on **Russ Abbot's Madhouse**, where they delighted audiences with their impersonations of two *Coronation Street* characters, Vera Duckworth and Mavis Riley. Such successes persuaded Dennis and Gee to form a partnership, and they were the stars of this BBC show. In the first series they were helped out by future stars Hale and Pace, and by the strange comic Roy Jay, whose act chiefly comprised his punctuation of stories with the words 'slither', 'hither' and 'spook', said in an unsettling way. Dennis and Gee then carried the second and third series (the latter was retitled *Les And Dustin's Laughter Show*), with different guest stars, including a couple more appearances by Jay.

Gee and Dennis were a likeable and popular pairing but the double-act came to a premature end in January 1986 when the 43-year-old Gee suffered a fatal heart attack. After the opening edition the third series was put on hold for two weeks before Dennis returned with six final shows. After a further 18-month absence, the premise continued as **The Les Dennis Laughter Show**.

Laura And Disorder

UK · BBC · SITCOM

6 × 30 mins · colour

19 Feb–26 Mar 1989 · BBC1 Sun 7.15pm

MAIN CAST
Laura Kingsley · · · · · · · · · · · · Wendy Craig
Oberon · · · · · · · · · · · · · · · Stephen Persaud
Howard Kingsley · · · · · · · · Graham Sinclair
Helen Kingsley · · · · · · · · · · · Sally Hughes

CREDITS
writers Jonathan Marr (Wendy Craig)/Ross Bentley · *director/producer* John B Hobbs

Recently divorced Laura Kingsley leaves California, where she has lived for the last ten years, and returns to England, visiting her unsuspecting son Howard. Laura is an adventurous, barnstorming, incident-prone woman, slightly out of step with the rest of the world – wherever she goes, an air of chaos follows, and she is soon disrupting her son's well-ordered life.

Jonathan Marr, the series' co-writer, was really the starring player Wendy Craig (using the pseudonym she had previously employed to script *... And Mother Makes Five*) and yet, despite this involvement in the shaping and development of her character, the persona was oddly unsuitable for her and the series seemed forced and contrived as a result. It bowed out after six episodes; a pity, since talent like Craig's deserved better.

Laverne And Shirley

USA · ABC (MILLER-MILKIS PRODUCTIONS/HENDERSON PRODUCTIONS) · SITCOM

178 × 30 mins · colour

US dates: 27 Jan 1976–9 May 1983

*UK dates: 1 July 1978–2 June 1979 (12 episodes) ITV Sat around 5pm

MAIN CAST
Laverne DeFazio · · · · · · · · · Penny Marshall
Shirley Feeney · · · · · · · · · · · Cindy Williams
Frank DeFazio · · · · · · · · · · · · · Phil Foster
Andrew 'Squiggy' Squiggman · · · · · · · · · · ·
· David L Lander
Lenny Kosnowski · · · · · · · Michael McKean
Carmine Ragusa · · · · · · · · · · · Eddie Mekka

CREDITS
creators Garry Marshall, Lowell Ganz, Mark Rothman · *writers* various · *directors* Garry Marshall, Alan Rafkin and others · *executive producers* Garry Marshall, Thomas L Miller, Edward K Milkis · *producers* Mark Rothman, Lowell Ganz, Tony Marshall, Arthur Silver, Nik Abdo

The **Happy Days** creator/producer Garry Marshall introduced two female Fonz-like characters (that is, tough and cool) into that series to see if they would prove popular and merit a run of their own. They were and they did: *Laverne And Shirley* ran contemporaneously with its parent programme and the two were nip and tuck at the top of the US TV ratings for a while, holding down positions one and two, in either order.

The series, like *Happy Days*, was set in Milwaukee in the late 1950s, where Laverne and Shirley work as bottle-cappers on the assembly line at Shotz brewery, and live together in an apartment. Neither has been endowed with much money, or education, and – like a chocolate assortment – while Laverne appears to be tough, she has a soft centre, and while Shirley appears to be soft-centred, she is tough. In short, although *Laverne And Shirley* was rare in that it starred two women and was also distinctly blue-collar, it was stereotypical and rode easy laughs, based on goofy, scarcely believable situations. Henry Winkler – the real Fonz – appeared as a guest in the premiere episode. To combat flagging ratings, the sixth US season of *Laverne And Shirley* saw everything switch from Wisconsin (where it had been for 113 episodes) to California (where it remained for 65 more), and, near to the end, the character of Shirley was phased out after a pregnant Cindy Williams failed to persuade the producers to reduce working hours – at this point the programme began with the title *Laverne*. (There were no such problems with her actress, Penny Marshall, who was the real-life sister of Garry.)

There were two spin-offs – children's animated series *Laverne And Shirley In The Army* (1981–82) and *Laverne And Shirley With The Fonz* (1982–83), with Penny Marshall voicing Laverne in both, Cindy Williams voicing Shirley in the former and Lynn Marie Stewart in the latter. Penny Marshall then went on to become a successful film director, specialising in comedies like *Big*, starring Tom Hanks, in 1988. Twelve years after the final US episode, Penny Marshall and Cindy Williams came together once more for *The Laverne And Shirley Reunion*, a one-hour special networked by ABC on 22 May 1995.

*Note. London-area ITV screened a dozen *Laverne And Shirley* episodes in 1978–79. Then, from 11 January to 12 October 1988, BBC1 broadcast 32, in weekday morning slots.

Law And Disorder

UK · ITV (THAMES FOR CENTRAL) · SITCOM
6 × 30 mins · colour
17 Jan–21 Feb 1994 · Mon 8pm
MAIN CAST
Phillippa Troy · · · · · · · · · · · · Penelope Keith
Gerald Triggs · · · · · · · · · · · · Simon Williams
Judge Wallace · · · · · · · · · · · Charles Kay
Arthur Bryant · · · · · · · · · · · Eamon Boland
Steven · · · · · · · · · · · · · · · · · John Junkin
Susan · · · · · · · · · · · · · · · · · Emma Davies

CREDITS
writer Alex Shearer · *director/producer* John Howard Davies

The fourth Thames/ITV sitcom for Penelope Keith inside nine years – following *Moving*, *Executive Stress* and *No Job For A Lady*. *Law And Disorder* cast her as Law Courts barrister Phillippa Troy, a widowed and bewigged fighter for justice, employing a no-nonsense approach to case-winning that was not always itself above the law. But win she always did, out-manoeuvring her usual barrister opponent, the God-fearing Gerald Triggs, with an acid-tongued statement or a withering glare cast over her half-glasses. Troy was also wont to correct others' bad grammar; hers was faultless because, as well as being a barrister, she was the author of a series of *Prickly Peter* children's books. The

worlds of justice and publishing had evidently done Phillippa Troy's bank balance proud, for she drove around the countryside in an open-top sports car.

In yet another imperious role, Penelope Keith – for whom the part was written – gave her usual good value as Troy, served by her instructing solicitor Arthur, her clerk Steven and her junior Susan. But *Law And Disorder* was too unrealistic and too middle-of-the-road to succeed: the court scenes didn't ring true – the witty Judge Wallace was a particularly unlikely character – and Troy's cases were crazy, having to defend a sleepwalker, a football fan given the wrong tattoo, and others of that ilk.

Lazarus And Dingwall

UK · BBC · SITCOM
6 × 30 mins · colour
1 Feb–8 Mar 1991 · BBC2 Fri 9pm
MAIN CAST
Lazarus · · · · · · · · · · · · · · · · · Stephen Frost
Dingwall · · · · · · · · · · · · · · · · · Mark Arden
Chief · · · · · · · · · · · · · · · · · · Peter Bland
Plainclothes 1 · · · · · · · · · · · · Simon Godley
Plainclothes 2 · · · · · · · · · · · · Neil Mullarkey
Clinton · · · · · · · · · · · · · · · · · Jim Findley
Armitage · · · · · · · · · · · · · · · · Race Davies

CREDITS
writers Kim Fuller/Vicky Pile · *directors* Bob Spiers (5), Geoff Posner (1) · *producer* Geoff Posner

A cop comedy that mixed the anything-goes, joke-laden style of *Police Squad* with the spot-on satire of *The Comic Strip Presents ...* The comedy double-act Arden and Frost (formerly called the Oblivion Boys) had become well known to TV viewers in a series of hilarious lager commercials and here they were cast as police partners Lazarus and Dingwall, members of the Really Serious Crime Squad. The partnership was part Starsky and Hutch, part Bodie and Doyle and part Abbott and Costello, and they investigated wildly improbable cases with the help and hindrance of a mixed bunch of incompetents, presided over by their equally lacklustre 'chief'.

Some of the smaller, regular roles and guest parts were played by faces well known on the comedy cabaret circuit, while the writers, Kim Fuller and Vicky Pile, were dab hands at the sort of anarchic comedy that delineated the 'alternative' scene. The pair added a new twist here, borrowed from the *Airplane!* movie (made by the people behind *Police Squad*), in which normal 'reality' and the conventions of a genre were breached for the sake of a good joke. This was a risky departure and needed some skill to carry off; the result was moderately successful, but with faster pacing and more brashness it could have succeeded enough to warrant a second series.

Leave It To Charlie

UK · ITV (GRANADA) · SITCOM
26 × 30 mins · colour
Series One (7) 13 July–24 Aug 1978 · Thu 7.15pm
Series Two (7) 10 Jan–7 Mar 1979 · Wed 8pm
Series Three (6) 12 Apr–24 May 1979 · Thu 8pm
Series Four (6) 19 Feb–25 Mar 1980 · Tue 8.30pm
MAIN CAST
Charlie Fisher · · · · · · · · · · · · · David Roper
Arthur Simister · · · · · · · · · · · · Peter Sallis
Alice Simister · · · · · · · · · · · Gwen Cherrell
Florence McGee · · · · · · · · · · · Jean Heywood
Jennifer Padgett · · · · · · · · · · Sally Kinghorn
Harry Hutchins · · · · · · · · · · · · David Ross
Mr Ffolliott · · · · · · · · · · · · · · · John Horsley

CREDITS
writers H V Kershaw (24), Barry Hill (2) · *director/producer* Eric Prytherch

Two comic actors well known for their northern parts – David Roper, who had appeared in *The Cuckoo Waltz*, and Peter Sallis from *Last Of The Summer Wine* – were the mainstays of this run-of-the-mill Granada sitcom which, despite its simplistic premise, ran for four series.

Roper starred as Charlie Fisher, a young, cheerful and optimistic agent for the Bolton-based Lancastrian Insurance company. His willingness to help is unceasing, and his clients tend to lean upon him for all sorts of assistance – which, inevitably, causes him all sorts of problems. Sallis was cast as Charlie's boss, Mr Simister, a gloomy pessimist whose wife Alice is so vague that she cannot recall his name.

See also *The Life Of Riley* [2].

Leave It To Pastry

see Mr Pastry

Leaving

UK · BBC · SITCOM
12 × 30 mins · colour
Series One (6) 20 June–25 July 1984 · BBC2 Wed 9pm
Series Two (6) 2 May–13 June 1985 · BBC2 Thu 9pm
MAIN CAST
Daniel Ford · · · · · · · · · · · · · · Keith Barron
Martha Ford · · · · · · · · · · · Susan Hampshire
Mr Chessington · · · · · · · · · · · Richard Vernon
Gina Ford · · · · · · · · · · · · · · · · Lucy Aston
Matthew Ford · · · · · · · · · · · · · Gary Cady
Mrs Ford · · · · · · · · · · · · · Elizabeth Bradley

CREDITS
writer Carla Lane · *director/producer* John B Hobbs

Daniel Ford and his wife Martha wish to have an amicable divorce, neither wishing to cause the other any unnecessary anguish. But such traumatic transactions rarely run smoothly and the Fords find numerous personal problems interfering with their plans.

Leaving represented more bitter-sweet fare from writer Carla Lane, who had started to invent a new genre, moving further and further away from conventional sitcom towards serial humorous drama. Some critics bemoaned the paucity of laughs, ignoring the series' intentionally serious premise and the writer's attempt to try something new. The low-key comedy element was no real problem, it just acquired an attitude adjustment on the part of the viewer; but the series suffered a more fundamental flaw in that its characters, while believable, were, unfortunately, rather dull.

The Lee Evans Show

UK · ITV (LITTLE MO FILMS FOR YORKSHIRE) · STANDUP

1 × 60 mins · colour
26 Dec 1996 · Thu 10.40pm

MAIN CAST
Lee Evans

CREDITS
writer Lee Evans · *director* John Birkin · *producer* Miles Ross

A Christmas special for the hard-working, effervescent standup comic. Actors Richard E Grant, Lesley Ash and American singer Tony Bennett were his guests.

See *An Evening With Lee Evans* for career details, and also *The World Of Lee Evans*.

The Leeds series

UK · ITV (YORKSHIRE) · SITCOMS

5 × 30 mins · colour
Return To Leeds 1 Aug 1972 · Tue 10.30pm
Deadline Leeds 31 July 1973 · Tue 10.30pm
The Play's The Thing (Juvenile Leeds) 28 Aug 1973 · Tue 10.30pm
Leeds Athletic 16 July 1974 · Tue 11pm
Le Prix de Leeds 23 July 1974 · Tue 11pm

MAIN CAST
John Wells
John Bird

CREDITS
writers John Wells/John Bird · *directors* Ian Davidson (ed 1), Len Lurcuck (eds 2–5), David Mallet (ed 5) · *producer* John Duncan

An irregular collection of single comedies in which every one of the many roles was portrayed by the two writers, John Wells and John Bird. Key players in the 'satire' boom of the early 1960s, their aim was to send-up the machinations of TV production, vouchsafing the viewer at home glimpses behind-the-scenes in TV Land, not merely to illustrate why the medium so often fails to deliver its message but to show, miraculously, how it sometimes does.

Ironically, these programmes were themselves beset with problems. Yorkshire first announced that four would be screened, focusing on documentary, drama, sports and current affairs/magazine departments. But the second transmission was badly delayed, from January to July 1973, so there was a year between this and its predecessor. The third programme was then announced as being the last, and so it seemed until, 12 months later, the sports send-up was broadcast, followed closely by a fifth and final script, showing the goings-on (and walkings-out) at the Leeds First International Festival Of Television.

As Wells and Bird would have realised, there was a story in all of this mucking about, but they resisted – perhaps wisely – the opportunity to write it up as a sixth programme.

Legacy Of Murder

see EMERY, Dick

The Legacy Of Reginald Perrin

see *The Fall And Rise Of Reginald Perrin*

Lennie And Jerry

UK · BBC · STANDUP/SKETCH

18 editions (7 × 50 mins · 6 × 35 mins · 4 × 45 mins · 1 × 40 mins) · colour
Series One (3 × 45 mins) 17 June–1 July 1978 · BBC1 Sat 7.50pm then 9pm
Special (50 mins) *Lennie And Jerry's Holiday Special* 28 Dec 1978 · BBC1 Thu 7.40pm
Series Two (6 × 50 mins) 26 Feb–2 Apr 1979 · BBC1 Mon 8.10pm
Special (45 mins) 7 July 1979 · BBC1 Sat 8.15pm
Special (40 mins) 30 Dec 1979 · BBC1 Sun 7.15pm
Series Three (6 × 35 mins) 28 Feb–10 Apr 1980 · BBC1 Thu mostly 7.55pm

MAIN CAST
Lennie Bennett
Jerry Stevens

CREDITS
writers Peter Vincent (15), Dennis Berson (12), Brad Ashton (10), Neil Shand (8), Howard Imber (8), Tony Hare (7), Terry Ravenscroft (6), Peter Spence (3), Tom Magee-Englefield (3), Barry Cryer (1) · *additional material* Lennie Bennett/Jerry Stevens · *producer* Ernest Maxin

With Morecambe and Wise en route to ITV, the BBC was keen to find other popular double-acts. They struck lucky with Little and Large and, around the same time, groomed Lennie and Jerry to follow the same path to success. This series utilised many of the writers who worked on *Little And Large*, but although the formula and quality were similar, this particular double-act failed to create a lasting impression.

Lenny Henry … [various shows]

see HENRY, Lenny

Leonard Henry

UK · BBC · STANDUP

7 editions (6 × 10 mins · 1 × 20 mins) · b/w
17 Nov 1936 · Tue 3.40pm (20 mins)
11 Jan 1937 · Mon 3.35pm (10 mins)
30 Apr 1937 · Fri 3.50pm (10 mins)
7 Mar 1938 · Mon 3.20pm (10 mins)
11 Mar 1938 · Fri 9pm (10 mins)
25 Aug 1938 · Thu 2.30pm (10 mins)
26 Aug 1939 · Sat 3.50pm (10 mins)

MAIN CAST
Leonard Henry

CREDITS
writer Leonard Henry

Lenny Henry is not the first comic of that name to become a star in Britain. Born Leonard H Ruming in Kensington, London, in 1890, the cockney comedian Leonard Henry was an early exponent of zany humour and became renowned as the first man to blow a raspberry on radio. His act combined bizarre routines with weird comic songs and a clutch of funny voices, all presented as if they had just that moment popped into his head. (He did indeed write his own material.)

Standing tall at five feet nothing – play was made of the fact that microphones had to be lowered for him – Henry made his debut broadcast on radio in September 1926 and first appeared on TV in its experimental days, prior to the launch of the service. He then made a succession of pre-war programmes (the first three of which aired under the *Starlight* banner) to delight the few hundred viewers then able to tune in. Henry died on 6 January 1973, aged 82.

Les And Dustin's Laughter Show

see *The Laughter Show*

The Les Dawson Show
Les Dawson's Christmas Box

see DAWSON, Les

The Les Dennis Laughter Show

UK · BBC · SKETCH

35 editions (19 × 30 mins · 15 × 35 mins · 1 × 40 mins) · colour
Series One (6 × 35 mins) 13 June–18 July 1987 · BBC1 Sat 6.25pm then 8.20pm
Series Two (8 × 35 mins) 28 May–16 July 1988 · BBC1 Sat around 7.45pm
Special (40 mins) 27 Dec 1988 · BBC1 Tue 6.50pm

Series Three (6 × 30 mins) 10 June–15 July
1989 · BBC1 Sat 7.05pm

Special (35 mins) 23 Dec 1989 · BBC1
Sat 7.55pm

Series Four (6 × 30 mins) 9 June–21 July 1990 ·
BBC1 Sat around 7pm

Special (30 mins) 22 Dec 1990 · BBC1
Sat 7.30pm

Series Five (6 × 30 mins) 22 June–27 July 1991 ·
BBC1 Sat 7pm

MAIN CAST
Les Dennis
Lisa Maxwell
Joe Longthorne (series 1 & 2)

OTHER APPEARANCES
Martin P Daniels
Jeffrey Holland
Bella Emberg

CREDITS
writers Paul Minett/Brian Leveson (20), Neil Shand
(13), Paul Alexander/Gavin Osbon (13), Russel
Lane (10), Peter Robinson (10), Geoff Atkinson (8),
Dennis Berson (7), Garry Chambers (6), Jamie
Rix/Nick Wilton (6), Colin Bostock-Smith (5),
Davies/Woolnough (4), Dix/Gibson/Measures (4),
Peter Vincent (4), Rosser/Davies (4),
Charlie Adams (3), Mark Landon/Nick Donaldson
(3), Hugh Smith (3), James Bibby (2), Terry Corrigan
(2), Andrew Hastings (2), Matthew King (2), Gordon
McPherson (2), Steve Punt (2), Kenneth Rock (2),
Laurie Rowley (2) and others · *script associates*
Paul Minett/Brian Leveson, Paul Alexander/Gavin
Osbon · *directors* Geoff Miles (13), Michael Leggo
(12), Kevin Bishop (10) · *producers* Kevin Bishop
(22), Geoff Miles (13)

After Dustin Gee's untimely death, Les
Dennis continued **The Laughter Show**
idea, initially with impressionist Joe Longthorne as a partner. Longthorne specialised in
'drag' roles and was particularly effective
when he appeared in the guise of music icons
Tina Turner and Shirley Bassey. Also on
hand was the young actress Lisa Maxwell,
who had made her TV debut, aged 11, in **The
Many Wives Of Patrick**. Here she added
impersonation to her illustrious list of credits
(actress/dancer/singer/host), with the Australian pop idol Kylie Minogue among her
repertoire. Dennis himself kept on his toes by
creating a fresh set of impersonations each
week for regular sketches based on films;
hence he appeared as Paul Hogan in a spoof
of *Crocodile Dundee*, *Raiders Of The Lost Ark*
hero Indiana Jones, and others. The regular
cast was joined by guest stars from the world
of comedy, notably Shane Richie, who
appeared in the very first show, capitalising
on his success in the stage musical *Grease*.

Note. This series was sometimes titled *Les
Dennis's Laughter Show*.

Les Girls

UK · ITV (CENTRAL) · SITCOM

7 × 30 mins · colour

15 May–10 July 1988 · Sun mostly 9.30pm

MAIN CAST
Jo-Ann · · · · · · · · · · · · · · · · · · Debby Bishop
Veronica · · · · · · · · · · · · · · · Rachel Fielding
Amanda · · · · · · · · · · · · · · · · · · · Sadie Frost
Susan · · · · · · · · · · · · · · · · · · · Janet McTeer
Maggie · · · · · · · · · · · · · · · · · Annie Lambert
Polly · · · · · · · · · · · · · · · · · · · Arabella Weir
Reg · · · · · · · · · · · · · · · · Thomas Wheatley
Conrad · · · · · · · · · · · · · · · Tom Georgeson
Mervyn · · · · · · · · · · · · · · · · · · Gerard Horan

CREDITS
writers Margaret Phelan (2), Guy Andrews (1),
Helen Leadbeater (1), Joanna Toye (1), Linda
Kearnan (1), not known (1) · *script editor* Diana
Culverhouse · *directors* Anthony Garner (4), Sharon
Miller (3) · *executive producer* William Smethurst ·
producer Patrick Harbinson

An unremarkable ITV series with a few
laughs but bordering on drama, charting the
careers of some young women working for
the agency Maggie's Models. It suffered from
erratic scheduling: there was a fortnight's gap
after the first two shows, and the remaining
episodes were screened at varying times,
being demoted from primetime to late-night.
Indeed, it was really only worthwhile watching to catch the cameo appearances from Neil
Pearson, Alexei Sayle, John Gordon-Sinclair,
Mark McGann, Bryan Pringle and Hugh
Laurie.

Les Lives

UK · BBC · SKETCH

8 × 5 mins · colour

11 Oct–13 Dec 1993 · BBC2 Mon mostly 6.25pm

MAIN CAST
Les · · · · · · · · · · · · · · · · · · · Fred Aylward
Bloody Nora · · · · · · · · · · · · · · Karen Beeny

CREDITS
writer Fred Aylward · *director* Neil MacKenzie
Matthews · *producer* Graham K Smith

Reeves and Mortimer weren't the only defectors to cross channels from C4 to the BBC
following *Vic Reeves Big Night Out* –
their silent assistant Les also made the trip
and starred in his own series of five-minute
wordless shorts, which charted his bizarre
adventures in his strange fantasy world. The
programmes were screened within the BBC2
youth strand *DEF II*.

Les Sez

see DAWSON, Les

The Leslie Crowther Show
Leslie Crowther's Scrapbook

see CROWTHER, Leslie

Leslie Randall Entertains

see *Joan And Leslie*

Leslie Weston

UK · BBC · STANDUP

1 × 10 mins · b/w

26 Jan 1937 · Tue 9.30pm

MAIN CAST
Leslie Weston

CREDITS
writer Leslie Weston · *producer* Dallas Bower

A single TV shot for the music-hall star Leslie
Weston – nicknamed the 'Cheery Chatterbox'
through his many broadcasts on BBC radio –
in which sang a pair of comedy songs.

Let The Blood Run Free

AUSTRALIA · 10 NETWORK (MEDIA ARTS) ·
SITCOM

26 × 30 mins · colour

Australian dates: 20 Aug 1990–22 Jan 1994

UK dates: 29 Aug 1992–7 Jan 1995
(26 episodes) C4 Sat 10pm then various days
around 12 midnight

MAIN CAST
Nurse Pam Sandwich · · · · · · · · · Jane Kittson
Dr Raymond Good · · · · · · · · Brian Nankervis
Nurse Effie Shunt · · · · · · · · · · · Helen Knight
Dr Richard Lovechild · · · · · · · · · David Swann
Orderly Warren Cronkshonk · · · · · · · · · · · ·
· Peter Rowsthorn
Matron Dorothy Conniving-Bitch · · · · · · · · · ·
· Linda Gibson

CREDITS
creator/writers The Blood Group (cast and Mark
Cutler, John Thomson) · *director* John Thomson ·
executive producer Ian McFadyen · *producer*
Bobbie Waterman

A kitsch-crammed Australian melodrama/
soap opera spoof set in a shambolic hospital,
St Christopher's. The character names should
give a clue as to the general level of the farce
here – suffice to say it wasn't subtle stuff.

The relationship between the characters
was typically complex, neatly parodying
similar structures in the genre it attempted
to lampoon. Dr Raymond Good (our hero) is
infatuated with new nurse Pam Sandwich, an
innocent, well-meaning, good-hearted woman;
but she is also desired by the lecherous
Lothario, Dr Lovechild, a suave and selfish
womaniser; he in turn is pursued by the evil
Matron Dorothy Conniving-Bitch, a murderous gargoyle who lives up to her name (Linda
Gibson's spectacularly over-the-top performance was quite brilliant); Lovechild is also
lusted after by Nurse Effie Shunt, with whom
he has toyed sexually but since jilted; Effie,
a passionate and romantic woman is herself
courted by the dense, inarticulate, ugly
orderly Warren Cronkshonk.

Based on a stage-play by the Blood Group
(the creative crew here), *Let The Blood Run
Free* was a loud, boisterous, basic brute from
Down Under that existed solely to create
laughs and had no pretensions towards satire,

moralising or messages. Gruesomely gory and full of violent slapstick, it came over like a cross between *The Young Ones*, *Dr Kildare* and an Italian horror movie. The series never fully escaped its stage origins and the cast hammed it up to the highest level as if making sure that people at the back of the theatre would get the joke. It could have all been a horrible mess (and, indeed, some critics thought it was) but the series was rescued from the TV rubbish bin by its sheer energy and determination to make audiences laugh. In the UK, it developed into a small cult and proved popular elsewhere beyond its home country – so much so, that the second series of 13 episodes was produced on the strength of its sales success. Not to everyone's taste perhaps, but a decent enough accompaniment to six tubes of Foster's.

Let There Be Love

UK · ITV (THAMES) · SITCOM

12 × 30 mins · colour

Series One (6) 4 Jan–8 Feb 1982 · Mon 8pm
Series Two (6) 10 Mar–21 Apr 1983 · Thu mostly 8pm

MAIN CAST

Timothy · · · · · · · · · · · · · Paul Eddington
Judy · · · · · · · · · · · · · · Nanette Newman
Dennis · · · · · · · · · · · · · · Henry McGee
Charles · · · · · · · · · · · · · Stephen Nolan
Edward · · · · · · · · · · · · · Ian Morrison
Elizabeth · · · · · · · · · · · Claudia Gambold
Mother · · · · · · · · · · · · · Elspeth March
Father · · · · · · · · · · · · · · · John Welsh

CREDITS

creators Johnnie Mortimer/Brian Cooke · writers Johnnie Mortimer/Brian Cooke (8), John Seaton (2), John Chapman (2) · director/producer Peter Frazer-Jones

Middle-aged, middle-class Timothy Love is a confirmed bachelor (although not in the *Private Eye* sense of the expression) who is happy with his lot: he has a good job, money, girlfriends when he wants them, and cherished freedom. Until a mother-of-three widow named Judy enters his life, that is. Judy is different, the type of woman with whom he can comfortably 'settle down'. They become engaged … and that's when the fun begins, Timothy having to share his life and do away with the old individualism.

The pair were married at the end of the first series, and in the second Timothy had to adapt to step-fatherhood, helping to parent Charles, Edward and Elizabeth as well as care for Judy's German-shepherd dog. Help/hindrance was supplied, in the usual sitcom measure, by Dennis Newberry, Timothy's partner in their advertising business.

Let There Be Love provided Nanette Newman's first sitcom role, while Paul Eddington recorded the dozen unspectacular

episodes either side of the third series of the BBC's *Yes Minister*.

Let's Laugh

UK · BBC · STANDUP

6 × 30 mins · b/w

10 May–2 Aug 1965 · BBC1 Mon 6.30pm

MAIN CAST

host · · · · · · · · · · · · · · · · · Johnny Hackett

CREDITS

writers various · producer Barney Colehan

A six-week standup series, hosted by the Liverpool comedian Johnny Hackett, in which each programme highlighted three different club comedy acts, all said to be from the North. (Some were not, however.) Mike Yarwood appeared in the first show and subsequent editions offered airtime to, among others, Hope and Keen, Mrs Shufflewick (Rex Jameson), Norman Collier, Frank Carson, Felix Bowness, Keith Harris, Freddie Sales, the Scaffold, Colin Crompton and Mike Burton.

Let's Parlez Franglais

UK · C4 (NORTH WEST TELEVISION) · SKETCH

10 × 20 mins · colour

6 Aug–8 Oct 1984 · Mon 6.40pm

MAIN CAST

Miles Kington

CREDITS

writer Miles Kington · director Maurice Kanareck · producer Tony Sutcliffe

Le TV version of Miles Kington's witty 'Franglais' articles and livres. A humorous daily quality-newspaper columnist (during this period at *The Times*, latterly *The Independent*), Kington first combined French and English into a whole new language for a feature in *Punch* magazine; it then took off, leading to books devoted to the ingenious vocabulary.

Each edition of the TV series comprised *trois* sketches, generally sending-up the type of situations prevalent in language-school textbooks. Kington himself appeared in *tout* programmes, and each one featured at least half a dozen guest stars, a series total of more than *soixante* top broadcasting names, among them John Barron, Melvyn Bragg, Dora Bryan, Leslie Crowther, Clive Dunn, Judy Geeson, Peter Jeffrey, Rosemary Leach, Maureen Lipman, Hugh Lloyd, Fulton Mackay, Peter O'Sullevan, Nicholas Parsons, Leslie Phillips, Cliff Richard, Willie Rushton, Prunella Scales, Lynn Seymour, Janet Street-Porter, Janet Suzman, and a couple of native French speakers, Petula Clark and Sacha Distel.

Note. With the assistance of Alison Steadman, Enn Reitel and Jon Glover, Miles Kington later presented his Franglais wit in a BBC Radio 4 series of that title, broadcast as five

ten-minute editions from 22 August to 19 September 1985.

Let's Stay Home

UK · ITV (ASSOCIATED-REDIFFUSION) · SKETCH

8 × 30 mins · b/w

4 June–23 July 1956 · Mon 9.30pm

MAIN CAST

Reg Dixon
The Wife · · · · · · · · · · · · · Rosemary Squires

OTHER APPEARANCES

Austin Melford
Henry McGee
Tony Sympson
Anita Sharp-Bolster
A J Dean
Muriel Young

CREDITS

writers Austin Melford (8), Steve Stephenson (3), Andrew Gray (2), Len Astor (1) · director Milo Lewis

Self-styled northern comedian Reg Dixon continued to feel 'proper poorly' in *Let's Stay Home*, his second series for the new commercial channel. Like the first (*Confidentially*) it featured someone as the Wife (here it was Rosemary Squires) and a team of regulars, including writer/performer Austin Melford and Henry McGee, who would go on to become an esteemed sideman to Benny Hill.

See also *Reg Dixon*.

Life After Birth

UK · C4 (TIGER ASPECT) · SITCOM

6 × 30 mins · colour

17 May–21 June 1996 · Fri 9.30pm

MAIN CAST

Alison · · · · · · · · · · · · · · · Emma Cunniffe
Judith · · · · · · · · · · · · · · · · Paula Bacon
Sylv · · · · · · · · · · · · · · · · · Paula Wilcox
Trish · · · · · · · · · · · · · · · · Jackie Downey
Gabriel · · · · · · · · · · · · · · · Fraser James
Alison's mum · · · · · · · · · · · Rachel Davies

CREDITS

writers Simon Block/Teresa Poland · director Liddy Oldroyd · producer Rachel Swann

Twenty-year-old Alison goes to a party, gets drunk, laid and falls pregnant. Nine months later she becomes a single mother, struggling against the system to bring up her baby boy, and *Life After Birth* charted her tribulations. Lending Alison a helping hand was her best friend and flatmate Judith, a struggling musician who, like Alison, is sexually promiscuous but too smart to fall into the same trap. Also on hand was Judith's boyfriend Gabriel, an amiable chap, genuinely fond of Alison. More of a hindrance than a help were the nosey neighbours – Sylv, a brash cockney woman, and Trish, gormless, gauche but well meaning. Both are mothers themselves and quick to offer Alison advice, but mostly the generation gap renders such pointers useless.

Life After Birth was an odd mix of comic and serious themes. Its trendy, archly contemporary, urban credit sequence – complete with fuzzy titles – belied the old-fashioned nature of the piece which, although unmistakably of the 1990s in its colourful language and themes, still featured many of the stereotypes (prying neighbours, cloying mother) that had dogged the sitcom genre for too long. Although a worthwhile attempt, the series never fully recovered from the downbeat nature of the premise, which made it hard to raise persistent laughs from what was often quite a depressing situation.

Life After Life

UK · ITV (LAWSON PRODUCTIONS FOR LWT) · SITCOM

1 × 75 mins · colour
30 Dec 1990 · Sun 8.15pm

MAIN CAST
Eric Burt · · · · · · · · · · · · · · · · · George Cole
Pat Sweeney · · · · · · · · · · · · · · · Gudrun Ure
Rosie Treadwell · · · · · · · · · Renee Asherson
Lord Deeds · · · · · · · · · · · · · · · William Fox
Lady Deeds · · · · · · · · · · · · · Mary Wimbush
Wing Commander Boyle · · · · · Leslie Phillips
Dr Trump · · · · · · · · · · · · · · · · · John Cater
Freda Neely · · · · · · · · · · · · · Gillian Raine
Det Insp Curtin · · · · · · · · · · · · John Fortune
Alice McCrum · · · · · · · · · · · · · · Helen Burns
Mrs Nuttall · · · · · · · · · · · Elizabeth Bennett

CREDITS
writer Jonathan Lynn · director Herbert Wise · producer Sarah Lawson

Scripted by Jonathan Lynn (*Yes Minister* and much else), this single but long comedy was intended to serve as the pilot for a full series, although no further episodes were made. George Cole starred, cast as Eric Burt, a 70-year-old made redundant from his job as a butler and forced, much against his wishes, to lie down in Green Pastures, a retirement home for the 'active elderly'. But here he meets two sisters, Rosie and Pat, one of whom is psychic, the other having healing powers. As the three team up to solve a murder mystery Burt realises that his adventures are only just beginning.

Note. Gary Webster, set to follow Dennis Waterman as the actor playing Arthur Daley's cohort in Thames TV's light-drama *Minder* when it returned for its eighth series in 1991, first worked with Cole in this production – he had a minor role as a removal man.

Life And Al Read

UK · ITV (ABC) · SKETCH

6 × 30 mins · b/w
29 Sep–3 Nov 1963 · Sun 3.30pm

MAIN CAST
Al Read

CREDITS
writer Al Read · directors Helen Standage (3), David Main (3) · producer Ronnie Taylor

Another rare TV excursion for the brilliant North Country standup comic Al Read, repeating the presentational style that was making his long-running BBC radio series (1951–68) such a success: philosophising to himself about the British way of life, dwelling on such topics as a picnic with the family, a visit to the barber, buying beer in a pub, buying a dress for 'the wife', and going to a football match. Each edition featured three or four such sketches. Ronnie Taylor, who had scripted or produced all of the radio series, produced again.

Note. A half-hour presentation of Al Read's stage-show *Such Is Life* was broadcast live from the Adelphi Theatre, London, on ITV on 27 July 1956.

See also *It's All In Life* and *Al Read Says What A Life!*

Life Begins At Forty

UK · ITV (YORKSHIRE) · SITCOM

14 × 30 mins · colour
Series One (7) 13 June–25 July 1978 · Tue 8.30pm
Series Two (7) 8 Feb–21 Mar 1980 · Fri 8pm

MAIN CAST
Chris Bunting · · · · · · · · · · · · · Derek Nimmo
Katy Bunting · · · · · · · · · · · Rosemary Leach
Jill Simpson · · · · · Rosemary Martin (series 1);
· · · · · · · · · · · · · · · Anna Dawson (series 2)
Gerry Simpson · · · · · · · Michael Graham Cox
Mrs Bunting · · · · · · · · · · · · · · Fanny Rowe
Priscilla · · · · · · · · · · · Angela Piper (series 2)
Horace the milkman · · · · · · · Gordon Rollings
· (series 2)

CREDITS
writer Jan Butlin · director/producer Graeme Muir

Life Begins At Forty pitched together the well-established TV comics (and serious actors) Derek Nimmo (cast as Chris Bunting) and Rosemary Leach (Katy), co-starring as a quintessentially comfortable middle-class couple, married for 17 years and heading happily down the highway of life. Then, suddenly, Katy discovers that she is pregnant and merry hell breaks loose, with Chris (in best Nimmo sitcom style) dithering and flapping about what to do. The baby was born at the end of the first series, ensuring a follow-up in which the new parents faffed about all over again, coping and worrying in equal measures. They were, at least, guided in their fumblings by friends Jill and Gerry Simpson, and by Chris's mum. Moira Lister made a guest appearance in the final episode, as Katy's sister, turning up for the christening.

For a similar series see the entry for *Late Expectations*.

A Life In Pieces

UK · BBC (TALKBACK PRODUCTIONS) · SKETCH

12 × 5 mins · colour
26 Dec 1990–6 Jan 1991 · BBC2 daily 9.50pm

MAIN CAST
Sir Arthur Streeb-Greebling · · · · · Peter Cook
Ludovic Kennedy · · · · · · · · · · · · · · himself

CREDITS
writer Peter Cook · script editor Rory McGrath · director John Lloyd · producer Peter Fincham

Peter Cook's dotty creation Sir Arthur Streeb-Greebling was first seen in the premiere episode of *Not Only ... But Also* in 1965 and here he was, 26 years later, being interviewed by Ludovic Kennedy about his 12 favourite Christmas presents (based on the gifts in the carol: three French hens, two turtle doves, and so on). In each segment Sir Arthur ranted on about a particular gift in the inimitable Cook style that appeared to be nothing more than an improvised ramble but which was scripted and invariably found a satisfying ending. Throughout his TV and stage life Streeb-Greebling made for a cantankerous and contrary figure, and when people happened to pronounce his name correctly he often countered that it was actually Greeb-Streebling.

Notes. Later in 1991 Cook was heard, but not seen, when he provided the voice for the C4 escapades of the *Viz* comic-strip character *Roger Mellie – The Man On The Telly*. Cook was an inspired choice to play this insensitive, egocentric buffoon whose compulsion to swear – his catchphrase was 'bollocks!' – made him the worst possible choice as a TV personality. The TV cartoon series, *It's Roger Mellie – The Man On The Telly*, ran for five consecutive nights from 30 December 1991 to 3 January 1992, for five minutes a time. A second C4 series, titled just *Roger Mellie*, aired from 29 December 1992 to 1 January 1993, with programmes varying in length from five to 25 minutes. Harry Enfield provided all the other voices in both series. Cook also appeared as Mellie in **Comic Relief** 1991.

Peter Cook made several other TV appearances following these series. He still made for a good chat-show guest, twice turned up in the biting news quiz *Have I Got News For You* on BBC2, and appeared in the same channel's pet-hates series *Room 101* (25 July 1994). He also acted in the light-drama series *Gone To Seed* (ITV, 13 November to 18 December 1992) and guested in a *One Foot In The Grave* special (BBC1, 26 December 1993). Cook died suddenly on 3 January 1995, leaving a huge hole in the comedy pantheon. An *Omnibus* special, *Some Interesting Facts*

About Peter Cook (BBC1, 19 December 1995), paid tribute to this remarkable man with clips and appreciations/reminiscences from his colleagues and friends.

A Life Of Bliss

UK · BBC · SITCOM

20 × 30 mins · b/w

Series One (10) 21 Jan–24 Mar 1960 · Thu 7.30pm

Series Two (10) *A Life Of Bliss!* 15 Feb–19 Apr 1961 · Wed mostly 8.30pm

MAIN CAST

David Bliss · · · · · · · · · · · · · · · · George Cole
Anne Fellows · · · · · · · Isabel Dean (series 1)
Tony Fellows · · · · · · · Colin Gordon (series 1)
Zoe Hunter · · · · · · · · · · · Pat Grove (series 1)
Pam Batten · · · · · Frances Bennett (series 2)
Bob Batten · · · · · · · · Hugh Sinclair (series 2)

CREDITS

writer Godfrey Harrison · *producers* Graeme Muir, Godfrey Harrison

The famous BBC radio sitcom *A Life Of Bliss*, which had first starred David Tomlinson, came to TV in 1960 bringing along its then star George Cole. He played David Alexander Bliss, an 'absurdly awkward, naïve, stumbling, fumbling, bachelor' whose dreamy personality invariably causes him to land in the soup.

Bliss strolled through a series of gentle adventures – usually centred around verbal gaffes and the usual sitcom misunderstandings – aided by his sister and brother-in-law, the Fellows, and his patient girlfriend Zoe. His true soul-mate, however, was his confidante Psyche the Dog, played by 'Mady', a wire-haired fox terrier whose expressive bark was provided by that ace animal impersonator Percy Edwards (he had also filled this role in the radio version). The second series brought cast changes as Bliss moved in with the Fellows' replacements, the Battens (also David's sister and brother-in-law), who lived in the fictional coastal resort of Havenville.

The BBC radio version ran for 118 episodes between 29 July 1953 and 3 March 1969.

The Life Of Riley   1

USA · NBC (IRVING BRECHER/DUMONT) · SITCOM

238 × 30 mins · b/w

US dates: 4 Oct 1949–22 Aug 1958

UK dates: 3 Apr–11 July 1956 (13 episodes) BBC mostly Tue 7.30pm

MAIN CAST

Chester A Riley · · Jackie Gleason (1949–50);
· · · · · · · · · · · · · · William Bendix (1953–58)
Peg Riley · · · Rosemary DeCamp (1949–50);
· · · · · · · · · · · · · · Marjorie Reynolds (1953–58)
Junior Riley · · · · · · · Lanny Rees (1949–50);
· · · · · · · · · · · · · · Wesley Morgan (1953–58)

Babs Riley Marshall · · · · · · · Gloria Winters
· (1949–50);
· · · · · · · · · · · · · Lugene Sanders (1953–58)
Jim Gillis · · · · · · · · · Sid Tomack (1949–50);
· · · · · · · · · · · · · · Tom D'Andrea (1953–58)

CREDITS

writers various · *directors* various · *producers* Tom McKnight, Irving Brecher

Very popular on US radio (NBC, 1944–51), *The Life Of Riley* was translated to the cinema screen in 1949 with William Bendix re-creating his radio role as the bumbling family man Chester A Riley, a well-meaning sort given to malapropisms and behaving like a bull in a china shop, intervening in problems only to make them worse, and working as an aircraft riveter in Los Angeles. Most episodes took place at home, where Riley tested the patience of his wife Peg and their children Junior and Babs.

Filming commitments prevented Bendix from taking the role when the series transferred to TV the same year, and Jackie Gleason snagged the part – his first TV series. However the Gleason version (screened in the USA by NBC from 4 October 1949 to 28 March 1950) wasn't a success and was cancelled after 26 episodes. But a second TV series with an all new cast – first imported on to UK television by the BBC, and then later shown by some ITV regions, although not in London – was made when Bendix was available once more. This time *The Life Of Riley* was a ratings hit and remained one of the most popular American TV comedies for five years.

The first series followed two test transmissions of *The Life Of Riley* on US television, with different actors trying out in the title roles – Herb Vigran on 13 April 1948 and Buddy Grey on 20 April 1948.

The Life Of Riley   2

UK · ITV (GRANADA) · SITCOM

7 × 30 mins · colour

6 Jan–17 Feb 1975 · Mon 8pm

MAIN CAST

Frank Riley · · · · · · · · · · · · · · · Bill Maynard
Brian Riley · · · · · · · · · · · · · · · Frank Lincoln
George Pollitt · · · · · · · · · · · · · John Comer
Ethel Goodchild · · · · · · · · · · Eileen Kennally
Janice Butcher · · · · · · · · · · · · Susan Littler
Clifford Pringle · · · · · · · · · · · John McKelvey
Mrs Pringle · · · · · · · · · · · · · · Pearl Hackney

CREDITS

writers H V Kershaw (5), Brian Finch (2) · *director/producer* Eric Prytherch

After voluntary quitting 1950s TV stardom to pursue an ultimately unspectacular stage career, Bill Maynard returned to the small-screen in this mediocre single series for Granada – a year later, however, he would

strike oil with *Oh No – It's Selwyn Froggitt*, made by Yorkshire Television.

In *The Life Of Riley* Maynard was cast as Frank Riley, by day an agent for the Lancastrian Assurance Company, by day *and* night a widower of some 18 years standing with a general hunger for women and a particular passion for Ethel Goodchild. Frank's biggest problem was his puritanical son, Brian, who – together with his saintly girlfriend, Janice – suddenly returned to the fold from the Welsh valleys, where he had been raised by his grandparents. In a reversal of the traditional father-son comedies, Brian usually managed to catch his father in the act of (at the very least) pursuance, and clearly disapproved, hampering his style.

Writer H V (Harry) Kershaw – a guiding light behind *Coronation Street* – later set another sitcom, *Leave It To Charlie*, around an agent for the almost identically named Lancastrian Insurance Company.

Life With Cooper

see COOPER, Tommy

Life With The Lyons

UK · BBC · *ITV (ASSOCIATED-REDIFFUSION) · SITCOM

40 × 30 mins · b/w

Series One (4) 29 June–10 Aug 1955 · fortnightly Wed mostly 8.15pm

Series Two (4) 31 May–12 July 1956 · fortnightly Thu 7.30pm

*Series Three (10) 17 Sep 1957–21 Jan 1958 · fortnightly Tue mostly 8.30pm

*Series Four (9) 19 Sep 1958–23 Jan 1959 · fortnightly Fri 6.10pm

*Series Five (13) 1 Jan–25 Mar 1960 · Fri 6.30pm

MAIN CAST

Ben Lyon · himself
Bebe Daniels · · · · · · · · · · · · · · · · herself
Barbara Lyon · · · · · · · · · · · · · · · · herself
Richard Lyon · · · · · · · · · · · · · · · · himself

OTHER APPEARANCES

Aggie MacDonald · · · · · · · · · · · Molly Weir
Florrie Wainwright · · · · · · · · · · Doris Rogers
Mr Wimple · · · Horace Percival (series 1 & 2)
Robin · · · · · · Richard Bellaers (series 1 & 2)

CREDITS

writers Bebe Daniels (40), Bob Block (40), Ronnie Hanbury (25), Bob Ross (13), Richard Waring (8), Bill Harding (4) · *ITV directors* John Phillips, Joan Kemp-Welch · *BBC producers* Bryan Sears, Barry Lupino

The TV version of the famous BBC radio series (1951–61) that starred the American film actors and real-life husband-and-wife team Ben Lyon and Bebe Daniels. The pair gained great popularity when they made London their home during the Second World War and featured with comedian Vic Oliver (*Hotel Imperial*) in the hit radio series

Hi, Gang! that spanned 1940–49. *Life With The Lyons* followed immediately and differed from most family sitcoms in that it was peopled by an actual family, with children Richard and Barbara Lyon re-creating their real-life selves, and the stories merely exaggerated, albeit in a humorous fashion, true events. In the TV series, as with the radio version, Molly Weir was cast as the Lyons' housekeeper Aggie MacDonald, Doris Rogers was their nosey next-door neighbour Florrie Wainwright, and, in the BBC TV run, Horace Percival appeared as the nebulous Mr Wimple. Before switching to the small-screen there had been three cinema feature films, *Life With The Lyons* (1954) and *The Lyons In Paris* (same year), both directed by Val Guest for Hammer Films; a *Hi, Gang!* movie in 1941; and a *Life With The Lyons* summer stage-play that ran in Blackpool and included a role for the up-and-coming young actress Diana Dors.

After the BBC TV series the Lyons enjoyed three further outings on ITV, aired while the BBC radio series was still on air. These 32 new TV programmes depicted further *sort of* true-to-life mishaps and adventures that befell the Lyons, at the time described as Britain's best-loved clan. Indeed, such was the degree of accuracy that when, in real life, the Lyons moved home from Marble Arch to Holland Park, the third ITV series also had them in a new home, the studio sets matching reality as closely as possible, right down to colour schemes, decorations and furniture. As ever, Bebe was the brains in the husband-and-wife partnership, co-writing every show and acting as chief scriptwriter throughout. A number of guest players appeared here and there, among them Jack Buchanan, Alfred Marks, Leslie Randall and Wilfrid Brambell (three times), while youngsters Barry Took and Geoffrey Palmer appeared once and twice respectively.

See also *Bebe Daniels And Ben Lyon.*

Life Without George

UK · BBC · SITCOM

20 × 30 mins · colour

Series One (6) 12 Mar–16 Apr 1987 · BBC1 Thu 9.30pm

Series Two (7) 6 Mar–24 Apr 1988 · BBC1 Sun 10pm

Series Three (7) 23 Mar–11 May 1989 · BBC1 Thu 9.30pm

MAIN CAST

Larry Wade · · · · · · · · · · · · · · Simon Cadell
Jenny Russell · · · · · · · · · · · · · · Carol Royle
Mr Chambers · · · · · · · · · · · · · Ronald Fraser
Amanda · · · · Rosalind March (series 1 & 2),
· · · · · · · · · · · Elizabeth Estensen (series 3)
Ben · · · · · · · · · · · · · · · Michael Thomas
Sammy · · · · · · · · · Kenny Ireland (series 1);
· · · · · · · · · · · Campbell Morrison (series 2)
Carol · · · · · · · · · · · · · · · Cheryl Maiker

CREDITS

writers Penny Croft (14), Penny Croft/Val Hudson (6) · *director/producer* Susan Belbin · *executive producer* Robin Nash

A sitcom that kept the business in the family: it was written (sometimes co-written) by Penny Croft, the daughter of David Croft who had co-authored *Hi-de-Hi!*, a series that had starred Simon Cadell who was married to Rachel Croft, Penny's sister.

But *Hi-de-Hi!* was less complex than *Life Without George*, which, ostensibly, was all about obsessional desire. Larry Wade (played by Cadell) is infatuated with dance teacher Jenny Russell; she, in turn, is still under the spell of George, her live-in lover of many years who has recently left in pursuit of another woman. Larry chases Jenny hard and fast but matters come to a head when she falls pregnant after a brief reunion with George. Despite her wish to retain independence, Jenny finally sees the worth in dependable Larry and agrees to marry him.

This was an intriguing series with soap opera overtones, that moved away from traditional sitcom to character comedy as it progressed. As for George, whose name featured in the title, he remained absent throughout.

Lift Off! With Coppers And Co!

UK · BBC · CHILDREN'S SKETCH

9 × 25 mins · colour

14 Apr–9 June 1987 · BBC1 Tue 4.30pm

MAIN CAST

David Copperfield
Sally Dewhurst
Anthony Howes
Wendy Leavesley
Michael Seraphim

CREDITS

creator Frank Hopkinson · *writers* Barry Faulkner (9), Terry Ravenscroft (9), Andy Cunningham (6), Dominic MacDonald (4), John Langdon (3), Kjartan Poskitt (3), Steve Punt (3), Wendy Leavesley (3), Judy Whitfield (2), Steve Womack (2), David Copperfield (1), Jeremy Hardy/John Langdon (1), Michael Omer (1), Phil Sadler (1) · *director* Steve Smith · *producer* Judy Whitfield

A previous children's series, *Lift Off!* (15 editions, 28 May 1985 to 17 June 1986) used the device of a talking lift, and lift operators, to introduce guest acts. Although it featured moments of zany comedy, it was mainly dominated by pop acts and variety turns. But when the series returned in 1987, adding the talents of *Three Of A Kind* co-star David Copperfield to the mix, the emphasis switched firmly to humour and the comedian's array of regular characters (including 'Medallion Man') and the title changed accordingly.

The idea then returned in 1988 as a sitcom, *Coppers And Co!*

Light Relief

UK · BBC · SKETCH

1 × 15 mins · b/w

16 Feb 1938 · Wed 9.40pm

MAIN CAST

Frank Napier
Anthony Cope
Hugh Burden
Cicely Paget Bowman
Queenie Leonard

CREDITS

writers various · *producer* Eric Crozier

Described as 'a programme of English humour', this 15-minute aggregation doubtless delighted the well-to-do Londoners who comprised the TV viewing audience during the pre-war years. Collectively and individually, Frank Napier, Anthony Cope, Hugh Burden and Cicely Paget Bowman performed comic recitations and fables, read humorous newspaper cuttings (as compiled by D B Wyndham Lewis in the book *The Non-Sensibles*) and performed two sketches from J B Morton's *By The Way*. Queenie Leonard sang two songs, 'Don't Dilly Dally On The Way' and Noël Coward's 'Don't Put Your Daughter On The Stage, Mrs Worthington'.

The Lighter Side

UK · BBC · SKETCH

3 × 30 mins · b/w

1 Aug–12 Sep 1951 · Wed around 8.30pm

MAIN CAST

see below

CREDITS

writer Godfrey Harrison · *additional material* Gordon Crier/Dick Pepper (show 2), Lawrie Wyman (shows 2 & 3) · *producer* Gilchrist Calder

Subtitled 'A Humorous Slant On Current Affairs', this sketch show addressed a different topic each week – food, sport and holidays – as would, much later, such series as *Moody, Scott On ...* and *The Frost Report*. Each edition of *The Lighter Side* featured a different cast, the contributors including Tony Hancock (who appeared in the first show as a civil servant), Gordon Crier, Dick Pepper, Irene Handl, Humphrey Lestocq, Molly Weir and Ernest Maxin.

The Likely Lads

UK · BBC · SITCOM

21 episodes (12 × 25 mins · 8 × 30 mins · 1 × short special) · b/w

Series One (6 × 25 mins) 16 Dec 1964–20 Jan 1965 · BBC2 Wed mostly 9.55pm

Short special · part of *Christmas Night With The Stars* 25 Dec 1964 · BBC1 Fri 7.15pm

Series Two (6 × 25 mins) 16 June–21 July 1965 · BBC2 Wed around 9pm

Series Three (8 × 30 mins) 4 June–23 July 1966 · BBC2 Sat around 9pm

MAIN CAST

Terry Collier · · · · · · · · · · · · · James Bolam
Bob Ferris · · · · · · · · · · · · · Rodney Bewes
Audrey Collier · · · · · · · · · · · · Sheila Fearn

OTHER APPEARANCES

Mrs Ferris · · · · · · · · · · · · · Irene Richmond
Mrs Collier · · · · · · · · · · · · Olive Milbourne
Mr Collier · · · · · · · · · · · · · Alex McDonald

CREDITS

writers Dick Clement/Ian La Frenais · producer Dick Clement

One of the very best British TV sitcoms – a delight in the 1960s, simply wonderful in its 1970s return, and still much appreciated and admired today. *The Likely Lads* focused on the friendship between two working-class blokes living in the north-east of England: Terry Collier, an Andy Capp-type, comfortable in his class, sharp but dour, with a quick wit and an eye for the main chance, and Bob Ferris, a more cautious, down-to-earth, less volatile but nonetheless ambitious individual who is easily tempted into tricky situations by Terry's barnstorming personality. The scripts crackled not only with great dialogue but with excellent observations and truisms about working-class life and young peoples' aspirations in the 1960s.

The brilliant casting of the reasonably high-profile James Bolam (as Terry) and Rodney Bewes (as Bob) continued the BBC's *Steptoe And Son*-inspired policy of employing straight actors in sitcoms rather than comedians, and once again the device paid off, the pair giving a more realistic reading of the scripts' robust dialogue. (As the series progressed, the friendship and professional regard between the writers and actors allowed the two stars to exercise a greater creative input.) The storylines were quite earthy for the period, following the path emblazoned by *Steptoe And Son*, but with a lighter, more uplifting appeal that owed to the characters' youth (they were approximately 21 at the start) and expectations. There was a rare honesty about how the lads reacted to recognisable true-to-life dilemmas such as cash shortages, the pursuit of the opposite sex (a constant theme), their work in an electrical components factory and their support of a struggling football team. Sheila Fearn was the next most regular actor, cast as Terry's sister Audrey, who, despite having the usual sibling disagreements with her incorrigible brother, nevertheless treated him with underlying affection, although she reserved the most sympathy for Bob, understanding how difficult it could be to go around with Terry. By the last series Audrey had

married and Terry and Bob were, at the ripe old age of 22, becoming concerned about the passing years and their own inactivity. In the final episode, succinctly titled 'Goodbye To All That', Bob decided to see the world by joining the British Army and Terry, initially aghast at the idea, decided to enlist with him. In a final, dramatic twist, Bob was rejected because of flat feet but Terry was signed on and the partnership was broken.

The Likely Lads was born in unusual circumstances. A radio producer, Dick Clement, was taking a BBC trainee directors course in television that granted him a budget of £100 and limited use of a studio in order to mount a production. Needing a script on the cheap, but having no contacts in TV circles, Clement approached a friend, Ian La Frenais, whom he had first met in a pub in Earls Court, London; the pair wrote a script about two friends – based on a sketch they had conceived for the BBC's staff-club drama group, the Ariel Players, in 1961 – that used a naturalistic style and featured 'normal' human beings rather than exaggerated TV 'personalities'. The BBC liked Clement's production, offered him a job on the staff and asked him to consider turning the idea into a series. When it was made, BBC2 executive Michael Peacock grabbed it for the newly launched second channel and it arrived on screen on 16 December 1964. Although the series quickly became greatly loved by its viewers these were few in number since, at this time, the channel was still only available in a minority of homes (those in London and the Midlands who had the appropriate receivers); for the majority of British TV watchers the first glimpse of Terry and Bob came in the 1964 *Christmas Night With The Stars* segment on BBC1. It wasn't until all of the episodes were repeated on BBC1 (series one 5 March–9 April 1965, series two 23 August–27 September 1965, series three 4 October–22 November 1966) that *The Likely Lads* enjoyed national exposure, at which time much of Britain was talking about it.

Note. The main cast re-created their roles for a BBC radio version, with scripts adapted by James Bolam, which ran for 16 episodes (eight from 6 August to 24 September 1967, eight more from 19 May to 7 July 1968).

Whatever Happened To The Likely Lads

UK · BBC · SITCOM

27 episodes (26 × 30 mins · 1 × 45 mins) · colour

Series One (13) 9 Jan–3 Apr 1973 · BBC1 Tue mostly 8.30pm

Series Two (13) 1 Jan–9 Apr 1974 · BBC1 Tue 8.30pm

Special (45 mins) 24 Dec 1974 · BBC1 Tue 7.45pm

MAIN CAST

Terry Collier · · · · · · · · · · · · · James Bolam
Bob Ferris · · · · · · · · · · · · · Rodney Bewes
Thelma Chambers/Ferris · · · · Brigit Forsyth
Audrey · · · · · · · · · · · · · · · · Sheila Fearn

OTHER APPEARANCES

Mrs Chambers · · · Joan Hickson (series 1);
· · · · · · · · · · · · · · · · Noël Dyson (series 2)
George Chambers · · · · · · · · · · · · Bill Owen
Susan Chambers · · · · · · · · · · · Anita Carey
Mrs Collier · · · · · · · · · · · · Olive Milbourne
Mrs Ferris · · · · · · · · · · · · Barbara Ogilvie
Les · · · · · · · · · · · · · · · · · Tony Haygarth

CREDITS

writers Dick Clement/Ian La Frenais · producers James Gilbert (series 1), Bernard Thompson (series 2 & special)

Dick Clement and Ian La Frenais' crowning achievement here was not that, with this sequel, they were able to match the quality of the earlier series but that they were able to better it, cementing *The Likely Lads* for all time as a truly outstanding British sitcom.

More than six years after the first series ended, Terry Collier returned from his stint in the army to find his north-east home-town and its inhabitants changed beyond recognition. His best friend Bob, with whom he has had no contact in the intervening years, has settled into a respectable white-collar job and is engaged to his boss's daughter, Thelma, a level-headed, prim librarian with aspirations – shared by Bob – to a better, brighter future. With distaste, Thelma remembers Terry from the past and she is aghast that he has returned to interrupt their cosy new lives and exert what can only be his customarily poor influence over her easily led fiancé.

Terry's globetrotting adventures intrigue Bob at first but he soon discovers that most of the exploits and alleged feats of derring-do have been fabricated, and that Terry's life – past, present and doubtless future – is destined to be tainted with the same misfortune and sense of failure. Although the years have changed Bob beyond all recognition – he's a member of the badminton club, wears a suit and tie for his desk job, drives a car, lives in a new semi-detached estate house and takes holidays on the Costa Brava – Terry is exactly the same as he ever was and always will be: lazy, arrogant, bigoted (not racially but by area: he loathes anyone not from the north-east), a gambler, a heavy drinker and virtually unemployable. But despite his resistance, Bob soon finds himself once again coming under his friend's sway. Appalled at Bob's forthcoming wedding, his attempts to turn his back on his class by marrying Thelma, and his deluded bourgeoisie notions, Terry tries his best to undermine the relationship, considering it his duty to remind Bob of the real necessities in life: birds, booze and football. But Terry's attempts are to no avail and at the end of the first series Thelma and Bob marry (with, of course, Terry as best man). In the second series Terry continues to cause tension and finally Thelma leaves Bob to go back to her mother's, remaining separated for a few episodes before a reconciliation takes place. In the final television offering, a Christmas special, Bob and Thelma's often rocky relationship was once more put to the test by the presence of Terry Collier, but it managed, just, to withstand the pressure.

In 1976 the cast and writers reunited for a feature film version of the series, titled simply *The Likely Lads* (directed by Michael Tuchner). The movie touched upon some of the themes of change and alienation covered in the series before following a more trad-itional sitcom spin-off route by taking its protagonists on holiday, away from their environment. It wasn't a patch on the TV episodes, some of which rank among the best British TV half-hours.

Notes. Like its predecessor, *Whatever Happened To The Likely Lads* also spawned a BBC radio version (12 episodes, 30 July to 15 October 1975), once again featuring the TV cast.

A US TV comedy, combining aspects of both *The Likely Lads* and *Whatever Happened To The Likely Lads*, was attempted. Called *Stuebenville* it was produced and written by Clement and La Frenais and featured two brothers (one hard working, one lazy, working in a steel mill) and their father, an opinionated widower. A pilot episode was made but it was not transmitted.

The Likes Of Sykes

see SYKES, Eric

Lil

UK · BBC · SITCOM

13 × 25 mins · b/w

Series One (6) 7 July–11 Aug 1965 · BBC1 Wed 6.30pm
*Series Two (7) 24 Dec 1965–11 Feb 1966 · BBC Wales Tue 9pm

MAIN CAST
Lil Thomas ················· Jessie Evans
Blod ····················· Joan Newell

CREDITS
writer Elaine Morgan · *producer* David J Thomas

The character of Lil Thomas first appeared on BBC TV five years before this sitcom, in

the drama series *A Matter Of Degree* (16 May–20 June 1960). Also written by Elaine Morgan, it depicted the conflicts within a Welsh mining family when one of the daughters, Doreen, wins a scholarship to Oxford. Lil was her sister, who stayed at home to keep house. Although not the lead character she made most impact and, as a consequence, was the focus of this sitcom, the only other regular being her friend Blod.

*Note. Before being broadcast by all BBC transmitters across Britain, the first series was seen in Wales (23 April–28 May 1965). The second series appeared *only* on BBC Wales, dates as shown.

Lily Savage Live: Paying The Rent

The Lily Savage Show

see SAVAGE, Lily

The Lisa Maxwell Show

UK · BBC · SKETCH/IMPRESSIONISM

6 × 30 mins · colour

25 July–29 Aug 1991 · BBC1 Thu 8.30pm

MAIN CAST
Lisa Maxwell

CREDITS
writers Paul Alexander/Gavin Osbon, Sue Teddern · *additional material* Lynn Peters (5), Ann Fletcher (3), Tim Goldstone (3), Gary Brown (2), Jeffrey Caunt (2) and others · *script associates* Paul Alexander/Gavin Osbon · *director/producer* Geoff Miles

Lisa Maxwell first tasted fame as a presenter of BBC children's series *Splash*, *The Bizz* and *No Limits*, but she had been working since her TV debut, aged 11, in *Father, Dear Father*, and later her prowess as a comedian/impressionist came to the fore with regular appearances on *The Les Dennis Laughter Show*, *The Joe Longthorne Show* and *The Russ Abbott Show*. In her own series, *The Lisa Maxwell Show*, she mixed contemporary impressions with period-costume pieces and was joined in the sketches by weekly guest stars, many (Jayne Irving and Terry Wogan among them) better known as presenters than as comedy actors.

Little And Large

Comedy double-act Syd Little (the thin one with glasses, born Cyril Mead, in Manchester, 19 December 1942) and Eddie Large (the more rotund one without specs, born Eddie McGinnis, in Glasgow, 25 June 1942) spent years guesting on other people's

TV shows before, in 1976, they were offered one of their own. Then, to quote the familiar cliché, they never looked back, enjoying a long run on the BBC throughout the 1980s, putting across their brand of uncomplicated, good-clean-fun, knockabout material.

Little and Large formed their partnership around 1962, starting out as pub singers in the north-west of England. They turned to comedy as the decade wore on and success was passing them by, and came out winners in a 1971 edition of *Opportunity Knocks*. From here they continued to make slow but steady progress until Royston Mayoh, a producer at Thames, persuaded his bosses to give the pair their own show.

Little and Large made their mark, but – without wishing to be unkind – the oft-mentioned comparisons between them and Laurel and Hardy must be restricted only to their build rather than to their legacy to the world of comedy.

See also Comic Relief.

The Little And Large Tellyshow

UK · ITV (THAMES) · STANDUP/SKETCH

8 editions (7 × 45 mins · 1 × 30 mins) · colour

Pilot (30 mins) 20 Dec 1976 · Mon 8.30pm
One series (7 × 45 mins) 18 Apr–30 May 1977 · Mon 6.45pm

MAIN CAST
Syd Little
Eddie Large

CREDITS
writers Tony Hawes, Syd Little, Eddie Large (pilot); Syd Little, Eddie Large, Neil Shand, Bernie Sharp, Gavin Osbon, Dave Dutton, Eddie Braben (series) · *director/producer* Royston Mayoh

L&L's first starring vehicle. The producer, Royston Mayoh, had previously cast them in a one-off Thames sitcom, *Three In A Bed*.

The Little And Largest Show On Earth

UK · BBC · STANDUP

1 × 45 mins · colour

27 Dec 1977 · BBC1 Tue 7.55pm

MAIN CAST
Syd Little
Eddie Large
Marti Caine

CREDITS
writers Mike Craig/Lawrie Kinsley, Ron McDonnell, David Renwick, Gavin Osbon, Tony Hawes, Syd Little/Eddie Large · *producer* Michael Hurll

A switch to the BBC and a Christmas special for the major and minor of mirth, filmed under the Big Top at Belle Vue, Manchester, and featuring Marti Caine as a guest.

Little And Large

UK · BBC · STANDUP/SKETCH

76 editions (57 × 35 mins · 13 × 30 mins · 3 × 40 mins · 2 × 45 mins · 1 × 50 mins) · colour

Special (45 mins) 1 May 1978 · BBC1 Mon 7.15pm

Series One (6 × 30 mins) 30 Sep–4 Nov 1978 · BBC1 Sat 8.30pm

Special (40 mins) *The Little And Large Christmas Show* 23 Dec 1978 · BBC1 Sat 6.40pm

Special (40 mins) 7 May 1979 · BBC1 Mon 7.40pm

Special (45 mins) 1 Jan 1980 · BBC1 Tue 8.10pm

Series Two (6 × 35 mins) 23 Feb–29 Mar 1980 · BBC1 Sat mostly 7.55pm

Special (40 mins) *The Little And Large Holiday Special* 5 May 1980 · BBC1 Mon 6.30pm

Special (50 mins) 20 Dec 1980 · BBC1 Sat 7.40pm

Series Three (6 × 35 mins) 21 Feb–28 Mar 1981 · BBC1 Sat around 8.10pm then around 6.55pm

Special (30 mins) 24 Dec 1981 · BBC1 Thu 6.05pm

Special (35 mins) 30 May 1983 · BBC1 Mon 7.20pm

Series Four (6 × 35 mins) 17 Dec 1983–21 Jan 1984 · BBC1 Sat mostly 5.55pm

Series Five (6 × 35 mins) 5 Jan–9 Feb 1985 · BBC1 Sat 6.40pm

Series Six (6 × 35 mins) 1 Mar–5 Apr 1986 · BBC1 Sat 7.05pm

Series Seven (6 × 35 mins) 21 Feb–28 Mar 1987 · BBC1 Sat 6.20pm

Series Eight (6 × 35 mins) 6 Feb–12 Mar 1988 · BBC1 Sat 6.20pm

Series Nine (8 × 35 mins) 11 Feb–1 Apr 1989 · BBC1 Sat 6.40pm

Series Ten (6 × 35 mins) 3 Feb–10 Mar 1990 · BBC1 Sat 6.40pm

Series Eleven (6 × 30 mins) 16 Mar–20 Apr 1991 · BBC1 Sat mostly 7pm

MAIN CAST

Syd Little
Eddie Large

CREDITS

writers Russel Lane (27), Eric Davidson (24), Gavin Osbon (23), Brad Ashton (14), Wyn Edwards (12), Gary Clapperton (11), Raymond Allen (9), Eddie Braben (9), Paul Minett/Brian Leveson (7), David Renwick (7), Garry Chambers (6), Colin Edmonds (6), Wally Malston (6), Mick Shirley (6), David Walton (6), Art Lamb (5), Eric Merriman (5), Laurie Rowley (5), Andrew Hastings (4), Clive Whichelow (4), Barry Cryer (3), John Junkin (3), Matthew King (3), Ron McDonnell (3), E H McGinnis (Eddie Large) (3), Ronnie Barbour (2), Rodney Dix (2), Rob Gotobed (2), Roy Granville (2), Robert E Gray (2), John N Lindley (2), David Page (2), Jim Pullin (2), Glyn Rees (2), Kenneth Rock (2), Hugh Smith (2), Terry Vincent (2) and others · *script associate* Russel Lane · *directors* Martin Shardlow (series 9), Peter Laskie/Barbara Jones (series 11) · *producers* Bill Wilson (41), Michael Hurll (24), David Taylor (6), Bill Wilson/Brian Whitehouse (3), John B Hobbs (1), Brian Penders (1)

In Little and Large, the BBC found the perfect comedy act to fill its early-Saturday-evening slot, and the duo enjoyed a long run with this show that firmly established them as major TV stars. While never ground-breaking, they provided consistent and durable middle-of-the-road entertainment aimed at and pleasing a specific type of audience.

Note. The programmes were titled *The Little And Large Show* from 7 May 1979.

Little Armadillos

UK · C4 (TVS) · SKETCH/SITCOM

7 × 30 mins · colour

13 Sep–25 Oct 1984 · Thu mostly 11.05pm

MAIN CAST

Donny · · · · · · · · · · · · · · · · · Jim Sweeney
Wayne · · · · · · · · · · · · · · · · · Steve Steen
Lars · · · · · · · · · · · · · · · · · · · Mark Arden
Amanda · · · · · · · · · · · · · · · Helen Lederer
Peter Wear
Phil Nice
The Flatlets

OTHER APPEARANCES

Rosamund Best
Stephen Frost
Alison Gunn
Daniel Peacock
Pat Senior
Suzanne Walsingham

CREDITS

writers Pete Richens/Colin Gibson (7), Dick Fiddy/Mark Wallington (3) · *additional material* Dick Fiddy/Mark Wallington (4), Andrea Solomons/Bob Sinfield (1) · *director/producer* Bob Spiers · *executive producer* Tony McLaren

Another outlet for the early-1980s so-called 'alternative comedy' set, *Little Armadillos* was a sketch show within which lived a recurring sitcom-style premise, wherein Wayne and Donny Armadillo, a pair of sibling psychopaths – referred to as identical twins, but clearly not – own and run a decaying niterie, the Seal Club, in the Docklands area of London. All of the action took place within the club, the TV set behind the bar being used as a device for cutting away to sketches.

The hands of Pete Richens (involved in the writing of many of the **Comic Strip Presents ...** productions), Bob Spiers (who had directed the *Strip*'s early films and later worked extensively with French and Saunders), and the presence of Stephen Frost, Mark Arden, Helen Lederer et al, coloured *Little Armadillos*' shade of comedy darker than the norm, and while as many ideas missed as they did hit, the show was always worth watching.

A Little Big Business

UK · ITV (GRANADA) · SITCOM

15 × 30 mins · b/w

Pilot · 8 Aug 1963 · Thu 7.30pm

Series One (5) 27 Feb–2 Apr 1964 · Thu 7.30pm

Series Two (9) 14 Jan–11 Mar 1965 · Thu 7.30pm

MAIN CAST

Marcus Lieberman · · · · · · · · David Kossoff
Simon Lieberman · · · · James Maxwell (pilot);
· · · · · · · · · · · · · · · Francis Matthews (series)
Lazlo · · · · · · · · John Cater (pilot, as Laslo);
· · · · · · · · · · · · · · · · Martin Miller (series)
Charlie · · · · · · · · · · · · Charles Lamb (pilot);
· · · · · · · · · · · · · Billy Russell (series 1);
· · · · · · · · · · · · · · Jack Bligh (series 2)
Basil Crane · · · · · · · · · David Langton (pilot);
· · · · · · · · · · · · · · David Conville (series)
Miss Stevens · · · · · · · · · · · · · Joyce Marlow
Naomi Lieberman · · · · · · · · Diana Coupland
· · · · · · · · · · · · · · · · · · (series 1);
· · · · · · · · · · · · Constance Wake (series 2)

OTHER APPEARANCES

Mrs Goldoni · · · · · · · · · · · · · Isa Miranda

CREDITS

writers Jack Pulman (14), Paul Jackman (1) · *directors* Milo Lewis (9), Cliff Owen (3), Herbert Wise (2), Graeme McDonald (1) · *producer* Peter Eton

David Kossoff returned to TV after a two-year absence following the end of **The Larkins**, appearing in a role written especially for him, that of Marcus Lieberman, a sagely but stubborn Jewish furniture maker and master craftsman, an immigrant from Latvia. Granada produced a single episode in August 1963 and then delivered a full series six months later, when most of the remaining cast changed. In particular, Francis Matthews took over from James Maxwell as Marcus's educated, ambitious and go-ahead son Simon, the generation gap – that useful staple for comedy ideas – forming the basis for many of the episodes. Many of the stories for the episodes were based on Kossoff's own experiences from a time years earlier when he worked in the furniture trade.

Note. Although it began as *A Little Big Business*, the 1965 series dropped the indefinite article.

The Little Big Show

UK · ITV (LWT) · SKETCH

1 × 45 mins · colour

12 Aug 1978 · Sat 9pm

MAIN CAST

Grahame Bond
Nick Edmett
Tricia George
Maggie Henderson
Robert Longden
Robin Nedwell
Norman Beaton

CREDITS
writers Grahame Bond, Geoffrey Atherden, Maurice Murphy · *director/producer* Maurice Murphy

The single programme was like a cross between *Opportunity Knocks* (showcasing new talent) and *Comedy Playhouse* (in which new ideas were tried out), comprising ten individual elements – comedy sketches, slapstick and music – with viewers invited to write and state which ones they thought could be developed into full series. There is no record of the response but, to be sure, no further programmes materialised.

A Little Bit Of Wisdom

see WISDOM, Norman

A Little Learning

UK · BBC · SITCOM

1 × 30 mins · b/w
31 May 1966 · BBC1 Tue 7.30pm

MAIN CAST
The Dean · · · · · · · · · · · · · · · · Jack Hulbert
The Bursar · · · · · · · · · · · Cicely Courtneidge

CREDITS
writer Christopher Bond · *producer* Eric Fawcett

Jack Hulbert and Cicely Courtneidge, the long-established British film stars and real-life husband and wife, starred in this *Comedy Playhouse* pilot that Hulbert himself developed.

Frank Muir – at this time the BBC's Assistant Head of Light Entertainment Group (Comedy) – suggested that Christopher Bond, one of the writers of Brian Rix's TV farces, should pen the script. In this, the Dean of Sheridan College at the co-educational University of Wessex has his pleasant existence shattered by the appointment of a new bursar, an attractive middle-aged woman whom the Dean has known 'not wisely but far too well' for his peace of mind.

Live At Jongleurs

UK · ITV (YORKSHIRE/IMWP PRODUCTIONS) · STANDUP

6 × 30 mins · colour
18 June–23 July 1997 · Wed mostly 11.10pm

MAIN CAST
host · Rick Wakeman

CREDITS
writers cast and others · *director* Ron Kanton · *producer* Ian Wilson

In the late 1990s TV schedulers filled many late-night slots with standup 'live-act' shows on the basis that they provided cheap-ish fodder. *Live At Jongleurs* – seen on cable/satellite before being screened by terrestrial TV – was much the same as the others, except perhaps that its makers took the adage

'comedy is the new rock and roll' somewhat too literally, utilising flashy *Top Of The Pops*-style backdrops and camerawork (slow motion zooms, cuts to b/w) and employing rock musician Rick Wakeman as host. The ITV series featured many comics from Britain, America, Canada and Australia, including Sean Meo, Judith Lucy, Steve McGrew, Matt Welcome, Rudy Lickwood, Arj Barker, Simon Bligh, Greg Fleet, Phill Jupitus, John Moloney, John Mann, Corky and the Juice Pigs, Mark Hurst, Ricky Grover, Russell Peters, Tim Clark, Graham Norton and Steve McGrew.

See also *Cabaret At The Jongleurs*.

The Liver Birds

UK · BBC · SITCOM

87 episodes (83 × 30 mins · 2 × 40 mins · 1 × 35 mins · 1 × short special); 5 × b/w · 82 × colour

Pilot (b/w) 14 Apr 1969 · BBC1 Mon 7.30pm

Series One (4 × b/w) 25 July–15 Aug 1969 · BBC1 Fri 8.20pm

Series Two (12 × colour) 7 Jan–25 Mar 1971 · BBC1 Thu 7.45pm

Series Three (13 × colour) 11 Feb–12 May 1972 · BBC1 Fri 7.40pm

Short special · part of *Christmas Night With The Stars* 25 Dec 1972 · BBC1 Mon 6.55pm

Series Four (13 × colour) 2 Jan–3 Apr 1974 · BBC1 Wed 7.40pm

Series Five (7 × colour) 5 Sep–17 Oct 1975 · BBC1 Fri mostly 8.30pm

Special (40 mins · colour) 23 Dec 1975 · BBC1 Tue 8.25pm

Series Six (5 × colour) 13 Feb–12 Mar 1976 · BBC1 Fri 8pm

Series Seven (8 × colour) 17 Oct–5 Dec 1976 · BBC1 Sun 8.15pm

Special (40 mins · colour) 22 Dec 1976 · BBC1 Wed 10pm

Series Eight (7 × colour) 23 Sep–4 Nov 1977 · BBC1 Fri 8.30pm

Special (35 mins · colour) 23 Dec 1977 · BBC1 Fri 8.25pm

Series Nine (6 × colour) 24 Nov 1978–5 Jan 1979 · BBC1 Fri 8.30pm

Series Ten (7 × colour) 6 May–24 June 1996 · BBC1 mostly Mon 8.30pm

MAIN CAST
Beryl Hennessey · · · · · · · · Polly James (pilot, · · · · · · series 1–4 & 10 & specials to 1972)
Dawn · · · · · Pauline Collins (pilot & series 1)
Sandra Hutchinson · · · · · · · · Nerys Hughes
· · · · · · · · · · · · · · · · · · (series 2 onwards)
Carol Boswell · · · · · · · · Elizabeth Estensen
· (series 5–9)

OTHER APPEARANCES
Mrs Hutchinson · · · · · · · · · · · Mollie Sugden
Mr Hutchinson · · · · · · · · · · · · · · Ivan Beavis
· · · · · · · · · · · · · (series 1–3 & 1 special);
· · · · · · · · · · · · John McKelvey (series 4);
· · · · · · · · · · · · William Moore (series 8 & 9)
Mrs Hennessey · · · Sheila Fay (series 1 & 2);
· · · · · · · · · · · Carmel McSharry (series 10)
Mr Hennessey · · · · Cyril Shaps (series 1 & 2)
Joe · · · · · · · · · George Leyton (series 1 & 2)

Gerry · · · · · · · · · · · · · Mike Lucas (series 2)
Paul · · · · · · · · · · · · · John Nettles (series 3–6)
Robert · · · · · · · · · · · Jonathan Lynn (series 4)
Mrs Boswell · · · Eileen Kennally (series 5–7);
· · · · · · · · · · · · · Carmel McSharry (series 8)
Mr Boswell · · · · Ray Dunbobbin (series 5–9)
Lucien · · · · · · · Michael Angelis (series 5–9)
Derek Paynton · · · · · · · · · · · · Tom Chadbon
· (series 8 & 9)

CREDITS
writers Carla Lane (64), Carla Lane/Myra Taylor (9), Carla Lane/Myra Taylor/Lew Schwarz (8), Jack Seddon/David Pursall (6) · *script editor* Eric Idle (series 2) · *main directors* Ray Butt (1969–79 series), Douglas Argent (1969–79), Angela deChastelai Smith (1996) · *producers* Sydney Lotterby (48), Douglas Argent (19), Roger Race (14), Philip Kampff (1996 series)

The Liver Birds – the key word is pronounced 'lie-va' – was the distaff answer to ***The Likely Lads***, charting the exploits of two young female friends in Liverpool, sharing a flat in Huskisson Street and a keen interest in the opposite sex. The city was still, just, exuding a certain glamour from the boom period that followed the success of the Beatles and other pop groups earlier in the 1960s (indeed the series' theme song was sung by the Scaffold, a pop/poetry trio that included Paul McCartney's brother, Mike). The series' title originated in the name given to two sculpted birds perched atop the Royal Liver Building at the city's Pier Head.

Originally the two 'liver birds' were Dawn (Pauline Collins) and Beryl (Polly James), but after five episodes Dawn moved on (or, rather, moved out) and was replaced by Sandra (Nerys Hughes), a pairing that resulted in the series' most popular period. At the end of the fourth series James left the cast (Beryl got married) and she was replaced by Carol (Elizabeth Estensen) who stayed throughout the remaining 1970s episodes.

Launched as a *Comedy Playhouse* pilot, *The Liver Birds* was the creation of first-time writers Carla Lane and Myra Taylor, Liverpool housewives who loosely based the characters and storylines upon their own experiences. The BBC initially teamed them with veteran writer Lew Schwarz, whose mission was explain sitcom-writing technique, and then employed Eric Idle as script editor, but from the third series the women were left alone; Taylor then departed soon after and Lane took sole charge of the writing.

The episodes concentrated on the relationship between the two lead players as they went about their everyday life, dealing with boyfriends, jobs, parents, lack of money and the quest for a more comfortable standard of living. This was a breakthrough period for young, single women following centuries of repression – they had independence, both sexual and financial, and the opportunity to live life as they wanted it, and Carla Lane's scripts reflected this admirably, as well as sketching the uncertainties and philosophies of being single when everyone else seemed to be married. (Although liberated, none of the main characters indulged in casual sex.) *The Liver Birds* was only the start of Lane's remarkable sitcom career but her ability to conjure laughs out of pathos and, as she called them, 'little tragedies', was apparent even here.

During its heyday, with Beryl and Sandra, there was a robust energy about the desperation in which the girls went to parties, trawled for 'talent' and threw themselves into relationships. Beryl was the more common one, spontaneous, scatty and with a voice so staggeringly piercing that you could hear it on the other channel; Sandra was quieter, more cautious, optimistic and refined, mainly thanks to the influence of her snobbish and overbearing mother (played in exaggerated music-hall style by Mollie Sugden). In hindsight, however, the series seems to have made as much impression for its reflections of fashion trends as for its humour, the young women wearing everything from caftans, maxi-coats and mini-skirts to trouser-suits, hot-pants and platform shoes. Carol, who replaced Beryl, dressed particularly loudly.

The arrival of scatty Carol was also used to introduce a wider circle of characters, including her larger-than-life Catholic parents and rabbit-obsessed brother Lucien. (Their family name, Boswell, reappeared in Carla Lane's 1980s series *Bread*.) *The Liver Birds* continued much as before until the eighth series, when the women worked as kennel maids and Sandra became romantically involved with a vet, Derek Paynton. They eventually married, and Derek narrowly avoided having to move to Africa to study wildlife. In the ninth series Sandra fell pregnant and Carol returned to live with her parents, but after the Boswells were evicted from their home she moved in with Sandra and her husband.

That should have been the end of it, for by this time the format had moved far away from the concept of two wacky young women sharing a flat, and with the greater emphasis on the fringe characters and Carol's family *The Liver Birds* was moving closer to the area that Carla Lane would explore in the extended-family sitcom *Bread*. Although fondly remembered, the series did not age well and (apart from screenings on cable/satellite nostalgia channels) has never enjoyed the mainstream re-run appeal of, say, *Dad's Army* or *Are You Being Served?* But in the 1990s, following the US trend of resurrecting old sitcoms, the BBC recommissioned three former hits for a new generation of viewers: the *Doctor* series (*Doctor At The Top*), Reginald Perrin (*The Legacy Of Reginald Perrin*) and *The Liver Birds*. Back came Polly James and

Nerys Hughes from the show's golden period, playing their characters nearly 20 years on. There was some liberty taken with continuity (Lucien, who had been Carol's brother, was now Beryl's brother; and Carmen McSharry, who had played Carol's mother Mrs Boswell, now appeared as Beryl's mother Mrs Hennessey) but the two lead characters were believable developments of their earlier selves: wiser, sadder, perhaps even more desperate – but both bouncing back from failed relationships and marriages to throw themselves into the maelstrom of middle-aged single life. The new series was not a great success, however – while the public might nostalgically reminisce about old television comedies, it rarely takes to updated revivals.

Note. Nerys Hughes and Polly James appeared in *The Last Waltz*, a specially scripted celebration that brought together the key characters from four Carla Lane series (*The Liver Birds*, **Solo**, *Bread* and **Butterflies**), screened by BBC1 on 10 March 1989 as part of **Comic Relief**.

Living It Up

see ASKEY, Arthur

Loitering With Intent

UK · BBC · SITCOM

1 × 30 mins · b/w

23 June 1967 · BBC1 Fri 7.30pm

MAIN CAST

Charles Pinfold	David Tomlinson
Louise Pinfold	Daphne Anderson
Vin	Barry Fantoni
Norm	Madeline Mills
Mr Griffiths	John Nettleton
Police constable	Rudolph Walker

CREDITS

writer Myles Rudge · producer Stuart Allen

A *Comedy Playhouse* pilot for a series that never materialised. Charles Pinfold and his wife Louise are a socially aware London couple who do their best to support 'green' causes, but when two refugees from Kilburn start camping on the lawn of their luxury house in Swiss Cottage they are saddled with a moral dilemma. Film star David Tomlinson was cast as Charles Pinfold.

Lollipop Loves Mr Mole

UK · ITV (ATV) · SITCOM

14 episodes (13 × 30 mins · 1 × short special) · colour

Series One (6) 25 Oct–29 Nov 1971 · Mon 8.30pm

Short special · part of *Mike And Bernie Winters' All-Star Christmas Comedy Carnival* 25 Dec 1971 · Sat 6.05pm

Series Two (7) *Lollipop* 17 July–4 Sep 1972 · Mon 8.30pm

MAIN CAST

Maggie Robinson	Peggy Mount
Reg Robinson	Hugh Lloyd
Violet Robinson	Pat Coombs
Bruce Robinson	Rex Garner

CREDITS

writer Jimmy Perry · directors David Askey (series 1 & special), Shaun O'Riordan (series 2) · producer Shaun O'Riordan

Dad's Army co-author Jimmy Perry was asked by Peggy Mount and Hugh Lloyd to come up with a sitcom in which they could co-star. (Previously, Perry had scripted the BBC2 series **The Gnomes Of Dulwich** in which Lloyd had appeared with Terry Scott.) *Lollipop Loves Mr Mole* was the result (the second series, for reasons of abbreviation only, was titled *Lollipop*), casting the comedy veterans as lovey-dovey husband-and-wife Maggie and Reg, as secure in their pet names 'Lollipop' and 'Mr Mole' as they are in their comfortable cottage in Fulham, south-west London. They're opposites, of course: Maggie (as with virtually all of Peggy Mount's TV roles) is as strong mentally as she appears to be physically, while Reg (Lloyd also being a victim of typecasting) is portrayed as timidity and kindness personified. Their cosy domestic set-up is brutally interrupted in the very first episode, however, when Reg's brother, Bruce, together with his fragile wife Violet, arrived back in England from Africa, ostensibly for just a few days but, in reality, for a prolonged stay as lodgers. Reg is accommodating – even finding Bruce a job at his office – but Maggie does not take kindly to Bruce's sponging and his shrinking Violet.

The company of actors who distinguished a number of Perry sitcoms cropped up here too: Bill Pertwee (from *Dad's Army*) was in one episode, while Michael Knowles, John Clegg and Michael Bates (all to star in *It Ain't Half Hot Mum* from 1974) also appeared.

London Comedy Festival

UK · ITV (ASSEMBLY FILM & TELEVISION FOR CARLTON) · STANDUP

2 × 60 mins · colour

12 & 19 Dec 1994 · Mon 10.40pm

MAIN CAST

Craig Ferguson

CREDITS

executive producer William Burdett-Coutts · producer Rosemary McGowan

Two hours of highlights from the first London Comedy Festival at the Riverside Studios in Hammersmith, west London, that ran from 4 to 18 December. Craig Ferguson was the host. Comics seen in the first programme were Jack Dee, Dave Schneider,

Felix Dexter, Rhona Cameron, Tony Hawks, Hattie Hayridge and Paul Morocco. The second featured Lee Evans, Jeff Green, Greg Proops, Ardal O'Hanlon, Moray Hunter and Jack Docherty, and Phil Kay. The programmes were screened by London-area ITV but not networked.

London Underground

UK · BBC (ENGLISH CHANNEL) · STANDUP
5 × 40 mins · colour
5 Oct–2 Nov 1992 · BBC2 Mon 11.55pm
MAIN CAST
host · Denis Leary
CREDITS
writers cast · *producers* Juliet Blake, Trevor Hopkins

A late-night standup show that featured comedians (and musical talent) from both sides of the Atlantic; the series' style suggested that it was made with a US sale in mind.

The fast-talking acidic American comedian Denis Leary, popular in the UK at this time, was the host, introducing on stage Caroline Aherne, John Thomson, 'Tommy Cockles' (Simon Day), Frank Skinner, Jeremy Hardy, Paul Provenza, Lee Evans, Steve Coogan, Bruce Morton, The Higgins Boys and Gruber, Colin Quinn, Bill Hicks, Jon Stewart, Helen Lederer, Jim Tavaré and John Sparkes.

The Lonelyhearts Kid

UK · ITV (THAMES) · SITCOM
6 × 30 mins · colour
17 July–21 Aug 1984 · Tue 8.30pm
MAIN CAST
Ken · · · · · · · · · · · · · · · · · Robert Glenister
Ray · · · · · · · · · · · · · · · · · · · George Winter
Ros · · · · · · · · · · · · · · · · · · Julia Goodman
Judy · · · · · · · · · · · · · · · Deborah Farrington
CREDITS
writer Alex Shearer · *director* Douglas Argent · *producer* Anthony Parker

Ken and Judy have been live-in lovers since schooldays but it is a relationship well beyond its 'sell by' date, not least because, while Judy has matured, Ken remains a spoilt and easily hurt boy. (He even takes teddy bears to bed.) They split up and Ken seeks solace in his sister Ros, and – unexpectedly – his former school adversary Ray.

The Lonelyhearts Kid provided a second major role for Robert Glenister in an Alex Shearer sitcom, following the three BBC series of *Sink Or Swim*.

The Loner

see DAWSON, Les

The Long Johns

UK · C4 (VERA) · SATIRE
20 × 15 mins · colour
Series One (6) 30 Aug–4 Oct 1995 · Wed 10.55pm
Series Two (5) 21 Feb–3 Apr 1996 · Wed 9.45pm
Series Three (6) 9 Jan–20 Feb 1997 · Thu 9.45pm
Series Four (3) *The Long Johns Election Specials* 3 Apr–24 Apr 1997 · Thu 9.45pm
MAIN CAST
John Bird
John Fortune
CREDITS
creators/writers John Bird/John Fortune · *directors* Juliet May (series 1), David Crean/Juliet May (series 2), Steve Smith (series 3 & 4) · *producers* Geoff Atkinson/Elaine Morris (series 1 & 3), Geoff Atkinson (series 2 & 4)

Sharp, top-quality verbal comedy, seen in *Rory Bremner … Who Else?* in edited form, *The Long Johns* comprised extended satirical snipes at aspects of British business or political life, presented in the form of face-to-face TV interviews. Bird and Fortune – truly, masters of their art – took it in turns to be the interviewer and interviewee, the former putting a number of forthright questions, the latter – usually given the name George Parr – either avoiding an answer in the manner to which politicians and businessmen have been trained, or responding, without shame, in a way that revealed startling hypocrisy, greed or inefficiency. Bird and Fortune studied their all-too-real topics in advance (huge payouts to company directors, privatisation, the cynicism behind Budget announcements, and so on) and worked out the bare bones of what they wanted to say, but the pieces as recorded were unscripted and improvised before a studio audience.

Although occupying a 15-minute slot in the schedules, the programmes only lasted between seven and ten minutes. This relatively short running time was proof indeed that quality, not size, is what matters.

Bird and Fortune have worked together for several decades – for other examples of their collaborations see *BBC-3*, *After That, This*, *The End Of The Pier Show*, *The Late Show*, *My Father Knew Lloyd George*, *Not So Much A Programme More A Way Of Life*, *Our Hands In Your Safe*, *A Series Of Bird's*, and *Well Anyway*.

Look At It This Way

UK · BBC · SATIRE
6 × 30 mins · b/w
16 Feb–27 Apr 1955 · fortnightly Wed mostly 9.30pm
MAIN CAST
Eric Barker

Pearl Hackney
Nicholas Parsons
Sheila McCormack
Robin Willett
Cameron Hall
CREDITS
writer Eric Barker · *producer* Graeme Muir

Described as 'a broad satirical revue' by Eric Barker, *Look At It This Way* turned its comic vision to a different subject each week: sport, industry, transport and so on. Barker was supported by his real-life wife Pearl Hackney and a regular team including Nicholas Parsons.

See also *Merry-Go-Round*, *The Newcomer*, *The Eric Barker Half-Hour* and *Something In The City*.

Look At The State We're In!

UK · BBC (VIDEO ARTS/SISYPHUS) · SATIRES
6 × 10 mins · colour
20 May–4 June 1995 · BBC2 Sat mostly 10.30pm/Sun mostly 7.20pm

The rights of the citizen were frequently in the headlines in 1995 with the then government's Criminal Justice Act and other legislation threatening to bring greater than ever restrictions to civil liberties. An informal public debate ensued in which the mysteries of the British constitution and the possibilities of a British Bill of Rights were discussed. BBC2's contribution was a 50-minute documentary, *Standing Up To The State* (20 May 1995), which took a global overview of human rights, followed by these six short satires, *Look At The State We're In!*, which used the views of pressure group Charter 88 as a provocative basis for a humorous look at the state. The season was concluded by a studio discussion, *Look At The State We're In! – The Debate*, which aired on BBC2 on 5 May 1995.

The Organisation   20 MAY

MAIN CAST
The Don · · · · · · · · · · · · · · · · · · Antony Sher
Marty · Ben Miller
Dewhurst · · · · · · · · · · · Adrian Edmondson
Rattner · · · · · · · · · · · · · · · · · · · Rik Mayall
CREDITS
writer Chris Langham · *director* Robert Knights · *executive producer* John Cleese · *producers* Roger Graef, Margaret Tree

The seemingly unlimited powers of two VAT inspectors from Her Majesty's Customs and Excise department shock even a Mafia Don.

Secrecy   21 MAY

MAIN CAST
Harold Kingsley · · · · · · · · · · · · John Cleese
Government Official · · · · · · · · Dawn French

CREDITS
writer Chris Langham · *director* Robert Knights · *executive producer* John Cleese · *producers* Roger Graef, Margaret Tree

An ordinary man is confounded by the Machiavellian rules concerning information held about him by the government.

Local Government 27 MAY

MAIN CAST
Mrs Peabody · · · · · · · · · · · · · Karen Tomlin
Local Councillor Johnson · · Imelda Staunton
Sir Michael Jaffa · · · · · · · · · · · Hugh Laurie

CREDITS
writer Chris Langham · *director* Robert Knights · *executive producer* John Cleese · *producers* Roger Graef, Margaret Tree

A local councillor is horrified at the powers that have been transferred from local government to the state.

Legal System 28 MAY

MAIN CAST
Jeff Jarndyce · · · · · · · · · · · · · · · Jeff Rawle
Sally · Ingrid Lacey
Judge Sutcliffe · · · · · · · · · · · Robert Hardy
Dr Smith · · · · · · · · · · · · · · · John Standing
Dr Jones · · · · · · · · Michael Fenton Stevens
Lisa Boon · · · · · · · · · · Alphonsia Emmanuel
Howard QC · · · · · · · · · Geoffrey Whitehead
Lilley QC · · · · · · · · · · · · · · · · · · Jack Klaff

CREDITS
writer Guy Jenkin · *director* Liddy Oldroyd · *executive producer* John Cleese · *producers* Roger Graef, Margaret Tree

An average man is unable to afford his legal costs. (This programme featured the writer Jenkin and actors Rawle and Lacey from *Drop The Dead Donkey*.)

Nanny Knows Best 3 JUNE

MAIN CAST
Storyteller · · · · · · · · · · · · · Prunella Scales
Ruler · · · · · · · · · · · · · · · · · Geoffrey Palmer
Frank · · · · · · · · · · · · · · · · · · Alex Langdon
Aide · Gina Moxley
Businessman · · · · · · · · · · · Philip McGough
Policemen · · · · · · · · · · · · Dicken Ashworth
· · · · · · · · · · · · · · · and Oliver Montgomery

CREDITS
writer/director Sean Hardie · *executive producer* John Cleese · *producers* Roger Graef, Margaret Tree

A fairy story setting for a *Yes Minister*-style view of the wide-ranging royal prerogative.

The Status Quo 4 JUNE

MAIN CAST
Politician · · · · · · · · · · · · · · · · John Cleese
Director · · · · · · · · · · · · · · · · · Hugh Laurie
Writer · · · · · · · · · · · · · · · · Chris Langham
Make-up Girl · · · · · · · · · · · Sara Stockbridge

CREDITS
writer John Cleese · *director* Hugh Laurie · *executive producer* John Cleese · *producers* Roger Graef, Margaret Tree

A meditation on apathy from John Cleese that took a look behind the scenes of a party political broadcast on behalf of 'the status quo'.

Look – Mike Yarwood!

see YARWOOD, Mike

Lord Tramp

UK · ITV (SOUTHERN) · CHILDREN'S SITCOM

6 × 30 mins · colour

1 Aug–12 Sep 1977 · Mon 4.45pm

MAIN CAST
Hughie Wagstaff · · · · · · · · · · · Hugh Lloyd
Miss Pratt · · · · · · · · · · · · · · · · Joan Sims
Tipping · · · · · · · · · · · · · · · · George Moon
Lucy · Lally Percy

CREDITS
creator Hugh Lloyd · *writer* Michael Pertwee · *producer* Peter Croft

Comic actor Hugh Lloyd created and starred in this series, which depicted a happy, carefree tramp, Hughie Wagstaff, who suddenly finds that he has inherited a title, a fortune, a huge estate and a 50-room mansion with staff in tow. He becomes, in effect, a most unlikely aristocrat, not altogether certain that he prefers his new lifestyle over the old. Leslie Dwyer and Jack Watling guested in three episodes apiece; also seen in addition to the regular cast were Alfie Bass and Aubrey Woods.

Lorry

SWEDEN · SVERIGES TELEVISION · SKETCH

1 × 35 mins · colour

25 Dec 1991 · C4 Wed 2.05am

MAIN CAST
not known

CREDITS
writers Peter Dalle, Rolf Borjlind, Sven-Hugo Persson · *director* Kjell Sundrall · *executive producer* Tommy Bennvik

A single British broadcast of a Swedish TV sketch/satire show with an adult feel.

The Losers

UK · ITV (ATV) · SITCOM

6 × 30 mins · colour

12 Nov–17 Dec 1978 · Sun 9.15pm

MAIN CAST
Sydney Foskett · · · · · · · · · Leonard Rossiter
Nigel · · · · · · · · · · · · · · · · · · Alfred Molina
Dennis Breene · · · · · · · · · · · · Joe Gladwin

CREDITS
writer Alan Coren · *director/producer* Joe McGrath · *executive producer* Terence Baker

It is one of life's mysteries how all the top-grade ingredients for a successful TV comedy can amount to, if not quite naught, then very little. *The Losers* starred Leonard Rossiter – magnificent at this time in both *Rising Damp* and *The Fall And Rise Of Reginald Perrin* – in a series written by Alan Coren, the great wit, writer and columnist, and then the editor of *Punch*, and directed/produced by Joe McGrath, whose work on *Not Only ... But Also* and scores of other TV plays, series and feature films had given him a comedy CV second to none. And yet *The Losers* was lacerated by the critics and viewers stayed away in droves.

Rossiter was cast as Sydney Foskett, in the business of managing wrestlers, who discovers and sets out to promote a new young charge, 'The Butcher', with an unusual tactic. Recognising that the public loves a loser, and that a large purse can be the reward for negotiating defeat in a rigged match, Foskett devises strategies for the Butcher to lose, and keep losing. For his part, the wrestler, an illiterate by the name of Nigel, is too dim-witted to realise what's going on.

Although Foskett was a cockney rather than a north-countryman, there were similarities between this character and Rigsby from *Rising Damp*: both men were seedy, both were connivers, with perhaps Foskett being the *nastier* of the two. But any other comparison between the two series must end there. *Rising Damp* will live forever, *The Losers* has been forgotten.

The Louie Anderson Show

USA · HBO (TALL PONY/LOUZELL) · STANDUP

1 × 30 mins · colour

US date: 10 Sep 1988
UK date: 14 Dec 1990 · C4 Fri 10.30pm

MAIN CAST
Louie Anderson

CREDITS
writer Louie Anderson · *director/producer* Anthony Eaton

A one-off cable TV special for the large and loud American comic, sharing his observations on human behaviour.

Raised in Minnesota, Anderson made his stage debut in an 'open mike' night at a local comedy club, performing so impressively that he was soon invited to appear as a guest on the principal US TV chat-shows. As a child, Anderson had used humour to defend himself against school bullies who taunted him for his oversized build, and these jokes became a staple of his act, but his material remains 'clean'. The author of two best-selling self-help books about his parents (his father was an alcoholic), material about his family is the backbone of Anderson's stage act and it also provided the stories for his Emmy Award-winning Saturday-morning animated children's television series *Life With Louie* (Fox, from 9 September 1995).

Love & War

USA · CBS (SHUKOVSKY ENGLISH ENTERTAINMENT) · SITCOM

58 episodes (57 × 30 mins · 1 × 60 mins) · colour

US dates: 21 Sep 1992–1 Feb 1995

UK dates: 15 Jan 1993–17 Dec 1994 (24 × 30 mins) ITV Fri mostly 10.40pm then Sat around 1am

MAIN CAST

Wallis 'Wally' Porter · · Susan Dey (1992–93)
Dana Palladino · · · · · Annie Potts (1993–95)
Jack Stein · · · · · · · · · · · · · · · · Jay Thomas
Nadine Berkus · · · · · · · · · · · Joanna Gleason
Ike Johnson · · · · · · · · · John Hancock (1992)
Abe Johnson · · · · · · · · · · · Charlie Robinson
Ray Litvak · · · · · · · · · · · · · · · · Joel Murray
Kip Zakaris · · · · · · · · · · · · · Michael Nouri
Mary Margaret 'Meg' Tynan · · Suzie Plakson

CREDITS

creator Diane English · *writers* various · *directors* various · *executive producers* Diane English, Joel Shukovsky · *producers* Elaine Pope, Shannon Gaughan and others

Although it failed to catch on in Britain, *Love & War* was the most popular new sitcom on US TV in 1992–93 – jokingly described as '*LA Law* meets *Cheers*' owing to the presence of Susan Dey (Grace Van Owen in the legal drama *LA Law*, as well as, years earlier, Laurie Partridge in *The Partridge Family*) and the ensemble setting in a restaurant/bar.

Dey co-starred as Wallis 'Wally' Porter, an attractive and upmarket businesswoman/chef who loses not only her husband but also her swanky New York restaurant, Chez Wally, when she is divorced. Desperate for a few double vodkas after the settlement hearing, she stops by the Blue Shamrock, a downmarket Manhattan bar and grill, and, on impulse, buys the majority share in the place from its current owner, big Ike Johnson (who nonetheless agrees to stay on as manager), vowing to turn it into a chic venue. The Blue Shamrock swiftly brings Wally together with one of the bar's principal habitués, Jack Stein, an intolerant and opinionated reporter for the *New York Register* newspaper, and, although complete opposites, they waste little time in cementing a relationship, going to bed in the second episode (the sitcom aired in the US after the watershed); their alliance forms the bedrock of the series from this point on. Other bar regulars include timid refuse-collector Ray Litvak; forthright and feminist *Register* sports journalist 'Meg' Tynan, who

disapproves of the Porter/Stein axis; and none-too-bright waitress Nadine Berkus, who needs the wage to finance her own and her children's education because her husband has been sent to jail for fraud.

John Hancock, the actor playing Ike Johnson (he had also played opposite Susan Dey in *LA Law*), died soon after the series began and was replaced by his character's ill-natured brother, Abe, an unemployed car worker from Detroit who becomes the new Blue Shamrock barman. Also seen regularly is Wally's ex-husband, Kip Zakaris, an egomaniacal B-movie actor.

The '*LA Law* meets *Cheers*' scenario ended after one year when the producers failed to renew Susan Dey's contract, reportedly because they felt there was insufficient chemistry between her and co-star Jay Thomas (who played Jack Stein). Replacing Wally – who was said to have gone to Paris – came another chef, Dana Palladino (played by Annie Potts), who stood up to Jack and didn't become his love interest for a year. Wally sold her interest in the Blue Shamrock to Abe.

Unusually, harking back to *The Burns And Allen Show*, the key characters in *Love & War* directly addressed comments to the camera while others around them were oblivious to 'the fourth wall'.

Love And Kisses

see ASKEY, Arthur

Love And Marriage · 1

see The Montreux Festival

Love And Marriage · 2

see CROWTHER, Leslie

A Love Letter To Jack Benny

see BENNY, Jack

The Love Of Mike

UK · ITV (ASSOCIATED-REDIFFUSION) · SITCOM

30 × 30 mins · b/w

20 Apr–7 Nov 1960 · Wed 7.55pm then Mon 8pm

MAIN CAST

Mike Lane · · · · · · · · · · · · · Michael Medwin

WITH

Carmel McSharry
George Roderick
Brian Wilde (7 episodes)
Bernard Fox (23 episodes)

CREDITS

writers Gerald Kelsey/Dick Sharples, James Kelly/Peter Miller and others · *directors* John Phillips (10), Bill Hitchcock (7), Ronald Marriott (4), Cyril Butcher (4), Bill Turner (4), Christopher Hodson (1)

Launched as a 26-week series but extended to 30, *The Love Of Mike* was an easy-going sitcom that related the philandering adventures of one Mike Lane, trumpeter with a dance band. Always on his uppers, Lane was usually unable to pay his rent, but avoidance of eviction was paramount because his flat was also his lair: the record-player volume was set as low as the lights, and he padded around in his dressing-gown, dangling a cigarette-holder, awaiting the arrival of his next conquest. Most episodes showed Mike plotting for the attention of a different girl – yet, like that other super-sharp schemer Ernie Bilko, he never quite managed to come out on top. (Literally – this was 1960.)

Mike Lane was played by Michael Medwin, who had recently left *The Army Game* and was held in high esteem not only for his talents as a comic actor but also as a good-looking, eligible young bachelor, so he was considered perfect for the role (although, ironically, during the series' run he got married in real life). Brian Wilde appeared as Mike's flat-mate and friend (he dropped out after seven episodes and was replaced by Bernard Fox), George Roderick (Sam Prout in *The Larkins*) was cast as a wife-dominated neighbour and Carmel McSharry was Mike's char-woman.

Medwin, Roderick and Fox teamed up again in 1961 for a 26-part series, *Three Live Wires*.

Love On A Branch Line

UK · BBC (THEATRE OF COMEDY/D L TAFFNER UK/NEW PENNY) · COMEDY SERIAL

4 × 50 mins · colour

12 June–3 July 1994 · BBC1 Sun around 8.45pm

MAIN CAST

Jasper Pye · · · · · · · · · · · · · Michael Maloney
Lord Flamborough · · · · · · · · · · Leslie Phillips
Lady Flamborough · · · · · · · · · · · Maria Aitken
Professor Pollux · · · · · · · · · Graham Crowden
Belinda Flamborough · · · · Abigail Cruttenden
Matilda Flamborough · · · · Charlotte Williams
Chloe Virley · · · · · · · · · · · · · Cathryn Harrison
Lionel Virley · · · · · · · · · · · · · · · · David Haig
Jones · Joe Melia
Quirk · · · · · · · · · · · · · · · · · Stephen Moore
Miss Mounsey · · · · · · · · · · · · · Amanda Root
Miss Tidy · · · · · · · · · · · · · · · · Gillian Raine

CREDITS

creator John Hadfield · *adapter/writer* David Nobbs · *director* Martyn Friend · *executive producers* John Reynolds, Alan Strachan · *producer* Jacqueline Davis

A fine adaptation of John Hadfield's 1959 comic novel, sympathetically written for TV by David Nobbs to retain much of the oh-so-English charm of the original. The story concerns a staid civil servant, Jasper Pye, who is sent out from London to report on a long-forgotten research institute set up by his government ministry in a stately home,

Arcady Hall, in East Anglia. The huge house is owned by the wildly eccentric double-amputee Lord Flamborough, who lost both legs through the carelessness of a railway footplateman and who now virtually lives in a train, named the *Flamborough Flier*. To the accompaniment of vintage jazz records, the train chugs up and down the otherwise closed branch line from Arcady to Flaxfield Junction. Flamborough's family – equally eccentric wife Lady Flamborough and their three uninhibited daughters Chloe, Belinda and Matilda – live in the stately home.

Pye arrives full of good intentions, determined to file an accurate report on the Department of Output Statistics, which was created to collate and analyse foreign publications but which has produced almost nothing. The Institute is run by the larger-than-life Professor Pollux and his archivist Quirk, both of whom view Pye's visit with trepidation. Their assistant Miss Mounsey is less perturbed, however; indeed, she is quite taken with him. But then, *most* of the women at Arcady Hall fall for Pye and his duties soon start to be forgotten as he falls under the spell of the beautiful stately home, its rural surroundings and intoxicating inhabitants. Within days of his arrival Pye is amorously involved with all three of the Flamborough daughters, a situation seemingly encouraged by the local residents, even by Lionel, Chloe's perpetually tipsy husband.

Location filming (at Oxburgh Hall in Suffolk) and a well-measured tone, combined with the whimsically humorous script and a romantic story, made *Love On A Branch Line* an enchanting comic production. Maloney fared admirably well as straight-man to the many eccentrics who roamed throughout the plot, and all of the cast acquitted themselves well, with particular merits for Abigail Cruttenden as the sexually promiscuous Belinda, and Graham Crowden as Pollux, while Leslie Phillips turned in a splendidly over-the-top performance to match his equally eccentric college master in *Honey For Tea*, which had just finished its run on BBC1.

Love, Sidney

USA · NBC (RG PRODUCTIONS/WARNER BROS) · SITCOM

44 × 30 mins · colour

US dates: 28 Oct 1981–29 Aug 1983
UK dates: 19 Jan–7 Sep 1984 (22 episodes) C4 Thu around 11pm then Fri 10pm

MAIN CAST

Sidney Shorr	Tony Randall
Laurie Morgan	Swoosie Kurtz
Patti Morgan	Kaleena Kiff

CREDITS

creator Oliver Hailey · *writers* various · *directors* various · *producers* George Eckstein, Rod Parker, Hal Cooper

A disappointing series that developed from a promising if bittersweet 110-minute US TV movie, *Sidney Shorr: A Girl's Best Friend* (screened in the USA on 1 February 1980 and in the UK by C4 on 23 August 1983). In this, Tony Randall – Felix Unger in **The Odd Couple** – played a lonesome 40-year-old homosexual commercial artist who meets a vivacious young actress, Laurie Morgan (played by Lorna Patterson), and ends up sharing his eight-room New York apartment with her, only to become shocked when she is impregnated by a man she does not love, and follows her term through to the delivery of a baby girl, Patti. Five years later, when Laurie wants out, to go to LA and marry, Sidney fights her in court for custody of the child he has helped to raise, the judgement giving him summer access to the young girl (played by Kaleena Kiff).

This was the starting-off point for the weekly sitcom. Laurie (now played by Swoosie Kurtz – actually her real name) has left her husband and returned to New York to share, with Patti, Sidney's apartment. However, and this is the crux of this sitcom's problem, Sidney is no longer gay – indeed, his sexuality is no longer referred to any which way. NBC executives, while content (just about, one suspects) to feature a gay lead character in a single TV movie bowed to the great moral majority and were not so keen to portray one in a weekly primetime series. Without this gay-man/heterosexual-woman axis the essence of the series was gone. Sure, the prim Sidney still mothered his two females, Laurie continued the cutting remarks and Patti was the kind of wisecracking pig-tailed brat usually seen in US sitcoms, but that was all.

Love Thy Neighbour

UK · ITV (THAMES) · SITCOM

56 episodes (54 × 30 mins · 1 × 45 mins · 1 × short special) · colour

Series One (7) 13 Apr–25 May 1972 · Thu 9pm
Series Two (6) 11 Sep–16 Oct 1972 · Mon 8.30pm
Short special · part of *All-Star Comedy Carnival* 25 Dec 1972 · Mon 5.45pm
Series Three (6) 19 Mar–30 Apr 1973 · Mon mostly 8pm
Series Four (7 × 30 mins · 1 × 45 mins) 12 Dec 1973–4 Feb 1974 · mostly Mon 8.30pm
Series Five (7) 18 Feb–1 Apr 1974 · Mon 8pm
Series Six (7) 2 Jan–13 Feb 1975 · Thu 8pm
Series Seven (7) 17 Apr–29 May 1975 · Thu 8pm
Series Eight (7) 11 Dec 1975–22 Jan 1976 · Thu mostly 8.30pm

MAIN CAST

Eddie Booth	Jack Smethurst
Joan Booth	Kate Williams
Bill Reynolds	Rudolph Walker
Barbie Reynolds	Nina Baden-Semper
Arthur	Tommy Godfrey
Jacko	Keith Marsh
Nobby Garside	Paul Luty (series 4–8)
Cyril	Ken Parry (series 3)

CREDITS

writers Vince Powell/Harry Driver (series 1–4 & special), Vince Powell (series 5 & 6), Sid Colin (2 eps), H V Kershaw (2), George Evans/Lawrie Wyman (2), Spike Mullins (2), Brian Cooke (1), Jon Watkins (1), Colin Edmonds (1), Johnnie Mortimer (1), Brian Cooke (1), Adele Rose (1) · *directors/producers* Stuart Allen (series 1 & 2 & special), Ronnie Baxter (series 3 & 4), Anthony Parker (series 5, 6 &, except one ep, 8), William G Stewart (series 7 & one ep in 8)

Having previously explored ethnic disharmony in **Never Mind The Quality, Feel The Width**, writing partners Powell and Driver followed Johnny Speight down the path of employing bigotry as humour and created *Love Thy Neighbour* for ITV. Unfortunately, whereas **Till Death Us Do Part** and **Curry And Chips** (however misunderstood they may have been) had highlighted the ignorance endemic in racism, *Love Thy Neighbour* rarely rose above indiscipline name-calling and crude stereotyping. If viewing the series again now, one recoils at the list of cheap, gratuitous insults flung in the faces of the black characters – although, of course, one must bear in mind that what is politically incorrect now has not always been so.

The premise of *Love Thy Neighbour* was simple: Eddie Booth is a staunch Union Jack-waving socialist, living with wife Joan in Maple Terrace and drinking down the Lion And Lamb with his mates Arthur, Nobby and flat-capped Jacko ('I'll 'ave 'alf'). Suddenly, new neighbours move in next door, Bill and Barbara ('Barbie'), who – pause for sharp intake of breath – are West Indian. Worse, Bill is a dyed-in-the-wool Tory. The name-calling begins immediately and, in truth, Bill is just as racist as Eddie, slinging 'whitey' epithets back at his neighbour. (Interestingly, these never seemed as derogatory.) The wives, by the way, seem to get along perfectly well; it is only the men who have the problems.

Black actors Rudolph Walker and Nina Baden-Semper both claimed not to be offended by the racism in the scripts and, like the writers, hoped that *Love Thy Neighbour* would break down barriers. Sadly, it did no such thing. It was, however (perhaps even more sadly), a rip-roaring success, leading to a spin-off 1973 feature film (directed by John Robins), a further TV series made and screened only in Australia (see next entry), and an American version. This was titled (subtle but necessary spelling difference) *Love Thy Neighbor* and starred Ron Masak and Joyce Bulifant as Democrat-voting Charlie and Peggy Wilson (the whites) and Harrison Page and Janet MacLachlan as Republican-voting Ferguson and Jackie Bruce (the blacks), living in disharmony in San Fernando, California. Unlike the British model, the US series was not a success and lasted for only 12 episodes, aired by ABC from 15 June to 19 September 1973.

Note. Harry Driver died, aged just 43, in November 1973, and Vince Powell carried on writing the British scripts alone until the end of the sixth season. He also wrote *A Proper Charlie*, a radio sitcom that starred Jack Smethurst as Charlie Garside, a factory-working union man, broadcast in eight episodes by BBC Radio 2 from 3 November to 22 December 1985.

Love Thy Neighbour In Australia

AUSTRALIA · 7 NETWORK · SITCOM

7 × 30 mins · colour

Australian dates: 4 May–15 June 1980
UK dates: 15 Sep–15 Dec 1982 (7 episodes) ITV
Wed around 12 midnight

MAIN CAST

Eddie Booth	Jack Smethurst
Bernard Smith	Robert Hughes
Jim Lawson	Russell Newman
Joyce Smith	Sue Jones
Cyril	Graham Rouse
Joe Marley	Ken Goodlet

CREDITS

creators Vince Powell/Harry Driver · *writers* Vince Powell/Ken Sterling · *director/producer* William G Stewart

A short-lived and not-at-all-clever Australian version of the popular British sitcom *Love Thy Neighbour*, in which our racist 'friend' Eddie Booth, having temporarily gone Down Under to work, moves into the Sydney suburb of Blacktown (clearly, it was not at all subtle either) and – surprise, surprise – has a problem with his neighbours.

Loved By You

UK · ITV (CARLTON/COLUMBIA TRISTAR) · SITCOM

7 × 30 mins · colour

11 Mar–22 Apr 1997 · Tue 8.30pm

MAIN CAST

Michael Adams	John Gordon-Sinclair
Kate Adams	Trevyn McDowell
Lander	Gary Love
Becky	Kim Thomson
Ruth	Gillian Bevan
Tom	Steven Alvey

CREDITS

creators Danny Jacobson/Paul Reiser · *writers* Danny Jacobson (1), Danny Jacobson/Paul Reiser (1), Danny Jacobson/Steve Paymer (1), Steve Paymer (1), Billy Grundfest (1), Daryl Rowland/Lisa DeBenedictus (1), Sally Lapiduss/Pamela Eells (1) · *script associate* Gary Sinyor · *directors* Richard Boden (5), Michael Owen Morris (2) · *executive producer* Richard Boden · *producer* Steve Bailie

Michael Adams is a documentary film-maker with a patchy track record and ambitions to work in the movies. His wife Kate is a far more successful career woman, employed in PR. Wed only for a few months, the story of their early married life is related in *Loved By You*, a slick, witty British adaptation of the equally slick and witty US hit *Mad About You* (NBC, from 23 September 1992).

The American standup comedian Paul Reiser co-created and starred in the original version, with Helen Hunt playing his wife Jamie; John Gordon-Sinclair and Trevyn McDowell were wise choices for the UK model, both bringing believability and affability to their roles. Supporting them were Gary Love as Michael's friend and confidante Lander (in the US version this character was Selby, played by Tommy Hinkley) and Kate's sister Becky (US version Lisa, played by Anne Ramsey). Rounding out the cast were the Adams' dull but loyal friends Ruth (US version Fran, played by Leila Kenzle) and her husband Tom (US version Mark, played by Richard Kind).

Loved By You was faithful to its antecedent, utilising the American scripts, anglicised where appropriate by Gary Sinyor, the writer/director of the hit British movie of 1993, *Leon The Pig Farmer*. Despite these credentials, and the successful American blueprint, the series was at times strangely uninvolving, and almost sterile. However, although not as popular – with viewers or critics – as *Mad About You* (itself not seen on British terrestrial TV at time of writing, but a staple of the Sky One satellite/cable channel), *Loved By You* promised enough in its first run of seven episodes to encourage Carlton to invest in a second series, expected to air in 1998.

Lovely Couple

UK · ITV (LWT) · SITCOM

13 × 30 mins · colour

7 Apr–30 June 1979 · Sat mostly 8.30pm

MAIN CAST

June Dent	Elaine Donnelly
David Mason	Anthony O'Donnell
Mr Hector Dent	David Lodge
Mrs Madge Dent	Geraldine Newman
Mrs Mason	Maggie Jones
Allan Brown	Nick Edmett
Carole Richards	Pauline Quirke
Jack 'Rollo' Dent	Roger Sloman

CREDITS

writer Christopher Wood · *director/producer* Derrick Goodwin

A single series charting the less-than-smooth running course of love between David Mason, a shaggy-haired clerk with a local engineering concern, and June Dent, whose family live slightly further up the suburban social scale. In order to be allowed a holiday together, David and June suggest engagement, only to

find that June's mother swiftly latches on to the idea of a wedding and won't let it drop. The 13 episodes focused on the doubts that David and June experienced in turn, and their lamentable efforts to get to the altar. They almost made it too, but June slipped a disc and David broke his ankle, and the celebration was postponed.

The Lovers

UK · ITV (GRANADA) · SITCOM

15 episodes (13 × 30 mins · 2 × short specials) · colour

Series One (6) 27 Oct–1 Dec 1970 · Tue mostly 8.30pm
Short special · part of *All-Star Comedy Carnival* 25 Dec 1970 · Fri 6pm
Series Two (7) 7 Oct–25 Nov 1971 · Thu 9pm
Short special · part of *Mike And Bernie Winters' All-Star Christmas Comedy Carnival* 25 Dec 1971 · Sat 6.05pm

MAIN CAST

Beryl	Paula Wilcox
Geoffrey	Richard Beckinsale
Beryl's mum	Joan Scott
Roland	Robin Nedwell

CREDITS

creator Jack Rosenthal · *writers* Jack Rosenthal (series 1 & special 1), Geoffrey Lancashire (series 2 & special 2) · *directors* Michael Apted (series 1 & special 1), Les Chatfield (series 2 & special 2) · *producers* Jack Rosenthal (series 1 & special 1), Les Chatfield (series 2 & special 2)

The Lovers was a fine and timely comedy sitcom, fine because it was written by Jack Rosenthal, timely because it appeared just after the 1960s, when the boundaries of permissiveness in all walks of life (most certainly television) had been greatly extended. Acceptable in 1970, it is inconceivable that *The Lovers* could have been screened in 1960.

The series related the lives of a young Manchester couple, boyfriend and girlfriend for two years, on and off, inexperienced by age and with sex hanging over their relationship like the sword of Damocles, yet pursuing what society dictated they ought. Modern-girl Beryl dreams of marriage and a white wedding (in its fullest sense), and wants none – yet – of what she and her partner call 'Percy Filth', the *ultimate* admission. Geoffrey wants what all young men want (besides football, that is), and is forever trying to get inside Beryl's knickers and stake a claim to what he feels is rightfully his – except that he is secretly scared by the prospect. Beryl, too, has mixed feelings, and the two play a continual game of verbal sexual-cat-and-mouse that goes nowhere but is as exhausting as the act itself.

As he had done with *The Dustbinmen* before it, Jack Rosenthal withdrew from his creation once it was established. In the second series, scripted by Geoffrey Lancashire, the lovers decide to take the plunge and become engaged, although it remains an on-off relationship at best.

The Lovers conferred fame on both its leading players. Paula Wilcox, then 20, went on to feature in **Man About The House**; Richard Beckinsale, 23, moved on to **Porridge** and **Rising Damp** and would undoubtedly have had a long and fruitful career were it not for his appallingly early death from a heart attack at the age of 31. Robin Nedwell also appeared regularly in *The Lovers*, as Geoffrey's best friend, and Rosenthal's wife, Maureen Lipman, then unknown to TV viewers, appeared in one episode.

A feature film version, *The Lovers!*, was released in 1972. This was better than most of the small-to-big-screen transfers, with both the stars reprising their TV roles, and Jack Rosenthal returning as writer; Herbert Wise directed.

The Loves Of Larch Hill

UK · BBC · SITCOM

1 × 30 mins · b/w
12 May 1969 · BBC1 Mon 7.30pm

MAIN CAST
Robert Love · · · · · · · · · · · · Robert Dorning
Liz Love · · · · · · · · · · · · · · · · · Jan Holden
Alison Love ('Smudge') · · · · · · · Gillian Blake
Keith Love · · · · · · · · · · · · · · David Munro
Rosemary Love · · · · · · · · · Marigold Russell
Mrs Love Sr · · · · · · · · · · · · · Nan Braunton

CREDITS
writer Anne Burnaby · producer Eric Fawcett

A single-episode *Comedy Playhouse* tale of an eccentric family, the Loves, who live in the Conservative community of Larch Hill. Husband Robert and his much younger wife Liz head the oddball household, which remains a constant source of irritation to their neighbours.

The LP Show With Victor Borge

see BORGE, Victor

Lucille Ball ...   [various shows]

see BALL, Lucille

Lucky Feller

UK · ITV (LWT) · SITCOM

13 × 30 mins · colour
3 Sep–26 Nov 1976 · Fri 7pm

MAIN CAST
'Shorty' Mepstead · · · · · · · · · · David Jason
Randolph Mepstead · · · · · · Peter Armitage
Mrs Mepstead · · · · · · · · · · · · Pat Heywood
Kathleen 'Kath' Peake · · · · · · · · Cheryl Hall
Mr Peake · · · · · · · · · · · · · · · Glynn Edwards

Mrs Peake · · · · · · · · · · · · · Maggie Jones

CREDITS
writer Terence Frisby · directors Mike Vardy (7), Gerry Mill (6) · producer Humphrey Barclay

Still endeavouring to find *that* role for his 'discovery' David Jason (see **Do Not Adjust Your Set**), producer Humphrey Barclay invited Terence Frisby (the author of the highly successful stage-play and movie *There's A Girl In My Soup*) to tailor a sitcom for the comic actor's talents. The result, the 13-part *Lucky Feller*, cast Jason in a tragic-comic role, as the girl-shy Shorty (5ft 6in, to be exact), who lives at home with his mum and brother in south-east London. The brother, Randolph, is the opposite of Shorty: endowed with the gift of the gab, he has no trouble chatting up women. Shorty and Randolph run a small-time plumbing and all-purpose repair business together.

During the first episode Shorty meets Kath; initially, at least, she fancies Randolph, and a sorry love-triangle ensues in which Shorty loves Kath, she loves his brother and his brother loves himself but, oblivious to his predicament, Shorty simply considers himself 'a lucky feller'. The final episode saw it all come right, though, when Shorty and Kath tied the proverbial knot.

Lucy ...   [various shows]

see BALL, Lucille

Luna

UK · ITV (CENTRAL) · CHILDREN'S SITCOM

12 × 30 mins · colour
Series One (6) 22 Jan–26 Feb 1983 · Sat 5.15pm
Series Two (6) 15 Feb–21 Mar 1984 · Wed 4.20pm

MAIN CAST
Luna · · · · · · · · · · · · Patsy Kensit (series 1);
· · · · · · · · · · · · · · · · · Joanna Wyatt (series 2)
Brat · · · · · · · · · · · · · · · · · · · Aaron Brown
Gramps · · · · · · · · · · · · · · · · Frank Duncan
Andy · · · · · · · · · · · · · · · · · · Colin Bennett
80H · · · · · · · · · · · · · · · · · · Roy Macready
Mother · · · · · · · · · · · · · · · · · · Linda Polan
Mr Efficiecity · · · · · · David Gretton (series 1);
· · · · · · · · · · · · · · · Russell Wootton (series 2)
40D · · · · · · · · · · · · · · Natalie Forbes (series 1)
32C · · · · · · · Vanessa Knox-Mawer (series 2)
Jazzmine · · · · · · · · · · · · · · · · · Hugh Spight

CREDITS
creator Michael Dolenz · writers Colin Bennett/ Colin Prockter · directors Michael Dolenz (9), Chris Tookey (3) · executive producer Lewis Rudd · producer Michael Dolenz

A futuristic children's sci-fi sitcom in which the characters spoke a language called Techno Talk. While clearly rooted in English (just as well, really) it had been tailored to suit the needs of the time, thus viewers had to get

used to such words as computerbodge, culturoid, bureaubureau, transitisation, totaloke, habiviron, nervidipso and absonoke; children were known as dimi males and dimi females, families were nabiviron groups and if you lost your egothenticity card then you disappeared.

The series was created/part-directed/ produced by the former Monkee Michael (Micky) Dolenz, who had been closely involved in **Metal Mickey** before this. Based on a story he wrote as a teenager, Dolenz described *Luna* as a 'science-fiction-comedy-adventure-drama', the action taking place in the next century, circa 2033. The teenage starring role (in the first series only) was played by Patsy Kensit, while Robbie Coltrane appeared in a minor role in one of the episodes.

Lunch In The Park

see BAXTER, Stanley and *Paul Merton In Galton & Simpson's ...*

Lust For Glorious

UK · C4 (ELLA COMMUNICATIONS) · SATIRE

1 × 40 mins · colour
20 Dec 1997 · Sat 9.30pm

MAIN CAST
Eddie Izzard · · · · · · · · · · · · · · · · · · himself
TJ · Mark Caven
Promo director · · · · · · · · · · · · · · · Phil Kay
Al · · · · · · · · · · · · · · · · · · · Mac McDonald
Mel · · · · · · · · · · · Deborah Sheridan-Taylor
1st French babe · · · · · · · · · · · Rhona Mitra
2nd French babe · · · · · · · · · · · Debbie Flett

CREDITS
writer Eddie Izzard · director Peter Richardson · executive producer Eddie Izzard · producer Ben Swaffer

A mock documentary purporting to show an attempt to turn Eddie Izzard into a comedy superstar for the USA. Shot fly-on-the-wall style, the spoof explored the adage that 'comedy is the new rock and roll' by showing Izzard behaving like a rock superstar, with all the attendant trappings of groupies, drugs, fast cars, hotel trashing and general bad behaviour thrown in. Director Peter Richardson brought more than a touch of his old **Comic Strip Presents ...** style to the piece which, although hardly original, had its fair share of quirky, humorous moments.

Lust For Glorious was screened within an entire evening (9pm to 1.35am) given over to Izzard by C4 and screened under the overall title *Channel Izzard*. A brilliantly inventive, surrealistic standup artist, Izzard is renowned for limiting his TV appearances (and for his tendency to cross-dress and wear make-up), and is one of the few major standup acts to achieve national popularity without small-screen exposure. Videos of his stage-shows sell extremely well, though, and one of these, *Eddie Izzard – Unrepeatable*, was screened by C4 on 11 April 1997. A pre-credit sequence for *Channel Izzard* showed the comedian with a psychiatrist (played by Jim Broadbent), who explained that the comic's spiralling ego was such that it was essential he finally tackle television, but that a series wouldn't be enough, he had to have an entire channel at his disposal.

The comic linked the evening from a control centre, where he addressed a studio audience and, by studying monitors, kept a bizarre watch on three rubbish skips that he had placed at various spots around London. In a recurring sequence called *Skipwatch* the comedian checked what was happening to the skips through the evening. The first sequence after the introduction was *Panic Shopping*, a filmed insert in which Izzard demonstrated how to undertake all of your Christmas shopping in just two hours on Christmas Eve. He then introduced a repeat airing of one of his favourite C4 comedy shows, the Canadian sketch series **Kids In The Hall**. After *Lust For Glorious* viewers were treated to the first TV screening of another of Izzard's concert videos, *Definite Article*, a record of his 1995–96 tour. Following a further look back at *Kids In The Hall* was another filmed insert, *Speed Archaeology*, dealing with an impatient archaeologist, and then a humorous twist on the German TV police series *Derrick* (screened late-nights by London-ITV 1987–93), in which an original version was redubbed (by Izzard, Phil Cornwell and Ronnie Ancona) for comic effect. The evening finished with Izzard introducing his favourite film, Woody Allen's early sci-fi comedy *Sleeper*.

Luv

UK · BBC · SITCOM

18 × 30 mins · colour

Series One (10) 9 Mar–11 May 1993 · BBC1 Tue 8pm

Series Two (8) 2 Mar–20 Apr 1994 · BBC1 Wed 8.30pm

MAIN CAST

Harold Craven	Michael Angelis
Terese Craven	Sue Johnston
Hannah Craven	Sandy Hendrickse
Victor Craven	Russell Boulter
Darwin Craven	Stephen Lord
Lloyd	Peter Caffrey
Eden	Julie Peasgood
Bernie	Jackie Downey

OTHER APPEARANCES

Antonio	Zubin Varla
Stephen	Derek Howard

CREDITS

writer/executive producer Carla Lane · *director/producer* Mike Stephens

Yet another serio-comedy from Carla Lane. This one dealt with the problems of a couple who, on the surface, seem to have everything but, underneath, remain unfulfilled. The lead character, Terese Craven, was a Lane heroine in the mould of Rea from **Butterflies** – indeed, comparisons between the two series are hard to avoid, but *Luv* was a harder, harsher idea and made for uncomfortable viewing at times.

Terese is in a comfortable marriage with a loving if distant husband, but inside she is being eaten alive by a desire to get more from life. She is unsure what she wants to do, and this uncertainty – combined with her dissatisfaction – results in extreme behaviour and a skewed viewpoint on life. Terese is married to a real-life 'flowerpot man', Harold – a wealthy, self-made businessman who became rich from the success of his flowerpot factory. Harold has lived to earn money and, now that they have plenty, cannot understand his wife's dissatisfaction; but, typically for a man, he finds it easier to run away from the issue rather than confront it. Harold's low sperm-count has meant that the couple could not conceive children so they adopted three: Hannah, Victor and Darwin. The first two have left home, Hannah to live with her Italian boyfriend Antonio, the gay Victor to reside with his lover Stephen. But Darwin, the youngest, has stayed at home, where he seems to be wasting away, spending long, miserable periods in bed and only really being motivated by his membership of an animal-rights group (a subject close to Carla Lane's heart). Harold has tried hard as a father, but has shown his love by gifts of money and lavish presents rather than personal investment. This is how he treats Terese too, and this inability to give of himself rather than of his pocket is likely the root cause of all their problems.

From this structure Lane wove a complex, intense series that, despite its seriousness, still featured many witty lines. As ever, she was not afraid to take the characters into some difficult areas – Harold had a brief but damaging affair with his secretary Eden, and Terese, well, she was in the thick of it: she found a lump in her body that she thought might be cancerous, she moved out to live alone at one point, and she contemplated divorce. Then Harold suffered financial problems and faced the collapse of his empire. The arrival of a grandchild, Hannah and Antonio's baby, did little to heal the wounds, but an attempt by the jilted Eden to gain revenge by seducing Darwin was thwarted.

Mac

UK · BBC (STONEYBRIDGE PRODUCTIONS) · SITCOM

1 × 30 mins · colour
1 Sep 1995 · BBC2 Fri 9.30pm

MAIN CAST
Mac · · · · · · · · · · · · · · · · Jack Docherty
Findlay · · · · · · · · · · · · · · Gordon Kennedy
Van Webster · · · · · · · · · · · · Nick Hancock
Aileen · · · · · · · · · · · · · · Elaine Collins
Mrs Hunter · · · · · · · · · · · Primrose Milligan

CREDITS
writer Jack Docherty · director Caroline Roberts · executive producer Colin Gilbert · producers Caroline Roberts, Jack Docherty

An earthy *Comic Asides* sitcom pilot from BBC Scotland, written by and starring comedian Jack Docherty as Mac, a rabid anti-English Scottish nationalist. Mac is an articulate, long-haired man who finds it difficult to hold down a job owing to his tendency to go ballistic at the mere mention of anything English. To Mac's shame, his brother Findlay runs Scotch Sales Limited, a shop that sells tatty souvenirs of Scotland to tourists from south o' the border. Even the name of the company irritates Mac, who is quick to point out that Scotch is something you drink, not a description of Scottish goods. He would completely avoid his brother's shop if it wasn't for the fact that he is lusting after Findlay's assistant Aileen. In this pilot episode Mac finds that he has a rival when the shop employs Van Webster, a spaced-out air-head who is not only terminally vague but also, horror upon horror, English. Even worse, Aileen seems to fancy him.

Broadening the character he regularly portrayed in the C4 sketch series *Absolutely*, this was an energetic offering from Docherty, but one that failed to graduate to a series. While not bursting with laughs it was nevertheless easy to watch, and Mac proved to be an oddly appealing character; in some ways this worked against the central premise, however, because it became difficult to believe that Aileen, a sharp woman, would

prefer the dopey Van to the flawed but passionate Mac.

See also *Mr Don And Mr George*.

Mad In Austria!

see The Montreux Festival

Maggie And Her

UK · ITV (LWT) · SITCOM

14 × 30 mins · colour
Pilot *Poppy And Her* 13 Aug 1976 · Fri 7pm
Series One (7) 13 Jan–24 Feb 1978 · Fri 7.30pm
Series Two (6) 22 Apr–27 May 1979 · Sun 7.15pm

MAIN CAST
Maggie (Poppy in the pilot) · · Julia McKenzie
Mrs Perry · · · · · · · · · · · · · · · Irene Handl

OTHER APPEARANCES
Miss Cartwright · · · · · · · · · · · Carol Gillies
Dicky · · · · · · · · · · · · · · · · · Eric Flynn
Tommy · · · · · · · · · · · · · · · · Peter Hale
Virginia · · · · · · · · · · · · · · · Moira Foot
Mabel · · · · · · · · · · · · · · · Olivia Breeze
Mrs Young · · · · · · · · · · · · · · · Anna Wing

CREDITS
writer Leonard Webb · directors Alan Wallis (pilot), David Askey (series 1), John Reardon (series 2) · producers Humphrey Barclay (pilot), David Askey (series 1), Simon Brett (series 2)

Julia McKenzie and loveable cockney Irene Handl, aged 35 and 76 respectively when the first full series began, starred in this LWT sitcom, the former as a divorced school-teacher, Maggie, living alone in a flat, and the latter as her good-intentioned but impossibly nosey neighbour Mrs P, a widow. Maggie is very eligible – there's a different man wooing or being wooed in virtually every episode – but, of course, Mrs P manages to stick her oar into every situation and influence, usually negatively, Maggie's chances.

The first series followed 17 months after the pilot, at which point Julia McKenzie's character was changed from Poppy to Maggie, and the series' title was altered accordingly.

Maggie – It's Me!

UK · BBC · SITCOM

1 × 30 mins · colour
3 May 1977 · BBC1 Tue 7.40pm

MAIN CAST
Maggie · · · · · · · · · · · · · Frances de la Tour
Allie · · · · · · · · · · · · · · · Rosemary Martin

CREDITS
writer Bernard Taylor · producer Graeme Muir

The last episode in the series *Comedy Special*, a successor to *Comedy Playhouse*. In *Maggie – It's Me!* Allie leaves her boyfriend in order to 'teach him a lesson', and seeks solace with her friend Maggie (played by the excellent Frances de la Tour). No series developed.

The Magic Box

see The Montreux Festival

The Magnificent Evans

UK · BBC · SITCOM

6 × 30 mins · colour
13 Sep–11 Oct 1984 · BBC1 Thu 8pm

MAIN CAST
Plantagenet Evans · · · · · · · · Ronnie Barker
Rachel · · · · · · · · · · · · · · Sharon Morgan
Bron · · · · · · · · · · · · · · · Myfanwy Talog
Willie · · · · · · · · · · · · · · · Dickie Arnold
Probert · · · · · · · · · · · · · · William Thomas

CREDITS
writer Roy Clarke · director/producer Sydney Lotterby

Writer Roy Clarke first toyed with using a photographer as the focal point in a sitcom with the *Comedy Playhouse* episode *Pygmalion Smith*; this had starred Leonard Rossiter as a character who, like Plantagenet Evans here, possessed a common surname and an uncommon first name.

Situated in deepest rural Wales, Evans was depicted as 'a grandiose, hectoring scaramouch driven by sordid motive and lust' – a witty and strangely likeable bully with a finely developed ego and an intolerance towards fools – and Ronnie Barker played the role like a cross between Orson Welles and Oscar Wilde. Evans's long-time fiancée, Rachel, also doubled as his assistant and she had a full-time job steering his lusting eyes away from other women and back to his viewfinder.

This was a quality product, with beautiful location shooting and another memorable performance from Barker, relishing the Welsh accent in which he delivered Clarke's sharp lines. But only one series was made and neither the character nor the premise had the chance to develop further.

The Magnificent One

UK · C4 (ROCKING HORSE PRODUCTIONS) · COMEDY FILM

1 × 45 mins · colour
6 Nov 1982 · Sat 9.15pm

MAIN CAST
Larry · · · · · · · · · · · · · · Adrian Edmondson
Mr Ho · · · · · · · · · · · · · · · · Burt Kwouk
The Samurai · · · · · · · · · · · · Simon Deerling

CREDITS
writer/director Sandy Johnson · producer Michael Hamlyn

An early TV venture for Adrian Edmondson, written and directed by the director of some of the *Comic Strip Presents ...* films. This single-episode comedy was set in Fulham and involved a Chinese family and a samurai.

Maid Marian And Her Merry Men

UK · BBC · CHILDREN'S SITCOM

26 episodes (25 × 25 mins · 1 × 50 mins) · colour

Series One (6) 16 Nov–21 Dec 1989 · BBC1
Thu 4.35pm

Series Two (6) 15 Nov–20 Dec 1990 · BBC1
Thu 4.35pm

Series Three (6) 7 Jan–11 Feb 1993 · BBC1
Thu 4.30pm

Special (50 mins) 24 Dec 1993 · BBC1
Fri 5.10pm

Series Four (7) 5 Jan–16 Feb 1994 · BBC1
Wed 5.10pm

MAIN CAST

Marian · · · · · · · · · · · · · · · · · Kate Lonergan
Robin · · · · · · · · · · · · · · · · · · · Wayne Morris
Barrington · · · · · · · · · · · · Danny John-Jules
Rabies · · · · · · · · · · · · · · Howard Lew Lewis
Little Ron · · · · · · · · · · · · · · · Mike Edmonds
King John · · · · · · · · · · · · · · Forbes Collins
The Sheriff of Nottingham · · · Tony Robinson
Gary · · · · · · · · · · · · · · · · · Mark Billingham
Graeme · · · · · · · · · · · · · · · · · David Lloyd
Gladys · · · · · · · · · · · · · · · · · Hilary Mason
Guy of Gisborne · · · · · · · · Ramsay Gilderdale
· (series 2–4)
Rotten Rose · · · Siobhan Fogarty (series 2–4)
Snooker · · · · · · Robin Chandler (series 2–4)

CREDITS

writer Tony Robinson · director David Bell ·
producer Richard Callanan

Familiar with period-piece costume comedy from his stint as Baldrick in **Blackadder**, Tony Robinson took centre-stage here as the writer and one of the stars of this deservedly popular children's sitcom, which put a feminist spin on the Robin Hood legend. In Tony Robinson's series, Hood is an ineffectual wimp, whereas the formidable idealist Marian is the true leader of the resistance against the evil monarch King John. Marian terrorises the forest-dwelling peasants into following her commands as she plots to rob from the rich to feed the poor. But, courageous and capable though she is, her plans rarely turn out as she envisages, being derailed either by her naïve idealism or the sheer incompetence of the mentally challenged nincompoops who comprise her Merry Men, including Rabies (a Rastafarian) and the appropriately diminutive Little Ron.

With its sharp scripts and outrageous, purposefully anachronistic plots, Robinson's refreshingly earthy series was good enough not only to amuse children; it could have entertained adults too had it been scheduled in a later slot. The first series made an immediate impression, winning awards from Bafta and the Royal Television Society and picking up the coveted Prix Jeunesse Variety Award at the International Children's Programme Festival in Munich.

Robinson has also taken a stage version of his show around British provincial theatres.

The Main Attraction

UK · BBC · STANDUP

12 × 45 mins · colour

Series One (7) 16 July–27 Aug 1983 · BBC1
Sat mostly 8.40pm

Series Two (5) 28 July–25 Aug 1984 · BBC1
Sat mostly 8.15pm

MAIN CAST

see below

CREDITS

directors Stanley Appel (8), John Bishop (4) ·
producers John Fisher (series 1), Stanley Appel
(series 2)

A Saturday-night entertainment show in which comedians featured extensively. Most editions in the first series included a 'comedy classic' feature in which a guest re-created a once famous routine.

Those appearing in the first series were Warren Mitchell (as Alf Garnett), David Copperfield, Tommy Cooper, Chas and Dave, Pam Ayres, Larry Grayson, Roy Jay, John Junkin, Shields and Yarnell, Charlie Drake, Bernard Manning, James Casey and Eli Woods (in a tribute to Jimmy James), Dickie Henderson, Janet Brown, Ted Rogers, Jimmy Cricket, Richard Stilgoe, Leslie Crowther and Bernie Winters (as Flanagan and Allen), Tessie O'Shea, Max Wall, Les Dennis and Dustin Gee.

The second series featured Norman Collier, David Copperfield, Duncan Norville, Gary Wilmot, Tom O'Connor, Brian Conley, Roy Walker, Chas and Dave, Marti Caine, Dave Wolfe, Mike Newman, Lew Lewis, Aiden J Harvey, Mike Reid, Charlie Daze, Roy Jay, Adrian Walsh, Les Dawson, Bobby Knutt, Bobby Davro, and the Roly Polys.

Mainly Millicent

see MARTIN, Millicent

Major Dad

USA · CBS (SSB PRODUCTIONS/SPANISH TRAIL PRODUCTIONS/UNIVERSAL TELEVISION) · SITCOM

96 × 30 mins · colour

US dates: 17 Sep 1989–13 Sep 1993

UK dates: 8 Jan 1990–11 Sep 1992 (26 episodes) BBC1 Mon 7.35pm then daily 11.35am

MAIN CAST

Major John D 'Mac' MacGillis · · · · · · · · · · ·
· Gerald McRaney
Polly Cooper/MacGillis · · · · · · Shanna Reed
Elizabeth Cooper · · · · · · · · · · · Marisa Ryan
Robin Cooper · · · · · · · · · · · · · Nicole Dubuc
Casey Cooper · · · · · · · · · · · Chelsea Hertford
Lt Gene Holowachuk · · · · · · · · Matt Mulhern
Merilee Gundersen · · · · · · Whitney Kershaw
· (1989–90)
Sgt Byron James · · Marlon Archey (1989–90)
Gunnery Sgt Alva Bricker · · · · · Beverly Archer
· (1990–93)
Maj Gen Marcus Craig · · · · · · · · · Jon Cypher
· (from 1990)
Jeffrey · · · · · · · · · · · · Chance Michael Corbitt

CREDITS

main writers Earl Pomerantz/Richard C Okie ·
directors Will MacKenzie, Linda Day, Ellen Falcon
and others · producer Will MacKenzie

Another variation on the familiar sitcom theme of mismatched-couple-survive-despite-their-differences. This time the unlikely lovebirds were the stereotypical hard-nosed conservative marine Major John 'Mac' MacGillis, and the liberal, idealistic investigative journalist Polly Cooper. They first meet when Cooper, a widow, visits Camp Singleton, near San Diego, to write an article for the local newspaper *The Oceanside Chronicle*. Despite their opposing views on almost everything, love blossoms, and after a whirlwind romance they marry and set up home with Polly's three children, teenager Elizabeth, 11-year-old Robin and six-year-old Casey. Later, Mac transfers to Camp Hollister, in Virginia, and Polly obtains a job editing the camp's newspaper *The Bulldog*, this new role bringing her into closer contact with the professional side of Mac's life and his brusque colleagues.

The comedy arose not only from the conflict between the couple but also from Polly's clashes with Mac's colleagues, naturally wary of a liberal journalist, and from her children, understandably opposed to the disciplinary attitudes of their stepfather. Of course, both sides learned to make allowances and the moral of the show seemed to be that, with love on your side, most differences can be ironed out by reasoned compromise.

The series was not shy of incorporating real-life events (like government cuts and the Gulf War) into its storylines, and Dan Quayle, then the US vice-president, appeared in an episode that marked the Marine Corps' 215th anniversary.

Makin' It

USA · ABC (MILLER-MILKIS PRODUCTIONS/ HENDERSON PRODUCTIONS/THE STIGWOOD GROUP) · SITCOM

9 × 30 mins · colour

US dates: 1 Feb–16 Mar 1979 (8 episodes)

UK dates: 25 Apr–13 June 1979 (8 episodes) ITV
Wed 5.15pm

MAIN CAST

Billy Manucci · · · · · · · · · · · · David Naughton
Tony Manucci · · · · · · · · · · · · Greg Antonacci
Tina Manucci · · · · · · · · · · · · · Denise Miller
Dorothy Manucci · · · · · · · · · · Ellen Travolta
Joseph Manucci · · · · · · · · · · · · · Lou Antonio

CREDITS

creators Mark Rothman, Lowell Ganz, Garry
Marshall · writers various · directors Lowell Ganz,

Joel Zwick, John Tracy · *executive producers* Thomas L Miller, Edward K Milkis, Lowell Ganz, Mark Rothman · *producers* David W Duclon, Deborah Leschin, Jeffrey Ganz

Cashing in on the disco craze of the period, *Makin' It* amounted to little more than an episodic clone of the hit movie *Saturday Night Fever*, the episodes focusing on the turbulent teen life of an Italian-American college boy, Billy Manucci, who lives for the dance floor of the Inferno disco and the only chance he can get to outshine his brother Tony.

Quite apart from the TV storylines, Robert Stigwood (who produced the movie) was involved here too; it also featured John Travolta's sister Ellen as Billy's mother and a good deal of Bee Gees music.

Making Faces

UK · BBC · SITCOM

6 × 30 mins · colour
25 Sep–30 Oct 1975 · BBC2 Thu 10.35pm

MAIN CAST
Zoya Hirst · · · · · · · · · · · · · · · Eleanor Bron
Stuart · · · · · · · · · · · · · · · · · · · Tim Preece

CREDITS
writer Michael Frayn · *director* Gareth Gwenlan · *producer* Robert Chetwyn

Not so much a sitcom, more a series of comedy playlets featuring the same main character. Eleanor Bron was cast as Zoya Hirst, a role written with her in mind by Michael Frayn, whose idea was to create a chameleon-like Jewish character who changed with every new environment and with every new person she met.

The series looked at six different moments in Zoya's life (Spring 1970; Trinity Term 1960; Packaging Industry Convention 1963; Summer 1966; April 1968; December 1974). Zoya and her contemporaries were from the affluent, academic world that Frayn and Bron had both experienced in real life and the pieces were deliberately designed so that Frayn could pass comment on the people and those times. Tim Preece played Stuart, Zoya's boyfriend.

The Making Of Peregrine

UK · BBC · SITCOM

1 × 30 mins · b/w
19 May 1969 · BBC1 Mon 7.30pm

MAIN CAST
Stanley Mold · · · · · · · · · · · · · · Dick Emery
Minerva Mold · · · · · · · · · · · · · Pat Coombs
Peregrine Mold · · · · · · · · · · · · Andrew Ray
Rory · Sam Kydd

CREDITS
writers Marty Feldman/Barry Took · *producer* Barry Lupino

A rare sitcom venture for Dick Emery, starring in a Feldman and Took script that

had been written years earlier. This *Comedy Playhouse* story concerned Stanley Mold's desire to make a man out of his rather drippy son, Peregrine. To assist him on his way to adulthood, Stanley takes Peregrine to a shady bar and tries to introduce him to some members of the opposite sex. No series developed but Emery continued to star on BBC1 in his own hugely successful sketch series.

Making Whoopee

see EVERETT, Kenny

The Maladjusted Busker

see HUDD, Roy

Malc Up Market

UK · BBC · STANDUP

1 × 30 mins · colour
4 Jan 1985 · BBC2 Fri 10.45pm

MAIN CAST
Malc Stent

CREDITS
producer Mike Derby

A one-off special featuring chubby Brummie raconteur Malcolm Stent, a folk-singing humorist with a guitar who was resident at the Boggery Club in Solihull (from where Jasper Carrott had been catapulted to fame and fortune). In this programme – previously broadcast in the Midlands only – Stent took his road show 'up market' to the Library Theatre, Solihull.

See also *Funnybone*.

The Mallard Imaginaire

see *The Whitehall Worrier*

Mama Malone

USA · CBS (BARRY/ENRIGHT/LEWIS PRODUCTIONS/CPT) · SITCOM

13 × 30 mins · colour
US dates: 7 Mar–21 July 1984
UK dates: 18 Feb–12 May 1984 (13 episodes)
C4 Sat 4.35pm

MAIN CAST
Renate Malone · · · · · · · · · · · · · Lila Kaye
Connie Karamakopoulos · · · · Randee Heller
Frankie Karamakopoulos · · · Evan Richards
Austin · · · · · · · · · · · · · · Raymond Singer
Ken · · · · · · · · · · · · · · · Pendleton Brown
Dino Forresti · · · · · · · · · · · Don Amendolia
Padre Guardiano · · · · · · · · · · Ralph Manza
Father Jose Silver · · · · · · · · Richard Yniguez

CREDITS
writers Bernard Dilbert, Sid Dorfman, Richard Freiman, Lynn Marie Latham, Bernard Lechowick, Terrence McNally, Leonard Melfi, Patt Shea,

Robert Van Scoyk, Harriet Weiss, Harvey Weitzman · *directors* various · *producers* Jack Barry, Dan Enright, Richard Lewis, Paul Bogart

The English actress Lila Kaye starred here as Mama Malone, an Italian-New Yorker widow of a Irish policeman who transmits a cable TV cookery show – *Cooking With Mama Malone* – direct from her cluttered sixth-floor apartment in Brooklyn, utilising recipes from her Mediterranean heritage. She not only prepares food, however: with a pre-warmed heart and a bowl full of ideas she cooks up solutions to her family's and neighbours' problems, the TV shows sometimes becoming more of a help-meeting than a guide to healthy eating, much to the annoyance of her director, Austin. Mama is also the object of an over-bearing daughter, Connie, who married a Greek named Karamakopoulos but is divorced and raising their child Frankie, and she commands too the attentions of her younger brother Dino, a lounge singer.

Proving her versatility, Lila Kaye switched here from Jewish momma to Italian mama: for nine years before appearing in this new role she had starred as Fay Greenberg in Thames TV's Yiddisher comedy series *My Son Reuben*. The daughter of a London book-maker, Kaye spent four months on Broadway in the Royal Shakespeare Company's production of Dickens' *Nicholas Nickleby* in 1982–83, also appearing in the acclaimed US TV version, and was preparing to return to England when she was invited to adopt an American accent and record the pilot edition of *Mama Malone*. A series developed, requiring her to fly to Hollywood, although it then sat on the shelf for the best part of a year before CBS aired it. Kaye's worst fears were realised when C4 imported *Mama Malone* for UK television, however: she had only taken the role in the knowledge that none of her British friends would be able to see it.

Mama's Back!

UK · BBC · SITCOM

1 × 30 mins · colour
6 Dec 1993 · BBC1 Mon 8.30pm

MAIN CAST
Tamara Hamilton · · · · · · · · · · · Joan Collins
Ian Hamilton · · · · · · · · · · · Michael Gambon
Stephen · · · · · · · · · · · · · · · Rupert Everett
Clive James · · · · · · · · · · · · · · · · himself
Maureen · · · · · · · · · · · · · · · · · · Dana Ivey
Sharon Emanuel · · · · · · · · Samantha Janus

CREDITS
writer Ruby Wax · *director* Ed Bye · *producer* Justin Judd

Joan Collins parodied herself (at least partially) in this comedy by Ruby Wax. The star was cast as Tamara Hamilton, a glamor-ous English actress in Hollywood who, after one tantrum too many, is unemployable and so returns to return to England to face the family she left behind.

Originally intended as a pilot for a series to be called *Next*, this remained an intriguing one-off with a heavyweight cast. The director, Ed Bye, is Wax's husband.

Man About The House

UK · ITV (THAMES) · SITCOM

40 episodes (39 × 30 mins · 1 × short special) · colour

Series One (7) 15 Aug–26 Sep 1973 · Wed 8.30pm
Short special · part of *All-Star Comedy Carnival* 25 Dec 1973 · Tue 6.30pm
Series Two (6) 9 Jan–13 Feb 1974 · Wed 8pm
Series Three (7) 9 Oct–20 Nov 1974 · Wed 8pm
Series Four (6) 6 Mar–10 Apr 1975 · Thu 8pm
Series Five (6) 4 Sep–9 Oct 1975 · Thu 8.30pm
Series Six (7) 25 Feb–7 Apr 1976 · Wed 8pm

MAIN CAST

Robin Tripp · · · · · · · · · · · Richard O'Sullivan
Chrissy Plummer · · · · · · · · · · · Paula Wilcox
Jo · · · · · · · · · · · · · · · · · Sally Thomsett
Mildred Roper · · · · · · · · · · · · Yootha Joyce
George Roper · · · · · · · · · · · · Brian Murphy

OTHER APPEARANCES

Larry Simmonds · · · · · · · · · · · Doug Fisher
Norman Tripp · · · · · Norman Eshley (series 6)

CREDITS

writers Johnnie Mortimer/Brian Cooke (37 episodes & special), Brian Cooke (2 episodes) · *director/producer* Peter Frazer-Jones

Chrissy (the dark-haired one) and Jo (the blonde one, prone to rambling illogicalities) share a bedsit flat at 6 Myddleton Terrace in the Earls Court district of London. The morning after a farewell party for a third (female) flatmate, and in sore need of the extra financial contribution, they prepare to start looking for her replacement. Unbeknownst to them, asleep in the bath after drinking too much of an appalling concoction they called punch, is Robin Tripp, the friend of a friend of a friend of a friend, and a catering student to boot. Since he can cook, they invite him to become the third flatmate, offering him the spare bedroom and warning him to keep out of theirs.

So began this enormously successful ITV sitcom, popular throughout the early 1970s and precursor of two direct sequels, *George And Mildred* and *Robin's Nest*. The first of these featured the *Man About The House* husband-and-wife landlords, who began this original series as very much the lesser characters and wound up as arguably the most popular. Their roles here set the moulds: Mildred is all for permitting the permissive society, especially if it will improve her social standing and allow her to flirt; George is petty-minded and as mean with his money as he is with his sexuality (which is dormant) – although he remains lecherous with women

other than his wife. Despite the *ménage-à-trois* situation there was very little overt naughtiness in *Man About The House*; rather, in the ribald manner of British humour, most of the jokes centred on parents' misunderstandings, friends' misunderstandings, girlfriends' misunderstandings, boyfriends' misunderstandings, ill-timed interruptions, wrong bedrooms, smalls hanging on the line, people *seeing* the smalls hanging on the line, and many other 'embarrassing' situations. There were some good lines and very funny situations, however.

Busy scripting the two sequels, writers Cooke and Mortimer seemed to hasten the demise of *Man About The House* – three episodes from the end of what turned out to be the last series, viewers were suddenly introduced to Robin's brother, Norman. Having unsuccessfully chased Chrissy's affections for some three years, and had all his advances spurned, coyly or firmly, Robin was upset to see Norman join the pursuit. Norman won, with rapid results: in the final programme he and Chrissy were married.

Man About The House by-products were many. First there was the feature film for cinemas, made by Hammer in 1974 (director John Robins) with the usual cast supported by a wealth of familiar faces (including Spike Milligan and Arthur Lowe). Then there were the two UK TV sequels, as mentioned above. Then the format was also sold to America, surfacing there as *Three's Company*, which ran for 169 episodes from 1977 to 1984. (Here the flatmates were Jack Tripper, Janet Wood and Chrissy Snow and the Ropers were Helen and Stanley.) It gets confusing, but *Three's Company* itself then had two sequels: *The Ropers*, which was the US version of *George And Mildred*, and *Three's A Crowd*, the US adaptation of *Robin's Nest*.

Man And Music

see MILLIGAN, Spike

The Man From Auntie

see *Ben Elton – The Man From Auntie*

Man O' Brass

see *Bold As Brass*

Man With A Mission

UK · ITV (ATV) · SITCOM

1 × 30 mins · b/w

8 Sep 1965 · Wed 9.10pm

MAIN CAST

Wilfred Hicks · · · · · · · · · · · · · Ronald Lacey
Forbes-Glanville · · · · · · · · · Thorley Walters

Mrs Whittaker · · · · · · · · · · · Avis Bunnage
Hope-Weston · · · · · · · · · · · · Derek Nimmo
Security Guard · · · · · · · · · · · · Harry Locke
Carol · · · · · · · · · · · · · · · · Denise Buckley

CREDITS

writers Richard Harris/Dennis Spooner · *director* Dicky Leeman · *producer* Alan Tarrant

Another of ATV's *Comedy Playhouse*-style series *Six Of The Best*, this single-episode comedy was written by Richard Harris and Dennis Spooner, later to find their niche with many of the ITV/ITC adventure series such as *Man In A Suitcase*, *Randall And Hopkirk (Deceased)*, *Department S* and *The Champions*.

The Management

UK · C4 (LWT) · SITCOM

6 × 30 mins · colour

27 Jan–2 Mar 1988 · Wed 10pm

MAIN CAST

Ron · · · · · · · · · · · · · · · · · · · Gareth Hale
Ron · · · · · · · · · · · · · · · · · · · Norman Pace
Mr Crusty · · · · · · · · · · · · · · · Bryan Pringle
Naomi · · · · · · · · · · · · · · · · · Kate McKenzie
Typhus Los Bentos, the chef · · · Andy Linden
Mrs Crusty · · · · · · · · · · · · Vilma Hollingbery
Fiona · · · · · · · · · · · · · · · · · Serena Evans

CREDITS

writers Gareth Hale/Norman Pace (5), Geoff Atkinson/Gareth Hale/Norman Pace (1) · *director* John Gorman · *producer* Charlie Hanson

A sitcom outing for the Two Rons, Hale and Pace's overtly tough tuxedo-clad bouncers, who brook no nonsense but talk heaps of it. Here, Ron and Ron take possession of a London night-club, left to them in his will by their late Uncle Albert. They style it as the Management Club and run it as only a pair of thick-as-two-short-planks bullies would, managing to liquidate it by the end of the six episodes.

In addition to the regular cast, a number of familiar faces turned up once apiece during the series, including Bryan Pringle, Norman Lovett, sex entrepreneur Paul Raymond (as himself), and Barbara Windsor, who was cast as Aunt Vicky, who sets up premises for dubious entertainment in Streatham. Any similarity between this and an establishment operated by Cynthia Payne was entirely intentional – indeed Ms Payne turned up in the episode.

The Management was home to the last TV recording made by the great Irene Handl, who appeared as a judge, trying the Two Rons after they had broken the law while driving their pink bubble car. She died, aged 85, on 29 November 1987, before the episode was broadcast.

See *Hale And Pace* for Gareth Hale and Norman Pace's sketch/standup work.

Mann's Best Friends

UK · C4 (THAMES) · SITCOM

6 × 30 mins · colour

15 Apr–20 May 1985 · Mon 8.30pm

MAIN CAST

Hamish James Ordway · · · · · Fulton Mackay
Henry Mann · · · · · · · · · · · · · Barry Stanton
Duncan · · · · · · · · · · · · · · Bernard Bresslaw
Dolly 'Doll' Delights · · · · · · · · Patricia Burke
Mrs Mann · · · · · · · · · · · · · · Barbara Hicks
Mrs Anstruther · · · · · · · · · · · · · · Liz Smith
Irvin · · · · · · · · · · · · · · · · · Clive Merrison
Phoebe · · · · · · · · · · · · · · · · Sara Corper

CREDITS

writer Roy Clarke · director/producer Derrick Goodwin

Literate, yes, but one of the more obscure sitcom offerings from Roy Clarke, the six episodes painting an almost surreal landscape of odd-bods and vagueness.

The series starred Fulton Mackay as Hamish James Ordway, a Scotsman who has retired from his job at the water board. He's fussy, interfering and nosey in the extreme, and – in need of accommodation – finds himself holed up at the Laurels, a dilapidated and very disorganised abode. Promised free board by the owner Henry Mann if he can sort everything and everyone out, Ordway sets about getting involved with the assortment of its unlikely occupants, including six Chinese waiters, livestock, the hostile and alcoholic Duncan, and a blonde named Dolly Delights – Doll to her friends – who announces herself as a drama tutor but is very probably a prostitute, judging by the number of male visitors who arrive for private lessons in her room and the fact that she's usually only seen in her under garments.

Not that the officious Hamish was much better: as he said of his organisational abilities, 'If I'd been Hitler, Germany would have won the war'. Just as well he wasn't.

Many Happy Returns

USA · CBS (MGM TV/LINDABOB PRODUCTIONS) · SITCOM

26 × 30 mins · b/w

US dates: 21 Sep 1964–12 Apr 1965

UK dates: 21 Jan–14 July 1965 (26 episodes) BBC2 mostly Wed 8.25pm

MAIN CAST

Walter Burnley · · · · · · · · · · · John McGiver
Joan Randall · · · · · · · · · · · Elinor Donahue
Bob Randall · · · · · · · · · · · · Mark Goddard
Harry Price · · · · · · · · · · · · Richard Collier
Wilma Fritter · · · · · · · · · · · · · Jesslyn Fax
Owen Sharp · · · · · · · · · · · · Russell Collins
Joe Foley · · · · · · · · · · · · · Mickey Manners
Lynn Hall · · · · · · · · · · · · · · Elena Verdugo

CREDITS

producer Parke Levy

A terribly corny title for a series that followed the escapades of a widower, Walter Burnley, who manages the complaints department at Krockmeyer's Department Store in Los Angeles. Burnley's tact and fairness in dealing with complaints enabled him to sort out the problems in his personal life, especially those of his daughter Joan and her husband Bob.

A few months after the finish of *Many Happy Returns* Mark Goddard, who played Bob, was rocket-shipwrecked as Major Don West in *Lost In Space*.

The Many Loves Of Dobie Gillis

USA · CBS (MARTIN MANULIS PRODUCTIONS/ 20TH CENTURY-FOX TV) · SITCOM

147 × 30 mins · b/w

US dates: 29 Sep 1959–18 Sep 1963

UK date: 30 Aug 1993 (1 episode) BBC2 Mon 12 noon

MAIN CAST

Dobie Gillis · · · · · · · · · · · · Dwayne Hickman
Herbert T Gillis · · · · · · · · · · · · Frank Faylen
Winifred 'Winnie' Gillis · · · · · · Florida Friebus
Maynard Krebs · · · · · · · · · · · · Bob Denver
Zelda Gilroy · · · · · · · · · · · · Sheila James
Thalia Menninger · · · · · · · · · Tuesday Weld
· (1959–60)
Milton Armitage · · Warren Beatty (1959–60)
Davey Gillis · · · · · Darryl Hickman (1959–60)
Chatsworth Osborne Jr · · · · · · Steve Franken
· (1960–63)
Duncan 'Dunky' Gillis · · · · · · Bobby Diamond
Professor Leander Pomfritt · · · · · · · · · · · · ·
· · · · · · · · · · · · · · · · · · William Schallert
Clarice Armitage · · · Doris Packer (1959–60)
Clarissa Chatsworth Osborne Sr · · · · · · · · · ·
· · · · · · · · · · · · · · · · · Doris Packer (1960–63)
Leander Pomfritt · · · · · · · · William Schallert
Riff Ryan · · · · · · · · · · · · · · Tommy Farrell
Melissa Frome · · · · · · · · · · · · Yvonne Lime

CREDITS

creator Max Shulman · writers various · directors Rod Amateau, David Davis, Ralph Murphy, Guy Scarpitta, Stanley Z Cherry, Thomas Montgomery · executive producer Martin Manulis · producers Rod Amateau, Joel Kane, Guy Scarpitta

One of the most discussed and influential early American sitcoms is scarcely known in Britain (see footnote). *The Many Loves Of Dobie Gillis* – aka simply *Dobie Gillis* – was the first US TV series to show the world through a teenager's eyes. It was a sitcom that depicted the lives and thoughts of teenagers at a time when, by and large, America was not yet ready to give them their voice. The characters were boldly new, it broke rules and was even surreal in places. It wasn't outstandingly funny, and it won't feature in many all-time-favourites lists, but it scored several firsts.

The series was based on a novel by the humorist and satirist Max Shulman, which in 1953 was made into a musical feature film, *The Affairs Of Dobie Gillis*, starring Bobby

Van. At this point Dobie was a college student, but the TV series knocked a few years off his age so that he was about 16. (The actor who played him, Dwayne Hickman, was 25 when the series began.) In the words of the signature tune, Dobie 'wants a gal who's dreamy, wants a gal who's creamy, wants a gal to call his own' – he's girl-hungry (but still virginal, this being 1959) and he has also realised that his father, Herbert, has worked hard all his life and for what? – a grocery store. (Herbert and Dobie's mother, Winnie, run Gillis Groceries in the quiet backwater town Central City, and the family live over the shop.) Dobie's horizons are set on a wider plain: he wants a beautiful woman by his side and a wallet permanently stuffed with bank notes, although how he intends to derive such wealth he does not know.

A perpetual dreamer and romantic, Dobie drools over the ultra sexy but materialistic Thalia Menninger (played by Tuesday Weld), who wants to find him a job that will earn him 'oodles and oodles of money' in order, she says, to improve the lot of her struggling family. Unfortunately for Dobie, he is regularly frustrated by fellow schoolboy Milton Armitage, who seems to steal away all of Dobie's favourite girls from under his nose. (When Milton left the series – the actor, the as yet unknown Warren Beatty, quit, claiming that the role was absurd – he was replaced by a similar figure, Chatsworth Osborne Jr, who did likewise. Bizarrely, Doris Packer, who had played Milton's mother Clarice, was re-cast as Chatsworth's mother, Clarissa.) It is Zelda Gilroy, however, who desperately wants to be married to Dobie, and who finally (viewers learned in a pair of sequels) got her man.

While Dobie is a scrubbed, crew-cut, red-blooded, fun-loving, non-smoking, non-drinking all-American boy, his buddy Maynard (played by Bob Denver) is a beatnik, with a goatee beard and sweatshirt, who thinks fast, speaks loose ('daddy-o') and shudders when someone mentions the word 'work' in his presence. Maynard is a surrealist who abides by values and a wacky creed hitherto unseen on American television. Dobie and Maynard are in the same class at school and, despite all their differences, they permanently hang out together.

The series had several unusual aspects. Many of the cast, especially the youngsters, employed a slightly staccato way of talking. The key father–son relationship of Dobie and Herbert was different to typical sitcoms: it was rocky and they even yelled at one another, usually because Dobie wanted his father to lend (give) him money, but Herbert – who did not necessarily know best – was a tightwad and wouldn't part with a cent. Herbert frequently called Dobie 'a bum' when he refused to perform particular in-store chores. Dobie spoke straight to camera – the audience at home – and when the time came for him to receive his compulsory American-sitcom moral lesson, he delivered it upon himself, in front of Rodin's statue the Thinker in the Central City park, in the same pose: crouching, fist tucked under chin. Some sitcom clichés remained, however: episodes were full of people telling frustrating, easy fibs instead of revealing possibly uncomfortable truths, and, as the episode count soared, dramatic changes in the storyline were introduced to inject fresh impetus – in the 1961–62 season Dobie and Maynard enlisted in the army, where they were well out of place and the episodes suffered accordingly, and in 1962–63 they enrolled in college. Apart from the sequels, this was as far as *The Many Loves Of Dobie Gillis* went.

Big names of the future abounded in the series. Warren Beatty and Tuesday Weld became movie stars, Bob Denver went on to star in *Gilligan's Island* and recurring small-role players Jo Anne Worley, Jack Albertson and Ron Howard in *Rowan And Martin's Laugh-In*, *Chico And The Man* and *Happy Days* respectively. The one man whose career stalled after Dobie Gillis was Dwayne Hickman – he never again appeared in any regular series, and after the guest spots more or less dried up he went behind the cameras with an executive position at CBS, resurfacing most notably to appear in a pair of Dobie Gillis sequels.

A one-off special, *Whatever Happened To Dobie Gillis?* (actually a pilot that failed to be promoted to a full series), screened by CBS on 10 May 1977, showed Dobie, now 40, in partnership with his father in the grocery business. Dobie is married to Zelda and they have a 16-year-old son, Georgie, at high school, while Maynard has become a successful businessman. This was followed by a two-hour CBS TV movie, *Bring Me The Head Of Dobie Gillis*, aired on 21 February 1988, again intended as the springboard for a revival of a weekly half-hour series – and failing. In this, Dobie and Zelda run the store and Georgie attends high school (he had obviously stopped ageing for the last 11 years). Unless death ruled them out, all of the key actors from the 1959–63 series returned to resume their roles, except Warren Beatty and Tuesday Weld; Connie Stevens played Thalia.

Note. Despite its cult status in the USA, *The Many Loves Of Dobie Gillis* was never screened at the time on British television. One episode was shown within BBC2's themed *One Day In The 60s* extravaganza, however, broadcast day-long on August Bank Holiday 1993.

The Many Wives Of Patrick

UK · ITV (LWT) · SITCOM

20 × 30 mins · colour

*Series One (7) 4 Sep–23 Oct 1976 · Sat mostly 10pm

*Series Two (7) 27 May–8 July 1977 · Fri mostly 7.30pm

*Series Three (6) 21 Apr–19 May 1978 · Fri 7.30pm; 16 Mar 1980 · Sun 4.30pm

MAIN CAST

Patrick Woodford	Patrick Cargill
Harold	Robin Parkinson
Wife 1: Elizabeth Woodford	Ursula Howells
Wife 2: Nancy Grenville	Elspet Gray
Wife 3: Josephine Fabre	Wendy Williams
Wife 4: Laura Ryder	Bridget Armstrong
Wife 5: Betsy Vanderhoof	Lorna Dallas (series 3)
Wife 6: Helen Woodford	Elizabeth Counsell
Mother: Marian Woodford	Agnes Lauchlan
Daughter: Amanda Woodford	Wendy Padbury (series 1)
Daughter: Madeleine Woodford	Julie Dawn Cole (series 2 & 3)

CREDITS

writer Richard Waring · director/producer William G Stewart

Patrick Woodford is a successful and moneyed Bond Street antiques dealer, moving in society circles, who, in a Henry VIII-esque move, has been clumsy enough to marry six times. As the first series begins he is planning to divorce his sixth wife (Helen, played by Elizabeth Counsell) because she drives him mad. However, Patrick's solicitor advises him that he no longer has sufficient funds to foot the bill and suggests that, instead, he persuades this one to divorce him. She is reluctant to do so, and succeeding episodes find Patrick seeking the counsel of other previous wives – in particular Elizabeth, the first (played by Ursula Howells who had also been the ex-wife of Patrick Cargill's character in *Father, Dear Father*). Having realised that he made a mistake by divorcing Elizabeth in the first place – and perhaps because she is the only ex-wife who has not since remarried – Patrick would also like to remarry her.

Considering that the relationships have failed, it is remarkable – but so very convenient for the TV premise – to note how much Patrick sees of his former wives, and they pop up with great regularity throughout the three series. Elspet Gray (married in real life to Brian Rix) played Nancy, the dominating second wife; Wendy Williams was third wife Josephine, a French woman (ooh la la); and Bridget Armstrong played fourth wife Laura, a sexy glamour gal. Throughout the first two series, the fifth wife, Betsy, was referred to but never seen – however, she appeared right at the last, remarried to an American and realising, with

a horror shared by Patrick, that their 'quickie' Las Vegas-style divorce was not legal, indicating that they had both been committing bigamy ever since. Robin Parkinson appeared throughout as Harold, Patrick's all-purpose assistant at work and at home, and a number of Patrick's nine children and handful of grandchildren appeared from time to time.

With his upper-class life and notions, the Patrick Woodford character was something of a departure for writer Richard Waring, who had hitherto depicted the ups and downs of strictly middle-class relationships in such series as *Marriage Lines*, *Not In Front Of The Children*, *... And Mother Makes Three* (and its sequel *Five*), *My Wife Next Door*, *Bachelor Father* and *Second Time Around*.

Of passing interest is an American TV pilot screened by NBC on 1 August 1979 which may have been an adaptation of *The Many Wives Of Patrick*, although no specific acknowledgement of a British ancestor was apparent. Titled *The Three Wives Of David Wheeler*, it starred Art Hindle in the title role, whose third marriage is troubled by the permanent presence of his former wives. Written and produced by Jay Folb, and put into production by Filmways, it did not develop into a full series. With a clearer nod to the British version, CBS financed a pilot – actually titled *The Many Wives Of Patrick* – for its 1980–81 season. Here the focus was on an insurance agent married and divorced six times. It was never screened and no series followed.

*Note. These dates reflect London-area ITV screenings. They differed considerably elsewhere, with other areas not broadcasting the full quantity. Also, the first episode of the third series (seen in London on 21 April 1978) went out elsewhere as the last episode of the second (26 July 1977). The very last episode, screened in the capital on 16 March 1980 (almost two years after the last series finished) was shown in other regions on 7 August 1978.

Marblehead Manor

USA · SYNDICATION/NBC (DAMES/FRASER-GRAY/NARDINO PRODUCTIONS/PARAMOUNT) · SITCOM

24 × 30 mins · colour

US dates: 13 Sep 1987–29 May 1988

UK dates: 17 Jan–27 June 1989 (24 episodes) C4 Tue 6pm

MAIN CAST

Albert Dudley	Paxton Whitehead
Hilary Stonehill	Linda Thorson
Randolph Stonehill	Bob Fraser
Rick	Michael Richards
Jerry Stockton	Philip Morris
Dwayne Stockton	Rodney Scott Hudson
Lupe Lopez	Dyana Ortelli
Elvis Lopez	Humberto Ortiz

CREDITS

creators Bob Fraser/David Lloyd · *writers* various · *directors* various · *producers* Bob Fraser, Gary Nardino, Rob Dames

A pratfall-full sitcom set in a large mansion in Marblehead, Massachusetts, owned by Randolph Stonehill (played by the series co-creator and co-producer Bob Fraser). An oddball, hot-tempered millionaire who has made his fortune by marketing vegetable oil, Randolph and his sexy wife Hilary employ a peculiar bunch of servants, led by the British head butler Albert Dudley and including various clumsy nincompoops, bimbos and non-English-speaking foreigners, such as gardener Rick, odd-job-man Dwayne, chauffeur Jerry, cook Lupe and her young brattish son Elvis. Such is their ineptitude that Hilary frequently has to intervene between her husband and the staff.

Marblehead Manor was unusual for two reasons. The first was to do with content: it is very rare for US sitcoms to be rooted in farce, normally the province of the London stage and some British TV comedies. The second was to do with business: although the series was independently made for first-run syndication, *Marblehead Manor* was one of five sitcoms that NBC chose to 'checkerboard' across its weekday schedules in autumn 1987 as a means of combating the game-show *Wheel Of Fortune*, which was sweeping the ratings. (The other four included *Out Of This World* and *She's The Sheriff*.) The effort was unsuccessful. Indeed, if one considers that, to no great effect, NBC had already aired a pilot for a series set in what was then called Stonehill Manor (1 August 1984, under the title *Help!* – also known as *At Your Service*), then it's clear that *Marblehead Manor* was likely to fail, albeit not without raising a few laughs first.

Two members of the cast had British roots: Linda Thorson – although born in Canada she lived in England – best known for her role as Tara King in *The Avengers*; and Paxton Whitehead, the Shakespearean actor who left England for America in 1963 and never returned. (One of Whitehead's earliest Broadway roles was as replacement for Jonathan Miller in the revue *Beyond The Fringe '64*, alongside Peter Cook, Dudley Moore and Alan Bennett.)

Margie And Me

UK · ITV (YORKSHIRE) · SITCOM

1 × 30 mins · colour

6 July 1978 · Thu 7.15pm

MAIN CAST

Arthur	Arthur Mullard
Margie	Betty Marsden
Lilian	Vanessa Ford
Dennis	Nigel Lambert
Cheeseman	Norman Bird

CREDITS

writer John Graham · *director/producer* Stuart Allen

A single-episode comedy starring cockney comedy heavyweight Arthur 'Arfur' Mullard as a beer-swilling widower needing to find himself a new council flat. He turns for help to his loving daughter Lilian but she is less keen to assist when Arthur declares that he also wants his girlfriend Margie (Betty Marsden) to figure in the plans. Any hopes that this pilot may have led to a full series came to nothing.

Marjorie And Men

UK · ITV (ANGLIA) · SITCOM

6 × 30 mins · colour

28 June–2 Aug 1985 · Fri 8pm then 8.30pm

MAIN CAST

Marjorie Belton	Patricia Routledge
Alice Tripp	Patricia Hayes
Henry Bartlett	James Cossins
Sid Parkin	Ronnie Stevens
Beryl	Jeanne Watts

CREDITS

writers John Gorrie (3), Peter Spence (3) · *director* John Gorrie · *producer* John Rosenberg

The first starring sitcom role for RSC actress Patricia Routledge cast her as Marjorie Belton, a divorcee eagerly questing a new man in her life. Ever optimistic and adventurous, but with a necessary sense of humour, she goes about her man-chasing with what might in more innocent times have been called gay abandon, for despite being put through the mill by a hurtful divorce, her zest for men and Mills and Boon-style romance has not been curbed.

In the meantime, Marjorie has returned to living with her mother Alice, a super-smart but interfering busy-body intent not on stopping any romance but on starting one; indeed, if anything, Alice's eyes are peeled even more determinedly for a new son-in-law than her daughter's are for a husband. In the daytime, Marjorie holds down a responsible clerical post at a bank, where the under-manager Henry Bartlett has designs on her, and her closest colleague and confidant is Sid Parkin, a married man who cares for Marjorie but, holding steadfast to the sanctity of his own marriage, contains his feelings. In the evenings, she's most likely to be found frequenting the local 'singles' bar.

Each episode of the six-part series showed Marjorie pursuing a different man, which not only got the production out and about – location filming took place all over East Anglia – but was a handy way of introducing guest actors. She meets greengrocer George Banthorpe (Timothy West), who talks of nothing but his vegetables; glib-talking Frank Aston (John Quayle), with whom she tries out

sidecar racing; Norton Phillips (George Baker) at a dancing class her mother has persuaded her to attend; the charming Kenneth Beresford (Mark Kingston) at a hotel; and the bank's earthy painter and decorator Andy Ellis (John Judd).

Only the second networked sitcom to be made by ITV's East of England franchise Anglia (the first was *Backs To The Land*), *Marjorie And Men* pitched together two great Patricias: Routledge and Hayes. And while the series was not an unqualified success, it was certainly an interesting and worthwhile venture.

The Mark Thomas Comedy Product

UK · C4 (LAWLESS FILMS) · STANDUP

6 × 35 mins · colour

23 Feb–29 Mar 1996 · Fri 10.30pm

MAIN CAST

Mark Thomas

CREDITS

writer Mark Thomas · *director* Andy de Emmony · *producer* Geoff Atkinson

From his stage debut at the Fat Cats Club, at the White Lion pub in Putney, London, on 19 November 1985, Thomas has never turned his back on his socialist roots and beliefs, unashamedly performing as a politically angry lefty. Passionate though he is, a grin is never far from his lips, and his wide-boy personality makes his agitprop material more credible than many of his contemporaries. Thomas is also very funny, having a Ben Elton-like knack to worry away at a subject and reveal its lunacies. Though toning down his language, he makes no other concessions for television.

The series mixed standup (recorded in a pub the previous night) with satirical routines, such as revamping a tank as an ice-cream van and trying to get an export licence for it, or recruiting a band of Ethiopians to make a Band Aid-style record to raise money for drought-hit Britain.

A second series was scheduled for early 1998.

Marlene Marlowe Investigates

UK · BBC · CHILDREN'S SITCOM

30 × 20 mins · colour

Series One (15) 25 Sep 1993–1 Jan 1994 · BBC1 mostly Sat 8.15am

Series Two (15) 24 Sep–31 Dec 1994 · BBC1 mostly Sat 7.45am

MAIN CAST

Marlene Marlowe	Kate Copstick
Aunt Maud	Jo Kendall

CREDITS

writer Roy Apps · *executive producer* Christopher Pilkington · *producer* Martin Hughes

Marlene Marlowe was the world's worst private detective but thought of herself as the Puddlethorpe-On-Sea (her hometown) version of her US 'tec namesake Philip Marlowe. To accentuate this supposed similarity, Marlene talked to herself in a fake American accent. But it was Marlene's Aunt Maud – owner of a 750cc motorbike known as the Mighty Moped – who did most of the detecting and solved most of the crimes.

Slapstick comedy for the very young, combining live action with animation in stories written by the acclaimed children's author Roy Apps. (The characters originally appeared in a five-episode story, *The Puddlethorpe Carnival Coup*, broadcast by BBC Radio 4 within the children's strand *Cat's Whiskers* from 20 May to 17 June 1990.)

Marmalade Atkins In Space

see *Educating Marmalade*

Marriage Lines

UK · BBC · SITCOM

45 episodes (36 × 25 mins · 7 × 30 mins · 2 × short specials) · b/w

Series One (10 × 25 mins) 16 Aug–18 Oct 1963 · Fri mostly 8pm

Short special · part of *Christmas Night With The Stars* 25 Dec 1963 · Wed 8.05pm

Series Two (13 × 25 mins) 22 May–9 Aug 1964 · BBC1 Fri mostly 8.50pm then Sun around 8pm

Short special · part of *Christmas Night With The Stars* 25 Dec 1964 · BBC1 Fri 7.15pm

Series Three (7 × 25 mins) 5 Jan–16 Feb 1965 · BBC1 Tue 8pm

Series Four (6 × 25 mins) 22 Aug–26 Sep 1965 · BBC1 Sun mostly 7.25pm

Series Five (7 × 30 mins) 22 Apr–3 June 1966 · BBC1 Fri 7.30pm

MAIN CAST

George Starling · · · · · · · · · · Richard Briers
Kate Starling · · · · · · · · · · · Prunella Scales
Miles · · · · · · · · · · · · · · Edward de Souza
Peter · · · · · · · · · · · Ronald Hines (series 1)
Norah · · · · · · · · · · · Christine Finn (series 1)

OTHER APPEARANCES

Kate's mother · · · · · · · · · · · · Dorothy Black
George's mother · · · · · · · · · · · Diana King
George's father · · · · · · · · · Geoffrey Sumner

CREDITS

writer Richard Waring · *producers* Graeme Muir (series 1, 2 & first special), Robin Nash (series 3–5 & second special)

Subtitled for its first series 'A Quizzical Look At The Early Days Of Married Life', *Marriage Lines* (written in its early days as *The Marriage Lines*) reunited producer Graeme Muir, actor/writer Richard Waring and actor Richard Briers, all of whom had worked together on *Brothers In Law*. Waring devised the new show with Briers in mind and he was well served not only by the young comedy actor but also by co-star

Prunella Scales. As Mr and Mrs Starling, the two leads tackled the scripts of marital ups-and-downs with gusto and brought a charming amiability to the series that made it very popular in its day.

Episodes revolved around ordinary situations: money problems, retrospective jealousy, cookery crises, and so on, but the main comedy dynamic arose from George's yearning for the pub camaraderie of the single chaps at work (he was a junior clerk in an office) and Kate's increasing frustration at her domestic bondage. They argued regularly but their relationship was rarely threatened by these everyday pressures. In the third series Kate fell pregnant, eventually giving birth to a baby girl, Helen. The fourth series was thought to be the last and writer Waring tied up the show in an episode titled 'Goodbye George, Goodbye Kate', which ended with the couple leaving England to pursue George's new job in Lagos. However, a fifth series was then commissioned, and because Prunella Scales was pregnant in real life, it was decided to have Kate expecting again and use this to explain the Starlings' return to the UK. The second 'happy event' occurred in the final episode.

Two series of a radio version were made, again with Briers and Scales in the lead roles, acting scripts adapted by Waring. The first, 13 episodes, ran from 21 May to 13 August 1965; the second, also 13 episodes, from 19 March to 11 June 1967. Both were broadcast by the BBC Light Programme.

Married

see *United States*

Married For Life

UK · ITV (COLUMBIA TRISTAR/CARLTON FOR CENTRAL) · SITCOM

7 × 30 mins · colour

5 Mar–16 Apr 1996 · Tue 8.30pm

MAIN CAST

Ted Butler · · · · · · · · · · · · · · · Russ Abbot
Pam Butler · · · · · · · · · · · · · · · Susan Kyd
Nikki Butler · · · · · · · · · · · · · Lucy Blakely
Lee Butler · · · · · · · · · · · · · · Peter England
Steve Hollingsworth · · · · · · · Hugh Bonneville
Judy Hollingsworth · · · · · · · · Julie Dawn Cole

CREDITS

creators Michael G Moye/Ron Leavitt · *writers* various · *adapters* Carl Gorham/Michael Hatt · *director* Terry Kinane · *executive producer* Richard Boden · *producer* Paula Burdon

The British adaptation of the hit US series *Married ... With Children*, the dysfunctional family sitcom which, by February 1995, had notched up 200 episodes and was the longest-running sitcom in current production. *Married For Life* notched (if that's still the

right word) all of seven episodes before the plug was pulled – and rightly so too.

Russ Abbot starred as the unlikeable Mike Butler (Al Bundy in the US version), the sorry shoe salesman whose life is far from what he wishes it to be. His Barbie Doll-like, sex-hungry wife here was Pam (not Peggy), his children were Nikki and Lee (for Kelly and Bud), the dog was Clive (not Buck) and the neighbours Steve and Judy Hollingsworth (instead of Steve and Marcy Rhoades).

In adapting *Married ... With Children* Carlton was clearly hoping to repeat the success of **The Upper Hand**, the UK adaptation of the US series **Who's The Boss?** But this particular comedy just didn't translate and, surprisingly, giving the prowess of Abbot and Kyd, the acting was worryingly flat.

The failure of *Married For Life* did not deter Carlton from trying another translation, **Loved By You**, the UK version of *Mad About You*, screened in 1997.

Married ... With Children

USA · FOX (EMBASSY COMMUNICATIONS) · SITCOM

251 episodes (245 × 30 mins · 6 × 60 mins) · colour

US dates: 5 Apr 1987– 5 May 1997

*UK dates: 9 June 1989–18 Dec 1984 (77 × 30 mins · 3 × 60 mins) ITV weekends around 12 midnight

MAIN CAST

Al Bundy · · · · · · · · · · · · · · · · · Ed O'Neill
Peggy Bundy · · · · · · · · · · · · · Katey Sagal
Kelly Bundy · · · · · · · · · · Christina Applegate
Bud Bundy · · · · · · · · · · · · · David Faustino
Marcy Rhoades/D'Arcy · · · · Amanda Bearse
Steve Rhoades · · David Garrison (1987–90)
Jefferson D'Arcy · · · Ted McGinley (1990–97)
Luke Ventura · · · · · · · · Ritch Shydner (1987)
Seven Bundy · · · · · Shane Sweet (1992–93)

CREDITS

creators Michael G Moye/Ron Leavitt · *writers* Michael G Moye/Ron Leavitt, Sandy Sprung/Marcy Vosburgh, Kevin Curran, Ralph R Farquhar, Ellen L Fogle, Katherine D Green, Larry Jacobson, Stacie Lipp, Richard Gurman, Kim Weiskopf and others · *directors* Gerry Cohen, Linda Day, Tony Singletary, Amanda Bearse, Sam W Orender and others · *executive producers* Michael G Moye, Ron Leavitt, Katherine D Green, Richard Gurman, Kim Weiskopf · *producers* Katharine D Green, Richard Gurman, John Maxwell Anderson, Sandy Sprung, Marcy Vosburgh, Kevin Curran, Barbara Blachut Cramer, Stacie Lipp, Larry Jacobson

Along with **The Simpsons**, *Married ... With Children* was a key ingredient in the establishment of Fox as a viable 'fourth network' on US television. Ironically, it was the brouhaha surrounding the condemnation of the show by moral watchdogs that alerted many viewers to its existence and ensured that it became Fox's biggest hit.

Married … With Children was designed as an antidote to popular, somewhat anodyne series (like *The Cosby Show*) that depicted near-perfect families. The Bundys of *Married … With Children* were far from perfect. They were 'poor white trash' and unashamedly proud of the fact. For Al Bundy, life was hell. A born loser, he worked long hours for little money as a salesman in a shoe shop. And if there was one thing he hated, it was feet. Especially women's feet. Especially *fat* women's feet, which he seemed to have to handle more than any other kind. Al was married to the sexually voracious, shopaholic, sweet-addicted Peggy, a statuesque redhead who viewed her husband as a lifelong meal-ticket and had no qualms about rifling through his pockets for cash or spending recklessly on his credit cards. Al took all the indignities his wife heaped upon him with the air of one who knew too well that this was his lot in life. Al and Peggy had two children: the attractive and sexually promiscuous 'air-head' Kelly; and the sexually frustrated, academically bright Bud. They also had a large, soppy dog, Buck, whose thoughts were occasionally shared with the viewers (voiced by series' producer Kevin Curran). Then there were the Bundys' neighbours: Steve (initially) and Marcy, well-to-do professional people who, oddly, befriended the Bundys despite the yawning chasm between them in social standing. Steve was a normal enough chap but Marcy, although fine on the surface, had a raft of volatile layers bubbling just underneath, so that, when pushed, she exhibited a number of different personalities, from a violent madwoman to an oversexed animal. Later in the series Steve left her, and she remained a lonely single person until waking up one morning next to a thick-headed but handsome man, Jefferson D'Arcy, whom, it transpires, she married the evening before while drunk.

These then were the main players, but it was the raunchy content of *Married … With Children* that made it unique. On Fox, which liked to test the limits of acceptability on mainstream US TV, the series was permitted to poke about in mucky areas from which other networks would have shied away. Entire episodes revolved around themes of dubious taste (menstruation, strip-joints, murder) while much fun was wreaked from equally off-colour subjects in almost every episode (Bud's masturbating, Al's smelly feet, Al's toilet-blocking ablutions, Al's lack of prowess in the bedroom, Kelly's prowess in the bedroom). And the show wasn't above drawing cheap laughs from funny names, especially Peggy's maiden name (still the name of the rest of her family), Wanker (a joke appreciated more by a British audience than the American). In fact the series' desire to go to any lengths to raise a laugh was one

of its strengths – no subject was deemed too precious, no gag considered too low, and the writers made a virtue out of the bad taste by playing the vulgarity card with unabashed relish. Ed O'Neill was exceptional as the luckless, truly tormented Al, and Katey Sagal (formerly a member of the Harlettes, Bette Midler's backing group) was perfect as his appalling but appealing wife. And the show was often truly funny, full of great lines, squirmingly embarrassing scenes, outrageous plots and memorable characters. *Married … With Children* outlived all of its contemporary series and sustained a high-quality level of low humour throughout its run.

Notes. The episode of 17 March 1991 (US date) introduced two new characters, Charlie Veducci and his son Vinnie (played by future *Friends* star Matt LeBlanc). The pair then graduated to a short-lived spin-off sitcom, *Top Of The Heap* (Fox, 14 April–21 July 1991) and the character of Vinnie returned the following year in another brief series, *Vinnie And Bobby* (Fox, 30 May–5 September 1992).

A British version of *Married … With Children* was attempted – called *Married For Life*, it starred Russ Abbot, who had a similarly long face to Ed O'Neill. But the UK model, shorn of most of its vulgarity, flopped. Three May 1992 US episodes of *Married … With Children* were set in England and guest starred Bill Oddie, Alun Armstrong, Steven Hartley and Tony Steedman.

*London-area ITV screened 80 episodes over five years, and a number of other ITV regions screened the series at various times, but *Married … With Children* has been seen much more extensively on the satellite/cable channel Sky One, which stripped the episodes every week-night in the mid- to late-1990s.

Marry The Girls

UK · BBC · SITCOM

1 × 30 mins · colour

1 Feb 1973 · BBC1 Thu 8pm

MAIN CAST

Luke Elms	John Le Mesurier
Lottie Elms	Barbara Murray
Sarah Elms	Sally Stephens
Miranda Elms	Sally Thomsett
Julie Elms	Briony McRoberts
Emma Elms	Yvette Vanson
Kate Elms	Heather Bell

CREDITS

writer Godfrey Harrison · *producer* Graeme Muir

A *Comedy Playhouse* pilot for a proposed series focusing on the trials of Luke Elms, a highly paid executive who nevertheless finds it a financial and emotional strain to support a wife and five unmarried daughters. His solution? Marry off the girls.

The idea failed to develop into a series, but for one of the cast, former child star Sally

Thomsett, sitcom success was just a few months away in the shape of *Man About The House*.

The Marshall Chronicles

USA · ABC (SWEETUM PRODUCTIONS/VIACOM TELEVISION) · SITCOM

7 × 30 mins · colour

US dates: 4 Apr–22 July 1990 (6 episodes)

UK dates: 11 July–22 Aug 1991 (7 episodes) C4 Thu 6pm

MAIN CAST

Marshall Brightman	Joshua Rifkind
Johnny Parmetko	Gabriel Bologna
Melissa Sandler	Nile Lanning
Leslie Barash	Meredith Scott Lynn
Cynthia Brightman	Jennifer Salt
Michael Brightman	Steve Anderson
Sean Bickoff	Bradley Gregg
Ira Resnick	Brad Bradley
Vincent	Todd Graff

CREDITS

creator Richard Rosenstock · *writers* Richard Rosenstock (3), Lee Aronsohn (1), Ken Levine/David Isaacs (1), Jordan Moffet (1), not known (1) · *directors* James Burrows (2), Matthew Diamond (2), Michael Lembeck (2), not known (1)

A Jewish rites of passage sitcom neatly summed up by one US critic as 'Woody Allen meets *The Wonder Years*'. Joshua Rifkind (aged 24) played the 17-year-old Marshall Brightman, a thin, bespectacled angst-ridden adolescent who bore a physical resemblance to the young Woody Allen and sported a similar personality (to Allen's screen and stage persona at least). Marshall was a bright but awkward high school pupil who lived with his parents in Manhattan and lusted after fellow student Melissa, as did his classmate Johnny Parmetko. This rivalry provided the backdrop to most of the episodes.

Unfortunately, the low-key *Marshall Chronicles* failed to charm audiences to the same degree as *The Wonder Years* and it disappeared from US screens after only a few weeks.

Marti Caine … [various shows]

see CAINE, Marti

Millicent Martin

The versatile singer/comedian/actress Millicent Martin was born in Romford on 8 June 1934. Her vocal talents were soon evident and she appeared in the children's chorus of *The Magic Flute* at the Royal Opera House when 14 years of age. Later, she trod the boards as a chorus girl, and in her early twenties (1954–57) toured the USA for three years in a production of *The Boy Friend*. Back in London, Martin began attracting bigger and better roles, both on stage (notably in *Expresso Bongo*, 1959) and in feature films, but it was her weekly stint in the famous satire programme *That Was The Week That Was*, in which she sang a song pertaining to the week's news and appeared in short sketches, that propelled Martin's name to the top and led to her own TV series as well as a major and memorable role in the British film *Alfie* in 1966. But the stage seemed to remain Martin's first love and as her film and TV appearances became more rare she increased her theatre work, starring in many productions in London and on Broadway.

Not all of Millicent Martin's television appearances fall within the comedy category, so the following is not fully representative of her small-screen career.

Mainly Millicent

UK · ITV (ATV) · SKETCH

19 editions (7 × 35 mins · 6 × 30 mins) · b/w

Series One (6 × 30 mins) 12 June–24 July 1964 · Fri 10.05pm

Series Two (7 × 35 mins) 10 Apr–22 May 1965 · Sat 8.25pm

Series Three (6 × 30 mins) *Millicent* 25 May–29 June 1966 · Wed 9.10pm

MAIN CAST
Millicent Martin

CREDITS
writers Keith Waterhouse/Willis Hall (8), John Warren/John Singer (5), Sid Green/Dick Hills (4), Bryan Blackburn (2) · *directors/producers* Francis Essex (series 1 & 2), Jon Scoffield (series 3)

Three starring series for the woman who had become a household name in Britain through her appearances in *That Was The Week That Was*. She was joined each week by guest stars to help out in the comedy sketches, including Roy Castle (twice), Ron Moody, Kenneth Cope and Roger Moore in the first series; Castle again, Willie Rushton, Jack Douglas, Lance Percival and Dickie Henderson in the second.

The third series had a shortened title – *Millicent* – a new producer and new resident writers in Keith Waterhouse and Willis Hall. Otherwise the format remained much as before, Martin's guest stars including Bernard Cribbins, Kenneth Connor, Dudley Foster, Kenneth Cope, Bill Fraser and Henry McGee.

Note. Martin also had two starring TV shows on the BBC in 1963, but the accent in both was on music rather than humour. The first, *Millicent Martin Sings*, was a 15-minute programme screened on 3 May. The second, *Millie*, was a song and dance show broadcast on 4 August.

Millicent And Roy

UK · ITV (REDIFFUSION) · STANDUP/SKETCH

1 × 60 mins · b/w

5 Oct 1966 · Wed 9.15pm

MAIN CAST
Millicent Martin
Roy Castle

CREDITS
writers Ronnie Cass, Alec Grahame, Barry Cryer, Dick Vosburgh · *director* Bill Turner · *executive producer* Buddy Bregman

A one-hour special for Martin and Castle, combining comedy sketches with musical numbers.

From A Bird's Eye View

UK/USA · ITV (ITC FOR ATV)/NBC (SHELDON LEONARD PRODUCTIONS) · SITCOM

15 × 25 mins · colour

US dates: 29 Mar–16 Aug 1971

*UK dates: 16 Sep 1973–29 Mar 1975 (15 episodes) mostly Sun around 12 midnight

MAIN CAST
Millie Grover · · · · · · · · · · · Millicent Martin
Maggie Ralston · · · · · · · · · · · · Patte Finley
Clyde Beauchamp · · · · · · · · · · Peter Jones

CREDITS
writers T E B Clarke (2), Pat Dunlop (2), John Muir/Eric Geen (1), R S Allen/Harvey Bullock (1), Anthony Marriott/Scott Finch (1), Carl Kleinschmitt (1), Bernie Rothman (1), Tom Brennand/Roy Bottomley (1), Brad Ashton (1), Lew Schwarz (1), John Warren/John Singer (1), Stan Cutler (1), Sid Dorfman (1) · *directors* Ralph Levy (11), John Robins (2), Peter Duffell (2) · *producer* Jack Greenwood

A sitcom vehicle for Millicent Martin, who starred as Millie, a somewhat scatterbrained stewardess for International Airlines, who could never resist helping people even though it usually ended in trouble. She flew the London–America route with her more sensible American colleague Maggie (played by Patte Finley). Peter Jones appeared as their harassed boss.

The series was an international co-production, funded jointly by the then Sir Lew Grade's ITC and a US company which sold the series to NBC, but was shot in England (hence the call for such supporting players as Arthur Mullard, Jess Conrad, Richard Briers, Frank Thornton, Carmen Munro, Clive Dunn and John Laurie). The director was an American, Ralph Levy, who had worked with Jack Benny and George Burns.

Shortly after *From A Bird's Eye View* finished on US screens came a similar series, *Shirley's World*. This too starred a top name (Shirley MacLaine) gallivanting around the globe, was made in England by Lew Grade for the American executive producer Sheldon Leonard, and shared

many of the same writers and crew as the earlier series.

*Note. These dates refer to London-ITV screenings. The series suffered from inconsistent UK scheduling: Lew Grade's ATV broadcast 15 episodes between 18 September 1970 and 1 January 1971 but it wasn't shown in London until September 1973, when 12 programmes went out very late on Sunday nights. The remaining three were not seen in the capital until they were included in a repeat run in early 1975.

Martin Mull In Concert

UK · BBC · STANDUP

1 × 30 mins · colour

19 Apr 1973 · BBC1 Thu 10.10pm

MAIN CAST
Martin Mull

CREDITS
writer Martin Mull · *producer* Stanley Dorfman

A BBC one-off for American comic. Born in Chicago in 1943, Mull proved to be something of an acquired taste for audiences on both sides of the Atlantic, never quite achieving the elevated status of his contemporaries Steve Martin, John Belushi, Robin Williams and others. Mull divided his time between comedy acting (*Mary Hartman, Mary Hartman* and *Roseanne*) and a standup act that often drew humour from musical instruments – he enjoyed a minor success with 'Duelling Tubas', his brass version of the hit instrumental 'Duelling Banjos'.

Marty Feldman ... [various shows]

see FELDMAN, Marty

Mary

USA · CBS (MTM ENTERPRISES) · SITCOM

13 × 30 mins · colour

US dates: 11 Dec 1985–8 Apr 1986

UK dates: 6 Sep–6 Dec 1987 (13 episodes) ITV Sun 12.30am

MAIN CAST
Mary Brenner · · · · · · · · · · Mary Tyler Moore
Frank DeMarco · · · · · · · · · · James Farentino
Ed LaSalle · · · · · · · · · · · · · · · · · John Astin
Jo Tucker · · · · · · · · · · · · · · · · Katey Sagal
Vincent Tully · · · · · · · · · · · · · · David Byrd
Lester Mintz · · · · · · · · · · · · · James Tolkan
Susan Wilcox · · · · · · · · · · · Carlene Watkins
Harry Dresden · · · · · · · · · Harold Sylvester
Ronnie Dicker · · · · · · · · · · · Derek McGrath

CREDITS
creators Ken Levine/David Isaacs · *writers* David Isaacs, Dennis K Koenig, Douglas Koenig, Ken Levine, Merrill Markoe, Gary Markowitz, Emily

Prudum Marshall, Tom Patchett, Patrick Proft, Donald Reiker, Tom Straw, Phoef Sutton, Jay Tarses, Jennifer Tilly, Douglas P Wyman, Shelley F Zellman · *directors* various · *producers* Ken Levine/David Isaacs

A vehicle for Mary Tyler Moore that cast her back into familiar territory: newsrooms. *The Mary Tyler Moore Show* had been set at a TV station, *Mary* was based at a newspaper. But there was one major difference between the two series: *The Mary Tyler Moore Show* was one of the best and most influential sitcoms of all time, blessed with some superb scripts; *Mary* was not. Few watched it and it was cancelled by CBS after one short season.

Moore starred as Mary Brenner, a divorcee in her forties, happily writing for a fashion/glamour magazine, *Woman's Digest*, until, following an executive shuffle, it folds and she is forced to look for another job. She lands one as consumer-issues correspondent for a piffling low-brow tabloid daily newspaper, the *Chicago Eagle*, recognising that the post is beneath her dignity but being in no position to refuse. There she works alongside a gaggle of characters such as one meets in any sitcom. As managing editor Frank DeMarco rules the roost – a sensation-seeker in all that he does, he also happens to fancy Mary, which is why he has given her a job; conceited Ed LaSalle (played by John Astin, Gomez in *The Addams Family*) is the theatre correspondent; Ronnie Dicker is the sports writer; cynical Jo Tucker (played by Katey Sagal, future star of *Married ... With Children*) is a feature writer whose chain-smoking causes Mary anguish because she sits opposite; Harry Dresden is the crime reporter; and Vincent Tully is the sub editor, appalling at his job (not surprising, because he's blind) but union protected.

At home, Mary is friendly with her neighbour Susan, who is engaged to a Mafioso, Lester. These two characters were quickly cut out of the storyline after CBS realised that the series needed emergency surgery. In the end, though, the body passed away after just 13 episodes.

Mary Hartman, Mary Hartman

USA · SYNDICATION (TAT PRODUCTIONS) · SITCOM

325 × 30 minutes · colour

US dates: 5 Jan 1976–July 1977

UK dates: 20 June–22 Aug 1980 (9 episodes) ITV Fri mostly 10.30pm

MAIN CAST

Mary Hartman	Louise Lasser (1976–77)
Tom Hartman	Greg Mullavey
Martha Shumway	Dody Goodman
George Shumway	Phil Bruns (1976–77);
	Tab Hunter (1977–78)
Cathy Shumway	Debralee Scott
Loretta Haggers	Mary Kay Place
Steve Fletcher	Ed Begley Jr

Mayor Merle Jeeter	Dabney Coleman
Garth Gimble	Martin Mull

CREDITS

writers various · *directors* various · *executive producer* Norman Lear · *producers* Lew Gallo, Eugenie Ross-Leming, Perry Krauss, Vivi Knight, Brad Buckner

A real novelty and pacesetter in the annals of US television, *Mary Hartman, Mary Hartman* was a daily afternoon pastiche of daily afternoon soap operas, high on comedy but decidedly dark with it, a black comedy in the original sense of the word. It ran in syndication (meaning that it was independently produced and not affiliated to any of the major US networks) for some 18 months, amassing 325 episodes in the process. Sequels took this figure into the stratosphere. In the UK *MHMH* received only a limited screening – London ITV began showing it in June 1980, one episode per week. At that rate it would have taken in excess of six years to get through the lot, but the UK run petered out after just nine episodes.

MHMH was produced by Norman Lear, the most successful US TV producer of the 1970s, with *All In The Family* (the US translation of *Till Death Us Do Part*) and *Sanford And Son* (the US *Steptoe And Son*) having made their mark in a major way, not only by causing audiences to laugh but also by forcing US TV comedy into new and much more controversial territory, embracing as they did bigotry, racism, homosexuality and other topics hitherto considered taboo by the sensitive US TV market. Controversy also walked hand-in-hand with *MHMH*: many of its characters and storylines were bad-taste exaggerations of the already sensationalist soaps it spoofed: Mary's husband Tom suffered from impotence, her sister Cathy was promiscuous, her grandfather Raymond Larkin was a flasher, an eight-year-old evangelist was electrocuted, a local wife-beater was impaled on a Christmas tree and another was drowned in a bowl of chicken soup. The heroine herself, Mary Hartman (played by Louise Lasser, former wife of Woody Allen), was a youthful 34-year-old housewife addicted to – and an absolute believer in – TV commercials.

MHMH came to end in the summer of 1977, the pressure of producing five episodes every week having proved too great. Louise Lasser quit and a sequel began without her, *Forever Fernwood* (this and the original series were both set in the fictional town of Fernwood, Ohio), which ran for 130 episodes. *Fernwood 2-Night* – which then became *America 2Night* – was another 130-episode spin-off, this time parodying talk-shows rather than soaps; a similar British series was written by Ruby Wax and screened by C4 in 1983 as *For 4 Tonight*. The best *MHMH* legacy of all,

though, was *Soap*, unrelated in terms of production company or actors but clearly picking up the *MHMH* spoof-serial baton.

The Mary Tyler Moore Show

USA · CBS (MTM ENTERPRISES) · SITCOM

168 × 30 mins · colour

US dates: 19 Sep 1970–19 Mar 1977

UK dates: 13 Feb 1971–29 Dec 1972 (34 episodes) BBC1 Sat 5.50pm then Fri 6.50pm

MAIN CAST

Mary Richards	Mary Tyler Moore
Lou Grant	Edward Asner
Ted Baxter	Ted Knight
Murray Slaughter	Gavin MacLeod
Rhoda Morgenstern	Valerie Harper (1970–74)
Phyllis Lindstrom	Cloris Leachman (1970–75)
Bess Lindstrom	Lisa Gerritsen (1970–75)
Sue Ann Nivens	Betty White
Georgette Franklin/Baxter	Georgia Engel

CREDITS

creators/executive producers James L Brooks/ Allan Burns · *writers* David Lloyd (31), Bob Ellison (15), Treva Silverman (15), Ed Weinberger/Stan Daniels (12), Ed Weinberger (8), Martin Cohan (8), Steve Pritzker (8), David Davis/Lorenzo Music (7), James L Brooks/Allan Burns (6) and others · *directors* Jay Sandrich (118) and others · *producers* Ed Weinberger/Stan Daniels, David Davis/Lorenzo Music

A landmark US sitcom that returned *Dick Van Dyke Show* star Mary Tyler Moore triumphantly to the small-screen and gave a generation of single American women a TV character in whom they could finally believe. It is virtually impossible to describe to British readers the place that *The Mary Tyler Moore Show* occupies in the hearts of a certain generation of Americans, but even without a knowledge of the social revolution in the US, and the ripples that the women's movement was causing at the time, it is not difficult to understand why the series was such a huge success: it had 'class' written all over it. Tight writing, spot-on characterisations and fast-paced plots lifted the series piece out of the norm and into the rarefied heights of sitcom heaven. The production evidently functioned as a hothouse, nurturing, developing and honing talent to the extent that virtually all of the creative crew went on to further triumphs with such series as *Taxi*, *The Bob Newhart Show* and *Cheers*.

The format was straightforward enough: Mary Richards was the lead character, a single woman (she was to have been a divorcee, but the writers then decided to depict her as unmarried) who leaves New York following the break-up of a relationship and arrives in Minneapolis, with its freezing temperatures and biting winds. Here she gets a job in the newsroom at a local TV station, WJM, reporting to the news producer Lou

Grant, a man who, at first, seems frostier than the weather but soon thaws to become a close friend – albeit a hard-edged and deeply cynical one. Mary's newsroom colleagues include the nervy but delightfully witty Murray Slaughter, the station's sole news writer; and the TV newsreader/anchorman Ted Baxter whose colossal stupidity is perfectly balanced by his colossal ego; among the other staff at WJM is Sue Ann Nivens, the catty presenter of *The Happy Homemaker Show*. Away from the office, Mary rents an apartment from the awful snob Phyllis Lindstrom (mother of Bess and wife of the never-seen Lars) but finds true female friendship – following a rocky start – with her upstairs neighbour Rhoda Morgenstern. Episodes concerned Mary's attempts to do well at work and remain loyal to her friends and colleagues even though she often seemed to be used by others.

While all of this added up to a robust premise, it wasn't the situation that made the series a hit so much as the marvellous ensemble playing that brought the characters to life. Mary Tyler Moore was especially good in a difficult role that could have so easily become bland in less adept hands, and she had generous support, most notably from Ed Asner as the irascible Lou, and Valerie Harper as the fiery Rhoda. The relationships between all the key characters seemed more real than was the norm for such fare, credit for which must go to Moore herself.

Following the demise of *The Dick Van Dyke Show*, Mary Tyler Moore had struggled to maintain her position as a major player, being particularly disappointed with the reaction to the feature film *Thoroughly Modern Millie*, which she had hoped would pave the wave to movie stardom. Impressed by another TV appearance with Dick Van Dyke in 1969 (*Dick Van Dyke And The Other Woman*), CBS decided that Moore might be just the star they needed to front a sitcom of appeal to a sophisticated audience. Moore was unsure and unwilling to commit, fearing any new role might suffer in comparison with her Laura character in *The Dick Van Dyke Show*, already cemented as one of the most popular parts in US TV history. However, when she talked the idea over with her husband, 20th Century-Fox executive Grant Tinker, they came up with a deal to offer CBS: she would do the series only on the condition that she and Tinker were given total control over the creation, casting and production, arguing that in a climate free from network interference they would have a better chance of coming up with a true original. CBS agreed, a wise decision as it turned out. To create the format, Tinker brought in James L Brooks and Allan Burns, with whom he had worked previously on the US schoolroom drama series *Room 222*

(1969–74) and they all set about the task of gathering together a group of keen young writers. Next, they took another bold step, casting a group of relatively unknown actors to play the main cast, rather than choosing more recognisable faces from the usually incestuous world of TV comedy. This ploy proved successful and became the norm later when casting for such ensemble shows as *Taxi* and *Cheers*. With the full team in harness and artistic control in their hands, they put *The Mary Tyler Moore Show* into production.

While not an instant success, the series did well enough in its early days to ensure its survival and then benefited from being scheduled as part of CBS's Saturday comedy night, guaranteed good viewing figures by the presence of ratings phenomenon *All In The Family* which kick-started the quintet of series that comprised most of that evening's schedule. In the 1973–74 season it became part of what is arguably the strongest line-up of comedy ever aired in the US: *All In The Family*, *M*A*S*H*, *The Mary Tyler Moore Show*, *The Bob Newhart Show* and **The Carol Burnett Show**. After 168 episodes, Moore and Tinker decided that the time had come to pull the plug, rightly figuring the wisdom of quitting while they were still ahead; *The Mary Tyler Moore Show* won 29 Emmy Awards, still (at 1997) a record for a US TV series, irrespective of genre.

Although the series was consistently funny, one episode stands out in sitcom lore, 'Chuckles Bites The Dust', in which Chuckles, a clown known by everyone at WJM, is killed (in costume as Peter Peanut, he is crushed when an elephant attempts to shell him). Mary is distraught, and angry that her colleagues – laughing hysterically about some of the funny incidents and accidents in Chuckles' life, and the manner of his death – seem disrespectful at his passing. Mary embarrasses them all into paying proper respect but at the funeral service memories of Chuckles flood into her mind and, despite desperate attempts to stifle her giggling, she finally explodes into laughter. The episode is a gem and features many of the attributes that graced the whole series.

The Mary Tyler Moore Show spawned two spin-offs during its long run: *Rhoda* and *Phyllis* and also gave belated birth to three more, the comedies *The Ted Knight Show* (CBS, 1978) and **The Betty White Show** and the drama series *Lou Grant* (CBS, 1977–82). (Additionally, comedy actor Paul Sand was given a series, *Paul Sand In Friends And Lovers*, on the strength of a single appearance as an income tax auditor in *The Mary Tyler Moore Show*; and there was another pilot – screened by CBS on 4 March 1972 – for a sitcom that failed to develop: titled *The Councilman* it featured two non-

MTM characters but Mary, in the role of Mary Richards, and Ted Knight, as Ted Baxter, both appeared to give it a helpful shove.) More importantly, however, *The Mary Tyler Moore Show* resulted in the founding of MTM Enterprises, which quickly went on to become one of the most creative and innovative independent production companies in the USA and gave rise to, among other series, **WKRP In Cincinnati** and dramas *Remington Steele*, *St Elsewhere* and *Hill Street Blues*.

Notes: *The Mary Tyler Moore Show* was first seen in Britain on BBC1, which showed 34 episodes concurrent with the US run. A decade later, between 30 January 1984 and 23 August 1985, C4 screened 39 episodes, commencing again with the pilot. The vast majority of the episodes, therefore, have never been seen on British TV, an oversight that requires remedy.

On 18 February 1991, CBS aired *Mary Tyler Moore: The 20th Anniversary Show*, a 90-minute special that reunited the principal cast members for a nostalgic look back at the series.

See also the **All In The Family** footnote.

The Mary Whitehouse Experience

UK · BBC (*SPITTING IMAGE PRODUCTIONS) · SKETCH

13 × 30 mins · colour

*Pilot · 3 Oct 1990 · BBC2 Wed 9pm

*Series One (6) 3 Jan–7 Feb 1991 · BBC2 Thu 9pm

Series Two (6) 2 Mar–6 Apr 1992 · BBC2 Mon 9pm

MAIN CAST
Steve Punt
Hugh Dennis
Rob Newman
David Baddiel

CREDITS
writers cast · director/producer Marcus Mortimer

The TV version of a sketch series originally broadcast under the same title and performed by the same quartet on BBC Radio 1.

The irreverent, hip humour of *The Mary Whitehouse Experience* came across to TV viewers as fresh and energetic, even though many of the routines were quite traditional in approach. Items were usually linked by one of the team setting the scene and the sketches varied from full-costume pieces on tailor-made sets to simple two-handers on a couch with no pretence at situation. Although the comedy covered universal themes, the sketches were quick-paced, being kept as short as possible to give the series a breath-less dynamic and a 1990s edge. Added to the mix were computer graphics, a stylish, rock-show-type industrial setting and other

contemporary motifs. The two double-acts complemented each other and the four worked well as a group.

The Mary Whitehouse Experience had its detractors, though, critics who found the humour occasionally tasteless and juvenile, but for its core group of young admirers at whom the show was aimed it scored heavily. Newman and Baddiel proved particularly popular and became major headlining artists during the run of the series, accorded pop star status and gaining their own series, *Newman And Baddiel In Pieces*. Punt and Dennis also progressed to their own series (*The Imaginatively-Titled Punt & Dennis Show*) as well as the ITV sitcom *Me, You And Him*.

The title *The Mary Whitehouse Experience* was, of course, a flippant reference to Mary Whitehouse, the tireless 'clean-up TV' campaigner who waged war against the excesses of television (and the BBC in particular) from the 1960s to 1990s.

Note. There were three series of *The Mary Whitehouse Experience* on Radio 1. The first, spanning 24 editions, ran from 7 April to 6 October 1989; the second, 11, aired from 6 January to 24 March 1990; the last, nine, spanned 20 October to 15 December 1990.

The Mascot

UK · BBC · SITCOM

1 × 25 mins · b/w
24 Jan 1964 · Fri 7.35pm

MAIN CAST
Mr Gibson · · · · · · · · · · · · · Dudley Foster
Billy Carter · · · · · · · · · · · · · Robert Dorning
Arnold Birtwistle · · · · · · · · · · · Joe Gladwin
Doris Birtwistle · · · · · · · · · · · · Clare Kelly

CREDITS
writers Vince Powell/Frank Roscoe · *producer* John Ammonds

A *Comedy Playhouse* episode featuring north-country comedy favourite Joe Gladwin as Arnold Birtwistle, a life-long fanatical supporter of – and club mascot for – Northtown Football Club, known as 'The Reds'. The dry Dudley Foster played Mr 'Moneybags' Gibson, Northtown's new chairman, who is determined to change the club's image regardless of the fans' wishes. His first job is to get rid of the mascot and from that clash sprang the comedy in this pilot, which never gained promotion to a series. However, the show's theme of sport versus commerce remains forever pertinent.

M*A*S*H

USA · CBS (20TH CENTURY FOX-TELEVISION) · SITCOM

251 episodes (247 × 30 mins · 3 × 60 mins · 1 × 150 mins) · 250 × colour · 1 × b/w

US dates: 17 Sep 1972–28 Feb 1983
UK dates: 20 May 1973–9 Mar 1988 (249 × 30 mins · 2 × 60 mins · 1 × 150 mins) BBC2 various days and times

MAIN CAST
Capt Benjamin Franklin 'Hawkeye' Pierce · Alan Alda
Capt John 'Trapper' McIntyre · Wayne Rogers (1972–75)
Capt B J Hunnicut · · · Mike Farrell (1975–83)
Maj Margaret 'Hot Lips' Houlihan · Loretta Swit
Lt-Col Henry Blake · · · · · · · McLean Stevenson · (1972–75)
Col Sherman T Potter · · · · · · · Henry Morgan · (1975–83)
Maj Frank Burns · · · Larry Linville (1972–77)
Maj Charles Emerson Winchester III · · · · · · · · · · · · · · · David Ogden Stiers (1977–83)
Cpl Walter 'Radar' O'Reilly · · · · Gary Burghoff · (1972–79)
Cpl Maxwell Klinger · · · Jamie Farr (1973–83)
Fr John Francis Patrick Mulcahy · George Morgan (pilot); · · · · · · · · · · · William Christopher (series)

OTHER APPEARANCES
'Spearchucker' Jones · · · · · · Timothy Brown · (1972)
Lt Maggie Dish · · · · · · · Karen Philipp (1972)
Ho-John · · · · · · · · · · · Patrick Adiarte (1972)
Nurse Margie Cutler · · · · · Marcia Strassman · (1972–73)
Ugly John · · · · · · · · John Orchard (1972–73)
Gen Brandon Clayton · · · · · · · · Herb Voland · (1972–73)
Lt Ginger Ballis · · · · · · · · Odessa Cleveland · (1972–74)
Gen Mitchell · · · · Robert F Simon (1973–74)
Nurse Kellye · · · Kellye Nakahara (1974–83)
Igor · · · · · · · · · · · · Jeff Maxwell (1976–83)
Sgt Rizzo · · · · · · · · · · G W Bailey (1981–83)

CREDITS
*M*A*S*H creator* Richard Hooker · *TV series creators* Larry Gelbart/Gene Reynolds · *main writers* Larry Gelbart, Laurence Marks, Ken Levine/David Isaacs, Jim Fritzell/Everett Greenbaum, Linda Bloodworth, Alan Alda, Thad Mumford/Dan Wilcox, Dennis K Koenig, David Pollock/Elias Davis · *main directors* Gene Reynolds, Hy Averback, Jackie Cooper, Don Weis, William Jurgensen, Larry Gelbart, Burt Metcalfe, Charles S Dubin, Alan Alda, George Tyne, Harry Morgan · *executive producers* Gene Reynolds (1976–77 season), Burt Metcalfe (1979–80, 1981–82, 1982–83) · *producers* Gene Reynolds (1972–73), Gene Reynolds/Larry Gelbart (1973–74, 1974–75, 1975–76), Don Reo/Alan Katz/Burt Metcalfe (1976–77), Burt Metcalfe (1977–78, 1978–79), John Rappaport/Jim Mulligan (1979–80), Thad Mumford/Dan Wilcox (1981–82, 1982–83)

A giant sitcom – undoubtedly one of the finest ever – that remains much revered around the world, where it is still screened in re-runs.

In his successful novel *MASH*, Dr Richard Hornberger – writing under the pseudonym Richard Hooker, and assisted by writing partner W C Heinz – turned his real-life Korean War experiences as a surgeon at the 8055 Mobile Army Surgical Hospital

(colloquially known as MASH) into the fictional adventures of a trio of medics at the 4077 MASH. (The trio were 'Trapper' John McIntyre, Walter Waldowski and 'Hot Lips' Houlihan.) It was the first in a long series of books featuring the characters, and Ingo Preminger, brother of film director Otto, purchased the screen rights, employing the one-time blacklisted writer Ring Lardner Jr to adapt it for the cinema. Lardner created a dark, bitter screenplay that brought out the anti-establishment, anti-authoritarian flavour of the premise, making it far more savage than the original books. The perceived anti-Americanism of the script worried many of those approached to direct the movie but eventually Hollywood maverick Robert Altman – an uncompromising individual with a distinctive film-making philosophy – was engaged, and the resulting film (starring Donald Sutherland, Elliott Gould, Tom Skerritt and Sally Kellerman) was an unexpected financial and critical success, even winning an Oscar for Best Screenplay. William Self, president of the film's production company 20th Century-Fox, then hit upon the idea of turning the movie into a TV series, figuring they could cut production costs by using the still-standing *M*A*S*H* sets in the studio and nearby Malibu Hills. ABC and CBS both expressed interest in such a project, but with reservations. In the end CBS were the first to commit the money for a pilot and William Self hired the producer Gene Reynolds to oversee the project. It was an exciting prospect, but one that seemed doomed – just how would a TV version of a film that pivoted on profanity, sexual situations, nudity, gruesome man-inflicted injuries and perceived anti-patriotism be acceptable to the rigidly controlled, controversy-shy broadcast industry?

But US TV was changing. *All In The Family* had broken through many of the networks' taboos and proved the existence of an audience for adult-orientated sitcoms. Gene Reynolds flew to London and convinced the American producer Larry Gelbart (who was working with Marty Feldman at the time) to come on board. Both were convinced that the only way to make *M*A*S*H* work was to keep it as tough as possible and to give it a classy air by shooting on film rather than video, utilising more exterior scenes than was the norm for a sitcom. They cast anew, retaining from the film only Gary Burghoff, as 'Radar', and slightly altering the emphasis to give the principal roles to two doctors, 'Trapper' and the newly invented 'Hawkeye' Pierce (who was much like the original Walter Waldowski). The casting was excellent right down the line but the inspired choice of Alan Alda as Hawkeye was one of the major factors in the show's fantastic successes in the ensuing years.

The TV series initially mirrored the format of the film, which itself had been somewhat episodic, relaying the sheer horror of the war in Korea as seen by the medics, nurses and support staff working at a MASH. Their non-militaristic backgrounds – coupled with the intense pressures under which they worked – made them a flippant, irreverent bunch who responded to the day-to-day real-life nightmarish scenes by taking refuge in illicit alcohol, mortuary humour, authority-baiting and casual sex. The central figure in all of this was Hawkeye, a cross between Groucho Marx and Dr Kildare, whose rapier wit was matched only by his skill with a scalpel and his humanity. Pierce kept up a constant stream of wisecracks beneath his surgical mask while his hands battled deftly to save the life of his bullet-torn and blown-apart patients on the operating table. Pierce's tent-mate and best pal was Trapper, a doctor with a similar sense of humour. Adding colour was Klinger, a man who constantly dressed in women's clothing in the hope that affecting transvestism would convince the authorities that he wasn't fit to serve and should be sent home to America. (It failed to work.) The commanding officer was the laid-back Henry Blake, whose assistant, O'Reilly, was given the nickname Radar on account of his twin abilities to hear incoming helicopters (carrying more wounded soldiers) before anyone else and pre-guess the needs of his colleagues. The head nurse was 'Hot Lips' Houlihan, a formidable woman who considered the behaviour of Hawkeye, Trapper, Klinger and others to be childish and unprofessional. Her opinions were shared by the man with whom she was conducting a discreet affair, Major Frank Burns, a loathsome, spineless weasel of a man who considered Hawkeye's antics worthy of court-martial – and he knew them better than most because he shared a tent with Hawkeye and Trapper. Also among the main cast was Father Mulcahy, a gentle 'man of the cloth' who was not above a good laugh and endeared himself to everyone with his common sense and the self-doubt that crept into his beliefs as he witnessed, day after day, soldiers and innocent victims alike being killed and mutilated in a senseless war.

The Korean War (actually, it wasn't even classified as a war but a 'police action') ran from June 1950 to July 1953 and was responsible for the deaths of 2,151,763 people, of which 71,500 were members of the UN forces (with a further 83,263 missing in action and 250,000 wounded) and made three million Koreans homeless. M*A*S*H not only reflected the futility and sheer madness of the war but, crucially, was made at a time when US soldiers were engaged in another senseless, prolonged and deeply damaging action in the Far East: the Vietnam War.

Although viewers recognised that the TV series was set in Korea, the parallels were blindingly obvious, and the series undoubtedly made a significant contribution to the anti-Vietnam War thinking that was growing in the USA in the early 1970s.

At first, M*A*S*H concentrated on the crew's lighter adventures, exploring the sexual situations, gambling and drinking escapades that had featured in the film, but even in the first season there were some bold new storylines that indicated the darker areas into which the series was prepared to venture. At the end of the first season it had performed just well enough in the ratings to escape cancellation, but CBS's programmer-in-chief, Fred Silverman, thought the series had greater potential and scheduled it in a dream position, between established smashes *All In The Family* and **The Mary Tyler Moore Show**. The second season saw M*A*S*H prove Silverman right, becoming a huge commercial and critical success. With a blossoming confidence, the producers further propelled the show into hitherto unexplored areas for television: unashamed anti-war viewpoints, heroic anti-establishment characters, the moral questioning of the government and, most groundbreakingly of all, the sympathetic portrayal of 'the enemy' as ordinary, helpless people and the implication that 'authority' was the real adversary. That all this was pushed forward along with – not instead of – some superbly funny scripts underlines the brilliant writing and majestic performances that marked out every episode as unmissable.

Behind the scenes there were certain areas of discord, however. The elevation of Hawkeye to centre-stage meant that Wayne Rogers (Trapper) and McLean Stevenson (Blake) had reduced roles, and, reportedly, they made their disappointment clear. They both left at the end of the third series, Trapper abruptly, with no explanation given until the following season, Henry Blake to go home. Chillingly, he never made it, the 4077th learning of his death in a helicopter crash. (Stevenson was convinced this was a spoiling ploy, to prevent him from returning or exploiting the character in a different series – the producers claim the demise was consistent with M*A*S*H sensibilities.) A new character, B J Hunnicut, was Trapper's replacement, a slightly more serious type perhaps but equally susceptible to Pierce's influence and equally at home with the wilder antics. The new camp commander was Colonel Sherman Potter, more establishment than Blake but similarly tolerant of Pierce's capers, recognising his worth as a surgeon and that the incredible pressures under which his doctors and nurses were working needed an outlet. Frank Burns left at the end of the fifth season, finally snapping mentally following

the marriage of Hot Lips (whom he had treated terribly) to Donald Penobscott (rarely seen in the series). Burns' replacement was the supremely snobbish Winchester, a surgeon whose wit and skills were the equal of Hawkeye's but whose class-consciousness prevented him from joining in and becoming one of the boys.

By this time changes were occurring to the main characters too: in particular, Hawkeye was becoming a more rounded, less jokey character than before – the war was clearly wearing him down. Hot Lips also mellowed, beginning to come around to Pierce's way of thinking and questioning the morality of the war. Her marriage ended in divorce and in one memorable two-parter, she and Pierce – caught behind enemy lines – were driven into each other's arms and a brief but liberating sexual liaison. Klinger eventually stopped wearing dresses and Radar returned home, his tour of duty at an end. Even Winchester was gradually reshaped into a rounder, slightly more likeable character and towards the end of M*A*S*H virtually the only conflict was the ongoing war itself.

During the run, the main cast became increasingly involved with the development of the series, Alan Alda writing and directing many episodes, other members writing, directing or suggesting storylines. But there was no doubt that the longevity of the series was taking its toll and Alda, among others, thought that it was diminishing in quality by the ninth season. They decided that the tenth would be the last, but CBS, desperate to keep it going for one more money-making year, offered them a tempting carrot if they agreed to just one more season – the chance to finish with a two-hour blockbuster, bringing the groundbreaking series to a memorable finish. Alda, who was to direct the episode, could see the merit in the idea and his vote swung it, thus an eleventh season went into production.

And so it came down to the famous finishing episode, a mammoth two-and-a-half-hour US TV slot (Alda was reluctant to cut it shorter and CBS was keen to sell the extra half hour advertising space) that was seemingly awaited by all of America. It paid off – the extended edition was akin to the very best of M*A*S*H, combining comedy, drama, emotional trauma and anti-war propaganda in a devastating brew, with Father Mulcahy suffering permanent blindness, Hawkeye a nervous breakdown and the cast members, one by one, leaving Korea for home (except for Klinger, that is, who married a local woman; ironically, the man who, visibly at least, had seemed the most desperate to leave was the only one not to do so). The episode was seen by 125 million Americans (a 77 per cent share), easily the most-watched US television programme to that time.

The inevitable spin-offs and sequels duly followed. *Trapper John MD* (CBS, 1979–86, some episodes screened by London-ITV from 26 June 1983) was a medical drama series set in contemporary times and featured Pernell Roberts as an older, wiser John McIntyre. *AfterMASH* (CBS, 1983–84) continued the adventures of Klinger, Potter and Father Mulcahy in civvy street, with the *M*A*S*H* actors reprising their roles. And *Walter* (aka *Radar*), with Gary Burghoff, was a pilot that aired on CBS on 17 July 1984 but failed to develop further. It is fair to say that none of these ventures came anywhere close to matching the majesty of the original series, which garnered 109 Emmy Award nominations, winning 14. On 25 November 1991, CBS aired a 90-minute special, *Memories Of M*A*S*H*, which looked back at the series with clips and cast interviews.

M*A*S*H was also a success in the UK, where – to its eternal credit – the BBC transmitted the series without the absolutely unnecessary 'canned' laugh-track that blighted the US version. The *M*A*S*H* film director Robert Altman is on record as saying that he thought the TV series was terrible, the 'most insidious form of propaganda … they don't show the blood, the horror. They don't make you pay for the laugh.' Although these sentiments may hold true for early episodes, they seem less pertinent for the middle and later years when, in some people's eyes, the TV writers might have been accused of making viewers pay too much for the laughs. These very few detractors aside, *M*A*S*H*, entirely deservedly, is a highly regarded series with truly remarkable episodes screened throughout its tenure. At its best it was ensemble TV of the very highest order: brilliant writing, acting and production combining to make audiences laugh, cry and, after episodes had finished, dwell on the issues raised. A series can do no more.

The Mate Market

UK · BBC · SITCOM

1 × 25 mins · b/w

3 Jan 1964 · Fri 7.35pm

MAIN CAST

John Cook	Lance Percival
Ann	Francesca Annis
Mr Steel	Richard Caldicot
Jean	Dilys Laye
Mrs Steel	Betty Huntley-Wright

CREDITS

writer Gerry Jones · *producer* Dennis Main Wilson

A *Comedy Playhouse* pilot for a proposed series intended to exploit the comedic talents of Lance Percival, who had impressed in *That Was The Week That Was*. In *The Mate Market* he played John Cook, a Mayfair socialite who maintains his lifestyle by running a marriage bureau. His 'leading lady' was played by the 18-year-old actress Francesca Annis, one of her earliest TV roles.

No series materialised but Percival reappeared with his own sketch series, *The Lance Percival Show*, the following year.

The Mating Machine

UK · ITV (LWT) · SITCOMS

7 × 30 mins · colour

9 Oct–20 Nov 1970 · Fri 8.30pm

A series of individual comedies united by a common theme: relationships brought together by a computer-dating agency (a headline-grabbing innovation in 1970).

Who Sleeps On The Right? 9 OCT

MAIN CAST

Dr Crow	John Cater
Foulkes	Jonathan Elsom
Elizabeth	Pauline Collins
Frank	Martin Shaw

CREDITS

writers John Esmonde/Bob Larbey · *director* Howard Ross · *producer* Bill Turner

Elizabeth and Frank look to be the ideal couple, and with a computer playing Cupid and a sea cruise in the offing, what can go wrong?

Flo And Monty And Henry … And Henry 16 OCT

MAIN CAST

Flo	Miriam Karlin
Monty	Norman Bird

CREDITS

writers Graeme Garden/Bill Oddie · *director* Howard Ross · *producer* Bill Turner

Bored with her marriage, Flo decides to find a lover via the computer, but instead she gets a multitude of would-be courtiers, all with cloth-caps, long coats and red carnations – and all called Henry. (There were ten Henrys all told, the actors including David Suchet and Roger Brierley.)

Only Three Can Play 23 OCT

MAIN CAST

Mrs Twiss	Eleanor Summerfield
Janet	Sarah Atkinson
Ronald	David Wood
Angus	Duncan Lamont

CREDITS

writers Johnnie Mortimer/Brian Cooke · *director* Howard Ross · *producer* Bill Turner

The clever matchmaking computer even reserves a cosy restaurant table for its clients. But, owing to a glitch, Janet's date turns out to be with *two* gentlemen looking for romance.

All About Little Eve 30 OCT

MAIN CAST

Eve Prosser	Gillian Bailey
Edgar Prosser	David Lodge
Phyllis Prosser	Jane Hylton

CREDITS

writers Ken Hoare/Mike Sharland · *director* Howard Ross · *producer* Bill Turner

Edgar and Phyllis, the parents of ten-year-old television star Eve, have grown apart. Eve, distressed at her father's loneliness, enrols him in a computer dating agency, unaware that her mother has also recently enrolled.

Sealed With A Loving Kiss 6 NOV

MAIN CAST

Arnold Biggs	Norman Rossington
Freda	Sheila Hancock
Mrs Biggs	Marjorie Rhodes
Waitress	Sheila Gill

CREDITS

writers Ray Galton/Alan Simpson · *director* Howard Ross · *producer* Bill Turner

The computer pairs Tarquin, an architect, with Michelle, a successful model. They are to meet under the clock at Waterloo Station. But who are Freda and Arnold, and how did they become involved?

See also the separate entry for *Sealed With A Loving Kiss*, and *Paul Merton In Galton & Simpson's …*

As The Bishop Said To The Actress 13 NOV

MAIN CAST

Paul Graham	Gerald Flood
Veronica West	Jan Waters

CREDITS

writers David Cumming/Derek Collyer · *director* Howard Ross · *producer* Bill Turner

Paul, a bachelor Bishop with a weakness for women, is enrolled by his chaplain in a dating agency, with a view to making the philanderer finally choose a partner for life. His chosen date, however, fed up with men wanting her for her body, decides to teach the bonking Bishop a lesson …

Ada's Last Chance 20 NOV

MAIN CAST

Lomax	Sam Kydd
Major Whitestone	William Mervyn
Mrs Ferzani	Stella Tanner
Miss Jones	Petronella Barker
Dr Bundy	Michael Lees

CREDITS

writer Donald Churchill · *director* Howard Ross · *producer* Bill Turner

The Daphne Dilke's Data Dating Agency is renowned for its success in bringing unlikely couples together. When new system ADA is brought in to take over the work, the results are explosive … literally.

Note. This episode featured an appearance by Petronella Barker, daughter of veteran husband and wife comedy team Eric Barker and Pearl Hackney.

Matt And Gerry Ltd

UK · ITV (THAMES) · CHILDREN'S SKETCH

4 × 15 mins · colour

27 May–17 June 1975 · Tue 12.15pm

MAIN CAST

Matthew Corbett
Gerry Marsden

CREDITS

deviser Matthew Corbett · *director/producer* Daphne Shadwell

Four slices of slapstick, served up for lunchtime-viewing toddlers by Matthew Corbett, son of Sooty-wielding Harry (and future manipulator of the puppet himself), with Gerry Marsden (former pop star) and a contraption they called Bobo the Computer. Corbett and Marsden had latterly been appearing together in *The Sooty Show*.

Max Boyce …   [various shows]

see BOYCE, Max

Max Bygraves …
                         [various shows]

see BYGRAVES, Max

The Max Wall Show

see WALL, Max

May To December

UK · BBC (CINEMA VERITY) · SITCOM

39 episodes (38 × 30 mins · 1 × 55 mins) · colour

Series One (6) 2 Apr–7 May 1989 · BBC1 Sun 8.35pm

Series Two (7) 4 Jan–15 Feb 1990 · BBC1 Thu 8.30pm

Special (55 mins) 31 Dec 1990 · BBC1 Mon 8pm

Series Three (7) 7 Jan–25 Feb 1991 · BBC1 Mon 8pm

Series Four (6) 8 Mar–19 Apr 1992 · BBC1 Sun 7.15pm

Series Five (6) 10 Mar–14 Apr 1993 · BBC1 Wed 8pm

Series Six (6) 22 Apr–27 May 1994 · BBC1 Fri 8.30pm

MAIN CAST

Alec Callender · · · · · · · · · · · Anton Rodgers

Zoe Angell · · · · Eve Matheson (series 1 & 2);
· · · · · · · · · Lesley Dunlop (special onwards)
Miles Henty · · · · · · · · · Clive Francis (series 1 & 2)
Jamie Callender · · · · · · · · · · Paul Venables
Miss Vera Flood ·
(later Mrs Tipple) · · · · · · · · · · Frances White
Hilary · · · · · · · · Rebecca Lacey (series 1–5)
Rosie MacConnachy · · · · · · · · Ashley Jensen
· (series 6)

OTHER APPEARANCES

Simone · · · · · · · · · · · · · · · Carolyn Pickles
Zoe's mother (Dot) · · · · · · · · Kate Williams
Zoe's father · · · · · · · · · · · · Ronnie Stevens
Zoe's sister (Debbie) · · · · · Chrissie Cotterill

CREDITS

creator Paul A Mendelson · *writers* Paul A Mendelson (29), Paul A Mendelson/Geoff Deane (1), Geoff Deane (7), Paul Minett/Brian Leveson (2) · *directors* Paul Harrison (20), Sydney Lotterby (13), John Kilby (6) · *executive producer* Verity Lambert · *producers* Sydney Lotterby (series 1 & 2), Sharon Bloom (series 3–6 & special)

The seemingly thin premise of *May To December* proved remarkably durable, with 39 episodes sprung from its theme of a generation-gap romance. It garnered reasonable ratings too, even reaching the Top 20 on occasions, although the episodes tended to warm viewers rather than cause them to guffaw.

Middle-aged solicitor Alec Callender – a partner in Semple, Callender and Henty – is a suburbanite dreamer, pining for Perry Mason-style cases but rarely working on anything more exciting than simple house conveyancing. In the course of his work he meets Zoe Angell, a 26-year-old PE teacher befuddled by her impending divorce; although neither is looking for romance there is an unmistakable spark and soon they embark on the rocky road of a 'spring and autumn' romance. Every variation and pitfall of such a relationship was explored over the course of six series, with the central romance overcoming every obstacle. Alec gets on unexpectedly well with Zoe's parents because, being of virtually the same age, they have much in common. Zoe and Alec themselves share an affection for old musicals and detective stories, their love doing the rest, and after living together for a year they marry and produce a baby daughter, Fleur. At work, Alec's colleagues include his son Jamie and the prim Miss Flood (who then marries and becomes Mrs Tipple).

The creator/writer Paul A Mendelson did not write the series specifically for Anton Rodgers but, coincidentally, there were many parallels with the actor's real life, not least the fact that he was in a second marriage to a much younger woman.

The prolific Mendelson scored a notable double during the fourth series when, an hour after *May To December*, his next sitcom *So Haunt Me* was scheduled on the same channel.

McHale's Navy

USA · ABC (STO-REV COMPANY FILMS) · SITCOM

139 episodes (138 × 30 mins · 1 × 60 mins) · b/w

US dates: 11 Oct 1962–30 Aug 1966

UK dates: 22 July–24 Oct 1963 (13 episodes) BBC Mon 8pm then Thu 9pm

MAIN CAST

Lt Quinton McHale · · · · · · · · Ernest Borgnine
Capt Wallace Binghamton · · · · · · · · Joe Flynn
Ensign Charles Parker · · · · · · · · Tim Conway
Lt Elroy Carpenter · · · · · · · · · · Bob Hastings
Lester Gruber · · · · · · · · · · · · Carl Ballantine
George 'Christy' Christopher · · · Gary Vinson
Harrison 'Tinker' Bell · · · · · · · · · · Billy Sands
Joe 'Happy' Haines · · · · · · · · Gavin MacLeod
· (1962–64)
Virgil Edwards · · · · · · · · · · · · · · Edson Stroll
Nurse Molly Turner · · · · Jane Tulo (1962–64)

CREDITS

writers Ralph Goodman, Walter Kempley, Joel Rapp, Marty Roth and others · *directors* Edward J Montague, Sidney Lanfield, Jean Yarbrough and others · *producers* Edward J Montague, Si Rose

A Bilko-type premise of military men aboard a ship – led by Lieutenant Quinton McHale – indulging in a number of unorthodox procedures to make life easier. They are stationed on Taratupa, a beautiful island in the Pacific, during the Second World War (later episodes saw the entire platoon very much in the thick of it, however, in Italy). But the main threat came not in the form of Japanese or Nazi aggression but rather in the shape of Captain Binghamton and his 'number one' Elroy Carpenter, who were forever out to catch McHale in the act.

The series began life as *Seven Against The Sea*, a 60-minute comedy/drama segment of *Alcoa Premiere* aired in the USA by ABC on 3 April 1962. Borgnine and Flynn starred and reprised their roles when the idea became a half-hour sitcom. It proved to be a durable premise, running for four years and spawning two feature film spin-offs, *McHale's Navy* (1964) and *McHale's Navy Joins The Air Force* (1965). Borgnine was absent for the latter and the main role was taken by Tim Conway as the naïve, gauche Parker. Popular though the series was in the USA, British audience response was lukewarm, possibly because the series made light of a war that had been experienced very differently in the UK.

Twenty-one years after the series ended, *McHale's Navy* was revived for a third feature film of that title, released theatrically in the USA in 1997 (but issued straight to video in the UK). Tom Arnold starred as Quinton McHale and Dean Stockwell as Wallace Binghamton, and Ernest Borgnine made a cameo appearance. Directed by Bryan Spicer, the movie was set in the present day, and was so resolutely up-to-date that its storyline embraced the subject of terrorism.

Me & My Girl

UK · ITV (LWT) · SITCOM

52 × 30 mins · colour

Series One (6) 31 Aug–5 Oct 1984 · Fri 8pm
Series Two (7) 18 Jan–1 Mar 1985 · Fri 7pm
Series Three (13) 6 Oct–27 Dec 1985 · mostly Fri 7pm
Series Four (13) 10 Jan–4 Apr 1987 · Sat 7.15pm
Series Five (6) 8 Jan–12 Feb 1988 · Fri 8pm
Series Six (7) 23 Sep–4 Nov 1988 · Fri 7.30pm

MAIN CAST

Simon Harrap · · · · · · · · · Richard O'Sullivan
Derek Yates · · · · · · · · · · · Tim Brooke-Taylor
Nell Cresset · · · · · · · · · · · · · Joan Sanderson
Samantha Harrap · · · · · · · · · · Joanne Ridley
Liz · · · · · · · · · · · · · · · · · · Joanne Campbell
Maddie · · · · · · · · · Leni Harper (series 1 & 2)
Isobel McClusky · · Sandra Clark (series 3–6)

OTHER APPEARANCES

Fergus Appleby · · Jon Cartwright (series 1–4)

CREDITS

creators Keith Leonard/John Kane · writers Colin Bostock-Smith (23), John Kane (19), Bernard McKenna (9), Mike Walling/Ian Whitham (1) · script editor Bernard McKenna · directors John Reardon (series 1 & 2, 6 eps in series 3, series 4 & 5, 4 eps in series 6), Malcolm Taylor (7 eps in series 3), Nic Phillips (3 eps in series 6) · executive producer Humphrey Barclay · producers John Reardon (series 1 & 2, 6 eps in series 3, series 4–6), Malcolm Taylor (7 eps in series 3)

A long-running but unexceptional hit vehicle for Richard O'Sullivan, in which he portrayed a widower, Simon Harrap, facing the triple challenge of raising his bubbly adolescent daughter, Samantha, winning business for his advertising agency, Eyecatchers, and exercising his libido by way of a succession of romantic dalliances. The first and third of these formed the nub of the series: how could Simon, as a caring and protective parent, expect his daughter to exercise caution and restraint with the opposite sex when he was so clearly interested in gallivanting?

Simon's long-time business partner and brother-in-law, Derek – himself a husband and father but, towards the end, footloose and free with his fancies – was involved in all aspects of Simon's life, and problems were further created, as much as they were solved, by Nell, the indomitable mother of Simon's late wife, Ruth, who – together with secretary Liz – also worked at Eyecatchers. On hand as salve were housekeepers Maddie (she left to get married at the end of the second series) and (from series 3) Isobel, an amiable if accident-prone Scots woman who became a confidante to Samantha.

The swift production of the first three series – 26 episodes were screened inside 16 months – was a response to a fear within the production camp that Joanne Ridley, who played Samantha, would, in real life, obviously outgrow her early-teenage role.

With nature taking its expected course, later episodes depicted Sam as more mature, gaining independence in her movements and relationships.

The creator of the series, Keith Leonard (his idea was then developed for TV by John Kane) was himself divorced and raised his daughter from the age of three. Her name was Samantha.

Me 'n' Meep

UK · ITV (THAMES) · CHILDREN'S SITCOM

1 × 30 mins · colour

28 June 1974 · Fri 4.50pm

MAIN CAST

Grandad · · · · · · · · · · · · · · · · · · · Jack Haig
Mr Tomlin · · · · · · · · · · · · · Roy Barraclough
Mr Trench · · · · · · · · · · · · · · Alec Bregonzi
Meep · John Kane

CREDITS

writer John Kane · director Leon Thau · producer Ruth Boswell

The final edition of Thames' Funny Ha Ha season of comedies for children. It depicted a purple-spotted mechanical character named Meep, visiting Earth on a research mission from the planet of Alphadalpha and befriended by two children who live with their grandfather. As they are about to be evicted Meep decides to lend some support. Writer John Kane appeared as the alien.

Me And My Big Mouth

UK · ITV (ATV) · SITCOM

1 × 30 mins · b/w

18 Aug 1965 · Wed 9.10pm

MAIN CAST

Alfie Smith · · · · · · · · · · · · · · · · Alfie Bass
Tom Brown · · · · · · · · · · · · · Peter Bowles

CREDITS

writer Fred Robinson · director Shaun O'Riordan · producer Alan Tarrant

The second of ATV's Comedy Playhouse-style series Six Of The Best gave a starring role to Alfie Bass, famed as Bootsie in The Army Game and its spin-off Bootsie And Snudge, with lead support from the up-and-coming young actor Peter Bowles.

Me And The Chimp

USA · CBS (PARAMOUNT) · SITCOM

13 × 30 mins · colour

US dates: 13 Jan–18 May 1972
UK dates: 16 Sep 1974–29 Jan 1975 (13 episodes) ITV Mon then Wed 5.20pm

MAIN CAST

Mike Reynolds · · · · · · · · · · · · · Ted Bessell
Liz Reynolds · · · · · · · · · · · · · Anita Gillette
Scott Reynolds · · · · · · · · · · · · Scott Kolden
Kitty Reynolds · · · · · · · · · · · Kami Cotler
Buttons · Jackie

CREDITS

creator Garry Marshall · director/producer Alan Rafkin · executive producer Garry Marshall

Before going on to launch Happy Days (and then Laverne And Shirley) with great success, US producer Garry Marshall came up with this stinker of a sitcom, which lasted just 13 episodes before being cancelled by CBS. Ted Bessell starred as Mike Reynolds, a dentist in Southern California who is persuaded by his children Scott and Kitty (can't you just picture them?) to keep, as a pet, a chimpanzee they have found in a park. The chimp has escaped from an air-force testing laboratory and is called Buttons because, yes, he just loves to press buttons, landing everyone – especially the dentist, do you know how many buttons there are in a dentist's surgery? – deep in monkey doo-doo.

Me Mammy

UK · BBC · SITCOM

21 × 30 mins (7 × b/w · 14 × colour)

Pilot (b/w) 14 June 1968 · BBC1 Fri 8.20pm
Series One (6 × b/w) 15 Sep–27 Oct 1969 · BBC1 Mon 10pm
Series Two (7 × colour) 7 Aug–18 Sep 1970 · BBC1 Fri 8.20pm
Series Three (7 × colour) 23 Apr–11 June 1971 · BBC1 Fri 8pm

MAIN CAST

Bunjy Kennefick · · · · · · · · · · · · Milo O'Shea
Mrs Kennefick · · · · · · · · · · · Anna Manahan
Miss Argyll · · · · · · · · · · · · · · · Yootha Joyce
Father Patrick · · · · · · · · · · · · · Ray McAnally
Cousin Enda · · · · · · · · · · · · · · · David Kelly

CREDITS

writer Hugh Leonard · producers James Gilbert (pilot, series 1 & 2), Sydney Lotterby (series 3)

The adventures of an Irishman, Bunjy Kennefick, a top executive with a London company. His jet-set bachelor lifestyle of fast cars and faster women makes him the envy of his friends – until, that is, they meet his ever-present mother. Her old-fashioned, traditional Irish morals, coupled with a devotion to her son's spiritual development, severely dent most of his more lecherous plans, especially where his regular girlfriend and secretary, the smouldering Miss Argyll, is concerned.

First seen as a Comedy Playhouse pilot, and created by Hugh Leonard (a good friend of the star Milo O'Shea), Me Mammy was a likeable slice of Irish whimsy that managed to incorporate true-life Irish incidents into the plots. The series had a gentle, mocking edge that took in most institutions and people, from the Roman Catholic church to traditional English misconceptions of the Irish. The series was a personal success for star O'Shea, who was actually a few years older than Anna Manahan, cast as his mother. O'Shea was enjoying a purple patch in his career at this time, following his remarkable performance as Bloom in the controversial film version of James Joyce's *Ulysses*. After the third series, *Me Mammy* was terminated by Leonard and O'Shea while it was still popular, both men agreeing that they had explored the subject sufficiently and that it was time to move on.

O'Shea later went to America, and a quarter of a century after this BBC series turned up in a 1995 episode of *Frasier*.

See also *Milo O'Shea* and *Tales From The Lazy Acre*.

Me, You And Him

UK · ITV (THAMES) · SITCOM
6 × 30 mins · colour
30 July–3 Sep 1992 · Thu 8.30pm

MAIN CAST
John · Nick Hancock
Mark · Steve Punt
Harry · Hugh Dennis
Helen · · · · · · · · · · · · · · · · Harriet Thorpe
Todd · · · · · · · · · · · · · · · · · · Ron Donachie

CREDITS
writers Steve Punt/Hugh Dennis/Nick Hancock · director/producer John Stroud

An occasionally surreal sitcom written by and starring the slowly becoming famous Nick Hancock with Steve Punt and Hugh Dennis, half of the team behind *The Mary Whitehouse Experience*. They cast themselves as friends from primary school days, having passed through the 11-plus and the 1960s, O-levels and the glam years, and college and the punk years, but the bond seems to be based on nothing more than familiarity and longevity, for the three have nothing in common and little sense of brotherhood. John is a schoolteacher whose way of marking homework is to accord his pupils' efforts whatever number he manages to throw on a dart board, or whatever is indicated by a dice. Harry is a sober-suited business executive, newly returned to England after three years working in Paris, and consumed with his own interests and the pursuance of promotion. Mark is a sad individual, unemployed, short of money and looking for someone to hold his hand through life. Husband and wife Todd and Helen live in the flat above and frequently pop into the storylines.

Despite the impressive credentials of the writers/leading players, *Me, You And Him* was a curious sitcom, stuffed with unfunny lines flatly delivered. The inclusion of some bizarre visual ideas, usually aligned with Nick Hancock's character, suggests that perhaps the writers intended their creation to be part domestic comedy and part spoof, but the net result was unsuccessful on both counts, and only one series was made.

Meet Janet Brown

UK · ITV (THAMES) · SKETCH/STANDUP
1 × 30 mins · colour
10 June 1980 · Tue 9pm

MAIN CAST
Janet Brown
Tim Barrett

CREDITS
director/producer Keith Beckett

A single special for the skilled Scots-born impressionist, expertly mimicking a posse of women, including Cilla Black, Barbara Cartland, Nana Mouskouri, Barbara Woodhouse, Esther Rantzen, the Hilda Ogden and Annie Walker characters from *Coronation Street* and, of course, Prime Minister Thatcher.

See also *Janet And Company*.

Meet Libby Morris

UK · ITV (ASSOCIATED-REDIFFUSION) · STANDUP
1 × 10 mins · b/w
19 Apr 1956 · Thu 7.20pm

MAIN CAST
Libby Morris

CREDITS
director Trafford Whitelock

Libby Morris had been appearing with Harry Secombe on BBC TV, and in ATV's *The Jack Jackson Show*, clowning and miming in between the discs and Jackson's inspired disc-jockeying style (similar to the later antics of Kenny Everett), when she was offered the chance to shine in A-R's weekly ten-minute slot for solo entertainers.

It was all going right for the Toronto-born actress and comedian at this time: she was also booked by Granada for a starring role in the sketch series *Two's Company*.

Meet Max Wall

see WALL, Max

Meet Phyllis Diller

UK · BBC · STANDUP
1 × 45 mins · colour
3 May 1968 · BBC2 Fri 9.55pm

MAIN CAST
Phyllis Diller

CREDITS
writer Phyllis Diller · producer Robin Nash

Phyllis Diller (born Phyllis Driver in Ohio in 1917) was a well-known face to TV audiences on both sides of the Atlantic. Her comedic style was to deliver a stream of one-liners mostly aimed at her own physical appearance: she had exaggeratedly sharp features and a shock of uncontrollable hair.

Diller entered the comedy world at the relatively late age of 37, when she was already a mother of five, but she made good almost immediately, hitting a rich vein of form with her good-natured self-deprecating humour. This BBC2 show was part of a series (with no generic title) headlining stars from home and abroad.

Meet The Champ

UK · BBC · SITCOM
6 × 30 mins · b/w
22 Sep–27 Oct 1960 · Thu 8pm

MAIN CAST
Bernie · · · · · · · · · · · · · · Bernard Bresslaw
J J · Jimmy James
Essie · · · · · · · · · · · · · · · Vilma Ann Leslie
Sammy · · · · · · · · · · · · · · Peter Butterworth

CREDITS
writer Sid Colin · producer Barry Lupino

An early BBC sitcom starring Bernard Bresslaw, who had shot to fame in *The Army Game* (also created by Sid Colin). In *Meet The Champ* he was cast as a gormless boxer whose girlfriend, Essie, wants him to give up the fight game and become a park-keeper or a car-park attendant. But his unscrupulous manager, J J, feels that his boy can become a champ, with enormous earning potential, a view echoed by the boxer's trainer, Sammy. A weekly battle of wills ensued.

Originally intended to run for nine episodes, only six were screened.

Meet The Wife

UK · BBC · SITCOM
40 episodes (20 × 30 mins · 19 × 25 mins · 1 × short special) · b/w
Pilot (30 mins) *The Bed* 28 Dec 1963 · Sat 9.35pm
Series One (7 × 25 mins) 21 Apr–2 June 1964 · BBC1 Tue 8pm
Series Two (6 × 25 mins) 12 Nov–17 Dec 1964 · BBC1 Thu 8pm
Short special · part of *Christmas Night With The Stars* 25 Dec 1964 · BBC1 Fri 7.15pm
Series Three (6 × 25 mins) 18 Apr–23 May 1965 · BBC1 Sun 7.25pm
Series Four (6 × 30 mins) 22 Nov–27 Dec 1965 · BBC1 Mon mostly 7.30pm
Series Five (13 × 30 mins) 26 Sep–19 Dec 1966 · BBC1 Mon 7.30pm

MAIN CAST
Thora Blacklock · · · · · · · · · · · · · · Thora Hird
Freddie Blacklock · · · · · · · · Freddie Frinton

CREDITS
writers Ronald Wolfe/Ronald Chesney · producers John Paddy Carstairs, Graeme Muir, Robin Nash

Having already authored the smash-hit sitcom *The Rag Trade*, writers Ronald Wolfe and Ronald Chesney turned in a second successful BBC success in *Meet The Wife*, which was blessed not only with good scripts but the top-notch casting of Thora Hird and Freddie Frinton.

Frinton played Freddie Blacklock, a north-country master-plumber. He is a man of simple pleasures who tends to like, and take, life easy. His wife Thora, however, is more forward-looking and has aspirations above her station. Actually, she's something of a snob, concerned with the way that other people view them and preferring to give a better but false impression than a truer one. In mixed company, for example, she affects a more refined voice, pronouncing her husband's name 'Fray-d', to which, in his sarcastic down-to-earth manner, he responds 'Yayss?'

The episodes centred on the simple problems of everyday life, Thora's attempts to better themselves and Freddie's to lead a quiet life. The sum total meant that *Meet The Wife* – sprung from a *Comedy Playhouse* pilot entitled *The Bed* – was a gentle if unambitious comedy that rang true and was a staple of the BBC's schedules for nearly three years.

Notes. *Meet The Wife* is the only TV comedy to be mentioned in the lyric of a Beatles song. It is cited in 'Good Morning Good Morning', on the album *Sgt Pepper's Lonely Hearts Club Band*, where John Lennon (the song's composer) sings 'It's time for tea and *Meet The Wife*'. The song was written in late 1966.

As early as 1966, a Dutch adaptation of *Meet The Wife* was being screened on Netherlands TV.

Since his death at the age of 53 on 16 October 1968, Freddie Frinton has achieved phenomenal cult status as a comedian in Scandinavia, by way of a 1963 West German TV film of a British music-hall sketch 'Dinner For One', adapted for TV as *Same Procedure As Last Year*. (A German director saw the piece being performed in Blackpool and realised that audiences in his home country would enjoy it.) Screened annually around New Year's Eve in Sweden, Norway and Denmark, the 18-minute skit, with English dialogue, depicts Frinton as an ageing butler serving a birthday dinner for his mistress Miss Sophie (May Warden), and becoming increasingly drunk as he consumes the drinks served for her now-deceased former friends. Oddly, with the possible exception of a performance by Frinton in a Swiss TV show screened by the BBC, also in 1963 (see **The Montreux Festival**), it is thought that the sketch has not been shown on British TV.

The Melting Pot

see MILLIGAN, Spike

Memoirs Of A Chaise Longue

UK · BBC · SITCOM

1 × 30 mins · b/w

2 July 1965 · BBC1 Fri 8pm

MAIN CAST
Alan Melville (voice only)
Fenella Fielding ('Mixed Doubles')
Jack Watling ('Mixed Doubles')
Betty Marsden ('Creature Of Habit')
John Le Mesurier ('Creature Of Habit')
J G Devlin ('A Warm Reception')
Shay Gorman ('A Warm Reception')

CREDITS
writers Marty Feldman/Barry Took · *executive producer* Graeme Muir · *producer* Graeme Muir

Writer/presenter Alan Melville returned to TV as the voice of a piece of furniture, the chaise longue in the title of this *Comedy Playhouse* idea. Writers Barry Took and Marty Feldman came up with the idea as a spoof on *The Yellow Rolls Royce*, a current feature film that followed three incidents in the life of the canary-coloured car. Originally they thought of making the linking device a commode but soon rejected that in favour of a chaise longue (which they initially wanted to be voiced by Kenneth Williams). Both were very pleased with the finished production, considering that it contained some of their best, cleverest and funniest writing.

The half hour, like the film, was split into three segments – 'Mixed Doubles', 'Creature Of Habit' and 'A Warm Reception' – each one featuring an incident in the life of the couch. 'Mixed Doubles' took place in the 1890s and concerned two married couples, each wife being the mistress of the other's husband; 'Creature Of Habit', set in the 1930s, focused on a predatory widow who, as she sat on the couch with her latest suitor, regaled him with strange stories of how her previous husbands had met their untimely deaths; 'A Warm Reception' was a twist on *Romeo And Juliet*, the offspring of two feuding Irish families consummating their passion on the chaise longue and consequently having to marry in a hurry.

Men Behaving Badly

UK · *ITV THEN BBC (HARTSWOOD FILMS FOR THAMES) · SITCOM

41 episodes (38 × 30 mins · 1 × 45 mins · 2 × short specials) · colour

*Series One (6) 18 Feb–24 Mar 1992 · ITV Tue 8.30pm

*Series Two (6) 8 Sep–13 Oct 1992 · ITV Tue 8.30pm

Series Three (6) 1 July–5 Aug 1994 · BBC1 Fri 9.30pm

Series Four (7) 25 May–13 July 1995 · BBC1 Thu 9.30pm

Short special · part of Children In Need 24 Nov 1995 · BBC1 Fri approx 12 midnight

Series Five (7) 20 June–1 Aug 1996 · BBC1 Thu mostly 9.30pm

Short special *Men Behaving Very Badly Indeed* · part of Comic Relief 14 Mar 1997 · BBC1 Fri 10.05pm

Series Six (6) 6 Nov–11 Dec 1997 · BBC1 Thu 9.30pm

Special (45 mins) 25 Dec 1997 · BBC1 Thu 10.20pm

MAIN CAST

Gary Strang	Martin Clunes
Dermot	Harry Enfield (series 1)
Tony	Neil Morrissey (series 2 onwards)
Deborah	Leslie Ash
Dorothy	Caroline Quentin
George	Ian Lindsay
Anthea	Valerie Minifie
Les	Dave Atkins (series 3 & 4)
Ken	John Thompson (series 5 onwards)

CREDITS
creator/writer Simon Nye · *director* Martin Dennis · *producer* Beryl Vertue

Whether making viewers chuckle or chunder, *Men Behaving Badly* has undeniably, and unapologetically, become *the* British sitcom of the 1990s, rivalled only by **Absolutely Fabulous**. The antidote to all that 1980s talk of the New Man, *MBB* has made the New Lad into a *cause célèbre*, crystallising 'traditional' male behaviour that had never really gone away but had certainly been out of vogue for a while. To be what the media categorised as a New Man, you had to care and share with your partner, and children if you had them, be responsible and recognise your place in the home and the community. To be a New Lad meant saying 'bollocks' to all of that, being self-centred, rude, crude and boorish, getting pissed on beer, swearing, bragging, belching, farting, fantasising, spewing and publicly rearranging the position of your genitals. Not surprisingly, plenty of men love *MBB*, identifying with the two male lead characters, while a good many women tend to like it because it proves what they have always known: that men can be sad berks, interested only in alcohol and sex (or, to quote *MBB* vernacular, boozing and shagging) – although, inevitably, the two male leads get plenty of the former and little of the latter. Martin Clunes, speaking before the first series aired, got it about right when he described *MBB* as 'the comedy of the locker-room, that rowdy male behaviour that we try to suppress in public'. Neil Morrissey, his subsequent co-star, has also summed it up by stating, 'Like most blokes we resolve all our problems by having a lager in front of the TV and not talking about anything'. Most of the episodes indeed ended in this non-reflective, inconsequential way, with the two guys sprawled on the couch, licking their wounds by guzzling from a can of lager, having advanced not a whit from the Neanderthal.

Men Behaving Badly was based around the antics of Gary and Dermot (series one) or

Tony (subsequent series), who share a shambolic London flat. Gary owns the apartment but takes in a lodger to help him pay the bills. (He's not short of money but is thrifty. One also suspects that he needs approving male company.) A pair of thirty-somethings, Gary and Tony cheerily indulge in their beer-swilling existence, talking out their fantasies – sexual and otherwise – and trying to avoid commitment or hard work by opening up another tin or by heading off to their rooms for a spot of private pleasure with a top-shelf magazine. A glamorous blonde, Deborah, owns the flat above Gary's, and is well aware that Tony fancies her, but she usually decides that being single is preferable to being Tony's. Gary has an on-off girlfriend, Dorothy, a sharp-minded hospital nurse who mostly loves Gary but would certainly *like* him more if his mental age advanced beyond 14. Usually embroiled in the lads' messy pranks, the 'girls' despair over these male specimens but, perhaps sensing that they'd be no better off elsewhere, stay put and try to make the best of a bad situation. Gary owns a small security firm, where his colleagues are George and Anthea; Tony doesn't work. The status quo shifted for the 1997 series (apparently the last, although one-off specials are planned for the future) when Dorothy and Gary almost made it to the altar, and Tony finally eroded Deborah's resistance and became her boyfriend (a relationship that was already foundering by the 1997 Christmas special).

Men Behaving Badly was written by Simon Nye, based on his 1989 novel of the same name. The author himself is anything but a New Lad – more of a New Man, really, if pigeon-holing is your thing – but he invented the Gary and Dermot/Tony characters based upon students he knew at London University. *MBB* producer Beryl Vertue – who started out in TV at Associated London Scripts in the 1950s, working with Galton and Simpson, Hancock, Milligan, Sykes, Speight and others – read Nye's relatively obscure novel and recognised its TV potential, tracking down the author to his job as a translator in a bank. (Born in 1958, Nye, as a linguist, had translated books about Wagner, Matisse and Braque before writing TV comedy.) Unusually, both Nye and Vertue have appeared in *MBB* – in the best Hitchcock tradition, Beryl Vertue usually makes one fleeting non-speaking appearance in each series; Nye had a non-speaking role in the first episode of series two, when Gary was casting around for a new flatmate after Dermot had gone off on an around-the-world trip. (This was the excuse for Harry Enfield, the brilliant comic oddly miscast in *MBB*, to leave the series; ironically, it was Enfield who had talked a reluctant Martin Clunes into taking the part of Gary, after both had

appeared in ITV's light-drama series *Gone To The Dogs* in 1991.)

While *Men Behaving Badly* is now known as a BBC sitcom, the groundwork for its stupendous success was laid on ITV, where it resided for its first two series. But although it won a prize in 1992 as the Best ITV Sitcom of the year (to be truthful, it had little competition), ITV Network Centre rejected a third series and Hartswood Films, *MBB*'s maker, promptly found a slot for it on BBC1 instead. Screened in a post-watershed slot, permitting more colourful language and behaviour, the BBC series won *MBB* many further awards, as did, individually, Martin Clunes, Caroline Quentin and Simon Nye, and ITV came to bitterly regret its decision.

The success of *MBB* has given Nye the freedom to extend his career as a TV writer, creating (all for ITV) the witty drama series *Frank Stubbs Promotes* (based on *Wideboy*, Nye's follow-up novel to *MBB*) and the sitcoms *Is It Legal?* and *My Wonderful Life* (based on a one-off light-drama *True Love*, 25 February 1996). He has also been working with Beryl Vertue on a feature film version of *MBB* (at the planning stage at the time of writing this entry but likely to cast all the principal TV players) and, again with Beryl Vertue, spent some time in America overseeing the US adaptation of *MBB*, produced by The Carsey-Werner Company and premiered by NBC on 18 September 1996.

The US *Men Behaving Badly* got off to a shaky start, and in content was inevitably less raunchy than the UK original – it had to be for scheduling in a primetime network slot; latter transmissions went out at eight o'clock on Sunday nights, prompting Vertue to comment that it was a time at which 'you cannot behave very badly'. Ron Eldard and Rob Schneider starred as the two lads, renamed Kevin Murphy and Jamie Coleman, while Justine Bateman (from *Family Ties*) was Sarah Stretten, Kevin's nurse girlfriend, and Dina Spybey played Brenda Mikowski, the object of Jamie's lusting. Eldard and Bateman dropped out after the first series, however, and were replaced by Ken Marino (as Steve) and Jenica Bergere (as Katie) but, underachieving, the show was soon cancelled, the last of just 28 episodes being screened in the US on Christmas Day 1997. In the 28 November 1996 edition of the BBC2 arts and popular culture series *The Works*, Beryl Vertue looked at the making of the American version and examined the differences between the two productions. (To avoid complication with the British original, the US version of *Men Behaving Badly* is retitled *It's A Man's World* for export sales.)

Notes. The 1997 **Comic Relief** short special, *Men Behaving Very Badly Indeed*, focused on the lads' fixation with Kylie Minogue,

reminiscing about their long-lasting lust for the Australian singer/actress by linking clips from previous shows. But when the real Kylie turned up at their flat the boys strangely failed to recognise her.

Martin Clunes and Caroline Quentin also appeared together in the TV adaptation of the hit stage-play *An Evening With Gary Lineker* (first staged in the theatre in December 1991), networked by ITV on 14 June 1994. Paul Merton (Quentin's then husband), Clive Owen, Lizzy McInnerny, co-authors Arthur Smith and Chris England, and former football star Lineker himself also appeared.

While this book was going to press it was announced that *Men Behaving Badly* would conclude with a three-part special series to air at Christmas 1999.

Men Of Affairs

UK · ITV (HTV) · SITCOM

*13 × 30 mins · colour

3 Oct 1973–23 Jan 1974 · Wed mostly 10.30pm

MAIN CAST

Barry Ovis MP	Brian Rix
Sir William Mainwaring-Brown MP	Warren Mitchell

OTHER APPEARANCES

Lady Mainwaring-Brown	Joan Sims

CREDITS

creator/writer Michael Pertwee · director Derek Clark · executive producer Patrick Dromgoole · producer Wallace Douglas

HTV (the ITV programme provider for Wales and the West) produced this networked sitcom based on Michael Pertwee's London stage farce *Don't Just Lie There, Say Something*, which had co-starred its producer Brian Rix with Alfred Marks and spanned more than 600 performances. Rix shared top billing in the series too, along with Warren Mitchell, who was relishing the opportunity to stretch his comedy talents beyond the role of Alf Garnett.

Both actors were cast as MPs, Mitchell as the bewigged, bewhiskered but never bewildered Minister for European Affairs, Sir William Mainwaring-Brown. This was a punning title if ever there was one, for Brown was a smooth-talking sex-mad womaniser, totally without integrity and permanently risking public humiliation through his philandering. Rix was cast as the minister's Parliamentary Private Secretary, Barry Ovis, whose task it was to cover up for Sir William's many transgressions.

Guest appearances in the series were made by, among others, Derek Royle (twice), Sam Kydd, Richard Hearne, Alfie Bass, Geoffrey Bayldon, Kate O'Mara (as a KGB agent), Alexandra Bastedo, Rix's long-time partner in farce Leo Franklyn, Bernard Bresslaw, Victor Maddern and Wallas Eaton. The series was written by Michael Pertwee, the brother of comic actor Jon and the son of writer Roland, with whom Michael wrote *The Grove Family* (the second – but first major – soap on British TV, from 1954) and many episodes of *The Saint*, *The Persuaders* and *Sergeant Cork*.

*Note. Seventeen episodes of *Men Of Affairs* were written but only 13 appear to have been screened.

Men Of The World

UK · BBC (ALOMO PRODUCTIONS) · SITCOM
12 × 30 mins · colour
Series One (6) 14 Mar–25 Apr 1994 · BBC1
Mon 8.30pm
Series Two (6) 19 Jul– 30 Aug 1995 · BBC1
Wed 8.30pm

MAIN CAST
Lenny Smart · · · · · · · · · · · · David Threlfall
Kendle Bains · · · · · · · · · · · · · · John Simm
Gilby Watson · · · · · · · · · · · · Daniel Peacock
Becky · · · · · · · · · · · · · · Eva Pope (series 2)

CREDITS
writer Daniel Peacock · *director* Terry Kinane · *executive producer* Allan McKeown · *producers* Laurence Marks/Maurice Gran, Claire Hinson

Best known for dramatic roles, David Threlfall returned to TV comedy (he had appeared in the C4 series *Nightingales*) cast as Lenny Smart, a thirty-something Manchester travel agent anxious to pass on his worldly wisdom to his colleague and flatmate Kendle Bains, aged 23. Lenny behaves like a big brother to Kendle and is determined to ensure he is well versed in all things masculine: sport, drinking and the pursuit of women. Lenny and window-cleaner Gilby – his friend since boyhood – are scarcely good role models, however, often behaving in a more juvenile fashion than the much younger yet immeasurably more sensible and sensitive Kendle. In the second series Kendle courted the lovely Becky (played by Eva Pope).

The series' writer Daniel Peacock – who also played Gilby – created a comedy that played on the tension between a 'new man' and the hitherto fashionable ways of adult masculinity. Kendle Bains tried to behave in a modern, politically correct fashion but acknowledged the existence of his baser instincts, behaviour that Lenny encouraged Kendle to follow. This was one of a number of series (including *Men Behaving Badly* and *Absolutely Fabulous*) that challenged the notions of 'political correctness', a movement that began with noble intentions and had done much good before being taken to ridiculous lengths.

Note. *Mud*, a children's light-drama series written by Daniel Peacock and his sometime partner Mickey Hutton, was running at the same time as *Men Of The World* (BBC1, 17 February 1994–30 March 1995).

The Mermaid Frolics

see The Amnesty Galas

Merry With Medwin

UK · ITV (ASSOCIATED-REDIFFUSION) · STANDUP/SKETCH
1 × 55 mins · b/w
24 Dec 1959 · Thu 9.35pm

MAIN CAST
Michael Medwin
Sidney James
Betty Marsden
Ron Moody

CREDITS
writer Neville Phillips · *director* Peter Croft

A one-off Christmas special that combined comedy with music (Shirley Bassey and Vince Eager contributed) and starred the man who had been around on stage since 1940 and in films since 1946 but was familiar to the nation as Corporal Springer from *The Army Game*.

Merry-Go-Round

UK · BBC · SITCOM
2 editions (1 × 65 mins · 1 × 40 mins) · b/w
14 Jan 1947 · Tue 8.30pm (65 mins)
10 Oct 1947 · Fri 9pm (40 mins)

MAIN CAST
Sub-Lieutenant Eric 'Hearthrob' Barker · · · · · ·
· Eric Barker
WREN Hackney · · · · · · · · · · · Pearl Hackney
Flying Officer Kyte · · · · · · Humphrey Lestocq
Commander Highprice/ · · · · · · · · · · · · · · · ·
Robin Fly · · · · · · · · · · · · · · · · · · Jon Pertwee

CREDITS
writer Eric Barker · *radio producer* Leslie Bridgmont

One of the most popular BBC radio comedy series of its time, *Merry-Go-Round* was a wartime show (on air from March 1944 to June 1948) that gave birth to the equally successful series *Stand Easy*, *Much-Binding-In-The-Marsh* and *Waterlogged Spa*, each of which encapsulated a different arm of the services – the Army, the RAF and the Royal Navy respectively.

So loved was *Merry-Go-Round* that BBC TV cameras dropped-in on two of the radio recordings. (The second was performed before an audience at the annual radio and TV equipment festival in London, Radiolympia.)

See also The Newcomer, The Eric Barker Half-Hour, Look At It This Way and Something In The City.

Mess Mates

UK · ITV (GRANADA) · SITCOM
40 × 30 mins · b/w
Series One (13) 28 June–20 Sep 1960 · Tue 8pm

Series Two (27) 12 Sep 1961–13 Mar 1962 · Tue 8.55pm then 7.30pm

MAIN CAST
'Croaker' Jones · · · · · · · · · · · · · · Sam Kydd
Captain Biskett · · · · · · · · · · · Archie Duncan
'Tug' Nelson · · · · · Victor Maddern (series 1)
Willie McGinniss · · · Fulton Mackay (series 1)
'Blarney' Finnigan · · · Dermot Kelly (series 1)
'Dapper' Drake · · · · · Ronald Hines (series 2)
'Twinkle' Martin · · · Michael Balfour (series 2)
'Fry-Up' Dodds · · · · Frank Atkinson (series 2)

CREDITS
writers Talbot Rothwell (series 1), Talbot Rothwell/Lew Schwarz (26 eps in series 2), David Cumming/Derek Collyer (1 ep in series 2) · *directors* Kenneth Carter (series 1), Graeme McDonald (series 2) · *producers* Kenneth Carter (series 1), Eric Fawcett (series 2)

Running at the same time (indeed sometimes on the same evening) as *Glencannon*, Granada's *Mess Mates* was a very popular sitcom of the high seas.

The first series set the course: the battered old cargo-boat SS *Guernsey* is sailing around Britain, skippered by Captain Biskett, a Scotsman whose lofty ambition of commanding a splendid ocean-going liner has been crushed. Worse, Biskett is led a sequence of merry dances by his crew, led by the Mate, 'Tug' Nelson, the *real* master of the men. Ever attempting to outwit the pleasant Captain, Nelson is a schemer, money-maker and womaniser (he knows one in every port) of Bilko-type proportions, endowed with that same gift-of-the-gab talent for talking himself out of sticky situations. As for the rest of the crew, who refer to the *Guernsey* as 'The Old Cow', there is the father-of-seven bosun and eternal worrier 'Croaker' Jones, the happily romantic Scot Willie McGinniss and the Irishman 'Blarney' Finnigan, fond – as his nickname suggests – of telling outlandish stories.

The second series drew upon the same type of humour but featured a substantially different crew – only Biskett and Croaker, newly promoted to Chief Engineer, remained – and a new vessel, *The Jersey Lily*, that boasted more comfortable quarters. The new Mate was 'Dapper' Drake.

Message To Major

UK · BBC (TOTFM PRODUCTIONS) · SATIRE
1 × 55 mins · colour
11 Sep 1991 · BBC2 Wed 9pm

MAIN CAST
Evita Bezuidenhout · · · · · · · · Pieter-Dirk Uys

CREDITS
writer Pieter-Dirk Uys · *director/producer* Francis Gerard

The South African satirist Pieter-Dirk Uys was a thorn in the side of the authorities during the apartheid years (and he continued to take a withering look at the politics and social situation of his country under its new government). Here, in drag as Evita Bezuidenhout, ambassador to the fictitious black homeland of Bapetikosweti, he presented a 'video postcard' to the newly installed British prime minister John Major, offering advice and commenting on the recent turbulent history of South Africa. Like all the best satire, Uys' material, although funny, bore a savage and sometimes bleak edge, employing an uncompromising style that led to many clashes with the SA government. With his country finally breaking free of apartheid, Uys' act – although still shocking – was tinged with optimism, as the monstrous creatures and system he lampooned seemed at last to be receding into history.

On a purely technical level, Uys' characterisations and impersonations were reminiscent of Barry Humphries (Bezuidenhout compares with Dame Edna Everage), but his more concentrated targets and the volatile nature of the subjects he covered, allied to the personal animosity felt towards him by the authorities, combined to give his comedy a dangerous edge. He may have made many enemies in his time but as Evita Bezuidenhout said, 'Prejudice is nothing more than a pigment of the imagination'.

See also *You ANC Nothing Yet.*

Metal Mickey

UK · ITV (LWT) · CHILDREN'S SITCOM
39 × 30 mins · colour
Series One (7) 6 Sep–25 Oct 1980 · Sat 5.15pm
Series Two (6) 4 Apr–2 May 1981 & 19 Sep 1981 · Sat 5.05pm
Series Three (7) 5 Sep–24 Oct 1981 · Sat 5.05pm
Specials (2) 19 & 26 December 1981 · Sat 5.05pm
Series Four (17) 18 Sep 1982–15 Jan 1983 · Sat mostly 5.10pm
MAIN CAST
Granny · · · · · · · · · Irene Handl (not series 3)
Mr Wilberforce · · · · · · · · · Michael Stainton
Mrs Wilberforce · · · · · · · · Georgina Melville
Ken Wilberforce · · · · · · · · · · · Ashley Knight
Haley Wilberforce · · · · · · · Lucinda Bateson
Steve Wilberforce · · · · · · · · · · · Gary Shail
Janey Wilberforce · · · · · · · · · · · Lola Young
CREDITS
writer Colin Bostock-Smith · *directors* Michael Dolenz (20), David Crossman (12), Nic Phillips (7) · *producer* Michael Dolenz

Mirth with a walking, talking mechanical man named Metal Mickey, a five-feet-tall rotund robot with red eyes, blue ears and a dazzling display of multi-coloured lights and buttons on his chest control-panel. Mickey is the invention of Ken Wilberforce, a precocious science boffin who has assembled the automaton to assist with the household

chores. But not everything deep down inside the metallic man is functioning as well as it ought and he just won't do what's expected of him. Mickey means well, but wreaks havoc and soon shows alarming tendencies towards summoning aliens, transporting people back in time and, worst of all, pop music. (He trundles around saying 'boogie boogie' half the day.) The extended Wilberforce family – four children, parents and dear old Granny – are the victims of Mickey's antics.

Metal Mickey first appeared on television in the ITV children's magazine show *The Saturday Banana*, and was then produced in his own series by a famous namesake from the past: Michael (Micky) Dolenz, the actor who had become a member of *The Monkees* and was now turning his hand to work behind the camera. The star of the series, though, apart from the android, was undoubtedly the great Irene Handl, as Granny, although her appearances became sporadic towards the end.

As a character in his own right, Metal Mickey enjoyed many TV appearances outside the scope of his own series.

Meter Maids

UK · BBC · SITCOM
1 × 30 mins · colour
5 Aug 1970 · BBC1 Wed 7.30pm
MAIN CAST
Polly · · · · · · · · · · · · · · · · Barbara Windsor
Smythe · · · · · · · · · · · · · · Joan Sanderson
Crocker · · · · · · · · · · · · · · · · · Pat Coombs
Supt Craddock · · · · · · · · · · Martin Wyldeck
Sgt McKenzie · · · · · · · · · · · · · · · Bob Todd
West · · · · · · · · · · · · · · · · Queenie Watts
Ruxton · · · · · · · · · · · · · · · Hilary Pritchard
CREDITS
writers Louis Quinn/Robin Hawdon · *producer* Douglas Argent

On paper, this looks like a winning formula for a typically broad British sitcom, boasting a pronounced female-led cast and a situation – a group of traffic wardens – immediately recognisable to viewers. But this *Comedy Playhouse* pilot was never developed into a series, suggesting, perhaps, that people saw enough of wardens on the street and did not wish to watch them at home too.

Robin Hawdon, co-author of the piece, was also an actor (*Chalk And Cheese*).

MH & 5p

see HARDING, Mike

Michael Barrymore
The Michael Barrymore Special

see BARRYMORE, Michael

Michael Bentine ...
[various shows]

see BENTINE, Michael

Michael Howard

UK · BBC · STANDUP
1 × 15 mins · b/w
26 Apr 1952 · Sat 8.20pm
MAIN CAST
Michael Howard
CREDITS
writer Lawrie Wyman · *producer* Michael Mills

A 15-minute filler for the humorous story-teller Howard – the programme was subtitled 'Talking About That' – in which he recounted a curious yarn about a man whose TV viewing is continually interrupted by the image of his brother sailing across the screen on a yacht.

See also *Here's Howard.*

Mick And Mac

UK · BBC · CHILDREN'S SKETCH
13 × 10 mins · colour
3 Jan–28 Mar 1990 · BBC1 Wed 4pm
MAIN CAST
Mick · · · · · · · · · · · · · · · Michael Barrymore
Mac · · · · · · · · · · · · · · · · · · · David Jarvis
CREDITS
writers Andy Walker/Geoff Atkinson · *director* Nigel Douglas · *producer* Judy Whitfield

A series of ten-minute sketches on different themes (decorating, changing a light bulb, making a phone call, etc) featuring the physical and verbal comedic talent of Michael Barrymore and David Jarvis. Mick was a cartoonist, using his adventures with the bucket-headed Mac (in full body costume) as the inspiration for a comic strip.

Mick And Montmorency

see DRAKE, Charlie

Mighty Moments From World History

see *The National Theatre Of Brent Presents ...*

Mike & Angelo

UK · ITV (THAMES · *TETRA FILMS FOR CARLTON) · CHILDREN'S SITCOM
93 × 25 mins · colour
Series One (10) 16 Mar–18 May 1989 · Thu 4.25pm
Series Two (10) 14 Sep–16 Nov 1989 · Thu 4.25pm
Series Three (13) 14 Nov 1990–13 Feb 1991 · Wed mostly 4.15pm

Series Four (10) 17 Oct–19 Dec 1991 ·
Thu 4.20pm

*Series Five (10) 7 Jan–11 Mar 1993 ·
Thu mostly 4.20pm

*Series Six (10) 22 Feb–26 Apr 1994 ·
Tue 4.15pm

*Series Seven (10) 5 Jan–9 Mar 1995 ·
Thu 4.15pm

*Series Eight (10) 4 Jan–7 Mar 1996 ·
Thu mostly 4.20pm

*Series Nine (10) 9 Jan–20 Mar 1997 ·
Thu mostly 4.15pm

MAIN CAST
Mike King · · · · · · · Matt Wright (series 1–3);
· · · · · · · · · · · · · Michael Benz (series 5–9)
Angelo · · · · · Tyler Butterworth (series 1 & 2);
· · · · · · · · · · · · · Tim Whitnall (series 3–9)
Rita King · · · Shelley Thompson (series 1–6)
Ellie · · · · · · · · · · · · · Jade Magri (series 4)
Melanie · · · · · · · Alexandra Milman (series 6)
Katy Andrews · · · · · Katy Murphy (series 7–9)

OTHER APPEARANCES
Philippa Fraser · · · · · · · · · · Alessia Gwyther
Cyril Pinner · · · · · · · · · · · · · · · John Levitt
Nancy · · · · · · · · · · · · · · · · · · Libby Morris
Brett Douglas · · · · · · · · · · · Gavin Richards
Sam · · · · · · · · · · · · Katie Pearson (series 7)
Uncle Bob · · · · · · · · · Ron Berglas (series 7)

CREDITS
writers Lee Pressman/Grant Cathro (series 1–6); Lee Pressman, Alex Bartlette, David Collier, James Stevenson (series 7); Lee Pressman, Grant Cathro/Alex Bartlette, Ken Allen Jones (series 8 & 9) · directors Neville Green (87), John Darnell (6) · executive producer Alan Horrox · producers Charles Warren, Alan Horrox, Neville Green

An extraordinarily long-running children's sitcom – extraordinary because it seems incomprehensible how any children can find it funny. But, despite being dogged by inappropriately superimposed canned laughter and visual effects that could doubtless be bettered if the budget was greater, Mike & Angelo continues to air – indeed, it is rarely off screen, repeats running in between original series. A 1998 series, in production at the time of writing, was expected to take the episode count beyond 100.

This is the premise. A writer, Rita King, divorces her husband Tony, quits America and comes to live in England with their son Mike, moving into a large, rambling old house in Larkswood Lane, somewhere in the Home Counties. Wandering lonely around the house Mike discovers Angelo, a mysterious humanoid from 'another dimension, a different universe beyond infinity' who is living in his wardrobe. Angelo, who left his home planet in a hurry when it began to self-destruct, turns everyone's life upside down by performing all kinds of magical tricks. Prone to walking up walls, dancing on the ceiling and rustling up historic figures, he nonetheless strikes up a friendship with Mike. For their part, Mike and his mother attempt – at first – to keep Angelo's presence a secret.

The cast has changed considerably over the years: the original Mike left (his character returned to America) but then returned (with a new actor). Rita also left and Angelo has been played by two different actors.

Writers Pressman and Cathro have enjoyed a similarly durable ITV children's run with the light-dramas based on the character T-Bag – as in the series *T-Bag Strikes Again* (1986), *T-Bag Bounces Back* (1987), *T-Bag And The Revenge Of The T-Set* (1989), *T-Bag And The Pearls Of Wisdom* (1990), *T-Bag And The Rings Of Olympus* (1991), *T-Bag And The Sunstones Of Montezuma* (1992) and *Take Off With T-Bag* (1992). They also created the sitcom **Cone Zone**. With Alex Bartlette, Pressman wrote episodes of the children's light-drama series *Snap* (ITV, 1997, returning in 1998).

Mike And Bernie Winters … [various shows]

see WINTERS, Mike and Bernie

Mike Harding In Belfast
The Mike Harding Show

see HARDING, Mike

Mike, Phil And Albert

see BENTINE, Michael

The Mike Reid Show

UK · BBC · STANDUP

6 × 45 mins · colour
Special · 4 Feb 1976 · BBC2 Wed 9pm
One series (4) 31 Jan–11 Mar 1977 · BBC2 fortnightly Mon 8.15pm
Special · 3 Mar 1978 · BBC2 Fri 9.30pm

MAIN CAST
Mike Reid

CREDITS
writers Dick Hills (4), Johnny Speight (3), Alex Brown/Pat Murray (3), Ernest Maxin (1), Eric Davidson (1), Larry Forrester (1), Hugh Stuckey/Peter Robinson (1), Mike Craig/Lawrie Kinsley (1), Ron McDonnell (1) · producers Ernest Maxin (4), Peter Whitmore (1), James Moir (1)

Starring shows for the London comedian who had risen to fame as one of the resident joke-tellers in *The Comedians*. Reid's style was to efficiently tell long, rambling jokes, most of which had strong punchlines that made the journey worthwhile. His gimmick was his cockney accent, somewhat exaggerated body language and the slang phrases with which he peppered his gags. In later years Reid demonstrated his acting prowess by becoming a regular character in the BBC1 soap *EastEnders*.

Mike Reid's Mates And Music

UK · ITV (CENTRAL) · SKETCH/STANDUP

4 × 60 mins · colour
20 June–11 July 1984 · Wed 8pm

MAIN CAST
Mike Reid
Gary Wilmot
Duncan Norvelle
Ray Alan and Lord Charles
Kenny Lynch
Harry Fowler
Patricia Brake

CREDITS
script associate Trevor McCallum · producer Nigel Lythgoe · director/executive producer Jon Scoffield

The cockney geezer from *The Comedians* starred in these four weekly programmes that embraced humour, song and dance. Each show featured a lengthy supporting cast and visiting guest artists. When the *Mates And Music* series ended Reid then hosted a weekly variety show, *Entertainment Express*.

Mike Yarwood … [various shows]

see YARWOOD, Mike

Mild And Bitter

UK · BBC · SKETCH

6 × 30 mins · b/w
19 Mar–23 Apr 1966 · BBC2 Sat around 9.30pm

MAIN CAST
Eric Merriman
June Whitfield
Peter Jones
James Beck

CREDITS
writer Eric Merriman · producer John Street

Eric Merriman – co-writer with Barry Took of the brilliant BBC radio sketch series *Beyond Our Ken* – penned and presented this TV sketch-show for the star pairing of Whitfield and Jones. James Beck (later to become famous as Walker in *Dad's Army*) was a regular support, and there were musical guest stars.

Miles Better

UK · C4 (CHILDSPLAY) · SITCOM

1 × 30 mins · colour
1 July 1992 · Wed 10.30pm

MAIN CAST
Michael Miles · · · · · · · · · · · · · · · Andy Gray
Gran · · · · · · · · · · · · · · · · · Ann Scott-Jones
Nita · · · · · · · · · · · · · · · · Jenny McCrindle
Linda · · · · · · · · · · · · · · · · Alison Peebles

CREDITS
writers Peter Arnott/Peter Mullan · director David G Hillier · executive producer Esta Charkham · producer Peter Tabern

The last of C4's *Bunch Of Five* sitcom pilots was a broad comedy featuring Andy Gray as a Glaswegian, Michael Miles, an obsessive security-systems salesman. A gauche man with an aggressive streak, Michael lives with, and torments, his Stalinist granny, whom he uses as a guinea-pig to experiment with new security devices. When he catches a burglar, Nita, ransacking his house, Miles sees her potential as a would-be partner and, after a few mishaps, she joins him in the firm. Their first victory is convincing the local community centre, run by career woman Linda, to buy their system.

Miles Better was a loud, far-fetched sitcom with larger-than-life characters and situations. The central figure, Miles, was a decent enough small-screen grotesque but, overall, the show may have lacked the necessary charm to ensure expansion to a series.

Milk-O

UK · ITV (ATV) · SITCOM

1 × 30 mins · colour

26 Nov 1975 · Wed 8pm

MAIN CAST

Jim Wilkins	Bob Grant
Rita Wilkins	Anna Karen
Dad	Leslie Dwyer
Norman Fish	Alan Curtis

CREDITS

writers Anthony Marriott/Bob Grant · *director/producer* John Scholz-Conway

Another of ATV's *Comedy Premiere* pilots, none of which was developed into a full series. *Milk-O* featured two of the stars of **On The Buses** – the jack-the-lad Jack (Bob Grant) and the dowdy Olive (Anna Karen) – as husband and wife, Grant swapping his busman's uniform for that of a milkman. Sadly for him, he oversleeps on the morning of the great Empty Milk Bottle Competition, which carries a £10 prize. Chaos, very predictably, ensues …

Millicent
Millicent And Roy

see MARTIN, Millicent

Spike Milligan

The son of an Irish officer serving in the British Army, Terence Milligan was born in Ahmednugar, India, on 16 April 1918. As 'Spike' Milligan, he became perhaps the most famous British humorist of the 20th-century, a man who, in the 1950s, revolutionised British comedy, influencing generations of comedians in the process.

Educated in India but living in England, in south London, from the age of 15, Milligan joined the army in 1940, serving as a gunner in the Royal Artillery; this was a crucial period in his comedic development, as documented in a number of hilarious best-selling memoirs, beginning with *Adolf Hitler: My Part In His Downfall* (1971). Like many comedians, Milligan also demonstrated a talent for musicianship, and played in an informal military band, the Boys Of Battery D. The links between the rhythms of music and humour have often been made, and it was telling that Milligan's penchant was for the more manifold, sometimes avant-garde world of jazz, for his humour was already developing upon similarly complex grounds. While serving in the army Milligan met Harry Secombe, and when they reunited after the Second World War Secombe took Milligan along to the Grafton Arms, a London pub run by Jimmy Grafton, a scriptwriter. Grafton recognised Spike's surreal comic vision and encouraged him to commit his humour to paper, a move that proved pivotal in his career.

After middling success co-writing with Grafton for a number of BBC radio shows, Spike Milligan – with Harry Secombe and two similarly wacky friends of Secombe's, Peter Sellers and Michael Bentine – pitched to the BBC the idea of a zany radio sketch programme which they wanted to call *The Goon Show*. The Corporation accepted the idea but not the title, and the first series (edited by Grafton and co-written by Milligan with Larry Stephens) aired on the Home Service from 28 May 1951 as *Crazy People*. After a slow start – and the desired name change to *The Goon Show* – the series became a national institution. Under the guidance of BBC radio producers Pat Dixon and the highly influential Dennis Main Wilson, *The Goon Show* ran for 241 editions, ending on 28 January 1960. Its influence in what, for most, was still the pre-TV age, is incalculable – the surreal, irreverent, barnstorming, rapid-paced series, most of which sprang from Milligan's mind-boggling imagination, made a profound impression upon millions of listeners, not only then but, in repeats, decade after decade. It made a particular impact upon younger listeners, some of whom – the *Monty Python's Flying Circus* comics, for example – were inspired to create similar free-flowing zany humour. Although the adjective is often over-used, *The Goon Show* was a truly seminal programme.

With varying degrees of success, numerous attempts were made to re-create the style of *The Goon Show* on TV, but Milligan enjoyed greater success on the small-screen when allowed free rein to create completely new formats and styles. Although he has been dogged with recurring depression and mental problems since 1956, his output has been prodigious – in addition to much radio and TV work, Milligan has written novels, books of poetry and humorous anthologies, appeared in a great number of movies and, through it all, remained a staunch campaigner for ecological issues and a virulent opponent of man's inhumanity to man and disregard for nature.

It is a popular but tragic contention that Milligan's comic genius is sparked by the passion and madness that rage in his brain; over the years, several documentaries have investigated the Milligan enigma, the 15 April 1996 edition of *Omnibus* (BBC1), narrated by Spike, arguably presenting the closest and most candid view of its subject.

Note. This entry includes Milligan's own TV series and programmes but excludes the Peter Sellers vehicles for which Spike was principally responsible (so see separate entries for **The Idiot Weekly, Price 2d**, **A Show Called Fred**, **Son Of Fred**) and the literally hundreds of TV appearances made by Milligan in chat-shows, game-shows and documentaries.

See also *Christmas Cracker* and *Supergran*.

Goonreel

UK · BBC · SKETCH

1 × 45 mins · b/w

2 July 1952 · Wed 8.45pm

MAIN CAST

Michael Bentine
Peter Sellers
Spike Milligan
Harry Secombe
Graham Stark
Sam Kydd
Eunice Gayson
Leslie Crowther

CREDITS

writers Michael Bentine, Jimmy Grafton, Spike Milligan · *producer* Michael Mills

A 'Goon' version of a television newsreel, with the famous radio comics bringing their particular brand of surreal mayhem to the small-screen. The programme publicity announced, in true Goon style, that the show was 'devised, presented, directed and produced by Mr Claude Boote assisted by Michael Mills'.

There had been a previous plan to bring the Goons' humour to the small-screen, with a show titled *Trial Gallop*, scheduled to air on 13 February 1952. But it was cancelled owing to the death of King George VI.

Man And Music

UK · BBC · SKETCH

1 × 30 mins · b/w

24 June 1957 · Mon 9.15pm

MAIN CAST

Spike Milligan
Dick Emery
Valentine Dyall
Graham Stark
Kenneth Connor
Mario Fabrizi
The Alberts
Johnny Vyvyan

CREDITS

writer Spike Milligan · *producer* Christian Simpson

Typical Milligan humour, relating the history of man and music using film clips and sketches. The show, also titled *A Short History Of Man And Music*, was billed as Part 2 with the explanation 'Part 1 was not accepted'.

Spike Milligan

UK · BBC · SKETCH

1 × 30 mins · b/w

5 Sep 1961 · Tue 8.55pm

MAIN CAST

Spike Milligan
Graham Stark
Bill Kerr
Mario Fabrizi
Valentine Dyall
The Alberts
Alec Bregonzi
Bob Todd

CREDITS

writer Spike Milligan · *producer* Barry Lupino

Subtitled 'A Series Of Unrelated Incidents At Current Market Value', this was an energetic half-hour of Milligan mayhem comprising the sort of bizarre prop-festooned sketches that would litter the *Q* series (1969–82).

The Telegoons

UK · BBC (GROSVENOR FILMS) · ANIMATION

26 × 15 mins · b/w

Series One (11) 5 Oct–21 Dec 1963 · Sat 5.40pm
Series Two (15) 28 Mar–1 Aug 1964 · BBC1 Sat around 5.15pm

MAIN CAST (VOICES ONLY)

Spike Milligan
Peter Sellers
Harry Secombe

CREDITS

writer Spike Milligan · *script editor* Maurice Wiltshire · *producer* Tony Young

A bizarre puppet-animated version of *The Goon Show* that, surprisingly, coped fairly well in putting images to the surreal audio

zaniness. String-and-rod puppets (designed by Ralph Young, the series' producer's father) combined to bring the famous characters to life – Eccles, Bluebottle, Neddie Seagoon, Brigadier Grytpype-Thynne, Major Denis Bloodnok, Henry Crun, Minnie Bannister and others – and traditional, simple cartoon animation and library footage was added to the mix to give the programmes a unique look.

The puppets' characteristics were based on Spike Milligan's doodled impressions of how they might look, creating a somewhat grotesque but worthwhile visual interpretation. Although the original team reassembled to record certain passages where necessary, it is thought that the soundtracks also utilised extracts from original BBC radio recordings.

Milligan's Wake

UK · ITV (ATV) · SKETCH

11 editions (7 × 30 mins · 4 × 20 mins) · b/w

Series One (4 × 20 mins) 5 Sep–26 Sep 1964 · Sat 11.05pm
Series Two (7 × 30 mins) 3 July–14 Aug 1965 · Sat 11.05pm

MAIN CAST

Spike Milligan

CREDITS

writers Ray Galton/Alan Simpson (series 1), Reuben Ship/John Bird (series 2), Spike Milligan (series 1 & 2) · *director* Gordon Reece (series 2) · *producer* Anthony Firth (series 1 & 2)

Mining the late-Saturday-night slot for irreverent comedy that was established by *That Was The Week That Was*, Spike Milligan here produced the kind of unpredictable, free-form sketch comedy that would later result in the BBC2 *Q* series. *Milligan's Wake* failed to scale such heights, however, although much of the material was very good, with Galton and Simpson contributing the bulk of the scripts in the first series, and Reuben Ship and John Bird adding a left-wing political edge in the second.

Spike's next major TV work was back on the BBC, in the 12-part *Muses With Milligan* (BBC2, 6 January to 24 March 1965). Not a comedy series as such, Milligan and weekly guests read poetry – including some of his own material.

Spike Milligan's Sad/Happy Ending Story Of The Bald Twit Lion

UK · BBC · SKETCH

1 × 30 mins colour

26 Dec 1967 · BBC2 Tue 4.35pm

MAIN CAST

Spike Milligan

CREDITS

writer Spike Milligan · *producer* Francis Coleman

A one-off seasonal special that told 'a story for the very all ages' and featured 'a cast of one-and-a-half in the Jungle of Bozzollika-Dowser'. The tale's telling was aided by pictures from Carol Barker and animation by Colin Whitaker.

The World Of Beachcomber

UK · BBC · SKETCH

19 × 30 mins · colour

Series One (13) 22 Jan–22 Apr 1968 · BBC2 Mon 8pm
Series Two (6) 22 Sep–27 Oct 1969 · BBC2 Mon 9.10pm

MAIN CAST

Spike Milligan
Frank Thornton
Leon Thau
Patricia Hayes
Julian Orchard
Michael Redgrave (series 1)
George Benson (series 1)
Clive Dunn (series 1)
Sheila Steafel (series 1)
Hattie Jacques (series 1)
Betty Marsden (series 1)
Lionel Wheeler (series 1)
Ann Lancaster (series 2)
Paul McDowall (series 2)
Fred Emney (series 2)
Bill Pertwee (series 2)
Charlie Atom (series 2)
Thelma Taylor (series 2)
Bernard Jamieson (series 2)

OTHER APPEARANCES

Arthur Mullard (series 1)
Gerald Campion (series 1)

CREDITS

writers Barry Took (6 eds in series 1, all series 2), John Junkin/Barry Took (2 eds in series 1), Neil Shand (7 eds in series 1) · *additional material* Ken Hoare (series 1), Spike Milligan (series 2) · *director* John Howard Davies · *producers* Duncan Wood (5 eds of series 1, all series 2), John Howard Davies (8 eds of series 1)

A TV adaptation of J B Morton's famous Beachcomber columns, which had run in the *Daily Express* from 1924. Milligan claimed that the columns, with their unlikely larger-than-life characters and bizarre humour, were a major influence when he created *The Goon Show* for radio. Although Milligan had less to do with the scripts here than with his other series, *The World Of Beachcomber* nevertheless embraced a style that was unmistakably his.

The series featured monologues, odd dances, filmed sketches, spoof advertisements and strange readings, such as *The Anthology Of A Huntingdonshire Cabman*, read out in the early episodes by Michael Redgrave. The shows, fronted and linked by Milligan as the dressing-gowned, pipe-smoking Dr Strabismus, included regular practical demonstrations of well-known phrases (eg, the contention 'When one door closes, another opens' was tested in a field full of doors) and advertisements for useless products from the Threadgold company, such as 'Threadgold's Thoroughgrip Garterettes'. As the series progressed, the items became increasingly bizarre and in between the two seasons Milligan launched his *Q* series which pushed still further the limits of surrealism and craziness on television, paving the way for *Monty Python's Flying Circus* which began in October 1969.

Note. The Beachcomber humour was brought to BBC Radio 4 by Richard Ingrams, John Wells, Patricia Routledge and John Sessions in the first of several series starting 18 March 1989.

See also *Grubstreet.*

The Goon Show

UK · ITV (THAMES) · SKETCH

1 × 30 mins · b/w

8 Aug 1968 · Thu 8pm

MAIN CAST

Hercules Grytpype-Thynne/Bluebottle/ · · · ·
Major Denis Bloodnok/ · · · · · · · · · · · · · ·
Henry Crun · · · · · · · · · · · · · · Peter Sellers
Neddie Seagoon · · · · · · · · Harry Secombe
Eccles/Minnie Bannister/ · · · · · · · · · · · · ·
Count Jim Moriarty · · · · · · · · Spike Milligan
The announcer · · · · · · · · · · · · · John Cleese
The effects · · · · · · · · · · · · John Hamilton
The bikini girl · · · · · · · · · · · Christine Pryor

CREDITS

writer Spike Milligan · *director* Joe McGrath · *producer* Peter Eton

Although Spike Milligan had been involved in numerous attempts to capture on TV the flavour of *The Goon Show*, this 1968 TV broadcast was the first time that a full *Goon* programme – as presented on radio, with the three leading players at the microphone, scripts in hand – had been tried. (See **Secombe And Friends** for an earlier but incomplete attempt.) Oddly, the show was made not by the BBC but by Thames, for ITV, screened just a few days after the launch of this new London franchise.

Spike was invited to write a new script especially for the show but couldn't come up with one in time, so – with John Cleese as the announcer – Milligan, Sellers and Secombe performed 'The Tale Of Men's Shirts', originally aired on 31 December 1959 during the tenth and final radio series. (This no-frills radio-to-TV translation method was employed again for *The Last Goon Show Of All* in 1972.)

The programme was deemed unsuccessful, scuppering Thames' plans to present a full series of TV *Goon Shows*.

Q ...

UK · BBC · SKETCH

38 × 30 mins colour

Series One (7) *Q5* 31 Mar–5 May 1969 · BBC2 Mon 8.50pm

Series Two (6) *Q6* 6 Nov–11 Dec 1975 · BBC2 Thu 9pm

Series Three (7) *Q7* 3 Jan–14 Feb 1978 · BBC2 Tue 9pm

Series Four (6) *Q8* 4 Apr–9 May 1979 · BBC2 Wed 9pm

Series Five (6) *Q9* 17 June–22 July 1980 · BBC2 Tue 9pm

Series Six (6) *There's A Lot Of It About* 20 Sep–25 Oct 1982 · BBC2 Mon 9pm

MAIN CAST

Spike Milligan
John Bluthal
Alan Clare
Richard Ingrams (*Q5*)
John Wells (*Q5*)
Philippe Le Bars (*Q5*)
Fanny Carby (*Q5*)
Anthony Trent (*Q5*)
Robert Dorning (*Q6, Q7*)
David Lodge (*Q6, Q7, Q8 & TALOIA*)
Julia Breck (*Q6, Q7, Q8, Q9 & TALOIA*)
Stella Tanner (*Q6, Q7, Q8*)
Peter Jones (*Q6*)
Alec Bregonzi (*Q6*)
Chris Langham (*Q6*)
Margaret Nolan (*Q6*)
Rita Webb (*Q6, Q8*)
Neil Shand (*Q7*)
Keith Smith (*Q7, Q8, Q9 & TALOIA*)
Sheila Steafel (*Q7*)
John D Collins (*Q7, Q8*)
Bob Todd (*Q8, Q9*)
Jeanette Charles (*Q8, Q9*)
David Rappaport (*Q9*)
David Adams (*TALOIA*)
Suzanne Sinclair (*TALOIA*)
Mike O'Malley (*TALOIA*)
Linzi Drew (*TALOIA*)
Susan Jack (*TALOIA*)

CREDITS

writers Spike Milligan/Neil Shand, Andrew Marshall/David Renwick (*TALOIA*) · *additional material* Philippe Le Bars, John Antrobus · *director* Ray Butt (*Q8, Q9*) · *producers* Ian MacNaughton (*Q5, Q6, Q7*), Douglas Argent (*Q8, Q9*), Alan J W Bell (*TALOIA*)

Classic TV anarchy from Milligan who, with writing partner Neil Shand, liked to present material that crossed lines of decency and taste in a quest to take comedy into unexplored territory. With their surreal sketch ideas, costumes that still bore the BBC prop department tags, half constructed sets, often bizarre make-up and air of uncontrolled chaos, the *Q* series were certainly groundbreaking and pipped *Python* to the post with their deliberate avoidance of punchlines, many of the sketches segueing into the next routine or simply being abandoned half way through.

Television scarcely seemed able to contain the sprawling scope of the *Q* series, and the shows baffled and angered as many viewers as they entertained. Milligan's relationship with his BBC masters was fraught during much of the run: he always wanted to direct the shows himself, propelling them into ever weirder areas, but the executives thought that he needed a strong hand on the tiller. Reputedly (but oddly), they refused to allow the final series to be titled *Q10*, thinking that the baffling *Q* prefix had been around for long enough, so Milligan – possibly with a nod towards such 'official' thinking – renamed it *There's A Lot Of It About.*

Although their importance within the development of the genre is recognised, the *Q* series do not enjoy the same posthumous reverence among fans and critics that is reserved for *Monty Python's Flying Circus*. There are, arguably, three main reasons for this. Firstly, the *Q* series were comedically less consistent, with moments of genius squeezed in between bouts of charmless corn. (This was probably because Milligan himself, with Shand, did the bulk of the writing, and his own idiosyncratic flights of fancy could be hit and miss, whereas the Pythons *all* wrote, the members exercising a kind of quality control mechanism over the others' writing, ensuring that flimsy material was rejected.) Secondly, there is the question of taste – Milligan's rather old-fashioned shock value usage of racial abuse (jokes about 'wogs' and 'Pakis') and sexual situations (the semi-clad, mammoth-breasted Julia Breck as sexual predator) were acceptable in the climate of the 1970s but don't age as well as the Pythons' shock material (homosexual brigadiers, cannibal undertakers) where authority figures bear the brunt of the humour. Lastly, there is the construction of the programmes – whereas both *Q* and *Python* had almost limitless freedom to leave a sketch at any point and play with the reality of the show and the genre of television, Terry Gilliam's brilliant animations permitted *Python* to effect seamless transitions from one sketch to the next, which, when coupled with the Pythons' faultless sense of programme continuity, gave their shows a greater all-round balance.

Notwithstanding all of this, the *Q* series provided Spike Milligan with his longest TV run and brought his humour firmly into the 1970s, delighting old and new fans alike.

Curry And Chips

UK · ITV (LWT) · SITCOM

6 × 30 mins · colour

21 Nov–26 Dec 1969 · Fri 8.30pm

MAIN CAST

Kevin O'Grady · · · · · · · · · · · · Spike Milligan
Arthur · · · · · · · · · · · · · · · · · · · Eric Sykes

Kenny	Kenny Lynch
Norman	Norman Rossington
Smellie	Sam Kydd
Dick	Geoffrey Hughes
Landlady	Fanny Carby

CREDITS
writer Johnny Speight · *director/producer* Keith Beckett

Written by Johnny Speight in the midst of the BBC's *Till Death Us Do Part*, this equally controversial, chaotic and memorable sitcom – ironically, LWT's first in colour – was short-lived. It had to be, such was the high feeling it stirred up, although Speight's undoubted intention, as with *Till Death*, was to highlight discrimination, not fuel it.

Set in the staff canteen and on the factory floor at Lillicrap Ltd, makers of seaside novelties, *Curry And Chips* starred a blacked-up Spike Milligan as 'Paki Paddy' Kevin O'Grady, who claimed to be Irish on his father's side; Eric Sykes, as the liberal-minded factory foreman often springing to the defence of the much-maligned O'Grady; Sam Kydd as the malodorous Smellie; Norman Rossington and Geoffrey Hughes as racist white Liverpudlians; and singer/actor Kenny Lynch as a black anti-Pakistani. In addition to the liberal slinging about of racist terms there was a good deal of (mostly harmless) swearing, one viewer noting that the word 'bloody' was said 59 times in a single episode. (Only Eric Sykes didn't swear – he refused to do so.)

Political-correctness ensured that two similar series – *The Melting Pot*, also starring Milligan as a Pakistani, six episodes of which were made in 1975, and *Jewel In The Crown*, for which a pilot was shot in 1985 – were scrapped, although one episode of the former was shown. (See below.)

Oh In Colour

UK · BBC · SKETCH

6 × 30 mins · colour
29 Sep–1 Nov 1970 · BBC2 Sun around 10.50pm

MAIN CAST
Spike Milligan
John Bluthal
Julia Breck
Arthur Mullard
Rita Webb

CREDITS
writers Spike Milligan/John Antrobus · *producers* Joe McGrath (3), John Howard Davies (2), Duncan Wood (1)

Another series of surrealistic sketches sprawling into each other and linked by no more than Milligan's unfettered imagination. Guest artists appeared each week, notably Eleanor Bron in the first show and Chic Murray in the fifth.

Follies Of The Wise

UK · BBC · STANDUP

1 × 35 mins · colour
3 Jan 1972 · BBC1 Mon 11.15pm

MAIN CAST
Spike Milligan

CREDITS
creator R G Payne · *writers* Sandy Brown/Martin Pawley · *director* Jim Franklin

A comedy travelogue with Milligan looking at, and commenting upon, some notable follies.

Milligan In …

UK · BBC · SKETCH

4 × 30 mins · colour
Autumn 1 Oct 1972 · BBC2 Sun 9pm
Winter 24 Dec 1972 · BBC2 Sun 9.30pm
Spring 13 May 1973 · BBC2 Sun 10pm
Summer 27 Aug 1973 · BBC2 Mon 9.25pm

MAIN CAST
Spike Milligan
John Bluthal
John Antrobus
John Wells (shows 1 & 4)
Cardew Robinson (show 1)
Madeline Smith (show 1)
Ray Ellington (show 1)
Fanny Carby (show 2)
Chris Langham (show 3)

CREDITS
writers Spike Milligan, John Antrobus (2), Chris Langham (1), Dick Vosburgh (1), Roy Tuvey/Maurice Sellar (1) · *producers* Roger Race (2), Ian MacNaughton (1), Michael Mills (1)

Seasonal thoughts from Milligan, with the usual suspects as guest stars, which combined to form a typically surreal mix of sketches, routines, songs and poems.

The shows marked Milligan's return to the BBC following a stint at ITV in *The Marty Feldman Comedy Machine* and two specials in Australia: *Spike Milligan Takes A Made-Up Look At Australia* (ABC, 26 January 1972) and *Carry On Spike In Australia* (Nine Network, 24 March 1972).

The Last Goon Show Of All

UK · BBC · STANDUP

1 × 40 mins · colour
26 Dec 1972 · BBC1 Tue 8.20pm

MAIN CAST

Hercules Grytpype-Thynne/Bluebottle/ Major Denis Bloodnok/ Henry Crun	Peter Sellers
Neddie Seagoon	Harry Secombe
Eccles/Minnie Bannister/ Count Jim Moriarty	Spike Milligan

CREDITS
writer Spike Milligan · *producers* John Browell (radio), Douglas Hespe (TV)

A TV recording of a radio broadcast from 5 October 1972, reuniting the Goons as part of the BBC's 50th anniversary celebrations. The event was a wonderful occasion, for – even if the humour was not quite on a par with the *Goon Shows* of old – this was clearly a much-loved old pals reunion for Sellers, Milligan and Secombe, with Prince Philip and Princess Anne among the enthusiastic studio audience. (The show's biggest royal fan, Prince Charles, couldn't attend but sent a telegram read out at the start of the show.) A BBC record album of the event (actually a different edit from both the radio and TV versions) was awarded a silver disc, racking up highly impressive sales figures for a comedy album.

A few days after this TV presentation the Goons reunited again as the hosts of *Festival Of Entertainment* (BBC1, 31 December 1972), an international variety spectacular.

The Goons were celebrated in C4's series *Heroes Of Comedy*, screened on 7 May 1997.

The Last Turkey In The Shop Show

UK · BBC · SKETCH

1 × 35 mins · colour
23 Dec 1974 · BBC2 Mon 8.30pm

MAIN CAST
Spike Milligan
John Bluthal
Carol Cleveland
Chris Langham
Rita Webb
Neil Shand
Johnny Vyvyan
Julia Breck
Fanny Carby

CREDITS
writers Spike Milligan/Neil Shand · *additional material* Chris Langham · *director* Ray Butt · *producer* Sydney Lotterby

A seasonal special for the arch Goonster, up to his usual anarchic mayhem. The title was a cheeky reference to an obscene impression perpetrated with the male genitalia that Milligan had probably witnessed, or performed, while serving in the army.

The Melting Pot

UK · BBC · SITCOM

1 × 30 mins · colour
11 June 1975 · BBC1 Wed 9.25pm

MAIN CAST

Mr Van Gogh	Spike Milligan
Mr Rembrandt	John Bird
Paddy O'Brien	Frank Carson
Nefertiti Skupinski	Alexandra Dane
Luigi O'Reilly	Wayne Brown
Eric Lee Fung	Harry Fowler
Richard Armitage	John Bluthal
Sheik Yamani	Anthony Brothers
Colonel Grope	Robert Dorning
Bluey Notts	Bill Kerr

CREDITS

writers Spike Milligan/Neil Shand · *producer* Roger Race

Six years after Johnny Speight's controversial *Curry And Chips* (see above) Spike Milligan once more appeared blacked-up, this time as an illegal immigrant to boot. He and John Bird were cast as a Pakistani father and son who enter Britain illegally by rowing boat, believing it to be the milk and honey land of free speech and no racism. Arriving via Amsterdam, where they have naïvely picked up the 'discreet' pseudonyms Mr Van Gogh and Mr Rembrandt, they end up living at 7 Piles Road, London, in the dingy lodgings of an Irish Republican coalman, Paddy O'Brien, and his sensual, South African-raised daughter Nefertiti Skupinski. The house is pandemonium, and the two Asians are true innocents abroad, mixing it with the other lodgers and regular visitors: black Yorkshireman Luigi O'Reilly, Chinese cockney spiv Eric Lee Fung, Orthodox London Jew Richard Armitage, the alcoholic, racist ex-Indian army officer Colonel Grope, the crude, racist Australian bookie's runner Bluey Notts, and the Orthodox Arab with a Scots accent (he works at the Bank of Scotland, Peckham branch) Sheik Yamani.

The idea, as with *Curry And Chips*, was to ridicule racism and highlight the ignorance of the issue but the style was misjudged and the ingredients constituted *way* too much of a heady brew for the BBC to handle – the five remaining episodes of the six-part series, all in-the-can, were never shown. All six scripts for *The Melting Pot* were published in a book of that title in 1983.

The Last Laugh Before TV-am

UK · C4 (RAVEL PRODUCTIONS) · SKETCH

1 × 30 mins · colour

2 Dec 1985 · Mon 9.25pm

MAIN CAST
Spike Milligan
Chris Langham
Emil Wolk
Mark Steel
Ra Ra Zoo

CREDITS

writers Spike Milligan/John Antrobus · *director* John Stroud · *producer* Alan Wright

A one-off show on C4, Milligan's first for Britain's new, fourth channel. Support/guest acts were drawn from the burgeoning 'alternative' comedy/cabaret circuit; TV-am was the then provider of breakfast television on ITV.

Milligan was next seen on C4 on 19 April 1986, when the channel aired *Spike*, a one-hour tribute made by Granada and presented by Shelley Rohde. Milligan

remembered his early days and various people came on to pay tribute, among them Richard Lester, Harry Secombe, Denis Norden, Michael Palin and Michael Foot MP.

An Evening With Spike Milligan

UK · ITV (WATCHMAKER PRODUCTIONS FOR CARLTON) · STANDUP

1 × 60 mins · colour

24 Feb 1996 · Sat 9pm

MAIN CAST
Spike Milligan

CREDITS

executive producer Elaine Bedell · *producer* Carolyn Longton

Carlton chose Milligan to kick-off its *An Evening With …* series (virtually a replica of LWT's long-running *An Audience With …*) A studio packed with celebrities – Sir Harry Secombe was among them – was delightfully entertained by Spike's reminiscences, poetry and song.

Milly

see **MARTIN, Millicent**

Milo O'Shea

UK · BBC · STANDUP

1 × 30 mins · colour

16 Mar 1970 · BBC2 Mon 9.40pm

MAIN CAST
Milo O'Shea

CREDITS

writer Hugh Leonard · *producer* Ian MacNaughton

An eve of St Patrick's Day 1970 special for the Irish character actor Milo O'Shea, then enjoying great popularity in the BBC1 sitcom *Me Mammy*. He performed sketches, read humorous poetry · and sang Irish songs. The full title of the programme was *Milo O'Shea Offers You A Small Irish For St Patrick's Day*.

The Milton Berle Show

USA · NBC · STANDUP/SKETCH

1 × 60 mins · b/w

US date: 11 Jan 1959

UK date: 19 May 1960 · BBC Thu 8.05pm

MAIN CAST
Milton Berle
Lucille Ball
Desi Arnaz

CREDITS

writer Lou Derman · *director* Desi Arnaz · *producer* Irving Starr

Milton Berle, born Milton Berlinger in New York on 12 July 1908, was the first comedy superstar of American television. Affection-

ately nicknamed 'Uncle Miltie' or 'Mr Television', his Tuesday-night series for NBC, *The Milton Berle Show* (from 1948), was a viewer magnet, and he is accredited with the sudden rise in sales of television receivers in the USA much in the way that the Queen's Coronation of 1953 is said to have dramatically increased TV sales in the UK.

Berle's style was that of a wisecracking, fast-talking gag machine, and, while his TV shows were rarely renowned for their subtlety, viewers loved the fact that they were never more than a few seconds away from the next punchline. The series finally floundered in 1956 when viewers were lured away by a sensational sitcom launched by rival network CBS, *The Phil Silvers Show*. But Berle survived to fight another day, appearing on TV in a number of subsequent series and specials.

This particular TV special was set in Las Vegas and featured Lucille Ball and Desi Arnaz in their *I Love Lucy* characters. (This probably prompted the BBC to buy it from America: Ball was well known in Britain whereas Berle was not.)

Mincemeat

UK · BBC · SKETCH/SATIRE

1 × 60 mins · b/w

20 Dec 1947 · Sat 8.30pm

MAIN CAST
Richard Hearne
Henry Oscar
Joan Hickson
Maxine Audley
John Salew
Richard Goolden

CREDITS

writers A E Wilson, Archie Harradine · *producer* John Glyn-Jones

A star-studded Christmas special that featured comedy sketches on a single theme: 'the incriminating letter, circumstantial or otherwise, that gets into the wrong hands'. The sketches parodied the style of a number of famous writers, from Shakespeare to Noël Coward, all drawn from theatre-critic and writer A E Wilson's book *Playwrights In Aspic*.

Other parts of the programme – which was subtitled 'How To Plan An Evening's Television' – included Richard Hearne causing mayhem while demonstrating how to mend a hole in a wall, and producer John Glyn-Jones, in full Russian Grand Duke costume, attempting to perform a Russian folk song.

Mind Your Language 1

UK · ITV (LWT) · SITCOM

29 × 30 mins · colour

Series One (13) 30 Dec 1977–24 Mar 1978 · Fri 7pm

Series Two (8) 7 Oct–25 Nov 1978 · Sat mostly 6pm

Series Three (8) 27 Oct–15 Dec 1979 · Sat mostly 6.45pm

MAIN CAST

Jeremy Brown	Barry Evans
Miss Courtney	Zara Nutley
Ali Nadim	Dino Shafeek
Giovanni Capello/Cuppello	George Camiller
Maximillian Papandrious	Kevork Malikyan
Taro Nagazumi	Robert Lee
Anna Schmidt	Jacki Harding
Jamila Ranjha	Jamila Massey
Juan Cervantes	Ricardo Montez
Ranjeet Singh	Albert Moses
Danielle Favre	Françoise Pascal
Chung Su-Lee	Pik-Sen Lim
Gladys	Iris Sadler
Sid	Tommy Godfrey
Zoltan Szabo	Gabor Vernon (series 2)
Ingrid Svenson	Anna Bergman (series 2)

CREDITS

writer Vince Powell · director/producer Stuart Allen

A return to TV for Barry Evans, who had virtually vanished from it after leaving the *Doctor* series. *Mind Your Language* cast him as Jeremy Brown, the teacher of an English evening class for foreign students whose ages ranged from twenties to pensionable. Mostly, the comedy derived from misunderstandings, and with a class full of non-English speakers these were plentiful, whether Brown was protectively saving his students from trouble or finding himself the victim of their trivial pursuits. Problems also came courtesy of the frostily formidable college principal Miss Courtney, who, in best authoritarian sitcom style, always seemed to find Brown in compromising positions.

The scripts ensured that every possible foreign stereotype was milked, and to this effect the class included representatives from China, France, Germany, Greece, India (both Sikh and Muslim), Italy, Japan, Pakistan, Spain and Sweden. 'Please, let us have no racialism,' teacher Brown pleaded of his pupils in the opening episode, 'in this class all are equal.' All things being equal, then, it is fair to say that this was still *very* dodgy comedy, deriving easy laughs from 'foolish foreigners' and their linguistic difficulties. It may not have been racist, as some claimed, but it certainly wasn't clever.

In 1985 another 13 episodes were made – see following entry – and then the format of *Mind Your Language* was sold to American TV where it was re-made as *What A Country!* and syndicated in 1986–87 for 26 episodes. Soviet comedian/defector Yakov Smirnoff (yes, really) starred as a Russian immigrant taxi driver, studying in Los Angeles to become an American citizen, together with Hungarian, Pakistani, Chinese, African and Mexican classmates. The Pakistani was played by the Indian tennis star Vijay Amritaj. Garrett M Brown was Taylor Brown,

the teacher, and Gail Strickland was cast as the principal.

Mind Your Language 2

UK · TRI FILMS · SITCOM

13 × 30 mins · colour

4 Jan–12 Apr 1986 · ITV Sat 2.15pm

MAIN CAST

Jeremy Brown	Barry Evans
Ingrid Svenson	Anna Bergman
Rita	Sue Bond
Giovanni Capello/Cuppello	George Camiller
Michelle Dumas	Marie-Elise Grepne
Anna Schmidt	Jacki Harding
Maria Papandrious	Jenny Lee-Wright
Juan Cervantes	Ricardo Montez
Ranjeet Singh	Albert Moses
Miss Courtney	Zara Nutley
Fu Wong Chang	Vincent Wong
Farrukh Azzam	Raj Patel
Henshawe	Harry Littlewood

CREDITS

writer Vince Powell · director Stuart Allen · executive producer Bachu Patel · producer Albert Moses

Six years after LWT brought down the curtain on *Mind Your Language*, viewers in four ITV regions were 'treated' to a new series. This was not made by London Weekend, however, but by an independent company, Tri Films, and it was produced by Albert Moses, who played one of the foreign students in the show. Writer Vince Powell, director Stuart Allen and most of the old cast were back on board, with some additions and replacements to cover the exits, and the programmes were shot on location and in a converted warehouse behind Waterloo Station in London.

The humour, safe to say, was much as before, with the same set-up in the same school. LWT declined to screen the new production but Central, HTV and Ulster broadcast a few episodes, and the series' best exposure was in the north-west, where Granada screened all 13 in one swoop. (Accordingly, the dates above refer to Granada's transmissions.) The series also sold well overseas.

Mind Your Manners

UK · BBC · CHILDREN'S SKETCH

7 × 10 mins (approx) · b/w

13 Jan–7 Apr 1951 · fortnightly Sat around 5pm

MAIN CAST

Elsie	Harry Hemsley
Peter	Peter Madden
Irene	Irene Prador

CREDITS

deviser Cecil Madden · writers Jill Allgood/Harry Hemsley · producer Jill Allgood

A series of TV appearances for the mimic Harry Hemsley, who scored on BBC radio

with his 'imaginary family' of children: Elsie, Winnie, Johnny and baby Horace. (Hemsley's impressions of youngsters were so accurate that they fooled many radio listeners.) In *Mind Your Manners* he brought Elsie, one of his 'children', to the small-screen for seven fortnightly visits, presented as part of the *For The Children* strand *Telescope*. The theme was role-reversal: parents Peter and Irene behaved badly and were rebuked by their small daughter.

Note. Harry Hemsley suffered a heart attack two days before the final edition in the series, and was hospitalised as a result; he then died on 8 April 1951. Despite his absence, this last programme was still made (broadcast live, as were all TV shows at the time), with someone else – unidentified in BBC paperwork – providing the voice of Elsie, out-of-vision. This particular edition of *Mind Your Manners* was unusual in one other respect, too: in a move to involve the viewers (and possibly overcome a touch of writer's block), youngsters watching the previous edition had been invited to send in their suggestions for a plot, upon which the script would be written. Two children came up with the same idea and, as joint winners, they were interviewed on air by Cliff Michelmore and asked to give their opinions of the piece.

Mind Your Own Business

UK · BBC · SITCOM

1 × 30 mins · colour

8 July 1970 · BBC1 Wed 7.30pm

MAIN CAST

Bill	Tony Selby
Ernie	Derek Griffiths
Dad	Norman Bird
Mum	Hilda Fenemore
Audrey	Cheryl Hall
Muriel	Adrienne Posta

CREDITS

writers Tony Bilbow/Mike Fentiman · producer Dennis Main Wilson

A *Comedy Playhouse* pilot about a cockney family trying to make ends meet as window-cleaners. The nub of the piece was that the two sons had different skin colour: Bill was white and Ernie black, the result of Mum's wartime fling with an American GI. No series developed.

Minding The Shop

UK · BBC · SITCOM

1 × 30 mins · colour

19 Aug 1968 · BBC2 Mon 8pm

MAIN CAST

George	Brian Cox
American lady	Margaret Tyzack
Shop owner	Ivor Dean

CREDITS
writer Alun Owen · producer James Gilbert

An sitcom oddity from the droll dramatist Alun Owen (*No Trams To Lime Street*; *Lena, O My Lena*; *A Hard Day's Night*) whose sometimes bleak scenarios were often laced with veins of black comedy. *Minding The Shop* – about an American customer encountering a bizarre brand of salesmanship from a shop assistant, George, in charge while his boss is out – stood alone on BBC2 and was not presented under the banner of any existing series. This is perhaps because it was felt too comedic for that period's series *Thirty Minute Theatre* (to which Owen contributed) yet too offbeat for *Comedy Playhouse*. Its status as 'quasi-sitcom' merits its inclusion here.

The Misfit

UK · ITV (ATV) · SITCOM

13 × 60 mins · colour

Series One (6) 3 Mar–7 Apr 1970 · Tue 9pm

Series Two (7) 1 Mar–12 Apr 1971 · Mon mostly 9pm

MAIN CAST
Basil Allenby-Johnson · · · · · · · Ronald Fraser
Stanley Allenby-Johnson · · · · · Patrick Newell
· (series 2)

OTHER APPEARANCES
Alicia Allenby-Johnson · · · · Susan Carpenter
· (series 1)
Ted Allenby-Johnson · · · · · · · · · Simon Ward
· (series 1)

CREDITS
writer Roy Clarke · directors James Gatward (8), Dennis Vance (5) · producer Dennis Vance

Written by Roy Clarke – later to score huge success with *Open All Hours*, *Last Of The Summer Wine*, *Keeping Up Appearances* and other fine series – *The Misfit* related the incidents and accidents of Basil 'Badger' Allenby-Johnson, a stiff-upper-lip middle-aged chappie who returns to England after living the colonial life as a rubber planter out in Malaya. He likes a drink … but he doesn't care for the old country now that it has undergone the Swinging Sixties. For a start, there's his trendy daughter-in-law Alicia, married to his son Ted; then there's the feminist issue, the long-haired younger generation's tendency to take to the streets and demonstrate against things they don't like, and the fact that he is the wrong side of an employable age. Each episode saw Badger looking uneasily at these and other issues at home and play in Britain in 1970, with a different support cast featured each week. Only in the second series was there a regular second player – Patrick Newell, who was cast as Basil's brother Stanley.

Misfits

UK · ITV (YORKSHIRE) · SITCOM

7 × 30 mins · colour

5 June–17 July 1981 · Fri 8.30pm

MAIN CAST
Liz Ridgeway · · · · · · · · · · · Anne Stallybrass
Skinner · · · · · · · · · · · · · · · · · · Enn Reitel
Oscar · · · · · · · · · · · · · · · · · · Kevin Lloyd
Monica Forbes · · · · · · · · · · · Marcia Ashton

CREDITS
writer Eric Chappell · director/producer Ronnie Baxter

Skinner and Oscar are a pair of misfits, intent, oddly, on journeying to Kathmandu, but without the wherewithal within. They get as far as Yorkshire and come upon a seemingly well-to-do woman, Liz Ridgeway. Liz is a divorcee, a plain-speaker, a free spirit happy to share her soul with wayfarers and life's outcasts. An unlikely trio is formed, witnessed by Liz's friend Monica.

Written by Eric Chappell, the author of **Rising Damp**, *Misfits* provided a much-sought-after comedy role for Anne Stallybrass, who had hitherto appeared in BBC heavyweight dramas and (as Anne Onedin) in the popular sailing-serial *The Onedin Line*.

Misleading Cases

UK · BBC · SITCOM

19 × 30 mins (13 × b/w · 6 × colour)

Series One (6 × b/w) *A P Herbert's 'Misleading Cases'* 20 June–25 July 1967 · BBC1 Tue 7.30pm

Series Two (7 × b/w) 18 Sep–30 Oct 1968 · BBC1 Wed 8.20pm

Series Three (6 × colour) *A P Herbert's Misleading Cases* 30 July–10 Sep 1971 · BBC1 Fri 8.30pm

MAIN CAST
Mr Justice Swallow · · · · · · · · · · Alastair Sim
Albert Haddock · · · · · · · · · · · · · Roy Dotrice
Sir Joshua Hoot · · · · · · · · · Thorley Walters
Mrs Haddock · · · · · · · · · · · · Avice Landon

CREDITS
creator A P Herbert · writers Alan Melville, Henry Cecil, Christopher Bond, Myles Rudge, Geoffrey Lumsden, Michael Gilbert · producers Michael Mills, John Howard Davies

High-class verbal comedy based on stories by A P Herbert, using the arena of a courtroom to debate moral issues such as 'Are Englishmen really free?' and 'Is every man's home his castle?' Each week, eternal litigant Albert Haddock appeared before the court involved in a small case of his own making, the crux of which hinged on one such moral question. The magnificent Alastair Sim – in a rare TV role – presided as Justice Swallow, who hovered between delight and frustration at Haddock's antics but could always be relied

upon to bring in a fair judgement. Sir Joshua Hoot was usually the opposing QC.

Born in 1890, A P (Alan Patrick) Herbert delighted generations of readers with his humorous writings. An Oxford law graduate, he never practised at the bar but used his studies to write six books on the subject (beginning with *Misleading Cases*, 1927), the first appearance in print of any such story occurring in *Punch* magazine in 1924. After a greatly varied and prolific career, Herbert died in 1971, aged 81.

The TV series boasted a galaxy of guest stars during its run, including comedy stalwarts Irene Handl, Fred Emney, Warren Mitchell, Jimmy Hanley, Arthur Mullard, Patricia Hayes, John Le Mesurier, Sam Kydd and, in the final episode, John Cleese, who appeared in a surprisingly low-key role as a financial expert, a part which, he admitted, he took solely for the opportunity to work with Alastair Sim.

Note. Credits for the first two series stated 'adapted by Alan Melville with some assistance from Henry Cecil', with the 'courtroom scenes' written by one or two of the other writers named above. The third series was credited entirely to Christopher Bond and Michael Gilbert.

Miss Jones And Son

UK · ITV (THAMES) · SITCOM

12 × 30 mins · colour

Series One (6) 18 Apr–30 May 1977 · Mon 8pm

Series Two (6) 9 Jan–13 Feb 1978 · Mon 8pm

MAIN CAST
Elizabeth Jones · · · · · · · · · · · Paula Wilcox
Geoffrey · · · · · · · · · · · · Christopher Beeny
· (first 8 episodes)
Dad · · · · · · · · · · · · · Norman Bird (series 1)
Mum · · · · · · · · · Charlotte Mitchell (series 1);
· · · · · · · · · · · · · · · · · · · Joan Scott (series 2)
Baby · · · · · · · · · · · · · · · · · · · Luke Steensil
David · · · · · · · David Savile (last 3 episodes)

OTHER APPEARANCES
Rose Tucker · · · · · · · · · · · · · · · · Cass Allen

CREDITS
writer Richard Waring · directors Peter Frazer-Jones (10), Robert Reed (2) · producer Peter Frazer-Jones

Born in the spirit of adventure that was the late 1970s, *Miss Jones And Son* was the first British sitcom to find laughter in the hitherto shaming trials and, yes, tribulations of an unmarried mother. How times had moved on.

Well, sort of – the parents of this particular unmarried mother were indeed ashamed of their daughter's plight. Even worse (as they saw it), the father – Fleet Street reporter Alan Sadler – wasn't even aware of the existence of his offspring, and was never seen. After four years together, within sound of the wedding bells, he had yearned for freedom and departed, just before Elizabeth Jones was pronounced pregnant. Shackled by her parents' attitude (although they did relent after a while), Miss Jones and son Roland Desmond Geoffrey, nicknamed 'Roly', found a small pad of their own, in Pimlico (London), where she discovered Geoffrey, a neighbour and platonic friend.

Never quite as adventurous as it could have been – there was no sign of any strike for independence or radical feminism in her thoughts or deeds – most episodes in the two series revolved around Miss Jones's hunt for a man. But could she be fancy-free without being footloose? At first the answer was no; however, by the end of the second series she seemed to have found her grail in David, a book-author-cum-widower with baby daughter. As she was a freelance book illustrator, the match seemed too good to ignore.

The format of *Miss Jones And Son* was sold by impresario Don Taffner to American TV, where it was remade as *Miss Winslow And Son* and networked by CBS in 1979. Darleen Carr starred as Susan Winslow, mother of baby Edmund Hillary Winslow. It lasted just six episodes, screened 28 March to 2 May.

The 'single mum' premise was explored again 16 years on, in **The Gingerbread Girl**.

Mister Ed

USA · SYNDICATION THEN CBS (FILMWAYS) · SITCOM

144 × 30 mins · b/w
US dates: early 1961–4 Sep 1966
*UK dates: 9 July 1964–27 July 1965
(26 episodes) ITV various dates and times

MAIN CAST
Wilbur Post · · · · · · · · · · · · · · · Alan Young
Carol Post · · · · · · · · · · · · · Connie Hines
The voice of Mister Ed · · · Allan 'Rocky' Lane
Roger Addison · · · · Larry Keating (1961–64)
Kay Addison · · · · · · Edna Skinner (1961–64)
Gordon Kirkwood · · · · Leon Ames (1964–66)
Winnie Kirkwood · · · · · Florence MacMichael
· (1964–66)

CREDITS
writers Larry Rhine, Ben Starr, Lou Derman · director Arthur Lubin · producers Arthur Lubin, Al Simon

After moving into their new home in Los Angeles, newly married couple Wilbur and Carol Post find something in the barn – a palomino horse named Mister Ed – left behind by the previous owners. To his astonishment, Wilbur discovers that Mister Ed can talk, but only to him because he's the first and only human Ed has liked enough to converse with. He's a cultured horse too: he likes music, the arts and, especially, fillies. A freelance architect, Wilbur sets up office in the barn, and enjoys exchanging tales (stories,

that is) with the horse – except, of course, everyone else thinks that he is mad to be talking to an animal and refuse to consider that the animal talks back to him.

From such an apparently weak and silly premise came a much-loved sitcom, which owed largely to the interplay between man (the English-born comic actor Alan Young – see **Alan Young**, **It's Young Again**, **Personal Appearance** and **Coming Of Age**) and beast, with Mister Ed becoming friend, confidant and a valued escape from reality for Wilbur, qualities not so easily available to him outside of the barn. Critics hated the series but not so the public, whose numbers kept it on screen for five years – despite a rocky start. Having directed seven 1950s movies about a talking donkey named Francis (with Donald O'Connor starring in six of them and Mickey Rooney the other), Arthur Lubin had been trying since 1954 to launch such a premise on TV. Even after receiving backing from Al Simon, the producer of **The Burns And Allen Show**, Lubin had little luck. An unaired pilot – *The Wonderful World Of Wilbur Pope*, with Scott McKay as Wilbur – was made but the networks wouldn't bite. It was only when Alan Young stepped into the role and *Mister Ed* lucked into syndication that CBS, which had been vocal in dismissing the series when it was first offered to them, decided to give it a network airing. The rest is equine history.

*Note. C4 gave *Mister Ed* its most extensive UK run, screening 78 episodes from 20 March 1987 to 24 May 1989. Perhaps it was these that were seen by Harry Enfield and Paul Whitehouse, inspiring their spot-on weekly 'Mr Dead' pastiches in the 1997 series of **Harry Enfield And Chums**.

Mistero Buffo

see **Robbie Coltrane In Mistero Buffo**

The Mistress

UK · BBC · SITCOM

12 × 30 mins · colour
Series One (6) 17 Jan–21 Feb 1985 · BBC2 Thu 9pm
Series Two (6) 22 Jan–26 Feb 1987 · BBC2 Thu 9pm

MAIN CAST
Maxine · · · · · · · · · · · · · · · · Felicity Kendal
Luke · · · · · · · · · · · Jack Galloway (series 1);
· · · · · · · · · · · · · · · · Peter McEnery (series 2)
Helen · · · · · · · · · · · · · · · · · · · Jane Asher
Jamie · · · · · · · · · · · · Tony Copley (series 2)

CREDITS
writer Carla Lane · director/producer Gareth Gwenlan

After exploring the mind of a woman contemplating but never committing adultery

(**Butterflies**), and a woman discovering that her long-term live-in lover was having an affair (**Solo**), writer Carla Lane here turned her attention to a fully fledged 'other woman' comedy, depicting a man's mistress. This is Maxine, who manages a florist shop and is having an affair with Luke (whose wife, Helen, is unsuspecting).

This series came at a time when Carla Lane was writing increasingly downbeat comedies, intentionally moving away from gags and utilising humour as a pressure valve in situations tinged with angst, disillusionment and melancholy. But the character of Maxine – despite suffering understandable pangs of guilt and worries regarding her insecure relationship – remained chirpy, liberated and optimistic. This appeared to indicate that, superficially at least, the advantages of conducting an affair outweigh the disadvantages. As Lane also realised, however, one's viewpoint on dangerous liaisons depends entirely upon one's role in the scenario.

A Mixed Bag

UK · BBC · SKETCH

1 × 15 mins · b/w
28 Apr 1952 · Mon 8.15pm

MAIN CAST
Bernard Miles

CREDITS
writer Bernard Miles · producer Gilchrist Calder

A short programme in which the actor/director/screenwriter Bernard Miles presented four sketches peopled by his humorous character inventions – a bus conductor discussing Greek mythology, an old woman giving a first-aid demonstration, a sailor, and a country yokel.

Miles was enjoying much small-screen popularity at the time: his portrayal of Long John Silver in a 1951 children's television dramatisation of *Treasure Island* was so well received that the serial was re-staged in an adult Saturday-night slot.

Mixed Blessings

UK · ITV (LWT) · SITCOM

22 × 30 mins · colour
Series One (7) 3 Mar–14 Apr 1978 · Fri 7.30pm
Series Two (6) 6 Oct–10 Nov 1978 · Fri 7pm
Series Three (9) 12 Apr–21 June 1980 · Sat mostly 7.30pm

MAIN CAST
Thomas Simpson · · · · · · · Christopher Blake
Susan Lambert/Simpson · · · Muriel Odunton
Matilda Lambert · · · · · · · · · Carmen Munro
William Lambert · · · · · · · · · · Stefan Kalipha
Winston Lambert · · · · · · · · Gregory Munroe
Annie Simpson · · · · · · · · · · · · · Sylvia Kay
Edward Simpson · · · · · · · · · George Waring
Aunt Dorothy · · · · · · · · · · · Joan Sanderson
Mrs Beasley · · · · · · · · · · · · Pauline Delany

CREDITS
writers Sid Green (series 1 & 2), Sid Green/Derrick Goodwin (series 3) · *directors* Derrick Goodwin (series 1 & 2), Pennant Roberts (series 3) · *producer* Derrick Goodwin

Love Thy Neighbour had placed black alongside white and set the stage for racial insults. *Mixed Blessings* merged black and white in harmony – or at least appeared to. The series centred on a newly married couple, Thomas and Susan, both university graduates and both born in England. Thomas is white, though, and Susan is black, and the two sets of parents – his are Annie and Edward Simpson, hers are Matilda and William Lambert – don't like it, or each other, one tiny bit. Thomas and Susan have to honeymoon in secret and then live for a while at Thomas's matter-of-fact Aunt Dorothy's before finding a place of their own. To add insult to what the parents see as injury, Susan is employed as a social worker but Thomas is unemployed (until midway through the second series) and so she supports the partnership financially. At the end of the second series Susan announced that she was pregnant, and she carried throughout the third, delivering at the end.

Mixed Blessings aired in the UK to a mixed reaction, but it was essentially harmless stuff – a point reflected by the fact that the series was sold by ITV for screening in the West Indies.

Note. Thomas – Christopher Blake – also sang the theme song, which was written by the actor Peter Davison. The part of Susan's brother, Winston, was played by Gregory Munroe, the real-life son of Carmen Munro (who played Matilda), despite the different surname spelling.

Moesha

USA · UPN (REGAN JON/BIG TICKET TELEVISION) · SITCOM
─────────────
49 episodes (48 × 30 mins · 1 × 60 mins to 31/12/97 · continuing into 1998) · colour
US dates: 23 Jan 1996 to date
UK dates: 30 Mar 1997 to date (13 × 30 mins to 31/12/97) C4 Sun mostly 9.50am

MAIN CAST
Moesha Mitchell · · · · · · · · · Brandy Norwood
Frank Mitchell · · · · · · · · · William Allen Young
Dee Mitchell · · · · · · · · · · · Sheryl Lee Ralph
Kim Parker · · · · · · · · · · · · Countess Vaughn
Myles Mitchell · · · · · · · · · · · Marcus T Paulk
Hakeem Campbell · · · · · · · · Lamont Bentley
Andell · · · · · · · · · · · · · · · · · Yvette Wilson
Niecy · · · · · · · · · · · · · · · · · Shar Jackson
'Q' Quinton · · · · · · · Fredro Starr (1996–97)

CREDITS
creators/executive producers Ralph R Farquhar, Sara V Finney, Vida Spears · *writers* Mara Brock and others · *directors* Henry Chan and others · *producers* Mary Ellen Jones, Leo J Clarke

For the three years following the death of her mother, Moesha Mitchell (15 at the start of the series but soon turning 16) has acted as the woman of the house for her younger brother, Myles, and salesman father, Frank. When Frank remarries, Moesha finds it difficult to come to terms with her stepmother, Dee, who also happens to be a teacher at Moesha's school. (Frank met Dee at a single-parents meeting there.) Despite these initial difficulties, Dee and Moesha arrive at an understanding and manage to co-exist in an uneasy peace.

Moesha is smart – very smart – yet despite her wisecracking mouth, usage of street-slang, yearning for a date and adult outlook on life, she is also a good girl in the old-fashioned sense of the phrase. She seems more than happy to follow her dad's rule about not dating until she turns 16, and even after reaching that age her first dates are harmless. Also seen in the episodes were teen neighbour Hakeem, who spends most of his time at the Mitchells', eating them out of house and home; and Moesha's boy-obsessed, plump, full-of-fun friend, Kim. Storylines concerned Moesha's rites of passage as she tried to be cool with her friends while avoiding drugs, sex and hanging out with a bad crowd.

Brandy Norwood was already a multi-million selling, Grammy Award-winning singer when she demonstrated further talents by starring here as Moesha Mitchell. The series was designed specifically to appeal to other African-American teens, and while it was amiable enough entertainment it suffered from a sugary cuteness and – the usual problem – too much sentimentality. Most episodes ended with Moesha (or one of the other cast) Learning A Valuable Lesson, and this moralising was heavy-handed at times. The series' good intentions were clear, though.

Mog

UK · ITV (WITZEND PRODUCTIONS FOR CENTRAL) · SITCOM
─────────────
13 × 30 mins · colour
Series One (6) 26 May–30 June 1985 · Sun 10pm
Series Two (7) 5 July–16 Aug 1986 · Sat around 11.30pm

MAIN CAST
Mog · · · · · · · · · · · · · · · · · · · Enn Reitel
F K Henderson · · · · · · · · · · · · · Tim Wylton
Mrs Mortensen · · · · · · · · · Catherine Schell
Oliver · · · · · · · · · · · · · Christopher Villiers
Capt Greenaway · · · · · · · · · Alan Shearman
Earl · · · · · · · · · · · · · · · · Malcolm Frederick
Mrs Williams · · · · · · · · · · · · · Toni Palmer
Miranda · · · · · · · · · · · · Abigail Cruttenden
Sir Peter Wakefield · · · · · · · · · · · John Grillo
Tom Manners · · · Jeremy Nicholas (series 2)

CREDITS
creator Peter Tinniswood · *adapters/writers* Dick Clement/Ian La Frenais (3), Dick Clement (3), Ian La Frenais (1), Paul Makin (4), Alan Shearman/Tony Charles (1), Paul Minett/Brian Leveson (1) · *director* Nic Phillips · *executive producer* Allan McKeown · *producers* Glen Cardno/Tony Charles

A series with the highest pedigree – it was based on the 1970 novel of the same title by Peter Tinniswood, the creator of 'Uncle Mort' (*I Didn't Know You Cared*), and most of the scripts were written by Clement and La Frenais, authors of *The Likely Lads* and *Porridge*. But, somehow, *Mog* failed to hit the right comedic spot, its gentle humour not helped by the absence of a studio audience.

Everything revolved around the central character, Mog, a burglar by trade whose word is never his bond, who seeks refuge from the police in Briardene, a mental hospital, from where he hops out for his nightly work, and then hops back again to live with his odd group of comrades. Although a far from usual setting for a comedy series, the inmates were not too problematic; indeed – like Mog – they were not insane but merely a ragtag of eccentrics who had opted out of life.

The Molly Wopsies

UK · ITV (THAMES) · CHILDREN'S SITCOM
─────────────
7 × 30 mins · colour
Pilot *The Molly Wopsy* 21 June 1974 · Fri 4.50pm
One series (6) 17 Mar–21 Apr 1976 · Wed 4.50pm

MAIN CAST
PC Berry · · · · · · · · · · · · · · · · · Aubrey Morris
Sgt Needler · · · · · · · · · · Walter Gotell (pilot);
· · · · · · · · · · · · · · · · · George Innes (series)
Dinky Dunkley · · · · · · · · Tony Maiden (pilot);
· · · · · · · · · · · · · · · · · · · Ben Forster (series)
Alan Musgrove · · · · · · · · · · · · Phil Daniels
Dotty Minton · · · · · · · · · · · · · · Julie Taylor
Norman Yates · · · · · · · · · Matthew Whiteman

CREDITS
writer Ron Smith · *director* Stan Woodward · *producer* Ruth Boswell

The fifth of Thames' *Funny Ha Ha* children's comedies was written (so it was announced) by a 50-year-old machine-line worker at the Morris car factory in Oxford, a Mr Smith, who speculatively submitted a script to the TV company. His story was set in wartime Oxfordshire, in the village of Heathcote, and centred on two child evacuees who gave the local ghost the name Molly Wopsy and proceeded to form a gang, also with that name. Led by Dinky Dunkley, the outfit had one major adversary: the village copper PC Berry.

Close on two years after the original pilot episode (titled simply *The Molly Wopsy*) Thames screened a full series of such adventures, utilising Arthur Askey's recording of 'Run, Rabbit, Run' as the theme tune.

The Money Or The Gun

AUSTRALIA · ABC · SATIRE

23 × 60 mins (plus specials) · colour

Australian dates: 26 Aug 1989–19 Nov 1990 (and specials to 1994)

UK date: 16 Oct 1991 (1 × 30 mins) BBC2 Wed 7.40pm

MAIN CAST

Andrew Denton

CREDITS

writer Andrew Denton · *producer* Mark Fitzgerald

Screened in Britain one time only (in BBC's *DEF II* youth slot *Gimme 8*, in which cult TV programmes from around the world of particular appeal to young people were highlighted), this show featured the bespectacled Australian satirist Andrew Denton presenting a wry look at anxiety. Born on 4 May 1961, the son of writer Kit Denton, Andrew Denton burst on to the Aussie scene in the late 1980s with his trademark style of ad-libbed satire. His long-running TV series *The Money Or The Gun* took a different subject each week and mixed comedy with documentary and music – every musical guest had to perform Led Zeppelin's 'Stairway To Heaven'. (This led to an album of assorted such novelty versions and the hit-single release of Rolf Harris's rendition, a surprise Top Ten success on the British chart, his first such placing for 23 years.)

The Monkees

USA · NBC (RAYBERT PRODUCTIONS/SCREEN GEMS) · SITCOM

58 × 30 mins · colour

US dates: 12 Sep 1966–25 Mar 1968

UK dates: 31 Dec 1966–13 June 1968 (56 episodes · b/w) BBC1 Sat around 6.15pm

MAIN CAST

Davy Jones	himself
Micky Dolenz	himself
Peter Tork	himself
Michael Nesmith	himself

CREDITS

creators/producers Bob Rafelson/Bert Schneider · *writers* Peter Mayerson, Treva Silverman, Dave Evans, Gerald Gardner/Dee Caruso, Coslough Johnson, Bernie Orenstein, Jack Winter and others · *directors* James Frawley, Bob Rafelson, Ralph Riskin, Bruce Kessler, Alex Singer, Ward Sylvester and others

'Hey-hey we're the Monkees!' sang the four mop-topped, assembly-line pop stars of this wacky US comedy. What they could have been singing was 'Hey-hey we're aping the Beatles!', and they certainly made a good go at it, with their *Help!*-influenced antics, catchy songs, modelled personalities and even the deliberate misspelling of their animal-name.

This is the story: two young TV producers (Bob Rafelson and Bert Schneider) decide to create a Beatles-like group to star in their own TV series and, hopefully, become as popular as the original act. To this end they place an advertisement in *Variety* (9 September 1965) calling for 'four insane boys, age 17–21', hold open auditions, gather much free publicity and, after turning down many hopefuls – including the singer Stephen Stills – they settle on their band: American former child-actor Micky Dolenz (The Manic One, an approximation of Ringo Starr), Peter Tork (The Gormless One, meant to be something like George Harrison), Michael Nesmith (The Deep And Deadpan One, a sort of John Lennon) and their very first choice, Davy Jones (The Short One, also The English One, intended to be like Paul McCartney). Mimicking Richard Lester's directorial style of jump cuts, slow- and fast-motion film and odd camera angles prevalent in *A Hard Day's Night* and *Help!*, Rafelson and Schneider crafted a fast-paced, frenetic TV show combining slapstick, engaging personalities and pop music in roughly equal quantities.

This cynical attempt to manufacture a youth cult had all the hallmarks of unmitigated disaster, and yet … *The Monkees* was actually likeable stuff. The obvious mistakes were avoided: the songs, many of them especially written for the band by top composers, were of a uniformly high standard, and the naturalistic playing of the stars prevented the series from becoming too slick. And by the end of its TV life a healthy dose of cynicism had crept into the proceedings too, enough to allow Frank Zappa a guest spot in the penultimate episode ('Monkees Blow Their Minds') and for the storyline of the last episode ('Mijacogeo') to centre on the exploitative power of television. A Monkees movie, *Head* (1968, director Bob Rafelson), continued this satirical tone and added a druggy psychedelic twist to the usual blend. Although the band were about to split, *The Monkees* had been an unqualified success story, for while the Beatles themselves, the Fab Four, had moved on from being the loveable mop-tops enjoying *Help!*-style hi-jinks, the Prefab Four filled in the void they left behind, and plenty of teenies were taken in by the invention and had a good time with some irresistible pop music and new opportunities to scream.

After the TV series came to an end the Monkees returned for a one-off hour-long music special, subtitled '33⅓ Revolutions Per Monkee' (screened in the USA on 14 April 1969 and in the UK by BBC1 – still in monochrome – on 24 May 1969). And on 28 December 1977 BBC1 presented *The Great Golden Hits Of The Monkees By The Guys Who Sang 'Em And The Guys Who Wrote 'Em*, produced by Micky Dolenz (he had become a successful TV producer, and for a while worked on ITV children's series detailed in this book). In this TV special, a studio recording of a 1975–76 stage act that toured US amusement parks and night-clubs, Dolenz, Davy Jones and two of the group's songwriters, Tommy Boyce and Bobby Hart, reminisced about the original TV series and the hit songs. In 1987 a misguided attempt to repeat the old formula resulted in the short-lived and undistinguished syndicated US TV series *The New Monkees*, with none of the original four participating. (This series has not been seen in Britain.)

Since then the 1960s TV series has been re-shown on umpteen different occasions, on a variety of British TV channels, and the band has reunited on several occasions for concert tours, the most notable occasion being the 1997 world trek that saw Michael Nesmith, hitherto reluctant to get back together with the other three – he had a career to pursue, and the others simply toured without him – complete the original unit for the first time in almost 30 years. Such was the media interest in the event that a new hour-length TV special, titled simply *The Monkees*, was networked in the USA by ABC on 17 February 1997 (screened in a 45-minute slot in the UK by C4 on 12 April 1997). This show featured contemporary videos and performance footage of the band interwoven with a new but terribly corny fictional story shot in true Monkees style.

Bob Monkhouse

Born in Beckenham on 1 June 1928, Robert Alan Monkhouse was educated at Dulwich College and, precociously talented, at the age of 12 was drawing strip-cartoons for children's comics. At about the same time, he also tried his hand at selling jokes to comedians, but with no initial success. After leaving school he became a cartoon film animator, developed a comedy act and began to be paid for gags that he provided to comedians (including the great Max Miller). Another source of income came from writing a number of salacious 'pulp fiction' books. In 1947 the young Monkhouse (now enlisted through National Service as a corporal) made his radio debut with Ralph Reader's BBC *Gang Show* series, and the following year (29 January 1948) he made his TV debut in the Corporation's fresh-talent showcase *New To You*.

Later in 1948, Monkhouse performed a formal audition for BBC radio, making such an impact with producer Dennis Main Wilson that he was immediately signed up for a number of appearances. (By this time, Monkhouse had met his long-term writing and sometime performing partner Denis Goodwin, but the two continued to work separately as well as a team.) Monkhouse quickly became a star, appearing regularly in popular programmes like *Variety Bandbox* and *Workers' Playtime*, and contributing scripts to even more shows. In 1949 he became the first comedian to be put under exclusive contract by the BBC and he began to make regular guest appearances in TV shows – including *Rooftop Rendezvous*, *Café Continental*, *Variety Parade*, *Geraldo's Band Show*, *Vic Oliver's Show Business*, *This Is Show Business* and *Garrison Theatre*.

It was the start of a long, long career on British TV, still running at the time of writing, that has seen the comic appear as a standup performer, sketch participator, chat-show guest, chat-show host, quiz-show host, serious dramatic actor and more. Although somewhat derided for a while – as a result of his hosting banal game-shows, and for what some viewers perceive as insincerity – Monkhouse is currently back in vogue, his quick and ready wit, pleasing personality and sheer longevity gaining respect from all quarters, especially young comedians coming through the ranks, very few of whom (if any) are likely to have top-rated careers that span, as Monkhouse's has, fully 50 years.

The following entry includes all of Bob Monkhouse's principal TV comedy appearances (aside from guest spots); in addition to these he has hosted *Val Parnell's Sunday Night At The London Palladium*, *Candid Camera* and *Bob Says Opportunity Knocks*, guested in a number of American shows, made a number of feature films, and written about film comedy and attempted to resurrect public interest in the great silent-film comedians with his memorable TV series *Mad Movies*. His stints as quiz- and game-show host have included *Do You Trust Your Wife?* (1956), *For Love Or Money* (1950s), *The Golden Shot* (1967–71, 1975), *Quick On The Draw* (1973–74), *Celebrity Squares* (1975–79, 1993–95), *Family Fortunes* (1980–83), *Bob's Full House* (1984–89), *$64,000 Question* (1990–91), *Bob's Your Uncle* (1991), *Gagtag* (1993) and *Monkhouse's Memory Masters* (1994–95).

See also *Christmas Box*.

Fast And Loose

UK · BBC · SKETCH
10 editions (5×45 mins · 5×30 mins) · b/w
Special (45 mins) 12 May 1954 · Wed 9.25pm
Series One (4×45 mins) 29 Sep–22 Dec 1954 · monthly Wed mostly 9.15pm
Series Two (5×30 mins) 20 Oct–15 Dec 1955 · fortnightly Thu around 9pm
MAIN CAST
Bob Monkhouse
Denis Goodwin

CREDITS
writers Bob Monkhouse/Denis Goodwin ·
producers Kenneth Carter, Brian Tesler

Workaholics Monkhouse and Goodwin fronted as well as scripted this sketch series, which came at a time when, together and separately, they were working in the fields of TV, radio, stage and cinema. (In his 'spare time' Monkhouse was even plying his trade in the USA too.)

The writers worked particularly hard on the first of these shows, announced as being the first in a series, and soon realised that they wouldn't be able to maintain the quality, especially with their other commitments. So Monkhouse faked a dead-faint at the end of the show which bought them precious breathing space – the programme did not return for another four months. When it did eventually get into a stride *Fast And Loose* had more than its fair share of the mishaps common to such live shows at this time, and in one sketch Monkhouse somehow contrived to blow off part of guest star Charlie Drake's ear during a sketch. One recurring slapstick routine featured Monkhouse as Osbert the Suitor, an accident-prone dolt endlessly bringing disaster upon the heads of his potential in-laws (played by Irene Handl and William Gauge) during his courtship of their daughter (sometimes Sheila Sweet, other times June Whitfield).

The Bob Monkhouse Show 1

UK · ITV (ITP PRODUCTIONS FOR ATV/ABC · *ATV) · SKETCH/STANDUP
2 editions (1×55 mins · 1×45 mins) · b/w
8 Dec 1956 · Sat 9pm (45 mins)
*20 Sep 1958 · Sat 8pm (55 mins)
MAIN CAST
Bob Monkhouse

CREDITS
producers Bill Lyon-Shaw (show 1), Albert Locke (show 2)

Two ITV specials for Bob Monkhouse, aired in the *Saturday Spectacular* strand. Guests included Sid Millward and Irene Handl in the first show, and Joan Savage and Kenneth Connor in the second. Monkhouse was to remain a staple of the commercial channel for some 30 years from this point, most of his appearances being as the host of game-shows and quizzes.

My Pal Bob

UK · BBC (*MONKHOUSE/GOODWIN PRODUCTIONS) · SITCOM
10×30 mins · b/w
Series One (4) 17 Jan–28 Feb 1957 · fortnightly Thu mostly 7.45pm

*Series Two (6) 28 Jan–7 Apr 1958 · fortnightly mostly Tue 7.30pm
MAIN CAST
narrator · · · · · · · · · · · · · · · Denis Goodwin
Bob Monkhouse · · · · · · · · · · · · · himself
Jill · · · · · · · · · · · Billie Whitelaw (series 1);
· · · · · · · · · · · · · · · · · · Jill Adams (series 2)
Terry · · · · · · · · · · · · · · · Terence Alexander
various roles · · · Kenneth Connor (series 2)

CREDITS
writers Bob Monkhouse/Denis Goodwin ·
producers Francis Essex, Ronald Marsh

Glimpses into the (fictional) life of Bob Monkhouse, related to the camera by his 'friend, partner and chief victim' Denis Goodwin. In the first series the role of Jill, Bob's wife, was played by Billie Whitelaw, already becoming established as a first-rate dramatic actress; in the second it was played by Jill Adams. Terence Alexander was cast as Terry, Bob's drunken next-door neighbour. For the second series, Monkhouse and Goodwin shot the episodes on film and leased them to the BBC for one screening, thus managing to maintain rights and prints. This approach was not only years before its time but it also, happily, ensured that these episodes survive intact in Monkhouse's own archive, a rarity with material of this period.

The Bob Monkhouse Hour

UK · ITV (ATV) · SKETCH/STANDUP
6×60 mins · b/w
18 Oct 1958 · Sat 7.55pm
15 Nov 1958 · Sat 7.55pm
14 Mar 1959 · Sat 7.55pm
4 Apr 1959 · Sat 7.55pm
27 June 1959 · Sat 7.55pm
7 July 1963 · Sun 8.25pm
MAIN CAST
Bob Monkhouse
Denis Goodwin (shows 1–5)

CREDITS
deviser Denis Goodwin · *writers* Bob Monkhouse/Denis Goodwin (shows 1–5), Sid Green/Dick Hills (show 6) · *additional material* Bob Monkhouse/Denis Goodwin (show 6) · *producers* Albert Locke (shows 1 & 2), Alan Tarrant (shows 3–5), Francis Essex (show 6)

Six single specials featuring Bob Monkhouse and (in the first five) professional partner Denis Goodwin. Kenneth Williams made a rare early guest TV appearance in the first of the bunch, Diana Dors and Tony Hawes appeared in the last.

The final show followed the end of Bob Monkhouse and Denis Goodwin's creative partnership, which had been disintegrating for a while and finally concluded in 1962 when Goodwin was offered work in the USA as one of Bob Hope's team of writers. He later returned to the UK and, facing deep personal crises, committed suicide in March 1975.

The Big Noise

UK · BBC · SITCOM

6 × 25 mins · b/w

18 Sep–23 Oct 1964 · BBC1 Fri mostly 8pm

MAIN CAST

Bob Mason · · · · · · · · · · · Bob Monkhouse
Kim Hunter · · · · · · · · · Norman Rossington

CREDITS

creators Bob Monkhouse/Denis Goodwin ·
writers Frank Muir/Denis Norden · executive
producer James Gilbert · producer Joe McGrath

Subtitled 'Episodes In The Uneasy Life Of A Top Pop Disc Jockey', this sitcom starred Monkhouse as Bob Mason, a typical product of the contemporary pop scene. Plots included Mason having to interview world famous pop stars the Heartbeats at his Auntie Lil's house in order to escape their manic fans; and talking a would-be suicide victim down from a ledge when the young man refused to talk to anyone else.

Occasional appearances from real-life pop DJs Jimmy Savile and David Jacobs, and the film journalist Peter Noble, added a touch of authenticity to the series, which also featured among its guest actors Warren Mitchell, David Hemmings, Sheila Steafel, Roy Hudd, Irene Handl and John Fortune. *The Big Noise* was reputedly harder-edged than similar product of the time, with Mason sporting a brash personality. It nevertheless failed to capture the public's imagination and lasted for only one series.

The Bob Monkhouse Comedy Hour

UK · ITV (THAMES) · SKETCH/STANDUP

4 editions (3 × 60 mins · 1 × 30 mins) · colour

19 Apr 1972 · Wed 8pm (60 mins)

The Bob Monkhouse Disturbance 22 Nov 1972 · Wed 8pm (60 mins)

The Bob Monkhouse Offensive 18 Apr 1973 · Wed 11pm (30 mins)

The Bob Monkhouse Breakdown 12 July 1973 · Thu 9pm (60 mins)

MAIN CAST

Bob Monkhouse

CREDITS

writers Bob Monkhouse/Wally Malston/Eric Davidson (show 1), Bob Monkhouse/Tony Hawes (shows 2–4) · additional material Wally Malston (show 2), Dick Vosburgh, Barry Cryer, Tony Hare (show 4) · directors Stuart Allen (show 1), Terry Henebery (shows 2 & 3), Ronald Fouracre (show 4) · producers Stuart Allen (show 1), Terry Henebery (shows 2 & 3), David Clark (show 4)

Having been dismissed as host of the popular quiz-show *The Golden Shot* (over a storm-in-a-teacup alleged bribing incident) and so freed from an exclusive contract with ATV, Bob Monkhouse signed up with Thames for a single hour-long special which, if it proved successful, would lead to an option on five more. The first show *was*

successful, and so was the second; the problem was that the third absolutely wasn't, and while the fourth was fine, that was deemed to be the end of the matter. Stuffed with guests, the shows were themed around specific subjects; the third was a censorship satire that was so poor that it went out at half the usual hour length and at 11pm when, it was hoped, no one was watching. Keen to keep their relationship going, Thames offered Monkhouse a celebrity quiz series *Quick On The Draw* instead.

Guests appearing in these four shows included Joe Baker, Clive Dunn, David Nixon, William Franklyn, Barbara Mitchell, Clement Freud, Bob Todd, Melvyn Hayes, Katie Boyle, Stanley Unwin, Diana Dors, Alfred Marks, Barbara Windsor, Jack Douglas, Bernard Hepton, Ronald Fraser, Diana Coupland and Rosemary Leach.

Monkhouse later returned to *The Golden Shot*, replacing Charlie Williams as host (who, in turn, had replaced Monkhouse's original successor Norman Vaughan).

I'm Bob, He's Dickie

UK · ITV (ATV) · SKETCH/STANDUP

3 × 60 mins · colour

6 July 1977 · Wed 8pm

1 Feb 1978 · Wed 8pm

6 Sep 1978 · Wed 8pm

MAIN CAST

Bob Monkhouse
Dickie Henderson

CREDITS

writers Dick Vosburgh (3), Garry Chambers (3), Bob Monkhouse (1) · director/producer Paul Stewart Laing

The twin comedic talents of Bob Monkhouse and Dickie Henderson, joking, singing and dancing their way through three one-hour specials, with guests.

See Dickie Henderson's combined entry for his other TV work.

Bonkers!

UK · ITV (ATV/ITC) · SKETCH/STANDUP

*24 × 30 mins · colour

*14 July–4 Aug 1979 · Sat mostly 5.15pm

MAIN CAST

Bob Monkhouse
The Hudson Brothers

CREDITS

writers Jack Burns, David Pollock/Elias Davis, Bob Monkhouse · director Peter Harris · executive producer Thomas M Battista · producer Jack Burns

Promoted as being full of 'furious knockabout fun' and 'music and madness', *Bonkers!* was an unabashed attempt at producing a real-person, slapstick version

of *The Muppet Show* – it was made in England by the same production company, Sir Lew Grade's ATV/ITC, with the same producer, Jack Burns, and with one if not both eyes cast firmly on the American TV market. The appeal for British viewers was Bob Monkhouse, the appeal for Americans were the Hudson Brothers, a trio of knockabout comics who never managed to live up to their billing as 'the new Marx Brothers' but tried very, very hard. (Dance routines were provided by the memorably named Bonkettes.)

*Note. In Britain the series was cut off in its 'prime' when – four editions into the run – ITV was blanked out by a long industrial action, but programmes continued to be made for syndication in America, where 24 were shown to no great reception.

The Bob Monkhouse Show   2

UK · BBC · STANDUP

31 editions (10 × 55 mins · 10 × 50 mins · 10 × 40 mins · 1 × 45 mins) · colour

Series One (10 × 55 mins) 24 Oct–25 Dec 1983 · BBC2 Mon 8.30pm

Series Two (10 × 50 mins) 7 Jan–11 Mar 1985 · BBC2 Mon 8.10pm

Special (45 mins) 3 May 1985 · BBC2 Fri 9pm

Series Three (8 × 40 mins) 13 Jan–3 Mar 1986 · BBC2 Mon 9.30pm

Series Four (2 × 40 mins) 7 June & 14 June 1986 · BBC1 Sat 9.10pm & 8.55pm

MAIN CAST

Bob Monkhouse

CREDITS

writers various · script associates Dennis Berson, Spike Mullins (series 1) · directors Geoff Miles (27), David Taylor (3), John Bishop (1) · producer John Fisher

An all-comedy standup series that forms an important visual record of many of the acts operating in the 1980s. Monkhouse introduced his guests, gave them space to perform extracts from their stage-shows and then participated in 'scripted' interviews in which he generously played straight-man, allowing them to air more of their material. The series introduced British TV viewers to a good deal of new talent from across the Atlantic – in particular it made Joan Rivers a success in the UK, her appearances on this show leading directly to her own series for BBC2.

In short, *The Bob Monkhouse Show* was an invaluable window on its time, the comics and comedy-actors appearing in the series including Russ Abbot, Ray Alan, Byron Allen, Pam Ayres, Pete Barbutti, Ronnie Barker, Michael Barrymore, Michael Bentine, Sandra Bernhard, Bob And Ray, Max Boyce, Janet Brown (twice), Max Bygraves, Jim Carrey, Sid Caesar, Lorraine

Chase, Peter Cook, Tommy Cooper, Professor Irwin Corey, Jimmy Cricket, Paul Daniels, Les Dawson, Phyllis Diller, Charlie Drake, Kenny Everett, Fascinating Aïda, Derek Griffiths, Robert Guillaume, Hale And Pace (twice), Mike Harding, Bob Hope, Frankie Howerd, Victoria Jackson, Roy Jay, Karen Kay, Kit And The Widow, Danny La Rue, Steve Landesberg, Rich Little, Little And Large, Ronn Lucas, Julia McKenzie, Ruth Madoc, Bernard Manning, Larry Miller, Spike Milligan, Warren Mitchell, Kelly Monteith, Monteith & Rand, Libby Morris, Martin Mull, Denis Norden, Duncan Norvelle, Tom O'Connor, Emo Philips, Su Pollard, Jan Ravens, Mike Reid, Joan Rivers (twice), Ted Rogers, Rita Rudner, Gerard Sety And Mac Ronay, Yakov Smirnoff, Paul Squire, Pamela Stephenson, 'The Unknown Comic' (Murray Langston), Gary Wilmot, Bernie Winters, Norman Wisdom, Victoria Wood and Steven Wright.

An Audience With Bob Monkhouse

UK · ITV (LWT) · STANDUP

1 × 60 mins · colour

21 May 1994 · Sat 9pm

MAIN CAST
Bob Monkhouse

CREDITS
writer Bob Monkhouse · director Patricia Mordecai · producer Lorna Dickinson

In the 1990s Monkhouse's career underwent a remarkable change. Moving away from hosting game-shows, he resurrected his standup reputation (which he had maintained on stage and as an after-dinner speaker) and won over a new generation of TV viewers with his sharp wit and clever one-liners. A measure of his newly revived acceptance was his invitation to appear on BBC2's satirical panel-game *Have I Got News For You*, in which he effortlessly managed to outshine his (admittedly generous) younger colleagues.

TV was now ready for Monkhouse's racier stage act and in this ITV special he blended material new and old. (For more information on *An Audience With ...*, see separate entry.)

Bob Monkhouse On The Spot

UK · BBC · STANDUP

12 × 30 mins · colour

Series One (6) 22 July–26 Aug 1995 · BBC1 Sat 9.25pm

Series Two (6) 22 June–27 July 1996 · BBC2 Sat mostly 9.15pm

MAIN CAST
Bob Monkhouse

CREDITS
writer Bob Monkhouse · directors Ian Hamilton (series 1), John Kilby (series 2) · producers Alan Nixon (series 1), Phil Clarke (series 2)

Two series in which Monkhouse was given full rein in which to display his brilliant technical style, encyclopedic memory of jokes and quicksilver comedic brain. Now fully established as one of the godfathers of British comedy, Monkhouse spun stories full of gags and humorous situations and, amazingly, finished with an improvisational tour-de-force in which he linked different subjects suggested by the audience. Known in the business for his incredible memory and lightning recall, Monkhouse obviously relished this tricky but rewarding challenge.

Monster Café

UK · BBC · CHILDREN'S SITCOM

30 × 15 mins · colour

Series One (15) 12 Sep–19 Dec 1994 · BBC1 Mon 3.45pm

Series Two (15) 14 Sep–21 Dec 1995 · BBC1 Thu 3.55pm

MAIN CAST
Frankie · · · · · · · · · · · · · · · Isobel Middleton
Igor · · · · · · · · · · · · · · · · David Shimwell
Mummy · · · · · · · · · · · · · · Toby Sedgwick
Baroness · · · · · · · · · · · · · · · · · · Peta Lily

CREDITS
writer Simon Davies · director Philippa Langdale · producer Alison Stewart

A spirited children's TV romp set in the Monster Café, an establishment staffed by a female Frankenstein-lookalike named Frankie (dressed in punk chic gear), an accident-prone and mumbling Mummy, and a Transylvanian odd-job man named Igor. Wielding control over the gruesome trio was the villainous Baroness, the owner of the castle that housed the café and the creator of Frankie (whom she called Frances).

The subtext here – similar to that of *The Munsters* – was that even monsters are human and need companionship to see them through life. The series was pleasingly garish and the cast hammed it up appropriately.

The Montreux Festival

The Golden Rose Of Montreux is an annual international contest for light entertainment TV shows, organised by the Swiss Broadcasting Corporation in co-operation with the town of Montreux and with the patronage of the European Broadcasting Union. It has been held since 1961 as part of the Montreux TV Festival, an industry event attended by programme-makers from all over the world.

Dozens of the non-British comedy entries from the competition have been screened on UK television, brief details of which follow. (Some were edited for UK broadcast; a few of the latter titles were entries for other Montreux prizes.)

Einfach Lächerlich (*Strictly For Laughs*), a sketch-show from West Germany, screened by the BBC on 17 August 1961.

La Revue Perdue (*The Lost Revue*), a mime and musical humour show from Czechoslovakia, screened by the BBC on 15 August 1962.

Zu Jung Um Blond Zu Sein (*Too Young To Be Blonde*), a musical humour show from West Germany, screened by the BBC on 24 August 1962.

Hocus Focus, a sketch-show from Belgium, screened by the BBC on 19 May 1963.

Silence, Silence, Silence, a sketch-show from Czechoslovakia, screened by the BBC on 19 May 1963.

Night Club, a sketch-show from Switzerland, screened by the BBC on 9 June 1963. (The British comic-actor Freddie Frinton – see **Meet The Wife** – was among the cast.)

Happy End, a musical humour show from Switzerland, screened by BBC1 on 31 May 1964.

The Rudi Carrell Show, a sketch-show from the Netherlands, screened by BBC1 on 7 June 1964.

The Jackie Gleason Show (aka *Jackie Gleason And His American Scene Magazine*), a comedy-variety show from the USA, screened by BBC1 on 18 June 1964 (see **The Honeymooners**).

Les Raisins Verts (*Sour Grapes*), a satire from France, screened by BBC1 on 17 July 1964.

The Wayne And Shuster Show, a standup show from Canada, screened by BBC2 on 17 July 1965 (see **Wayne and Shuster**).

The Cold Old Days, a sketch-show from Finland, screened by BBC2 on 24 July 1965

Sandy – The Noble-Minded Cowboy, a sketch-show from Czechoslovakia, screened by BBC2 on 7 September 1965.

Collages '65, a satire from Norway, screened by BBC2 on 21 September 1965.

The Bernard Show, a sketch-show from Switzerland, screened by BBC2 on 14 June 1966.

That's Entertainment, a sketch-show from Norway, screened by BBC2 on 21 June 1966.

L'arroseur Arrosé (*The Sprinkler Sprinkled*), a sketch-show from France, screened by BBC2 on 5 July 1966.

Dorus, a sketch-show from the Netherlands, screened by BBC2 on 4 May 1967.

Bedside Story, a sketch-show from Norway, screened by BBC2 on 17 May 1970.

Six Escapees, a sketch-show from Czechoslovakia, screened by BBC2 on 31 May 1970.

Haddimassa (*Hello Masses*), a satire from the Netherlands, screened by BBC2 on 7 June 1970.

HurRah, a sketch-show from Norway, screened by BBC2 on 4 June 1971.

Love And Marriage, a sketch-show from Finland, screened by BBC2 on 3 September 1971.

The Magic Box, a sketch-show from Sweden, screened by BBC2 on 17 September 1971.

Allitälli, a sketch-show from Finland, screened by BBC2 on 31 July 1972.

Mad In Austria!, a sketch-show from Austria, screened by BBC2 on 6 July 1975.

Do You Dig Dogs?, a sketch-show from Norway, screened by BBC2 on 6 July 1975.

The Nor-Way To Broadcasting, a sketch-show from Norway, screened by BBC2 on 30 August 1976.

The Sören Kierkegaard Road Show, a satire from Denmark, screened by C4 on 26 August 1990.

Neutral Policy, a sitcom from Finland, screened by C4 on 26 August 1990.

Chateaux du Dracula, a satire from Romania, screened by C4 on 2 September 1990.

East Of Sweden, a satire from Finland, screened by C4 on 25 August 1993.

Un Peu de Tout, a sketch-show from Belgium, screened by C4 on 1 September 1993.

Monty Python's Flying Circus

UK · BBC · SKETCH

46 × 30 mins · colour

Series One (13) 5 Oct 1969–11 Jan 1970 · BBC1 Sun around 11pm

Series Two (13) 15 Sep–22 Dec 1970 · BBC1 Tue around 10.10pm

Series Three (13) 19 Oct 1972–18 Jan 1973 · BBC1 Thu 10.15pm

Special *Monty Python's Fliegende Zirkus* 6 Oct 1973 · BBC2 Sat 9.45pm (a Bavaria Atelier, Munich production for WDR)

Series Four (6) *Monty Python* 31 Oct–5 Dec 1974 · BBC2 Thu 9pm

MAIN CAST

Graham Chapman
John Cleese (not series 4)
Terry Gilliam
Eric Idle
Terry Jones
Michael Palin

OTHER APPEARANCES

Carol Cleveland
Connie Booth
Ian Davidson

CREDITS

writers John Cleese/Graham Chapman, Terry Jones/Michael Palin, Eric Idle, Terry Gilliam · *additional material (series 4)* Douglas Adams/Graham Chapman, Neil Innes/Graham Chapman · *animations* Terry Gilliam · *producers* Ian MacNaughton (41), John Howard Davies/Ian MacNaughton (4), Thomas Woitkewitsch (German special)

A series of crucial importance in the development of comedy, not just on British TV but on a global scale and in various media. But although *Monty Python's Flying Circus* is the most analysed comedy programme of all time

it remains difficult to convey in print the sheer bombastic vitality of a show that seemed to break all the rules and then establish completely new ones. Quite simply, the Pythons (as the team's six members became known) invented a new genre.

Brought together by Barry Took (then a comedy adviser at the BBC), who had seen the various players in *At Last The 1948 Show* and *Do Not Adjust Your Set*, the *Python* team had many strengths but perhaps none more important than their understanding of continuity and symmetry, which meant that their seemingly aimless, stream-of-consciousness ideas and sketches were prevented from dissolving into anti-climax by being contained within a rigid, but flamboyant, structure. Once the Pythons decided to virtually do away with the traditional idea of using punchlines to finish a sketch – instead preferring to segue from one segment to the next – they unleashed their full writing potential, since ideas that were funny yet would hitherto have been rejected because of having a weak ending could now be joyously accommodated. Spike Milligan had also trod this route in his *Q* series but less successfully, although it was no surprise that his producer, the former actor Ian MacNaughton, kept his hand on the tiller during *Python*'s run. Further, it is impossible to overestimate the value of Terry Gilliam's animation to the show's successful use of the segue technique. An American who had first met John Cleese in New York and then worked on *Do Not Adjust Your Set*, Gilliam provided simple cut-out animations that tended to feature grotesque characters and situations which, as often as not, were used as linking devices to move the show from one area to another. Because of the nature of animation, Gilliam's inspired work made it possible to link two bizarrely different ideas without spoiling the continuous flow that gave the show its strength.

All of the *Monty Python* team wrote their own material and were their own fiercest critics, ensuring a very high standard for the finished product, and their different writing approaches meant that a wide variety of material was featured, subverting the genre well away from the standard 'two men at a desk' sketch format much in evidence elsewhere on television. They also toyed with the established structure of TV, sometimes running the closing credits of the show half-way through, or being announced as a completely different programme altogether and starting with a mocked-up false title sequence. This did not mean that they *completely* rejected the traditional styles, however, indeed some of *Python*'s most memorable sketches (like 'The Argument Sketch', wherein a man pays to argue; 'The

Dead Parrot Sketch', where a dissatisfied customer seeks recompense from the pet-shop dealer who sold him a deceased feathered-friend; and 'The Cheese Shop Sketch', where a man tries to buy cheese from a dedicated store that is nonetheless entirely devoid of the stuff), all featuring Michael Palin and John Cleese, are classic 'two men at a desk' sketches.

Mostly, however, the show ranged far further afield, with sketches taking place on the top deck of a moving double-decker bus, in the sea, in forests and so on. The series even spawned a collection of catchphrases which belied its innovative style, the most famous being the link line 'And now for something completely different', and others including 'My brain hurts' (delivered by Mr Gumby, a brain-challenged individual with a knotted handkerchief on his head) and lines associated with individual sketches like 'Nobody expects the Spanish Inquisition!' and 'Nudge-nudge, wink-wink, say no more!' All told, the programmes featured a fantastically oddball set of characters: manic game-show hosts, homosexual brigadiers, exaggerated stereotyped Australians, aspirant lumberjacks, men with tape recorders up their noses, lecherous virgins, heroic bicycle repairmen, extra-terrestrial tennis-playing blancmanges and *many* more of that wonderfully inventive ilk. And then there were the female characters, who (with the honourable exception of resident glamorous woman Carol Cleveland, who portrayed the sexier females in the scripts – especially for kissing scenes) were played by the all-male Pythons: the awful shrill-voiced, bigoted Pepperpots (Cleese, Graham Chapman, Eric Idle); the dinosaur theorist Anne Elk (Cleese); mother figures (Terry Jones); housewives (Idle or Chapman); gangster's moll (Cleese); coy young women (Palin, Idle) and so on.

The first series began quietly enough, late on Sunday nights, with no indication of what it was to become. The title, *Monty Python's Flying Circus*, revealed and meant nothing. (Other ideas for the title had included *Gwen Dibley's Flying Circus*, *Vaseline Review*, *Owl-Stretching Time* and *Arthur Megapode's Cheap Show*.) The series soon built up a cult following, however, appealing to a youthful audience hitherto more interested in rock music than TV comedy. As its popularity grew so too did the controversy surrounding much of the material, which was often of an adult nature. (This led to clashes within the BBC itself and the Pythons, although probably the last people to prosper from the liberal attitudes of one-time BBC director-general Sir Hugh Greene, were also the first to suffer from the more rigid regime that followed. Having noted this, however, it is germane to point out that the Pythons won most of their battles over script content and it remains doubtful that they would have been given as much freedom on ITV or anywhere else in the world.) Following the second series, the Pythons made their first feature film, the modestly successful *And Now For Something Completely Different* (1971, directed by Ian MacNaughton) which was filmed on a minuscule budget in a disused milk depot in north London and consisted of newly shot versions of their favourite TV sketches. By the third TV series the show had amassed a huge following and won the coveted Silver Rose at the Montreux Festival. Anticipation and expectations were now running very high but the Pythons managed to maintain their ultra high standards, even if, below the surface, cracks within the unit were beginning to show and John Cleese, becoming dissatisfied with the production, was keen to move on to something completely different.

A hint of *Python*'s future international popularity came when the team were asked to make two shows for West German TV, the first actually performed in (phonetic) German, the second dubbed from a British-made show. The former (*Monty Python In Deutschland*, WDR 1971) has not been shown on terrestrial British TV to the present time but the latter (*Monty Python's Fliegende Zirkus*, aka *Monty Python Blodeln Fur Deutschland*, WDR 1972) first aired on BBC2 on 6 October 1973 and features Cleese's last TV work with the group. A short fourth BBC series, screened under the reduced title of *Monty Python*, was made without Cleese and for the first time there was a lack of consistency within the production, although it finished on a high with the last ever edition featuring one of *Python*'s most memorable creations, the horrible Garibaldi clan, living a disgusting life in a grotesque parody of the BBC2 fly-on-the-wall documentary series *The Family*, with Gilliam particularly unpleasant as the Garibaldis' baked-beans-obsessed son Kevin. The hard-hitting, loud, over-the-top style of this sketch was a precursor of the next groundbreaking British comedy series, **The Young Ones**, which followed in 1982. Thus, after 45 UK editions the TV show, *Monty Python's Flying Circus* ended … but for the six *Python* players the story had only just begun.

In July 1974, while the Pythons were working on the scripts for the final series, *Monty Python's Flying Circus* was shown for the first time on American television (in Dallas, on local public broadcasting station KERA). From this humble beginning a monster grew, the series quickly becoming the most popular programme on the channel, which in turn alerted programmers at other stations. Popular UK belief that the 'Britishness' of *Python* would bemuse and

possibly even alienate US audiences proved groundless and a cult began to build in a similar way, and with a similar audience, to the way it had blossomed in the UK in 1969 and 1970. Back in Britain, meanwhile, the Pythons (with a returned John Cleese) completed their second feature film, *Monty Python And The Holy Grail* (1975, directors Terry Gilliam and Terry Jones), which featured all-new material woven around the single theme of King Arthur's quest for the Holy Grail. Made on a slightly bigger budget than their first movie, *Grail* was a huge hit and when it was released in America added to the interest that was building up around the TV series. By the summer of 1975 the BBC series were airing on 130 public broadcasting stations and even on a couple of local commercial stations in Las Vegas and Houston. The US networks, never slow to pick up on a trend, wanted a piece of the action too and ABC acquired the series from the BBC's US distribution agent Time-Life Films. When ABC ran the series in its *Wide World Of Entertainment* slot in October 1975 the Pythons were horrified that the shows had been haphazardly re-edited, thus losing the essential continuity. When ABC refused to stop treating the series in this manner the Pythons, in an unprecedented move, took them to the US courts in a battle for artistic rights. The historic court case ended in mixed fortunes for the Pythons when the judge agreed that their artistic rights had been violated but refused to halt the ABC broadcasts owing to the complex nature of the BBC's US distribution rights. The Pythons then won on appeal which – although too late to stop ABC's original broadcasts – meant that they gained control over subsequent US broadcasting of the programmes. They also won back the rights to the series from the BBC once their original contract with the Corporation expired, so from 31 December 1980 the Pythons themselves became owners of their series – a groundbreaking arrangement.

Although they all took time out to pursue individual endeavours, the team reunited once more in the late 1970s to make easily their most controversial big-screen outing, a spoof on organised religion set in biblical times and concerning an ordinary bloke who is mistaken for the Messiah. *Monty Python's Life Of Brian* (1979, directed by Terry Jones) was a massive success and probably represents the *Python* team at the height of their collaborative creative powers. Most noticeable is the improved acting skills of the troupe, making them, as if it were not already clear, the only true interpreters of their own dazzling writing. In the ten years since they formed their partnership, the Pythons had become by far the most important and influential comedy team in the world.

Throughout the 1970s *Monty Python* records and spin-off books had been selling in abundance, and the team was also gaining a reputation for their stage presentations of the TV sketches. The Pythons first performed their TV material in theatres as early as 1971 (in Coventry) and went on to play full British tours. But they became an attraction of rock star magnitude in the USA, culminating in a four-night performance at the Hollywood Bowl (26–29 September 1980) in Los Angeles. The shows were videotaped and certain segments transferred to film and released as a movie in America (*Monty Python Live At The Hollywood Bowl*, 1982, director Terry Hughes). The Pythons agreed to perform these shows as a break from writing the script for their next and (to date) last film, *Monty Python's The Meaning Of Life* (1983, directed by Terry Jones). This feature film, like their first, was a collection of sketches, but unlike *And Now For Something Completely Different* all these pieces were especially written for the big screen and slotted together with the group's usual structural skills. Once again, controversy surrounded the production, with two particular sketches ('Every Sperm Is Sacred', a satire on the Catholic church's attitude to birth control; and 'The Restaurant Sketch', in which a constantly vomiting glutton finally explodes, showering restaurant diners with entrails) meriting the most attention. This was the last time that the Pythons worked together creatively as a full team, although the members reunited to film segments for a twentieth-anniversary tribute, *Parrot Sketch Not Included* (a Tiger Television production for Python (Monty) Pictures, screened by BBC1 on 18 November 1989) that was hosted by the US comedian Steve Martin. On 4 October 1989, shortly after filming these segments, and one day before the actual anniversary of the first *Python* programme, Graham Chapman died of cancer, aged 48. The others praised his impeccable timing.

Individually, the Pythons have continued to wield a huge influence in the worlds of comedy and beyond, creating a number of memorable TV or film projects: **Fawlty Towers** (Cleese); **Rutland Weekend Television, Nearly Departed**, *The Rutles, Nuns On The Run* (Idle); *Around The World In 80 Days, Pole To Pole, Full Circle, The Missionary, The American Friend* (Palin); *Eric The Viking* (Jones); *Time Bandits, Brazil, The Adventures Of Baron Munchausen, The Fisher King, Twelve Monkeys* (Gilliam). Occasionally, individual Pythons have combined for projects too: Cleese and Idle (*Splitting Heirs*); Palin and Jones (**Ripping Yarns**); and, perhaps most notably, Cleese and Palin for the feature films *A Fish Called Wanda* and *Fierce Creatures*.

In essence, the *Monty Python* team are the comedy equivalent of the Beatles. Both started off in the UK but refused to bow to the conventions of, or be limited by, the constraints of a then-staid British organisation (for the Beatles it was EMI, for the Pythons the BBC). Both were resolutely and uncompromisingly British yet became internationally famous and managed the previously unattainable task of conquering the USA in their respective spheres. Like the Beatles, the Pythons moved individually into a number of diverse creative areas after the collective was disbanded. Like the Beatles, despite whatever contemporary successes they enjoy, the Pythons are always referred to by the media in terms of the original group (ie, 'ex-Beatle George Harrison' and 'ex-Python John Cleese'). Like the Beatles, the Pythons are often the subject of 'reunion' rumours ... even though one of their members is dead. (An April 1998 one-off stage reunion of the surviving Pythons, likely to yield an HBO TV special, was announced in late 1997.) Like the Beatles, *Monty Python* continues to entertain and influence new generations and inspire emerging creative talents. Like the Beatles, the Pythons have been able wrest control over their artistic output and do not hesitate to use the courts to justify their legal rights. And, like the Beatles in the field of music, while other new acts come along and temporarily grab the headlines, none can challenge *Monty Python*'s everlasting supremacy in the field of TV comedy.

Moody And Pegg

UK · ITV (THAMES) · SITCOM

12 × 60 mins · colour

Series One (6) 29 July–9 Sep 1974 · Mon 9pm
Series Two (6) 24 July–28 Aug 1975 · Thu 9pm

MAIN CAST

Roland Moody	Derek Waring
Daphne Pegg	Judy Cornwell

OTHER APPEARANCES

Monica Bakewell	Frances Bennett
Auntie Ethel	Sheila Keith
George	Peter Denyer
Sid	Tony Selby
Iris	Adrienne Posta
Jim	Denis Lill
Miranda	Louise Hall Taylor
Rowena Moody	Lea Dregorn

CREDITS

writers Julia Jones/Donald Churchill · directors Jonathan Alwyn (4), Mike Vardy (4), Richard Martin (2), Baz Taylor (1), Roger Tucker (1) · producer Robert Love

Derek Waring and Judy Cornwell starred in this interesting Thames series that accented comedy but also had moments of drama. Waring played Roland Moody, a newly divorced 42-year-old junk/antique dealer

greatly anticipating freedom from matrimonial ties. Cornwell was cast as Daphne Pegg, plain spinster and dedicated civil servant in her early thirties who leaves her home in Bolton after realising that her office boss will never agree to marry her. She heads for London and a clean break, but, owing to a rogue estate agent's dealings, finds that a man – Moody – also has a valid lease arrangement for the property she acquires. Unable to work out who is the squatter, they agree to be feuding partners and share, forging a very uncomfortable situation that is exacerbated by Moody's prodigious line of visiting girlfriends. Eventually, Moody loses in a winner-takes-all poker game and leaves, only to return in the second series.

Moody In ...

UK · BBC · MUSICAL SITCOM

6 × 30 mins · b/w

7 June–12 July 1961 · Wed mostly 8.30pm

MAIN CAST

Ron Moody
David Kernan
Peter Gilmore
Richard Caldicot
Tom Clegg
Tony Sympson
Vivienne Martin
Amanda Barrie
Brian Oulton
Greta Hamby
Pamela Conway
Una Stubbs

CREDITS

writer Ron Moody · producer James Gilbert

Ron Moody and a small company of actors, singers and dancers in an unusual musical sitcom, with a different setting each week. The talented actor/writer Moody was enjoying huge success on the London stage at this time, appearing as Fagin in the musical *Oliver!*

Note. The last word of each edition in the series always gave away the subject, hence the six programmes were actually titled, respectively, *Moody In Storeland*, *Moody In Tin Pan Alley Land*, *Moody In Clock Factory Land*, *Moody In Theatreland*, *Moody In Musketeerland* and *Moody In Teleland*.

Mooney And Magee

UK · ITV (CARLTON) · CHILDREN'S SITCOM

2 × 10 mins · colour

6 Aug & 13 Aug 1997 · Wed 4pm

MAIN CAST

Steve Mooney
Karl Magee

CREDITS

writer/director/producer Paul Cole · executive producer Michael Forte

Slapstick to the fore with bungling odd-job men Mooney and Magee in a brace of comic escapades. In the first story the pair came to grief when they tried to repair the beloved Jaguar car of a well-to-do gent; in the second they proved they were just as inept at house decorating.

This was unashamed physical comedy for younger viewers, with ex-British gymnast Karl Magee particularly effective at the pratfalls and stunt work. Another in the long line of clown-like double-acts for kids, following *Mick And Montmorency*, **Hope and Keen** (also real-life gymnasts) and the Chuckle Brothers of the long-running *Chucklevision*.

More Before The Fringe

see *Before The Fringe*

More Faces Of Jim

see *Faces Of Jim*

The More We Are Together

UK · ITV (YORKSHIRE) · SITCOM

6 × 30 mins (5 × colour · 1 × b/w)

*30 Jan–6 Mar 1971 · Sat 5.10pm

MAIN CAST

Norma Dunk	Betty Marsden
Doris Tingle	Avril Angers
Wally Dunk	Victor Brooks (4 eps);
	Kenneth Watson (last 2 eps)
Frank Wilgoose	Roy Barraclough

CREDITS

writer Robert Storey · director Mike Bevan · executive producer John Duncan · producer Ian Davidson

A bizarre sitcom – pitifully light on laughs – that focused upon middle-age sex antics, with a friend, lodger, relation and neighbour indulging in a series of passions for one another that may have confused them and certainly befuddled the viewers at home who did not warm to *The More We Are Together* one little bit.

Remarkably, the series was scheduled by ITV for the post-sports slot on Saturday afternoons, even though episode titles like 'The Lodger And The Pill', 'I Love Little Pussy' (about a cat, *of course*) and 'Crumpet Voluntary' left little to the imagination. The upshot was that only four of the six episodes were screened by London-area ITV. Other regions too showed either an incomplete series or rescheduled latter episodes late at night.

*Note. These dates relate to the complete run, screened by Yorkshire TV. In London, the last episode to be screened, the fourth, went out on 20 February.

Morecambe And Wise

In the upper echelons of the (imaginary) British TV comedy hall of fame, a quartet of acts stand above the rest at the acme of their profession: Tony Hancock, Benny Hill, Tommy Cooper and the legendary team of Morecambe and Wise. All were hugely beloved by the British public and enjoyed careers that spanned decades, but for sheer consistency M&W reign supreme.

Eric Morecambe was born John Eric Bartholomew on 14 May 1926 and took his stage surname by adopting the town of his Lancashire birthplace; Ernie Wise was born Ernest Wiseman in Leeds on 27 November 1925. Wise was a comic child prodigy: he began his career in a double-act with his father (called Carson and Kid, later Bert Carson and The Little Wonder) while still in his pre-teens. In 1939, age 13, Wise was put under contract to impresario Jack Hylton and, following an appearance in the stage-show *Band Waggon* (starring Arthur Askey, based upon his radio series), was hailed in the press as a major discovery. Morecambe, meanwhile, was appearing in talent shows, his winning prize at one such contest being to audition for Jack Hylton – and this is where he first crossed paths with Wise.

Eventually, the two joined the touring talent show *Youth Takes A Bow*, and during its run Eric's mother, Sadie Bartholomew, coerced the pair into becoming a double-act, with Eric as the funny one and Ernie as his feed. The act was dissolved when Second World War service sent them their separate ways. After the war, the pair individually re-entered variety but crossed paths again when Eric, auditioning for a job as comic in a circus/variety show, was told that they already had one but that he could fill-in as the comedian's feed. The comic was Ernie and the double-act was reborn, now in a mirror image to its previous incarnation. Yet still the pair weren't committed to being a partnership and at the end of the tour they went their separate ways once more.

Another, third chance meeting led to them sharing accommodation in London and, once again at Sadie Bartholomew's urging, they formed a double-act. A tough period bottomed out after a stint at the famous Windmill Theatre when they were 'let go' because they failed to attract as many laughs as a similar act, Hancock and Scott (Tony Hancock and his partner Derek Scott). Spurred on rather than discouraged by this setback, they wrote to hordes of variety agents informing them that they were 'free', almost immediately began to get work and

in this period began polishing their act. On 28 September 1951 Morecambe and Wise made their TV debut in the BBC's young talent show *Parade Of Youth*, having already been heard on radio on *Workers' Playtime* and *Variety Fanfare* (BBC north's equivalent of *Variety Bandbox*). They then became regulars on *Variety Fanfare* and, in 1954, were given their own BBC national radio series (the first of several, extending to 1979), *You're Only Young Once*, followed immediately by their first real chance to break into television with the series *Running Wild*.

After that …

Running Wild

UK · BBC · STANDUP

6 × 30 mins · b/w

21 Apr–30 June 1954 · fortnightly Wed around 9.30pm

MAIN CAST
Eric Morecambe
Ernie Wise
Alma Cogan

CREDITS
writers Len Fincham/Lawrie Wyman (shows 1–3), Maurice Rodgers/Alan Blain (show 1), Ronnie Hanbury (shows 3–6), Denis Gifford/Tony Hawes (shows 4–6) · *director* Ernest Maxin · *producer* Bryan Sears

Broadcast live every fortnight from the BBC's new Television Theatre in Shepherd's Bush, London, this first starring series for comedy double-act Morecambe and Wise didn't strike any chords with critics or the public and is considered one of the low points in the duo's career. Indeed, after three editions the critical mauling they were receiving was so savage that M&W begged the BBC to drop the series, but Ronnie Waldman, the Head of Light Entertainment, thought the criticisms unfair and persevered with the three remaining shows.

By the end of *Running Wild*, Morecambe and Wise felt that they had blown their big chance for TV stardom, but they were (of course) wildly wrong – although taking two years to re-establish themselves, they fared much better in their next TV appearances, on ITV, as the resident comedy act on *The Winifred Atwell Show* over ten weeks in 1956 (21 April-23 June). These scripts were written by Johnny Speight and he was the first to really utilise the double-act's TV potential.

Double Six

UK · BBC · STANDUP

5 × 30 mins · b/w

11 Aug–8 Sep 1957 · Sun mostly 9.30pm

MAIN CAST
Eric Morecambe

Ernie Wise
Ted Lune

CREDITS
writers Eric Morecambe/Ernie Wise · *producer* Ronnie Taylor

Having resurrected their TV career via their appearances on *The Winifred Atwell Show*, Morecambe and Wise returned to the BBC by fronting this fast-moving revue. In the period of live TV it was customary for such shows to be broadcast on Sundays, when theatres were closed and the acts were not needed elsewhere. (In their case, during the run of *Double Six*, Morecambe and Wise were appearing Mondays to Saturdays in *Let's Have Fun* at the Central Pier, Blackpool.)

The Morecambe And Wise Show 1

UK · ITV (ATV) · SKETCH/STANDUP

67 editions (57 × b/w [35 × 30 mins · 22 × 35 mins] · 10 × 60 mins · colour)

Series One (9 × 30 mins · b/w) 12 Oct–7 Dec 1961 · Thu 8pm

Series Two (13 × 30 mins · b/w) 30 June–22 Sep 1962 · Sat 9.30pm

Series Three (13 × 30 mins · b/w) 15 June–7 Sep 1963 · Sat mostly 9.30pm

Series Four (13 × 30 mins · b/w) 4 Apr–26 June 1964 · mostly Sat 8.25pm

Series Five (9 × 35 mins · b/w) 22 Jan–19 Mar 1966 · Sat 9.20pm

Series Six (10 × 60 mins · colour but screened in b/w) 1 Oct 1967–31 Mar 1968 · Sun mostly 8.25pm

MAIN CAST
Eric Morecambe
Ernie Wise
Sid Green
Dick Hills

OTHER APPEARANCES
Millicent Martin (series 6)

CREDITS
writers Sid Green/Dick Hills · *directors* Colin Clews/Philip Casson (series 6) · *producer* Colin Clews

The theatrical/TV impresario Bernard Delfont gave Morecambe and Wise their own ITV series after the pair appeared frequently on the small-screen in 1960 without a show of their own, notching up 12 spots on *Val Parnell's Sunday Night At The London Palladium*. Now the same network pitched them into a series of their own, teaming the comedians with another double-act, the writers Sid Green and Dick Hills. Sid and Dick, as they soon became known to the nation, also ventured out from behind-the-scenes to feature in front of the cameras with the comics.

The first ATV series – broadcast live each week from the Wood Green Empire in north London – was so successful that a second run was commissioned and given a

Saturday primetime slot; from here on, after seven years of irregular TV appearances, M&W were firmly established as stars of the medium and Britain's best comedy double-act. Catchphrases soon developed, with Eric as the wag and Ernie the butt of all jokes: Morecambe would grab Wise by the throat and remark 'Get out of that!'; Morecambe would claim that Wise possessed 'short fat hairy legs'; the two comics, with their scriptwriters, sang a catchy comedy song that attained national fame, 'Boom Oo Yatta Ta Ta'; and every programme ended with the first line – but never more – of the age-old dirty joke 'There were these two old men sitting in deckchairs …'.

As a result of these extremely funny ITV series, Morecambe and Wise branched out into the cinema with three starring feature films, released in 1964, 1966 and 1967 respectively – *The Intelligence Men*, *That Riviera Touch* and *The Magnificent Two*. Some fine moments occurred in these movies but there can be little argument that the transition from small-screen to big was far from successful – the comics found it hard to sustain the laughs without a live audience, and the critics had few kind words to impart.

Although screened in the UK in monochrome, the sixth ITV series was taped in colour especially for the US market, and so American/international guests starred in each edition. It was aired in the States by the ABC network under the title *The Piccadilly Palace*, ahead of the UK transmissions, from 20 May to 9 September 1967, as a summer replacement for *The Hollywood Palace*. Morecambe and Wise had long wished to crack the American market (and had appeared there on *The Ed Sullivan Show*) but would not commit themselves to the 16 shows that ABC wanted and were negotiating for via ATV's Lew Grade. Although warmly received by those viewers who tuned in – especially in Canada, where Morecambe and Wise had just appeared on stage, in Toronto – the American audience ratings were not high enough to warrant a further US run, a fault that Grade, in his autobiography, blamed on the comedians' refusal to slow down their fast-paced act.

By this time, Morecambe and Wise were growing dissatisfied with their ATV contract, and working in colour was something that had appealed to them. The obvious step, therefore, was to switch channels, launching a season of shows on BBC2 (the only colour channel in Britain until late 1969) in September 1968. They wouldn't return to ITV for another ten years – ten *golden* years.

The Morecambe And Wise Show · 2
UK · BBC · SKETCH/STANDUP

69 editions (50 × 45 mins · 3 × 65 mins · 5 × 60 mins · 4 × 50 mins · 7 × 30 mins) · colour

Series One (7 × 30 mins) 2 Sep–21 Oct 1968 · BBC2 Mon mostly 8.50pm

Series Two (4 × 50 mins) 27 July–7 Sep 1969 · BBC2 fortnightly Sun around 10.20pm

Special (60 mins) 25 Dec 1969 · BBC1 Thu 8.15pm

Series Three (7 × 45 mins) 14 Jan–22 Apr 1970 · BBC2 fortnightly Wed 9.10pm

Series Four (5 × 45 mins) 1 July–26 Aug 1970 · BBC2 fortnightly Wed 9.10pm

Special (45 mins) 8 Oct 1970 · BBC1 Thu 8.15pm

Special (60 mins) 25 Dec 1970 · BBC1 Fri 8.15pm

Series Five (7 × 45 mins) 8 Apr–15 July 1971 · BBC2 fortnightly Thu 9.20pm

Series Six (6 × 45 mins) 19 Sep–24 Oct 1971 · BBC1 Sun 7.25pm

Special (65 mins) 25 Dec 1971 · BBC1 Sat 8pm

Special (60 mins) 25 Dec 1972 · BBC1 Mon 8.15pm

Series Seven (12 × 45 mins) 5 Jan–23 Mar 1973 · BBC1 Fri 8.15pm

Special (60 mins) 25 Dec 1973 · BBC1 Tue 7.35pm

Series Eight (6 × 45 mins) 27 Sep–1 Nov 1974 · BBC1 Fri 8.15pm

Special (65 mins) 25 Dec 1975 · BBC1 Thu 7.40pm

Series Nine (6 × 45 mins) 7 Jan–19 Apr 1976 · BBC1 irregular Wed 8.15pm

Special (60 mins) 25 Dec 1976 · BBC1 Sat 7.45pm

Special (65 mins) 25 Dec 1977 · BBC1 Sun 8.55pm

MAIN CAST
Eric Morecambe
Ernie Wise

OTHER REGULAR APPEARANCES
Janet Webb (series 2–7)
Arthur Tolcher (series 8 & 9 and 4 specials)

CREDITS
writers Sid Green/Dick Hills (series 1), Eddie Braben (series 2 onwards) · *additional material* Mike Craig/Lawrie Kinsley, Barry Cryer, John Junkin, Ron McDonnell · *producers* John Ammonds (series 1–8 and 6 specials), Ernest Maxin (series 9 and 3 specials)

Morecambe and Wise returned to the BBC in triumph, their phenomenal success on ITV taking them from reliable guest-artist status to full-blown superstars. Incredibly, these BBC shows not only confirmed their progress but succeeded in bettering the ITV period. Famous name celebrities virtually queued up to face ridicule in guest spots (Peter Cushing, Glenda Jackson, André Previn, Diana Rigg, Shirley Bassey and Eric Porter, to name but a few) and M&W, at the height of their powers and supremely confident, executed their flawless comedy seemingly effortlessly. This is not to suggest that the shows were slick and mechanical – far from it, they were full of ad-libs and asides (or seemed to be – many were actually scripted) and Morecambe's laddish buffoonery was as amiable and natural as ever.

After the first series, however, Eric Morecambe suffered a heart attack, and there were real fears that the act would have to finish. Sid Green and Dick Hills may have thought so, leaving a clearly uncertain future to sign an exclusive writing contract with ATV that brought their hugely successful relationship with Eric and Ernie to an end. So the first priority, upon Eric's return to fitness, was for the pair to find a new writer. The man they chose, principally because of his work for Ken Dodd, was former dustman Eddie Braben, and it was Braben who propelled Morecambe and Wise into the comic stratosphere, guiding them away from the cross-talk of the traditional double-act and re-creating their relationship, giving Ernie quite a few laughs with his exaggerated pomposity and literary ambitions (casting big-name guests in 'plays what I wrote') while still allowing Eric to cap him comedically (despite being portrayed as the less bright of the two). Morecambe's child-like attention-seeking ploys – like tossing non-existent stones into a paper bag, or insisting that Ernie was wearing a wig so good that 'you couldn't see the join' – never failed to prick Ernie's pomposity. A running gag through most of the series had the amply proportioned Janet Webb appearing at the end of each programme, thanking viewers for watching *her* show. Later series had a similar recurring joke, with Arthur Tolcher appearing throughout the show to play a fast tune on his harmonica, only to be told 'Not now, Arthur' and be hustled off; when, at the end of a programme, he was finally free to play, the screen would cut to black almost immediately.

So enormous was Morecambe and Wise's popularity that their fabulously funny Christmas shows became quintessential seasonal viewing in Britain, even replacing the BBC's long-time seasonal stalwart *Christmas Night With The Stars* (which the pair hosted in 1968). Now settling comfortably into middle-age, and despite Eric's delicate heart condition, they still managed energetic song and dance routines and superbly timed visual comedy. Indeed, they worked tirelessly, still appearing on stage for series and adapting many of the TV routines for series after series of BBC radio shows. During this period Eric and Ernie's genuine affection for one other shone through the material and their own enjoyment of their work was picked up by the audience who regarded them as their 'pals' as well as their entertainers. To be sure, Morecambe and Wise, at this time, were *loved* by the British people, capturing the heart and soul of their legions of fans much in the way that Laurel and Hardy inspire deep affection.

Eventually, Thames Television, which had enjoyed huge success with Benny Hill – who had gone to ITV just as M&W crossed to the BBC – decided that they needed the double-act as part of their line-up and in a well-publicised coup enticed them back to ITV in 1978.

The Morecambe And Wise Show 3

UK · ITV (THAMES) · SKETCH/STANDUP

33 editions (26 × 30 mins · 6 × 60 mins · 1 × 75 mins) · colour

Special (60 mins) 18 Oct 1978 · Wed 8pm

Special (75 mins) 25 Dec 1978 · Mon 9pm

Special (60 mins) 25 Dec 1979 · Tue 8.45pm

Series One (6 × 30 mins) 3 Sep–8 Oct 1980 · Wed 8pm

Special (60 mins) 25 Dec 1980 · Thu 8.30pm

Series Two (7 × 30 mins) 1 Sep–13 Oct 1981 · Tue 8pm

Special (60 mins) 23 Dec 1981 · Wed 8pm

Series Three (7 × 30 mins) 27 Oct–8 Dec 1982 · Wed 8.30pm

Special (60 mins) 27 Dec 1982 · Mon 9pm

Series Four (6 × 30 mins) 7 Sep–19 Oct 1983 · Wed 8pm

Special (60 mins) 26 Dec 1983 · Mon 8.45pm

MAIN CAST

Eric Morecambe
Ernie Wise

CREDITS

writers Barry Cryer/John Junkin (1978 specials), Eric Morecambe/Ernie Wise (1979 special), Eddie Braben (1980–82 series & specials, 1983 series), Eric Green/Dick Hills (1983 special) · *additional material* Eric Morecambe/Ernie Wise (1978 specials & 1980 series) · *directors/producers* Keith Beckett (1978 specials), John Ammonds (1979 special, 1980–82 series & specials), Mark Stuart (1983 series and special)

It is regrettable that after such a glittering period, the final years of Morecambe and Wise registered them in decline. Right from the October 1978 relaunch of their ITV career it was clear that they had made a mistake in leaving the BBC. Their first special for Thames featured the usual array of star guests (in this case Donald Sinden, Judi Dench, Leonard Sachs and Peter Cushing), all waiting in line to be made figures of fun, but the comic material was thin. This was due – in part if not whole – to the fact that scriptwriter Eddie Braben remained contractually bound to the BBC for a while longer and could not yet make the switch. But by the time that Braben was able to join M&W on ITV, in 1980, the comedians had somehow lost the thread, and

their shows were firmly on the slide. Not even the engagement of their former BBC producer John Ammonds and a reappearance by Glenda Jackson, reprising her rightly famous BBC appearance with M&W, could resuscitate the flagging partnership. Sadly, the comics were no longer compulsive viewing and their shows stopped being the talk of the country.

Where ITV really hoped to use Morecambe and Wise, and so trounce the BBC, was in the Christmas-night ratings battle. To this end, Thames utilised the same style of show that the comics had created so marvellously for the Corporation in preceding years, and which had attracted in excess of 20 million viewers. Alas, the chemistry was now wrong and the shows were a pale imitation of what had gone before. After the first year (1978) M&W's ITV seasonal specials failed to top the ratings, attracting some eight million viewers fewer than in previous years. Indeed, after 1980, ITV seemed unwilling to enter the battle, screening the programmes around but never on 25 December.

Ironically, Sid Green and Dick Hills returned to the fold for the 1983 Christmas special, joining Eddie Braben as writers, but it turned out to be Morecambe and Wise's very last TV show because Eric died on 28 May 1984, shortly after leaving the stage at a charity concert in Gloucestershire. Ernie lost his friend and partner of some 40 years and – no exaggeration – the country lost its best-loved comic and went into collective mourning. The latter ITV years may have been a disappointment but the overall effect of M&W's career together was one of deep, lasting joy.

Scores of compilations of M&W's best material have been screened on TV since, as have many glowing tributes. Five special programmes also merit mention here and form part of the M&W television canon.

Fools Rush In, the 18 February 1973 edition of the BBC1 arts strand *Omnibus*, followed the two weeks of rehearsal that had led up to the comics' BBC show screened two days earlier.

Morecambe and Wise made an unlikely appearance, as themselves, in an edition of Thames' tough-cops series *The Sweeney* (episode titled 'Hearts And Minds', screened 23 November 1978). The story goes that when M&W asked *Sweeney* stars John Thaw and Dennis Waterman to appear in their 1976 BBC Christmas show, they responded that they would only do so if M&W appeared in *their* programme. Two years later the debt was repaid – doubtless helped by the fact that, by this time, M&W had switched from the BBC to Thames.

The duo remembered their earliest times on stage, travelling the country and playing the halls, in an hour-long special, *Eric And Ernie's Variety Days* (Thames for ITV, 2 March 1983).

Eric and Ernie's final work together was a real departure: *Night Train To Murder*, a 90-minute made-for-TV comedy thriller play that they wrote together with Joe McGrath (who also directed/produced, for Thames). The film harked back, in more ways than one, to their disappointing 1960s movies, and was screened by ITV seven months after Eric's death, on 3 January 1985.

Morecambe And Wise On Stage is a film of a concert the double-act performed at the Fairfield Halls in Croydon in October 1973. Intended then only for the archive, it was edited by Thames into an hour-long TV special, screened by ITV on 17 February 1987.

Mork And Mindy

USA · ABC (MILLER-MILKIS PRODUCTIONS/ HENDERSON PRODUCTIONS/PARAMOUNT) · SITCOM

95 episodes (92 × 30 mins · 3 × 60 mins) · colour

US dates: 14 Sep 1978–12 Aug 1982

UK dates: 10 Mar 1979–11 July 1981 (58 × 30 mins · 1 × 60 mins) ITV various days and times

MAIN CAST

Mork	Robin Williams
Mindy McConnell	Pam Dawber
Frederick McConnell	Conrad Janis
Cora Hudson	Elizabeth Kerr
Orson	Ralph James (voice only)
Mearth	Jonathan Winters (1981–82)
Franklin Bickley	Tom Poston
Remo DaVinci	Jay Thomas (1979–81)
Jean DaVinci	Gina Hecht (1979–81)

CREDITS

creators Garry Marshall/Dale McRaven/Joe Gauberg · *writers* various · *directors* Howard Storm, Harvey Medlinsky, Joel Zwick, Jeff Chambers · *executive producers* Garry Marshall, Tony Marshall · *producers* Dale McRaven, Bruce Johnson, Tom Tenowich, Ed Scarlach

Forget Mork, forget Mindy, forget the 'plot'. This series was all about Robin Williams, and he turned, literally overnight, when the first episode went out, from a little-known actor into a superstar. Williams' prodigious comic talent stunned viewers. Frenetic, breathtaking, awesome – all the adjectives applied as Williams dazzled audiences with his machine-gun humour, and mental, verbal and physical dexterity. Williams insisted he be allowed space to improvise, claiming to make up around a third of all the dialogue as he went along, and the series profited from this enormously, leaping to the top of the ratings. (Ironically, though, its fall was almost as swift.)

Mork And Mindy was created out of a single February 1978 episode of **Happy Days** ('My Favorite Orkan', first screened in the UK by ITV on 22 July 1978), in which Richie Cunningham dreams that an alien (Mork) arrives in Milwaukee and tries to capture him as a specimen of Earthlings. In the series proper Mork is a friendly, easy-going alien, something of an outcast on Ork, his home planet, because he possesses a sense of humour. So he is sent to 'an insignificant planet', Earth, charged with the job of studying its unfathomable humans and reporting his findings and conclusions back to the spirit of Orson, leader of Ork. (This Mork does by mind transference at the end of each episode, these homilies casting thought-provoking light on human frailties and foibles.) As soon as he lands on Earth, Mork is befriended by Mindy McConnell, a pretty university student, and so he ends up back at her place, 1619 Pine Street in Boulder, Colorado, and sets about making his studies from there in the aforementioned mega-loopy manner. Mork's favourite phrase from his old planet is 'na-no, na-no' – and it soon became a catchphrase for all of America. Eventually, inevitably, M&M fall in love and marry; Mork (yes, *Mork*) then lays an egg which hatches into a fully grown adult 'baby', Mearth (played by the veteran comedy improviser Jonathan Winters, Robin Williams' real-life idol in the field – see **You're Invited**).

In common with a number of other top US sitcoms, *Mork And Mindy* transferred to animated form when the real series ended, Williams and Dawber voicing their roles in a Hanna-Barbera series screened in America from September 1982 to September 1983.

Following its initial exposure in Britain on ITV from 1979 to 1981 C4 thrice screened extended runs of *Mork And Mindy*, beginning with the premiere episode (which, emphasising the *Happy Days* link, featured Henry Winkler as the Fonz) – from 15 June 1988 (94 episodes), 16 March 1993 (92 episodes) and 27 June 1995 (93 episodes) respectively. The premise of sending aliens to Earth to study our ways has proved a useful comedic device, giving rise to much sitcom mirth (*My Favorite Martian*, *ALF* and *3rd Rock From The Sun*).

See also Robin Williams: An Evening At The Met.

Mornin' Sarge

UK · BBC · SITCOM

7 × 30 mins · colour

Pilot · 16 June 1989 · BBC2 Fri 9pm

One series (6) 17 Nov–22 Dec 1989 · BBC2 Fri 9pm

MAIN CAST
Ted · Robin Driscoll
Ben · Tony Haase

Kevin · · · · · · · · · · · · · · · · · Pete McCarthy
Wendy · · · · · · · · · · · · · · Rebecca Stevens
'Sarge' · · · · · · · · · · · · · · · · · Paul Brooke

CREDITS
writers Tony Haase/Pete McCarthy/Rebecca Stevens · *directors/producers* John Kilby/Jamie Rix

The comings and goings at Middleford Police Station formed the background to this *Comic Asides* pilot and subsequent series, following the adventures of a group of constables (Kevin, Wendy, and the plainclothes copper Ted), their inspector (Ben) and their sergeant ('Sarge').

This was the first of the *Comic Asides* programmes to be developed into a series but, eventually, four of the first six (the others being **KYTV**, **Tygo Road** and **I, Lovett**) were taken up.

See also They Came From Somewhere Else.

Morris Minor's Marvellous Motors

UK · BBC (NOEL GAY TELEVISION) · CHILDREN'S SITCOM

6 × 25 mins · colour

8 Apr–13 May 1989 · BBC1 Sat around 6pm

MAIN CAST
Morris · · · · · · · · · · · · · · · · · · · Tony Hawks
Crawford · · · · · · · · · · · · · · Timothy Bateson
Angus Head · · · · · · · · · · · · · · · Tony Haase
Sonia Head · · · · · · · · · · · · · Camille Coduri
Mrs Plugg · · · · · · · · · · · · · · · · Una Stubbs
Sedgefield · · · · · · · · · · · · · · · Carl Gorham
Martin · · · · · · · · · · · · · · · · · Philip Herbert
Sparky Plugg · · · · · · · · · · · · · Andy Serkis
Winkworth · · · · · · · · · · · · · Donald Hewlett
Helen · · · · · · · · · · · · · · Bridget Thornborrow

CREDITS
writers Tony Hawks/Neil Mullarkey · *director* Juliet May · *producer* Nick Symons

A comedy-fantasy series for younger viewers centred on Morris Minor's Marvellous Motors, a car workshop in Normalton that repairs Morris Minor cars but, as a result of there being very few in the town, has next to no business. The leaseholder of the property, Mrs Plugg, puts a young man – whose name happens to be Morris Minor – in charge of the garage, and among his many distractions is the dastardly local restaurant owner Angus Head, who – with his henchman Martin – hatches nefarious schemes in order to gain control of the business (where, incidentally, his daughter Sonia works as a trainee mechanic). Morris is aided by his two employees, Sparky Plugg, the leaseholder's son, and Sedgefield.

The comedy musician Tony Hawks co-wrote the series, and his band Morris And The Minors provided the music that was integral to the storylines – they become Normalton's biggest band (which wasn't saying much).

The Mort Sahl Show

UK · BBC · STANDUP

1 × 50 mins · b/w

19 July 1961 · Wed 8.30pm

MAIN CAST
Mort Sahl

CREDITS
writer Mort Sahl · *producer* Bill Cotton Jr

The US comedian Mort Sahl was born in Canada in 1927, but his family returned to their native New York when he was four. Sahl first burst on to the American standup scene in the 1950s with a refreshing brand of social comedy based around contemporary issues, issuing a very popular record album of his act. Sahl was a frequent guest star on US TV shows but this BBC recording was masterminded by Frank Muir and Denis Norden who had met Sahl in Los Angeles and took pleasure in encouraging his trip to London and escorting him around. Such was the esteem of Sahl's album in the UK that London's intellectual élite clamoured to be among the TV studio audience (although they were not seen on camera).

Sahl's material at the time of the show ranged over such diverse topics as sports cars, psychiatry, 'red' China, President Kennedy, Fidel Castro, stereophonic jazz, menthol cigarettes, Billy Graham, beards, the hydrogen bomb and, of course, 'chicks'. But in this BBC show Sahl performed his typical US standup act, as released on his album; this disappointed many of the cognoscenti in the audience, who hoped that they might hear something new, including perhaps shrewd observations on the British.

The Most Likely Girl

UK · ITV (ATV) · SITCOM

4 × 30 mins · b/w

23 Sep–4 Nov 1957 · fortnightly Mon 8.30pm

MAIN CAST
Arethusa Wilderspin · · · · · · · · · · · Beryl Reid
Eve Edwards · · · · · · · · · · · · · Noele Gordon
Madge Dresswell · · · · · · · · · Barbara Couper

CREDITS
writer Robert Bishop · *director/producer* Cecil Petty

Gaining fame for her comic character creations Marlene, the dim Birmingham gal, and the schoolgirlish Monica, Beryl Reid starred in this early ITV sitcom as Arethusa Wilderspin, a likely lass, brimming with confidence and on the lookout for a man. She met one – called a 'victim' – in each episode, being aided in the pursuit by her witty and worldly friend Eve. Six episodes of *The Most Likely Girl* were announced but only four were screened.

Eve was played by Noele Gordon, the future *Crossroads* soap star. She was already a champion in the eyes of ATV executives, hosting an afternoon chat-show, *Tea With Noele Gordon*, in 1956, and a magazine programme, *Lunch Box*, in 1957.

Mostly Maynard

UK · BBC · SKETCH

5 × 30 mins · b/w

26 Feb–26 Mar 1957 · Tue 8pm

MAIN CAST
Bill Maynard
Betty Marsden
Len Lowe

CREDITS
writer Eric Merriman · *producer* Albert Stevenson

A showcase for the talented Bill Maynard, who had scored a hit with Terry Scott in **Great Scott – It's Maynard!** and was rewarded with a solo starring series, also on the BBC. Maynard's style of talking straight to camera was considered 'intimate' at the time and his habit of 'owning up' when lines were forgotten, props dropped or gags flopped endeared him to the viewing audience.

Mother And Son

AUSTRALIA · ABC · SITCOM

42 × 30 mins · colour

Australian dates: 16 Jan 1984–21 Mar 1994

UK dates: 9 Apr 1986–6 May 1987 (14 episodes) C4 Wed mostly 5.55pm

MAIN CAST
Maggie Beare ············· Ruth Cracknell
Arthur Beare ············· Garry McDonald
Robert Beare ············· Henri Szeps
Liz Beare ··············· Judy Morris
Deidre ················ Suzanne Roylance

CREDITS
writer Geoffrey Atherden · *director/producer* Geoff Portman

An Australian sitcom imported by C4 on the strength of its successes with Garry McDonald's 'little Aussie bleeder' character **'Norman Gunston'**. Here, McDonald was cast as Arthur Beare, a writer in his mid-thirties who has separated from his wife Deidre – they are later divorced – and returns to live with his elderly widowed mother, Maggie. Mum is not at all well, indeed she is dissolving into senility, but she exploits this ill-health to keep Arthur shackled at home. She also has another son, Robert – a dentist, married to Liz – who is determined not to become entrapped by his mother's wiles and genuine difficulties.

There wasn't much to it – and what there was somewhat contrived – but Aussie audiences really took to *Mother And Son* and it ran there for six series over nine years, ending in 1994. At this point, the writer Geoffrey Atherden was invited to adapt his

creation for a British version, **Keeping Mum**, aired by BBC1 in 1997.

Mother Came Too

UK · BBC · SITCOM

1 × 25 mins · b/w

4 June 1965 · BBC1 Fri 8pm

MAIN CAST
Mrs Pratt ················ Peggy Mount
Arthur Pratt ············· Graham Stark

CREDITS
writer John Waterhouse · *executive producer* Graeme Muir · *producer* Philip Barker

A *Comedy Playhouse* segment that offered yet another variation on Peggy Mount's formidable female character, cast this time as timid Graham Stark's overbearing mother.

Mother Came Too marked the solo TV script debut for radio, film and stage writer John Waterhouse, whose only previous small-screen work had been collaborating with Ronald Wolfe on **Here's Archie**.

Mother Nature's Bloomers

see *Get The Drift*

Mother's Ruin

UK · ITV (GRANADA) · SITCOM

6 × 30 mins · colour

29 May–10 July 1994 · Sun 7pm

MAIN CAST
Leslie Flitcroft ·········· Roy Barraclough
Kitty Flitcroft ············· Dora Bryan
Brucella Pashley ·········· Julia Deakin
Wendy Watson ············ Kay Adshead
Clive Watson ············· Jason Done

CREDITS
writer John Stevenson · *director* John Stroud · *executive producer* Andy Harries · *producer* Antony Wood

Sorry!-like (and, frankly, just plain sorry) sitcom written especially for Roy Barraclough. He was cast as Leslie Flitcroft, the henpecked 50-year-old son of maddening mother Kitty, on whose behalf he manages the family-owned health and homeopathic food store Nurse Nature. Leslie is desperate to run off with his woman-friend of some ten years' standing, Wendy Watson, but his mother perpetually destroys his plans and keeps him under her wing.

Kitty, meanwhile, a former stage actress, denies old age with a combined diet of primrose oil and gin; Wendy, the single mother of teenage son Clive, is tired of waiting for Leslie to confront his mother; and Brucella, the lank-haired plain-Jane shop assistant, is considered by Kitty as ideal daughter-in-law material.

John Stevenson had already written for Roy Barraclough when the comic actor played

Alec Gilroy in *Coronation Street*. But *Mother's Ruin* – a broad, obvious, innuendo-laden northern sitcom – reeked of the bad old days of 1970s ITV comedy and was decidedly anachronistic in the more slick 1990s.

The Mothers-In-Law

USA · NBC (UNITED ARTISTS) · SITCOM

54 × 30 mins · colour

US dates: 10 Sep 1967–7 Sep 1969

UK dates: 19 July 1968–27 Mar 1969 (29 × b/w) BBC1 Fri 6.40pm then Thu 6.15pm

MAIN CAST
Eve Hubbard ············· Eve Arden
Kaye Buell ············· Kaye Ballard
Roger Buell ···· Roger C Carmel (1967–68);
············· Richard Deacon (1968–69)
Herb Hubbard ··········· Herbert Rudley
Jerry Buell ··············· Jerry Fogel
Suzie Hubbard Buell ······ Deborah Walley

CREDITS
writers Madelyn Davis/Bob Carroll Jr, Fred S Fox/Seaman Jacobs, William O'Hallaren and others · *director/producer* Desi Arnaz

A feuding families sitcom saved from purgatory by the inspired casting of its female leads. Eve Arden, an American sitcom legend following her long-running series *Our Miss Brooks* (radio 1948–57, TV 1952–56, but never heard/screened in the UK), attacked her lines with gusto and was matched in the quickfire-delivery department by singer-comedian Kaye Ballard. These two neighbours (the series was set in Los Angeles) clashed over virtually everything, both claiming to have the interests of their respective offspring at heart.

The Hubbards were the more staid family: husband Herb was a lawyer and Eve an ex-golf pro, whereas Roger Buell was a TV scriptwriter and Kaye a bored housewife adept at interfering in other people's lives. Cementing the neighbourly relationship, the Hubbards' daughter Suzie married the Buells' son Jerry, and they lived in Herb and Eve's garage.

The series was produced by Desi Arnaz (*I Love Lucy*), who also turned up in the episodes from time to time in the guise of a bullfighter, Raphael del Gado.

Moving

UK · ITV (THAMES) · SITCOM

6 × 30 mins · colour

9 Jan–13 Feb 1985 · Wed 8.30pm

MAIN CAST
Sarah Gladwyn ·········· Penelope Keith
Frank Gladwyn ··········· Ronald Pickup
Liz Ford ··············· Prunella Gee
Eileen Lewis ············· Natalie Slater
Jimmy Ryan ············ Roger Lloyd Pack
Bill Lomax ·············· David Ashford
Beryl Fearnley ············· Eliza Hunt
Jane Gladwyn ·········· Barbara Wilshere

CREDITS

writer Stanley Price · director/producer Les Chatfield

Sarah and Frank Gladwyn have weathered the storm: they've created a new generation of Gladwyns and now they're alone again, rattling around their big family house like the proverbial peas in a biscuit tin. The time has come for them to realise their capital, move to a flat and put the surplus cash to good use, like investing in a new career for Sarah. First, however, they need someone to buy their 'des res' – and not just anyone: Sarah wants it to be 'the right person'. As it turns out, this is the last of their concerns, for sales fall through, purchases fall through, cracks appear in the house and in the marriage, daughter Jane returns unexpectedly from college, Sarah's sister Liz is a Valium-popper and everything is quite some distance from being sweetness and light.

Written by Stanley Price – adapted from his comedy play of the same name which had enjoyed a successful run on the London stage – and taped without a studio audience, *Moving* was the first of four starring roles for Penelope Keith in Thames sitcoms, leading to *Executive Stress*, *No Job For A Lady* and *Law And Disorder* (as well as her hosting of Thames' game-show *What's My Line?* in 1988, and Thames' gardening series *Growing Places With Penelope Keith* in 1989).

The six episodes were abridged into a single 90-minute repeat, networked on 2 September 1987.

Moving Furniture

UK · BBC · SKETCH

1 × 10 mins · b/w

9 Mar 1938 · Wed 3pm

MAIN CAST

Richard Hearne
Lily Palmer
George Nelson

CREDITS

writer Richard Hearne · producer Reginald Smith

A one-off comedy sketch, presented under the *Starlight* banner, starring Richard Hearne in pre-**Mr Pastry** mode.

See also Bath H&C, S-s-s-h! The Wife! and Take Two Eggs.

Mr Aitch

UK · ITV (REDIFFUSION) · SITCOM

15 × 30 mins · b/w

6 Jan–21 Apr 1967 · Fri 9.10pm

MAIN CAST

Harry Aitch	Harry H Corbett
Albie	Norman Chappell
Lefty	Gordon Gostelow

CREDITS

writers Dick Clement/Ian La Frenais (9), Ray Galton/Alan Simpson (4), Dave Freeman (1), John Junkin (1) · directors Christopher Hodson, John Robins, Bill Turner · producer Peter Eton

With *Steptoe And Son* presumed dead – it had ended in 1965 and the 1970 revival was not yet on the cards – Harry H Corbett set about finding himself another starring role. *Mr Aitch* was meant to be it, and certainly the calibre of the team behind the series was A1: writers Dick Clement and Ian La Frenais were fresh from *The Likely Lads* and *Lucky Jim*; and Ray Galton and Alan Simpson had, of course, scaled the highest heights with *Hancock* and *Steptoe*. Still, *Mr Aitch* failed to take off, and only one series was made.

Harry H Corbett let it be known that he considered himself Mr Harry Aitch in more than name – he made it clear that he identified strongly with the part, that it had been within him for a number of years and that he was relishing the opportunity to step out of the Harold Steptoe character. Mr Aitch wanted status more than he wanted money, he wanted to live on his wits, to pander to his ego, he wanted to be a Londoner and enjoy 'birds galore', yet he spent most of the time conning himself.

Norman Chappell (as Mr Aitch's chauffeur-cum-valet) and Gordon Gostelow were the only other regular members of the cast, although Al Mancini, Bernard Cribbins, John Junkin (who wrote one of the episodes) and Rita Webb (wonderfully cast as a French au pair!) made guest appearances, and there was a double role for the then little-known comic Barry Cryer: he appeared in one episode as a policeman, and was also the studio audience warm-up act before the recordings began.

Mr And Mrs

see BALL, Lucille

Mr Bean

Even before *Not The Nine O'Clock News*, Rowan Atkinson's earliest TV appearances – in the worth-watching LWT one-off *Rowan Atkinson Presents … Canned Laughter* and in the first presentation of *The Secret Policeman's Ball* (The Amnesty Galas) – pinpointed this hitherto unknown comic actor's ability to draw laughs from dialogue-free comedy and his remarkably flexible face. *Not The Nine …* compounded this to the point where, during his 1981 stage tour (resulting in the *Live In Belfast* album), Atkinson mocked himself as 'that rubber-faced twat from *Not*

Now Nationwide'. So, after the long dialogue-rich *Blackadder* series, which gave Atkinson a welcome opportunity to broaden his acting style, he was happy to consider a return to mime.

In both *Canned Laughter* and the 1981 tour Atkinson portrayed male characters who were complete and utter twerps – gormless, hapless, clueless, shiftless individuals who not only were born losers but were destined to remain that way. A new character was developed from here, Atkinson knowing that his surname must be a vegetable. After dismissing Mr Cauliflower and Mr Cabbage, Mr Bean was given the go ahead – destined to stumble his way into the comedy hall of fame. Crucially, the decision was taken to make the *Mr Bean* episodes virtually dialogue-free. In *Mr Bean* one rarely hears anything above a grunt or a muffled, almost wholly swallowed word; these are silent comedies in the tradition of French pantomimist Jacques Tati's *Monsieur Hulot* films, which Atkinson has acknowledged as a major influence.

To describe Mr Bean in a few words is problematic. He's a berk in a sports jacket with leather elbow-pads. He goes about life with a childlike innocence and wonderment. Perpetually curious but exasperatingly clumsy, he's guaranteed to touch, and break, everything around him. He can be alternately brash and meek, forward and shy, sensitive and insensitive; dazzlingly clever but mostly stupefyingly stupid. He can be hurt but, incongruously, has pronounced malicious, devilish and deceitful streaks. Richard Curtis, who co-authored many Bean scripts, had a passable bash at summing up Bean when he said, 'My theory is that he was abandoned at the age of six for being too annoying and had to bring himself up.' One might also say, bluntly, that, in Mr Bean, Atkinson has found A Million Ways To Be A Prat. Intriguingly, each episode of *Mr Bean* began with the man falling to the ground from a great height and into a narrow beam of light – as if he was an alien dumped from a craft in outer space, or (as the heavenly theme music seemed to corroborate) a God-sent missionary whose task was to irritate humankind.

The plan all along was to make – or at least screen – the *Mr Bean* episodes sporadically, never as a weekly or regular series, to slowly build momentum and not splurge all the comedic ideas in one go. As such, only 13 episodes were made for television; typically 24 minutes long, for a commercial TV half-hour, each includes three or more distinct sketches. (A number of the episodes have been re-edited for compilation programmes and video releases, some tapes including newly performed linking material and even a full fourteenth programme not screened on TV.)

With his mouth agape and his hands twiddling, Mr Bean has become perhaps Britain's best loved comedy export, sold to 82 countries, the virtually silent humour giving the series *massive* international appeal – assisted, in the first instance, by clever placing of the episodes on in-flight aeroplane screens. But with those 13 TV episodes under his belt – the number he always predicted he would make – Rowan Atkinson turned Mr Bean's attention from small-screen to big: a full-length feature, *Bean – The Ultimate Disaster Movie*, being a worldwide box-office hit in 1997. The film was built around a case of mistaken identity – in the guise of an international art expert, Bean flies to Los Angeles where he destroys not only a priceless painting but the unity of the family who serve as his hosts. The movie was co-written by Richard Curtis and Robin Driscoll and directed by Atkinson's former *Not The Nine O'Clock News* colleague Mel Smith. (To promote its release, ITV screened a one-hour special on 31 July 1997, *The Story Of Bean*, in which Rowan Atkinson reflected on his career to date, with particular emphasis on the Mr Bean character.)

See also *Rowan Atkinson – On Location In Boston.*

Mr Bean

UK · ITV (TIGER TELEVISION FOR THAMES) · SITCOM

1 × 30 mins · colour

1 Jan 1990 · Mon 8pm

MAIN CAST
Mr Bean · · · · · · · · · · · · · · Rowan Atkinson
OTHER PARTS PLAYED BY
Paul Bown, Rudolph Walker, Roger Sloman, Richard Briers, Howard Goodall

CREDITS
writers Richard Curtis/Rowan Atkinson/Ben Elton · *director/producer* John Howard Davies

Mr Bean sits an exam and is blissfully happy until, too late, he realises that he has studied the wrong maths equations; tries to change into his swimming trunks at the beach without anyone seeing his bits; and tries to stifle a sneeze in church.

So entered a new TV hero on New Year's Day 1990. The episode collected three major prizes at the Montreux TV Festival, including the prestigious Golden Rose.

The Return Of Mr Bean

UK · ITV (TIGER TELEVISION FOR THAMES) · SITCOM

1 × 30 mins · colour

5 Nov 1990 · Mon 8pm

MAIN CAST
Mr Bean · · · · · · · · · · · · · · Rowan Atkinson
OTHER PARTS PLAYED BY
Dave O'Higgins, Paul McDowell, William Van Dyck, John Junkin, Roger Lloyd Pack, Steve McNicholas, Robin Driscoll, Matilda Ziegler, Tina Maskell

CREDITS
writers Robin Driscoll/Richard Curtis/Rowan Atkinson · *director/producer* John Howard Davies

Mr Bean goes department-store shopping with his new American Express card; treats himself to a slap-up birthday meal for one; and waits at a cinema for the Queen to arrive for a Royal Film Premiere.

The Curse Of Mr Bean

UK · ITV (TIGER TELEVISION FOR THAMES) · SITCOM

1 × 30 mins · colour

1 Jan 1991 · Tue 8.30pm

MAIN CAST
Mr Bean · · · · · · · · · · · · · · Rowan Atkinson
OTHER PARTS PLAYED BY
Angus Deayton, Matilda Ziegler

CREDITS
writers Robin Driscoll/Richard Curtis/Rowan Atkinson · *director/producer* John Howard Davies

Mr Bean negotiates a tricky car park barrier; goes for a swim; has a park bench lunch; and escorts his girlfriend to a horror movie.

This episode won an International Emmy Award.

Mr Bean Goes To Town

UK · ITV (TIGER TELEVISION FOR THAMES) · SITCOM

1 × 30 mins · colour

15 Oct 1991 · Tue 8.30pm

MAIN CAST
Mr Bean · · · · · · · · · · · · · · Rowan Atkinson
OTHER PARTS PLAYED BY
Nick Hancock, Robin Driscoll, Dursley McLinden, Matilda Ziegler, Alan Shaxon, Julia Howson, Howard Goodall, Richard Marcangelo, Mark Kahn, Phil Nice

CREDITS
writers Robin Driscoll/Richard Curtis/Rowan Atkinson · *directors* John Birkin, Paul Weiland · *executive producers* Peter Bennett-Jones, John Howard Davies · *producer* Sue Vertue

Mr Bean buys a television; has his camera stolen; finds it hard to install the TV correctly; endures an itchy foot; and spends the evening romantically entertaining his girlfriend, and annoying people, at a disco.

The Trouble With Mr Bean

UK · ITV (TIGER TELEVISION FOR THAMES) · SITCOM

1 × 30 mins · colour

1 Jan 1992 · Wed 8pm

MAIN CAST
Mr Bean · · · · · · · · · · · · · · Rowan Atkinson
OTHER PARTS PLAYED BY
Richard Wilson, Caroline Quentin, Sam Mead, Nathan Lewis, Bridget Bramman, Hugo Mendez, Michael Godley, Christine Ellerbeck

CREDITS
writers Robin Driscoll/Richard Curtis/Rowan Atkinson · *directors* John Birkin, Paul Weiland · *executive producers* Peter Bennett-Jones, Richard Willmore · *producer* Sue Vertue

Mr Bean oversleeps but manages, ingeniously, to drive to the dentist in time for his appointment, although the dentist comes to regret this; he then eats lunch in the park and tries to help a boy repair his remote-control boat.

Mr Bean Rides Again

UK · ITV (TIGER TELEVISION FOR THAMES) · SITCOM

1 × 30 mins · colour

17 Feb 1992 · Mon 8pm

MAIN CAST
Mr Bean · · · · · · · · · · · · · · Rowan Atkinson
OTHER PARTS PLAYED BY
Roger Sloman, Su Douglas, John Rolfe, Stephen Frost, Nick Hancock, Eryl Maynard, Hugo Mendez

CREDITS
writers Robin Driscoll/Richard Curtis/Rowan Atkinson · *directors* Paul Weiland, John Birkin · *executive producer* Peter Bennett-Jones · *producer* Sue Vertue

Unwilling to attempt mouth-to-mouth resuscitation, Mr Bean revives a heart-attack victim with car-battery jump leads but then electrocutes him instead; tries to post a letter but ends up posting himself; packs for a holiday; travels to the airport by train; and proves immensely irritating to the poorly child sitting next to him on the aeroplane.

Merry Christmas Mr Bean

UK · ITV (TIGER TELEVISION FOR THAMES) · SITCOM

1 × 30 mins · colour

29 Dec 1992 · Tue 8.30pm

MAIN CAST
Mr Bean · · · · · · · · · · · · · · Rowan Atkinson
Irma Gobb · · · · · · · · · · · · · · Matilda Ziegler
OTHER PARTS PLAYED BY
C J Allen, Owen Brenman, John Warner, Lee Barrett, Jonathan Stratt

CREDITS
writers Robin Driscoll/Richard Curtis/Rowan Atkinson · *director* John Birkin · *executive producer* Peter Bennett-Jones · *producer* Sue Vertue

Mr Bean purchases his Christmas decorations at Harrods; collects money for and then conducts a Salvation Army band;

steals the town centre Christmas tree; enjoys the free entertainment provided by carol singers; stuffs himself inside the biggest turkey in the world; and manages to upset his woebegone girlfriend Irma over Christmas Day lunch.

Mr Bean In Room 426

UK · ITV (TIGER ASPECT PRODUCTIONS/ THAMES FOR CENTRAL) · SITCOM

1 × 30 mins · colour

17 Feb 1993 · Wed 8pm

MAIN CAST
Mr Bean · · · · · · · · · · · · · · Rowan Atkinson

OTHER PARTS PLAYED BY
Michael Fenton Stevens, Roger Brierley, Matthew Ashford, Danny La Rue

CREDITS
writers Robin Driscoll/Rowan Atkinson · *director* Paul Weiland · *producer* Sue Vertue

Mr Bean checks into an elegant hotel; tries to win a battle of wits with the man in the adjacent room; and makes a brief foray into cross-dressing, much to the chagrin of Danny La Rue (appearing as himself).

Note. In the can but not yet scheduled for screening, this episode was shown in place of the advertised *Mind The Baby, Mr Bean*, which was postponed on grounds of sensitivity following the murder of a child that was distressing the British nation.

Do-It-Yourself, Mr Bean

UK · ITV (TIGER ASPECT PRODUCTIONS/ THAMES FOR CENTRAL) · SITCOM

1 × 30 mins · colour

10 Jan 1994 · Mon 8pm

MAIN CAST
Mr Bean · · · · · · · · · · · · · · Rowan Atkinson

OTHER PARTS PLAYED BY
Robert Austin, Simon Godley, Helen Burns, David Stoll, Rupert Vansittart, Andy Greenhalgh

CREDITS
writers Robin Driscoll/Rowan Atkinson · *director* John Birkin · *producer* Peter Bennett-Jones

Mr Bean hosts the flattest New Year's Eve party of all time; in the morning he replaces the dummy of himself he had positioned at the head of the queue of people waiting outside Arding and Hobbs department store for its New Year's Day sale to begin; invents a clever way of transporting home his purchases; then wreaks havoc with a spot of domestic DIY.

Mind The Baby, Mr Bean

UK · ITV (TIGER ASPECT PRODUCTIONS/ THAMES FOR CENTRAL) · SITCOM

1 × 30 mins · colour

25 Apr 1994 · Mon 8pm

MAIN CAST
Mr Bean · · · · · · · · · · · · · · Rowan Atkinson

OTHER PARTS PLAYED BY
Susie McKenna, Andy Bradford, Nick Scott, Lydia Henderson-Boyle, Anthony Hambling

CREDITS
writers Robin Driscoll/Rowan Atkinson · *additional material* Richard Curtis, Paul Weiland · *director* Paul Weiland · *executive producer* Peter Bennett-Jones · *producer* Sue Vertue

Down at Southsea, and on his way to the funfair, Mr Bean finds himself with baby in tow – his yellow Mini car has hooked on to a pram. Despite the inhibiting presence of the infant, Mr Bean is determined to enjoy every one of the attractions. When the baby is finally returned safely to its mother Mr Bean finds that he has collected a stray dog.

See the second paragraph of *Mr Bean In Room 426*, above.

Back To School, Mr Bean

UK · ITV (TIGER ASPECT PRODUCTIONS FOR CENTRAL) · SITCOM

1 × 30 mins · colour

26 Oct 1994 · Wed 8pm

MAIN CAST
Mr Bean · · · · · · · · · · · · · · Rowan Atkinson

OTHER PARTS PLAYED BY
Suzanne Bertish, Lucy Fleming, Al Hunter-Ashton, David Schneider, John Barrard, John Clegg, Sam Driscoll, Tracey Roberts, Harriet Eastcott, Sarah Milo, Chris Ryan, Rupert Bates, Chris Driscoll

CREDITS
writers Robin Driscoll/Rowan Atkinson · *director* John Birkin · *producer* Peter Bennett-Jones

Mr Bean drills some cadets; attends the open-day of an adult education college; gets a rare stamp stuck on his forehead; becomes over-enthusiastic in the chemistry and judo demonstrations; stumbles across a nude model in the Life Class; and manages to lose his trousers.

Tee Off, Mr Bean

UK · ITV (TIGER ASPECT PRODUCTIONS FOR CENTRAL) · SITCOM

1 × 30 mins · colour

20 Sep 1995 · Wed 8pm

MAIN CAST
Mr Bean · · · · · · · · · · · · · · Rowan Atkinson

OTHER PARTS PLAYED BY
Jacqueline Defferary, Grant Masters, David Battley, Marilyn Finlay

CREDITS
writers Robin Driscoll/Rowan Atkinson · *additional material* Andrew Clifford · *director* John Birkin · *producer* Sue Vertue

Doing his laundry, Mr Bean manages once again to lose his trousers; then he plays a particularly crazy game of crazy golf where he loses his ball in all the wrong places.

Goodnight Mr Bean

UK · ITV (TIGER ASPECT PRODUCTIONS FOR CENTRAL) · SITCOM

1 × 30 mins · colour

31 Oct 1995 · Tue 8.30pm

MAIN CAST
Mr Bean · · · · · · · · · · · · · · Rowan Atkinson

OTHER PARTS PLAYED BY
Suzy Aitchison, Elizabeth Bennett, Rupert Bates, Penelope Nice, Rupert Vansittart

CREDITS
writers Robin Driscoll/Rowan Atkinson · *director* John Birkin · *executive producer* Peter Bennett-Jones · *producer* Sue Vertue

With his hand stuck inside a teapot, Mr Bean goes to the outpatients department at hospital but loses his own patience while awaiting his turn; out with his camera he seizes a photo opportunity by re-dressing and enormously irritating an immobile sentry guard; back home, he prepares for bed but has trouble falling asleep.

This was the last *Mr Bean* programme to appear on British television. A fourteenth half-hour, *Hair By Mr Bean Of London*, has been released exclusively on video (written by Robin Driscoll/Rowan Atkinson/Richard Curtis, directed by John Birkin, executive produced by Peter Bennett-Jones and produced by Sue Vertue).

Miscellaneous Mr Bean TV appearances have included

Comic Relief 1991
BBC1 · 15 March 1991

Seeking to raise money while having the traditional 'stonking' good time, Mr Bean takes part in sponsored silence, tea drinking, codpiece wearing and impersonating Madonna activities.

Total Relief
BBC1 · 12 March 1993

The 1993 Comic Relief telethon married up Mr Bean with Cilla Black's game-show *Blind Date*. Mr Bean's antics prove popular with the studio audience, their applause misleading the woman on the other side of the screen to select him for her date. We then see them out together, a night that he alone thoroughly enjoys.

Live & Kicking
BBC1 · 16 October 1993

Promoting the release of a *Mr Bean* video, Rowan Atkinson appeared as Bean on this Saturday morning children's magazine show, making mayhem in the studio.

The Night Of Comic Relief
BBC1 · 17 March 1995

In a segment titled *Torvill and Bean*, Mr Bean replaced Christopher Dean to join up with Jayne Torvill in their ice-skating show.

National Lottery Live
BBC1 · 2 August 1997

Mr Bean ran amok during the weekly National Lottery presentation, in one of a number of personal appearances around this time aimed to promote the release of *Bean – The Ultimate Disaster Movie.*

Chat-shows and TV commercials

Rowan Atkinson has sometimes appeared in these in the character of Mr Bean. One commercial was for the Norwegian grocery store REMA 1000, where he compared the numbers of sweets from two packets, and squirted mayonnaise into a long line on the floor to find out which of two tubes contained the most. Another was for the chocolate sweets M&Ms, in which he sent one of the M&M characters skittling down the lane at a bowling alley.

Mr Big

UK · BBC · SITCOM

14 × 30 mins · colour

Pilot *The Big Job* 21 May 1974 · BBC1 Tue 8.30pm

Series One (6) 7 Jan–11 Feb 1977 · BBC1 Fri 7.40pm

Series Two (7) 23 June–4 Aug 1977 · BBC1 Thu 8.30pm

MAIN CAST

Eddie · Peter Jones
Dolly · · · · · · · · · · · · · · · · · · · Prunella Scales
Ginger · · · · · · · · · · · · · · Nick Brimble (pilot);
· · · · · · · · · · · · · · · · · · Ian Lavender (series)
Norma · · · · · · · · · Andonia Katsaros (pilot);
· · · · · · · · · · · · · · · · Carol Hawkins (series)

CREDITS

creator Peter Jones · *writers* Peter Jones (pilot), Peter Jones/Christopher Bond (series) · *directors* Gareth Gwenlan (pilot), Ray Butt (series) · *producer* Dennis Main Wilson

The comic adventures of a family of crooks – led by the bumbling dad, Eddie. The actor/writer Peter Jones came up with the idea, which first aired as *The Big Job*, a *Comedy Playhouse* pilot; it took nearly three years to translate into a series.

Jones himself played Eddie, a small-time crook with big ideas and an uncanny knack for bungling his crimes, and he was aided by his light-fingered wife Dolly and their children Norma and Ginger. Crime was an integral part of the family's history – Eddie's mother had already had her collar felt and was serving time at Her Majesty's pleasure.

Despite stretching to two series, *Mr Big* failed to catch on to any great degree, representing a rare blip in the successful careers of Jones and the producer Dennis Main Wilson.

Mr Deeds Goes To Town

USA · ABC (SCREEN GEMS) · SITCOM

17 × 30 mins · colour

US dates: 26 Sep 1969–16 Jan 1970

UK dates: 8 Feb–12 Apr 1975 (17 episodes) BBC1 Sat 12 noon

MAIN CAST

Longfellow Deeds · · · · · · · · Monte Markham
Tony Lawrence · · · · · · · · · · Pat Harrington Jr
Henry Masterson · · · · · · · · · · · · Herb Voland
The Butler (George) · · · · · · · · · · · Ivor Barry

CREDITS

creator Clarence Budington Kelland · *writers* various · *directors* various · *producers* Harry Ackerman, E W Swackhamer

A television version of the famous 1936 movie of the same title, directed by Frank Capra. The original story – based on a stage-play, *Opera Hut*, by Clarence Budington Kelland – focused on a small-town poet, Longfellow Deeds, who inherits his uncle's multi-million-dollar business and shocks New York by taking over the corporation with the express purpose of helping people rather than taking advantage of them. Gary Cooper played the lead in the movie and Monte Markham took the TV honours, the character this time starting out as a newspaper editor.

The simple moral of generosity and making the world a better place failed to cut much ice with US TV viewers in 1969 and, faring poorly in the ratings, the series was cancelled after only 17 episodes.

Mr Digby, Darling

UK · ITV (YORKSHIRE) · SITCOM

20 episodes (10 × 30 mins · colour; 9 × 30 mins · b/w; 1 × short special · colour)

Series One (6 × b/w) 6 Jan–10 Feb 1969 · Mon 9.30pm

Series Two (3 × b/w · 4 × colour) 27 Oct–22 Dec 1969 · mostly Mon 9.30pm

Short special (colour) · part of *All-Star Comedy Carnival* 25 Dec 1969 · Thu 6pm

Series Three (6 × colour) 21 Dec 1970–25 Jan 1971 · Mon mostly 9.30pm

MAIN CAST

Roland Digby · · · · · · · · · · · · · · Peter Jones
Thelma Teesdale · · · · · · · · Sheila Hancock

OTHER APPEARANCES

Chambers · · · · · Norman Chappell (series 1)
Olive · · · · · · · · · · · · · Beryl Cooke (series 1)
Mr Trumper · · · · · · · · Brian Oulton (series 1)
Joyce · · · · · · · · · · · · Janet Brown (series 2)
Mr Bailey · · · · · · · · Peter Stephens (series 2)
Norman Stanhope · · · · · · · · Michael Bates
· (series 3)

CREDITS

writers Ken Hoare/Mike Sharland · *directors* Christopher Hodson (14 & special), Bill Hitchcock (5) · *executive producer* John Duncan (series 3) · *producers* Christopher Hodson (14), Bill Hitchcock (5), Sid Colin (special)

With his wife and children at home, the office at pesticide manufacturers Rid-O-Rat is where Roland Digby finds peace and quiet. And this is not just because his spouse and sprogs are missing – the office is where awaits faithful Thelma. She is a secretary/PA par excellence, the perfectionist's perfectionist determined to make life as easy as it can be for her boss, whether by smoothing the paths of industry or his tailored suit, darning his socks or providing slippers and kippers. Unmarried, Thelma has all the time in the world to devote to the extremely incompetent Mr Digby, provided that it is between nine and five.

Mr Digby, Darling not only reunited Peter Jones and Sheila Hancock, previously together in **The Rag Trade**, but also brought Jones back together with writers Hoare and Sharland, who had scripted **Beggar My Neighbour**. A pleasing and lightly funny sitcom, it extended easily to three series.

Mr Don And Mr George

UK · C4 (ABSOLUTELY PRODUCTIONS) · SITCOM

6 × 30 mins · colour

25 Aug–29 Sep 1993 · Wed 10.35pm

MAIN CAST

Mr Donald McDiarmid · · · · · · Moray Hunter
Mr George McDiarmid · · · · · · · Jack Docherty

CREDITS

writers Moray Hunter/Jack Docherty · *director/producer* Alan Nixon

One by-product of the 1980s comedy revolution was the surreal, post-modern sitcoms developed by its players. These shows differed greatly from traditional sitcoms in their willingness to forsake reality, acknowledge the audience (both in the studio and at home) and eschew accepted ideas of plot in order to revolve around the stage personas of their stars. The collection included **Sean's Show**, **Terry And Julian**, **Newman And Baddiel In Pieces** (virtually a sitcom) and Reeves and Mortimer's one-off **The Weekenders**, all of which diverged from the norm. Another example was *Mr Don And Mr George*.

The series was based on two characters Hunter and Docherty developed for the sketch series **Absolutely**, and, indeed, the episodes had the feel of extended sketches rather than fully structured comedy half-hours. Although not related, the two characters shared a surname and each week hared about the deliberately cheesy studio sets in all sorts of surreal adventures. Funny in places, downright weird in others.

Mr Gillie Potter

see *Gillie Potter*

Mr H Is Late

see SYKES, Eric

Mr John Jorrocks

UK · BBC · COMEDY SERIAL

8 × 25 mins · b/w

23 July–10 Sep 1966 · BBC2 Sat 8.15pm

MAIN CAST

John Jorrocks	Jimmy Edwards
Mrs Jorrocks	Angela Baddeley
Betsy	Ann Penfold
Benjamin	Alan Baulch
James Pigg	Walter Carr
Belinda	Heather Bell
Lady Barnington	Moyra Fraser
Duke of Donkeyton	Michael Bates

CREDITS

creator R S Surtees · writer Michael Voysey · director Peter Dews · producer David Conroy

An eight-part series in which Jimmy Edwards – minus his trademark handlebar moustache – portrayed R S (Robin Smith) Surtees' famous 'sporting Falstaff' Mr John Jorrocks, a rambunctious cockney who leaves his job as a grocer to become squire and Master of Foxhounds at Handley Cross. Here, he and his wife make waves as their broad East End ways, manners and accents clash sharply with the countrified sensibilities of the local gentry.

John Jorrocks first appeared in a long series of stories in *New Sporting Magazine* in 1831, edited by Surtees – the character was also published in book form in 1838 and 1843 – and the television version returned to this original period for its richly comic adaptation. The series was full of larger-than-life characters and comedic situations, and Edwards was a perfect choice to play the barnstorming Jorrocks, using all of his customary bluster to create a character that, to all intents and purposes, was Pa Glum on a horse.

The TV series followed on the heels of a stage musical, *Jorrocks*, mounted in London in 1966, with Joss Ackland in the title role and Thelma Ruby as his wife. (Paul Eddington and Richard Stilgoe were also among the cast.)

Mr Justice Duncannon

UK · BBC · SITCOM

6 × 25 mins · b/w

18 Jan–22 Feb 1963 · Fri mostly 8.50pm

MAIN CAST

Mr Justice Duncannon	Andrew Cruickshank

CREDITS

writers Frank Muir/Denis Norden, Henry Cecil · producer Graeme Muir

A full series for the stern but humane judge Justice Duncannon, a wryly humorous Scotsman in London who made a popular appearance in the final episode of *Brothers*

In Law. His professional intransigence was tempered by two weaknesses – his fondness for women and whisky.

Andrew Cruickshank (of *Dr Finlay's Casebook* fame) took the title role and the *Brothers In Law* production team reunited for these six episodes.

Mr Little At Large

see Reggie Little

Mr Majeika

UK · ITV (TVS) · CHILDREN'S SITCOM

20 episodes (19 × 30 mins · 1 × 60 mins) · colour

Series One (6) 13 Mar–17 Apr 1988 · Sun mostly 4.30pm

Special (60 mins) 25 Dec 1988 · Sun 1.15pm

Series Two (6) 7 Jan–11 Feb 1989 · Sat 4.15pm

Series Three (7) 3 Jan–14 Feb 1990 · Wed 4.40pm

MAIN CAST

Mr Majeika	Stanley Baxter
Melanie Brace-Girdle	Claire Sawyer
Thomas Grey	Andrew Read (not series 3)
Hamish Bigmore	Simeon Pearl
Headmaster (Mr Dudley Potter)	Roland MacLeod
Mrs Bunty Brace-Girdle	Fidelis Morgan
Mrs Pam Bigmore	Eve Ferret
The Worshipful Wizard of Walpurgis	Richard Murdoch (mostly voice only)
Prince	Sanjiv Madan (series 3)

OTHER APPEARANCES

Wilhelmina Worlock	Miriam Margolyes (series 1 & 2)
Miss Flavia Jelley	Pat Coombs (series 1 & 2)
Miss Lammastide	Sonia Graham (special & series 2)
Mrs Fenella Fudd	Adele Silva (special & series 3)
Ron Bigmore	Chris Mitchell (series 1 & 2)
Sgt Sevenoaks	Robin Driscoll (special & series 2 & 3)

CREDITS

creator Humphrey Carpenter · adapter/writer Jenny McDade · directors Michael Kerrigan (11), Derek Banham (6), Roger Cheveley (2), Terry Marcel (1) · executive producer J Nigel Pickard · producers Roger Cheveley (series 1), John Price (series 2 & 3 & special)

Mr Majeika is an irrepressible wizard, sent to England (called 'Britland') from the planet Walpurgis because he has failed his O-level sorcery exam for the seventeenth time. He drops into the sleepy village of Much Barty, finding a post at St Barty's School as Class Three's new form-teacher, where he quickly befriends two of the children, Melanie Brace-Girdle (daughter of Bunty Brace-Girdle, a busy-body local councillor) and Thomas Grey (later replaced by an Asian boy, Prince). Only they realise his ability to produce weird and wonderful sorcery.

Majeika enters into his magic with reluctance, however, because he is trying hard to behave himself on Earth, and because the Worshipful Wizard of Walpurgis is keeping an eye on him from above. (His reprimanding voice is frequently heard.) All the same, trickery becomes more and more necessary, leading Majeika, Melanie and Thomas (then Prince) into some remarkable adventures. Their fun is despised – but usually prompted – by the horribly spoilt Hamish Bigmore, a pupil so ghastly that his mere presence had caused the resignation of the previous class teacher and frightened off the 79 applicants for the post. But one waggle of Mr Majeika's oddly tufted grey hair is all that it takes for the fun to start and for Bigmore to be put firmly in his place.

Mr Majeika prompted a surprising but most welcome return to television for one of its most talented exponents, the Scottish comic actor Stanley Baxter. The series was written by Jenny McDade, who had so successfully turned the *Supergran* books into a TV series. Here she adapted three children's books written by Humphrey Carpenter (who appeared in one of the TV episodes), *Mr Majeika*, *Mr Majeika And The Music Teacher* and *Mr Majeika And The Haunted Hotel*. Carpenter then went on to write a fourth book based on McDade's scripts, *The Television Adventures Of Mr Majeika*.

Mr Merlin

USA · CBS (LARRY LARRY CO PRODUCTIONS/ CPT) · SITCOM

22 × 30 mins · colour

US dates: 7 Oct 1981–18 Aug 1982

UK dates: 4 Jan–12 July 1982 (22 episodes) ITV mostly Wed 5.15pm

MAIN CAST

Max Merlin	Barnard Hughes
Zachary Rogers	Clark Brandon
Leo Samuels	Jonathan Prince
Alexandra	Elaine Joyce

CREDITS

writers various · producers Larry Rosen, Larry Tucker

A very silly sitcom, in which Merlin – the fictional King Arthur wizard character, now aged 1600 years – arrives in the present and, to front his sorcery business, runs a car-repair workshop in San Francisco under the name of Max Merlin. Having been somewhat lax in his doing of good deeds recently, Max is under instruction to train a new magician, but said teenage garage apprentice, Zachary Rogers, would rather spend his time chasing young women than waving a wand.

Somehow, this one managed to get past the commissioning stage – by magic, perhaps.

'Mr Pastry'

Richard Hearne's much loved alter ego Mr Pastry made a great many TV appearances following his small-screen debut in 1946, endearing himself to more than one generation of viewers in the process. Pastry was a bumbling, accident-prone old man forever involved in elaborate slapstick and physical comedy, with a definite touch of pathos. But although he was Richard Hearne's most famous comic creation, he was by no means the only character in his arsenal, and Hearne also had another claim to fame: he was the first television comic to be allowed to use a signature tune, a recording of 'Pop Goes The Weasel' by the Folk Dance Band (as released on disc by HMV).

Hearne was born in Norwich on 30 January 1908 and made his first stage appearance at the age of six weeks. His father was a circus acrobat, and *his* father a circus groom, while baby Hearne's mother was an actress, so the youngster quickly became familiar with living the life of a travelling performer, working from the age of ten not only in the circus but in revue, pantomime, ballet, variety and musical comedy. Hearne learned scores of different methods of falling over, and all of his skills crystallised in the character of Mr Pastry, invented circa 1945. Although aged only 37, Hearne put on 'granny' glasses, a bowler hat, a white moustache, sprinkled flour in his hair and fell into the role of the old man as easy as falling off ... well, in Hearne's case, just about anything. (The name Pastry, incidentally, and certain of the mannerisms, were based on a character Hearne had played in a Fred Emney stage production, *Big Boy*.)

Through his TV work and appearances in a number of feature films, Mr Pastry became a firm favourite in many countries, popular with children and adults alike; in France he was known as Papa Gateau, in Germany Mr Sugar Tart. Hearne also held the record for the number of appearances on the American TV variety series *The Ed Sullivan Show*. Reputedly, he was keen to remind people that there were other aspects to his career, but Mr Pastry tended to swamp other endeavours. The final Mr Pastry TV series ran in 1962 and, although he was seen regularly thereafter in guest spots, he gradually retired during the 1960s, bemoaning the decline of 'clean' humour as the decade wore on. Awarded the OBE for his services to charity, he then suffered heart attacks in 1969 and again ten years later, dying from the last on these on 25 August 1979.

The following details Mr Pastry's series and one-off own TV shows in his home country. In addition, the character turned up in a number of variety programmes, one of his last being in BBC1's *The Good Old Days* on 18 March 1976. Hearne looked back on his long career in one of BBC2's *Suddenly It's ...* series (*Suddenly It's Richard Hearne*, 14 August 1967). For further Hearne TV work see *Bath H&C*, *Comedy Bandbox*, *Half An Hour*, *The Handle Bar*, *Kaleidoscope*, *Men Of Affairs* (one of his final TV appearances), *Mincemeat*, *Moving Furniture*, *Paging You*, *S-s-s-h! The Wife!* and *Take Two Eggs*.

The Village Store

UK · BBC · SKETCH

1 × 10 mins (approx) · b/w

19 Aug 1946 · Mon 8.30pm

MAIN CAST
Mr Pastry · · · · · · · · · · · · · · · Richard Hearne
Yvonne Hearne

CREDITS
writer Richard Hearne · *producer* Harry Pringle

Mr Pastry made his TV debut in this segment of the *Variety* strand. Yvonne Hearne, Richard's wife, was his regular comedy cohort. The piece was performed again a few months later as *Mr Pastry's Emporium*, a single sketch within *Variety* that was screened on 16 December 1946.

Just For Fun

UK · BBC · SKETCH

1 × 70 mins · b/w

5 July 1947 · Sat 8.50pm

MAIN CAST
Mr Pastry · · · · · · · · · · · · · · · Richard Hearne
Yvonne Hearne
Jean Kent
Henry Oscar
Joan Heal

CREDITS
deviser Richard Hearne · *producer* Walton Anderson

An epic length for a comedy show of its period – the usual running time for such shows was 45 minutes. But Richard Hearne was a popular performer with much TV experience and producer Walton Anderson had worked in the medium since 1939; also, live drama productions of the time ran to a similar length, so it was considered an acceptable risk.

Richard Hearne

UK · BBC · CHILDREN'S SKETCH

1 × 15 mins · b/w

11 Apr 1948 · Sun 4.45pm

MAIN CAST
Mr Pastry · · · · · · · · · · · · · · · Richard Hearne

CREDITS
writer Richard Hearne · *producer* Caryl Doncaster

Mr Pastry is ejected from a children's party he has gatecrashed, but returns – minus his moustache – in the guise of a little girl, and stays to assist the conjuror. The sketch was screened within the strand *For The Children*.

Mr Pastry At Home!

UK · BBC · SKETCH

1 × 20 mins · b/w

15 June 1949 · Sun 8.40pm

MAIN CAST
Mr Pastry · · · · · · · · · · · · · · · Richard Hearne
Yvonne Hearne

CREDITS
writer Richard Hearne · *producer* Henry Caldwell

The premise: Mr Pastry is about to take delivery of his long-awaited television set ...

Mr Pastry Gets A Job

UK · BBC · SKETCH

8 × 15 mins approx · b/w

14 Apr–21 July 1950 · fortnightly Fri approx 8.30pm

MAIN CAST
Mr Pastry · · · · · · · · · · · · · · · Richard Hearne

CREDITS
writer Richard Hearne · *producer* Graeme Muir

A resident comedy segment within the fortnightly TV magazine *Kaleidoscope*.

Camping

UK · BBC · CHILDREN'S SKETCH

1 × 10 mins · b/w

18 June 1950 · Sun 5.30pm

MAIN CAST
Mr Pastry · · · · · · · · · · · · · · · Richard Hearne

CREDITS
writer Richard Hearne · *producer* Peter Thompson

'Scoutmaster Pastry' shows five boy-scouts how to erect a tent.

Mr Pastry's Progress　　　　　1

UK · BBC · SITCOM

6 × 15 mins · b/w

31 Dec 1950–4 Feb 1951 · Sun 8.15pm

MAIN CAST
Mr Pastry · · · · · · · · · · · · · · · Richard Hearne

CREDITS
writer Richard Hearne · *producer* Ian Carmichael

The first weekly glimpse into the fortunes of television's favourite handyman. The producer, Ian Carmichael, went on to become an internationally renowned actor; at this time he was on the BBC staff.

April Fool's Day

UK · BBC · CHILDREN'S SKETCH

1 × 15 mins · b/w

1 Apr 1951 · Sun 5pm

MAIN CAST

Mr Pastry · · · · · · · · · · · · · · Richard Hearne

CREDITS

writer Richard Hearne · producer Michael Westmore

Mr Pastry makes pastry. The programme appeared in the strand *For The Children*.

Mr Pastry's Holiday Show

UK · BBC · SITCOM

1 × 30 mins · b/w

5 Aug 1951 · Sun 8.15pm

MAIN CAST

Mr Pastry · · · · · · · · · · · · · · Richard Hearne

CREDITS

writer Richard Hearne · producer Bill Lyon-Shaw

A one-off special with the unhandy handyman.

By Request

UK · BBC · SKETCH

3 × 15 mins · b/w

15 June–13 July 1952 · fortnightly Sun around 9pm

MAIN CAST

Mr Pastry · · · · · · · · · · · · · · Richard Hearne

CREDITS

writer Richard Hearne · producer Bill Lyon-Shaw

A short series. Hearne was supported in the first show by his wife Yvonne, in the second by Benita Lydel, and in the third by a bigger cast: Carl Lacey, Pauline Loring, Richard Waring, Don Bryant, Bob Vossler and Laurence Hepworth.

With the gradual expansion of television, these three programmes were the first opportunity for viewers in Scotland and the north of England to see Mr Pastry on the small-screen.

The Mr Pastry Show

UK · BBC · SKETCH

1 × 30 mins · b/w

12 Nov 1952 · Wed 8.15pm

MAIN CAST

Mr Pastry · · · · · · · · · · · · · · Richard Hearne

CREDITS

writer Richard Hearne · producer Bill Ward

Another one-off for the blustering clown.

Mr Pastry Takes A Holiday

UK · BBC · CHILDREN'S SKETCH

1 × 15 mins (approx) · b/w

23 Dec 1952 · Tue approx 5.55pm

MAIN CAST

Mr Pastry · · · · · · · · · · · · · · Richard Hearne
narrator · · · · · McDonald Hobley (voice only)

CREDITS

writer Richard Hearne · commentary writer J C Tobin · producer D A Smith

A special film for Christmas showing Mr Pastry playing winter sports in Norway. The programme, which appeared in the strand *Children's Television*, was screened again on 28 January 1956 as *Mr Pastry Learns To Ski*.

Mr Pastry's Spicy Life   1

UK · BBC · SKETCH

1 × 60 mins · b/w

4 Dec 1954 · Sat 9.15pm

MAIN CAST

Mr Pastry · · · · · · · · · · · · · · Richard Hearne
McDonald Hobley

CREDITS

writers Richard Hearne/Talbot Rothwell · producer Bill Ward

A special comedy variation of *Spice Of Life*, a BBC series in which celebrities reminisced about the people who added spice to their lives. It also went out under the title *Richard Hearne In Mr Pastry's Spicy Life*.

Richard Hearne As Mr Pastry

UK · ITV (ATV) · SKETCH

6 × 45 mins · b/w

17 Dec 1955–21 Jan 1956 · Sat 8.15pm

MAIN CAST

Mr Pastry · · · · · · · · · · · · · · Richard Hearne
Howard Jones
Reg Arnold
Guy Fame

CREDITS

writer Richard Hearne · director/producer Bill Lyon-Shaw

Six weekly programmes aired under the *Saturday Showtime* banner by ITV soon after the channel was launched, with other guests filling out the bills.

Highland Fling

UK · ITV (ASSOCIATED-REDIFFUSION) · SITCOM

6 × 30 mins

5 Aug–9 Sep 1957 · Mon 9.30pm

MAIN CAST

Richard Hearne
James Hayter
Charles Heslop
Nicolette Roeg
Jean Bayless
David Williams

Charles Lamb
Rufus Cruickshank

CREDITS

creator Richard Hearne · adapter/writer Richard Waring · director John Phillips · producer Henry Kendall

Back in the 1930s, Richard Hearne came up with an idea for a musical comedy that he planned to mount on the London stage. He never succeeded, but 20 years later Associated-Rediffusion agreed to turn the story into a six-part sitcom (still with music) and brought in Richard Waring to adapt it for TV. The comedic premise revolved around an ancient Scottish castle being offered for sale by an old-fashioned Mayfair estate firm, Nutty, Dime and Wormy. When a millionaire, Augustus Trim, makes an offer they seem reluctant to sell it to him, and matters are complicated when the hero's best friend falls in love with the millionaire's beautiful daughter. Richard Hearne played two roles: that of a Mr McQuirtle and his friend – one requiring a 'straight' perform- ance, the other the clownish Mr Pastry.

Shortly after this series BBC cameras paid a visit to Platt Farm in Borough Green, Kent, for the 24 September 1957 programme *Meet Richard Hearne Alias Mr Pastry*. This was one segment in a continuing BBC series visiting the homes of stars.

Mr Pastry's Spicy Life   2

UK · BBC · SKETCH

1 × 60 mins · b/w

23 Nov 1957 · Sat 8pm

MAIN CAST

Mr Pastry · · · · · · · · · · · · · · Richard Hearne
Alex Macintosh

CREDITS

writers Richard Hearne/Talbot Rothwell · producer Bryan Sears

Further anecdotes and reminiscences from Mr Pastry in a second spoof edition of *Spice Of Life*.

The Adventures Of Mr Pastry

UK · ITV (ATV) · SITCOM

1 × 30 mins · b/w

21 June 1958 · Sat 6pm

MAIN CAST

Mr Pastry · · · · · · · · · · · · · · Richard Hearne
Professor · · · · · · · · · · · · · · Buster Keaton
Landlady · · · · · · · · · · · · · · · Peggy Mount

CREDITS

director Ralph Smart

This single TV production, made in London, brought together two masters of slapstick – Richard Hearne and the celebrated Ameri can film star and director Buster Keaton. The premise had Mr Pastry as an enthusiastic pupil, going to learn method-acting from a professor (Keaton). But the teacher is a sham, in it only for the money.

This was meant to be the first episode in a full series, but Keaton (63 at the time) fell ill and had to return home.

Mr Pastry

UK · BBC · CHILDREN'S SKETCH

1 × 10 mins · b/w
21 Dec 1958 · Sun 5.15pm

MAIN CAST
Mr Pastry · · · · · · · · · · · · · Richard Hearne

CREDITS
writer/producer Richard Hearne · director Bill Parry Jones

Also known as *How Mr Pastry Joined The Circus* and *Mr Pastry At The Circus*.

Leave It To Pastry

UK · BBC · CHILDREN'S SITCOM

4 × 25 mins · b/w
14 May–4 June 1960 · Sat 5.25pm

MAIN CAST
Mr Pastry · · · · · · · · · · · · · Richard Hearne
Jill Connors · · · · · · · · · · · · Dorothy White
Buster · · · · · · · · · · · · · · Ronnie Raymond
Mrs Trench · · · · · · · · · · · · · Margot Boyd

CREDITS
writers Hugh Woodhouse/Ken Hoare · producer Johnny Downes

This series was made after Hearne returned from another of his successful forays into the American entertainment scene.

Ask Mr Pastry

UK · BBC · CHILDREN'S SITCOM

8 × 25 mins · b/w
25 Mar–13 May 1961 · Sat 5.25pm

MAIN CAST
Mr Pastry · · · · · · · · · · · · · Richard Hearne
Miss Print · · · · · · · · · · · · · Barbara Hicks
Mrs Spindle · · · · · · · · · · · · Dandy Nichols
Miss Moss · · · · · · · · · · · · · Amy Dalby
Stoker · · · · · · · · · · · · · · Barry Henderson
Vicar · · · · · · · · · · · · · · · John Kidd
Constable · · · · · · · · · · · · · John Brittany
Susan Bell · · · · · · · · · · · · Patricia Sinclair
Farmer Tony Young · · · · · · · · · · · Ian Shand

CREDITS
writers Patrick Campbell/Vivienne Knight · producer David Goddard

Eight Pastry adventures set in the fictional English village of Little Wotting.

Mr Pastry Hooks A Spook

UK · BBC · CHILDREN'S SITCOM

1 × 25 mins · b/w
28 Oct 1961 · Sat 5.25pm

MAIN CAST
Mr Pastry · · · · · · · · · · · · · Richard Hearne

John Groom · · · · · · · · · · · · Melvyn Hayes
PC Tom · · · · · · · · · · · · · · John Brittany

CREDITS
writer Richard Hearne · producer David Goddard

Mr Pastry goes hunting spooks but instead uncovers a couple of crooks.

Mr Pastry's Progress

UK · BBC · CHILDREN'S SITCOM

6 × 25 mins · b/w
14 Apr–19 May 1962 · Sat 5.25pm

MAIN CAST
Mr Pastry · · · · · · · · · · · · · Richard Hearne
Miss Print · · · · · · · · · · · · · Barbara Hicks

CREDITS
writer James Cairncross · additional material Richard Hearne · producer David Goddard

A six-week series, featuring all new material, in which Mr Pastry reminisces with children about his past adventures.

Mr Pastry's Pet Shop

UK · BBC · CHILDREN'S SITCOM

6 × 25 mins · b/w
17 Nov–22 Dec 1962 · Sat 5.25pm

MAIN CAST
Mr Pastry · · · · · · · · · · · · · Richard Hearne
Miss Print · · · · · · · · · · · · · Barbara Hicks

CREDITS
writers James Cairncross/Richard Hearne · producer David Goddard

Following a holiday in Jersey, where he is much taken with the zoo (the same one that featured in the 1997 John Cleese movie *Fierce Creatures*), Mr Pastry decides to open his own. When these plans fall flat, he settles for a pet shop instead.

Mr Smith

USA · NBC (PARAMOUNT/WEINBERGER-DANIELS PRODUCTIONS) · SITCOM

13 × 30 mins · colour
US dates: 23 Sep–16 Dec 1983
UK dates: 2 Nov 1985–15 Feb 1986 (13 episodes) ITV Sat 11.30am

MAIN CAST
Mr Smith · · · · · · · · · · · · · · C J (animal),
· · · · · · · · · · · · · · · · · · Ed Weinberger (voice)
Tommy Atwood · · · · · · · · · · · · Tim Dunigan
Ellie Atwood · · · · · · · · · · · · Laura Jacoby
Raymond Holyoke · · · · · · · · · · Leonard Frey
Dr Judy Tyson · · · · · · · · · · · Terri Garber
Dr Kline · · · · · · · · · · · · · Stuart Margolin

CREDITS
writers Michael J Ahnemann, Dari Daniels, George Kirgo, David Lloyd, Douglas P Wyman · directors various · executive producers Stan Daniels/ Ed Weinberger

Everything was going great for C J, the orang-utan, as the late 1970s slid into the early 1980s. He didn't get where he was then without appearing with Clint Eastwood in *Every Which Way But Loose* and silver-screen nymphet Bo Derek in her remake of *Tarzan The Ape Man*. This monkey was hot property, and – doubtless thinking of previous animal successes, including *Me And The Chimp* and *Mister Ed* – NBC decided to capitalise and make him a sitcom star too. *Mr Smith* was the result.

In the opening episode, the orang-utan (then known simply as Cha Cha) was left alone in a government research laboratory, mixed himself a bunch of various chemicals, drank it and was transformed into a genius level (IQ 256), walking (well, scrabbling), talking government consultant, asked to profess his opinion about everything from missile policy to tough legal problems. Named Mr Smith, he was kitted out with serious spectacles, briefcase and dressed in expensively tailored suits and had a disdainful human assistant, Raymond Holyoke. After work and at weekends Smith lived the good life out in pleasant valley suburbia with his old trainer Tommy and his annoying little sister Ellie, and a common or garden regular non-special other orang-utan, Bobo, whom he rescued from being sent to a zoo in France.

Humour was wrought – just – from little more than the basically amusing sight of a monkey dressed in human clothes going about human business. But, good though C J was good at acting, he couldn't do it all, so, reportedly, a midget actor in an orang-utan suit did some of his work for him.

Pitiful stuff, really, and one of the worst sitcoms of all time. Viewers at home, who certainly did not go bananas for *Mr Smith*, voted with their 'off' switches and C J's sitcom career was over in 13 weeks.

Mr Wodehouse Speaking

UK · BBC · SKETCH

1 × 60 mins · colour
26 Dec 1972 · BBC1 Tue 11.10pm

MAIN CAST
P G Wodehouse · · · · · · · · · · William Mervyn
Young Wodehouse · · · · · · · · · · Sean Arnold

CREDITS
writers Gerry Davis/Rex Tucker · director Rex Tucker · producer Gerald Savory

Dramatisations of incidents, and readings, from the works of the great British humorist. William Mervyn was the guide to 'the comic and idyllic world of P G Wodehouse'.

See also *The World Of Wooster*, *Blandings Castle*, *Jeeves And Wooster*, *Ukridge*, *Uncle Fred Flits By*, *Wodehouse Playhouse* and *The Reverent Wooing Of Archibald*.

Mrs Feather

UK · BBC · SKETCH/STANDUP

2 editions (1 × 10 mins · 1 × 60 mins) · b/w

25 Oct 1937 · Mon 9pm (10 mins)
Mrs Feather's Christmas Party 24 Dec 1948 ·
Fri 8pm (60 mins)

MAIN CAST
Mrs Feather · · · · · · · · · · Jeanne de Casalis

CREDITS
writer Jeanne de Casalis · *producers* Reginald
Smith (show 1), Walton Anderson (show 2)

One of the most loved comedy characters of
the time, Mrs Feather was a light-headed
society woman and housewife forever getting
into verbal contortions on the telephone (at
this time still quite a novelty instrument).
Radio listeners – and, in these two TV
programmes, viewers of an even more new-
fangled device – eavesdropped on her one-
way discussions, hearing her get into trouble
with one verbal gaffe after another.

Mrs Feather was the invention of the comic
actress and dramatic writer Jeanne de Casalis,
born in Basutoland, South Africa, on 22 May
1897. Educated in France, she began her show
business career in music before, eventually,
settling in London, playing many West End
stage parts and marrying the English actor
Colin Clive. She died on 19 August 1966.

The sketch 'Mrs Feather's Motor Repairs'
was enacted in the first of the two TV shows
– viewers witnessed her side of a phone
conversation with a Mr Ozmond; the second
was an hour-length Christmas special with
an array of famous comedy stars on hand as
guests, including married double-act Nan
Kenway and Douglas Young, Claude Hulbert,
Enid Trevor, Kenneth Horne and Sam Costa.

The Mrs Merton Show

UK · BBC (GRANADA) · SATIRE

**25 editions (24 × 30 mins · 1 × short special) ·
colour**

Series One (6) 10 Feb–24 Mar 1995 · BBC2
Fri 11.15pm
Series Two (6) 12 Nov–17 Dec 1995 · BBC2
Sun 9.30pm
Special · 24 Dec 1995 · BBC2 Sun 8.45pm
Short special · part of *Children In Need* 22 Nov
1996 · BBC1 Fri around 12.30pm
Special · 24 Dec 1996 · BBC1 Tue 11pm
Series Three (6) 14 Feb–28 Mar 1997 · BBC1
Fri mostly 10.20pm
Series Four (3) *Mrs Merton In Las Vegas*
10 Apr–24 Apr 1997 · BBC1 Thu 10pm
Special · 27 Dec 1997 · BBC1 Sat 10.15pm

MAIN CAST
Mrs Merton · · · · · · · · · · · · Caroline Aherne
· · · · · · · · · · · · · · · · · · (aka Caroline Hook)

CREDITS
writers Caroline Aherne, Craig Cash, Henry Normal,
Dave Gorman · *directors* Pati Marr (16), Dominic
Brigstocke (6), Philippa Robinson (1), Tom

Prescott (1), not known (1) · *executive producers*
Andy Harries, Clive Tulloh · *producers* Peter
Kessler (13), Mark Gorton (9), Philippa Robinson
(1), Kenton Allen (1), not known (1)

The Manchester-based comedian Caroline
Aherne (later Hook then back to Aherne
again) first brought her Mrs Merton creation
to the public in a number of broadcasts on
Stockport local radio. The character, a spoof
agony aunt, dished out dubious advice in
answer to various dilemmas put to her. When
Mrs Merton graduated to her own TV chat-
show series, Aherne, then 30, had to undergo
a complex make-up procedure to age herself
into the perky pensioner.

Mrs Merton is a down-to-earth, seemingly
prim aunt whose harmless looks and demure
demeanour make all the more shocking her
sudden excursions into sexual matters and
other areas of dubious taste. Guests (real-life
celebrities, not actors) are quizzed about their
lives and careers and find themselves on the
receiving end of questions that are outrageous
double entendres. In much the same way that
Barry Humphries can get away with the most
shocking impertinence as his alter ego Dame
Edna, so Aherne manages to 'slip the knife
in' while safely disguised as an elderly
matriarch. Her hand-picked audience –
always the same gang of real-life pensioners
(some are in their eighties), most of whom
are known personally to Aherne – help to
maintain the illusion. In her exchanges with
these real-life stooges – bemoaning modern-
day mores, reminiscing about wartime,
harking back to a long-gone youth – Merton
seemed uncannily real. Each week the
audience was invited to join in a studio
discussion ('Let's have a heated debate!') and
here Aherne worked her charges superbly,
effortlessly scoring laughs while never letting
her guise slip.

The series started as a late-night venture
on BBC2 but made such waves that it
graduated to a peak-time slot on BBC1. Many
of Merton's guests revealed themselves as
good sports, willing to take the ribbing, but
some seemed baffled by her insolence and
others merely out of their depth. It must have
seemed a good idea to move the production –
lock, stock and audience – to Las Vegas for a
trio of specials featuring American guests,
but these particular shows were poorly
received in comparison with the domestically
taped ones, and it was beginning to appear
that the format's value was wearing thin. All
the same, a new series was commissioned for
screening in spring 1998.

Mrs Mulligan's Private Hotel

UK · BBC · SKETCH

1 × 45 mins · b/w

28 June 1948 · Mon 8.45pm

MAIN CAST
Jimmy O'Dea
Harry O'Donovan
Maureen Potter
George Arnott
Brian Duffy
Vernon Hayden
Tom Donovan
Rex Ramer

CREDITS
writer Harry O'Donovan · *producer* Richard Afton

Mrs Mulligan, the tipsy alter ego of Irish
comedian Jimmy O'Dea, starred in a number
of BBC radio series at this time, such as *Over
To Mulligan's* (1944) and *At The Mulligan
Inn* (1946), written by his former double-act
partner Harry O'Donovan. The popular
character crossed over to TV (and cross-
dressed for the cameras) for this special one-
off, with George Arnott and Maureen Potter
re-creating their radio roles as, respectively,
Mr Ormerod and Mrs Mulligan's daughter
Maureen.

Mrs Wilson's Diary

UK · ITV (LWT) · SITCOM

1 × 60 mins · b/w

4 Jan 1969 · Sat 9.55pm

MAIN CAST
Gladys Wilson · · · · · · · · · · · · · Myvanwy Jenn
Harold Wilson · · · · · · · · · · · · · · · Bill Wallis
Inspector Trimfitting · · · · · · Stephen Lewis
Gerald Hoffman · · · · · · · · · · · · Peter Reeves
Roy Jenkins · · · · · · · · · · · · Nigel Hawthorne
George Brown · · · · · · · · · · · · · · · Bob Grant
David Frost · · · · · · · · · · · · · · David Battley
Robot Heath · · · · · · · · · · · · · · Reg Templar

CREDITS
writers Richard Ingrams/John Wells · *cartoons*
William Rushton · *director/producer* Stuart Allen

Its influence and value to the nation almost
unparalleled since being launched in 1961,
the magazine *Private Eye* has made few
excursions into the realm of television – and
most of the few have been of a documentary
nature in which it is the subject. But following
the successful London stage run of a musical
version of Richard Ingrams and John Wells'
political satire *Mrs Wilson's Diary* (music
composed by Jeremy Taylor, the play directed
by Joan Littlewood, staged from September
1967), the production was transferred to the
TV studio by LWT. Like most things *Private
Eye*, it happened not without problems.
The programme was originally due for
transmission on 23 November 1968 but was
pulled at the eleventh hour when controversy
arose over a scene depicting the cabinet
minister George Brown in a state of alcoholic
confusion (or, as the magazine has it, being
'tired and emotional'). With a re-recording of
the offending section in place, the production
was finally screened on 4 January 1969.

Mrs Wilson's Diary had been running for some years in *Private Eye* and was the forerunner of the *Heathco* column published in the magazine when Edward Heath was Prime Minister, the *Dear Bill* letters when Margaret Thatcher was in Number 10 (see **Anyone For Denis?**), *The Secret Diary Of John Major aged 47¾* that ran when her successor was PM, and, presently, Tony Blair's *St Albion Parish News*.

See also **Grubstreet** and **Private Eye TV**.

Mulberry

UK · BBC · SITCOM

13×30 mins · colour

Series One (6) 24 Feb–30 Mar 1992 · BBC1 Mon 8pm

Series Two (7) 8 Apr–25 May 1993 · BBC1 mostly Thu 8pm

MAIN CAST

Mulberry	Karl Howman
Miss Farnaby	Geraldine McEwan
Bert Finch	Tony Selby
Alice Finch	Lill Roughley
The Stranger	John Bennett

CREDITS

writers John Esmonde/Bob Larbey · *directors* John B Hobbs, Clive Grainger (2) · *producer* John B Hobbs

An offbeat fantasy sitcom starring Karl Howman as the mysterious Mulberry, a man who appears at the household of a cantankerous spinster, Miss Farnaby, and inveigles himself on to the staff as her manservant. Her other staff are Bert and Alice Finch, who have served her since they were children, but a sullen disregard has developed between mistress and servants, Miss Farnaby viewing them as lazy, inefficient and untrustworthy, the Finches viewing her as bitter and twisted. Mulberry's arrival brings a jolt of freshness to the place and he gradually begins to bring Miss Farnaby out of herself and repair the broken relationship that exists. He seems to dote on his wealthy employer and his concern and natural charm wears down her harsh exterior.

But Mulberry is not all he seems; in fact, he is an apprentice Grim Reaper who has come to the house to escort Miss Farnaby to the next world. A sentimental streak causes him to dedicate himself to making her last days on Earth happy; thus he has taken the position as servant to put his plans into motion. This sensitivity is viewed with scorn by Mulberry's father, a fully fledged Grim Reaper who sees no such need to pander to human emotions. He appears to Mulberry as a mysterious stranger ('The Stranger') in a black hat and dark clothes, constantly urging him to get on with the job and attempting to prise him away from the Farnaby estate. In one episode, Mulberry's sympathetic nature is

championed by Springtime (Sylvia Sims), Mulberry's mother, who materialises as an elegant lady. She buys Mulberry more time to spend with his employer.

An intriguing series, *Mulberry* was a brave attempt at stretching the sitcom genre. The scenes between Howman and McEwan were winningly underplayed (although the rather more obvious sitcom style of the Finches seemed at odds with the overall subtlety of the piece).

Mum's Boys

UK · BBC · SITCOM

7×30 mins · b/w

3 Apr–22 May 1968 · BBC1 Wed 8.20pm

MAIN CAST

Crystal Pallise	Irene Handl
Leonard Pallise	Bernard Bresslaw
Robin Fosdyke	Pete Murray

CREDITS

writers Jimmy Grafton/Jeremy Lloyd · *producer* Eric Fawcett

A single series in which comedy trooper Irene Handl was the mum of the title, with Bernard Bresslaw and Pete Murray cast as her adult sons from separate marriages.

Mrs Pallise makes a living out of renting rooms in her terraced house, while her dullard son Leonard tries to find work as an actor. Into this environment walks her other son, Robin Fosdyke, the result of a short-lived marriage to the Hon Bertram Fosdyke. The humour arose from the class conflicts between the two Pallises and their 'cuckoo in the nest'.

The Munsters

USA · CBS (KAYRO-VUE PRODUCTIONS) · SITCOM

70×30 mins · b/w

US dates: 24 Sep 1964–12 May 1966

*UK dates: 1 Apr 1965–25 Sep 1967 (39 episodes) BBC2 Thu 8.50pm · then BBC1 Sat around 6.30pm · then various days/times

MAIN CAST

Herman Munster	Fred Gwynne
Lily Munster	Yvonne De Carlo
Grandpa (Sam Dracula)	Al Lewis
Marilyn	Beverley Owen (1964);
	Pat Priest (1964–66)
Eddie Wolfgang Munster	Butch Patrick

CREDITS

creators Norman Liebmann/Ed Haas, Al Burns/Chris Hayward · *writers* Norman Liebmann/Ed Haas, Joe Connelly/Bob Mosher, James Allardice/Tom Adair, Doug Tibbles/George Tibbles, Dick Conway, Ted Bergman, Richard Baer, Dennis Whitcomb · *directors* Ezra Stone, Charles Rondeau, Donald Richardson, Norman Abbott, Gene Reynolds, Jerry Paris, Charles Barton, Seymour Berns, Joseph Pevney, Lawrence Dobkin, Earl Bellamy · *producers* Joe Connelly/Bob Mosher

At 1313 Mockingbird Lane, Mockingbird Heights, lived one of America's strangest sitcom families, *The Munsters*. Strangest looking, that is, for beneath Herman's Frankensteinian facial features, Lily's vampiric visage, Grandpa's Dracula countenance and Eddie's Wolfman looks, lurked possibly the sweetest and most sensitive sitcom family ever to grace the small-screen. This, of course, was the nub of the series: that a family so weird could overcome the everyday problems of modern living – and the fact that people ran away from them, screaming – by their generosity, gentleness and belief in traditional American values.

Herman Munster was the breadwinner, working in a local funeral parlour (Gateman, Goodbury And Graves). He was a massive and clumsy oaf with a heart of gold and a desire only to be a good husband and father; Lily, his doting wife, wanted only to keep the family happy; Grandpa, Lily's father, had a touch of the mad scientist about him, always brewing up spells in his cellar laboratory, lamenting the loss of the old lore and 'old country' Transylvania; and Eddie, Lily and Herman's son, was a typical healthy schoolboy, albeit with fangs, a pet dinosaur and a penchant for hanging upside-down. The odd-one-out was Marilyn, whose traditional all-American beauty was a cause of constant heartache for the others, who loved her despite what they – with their reverse psychology – considered her horrific looks. Marilyn (originally played by Beverley Owen, who quit after 13 episodes to be replaced by Pat Priest) is Lily's sister's daughter whom the Munsters, with typical benevolence, have taken in and are raising as their own. (Subsequent literature sometimes names her Marilyn Munster, which she could only be if Lily's sister also married a Munster, or if Lily and Herman officially adopted her.)

Storylines in *The Munsters* were of simple domestic, familial and work situations that could have appeared in any US family-orientated sitcom, but with the added edge of happening to a family that other people were hugely frightened by – the Munsters, of course, not recognising that they were different, never understood why people reacted in this way. As for the lead actors, Fred Gwynne and Al Lewis had teamed up previously in the great US sitcom **Car 54, Where Are You?**, and the glamorous Yvonne De Carlo had enjoyed a notable Hollywood film career, so there was no shortage of pedigree about the series.

Munsters spin-offs have been many. A feature film, *Munsters Go Home* (1966, directed by Earl Bellamy), was originally intended as a TV movie but was given theatrical release when the series proved such a huge domestic and international success. (This featured the original TV cast but with Debbie Watson in the role of Marilyn.) ABC TV aired a one-hour animated special, *The Mini-Munsters*, in 1973 (with Al Lewis voicing Grandpa). A badly received TV movie, *The Munsters' Revenge* (NBC, screened in the USA on 27 February 1981), reunited the three principal original cast members, supported by Jo McDonnell as Marilyn and K C Martel as Eddie. And in 1988 – following a two-hour TBS cable TV special *The Best Of The Munsters* that showed Lewis, Priest and Patrick, in character, looking back at some of their favourite 1960s episodes – began a disastrous new syndicated series, *The Munsters Today*. All was then quiet until the appearance of a Fox TV movie on 31 October 1995, *Here Come The Munsters*, that was akin to a 'prequel' to the original TV series, showing how the Munster family, having been driven from their home in Transylvania, came to settle in Mockingbird Heights. (It was set in the 1990s, however.) Clear reference was made to the 1960s TV series, with the actors chosen and made up to look as much like the original Herman, Lily, Grandpa, Eddie and Marilyn as possible. (Moreover, it included special appearances by Yvonne De Carlo, Al Lewis, Butch Patrick and Pat Priest. Fred Gwynne could not appear – he died in 1993 and, reportedly, in his final years, had refused to even talk about his *Munsters* role.) The movie's director was Robert Ginty and, appropriately enough, Edward Herrmann was cast as Herman Munster. This was followed on 17 December 1996 by *The Munsters' Scary Little Christmas*, another TV movie, also made and screened in the USA by Fox, in which Grandpa accidentally magics Santa Claus and some elves into his laboratory and has difficulty in returning them.

*Note. *The Munsters* was first screened in the UK by BBC2 on 1 April 1965, when that channel was scarcely available outside of the London area. BBC1 repeats, and then first-runs, followed from 9 October the same year. C4 three times re-ran the complete series of 70 episodes, from 5 November 1982, 31 August 1987 and 9 February 1991; latterly, from 5 May 1995, episodes have aired again on BBC2.

The Munsters Today

USA · SYNDICATION (THE ARTHUR COMPANY/ MCA) · CHILDREN'S SITCOM

66 × 30 mins · colour

US dates: 8 Oct 1988–16 June 1991

UK dates: 6 Jan 1990–24 Mar 1996 (54 episodes) ITV mostly Sat 12.30pm

MAIN CAST

Herman Munster · · · · · · · · · · · John Schuck
Lily Munster · · · · · · · · · · · · Lee Meriwether
Grandpa · · · · · · · · · · · · · · · Howard Morton
Marilyn · · · · · · · · · · · · · · · Hilary Van Dyke
Eddie · · · · · · · · · · · · · · · · · Jason Marsden

CREDITS

creators Norman Liebmann/Ed Haas, Al Burns/ Chris Hayward · *writers* Bill Rosenthal/Noah Taft, Michael Davidoff, Andrew Boracove, Bryan K Joseph, Mark Miller and others · *directors* Peter Isacksen, Lee Lochhead, Bonnie Franklin, Scott Redman, Russ Petranto · *executive producer* Arthur Annecharico · *producers* Lloyd J Schwartz, Bryan K Joseph

Twenty years after Grandpa has placed the Munster family in suspended animation they reawaken in the late 1980s. So explained the opening credits of *The Munsters Today* (conveniently ignoring TV movie *The Munsters' Revenge* in their time scale of events).

Although the family still lived at 1313 Mockingbird Lane and looked faintly similar to their 1960s selves, this low-budget colour video-taped follow-up was only a ghostly, shockingly poor imitation of the original monochrome series. Aimed fairly and squarely at the pre-teen market, with hardly any consideration towards adult viewers, it was a poor appendix to the *Munsters* story. The cast, especially John Schuck, put a lot of energy into their roles but were ultimately defeated by the virtually non-existent production values.

The Muppet Show

UK · ITV (ATV/ITC) · SKETCH

120 × 30 mins · colour

*Series One (24) 24 Oct 1976–2 Apr 1977 · Sun 5.35pm then Sat 5.15pm

Series Two (30) 30 Sep 1977–23 Apr 1978 · Fri 7pm then Sun 7.15pm

Series Three (18) 17 Nov 1978–9 Mar 1979 · mostly Fri 7pm

Series Four (24) 24 Oct 1979–4 Apr 1980 · Fri mostly 7pm

Series Five (24) 5 Oct 1980–15 Mar 1981 · Sun 5.30pm

MAIN CAST (PUPPETEERS/VOICES)

Kermit/Rowlf/Waldorf/ Dr Teeth/ · · · · · · · · ·
Captain Link Heart-throb · · · · · · · · · Jim Henson
Miss Piggy/Fozzie Bear/ · · · · · · · · · · · · ·
Animal/Sam The Eagle · · · · · · · · · Frank Oz
Floyd Pepper/Uncle Deadly/ · · · · · · · · · · · ·
Robin/ Fleet Scribbler/J P Grosse/ · · · · · · · ·
Crazy Harry/Floyd/Pops/ · · · · · · · · · · · · · ·
The Electric Mayhem Band/ · · · · · · · · · · · · ·
Dr Strangepork/Lew Zealand · · · Jerry Nelson
Scooter/Sweetums/ Statler/ · · · · · · · · · · · ·
Beaker/Thog/Janis · · · · · · · · Richard Hunt
Gonzo The Great/Bunsen Honeydew/ · · · · · · · ·
Zoot/Muppy/ Beauregard · · · · · · Dave Goelz
Annie Sue · · · · · · · · · · · · · · · Louise Gold
Rizzo The Rat · · · · · · · · · · · · Steve Whitmire

CREDITS

writers Jerry Juhl (all series), Jim Henson (all series), Jack Burns (series 1), Marc London (series 1), Don Hinkley (series 2–5), Chris Langham (series 2, 3 & 5), Joseph A Bailey (series 2), David Odell (series 4 & 5) · *directors*

Peter Harris (77), Philip Casson (43) · *executive producers* David Lazer (all series), Jim Henson (series 1) · *producers* Jack Burns (series 1), Jim Henson (series 2–5)

Arguably the most successful TV comedy series of all time – certainly so in terms of international sales: it has been screened in more than 100 countries – *The Muppet Show* was the brilliant realisation of Jim Henson, an American puppeteer with a wild imagination and sense of humour that was both childlike and of appeal to adults. Embracing the same simple theme as *The Jack Benny Program* in earlier decades – a show about putting on a show – *The Muppet Show* depicted the antics of some wacky marionette puppet (hence the word Muppet) troupers onstage and backstage as they inter-related, hurried about their show business, overcame difficulties by the thousand and dealt with interfering or awkward or in any other sense problematic guest stars.

Despite the impressive roll-call of human guests, *the* star of the Muppets was Kermit, a kindly frog whose job as MC was to keep the show on the tracks while boosting the wavering confidence of his players, trying to live with their insufferably large egos, put up with their occasionally off-beam pranks and thwart the amorous advances of the show's *sow fatale*, Miss Piggy. Without any redeeming features save her irrepressible self-absorption, Miss Piggy considered herself the principal star of the show, and her aggressive or fawning treatment of guests was as unpredictable as her unrequited affection for Kermit was constant.

In all, there were scores of Muppet characters, but the other chief players were the hopelessly unfunny comedian Fozzie Bear; Gonzo The Great, a failed trumpeter with a fetish for chicken; Rowlf, an unkempt piano-playing canine; Scooter, who served as Kermit's factotum; a huge rat named Rizzo; loony scientist Bunsen Honeydew; a mighty monster called Sweetums; resident rock band the Electric Mayhem, with out-of-his-head guitarist Floyd and mad drummer Animal; and, up in a private box at the Vaudeville Theatre, two ageing hecklers called Statler and Waldorf who liked to think that their put-downs of the stage-show were witty. There were recurring sketches like the *Star Trek* send-up *Swine Trek*; and, without fail, every human guest star was ignobly treated or put into surreal situations – Rudolf Nureyev danced to new ballet *Swine Lake*, for example, Elton John duetted with Miss Piggy on 'Don't Go Breaking My Heart' and sang 'Crocodile Rock' with a choir of crocodiles, and Peter Sellers performed from *Richard III* in the manner of Sir Laurence Olivier while holding clucking chickens under his arms.

One of the great strengths of *The Muppet Show* was that no guest intimated that the puppet characters were anything other than human, conversing and interacting with the furry creatures as if it was perfectly normal. By placing a strong emphasis on its American TV exposure as well as global sales, the biggest names in show business accepted invitations to appear: among those to guest in the 120 editions were Julie Andrews, Shirley Bassey, Milton Berle, Victor Borge, Carol Burnett, George Burns, Ruth Buzzi, Johnny Cash, John Cleese, James Coburn, Alice Cooper, Dom DeLuise, Marty Feldman, Bruce Forsyth, Valerie Harper, Debbie Harry, Bob Hope, Glenda Jackson, Elton John, Danny Kaye, Gene Kelly, Chris Langham (the British comic actor who also co-wrote many editions), Cloris Leachman, Liberace, Rich Little, Steve Martin, Ethel Merman, Spike Milligan, Liza Minnelli, Dudley Moore, Roger Moore, Zero Mostel, Rudolf Nureyev, Vincent Price, Gilda Radner, Tony Randall, Lynn Redgrave, Leo Sayer, Peter Sellers, Paul Simon, Sylvester Stallone, Jean Stapleton, Loretta Swit, Peter Ustinov, Nancy Walker, Raquel Welch and Jonathan Winters. Quite a roll-call. On the back of *The Muppet Show*, Jim Henson's creations quickly permeated every aspect of show business – not only TV but films, books, magazines, records (a British number one album and two hit singles), audio and video tapes, commercials and every conceivable kind of merchandise item, with particular emphasis on the green-felt frog Kermit and the 'glam' Miss Piggy.

While *The Muppet Show* was, by all appearances, an American series – the accents, the characters, the majority of the writers – it was, in fact, a British production. The American TV networks were unconvinced that Jim Henson's idea would have any adult appeal and, after ABC aired a single half-hour pilot episode there on 19 March 1975, and NBC failed to realise the possibilities after Henson's Muppets appeared in early editions of **Saturday Night Live**, they passed up the opportunity to produce a series, much to Henson's frustration. It was then that the British impresario Sir Lew Grade, the chairman of ATV, stepped in. Henson's creatures had appeared in three light entertainment specials made by ATV for American sale (two starring Julie Andrews, the other featuring musician Herb Alpert) and Grade could see the Muppets' wider appeal where the American TV executives could not. Grade invited Henson to move his entire production workshop to Britain – writers, puppeteers, producers and more – to make *The Muppet Show* at ATV's studio in Borehamwood, just north of London, working with British designers and directors. Most of the 120 guest stars were American but they too flocked to Borehamwood to tape their contributions. Shrewdly, Grade was then able

to sell *The Muppet Show* back to America, where, vastly popular with children and adults, it was screened in first-run syndication from late September 1976, proving that the network executives, not for the first or last time, had made a costly error of judgement.

But although one can lay a good deal of credit at Sir Lew Grade's door, and tip the hat to the major creative contribution of Frank Oz (who voiced Miss Piggy and several other characters), *The Muppet Show* owed it all to Jim Henson, who ranks alongside Walt Disney in terms of creative genius. Born in Greenville, Mississippi, on 24 September 1936, Henson was fascinated at an early age by TV and puppetry in equal measure, and first combined the two in *Sam And Friends*, a series of a five-minute shows that aired locally on WRC-TV in Washington DC from 1955 to 1961. Henson introduced Muppet characters, including Kermit, for the first time in this programme. *Sam And Friends* led to Henson and his then colleague Jane Nebel producing 160 Wilkins Coffee TV commercials and then making guest appearances for the Muppet characters on *The Tonight Show, The Jimmy Dean Show, The Ed Sullivan Show* and other top series. But it was in 1969 that the Muppets became internationally famous, when Jim Henson was invited to bring his puppets into a new entertainment and education series for pre-school children, *Sesame Street*, made by the Children's Television Workshop, an American non-profit organisation established to provide informative, fun TV programming for young children, particularly the financially and racially disadvantaged. Still on air at the time of writing – after almost 30 years and thousands of episodes – *Sesame Street* has provided a perfect platform for Muppet characters like Big Bird, the Cookie Monster, the Count, Fozzie Bear (the only original *Sesame Street*er to graduate to *The Muppet Show*), Bert, Ernie and Grover. *The Muppet Show* grew out of Henson's desire to produce, alongside *Sesame Street*, less didactic and more mature material, and its success, in turn, allowed Henson to branch out into other TV enterprises and the movies. Jim Henson died on 16 May 1990, age 53, but his creative spirit lives on and his son Brian is at the helm of the still ultra-busy Jim Henson Productions.

*Notes. These dates refer to the London-area ITV transmissions – however only 23 of the 24 first series episodes were screened in the capital. All 24 were broadcast in the Midlands (ATV's own area), beginning on 5 September 1976, seven weeks ahead of London, but ending on 23 April 1977, three weeks after. Forty-five of the 120 episodes were screened by BBC1 from 8 February 1986 to 7 October 1987.

The remainder of this entry provides a thumbnail sketch (a large thumbnail, admittedly) of some of the other work by Jim Henson and, subsequent to his death, his production company, beginning with TV. Most programmes are rooted in humour, many are educational in approach, all bear Henson's trademark touch, especially his ability to treat a familiar subject, like nursery rhymes, in a uniquely accessible manner. But this is by no means a complete list – Muppet characters have cropped up in countless other programmes other the years, from chat-shows to, even, the 1977 *Royal Variety Show* (for this one year only renamed *The Silver Jubilee Variety Gala*, televised by ITV on 4 December 1977).

Sam And Friends (USA, 1955–61, see above).

Sesame Street (USA, 1969 to date, see above; UK, ITV [London area] from 25 September 1971 and now daily on C4).

The Muppet Musicians Of Bremen (USA, one-hour special, 1972; UK BBC1 as two programmes, 10 and 17 April 1973). Kermit introduces various Muppet characters as they set out on a musical journey.

Fraggle Rock (85 episodes, USA 1983–87; UK, ITV from 7 January 1984 to 22 August 1990), designed to explain to children how the world can live peacefully. Set on a rock, where a lonely lighthouse keeper (first Fulton Mackay then John Gordon-Sinclair then Simon O'Brien) is kept company by his dog and Muppet characters Wembley, Red, Mokey, Gobo, Boober and others.

Muppet Babies (aka *Jim Henson's Muppet Babies* and *Jim Henson's Muppets, Babies and Monsters*; USA 1984–92; UK, BBC1 from 25 December 1985 to 28 August 1991, ITV from 2 January 1993). Cartoon baby versions of Kermit, Miss Piggy, Rowlf, Fozzie Bear, Scooter and Gonzo, living in a nursery under the supervision of Nanny (voiced by Barbara Billingsley).

Jim Henson Presents (USA, 1985), series in which Henson interviews five puppet artists from around the world.

Fraggle Rock (cartoon version, USA 1987–88; UK, ITV from 2 January 1990).

Jim Henson's The Storyteller (nine episodes, USA, 1987; UK, C4 from 29 September 1991). John Hurt recounts folk tales, fables and legends in the company of a cynical dog, actors and puppets from the Jim Henson's Creature Shop.

Jim Henson's Greek Myths (four episodes, USA 1987; UK, C4 from 1 December 1991). In the company of another cynical dog, Michael Gambon narrates stories from ancient Greece.

The Jim Henson Hour (USA, 1989). A Henson jamboree bag: the excitement of 'MuppeTelevision', Miss Piggy's Hollywood, Storytelling and more. Included several specials.

The Ghost Of Faffner Hall (13 episodes, USA, 1989; UK, ITV 16 August to 8 November 1989). The adventures of some music-loving residents at Faffner Hall, a music conservatory haunted by the ghost of its founder, Fughetta Faffner.

Jim Henson's Mother Goose Stories (13 episodes; USA, 1990; UK, ITV from 5 September 1988 to 28 November 1988). Nursery rhymes.

Dinosaurs (USA, 1991–94; UK, ITV from 3 November 1991 to 19 December 1992).

Jim Henson's Dog City (26 episodes; USA, 1992–94; UK, C4 from 7 May to 3 September 1995). Puppetry and animation depicting the adventures of a dog private detective, Ace Hart.

CityKids (USA, 1993–94), a music, comedy and drama series addressing problems faced by teenagers from racial and ethnic backgrounds.

Jim Henson's Secret Life of Toys (USA, 1994). Toys come to life.

Jim Henson's Animal Show With Stinky And Jake (USA, 1994 to date; UK, BBC1/2 1996–97). A puppet animal TV chat-show promoting the preservation of wildlife.

Muppets Tonight (USA, 1996 to date; UK, BBC1 from 6 September to 31 December 1996).

Aliens In The Family (USA, 1996). A human man and an alien women marry and raise extraterrestrial children.

The Wubbulous World Of Dr Seuss (USA, 1996 to date). Dr Seuss's children's stories brought to life via 3D computer animation and Jim Henson puppets.

The Bear In The Big Blue House (USA, 1997 to date). New Muppet characters educate and entertain pre-school children.

Muppet Classic Theatre (USA, 1997 to date). More wackily presented fairy tales.

TV specials featuring the Muppets and/or other Jim Henson creations have included, in alphabetical order, *The Best Of The Muppets* (a compilation from the first series made for entry into the Montreux TV Festival, where it won the Golden Rose, screened in the UK by ITV on 9 April 1977), *CityKids*, *The Cube*, *Down At Fraggle Rock – Behind The Scenes*, *Emmet Otter's Jug-Band Christmas* (UK, ITV on 26 December 1981), *The Fantastic Miss Piggy Show*, *The Frog Prince*, *The Great Santa Claus Switch*, *Gulliver's Travels*, *Here Come The Puppets!* (UK, ITV on 2 January 1988), *Hey Cinderella*, *Inside The Labyrinth*, *Jim Henson's The Christmas Toy*, *John Denver And The Muppets: A Christmas Together* (UK, BBC1 15 December 1979), *John Denver And The Muppets: A Rocky Mountain Holiday*, *Mr Willowby's Christmas Tree*, *A Muppet Family Christmas* (UK, BBC1 26 December 1989), *The Muppet Show: Sex And Violence*, *The Muppet Valentine Special*, *The Muppets: A Celebration Of 30 Years*, *The Muppets At Walt Disney World* (UK, ITV 26 May 1991), *The Muppets Celebrate Jim Henson* (UK, C4 6 May 1991), *The Muppets Go Hollywood*, *The Muppets Go To The Movies* (the first Muppets special, screened in the UK by ITV on 10 July 1981, with Dudley Moore and Lily Tomlin and featuring clips from the movie *The Great Muppet Caper*), *The Muppets On Puppets*, *Of Muppets And Men* (UK, ITV 27 December 1981), *Puppetman*, *Sesame Street … 20 And Still Counting*, *The Tale Of Bunny Picnic*, *Tales From Muppetland*, *Tales Of The Tinkerdee*, *The World Of Jim Henson* (a two-hour celebration, screened in the UK by C4 on 26 December 1995), *The World Of The Dark Crystal* and *Youth '68*.

Movies featuring the Muppets and/or other Jim Henson creations/productions have included *The Muppet Movie* (1979), *The Great Muppet Caper* (1981), *The Dark Crystal* (1982), *The Muppets Take Manhattan* (1984), *Labyrinth* (1986), *The Witches* (1990), *The Muppet Christmas Carol* (1992), *Muppet Treasure Island* (1996) and *Buddy* (in production at the time of writing).

Muppets Tonight

USA · ABC THEN THE DISNEY CHANNEL (JIM HENSON PRODUCTIONS) · SKETCH

20 × 30 mins (to 31/12/97 · continuing into 1998) · colour

US dates: 8 Mar 1996 to date

UK dates: 6 Sep 1996–31 Dec 1996 (13 episodes) BBC1 Fri 7pm then various days and times

MAIN CAST (PUPPETEERS/VOICES)

Kermit/Rizzo The Rat/	
Andy Pig/Beaker/	Steve Whitmire
Miss Piggy/Fozzie Bear/	
Sam The American Eagle/Animal/	Frank Oz
Spamela Hamderson	Leslie Carrara
Gonzo/Randy Pig/	
Waldorf/Bunsen Honeydew/	
Bill The Bubble Guy	Dave Goelz
Sal The Monkey/Seymour The Elephant/	
Dr Phil Van Neuter/Nigel	Brian Henson
Bobo The Bear/	
Johnnie Flama/ Pepe The Prawn/	
Big Mean Carl	Bill Barretta
Statler	Jerry Nelson
Clifford/Mulch	Kevin Clash

CREDITS

writers Dick Blasucci, Paul Flaherty, Darin Henry, Jim Lewis, Kirk R Thatcher, Patric M Verrone and others · *directors* Gary Halvorson, Greg V Fera, Brian Henson, Tom Trbovich · *executive producers* Brian Henson, Dick Blasucci · *producer* Martin G Baker

Fifteen years after **The Muppet Show** ended, Jim Henson Productions – under the direction of the late founder's son, Brian – revived the idea for an all-new series, *Muppets Tonight*. Made in the USA, primarily for American screening but with both eyes, as ever, on its international appeal, the series included all the hallmarks of the earlier, British-made production. The original series had been based in a theatre, with the cast busy putting on a variety show. The new premise was similar: they still had shows to put on, but here the setting was their own TV station, KMUP-TV.

Some of the old characters returned, including – when Frank Oz was around, but not in every edition – Miss Piggy, Fozzie Bear and Animal, as well as the ever loveable Kermit, Rizzo The Rat and, sitting in armchairs criticising the TV fare (and also winding up their nurse at a geriatric home), Statler and Waldorf. There was a bunch of

new characters too, including Clifford, the new host of the show, a dreadlocked, streetwise dude who, quietly, suffers from insecurity; Johnnie Flama, a Mafioso-type crooner, with his bodyguard Sal; two brainless pigs called Randy and Andy (the word randy has no sexual connotation in the USA), nephews of Miss Piggy; Bobo, the hungry security guard bear; Seymour and Pepe, an elephant and prawn respectively who operate the elevator and want to be famous; and Bill The Bubble Guy, a relentless volunteer whose sole talent is to be able to blow bubbles from the top of the head. Additionally, two glam pigs, Spamela Hamderson and David Hoggselhoff – obviously pastiching Pamela Anderson and David Hasselhoff – appeared in the regular *Baywatch*-style beach serial *Bay Of Pigswatch*.

Among those lining up as guest stars, or in walk-on spots, were Paula Abdul, Jason Alexander, Tony Bennett, Garth Brooks, Pierce Brosnan, Cindy Crawford, Billy Crystal, Micky Dolenz, Whoopi Goldberg, John Goodman, Evander Holyfield, Larry King, Jay Leno, Johnny Mathis, Leonard Nimoy, Penn and Teller, Michelle Pfeiffer, Prince, Dennis Quaid, Little Richard and William Shatner.

Note. Some UK programmes included sketches additional to the original US editions.

Murder Most Horrid

UK · BBC (TALKBACK PRODUCTIONS) · SITCOMS

18 × 30 mins · colour

Series One (6) 14 Nov–19 Dec 1991 · BBC2 Thu mostly 9pm

Series Two (6) *Murder Most Horrid II* 3 Mar–7 Apr 1994 · BBC2 Thu 9pm

Series Three (6) 10 May–14 June 1996 · BBC2 Fri 9pm

A bunch of deliciously jet-black comedies in the style of *Alfred Hitchcock Presents*, each with murder as the theme and each pastiching a style of murder storytelling. Dawn French starred in 18 different roles, demonstrating her versatility as an actress by switching effortlessly from – in the first series alone – domineering *femme fatale* to shy policewoman to hapless Brazilian au pair to a determined scientist.

Note. Dawn French took her television acting roles into a new area on 3 October 1993 when she appeared in the BBC1 *Screen One* drama *Tender Loving Care*. In this chilling film, she played a nurse, Elaine Dobbs, who belies her benevolent demeanour by killing off awkward patients. Based on a true-life story, this really was a murder most horrid.

The Case Of The Missing
14 NOV 1991

MAIN CAST

WPC Diane Softly	Dawn French
Chief Inspector	Bill Paterson
Pathologist	Timothy Spall
Editor	Peter Bland
Sgt Dobson	Stephen Frost

CREDITS

writers Ian Hislop/Nick Newman · director Bob Spiers · executive producer Peter Fincham · producer Jon Plowman

WPC Softly is mysteriously promoted to Inspector and transferred from the Traffic Division to head a murder investigation.

The Girl From Ipanema
21 NOV 1991

MAIN CAST

Maria	Dawn French
Lydia Howling	Jane Asher
Maurice Howling	Martin Jarvis

CREDITS

writers Paul Smith/Terry Kyan · director Bob Spiers · executive producer Peter Fincham · producer Jon Plowman

Maria, a Brazilian au pair, discovers that her Hampstead employers, a parliamentary candidate and a liberal multinational businesswoman, are embroiled in a hotbed of sexual and political intrigue.

He Died A Death
28 NOV 1991

MAIN CAST

Judy Talent	Dawn French
Tony Sparkle	Tony Slattery
Insp Salford	Kenneth Cranham
Insp Turner	Kevin McNally
Basil Hampton	Stephen Moore
Beryl	Gwen Taylor

CREDITS

writers Ian Hislop/Nick Newman · director Bob Spiers · executive producer Peter Fincham · producer Jon Plowman

Fading TV soap star Judy Talent becomes involved in a real-life mystery while acting in *The Catflap*, a stage whodunit.

A Determined Woman
5 DEC 1991

MAIN CAST

Rita Proops	Dawn French
Selwyn Proops	Jim Broadbent
Helen	Kathy Burke
Dr Rachel Vine	Caroline Blakiston

CREDITS

writer/director James Hendrie · director James Hendrie · executive producer Peter Fincham · producer Jon Plowman

When quantum physicist Rita Proops is made redundant by her university she determines to continue her experiments into time-travel at home, and hopes to use the process to avert the day she murdered her husband Selwyn.

Murder At Tea Time
12 DEC 1991

MAIN CAST

Bunty Breslaw	Dawn French
Colin	Dexter Fletcher
Mrs Grove	Diane Bull
Simon Grove	Ben Davis
Sally	Jane Booker
Charlie Dunn	Andy Parsons
Lizzie	Rebecca Stevens

CREDITS

writers Graham Alborough/Jez Alborough · director Bob-Spiers · executive producer Peter Fincham · producer Jon Plowman

Bunty Breslaw, award-winning presenter of the popular children's TV show *Write Away*, becomes insanely jealous of her younger colleague, Colin. In order to dispose of him, she contrives more and more dangerous stunts for him to perform.

Mrs Hat And Mrs Red
19 DEC 1991

MAIN CAST

Katie Hatcliffe/	
Sonia Redcliffe	Dawn French
Roy Redcliffe	Jim Carter
Jemima Redcliffe	Kate McEnery

CREDITS

writers James Hendrie/Ian Brown · director Bob Spiers · executive producer Peter Fincham · producer Jon Plowman

A tale of two vastly different women who look exactly alike. Mrs Hat takes the place of Mrs Red after the latter walks out on her husband Roy and daughter Jemima, but when Mrs Red returns Roy has to decide who to keep as his wife, a murderous decision …

Overkill
3 MAR 1994

MAIN CAST

Tina Mellish	Dawn French
Carmela Vezza	Amanda Donohoe
Doverson	Peter Vaughan
Lambert	Colin Salmon

CREDITS

writer Steven Moffat · director Bob Spiers · executive producer Peter Fincham · producer Jon Plowman

While trying to commit suicide in a hotel room, social worker Tina Mellish meets an international hit-woman. The first episode in the second series.

Lady Luck
10 MAR 1994

MAIN CAST

Denise Cunningham	Dawn French
Sean Lacey	Sean Gallagher
Gary	Jo Dow
Sheena	Ann Bryson

CREDITS

writers Paul Smith/Terry Kyan · director Bob Spiers · executive producer Peter Fincham · producer Jon Plowman

Denise Cunningham, a hairdressing salon proprietor, is taken hostage by an escaping bank robber.

A Severe Case Of Death
17 MAR 1994

MAIN CAST

Maude Jenkins	Dawn French
Squire Thorpe	John Fortune
Old Dr Adams	Timothy West

CREDITS

writer Chris England · director Marcus Mortimer · executive producer Peter Fincham · producer Jon Plowman

Maude Jenkins, a housekeeper, has to dress up as a man in order to be accepted as a doctor in the 19th-century.

We All Hate Granny
24 MAR 1994

MAIN CAST

Granny Lily Gibbons	Dawn French
Tom	James Fleet
Jocasta	Victoria Wicks

CREDITS

writer James Hendrie · director Dewi Humphreys · executive producer Peter Fincham · producer Jon Plowman

A young couple decide that their lives would be much better if their children's granny was dead. But she, randy old Lily Gibbons, is quite an unusual old woman.

Mangez Merveillac
31 MAR 1994

MAIN CAST

Verity Hodge	Dawn French
Patron	Philip Jackson
Mrs Templecombe	Patricia Hayes

CREDITS

writers Ian Hislop/Nick Newman · director Bob Spiers · executive producer Peter Fincham · producer Jon Plowman

Verity Hodge, a vicious, money-hungry travel/cookery writer, discovers a corner of France hitherto unknown to her rivals, but destroys it by writing a book.

Smashing Bird
7 APR 1994

MAIN CAST

Vikki	Dawn French
Clancy	Hywel Bennett
Terry	Ray Winstone
Ray	David Bamber
Psycho	Philip Martin Brown
Tommy	Mark McGann

CREDITS

writer Jon Canter · director Dewi Humphreys · executive producer Peter Fincham · producer Jon Plowman

In the East End of London in the 1960s, a crime getaway driver, Ray, and his night-club torch-singing fiancée, Vikki, plan to give up a life of crime. Then Vikki becomes a killer.

Girl Friday

10 MAY 1996

MAIN CAST

Sally Fairfax · · · · · · · · · · · · · Dawn French
Harvey Stafford · · · · · · · · · · · Nigel Havers
Karen · · · · · · · · · · · · · · Geraldine McNulty
DC Jobson · · · · · · · · · · · · · Paul Moriarty

CREDITS

writer Paul Smith · director Dewi Humphreys · executive producer Peter Fincham · producer Sophie Clarke-Jervoise

Sally Fairfax, a doting and super-efficient PA, witnesses her boss commit a murder. The first episode in the third series.

A Life Or Death Operation

17 MAY 1996

MAIN CAST

Kate Marshall · · · · · · · · · · · Dawn French
Mrs Osman · · · · · · · · · · · · · Brigit Forsyth
Duncan Japp · · · · · · · · · · · · · · John Bird
Hilary · · · · · · · · · · · · · · · · · Jo Unwin
Giles · · · · · · · · · · · · · · · Peter Wingfield
Sister Debbie · · · · · · · · · · · Llewella Gideon

CREDITS

writers Mark Burton/John O'Farrell · director Dewi Humphreys · executive producer Peter Fincham · producer Sophie Clarke-Jervoise

Kate Marshall, esteemed surgeon and the host of the hit TV series *Accident & Emergency*, is willing to kill to keep secret a past indiscretion.

Dying Live

24 MAY 1996

MAIN CAST

Daisy Talwinning · · · · · · · · · · Dawn French
General Alberto · · · · · · · · · · · · Jim Carter
Daniel Hoffmeyer · · · · · · · · · · John Thomson
Yvonne Quail · · · · · · · · · · · Helen Lederer
Marcos · · · · · · · · · · · · · Alistair McGowan
Mr Maddox · · · · · · · · · · · · · Stratford Johns
Driver · · · · · · · · · · · · · · · · Kevin Allen
Franklin · · · · · · · · · · · · · · · Bryan Pringle

CREDITS

writer Steven Moffat · director Dewi Humphreys · executive producer Peter Fincham · producer Sophie Clarke-Jervoise

Abattoir employee Daisy Talwinning ('I love working with animals') is mistaken for an executioner, being broadcast live on TV, while on holiday in the South American country Panador.

The Body Politic

31 MAY 1996

MAIN CAST

Linda Bryce · · · · · · · · · · · · · Dawn French
Jerry Bryce · · · · · · · · · · · · · Hugh Laurie
Brian · · · · · · · · · · · · · · Paul Mark Elliott
Barlow · · · · · · · · · · · · · · · John Bennett

CREDITS

writer Anthony Horowitz · director Ferdinand Fairfax · executive producer Peter Fincham · producer Sophie Clarke-Jervoise

Jerry Bryce, the Leader of the Opposition, and his wife Linda, a primary-school teacher, make a grisly discovery – three bodies are buried under their kitchen floor.

Confess

7 JUNE 1996

MAIN CAST

Sgt Wendy Hodge · · · · · · · · · · Dawn French
Sgt Val Cole · · · · · · · · · · · · · Minnie Driver
Frank Foster · · · · · · · · · · · Roger Lloyd Pack
DCI Dave Jones · · · · · · · · · George Costigan
DCS Barratt · · · · · · · · · · · · · Clive Russell

CREDITS

writer Jon Canter · director Coky Giedroyc · executive producer Peter Fincham · producer Sophie Clarke-Jervoise

Two unorthodox policewomen, Sergeants Hodge and Cole, clumsily interrogate Frank Foster, a former Essex gangland boss, about the murder of a policeman.

Dead On Time

14 JUNE 1996

MAIN CAST

Grim Reaper · · · · · · · · · · · · · Dawn French
Tony Smedley · · · · · · · · · · · · Danny Webb
Alison Smedley · · · · · · · · · Regina Freedman
Rachel · · · · · · · · · · · · · · Sophie Okonedo
Chris Bastable · · · · · · · · · · · · Brian Capron

CREDITS

writers Ian Hislop/Nick Newman · director Ferdinand Fairfax · executive producer Peter Fincham · producer Sophie Clarke-Jervoise

A pink-dress-wearing Grim Reaper, desperate for promotion to a position with the cherubim, has to rescue her failing reputation by despatching one more human.

Murphy Brown

USA · CBS (SHUKOVSKY-ENGLISH/WARNER BROS) · SITCOM

231 episodes (226 × 30 mins · 5 × 60 mins to 31/12/97 · continuing into 1998) · colour

US dates: 14 Nov 1988 to date

UK dates: 5 Sep–24 Oct 1994 (8 episodes) BBC2 Mon 6pm

MAIN CAST

Murphy Brown · · · · · · · · · · Candice Bergen
Jim Dial · · · · · · · · · · · · · Charles Kimbrough
Frank Fontana · · · · · · · · · · · · Joe Regalbuto
Miles Silverberg · · · Grant Shaud (1988–96)
Corky Sherwood/Forrest · · · · · · · Faith Ford
Phil · · · · · · · · · · · · · · Pat Corley (1988–96)
Audrey · · · · · · · · · · · Jane Leeves (1992–93)
Eldin Bernecky · · · · · · · · · Robert Pastorelli
· (1988–94)
Miller Redfield · · Christopher Rich (1995–97)
Kay Carter-Shepley · · Lily Tomlin (from 1996)
Avery Brown · · · · · · · · · · Haley Joel Osment
· (from 1997)

OTHER APPEARANCES

Eugene Kinsella · · · · · · · · Alan Oppenheimer
· (1988–92)
Jake Lowenstein · · · Robin Thomas (1988–96)
Jerry Gold · · · · · · · · · Jay Thomas (1989–96)
John · · · · · · · · · · · John Hostetter (1990–96)
Peter Hunt · · · · · · · · · Scott Bakula (1993–96)
Stan Lansing · · · Garry Marshall (from 1994)
McGovern · · · · · · · · · · Paula Cale (1995–96)

CREDITS

creators Diane English/Joel Shukovsky · writers Diane English and others · directors Barnet Kellman, Peter Bonerz, Alan Rafkin, Lee Shallat, Steve Zuckerman and others · executive producers Diane English, Joel Shukovsky, Candice Bergen, Markus Flanagan · producers Frank Pace, Rob Bragin, Ned E Davis, Bill Diamond, Bob Jeffords, Deborah Smith

A TV news-magazine show, *FYI*, was the setting for this classy series that put a late-1980s spin on *The Mary Tyler Moore Show*. Murphy Brown was the star interviewer of *FYI* and her uncompromising questioning and acerbic wit had turned her into a media icon. In the opening episode, she has just returned from a stint at the Betty Ford Clinic, where she has been weaned off alcohol and tobacco. She has, however, lost none of her bite and is soon causing waves and making life tough for the show's new and impossibly young executive producer Miles Silverberg. In her forties, Murphy has divorced husband Jake and channelled all of her energies into work. She is purely and simply a driven career-woman and every-thing else takes second place.

Outside of work, Murphy's home is being painted by a hugely imaginative artist, Eldin (he would eventually spend six years on the job) and her social activities take place mainly at Phil's bar, a nearby watering hole frequented by media people. The gravel-voiced bar-owner Phil dispenses drink and advice in about equal measure and is like a father figure to her.

Staffing the front-end of *FYI* are stiff anchorman Jim Dial, bimbo Corky Sherwood and investigative journalist Frank Fontana, who – bowing to pressure from his bosses – always wears a wig on camera, although content to be without it the rest of the time. A veneer of reality was added to the plots with the name-dropping of real-life celebrities and occasional appearances from well-known movers and shakers, cast as themselves. *Murphy Brown* took great pains to keep abreast of the times and many of the storylines – such as the threats of job loss for the *FYI* staff following a takeover of their host network – mirrored actual events.

The sitcom, always smoothly produced, may have remained an average achieving production had not a national controversy blown up over one of its storylines. In the 1991–92 season Murphy discovered that she was pregnant after a fling with her ex-husband Jake. Although both Jake and Murphy's current boyfriend Jerry Gold offered themselves as father to the baby boy, Murphy – independent to the end – decided to raise the child alone. The day after this episode was aired, US vice-president Dan Quayle, in a speech addressing the 'poverty of values' in America, singled out the show, and this particular storyline, as setting a poor example. This rather ill-judged criticism – Quayle had a reputation for shooting himself in the foot – drew a sharp response from the show's creator/executive producer Diane English who pointed out that if the vice-president truly believed that a woman couldn't adequately raise a child on her own, he should actively campaign for easily obtainable, safe abortions. Other TV producers leapt to the show's defence and the only noticeable outcome to the attack was the show's sudden rise in the ratings. The series got its own back on Quayle with an hour-length episode ('You Say Potatoe, I Say Potato', aired in the USA on 21 September 1992) that made numerous mocking references to him. By 1993, Quayle had gone but *Murphy Brown* was still around.

Note. Film-star comic actress Lily Tomlin joined the cast of *Murphy Brown* in 1996, her first regular sitcom role.

Murray And Me

UK · BBC · SITCOM

1 × 25 mins · b/w

8 July 1965 · BBC1 Thu 8.50pm

MAIN CAST

Murray · · · · · · · · · · · · · · · · · · Chic Murray
Tommy Penn · · · · · · · · · · · · · · · Alan Baulch

CREDITS

writer John Law · executive producer Graeme Muir · producer Philip Barker

A *Comedy Playhouse* pilot written especially for the great Scottish standup comedian Chic Murray. He was cast as a 'knowledge boy' (an epithet given to a man of any age), training his memory to study all of the streets and places in London in order to become a taxi driver. Invited to spend the day looking after a young child, Tommy Penn, he devotes the time to showing the boy the various uses of total recall. No series developed.

My Brother's Keeper

UK · ITV (GRANADA) · SITCOM

13 × 30 mins · colour

Series One (7) 7 Sep–19 Oct 1975 · Sun 7.25pm
Series Two (6) 10 May–21 June 1976 · Mon 8pm

MAIN CAST

Brian Booth · · · · · · · · · · · · · · · George Layton
Pete Booth · · · · · · · · · · · · · · · Jonathan Lynn
Mrs Booth · · · · · · · · · · · · · · · · Hilary Mason
Sgt Bluett · · · · · · · · · · · · · · · · Tenniel Evans

CREDITS

writers George Layton/Jonathan Lynn · director/producer Bill Gilmour

Having written and appeared together in LWT's various *Doctor* series, George Layton and Jonathan Lynn did likewise in this Granada sitcom, casting themselves as twin brothers identical neither in appearance nor personality. Indeed, they could scarcely have been more different: Brian was a clean-cut eager-beaver police constable, intent on vaulting up the ladder of success; Pete was a bearded, fiery, militant student at the local technical college. They also held completely opposing views on life, except that they both shared a passion for women.

The series – inspired by an article about twins that Layton read in *The Times* – was set in the fictional northern town of West Hockley, with Hilary Mason cast as the lads' exasperated mother.

My Dad's A Boring Nerd

UK · ITV (GRANADA) · CHILDREN'S SITCOM

1 × 30 mins · colour

28 Aug 1997 · Thu 4.40pm

MAIN CAST

Mr Burton · · · · · · · · · · · · · · · David Bamber
Mrs Burton · · · · · · · · · · · · · · Michelle Holmes
Kevin Burton · · · · · · · · · · · · · Anthony Lewis
Sophie Burton · · · · · · · · · · · · Julia Howarth
Brian · · · · · · · · · · · · · · · · · · Alan Halsall

CREDITS

writer Joe Turner · director Beryl Richards · executive producers Danielle Lux, Kieran Roberts · producer Yvon Grace

Thirteen-year-old Kevin Burton is a compulsive daydreamer whose exciting flights of fantasy seem to be a reaction to his embarrassment at having a colossally boring dad. Mr Burton (David Bamber from *Chalk*) is a British Safety Standards officer totally obsessed with accidents and their causes, a man whose only line of conversation concerns the everyday dangers that people face, a man who feels cutlery is too dangerous to have in the home. Not surprisingly, Kevin's embarrassment is also shared by his mother (Michelle Holmes from *Goodnight Sweetheart*) and his big sister Sophie, and the siblings have made a pact not to allow any of their friends to meet their father in case word gets out at school about his spectacularly tedious nature.

But a timing slip-up results in Kevin's school-friend Brian being in the house when Kevin's dad returns home from work, and, indeed, Brian learns of Mr Burton's stupefying dullness. But Brian is more concerned with Sophie, on whom he has a passionate crush. For Kevin, things go from bad to worse when he learns in a biology lesson that he may inherit many of his father's traits. Kevin's daydreams become wilder and he experiences difficulty (as do the viewers) in differentiating fantasy from reality. In the end however, Mr Burton's reactions to a fire in the

house, caused by Kevin, give the lad cause to re-evaluate his dad.

This was a classy, witty and well-acted one-off sitcom, shot on film, with more than enough potential to be developed into a series.

My Dead Dad

UK · C4 (SCOTTISH) · SITCOM

6 × 30 mins · colour

28 July–1 Sep 1992 · Tue 8pm

MAIN CAST

William Farquhar Dundee · · · · · · Roy Hanlon
Alexander 'Eck' Dundee · · · · Forbes Masson
Jools · · · · · · · · · · · · · · · · · Debra Gillett

CREDITS

writer John McKay · director/producer Alan Nixon · executive producer Sandy Ross

In spite of being on the dole, Alex 'Eck' Dundee has a reasonably pleasant life, a decent room in a shared flat, an embryonic romance with the sexually permissive Jools, and a winning optimism about his job prospects that carries him through his many interviews. But all of this is disrupted by the arrival of Eck's late father, spirited down from heaven for reasons that neither of them understands. Said dad, Willie, who died 14 years earlier, surmises that he must have been sent down to help his son through a particularly difficult patch, but actually all of Alex's problems arise *from* his father's presence. Unlike most screen ghosts, Willie can be seen by everyone, not just the hauntee, and, by way of an apparent supernatural tradition, he is linked to his son by an invisible umbilical chord that prevents them from straying more than a few feet from one another. This causes Alex untold problems, as his dad – garishly dressed, heavily cologned and with forthrightly expressed old-fashioned views – is not the ideal companion for a would-be dashing young man about town.

My Dead Dad was a bit of an odd fish and not just because of its supernatural storyline. Forbes Masson (former half of the comedy double-act Victor and Barry) was a dependable lead but the whole thing just didn't seem to gel. It also had a hard job playing down its stage origins, the premise having first appeared as a theatre play, *Dead Dad Dog*.

My Father Knew Lloyd George

UK · BBC · SATIRE

1 × 70 mins · b/w

18 Dec 1965 · BBC1 Sat 10pm

MAIN CAST

John Bird
Alan Bennett
John Fortune
Eleanor Bron

CREDITS
writer John Bird · *additional material* Alan Bennett, Eleanor Bron, John Fortune · *director* Jack Gold · *producers* Jack Gold, Ned Sherrin

John Bird's complex tale of a Victorian scandal was made by the **BBC-3** team, with all of the cast undertaking multiple roles; particularly amusing were Bird himself as Queen Victoria and Alan Bennett as an oily Victorian villain. The storyline involved the quest of a young man (Fortune) attempting to clear his grandfather (also Fortune) from a scandal involving the wife of the Prime Minister.

Bird was named Television Personality Of The Year by the Society Of Film And Television for the production.

My Favorite Martian

USA · CBS (JACK CHERTOK TELEVISION) · SITCOM

107 × 30 mins (75 × b/w · 32 × colour)
US dates: 29 Sep 1963–4 Sep 1966
UK dates: 7 Nov 1963–7 Oct 1964
(37 episodes · b/w) ITV various days and times

MAIN CAST
'Martin O'Hara' · · · · · · · · · · · Ray Walston
Tim O'Hara · · · · · · · · · · · · · · · · Bill Bixby
Lorelei Brown · · · · · · · · · · · Pamela Britton
Bill Brennan · · · · · · · · Alan Hewitt (1964–66)
Harry Burns · · · · · · · J Pat O'Malley (1963–64)
Angela Brown · · · · · Ann Marshall (1963–64)

CREDITS
creator John L Greene · *writers* John L Greene, Al Martin/Bill Kelsay, James Komack, William Blinn/Michael Gleason, Elroy Schwartz/Austin Kalish, Albert E Lewin/Burt Styler, Ben Gershman/Bill Freedman and others · *directors* Alan Rafkin, Oscar Rudolph, Sidney Miller and others · *producer* Jack Chertok

A Martian spaceship crash-lands on Earth and from it emerges a middle-aged (that is, 450-year-old), remarkably human-looking and English-speaking anthropologist, known on his home planet as X-Idgius 12½. The crash is witnessed by a *Los Angeles Sun* reporter, Tim O'Hara, and the Martian moves into the journalist's rented apartment until his spaceship – which is kept in the garage – is repaired. In the meantime, no one can know who or what he is, so the Martian passes himself off as Martin O'Hara, the reporter's uncle. Predictably, 'Uncle Martin' gets Tim into all sorts of inexplicable trouble – which, considering that the journalist resists the idea of scooping the newspaper story of the century – seems a bit tough. (Although, of course, this is where the fun comes in.) Capable of extending antennae from his skull, becoming invisible and exercising his telepathy and levitation skills, the Martian constantly arouses the suspicion of a local LAPD cop, Bill Brennan, as well as befuddling O'Hara's landlady, Lorelei Brown.

My Favorite Martian remains a much-loved and fondly recalled sitcom in America but no sequel or revival has emerged except *My Favorite Martians*, a 1973–75 animated series (with Jonathan Harris and Howard Morris voicing the Uncle Martin and Tim parts). However, in production during the writing of this book was a Hollywood feature-film version, being directed by Donald Petrie for Warner Bros and starring Jeff Daniels and Christopher Lloyd.

The fish-out-of-water alien-on-Earth premise has served sitcoms remarkable well, *viz* **Mork And Mindy**, **ALF** and **3rd Rock From The Sun**.

My Gay Dads

see Sitcom Weekend

My Good Friend

UK · ITV (HARTSWOOD FILMS FOR ANGLIA) · SITCOM

14 × 30 mins · colour
Series One (7) 4 Apr–16 May 1995 · Tue 8.30pm
Series Two (7) 27 Aug–8 Oct 1996 · Tue 8.30pm

MAIN CAST
Peter Banks · · · · · · · · · · · · · · · George Cole
Harry King · · · · · · · · · · · · · Richard Pearson
Ellie · · · · · · · · · · · · · Minnie Driver (series 1);
· · · · · · · · · · · · · · Lesley Vickerage (series 2)
Brian · · · · · · · · · · · · · · · Michael Lumsden
Betty · · · · · · · · · · Matilda Ziegler (series 1);
· · · · · · · · · · · · · Annabelle Apsion (series 2)
Neil · · · · · · · · · · · · · Caleb Lloyd (series 1);
· · · · · · · · · · · · · · Jamie O'Brien (series 2)
David · · · · · · · · · · · · · · · Ian Keith (series 1)
Tim · · · · · · · Matthew Lloyd Davies (series 1)
Maria · · · · · · · · · · · Nimmy March (series 2)

OTHER APPEARANCES
Miss Byron · · · · · · · · · · · · · · · · Joan Sims

CREDITS
writer Bob Larbey · *directors* Martin Dennis (series 1), Jeremy Ancock (series 2) · *producer* Beryl Vertue

Peter Banks, a pensioner, is lonely following the death of his wife Margaret and the premature retirement thrust upon him, a postman, by the Post Office. Reluctantly, he has moved in with his fussy daughter, Betty, and her dull and infertile husband Brian because he cannot afford to live on his own. Betty's punctiliousness and house-cleanliness drive Peter mad; in turn, his strong rebellious streak and disobeying of her house orders get under her skin. Truth be admitted, though they're not cruel people, neither Betty nor Brian would mind Peter dying so that they can get their life back. But just as they begin discussing putting him into a home Peter meets retired librarian Harry King in a wine bar and they quickly become agreeable company for one another.

Harry lives in a large house owned and run by an attentive young landlady, Ellie, single mother of an eight-year-old boy, Neil. Ellie encourages Harry's friendship with Peter because she doesn't like to see him lonely and because, from the off, she develops a fond spot for Peter, enjoying his sharp sense of irony and fighting spirit. Unlike most of the people in the men's lives, Ellie doesn't regard growing old as a problem. Eventually, Peter moves into the house too, also shared by a slightly loopy spinster, Miss Byron, and the pair feel free to reject society's expectations by acting up. Peter is a mischievous man who likes to pokes fun at everything and everyone, and he usually leads the genteel and forgetful Harry into temptation, but not, one suspects, to the latter's regret. (Beryl Vertue, the series' producer, also made **Men Behaving Badly**, so *My Good Friend*, again depicting the friendship of two males, could be interpreted as *Old Men Behaving Fairly Badly*.)

Through two fine series, *My Good Friend* was excellently played by both George Cole and Richard Pearson, and well written by Bob Larbey, who created a poignant comedy that didn't look down upon old age but blended pathos and wit into realistic dialogue and situations. Minnie Driver, cast as Ellie, quit after the first series, pursuing a film career in Hollywood, and Matilda Ziegler also left. They were replaced by Lesley Vickerage and Annabelle Apsion, both of whom had appeared in ITV's hit drama series *Soldier, Soldier* (as Kate Butler and Joy Wilton respectively). In between the two series, George Cole starred in a seven-part light-drama for ITV, *An Independent Man* (from 10 June 1996).

My Good Woman

see CROWTHER, Leslie

My Hero

USA · NBC (SHARPE-LEWIS PRODUCTIONS) · SITCOM

33 × 30 mins · b/w
US dates: 8 Nov 1952–1 Aug 1953
UK dates: 24 Sep 1955–17 Mar 1956
(27 episodes) ITV mostly Sat 3.30pm

MAIN CAST
Robert S Beanblossom · · · · · Bob Cummings
Julie Marshall · · · · · · · · · · · · · Julie Bishop
Willis Thackery · · · · · · · · · · · · · · John Litel

CREDITS
writers various · *director* Harold Daniels · *producer* Mort Green

The first American sitcom screened by ITV, preceding *I Love Lucy* by a day, and only the second sitcom import to be shown on British TV, following the BBC's run of **Amos 'n' Andy**.

My Hero depicted the life and adventures of Robert (Bob) Beanblossom, an estate agent for the Thackery Realty Company in Los Angeles. His pleasant, easy-going personality and good looks just about manage to secure him successful deals despite the lack of any particular talent for his work; these bumbling victories are aided by his secretary, Julie Marshall – she sees Beanblossom as the hero in the series' title – who, enamoured by his charm, is happy to smooth over the errors that he makes along the way. Just as important, Marshall also keeps things sweet between Beanblossom and his irascible boss, ol' Mr Thackery himself.

My Honourable Mrs

UK · BBC · SITCOM

7 × 30 mins · colour

14 July–26 Aug 1975 · BBC1 mostly Mon 8pm

MAIN CAST

Henry Prendergast · · · · · · · · · Derek Nimmo
Jane Prendergast · · · · · · · · · · Pauline Yates
Trevor Crichton · · · · · · · · · · · Aubrey Woods
Eric Forbes · · · · · · · · · · · · · · · Alan Curtis
Tim · · · · · · · · · · · · · · · · · Anthony Howden
Sarah · · · · · · · · · · · · · · Sylvestra le Touzel
William · · · · · · · · · · · · · · Nicholas Drake

CREDITS

writer Richard Waring · producer Graeme Muir

Socio-political problems develop for businessman Henry Prendergast when his wife's interest in politics suddenly becomes more than just a hobby: she is selected as the Tory candidate for Brinkley and duly wins a seat in Parliament. The comedy centred on her suddenly diminished role in their relationship and family life, and the complications that her new standing caused in their lives.

Nimmo and Yates were well cast and both were formidable in this kind of comedy, but the idea failed to appeal to viewers to any great degree. Andrew Faulds MP was the series' political adviser.

My Husband And I   1

UK · ITV (JACK HYLTON TV PRODUCTIONS FOR ASSOCIATED-REDIFFUSION) · SITCOM

7 × 30 mins · b/w

20 July–12 Oct 1956 · fortnightly Fri 8.30pm

MAIN CAST

Evelyn Laye · · · · · · · · · · · · · · · · · · herself
Frank Lawton · · · · · · · · · · · · · · · · himself
Molly · · · · · · · · · · · · · · · · · · · Linda Gray
Jennings · · · · · · · · · · · · Peter Collingwood
Jane · · · · · · · · · · · · Alicia Massy-Beresford

CREDITS

writers Geoffrey Kerr, James Leasor · producer Eric Fawcett

A short-lived domestic sitcom tailored (in Savile Row, one suspects) for the refined

husband-and-wife stage stars Evelyn 'Boo' Laye and Frank Lawton. The oft-bejewelled Laye had entered the acting profession in 1915, aged 15, and enjoyed a long and successful career in musicals and films, British and American. Four years her junior, Lawton was also a major stage and film figure. Combining laughlines with humorous songs, *My Husband And I* focused on the crises that typically afflicted such characters: he doesn't notice her new dress, she doesn't want him to grow a moustache … and other such gritty realisms.

My Husband And I   2

UK · ITV (YORKSHIRE) · SITCOM

15 × 30 mins · colour

Series One (7) 9 Jan–20 Feb 1987 · Fri 8.30pm

Special · 18 Dec 1987 · Fri 9pm

Series Two (7) 8 Apr–20 May 1988 · Fri 8pm

MAIN CAST

Nora Powers · · · · · · · · · · · · · Mollie Sugden
George Powers · · · · · · · · · · · William Moore
Bambi Bamber · · · · · · · · · · · Deddie Davies
Tracy Cosgrove · · · · · · · · · · · Carol Hawkins
Mr Mundy · · · · · · · · · · · · · · · John Horsley
Pearl · · · · · · · · · · · · · · · · Isabelle Lucas
Samantha · · · · · · · · · · · · · · Roberta Tovey
Anita · · · · · · · · · · · · · · · · · Natasha Gray
Henrietta · · · · · · · · · · · · · · · · Jane Ashton

CREDITS

writers Pam Valentine/Michael Ashton · director/producer Graham Wetherell

As soon as the last of the five series of *That's My Boy* concluded, the teaming of star Mollie Sugden, writers Pam Valentine and Michael Ashton and production company Yorkshire Television came up with what they hoped would be another winning sitcom, *My Husband And I*. Granted, this new creation stretched to two series, but one can only wonder by what miracle decision this was permitted.

Sugden was cast in yet another blowsy character, this time as Nora Powers, the head of personnel at Ashvale Advertising, a place that must have boasted the oldest staff ever to work in such a company. (Ad agencies are usually populated by young thrusting types.) Like all Sugden's other TV roles Nora liked to maintain her dignity, so she was embarrassed when her retired husband George returned to work – as chief commissionaire at Ashvale Advertising. (George was played by Sugden's real-life spouse William Moore; they had previously played together in *The Liver Birds*.) Very little happened in any of the 15 half-hour episodes of *My Husband And I* and the scripts were so wooden they could have been written on raw tree instead of its paper derivative.

My Man Joe

UK · ITV (ATV) · SITCOM

6 × 30 mins · b/w

24 Feb–31 Mar 1967 · Fri around 10pm

MAIN CAST

Joe · Joe Baker
Lord Peregrine Hansford · · Francis Matthews

CREDITS

writer Godfrey Harrison · director Dennis Vance · producer Alan Tarrant

In between making *The Joe Baker Show* and *Baker's Half-Dozen*, London-born comic actor Joe Baker starred in this single-series sitcom for ATV. He appeared as simply Joe, a clumsy oaf forever inventing crazy (but ultimately unsuccessful) schemes to make a pile of money for a faded aristocrat, Lord Hansford.

My Name Is Harry Worth

see WORTH, Harry

My Old Man

UK · ITV (YORKSHIRE) · SITCOM

13 × 30 mins · colour

Series One (7) 3 May–21 June 1974 · Fri 8.30pm
Series Two (6) 19 Mar–23 Apr 1975 · Wed 8pm

MAIN CAST

Sam Cobbett · · · · · · · · · · · · · · · Clive Dunn
Doris · · · · · · · · · · · · · · · · Priscilla Morgan
Arthur · · · · · · · · · · · · · · Edward Hardwicke

OTHER APPEARANCES

Willie · · · · · · · · · · · · · · · · · · George Tovey
Cyril · · · · · · · · · · · · · · · · · · Peter Mayock
Andrew · · · · · · · · · · · · · · · Jon Laurimore
Ron · · · · · · · · · · · · · Keith Chegwin (series 1)

CREDITS

writer Gerald Frow · director Paddy Russell · producers John Duncan (series 1), Paddy Russell (series 2)

Still only 53 when it began, *My Old Man* created another aged role for its star Clive Dunn. After just 20 minutes in make-up each week he emerged from the dressing-room as Sam Cobbett, veteran complainer – sorry *campaigner* – of two world wars. If Dunn was concerned about being typecast – he had also been old before his time in many previous TV roles, including those in *Bootsie And Snudge* and *Dad's Army* and, of course, reached number one with his pop single 'Grandad' – he was at least finally reaping the rewards of a long career. (Proving how much Dunn aged himself for the role, the part of his daughter Doris was played by his real-life wife Priscilla Morgan – albeit she was 38 to his 53.)

My Old Man cast Dunn as a lively old dog, evicted from his house in Ironmonger Row so that it could be demolished, and who, with his flat cap, woollen scarf and battered suitcase, moves into Doris's new 13th-storey tower-block flat. Like a prototype of Harry Enfield's 'Mr Don't Wanna Do It Like That' nuisance, Sam can always see a better way of doing something and proceeds to disrupt her family's life in unimaginable ways. Edward Hardwicke (recently on TV as Captain Pat Grant in the BBC drama series *Colditz*) gave good value as Doris's husband, while Ron, one of their children, was played by Keith Chegwin, then 17 and still unknown.

The series came about after the BBC failed to develop Gerald Frow's original single-episode script, screened by BBC2 on 8 April 1973 in Ronnie Barker's series **Seven Of One**.

My Pal Bob

see MONKHOUSE, Bob

My Son Reuben

UK · ITV (THAMES) · SITCOM

6 × 30 mins · colour
8 Sep–13 Oct 1975 · Mon 8pm

MAIN CAST
Fay Greenberg · · · · · · · · · · · · · · · · Lila Kaye
Reuben Greenberg · · · · · · · · · Bernard Spear
Vera Caplan · · · · · · · · · · · · · · Stella Tanner
Betty Smith · · · · · · · · · · · · · · Jo Rowbottom

OTHER APPEARANCES
Rabbi Jackson · · · · · · · Christopher Benjamin

CREDITS
writer Vince Powell · director/producer Anthony Parker

There was more cheek-pulling than leg-pulling in this short-lived kosher comedy, which co-starred Bernard Spear as a middle-aged laundry-working bachelor, Reuben, and Lila Kaye as his smothering Yiddisher momma, Fay, whose 'No one is too good for my son' statements could also have been read as 'No one will have my son unless I arrange it'.

Warning Reuben that her present for any wedding planned without her express personal involvement will be an invitation to her funeral, Fay endeavours to spike his few romantic attachments, especially if – *oy gevalt!* – they involve any *shikseh* (gentiles). When Reuben finally decides that enough is enough and packs his bags, momma feigns illness to bring him home again and Reuben realises that he is trapped.

My Son Reuben was another ethnic/cross-cultural comedy from Vince Powell, the final two episodes overlapping with the launch of yet another, **Rule Britannia!** (See also **Father Charlie, Love Thy Neighbour, Mind Your Language, The Wackers** and **Never Mind The Quality, Feel The Width**.)

My Three Sons

USA · ABC THEN CBS (DON FEDDERSON PRODUCTIONS) · SITCOM

380 × 30 mins (184 × b/w · 196 × colour)
US dates: 29 Sep 1960–24 Aug 1972

UK dates: 26 May 1961–25 June 1968 (105 episodes · b/w) ITV various days and times

MAIN CAST
Steve Douglas · · · · · · · · · · · Fred MacMurray
Mike Douglas · · · · Tim Considine (1960–65)
Robbie Douglas · · · · · · · · · · · · · Don Grady
Richard 'Chip' Douglas · · · Stanley Livingston
Ernie Thompson Douglas · · · Barry Livingston
Michael 'Bub' O'Casey · · · · · William Frawley
· (1960–65)
'Uncle' Charley O'Casey · · William Demarest
· (1965–72)
Barbara Harper/Douglas · · · Beverly Garland
· (1969–72)
Dodie Harper/Douglas · · · · · · · · · Dawn Lyn
· (1969–72)
Polly Williams/Douglas · · · · · Ronnie Troupe
· (1970–72)

CREDITS
writers various · director James V Kern · executive producer Don Fedderson · producers Don Fedderson, Edmund Hartmann, Fred Henry, George Tibbles

An honest-to-goodness middle-class middle-America sitcom that typified the period in which it began, 1960, and was sadly outmoded by the time it came to an end, a massive 380 episodes later in 1972.

The established Hollywood film star Fred MacMurray was the pivot – as aviation engineer and widower Steve Douglas he is the sole parent of three clean-cut boys, Mike (18 when the first series began), Robbie (14) and 'Chip' (seven). The four are also aided by a fifth male, Irish 'Bub' O'Casey, Steve's irascible father-in-law who uses his retired status to move in as cook of the house and its dominating force. ('Bub' was played by William Frawley, who had excelled as the grumpy Fred Mertz in *I Love Lucy*; this was his last major role before his death in March 1966.) The cast changed a number of times over the years and the storylines were somewhat tortuous: by the end, all the kids had flown the roost and started families of their own, extending the players in a soap-like fashion, and Steve had remarried, to Barbara Harper.

A total of 105 episodes were screened by London-area ITV, principally in 1964 and 1965. In the USA the series ran on the ABC network from 1960 to 1965 then aired on CBS from 1965 to 1972. An attempt to float a spin-off series, *Robbie*, focusing on the exploits of the middle Douglas son after he married and moved to San Francisco with his family, foundered after the pilot was screened by CBS on 20 March 1971.

My Two Dads

USA · NBC (MICHAEL JACOBS PRODUCTIONS/COLUMBIA-TRISTAR) · SITCOM

60 × 30 mins · colour
US dates: 20 Sep 1987–30 Apr 1990

UK dates: 10 May 1990–9 Sep 1991 (60 episodes) C4 Thu then Mon mostly 8.30pm

MAIN CAST
Michael Taylor · · · · · · · · · · · · · · Paul Reiser
Joey Harris · · · · · · · · · · · · · · · · Greg Evigan
Nicole Bradford · · · · · · · · · · · · Staci Keanan
Judge Margaret Wilbur · · · · Florence Stanley
Zach Nichols · · · · · · · Chad Allen (1989–90)
Ed Klawicki · · · · · · · · · Dick Butkus (1987–89)
Cory Kupkus · · · · · · · · · · · · · · Vonni Ribisi
Shelby Haskell · · · · · · · · · · · · Amy Hathaway

CREDITS
creators Michael Jacobs, Danielle Alexandra · writers various · directors various · producers David Steven Simon, Roger Garrett, Mark Brull and others

Joey Harris and Michael Taylor are two long-term friends who both had affairs with the same woman, Marcia Bradford, at about the same time some 13 years ago. When she dies, her will reveals that one of the two is the father of her daughter Nicole, but she had no idea which. Biological testing fails to come up with a satisfactory answer so Judge Margaret Wilbur appoints the two men joint guardians of the girl. They duly agree to the parental responsibility but are kept under the watchful eye of the judge who, conveniently, owns the building in which they reside.

This scarcely plausible plot provided the background for *My Two Dads*, an unchallenging and harmless sitcom that somehow managed to draw 60 episodes out of its contrived situation. The comedy arose from the difficulties experienced by the two guys in being both father and 'mother' to the girl, and the disputes arising from their different personalities: Joey, an artist and art teacher, was more laid-back and took a more relaxed view of child-rearing, whereas Michael, a financial adviser (and later marketing manager) held more traditional values. However, their long friendship and earnest desire to do the best for Nicole meant that, in most instances, a positive compromise was reached. As the girl became older the two fathers worried less about her education and spiritual upbringing and more on her romantic life, especially her relationships with boyfriends Cory and Zach.

Despite the hint of danger in the series' premise, *My Two Dads* was an unremittingly middle-of-the-road series that used a heavy hand when dishing out the morals that accompanied most episodes. Bit-part characters were treated as mere ciphers, their only function being to propel the plot, while the determination of the producers to portray the main protagonists as exceptionally-nice-people-only-trying-to-do-what's-best left a sickly sweet taste in the mouth. Even the presence of the fine and formidable character-actress Florence Stanley (who also took on some directorial duties) couldn't lift the series out of the mush.

My Wife And I

UK · ITV (ASSOCIATED-REDIFFUSION) · SITCOM

11×30 mins · b/w
30 June–10 Sep 1958 · mostly Wed 8pm

MAIN CAST

Phyllis Finley	Mai Zetterling
David Finley	Rex Garner
The secretary	Joan Benham

CREDITS

writer Pamela Craig · *director* Eric J Croall · *producer* Michael Westmore

The Swedish-born (but British resident) actress Mai Zetterling, best known at this time for her dramatic roles, co-starred in this 11-part series, her first comedy outing, playing what she described as a 'dizzy, mad, crazy woman' Phyllis Finley.

Phyllis was the wife of David (played by Rex Garner, famous at this time as the private eye Vic Steele in Associated-Rediffusion's 1957–59 detective series *Shadow Squad*), who was surrounded by women – not only Phyllis but also his secretary, mother-in-law and charlady.

My Wife And I was based on an American radio series. Zetterling went on to become an acclaimed TV and movie director in later years.

My Wife Jacqueline

UK · BBC · SITCOM

6×30 mins · b/w
30 July–22 Oct 1952 · fortnightly Wed around 8.30pm

MAIN CAST

Tom Bridger	Leslie Phillips
Jacqueline Bridger	Joy Shelton
Margaret	Anthea Holloway

CREDITS

writer A P Dearsley · *producer* Dicky Leeman

A comedy series that was described at the time as 'serial play' because the term situation comedy was not yet a comfortable one. Former child actor Leslie Phillips, though still in his twenties, was an old hand at the game, and Joy Shelton, who was married to the comedy actor Sydney Tafler, went on to enjoy many years of popularity with British film and TV viewers.

My Wife Next Door

UK · BBC · SITCOM

13×30 mins · colour
19 Sep–12 Dec 1972 · BBC1 Tue mostly 8.30pm

MAIN CAST

George Bassett	John Alderton
Suzy Bassett	Hannah Gordon
Henry	Tim Barrett
Suzy's mother	Diana King
George's mother	Mollie Sugden
Liz	Paddy Frost

CREDITS

creators Brian Clemens/Richard Waring · *writer* Richard Waring · *producer* Graeme Muir

An entertaining and worthwhile romantic sitcom given added class by the first-rate lead performers.

Following their divorce, both Suzy and George Bassett head out into the country to start afresh, only to discover, too late, that they have moved into adjoining cottages. The ensuing conflicts and complications kept the series buoyant for 13 episodes, most of them concentrating on George's canny attempts to woo back his wife. Although the variations on the theme woven by writer Richard Waring were ingenious they were not endless, and by the end of the run the idea seemed to have been fully explored. So in spite of winning the Society Of Film And Television award for the year's best sitcom, *My Wife Next Door* did not reappear for a second season.

CBS made two unsuccessful attempts at launching a US adaptation, both using the British title and directed by Bill Persky. The first, written and produced by Persky with Sam Denoff, screened in America on 31 December 1975 and starred James Farentino and Julie Sommers. The second, aired on 11 September 1980, starred Granville Van Dusen and Lee Purcell. This one was written by Dick Clement and Ian La Frenais, who also co-produced with Allan McKeown for Marble Arch Productions.

My Wife's Sister / Our Dora

UK · ITV (GRANADA) · SITCOM

39×30 mins · b/w
18 Sep 1956–11 June 1957 · Tue mostly 8pm
(4 episodes as *Our Dora* · 35 as *My Wife's Sister*)

MAIN CAST

Dora	Dora Bryan (episodes 1–4 only)
Ellie Martin	Eleanor Summerfield (episodes 5–39)
Clara Hackett	Helen Christie
Charlie Hackett	Martin Wyldeck

OTHER APPEARANCES

Mavis	Fanny Carby

CREDITS

writer Reuben Ship · *directors* Milo Lewis (20), Henry Kaplan (16), Guy Nottingham (3) · *producer* Eddie Pola

A long-running Granada sitcom – the first from the new north of England TV franchise which had taken to the air on 3 May 1956 – that was not itself without drama. The series began as *Our Dora*, a vehicle for the stage and screen personality Dora Bryan, but after just four weeks the star suddenly quit, following the death of her first child. With the scripts swiftly amended, the series carried on, without skipping so much as a week, as *My Wife's Sister*, Eleanor Summerfield having been drafted in to replace Bryan. If anything, it enjoyed greater fortune in its second life, many critics comparing *My Wife's Sister* favourably with the imported American comedies of the period – high praise indeed. (There was a North American connection; writer Reuben Ship was Jewish-Canadian and scripted with a noticeable 'American' style.)

The original premise of *Our Dora* cast Bryan as a GI bride, returning to England from America after the unexpected death of her husband. She moves in with her sister Clara (with whom she had once appeared in a theatrical variety act) and her husband Charlie, a no-nonsense businessman who is far from welcoming and would rather not set the home fires burning for his guest. Summerfield filled the same role – whose first name was altered, appropriately enough, to Ellie – and she successfully continued to emphasise the screwball nature of the lead character.

Collectively, the series ran for 39 straight weeks, and when it ended it was immediately replaced by Granada's new service sitcom, **The Army Game**.

My Wonderful Life

UK · ITV (GRANADA) · SITCOM

7 episodes (1×60 mins · 6×30 mins) · colour
Pilot (60 mins) *True Love* 25 Feb 1996 · Sun 8.45pm
One series (6×30 mins) 1 May–5 June 1997 · Thu 8.30pm

MAIN CAST

Donna	Emma Wray
Phil	Philip Glenister
Lawrie	Gary Webster (series)
Roger	Hamish Clark (series)
Marina	Elizabeth Berrington (series)
Alan	Tony Robinson (series)
Rhiannon	Hannah McVeigh (pilot); Amanda Riley (series)
Shirley	Elizabeth Earl (pilot); Vicky Connett (series)

CREDITS

creator Simon Nye · *writers* Simon Nye (3), Amanda Swift (2), Paul Dornan (2) · *directors* Simon Massey (pilot), Sid Roberson (series) · *executive producer* Andy Harries · *producers* Brian Park (pilot), Mark Redhead (series)

Conceived as a one-off comedy-drama, *True Love* contained sufficient promise for a full sitcom series to be commissioned, focusing on the lead character. The writer of the original piece, Simon Nye, was in the USA at the time, adapting **Men Behaving Badly** for American TV, so four episodes of the resulting series, retitled *My Wonderful Life*, were scripted by other writers. (The same arrangement looked certain to apply for a second series too, scheduled for screening from the spring 1998.)

Episodes focused on the plight of Donna, a nurse who has finally managed to oust her useless husband, Phil, and is raising their two children, Rhiannon and Shirley, on her own. But she does have two new men in her life – Lawrie, a sparky ambulance driver, and Roger, a reliable but unexceptional doctor. Donna is torn between the two and, ideally, would like a mixture of them both: Roger's reliability crossed with Lawrie's brashness. Next-door neighbours Marina and her 'new man' husband Alan are also around to lend a helping hand when they can.

My Wonderful Life was an intentionally low-key series, shirking the normal sitcom fallbacks of broad jokes and physical comedy in favour of a gentler, warmer approach, the absence of a studio audience or a 'canned' laugh-track adding to the atmosphere. The series was moderately well received, with Emma Wray (who had made a splash in *Watching* when portraying an equally feisty character) in good form as Donna and Tony Robinson attracting especial kudos for his portrayal of Alan, a muesli-eating, new-age, urban eco-warrior.

Note. The series' planned launch on 3 April 1997 was postponed owing to live soccer coverage.

My World ... And Welcome To It

USA · NBC (SHELDON LEONARD PRODUCTIONS) · SITCOM

26 × 30 mins · colour

US dates: 15 Sep 1969–9 July 1970

*UK dates: 12 Nov 1969–13 May 1970 (26 episodes) BBC2 Wed mostly around 10.30pm

MAIN CAST

John Monroe	William Windom
Ellen Monroe	Joan Hotchkis
Lydia Monroe	Lisa Gerritsen
Hamilton Greeley	Harold J Stone
Philip Jensen	Henry Morgan

CREDITS

creator James Thurber · *writers* various · *directors* various · *executive producer* Sheldon Leonard · *producer* Danny Arnold

A witty and exceptional sitcom that mixed animation, satire and fantasy to good effect in its stories of John Monroe, a cartoonist for *Manhattanite* magazine. The series was based on *drawings, stories, inspirational pieces and things that go bump in the night*, a book by James Thurber (who also created Walter Mitty), and it retained much of the quirky angst that characterised the author's acerbic work. Popular with critics and hailed as a trend-setter by TV viewers who liked to consider themselves more discerning, the

series was cancelled after 26 episodes owing to low ratings.

John Monroe was a stylised version of Thurber (who was a cartoonist for *New Yorker* magazine), with a tendency to escape into a fantasy world (represented in the series as animation) when the real one became too much for him. He was the put-upon partner in his marriage to Ellen, but this was due entirely to his own neuroses rather than any problems presented by his wife. Ellen was devoted to John but showed concern for his generally jaundiced view of life (a downbeat attitude virtually unknown on US TV at the time). Their daughter, Lydia, was ten going on 55 and had her future totally mapped out.

The idea first appeared on US TV ten years before this, as *Christabel* (NBC, 8 June 1959), a segment of *Goodyear Playhouse* that was intended as the pilot episode for a full series, *The Secret Life Of John Monroe*. In this earlier version, which also utilised the device of animation to represent Monroe's fantasy world, Arthur O'Connell played John and Georgann Johnson was cast as Ellen. A second pilot, *The Secret Life Of James Thurber*, again with a similar format, aired in the USA as a segment of *The June Allyson Show* (CBS, 20 March 1961), with Orson Bean as James Thurber. Many years later, a similar idea formed the basis of two CBS sitcoms, *Pen 'n' Inc* (1981) and *The People Next Door* (1989). But none of these attempts matched the wit and charm of *My World ... And Welcome To It*, which remains something of a buried treasure.

*Note. After the BBC2 run in 1969–70, the series was repeated for a wider audience on BBC1. Then, 14 years after it first aired, C4 screened 24 episodes, between 10 September 1983 and 23 September 1987.

N7

UK · BBC · SITCOM

1 × 30 mins · colour

25 Aug 1995 · BBC2 Fri 9.30pm

MAIN CAST

Nick	James Larkin
Craig	John Stratton
Shonagh	Louise Beattie
James	David Westhead
Alvin	Cliff Parisi
Vince	Phil Daniels
Andy	Andrew Lincoln
Brian	Simon Clayton
Denis	Charles McKeown

CREDITS

writer Nick Revell · *director* Angela deChastelai Smith · *executive producer* Susan Belbin

A *Comic Asides* pilot. Nick is a writer going through a bad patch. On the same day that his flat caught fire his girlfriend ran off with a Brazilian toyboy. Now he is staying with friends, Craig and Shonagh, until his place is habitable once again. The only things Nick managed to salvage from the fire were his two potted geraniums, Alvin and Vince, who talk to one another, discussing philosophical issues. Only Nick can hear them talking (although, occasionally, they place suggestions in other human's minds). This one-off episode dealt with Nick's attempts to rebuild his life and find a new girlfriend, helped in the latter quest by Craig and a gay pal, James.

N7 (this being the postal area of Holloway, north London) was a real curio piece. Other writers might have focused their work on the device of the talking geraniums (*à la Mister Ed*), but in Nick Revell's thoughtful script this was merely a diversion, the central theme being a rather low-key look at modern-day single life from the perspective of a downbeat thirty-something male. The result was intriguing rather than amusing but eminently watchable.

The Naked Truth

USA · ABC (BRILLSTEIN-GREY COMMUNICATIONS/ CHRIS THOMPSON PRODUCTIONS/COLUMBIA)

THEN NBC (BRILLSTEIN-GREY COMMUNICATIONS/COLUMBIA) · SITCOM

43 × 30 mins (to 31/12/97 · continuing into 1998) · colour

US dates: 13 Sep 1995 to date

UK dates: 26 June 1996 to date (20 episodes to 31/12/97) C4 various days around 12 midnight

MAIN CAST

Nora Wilde	Téa Leoni
Camilla Dane	Holland Taylor
Nicky Columbus	Jonathan Penner (1995–97)
Stupid Dave	Mark Roberts
Chloe Banks	Amy Ryan
Earl Donner	Jack Blessing (1995–96)
T J	Darryl Sivad (1995–96)
Les	George Wendt (1996–97)
Bradley Crosby	Chris Elliott (from 1997)
Suji	Amy Hill (from 1997)
Jack Sullivan	Tom Verica (from 1997)
Harris Van Doren	Jim Rash (from 1997)

CREDITS

creator Chris Thompson · *writers* Chris Thompson, Paul Lieberstein, Gary Janetti and others · *directors* Peter Bonerz, Michael Lessac, Arlene Sanford and others · *executive producers* Chris Thompson (ABC), Jay Daniel (NBC), Brad Grey, Bernie Brillstein, Maya Forbes · *producer* Nancy Haas

Téa Leoni's previous sitcom, *Flying Blind*, endured a credibility problem because it seemed unlikely that her character – a super-sexy free spirit – would fall for an essentially dull guy, and in *The Naked Truth* there was a similar dilemma. This time she played a smart, Pulitzer Prize-winning photo-journalist, forced by circumstances to whole-heartedly embrace the sleazy world of tabloid journalism by becoming a paparazzo. If you could buy this unlikely premise then the show was a decent reward: a bright, breezy and, at times, surprisingly hard-edged comedy.

Leoni was cast as Nora Wilde, newly divorced from her mega-rich, two-timing husband in a settlement in which, in a moment of reckless pride, she passed up an offer of $1.8m in favour of total freedom. After her initial euphoria dies down she realises that she is penniless and in dire need of a job. Of the 200 periodicals and news-papers she approaches for work, only one replies: *The Weekly Comet*, a downmarket supermarket tabloid in the *National Enquirer* mould. Despite her initial misgivings, Wilde is soon on the *Comet* payroll as a celebrity stalker, slugging it out with the pros for the sleaziest star shots, encouraged all the while by her shameless editor, Camilla Dane, and the veteran photographer Nicky Columbus. And the stars were genuine – real-life celebrities appeared in the series every week, willing to mock their own screen image by appearing in all manner of degrading situations.

These guest appearances were the icing on an already rich cake, but somehow the ingredients didn't quite mix. Perhaps it was the dubious moral tone of the series that prevented it from reaching the dizzy heights, or simply the sight of the uncommonly attractive Leoni undertaking such an unattractive occupation. Whatever the cause, after the first season, and in spite of critical acclaim for the show, ABC were pondering whether to cancel or renew when NBC stepped in and took it from them. The new owners brought in Jay Daniel (from *Moonlighting* and *Roseanne*) as executive producer and he instigated a number of changes, moving Wilde from the sleaze-beat to the agony pages and giving cause for the character to show some compassion. Then George Wendt (Norm in *Cheers*) was added to the cast as the *Comet*'s new boss, an idealist who wanted the paper to move upmarket (much to the annoyance of Camilla). These changes were intended to move the show away from its celebrity base towards a character-comedy, where the interplay between the main protagonists became the main focus.

Naked Video

UK · BBC · SKETCH

30 × 30 mins · colour

Series One (6) 12 May–16 June 1986 · BBC2 Mon 9.30pm

Series Two (6) 16 Apr–21 May 1987 · BBC2 Thu 9pm

Series Three (6) 19 Jan–23 Feb 1989 · BBC2 Thu 9pm

Series Four (6) 29 Sep–3 Nov 1989 · BBC2 Fri 9pm

Series Five (6) 14 Oct–18 Nov 1991 · BBC2 Mon 10pm

MAIN CAST

Gregor Fisher
Andy Gray
Helen Lederer
Tony Roper
Elaine C Smith
Jonathan Watson
Ron Bain (series 1 & 2)
John Sparkes (series 1–3)
Kate Donnelly (series 4)
Louise Beattie (series 5)

CREDITS

writers cast and others · *script editor* Philip Differ · *director* Brian Jobson · *producers* Colin Gilbert (series 1–4), Colin Gilbert/Philip Differ (series 5)

The BBC Radio Scotland series *Naked Radio* proved to be a popular part of the local schedule (it wasn't heard nationally until being given a one-off airing by Radio 4 on 26 April 1982), and in 1985 the cast successfully mounted the show on stage at the Edinburgh Festival Fringe. Radio producer Colin Gilbert realised that the series had the visual potential for television and so *Naked Video* was born, shown on national BBC2.

For this TV version the radio cast was swelled by two Sassenachs, Helen Lederer and John Sparkes, and the result was a fast-moving, irreverent and lively production that featured a number of recurring characters and situations. Gregor Fisher's scatological scallywag Rab C Nesbitt was first unveiled to a national audience here, as was his other invention, the gormless Baldy Man. Lederer performed her own monologues from a wine bar, and John Sparkes appeared as Welsh poet Siadwell (pronounced Shadwell). The series had a creditable run, was never less than entertaining and its influence lasted even longer, with Fisher's characters re-appearing in their own series (*Rab C Nesbitt* and *The Baldy Man*) and Lederer utilising her character in subsequent projects.

See also *Only An Excuse*.

Nanny And The Professor

USA · ABC (20TH CENTURY-FOX TV) · SITCOM

54 × 30 mins · colour

US dates: 21 Jan 1970–27 Dec 1971
UK dates: 7 Apr 1970–23 Feb 1973 (54 episodes) ITV various days and times

MAIN CAST

Phoebe Figalilly · · · · · · · · · · · · · · Juliet Mills
Professor Howard Everett · · · · · Richard Long
Prudence Everett · · · · · · · · · · · Kim Richards
Howard Jr 'Hal' Everett · · · · · David Doremus
Bentley 'Butch' Everett · · · · · · Trent Lehman

CREDITS

creators Thomas L Miller, A J Carothers · writers various · directors various · producers David Gerber, Charles FitzSimmons, Wes McAffe

In keeping with the United States' fascination for all things British that followed the Beatles' cultural breakthrough, *Nanny And The Professor* starred a well-enunciated and pretty young Englishwoman who breezes into the lives of an American family struggling to cope with the departure of their fifth nanny inside a year. Where all others have failed, Phoebe Figalilly – for it is she – brings order and calm to their muddled existence and chaotic personalities. Since Nanny can also talk to their coterie of animals (including sheepdog, goats, rooster and guinea pig) she is, in effect, like Mary Poppins and Doctor Dolittle rolled into one, with perhaps a little bit of Samantha (from *Bewitched*) thrown in. The family were your everyday tragic American sitcom lot – a good-looking widowed professor of maths, Howard Everett, with three rascally offspring: 12-year-old 'Hal', eight-year-old 'Butch', and dear Prudence, five. Together they could flash the whitest teeth you ever did see, especially when Nanny won their hearts, attributing her special powers to 'a little bit of faith and lots of love'.

This was, in other words, a relentlessly nice sitcom, with Juliet Mills – daughter of John, Hayley's older sister – good value in the lead role. Jay Sandrich (later to lend his talents to *The Mary Tyler Moore Show*, *The Bob Newhart Show*, *Soap* and other top US sitcoms) was among the directors, the theme song was sung by Harry Nilsson and all 54 episodes were screened in the UK, with repeats keeping it visible until 1976 (with some seen again in 1988 in ITV's TV-am slot).

Note. All five principal cast members voiced their roles in a one-off hour-length animated version of *Nanny And The Professor*, networked by ABC on 15 September 1973 as a possible prelude to a series that never occurred.

Nanny Knows Best

UK · ITV (GRANADA) · SITCOM

1 × 30 mins · colour

14 Oct 1980 · Tue 7pm

MAIN CAST

Nanny Price · · · · · · · · · · · · · · · · Beryl Reid
Lucinda Botsky · · · · · · · · · · Wanda Ventham
Billy Benson · · · · · · · · · · · · · Peter Bowles
Perry · · · · · · · · · · · · · · · · · Matthew Fryer
Pandora · · · · · · · · · · · Emma Jane Kennedy

CREDITS

writer Anne Valery · director Bob Hird · producer Susi Hush

A single-episode sitcom, never developed further, that starred the great Beryl Reid as a professional nanny, her terms of employment being payment in cash, a 21-inch colour telly, a family holiday in Bognor Regis and a regular newsagent's order of the *News Of The World*, *The Psychic* and (every nanny's source of work) *The Lady*. Nanny duly acquires a new post in the swanky London district of Kensington, looking after the two children of Lucinda Botsky – who think her a witch – and Botsky's live-in partner Billy Benson, a property dealer.

Nat's In The Belfry

UK · BBC · STANDUP

2 × 45 mins · b/w

11 Apr 1956 · Wed 8.45pm
9 May 1956 · Wed 8.45pm

MAIN CAST

Nat Jackley
Marianne Lincoln

CREDITS

deviser/producer Richard Afton · writers David Jenkins (show 1), Marianne Lincoln (show 1), Freddie Robertson (show 2)

Two starring shows for the long-faced, 'rubber-necked' and loose-limbed variety star Nat Jackley, a physical comedian who started out in show business in the 1920s with the

clog-dance troupe the Eight Lancashire Lads (which had once counted Charlie Chaplin among its number). He later invented a vocal comic style in which he appeared to suffer from a strange speech impediment: part lisp, part toffee-stuck-to-the-roof-of-the-mouth.

Jackley was born Nathaniel Jackley-Hirsch, in Sunderland in 1909. His first wife, Marianne Lincoln, with whom, reportedly, he had a stormy relationship, worked with him professionally for a time, and indeed appeared in these two TV specials. He died in September 1988.

Nathaniel Titlark

UK · BBC · SITCOM

10 × 30 mins · b/w

Series One (4) 21 Feb–3 Apr 1956 · fortnightly Tue mostly 9.30pm
Series Two (6) 3 Apr–8 May 1957 · Wed mostly 8.30pm

MAIN CAST

Nathaniel Titlark · · · · · · · · · · · Bernard Miles
Jessie Titlark · · · · · Megs Jenkins (series 1);
· · · · · · · · · · · · · · · Maureen Pryor (series 2)

CREDITS

creator Bernard Miles · writers James Lansdale Hodson (series 1), Bill Naughton (series 2) · producers Adrian Waller (series 1), Andrew Osborn (series 2)

The first TV sitcom role for the great stage and film actor Bernard Miles. It was based on an earthy country character whom he created, Nathaniel Titlark, described as 'a rare combination of poet, peasant, poacher, bird-watcher and connoisseur of fine beer'.

The character was developed by writer James Lansdale Hodson but Hodson died after the first series so Miles collaborated with Bill Naughton for the second. The episodes were set in a village in the Chiltern Hills (north-west of London), allowing Miles ample scope to exercise a country dialect.

The National Theatre Of Brent Presents ...

UK · C4 (ARTIFAX) · BBC · SATIRE

6 editions (3 × 60 mins · 2 × 50 mins · 1 × 50 mins) · colour

1. 18 Jan 1984, *Messiah*, C4 Wed 9pm (60 mins)
2. 13 Nov 1985, *Arthur And Guinevere*, C4 Wed 9pm (60 mins)
3. 20 Nov 1985, *Lawrence Of Arabia*, C4 Wed 9pm (60 mins)
4. 27 Nov 1985, *Dawn Of Man*, C4 Wed 9pm (50 mins)
5. 4 Dec 1985, *Boadicea*, C4 Wed 9pm (50 mins)
6. 9 July 1989, *Revolution!!*, BBC2 Sun 10.15pm (55 mins)

MAIN CAST (PROGRAMMES)
Desmond 'Olivier' Dingle · · · · Patrick Barlow
· (all)
Wallace · · · · · · · · · · · · Jim Broadbent (1 & 6)
Bernard · · · · · · · · · · · · · Robert Austin (2–5)

CREDITS (PROGRAMMES)
writers Patrick Barlow/Jim Broadbent (1), Patrick Barlow/Jude Kelly (2–5), Patrick Barlow/Jim Broadbent/Martin Duncan (6) · directors Geoffrey Sax (1), Jude Kelly/John Stroud (2–5), Jonathan Stedall (6) · executive producer Andrew Snell (1) · producers Jenny Reeks (1), Andrew Snell (2–5), Margaret Windham Heffernan/George Faber (6)

With considerable experience in theatre production, Patrick Barlow turned to standup comedy in the late 1970s, creating characters such as the middle-aged Lancashire housewife Henrietta Sluggett and the dodgy magician Doctor Denis Dugdale. But Barlow's third creation, in 1980, was to become his best known alter ego: Desmond 'Olivier' Dingle, a megalomaniac academic (of sorts) with a rare ability to get to the crux of the planet's pivotal moments and greatest stories and to regurgitate them in severely abbreviated form. Dingle is also the founder/artistic director/chief executive of the National Theatre Of Brent (Brent being the north London area famed by its left-wing council). The beneficiaries of a £250 arts grant, the two-man NTOB – staffed by Dingle and an assistant, either Wallace or Bernard – was launched with a production of *The Charge Of The Light Brigade* in the Piazza at Covent Garden, venue for assorted street entertainers. From here the NTOB moved into theatres, with productions such as *Zulu, The Complete Guide To Sex, The Greatest Story Ever Told* and Wagner's opera *Götterdämmerung* (the *Ring* cycle, truncated to 75 minutes), all performed in their trademark ill-fitting grey suits.

C4 brought the NTOB to television for a one-off special performance of *Messiah* in 1984 and then broadcast four further productions in 1985 under the generic series title *Mighty Moments From World History*. A later programme, *Revolution!!*, was screened by BBC2 during celebrations for the 200th anniversary of the French Revolution, while Barlow stepped out of the Dingle character for the four-part *The True Adventures Of Christopher Columbus*, aired by BBC2 during the 500th anniversary celebrations of Columbus's discovery of America.

Barlow has continued to espouse the theories of Desmond 'Olivier' Dingle by way of books, public lectures, stage-shows and radio series. These have included the eight-part reading of his NTOB book *All The World's A Globe* on BBC Radio 3 (13 May–7 June 1990) and the neatly worded *Desmond Olivier Dingle's Compleat Life And Works Of William Shakespeare By Desmond Olivier Dingle* (six editions on BBC Radio 4,

6 September to 11 October 1995) in which, assisted by Duncan Preston, Barlow condensed the works of the Bard. Back once more with Jim Broadbent, Barlow used the wireless medium to re-enact the life of Christ, *The Greatest Story Ever Told*, broadcast by BBC Radio 4 on 16 December 1996. In 1997, he toured with the NTOB stage-show *The Mysteries Of Sex*.

See also **Cabaret** and The Amnesty Galas (for **The Secret Policeman's Biggest Ball**).

Naught For Thy Comfort

UK · ITV (YORKSHIRE) · SITCOM

1 × 30 mins · colour
10 Mar 1977 · Thu 9pm

MAIN CAST
Richard Burton · · · · · · · · · · · · Roy Kinnear
WITH
Fanny Carby
John Clive
Claire Faulconbridge
Frank Gatliff
Robert Gillespie
Robin Hunter
Edward Kemp
David Rowlands
Alan Freeman (voice only)

CREDITS
writers/associate producers Ray Galton/Alan Simpson · director/producer Ronnie Baxter · executive producer Duncan Wood

A single-episode comedy within Yorkshire's series of *The Galton & Simpson Playhouse*. It starred Roy Kinnear as the unlikely-named Richard Burton, an airline steward who returns home from work to find that his wife has left him, a situation that provokes a variety of reactions from his family and friends.

Kinnear and Claire Faulconbridge had previously appeared together in another Ronnie Baxter-produced Yorkshire TV series, *N.U.T.S.*

Naunton Wayne

UK · BBC · STANDUP

2 editions (1 × 5 mins · 1 × 10 mins) · b/w
24 Nov 1937 · Wed 9pm (5 mins)
23 Aug 1939 · Wed 9.30pm (10 mins)

MAIN CAST
Naunton Wayne

CREDITS
writer Naunton Wayne · producers J Royston Morley (show 1), Philip Bate (show 2)

Born in Glamorganshire in 1901, the comedian Naunton Wayne is best remembered as Caldicott, one half of the cricket-mad duffers **Charters And Caldicott**. A year before first appearing in this guise, he starred solo in a five-minute standup slot on the new and scarcely

available television service. He returned for a second dab two years later, just before transmissions closed down for the duration of the Second World War.

Nearest And Dearest

UK · ITV (GRANADA) · SITCOM

46 episodes (33 × 30 mins · colour; 11 × 30 mins · b/w; 1 × 50 mins · colour; 1 × short special · colour)

Series One (6 × 30 mins · b/w) 15 Aug–19 Sep 1968 · Thu 8pm
Series Two (5 × 30 mins · b/w) 8 July–5 Aug 1969 · Tue 8.30pm
*Series Three (6 × 30 mins · colour) 9 Oct–13 Nov 1969 · Thu 9pm
Special (50 mins · colour) 26 Dec 1969 · Fri 6.10pm
Series Four (5 × 30 mins · colour) 14 May–11 June 1970 · Thu around 7pm
Series Five (8 × 30 mins · colour) 17 Dec 1970–25 Feb 1971 · Thu around 7pm
Series Six (7 × 30 mins · colour) 1 June–20 July 1972 · Thu 9pm
Short special (colour) · part of *All-Star Comedy Carnival* 25 Dec 1972 · Mon 5.45pm
Series Seven (7 × 30 mins · colour) 21 Dec 1972–7 Feb 1973 · Thu around 8.45pm

MAIN CAST
Nellie Pledge · · · · · · · · · · · · · · Hylda Baker
Eli Pledge · · · · · · · · · · · · · · · · · Jimmy Jewel
Lily · Madge Hindle
Walter · · · · · · · · · · · · · · · · · · · Eddie Malin
Stan · · · · · · · · · · · · · · · · · · · Joe Gladwin
Grenville · · · · Freddie Rayner (from series 3)
Bert · · · · · · · · · · · · · · Bert Palmer (series 1)
OTHER APPEARANCES
Joshua Pledge · · · · · · · · · · · · · John Barrett
· · · · · · · · · · · · · · · · · · (first episode only)

CREDITS
creators Vince Powell/Harry Driver · writers Tom Brennand/Roy Bottomley (18 & both specials), John Stevenson (19), Vince Powell/Harry Driver (4), Rex Howard Arundel (1), George Layton/Jonathan Lynn (1), Lew Schwarz (1) · script editors John Stevenson, Lew Schwarz · directors June Howson (series 1 & 2), Bill Podmore (series 3–6 & both specials) · producers Peter Eckersley (series 1–3 & special 1), Bill Podmore (series 4–7 & special 2)

Upon the death of Joshua Pledge, a veteran pickle-magnate, his two unmarried middle-aged-plus children, Nellie and Eli, jointly inherit their father's assets: £9 17s 6d and Pledge's Purer Pickles – the old man's condiment company, with its decrepit factory, ragbag staff, 12 tons of pickled onions, and stores of gherkins, cauliflower and beetroot. Endowed with the responsibility of keeping the concern afloat, the pair are hindered by the fact that they cannot abide each other's company – let alone the company they have to keep – and bicker constantly.

Set in Colne, Lancashire, this North Country comedy was rooted in Blackpool-style humour and worked well because of its strong scripts and the prowess of its two major stars, 4ft 10in battler Hylda Baker (Nellie), complete with her 'He knows, you know' catchphrase and armoury of double entendres and malapropisms, and Jimmy Jewel (Eli), the veteran comic (he had bravely broken his double-act with Ben Warriss in 1967), cast as a leering Lothario who inexplicably manages to pull all the blonde young beauties. (Julie Goodyear, about to take off as brassy Bet Lynch in *Coronation Street*, was one such conquest.)

In the show – and reputedly off-stage too – Baker and Jewel hurled insults at one another with good aim and hilarious regularity. Eli liked a drink (although, in real life, Jewel did not imbibe), being one Pledge who had no wish to sign the pledge; prudish Nellie was untouched by the male hand and seemed determined to stay that way. Nellie and Eli shared a large rambling house and socialised with Pledge's Purer Pickles' foreman, Stan, their cousin Lily and her nervous husband, Walter, who was always rushing to the toilet.

There were two British spin-offs from the series: a summer 1970 *Nearest And Dearest* stage-show at the Grand Theatre in Blackpool, and a 1972 *Nearest And Dearest* feature film (written by Tom Brennand and Roy Bottomley and directed by John Robins for Hammer Films) that starred the usual cast. Quite bizarrely, though, a US TV adaptation of *Nearest And Dearest* was titled *Thicker Than Water*, which happened to have been the name of a 1969 BBC sitcom starring Jimmy Jewel that was otherwise unrelated. The US *Thicker Than Water* (not screened in Britain) starred Julie Harris and Richard Long as Nellie and Ernie Paine, squabbling siblings who run Paine's Pure Pickles at the suggestion of their still-living but aged father, Jonas. The series ran for 13 episodes in 1973, networked by ABC.

*Note. This series was taped in colour but first screened in black and white because ITV still broadcast in monochrome at that time.

See also **Be Soon, Not On Your Nellie** and the combined entry for Jewel and Warriss.

Nearly Departed

USA · NBC (LORIMAR TELEVISION/BASKIN-SHULMAN PRODUCTIONS) · SITCOM

6 × 30 mins · colour

US dates: 10 Apr–1 May 1989 (4 episodes)
UK dates: 11 Oct–20 Dec 1990 (6 episodes)
BBC1 Thu 11.50pm

MAIN CAST

Grant Pritchard · · · · · · · · · · · · · · · · · Eric Idle
Claire Pritchard · · · · · · · Caroline McWilliams
Mike Dooley · · · · · · · · · · · · · · Stuart Pankin
Liz Dooley · · · · · · · · · · · · · · · Wendy Schaal
Derek Dooley · · · · · · · · · · · · · · · Jay Lambert
Grandpa (Jack Garrett) · · · · · · · · · · · · · · ·
· · · · · · · · · · · · · · · · · · Henderson Forsythe

CREDITS

creators John Baskin/Roger Shulman · writers John Baskin/Roger Shulman, Sy Dukane/Denise Moss, Neil Alan Levy · director John Rich · executive producers John Baskin/Roger Shulman · producer Jack Seifert

This modern-day cross between Oscar Wilde's *The Canterville Ghost* and Thorne Smith's *Topper* featured Eric Idle and Caroline McWilliams as Grant and Claire Pritchard. The couple are killed in a car crash and return to their house as ghosts, where they try to adjust to the after-life. Their situation is further exacerbated by the arrival of the Dooley family, the ill-mannered new owners of the Pritchards' elegant home, who commence to 'redesign' the place in a style which the snobbish Grant abhors. As the Dooleys settle into their new home Grant's ire increases, a rage stoked by the fact that Claire likes the new family. Then, much to the Dooleys' chagrin, their Grandpa Jack moves in, having been evicted from his previous home. It transpires that he is the only human who can see and hear the two ghosts, and he becomes their sole link with the terrestrial plain, the three forming a reluctant mutual-help society.

Nearly Departed was very short-lived, snuffed from the US schedules after only four episodes (six had been made to this point). Eric Idle considered the decision premature since the series was improving with each episode; indeed, he contended that the funniest two were the pair that had not yet aired. (All six were shown in the BBC run.) Idle may have had a point – many TV shows need time to settle down – but, on the negative side, *Nearly Departed* was charmless stuff.

Nelson's Column

UK · BBC · SITCOM

12 × 30 mins · colour

Series One (6) 17 Feb–24 Mar 1994 · BBC1 Thu 8pm
Series Two (6) 26 June– 31 July 1995 · BBC1 Mon 8.30pm

MAIN CAST

Gavin Nelson · · · · · · · · John Gordon-Sinclair
Clare · · · · · · · · · · · · · · · · · Sophie Thompson
Mike · · · · · · · · · · · · · · · · · Steven O'Donnell
Jackie · · · · · · · · · · · · · · · · Elizabeth Counsell
Lorraine Wilde · · · · Camille Coduri (series 2)

CREDITS

writer Paul Mayhew-Archer · directors Susan Belbin (series 1), Nick Wood (series 2) · producer Susan Belbin

Following their collaboration on **An Actor's Life For Me**, writer Paul Mayhew-Archer and actor John Gordon-Sinclair teamed again for this commendable series set in a local newspaper office.

The star played Gavin Nelson, a journalist on a small-town rag, *The Weekly Herald*, edited by a devoted career woman, Jackie, who had a tabloid mentality when it came to news reporting. Gavin covered local issues such as noise pollution and neighbourhood disputes, but most of his time was spent pursuing the woman of his dreams (literally), the paper's cub reporter Clare. Such was his affection for her that he even moved into the same house, renting the room adjacent to her's. But although fond of Gavin, Clare was determined not to become involved with anyone at work, and thus the battle-lines were drawn. In between them was the paper's photographer, Mike, and the plots were spiced by the rivalry of the town's other newspaper, *The Courier*. In the second series Gavin moved away from Clare but continued his pursuance, even though his old flame Lorraine also turned up to work at the paper.

The Nesbitts Are Coming

UK · ITV (YORKSHIRE) · SITCOM

6 × 30 mins · colour

17 Apr–22 May 1980 · Thu mostly 9pm

MAIN CAST

Ernie Nesbitt · · · · · · · · · · · · · · Clive Swift
Mrs Nesbitt · · · · · · · · · · · · · Maggie Jones
Marlene Nesbitt · · · · · · · · · Deirdre Costello
Len Nesbitt · · · · · · · · · · · · · · John Price
Tom Nesbitt · · · · · · · · · · · · Christian Rodska
Det-Sgt Arnold Nixon · · · · · · · · · · · Ken Jones
Station-Sgt Billy Machin · · · · · · · Tony Melody
PC Elwyn Harris · · · · · · · · · · · · · John Clive
WPC Kitty Naylor · · · · · · · · · Patsy Rowlands
PC Crowther · · · · · · · · · · · · · · Arthur White

CREDITS

writer Dick Sharples · director/producer Ronnie Baxter

An unusual sitcom that blended dialogue with music especially composed to advance the humour.

The Nesbitts are a family of unruly roving crooks, wandering from northern town to northern town in an open-top van (like a terrifying **Beverly Hillbillies**) to avoid the problems they leave behind and happily cause anew elsewhere. They can't abide the law and people can't abide them, especially local police divisions, who dread the Nesbitts' arrival in their towns, fearing for the crime statistics. The family are a terrible bunch: the patriarchal father, Ernie Nesbitt, has a prison record that's almost as bad as his cough. Mum schemes for the ultimate big crime, son Len swans around in a cowboy hat thinking that he is the next Clint Eastwood, Marlene chases anything in trousers, and Tom is a punk-rocker. Sadly, the officers at the Viaduct Police Station are too inept to make a conviction stick.

The series was very much the creation of Dick Sharples: he not only wrote the scripts but also crafted the song lyrics (put to music composed by Laurie Holloway). Sharples originally created the ghastly family for a two-part story in the BBC1 police drama series *Z Cars* ('The Nesbitts Are Back', screened 1 and 2 May 1967), knowing then that, if seen in a comedic light, they were ripe for further exploitation.

Neutral Policy

see The Montreux Festival

Never A Cross Word

UK · ITV (LWT) · SITCOM

13 episodes (6×45 mins · b/w; 7×30 mins · colour)

Series One (6×45 mins · b/w) 10 Aug/27 Sep–25 Oct 1968 · Fri 8.30pm

Series Two (7×30 mins · colour) 20 Dec 1969–31 Jan 1970 · Sat mostly 7.35pm

MAIN CAST

Ronald Baldock · · · · · · · · · · Paul Daneman
Deirdre Baldock · · · · · · · · Nyree Dawn Porter
· (series 1);
· · · · · · · · · · · · · Barbara Murray (series 2)

CREDITS

writers Donald Churchill (series 1), Michael Pertwee (series 2, one ep with Jack Watling) · *directors/producers* Stuart Allen (series 1), David Askey (series 2)

A good-value sitcom that aired soon after LWT was launched. Very soon after, in fact: the first episode was screened without notice on 10 August 1968 when an ITV dispute caused it to be pulled off the shelf and transmitted instead of another programme. It was then broadcast again in its proper place, seven weeks later, as the opening episode in a six-week run.

The first series of *Never A Cross Word* co-starred Paul Daneman – the Shakespearean actor equally at home with comedy, as in the BBC's *Not In Front Of The Children* – and Nyree Dawn Porter, whose performance as Irene in *The Forsyte Saga* in 1967 had endeared her to the nation. Together, they portrayed a comfortable, middle-class, middle-income couple, no children, living in semi-detached suburbia, he with an important job in a big organisation, she – sexy and scatterbrained – with time on her hands and a talent for getting into scrapes. Everything changed in the second series, however, with a reduced programme length (the idea of the 45-minute ITV sitcom advanced by LWT had not caught on), a different director/producer and new leading lady: Nyree Dawn Porter dropped out and was replaced by Barbara Murray, best known as Lady Wilder in ITV drama series *The Power Game*. Ronald had a better job too, and they lived in a bigger house.

John Alderton snagged the lead role in *Please, Sir!* as a result of his hilarious guest appearance as an asthmatic teacher-cum-lodger, Anthony Deepcut, in the opening episode of the first series. Indeed, there were guest actors in most episodes of *Never A Cross Word*, with Roy Kinnear, Barry Fantoni, Bill Fraser, Hattie Jacques, Charlotte Mitchell, Lana Morris, Kate O'Mara, Jack Watling, June Whitfield, Vic Wise and Pauline Yates among those who popped up.

Never Mind The Horrocks

UK · C4 (HAT TRICK PRODUCTIONS) · SKETCH

1×50 mins · colour

19 Sep 1996 · Thu 10pm

MAIN CAST

Jane Horrocks
Martin Clunes
Rebecca Front
Philip Pope
Mel Giedroyc
David Haig

CREDITS

writers Ian Brown, Mark Burton/John O'Farrell, Andy Hamilton, Graham Linehan/Arthur Mathews, Georgia Pritchett, Steve Punt, Pete Sinclair · *director* John Birkin · *executive producer* Denise O'Donoghue · *producer* Dan Patterson

A one-off special highlighting the versatility of comedy actress Jane Horrocks, who had impressed as Bubble, Edina's scatty secretary, in *Absolutely Fabulous*. Here, she was given the time, material and support to appear in some fine sketches, including spoofs of US breakfast TV and a BBC costume drama. She also pulled off some neatly observed impersonations, including Cilla Black, Marlene Dietrich and, most impressively, Shirley Bassey.

Good though the show was, however, the 50-minute slot perhaps stretched the concept a mite too far.

Never Mind The Quality, Feel The Width

UK · ITV (*ABC · THAMES) · SITCOM

40 episodes (20×30 mins · colour; 18×30 mins · b/w; 1×60 mins · b/w; 1×short special · colour)

*Pilot (60 mins · b/w) 18 Feb 1967 · Sat 10.30pm

*Series One (6×30 mins · b/w) 25 Nov–30 Dec 1967 · Sat mostly 7pm

*Series Two (5×30 mins · b/w) 3 Sep–17 Sep 1968 · Tue around 8.30pm; 6 & 20 Aug 1970 · Tue around 7pm

Special (30 mins · b/w) 26 Dec 1968 · Thu 6.30pm

Series Three (6×30 mins · b/w) 21 Aug–25 Sep 1969 · Thu 9pm

Short special (colour) · part of *All-Star Comedy Carnival* 25 Dec 1969 · Thu 6pm

Series Four (6×30 mins · colour) 25 June–30 July 1970 · Thu mostly 7pm

Series Five (7×30 mins · colour) 15 Dec 1970–26 Jan 1971 · Tue 8.30pm then around 7pm

Series Six (7×30 mins · colour) 3 Aug–14 Sep 1971 · Tue 6.55pm

MAIN CAST

Emmanuel Cohen · · · · · · · · · · John Bluthal
Patrick Kelly · · · · · · · · · · Frank Finlay (pilot);
· · · · · · · · · · · · · · · · · · Joe Lynch (all series)
Rabbi Levy · · · · Christopher Benjamin (pilot);
· · · · · · · · · · · · · · Cyril Shaps (series 1–5)
Father Ryan · · · · · · · · · · Denis Carey (pilot);
· · · · · · · · · · · · · · Eamon Kelly (series 1–5)

OTHER APPEARANCES

Lewtas · · · · · · · · · · · · · · · · · Bernard Spear

CREDITS

writers Vince Powell/Harry Driver (38), Dick Sharples (2) · *directors* Patrick Dromgoole (pilot), Ronnie Baxter (26 & both specials), Stuart Allen (7), Alan Tarrant (4) · *producers* Leonard White (pilot), Ronnie Baxter (26 & both specials), Stuart Allen (7), Alan Tarrant (4)

For 15 years, Irish-Catholic trousermaker Patrick Michael Kevin Aloysius Brendan Kelly has been working for Emmanuel (Manny) Cohen, a Jewish jacketmaker, in their back-street workroom in Whitechapel, in the East End of London. Then the two decide to combine forces and form a partnership, recognising that each requires the other's skill. More than ever before they become argumentative sparring partners, needling each other as well as the cloth, each being incapable of understanding the other's religious beliefs, his patriotism (Cohen is for Israel, Kelly for Ireland) and philosophies about life in general. Rabbi Levy and Father Ryan often visit to separate the quarrelling pair (and while they're at it, order new suits).

Written by Vince Powell and Harry Driver, this was a clever idea for a series: despite their many differences the two main characters need each other, just as a suit-jacket needs a pair of trousers, and vice versa. Powell, a churchgoing Catholic, had been a tailor for a while and once heard an Irishman say the words in the title. Driver, although agnostic, was brought up in a Jewish area of Manchester and had worked for Marks & Spencer. So both were well qualified to write about the twin topics of religion and the rag trade, producing scripts that crackled with good lines yet stopped short of arousing religious controversy. (One episode was shown to the World Council Of Churches as an example of unity and then entered into a religious TV festival, only to be beaten by porky puppets Pinky And Perky – even a rabbi would have to concede that there might have been a message in there somewhere!)

The first screening of *NMTQ* occurred as a single comedy-drama in the *Armchair Theatre* strand, at which point its potential was recognised and a series commissioned. The first episode of the first series reprised the storyline of the *Armchair Theatre* premiere but – with the exception of John Bluthal as Manny Cohen – sported a different cast. During its four-year run a number of guests appeared in single episodes of *NMTQ*, among them Leslie Noyes, Dennis Price, Fred Emney, David Kossoff (appearing as himself), Rupert Davies, Dick Bentley, and Chelsea footballer Peter Osgood. Bernard Stone, David Kelly, Yootha Joyce and Bill Maynard were among the actors supporting the main TV cast in a 1972 *Never Mind The Quality, Feel The Width* feature film, directed by Ronnie Baxter.

*Note. *NMTQ* was originally made by ABC, and was then taken over by the new London ITV franchise, Thames. The second series is particularly curious – ABC produced six episodes but none was screened before the company left the TV business; three were shown soon after Thames took over, and these were erroneously ascribed to the new company in records of the period. Of the remainder, two were screened in August 1970, incorrectly announced as repeats. The one remaining episode ('And A Yarmulka To Match') appears never to have been shown.

Never Say Die   1

UK · ITV (YORKSHIRE) · SITCOM

6 × 30 mins · colour
4 Aug–8 Sep 1970 · Tue 8.30pm

MAIN CAST

Mr Hebden	Reginald Marsh
Mr Oliphant	Patrick Newell
Mr Finucane	Noel Purcell
Corker	Teddy Green
Mr Bridge	Larry Noble
Albert	Wilfrid Brambell
Sister Ringstead	Ken Parry
Poniatowski	Hugh Walters
Nurse Whitethroat	Mary Healey

CREDITS

writer Peter Tinniswood · *director* Derrick Goodwin · *executive producer* John Duncan

Never Say Die – an ideally titled hospital comedy – was the first TV series written by Peter Tinniswood, aged 33 at the time and just beginning to find success as a novelist and playwright. Harking back to his student days as a hospital porter, it was set in the men's ward of a fictitious North Country hospital, the Victoria Memorial, and drew its humour from the disparate variety of patients and their skirmishes with the staff. (Wilfrid Brambell played one of the patients, Albert, the namesake of his *Steptoe And Son* role.)

Never Say Die   2

UK · C4 (HUMPHREY BARCLAY PRODUCTIONS) · SITCOM

6 × 30 mins · colour
16 Nov–21 Dec 1987 · Mon 9.30pm

MAIN CAST

Jenny	Janette Legge
Dorothy	Irene Handl
Sid	Arthur English
Jack	Tommy Eytle
George	Peter Copley
Danny	Nicholas Delve
Connie	Constance Chapman
Muriel	Helena McCarthy
Soozie	Lusha Kellgren
Joan	Margery Mason
Fred	Charlie Chester
Chingascook	Christopher Malcolm
Gajmukhi	Zohra Segal
Mrs Danvers	Carole Hayman
Mr Danvers	Michael Attwell

CREDITS

writer/director Lou Wakefield · *producer* Humphrey Barclay

The Arthur Smuggins block of sheltered flats for nine elderly citizens is appointed a new warden, Jenny, herself desperately in need of a place to rest her head, being a stony-broke single parent with dog and kids in tow. The nine are a zesty bunch, determined to prove that they have plenty of life to live: Jack and Connie get engaged, Dorothy likes to consult a spirit guide (Chingascook) and Muriel instigates a die-in for peace.

While it was good to see the likes of Irene Handl, Constance Chapman, Arthur English, Charlie Chester and Peter Copley again, *Never Say Die* suffered an early death itself, surviving for just one series.

Never Talk To Strangers

UK · ITV (LWT) · SITCOM

1 × 30 mins · b/w
3 May 1969 · Sat 9.20pm

MAIN CAST

Basil	Harry H Corbett
Olive	Rosemary Leach
Landlady	Dorothy Frere

CREDITS

writers Ray Galton/Alan Simpson · *director/producer* David Askey

Another single-episode production in LWT's *The Galton & Simpson Comedy* season. This one paired Harry H Corbett (who attained fame in Galton and Simpson's **Steptoe And Son**) and Rosemary Leach as two lonely people who see in each other the chance of finally securing happiness.

Never The Twain

UK · ITV (THAMES) · SITCOM

67 × 30 mins · colour
Series One (6) 7 Sep–19 Oct 1981 · Mon 8pm
Series Two (6) 7 Sep–12 Oct 1982 · Tue 8pm
Series Three (6) 10 Oct–14 Nov 1983 · Mon 8pm
Series Four (6) 8 Nov–13 Dec 1984 · Thu 8pm
Series Five (6) 8 Jan–12 Feb 1986 · We 8.30pm
Series Six (6) 15 Jan–19 Feb 1987 · Thu mostly 8pm
Series Seven (6) 27 Jan–2 Mar 1988 · Wed 8.30pm
Series Eight (6) 24 Oct–28 Nov 1988 · Mon 8pm
Series Nine (6) 6 Sep–11 Oct 1989 · Wed 7pm
Special · 28 Dec 1989 · Thu 8.30pm
Series Ten (6) 5 Sep–10 Oct 1990 · Wed 7pm
Series Eleven (6) 4 Sep–9 Oct 1991 · Wed 7pm

MAIN CAST

Simon Peel	Donald Sinden
Oliver Smallbridge	Windsor Davies
David Peel	Robin Kermode (series 1–3); Christopher Morris (series 8)
Lyn Smallbridge/ Peel	Julia Watson (series 1–3); Tacy Kneale (series 8)
Ringo	Derek Deadman
Banks	Teddy Turner (series 1–7)
Mrs Sadler	Maria Charles (series 2–7)
Aunt Eleanor	Zara Nutley (series 8–11 & special)

OTHER APPEARANCES

Veronica Barton	Honor Blackman (series 1 & 2)
Dr Brown	Gordon Peters (series 9)

CREDITS

creator Johnnie Mortimer · *writers* Vince Powell (32), Johnnie Mortimer (18), John Kane (12), Brian Platt (2), Dick Hills (2), Peter Tilbury (1) · *directors* Peter Frazer-Jones (series 1–3), Robert Reed (series 4–7), Douglas Argent (series 8), Nick Hurran (series 9 & 10 & special), Anthony Parker (series 11) · *producers* Peter Frazer-Jones (series 1–7), Anthony Parker (series 8–11 & special)

Simon Peel and Oliver Smallbridge contest a bitter rivalry in all that they do. Not only are they next-door neighbours, they are also rivals in the antiques market (formerly business partners, they are now pursuing trade individually). Typifying his character, Peel believes that he deals in the best end of the business, Smallbridge the tatty end.

Like all people in sitcoms who cannot stand the sight of each other, this loathing is manifested in the form of wisecracks rather than undiluted vitriol. Common sense would dictate that the men go their separate ways and never again darken each other's doorstep; a sitcom, however, requires them to remain together and maintain the festering relationship. In the early days of *Never The Twain*, up to series three, this was done by uniting the children of the warring men. Peel is divorced from his wife Stephanie and raising his son David as a single parent. Smallbridge is a widower raising his daughter Lyn. In the opening episode the children astound their respective fathers by revealing that they're having a relationship and intend to marry. (This they did in the last episode of the first series.) When the newly-weds emigrated to Canada (after series three) the writers contrived to have Peel and Smallbridge renew their business partnership, which lasted for three more series. David and Lyn returned from Canada in series seven (with different actors in the roles) having produced a grandson, Martin. The baby, of course, introduced yet another feuding topic: who is the better and more doting grandparent? Hereafter it was left to tried and trusted sitcom diversions to keep the kettle boiling – battles for the attention of women, burglaries in the antique shops, and so on – and the introduction of new characters, like Simon's Aunt Eleanor, who came to live among the men in the town of Deveraux Dale.

This, then, was the nub of *Never The Twain*, each man scoring petty victories over the other, tossing verbal brickbats around if no real bricks were to hand. Ex-public-schoolboy Peel assumed the intellectual high ground, the state-educated Smallbridge, proud of his working-class roots, aimed lower. And yet, there was something special about the series, something that sustained its interest for fully ten years. It may have been the scripts – it is remarkable how the writers (Johnnie Mortimer wrote all of the first two series and most of the eighth, Vince Powell wrote all of the last three series) could invent so many witty put-downs and so many ways for one man to score points over the other, like an infinite version of Stephen Potter's *One-upmanship*. More likely, though, the strength of the series owed to the chemistry between the two leading players. Windsor Davies was building upon the success that came relatively late in his career via his part in *It Ain't Half Hot Mum*. Donald Sinden, the theatrical 'actorrrr' whose plummy voice seemed to increase in 'rrrrichness' and 'rrrresonance' in latter years, had been a hit as the very English butler in *Two's Company*. Indeed, *Never The Twain* was a hit with *all* the Sinden family: Donald's sons Marc and Jeremy appeared in the final programme of the tenth series and his wife Diana had a role in the last episode of all.

New Attitude

USA · ABC (CASTLE ROCK ENTERTAINMENT) · SITCOM

8 × 30 mins · colour

US dates: 8 Aug–7 Sep 1990 (5 episodes)
UK dates: 29 Oct–17 Dec 1990 (8 episodes)
BBC2 Mon mostly 7.05pm

MAIN CAST

Vicky St James	Sheryl Lee Ralph
Yvonne St James	Phyllis Yvonne Stickney
Lamarr	Morris Day
Taylor	Karen Bankhead
Leon	Earl Billings
Irma	Ja'net Dubois
Bebe	Bebe Drake-Massey
Chilly D	Larenz Tate

CREDITS

creator Shelly Garrett · *writers* Jack Elinson, Maiya Williams, Tom Straw, Ralph R Farquhar

Based on a US stage-play – *Beauty Shop*, by Shelly Garrett – this all-black sitcom was set in an inner-city salon, New Attitude, operated by sisters Vicky and Yvonne St James. The two were like chalk and cheese: Vicky was sensible, Yvonne was wild. Apart from their parentage, about the only thing they had in common was the salon, into which they had poured all their money and for which they cared deeply. The business's chief asset was its flamboyant stylist Lamarr, a strutting, macho egotist with ambitions to become a rock star. (He was played by a real-life rock star, Morris Day, who had been in Prince's band, appeared in his two movies *Purple Rain* and *Graffiti Bridge*, and, at this time, had his own band, the Time.)

In the USA the series was snipped from the schedules after only five episodes; in the UK, the eight that had been made prior to cancellation were screened within *DEF II*, the 'yoof' strand on BBC2.

The New Dick Van Dyke Show

USA · CBS (CAVE CREEK ENTERPRISES) · SITCOM

72 × 30 mins · colour

US dates: 18 Sep 1971–2 Sep 1974
UK dates: 8 Oct 1971–4 Aug 1972 (24 episodes)
ITV Fri 6.30pm

MAIN CAST

Dick Preston	Dick Van Dyke
Jenny Preston	Hope Lange
Annie Preston	Angela Powell
Lucas Preston	Michael Shea
Michele 'Mike' Preston	Fannie Flagg (1971–73)
Bernie Davis	Marty Brill (1971–73)
Carol Davis	Nancy Dussault (1971–73)
Ted Atwater	David Doyle (1972–73)
Dennis Whitehead	Barry Gordon (1973–74)
Max Mathias	Dick Van Patten (1973–74)
Margot Brighton	Barbara Rush (1973–74)

CREDITS

creator/writer/producer Carl Reiner · *executive producers* Bernie Orenstein, Saul Turteltaub

Five years after the concluding episode of the truly brilliant sitcom **The Dick Van Dyke Show**, its star and its creator/producer Carl Reiner tried to replicate its success with a revival along similar grounds, which they called (without much originality but typical of US TV) *The New Dick Van Dyke Show*.

Whereas before our man had been TV scriptwriter Rob Petrie now he was TV talk-show host Dick Preston, fronting his own show – *The Dick Preston Show* – at the (fictional) station KXIU-TV in Phoenix, Arizona. And whereas, before, the focus was split between office and home life, now the focus was split between … studio and home life. Once again, Dick had a wife, Jenny, and a young child, Annie. (They also had an older son, Lucas, who was mostly away at college.)

Thankfully, one further old-to-new comparison could also be drawn: this new series, like its predecessor, was good stuff. Not *as* good, of course – it could scarcely have bettered the original – but there were some fine moments. Viewers in Britain saw all 24 episodes of the first US season, so they would have been unaware that, for its third and final season on American TV (1973–74), the scenario radically altered, with Dick and his family upping sticks to Hollywood, where he became the star character, Dr Brad Fairmont, of a daytime hospital soap opera titled *Those Who Care*. Most of the supporting cast changed accordingly.

New Look

UK · ITV (ATV) · SKETCH

11 editions (10 × 60 mins · 1 × 45 mins) · b/w

11 Dec 1958–24 June 1959 · mostly tri-weekly
Thu 9pm

MAIN CAST

Roy Castle
Joe Baker
Jack Douglas
Ronnie Stevens
Gillian Moran
Joyce Blair

OTHER APPEARANCES

Bruce Forsyth

CREDITS

deviser/producer Brian Tesler · *writers* Jimmy Grafton, Alan Fell, Jeremy Lloyd

Aiming to develop fresh young stars for the TV medium, ATV managing director Val Parnell launched *New Look* toward the end of 1958. The talent show idea was far from new, of course; indeed, by this time there were already been many of them on television, their pronounced variety element putting them beyond the scope of this book. *New Look* was different: the focus here was firmly on comedy – so much so, in fact, that rather than have the artists provide their own material, three writers provided all of the scripts.

New Look was undoubtedly an outstanding success – even before it went on air. Two of producer Brian Tesler's earliest signings were Roy Castle, aged 26, and Bruce Forsyth, 30, and the promise they showed in an unscreened pilot edition greatly impressed ATV executives, as a result of which Castle, still unknown, was added to the bill of the 1958 *Royal Variety Show* and Forsyth was appointed the MC of *Val Parnell's Sunday Night At The London Palladium*. Both were surefootedly on their way to stardom (indeed, Forsyth's burgeoning fame took him away from *New Look* after the opening editions). *New Look* also gave the first regular TV exposure to comic double-act Joe Baker, 29, and Jack Douglas, 31, following their small-screen debut on the BBC in January 1954 (they would arguably enjoy greater success as individuals). Of the three women in the show, Joyce Blair was the sister of Lionel, who provided the show's dance direction.

The New Phil Silvers Show

USA · CBS (GLADASYA PRODUCTIONS/UA-TV) · SITCOM

30 × 30 mins · b/w

US dates: 28 Sep 1963–27 June 1964

UK dates: 23 Sep 1964–23 Apr 1965 (25 episodes) ITV mostly Wed 6.30pm

MAIN CAST

Harry Grafton	Phil Silvers
Mr Brink	Stafford Repp
Louise	Elaine Gardner
Mr Osborne	Douglass Dumbrille
Waluska	Herbie Faye
Lester	Jim Shane
Grabowski	Norman Grabowski
Roxy	Pat Renella
Starkey	Steve Mitchell
Audrey	Elena Verdugo
Susan	Sandy Descher
Andy	Ronnie Dapo

CREDITS

writers Ben Starr, Phil Sharp and others · directors Rod Amateau and others · producer Rod Amateau

Four years after **The Phil Silvers Show** – the all-time-great *Sergeant Bilko* series – the star was launched in a second major TV production, called (no prizes for ingenuity) *The New Phil Silvers Show*. In this, Silvers was cast as Harry Grafton, a maintenance fixer and foreman in a Los Angeles factory, Osborne Industries. (The series was taped in Hollywood whereas its forerunner had been recorded in New York.) There were clear similarities between the Grafton and Bilko characters: both were con-artists, both were manipulators and both wanted to beat the system. Grafton operated the Osborne coffee trolley, owned the vending machines and, unknown to all, ran his own business, Grafton Enterprises, from his office. Stafford Repp, as the boss Mr Brink, was the Colonel Hall-type figure of authority who had to be outflanked, and as Bilko had his platoon so Grafton had put-upon factory-floor workers (one of whom was played by Herbie Faye, who had taught Phil Silvers the art of comedy back in 1932 and was cast as Fender in *Bilko*). Evelyn Patrick, Silvers' wife, appeared in occasional episodes, as Mr Osborne's niece.

A few episodes stood out from the crowd as being of near-*Bilko*-like quality but the others were not so good, and it was obvious that everyone was trying too hard to make the show as good as its predecessor – which, of course (as pretty much every sitcom writer has discovered), was nigh on impossible. And there was one fatal flaw in the Grafton make-up: while Bilko was trying to swindle the

system, the government, the US Army, but deep, deep down had a soft centre, Grafton's battles were against honest men: the company boss and his fellow blue-collar workers, and underneath the nastiness was … more nastiness. Soon enough Silvers and the production team were receiving mail from irate viewers wondering why Grafton didn't stop trying to buck industry and do an honest day's work for a decent day's pay.

To side-step the problem, and to resuscitate the already flagging series, it was decided in February 1964 to give Harry Grafton a family background – a widowed sister Audrey and her two children Susan and Andy – the plan being to gradually shift the emphasis away from the factory and on toward domestic issues. But it was to no avail: after just 30 episodes CBS pulled the plug. From here on, Phil Silvers' TV appearances were restricted to guest spots or further attempts to relaunch Bilko in a new guise, such as a CBS pilot, *Eddie*, that aired in the USA on 5 September 1971. In this, Silvers was cast as Eddie Skinner, a patrolman for a Bel Air residential community who liked to manipulate his colleagues for personal gain.

The New Statesman   1

UK · BBC · SITCOM

7 × 30 mins · colour

Pilot · 3 Dec 1984 · BBC2 Mon 8.30pm

One series (6) 12 Sep–17 Oct 1985 · BBC2 Thu 9pm

MAIN CAST

George Vance	Colin Blakely (pilot); Windsor Davies (series)
Enid Vance	Gwen Taylor (pilot); Anna Dawson (series)
Owen Thomas (Owen Vance in the pilot)	Eilian Wyn
Phillip Thomas	Ivor Roberts
Clementine Vance	Madeline Adams (series)
Robert Vance	Sean Chapman (series)

CREDITS

writer Douglas Watkinson · director/producer David Askey

George Vance is the custodian of an agricultural museum near Aylesbury. A fiercely proud Welshman but marooned in England, he nevertheless has a relatively easy life running his exhibition. The situation changes wildly, however, when he inherits an Earldom, entitling him to take a seat in the House of Lords and acceptance into aristocracy. Vance sets out to change the world but events conspire against him, and the life of a blue-blood is revealed to be not as good as it is cracked up to be. But, while irritating and pompous, George has a winning, indomitable spirit that allows him to bounce back from any catastrophe.

The New Statesman   2

UK · ITV (YORKSHIRE); *ITV (ALOMO PRODUCTIONS FOR YORKSHIRE); **BBC; ***BBC (ALOMO PRODUCTIONS) · SITCOM

29 episodes (27 × 30 mins · 1 × 70 mins · 1 × short special) · colour

Series One (7 × 30 mins) 13 Sep–25 Oct 1987 · Sun mostly 10pm

**Short special *Alan B'Stard Closes Down The BBC* · part of Comic Relief 5 Feb 1988 · BBC1 Fri approx 11.50pm

Series Two (7 × 30 mins) 15 Jan–26 Feb 1989 · Sun mostly 10pm

Special (70 mins) *Who Shot Alan B'Stard?* 14 Jan 1990 · Sun 10.05pm

Series Three (6 × 30 mins) 6 Jan–10 Feb 1991 · Sun mostly 9.55pm

*Series Four (6 × 30 mins) 22 Nov – 26 Dec 1992 · mostly Sun 10.05pm

***Special (30 mins) *A B'Stard Exposed* 30 Dec 1994 · BBC1 Fri 10.10pm

MAIN CAST

Alan B'Stard	Rik Mayall
Piers Fletcher-Dervish	Michael Troughton (all but 1994 special)
Sarah B'Stard	Marsha Fitzalan (all but 1994 special)
Beatrice Protheroe	Vivien Heilbron (series 1)
Norman Bormann	Rowena (R R) Cooper (series 1)
Sir Stephen Baxter	John Nettleton (series 1 & 2)
Bob Crippen	Nick Stringer (series 1 & 2)
Geoff Dicquead	Berwick Kaler (series 2 & 1990 special)

OTHER APPEARANCES

Mrs Thatcher	Stephen Nallon (series 1 & 2 & 1990 special)
Mr Speaker	John Carlin (series 1); Victor Lucas (series 2); David Beale (1990 special); Martin Friend (series 3)
Sir Greville McDonald	Terence Alexander (1990 special, series 3 & 4)
Roland Gidleigh-Park	Charles Gray (series 1)

CREDITS

writers Laurence Marks/Maurice Gran · directors Geoffrey Sax (1987–90), Graeme Harper (series 3 & 4), Marcus Mortimer (1994 special) · executive producers David Reynolds (series 2), Michael Pilsworth (series 4) · producers David Reynolds (series 1 & 1990 special), Tony Charles (series 2), Andrew Benson (series 3), Bernard McKenna (series 4), Claire Hinson (1994 special)

It is May 1987 and Alan Beresford B'Stard is elected – at the age of 31 – as the Conservative MP for the North Yorkshire constituency of Haltemprice. His majority, 26,738, is the largest in the House of Commons, a fact not unconnected to the head-on car crash involving his two principal election opponents, the Labour and SDP candidates, who are presently in hospital instead of on the hustings. To prevent the police from revealing that their cars had been tampered with, B'Stard promises to push through

Parliament a bill enabling the boys in blue to pack pistols instead of truncheons. What he doesn't explain is that he can get the weapons for them, wholesale, made from recycled frying pans, and that they may not work very well.

So began one of the best, and certainly the most outrageous, British sitcoms of the late 1980s. While *Yes Minister* draw plaudits for its wittily accurate portrayal of Whitehall machinations, *The New Statesman* bludgeoned and appalled – in the most uproarious of ways. But even as the most unscrupulous, wickedest, greediest, nastiest politician of all time, Alan B'Stard seemed to reflect some truths of 1980s Britain. The phrase 'political sleaze' could have been invented for him but it was carried through into reality by others of his generation.

The New Statesman came about after Rik Mayall, impressed by **Shine On Harvey Moon**, invited writers Marks and Gran to concoct a vehicle for him. As to what type of role of wanted, Mayall later commented, 'I think that selfish, vain people are very, very funny. I wanted to play someone grown up, powerful and a complete and utter bastard.' Marks and Gran did Mayall proud: the spleen of their wit fully vented, they unleashed the most depraved character imaginable, and so brilliantly named too. (B'Stard, as well as being apposite, might have been taken by Marks and Gran from a vintage Cook and Moore sketch, 'Dud And Pete On Sex'.) So rich in ideas was *The New Statesman*, and so fond of the series were Marks and Gran, that it remains their only latter-day creation they have kept entirely to themselves, writing every episode. Created upon their return from an unhappy stint in Hollywood, where Marks and Gran worked for nine months as staff writers for US TV, the first series was so funny that it won an International Emmy Award, while the extended laughs of the studio audience meant that all the programmes overran, and gags had to be cut. From then on, the pair wrote 19-minute scripts, allowing for almost five minutes of laughs per episode. ITV, for its part, screened the series at 10pm on Sunday nights, a tried and trusted slot for its more subversive comedies, which, to 1987, included **Spitting Image, Whoops Apocalypse, Mog, Hot Metal, Room At The Bottom** and **Hale And Pace**.

Mayall was consistently superb as the suave, pin-striped B'Stard, the principal power operator in a system devoid of scruples. Although his personality matched his name he nevertheless exuded a certain boyish charm which allowed him to get away with his more monstrous statements and schemes. In a *Who's Who* entry B'Stard described his recreational activities as 'Making money, Drinking, Driving, Dining out on other people's expenses, Boogying,

Bonking, Droit du Signeur, Grinding the faces of the poor'. As treasurer of the Keep Britain Nuclear pressure group, he was behind the dumping of nuclear waste in a children's playground. Before becoming an MP he was secretary of the Friends of South Africa, a position he resigned in protest at left-wing infiltration of the group; his interests declared in the MPs register (and there were plenty not declared) were chairman/managing director of B'Stard Residential Developments Ltd and director of Advance Missile Systems Ltd. Committees formed by B'Stard usually had the initials CASH, to whom, he insisted, donors should make their cheques payable. He was the ultimate income-tax defrauder.

His marriage, too, was a sham: B'Stard's wife Sarah was as money-motivated as her husband and, despite having lesbian tendencies (she had an affair with B'Stard's political agent, Beatrice) would sleep with anyone (even B'Stard) for her own ends. He married her, of course, purely for her respectability and money, although Roland Gidleigh-Park, her despicable father, from whom she would ultimately inherit everything, hated B'Stard with a vengeance, a feeling mutually expressed. B'Stard and Sarah had one daughter (loyally named Margaret Hilda). B'Stard committed adultery at every turn, charming women with talk of his 'enormous majority', although the fun rarely lasted more than a few seconds.

At work, B'Stard was permanently beastly to Piers Fletcher-Dervish, his parliamentary assistant, a young MP recently elected member for South Wiltshire but decidedly one of the old-school 'upper-class-twit' Conservatives. As Baldrick was to Blackadder so Fletcher-Dervish was a hapless ingredient in B'Stard's devilish schemes and indulgences, a permanent whipping boy who never had the sense to run a mile in the opposite direction. Others became embroiled in B'Stard's evil doings, too. In the first series, B'Stard's political/financial consultant Norman Bormann was slowly revealed to be changing sex, from male to female. (The actor, originally billed as R R Cooper, was eventually credited to her full name, Rowena Cooper.) B'Stard's toughest opponent on the benches was the dour, whining Labour MP Bob Crippen, who was singularly unsuccessful in unmasking B'Stard as the perpetrator of so many immoral practices. B'Stard styled himself as a Thatcherite toyboy, and the Leaderene herself was seen in the series, played by a man, Steve Nallon, also the voice of her latex puppet in *Spitting Image*. Various TV personalities appeared as themselves in *The New Statesman*; additionally, seen in character roles, were Stephen Fry, Hugh Laurie, Helen Lederer, Celia Imrie, Don Henderson and John Sessions, the latter as a cocaine-addicted

peer who was accidentally killed when someone tried to assassinate B'Stard.

A spoof shooting incident at the end of the second series, staged by B'Stard, led to a single 70-minute *Dallas*-like special, *Who Shot Alan B'Stard?*, which combined surrealistic gun footage with the usual political skulduggery. B'Stard, of course, could not be killed off, or silenced. Even when he was held prisoner in a Siberian gulag he managed to orchestrate his release. When he returned to England to find that everything he had ever corrupted for was now lost, including his parliamentary seat, he quickly became a Euro MP, representing the German constituency of Obersaxony. Finally (in a 1994 BBC1 special), B'Stard was interviewed by Brian Walden following his victory in a recent Welsh by-election that had returned him to domestic parliament. (His rivals were found after polling day at the bottom of a coal mine.)

For its first series, authenticity was added to *The New Statesman* by way of a remarkably realistic studio set representing the inside of the House of Commons. (The set had been created by Granada for its dramatisation of Jeffrey Archer's parliamentary novel *First Among Equals*, screened September to December 1986, and was bought by Yorkshire when they heard that it was destined for the scrap heap.) The set was particularly effective because, when *The New Statesman* began, the British electorate was not yet familiar with the inside of their parliament, TV coverage only starting in November 1989. And when such images did begin to prevail on the nightly news bulletins they served only to underline the accuracy of *The New Statesman*'s portrayal of Parliament as a yah-boo playground for spoiled brats. Further realism was guaranteed by the enlisting of Mrs Renee Short, Labour MP for Wolverhampton 1964–87, as political adviser to the writers.

Screened at a time when the Conservative government was free to indulge its whims by virtue of a three-figure parliamentary majority, *The New Statesman* provided a necessary slice of biting satire to British political life. But while, for most, it raised cackles, for others it raised hackles: many MPs were grossly offended at their kind being portrayed in such a gratuitously offensive manner. Teddy Taylor, Conservative member for Southend, commented, in a line worthy of B'Stard himself, 'It was so immature and childish it reminded me of a Neil Kinnock speech'. Right on.

New Who Do You Do?

see *Who Do You Do?*

The Newcomer

UK · BBC · SKETCH

1 × 15 mins · b/w

4 Feb 1950 · Sat 9.10pm

MAIN CAST
Eric Barker
Pearl Hackney
Joe Linnane

CREDITS
producer Richard Afton

A one-off 15 minute sketch for husband-and-wife radio favourites Eric Barker and Pearl Hackney, screened when they were at the height of their popularity.

See also *Merry-Go-Round, The Eric Barker Half-Hour, Look At It This Way* and *Something In The City*.

Newhart

USA · CBS (MTM ENTERPRISES) · SITCOM

184 episodes (183 × 30 mins · 1 × 60 mins) · colour

US dates: 25 Oct 1982–21 May 1990

*UK dates: 27 Jan 1983–30 Jan 1987 (64 × 30 mins · 1 × 60 mins) ITV/C4 various days and times

MAIN CAST
Dick Loudon · · · · · · · · · · · · · · Bob Newhart
Joanna Loudon · · · · · · · · · · · · · Mary Frann
George Utley · · · · · · · · · · · · · · Tom Poston
Michael Harris · · · · Peter Scolari (1984–90)
Stephanie Vanderkellen · · · · · · · · Julia Duffy
· (1983–1990)
Leslie Vanderkellen · · · · · · · Jennifer Holmes
· (1982–83)
Kirk Devane · · Steven Kampmann (1982–84)
First Darryl · · · · · · · · · · · · · Tony Papenfuss
Second Darryl · · · · · · · · · · · · John Voldstad
Larry · · · · · · · · · · · · · · · · William Sanderson

CREDITS
creator/executive producer Barry Kemp · *writers* various · *directors* various · *producer* Sheldon Bull

The Bob Newhart Show (142 episodes, 1972–78) was never networked on UK television. Had it been, British viewers would be familiar with what has long been widely acclaimed as one of the all-time great American sitcoms, in which the star was cast as a psychologist, Bob Hartley, living and working among a cast of wacky characters. For most British people, Bob Newhart is still best known as the self-styled 'button-down' comedian of the early 1960s, who built an international reputation with his standup act, distinguished by hilarious one-sided dialogues like his phone conversation with Sir Walter Raleigh after the latter had discovered tobacco.

Newhart, which premiered in the USA four years after *The Bob Newhart Show*, was screened in the UK. This series – like its predecessor, made by Mary Tyler Moore's company MTM – came about after Newhart stayed at a country inn, observed the comings and goings and realised that there was the makings of a sitcom in there somewhere. Not that *Newhart* was in any sense a *Fawlty Towers Mark II*: the show was not itself about the running of a hotel. (Indeed, the place rarely seemed to accommodate guests.) Rather, as with *The Bob Newhart Show*, the humour was drawn from the star's reactions to the situations and people around him. As Newhart told the *New York Times*, 'The recurring theme is that the person [himself], through no fault of his own, is put in the middle of a situation and forced to sort it out'. And, once again, the series was aimed at a slightly older and perhaps more sophisticated audience than most sitcoms.

This was the premise: Dick Loudon is a happily married man, living in New York, who indulges his passion for American history by buying the Stratford Inn in River City, Vermont, built in 1774. The old place has been dark for years and is in drastic need of renovation, but Dick and his wife Joanna (overcoming her initial reluctance to become a hotelier) knuckle down, refurbish and re-open the inn for business. Dick is the author of *How To* books, such as *How To Make Your Dream Bathroom* and *How To Panel In Hard-To-Reach Places*, and intends to live and work at the inn, broadening his horizon to include novels.

Upon arrival in River City the Loudons encounter the locals, New Englanders set square in their smalltown ways. There is Leslie Vanderkellen, a snootily superior and wealthy university student who becomes a maid at the inn in order to experience everyday life for 'average' people. When Leslie left (it was said that she went to Oxford to continue her studies) she was replaced by her self-obsessed cousin Stephanie. There is the inn's slow-moving janitor, George Utley, whose family have been in employment there for two centuries. There is Kirk Devane, who runs the neighbouring Minuteman Cafe and souvenir store. Kirk is a pathological liar, forever fibbing and then apologising for having done so. Most bizarrely of all, there are three mangy odd-job men, all brothers – Larry, Darryl and, confusingly, another Darryl. Although claiming to be university-educated (again, in England) neither Darryl speaks, not even when they take over the running of the Minuteman Cafe after Kirk has moved in to pastures new. As one of the sanest people around, Dick is approached with all these characters' problems.

Typically for a long-running American sitcom, fresh impetus was introduced mid-run in order to extend the storylines and cast. Dick Loudon hosted a chat-show on a local Vermont TV station which brought him into regular contact with snobbish yuppie producer Michael Harris whose girlfriend was Stephanie Vanderkellen. Later still, after Michael was sacked from the TV station, and after splitting up with Stephanie, they reunited, married, and took up residence at the inn, with Stephanie heavily pregnant.

The concluding episode of *Newhart* is one of the best known half-hours in US TV history. Investing awesome sums of money, Mr Takadachi, a Japanese businessman, buys the whole town of River City so that he can develop it into a golf course. Dick and Joanna won't sell and, in a swift passage of time, viewers see the inn five years on: as a Japanese-styled hotel situated on the 14th fairway of the course. There is a rowdy reunion of local folk from the old days, the two Darryls having married women who never stop talking. Viewers finally hear them speak for the first time when they order their wives 'Quiet!', their brother Larry explaining, 'They never spoke before because nothing ever pissed them off before'. During the re-union Dick is knocked unconscious by a golf ball; when he awakes he is in bed with Emily (his wife in *The Bob Newhart Show*, again played by Suzanne Pleshette) and (now back as Bob Hartley) he tells her about his most extraordinarily realistic dream, in which he had been married to a blonde named Joanna and together they had run a Vermont inn.

*Note. British screenings of *Newhart* began on ITV, which (in the London area, and sometimes under the simplified title *Bob Newhart*) broadcast 21 episodes from 27 January 1983 to 14 June 1984, Thursdays at 10.30pm and then at midnight. The series then switched to C4, which screened 43 half-hours and the one hour-length episode from 9 November 1984 to 30 January 1987 (various days and times). The final episode, despite its fame in the US, has not been seen on British TV.

Newman And Baddiel In Pieces

UK · BBC · STANDUP/SKETCH

7 × 30 mins · colour

One series (7) 27 Sep–25 Oct 1993 · BBC2 Mon 10pm

Special *Newman And Baddiel Christmas In Pieces* 20 Dec 1993 · BBC2 Mon 9pm

MAIN CAST
Rob Newman
David Baddiel

CREDITS
writers Rob Newman/David Baddiel · *director* Babara Jones · *producer* Harry Thompson

With the radio and TV series of *The Mary Whitehouse Experience* (in which they appeared alongside Punt and Dennis), comedy double-act Newman and Baddiel enjoyed a meteoric rise to pop-star-like status, going on to fill massive auditoriums (Wembley Arena, for one) for their live shows. It was as if, single-handedly, they were making true the adage that 'comedy is the new rock and roll'. Inevitably, the pair were also given their own starring TV series.

Whereas *The Mary Whitehouse Experience* had blended traditional comedy ideas with its more radical departures, in *Newman And Baddiel In Pieces* the double-act experimented in a refreshingly new, darker area of comedy. The pair appeared separately in two locations – Baddiel in a flat that he shared with his girlfriend; Newman in a bizarrely palatial set – and from here they delivered monologues that introduced the week's themes and linked the sketches. The solo pieces were quite moody and satirical, eschewing cheap jokes in order to establish a darker comedic framework.

The main theme of each edition was complemented by recurring set-pieces that featured returning characters, especially Newman and Baddiel's old favourites the two history professors – elderly academics who fronted a TV programme titled *History Today* and who drifted away from their subject to indulge in a puerile and infantile name-calling feud, using schoolboy taunts to ridicule one another. The characters had struck a particular chord with younger viewers, at whom the comics also addressed other material, such as a spoof of the MTV show *Unplugged* (wherein musicians and singers perform without electric instrumentation) in which they showed what would happen if the then trendy all-electric bands such as the Orb and Utah Saints performed on the show – an embarrassed silence.

Note. On 13 December 1993 BBC2 presented *Newman And Baddiel On The Road To Wembley*, a documentary (of sorts) that looked at the double-act making their TV series and going on tour, building from a gig in front of 100 fans at Norwich to a massive turn-out at Wembley Arena. A 60-minute tape of the Wembley concert, released on video, was screened by BBC2 on 29 December 1994 as *Newman And Baddiel Live And In Pieces*.

News At Twelve

UK · ITV (CENTRAL) · CHILDREN'S SITCOM

6 × 30 mins · colour

22 Feb–28 Mar 1988 · Mon 4.45pm

MAIN CAST

Kevin Doyle	Ewan Phillips
Doris Doyle	Julia Foster
Arthur Starkey	Patrick Malahide
Iris Swindley	Sheila Fearn
Granny Doyle	Constance Chapman
Wayne Harris	Mark Billingham
Sharon Doyle	Rebecca Lacey
Tina Swindley	Lisa Brice
Liz Wilde	Louise Head
Mr Doyle	Jackie McDee
Harry Patel	Tariq Yunus
Barry Sykes	Richard de Sousa
Gavin Bates	Darren Bastable

CREDITS

writer Francis Sinclair · *director* Alex Kirby · *executive producer* Lewis Rudd · *producer* Pamela Lonsdale

A children's sitcom set in and around the bedroom at 13 Tindale Close, Biddlecombe, wherein, every evening, 12-year-old Kevin Boyle broadcasts an imaginary TV news bulletin to viewers near and far. His news stories tend to focus on local events, and are usually based upon fantasies involving his mother, relatives and schoolfriends.

Most unusually for a British children's sitcom, the format rights to *News At Twelve* were picked up by an American production company, which proceeded to make a pilot for screening there (with the same programme title) by NBC. Produced by Bill Persky, the adaptation starred Danny Gerard as 12-year-old Danny Peterson, but its scheduled airing on 19 August 1991 was postponed at the last moment and it never went out.

Next Of Kin

UK · BBC · SITCOM

22 × 30 mins · colour

Series One (6) 15 May–19 June 1995 · BBC1 Mon 8.30pm

Special · 21 Dec 1995 · BBC1 Thu 8.30pm

Series Two (7) 2 Jan–13 Feb 1996 · BBC1 Tue 8.30pm

Series Three (8) 2 Jan–20 Feb 1997 · BBC1 Thu 8.30pm

MAIN CAST

Maggie Prentice	Penelope Keith
Andrew Prentice	William Gaunt
Georgia Prentice	Ann Gosling
Philip Prentice	Matthew Clarke
Jake Prentice	Jamie Lucraft
Liz	Tracie Bennett (series 1 & 2)
Tom	Mark Powley (series 1 & 2)

CREDITS

writers Jan Etherington/Gavin Petrie · *director/producer* Gareth Gwenlan

Maggie and Andrew Prentice have taken early retirement and are looking forward to spending their last decades sipping good wine and enjoying the fine cuisine and clement climate at their new home in France. But their plans are shelved by the death in a car crash of their estranged son Graham and his humourless wife. As the next of kin, the Prentices become the legal guardians of their three grandchildren, Georgia (13), Graham (11) and Jake (5), and their menagerie of pets. It's a rum do, especially for Maggie who readily admits that she loathes children and was never cut out for motherhood. To make matters worse, the sprogs are essentially miniature versions of their parents, indoctrinated as haters of humankind, virulent anti-smokers and champions of various modern-day concerns: whales, trees,

the environment, sexual politics, and so on. (The original cast was rounded off by the Prentices' house-cleaner, Liz, who has a crush on Tom, a Lothario builder employed by the family.) After the 1995 Christmas special the Prentices officially adopt their young charges.

This was another variation on the elder-couple-unexpectedly-recast-in-the-role-of-parents theme (William Gaunt had trod similar ground in *No Place Like Home*), but laughs were harder to come by in this version, perhaps because the situation seemed so awful, with three children made orphans in a fraction of a second (although the writers did not dwell on this) and Maggie genuinely suffering in her new situation. It was only in latter episodes that the series really clicked, as the premise bedded down and the generation-gap interplay was promoted to the fore.

Nice Day At The Office

UK · BBC · SITCOM

6 × 30 mins · colour

26 Sep–31 Oct 1994 · BBC1 Mon 10.10pm

MAIN CAST

Phil Bachelor	Timothy Spall
Tippit	John Sessions
Janice Troutbeck	Anna Massey
Chris Selwyn	David Haig
Dave Morrison	Brian Pettifer
Lizzie Kershaw	Nicola Stephenson

CREDITS

writers Paul Shearer/Richard Turner · *director* John Kilby · *producer* Stephen McCrum

The petty squabbles, inter-departmental wrangles and complex politics of office life formed the basis for this energetic sitcom that, owing to its colourful language, was screened in a post-watershed slot.

Timothy Spall played the monstrous Phil Bachelor, a swaggering. loud-mouthed lager-lout hopelessly bored by his job and so seeking solace in the bottle and any other outside diversions. His boss was senior manager Chris Selwyn, who constantly attempted to indicate his seniority but was treated disrespectfully by Phil and his co-workers in the data processing department. Those colleagues were: the demure but occasionally acerbic Janice Troutbeck (Anna Massey in her first regular sitcom role); hapless, unambitious Dave Morrison; and young secretary Lizzie Kershaw, who was more interested in finding a boyfriend than in processing data. Also among the regular cast was Tippit, a Scots security guard (played by John Sessions) who was a stickler for rules and gained pleasure by harassing the office staff.

The series had some good moments, and office workers would have recognised plenty of familiar situations in the storylines, but it failed to materialise for a second run.

Nice Time

UK · ITV (GRANADA) · SKETCH

28 × 30 mins · b/w

*Series One (14) 11 Aug–16 Nov 1968 ·
Sun 5pm then Sat around 5.30pm

Series Two (14) 9 Mar–8 June 1969 ·
Sun 5.30pm

MAIN CAST

Kenny Everett
Germaine Greer
Jonathan Routh
Sandra Gough (series 2)

CREDITS

directors Bill Podmore (20), Bill Podmore/
Anton Bowler (8) · *producer* John Birt

A memorably riotous programme that combined anarchic, anything-goes humour with an assortment of archive film and TV clips screened in response to viewers' requests. Originally produced by Granada purely for local consumption, *Nice Time* soon spread to other ITV regions (albeit not all), with viewers delighting in the saucy humour conjured up by the three – then four – presenters. Kenny Everett was already known to millions as the wacky radio DJ, Jonathan Routh ditto as the prankster dodging out from behind the *Candid Camera*, while Germaine Greer, hitherto a lecturer at Warwick University, went on from *Nice Time* to become the best-selling author of *The Female Eunuch* and the nation's most remarked-upon feminist. (How comfortable she was with many of the sexist *Nice Time* jokes is debatable.) Sandra Gough was added to the brew in the 1969 series. John Birt, then a staff producer at Granada, now BBC director-general, was at the helm throughout.

*Note. These dates refer to the London-area screenings; a truer picture of this first series can be gathered by referring to Granada's local transmissions in the north-west of England, where the first 14 editions were broken down into two series: five programmes screened on Fridays from 7 June (the premiere) to 5 July 1968 and nine more on Sundays from 1 September to 3 November 1968.

See Kenny Everett's combined entry for his other TV work.

Nice To See You!

see *The Bruce Forsyth Show*

Nice Work   1

UK · BBC · SKETCH

2 editions (1 × 30 mins · 1 × 50 mins) · b/w

Nice Work 1 Apr 1938 · Fri 3.10pm (30 mins)

If You Can Get It 1 Apr 1938 · Fri 9.10pm
(50 mins)

MAIN CAST

Charles Heslop
The Bashful Boys
Cyril Fletcher
Guy Glover
The Three Romps
The Narkover Gang
Campbell and Rogerson

CREDITS

deviser/producer Cecil Madden

A two-part April Fool's Day special presented either side of the early-evening break in transmissions that operated at the time. Described as 'a crazy programme', the comedy cast was also supplemented by television presenters Leslie Mitchell and Joan Miller.

Nice Work   2

UK · BBC · SITCOM

8 × 30 mins · colour

One series (7) 15 Oct–26 Nov 1980 · BBC1
Wed 8.30pm

Special · 22 Dec 1980 · BBC1
Mon 9.25pm

MAIN CAST

Edwin Thornfield	Edward Woodward
Monica Thornfield	Hilary Tindall
Mr Blundell	John Comer
Frank Lazenby	Aubrey Woods
Granville Walker	Christopher Godwin
Alice Morrison	Amanda Kemp
Robert Thornfield	Russell Lewis

CREDITS

writer Anthony Couch · *producer* Bernard Thompson

Viewers were familiar with seeing Edward Woodward as the tortured assassin in *Callan*, or as the justice-seeking hero of *The Equalizer*, than in comedy roles, but the actor demonstrated his versatility by taking the lead in this series built around the tricky and fraught relationships between management and workers at the British factory of a German-owned kitchen unit manufacturing concern, Hoffman Pressburger.

Woodward was cast as Edwin Thornfield, a labour relations officer whose job it is to keep the peace between the management (in the form of Frank Lazenby, a pompous snob who privately refers to the workers as 'swine') and the workers (represented by an unpleasant and militant, regulation-quoting union shop-steward Mr Blundell). The series also showed Edwin's life at home with his wife Monica (who runs an art gallery) and son Robert.

The screening of a Christmas special probably indicates that the BBC believed the series had the potential to be a long-runner, but it never returned after this, ending after just eight episodes.

'Nicholas Craig'

A more cynical twist on a subject previously explored in Michael Green's book *The Art Of Coarse Acting*, Nicholas Craig was a (hoax) pompous, egotistical, self-absorbed thespian character – a real 'luvvie' who knows how to make a drama out of a drama.

The character was created for a book of 'autobiographical' theatrical memoirs (*I, An Actor*, 1988), and it was only when this was developed into a six-part series of 15-minute readings and performances for BBC Radio 4 (29 April–3 June 1989) that Craig was revealed to be the writer/comic actor Nigel Planer, who created the character in conjunction with fellow writer Christopher Douglas.

Although the mask was gone, Planer continued to enact Craig in a series of spot-on, spoof TV 'mockumentaries' and on stage in *Acting, Acting, Acting*.

Nicholas Craig – The Naked Actor

UK · BBC · SATIRE

6 × 20 mins · colour

22 Nov–27 Dec 1990 · BBC2 Thu 10.10pm

MAIN CAST

Nicholas Craig ············ Nigel Planer

CREDITS

writer Christopher Douglas · *director* Charles Miller · *producer* Caroline Wright

A six-part exploration of the art of acting, fronted by the appallingly affected Craig. Planer's alter ego explained, among other things, the use of props, the importance of rehearsals, how to act for television and the right way to collect awards. So accurate was Planer's impersonation, and so deadly serious was the satire, that some viewers, unaware of the premise, believed they were watching the real thing.

Nicholas Craig's Interview Masterclass

UK · BBC · SATIRE

1 × 15 mins · colour

23 June 1990 · BBC2 Sat 9.40pm

MAIN CAST

Nicholas Craig ············ Nigel Planer

CREDITS

writer Christopher Douglas · *producers* Charles Miller, Caroline Wright

Classical actor Nicholas Craig discusses how to make a successful appearance on a TV chat-show – 'when one finds oneself playing the hardest role of all: oneself'. Cheekily, BBC2 screened this spoof during the interval of its four-hour presentation of the Royal Shakespeare Company's *Othello*.

The Nicholas Craig Masterclass

UK · BBC · SATIRE

5 × 20 mins · colour
12 Mar–16 Apr 1992 · BBC2 Thu 10.10pm

MAIN CAST
Nicholas Craig · · · · · · · · · · · Nigel Planer

CREDITS
writer/director Christopher Douglas · *directors*
Janet Fraser Crook, Christopher Douglas ·
producer Caroline Wright

More top tips from Craig, this time advising
aspiring TV celebrities on how to host TV
travel programmes, cook on camera and
appear on the political programme *Question
Time*.

Nigel Planer was assisted by a changing
cast, including Michael Palin, appearing as
himself, in the travel episode.

Nicholas Craig's Masterpiece Theatre

UK · BBC · SATIRE

1 × 15 mins · colour
31 Aug 1992 · BBC2 Mon 9.30pm

MAIN CAST
Nicholas Craig · · · · · · · · · · · Nigel Planer

CREDITS
writer/director Christopher Douglas

A one-off look at costume drama, screened
as part of BBC2's themed night of atrocious
television, *TV Hell*.

Nick Revell

UK · BBC · STANDUP

1 × 50 mins · colour
24 June 1989 · BBC1 Sat 10.20pm

MAIN CAST
Nick Revell
John Stapleton

CREDITS
writer Nick Revell · *director/producer* John Kaye
Cooper

Born in 1957, in Enfield, north of London,
Nick Revell was another talented newcomer
to emerge during the 'alternative' comedy
boom of the early 1980s. He worked
frequently on BBC radio and as one of the
comedy stage-team Brave New Comedy
before appearing in *Cabaret At The
Jongleurs* and securing this one-off
programme in which to expand his act.
Revell's material at this time, mostly
observational and self-written, allowed him
to shuffle from character to character,
finding humour in showing how different
people react to different situations. (John
Stapleton, who joined the comic here, is a
current-affairs TV presenter.)

For Revell's other TV work see *Friday
Night Live*, *Just For Laughs*,
Paramount City, *Pyjamarama*, *Stand
Up* and *Off The Wall*. He wrote the last of
these, and his writing has also contributed
to programmes made by Dave Allen, Rory
Bremner, Jasper Carrott, the series *Drop The
Dead Donkey* and *Three Of A Kind*, and
the one-off sitcom *N7*.

Nicked At The Bottle

UK · BBC · SITCOM

1 × 30 mins · b/w
16 Nov 1963 · Sat 9.25pm

MAIN CAST
Mossy · · · · · · · · · · · · · · · · · · George Cole
Mrs Emily Trout · · · · · · · · · Margaretta Scott
Mrs Martin · · · · · · · · · · · · · · · · Doris Hare
Jeremy Trout · · · · · · · · · · · · James Villiers
Mr McMurtrie · · · · · · · · · · · Charles Heslop
Samantha Trout · · · · · · · · · Gabriella Licudi

CREDITS
writer Marty Feldman · *producer* Michael Mills

A *Comedy Playhouse* pilot from Marty
Feldman, enlivened by its liberal use of
Yiddish and criminal slang. George Cole was
cast in the lead role, as Mossy, the leading
crooked lawyer in London, advising his client,
Emily Trout, the matriarch of a larcenous
family. Good stuff, but no series developed.

Night Beat News

UK · C4/S4C (WP PRODUCTIONS) · SITCOM

13 × 30 mins · colour
5–25 Mar 1984 · Mon to Thu mostly 5pm

MAIN CAST
Vicky · · · · · · · · · · · · · · · · · · Nia Ceidiog
Monique · · · · · · · · · · · · · · Carys Llywelyn
Simon · · · · · · · · · · · · · · · · · · Dewi Morris
David · · · · · · · · · · · · · · · · · Dyfed Thomas
Owen Lewis · · · · · · · · · · · John Pierce Jones
Greg Phillips · · · · · · · · · · · William Thomas
Freda Phillips · · · · · · · · Christine Pritchard
Emlyn · · · · · · · · · · · · · · · Cadfan Roberts
Gareth · · · · · · · · · · · · · · · · Robin Griffith
Annie Aubrey · · · · · · · · Lowri Anne Richards
Derec Edwards · · · · · · · · · · · · · Wynn Rees
Garfield · · · · · · · · · · · · · · Timothy Bateson
Milwr · · · · · · · · · · · · · · Richard Clay Jones

CREDITS
writer Bill Keenan · *director* Jan Darnley-Smith ·
producer Peter Miller

Written by an American, Bill Keenan, this
was one of the first British 'media' sitcoms
of the age – *Hot Metal* (set in a newspaper
office), *Kit Curran* (radio) and *Drop The
Dead Donkey* (TV news) all followed.

As well as being the title of the series,
Night Beat News was the name of a nightly
TV magazine programme set in the fictitious
Channel 9 station in Wales. It is a place
where everything can and does go wrong,
consistently, and where love blooms, rugby

match and eisteddfod reports go awry, the
advent of computer technology causes strikes,
and more.

Unusually, but appropriately, the series
was screened daily by C4 Mondays to
Thursdays, over three weeks in 1984, with
one final Monday screening rounding off the
13 episodes. The series aired in Wales much
earlier, however, in 1983, for it was made
for S4C (Sianel Pedwar Cymru), C4's Welsh-
language service. The cast was bi-lingual
and each scene was taped twice over, first in
Welsh and then in English.

Night Club

see *Meet The Wife* and The Montreux Festival

Night Court

USA · NBC (WARNER BROS/STARRY NIGHT
PRODUCTIONS) · SITCOM

193 × 30 mins · colour
US dates: 4 Jan 1984–13 Apr 1992
UK dates: 10 Jan–21 Mar 1985 (13 episodes)
BBC1 Thu 11.15pm

MAIN CAST
Judge Harry T Stone · · · · · · · Harry Anderson
Assistant DA Dan Fielding · · · · · · · · · · · · · ·
· John Larroquette
Bailiff 'Bull' Shannon · · · · · · · · · Richard Moll
Bailiff Selma Hacker · · · · · · Selma Diamond
· (1984–85)
Court Officer Rosalind 'Roz' Russell · · · · · · ·
· · · · · · · · · · · · Marsha Warfield (1986–92)
Court Officer Florence Kleiner · · · · · · · · · · ·
· · · · · · · · · · · · · Florence Halop (1985–86)
Court Clerk Lana Wagner · · · · · Karen Austin
· (1984)
Court Clerk Mac Robinson · · · · · · · · · · · · · ·
· · · · · · · · · · · · Charlie Robinson (1984–92)
Public Defender Liz Williams · · · · Paula Kelly
· (1984)
Public Defender Billie Young · · · · Ellen Foley
· (1984–85)
Public Defender Christine Sullivan · · · · · · · ·
· · · · · · · · · · · · · · · · · Markie Post (1985–92)
Stenographer Lisette Hocheiser · · · · · · · · · ·
· · · · · · · · · · · · · · · · · Joleen Lutz (1990–92)
Buddy Ryan · · · · · · · · · John Astin (1990–92)

CREDITS
creator/producer Reinhold Weege · *writers*
Reinhold Weege and others · *directors* James
Burrows and others

A sitcom set in a Manhattan night court. The
creator, Reinhold Weege, had been involved
in *Barney Miller* and, in the pace and
plotting, there was some similarity between
the two series. The main difference between
them was that *Night Court* had an unreal and
sometimes surreal quality that enabled the
style to veer between vaudevillian slapstick
and wacky but sharp dialogue, the production
having something of a dream-like quality to it
which seemed in keeping with its nocturnal
setting. To add to the overall weirdness, the
lead character, Judge Harry Stone, was an

unorthodox man passionately interested in magic and occasionally performing tricks in court. Initially, this flippant behaviour outraged the court officials but gradually most of them came to admire Harry for his essential worthiness and off-centre but effective common-sense attitudes. Many cast changes took place during the show's run but, from 1986, with Markie Post established as Christine Sullivan, Charlie Robinson on the team as Mac, and Marsha Warfield installed as Roz Russell, the mix really worked.

Judge Harry Stone was played by Harry Anderson, who graduated from being a back-street side-show hustler (three-card tricks etc) to a standup act combining comedy and magic. His TV break came when he was invited to make occasional appearances in **Cheers** as Harry, an amiable con-man. The producers of *Night Court* cast Anderson on the strength of those performances, and the role of Harry Stone turned him into a major TV star. The judge's interplay with the other court staff formed the basis of the sitcom. Dan Harding was the sleazy, sex-starved District Attorney who harboured desires for the sexy Christine, although she was more than capable of fending him off; instead, after her marriage failed, she had a brief affair with Harry. The male bailiff was Bull Shannon, a huge, bald, fearsome man whose IQ of 181 was belied by his looks, which made people think of him as an oaf. Court Officer Rosalind 'Roz' Russell was a former air stewardess who quit her job because she couldn't bring herself to kow-tow to rude and unpleasant customers, and instead enjoyed being mean in court.

Night Court failed to make any mark in the UK and so the BBC did not buy in any more episodes after screening an initial 13. But in the USA the series was a monster success. It may have lacked the in-depth characterisation of *Cheers* or the realistic, understated dialogue of *Barney Miller*, but it was another in a long line of polished American ensemble comedies that rarely fail to deliver. When the end came, in 1992, the production crew gave full vent to the whimsical and surreal nature of the show by having Bull kidnapped by aliens and taken to the planet Jupiter. Predictable, *Night Court* was not.

A Night In The Life Of ...

see *The Bruce Forsyth Show*

A Night On Mount Edna

see HUMPHRIES, Barry

Night Stand

USA · SYNDICATED (RC ENTERTAINMENT/BIG TICKET TELEVISION/SPELLING ENTERTAINMENT) · SATIRE

96 × 30 mins · colour
US dates: Sep 1995–Mar 1997
*UK dates: 5 Apr 1997 to date (18 editions to 31/12/97) C5 various days around 4.30am

MAIN CAST
Dick Dietrick · · · · · · · · · · · · · Timothy Stack
Miller · · · · · · · · · · · · · · · · Peter Siragusa

CREDITS
creators/executive producers Paul Abeyta, Peter Kaikko, Timothy Stack · *writers* Timothy Stack, David Morgasen and others · *directors* various · *producers* various

Alternatively titled *Night Stand With Dick Dietrick*, this was an inventive and at times uproariously funny spoof of the sensationalist and sleazy 'real people' confrontational TV shows that became big business in the USA in the 1990s: *Ricki Lake*, *The Jerry Springer Show*, *Sally Jessy Raphael*, *Geraldo* and others. The series' co-creator, former **Saturday Night Live** writer Timothy Stack, starred as the host of *Night Stand*, Dick Dietrick, a hapless, shallow man devoid of any emotional depth, and he was aided by Miller, a general dogsbody who mostly kept behind the scenes. Actors played the volatile guests and the highly reactive speaking audience members.

*Note. C5 screenings varied in length, some of the shows being rather clumsily edited to as little as 15 minutes in order to fit into available late-night slots. The series had much to enjoy, however, and deserved better treatment and more accessible scheduling – as, indeed, it has received on British cable/satellite TV. Typically, on American TV, two half-hour editions were screened back to back, for an hour's viewing.

Nightingales

UK · C4 (ALOMO PRODUCTIONS) · SITCOM
13 × 30 mins · colour
Series One (6) 27 Feb–3 Apr 1990 · Tue 10pm
Series Two (7) 30 Dec 1992–10 Feb 1993 · Wed 10.30pm

MAIN CAST
Carter · · · · · · · · · · · · · · · · · Robert Lindsay
Bell · · · · · · · · · · · · · · · · · · David Threlfall
Sarge · · · · · · · · · · · · · · · · · · James Ellis

OTHER APPEARANCES
Eric 'The Werewolf' Swan · · · · · · · · Ian Sear

CREDITS
writer Paul Makin · *director* Tony Dow · *executive producer* Laurence Marks · *producers* Esta Charkham (series 1), Rosie Bunting (series 2)

In the dizzying heights of a high-rise tower block, three security guards wile away the night shift in a variety of bizarre ways.

Writer Paul Makin had been an important member of the team on a number of Laurence Marks and Maurice Gran comedies, but here he scripted the strangest offering yet from their Alomo company. (Incidentally, they coined the name Alomo Productions to mean

'A Lo [for Laurence] Mo [for Maurice] production'.) *Nightingales* unashamedly did away with the traditional realism of most sitcoms to delight in a fantasy world of its own making. The three security guards were quite at home in this off-centre environment and took most of the surreal happenings in their stride. The eldest member of the trio was Sarge, a friendly, optimistic man with the air of a friendly uncle. He was completely happy with his position – unlike his cohorts, the articulate but frustrated Carter, and the dense and violent Bell. Carter wanted more out of life whereas Bell's disposition was naturally grumpy and easily provoked.

The heavyweight acting talent seemed to relish their parts, which, in all honesty, had more in common with characters from a Pinter play than a sitcom. Indeed, a recurring joke was trio's obsession with this particular playwright. In the course of the two series the topics of conversation embraced a real (albeit friendly) werewolf, a murderous poisoning attempt, both the Pope and Harold Pinter leaving the trio's Christmas party on a tandem and (in the same episode) the failed attempts of our heroes to escape being drawn into a Christmas allegory.

Nightingales was a novel and commendable attempt to create something strikingly different within the sitcom format – · a not wholly successful but brave and worthy effort nonetheless. Surprisingly, given its 'difficult' and dark nature, a US version was mooted. An unaired pilot episode, made in 1992, was written by Tony Sheehan, produced by Allan McKeown, directed by James Burrows and starred the British actor Trevor Eve. Predictably, it failed to find a buyer and no series developed.

Nights

UK · C4 (STEPHENS KERR) · SITCOM
5 × 15 mins · colour
10 Feb–14 Feb 1993 · Wed to Sun mostly 11.05pm

MAIN CAST
Carol · · · · · · · · · · · · · · · · · Lesley Sharp
Bob · · · · · · · · · · · · · · · · · · Nick Hancock

CREDITS
writer Sarah Ann Kennedy · *directors* Cindy Irving, Dominic Brigstocke · *executive producer* Eleanor Stephens · *producer* Jonathan Bairstow

Five short comedies charting the birth, growth and collapse of a romance. The series mixed live action with animation (also created by writer Sarah Ann Kennedy) and the humour arose from the disparity of events as told by the couple with the more accurate versions depicted by the animation.

The shows were screened to bookend C4's *Love Weekend*, three evenings of programmes relating to the theme of love and romance.

The Nightwatchman

UK · C4 (C4) · SATIRE

1 × 50 mins · colour

9 June 1983 · Thu 11.40pm

MAIN CAST

Gerry Arkwright · · · · · · · · · · · · · Keith Allen

CREDITS

director Chris Gage · producer Peter Berry

A single programme, broadcast live on the night of the General Election, 1983, as the results came in. Standup comic Keith Allen – who had previously made *Whatever You Want*, a dangerous topical series for C4 in the network's earliest days – took on the role of Gerry Arkwright, a gay northerner ('my father was gay and his father before him was gay') whose job, as indicated by the title, was to man a building in the dead of night. It was a disused factory and Arkwright, watching the election results as they came in, mused bitterly on democracy and southerners.

9 To 5

USA · ABC (IPC) THEN SYNDICATION (20TH CENTURY-FOX) · SITCOM

118 × 30 mins · colour

US dates: 25 Mar 1982–27 Oct 1983 (33 ABC episodes); Sep 1986–Sep 1988 (85 syndicated episodes)

UK dates: 15 Oct 1982–28 Apr 1984 (21 ABC episodes) ITV mostly Fri 10.30pm; 8 Apr 1988–16 June 1989 (25 syndicated episodes) ITV mostly Fri 2.30pm then 1.30pm

MAIN CAST

Violet Newstead · · · · Rita Moreno (1982–83)
Doralee Rhodes · · · · · · · · Rachel Dennison
Judy Bernly · · · · · · · · · · · · · · Valerie Curtin
Franklin Hart · · · · · · · Jeffrey Tambor (1982);
· · · · · · · · · · · · · · · · Peter Bonerz (1982–83)
Roz Keith · · · · · · · · · Jean Marsh (1982–83)
Harry Nussbaum · · Herb Edelman (1982–83)
Clair · · · · · · · · · · · · Ann Weldon (1982–83)
Michael Henderson · · · George Deloy (1983)
Tommy · · · · · · · · · · · · Tony LaTorra (1983)
Linda Bowman · · · · · · · · · Leah Ayres (1983)
Marsha McMurray Shrimpton · · · · · · · · · · ·
· · · · · · · · · · · · · · · Sally Struthers (1986–88)
William 'Bud' Coleman · · · · · Edward Winter
· (1986–88)
Charmin Cunningham · · · · · · · Dorian Lopinto
· (1986–87)
Morgan · · · · · · · · · · · · Art Evans (1986–88)
Russ Merman · · · · · · Peter Evans (1986–88)
E Nelson Felb · · · Fred Applegate (1987–88)
James · · · · · · · · James Martinez (1986–88)

CREDITS

creator Patricia Resnick · writers various · directors various · producers 1982–83 Jane Fonda, James Komack, Bruce Gilbert; 1986–88 Michael Kagan, Ava Nelson

A series spun-off from the 1980 hit comedy movie of the same name, which starred Jane Fonda, Lily Tomlin and Dolly Parton as top-flight secretaries exasperated by and then exacting revenge on their chauvinistic male

boss. Fonda was the producer of the TV version – initially at least – and briefly appeared on camera in one episode as a security guard, and while the three leading players were all new, Parton's younger sister (by 13 years) Rachel Dennison – similar face and hair but not *quite* so busty – took her role, so a kind of continuity was effected.

The office setting (again, only utilised at first) was Consolidated Companies in Cleveland, Ohio, where tempestuous single-parent Violet (Lily Tomlin in the movie), on the staff for 12 years, is always having to train the new staff but is keen to move on up; Doralee is a kind-natured but crafty country gal; Judy (Jane Fonda in the movie) is a college graduate, impeccably dressed but lacking in smarts. The spineless boss (at first) is Franklin Hart, vice-president of sales for the Midwest, a man who views all the secretaries as lackeys and sex objects. Roz (played by the British actress Jean Marsh, co-creator of and star of *Upstairs, Downstairs*) is his ally in the outer office, snitching on the three principal secretaries. (At first, Hart was played by Jeffrey Tambor, later to appear in **The Larry Sanders Show**.)

Judy left before the start of the second ABC season, in September 1983, and was replaced by a new secretary, Linda, and a new corporate identity: Consolidated Companies of Cleveland was out, American Household Products of New York was in. Actually, there was much turmoil behind the cameras by this time, with cast and crew changes occurring with great rapidity. Sure enough, just four episodes into the second season ABC cancelled. After a lengthy intermission, however, 20th Century-Fox put a new batch of 85 episodes into production for 'first-run syndication'. Whereas the ABC production had been shot on film these new episodes were shot on video, looking far less classy – and being much less funny – than their forebears. Indeed, there was also a significant switch in direction: while the ABC episodes had been a little less feminist in tone than the movie, these syndicated ones ditched the premise altogether, trading simply as an office sitcom. Doralee and Judy were the only ones to remain from the original cast, newly joined by Marsha, a dizzy divorcee. The company name was now Barkley Foods International, and the three mainstays had (in the original sense of the word) a boss apiece.

The 1977 Cambridge Footlights Revue

see The Cambridge Footlights

The 1986 Golden Egg Awards

UK · BBC · OUTTAKES COMEDY

1 × 25 mins · colour

28 Mar 1986 · BBC1 Fri 7.40pm

MAIN CAST

Noel Edmonds
Mike Smith

CREDITS

writers/compilers Julia Knowles/Caroline Thomas · producer Michael Hurll

Growing out of a regular slot on Noel Edmonds' *Late Late Breakfast Show* (79 editions on BBC1, 4 September 1982 to 8 November 1986), the Golden Egg Awards were presented to the perpetrators of foul-ups, Colemanballs (a *Private Eye* name for silly things said on radio and TV), Spoonerisms, pratfalls and other cock-ups caught on camera. In the series, the winner of the most awards had been motor racing TV commentator Murray Walker, famous as the man whose excited declarations that a driver 'cannot lose!' was invariably followed by said driver spectacularly crashing out of a race.

The Nineteenth Hole

see SYKES, Eric

No Appointment Necessary

UK · BBC · SITCOM

7 × 30 mins · colour

10 June–22 July 1977 · BBC1 Fri 8.30pm

MAIN CAST

Alf Butler · · · · · · · · · · · · · · · · · · Roy Kinnear
Penelope Marshall · · · · · · Josephine Tewson
Beryl Armitage · · · · · · · · · · · · · · Avril Angers
Colonel Marshall · · · · · · · · · · Robert Dorning
Sandra · · · · · · · · · · · · · Claire Faulconbridge
Mervyn · · · · · · · · · · · · · · · · · · · Denis Bond

CREDITS

writers Peter Robinson/Hugh Stuckey · producers Douglas Argent (6), Harold Snoad (1)

The likeable comedy actor Roy Kinnear starred here as Alf Butler, a greengrocer who also owns a ladies hairdressing salon. The latter establishment provided the setting for most of the comedy, which arose from Butler's clashes with the women who ran it for him.

No Cure For Cancer

UK/USA · C4 (SHOWTIME/FULL CIRCLE/C4) · STANDUP

1 × 75 mins · colour

US date: 20 Feb 1993

UK date: 3 Feb 1993 · Wed 11.05pm

MAIN CAST

Denis Leary

CREDITS

writer Denis Leary · director Ted Demme · producer Forest Murray

Fuelled by adrenalin, nicotine and sheer anger, the fine American comedian Denis Leary was already known to British

TV audiences from his appearances on *Paramount City*, *London Underground* and in the *Just For Laughs* festival. Here, viewers had a chance to see his blistering one-man show attacking modern-day American living. Stalking the stage like a crazed, chain-smoking tiger, Leary railed against anti-smokers, the National Rifle Association, vegetarians, political correctness, American morals, big-business hypocrisy and John Denver. The award-winning show captured the tongue-in-cheek comedian at full throttle in a hilarious and exhausting performance.

Leary later became even more of a familiar face on British TV via a series of filmed inserts in Jonathan Ross's live variety show *Saturday Zoo* (C4, 16 January–10 April 1993) and in a series of abrasive commercials for Holsten lager.

No Frills

UK · BBC · SITCOM

7 × 30 mins · colour

5 Sep–17 Oct 1988 · BBC1 Mon 8.30pm

MAIN CAST

Molly Bickerstaff · · · · · · · · · · · Kathy Staff
Kate · · · · · · · · · · · · · · · Belinda Sinclair
Suzy · · · · · · · · · · · · · Katherine Schlesinger
Nicky · · · · · · · · · · · · · · · · · Jan Ravens
Grant · · · · · · · · · · · · · · · · Freddie Brooks

CREDITS

writer Janey Preger · director/producer Mandie Fletcher

The recently widowed Molly Bickerstaff moves from Oldham to live in London with her divorced daughter Kate and granddaughter Suzy. Her arrival brings a clash of ideas and cultures, the comedy arising from the continuing conflict.

Critics at the time pointed out that *No Frills* was similar in theme to Simon Brett's BBC radio series *After Henry* (yet to transfer to TV), which also dealt with three generations of women living under the same roof. But this was an unfair accusation: *No Frills* was as much about the north/south divide as it was the generation-gap blues. And it had a harder edge, with the protagonists less well-off than the characters in *After Henry* and beset with darker dilemmas.

Although Kathy Staff took top billing (she was enjoying huge popularity through her portrayal of Nora Batty in *Last Of The Summer Wine*), the series centred as much around Kate, trying to bring up a rebellious 16-year-old daughter while working as an art lecturer and having to deal with a well-meaning but disruptive mother who held what she saw as old-fashioned ideas and values.

No – Honestly

UK · ITV (LWT) · SITCOM

13 × 30 mins · colour

4 Oct 1974–5 Jan 1975 · Fri 8.30pm then Sun mostly 9.45pm

MAIN CAST

Charles Danby · · · · · · · · · · · · John Alderton
Clara Burrell/Danby · · · · · · · Pauline Collins

CREDITS

writers Terence Brady/Charlotte Bingham · directors David Askey (12), Bill Turner (1) · producer Humphrey Barclay

Charles Danby, affectionately known as C D (also short for Clever Drawers), is an orphan-turned-actor of irregular employ who meets Clara – a debutante of ennobled parentage – at a Hampstead party. They begin a relationship and then (halfway through the series) marry, the final episode marking their first anniversary.

But this is only half of the story of *No – Honestly*, for the premise of the series was that all of this took place ten years ago, and each episode was seen in a flashback to those earlier, unsteady times, when the couple were not only younger but much more innocent. Consequently, each programme opened and closed with C D and Clara sitting together, in the present, talking directly to the viewer as they cast their fond look back. By this time, a decade on, she has become a successful author of children's books about a character named Ollie the Otter (odd, considering that she is prone to malapropisms) and he is an actor of thankfully steadier employ.

Appropriately enough, the series starred real-life husband and wife John Alderton and Pauline Collins and was written by spousal-team Terence Brady and Charlotte Bingham – she being the daughter of a Lord and Lady. The series was based on the second volume of Bingham's autobiography, *Coronet Among The Grass*, published in 1972.

Lynsey de Paul wrote and sang the *No – Honestly* theme tune, which became a hit single. There was also an attempt to sell an adaptation of *No – Honestly* to American television: a pilot was made by CBS in 1987, never aired or developed, which depicted Charles and Clara, their surname now Douglas, he being an orphan from the Bronx, she being educated at the finest US schools.

See also the sequel, *Yes – Honestly*.

No Job For A Lady

UK · ITV (THAMES) · SITCOM

18 × 30 mins · colour

Series One (6) 7 Feb–14 Mar 1990 · Wed 8pm
Series Two (6) 7 Jan–11 Feb 1991 · Mon 9pm
Series Three (6) 6 Jan–10 Feb 1992 · Mon 8pm

MAIN CAST

Jean Price · · · · · · · · · · · · · Penelope Keith
Godfrey Eagan · · George Baker (series 1 & 2)
Geoff Price · · · · · · · · · · · · · Mark Kingston
Norman (Whip) · · · · · · · · · · Garfield Morgan
Ken Miller · · · · · · · · · · · · · · · Paul Young
Freddy · · · · · · · · · · · · · · · Brogden Miller
Policeman · · · · · Nigel Humphreys (series 1)
Tim · · · · · · · · · · · · Jonathan Dow (series 1)
Mark · · · · · · · · · · · · · Paul Rattigan (series 2)
Harry · · · · · · Nigel Humphreys (series 2 & 3)
Richard · · · · · · · Michael Cochrane (series 3)

CREDITS

writer Alex Shearer · director/producer John Howard Davies

Another Thames sitcom for Penelope Keith, cast this time as a newly elected Labour MP, Jean Price, making her first footings inside the House of Parliament and rapidly becoming immersed in the world of whips, leaks, committees, speeches and cold shoulders. Life was far from glamorous for this peoples' representative. As the MP for an inner-city seat she was extensively lobbied by her constituents and as a woman she also had to hold down three other positions: mother to her children, wife to her husband Geoff and running the family home. *No Job For A Lady* was an apt title – at this time there were only 42 women MPs, despite (or perhaps because of) the presence of a female prime minister throughout the 1980s.

The series focused mostly on parliamentary activities outside the main chamber – the interior was not seen, a ploy that must have helped keep the budget down – with most of the action taking place inside Jean Price's office (which she shared with Scots colleague Ken Miller), in the lobby and in the various Westminster lounges. Representing 'the caring face of politics', Price was an idiosyncratic soul, her rebellious tendencies ensuring that her political friends and foes were sometimes indistinguishable. Her most recognisable opponent (in the first two series only) was Tory MP Godfrey Eagan (played by George Baker).

While nowhere near as good as the majestic *Yes Minister*, the series was well crafted by Alex Shearer. The writer did not have Penelope Keith in mind for the lead role but Thames continued to see her as their sitcom saviour, and again teamed her with director/producer John Howard Davies, with whom she had worked on *The Good Life* and *Executive Stress*. The threesome of Keith, Shearer and Davies then reunited in 1994 for *Law And Disorder*.

No Peace On The Western Front

UK · BBC · SITCOM

1 × 30 mins · colour

30 Aug 1972 · BBC1 Wed 9.25pm

MAIN CAST

Fritz von Scharngnau · · · · · · Warren Mitchell
Jock MacMillan · · · · · · · · · · · Ronald Fraser

CREDITS

writer Denis Pitts · *producer* Dennis Main Wilson

A *Comedy Special* one-off that focused on a meeting between two opposing soldiers: a Prussian private and a Glaswegian Seaforth Highlander, at the Somme in 1916.

No Place Like Home

UK · BBC · SITCOM

43 × 30 mins · colour

Series One (6) 13 Dec 1983–24 Jan 1984 · BBC1 Tue 7.40pm

Series Two (8) 12 Sep–31 Oct 1984 · BBC1 Wed 8pm

Special · 26 Dec 1984 · BBC1 Wed 5.50pm

Series Three (13) 8 Jan–23 Apr 1986 · BBC1 Wed 7.40pm

Series Four (7) 14 Oct–25 Nov 1986 · BBC1 Tue 8pm

Series Five (7) 8 Sep–20 Oct 1987 · BBC1 Tue 7pm

Special · 22 Dec 1987 · BBC1 Tue 7pm

MAIN CAST

Arthur Crabtree · · · · · · · · · · · William Gaunt
Beryl Crabtree · · · · · · · · · · Patricia Garwood
Nigel Crabtree · · Martin Clunes (series 1–3);
· · · · · Andrew Charleson (series 4 onwards)
Tracy Crabtree · · · · · · · · · · · · Dee Sadler
Paul Crabtree · · · · · · · · · · Stephen Watson
· (series 1–4)
Lorraine Codd · · · · · · · · · · Beverley Adams
Raymond Codd · · · · · · · · · · · · · Daniel Hill
Vera Botting · · · Marcia Warren (series 1–4);
· · · · · · · · · · Ann Penfold (series 5 onwards)
Trevor Botting · · · · · · Michael Sharvell-Martin
Baby Timothy · · David Strange (series 2 & 3)

CREDITS

writer Jon Watkins (John E Watkins) · *directors* Robin Nash (30), Susan Belbin (8), Martin Shardlow (5) · *producer* Robin Nash

When Arthur and Beryl Crabtree marry off their daughter Lorraine they are finally free of children, their three other offspring having already flown the nest. But their blissful liberty is short-lived because, almost immediately, financial and other crises cause Nigel, Tracy and Paul to move back home; soon afterwards, Lorraine has marital problems and she too returns. Her dolt of a husband, Raymond, desperate to patch things up, then becomes a regular visitor, as do the Crabtrees' neighbours Vera and Trevor Botting, so every last scrap of peace and tranquillity well and truly vanishes from Arthur and Beryl's lives. Their offspring interfere constantly and the house degenerates into chaos, with unsuitable suitors calling around and marital unrest, unemployment, dubious behaviour and indolence being par for the course.

A steady if unspectacular series, *No Place Like Home* starred William Gaunt and Patricia Garwood in the lead roles, and (in the first three series) future **Men Behaving**

Badly star Martin Clunes (cast as Nigel). The actor Stephen Watson (who played Paul) died, aged 24, while on his honeymoon in Spain, just before the fourth series was screened but after most of the episodes had been recorded.

Note. The writing credit for the final eight episodes changed from Jon Watkins to John E Watkins.

No Problem!

UK · C4 (LWT) · SITCOM

27 × 30 mins · colour

Series One (10) 7 Jan–11 Mar 1983 · Fri 9pm then 9.30pm

Series Two (11) 14 Jan–31 Mar 1984 · Sat 7pm then 6pm

Series Three (6) 27 Apr–1 June 1985 · Sat 6.30pm

MAIN CAST

Toshiba · · · · · · · · · · · · · · Chris Tummings
Angel · · · · · · · · · · · · · · · · · · · Janet Kay
Bellamy · · · · · · · · · · · Victor Romero Evans
Sensimilia · · · · · · · · · · · · · · Judith Jacob
Beast · · · · · · · · · · · · · · Malcolm Frederick
Terri · · · · · · · · · · · · · · · Shope Shodeinde
Susannah · · · · · · · Sarah Lam (series 1 & 2)
Melba · · · · · · · · · · · · · · · · Angela Wynter

OTHER APPEARANCES

Isaiah · · · · · · · · · · · Alan Igbon (series 1 & 2)

CREDITS

writers Mustapha Matura/Farrukh Dhondy (26), Carol Williams (1) · *directors* Nic Phillips (14), Nic Phillips/Charlie Hanson (1), Michael Dolenz (6), Graham C Williams (6) · *producers* Charlie Hanson (26), Charlie Hanson/Michael Dolenz (1)

No Problem! was not only the first British-made sitcom on C4 but also the first black-made sitcom created for British TV. (The only preceding example, **The Fosters**, was a UK adaptation of an American series.) The cast were members of the Black Theatre Co-operative, which staged plays in and around London in the early 1980s. Unbeknown to them, LWT's Head of Comedy Humphrey Barclay had been along to see many (if not all) of the BTC events and he duly commissioned the series, financing a four-week drama-and-writing workshop in which writing ideas and acting talent could be assessed. Co-writer Farrukh Dhondy – born in India, university-educated in England and the author of five BBC1 plays later in 1983, the first drama series about British-Asian life – became co-writer of *No Problem!* with Mustapha Matura.

The idea was *not* to make *No Problem!* into a vehicle for racial complaint but to make the programme as funny as possible. This did not suit various black causes which actively came to dislike the series and criticised its lack of a 'stance'.

No Problem! drew its comedy in ensemble fashion. Set in a council house in Willesden Green, north London, episodes focused on the young-adult Powell children, whose parents

(never seen) have returned to Jamaica, leaving their offspring to fend for themselves. Terri is hoping to become established as a model; her boyfriend, Beast, opens a night-club; Toshiba runs a pirate radio station (Radio Runnings) and later releases his own hit record; Melba is their cousin, visiting from Jamaica; and so on. Even if *No Problem!* was not radical, black culture was embraced from first to last, right through to the reggae band Aswad appearing in the final episode. The series ended, incidentally, when Farrukh Dhondy, in a feat of great integrity, was appointed Commissioning Editor of Multicultural Programmes at C4 and axed his own show. He returned in July 1985 with **Tandoori Nights**, however.

Note. The principal cast of *No Problem!* – Chris Tummings, Janet Kay, Victor Romero Evans, Judith Jacob, Malcolm Frederick and Shope Shodeinde – turned up together in C4's 1983/84 New Year's Eve hour-long special *Party At The Palace*, performing especially written material in character. Romero Evans was also appearing regularly at this time on C4's magazine programme *Black On Black*.

No Soap, Radio

USA · ABC (ALAN LANDSBURGH PRODUCTIONS) · SITCOM

* 5 × 30 mins · colour

US dates: 15 Apr–13 May 1982

UK dates: 10 May–7 June 1983 (5 episodes) · BBC2 Thu 9.25pm

MAIN CAST

Roger · · · · · · · · · · · · · · · · Steve Guttenberg
Karen · · · · · · · · · · · · · · · · · Hillary Bailey
Mr Plitzky · · · · · · · · · · · · · · · · · Bill Dana
Mrs Belmont · · · · · · · · · · · · · · · Fran Ryan
Morris · · · · · · · · · · · · · · · · · Jerry Maren
Tuttle · · · · · · · · · · · · · · · · Stuart Pankin
Sharon · · · · · · · Brianne Leary (first episode)

CREDITS

writers Les Alexander, Dick Smith, Ron Richards, Michael Jacobs · *directors* John Robins, Charles W Hobin, Bill Hobin · *producers* Les Alexander, Dick Smith

Seemingly an American attempt to cross **Fawlty Towers** with **Monty Python's Flying Circus**, this deliberately zany series was set (loosely) around the seedy Pelican Hotel in Atlantic City. Visual gags abounded, usually unconnected to the storyline – the hotel elevator opened its doors to various different locations: Miami Beach, a student protest in San Francisco, and so on; when people walked into rooms they found themselves in woods and other strange places; and even if they managed to stay in the hotel they might suddenly encounter a Western gunslinger or be pursued by a man-eating chair. All of these phenomena went unremarked upon by the hotel staff: the manager Roger, his assistant Karen, the house detective Tuttle, and others.

The actor Steve Guttenberg, cast as Roger, went on to forge a successful career in crazy comedy movies (the *Police Academy* films, *3 Men And A Baby* and many others) but his likeable presence was not enough to prevent *No Soap, Radio* from being cancelled by ABC after just five outings; while the series was an ambitious attempt at creating something out of the ordinary, such experiments are difficult to maintain in the hothouse atmosphere of US primetime TV, where immediate success and the blessing of advertisers is usually the key to survival.

*Note. Although only five episodes aired, 13 were made.

No Strings 1

UK · BBC · SITCOM

7 × 30 mins · colour

Pilot · 16 Apr 1974 · BBC1 Tue 8.30pm

One series (6) 4 Oct–8 Nov 1974 · BBC1 Fri 7.45pm

MAIN CAST

Leonora	Rita Tushingham
Derek	Keith Barron

CREDITS

writer Carla Lane · *producers* Roger Race (pilot), John Howard Davies (series)

When Derek advertises for a flatmate he gets more than he bargained for: Leonora, who, albeit unintentionally, disrupts his life in a major way.

Carla Lane's comedy made the successful transition from *Comedy Playhouse* pilot to full series with this direct but amiable premise. Rita Tushingham was cast as the lonely Leonora, whose quirky charm was bound, eventually, to creep through Derek's defences.

No Strings 2

UK · ITV (YORKSHIRE) · SITCOM

7 × 30 mins · colour

12 Apr–31 May 1989 · Wed 8.30pm

MAIN CAST

Sam Jessop	Edward Petherbridge
Rosie Tindall	Jean Marsh
Sally Tindall	Amanda Waring
Joe Jessop	John McAndrew
Nick Jessop	Graham McGrath
Grandad	Robert Fyfe
Sonia	Alison Bettles
Darren	Sam Smart

CREDITS

writer Jan Butlin · *director/producer* Ronnie Baxter

Seven episodes of love, sex and infidelity in suburbia. A man, Sam, and a woman, Rosie, meet in unusual circumstances: his wife is having an affair with her husband, leaving the spouses devastated, hurt and lonely. When the two chance to meet they find that

their partners' fraternising is not all that they have in common, and a relationship slowly develops, along with other mid-life crises. A schoolteacher, Sam already has two sons, Joe and Nick. Rosie has a daughter, Sally. The three offspring added the usual complications.

Working on the premise that some of the best sitcoms feature actors rather than comedians, *No Strings* cast a heavyweight pair in the lead roles, Edward Petherbridge and Jean Marsh, both more familiar with straight drama. This was Marsh's first regular part in a British TV series since her role in the series she co-created, *Upstairs, Downstairs* (although she was also seen in Britain in the US sitcom *9 To 5*). A similar theme was explored in the later BBC sitcom *Ain't Misbehavin'*.

No Sweat

UK · BBC (INITIAL FILM AND TELEVISION/BMG ENTERTAINMENT INTERNATIONAL) · CHILDREN'S SITCOM

9 × 25 mins · colour

3 Apr–29 May 1997 · BBC1 Thu 5.10pm

MAIN CAST

Jimmy Osman	James Hurst
Greg Fuggle	Lee Otter
Miles Smith-Jones	Tom Lowe
Giles Beamish	Sam Chapman
Bev Osman	Harriet Thorpe
Jassy Pinkerton	Scarlett Strallen
Lucy Shaw	Keisha Atwell
Teacher	Peter Corey
Janis	Gemma McCluskie
Carly	Jessica Meyer
Romey Pinkerton	Georgia Neville
Jason 'Belch' Belcher	Daniel Smith
Greebo	Stefan Wectawek
Colin Crabbe	Michael Hobbs

CREDITS

writer Roy Apps · *director* Alex Kirby · *executive producers* Christopher Pilkington, Malcolm Gerrie · *producer* Esta Charkham

All-boy pop group North And South (Hurst, Otter, Lowe and Chapman) starred in this stirring sitcom charting the rise to fame of a school band called, er, North And South.

Hurst played Jimmy Osman (a name dangerously similar to Jimmy Osmond), a green-haired lad who arrives in Brighton having left his previous school after an incident that involved his teacher, a concrete mixer and a lorry-load of Cadbury's Flake. Osman enrols at Peabody School and makes friends with Greg Fuddle, a hapless but genial youngster. He also encounters the local bully, Janis, a diminutive girl with a mean streak, and her gormless sidekick Carly. The girls terrorise Jimmy and Greg, who, as a consequence, have to expend much energy dodging them. Jimmy convinces Greg that they should form a rock band and so become overnight millionaires with fast cars and

access to pretty young women. Greg falls in with the plan and the two then try to recruit a pair of beautiful but stuck-up girls from rival St Ethelburga's School – Jassy (played by Scarlett Stratten, the niece of singer/actress Bonnie Langford) and Lucy – to sing with the band. While they struggle to persuade the girls, two posh St Ethelburga boys, Miles and Giles, form their own group Doctor B, in direct competition to North And South. *No Sweat*, a serial comedy, followed the struggles of Jimmy and Greg to overcome their friendly rivals, escape the clutches of Janis and Carly (and lesser bullies Belcher and Greebo) and achieve fame and fortune. Further complications came from Jimmy's overbearing mother, Bev, who, although supportive of the band, was adamant that her son should have nothing to do with the girls.

No Sweat was an energetic production with good performances from its young leads, although it was flawed slightly by the nature of some of the comedy – the story was intriguing enough without some of the more imposing moments of slapstick and verbal japery. Moreover, episodes ought to have carried a caveat: BMG Entertainment's financial stake in the series (and the involvement of pop TV producer Malcolm Gerrie) indicates that *No Sweat* was designed not just to entertain TV viewers but to sell records and, thus it was hoped, create a cross-media marketing phenomenon. It worked: the band scored an immediate top ten single, made videos and went on tour, events captured in a documentary, *No Sweat Christmas Special*, screened by BBC1 on 26 December 1997. A second series was being made as this book was completed, for screening in spring 1998.

No – That's Me Over Here!

UK · ITV (REDIFFUSION · *LWT) · SITCOM

25 × 30 mins (13 × colour · 12 × b/w)

Series One (6 × b/w) 14 Nov–19 Dec 1967 · Tue mostly 8.30pm

Series Two (6 × b/w) 15 May–17 June 1968 · mostly Wed 9pm

*Series Three (13 × colour) 12 Sep–5 Dec 1970 · Sat 6.45pm then 7pm

MAIN CAST

Ronnie	Ronnie Corbett
Laura	Rosemary Leach
Henry	Henry McGee
Secretary	Jill Mai Meredith
The boss	Ivor Dean

CREDITS

writers Barry Cryer/Graham Chapman/Eric Idle (series 1), Barry Cryer/Graham Chapman (series 2 & 3) · *directors* Mark Stuart, Ronald Fouracre (series 3) · *executive producer* David Frost · *producers* Bill Hitchcock/Marty Feldman (series 1), Bill Hitchcock (series 2 & 3)

In a position of some power within London ITV – both Rediffusion and its successor LWT – David Frost was consistent in his promotion of the three comedic talents who had helped elevate his BBC series **The Frost Report**, serving as executive producer on **At Last The 1948 Show** (starring John Cleese and others), **The Ronnie Barker Playhouse** and this, the first starring vehicle on TV for Ronnie Corbett, *No – That's Me Over Here!*

Corbett appeared as a little man (what else?) who thinks big thoughts and will do anything to improve his status. Dressed sharply in his pin-striped suit, bowler hat, and with his briefcase, umbrella and copy of *The Times*, Ronnie commutes from suburbia into work each day on the train, together with his sniffy neighbour Henry (McGee) who also works at the same place and for whom the term 'office politics' might have been invented. Barry Cryer, together with future Pythons Graham Chapman and Eric Idle, wrote the first series, Chapman and Cryer (along with Tim Brooke-Taylor) appearing in its final episode. Idle dropped out at this point and, after a second run, the programme lay dormant when Rediffusion lost its franchise. Two years later, however, LWT gave it another spin.

Corbett and Rosemary Leach went on to reprise their spousal relationship in a couple of further Cryer/Chapman series for the BBC – *Now Look Here ...* and its sequel *The Prince Of Denmark*.

No Time For Sergeants

USA · ABC (PENCAM PRODUCTIONS/WARNER BROS) · SITCOM

34 × 30 mins · b/w

US dates: 14 Sep 1964–6 Sep 1965

*UK dates: 16 Feb 1965–8 Nov 1969 (34 episodes) ITV various days and times

MAIN CAST

Pvt Will Stockdale · · · · · · · · Sammy Jackson
Sgt King · · · · · · · · · · · · · · · · · · Harry Hickox
Capt Martin · · · · · · · · · · · · · · · Paul Smith
Col Farnsworth · · · · · · · · · · Hayden Rorke
Pvt Ben Whitledge · · · · · · · · · · Kevin O'Neal
Millie Anderson · · · · · · · · · · · Laurie Sibbald

CREDITS

creator Mac Hyman · *writers* Norman Paul, John L Greene, Elon Packard, William Burns · *director* Richard Crenna · *executive producer* William T Orr

The stories of Will Stockdale, a country yokel from Georgia drafted into the American Air Force, whose naïvety, innocence and natural honesty is totally at odds with the rigid USAF base community and officers; they usually find, however, that his hillbilly philosophies are nearer the target than their military ones.

Before ABC produced this short-lived TV series *No Time For Sergeants* had already been around as a novel and then as a one-shot

US TV drama (1955), Broadway stage-play (adapted by Ira Levin) and feature film (1958) – all three starring Andy Griffith.

*Note. Twenty-six of the 34 episodes were screened by London-area ITV between 16 February and 14 September 1965.

Nobody Does It Like Marti

see CAINE, Marti

Nobody Is Norman Wisdom

see WISDOM, Norman

Nobody's Perfect   UK

UK · ITV (LWT) · SITCOM

14 × 30 mins · colour

Series One (7) 28 Sep–9 Nov 1980 · Sun 8.15pm
Series Two (7) 25 July–12 Sep 1982 · Sun mostly 10pm

MAIN CAST

Bill Hooper · · · · · · · · · · · · · · · Elaine Stritch
Sam Hooper · · · · · · · · · · · · Richard Griffiths
Mrs Whicker · · · · · · · · · · · · · · · Ruby Head
Henry Armstrong · · · · · · · · · Moray Watson
Liz Parker · · · · · · · · · · · · · · · · Kim Braden
Sammy · · · · · · · · · · · · · · · · · · Simon Nash

CREDITS

Maude script adapters Elaine Stritch (13), Richard Griffiths (1) · *director* Christopher Baker · *producer* Humphrey Barclay

Nobody's Perfect was the British adaptation of the highly successful American sitcom *Maude* (CBS, 141 episodes, 1972–78), which starred Bea Arthur (Dorothy in **The Golden Girls**) as a loud-mouthed liberal and was itself spun-off from **All In The Family**, the US version of **Till Death Us Do Part**. Humphrey Barclay, producer and deputy controller of entertainment at LWT, had acquired the option on a British version of *Maude* and wanted the strident-voiced British-based American actress Elaine Stritch for the role, to follow her success in **Two's Company**. But, upon the reading the scripts, Stritch felt that Maude's character, four-times married, did not suit her style. Various British writers were asked to adapt the scripts but still none of them suited until one day the talented Stritch, with no prior experience of writing, said that she would have a go herself. Given an office at LWT, and then working from her Savoy Hotel apartment, she managed the job without too much difficulty and the series took to the air.

Some ITV regions had screened a few episodes of *Maude* in the mid-1970s but it was never networked or seen in the London area, so the premise of *Nobody's Perfect* was fresh to virtually all viewers. Stritch played the part of Bill, an American woman eight years into her second marriage. Her husband,

Sam Hooper, is also in his second marriage. Sam has a divorced daughter, Liz, who has delivered him a grandson, (confusingly named Sammy). Bill exercises a biting liberal wit, usually aimed at Sam but sometimes at their neighbour Henry Armstrong or their woman 'who does', Mrs Whicker. The 14 episodes depicted the Hoopers' at times bumpy marriage and the usual crop of marital misunderstandings.

On balance, it must be said, the British version was no match for the American one, even allowing for a fine opening sequence that featured cartoons drawn by the noted American caricaturist Al Hirschfeld, a personal friend of Stritch's.

Nobody's Perfect   USA

USA · ABC (UNIVERSAL TV) · SITCOM

8 × 30 mins · colour

US dates: 26 June–28 Aug 1980
UK dates: 3 Sep 1980–5 Jan 1981 (8 episodes) ITV mostly Wed 7pm

MAIN CAST

Det Insp Roger Hart · · · · · · · · · · Ron Moody
Det Jennifer Dempsey · · · · · · · Cassie Yates
Lt Vince DeGennaro · · · · · · · Michael Durrell
Det Jacobi · · · · · · · · · · · · · · · Victor Brandt
Det Grauer · · · · · · · · · · · · · · · Tom Williams
Det Ramsey · · · · · · · · · · · · · · · Renny Roker

CREDITS

creators Arne Sultan/Chris Hayward · *writers* Arne Sultan, Chris Hayward, Ken Hecht, Mike Marmer, Peter Galley, Donald Harris · *directors* Robert Douglas, Norman Abbott, Tony Mordente · *executive producer* Norman Barasch · *producers* Arne Sultan, Chris Hayward, Lew Gallo, Edward J Montagne

A short-lived and ill-fated American sitcom that starred the British actor (and singer/ songwriter) Ron Moody as a very English detective who is temporarily assigned from Scotland Yard to the 22nd precinct of the San Francisco Police Department in a foreign-exchange programme. Here, Hart reports to Lieutenant Vince DeGennaro and is teamed up with a junior detective, Jennifer Dempsey.

The main basis of the comedy was Hart's absent-mindedness, persistent clumsiness and the juxtaposition of his English urbanity and the American cops' (comparative) uncouthness; despite this, and indeed despite himself, Hart always managed to solve his cases. One can gauge the level of humour from an incident in the opening episode, however, when Hart so startles a man planning to leap from the Golden Gate Bridge that the would-be suicide topples over the edge and plummets into the water.

The eight episodes were filmed by ABC in 1979 but the series' planned launch that September was postponed. The first problem was the proposed title, *Hart In San Francisco*, which was deemed too close to the popular crime series *Hart To Hart*. The main problem, though, was the content: the series simply was not funny – and when it finally reached the screen, a year later, viewers agreed. In Britain it was retitled *Hart Of The Yard* when screened by ITV because, within four weeks of the premiere episode, the network was due to screen a new British-made sitcom titled *Nobody's Perfect* (see previous entry). These and other problems dogged the show, and the level of humour was such that it had no chance of fighting back.

The Nor-Way To Broadcasting

see The Montreux Festival

Norbert Smith – A Life

UK · C4 (HAT TRICK PRODUCTIONS) · SITCOM

1 × 60 mins · colour

3 Nov 1989 · Fri 10.30pm

MAIN CAST

Sir Norbert Smith · · · · · · · · · · · Harry Enfield
Melvyn Bragg · · · · · · · · · · · · · · · · · himself

CREDITS

writers Harry Enfield/Geoffrey Perkins · *director* Geoff Posner · *executive producer* Denise O'Donoghue · *producer* Geoffrey Perkins

A glorious, Montreux Silver Rose-winning 'mockumentary' co-written by and starring Harry Enfield. He appeared in the guise of one of his first comic creations, Sir Norbert Smith, actor and stalwart of the British film industry, now in his eighties and completely forgetful but looking back upon his career in the movies with interviewer Melvyn Bragg (who appeared as himself, as if this was an edition of his arts series *The South Bank Show*).

As Smith, the programme gave Enfield the opportunity to lovingly lampoon a raft of famous films over several decades and appear in a range of roles (including a spot-on *Carry On* spoof, and a fine impression of a Will Hay film in which he imitated Graham Moffatt), emphasising his mastery of comic characterisation. One such invention was Mr Greyson, delivering a wartime Ministry Of Information film about the perils of venereal disease ('caused by ghastly horridness, beastly nastiness and sordid frightfulness') that led to the series of Mr Chomondley-Warner sketches in *Harry Enfield's Television Programme*.

Very similar in approach to *The Rutles*, Eric Idle and Neil Innes's spoof on the Beatles' story (see *Rutland Weekend Television*), *Norbert Smith – A Life* featured a lengthy cast, including Peter Goodwright, Josie Lawrence, Renee Asherson and three of the *Carry On* alumni, Jack Douglas, Barbara Windsor and Kenneth Connor.

The Norman Evans Show

UK · BBC · STANDUP

4 × 60 mins · b/w

One series (3) 21 Apr–16 June 1956 · monthly Sat around 9pm

Special · 13 Oct 1956 · Sat 8.30pm

MAIN CAST

Norman Evans
Betty Jumel
Mrs Shufflewick · · · · · · · · · · · Rex Jameson

CREDITS

writers Norman Evans, Richard Afton, Ronnie Hanbury, Len Lowe · *producer* Richard Afton

Born in Rochdale in 1901, comedian Norman Evans was encouraged to enter show business in 1934 by the town's most famous entertainer, Gracie Fields. His forte was appearing in drag as a hatchet-faced, toothless old woman leaning over a garden wall and gossiping with a fictitious neighbour. (In other words, the discussions were one-sided.) These conversations embraced everything from local scandal to the price of groceries, but 'she' gained most mileage from descriptions of medical problems and operations. Evans endowed the character with a wonderful array of exaggerated facial contortions and embroidered every routine with quick glances around, as if to check for eavesdroppers, before launching into the most intimate revelations. These usually involved the silent mouthing of words deemed particularly embarrassing. This entire act was faithfully continued after Evans's death in 1962 by Les Dawson – it was not plagiarism, however, but an act of homage: the young Manchester-born comic was the first to admit that Evans did it first.

These four shows were presented under the *Saturday Comedy Hour* banner; notably, the edition of 13 October 1956 featured as guests the wonderfully surreal comedy of sand-dancers Wilson, Keppel And Betty. Another star guest in the series was Mrs Shufflewick, a cockney comic character also played by a man in drag, Rex Jameson.

See also *Evans Abode*, which followed immediately after *The Norman Evans Show* came to an end.

The Norman Gunston Show

see GUNSTON, Norman

The Norman Vaughan Show

UK · BBC · STANDUP/SKETCH

9 editions (3 × 45 mins · 6 × 25 mins) · b/w

Special (45 mins) *Norman Vaughan* 1 Feb 1966 · BBC2 Tue 8.50pm

Special (45 mins) 30 Apr 1966 · BBC1 Sat 8.25pm

Special (45 mins) 12 June 1966 · BBC1 Sun 9pm

One series (6 × 25 mins) 6 Oct–10 Nov 1966 · BBC1 Thu 9.05pm

MAIN CAST

Norman Vaughan
Bill Pertwee (series)

CREDITS

writers Eric Merriman (specials 1 & 2), Barry Took (special 3 & series) · *producers* Kenneth Carter (8), Michael Hurll (1)

Born in Liverpool on 10 April 1927, the comedian Norman Vaughan became famous as the compere of the ITV variety series *Val Parnell's Sunday Night At The London Palladium* (1961–62 and 1964–65), and went on to further success as the host of ATV's game-show *The Golden Shot* (1972).

After entering show business in 1941, Vaughan's first TV appearance was in the BBC new-talent series *Showcase* on 13 September 1954, and the producer of that show, Kenneth Carter, was still around when Vaughan had made his name and was offered these three primetime specials with a series to follow. The young comedian – whose buzz words were 'swinging' and 'dodgy', accompanied by an extension of his thumb – appeared in a collection of standup and filmed sketches written by his long-term collaborator Eric Merriman and by Barry Took. Support in the series was provided by the long-time comedic foil Bill Pertwee (later to make his name in *Dad's Army*).

See also *Scott Free* and *A Touch Of The Norman Vaughans*.

Norman Wisdom ... [various shows]

see WISDOM, Norman

Not In Front Of The Children

UK · BBC · SITCOM

39 episodes (38 × 30 mins · 1 × short special) · 21 × b/w · 17 × colour

Pilot *House In A Tree* 26 May 1967 · BBC1 Fri 7.30pm

Series One (6) 25 Aug–29 Sep 1967 · BBC1 Fri 8.20pm

Series Two (8) 23 Feb–12 Apr 1968 · BBC1 Fri 8.20pm

Series Three (6) 25 Oct–29 Nov 1968 · BBC1 Fri 7.55pm

Short special · part of *Christmas Night With The Stars* 25 Dec 1968 · BBC1 Wed 6.40pm

*Series Four (17 × colour) 12 Sep 1969–9 Jan 1970 · BBC1 Fri 7.55pm

MAIN CAST

Jennifer Corner · · · · · · · · · · · · Wendy Craig
Henry Corner · · · · · · · · · · · · Paul Daneman
· · · · · · · · · · · · · · · · · · · (pilot & series 1);
· · · · · · · · · Ronald Hines (series 2 onwards)
Trudi Corner · · · · Roberta Tovey (series 1–3);
· · · · · · · · · · · · · Verina Greenlaw (series 4)
Robin Corner · · · · · · · · Hugo Keith-Johnston
Amanda Corner · · · · · · · · · · · · · Jill Riddick

CREDITS
writer Richard Waring · *producer* Graeme Muir

A middle-class, middle-of-the-road but nonetheless competent sitcom, first unveiled within the *Comedy Playhouse* strand, in which Wendy Craig struck a chord with her performance as a harassed housewife and mother of three, coping with the rigours of everyday life.

Very popular at the time, but criticised by those who liked their comedy a little more thoughtful (there was a hilarious reference to the series' perceived naffness in the radio comedy *I'm Sorry, I'll Read That Again*), *Not In Front Of The Children* was easy, uncomplicated domestic humour, quite unrealistic with its absence of *real* family strife, but packed full of misunderstandings, light arguments and little problems caused by three nice, clean-cut but maddening children. Craig starred as Jennifer Corner and her husband, Henry, was portrayed first by Paul Daneman and then Ronald Hines. Roberta Tovey – best known at the time for her role as the Doctor's granddaughter in the two 1960s *Doctor Who* feature films – appeared as Trudi Corner in the first three series.

Craig went on to carve out quite a career for herself in such house-bound wife/mother roles and, despite often having to work within clichéd and restraining scripts, always gave of her best. But it wasn't until she worked for Carla Lane, in *Butterflies*, that she was able to explore in greater depths the frustrations, disappointments and melancholy of such a character. Before that, however, she starred in other, similar series from the writer Richard Waring: *... And Mother Makes Three* and its sequel *... And Mother Makes Five*.

Notes. Richard Waring adapted 26 episodes of *Not In Front Of The Children* for broadcast by BBC Radio 4 between 30 September 1969 and 27 December 1970. All of the TV cast re-recorded their roles with the exception of Ronald Hines; Henry Corner was voiced by Francis Matthews.

*Although made in colour, the first ten episodes of the fourth series aired in b/w because BBC1 did not begin colour broadcasting until 15 November 1969. When the series was repeated all the episodes were shown in colour.

Not On Your Nellie

UK · ITV (LWT) · SITCOM

17 × 30 mins · colour
Series One (7) 15 Mar–26 Apr 1974 · Fri 8.30pm
Series Two (6) 24 Jan–28 Feb 1975 · Fri 8.30pm
Series Three (4) 3 Aug–24 Aug 1975 · Sun 7.25pm

MAIN CAST
Nellie Pickersgill · · · · · · · · · · · Hylda Baker
Jed Pickersgill · · · John Barrett (series 1 & 2)
Stanley Pickersgill · · Jack Douglas (series 3)
Charlie · · · · · · · · · · · · · · · · · Leo Dolan
Gilbert · · · · · · · · · · · · · · Roger Howlett
Beryl · · · · · · · · · · Alexandra Dane (series 1)
Doris · · · · · · · · · · Wendy Richard (series 2)
Big Brenda · · · · · · · · Sue Nicholls (series 3)
Ali · · · · · · · · · · · · · · · · · · Ashiq (series 1);
· · · · · · · · · · · · · · · · · · · Azad Ali (series 2)
George · · · · · · · David Rayner (series 1 & 2)

CREDITS
writers Tom Brennand/Roy Bottomley · *director/producer* Bryan Izzard

Wielding her boa, and mouthing more malapropisms per sentence than old Mrs Malaprop herself, Hylda Baker in *Not On Your Nellie* all but reprised the blunt, trussed-up, virginal northern-woman role she had effected so well in **Nearest And Dearest** and in much of her stage career. In that earlier series she had been cast as Nellie Pledge, heiress to a pickle factory; here she was Nellie Pickersgill, daughter of a London publican, summoned down from Bolton to Fulham to help out in his hour of need.

Although written by Brennand and Bottomley, who had scripted most episodes of *Nearest And Dearest*, *Not On Your Nellie* was no sequel, for, if anything, spinster Miss Pickersgill was even more resilient, even more brusque, even more virginal, even more battling than Miss Pledge had been, disapproving of drinking in general and the habitués of the Brown Cow in particular (notably window cleaner Charlie, London Underground tube train guard Ali and stereotypical gays from the fashion world George and Gilbert). For that matter, Nellie also disapproved of her father, Jed, who only put down his pint and moved from his bar stool to gamble on the horses and pinch women's bottoms, and she certainly didn't have time for the 'loose' barmaids Beryl (the first series), Doris (second) and Big Brenda (third).

In the shortened, final series Nellie's dad was said to have returned north and was replaced by his cousin Stanley, played by Jack Douglas. The final episode gave the *Carry On* star an opportunity to perform his famous twitchy Alf Ippititimus character, when he appeared in two roles, as cousin Stanley and as *his* cousin, the accident-prone Alf.

See also *Be Soon*.

Not Only ... But Also   UK

UK · BBC · SKETCH

22 editions (7 × 45 mins · b/w; 7 × 45 mins · colour; 7 × 30 mins · b/w; 1 × 50 mins · b/w)
Series One (7 × 45 mins · b/w) 9 Jan–3 Apr 1965 · BBC2 fortnightly Sat mostly 9.25pm
Series Two (7 × 45 mins · b/w) 15 Jan–26 Feb 1966 · BBC2 Sat mostly 9.35pm
Special (50 mins · b/w) 26 Dec 1966 · BBC2 Mon 9pm
Series Three (7 × 45 mins · colour) 18 Feb–13 May 1970 · BBC2 fortnightly Wed mostly 9.10pm

MAIN CAST
Dudley Moore
Peter Cook

CREDITS
writers Peter Cook/Dudley Moore · *additional material* Robert Fuest, John Law, Dick Clement, Joe McGrath, Robert Sale, Jonathan Abbott and others · *producers* Joe McGrath (series 1), Dick Clement (series 2), John Street (special), James Gilbert (series 3)

A true television comedy classic – not only Peter Cook but also Dudley Moore combining to provide three brilliant series of sketch comedy, beginning in 1965 and ending in 1970. The two made a perfect double-act, the tall, elegant, rapier-witted Peter Cook contrasting with the small and more intense Moore.

The series had scores of high points, but the wonderful 'Dagenham Dialogues' – in which 'Pete', as a confident but ill-informed bore, held forth to 'Dud', a scruffy, even less informed herbert – were triumphs of surreal writing and dazzling improvisation that brought tears to the eyes of the audience – and occasionally to Moore too, flummoxed into a stifled hysteria by one of Cook's delicious ad-libs or flights of humorous fancy; miraculously, Moore always returned from the brink of disaster to get the sketch back on track. Many of the Dud and Pete sequences are rightfully regarded as classics of the genre, from the first – informally titled 'Sex Fantasies' – in which they recounted how they had brutally despatched Greta Garbo and Jane Russell from their bedrooms and ordered them never to come back, through 'Dud And Pete At The Zoo', 'Dud And Pete On Sex', 'Religions', 'Superstitions' and 'Dud Dreams', to arguably the greatest British TV comedy sketch of all time, 'Dud And Pete At The Art Gallery', in which the pair meet up to eat their sandwiches and discuss the paintings in their quasi-knowledgeable but blissfully ill-informed manner.

If *Not Only ... But Also* had merely given viewers the Dud and Pete sketches, this would have been enough, but there was so much more to enjoy. It also featured the surrealistic ramblings of Sir Arthur Streeb-Greebling (Cook, explaining how to teach ravens to fly underwater, and run a restaurant called 'The Frog And Peach') and a slew of great sketches including several memorable father-and-son sequences (in which, characteristic of all their comedy, Cook was the dominant force); a film showing an order of leaping nuns who take to the trampoline after prayers; 'Bo Dudley', in which blues pianist Moore innocently explained away a song lyric that was clearly stuffed with sexual references; and a fine spoof on the puppet adventure series *Thunderbirds*. There were also some excellent musical moments from Moore (with and without and his modern-jazz group, the Dudley Moore Trio) and, on the same melodic theme, inspired opening and closing sequences for every programme. In the introductions Moore and Cook were shown at a piano and then the camera would pull back to reveal the more and more unlikely settings in which they were being filmed: underwater, on board an aircraft carrier, in a car wash, and so on. At the end of every show Moore played piano and sang with Cook the song (composed by Moore) that became their theme music, 'Goodbye-ee'.

There were many guest appearances in the three series, most notably from John Lennon (in the first show and again in the 1966 Christmas special), Barry Humphries, Spike Milligan, Ronnie Barker, Norman Rossington, Sheila Steafel, Anna Quayle, Eric Sykes and Alan Bennett. In the 1970 series – which followed a gap of four years and was the only one made in colour – guests were encouraged to participate in 'Poets Cornered', a nerve-wracking showcase for ad-lib raconteuring: those who deliberated or failed were dumped headlong into a pool of foamy sludge. (In so doing, *Not Only … But Also* became a forerunner of *Tiswas* and all the other shows of the 1970s and onwards that delighted in such visual excesses.)

In an act of appalling corporate blunder, the BBC wiped or junked many editions of *Not Only … But Also* from its archives in the late 1960s and early 1970s, as it did, so indiscriminately, with many hundreds of other series and programmes. Some editions therefore no longer exist, but surviving sequences were compiled into a one-off 40-minute programme, *The Best Of Not Only … But Also*, screened by BBC2 on 24 December 1974, for which Cook and Moore added new wraparound sequences, shot in New York where they were touring with the stage-show *Good Evening* (see **Behind The Fridge**). Enough old shows were then scraped together (some were rescued from the archives of overseas TV companies to which, fortunately, the BBC had sold copies in the 1960s) to enable the BBC to piece together six half-hour compilation shows, screened on BBC2 from 4 November to 9 December 1990 as *The Best Of … What's Left Of … Not Only … But Also* (the highlights from which were released on video). Their partnership broken for more than a decade to this point, Cook and Moore reunited to promote the series and video in trailers and chat-show appearances.

Notes. *Not Only … But Also* was originally conceived as a showcase for Dudley Moore, with Peter Cook in a subsidiary role, but by the second programme the two were firmly established as joint leads. (The first series was actually titled *Not Only … But Also …* but the second ellipsis was dropped after this.) Most of the sketches were written by Cook but were credited to Peter Cook/Dudley Moore.

Not Only … But Also originated as a BBC2 series but the channel was not available nationally at this time (and where it was transmitted, it was only receivable on new or adapted older sets). So all three series were repeated on the fully available BBC1, usually quite soon afterwards. The first series (only six of the seven editions) was repeated from 20 May to 24 June 1967; the second was screened by BBC1 from 21 May 1966 to 2 July 1967 in a primetime Saturday-night slot; the special was repeated on 7 February 1967; and the third and final series (the seven editions were edited from 45 to 30 mins) went out from 18 September to 30 October 1970.

Peter Cook and Dudley Moore's screen ventures around this time were many, most but not all featuring them as a pair. Cook played the Mad Hatter in his fellow revue star Jonathan Miller's weird and wonderful adaptation of *Alice In Wonderland* (BBC1, 28 December 1966). Moore appeared in many music shows on radio and television. Both men appeared together on ITV in *The New London Palladium Show* on 26 September 1965, on that year's *Royal Variety Show* (broadcast by ITV on 14 November 1965 and leading to an excellent EP record of the Dud and Pete sketch they performed, 'By Appointment') and, through some success with their Decca singles, on such pop shows as *Ready, Steady, Go!* The pair also acted together in a number of feature films at this time (*Bedazzled, The Wrong Box, The Bed Sitting Room* and *Monte Carlo Or Bust*) and on TV in John Antrobus's absurdist comedy *An Apple A Day*.

See also **Goodbye Again**.

Not Only … But Also   Australia

AUSTRALIA · ABC · SKETCH
....
2 × 30 mins · colour

Australian dates: 8 & 15 Feb 1971

UK dates: 18 & 25 June 1971 · BBC1 Fri 8pm

MAIN CAST

Peter Cook
Dudley Moore
Barry Humphries

CREDITS

writers Peter Cook/Dudley Moore

Two shows recorded in Australia. The BBC series of *Not Only … But Also* was very popular there and ABC paid for Cook and Moore to fly Down Under to tape the programmes in its own studios, where they were joined by special guest Barry Humphries. Apart from a few new items (including another Sir Arthur Streeb-Greebling interview, in which he talked of domesticating a funnel-web spider), most of the sketches were oldies, including the classic 'audition', first seen in **Beyond The Fringe**, in which Moore, hopping maniacally as a one-legged man ('a unidexter'), applies for an audition for the part of Tarzan in an forthcoming film.

Both shows were imported by the BBC and screened under the title *Peter Cook And Dudley Moore In Australia*.

Not So Much A Programme More A Way Of Life

UK · BBC · SATIRE

62 × 45 mins · b/w

13 Nov 1964–11 Apr 1965 · BBC1 Fri · Sat and Sun around 10.30pm

MAIN CAST

John Bird
Eleanor Bron
Michael Crawford
John Fortune
David Frost
Roy Hudd
Cleo Laine
P J Kavanagh (early editions)
William Rushton (early editions)
Brian Murphy (Feb 1965 onwards)

CREDITS

writers cast · *additional material* Peter Lewis/Peter Dobereiner · *producer* Ned Sherrin

Not So Much A Programme More A Way Of Life was the BBC's second entry in the early 1960s 'satire boom', following the demise of **That Was The Week That Was**. That series had been cancelled because of the impending 1964 General Election; now the way was clear once more for some late-evening satirical comedy – to be screened not once a week but three times, on Fridays, Saturdays and Sundays. This time, however, the BBC was determined that it would exercise more control over the content, and hopefully attract less controversy in the process.

The executives were proved wrong – right from the start, the new series demonstrated that it could pack the same savage punch that had characterised *TW3*. Probably its most contentious sketch featured John Bird as President Jomo Kenyatta of Kenya, which drew scathing criticism and an official complaint from its High Commission. Another popular but sometimes controversial feature was a regular Sunday spot in which young actor Michael Crawford, as Byron, sounded off about aspects of British life: the National Health Service, religion, attitudes to sex and so on. (These sketches were written by Peter Lewis/Peter Dobereiner.)

Although the experiment of running the show thrice weekly was a bold one, it became the series' downfall. Exhaustion set in relatively quickly and the mix of music, sketch, monologue and studio discussion began to unravel, the discussion elements becoming increasingly longer in duration. Arguably the series' most significant achievement was that it provided a vehicle for the emergence of Eleanor Bron as a force to be reckoned with in what was otherwise an oppressively male domain.

Not The Nine O'Clock News

UK · BBC · SKETCH

27 × 25 mins · colour

Series One (6) 16 Oct–20 Nov 1979 · BBC2
Tue 9pm

Series Two (7) 31 Mar–12 May 1980 · BBC2
Mon mostly 9pm

Series Three (8) 27 Oct–15 Dec 1980 · BBC2
Mon 9pm

Series Four (6) 1 Feb–8 Mar 1982 · BBC2
Mon 9pm

MAIN CAST

Rowan Atkinson
Pamela Stephenson
Mel Smith
Griff Rhys Jones
Chris Langham (series 1)

CREDITS

writers Rowan Atkinson, Mel Smith, Griff Rhys Jones, Andy Hamilton, Guy Jenkin, Richard Curtis, Andrew Marshall/David Renwick, Rory McGrath, Simon Woodham, Colin Bostock-Smith, Vicky Pile, Guy Meredith, Kim Fuller, Laurie Rowley, Mark Wallington/Dick Fiddy, Paul Smith/Terry Kyan, Howard Goodall, Tony Mather, Jim Hitchmough, Philip Pope, Mike Radford, Paul Newstead, Janey Preger, Colin Gilbert, Peter Richardson, Nigel Planer/Roger Planer, Peter Brewis, Clive Anderson, Ruby Wax, Douglas Adams, Mick Deasey, John Lloyd, Sean Hardie and others · *songs* Howard Goodall, Philip Pope, Peter Brewis, Chris Judge Smith · *directors* Bill Wilson, Geoff Posner · *producers* John Lloyd/Sean Hardie

A forthright, irreverent, tart, often controversial and extremely funny sketch series that made the biggest splash in the genre since the heady days of *Monty Python's Flying Circus* and neatly bridged the gap between the zany mania of the 1970s and the anarchic cynicism of the 'alternative' comedy of the 1980s.

By 1978, BBC radio producer John Lloyd was becoming frustrated that many of the medium's shows were being adapted for television without his or his colleagues' input. So he approached two heads of department in TV – John Howard Davies (comedy) and James (Jimmy) Gilbert (light entertainment) – pitching the idea of a contemporary sketch show, the like of which hadn't been tried for some years. They offered Lloyd a six-slot series with no real brief beyond the proviso

that he collaborate with Sean Hardie, a BBC current-affairs expert recommended to the comedy department because of his quirky sense of humour. Together, Lloyd and Hardie set about discussing formats, considering and rejecting many ideas (such as *Sacred Cows*, which would have dissected modern-day trends in a method similar to that used in *The Frost Report*). Eventually, the two agreed upon a contemporary, fast-paced sketch show loosely based around the concept of a news bulletin and utilising a scatter-gun approach to take pops at its many targets.

Looking around for likely participants, Lloyd and Hardie picked a team that comprised Rowan Atkinson, Chris Emmett, Christopher Godwin, John Gorman, Chris Langham, Willoughby Goddard and Jonathan Hyde, and duly embarked upon recording the first edition of *Not The Nine O'Clock News* (directed by Bob Spiers). This was scheduled to air on 2 April 1979, replacing *Fawlty Towers* in the schedules, and to this end the show began with a recording of John Cleese, as Basil Fawlty, explaining to a phone caller (clearly, someone at the BBC) that he had no show ready for that week so why didn't they fill the slot with something else, 'a tatty revue' perhaps. But when BBC executives viewed an advance copy of the show they fretted that its overtly political nature was uncomfortable so close to the imminent General Election, and considered too that the programme's mix wasn't quite right. The series was promptly pulled from the schedules (too late to prevent it from being listed for two weeks in *Radio Times*) and the BBC gave Lloyd and Hardie six months to have another go. In hindsight, both producers realised that this was a stroke of luck – they went back to the drawing board and came up with something altogether better.

In the new team Lloyd was determined to include a funny woman. Victoria Wood declined his invitation to join up, feeling that her future lay in solo performance. Lloyd also considered Alison Steadman and Susan George, but then he met an Australian actress, Pamela Stephenson, at a party and became convinced that she was the one for the job. Rowan Atkinson and Chris Langham remained from the original show and the final member of the reduced team was a comedy actor, Mel Smith. All four members were virtual unknowns, which was what Lloyd wanted.

The revised shows worked well, and the first series of *Not The Nine O'Clock News* – it was scheduled opposite the *Nine O'Clock News* on BBC1 – drew just about enough viewers to gain a second run. But it was felt that Chris Langham did not quite fit in so he was let go and replaced by a comedy performer and BBC radio producer, Griff Rhys Jones, who had appeared occasionally

as support in the first series. These four then became *the* team of *Not The Nine O'Clock News*, the most talked-about comedy quartet in Britain for the next three years. Pamela Stephenson tapped a hitherto undiscovered talent for mimicry, her impressions of women newsreaders proving to be one of the series' many highlights. Rowan Atkinson excelled at visual comedy as well as verbal gymnastics, and Mel Smith and Griff Rhys Jones brought a naturalistic acting style to the sketches. The second series firmly established the show as a great success, winning the Silver Rose at the Montreux Festival.

Some of the material for the series came from a central team of regular writers – and the cast themselves were also involved in the development of the material – but it benefited from an 'open-door' policy, which meant that virtually anyone could send in sketches and have them evaluated. This created a fertile training ground for new talent, many budding writers enjoying their first TV exposure in the series. The producers did lay down some important parameters, however: the show had to be contemporary rather than topical, although its recording schedule (it was taped on Sunday evenings for transmission the next night) meant that some last-minute material could be added; short sketches were preferred to long ones (in its entire run only a handful of sketches ran for more than two minutes); and the show was unashamedly modern – if a sketch took place in a pub it had to be a noticeably modern pub with Space Invaders being played instead of dominoes, or if it was set in a hospital it had to be a modern, under-staffed one with harassed doctors and nurses. These rules – combined with re-voiced news footage and employment of new video equipment and techniques like Quantel – gave the series a distinctive visual appearance.

The fast pacing and density of the material meant that a lot of ground was covered in the 27 editions, and there were dozens of memorable skits. Every viewer had their particular favourites, the highlights including a parody of the newly emerging pop-video industry, 'Nice Video, Shame About The Song'; a send-up of Abba; the team's satirical comment on the religious furore surrounding *Monty Python's Life Of Brian*, in which Pythonists accused the church of blaspheming against the Flying Circus; a beauty-contest sketch featuring an unusually candid contestant (host: 'And why do you want to be Miss World?', contestant: 'I want to get laid by someone famous'); and an interview with Gerald, an intelligent and urbane talking gorilla (trainer: 'When we captured Gerald he was wild', gorilla: 'Wild? I was absolutely *livid*'). Two of the most controversial sketches were about the Ayatollah of Iran and the Polish communist leader Lech Walesa, prompting irate viewers (as they always seem to do in such cases) to research the phone number of the *Daily Mirror* – or some other such worthy paper – and call in such numbers that they 'blocked the switchboard'.

In 1982 – after the team mounted a *Not The Nine O'Clock News* stage-show in Oxford and London – the quartet decided, amicably, to call it a day, figuring that they had exploited the format for all it was worth and that it was time to move on to other, individual projects. Pamela Stephenson pursued a successful Hollywood film career, Rowan Atkinson went into **Blackadder** and **Mr Bean**, and Mel Smith and Griff Rhys Jones stayed together for their own series (see **Smith and Jones**).

Notes. An American adaptation, *Not Necessarily The News* (1983–89, following a pilot on 14 September 1982), was able to replicate much of the bite of the original British series because it was transmitted by cable channel Home Box Office, less regulated than the main networks.

On 10 September 1981, the BBC1 series *Behind The Scenes With ...* focused on Pamela Stephenson, watching her rehearse various routines and characterisations from *Not The Nine O'Clock News*. It also featured some original comedy material.

See also **Fundamental Frolics**.

Not With A Bang

UK · ITV (LWT) · SITCOM

7 × 30 mins · colour

25 Mar–6 May 1990 · Sun mostly 10.05pm

MAIN CAST

Brian Appleyard	Ronald Pickup
Colin Garrity	Stephen Rea
Graham Wilkins	Mike Grady
Janet Wilkins	Josie Lawrence

CREDITS

writers Tony Millan/Mike Walling · *director/producer* Robin Carr

If the world has to end, then let it be like this: Judith Hann (appearing as herself) is displaying the contents of a beaker in BBC1's science show *Tomorrow's World* when a splash of the volatile liquid lands on her arm. Within seconds she is reduced to a pile of ash on the floor, followed by everyone else in the TV studio followed by all of London, all of Britain and, pretty soon, all of the world. No pain, no conflagration, just ash.

This was how the appropriately titled *Not With A Bang* started, a series that aired in what, for about a decade, was ITV's slot for slightly subversive comedies, late Sunday evenings. The remaining scenes and episodes took place perhaps a year on, when viewers come across two survivors of the holocaust, Colin and Brian, who have teamed up and are trying their best to make sense of what has

happened while still enjoying their old habits, like going to the pub. Naturally, they believe they are the only survivors, but then they meet a young married couple, Janet and Graham, who had also assumed themselves the only human remnants. The four build a mini-community in a country cottage and immediately run into problems of the human kind. For one, with a married couple, the continuation of the race seems assured, but Graham is reluctant to pursue the idea. Colin, meanwhile, is obsessed with rugby league and talks about little else.

Although not acknowledged as an adaptation, a similar sitcom was screened in the USA by Fox in 1992. Titled *Woops!* it depicted the six survivors of a nuclear holocaust who form a community in a countryside farmhouse. It has not been screened in Britain. Ray Galton and Alan Simpson also came up with a similar plotline for a 1974 *Comedy Playhouse* half-hour, **The Last Man On Earth**, and a similar premise was explored in a sci-fi adventure series, *Survivors*, screened by BBC1 1975–77.

Nothing Like A Royal Show!

UK · ITV (LWT) · STANDUP

1 × 135 mins · colour

14 Apr 1990 · Sat 9pm

MAIN CAST
see below

CREDITS

writers cast · *director* Terry Kinane · *executive producer* Marcus Plantin · *producer* Paul Lewis

A one-off charity show taped at the Hackney Empire in east London and compered by Jools Holland that raised money for the Entertainment Artistes' Benevolent Fund. Several musical and other non-comedy acts appeared, but the emphasis was on humour, with a lengthy cast of names including Gareth Hale, Norman Pace, Julian Clary, Steve Coogan, Kit Hollerbach, Jeremy Hardy, Steve Nallon, Jack Dee, Steve Rawlings, Doon Mackichan, Patrick Marber, John Lenahan, Vic Reeves, Bob Mortimer, Chris Luby and Richard Morton.

Now And Then

UK · ITV (LWT) · SITCOM

13 × 30 mins · colour

Series One (7) 24 July–4 Sep 1983 · Sun mostly 9.15pm

Series Two (6) 8 July–12 Aug 1984 · Sun 9.30pm

MAIN CAST

NOW:

Peter Elston	Bernard Holley
Jill Elston	Jill Kerman
Alan Elston	Marc Gilbey
Amanda Elston	Polly Bell

THEN:

Peter Elston	John Alford
Norman Elston	Sam Kelly
Bet Elston	Marcia Warren
Gran	Liz Smith
Grandad	Arthur Lovegrove (series 1)
Mary Elston	Tracy Hyde
Sonia Elston	Cindy O'Callaghan
Randall	Ray Burdis
Aunt Sadie	June Brown
Uncle Gordon	Barry Stanton
Rene Manderville	Carol Harrison (series 2)
Mr Pluckrose	John White (series 2)

CREDITS

writers John Esmonde/Bob Larbey · *director* Derrick Goodwin · *producers* Derrick Goodwin (10), Humphrey Barclay (3)

An unusual Esmonde and Larbey sitcom, with drama roots, the premise of *Now And Then* was the planned sale of a south London house where a middle-aged husband and father of two, Peter Elston, had spent his entire life. The potential move awoke in him a scrapbook of memories, so part of each episode was spent in the past – during the Second World War, when Peter was seven/eight years old – and part in the present, where Peter's rebellious son Alan reminded him of how he used to be.

It was the war years – as seen through the eyes of a small boy – that shone through the mist, however. As Peter saw it, his father, Norman, was a great sage; Mum was a heroine; Grandad (who had died by the second series) and Gran doted upon him; psychic Aunt Sadie and Uncle Gordon, who owned a surgical appliances shop, caused plenty of merriment; elder sister Sonia married a GI named Nelson and fell pregnant; another sister, Mary, joined the ATS and went about with a boyfriend named Randall; and brother Ted was away in the forces. For young Peter, wartime meant exciting uncertainty, blackouts, the Anderson Shelter, food shortages and a doodlebug bomb interrupting one of his piano lessons.

Now Look Here ...

UK · BBC · SITCOM

13 × 30 mins · colour

Series One (7) 5 Nov–17 Dec 1971 · BBC1 Fri 8pm

Series Two (6) 24 Jan–7 Mar 1973 · BBC1 Wed 7.30pm

MAIN CAST

Ronnie	Ronnie Corbett
Mother	Madge Ryan (series 1);
	Gillian Lind (series 2)
Laura	Rosemary Leach
Col Sutcliffe	Donald Hewlett
Keith	Richard O'Sullivan (series 1)
Miss Blyton	Pat Hamilton (series 1)
Bobby	Wallas Eaton (series 1)
Sally	Linda Hayden (series 1)

CREDITS

writers Graham Chapman/Barry Cryer · *producers* Bill Hitchcock (series 1), Douglas Argent (series 2)

Another sitcom for Ronnie Corbett, who was enjoying great success at this time as half of **The Two Ronnies** partnership.

The first series of *Now Look Here …* cast Corbett as a mother-dominated man (much like his role in **Sorry!**), desperate to spread his wings, and by the end of those seven episodes he had indeed found a soul-mate, Laura. By the start of the second series they had married and the format changed to reflect husband-and-wife storylines, split between domestic situations and Ronnie's job in insurance.

Now Look Here … was written by Graham Chapman and Barry Cryer, who had also scripted Corbett's earlier sitcom **No – That's Me Over Here!**, in which he was also married to a woman named Laura, also played by Rosemary Leach. Gradually, it seems, the two premises began to merge, the fifth episode in the second series going as far as re-introducing Henry McGee from the earlier show, once again cast as Ronnie's oily neighbour.

After *Now Look Here …* ended there was a further change of format, Corbett and Leach returning a year later in **The Prince Of Denmark**.

Now – Something Else

see BREMNER, Rory

Now Take My Wife

UK · BBC · SITCOM

14 episodes (1 × 35 mins · 13 × 30 mins) · colour

Pilot (35 mins) *Just Harry And Me* 1 Apr 1971 · BBC1 Thu 7.40pm

One series (13) 13 Sep–6 Dec 1971 · BBC1 Mon 7.30pm

MAIN CAST
Claire Love · · · · · · · · · · · · · Sheila Hancock
Harry Love · · · · · · · · · · · · · Donald Houston
Jenny Love · · · · · · · · Lynne Frederick (pilot);
· · · · · · · · · · · · · · · · · · · Liz Edmiston (series)

CREDITS
writer Charles Laurence · *producers* Duncan Wood (7), Sydney Lotterby (6), Douglas Argent (1)

A series developed from a single *Comedy Playhouse* episode, *Just Harry And Me*.

The pilot concentrated on generation-gap blues between the upper-middle-class Loves, Claire and Harry, and their teenage daughter Jenny. Between the pilot and the full series, however, the format altered slightly, the 13 weekly episodes focusing on the comical situations caused by the zany Claire and her rather peculiar outlook on life, and the reaction of her exasperated parents.

Note. Young actress Lynne Frederick, who played Jenny Love in the pilot, went on to marry David Frost and, later, Peter Sellers.

Now What

UK · ITV (CRUCIAL FILMS FOR CARLTON) · SKETCH

1 × 30 mins · colour

14 Aug 1995 · Mon 8pm

MAIN CAST
Fiona Allen
Don Gilét
Alan D Marriott
Curtis Walker
Angela Wynter

CREDITS
writers Andrew Barclay, Will Buckley, Jane Bussman, David Coe, Geoff Deane, Carlton Dixon, Sharon Foster, Jeremy Front, Tony Gardiner, Paul Henry, Paul Johnson, Jo Martin, David Quantick · *script editor* Jim Pullin · *director* Chris Bould · *executive producers* Lenny Henry, Polly McDonald · *producer* Lenny Barker

The sixth and last programme in ITV's 1995 pilot launch-pad *Comedy Firsts* was the only one to feature sketch comedy as opposed to situation. *Now What* was a Lenny Henry-sponsored programme – performed by a mostly black quintet of young comics – which, to be blunt, rarely rose above the juvenile, with characters like Triviaman, who arrives in a puff of smoke to spout very boring minutiae, and a deliberately wooden spoof of the BBC medical drama series *Casualty*, called *Casually*, failing to raise many laughs. ITV has been a no-man's-land for sketch comedy since the late 1960s – all the best shows in the genre have been BBC- or C4-made – and, regrettably, *Now What*, which developed out of a workshop for budding new comedy writers, did nothing to rectify this.

Now Who Do You Do?

see *Who Do You Do?*

Nurses

USA · NBC (WITT-THOMAS-HARRIS PRODUCTIONS/TOUCHSTONE TELEVISION) · SITCOM

68 × 30 mins · colour

US dates: 14 Sep 1991–7 May 1994

UK dates: 28 Aug 1992–7 May 1996 (68 episodes) C4 Fri 10pm then Tue around 12 midnight

MAIN CAST
Nurse Sandy Miller · · · · · · · Stephanie Hodge
· (1991–93)
Nurse Annie Roland · · · · · · · · Arnetia Walker
Nurse Julie Milbury · · · · · · · · Mary Jo Keenen
Gina Cuevas · · · · · · · · · · · · · · · Ada Maris
Paco Ortiz · · · · · · · · · · · · · Carlos LaCamara
Greg Vincent · · · · · · · Jeff Altman (1991–92)
Dr Hank Kaplan · · · · · Kenneth David Gilman
Nurse Luke · · · · · · · · · · · · Markus Flanagan
Jack Trenton · · · · · David Rasche (1992–94)
Casey MacAfee · · Loni Anderson (1993–94)

CREDITS
creator Susan Harris · *writers* Susan Harris and others · *directors* Terry Hughes and others · *executive producers* Paul Junger Witt, Tony Thomas, Susan Harris · *producers* Nina Feinberg and others

A female-led ensemble comedy, set in the Miami Community Medical Center – the third sitcom from Susan Harris to be based in this Florida city (the others being **The Golden Girls** and **Empty Nest**). The series examined the working lives of a group of nurses-with-attitude and, as with *The Golden Girls*, made verbal exchanges, rather than physical comedy, the focus of the humour. The five-strong nursing team comprised four women and one man: Sandy, a throaty-voiced, world-weary divorcee; Annie, a wife and mother harassed both at home and at work; Gina, a virginal, sharp-tongued Latin American immigrant; Julie, a naïve, multi-phobic new arrival; and Greg, a slightly unhinged, anti-authoritarian male.

The relationship and rapport between this quintet formed the fulcrum of the series, with frank discussions about sex lives (a Susan Harris speciality) providing the basis of much of the humour. The nurses' antagonism towards the arrogant and mostly incompetent staff doctors (with the exception of the hard working Dr Kaplan) was also a constant factor in the storylines. In later seasons the comedy character actors David Rasche (from **Sledge Hammer!**) and Loni Anderson (**WKRP In Cincinnati**) were added to the cast, the former as a convicted embezzler, Jack Trenton, performing community service at the Medical Center, the latter as hospital administrator Casey MacAfee.

By Susan Harris's high standards, *Nurses* was fairly mediocre fare, but it certainly had good moments and, typically for one of her creations, did not shirk from facing up to adult topics. Harris's constant determination to give women a strong yet emotional voice, and allow women space and time to deal with subjects of a sensitive (some may think non-comedic) nature, makes her the US equivalent of the British writer Carla Lane.

N.U.T.S.

UK · ITV (YORKSHIRE) · SKETCH

6 × 30 mins · colour

14 Oct–18 Nov 1976 · Thu 9.30pm

MAIN CAST
Barry Took
Roy Kinnear
Frederick Jaeger
Dave Evans
Claire Faulconbridge
Chris Emmett

CREDITS
deviser Barry Took · *writers* Chris Emmett (6), Dave Evans (6), Harry Lovelock (6), Geoff Rowley (6),

Alan Coren (3), Tony Bilbow (1) · *producer* Ronnie Baxter

A series of comedy sketches, some of which hit well while others missed badly. The skits were written by good writers, put across with enthusiasm and linked by the amiable and witty Barry Took. The final edition included a collection of filmed outtakes that had gone hilariously wrong, an idea mined with great effect by LWT in *It'll Be Alright On The Night*, the first edition of which was screened by ITV a year later.

See also **Took And Co**.

Nuts In May

see **HOWERD, Frankie**

The Nutt House

USA · NBC (BROOKSFILMS TELEVISION/ALAN SPENCER PRODUCTIONS/TOUCHSTONE TELEVISION) · SITCOM

10 × 30 mins · colour

US dates: 20 Sep–1 Nov 1989 (7 episodes)
UK dates: 14 Oct–16 Dec 1989 (10 episodes)
BBC2 Sat 9.50pm

MAIN CAST

Reginald J Tarkington	Harvey Korman
Ms Frick/Mrs Nutt	Cloris Leachman
Freddy	Mark Blankfield
Charles Nutt III	Brian McNamara
Sally Lonnaneck	Molly Hagan

CREDITS

creators Mel Brooks/Alan Spencer · *writers* Mel Brooks/Alan Spencer, Richard Day, Jim Geoghan, Alicia Marie Schudt · *directors* Gary Nelson, Bruce Bilson, Roger Duchovny · *executive producers* Mel Brooks/Alan Spencer

A certifiably crazy US sitcom centred around the Nutt House, a New York hotel of much-faded grandeur. The establishment is staffed by a bunch of ludicrous incompetents under the leadership of the prissy and oily manager Reginald J Tarkington, who is answerable to the eccentric owner Mrs Nutt (played by Cloris Leachman, one of two roles she had in the series) and her son and heir Charles. Completing the staff was the near-blind lift operator, Freddy, secretary Sally (normal, compared to the others) and the formidable Mrs Frick (Leachman again), a voluminous, over-sexed Teutonic with a broad accent and carnal designs on Tarkington.

Clearly, subtlety was not part of the comedic tapestry in this combination of wacky plots, madcap characters, OTT slapstick and surreal sight gags. The result was as if **Fawlty Towers**, **Police Squad**, Arthur Hailey's *Hotel* and Mel Brooks' *Blazing Saddles* had been put into a blender, yielding a colourful concoction, hard to swallow but with a few nuggets of gold amid the sprawling mess. (Harvey Korman and Cloris Leachman had previously appeared together in Brooks' 1977 movie *High Anxiety*.)

Mel Brooks' stamp was all over *The Nutt House* – he co-created, co-wrote and co-executive-produced the series and his characteristic comedy style was evident in the screeched high-volume exchanges and violence between the main protagonists. *The Nutt House* was not a place for a long stay and NBC evidently agreed, cancelling the series after only seven episodes had been screened. (Ten had been made to this point, and all were shown by BBC1.)

Des O'Connor

Concerning himself, as he has in recent years, with chat-shows (albeit humorous ones), game-shows and music, it is easy to forget that Des O'Connor started out as a comic, and that his TV sketch series, with Jack Douglas cast as his foil, aired for most of the 1960s. And in the light of the unrelenting ribbing that O'Connor suffered at the hands of Morecambe and Wise, which caused him to suffer a 'joke' standing quite distinct from his comic prowess, it is also easy to forget that O'Connor is and has always been a polished performer.

Born on 12 January 1932 in Stepney, in the East End of London, O'Connor pushed himself to the top the hard way, working as a Butlin's Redcoat and playing the dying stages of 1950s variety theatres after his stint of National Service had ended. Although he made his TV debut on the BBC on 2 October 1954, it was in 1957, on ITV, that O'Connor made his first regular small-screen appearances, as the host of game-show *Spot The Tune!* (for which he was billed as Desmond O'Connor), and from here he performed frequently on the top-rated variety series *Val Parnell's Sunday Night At The London Palladium*, either as an act or as host when the regular MCs were unavailable. O'Connor made a big deal out of the fact that he was a plain, ordinary man who happened to tell jokes, and his decision to keep his own name, rather than adopt a stage pseudonym, was a key part of this process: he wanted it to be seen that he had no 'side' and was squeaky clean. As such, O'Connor became much loved by the mums at home, and this same audience ensured that his career as a ballad singer was an immediate success – he has scored eight chart singles to date, including the number one 'I Pretend' in 1968, and sold albums by the million. (In truth, it was O'Connor's singing that Morecambe and Wise loved to send up, not his comedy act.)

The entry that follows focuses solely on O'Connor's comedy work within TV, omitting *Des O'Connor Now!* (a music show for Thames, from 10 June 1985), *Des O'Connor Tonight* (a comedy chat-show with music, first BBC then Thames then Central, 1977 to date) and the game-shows he has hosted, such as *Pot Of Gold* and, from 24 February 1992, the revived *Take Your Pick*.

The Des O'Connor Show

UK · ITV (ATV) · STANDUP/SKETCH

72 editions (8 × 25 mins · b/w; 33 × 30 mins · b/w; 1 × 50 mins · b/w; 29 × 60 mins · colour; 1 × short special · colour)

Series One (6 × 30 mins · b/w) 29 May–19 July 1963 · Wed 9.15pm then Fri 10.15pm

Series Two (6 × 30 mins · b/w) 23 June–4 Aug 1965 · Wed 9.10pm

Series Three (6 × 30 mins · b/w) 30 Mar–18 May 1966 · Wed 9.10pm

Series Four (6 × 30 mins · b/w) 20 Oct–25 Nov 1966 · Thu 9.40pm then Fri 9.35pm

Series Five (8 × 25 mins · b/w) 30 Sep–18 Nov 1967 · Sat 10.20pm

Series Six (9 × 30 mins · b/w) 20 Apr–15 June 1968 · Sat mostly 7pm

Special (50 mins · b/w) 2 Nov 1968 · Sat 6.15pm

Series Seven (14 × 60 mins · colour) 9 May–8 Aug 1970 · Sat 6.15pm

Short special (colour) · part of *All-Star Comedy Carnival* 25 Dec 1970 · Fri 6pm

Series Eight (14 × 60 mins · colour) 26 June–25 Sep 1971 · Sat mostly 6.45pm

Special (60 mins · colour) 28 Dec 1973 · Fri 9pm

MAIN CAST

Des O'Connor
Jack Douglas (series 1–5, 7–8)
Jim Couton and Rex (series 7 and second special)
The MacGregor Brothers (series 7)
Dom DeLuise (series 8)
Connie Stevens (series 8)
Charlie Callas (series 8)
Joe Baker (series 8)

CREDITS

writers Alan Fell, Stanley Myers, Johnny Whyte, Des O'Connor (series 1); Tony Hawes (series 2–6 and first special); Tony Hawes, Bill Larkin, Paul Wayne, Michael Magee, John Muir/Eric Geen, Charles Lee, Gig Henry, Bryan Blackburn (series 7); Tony Hawes, Barry Cryer, Ronnie Cass, Stan Dreben, Lila Garrett, David Pollock/Elias Davis (series 8); Bryan Blackburn, Mike Craig, Lawrie Kinsley, Ron McDonnell (second special) · *additional material* Spike Mullins (series 5 & 6) · *directors* Brian Bartholomew (series 1), Philip Casson/Bill Hitchcock (series 5), Bill Hitchcock (series 6), Robert Fleming, Bill Hitchcock, John Robins (series 7), Jon Scoffield (series 8), Colin Clews (second special) · *producers* Albert Locke (47), Alan Tarrant (17), Dicky Leeman (6), Colin Clews (1) · *executive producer* Mort Lachman (series 7 & 8)

It was *The Des O'Connor Show* that firmly established the London comic as a top-rated act, with Jack Douglas (perhaps best known now as a *Carry On* actor) by his side in seven of the first eight series, playing the foil.

Of particular interest are the 28 programmes that aired 1970–71, which were made expressly with the export (primarily the US) market in mind. ATV chief Sir Lew Grade wanted to make O'Connor a star turn in the USA, and all of these shows were transmitted primetime by NBC virtually simultaneously with the UK transmissions. They did quite well there, too – O'Connor was known to the US audience by way of three early 1960s appearances he made on *The Ed Sullivan Show* and his occasional Las Vegas stage seasons. For these two 1970–71 series American writers were brought on board (Bill Larkin, Charles Lee and Gig Henry wrote for Bob Hope; Paul Wayne and Michael Magee for the Smothers Brothers), an American executive producer (Mort Lachman) was appointed and US guest stars (among them Liberace, Phyllis Diller, Sid Caesar, Phil Silvers, Dom DeLuise and Jack Benny) were an integral part of the weekly casts. Ultimately, however, O'Connor gave up trying to crack this hardest of markets and focused solely on his home country.

Des O'Connor On Stage

UK · ITV (ATV) · STANDUP/SKETCH

4 × 45 mins · b/w

3 May–24 May 1969 · Sat mostly 6.15pm

MAIN CAST

Des O'Connor

CREDITS

writer Tony Hawes · *producer* Albert Locke

This short series featured Des in sketch and song, with star guests galore.

Des

UK · ITV (ATV) · STANDUP/SKETCH

16 × 30 mins · colour

Series One (8) 7 Mar–31 May 1972 · mostly Tue around 7pm

Series Two (8) 26 Oct–14 Dec 1972 · Thu around 7pm

MAIN CAST

Des O'Connor
Johnny Vyvyan (series 1)

CREDITS

writers Tony Hawes, Des O'Connor (series 1); Mike Craig, Lawrie Kinsley, Ron McDonnell (series 2) · *producer* Albert Locke

O'Connor was now well on his way to variety, with the accent here as much on song as on comedy.

Des O'Connor Entertains

UK · ITV (ATV) · STANDUP/SKETCH

18 editions (14 × 30 mins · 4 × 60 mins) · colour

Series One (7 × 30 mins) 19 Feb–2 Apr 1974 · Tue 7.05pm

Special (60 mins) 27 Dec 1974 · Fri 9pm

Series Two (7 × 30 mins) 7 Mar–18 Apr 1975 · Fri mostly 8.30pm

Special (60 mins) 27 Feb 1976 · Fri 9pm

Special (60 mins) 4 June 1976 · Fri 9pm

*Special (60 mins) 10 Dec 1976 · Fri 9pm

MAIN CAST
Des O'Connor
Johnny Vyvyan
Eli Woods (specials 1, 3, 4 & series 2)
Mike Burton (special 1 & series 2)
Sandra Dickinson (series 2)

CREDITS
writers Mike Craig, Lawrie Kinsley, Ron McDonnell, Des O'Connor · *director/producer* Colin Clews

Two series and four specials of humour and music, with weekly comic guests.

*Note. This final special was not screened by London-area ITV.

Tom O'Connor

Born in Bootle on 31 October 1939, Tom O'Connor was a maths and music teacher when he won an edition of the talent-spotting ITV series *Opportunity Knocks* and went on to become a star standup as a contributor to **The Comedians**.

O'Connor has appeared in a number of shows as a comedian in his own right but the majority of his TV work has been in variety programmes (*Wednesday At Eight, London Night Out, Night Out At The London Casino*) and as the host of quiz- and panel-games (*Name That Tune, Zodiac, Password, Gambit, Cross Wits, I've Got A Secret*, the travelling daytime magazine programme *The Tom O'Connor Roadshow* and others).

The Tom O'Connor Show

UK · ITV (THAMES) · STANDUP

1 × 30 mins · colour

12 Oct 1976 · Tue 8pm

MAIN CAST
Tom O'Connor

CREDITS
writers Spike Mullins, Pat Finan · *director/producer* Keith Beckett

A half-hour special starring the comedian whose uncontroversial material made him a safe bet for family viewing. This single show led to a full series …

Tom O'Connor   1

UK · ITV (THAMES) · STANDUP

6 × 30 mins · colour

1 Mar–5 Apr 1977 · Tue 8.30pm

MAIN CAST
Tom O'Connor

CREDITS
writers Dick Hills, Spike Mullins, Pat Finan · *directors/producers* William G Stewart (5), Dennis Kirkland (1)

Following his appearance in the 1976 *Royal Variety Show* (screened by BBC1 on 15 November) and his hosting of the first series of Thames' variety programme *Wednesday At Eight* (networked 10 November–22 December 1976), O'Connor was given his own starring series by the London-ITV station, in which he cast a shrewd, scripted eye over burning issues of the day.

The final show in the series, recorded at the Casino Theatre in London, led directly to another, much more variety-accented one: *Night Out At The London Casino*, networked by Thames from 20 July to 1 August 1977. Tom O'Connor was the wise-cracking MC in all of those seven programmes.

Tom O'Connor   2

UK · BBC · STANDUP/SKETCH

16 editions (10 × 30 mins · 6 × 35 mins) · colour

Series One (4 × 30 mins) 14 Aug–4 Sep 1984 · BBC2 Tue mostly 9pm

Series Two (6 × 35 mins) 10 Jan–14 Feb 1986 · BBC2 Fri 9pm

Series Three (6 × 30 mins) 9 Dec 1986–27 Jan 1987 · BBC1 Tue 8.30pm

MAIN CAST
Tom O'Connor
Andrew Sachs (series 1)
Derek Griffiths (series 1 & 2)
Cherry Gillespie (series 2)
Mike Berry (series 2)
Chris Emmett (series 2 & 3)
Caroline Gruber (series 3)
Jeff Stevenson (series 3)
Mick Walker (series 3)

CREDITS
script associate Barry Faulkner · *producer* Rick Gardner

A sketch-led comedy show for the self-styled 'Mr Clean' of comedy, who had given up hosting ITV's *Name That Tune* to make this series for the BBC. The familiar and proven format was to take a different subject each week and base the sketches and routines around that single theme (schooling, cinema, hobbies and so on).

The Odd Couple

USA · ABC (PARAMOUNT) · SITCOM

114 × 30 mins · colour

US dates: 24 Sep 1970–4 July 1975

*UK dates: 11 July 1971–22 Dec 1973 (24 episodes) ITV various days and times

MAIN CAST
Felix Unger · · · · · · · · · · · · · · · Tony Randall
Oscar Madison · · · · · · · · · · · · Jack Klugman
Murray Greshner · · · · · · · · · · · · Al Molinaro
Speed · · · · · · · · · · Garry Walberg (1970–74)
Vinnie · · · · · · · · · · · · · · · · · Larry Gelman
Roger · · · · · · · · · · · · Archie Hahn (1973–74)
Roy · · · · · · · · · · Ryan McDonald (1970–71)
Cecily Pigeon · · · · · · · · · · · · · Monica Evans
Gwendolyn Pigeon · · · · · · · · · · · Carol Shelly

CREDITS
creator Neil Simon · *writers* Harvey Miller and others · *director* Harvey Miller · *executive producers* Garry Marshall, Sheldon Keller · *producers* Garry Marshall, Jerry Belson

Neil Simon's fabulously funny creation *The Odd Couple* started out in 1965 as a Broadway play, became a movie in 1968 (with Jack Lemmon and Walter Matthau) and then was adapted for TV by ABC in 1970, remaining on screen for five years and more than a hundred episodes. Throughout, comedy of the highest quality was served up.

Although new scripts were written (not by Neil Simon, who distanced himself from the TV version), the series followed the original Broadway premise pretty closely. The cornerstone of the comedy was the relationship between two very different men: the fastidiously neat, precise and thin Felix Unger, and his fat, lazy slob of a childhood friend Oscar Madison, the two sharing Oscar's Park Avenue apartment after becoming divorced from their respective loved ones. But if you think that *The Odd Couple* was another 'fat-and-thin' comedy you'd be wildly wrong. There was nothing traditional about this creation: neither man was stupid, and neither man was funnier than the other. Rather, because the comedy was drawn on the fundamental differences and conflicts in *character* between the two, the humour was not physical but cerebral: Felix is a photographer, a hypochondriac and an obsessive; Oscar is a sports journalist for the (fictitious) newspaper the *New York Herald* and a slob supreme. They may live together but it's a match made in hell.

While there were other parts – Murray, Speed, Roy and Vinnie were Felix and Oscar's poker-playing pals, and Cecily and Gwendolyn were their super-dotty English neighbours/girlfriends (Monica Evans and Carol Shelly reprising the roles they had played on Broadway and in the movie) – it was Tony Randall and Jack Klugman who were the undoubted stars of *The Odd Couple*, forming a wonderful interplay and comic understanding that enriched every script. Art Carney and Martin Balsam were originally intended for the roles, and then Tony Randall and Mickey Rooney were considered, but eventually Randall and Jack Klugman, both of whom had appeared in touring versions of the play, were selected. Even taking into the account the brilliant Lemmon/Matthau movie, it seems hard to imagine anyone else in the roles. Indeed, although the TV series ended more than 20 years ago, Randall and Klugman continue to play Felix and Oscar on stage, and they starred in a London theatrical revival in 1996.

In Britain, ITV screened all of the opening 24 episodes – the first US season – but no more. (These were marred by ABC's ludicrous 'canned' laugh-track that was eventually replaced by the laughter of a real studio audience.) Subsequently, BBC1 screened 44 episodes of *The Odd Couple* from 10 September 1988 to 30 April 1992, but the final episode has never been shown in the UK, showing Felix reuniting with his ex-wife and moving out of Oscar's apartment, leaving him to revel in his own mess once again.

There have been two further attempts to put *The Odd Couple* on TV. American ABC's *The New Odd Couple*, never shown on British TV, cast black actors in the parts for the first time, but it lasted only 13 episodes. Ron Glass played Felix and Desmond Wilson was Oscar. (Previously, ABC had also failed to convince with a black sitcom based on Neil Simon's *Barefoot In The Park*, never screened in the UK.) And the animators dePatie/Freleng came up with a Saturday-morning TV cartoon version for children, *The Oddball Couple*, which ran for one US season from September 1975. This starred a just-so cat called Spiffy (the Felix part – it's obvious why they couldn't use this name) and a dishevelled dog Fleabag (the Oscar role) sharing an office as freelance magazine writers. Paul Winchell and Frank Nelson voiced the roles.

Odd Man Out

UK · ITV (THAMES) · SITCOM

7 × 30 mins · colour

27 Oct–8 Dec 1977 · Thu 9pm

MAIN CAST

Neville Sutcliffe · · · · · · · · · · · · · John Inman
Dorothy · · · · · · · · · · · · · Josephine Tewson
Ma · · · · · · · · · · · · · · · · · · · Avril Angers
Wilf · · · · · · · · · · · · · · · · Peter Butterworth

CREDITS

writer Vince Powell · *director* Anthony Parker · *producer* Gerald Thomas

In a typical example of a BBC comedy star going to ITV and falling flat on his face, John Inman was awarded this part – his first starring role – after shooting to fame as the mincing Mr Humphries in the BBC sitcom

Are You Being Served? He probably wished that he hadn't bothered. Flouncing and pouting his way through the murky *Odd Man Out* scripts in a manner which, surely, indefensibly, maintained the tainted homosexual TV image of old, Inman played Neville Sutcliffe, owner of a Blackpool fish and chipperie who inherits half ownership (with step-sister Dorothy) of his father's stick-rock factory in Sussex. (Shades of *Nearest And Dearest* here.) Sutcliffe duly departs Blackpool and moves down to Littlehampton (ho-ho) and launches into whole new sorry episodes in his life. Among his staff at the factory is Wilf (played by Peter Butterworth) whose favourite saying is 'How's your rock, cock?'. Quite.

Vince Powell, *Odd Man Out* writer, had done much better work elsewhere, as had producer Gerald Thomas, best known for his *Carry On* films. In the form of seaside rock, indeed, this series had 'appalling' running all the way through it.

See also *Take A Letter, Mr Jones ...*

Oddballs

see *Auntie's Sporting Bloomers*

Of Mycenae And Men

UK · BBC · SITCOM

1 × 30 mins · colour

23 Mar 1979 · BBC2 Fri 10.15pm

MAIN CAST

Helen of Troy · · · · · · · · · · · · · · · Diana Dors
Menelaus · · · · · · · · · · · · · · · · Freddie Jones
Kassandra · · · · · · · · · · · · · Annette Crosbie
The Messenger · · · · · · · · · · · Derek Godfrey
Mr Taramasalatopoulos · · · · · · Bob Hoskins

CREDITS

writers Frederick Raphael/Kenneth McLeish · *director* Hugh David · *producer* Richard Broke

A good cast, neat title and the sort of punning character name (Mr Taramasalatopoulos) that wouldn't have been out of place in an episode of *Up Pompeii!*, all featured in this one-off oddity that took a comedic look at what might have happened to Helen of Troy after the Trojan War.

Off Beat ...

UK · BBC · MUSICAL HUMOUR

3 × 30 mins · b/w

29 Jan–12 Feb 1965 · BBC2 Fri 9.15pm

MAIN CAST

Dudley Moore (show 1)
Ivor Cutler (show 2)
Joan Turner (show 3)

CREDITS

director/producer Francis Coleman

Also known as *Off Beat For Tired Music Lovers*, this curious mix of comedy and music

was typical of the sort of format experimentation that new channel BBC2 attempted in its infancy. Each of the three shows was built around a different star.

Off The Rack

USA · ABC (BROWNSTONE PRODUCTIONS/ MUGWUMP PRODUCTIONS/WARNER BROS) · SITCOM

8 × 30 mins · colour

US dates: 7 Dec 1984 (pilot) · 15 Mar–26 Apr 1985 (series)
UK dates: 6 Nov–18 Dec 1987 (7 episodes) ITV Fri 12.30am

MAIN CAST

Sam Waltman · · · · · · · · · · · · · Edward Asner
Kate Halloran · · · · · · · · · · · Eileen Brennan
Shannon Halloran · · · · · · · · · Claudia Wells
Timothy Halloran · · · · · · · R J Williams (pilot);
· · · · · · · · · · · · · · · · · · Corey Yothers (series)
Brenda Patagorski · · · · · · · · · · · Pamela Brull
Cletus Maxwell · · · · · · · · · Dennis Haysbert
Skip Wagner · · · · · · · · · · · · Sandy Simpson

CREDITS

writers Dan Guntzelman/Steve K Marshall, Richard Baer, Lissa A Levin, Bob Randall · *director* Jay Sandrich · *executive producers* Dan Guntzelman/Steve K Marshall, Marc Merson · *producer* Frank Badami

Sam Waltman is a crusty old chauvinist who owns half of an almost-bankrupt fashion business in Los Angeles, H&W Garments. Upon the death of his partner, Dan, Sam is horrified to discover that the other share of the enterprise has been left to his late associate's feisty wife Kate. Sam and Kate now have to try to get along, not only for the good of the business but also her two children Shannon (16) and Timothy (7), employees Patagorski and Maxwell, and fashion designer Wagner. The scene is set for a good fight, Sam doing his best to resist Kate's ideas and business changes, Kate railing against Sam's old-fashioned ways, his cigar smoke and much else.

The casting was excellent, with both Eileen Brennan (Kate) and Edward Asner (Sam) renowned for their sharp-tongued TV personas, but the series was cancelled and failed to progress beyond eight episodes.

Off The Wall

UK · BBC · SKETCH

1 × 30 mins · colour

2 Dec 1989 · BBC1 Sat 10.05pm

MAIN CAST

Nick Revell
Doon Mackichan
Owen Brenman
John Hegley

CREDITS

writers Nick Revell, John Langdon, Barry Cryer, James Hendrie · *director/producer* Marcus Mortimer · *executive producer* John Kaye Cooper

A topical sketch show, possibly intended as a pilot for a series that failed to materialise.

The Offer

see *Steptoe And Son*

The Office

UK · ITV (RICHMOND FILMS & TELEVISION FOR CARLTON) · SITCOM
1 × 30 mins · colour
2 July 1996 · Tue 8.30pm

MAIN CAST
Norman Platt · · · · · · · · · · · · Robert Lindsay
Hillary Drummond · · · · · · · · · · · · · Isla Blair
Pru · · · · · · · · · · · · · · · · · · Rebecca Front
Nigel · · · · · · · · · · · · · · · · · Stefan Dennis
Gordon · · · · · · · · · · · · · · Toby Longworth
Joan · · · · · · · · · · · · · · · · · Sara Powell
Chief Executive Officer · · · · · · · Clive Graham
Mrs Platt · · · · · · · · Belinda Lang (voice only)

CREDITS
writer Steven Moffat · *director* Paul Jackson · *executive producer* Bill Ward · *producer* Sandra Hastie

An impeccably cast one-off. Robert Lindsay starred as Norman Platt, a middle-manager at Trans Atlas International who is due in the conference hall to address the company's divisional managers. Beforehand, though, he is summoned to the office of his new boss, an intimidating woman named Hillary Drummond. She hints that he is her preferred candidate for a senior executive position but, through a simple misunderstanding, he arrives at the conclusion that this promotion is dependent on their having sex, on the desk, immediately. Shedding his doubts, and then his clothes, until he's stretched out stark naked among her paper clips, Platt then realises that she meant for nothing of the kind. As the truth dawns and his clothes come to rest behind a locked door, he is dragged deeper and deeper into the mire in order to get himself dressed and to the meeting, a task in which he is aided, just, by his dippy temporary secretary Pru and some motor-bike couriers. He succeeds, however, delivering his speech in a woman's pink jacket and skirt – and because the subject is gender stereotyping in the workplace he is applauded for his apparent initiative.

This single comedy farce (Carlton preferred to see it labelled thus rather than as a sitcom) was one of ITV's entries for the Golden Rose of Montreux 1996, but it did not win. And if it was a pilot, no series has followed – possibly because all the comedic eggs were put into this one, only fairly amusing basket.

An Officer And A Gentleman

UK · BBC · SITCOM
1 × 30 mins · colour

8 Jan 1970 · BBC1 Thu 7.30pm

MAIN CAST
Major Gissing · · · · · · · · · · · · · James Grout
Sid Coil · · · · · · · · · · · · · · · · Ken Wynne
Mrs Telfer · · · · · · · · · · · · · Patricia Hayes
Miss Jellicoe · · · · · · · · · · · · · Diana King
Dimitri Yevgenyvitch · · · · Raymond Westwell

CREDITS
writer Myles Rudge · *producer* Robin Nash

Character actor James Grout flexed his comedy muscles in the role of military man Major Gissing, but his usual sterling performance failed to rescue this *Comedy Playhouse* project from the one-off file.

Oh Brother!

UK · BBC · SITCOM
20 episodes (19 × 30 mins · 1 × short special) · 13 × b/w · 7 × colour
Series One (6 × b/w) 13 Sep–18 Oct 1968 · BBC1 Fri 7.55pm
Short special (b/w) *Oh Brother!* and *All Gas And Gaiters* combination as part of *Christmas Night With The Stars* 25 Dec 1968 · BBC1 Wed 6.40pm
Series Two (6 × b/w) 11 Apr–16 May 1969 · BBC1 Fri 8.20pm
Series Three (7 × colour) 16 Jan–27 Feb 1970 · BBC1 Fri 7.55pm

MAIN CAST
Brother Dominic · · · · · · · · · · · Derek Nimmo
The Prior, Father Anselm · · · · · · Felix Aylmer
Master of Novices · · · Colin Gordon (series 1)
Sub-Prior Father Matthew · · · · Derek Francis
· (series 2 & 3)

CREDITS
writers David Climie/Austin Steele · *director* Harold Snoad · *producers* Duncan Wood (10), Johnny Downes (7), Harold Snoad (3)

More religious revelry and another naïf character for Derek Nimmo. In *All Gas And Gaiters* he had been Reverend Noote; now he was a monk, Brother Dominic. Names and rank notwithstanding, however, there was little to distinguish between the two.

Designed as a showcase for Nimmo, the premise of *Oh Brother!* was simple: Brother Dominic is a well-meaning but accident-prone novice at Mountacres Priory, who treads the thin line between acceptance within the order and expulsion from it, according to his mishaps and the prevailing judgement of his peers: Father Anselm is kindly and accommodating, Father Matthew is exasperated with Dominic's clumsiness.

Oh Brother! was an unremarkable sitcom, but it prospered because of Nimmo's ability to bring the best out in his material and his great popularity at the time. (This also accorded him his own chat-show, *If It's Saturday It Must Be Nimmo*, screened by BBC1 from 24 October to 19 December 1970.)

Oh Brother! also spawned a sequel, *Oh Father!*

Oh, Doctor Beeching!

UK · BBC · SITCOM
19 × 30 mins · colour
Pilot · 14 Aug 1995 · BBC1 Mon 8.30pm
Series One (8) 8 July–27 Aug 1996 · BBC1 mostly Mon 8.30pm
Series Two (10) 29 June–28 Sep 1997 · BBC1 Sun mostly 6.45pm

MAIN CAST
Jack Skinner · · · · · · · · · · · · · · Paul Shane
Ethel Schumann · · · · · · · · · · · · · Su Pollard
Cecil Parkin · · · · · · · · · · · · Jeffrey Holland
May Skinner · · · · · · · Sherrie Hewson (pilot);
· · · · · · · · · · · · · · · · · Julia Deakin (series)
Vera Plumtree · · · · · · · · · · · · Barbara New
Harry Lambert · · · · · · · · · · · Stephen Lewis
Arnold · · · · · · · · · · · · · · · · · Ivor Roberts
Ralph · · · · · · · · · · · · · · · · · Perry Benson
Percy · · · · · · · · · · · · · · · · · · Terry John
Gloria Skinner · · · · · · · · · Lindsay Grimshaw
Wilfred Schumann · · · · · · · · · · · Paul Aspden
Amy Matlock · · · · · · · Tara Daniels (series 2)
Mr Orkindale · · Richard Spendlove (series 2)

CREDITS
creators David Croft/Richard Spendlove · *writers* David Croft/Richard Spendlove (13), John Stevenson (3), Paul Minett/Brian Leveson (2), John Chapman (1) · *director* Roy Gould · *producers* David Croft (series 1), David Croft/Charles Garland (series 2)

Britain was once traversed by a network of railway lines that reached even the smallest towns. Over the years some of these lines were allowed to deteriorate or be abandoned, but in 1963 Doctor Beeching – commissioned by the government to recommend a course of action that would save the exchequer millions of pounds – called for the closure of 2128 stations in one sweep, and the ripping up of hundred of lines perceived to be uneconomic. The execution of his suggestions decimated the service, all but erasing the rural railways that served the less populous communities in Britain. Throughout 1963, virtually every town in Britain feared that it would lose its local service, and railway staff spent the year worrying about redundancy. This situation provided the background for *Oh, Doctor Beeching!*, a sitcom created and written by ensemble comedy maestro David Croft in collaboration with Richard Spendlove (who had worked on the railways for 30 years).

The series was set at Hatley Station, a shabby but nonetheless picturesque halt servicing a sleepy local line. Awaiting the arrival of his new boss, Jack Skinner, who sports a pronounced limp, is the acting stationmaster. He's an average man – not too bright, not over-ambitious – but is delighted to have a beautiful wife, May, who runs the station buffet. Her looks and his insecurity makes him prone to jealousy, however, and he always imagines that she is seeing other men. Jack and May live at the station with their daughter Gloria, who attends college.

The other local residents and staff include ticket saleslady Ethel and her son, the odd-job man Wilfred (the product of Ethel's involvement with a US serviceman during the Second World War); Vera Plumtree, the widow of a respected train driver; signalman Harry Lambert who is sufficiently underworked to operate several sidelines from his signalbox, including hairdressing and selling fruit and vegetables; and train drivers/guards Arnold, Ralph and Percy.

The arrival of the efficient and officious new stationmaster Cecil Parkin causes waves among the staff, however – especially May, who had a passionate affair with him before her marriage to Jack; according to the calendar, it transpires that Cecil is Gloria's real father. But the complex relationships between the protagonists fade into the background when Beeching's report is published and Hatley is threatened with closure. As the staff stare redundancy in the face only one thing matters: survival.

Most of the major actors in *Oh, Doctor Beeching!* came from David Croft's informal rep company, some playing variations of characters they had portrayed before (principally in *Hi-de-Hi!*). And, cast as Harry Lambert, Stephen Lewis intentionally gave his character most of the mannerisms of his most famous TV portrayal, 'Blakey' in *On The Buses*. Although set in 1963 the sitcom had a much earlier period feel – possibly to accentuate the quaintness of the line and its handsome but troublesome steam engines – and thus *Oh, Doctor Beeching!* invited comparisons with earlier feature films on a similar theme, such as Will Hay's similarly titled *Oh Mr Porter* (1937, directed by Marcel Varnel) and *The Titfield Thunderbolt* (1952, Charles Crichton). But arguably its closest antecedent was the earlier TV sitcom *The Train Now Standing*, and, coincidentally or otherwise, this title was used for one of the first series' episodes.

Note. *Oh, Doctor Beeching!* was launched on 14 August 1995 as a single-episode pilot. On 1 July 1996, a week before the first full series began, this was repeated with newly filmed, revised elements.

Oh Father!

UK · BBC · SITCOM

7 × 30 mins · colour

12 Sep–24 Oct 1973 · BBC1 Wed 6.50pm

MAIN CAST

Father Dominic · · · · · · · · · · · · Derek Nimmo
Father Harris · · · · · · · · · Laurence Naismith
Mrs Carr · · · · · · · · · · · · · · · Pearl Hackney
Walter · · · · · · · · · · · · · · · · · · David Kelly

CREDITS

writers David Climie/Austin Steele · producer Graeme Muir

A sequel to *Oh Brother!* in which the unthinkable happened: Brother Dominic was promoted to become Father Dominic, curate to Father Harris. The elevation in status did nothing to temper his penchant for disaster, though, and the comedy continued much as before. Felix Aylmer and Derek Francis reappeared as their *Oh Brother!* characters in a couple of episodes but there was no doubting that the format had run its course and, finally, Nimmo's meteoric rise through the ecclesiastical hierarchy was ended. (A pity really, because one could have imagined seeing him go all the way, becoming a deity in an ultimate series *Oh God!*)

Capitalising on his continuing popularity, Nimmo fronted another long-running chat and miscellany show, *Just A Nimmo*, in which he, his guest of the week and the studio audience light-heartedly discussed a number of topics. The series opened on BBC2 on 11 February 1974 and 28 editions aired before it bowed out on 27 March 1978.

See also *Hell's Bells*.

Oh Happy Band!

see WORTH, Harry

Oh In Colour

see MILLIGAN, Spike

Oh, Madeline

USA · ABC (THE CARSEY-WERNER COMPANY) · SITCOM

19 × 30 mins · colour

US dates: 27 Sep 1983–13 Mar 1984
UK dates: 18 Sep–11 Dec 1986 (13 episodes) C4 Thu 9pm

MAIN CAST

Madeline Wayne · · · · · · · · · Madeline Kahn
Charlie Wayne · · · · · · · · · · · James Sloyan
Robert Leone · · · · · · · · · · · Louis Giambalvo
Doris Leone · · · · · · · · · · · · · Jesse Welles
Annie McIntyre · · · · · · · · · · Francine Tacker

CREDITS

writers Terence Brady/Charlotte Bingham and others · directors various · producers Marcy Carsey/Tom Werner

This American adaptation of the LWT sitcom *Pig In The Middle* starred film actress Madeline Kahn (best known for her roles in movies *What's Up Doc?*, *Paper Moon*, *Blazing Saddles*, *Young Frankenstein* and *High Anxiety*). She was cast as a bored, middle-aged, middle-class housewife living in a Chicago suburb, determined to introduce some zest into what she perceives as her lacklustre ten-year marriage to Charlie (who writes steamy novels under the pen name Crystal Love) and her pedestrian lifestyle in general. Other parts were Charlie's friend

Robert, Madeline's friend Doris (also Robert's ex-wife) and Annie, Charlie's amorous publishing editor.

This was the first series from Marcy Carsey and Tom Werner, who went on to produce *The Cosby Show*, *Roseanne* and many other respectable hits, but *Oh, Madeline* made little impact and was cancelled after 19 episodes, despite the unusual blend of sharp lines, sight gags and slapstick reminiscent of *I Love Lucy*.

Oh No – It's Selwyn Froggitt

UK · ITV (YORKSHIRE) · SITCOM

29 × 30 mins · colour

Pilot · 30 Sep 1974 · Mon 8pm
Series One (6) 7 Jan–11 Feb 1976 · Wed 8.30pm
Series Two (7) 21 Feb–4 Apr 1977 · Mon 8pm
Series Three (8) 8 Nov–27 Dec 1977 · Tue mostly 7.30pm
*Series Four (7) *Selwyn* 5 Sep–17 Oct 1978 · Tue mostly 8.15pm

MAIN CAST

Selwyn Froggitt · · · · · · · · · · · · Bill Maynard
Mrs Froggitt (Mum) · · · · · · · · Megs Jenkins
· (series 1–3)
Maurice Froggitt · · · · · · · · · · Robert Keegan
· (series 1–3)
Clive · · · · · · · · Richard Davies (series 1–3)
Ray · · · · · · · · · · · · · · Ray Mort (series 1–3)
Jack · · · · · · · · · · · · · · Bill Dean (series 1–3)
Harry · · · · · · · · Harold Goodwin (series 1–3)
Vera Parkinson · · · · · · · · · · Rosemary Martin
· (series 1);
· · · · · · · · · · · · · Lynda Baron (series 2 & 3)
Mervyn Price · · · Bernard Gallagher (series 4)

CREDITS

creator Alan Plater · writers Alan Plater (16), Mike Craig/Lawrie Kinsley/Ron McDonnell (3), Bernie Sharp (2), H V Kershaw (1); *Selwyn*: Lawrie Kinsley/Ron McDonnell (4), Richard Knight (2), Jon Glover/Jeremy Nicholas (1) · director/producer Ronnie Baxter

Having returned to TV with *The Life Of Riley*, Bill Maynard scored a major success with *Oh No – It's Selwyn Froggitt*, produced by Yorkshire TV and set in that county. Froggitt is an excessively boisterous double-sized half-wit dogged by disaster, the type of person people cross roads to avoid, a deeply jovial man who has somehow deluded himself into thinking that he can fix anything but, rather, breaks everything.

Daytime finds Selwyn working as a labourer for the local council's Public Works department – so inept that he cannot dig a hole in the ground without simultaneously filling it in. Evenings find him, a copy of *The Times* tucked under the sleeve of his donkey-jacket, down at the Scarsdale Working Men's Club And Institute where, foolishly, the committee has appointed him secretary. Most of the series' humour was generated at two locations: here at the club, where Selwyn's well-intentioned problems are felt most keenly by the barman Ray and the drinking regulars Clive, Jack and Harry, and at home, where Selwyn exasperates his ever-loving mum and his brother Maurice.

Oh No – It's Selwyn Froggitt was created by the esteemed television playwright Alan Plater, and the pilot – in which, incidentally, the character's name was spelled Froggit and the title reflected this – was aired as one of six single-edition comedies networked by Yorkshire TV around September 1974, with one other (*Rising Damp*) also becoming a full series. The role was fashioned especially for Bill Maynard, who came up with the original idea of an uncouth yet bizarrely cultured character, and it soon attained great popularity, scoring highly in the ratings while Froggitt's catchphrase – 'magic', uttered while sticking up one or both thumbs – contributed to the popular vernacular of the era.

The final series of *Oh No – It's Selwyn Froggitt* was followed by a pantomime stage production featuring the character, and then by an incredibly weak TV sequel, titled simply *Selwyn*, in which, having seen the post advertised in *The Times*, Froggitt is appointed Entertainments Officer at Paradise Valley holiday camp, where his lumbering, bumbling mishaps impact most upon the camp's exasperated manager, Mervyn Price. The Scarsdale regulars did not appear in this series, and, tellingly, Alan Plater was not a contributor. Maynard was probably significant in the change of setting from village to holiday camp: as Billy Williams, he had made his professional stage debut at Butlin's, Skegness, in 1951, as support to Terry Scott. (They both played the Butlin's camp at Filey in 1952, toured together and were given their own sketch-comedy series by the BBC in 1955–56, *Great Scott – It's Maynard!*)

Note. On the back of his success with the *Selwyn* series, Bill Maynard starred in a one-off, hour-long variety special, *Bill Maynard In Person*, networked by Yorkshire TV on 3 January 1979. The star appeared in a number of sketches (written by Dick Hills, Mike Craig, Spike Mullins, Ron McDonnell and Lawrie Kinsley) and introduced musical acts.

The Old Boy Network

UK · BBC · STANDUP

22 editions (17 × 40 mins · 5 × 45 mins) · colour

Special (40 mins) *Arthur Askey In The Old Boy Network* 31 Dec 1978 · BBC2 Sun 7.20pm

Series One (5 × 40 mins) 14 Sep–19 Oct 1979 · BBC2 Fri 8.20pm

Series Two (6 × 40 mins) 2 Sep–7 Oct 1981 · BBC2 Wed 9pm

Special (45 mins) *Eric Sykes: One Of The Great Troupers* 10 Dec 1981 · BBC2 Thu 9pm

Series Three (4 × 45 mins) *Spotlight* 16 May–6 June 1983 · BBC2 Mon 9.25pm

Series Four (5 × 40 mins) *Spotlight* 27 June–25 July 1984 · BBC2 Wed 7.50pm

MAIN CAST
see below

CREDITS
script associate Jimmy Perry · *producer* Don Sayer

Programmes highlighting some of the elder statesmen of British comedy. In each edition, filmed in theatres, the chosen comic performed anew some of his old routines, showed film clips where possible, and recounted anecdotes from his life. Although the 1983–84 editions had a different title (*Spotlight*) the format was, essentially, the same as *The Old Boy Network*.

Featured were Arthur Askey (31 December 1978), Sandy Powell (14 September 1979), John Laurie (21 September 1979), Tommy Trinder (28 September 1979), Jack Warner (12 October 1979), Fred Emney (19 October 1979), Leslie Sarony (2 September 1981), Percy Edwards (9 September 1981), Chesney Allen (16 September 1981), Doris Hare (23 September 1981), Nat Jackley (30 September 1981), Richard Murdoch (7 October 1981), Eric Sykes (10 December 1981), Alfred Marks (16 May 1983), Dickie Henderson (23 May 1983), Jimmy Edwards (30 May 1983), Spike Milligan (6 June 1983), Bill Maynard (27 June 1984), Peter Goodwright (4 July 1984), Leslie Crowther (11 July 1984), Jack Douglas (18 July 1984) and Ray Alan (25 July 1984).

Note. A similar show, *A Chance To Meet …*, originally broadcast by BBC North East transmitters, aired nationally on BBC1 in 1989. This again concentrated on veteran stars and the comedy names of interest included Ian Carmichael (4 July), Jimmy Jewel (5 July) and the not-so-veteran Barry Cryer (6 July).

Old Boy Network

UK · ITV (CLEMENT-LA FRENAIS/SELECTV FOR CENTRAL) · SITCOM

7 × 30 mins · colour

16 Feb–12 Apr 1992 · Sun mostly 10.05pm

MAIN CAST
Lucas Frye · · · · · · · · · · · · · · · · · · Tom Conti
Peter Duckham · · · · · · · · · · · · John Standing
Sir Roland White · · · · · · · · · · · · Robert Lang
Tamsin · · · · · · · · · · · · · · · · · Georgia Allen
Parker Morrow · · · · · · · · · · · · · Jayne Brook

CREDITS
creators Dick Clement/Ian La Frenais · *writers* Dick Clement/Ian La Frenais (6), Steve Coombes/Dave Robinson (1) · *director/producer* Sydney Lotterby · *executive producers* Allan McKeown, Tony Charles

Spy humour from Clement and La Frenais, forever saddled with the stiff task of trying to better their brilliant sitcoms *The Likely Lads* and *Porridge* and light-drama series

Auf Wiedersehen, Pet. Old Boy Network was not in the same league as these esteemed series, but, in truth, it aimed to raise a smile rather than loud guffaws.

Making his sitcom debut, Tom Conti was one of the two old boys in the title, cast as Lucas Frye, a former MI5 agent disgraced when his old public-school rival Peter Duckham, an MI6 adversary whose loathing for Frye had become an obsession, exposed him as a Soviet double-agent, betraying Britain to the Ruskies. With the Cold War melting, Frye begs to leave Moscow and be allowed home, where, keen to embrace his old ways, he rejoins his old London gentleman's club. It is here that Frye is seen by a horrified Duckham (played by John Standing), and they fall into contemptuous conversation which, nonetheless, soon turns to their advantage: Frye requires work and money while Duckham has been retired early and has similar needs, so they decide to go into business together, as Frye-Duckham Associates, opening up a private espionage agency in Mayfair. But their mutual distrust is so great that FDA is doomed to fail – Frye, the more assured character, teases Duckham by reminding him that he once slept with Duckham's ex-wife Sophie; and, although officially retired, Duckham still reports on Frye to his former MI6 boss Sir Roland White. Matters are not helped when they take on a couple of employees: a daffy secretary, Tamsin, and, to help ease their spying burden, Parker Morrow, a former American CIA agent who plays mind games with both Frye and Duckham. FDA's assignments are small fry compared to working for the MI5, MI6, CIA and KGB, but the pair, assisted by Morrow, carry out their tasks with an almost reluctant energy and dry wit, usually with success but not always resulting in payment.

The net result was an entertaining seven episodes suggestive of *Randall And Hopkirk (Deceased)* but more wry, crisp and dry than that light 1960s crime-show. Only one series was made, however and, following the disappointment of their previous sitcom *Freddie And Max*, Clement and La Frenais were clearly finding it tough to regain their Midas touch. Their next major TV writing venture was *Full Stretch*, another light-drama series – not a comedy, as such – made by WitzEnd for Meridian and screened by ITV from 5 January to 9 February 1993.

The Old Campaigner

UK · BBC · SITCOM

7 × 30 mins · b/w

Pilot · 30 June 1967 · BBC1 Fri 7.30pm

One series (6) 6 Dec 1968–10 Jan 1969 · BBC1 Fri 7.55pm

MAIN CAST
James Franklin-Jones ('F J') · · · Terry-Thomas

Peter Clancy · · · · · · · · Derek Fowlds (pilot);
· · · · · · · · · · · · · · · · Jonathan Cecil (series)
Miss Pinto · · · · · · · · · · · · · · · Lois Penson
'L B' · · · · · · · · · · · Norman Claridge (pilot);
· · · · · · · · · · · · · · · · Reginald Marsh (series)

CREDITS
writer Michael Pertwee · producers Robin Nash (pilot), James Gilbert (series)

The adventures of James Franklin-Jones – known as 'F J' to his colleagues – a globetrotting salesman for Balsom Plastics. Each week F J jets about the world on the firm's business, never letting work interfere with his true vocation: the quest for 'crumpet', a pursuit he follows with military precision, using, as ammunition, a fund of chat-up lines, invented pasts and cunning tricks. In the Comedy Playhouse pilot the wily 'old campaigner' was confronted with Peter Clancy, a young and naïve assistant who, to learn the ropes, was assigned to accompany him on his travels. Although F J was initially horrified by his young charge's highly developed set of morals and ethics, he soon managed to open the young man's eyes to a wide world of rich food, strong drink and willing women.

Portraying yet another variation on his rakish cad persona, this was a brisk, seemingly effortless role for Terry-Thomas. In the pilot episode, Clancy was played by Derek Fowlds, soon (from March 1969) to become well-known to children as straightman to the witty puppet fox Basil Brush. Fowlds later achieved even greater success, again playing an assistant, in **Yes Minister**.

The Old Contemptible

UK · BBC · SITCOM
1 × 30 mins · colour
15 July 1970 · BBC1 Wed 7.30pm
MAIN CAST
Sam Oakley · · · · · · · · · · · · · · Billy Russell
Arthur Oakley · · · · · · · · · · · · Arthur English
Lily Oakley · · · · · · · · · · Gretchen Franklin
Josie Oakley · · · · · · · · · · · Tamara Ustinov

CREDITS
writer Keith Waterhouse · director Vere Lorrimer · producer Dennis Main Wilson

A Keith Waterhouse-written Comedy Playhouse episode centred around a First World War survivor, Sam Oakley, the 'old contemptible' of the title, who tries to bring a sense of old-fashioned values to the modern world.

Olive Fox

UK · BBC · MUSICAL HUMOUR
1 × 5 mins · b/w
24 Feb 1937 · Wed 9pm
MAIN CAST
Olive Fox
Evel Burns

CREDITS
producer Harry Pringle

Olive Fox was best known as one half of the concert-party double-act Fox and Rose. Born in Brixton, south London, she went to school in Boulogne and, upon returning to England, followed her mother (a professional contralto) into concert parties and the music-hall. After marrying the pantomime dame and concert-party artist Clarkson Rose they mounted a long-running stage revue Twinkle; she also continued to appear solo, presenting her humour in a style similar to Cicely Courtneidge, and in this very early TV presentation performed 'Life In The Old Girl Yet' and 'An Ordinary Woman Like Me', accompanied by Evel Burns.

The significance of this performance is that it made Olive Fox the first comedienne to appear in her own starring slot on British television. The grand antecedent of Joyce Grenfell, Beryl Reid, Sheila Hancock, Victoria Wood, French and Saunders and all the other funny-women who have since made their mark on the small-screen, Olive Fox died on 25 September 1964.

On The Air

USA · ABC (LYNCH-FROST PRODUCTIONS) · SITCOM
7 × 30 mins · colour
US dates: 20 June–4 July 1992 (3 episodes)
UK dates: 24 July–4 Sep 1993 (7 episodes)
BBC2 Sat 1.55am
MAIN CAST
Lester Guy · · · · · · · · · · · · · · · Ian Buchanan
Vladja Gochktch · · · · · · · · · · · David L Lander
Ruth Trueworthy · · · · · · · · Nancye Ferguson
Bert Schein · · · · · · · · · · · · · Gary Grossman
Betty Hudson · · · · · · Marla Jeanette Rubinoff
Dwight McGonigle · · · · · · · · · Marvin Kaplan
Mickey · · · · · · · · · · · · · · · Mel Johnson Jr
Buddy Budwaller · · · · · · · · · · Miguel Ferrer
'Blinky' Watts · · · · · · · · · · · · Tracey Walter
The Hurry Up Twins · · · · · · · · · · Raleigh and
· · · · · · · · · · · · · · · · · · · Raymond Friend

CREDITS
creators David Lynch/Mark Frost · writers David Lynch, Mark Frost, Robert Engels · director Jack Fisk · executive producers David Lynch/Mark Frost, Robert Engels · producer Deepak Nayar

Following the success of their fantastical soap noir series Twin Peaks (screened in the USA 8 April 1990 to 10 June 1991 and in the UK, by BBC2, 23 October 1990 to 18 June 1991), film director David Lynch and his production partner Mark Frost were hot property. So they combined with other production personnel from that earlier series (including writer Robert Engels and composer/arranger Angelo Badalamenti) to put together On The Air, an equally bizarre and off-centre idea, this time undermining the genre of sitcom.

The series was set in 1957 and centred around TV channel ZBC (Zoblotnick Broadcasting Corporation), home of a live variety programme titled The Lester Guy Show. Guy is an insipid, young but already jaded star trying desperately to revive his flagging career but cursed with an inept production team, shoddy sets, cheesy dancers, clumsy and dangerous scene-shifters and supernaturally bad luck. The other major characters included Guy's incomprehensible director Gochktch, his assistant Ruth (the only person on the set able to understand her boss), nervous producer Dwight McGonigle and the vacuous glamour-queen Betty Hudson – the target for Guy's blistering professional jealousy. Each week, events conspired against Guy and the crew's attempts to produce a good show.

However, as those who watched Lynch and Frost's Twin Peaks will readily believe, this simple explanation of On The Air does little to suggest the real flavour of the piece, which was, quite simply, absurdist. Visual gags combined with wild sound effects and violent slapstick to give the series a style quite unlike other television programmes – coming across as something like a blend of Olsen and Johnson's surreal theatrical comedy Hellzapoppin, a Three Stooges routine and a Warner Bros cartoon. Seven out of ten for effort. Ten out of ten for weirdness.

Note. On American TV, On The Air lasted for just three episodes before network ABC pulled the plug. Seven episodes had been made, however, and all of these were screened in the UK by BBC2.

On The Bright Side

see BAXTER, Stanley

On The Buses

UK · ITV (LWT) · SITCOM
76 episodes (60 × 30 mins · colour; 14 × 30 mins · b/w; 2 × short specials · colour)
Series One (7 × b/w) 28 Feb–12 Apr 1969 · mostly Fri 7.30pm
Series Two (6 × b/w) 31 May–5 July 1969 · Sat 7pm
Short special (colour) · part of All-Star Comedy Carnival 25 Dec 1969 · Thu 6pm
Series Three (13 × colour) 2 Jan–27 Mar 1970 · Fri 8.30pm
Series Four (12 × colour · 1 × b/w) 27 Nov 1970–21 Feb 1971 · Fri 8.30pm then Sun mostly 7.25pm
Series Five (15 × colour) 19 Sep–26 Dec 1971 · Sun 7.25pm
Series Six (7 × colour) 20 Feb–2 Apr 1972 · Sun 7.25pm
Short special (colour) · part of All-Star Comedy Carnival 25 Dec 1972 · Mon 5.45pm

Series Seven (13 × colour) 9 Feb–6 May 1973 ·
Fri 8.30pm then Sun 7.25pm

MAIN CAST

Stan Butler	Reg Varney
Mrs Butler	Cicely Courtneidge (series 1);
	Doris Hare (series 2 onwards)
Arthur	Michael Robbins (not series 7)
Olive	Anna Karen
Inspector Blake	Stephen Lewis
Jack Carter	Bob Grant

OTHER APPEARANCES

Doreen	Pat Ashton

CREDITS

writers Ronald Wolfe/Ronald Chesney (55 &
special 1), Bob Grant/Stephen Lewis (11 &
special 2), George Layton/Jonathan Lynn (6),
Garry Chambers/Wally Malston (1), Myles Rudge
(1) · directors/producers Stuart Allen (series 1–4
& special 1), Derrick Goodwin (series 5 & 3 eps in
series 6), Bryan Izzard (4 eps in series 6, all of
series 7 & special 2)

Within six months of its launch, LWT was
the grateful recipient of a new sitcom from the
writing Two Ronnies, Wolfe and Chesney.
Having previously created **The Rag Trade**
and **Meet The Wife** for the BBC, the pair
came up with On The Buses (rejected by the
BBC) and it turned out to be the ace in the
pack, giving ITV the kind of long-running
production upon which networks thrive. Yes,
it was vulgar; yes, it scored easy, cheap and
cheerful laughs; yes, all the characters
shouted their lines instead of talking them;
yes, Stan said 'Cor blimey' at least a dozen
times in every episode; and, yes of course,
the critics disliked it – but viewers loved it.

On The Buses was, in both senses of the
word, a vehicle for Reg Varney, age 47 when
it began, and previously best known for his
role in The Rag Trade. Here he drew upon his
working-class background to portray the wily
bachelor bus driver Stan Butler, and scenes
took place mostly in three locations. The first
was home, where Stan still lived with his
bingo-loving, widowed, super-smothering
mum, his unglamorous and almost
permanently unemployed sister Olive and her
layabout sponger of a husband Arthur. The
others locations were out on the road, where
Stan drove his green double-decker Bus 11
to the Cemetery Gates, and the depot of the
Home Counties-based Luxton and District
Traction Company, where Stan formed a
jack-the-lads pals act with bus conductor
companion Jack Carter. Their antics never
failed to rile the petty-minded Inspector
'Blakey' Blake, whose lip-quivering
expostulation 'I 'ate you, Butler!', usually
uttered after Stan had caused the Inspector
to come a cropper, soon became a national
catchphrase. Stretching the viewers'
(dis)belief was the fact that, in many of the
storylines, beautiful bus-working 'clippies'
seemed to find the larksome Stan and Jack
very fanciable and were not averse to nipping
up to the top deck for some slap and tickle.

(They'd have been better off going to see
an optician.)

Although it's scarcely credible to consider
that the premise could have been stretched
so far, On The Buses was a primetime
ITV sitcom for 74 half-hour episodes and,
moreover, was spun-off into no less than three
cinema feature films made by Hammer (On
The Buses, 1971; Mutiny On The Buses, 1972;
Holiday On The Buses, 1973; all written and
produced by Wolfe and Chesney, the first two
directed by Harry Booth, the last by Bryan
Izzard). The TV series' huge popularity can
be gauged from the fact that the first of these
movies was the top British box-office film in
1971, surpassing even the James Bond movie
Diamonds Are Forever.

Michael Robbins quit On The Buses before
the final series – his skiving character Arthur
was said to have finally walked out on Olive,
and divorce talk was in the air. And even Reg
Varney failed to see it out, leaving after seven
episodes of the final 13 – reputedly, Stan went
to the Midlands to work in a bus-making
factory. At this point 'Blakey' – who had risen
from bit-part player to the series' primary
attraction – moved into the Butler household
as lodger. Wolfe and Chesney had also
relinquished their role as exclusive writers
by this time: as well as acting in the series,
Bob Grant (Jack) and Stephen Lewis (Blakey)
began contributing scripts, as did Jonathan
Lynn and George Layton. When it all finally
finished Blakey's character was spun-off
into a new Wolfe and Chesney sitcom, **Don't
Drink The Water**, while plain Olive's
character, once again played by (the actually
far from plain) Anna Karen, resurfaced in the
writers' 1977–78 LWT revival of The Rag
Trade.

Like several other London-made ITV
sitcoms of the era, the format of On The
Buses was sold to American television, where
it was remade by NBC as Lotsa Luck, running
for 24 episodes in 1973–74. This starred Dom
DeLuise as Stan Belmont, a lost property
clerk for the New York bus department, living
at home with mum Iris (Kathleen Freeman),
sister Olive (Beverly Sanders) and her good-
for-nothing Arthur (Wynn Irwin). Despite a
top-notch production team of Carl Reiner, Bill
Persky and Sam Denoff (they had made **The
Dick Van Dyke Show**) Lotsa Luck failed
to succeed and has never been screened in
Britain. Another no-show was an early 1990s
plan to revive the Stan Butler character for
an ITV series, with Reg Varney reprising
his role but in an elevated position: that of a
businessman operating his own fleet of buses
in the newly deregulated market.

On The House

UK · ITV (YORKSHIRE) · SITCOM

12 × 30 mins · colour

Series One (6) 24 Sep–29 Oct 1970 ·
Thu around 7pm

Series Two (6) 22 Apr–27 May 1971 · Thu 7pm

MAIN CAST

Gussie Sissons	Kenneth Connor
Charlie Cattermole	John Junkin
'Old' Fred Spooner	John Normington
Arnold Pugh	Tommy Godfrey
Walter	Gordon Rollings (series 1)
Stanley	Peter Attard (series 1)
Derek	Derek Griffiths (series 2)
Harvey	Robin Askwith (series 2)

CREDITS

writer Sid Colin · director/producer David Mallet ·
executive producer John Duncan

In the manner of **The Rag Trade**, On The
House depicted the classic 'them-against-us'
situation rife in blue-collar trades in Britain
in the post-war years. Kenneth Connor
co-starred, appearing as Gussie Sissons,
chief labourer for house builders Thomas
Clackwood and Sons, who pitches his
comrades into a series of 'what-about-the-
workers?' skirmishes with the bane of his
life, the exasperated site foreman Charlie
Cattermole (played by co-star John Junkin).

Hermione Baddeley, Brian Glover,
Imogen Hassall, Patrick Newell, Milo O'Shea,
Madeline Smith, Patrick Troughton and
Paula Wilcox were among those who popped
up in an episode apiece while the second
series added to the regular cast Play School
presenter Derek Griffiths as a carpenter
and Robin Askwith as a long-haired idler.
'Nuff said.

On The Knocker

UK · BBC · SITCOM

1 × 30 mins · b/w

28 Sep 1963 · Sat 9.45pm

MAIN CAST

Ronnie Fender	Ronald Fraser
Frank	Alfred Burke
Carole Lewisham	Diana Hope
Arthur Lewisham	Noel Johnson
Mrs Soames	Betty England

CREDITS

writers Harry Driver/Jack Rosenthal · producer
Douglas Moodie

A one-off Comedy Playhouse presentation
featuring Ronnie Fraser as door-to-door
salesman Ronnie Fender who has an
'individual approach' to his clients. The
BBC had high hopes that a series would
follow but it never materialised.

On The Margin

UK · BBC · SKETCH

6 × 30 mins · b/w

9 Nov–14 Dec 1966 · BBC2 Wed 8.05pm

MAIN CAST

Alan Bennett
John Sergeant

Roland MacLeod
Madge Hindle
Virginia Stride
Yvonne Gilan

CREDITS
writer Alan Bennett · *director* Sydney Lotterby ·
producer Patrick Garland

The brilliant Alan Bennett was allowed full
rein in this short-lived but well-remembered
series. Comedy sketches, poems and songs
featured each week, as did archive clips of
famous music-hall acts. A recurring sketch,
'Streets Ahead', eavesdropped on the 'life and
times in NW1', dwelling on two couples, Nigel
and Jane Knocker-Threw, and the Touch
Paceys, resident in that London district.
Bennett's ability to weave deceptively savage
satire into apparently innocuous sketches,
and his delight in 'camping up' his characters,
were both apparent in this clever series. In
addition to a regular supporting cast,
Jonathan Miller (Bennett's former **Beyond
The Fringe** colleague) and John Fortune
made guest appearances during the six
editions.

The BBC liked *On The Margin* so much
that it was twice repeated within six months
of the original run (BBC2, 1 January to
12 February 1967; BBC1, 27 May to 1 July
1967) but then, in a colossally stupid move, it
saw fit to destroy the only existing prints, by
no means the Corporation's only such act of
vandalism at this time but definitely one of
its worst. Years later, on 1 January 1990, a
television archive celebration mounted by
C4, *The A–Z Of Television*, featured a section
lamenting the wiping of so much of the
medium's past; utilising the original script,
Bennett re-performed a skit from *On The
Margin*.

On The Rocks

UK · ITV (TYNE TEES) · CHILDREN'S SITCOM
8 × 30 mins · b/w
8 July–26 Aug 1969 · Tue 5.20pm
MAIN CAST
Arthur Mullard
Pip Hinton
Billy McComb
Bryan Burdon

CREDITS
writers Larry Parker (6), Guy Rowston (2) · *script
editor* Guy Rowston · *directors* Peter Webb,
Roy Match · *producer* Penny Wootton

A children's adventure-comedy series
starring Billy McComb (a veteran of BBC
children's TV shows) as the mad producer at
SeaView Television, the smallest station in
Britain. The company transmits its signals –
provided the wind is blowing in the right
direction – from a lighthouse, aiming its
ramshackle programming at the handful of
residents in Kipper Cove and Mumbling Bay.

Big Arthur Mullard was McComb's
assistant, as was Pip Hinton, who was prone
to break into song, and Bryan Burdon played
'the new boy'. A young Warren Clarke –
much later to achieve fame in *The
Manageress, Nice Work, Dalziel And Pascoe*
and many other top drama series – appeared
in one episode.

On The Up

UK · BBC · SITCOM
19 × 30 mins · colour
Series One (7) 4 Sep–16 Oct 1990 · BBC1
Tue 8.30pm
Series Two (6) 6 Sep–11 Oct 1991 · BBC1
Fri 8.30pm
Series Three (6) 28 Sep–2 Nov 1992 · BBC1
Mon 8pm

MAIN CAST
Tony Carpenter	Dennis Waterman
Sam	Sam Kelly
Fiona Wembley	Joan Sims
Maggie	Jenna Russell
Ruth Carpenter	Judy Buxton
Dawn	Michelle Hatch
Mum	Dora Bryan (series 1);
	Pauline Letts (series 2)

OTHER APPEARANCES
Stephanie Carpenter	Vanessa Hadaway
Jane Webster	Fiona Mollison
	(from series 2)

CREDITS
writer Bob Larbey · *directors* Gareth Gwenlan (13),
Paul Harrison (6) · *producer* Gareth Gwenlan

Dennis Waterman carved a career out of
portraying likeable cockney characters with
a heart of gold beating 'neath their rough
exteriors, and in *On The Up* he played yet
another version: Tony Carpenter, who had
elevated a small taxi-cab company into a
thriving executive car-hire business and made
himself a millionaire in the process. While
doing so, and in spite of his wealth, Carpenter
had also managed to keep his East End
sensibilities and outlook. He does, however,
live in a big house, which requires a
permanent staff, although his friendly 'we're-
all-mates-together' attitude permits them
to treat him as an equal rather than in the
customary deferential manner. Carpenter's
secretary, Maggie, has a sharp line in
backchat; the cook, Mrs Wembley, works to
her own agenda; and the butler, Sam, is just
plain insolent. Tony tolerates the uppity
nature of his staff and their surly attitude
towards him mainly because they are the
closest he has to real friends, people who 'tell
it like it is' without deference to his fortune.
But Ruth Carpenter, Tony's wife, has
vastly a different take on life – she is a snob
and disapproves of Tony's downmarket
tastes and unbecoming familiarity with the
staff. Inevitably, these differences take their
toll and the couple spend much of the time
drifting apart and coming (grudgingly) back

together again. These conflicts formed the
bedrock of *On The Up*.

The writer Bob Larbey was an old hand at
this sort of relationship comic interplay, but
although there were some telling moments
and amusing dialogue, the series rarely
exploited the full potential of the class and
marital conflicts that it featured.

On With The Show

UK · ITV (JACK HYLTON TV PRODUCTIONS FOR
ASSOCIATED-REDIFFUSION) · SKETCH
6 editions (5 × 60 mins · 1 × 45 mins) · b/w
5 June–14 Aug 1958 · fortnightly Thu mostly 9pm
MAIN CAST
June Whitfield
Alan White
OTHER APPEARANCES
Harry Fowler
Barbara Windsor

CREDITS
director Douglas Hurn · *executive producer* Jack
Hylton

The Australian actor Alan White, based in
Britain, co-starred with the fast-rising British
star June Whitfield in this series of six shows,
mixing unrelated comedy sketches with
musical interludes from guest artists.

The shows were broadcast live from the
Hackney Empire, in the East End of London,
and guest MCs included Sid James, George
Baker, Evelyn Laye and Dennis Price. A still
unknown Barbara Windsor, then 21, made
minor appearances in the series while some of
the scripts had been purchased · – lock, stock
and punctuation marks – from the USA by
the producing impresario Jack Hylton; there,
they had been used in TV shows and stage
appearances by Sid Caesar.

Once In A Lifetime

UK · ITV (NOEL GAY TELEVISION FOR CARLTON) ·
SITCOM
1 × 30 mins · colour
23 Mar 1993 · Tue 8.30pm
MAIN CAST
Matron	Pam Ferris
Mojo	Lisa Maxwell
Helen	Maria McErlane
Bella White	Kate Robbins
Roger	Ramsay Gilderdale

CREDITS
writers Nick Symons/Sandi Toksvig/Joolz · *script
editor* Nick Revell · *director* Sylvie Boden ·
executive producer Charles Armitage · *producer*
Nick Symons

A single-episode pilot screened by Carlton as
part of its *Comedy Playhouse* season in 1993,
and perhaps the one most ripe for further
development. The powers that be must have
thought otherwise, however, for no series
followed.

The plot was somewhat convoluted, but the nub was that two disparate women – one well-spoken, tidy, strait-laced and middle-class, the other a tattooed, pierced, earthy punk with baby in tow – discover that not only were they resident together, as babies, at an orphanage but that they are twin sisters, separated at six months when Helen was fostered by a well-to-do couple who founded a grand private music school. Despite being shocked by the discovery that she has a twin, let alone someone as alien to her as Mojo, Helen comes to realise that they share the same phobias, dreams, likes and dislikes, and speak certain lines at the same time, and they immediately form a tight bond that makes perfect sense to them both, as if they had realised that, hitherto, a part of life's jigsaw puzzle had been missing.

Their sisterhood is revealed on the TV show *Once In A Lifetime* (strongly reminiscent of ITV's *Surprise, Surprise*) hosted by the toothy Liverpudlian Bella White (bearing every resemblance to Cilla Black – a role played by Ms Black's premiere impersonator Kate Robbins). Helen is taken to the TV taping by her boyfriend Roger, a wet solicitor, and by 'Matey', for 25 years the Matron at Helen's late parents' Fountain Musical Academy, a strikingly sexual woman who, alone among the characters in the sitcom, talked straight to the camera.

Although *Once In A Lifetime* was not developed, the plot was similar in concept to Victoria Wood's *Screen One* drama *Pat And Margaret*, broadcast by BBC1 on 11 September 1994.

Once Upon A Time In The North

UK · BBC (PHILIP PARTRIDGE PRODUCTIONS) · SITCOM

6 × 30 mins · colour

3 May–7 June 1994 · BBC1 Tue 8.30pm

MAIN CAST

Len Tollit	Bernard Hill
Pat Tollit	Christine Moore
Mr Bebbington	Bryan Pringle
Siobhan Tollit	Susan McArdle
Sean Tollit	Andrew Whyment
Morris Tollit	Bob Mason
Bob Carling	Bill Stewart

CREDITS

writer Tim Firth · directors Phil Partridge, John Clive · producer Phil Partridge

Whimsical tales of the Tollit family, who live in the picturesque Yorkshire town Sutton Moor. The husband, Len, is a soft-hearted, well-meaning chap who holds strong views on certain subjects and is fiercely proud of his working-class roots. But his determination to prove himself the equal of those who may consider themselves his betters often leads to confrontation and infuriates his wife, Pat. They have two children, the pre-teen Sean

and the sexually-maturing Siobhan, who, at 15, is at that 'awkward age'. Living in the granny flat in their yard is Mr Bebbington, who had been Len's late mother's boyfriend but has remained with them for six months since her death. Pat constantly cajoles Len into getting Bebbington out but he is quite content to let him stay and treats him as one of the family. Len's brother, Morris, who lives nearby, is a spiritual man who comes across as half-hippy and half-witted.

In the opening segment we find that Len has been made redundant from North Cheshire Lubricants and is spending his redundancy money on starting up a new business, selling cellular phones. He is optimistic about the success of the venture but the rest of the family are convinced that the project is a folly. The scheme does indeed fail and subsequent episodes detailed the everyday tribulations that confront modern-day families in a changing world.

Once Upon A Time In The North looked strikingly handsome, being shot on film on location, which added to its quaint charm. But, despite its merits, the series failed to materialise for a second run and viewers were left to assume that the Tollits lived moderately happily ever after. The writer, Tim Firth, did return however, with the BBC1 light-drama series (not a comedy, but close) *All Quiet On The Preston Front* (six episodes 4 January to 8 February 1994) and successor *Preston Front* (six episodes, 16 July to 27 August 1995 and, finally, seven more, 21 July to 8 September 1997).

One Foot In The Grave

UK · BBC · SITCOM

37 episodes (29 × 30 mins · 3 × 60 mins · 1 × 90 mins · 1 × 70 mins · 1 × 50 mins · 1 × 40 mins · 1 × short special) · colour

Series One (6 × 30 mins) 4 Jan–8 Feb 1990 · BBC1 Thu 9.30pm

Series Two (6 × 30 mins) 4 Oct–15 Nov 1990 · BBC1 Thu 9.30pm

Special (60 mins) 27 Dec 1990 · BBC1 Thu 9.30pm

Special (50 mins) 30 Dec 1991 · BBC1 Mon 9.30pm

Series Three (6 × 30 mins) 2 Feb–8 Mar 1992 · BBC1 Sun 9.05pm

Series Four (6 × 30 mins) 31 Jan–7 Mar 1993 · BBC1 Sun 8.55pm

Short special · part of *Total Relief* 12 Mar 1993 · BBC1 Fri 10.30pm

Special (90 mins) *One Foot In The Algarve* 26 Dec 1993 · BBC1 Sun 9.05pm

Special (40 mins) 25 Dec 1994 · BBC1 Sun 9pm

Series Five (5 × 30 mins) 1 Jan–29 Jan 1995 · BBC1 Sun 9pm

Special (60 mins) 25 Dec 1995 · BBC1 Mon 9pm

Special (60 mins) 26 Dec 1996 · BBC1 Thu 9pm

Special (70 mins) 25 Dec 1997 · BBC1 Thu 9pm

MAIN CAST

Victor Meldrew	Richard Wilson
Margaret Meldrew	Annette Crosbie
Mrs Warboys	Doreen Mantle

OTHER APPEARANCES

Patrick	Angus Deayton
	(series 2–1996 special)
Pippa	Janine Duvitski
	(series 2–1996 special)
Nick Swainey	Owen Brenman
	(series 2 onwards)
Derek McVitie	Tim Brooke-Taylor
	(1997 special)
Betty McVitie	Marian McLoughlin
	(1997 special)

CREDITS

writer David Renwick · directors Susan Belbin (35), Sydney Lotterby (1), Christine Gernon (1) · producers Susan Belbin (36), Esta Charkham (1)

Born Iain Colquhoun Wilson in Greenock on 9 July 1936, Richard Wilson had a long and unspectacular career as a TV comedy-actor, with hundreds of bit-part and supporting roles, before – in his mid 50s, and probably much to his own surprise – being elevated to superstardom. The transformation, after years of slogging away, came through his portrayal of the cantankerous Victor Meldrew in *One Foot In The Grave*, and from being a recognisable face to which few viewers could put a name, Richard Wilson was suddenly an award-winning and greatly popular actor.

It all started quietly. At the beginning of the first series Victor Meldrew is forced into taking early retirement, and tries to adjust to an unwanted final years of leisure with his wife Margaret. Refusing to believe that he is no longer of any use to society, he takes odd jobs, helps out with good causes and generally tries to make himself busy. Although glum of expression, and generally fed up with the inanities of life, he nevertheless maintains an air of optimism – feeling, despite all evidence to the contrary, that things will turn out all right. He is invariably wrong about this, and all manner of events conspire against Meldrew to send him into increasingly stranger and wilder situations. These consequences are rarely of his own making but are instigated by wild coincidences, complex misunderstandings, bureaucratic inefficiencies and sheer, awesome bad luck. As Victor becomes embroiled in such shenanigans, his volcanic temper – which tends to simmer at the best of times – erupts in a torrent of verbal vitriol against the unfairness of it all, such onslaughts usually being preceded by his bemoaning exclamation 'I don't be-lieve it!'.

Throughout it all, Margaret tries to keep her patience and rise above her husband's frustrations, but, because she is often caught up in the same maelstrom engulfing Victor, she too sometimes vents her anger – unfairly blaming Victor, who is usually an innocent pawn in the Machiavellian plot that has them ensnared. It is not Victor's fault that he suddenly finds himself in possession of a huge mountain of radioactive compost; it is not his fault that he is caught by his wife in bed with an old woman, someone whom he *assumed* was Margaret but is actually a stranger from a nursing home, dumped there owing to a clerical error; it is not his fault that, while awaiting an operation in hospital, his pubic hair is shaved by someone he assumes is a doctor but who turns out, mid-shave, to be a dangerous escaped lunatic …

Richard Wilson became a star because of the role written for him, and because he perfectly captured the stupefied disbelief with which the Scotsman Meldrew confronted each and every surreal turn in his life. He was also blessed to be working with Annette Crosbie, who turned in a brilliant and underrated performance as Margaret, a Scotswoman whose expressions and eloquent silences could speak volumes. Rounding out the cast was Margaret's friend Mrs Warboys, an irritating widow who has attached herself to the couple; and neighbours Nick Swainey, an annoyingly cheerful, slightly mad individual looking after his senile mother; and (neighbours on the other side) young couple Patrick and Pippa. The last-mentioned becomes good friends with Margaret but Patrick, always catching Victor in the most preposterous situations, believes him to be certifiably insane and malicious. Patrick and Pippa eventually move away but the Meldrew curse casts a long shadow from which they never fully escape.

One Foot In The Grave attracted only moderate ratings to begin with, and critics were lukewarm (or worse) to its appeal. Perhaps it was the very premise – the grumblings of an irascible malcontent – that failed, yet, to appeal. But as the series developed it began to attract increasing numbers of fans, and word-of-mouth testimony lured new viewers into watching repeated episodes. However they arrived at it, all who saw *One Foot In The Grave* were in for a treat. David Renwick's extraordinary scripts combined intricate plots with wonderfully colourful dialogue and black humour. Renwick said he had been inspired to create Meldrew after watching an embittered character whom Walter Matthau had portrayed in a Neil Simon film (presumably, Willy Clark in Herbert Ross's 1975 movie *The Sunshine Boys*) but it was the extreme, almost surreal nature of the piece as much as the characterisations that made the series so successful. Renwick was never afraid to take chances with his ideas, setting almost entire episodes in a bed or a traffic jam. The series' jaunty title song – written and performed by Eric Idle – indicated too that there was more to this series than first met the eye. Meldrew was a tragi-comic

character, who thought himself a sane man living in a mad modern world. His relationship with his wife seemed framed more by habit than by love or affection, yet their past held a bonding secret: they had lost a child and remained somehow unfulfilled.

By the third series, *One Foot In The Grave* was making the Top 20 ratings, with some episodes seen by more than 16 million viewers. Meldrew – and Wilson – had finally made their mark, earning them a place in the UK sitcom hall of fame. The episodes maintained a mad momentum, with seasonal specials faring particularly well: the Christmas 1993 edition topped 20 million viewers and the 1996 Boxing Day special was only pipped in the ratings by the record-breaking final series of **Only Fools And Horses**. The 1997 special introduced the Meldrews' new neighbours, Derek and Betty McVitie, who moved into the house vacated by Patrick and Pippa.

Notes. A US adaptation of *One Foot In The Grave*, retitled *Cosby*, was produced by Carsey-Werner and launched by CBS on 16 September 1996, starring Bill Cosby as Hilton Lucas and Phylicia Rashad as his wife Ruth (she had been his wife in **The Cosby Show** too), with Madeline Kahn playing Ruth's friend, Pauline. Reaction from US viewers was lukewarm during the series' initial 12 months on screen but the network committed itself to giving it a long run, and by 31 December 1997 it had already clocked up 36 episodes.

Four *One Foot In The Grave* TV scripts were adapted for radio by David Renwick and re-recorded by the cast – the programmes were aired by BBC Radio 2 from 21 January to 11 February 1995.

One For The Road

UK · C4 (CHANNEL X/ALTMAN INTERNATIONAL PRODUCTIONS) · SATIRE
....
6 × 30 mins · colour
....
4 Sep–9 Oct 1995 · Mon 8pm

MAIN CAST
Simon Treat · · · · · · · · · · · · · · Alan Davies

CREDITS
writer Gary Sinyor · *additional material* Iain Coyle, Alan Davies · *director/producer* Steven Bawol · *executive producer* Robert Altman

An unusual travelogue-spoof that charted the globetrotting adventures of timeshare sales-man Simon Treat. Each episode was present-ed as a video-tape that Simon mailed back to England detailing his current exploits.

In the opener, the tape is sent to Simon's boss, who is expecting to see details of virgin land that they plan to develop in Israel. Instead, he witnesses a comedy of errors in which Simon screws up his boss's chance of becoming a millionaire. At first, Simon is a

cynical manipulator of people, with only the job on his mind, but he gradually unwinds and by the end of the tape announces that he is taking off in a motorcycle and sidecar to experience adventures anew, the ensuing episodes following his progress.

One For The Road was a neat idea, quietly humorous rather than broadly funny. The location shooting and performance by the likeable Davies neatly captured the flavour of the celebrity TV travelogues the series set out to lampoon, and it gained an added dimension via the device of presenting the stories as the product of a hand-held camera, complete with jump-cut editing.

One Jasper Carrott

see CARROTT, Jasper

One Night In Lincoln

see HARDING, Mike

One Night Stand

USA · HBO · STANDUP
....
55 × 30 mins · colour
....
US dates: 15 Feb 1989–15 Nov 1992
UK dates: 5 Dec 1989–9 Nov 1993 (20 editions)
C4 various days and times

MAIN CAST
see below

CREDITS
writers cast · *directors* Peter Calabrese, David Grossman, Sue Wolf, Robin Shlien/Sue Wolf, Steve Santos, John Fortenberry and others · *executive producers* Robin Shlien/Sue Wolf, Peter Calabrese · *producers* Robin Shlien/Sue Wolf

A series spotlighting 55 of America's prime standup comics, caught in the act, usually at the Vic Theatre in Chicago. Each edition showed a single performer working an enthusiastic live audience; the fact that the broadcasts were made for screening by cable company HBO ensured that the comedians could be liberal with their vocabulary and choice of subject matter.

The following 20 programmes were screened in the UK by C4, mostly late at night and usually more than once (the dates in parentheses reflect US date/first UK broadcast). Rita Rudner (29 March 1989/5 December 1989), Bob Nelson (8 March 1989/12 December 1989), Kevin Meaney (22 February 1989/19 December 1989), Joy Behar (1 March 1989/22 May 1990), Judy Tenuta (15 February 1989/6 September 1991), Blake Clark (15 March 1989/13 September 1991), Paula Poundstone (12 April 1989/20 September 1991), Kevin Pollak (22 March 1989/27 September 1991), Bill Maher (5 April 1989/11 October 1991), Ellen DeGeneres (24 February 1990/5 March 1992), Jake

Johannsen (31 March 1990/12 March 1992), Norm MacDonald (4 May 1991/19 March 1992), Dom Irrera (19 April 1989/2 April 1993), Diane Ford (21 April 1990/19 April 1993), Mike Binder (10 March 1990/16 June 1993), Allan Havey (2 March 1991/17 June 1993), Will Durst (14 April 1990/23 June 1993), Brian Haley (11 May 1991/30 June 1993), Jimmy Tingle (6 April 1991/7 July 1993) and Bill Hicks (27 April 1991/9 November 1993).

Note. Additionally, these 35 editions of *One Night Stand* have shown in the USA but not the UK. Barry Sobel (26 April 1989), Damon Wayans (3 May 1989), Larry Miller (10 February 1990), Tom Parks (17 February 1990), Robin Harris (3 March 1990), Charles Fleischer (17 March 1990), Ritch Shydner (24 March 1990), Bobby Slayton (7 April 1990), Dennis Wolfberg (28 April 1990), Rick Overton (9 February 1991), Rick Aviles (16 February 1991), Mark Curry (23 February 1991), Jeff Marder (9 March 1991), Taylor Negron (16 March 1991), Martin Lawrence (23 March 1991), The Higgins Boys and Gruber (30 March 1991), Cathy Ladman (13 April 1991), George Wallace (20 April 1991), Michael Colyar (18 May 1991), Bill Maher (second appearance, 19 July 1992), Mario Joyner (26 July 1992), Lew Schneider (2 August 1992), John Riggi (9 August 1992), Eddie Griffin (16 August 1992), Ellen DeGeneres (second appearance, 23 August 1992), Allan Havey (second appearance, 6 September 1992), Susie Essman (20 September 1992), Colin Quinn (27 September 1992), Dana Gould (4 October 1992), D L Hughley (11 October 1992), Diane Ford (second appearance, 18 October 1992), Dom Irrera (second appearance, 25 October 1992), Gilbert Gottfried (1 November 1992), Jon Hayman (8 November 1992) and Joe Bolster (15 November 1992).

One Of The Boys

USA · NBC (TOY PRODUCTIONS/CPT) · SITCOM

13 × 30 mins · colour

US dates: 23 Jan–20 Aug 1982

UK dates: 4 Jan–26 Apr 1983 (12 episodes) ITV Tue 3.30pm

MAIN CAST

Oliver Nugent · · · · · · · · · · · · Mickey Rooney
Adam Shields · · · · · · · · · · · · · Dana Carvey
Mrs Green · · · · · · · · · · · · · · Francine Beers
Jonathan Burns · · · · · · · · · · · Nathan Lane
Bernard Solomon · · · · · · · Scatman Crothers
Jane · Meg Ryan

CREDITS

writers Richard G Albrecht, Norman Barasch, Michael Di Gaetano, Lawrence Gay, Casey Keller, Dinah Kirgo/Julie Kirgo, Laurie Newbound, Bernie Orenstein, Toni Palmer, Brad Rider, Saul Turteltaub, Gina Wendkos · *producers* Saul Turteltaub, Bernie Orenstein

Mickey Rooney's third sitcom, but the only one to be screened in Britain and the only one in which his character name was not Mickey. (The other two were *The Mickey Rooney Show*, in 1954–55, and *Mickey*, 1964–65.) He starred here as Oliver Nugent, a feisty 66-year-old rescued by his grandson Adam from the ignominy of spending his final years at a retirement home, Bayview Acres. Adam suggests (if you can believe this) that Oliver join him and his room-mate Nathan in their New Jersey college student apartment.

A loveable rogue, Oliver is popular with the other kids and especially with Jane, Adam's girlfriend; he has a date with Mrs Green, the landlady of the student rooms, takes a part-time job to make money and is more than happy to join fellow OAP and friend Bernard Solomon in putting on the occasional dancing show for the kids' entertainment.

The most striking aspect of *One Of The Boys* was the players: Dana Carvey (Adam) became a big star in **Saturday Night Live** while Jane was played by a then-unknown young actress, Meg Ryan.

One On Two

UK · BBC · MONOLOGUE

5 × 10 mins · colour

18 June–3 July 1990 · BBC2 various days 11.45pm

MAIN CAST

see below

CREDITS

writers see below · *executive producer* Michael Jackson · *producer* Juliet Blake

A short series of comedy monologues performed by comedians.

18 June: *The Man I Was*, with Chris Lynam; writers Paddy Fletcher/Chris Lynam. A celebrity reminisces about his early days.

19 June: *Dead Good Friends*, with Jo Brand; writer Jo Brand. A mortuary assistant really enjoys her work.

20 June: *Nine Lives*, with Andrew Bailey; writers John Dowie/Andrew Bailey. A suspicious message in a bottle – joke or death threat?

2 July: *Dirty Weekend*, with Caroline Quentin; writer Arthur Smith. A doctor and nurse set off for a dirty weekend.

3 July: *Optical Allusions*, with and written by John Hegley. John falls in love with his optician.

Note. In 1996, Carlton aired *First Sign Of Madness*, a four-part ITV series of half-hour monologues. Although performed by actors known for their comedy work – Jim Broadbent, Stephen Tompkinson, Brenda Blethyn and Pauline Quirke – and although vaguely humorous, these were closer in style to Alan Bennett's intense *Talking Heads* monologues (BBC1, 19 April to 24 May 1988), being more dramatic in content than comedic.

One-Upmanship

UK · BBC · SKETCH

18 × 30 mins · colour

Special *Christmas Oneupmanship* 19 Dec 1974 · BBC2 Thu 9pm

Series One (6) 10 Mar–14 Apr 1976 · BBC2 Wed 9.45pm

Series Two (6) 9 Nov–14 Dec 1976 · BBC2 Tue 9pm

Series Three (5) 7 Aug–4 Sep 1978 · BBC2 Mon 9.45pm

MAIN CAST

Richard Briers
Peter Jones
Frederick Jaeger

CREDITS

creator Stephen Potter · *adapter/writer* Barry Took · *producers* Bernard Thompson (special & series 1), Graeme Muir (series 2), Douglas Argent (series 3)

Stephen Potter's humorous manuals for a smoother life had long been turned into radio programmes; here they were adapted for television by Barry Took and brought to life by comedy actors Richard Briers and Peter Jones.

In each programme, a different aspect of modern living – from health to golf – was given the Potter treatment at the mythical Yeovil College of Lifemanship. Jones was no stranger to this excellent comic material, having appeared in the 1960 British comedy film *School For Scoundrels* (director Robert Hamer) which had been based on Potter's works.

In all, Potter, the former BBC broadcaster and college lecturer, wrote six books that pertained to the subject: *Gamesmanship* (1947), *Lifemanship* (1950), *One-Upmanship* (1952), *Supermanship* (1958), *Anti-Woo* (1965) and *The Complete Golf Gamesmanship* (1968).

Only An Excuse

UK · BBC · SATIRE

1 × 30 mins · colour

13 June 1994 · BBC1 Mon 8.30pm

MAIN CAST

Jonathan Watson
Tony Roper

CREDITS

writers Jonathan Watson/Tony Roper · *director/producer* Philip Differ

With England, Scotland, Northern Ireland and Wales all failing to make the 1994 World Cup Finals in the USA, this one-off comedy took a satirical look at the state of British football. Comedians Watson and Roper (part of the **Naked Video** team) presented the show and impersonated a host of characters – including Kenny Dalglish, Eric Cantona, Ryan Giggs, Graeme Souness and soccer pundit Archie Macpherson – all trying to explain away the inadequacies of the national teams.

Only Fools And Horses

UK · BBC · SITCOM

63 episodes (35×30 mins · 1×35 mins · 13×50 mins · 4×60 mins · 1×65 mins · 2×75 mins · 1×80 mins · 2×85 mins · 1×90 mins · 1×95 mins · 2×short specials) · colour

Series One (6×30 mins) 8 Sep–13 Oct 1981 · BBC1 Tue 8.30pm

Special (35 mins) 28 Dec 1981 · BBC1 Mon 9.55pm

Series Two (7×30 mins) 21 Oct–2 Dec 1982 · BBC1 Thu 8.30pm

Short special · part of *The Funny Side Of Christmas* 27 Dec 1982 · BBC1 Mon 8.05pm

Special (30 mins) 30 Dec 1982 · BBC1 Thu 7.55pm

Series Three (7×30 mins) 10 Nov–22 Dec 1983 · BBC1 Thu 8.30pm

Special (30 mins) 25 Dec 1983 · BBC1 Sun 9.35pm

Series Four (7×30 mins) 21 Feb–4 Apr 1985 · BBC1 Thu 8pm

Special (90 mins) 25 Dec 1985 · BBC1 Wed 7.30pm

Series Five (6×30 mins) 31 Aug–5 Oct 1986 · BBC1 Sun 8.35pm

Special (75 mins) 25 Dec 1986 · BBC1 Thu 7.05pm

Special (60 mins) 25 Dec 1987 · BBC1 Fri 6.25pm

Special (80 mins) 25 Dec 1988 · BBC1 Sun 5.05pm

Series Six (6×50 mins) 8 Jan–12 Feb 1989 · BBC1 Sun 7.15pm

Special (85 mins) 25 Dec 1989 · BBC1 Mon 4.05pm

Special (75 mins) 25 Dec 1990 · BBC1 Mon 5.10pm

Series Seven (6×50 mins) 30 Dec 1990–3 Feb 1991 · BBC1 Sun 7.15pm

Specials (1×50 mins · 1×95 mins) 24 Dec 1991 · BBC1 Wed 7.30pm · & 25 Dec 1991 · BBC1 Thu 3.10pm

Special (65 mins) 25 Dec 1992 · BBC1 Fri 6.55pm

Special (85 mins) 25 Dec 1993 · BBC1 Sat 6.05pm

Series Eight (3×60 mins) 25 · 27 & 29 Dec 1996 · BBC1 Wed 9pm · Fri & Sun 8pm

Short special · part of Comic Relief 14 Mar 1997 · BBC1 Fri 7.40pm

MAIN CAST

Derek ('Del') Trotter · · · · · · · · · David Jason
Rodney Trotter · · · · · · · · Nicholas Lyndhurst
Grandad · · · · · · Lennard Pearce (series 1–3)
Uncle Albert · · · · · · · · · · · Buster Merryfield
· (series 4 onwards)
Trigger · · · · · · · · · · · · · · Roger Lloyd Pack
Cassandra · · · · · · · · · · · · · Gwyneth Strong
· (series 6 onwards)
Raquel · · · · · · · · · · · · Tessa Peake-Jones
· · · · · · · · · · · · · · · · · · · (regular from series 7)

OTHER APPEARANCES

Boycie · · · · · · · · · · · · · · · · · · · John Challis
Marlene · · · · · · · · · · · · · · Sue Holderness
Denzil · · · · · · · · · · · · · · · · · · Paul Barber
Mickey Pearce · · · · · · · · · · · Patrick Murray
Mike · · · · · · · · · · · · · · Kenneth MacDonald

CREDITS

writer John Sullivan · *directors* Ray Butt (24), Tony Dow (18), Susan Belbin (7), Martin Shardlow (6), Mandie Fletcher (4) · *producer* Ray Butt (39), Gareth Gwenlan (18), Bernard Thompson (1) other credits not available

The sublime comic adventures of the Trotter brothers, Del and Rodney, as they duck and dive through the streets of south London, eking out a living. From humble beginnings, *Only Fools And Horses* grew to be a national favourite, with its beautifully drawn, superbly cast characters endearing themselves to the mass public. In the process, it became one of the very best British sitcoms of all time.

John Sullivan had proved adept at writing realistic earthy dialogue with **Citizen Smith** and it was while chatting to the producer of that series, Ray Butt, that the idea of *Only Fools And Horses* took seed. Sullivan discovered that he and Butt had both worked in street markets, where, they agreed, the most interesting characters were the fly-pitchers, men who turn up and sell all manner of dodgy items from a suitcase. Sullivan wondered where such people came from and what their life was like and he turned his musings into a pilot script for a series he planned to call *Readies*. The BBC's Head of Comedy, John Howard Davies, who had expressed reticence when hearing of the idea verbally, quickly recognised the script's potential and decided to commission a series then and there. Nicholas Lyndhurst was signed up as the younger brother, Rodney, and Lennard Pearce came on board as Grandad, but the casting of the elder Trotter brother, Derek, was more problematic. Enn Reitel was considered – one advantage being that he looked a little like Lyndhurst – but other commitments caused him to turn down the job. Jim Broadbent passed it up for the same reason. Roger Lloyd Pack was also considered, but he looked so much like Trigger (a character so named by Sullivan because he had a face like a horse) that he was offered that role instead. Butt finally decided upon David Jason while watching a repeat episode of **Open All Hours**; Sullivan, though, had serious misgivings – he associated Jason with **A Sharp Intake Of Breath** and **The Top Secret Life Of Edgar Briggs** and could not imagine him as the sharp-talking, tough, streetwise Derek Trotter. Ray Butt persevered, however, and persuaded Sullivan to let Jason attend a script read-through with Lyndhurst. Happily, Jason 'got' the character immediately, and his rapport with Lyndhurst was electric. Sullivan concurred and one of British TV's most pleasing partnerships was born.

In part, Jason's depiction of Derek Trotter was based on a builder, Derek Hockley, for whom he had worked in his days as an electrician. Hockley had many of the

affectations outlined by Sullivan in his characterisation of Del (gold jewellery, camel-hair coat) and Jason added others, like his habit of twitching his neck. Renowned as a perfectionist, Jason worked extremely hard on developing the character and this, allied with Sullivan's scorching scripts, resulted in a solid, well-rounded, highly humorous figure who was in top gear right from the start. The public was slow to react, though, and ratings for the first series were mediocre. Had *Only Fools And Horses* been an ITV series, where long-term promise has to be shown quickly, it might never have returned, but the BBC has a history of allowing shows time to settle and so a second series was commissioned. Once again, the ratings were unremarkable – but, magically, when it was repeated, word of mouth caused it to notch up massive viewing figures and its future was assured.

Like Thames' successful light-drama series *Minder*, *Only Fools And Horses* was set in south London – its base was Peckham – and it featured likeable dodgy characters who want to take your money but won't hit you on the head to do so. Derek Trotter is a streetwise chancer always looking to make a fast buck; with a never-ending supply of get-rich-quick schemes, and an inner belief in his ability to sell anything to anyone, Derek – or Del Boy', as he is known to one and all – embroils 'the firm' (as he calls the family business) in all sorts of improbable situations. His brother is different: a tall, thin, worried individual, Rodney – or 'Rodders' as Del calls him – looks upon all of Derek's dealings with an air of pessimism, usually well-founded, yet he is always cajoled into the capers. Academically, Rodney is much brighter than Del but he lacks his elder brother's street-smart, blinding confidence and self-assurance. The third member of the team is their Grandad, an indolent, scruffy man constantly moaning about his lot in life. What little use he is to the firm, however, is never questioned – Grandad is family, and in Derek's philosophy that is that: he is part of the team.

These touches of loyalty and the adherence to their own peculiar morality gave the characters some depth and allowed them to discuss serious and emotional subjects in a believable way without becoming mawkish. When the actor Lennard Pearce died, John Sullivan didn't just replace him with another actor, he wrote Grandad's death into the plot, to face the issue of the family's loss in a touching yet comic way. Then, to keep the sturdy triangle of characters intact, he introduced Uncle Albert, a shifty, boastful ex-sea-dog who inveigles his way into the Trotters' lives, managing to stay with them – despite some early efforts to oust him – in their high-rise council flat in Nelson Mandela House. Ultimately, Albert is accepted as part of the team, mostly because of Del's unfailing sense of family loyalty and duty.

The texture of the writing was enlivened enormously by Sullivan's colourful dialogue, liberally peppered with malapropisms, abbreviations, slang and delightful expressions ('dipstick', 'plonker', 'luvverly jubberly'). The show also benefited from some marvellous support characters, including the suave villain Boycie and his vacuous wife Marlene, who is desperate to have a baby; the glum Denzil, who is often roped in on Del's schemes; the pub landlord, Mike; and, most memorably, Trigger, a long-faced, mentally-challenged individual who, throughout the entire run of the series, thinks that Rodney's name is Dave.

The sudden popularity of *Only Fools And Horses* led to the making of annual Christmas specials, and Sullivan's wish to give the characters more room to stretch was granted so that, for two series, the episodes were 50 minutes long instead of the standard half-hour. Later still, this was extended to 60. As the series progressed Del and Rodney – who were single in the earliest episodes – began to settle down with respective partners, but both experienced women problems; Rodney, who married the bright Cassandra, became intimidated by her career and friends; Del endured a volatile relationship with Raquel, an aspiring actress who, when they first met, was moonlighting as a stripagram. Eventually, however, Del and Raquel cemented their relationship with the birth of a baby. By this time, the series had moved on from its initial premise of the two roguish but likeable brothers, to cover wider themes. It also kept pace with real-life events: for example, during the 1980s Del became a yuppie and tried to move up in society. But at no time did *Only Fools And Horses* lose its heart and soul: the realistic and hilarious relationship between the brothers.

The series ended with a bang, in the shape of three hour-long episodes that introduced Raquel's long-lost parents and culminated in a glorious triumph for Del and Rodney when an antique watch Del has had hanging around for years turns out to be a rarity of enormous historical value. It sells at auction for over £6m and the Trotters finish the series rich beyond even Del's wildest dreams. Despite this, there still remained a sense of irony as Del admitted to Rodney that he missed the ducking and diving. For the public, who had long since taken the Trotter brothers to heart, the ending was an unexpected treat and seemed just reward for the amount of laughter the family had provided. The viewing figures for the final three episodes were awesome – over 21 million for each of the first two and a mammoth 24.35 million for the final outing. This smashed the previous best British record

for a TV programme (excluding, that is, state and royal events), topping by 400,000 the figure generated by the last episode of *To The Manor Born*. (Also, *To The Manor Born* only had two channels to oppose whereas *Only Fools* triumphed against three terrestrial channels and a host of cable and satellite stations.) The Trotters made one final appearance in a segment for **Comic Relief** 1997; set before their windfall, Del and Rodney discussed their financial problems but agreed (charitably) that there were many people worse off than they. In a clever piece of dialogue, the pair also alluded to Lyndhurst's and Jason's other successful screen personae, Gary Sparrow (from **Goodnight Sweetheart**) and the dour detective Inspector Frost.

From *Only Fools And Horses'* many memorable moments, three images linger longest in the memory. The first was when, while renovating a house, Rodney and Del Boy, with Grandad's 'assistance', cause a priceless crystal chandelier to smash to smithereens on the floor below. The second was a wonderful piece of physical comedy involving Del and Trigger at the bar in the Nag's Head, their customary watering-hole; eyeing up a couple of girls, Del goes to lean on a bar flap which, unbeknownst to him, has just been raised, and with a perfect pratfall, drops clean out of shot. The final and perhaps most abiding memory is that of the dilapidated vehicle that served as the Trotters' company transport: an ancient yellow Reliant Robin three-wheeler with the legend – one that encapsulated Del's entire business philosophy – 'New York, Paris, Peckham'.

Only Jerks And Horses

see Sitcom Weekend

Only On Sunday

UK · BBC · SITCOM
....
1 × 30 mins · colour
18 June 1975 · BBC1 Wed 9.30pm

MAIN CAST
Geoffrey · · · · · · · · · · · · · · · Trevor Bannister
Patrick · · · · · · · · · · · · · · · · Peter Bowles

CREDITS
writers Dick Clement/Ian La Frenais · *producer* Gareth Gwenlan

The second of five unrelated, one-off sitcom episodes that aired independently following the demise of *Comedy Playhouse*. This effort, written by **Porridge** creators Clement and La Frenais, was set in the world of village cricket. No series developed.

Only When I Laugh

UK · ITV (YORKSHIRE) · SITCOM
....
29 × 30 mins · colour

Series One (7) 29 Oct–10 Dec 1979 · Mon 8pm
Series Two (7) 29 Apr–10 June 1980 · Tue 8.30pm
Series Three (7) 2 Sep–14 Oct 1981 · Wed mostly 8pm
Special · 24 Dec 1981 · Thu 7.30pm
Series Four (7) 4 Nov–16 Dec 1982 · Thu 7.30pm

MAIN CAST
Roy Figgis · · · · · · · · · · · · · · · James Bolam
Archie Glover · · · · · · · · · · · · · Peter Bowles
Norman Binns · · · · · · · · · Christopher Strauli
Dr Gordon Thorpe · · · · · · · · Richard Wilson
Gupte · · · · · · · · · · · · · · · · Derrick Branche

CREDITS
writer Eric Chappell · *director/producer* Vernon Lawrence

James Bolam's first comedy since **Whatever Happened To The Likely Lads** (in the interim he had scored great acclaim as tough Jack Ford in the BBC1 drama *When The Boat Comes In*) pitched him into this happy ensemble that frequently topped the ratings.

Only When I Laugh was set in an NHS hospital wherein a trio of very different patients was forever playing the art of one-upmanship and getting into scrapes with each other, at the same time causing grief to the irritable surgeon Thorpe (Richard Wilson) and Gupte (Derrick Branche), the luckless and easily flustered ward orderly from Delhi. Bolam played Figgis, a lorry driver who, one sensed, revelled in the confines of the hospital ward, stirring up bad odour and using his limited medical knowledge and broad-ranging working-class opinions to wind up the other patients. In particular, he enjoyed teasing Binns (Christopher Strauli), a hapless, innocent middle-class mummy's boy, and Archie Glover (Peter Bowles), a cultivated upper-class hypochondriac who enjoys having everyone running around for him.

Most episodes were set in the ward – there wasn't much wrong with them, but the three leading players seemed destined to remain hospital- and dressing-gown-bound for the duration – with young nurses and a succession of visitors providing writer Eric Chappell (who, with director/producer Vernon Lawrence, was following on from the great **Rising Damp**) opportunities to bring in other actors when necessary.

Only When I Laugh enjoyed a second lease of life when C4 began two series of repeats, from 28 March 1994 and 9 January 1995, that fared unexpectedly well.

Ooh La La!

UK · BBC · FARCE
....
18 episodes (12 × 30 mins · 6 × 60 mins) · colour

Series One (6 × 30 mins) 6 Apr–11 May 1968 ·
BBC2 Sat 9.30pm

Series Two (6 × 30 mins) 1 July–12 Aug 1968 ·
BBC2 Mon 8pm

Series Three (6 × 60 mins) 12 May–16 June
1973 · BBC2 Sat around 10pm

MAIN CAST
Patrick Cargill
Amanda Barrie (series 1)
Fenella Fielding (series 2)

CREDITS
original writers Georges Feydeau (13),
Sacha Guitry (2), Eugene Labiche/Marc Michel (2),
Eugene Labiche (1) · *adapters/translators*
Ned Sherrin/Caryl Brahms · *producers* Stuart Allen
(series 1), Barry Lupino (series 2), Douglas Argent
(series 3)

TV adaptations of French farces translated
by Ned Sherrin and Caryl Brahms and
starring the light-comedy actor Patrick
Cargill, who was a regular performer in such
farces on stage. The short Feydeau farcettes
were originally written as curtain-raisers for
Parisian audiences who expected more for
their money than one straight play. The
third, final TV series – titled *Patrick Cargill
In Ooh La La!* – tackled some of Feydeau's
longer pieces.

Every edition featured all of the classic
elements of farce: rakish men, comely
wenches and formidable wives enduring
mistaken identities and misunderstandings,
making break-neck entrances and exits,
hiding in cupboards and so on, but the genre
has always suffered in its transportation
to TV, losing the audience's thrill at the
frantic, split-second timing of the live stage
performance. Despite being a praiseworthy
effort, *Ooh La La!* also failed to overcome
this fundamental shortcoming.

Open All Hours

UK · BBC · SITCOM

**27 episodes (26 × 30 mins · 1 × short special) ·
colour**

Pilot · 25 Mar 1973 · BBC2 Sun 8.15pm

Series One (6) 20 Feb–26 Mar 1976 · BBC2
Fri 9pm

Series Two (7) 1 Mar–19 Apr 1981 · BBC1
Sun 7.15pm

Series Three (6) 21 Mar–25 Apr 1982 · BBC1
Sun 7.15pm

Short special · part of *The Funny Side Of
Christmas* 27 Dec 1982 · BBC1 Mon 8.05pm

Series Four (6) 1 Sep–6 Oct 1985 · BBC1
Sun 7.15pm

MAIN CAST
Arkwright · · · · · · · · · · · · · · · Ronnie Barker
Granville · · · · · · · · · · · · · · · · David Jason
Nurse Gladys Emmanuel · · · · Sheila Brennan
· (pilot);
· · · · · · · · · · · · · · · · · · Lynda Baron (series)

OTHER APPEARANCES
Mrs Blewitt · · · · · · · · · · · · · · · Kathy Staff
Mavis · · · · · · · · · · · · Maggie Ollerenshaw
Milkwoman · · · · · · · · · · · · · Barbara Flynn

Mrs Featherstone · · · · · · · · Stephanie Cole
Julie · · · · · · · · · · · · · · · · · Helen Cotterill

CREDITS
writer Roy Clarke · *producers* Sydney Lotterby (26),
Robin Nash (1)

First seen in *Seven Of One*, the series
of Ronnie Barker pilots, *Open All Hours*
provided more memorable slices of northern
life from *Last Of The Summer Wine*
creator Roy Clarke. A schoolteacher when
he began writing in earnest, Clarke had been
employed in several occupations before this,
including spells as a policeman (he used the
experience to write the sitcom *Rosie*) and
in a corner-shop, from which he drew the
inspiration for *Open All Hours*. However, the
series' lead character – the stuttering, miserly,
lustful shopkeeper Arkwright – was the
invention of actor/writer Ronnie Barker;
Clarke developed the equally strongly drawn
contrasting characters, created the plots and
wrote the scripts, imbuing them with the
naturally humorous linguistic rhythm that
is his trademark.

A comic actor par excellence, Ronnie
Barker's performance as the old-fashioned
Arkwright was wonderfully judged, with the
stutter used to fine comic effect and not over-
used for cheap laughs. A few complaints were
registered over the humorous use of a speech
impediment but Arkwright was so amiable
and the humour so good-natured that it was
deemed by most people to be a portrayal
without malice. But although most of the
humour was verbal, Barker also showed his
aptitude for physical comedy in a wonderful
double-act with the shop's till, which grabbed
the money from his fingers with a speed
and ferocity more commonly associated with
a shark. Barker worked up the routine
impressively, often hesitating before the till,
weighing up the options, before risking his
fingers in the guillotine-like drawer. Dour, sour-
faced customers popped into Arkwright's
shop, usually for single items, and the
owner's meanness and greed – coupled with
the paucity of the local custom – caused him
to open the premises for longer and longer
hours and to invent countless brilliant
schemes to increase business.

Equally adept at both the verbal and
physical comedy was Barker's principal
support, David Jason. He was cast as
Granville, Arkwright's dreamer of a nephew,
who wiles away his hours as shop assistant
and delivery boy (with trusty bicycle) sighing
heavily, feeling – indeed, knowing – that
his life is slipping away without romance,
foreign travel, glamour and exotic or erotic
experiences. His unconsummated relationship
with the milkwoman, played with a smouldering air by Barbara Flynn, was a metaphor
for all his missed opportunities. Arkwright
himself also has a dream to follow: marriage

to the buxom nurse Gladys Emmanuel, who
lives across the road but is tied into caring for
her aged mother. Nurse Gladys – in a finely
judged, very real performance by the underrated Lynda Baron – never ceases to drive
Arkwright into paroxysms of lust with her
ample charms. She is an honest, down-to-
earth woman seemingly unaffected by
Arkwright's intentions but occasionally
letting her guard down enough to suggest
that if the circumstances are right … who
knows? But even by the last episode, her
affection for Arkwright was never shown to
be carnal – as his certainly was – and the
relationship remained unrequited.

Note. The location of Arkwright's corner shop
– Lister Avenue in Doncaster – has become
a tourist landmark since the series began. It
was not a grocery store in real life, however,
but a hairdressing salon that the BBC
designers altered to suit their purpose.

The Open Mic Awards

UK · C5 (AVALON TELEVISION) · STANDUP

1 × 60 mins · colour

2 Oct 1997 · Thu 11.05pm

MAIN CAST
host · · · · · · · · · · · · · · · · · Boothby Graffoe

CREDITS
writers various · *director* Peter Orton · *producer*
Sam Pinnell

A TV presentation of the prestigious
Edinburgh Festival Fringe award for new
standup comedy talent. The event was hosted
by Boothby Graffoe (who took his name from
a town in Lincolnshire) and the ten featured
acts were Paul Foot, Simon Evans, Anton,
Alex Boardman, Daryl Martin, Harpie,
Stephen Keyworth, Michael Toombs,
T J Murphy and Nick Hoare.

Paul Foot won, completing a notable
double: he also picked up the similar BBC
New Comedy Award at the same Festival,
shown in a special edition of *The Stand
Up Show* (BBC1, 27 September 1997).

Opening Night

see SYKES, Eric

Operation Good Guys

UK · BBC (FUGITIVE GROUP/BBC) · SITCOM

7 × 30 mins · colour

29 Dec 1997–7 Feb 1998 · BBC2
mostly Sat 9.30pm

MAIN CAST
DI Beach · · · · · · · · · · · · · · · David Gillespie
DS Raymond Ash · · · · · · · · · · · Ray Burdis
Sgt Dominic de Sade · · · · · Dominic Anciano
'Smiler' McCarthy · · · · · · · · · · · Hugo Blick
Gary Barwick · · · · · · · · · · · · · Gary Beadle
Mark Kemp · · · · · · · · · · · · · · · Mark Burdis

Roy Leyton	Roy Smiles
Kim Finch ('Boo-Boo')	Kim Taylforth
'Bones'	Perry Benson
'Strings'	John Beckett

CREDITS
creators Dominic Anciano/Ray Burdis · *writers/directors/producers* Dominic Anciano/Ray Burdis/Hugo Blick · *executive producers* Jim Beach, Geoffrey Perkins

A sparkling fly-on-the-wall documentary spoof, ostensibly covering a police action code-named 'Operation Good Guys'. The initiative is designed to bring down crime-lord 'Smiler' McCarthy, known to the force as 'Teflon Don' because 'nothing sticks to him'.

The head of operations, DI Beach, has hand-picked his task squad from across the board, the team being his long-term sidekick DS Ash; armed-response expert Sgt de Sade; undercover vice-squad operative Kim Finch (who spends much of her time in the guise of a prostitute/stripper named Boo-Boo); undercover drugs-squad man 'Bones'; deep undercover officer Gary Barwick; another undercover man, the 1960s-throwback and would-be rock musician 'Strings'; civilian accountant Roy Leyton; and naïve new recruit Mark Kemp, who just happens to be the Commissioner's nephew.

Beach has permitted a documentary unit to film every step of the operation, surmising that the successful outcome of the venture will reflect well upon him. But his faith is misplaced – the team is excruciatingly inept, bungling even the simplest of tasks and, embarrassingly, often embroiling famous faces in their foul-ups (including the Arsenal and England goalkeeper David Seaman, and the entrepreneur Victor Kiam, both of whom appeared in episodes as themselves). McCarthy, on the other hand, goes about his dirty business in the same old way, constantly keeping one or several steps ahead of the boys in blue. As the operation continues, the lawsuits against the squad mount up, and general over-expenditure forces Roy Leyton to tighten the purse strings, leading to a cash-flow crisis that jeopardises still further the integrity of the mission.

Operation Good Guys was a marvellously inventive satire, overflowing with good ideas and memorable characters. Any thoughts that the initial premise might be too thin were dispelled by the creativity of the actors and the strength of the ongoing plot (which could easily have stood on its own without the fly-on-the-wall-film gimmick). The fact that the dialogue within the structured storylines was mainly improvised also added to the spontaneous, 'real-life' feel of the series. Executive producers Jim Beach and Geoffrey Perkins themselves turned up in episodes, Beach as the Commissioner, Perkins as the Head of Interpol.

The Optimist

UK · C4 (*NEW CENTURY FILMS/CHARISMA FILMS · **OPTIMIST COMPANY FOR CHARISMA FILMS) · SITCOM

13 × 30 mins · colour
*Series One (7) 14 Apr–26 May 1983 · Thu 8pm
**Series Two (6) 31 Dec 1984–5 Jan 1985 · Mon to Sat mostly 7.30pm

MAIN CAST
The Optimist .... Enn Reitel

CREDITS
writers Richard Sparks (series 1), Enn Reitel/Robert Fuest/Robert Sidaway (series 2) · *directors* Peter Ellis (series 1), Robert Fuest (series 2) · *executive producer* John Brittany · *producer* Robert Sidaway

Although British-made, the first of these two series was filmed out and about on location in Hollywood, and it was entirely silent. Enn Reitel – his unusual name owes to his Baltic parentage – was cast as the dreamy optimist in the title, despising people who represented hurdles in his life, and failing in most things he set out to achieve. The second series – first screened by C4 in daily episodes – was *mostly* silent and shot in London. As before, other actors appeared with the optimist in each programme but he was the only ever-present.

Much of the humour was based in wild fantasy sequences and bizarre occurrences that boggled the eyes but cannot adequately be represented on the printed page. Suffice to say that *The Optimist* was one creation that stood out from the crowd.

The Orchestra

ISRAEL (UNITED STUDIOS OF ISRAEL) · SITCOM

10 × 30 mins · colour
Israel dates: not known
UK dates: 22 May 1986–17 Jan 1987 (10 episodes) C4 Thu 9pm then Sat mostly 8.30pm

MAIN CAST
The Maestro .... Julian-Joy Chagrin
The Valet .... Sephy Rivlin

CREDITS
writer/director Julian-Joy Chagrin · *producers* David Goldstein, Eliezer Dorot

This first (and, to date, only) comedy programme imported on to British TV from Israel featured the acclaimed mime comic Julian-Joy Chagrin, drawing humour from and parodying the ways of classical music with his unique combination of music-hall slapstick and the serious.

The great conductor Zubin Mehta appeared in the third programme. 'The Dance Of The Hours' – one of the first five episodes screened by C4 from 22 May to 19 June 1986 – won the Independent Programme Golden Rose award at the 1985 Montreux TV Festival.

The Other 'Arf

UK · ITV (WITZEND PRODUCTIONS FOR ATV · *WITZEND PRODUCTIONS FOR CENTRAL) · SITCOM

26 × 30 mins · colour
Series One (7) 30 May–11 July 1980 · Fri 7.30pm
Special · 4 Jan 1981 · Sun 8.15pm
Series Two (6) 24 Apr–29 May 1981 · Fri 8.30pm
*Series Three (6) 12 Nov–17 Dec 1982 · Fri 8.30pm
*Series Four (6) 24 Feb–30 Mar 1984 · Fri 8.30pm

MAIN CAST

Lorraine Watts	Lorraine Chase
Charles Latimer MP	John Standing
George Watts	John Cater (series 1–3)
Lord Freddy Apthorpe	James Villiers (series 1–3)
Sybilla Howarth	Patricia Hodge (series 1 & 2)
Brian Sweeney	Steve Adler (series 1 & 2)
Astrid Lindstrom	Natalie Forbes (series 1)
Bassett	Richard Caldicot (series 4)
Mrs Lilley	Sheila Keith (series 4)

CREDITS
creator Terence Howard · *writers* Terence Howard (23), Paul Makin (2), Ian La Frenais (1) · *script editors* Dick Clement/Ian La Frenais · *directors* John Kaye Cooper (series 1 & special), Alan Wallis (series 2 & 3), Douglas Argent (series 4) · *executive producer* Allan McKeown · *producers* Tony Charles/John Kaye Cooper (series 1), Tony Charles/Alan Wallis (series 2 & 3), Tony Charles/Douglas Argent (series 4)

The Other 'Arf depicted an unlikely long-term relationship between a 'fick down-to-erf cockney gel' model and a groomed true-blue Tory MP, after their chance meeting in a restaurant, and drew upon the sudden, unexpected fame that befell the attractive Lorraine Chase when she appeared in a TV commercial for the alcoholic drink Campari, uttering a phrase about Luton Airport. As preposterous as these things always seem with hindsight, the phrase – and hence Lorraine – attained national fame at the time.

The comedy, of course, focused on the culture clash – culture shock, even – when the two lovers tried to fraternise socially, the urbane Charles Latimer MP being more at home in Belgravia and the winners' enclosure at Royal Ascot; Lorraine Watts among the hot-dog wrappers and beer-in-a-plastic-glass crowd at Catford greyhound track. The relationship had additional obstacles too: Charles was already engaged, to the awfully-awfully Sybilla Howarth, and Lorraine had her football-mad Brian, so it was very much an on-off affair at first – Charles could scarcely have afforded to sever his ties with Sybilla (or, more precisely, with her rich father), and while Lorraine was a beautiful companion to sit beside in his private box at the opera, there was always the horrible chance that she might open her mouth to talk and, with her 'cor blimey, stone the bleedin' crows' manner, embarrass him.

In order to maintain topicality, Charles decided to switch colours from Conservative to SDP during the 1982 series, by which time Lorraine had forced Charles to abandon his engagement to Sybilla and they were now married. When the final series began, in 1984, Charles was out of politics altogether and the couple turned his old family seat into a hotel, maintaining its old staff (Bassett and Mrs Lilley).

One of the first independent productions of the era (WitzEnd being Dick Clement and Ian La Frenais' company, indeed the pair scripted one of the final episodes), *The Other 'Arf* was created especially for Lorraine Chase by Terence Howard, who worked in the advertising world and had been involved in her TV commercials. And there really was a culture difference between Lorraine and her co-star: she hailed from Deptford, south London, and John Standing was the stage name for an Old Etonian, Sir John Leon.

The Other One

UK · BBC · SITCOM

13 × 30 mins · colour

Series One (7) 11 Nov–30 Dec 1977 · Fri 8.30pm
Series Two (6) 23 Feb–30 Mar 1979 · Fri 8.30pm

MAIN CAST
Ralph Tanner · · · · · · · · · · · · Richard Briers
Brian Bryant · · · · · · · · · · · Michael Gambon
Manolo · · · · · · · Michael Chesden (series 1)

CREDITS
writers John Esmonde/Bob Larbey · *producers* John Howard Davies (series 1), Roger Race (series 2)

Following hot on the heels of the last series of **The Good Life** (although two further specials followed), this was another sitcom written for Richard Briers by John Esmonde and Bob Larbey. It could not have been much more different, though, and garnered none of the affection of that earlier show.

Briers was cast as Ralph Tanner, a rather sad character who presents the world with a wholly artificial front. A compulsive liar, he uses any means, no matter how embarrassing, to portray himself as a worldly, 'been there, seen it, done it all' chap, whereas, in reality, he is an inexperienced incompetent. Nevertheless, his brash front is enough to impress the gullible, timid Brian when they first meet in an airport, awaiting the same flight to Spain. There, they hope to conquer the fillies. Inevitably, they fail.

The majority of the first series was set in Spain, with Ralph loping about with the confidence of a native and Brian following him, invariably into chaos. Ralph constantly proclaims himself a 'lone wolf' who needs no-one but actually he is lonely and needs

Brian's company and friendship. On their return to England, Ralph seeks out Brian once more and the second series depicted them as travelling salesmen.

The Other Reg Varney

see **VARNEY, Reg**

O.T.T.

UK · ITV (CENTRAL) · SKETCH/STANDUP

*13 × 60 mins · colour

*2 Jan–3 Apr 1982 · Sat around 11pm

MAIN CAST
Chris Tarrant
Lenny Henry
Bob Carolgees
John Gorman
Helen Atkinson Wood
Alexei Sayle

OTHER APPEARANCES
Colette Hillier (one edition)

CREDITS
writers Howard Imber and cast · *director* Peter Harris · *producer* Chris Tarrant

A bizarre occurrence took place between 1979 and 1981: a generation of adults, principally in the 18–25 age group, discovered the delights of ATV's newly networked (but on screen in the Midlands since 5 January 1974) Saturday-morning children's show *Tiswas*, either steadfastly watching the entire two hours – getting up for the start, bleary-eyed, at 10.30am – or clamouring to take part in the viewer-participation elements of this fabulously anarchic show, like the cage, where gunge or water was thrown over its inhabitants. Soon enough, the show's principal talents – Chris Tarrant, Lenny Henry, Bob Carolgees, John Gorman and Sally James – went out on tour (as the Four Bucketeers, under which name, with a little help from Lenny Henry, they had also released an album and hit single), playing night-clubs and aiming their hilarious stage-show, which included much risqué material, squarely at this same audience. The adulation was stunning, and it became a veritable badge-of-honour to be doused, sprayed or abused by the *Tiswas* teamsters in these strictly adult shows.

The obvious move, then, was for these arch-pranksters to quit *Tiswas* (which they did on 28 March 1981; it carried on with new players though much less successfully) and start their own adult programme – adult, that is, in both senses of the word. *O.T.T.* was the result, and it was very poor stuff. The titular abbreviation, of course, stood for Over The Top and this was a policy that the cast endeavoured to pursue with full vigour. Inexplicably, though, the very type of material that had worked so well in the Four Bucketeers concerts bombed on TV, and its

extreme attempts to take television down new avenues of humour drew very considerable and mostly deserved flak not only for the cast but also for Central TV, which launched the series on only its second day of operations. For sure, *O.T.T.* did not give the new ITV franchise an auspicious start.

Of the five Four Bucketeers, only Sally James did not make the move, remaining with *Tiswas*. Bob Carolgees brought with him his gobbing punk puppet Spit the Dog and dense alter ego Houdi-Elbow, Lenny Henry reprised his Rasta character Algernon, Chris Tarrant was the slightly dangerous but seemingly affable host, former Scaffold singer John Gorman reprised his dim-policeman character, and new members of the team included Helen Atkinson Wood, the fast-rising 'Albanian' comedian Alexei Sayle (uncomfortable with much of the non-PC material in the show, he pulled out of the latter editions), the pie-flinging Count Custard (a logical successor to the *Tiswas* Phantom Flan-Flinger) and, unforgettably, three naked blokes who deftly swapped around the balloons that covered their private parts. Apart from the odd pre-recorded insert, everything went out live, so this was dangerous television. Most viewers couldn't reach their 'off' button fast enough.

*Note. The series extended to 12 programmes. The thirteenth and final edition compiled the highlights (*sic*) of the previous dozen.

See also **Saturday Stayback**.

Our Brian

see **Hey Brian!**

Our Dora

see **My Wife's Sister**

Our Hands In Your Safe

UK · ITV (GRANADA) · SATIRE

1 × 35 mins · colour

27 Aug 1995 · Sun 11.15pm

MAIN CAST
John Bird
John Fortune

CREDITS
writers John Bird/John Fortune · *director* Sarah Harding · *producer* Vicky Matthews

A wonderfully titled one-off in which master satirists Bird and Fortune mocked up a year in the life of an NHS trust, depicting managers whose primary concern is no longer healthcare but the balance sheet.

They visited the same subject in a 1994 edition of **Rory Bremner … Who Else?**, later re-screened (on 13 September 1995) in **The Long Johns**.

Our House

UK · ITV (ABC) · SITCOM

39 episodes (26 × 45 mins · 13 × 55 mins) · b/w

Series One (13 × 55 mins) 11 Sep–4 Dec 1960 ·
Sun 3.25pm

*Series Two (26 × 45 mins) 16 Sep 1961–21 Apr
1962 · fortnightly then weekly Sat 7.40pm

MAIN CAST

Georgina Ruddy · · · · · · · · · · Hattie Jacques
Simon Willow · · · · · · · · · · · Charles Hawtrey
Herbert Keene · · · · · · · · · Frederick Peisley
Marcia Hatton · · · · · · · · · · · Leigh Madison
Stephen Hatton · · Trader Faulkner (series 1)
Daisy Burke · · · · · · · · · · Joan Sims (series 1)
Gordon Brent · · · · · · · · Norman Rossington
· (series 1)
Captain Iliffe · · · · · Frank Pettingell (series 1)
Mrs Iliffe · · · · · · · · Ina de la Haye (series 1)
William Singer · · Bernard Bresslaw (series 2)
Henrietta · · · · · · · · · · Hylda Baker (series 2)
Marina · · · · · · Eugenie Cavanagh (series 2)

WITH

Johnny Vyvyan (series 2)
Harry Korris (series 2)

CREDITS

creator/main writer Norman Hudis · other writers
Brad Ashton, Bob Block · producer Ernest Maxin

If you like Carry On movies, especially the
earlier and more subtle ones – then chances
are you would have loved Our House. Created
and principally written by Norman Hudis –
'fresh' from scripting the first five Carry On
films: Sergeant, Nurse, Teacher, Constable
and Regardless, and just before penning the
sixth, Cruising – the series reunited Carry On
actors Hattie Jacques, Charles Hawtrey and
Joan Sims, and featured Bernard Bresslaw,
who would become a staple of the movie
series from 1965. Hudis's TV idea was to
bring together under one roof nine people
of varying backgrounds and develop the
interplay accordingly, so the opening episode
found the nine – two couples and five
individuals – all with an urgent need to
find a place to live, meeting up in an estate
agent's office and realising that if they
pooled their finances they could buy a
huge house together.

Hattie Jacques was arguably the main star
of this riotous assembly, playing the role of a
librarian who, forced to keep hushed at work,
loved to make lots of noise at home. Charles
Hawtrey played another prissy role, as an
amiable loner working in the local council's
rates office. Sims flitted in and out of jobs and
was the bane of the local Labour Exchange;
Rossington was a law student whose life was
dictated by his father's wishes; Peisley was a
shy and persecuted bachelor bank clerk;
Captain Iliffe was a retired naval captain
whose wife was a violinist; and Stephen and
Marcia Hatton were newly-weds. The second
series (see footnote) featured a drastically
changed cast, adding Hylda Baker, Bernard
Bresslaw and others but losing many stars

from the first, while among those who
appeared once apiece in Our House were
McDonald Hobley, Jill Day, Deryck Guyler
and a very young holiday-camp entertainer,
Roy Hudd.

*Notes. Our House lost its network status
after seven fortnightly episodes of the second
series. The remaining 19 episodes, aired
weekly, were not shown by London-area ITV,
which screened its last on 9 December 1961.

Three episodes of the 39 are believed to
have survived the years as tele-recordings
(the others have been junked) but none has
been seen on British television since 1962.

See also **Carry On ...**

Our Kid

UK · ITV (YORKSHIRE) · SITCOM

6 × 30 mins · colour

8 Apr–20 May 1973 · Sun 9.30pm

MAIN CAST

Bob Buslingthorpe · · · · · · · · · · Barrie Rutter
Ben Buslingthorpe · · · · · · · · · · · · Ken Platt
Lynda · · · · · · · · · · · · · · · · Sylvia Brayshay

CREDITS

creators Keith Waterhouse/Willis Hall · writers Eric
Geen (2), Anthony Couch (2), Keith Waterhouse/
Willis Hall (1), David Nobbs (1) · director/producer
Ian Davidson

Prolific writers Waterhouse and Hall created
and part-scripted this single Yorkshire series
that, unusually, focused on a fraternal
relationship – our kid being a northern term
for brother.

Ever since his mother died, leaving them
her house at 59 Spring Street, Halifax, Ben
Buslingthorpe has taken care of his baby
brother Bob. Now middle-aged, Ben still does
all of the household chores and takes care of
Bob's every domestic need. Bob, who is a man
of industry – he does daily hard labour down
at the local factory – relies heavily upon Ben,
but he has also caught the attention of a
local lass, Lynda, and the two have become
engaged. But can Lynda prise the brothers
apart, and will Ben let go of the umbilical
cord?

Our Man At St Mark's

UK · ITV (*ASSOCIATED-REDIFFUSION ·
REDIFFUSION) · SITCOM

46 × 30 mins · b/w

*Series One (7) 25 Sep–27 Nov 1963 ·
Wed mostly 9.15pm

Series Two (13) 16 Apr–29 July 1964 ·
mostly Thu 7.30pm

Series Three (13) 26 Apr–2 Aug 1965 ·
Mon 9.10pm

Series Four (12) Our Man From St Mark's
4 July–19 Sep 1966 · Mon mostly 9.10pm

Special Our Man From St Mark's 28 Dec 1966 ·
Wed 10.40pm

MAIN CAST

The Rev Andrew Parker · · · · · · Leslie Phillips
· (series 1)
The Rev/Venerable Stephen Young · · · · · · ·
· · · · · · · · · · · Donald Sinden (from series 2)
Mrs Peace · · · · · · · · · · · · · · · Joan Hickson
Anne Gibson · · · · · · · · Anne Lawson (series 1)
Harry Danvers · · · Harry Fowler (series 3 & 4)
The Bishop · · · · · · · · · Clive Morton (series 4)
The Rev John Spencer · · · · · · Peter Vaughan
· (series 4)

CREDITS

creators/writers James Kelly/Peter Miller ·
directors Bill Turner (18), Richard Doubleday (14),
Christopher Hodson (10), Geoffrey Hughes (3),
Cyril Coke (1) · producer Eric Maschwitz

At first an amiable and even sentimental
comedy, Our Man At St Mark's set out to
depict the gently humorous incidents that
can befall a country village vicar as he works
his flock of parishioners and weaves his way
in and out of their daily lives.

Leslie Phillips – usually typecast as a
woman-hungry cad – was the man of the
cloth in the first series, being somewhat
unusual in that he had a girlfriend. (Not, of
course, of the live-in variety.) In the second
series, however, his fictitious parish, Felgate
(location shooting was done in Denham
Village, Bucks), was sent a replacement, the
dog-loving Stephen Young, who – like his
predecessor – depended to a great extent on
the support of the loyal but sometimes stern
vicarage housekeeper Mrs Peace who, in
reality, was the backbone of the community.
(Young was played by Donald Sinden, an apt
role since, in real life, he was a renowned
lover of churches, going on to wax lyrical
about their architecture in the late-1970s
BBC1 series Discovering English Churches.)

The first two series of Our Man At St
Mark's, then, were quite light-hearted, but
the humour went a shade darker in the third
when more serious social issues became the
focus, causing the episodes to be screened
later in the evening. Some light relief was
added, however, in the shape of Harry Fowler
– cast yet again as a cockney scallywag –
who reformed from being Harry The Yo-Yo –
so called because he was always bouncing in
and out of jail – to becoming Young's scooter-
riding sexton and gravedigger.

There was another change of direction in
the final series, literally: Stephen Young was
promoted from Reverend to Archdeacon and,
with Mrs Peace, moved from Felgate to
Lynchester. (The cathedral scenes were filmed
in Lincoln.) Appropriately, the series' title
altered subtly to Our Man From St Mark's.

Our Man In Moscow

UK · BBC · SITCOM

1 × 30 mins · b/w

1 Mar 1963 · Fri 8.45pm

MAIN CAST

Sir William Hunter	Robert Morley
Nicolai	Patrick Wymark
Mortimer	Frank Thornton
Kulkinoff	Anthony Newlands

CREDITS

writers Ray Galton/Alan Simpson · producer Duncan Wood

The second series of the BBC's *Comedy Playhouse* was once again written exclusively by Ray Galton and Alan Simpson. In this opening one-off episode they introduced viewers to Sir William Hunter, HM Government's ambassador to Moscow, who faces a delicate situation when Nicolai, a Russian tuba-player, applies for political asylum. The ambassador's secretary, Mortimer, and the Russian minister of culture, Kulkinoff, also become embroiled in the events.

Ours Is A Nice House

UK · ITV (LWT) · SITCOM

13 × 30 mins · colour

*Series One (6) 10 Oct–14 Nov 1969 · Fri 8.30pm

Series Two (7) 25 July–5 Sep 1970 · Sat 6.45pm

MAIN CAST

Thora Parker	Thora Hird
Alan Parker	Leslie Meadows
Vera Parker	Caroline Dowdeswell
Alf Whittle	Harry Littlewood
Elsie Crabtree	Ruth Holden
Gran	May Warden
Brandon Bailey	David Stoll (series 1)
Mrs Orpington-Hunt	Beatrix Mackey (series 1)
Dudley Banks-Smith	Ray Fell (series 2)
Lottie Bottomley	Damaris Hayman (series 2)

CREDITS

writer Harry Littlewood · directors Stuart Allen (8), Howard Ross (5) · producer Stuart Allen

The great Thora Hird starred in this series as a Lancashire boarding-house landlady named (what else?) Thora. A widowed mother of two teenagers – son Alan and daughter Vera – she runs a clean, respectable house ('nice, you know, none of your tat'). The comedy was sprung from the ensemble of resident boarders (one of whom, Alf Whittle, was played by the series' writer Harry Littlewood), itinerant lodgers who flitted into and then out of the weekly episodes, and friends and neighbours, like next door's Elsie Crabtree, who was always popping around to borrow something or other and have a natter about this or that.

*Note. The first series was shown in black and white on the still-monochrome ITV, but a repeat airing (28 February to 4 April 1970) was screened in colour.

Out Of The Trees

UK · BBC · SKETCH

1 × 30 mins · colour

10 Jan 1976 · BBC2 Sat 10pm

MAIN CAST

Graham Chapman
Maria Aitken
Roger Brierley
Jennifer Guy
Maggie Henderson
Marjie Lawrence
Simon Jones
Tim Preece
Mark Wing-Davey

CREDITS

writers Graham Chapman/Bernard McKenna/Douglas Adams · producer Bernard Thompson

Following the demise of **Monty Python**, Graham Chapman – like the other members of that troupe – was looking for fresh outlets, and with this one-off broadcast he was hoping to realise his own sketch series.

Chapman was beginning to write with Bernard McKenna and he had already collaborated with Douglas Adams for the last series of *Python*, and so the sketches were not dissimilar in style of that show. The general consensus was that *Out Of The Trees* lacked cohesion, though, and no series developed.

But at least one good thing came of the programme: Adams went on to cast Mark Wing-Davey in one of the key roles (Zaphod Beeblebrox) in his pioneering radio, and later TV, comedy series **The Hitch-Hiker's Guide To The Galaxy**.

Out Of This World   UK

UK · BBC · SKETCH

1 × 30 mins · b/w

15 Nov 1950 · Wed 8.30pm

MAIN CAST

Bobby Howes
Hattie Jacques
Zena Marshall

CREDITS

writers Ted Kavanagh, Carey Edwards · producer Michael Mills

The team behind **Such Is Life** reunited for this proposed series of which only this first episode, subtitled 'The Adventures Of Sir Percy Howsey', appeared. Publicity for *Out Of This World* stated, 'The hero of this new fortnightly series will appear in the most extraordinary guises, burlesquing characters from fiction'. The remaining guises, clearly, were invisible.

Out Of This World   USA

USA · SYNDICATION/NBC (BOB BOOKER PRODUCTIONS/MCA) · SITCOM

96 × 30 mins · colour

US dates: 17 Sep 1987–26 May 1991

UK dates: 9 Apr 1990–24 Apr 1992 (96 episodes) ITV weekdays 10am

MAIN CAST

Donna Garland	Donna Pescow
Evie Garland	Maureen Flannigan
Kyle Applegate	Doug McClure
Uncle Beano Froelich	Joe Alaskey (1987–90)
Lindsay Selkirk	Christina Nigra
Troy	Burt Reynolds (voice only)
Buzz	Buzz Belmondo

CREDITS

creators John Boni, Bob Booker (based on a format by D L Wood) · writers various · directors various · executive producers Bob Booker, John Boni, Barbara Booker · producers John Boni, Barbara Booker

Celebrating her 13th birthday, goody-two-shoes Californian gal Evie Garland makes three shattering discoveries: her father is not dead, as presumed; he is not human but an alien from the planet Anterias (he and Evie's mother had married and 'blended life forms' when he was on an extended interplanetary visit); and that, being half-alien, she has the power to perform humanly impossible deeds. These include freezing motionless people around her, simply by placing together her two index fingers, 'gleeping' – making things materialise by the power of thought – and teletransportation. From this point on, Evie's life is never the same again, and she and her mother Donna, who runs a school for gifted children of rich 'Californny' parents, have to adjust to the change as best they can. Meanwhile, Evie's alien father, Troy, communicates with his daughter by voice (belonging to none other than Burt Reynolds), his words issuing from a blue crystal on Evie's bedside cabinet. A gaggle of sitcom-style characters populated the remaining roles, one being the self-centred local mayor (and later the police chief) – played by Doug McClure, Trampas in the western series *The Virginian* – a former TV actor who likes to think of himself as Clint Eastwood, not least because the town in which the series was set, Marlowe, is nearby Carmel, where Eastwood was indeed mayor.

Out Of This World was another of NBC's attempts to overturn the triumphant ratings winner *Wheel Of Fortune* by 'checkerboarding' a different low-budget sitcom each evening in the same slot (see **Marblehead Manor** for further details, and also **She's The Sheriff**). Inexplicably successful, and a real favourite among younger viewers, NBC extended the life of *Out Of This World* to four seasons, during which time the storylines became pretty well exhausted. In the final episode Troy returned to Earth, except that he was transparent; then, when a piece of equipment malfunctioned, he was stranded in California while Evie was sent back to Anterias.

The series was imported to Britain by ITV and, like all imports, was screened differently from region to region; in London and several other areas it was 'stripped', daily, Mondays to Fridays at 10am, when audience-participation talk-show *The Time … The Place* was off-air.

Out Of Tune

UK · BBC · CHILDREN'S · SITCOM

30 × 25 mins · colour

Series One (17) 14 Feb–4 June 1996 · BBC1
Wed 4.35pm then Tue 4.35pm
Series Two (13) 24 Sep–17 Dec 1997 · BBC1
Wed 4.35pm

MAIN CAST

Street	Tim Downie
Ice D	Jotham Annan
Sheri	Louise Sullivan
Mickey	Thomas Maher
Frankie	John Waterhouse
Rev Worthington	Nick Maloney
Tony	John Labanowski
Chas	Jane Danson (series 1)
Carol	Charlene Brooks (series 1)
Natalie	Tonatha Davis (series 2)
Midge	Rebecca Clarke (series 2)
Lenny	Joe Murphy (series 2)
James	Jonathan Praeger (series 2)
Rachel	Lianne Islin (series 2)

CREDITS

writers John Sayle (8), Rory Clark/Robert Taylor (8), Brian Jordan (7), Gail Renard (4), Johnny Meres (3) · *executive producer* Christopher Pilkington · *director/producer* Martin Hughes

A children's sitcom focusing on the motley bunch who comprise a church choir in the village of Broughton. The place doesn't have much going for it by way of excitement, apart from occasional activities at the village hall, so the best place for the local youngsters to meet, mingle, gossip and romantically liaise is at choir practice, hence the meetings are well attended. Few of the number are there because they possess a good voice, though, which means that the choir is bad – very, very bad – the combination of the youngsters' vocal 'talents' resulting in a sound that is pitched somewhere between a strangled cat and the mating call of a bull elephant. The patient vicar tries his best to improve them, but to no avail.

The central characters within the choir are Street, a rakish boy slightly order than the others; the bossy Chas, who leads the girls and is the object of Street's passion; Ice D, a streetwise, village newcomer from an urban environment; and Frankie, an aspiring wheeler-dealer whose uncle can get hold of anything, 'no questions asked'.

All told, *Out Of Tune* was a competent comedy that occasionally hit the right note,

with fair acting from the young cast and some shameless hamming from the older members. Enjoyable but untaxing. A third series, for screening in spring 1998, was being made as this book went to press.

Outside Edge

UK · ITV (CENTRAL) · SITCOM

22 episodes (21 × 30 mins · 1 × 60 mins) · colour

Series One (7 × 30 mins) 24 Mar–5 May 1994 · Thu 8.30pm
Series Two (7 × 30 mins) 5 Jan–6 Feb 1995 · Thu 8.30pm
Special (60 mins) 25 Dec 1995 · Mon 10pm
Series Three (7 × 30 mins) 2 Jan–13 Feb 1996 · Tue 8.30pm

MAIN CAST

Miriam Dervish	Brenda Blethyn
Roger Dervish	Robert Daws
Maggie Costello	Josie Lawrence
Kevin Costello	Timothy Spall
Dennis Broadley	Denis Lill
Bob Willis	Jeremy Nicholas (series 1); Michael Jayston (from series 2)
Alex Harrington	Ben Daniels (series 1); Christopher Lang (from series 2)
Nigel	Nigel Pegram

OTHER APPEARANCES

Ginny	Tracy Brabin (not series 3)
Fred	Roy Holder (series 2)
Sonia	Rosemary Martin (series 2)
Clive	Duncan Knowles (series 3)
Arnold	Howard Jacks (series 3)
Shirley Broadley	Hilary Crane (series 3)
Vicar	David Belcher (series 3)
Sophie	Amanda Waring (series 3)

CREDITS

writer Richard Harris · *director* Nick Hurran · *executive producer* Paul Spencer · *producer* Paula Burdon

A multi-award-winning piece in 22 delightfully written, performed and directed episodes, shot on film without an audience. The sum added up to an all-too-rare occurrence: an ITV comedy which was so good that it could scarcely have been bettered by the BBC.

The landscape for *Outside Edge* is village cricket, played to a low standard but in deadly earnest by its white-flannelled protagonists. The principal focus, however, is on marital harmony, and two relationships in particular: Roger Dervish, cricket club captain, with his mousy wife Miriam, and their social inferiors Kevin, a slob, and his zesty wife Maggie. Author Richard Harris drew out these four characters to perfection, and his script – laden with awkwardness, pregnant pauses, sly asides, digs and despatches – brilliantly encapsulated the repressed discomfort of middle-class middle-England.

The key relationship is between Roger and Miriam (Mim) Dervish. Roger plans his Brent

Park Cricket Club campaigns like a military director, even wearing the club blazer at home. Chauvinistic and self-important, he speaks brusquely and patronisingly to Mim because, bereft of sensitivity, he knows no other way. Besides, he probably reasons, Mim not only expects him to crack the whip but *respects* it. Roger demands maximum spousal co-operation in exchange for only the very occasional cheek-peck or 'Love you' sentiment called out in her general direction. (When angry, this becomes 'love you, okay, fair enough' through gritted teeth.) To hurry Mim along, Roger barks 'chop chop', oblivious to her annoyance. Mim's problem is that she is so repressed that this anger stands no chance of being forcefully expressed. She knows her place: she makes the cricket-match teas (meaning not just tea but sandwiches and much more), serving the food on trestle tables she herself has erected. She rushes around as Roger's lap-dog, doing his bidding while perpetually biting her lip to help keep the wheels oiled. Sex between Roger and Mim, one suspects, is performed rarely and with the light off. They have two children, both away at university.

For all its apparent eddies, Kevin and Maggie's relationship is much the more fulfilling and mutual, each recognising the other's strengths and weaknesses. Kevin is a beer-swilling slob par excellence. Down-to-earth, he refers to his wife disparagingly whether angry or as a term of endearment. Maggie loves Kevin to pieces and is his biggest fan, realising and indeed nurturing the little boy trapped inside her man. Nothing defeats Maggie – she's a massively capable, busty woman in a massive furry coat, with boundless energy and a huge capacity for hugs and sex (she even tempts Kevin into sex in the Dervish's garden shed). Rewardingly, Mim and Maggie become friends, the former gaining her voice vicariously through the latter. Although looked down upon as uncouth by the other players, Kevin has the best relationship of all the cricket team, a bunch of ageing Lotharios, wife-cheaters and drinkers who care little for their captain Roger's fussy organising, fight among themselves, hold out for the batting positions of their choice and are not averse to running one another out while at the wicket.

The author Richard Harris adapted and extended his original long-running and much-travelled stage-play of *Outside Edge* for this excellent TV version. It had already been seen on the small-screen in its original form, a 105-minute LWT dramatic production broadcast on 19 December 1982, with Prunella Scales cast as Miriam, Paul Eddington as Roger, Maureen Lipman as Maggie and Jonathan Lynn as Kevin.

Over The Rainbow

UK · ITV (CLEMENT-LA FRENAIS/SELECTV FOR MERIDIAN) · SITCOM

8 × 30 mins · colour

11 July–29 Aug 1993 · Sun mostly 10.20pm

MAIN CAST

Finnoula ('Finn') · · · · · · · · · · · Angeline Ball
Michelle · · · · · · · · · · · · · Bronagh Gallagher
Neil · · · · · · · · · · · · · · · · · · · Peter Sullivan
Spence · · · · · · · · · · · · · · · · · · · Ian Targett
Uncle Roddy · · · · · · · · · · · Eamon Morrissey

CREDITS

creators Dick Clement/Ian La Frenais · writers Dick Clement/Ian La Frenais (7), Geoff Rowley (1) · director Declan Lowney · executive producers Allan McKeown, Tony Charles · producer Bernard McKenna

A spin-off from the very successful Dublin-based movie *The Commitments*, with two of the cast members reprising their roles, as young Irish women Finnoula ('Finn') and Michelle. While the movie was based on the book written by award-winning author Roddy Doyle, Dick Clement and Ian La Frenais wrote its screenplay and this eight-episode series, which borrowed – in concept as well as some specific dialogue – from their eight-part 1974 sitcom *Thick As Thieves*. (Indeed, this series was made with that title before being altered to *Over The Rainbow*.)

Thick As Thieves had focused on three people: a married couple and the man's best friend, and what happens when the male spouse comes out of jail to find his pal shacked up with his wife, leading to an unlikely but surprisingly not too uncomfortable *ménage à trois*. In *Over The Rainbow* the likely lads are best mates Neil and Spence. Despite Neil's reluctance, the pair participate in a spot of safe-blowing during Neil and Finn's wedding reception – it was to have been the perfect alibi – which goes disastrously wrong: Spence, the lookout, gets away from the scene of the crime but Neil, driver of the getaway car, is trapped inside the vehicle. With her husband in prison, Finn quits London and moves into a flat over a Brighton pub, the Rainbow, where, after a few months, she begins a relationship with Spence. He moves in, albeit into the spare room, and then, one year after their wedding, Neil is released from jail on probation, to find his best mate living with his divorce-seeking wife. As with *Thick As Thieves*, the two pals quickly reconcile themselves to the unusual situation and settle down to make the best of their lot, sharing their desire for Finn. She, on the other hand, wants nothing to do with either of them.

Finn is lead singer and her friend Michelle is singer/guitarist with the rock/soul band Static Cling (so named by Spence), rehearsing and performing in the Rainbow, a pub owned by Finn's Irish Uncle Roddy, something of a crime 'godfather' – he 'masterminded' the wedding reception burglary. (A lecherous sort, Roddy also lusts after Finn, unhindered by family ties – he married her aunt, so he's not a blood relative.) Eyeing up Static Cling's talent, and always looking for their next scam, Neil and Spence fancy themselves as music-business moguls and the series depicted their attempts at rock management: Static Cling are renamed Wicked Cleavage and, eventually, with a little 'help' from Uncle Roddy, they hit the road for their first tour.

Over The Rainbow never returned for a second series; while the storyline and some of the dialogue was of a good class, the characters were probably too unsympathetic to win over the viewing public.

Oxford Accents

UK · BBC · SKETCH

1 × 45 mins · b/w

26 Feb 1954 · Fri 9.10pm

MAIN CAST

Gareth Wigan
Henry White-Smith
Margaret Smith
Jeanne Lewis

CREDITS

director Antony Craxton

A televised version of an 'intimate revue' presented by the Experimental Theatre Club in collaboration with the Oxford University Dramatic Society. The show was broadcast direct from the Newmann Room of the Old Bishop's Palace in Oxford by the BBC's new-fangled 'mobile television unit', and Brian Johnston was on hand to introduce the proceedings for the viewers at home.

The show was devised and directed by Ned Sherrin (reading Law at Exeter College), who told *Radio Times* that his show aimed at laughs but was not parochial: such universal themes as looking for a job were dealt with, which should appeal to a wide public, he said.

After his studies, Sherrin decided not to pursue a career in the legal profession and instead became a film, theatre and TV producer, presenter, director and writer, still very active at the time of writing. From 1957 to 1966 he was on the staff at the BBC, where he formulated the perfect marriage of university revue and television entertainment with *That Was The Week That Was*.

See also The Cambridge Footlights.

Pacific Station

USA · NBC (KTMB PRODUCTIONS/TOUCHSTONE TELEVISION) · SITCOM

10 × 30 mins · colour

US dates: 15 Sep 1991–3 Jan 1992

UK dates: 27 July–5 Oct 1993 (10 episodes) C4 Tue 8.30pm

MAIN CAST

Det Bob Ballard · · · · · · · · Robert Guillaume
Det Richard Capparelli · · · · · Richard Libertini
Capt Kenny Epstein · · · · · · · · · · Joel Murray
Det Al Burkhardt · · · · · · · · · · · Ron Leibman
Deputy Commissioner Hank Bishop · · · · · · ·
· John Hancock
Det Sandy Calloway · · · · · Megan Gallagher

CREDITS

creators/writers/executive producers Barry Fanaro/Mort Nathan, Kathy Speer/Terry Grossman · director James Burrows · producer Rita Dillon

A police sitcom that saw a welcome return of comedy-actor Robert Guillaume, who had progressed from *Soap* to his own starring show *Benson*. Guillaume was cast as Bob Ballard, an easy-going but hard-working 'by-the-book' detective who has devoted his life to the force. When his superior, Captain Phil Dunbar, is arrested on criminal charges, Ballard (and his station colleagues) assume he will be promoted to fill the vacancy. Instead, however, the youthful, inexperienced and generally thick Kenny Epstein arrives to take up the post – in a changing world, he has been employed because he has majored in journalism and knows how to handle the press. To add to Ballard's woes, on this same day he is assigned a new partner, the spaced-out, sensitive Richard Capparelli, who, it transpires, has just returned to work after extended psychiatric leave. Completing the main corps of characters are lecherous Detective Al Burkhardt (played by Ron Leibman, who made a career out of portraying such characters) and portly deputy commissioner Hank Bishop. In later episodes Megan Gallagher joined the cast as Ballard's new partner Sandy Calloway. The station was based in Venice Beach, California,

a well-known hang-out for those who like to live a more offbeat lifestyle.

A generally intelligent sitcom, *Pacific Station* was a little too innocuous for its own good. After just 10 episodes (with a two month gap in the middle of the 'run'), NBC turned out the lights.

Packet Of Three

UK · C4 (JON BLAIR FILM COMPANY · FINE TIME FILM AND TELEVISION) · SITCOM/STANDUP

16 × 45 mins · colour

Series One (8) 2 Aug–20 Sep 1991 · Fri 10.30pm

Series Two (8) *Packing Them In* 9 Sep–4 Nov 1992 · Wed 10.40pm

MAIN CAST

Frank · · · · · · · · · · · · · · · · · Frank Skinner
Jenny · · · · · · · · · · · · · · · · · · Jenny Eclair
Henry · · · · · · · · · · · Henry Normal (series 1)
Reg · · · · · · · · · · · · · Roger Mann (series 2)
Boyle · · · · · · · · · · · · · Kevin Eldon (series 2)

CREDITS

writers cast and others · directors John Stroud (series 1), Juliet May (series 2) · executive producer Jon Blair (series 2) · producers Jon Blair (series 1), Jo Sargent (series 2)

A not entirely successful but nevertheless intriguing attempt to combine sitcom with standup comedy. The series was set at the fictitious Crumpsall Palladium, run by theatre owner Henry with help from his kiosk assistant and ticket seller Jenny and the stage manager and compere Frank. The backstage plots were supplemented each week by guest appearances from real-life comedy acts who performed on the stage. The first series featured three acts per show, hence its roguish title, but with differing numbers of guest stars in the second series' editions, the title changed to the more flexible *Packing Them In*.

The sitcom side of the show worked quite well and was far more risqué than most of the genre's offerings – Jenny Eclair and Frank Skinner are renowned for their respective no-holds-barred live acts and they brought some of that style to the show. But the standup acts, although often very funny, seemed to interrupt the flow of the storylines and undermined the fictional elements. In retrospect, it is easy to see that the two styles didn't mix, but, at the time, the series served as a worthy attempt to do something different, and at least succeeded in serving up regular doses of acerbic wit.

Note. In 1995, Eclair became the first woman to win the prestigious Perrier Award at the Edinburgh Festival Fringe; two years later she landed her own TV series, *Jenny Eclair Squats* (C5, 10 editions, 3 October to 5 December 1997) in which she visited celebrities' houses and chatted in situ with various guests.

Paging You

UK · BBC · SKETCH

5 editions (2 × 35 mins · 1 × 30 mins · 1 × 45 mins · 1 × 60 mins) · b/w

3 Nov 1946 · Sun 3pm (30 mins)
12 Jan 1947 · Sun 3pm (35 mins)
2 Feb 1947 · Sun 3.25pm (35 mins)
12 Jan 1948 · Mon 3pm (45 mins)
25 Feb 1948 · Wed 3pm (60 mins)

MAIN CAST

Brian Reece
Phyllis Robins (show 1)
Richard Hearne (shows 2 & 5)
Humphrey Lestocq (show 3)
Bobby Howes (show 4)
Bill Fraser (show 4)
Claude Hulbert (show 5)
Enid Trevor (show 5)

CREDITS

writers Peter Dion Titheradge, Bob Probst and others · producer Walton Anderson

An occasional series set in a busy hotel foyer, where comedy sketches and musical items were presented. The flexible format allowed for different guest stars to appear in each edition.

Note. Both the 1948 shows were restaged in evening slots, on 17 January and 28 February respectively, for those who were unable to catch the afternoon transmissions. ('Second performances' were common practice at this time, not only for this reason but also because no method of recording TV shows, allowing a simple repeat airing, had yet been perfected.)

Palace Hill

UK · ITV (CENTRAL) · CHILDREN'S SITCOM

21 episodes (14 × 25 mins · 7 × 30 mins) · colour

Series One (7 × 25 mins) 9 Nov–21 Dec 1988 · Wed mostly 4.50pm

Series Two (7 × 25 mins) 5 Jan–16 Feb 1990 · Fri 4.45pm

Series Three (7 × 30 mins) 17 Apr–29 May 1991 · Wed 4.40pm

MAIN CAST

Prince William · · · Philip Wombwell (series 1)
Prince Harry · · · · Richard de Sousa (series 1)
Princess Beatrice · · Phoebe Wood (series 2)
Chas Slough · · · · · · · · Mark Dexter (series 3)
Di · · · · · · · · · · · · · · · Danielle Tilley (series 3)
Jimmy · · · · · · · · · · · · · · · · · · · Steven Ryde
Nick Knuckle · · · · · · · · · · · · · Oliver Hawker
Mandy · · · · · · · · · · Alison Dury (series 1 & 2)
Wendy · · · · · · · · Keeley Coxon (series 1 & 2)
Eskimo · · · · · Alison Hammond (series 1 & 2)
Maggie Thatcher · · · · · · · · · · Tessa Harrison
· (series 2 & 3)
Binky Spoon · · · · · · Gail Kemp (series 2 & 3)
Chelsea Bun · · · · · · · · · Ian Kirkby (series 2)

WITH (ALL SERIES 1)
Julian Aubrey, Mark Dexter, Ladene Hall, James Hooton, Amanda Loy Ellis, Katie McReynolds, Johann Myers, Julie Schatzberger, Tracie Stanley, Paul Stark

CREDITS
writers Peter Corey/Bob Hescott · directors Glyn Edwards (series 1), David Crozier (series 2), Brian Lighthill (series 3) · executive producer Lewis Rudd · producer Sue Nott

A spin-off from Central's award-winning children's sketch series **Your Mother Wouldn't Like It**, depicting (at first) the adventures of royal sprogs attending a comprehensive school, Palace Hill. Any similarity between this establishment and *Grange Hill* (the fictional school at the centre of a BBC1 children's drama series since 8 February 1978) was entirely coincidental – it was said.

Each of the three series had a different axis: in the first, Princes William and Harry enrolled in Class 1C; in the second they were gone but Princess Beatrice arrived in the school, with Binky Spoon – her maid – in tow, and there was a new headmistress, former head-girl Maggie Thatcher (Tessa Harrison imitating you-know-who); the third series was so far out it was set in an identical school floating in outer space, with William, Harry and Beatrice all gone but two additional characters on board the rocket ship, the Prince Charles-like Chas Slough and the woman for whom he was planning to neglect Maggie, the regal Di, a member of the Galactic Imperial Family. Other pupils included the Billy Bunter-like Jimmy and the nerdish Nick Knuckle, who was having an on/off relationship with Binky Spoon.

The *Palace Hill* humour was surreal and very much an acquired taste, especially in the far-fetched final run, but the series remained a hit over some three years. As with *Your Mother Wouldn't Like It*, the company of players was drawn from members of the Central Junior Television Workshop, based in Nottingham and sponsored by Central TV.

The Pall Bearer's Revue

UK · BBC · STANDUP
5 × 30 mins · colour
6 Jan–3 Feb 1992 · BBC2 Mon 10pm
MAIN CAST
Jerry Sadowitz

CREDITS
writer Jerry Sadowitz · director Stephen Stewart · producer Jamie Rix

Provocative comedian Jerry Sadowitz (his first name is sometimes written as Gerry) first came to public attention at the 1987 Edinburgh Festival Fringe, where his foul-mouthed stream-of-abuse comedy was startling even by post-'alternative' standards. Sadowitz takes a jaundiced view of life or, as he puts it, 'I ****ing hate everything, right'. His rapidly delivered venom and 'in-your-face' attitude would be unbearable were it not for the fact that he can be genuinely funny,

suddenly surprising audiences with a brilliant line slap in the middle of what had seemed pointless ranting. Also, occasionally, the seriousness of the subjects he tackles, and the way he confronts them, makes for challenging and dangerous comedy. Nothing is safe from Sadowitz's bile: politicians from all sides are rubbished, he attacks religious zealots along with agnostics, Catholics along with Protestants, Jews as well as Arabs – in fact, the whole world seems to be his scratching post. Famously, his opening greeting to a Canadian audience on one occasion was 'Hello moose ****ers!'.

Sadowitz is also a gifted magician and he has often combined comedy and magic in his stage act. For this series, the BBC bravely gave him a chance to see if the combination, and his uncompromising comedic style, could be adapted for the small-screen, but it was not a great success. Previously, he had presented his magical skills in a C4 series *The Other Side Of Gerry Sadowitz* (three editions, 23 to 26 December 1990) and hosted a spoof game-show, *The Greatest F****** Show On Earth* (C4, 26 March 1994), as part of a *Without Walls* special on swearing.

At the time of writing, Sadowitz was preparing a chat-show series to be aired by C5 in early 1998.

Pallas

UK · C4 (NOEL GAY TELEVISION) · SATIRE
13 episodes (6 × 10 mins · 4 × 5 mins · 3 × 25 mins) · colour
Series One (6 × 10 mins · 4 × 5 mins) 24 Dec–27 Dec 1991 · weekdays various times
Series Two (3 × 25 mins) *Pallas 2* 22 Dec–24 Dec 1992 · weekdays 10pm
MAIN CAST (VOICE ONLY)
narrator · · · · · · · · · · · · · · · · · Richard E Grant

CREDITS
writers Geoff Atkinson/Kim Fuller · producer Geoff Atkinson

Real-life news footage revoiced by actors for satirical effect, in a fashion similar to the earlier **Staggering Stories Of Ferdinand De Bargos**. This time the footage featured the Royal family and a wicked soap opera spoof was spun around the material, thus explaining the title – a pun on the US 'supersoap' *Dallas*.

See also **The Almost Complete History Of The 20th Century** and **Klinik!**

Paper Moon

USA · ABC (PARAMOUNT/THE DIRECTORS COMPANY) · SITCOM
13 × 30 mins · colour
US dates: 12 Sep 1974–2 Jan 1975
UK dates: 1 Oct 1974–31 Jan 1975 (13 episodes) BBC2 Tue mostly 9.10pm

MAIN CAST
Addie Pray · · · · · · · · · · · · · · · · Jodie Foster
Moze Pray · · · · · · · · · · · Christopher Connelly

CREDITS
creator Joe David Brown · writers various · directors various · executive producer Anthony Wilson · producer Robert Stambler

Based on Peter Bogdanovich's 1973 film of the same name, this TV series continued the adventures of an itinerant couple of con artists – father and daughter – working the American Midwest in the 1930s. The story was based upon a novel, *Addie Pray*, written by Joe David Brown.

The film had starred real-life father and daughter Ryan and Tatum O'Neal – she won an Oscar for her role, becoming, at the age of nine, the youngest to do so; the TV series featured adequate substitutes in the shape of Chris Connelly (who, ironically, had played Ryan O'Neal's brother in the long-running US soap *Peyton Place*) and 12-year-old Jodie Foster, already in her second sitcom following a spell in *The Courtship Of Eddie's Father* (ABC, 1969–72).

An introductory, behind-the-scenes documentary, filling in the background story and painting a picture of life in America in the 1930s, was aired as a prelude to the series by BBC2 on 24 September 1974. The device of turning successful feature films into TV series has often been used in America, but *Paper Moon* was no *M*A*S*H* and bowed out after just 13 episodes.

Para Handy

The Scottish folk hero Para Handy – the skipper of 'puffer' (small cargo boat) *The Vital Spark* – first appeared in the *Glasgow Evening News* on 16 January 1905 and eventually progressed to a weekly column in which his fictional anecdotal tales of a seafaring life delighted readers. As the years passed the stories grew in popularity, striking a chord with Scottish people. The author, Neil Munro, considered them lightweight fare compared with his main literary contribution, serious historical novels; indeed, when the columns were gathered together in book form he hid behind the pseudonym Hugh Foulis. But he had created a lasting and well-loved national icon that endured long after his other work had been forgotten.

The gentle drollery of Para Handy was considered ideal fare for television audiences and a number of series have brought the character and his cronies to life.

Para Handy – Master Mariner

UK · BBC · SITCOM

6 × 30 mins · b/w

11 Dec 1959–22 Jan 1960 · Fri 8.30pm

MAIN CAST

Para Handy ············· Duncan Macrae
Dan Macphail ·············· John Grieve
Dougie ··············· Roddy McMillan
Sunny Jim ················ Angus Lennie

CREDITS

creator Neil Munro · *writer* Duncan Ross · *director* James MacTaggart · *producer* Pharic Maclaren

Set in the very locations that *Para Handy* creator Neil Munro used in the original stories, and shot on a 'puffer' of a similar vintage to the one described, this BBC Scotland series benefited enormously from the filmed sequences, most of them directed by the esteemed James MacTaggart. Duncan Ross updated the stories to contemporary times figuring that the trials and tribulations of a working life on the sea had changed little since the period in which the original tales were set.

The Vital Spark

UK · BBC · SITCOM

21 episodes (20 × 30 mins · 1 × 50 mins) (14 × b/w · 7 × colour)

Pilot (30 mins · b/w) 12 Aug 1965 · BBC1 Thu 8.50pm

Series One (6 × 30 mins · b/w) 28 Jan–4 Mar 1966 · BBC1 Fri 7.30pm

Series Two (7 × 30 mins · b/w) 16 Aug–27 Sep 1967 · BBC1 Wed 7.30pm

Special (50 mins · colour) 5 Mar 1973 · BBC1 Mon 9.25pm [BBC Scotland only]

Series Three (6 × 30 mins · colour) 19 Sep–24 Oct 1974 · BBC2 Thu mostly 9pm

MAIN CAST

Para Handy ············· Roddy McMillan
Dan Macphail ·············· John Grieve
Dougie ········· Robert Urquhart (pilot);
················· Walter Carr (series)
Sunny Jim ················ Alex McAvoy

CREDITS

creator Neil Munro · *writer* Bill Craig · *executive producer* Graeme Muir (pilot) · *producer* Pharic Maclaren

More adventures with the Scottish salts, again shot in authentic locations and featuring some of the same crew from the earlier TV series – including producer Pharic Maclaren and actors John Grieve (cast once again as Dan Macphail) and Roddy McMillan (now promoted from Dougie, the mate, to skipper Para Handy). After a successful pilot in the *Comedy Playhouse* strand, a series arrived the following year.

This time the updated tales were affected by present-day influences, reflecting the way that the modern world was making a real impact upon the lives of Scottish seamen. To this end, the crew of the *Vital Spark* had to deal not only with the regular hardships of their life but also with a decade unsympathetic to their existence.

After the second series the 'puffer' seemed doomed to sail into the distance, never to return, but a one-off special, made as part of BBC Scotland's 50th anniversary celebrations in 1973, reunited the original cast and creative personnel and the success of that programme prompted a further series, aired by BBC2 the following year. This third series, the first in colour, recycled some of the earlier storylines.

The Tales Of Para Handy

UK · BBC · SITCOM

9 × 50 mins colour

Series One (6) 31 July–4 Sep 1994 · BBC1 Sun 8pm

Series Two (3) 31 July–21 Aug 1995 · BBC1 Mon 9.30pm

MAIN CAST

Para Handy ··············· Gregor Fisher
Dan Macphail ············· Rikki Fulton
Dougie ················· Sean Scanlan
Sunny Jim ··············· Andrew Fairlie

CREDITS

creator Neil Munro · *writers* Bob Black (5), Michael Russell (3), Colin MacDonald (1) · *director/producer* Colin Gilbert

Gregor Fisher, the star of **Rab C Nesbitt**, took the lead role in this 1990s adaptation of the famous tales. This time, the stories were set in the 1930s, but otherwise the style was much the same as the earlier TV adventures, albeit with slightly more of an 'edge'.

Paradise Island

UK · ITV (THAMES) · SITCOM

7 × 30 mins · colour

21 Apr–18 July 1977 · mostly Thu 7.10pm

MAIN CAST

Rev Alexander Goodwin ······· Bill Maynard
Cuthbert Fullworthy ······· William Franklyn

CREDITS

creator Michael Haley · *writers* Michael Haley (1), Vince Powell (1), Jon Watkins (1), Bernie Sharp (1), Brian Cooke (1), John Junkin (1), Alan Melville (1) · *directors/producers* William G Stewart (6), Stuart Allen (1)

The sole survivors of a Pacific Ocean shipwreck, two men are thrown up on a deserted desert island. One is the ship's entertainments officer, a lovelorn hedonist called Cuthbert Fullworthy, who immediately plans his escape, the other is the Reverend Alexander Goodwin, who, as one might expect, is more circumspect about his plight. Together they set about exploring the island, at the same time testing their ability to get along in spite of their disparate personalities.

The series was created by a design engineer, Michael Haley, whose single script was turned into the opening episode, with other writers handling it from there.

Paramount City

UK · BBC (*CONSOLIDATED COMEDY DIVISION PRODUCTIONS/ENGLISH CHANNEL PRODUCTIONS) · STANDUP

20 × 40 mins · colour

*Series One (10) 31 Mar–2 June 1990 · BBC1 Sat 10.30pm

Series Two (10) 25 May–3 Aug 1991 · BBC1 Sat 10pm

MAIN CAST

Arthur Smith (host, series 1)
Curtis Walker (co-host, series 2)
Ishmael Thomas (co-host, series 2)
'Tommy Cockles' (Simon Day) (resident, series 2)

CREDITS

writers cast and others · *directors* David G Croft (series 1), Stephen Stewart (series 2) · *executive producer* Janet Street-Porter · *producers* Juliet Blake/Trevor Hopkins (series 1), Alan Nixon (series 2)

A basic standup show filmed at a London venue, Paramount City. Stars from both sides of the Atlantic performed and occasionally comedians from even further afield appeared.

The uncomplicated premise allowed acts to perform short extracts from their live routines and thus the series operated as a showcase for the artist's talents, to encourage punters to turn up at their live shows or buy their videos or comedy recordings, or to impress watching impresarios and TV producers. But a good many of the comics were deeply unhappy with the show, bemoaning frequent last-minute script interference and what they saw as the series' ill-conceived sense of direction.

In addition to the hosts (above), the British acts seen in the two series included Angela Clarke, Jeremy Hardy, Helen Lederer, Steve Coogan, Jack Dee, Nick Revell, Julian Clary, Jo Brand, Mark Steel, John Hegley, Mark Thomas, Chris Langham, Jim Tavaré, Mark Hurst, Frank Skinner, Morwenna Banks, Alan Cumming and Forbes Masson, Jim Sweeney and Steve Steen, Roy Hutchins, Shane Richie, Hattie Hayridge and Caroline Aherne. Guests from overseas included Denis Leary, Monica Piper, Linda Smith, Richard Belzer, Stephanie Hodge, Chris Rock, Pamela Matteson, Mario Joyner, Rachel Berger, Will Durst, Cathy Ladman, Richard Jeni, Emo Philips, Fred Stoller, Danitra Vance, Charlie Fleischer, Paul Provenza, Allan Havey, Bill Hicks, Mark Curry and Janeane Garofalo.

Pardon My Genie

UK · ITV (THAMES) · CHILDREN'S SITCOM

26 × 30 mins · colour

Series One (13) 10 Apr–3 July 1972 ·
Mon mostly 5.20pm

Series Two (13) 29 Jan–23 Apr 1973 ·
Mon mostly 4.25pm

MAIN CAST

The Genie · · · · · · · · Hugh Paddick (series 1);
· · · · · · · · · · · · · · · · · · Arthur White (series 2)
Mr Cobbledick · · · · · · · · · · · Roy Barraclough
Hal Adden · · · · · · · · · · · · · · · · · Ellis Jones
PC Appleby · · · · · · · · · · · · · · · Joe Dunlop
Patricia Cobbledick · · · · · · · · Lynette Erving
Mrs Sibley · · · · · · · · · · · · · · · · Doris Rogers

CREDITS

creator Bob Block · writers Bob Block (25), Larry
Parker (1) · directors Daphne Shadwell (11),
Robert Reed (9), Vic Hughes (6) · producer Daphne
Shadwell

A young assistant in a hardware shop in the
fictitious town of Widdimouth – the lad goes
by the unlikely and painfully punful name
Hal Adden – happens to be polishing up some
watering cans when out pops a genie, 4000
years old and keen to serve his new master.
The only trouble is, his back's a bit stiff and
well, what with one thing and another, his
spells have a habit of going wrong. As for
the shop owner, Mr Cobbledick, he quickly
resigns himself to never coming out on top
in his skirmishes with the Magical One.

This deservedly popular children's series –
akin to a cross between **Open All Hours**
and US children's cartoon Shazzan! – enjoyed
a remarkable final episode, in which the Genie
caused mayhem at a TV studio. Because the
series was filmed at Thames, the stars on the
receiving end of the bad magic included the
station's biggest names: Eamonn Andrews,
Tony Bastable, Wendy Craig, Dickie Davies,
William Mervyn, Jack Smethurst, Susan
Stranks and, last but by no means least, Puff
The Pony.

Pardon The Expression

UK · ITV (GRANADA) · SITCOM

*36 × 30 mins · b/w

Series One (12) 2 June–18 Aug 1965 · Wed 7pm

Series Two (24) 10 Jan–27 June 1966 ·
Mon 9.10pm then Fri mostly 9.40pm

MAIN CAST

Leonard Swindley · · · · · · · · · · · Arthur Lowe
Mrs Edgeley · · · · · · · · · · · · · · · Betty Driver
Miss Sinclair · · · · · · · · · · · · · · Joy Stewart
Ernest Parbold · · · · · Paul Dawkins (series 1)
Wally Hunt · · · · · · · Robert Dorning (series 2)

OTHER APPEARANCES

Mavis Foster · · · · · · · · Holly Doone (series 1)
Pam Plummer · · · · Barbara Young (series 1)
Miss Buxton · · · · · · · · Judith Furse (series 1)

CREDITS

writers Vince Powell/Harry Driver (16), Vince
Powell (3), Harry Driver/Jack Rosenthal (3), Jack

Rosenthal (2), Jack Rosenthal/Geoffrey
Lancashire (1), Geoffrey Lancashire (1), Charles
Hart/Peter Bishop (5), Christopher Bond (4),
Richard Harris/Dennis Spooner (1) · directors
Wally Butler (series 1), Michael Cox (series 2) ·
executive producer H V Kershaw · producers Harry
Driver (series 1), Derek Granger (series 2)

Not so much a sequel but definitely a spin-off
from Coronation Street – remarkably, in the
soap's 38 years history (to the time of writing),
its only spin-off (although see footnote).

Bankrupted at Gamma Garments, defeated
on the hustings (when he formed the Property
Owners And Small Traders Party and fought
the local election) and finally jilted at the altar
by Emily Nugent, it seemed right and proper
that the fastidious fusspot teetotaller Leonard
Swindley (Arthur Lowe) should leave the
environs of the Street and take refuge
elsewhere. In Pardon The Expression – so
called because, in the Street scripts, he was
prone to beginning his dialogue with 'If
you'll pardon the expression' – Swindley's
experience of running a haberdashery
was sorely tested when he was appointed
assistant manager at a northern branch of a
national chain of department stores, Dobson
And Hawks, in charge of around three dozen
staff, mostly young women. Attempting
desperately to pass muster, and at the same
time to climb his way up the social ladder,
Swindley was constantly out of his depth.
Wearing a Homburg hat and an air of
harassment, he just managed to avoid total
humiliation, although the later scripts
changed this, and the end of each programme
usually found Swindley the ultimate victim of
his own ineptitude.

Arthur Lowe – who would repeat
Swindley's red-cheeked pomposity in his roles
as Mainwaring in **Dad's Army**, and in
Potter – was by no means the only player in
Pardon The Expression, however. There were
major roles for Joy Stewart, cast as the store's
staff manageress, and Betty Driver, who
appeared as the manageress of the staff
canteen. And there was a boss for Swindley
to report to: in the first series this was Paul
Dawkins (as the laid back Ernest Parbold)
but, following a real-life car crash, he was
replaced in the second by Robert Dorning
as Wally Hunt.

The Coronation Street links were many.
Betty Driver went on to appear in the soap
as Betty Turpin, while Amanda Barrie (Alma
Sedgewick/Baldwin) and Julie Goodyear (Bet
Lynch/Gilroy) appeared in one episode apiece.
The writers and production team also had
strong links with the Street (and producer/
chief writer Harry Driver had once worked as
assistant manager for a chain store, so was
well placed to give the fictitious Dobson And
Hawks a touch of reality). The first series of
Pardon The Expression was even screened in
the slot immediately before the Street, giving

aficionados of the soap an hour of the
characters with which they were familiar.
Like the Street, a number of well-known faces
graced the cast of Pardon The Expression for
one or a few episodes apiece, among them
John Laurie and John Le Mesurier (who would
go on to join Lowe in Dad's Army), Dandy
Nichols and Warren Mitchell (who would
team up in **Till Death Us Do Part**),
youngsters Pauline Collins, Warren Clarke,
Geoffrey Palmer, Wendy Richard and Ben
Kingsley, and established actors Milo O'Shea,
Jerry Desmonde, Fanny Carby and John
Barron.

Clearly, Pardon The Expression had plenty
going for it, which is why, after Leonard
Swindley and Wally Hunt were sacked from
Dobson And Hawks in the final episode, the
characters were revived for a further spin-off,
Turn Out The Lights.

*Notes. Screening dates for Pardon The
Expression varied around the ITV regions,
but no station, including Granada, showed
more than 36 episodes; negatives held in
Granada's film library, however, suggest
that 39 were made.

A later Granada sitcom, **The Brothers
McGregor** (screened 1985–88), featured
minor characters who had appeared in one
episode of Coronation Street, but different
actors portrayed the roles and so, unlike
Pardon The Expression, it cannot be
classified as a true spin-off.

Parent-Craft

UK · BBC · CHILDREN'S SITCOM

6 × 25 mins · b/w

19 July–27 Sep 1951 · fortnightly Thu 5.10pm

MAIN CAST

Mrs Pebble · · · · · · · · · · · · · · · Janet Burnell
Mr Pebble · · · · · · · · · · · · · · William Mervyn
Anne Pebble · · · · · · · · · · · · · Shirley Eaton
Irving Pebble · · · · · · · · · · · · · · William Fox
R Cressington-Tallboy · · · · · · · Robert Morley

CREDITS

writer Robert Morley · producer Alan Bromly

A fascinating children's sitcom written by big
bluff Robert Morley, who also appeared in his
creation along with, among others, the noted
character actor William Mervyn and the
imminently famous British actress and sex
symbol Shirley Eaton. The premise was 'how
o handle your parents', and in each of the
six episodes the Pebble children, Anne and
Irving, had to deal with the nitty-gritty of
adolescent life, 1950s-style: mum, dad,
homework, pocket money and school friends.

Parenthood

USA · NBC (IMAGINE TELEVISION) · SITCOM

**12 episodes (1 × 60 mins · 11 × 30 mins) ·
colour**

US dates: 20 Aug–10 Nov 1990
UK dates: 4 June–10 Sep 1993 (1 × 60 mins ·
11 × 30 mins) BBC2 Fri 7pm

MAIN CAST

Gil Buckman	Ed Begley Jr
Karen Buckman	Jayne Atkinson
Kevin Buckman	Max Elliott Slade
Taylor Buckman	Thora Birch
Justin Buckman	Zachary LaVoy
Helen Buckman	Maryedith Burrell
Garry Buckman	Leonardo DiCaprio
Julie Hawks	Bess Meyer
Tod Hawks	David Arquette
Susan Merrick	Susan Norman
Nathan Merrick	Ken Ober
Patty Merrick	Ivyann Schwan
Frank Buckman	William Windom
Marilyn Buckman	Sheila MacRae
Great Grandma Greenwell	Mary Jackson

CREDITS

creators Lowell Ganz, Babaloo Mandel, Ron Howard · *writers* David Tyson King, Ron Howard and others · *director* Allan Arkush · *executive producers* Carla Fry, Allan Arkush, David Tyson King, Lowell Ganz, Babaloo Mandel, Russ Woody, Brian Grazer, Ron Howard · *producers* April Smith, Sascha Schneider

An ultra-slick ensemble comedy-drama based on the successful 1989 movie of the same name. The strengths of the film were its realistic but highly humorous look at the joys and pitfalls of parenthood, and the fact that it embraced a family-wide perspective on the subject, concentrating on three generations. These strengths were transferred to the series and proved a rich source of comedy and light-drama. If it had a fault, it was that its characters were prone to introverted self-analysis, which, beyond the length of a movie, began to irritate and made the TV viewer long for the characters to concentrate more on the world beyond their extended family. For the record, the parents were Gil and Karen, their children were Kevin, Taylor and Justin. Helen was one of Gil's two sisters, with children Garry and Julie (who was married to Tod); Susan was his other sister, married to Nathan and mother of Patty. Gil's parents were Frank and Marilyn; Marilyn's mother was Great Grandma Greenwell. The role of Garry was played by the up-and-coming young actor Leonardo DiCaprio.

The feature film was directed by Ron Howard (Richie Cunningham in **Happy Days**) and written by Howard, Lowell Ganz and Babaloo Mandel, all of whom worked on this television follow-up. Max Elliott Slade, Zachary LaVoy and Ivyann Schwan reprised their film roles but different actors took the other parts with, notably, Ed Begley Jr in the role originally played by Steve Martin, Ken Ober replacing Steve Moranis, Bess Meyer replacing Dianne Weist and William Windom replacing Jason Robards.

Paris

UK · C4 (TALKBACK PRODUCTIONS) · SITCOM
6 × 30 mins · colour
14 Oct–18 Nov 1994 · Fri 9.30pm

MAIN CAST

Alain Degout	Alexei Sayle
Paul Rochet	Neil Morrissey
Minotti	Allan Corduner
Madame Ovary	Beverley Klein
Hugo	Walter Sparrow
Pilo	Simon Godley
Belunaire	James Dreyfus

CREDITS

writers Graham Linehan/Arthur Mathews · *director* Liddy Oldroyd · *executive producer* Peter Fincham · *producer* Sioned Wiliam

A sitcom depicting the misadventures of a struggling artist, Alain Degout, in the volatile setting of 1920s Paris. Degout is a hopeless painter of simplistic nostalgia-fodder (baskets of puppies, wide-eyed orphans, kittens playing with wool) who longs to be famous. His friends are the stupendously stupid Paul Rochet, an indecisive and impressionable fop; and the quack psychiatrist Minotti, a Freud lookalike who delights in tormenting his most regular client, the woefully confused Madame Ovary. An assortment of atmospheric Parisian characters (gendarmes, prostitutes, innkeepers, fellow artists, anarchists, communists and fascists) provided the background colour.

Predictably, considering its writers (future **Father Ted** creators Linehan and Mathews) and cast (Sayle, Morrissey), *Paris* was a far from traditional piece, being pitched as somewhere between a French farce and an exaggerated satire. The scripts were perky and the overplaying of the actors well judged, but, overall, it never quite achieved the right blend of anarchic slapstick and character-driven comedy.

Partners   UK

UK · BBC · SITCOM
6 × 30 mins · colour
29 Jan–5 Mar 1981 · BBC1 Thu 8.30pm

MAIN CAST

Rupert Bannister	Derek Waring
Diana Bannister	Mel Martin
Brenda	Jacqueline Clarke
Pamela Heslop	Elizabeth Counsell
George Gilkes	Derek Francis
Mr Matheson	Derek Farr

CREDITS

writer Richard Waring · *producer* Harold Snoad

More domestic dilemmas from writer Richard Waring, this time in a series that carried echoes of his co-creation from a decade earlier, **My Wife Next Door**. The main star in the series was the writer's brother, actor Derek Waring.

Rupert Bannister's downtrodden business enterprise, Bannister Bathroom Fittings, is suddenly given a chance to expand thanks to a potential investor. However, to obtain the capital, Rupert has to retrieve the shares that he spontaneously gave to his wife on their wedding night. This is tricky because, just as the deal is entering the pipeline, they are going through a divorce and experiencing, obviously, very strained relations. When Diana realises the true value of her shares she decides to hang on to them, thus remaining 'partners' with Rupert despite their marital estrangement.

Just as becoming neighbours forced the divorcees in *My Wife Next Door* back together, so here the business angle kept Rupert and his ex-wife Diana in close proximity, giving rise to a faint hope that they might rescind their divorce on the last day before it became absolute.

Partners   USA

USA · FOX (JEFF & JEFF PRODUCTIONS/ UNIVERSAL TELEVISION) · SITCOM
22 × 30 mins · colour
US dates: 11 Sep 1995–1 Apr 1996
UK dates: 22 Sep–4 May 1997 (22 episodes) C4 Sun around 12 midnight

MAIN CAST

Bob	Jon Cryer
Owen	Tate Donovan
Alicia	Maria Pitillo
Heather	Catherine Lloyd Burns

OTHER APPEARANCES

Lolie	Corrine Bohrer

CREDITS

creators/executive producers Jeff Greenstein/Jeff Strauss · *writers* Jeff Greenstein/Jeff Strauss (4), Adam Belanoff (3), Oliver Goldstick (3), Bernadette Luckett (3), Ari Posner/Eric Preven (3), Paul Redford (3), Douglas Leiblien (1), Margaret Malleon (1), Maryanne Melloan (1) · *directors* James Burrows (10), Max D Tash (4), Paul Lazarus (3), Ellen Gittelsohn (2), Stan Daniels (1), Dennis Erdman (1), Jay Kleckner (1) · *producers* Jay Kleckner, Adam Belanoff

Friends since childhood, Bob and Owen are partners in a San Francisco architecture business. Bob is the witty, spontaneous one of the two, Owen is less articulate and more measured in his responses. Owen is going out with the sexy and passionate Alicia, a romance that has been growing happily for quite some time, and the series began with Owen proposing to Alicia, subsequent episodes charting the effect of their forth-coming marriage on the three protagonists. Basically, what transpired was a tug of love, with Owen in the middle. The demanding Bob was anxious to keep his male friendship, and Alicia was worried that she would end up playing second fiddle to him.

Beyond the storylines, however, it was the characters who made *Partners* work and the writers refused to go for the easy option of making either Bob or Alicia the villain of the piece, instead showing how each was sensitive to the other's feelings. The dialogue was cute and snappy (writer/creators Greenstein and Strauss had worked on **Dream On** and **Friends)** and the cast worked hard to make the show click. Catherine Lloyd Burns was particularly funny as Heather, Bob and Owen's accident-prone office employee.

It all added up to a pleasing, modern construction, well designed and with a firm comic foundation. But despite these attributes US public response was lukewarm and no second season ensued.

The Partridge Family

USA · ABC (SCREEN GEMS) · SITCOM

96 × 30 mins · colour

US dates: 25 Sep 1970–31 Aug 1974

*UK dates: 17 Sep–31 Dec 1971 (12 episodes) BBC1 Fri 5.20pm then Sat 5.10pm · and 21 Oct 1972–7 Sep 1974 (80 episodes) ITV Sat mostly 12 noon

MAIN CAST

Shirley Partridge · · · · · · · · · · · Shirley Jones
Keith Partridge · · · · · · · · · · · · David Cassidy
Laurie Partridge · · · · · · · · · · · · · Susan Dey
Danny Partridge · · · · · · · · · Danny Bonaduce
Christopher Partridge · · · · · Jeremy Gelbwaks
· (1970–71);
· · · · · · · · · · · · · · Brian Forster (1971–74)
Tracy Partridge · · · · · · · · · · Suzanne Crough
Reuben Kinkaid · · · · · · · · · · · Dave Madden

CREDITS

creator Bernard Slade · writers Bernard Slade, Richard Deroy, Ron Friedman, Dale McRaven, William Bickley, Susan Harris, Steve Zacarias, Michael Leeson, Lloyd Turner, Gordon Mitchell, Dick Bensfield, Perry Grant and others · directors Jerry Paris, Bob Claver, Peter Baldwin, Ralph Senesky, Richard Kinon, Lou Antonio, Jerry London, Bruce Bilson, E W Swackhamer · producers Bob Claver, Paul Junger Witt

The adventures of the Partridge Family, a singing group that made **The Monkees** look like dangerous punk rockers. Despite its saccharine spin on the world of pop, however, the series reached its target audience in a big way, making an international star of young heart-throb David Cassidy and selling many millions of albums and singles worldwide.

Loosely based on the real-life story of the popular 1960s band the Cowsills, *The Partridge Family* starred Shirley Jones (Cassidy's real-life stepmother) as the widowed Shirley Partridge, raising her family of five in San Pueblo, California. When 16-year-old Danny organises them into a singing group, they surprisingly score a sizeable hit with their first single, 'I Think I Love You' (also a hit in the real world), and then take to the road and the life of travelling pop stars. They are accompanied by their

agent/manager, Reuben Kinkaid, who, ironically, dislikes children and so is less than enamoured with his task of corralling not just Shirley and Keith but Keith's younger siblings – Laurie (15, keyboards), Danny (10, guitar), Christopher (7, drums) and Tracy (5, tambourine) – all of whom, as one would expect, have such super-white teeth as to bring tears to the eyes of even the most jaded toothpaste executive.

The mix of pop, comedy and teenybopper sex symbols in the shape of Cassidy and Susan Dey (later to star in *LA Law*) proved irresistible, and the series enjoyed a major teen following on both sides of the Atlantic. It also gave rise to an animated spin-off *Partridge Family 2200 AD* (CBS, 1974–75) which followed the adventures of a futuristic Partridge Family as they toured different planets with their songs. Some of the original cast members (Dey, Bonaduce, Forster, Crough, and Madden) provided the voices.

*Note. LWT additionally screened 61 episodes of *The Partridge Family* between 12 March 1988 and 23 November 1990, mostly in post-midnight slots.

Pastoral Care

UK · C4 (REGENT PRODUCTIONS) · SITCOM

1 × 60 mins · colour

24 Feb 1988 · Wed 10.30pm

MAIN CAST

Rev Timothy White · · · · · · · · Tony Robinson
Rev David Williams · · · · · · · · · Jack Shepherd
Tom · · · · · · · · · · · · · · · Richard O'Callaghan
Osgood · · · · · · · · · · · · · · Benjamin Whitrow
Arbuthnot · · · · · · · · · · · · · · Victoria Wicks
Simon · · · · · · · · · · · · · · · · · Derek Waring

CREDITS

writer Andy Hamilton · director Roger Bamford · producer William G Stewart

The fourth of six single comedies screened under the banner *Tickets For The Titanic*. Tony Robinson starred in this Andy Hamilton creation, cast as a vicar whose employment in the quiet parish of St Peter's, in the village of Wandlesham, is abruptly overtaken by events after he pays a visit to a nearby nuclear-missile base and meets up with the campaigners camped outside the fence. (Clear shades of Greenham Common here.) Suddenly, our unassuming man of the cloth finds himself under intelligence surveillance.

Patter Merchants

UK · ITV (SHIHALLION FOR GRAMPIAN) · STANDUP

8 × 30 mins · colour

30 May–19 July 1990 · mostly Wed 1.30am

MAIN CAST

Allan Stewart

CREDITS

director/producer Martin Cairns

Eight half-hours of standup comedy taped at the Stakis Tree Tops Hotel in Aberdeen and hosted by the Scottish impressionist Allan Stewart, previously seen in *Go For It*, *Copy Cats* and *The Comedy Crowd* as well as series under his own name. London-ITV company Thames screened *Patter Merchants* in the early hours, rightly recognising that its phalanx of regional comics, unknown in the capital, would draw few viewers. Among those seen in the series were Mike Lancaster, Jethro, Clem Dane, Steve Womack, Gary Denis, Adrian Walsh, Billy Jeffrey, Jim Rosie, Rikki Stevens, Cheryl Taylor, Mia Carla, Bill Barclay, Eddie Rose, Hilary O'Neil, Dean Park, Dave Wolfe, Johnnie Adam, Gerald Fitzpatrick, Boothby Graffoe (who went on to other TV shows) and perhaps the series' best known participators (but still scarcely 'famous') Aiden J Harvey and Duggie Brown.

Aberdeen was also the setting for *Scotch And Irish*, an eight-part music-and-comedy series screened (again, London-ITV dates) even deeper into the twilight hours, from 8 January to 26 February 1996.

The Paul Calf Video Diary

see COOGAN, Steve

The Paul Hogan Show

AUSTRALIA · 7 NETWORK · 9 NETWORK (JP PRODUCTIONS) · SKETCH

48 × 50 mins · colour

Australian dates: 11 May 1973–21 Sep 1982

UK dates: 2 Nov 1982–30 Dec 1983 (27 × 30 mins · 2 × 60 mins) C4 mostly Fri 10pm

MAIN CAST

Paul Hogan
John Cornell
Andrew Harwood
Marguerite Frewin
Delevene Delaney
John Blackman
Sue McIntosh
Roger Stephen
Graham Mathrick
Marion Edward

CREDITS

writer Paul Hogan · producers John Cornell, Peter Faiman

The best known comic to emerge from Australia, Paul Hogan's career, which began as little more than a stunt, has scaled the highest heights internationally, with his starring appearances (as a talented straight actor) in the movie *Crocodile Dundee* and its sequel *Crocodile Dundee 2*. Before C4 imported *The Paul Hogan Show* to UK TV, however, it is fair to say that Hogan was only really known in Britain through his commercials for Foster's lager. That soon changed.

In 1971, when aged 32, Hogan was a rigger working on Sydney Harbour bridge, and one day, moaning about the harsh treatment accorded would-be stars on the talent spotting TV series *New Faces* (clearly, the Australian version of this show could be as vicious as the British equivalent), he decided, just for a joke, to enter the programme himself, as a knife-throwing tap-dancer. He intended to be bad but something caught the eye and he was invited back, again and again. He was then engaged by journalist Mike Willesee to appear regularly on the daily show *A Current Affair*, which led to him being awarded the Best New Talent honour in 1972. His own dedicated programmes soon followed but Hogan was clever: instead of tying himself down to a series, and perhaps becoming too familiar too quickly, he entered into a lengthy run of occasional specials, first for the Nine Network, then Seven and finally, in 1977, tempted by a very large sum of money, back to Nine again.

The essence of Hogan's humour in these sketch shows was his cast of invented characters, most of whom caught the public's imagination. First and foremost was Hoges, the know-it-all in shorts, football boots and a sleeveless shirt, always knocking authority. Others included the failed Italian entertainer Luigi The Unbelievable, the neatly named Leo The Wanker, Perc The Wino, the thug Slug and the western hero Clunk Eastwood. Hogan's long-time producer John Cornell went in front of the cameras too, as the numskull and womanless Strop, and a core supporting cast evolved.

Combining all this, and impersonations, send-ups and political satire, Hogan's programme were 50-minute shows. What C4 screened in Britain, mostly, were half-hour programmes, re-edited and packaged especially for syndication at home and abroad from the editions screened by Network Nine in Australia from 1977. Under the title *Paul Hogan's England*, C4 also screened two such full-length programmes in their entirety (4 November and 30 December 1983), both of which were shot in London.

Paul Merton In Galton & Simpson's ...

UK · ITV (CARLTON FOR CENTRAL) · SITCOMS

15 × 30 mins · colour

Series One (8) 26 Jan–15 Mar 1996 · Fri 8.30pm
Series Two (7) 2 Sep–21 Oct 1997 · Tue 8.30pm

Musical analogies help explain this project. To the comedian Paul Merton, the writing of Ray Galton and Alan Simpson is the best there has been in British comedy. He sees the two men – responsible for **Steptoe And**

Son, Tony Hancock's memorable work, and for much else – as the best, as pivotal to comic scriptwriting as Lennon and McCartney were to rock music. And just as any singer or musician can 'cover' a Lennon and McCartney song so Merton set out here to 'cover' a selection of Galton and Simpson scripts.

With his deadpan comic delivery, and broad knowledge of – and love for – British comedy evident in some of his devastating witticisms in BBC2's panel-game *Have I Got News For You* (as well as in *Paul Merton's Life Of Comedy*, a six-part series for BBC1, 4 May to 8 June 1995, in which he paid tribute to the TV shows that had loomed large in his life), Merton was the clear choice when Ray Galton and Alan Simpson decided to dust off and update some of their old scripts and seek out someone new to put them across. The mutual admiration was aided further when conversations uncovered the fact that Merton had attended Simpson's old school, in the south London district of Mitcham, and he had grown up half a mile away from where Galton had lived.

Of the 15 scripts that he tackled, six were first performed (and made famous) by Tony Hancock. In these programmes, specific Hancockisms like 'stone me' were excised; and whereas Tony always the played the part of Tony so, here, Paul was always Paul. Sid James's roles were played by Sam Kelly and, once, Merton's (then) wife Caroline Quentin. But homage was paid to Hancock when, in one of the programmes, a black Homburg hat and astrakhan coat were visible hanging on a hook.

Merton's main worry in performing Hancock's material – similar to that felt by any rock band performing Beatles songs, to continue the musical analogy – was that he would come off second best, since he is no great actor and Hancock is recognised as a comic actor without parallel in Britain. And, to be honest, such fears turned out to be the series' downfall; the inevitable comparisons with Hancock stacked the odds against Merton and he failed to overcome them – it was uncomfortable watching someone else toying with the crown jewels. Rather, the best episodes were those in which Merton re-enacted less familiar Galton and Simpson scripts, those not written for Hancock, like *Impasse*, not seen on TV for 30 years or more. The two series drew a mixed reaction, but, Merton, the comedy fan, appeared not to care when he commented, 'Even if it was a disaster at least I could say I did it – I worked with Galton and Simpson.'

Note. Obviously, and to avoid repetition, the writing credit for all of the following is Ray Galton/Alan Simpson.

Twelve Angry Men · 26 JAN 1996

MAIN CAST

Paul	Paul Merton
Sam	Sam Kelly
The Judge	Peter Jeffrey
Military gentleman	Geoffrey Whitehead
Company director	Gary Waldhorn
Farmer	David Daker
Prosecuting counsel	Michael Fenton Stevens
Defence counsel	Adjoa Andoh
Sergeant	Nick Maloney
Usher	Peter Waddington
Bank clerk	Rob Brydon

CREDITS

director Martin Dennis · *producer* Richard Boden

Originally screened in the BBC's *Hancock's Half Hour* on 16 October 1959. In a pastiche of the stage-play/movie *Twelve Angry Men*, Paul (in Hancock's role) digs in his heels and insists that a petty criminal is innocent. At first he is on his own but Sam (in Sid James's role) soon joins him, lured by the daily payment rate given to jurors. One by one they persuade the others to agree to the man's innocence but then, at the end, Paul changes his mind and declares the man guilty after all.

Impasse · 2 FEB 1996

MAIN CAST

Dave Kettle	Paul Merton
Charles Ferris	Geoffrey Whitehead
AA man	Sam Kelly
RAC man	Denis Lill
Celia Ferris	Phyllida Law
Kirsty Kettle	Tilly Vosburgh
Police Constable	Roger Lloyd Pack

CREDITS

director Martin Dennis · *producer* Richard Boden

Impasse (see separate entry under that title for the storyline précis) was originally a BBC *Comedy Playhouse*, screened on 15 March 1963.

The Radio Ham · 9 FEB 1996

MAIN CAST

Paul	Paul Merton
Albert	Al Hunter Ashton
Phyllis	Stella Tanner
Constable/Russian	Jim Sweeney
Sergeant	Geoffrey McGivern
Yachtsman	Michael Jayston
Englishman/actor/man	Owen Brenman
Actress	Caroline Bernstein
Indian gentleman	Arif Hussein

CREDITS

director Martin Dennis · *producer* Richard Boden

Originally screened in the BBC series *Hancock* on 9 June 1961. Paul sits at home, playing with his latest hobby: amateur radio, chatting with other 'DX-ers' around the world. They exchange useless information until Paul suddenly picks up a genuine 'mayday' alert.

Jealously guarding the distress call as his own, events conspire against his organising a rescue.

Sealed With A Loving Kiss   16 FEB 1996

MAIN CAST
Arnold · Paul Merton
Primrose · · · · · · · · · · · · · · · Josie Lawrence
Arnold's mother · · · · · · · · · Rosemary Leach
Station porter · · · · · · · · · · · · · · · Paul Bigley

CREDITS
director Martin Dennis · producer Richard Boden

Sealed With A Loving Kiss (see separate entry under that title for the storyline précis) was originally a BBC *Comedy Playhouse*, screened on 9 February 1962. It was also reworked in the 1970 series *The Mating Machine*.

The Missing Page   23 FEB 1996

MAIN CAST
Paul · Paul Merton
Caroline · · · · · · · · · · · · · Caroline Quentin
Librarian · · · · · · · · · · · · · · Patrick Barlow
Mr Proctor · · · · · · · · · · · · · · · Jim Sweeney
Curator · · · · · · · · · · · · · · · · · David Hatton

CREDITS
director Martin Dennis · producer Richard Boden

Originally screened in the BBC's *Hancock's Half Hour* on 11 March 1960. Paul is enjoying a murder-mystery book borrowed from the library, but, when he arrives at the cliff-hanging end of the story, the last page appears to be missing. He takes drastic steps to establish 'whodunit', until, eventually, the British Library informs him that all copies were incomplete in this way. So Paul and Caroline (Merton's then real-life wife Caroline Quentin playing the original Sid James role) set out to track down the author.

Don't Dilly Dally On The Way   1 MAR 1996

MAIN CAST
Kevin · · · · · · · · · · · · · · · · · · · Paul Merton
Joyce · · · · · · · · · · · · · · · Gwyneth Strong
Father · · · · · · · · · · · · · · · · · · · Sam Kelly
Mother · · · · · · · · · · · · · · · · · · · Anne Reid
Gordon · · · · · · · · · · · · · Matthew Ashforde
Avril · · · · · · · · · · · · · · · · · · Emma Cunliffe

CREDITS
director Martin Dennis · producer Richard Boden

Don't Dilly Dally On The Way (see separate entry under that title for the storyline précis) was originally screened in ITV's *The Galton & Simpson Comedy* on 10 May 1969.

The Lift   8 MAR 1996

MAIN CAST
Paul · Paul Merton
Maintenance man · · · · · · · · · · · · Sam Kelly
Air Marshall · · · · · · · · · Geoffrey Whitehead
Doctor · · · · · · · · · · · · · · · · Gary Waldhorn

Vicar · Peter Jones
Producer · · · · · · · · Michael Fenton Stevens
Secretary · · · · · · · · · · · · · Sheridan Forbes
Gwen Humphries · · · · · · · · · · · · · Anne Reid
George Humphries · · · · · · · · John Baddeley
Fireman · · · · · · · · · · · · · · · Mike Sherman
PR Man · · · · · · · · · · · · · · · Guy Nicholls

CREDITS
director Martin Dennis · producer Paul Spencer

Originally screened in the BBC series *Hancock* on 16 June 1961. Paul steps into a lift at the BBC, the ninth passenger when the limit is eight. Sure enough, on its journey, it becomes stuck in the shaft. Faced with the prospect of an all-night vigil Paul sets out to provide the entertainment.

The Bedsitter   15 MAR 1996

MAIN CAST
Paul · Paul Merton

CREDITS
director Martin Dennis · producer Richard Boden

Originally screened in the BBC series *Hancock* on 26 May 1961 (the first edition of that series). A true single-hander: Paul spends the night alone in his London bedsit flat, doing his best, unsuccessfully, to bide his time.

The Clerical Error   2 SEP 1997

MAIN CAST
Paul · Paul Merton
Vicar · · · · · · · · · · · · · Geoffrey Whitehead
Wife · Sally Giles
Sandra Evans · · · · · · · · · · Katy Carmichael
Reporter · · · · · · · · · · · · · · · · Nick Wilton

CREDITS
director Martin Dennis · executive producer Richard Boden · producer Jamie Rix

The Clerical Error (see Les Dawson's combined entry for the storyline précis) was originally screened by ITV on 22 July 1975 in *Dawson's Weekly*.

The Wrong Man   9 SEP 1997

MAIN CAST
Paul · Paul Merton
Sergeant · · · · · · · · · · · · · Roger Lloyd Pack
CID officer · · · · · · · · · · · · · Nicky Henson
Sprott · · · · · · · · · · · · · · · · · · · Cliff Parisi
Mrs Haggerty · · · · · · · · · · · Gabrielle Blunt
Mr Hardacre · · · · · · · · · · · · Walter Sparrow

CREDITS
director Martin Dennis · executive producer Richard Boden · producer Jamie Rix

Originally screened by the BBC in *Hancock's Half-Hour* on 6 March 1959. Paul sights a flying-saucer (thrown by a neighbour) and reports it to the police as a possible UFO. While he's at the station the duty sergeant

asks him to make up the numbers in an identification parade and Paul is suddenly the prime suspect in a robbery investigation. He sets out to track down the real thief.

I Tell You It's Burt Reynolds   16 SEP 1997

MAIN CAST
Paul · Paul Merton
Gavin · · · · · · · · · · · · · · · · · Nigel Planer
Jill · · · · · · · · · · · · · · · · · Maria McErlane
Steve · · · · · · · · · · · · · · · · · · Jim Sweeney
Granny · · · · · · · · · · · · · · · · Jean Heywood

CREDITS
director Martin Dennis · executive producer Richard Boden · producer Jamie Rix

I Tell You It's Burt Reynolds (see separate entry under that title for the storyline précis) was originally screened by ITV in *The Galton & Simpson Playhouse* on 31 March 1977.

Visiting Day   30 SEP 1997

MAIN CAST
Paul · Paul Merton
Mother · · · · · · · · · · · · · · · · · Lynda Baron
Father · · · · · · · · · · · · · · · · Brian Murphy
Mrs Thompson · · · · · · · · · · · · · Anne Reid
Nurse Barnes · · · · · · · · · · Nicole Arumugam
Mr Thompson · · · · · · · · · · · Philip Aldridge

CREDITS
director Martin Dennis · executive producer Richard Boden · producer Jamie Rix

Visiting Day (see separate entry under that title for the storyline précis) was originally screened by the BBC in *Comedy Playhouse* on 2 February 1962.

The Suit   7 OCT 1997

MAIN CAST
Paul · Paul Merton
Penny · · · · · · · · · · · · · · · · Katy Carmichael
Wife · Louisa Rix
Jimmy · · · · · · · · · · · · · · · · Fred Wakefield
Burglar · · · · · · · · · · · · · · · · Nigel Peever

CREDITS
director Martin Dennis · executive producer Richard Boden · producer Jamie Rix

The Suit (see separate entry under that title for the storyline précis) was originally screened by ITV in *The Galton & Simpson Comedy* on 19 April 1969.

Being Of Sound Mind   14 OCT 1997

MAIN CAST
Paul · Paul Merton
Solicitor · · · · · · · · · · · · Geoffrey Whitehead
Aunt Freda · · · · · · · · · · · · · · · Toni Palmer
Uncle Arthur · · · · · · · · · · · · Brian Murphy
Aunt Fanny · · · · · · · · · · · · Pamela Cundell
Uncle George · · · · · · · · · · · Reginald Marsh
Evelyn Duckworth · · · · · · · · · · · Sam Kelly
Agency woman · · · · · · · · · · · Helen Lederer
Agency man · · · · · · · Michael Fenton Stevens

CREDITS
director Martin Dennis · *executive producer* Richard Boden · *producer* Jamie Rix

Being Of Sound Mind (see Les Dawson's combined entry for the storyline précis, under the original title *Where's There's A Will*) was originally screened by ITV on 19 June 1975 in *Dawson's Weekly*.

Lunch In The Park   21 OCT 1997

MAIN CAST
Geoffrey Tupper · · · · · · · · · · · · Paul Merton
Sarah Tiptree · · · · · · · · · · · Josie Lawrence

CREDITS
director Martin Dennis · *executive producer* Richard Boden · *producer* Jamie Rix

Lunch In The Park (see Stanley Baxter's combined entry for the storyline précis) was originally screened by the BBC in *Comedy Playhouse* on 22 December 1961.

The Paul Merton Show

UK · BBC · SKETCH

1 × 30 mins · colour
21 Oct 1996 · BBC2 Mon 9.30pm

MAIN CAST
Paul Merton
Leslie Ash
Richard Vranch

CREDITS
writers Paul Merton, John Irwin, Lee Simpson/Jim Sweeney, Richard Vranch · *director* Julia Knowles · *producers* Phil Clarke, Emma Gage

The post-modern tone of C4's *Paul Merton – The Series* (next entry) was ditched in this BBC one-off, in favour of a more traditional comedy/variety setting – closer, in fact, to *The Morecambe And Wise Show* than the cutting-edge product of his contemporaries.

Although any attempt to explore new avenues and stretch talents must be commended, the switch was not an unqualified success. The quirky, surrealistic ramblings of Merton's standup material seemed at odds with the 'showbiz' environment; also, his attempts at Eric Morecambe-style asides to the audience during sketches and routines seemed less than convincing. Particularly telling was the fact that the most memorable and hilarious part of the show, a monochrome sketch in which fluffy glove puppets enacted a classic scene from *Casablanca*, was the least traditional item in the show.

See also *Does China Exist?*

Paul Merton – The Series

UK · C4 (HAT TRICK PRODUCTIONS) · SKETCH

12 editions (6 × 30 mins · 6 × 35 mins) colour

Series One (6 × 30 mins) 25 Sep–30 Oct 1991 · Wed 10.30pm

Series Two (6 × 35 mins) 3 Sep–8 Oct 1993 · Fri 10.30pm

MAIN CAST
Paul Merton
John Irwin
Robert Harley

CREDITS
writers Paul Merton, John Irwin · *directors* Geoff Posner (series 1), Liddy Oldroyd (series 2) · *executive producer* Denise O'Donoghue · *producer* David Tyler

The deeply deadpan standup star Paul Merton caused ripples as a regular in C4's improv parlour-game series *Whose Line Is It Anyway?* and then made a huge splash as one of the two resident team captains in BBC2's satirical panel-game *Have I Got News For You*, both series made by Hat Trick Productions. In the latter, Merton's stream-of-consciousness patter, poking into bizarre and surreal areas, became so popular that he was offered his own Hat Trick series, commissioned by C4.

Paul Merton – The Series was an odd fish – but what else could one expect from such an exponent of weirdness? One recurring linking sketch showed him behind the counter at a railway-station newspaper kiosk, serving the occasional customer but mostly just spouting his unusual philosophy, or rambling on aimlessly about whatever subject seemed to come into his head, until, more often than not, he finished with the resigned catchphrase 'innit marvellous?'. This verbal torrent of random ideas and non-sequiturs sometimes led, coherently, into a series of sketches but on occasion went nowhere at all. The miscellaneous sketches – some studio-bound, some on film – had no real relation to one another but they all followed a pattern, of sorts, in which ludicrous ideas were exploited to outrageously zany levels; hence a sketch about POWs taking a dummy to a head-count, in order to cover up the escape of one of their number, ended with Merton, as the last man in the camp, carting around an elaborate assembly of dozens of badly-made dummies in order to continue fooling the Germans – who, it transpires, are also down to one man and are using dummies to create the illusion of a whole guard force.

The first run of *Paul Merton – The Series* drew a mixed reaction from critics who, perhaps, expected too much from the *Have I Got News For You* favourite. Certainly, Merton was funnier in that BBC2 series, but this was because it played to his ultimate strength: his ability to march into unscripted territory without a safety net. (The programmes *were* pre-recorded, but Merton's contributions were true spur-of-the-moment improvisations.) Strangely, without this 'live-show' danger, the surrealism carried less bite.

Still, *Paul Merton – The Series* had some fine ideas and genuinely hilarious moments – *and* it was all achieved without the coarse language, violent slapstick and in-yer-face shock tactics that had become *de rigeur* for so many of his contemporaries.

Paul Squire, Esq

UK · BBC · SKETCH/STANDUP

6 × 35 mins · colour
26 Feb–2 Apr 1983 · BBC1 Sat 8.20pm

MAIN CAST
Paul Squire

CREDITS
writers Kim Fuller, Rob Grant/Doug Naylor, Terry Ravenscroft, Neil Shand, Helen Murry/Jamie Rix/Nick Wilton · *director/producer* Geoff Posner

Following his ITV series *The Paul Squire Show* (next entry), the likeable young comic switched to BBC1, combining the usual impressions (Frank Spencer and so on) with more unusual ones (Tom Baker's Doctor from *Doctor Who*, Spiderman and more). By August 1983, though, he was back on ITV, in *PS It's Paul Squire*.

The Paul Squire Show

UK · ITV (ATV · *CENTRAL) · SKETCH/STANDUP

11 × 30 mins · colour
Series One (6) 2 Sep–14 Oct 1981 · Wed 7pm
*Series Two (5) 15 July–12 Aug 1982 · Thu 7.15pm

MAIN CAST
The star · · · · · · · · · · · · · · · · · Paul Squire
The music director · · · · · · · · Bernard Spear
The writer · · · · · · · · · · · · · · · Bobby Knutt
The producer · · · · · · · · · · · · Anna Dawson
The temporary secretary · · · · · Debbie Arnold
· (series 1)

CREDITS
creator Royston Mayoh · *writers* Garry Chambers, Paul Squire, Wally Malston, Bill Martin, Max Sherrington (series 1); David Hansen, Paul Owen (series 2) · *director/producer* Royston Mayoh

Hailing from a show-business background, Paul Squire first entered variety at the age of nine as one of the Millionaires, a musical comedy group he formed with his brother and sister. They toured northern working men's clubs and then Europe and Africa, which meant that Squire, still of school age, received his education in the various places they toured. The group split up amicably in 1977 and Squire started performing songs and comedy on his own, achieving moderate success and making a name for himself in pantomime. When he added impressionism to his roster of talents he attracted the attention of ITV companies and made a number of appearances in variety series like *Search For A Star* and *Starburst*. His increasing popularity led to a guest appearance in the 1980 *Royal Variety Show* (BBC1, 23 November) and then this starring series for ATV.

The theme of the series was, oddly, the making of a TV series, with Bobby Knutt appearing as the scriptwriter, Anna Dawson cast as the producer, Debbie Arnold playing a temp sec and Bernard Spear the show's musical director.

Paul Squire's next production was for the BBC (previous entry, **Paul Squire, Esq**).

Pauline's Quirkes

UK · ITV (THAMES) · CHILDREN'S SKETCH

6 × 30 mins · colour

15 Nov–20 Dec 1976 · Mon 4.45pm

MAIN CAST

Pauline Quirke
Linda Robson
Philip Elsmore
Nula Conwell
Flintlock

CREDITS

writers Charles Verrall/Bill Rice · *director/producer* Roger Price

Such was her promise that, following the success of **You Must Be Joking!**, 17-year-old Pauline Quirke was pitched by Thames TV into her first self-titled series. As before, she was accompanied by Linda Robson – both were students at the Anna Scher Children's Theatre in Islington, north London, the co-owner of which, Charles Verrall, co-scripted this series. In *Pauline's Quirkes* the two teenies, with Nula Conwell, constantly indulged in boy-chasing with the members of pop group Flintlock, who appeared throughout (despite Pauline's on-screen confession that she was really a Bay City Rollers fan). One edition featured two DJs – Mike Read and Steve Wright – from Radio 210, the station based in Reading, Berkshire.

Quirke's next venture for Thames TV's children's programming was *Pauline's People*, a weekly teenage magazine show which – along with chat, sketches, music and consumer complaint investigations – took a humorous and unconventional look at activities in the London area. Once again, she was joined by chum Linda Robson, and two series were broadcast, beginning 9 January 1978 and 3 January 1979.

Pearl

USA · CBS (IMPACT ZONE/JUNGER WITT/ WARNER BROS) · SITCOM

22 × 30 mins · colour

US dates: 16 Sep 1996–19 Feb 1997 (18 episodes)
UK dates: 12 July–13 Dec 1997 (22 episodes) C4 Sat around 3am

MAIN CAST

Pearl Caraldo ············· Rhea Perlman

Professor Stephen Pynchon ············
···················· Malcolm McDowell
Annie Carmen ············· Carol Kane
Frankie Spivak-Tuch ········ Kevin Corrigan
Joey Caraldo ················ Dash Mihok
Amy Li ··················· Lucy Alexis Liu

CREDITS

creator Don Reo · *writers* various · *directors* various · *executive producers* Don Reo, Rhea Perlman, Paul Junger Witt, Tony Thomas, Gary S Levine

A first post-*Cheers* series for Rhea Perlman, who had shot to fame in that esteemed series as the fiery barmaid, Carla; *Pearl* was very much a vehicle for that same combustible screen persona.

She was cast as Pearl Caraldo, an under-educated blue-collar widow and mother who, in an attempt to better herself, enrols as a mature humanities student at Swindon University in New York, a subject with the highest failure rate. Her lecturer is Professor Pynchon, a self-obsessed British man and a snob of the first order. The two clash immediately: Pearl, although bright and willing to learn, is a fish out of water in the world of academia (she works at the docks) and Pynchon (deliciously played by Malcolm McDowell) is a raving egomaniac with a barbed wit. Pynchon sets out to humiliate Pearl, as he does all to all 'inferiors', but, being older than his usual students, and a tough battler who has experienced the hardships of life, she is made of sterner stuff and gives as good as she gets. As time passes, a grudging mutual respect develops.

This antagonistic relationship was at the core of *Pearl*, and the other characters were little more than accessories – Carol Kane, as Annie, played yet another variation of her scatty weirdo screen-persona; Joey was Pearl's single-parent son; the student Frankie Stevac was hapless and socially awkward; and Amy Lee was a fiercely intelligent but virtually humourless Chinese-American student. The series also called upon the favours of others to help out: Billy Connolly made a guest appearance in one episode, cast as Pynchon's estranged brother; Danny DeVito (Rhea Perlman's real-life husband) appeared once, as did Ted Danson (Sam Malone in *Cheers*).

Pearl had some good moments – the dialogue was snappy and the two lead actors seemed to relish their verbal sparring – but it was flawed, not least because the central premise did not permit enough storyline variations. Even the occasional flashes of sexual tension between Pearl and the professor couldn't disguise the fact that the plots followed much the same route, week after week. Keenly anticipated in the USA, the series was a major disappointment and was cancelled after 18 episodes had been screened. In the UK, where all of the 22 that had been

made were aired, it passed by virtually unnoticed owing to C4's odd decision to schedule it deep into the night; granted, *Pearl* wasn't brilliant, but it deserved better than this.

The Pee Wee Herman Show

USA · HBO · SATIRICAL SITCOM

1 × 60 mins · colour

US dates: 11 Sep 1981
UK dates: 29 May 1989 · BBC2 Mon 8.50pm

MAIN CAST

Pee Wee Herman ··········· Paul Reubens
Kap'n Karl ················ Phil Hartman
Miss Yvonne ············· Lynne Stewart
Hammy ··················· Tito Larriva
Susan ··················· Nicole Panter
Mailman Mike ·············· John Moody
Jambi ··················· John Paragon
Hermit Hattie ············· Edie McClurg
Mrs Jelly Donut ··········· Monica Ganas
Mr Jelly Donut ············· Brian Seff

CREDITS

writers Paul Reubens, Marty Callner, Bill Stein, Lynne Stewart, Phil Hartman, John Paragon, Edie McClurg · *director* Marty Callner · *producers* Paul Reubens, Marty Callner

The character of Pee Wee Herman – a camp, high-voiced, pasty-faced, eye-rolling, bow-tie-wearing naïf, as invented and played by Paul Reubens – became a cult phenomenon in America. In this one-off special, Reubens satirised US TV children's shows of the late 1950s, his Herman persona hosting a wacky, manic and somewhat vulgar entertainment for kids, with garishly coloured sets, talking furniture and various characters spoofing children's favourites from that period.

This show, and Herman's guest appearances on cult hits like *Late Night With Letterman* and **Saturday Night Live**, led to a feature film, *Pee Wee's Big Adventure* (1985, director Tim Burton), which was a smash hit in the USA. In turn, this led to a TV series, *Pee Wee's Playhouse* (CBS 13 September 1986–27 July 1991), which, ironically, aired in the same Saturday-morning slot that was home to the shows he spoofed. The series was a huge success – appealing as much to children taking the show at face value as it did to adults, who appreciated its knowing humour on a different level – and it carried an overriding message, imploring children to explore the wildest corners of their imagination and reach for areas they may have thought inaccessible. A second feature film followed in 1988 (*Big Top Pee Wee*, director Randal Kleiser) but then Reubens was arrested over an alleged indecent exposure incident in a porn cinema. He denied the charge but the resulting publicity caused CBS to cancel the series mid-run and Pee Wee Herman disappeared from public view while Reubens, his confidence reportedly shaken, contemplated his future. In 1992 he received a major boost when, at an MTV awards event, he was greeted by a standing ovation.

Peggy Ryan

UK · BBC · STANDUP

1 × 25 mins · b/w

20 July 1947 · Sun 3.35pm

MAIN CAST
Peggy Ryan

CREDITS
producer Henry Caldwell

The American comedian and dancer Peggy Ryan had been a child star in vaudeville and began acting in movies while still in her teens. Here she took time off from her film career – where she successfully partnered song-and-dance man Donald O'Connor – to make her British TV debut in a 'Beach Party' miscellany of comedy and music. The show also featured the talents of Jimmy Cross, singing group the Radio Revellers and Eric Robinson's Orchestra.

People Like Us

UK · ITV (JACK HYLTON TV PRODUCTIONS FOR ASSOCIATED-REDIFFUSION) · SITCOM

3 × 30 mins · b/w

7 Oct–4 Nov 1957 · fortnightly Mon 9.30pm

MAIN CAST
Reg Dixon
Sally Barnes

CREDITS
writers Sid Colin/Talbot Rothwell · *director* Kenneth Carter

This short series (just three programmes) failed to hit the mark, if the critics of the day were anything to go by.

Dixon and Barnes had appeared together in *Jump For Joy*, a pier show at Southsea that impresario Jack Hylton televised on A-R on 4 July 1957. Here, the pair were inside a TV studio, ensconced at 'Sunnyholme', a nondescript boarding house in an anonymous, medium-sized provincial town; Dixon played a librarian and Barnes a shop assistant. The humour, such as it was, was drawn out of their everyday situations and their abilities as entertainers. The critics hated it.

See also Just Sally.

Percy Ponsonby …

UK · BBC · SKETCH

10 × 10 mins · b/w

One series (6) *In The Barber's Chair* 6 Mar–15 May 1939 · various days and times

Special *Percy Ponsonby Goes To The Test Match* 24 June 1939 · Sat 3.30pm

Special *Percy Ponsonby Goes To Wimbledon* 1 July 1939 · Sat 3.20pm

Special *Percy Ponsonby Packs For A Bank Holiday* 1 Aug 1939 · Tue 9.55pm

Special *Percy Ponsonby Catches The 9.15* 18 Aug 1939 · Fri 10.15pm

MAIN CAST
Percy Ponsonby · · · · · · · · · · Charles Heslop

OTHER APPEARANCES
*The Customer/*other roles · · · Harry Atkinson

CREDITS
writer Reginald Arkell · *producers* Fred O'Donovan (5 eds of series), Jan Bussell (1 ed of series), Eric Fawcett (special 1), not known (special 2), S E Reynolds (special 3), George More O'Farrell (special 4)

This was a clear attempt at inventing the first recurring comic character for television, someone who might garner the appeal of radio creations like **Mrs Feather**. The comedian Charles Heslop starred as Percy Ponsonby, a barber who works dutifully in his shop, lather and brush in hand. Following a six-part series *In The Barber's Chair*, screened irregularly over some two months, Heslop returned to the small-screen for four further specials over a similar period. All was shaping up well for the comic, who seemed destined to become the first TV comedy star, when – 14 days after the fourth special was transmitted – the television service closed down for the duration of the Second World War (it was halted because it was feared that German bombers would use the transmissions to home in on London). And that was the end of Percy.

See also Charles Heslop.

A Perfect State

UK · BBC (CINEMA VERITY) · SITCOM

7 × 30 mins · colour

27 Feb–13 Apr 1997 · BBC1 Thu 8.30pm then Sun around 3.30pm

MAIN CAST
Deputy Mayor Laura Fitzgerald · · Gwen Taylor
Julie Fitzgerald · · · · · · · Jacqueline Defferary
Malcolm Batley · · · · · · · · · · Matthew Cottle
Mayor Winston Wainwright · · Rudolph Walker
Gareth Jones · · · · · · · · · · · · · · · Alan David
Simon Watson · · · · · · · · · · · Richard Hope
Bert Figgis · · · · · · · · · · · · · · Trevor Cooper
Johnny Pearce · · · · · · · · · · · · Danny Webb
Deidre Pearce · · · · · · · · · · · · · Emma Amos

CREDITS
writer Michael Aitkens · *director* Dewi Humphreys · *executive producers* Verity Lambert, Geoffrey Perkins · *producer* Sharon Bloom

Flatby-on-the-Bog is a nondescript coastal town whose main industry is fishing (although it's virtually a one-man-and-his-boat operation). The locals would prefer the main industry to be tourism but Flatby just isn't the type of place that attracts outside visitors; indeed, the locals themselves don't seem to like it very much. Even the town's principal activist, its deputy mayor Laura Fitzgerald, who is determined to champion local fishermen against destructive European Union legislation, unleashes many barbs about the town's unattractiveness and its inhabitants' tendency to inbreed. As a relentless crusader, and manager of the local pub, she knows everything about everyone.

Laura's daughter, Julie, a solicitor, is involved (although seemingly non-sexually) with the boring Malcolm Batley, an expert on local history and a fiercely left-wing political idealist. Malcolm singularly fails to impress Julie's mother until he discovers that, owing to the occasional submergence of the Flatby peninsula, it has never been formally ratified as part of the British mainland. This information, interpreted legally by Julie, means that Flatby could, in theory, declare independence. Laura immediately seizes upon the idea, seeing it as a way to flaunt EU regulations and thumb the town's collective nose at Whitehall. First, however, she has to convince her fellow councillors, which she does by persuasion (she tells wide-boy estate agent Johnny that Flatby will become a tax haven, attracting the super-rich), threat (she tells Bert, a local butcher, that EU regulations will prevent him from selling much of his best produce), and blackmail (she tells the golf-fanatic mayor that she will reveal details of their wild affair 20 years earlier; when this fails to convince him, she threatens to disclose his recent affair with a woman whose husband is in an oxygen tent). Flatby's declaration of independence and its erection of a border post brings it to the attention of two Whitehall civil servants, the creepy but ferocious Gareth Jones and the kind-hearted Simon Watson, whose eventual role as go-between between the new state and the government is complicated by his passionate feelings towards Laura.

The notion of claiming independence for a tiny village or town, able to make its own rules, resulted in a delightful Ealing comedy, *Passport To Pimlico* (1949), but *A Perfect State*, made almost 50 years later, singularly failed to do the theme justice, and its embracing of British tabloid newspaper 'scare' stories about the EU insisting upon 'regulation-shaped cucumbers' and 'threats to the sanctity of the British sausage' was clumsy. Disliked by critics, and watched by few viewers compared with other shows in its primetime slot, the series was relegated to Sunday afternoons for the final two episodes.

Perfect Strangers

USA · ABC (MILLER-BOYETT PRODUCTIONS/LORIMAR TELEPICTURES/TAL PRODUCTIONS) · SITCOM

150 × 30 mins · colour

US dates: 25 Mar 1986–6 Aug 1993
UK dates: 3 Jan 1987–9 June 1992
(71 episodes) BBC1 Sat 5.20pm then
weekdays 9.05am

MAIN CAST

Balki Bartokomous	Bronson Pinchot
Larry Appleton	Mark Linn-Baker
Jennifer Lyons	Melanie Wilson
Mary Anne Spencer	Rebeca Arthur
Harriette Winslow	JoMarie Payton-France (1987–89)
Donald 'Twinkie' Twinkacetti	Ernie Sabella (1986–87)
Edwina Twinkacetti	Belita Moreno (1986–87)
Susan Campbell	Lise Cutter (1986)
Lydia Markham	Belita Moreno (1987–93)
Mr Gorpley	Sam Anderson (1987–92)

CREDITS

writers Chip Keyes/Doug Keyes, Bob Keyes, William Bickley/Michael Warren, Paula A Roth and others · director Joel Zwick · executive producers Thomas L Miller, Robert L Boyett, Dale McRaven · producers Mark Fink and others

In the mid-1980s there was a mini-trend in American TV and movies in which US society and customs were made funny by viewing them through the eyes of a foreigner. *Taxi* had its constantly baffled East European immigrant Latka; an Aussie, Paul Hogan, tried to come to terms with New York in *Crocodile Dundee*; and in *Coming To America* Eddie Murphy was a visitor from Africa. The TV sitcom *Perfect Strangers* explored the same theme, wherein a man named Balki Bartokomous travels to America from his Mediterranean Island (Mypos) in search his distant cousin, Larry, in Chicago.

Like Latka in *Taxi*, Balki derived big guffaws by strangling the English language with a bizarre accent and his odd phrasing. Admittedly this might be a 'cheap' method of getting laughs, but the actor Bronson Pinchot proved brilliant at doing it, squeezing every ounce of humour from his lines. Larry (played by Louie Anderson in an unaired pilot and Mark Linn-Baker in the series) was usually straight-man to Balki, enhancing the situation by developing a wide-eyed look to greet Balki's excesses and displaying fine comic timing with his pauses and eventual reactions.

The characters went through various changes in their situation but for the bulk of the run they worked at the *Chicago Chronicle*, Larry as an assistant to the city editor, Balki in the mailroom. Also employed there was a wisecracking lift attendant, Harriette Winslow – she proved so popular that she graduated to her own spin-off series, *Family Matters* (ABC, 22 September 1989 to date).

Perils Of Pendragon

UK · BBC · SITCOM

6 × 50 mins · colour

18 Jan–7 Mar 1974 · BBC2 mostly Fri 8.10pm

MAIN CAST

Isaac	Kenneth Griffith
Rosko	John Clive
Aunt Angharad	Lally Bowers
Rev Murchison Mort	Aubrey Richards
Aunt Floss	Olive Mercer
Mrs Magwitch	Rhoda Lewis
Myfanwy	Beth Morris
Uther Jacobs	Trevor Ray

CREDITS

writer Peter Draper · directors Michael Ferguson (4), George Spenton-Foster (2) · producer Derrick Sherwin

Described as '*Clochemerle* in Wales' this fine, six-part filmed series was a rural satire with a strong emphasis on black comedy. Pendragon represented a microcosm of the world and was used to explore the classic themes of marriage, friendship, greed and politics. One episode, 'Marx And Sparks', was postponed for three weeks because its storyline, involving philosophical political arguments, was deemed too sensitive to be screened within sight of the General Election on 28 February 1974.

Note. The 1 February episode, 'A Persistent Coffin', was a remake of an earlier BBC1 play of the same title, screened in the drama anthology *The Man Outside* on 2 June 1972, with both Kenneth Griffith and John Clive in the same principal roles. Here the tiny Welsh town was called Pswllab.

Personal Appearance

UK · ITV (GRANADA) · STANDUP

17 × 30 mins · b/w

*18 June–10 Oct 1957 · Tue then Thu 8.30pm

MAIN CAST

Alan Young

CREDITS

director Philip Jones

The British-born comedian Alan Young returned home from North America to appear in this Granada series. He was no stranger to TV: his US series *The Alan Young Show* (never screened in the UK) had aired from 1950 to 1953 and he went on to even greater small-screen exposure a decade later as the straight man to talking horse *Mister Ed*.

*Note. *Personal Appearance* started one week before this but with a variety of guests and no emphasis on comedy. These dates refer only to Alan Young's tenure.

See also *It's Young Again*, *Alan Young* and *Coming Of Age*.

Pet Pals

UK · BBC · CHILDREN'S SITCOM

6 × 30 mins · b/w

21 May–25 June 1965 · BBC1 Fri 5.05pm

MAIN CAST

Jim	Jim Dale
Mr Potter	Richard Caldicot
Charlie	Sydney Bromley

CREDITS

creator James Green · writers George Evans/Derek Collyer · producer Barry Lupino

A children's series for the comedian/actor/singer Jim Dale. He was cast here as a young-ish man who owns a pet shop but becomes so attached to his critters that he refuses to sell them, so that the place, eventually, comes to resemble a menagerie.

See also *Join Jim Dale*.

Peter Cavanagh

UK · BBC · IMPRESSIONISM

5 editions (4 × 15 mins · 1 × 20 mins) · b/w

One series (4) 14 Nov–19 Dec 1955 · Mon 4pm
Special (20 mins) 31 Jan 1957 · Thu 5.25pm

MAIN CAST

Peter Cavanagh
Terry Scott (special)

CREDITS

writer Peter Cavanagh · producers Kenneth Milne-Buckley (series), Johnny Downes (special)

Impressionist Peter Cavanagh was billed as 'the voice of them all' and enjoyed much success on BBC radio before turning his attention to television. In these shows, the last of which was aired as part of the strand *Children's Television*, he aimed to analyse the style of certain comics by his impersonations, hoping that some of those he was featuring would join him on the set. (This followed a famous 1950 radio broadcast in which Cavanagh had duetted *as* and *with* Arthur Askey, with each of them singing alternate lines in Askey's famous theme 'The Bee Song'.)

Peter Cook & Co

UK · ITV (LWT) · SKETCH

1 × 65 mins · colour

14 Sep 1980 · Sun 10.30pm

MAIN CAST

Peter Cook
Rowan Atkinson
John Cleese
Terry Jones
Robert Longden
Beryl Reid
Paula Wilcox

CREDITS

writer Peter Cook · script associate Bernard McKenna · director/producer Paul Smith · executive producer Humphrey Barclay

The point of this so-called 'spectacular', one suspects, was to glory in and revive Cook's dazzling comedy genius. Unfortunately, it only reflected his decline, even when he slipped into one of his best characters of old, the monotonous bore E L Wisty. The new comic personas – Manhattan cabbie Herb Natky (these elements were taped in New York) and the ant expert Professor Henreich Globnick – were decidedly unspectacular, and Cook never was much of an actor. Although written by him, two sketches failed to show Cook at all, being played by members of the fine guest cast.

It wasn't all bad, though, and a fine spoof of Roald Dahl's then-current ITV drama series *Tales Of The Unexpected* was among the highlights.

For Cook's principal TV work see *An Apple A Day*, *Behind The Fridge*, *Beyond The Fringe*, *Goodbye Again*, *A Life In Pieces* (this entry also includes details of Cook's final TV appearances), *Not Only … But Also*, *The Two Of Us*[1], *What's Going On Here?* and *Where Do I Sit?*

The Peter Principle

UK · BBC (HAT TRICK PRODUCTIONS) · SITCOM

7 × 30 mins · colour

Pilot · 4 Sep 1995 · BBC1 Mon 8.30pm

One series (6) 2 June–7 July 1997 · BBC1 Mon 8.30pm

MAIN CAST

Peter Duff (pilot)/	
Peter Duffley (series)	Jim Broadbent
Susan Harvey	Lesley Sharp (pilot);
	Claire Skinner (series)
Iris	Linda Bassett (pilot);
	Janette Legge (series)
Geoffrey	David Gant (pilot);
	Stephen Moore (series)
Brenda	Zoe Hayes (pilot);
	Tracy Keating (series)
David	Stuart McQuarrie (pilot);
	Daniel Flynn (series)
Bradley	David Schneider
Mrs Parkes	Helena McCarthy
Kevin Mott	Clive Russell
Milton Macrae	Michael J Shannon

CREDITS

writers Mark Burton/John O'Farrell/Dan Patterson · *directors* Terry Kinane (pilot), Nick Wood (series) · *executive producer* Denise O'Donoghue · *producer* Dan Patterson

Peter Duffley (Peter Duff in the pilot episode) is a buffoon. He is a sycophantic, self-important, pompous, clumsy and utterly inept dolt who has somehow (only in sitcoms does this happen) become the manager of a forward-looking bank, County and Provincial (C&P) – the Aldbridge branch, to be precise. The brighter members of his staff easily see through his transparent attempts to bluff his way through problems, and they treat him with barely disguised contempt. Most active in this field is his assistant manager, the sharp and efficient Susan, who feels – with full justification – that she would make a far

better boss. Then there is David, their link to head office, an ambitious, forceful area manager who can see Susan's obvious merits but, at the same time, is remarkably tolerant with Peter's shortcomings.

A cracking pilot episode with lots of good lines and a masterful · performance from the accomplished Jim Broadbent, ably demonstrated the potential for a series but this didn't arrive for nearly two years – and then carried considerable cast changes. These six new episodes were received not nearly so well, with criticism levelled against the predictability of the humour (Duffley was always bound to fail in the most excruciatingly embarrassing of ways) and the similarity of his character – in his bumbling, repressed English ineptitude – to a combination of Basil Fawlty and Harry Worth.

The Peter Sellers Show

UK · ITV (ATV) · SKETCH/STANDUP

1 × 60 mins · b/w

8 Feb 1958 · Sat 10.20pm

MAIN CAST

Peter Sellers
Eric Sykes

CREDITS

writer Eric Sykes · *producer* Bill Lyon-Shaw

One year after ITV screened two programmes as *Eric Sykes Presents Peter Sellers*, this show, reuniting the two top-line comic stars, was aired in the strand *Val Parnell's Saturday Spectacular*.

Peter's Troubles

see BUTTERWORTH, Peter

Petticoat Junction

USA · CBS (FILMWAYS) · SITCOM

212 × 30 mins (64 × b/w · 148 × colour)

US dates: 24 Sep 1963–12 Sep 1970

*UK dates: 23 Jan–25 Dec 1964 (37 episodes · b/w) ITV Thu then Tue 8.30pm

MAIN CAST

Kate Bradley	Bea Benaderet (1963–68)
Uncle Joe Carson	Edgar Buchanan
Betty Jo Bradley Elliott	Linda Kaye Henning
Billie Jo Bradley	Jeannine Riley (1963–65);
	Gunilla Hutton (1965–66);
	Meredith MacRae (1966–70)
Bobbie Jo Bradley	Pat Woodell (1963–65);
	Lori Saunders (1965–70)
Floyd Smoot	Rufe Davis (1963–68)
Charlie Pratt	Smiley Burnette (1963–67)
Homer Bedloe	Charles Lane (1963–68)
Steve Elliot	Mike Minor
Dr Janet Craig	June Lockhart (1968–70)
Sam Drucker	Frank Cady
Newt Kiley	Kay E Kuter (1964–70)

CREDITS

creator Paul Henning · *writers* various · *directors* various · *executive producer* Paul Henning · *producers* Dick Wesson, Charles Stewart, Al Simon

Petticoat Junction was almost but not quite a spin-off from *The Beverly Hillbillies*, and both were born of the same clever creator, Paul Henning, the doyen of rural comedy. Its main star was Bea Benaderet, who had occasionally featured in *The Beverly Hillbillies* as Pearl, Jethro's mother. Here she played a similar character, Kate Bradley, the widowed owner of a small hotel, the Shady Rest, in the rural, sleepy town of Hooterville. The series brought deserved top-billing to this actress, who had become familiar to US TV viewers as next-door neighbour Blanche in *The Burns And Allen Show*, and voiced Betty Rubble in *The Flintstones* (which was an unacknowledged but obvious cartoon version of another great 1950s US sitcom, *The Honeymooners*). Most of the *Petticoat Junction* comedy was set in Sam Drucker's general store, the railway station – where the Hooterville Cannonball, a decrepit steam train, was driven by Floyd and Charlie – and around the Shady Rest, where Kate was helped out by her three gorgeous daughters Billie Jo, Bobbie Jo and Betty Jo (the latter was played by Paul Henning's daughter, Linda Kaye Henning) and by Uncle Joe Carson, who pronounced himself the hotel's manager.

Like *The Beverly Hillbillies* before it and *Green Acres* after it – the latter was also set in and around Hooterville, and there was much cast-swapping as a result – most of the humour came from the wonderful ensemble playing and the characters' bizarre ways of life. Sadly, the series dropped a notch or two when Benaderet missed many latter episodes through ill-health and then died before the sixth US season (at which point June Lockhart was brought in), but its place as one of the best-loved and most durable of US sitcoms was already assured.

*Note. Following the initial ITV screenings, BBC1 acquired *Petticoat Junction* and broadcast 25 colour episodes on Tuesday afternoons from 11 September 1973 to 16 April 1974.

Un Peu de Tout

see The Montreux Festival

Phenom

USA · ABC (GRACIE FILMS/COLUMBIA TELEVISION) · SITCOM

22 × 30 mins · colour

US dates: 14 Sep 1993–31 Aug 1994

UK dates: 8 Mar–2 Aug 1994 (22 episodes) C4 Tue 6.30pm

MAIN CAST

Dianne Doolan	Judith Light
Angela Doolan	Angela Goethals
Mary Doolan	Ashley Johnson
Brian Doolan	Todd Louiso
Roanne	Jennifer Lien
Lou Del La Rosa	William Devane

CREDITS

creators Dick Blasucci/Marc Flanagan/ Sam Simon · writers various · directors various · executive producers James L Brooks, Dick Blasucci, Danny Kallis · producers Kathy Ann Stumpe, Richard Sakai, Hudson Hickman

A youth-aimed sitcom about a tennis wunderkind, Angela Doolan, the 'phenom' of the title. Fifteen years old, she has the potential to be a sports superstar but worries about losing her normality and severing her family ties. Angela's father has deserted the family, to rediscover his youth and dally with younger women, leaving her mother Dianne to raise the family and to try to keep a lid on her bitterness. There were attempts to portray the family as dysfunctional, with older brother Brian depicted as inarticulate and introverted, and younger sister Mary as undisciplined and prone to mischief, but the group was too cute to pull it off. Even the obsessive tennis coach Lou, who was determined to bring out the champion in Angela regardless of the cost to her growth as a human, didn't come across as the one-track minded monster that he was obviously intended to be – instead he was like a smart-talking, boastful uncle who had made good. Although he did lust after Angela's mother, he was quite upfront about it and didn't attempt to hide his desires behind innuendo.

The occasional acid line (usually from Dianne) failed to give the series any sort of edge and it lacked the cool of Borg, the fire of McEnroe and the sex appeal of Agassi. Worse, it wasn't even as funny as Nastase.

Phil Cool

UK · ITV (CENTRAL) · IMPRESSIONISM

5 × 30 mins · colour

1 Aug–29 Aug 1992 · Sat around 11pm

MAIN CAST

Phil Cool
Jon Glover
Chris Emmett
Sophie Thompson
Zoe Greig

CREDITS

director Alistair Clark · producer Paul Spencer

Another series for the skilled but unusual impressionist, recorded in live performance at the Belgrade Theatre in Coventry. Here the comic exercised his usual dexterity in taking on impersonations of everyone from John Major to Minnie Mouse.

Note. Soon after this ITV series, on 7 January 1993, Cool was featured in C4's A Day In The Life … series, taped backstage at the Victoria Hall, Hanley, as he prepared for a concert.

See also Cool It and Cool Head.

Phil Kay Feels …

UK · C4 (URPH PRODUCTIONS/CHANNEL X) · STANDUP

6 × 35 mins · colour

18 Apr–23 May 1997 · Fri 10.30pm

MAIN CAST

Phil Kay

CREDITS

writer Phil Kay · additional material Martin Trenaman · director Mark Mylod · executive producer Alan Marke · producer Jo Sargent

Scottish comic Phil Kay first came to prominence in 1989 when he won 'So You Think You're Funny', the newcomer's competition at the Edinburgh Festival Fringe. A hairy, thin, hyper-energetic individual, Kay has a nervy, rapid-fire delivery in which words seem to tumble out of his mouth in a dash to appear in the right order, his sentences often seeming to run into one another. This babbling style means that Kay seems to get through much more material per minute than other comedians, and the overall impression is that he is spouting forth a stream-of-consciousness rant that seems totally improvised; really, however, there is a guiding structure beneath the flow.

The technique was in full view in this C4 series Phil Kay Feels …, in which, each week, the comedian explored a suffixed theme ('Natural', 'Technical', 'Lovely', 'Entertaining', 'Sporty', 'Wet'), although the subjects were very loosely interpreted and seemed only to serve as a launching pad for his rambling meanderings. These were enjoyable slices of off-the-wall comedy, with a small degree of audience participation, and the routines were punctuated by short film clips intended to illustrate particular points.

Phil Kay Feels … provided Kay with well-deserved TV exposure. Perhaps a little too much, actually – in the first programme, exploring the 'Natural' theme, he ran on stage stark naked, providing not only the studio audience but also viewers at home with an unexpected and unexpurgated full-frontal eyeful.

The Phil Silvers Show

USA · CBS · SITCOM

143 episodes (142 × 30 mins · 1 × 60 mins) · b/w

US dates: 20 Sep 1955–19 June 1959

*UK dates: 20 Apr 1957–2 June 1960 (129 × 30 mins · 1 × 60 mins) BBC various days and times

MAIN CAST

Sgt Ernest G 'Ernie' Bilko	Phil Silvers
Cpl Rocco Barbella	Harvey Lembeck
Cpl Steve Henshaw	Allan Melvin
Col John T Hall	Paul Ford
Sgt Joan Hogan	Elisabeth Fraser (1955–58)
Sgt Francis Grover	Jimmy Little
Sgt Andrew Pendleton	Ned Glass (1955–56)
Sgt Stanley Sowici	Harry Clark (1955–56)
Sgt Rupert Ritzik	Joe E Ross (1956–59)
Mrs Emma Ritzik	Beatrice Pons (1956–59)
Pvt Duane Doberman	Maurice Gosfield
Pvt Sam Fender	Herbie Faye
Pvt Fleischman	Maurice Brenner
Pvt 'Stash' Kadowski	Karl Lukas
Pvt Mullen	Jack Healy
Pvt Dino Paparelli	Billy Sands
Pvt Fielding Zimmerman	Mickey Freeman
Pvt Sugarman/Thompson	Terry Carter

OTHER APPEARANCES

Mrs Nell Hall	Hope Sansberry
Capt Barker	Nick Saunders
Lt Anderson	Jim Perry (1955–56)
Chaplain	John Gibson
Pvt Claude Dillingham	Walter Cartier
Pvt Gander	Tige Andrews
Pvt Gomez	Bernie Fein
Pvt Palmer	P J Sidney
WAC Edna	Louise Golden
WAC Billie	Billie Allen

CREDITS

creator Nat Hiken · writers Nat Hiken (71, seven of these alone and the remainder in conjunction with, variously and principally, Billy Friedberg, Tony Webster, Terry Ryan, Barry Blitzer, Arnie Rosen, Coleman Jacoby, Leonard Stern, Arnold Auerbach and Harvey Orkin); remaining episodes mostly written by Terry Ryan (some with Phil Sharp), Arnie Rosen/Coleman Jacoby, Neil Simon, Sydney Zelinka/A J Russell, Billy Friedberg · directors Al De Caprio, Aaron Ruben · producers Nat Hiken (1955–57), Edward J Montagne (1957–59)

Phil Silvers had been around for years as the perennial 'second fiddle', first in vaudeville and then on Broadway and in the movies, when, after bringing the house down as MC of a CBS dinner in 1954, the network invited him to star in his own television comedy series. Silvers was reluctant but agreed to the proposal when CBS brought Nat Hiken into the picture. Hiken was immensely regarded in the comedy business as a radio writer for Fred Allen and Milton Berle, and for penning Martha Raye's 1953–55 TV specials. The star and the writer duly set to thinking up ideas for their series. Hiken's initial thought was to cast Silvers as a scheming army sergeant, and it was only some months later, with a table full of alternative ideas in front of them, that they returned to this and realised it could succeed. The Phil Silvers Show – also titled You'll Never Get Rich and, informally, Bilko and Sgt Bilko – was born, destined to win honours by the score, including three consecutive Emmy Awards for Best Comedy Series, and become, unarguably, one of the all-time great sitcoms. Many consider it *the* best.

Fleshed out, Ernest G Bilko, known to one and all as Ernie, was a master sergeant who would go to any lengths to beat the system, be it by conniving, bluffing, bribing, cheating, gambling, lying, finagling or any other devious device known only to him. No sharper operator ever existed than Bilko, no one more capable of fleecing his fellow man or forcing even the top brass at the Pentagon to quake. No one was beyond or safe from a Bilko operation – he could *smell* money, and he had all human life worked out, being capable not only of predicting the thoughts of others but calculating how long it would take people to think them. But Bilko had two crucial weaknesses: like all addicted gamblers, he could not resist one last flutter, and, down, deep down, *deep* deep down, resided a conscience that prevented him from making the final, ultimate move which would garner him his life's goals: wealth and physical comfort. For all his grasping, indeed *because* of his grasping, Bilko would never be a winner.

Ernie Bilko ran the motor-pool platoon at Fort Baxter, a US Army post in Roseville, Kansas, so remote that Washington scarcely remembered it was there. Nominally, the post was run by Colonel Hall but he recognised that Bilko was really in charge, the one man who could make the post work with clockwork precision or at the speed of molasses with a mere click of his fingers. A bumbler who was both anxious for Fort Baxter to be recognised by the top brass but keen too on the quiet life that resulted from its remoteness, Hall longed to be rid of Bilko, but, when this occasioned, he recognised immediately that Bilko was an essential part of the status quo that granted him, mostly, an easy life. Colonel Hall, and his wife Nell who was sublimely manipulated by the arch-flatterer Bilko, were but putty in the master sergeant's hands.

Bilko's principal 'pigeons', though, were the members of his platoon. Usually, US Army personnel are depicted on TV or in the movies as smart, fit, tall, handsome, virile men, eager to fight for their country and ever at the ready. Bilko's motor-pool privates were scruffy, lazy, unattractive slobs who liked to do as little work as possible, never paraded and were almost fearful of weaponry. While they dreaded Bilko's fantastic array of ideas to part them with their pay-packets they realised that resistance was useless. They knew too that although he would only just stop short of selling them into slavery, Bilko would also include them in his countless get-rich-quick schemes and protect them from the harsh realities of army life. Just like Colonel Hall, while the men were unhappy with what Bilko offered, they took comfort from knowing where they stood. (Incidentally, Nat

Hiken had named Bilko after a minor league US baseball player, Steve Bilko, whom he admired, happy with the connotation that it also gave of being bilked – that is, cheated. So too were Bilko's platoon members named after sportsmen – Paparelli was a baseball umpire, Barbella was the real name of the boxer Rocky Graziano, and other boxing names, as well as genuine boxers, populated the cast.) Of all Bilko's platoon of hapless wonders, Pvt Duane Doberman, played by Maurice Gosfield, stood out as the ultimate in slobbery – a short, appallingly-dressed fat man with an embarrassed, round, sweaty face and high, squeaky voice. Doberman failed to grasp the ways of the world, the ways of the barracks even, and became the ultimate 'patsy' in Bilko's schemes. Mostly, he arrived in a scene a few seconds late or spoke his line a few seconds late because he was supposed to; at other times it was because Gosfield's sense of timing was awry. As the series progressed so more and more the plotlines revolved around Doberman. Naturally, he became a huge star.

Elsewhere, Bilko had less affection for the other targets of his wiles: fellow sergeants Grover, Sowici, Pendleton and, best of all, Ritzik, the klutz of a cook who perpetually lost to Bilko, causing his volatile wife Emma to become even more fractious. Also on the post were a number of WACs, including Sgt Joan Hogan with whom Bilko enjoyed/endured an on-off relationship – it was on provided that she was willing to put up with his lies and conniving, it was off if she was not.

The Phil Silvers Show hit the ground running in the autumn of 1955 – the first two episodes were sensationally good, and within a short time it was heading the ratings and ranked as the number one comedy series in the USA. In Britain, where the series was unveiled 18 months later and screened out of sequence, Ernie Bilko became second only to Tony Hancock as a comedy figure of great significance in that period. The British people loved Bilko from the start and, while the series became inexplicably forgotten in America in the 1970s and 1980s, it has remained a staple of the BBC's programming, much cherished and discussed to the present day.

Although the series has plenty to admire in all directions, it owes this long-lasting success to two essential factors. The first is the performance of Phil Silvers. Never has a comic actor been so completely identifiable with his TV persona as Silvers was with Bilko. And never before or since has a man dominated a sitcom with such comedic power. The series was written to Silvers' strengths: fast-talking, quick-witted, razor-sharp, a gambler, a leader of men. As Bilko, Silvers was never less than sensational, delivering his lines with speed and guile and marvellously ad-libbing when the situation

required it. Silvers was the quintessential New York Jewish comedian, and the series – written and filmed in Manhattan – was blessed with all of the sharpness that typifies these twin centres of humour.

The second reason is Nat Hiken, another New York Jew and justifiably dubbed a genius by Silvers. Virtually all of the 71 episodes written during Hiken's tenure at the helm of *The Phil Silvers Show* represent TV comedy at its finest. What distinguished his work from that of other TV writers was his economy: what they would take sentences to express, Hiken could put across in just a few words. He also had an ability to maintain several storylines simultaneously within an episode, and the delightful knack of introducing bizarre denouements into his scripts – almost, one senses, as a challenge to himself, as if he found writing so easy that he needed to make the job harder by thinking of an improbable solution to which he must find an even more absurd premise. Hiken's *Bilko* scripts were awesome, and probably twice the length of any other US half-hour sitcom, so densely packed were the words and ideas. Among British sitcoms, only **Fawlty Towers** can rival *The Phil Silvers Show* in this regard.

Recognising that the pressure of producing such scripts on a weekly basis, 35 weeks a year, would probably kill him, Nat Hiken withdrew from *The Phil Silvers Show* at the end of its second season, going to on score another notable success in 1961 with **Car 54, Where Are You?** While it carried on for a further two years, *Bilko* was not the same without him. Indeed, one could argue that it merits its five-star status not because all 143 episodes were superb but because, during Hiken's reign, his shows rated *eight* out of five whereas the subsequent episodes deserve two out of five, despite Silvers' unwavering brilliance and scripts from an up-and-coming young writer named Neil Simon. In an attempt to inject fresh impetus, the fourth year was based not at Fort Baxter but in a new location, Camp Fremont in Grove City, California. The end came a few months later, in the summer of 1959, when CBS executives pulled the plug so that they could sell the series into syndication while it was still 'hot'. (The last scene in the final episode has Bilko in jail, finally landed there by Colonel Hall, stuttering 'Th-th-that's all folks!') Although some consider this to have been a mistake, believing *The Phil Silvers Show* to have been good for another few years, the cancellation came not a moment too soon, for the series was well past its peak and the glory days of the Hiken era and Emmy Awards supremacy. Silvers' post-*Bilko* career went downhill rapidly and, apart from spots in *Car 54*, few of the remaining cast were ever seen again. Alan Alda, Fred Gwynne and Dick Van Dyke all went on from *Bilko* guest appearances when unknown to greater fame, however.

Of the modern-day sitcoms only **Seinfeld** and **Frasier** come close to matching the impeccable qualities of the early *Bilko* episodes – especially *Seinfeld*, which, à la Hiken's work, intentionally adds seemingly irrelevant plot strands into a storyline and then neatly ties them all up at the end. And yet … these throne-pretenders may not stand the test of time as *Bilko* has, for the best Hiken-written episodes are already more than 40 years old. For its legions of dedicated fans, watching a great *Bilko* episode is like spending half an hour in the company of an old and dear friend: you may know the lines by heart, you may know the plots, you may remember where the boom microphone accidentally drops into the camera's view – speed and *feel*, not technical perfection, were the bywords in the 1950s – but you sit there and laugh every time, admiring Silvers' breathtaking performance and gasping at the speed of the action and the sheer brilliance of it all. Although it finished in 1959, *The Phil Silvers Show* remains the benchmark against which all great sitcoms must be measured.

Spin-offs have been surprisingly few. The Hanna-Barbera children's cartoon series *Top Cat* (USA, 1961–62; screened as *Boss Cat* in the UK by the BBC from 16 May 1962) is clearly fashioned on *The Phil Silvers Show*, depicting the adventures of a bunch of alley cats led by the wily and opportunistic Top Cat, always outsmarting the local policeman Officer Dibble (the Colonel Hall figure) but never able to grab the supreme prize: money, luxury and an escape from pavement life. Emphasising the similarity between *Top Cat* and *Bilko*, Maurice Gosfield voiced the part of Benny The Ball, a dumb moggy modelled closely on Duane Doberman. In 1995 the British actor/writer/director Jonathan Lynn (the co-writer of **Yes Minister**, among numerous other credits) went to Hollywood to direct a feature film version, titled *Sgt Bilko*, which starred Steve Martin in the lead role and updated the format to a modern-day army post. Compared with the original, the film was destined to be found wanting, but it did have a few high spots and, at the very least, its release finally rejuvenated US interest in what had become virtually a forgotten series there, with cable TV station Nick At Nite screening original 1950s episodes to perhaps three generations of Americans who had never before set eyes on arguably their country's finest comedy series.

*Notes. The BBC has several times programmed extended runs of *The Phil Silvers Show* repeats – beginning 23 October 1966, 14 April 1973, 31 August 1979, 7 November 1984 and 3 October 1993 – but one episode, 'Bilko's Merry Widow', remains

unseen on British TV (although it has been issued in the UK on video). A one-hour *Bilko* TV special, *Keep In Step*, screened in the USA on 23 January 1959, with Sidney Chaplin and Diana Dors as guest stars, has been shown just once by the BBC, on 8 August 1959, with an introduction recorded especially for Britain by Silvers. Phil Silvers and Maurice Gosfield appeared together, in character, in a specially recorded greeting to the BBC, screened by the channel on the twenty-first anniversary of the launch of British television, 2 November 1957, during a programme titled *The World Our Stage*. The Bilko Platoon, so called, were guests in an edition of the US TV series *The Perry Como Music-Hall*, screened by the BBC on 6 January 1960. On 31 December 1984, BBC2 paid homage to *The Phil Silvers Show* with the celebratory salute *Bilko On Parade*, narrated by Kenneth Williams and featuring clips from the series and reminiscences from Phil Silvers. The star died ten months later, on 1 November 1985, age 74, by all accounts a broken man. For four years in the 1950s he had caught the lightning but then it had slipped through his fingers.

See also **The New Phil Silvers Show**, **The Slowest Gun In The West** and **Just Polly And Me**.

Phyllis

USA · CBS (MTM ENTERPRISES) · SITCOM

49 × 30 mins · colour

US dates: 8 Sep 1975–30 Aug 1977

UK dates: 21 Oct 1976–5 Jan 1978 (22 episodes) ITV various days and times

MAIN CAST

Phyllis Lindstrom	Cloris Leachman
Bess Lindstrom	Lisa Gerritsen
Julie Erskine	Barbara Colby (1975);
	Liz Torres (1975–76)
Leo Heatherton	Richard Schaal
Audrey Dexter	Jane Rose
Judge Jonathan Dexter	Henry Jones
Sally Dexter	Judith Lowry

CREDITS

writers various · *directors* Jay Sandrich, Joan Darling, James Burrows, Harry Mastrogeorge, Asaad Kelada · *executive producers* Ed Weinberger, Stan Daniels

Out of **Rhoda**, *Phyllis* and *Lou Grant* (the latter being more dramatic than comedic), *Phyllis* was the least convincing and successful of the direct spin-offs from **The Mary Tyler Moore Show**. As before, Phyllis Lindstrom was played by Cloris Leachman, but no longer was she Mary's interfering, egocentric landlady in Minneapolis whose husband was the heard-of-but-never-seen Lars. In *Phyllis* Lars is dead and the widowed Mrs Lindstrom, with daughter Bess, has taken off for San Francisco to begin a new life, moving in with her late husband's mother, Audrey Dexter,

and Audrey's second husband, Judge Jonathan Dexter. The two US seasons followed Phyllis's painful attempts to adjust to drastically reduced financial circumstances, single-parenthood and a working career that saw her employed as secretarial assistant to a photographer, Julie Erskine, at Erskine's Commercial Photography, and then in Bay Area local government.

As with the other series mentioned above, MTM Enterprises – Mary Tyler Moore's company – produced.

Pickersgill People

UK · BBC · SITCOM

5 × 55 mins · colour

17 Apr–15 May 1978 · BBC2 Mon mostly 9pm

MAIN CAST
see below

CREDITS

writer Mike Stott · *script editor* Michael Wearing · *directors* Alan Dossor (3), Pedr James (2) · *producer* Tara Prem

Comic comings and goings centred on the fictitious northern town of Pickersgill. Each episode looked at a different aspect of life there and so featured a different set of characters, although the police, in the shape of PC Shane Pritchard (Nick Stringer), turned up in a few stories.

Some criticism was levelled at writer Mike Stott for portraying northerners as 'thick' but the series also had its supporters who enjoyed the zany situations and posse of eccentric characters. The casts were strong throughout, with Prunella Scales, Bernard Hill, George Costigan, Matthew Kelly, Richard Wilson, Antony Sher, Philip Jackson, Bryan Pringle, Roger Sloman and Sam Kelly among those appearing.

The Picnic

see **The Two Ronnies**

A Picture Of Innocence

UK · BBC · SITCOM

1 × 30 mins · b/w

9 Nov 1963 · Sat 9.40pm

MAIN CAST

Bette Berry	Patricia Burke
Arthur Berry	Frederick Peisley
Ada Stringer	Marian Spencer
Arnold Slater	Charles Lloyd Pack

CREDITS

writers Harry Driver/Jack Rosenthal · *director* Douglas Argent · *producer* Douglas Moodie

The prolific writing team of Harry Driver and Jack Rosenthal came up with this *Comedy Playhouse* tale of a Preston man, Arthur Berry, whose love of fine art is not shared by his family or friends, and threatens to cause a rift between them. Their insurance collector, Arnold Slater (played by the ever dependable Charles Lloyd Pack), does share Arthur's taste, however.

Pig In The Middle

UK · ITV (LWT) · SITCOM

20 × 30 mins · colour

Series One (7) 27 Jan–9 Mar 1980 · Sun 8.45pm
Series Two (6) 13 Sep–18 Oct 1981 · Sun mostly 8.15pm
Series Three (7) 4 Mar–22 Apr 1983 · Fri 8.30pm

MAIN CAST

Bartholomew ('Barty') Wade · · · · · · · · · · · ·
· · · · · · · · · · · · Dinsdale Landen (series 1);
· · · · · · · · · · · · Terence Brady (series 2 & 3)
Susan Wade · · · · · · · · Joanna Van Gyseghem
Nellie Bligh · · · · · · · · · · · · · Liza Goddard
Andy Trubshaw · · · · · · · · · · · · John Quayle
Alice Boocock · · · · · · · · · Nichola McAuliffe

OTHER APPEARANCES

Mrs Bligh · · · · · · · · · · Eleanor Summerfield

CREDITS

writers Terence Brady/Charlotte Bingham · director/producer Les Chatfield

The marriage of Bartholomew 'Barty' Wade and Susan Wade, no longer thirty-somethings, is proving something of a strain. He is the archetypal little boy turned civil servant who has never quite got around to growing up; she likes to maintain a certain middle-class standard, keeping house and husband trim; between them, they can reel off a list of mutual frustrations as tall as a church spire. Susan also likes to throw parties at their East Sheen (south-west London) home, and it is at one such gathering that Barty meets the easy-going, footloose and freely fanciable Nellie, for whom he falls hook, line and sinker, becoming the title's 'pig in the middle'. He is a celibate one, however, for – while he can fulfil with Nellie all the things that he cannot do with Susan – they do not get into bed.

The three series of this funny sitcom handled well such a farcical juggling act, with Barty, the survivor, usually managing to get out of the scrapes that befall those leading such a triangular life. In the final series Barty finally leaves Susan – even then, he still only moves next door to Nellie – only to find that, now part of a permanent fixture, his new partner adopts some of his ex-wife's most irritating traits, and that the allure of the relationship – being no longer extramarital – had passed.

Terence Brady, co-author of *Pig In The Middle* with wife Charlotte Bingham, appeared in a first-series episode as one of Barty's old school chums but then took over the main role of Barty himself in the second and third runs after Dinsdale Landen declared himself unable to proceed.

The format of *Pig In The Middle* was sold to the American ABC network where it was reworked with substantial plot changes as the 19-episode sitcom *Oh, Madeline*.

The Piglet Files

UK · ITV (LWT) · SITCOM

21 × 30 mins · colour

Series One (7) 7 Sep–19 Oct 1990 · Fri 8pm
Series Two (7) 3 May–14 June 1991 · Fri 8.30pm
Series Three (7) 29 Mar–10 May 1992 · Sun 7.15pm

MAIN CAST

Peter Chapman · · · · · · · · Nicholas Lyndhurst
Major Maurice Drummond · · · · · Clive Francis
Major Maxwell · · · · · · · · · · · John Ringham
Dexter · · · · · · · · · · · · · Michael Percival
Lewis · · · · · · · · · · · · · · · · · Steven Law
Sarah Chapman · · · · · · · · · · · Serena Evans
Trueman · · · · · · · · · · · · · · · Paul Cooper
Flint · · · · · · · · · · · · · · · · · Louise Catt

CREDITS

writers Paul Minett/Brian Leveson · director/producer Robin Carr

A sitcom starring Nicholas Lyndhurst as plain ordinary Peter Chapman, a young electronics whiz and college lecturer at a local polytechnic, who is suddenly recruited by an MI5 supremo, Major Drummond, to teach spies about the espionage equipment they'll be handling. Such is the secrecy surrounding his mission that MI5 prohibits Chapman – given the code-name Piglet – from telling his wife Sarah about his new job. Naturally, with all the cloak-and-dagger manoeuvrings, she assumes that he is having an extramarital affair, and it proves especially difficult for him to persuade her why his life is suddenly revolving in different circles, having their home become an MI5 'safe house' for harbouring defectors, for example.

Television has long thrived on espionage thrillers, but, while many a comedy sketch has sent up the genre, few sitcoms – *Get Smart* being the best-known exception – have used it as the central theme. Like that classic US series, *The Piglet Files* showed the humdrum, humorous and inept side of espionage, far removed from the world of Le Carré novels, with Peter's MI5 colleagues, from the majors to spies Dexter and Lewis, all dunderheads. The series also provided a beefier role for Lyndhurst, no longer a pimply teenage son (*Butterflies*) or a hapless 'plonker' (*Only Fools And Horses*). Here he liked to think of himself as the new 007, getting to shoot guns, fly planes and run the gauntlet of glamorous East German spy women.

LWT enjoyed steady success with three series of *The Piglet Files* whereas it was originally commissioned as a single three-episode mini-series, at which point

Lyndhurst's character was to have been called Peter Lynford.

Pigsty

UK · BBC · CHILDREN'S SITCOM

18 × 10 mins · colour

Series One (9) 10 Sep–5 Nov 1990 · BBC1 Mon 4.25pm
Series Two (9) 9 Sep–4 Nov 1991 · BBC1 Mon 4.25pm

MAIN CAST

Troyboy · · · · · · · · · · · · · Richard Gauntlett
Pinks · · · · · · · · · · · · · · · Tessa Crockett
Little Pig · · · · · · · · · · · · · Peter Mandell
M T · · · · · · · · · · · · · · · · Mark Hadfield

CREDITS

creator/producer Pippa Dyson · writer Paul A Mendelson · director Steven Andrew

A basic children's comedy, with music, set in the Pizza Café, an establishment run by a family of pigs (humans in pig outfits, obviously). The venue catered for human clientele and some of the regulars befriended their porcine hosts, joining in the japery and songs.

Pilgrims Rest

UK · BBC (TIGER ASPECT) · SITCOM

6 × 30 mins · colour

31 July–4 Sep 1997 · BBC1 Thu 8.30pm

MAIN CAST

Bob Payne · · · · · · · · · · · · · · Gary Olsen
Tilly · · · · · · · · · · · · · · · · · Gwen Taylor
Quentin · · · · · · · · · · · · · · Jonathan Aris
Drew Dunstable · · · · · · · · · · · · John Arthur
Didier · · · · · · · · · · · · · · · Pierre Forest
Ronnie Barrett · · · · · · · · · · · · Jay Simpson
Pamela · · · · · · · · · · · · · · · Nina Young
Mo Grant · · · · · · · · Michael Fenton Stevens

CREDITS

creator Bernard McKenna · writers Bernard McKenna (2), Simon Block (2), Paul Mayhew-Archer (2) · director Gareth Carrivick · producer Mark Chapman

The formidable talents of comedy actors Gary Olsen and Gwen Taylor combined for this series that centred around the comings and goings at a transport café. It was Taylor's second new BBC sitcom of the year, following *A Perfect State*.

Olsen played Bob Payne, a former rock and roll roadie who, some six years previously, bought Pilgrims Restaurant, a thriving Kent truck-stop. A £50,000 loan from his sister Tilly (married to a successful Mancunian businessman) helped pay for the joint – she willingly put up the money because the place seemed a good investment and likely to settle her flaky brother. But one year after the purchase a new by-pass took most of the traffic away from the road and the café's customers went with it; subsequently, it fell into decline and only managed to stay open thanks to the patronage of a few dogged regulars. The most obvious visual pointer to the deterioration was the malfunctioning neon roof sign which should have read Pilgrims Restaurant but mostly said 'Pilgrims Rest' (thus the series' title) and, variously, 'grim Rest', 'pigs aunt' and other words accrued by illuminating only certain letters. (This device was also used for the opening shots of *Fawlty Towers*.)

Despite all this, Bob seems happy enough with his business: he's hardly money-motivated and his ambitions lie elsewhere – in his low-key pursuit of the café's beautiful antipodean waitress Pamela, for instance. But then Tilly arrives on the scene. Her husband Duncan has ditched her, causing her to lose their house, her income and all of her belongings, and now she wants to recoup her £50,000 loan from Bob. Naturally, he cannot pay it; Tilly insists he sell the café but then relents, anticipating the problems this would cause her brother, who would probably end up living with her anyway. So she decides to stay on at Pilgrims Restaurant while she gets her life back on track, the clashes between brother and sister forming the basis for the storylines.

The café's regular customers were policeman Drew Dunstable (Constable Dunstable) and his academic and keen new cop partner Quentin; wide-boy cab driver Ronnie; French trucker Didier; and a suave businessman, Mo, who, much to Bob's chagrin, hopes to rekindle a romance with Pamela. She causes most of the male pulses to quicken, not least with stories of her other job: a nude model at the local college where she is a part-time student. Tilly's errant husband Duncan (played by John Duttine) turned up in the final episode.

Given a distinct American look, *Pilgrims Rest* had likeable characters and a fine, believable location, but for all its plus-points it distinctly failed to spark. The potential was there, and a second series – should there be one – might yet consolidate the good ideas and make the show a going concern.

The Pink Medicine Show

UK · ITV (LWT) · SKETCH

6 × 30 mins · colour

9 June–14 July 1978 · Fri 7.30pm

MAIN CAST

Chris Beetles
Rob Buckman
Lynda Bellingham
Nickolas Grace
Peter John

CREDITS

writers Chris Beetles, Rob Buckman · *director/producer* Paul Smith

Young medical doctors turned humorists Chris Beetles and Rob Buckman collated

dozens of short sketch ideas and wrote this series that took an irreverent view of their practise; typical skits showed what happened to Rudyard Kipling's poetry when his tonsils were removed, and the workings of the Maurice Chevalier School Of Surgery. The two writers also performed their work, assisted by, among others, the fast-rising young actress Lynda Bellingham.

Pinkerton's Progress

UK · BBC · SITCOM

6 × 30 mins · colour

18 May–22 June 1983 · BBC2 Wed 9pm

MAIN CAST

Mr Pinkerton	Geoffrey Whitehead
Miss Shilling	Eleanor Bron
Mr Renfrew	Michael Elwyn
Mr Davies	Clive Merrison
Mr Beech	Derek Francis
Mr Flax	Alan Parnaby
Mr Parsons	David Sibley
Bursar	Paul Hardwick
Mr Clifford	Andrew Robertson
Headmaster Grinwell	Derek Farr

CREDITS

writer Charles McKeown · *director* John B Hobbs · *producer* Gareth Gwenlan

A school-based sitcom centring on the masters of Lyttleton Old School. Geoffrey Whitehead was cast as Pinkerton, the newly arrived Deputy Head who soon realises that the establishment is run solely for the benefit of the teachers and not the pupils. He sets about trying to bring an end to this situation, determined that the school should not be run for the masters *or*, for that matter, the pupils, but for Pinkerton himself.

The plots unfolded mostly in the teachers' staff room, where the school politics were fought and schemes hatched. Pinkerton often had to juggle the egos and ambitions of his colleagues in order to maintain peace and a sense of balance, albeit one that weighed in his favour. Meanwhile, Miss Shilling (Eleanor Bron) was the object of the lustful attentions of both Mr Davies and Mr Renfrew, a situation that proved another obstacle to Pinkerton's progress.

Pinwright's Progress

UK · BBC · SITCOM

10 × 30 mins · b/w

29 Nov 1946–16 May 1947 · fortnightly Fri around 9pm

MAIN CAST

Mr J Pinwright	James Hayter
Aubrey	Clarence Wright
Miss Doolittle	Sara Gregory
Miss Peabody	Daphne Maddox
Mrs Sigsbee	Doris Palmer
Ralph	Leonard Sharp
Salesman	Charles Irwin

CREDITS

writer Rodney Hobson · *script editor* Ted Kavanagh · *producer* John Glyn-Jones

British television's first authentic half-hour situation comedy series.

Mr J Pinwright (played by James Hayter) is the proprietor of the smallest multiple-store in the world, Macgillygally's Stores. He has a pretty daughter and a hated rival, and his difficulties are increased by his staff's irritating efforts to be helpful (one of the staff, the outrageous Mrs Sigsbee, was like an early version of Mrs Slocombe from *Are You Being Served?*). Further complications arose through the inadequacies of Ralph, a deaf, octogenarian messenger boy.

Ted Kavanagh, writer of the highly esteemed BBC radio series *It's That Man Again* (fondly abbreviated to *ITMA*) edited the scripts for writer Rodney Hobson.

Pirates

UK · BBC (CHILDSPLAY PRODUCTIONS) · CHILDREN'S SITCOM

24 × 25 mins · colour

Series One (5) 6 Oct–3 Nov 1994 · BBC1 Thu 4.35pm

Special · 22 Dec 1994 · BBC1 Thu 4.30pm

Series Two (6) 4 Oct–8 Nov 1995 · BBC1 Wed 4.35pm

Series Three (12) 18 Mar–6 May 1997; 5 Aug–26 Aug 1997 · BBC1 Tue 4.35pm

MAIN CAST

Lawrence Kitten	Benjamin Rennis
Helen Kitten	Debby Bishop
Gran (Abigail Blood)	Liz Smith
Roger Bones	Paul Bown
Lambkin Bones	Hayley Elliot
Man-In-The-Sack	Toby Sedgwick (movement director series 1); Paul Filipiak (from series 2)
Mr Neville Jones/ Basmati Bill	Andrew Sachs
Mrs Mildred Jones	June Brown (series 1); Jillie Meers (from series 2)
Grog Blossom Kate	Rebecca Stevens (from series 2)

OCCASIONAL APPEARANCES

Jill Crutchworthy	Helen Lederer
Molly Blood	Buffy Davis (series 2)

CREDITS

writers Rebecca Stevens/Peter Tabern (18), Rebecca Stevens/Matthew Tabern/Peter Tabern (1), David Freeman/Alan Gilbey/Peter Tabern (2), Matthew Tabern/Peter Tabern (1), Michael Malaghan/Matthew Tabern/Peter Tabern (2) · *executive producers* Albert Barber, Jeremy Swan · *directors* Peter Tabern (series 1–2), John Hay (series 3) · *producer* Peter Tabern

A swashbuckling fantasy comedy in which a family of pirates turned into landlubbers when they moved into a normal house in the twee town of Little-Wheedling-In The-Vale.

After the move, said pirates, the Bones family, continue to live their life exactly as if they were still plundering on the high seas: firing cannons, flying the Skull And Crossbones, making captives walk the plank, and so on. The Bones are an all-round odd bunch, comprising handsome ladies' man Roger; his eccentric mother-in-law, the pistol-packing and sword-wielding Abigail Blood, who goes around with a parrot, Pustule, on her shoulder; Lambkin Bones, Roger's daughter, a youngster being brought up on pirate ways; Man-In-The-Sack, their willing servant who is, literally, a man in a sack; and a baby, a hideous green-skinned violent creature who remains unseen within a pram.

The Bones' arrival causes mixed reactions among the neighbours in their suburban cul-de-sac. Next-door single mum Helen Kitten and her son Lawrence welcome them: the youngster is glad to play with Lambkin and Helen begins a romance with Roger. But, from across the road, Mr and Mrs Jones take a very different view: Mrs Jones, head of the local community group, worries about the piratical carryings-on, and Mr Jones has to fend off the attentions of Abigail, given that he is a dead-ringer for her old flame Basmati Bill (who does eventually turn up in the story, played by Andrew Sachs). In the second series, co-writer Rebecca Stevens joined the cast as the hygienically-challenged Grog Blossom Kate. Also appearing occasionally were Roger's estranged wife, the awful Molly, mother of Lambkin and the hideous baby; and the health visitor Jill Crutchworthy (Helen Lederer).

It all added up to anarchic and surreal fun for younger viewers, with an impressive cast and an equally strong roster of special guest stars, including 'Lily Savage', Patrick Barlow, Windsor Davies, Roger Sloman, Charlotte Cornwall, Nicholas Parsons, Tony Slattery, Michael Elphick and Pauline McLynn.

'Pity Poor Edie ... Married To Him'

UK · ITV (LWT) · SITCOM

1 × 30 mins · b/w

17 May 1969 · Sat 7.30pm

MAIN CAST

Alec Hentill · · · · · · · · · · · · · · · · · Milo O'Shea
Edie Hentill · · · · · · · · · · · · · Gwendolyn Watts

CREDITS

writers Ray Galton/Alan Simpson · director/producer David Askey

Another in the series of individual comedies presented under the banner of *The Galton & Simpson Comedy*. This one starred Milo O'Shea and Gwendolyn Watts as a married couple, with the woman being the breadwinner.

The Plan

UK · BBC · SITCOM

1 × 30 mins · b/w

2 Nov 1963 · Sat 9.50pm

MAIN CAST

Albert Fawkes · · · · · · · · · · · · · Peter Cushing
Seamus McMichael · · · · · · · · · P G Stephens
Lieutenant Mills · · · · · · · · · · · · Graham Stark
Captain Hawkins · · · · · · · · Francis Matthews

CREDITS

writers Richard Harris/Dennis Spooner · producer Sydney Lotterby

A *Comedy Playhouse* offering from Richard Harris and Dennis Spooner, both of whom went on to become closely associated with action-drama TV series. This perhaps explains the somewhat dramatic plot of *The Plan*, which, in hindsight at least, seems to have employed a rather dubious subject for a comedy. Peter Cushing played Albert Fawkes, a man who – teased to breaking point by the historic significance of his name – decides to retaliate by repeating the gun-powder plot and blowing up the present-day Houses of Parliament, enlisting as his assistant a former IRA bomber, Seamus McMichael. Needless to say, no series followed.

Planet Mirth

UK · ITV (CARLTON/SCI-FI CHANNEL) · SKETCH

*19 × 30 mins · colour

14 Aug–18 Dec 1997 · Thu around 1am

MAIN CAST

Emma Kennedy
Rudy Lickwood
Milton Jones
Ben Moor

CREDITS

writers cast and Debbie Barham, Matt Bell, Paul Chronnell, Nathan Cockerill, Richard Easter, Dan Evans, Ash Friedlein, Miles Moss, Dan O'Brien · script editor Andrew Whelan · director Andrew Nicholson · executive producer Nick Symons · producer Fiona Jennison

A sci-fi-themed sketch show featuring standup comics Milton Jones and Rudy Lickwood, and actor/writers Emma Kennedy and Ben Moor. Regular set pieces and characters were mixed alongside more traditional one-off sketches. Recurring segments included spoof galactic breakfast show *Every Single Morning*, in which viewers from other planets phoned in with their problems; the adventures of four mismatched people on a space caravan holiday; alien beings manipulating Earthlings in a bizarre game of Earth Invaders; and a documentary slot focusing on Susan Snape, a Venusian stranded on Earth at the age of two and who is still trying to adjust to life here.

Using sketch shows to introduce screen and writing talent is a tried-and-tested method of breeding new generations of programme creators, and so is commendable, but *Planet Mirth*, for all its undoubted good intentions, was fairly hopeless. The series looked like it was made on a shoestring budget (almost certainly a reflection of the truth), and sketches were often overlong or badly focused and sometimes seemed to lack a humorous centre altogether. The four cast members struggled as best they could with the thin material but they couldn't save this show from being, frankly, a waste of space.

*Note. Although the series was intended to run for 20 editions, only 19 had been screened by London-area ITV by 31 December 1997.

The Plank

see SYKES, Eric

Platypus Man

USA · UPN (FANARO-NATHAN PRODUCTIONS/ PARAMOUNT) · SITCOM

13 × 30 mins · colour

US dates: 23 Jan–15 May 1995

UK dates: 5 Aug 1997–4 Sep 1997 (13 episodes) BBC2 various weekdays 12.05am

MAIN CAST

Richard Jeni · · · · · · · · · · · · · · · · · · himself
Lou Golembiewski · · · · · · · · · · · Ron Orbach
Paige McAllister · · · · · · · · · · · Denise Miller
Tommy Jeni · · · · · · · · · · · · · David Dundara
Vern Tuttle · · · · · · · · · · · · · · Ethan Phillips

CREDITS

creators/executive producers Barry Fanaro/Mort Nathan · writers various · script supervisor Susan Harris · directors various · producers Marica Govons, Michael Rotenberg

Another example of a standup comedian turning his stage routine into a sitcom – *à la Roseanne*, *Seinfeld* and *All-American Girl* – Richard Jeni's *Platypus Man* stage-show was filmed by HBO and screened by the US cable channel in January 1993. Basically, the thrust of the piece was the dating problems experienced by a single male in a city. Jeni coined the term Platypus Man because (he claimed) the Platypus 'lives alone, is short-legged, and tries to mate a lot but can't', a description that pretty much summed up his own situation.

In the series – screened by one of the new networks on US television, Paramount's UPN – Jeni portrayed a cable-TV-channel chef, hosting a 'cooking show for morons', aided by the dull Vern Tuttle. Jeni spends much of his spare time hanging out at the bar where his brother Tommy works, and where he meets his friend Lou. The other regular cast member was Jeni's female neighbour, Paige, a former pro golfer who has become a sportswriter and seems to have as much trouble dating as Jeni. The obvious solution, of course, would be for the two of them to hook up, but in this particular corner of sitcomland the obvious isn't always done, and they remain just good friends.

The series was easy to watch but offered few surprises and became somewhat repetitious. Jeni acquitted himself reasonably well but Denise Miller, as Paige, was the one who really caught the eye.

Playing For Real

UK · BBC · COMEDY SERIAL

6 × 45 mins · colour
29 July–2 Sep 1988 · BBC1 Fri 9.30pm

MAIN CAST

Chrissie Buchan ········· Patricia Kerrigan
Sam Montgomery ··········· Alec Heggie
Dougie Kemp ··············· Jake D'Arcy
Mo Maconachie ············· Iain Andrew
Bern McAvennie ·········· David Meldrew
Toni Rossi ··············· Lawrie McNicol
Perry Gilbert-Walker ········· Sandy Welch
Agnes Buchan ············· Anne Kristen
Teresa Kelly ············· Juliet Cadzow
Elton Trelford ············ Michael Garner

CREDITS

writers Julie Welch (4), Graham Baird (1), Daniel Boyle (1) · director Jim Hill · producer Tim Aspinall

A BBC Scotland comedy series set in the pulsating world of Subutteo football. Upon the death of Billy Buchan – 'the Bill Shankly of table football' – the battle begins to see who will replace him as player/manager of Real Falkirk, the table-football club that he founded and controlled. But his would-be successors have reckoned without Billy's daughter, Chrissie, who returns from London to claim the spot as hers. At first there is strong opposition from her male-chauvinist rivals but Chrissie's fabulous finger-flicking skills quickly win them over and soon she is in the forefront of the team that, in the words of journalist Elton Trelford from *Subutteo Scene* magazine, 'are dragging what is no longer a kid's pastime kicking and screaming into the 20th-century'. With the aid of her favourite player, a miniature Charlie Nicholas (complete with earring), Chrissie leads Real Falkirk on a glorious cup run against the likes of the all-women Cosmopolitan Manchester and the mighty Ajax Ramsgate.

The sportswriter Julie Welch set up the situation and wrote four of the episodes, neatly bringing a female perspective to this predominantly (though not exclusively) male recreation. The series was meant to be played entirely for laughs but when the director and producer went on research missions to meet real table-top fanatics and attend their matches, they realised that those involved, although having a sense of humour, took the game deadly seriously. Reflecting this, the scripts embraced some dramatic elements, although they maintained the humorous irony

that the table game is but a microcosm of professional soccer played on grass.

The Play's The Thing

see The Leeds series

Plaza Patrol

UK · ITV (YORKSHIRE) · SITCOM

6 × 30 mins · colour
15 July–19 Aug 1991 · Mon 7pm

MAIN CAST

Bernard Cooney ········· Tommy Cannon
Trevor Purvis ············· Bobby Ball

CREDITS

writers Richard Lewis/Louis Robinson · director/producer Graham Wetherell

Having played a couple of dozy coppers in the feature film *The Boys In Blue*, Cannon and Ball moved into sitcom territory here, cast as dozy night-security men at a shopping mall, Margaret Thatcher Plaza, in a series created especially for them. Cooney was a hard worker with brains, Purvis was hopeless and without, and the bosses at H&L Security were rarely pleased with their results.

Although tailored for their audience, Cannon and Ball's antics once again came across as third-class Abbott and Costello, or tenth-class Laurel and Hardy, and the six episodes were woefully predictable stuff. Even allowing for variations in public taste, how did ITV bosses think the public would wear it?

Please, Sir!

UK · ITV (LWT) · SITCOM

57 episodes (46 × 30 mins · colour; 7 × 45 mins · b/w; 2 × 30 mins · b/w; 2 × short specials · colour)

Series One (7 × 45 mins · b/w) 8 Nov–20 Dec 1968 · Fri mostly 8.30pm

*Series Two (13 × 30 mins · colour) 20 Sep–13 Dec 1969 · Sat 7.30pm

Short special (colour) · part of *All-Star Comedy Carnival* 25 Dec 1969 · Thu 6pm

Series Three (12 × 30 mins · colour · 1 × 30 mins · b/w) 20 Sep–13 Dec 1970 · Sun 7.25pm

Special (30 mins · b/w) 27 Dec 1970 · Sun 7.25pm

Series Four (21 × 30 mins · colour) 18 Sep 1971–13 Feb 1972 · Sat mostly 6.30pm then Sun 7.25pm

Short special (colour) · part of *Mike And Bernie Winters' All-Star Christmas Comedy Carnival* 25 Dec 1971 · Sat 6.05pm

MAIN CAST

STAFF:
Bernard Hedges ············ John Alderton
Norman Potter ············· Deryck Guyler
Mr Morris Cromwell ········· Noel Howlett
Doris Ewell ············· Joan Sanderson
Mr Price ············· Richard Davies
Mr Smith ················· Erik Chitty

Mr Sibley ············· Lindsay Campbell
Penny Wheeler/Hedges ········ Jill Kerman
·············· (series 3 & 1970 special)
Gregory Dix ····· Glynn Edwards (1971–72)
David Ffitchett-Brown ····· Richard Warwick
························· (1971–72)
Miss Petting ···· Vivienne Martin (1971–72)

PUPILS:
Peter Craven ············· Malcolm McFee
····················· (to end 1970)
Eric Duffy ······· Peter Cleall (to end 1970)
Maureen Bullock ············ Liz Gebhardt
····················· (to end 1970)
Sharon Eversleigh ········· Penny Spencer
····················· (to end 1970)
Frankie Abbott ··· David Barry (to end 1970)
Dennis Dunstable ··········· Peter Denyer
····················· (to end 1970)
Gobber ········· Charles Bolton (1971–72)
Terry Stringer ···· Barry McCarthy (1971–72)
Des ············· Billy Hamon (1971–72)
Celia ············· Drina Pavlovic (1971–72)
Daisy ········· Rosemary Faith (1971–72)

CREDITS

creators John Esmonde/Bob Larbey · writers John Esmonde/Bob Larbey (45), Geoff Rowley/Andy Baker (7), Tony Bilbow (5) · directors Mark Stuart (29 & first two specials), Howard Ross (11 & 1971 special), Alan Wallis (5) other episodes unaccredited · executive producer Mark Stuart (1971–72) · producers Mark Stuart (all episodes to Dec 1970), Philip Casson (8), other episodes unaccredited

Complicated it was not – rowdy it certainly was – but *Please, Sir!* was the top ITV sitcom in its time. Created by Esmonde and Larbey, it starred John Alderton as Bernard Hedges, a happy naïf whose first job as a newly qualified teacher is at a tough south London school, Fenn Street Secondary Modern. Here he is handed the daunting task of being the form teacher for the ineducable Class 5C, a mob of rowdy, unruly adolescent boys and startlingly mature mini-skirted young women. Hedges – wittily nicknamed 'Privet' by the kids – soon finds his lofty idealism blunted. Whether the writers were influenced by the 1967 movie *To Sir With Love* is not known; what is known is that they went to school together in south London and the experience was sufficiently fresh in their memory to create a comedy in the same surroundings.

Most of the *Please, Sir!* action took place in the classroom and the staffroom, where, in this latter location, there was enmity and/or a sense of beleaguered exhaustion and resignation among the staff. Among Hedges' colleagues at Fenn Street were Morris Cromwell, the well-meaning but vapid headmaster; Doris Ewell, his formidable but smarmy assistant; the decrepit sports master Smith; and the canny Welsh maths and science teacher Price. The real power, though, was held by the school janitor, Potter, a former Desert Rat who put the protection of his own back before all else.

Neatly bridging the gap between *Blackboard Jungle* and **Whack-O!**, *Please, Sir!* was a remarkably popular series. Frank Muir (then LWT Head of Entertainment) deserved applause for casting John Alderton in the lead role (this was as a result of Alderton's appearance as a teacher in the opening episode of **Never A Cross Word**) and the actor never looked back from here. Further, although 56 when the series began, Joan Sanderson's career blossomed as a result of *Please, Sir!*, as did Deryck Guyler's, who, incidentally, was originally cast in the role of the headmaster. (Guyler and Sanderson had appeared together in a Spring 1968 Esmonde and Larbey sitcom for BBC radio, *You're Only Old Once*.) Ironically, it was the 5C pupils who failed to shine beyond the confines of Esmonde and Larbey's scripts. Most were actually in their early 20s when the series began (which is why they looked like the most developed fifth-formers you'd ever seen), and when they finally left school (oddly, at Christmas time) most went immediately into a sequel, **The Fenn Street Gang**. Beyond that, little was heard of the young actors, most going into writing or the theatre and some leaving the profession altogether.

The Fenn Street Gang marked a turning point in the fortunes of *Please, Sir!* The first *Fenn* series ran simultaneously with the last of *PS!* (indeed there was considerable character swapping between the two) and Esmonde and Larbey were at full stretch to script all of the episodes; eventually they handed a dozen *Please, Sir!* programmes over to other writers. With the old 5C disbanded, new pupils were brought into the cast but they did not capture the viewers as before. Worse, John Alderton wanted out. His character, Hedges, had become engaged to Penny Wheeler during the third series and they were married in the 1970 Christmas special; now he was written out (appearing in three episodes of *The Fenn Street Gang* and two of the final series of *Please, Sir!* before doing so) to take a year's course in sociology. He too was replaced but, again, the formula that had made the series so successful was now lost, and the series somewhat fizzled out from here, the final episode seeing the perpetual spinster Miss Ewell marrying Mr Sibley.

In addition to spawning *The Fenn Street Gang* (which, in itself, begat **Bowler**), there was a *Please, Sir!* feature film released to cinemas in 1971. All the usual cast appeared, Esmonde and Larbey wrote the script and Mark Stuart directed. Then, in 1975, a series titled **Welcome Back, Kotter** was unveiled on American TV, depicting the stories of a teacher struggling to maintain control over a class of rough, tough but funny kids in a Brooklyn school. The parallels between this series and *Please, Sir!* were

obvious but the US producers did not acknowledge the British predecessor and it was impossible for anyone to prove otherwise.

*Note. The second series of *Please, Sir!* straddled ITV's switch from black and white to colour transmissions, the first eight episodes being screened in monochrome, the remaining five in colour. They were all made in colour, however, as subsequent repeats proved.

Pleasure At Her Majesty's

see The Amnesty Galas

Plum's Plots And Plans

UK · BBC · CHILDREN'S SITCOM

3 × 30 mins · colour

9 Dec–23 Dec 1977 · BBC1 Fri 4.40pm

MAIN CAST

Cornelius Plum	Arthur Howard
Major Huffin	Aubrey Woods
Dr Pretzel	William Hootkins

CREDITS

creator Kay King · *writer* Peter Robinson · *director* Jeremy Swan · *executive producer* Anna Home

The crackpot adventures of the well-meaning schemer Cornelius Plum and his hopeless assistants Major Huffin and Dr Pretzel. A short-lived series for children in the mould of another wacky threesome, *The Goodies*.

Police Squad

USA · ABC (PARAMOUNT) · SITCOM

6 × 30 mins · colour

US dates: 4 Mar–8 Apr 1982

*UK dates: 5 Oct–2 Nov 1985 (5 episodes) ITV Sat around 1am

MAIN CAST

Det Frank Drebin	Leslie Nielsen
Capt Ed Hocken	Alan North
Ted Olsen	Ed Williams
Shoe-shine Johnny the Snitch	William Duell

CREDITS

creators/executive producers Jim Abrahams/David Zucker/Jerry Zucker · *writers* Tino Insana/Robert L Wuhl (2), Nancy Steen/Neil Thompson (2), Patrick Proft (1), Jim Abrahams/David Zucker/Jerry Zucker (1) · *directors* Joe Dante (2), Georg Stanford Brown (1), Paul Krasny (1), Reza S Badiyi (1), Jim Abrahams/David Zucker/Jerry Zucker (1)

A cut-glass gem of a comedy series that ran for just six episodes but which launched an incredibly successful string of movies.

Creators Abrahams, Zucker and Zucker (the last two are brothers) first came to prominence with a film version of their successful *Kentucky Fried Theatre* touring stage revue. *Kentucky Fried Movie* (1977) was a high-quality collection of sketches, many of which employed film and TV genres as

targets. They followed it with the zany disaster-movie spoof *Airplane!* (1980), in which well-known actors played their roles deadly straight while the most lunatic things happened around them. The most deadpan of them all was the star, Leslie Nielsen, a Canadian who had worked in the business for many years but, hitherto, always as a second-string. He was so good in *Airplane!* that the team kept him on board for their next project, the TV series *Police Squad*, which – employing the same anything-goes, scatter-gun mixture of bizarre verbal jokes and outrageous visual gags – resulted in six miniature masterpieces of classy comedy.

Police Squad was a spoof on TV cop shows – not the more trendy, modern shows of the period like *Starsky And Hutch*, but the classic police procedural series of the past, such as *Dragnet*, *Highway Patrol* and, in particular, Lee Marvin's *M Squad* (1957–60). Nielsen starred as Frank Drebin, a plain-clothes detective of indeterminate rank who worked a precinct in a 'large American city'. His boss was Captain Ed Hocken, a veteran officer; other regulars were forensic scientist Ted Olsen (who had a dubious fascination with young boys) and a shoe-shine man, Johnny, a remarkable font-of-all-knowledge who, for a fee, spilled all he knew to Drebin. Johnny seemed to know everything about everything, and as Drebin arrived to ask him for information, the shoe-shiner would be slipping knowledge to other people in their walks of life too, giving complicated structural information to a fireman about to enter a blazing building, offering vital surgical advice to a doctor about to perform an operation, and so on. Such recurring jokes littered *Police Squad*: the show's opening title, given on screen, was always different to the one being announced; Drebin was a terrible driver, never failing to knock over dustbins; and the final frame-freeze, so typical of US crime dramas, was not a freeze-frame at all but a period in which the actors had to remain completely motionless in the middle of whatever they were doing, no matter how painful or awkward the consequences. Best of all, though, was the series' treatment of guest stars (traditional in every US TV crime show): in each episode a famous face appeared only to be killed off in the opening pre-credit sequence. (The six victims were Lorne Greene, Georg Stanford Brown, Robert Goulet, William Shatner, Florence Henderson and William Conrad.)

Leslie Nielsen was an inspired choice as Drebin, turning in the same level and style of performance he had employed years before in genuine police shows such as *The New Breed* and *The Protectors*. But, despite its brilliance, *Police Squad* was soon off the air. Its cancellation was partly explained by an ABC programming executive, who claimed that the show required 'too much attention' from viewers. He had a point (*up* to a point) – *Police Squad* episodes were indeed stuffed full of blink-and-you'll-miss-them sight gags and clever dialogue, but those viewers who were able to concentrate were amply rewarded. The cancellation of the series is a real indictment of where US TV was at in the early 1980s.

Fortunately, the story didn't end there. In 1988, Abrahams, Zucker and Zucker resurrected the premise for a feature film, *The Naked Gun: From The Files Of Police Squad*, which re-introduced Drebin (now officially a Lieutenant). Ed Williams returned as Ted Olsen and George Kennedy took the role of Captain Hocken. The movie was a monster hit and demonstrated that, just as good TV shows can lead to bad movies (witness *Car 54, Where Are You?*), so failed TV shows can lead to successful movies. The enormous revenue generated by the film led to a pair of sequels, *The Naked Gun 2½: The Smell Of Fear* (1991) and *The Naked Gun 33⅓: The Final Insult* (1994), both being major box-office winners. The movies made Nielsen a bankable star, and he professed himself more than happy with his new 'comedy-icon' status, even though it undermined his ability to return to straight acting.

*Note. Some ITV regions screened the series in March 1983, but in this first run only five of the six episodes were shown in the London-area. The omitted episode ('Revenge And Remorse') finally turned up when BBC2, nationally, re-ran the full set of six from 7 September to 12 October 1989. Subsequently, BBC2 has screened all half-dozen episodes on several further occasions.

A Policeman's Lot

see SYKES, Eric

Pookiesnackenburger In …

UK · C4 (AFTER IMAGE) · MUSICAL HUMOUR
5 × 30 mins · colour
4 Apr–2 May 1985 · Thu 9pm
MAIN CAST
Pookiesnackenburger (Sue Bradley, Paul Clare, Luke Cresswell, Nick Dwyer, John Helmer, Steve McNicholas)

CREDITS
writers cast · *producers* Jane Thorburn, Mark Lucas, Anne McGeoch

Five programmes of scripted prose and musical zaniness – each pursuing a different comedic idea. All of the material was written, composed and performed by Pookiesnackenburger, a six-piece group of musical entertainers, with the emphasis on comedy, who formed in Brighton in 1981 and were 'discovered' while busking in Covent

Garden, London, a year later. (The name Pookiesnackenburger was coined after a character heard by the band on a compilation album of 1960s American radio recordings.)

Twelve months in the making, the series was commissioned by C4 after the group had taken part in lively 'filler' items in 1983.

Poor Little Rich Girls

UK · ITV (GRANADA) · SITCOM
7 × 30 mins · colour
12 July–23 Aug 1984 · Thu 9pm
MAIN CAST
Daisy Troop · · · · · · · · · · · · · · Jill Bennett
Kate Codd · · · · · · · · · · · · · · · Maria Aitken
Dave Roberts · · · · · · · · · · · · Richard Walker
Larry Codd · · · · · · · · · · · · · Lewis Fiander
Lady Harriet · · · · · · · · · · · · · · Joan Hickson

CREDITS
writer Charles Laurence · *director* Nicholas Ferguson · *producer* Pieter Rogers

Maria Aitken and Jill Bennett – established stars of the theatre, and personal friends – concocted the idea for *Poor Little Rich Girls* over lunch, and it was brought to the screen by Granada in a classy, adult presentation that tried to score with wit and sophistication rather than easy laughs; although it was mostly shot in the studio, there was no audience.

Kate Codd (Aitken) and Daisy Troop (Bennett) are cousins who haven't met for 15 years but decide to spend some time together following the death of Daisy's husband and the hostile divorce Kate has just endured from her second husband, Larry. Each woman believes the other to be affluent, with Kate considering Daisy 'England's answer to Jackie Onassis'. The truth, however, is that both are virtually penniless – save for the £3000 a year each receives from their grandfather's trust fund – and Kate is holed up in a pleasant but inglorious basement flat in Manchester. Three times married, three times widowed (her last husband, Gerald, lost their fortune before being trampled to death by a giraffe), and once a countess, Daisy likes to play the wide-eyed little-girl-lost routine, looking out for husband number four and a swift return to the first-class travel and champagne life to which she aspires.

The nub of the series was that, despite their differences, the two cousins found comfort and refuge in each other's presence, and set about rebuilding their lives. Joan Hickson appeared in several episodes as Lady Harriet and Richard Walker played the part of Kate's reliable friend Dave Roberts, a builder and decorator who lived in a flat at the bottom of the garden.

Poppy And Her

see *Maggie And Her*

Porkpie

UK · C4 (HUMPHREY BARCLAY PRODUCTIONS) · SITCOM
12 × 30 mins · colour
Series One (6) 13 Nov–18 Dec 1995 · Mon 8.30pm
Series Two (6) 22 Aug–26 Sep 1996 · Thu 8.30pm
MAIN CAST
Augustus Neapolitan Cleveland 'Porkpie'
Grant · · · · · · · · · · · · · · · Ram John Holder
Benji · · · · · · · · · · · · · · · · Derek Griffiths
Leone · · · · · · · · · · · · · · · Llewella Gideon
Michael Ambrose · · · · · · · · · · · Geff Francis
Mandy Ambrose · · · · · · · · · · Matilda Thorpe
Aloysius · · · · · · · · · Robbie Tucker (series 1)
Susu · · · · · · · · · · Mona Hammond (series 2)

CREDITS
creator/writer Trix Worrell · *director* Charles Lauder · *executive producers* Al Mitchell, Trix Worrell · *producers* Humphrey Barclay (series 1), Paulette Randall (series 2)

A series of his own for 'Porkpie' Grant, one of the regulars in the barber-shop sitcom *Desmond's*. In the opening episode, lollipop-man Porkpie is finding life tough and lonely, but winning the £10m jackpot on the brand new National Lottery changes everything and he moves out of his high-rise council tower block and into a spacious cottage. The rest of the series looked at how the sudden influx of such a huge sum of money affected the life of the likeable rascal, who, although fit and healthy, was the first to admit that he was past his prime.

On hand to offer Porkpie advice and friendship were Desmond's son Michael (once again played by Geff Francis), who was transfixed by the thought of all that loot, and his less mercenary wife Mandy. Then there was Benji, a stranger with a dubious past whom Porkpie befriended and employed as a general factotum. Finally (joining the cast halfway through the first series) there was Leone, a sprightly, talkative maid with a neat line in sarcasm. Together they comprised a new, surrogate family for Porkpie, who came to realise that (with the possible exception of Michael) their genuine friendship was worth more than the money he had won.

Although used to being careful with money, Porkpie often showed his generosity with his new-found wealth, his most extravagant gesture being to finance a Brixton community centre in tribute to his old friend Desmond. In the second series, Porkpie returned from a Caribbean cruise to be confronted by his childhood sweetheart, Susu, who soon worked her way back into his affections. Eventually Benji found romance too, of a sort, with Leone.

With *Porkpie*, the writer Trix Worrell demonstrated once again his talent for inventing likeable larger-than-life characters and for striking a credible balance between accent and patois within the dialogue. Although, regrettably, it tended toward the inclusion of simplistic moralising, *Porkpie* was nevertheless unassuming, easy-going, good entertainment.

Porridge

UK · BBC · SITCOM

21 episodes (19 × 30 mins · 1 × 45 mins · 1 × 40 mins) · colour

Pilot · 1 Apr 1973 · BBC2 Sun 8.15pm

Series One (6) 5 Sep–10 Oct 1974 · BBC1 Thu 8.30pm

Series Two (6) 24 Oct–28 Nov 1975 · BBC1 Fri 8.30pm

Special (45 mins) 24 Dec 1975 · BBC1 Wed 8.25pm

Special (40 mins) 24 Dec 1976 · BBC1 Fri 8pm

Series Three (6) 18 Feb–25 Mar 1977 · BBC1 Fri 8.30pm

MAIN CAST

Norman Fletcher · · · · · · · · · · Ronnie Barker
Lennie Godber · · · · · · · · Richard Beckinsale
Mr MacKay · · · · · · · · · · · · · Fulton Mackay
Mr Barrowclough · · · · · · · · · · · Brian Wilde

OTHER APPEARANCES

'Blanco' · · · · · · · · · · · · · · · · David Jason
Heslop · · · · · · · · · · · · · · · Brian Glover
Ives · · · · · · · · · · · · · · · · · Ken Jones
'Lukewarm' · · · · · · · · · Christopher Biggins
Harris · · · · · · · · · · · · · · · Ronald Lacey
Governor · · · · · · · · · · · Michael Barrington
McLaren · · · · · · · · · · · · · · · Tony Osoba
Harry Grout · · · · · · · · · · · · Peter Vaughan
Warren · · · · · · · · · · · · · · · · Sam Kelly
'Gay' Gordon · · · · · · · · · · · Felix Bowness
Ingrid Fletcher · · · · · · · · · · · Patricia Brake

CREDITS

writers Dick Clement/Ian La Frenais · *producer* Sydney Lotterby

The first episode of Ronnie Barker's *Comedy Playhouse*-like **Seven Of One** introduced the northern shopkeeper Arkwright, who went on to become a firm TV favourite in **Open All Hours**. But the following week's edition, *Prisoner And Escort*, provided viewers with their first sight of the Londoner lag Norman Stanley Fletcher, who accrued an even greater popularity. Fletcher was a marvellous creation – a bona-fide TV comedy icon, one of an elite number that also includes Alf Garnett, the Steptoes, Basil Fawlty and Victor Meldrew – and Ronnie Barker, who by the mid-1970s was at the acme of his profession, was sensationally good in the role.

Following their *Seven Of One* pilot, the writers Clement and La Frenais waited, and waited, for the BBC to decide whether or not to develop the idea into a full series. So long was the wait that, in the meantime, they went to LWT and developed a variation on the comedy-crime theme, **Thick As Thieves**, which starred Bob Hoskins and John Thaw. When that folded after one season, the BBC were at last persuaded to go ahead and create

a series around the character of Fletcher. Various titles such as *Bird* and *Stir* were banded about for the prison-based series before the writers settled on yet a third epithet used by criminals to mean incarceration: *Porridge*. The resulting series immediately became one of the all-time greats, with memorable, believable characters, richly comic dialogue and cunning plots.

Each episode began with the noise of prison doors slamming shut and the ringing tones of a judge (voiced by Barker) sentencing Fletcher to prison for five years. This set the tone: habitual criminal Fletcher is returning to jail for yet another stretch, although this time he is determined that it will be his last. Hoping his senior status will snag him a single cell, Fletcher is forced to share with a first-time offender, Lennie Godber, a naïve, scared Birmingham lad. Unintentionally, Fletcher becomes a father-figure to the young man, steering him through the choppy waters of prison life. Although the pair aim for a quiet time, they invariably clash with authority in the shape of the kindly, well-meaning and easily swayed guard Mr Barrowclough, and the harsh and suspicious, everything-by-the-book Scots warden Mr MacKay. Sometimes it is Fletcher's sharp tongue that gets them into trouble, or his incorrigible criminal leanings, at other times it might be Godber's naïvety – but, whatever the cause, more often than not it is fate and circumstance that lands them in trouble with the officious MacKay. But, by using all his guile and prison experience, Fletcher usually manages to extricate them, hoping – and usually succeeding – to score 'a little victory' along the way, something to cling to in the long, dark hours behind bars. In essence, Fletcher's advice to Godber, born of his long prison experience, is the two-fold 'bide your time' and 'don't let the bastards grind you down'.

Fletcher's common-sense and reluctant humanity mean that he is held in some regard by many of his fellow prisoners, but his guile cuts no ice with Harry Grout, the Mr Big among the convicts, who seems to have as much say in the running of Slade Prison as the governor and wardens. Some of the sharpest plots found Fletcher treading a tightrope between Grout and MacKay, having somehow to find a way to appease both parties. Other recurring characters in the series included the dithery Alzheimer-suffering old man 'Blanco' (brilliantly portrayed by the young David Jason); the thick-headed Yorkshireman Heslop; the gay 'Lukewarm'; the antagonistic black Scotsman McLaren; the guileless Warren; the disgraced dentist Harris; the weasely and conniving Ives (who always began speaking with the words ''ere listen!'); and, of course, the Slade Prison governor, a somewhat over-gentle soul whom Fletcher had wrapped around his finger.

Porridge was so successful that people wondered why prison hadn't been used before as a situation for comedy, the general explanation being that jail was such a sensitive setting that only the finest-judged writing and performances could make it acceptable. But, actually, *Porridge* did have antecedents: an earlier ITV series, *Her Majesty's Pleasure*, and the 1960 feature film comedy *Two Way Stretch* (director Robert Day) which featured Peter Sellers as a cockney character akin to Fletcher, Bernard Cribbins as a Godber type and Lionel Jeffries as an officious warden, much like MacKay. But writers Clement and La Frenais cited sitcom maestros Galton and Simpson as their inspiration, explaining that the **Hancock** episode 'The Lift' had impressed upon them how it was possible to create great comedy in very confined spaces. Since first viewing that 25-minute gem in 1961, Clement and La Frenais had been trying to invent a series that was, basically, two men talking in a room. In creating *Porridge*, and writing 21 sumptuous comedy scripts, the writers arguably eclipsed their previous wonder-creation **The Likely Lads** and its even better sequel **Whatever Happened To The Likely Lads**, all the episodes of *Porridge*, bar none, were brilliantly written and acted, but perhaps the best, 'A Night In' was a straight two-hander for Barker and Beckinsale and one of the finest examples of sitcom writing in a British series.

In keeping with the series' general optimism regarding Fletcher and Godber's future, a sequel, **Going Straight**, showed them back in the outside world after they had been released on parole. But the characters were back in mufti in 1979 for the feature film *Porridge* (director Dick Clement) which, while not as good as the TV episodes, was better than most British sitcom-to-movie adaptations.

At the height of its UK success, Clement and La Frenais instigated an American adaptation of *Porridge*, titled *On The Rocks*, which was screened by ABC. After weathering initial criticism from the US National Association For Justice, which worried that it was painting too rosy a picture of prison life, the series – set in Alamese Minimum Security Prison – enjoyed some success, especially with its employment of real-life inmates as extras and walk-ons. (The UK series had done likewise.) Running to 22 episodes, from 11 September 1975 to 17 May 1976, the US version starred José Perez as the scheming Hector Fuentes, and Mel Stewart as his adversary, the stern prison officer Gibson. (A proposed spin-off series from the US version, *I'll Never Forget What's Her Name*, which was to feature Rosa Dolores [Rita Moreno] as the cousin of Hector Fuentes, never made it beyond a pilot, however, which aired on ABC on 29 March 1976.)

Porterhouse Blue

UK · C4 (PICTURE PARTNERSHIP PRODUCTION) ·
COMEDY SERIAL

4 × 60 mins · colour

3–24 June 1987 · Wed mostly 10pm

MAIN CAST

Skullion	David Jason
Sir Godber Evans	Ian Richardson
Lionel Zipser	John Sessions
Dean	Paul Rogers
Senior Tutor	John Woodnutt
Bursar	Harold Innocent
Mrs Biggs	Paula Jacobs
Lady Mary	Barbara Jefford
Sir Cathcart De'Ath	Charles Gray
Cornelius Carrington	Griff Rhys Jones
Praelector	Ian Wallace
Professor Siblington	Willoughby Goddard
Chaplain	Lockwood West
Chef	John Rogan
Arthur	Roy Evans
Dr Messmer	Tim Preece

CREDITS

creator Tom Sharpe · *adapter/writer* Malcolm
Bradbury · *director* Robert Knights · *producer* Brian
Eastman

Two years after the BBC's successful
adaptation of **Blott On The Landscape**,
another of Tom Sharpe's witty works, the
1974 novel *Porterhouse Blue*, was brought to
the small-screen, this time by C4.

Porterhouse College, Cambridge, is famous
for three principal reasons: its haute cuisine,
shockingly poor academic results and rowing
prowess. Suddenly, a new Master, Sir Godber
Evans, arrives on the scene, determined to
sweep out the old and usher in the new:
women students, successful scholars, condom
vending machines, a self-service lunch
canteen and a profit line. Worse than all
of this, though, the crusty old gents at
Porterhouse are shocked to the marrow by
Sir Godber's background: he was a grammar-
school boy. But, for all of Evans's many foes,
none is as cunning, or as inarticulate, as the
Porterhouse porter, Skullion, who will stop
at nothing to preserve tradition, and his job.
Inside this richly woven story were the usual
well-drawn cast of Tom Sharpe characters
exercising their eccentricities and
perversions.

Principal among these is the student
Zipser, who is sexually obsessed by the ample
charms of his dorm cleaner Mrs Biggs and
who meets his death in an utterly bizarre
circumstance that simultaneously sends
thousands of gas-filled condoms floating up
into the Cambridge sky. The story concludes
with Sir Godber Evans murdered and
Skullion not only reappointed at Porterhouse
but made the new Master.

A sequel to *Porterhouse Blue*, *Grantchester
Grind*, was published in 1995 and may make
a future TV serial.

Porterhouse – Private Eye

UK · ITV (ATV) · SITCOM

1 × 30 mins · b/w

1 Sep 1965 · Wed 9.10pm

MAIN CAST

Edwin Porterhouse	Peter Butterworth
Daffodil	June Whitfield
Otto Mulchrone	Dudley Foster

CREDITS

writer Maurice Wiltshire · *director* Albert Locke ·
producer Alan Tarrant

Peter Butterworth starred as Porterhouse, a
clumsy amateur detective, in this single-
episode production screened as part of ATV's
Six Of The Best season of pilots.

Porterhouse's task, to guard a precious
snuff box, was 'aided' by his equally inept
daughter Daffodil (June Whitfield), a
bespectacled woman dressed in judo costume
and obsessed with practising the martial art
at every opportunity. No series developed.

Posh

UK · ITV (WITZEND PRODUCTIONS FOR
CENTRAL) · SITCOM

1 × 30 mins · colour

5 Apr 1982 · Mon 8pm

MAIN CAST

Jack Scratch	John Cater
Steve Martini	Steve Alder
Mr Vicarage	Ronald Lacey
Mr Poppy	Michael Cashman
Ronnie Strumper	Kevin Lloyd
Rosie O'Grady	Patrick Durkin
Miss Humphreys	Lesley Duff

CREDITS

writer Terence Howard · *script editors* Dick
Clement/Ian La Frenais · *director* Christopher
Baker · *executive producer* Allan McKeown ·
producer Tony Charles

A single-episode sitcom which may have been
a pilot for a full series that failed to develop.
POSH was named after the phrase used by
British travellers sailing to and from India in
the days of the Raj: to avoid the blistering sun,
passengers would request the location of their
cabins as 'port out, starboard home'. This
sitcom, obviously, was set on board a ship, the
luxury cruise liner *Lord Fordingham*, wherein
Jack Scratch, the Acting Senior Cabin Steward,
finally manages to secure a C Deck cabin for
himself but is alarmed to find that he must
share it with the newly employed ship's waiter
Steve Martini.

The Posse –
Armed And Dangerous

UK · C4 (LWT) · SKETCH

1 × 65 mins · colour

21 May 1993 · Fri 11.10pm

MAIN CAST

Victor Romero Evans
Robbie Gee
Roger Griffiths
Gary McDonald
Eddie Nestor
Sylvester Williams
Michael Buffong

CREDITS

writer various · *director* Liddy Oldroyd · *producer*
Nadine Marsh Edwards

Young comics and actors performing satirical
sketches that looked at black life in modern-
day Britain.

In addition to this one-off TV special, the
Posse performed occasional revue shows on
the fringe theatre circuit – ironically, when
fed up at their inability to find television
work. Such shows embraced satires of a
broad range of black topics, from Jamaican
gangster culture to TV talk-show hosts.

Potter

UK · BBC · SITCOM

20 × 30 mins · colour

Series One (6) 1 Mar–5 Apr 1979 · BBC1
Thu 8.30pm

Series Two (7) 27 Feb–9 Apr 1980 · BBC1
Wed mostly 8.30pm

Series Three (7) 17 July–28 Aug 1983 · BBC1
Sun around 10pm

MAIN CAST

Redvers Potter	Arthur Lowe (series 1 & 2); Robin Bailey (series 3)
Aileen Potter	Noël Dyson
Vicar	John Barron
'Tolly' Tolliver	John Warner
Harriet	Sally Bowers (series 1)
Willy	Ken Wynne (series 1)

CREDITS

writer Roy Clarke · *producers* Peter Whitmore
(series 1 & 2), Bernard Thompson (series 3)

Arthur Lowe portrayed several memorable
TV characters in his time, including Leonard
Swindley in *Coronation Street*, **Pardon The
Expression** and **Turn Out The Lights**,
Captain Mainwaring in **Dad's Army**, Father
Duddleswell in **Bless Me, Father** and, here,
the incorrigible meddler Redvers Potter.

As *Potter* begins, Redvers Potter is retiring
from his job at the helm of the confectionery
company that has given Britain the famous
'Potter Mints' ('The Hotter Mints'). Thus, this
captain of industry, a man used to organising
people and things, suddenly has time on his
hands, a commuter no more and somewhat
at a loose end in the leafy suburbs of south
London. Rather than sit back and take it easy,
Potter determines to lead a full life by making
himself useful and wandering around
'assisting' people, whether or not they have
asked for or require his help. A bombastic
man with set ways and an outlook shaped by
50 years of reading *The Daily Telegraph*,

Potter is permanently at odds with those he is trying to help and his presence usually exacerbates the situations.

Potter had the traditional sitcom support system: a wife (Aileen) who somehow put up with his eccentricities; a young neighbour, 'Tolly' – a man whom Potter felt needed the benefit of his advice and experience (but who palpably did not); and a like-minded drinking buddy and confidant (the local vicar) with whom to share his philosophy. Such characters have almost become clichés in sitcoms yet they seemed less so in the skilled hands of writer Roy Clarke, who had already proved a master of naturally humorous dialogue with *Last Of The Summer Wine* and *Open All Hours*.

When Lowe died in 1982, plans were already advanced for a third series of *Potter*, so Robin Bailey – impressive as Uncle Mort in *I Didn't Know You Cared* – took over the role, and, considering the exacting task, fared exceedingly well.

Potter's Picture Palace

UK · BBC · CHILDREN'S SITCOM

13 × 25 mins · colour

Series One (7) 13 Sep–25 Oct 1976 · BBC1 Mon mostly 5.15pm
Series Two (6) 14 Apr–19 May 1978 · BBC1 Fri 4.40pm

MAIN CAST
Peter Potter · · · · · · · · · · · · · · Eden Phillips
Melvyn Didsbury · · · · · · · · · · Melvyn Hayes
Sidney Bogart · · · · · · · · · · · · · John Comer
Joan Biddie · · · · · · · · · · · · · · Angela Crow
Frank Plank · · · · · · · · · · · · · · Colin Edwynn
Reggie Turpin · · · · · · · David Lodge (series 1)
The Kid · · · · · · · · · · · · Bruce Watt (series 1)
Desmond Bagshaw · · · · · · · · Mark Dempsey
· (series 2)

CREDITS
writers Brian Finch (10), Phil Redmond (2), Dick Sharples (1) · directors Tony Harrison (series 1), Jeremy Swan (series 2) · producer John Buttery

Comedy misadventures centred around an old-fashioned cinema, Potter's Picture Palace. Upon the death of his Aunt Mattie, her nephew Peter Potter expects to inherit the old cinema, but villainy (in the shape of cousin Reggie) seeks to thwart him. Reggie had disappeared by the second series but the cinema's staff returned for a second performance.

Potty Time

see BENTINE, Michael

The Powers That Be

USA · NBC (ACT III TELEVISION/CASTLE ROCK ENTERTAINMENT/COLUMBIA PICTURES TELEVISION) · SITCOM

19 episodes (17 × 30 mins · 2 × 60 mins) · colour

US dates: 7 Mar 1992–16 Jan 1993
UK dates: 17 Oct 1994–22 July 1995 (21 × 30 mins) ITV mostly Thu 11.40pm

MAIN CAST
Senator William Powers · · · · · · John Forsythe
Margaret Powers · · · · · · · · · · Holland Taylor
Jordan Miller · · · · · · · · · · · · · · · Eve Gordon
Bradley Grist · · · · · · · · · · · · Peter MacNicol
Caitlyn Van Horne · · · · · · · · Valerie Mahaffey
Theodore Van Horne · · · · · David Hyde Pierce
Charlotte · · · · · · · · · · · · Elizabeth Berridge
Pierce Van Horne · · · · · Joseph Gordon-Levitt
Sophia Lipkin · · · · · · · · · · · · · Robin Bartlett

CREDITS
creators Marta Kauffman/David Crane · writers Charlotte Brown, Ron Burla, Anne Convy, Marta Kauffman/David Crane, Rod Parker, Bob Sand, Graham Yost · directors Hal Cooper, Art Wolff, Norman Lear · executive producers Norman Lear, Charlotte Brown, Mark E Pollack · producer Patricia Fass Palmer and others

A vaguely satirical US comedy set in Washington DC and focusing on the political career of an inept senator, William Powers, and his dysfunctional family. Like so many sitcoms, the lack of any sustaining wit in *The Powers That Be* was over-compensated for by the creation of a phalanx of unreal characters, to the point where the ensuing mix managed to eliminate reality.

William 'Bill' Powers (played by John Forsythe, Blake Carrington in *Dynasty*) is a clueless US senator of the Democrat persuasion. Now 65, he has been in such a position for 26 years. Margaret, his dominating wife, is obsessed with status, power-playing and party invitations, and harbours ambitions – which will surely go unfulfilled – of being First Lady. Younger than her husband, Margaret pushes for his career advancement, usually in the face of his ineptitude. Caitlyn Van Horne is their pathetic, vain daughter, married to a weak and ineffective Republican congressman, Theodore Van Horne (excellently played by David Hyde Pierce, later to shine as Niles Crane in *Frasier*) who is always mumbling contemplations of suicide – probably in the hope that the act will gain him some attention. Caitlyn and Theodore's young son, Pierce, is always being dressed up in his smartest clothes in case a photo opportunity should arise. Jordan Miller is William Powers' efficient chief administrative assistant, au fait with the palm-greasing necessary to proceed in the capital. She's also his mistress – they have secret assignations every Sunday morning. Sophia Lipkin is William Powers' illegitimate daughter from a wartime dalliance, who now serves him as a political aide. Her down-to-earth (well, New York) views cut through the middle-of-the-road gush talked by most of the others. Bradley Grist is William Powers' press secretary and

Charlotte is the Powers' housemaid, scared of Margaret's patronising put-downs and power games but possessing a crush on (of all people) the wimpish Theodore.

Well-mannered, and distinguished by appearance, Bill Powers suggested an older version of Bill Clinton (whose name was often voiced in the series although he was, of course, never seen). But neither this nor anything else could prevent *The Powers That Be* from being axed after a year of sporadic US screenings. Marta Kauffman and David Crane, who had already created *Dream On*, found greater success with their next venture, *Friends*.

A Present For Dickie

see HENDERSON, Dickie

The Preventers

UK · ITV (ABSOLUTELY PRODUCTIONS FOR CARLTON) · SITCOM

1 × 30 mins · colour

16 Dec 1996 · Mon 10.40pm

MAIN CAST
Penelope Gold · · · · · · · · · · Morwenna Banks
Craig Sturdy · · · · · · · · · · · · · · Robert Harley
Mike Stallion · · · · · · · · · · · · · Chris England
The Controller · · · · · · · · · · · · William Gaunt
Lord Timothy Belvoir St Nash · · · · · · · · · · · ·
· Simon Williams
Roger Stavro Mordick · · · · · · · Ed Devereaux
Dr Keelover · · · · · · · · · · · · · · Chris Langham
Croupier · · · · · · · · · · · · · · · · Neil Mullarkey

CREDITS
writers Morwenna Banks/Chris England/Robert Harley · director Liddy Oldroyd · executive producer Miles Bullough · producer Nick Symons

Someone had to do it. *The Preventers* was an excellent spoof of the high-action adventure programmes that proliferated on British TV in the 1960s and early 1970s, series such as *The Avengers*, *The Baron*, *The Champions*, *Department S*, *Jason King*, *The Persuaders* and *The Protectors*, several of which had been shown again in the mid-1990s and so were fresh in the minds of viewers. All the classic ingredients of those cult series were here in *The Preventers*: an expensive car hurtling off a cliff, a ridiculous but exotic mission, a mysterious organisation of evil-doers, dialogue peppered with 'What the …?', 'How the …?' and 'Who the …?' expostulations, dynamic music, crazy gadgets, cheap sets and an all-laughing finale.

Screened as a pilot for a full series that (to the time of writing) has yet to appear, *The Preventers* depicted the exploits of an elite team of international troubleshooters: the suave but thick Craig Sturdy and the mysteriously enigmatic Penelope Gold. Oh, and a third one, Mike Stallion. Sent on a mission by the Controller, head of their top-secret movement, known as the Movement, the trio's task is to prevent an evil consortium, known as the Consortium and headed by the evil Australian media tycoon Roger Stavro Mordick, from using TV to brainwash viewers into thinking that they're back in the 1960s. Events unfold dramatically at Popstock, a hippy pop festival being held in the grounds of the ancestral pile owned by Lord Timothy Belvoir St Nash (pronounced Beaversnatch).

First staged on the Edinburgh Festival Fringe, *The Preventers* was initially broadcast by BBC Radio 4, as two half-hour stories, on 13 and 20 March 1996, with all principal parts played by the same actors. (These were followed by two further pastiche stories, the four-week season airing under the generic title *Fab TV*.) The writer/performers all knew their TV adventure series well and brought good comedy experience to the production: Banks was part of *Absolutely*, England co-wrote the hit stage-play (and TV production) *An Evening With Gary Lineker*, and Harley wrote *You Cannot Be Serious*, a series for BBC Radio 5 Live. Adding a real link with the past, The Controller was played by William Gaunt, who had starred as Richard Barrett in *The Champions*.

A Prince Among Men

UK · BBC · SITCOM

6 × 30 mins · colour
15 Sep–20 Oct 1997 · BBC1 Mon 8.30pm

MAIN CAST
Gary Prince · · · · · · · · · · · · · · · Chris Barrie
Lisel Prince · · · · · · · · · · · · · Francesca Hunt
Sonia Trent · · · · · · · · · · · · Samantha Power
Beverly Baker · · · · · · · · · · · · · · Susie Blake
Mark Fitzherbert · · · · · · · · Timothy Bentinck
Vince Hibbert · · · · · · · · · · · · Bryan Pringle
Dave Perry · · · · · · · · · · · · · · · · Cliff Parisi

CREDITS
writers Tony Millan/Mike Walling · director/producer Mike Stephens

The talented Chris Barrie had already starred as Rimmer in *Red Dwarf* and Gordon Brittas in *The Brittas Empire*; here, he portrayed another ghastly creation, an egocentric ex-football star turned businessman/entrepreneur, Gary Prince.

The totally self-obsessed Prince has a raging superiority complex and treats all those around him as lesser mortals. This includes his beautiful German wife Lisel (whom Gary met while he was playing for Bayern Munich), now a successful book translator working from their gimmick-laden Cheshire home; secretaries Beverly, who sees right through Gary's posturing, and Sonia, who still hero-worships him; right-hand-man Dave, Gary's rough and ready but conscientious personal manager, a former East End of London barrow-boy; and

business manager Mark, an arrogant, upper-class young man whose innate superiority rankles Gary. There's also the local publican, Vince Hibbert, who – as manager of the tiny Pennine League amateur club Ferny Heath – first discovered Gary as a precocious teenager. Then, Vince considered that Gary was a spoiled kid with a rich talent, and, all these years on, his opinion has not altered. Prince's footballing prowess was beyond question but his swaggering big-headedness and inept people-management skills ensure that he remains an unpleasant companion.

While Barrie proved once again how adept he is at portraying unlikeable men, Gary Prince failed to sparkle in the manner of his previous characters. Oddly, this was probably because he wasn't extreme enough – for, despite his surface flaws, he seemed a decent sort underneath, someone who truly wanted to be liked. This visible soft-centre worked against Prince's most outrageous moments of bad taste, limiting his comic potential. But, in the face of stern objections by some critics, the BBC thought the series worth persevering with and a new batch of episodes was promised for spring 1998.

The Prince Of Denmark

UK · BBC · SITCOM

6 × 30 mins · colour
10 Apr–15 May 1974 · BBC1 Wed 7.40pm

MAIN CAST
Ronnie · · · · · · · · · · · · · · · · · Ronnie Corbett
Laura · · · · · · · · · · · · · · · Rosemary Leach
Steve · · · · · · · · · · · · · · · · · David Warwick
Mr Yates · · · · · · · · · · · · · · · · Roger Booth

CREDITS
writers Barry Cryer/Graham Chapman · producer Douglas Argent

A sequel to *Now Look Here ...* For this series, Laura inherited a pub, The Prince Of Denmark, and Ronnie said goodbye to insurance and began a new career as a publican.

Until *Cheers*, sitcom writers found it difficult to mount a successful sitcom in a bar setting. *The Prince Of Denmark*, written by Barry Cryer with Graham Chapman (from *Monty Python*) was a moderately good series, the best episode being where Ronnie had to deal with soccer and rugby union supporters in his bar, the former – against his prejudiced expectations – being quiet and unobtrusive, the latter, ditto, boisterous and uncontrollable.

Private Benjamin

USA · CBS (WARNER BROS) · SITCOM

39 × 30 mins · colour
US dates: 6 Apr 1981–5 Sep 1983
UK dates: 13 Sep 1982–28 Aug 1984
(39 episodes) ITV mostly Mon 5.15pm

MAIN CAST
Pvt Judy Benjamin · · · · · · · Lorna Patterson
Capt Doreen Lewis · · · · · · · · Eileen Brennan
Col Lawrence Fielding · · · · · · · Robert Mandan
Sgt Lucien C 'Ted' Ross · · · · · · Hal Williams
Pvt Stacy Kouchalakas · · Wendie Jo Sperber
· (1982–83)
Pvt Maria Gianelli · · · · · · · · · · · · Lisa Raggio
Pvt Rayleen White · · · · · · Joyce Little (1981)
Pvt Lu Ann Hubble · · · · · Lucy Webb (1981–82)
Pvt Jackie Simms · · · · · · Damita Jo Freeman
· (1981–83)
Pvt Carol Winter · · · · Ann Ryerson (1981–82)
Pvt Barbara Ann Glass · · · · · · · · Joan Roberts
· (1981)
Pvt Harriet Dorsey · · · · · Francesca P Roberts
· (1981)

CREDITS
creators Nancy Meyers/Charles Shyer/Harvey Miller · writers various · directors various · executive producers Bob Brunner, Ken Hecht · producers Madelyn Davis, Bob Carroll Jr, Don Reo, Nick Arnold

*M*A*S*H* had been turned, with most spectacular success, from a comedy movie into a sitcom. Why not, some top producers reckoned, do the same with *Private Benjamin*? The 1980 feature film – starring Goldie Hawn as a Jewish 'princess' widow, kidded into joining the US Army and so leaving behind wealth for an altogether different life – had certainly been a box-office smash. And indeed, it wasn't a bad TV series either, not in the same league as *M*A*S*H* (very few programmes are) but quite watchable and, in places, very funny.

Hawn was not prepared to play the part again so Lorna Patterson (the singing stewardess in the movie *Airplane!*) was cast in the lead role. Eileen Brennan and Hal Williams (as Lewis and Ross) did carry through their parts from the *Private Benjamin* movie, however, resolute in their attempts to make a soldier out of the pampered ex-socialite, and countering Benjamin's attempts to have the army do things her way.

This was at least the third, but the only successful, attempt to transfer *Private Benjamin* (or something similar) to a TV sitcom: Paramount made a single pilot, *Hot WACS* (otherwise known as *Soldier Girls*), that aired in America on 1 June 1981; NBC tried to get *Wendy Hooper – US Army* off the ground two months later, on 14 August.

Private Eye TV

UK · BBC · SATIRE

1 × 45 mins · colour
28 Dec 1971 · BBC2 Tue 10.30pm

MAIN CAST
John Bird
Eleanor Bron
Spike Milligan
William Rushton
John Wells

Christopher Booker
Barry Fantoni
Paul Foot
Richard Ingrams

CREDITS
compiler Barry Took · *producer* Dennis Main Wilson

A TV compilation of ten years of humorous material published in the famous satire magazine *Private Eye*. Familiar faces from the world of TV satire interpreted the written word for the small-screen.

Note. The thirtieth anniversary of the publication was marked by an edition of the LWT/ITV arts series *The South Bank Show* on 15 September 1991, in which John Wells read from *Dear Bill* and other contributors included Peter Cook, Barry Humphries, Auberon Waugh, Paul Foot, Richard Ingrams and Ian Hislop.

See also Anyone For Denis?, Grubstreet and Mrs Wilson's Diary.

The Private Lives Of Edward Whiteley

UK · BBC · SITCOM

1 × 30 mins · b/w
29 Dec 1961 · Fri 8.45pm

MAIN CAST
Edward Whiteley · · · · · · · · · · · · Tony Britton
Hargreaves · · · · · · · · · · · Raymond Huntley

CREDITS
writers Ray Galton/Alan Simpson · *producer* Duncan Wood

Another of the Galton and Simpson editions of *Comedy Playhouse* – this one was a period piece about a dedicated bigamist, Edward Whiteley.

Private Secretary

USA · CBS THEN NBC (JACK CHERTOK PRODUCTIONS) · SITCOM

103 × 30 mins · b/w
US dates: 1 Feb 1953–10 Sep 1957
UK dates: 19 Jan 1959–20 Dec 1960 (52 episodes) ITV various days and times

MAIN CAST
Susie MacNamara · · · · · · · · · · · Ann Sothern
Peter Sands · · · · · · · · · · · · · · · Don Porter
Violet Praskins · · · · · · · · · · · · · Ann Tyrrell
Mickey 'Cagey' Calhoun · · · · · · · Jesse White
Sylvia · Joan Banks

CREDITS
director Christian Nyby · *producer* Jack Chertok

Established Hollywood comedian Ann Sothern was a rarity in 1950s US television: a woman not prepared to play the subordinate female roles that were typical of the era. As the audacious former stage actress Susie MacNamara, private secretary to theatrical agent Peter Sands, Sothern dominated this series (which was repeated in the USA under

a different title, *Susie*), her extrovert and witty personality being the fulcrum of life at the New York theatrical agency International Artists Inc. Susie's only problem was that her efficiency sometimes went too far and she became embroiled in Sands' private life. Her best friend was the firm's switchboard operator Vi Praskins; 'Cagey' Calhoun was Sands' cigar-chomping rival.

Sothern, Porter and Tyrrell teamed up again in *The Ann Sothern Show* (1958–61) in which they ran a big-city hotel. (This series has not aired on British TV.)

Le Prix de Leeds

see The Leeds series

PS It's Paul Squire

UK · ITV (CENTRAL) · SKETCH/STANDUP

9 × 30 mins · colour
20 June–22 Aug 1983 Mon 5.15pm

MAIN CAST
Paul Squire
Michael Robbins
John Sharp
Eli Woods
Helene Hunt
Lance Ellington
Tony Burrows

CREDITS
writers Paul Owen, David Hansen, Royston Mayoh · *director/producer* Royston Mayoh

More humour from the fresh-faced funster. (See **The Paul Squire Show** for biographical information.)

Psst!

UK · ITV (GRANADA) · SKETCH

13 × 30 mins · b/w
11 Jan–5 April 1969 · Sat around 11pm

MAIN CAST
Keith Dewhurst
Jeremy Taylor
Richard Stilgoe
Kenny Lynch
Jean Hart (editions 1–6)
Julie Covington (editions 8–13)

CREDITS
writers cast · *directors* Wally Butler, Bill Podmore, Pat Johns · *executive producer* Michael Scott · *producers* Nick Elliott, David Warwick

A weekly series that cast a humorous and sometimes satirical light on the topics of the week, in the manner born of **That Was The Week That Was**. The shows were linked by Keith Dewhurst – some time *Z Cars* writer and author of stage-plays – and ideas were also contributed by members of the cast, one of whom, the young singer Julie Covington, went on to stage, screen and recording successes in the late 1970s.

A sequel to a weekly news review, *At Last It's Friday*, which was screened only in Granada's north-west territory towards the end of 1968, *Psst!* was not networked – it was shown in the north-west and in the London-area (although only 12 of the 13 editions were seen in the capital).

Pull The Other One

UK · ITV (CENTRAL) · SITCOM

6 × 30 mins · colour
15 June–20 July 1984 · Fri 8.30pm

MAIN CAST
Sidney Mundy · · · · · · · · · · · Michael Elphick
Sadie Mundy · · · · · · · · · · · · · Susan Tracy
Grandma · · · · · · · · · · · · · · · · · · Lila Kaye
Terry · Tim Preece
Barmaid · · · · · · · · · · · · · · Diana Goodman
Kevin · · · · · · · · · · · · · · · · · · Lucas Penn
Dawn · · · · · · · · · · · · · · · · Tessa Harrison

CREDITS
writer Michael McStay · *director* Peter Ellis · *producer* Joan Brown

A new series with an interesting cast – Michael Elphick, Lila Kaye from **Mama Malone**, and Tim Preece, the dull, wine-making Tom in **The Fall And Rise Of Reginald Perrin** – which ought to have added up to something memorable but did not. Most of the action stemmed from the indomitable Grandma and her encounters with the Mundy family, with whom she lived. Her daughter, Sadie, thinks the world of her, but Sadie's husband, Sidney, cannot abide the old woman in his abode. The family's refuge, in their many times of stress, was their good friend Terry. The series was set in Birmingham and a good deal of 'Brummie' humour ensued.

This was the first TV series from writer Michael McStay who, hitherto, had been an actor, appearing in the popular ITV crime series *No Hiding Place* (Associated-Rediffusion, 1959–67). He had previously written about Sid, Sadie, Grandma and Terry in the BBC Radio 4 play *Grandma Goes West*, broadcast within the *Thirty-Minute Theatre* strand on 19 February 1983. On this occasion the roles were taken by, respectively, Michael Graham Cox, Frances Jeater, Liz Smith and Stuart Organ.

Pulp Video

UK · BBC · SKETCH

7 × 30 mins · colour
Pilot · 18 Aug 1995 · BBC2 Fri 9.30pm
One series (6) 16 Aug–20 Sep 1996 · BBC2 Fri 9.30pm

MAIN CAST
Andrew Fairlie
Greg Hemphill
Jane McCarry
David McGowan

Gavin Mitchell
Ford Kiernan
Fred MacAulay
Alan Francis (series)
Julie Wilson Nimmo (series)
Ronnie Ancona (series)
Veronica Leer (pilot)
Mark Radcliffe (pilot)
Marc Riley (pilot)
Parrot (pilot)
Nicola Park (pilot)

CREDITS

writers Rab Christie/Greg Hemphill, Garry Johnston, Ford Kiernan, Fred MacAulay, John McGlade, Parrot, Mark Pierson, Mark Radcliffe/Marc Riley, Colin Russell, Rikki Brown, Iain Campbell, Mitch Benn, Andy Pollen, William Docherty, John Douglas, Cathy Dunning/Fintan Coyle, Brian Morgan, Brian Morrison, Malcolm Morrison, Gordon McPherson, George Poles, David Walton, Fraser Watt, Mark Wilk and others · *executive producers* Colin Gilbert (pilot), Mike Bolland (series) · *directors/producers* Dave Behrens/Philip Differ (pilot), Ron Bain (series)

A fast-paced contemporary sketch show from the *Naked Video* creative team, first screened within the *Comic Asides* season. A huge list of script contributors may have accounted for the rather strange mélange of sketches, some of which were sophisticated while others were quite basic. Although the team members threw themselves wholeheartedly into the pieces the mix seemed cumbersome at times; however, the sheer speed and vitality of the show managed to paper over many of the cracks.

Punch And Judex: Mr Potter's Joyous Judicial Joke

see Gillie Potter

Punch Drunk

UK · BBC · SITCOM

6 × 30 mins · colour

4 Jan–8 Feb 1993 · BBC1 Mon 8.30pm

MAIN CAST

Vinnie Binns · · · · · · · · · · · · · · Kenny Ireland
Hance Gordon · · · · · · · · · · · · · · John Kazek
Vikki Brown · · · · · · · · · · · · Diana Hardcastle
Pat Hunter · · · · · · · · · · · · · · · Sean Scanlan
Neillie · · · · · · · · · · · · · · · · · Jake D'Arcy
Norman Banks · · · · · · · · · · · Jonathan Kydd
Slug · · · · · · · · · · · · · · · · · · Gilbert Martin
Mrs Gordon · · · · · · · · · · · · · Claire Nielson
Danny Boyle · · · · · · · · · · · · Grant Smeaton

CREDITS

writer Clayton Moore · *director* Ron Bain · *producer* Colin Gilbert

A BBC Scotland sitcom about professional boxing in Glasgow, following the fortunes of a manager, Vinnie Binns, and his protégé, Hance Gordon. A veteran of the fight game, Binns realises that his young charge has the potential to be a champ, if handled correctly,

but they face opposition not only from rival managers, crooked promoters and ring opponents but also from Doctors Against Boxing, an organisation led by Norman Banks. Initially, Banks's partner, medic Vikki Brown, is a participant in the anti-boxing alliance but then she becomes involved with Hance and, although she maintains many of her moral objections to the sport, she switches her allegiance to Hance and Vinnie.

This device, of getting Vikki Brown in the opposition camp, was a neat one and should have given rise to a strong central premise, but *Punch Drunk* never realised its potential, suffering from weak punchlines and failing to score many points with its audience. This was a shame because Diana Hardcastle impressed as the spiky Vikki, and if the rest of the production had shaped up just as well then the show could have been a contender.

The Punch Review

UK · BBC · SATIRE

7 × 30 mins · colour

Special · 21 Dec 1975 · BBC2 Sun 9pm
One series (6) 4 Jan–15 Feb 1977 · BBC2 Tue around 10.40pm

MAIN CAST

Robin Bailey
Julian Holloway
John Bird (special)
Chris Emmett (special)
Patricia Hayes (special)
Roy Kinnear (special)
Sheridan Morley (special)
Gwen Taylor (special)
Bill Grundy (special & one edition in series)

CREDITS

original material Alan Coren, Basil Boothroyd, Miles Kington, Keith Waterhouse, Michael Palin/Terry Jones, E S Turner, Spike Milligan · *adapter* Barry Took · *producers* Gareth Gwenlan (special), Roger Race (series)

The first of these seven programmes was an end-of-year comedy special in which written material from the famous humour magazine *Punch* was enacted, with a large ensemble cast assembled to translate the words into action. The format proved successful enough for a series to follow just over a year later.

Punky Brewster

USA · NBC THEN SYNDICATION (LIGHT KEEPER PRODUCTIONS/COLUMBIA) · SITCOM

88 × 30 mins · colour

US dates: 16 Sep 1984–May 1989
UK dates: 30 Aug 1986–9 Aug 1987
(26 episodes) ITV mostly Sat 11.30am

MAIN CAST

Penelope 'Punky' Brewster · · · · · · · · · · · · · ·
· Soleil Moon Frye
Henry Warnimont · · · · · · · · · · George Gaynes
Cherie Johnson · · · · · · · · · · · Cherie Johnson
Betty Johnson · · · · · · · · · · · · · Susie Garrett

Eddie · · · · · · · · · · · · · Eddie Deezen (1984)
Margaux Kramer · · · · · · · · · · · · · Ami Foster

CREDITS

writers David W Duclon, Jim Everling, Carmen Finestra, Joe Fisch, Jim Geoghan, Rick Hawkins, Christine Houston, Neil Lebowitz, Gary Menteer, Liz Sage, David N Titcher, Dorothy Van, Barry Vigon · *directors* various · *producers* David W Duclon, Gary Menteer, Rick Hawkins, Liz Sage

Depending on your viewpoint, this was either a ghastly, sickly-sweet, cheaply made sitcom of the worst kind, or a harmless slice of apple-pie America. Most adults tended towards the former view, which is why (in London, at least) ITV scheduled *Punky Brewster* on Saturday mornings. In America, it went out in the Sunday evening 'family hour', between 7 and 8pm, which must have sent many a kiddie off to bed with a warm tingle, and many a parent scurrying for a stiff drink.

'Punky' – real name Penelope – is a sugary seven-year-old, deserted by her father and abandoned by her mother, who makes her home in a vacant Chicago apartment. With only her puppy dog Brandon (named, incidentally, after NBC executive Brandon Tartikoff) as solace, she is discovered and subsequently adopted by Henry Warnimont, part-time manager of the building, part-time photographer. (In this era of paedophilia scares, this premise surely wouldn't be allowed today.) Henry is a salty old widower, but one with redeeming features. Most episodes, indeed, ended up with the old grouch being redeemed by his big-eyed, big-hearted, perennially optimistic young chum. Although these were the two main characters other parts included Punky's best friend Cherie Johnson (played a young girl of the same name), her grandmother Betty, Punky's rich and spoiled friend Margaux, and building maintenance man Eddie.

NBC networked 44 episodes of *Punky Brewster* from 1984 to 1986, whereupon the programme continued to be produced for 'first-run syndication', finally ceasing in 1989. NBC also aired a Saturday-morning cartoon series, *It's Punky Brewster* (88 episodes, 14 September 1985 to 2 September 1989), voiced by all the main players. (Nine of these animated episodes were screened in Britain between 1988 and 1990 within the ITV breakfast strand TV-am.) NBC also attempted to float a spin-off from *Punky Brewster*, airing a pilot titled *Fenster Hall* in the USA on 31 March 1985 – this time, no series developed.

Punt And Dennis

see *The Imaginatively-Titled Punt & Dennis Show*

A Puppet Lives In My House

see Sitcom Weekend

Pure Goldie

USA · NBC (GEORGE SCHLATTER-ED FRIENDLY
PRODUCTIONS) · STANDUP/SKETCH

1 × 60 mins · colour

US date: 15 Feb 1971

UK date: 17 June 1971 · BBC1 Thu 8.10pm

MAIN CAST

Goldie Hawn
Ruth Buzzi
Johnny Carson

CREDITS

writers Bill Persky/Sam Denoff · *director* Marty
Passetta · *producers* Bill Persky/Sam Denoff

A one-off special showcasing the talents of
Rowan And Martin's Laugh-In star
Goldie Hawn who, at this time, was in the
early stage of her meteoric rise to stardom.
Helping her out in this NBC show was fellow
Laugh-In regular Ruth Buzzi and America's
premier TV chat-show host Johnny Carson.

Pushful And Pieface

UK · BBC · CHILDREN'S SKETCH

**3 episodes (1 × 5 mins · 1 × 10 mins · 1 × 15
mins) · b/w**

29 Mar 1957 · Fri 5.50pm (5 mins)

10 July 1957 · Wed 5.45pm (10 mins)

4 Oct 1957 · Fri 5.45pm (15 mins)

MAIN CAST

Sir Hugh Pushful PTO RSVP · · · · · · · · · · · · · ·
· · · · · · · · · · · · · · · · · Peter Howell (show 1);
· · · · · · · · · · · · · Raymond Rollett (show 2);
· · · · · · · · · · · · · · · · · · Bill Fraser (show 3)
Pieface · · · · · · · · · · · · · · · · · · · Bob Harris

CREDITS

writer David Edwards · *producers* Vere Lorrimer
(shows 1 & 2), Richard West (show 3)

Described as adventures with 'the champ of
the chumps', these slapstick playlets aired
within the strand *Children's Television*. The
last of the three was intended for viewing by
deaf children.

Pushing Up Daisies / Coming Next ...

UK · C4 (LWT · *PAUL JACKSON PRODUCTIONS) ·
SKETCH/STANDUP

13 × 30 mins · colour

Series One (7) *Pushing Up Daisies* 3 Nov–15 Dec
1984 · Sat mostly 11pm

*Series Two (6) *Coming Next ...* 14 Sep–19 Oct
1985 · Sat 11pm

MAIN CAST

Chris Barrie
Gareth Hale
Norman Pace
Carla Mendonça

CREDITS

writers Gareth Hale/Norman Pace (12), Geoff
Atkinson (11), Kim Fuller (6), James Hendrie (5),
Chris Barrie (4), Vicky Pile (4), Stephen Fry (3),
Terry Morrison (3), Bob Sinfield/Andrea Solomons

(3), Tony Sarchet (2), Andrea Solomons (1) · *script
editor* Kim Fuller · *directors* Terry Kinane (*Pushing
Up Daisies*), Geoff Posner (*Coming Next ...*) ·
producers Paul Jackson (*Pushing Up Daisies*),
Geoff Posner/Paul Jackson (*Coming Next ...*)

Two series of sketch shows – with different
titles – featuring the fast-rising talents of, in
particular, Chris Barrie and Hale and Pace.
Best known as an impressionist at this time –
his talents were considerably aiding *Spitting
Image* – Chris Barrie performed a more than
passable imitation of Bjorn Borg while, not
to be left out, Carla Mendonça delivered an
unctuously sympathetic impersonation of the
TV doctor Miriam Stoppard.

Pygmalion Smith

UK · BBC · SITCOM

1 × 30 mins · colour

25 June 1974 · BBC1 Tue 8.30pm

MAIN CAST

Pygmalion 'Smithy' Smith · · · · · · · · · · · · · · ·
· Leonard Rossiter
Brewster · · · · · · · · · · · · · · · · · T P McKenna
Auriol Pratt · · · · · · · · · · · · Barbara Courtney
Mrs Kintoul · · · · · · · · · · · · Margaret Burton

CREDITS

writer Roy Clarke · *producer* Roger Race

A *Comedy Playhouse* segment starring the ace
comedy actor Leonard Rossiter as Pygmalion
Smith, the 'Happy Snaps' photographer at an
out-of-season holiday resort. Always with
an eye for the main chance, Smith meets a
beautiful girl from the local fish-filleting
sheds and sets about making her a cover
star – and, in the process, gaining fame and
fortune for himself.

Despite Rossiter's presence, and with
reliable Irish actor T P McKenna in a
supporting role, no series followed. But
writer Roy Clarke returned to the theme of
photography years later with the Ronnie
Barker sitcom *The Magnificent Evans*.

Pyjamarama

UK · ITV (LWT) · STANDUP

6 editions (5 × 30 mins · 1 × 45 mins) · colour

6 Jan–10 Feb 1984 · Fri mostly 11.30pm

MAIN CAST

host · Arthur Smith

CREDITS

writers cast · *executive producers* Melvyn Bragg/
Nick Evans · *director/producer* Ken O'Neill

A late-night LWT series, screened only by
London-area ITV, in which Arthur Smith
introduced comedy acts new to TV, usually
two per show, generously giving all but half
a programme of airtime to each performer.
Among those venting their acts, and
sometimes their spleens, were Jenny Lecoat
and Norman Lovett (programme one), Nick
Revell, the Chevalier Brothers and John Dowie

(two), the Joeys and Ronnie Golden (three),
Clive Anderson and Harvey And The
Wallbangers (four), Chris Barrie (still calling
himself Christopher Barrie), Fascinating Aïda
and Mac McDonald (five), Helen Lederer,
Mark Steel, John Hegley and the Popticians
(programme six).

See also *1st Exposure* and *291 Club*.

Six months after the end of *Queenie's Castle* Dors was cast as another sassy brassy lassie in YTV's ***All Our Saturdays***.

Q ...   [various shows]

see **MILLIGAN, Spike**

Queenie's Castle

UK · ITV (YORKSHIRE) · SITCOM

18 × 30 mins · colour

Series One (6) 5 Nov–10 Dec 1970 ·
Thu around 7pm

Series Two (6) 3 June–8 July 1971 · Thu 9pm

Series Three (6) 1 Aug–5 Sep 1972 · Tue 7.05pm

MAIN CAST

Queenie Shepherd · · · · · · · · · · ·	Diana Dors
Jack · · · · · · · · · · · · · · · · · ·	Tony Caunter
Douglas Shepherd · · · · · · · · ·	Barrie Rutter
Raymond Shepherd · · · · · · ·	Freddie Fletcher
Bunny Shepherd · · · · · · · · · ·	Brian Marshall
Mrs Petty · · · · · · · · · · · · · · ·	Lynne Perrie

CREDITS

creators Keith Waterhouse/Willis Hall · *writers*
Keith Waterhouse/Willis Hall (12), Stuart Harris
(2), John Junkin (1), Brian Marshall (1), Oliver Free
(1), Peter Robinson/David Rutherford (1) ·
directors/producers Graham Evans (series 1), Ian
Davidson (series 2 & 3) · *executive producer* John
Duncan (series 1 & 2)

A popular North Country vehicle for Diana
Dors, who starred as the indomitable and
downright blunt Queenie Shepherd, drinker of
light ale by the crate, owner of a stout
Yorkshire accent and bitter ruler of the roost
in her own castle: a tower-block named
Margaret Rose House, situated in the regally
named Buckingham Flats.

Created by Waterhouse and Hall, who
wrote the first two series, *Queenie's Castle*
also starred Freddie Fletcher, Barrie Rutter
and Brian Marshall as Queenie's three dodgy-
dealing sons Raymond, Douglas and Bernard
('Bunny'), Tony Caunter as brother-in-law
Jack, and Lynne Perrie (later Ivy Tilsley/
Brennan in *Coronation Street*) as the
Shepherds' neighbour Mrs Petty, who, as
secretary of the Residents' Association, was
viewed as the arch-enemy and treated
abominably.

Rab C Nesbitt

UK · BBC · SITCOM

41 episodes (36 × 30 mins · 2 × 45 mins · 2 × 50 mins · 1 × short special) · colour

Special (45 mins) *Rab C Nesbitt's Seasonal Greet* 31 Dec 1989 · BBC2 Sun 9.30pm

Series One (6) 27 Sep–1 Nov 1990 · BBC2 Thu 9pm

Special (45 mins) *Fitba* 15 July 1991 · BBC2 Mon 9.45pm

Series Two (6) 14 May–18 June 1992 · BBC2 Thu 9pm

Special (50 mins) 31 Dec 1992 · BBC2 Thu 11.30pm

Series Three (6) 18 Nov–23 Dec 1993 · BBC2 Thu 9pm

Series Four (6) 19 Sep–24 Oct 1994 · BBC2 Mon 9pm

Short special · part of *Fry And Laurie Host A Christmas Night With The Stars* 27 Dec 1994 · BBC2 Tue 9pm

Special (50 mins) 29 Dec 1994 · BBC2 Thu 9pm

Series Five (6) 5 Jan–9 Feb 1996 · BBC2 Fri 9pm

Series Six (6) 1 Aug–5 Sep 1997 · BBC2 Fri 9.30pm

MAIN CAST

Rab C Nesbitt · · · · · · · · · · · · · Gregor Fisher
Mary Nesbitt · · · · · · · · · · · · · Elaine C Smith
Gash Nesbitt · · · · · · · · · · · · · Andrew Fairlie
Burney Nesbitt · · · · · Eric Cullen (series 1–4)
Screech Nesbitt · · · · · · · · · · · David McKay
· · · · · · · · · · · · · · · · · · · (series 5 onwards)
Jamesie Cotter · · · · · · · · · · · · Tony Roper
Ella Cotter · · · · · · · · · · · · Barbara Rafferty
Andra · · · · · · · · · · · · · · · · Brian Pettifer
Dougie · · · · · · · · · Charlie Sim (series 1–4)
Dodie · · · · · · · · · · · · · · · · · Iain McColl
Norrie · · · · · · · · · · · · · · · · · John Kazek

CREDITS

writer Ian Pattison · *directors* Colin Gilbert (40), Ron Bain (1) · *producer* Colin Gilbert

Ian Pattison's monstrous creation Rab C Nesbitt was made flesh by the wonderful performance of Gregor Fisher. Nesbitt had first gained national exposure in **Naked Video** but he graduated to his own series following a 1989 Hogmanay special, *Rab C Nesbitt's Seasonal Greet*. A dirty, skiving, foul-mouthed, sexist drunkard, Nesbitt

represents an odd choice for a Scots comedy icon, but Fisher managed to make the character live, even suggesting the vulnerability and humanity beneath the appalling surface.

Liberated from the strictures of the short sketches in *Naked Video*, the series could treat viewers to a wider view of Rab's family and friends – his wife Mary ('weak in a strong sort of way'), teenage sons Gash and Burney, devious drinking buddy Jamesie, and Jamesie's wife, the baby-craving Ella. When not on a binge, Rab could be found pursuing nefarious deeds, pursuing other women or spending time in the local police cells for drink-related misdemeanours (and, one time, an accusation of murder). The string-vested philosopher remained an incorrigible slob throughout, neither learning from his mistakes nor acknowledging that he had made any. His speech – slurry and littered with slang – and strong Glasgow accent never made allowances for the fact that it was impenetrable to most viewers, but those who missed out on the dialogue were still able to comprehend that this was an oddball character. Besides, just the *sound* of Nesbitt cursing was funny enough. Many famous names guest-starred in the series, including Scots comedians Stanley Baxter and Rikki Fulton, aggressive comedy magician Jerry Sadowitz and Anita Dobson.

In the sixth series Rab's drink-sodden lifestyle was given a severe jolt when he was diagnosed with cancer and battled for his life. A two-parter in which, while hospitalised, he mused on his own mortality, was a high point of the 41 episodes made thus far, managing to pull off the difficult trick of combining humour with this gravest of subjects. But Rab rallied, and, at the time of writing, a seventh season of stories was likely to air in 1998.

See also **The Baldy Man.**

Radio Roo

UK · BBC · CHILDREN'S SITCOM

31 × 15 mins · colour

Series One (5) 25 Feb–25 Mar 1991 · BBC1 Mon 3.50pm

Series Two (13) 6 Jan–30 Mar 1992 · BBC1 Mon 3.55pm

Series Three (13) 4 Jan–29 Mar 1993 · BBC1 Mon 3.55pm

MAIN CAST

Dennis · · · · · · · · · · · · · · · Wayne Jackman
Clive · · · · · · · · · · · · · · · · Ian Tregonning
Margaret · · · · · · · · · · · · · Caroline O'Connor

CREDITS

writer Wayne Jackman · *director* David Coyle · *producer* Christine Hewitt

The adventures of Dennis and Clive, who run a radio station, Radio Roo. Each week the pair became involved in escapades rooted in confusion and slapstick – a situation shared

by many other children's series except that, here, Clive was a kangaroo.

Being that there aren't too many kangaroos within the vicinity of the BBC studios in west London, and even fewer who can talk, Clive The Kangaroo was – yes – a life-sized puppet, given a broad Australian accent by Ian Tregonning.

Strictly speaking, Clive owned Radio Roo – he was bequeathed it – but his tendency to break things through his jumpy, boisterous behaviour meant that Dennis and his friend, the scatty Margaret, assumed nominal responsibility.

The Rag Trade 1

UK · BBC · SITCOM

37 episodes (23 × 30 mins · 13 × 25 mins · 1 × short special) · b/w

Series One (10 × 30 mins) 6 Oct–8 Dec 1961 · Fri mostly 8.45pm

Series Two (13 × 30 mins) 6 Apr–29 June 1962 · Fri 8.45pm then 7.30pm

Short special · part of *Christmas Night With The Stars* 25 Dec 1962 · Tue 7.15pm

Series Three (13 × 25 mins) 5 Jan–30 Mar 1963 · Sat mostly 8pm

MAIN CAST

Harold Fenner · · · · · · · · · · · · · · · Peter Jones
Paddy · · · · · · · · · · · · · · · · · · · Miriam Karlin
Reg · Reg Varney
Lily ('Little Lil') · · · · · · · · · · · · · Esma Cannon
· (series 1 & 2)
Carole · · · · · · Sheila Hancock (series 1 & 2)
Judy · · · · · · · · · · Barbara Windsor (series 3)
Shirley · · · · · · Wanda Ventham (series 2 & 3)
Myrtle · · · · · · · · Claire Davenport (series 3)
Janet · · · · · · · · · · · Amanda Reiss (series 3)
Sandra · · · · · · · · · Sheena Marshe (series 3)
Olive · · · · · · · · · · · · · Stella Tanner (series 3)
Betty · · · · · · · · · · · Patricia Denys (series 3)
Gloria · · · · · · · · · · · Carmel Cryan (series 3)
Reg's mum · · · · · · · · Irene Handl (series 3)

**OTHER APPEARANCES
(UNNAMED ENSEMBLE CHARACTERS)**

Barbara Windsor (series 1)
Judy Carne (series 1)
Ann Beach (series 1)
Toni Palmer (series 1)
Rita Smythe (series 1)
Gwendolyn Watts (series 2)
Jan Williams (series 2)
Julia Samuel (series 2)
Elaine Kagan (series 2)

CREDITS

writers Ronald Wolfe/Ronald Chesney · *director/producer* Dennis Main Wilson

A classic early 1960s sitcom, set in the workshop of Fenner Fashions and focusing on a battle of wills between the management – Harold Fenner – and the workers, led by the trade union shop-steward, Paddy, who used any excuse to blow her whistle and bellow her catchphrase 'Everybody out!' The series was hugely popular and the energetic and rowdy performances from the cast, especially Peter

Jones and Miriam Karlin in these two leading roles, carried the audience along with such gusto that the groundbreaking nature of the programme was all but ignored at the time. For, unusually, this was a show predominantly populated by strong-of-character working women and was set in a working-class environment, well away from the cosy middle-class, male-dominated domesticity of other British sitcoms of the period. Giving the female members of the cast all the funny lines was unprecedented, but the enormous ratings proved how successful the writers Wolfe and Chesney were in their enterprise. Although Karlin received top billing among the women, she was not the only one to shine – Carole, played by Sheila Hancock, also caught the eye, and the waif-like eye-rolling Esma Cannon invariably stole the show with her fluttery antics.

Although most episodes involved a conflict between the boss and the staff, the plots were usually resolved by having everyone pull together, which kept the atmosphere at Fenner Fashions comfortable rather than hostile. Peter Jones's role, typically, was as straight-man to the women, and Reg Varney (later to star in Wolfe and Chesney's *On The Buses*) fared little better as his foreman, stuck in the dichotomous position of having a foot in both camps, management and workforce. Minor cast changes occurred from series to series but major restructuring was necessary for the third, after the departures of Cannon and Hancock. Barbara Windsor, who had played a minor role in the first series, returned to become Judy, Reg's love interest; and Irene Handl was cast as Reg's chatty mum, who came to work as Fenner's book-keeper. This third season, it has to be acknowledged, rarely matched the quality of the first two.

A stage version of *The Rag Trade* (with most of the TV cast) ran at the Piccadilly Theatre in London from December 1962 to February 1963 but – like all West End productions at the time – made little impression because of the particularly savage weather experienced that winter. The series has proved far more durable in a number of foreign versions, however, including Belgian version *FreddyTex* (1994), the Portuguese *Trapos And Company* (1995), and a massively successful Scandinavian TV adaptation, *Fredericksson's Fabriks* (1989–94), which, when it concluded, spawned *Fredericksson's Fabriks – The Movie!* But a US adaptation, *The Rag Business*, made by ABC and screened there on 8 July 1978, failed to get beyond the pilot episode. Undeterred, around the same period, Wolfe and Chesney sensed the time might be right for a British revival of their creation and took the idea back to the BBC. After producing a pilot (never transmitted) the BBC turned the writers

down, though, and so they took it instead to LWT, who picked up the option.

See also *Wild, Wild Women*.

The Rag Trade   2

UK · ITV (LWT) · SITCOM

22 × 30 mins · colour

Series One (15) 11 Sep–24 Dec 1977 ·
Sun mostly 7.15pm

Series Two (7) 8 Sep–20 Oct 1978 · Fri 7.30pm

MAIN CAST

Harold Fenner · · · · · · · · · · · · · Peter Jones
Paddy · · · · · · · · · · · · · · · · · Miriam Karlin
Tony · · · · · · · · · · · · · · · Christopher Beeny
Olive · · · · · · · · · · · · · · · · · Anna Karen
Kathy · · · · · · · · · · · · · · · Diane Langton
Lyn · · · · · · · · · · · · · · · · Gillian Taylforth
Mabel · · · · · · · · · · · · · · · Deddie Davies
Jo-Jo · · · · · · · · · · · · · · Lucita Lijertwood
Mrs Fenner · · · · · Rowena Cooper (series 1);
· · · · · · · · · · · · · · · · · Joy Stewart (series 2)

CREDITS

writers Ronald Wolfe/Ronald Chesney ·
director/producer Bryan Izzard

The decade had changed but things were much as before at Fenner's (including some of the storylines) and the central premise still revolved around the conflict between Fenner and Paddy. Reg was replaced here by the young and naïve Tony (Christopher Beeny) and a Barbara Windsor type (Diane Langton) played the buxom Kathy. Anna Karen was drafted in as Olive, a character only inches away from the Olive she had portrayed in the same writers' *On The Buses*. Extra spice was added by the occasional appearance of Mrs Fenner, upon whom the girls were not keen.

In one episode, in a rare moment of détente, Paddy and Fenner reminisced on their past and we discovered that they had once had a fling, which went some way to explaining the affection that undercut their disputes. Viewed overall, however, this revival of *The Rag Trade* was an unexceptional off-the-peg offering, a long way from the quality, designer item that the BBC had fashioned in the 1960s.

Raise Your Glasses

UK · BBC · SKETCH/STANDUP

6 editions (5 × 45 mins · 1 × short special) · b/w

One series (5) 14 Oct–16 Dec 1962 · fortnightly
Sun 7.25pm

Short special · part of *Christmas Night With The Stars* 25 Dec 1962 · Tue 7.15pm

MAIN CAST

Alan Melville
Arthur Askey
Pip Hinton
David Kernan

CREDITS

writer Alan Melville · producer Bryan Sears

Melville and long-term collaborator Bryan Sears were the creative forces behind this comedy pot-pourri, linked each week to a particular anniversary. Melville co-starred with Arthur Askey – both wore spectacles, hence the title – but neither was satisfied with the product, and the BBC bosses were also less than impressed, withdrawing an option that would have extended the series to 13 editions.

Les Raisins Verts

see The Montreux Festival

The Ramona Stories

USA · PBS (ATLANTIS FILMS/LANCIT MEDIA/
REVCOM TELEVISION) · CHILDREN'S SITCOM

20 × 30 mins · colour

US dates: 10 Sep 1988–21 Jan 1989

UK dates: 27 Aug 1989–9 Sep 1990
(20 episodes) C4 Sun 8.30am then 8.55am

MAIN CAST

Ramona Quimby · · · · · · · · · · · Sarah Polley
Beatrice 'Beezus' Quimby · · · · Lori Chandos
Dory Quimby · · · · · · · · Lynda Mason Green
Bob Quimby · · · · · · · · · · · · · Barry Flatman

CREDITS

creator Beverly Cleary · writer Ellis Weiner · director Randy Bradshaw · executive producers Michael Macmillan, Cecily Truett, Seaton McLean, Hugh Martin · producer Kim Todd

An American series, produced for the Public Broadcasting Service, which adapted the humorous children's books written by Beverly Cleary. The star turn was an eight-year-old girl, Ramona Quimby, who lived with her mother Dory, father Bob and elder sister Beezus. Episodes centred on Ramona's epochal childhood moments: vomiting in front of the class at school, being an object of fun, being able to afford only the salon's student to cut her hair, and fearing that the arrival of a baby sister would mean her own presence was overlooked.

The series was screened in the UK as *Ramona*, during C4's Sunday *Early Morning* strand for younger viewers.

The Randall Touch

UK · ITV (ATV) · SITCOM

12 × 30 mins · b/w

20 June–8 Sep 1958 · Fri 8.30pm then
Mon 10.15pm

MAIN CAST

Leslie · · · · · · · · · · · · · · · · Leslie Randall
Joan · · · · · · · · · · · · · · · · · Joan Reynolds

OTHER APPEARANCES

Mike Kelly · · · · · · · · · · · · · · · Harry Towb
Mrs Henshawe · · · · · · · · · · · · · Noël Dyson

CREDITS

writers Gerald Kelsey/Dick Sharples (7),
Bill Craig/John Law (5) · producer Hugh Rennie

Following virtually three years of *Joan And Leslie*, viewers were promised 'an entirely different' series in *The Randall Touch*. In truth, it was more of a sequel, with certain elements of the former being continued. True, Leslie Randall was no longing writing the Dorothy Goodheart column, but he *was* writing – interviewing crooks, spies and other adventuresome folk. This meant that, instead of being apron-tied to the home, Joan and Leslie finally got out and about beyond the studio, with a series of mini-stories – four of them spanning the 12-week run – being shot on location. Harry Towb and Noël Dyson still appeared in their respective roles as friend and charlady, but only occasionally.

Rap Master Ronnie: A Report Card

USA · HBO · SATIRE

1 × 50 mins · colour
US date: 1988
UK date: 18 Nov 1988 · BBC2 Fri 9.30pm

MAIN CAST
Jim Morris
Carol Kane
Jon Cryer
Tom Smothers
Dick Smothers

CREDITS
writer Garry Trudeau · *additional lyrics* Liz Swados · *director* Jay Dublin · *producer* Timothy Marx

A collection of satirical musical sketches looking back upon Ronald Reagan's eight years as president of the USA.

Masterminded by lyricist Elizabeth Swados and Pulitzer Prize-winning cartoonist Garry Trudeau – creator of the famous and long-running (1970 to date) *Doonesbury* satirical comic strip – the show was originally written for the 1984 election, being premiered that year at the Village Gate in New York. Updated regional productions ran continuously until 1988 at which time HBO put it on TV.

The show's suffixed title, *A Report Card*, sums up the overall approach: it was an end of (two) term(s) account on Reagan's record on the war against drugs, inner city social problems, foreign affairs and more. Impressionist Jim Morris starred as Reagan, rapping with a couple of secret-service men.

The Ray Stevens Show

CANADA · CTV · SKETCH

8 × 60 mins · colour
Canadian dates: not known (US dates · 20 June–8 Aug 1970)
UK dates: 18 Sep–6 Dec 1970 (7 editions) BBC2 Sun 7.25pm

MAIN CAST
Ray Stevens
Steve Martin

Dick Curtis
Billy Van

CREDITS
writers Jack Hanrahan, Phil Hahn · *executive producers* Allan Blye, Chris Beard, Murray Chercover

An international line-up – the regular cast included Ray Stevens, the American comic singer; Lulu, the Scottish singer; Mama Cass Elliot, the American singer; and Steve Martin, the American comic – gathered for this Canadian sketch series, taped in Toronto and screened not only domestically but in the USA by NBC and UK by the BBC.

Stevens was very popular at the time for his novelty comedy records, scoring two US Top 10 records in the 1960s, and a number one in 1970 with 'Everything Is Beautiful'. (He also had another number one in 1974, with 'The Streak'.) But the series is perhaps most interesting in hindsight, affording an early view of the movie comedy superstar-to-be Steve Martin.

Ted Ray

The son of a comic, Ted Ray – born George Olden in Wigan on 21 November 1905 – entered show business as a violinist, performing for a time as Nedlo The Gypsy Violinist – Nedlo being a palindrome of Olden. In 1930 he changed the name again, to Ted Ray, in honour of a famous British golfer of the period. After making his stage debut that same year, at the London Music Hall in Shoreditch, the young Ray enjoyed some pre-war success combining violin playing and comedy (he called it 'fiddling and fooling'), making his film debut in 1935. After the war, however, he abandoned the violin in favour of 'patter', admiring the talking style of American comedians, and he became a household name in 1949 when he was given his own BBC radio show, *Ray's A Laugh* – the series ran until 1961, and Ray's fame was such that he appeared in several feature films of the period. Throughout his career he was renowned as a reliable raconteur and a clever exponent of off-the-cuff comedy.

Ray's frequent excursions into television consolidated this popularity, and his easygoing conversational style of humour, liberally sprinkled with punchlines, assured him regular small-screen work until into the 1970s. He died of a heart attack on 8 November 1977, aged 71, leaving a wife and two children who also entered the entertainments business: Andrew Ray, an actor, and Robin Ray, actor turned classical music expert and radio presenter.

Note. In addition to the programmes listed below, Ted Ray appeared on TV on scores of other occasions, as a variety show guest, in numerous panel-game programmes, and also in a couple of informal specials in which he reminisced about and assessed fellow artists: *One Good Turn* (BBC2, 10 March 1965) and *Ted's Turn Again* (BBC2, 20 November 1965). He looked back on his own career in *Suddenly It's Ted Ray* (28 August 1967), one of BBC2's *Suddenly It's … series*.

See also *I Object*.

The Ted Ray Show

UK · BBC · SKETCH/STANDUP

29 editions (28 × 60 mins · 1 × short special) · b/w

Series One (4) 21 May–13 Aug 1955 · monthly Sat mostly 9.15pm
Series Two (4) 28 Apr–21 July 1956 · monthly Sat mostly 9.15pm
Series Three (8) 19 Jan–3 Aug 1957 · monthly Sat mostly 8pm
Series Four (5) 25 Jan–10 May 1958 · monthly Sat 8pm
Series Five (3) 27 Sep–22 Nov 1958 · monthly Sat 8pm
Short special · part of *Christmas Night With The Stars* 25 Dec 1958 · Thu 6.25pm
Series Six (4) 31 Jan–2 May 1959 · monthly Sat mostly 7.30pm

MAIN CAST
Ted Ray
Kenneth Connor (series 4)
Diane Hart (series 4)

CREDITS
writers Sid Colin/Talbot Rothwell/George Wadmore (series 1–4), John Junkin/Terry Nation (series 5 & 6 and special) · *additional material* Dave Freeman (3 shows) · *producers* George Inns (series 1–5), Bill Ward (2 shows), Ernest Maxin (1 show), Barry Lupino (1 show)

A long-running starring show that underwent various changes over the years. The first series accented variety, with international guests appearing; the second and third series had a greater emphasis on standup comedy; the fourth featured domestic routines (with Diane Hart as Ted Ray's wife and Kenneth Connor as 'that interfering brother-in-law'); the fifth and six – with new writers on board – concentrated on sketch comedy and were branded 'New Edition' and '1959 Edition' respectively to underline the difference in approach.

Hip Hip Who Ray

UK · ITV (ATV) · STANDUP

6 × 45 mins · b/w
25 Aug–29 Sep 1956 · Sat 8.15pm then 9pm

MAIN CAST
Ted Ray

CREDITS
writers Sid Colin/George Wadmore · *director/producer* Albert Locke

Ted Ray built upon his success in the new medium of television, gained through his monthly BBC series *The Ted Ray Show*, by jumping ship to 'the other side' during an interlude in the Corporation's scheduling. Bringing with him the writers Sid Colin and George Wadmore, he hosted a swift series of six Saturday-night programmes featuring his very popular standup act.

Note. The title should not be confused with the popular radio comedy series of the period, *Hip-Hip-Hoo-Roy!*, which starred Derek Roy and had featured among the cast the up-and-coming youngsters Spike Milligan, Peter Sellers and Alfred Marks.

Ray's A Rat

UK · BBC · STANDUP

1 × 30 mins · b/w

22 Sep 1957 · Sun 8pm

MAIN CAST
Ted Ray
Joan Turner
Morris and Cowley
Billie Carlyle

CREDITS
writers George Wadmore, Ted Ray · *producer* George Inns

The Grand Order Of Water Rats is a British show-business organisation dedicated to using the appeal of its celebrity members to raise money for charity. (It takes its name from a racehorse, The Water Rat, owned by the founder members at the turn of the 20th-century – much of the horse's winnings were given to charitable causes.)

In addition to this special programme featuring Ted Ray, other Water Rats celebrity presentations were televised by the BBC in late 1957: Charlie Chester (*The Water Rat Rag*) on 15 September; Nat Jackley, 6 October; Cyril Dowler, 13 October; Jimmy Wheeler, 20 October; Vic Oliver, 27 October; Jimmy O'Dea, 3 November; Cyril Dowler again, 1 December.

Friday The 13th

UK · BBC · SKETCH

1 × 30 mins · b/w

13 Dec 1957 · Fri 7.30pm

MAIN CAST
Ted Ray

CREDITS
writers John Junkin/Terry Nation · *producer* George Inns

A Friday the 13th sketch show in which Ted Ray posed the question 'Are you super-stitious?', scripted by his current writing team of Junkin and Nation.

It's Saturday Night

UK · BBC · STANDUP

4 × 45 mins · b/w

19 Sep–12 Dec 1959 · monthly Sat 7.45pm

MAIN CAST
Ted Ray
Robin Ray
June Whitfield (shows 1 & 3)
Alec Bregonzi (show 2)

CREDITS
writers Ray Enterprises · *additional material* Pete Davis/Johnnie McGregor (show 1), Bill Kelly/Arthur Laye (shows 2 & 4), Bernard Botting/Charlie Hart (show 3) · *producer* Albert Stevenson

A short series in which Ted Ray provided the quips in between other comedy acts. His son Robin, just starting out as an actor, was among the guests. (The main writing credit was given to Ray's company, Ray Enterprises – the identities behind this were not stated.)

Happy Family

UK · BBC · SITCOM

1 × 25 mins · b/w

18 June 1965 · BBC1 Fri 8pm

MAIN CAST
Ted · Ted Ray
Marian · · · · · · · · · · · · · · Daphne Anderson
Freddie · · · · · · · · · · · · · Patrick Westwood
Jack · · · · · · · · · · · · · · · · · · · Robert Raglan
Milly · · · · · · · · · · · · · · · · · · · Lyn Pinkney
Jenny · · · · · · · · · · · · · · · · · Mary Maude
Jill · Judy Geeson
Deborah · · · · · · · · · · · · · Carla Challoner
Mandy · · · · · · · · · · · · · Janet Hannington

CREDITS
writers Sid Green/Dick Hills · *executive producer* Graeme Muir · *producer* Bryan Sears

This *Comedy Playhouse* pilot was the first attempt at a 'legit' TV sitcom for the veteran comedian Ted Ray, although he had appeared in a recurring domestic sketch in the 1958 series of *The Ted Ray Show*, and his famous BBC radio series *Ray's A Laugh* was essentially a sitcom.

In *Happy Family* he played the only man in a house full of women: his wife Marian and four young daughters, Jenny, Jill, Deborah and Mandy. (Jill was played by the 16-year-old future film star Judy Geeson.) Ray's only male companion at home was a dog. No series developed.

Notes. Ending just two days before *Happy Family*, Ray was one of three comics appearing each week in an improvisational parlour-game show, *I Object* (ten editions, BBC1, 14 April to 16 June 1965). The programmes had a courtroom setting, and Ray and Charlie Chester (who co-devised the show with his long-time collaborator Charles Hart) appeared as counsels for or against propositions put before the jury (12 members of the public), with Jimmy Edwards acting as the judge. There were four issues debated per programme, each sparked by an 'I Object' statement – for example, 'I object to the confusing number of traffic signs on the road'.

Nearly two years later, Ray starred in *Hooray For Laughter*, a one-off sketch/standup show screened on 12 March 1967 (but not in London) by the Midlands/North ITV company ABC. The programme was co-written by Ray with John Junkin, produced by Peter Frazer-Jones, and the supporting cast included Junkin, Reg Varney, Ray Alan, Mike Felix and singer Rosemary Squires.

Re-Joyce

see GRENFELL, Joyce

Re-Turn It Up!

see JEWEL, Jimmy and Ben Warriss

Ready Freddie Starr

see STARR, Freddie

The Real McCoy

UK · BBC · SKETCH/STANDUP

31 editions (30 × 30 mins · 1 × short special) · colour

Series One (6) 10 May–14 June 1991 · BBC2 Fri 9pm

Series Two (6) 6 July–10 Aug 1992 · BBC2 Mon 10pm

Series Three (6) 7 May–11 June 1993 · BBC2 Fri 9pm

Series Four (6) 9 Aug–13 Sep 1994 · BBC2 Tue 9pm then 10pm

Short special · part of *Fry And Laurie Host A Christmas Night With The Stars* 27 Dec 1994 · BBC2 Tue 9pm

Series Five (6) 5 Jan–9 Feb 1996 · BBC2 Fri 10pm

MAIN CAST
Llewella Gideon
Curtis Walker (series 1 & 2)
Ishmael Thomas (series 1 & 2)
Collette Johnson (series 1 & 2)
Felix Dexter (series 3–5)
Perry Benson
Leo Chester
Meera Syal
Robbie Gee
Fraser Downie
Leon Black
Judith Jacob
Eddie Nestor
Kulvinder Ghir (series 4 & 5)

CREDITS
writers cast and others · *directors* Terry Jervis (12), Jo Johnson (6), Angela deChastelai Smith (6), Charlie Hanson (5), John Kilby/Charlie Hanson (1), Geoff Posner (special) · *producers* Charlie Hanson (12), Bill Wilson (12), Paulette Randall (6), Claudia Lloyd (special)

A sketch series featuring an array of talented black comedy stars performing material aimed unashamedly at an across-the-board black audience. Central in the first two series was the comedy double-act of Curtis and Ishmael, who had established themselves as viable TV stars with their residency on **Paramount City**. They built on that reputation here, given space to delve deep into the black experience for their humour. As talented vocal impressionists, they spoofed many identifiable targets, including rambling elder Jamaican characters, rap artists and smooth-talking Lotharios. This area had been touched upon by Lenny Henry but, nonetheless, the comedic exploration of such black stereotypes on TV was extremely rare. Curtis and Ishmael were joined by Collette Johnson and Llewella Gideon, who provided their own spot-on character impersonations drawn from the black female perspective. Also featured was Indian standup Meera Syal, who provided a similar comedy service aimed at the series' Asian viewers. By series three, Curtis and Ishmael and Collette Johnson had moved on, and the support cast took centre stage, proving reasonably adept at the task.

Although not black himself, the producer of the first two series, Charlie Hanson, was the co-founder of the Black Theatre Co-operative and had often worked on black-themed shows, producing **No Problem!** and **Desmond's** before creating *The Real McCoy*. He was working with Curtis and Ishmael on **The 291 Club** at the Hackney Empire and suggested making a television version, but, instead, the BBC opted for a totally new sketch series, launching *The Real McCoy*. (Ultimately, LWT mounted a series from the 291 Club.) Hanson brought the team together but realised, after the first six editions, the limitations of the series: although the cast were excellent at characterisation and standup, they found it hard to maintain a high quality of humour in longer sketches. This problem was addressed in the second batch of six editions, at which point the series noticeably improved. Subsequently, with the cast upheavals and Hanson's departure, it suffered from inconsistency, but it seems churlish to level much criticism at something that tried hard – and often succeeded – to fill an obvious and shamefully neglected gap in the UK television landscape. (Incidentally, later in its run, the series often included black guest stars from the worlds of entertainment and sport.)

Black comedy in the UK was enjoying a boom period at this time, much like the 'alternative' scene a decade earlier, and once again Britain seemed to be following the US lead, where Eddie Murphy, Arsenio Hall, Whoopi Goldberg, Robert Townsend and others were in the vanguard of a revolution. A year before *The Real McCoy* first appeared, Keenen Ivory Wayans' series *In Living Color* (1990–94) presented a similarly slanted show in the USA, its posse of comedians humorously reflecting the US experience. *In Living Color* was a huge success for the Fox network, which proclaimed it a 'black **Saturday Night Live**'; perhaps if the BBC had described *The Real McCoy* as a 'black **Not The Nine O'Clock News**' (a series that it did resemble in some ways) it might have found a wider audience.

See also Felix Dexter On TV.

The Real Mike Yarwood?

see YARWOOD, Mike

Red Dwarf

UK · BBC (PAUL JACKSON PRODUCTIONS · *GRANT NAYLOR PRODUCTIONS) SITCOM
44 × 30 mins · colour

Series One (6) *Red Dwarf* 15 Feb–21 Mar 1988 · BBC2 Mon 9pm
Series Two (6) *Red Dwarf II* 6 Sep–11 Oct 1988 · BBC2 Tue 9pm
Series Three (6) *Red Dwarf III* 14 Nov–19 Dec 1989 · BBC2 Tue 9pm
*Series Four (6) *Red Dwarf IV* 14 Feb–21 Mar 1991 · BBC2 Thu 9pm
*Series Five (6) *Red Dwarf V* 20 Feb–26 Mar 1992 · BBC2 Thu 9pm
*Series Six (6) *Red Dwarf VI* 7 Oct–11 Nov 1993 · BBC2 Thu 9pm
*Series Seven (8) *Red Dwarf* 17 Jan–7 Mar 1997 · BBC2 Fri 9pm

MAIN CAST
Ace/Arnold Rimmer · · · · · · · · · Chris Barrie
David Lister · · · · · · · · · · · · · · Craig Charles
Cat · · · · · · · · · · · · · · · · · · Danny John-Jules
Holly · · · · · · · Norman Lovett (series 1 & 2); · · · · · · · · · · · · Hattie Hayridge (series 3–6)
Kryten 2X4B 523P · · · David Ross (series 2); · · · · · · · · · · · Robert Llewellyn (series 3–7)

OTHER APPEARANCES
Christine (Kristine) Kochanski · · · · · · · · · · · · · · · · · · · C P (Clare) Grogan (series 1, 2 & 6); · · · · · · · · · · · · · · · · · Chloë Annett (series 7)

CREDITS
writers Rob Grant/Doug Naylor (36), Doug Naylor/Paul Alexander (3), Doug Naylor (2), Doug Naylor/Kim Fuller (1), Doug Naylor/Robert Llewellyn (1), Doug Naylor/Paul Alexander/James Hendrie (1) · *directors* Ed Bye (32), Juliet May (6), Andy de Emmony (6) · *executive producers* Paul Jackson (series 1–3), Rob Grant/Doug Naylor (series 4–6), Doug Naylor (series 7) · *producers* Ed Bye (32), Hilary Bevan Jones (6), Justin Judd (6)

A long-running sci-fi space sitcom that became BBC2's biggest comedy export and developed a strong, national and international cult following, *Red Dwarf* is a perfect example of the benefits achievable by the BBC's patience in giving a rocky production time to find its feet.

Created and written by Rob Grant and Doug Naylor (whose previous TV experience included contributions to **Carrott's Lib**, 1982–83, and then **Spitting Image**), *Red Dwarf* got off to an auspicious start – five million viewers saw the premiere episode – but this dwindled to two million by the end of the initial series as viewers tired of the wobbly sets, and everyone involved in the creative process needed time to get into their stride. But by the second series all the ingredients gelled, audience figures were up again and the BBC found themselves with a very popular comedy destined to outlive most other series.

This is the premise: the crew of a 21st-century deep-space mining ship, the *Red Dwarf*, are all – bar one – wiped out following a radiation leak. The sole survivor is David Lister, who has been placed in suspended animation for 18 months as punishment for smuggling aboard a pet pregnant cat. Lister remains in stasis for three million years, and when he awakes he has some unexpected company: a hologram of his former shift leader Rimmer, who has retained all the foibles of the master material; the shipboard computer Holly, now showing definite signs of senility; and 'Cat' a strange human-like creature who turns out to have evolved, over the past three million years, from the pregnant moggy – resulting in a sort of feline-sapien. This mismatched assortment proceed to roam the universe, becoming involved – despite their reluctance – in a fantastic variety of weird and wonderful adventures. By the third series the computer personality had been replaced by a new, sparkier version and the crew were joined by an all-too-human-like android, Kryten.

The series was developed by Grant/Naylor out of an earlier comedy creation, 'Dave Hollins – Space Cadet', a recurring skit in their BBC Radio 4 comedy series Son Of Cliché (eight editions, 23 August–11 October 1983, this being the sequel to a 1981 series by the same writers). Hollins was the last man alive in the universe, whose only companion was his computer, Hab (voiced by Chris Barrie). Later, when the writing duo were exploring ideas for possible TV sitcoms, they returned to Hollins, expanded him into Dave Lister and created partners to accompany him in his space rambles, re-employing Barrie in the key role of Rimmer.

Ostensibly, despite its futuristic trappings, *Red Dwarf* has all the aspects of a traditional sitcom: a closed set, the clash of opposing personalities forced to share the same space, a surrogate family set-up and the continuing possibility that their dilemma might be resolved at any moment. But as the series progressed it called upon different strengths to propel it away from traditional orbits towards more uncharted areas. Although the plots embraced many typical sci-fi themes (parallel universes, black holes, time warps, alternative histories, matter transportation and so on), when wedded to the comedy format some truly original television was created. Grant and Naylor refused to underestimate their audience and assumed that viewers would have had sufficient grounding in sci-fi to make elaborate explanations unnecessary. And even if the science did leave the audience behind, the writers realised that the comedy would carry the day. Vulgar, occasionally crude but always witty, the dialogue more than matched the crazy plots – Rimmer was a whiny, shallow, self-centred hologram who had a sharp tongue and considered himself above the others; Lister was an everyman with a 'laddish' outlook on life; Cat was a fashion victim who often displayed aspects of his feline past; the admirable Kryten was an android servant who, like Jeeves, often operated beyond the call of duty but who, unlike Wodehouse's creation, often dropped his masters into difficulties rather than saving them. The computer, Holly, was at first morose and senile (in the person of Norman Lovett); a later personality (interpreted by Hattie Hayridge) was more efficient but had a flippant attitude and a mischievous streak.

The seventh series followed a gap of three years, with Chris Barrie announcing that he had taken Rimmer as far as he wanted and amicably leaving the production, bowing out in the episode aired on 14 February 1997. (This event led to the reappearance of Christine/Kristine Kochanski, Rimmer's ex-girlfriend, originally played by Clare Grogan but now by Chloë Annett.) Otherwise, the exploits continued much as before with perhaps an even greater freedom to explore extreme plot ideas and uncharted territories: to badly go where none had gone before.

Although not attracting the same number of fans as *Star Trek* or *Doctor Who*, *Red Dwarf* has a strong, dedicated following, its fans being known as Dwarfers. The series is particularly popular in the USA, and in 1992 a pilot episode of an American adaptation was made by Universal for NBC. Robert Llewellyn from the British series re-created his role as Kryten but the rest of the cast were different, and included Jane Leeves (later Daphne Moon in *Frasier*) as Holly. The pilot never aired, however, and was not developed into a series. A second attempt, *Red Dwarf USA*, steered by Grant and Naylor, changed the format and cast somewhat but retained Leeves and Llewellyn; this too failed to get picked up.

At the time of writing, an eighth UK series, and possible feature-film version, were in the pipeline for 1998.

Note. As an aid to international sales, early episodes of *Red Dwarf* were revisited in the late 1990s, with computer-generated imagery, digital video effects and digital stereo sound replacing the suddenly very dated mechanical effects and mono sound of old. This is the first time that a British comedy series has been treated to retrospective improvements, but it is typical of the forward-thinking that sets *Red Dwarf* apart from most of its contemporaries.

Reeves And Mortimer

Vic Reeves (born in Darlington, 24 January 1959; real name James/Jim Moir) and Bob Mortimer (born in Middlesbrough, 23 May 1959) first joined forces at the Albany Empire in Deptford, south London, where Reeves ran comedy nights and Mortimer, a practising Legal Aid solicitor, was a regular heckler. They combined together on a stage-show, *Vic Reeves Big Night Out*, which constituted a blend of bizarre acts and surreal standup, and toured universities with the production. The TV presenter Jonathan Ross then persuaded C4 chief executive Michael Grade to see the show, which led to a TV version in 1990.

Both Reeves and Mortimer had been failed punk rockers in the late 1970s, and an element of that same style of anarchy permeates their comedy act and gives them limited but intensely dedicated appeal: they employ the violent slapstick of the alternative 'new wave' comedy, mixed with Pythonesque absurdity and, most importantly of all, a vaudevillian style reminiscent of traditional stage pairings. Their knowing, exaggerated performance and deconstruction of style allow them to embroil their audience in what, to all intents and purposes, are private jokes, and the sum total makes for intelligent and totally unpredictable humour that surprises as much as it delights. Weird, but with undoubted charm, the pair's plundering of styles and awareness of comedy history could arguably present them with the claim of being Britain's first truly post-modernist double-act. Such is their status, the pair were the subject of a BBC1 *Omnibus* arts documentary, *The Film Of Reeves And Mortimer*, screened on 21 September 1997.

See also Comic Relief and *It's Ulrika!*

Vic Reeves Big Night Out

UK · C4 (CHANNEL X) · STANDUP/SKETCH

16 editions (14 × 30 mins · 1 × 45 mins · 1 × 60 mins) · colour

Series One (6) 25 May–29 June 1990 · Fri 10.30pm

Special (45 mins) *Vic Reeves New Year's Eve Big Night Out* 31 Dec 1990 · Mon 11.35pm

Series Two (8) 27 Feb–17 Apr 1991 · Wed 10.30pm

Special (60 mins) *Vic Reeves Big Night Out On Tour* 27 Dec 1991 · Fri 10.35pm

MAIN CAST
Vic Reeves
Bob Mortimer

CREDITS
writers Vic Reeves/Bob Mortimer · *director/producer* Peter Orton

A contagious, comical mix of violent slapstick, weird characters, surreal ideas and twisted variations on traditional music-hall offerings. The whole collection was presented in a free-form, sprawling style that seemed randomly programmed but which, although unstructured, was rarely undisciplined within its own boundaries.

Vic Reeves Big Night Out had been an ever-changing show appearing at a number of venues on the 'alternative' comedy circuit. The hours of inspired lunacy that Reeves and Mortimer concocted amused their loyal following but failed to make much impact on the comedy business in general, and C4 took a risk in mounting it on television. It paid off – the pair quickly gathered a cult following, bringing the 'right type' of audience to the channel.

On TV, *Vic Reeves Big Night Out* was certainly different from other fare the small-screen offered at this time, being an odd and constantly surprising amalgam of bizarre comedy vignettes, including the strange scientist Les; The Man With A Stick, who was literally a chap with a stick which bore an enigmatic message; the Kangaroo Court of Judge Nutmeg; Novelty Island, a specially set-aside area for guest objects; and Wavy Davy, a bloke who waved.

The final edition, screened on 27 December 1991, was a recording of a stage performance, taped at the City Hall in Newcastle upon Tyne, with all the best-loved bits from the TV series worked into the show.

See also *Les Lives*.

The Weekenders

UK · C4 (GRANADA) · SITCOM

1 × 30 mins · colour

17 June 1992 · Wed 10.30pm

MAIN CAST
Jim · Vic Reeves
Bob · Bob Mortimer

CREDITS
writers Bob Mortimer/Jim Moir (Vic Reeves) · *director* Sandy Johnson · *producer* Mark Robson

A surreal offering, broadcast as part of C4's comedy pilots series *Bunch Of Five*. Here, Vic (writing and appearing under his real name Jim) and Bob played two strange friends who live in a truly bizarre world. They take a bus trip to a meat festival (held in an open field) where they purchase a speciality meat product (a sausage) that is badly wanted by aliens who need it to feed their monstrous queen. At first the lads resist but then they help the aliens to achieve their aim.

This one is hard to sum up in words. Basically, however, *The Weekenders* was *way* weird, combining echoes of the Beatles' *Magical Mystery Tour* with Pythonesque and Milliganesque lunacy and moments of utter Reeves and Mortimer-style nonsense. The programme also included cameo appearances from 'Tommy Cockles' (Simon Day) as a slow-motion policeman, Paul Whitehouse as a bus driver with attitude, Human League vocalist Phil Oakey as a meat salesman, and John Thomson (appearing as John Patrick Thomson) as a police constable. (Whitehouse, Day and Thomson all teamed again in *The Fast Show* from 1994.)

Delightfully uninhibited, this was outrageous, intriguing stuff – effortlessly watchable and, in places, hilariously funny.

The Smell Of Reeves And Mortimer

UK · BBC (CHANNEL X) · STANDUP/SKETCH

13 editions (12 × 30 mins · 1 × short special) · colour

Series One (6) 21 Sep–26 Oct 1993 · BBC2 Tue 9pm

Short special · part of *Fry And Laurie Host A Christmas Night With The Stars* 27 Dec 1994 · BBC2 Tue 9pm

Series Two (6) 5 May–9 June 1995 · BBC2 Fri 9.30pm

MAIN CAST
Vic Reeves
Bob Mortimer

CREDITS
writers Vic Reeves/Bob Mortimer · *executive producers* Alan Marke, Charlie Higson · *director/producer* John Birkin

Switching from C4 to BBC2, the duo continued to mix anarchy and surrealism, much as before, delighting their loyal following. The studio-set featured the huge letters 'R' and 'M' and various columns, and once again there was a desk, from which the pair launched many of the skits. They introduced new characters, including the bra-wearing men Pat Wright and Dave Arrowsmith; awful folk duo Mulligan and

O'Hare; flatulent farceurs the Petomanes; and the Max Wall-ish Uncle Peter, played by Charlie Chuck. Among the many other highlights were occasional visits with Slade, the 1970s glam-rock group, brilliantly imitated by Reeves, Mortimer, Paul Whitehouse and Mark Williams.

Note. On 27 December 1993, again on BBC2, Reeves and Mortimer presented *At Home With Vic And Bob*, an entire evening's programming in which the double-act linked a night of their favourite old shows. In between the nostalgic programmes the pair presented vignettes featuring some of their characters including the Bra Men, Slade At Christmas, and Mulligan and O'Hare. The evening also included the debut of what would soon become the pair's ultra-successful anarchic game-show *Shooting Stars* (BBC2, eight editions, 22 September–10 November 1995; special, 29 December 1995; 14 editions, 27 September–27 December 1996; seven editions, 26 September–7 November 1997; special 22 December 1997).

The Refuge

UK · C4 (YORKSHIRE) · SITCOM

14 × 30 mins · colour

Series One (7) 21 Sep–9 Nov 1987 · Mon mostly 9.25pm

Series Two (7) 22 June–3 Aug 1988 · Wed mostly 11pm

MAIN CAST
Helen Crichton-Crick · · · · · Caroline Blakiston
Julia · · · · · · · · · · · · · · · · · Julia Hills
Dee Dee · · · · · · · · · · · · · · · Lou Wakefield
WPC Brenda Bollard · · · · · · · Carole Hayman
Cyril · · · · · · · · · · · Louis Mahoney (series 1)

CREDITS
writers Sue Townsend/Carole Hayman · *director* Les Chatfield · *producers* Vernon Lawrence (series 1), Les Chatfield (series 2)

Sue Townsend, the creator of *The Secret Diary Of Adrian Mole*, co-scripted this C4 sitcom that espoused feminism, albeit with a wry and occasionally self-mocking touch. Her co-author, Carole Hayman, appeared before the cameras, as WPC Brenda Bollard, one of four people living in a refuge for women. The flat belonged to Dee Dee, a local radio broadcaster endowed with strong social responsibilities, her original intention being to open its doors 24 hours a day to life's waifs and strays – two of whom were her mother, Helen, and her best friend from university, the seriously feminist barrister Julia, a Sloane Ranger-type still smarting from a recent divorce. But after experiencing teething troubles with a couple of oddballs (the black chauvinist Cyril, and a filthy-minded vagrant nicknamed Rum Weather), the women decided to restrict membership of the sanctuary to male-

oppressed females. Still, The Refuge attracted an odd bunch, including a sex-change woman and someone who chopped through the door with an axe, and the co-operative had to grapple with knotty problems such as whether they should permit inside the house a male repairman to fix their TV.

Reg Dixon

UK · BBC · STANDUP

1 × 15 mins · b/w

21 July 1953 · Tue 8.15pm

MAIN CAST
Reg Dixon

CREDITS
writer Reg Dixon · *producer* Kenneth Carter

Although born in Coventry, Reg Dixon was classified as a 'northern comedian' because of the accent he developed for his act, especially in the delivery of his catchphrase 'I've been proper poorly'. Dixon was well known through his radio work but stage audiences – and, here, television viewers of the long-running *Starlight* series – familiar with his gentle voice, were surprised by his six-foot, 16-stone stature.

See also *Confidentially* and *Let's Stay Home*.

Reg Varney ...   [various shows]

see VARNEY, Reg

Reggie

USA · ABC (FOX UNICORN/CAN'T SING CAN'T DANCE PRODUCTIONS/COLUMBIA PICTURES) · SITCOM

6 × 30 mins · colour

US dates: 2 Aug–1 Sep 1983

UK dates: 14 Sep–19 Oct 1984 (6 episodes) C4 Fri 10pm

MAIN CAST
Reggie Potter · · · · · · · · · · Richard Mulligan
Elizabeth Potter · · · · · · · · · · · Barbara Barrie
C J Wilcox · · · · · · · · · · · · · · · · · Chip Zien
Joan Reynolds · · · · · · · · · · · · · · · Jean Smart
Linda Potter Lockett · · · · · · · · · · Dianne Kay
Tom Lockett · · · · · · · · · · · · · Timothy Stack
Mark Potter · · · · · · · · · · · · · · Tim Busfield

CREDITS
creator David Nobbs · *writers* Sylvia Alan, Lorin H Dreyfuss, Ken Hecht, Dinah Kirgo/Julie Kirgo, Bernie Kukoff, David Landsberg, Stephen Nathan, Paul B Price · *executive producers* Barbara Corday, Bernie Kukoff · *producers* Dinah Kirgo, Julie Kirgo

This American adaptation of *The Fall And Rise Of Reginald Perrin* ought to have worked. Not only was the original BBC version a brilliant treat but the US model cast Richard Mulligan – the loveable loose-limbed buffoon Burt Campbell from *Soap* – in the starring role. Yet *Reggie* (so titled) was as unfunny as the original was hilarious, and as slow and unremarkable as the original was brilliantly paced and delightful. American viewers usually recognise a bummer when they see one, and so it proved: the show was cancelled after just six episodes, a rare example of a UK series running longer than its US counterpart.

In *Reggie*, the first names were the same but the surnames were changed. Reggie Potter works at the Funtime Ice Cream Company, where he is perpetually frustrated by his boss C J (now portrayed as a younger man). At home, Reggie lusts after his son Mark's girlfriend (in the British series Mark had no girlfriend and was only seen occasionally) and confides in a Basil Brush-like stuffed fox (in the original, a live cat, Ponsonby, was given access to Perrin's confidences). A good deal of each episode was given over to Reggie's fantasy dreams but these failed to elevate the show out of the mediocre.

'Reggie Little'

A bright and breezy though luckless individual, invented by the TV writer Godfrey Harrison and portrayed by actor Desmond Walter-Ellis in a number of TV appearances. The moral inherent in all of Little's adventures was 'more haste less speed' as the character's own enthusiasms and eagerness often tripped him up.

These Are The Days

UK · BBC · SKETCH

7 × 15 mins approx · b/w

12 Jan–20 Apr 1951 · fortnightly Fri approx 8.30pm

MAIN CAST
Reggie Little · · · · · · · Desmond Walter-Ellis

CREDITS
writer Godfrey Harrison · *producer* Graeme Muir

A resident comedy segment within the fortnightly TV magazine *Kaleidoscope*.

When Desmond Walter-Ellis left the series to return to fulfil a stage engagement, Godfrey Harrison invented a new comedy spot, *Fools Rush In*, for the miscellany programme, which gave up-and-coming young comedian Tony Hancock his first regular TV work.

Mr Little At Large

UK · BBC · CHILDREN'S SKETCH

10 × 15 mins · b/w

Series One (4) 27 Feb–19 Mar 1952 · mostly Wed 5.55pm

Series Two (6) 30 Apr–29 June 1952 · mostly fortnightly Wed around 5.30pm

MAIN CAST
Reggie Little · · · · · · · Desmond Walter-Ellis

CREDITS
writer Godfrey Harrison · *producers* Michael Westmore (series 1), Douglas Hurn (series 2)

Two series for younger viewers, screened within the strand *Children's Television*.

Reggie Little At Large

UK · BBC · SITCOM

6 × 30 mins · b/w

6 May–15 July 1953 · fortnightly Wed around 9pm

MAIN CAST
The Commentator · · · · · · · Godfrey Harrison
Reggie Little · · · · · · · Desmond Walter-Ellis
Maynard Withering · · · · · Richard Caldicot
Pauline Dear · · · · · · · · Sheila McCormack

CREDITS
writer Godfrey Harrison · *producer* Graeme Muir

An adult sitcom slot for Reggie Little – cast here as 'the well-meaning but somewhat inefficient estate agent'. Richard Caldicot played his boss and Sheila McCormack was his ever-helpful secretary. Writer Godfrey Harrison appeared as the commentator on the proceedings.

Reginald Purdell

UK · BBC · STANDUP

1 × 10 mins · b/w

17 Apr 1937 · Sat 9pm

MAIN CAST
Reginald Purdell

CREDITS
producer Gordon Grier

An early TV comedy performance by Reginald (Reggie) Purdell, who had shown remarkable versatility since his stage debut as a child entertainer in 1911, going on to write, direct and appear in projects for film and theatre and scoring acclaim as a comedian and comedy-actor. However, he was probably best known at this time as the voice of the Magician in the popular BBC children's radio series *Toytown*, featuring Larry The Lamb.

In this TV appearance, Purdell performed three comic songs, 'Knocked 'Em In The Old Kent Road', 'Mrs Henry Hawkins' and 'My Old Dutch'.

See also *Kaleidoscope*.

Relative Strangers

UK · C4 (HUMPHREY BARCLAY PRODUCTIONS) · SITCOM

19 × 30 mins · colour

Series One (12) 14 Jan–1 Apr 1985 · Mon 8.30pm

Series Two (7) 26 Jan–9 Mar 1987 · Mon 9.30pm

MAIN CAST
Fitz · · · · · · · · · · · · · · · · · · · Matthew Kelly
John · · · · · · · · · · · · · · · · · · · Mark Farmer
Percy Fisher · · · · · · · · · · Bernard Gallagher
Gerald · · · · · · · · · · · · · · · · · David Battley
Heather · · · · · · · · · · · · · June Page (series 1)
Carol · · · · · · · · · Jacqueline Beatty (series 2)

CREDITS
creators/script editors Laurence Marks/Maurice Gran · *writers* Laurence Marks/Maurice Gran (7), Paul Makin (4), Geoff Rowley (2), Richard Maher/ Roger Michell (2), Gary Lawson/John Phelps (2), Mike Walling/Ian Whitham (2) · *directors* John Kaye Cooper (series 1), Nic Phillips (series 2) · *executive producer* Al Mitchell · *producers* Humphrey Barclay/John Kaye Cooper (series 1), Humphrey Barclay (series 2)

Best known for hosting game-shows and being a perpetrator of *Game For A Laugh*, Matthew Kelly – who started out as an actor – reprised the role of Fitzroy ('Fitz') that he had played in **Holding The Fort**, five years earlier, in this successful Marks and Gran spin-off.

Now 36 and working in a hardware shop owned by Percy Fisher, Fitz remains a wisecracking, free-spirited bachelor, anxious to be free of any ties. But he receives a severe jolt in the opening episode: a 17-year-old boy, John, wanders into the hardware shop with proof that Fitz is his father – the result of a single-night dalliance with one Donna Appleton at a Butlin's holiday camp back in 1966. John's mother has recently been killed in a road accident and so the teenager descends upon his dad, feeling that his father owes him a favour or two. John and Fitz become something of a double-act, stepping out together for nights on the tiles, but the father is occasionally shocked by the sight of his son doing the things that he himself likes to do, like picking up a different woman every night. Fatherhood, indeed, is the most sobering and anchoring experience of Fitz's hitherto footloose and hedonistic existence.

A decent sitcom this, and not a million miles away in premise from **Home To Roost**, which ran on ITV at almost the same time, with young son arriving on the scene to show father that behavioural patterns can be passed on in the genes.

The Reluctant Romeo

see CROWTHER, Leslie

Rentaghost

UK · BBC · CHILDREN'S SITCOM

58 episodes (38 × 25 mins · 19 × 30 mins · 1 × 40 mins) · colour

Series One (5 × 25 mins) 6 Jan–3 Feb 1976 · BBC1 Tue 5.15pm

Series Two (6 × 25 mins) 18 May–22 June 1976 · BBC1 Tue 5.15pm

Series Three (6 × 25 mins) 22 Feb–29 Mar 1977 · BBC1 (1 episode on BBC2) Tue 4.40pm

Series Four (6 × 25 mins) 14 Sep–19 Oct 1978 · BBC1 Thu 4.35pm

Special (40 mins) *Rentasanta* 21 Dec 1978 · BBC1 Thu 4.30pm

Series Five (5 × 25 mins) 7 Mar–21 Mar 1980 · BBC1 Fri then Tue around 5.10pm

Series Six (6 × 30 mins) 24 Apr–29 May 1981 · BBC1 Fri 5.05pm

Series Seven (13 × 30 mins) 5 Oct–29 Dec 1982 · BBC1 Tue 5.10pm

Series Eight (5 × 25 mins) 18 Oct–15 Nov 1983 · BBC1 Tue 4.40pm

Series Nine (5 × 25 mins) 9 Oct–6 Nov 1984 · BBC1 Tue 4.35pm

MAIN CAST
Timothy Claypole · · · · · · · · Michael Staniforth
Harold Meaker · · · · · · · · · · Edward Brayshaw
Fred Mumford · · · · · · · · · · · Anthony Jackson
· (series 1–4)
Hubert Davenport · · · · · · Michael Darbyshire
· (series 1–4)

OTHER APPEARANCES
Ethel Meaker · · · · · · · · · · · · · · · Ann Emery
Mrs Mumford · · · · · · · · · · · · · Betty Alberge
Mr Mumford · · · · · · · · · · · · · · John Dawson
Catastrophe Kate · · · · · · · · · · · Jana Shelden
Hazel the McWitch · · · · · · · · · · · Molly Weir
Nadia Popov · · · · · · · · · · · · · · Sue Nicholls
Rose Perkins · · · · · · · · · · · · · · · · Hal Dyer
Arthur Perkins · · · · · · · · · · · · Jeffrey Segal
Susie Starlight · · · · · · · · · · Aimi Macdonald
Adam Painting · · · · · · · · Christopher Biggins
Queen Matilda · · · · · · · · · · · · Paddie O'Neil

CREDITS
writer Bob Block · *director* David Crichton · *producers* Paul Ciani (series 1), Jeremy Swan (series 2–9)

A ghostly fantasy comedy that proved irresistible to – and durable with – younger viewers.

Writer Bob Block's original concept featured ghosts who have come back from the spiritual world to make amends for failing in their previous existence, but although the spectres had magical powers they still tended to be hidebound by the same ineptness that had dogged them during their earthly lives. In the opening episode, Fred Mumford returns from the spirit world and opens the agency Rentaghost, which offers ghosts and poltergeists for hire on a daily or weekly rental. He is helped (and hindered) in these plans by a fussy Victorian ghost, Davenport, and mischievous medieval poltergeist Claypole. Initially, Mumford enlists the additional support of his still-living parents, but things really take off when he links up with wheeler-dealer Mr Meaker, who becomes their agent.

The four had many comically spooky adventures before Davenport and Mumford moved on, leaving Meaker and Claypole to run the show. Following their departure (from series five) the format changed, becoming more domestic, and other characters were

brought in and began to share centre stage, notably Hazel the McWitch and, in later episodes, Nadia Popov. Like many other children's series, *Rentaghost* was able to attract more than decent actors to its ranks.

Rep

UK · ITV (GRANADA) · SITCOM
....
4 × 30 mins · colour
....
9 July–30 July 1982 · Fri 8.30pm
....
MAIN CAST
J C Benton · · · · · · · · · · · · · Iain Cuthbertson
Royston Flagg · · · · · · · · · · · · Stephen Lewis
Flossie Nightingale · · · · · · · · Patsy Rowlands
Angela Soames · · · · · · · · · Caroline Mortimer
Dr Crombie · · · · · · · · · · · · · · · John Fraser
Violet Littlejohn · · · · · · · · · · · · · Clare Kelly
Wyndham Carter · · · · · · · Richard Hurndall
Dudley Blake · · · · · · · · · · · · · Clive Carter
Wendy Meadows · · · · · · · · · · Lucy Hornak
Stewart Sterne · · · · · · · · · · · · Brian Carter
Flick Harold · · · · · · · · · · · Susan Wooldridge

CREDITS
writers Digby Wolfe/Ray Taylor · *director/producer* Bryan Izzard

A short-series sitcom depicting the J C Benton Players, a touring repertory company led by the forenamed manager and playing a season in Lytham St Annes, near Blackpool, back in days gone by. All the usual trials and tribulations ensue: takings are down, the leading lady is temporarily voiceless, the theatre manager is threatening closure, the landlady at the 'digs' is troublesome, the local Watch Committee is unhappy at the chosen plays, an important film producer is rumoured to be in the audience, and so on.

As a performer, *Rep* co-author Digby Wolfe had been a British TV star in the late 1950s before moving to the USA to become a top writer on such shows as **Rowan And Martin's Laugh-In** (see **Sheep's Clothing** for details).

The Rescue

UK · BBC · SITCOM
....
1 × 30 mins · colour
....
11 Jan 1973 · BBC1 Thu 8pm
....
MAIN CAST
Clive · Peter Jones
Guy Shelmerdine · · · · · · · · Nicholas Parsons
Connie Shelmerdine · · · · · · · · · Moyra Fraser
Mrs Harris · · · · · · · · · · · · Lucita Lijertwood

CREDITS
writer Peter Jones · *producer* John Howard Davies

Peter Jones scripted and starred in this *Comedy Playhouse* tale of a would-be suicide and the problems he causes his rescuer. It was a contemporary spin on Jean Renoir's classic 1932 black comedy film *Boudu Sauvé Des Eaux* (*Boudu Saved From Drowning*), in which a tramp rescued from drowning plagues the family who saved him.

The Return Of Shelley

see *Shelley*

Return To Leeds

see The Leeds series

The Reunion

UK · BBC · SITCOM
....
1 × 30 mins · b/w
....
12 Jan 1962 · Fri 8.45pm
....
MAIN CAST
Maurice Woolley · · · · · · · · · · · Lee Montague
Paddy O'Hanahan · · · · · · · · · · · · J G Devlin
Arthur Clench · · · · · · · · · · · · · · Dick Emery
'Bow-Tie Bertie' · · · · · · · · · · · Patrick Cargill
Sammy Burton · · · · · · · · · · · · · Jerold Wells
Johnny Burton · · · · · · · · · Bernard Goldman
Tommy Whitelaw · · · · · · · · · · David Gregory
Colonel Yateley · · · · · · · · · · · Cameron Hall

CREDITS
writers Ray Galton/Alan Simpson · *producer* Duncan Wood

Another Galton and Simpson comedy playlet from their first season of *Comedy Playhouse*. This one showed a reunion of old friends, and the unfortunate consequences that resulted.

The writers clearly found the subject of reunions a rich source of comedy, for they also used the situation as the basis for one of the best-loved episodes of *Hancock's Half Hour*, screened on 25 March 1960.

The Reverent Wooing Of Archibald

UK · BBC · SITCOM
....
1 × 30 mins · colour
....
9 July 1974 · BBC1 Tue 8.30pm
....
MAIN CAST
Mr Mulliner · · · · · · · · · · · · · William Mervyn
Archibald Mulliner · · · · · · · · Julian Holloway
Aurelia Cammerleigh · · · · · · Madeline Smith
Aunt Cora · · · · · · · · · · · · · · · Joan Benham

CREDITS
creator P G Wodehouse · *adapter/writer* David Climie · *producer* Graeme Muir

A *Comedy Playhouse* episode presenting another slice of Wodehouse wit for the small-screen.

Archibald Mulliner – a feckless individual with little to offer beyond his sock collection and ability to imitate an egg-laying hen – has fallen headlong for the delightful Aurelia Cammerleigh, and enlists the aid of his sage uncle (William Mervyn) in his pursuit of romantic fulfilment.

See also **The World Of Wooster, Mr Wodehouse Speaking, Wodehouse Playhouse, Ukridge, Blandings Castle, Uncle Fred Flits By** and **Jeeves And Wooster**.

Revolting Women

UK · BBC · SKETCH/STANDUP

6 × 25 mins · colour

Special · 22 Jan 1981 · BBC2 Thu 10.20pm

One series (5) 18 Sep–16 Oct 1981 · BBC2
Fri 9.55pm

MAIN CAST
Jeni Barnett
Philip Bird
Linda Broughton
Alison Skilbeck
Linda Dobell (series)
Marcella Evaristi (special)
Helen Glavin (special)

CREDITS
writers cast · directors Geoff Posner (special), Lou
Wakefield (series) · producer Lyn Webster

A humorous, feminine view of life, created by
an almost totally female cast.

The show was created as a response to
the stereotyping of women on mainstream
television, its producer, Lyn Webster, noting
that even in shows starring women – she
cited **The Liver Birds** as an example – the
storylines tended to revolve around their men.
In *Revolting Women* the team set out to forge
a comedy series that reflected women's values
and virtues. The programmes featured a
running serial 'Bogwomen', about an ancient
matriarchal tribe.

The only male in *Revolting Women* was the
actor Philip Bird, who performed in a variety
of male roles in the sketches. The cast were
quick to point out that the humour was
'feminine' rather than 'feminist', though, and
that Bird's characters weren't all villains.

La Revue Perdue

see The Montreux Festival

Rhoda

USA · CBS (MTM ENTERPRISES) · SITCOM

**108 episodes (106 × 30 mins · 2 × 60 mins) ·
colour**

US dates: 9 Sep 1974–9 Dec 1978

UK dates: 19 Nov 1974–24 June 1981
(106 × 30 mins · 2 × 60 mins) BBC2 various days
mostly 9pm

MAIN CAST
Rhoda Morgenstern/Gerard · · Valerie Harper
Brenda Morgenstern · · · · · · · · Julie Kavner
Ida Morgenstern · · · · · · · · · · Nancy Walker
· · · · · · · · · · · · · · · · · (not 1976–77 season)
Martin Morgenstern · · · · · · · · Harold J Gould
· · · · · · · · · · · · · · · · · (not 1976–77 season)
Joe Gerard · · · · · · · · · David Groh (1974–77)
Myrna Morgenstein · · · · · · · Barbara Sharma
· (1974–76)
Sally Gallagher · · · · · Anne Meara (1976–77)
Carlton The Doorman · · · · · · · Lorenzo Music
· (voice only)

CREDITS
creators Allan Burns, James L Brooks · writers
Charlotte Brown, Coleman Mitchell/Geoffrey

Neigher, Pat Nardo/Gloria Banta, David Lloyd,
Allan Katz, Deborah Leschin, Michael Leeson,
Norman Barasch/Carroll Moore and others ·
main directors Tony Mordente, Robert Moore ·
other directors Asaad Kelada, Howard Storm,
Doug Rogers, James Burrows, Nancy Walker and
others · executive producer James L Brooks, Allan
Burns · producers Lorenzo Music, David Davis,
Charlotte Brown, Don Reo, Allan Katz

Cast as the 'Jewish American Princess' Rhoda
Morgenstern in **The Mary Tyler Moore
Show**, the sharp, perfectly judged
performance by Valerie Harper had made the
promotion of the character to her own series
seem inevitable. *Rhoda* was that successful
spin-off, depicting what happened to Mary
Richards' friend after she returned to her
native New York from Minneapolis for a two-
week holiday ... that became permanent.
The result was another first-rate winner, not
as good as *The Mary Tyler Moore Show* (few
series have been) but eminently watchable
nonetheless.

During this fortnight's vacation back home,
33-year-old Rhoda is sent on a blind date by
her mother and promptly falls in love with
her companion, Joe Gerard, the owner of a
demolition company and father of a ten-year-
old son (Donny) from his first marriage. Their
romance quickly develops and they are
married in an hour-long episode (screened in
the USA on 28 October 1974 and the UK on
12 March 1975). Featuring all of the cast from
The Mary Tyler Moore Show as wedding
guests, the programme was the top-rated
special of the year in the USA, and the
episodes that followed over the next two
years were also particularly well watched.

Rhoda and Joe have a fun, adult relationship but the street-smart Rhoda is not cut out
to be a housebound wife and so she starts her
own window-dressing business, Windows By
Rhoda, with a former school friend, the shy
Myrna (who shares a similar surname). All
seems to be going well, however, and Rhoda
and Joe set up together in a Manhattan
apartment; Rhoda's younger sister, Brenda,
a bank-teller, lives in the same building.
A recurring joke in the series was provided
by the doleful voice of the front-desk man,
forever announcing himself over the
intercom as 'Uh, hi ... this is Carlton ...
your doorman ...' before enquiring whether
or not to allow someone up. (The real joke
was that, contrary to the given impression,
the owner of the voice was no dolt: it
belonged to the oddly named Lorenzo Music
who wrote and produced many of the
episodes.)

Eventually, however, it transpires that
Rhoda and Joe's marriage is in trouble and, in
a bold move for US TV, they agree to divorce
and Rhoda starts to live as a single woman
again, spending more time with Brenda and a
new friend, air stewardess Sally Gallagher. It

seemed that, at long last, the creators of the
show were getting their wish to feature a
divorcee – the original plan for *The Mary
Tyler Moore Show* had been to cast Mary
Richards in such a position – but the idea
proved as unpopular with viewers of *Rhoda*
as the wedding had been successful, and the
ratings dropped off rapidly after this.

Much of the comedy in the series centred
on Rhoda's relationships with Brenda and
their parents Ida and Martin. Rhoda's
relationship with Mary Richards had been
one of the many joys of *The Mary Tyler
Moore Show*; in *Rhoda* a similar alliance
was created between Rhoda and Brenda, a
downtrodden young woman totally lacking in
self-esteem. In the earlier series, Rhoda had
been dumpy and lacked confidence; now she
was veritably brimming with it, being in
greater control of her life. Her attempts to
inspire the equally dumpy Brenda to be a
more complete person was a recurring theme.
But, neither Rhoda nor Brenda had any
control over Ida, their hugely manoeuvring
and oh-so-Jewish mother, a veritable
diminutive dynamo played to perfection by
Nancy Walker. (She was also, at this time,
cast as the wacky housekeeper Mildred in the
police drama *McMillan And Wife*.) Walker
made such an impact in *Rhoda*, indeed, that
she was given her own sitcom *The Nancy
Walker Show* (not screened in Britain), a
short-lived series aired by ABC in 1976. The
always excellent Harold J Gould played
Martin, who didn't have a lot to do except
support his daughters and agree with his
domineering wife. But while Valerie Harper
went on to star in another sitcom (**Valerie**) it
was Julie Kavner – cast here as Brenda – who
went on to the greatest success, appearing
regularly in **The Tracey Ullman Show**
and then achieving sitcom immortality as the
voice of Marge Simpson (and others) in **The
Simpsons**.

Note. In 1974–75, BBC2 screened *Rhoda* as
part of a *Yankee Treble* series of alternating
US sitcoms, the other two in the cycle being
Chico And The Man and *Paper Moon*.

Rhubarb Rhubarb!

see SYKES, Eric

Rich Little's A Christmas Carol

USA · HBO · SITCOM

1 × 60 mins · colour

US date: 9 Dec 1982

UK date: 24 Dec 1989 · ITV Sun 12.30am

MAIN CAST
Rich Little

CREDITS
writer Rich Little · director Trevor Evans · producer
Norman Sedawie

A virtuoso one-man display of talent from the comic impressionist Rich Little, not only portraying all the 14 major characters in Dickens' *A Christmas Carol* but doing them in the guise of Humphrey Bogart, W C Fields, Groucho Marx, John Wayne and Laurel and Hardy.

Apart from his appearances in variety and chat-shows, this was the first long-form exposure of Little's great comedic talent to the British TV audience – although few would have seen this post-midnight transmission. Born 26 November 1938 in Ottawa, Canada, Little has long been famous as perhaps the foremost comic impressionist in North America, and certainly the most adventurous – his range is said to extend to 160 characters. Such a broad palette has ensured Little's longevity while other mimics have fallen by the wayside along with the demise of their most associated public figures. Unlike, say, Rory Bremner, however, Little deliberately avoids politicising his characters, and so while his shows remain full of fun they can lack bite.

Having, it seems, bought a job lot, ITV screened a second Rich Little TV special 24 hours after this one. See the following entry.

Rich Little's Robin Hood

USA · HBO · SITCOM

1 × 60 mins · colour

US date: 26 Feb 1983

UK date: 25 Dec 1989 · ITV Mon 4.50am

MAIN CAST
Rich Little

CREDITS
writers Rich Little, Mel Bishop · director Trevor Evans · producers Rich Little, Ken Kragen

Another dazzling display of impressionism from Little, playing the parts of 16 characters from the *Robin Hood* story in the guise of more American show business personalities.

Rich Tea And Sympathy

UK · ITV (YORKSHIRE) · SITCOM

6 × 60 mins · colour

5 July–9 Aug 1991 · Fri 9pm

MAIN CAST

Julia Merrygrove	Patricia Hodge
George Rudge	Denis Quilley
Grandpa Rudge	Lionel Jeffries
Granny Trellis	Jean Alexander
Sally	Anne Reid
Steve Merrygrove	Ray Lonnen
Nikki	Tracie Bennett
Colin Pink	James Warrior
Samantha Merrygrove	Claudia Bryan
Warren Rudge	Chris Garner
Karen Rudge	Lorraine Ashbourne
Tracey Rudge	Sara Griffiths
John Merrygrove	Jason Flemyng

CREDITS
writer David Nobbs · directors Michael Simpson (4), David Reynolds (2) · executive producer Vernon Lawrence · producer David Reynolds

More finely drawn entanglements of two very different Yorkshire families courtesy of writer David Nobbs – perhaps not as good as *A Bit Of A Do* but excellent entertainment all the same.

The series delved into the ramifications of a love affair between a Labour-voting divorcee, Julia Merrygrove, and an urbane Tory widower, George Rudge, who become enmeshed after their supermarket trolleys have done likewise. It is not only their politics that oppose but their lifestyles, and their subsequent relationship has a dramatic effect on their self-seeking families.

Julia Merrygrove is an attractive, intelligent, kind-hearted and partly liberated woman with two teenage children, John and Samantha, a job and a position on the local council. Her mother (Granny Trellis) is a blunt-speaking Yorkshirewoman addicted to watching snooker on TV. George Rudge, meanwhile, is the head of Rudge Brothers biscuit factory, a chauvinistic, rude, macho sweetmeat magnate who 'tells it like it is', no matter who may get hurt in the process. His three children – Warren, Karen and Tracey – are as selfish as Julia's pair, and he too has an oddball parent: a sex-mad father (Grandpa Rudge). Typical of David Nobbs' work, the funny if bittersweet humour came from being able to witness the fantastic jostling for positions that ensued.

Denis Quilley was cast as the dreadful George Rudge, while the principal mother and daughter relationship of Julia Merrygrove and Granny Trellis was enacted by the bizarre combination of Jean Alexander – known and loved by millions as Hilda Ogden in *Coronation Street*, a role she quit in December 1987 – and the English Rose actress, Patricia Hodge.

Richard Digance ... [various shows]

see DIGANCE, Richard

Richard Hearne
Richard Hearne As Mr Pastry

see Mr Pastry

The Richard Stilgoe Show

UK · ITV (THAMES) · SKETCH/STANDUP

1 × 60 mins · colour

2 May 1988 · Mon 11.30pm

MAIN CAST
Richard Stilgoe

Maureen Lipman
Peter Skellern

CREDITS
writer Richard Stilgoe · director Mark Stuart · producer James Gilbert

A bank holiday special for wry entertainer Stilgoe with his guests, recorded at the Questors Theatre in Ealing, west London.

See also *A Class By Himself*, *And Now The Good News* and *Psst!*

Right Charlie

UK · BBC · CHILDREN'S SKETCH

24 editions (19 × 25 mins · 5 × 15 mins) · colour

Series One (6) 19 May–23 June 1972 · BBC1 Fri 5.20pm

Series Two (6) 7 Feb–14 Mar 1973 · BBC1 Wed 4.50pm

Series Three (5 × 15 mins) 25 Nov–30 Dec 1974 · BBC1 Mon 5.25pm

Series Four (7) 2 Apr–21 May 1976 · BBC1 Fri 4.45pm

MAIN CAST
Charlie Cairoli ('the clever comical clown')
Paul Connor ('the master of musical melodies')
Jimmy Buchanan ('the fantastic frozen-face phenomenon')
Charlie Cairoli Jr ('in his father's footsteps')

CREDITS
producers Nick Hunter (series 1), Tony Harrison (series 2–4)

Circus-style slapstick for younger viewers with the famous clown Charlie Cairoli. Hinging on a loose theme every week – a new car, decorating the house, and so on – Charlie and his team threw themselves into the physical comedy with gusto, resulting in the sort of frantic antics that adults find tedious but children love enormously.

Rik Mayall Presents

UK · ITV (GRANADA) · SITCOMS

6 × 60 mins · colour

Series One (3) 20 May–3 June 1993 · Thu 9pm

Series Two (3) 29 Jan–12 Feb 1995 · Sun 9.45pm

Two series created especially for Mayall, conceived by Granada TV, which had been impressed by the comic's acting abilities. Although classifiable as comedy-dramas, embracing high production values and shot expensively on film, the six programmes were made by the ITV company's comedy department and were essentially comedic in content, albeit of a dark nature. Mayall welcomed them as a handy opportunity to expand his style and show TV viewers that there was more to him than the revolting Rik in *The Young Ones*, the repulsive Richie in *Bottom* and the despicable B'Stard in *The New Statesman*. He had a point (as well as a degree in drama from Manchester University), and had already made a similar departure with his theatre work. Both series were excellent, and the first won Mayall Best Comedy Performer at the British Comedy Awards.

Note. In between the two series, Mayall demonstrated still greater versatility by appearing in *Horse Opera* (13 February 1994), the last in a series of new operas especially commissioned for television by C4. He played an office clerk who, after a blow on the head, finds himself embroiled in a Wild West adventure.

Micky Love   20 MAY 1993

MAIN CAST
Micky Love · · · · · · · · · · · · · · · · · Rik Mayall
Adele Franklin · · · · · · · · · · · · · Eleanor Bron
David Critchley · · · · · · · · · · · · Peter Capaldi
Greg Deane · · · · · · · · · · · · · Alan Cumming
Tamsin · · · · · · · · · · · · · · · · · Jennifer Ehle
Martin Bowen · · · · · · · · · · · · Nicky Henson
Tony Scott · · · · · · · · · · · · Michael Maloney

CREDITS
writer Peter Morgan · director Nick Hamm · producer Andy Harries

Micky Love, ageing northern presenter of the quiz-show *Family Values*, Vista TV's number one rated programme for 13 series, is rocked by the arrival of Greg Deane, a fast-rising youthful Scotsman with an idea for a live and dangerous peak-time game-show. A reformed alcoholic who has battled to keep his career going, Love hears an incorrect rumour, emanating from the tea-lady, that his show will be axed to make way for Deane's – and takes action that results in his drink-sodden downfall on live TV.

Micky Love included cameo appearances by Nick Hancock, Duggie Brown, Malcolm McLaren, Hughie Green, Stuart Hall, William Roache and Anne Reid (Ken and Valerie Barlow in *Coronation Street*) and the once-big TV comic Freddie 'Parrot Face' Davies.

Briefest Encounter   27 MAY 1993

MAIN CAST
Greg · Rik Mayall
Siobhan · · · · · · · · · · · · · Amanda Donohoe

CREDITS
writer Peter Learmouth · director Nick Hamm · producer Andy Harries

Greg, a smooth-talker, thinks that he has hit it off when a beautiful journalist, Siobhan, whom he meets at a party he has gatecrashed, invites him back to her flat. But his ardour is cooled by the frequent interruptions of her pet dog Brumus, and Greg's determination to win the battle for her affections steers the evening towards a different climax from the one he expected – an inferno.

Amanda Donohoe – C J Lamb in the US drama series *LA Law* – played Siobhan.

Dancing Queen   3 JUNE 1993

MAIN CAST
Neil · Rik Mayall
Pandora/Julie · · · · · · Helena Bonham-Carter
Sophie · · · · · · · · · · · · · · · · Serena Gordon
Margaret · · · · · · · · · · · · · · · Dorothy Tutin
Nigel · · · · · · · · · · · · · · · · Nathaniel Parker
Donald · · · · · · · · · · · · · · · · Martin Clunes
Policeman · · · · · · · · · · · · · · Bill Cashmore

CREDITS
writer Nick Vivian · director Nick Hamm · producer Andy Harries

An eve-of-wedding stag-night prank finds the bridegroom, Neil, drunk, without trousers and stranded on a train bound for Scarborough together with the strippagram girl, Pandora, hired to titillate him and his pals. With no chance of getting back to Maidstone to attend his wedding, Neil, something of an upper-class-twit, reflects on what he's missing, and finds himself drawn to the warm-hearted stripper.

The Big One   29 JAN 1995

MAIN CAST
Lewis Fox · · · · · · · · · · · · · · · · · Rik Mayall
Mrs Wilde · · · · · · · · · · · · · · Phyllis Logan
Miles · · · · · · · · · · · · · · · · · · · Phil Daniels
Jeff · · · · · · · · · · · · · · · · · Cal MacAninch
Peter McCrane · · · · · · · · Edward Tudor Pole
Leon · · · · · · · · · · · · · · · · Philip McGough
Jules · · · · · · · · · · · · · · · Saffron Burrows
John Wilde · · · · · · · · · · · · · · · David Sibley
Security Guard · · · · · · · · · · · · · Paul Barber

CREDITS
writer Piers Ashworth · director Simon Cellan Jones · executive producer Andy Harries · producer Mark Redhead

A compulsive liar, estate agent Lewis Fox harbours dreams of becoming rich by perpetrating the ultimate swindle – 'the lie that changes everything' – and sets out to achieve it, assuming the identity of a rich dead gangster and enjoying the attentions of his widow (played by Phyllis Logan). His fantasies then begin to come alarmingly true when a pair of hoods come looking for him, but the villa in Spain beckons …

Dirty Old Town   5 FEB 1995

MAIN CAST
Raymond · · · · · · · · · · · · · · · · · Rik Mayall
Sally · · · · · · · · · · · · · · · · · Frances Barber
Jeremy Swain · · · · · · · · · · · Michael Kitchen
Vic Leigh · · · · · · · · · · · · · · Brian McCradie
Michael · · · · · · · · · · · · · · · Sean McGinley
Claire · · · · · · · · · · · · · · · · Helen McCrory
Rik Powers · · · · · · · · · · · · · · · Duncan Bell
Stefan · · · · · · · · · · · · · · · · · · Tom Russell
Klaus · · · · · · · · · · · · · · · · · · Metin Yenal

CREDITS
writers Paul Unwin/Stephen Ward/Nick Vivian · director Paul Unwin · executive producer Andy Harries · producer Mark Redhead

A bittersweet tale of a London street vagrant, Raymond, swept up into the world of high-powered, drink-heavy business lunches and international dealings after a film script literally falls into his possession and he is mistaken for its author.

Clair de Lune   12 FEB 1995

MAIN CAST
Toby · Rik Mayall
Clair · · · · · · · · · · · · · Serena Scott Thomas
Pete · Lee Evans
Terry Devane · · · · · · · · · · · · Mark Frankell
Annie · · · · · · · · · · · · · · · · · Leonie Sooke
Mrs Gaffney · · · · · · · · · · · · · Selina Cadell

CREDITS
writer Nick Vivian · director Paul Unwin · executive producer Andy Harries · producer Mark Redhead

Toby is a widowed single-parent, reluctantly working as a mini-cab driver to ease his cash-strapped state, raise his seven-year-old daughter Annie in a little comfort and put himself through law school. One day, en route to taking Annie to a birthday party, he picks up a customer, a beautiful but volatile *femme fatale* named Clair, armed with a gun and with both a malevolent lover and the police on her trail.

The Rikki Fulton Show

UK · BBC · STANDUP

2 × 45 mins · b/w
29 Oct 1960 · Sat 7.50pm
3 June 1961 · Sat 7.45pm

MAIN CAST
Rikki Fulton

CREDITS
writer Rikki Fulton · producers John Street (show 1), Eddie Fraser (show 2)

Rikki Fulton made a name for himself on BBC radio as the compere of *The Show Band Show* before returning home to Scotland to try his hand at being a comedian and impressionist. After making a successful transition he appeared in a few TV appearances as a guest before, at the age of 36, being given these two starring shows.

See also *Scotch And Wry*.

Rings On Their Fingers

UK · BBC · SITCOM

20 × 30 mins · colour
Series One (6) 13 Oct–17 Nov 1978 · BBC1 Fri 8.30pm

Special · 23 Dec 1978 · BBC1 Sat 9.50pm

Series Two (7) 5 Sep–17 Oct 1979 · BBC1 Wed 8.30pm

Series Three (6) 23 Oct–27 Nov 1980 · BBC1
Thu 8.30pm

MAIN CAST

Sandra 'Sandy' Bennett/Pryde · · Diane Keen
Oliver Pryde · · · · · · · · · · · · · · · Martin Jarvis

OTHER APPEARANCES

Victor · · · · · · · · · · · · · · · · · · · Tim Barrett
Edgar · John Kane
Mrs Bennett · · · · · · · · · · · · · · Barbara Lott
Mr Bennett · · · · · · · · · · · · · · · John Harvey
Mrs Pryde · · · · · · · · · · · Margaret Courtenay
Mr Pryde · · · · · · · · · · · · · · · · · Keith Marsh

CREDITS

writer Richard Waring · *director/producer* Harold
Snoad

Another dose of domestic double-trouble from
writer Richard Waring, *Rings On Their
Fingers* cast Diane Keen and Martin Jarvis
as Sandy Bennett and Oliver Pryde, a good-
looking unmarried couple in their late
twenties who have been co-habiting, quite
happily, for six years. But then Sandy begins
to become fixated by 'the urge' – desiring
bouquets, bridesmaids, a ring on her finger, a
bulge in her frontage. Oliver loves his Sandy
but he's perfectly happy in the state of
unwedded bliss, not least so that he can
continue to study the anatomies of other
women without too much guilt.

But the pressure is applied and, with the
greatest reluctance, Oliver recognises that
he is beaten: by the end of the first series
they are married and off on honeymoon.
Subsequent episodes showed the Prydes
adjusting to married life and discovering that
the existence of a formal contract somehow
altered their attitudes towards one another,
and their friends' and acquaintances'
attitudes towards them as a couple. As the
series wore on (and on) the stories usually
ending up in classic *Marriage Lines*
territory of light marital disharmony. By the
end of run, however, their union was soon to
be blessed by the arrival of their first born.

Ripping Yarns

UK · BBC · COMEDY FILMS

9 × 30 mins · colour

Special · 7 Jan 1976 · BBC2 Wed 9pm

Series One (5) 27 Sep–25 Oct 1977 · BBC2
Tue 9pm

Series Two (3) 10 Oct–24 Oct 1979 · BBC2
Wed 9.25pm

Nine lavishly filmed half-hour comedies,
spoofing the type of stirring adventure stories
found in boys' annuals of the early- to mid-
20th-century.

Following the demise of *Monty Python*,
BBC producer Terry Hughes invited Michael
Palin to come up with a new series. Palin and
his long-term writing partner, fellow Python
Terry Jones, duly pondered a range of ideas
but it was Jones's brother who pointed out
the comic potential of an old annual, *Ripping
Tales*, that Palin had given to Terry Jones as a
gift. (Jones's brother had also suggested their
earlier series *The Complete And Utter
History Of Britain*.)

The annual, and others of its ilk, did indeed
prove a fertile ground, but the resulting story
ideas were such that Palin and Jones felt
convinced that the series would have to be
shot on film in order to benefit from the
necessarily higher production qualities and
attention to period detail they envisaged.
They then wrote a pilot episode, *Tomkinson's
Schooldays*, which aired independently under
that title on 7 January 1976 and carried an
unmistakable Pythonesque edge, with its
intense cruelty (boys were nailed to walls),
marvellously ludicrous vignettes (Tomkinson
constructed a 14,000-ton ice-breaker ship in
the handicraft class) and the sort of idea-
reversal that the two writers relished (kids
caned the headmaster, parents expected their
children to get proper bullying, and so on).

A full series materialised in 1977, tapping
the boys' adventure annuals for its subjects:
triumph against adversity ('The Testing Of
Eric Olthwaite'), war ('Escape from Stalag
Luft 112B'), crime ('Murder At Moorstones
Manor'), exploration ('Across The Andes By
Frog') and black magic ('The Curse Of The
Claw'). As the writers had wished, the
production values were of a uniformly high
standard, but this meant that the costs were
significantly higher than normal for a comedy
half-hour. For this reason, when Palin and
Jones were planning a second series, the
BBC decided they could afford only three
more shows – a 1920s espionage thriller
('Whinfrey's Last Case'), a football story
('Golden Gordon') and a spoof of the overtly
racist yarns that passed unchallenged in old
schoolboy annuals, 'Roger Of The Raj'. All
nine programmes were superbly cast, with
Palin in the lead roles throughout. John Cleese
made an ultra-brief but wonderful cameo
appearance in 'Golden Gordon'.

Because it was shot on film, the series has
withstood the passing of time much better
than most other programmes of the period,
and Palin and Jones's excellent scripts mean
that there is still a wealth of comedy lurking
in these nine classic *Ripping Yarns*. Of the
nine episodes, at least half a dozen were quite
brilliant, and two in particular, 'The Testing
Of Eric Olthwaite' and 'Golden Gordon', are
magnificent, virtually without peer in the
realm of British TV comedy half-hours.

Tomkinson's Schooldays   7 JAN 1976

MAIN CAST

Tomkinson/Headmaster/ · · · · · · · · · · · · · · ·
Mr Craffit · · · · · · · · · · · · · · · · Michael Palin
Mr Ellis · · · · · · · · · · · · · · · · · · · Terry Jones
Mummy · · · · · · · · · · · · · · · · · Gwen Watford
School Bully · · · · · · · · · · · · · · · · Ian Ogilvy

CREDITS

writers Michael Palin/Terry Jones · *director* Terry
Hughes

Tomkinson, a schoolboy, seeks to escape from
the brutal regime of Graybridge, a public
boarding school. Set in 1912.

The Testing Of Eric Olthwaite   27 SEP 1977

MAIN CAST

Eric Olthwaite/ ·
Bank manager · · · · · · · · · · · · · Michael Palin
Vera Olthwaite · · · · · · · · · · · · · Barbara New
Mr Olthwaite · · · · · · · · · · · · · · John Barrett
Irene Olthwaite · · · · · · · · · · · · · Anita Carey
Mr Bag · Reg Lye
Mrs Bag · · · · · · · · · · · · · · · · · · · Liz Smith
Enid Bag · · · · · · · · · · · · · · · Petra Markham
Arthur · · · · · · · · · · · · · · · · · · · Ken Colley
Chauffeur · · · · · · · · · · · · · · · · · Roger Avon
Lord Mayor · · · · · · · · · · · · Clifford Kershaw

CREDITS

writers Michael Palin/Terry Jones · *director* Jim
Franklin

An important moment arrives in the life of a
stupefyingly boring Yorkshireman, Eric
Olthwaite. Set in 1934.

Escape From Stalag Luft 112B   4 OCT 1977

MAIN CAST

Major Phipps · · · · · · · · · · · · · Michael Palin
Herr Vogel · · · · · · · · · · · · · · · · Roy Kinnear
Colonel Harcourt Badger-Owen · · · · · · · · · · · ·
· John Phillips
Biolek · · · · · · · · · · · · · · · · · · · Julian Hough
Second Guard · · · · · · · · · · · · David English
'Buffy' Attenborough · · · · · · · · David Griffin
Nicolson · · · · · · · · · · · · · · · Timothy Carlton

CREDITS

writers Michael Palin/Terry Jones · *director* Jim
Franklin

A First World War British prisoner-of-war in
Germany is frustrated by the bureaucratic
channels blocking his escape plans. Set in
1917.

Murder At Moorstones Manor   11 OCT 1977

MAIN CAST

Charles Chiddingfold/ · · · · · · · · · · · · · · · · · ·
Hugo Chiddingfold · · · · · · · · · · Michael Palin
Lady Chiddingfold · · · · · · · · · · · Isabel Dean
Dora Chiddingfold · · · · Candace Glendenning
Ruth · Anne Zelda
Sir Clive Chiddingfold · · · · Frank Middlemass
Manners · · · · · · · · · · · · · · Harold Innocent
Dr Farson · · · · · · · · · · · · · Iain Cuthbertson

CREDITS

writers Michael Palin/Terry Jones · *director* Terry
Hughes

An Agatha Christie spoof with too many
people confessing to too few murders. Set in
1926.

Across The Andes By Frog
18 OCT 1977

MAIN CAST

Captain Walter Snetterton · · · · Michael Palin
Mr Gregory · · · · · · · · · · · · · Denholm Elliott
RSM Urdoch · · · · · · · · · · · Don Henderson
Peruvian mountain guide · · · · · · · Eileen Way

CREDITS

writers Michael Palin/Terry Jones · director Terry Hughes

A tale of a pioneering British amphibian assault on the Andes. Set in 1927.

Note. Michael Palin and Denholm Elliott reunited in Palin's 1982 comedy feature film *The Missionary*.

The Curse Of The Claw
25 OCT 1977

MAIN CAST

Sir Kevin Orr/Uncle Jack · · · · · Michael Palin
Grosvenor · · · · · · · · · · · · · · Aubrey Morris
Captain Merson · · · · · · · · · · · Keith Smith
Kevin's mother · · · · · · · · · · · Hilary Mason
Kevin's father · · · · · · · · · · · Tenniel Evans

CREDITS

writers Michael Palin/Terry Jones · director Jim Franklin

A black-magic ritual surrounds a strange Burmese 'sacred claw' which brings misfortune to all who possess it. Set in 1926.

Whinfrey's Last Case
10 OCT 1979

MAIN CAST

Gerald Whinfrey · · · · · · · · · · · Michael Palin
Mrs Otway · · · · · · · · · · · · · · Maria Aitken
General Chapman · · · · · · · · · · · · · Jack May
Lorry driver · · · · · · · · · · · · · Steve Conway
Lord Raglan · · · · · · · · · · · · · · Gerald Sim
Admiral Jefferson · · · · · · · · · Antony Carrick
Mr Girton · · · · · · · · · · · · Edward Hardwicke

CREDITS

writers Michael Palin/Terry Jones · director Alan J W Bell

Suave adventurer Gerald Whinfrey effortlessly thwarts a nefarious German plot to start the First World War before the British have made enough trestle tables. Set in 1913.

Golden Gordon
17 OCT 1979

MAIN CAST

Gordon Ottershaw · · · · · · · · · Michael Palin
Mrs Ottershaw · · · · · · · · · · · · Gwen Taylor
Barnstoneworth Ottershaw · · · · John Berlyne
Mr Dainty · · · · · · · · · · · · · · David Leland
Chairman · · · · · · · · · · · · · · Teddy Turner
Arthur Foggen · · · · · · · · · · · · · Bill Fraser
Neville Davitt · · · · · · · · · · · Roger Sloman

CREDITS

writers Michael Palin/Terry Jones · director Alan J W Bell

A football fanatic fights to save his local team, Barnstoneworth United, from being disbanded, while he makes his son learn the team players by heart ('Hagerty F, Hagerty R, Tomkins, Noble, Carrick, Dobson, Crapper, Dewhurst, MacIntyre, Treadmore and Davitt'). Set in 1935.

Note. David Leland, who played Barnstoneworth's excitable manager, went on to become a top film director.

Roger Of The Raj
24 OCT 1979

MAIN CAST

Roger Bartlesham · · · · · · · · · Michael Palin
Lord Bartlesham · · · · · · · · · Richard Vernon
Lady Bartlesham · · · · · · · · · Joan Sanderson
Colonel Runciman · · · · · · · John Le Mesurier
Miranda · · · · · · · · · · · · · · · Jan Francis
Hopper · · · · · · · · · · · · · · · Roger Brierley
Major Daintry · · · · · · · · · · · Allan Cuthbertson

CREDITS

writers Michael Palin/Terry Jones · director Jim Franklin

Tales from a British family in India, who are obsessed with maintaining the manners and morals of Britain. Set in 1914.

Rising Damp

UK · ITV (YORKSHIRE) · SITCOM

28 × 30 mins · colour

Pilot · 2 Sep 1974 · Mon 8pm
Series One (6) 13 Dec 1974–17 Jan 1975 · Fri 8.30pm
Series Two (7) 7 Nov–19 Dec 1975 · Fri 7.30pm
Special · 26 Dec 1975 · Fri 7.45pm
Series Three (7) 12 Apr–24 May 1977 · Tue 8.30pm
Series Four (6) 4 Apr–9 May 1978 · Tue 8pm

MAIN CAST

Rupert Rigsby · · · · · · · · · · · Leonard Rossiter
Ruth Jones · · · · · · · · · · · Frances de la Tour
Alan Moore · · · · · · · · · · · Richard Beckinsale
· (series 1–3)
Philip Smith · · · · · · · · · · · · Don Warrington

OTHER APPEARANCES

Brenda · · · · · · · · · · · · · Gay Rose (series 2)

CREDITS

writer Eric Chappell · directors/producers Ronnie Baxter (19), Vernon Lawrence (6), Len Lurcuck (2), Ian MacNaughton (pilot)

ITV's finest ever sitcom, distinguished by the magnificent acting of Leonard Rossiter, cast as Rigsby, the landlord of a run-down boarding-house in a northern university town. Rigsby was obnoxious – a nosey, bigoted, racist, lecherous but sexually frustrated, miserly, interfering wretch – but in Rossiter's hands he became somehow loveable.

Rossiter's performance, and Eric Chappell's excellent scripts, made *Rising Damp* an extra special creation, and the superb support from three other fine actors – Rigsby's trio of most regular tenants – elevated it to the highest level. Frances de la Tour was wonderful as the lovelorn spinster Ruth Jones; Richard Beckinsale (who, simultaneously, was appearing in *Porridge*) shone as the sexually inexperienced and generally immature medical student Alan; and Don Warrington was just right as the sage black student Philip, who never denied rumours that he was the son of a tribal chief, was the focus of Ruth's flirtatious suggestions and bore the brunt of Rigsby's regular racial taunts.

Rising Damp seemed to come out of nowhere. While justifiably acclaimed for his stage and TV dramatic roles, Rossiter had never before appeared in situation comedy. And Chappell was an equally unlikely source for a sitcom – he had been an Electricity Board accountant. Then, in 1973, Chappell wrote a play, *The Banana Box*, about a seedy bedsit landlord named Rooksby (*sic*). Magically, it all then fell into place – the play, which starred Wilfrid Brambell in its first run in Leicester and then Leonard Rossiter when it toured with Don Warrington, Frances de la Tour and Paul Jones – reached the Apollo Theatre in London, where its television potential was noticed by Yorkshire TV executives. With Beckinsale replacing Jones, YTV networked a one-off pilot episode in September 1974; three months later the first full series hit the screens and was an instant smash. Aside from scripting the pilot episode of *The Squirrels*, which had aired eight weeks earlier, *Rising Damp* was Chappell's first sitcom – and his best.

Owing to its regular repeat runs – which always attract high audience figures and rave reviews – it is easy to forget that *Rising Damp* extended to just 28 episodes over four series. And, in truth, the quality of the scripts varied; at their best, though, they were superb, and even when they were not Leonard Rossiter was *always* so, delivering his lines with masterful pace and timing and speaking volumes with a simple twitch or a roll of his eyes. Rigsby may have been an appalling character but, in perfectionist Rossiter's hands, he was a joy to behold: the way he clutched his mangy moggy Vienna, furtively stalked the house and barged into his tenants' rooms, showed that Rossiter had truly got 'inside' his character. That he was also starring at the same time in a totally different but equally fine creation, in the BBC's *The Fall And Rise Of Reginald Perrin*, is quite remarkable.

Gay Rose, as temporary lodger Brenda, who posed nude for art life-classes, briefly joined the second series when Frances de la Tour took a short leave of absence, but otherwise the cast remained constant until the final series, when Richard Beckinsale dropped out. Shortly afterwards – a true tragedy, for he was a mere 31 – Beckinsale died of a heart attack, following which a *Rising Damp* feature film (directed by Joe McGrath) was made, with Christopher Strauli in the role of Alan. Released in 1980, this brought Eric Chappell's creation to a slightly disappointing end.

Note. The format of *Rising Damp* was sold to America, where King-Hitzig Productions made a pilot episode for CBS, titled *27 Joy Street* – the address of the boarding-house, situated in Cambridge, Massachusetts. The programme starred Jack Weston as the landlord who involved himself in the lives of his tenants: two medical students, a nude model (based on Brenda) and a professional wrestler (one *Rising Damp* episode had indeed featured a wrestler). Although closely based on Eric Chappell's creation, the US episode was rewritten by Peter Stone and directed by Bill Persky. CBS was unimpressed and declined even to screen the pilot, let alone commission a series.

Rita Rudner

UK · BBC · SKETCH/STANDUP
6 × 30 mins · colour
18 Sep–23 Oct 1990 · BBC2 Tue 9pm
MAIN CAST
Rita Rudner
Martin Bergman

CREDITS
writers Rita Rudner/Martin Bergman · *director/producer* Kevin Bishop

US comedian Rita Rudner began her entertainment career as a dancer but, although reasonably successful, she grew weary of the limitations of the field. She then moved into comedy and honed her act by turning up at night-clubs just before they were due to close, begging a five-minute floor spot. Her comedy was observational and the stage persona she presented was of a waif-like ingénue, with a Gracie Allen-like, logic-defying outlook on life. Occasionally, nuggets of dark humour surfaced unexpectedly in an apparently innocent routine, sending a shockwave through her audience. These bolts were all the more surprising because Rudner's voice is deceptively sweet and airy, and her face that of an innocent child. But the portrayal of this somewhat dim persona belied her intelligence: in order to understand and achieve comedy she pored over video tapes and audio recordings of Jack Benny, George Burns, Woody Allen and other greats, working out, in infinitesimal detail, how they structured words and used pauses to effect maximum humour in a sentence, studying their rhythm and timing and the cadences of their speech.

In 1984, while performing at a US comedy club, Catch A Rising Star, Rudner was seen by British theatrical producer Martin Bergman, who immediately spotted her

potential and took her under his wing, polishing her presentation, teaching interview techniques and giving her other hints on dealing with the media. Under his tutelage, she quickly established herself as a headlining act and, later, the pair married.

Rudner first made a splash in Britain as one of a number of US comics who guested on British TV comedy or chat-shows in the 1980s. She particularly impressed on her debut, on the BBC1 chat-show *Wogan* on 2 August 1987. After further TV spots and some UK stage performances Rudner was given this starring series by the BBC, co-written with Bergman, who also appeared, playing her on-screen husband. The show blended standup, sketches and songs and each week featured British comedy guest stars, including Jennifer Saunders, Stephen Fry and Adrian Edmondson. In the final edition Rudner explained that she had to return to the USA because her visa had expired, and that the show was mounted as a campaign to prevent her ejection. But Rudner was moving on to different areas. Her book *Naked Beneath My Clothes* was a US best-seller, and in 1992 Bergman and Rudner co-wrote, and Rudner appeared in, the Kenneth Branagh-directed movie *Peter's Friends*.

The River

UK · BBC · SITCOM
6 × 30 mins · colour
20 Oct–24 Nov 1988 · BBC1 Thu 8.30pm
MAIN CAST
Davey Jackson · · · · · · · · · · · · · David Essex
Sarah MacDonald · · · · · · · · · Katy Murphy
Tom Pike · · · · · · · · · · · · · · · · Shaun Scott
Aunty Betty · · · · · · · · · · · Vilma Hollingbery
Colonel Danvers · · · · · · · · · · · · · David Ryall

CREDITS
writer Michael Aitkens · *director/producer* Susan Belbin

In his first TV acting role, actor/singer David Essex starred in this series as Davey Jackson, a cockney former wide-boy who fell in love with nature during a spell in open prison and now has settled as a lock-keeper in rural Chumley-on-the-Water. But Davey's quiet life changes when he falls in love with the tactless but vulnerable Sarah, a Scottish bargee who stays with him in his lock-keeper's cottage while her narrow-boat's broken propeller-shaft is repaired.

The series' director/producer, Susan Belbin, claimed that it was a love story, not a sitcom, and certainly the humour was of a gentle observational type, usually arising from the eccentric characters in Jackson's life, including his Aunty Betty, with whom he shares the cottage. All the same, *The River* was made by the BBC's comedy department and, despite outward appearances, was closer to being a sitcom than many others so

described – indeed, as for the paucity of belly-laughs, there have been plenty of sitcoms similarly but less intentionally bereft.

The Road And The Miles Of Max Boyce

see BOYCE, Max

Roamin' Holiday

see BYGRAVES, Max

The Robbie Coltrane Special

UK · ITV (POZZITIVE PRODUCTIONS FOR LWT) · SKETCH/STANDUP
1 × 60 mins · colour
16 Sep 1989 · Sat 10.10pm
MAIN CAST
Robbie Coltrane

CREDITS
writers Robbie Coltrane, Geoff Atkinson, Kim Fuller, Moray Hunter/Jack Docherty, Richard Curtis · *director* Geoff Posner · *producers* Geoff Posner, Geoffrey Perkins

A true once-only occasion: Robbie Coltrane in his own hour-long comedy special. It was far from being a one-man performance, with a long support cast (John Fortune among them), but Coltrane was the man to watch, appearing in a number of taped sketches, some of which hit the mark, others not.

The star appeared in a variety of roles – as Miss Burtingham, the redoubtable, boozing, mink-clad headmistress of St Botolph's, a St Trinian's-like 'academy for young ladies'; as Struan McLeish, a Border TV presenter; as a Jewish restaurateur complaining that he had to seat 12 men at The Last Supper 'all on one side of the table – I lost a dozen covers!'; as the film narrator Edgar Dustcarten (a play on the writer Edgar Lustgarten whom Coltrane had previously lampooned in *Laugh??? I Nearly Paid My Licence Fee*) introducing a *Scotland Yard* B-picture *Silent Stiffy Of Stanmore*; as Siegfried in a spoof of *All Creatures Great And Small*; and, in the most expansive piece, as rock singer Robbie Wilson, in a sketch charting Wilson's entire career in a style reminiscent of the celebrated rock comedy movie *This Is Spinal Tap*.

Note. From 5 to 26 April 1990, BBC2 screened *Robbie Coltrane In Mistero Buffo*, a four-part presentation of Dario Fo's satirical version of the medieval mystery plays, as staged by the Borderline Theatre Company in a Scottish touring production. On 31 March 1990, as an introduction to the series, the same channel screened a 20-minute profile of Coltrane that examined his relatively short but prolific career to date.

Robbins

UK · ITV (GRANADA) · SKETCH/STANDUP

1 × 30 mins · colour

27 Aug 1986 · Wed 8pm

MAIN CAST
Ted Robbins
Kate Robbins
Jane Robbins
Emma Robbins
Amy Robbins

CREDITS
director Tom Poole · *producer* Trish Kinane

The Robbins family from Merseyside are a remarkable bunch: all five children are talented stage performers, albeit not all with humour as the main thrust.

First-cousins of Paul McCartney (their mother, Bett, is his aunt), the quintet of Robbins youngsters starred in this one-off programme, their very own TV special, in August 1986, which was akin to a pilot for *Kate And Ted's Show*, launched 11 months later. Kate, who went on to become perhaps the most recognisably successful of the five, certainly as far as comedy is concerned, then progressed even further, to *The Kate Robbins Show* in 1988. But, notwithstanding her 1981 hit single ('More Than In Love') which followed an appearance in the ATV soap opera *Crossroads*, and her fine voice impressions in *Spitting Image*, the best-known Robbins in 1986 was probably Ted, who was appearing regularly in the ITV game-show *Some You Win*.

See also *Saturday Gang*.

The Robert Dhéry Show

UK · ITV (JACK HYLTON TV PRODUCTIONS FOR ASSOCIATED-REDIFFUSION) · SKETCH

6 editions (5 × 30 mins · 1 × 45 mins) · b/w

One series (4 × 30 mins) 22 Feb–29 Mar 1957 · Fri 8.30pm

Special (45 mins) 8 May 1958 · Thu 9.45pm

Special (30 mins) 19 May 1958 · Mon 10.15pm

MAIN CAST
Robert Dhéry
Colette Brosset
Pierre Olaf
Jacques Legras
Roger Caccia
Philippe Dumat

CREDITS
creator/writer Robert Dhéry · *directors/producers* Robert Dhéry/Eric Fawcett (series), Douglas Hurn (special 1), Bill Hitchcock (special 2)

Robert Dhéry – a tall, dark and handsome French comic entertainer – had been playing the Garrick Theatre in London for some 16 months in his saucy (there was some nudity) revue *La Plume de ma Tante*, when its producer Jack Hylton arranged for the less racy moments to be transferred into TV

programmes for Associated-Rediffusion. (Hylton was also charged with the duty of providing all A-R's entertainment programmes.) An extract from the production had already been performed in the 1955 *Royal Variety Show* (again, presented by Jack Hylton) so interest was high and the programmes – filmed in A-R's Wembley TV studios – certainly did not disappoint, standing out as perhaps the funniest of all Hylton's (sometimes dire) TV productions.

With his acute sense of comic timing, Robert Dhéry (real name Robert Fourrey) was the centrepiece of most of the sketches, and his wife Colette Brosset was also among the cast. The two 1958 programmes – one live, the other recorded – were made after *La Plume de ma Tante* had closed and the company, having returned to Paris, were on a short visit back to Britain. The first of these included Dhéry's comic observations on British life.

The Robert Horton Show

UK · ITV (ATV) · SKETCH

1 × 55 mins · b/w

23 Jan 1960 · Sat 8pm

MAIN CAST
Robert Horton
Dave King

CREDITS
writers Sid Green/Dick Hills · *director* Rita Gillespie · *producer* Albert Locke

A single show (screened in the weekly *Saturday Spectacular* strand) in which the British comic Dave King joined forces with the visiting American actor Robert Horton – famous at this time for starring as Flint McCullough in the western TV series *Wagon Train* – for a number of sketches and (with Joan Regan) songs. Horton was keen to break into comedy and later appeared on Broadway in *110 In The Shade*.

Robert's Robots

UK · ITV (THAMES) · CHILDREN'S SITCOM

14 × 30 mins · b/w

Series One (7) 12 Nov–24 Dec 1973 · Mon 4.50pm

Series Two (7) 11 Nov–23 Dec 1974 · Mon 4.50pm

MAIN CAST
Robert Sommerby · · · · · · · · · · · · John Clive
Eric · Nigel Pegram
KT · Brian Coburn
Marken · · · · · · · · · · · · · · · · · · · Leon Lissek
Aunt Millie · · · · · · · · · · · · · · · Doris Rogers
Gimble · · · · · · · · · · Richard Davies (series 1)
Angie · · · · · · · · · · · · Jenny Hanley (series 1)
Plummer · · · · · · · · · · · David Pugh (series 2)
Desiree · · · · · · · · · · · · April Olrich (series 2)
Robot George · · · · William Lawford (series 2)
Blabberbeak, the parrot · · · · · · Nigel Pegram
· · · · · · · · · · · · · · · · · · (series 2, voice only)

CREDITS
writer Bob Block · *director/producer* Vic Hughes

Having completed 26 episodes of *Pardon My Genie*, writer Bob Block created this new children's series for Thames, in which restaurateur-cum-mad inventor Robert Sommerby was financed by the British government to build a bunch of robots that looked and behaved in a distinctly human fashion and 'enjoyed' human traits, such as falling in love. (One of the robots, KT – nicknamed Katie – was so dense that he fell in love with a gas-stove.)

Keen to avoid the usual TV portrayal of robots as lumbering scraps of silvery metal, Robert's creations were so human-like that they had to be portrayed by human actors, which tested the ingenuity of Thames' special effects department – and doubtless the series' budget – to the limit. Most of the episodes centred on the misadventures of the robots and the lamentable efforts of the foreign spy Marken (assisted by Gimble in the first series and Plummer in the second) to steal the secrets of Robert's robots.

A number of familiar faces were among the cast, including Richard Davies (*Please, Sir!*), Jenny Hanley (*Magpie*) and Doris Rogers, who, decades earlier, had played Florrie Wainwright in both the radio and TV versions of *Life With The Lyons*, which Block had helped to script.

Robin Williams: An Evening At The Met

USA · HBO · STANDUP

1 × 60 mins · colour

US date: 11 Oct 1986

UK date: 29 Dec 1989 · C4 Fri 11pm

MAIN CAST
Robin Williams

CREDITS
writer Robin Williams · *director* Bruce Gowers · *executive producers* Buddy Morra, Larry Brezner · *producer* David Steinberg

A superlative standup performance from the manic Williams (born Chicago, 21 July 1952), staged in that most unlikely of settings, the Metropolitan Opera House in New York City. Instead of prima donnas prancing about the stage here was Williams in a loud Hawaiian shirt and baggy trousers, dashing around with unsurpassable energy, his quicksilver comic brain spouting forth rapid-fire thoughts on everything from drugs to being a father.

This was an all-too-rare opportunity for British TV viewers to see Williams' acclaimed standup act, the comic being best known outside of America for the sitcom *Mork And Mindy* and starring roles in movies that, to 1989, included *The World According To*

Garp, Dead Poets Society and *Good Morning, Vietnam*.

Note. On 23 April 1993, C4 preceded a season of Williams' movies with a 30-minute tribute, *Robin Williams – Acting Funny*, comprising clips from the actor's TV and film work with comments from his contemporaries.

Robin's Nest

UK · ITV (THAMES) · SITCOM

47 × 30 mins · colour

Series One (7) 11 Jan–22 Feb 1977 · Tue 8.30pm

Series Two (6) 23 Feb–30 Mar 1978 · Thu 8pm

Series Three (13) 25 Sep–18 Dec 1978 · Mon mostly 8pm

Series Four (7) 22 Feb–5 Apr 1979 · Thu 8pm

Special · 27 Dec 1979 · Thu 8.30pm

Series Five (5) 8 Jan–5 Feb 1980 · Tue 8.30pm

Special · 24 Dec 1980 · Wed 7pm

Series Six (7) 17 Feb–31 Mar 1981 · Tue 8pm

MAIN CAST

Robin Tripp · · · · · · · · · · · Richard O'Sullivan
Victoria ('Vicky') Nicholls/Tripp · Tessa Wyatt
James Nicholls · · · · · · · · · · · · Tony Britton
Albert Riddle · · · · · · · · · · · · · · David Kelly

OTHER APPEARANCES

Gertrude · · · · · Peggy Aitchison (series 5 & 6)

CREDITS

creators Johnnie Mortimer/Brian Cooke · *writers* Johnnie Mortimer/Brian Cooke (14), George Layton (12), Bernard McKenna (4), Adele Rose (4), David Norton/Roger Taylor (2), Terence Brady/ Charlotte Bingham (2), Jon Watkins (2), Terence Feely (1), Willis Hall (1), Ken Hoare (1), Dave Freeman (1), not known (3) · *director/producer* Peter Frazer-Jones

With *George And Mildred* successfully spun-off from *Man About The House*, writers Johnnie Mortimer and Brian Cooke turned their attentions to Richard O'Sullivan, the principal figure in that original series. There he had been Robin Tripp, a catering student, living (without sin, to his chagrin) with two girls. In *Robin's Nest* he was a newly qualified chef, living very much in sin with his girlfriend Vicky (Tessa Wyatt).

Keen to open up their own bistro, Robin and Vicky enter into a business partnership with her irascible father James. Being the co-owner, and a very protective parent who – initially, at least – disapproves of his daughter's choice of boyfriend, James is on the scene all the time. (This was Tony Britton's first regular sitcom role; occasional episodes also featured Vicky's mother, divorced from James, played by Honor Blackman and then by Barbara Murray.) Bestowing the series its title, the bistro – situated in the Fulham area of London – is called Robin's Nest; Robin and Vicky work there full-time, as does Albert Riddle, a one-armed Irishman with a criminal record, who does the washing-up more with blarney than bubble.

Robin and Vicky were almost married at the end of the first series, and they finally tied the knot at the conclusion of the second. Vicky then gave birth to twins in the fifth, by which time Mortimer and Cooke had long abdicated the writing role – in the series' final three years the pair scripted just one episode. All the same, by making it clear that Robin and Vicky were unwed yet living and indeed sleeping together, they had scored a first, the 'common-law marriage' situation having never been depicted before in a British sitcom. Special permission had to be sought from the Independent Broadcasting Authority before the writers were given the go-ahead.

Note. As *Man About The House* led to **Three's Company**, and *George And Mildred* led to *The Ropers*, so *Robin's Nest* also sported a US adaptation, **Three's A Crowd**.

Rock With Laughter

UK · ITV (YORKSHIRE) · SKETCH/STANDUP

6 × 30 mins · colour

21 June–26 July 1980 · Sat mostly 6.30pm

MAIN CAST

various

CREDITS

directors Ian Bolt, Len Lurcuck · *producer* Mike Goddard

Six slickly produced shows showcasing newly discovered artists from cabaret clubs. The emphasis was on comedy impressionism, and Phil Cool was among those getting his first big break. (Also seen in the series were Alan J Bartley, Beano, Bobby Sox and the Prize Guys, Ines Burn, the Don Juans, Dave Draper and Robert Shaw, the Druids, Greengage, the Ivy League and Terry Webster.)

The entire series was taped in five days and, in the style of **The Comedians**, the best bits were scattered around the six programmes in a no-pause-for-breath fashion.

Roger Doesn't Live Here Anymore

UK · BBC · SITCOM

6 × 30 mins · colour

24 Sep–29 Oct 1981 · BBC2 Thu 9pm

MAIN CAST

Roger Flower · · · · · · · · · · · · Jonathan Pryce
Emma Flower · · · · · · · · · · · · Diane Fletcher
Arabella Flower · · · · · · · · · · · · Alice Berry
Charles Flower · · · · · · · · · · Benjamin Taylor
Rose · Kate Fahy
Stanley · · · · · · · · · · · · · · Michael Elphick

CREDITS

writer John Fortune · *director* John B Hobbs · *producer* Dennis Main Wilson

A characteristically dark comedy from John Fortune, following the hapless Roger Flower as he undergoes an acrimonious divorce from his wife Emma.

Rarely has such a bitter marital break-up been presented as comedy, with Emma going to enormous lengths to turn the children of the marriage, Arabella and Charles, against their father – including, for example, showing them family home-movies to illustrate his bad points. Despite Emma's efforts, however, Roger gradually manages to win back his children's affections, and does so without having to besmirch his estranged wife.

In the meantime, Roger is having an affair with Rose, a woman who, it transpires, only truly enjoys intercourse when it is part of an adulterous affair. Thus, on the day that Roger's divorce is finalised, she marries a wrestler, Stanley, purely so that her relationship with Roger can continue to be illicit. Curiously touching though this is, Stanley's addition to the equation adds to Roger's mounting problems (as it were).

A classy series, but one caught uncomfortably between two genres, *Roger Doesn't Live Here Anymore* represents serio-comedy at its best, and it retained its suitably dramatic effect by usurping a studio audience or 'canned' laugh-track. Fortune and producer Main Wilson were insistent upon this point, convinced that the lack of obtrusive laughter would bring out the best in the actors. Both leading players, Pryce and Fletcher, were indeed excellent (although such talent will shine in any situation) but the series, perhaps because of its intriguing seriousness, did not make for comfortable viewing.

Roger Roger

UK · BBC · SITCOM

1 × 60 mins · colour

26 Aug 1996 · Mon 9pm

MAIN CAST

Phil · Neil Morrissey
Sam · Robert Daws
Chrissie · · · · · · · · · · · · · · Lesley Vickerage
Reen · Pippa Guard
Baz · David Ross
Marlon · · · · · · · · · · · · · · · · · Ricci Harnett
Barry · · · · · · · · · · · · · · · · · · John Thomson
Rajiv · · · · · · · · · · · · · · · · · · · Paul Sharma
Andre · · · · · · · · · · · · · · · Terence Maynard
Cambridge · · · · · · · · · · · · · · · Chris Larkin
Henry · · · · · · · · · · · · · · · · Jude Akuwudike
Pam · · · · · · · · · · · · · · · · · · · Sandra Payne

CREDITS

writer John Sullivan · *director* Tony Dow · *producer* Gareth Gwenlan

A one-off comedy by John Sullivan, intended as a pilot for a full series. (This was shot in 1997 for airing in early 1998.) Made under the working title *P O B* but screened as *Roger Roger*, the single 60-minute episode charted the goings-on at a London mini-cab firm, Cresta Cabs. The company is owned by Sam, permanently anxious that his team do not let down his company's good name, and it is largely because of the organisational abilities of his assistant, Reen, that punters are collected more or less at the time they have requested.

The setting allowed Sullivan the opportunity to play with a large number of diverse characters – the drivers – the principal one being Phil, nicknamed Bonio. Phil's desire to become a rock star is necessarily reined in by his common-law wife Chrissie when realities like feeding their children Madonna and Cher, and paying bills, seem to be passing him by. The other drivers include Baz, also a postman, and his dim son Marlon; Barry, who is scathing in his feelings about women, but only because they scare him; Henry, an immigrant from Nigeria whose sense of direction is somewhat wayward; a university graduate nicknamed 'Cambridge'; an ambitious and well-dressed Asian, Rajiv; and Andre, a laid-back West Indian who is very much a ladies' man.

Note. Indications during production of the 1998 series suggested that Neil Morrissey had been replaced by Philip Glenister, and that the role of Phil – pivotal in the pilot – had been diminished in importance to the central theme.

Roland Rat

see *Tales Of The Rodent Sherlock Holmes*

Roll Over Beethoven

UK · ITV (WITZEND PRODUCTIONS FOR CENTRAL) · SITCOM
*13 × 30 mins · colour

Series One (6) 25 Feb–1 Apr 1985 · Mon 8pm
Series Two (7) 15 Apr–27 May 1985 · Mon mostly 8pm

MAIN CAST
Belinda Purcell · · · · · · · · · · · · Liza Goddard
Nigel Cochrane · · · · · · · · · · · · · Nigel Planer
Oliver Purcell · · · · · · · · · · · · · Richard Vernon
Lem · · · · · · · · · · · · · · Desmond McNamara
Marvin · · · · · · · · · · · · Emlyn Price (series 2)

CREDITS
creators Laurence Marks/Maurice Gran · writers Laurence Marks/Maurice Gran (11), Paul Makin (2) · script editors Ian La Frenais (series 1), Laurence Marks/Maurice Gran (series 2) · directors Derrick Goodwin (series 1), Nic Phillips (series 2) · executive producer Allan McKeown · producer Tony Charles

Nigel Cochrane, whose career as bass guitarist and lead singer with the heavy-metal band Graf Spee has made him a multi-millionaire, quits at the age of 23 and moves into the Grange, the manor house in the quiet Surrey village of Churston Deckle. He intends

not only to make it his place of abode but to tape his first solo album there, in a newly installed home studio. Pride of place in the studio is an array of keyboards, courtesy of which, all by himself, Nigel will emulate the instruments of a full rock band. There is only one snag: he is clueless about how to play them.

Enter the local piano-tutor, and church organ-player, Belinda Purcell, whose musical interests have hitherto extended as far as the classics and who is asked to give Nigel keyboard lessons. Belinda is the daughter of Oliver Purcell, a widower, retired school headmaster and writer of letters to *The Times*, now more interested in flower shows, a peaceful life and finding a man for his demure and unblemished daughter, provided that she keeps her Victorian values intact. In no way, Oliver is certain, must that man be Nigel, whose lifestyle and values are anathema to him, and whom he considers as 'a semi-literate teddy boy' and 'that representative of the great unwashed'.

But, of course, Nigel becomes infatuated with Belinda, and – to the enormous chagrin of her father – she falls in love with him too. Soon they're writing hit songs together, recorded and released by Nigel on his first solo album. Belinda then starts to write with Nigel's pal Marvin, going on to record her own album and gaining her grudging father's approval.

Roll Over Beethoven deserved plaudits for managing to avoid the usual cringe-worthy pitfalls suffered when TV dramatically portrays the rock and roll world. Unquestionably a sitcom, it embraced moments of light-drama and was taped without a studio audience although, on balance, it may have been better served with one. Overall, though, it succeeded through its lead players: as Nigel Cochrane's general factotum Lem, Desmond McNamara rendered a great impression of a rock and roll roadie; Richard Vernon gave his usual fine value as the crusty gent; Nigel Planer (who did not appear in some latter episodes) was excellent as the immature Cochrane, expelled from school at 15 and living out 'rock star' behaviour to the hilt, yet with manners underneath; and Liza Goddard impressed as a sort of Jane Asher character whose head and lifestyle are turned around by the revolutionary company she keeps.

*Note. ITV screened the 13 episodes in virtually one blast but actually there were two distinct series, a first of six episodes and a second of seven.

The Rolling Stones

see *An Evening At Home With Bernard Braden and Barbara Kelly*

Romany Jones

UK · ITV (LWT · *THAMES) · SITCOM
27 × 30 mins · colour

*Pilot · 15 Feb 1972 · Tue 10.30pm
Series One (7) 25 May–6 July 1973 · Fri 7.30pm
Series Two (6) 14 Sep–21 Oct 1973 · Sun 7.25pm
Series Three (7) 16 Aug–27 Sep 1974 · Fri 8.30pm
Series Four (6) 6 June–11 July 1975 · Fri 7.30pm

MAIN CAST
Bert Jones · · · · · · · · James Beck (1972–73)
Betty Jones · · · · · · · Jo Rowbottom (1972–73)
Wally Briggs · · · · · · · · · Arthur English (pilot);
· · · · · · · · · · · · · · · · · Arthur Mullard (series)
Lily Briggs · · · · · · · Queenie Watts (all series)
Mr Gibson · · · · · · Kevin Brennan (1972–73)
Jeremy Crichton-Jones · · · · · · Jonathan Cecil
· (1974–75)
Susan Crichton-Jones · · · · · · · · · · Gay Soper
· (1974–75)
Eileen · · · · · · · Maureen Sweeney (1974–75)

CREDITS
creators Ronald Wolfe/Ronald Chesney · writers Ronald Wolfe/Ronald Chesney (13), Jon Watkins (6), Myles Rudge (3), Geoff Rowley/Andy Baker (2), Chris Boucher (1), George Layton/Jonathan Lynn (1), Peter Denyer/Graham Hooson (1) · director/producer Stuart Allen

While the writers Wolfe and Chesney can be loudly applauded for creating *The Rag Trade*, and be worthy of a tentative tap on the back for conceiving *On The Buses*, they could also be arrested for unleashing *Romany Jones* on to an unsuspecting British public. Not to mince words, this was an appalling sitcom, and how it lasted for four series beggars belief. The series depicted two couples living the life of gypsies on a rundown caravan site. And while it is not recorded how real-life gypsies took to being so stereotypically portrayed as argumentative, drinking, gambling, work-shy, dole-drawing, loud-mouthed simpletons, it is a fair bet that they were not amused. Nor indeed, were many other viewers.

Thames' pilot episode and LWT's series that followed a year later cast James Beck (Walker in *Dad's Army*) and Jo Rowbottom as Bert and Betty Jones; newly wed after seven years of going together, they spend their wedding night in their rickety caravan, which is natural to Bert but distinctly alien to Betty, who was born and bred in Streatham. Most of the 'comedy' then centred on life in theirs and a neighbouring caravan that housed Lily and Wally Briggs (Queenie Watts and Arthur Mullard, although Arthur English was cast in the pilot).

James Beck died on 6 August 1973, after completing the second series, following which his and Betty's characters were written out. In their place, fantastically, came a City gent, Jeremy Crichton-Jones, complete with bowler hat and his young debutante wife Susan.

They were poor and he was as sexually uneducated as he was gullible to Lily and Wally's schemes. (The new characters had to be called Jones otherwise the series' title would have meant nothing.)

Lily and Wally Briggs were also spun-off into their own series, *Yus My Dear*, which was even more dire.

Ronald Frankau

UK · BBC · STANDUP

1 × 10 mins · b/w
24 Jan 1939 · Tue 3.25pm

MAIN CAST
Ronald Frankau
Monte Crick

CREDITS
writer Ronald Frankau · producer Philip Bate

A short *Starlight* comedy slot for the comedian Ronald Frankau (1894–1951), who was enjoying a certain infamy at this time for his risqué songs (he sold over 100,000 records in 1932), books, cinema films and London cabaret engagements. Frankau and the BBC radio star Tommy Handley performed together many times, most famously as the mismatched couple 'Mr Murgatroyd and Mr Winterbottom', Frankau's Etonian accent oddly contrasting with Handley's Liverpudlian dialect as they humorously discussed topical items.

On this occasion Frankau's piano accompanist was Monte Crick, who went on to become one of the four actors to portray Dan Archer in the BBC's landmark radio drama serial *The Archers*.

The Ronnie Barker Playhouse

UK · ITV (REDIFFUSION) · SITCOMS

6 × 30 mins · b/w
3 Apr–8 May 1968 · Wed mostly 9pm

Having served a long apprenticeship in rep, on radio, TV and in films, Ronnie Barker was given this series, his first as a top star, at the age of 38. The break came courtesy of David Frost, who had long been featuring Barker in sketches within his BBC series *The Frost Report*.

The Ronnie Barker Playhouse was the launching-pad for a career that soon reached into the stratosphere of TV comedy. Each of the six episodes depicted the star in a different role. He later revisited the formula with *Six Dates With Barker* and *Seven Of One*.

Tennyson   3 APR

MAIN CAST
Tennyson Elias Williams · · · · · Ronnie Barker
Cecil · · · · · · · · · · · · · · · · · · Dudley Jones
Mrs Cecil · · · · · · · · · · · Gwendolyn Watts
Lecher Lewis · · · · · · · · · · · Talfryn Thomas

Shelley Longfellow Morgan · · · · · · · · · · · · · ·
· · · · · · · · · · · · · · · · · · Richard O'Callaghan

CREDITS
writer Alun Owen · director Michael Lindsay-Hogg · executive producer David Frost · producer Stella Richman

A failed Welsh poet, Tennyson The Tonsil, is prevented from taking part in a recitation competition.

Ah, There You Are   10 APR

MAIN CAST
Lord Rustless · · · · · · · · · · · · Ronnie Barker
Badger · · · · · · · · · · · · · · George A Cooper
Willy · Bill Shine
Jane · · · · · · · · · · · · · · · · Sandra Michaels

CREDITS
writer Alun Owen · director Michael Lindsay-Hogg · executive producer David Frost · producer Stella Richman

The eccentric Lord Rustless is prevented from pursuing his favourite hobby, roller-skating, by the arrival of a film crew making a TV commercial. (Rustless became the focus of two subsequent series, *Hark At Barker* and *His Lordship Entertains*.)

The Fastest Gun In Finchley   17 APR

MAIN CAST
Ronald Winterbourne · · · · · · Ronnie Barker
Tupper · · · · · · · · · · · · · · · · Glenn Melvyn
Jenkinson · · · · · · · · · · · Walter Horsbrugh
Gosling · · · · · · · · · · · · · · · · Colin Jeavons
Beatrice · · · · · · · · · · · · · Charlotte Mitchell
Mrs Granville · · · · · · · · · · · · · Sheila Keith

CREDITS
writers Johnnie Mortimer/Brian Cooke · director Michael Lindsay-Hogg · executive producer David Frost · producer Stella Richman

Winterbourne's wish to be the chairman of the Finchley And Hendon Cowpokes Association is thwarted by the claims of a rival candidate. Perhaps they should settle things the Wild West way …

The Incredible Mister Tanner   24 APR

MAIN CAST
Cyril Tanner · · · · · · · · · · · · · · Ronnie Barker
Peregrine · · · · · · · · · · · · · · · · Alec Clunes
Arthur · · · · · · · · · · · · · · · Richard O'Sullivan
Ma · Doris Hare
Official · · · · · · · · · · · · · · · · · Frank Gatliff

CREDITS
writers Johnnie Mortimer/Brian Cooke · director Michael Lindsay-Hogg · executive producer David Frost · producer Stella Richman

A busking escapologist, Cyril Tanner, decides to prove that he is on a par with the great Harry Houdini. (Tanner became the focus of two subsequent series, *The Incredible Mr Tanner* and *Kindly Leave The Kerb*.)

Talk Of Angels   1 MAY

MAIN CAST
The Monk · · · · · · · · · · · · · · Ronnie Barker
Matthew · · · · · · · · · · · · · · · · · David Kelly
Doreen · · · · · · · · · · · · · · · Maureen Toal
Nigel · · · · · · · · · · · · · · · Donald Hewlett
Deirdre · · · · · · · · · · · · · · · Liz Crowther
Ramona · · · · · · · · · · · · · Gillian Fairchild

CREDITS
writer Hugh Leonard · director Michael Lindsay-Hogg · executive producer David Frost · producer Stella Richman

An elongated sketch detailing the comic situations that arise when Matthew and Doreen play host to a monk from a silent order.

Alexander   8 MAY

MAIN CAST
Alexander · · · · · · · · · · · · · · Ronnie Barker
Mumsie · · · · · · · · · · · · · · Molly Urquhart
Lesley Crown · · · · · · · · · · · · Pauline Yates
Miss Craig · · · · · · · · · · · Pamela Ann Davy

CREDITS
writer Alun Owen · director Michael Lindsay-Hogg · executive producer David Frost · producer Stella Richman

At home, Alexander is a mother's boy. At work, the Scotsman has Casanova-like designs on a number of women.

The Ronnie Barker Yearbook

UK · BBC · SKETCH

1 × 45 mins · colour
20 Mar 1971 · BBC1 Sat 8.20pm

MAIN CAST
Ronnie Barker
Ronnie Corbett
John Cleese
Billy Dainty
Noël Dyson

CREDITS
writers Gerald Wiley (Ronnie Barker), Dick Vosburgh, Eric Idle, John Cleese/Graham Chapman · producer Terry Hughes

Made as an introduction to *The Two Ronnies*, this was the first of two specials screened on consecutive Saturdays; Corbett was a guest in this first show, which spotlighted Barker; Barker was then a guest in the second, showcasing Corbett.

Ronnie Barker's programme took the format of an almanac, looking at the months of the year, and was partly written by Barker under his pseudonym Gerald Wiley.

Ronnie Corbett In Bed

UK · BBC · SKETCH

1 × 45 mins · colour
27 Mar 1971 · BBC1 Sat 8.20pm

MAIN CAST
Ronnie Corbett
Ronnie Barker

CREDITS
writers John Antrobus, Barry Cryer, Doug Fisher, Eric Idle, David Nobbs, Spike Mullins, Dick Vosburgh · *producer* Terry Hughes

One week after Ronnie Barker's programme, Ronnie Corbett's show had the diminutive comedian introducing flights of fancy from the comfort of a large four-poster bed (a format suggested by writer Barry Cryer).

The Two Ronnies launched on Easter Saturday, 10 April 1971. Seven weeks later, on 27 May 1972, a single compilation embracing the best moments from both *The Ronnie Barker Yearbook* and *Ronnie Corbett In Bed* aired as a *Two Ronnies* special.

The Ronnie Corbett Show

UK · BBC · STANDUP/SKETCH

6 × 30 mins · colour

22 Sep–27 Oct 1987 · BBC2 Tue 9pm

MAIN CAST
Ronnie Corbett

CREDITS
writers Barry Cryer (6), Spike Mullins (5), Ian Davidson (3), Peter Vincent (3), Neil Shand (3), Rory Bremner/John Langdon (1), Laurie Rowley (1), Bryan Blackburn (1), Steve Punt (1) · *script associate* Neil Shand · *director/producer* Marcus Mortimer

The One Ronnie in his own series, featuring his familiar rambling monologues and characteristic sketches. He was supported each week by musical guest stars and comedy acts, including Rory Bremner, Hinge and Bracket, Kit And The Widow, Punt and Dennis, and Richard Digance. Actors Keith Barron, Frank Thornton, Philip Madoc and others also helped out in the sketches.

The Ronnie Corbett specials

UK · BBC · STANDUP/SKETCH

19 editions (15 × 45 mins · 4 × 40 mins) · colour

Series One (4) *All This And Corbett Too*
22 Nov–13 Dec 1975 · BBC1 Sat around 8.40pm

Series Two (6) *Ronnie Corbett's Saturday Special*
1 Jan–12 Mar 1977 · BBC1 fortnightly Sat mostly 8.25pm

Series Three (5) *Ronnie Corbett's Thursday Special* 6 Apr–4 May 1978 · BBC1 Thu 9.25pm

Series Four (4 × 40 mins) *The Ronnie Corbett Special* 13 Apr–4 May 1979 · BBC1 Fri mostly 7.50pm

MAIN CAST
Ronnie Corbett

CREDITS
writers Eddie Braben (14), Spike Mullins (4), Ronnie Taylor (1), Eric Davidson (1), Bob Hedley (1) · *producer* Michael Hurll

A comedy-led entertainment show. Corbett was joined each week by a guest star, those appearing during the 19 editions including Harry Secombe, Ted Rogers, Larry Grayson, Danny La Rue, Frank Carson, Jimmy Tarbuck, John Inman, Jim Davidson, Lennie Bennett, Lenny Henry, the Krankies, Beryl Reid, and Hinge and Bracket.

A Roof Over My Head

UK · BBC · SITCOM

8 × 30 mins · colour

Pilot · 5 Apr 1977 · BBC1 Tue 7.40pm

One series (7) 3 Aug–16 Sep 1977 · BBC1 Wed 8.30pm then Fri 7.40pm

MAIN CAST

James	Brian Rix
Sheila	Lynda Baron
Jack Askew	Peter Bowles (pilot);
	Francis Matthews (series)
Flamewell	Alfie Bass
Sir Phillip Comer	Richard Hurndall (pilot);
	Dennis Ramsden (series)
Bert	Michael Stainton
Gaye	Gail Harrison
Maureen	Deborah Watling (pilot);
	Louisa Rix (series)
Mrs Bagworth	Sheila Keith

CREDITS
creator Michael Green · *adapter/writer* Barry Took · *producer* Douglas Argent

The trials and tribulations of buying a new home, adapted from Michael Green's book *The Art Of Coarse Moving* and turned into a sitcom series by Barry Took after a pilot episode was successfully mounted in the BBC's new try-out strand *Comedy Special*.

James and Sheila were the couple trying to move, and all of the pitfalls of home buying were exploited for comic effect. Green made a cameo appearance in one of the episodes.

The same idea was explored in the 1985 ITV sitcom *Moving*.

Room At The Bottom   1

UK · ITV (ABC) · SITCOM

4 × 30 mins · b/w

7 June–28 June 1964 · Sun 3.35pm

MAIN CAST

Nesbitt Gunn	Lionel Jeffries
Mr Hughes	Dick Emery

OTHER APPEARANCES
Pamela Harrington
Ellen Pollock
Wendy Craig
Monty Landis
John Wood

CREDITS
writer John Antrobus · *director* Dick Lester

A short-run sitcom only part-networked and not screened by London-area ITV (but included here because of its 1980s revival – see following entry).

Subtitled 'Confessions Of A Television Producer', *Room At The Bottom* charted the exploits of Nesbitt Gunn, a drama turned light entertainment TV producer for the commercial channel, who likes to flex his ego on the studio floor, causing problems for both his junior and senior staff. The series ended with Gunn applying for a job with 'the other side', the BBC. Lionel Jeffries was cast as Gunn, and Dick Emery as his executive producer; Wendy Craig turned up in the first two episodes as a production secretary, the first episode also guest featured future *Dad's Army* stars John Le Mesurier and Clive Dunn.

Room At The Bottom was taped in September 1963 and sat on the shelf for nine months before a 'canned' laugh-track was added and the programmes were screened, primarily in the Midlands and the North. The series was directed by Richard (Dick) Lester, representing his last serious venture in TV production before concentrating his energies exclusively on the direction of feature films. (See also *The Dick Lester Show*.) But he teamed again with Antrobus in 1969 when he directed the movie *The Bed-Sitting Room* (Antrobus wrote the screenplay), and he worked with Jeffries again when making the 1975 movie *Royal Flash*.

Room At The Bottom   2

UK · ITV (YORKSHIRE) · SITCOM

13 episodes (12 × 30 mins · 1 × 55 mins) · colour

Series One (5 × 30 mins · 1 × 55 mins) 9 Nov–14 Dec 1986 · Sun mostly 10pm

Series Two (7) 15 May–3 July 1988 · Sun mostly 10pm

MAIN CAST

Nesbitt Gunn	James Bolam
Kevin Hughes	Keith Barron
Chaplain	Richard Wilson
Celia Pagett-Smythe	Deborah Grant
Tom	Oliver Cotton
Nancy	Erika Hoffman
Dr Barton	Malcolm Tierney (series 1)
Jeffrey	Martin Fisk (series 2)

CREDITS
creator John Antrobus · *writers* Ray Galton/John Antrobus · *director* David Reynolds · *producers* Vernon Lawrence (series 1), David Reynolds (series 2)

An outrageous exaggerated account of late 1980s media life, suitably updated from the 1964 series of the same title (see above). For this adaptation, the writer John Antrobus was joined by one of his greatest contemporaries, Ray Galton.

Megla Television is ruled by its power-crazed and mean-minded boss Kevin Hughes, weaver of deceit and lies, sender of dictatorial memos (which he pronounces 'mee-moes'), a man who controls the whip – and uses it to keep his staff in order. His principal whipping boy is Nesbitt Gunn, once a drama producer but demoted by Hughes to Light Entertainment, specifically to quiz- and game-shows – a position which, Gunn knows, is the last stop before the dole queue. Hughes finds any excuse, *every* excuse, in which to berate and belittle his minion, roasting his hide from his plush Mayfair HQ on a regular basis. To his credit, Gunn keeps up his morale with witty rejoinders.

Though dominated by its two leading players, *Room At The Bottom* was blessed with a fine ensemble cast, with Richard Wilson appearing as Megla TV's dodgy in-house chaplain Toby Duckworth (he also happens to be Hughes' brother-in-law); Oliver Cotton as Tom, the yuppie head of the drama department; Erika Hoffman as Hughes' sexy secretary Nancy; and Deborah Grant as Celia, the remarkably efficient production assistant who starts out as Nesbitt's girlfriend but is tempted away by Tom, much to the latter's mischievous delight, although she sometimes keeps a sympathetic eye for her ex.

Room At The Bottom 3

UK · BBC · SITCOM

8 × 30 mins · b/w

Pilot · 14 June 1966 · BBC1 Tue 7.30pm
One series (7) 14 Mar–25 Apr 1967 · BBC1 Tue 7.30pm

MAIN CAST

Gus Fogg	Kenneth Connor
Mr Powell	Deryck Guyler
Mr Dillington	Francis Matthews (pilot)
Happy Brazier	Richard Pearson (pilot);
	Gordon Rollings (series)
Horace Robinson	Kenny Lynch (series)
Mr Salisbury	Brian Wilde
Cyril Culpepper	Patrick Newell (series)

CREDITS

writers John Esmonde/Bob Larbey · producer David Askey

Esmonde and Larbey's first television sitcom depicted the exploits of a group of maintenance men working at Saracens Manufacturing Company. The men are led by their fiddler-in-chief Gus Fogg (Kenneth Connor).

The series' premise sprang from the writers' observation that 'basement maintenance men often exert considerable power over the wheels of British industry'. The scene was set up in the *Comedy Playhouse* pilot from which the series evolved – the men are still drawing the wages of a colleague who passed away four years earlier. When a keen new personnel manager, Mr Salisbury, insists on meeting all of the staff personally, Gus and his cronies are faced with a dilemma. The seemingly simple solution is to hire a stand-in, but owing to a misunderstanding two men show up, one elderly and one young.

Note. Following *Room At The Bottom*, Esmonde and Larbey's next TV sitcom was another pilot, screened only in local areas by the Midlands/North ITV weekend franchise ABC. Titled *Just Good Friends*, it aired late-night on 25 November 1967 within a *Comedy Playhouse*-style strand titled *Comedy Tonight* and starred Derek Nimmo and Amanda Barrie as an engaged couple having to overcome the jealousy she suffers owing to his part-time job as an art school nude model. The top British comedy film director John Paddy Carstairs directed, but no series developed.

Room Service

UK · ITV (THAMES) · SITCOM

7 × 30 mins · colour

2 Jan–13 Feb 1979 · Tue 8.30pm

MAIN CAST

Charles Spooner	Bryan Pringle
Aldo de Vito	Freddie Earlle
Mrs McGregor	Jeillo Edwards
Horace Murphy	Chris Gannon
Dick Sedgewick	Matthew Kelly
Gustav	Gertan Klauber
Mr Morris	Basil Lord
Freda	Judi Maynard
Marlene Barry	Penelope Nice
Fedros	Michael Petrovitch

CREDITS

writer Jimmy Perry · director/producer Michael Mills

Jimmy Perry has written some great situation comedies (**Dad's Army**, for instance) but this sorry affair isn't one of them. Like a disastrous cross between **Fawlty Towers** and his own **You Rang, M'Lord?**, *Room Service* was set in the room-service section of a fictitious five-star London hotel, the Prince Henry. The department was managed by Charles Spooner (Bryan Pringle), a fierce protector of his staff but a fierce opponent if they transgressed the rules, and said staff were the typical motley crew: short, tall, fat, thin, white, black and all shades in between, loyal, disloyal, punctual, sloppy and so on. The guests too, were the usual motley crew: gangsters, scantily-clad beauties, newly weds, dog owners et al …

Root Into Europe

UK · ITV (ASPECT FOR CENTRAL) · COMEDY SERIAL

5 × 60 mins · colour

17 May–14 June 1992 · Sun 8.45pm

MAIN CAST

Henry Root	George Cole
Muriel Root	Pat Heywood

CREDITS

creator William Donaldson · series developer Anthony Tancred · writers William Donaldson/Mark Chapman · director Mark Chapman · executive

producer Rod Henwood · producers Justin Judd/Mark Chapman

A five-part series that charted a trip around continental Europe by Henry Root, self-appointed protector of everything British in what, for him, was the alarmingly liberal and deregulated European Union; the year of its screening, 1992, was when all remaining trade barriers between EU member countries were abolished.

The Henry Root character was invented by the writer and one-time theatrical producer William Donaldson (co-author of the TV series with its co-producer Mark Chapman). Root sprang to fame as the apparent author of a barrage of robust letters sent – from his home at 139 Elm Park Mansions, Park Walk, London SW10 – to the most prominent figures in British life, the great, the good and the not-so-good but nonetheless powerful: everyone from the Prime Minister down (or up). These right-wing, jingoistic missives – imploring the return of capital punishment, the closing of borders, and more – and the replies they elicited from their addressees who believed them to be genuine, were compiled into book form in 1980 as *The Henry Root Letters*. Although he assiduously kept his name off the volume – the author's identity and even the copyright notice were ascribed to Root – Donaldson's cover as the Root architect was blown when the hilarious book became the number one UK best-seller that year.

This TV series, the first screen realisation of what Donaldson himself called 'a quite dreadful man, without a single redeeming quality', indicated that Root had lost none of his bombastic pomposity or self-righteousness in the 12 years since being published. (Even if the substantial royalties had enabled a move from SW10 to leafy Esher.) Root was, if you like, the barely acceptable face of bigotry – Alf Garnett made 'respectable' by a little education, a tweed jacket and a tie – traversing Europe to 'catch the continental at it' as he and his poor wife Muriel (Henry continually called her 'Mrs Root') investigated people, places and lifestyles in France, Belgium, Spain, Italy, Germany and the Netherlands.

Astonishingly blunt, completely oblivious to the fact that his opinions and rudeness might be alien or offensive to others, and gobsmackingly ignorant of any other point of view, Root staggered from one disastrous European situation to another, insulting and misunderstanding with equal measure. His spectacular *faux pas* were captured on video by Mrs Root, for not only had Henry appointed himself the country's European regulator in a letter to the Prime Minister, he had also written to the BBC chairman offering a TV series based on his travels with the camcorder. (The opening episode included cameo roles, as themselves, by publishing mogul Lord Weidenfeld and the entrepreneur Richard Branson.)

George Cole was the perfect TV encapsulation of the dreadful Root, sniffily towing his wife (played well by Pat Heywood) around Europe as he set out to 'know your enemy'. The producers' original plan was to place the pair among perfect strangers who would be unaware that they were being filmed, but it soon became obvious that the settings had to be scripted and bystanders alerted to the situation. Everyone agreed – the former Palermo mayor included – on the proviso that Root, not they, would be the only one to appear foolish in the final cut. He most certainly did.

Roots

UK · ITV (ATV) · SITCOM

6 × 30 mins · colour

*11 Sep–1 Nov 1981 · Fri 8pm then Sun 2pm

MAIN CAST

Melvin Solomons · · · · · · · · · Allan Corduner
Nettie Solomons · · · · · · · · · · · · Joy Shelton
Harry Solomons · · · · · · · · Stanley Meadows

OTHER APPEARANCES

Gilbert · · · · · · · · · · · · · · · · Anna Tzelniker
Melanie Goldblatt · · · · · · · · · Lesley Joseph

CREDITS

writers Laurence Marks/Maurice Gran · director/producer Keith Farthing

Following **Holding The Fort**, Marks and Gran's second sitcom was Roots – it was a great title but a poor series. Unrelated to the fine American TV drama of the same name, this Roots played on the fact that the series' hero is a dentist, experiencing problems with his Jewish family.

The dentist is Melvin Solomons, newly qualified and clearly in line for a prosperous, steady but uneventful life. The trouble is, he longs to leave behind the world of gums, fillings and root canals and become an artist. His parents – mother Nettie and father Harry, who works in the schmutter business – have other ideas, and are horrified when Melvin decides to take the plunge. The six episodes chart his progress in a territory unfamiliar to Jews, pitted against the all too familiar interfering family 'concern'.

Lesley Joseph was cast in the minor role of Melanie Goldblatt, Melvin's successfully married sister; eight years later Marks and Gran employed her again, much more successfully, in another of their creations, **Birds Of A Feather**.

*Note. Owing to audience apathy, the last three episodes were postponed by London-area ITV; intended to continue on Friday nights until 16 October they were rescheduled, when even fewer people were watching, to Sunday afternoons, concluding on 1 November.

Rory Bremner … [various shows]

see BREMNER, Rory

Roseanne

USA · ABC (WIND DANCER PRODUCTIONS/THE CARSEY-WERNER COMPANY/FULL MOON & HIGH TIDE PRODUCTIONS) · SITCOM

220 episodes (218 × 30 mins · 2 × 60 mins) · colour

US dates: 18 Oct 1988–20 May 1997

UK dates: 27 Jan 1989–18 June 1997 (218 × 30 mins · 2 × 60 mins) C4 mostly Fri 10pm

MAIN CAST

Roseanne Conner · · · · · · · · · · · · · · · · · · ·
· · · · · · · · · · · · · · *Roseanne (Barr/Arnold)
Dan Conner · · · · · · · · · · · · · John Goodman
Darlene Conner · · · · · · · · · · · · Sara Gilbert
Rebecca ('Becky') Conner/Healey
· · · · Lecy Goranson (1987–93 & 1995–97);
· · · · · · · · · · · · · · · Sarah Chalke (1993–95)
David Jacob (D J) Conner · · · · · · · Sal Barone
· (pilot);
· · · · · · · · · · · · · · · Michael Fishman (series)
Jackie Harris · · · · · · · · · · · · · Laurie Metcalf
David Healey · · · · Johnny Galecki (1992–97)

OTHER APPEARANCES

Bev Harris · · · · · · Estelle Parsons (1989–97)
Leon Carp · · · · · · · · · Martin Mull (1991–97)
Nancy Bartlett · · · · · · · · · · · Sandra Bernhard
· (1991–97)
Mark Healey · · · · · · · Glenn Quinn (1990–97)
Arnie Merchant (later Arnie Thomas) · · · · · · ·
· · · · · · · · · · · · · · · · Tom Arnold (1989–94)
Booker Brooks · · George Clooney (1988–89)
Crystal Anderson · · Natalie West (1988–92)
Bonnie Watkins · · · · · · · · · Bonnie Sheridan
· (1991–92)

CREDITS

creator Matt Williams · writers various · directors various · executive producers Roseanne Arnold, Tom Arnold, Jay Daniel, Marcy Carsey, Tom Werner, Dan Palladino and others · producers Jeff Abugov, Al Lowenstein, Brad Isaacs, Maxine Lapiduss and others

A major landmark on the US comedy landscape, Roseanne attracted huge controversy both on and behind the screen. At the centre of both was Roseanne herself, a brilliant standup comic here portraying Roseanne Conner, a variation of a character she developed for the stage.

Roseanne Conner is a sharp, wisecracking, powerful (but not overbearing) wife to husband Dan, her high-school sweetheart; she is also mother to children D J, Darlene and Becky; and sister to Jackie. Living at 714 Delaware Street in Lanford, Illinois, the family are strictly blue-collar and financially challenged but manage to carry on thanks to Dan's determination to make ends meet, Roseanne's own jobs (plastics factory, beauty salon, waitress and more) and her gallows humour. Their two daughters both experience the early trials of courtship and the youngest

child, the son, surrounded by dominant women, tends to bond closest with his father. Jackie is a neurotic individual who seems doomed to an unwanted single life and unsatisfactory affairs (although she does eventually marry, have a child and divorce). On the surface then, Roseanne could be mistaken for just another working-class sitcom. Actually, it was America's most groundbreaking 'seriously' funny series since **All In The Family**, made more than 15 years earlier.

What made Roseanne different was its jaw-dropping social realism, brutally naked honesty and uncomfortable depiction of a family. Both Roseanne and Dan were overweight, and their children were far from perfect: lying, keeping secrets from their parents and displaying anti-social traits. They loved each other but often they didn't seem to like each other very much, if at all. The strongest arguments ever spat out in a sitcom littered the plots, and subjects considered taboo for most US comedies (homosexuality, under-age sex, drug taking, infidelity and the like) were considered fair game for Roseanne. Only **Married … With Children** came anywhere close to this series' obsession with the dark side of the American dream.

During the long, long run of the series a huge amount of semi-regular characters were introduced, including long-term boyfriends for Becky and Darlene (Mark and David); Roseanne and Jackie's disagreeable mother, Bev; Dan's friend Arnie (played by Roseanne's real-life husband Tom Arnold); Roseanne's gay boss Leon; and her bisexual friend Nancy. The relationships and interplay between these and many other resident and visiting characters are way too complicated to detail here, suffice to say that, beneath the complexities, the core was the struggle of everyday life. However, although the show could be hysterically funny, with spot-on performances right down the cast, Roseanne just wouldn't have been Roseanne without Roseanne.

Roseanne Barr was born in Salt Lake City on 3 November 1953, but although she realised from an early age that she was funny, she didn't begin performing until the end of the 1970s, by which time she had long been married and mothered four children. She found success almost immediately, and her uncompromising, feminist material assured her of notoriety. In these early days she counted a sizeable lesbian contingent among her supporters, but as her act developed she appealed to a wider audience, one that, she herself was surprised to see, also comprised many males. She started appearing on TV in the mid 1980s, making the most impact with her enraged, working-class, no-nonsense housewife character – a towering creation that was a million miles away from the US domestic homemakers normally depicted. *Roseanne* was now only a step away.

From the off, there was friction on the set of *Roseanne* – for a start, head writer Matt Williams and Roseanne held widely differing opinions about the shape of the show, a clash that led to a well-publicised falling out. Reportedly, Roseanne was outraged that Williams alone received the 'creator' credit on the series, pointing out that the show was based fundamentally on the character she had developed for her standup act. (Her 1987 HBO special, which features this stage persona, seems to bear out the fact – see following entry.) But, she lost the battle, so much that even when she managed to force Williams off the series he still received his credit, the star having to be content with the secondary 'based on a character created by Roseanne Arnold' line.

This was just the tip of the iceberg, though: scores of other sensational clashes occurred between the star and her creative crew over the years, most of which, such as the dismissal of several teams of writers, were picked up gleefully by the press. One major incident was the collapse of Roseanne's real-life marriage to fellow cast member Tom Arnold; this was so dramatic, indeed, that it was turned into a 1994 US TV movie, *Roseanne And Tom: Behind The Scenes* (with Patrika Darbo and Stephen Lee in the lead roles). An edition of the BBC2 documentary series *Funny Business* (13 December 1992) – shot during the writing, planning and recording of a *Roseanne* episode – amply depicted the frustrations, anger and resentment that existed behind the scenes. Perhaps as a result of all these problems, *Roseanne* was veritably snubbed by those who decide the Emmy Awards – it wasn't even *nominated* for the honour Outstanding Comedy Series.

But – and it is important not to allow the problems to overshadow this – on-screen, *Roseanne* maintained a terrifically high standard. The series rarely wavered in quality and was also never afraid to experiment and innovate – with its annual gruesome Hallowe'en specials, for example, which featured truly gory special effects; its dream-sequence shows; its 'blooper' closing credit sequences; its episodes that spoofed other series, and, perhaps most remarkably, an entire episode that parodied the sugar-sweet black and white US domestic sitcoms of the 1950s ('The Fifties Show').

Because of all the creative problems, every new season of *Roseanne* was reckoned to be its last, but the series ran and ran. Its ninth and final season though, 1996–97, is considered by critics to have been one too many. The opening episode saw the Conners win $108m on the Illinois state lottery and the ensuing episodes attempted to show that,

despite the money, they all remained essentially the same people. (A similar ruse occurred in the British series *Only Fools And Horses*, but here the windfall came in the last episode. This allowed the series to end on a high note and prevented the writer, John Sullivan, from having to re-invent the format to feature the one-time strugglers in a grandiose environment.) By the show's high standards, the last season of *Roseanne* was a major disappointment – in the UK, C4 relegated it to a late-night slot, which spoke volumes considering that the channel had hitherto vigorously championed the series, with, including repeats, more than 400 transmissions inside eight years. But the final season did include a remarkable crossover episode in which Edina and Patsy from *Absolutely Fabulous* turned up, in character, in a story co-written by Jennifer Saunders, the first example of characters from a British series appearing in a completely different US production. This was no coincidence, though: Roseanne had purchased the American adaptation rights to *AbFab* and was planning its launch at this time.

Roseanne was finally laid to rest on 20 May 1997, ending a problematic programme that thrived despite, or perhaps because of, the creative differences behind the screen. There is no doubt that some of the criticisms levelled at Roseanne, and her refusal to compromise, were born of the sexist attitude that perceives a determined man as being 'strong' but a determined woman as 'difficult'. Her achievement in getting a smash-hit primetime network show that featured non-handsome (but not unattractive) characters facing real problems in an imperfect world was considerable, however, and its impact cannot be underestimated in the annals of US television.

*Notes. Early episodes credited the star as Roseanne Barr (her maiden name, even though she had married and subsequently divorced Bill Pentland in the early 1970s). In 1991, after her marriage to Tom Arnold, she changed her name to Roseanne Arnold, at which point the screen credits for the episodes of *Roseanne* already in syndication were retrospectively altered. From the seventh season onwards (September 1994), following her divorce from Arnold and marriage to Ben Thomas, she dropped her surname altogether for professional purposes, being credited simply as Roseanne.

The series also inspired the US Saturday-morning children's cartoon series *Little Rosey*, voiced by Roseanne and screened in the UK by C4 on Sundays in the *Early Morning* strand from 19 January 1992; and *Rosey And Buddy*, an animated cartoon voiced by Roseanne and Tom Arnold, first screened in the UK by C4 on 26 December 1992.

The Roseanne Barr Show

USA · HBO · STANDUP

1 × 55 mins · colour

US date: 19 Sep 1987

UK date: 10 June 1989 · C4 Sat 11pm

MAIN CAST
Roseanne Barr
Tom Arnold
Lois Bromfield
Heather Hopper
Erica Horn
Steve Morris
Bill Pentland

CREDITS
writers Roseanne Barr, Rocco Urbisci, Bill Pentland · *director* Rocco Urbisci · *producers* Syd Vinnedge, Tony Scotti

Such was the impact of *Roseanne* that, within five months of importing the US sitcom to Britain, C4 screened this one-off recording of the series' star in standup concert, taped by the US cable network HBO a year before the sitcom had begun in the USA. It was mostly a one-woman show, but Barr was joined by others for sketches that mocked family life and duly vented all of her feminist and sizeist ire.

The show was Roseanne's first major TV exposure on US TV beyond chat-show appearances, and she gave it full pelt. Men were clearly in the firing line, and this despite the fact that her then current husband Bill Pentland and her future husband Tom Arnold were among the cast.

It was this single appearance, indeed, that prompted Carsey-Werner to offer Roseanne her own sitcom. The fight was still most definitely on, but she would never be an 'unknown' again.

Rosie

UK · BBC · SITCOM

34 × 30 mins · colour

Series One (7) *The Growing Pains Of PC Penrose*
2 Sep–14 Oct 1975 · BBC1 Tue 9.25pm

Series Two (6) 5 Jan–9 Feb 1977 · BBC1
Wed mostly 7.40pm

Series Three (7) 18 May–6 July 1978 · BBC1
Thu 8pm

Series Four (7) 7 June–19 July 1979 · BBC1
Thu 8.30pm

Series Five (7) 18 Sep–30 Oct 1981 · BBC1
Fri 8.15pm

MAIN CAST
PC Michael Penrose ('Rosie') · · · · · · · · · · ·
· Paul Greenwood
Sgt W T Flagg · · · · · · Bryan Pringle (series 1)
PC Buttress · · · · · · · · David Pinner (series 1)
PC Toombs · · · · · · · · · · Alan Foss (series 1)
Insp Fox · · · · Christopher Burgess (series 1)
WPC Dean · · · · · · Catherine Chase (series 1)
Millie Penrose · · · · · · Avril Elgar (series 2–4);
· · · · · · · · · · · · · · Patricia Kneale (series 5)
Uncle Norman · · · Allan Surtees (series 2–5)
Aunt Ida · · · · · · · Lorraine Peters (series 2–5)

PC Wilmot · · · · · ·Tony Haygarth (series 2–5)
Chief-Insp Dunwoody · · · · · · · · · ·Paul Luty
· (series 2–4)
WPC Brenda Whatmough · · · · · · · · · · · · · ·
· · · · · · Penny Leatherbarrow (series 2–5)
Gillian · · · · · · · · Frankie Jordan (series 2–5)
Merv · · · · · · · · · Robert Gillespie (series 2);
· · · · · · · · · · · · · · · · John Cater (series 3–5)
Renata · · · · · · · · · · · Janet Dale (series 4);
· · · · · · · · · · · · · · · · Liz Goulding (series 5)
Englebert · · · · · · ·Albert Shepherd (series 5)
Bill · · · · · · · · · · Don McKillop (series 2–4)
Glenda · · · · · · · · Maggie Jones (series 2–4)

CREDITS
writer Roy Clarke · producers Douglas Argent
(series 1), Bernard Thompson (series 2–5)

The prolific writer Roy Clarke drew upon his earlier experiences as a policeman for this wistful sitcom, which followed the fortunes of a young, idealistic police constable.

The first series, titled *The Growing Pains Of PC Penrose*, was set in the Yorkshire town of Slagcaster, where probationary new recruit PC Penrose – who has 'escaped' from his home-town at the age of 19 to start a life on his own – and his colleague, the libidinous PC Buttress, fall under the wing of Sergeant Flagg. The veteran officer despairs of Penrose's naïvety but tries his best to school the lads in the ways of police work – albeit his own rather unorthodox methods.

The second (and subsequent) series was retitled *Rosie*, after Penrose's nickname. In this, Penrose departs Slagcaster and takes a compassionate posting back home, in the coastal town Ravensby, because – he is told – his widowed mother is at death's door. In fact, the manipulative, mascara-laden Millie simply wants him back, for, as the series' theme music (co-written and sung by Rosie actor Paul Greenwood) indicates, he is her pride and joy, and she will never let him go. Sure enough, Rosie returns to live with his mum, who unceasingly expresses her disappointment, born out of snobbery as much as a fear for his well-being, that he has joined the police force. Rosie's Uncle Norman and Aunt Ida live with the Penroses – Ida's feelings on the subject of Rosie's occupation are much like Millie's except that hers are born out of a genuine fear for his safety. (Actually, she has little to worry about – the crime rate in Ravensby is almost nil.) Uncle Norman is more supportive of Rosie, recognising the need for male-togetherness in their female-dominated world.

Rosie's return to Ravensby delights his long-standing girlfriend Gillian, the daughter of affluent, disapproving parents Bill and Glenda. Gillian wants marriage but Rosie doesn't, and he constantly has to temper her enthusiasms. Like Millie and Ida, she also feels that police work is no job for a delicate, almost pretty lad like Rosie. But, with no real evidence to support his view, he feels certain

that he has the potential to become a good copper, and duly perseveres. At the police station he strikes up a good friendship with PC Wilmot, a man of strange habits (like adjusting his genitals in public). Rosie is also assisted in his fight against crime by an informer, Merv. As Rosie sees it, 'proper' crime-fighters always seem to rely upon informants, so it is a relationship he must pursue; but Merv is deeply unreliable owing to his phenomenal short-sightedness. He always make spectacular entrances, crashing into tables, knocking cups of tea over vital evidence, and so on – so it is no wonder Rosie's senior officer, Dunwoody, is less than impressed by this conduit to the underworld. In the final series, Wilmot's role in the series was almost as great as that of Rosie's, and, to capitalise on the characters' rapport, Rosie moved out of the family home and the two of them shared accommodation.

Although it possibly overstayed its welcome, *Rosie* was another fine Roy Clarke creation, typically full of fascinating northern folk and delightfully idiosyncratic dialogue. For a police comedy, the episodes were remarkably free of criminal activity, leaving Clarke space to concentrate on what he does best, sketching out the characters in his own inimitable style.

The Rough With The Smooth

UK · BBC · SITCOM

7 × 30 mins · colour

Pilot · 22 Apr 1971 · BBC1 Thu 7.40pm
One series (6) 16 July–20 Aug 1975 · BBC1
Wed 9.55pm

MAIN CAST
Richard Woodville · · · · · · ·Tim Brooke-Taylor
Harold King · · · · · · · · · · · · · · · ·John Junkin

CREDITS
writers John Junkin/Tim Brooke-Taylor · producers
Leon Thau (pilot), Harold Snoad (series)

In 1971, soon after ending their working relationship with Marty Feldman (on the series *It's Marty*), Tim Brooke-Taylor and John Junkin co-wrote and appeared in a single-episode *Comedy Playhouse* pilot, depicting two flat-sharing bachelors – the 'rough' Harold King, and the 'smooth' Richard Woodville – rivals in the pursuance of women. Four years later the pilot evolved into a series which continued their exploits.

Round And Round

UK · BBC · SITCOM

6 × 30 mins · colour

25 June–30 July 1984 · BBC2 Mon 9.25pm

MAIN CAST
Maureen · · · · · · · · · · · · ·Bernadette Shortt
Mum Stevens · · · · · · · · · · · ·Eileen Kennally
Dad Stevens · · · · · · · · · · · · · · · ·Dave King
Francis · · · · · · · · · · · · · · · · ·James Lister

CREDITS
writer John Fortune · director Peter Hammond ·
producer Ray Butt

Further proof of John Fortune's refusal to be confined by the conventional strictures of situation comedy, this six-part series reflected the passage of 14 years in the life of a young woman, Maureen.

We first see Maureen in 1958, as she encounters adolescent love for the first time, meeting Robert Creasey (John Gordon-Sinclair). The second instalment takes place in 1961, where Maureen is at university and discovering the joys and dangers of sex (her partner, Patrick, was played by Nicholas Lyndhurst). Next it is 1964 and Maureen is getting married to Francis (James Lister). The fourth episode is set in 1967, with Maureen and Francis starting a family. In the fifth, set in 1970, the marriage crumbles into divorce. Finally, in 1972, Maureen falls in love again (with Malcolm, played by Tony Haygarth), thus fulfilling the series' title *Round And Round*.

A fine concept, giving Fortune a further landscape in which to sketch his fascination with, and the repercussions of, relationships. Among the actors appearing in the series were John Bird, a very young Kathy Burke, Joan Hickson and the writer himself.

Round The Bend

UK · BBC · SKETCH

5 × 60 mins · b/w

29 Oct 1955–17 Mar 1956 · monthly
Sat 8.30pm

MAIN CAST
Jon Pertwee
Lupino Lane (show 1)
Bill Pertwee (shows 2 & 3)
Dick Emery (shows 2, 4 & 5)

CREDITS
writers Jon Pertwee (3), Sid Green/Dick Hills (3),
Michael Pertwee (2), David Climie (2), Freddie
Robertson (1), Frank Driscoll (1) · producers John
Warrington (shows 1 & 2), Bryan Sears (shows
3–5)

The multi-voiced Jon Pertwee headlined all five editions of this hour-long comedy-accented entertainment series. His brother Michael was on hand with some of the writing duties and their cousin Bill (later to star in *Dad's Army*) turned up as guest star in a couple of the shows.

Round The Twist

AUSTRALIA · 7 NETWORK THEN ABC
(AUSTRALIAN CHILDREN'S TELEVISION
FOUNDATION) · CHILDREN'S SITCOM

26 × 30 mins · colour

Australian dates: 26 Aug–18 Nov 1990 (7
Network); 20 Mar–12 June 1993 (ABC)

UK dates: 6 Apr–18 May 1990; 16 Apr–9 July 1993 (26 episodes) BBC1 Fri 5.10pm

MAIN CAST

Linda Twist	Tamsin West (1990); Joelene Crnognorac (1993)
Pete Twist	Sam Vanderburgh (1990); Ben Thomas (1993)
Bronson Twist	Rodney McLennan (1990); Jeffrey Walker (1993)
Mr Twist	Richard Moir
Nell	Bunny Brooke
Mr Snapper	Esben Storm
Matron Gribble	Judith McGrath (1990)
Miss James	Robyn Gibbes (1993)
Mr Gribble	Frankie J Holden (1990); Mark Mitchell (1993)

CREDITS

creator Paul Jennings · *writers* Paul Jennings, Esben Storm · *directors* Steve Jodrell, Mark Lewis, Esben Storm · *producers* Antonia Barnard, Patricia Edgar

A weird and wonderful Australian children's sitcom based upon Paul Jennings' books *Unreal!*, *Unbelievable!* and *Quirky Tales*. The author provided most of the TV scripts.

The episodes featured the motherless Twist children, who live in a lighthouse on the bleak Victoria coastline, and whose lives are imbued with fantasy, mysticism and flights of fancy. Other characters included the nasty Mr Gribble, their nearest neighbour.

Three years after the first batch of 13 episodes, made by the 7 Network, a second series was made, this time for ABC. The young child actors having aged too much to repeat their roles, new children were brought in to play the parts of Linda, Pete and Bronson. (Also, Mark Mitchell replaced Frankie J Holden as Gribble.) But the barnstorming fun continued unabated.

Rowan And Martin's Laugh-In

USA · NBC (GEORGE SCHLATTER-ED FRIENDLY PRODUCTIONS/ROMART) · SKETCH/STANDUP

140 × 60 mins · colour

US dates: 9 Sep 1967 (pilot) · 22 Jan 1968–14 May 1973

UK dates: 8 Sep 1968–24 Oct 1971 (88 editions) BBC2 Sun various times

MAIN CAST

Dan Rowan
Dick Martin
Gary Owens
Ruth Buzzi
Alan Sues (1968–72)
Henry Gibson (1968–71)
Arte Johnson (1968–71)
Judy Carne (1968–70)
Goldie Hawn (1968–70)
Jo Anne Worley (1968–70)
Larry Hovis (1968, 1971–72)
Charlie Brill (1968–69)
Chelsea Brown (1968–69)
Dave Madden (1968–69)
Pigmeat Markham (1968–69)
Eileen Brennan (1968)
Roddy Maude-Roxby (1968)
Jeremy Lloyd (1969–70)
Lily Tomlin (1970–73)
Johnny Brown (1970–72)

CREDITS

creators Dan Rowan, Dick Martin, George Schlatter, Ed Friendly · *writers* Paul Keyes, Jim Abell, Chris Beard, Jim Carlson, John Carsey, Gene Farmer, Phil Hahn/Jack Hanrahan, Coslough Johnson, Jeremy Lloyd, Marc London, Allan Manings/Hugh Wedlock Jr, Jack Mendelsohn, Lorne Michaels/Hart Pomerantz, Jim Mulligan, David Panich, John Rappaport, Stephen Spears, Barry Took, Digby Wolfe and others · *executive producers* George Schlatter/Ed Friendly (1968–71), Paul Keyes (1971–73) · *producers* Paul Keyes, Carolyn Raskin

While the UK has a long heritage of crazy TV comedy – stretching back to Spike Milligan's *A Show Called Fred*, *Son Of Fred* and *The Idiot Weekly, Price 2d*, Michael Bentine's *It's A Square World* and the pre-*Python* series *At Last The 1948 Show* – there have been far fewer attempts to establish American TV sketch shows, producers perhaps being unwilling or unable to provide the creative freedom necessary for the genre to survive. Ernie Kovacs had made some inroads into producing original televisual zaniness, and Gracie Allen had treated audiences to her bizarre verbal imagery, but it wasn't until *Rowan And Martin's Laugh-In* that the genre truly flourished. *Laugh-In* (as it colloquially became known) was an anything-goes, scatological mish-mash of quickfire gags, micro-sketches, corn, puns, satire and slapstick. Its huge regular cast and battery-farm writing process worked in harness to produce a jam-packed hour of irreverent nonsense aimed unashamedly at the funny bone.

The hosts, Dan Rowan (suave-looking, with moustache) and Dick Martin (clean-cut and clean-shaven), met at a restaurant in the winter of 1951–52; and they immediately experimented with a double-act, one that served them passably well over the following years. Although both had experience as comedy writers, they found that they worked better at improvisation than with scripts, and so developed a relaxed style of crosstalk that seemed fresh to young American audiences jaundiced by the heavily scripted exchanges common among US TV comics. *Laugh-In*, and the more satirical *Smothers Brothers Show* which appeared at the same time in the late 1960s, appealed greatly to this new kind of US TV viewer, those who were actively seeking out programmes that reflected the enormous changes taking place in American society.

Created by Rowan, Martin, their manager George Schlatter and a former network vice-president, Ed Friendly, *Rowan And Martin's Laugh-In* bounced to the top of the US ratings within weeks of its launch. The series was stuffed full of recurring characters, skits and, in particular, catchphrases, all of which were soon ringing around the school-halls and workplaces of America. These included 'Sock it to me' (usually said by the American-domiciled British actress Judy Carne, who duly became known as the 'sock it to me girl'), upon which the person would usually be drenched by a bucket of water; the surreal poems by the flower-holding Henry Gibson; Martin's odd saying 'you bet your bippy'; Arte Johnson's German soldier, declaring 'Ver-r-r-ry interrresting … but shhtupid'; 'Here comes the judge', first used by Sammy Davis Jr but then the clarion call of Pigmeat Markham, who released a successful record of the same name; and the lexiconigraphical reference 'Look that up in your Funk and Wagnalls!' (sales of this particular dictionary reputedly soared as a result of the constant free plugs). Other enduring memories include the regular reminder that the show came from 'beautiful downtown Burbank'; Goldie Hawn, feigning to be a dumb-blonde to purposely fluff her lines; Lily Tomlin's brilliant skits as the irritating, nasal telephone operator Ermintrude; 'The Flying Fickle Finger Of Fate Award', presented to corrupt or inept industries or government offices; Ruth Buzzi, dressed up as Gladys, a virginal old spinster, knocking a similarly aged lecher (Arte Johnson) over the head with her handbag or umbrella as he shuffled up to her and suggested congress; cross-eyed Big Al's Sports Scene updates (performed by Alan Sues); Gary Owens' earnest, old-style radio announcements; and the 'Joke Wall', a set full of windows from which members of the cast popped out to shout one-liners. (The series had a huge cast list, and in addition to main members named above, the following also played regular parts: Dennis Allen, Tod Bass, Brian Bressler, Richard Dawson, Patti Deutsch, Moosie Drier, Ann Elder, Lisa Farringer, Byron Gilliam, Teresa Graves, Harvey Jason, Donna Jean Young, Sarah Kennedy, Mitzi McCall, Nancy Phillips, Pamela Rodgers, Barbara Sharma, Jud Strunk, Willie Tyler and the oddly named Dick Whittington.)

Laugh-In had a strong British input, not only the performers Judy Carne and Roddy Maude-Roxby, but performer/writer Jeremy Lloyd, but co-developer and writer Digby Wolfe (*Sheep's Clothing*), and scriptwriter Barry Took, who was given leave of absence by the BBC to take part in the project. The real spice in *Laugh-In*, though, was the array of unlikely guest stars who appeared each week, including John Wayne, Danny Kaye, Jack Benny, Johnny Carson, Rock Hudson, Ringo Starr, the Smothers Brothers and, remarkably, President Richard Nixon (who rather nervously delivered the 'Sock it to me' catchphrase).

The series was very well received in the UK too, although – airing on the minority channel BBC2 – it failed to become the ratings phenomenon that it was in the USA. In 1969, Rowan and Martin tried to capitalise on the series' popularity with a feature film, *The Maltese Bippy* (directed by Norman Panama), but while it was aimed at a similar audience it failed to achieve any great success. Without its two frontmen the series was revived by NBC in 1979 but it was soon cancelled, this particular run being notable only for the inclusion of Robin Williams among the regular cast. The time for *Laugh-In* was the late 1960s and that time had passed.

Note. Rowan and Martin appeared together in *Like Hep!*, a US variety special fronted by the singer Dinah Shore, produced by the *Laugh-In* team of George Schlatter and Ed Friendly and screened by BBC1 on 16 September 1969. The comics also jointly hosted *Double Bananas*, a 90-minute special (aired in the USA by HBO in 1979) that paid tribute to the golden days of variety and included guest appearances by such luminaries as Sid Caesar and Imogene Coca. It was screened in Britain by C4 on 2 May 1983. On 7 February 1993 NBC broadcast *Rowan And Martin's 25th Anniversary*, which reunited most of the original cast to take a nostalgic look back at the series. This was screened in Britain by BBC2 on 25 December 1994. (BBC2 also repeated 26 editions of the original series, from 31 October 1983 to 27 November 1984.)

See also *Pure Goldie* and *Ver-r-r-ry Interesting*.

Rowan Atkinson On Location In Boston

UK · BBC (TIGER TELEVISION/POLA JONES) · STANDUP

1 × 55 mins · colour

11 Apr 1992 · BBC1 Sat 10.30pm

MAIN CAST
Rowan Atkinson
Angus Deayton

CREDITS
writers Rowan Atkinson, Richard Curtis, Ben Elton · *director* Thomas Schlamme · *executive producer* Peter Bennett-Jones

Born in Newcastle upon Tyne on 6 January 1955, Rowan Atkinson first demonstrated an ability to entertain when he joined the Oxford Revue, while studying for a science degree at university. In 1977 he made a considerable impact as part of the Revue's show on the Edinburgh Festival Fringe, making his London stage debut in Hampstead the same year in *Beyond A Joke*. After further stage performances he wrote and starred in *Rowan Atkinson Presents ... Canned Laughter*, a one-off half-hour screened by ITV in 1979. Soon afterwards he was chosen

for the *Not The Nine O'Clock News* team, where he became a household name. Films, stage performances and the brilliant TV series *Blackadder* followed before *Mr Bean* opened the door to international fame.

By the beginning of the 1990s Atkinson had reached a point in his career when he was considering resting from, or giving up, stage performances; because of this, he decided to film his two appearances at the Huntingdon Theatre in Boston, USA, in December 1991, where he performed the best bits from his stage acts of the previous decade (including skits featuring a Mr Bean-like character). Angus Deayton played the straight-man, underscoring Atkinson's buffoonery, a role he had also served on tour. The finished film, produced by Atkinson's own company Tiger Television, was shown first on the US cable channel HBO on 1 March 1992, but it was then re-edited for UK transmission as the original programme contained material considered too risqué for a BBC1 audience.

Note. This same year, Tiger Television also produced *Funny Business*, a six-part mostly documentary series for BBC2 (22 November to 27 December) that looked at the art of comedy. Atkinson appeared in the first programme, subtitled 'Visual Comedy, A Lecture By Rowan Atkinson M Sc (Oxon)'. In demonstrating elements of the lecture he portrayed a physical comedian, given the name Kevin Bartholomew.

Rowan Atkinson Presents ... Canned Laughter

UK · ITV (LWT) · SKETCH

1 × 30 mins · colour

8 Apr 1979 · Sun 10pm

MAIN CAST
Robert Box/Dave Perry/
Mr Marshall · · · · · · · · · · · Rowan Atkinson
Lorraine · · · · · · · · · · · · · · Sue Holderness

CREDITS
writer Rowan Atkinson · *director* Geoffrey Sax · *producer* Humphrey Barclay

Screened six months before the start of *Not The Nine O'Clock News*, this single-episode LWT production marked the first major TV appearance of Rowan Atkinson, 24 and on the verge of a flourishing career. He played three roles: the pathetic accident-prone nerd Robert Box – a prototype *Mr Bean*, but with a voice – who finally plucks up the courage to ask a girl for a date; a moustachioed, frilly-shirted failed stage entertainer, Dave Perry; and the glassy, ghastly company boss Mr Marshall. All three end up in the final restaurant scene, Box and Perry consoling each other for their respective mishaps while Marshall looks on impassively. The canned laughter mentioned in the title was played throughout the half-hour, and most especially

at the end when its constant repetition made the use of this electronic forgery particularly obvious.

The Roy Castle Show

UK · BBC · SKETCH

5 × 45 mins · b/w

1 May–26 June 1965 · BBC1 fortnightly
Sat mostly 7.25pm

MAIN CAST
Roy Castle
Peter Butterworth
Pat Coombs

CREDITS
writers Sid Green/Dick Hills · *producer* Bill Lyon-Shaw

The talented all-round entertainer Roy Castle starred in scores of TV series over the years but this 1965 offering had comedy at its core and was scripted by Morecambe and Wise's writers Sid Green and Dick Hills.

The series was made at a time when Castle's career was blossoming in all fields, and he recorded it directly after filming his contribution to the first *Doctor Who* feature film (*Dr Who And The Daleks*), in which, as the Time Lord's grandson, he had added a touch of comedy to a role hitherto played straight on television.

Roy Hudd ...   [various shows]

see HUDD, Roy

Roy's Raiders

UK · BBC · SITCOM

6 × 30 mins · colour

20 July–24 Aug 1991 · BBC1 Sat 6.30pm

MAIN CAST
Roy · · · · · · · · · · · · · · · · · · · James Grout
Henry · · · · · · · · · · · · William Vanderpuye
Bazza · · · · · · · · · · · · · · Shane Withington
Jill · · · · · · · · · · · · · · · · Rebecca Stevens
Chris · · · · · · · · · · · · · · Edward Tudor Pole
Daisy · · · · · · · · · · · · · · · · · · Sara Crowe
Gavin Bailey · · · · · · · · · · · · · · Des McAleer
Winco · · · · · · · · · · · · · · · · Milton Johns
Jack · · · · · · · · · · · · · · · · · Mark Adams
Jessie · · · · · · · · · · · · · · · · · Pat Coombs

CREDITS
writer Michael Aitkens · *director* Sue Longstaff · *producer* Susan Belbin

An earthy ensemble comedy concerning the antics of a firm of motorcycle couriers, Roy's Raiders. James Grout was cast as the boss of the company, in charge of a disparate staff, most of whom are waiting for a better job to come along. This is especially true of Daisy, a frustrated actress who always seems on the verge of a big break. Episodes revolved around the relationships of the staff and the company's ongoing battle with a rival courier firm, Bailey's Comets.

This series didn't fare as well as Aitkens' concurrent sitcom *Waiting For God*, and it failed to return for a second series. The writer himself appeared in one episode.

Rude Health

UK · C4 (ELSTREE COMPANY/METROPOLITAN TV) · SITCOM

14 × 30 mins · colour

Series One (7) 16 Mar–27 Apr 1987 · Mon mostly 9.30pm

Series Two (7) 4 Jan–15 Feb 1988 · Mon 8.30pm

MAIN CAST

Dr Charles Sweet	· · · · · · · · · · · ·	John Wells
Dr Peter Pink	· · · · · · · · · · · · · · · · ·	John Bett
Dr Andrew Putter	· · · · · · · · · · · · · ·	Paul Mari
Sir Nigel Toft	· · · · · ·	Moray Watson (series 1)
Mrs Thorpe	· · · · · · · · · · · ·	Josephine Tewson
Caroline Toft	· · · · · · · ·	Judy Gridley (series 1)
Leonie	· · · · · · · · · · · · · ·	Susie Ann Watkins
Veronica Sweet	· · · · · · · · · · · · · · ·	Gay Soper
Lady 'Pig' Toft	· · ·	Yvonne Manners (series 1)
Mrs Joy	· · · · · · · · · · · · · ·	Liz Fraser (series 2)

CREDITS

writers Phil Gould/Quentin Brown · *director* David Macmahon · *executive producers* Greg Smith/Alan Janes

A sitcom vehicle for John Wells, whose long and distinguished career in the realm of satire had distilled down to one role for which he was best known: Denis Thatcher in *Anyone For Denis? Rude Health* did not change this perspective, for, although extending to two series, its acclaim was small, and this despite the additional casting of Angela Thorne (Margaret Thatcher in *Anyone For Denis?*).

The youthful-looking Wells played the part of Dr Sweet, who – upon the death of Dr Crabbe – becomes the senior partner of a doctors' surgery in a small town, and so takes over its control. Sweet is the sort of GP who is only happy so long as his patients are well and he can dispense with them after 35 seconds; keen, too, to maximise his income, he tries to persuade certain well-to-do NHS patients to register with him privately, in particular (in the first series) the upper-crust Tofts. Sweet is the eldest of the three general practitioners, and often despairs of his two younger partners, the eccentric Dr Pink and the imbecilic Dr Putter, as well as the glamorous receptionist, Leonie. Mrs Thorpe, the surgery manager, is the only calming influence.

Although vaguely subversive, *Rude Health* was an incurably unremarkable series, reliant upon surreal scenarios and a smattering of coarse language to raise laughs. It was better than lame, certainly … but not by much.

The Rudi Carrell Show

see The Montreux Festival

Rule Britannia!

UK · ITV (THAMES) · SITCOM

7 × 30 mins · colour

8 Oct–19 Nov 1975 · Wed mostly 8pm

MAIN CAST

George Bradshaw	· · · · · · · · · · ·	Tony Melody
Taffy Evans	· · · · · · · · · · · · ·	Richard Davies
Jock McGregor	· · · · · · · · · · ·	Russell Hunter
Paddy O'Brien	· · · · · · · · · · · · · · ·	Joe Lynch
Lil Bradshaw	· · · · · · · · · · · · · · · ·	Jo Warne
Maggie	· · · · · · · · · · · · · · · · · ·	Carol Mills

CREDITS

writer Vince Powell · *director/producer* Anthony Parker

Read the names George Bradshaw, Jock McGregor, Taffy Evans and Paddy O'Brien and you don't have to be a genius to work out that *Rule Britannia!* brought to the screens the ancient standup humour about the Englishman, the Scotsman, the Welshman and the Irishman. Truth is, the series rarely deviated from such corny stereotypes – boozing, bruising and carousing being the disorder of the day.

Bradshaw is the archetypal English bore, a man who has forgotten that life is for the living. He has also forgotten that, a quarter-century earlier, he made a pact with his three fellow Royal Navy sailors that they would all meet up 25 years on. When he remembers, he has to overcome the doubts of his wife Lil; when the lads stay together she has to pull him back from the brink.

Writer Vince Powell was no stranger to the 'ethnic' sitcom idea; indeed his Jewish comedy *My Son Reuben* was still airing when *Rule Britannia!* landed on ITV. Joe Lynch – Paddy O'Brien – was no stranger to them either: he had played the part of Patrick Kelly in Powell's *Never Mind The Quality, Feel The Width*.

Rumpus Point

UK · ITV (ASSOCIATED-REDIFFUSION) · CHILDREN'S SKETCH

13 × 15 mins · b/w

28 Sep–21 Dec 1955 · Wed 5pm

MAIN CAST

Allan Maxwell
Keith Smith

OTHER APPEARANCES

Clive Dunn
Dennis Clinton

CREDITS

writer Peter Ling

Later to co-create with long-time collaborator Hazel Adair the famous TV soaps *Compact* (BBC) and *Crossroads* (ITV), Peter Ling wrote these weekly bundles of fun for children, screened when ITV was broadcast only in the London area. Slapstick was the order of the day and *Rumpus Point*, by all accounts, did not pull its punches.

Run, Buddy, Run

USA · CBS (TALENT ASSOCIATES) · SITCOM

16 × 30 mins · colour

US dates: 12 Sep 1966–2 Jan 1967

UK dates: 1 Nov 1966–10 Jan 1968
(14 episodes · b/w) ITV various days and times

MAIN CAST

Buddy Overstreet	· · · · · · · · · · ·	Jack Sheldon
Devere	· · · · · · · · · · · · · · · · ·	Bruce Gordon
Junior	· · · · · · · · · · · · · · · · · ·	Jim Connell
Wendell	· · · · · · · · · · · · · · ·	Nick Georgiade
Harry	· · · · · · · · · · · · · · · · · ·	Gregg Palmer

CREDITS

writers Budd Grossman (3), Jack Elinson/Norman Paul (2), Myles Wilder (2), Ben Gershman/Bill Freedman (2), Mel Tolkin/Ernest Chambers (1), William Raynor (1), Seaman Jacobs/Ed James (1), Ray Singer (1), Jack Winter (1), Al Gordon/Hal Goodman (1), Izzy Elinson (1) · *producers* David Susskind, Leonard Stern, Dan Melnick, Jack Elinson

A spoof of the 'man on the run' adventure series of the period (such as *The Fugitive* and *Run For Your Life*), *Run, Buddy, Run* depicted the perilous life of a quiet everyday American accountant, Buddy Overstreet, who happens to overhear some gangsters talking while taking a Turkish bath. Their hip/hit vocabulary means nothing to him but the hoods assume it does and that, because he heard so much, he must be captured and eliminated. Overstreet duly takes to the streets, each episode placing him in a different situation – although, inevitably, the leader of the gang, Devere, always turns up.

Buddy Overstreet was played by Jack Sheldon, but perhaps the best part was Devere's – alias 'Mr D' – excellently played by Bruce Gordon as a spin on the Frank Nitti gangster role he created for the classic 1959–63 US crime series *The Untouchables*.

Note. The *Run, Buddy, Run* writer Budd Grossman (a veteran of many US series, including *Gilligan's Island* and *Diff'rent Strokes*) lived in Britain for three years at the end of the 1950s, during which time he created, and mostly wrote, *Time Out For Peggy*, an ITV sitcom starring Billie Whitelaw as Peggy Spencer, a blonde who inherits a decrepit boarding-house and struggles to make it a success. The series, made by the Midlands/North weekend station ABC, aired in these areas from 30 March to 29 June 1958 (12 episodes) and 14 September 1958 to 25 January 1959 (12 more) but was not screened in the London area.

Running The Halls

USA · NBC (STEVE SLAVKIN PRODUCTIONS/NBC PRODUCTIONS) · CHILDREN'S SITCOM

13 × 30 mins · colour

US dates: 11 Sep–4 Dec 1993

UK dates: 17 Mar–9 June 1994 (13 episodes) C4 Thu 6.30pm

MAIN CAST

Molloy Simpson	Lackey Bevis
Holiday	Laurie Fortier
Andy McBain	Richard Hayes
Taylor	Craig Kirkwood
Reese	Trevor Lissauer
Nikki	Senta Moses
Shark	Richard Speight Jr
Miss Gilman	Pamela Brown

CREDITS

creator/executive producer Steve Slavkin · *writers* various · *directors* various · *producers* Greg Gorden

The adventures of six new students at Middlefield Academy, a New England boarding school, constituted this woeful rites of passage sitcom featuring an array of typically toothy Americans finding out that friendship overcomes all. In opposition to the sparky sextet are the beautiful but officious Miss Gilman, and a serious-minded, gauche fellow student, Shark, hidebound by the rule book and determined to ensure that the others toe the line.

Like the more successful (but equally bad) *Saved By The Bell*, *Running The Halls* was a simplistic slice of moral majority propaganda. Each week the cast learned A Valuable Rule Of Life (ugly people need love too, fat people have feelings, honesty pays) which enriched their existence and caused all to end happily. And the series gleefully embraced the dumb side of American teenage philosophy, delighting in its portrayal of Shark as a nerd, proven by his interest in opera and European culture. One longed for an exchange student from *Grange Hill* to appear and bring an air of tension to their tedious lives. Compared to *Running The Halls*, indeed, even the ITV schoolyard sitcom *Please, Sir!* was a gripping and realistic social document.

Running Wild   1

see Morecambe and Wise

Running Wild   2

UK · ITV (LWT) · SITCOM

13 × 30 mins · colour

Series One (6) 6 Mar–10 Apr 1987 · Fri 8.30pm

Series Two (7) 23 Apr–4 June 1989 · Sun around 10.30pm

MAIN CAST

Max Wild	Ray Brooks
Babs Wild	Janet Key
Stephanie Wild	Michelle Collins
Rob	Peter Amory
Tom Coleman	Berwick Kaler (series 1)
Jenny	Brigit Forsyth (series 2)

CREDITS

writer Philip Trewinnard · *directors* Vic Finch (series 1), Derrick Goodwin (series 2) · *producers* Marcus Plantin (series 1), Derrick Goodwin (series 2)

Max Wild yearns to re-live his 1950s youth, when, as a rocking and rolling Teddy Boy, he jived in his crêpe-soled shoes to the jukebox sounds, and dropped out of art school to pursue the lifestyle of a bohemian. Now, alas, he is married and the nearest he gets to the fifties is his age – he's 45 and rising. However, with his student daughter Stephanie now an adult herself and no longer in need of a morally upright father, and bored with his job as an environmental health officer for the local council, Max sets out to recapture his golden days, donning his drainpipe trousers once more and leaving his family for garrets new and even loftier plans to write a rock opera, *Firestar*. But although he can wear bootlace ties he cannot break the ties that bind, often returning to his estranged wife Babs.

By the second series, set a year after the first, Max has tired of reliving his past and wants to return home to wife and daughter. But, with new men-friends and a blossoming career in PR, Babs has other plans. However, the sudden presence of her sister Jenny, who has moved in because her marriage has broken down, upsets the apple cart, as does Stephanie's announcement that she's pregnant with her boyfriend Rob's baby, news that infuriates her mother and so sends the daughter scurrying to her father.

A comedy that seemed to develop a dramatic edge as it progressed, *Running Wild* marked the sitcom debut of acclaimed actor Ray Brooks. He and Janet Key (cast as Babs) had previously worked together in a few episodes of the BBC1 drama series *Big Deal* (1984–86)

Rushton's Illustrated

UK · ITV (ATV) · SKETCH

5 × 30 mins · colour

18 Feb–17 Mar 1980 · Mon 8pm

MAIN CAST

William Rushton
Roy Kinnear
Hugh Paddick
Richard O'Brien
Norman Chappell
Caroline Villiers

CREDITS

writer William Rushton · *director/producer* Glyn Edwards

The witty cartoonist and writer William Rushton – most popularly associated with the early days of *Private Eye* magazine, a host of books, the TV series *That Was The Week That Was* and for appearing in every radio and TV panel-game imaginable – had the opportunity to stretch out in this ITV series, placing himself and his regular support cast in an array of bizarre comedy skits that required scores of costume changes. Six programmes were promised in ATV's promotional literature but only five were screened.

Note. Rushton died on 11 December 1996, aged 59.

Russ Abbot ...   [various shows]

see ABBOT, Russ

Rutland Weekend Television

UK · BBC · SKETCH

14 × 30 mins · colour

Series One (6) 12 May–16 June 1975 · BBC2 Mon 9pm

Special · 26 Dec 1975 · BBC2 Fri 10.55pm

Series Two (7) 12 Nov–24 Dec 1976 · BBC2 Fri mostly 9pm

MAIN CAST

Eric Idle
Neil Innes
David Battley
Henry Woolf
Gwen Taylor

CREDITS

writer Eric Idle · *songs* Neil Innes · *producer* Ian Keill

Following the (temporary) demise of *Monty Python's Flying Circus* at the end of 1974, its various members moved on to new projects. First out of the trap was Eric Idle with this clever sketch series centred on 'Britain's smallest television network'.

The title *Rutland Weekend Television* – both a reference to Britain's smallest county, Rutland, which had disappeared in 1974 with the redrawing of boundaries, and a pun on the ITV Friday–Sunday franchise for the capital, London Weekend Television – was suggested by John Cleese, who, according to Idle, was paid £1 for his trouble. The concept of using a television network as a launch-pad for the sketches allowed Idle a great deal of scope to tap various subjects and areas, but, ironically, his elaborate plans were undermined by the small budget allocated to the series by the BBC. To portray a TV station struggling with a paucity of cash, Idle had, indeed, a paucity of cash; typically, he worked the cheapness of the show into a running gag.

Among the *Monty Python* team, Eric Idle was the only person to write alone, so he had no problems adapting to post-*Python* work. He also invited the fine musical wit Neil Innes (a former member of the Bonzo Dog Doo-Dah Band) to provide comic songs. Some excellent work emerged – Idle was brimming with ideas and seemed to have learned different styles from the other Pythons: sketches ranged from spoof documentaries to parodies of period dramas and, indeed, send-ups of all aspects of television programming. Innes, David Battley, Henry Woolf and Gwen Taylor helped perform the material and there were occasional star guest appearances, notably George Harrison in the 1975 Christmas special.

The ex-Beatle and the ex-Python had become good friends around this period, and this probably sparked the creation of a super-successful spin-off from *Rutland Weekend Television*: the TV movie *The Rutles* (aka *All You Need Is Cash*). This began when Neil Innes wrote a song pastiching a circa 1964 Beatles track, which was then enacted in an edition of *RWT* utilising the same directorial style that Richard Lester had favoured in the Beatles' movie *A Hard Day's Night*. On 2 October 1976, Eric Idle hosted an edition of the US comedy show **Saturday Night Live**, right at the time when a long-running joke in that series centred on a possible re-formation of the Beatles on the show, in return for which, generously, the Fab Four would be paid $800 a man. Asked to bring over the Beatles with him from Britain, Idle responded that he couldn't, but he could bring a great new film of them – indicating the 'Rutles' clip from *RWT*. The response of *SNL* viewers was so great that the series' producer Lorne Michaels and Idle agreed to make a full-length 'mockumentary' detailing the history of the Rutles – essentially a spoof on the Beatles' entire career – with Michaels as the producer for NBC. Made, thankfully, on a much bigger budget, *The Rutles* aired in the USA on 22 March 1978 and on 27 March 1978 in the UK, on BBC2. Idle directed (together with *SNL* director Gary Weis), wrote and also appeared in the film – as the presenter and as the Paul McCartney-like Dirk McQuickly; Neil Innes was the John Lennon-like Ron Nasty; Rikki Fataar played the George Harrison-like Stig O'Hara; and John Halsey was the Ringo Starr-like drummer Barrington Womble, alias Barry Wom. George Harrison, Michael Palin, Ron Wood, Mick Jagger, Paul Simon, and *SNL* regulars John Belushi, Dan Aykroyd, Bill Murray and Gilda Radner were also in the cast, in cameo roles. The film was a triumph from the first frame to the last, and a resounding success not only for Idle but also for Innes, who provided a slew of spot-on Beatles song parodies, leading to a hit album and singles; a very-long-awaited sequel album was issued in 1996. (*RWT* had also generated spin-offs: the book *The Rutland Dirty Weekend Book* and the Innes album *The Rutland Weekend Songbook*.)

Notes. Just before launching *RWT*, Idle experimented with the idea of spoof broadcasting with his BBC Radio 1 series *Radio Five* (six hour-long editions, 30 March–4 May 1974). The title was a play on the BBC's national radio stations, Radios 1 to 4. An actual Radio 5 has subsequently come into existence.

Neil Innes later gained his own BBC2 series, *The Innes Book Of Records* (17 January–21 February 1979, 2 June–7 July 1980, and 28 September–9 November 1981, a total of 18 editions) that featured original songs and weekly guest artists. The series was whimsical, with more emphasis on music than straight humour, but it did feature some comedy guests, including Rowan Atkinson, Michael Palin, Ivor Cutler, Viv Stanshall and Stanley Unwin.

Ryan And Ronnie

UK · BBC · SKETCH

*20 editions (13 × 30 mins · 7 × 25 mins) · colour

Series One (7 × 30 mins) 18 June–30 July 1971 · BBC1 Fri mostly 5.20pm

Series Two (7 × 25 mins) 12 July–25 Aug 1972 · BBC1 Wed 7pm

Series Three (6 × 30 mins) 9 July–20 Aug 1973 · BBC1 Mon 7.30pm

MAIN CAST
Ryan Davies
Ronnie Williams
Myfanwy Talog
Bryn Williams
Margaret Williams (series 1)

CREDITS
writers Ryan Davies/Ronnie Williams · *producer* David Richards

With three Welsh-language TV series under their belts, comedians Ryan and Ronnie had already enjoyed great success in their home country before the BBC decided that their particular brand of humour could be appreciated by the nation as a whole. The comics admitted that, at first, they found it difficult to work in English, but they soon settled down to a style that crossed visual humour with some verbal clowning. The thin, long-faced Ryan provided a visual counterpoint to the round-faced Ronnie and, although something of an acquired taste, the duo counted many English fans among their following, impressing with odd characteristics like buttering a loaf of bread before it is sliced, and folding arms in an exaggeratedly defiant style.

*Note. This figure refers to the nationally broadcast English-language editions.

See also **How Green Was My Father**.

S And M

UK · C4 (HAT TRICK PRODUCTIONS) ·
IMPROVISATIONAL

7 × 30 mins · colour
6 Nov–18 Dec 1991 · Wed 10.30pm

MAIN CAST
Tony Slattery
Mike McShane

CREDITS
director Liddy Oldroyd · *executive producer* Denise
O'Donoghue · *producer* Dan Patterson

With the 'improv' boom in full swing, most of
the leading lights from C4's ad-libbed parlour-
game *Whose Line Is It Anyway?* graduated
to their own series. John Sessions, Josie
Lawrence and Paul Merton had all made the
transition and now it was the turn of Tony
Slattery and Mike McShane.

The teaming of the large, loud and
aggressive American (McShane) with
the dapper, quieter but mischievous Brit
(Slattery) was an obvious move and the pair
played off well against each other in a
number of sketches. The subjects to kick-start
their imagination were simple enough: 'at the
barber's', 'in a restaurant' and so on, and one
recurring theme, a leftover from *Whose Line
Is It Anyway?*, showed the couple giving
voices to two peas in a pod.

Sabrina The Teenage Witch

USA · ABC (FINISHING THE HAT PRODUCTIONS/
HARTBREAK FILMS) · CHILDREN'S SITCOM

**36 episodes (35 × 30 mins · 1 × 60 mins to
31/12/97 · continuing into 1998) · colour**
US dates: 25 Sep 1996 to date
UK dates: 23 Nov 1996 to date (25 × 30 mins to
31/12/97) ITV mostly Sat around 5.40pm

MAIN CAST
Sabrina Spellman · · · · · · · Melissa Joan Hart
Hilda Spellman · · · · · · · · · · · Caroline Rhea
Zelda Spellman · · · · · · · · · · Beth Broderick
Harvey Kinkle · · · · · · · · · · · · Nate Richert
Libby Chessler · · · · · · · · Jenna Leigh Green
Jenny Kelly · · · Michelle Beaudoin (1996–97)
Eugene Pool · · · · · · · · Paul Feig (1996–97)
Sabrina's father · · · · · · · · · · Robby Benson
Valerie · · · · · · · · Lindsay Sloane (from 1997)
Willard Kraft · · · · · · Martin Mull (from 1997)
Salem The Cat · · · · · · Nick Bakay (voice only)

CREDITS
creator Nell Scovell · *writers* Nell Scovell, Nick
Bakay, Carrie Honigblum/Renee Phillips, Frank
Conniff and others · *directors* Gary Halvorson,
Peter Baldwin, Robby Benson and others ·
executive producers Nell Scovell, Paula Hart,
Miriam Trogdon · *producers* Kenneth R Koch (from
1996), Gary Halvorson (from 1997)

Sabrina Spellman transforms into a witch on
her sixteenth birthday, which also happens to
be the day that she starts at a new school. At
first, Sabrina refuses to believe that she is
more than a mere mortal and is utterly
bemused by her newly developed talents, but
as time passes she recognises that her hexy
powers can prove useful – even though they
don't always allow her to snag what she most
desires and, sometimes, they can be her
undoing.

Sabrina lives with her two aunts, Hilda and
Zelda, who have been charged by Sabrina's
father with the job of teaching her the ways
of magic. (Dad himself – Edward Spellman –
lives inside a book, and Sabrina frequently
turns to him for help. Her mother, however,
is a mortal, and Sabrina is warned that if she
lays eyes upon her in the next two years she'll
turn into a ball of wax. Thus the living-with-
aunts scenario is explained.)

Episodes recounted Sabrina's life at home
and, most particularly, at school, Westbridge
High, where her best friend is Jenny, the boy
she fancies is Harvey and her prime enemy
is Libby, the school cheerleader who taunts
Sabrina and thus becomes the first victim of
her untutored witchcraft. At home, Sabrina
is comforted by her black cat Salem (an
animatronics puppet).

Sabrina The Teenage Witch was like a
teenage *Bewitched*, then – indeed, it was
very like *Tabitha*, and that same relentless
goodness was part and parcel of the episodes.
Sabrina is a nice girl and not one to ill-use her
powers for any deviant or illegal purpose. As
it is for any other 16-year-old, so life for this
teenage witch is problematic and confusing.

The lead part was played by Melissa Joan
Hart, the 20-year-old who came to the series
on the back of the successful *Clarissa
Explains It All*, and the series was the
work of the production company, Hartbreak
Films, which she formed with her real-life
mother Paula, one of the executive producers.
Popular in its Fridays 8.30pm slot on ABC,
Sabrina The Teenage Witch was quickly
bought by ITV for screening on British
television, the commercial station pitching it
against *The Simpsons* on BBC1, a ratings
battle that, surprisingly, *Sabrina* won hands-
down. Guest stars in the series included
magicians Penn and Teller (several times),
Debbie Harry, Randy Travis and Raquel
Welch.

The series followed closely on the heels of a
Showtime cable TV movie of the same title
(shown in the USA on 7 April 1996; first aired
terrestrially in the UK by C5 on 31 December
1997) that also starred Melissa Joan Hart but
with different actors in all other roles except
for Michelle Beaudoin. (The director was
Tibor Takacs.) But this was by no means the
first time that the teenage witch had appeared
on US TV: as a long-established regular in the
Archie Comics Publications comic-books,
Sabrina appeared from 1969 in Filmation's
Saturday-morning cartoon series *The Archie
Show* (the series that led to the Archies' 1969
hit single 'Sugar Sugar') before being
promoted to her own stand-alone cartoon
series from 1970 to 1974, and other
programmes throughout the rest of that
decade.

Sadie, It's Cold Outside

UK · ITV (THAMES) · SITCOM

6 × 30 mins · colour
21 Apr–25 June 1975 · mostly Mon 8pm

MAIN CAST
Sadie Potter · · · · · · · · · · · · Rosemary Leach
Norman Potter · · · · · · · · · · · Bernard Hepton

CREDITS
writer Jack Rosenthal · *directors/producers* Mike
Vardy (4), Les Chatfield (2)

The acutely observant and witty writer Jack
Rosenthal – noted for his single dramas as
well as his series – conceived *Sadie, It's Cold
Outside* while sitting in a café and watching a
middle-aged couple stop outside, peek
through the window at the customers, glance
at prices on the menu and shuffle off, feeling
that this was no longer their world. *Sadie*
achieved this same sense of
disenfranchisement but in a comedy setting.

Norman Potter is a shy, balding factory
worker, whose ambitions have amounted to
naught, who wants to change the world into
a nicer, kinder, more considerate place – the
type of world he hoped it would be when
youth was on his side – but who spends most
of his time changing only the channels on his
TV. Sadie Potter, his wife, has spent her
married years cooking, cleaning and
shopping. Together, they've been married
for 23 years and are now middle-aged
grandparents wondering how life has
managed to pass them by without them
realising it, and how other people seem to
find the modern ways perfectly acceptable.

Bernard Hepton and Rosemary Leach –
two actors equally at home in comedy and
straight drama – co-starred as Norman and
Sadie. Maureen Lipman, to whom Rosenthal
had been married for three years at this point,
was not in *Sadie, It's Cold Outside*, as she
would be in some of her husband's other
work, but there was a tiny role in the first

episode for a struggling young actress named Lesley Joseph.

Safe And Sound

UK · BBC (WITZEND PRODUCTIONS) · SITCOM

6 × 30 mins · colour

9 Aug–13 Sep 1996 · BBC1 Fri 8.30pm then 8pm

MAIN CAST

Tommy Delaney · · · · · · · · · · · Des McAleer
Dougy Flynn · · · · · · · · · · · · · Sean McGinley
Eleanor Delaney · · · · · · · · · Michelle Fairley
Maggie Delaney · · · · · · · · · · Gabrielle Reidy
Lena Delaney · · · · · · · · · · · Saoirse O'Dwyer
Hughie Delaney · · · · · · · · · · Conor O'Dwyer

CREDITS

writer Timothy Prager · director Bill Pryde · executive producers Robert Cooper, Geoffrey Perkins, Guy Slater · producer Joanna Willett

Comedy across the sectarian divide in Belfast, with chums since childhood Tommy (Catholic) and Dougy (Protestant) working together in the small 'Safe And Sound' motor-garage – Dougy is the management, Tommy his hardworking mechanic. The series' main strengths were the well-drawn and believable characters and the exceptionally fine perform-ances from the four lead actors.

In the opening episode Tommy fails in his attempt to restart his marriage to Maggie and so is forced to lodge with his sister Eleanor, a sexually hyperactive good time girl with whom Dougy is besotted. All the major protagonists have volatile relationships with one another, thus their encounters crackle with heated discussions and flaming arguments.

Filmed entirely on location and aired without a laugh-track, *Safe And Sound* was a quality comedy unafraid to tackle controversial issues. The 'troubles', while never the major theme, permeated the entire proceedings like a background wash.

Sailortown

UK · ITV (CENTRAL/ULSTER FOR CARLTON) · SITCOM

1 × 30 mins · colour

20 Apr 1993 · Tue 8.30pm

MAIN CAST

Skeeball · · · · · · · · · · · · · · · James Nesbitt
Danny · · · · · · · · · · · · · · · · · · Pat Laffan
Tamata · · · · · · · · · · · · · · Mark Mulholland
Billy · · · · · · · · · · · · · · · · Brendan Conroy
Brad · · · · · · · · · · · · · · · · · · Simon Magill
Father Francis · · · · · · · · · · · · John Rogan
Mrs Mac · · · · · · · · · · · · · · · · Olivia Nash
Gerry · · · · · · · · · · · · · · · · Joe McPartland

CREDITS

writers Martin Lynch/Mark Bussell · director Nick Hurran · executive producer Paul Spencer · producer Trevor McCallum

Barney Mulgrew, owner of a decrepit dockers' pub in the 'Sailortown' district of Belfast, has died, and two men – his young grandson/next-of-kin Skeeball, and middle-aged son-in-law Danny, who manages the pub – vie to take sole control. Barney had made out a will but the interested parties had come to believe that it was in the pocket of the suit in which he was buried. Hungover from the wake, all the pub's best customers gather for the funeral, which takes place amid Ulster's barbed wire and under the gaze of British soldiers. A couple of days later the will is suddenly found – the pub has been left jointly to Danny and Skeeball.

A brave if dour, hard-drinking comedy, as black as a pint of Guinness and as spirited as a whiskey, *Sailortown* was the eighth and final single-episode pilot screened by Carlton as part of its *Comedy Playhouse* season in 1993. While it may have appealed to Ulstermen, few outside of the province would have found much to laugh at, and no series developed.

Sam And Janet

UK · ITV (ATV) · SITCOM

15 × 30 mins · b/w

Series One (6) 27 June–4 Aug 1967 · mostly Fri 8.30pm

Series Two (9) 23 Jan–19 Mar 1968 · Tue mostly 7pm

MAIN CAST

Sam Marshall · · · · · · · · · · · · · John Junkin
Janet Marshall · · · · · · · Joan Sims (series 1);
· · · · · · · · · · · · · · Vivienne Martin (series 2)

CREDITS

writer David Cumming · director Paul Bernard (series 1) · producer Alan Tarrant

Sam And Janet depicted a friendly but determined battle of the sexes, as written by David Cumming and based, as he candidly admitted, upon his own real-life experiences.

The Marshalls have been married for 19 years, raised two children and live, quite comfortably off, in suburbia. Though all would seem cosy, their relationship is fre-quently stormy and has a habit of becoming bogged down in unnecessary complications. Sam runs his own company, manufacturing plastic table mats, and is placid only in between his frequent outbursts. Janet is a stoic: she puts up with Sam's moods, tempers what he sees as her feminine unreasonableness and, by her own methods, manages to get her way and live out hopes and fears of her own.

Sam And Janet arrived on TV after a successful run on BBC radio, with David Kossoff and Joan Sims in the two leading roles. Twenty episodes were aired on the Light Programme over two series – eight from 12 January to 2 March 1966 and 12 from 29 September to 15 December 1966. Of these 20 scripts, 15 were directly adapted for television, with Sims reprising her role and John Junkin playing the part of Sam. (Kossoff was older and, although this did not matter on the radio, he wouldn't have looked the part on TV.) Having played Janet for a year and a half in both mediums, Sims quit after the first television series and was replaced by Vivienne Martin.

Sam The Samaritan

UK · BBC · SITCOM

1 × 25 mins · b/w

5 Aug 1965 · BBC1 Thu 8.50pm

MAIN CAST

Sam Small · · · · · · · · · · · · · Wilfrid Brambell
Ginger Dick · · · · · · · · · · · · · · Roy Kinnear
Peter Russet · · · · · · · · · · · · · · John Junkin

CREDITS

creator W W Jacobs · adapter/writer David Climie · executive producer Graeme Muir · producer Michael Mills

A well-cast *Comedy Playhouse* period piece (set in 1910) that followed three stokers from the SS *Chesapeake* on shore leave, a practical joke threatening to jeopardise their friendship. No series followed this pilot.

The script was based upon a short story by W W (William Wymark) Jacobs (1863–1943), the prolific writer whose most famous creation was the horror story *The Monkey's Paw*. Jacobs wrote scores of sea-related short stories, published in a dozen collections from 1896 to 1926, and many of his works were produced for the stage and screen, including *The Money Box* (1903), adapted in 1936 as the Laurel and Hardy movie *Our Relations*.

Sandy – The Noble-Minded Cowboy

see The Montreux Festival

Sardines

UK · ITV (TALKBACK PRODUCTIONS FOR CARLTON) · SITCOM

1 × 30 mins · colour

24 July 1995 · Mon 8pm

MAIN CAST

Davy Kotowski · · · · · · · · · · · Griff Rhys Jones
Chris Cheese · · · · · · · · · · · · · William Ivory
Captain Alec McCleod · · John (Jack) Docherty
Roger Tench · · · · · · · · · · · · · Anthony Smee
Proudlove · · · · · · · · · · · · · · Paul Shearer
Lionel Pinner · · · · · · · · · · · Ian Bartholomew
Galloway · · · · · · · · · · · · · · Peter-Hugo Daly
Coxswain · · · · · · · · · · · · · · Perry Benson
Simon Adair · · · · · · · · · · · · · · Ben Miller
Alastair Simpson · · · · · Alexander Armstrong
Mickey Davis · · · · · · · · · · · · · Jake Abraham

CREDITS

writers Gareth Edwards/Chris Langham/Ben Miller · script editor Chris Langham · executive producer Peter Fincham · director/producer Charlie Hanson

David 'Davy' Kotowski is a petty officer aboard the submarine HMS *Wolverine* – a smart-aleck, charismatic, ingenious and incredibly crooked torpedo man, like a seafaring Sgt Bilko, with his fishy fingers in more pies than Captain Birdseye. But following a rigged arm-wrestling contest that leaves half the crew with their arms in slings and him with a few extra quid in his bell-bottom pockets, Kotowski is brought to kow-tow before the captain's disciplinary table for the ninth time. He has escaped punishment on eight previous visits but this time he is sentenced to a denial of shore leave and 20 hours' laundry duty. Delegating most of his punishment to the simple-minded sailor Chris Cheese, Kotowski plots revenge on his informant and arch rival, Petty Officer Lionel Pinner – a snide in a ginger wig – when Cheese accidentally challenges himself, on Kotowski's behalf, to a £100 grudge darts match. The trouble is, Cheese is only good at darts when he's angry (much like the episode of **The Phil Silvers Show** in which a champion boxer was only angry enough to fight if someone was rude about chrysanthemums).

Screened as a pilot in ITV's 1995 *Comedy Firsts* season, *Sardines* was Griff Rhys Jones's first sitcom role (apart from the single comedies in **Smith And Jones In Small Doses**) but it wasn't particularly good and no series developed.

Saturday Gang

UK · ITV (LWT) · STANDUP/SKETCH

12 × 30 mins · colour

Series One (6) 11 Oct–15 Nov 1986 · Sat 7.15pm

Series Two (6) 9 Apr–14 May 1988 · Sat 5.45pm

MAIN CAST
Gary Wilmot
Gareth Hale
Norman Pace
Kate Robbins

CREDITS
series 1 writers Charlie Adams, Geoff Atkinson, Jeremy Browne, Joe Griffiths, Gareth Hale/Norman Pace, Sonny Hayes, Paul Minett/Brian Leveson, Terry Morrison, Laurie Rowley, Gary Wilmot/Martin Beaumont · *series 2 writers* Charlie Adams, Geoff Atkinson, Ronnie Barbour, Joe Griffiths, Phil Hopkins, Terry Ravenscroft, Ted Robbins, Laurie Rowley, Stephen Sheridan, Alan Simmons/Keith Simmons · *directors* Vic Finch (series 1 & 2), John Gorman (series 2) · *producers* Marcus Plantin (series 1), Alan Nixon (series 2)

Straightforward but amusing mainstream Saturday-evening fare from LWT. The show gave early regular exposure to double-act Hale and Pace and the multi-talented Kate Robbins (see also *Robbins*, aired two months beforehand), while helping cement the future upward path of Gary Wilmot.

Saturday Live   1

UK · C4 (LWT) · STANDUP/SKETCH

21 editions (11 × 90 mins · 8 × 75 mins · 2 × 80 mins) · colour

Special (90 mins) 12 Jan 1985 · Sat 8.30pm

Series One (10 × 90 mins) 25 Jan–29 Mar 1986 · Sat 8.30pm

Series Two (8 × 75 mins · 2 × 80 mins) 7 Feb–11 Apr 1987 · Sat 10pm

MAIN CAST
various (see below)
host · · · · Ben Elton (show 8 and all series 2)

MOST REGULAR APPEARANCES
Stephen Fry/Hugh Laurie (every edition except special)
The Dangerous Brothers (Adrian Edmondson/Rik Mayall) (all series 1)
Ben Elton (series 1)
The Oblivion Boys (Mark Arden/Stephen Frost) (series 1)
Harry Enfield (show 4 of series 1 and all series 2)

CREDITS
regular writers Mark Arden/Stephen Frost, Geoff Atkinson, Garry Chambers, John Langdon, Pete McCarthy/Rebecca Stevens, Ben Elton, Adrian Edmondson/Rik Mayall, Stephen Fry/Hugh Laurie, Harry Enfield and others · *additional writers* Guy Jenkin, Laurie Rowley, Ricky Greene, Bernard McKenna and others · *directors* Paul Jackson (special), Paul Jackson/Geoff Posner (series 1), Ian Hamilton (series 2) · *executive producer* Marcus Plantin (series 2) · *producers* Paul Jackson (special), Paul Jackson/Geoff Posner (series 1), Geoffrey Perkins/Geoff Posner (series 2)

Such was the explosion of the so-called 'alternative comedy' movement that by the mid-1980s some 50 comedy clubs were operating in London and a galaxy of performers were working the venues, little known outside the capital. Virtually singlehandedly, the C4 series *Saturday Live* brought this burgeoning scene to a national TV audience, propelling several of the performers to stardom.

As with so many such programmes in this period, the guiding light here was Paul Jackson, already the man behind **The Young Ones** and **Three Of A Kind** on BBC1 and, on C4, **The Entertainers** and **Pushing Up Daisies**. Jackson had also been closely involved in the making of the BBC's **Carrott's Lib**, in which Jasper Carrott risked all by performing live every week. With an idea to merge the skill and adrenalin-pulsing excitement of live TV with the unpredictability and vigour of the London comedy/cabaret acts, Jackson persuaded LWT to produce a single programme (akin to a pilot but described above as a special) and commission first one and then another full series of 10 programmes each, to be beamed live to the nation from the company's studios on London's South Bank.

Although rarely climbing above 1.5 million viewers, *Saturday Live* was an instant,

massive hit with its staunch audience, particularly those in the 18–25/student age bracket. Being live, each and every show carried the scent of danger, the acts and audience never being certain what would develop. (A lawyer was on hand in the studio during the first series, although quite what he could have done after a slanderous statement had been uttered is unclear.)

Visiting musicians – usually rock bands – brought relief between the comedy acts and permitted time for changes in costume and scenery, and there were some pre-recorded inserts, including the first series' weekly Dangerous Brothers act from Rik Mayall and Adrian Edmondson, who performed all of their own stunts. Virtually anyone who was anyone on the current comedy scene appeared in *Saturday Live*: turning up twice or more were Chris Barrie, Craig Charles, Cliff Hanger (Pete McCarthy, Rebecca Stevens, Tony Haase, Robin Driscoll), Dawn French and Jennifer Saunders, Nick Hancock and Neil Mullarkey, Jeremy Hardy, Lenny Henry, Helen Lederer and Andy de la Tour, while among those popping up once apiece were Rowan Atkinson with Angus Deayton, Morwenna Banks, Julian Clary (as the Joan Collins Fan Club), Robbie Coltrane, Josie Lawrence, Jenny Lecoat, Norman Lovett, Paul Merton, Nigel Planer, Steve Punt and Hugh Dennis, Kate Robbins, Timothy Spall and Emma Thompson. There were also spots for visiting American comics, including Abby Stein, Emo Philips, Charles Fleischer, Rita Rudner, Louie Anderson and Will Durst, while Steven Wright hosted one of the editions in the first series, as did Ben Elton, Tracey Ullman, Lenny Henry, Pamela Stephenson, Chris Barrie, Michael Barrymore, Hale and Pace, Fascinating Aïda and Peter Cook.

Cook's appearance in *Saturday Live* underlines the fact that the programme – especially in its first series – was not given over exclusively to the young 'uns. During his show, Cook appeared in several politically pointed sketches with John Wells; John Bird also made a number of appearances, and Jasper Carrott, Frankie Howerd and Spike Milligan participated too. Carrott performed in one of the shows hosted by Ben Elton, telling a joke about women drivers. Elton followed him on-stage with the remark 'Nice one, Jasper, really taking on the dangerous, controversial issues in your comedy ...'

Ben Elton's star really came into the ascendant with *Saturday Live*. Although invited merely to write for the show – his writing prowess being long proven, courtesy of *The Young Ones* – Elton asked to perform too and was given an option of five shows. He quickly became the show's most seen face, however, hosting all of the second series. With his trademark sparkly suit, rapid-fire delivery and whole-hearted embrace of topics avoided by many other comedians as too dangerous or too political, Elton grabbed the series and its viewers by the throat and made everyone pay attention. That Mrs Thatcher (whom Elton called 'Thatch') was Prime Minister at the time, wielding a political sword that may have been the electorate's wish but was not necessarily in the nation's best interests, gave the comedian ample fuel for his straight-for-the-jugular humour, landing Elton in hot water with *The Sun* and other then loony-right newspapers. (As if he cared.) Many who saw Ben Elton's act on *Saturday Live* simply pronounced him – and the show – 'leftie', a guess, and not necessarily true at that. In fact, Elton and many of the other comics were simply railing against authority and what they saw as the misuse of power, and the fact that the Tories happened to be in government at the time made them the target.

Stephen Fry and Hugh Laurie, who appeared in all 20 editions of the two full series, were another act to gain great strength from *Saturday Live*, but the biggest leap to fame was afforded to Harry Enfield, who began it as an unknown and shot to stardom by producing the first of his remarkable array of created characters: Stavros, the Greek immigrant who runs a kebab shop in Hackney, east London, and has, at best, a faltering command of the English language. (The character was based on a real kebab shop owner, Adam Athanaffiou, who had a shop in Well Street, Hackney, where Enfield had been lodging with his friend Paul Whitehouse. This friend, shortly to become a major comic figure in his own right, helped Enfield create the Stavros character, although his contribution went publicly unnoticed at the time.) Enfield went on to become *the* star of *Saturday Live*'s follow-on series *Friday Night Live* where he added the brilliantly drawn Loadsamoney (again, with much inspiration from Whitehouse) to his portfolio of characters.

Notes. A specially reduced 35-minute version of the edition fronted by Hale and Pace was submitted as ITV's entry for the Golden Rose of Montreux award in 1986, and was screened by C4 on 22 April 1986. It did not win, however. In 1993 C4 screened a variety/general entertainment series, *Saturday Zoo* (13 editions, 16 January to 10 April), fronted by Jonathan Ross and featuring a weekly array of music, celebrity interviews and comics. The *Saturday Live* idea – which borrowed heavily from the US show *Saturday Night Live* – was reworked in Australia as *The Big Gig*, which ran there for 66 editions from 1989 to 1992, broadcast by ABC, and featured visiting guest comics, including Ben Elton and Craig Ferguson. Finally, a decade after its

first run of *Saturday Live*, LWT relaunched the series anew – see following entry.

Saturday Live 2

UK · ITV (LWT) · STANDUP/SKETCH

8 × 60 mins · colour

1 June–20 July 1996 · Sat mostly 10.10pm

MAIN CAST

host · Lee Hurst

MOST REGULAR APPEARANCES

Harry Hill
Alan Parker Urban Warrior

CREDITS

writers cast · *director* Ian Hamilton · *producer* Susie Dark

Exercising the TV maxim that goes (something like) 'there's no hit like an old hit', ITV sanctioned LWT's revival of *Saturday Live* fully ten years after the original production had been such a groundbreaker. The trouble with this 1996 version was, quite simply, that the ground was already broken. With 1990s TV continually pulling out all the stops to shock its audience, the new version of *Saturday Live* was no more, or less, valid than any other standup show. Revolutions in comedy, like lightning bolts, never strike twice in the same place.

Which is not to say that the attempt was worthless. The new series – broadcast live, like its predecessor, and similarly mixing comedy with live music acts – was put into the capable hands of a likeable host, Lee Hurst, the comic whose wit, like his bald pate, sparkled on the sporting quiz-show *They Think It's All Over* (BBC1 from 14 September 1995), in which he was an ever-present along with Rory McGrath, David Gower, Gary Lineker and chairman Nick Hancock. Hurst's standup act, with contributions from regulars Harry Hill and the oddly named Alan Parker Urban Warrior, were the staple of the series' eight shows. Guests included Tim Vine, Rich Hall, Alistair McGowan, Neil Mullarkey, Tony Hawks, 'Gayle Tuesday' (Brenda Gilhooly) and, from *Men Behaving Badly*, Caroline Quentin and Leslie Ash. But their efforts were mostly in vain – few viewers tuned in.

The Saturday Night Armistice

UK · BBC · SATIRE

16 editions (13 × 30 mins · 1 × 40 mins · 1 × 45 mins · 1 × 180 mins) · colour

Series One (6 × 30 mins) 24 June–5 Aug 1995 · BBC2 Sat around 9.50pm

Special (40 mins) *The Saturday Night Armistice Party Bucket* 22 Dec 1995 · BBC2 Fri 10.30pm

Series Two (6 × 30 mins) *Friday Night Armistice* 14 June–19 July 1996 · BBC2 Fri 10pm

Special (180 mins) *The Election Night Armistice* 1 May 1997 · BBC2 Thu 10.30pm

Special (45 mins) *The Christmas Armistice* 29 Dec 1997 · BBC2 Mon 10.50pm

Special (30 mins) *The Armistice Party Bucket* 2 Jan 1998 · BBC2 Fri 10.25pm

MAIN CAST

Armando Iannucci
Peter Baynham
David Schneider

CREDITS

writers cast, Kevin Cecil, Andy Riley, Graham Linehan/Arthur Mathews and others · *directors* Steve Bendelack, Andy de Emmony, John Kilby, John L Spencer · *producer* Sarah Smith

Late-night topical fun from some of the team from *The Day Today*, with those shows' Scottish producer Armando Iannucci stepping out from the shadows to act as host. (In fact, he had already attracted his own series on BBC Radio 1 in 1993–94.)

What was presented as an irreverent and idiosyncratic look at the week's news stories was actually much more than this, with items that started out in a traditional TV satire format eventually being exploited to surreal lengths and ending up as totally illogical but often hilarious absurdities. There were certain elements of *The Day Today* apparent in the series' make-up but the enhanced topicality (the programmes were recorded the night before transmission) and the informality of the presentation team ensured that *The Saturday Night Armistice* had enough individual style to distinguish it from its antecedents.

Recurring features included the travels of 'The Mr Tony Blair Puppet', a gonk caricature of the (then) Leader of the Opposition; 'Hunt The Old Woman', in which viewers were asked to phone in if they spotted the show's resident OAP inveigling herself on to other shows or into filmed news items; and 'The Miniaturised Area', a scaled-down set (complete with its own miniature Mr Tony Blair Puppet) from which the gang supposedly accessed the world's security cameras in order to see 'What Happened Next' after certain pieces of news footage ended.

The studio sections were augmented by filmed sketches and the re-editing or technical altering of recent news or programme items to score comedic points. This is an over-used and somewhat lazy way to attract cheap laughs but the *Armistice* team capitalised on the device better than most. Part of their success stemmed from their intelligence and refusal to talk down to the audience. The material often sprang from the inside pages of the quality press rather than the banner headlines of the tabloids, a stance rarely taken since *That Was The Week That Was* first established the blueprint for TV satire. Like the *TW3* team, the *Armistice* gang were at times dangerously close to being (and sometimes were) smug, but on the whole they got away with it, thanks to sheer wit and verve.

Notes. The 22 December 1995 special included highlights from the previous series along with some new material. Scheduling forced the change of name to *Friday Night Armistice* for the second series but the mix was much as before. (Repeat screenings on Sunday nights were billed *Last Friday Night's Armistice*.) The 1 May 1997 General Election special broadened the show to include live music and guest celebrities (including Steve Coogan as Alan Partridge). The seasonal specials of Christmas 1997 and New Year 1998 once again combined some new footage with repeated material. A third series (*The Friday Night Armistice*) was due to air in early 1998.

Saturday Night Live

USA · NBC · SKETCH/STANDUP

436 × 90 mins (to 31/12/97 · continuing into 1998) · colour

US dates: 11 Oct 1975 to date

UK dates: 16 Oct 1982–10 Mar 1984 (21 × 60 mins) ITV Sat around midnight

MAIN CAST (TO 1997)

Chevy Chase (1975–76), Dan Aykroyd (1975–79), John Belushi (1975–79), Jane Curtin (1975–80), Garrett Morris (1975–80), Laraine Newman (1975–80), Gilda Radner (1975–80), Bill Murray (1977–80), Harry Shearer (1979–80 & 1984–85), Gilbert Gottfried (1980–81), Gail Matthius (1980–81), Ann Risley (1980–81), Charles Rocket (1980–81), Denny Dillon (1980–82), Brian Doyle-Murray (1980–82), Eddie Murphy (1980–84), Joe Piscopo (1980–84), Christine Ebersole (1981–82), Tony Rosato (1981–82), Robin Duke (1981–84), Tim Kazurinsky (1981–84), Mary Gross (1981–85), Brad Hall (1982–84), Gary Kroeger (1982–85), Julia Louis-Dreyfus (1982–85), Jim Belushi (1983–85), Billy Crystal (1984–85), Christopher Guest (1984–85), Rich Hall (1984–85), Martin Short (1984–85), Pamela Stephenson (1984–85), Joan Cusack (1985–86), Robert Downey Jr (1985–86), Anthony Michael Hall (1985–86), Randy Quaid (1985–86), Terry Sweeney (1985–86), Danitra Vance (1985–86), Nora Dunn (1985–91), Jon Lovitz (1985–91), Jan Hooks (1986–91), Dennis Miller (1986–91), Dana Carvey (1986–92), Victoria Jackson (1986–92), Phil Hartman (1986–94), Kevin Nealon (1986–95), Mike Myers (1989–95), Rob Schneider (1990–94), Julia Sweeney (1990–94), Chris Farley (1990–95), David Spade (1990–96), Chris Rock (1991–93), Melanie Hutsell (1991–94), Ellen Cleghorne (1991–95), Adam Sandler (1991–95), Tim Meadows (1991 to date), Norm MacDonald (1993–97), Morwenna Banks (1994–95), Chris Elliott (1994–95), Janeane Garofalo (1994–95), Michael McKean (1994–95), Molly Shannon (1994 to date), Jim Breuer (1995 to date), Will Ferrell (1995 to date), Darrell Hammond (1995 to date), David Koechner (1995–96), Mark

McKinney (1995–97), Cheri Oteri (1995 to date), Chris Kattan (1995 to date), Colin Quinn (1995 to date), Nancy Walls (1995–96), Fred Wolf (1995–97), Ana Gasteyer (1996 to date), Tracy Morgan (1996 to date)

OTHER REGULAR APPEARANCES

George Coe (1975), The Muppets (1975–76), Michael O'Donoghue (1975–79), Andy Kaufman (occasional, 1975–82), Tom Davis (1977–80), Al Franken (1977–80, 1986, 1989–95), Don Novello (1978–80 & 1985–86), Paul Shaffer (1979–80), Peter Aykroyd (1980), Jim Downey (1980), Mitchell Kriegman (1980), Yvonne Hudson (1980–81), Matthew Laurance (1980–81), Patrick Weathers (1980–81), Harry Anderson (1982–84), Stephen Wright (1983–85), Sam Kinison (1985–86), Penn And Teller (1985–86), Dan Vitale (1985–86), Damon Wayans (1985–86), A Whitney Brown (1986–90), Ben Stiller (1989), Siobhan Fallon (1991–92), Robert Smigel (1991–93), Beth Cahill (1992–93), Jay Mohr (1993–95), Sarah Silverman (1993–95)

CREDITS

writers various (at least 130 people) · *directors* Dave Wilson and many others · *executive producers* Dick Ebersol and many others · *producers* Lorne Michaels (1975–80, 1985–93), Jean Doumanian (1980), Dick Ebersol (1980–85), James Downey (1994 to date)

It would take a whole book to write about the cause and effect of *Saturday Night Live* (indeed several have been written) but, in short, *SNL* has singlehandedly revolutionised sketch and standup comedy on American TV, establishing a strong foundation for intelligent, adult humour in the medium by way of a long-running and at times brilliant programme.

So for its evolution. The building blocks that led to *SNL* were **The Smothers Brothers Show, Rowan And Martin's Laugh-In** and **Monty Python's Flying Circus**; the first of these proved that 'hip' youth-orientated comedy could work on US television, but after its cancellation nothing substantial came along to replace it. Meanwhile, during this early 1970s, an explosion of 'new wave' comedy (or 'anti-comedy' as it was sometimes described) was erupting in clubs and theatres across the USA, like the Second City (Chicago and also Toronto), Channel One (New York) and Kentucky Fried Theatre (Madison, Wisconsin). These troupes had a healthy following, and when Channel One made a movie, *The Groove Tube*, featuring parodies of TV programmes, its cult success alerted TV producers that there was an untapped youth audience hooked on risky, untraditional comedy.

NBC was known for screening the fewest comedies of the three major US TV networks, but its president, Herb Schlosser, remained proud of its association with *Laugh-In* and was keen to invent a similarly 'in' show for the 1970s. Two of the junior writers on that

series had been Lorne Michaels, a Canadian, and his double-act partner Hart Pomerantz. Both became disillusioned by the experience, feeling that their material was often dismissed on a whim, and that the show was too 'establishment' and safe, the very opposite of what it purported to be. In 1969, Michaels and Pomerantz were commissioned by the Canadian network CBC to deliver four TV specials per year for the next few years, which aired under such titles as *The Hart And Lorne Terrific Hour* and *Today Makes Me Nervous*, shows that were clearly influenced by *Monty Python* (which aired on CBC from 1970, four years before its transmission in America). But although quite successful in his home country Michaels wanted to make it in the States and flew back and forth to Hollywood with programme suggestions. On one trip he pitched to NBC the idea of a comedy programme aimed at a generation raised on television. Although the idea was considered too revolutionary, NBC were looking for a creator/producer for a proposed Saturday-night series, and when Michaels was offered the job he envisaged a way of using the slot to create 'his' show.

The rest, as they say, is history. Michaels fought tooth and nail to persuade NBC to risk a number of radical ideas and allow him to book the most controversial comedy artists as guest hosts, including George Carlin, Richard Pryor and Lily Tomlin. Such acts might have been acceptable to the network with the wave of a hand were it not for Michaels' insistence that the show be broadcast live. This was considered sheer madness by his bosses, but Michaels insisted and, eventually, won the battle, all but one of the subsequent editions being screened live from New York. The single exception was a first series edition featuring Pryor: his reputation for bad language so worried NBC that they browbeat Michaels into accepting a five-second delay. In the event, nothing was bleeped. So conservative were the US networks at this stage that another major concern was whether George Carlin should be allowed to wear jeans and a tee-shirt on the show or, as NBC wanted, a suit. (Carlin won the battle.)

At this point the series was titled *Saturday Night*, because ABC had launched a show called *Saturday Night Live With Howard Cosell* a few weeks earlier. But, after the demise of the ABC series, Michaels' programme reverted to its originally intended title *Saturday Night Live*. The show was controversial from the start and has maintained its notoriety ever since, Michaels and his team determining, thanks to the influence of *Python*, to discard the rule-book and start afresh. The Cosell show had featured a regular comedy troupe (featuring Bill Murray) called the Primetime Players, so, in typically flip style, Michaels nicknamed his crew of comedy guerrillas the Not Ready For Primetime Players. The combination of the comics also owed something to *Python*, with Michaels particularly taken with an Eric Idle quote that the Pythons were 'the best comedy fighting team ever assembled'. Michaels was determined to assemble a similarly powerful force, with talent in depth. Over the many years of its life, this ever-evolving group of regular comedy-actors has defined the shape of the show, with the key members of the earliest gangs building the foundation: Chevy Chase (originally hired solely as a writer), John Belushi, Dan Aykroyd, Laraine Newman, Gilda Radner, Garrett Morris and, later, Bill Murray. Since then different combinations have carried the torch, many of its members (Billy Crystal, Martin Short) moving on to greater stardom.

The show always features a guest host, drawn from the full spectrum of public life, not just entertainers. The most regular host has been Steve Martin (12 times), whose personal popularity ensures the show significantly higher ratings whenever he appears. Other regulars have included Buck Henry (10), Tom Hanks (6), Elliott Gould (6), Candice Bergen (5), Danny DeVito (5) and John Goodman (5). Notable British-born (or based) hosts have included Peter Cook and Dudley Moore (24 January 1976), Dudley Moore alone (25 January 1986), Eric Idle (2 October 1976, 23 April 1977, 9 December 1978 and 20 October 1979), Michael Palin (8 April 1978, 27 January 1979, 12 May 1979 and 21 January 1984), Tim Curry (5 December 1981) and Miranda Richardson (20 March 1993), while Morwenna Banks and Pamela Stephenson have both had stints in the regular cast. Almost as important as the guest hosts have been the remarkable array of top musical guests playing live on the show, from Paul McCartney to the Rolling Stones; others, like Sting, Frank Zappa, George Harrison, Ringo Starr, Ray Charles, Stevie Wonder and others, have doubled as hosts, Paul Simon – a good friend of Lorne Michaels – doing so four times to date.

Memorable moments from the shows have included the appearance of the *Rutland Weekend Television*-filmed Rutles sketch, which – with *SNL*'s own $3200 offer for the Beatles to reunite on the show – led directly to the 1978 TV special *The Rutles* (aka *All You Need Is Cash*), produced by Michaels and featuring many of the *SNL* cast; Steve Martin and Dan Aykroyd's 'wild and crazy guys'; the news-like Weekend Update reports; John Belushi and Dan Aykroyd's Blues Brothers; Dana Carvey and Mike Myers' cable TV spoof *Wayne's World*; Chevy Chase's pratfalling President Ford impression; Don Novello's Father Guido Sarducci; the dozens of TV commercial spoofs; Toonces, the cat that can drive a car; John Belushi's

destructive Samurai character and brutal Joe Cocker impression; naff puppet Mr Bill; the Coneheads, an alien family stranded on Earth; Pat, a Julia Sweeney character of unspecified sexual denomination; and a veritable zoo of great characters: the Bees, Land Shark, Nick The Lounge Singer, the Nerds, Ed Grimley Jr and many others.

The eclectic mix of surreal sketches, satire, filmed oddities and rock music, linked by different guest hosts, has proved remarkably durable. The surreal and black edge to much of the humour may echo *Python*, and the 'live' broadcasts may allow the inclusion of topical satire reminiscent of *That Was The Week That Was*, but, overall, *Saturday Night Live* stands alone in its field and has consistently proven to be a brave showcase for talent in the otherwise highly restricted world of US network television.

Notes. There have been ten feature film spin-offs featuring characters or sketches created for or developed on *Saturday Night Live*: *The Blues Brothers* (1980, director John Landis) with John Belushi and Dan Aykroyd; *Gilda Live* (1980, director Mike Nichols) with Gilda Radner; *Wayne's World* (1992, director Penelope Spheeris) with Dana Carvey and Mike Myers; *Bob Roberts* (1992, director and star Tim Robbins); *Mr Saturday Night* (1992, director and star Billy Crystal); *Mo' Money* (1992, director Peter MacDonald) with Damon Wayans; *Coneheads* (1993, director Steve Barron) with Dan Aykroyd, Jane Curtin and David Spade; *Wayne's World II* (1993, director Stephen Surjik) with Dana Carvey and Mike Myers; *It's Pat* (1994, director Adam Bernstein) with Julia Sweeney; and *Stuart Smalley* (aka *Stuart Saves His Family*, 1995, director Harold Ramis) with Al Franken and Julia Sweeney.

Saturday Night Live has enjoyed two outings on British television. First, beginning late 1982, ITV screened 21 editions from 102 hour-length programmes of re-edited and re-packaged highlights produced by NBC for overseas sale and US syndication. Then, ten years later, BBC2 screened a further six editions, of varying lengths, from 7 November to 12 December 1992. (There was also a one-off special, *Saturday Night Live Goes Commercial*, a compendium of TV advert send-ups by Murphy, Murray, Aykroyd, Belushi, Chase and others, screened by London-area ITV on 28 November 1992.) In 1996 (from 17 to 31 January) C4 screened a series of three 60-minute programmes, *The Best Of Aykroyd, Belushi And Chase*, that compiled (actually in reverse order) the best *SNL* comedy moments from each of the three comics. Finally, two attempts to capture the same feel as *SNL* have been made in Britain: *Saturday Live* (1985–87 and 1996) and *Friday Night Live* (1988).

Saturday Stayback

UK · ITV (CENTRAL) · SKETCH/STANDUP

6 × 45 mins · colour

22 Jan–26 Feb 1983 · Sat 11.15pm

MAIN CAST
Chris Tarrant
Helen Atkinson Wood
Bob Carolgees
Tony Slattery
Timothy Davies
Suzanne Sinclair
Kevin Seisay
Trevor James
Phil Cool
David Adams

CREDITS
writers cast · director Peter Harris · producer Chris Tarrant

One year after the embarrassing but surprising failure that was *O.T.T.* Chris Tarrant returned to ITV with another 'adult' sketch series in the same slot. The very title (Saturday Stayback is an expression for an illegal extension of pub drinking hours) indicated the series' intent: it was aimed at those who were returning home from the pub but were willing to continue to party in the company of their TV. The assembled comics were definitely going to have a good self-indulgent time, come what may, and intended to bludgeon the viewers into having one with them.

Again, predictably perhaps, the result was a flop, although not as big a flop as *O.T.T.* had been. But at least two new TV talents – Phil Cool and Tony Slattery – were encouraged along the way. There was no further revival of the idea after this, but Chris Tarrant has continued to be a popular, funny and shrewd personality in numerous ITV 'people' shows since the mid-1980s.

'Lily Savage'

Lily Savage is a bottle-blonde, 6ft 2in trollop from Birkenhead, first unveiled on a pub stage in Vauxhall, south London, in 1985, by her creator Paul O'Grady, the man beneath the wig. At first glance, the scathing and bitchy Savage seems typical of the camp creations of previous cross-dressers, but it soon becomes obvious that she is a superior version, several notches above her predecessors. This owes to O'Grady's brilliant ability to think on his feet, his adeptness at working an audience and, most importantly, his skill in imbuing Lily with the fully developed, larger-than-life yet wholly believable personality of a former prostitute and mother of two ghastly kids.

All this, allied to a biting wit, ensures that the character has been quickly elevated to the status of a comedy icon; a phenomenon who, like Barry Humphries' Dame Edna Everage, seems to exist in the public mind as a wholly real person. What makes this mainstream popularity so unusual is that while Lily can be startlingly vulgar – using language and tackling topics more commonly explored by stag-night comics – the public is willing to accept such vulgarity when delivered in an exaggeratedly gay, vaudevillian fashion, whereas in less deft hands the same material might well be deemed offensive. This is equally true of Dame Edna (and, to a lesser extent, Caroline Aherne's Mrs Merton): the inventions permit the character to say and do things that would be impossible without the disguise. Interviewed in 1996 O'Grady revealed that he created Lily based upon someone he had seen in a Sheffield market, a hard-as-rocks peroxide-blonde who was pushing a pram, wearing stilettos and a micro skirt and stomping ahead of her 'all snot and ice cream' vile children. As for the surname, Savage is O'Grady's mother's maiden name.

In addition to the programmes listed below, Savage has appeared many other times on TV, sometimes as a presenter (especially on C4's *The Big Breakfast* in 1995–96) and as both interviewer and an interviewee. Other appearances have included a ten-minute slot in C4's marijuana-themed *Pot Night* (4 March 1995), and the successful variety series *Live From The Lilydrome* (ITV from 11 March to 22 April 1995, with a couple of postponements along the way). Beginning with a one-off special edition screened on 26 December 1997, the 'blonde bombsite' took over the host duties of BBC1's revived celebrity game-show *Blankety Blank*, with a full series set to follow in spring 1998.

Lily Savage Live: Paying The Rent

UK · C4 (CHATSWORTH TELEVISION) · STANDUP

1 × 60 mins · colour

29 Dec 1995 · Fri 11.35pm

MAIN CAST
Lily Savage · · · · · · · · · · · · · · · Paul O'Grady

CREDITS
writer Paul O'Grady · *director/producer* Gary Wicks · *executive producers* Tony Carne, Mike Esser

Recorded highlights of Lily's 'one-woman' performance in London in 1993. For TV audiences this was a first chance to see the unadulterated Savage, in a show long enough to fully exploit the depth of O'Grady's masterly creation.

An Evening With Lily Savage

UK · ITV (WATCHMAKER PRODUCTIONS FOR CARLTON) · STANDUP

1 × 60 mins · colour

6 Nov 1996 · Wed 9pm

MAIN CAST
Lily Savage · · · · · · · · · · · · · · Paul O'Grady

CREDITS
writer Paul O'Grady · *director* Brian Klein · *executive producer* Elaine Bedell · *producer* Martin Cunning

Similar to LWT's *An Audience With …* series, and filmed in the same London South Bank Studios, Carlton's *An Evening With …* specials placed comedians before celebrity audiences and let them off the leash. Lily Savage proved the perfect performer for such an occasion and the riotous stories, outrageous reminiscences and bawdy gossip she gave in answer to questions made for a memorable evening of top quality standup comedy. More than any other TV appearance, this one propelled Savage to stardom.

The Lily Savage Show

UK · BBC (WILDFLOWER) · STANDUP/SKETCH

6 × 30 mins · colour

16 Nov–12 Dec 1997 · Sun mostly 10pm

MAIN CAST
Lily Savage · · · · · · · · · · · · · · Paul O'Grady
Jason Savage · · · · · · · · · · · Daniel Newman
Bunty Savage · · · · · · · · · · · · · · · · · · Sonia
Vera Cheesman · · · · · · · · · · · · · · herself
Janet Street-Porter · · · · · · · · · · · · herself

CREDITS
writer Paul O'Grady · *executive producers* Waheed Ali, Geoff Miles, Brendan Murphy · *director* Alasdair Macmillan · *producer* Mark Linsey

A sparkling comedy show from Savage, now strutting her stuff for the BBC. For the first time we meet the Savage family in the flesh: son Jason – recently released from Borstal and now planning a career as a documentary film-maker; daughter Bunty, a petty criminal who sells dodgy gear in Oxford Street, London; and sister Vera, more often seen than heard. The series' other regular was Janet Street-Porter, cast as Lily's BBC studio floor-manager, a comparatively lowly position she has been forced to undertake owing to a sudden career decline.

In a variety of extravagant but tacky costumes, Lily delivered a fair amount of material straight to the audience from her lavish set, and the series also featured sketches (both filmed and in the studio), mostly spoofing other television programmes and conventions. Fly-on-the-wall documentary sections featuring the Savage family (shot as a video diary by Jason) revealed the sordid home life of the dubious clan.

The style of *The Lily Savage Show* – innuendo-laden comedy dialogues delivered as informal chats to the audience and leading to extended sketches, combined with Lily's penchant for making cracks at the 'tightness' of the BBC – was reminiscent of the excellent mid-1960s series *Frankie Howerd*. It also matched that earlier show for quality – rare praise indeed.

Saved By The Bell

USA · NBC (PETER ENGEL PRODUCTIONS/NBC PRODUCTIONS) · CHILDREN'S SITCOM

87 episodes (86 × 30 mins · 1 × 120 mins) · colour

*US dates: 30 Nov 1988–22 May 1993

**UK dates: 9 Aug 1992–1 June 1995 (86 × 30 mins · 1 × 120 mins) · ITV/C4; Sun 9am (ITV) · various days and times (C4)

MAIN CAST
Zachary 'Zack' Morris · · Mark-Paul Gosselaar
Lisa Marie Turtle · · Lark Voorhies (1989–93)
Samuel 'Screech' Powers · · Dustin Diamond
· (1988–93)
Kelly Kapowski · · · · · Tiffani-Amber Thiessen
· (1989–93)
Albert Clifford 'A C' Slater · · · · · Mario Lopez
· (1989–93)
Jessica 'Jessie' Myrtle Spano · · · · · · · · · · ·
· · · · · · · · · · · · · Elizabeth Berkley (1989–93)
Max · · · · · · · · · · · · · · · Ed Alonzo (1989–93)
Richard Belding · · · · · · · · · Dennis Haskins
· (1988–93)
'Ox' · · · · · · · · · · · · Troy Froman (1989–93)
Tori Scott · · · · · · · Leanna Creel (1992–93)
Karen · · · · · · · · · · · · · Carla Gugino (1988)
Nicole 'Nikki' Coleman · · · · · Heather Hopper
· (1988)
Mickey · · · · · · · · · · · · · Max Battimo (1988)

CREDITS
creator Sam Bobrick · *writers* various · *directors* various · *executive producers* Peter Engel, William Phillips, Gary Considine · *producers* Marica Govons, Franco E Bario

A really bad US Saturday-morning teenagers' sitcom and merchandising vehicle, unusual in that it was a live-action series rather than a cartoon – until 1988 the staple fare of that transmission slot. *Saved By The Bell* was cut of the same cloth as *Beverly Hills 90210* but was even more vacuous than that inexplicably popular teen drama (screened in Britain by ITV since 5 January 1991).

The series was based around the lives of a bunch of stereotypically 'Hollywood' teenies at Bayside High School, located in the fictional town of Palisades, California. The lead character is a good-looking blond charmer named Zack Morris; Kelly Kapowski, the most beautiful girl in the school, is Zack's girlfriend and captain of the cheerleaders and various sports teams; Lisa Marie is a rich black girl; 'Screech' is a gawky computer nerd whose facial appearance lands him fifth place in an *ALF* lookalike contest (see the entry for that sitcom to realise how hurtful this 'honour' is); 'A C' is a muscle-bound hunk keen on pursuing a wrestling scholarship; 'Jessie' is a lissom brunette; and Tori is a leather-clad biker girl. Together they form a wholesome bunch, displaying their dazzlingly white teeth, perfect hair and super-smart casual clothes and regularly getting under the skin of the school principal Richard Belding, a dumb ass of a headteacher. The storylines were wafer thin, there were lots of high-fives and the whole premise was phenomenally banal – although, it must be said, no more so than some British children's TV comedies.

Determined to switch *Saved By The Bell* to a conventional time slot, NBC produced a primetime special (*Saved By The Bell – Hawaiian Style*, a two-hour TV movie aired in the USA on 27 November 1992 and in the UK by C4 on 26 December 1994) as a warm-up towards a primetime spin-off, **Saved By The Bell: The College Years**, which was followed by a further Saturday-morning series, **Saved By The Bell: The New Class**.

*Note. *Saved By The Bell* emanated from a one-off pilot, aired by NBC on 11 July 1987 under the title *Good Morning, Miss Bliss*, starring British-born actress Hayley Mills as Miss Carrie Bliss, a sixth-grade teacher at a high school in Indianapolis. Unusually, with NBC acting as producer, the programme was then picked up by the Disney company, which launched a series of 13 programmes with this title on its dedicated cable channel, aired from 30 November to 21 December 1988. Disney then ceased its interest, Hayley Mills left and NBC announced that it would relaunch its property later in 1989 with a new title, *Saved By The Bell*, a new focus and a California location, taking to the air on 20 August 1989.

**Saved By The Bell* was first seen in Britain within ITV's TV-am strand, with 20 episodes aired between 9 August and 20 December 1992. Screenings switched to C4 from 9 January 1993, which showed all 87 episodes until the last on 1 June 1995.

Saved By The Bell: The College Years

USA · NBC (PETER ENGEL PRODUCTIONS/NBC PRODUCTIONS) · CHILDREN'S SITCOM

19 episodes (17 × 30 mins · 2 × 60 mins) · colour

US dates: 22 May 1993 (pilot) · 14 Sep 1993–8 Feb 1994 (series) · 7 Oct 1994 (special)

UK dates: 29 Dec 1994–4 May 1995 (19 × 30 mins) C4 Thu 6.30pm

MAIN CAST

Zachary 'Zack' Morris · · Mark-Paul Gosselaar
Kelly Kapowski · · · · · · Tiffani-Amber Thiessen
Albert Clifford 'A C' Slater · · · · · Mario Lopez
Samuel 'Screech' Powers · · Dustin Diamond

Leslie Burke · · · · · · · · · · · · Anne Tremko
Alex Taber · · · · · · · · · · · · Kiersten Warren
Danielle Marks · · · · · · · · · Essence Atkins
Michael Rogers · · · · · · · · · · · Bob Golic
Professor Jeremiah Lasky · · · · Patrick Fabian
Dean Susan McMann · · · · · · Holland Taylor
· (1994)

CREDITS

creator Sam Bobrick · *writers* various · *directors* various · *executive producer* Gary Considine · *producers* Marica Govons, Franco E Bario

And thus we followed 'Zack', Kelly, 'A C' and 'Screech' from Bayside High School to California University, and from (in America, at least) Saturday-morning TV to Tuesday-night primetime. The opening episode set the tone: the four made new friends, sharing rooms in a mixed-sex dorm with Alex, who wanted to become an actress; Leslie, a rich girl from San Francisco; and mature student, resident director of the dormitory and former American football pro Michael Rogers (played by former American football pro Bob Golic). On the teaching side there was Professor Lasky and Dean McMann.

New location aside, it was pretty much business as usual. Failing to capture viewers in its new time slot, *Saved By The Bell: The College Years* was cancelled after just one season, ending with a one-hour special in which Zack and Kelly married in Las Vegas. They deserved each other.

Saved By The Bell: The New Class

USA · NBC (PETER ENGEL PRODUCTIONS/NBC PRODUCTIONS) · CHILDREN'S SITCOM

111 × 30 mins (to 31/12/97 · continuing into 1998) · colour

US dates: 11 Sep 1993 to date

UK dates: 1 Jan 1995 to date (66 episodes to 31/12/97) C4 Sun mostly 10.45am

MAIN CAST

Richard Belding · · · · · · · · Dennis Haskins
Samuel 'Screech' Powers · · Dustin Diamond
· · · · · · · · · · · · · · · · · · · (from 1994)
Scott Erikson · · · · · Robert Sutherland Telfer
· · · · · · · · · · · · · · · · · · · (1993–94)
Hammersmith · · · · · · David Byrd (1993–94)
Tommy De 'Tommy D' Lucca · · · · · · · · · · · ·
· · · · · · · · · · · Jonathan Angel (1993–96)
Barton 'Weasel' Wyzell · · · · · · · Isaac Lidsky
· · · · · · · · · · · · · · · · · · · (1993–94)
Lindsay Warner · · Natalia Cigliuti (1993–96)
Megan Jones · · · · Bianca Lawson (1993–94)
Vicki Needleman · · · · · · · Bonnie Russavage
· · · · · · · · · · · · · · · · · · · (1993–94)
'Crunch' Grabowski · · Ryan Hurst (1993–95)
Brian Keller · · · · · Christian Oliver (1994–95)
Rachel Myers · · · · Sarah Lancaster (1994–97)
Bobby Wilson · · Spankee Rogers (1994–95)
Ryan Parker · · · · · · · · Richard Lee Jackson
· · · · · · · · · · · · · · · · · · · (from 1995)
R J 'Hollywood' Collins · · · · · · · Salim Grant
· · · · · · · · · · · · · · · · · · · (from 1995)
Maria Lopez · · · · · · · · · · Samantha Becker
· · · · · · · · · · · · · · · · · · · (from 1995)

Nicky Farina · · · · · · · Ben Gould (from 1996)
Eric Little · · · · · · Anthony Harrell (from 1996)
Katie Peterson · · · · · · · · · · Lindsey McKeon
· · · · · · · · · · · · · · · · · · · (from 1996)
Liz Miller · · · Ashley Lyn Cafagna (from 1997)

CREDITS

creator Sam Bobrick · *writers* various · *directors* various · *executive producers* Peter Engel, Gary Considine · *producers* Marica Govons, Franco E Bario, Sue Feyk, Chris Conte, Carl Kurlander, Renee Palyo

Oh, the pain of it all. *Saved By The Bell – The New Class* was the sequel to **Saved By The Bell** when the original, irritatingly banal pupils grew up (sort of) and went off to **Saved By The Bell – The College Years**. In an entirely predicable move, nearly all the new students in *The New Class* were role-for-role replicas of the originals. The new 'Zack'-like character was Scott Erikson, the new Karen was Vicki, the new Kelly was Lindsay, the new Mickey was 'Tommy D', the new Lisa Marie was more or less Megan, the new nerdy 'Screech' was the nerdy 'Weasel', the new 'Ox' was 'Crunch' and so on, and on, and on, and on. Why waste a bunch of scripts just because all the original characters are no longer present?

Of course, a new class is only a new class in its first year. Then other new classes come along. Which goes some way to explaining why, each succeeding September, new characters have been added to *Saved By The Bell – The New Class*. The only regulars have been principal Richard Belding and the original 'Screech', who returned to Bayside High as a young adult to become Belding's administrative assistant.

Scoop

UK · ITV (GRANADA) · SITCOM

1 × 30 mins · b/w

20 June 1963 · Thu 7.30pm

MAIN CAST

Maria · · · · · · · · · · · · · · · · · · Miriam Karlin
Albert · · · · · · · · · · · · · · · Warren Mitchell

CREDITS

writers Barry Took/Peter Miller/James Kelly · *director* Graeme McDonald · *producer* Peter Eton

Another of the single-episode productions in Granada's *Comedy Four* season. *Scoop* starred Warren Mitchell as a newspaper reporter who has a chance to score the ultimate journalistic coup, providing that he does not allow his honesty to get in the way. Miriam Karlin co-starred as Maria, an opera singer who was the source of the newsworthy item in question.

Note. Barry Took, who co-wrote this script, also adapted Evelyn Waugh's *Scoop* for the BBC (see next entry). Apart from the author and title connections, the two productions are unrelated.

Scoop
2

UK · BBC · COMEDY SERIAL

7 × 30 mins · colour

8 Oct–19 Nov 1972 · BBC2 Sun 9pm

MAIN CAST

William Boot	Harry Worth
Mrs Stitch	Sheila Hancock
Salter	Brian Oulton
Lord Copper	Kenneth J Warren
Baldwin	John Junkin
John Boot	Gerald Flood
Uncle Theodore	Meredith Edwards
Katchen	Sinead Cusack

CREDITS

creator Evelyn Waugh · *adapter/writer* Barry Took · *producer* Michael Mills

This TV adaptation of Waugh's hilarious satire on war and journalism featured Harry Worth as William Boot, a country bumpkin nature correspondent who is mistakenly sent by the London-based newspaper *The Daily Beast* to cover a civil war in an African republic. Boot's arrival in war-torn Ishmaelia is the catalyst for a series of disasters, misconceptions and misunderstandings.

Eyes were raised at the casting of Harry Worth in the sort of satire that was very different from the comedian's usual style, but the producer Michael Mills, who had recently resigned as the BBC's Head of Comedy to concentrate on producing, counted on the fact that Boot's accident-prone persona was similar to Worth's sitcom characterisations. The fact that Worth was obviously much older than the man portrayed in the book caused some problems, though, with Boot's relatives and his girlfriend Katchen having to be aged accordingly. All the same, the production was performed – like a sitcom – in front of a studio audience, many of whom were baffled by the storyline and presumably expected a typical Harry Worth comedy. Despite Barry Took's efforts to produce a worthy TV translation, the casting and style of the series worked against the production and it was not deemed a success.

A one-off LWT adaptation, aired as a two-hour film by ITV on 26 April 1987, was more faithful to the original 1938 novel, and the filming and locations were elegant and lavish, but this too was unable to capture the elusive comedic quality of the novel. Michael Maloney played Boot in this production.

Scotch And Wry

UK · BBC · STANDUP/SKETCH

1 × 40 mins · colour

1 Jan 1983 · Sat 11.20pm

MAIN CAST

Rikki Fulton
Gregor Fisher
Miriam Margolyes
Phyllis Logan
Pat Doyle

CREDITS

writers Laurie Rowley, Niall Clark, Mick Deasey, Neil MacVicar, Guy Jenkin, Rikki Fulton · *script editor* Colin Gilbert · *director* Rod Natkiel · *producer* Gordon Menzies

Scottish high-jinks for New Year's Day, featuring a worthy collection of comedy talent.

Scott Free

UK · BBC · SITCOM

6 × 30 mins · b/w

22 July–26 Aug 1957 · Mon mostly 8pm

MAIN CAST

Terry Scott	himself
Norman Vaughan	himself
Gribble	Wallas Eaton
Councillor Bland	Henry Longhurst
Bland's daughter	Marcia Ashton

CREDITS

writer Lew Schwarz · *producer* Harry Carlisle

Terry Scott's first television series as the sole main star. (He had shared top billing with Bill Maynard in the 1955–56 run *Great Scott – It's Maynard!*) He and support comic-actor Norman Vaughan played 'themselves' in this sitcom, cast as out-of-work actors sent by their despairing agent to the sleepy seaside town of Bogmouth to take up the hopeless jobs of Entertainment Officers. Storylines revolved around their attempts to liven up the place, ideas usually scuppered by the well-meaning but accident-prone local councillor, Bland. In the meantime, Scott falls both for the councillor's daughter (played by Marcia Ashton) and the confidence tricks of a local 'old salt', Gribble.

Also seen in the series, one episode apiece, were Percy Edwards, Gilbert Harding, Brian Johnston and Stanley Unwin.

Beside The Seaside, an ITV series with a similar theme, was launched one month before this BBC run.

Scott On …

UK · BBC · SKETCH

31 editions (30 × 45 mins · 1 × short special) (3 × b/w · 28 × colour)

Special (b/w) 19 Dec 1964 · BBC2 Sat 9.25pm

Series One (2 × b/w) 15 May & 5 June 1965 · BBC2 Sat 9.30pm/9.50pm

Special (colour) 29 Sep 1968 · BBC2 Sun 7.25pm

Series Two (6 × colour) 21 Sep–2 Nov 1969 · BBC2 Sun various times

Series Three (6 × colour) 2 Sep–8 Oct 1970 · BBC2 Wed 9.20pm then Thu 9.25pm

Short special (colour) · part of *Christmas Night With The Stars* 25 Dec 1970 · BBC1 Fri 6.45pm

Series Four (8 × colour) 23 Sep–30 Dec 1971 · BBC2 fortnightly Thu 9.20pm

Series Five (5 × colour) 9 Oct–11 Dec 1972 · BBC2 fortnightly Mon 9.25pm

Special (colour) 7 Feb 1974 · BBC2 Thu 9pm

MAIN CAST

Terry Scott
June Whitfield (from special 2)
Rita Webb (special 1 & series 1)

CREDITS

writers Marty Feldman/Barry Took (special 1 & series 1), Bryan Blackburn (special 2, series 2 & 3), Dick Vosburgh/Eric Davidson (series 2), Dave Freeman (series 3 & 4 & short special), John Kane (special 3 & series 5), Humphrey Ventnor (series 5) · *additional material* Eric Merriman and others · *producers* Dennis Main Wilson (special 1 & series 1), Kenneth Carter (special 2 & series 2), Peter Whitmore (short special, 1974 special, series 2–5)

A series of themed-sketch shows starring Terry Scott, which became one of the earliest comedy successes on BBC2.

Each show concentrated on a single topic, the name of the theme tacked on to the series' generic title *Scott On …*, for example *Scott On Marriage* and *Scott On Superstition* (see below for full list). Throughout the 31 editions, but especially in the early shows, the series benefited from top quality writing, and Scott's good-natured acceptance of dressing up in outrageous costumes or prancing about in drag. From the 29 September 1968 programme through to the end of the final series, Scott enjoyed strong comedic support from June Whitfield; this was the first time they had worked together and it led to a continuation of their screen partnership in the sitcom *Happy Ever After* which then became the even longer-running *Terry And June*. All editions of *Scott On …* included contributions from a changing company of supporting players in the minor roles.

Notes. The first programme was written as a showcase for Kenneth Williams but he backed out before filming began. His replacement then made the show his own.

The 28 colour editions, 1968–74, were screened under BBC2's *Show Of The Week* banner.

The *Scott On …* titles (shown here chronologically, series and specials appropriately divided) were *Birds*; *Money, Food; Marriage*; *Habits, Superstition, The Seven Deadly Sins, Leisure, The Body, Christmas; Progress, Law, Industry, Communication, History, Nature; Christmas Trees; Travel, Wealth, Dress, Entertainment, The Home, Rebellion, Supernatural, Food; The Sex War, Language, Culture, Success, The Permissive Society; Courage*.

Screaming

UK · BBC · SITCOM

8 × 30 mins · colour

15 Mar–3 May 1992 · BBC1 Sun 9.05pm

MAIN CAST

Annie	Gwen Taylor
Beatrice	Penelope Wilton

Rachael	Jill Baker
Ralph	Tim Berrington

CREDITS

writer Carla Lane · *director/producer* Mike Stephens

A serio-comedy piece looking at the relationships between women and the effect upon them of their relationships with men.

Screaming depicted three intelligent women, all aged about 40, who share a house. The trio are former schoolfriends and each, at the present, is without a male partner. But there is a further, fundamental link between them, one that, initially, they do not realise: they have all been sexually involved with the same man, Ralph. All three experienced their time with him differently: Beatrice's affair with Ralph was clandestine; Rachael now likes to think that he is dead; and Annie fondly recalls the joys of their sexual activity.

The naturally unfolding dialogue, melancholic situations and slow pace of *Screaming* immediately marked it out from the pack, but it was treated by the BBC as a traditional sitcom, scheduled in a peak-time BBC1 slot and recorded in front of a studio audience. The writer and at least one of her actresses (Wilton) tried to convince the Corporation that the series would work better without a live audience, and had the show been presented on BBC2 they might have won the point, but, post-**Bread**, Lane was considered hot stuff and the BBC decided, accordingly, that a hot slot was appropriate. This and other Lane tragi-comedy hybrids also seemed to confuse critics, who reviewed them as if they were standard sitcoms that were short on laughs. To this end, Lane's less-obvious work might have fared better if it was perceived as a new genre, like the Americans' 'dramady'.

Scrooge – A Christmas Sarah

UK · BBC · CHILDREN'S SKETCH

1 × 30 mins · colour

29 Dec 1990 · BBC1 Sat 10am

MAIN CAST

Sarah Scrooge	Sarah Greene
Phil Scratchit	Phillip Schofield
Mrs Scratchit	Emma Forbes
Tiny Gordon	Gordon The Gopher
Jacob Marley	Rowland Rivron
Ghost Of Christmas Past	Norman Lovett
Ghost Of Christmas Present	Susie Blake
Ghost Of Christmas Future	Normski

CREDITS

creator Charles Dickens · *adapters/writers* Trev Neal/Simon Hickson · *director* Peter Leslie · *producer* David Mercer

An extended sketch that put a comic spin on Dickens' *A Christmas Carol* and featured regulars from the BBC1 children's magazine show *Going Live!* with comedy guest stars.

Scully

UK · C4 (GRANADA) · SITCOM

7 episodes (6 × 30 mins · 1 × 60 mins) · colour

14 May–25 June 1984 · Mon 8pm

MAIN CAST

Francis 'Franny' Scully	Andrew Schofield
'Mooey' Morgan	Ray Kingsley
Mad Dog	Mark McGann
Joanna	Cathy Tyson
Snooty Dog	Richard Burke
Puppy Dog	Lucinda Scrivener
Gran	Jean Boht
Kenny Dalglish	himself
Mrs Scully	Val Lilley
Steve	David Ross
Bignall	Gary Bleasdale
Mrs Heath	Judith Barker
Isaiah	Tom Georgeson
Marie	Gilly Coman
Tony	Peter Christian
Dracula	Tony Haygarth
Arthur	Jimmy Gallagher
Florrie	Paula Jacobs
Henry	Elvis Costello
Rita	Angie Catherall

CREDITS

writer Alan Bleasdale · *director* Les Chatfield · *producer* Steve Morrison

A hard-headed 15-year-old Scouser, Francis 'Franny' Scully, daydreams about being a hero for Liverpool Football Club. He attends school, but – in his head – he's scarcely present, being off and away in a world of his own, running on to the Anfield pitch while the Kop sing 'one Franny Scully, there's only one Franny Scully'. Scully's idol – as he regularly informs the viewers via straight-to-camera asides – is the Reds' striker supreme Kenny Dalglish, who appears frequently in his visions … and so in real life in the series. Scully's best mate is Mooey, a relentlessly cheerful school friend whose nickname is 'Bungalow Head' because people reckon 'he's got nothing upstairs'. Together, and with other mates, the pair go about their daily lives in a mad whirl, out for the crack (the laughs, that is) and, particularly in Scully's case, escaping the madhouses of school and home. (Among the family characters are Gran, who guzzles pina coladas, train-obsessed brother Henry, who listens to railway recordings through headphones, and goody-goody brother Arthur.)

High on humour, but with moral elements, the TV series was adapted by Alan Bleasdale from his two previously published novels – *Scully* (1975) and its sequel *Who's Been Sleeping In My Bed?* (1977) – and was also furnished with additional script material. Undoubtedly, the author's passion for Liverpool FC was much in evidence, as was his teaching background (Bleasdale left the profession in 1975 to concentrate full-time on his writing), to the extent that the Scully and Mooey characters were based upon two boys

in a Huyton remedial school where Bleasdale had taught. Scully had first appeared on TV in a single *Play For Today* production screened by BBC1 on 3 January 1978, titled *Scully's New Year's Eve*. In that, as in the series, the title role was played by Andrew Schofield, far from 15 but convincing all the same.

Kenny Dalglish was not the only famous Liverpool footballer to appear in *Scully*: goalie Bruce Grobbelaar, manager Bob Paisley, old boy Ian St John and – in the title sequence as well as the series – the rest of the 1983–84 team all turned up, and there was a major role too for the Liverpool-born rock star Elvis Costello, who acted the part of Scully's train-mad brother Henry as well as singing the theme song, the self-composed 'Turning The Town Red'.

Sealed With A Loving Kiss

UK · BBC · SITCOM

1 × 30 mins · b/w

9 Feb 1962 · Fri 8.45pm

MAIN CAST

Arnold	Ronald Fraser
Freda	Avril Elgar
Arnold's mother	Gladys Henson
Station porter	Vic Wise
Trolley lady	Rita Webb

CREDITS

writers Ray Galton/Alan Simpson · *producer* James Gilbert

A Galton and Simpson *Comedy Playhouse* playlet about Arnold and Freda, who have conducted a romance through written correspondence. Now they meet for the first time, but the situation is complicated by the fact that neither of them has been entirely truthful.

The script was twice re-used: in **The Mating Machine** (1970), and **Paul Merton In Galton & Simpson's …** (1996).

Sean Hughes Is Thirty Somehow

UK · C4 (MY WORLD PRODUCTIONS) · STANDUP

1 × 65 mins · colour

22 Dec 1995 · Fri 10.10pm

MAIN CAST

Sean Hughes

CREDITS

writer Sean Hughes · *producer* Sylvie Boden

Celebrating his 30th birthday, this special recording saw the standup comic Sean Hughes reflect upon his growing responsibilities and anxieties, and dwell upon the ageless issues of sex, love and God.

The show was recorded at the Riverside Studios in London.

See also *Aah Sean* and *Sean's Show*.

Sean's Show

UK · C4 (CHANNEL X) · SITCOM

14 × 30 mins · colour

Series One (7) 15 Apr–27 May 1992 ·
Wed 10.30pm

Series Two (7) 17 Nov–29 Dec 1993 ·
Wed mostly 10.35pm

MAIN CAST
Sean Hughes

CREDITS
writer Sean Hughes · *director* Sylvie Boden ·
producer Katie Lander

A surreal sitcom in which the 'fourth wall'
was broken, allowing Hughes to address the
studio audience and discuss the sitcom world
in which he lives.

Hughes' flat – in Chelsea, London – was the
studio set in which most of the adventures
occurred, and in the first series serialised
storylines revolved around his rocky
relationship with girlfriend Susan. For the
second series he was chasing a different
woman, Lizzie, who worked with him at a
garage. Manic ideas littered the scripts (there
were appearances by God's brother Shaw;
a flatmate spider called Elvis; and Bosnian
refugee television addicts) and the whole
premise was whisked smoothly along by
the amiable – albeit sometimes confused –
Hughes.

Some critics accused *Sean's Show* of being
an unacknowledged rehash of the US series
It's Garry Shandling's Show which likewise toyed with the mechanics of reality
(and was itself a modern-day version of *The
Burns And Allen Show*). However, the
device of incorporating sitcom elements within a standup act had been used by Hughes for
many years, and was essentially the format
that won him the Perrier Award in 1990.

Note. Hughes later presented *Sean's Shorts*,
a series of six short light-hearted travelogues
screened by BBC2 from 4 January to 8
February 1993.

**See also *Aah Sean* and *Sean Hughes Is Thirty
Somehow*.**

Searching

UK · ITV (NOEL GAY TELEVISION FOR CARLTON) ·
SITCOM

7 × 30 mins · colour

8 June–20 July 1995 · Thu 9.30pm

MAIN CAST
'Mrs' Tilston · · · · · · · · · · · · · Prunella Scales
Chancy · · · · · · · · · · · · · · · · · · Julia St John
Lena · · · · · · · · · · · · · · · · · Victoria Carling
Dora · · · · · · · · · · · · · · · · · · Clare Cathcart
Milly · · · · · · · · · · · · · · · · Regina Freedman
Daniel Carter · · · · · · · · · · · · Robert Gwilym
Hetty · · · · · · · · · · · · · · · · Amanda Bellamy
Chancy's dad · · · · · · · · · · · · Reginald Marsh
Chancy's mum · · · · · · · · · · · Marcia Warren
April · · · · · · · · · · · · · · · · · · · Mabel Aitken

Mr Gillespie · · · · · · · · · · · David Gooderson
Gerald · · · · · · · · · · · · · · · · Mark Williams
Hetty's mum · · · · · · · · · · · · · · · Jo Warne
Hetty's dad · · · · · · · · · · · · · · John Rapley
Duncan · · · · · · · · · · · · · · · James Nesbitt

CREDITS
writer Carla Lane · *director* Robin Nash · *executive
producers* Bill Cotton Jr, Carla Lane · *producer*
John Bartlett

Carla Lane's first ITV comedy since contributing to *Bless This House* 20 years earlier.
The setting was Sunfield Voluntary Therapy
Centre for young women with special
psychological needs, an experimental venture
in its early days and the recipient of local
authority funding. Actually an ordinary if
largish house in a residential street, Sunfield
is run by one Mrs Tilston, for whom it is not
only the culmination of years of studying
and saving but also a personal crusade since,
to use her words, her own mother 'went
doolally'. Tilston, one is tempted to comment,
is not altogether together herself – a devout
Christian, she charges around the house
crying 'up and dashing!', wearing a green
sweatshirt with the legend 'I am His', singing
hymns, shaking a handbell to get the
attention of her five inmates and then either
fussily mothering, organising or criticising
them. She's not even married – she calls
herself Mrs Tilston to ward men off, although
she continues to hold a torch for her only true
love, a Mr Gillespie, who, during the series,
unexpectedly turns up at the house and puts
her in even more a spin than usual.

Sunfield's five residential charges are all
seeking refuge from a world they are unable
to handle. Chancy is a thrice-divorced man-
hater and aggressive husband-beater whose
problems emanate from her bulldozing father
and put-upon mother. (This doesn't stop her
from becoming obsessed with Daniel Carter,
a male counsellor/therapist on a six week
assignment at Sunfield.) Milly is a skimpily
dressed kleptomaniac who steals only useless
items and is locked into a dull and lifeless
marriage. Scotswoman Dora is suicidal,
cultured Lena is a compulsive puller of train
emergency cords and Hetty obsessively hides
herself under umbrellas, even inside the
house, claiming that 'she didn't do it'.

As could be expected, the scripts contained
a fair share of anti-male dialogue, with
particular emphasis on the loathing of
testicles and all that they produce. *Searching*,
indeed, is not easily classifiable as a sitcom –
Prunella Scales, who starred as Mrs Tilston,
endeavoured to slot it into a new category by
calling it a 'drama-doc-sit-trag'. Very clearly
the work of Carla Lane, the series might have
been given time to bed down on the BBC.
On ITV it was deemed an insufficiently
commercial prospect and hit the rocks after
a single series.

Seaview

UK · BBC · CHILDREN'S SITCOM

12 × 30 mins · colour

Series One (6) 5 Oct–9 Nov 1983 · BBC1
Wed 5.10pm

Series Two (6) 20 Feb–27 Mar 1985 · BBC1
Wed 5.05pm

MAIN CAST
Sandy Shelton · · · · · · · · · · · Yvette Fielding
George Shelton · · · · · · · · · · · · Aaron Brown
James · · · · · · · · · · · · · · · Chris Hargreaves
Mrs Shelton · · · · · · · · · · Maggie Ollerenshaw
Mr Shelton · · · · · · · · · · · · David Gooderson
Duncan · · · · · · · · · · · · · · · · · Lloyd Peters
Petra · · · · · · · · · · · · · · · · · Carla Rogerson
Ian · · · · · · · · · · · · · · Mark Jordan (series 2)

CREDITS
writer Chris Barlas · *director* Marilyn Fox · *executive
producer* Paul Stone

An up-to-the-minute sitcom for children, set
in a recognisable world of discos, teenage
romance, heavy-metal bands and Space
Invader machines.

The episodes centred on the Seaview
Private Hotel. Sandy and George Shelton are
teenagers helping their parents to run the
newly opened hostelry. A bright, modern girl,
Sandy has strong opinions and the courage to
see them through – when her parents refuse
to pay the children for their help, she urges
them to strike; when her father buys her
mother a real fur coat, Sandy campaigns
against it and sets up her own ecological
group; when her parents are taken ill, Sandy
and George take over the running of the hotel,
introducing their own money-making
schemes.

The first series also carried a sub-plot
about their friend Duncan's heavy-metal
band, which Sandy wants to join. Typically,
when she finally does so, she tries to persuade
them to perform her own compositions. In the
second series, Sandy – just about to turn 16 –
encounters romance when she is smitten by
Ian.

Yvette Fielding, who played Sandy, went
on to become a *Blue Peter* presenter
(September 1987–June 1992).

Harry Secombe

The Welsh Goon, Harry Secombe was born
in Swansea on 8 September 1921. He
entertained as a child at church social
gatherings, enacting celebrity impressions,
but did not perform with any great
regularity until serving King and Country in
the Royal Artillery during the Second World
War, when he appeared in Forces shows.
More intent on a career in comedy after the
war – his first billed BBC TV appearance

was on 11 November 1946 – Secombe went into partnership with his friend, writer and agent Jimmy Grafton, who ran the Grafton Arms pub in London. It was here that Secombe would soon gather with new pals Spike Milligan, Peter Sellers and Michael Bentine. Individually, all appeared frequently on BBC radio in the late 1940s and early 1950s, and in 1951, as a quartet, they launched *The Goon Show*, first broadcast under the title *Crazy People*. The series made stars of them all (when Bentine left, the other three carried on until 1960) and it gave Secombe free rein to display his fine line in comedic noises and voices. Inevitably, each of the three Goons were pigeon-holed by the public, and Secombe was considered an irrepressibly happy man. Rarely are such easy encapsulations true, but this one is.

At the same time as he was making giant strides in comedy, Harry Secombe developed a sideline as a singer, and this gradually took over from the humour when he gained major stage and film roles – notably *Pickwick* and the movie *Oliver!* – that required this particular talent. In recent years Secombe has focused almost entirely on religious TV programming (he hosted ITV's *Highway* from 1983 to 1993, travelling the country to chat with guests and sing hymns) and tends to venture into humour only in gala concerts and variety shows.

Harry Secombe's once-rotund figure suggested a jolly man, always laughing and blowing raspberries. Now much slimmer – he was forced to diet on health grounds – and knighted (in 1981) for his services to entertainment and charity, Secombe remains all of these things and is a much-loved personality.

The following in no way represents a complete list of Harry Secombe's TV work, but it focuses on his principal comedy broadcasts. See also *The Bruce Forsyth Show*, *Don't Spare The Horses*, **The Ronnie Corbett Specials**, *Television's Christmas Party* and, within Spike Milligan's main entry, *Goonreel*, *The Goon Show*, *The Last Goon Show Of All* and *An Evening With ... Spike Milligan*.

Secombe Here!

UK · BBC · SKETCH

3 × 60 mins · b/w

14 May 1955 · Sat 9.30pm

9 July 1955 · Sat 9pm

3 Sep 1955 · Sat 8.45pm

MAIN CAST
Harry Secombe
Johnny Vyvyan

CREDITS
writers Jimmy Grafton (shows 1–3), Eric Sykes (shows 1 & 2), Spike Milligan (shows 1 & 3), Harry Secombe (show 2) · *producers* Bill Lyon-Shaw (shows 1 & 2), Albert Stevenson (show 3)

Two of these three Secombe specials included further attempts to unleash on TV the zany brilliance of BBC radio's quintessential comedy series *The Goon Show*. The last was broadcast live from the National Radio Show at Earls Court, in London, and was immediately followed by a variety special (from the same event) titled *Arenascope Presents OB Parade* that included some additional clowning from Milligan and Sellers, joined by Secombe.

Harry's guests in *Secombe Here!* included, in the first show, Spike Milligan, Eric Sykes, Valentine Dyall and Shirley Eaton; Bill Kerr and Libby Morris in the second; Peter Sellers, Sam Kydd and Libby Morris again in the third.

The Harry Secombe Show 1

UK · ITV (ATV) · SKETCH/STANDUP

8 × 45 mins · b/w

One series (6) 24 Sep–29 Oct 1955 · Sat 8.15pm

Special · 22 Dec 1956 · Sat 9pm

Special · 23 Mar 1957 · Sat 8.30pm

MAIN CAST
Harry Secombe
Norman Vaughan (series)
Johnny Vyvyan (series)

CREDITS
writer Eric Sykes · *director/producer* Bill Lyon-Shaw

Beginning two days after the launch of ITV, Harry Secombe was the first star to attract his own weekly series on the new commercial network, screened in the *Saturday Showtime* strand. All of the comedy material was scripted by Eric Sykes, with Secombe appearing in sketches under his pseudonymous guise Fred Nerk.

The Secombe Saga

UK · BBC · SKETCH

1 × 60 mins · b/w

7 Dec 1957 · Sat 8pm

MAIN CAST
Harry Secombe
Terry-Thomas
Bill Fraser

CREDITS
writer Jimmy Grafton · *producer* Ernest Maxin

Subtitled 'Those Tarnished Years' and screened in the BBC's *Saturday Show* strand. Support this time came from the ever reliable Terry-Thomas and that master of the stern stare, Bill Fraser.

Secombe And Friends

UK · ITV (ATV) · SKETCH/STANDUP

5 editions (4 × 60 mins · 1 × 55 mins) · b/w

21 Feb 1959 · Sat 7.55pm (60 mins)

25 Apr 1959 · Sat 7.55pm (60 mins)

26 Sep 1959 · Sat 8pm (55 mins)

16 Oct 1966 · Sun 8.25pm (60 mins)

13 Nov 1966 · Sun 8.25pm (60 mins)

MAIN CAST
Harry Secombe

CREDITS
writers not listed (shows 1–3), Jimmy Grafton (shows 4 & 5) ('The Whistling Spy Enigma' by Spike Milligan) · *producers* Brian Tesler (shows 1–3), Jon Scoffield (shows 4 & 5)

Five single shows, aired over almost eight years, that depicted the star in comedy and musical modes. The programmes were particularly notable for the major comedic names helping out, including all of Secombe's fellow ex-Goons – Spike Milligan, Peter Sellers and Michael Bentine – and Tony Hancock. The intention of the fourth edition was to present the programme in the style of a *Goon Show* recording – the set was made up to look like a BBC radio studio – and one complete *Goon Show* script ('The Whistling Spy Enigma', first broadcast on the wireless on 28 September 1954) was enacted. It was not a success, however, and only some of the material was included in the taped broadcast.

Harry's friends in *Secombe And Friends* included Donald Houston (three shows), Spike Milligan (two), Bill Fraser (two), Peter Haigh (two), Joyce Blair (two), Lionel Blair (two), Glyn Houston (two), Stanley Baker (two), and one appearance apiece from Osian Ellis, the Peiro Brothers, Simon Kester, Harry Worth, Hattie Jacques, Patricia Lambert, Richard Burton, Roy Castle, Ray Ellington, Geraint Evans, Eric Rogers, Peter Sellers, Michael Bentine, Tony Hancock, Danny La Rue, Adele Leigh, Jeremy Lloyd and Nora Nicholson.

Secombe At Large

UK · BBC · STANDUP

2 editions (1 × 60 mins · 1 × 50 mins) · b/w

30 May 1959 · Sat 7.30pm (60 mins)

7 Nov 1959 · Sat 9.35pm (50 mins)

MAIN CAST
Harry Secombe
Mario Fabrizi

CREDITS
writer Jimmy Grafton · *script associates* Jeremy Lloyd, Alan Fell · *producer* Bill Cotton Jr

BBC specials featuring Secombe and guests in a mixed bag of comedy and musical items. Sam Kydd guested in the first show, Dora Bryan and Clive Dunn in the second.

Who Is Secombe?

UK · BBC · SKETCH/STANDUP

1 × 45 mins · b/w

26 Dec 1963 · Thu 8.20pm

MAIN CAST

Harry Secombe
Dora Bryan
Roy Castle
Jimmy Edwards
Fenella Fielding
Anton Rodgers
Amanda Barrie

CREDITS

deviser Jimmy Grafton · *writers* Jimmy Grafton,
Jeremy Lloyd, Sid Green/Dick Hills, David Climie,
Johnny Whyte · *producer* James Gilbert

An array of Secombe's friends assembled
here to present different comedic views of
the former Goon. Dora Bryan looked at
his comic artistry; Fielding dissected his
sex appeal; Jimmy Edwards recalled his
formative years as a scholar; Amanda Barrie
helped assess his dancing ability; and Anton
Rodgers considered his acting prowess.

The Harry Secombe Show   2

UK · BBC · SKETCH

**31 editions (27 × 45 mins · 2 × 50 mins · 1 × 55
mins · 1 × 60 mins) · colour**

Special (55 mins) 25 Dec 1968 · BBC2
Wed 10.30pm

Special (50 mins) 4 May 1969 · BBC2
Sun 7.25pm

Special (50 mins) 31 Aug 1969 · BBC2
Sun 10.20pm

Special (45 mins) 15 Nov 1969 · BBC1
Sat 7.30pm

Special (45 mins) 29 Nov 1969 · BBC1
Sat 7.30pm

Series One (6 × 45 mins) 12 Sep–17 Oct 1970 ·
BBC1 Sat 8.15pm

Series Two (8 × 45 mins) 11 Sep–30 Oct 1971 ·
BBC1 Sat mostly 8.15pm

Series Three (6 × 45 mins) 18 Nov–23 Dec
1972 · BBC1 · Sat 7.35pm

Special (60 mins) *A Royal Television Gala
Performance* 25 July 1973 · BBC1 Wed 8pm

Series Four (5 × 45 mins) 1 Dec–29 Dec 1973 ·
BBC1 Sat 7.15pm

MAIN CAST

Harry Secombe
Julian Orchard

CREDITS

writers Jimmy Grafton (31), Jeremy Lloyd (6),
David Climie (4), Lew Schwarz (4), Tony Hare (3),
Stan Mars (2), Gordon Clyde (1), John Law (1),
Marty Feldman/Barry Took (1) · *director* James
Moir (6) · *producers* Terry Hughes (26), Colin
Chapman (5)

Further shows for Secombe, aided in the
sketches by Julian Orchard and celebrity
guest stars. The humour content of the
shows varied considerably – some were
sketch-led while others were dominated by

musical acts. The most notable comedy
guest stars were Peggy Mount (25 December
1968), Arthur Askey (15 November 1969),
Spike Milligan (3 October 1970), Hattie Jacques
(25 September 1971), Beryl Reid (2 October
1971, 9 December 1972, 25 July 1973 and
22 December 1973), Dickie Henderson
(16 October 1971), Dick Emery (30 October
1971) and Arthur Lowe (2 December 1972).

Note. On 11 June 1969 BBC2 presented a TV
version of *Pickwick*, the highly successful
London stage musical based upon *The
Pickwick Papers*. Secombe starred in the
stage version and reprised the role for this
TV special, which was adapted by Jimmy
Grafton and James Gilbert, directed by
Terry Hughes and produced by James
Gilbert.

Bombardier Secombe Back Among The Boys

UK · BBC · STANDUP

1 × 30 mins · colour

22 Dec 1973 · BBC1 Tue 10pm

MAIN CAST

Harry Secombe

CREDITS

producer Kenneth Carter

A filmed record of Secombe entertaining the
troops in Northern Ireland for Combined
Services Entertainments. Karen Young and
the Karlins provided the glamour obligatory
for such occasions.

Note. One of Secombe's many musical TV
outings at this time was *Sing A Song Of
Secombe*, screened by BBC1 on 29 December
1974. Peter Sellers and Spike Milligan joined
their fellow ex-Goon for a couple of short,
pre-recorded sketches at the end of the
otherwise all-melodious extravaganza.

Have A Harry …

UK · ITV (YORKSHIRE) · SKETCH

2 × 60 mins · colour

Have A Harry Christmas 23 Dec 1977 · Fri 8pm

Have A Harry Birthday 11 Oct 1978 · Wed 8pm

MAIN CAST

Harry Secombe

CREDITS

writers Barry Cryer, Spike Mullins, Peter Vincent,
Peter Robinson · *director/producer* Vernon
Lawrence

Two hours of comedy and music on the
themes of Christmas and birthdays. Both
shows featured humorous and musical guest
stars.

Secombe's gradual shift of emphasis
towards music and away from comedy saw
the balance weigh in favour of melody from
this point on. So these following music-
dominated ITV programmes are beyond the

parameters of this book: *Secombe With
Music* (17 December 1980, 27 December
1981, 27 January 1982, 21 April 1982, 5 May
1982, 2 June 1982 and 15 September 1982)
and *Secombe At Christmas* (24 December
1982).

Second Thoughts

UK · ITV (LWT) · SITCOM

49 × 30 mins · colour

Series One (7) 3 May–14 June 1991 · Fri 8pm

Series Two (12) 3 Jan–20 Mar 1992 · Fri 8.30pm

Series Three (15) 18 Oct 1992–12 Feb 1993 ·
Sun 7.15pm then Fri 8.30pm

Series Four (7) 29 Oct–17 Dec 1993 · Fri 8.30pm

Series Five (8) 26 Aug–14 Oct 1994 · Fri 8.30pm

MAIN CAST

Bill Macgregor	James Bolam
Faith Grayshot	Lynda Bellingham
Liza Macgregor	Belinda Lang
Hannah Grayshot	Julia Sawalha
Joe Grayshot	Mark Denham

OTHER APPEARANCES

Hilary	Louisa Rix (series 1); Paddy Navin (series 2 & 3)
Richard	Geoffrey Whitehead
Marjorie	Georgina Melville
Callum	Ian Henderson (series 5)

CREDITS

writers Jan Etherington/Gavin Petrie ·
directors/producers David Askey (series 1), Robin
Carr (series 2–5) · *executive producer* Robin Carr
(series 1)

A good-value ITV comedy about two young-
middle-aged divorcees with very different
backgrounds, trying to build – and cling to –
a relationship despite the pressures pulling
it apart. The principal players were the ever-
excellent James Bolam, cast as Bill
Macgregor, the art editor of a style magazine,
and Lynda Bellingham, hitherto best known
as Mum in the Oxo TV commercials, cast as
freelance illustrator Faith Grayshot.

Faith has two teenage children from her
marriage – not 'problem teenagers' as such,
but endowed with every teenager's peculiar
sense of priorities and customary inability to
adopt tact and diplomacy. Bill, however, has
a definite problem: a glamorous, snooty and
most definitely bitchy ex-wife, Liza, who
seems determined to ruin his relationship
with Faith with her mischievous meddling.
When Bill and Faith are together, Bill's
eternal gripe is that she always puts the
children's, or her dog's, interests first, while
his unfamiliarity with kids is such that when
he is thrust into a paternal role it is like
watching a drowning man thrashing around
without a life-jacket.

As they strive to overcome the hurdles
placed before them, Faith and Bill endure
major rows in virtually every episode, and
break up several times. They twice try to

marry but both times stop short on the planned wedding day, making a mockery of the series' optimistic theme music, Gershwin's 'Our Love Is Here To Stay'. Meanwhile, the children grow up, jobs come and go and the arguments just keep on coming. All the while, Faith and Liza never meet – a situation rectified only in the very last TV episode. Liza is pregnant, but won't tell the two possible prospective fathers whose child it is. At the end, as she gives birth to a boy, Faith declares that it looks like Bill. This is never proven because the programme ends there, but the inference is that this allegation is the final breaking point in Bill and Faith's association.

Second Thoughts was based upon the real-life relationship of the writers, husband and wife Etherington and Petrie. Both had been journalists – Petrie was features editor at *TVTimes* and Etherington a regular freelancer for the same magazine, interviewing comedy writers and performers among other duties. Once they became partners a writing relationship developed alongside, and they won the first bi-annual *Radio Times* Radio Comedy Award, then titled 'Sounds Funny', in 1987. Created for BBC radio, *Second Thoughts* followed soon after, Petrie crafting the characters and storylines and Etherington adding the dialogue, recalling how, when they first met, Petrie was a wealthy bachelor while Etherington was up to her eyes in children and dogs. A success on the wireless for more than two years, *Second Thoughts* was the third major BBC radio sitcom of the 1980s to be adapted for TV – all of them ITV, oddly – following on from *After Henry* and *Up The Garden Path*. There could have been no questioning its radio origin: *Second Thoughts* came across as more wordy and situation-bound than most TV sitcoms.

The fifth series of *Second Thoughts* was weaker than the others (it was the first stretch of episodes not to have been written for radio), with a clear shift in emphasis away from Faith and Bill towards the lives of the children and other characters. Petrie and Etherington must have seen the writing on the wall and allowed the series to die, instead focusing their attention on what they would do with the sequel, *Faith In The Future*.

Note. There were 31 BBC Radio 4 episodes of *Second Thoughts*, broadcast as follows – series one (eight episodes, 1 November–20 December 1988), series two (eight episodes, 31 October–19 December 1989), series three (eight episodes, 9 April–28 May 1991), series four (six episodes, 18 June–23 July 1992) and, finally, a Christmas special (25 December 1992). Four of the principal actors in the subsequent TV series – Bolam, Bellingham, Lang and Denham – played the same roles in the radio version; Hannah was played on radio by Kelda Holmes (series one and two), Emma Gregory (three) and Julia Sawalha (four and the special); Hilary was played by Celia Imrie. Apart from the Christmas special, the scripts for the other 30 episodes of the radio *Second Thoughts* all translated directly to TV.

Second Time Around

UK · BBC · SITCOM

13 × 30 mins · colour

Series One (7) 23 Oct–4 Dec 1974 · BBC1
Wed 9.25pm

Series Two (6) 10 Jan–14 Feb 1975 · BBC1
Fri 8.30pm

MAIN CAST

Harry · · · · · · · · · · · · · · · · · · Michael Craig
Vicki · · · · · · · · · · · · · · · · · · Patricia Brake
Ronnie · · · · · · · · · · · · · · · · · Gerald Flood
Maggie · · · · · · · · · · · · · Jacqueline Clarke
Connie · · · · · · · · · · · · · · · Patricia Driscoll

CREDITS

writer Richard Waring · producer Graeme Muir

Writer Richard Waring claimed that life gave him the inspiration for his sitcoms – hence, when he first married he created *Marriage Lines*, when they had kids he wrote *Not In Front Of The Children*, his divorce inspired *My Wife Next Door*, his ensuing experiences as a single father he used for *Bachelor Father*, and his second marriage, to a woman some 20 years younger than he, begat this series, *Second Time Around*. Actually, this last fact is not the whole truth of the matter: Frank Muir had suggested the idea to Waring years earlier, and he had duly scripted a pilot episode with Leslie Phillips in his mind for the lead role, but Waring wasn't altogether happy with the result and shelved it until his own experiences gave him more insight into the theme.

In *Second Time Around*, Harry is 50-years-old, divorced for the last ten, who meets and begins a relationship with a much younger woman, Vicki – so young, in fact, her father is younger than Harry. The first series charted the alliance from their initial encounter through to their inaugural date, engagement, the inevitable clashes with her parents and his ex-wife Connie, Harry's stag night and, finally, their wedding. The second depicted the less-than-perfect honeymoon, the early days of the marriage, the problems caused by Vicki's inability to cook (this *was* the 1970s) and, finally, the possibility that Vicki had fallen pregnant.

Note. A pilot for a US adaptation, also titled *Second Time Around* (aka *Wild About Harry*), was aired by NBC on 26 May 1978. Written by Waring, the episode starred Efrem Zimbalist Jr as 45-year-old Harry Baxter and Andrea Howard as 20-year-old Vicki. Stephanie Zimbalist, Efrem's real-life daughter, was cast as his disapproving screen daughter, Jennie. It failed to graduate to a series.

Seconds Out

UK · BBC · SITCOM

13 × 30 mins · colour

Series One (6) 6 Jan–10 Feb 1981 · BBC1
Tue 8.30pm

Series Two (7) 3 Dec 1981–21 Jan 1982 · BBC1
Thu 8.30pm

MAIN CAST

Pete Dodds · · · · · · · · · · · · · Robert Lindsay
Tom Sprake · · · · · · · · · · · · · Lee Montague
Dave Locket · · · · · · · · · · · · · · · · Ken Jones
Hazel · · · · · · · · · · · · · · Leslie Ash (series 2)

CREDITS

writer Bill MacIlwraith · producer Ray Butt

One of only a handful of sitcoms that has taken sport as its central theme, *Seconds Out* charted the funny side of a boxer's life. In keeping with the theme, the episodes were sequentially titled 'Round One', 'Round Two' and so on.

Citizen Smith had demonstrated the star potential of Robert Lindsay and in this, his next major TV role, he was cast as the aspiring pugilist, Pete Dodds. The series followed his career as he moved up the ladder of success, graduating from small halls to become British Middleweight Champion and a competitor for the European Championship. Accompanying him on this dizzy rise were his manager Tom Sprake and trainer Dave Locket (played by the ever dependable Ken Jones). The series demonstrated a fair amount of cynicism towards the sport, with dodgy deals and unscrupulous promoters among the players.

The Secret Diary Of Adrian Mole, Aged 13¾

UK · ITV (THAMES) · SITCOM

12 episodes (11 × 30 mins · 1 × 60 mins) · colour

Series One (1 × 60 mins · 5 × 30 mins)
16 Sep–21 Oct 1985 · Mon 8pm

Series Two (6 × 30 mins) *The Growing Pains Of Adrian Mole* 5 Jan–9 Feb 1987 · Mon 8pm

MAIN CAST

Adrian Mole · · · · · · · · · · · · · Gian Sammarco
Pauline Mole · · · · · · Julie Walters (series 1);
· Lulu (series 2)
George Mole · · · · · · · · · · · · · Stephen Moore
May (Grandma) Mole · · · · · · · · · · · Beryl Reid
Pandora Braithwaite · · · · · · · · Lindsey Stagg
Bert Baxter · · · · · · · · · · · · · · · · · Bill Fraser
Queenie Baxter · · · · · · · · · · · · · · Doris Hare
Nigel · · · · · · · · · · · · · · · Steven Mackintosh
Mr Lucas · · · · · · · · · · · · · · Paul Greenwood
Doreen Slater · · · · · · · · · · · · · · · Su Elliott
Mr Scruton · · · · · · · · · · · · · · · Freddie Jones
Ivan Braithwaite · · · · · · · · · · · Robin Herford
Tania Braithwaite · · · · · · · · · Louise Jameson
Barry Kent · · · · · · · · · · · · · · Chris Gascoyne

OTHER APPEARANCES

Maxwell	Anthony Watson
Ms Fossington-Gore	Mary Maddox
Barbara Boyer	Shona Lindsay
Mrs Claricoates	Marian Diamond
Kev	Roger Fox
Mrs O'Leary	Maggie Shelvin (series 1)
Mr O'Leary	Walter McMonagle (series 1)
Mr Singh	Ahmed Khalil (series 1)
Mrs Singh	Feroza Syal (series 1)
Dr Gray	Bill Wallis (series 1)
Claire Neilson	Nikki Brooks (series 1)
Craig Thomas	Jeremy Austin (series 1)
Courtney Elliott	John Bird (series 2)

CREDITS

writer Sue Townsend · *script editor* Patrick Barlow (series 2) · *director/producer* Peter Sasdy · *executive producer* Lloyd Shirley

First publicly unveiled as *The Diary Of Nigel Mole, Aged 13¾* in BBC Radio 4's *Thirty-Minute Theatre* slot on 2 January 1982, a subsequent book, commissioned by Methuen on the strength of the broadcast, saw the principal's name change to Adrian and the word *Secret* added to the title. Duly published in volume form later in 1982 as *The Secret Diary Of Adrian Mole, Aged 13¾*, Sue Townsend's creation went on to become one of the literary delights of the decade, a best-seller for several years, and the springboard for a whole raft of *Mole* materials, including a touring stage musical, a songbook, further BBC radio readings, these two ITV series (the second of which was based upon the sequel book *The Growing Pains Of Adrian Mole*, 1984), and additional novels *The True Confessions Of Adrian Albert Mole etc* (1989) and *Adrian Mole: From Minor To Major* (1991). Each in turn plotted the staccato-style diary-entries of the growing Mole, raised in the author's home city Leicester, who starts out as a near 14-year-old adolescent schoolboy, his chief worries being acne and his parents' dwindling relationship and his primary interests being writing and poetry (with grand intellectual pretensions). He is misunderstood, unappreciated and unrecognised, his life is bewildering, and the adults within it are not only appalling as role models but appalling, period.

The TV cast of characters was considerable, but each played their part well, weaving in and out of Adrian's confused teenage years. His parents Pauline and George were forever embarrassing him and exhausting the realms of marital strife. Pauline found herself a new partner, Mr Lucas, whom Adrian considered creepy (indeed he nicknamed him 'Creep' Lucas) so George also acquired a new partner, Doreen Slater, whom Adrian nicknamed 'Stick Insect' on account of her slender figure – until, that is, she became pregnant and (in the second series) delivered a baby, finally bringing to an end Adrian's only-child status. Pauline, meanwhile, in a perfect example of how

Adrian was always an afterthought for his warring parents, threatened to dump him at the DHSS office if she didn't receive one of her Giro cheques. Adrian's grandmother (excellently played by Beryl Reid, once again affecting a Brummie accent) offered some stability but her befuddled, down-to-earth encouragement often caused him great discomfort. Pandora Braithwaite was Adrian's abiding passion (hence the TV theme music, Ian Dury's 'Profoundly In Love With Pandora', a minor hit on the charts); like all early teenage romances theirs was all talk and little action – he chased and she was chaste – Pandora refusing point blank to show Adrian one of her nipples, for example, after he realised, to his horror, that he'd never seen one before. ('This is what comes of living in a cul-de-sac,' he diarised.) Their mutual attempts at sincerity were nonetheless touching, and they were never discouraged by either set of parents, Pandora's being Ivan and Tania.

Pandora often helped Adrian to tend and shop for Bert Baxter, an 89-year-old to whom Mole was a reliable aide. The youngsters never seemed to mind Bert's earthy manner ('I'd give me right ball to go to Skeggy,' he once declared, choosing Skegness as his ideal choice of holiday venue) or his penchant for eating pickled beetroot straight from the jar. Bert's wife, Queenie, was similarly direct. At school, Adrian had a best friend, Nigel, but risked altercations with the bully Barry Kent (who was easily tamed by Adrian's grandma, however) and by Mr Scruton, nicknamed Popeye, the Thatcher-adoring headmaster.

The second series was a straightforward continuation of the first, but had one notable cast change, the singer Lulu replacing the excellent Julie Walters as Adrian's mum.

Although shot on film, without an audience, both series were high on laughs, and Sue Townsend's involvement in the production ensured that the episodes caught the books' infectious and often hilarious stream of narrative. They also carried over the author's gentle but nonetheless definite political barbs – for example, Adrian awoke one morning to find his country at war over the Falkland Islands, a place he had never known to have existed before; yet, encouraged by the tabloid media, and against his better judgement, he felt it was seemly to become a flag-waving jingoist.

Oddly, considering the success of these two TV series, no further small-screen adaptations of the remaining *Mole* books have transpired. Odder still, young Gian Sammarco, perfect in the Mole role, never seemed to capitalise on his success and was rarely seen again.

The Secret Life Of TV

UK · BBC · SATIRE

1 × 5 mins · colour

31 Aug 1992 · BBC2 11.10pm

MAIN CAST

Victor Lewis-Smith

CREDITS

writer Victor Lewis-Smith · *director* Richard Curson Smith

A five-minute sketch screened within a themed BBC2 evening of awful programmes, *TV Hell. The Secret Life Of TV* was a spoof look at the workings that TV tries to keep hidden from the viewer. (See **Credible Credits** for more information.)

See also ***Inside Victor Lewis-Smith*** and *TV Offal.*

The Secret Policeman's Ball

The Secret Policeman's Biggest Ball

see The Amnesty Galas

See How They Run

UK · C4 (TVS/THEATRE OF COMEDY PRODUCTIONS) · FARCE

1 × 90 mins · colour

25 Dec 1984 · Tue 8.30pm

MAIN CAST

Bishop of Lax	Michael Denison
Penelope Toop	Liza Goddard
Miss Skillon	Maureen Lipman
Rev Arthur Humphrey	Derek Nimmo
Lt Cpl Clive Winton	Christopher Timothy
The intruder	Peter Blake
Ida	Carol Hawkins
Rev Lionel Toop	Royce Mills
Sgt Towers	Bill Pertwee
Willie Briggs	Steven Mackintosh

CREDITS

writer Philip King · *adapter* Ray Cooney · *directors* Les Chatfield/Ray Cooney · *executive producer* Michael Blakstad · *producer* Martin Schute

A TV version of the stage farce popular since 1945 about the comings and goings of clerics in an English vicarage during the Second World War, one of whom is an escaped Nazi prisoner-of-war in disguise.

See You Friday

UK · ITV (YORKSHIRE) · COMEDY SERIAL

6 × 30 mins · colour

9 May–13 June 1997 · Fri 8.30pm

MAIN CAST

Greg	Neil Pearson
Lucy	Joanna Roth
Bernie	Mark Benton
Sophie	Hermione Norris
Fiona	Daisy Bates
Daniel	Hugh Bonneville
Vanessa	Denise Welch
Dave	Trevor Fox
Rob	Neil Armstrong

CREDITS
writer Alan Whiting · *director* Simon Massey · *executive producer* David Reynolds · *producer* Lizzie Taylor

A more than competent six-part comedy that charted the wobbly romance of Greg and Lucy, who fall in love on the last day of a Greek holiday and try to continue the relationship back in England, against all their friends' predictions that holiday romances never last the distance.

The biggest complication is the physical distance between them – Lucy is at college in London, Greg is a policeman in Newcastle, 250 miles away from the capital. Both are reluctant to move, but, equally, they are determined for the relationship to succeed. Greg's working hours are unpredictable and Lucy's tatty car regularly breaks down, so meeting becomes a real problem. And that's not all: Greg's snobbish sister Fiona causes further difficulties and his colleagues' only interest in the affair is in taking bets on how long the encounter will last; Lucy's best friend – the surly Sophie – also seems to be agin the idea, but she does receive unbridled support from her gay flatmate, Daniel.

Stylishly shot, and without a studio audience or laugh-track, *See You Friday* was a cut above the usual fare and purposefully steered clear of easy laughs and smutty innuendo. The acting was uniformly good and the dialogue carried a realistic edge. Six episodes just about stretched the premise to breaking point, however, so it is hard to see how it might run to a second series.

Seinfeld

USA · NBC (WEST-SHAPIRO PRODUCTIONS/ CASTLE ROCK ENTERTAINMENT) · SITCOM

160 episodes (154×30 mins · 6×60 mins to 31/12/97 · continuing into 1998) · colour

US dates: 5 July 1989 (pilot); 31 May 1990 to date

UK dates: 6 Oct 1993 to date (70×30 mins · 3×60 mins to 31/12/97) BBC2 various days around 11.30pm

MAIN CAST

Jerry Seinfeld	himself
Elaine Benes	Julia Louis-Dreyfus
George Costanza	Jason Alexander
Cosmo Kramer	Michael Richards

OTHER APPEARANCES

Newman	Wayne Knight (from 1992)
Morty Seinfeld	Phil Bruns (1990); Barney Martin (from 1991)
Helen Seinfeld	Liz Sheridan
Frank Costanza	Jerry Stiller (from 1993)
Estelle Costanza	Estelle Harris (from 1992)
Uncle Leo	Len Lesser (from 1991)
J Peterman	John O'Hurley (from 1995)

CREDITS

creators Larry David/Jerry Seinfeld · *writers* Larry David, Larry David/Jerry Seinfeld, Larry Charles, Peter Mehlman, Alec Berg/Jeff Schaffer, Tom Gammill/Max Pross, Gregg Kavet/Andy Robin and others including Carol Leifer, David Mandel, Spike Feresten, Marjorie Gross, Tom Leopold, Bill Masters, Bob Shaw, Bruce Kirschbaum, Elaine Pope, Jennifer Crittenden, Lawrence H Levy, Marc Jaffe, Matt Goldman, Steve O'Donnell, Tom Gammill · *directors* Tom Cherones, Andy Ackerman and others, including David Owen Trainor, David Steinberg, Jason Alexander, Joshua White · *executive producers* Larry David, Andrew Scheinman, George Shapiro/Howard West, Jerry Seinfeld · *producers* Jerry Seinfeld, Andy Ackerman, Tim Kaiser, Suzy Mamann Greenberg

The sitcom art has not been explored much better than this. The seminal 'show about nothing', *Seinfeld* began quietly enough but eventually triumphed to become perhaps the most popular sitcom of all time in the USA.

Born in Brooklyn, New York, on 29 April 1955, Jerry Seinfeld had a blossoming career as a standup comedian, appearing often on TV – especially on *The Tonight Show* – before this sitcom elevated him to superstardom. He created *Seinfeld* with fellow standup Larry David (who stayed on board until 1996), and the concept first aired as *The Seinfeld Chronicles* (NBC, 5 July 1989). The series then got off to a rickety start in 1990, first as a four-week trial then as a limited run often 'pre-empted' (taken off so that another show could air). NBC knew they had *something* but nobody could really figure out what.

Jerry Seinfeld's stage act chiefly comprises his observations about the madness of life's idiosyncrasies; the sitcom *Seinfeld*'s premise was to adapt these views into stories – to this end, the episodes were light on plot (prompting the famed 'show about nothing' tag), but heavy on character and comic dialogue. Essentially, the episodes are about the minutiae of daily living, as experienced by four unmarried New Yorkers who, without particular responsibilities, obsess about the small things in life – queuing for the theatre, getting caught in traffic jams, being banned from a soup kitchen or a greengrocer's store, urinating in a health spa shower, buying a new suit, selling old suits, getting together with friends, and so on.

To make it work, Jerry Seinfeld and Larry David created a trio of friends with whom the Seinfeld character could engage; all four – their storylines expertly interwoven – meet regularly, either in Jerry's apartment, where they routinely raid his fridge, or in their favourite hang-out, a Manhattan street-corner deli, Monk's.

The first in the trio is the feisty Elaine, an ex-girlfriend and still close platonic friend of Jerry's. The pair split up because there was no physical chemistry between them, but they still have a great deal in common, making each other laugh and enjoying each other's company. Once in a while they consider (and even have) a sexual fling with one another, but for the main they keep separate sex lives (both quite active) that each has no problem in discussing with the other.

George, an old friend of Jerry's (they went to school together), is an intense, nervy man utterly devoid of scruples and always causing enormous problems for himself by making promises that he cannot keep or saying one thing while meaning another. George likes hanging around with Jerry because the comic is recognised from his TV appearances; for George, this is celebrity by association, a sort of passive fame. He is an eternal worrier with wild mood swings, a man who is never happy with his lot in life and seems determined (at least subconsciously) to keep it that way with his gross behaviour.

The third other character is Kramer, a friend because he has the apartment opposite Jerry's in the Manhattan block. (Although set in New York, episodes were shot in Hollywood, with a specially constructed Manhattan street set.) A wild physical specimen, Kramer is the antithesis of George. Tall, thin and with a shock of hair (George is short, chunky and balding), Kramer is an eternally optimistic individual, completely at ease with his lot. A spontaneous, fearless streak causes him to become involved in wild situations that often spin out of control, but his natural acceptance to go with the flow and make the best of any given circumstance usually sees him in good stead at the end.

Compared to these three, the Jerry Seinfeld character makes less of an impact. Verbally funny of course, he is more often the catalyst or the passive central player in the unfolding events. This unselfish device by Seinfeld really gives the show its wings, with the comedian as the hub, able to observe the chaos around him but not always being a part of it. Until the 1996–97 season, virtually every show was bookended or just opened by a snippet of Seinfeld's live act, in which he'd present a routine about that week's theme – here the line between reality and fiction was blurred as it was possible to view the comedian on stage as the real Jerry Seinfeld introducing the show or the character Jerry Seinfeld with a routine based on the events in that week's story. Either way, it worked.

Within three years *Seinfeld* had risen to become one of the biggest comedy hits in the USA – it had taken a while for the public to pick up on the style of the show but now they had got it they were crazy about it. In 1996 the US magazine *TV Guide* ran an article arguing that *Seinfeld* was the best sitcom of all time, a testament to the genius of the self-effacing Jerry Seinfeld and his ace support team. Certainly, Julia Louis-Dreyfus and Jason Alexander were faultless in their parts, delivering their lines in a perfect quick-talking New York idiom, twisting the dialogue to reap its maximum potential. But it was Michael

Richards, as Kramer, who virtually stole the show with his repertoire of exaggerated double-takes and odd physical comedy. Richards had impressed as the gangly janitor turned TV star in the 1989 satire movie *UHF* (and he also appeared in an episode of *Mad About You*) but in *Seinfeld* he took the art to a new plane, much to the delight of the studio audiences who greeted his lightning-paced entrances with whoops of delight.

The series succeeds on every conceivable level. Although named after Jerry Seinfeld, he is not the star: the series has four of them, and each player, equal to the others, is given a specific plot-idea in every episode. This premise works not only because the actors are good but also because the production unit, and Jerry Seinfeld's team of writers, are the best in the business, able to turn out 24 superb scripts a year and ever putting themselves on the line by setting new challenges, such as one 1997 episode, 'The Betrayal', in which the entire half-hour was planned backwards, beginning with an up-to-date scene and then tracking back over the seconds, minutes, hours, days, weeks, months and, ultimately, years, to reveal how the final situation had developed. Not since the first two seasons of **The Phil Silvers Show**, when its brilliant creator Nat Hiken was the principal writer, has a sitcom been blessed with such fine, tight, economical writing. Like an early *Bilko* episode, the best *Seinfeld* half-hours are wonders to behold, with not one line – not one *word* – going astray, and with so many diverse and apparently irrelevant plot strands and ideas, obvious or discreet, being tied up joyfully within 22 minutes. Jerry Seinfeld's very edict about his series – 'no hugs, no learning' – makes it, and him, stand out from the pack as something special, knowing and intelligent.

When, on Christmas Eve 1997, news leaked out that Jerry Seinfeld was cancelling the series effective from May 1998, America suffered collective shock and newspapers published major, front-page obituaries. 'A stunned nation prepares for life without *Seinfeld*,' declared the cover of *People* magazine, while *Time* delivered a similar eulogy. Most distressed of all was NBC: *Seinfeld* delivered the network not only massive ratings but captured, like so very few other shows, the 18–49 adult above-average-intelligence viewers so desirable to advertisers. NBC reputedly offered Jerry Seinfeld $5m per episode to keep it going (*Forbes* magazine already estimated his 1996 earnings as $66m), but the star's mind was made up: it was not a question of money but of timing – he wanted to end *Seinfeld* when it was ahead, while it was still in its prime, not when it had turned into a faded, past-its-date show. Few stars would make such a pressurised, fiscally obdurate decision, let

alone on such principled grounds, but then, few sitcoms have been as brilliant as *Seinfeld*.

Selwyn

see *Oh No – It's Selwyn Froggitt*

Sergeant Bilko

see *The Phil Silvers Show*

A Series Of Bird's

UK · BBC · SITCOMS
8 × 25 mins · b/w
3 Oct–21 Nov 1967 · BBC1 Tue 9.05pm

MAIN CAST
John Bird
John Fortune

CREDITS
writers John Fortune/John Bird · *additional material/script associates* Michael Palin/Terry Jones · *producer* Dennis Main Wilson

Following his rise in the short-lived satire boom in the early 1960s, actor/writer John Bird was given his own series and allowed carte blanche to steer it any way he chose. Typically, he came up with something new in the TV comedy genre: a series of unrelated satirical playlets, some coming across like sharp but traditional sitcoms, others spoofing television themes and one being an extended conversation on the state of the nation. Acting support came from guest stars, including Eleanor Bron and Warren Mitchell, while producer Dennis Main Wilson recruited Michael Palin and Terry Jones to help with the scripts, giving the two their first valuable opportunity to write narrative instead of short sketches. (Palin also appeared on camera.)

The result was an intriguing and clever slice of television, described by Bird as 'satire by the back door'. Unfortunately, this type of programme didn't fit into any of the established pigeon-holes at the BBC, and Bird and Fortune's determination to explore unconventional themes in an unorthodox style seemed to perplex the Light Entertainment department, which wasn't even certain if the programmes fitted that category.

A Series Of Bird's lasted just one series. However, *The Eric Giddings Story*, a spoof that looked at how a television documentary is made, which spread over two weeks in the series, was more successful than the other episodes; Bird later returned to the theme of satirising the mechanics of programme making – *viz* **The Leeds series**.

The Day Of The Revolution   3 OCT

GUEST CAST
Eleanor Bron, Warren Mitchell, Roland MacLeod, John Mulgrew, Arthur Mullard

The Plot Of Land   10 OCT

GUEST CAST
Roddy Maude-Roxby, Roland MacLeod, John Mulgrew

Here Come The Trendies   17 OCT

GUEST CAST
Roddy Maude-Roxby, Eleanor Bron, Pat Coombs

The Eric Giddings Story   24 OCT

GUEST CAST
John Warner, Roland MacLeod, Annabel Leventon

The Eric Giddings Story – 2, The Plot Thins   31 OCT

GUEST CAST
John Warner, Roland MacLeod, Patricia Denys

Back To The Front   7 Nov

GUEST CAST
Peter Cook

Urban Renewal   14 NOV

GUEST CAST
Lucy Griffiths, Roland MacLeod, Michael Palin, Roy Denton, Richard King, Aubrey Danvers-Walker

Lucid Intervals   21 NOV

GUEST CAST
George Romanov, Jerry Wayne, Michael Palin

John Sessions

Born John Marshall in Largs, Ayrshire, on 11 January 1953, John Sessions studied at Bangor University before completing a PhD in Toronto, Canada. Upon his return to Britain he joined RADA at the age of 26 and first made waves in the world of entertainment at the 1983 Edinburgh Festival Fringe. Soon after, in 1983–84, he performed satirical sketches in LWT's Janet Street-Porter/Hunter Davies live miscellany *After Midnight* and then used his brilliant improvisational skills in a C4 series about madness, and in particular the one-hour programme *The History Of Psychiatry* (1 October 1986). During the next few years Sessions worked as an actor as well as a comedy performer (in 1987 he had a one-man show in London, *The Life Of Napoleon*, in which he portrayed more than 30 characters) before making a major impact on TV viewers: first as the condom-inflating Zipser in Tom Sharpe's **Porterhouse Blue** and then as a regular competitor in C4's comedy parlour-game *Whose Line Is It Anyway?*

(from 23 September 1988) in which standup stars and guest celebrities improvised sketches from audience suggestions in styles chosen by host Clive Anderson. After this, Sessions was a star, with several humorous TV series as well as straight parts in stage, radio, TV and film dramas coming his way.

See also *Laugh??? I Nearly Paid My Licence Fee, Nice Day At The Office* and *Stella Street*.

John Sessions

UK · C4 (PAUL JACKSON PRODUCTIONS) · IMPROVISATIONAL

1 × 60 mins · colour
1 Jan 1988 · Fri 10pm

MAIN CAST
John Sessions

CREDITS
director/producer Paul Jackson

A one-man TV programme in which Sessions improvised a witty tour of the ages as charted by blockbuster films like *West Side Story* and *Out Of Africa*. (The programme was repeated on 1 July 1990 as *John Sessions Solo*.)

John Sessions On The Spot

UK · BBC · IMPROVISATIONAL

6 × 25 mins · colour
26 June–31 July 1989 · BBC2 Mon 9.45pm

MAIN CAST
John Sessions

CREDITS
director/producer Geoff Posner

John Sessions' success in *Whose Line Is It Anyway?* (BBC Radio 4 then C4) led to this BBC2 solo series, which once again illustrated the man's quick-thinking, fast-talking improvisational skills that had so impressed C4 audiences. In *On The Spot* Sessions took suggestions from the audience and wove sketches and monologues from the ideas, playing all the characters himself, and using his talents of mimicry and voice characterisation to enhance the effect.

John Sessions's Tall Tales

UK · BBC · MONOLOGUE

6 × 25 mins · colour
19 Jan–23 Feb 1991 · BBC2 Sat 9.30pm

MAIN CAST
John Sessions

CREDITS
writer John Sessions · *director/producer* Geoff Posner

Moving away from improvisation, Sessions this time penned six one-man comic plays and performed them for the TV cameras at the Half-Moon Theatre in London. Each one

allowed the actor to display his full range of mimicry talents and demonstrated the extraordinary lengths of imagination he could tap as a writer – the themes ranged from the story of a middle-aged painter who is convinced that he is irresistible to women, to a link-up between D H Lawrence and the Australian TV soap *Neighbours*.

In order of screening, the six productions were *Harold's Night Out, The Glory And The Dream, Don Juan In Cornwall, Neighbours And Lovers, There's Nowt So Queer As Folk* and *The Toy Shop*. After *Tall Tales* Sessions appeared in *Life With Eliza*, a 12-episode series of 10-minute programmes screened by BBC2 (20–31 December 1992), a part-monologue, part-acted whimsical offering written and directed by Beryl Richards and based on Barry Pain's *Eliza* stories.

John Sessions's Likely Stories

UK · BBC (POZZITIVE PRODUCTIONS) · MONOLOGUE

6 × 30 mins · colour
8 May–12 June 1994 · BBC2 Sun mostly 9pm

MAIN CAST
John Sessions

CREDITS
writer John Sessions · *director/producer* Geoff Posner

Six more comic playlets performed by Sessions. Themes this time included Gothic horror stories and an actor's encounter with small furry animals. In order of screening, the six productions were *Honey I Shrunk My Ego, Handsome Ted Has His Day, Corinna Discovers The World, The End Of The Story, Robert And Jackie* and *Lord Of The Isles*.

Set Of Six

UK · C4 (CHANNEL X) · SITCOMS

6 × 30 mins · colour
12 June–17 July 1990 · Tue 11.50pm

MAIN CAST
The Scrote Sextuplets · · · · · · Rowland Rivron
narrator · · · · · · · · · · · · · · · · · · Tony Bilbow

CREDITS
writers Ian Brown/Rowland Rivron · *directors* John Stroud (3), Gerald Scarfe (3) · *producer* Katie Lander

As with *Happy Families*, this series was designed for its star to portray a number of different members of the same family. In this case the actor was Rowland Rivron and his subject was the Scrote sextuplets, a motley bunch of flawed individuals, each one the subject of a mock fly-on-the-wall-style documentary.

First up was Dr Martin Scrote, a dubious quack whom Rivron had previously

portrayed in C4's humorous late-night chat-show *The Last Resort With Jonathan Ross*. In *Set Of Six* viewers were able to witness the doctor performing further medical mishaps and surgical screw-ups.

Next was David 'Top Shot' Scrote, staff photographer at the *Bexhill On Sea Observer*. David has the usual Scrote family traits – insensitivity and incompetence – and is dismissed from the paper after a series of errors, one being when he is sent to cover a wedding but instead goes to a funeral, his photos being staged in the same way ('Just the immediate family with the coffin'). David then goes to London but returns after a run-in with the film director Michael Winner, pictures of which, ironically, make the front pages.

The third in the series depicted the punch-drunk boxer Terry Scrote, a poor pugilist who hopes that the documentary will act as his gateway into the glamorous world of tomato ketchup ads.

Fourth in the frame was Ronnie Scrote, a self-styled south London 'supergrass'. Ronnie hopes to fly to Rio de Janeiro in order to escape the wrath of those he has 'shopped', but – owing to a typical Scrote family cock-up – he ends up in Iceland. But when the cold becomes too much he returns to Bermondsey to face the music.

Farmer Giles Scrote came next, a fey, walking disaster zone who has to manage his 600-acre farm alone after his wife walks out on him. Soon the holding has dwindled to just six acres, with Giles using the TV documentary as a means of advertising the farm's sale.

Last of all was Tarquin Scrote, one-time Tory MP for Felchcombe and Thorpe, now a destitute gentleman of the road desperate for alcohol and cigarettes.

Set Of Six was elegantly shot on film (three of the episodes were directed by the noted cartoonist Gerald Scarfe) and, at times, the comedy was hilarious. Rivron proved adept at handling the different guises, imbuing each family member with individual characteristics alongside their collective odious Scrote traits. Quite a low-key series, it deserved better scheduling.

The Setbacks

UK · ITV (THAMES) · SITCOM

25 episodes (13 × 10 mins · 12 × 15 mins) · colour

Series One (6 × 10 mins) 12 Mar–16 Apr 1980 · Wed 6.25pm

Series Two (7 × 10 mins) *The Seven Setbacks Of The Setbacks* 12 Oct–23 Nov 1981 · Mon 6.25pm

Series Three (4 × 15 mins) 13 Aug–21 Aug 1984 · Mon/Tue 6.20pm

Series Four (4 × 15 mins) 29 July–19 Aug 1985 · Mon 6.20pm

Series Five (4 × 15 mins) *Barry Setback And The Big Wide World* 28 July–18 Aug 1986 · Mon 6.20pm

MAIN CAST

Lily Setback · · · · · · Patsy Byrne (series 1–3); · · · · · · · · · · Patsy Rowlands (series 4 & 5)
Larry Setback · · · · John Cater (series 1 & 2); · · · · · · · · · · · · Robin Parkinson (series 3); · · · · · · · · · · · · · · · · Patrick Connor (series 4)
Mary Setback · · · · · Clare O'Neill (series 1); · · · · · · · · · · · · · Stella Goodier (series 4)
Sylvia Setback · · · Kim Taylforth (series 1–3)
Barry Setback · · · Andrew Paul (series 1 & 2); · · · · · · · · · · · · Glyn Grimstead (series 3–5)
Tony · · · · · · · · · · · John Blundell (series 1)
Mr Everyman (series 1)/ · · · · · · · · · · · · · · ·
Mr Everybody (series 2)/ · · · · · · · · · · · · · ·
other roles (series 3 & 4) · · · Reginald Marsh
Gordon · · · · · · · · · · · Roger Martin (series 2)
Gran · · · · · · · · · · · Mollie Maureen (series 2); · · · · · · · · · · · Una Brandon-Jones (series 4)
Carry · · · · · · · · · · · Elizabeth Adare (series 2)
Denis · · · · · · · · · Ashley Gunstock (series 5)
Trish · · · · · · · · Jacqueline de Peza (series 5)
Deborah · · · · · · · · Kate O'Connell (series 5)
various roles · · · · · · · Derek Royle (series 5)

CREDITS

writers Charlie Stafford (series 1 & 2), David Stafford (series 3–5) · director Alan Afriat · producers Simon Buxton (series 1–4), Alan Afriat (series 5)

A novel idea from Thames, which utilised a series of short sitcoms to dispense community advice to viewers. The programmes depicted the accident-prone Setback family: as they suffered society's pitfalls, viewers learned how they could avoid them or, at least, know their rights if they were in the same boat. The family members were dogged by misfortune but the mother/wife, Lily, steered them through troubled waters, aided by her knitting-bag full of advisory leaflets. (Viewers, in turn, could send away to Thames for fact-sheets that repeated the advice given in the stories.) Episodes related information about all manner of rights – at work, dealing with the Inland Revenue, unemployment, credit checks, and the workings of the NHS.

Note. Some of the episodes were compiled into half-hour editions and broadcast nationally on C4 from 30 September 1986.

See also *Casting Off*.

704 Hauser

USA · CBS (ACT III TELEVISION/CASTLE ROCK ENTERTAINMENT/COLUMBIA) · SITCOM

6 × 30 mins · colour

US dates: 11 Apr 1994–9 May 1994 (5 episodes)
UK dates: 13 Sep–18 Oct 1994 (6 episodes) C4 Tue mostly 11.50pm

MAIN CAST

Ernest Cumberbatch · · · · · · · · · John Amos
Rose Cumberbatch · · · · · · · Lynnie Godfrey
Thurgood Marshall 'Goodie' Cumberbatch · T E Russell
Cherlyn Markowitz · · · · · · · · · Maura Tierney

CREDITS

creator/writer/director Norman Lear · executive producers Norman Lear, Mark E Pollack, Roger Shulman, John Baskin · producer Patricia Fass Palmer

More than 20 years after the address first became famous on US TV as the Bunkers' home in *All In The Family*, the producer Norman Lear used the house – in Queens, New York – as the setting for a 1990s variation on warring family generations. (The British equivalent would be a new sitcom set in Alf and Else Garnett's old house in Wapping.)

The political and racial balance was reversed this time, with the black parents Ernest and Rose Cumberbatch being liberals and their son 'Goodie' an ultra-right conservative, dating a white Jewish girl, Cherlyn Markowitz. Thus the scene was set for raging inter-family conflict, with extra ingredients (as if they were needed) coming from Rose's dedication to her church, and Cherlyn's determination to marry Goodie in spite of her own parents' rejection of him (on account of his politics, *not* his colour or religion).

The link with the Bunkers was marked by a guest appearance in the first episode by Archie's son-in-law Joey Stivic (played this time by Casey Siemaszko). However, although there were many similarities between the two series in terms of content, *704 Hauser* failed to make anything like the impact of *All In The Family* and disappeared from the US schedules after just five episodes. Six were shown in the UK (where the series was alternatively titled *704 Hauser Street*).

The Seven Faces Of Jim

see *Faces Of Jim*

Seven Of One

UK · BBC · SITCOMS

7 × 30 mins · colour

25 Mar–6 May 1973 · BBC2 Sun mostly 8.15pm

Seven comedy one-offs starring Ronnie Barker, who had fronted similar ITV series *The Ronnie Barker Playhouse* in 1968 and *Six Dates With Barker* in 1971. *Seven Of One* was a marvellously successful venture, leading to two long-lasting series, *Open All Hours* and *Porridge*.

Open All Hours   25 MAR

See that programme for information.

Prisoner And Escort   1 APR

See *Porridge* for information.

My Old Man   8 APR

MAIN CAST

Sam Cobbett · · · · · · · · · · · · · Ronnie Barker
Doris · Ann Beach
Arthur · · · · · · · · · · · · · · · · Graham Armitage

CREDITS

writer Gerald Frow · executive producer James Gilbert · producer Sydney Lotterby

How will Sam Cobbett survive in retirement after 30 years as an engine driver? (The BBC declined to develop this idea further so writer Gerald Frow took it to Yorkshire TV where it became a series for Clive Dunn – see *My Old Man*.)

Spanner's Eleven   15 APR

MAIN CAST

Albert Spanner · · · · · · · · · · · Ronnie Barker
Councillor Morgan Todd · · · · · · · Bill Maynard
Vera Spanner · · · · · · · · · · · Priscilla Morgan
Horace the Vet · · · · · · · · · · · · · · John Cater

CREDITS

writer Roy Clarke · executive producer James Gilbert · producer Harold Snoad

Albert Spanner is a football fanatic, whose team, Ashfield, is anchored at the bottom of the league.

Another Fine Mess   22 APR

MAIN CAST

Harry Norvel · · · · · · · · · · · · · · Ronnie Barker
Sydney Jefferson · · · · · · · · · · · · · Roy Castle
Doris Norvel · · · · · · · · · · · · · · Avis Bunnage
Cissie · · · · · · · · · · · · · · · · Margery Mason
Neighbour · · · · · · · · · · · · · · · Pearl Hackney
Edwina · · · · · · · · · · · · · · · · Pauline Delany

CREDITS

writer Hugh Leonard · executive producer James Gilbert · producer Harold Snoad

An opportunity for Ronnie Barker and Roy Castle to effect an impersonation of Laurel and Hardy. No series was intended by the stars here – they simply wanted to pay homage to the everlasting comic giants. (The surnames were appropriate: Norvel – actually Norvell – was Hardy's middle name, Jefferson was Laurel's real surname.)

One Man's Meat   29 APR

MAIN CAST

Alan Joyce · · · · · · · · · · · · · · · Ronnie Barker
Daily woman · · · · · · · · · · · · · · · Joan Sims
Marion Joyce · · · · · · · · · Prunella Scales
Police Sergeant · · · · · · · · · · Glynn Edwards
Police photographer · · · · · · · · · · Sam Kelly

CREDITS

writer Jack Goetz (Ronnie Barker) · executive producer James Gilbert · producer Harold Snoad

Alan Joyce is forced on a starvation diet by his wife. (The writer, Jack Goetz, was Ronnie Barker hiding under another pen name.)

I'll Fly You For A Quid 6 MAY

MAIN CAST
Evan Owen/Grandpa Owen · · · · Ronnie Barker
Rev Simmonds · · · · · · · · · · · · Emrys James
Mortlake Owen · · · · · · · Richard O'Callaghan
Mrs Owen · · · · · · · · · · · · · Margaret John
Mr Pugh · · · · · · · · · · · · · · Talfryn Thomas
April Owen · · · · · · · · · · · · · · · Beth Morris
Auntie · · · · · · · · · · · · · · · · Gwyneth Owen

CREDITS
writers Dick Clement/Ian La Frenais · executive producer James Gilbert · producer Sydney Lotterby

Gambling fanatic Evan Owen is distraught when his father dies – because he is certain that a winning betting slip is concealed somewhere on the corpse. The episode was set in a Welsh mining village, and Ronnie Barker played two roles – the dying old miner grandfather and his son Evan. (This was intended as the premiere episode in *Seven Of One* but was postponed and replaced by *Open All Hours*.)

Seven Year Hitch

UK · BBC · SITCOM
1 × 30 mins · b/w
28 June 1966 · BBC1 Tue 7.30pm
MAIN CAST
Ernest 'Ern' Conway · · · · · · Harry H Corbett
Isabel 'Is' Conway · · · · · · · · · · · Joan Sims
Deirdre · · · · · · · · · · · · · · · · · Dawn Beret
Mr Swann · · · · · · · · · · · · · · · Derek Royle

CREDITS
writer Fred Robinson · producer Vere Lorrimer

A *Comedy Playhouse* one-off by Fred Robinson (writer of **The Larkins**) starring Harry H Corbett as Ern, the somewhat pompous proprietor of an unsuccessful dance school. Joan Sims was cast as his wife, with whom Ern is constantly at loggerheads.

The previous time Corbett appeared in a *Comedy Playhouse* pilot it led to **Steptoe And Son**. He had no such luck this time.

Sez Les

see DAWSON, Les

Shall We Gather At The River

UK · C4 (ETC PRODUCTIONS) · SITCOM
1 × 30 mins · colour
24 June 1992 · Wed 10.30pm
MAIN CAST
Herbert Alcock · · · · · · · · · · · · Gwilym Cox
Mrs Alcock · · · · · · · · · · · Rosemary Leach
Gran · · · · · · · · · · · · · · · · · · Beryl Reid
Hedley · · · · · · · · · · · Michael Troughton
Mr Strathclyde · · · · · · · · · Francis Matthews

CREDITS
writer Timothy Keen · director John Henderson · producer Esta Charkham

One of C4's *Bunch Of Five* sitcom pilots. *Shall We Gather At The River?* (the title was taken from a hymn) was a downbeat comedy about a funeral-obsessed man, Herbert. His asthmatic mother despairs at what she considers to be his morbid fascination, whereas he claims that he gatecrashes funerals only to listen to the hymns. Herbert's virtually bedridden grandmother (played by Beryl Reid) empathises with him because she too has a somewhat unusual interest in the rituals of internment.

An oddball offering, reminiscent of the cult movie *Harold And Maude* (1971, director Hal Ashby), in which a death-obsessed teenager befriends a wacky octogenarian with a similar interest.

Shamrot

UK · BBC · SITCOM
1 × 30 mins · b/w
19 Oct 1963 · Sat 9.45pm
MAIN CAST
Dermot · · · · · · · · · · · · · · · Dermot Kelly
Woman · · · · · · · · · · · · · Kathleen Harrison
'Coloured boy' · · · · · · · · · Thomas Baptiste
Man in labour exchange · · · · · Arthur Mullard
First Irishman · · · · · · · · · · · Alan Simpson
Second Irishman · · · · · · · · · · · Tony Doyle

CREDITS
writer Johnny Speight · producer Philip Barker

A *Comedy Playhouse* one-off from Johnny Speight, characteristically imbued with more than a dab of controversy.

Dermot is a London-born but British-hating Irishman. He has never been to Ireland but this doesn't stop him being aggressively Irish, even to the extent that he refuses to get a job as it would help Britain's prosperity. Rather, he stays on the dole, reckoning that every penny he takes helps to destroy the British economy.

Sharon And Elsie

UK · BBC · SITCOM
12 × 30 mins · colour
Series One (6) 27 Jan–9 Mar 1984 · BBC1 Fri mostly 7.55pm
Series Two (6) 21 June–26 July 1985 · BBC1 Fri 8.30pm
MAIN CAST
Elsie Beecroft · · · · · · · · · · · Brigit Forsyth
Sharon Wilkes · · · · · · · · · · Janette Beverley
Stanley · · · · · · · · · · · · · · · · John Landry
Ivy · · · · · · · · · · · · · · · · · Maggie Jones
Elvis Wilkes · · · · · · · · · · · · · Lee Daley
Tommy Wallace · · · · · · · · · · · John Junkin
Roland Beecroft · · · · · · · · Bruce Montague
Ike · · · · · · · · · · · · · · · · Gordon Rollings
Wayne · · · · · · · · · · · · · · · · · John Wild
Mrs Tibbett · · · · · · · · · · · · Paula Tilbrook
Olive · · · · · · · · · · · · · · · Carmel McSharry
Enid · · · · · · · · · · · · · · · · · · Diana King

CREDITS
writer Arline Whittaker · executive producer Roger Race (series 2) · directors/producers Roger Race (series 1), Mike Stephens (series 2)

Elsie Beecroft is set in her ways. A Manchester lass, she believes that she is 'a cut above the rest', with a well-organised home and job at Blakes And Sons, printers of greeting cards and calendars. But she is shaken out of her complacency by the arrival of Sharon Wilkes, a young, spiky, 'punk like' school leaver, employed as the firm's new secretary. Elsie and Sharon have opposing views on almost everything, opinions formed by their respective ages and social backgrounds. Nevertheless, a friendship develops and both begin, albeit grudgingly, to see the other's point of view. Elsie soon comes to question the beliefs that she held firm, including such fundamentals as the nature of marriage, families and the work ethic.

Sharon And Elsie gave a starring role to Brigit Forsyth, who had offered sterling support as Thelma, a character endowed with similar attributes, in **Whatever Happened To The Likely Lads**. Elsie's husband was played by Bruce Montague (the would-be seducer in **Butterflies**) and John Landry played Sharon and Elsie's work colleague Stanley. Wayne was Sharon's on–off love interest and Lee Daley her handful of a brother, Elvis.

The Sharp End

UK · BBC · SITCOM
8 × 50 mins · colour
12 Apr–31 May 1991 · BBC1 Fri 9.30pm
MAIN CAST
Celia Forrest · · · · · · · · · · · · · Gwen Taylor
Carmichael · · · · · · · · · · · · · James Cosmo
Andy Barras · · · · · · · · · Philip Martin Brown
Celia's mother · · · · · · · · · · · · Clare Kelly
Wendy Forrest · · · · · · · · · · · · Rachel Egan
Crystal · · · · · · · · · · · · · · · · Gaynor Faye

CREDITS
writer Roy Clarke · directors Brian Parker (4), David Penn (4) · producer Fiona Finlay

A darker-in-tone sitcom from Roy Clarke, running 50 minutes per episode instead of the standard half-hour. Not entirely successful, it enjoyed plenty of good moments.

Gwen Taylor starred as Celia Forrest, who – upon her father's death – realises with horror that she has inherited his business, a dilapidated debt-collection agency. Neither her bereaved mother nor her stroppy teenage daughter, Wendy, believes that she can handle the task, and rival debt collector Andy Barras impresses upon her his belief that it is no job for a woman. But Celia is headstrong and determines to rise to the challenge. Taking on one of her debtors, the dyslexic Carmichael, as an assistant, she is soon out and about in the Yorkshire town of Rawthorne, in pursuance of those who fail to pay (leaving the office in the barely capable hands of a secretary, Crystal). The clashes and problems she encounters while doing so are almost outweighed by the quarrels she has with the fiery Carmichael, but gradually a grudging fondness grows between them.

A Sharp Intake Of Breath

UK · ITV (ATV) · SITCOM
22 × 30 mins · colour
Pilot · 28 July 1977 · Thu 7pm
Series One (6) 20 Feb–27 Mar 1978 · Mon 8pm
Series Two (6) 19 Feb–26 Mar 1979 · Mon 8pm
Series Three (3) 4 Jan–18 Jan 1980 · Fri 8.30pm
Series Four (6) 11 Jan–15 Feb 198 · Sun 7.15pm

MAIN CAST
Peter Barnes · · · · · · · · · · · · · David Jason
Sheila Barnes · · · · · · · · · Jacqueline Clarke
various roles · · · Richard Wilson (series 1–3)
various roles · · Alun Armstrong (series 1 & 2)

CREDITS
creator Ronnie Taylor · writers Ronnie Taylor (14), Vince Powell (6), Kenneth Cope (1), Leslie Duxbury (1) · cartoons Mel Calman · directors/producers Les Chatfield (series 1 & 2), Stuart Allen (series 3 & 4)

Following his success as support to Ronnie Barker in the BBC's **Open All Hours**, and just before taking off as Del Boy in **Only Fools and Horses**, David Jason starred in this ITV sitcom as Peter Barnes, a hapless Mr Average character, ever trying to beat officialdom and red tape. Sharing in his frustrations were his wife Sheila (Jacqueline Clarke) but against him were Richard Wilson and Alun Armstrong, the pair showing up each week in different roles that defeated Jason's incompetent war against bureaucracy.

First seen in the ITV pilots season *The Sound Of Laughter*, the series was created by comic stalwart Ronnie Taylor but his sudden and unexpected death caused the third series to be aborted after only three episodes. The final series was written by the equally venerable Vince Powell.

An American adaptation of *A Sharp Intake Of Breath* – titled *Harry's Battles* – was screened there as a pilot by ABC on 8 June 1981. It starred Dick Van Dyke as Harry Fitzsimmons, the manager of a Pittsburgh supermarket who is permanently entangled in bureaucracy. No series developed.

Sheep's Clothing

UK · BBC · SITCOM
7 × 30 mins · b/w
13 June–5 Sep 1957 · fortnightly Thu mostly 7.30pm

MAIN CAST
Digby Wolfe · · · · · · · · · · · · · · · · · himself
Lita Roza · · · · · · · · · · · · · · · · · · · herself

Valet · · · · · · · · · · · · · · · · · Ronnie Corbett
various roles · · · · · · · · · · · · · · Larry Taylor

CREDITS
writers Sid Green/Dick Hills · producer Russell Turner

In 1956, the fast-rising, enterprising comedian Digby Wolfe appeared in ATV's punningly titled *Wolfe At The Door*, a 12-part sketch series, not screened in London but which ran in the Midlands from 18 June to 10 September 1956. In this, Wolfe explored the comic situations that could be found by passing through doorways – into a theatrical dressing-room, for example. Charles Hawtrey and Hattie Jacques aided the fun, which was written by Tony Hawes (gags) and Richard Waring (situations). Among other ITV appearances this same year, Wolfe occasionally compered *Variety Startime*, and provided the humour while Edmundo Ros and his Orchestra delivered the melody in *Mirth And Maracas*, a one-off show screened on 14 March 1956.

One year on, the BBC networked a new programme, *Sheep's Clothing* (titled thus so that the screen announcer could introduce the editions as 'And now, Digby Wolfe in *Sheep's Clothing*'). A sitcom written by Sid Green and Dick Hills, Wolfe was cast as a 'rather genteel wide-boy', who, faced with the prospect of enforced employment, was determined to start at the top – where work was 'at a minimum and rewards were at a maximum'. The singer Lita Roza played Wolfe's girlfriend and Ronnie Corbett his 'gentleman's gentleman', a double-act routine that Corbett and Wolfe had first developed in *The Yana Show*, a BBC variety programme hosted by that particular singer.

British, but born in Norway, Wolfe eventually left the UK and established himself as a headlining star in Australia. A pay dispute there caused him to move on once more, this time to the USA, where he achieved further success in his chosen field, most notably as one of the backroom team behind **Rowan And Martin's Laugh-In**.

Sheila

UK · C4 (REGENT PRODUCTIONS) · SKETCH
1 × 60 mins · colour
4 Dec 1982 · Sat 7.15pm

MAIN CAST
Sheila Steafel

CREDITS
writers Keith Waterhouse, Barry Cryer, Dick Vosburgh/Frank Lazarus, Andy Hamilton, Alistair Beaton · director/producer William G Stewart

A richly merited solo special for the fine actress/comedian Sheila Steafel, born in Johannesburg (26 May 1935) but who has lived her adult life in Britain. Hitherto a sterling member of umpteen 'supporting

casts', here she portrayed a number of characters written for her by top writers, some leased from her one-woman stage-show (*Steafel*), others created especially for this programme.

Shelley

UK · ITV (THAMES) · SITCOM
71 × 30 mins · colour
*Series One (7) 12 July–2 Aug 1979; 17 Apr–1 May 1980 · Thu mostly 9.30pm
Series Two (6) 8 May–18 June 1980 · Thu around 10.40pm
Special · 22 Dec 1980 · Mon 8pm
Series Three (7) 29 Dec 1980–9 Feb 1981 · Mon 8pm
Series Four (6) 18 Feb–1 Apr 1982 · Thu 9pm
Series Five (6) 4 Nov–9 Dec 1982 · Thu 8pm
Series Six (6) 1 Dec 1983–12 Jan 1984 · Thu mostly 8pm
Series Seven (6) *The Return Of Shelley* 11 Oct–15 Nov 1988 · Tue 8.30pm
Series Eight (13) 17 Oct 1989–9 Jan 1990 · Tue 8.30pm
Series Nine (6) 24 Sep–29 Oct 1990 · Mon 9pm
Special · 1 Jan 1991 · Tue 10.15pm
Series Ten (6) 28 July–1 Sep 1992 · Tue 8.30pm

MAIN CAST
James Shelley · · · · · · · · · · · Hywel Bennett
Frances Smith/Shelley · · · · · Belinda Sinclair
· (series 1–6)
Edna Hawkins · · · · · · · · · Josephine Tewson
· (series 1–6)

OTHER APPEARANCES
Gordon Smith · · · · · · · · · · · Frederick Jaeger
· (series 1–6)
Isobel Shelley · · · · · · Sylvia Kay (series 1–6)
Paul England · · · · Warren Clarke (series 1–6)
Desmond · · · · · Garfield Morgan (series 1–6)
Carol · · · · · Caroline Langrishe (series 7 & 8)
Graham · · · · · · Andrew Castell (series 7 & 8)
Phil · · · · · · · · · · Stephen Hoye (series 8 & 9)
Ted Bishop · · · · · David Ryall (series 9 & 10)
George · · · · · · · James Grout (series 9 & 10)

CREDITS
creator Peter Tilbury · writers Peter Tilbury (22), Andy Hamilton (17), Andy Hamilton/Guy Jenkin (3), Guy Jenkin (16), Barry Pilton (10), Bernard McKenna (1), Colin Bostock-Smith (1), David Firth (1) · director/producer Anthony Parker

Among the longest-running of all ITV sitcoms, *Shelley* centred unmistakably on a single actor, Hywel Bennett. Despite the arrival and departure of many support characters, Bennett's Shelley remained the sharp focus: ever the idle philosopher, cynically rejecting or questioning the norm with witty one-liners delivered in a laconic, resigned, London accent. Shelley scored with the viewers – who, after a slow start, greatly warmed to the character – because his often profound views on everyday life, while rooted in laziness, struck a chord.

When the first series began, James Shelley was a 28-year-old undergraduate malcontent, whose determination not to pay income tax – even though it had funded his education for three years – caused him to resolve pursuance of a life of un- or under-employment. He and his girlfriend, Frances (Fran) had moved into a tiny north London bedsit where Shelley's verbal dexterity and jaded views failed to impress the stern landlady, Mrs Hawkins. From here on in the die was cast: whatever life threw at Our Hero he remained his same sardonic self, never considering that his slothful indifference to work should rob him of his right to have forthright opinions about the rights and wrongs of life and other people's existence. Like the famous poet of the same name, indeed, Shelley felt that he was being persecuted in his lifetime.

Fran then became pregnant, they married, moved home and, at the end of the third series, Fran delivered unto Shelley a baby, Emma (named after Bennett's own real-life daughter). But not even the arrival of a dependant could imbue in Shelley a sense of responsibility and, at the start of the fifth series, Fran kicked him out, insisting that he shouldn't return until he had proved himself capable of looking after his wife and child. Shelley, of course, was unchangeable and, after moving in temporarily with his best man, Paul, the series appeared to have ended when Shelley went off to America.

Although that seemed to be that, a long run of repeats kept *Shelley* in the public eye and, approaching five years on, the series was revived for what would become 32 new episodes. As before, with Shelley unable to stick a job for long enough to gather any savings (he had, for a short while, worked at the Foreign Office and then gone into temping), he had to live in shared accommodation (actually, a neat way of providing the scriptwriters with a changing cast of characters). Mrs Hawkins was now off the scene but, in her place were Graham and Carol, upwardly mobile yuppies of the type that Shelley was unfamiliar with, having quit Britain before the dawn of Thatcher's Eighties. Back in Blighty after five years of teaching English – first in America and then the Arab Emirates – Shelley was quite unprepared for what had befallen his home country, a place where money was everything (and he, of course, had none) and where crime was on the increase – he was even mugged in one of the episodes. Now over 40-years-old, Shelley had essentially the same views on life as before and, except for his landlords – in the final two series he lodged with the slightly kooky OAP widower Ted Bishop – he was truly alone. Fran and Emma, oft referred to and occasionally spoken to by phone, were now living in Canada.

Peter Tilbury created *Shelley* after experiencing life on the dole and finding that his education counted for little at that time. After writing the first three series, however, he went off to write *Sorry, I'm A Stranger Here Myself*, and write/appear in *It Takes A Worried Man*, and handed *Shelley* over to others. Andy Hamilton (who appeared in one episode), Guy Jenkin and Barry Pilton scripted the majority of the remainder. (Together, Hamilton and Jenkin would later create *Drop The Dead Donkey*.)

*Notes. The first series of *Shelley* was interrupted after four weeks by the strike that blanked out ITV in the late summer of 1979. The remaining three episodes were shown as a prelude to the second series, of six episodes, making for a nine-week run.

Five years after ending on TV, *Shelley* was revived by BBC Radio 2 in a six-part series broadcast 22 May–26 June 1997. Performing scripts especially adapted for the new medium, Stephen Tompkinson was cast as the philosophical idler and Gina McKee as Fran, with Maggie Steed appearing as landlady Mrs Hawkins and other parts taken by the likes of Kate Robbins, Phil Nice, Phil Cornwell and Howard Lew Lewis.

Shelley Berman

UK · BBC · STANDUP

3 × 45 mins (2 × b/w · 1 × colour)
3 Dec 1961 · Sun 9.15pm (b/w)
4 Jan 1966 · BBC1 Tue 8.50pm (b/w)
6 June 1968 · BBC2 Fri 9.05pm (colour)

MAIN CAST
Shelley Berman

CREDITS
writer Shelley Berman · *producers* Bryan Sears (shows 1 & 2), John Street (show 3)

Born in Chicago on 3 February 1926, Shelley Berman performed in 'legitimate' theatre before forming an improvisational comedy trio with Mike Nichols and Elaine May. In 1957 he went solo and quickly established himself as one of the finest practitioners of the art of the comedy monologue – his casual stage presence, allied to his acute sensitivity, enabling him to pick on subjects that struck an anxious chord with audiences, giving him the edge over his contemporaries.

These BBC shows, the first of which was made at the urging of Frank Muir and Denis Norden, gave the US comic a rare chance to present his material in long form rather than in the ten-minute slots available to him on US TV; this, he admitted, was the decisive factor in his coming to London.

She's The Sheriff

USA · NBC/SYNDICATED · (LORIMAR TELEPICTURES) · SITCOM

48 × 30 mins · colour
US dates: 15 Sep 1987–spring 1989

UK dates: 4 Sep 1989–31 Dec 1991 (21 episodes) BBC1 Mon 3.35pm then daily 8.40am

MAIN CAST

Sheriff Hildy Granger	Suzanne Somers
Deputy Max Rubin	George Wyner
Gussie Holt	Pat Carroll
Kenny Granger	Taliesin Jaffe
Allison Granger	Nicky Rose
Deputy Dennis Putnam	Lou Richards
Deputy Hugh Mulcahy	Guich Koock
Deputy Alvin Wiggins	Leonard Lightfoot

CREDITS
writers Mark Rothman, Mark Miller, Juliet Packer, Harry O'Brien · *directors* Alan Rafkin, Doug Smart · *executive producer* Alan Hamel · *producers* Mark Rothman, David Goldsmith

By the late 1980s, single mothers struggling to raise their children were commonplace in US sitcoms, whether they were divorcees or, as in this case, widows.

When her husband dies, Hildy Granger takes over his job as the sheriff of Lakes County, Nevada. Most of the male deputies accept her well enough, but one of them, Max Rubin, is bitterly resentful of the appointment and does his best to disgrace her. At home, the energetic Gussie, Hildy's mother, is on hand to look after children Kenny and Allison while mom is out upholding the law.

Notes. A pilot for *She's The Sheriff*, titled *Cass Malloy*, was aired in the USA by CBS on 21 July 1982, with Caroline McWilliams in the lead role. It took some years to progress the project further but the subsequent series was set to star Priscilla Barnes as the sheriff. Shortly before production began, however, Somers was brought in as her replacement. The move was ironic: Barnes had replaced Somers in *Three's Company* in 1981.

She's The Sheriff was one of the five sitcoms chosen by NBC to 'checkerboard' across its weekday schedules in autumn 1987 – see also *Out Of This World* and, for details, *Marblehead Manor*.

Shillingbury Tales

UK · ITV (ATV) · SITCOM

6 × 60 mins · colour
17 May–21 June 1981 · Sun 7.15pm

MAIN CAST

Peter	Robin Nedwell
Sally	Diane Keen
Jake	Jack Douglas
Mandy	Linda Hayden
Terry	Lilian Verner
Harvey	Joe Black
Rev Norris	Nigel Lambert

OTHER APPEARANCES

Cuffy	Bernard Cribbins
Marjorie Cavendish	Mona Washbourne

CREDITS
writer Francis Essex · *director* Val Guest · *producer* Greg Smith

Shot on 35mm film, without an audience or laugh-track, *Shillingbury Tales* was a comedy with a light-dramatic touch that depicted modern life in a typical English village: its pub, pond and people, its rumours, scandals and preservation campaigns. The main star was Robin Nedwell, cast as pop musician Peter Higgins who moves into the village of Shillingbury with his wife Sally. Their arrival threatens to upset the rustic apple cart but life goes on much as it had before.

The series followed a full-length made-for TV movie, *The Shillingbury Blowers*, produced by Sir Lew Grade's Inner Circle company and screened by ITV on 6 January 1980. Nedwell, Keen and Jack Douglas all featured, as did Trevor Howard. The writer of both film and series was Francis Essex, the music composer who had moved into TV production and then management; the director in both instances was Val Guest, the vastly experienced man behind all manner of British films since 1943.

As well as the regular cast, each episode of *Shillingbury Tales* – filmed on location in the Hertfordshire village of Aldbury, near Berkhamsted – featured one or more guest stars, including Diana King and Lionel Jeffries. Bernard Cribbins twice appeared as Cuffy, a tinker who resided in a ramshackle caravan. The character proved so interesting that a spin-off series evolved in 1983, *Cuffy*.

Shine A Light

UK · ITV (YORKSHIRE) · SITCOM

6 × 30 mins · colour

1 Apr–27 May 1970 · Wed mostly 10.30pm

MAIN CAST
Wally Trott · · · · · · · · · · · · · Timothy Bateson
Les Robinson · · · · · · · · · · · · · · · Tony Selby
OTHER APPEARANCES
Taffy Lewis · · · · · · · · · · · · · · · Howell Evans

CREDITS
writers David Nobbs/David McKellar/Peter Vincent · *director* Bill Hays · *executive producer* John Duncan

A series about two lighthousemen cooped up together, miles out at sea on (the fictitious) Bachelor Rock lighthouse, and the comedic situations that their unusual form of co-habitation force upon them. Wal is the senior of the two, Les his junior, they don't get on at all well and there are an *awful* lot of stairs to go down and up in order to fetch and carry.

Virtually all of the comedy was played out between the two, the only relief coming from the visiting captain of a supply ship, Taffy Lewis, and, in one episode, the appearance of a relief lighthouseman (played by John Le Mesurier). In the final episode Les was posted to another lighthouse.

Shine On Harvey Moon

UK · ITV (WITZEND PRODUCTIONS/CENTRAL · *WITZEND PRODUCTIONS/MERIDIAN) · COMEDY SERIAL

35 episodes (12 × 30 mins · 23 × 60 mins) · colour

Series One (6 × 30 mins) 8 Jan–12 Feb 1982 · Fri 8.30pm
Series Two (6 × 60 mins) 10 Sep–15 Oct 1982 · Fri 9pm
Series Three (9 × 60 mins) 1 June–27 July 1984 · Fri 9pm
Series Four (8 × 60 mins) 5 July–23 Aug 1985 · Fri 9pm
*Series Five (6 × 30 mins) 23 Apr–28 May 1995 · Sun 8.30pm

MAIN CAST
Harvey Moon · · · · · · · · · · Kenneth Cranham
· (series 1–4);
· · · · · · · · · · · · · Nicky Henson (series 5)
Nan · · · · · · · · · · · · · · Elizabeth Spriggs
Rita Moon · · · · · · · · · · · · · Maggie Steed
Maggie Moon · · · · · · · · · · · · Linda Robson
Stanley Moon · · · · · · · · · · · Lee Whitlock
Lou Lewis · · · · · · Nigel Planer (not series 4)

OTHER APPEARANCES
Harriet Wright · · · · · · Fiona Victory (series 1)
Reginald Merrick · · · · · · · Bernard Gallagher
· (series 2)
Monty Fish · · · · · · · · Linal Haft (series 2 & 3)
Aunt Hilda · · · · · · Monica Grey (series 2 & 3)
Mr Hartley · · Christopher Benjamin (series 2)
Connie Rosenthal · · Dudley Sutton (series 2)
Frieda Gottlieb · · · · · · · · · · · Suzanne Bertish
· (series 3 & 4)
Erich Gottlieb · · · · Leonard Fenton (series 3)
Dick Elliot · · · · · Clive Merrison (series 3 & 4)
Mr Compton · · · · · · Roger Brierley (series 3)
Leo Brandon · · Mark Kingston (series 3 & 4)
Mrs Brandon · · · · · · · Gwen Nelson (series 3)
Ryder · · · · · · · · · Albert Welling (series 3 & 4)
Miss Sprake · · · · Marlene Sidaway (series 3)
Kitty · · · · · · · · Maureen O'Farrell (series 3)
Veronica · · · · · · · · Pauline Quirke (series 3–5)
Janice · · · Michele Winstanley (series 3 & 4)
Geoff Barratt · · · · · Tenniel Evans (series 4)
Quentin Elliot · · · · · · David Garth (series 4)
Alfie · · · · · · · · · · · Glen Murphy (series 4)
Noah Hawksley · · · · Colin Salmon (series 5)
Avis · · · · · · · · · · · Marion Bailey (series 5)
Roy · · · · · · · · · · · · · · Lee Ross (series 5)
Derek · · · · · · · · · · · · · Ian Dunn (series 5)
Marjorie · · · · · · · Sophie Staunton (series 5)

CREDITS
creators Laurence Marks/Maurice Gran · *writers* Laurence Marks/Maurice Gran (series 1–3, 2 eps in series 4, 2 eps in series 5), Alan Clews (3 eps in series 4), Francis Megahy (2 eps in series 4), Barry Lamoto (1 ep in series 4), Dick Clement/Ian La Frenais (3 eps in series 5), Gary Lawson/John Phelps (1 ep in series 5) · *script editors* Dick Clement/Ian La Frenais (series 1 & 2) · *director* Baz Taylor · *executive producer* Allan McKeown · *producer* Tony Charles

This first great series from Marks and Gran was not *exactly* a sitcom. Rather, *Shine On Harvey Moon* was a humorous evocation of one family's life – the characters, the situations, the predicaments. No studio

audience was employed but, for sure, there was end-to-end humour and some scorching lines in every script. While the first and last series were sitcom-style half-hours, the remaining episodes were hour-length, allowing room for the writers to stretch out.

This is the premise: the Second World War has ended, and on 9 November 1945 Corporal Harvey Moon is demobilised and returns home to Hackney, east London, having served His Majesty's Forces in relative safety: as a stores clerk for the RAF in Bombay. Everyone believes him to be dead, killed in action, so plenty of goings-on have been going on in his absence: his wife Rita has been more than accommodating with American GIs; his 17-year-old daughter Maggie is going about with his pre-war pal, the spiv Lou; his infant son Stanley is a street-wise and precocious pre-pubescent youngster; and his home has been bombed flat. This is all a mighty come-down for Harvey, who had built himself up nicely before the war, earning a steady wage as a professional footballer for Clapton Orient.

Amid rationing and rubble, and as the calendar turns through to 1948 (the episodes were sequential), Harvey Moon sets about rebuilding his life, his mum (Nan) providing the only real rock of support. Harvey is elected a local Labour councillor, begins a relationship with Stanley's school head-mistress, Harriet Wright, and lives with Stanley and Nan in a prefab bungalow. Unfortunately, this too is blown up, by a hitherto unexploded wartime bomb, so he moves in as lodger with Erich Gottlieb and his sister Frieda.

By the end of the fourth series, Harvey and Rita had reunited, although their relationship remained shaky. But in a surprise revival, in 1995, they were apart once more. This last run carried the story through to 1953 – Maggie marries Lou; Stanley has grown up and been conscripted into the RAF; and Nan is bitterly opposed in general to the 'coloureds' that are 'invading Britain' and specifically opposed to Harvey's Jamaican friend Noah, who is lodging with them. As before, the episodes traced the changes in Britain – and British attitudes – after the war, reflecting the gloom but embracing the bright future engendered by the Festival Of Britain, the Queen's coronation and BBC radio comedy.

The series' title was a pun on the song 'Shine On Harvest Moon'; and one episode was titled 'Goodnight Sweetheart', after another popular number of the era – this, in turn, became the name of a second fine Marks and Gran exercise in wartime nostalgia. *Shine On Harvey Moon* is held in high esteem and warm affection by the viewing public, and it certainly had ramifications: Nigel Planer went on to appear in Marks and Gran's ***Roll Over***

Beethoven, and Linda Robson and Pauline Quirke went on to star in Marks and Gran's most famous sitcom creation of all, *Birds Of A Feather*, the two writers recognising the special relationship that existed between the two former school friends.

Shirley's World

UK/USA · ITV/ABC (ATV/SHELDON LEONARD PRODUCTIONS) · SITCOM

17 × 30 mins · colour
US dates: 15 Sep 1971–5 Jan 1972
UK dates: 21 Jan–14 May 1972 (17 episodes)
ITV Fri 10.30pm then Sun mostly 4.10pm

MAIN CAST
Shirley Logan · · · · · · · · · · Shirley MacLaine
Dennis Croft · · · · · · · · · · · · · John Gregson

OTHER APPEARANCES
Rodney, the office boy · · · · · · · · · Kim Smith

CREDITS
creators Frank Tarloff/Melville Shavelson · *writers* Peter Miller (5), Lew Schwarz (2), Frank Tarloff (1), John Muir/Brian Degas (1), Philip Mishkin/Bob Reiner (1), Tom Brennand/Roy Bottomley (1), Richard Deroy (1), Anthony Skene (1), T E B Clarke (1), Patrick Alexander (1), Jeremy Burnham (1), Jack Seddon/David Pursall (1) · *directors* Ralph Levy (5), Ray Austin (5), Charles Crichton (2), Frank Cvitanovich (1), Leslie Norman (1), Peter Hunt (1), Peter Sasdy (1), Sidney Hayers (1) · *executive producer* Sheldon Leonard · *producer* Barry Delmaine

Major Hollywood film actress Shirley MacLaine made her first (and, to date, only) foray into the world of regular TV work with *Shirley's World* – and the experience didn't last long: a uncomfortable vehicle for her talents, the series ended after just 17 episodes. Not even the support of another established film man, the Scottish actor John Gregson, theme music by John Barry and Laurie (*The Avengers*) Johnson, and a variety of exotic locales, could save the day.

Shirley's World portrayed MacLaine as a bubbly London-based photo-journalist writing for the (fictitious) magazine *World Illustrated*, her assignments taking her all over the world and into the variety of adventures that usually befall *all* lively sitcom heroines. Gregson played her despairing editor.

Like *From A Bird's Eye View*, which immediately preceded it (and wherein the same format of globetrotting international star with a British boss was employed), the series was made by the then Sir Lew Grade's ATV for his international distribution company ITC. Once more, Grade teamed up with the experienced US producer Sheldon Leonard who ensured that the product was well pitched for the US market, and indeed it screened there in its entirety before being shown in Britain. The Grade connection explains the appearance in *Shirley's World*, once apiece, of a number of British actors,

among them Joss Ackland, Joe Baker, Rodney Bewes, Brian Blessed, Erik Chitty, Graham Crowden, Cyril Cusack, Peter Dyneley, Derek Francis, Murray Head, Nicky Henson, Arthur Howard, Jeremy Lloyd, Charles Lloyd Pack, Roddy McMillan, Aimi Macdonald, Ron Moody, Bill Nagy, Patrick Newell, Dandy Nichols, Bill Owen, Una Stubbs and Sally Thomsett. British writers and directors (among them Charles Crichton, famous for his Ealing comedies and, much later, *A Fish Called Wanda*) were also involved.

A Shoe Fetishist's Guide To Bruce Morton

UK · C4 (BIG STAR IN A WEE PICTURE PRODUCTIONS) · STANDUP

1 × 30 mins · colour
4 Jan 1991 · Fri 10.30pm

MAIN CAST
Bruce Morton

CREDITS
writer Bruce Morton · *director* Don Coutts · *producer* Stuart Cosgrove

Recorded at the Third Eye Centre in Glasgow, this was a one-off special for somewhat surreal Scottish comedian Bruce Morton, born in that city.

Morton began his career by unsuccessfully attempting to write material for Kenny Everett and *The Two Ronnies*, before realising that, to get his material performed, he would have to do it himself – he went ahead and duly won the inaugural 'So You Think That's Funny' competition in his home city's arts festival, Mayfest. Morton then founded the Scottish comedy collective *The Funny Farm*, given their own show by Scottish Television, and in 1992 was short-listed for the Perrier Award at the Edinburgh Festival Fringe. Refreshingly, he has repeatedly refused to move to London to further his career, content with the success he has achieved in Scotland.

See also *Sin With Bruce Morton*.

A Show Called Fred

UK · ITV (ASSOCIATED-REDIFFUSION) · SKETCH

5 × 30 mins · b/w
2 May–30 May 1956 · Wed 9.30pm

MAIN CAST
Peter Sellers
Valentine Dyall
Kenneth Connor
Graham Stark
Patti Lewis
Max Geldray

CREDITS
writer Spike Milligan · *director/producer* Dick Lester

Following the six editions of *The Idiot Weekly, Price 2d* that finished only a month earlier, Spike Milligan and Peter Sellers returned with a further attempt to translate the surreal lunacy of *The Goon Show* to the small-screen. Again, only London-area viewers got to see it, and again the result was reasonably successful, creating a crazy visual style to match the bizarre audio antics that elevated the radio series above its contemporaries. Later still, also in 1956, the team returned to TV for a third time with a direct descendant of this series, *Son Of Fred*.

Note. A single half-hour programme, *Best Of Fred*, amalgamating the prime surviving bits of *A Show Called Fred* and *Son Of Fred*, was screened by ITV on 18 September 1963.

Show For The Telly

UK · BBC · SKETCH

1 × 30 mins · b/w
21 Sep 1956 · Fri 9.30pm

MAIN CAST
Kenneth Horne
Richard Murdoch

CREDITS
writers Kenneth Horne/Richard Murdoch · *producer* Graeme Muir

Following the demise of their famous BBC radio comedy smash *Much-Binding-In-The-Marsh*, the Corporation's television department gave Kenneth Horne and Richard Murdoch carte blanche to deliver their particular brand of affable humour in this one-off special.

Show Me A Spy!

UK · BBC · CHILDREN'S SITCOM

2 × 35 mins · b/w
1 Nov & 8 Nov 1951 · Thu 5.10pm

MAIN CAST
Peter Blythe · · · · · · · · · · · · Barry Macgregor
Paul Melvin · · · · · · · · · · · Michael Croudson
Sir Alexander Blythe · · · · · · John Le Mesurier
Margot Francis · · · · · · · · · · · Peggy Livesey
Professor Mahler · · · · · · · · · Hugo Schuster

CREDITS
writer Godfrey Harrison · *producer* Rex Tucker

A two-part comedy thriller for younger viewers, screened within the BBC's *For The Children* strand. The action took place in the British Embassy in Nimbus, the capital of Belgonia, a fictional Middle European country. Future *Dad's Army* star John Le Mesurier was among the cast.

The two episodes were performed a second time, on Sunday afternoons 4 and 11 November 1951.

A Show Of My Own

UK · ITV (YORKSHIRE) · IMPRESSIONISM

1 × 30 mins · colour
11 July 1977 · Mon 8pm

MAIN CAST
Dave Evans

CREDITS
writer Mike Goddard · director/producer Vernon Lawrence

The first starring show for impressionist Dave Evans, a regular TV guest who specialised in music spoofs. The following year he was given a second special, *An Evening With Dave Evans*.

Shut That Door!!

see GRAYSON, Larry

Sid Caesar Invites You

UK · BBC (SHELLRICK PRODUCTIONS) · SKETCH

13 × 30 mins · b/w
1 July–23 Sep 1958 · Tue 8pm

MAIN CAST
Sid Caesar
Imogene Coca
Jeremy Hawk

CREDITS
writers Mel Tolkin, Mel Brooks, Mike Stewart · producer Duncan Wood

The BBC scored a notable coup in 1958 by luring ace American funny man Sid Caesar to the UK for this series, which also featured his most famous partner, Imogene Coca, from the earlier *Your Show Of Shows*, an American TV classic.

Following the demise of *Your Show Of Shows* in 1954, the comic launched another series, *Caesar's Hour*, which ran until 1957 but, although successful, this missed the added sparkle of the marvellous Coca. The two reunited for the American version of *Sid Caesar Invites You* in January 1958 but, failing to live up to its promise, this ended after only five months, on 25 May. Its cancellation, however, allowed the BBC to woo Caesar over to London, hence this UK version of the series, which repeated much of the material from the American and so introduced British viewers to many of Caesar and Coca's classic character inventions.

Note. Mel Brooks, who wrote much of the material for this series, hosted a fine hour-length tribute to Caesar in 1985, made by LWT and screened by C4 that Christmas Day as *Mel Brooks Hails Sid Caesar*. In this, the pair reunited once more, along with fellow alumnus Carl Reiner.

The Sid Caesar Show

USA · NBC · SKETCH

1 × 60 mins · b/w
US date: 1958
UK date: 30 Nov 1958 · BBC Sun 8pm

MAIN CAST
Sid Caesar
Shirley MacLaine
Art Carney
Cliff Norton

CREDITS
writers various · producer Max Liebman

A Sid Caesar special, imported from the USA and screened by the BBC (trimmed from the hour-length to 45 minutes by BBC editor Philip Barker) shortly after the British-made series *Sid Caesar Invites You* (see previous entry). The zany American comic was joined here by his regular support Cliff Norton and guest stars Shirley MacLaine and Art Carney.

Sid Caesar's Show Of Shows

see *Your Show Of Shows*

The Sid James Show

UK · ITV (ATV) · SKETCH

2 × 50 mins · b/w
11 Mar 1961 · Sat 7.40pm
8 July 1961 · Sat 7.55pm

MAIN CAST
Sidney James

CREDITS
writers Sid Green/Dick Hills (show 1), Dave Freeman (show 2) · producer Colin Clews

Screened in the *Saturday Spectacular* strand, these two shows provided rare sketch-based outings for our pal with the 'ooter, usually seen only in films or TV sitcoms. Guests helped out, with Wilfrid Brambell and Kenneth Connor appearing in the second.

Side By Side

UK · BBC · SITCOM

13 × 30 mins · colour
Series One (6) 27 Apr–1 June 1992 · BBC1 Mon 8.30pm
Series Two (7) 18 Feb–1 Apr 1993 · BBC1 Thu 8.30pm

MAIN CAST
Vince Tulley · · · · · · · · · · · · · · · Gareth Hunt
Gilly Bell · · · · · · · · · · · · · · · · · · Louisa Rix
Stella Tulley · · · · · · · · · · · · · · Julia Deakin
Katie Bell · · · · · · · · · · · · · · Mia Fothergill
Terry Shane · · · · · · · · · · · · Alex Walkinshaw

CREDITS
writer Richard Ommanney · directors/producers Sue Bysh (12), Nic Phillips (1) · executive producer Martin Fisher

Following his success with *Three Up, Two Down*, writer Richard Ommanney again took the theme of a mismatched couple for a sitcom.

Side By Side told the tale of two neighbours in Kingston upon Thames, who hold opposing views on everything. Louisa Rix was cast as the recently widowed Gilly Bell, struggling to bring up her teenage daughter Katie; Gareth Hunt played Vince Tulley, her neighbour, a successful and relatively wealthy plumber. The clashes arose because Vince held ostentatious views about decor and design and was always attempting to create increasingly bizarre features (a mock Acropolis, a windmill, a rain-forest mural) both inside and outside his house. Most of these follies incurred the wrath of Gilly, who was loath to see the tone of the neighbourhood lowered. But it was a friendly rivalry, carried out in a civilised manner, for not only had they a grudging admiration for one another but there was no (well, very little) sexual attraction between them. Vince was happily married to Stella, who adored him, and she in turn got on very well with Ginny. Instead, the sexual tension existed between the two younger members of the cast, Katie and Vince's nephew and assistant Terry, who enjoyed a love–hate relationship.

Side By Side suffered from its lack of passion between the lead players – although its inclusion would have led critics to conclude it was a virtual remake of *Three Up, Two Down*. Without it, the series had a sterile quality.

The Siege Of Sydney's Street

UK · BBC · SITCOM

1 × 25 mins · b/w
17 Jan 1964 · Fri 7.35pm

MAIN CAST
Sydney Lord · · · · · · · · · · · · · · · · Roy Kinnear
Roger Matthews · · · · · · · · · · Gordon Rollings
Mr Wilkes · · · · · · · · · · · · · · · George Benson
Bailiff · · · · · · · · · · · · · · · · · · · Arthur Mullard

CREDITS
writers Richard Harris/Dennis Spooner · producer Dennis Main Wilson

Another *Comedy Playhouse* pilot from Harris and Spooner (following *The Plan* for Peter Cushing). This time their anti-authority figure was the 'flat-capped, fag-drooping, duffel-coated, bicycle-clipped' Sydney Lord, played by the fast-rising 28-year-old comedy-actor Roy Kinnear.

Lord is a man with an over-developed social conscience, a man determined to fight bureaucratic dictatorship wherever he finds it – which is practically everywhere. Alas, once again, no series materialised.

Silence, Silence, Silence

see The Montreux Festival

Silk, Satin, Cotton, Rags

UK · BBC · SITCOM

6 × 30 mins · b/w

10 May–14 June 1952 · Sat mostly 8.30pm

MAIN CAST

Stella Graham	Cécile Chevreau
Nick Nicholson	Barry K Barnes
Geoffrey Masters QC	Anthony Ireland
Max Rollo	Richard Murdoch
Sir William Heyward	Clive Morton
Phipps	Gladys Henson

CREDITS

writer M A Lonsdale · *producer* Douglas Moodie

An early six-part comedy featuring Cécile Chevreau as Stella Graham, an attractive-looking journalist who has four suitors: a barrister, a dress designer, a businessman and a journalist – hence the series' title.

Silver Spoons

USA · NBC THEN SYNDICATION (EMBASSY TV) · SITCOM

116 × 30 mins · colour

US dates: 25 Sep 1982–spring 1987

UK dates: 28 Dec 1984–7 Aug 1986 (22 episodes) ITV various weekdays mostly 5.15pm

MAIN CAST

Ricky Stratton	Ricky Schroder
Edward Stratton III	Joel Higgins
Kate Summers-Stratton	Erin Gray
Edward Stratton II	John Houseman
Leonard Rollins	Leonard Lightfoot (1982–83)
Dexter Stuffins	Franklyn Seales
Derek Taylor	Jason Bateman (1982–84)
Freddy Lippincottleman	Corky Pigeon (1983–85)
Alfonso Spears	Alfonso Ribeiro (1984–87)
Lulu Baker	Pearl Bailey

CREDITS

writers various · *directors* various · *producers* David W Duclon, Robert Illes, James R Stein

An agreeable reverse-trend sitcom starring Ricky Schroder, the child actor who had latterly starred in two major films, *The Champ* and *Little Lord Fauntleroy*.

Schroder played Ricky Stratton, the child of a marriage that ended in divorce after just six days – indeed he was born and raised by his mother Evelyn without his father's knowledge. Finding himself parent-less and adrift at boarding school, Ricky seeks out his father – named, in that curious American way, Edward III – they unite, fall in love and vow to stay together. The child has a wariness, intelligence and maturity that belie his young age (12 as the series begins) while his father, 35, is immature, being hooked on every video game ever invented, many of

which he plays around the house, together with his model railway. He's so into games, in fact, that he runs his own concern, Eddie's Toys Company, a branch of Stratton Industries, giving him millionaire status and a very pleasant Long Island home. The differences are complementary, however, and the pair enjoy that father–son 'bonding' relationship so favoured in 1980s TV series, discovering that they are able to learn life's lessons from one another. *Silver Spoons* also featured a number of other players, chief among them Kate Summers, Edward's secretary, whose keenness to be closer to her boss is eventually (in February 1985) realised with their marriage; and Edward II, III's domineering father and the ultimate owner of Stratton Industries, who appears from time to time and finds that the presence of his grandson Ricky finally helps him forge a decent relationship with his son.

If all this sounds gooey, well, it was. But it also carried a certain charm that brought a smile to the lips and left the viewer feeling fine about life for a few minutes. The good times for *Silver Spoons* lasted some four years and 94 episodes before NBC reached for the cancel button. This was short of the 116 figure that Embassy Productions had promised the US TV market would be available for syndication, so an additional 22 episodes were taped for first-run syndication.

Simply Sheila

UK · BBC · SKETCH

1 × 50 mins · colour

7 July 1968 · BBC2 Sun 8.15pm

MAIN CAST

Sheila Hancock
Roy Kinnear
Roddy Maude-Roxby
Joyce Grant
Lynda Marchal

CREDITS

writers Graham Chapman/John Cleese, Eric Idle, Bob Block, David Campton, Peter Cook, Ken Hoare, David Monico, Malcolm Taylor · *producer* Sydney Lotterby

A BBC2 *Show Of The Week* special for Sheila Hancock, the sketches and songs charting the theme 'The Woman And How To Treat It'. Along with Beryl Reid, Hancock was one of the few women to headline such shows on British TV at this time, and she consolidated her success with the series *But Seriously – It's Sheila Hancock*.

The Simpsons

USA · FOX (GRACIE FILMS/20TH CENTURY-FOX) · ANIMATED SITCOM

188 × 30 mins (to 31/12/97 · continuing into 1998) · colour

US dates: 17 Dec 1989 to date

UK dates: 23 Nov 1996 to date (53 episodes to 31/12/97) BBC1 Sat around 5.30pm then BBC2 Mon/Fri 6pm

MAIN CAST (VOICES)

Homer Simpson/Krusty The Klown/ Grandpa Abraham Simpson/ Barney/Groundskeeper Willy/ Mayor 'Diamond' Joe Quimby/ and others	Dan Castellaneta
Marge Simpson/Patty Bouvier/ Selma Bouvier	Julie Kavner
Bart Simpson/Nelson Muntz/ Todd Flanders and others	Nancy Cartwright
Lisa Simpson	Yeardley Smith
Montgomery Burns/Principal Skinner/ Ned Flanders/Smithers/ Otto The Bus Driver/Kent Brockman/ Dr Marvin Monroe/Rev Lovejoy/ and others	Harry Shearer
Moe/Apu/Chief Wiggum/ Dr Nick Riviera	Hank Azaria
Helen Lovejoy and others	Maggie Roswell
Milhouse and others	Pamela Hayden
Mrs Krabapple and others	Marcia Wallace

CREDITS

creator Matt Groening · *developers* James L Brooks, Matt Groening, Sam Simon · *writers* Matt Groening, John Swartzwelder, Sam Simon and others · *directors* Mark Kirkland, Jim Reardon, David Silverman, Rich Moore, Jeffrey Lynch and others · *executive producers* Bill Oakley, John Weinstein · *producers* Richard Sakai, Larina Jean Anderson, Jay Kogen, Wallace Wolodarsky · *supervising animation director* Gabor Csupo · *animation producers* Margot Pipkin, Sherry Gunthers, Mike Wolf · *animation company* Klasky Csupo

A two-dimensional comedy tour de force with more depth than most of its three-dimensional counterparts, *The Simpsons* rode in on the wave of an animation renaissance in the late 1980s. This stemmed, ostensibly, from the success of the feature film *Who Framed Roger Rabbit?* (1988, director Robert Zemeckis) but was also created from areas as diverse as commercials, pop videos and MTV's between-programme 'stings'. Previous attempts at animated sitcoms had met with mixed success and were either just children's cartoons in extended form – *The Flintstones, Top Cat, Wait Till Your Father Gets Home, The Jetsons, Wacky Races, Scooby Doo, Where Are You?* – or spin-offs from live action sitcoms. *The Simpsons*, however, an entirely original work with an absolute encompassment of traditional situation comedy qualities, is a bona fide sitcom. (And while children watch it in numbers, much of the humour is aimed fairly and squarely at adults, who do likewise.)

Cartoonist Matt Groening, the creator of a syndicated newspaper comic-strip, *Life In Hell*, first introduced the Simpson family in short segments within *The Tracey Ullman Show*. It was difficult to gauge the success of the pieces within this different setting, but when they were put into cinemas, to show before main features, audience responses alerted Groening and others to the potential of his creation. Working with James L Brooks and Sam Simon, Groening developed *The Simpsons* into a half-hour animated sitcom and the rest, to use the cliché that is perfectly applicable here, is TV history. America had a new sitcom clan – one every bit as memorable and believable as the Kramdens, the Bunkers, the Huxtables and the Bundys, and the 1990s had a new phrase to litter everyday speech: 'dysfunctional family'.

The nominal 'head' of the Simpson family is Homer, a thick-headed, lazy, beer-guzzling buffoon of simple pleasures. He is married to Marge, a sensible, down-to-earth woman who, in traditional sitcom fashion, acts as the fulcrum of the family, trying to keep them together and functioning despite their myriad problems. Homer and Marge have three children – Lisa, eight-years-old, is a hyper-intelligent, liberal-thinking, sax-playing prodigy, whose very intellect is the cause of most of her problems; the baby, Maggie, is a perpetual dummy-sucker; and Bart, ten, is an anti-establishment, hyper-active delinquent who glorifies in mischief and his position as a major under-achiever, encouraged by his dad. Bart and Homer are usually at the centre of whatever crisis the family is facing (and they face them all the time).

Peripheral family members include Grandpa Simpson, an aggressive, senile senior-citizen housed in a nearby old folks' home; and Marge's sisters – the gravel-throated, chain-smoking Bouviers Patty and Selma. There is also a huge list of support players, many of whom appear with surprising regularity. These major minor-players are Krusty The Klown, a dubious children's entertainer whose failings include fraud as well as alcohol, gambling and drug addictions; Principal Skinner, the headmaster at Bart and Lisa's school, a man still haunted by flashbacks to the Vietnam War; Ned Flanders and his family, the Simpsons' God-fearing and wimpish neighbours; the devilish Mr Burns, who runs the local nuclear power plant where Homer works; Smithers, Burns' gay, sycophantic assistant; the gun-toting Moe, owner of 'Moe's', Homer's favourite drinking bar; Apu, the Indian owner of the local convenience store; Mayor Quimby, a corrupt local official; and Wiggum, the corruptible police chief. These, then, are the residents of Springfield (an arch reference to the hometown in the classically twee 1954–63 US sitcom *Father Knows Best*). They're a motley bunch – the *motliest* of motley bunches – but each and every one packs a believability-factor belied by their cartoon nature.

From these characters the stories are played out – complex tales that feature mistrust, duplicity and flawed individuals

following the dictates of their character rather than their conscience. Unlike so many American TV series, there is no simple moralising in *The Simpsons*: good guys sometimes lose, bad acts are sometimes rewarded, drink is drunk, and joints are puffed in a grotesque but real mirror-reflection of American life. And, not forgetting that this is a comedy, the episodes are very, very funny. The sharp scripts, enhanced by brilliant voice characterisations and a distinctive animated style, make *The Simpsons* a true television classic.

The series became a major success virtually upon its 1990 launch and quickly blossomed into a phenomenon with all the incumbent media focus and spin-off merchandising. Harshly criticised at first by the moral majority, most protests were eventually forgotten as its genius came to be recognised with umpteen awards and the series became accepted as a vital part of US culture. Over the ensuing years it has continued to go from strength to strength, with famous celebrities signing up to voice guest roles, including Paul and Linda McCartney, Ringo Starr, George Harrison, Sting, Michael Jackson, Kelsey Grammer (as the murderous Bob), Jackie Mason, Elizabeth Taylor, Bob Hope, Larry King, Cloris Leachman, Tony Bennett, Dustin Hoffman, Michelle Pfeiffer, Albert Brooks, Penny Marshall, Danny DeVito (as Homer's erstwhile brother), Luke Perry, Barry White, James Brown and *X-Files* characters Scully and Mulder (David Duchovny and Gillian Anderson).

Along with *Married ... With Children*, *The Simpsons* presents a welcome antidote to the politically correct, mawkishly sentimental fare on offer in most (though not all) other series on American TV, both shows paving the way towards a less inhibited era. In the UK, the series aired for many years on the Sky satellite/cable channel before it made its terrestrial bow on the BBC in November 1996, with a deserved fanfare. A specially commissioned documentary, *The Simpsons Have Landed* (BBC1, 24 November 1996), was screened to introduce the series to British viewers, providing a definitive view of the Springfield world and its inhabitants.

Notes: Dan Castellaneta has revealed that Homer's distinctive cry of 'Doh!', to suggest frustration, is his shortened version of the longer 'Dooooouuh!', spat in similar circumstances by the Scottish screen actor James Finlayson in Laurel and Hardy films of the 1920s and 1930s.

The name Homer Simpson has long existed in American mythology – he was the ineffectual, emotionally crippled symbol of Protestant American manhood in Nathaniel West's bitter satire *The Day Of The Locust*.

Also, although the major members of the Simpsons – Homer, Margaret, Lisa and Maggie – were named after Matt Groening's own family, there, the creator swears, all resemblance ends.

Dan Castellaneta guest starred in an episode of the US legal drama series *LA Law*, in which – employed as a walking, talking Homer Simpson character at a California theme-park – he is dismissed for inappropriate (or perhaps all too appropriate) behaviour while in costume. (The episode was 'LA Lawless', screened in the USA on 22 October 1992.).

A feature-film version of *The Simpsons* was being planned as this book went to press.

See also *King Of The Hill*.

Sin With Bruce Morton

UK · C4 (BIG STAR IN A WEE PICTURE PRODUCTIONS) · STANDUP

4 × 35 mins · colour

2 June–23 June 1993 · Wed 10.30pm

MAIN CAST
Bruce Morton

CREDITS
writer Bruce Morton · *director* Don Coutts · *producer* Jo Sargent

A starring series for the Glaswegian comic who, shortly before this, had the thankless task of performing as warm-up man for *The Jack Dee Show*. Actually, Morton's style is as different from Dee's as it is possible to get – whereas Dee always dresses smartly and fuels his routines with inner angst, Morton appears casually dressed in sloppy jumpers and jeans, and his delivery is laidback and more conversational than confrontational. (For biographical details see *A Shoe Fetishist's Guide To Bruce Morton*.)

In each of the four programmes in this C4 series Morton delivered a standup routine themed by a deadly sin – sloth, lust, avarice and anger – but the other three got a look in as well, Morton straying into other territories when he could; the 'Sloth' edition, for example, also featured meditations on the nature of envy. The series was based on his successful one-man stage-show, *Sin*, which was nominated for the Perrier Award at the Edinburgh Festival Fringe in 1992.

Note. Morton explored Amsterdam's dope cafés for the documentary *Amsterdam By Night*, screened during C4's themed marijuana evening, *Pot Night*, on 4 March 1995.

Sing The Lady Out Of Bed

UK · BBC · SKETCH

1 × 30 mins · colour

12 Dec 1974 · BBC2 Thu 9pm

MAIN CAST
Peter Lambert
Willie Ross
Mary Miller
Tony Selby
Dennis Waterman

CREDITS
writer Peter Campbell/Roger Ordish · *producer* Dennis Main Wilson

A one-off sketch show. BBC producer Dennis Main Wilson had spotted the musical comedy duo Ross and Lambert on stage – the pair were a regular fixture on the northern club circuit. When the zany script for *Sing The Lady Out Of Bed* arrived on his desk, he decided it was perfect for them, engaging Tony Selby, Mary Miller and Dennis Waterman to flesh out the comic routines.

Singles

UK · ITV (YORKSHIRE · *THAMES) · SITCOM

22 editions (21 × 30 mins · 1 × 60 mins) · colour
*Pilot (60 mins) 19 June 1984 · Tue 9pm
Series One (7 × 30 mins) 27 Jan–9 Mar 1988 · Wed 8pm
Series Two (7 × 30 mins) 23 Jan–6 Mar 1989 · Mon 8pm
Series Three (7 × 30 mins) 10 July–21 Aug 1991 · Wed 9.30pm

MAIN CAST
Malcolm · · · · · · · · · · · Robin Nedwell (pilot);
· · · · · · · · · · · · · Roger Rees (series 1 & 2)
Dennis Duval · · · · · · Simon Cadell (series 3)
Pamela · · · · · · · · · · Angela Richards (pilot);
· · · · · · · · · · · · · · · · Judy Loe (all series)
Clive · · · · · · · · · · · · John Kavanagh (pilot);
· · · · · · · · · · · · · Eamon Boland (all series)
Jackie · · · · · · · · · · · · · · Jane Carr (pilot);
· · · · · · · · · · · · · · · Susie Blake (all series)

OTHER APPEARANCES
Di · · · · · · · · · · · · · Patricia Brake (pilot);
· · · · · · · · · · · · · · · · Gina Maher (series 1)

CREDITS
writers Eric Chappell/Jean Warr · *directors/ producers* Robert Reed (pilot), Vernon Lawrence (series 1), Nic Phillips (series 2), Graham Wetherell (series 3) · *executive producers* Lloyd Shirley (pilot), Vernon Lawrence (series 2)

Two men and two women meet in a singles' bar, during a local hotel's social evening for the unattached. Desirous of 'a good time', Malcolm is a cocksure market-trader who, although still a bachelor, has convinced himself that he understands all there is to know about women. His pal Clive is a single parent: his wife has deserted, leaving him to cope with their three children and hold down a job as a poorly paid hospital porter. Jackie is a recent divorcee keen on remarrying, hopefully to a professional man. (Her first husband, to her chagrin, was a lorry-driver.) Her best friend Pamela, the mother of an adult son, married young but the union has fallen apart and now she is close to bankruptcy.

Despite mutual deceit, low cunning and, for Pam and Jackie, many a hasty chat inside the ladies' lav, relationships gradually evolve: Malcolm is after Pam, Pam fancies Malcolm, Jackie hopes that Clive fancies her, Clive wants to know Jackie more intimately. As the third series started, the four had agreed on a double wedding, and Clive, Jackie and Pam were waiting at the register office for Malcolm. He fails to show, jilting the crestfallen Pam, but in walks a friend of Clive's, Dennis Duval, a pretentious out-of-work actor with three wives in his past and a larger than life ego in his present. (He calls himself 'the handsome, virile, Dennis Duval'.) Duval now begins to chase after Pam, overturning her reluctance as the episodes tick by. (Malcolm had to be written out of the series after actor Roger Rees swapped one bar for another, leaving Singles to join the cast of the American sitcom Cheers, where he played the English businessman Robin Colcord.)

Created and written by the *Duty Free* team of Eric Chappell and his erstwhile assistant Jean Warr, *Singles* was developed from their one-off 60-minute comedy-drama, *Singles' Night*, screened more than three years before the first series.

Sink Or Swim

UK · BBC · SITCOM

19 × 30 mins · colour
Series One (7) 4 Dec 1980–22 Jan 1981 · BBC1 Thu mostly 8.30pm
Series Two (6) 22 Oct–26 Nov 1981 · BBC1 Thu 8.30pm
Series Three (6) 9 Sep–14 Oct 1982 · BBC1 Thu 8.30pm

MAIN CAST
Brian Webber · · · · · · · · · · · · · Peter Davison
Steve Webber · · · · · · · · · · · Robert Glenister
Sonia · · · · · · · · · · · · · · · · · Sara Corper

OTHER APPEARANCES
Mike Connor · · · · Ron Pember (series 1 & 2)
Sandra · · · · · · · Amanda Orton (series 1 & 2)
Christine · · · · · · · · Gillian Taylforth (series 2)
Charlotte · · · · · · Briony McRoberts (series 3)
Douglas · · · · · · · · Russell Wootton (series 3)

CREDITS
writer Alex Shearer · *directors/producers* Roger Race (14), Gareth Gwenlan (5) · *executive producer* Gareth Gwenlan

A sibling-rivalry sitcom starring the versatile actor Peter Davison, equally at home in comedy and straight drama.

Davison was cast as Brian Webber, a northerner who has ventured south to seek his fame and fortune but ends up living, ingloriously, on a damp houseboat in London. A hard worker, he desperately wants to better himself but seems doomed to be unlucky; his girlfriend, Sonia, is an ecologically conscious vegetarian, a glum and earnest young woman involved in numerous causes. Into this far

from perfect life arrives Brian's younger brother, Steve – an indolent, cynical, forthright individual, obsessed with sex, who possesses many of the character 'attributes' that Brian has affected to leave behind. Steve's presence embarrasses his older brother and alienates Sonia, who views him as a northern lout. But blood is thicker than water and Brian tolerates his younger sibling, rediscovering aspects of his own character along the way.

The first two series ran in this vein; the third showed Brian attempting to improve his lot by studying as a mature student at university in Newcastle upon Tyne, accompanied, inevitably, by Sonia and Steve.

The writer Alex Shearer also explored the subject of mismatched characters forced together by circumstance or blood in *Chalk And Cheese* and *The Front Line*.

Sir Les And The Great Chinese Takeaway

see HUMPHRIES, Barry

Sir Yellow

UK · ITV (YORKSHIRE) · SITCOM

6 × 30 mins · colour
13 July–19 Aug 1973 · Fri 7pm then Sun 12.05am

MAIN CAST
Sir Yellow · · · · · · · · · · · · · Jimmy Edwards
Gregory · · · · · · · · · · · · · · · Melvyn Hayes
Sir Griswold · · · · · · · · · · · · · · Alan Curtis
Cedric · · · · · · · · · · · · · · Michael Ripper

CREDITS
writer Johnny Heyward · *script editor* David Nobbs · *director* Ian Davidson · *producer* Bill Hitchcock

Emulating the level of wit to which this series climbed, one cannot resist stating that *Sir Yellow* was joust awful. Set in the 13th-century but laced with contemporary 'jokes', it starred Jimmy Edwards – the blowsy, handlebar-moustachioed comic – as a cowardly knight who determinedly spends his time blustering around the country, guzzling alcohol, chasing busty wenches (ironically, Edwards had just revealed his homosexuality) and avoiding death at the hands of his enemy, Sir Griswold.

The first programme went out on a Friday the 13th and it was an ill omen: *Sir Yellow* began amid heightened expectations – Edwards had long been a major personality – but it fell from grace with alarming speed. By the third episode the series had been dropped from a Friday 7pm slot to a graveyard post-midnight placing on Sunday. Retrospectively, perhaps the only truly interesting thing about *Sir Yellow* is that an unknown youngish actor named Bob Hoskins had a minor role in one of the episodes.

Sister, Sister

USA · ABC THEN WB (DE PASSE
ENTERTAINMENT/PARAMOUNT) · CHILDREN'S
SITCOM

**87 × 30 mins (to 31/12/97 · continuing into
1998) · colour**

US dates: 1 Apr 1994–28 Apr 1995 (ABC) · 6 Sep
1995 to date

UK dates: 31 Mar 1996 to date (53 episodes to
31/12/97) C4 Sun mostly 9.45am

MAIN CAST

Tamera Campbell · · · · · · · · · Tamera Mowry
Tia Landry · · · · · · · · · · · · · · · · · Tia Mowry
Ray Campbell · · · · · · · · · · · · · · · · · Tim Reid
Lisa Landry · · · · · · · · · · · · · Jackée Harry
Roger Evans · · · · · · · · · · Marques Houston
Sarah · · · · · · · · Brittany Murphy (1994–95)
Terrence Winningham · · · · · · · Dorien Wilson
· (1995–96)

CREDITS

creators Kim Bass, Gary Gilbert, Fred Shafferman ·
writers Brian Pollack, Mert Rich and others ·
directors Jack Shea and others · executive
producers Mert Rich, Brian Pollack, Suzanne de
Passe, Leslie Ray, David Simon, Suzanne Coston,
Irene Dreayer · producer Joseph Scott

An unexceptional but harmless sitcom
following the lives of black twin sisters,
Tamera and Tia, separated at birth and
adopted by different families, the Campbells
and the Landrys. By chance, 14 years later,
they are reunited, immediately hit it off and
vow never to be separated again. As luck
would have it, they both have single parents
of the opposite sex – Tamera's foster-father,
Ray (Tim Reid from *Frank's Place*), is
a white-collar conservative who teaches
business studies, Tia's foster-mother, Lisa
(played by the busy and ever reliable Jackée
Harry), is brash and working-class. Sure
enough, they all move in together and,
despite the obvious culture clashes between
the two foster-parents, settle down to an
ordered life. Ray and Lisa even become
fond of one another.

Sister, Sister – sometimes written without
the comma – was made with a young
audience in mind, and it so clearly set out to
be middle-of-the-road that you could almost
see the white line running down the centre of
the set.

Sitcom Weekend Spoofs

UK · C4 (PARAMOUNT COMEDY CHANNEL) ·
SATIRE

4 × 5 mins · colour

24 & 25 May 1997 · Sat/Sun various times

CREDITS

writers Matt Lucas/David Walliams · director Edgar
Howard Wright Jr · executive producer Myfanwy
Moore · producer Nira Park

Over the bank holiday weekend of 24–26 May
1997 C4 screened *Sitcom Weekend*, a mixed
bag of sitcoms, films and documentaries that

filled the channel's schedules over three
nights. Among the programmes were these
four five-minute sitcom spoofs, made by
the Paramount Comedy Channel and
subsequently screened on that cable/satellite
station.

I'm Bland ... Yet My Friends Are Krazy!
24 MAY

MAIN CAST

Matt Lucas
David Walliams
Bob Mortimer
Anna Francolini
Steve Pemberton
Reece Shearsmith

A *Seinfeld* spoof that had only a superficial
resemblance to the original and way missed
its mark – it began as a mildly accurate
portrayal of Jerry Seinfeld and Kramer but
soon degenerated into a wild surrealistic farce
closer to a pastiche of *Crackerjack* than the
giant US series.

My Gay Dads
24 MAY

MAIN CAST

Matt Lucas
David Walliams
Jenny Evans
Simon Greenall
Reece Shearsmith

An over-the-top but amusing satire of the
lesser US sitcoms' patronising attitude
towards gays and family ties, utilising the
premise of *My Two Dads*.

A Puppet Lives In My House
25 MAY

MAIN CAST

Matt Lucas
David Walliams
Rebecca Front
Paul Putner

An effective sketch depicting a family who
live with a wisecracking, chaos-causing glove
puppet – effectively spoofing *ALF* and its ilk.

Only Jerks And Horses
25 MAY

MAIN CAST

Matt Lucas
David Walliams
Brian Bovell
Mark Gatiss
Paul Putner

A clever skit imagining a US adaptation of
Only Fools And Horses. Uncle Albert has
been replaced by a robot, and market-trader
Del now trades in the stock market – and is
hugely successful. Rodney (actually called
'Roderney' in this version) has been imported
from the British original but isn't considered
funny by the audience and is soon written
out. 'Good jubbly!'

Sitting Pretty
1

UK · BBC · SITCOM

1 × 30 mins · colour

11 June 1974 · BBC1 Tue 8.30pm

MAIN CAST

Nick Ransley · · · · · · · · · · · · Nicky Henson
Jo Ransley · · · · · · · · · · · · · · · · Una Stubbs

CREDITS

writers Pauline Devaney/Edwin Apps · producer
Graeme Muir

A single-episode *Comedy Playhouse* from
husband-and-wife writers Devaney and Apps,
the creators of *All Gas And Gaiters*. The
subject this time was the protected status of a
sitting tenant, Jo Ransley. No series
developed.

Sitting Pretty
2

UK · BBC · SITCOM

13 × 30 mins · colour

Series One (6) 19 Nov–24 Dec 1992 · BBC1
Thu 8.30pm

Special · 1 Jan 1993 · BBC1 Fri 8.30pm

Series Two (6) 24 Nov–29 Dec 1993 · BBC1
Wed 8.30pm

MAIN CAST

Annabel 'Annie' Briggs · · · · · · · · Diane Bull
Sylvie · · · · · · · · · · · · · · · · Heather Tobias
Tiffany · · · · · · · · · · · · · · · · Alison Lomas
Kitty · · · · · · · · · · · · · · · Vilma Hollingbery
George · · · · · · · · · · · · · · · · · · John Cater

CREDITS

writer John Sullivan · directors Susan Belbin (7),
Angela deChastelai Smith (6) · producer Susan
Belbin

Stage star Diane Bull took the lead role in this
John Sullivan sitcom about a pampered 'good-
time girl' who suddenly, aged around 40,
lands on hard times.

Bull was cast as Annie Briggs, a golden
girl in the Swinging Sixties who subsequently
lived off a succession of sugar-daddies drawn
to her good looks, firm figure and dizzy, light-
hearted personality. Annie has married the
latest of these suitors, a millionaire named
Boris, and settled down to the good life, but
they have been married for less than a year
when he dies while conducting an extramarital affair. Annie is devastated and worse
news follows: she is financially destitute.
Forced to return to the family home, a
ramshackle farm in Kent, she is welcomed by
her doting parents but resented by her dowdy
twin sister, Sylvie, who has enjoyed none of
the benefits that have fallen Annie's way.
Sylvie has stayed behind on the farm,
working hard, looking after her parents and
remaining, as far as possible, loyal to hippy
ideals. Both sisters are also unmarried
mothers – Annie has a daughter, Tiffany, the
result of an affair with a photographer; Sylvie

has a son, named Lone Star at birth but known as Andrew.

Episodes charted the flashy Annie's attempts to come to terms with her diminished new environment and settle in with her basic family once again. With her hybrid East-End/Home Counties accent, pampered pooch and affected airs and graces, she sticks out like the proverbial sore thumb but is accepted back into the fold all the same. Her presence also brings the others – especially Sylvie – out of themselves.

Conscious of the criticism over the lack of women in **Only Fools And Horses**, Sullivan restored the balance by focusing this time on sisters instead of brothers. And his dialogue remained as crisp and funny as ever, some of the lines (such as 'When you come from Bethnal Green an allotment and a rat counts as a farm') being redolent of the Trotter family at their best.

Six Dates With Barker

UK · ITV (LWT) · SITCOMS

6 × 30 mins · colour

8 Jan–12 Feb 1971 · Fri 7.30pm

Following the success of **The Ronnie Barker Playhouse**, LWT presented a second series of six single-episode comedies starring the versatile and brilliant Barker. Each was written by a different author, embracing a separate theme and era. Like that earlier series, and another in 1973, **Seven Of One**, screened by the BBC, several of the programmes had far-reaching consequences.

1937: The Removals Person   8 JAN

MAIN CAST

Fred · Ronnie Barker
Travers · · · · · · · · · · · · · Josephine Tewson
Albert · · · · · · · · · · · · · Christopher Timothy
Mrs Vaile · · · · · · · · · · · · · · · Joan Benham
Angela · · · · · · · · · · · · · · · · Gillian Fairchild

CREDITS

writer Hugh Leonard · director Maurice Murphy · producer Humphrey Barclay

A myopic removal man, Fred, carries out his business while the owner of the house is away watching the Coronation procession. This was, in essence, the pilot for **Clarence**.

1899: The Phantom Raspberry Blower Of Old London Town   15 JAN

MAIN CAST

Insp Alexander/Disraeli/ · · · · · · · · · · · · · · · ·
Home Secretary · · · · · · · · · Ronnie Barker
The Phantom · · · · · · · · · · · · · Alan Curtis
Sgt Bowles · · · · · · · · · · · · · · · Larry Noble
Butler · · · · · · · · · · · · · · · · · · · John Sharp
Maureen Body · · · · · · · · · · · · · Moira Foot
Duchess · · · · · · · · · · · · · Christine Ozanne

CREDITS

writer Spike Milligan · director Maurice Murphy · producer Humphrey Barclay

A typical Spike Milligan piece, about a Jack The Ripper-style raspberry blower on the loose in Victorian London, from whom no one is safe. This lunatic romp was later revived as an eight-part mini-serial within the fifth series of **The Two Ronnies**.

1970: The Odd Job   22 JAN

MAIN CAST

Arthur Harriman · · · · · · · · · · Ronnie Barker
Clive · · · · · · · · · · · · · · · · · · · David Jason
Kitty Harriman · · · · · · · · · · · · · · Joan Sims

CREDITS

writer Bernard McKenna · director Maurice Murphy · producer Humphrey Barclay

A particularly inventive black comedy, with a show-stealing acrobatic performance by David Jason. Feeling suicidal after his wife has left him, Arthur Harriman finds that he has no flair for the task and so employs an odd-job man, Clive, to do the deed. But when he changes his mind he is unable to call the hit man off …

The script was later adapted by Bernard McKenna, with Graham Chapman, for a feature film, *The Odd Job* (1978), which starred Chapman in the Ronnie Barker role. The writers intended to cast Keith Moon as the odd-job man but, in the end, David Jason was recruited to reprise his TV performance.

1915: Lola   29 JAN

MAIN CAST

Fritz Braun/Lola · · · · · · · · · · Ronnie Barker
Major Rupert Yappe · · · · · · · · Freddie Jones
Lord Kitchener · · · · · · · · · · · Valentine Dyall
Captain Otto von Diesel · · · Graham Armitage
Kaiser Wilhelm · · · · · · · · · Dennis Ramsden
Frenchman · · · · · · · · · · · · · Freddie Earlle

CREDITS

writers Ken Hoare/Mike Sharland · director Maurice Murphy · producer Humphrey Barclay

A First World War comedy in which two bumbling Germans – the head of espionage (von Diesel) and his shorthand typist (Braun) – get into trouble by failing to keep tabs on their country's top female agent. Disaster will be averted if Braun, in drag, can carry out a convincing impersonation of the missing Lola.

1971: Come In And Lie Down   5 FEB

MAIN CAST

Dr Swanton · · · · · · · · · · · · · Ronnie Barker
The Gasman · · · · · · · · · · · · Michael Bates

CREDITS

writer John Cleese · director Maurice Murphy · producer Humphrey Barclay

Another significant marker on the road to **Fawlty Towers**, this John Cleese-scripted episode cast Barker as a psychiatrist and Michael Bates as a repressed character so fearful of discovering any mental instability within himself that he poses as a gasman instead of a patient. Many of the mannerisms, nuances and concerns of Bates' character became recognisable traits of the manic Basil Fawlty.

2774 AD: All The World's A Stooge   12 FEB

MAIN CAST

Prince Boffo · · · · · · · · · · · · · Ronnie Barker
Arch Funster · · · · · · · · · · · Michael Hordern
Atlas · · · · · · · · · · · · · · · · Victor Maddern
Cheeky · · · · · · · · · · · · Lesley-Anne Down
Princess Hysteria · · · · · · · · · · · Joyce Grant

CREDITS

writer Gerald Wiley (Ronnie Barker) · director Maurice Murphy · producer Humphrey Barclay

In the far distant future, comedy has become the religion and jokes are compulsory. Grave consequences await those who do not join in the fun.

Six Escapees

see The Montreux Festival

Six More Faces Of Jim

see **Faces Of Jim**

Six Of The Best

UK · ITV (ATV) · SITCOMS

6 × 30 mins · b/w

A series of one-off sitcom pilots that ATV hoped would develop into series. None did. See individual entries for further details.

11 Aug 1965	Annie Doesn't Live Here Anymore
18 Aug 1965	Me And My Big Mouth
25 Aug 1965	Charlie's Place
1 Sep 1965	Porterhouse – Private Eye
8 Sep 1965	Man With A Mission
15 Sep 1965	Are There Any More At Home Like You?

The Sky Larks

UK · BBC · SITCOM

16 × 30 mins · b/w

11 July–24 Oct 1958 · Fri mostly 8pm

MAIN CAST

Vice-Admiral Sir Godfrey Wiggin-Fanshawe
KBE DSO DSC RN · · · · · · · · · A E Matthews
· · · · · · · · · · · · · · · · · (from episode 5)
Lt Gilmore RN · · · · · · · · · · · Anton Rodgers
Lt Stannard RN · · · · · · · · · Robert Chetwyn
Lt Copper · · · · · · · · · · · · · Roland Curram
Radio Comms Op (Air) N Reynolds · · · · · · · ·
· · · · · · · · · · · · · · · · · · John Southworth

Cmdr Morris DSC RN · · · · · · · Frank Shelley
Capt Crocker-Dobson DSO RN · · · · · · · · · · ·
· William Mervyn

CREDITS
creator John Warrington · *writers* Trevor Peacock/
Gavin Blakeney · *producer* John Warrington

Subtitled 'The Adventures And Misadventures Of A Naval Helicopter Crew', this rare British filmed comedy series was shot on location, mostly between Naples to Malta, on board the HMS *Ark Royal, Albion* and *Cavendish.* In the series the ship was called the HMS *Aerial* and authenticity was assured when the crew of the *Ark Royal* acted as extras.

Veteran actor A E Matthews joined the cast from the fifth episode, his character – Sir Godfrey Wiggin-Fanshawe, an ageing and irascible fitness freak who cycles around on deck – seeming to make the biggest splash with viewers and critics.

The 'Slap' Maxwell Story

USA · ABC (SLAP HAPPY PRODUCTIONS) · SITCOM

22 × 30 mins · colour
US dates: 23 Sep 1987–14 Sep 1988
UK dates: 21 Jan 1989–20 Oct 1990 (22 episodes) BBC2 Sat 9.15pm then Thu 8pm

MAIN CAST
'Slap' Maxwell · · · · · · · · · Dabney Coleman
Annie Maxwell · · · · · · · · · · · Susan Anspach
Judy Ralston · · · · · · · · · · · Megan Gallagher
The Dutchman · · · · · · · · · · · · · · Bill Cobbs
Nelson Kruger · · · · · · · · · · · · · Brian Smiar
Charlie Wilson · · · · · · · · · · · · Bill Calvert

CREDITS
creator/director Jay Tarses · *writers* Jay Tarses, Bob Brush and others · *producers* Bernie Brillstein, Jay Tarses

Following their excruciatingly funny sitcom *Buffalo Bill*, creator/writer Jay Tarses and star Dabney Coleman reunited for *The 'Slap' Maxwell Story*, which once again flew in the face of conventional US sitcom wisdom by having a thoroughly unlikeable and mean-spirited character as its lead.

'Slap' Maxwell is a gifted but heartless sportswriter working for Midwestern newspaper *The Ledger.* A cranky, impatient individual with absolutely no regard for the feelings of his fellow man, Maxwell is nevertheless hurt and amazed when people rail back against *him.* His ex-wife Annie is plagued by his unwanted attentions – they are divorced but Slap endlessly attempts reconciliation, usually in a cringingly embarrassing scene. Otherwise he courts Judy, a secretary at the newspaper, and makes life miserable for his editor, Nelson Kruger, and the copy-boy, Charlie Wilson. For recreation, Slap hangs out at a bar, tended by 'the Dutchman'.

In the USA the series was described as a 'dramady' in an attempt to explain the seriousness of the comedy (such programmes were becoming commonplace at the time). Once again, though, while the critics raved the public ran, *The 'Slap' Maxwell Story* disappearing after just one season.

Slapstick And Old Lace

see DRAKE, Charlie

Slater's Day

UK · ITV (YORKSHIRE) · SITCOM

1 × 30 mins · colour
3 Dec 1974 · Tue 7.05pm

MAIN CAST
Freddy Slater · · · · · · · · · · · · · · John Junkin
Jean Slater · · · · · · · · · · · · · · · Mary Miller
Jack · · · · · · · · · · · · · · · · · Peter Mayock
Muriel · · · · · · · · · · · · · · Maureen Sweeney
Frogley · · · · · · · · · · · · · James Cairncross

CREDITS
writer Chris Boucher · *producer* Paddy Russell

A single-episode comedy from Yorkshire TV that, unlike two others (*Rising Damp* and *Oh No – It's Selwyn Froggitt*) in the unnamed six-part pilots strand that aired in autumn 1974, failed to progress into a full series of its own. John Junkin starred as Slater, a PR man who, generally, is happy with his lot until he suddenly encounters the bad day to end all bad days.

Note. The programme was originally intended for screening on 7 October 1974 but this was cancelled because of the period's three-day week and its attendant power conservation.

Sledge Hammer!

USA · ABC (ALAN SPENCER PRODUCTIONS/NEW WORLD TELEVISION) · SITCOM

41 × 30 mins · colour
US dates: 23 Sep 1986–12 Feb 1988
UK dates: 26 Sep 1987–28 Aug 1992 (38 episodes) ITV weekend nights after 12 midnight

MAIN CAST
Inspector Sledge Hammer · · · · David Rasche
Det-Sgt Dori Doreau · · · · · Anne-Marie Martin
Captain Trunk · · · · · · · · · · · Harrison Page

CREDITS
creator Alan Spencer · *writers* Mert Rich/Brian Pollack (9), Mert Rich/Brian Pollack/Alan Spencer (1), Alan Spencer (5), Mark Curtiss/Rod Ash (5), Michael Reiss/Al Jean (5), David Ketchum/Tony Di Marco (4), Chris Ruppenthal (3), Jim Fisher/Jim Staahl (2), Gerard Gardner (2), Ron Friedman (1), Tino Insana/Robert L Wuhl (1), Alan Mandel (1), Deborah Raznick/Daniel Benton (1), Alicia Marie Schudt (1) · *directors* Seymour Robbie and others · *executive producer* Alan Spencer · *producers* Robert Lovenheime, William D'Angelo, Thomas Kane

In the same way that *Get Smart* was a pastiche of TV spy shows, *Sledge Hammer!* was a parody of TV cop shows and movies, especially those in the *Dirty Harry* mould.

American standup comic David Rasche starred as Hammer, an archetypal over-the-top celluloid cop, spouting brainless macho catchphrases intended to inspire fear in the bad and faith in the good ol' US justice system, hating wimps and pimps, shooting warning shots at jaywalkers and litter-bugs, and driving around in a car affixed to which is the sticker 'I Love Violence'. Hammer's boss, likely to hit the medicine pills whenever he has to deal with his square-jawed Rambo-like detective, is Captain Trunk; Hammer's sidekick is a beautiful woman, Dori, a martial arts expert whose prowess and detective nous land her most of the solutions. Dori's romantic interest in her hunky colleague is never reciprocated, however – Hammer is too interested in his .44 Magnum, which he names 'Gun', talks to, lovingly polishes and, yes, takes to his bed, where it rests on its own cream satin pillow.

The last episode of the first US season was unusual to say the least: expecting it to be the last episode *ever*, the writers gave Hammer the duty of defusing a primed nuclear device. After muttering his usual 'Trust me, I know what I'm doing' the bomb exploded, wiping out not only the cast but the entire city of Los Angeles. When, surprisingly, a second series was commissioned, it began with a replay of the incident, over which was superimposed an announcement stating that this new series was set five years before the first – a novel get-out.

Note. London-area ITV screened 38 of the 41 episodes sporadically over a five-year period. The missing three were shown during repeat runs in 1995 and 1996.

A Slight Case Of …

UK · BBC · SITCOM

6 × 30 mins · b/w
8 Sep–10 Oct 1965 · BBC2 Wed 8.20pm then Sun 10.05pm

MAIN CAST
H A Wormsley · · · · · · · · · · · · · Roy Kinnear
Mr Poliansky · · · · · · · · · · · · · · Joe Melia

CREDITS
writer Leon Griffiths · *producer* David Croft

The adventures of the resourceful H A Wormsley: chairman, executive president, managing director, staff and secretary of seven companies – to name but one example, he is a private eye for the Detective Bureau Of Great Britain. Whatever the endeavour, Wormsley hardly cuts a dashing figure, but what he lacks in physical élan he makes up for in verbal dexterity, using a 'gift of the gab' to talk his way out of tricky situations.

The writer Leon Griffiths returned to the theme of a dubious character with a silvery tongue a decade later, with his glorious invention of Arthur Daley for the ITV light-drama series *Minder*.

John Inman, Jon Pertwee, Bryan Pringle, Sydney Tafler and Hugh Lloyd were among the guest actors who turned up in one episode each.

A Slight Hitch

UK · ITV (THAMES) · SITCOM

1 × 30 mins · colour

28 Mar 1991 · Thu 8.30pm

MAIN CAST

Simon · · · · · · · · · · · · · · · · · Nigel Havers
Anna · · · · · · · · · · · · · · · · · Joanna Kanska
Katerina · · · · · · · · · · · · · · · Nancy Nevinson
Helen · · · · · · · · · · · · · · · · · Helen Christie
Susie · · · · · · · · · · · · · · · · · Sarah-Jane Varley

CREDITS

writer Adrienne Conway · *director/producer* John Howard Davies

A single-episode sitcom – perhaps a pilot that went no further – written by **Streets Apart** author Adrienne Conway. It starred Nigel Havers, so often the archetypal upper-crust Englishman, as a confirmed bachelor who finally yields to marriage, solely in order to help a young Polish woman remain in London as a student. The question is: how will they spend their wedding night?

Slinger's Day

see *Tripper's Day*

The Slowest Gun In The West

USA · CBS · SITCOM

1 × 60 mins · b/w

US date: 7 May 1960
UK date: 7 June 1962 · BBC Thu 7.55pm

MAIN CAST

Fletcher Bissell III · · · · · · · · · · · Phil Silvers
Chicken Farnsworth · · · · · · · · · · Jack Benny
Nick Nolan · · · · · · · · · · · · · · · Bruce Cabot
Carl Dexter · · · · · · · · · · · · · · Jack Albertson
Sam Bass · · · · · · · · · · · · · · · Lee Van Cleef

CREDITS

writer Nat Hiken · *director* Herschel Daugherty · *producers* William Frye, Nat Hiken

A one-off comedy 'spectacular' – aired on the BBC as *The Phil Silvers Special* – that reunited the star with Nat Hiken, the writer of **The Phil Silvers Show**. The setting here, silly but amusing, was a western, telling the tale of the cowardly Fletcher Bissell III, elected sheriff of the lawless town of Primrose, Arizona. To get rid of him, the local baddies hire a gunslinger, Chicken Farnsworth – played by Jack Benny – who turns out to be just as big a coward as Bissell.

Five months after this, Hiken and Silvers made a second CBS special – **Just Polly And Me**.

A Small Problem

UK · BBC · SITCOM

6 × 30 mins · colour

26 Jan–2 Mar 1987 · BBC2 Mon 9pm

MAIN CAST

Howard · · · · · · · · · · · · · · · Christopher Ryan
Roy Pink · · · · · · · · · · · · · · · · Mike Elles
Fred · · · · · · · · · · · · · · · · · · Dickie Arnold
Lily · · · · · · · · · · · · · · · · · Christine Ozanne
George · · · · · · · · · · · · · · · · David Simeon
Heather · · · · · · · · · · · · · · · Joan Blackham
Sid · Big Mick
Mr Motokura · · · · · · · · · · · · Tetsu Nishino
Mrs Motokura · · · · · · · · · · · · · Sayo Inaba

CREDITS

writers Tony Millan/Mike Walling · *director/producer* David Askey

Rarely has such a tiny sitcom caused such big problems as the ironically titled *A Small Problem*.

The series was conceived as a satire on the nature of prejudice, with 'heightism' used as the metaphor for all the universal 'isms' (racism, sexism, ageism and so on). The premise was a Britain where short people are discriminated against, height regulations stipulating that anyone under 5ft must live in tower-block ghettos south of the River Thames. In the first episode, a new EEC regulation height of 1.55 metres is enforced, and this means that Roy Pink, at 5ft ¼in, is suddenly designated 'short' and rounded up to live in the ghetto. For Roy, a 'heightist' who despises short people, being classified as one of them is a real body-blow. While in the ghetto he meets Fred, the timid leader of the residents' association, Howard, leader of the militant Small Liberation Front, and Japanese businessman Mr Motokura, who was in Britain to open a new factory when he was herded off to the ghetto. Through these acquaintances, Roy is gradually made aware of the plight of short people, and presumably – had the series continued – he would have come to see the stupidity of his own prejudice. But *A Small Problem* ended prematurely after just one series, partly because of the furore surrounding its transmission.

Writers Millan and Walling were actors who had been in their fair share of sitcoms (the former was a regular in **Citizen Smith**, the latter was a perennial in **Brush Strokes**) when they decided to use comedy to tackle the issue of prejudice. Their mistake was in picking 'heightism' as their theme (although, to be fair, any theme would have caused a furore). As soon as the first episode went out, the complaints flooded in – people of restricted height being outraged that smallness should be the object of comedy.

These complainants accused the writers of reinforcing height prejudices that already existed: many found the terms of abuse used in the show ('dwarf', 'midget') personally offensive, while others pointed out that such a series wouldn't have been tolerated had it been about a racial minority (which rather missed the point of using a metaphor). Millan and Walling went on the BBC's community-access programme *Open Air* to answer their accusers, arguing that all prejudice was stupid and that they could have taken anything – people with blue eyes, people with big ears – as the theme.

All the same, the writers would have done well to learn a lesson from the American singer/songwriter Randy Newman, who, in 1977, used the same trick of utilising 'heightism' as a metaphor for prejudice in his satirical hit 'Short People'. Although the song was intended to ridicule discrimination, the outcry was enormous and the furore dogged him for years.

Small Wonder

USA · SYNDICATION (METROMEDIA VIDEO PRODUCTIONS) · SITCOM

92 × 30 mins · colour

US dates: Sept 1985–Sept 1989
UK dates: 6 Apr–29 June 1986 (12 episodes) ITV Sun 1.30pm

MAIN CAST

Victoria Ann 'Vicky' Smith · · Tiffany Brissette
Ted Lawson · · · · · · · · · · · · · · Dick Christie
Joan Lawson · · · · · · · · · · · Marla Pennington
Jamie Lawson · · · · · · · · · · · · Jerry Supiran
Harriet Brindle · · · · · · · · · · Emily Schulman
Bonnie Brindle · · · · · Edie McClurg (1985–86)
Brandon Brindle · · William Bogert (1986–89)

CREDITS

creator Howard Leeds · *writers* various · *directors* various · *producers* Howard Leeds, Budd Grossman

Small Wonder is widely considered one of the worst low-budget sitcoms of all time, inexplicably stretched to 92 episodes and, equally curiously, imported to British television by ITV (well, by LWT at least, which screened it on Sunday afternoons).

The 'premise' was this: Ted Lawson, an engineer/inventor for United Robotronics, builds an android in an effort to assist handicapped children. The 11-year-old child robot is named VICI (Voice Input Child Identicant) – Vicky to others – and is taken home by Lawson so that it can mature within a family environment. Ted's wife treats Vicki as if it had been hatched inside her womb, and Jamie, the Lawsons' son (real 11-year-old flesh and bones) quickly befriends his new 'sister'. All of which is curious because Vicki is the essence of all ghastly sickly-sweet American sitcom children alloyed into one appalling metallic bundle; she's also super-strong, has a streak of logic that would make even (Leonard Nimoy's) Spock seem human and speaks in a boring monotone.

The Lawson family – berks, all – try to keep Vicky's existence a secret (begging the question of why she was made and then taken home in the first place), but their disagreeable neighbours, the Brindles, *will* keep on popping up at the most unexpected moments, especially nosey Harriet, who is keen on Jamie, and her mother Bonnie and her father Brandon, who just happens to be Ted Lawson's work boss.

The Small World Of Samuel Tweet

UK · BBC · CHILDREN'S SITCOM

12 × 25 mins · colour

Series One (6) 24 May–28 June 1974 · BBC1
Fri mostly 5.15pm (1 episode on BBC2)

Series Two (6) 5 June–10 July 1975 · BBC1
Thu mostly 5.15pm

MAIN CAST

Samuel Tweet ··········· Freddie Davies
Lord Chumpton ········ Cardew Robinson
Miss Doogoodie ········ Damaris Hayman
PC Wicketts ············· Colin Edwynn
Sandra Jones ······· Prue Clarke (series 2)
Russell Chumpton ····· Norman Turkington
···························· (series 2)

CREDITS

writer Gary Knight · *producer* Tony Harrison

Born in Brixton, south London, on 21 July 1937 and raised in the north, the standup comedian Freddie Davies began his career as a holiday-camp entertainer and turned pro in 1964, working the cabaret circuit and then gaining fame at the end of the decade after appearances on *Val Parnell's Sunday Night At The London Palladium* and *Opportunity Knocks*. Because his act featured corny jokes about budgerigars, and his face – pulled a certain way – resembled a tropical bird, Davies was given the nickname 'Parrot Face'. Henceforth, billings proclaimed him Freddie 'Parrot Face' Davies, but he didn't seem to mind.

Davies' stage persona was that of a gormless, bowler-hatted, bird-obsessed (the feathered kind), lisping dolt, an unusual act that proved popular with youngsters and adults alike, and in 1974 he was given this children's TV comedy series, written especially for a variation of his stage character, Samuel Tweet. Mr Tweet is a well-meaning but simple soul (a twit Tweet …) who works in a pet shop in Chumpton Green and becomes involved in a number of exploits with Lord Chumpton and other leading lights in the tiny village. Various animals – including, of course, budgies and parrots – appeared regularly in the storylines.

Smashie And Nicey – The End Of An Era

UK · BBC (TIGER ASPECT) · SKETCH

1 × 45 mins · colour

4 Apr 1994 · BBC1 Mon 9.55pm

MAIN CAST

Mike 'Smashie' Smash ··· Paul Whitehouse
Dave 'Nicey' Nice ·········· Harry Enfield

CREDITS

writers Harry Enfield/Paul Whitehouse · *director* Daniel Kleinman · *producer* Alison Owen

Enfield and Whitehouse's marvellous comedy creations, the ageing 'poptastic' DJs Mike 'Smashie' Smash and Dave 'Nicey' Nice, struck a chord with the public and graduated from sketches in *Harry Enfield's Television Programme* to (ironically) presenting *Top Of The Pops* and fronting a tribute to that durable chart show in *Smashie And Nicey's Top Of The Pops Party* (BBC1, 4 January 1994).

This Easter special, *Smashie And Nicey – The End Of An Era*, was a spoof documentary looking back over the careers of the glib, inanity-spouting DJs on the occasion of their retirement from Radio Fab FM. Landmark moments in the life of the pair were plundered from events in the careers of real-life DJs (especially Tony Blackburn and Alan Freeman, upon whom, respectively, the two characters were loosely based) which were sent-up with the aid of beautifully constructed 'archive' material. Seemingly happy to join in the fun, Freeman and Blackburn appeared as themselves in the show, as did Bob Geldof, Valerie Singleton and Angus Deayton.

The programme won the 1995 Silver Rose of Montreux. (Another British entry, Chris Evans's C4 game-show *Don't Forget Your Toothbrush*, won the Golden Rose.)

Note. 'Smashie and Nicey' introduced the first editions of C4's *Late Licence* strand, on 19 and 20 November 1993, providing the between-programmes linking material. They also appeared in character in **Comic Relief** in 1991, 1993 and 1997.

The Smell Of Reeves And Mortimer

see Reeves And Mortimer

Smith And Goody

UK · ITV (THAMES) · CHILDREN'S SKETCH

7 × 30 mins · colour

One series (6) 23 Sep–28 Oct 1980 · Tue 4.45pm

Special *Smith And Goody … On Ice!* 30 Dec 1980 · Tue 4.45pm

MAIN CAST

Mel Smith

Bob Goody
Peter Brewis

CREDITS

writers Mel Smith/Bob Goody · *director/producer* Roger Gale · *executive producer* John Hambley

Shortly before the third series of *Not The Nine O'Clock News* on BBC2, Mel Smith ventured over to ITV for a children's sketch production, co-written with and co-starring Bob Goody, with music provided by Peter Brewis. As well as being funny, the series had a specific aim: to advocate literature. Set in a flat in which books, newspapers and magazines were coming out of every crevice, the sketches were designed to encourage young people to enjoy reading, especially those kids whose families did not frequent bookstores or libraries.

Smith (rotund) and Goody (lanky) made for the archetypal double-act partnership, and had worked together since meeting at drama school, mounting a joint production at the 1977 Edinburgh Festival Fringe.

Smith And Jones

Mel Smith (born in London, 3 December 1952) studied experimental psychology at Oxford before becoming a theatre director for six years and then taking to the stage. Griff Rhys Jones (born in Cardiff, 16 November 1953) joined the comedy world by the more traditional post-war route: a stint with the Cambridge Footlights leading to employment as a BBC radio producer and stage performances with fellow Footlights contemporaries Clive Anderson and Rory McGrath.

When producer John Lloyd was putting together his team for *Not The Nine O'Clock News*, Smith was employed as a permanent fixture while Jones, initially, was utilised only in small roles, becoming a fully fledged member of the team for the second series. But as the four-man *Beyond The Fringe* team 20 years earlier had led to the forming of a long-lasting double-act in Peter Cook and Dudley Moore, so *Not The Nine …* generated a durable partnership in Mel Smith and Griff Rhys Jones, who clearly enjoyed a special comedic chemistry that was worthy of further exploration when the parent series ended. This they did, forming their own company (TalkBack Productions) which, in its earliest days, focused on the making of witty, innovative radio and TV commercials. Their first television sketch series followed in 1984 (after a short try-out in 1982), pitching their humour somewhere between traditional stage patter and the harder 'alternative' comedy of the period, and the partnership has continued to the time of writing.

See also *Sardines*, *Smith And Goody* and Comic Relief.

Alas Smith And Jones

UK · BBC · SKETCH

27 editions (25 × 30 mins · 1 × 40 mins · 1 × 5 mins) · colour

Short special (5 mins) part of *The Funny Side Of Christmas* 27 Dec 1982 · BBC1 Mon 8.05pm

Series One (6) 31 Jan–6 Mar 1984 · BBC2 Tue 9.30pm

Series Two (6) 31 Oct–5 Dec 1985 · BBC2 Thu 9pm

Series Three (6) 18 Sep–23 Oct 1986 · BBC2 Thu 9pm

Series Four (7) 15 Oct–26 Nov 1987 · BBC2 Thu 9pm

Special (40 mins) *Alas Sage And Onion* 21 Dec 1988 · BBC2 Wed 9pm

MAIN CAST
Mel Smith
Griff Rhys Jones

CREDITS
writers Mel Smith, Griff Rhys Jones, Andy Hamilton, Clive Anderson, Simon Bell, Jimmy Mulville, Rory McGrath, Mark Cullen, Colin Bostock-Smith, Laurie Rowley, Paul Smith/Terry Kyan, Roger Planer, Barry Bowes, Robin Driscoll, Moray Hunter/Jack Docherty, Paul Martin, John Irwin, Paul B Davies, Jon Canter, Dick Hills, Mark Steel, Terry Ravenscroft, Guy Jenkin, Andrew Hastings, Jamie Rix/Nick Wilton, John Kilby, Martin Booth, John Machin, Tony Sarchet, Ian Brown, Abi Grant, Phil Nice/Arthur Smith, Rob Grant/Doug Naylor and others · *script editor* Jimmy Mulville · *directors/producers* Martin Shardlow (series 1), Jimmy Mulville/John Kilby (series 2), John Kilby (series 3), Jamie Rix/John Kilby (series 4 & 1988 special)

Alas Smith And Jones – the title being a punning twist on the popular US cowboy series *Alias Smith And Jones* – was an unpretentious sketch show that, at times, touched the heights. Mel and Griff introduced the programmes as 'themselves', standing in front of a studio audience, before letting the (usually high quality) sketches unfold, one after another, with little or no further linking. Typically, as with *Not The Nine O'Clock News*, these sketches were contemporary rather than topical.

With some of the *Not The Nine O'Clock News* writing talent on board it was inevitable that, in parts, *Alas* echoed that earlier show in style and content, but there were enough innovations to give the new series its own identity. One of the differences was the inclusion of long-ish filmed sketches, usually spoofing a TV programme, film or, more likely, an entire genre. The principal difference, though, were the 'head to head' – sequences, in which the two men sat face-to-face and pursued abstract

conversations about any subject under the sun, Smith being the rather superior know-all (who actually knew very little), Jones, terminally dense, speaking with a 'thicko' voice and employing a bizarre logic and insatiable curiosity. The idea created for a series of radio advertisements, these conversations were often hysterically funny, comprising a litany of misunderstandings and misconceptions piled one on top of another – although, inevitably, they drew 'second best' comparisons with Peter Cook and Dudley Moore's fabulous 'Pete and Dud' excursions (the so-called 'Dagenham Dialogues').

Although a double-act, Smith and Jones were not typical of the genre: either – or both, or neither – could play the funny-man or the foil, depending on the material. In other words, unlike, say, Morecambe and Wise, or Little and Large, the pair didn't stick to a recognisable relationship or to familiar characteristics within the sketches but instead acted as different personae to suit the writing, a method already utilised by the Two Ronnies but pursued to even greater lengths here. A high standard of writing and performance throughout distinguished the series, reinforcing the already high reputations and standing of the two stars.

Note. In 1985, after the first series of *Alas Smith And Jones*, the stars appeared on the big screen in Mike Hodges' disappointing sci-fi comedy movie *Morons From Outer Space*.

The World According To Smith And Jones

UK · ITV (LWT) · SKETCH

12 × 30 mins · colour

Series One (6) 11 Jan–15 Feb 1987 · Sun 10pm

Series Two (6) 16 Jan–20 Feb 1988 · Sat mostly 10.40pm

MAIN CAST
Mel Smith
Griff Rhys Jones

CREDITS
writers Colin Bostock-Smith (7), Moray Hunter/Jack Docherty (4), Clive Anderson (1), Geoffrey Perkins (1) · *script editor* Nick Symons (series 2) · *director* Terry Kinane · *executive producer* Richard Drewett · *producer* Charles Brand

A novel idea for a sketch series, with Smith and Jones replaying old film clips in order to make sense of the world's history and so gain a fuller understanding of the meaning of life. Along the way, of course, they managed to prove that Queen Victoria was a vacuum cleaner, and that Britain won the Eurovision Song Contest in 1195.

Altering the concept slightly, programmes in the second series were

themed along specific lines: medicine, war, law, education, the arts and science.

The Home-Made Xmas Video

UK · BBC · SKETCH

1 × 30 mins · colour

23 Dec 1987 · BBC2 Wed 9.30pm

MAIN CAST
Griff Rhys Jones
Mel Smith
Diane Langton

CREDITS
writer Robin Driscoll · *director* Jamie Rix · *producer* John Kilby

A spoof of a family Christmas, as seen through the lens of a domestic video camera. All the expected dodgy close-ups, cock-ups and family crises were exploited, with strange angles and wobbly hand-held camera techniques that would have been familiar to many video-camera owners.

Smith And Jones In Small Doses

UK · BBC (TALKBACK PRODUCTIONS) · SITCOMS

4 × 20 mins · colour

19 Oct–9 Nov 1989 · BBC2 Thu 10.10pm

By way of a change, Smith and Jones temporarily departed the sketch formula for a short series of individual comedy playlets.

The Whole Hog   19 OCT

MAIN CAST
Giles · Mel Smith
Maurice · · · · · · · · · · · · · · · · Griff Rhys Jones

CREDITS
writer Graeme Garden · *director* Mike Newell · *producers* Peter Fincham, Trevor Evans

Giles meets his ex-wife after ten years and is shocked to find that she is now a man, and the chairman of his company.

The Boat People   26 OCT

MAIN CAST
Derek · Mel Smith
Colin · · · · · · · · · · · · · · · · Griff Rhys Jones

CREDITS
writer Griff Rhys Jones · *director* Kevin Billington · *producers* Peter Fincham, Trevor Evans

A weekend on Derek's yacht is no fun for the claustrophobic Colin.

Second Thoughts   2 NOV

MAIN CAST
Sam · Mel Smith
Boz · · · · · · · · · · · · · · · · · · Griff Rhys Jones

CREDITS
writer Anthony Minghella · *director* Paul Weiland · *producers* Peter Fincham, Trevor Evans

Two would-be suicides fight for the right to be the first to throw himself off a newly constructed bridge.

The Waiting Room

9 NOV

MAIN CAST

Rev Ben Bottomley · · · · · · · · · · Mel Smith
Rev Andrew Pennycuick · · · Griff Rhys Jones
Receptionist · · · · · · · · · · · Deborah Norton

CREDITS

writer John Mortimer · director Brian Gilbert · producers Peter Fincham, Trevor Evans

Two men of the cloth disagree about more than just the style of religious services.

Smith And Jones

UK · BBC (TALKBACK PRODUCTIONS) · SKETCH

30 × 30 mins · colour

Series One (6) 16 Nov–28 Dec 1989 · BBC1 Thu 9.30pm

Series Two (6) 22 Nov 1990–3 Jan 1991 · BBC1 Thu 9.30pm

Series Three (6) 22 Oct–3 Dec 1992 · BBC1 Thu 9.30pm

Series Four (6) 6 Sep–18 Oct 1995 · BBC1 Wed 9.30pm

Series Five (6) 19 June–24 July 1997 · BBC1 Thu mostly 10pm

MAIN CAST

Mel Smith
Griff Rhys Jones
Chris Langham (series 1)
Diana Quick (series 1)
Miranda Richardson (series 1)

CREDITS

writers Mel Smith, Griff Rhys Jones, Clive Anderson, Robin Driscoll, Graeme Garden, Simon Greenall, Chris Langham, Pete McCarthy, Paul Smith/Terry Kyan and others · directors Dominic Brigstocke (12), John Kilby (6), Graham C Williams (6), Chris Bould (6) · producers Jon Plowman (12), Jon Magnusson (12), Jamie Rix (6)

Smith and Jones switched to BBC1 and returned to the now *Alas*-less sketch format, the first series being launched one week after the final *Smith And Jones In Small Doses* playlet on BBC2.

Similar in format to *Alas Smith And Jones*, the pair were determined to maintain the new show's contemporary feel, and among the targets of the humour this time was the then current open-ended C4 chat-show *After Dark*, and modern phenomena such as squeegee-wielding windscreen washers at traffic lights and New Age travellers. The first series featured a recurring sketch about a mythological Greek soap opera (*Olympus*), and throughout the run the pair presented their dumb and dumber couple in more 'head to head' routines (often written by Clive Anderson). With the usual high quality writing and production values, Smith and Jones won a British Comedy Award for their efforts.

During this period both men maintained their individual careers too, such endeavours keeping *Smith And Jones* out of production for an extended period in 1991 and 1992 (although an eight-week run of compilation repeats, screened 19 September–14 November 1991, kept them in the public eye). Jones appeared in straight drama and stage work; Smith also took straight acting roles and directed moves – *The Tall Guy*, released in 1989, *Radioland Murders* in 1994 and *Bean – The Ultimate Disaster Movie* in 1997. After a three-year absence, the TV series returned in 1995, and a fifth season followed two years later still, with the duo demonstrating once again their determination to explore new characterisations and areas of comedy. This time around, however, the public and critical reaction was poor, and indications were afoot that the 1997 run may have been their final work in this format.

Note. Highlights from the pairing's many BBC TV shows were re-edited for a series of ten half-hour programmes on BBC Radio 2, *Smith And Jones Sound Off*, broadcast from 16 November 1996 to 18 January 1997.

The Smiths

UK · ITV (GRANADA) · SITCOM

1 × 30 mins · colour

7 Aug 1995 · Mon 8pm

MAIN CAST

Clive Smith · · · · · · · · · · · · · Kevin McNally
Carol Smith · · · · · · · · · · · · Rebecca Lacey
Wayne Smith · · · · · · · · · · · · · · Scott Neal
Debbie Smith · · · · · · · · · · · Heather Jones
Geoff · · · · · · · · · · · · · · · · Rowland Rivron
Linda · · · · · · · · · · · · · · · · Jackie Downey
Donna · · · · · · · · · · · · · · · · · Sonia Evans
Dooley · · · · · · · · · · · · · · · Geoffrey Hughes
Wilf · · · · · · · · · · · · · · · · · · Angus Lennie

CREDITS

writer Julian Roach · director Tom Poole · executive producer Andy Harries · producer Antony Wood

The fifth pilot in ITV's *Comedy Firsts* season was this Merseyside sitcom about the Smith family.

Clive and Carol Smith struggle to keep the wolf from the door and raise their two layabout teenagers Wayne and Debbie. Life is tough, and the walls of their small semi-detached so thin that Clive and Carol have to recline the seats of their ramshackle 1981 Ford Cortina for their moments of passion, just as they had in their courting days. When the car gearbox packs up they go without for a couple of weeks, but then, with his friend Geoff's help, Clive manages to fix it up. While they're celebrating down the pub, however, the car is bought by a passing stranger, so Clive and Carol purchase a garden shed instead.

Unusually, *The Smiths* was taped without an audience. (Either this or there was one but they found nothing to laugh at.) No series developed.

The Smothers Brothers Comedy Hour

USA · CBS (COMEDIC PRODUCTIONS) · SKETCH

71 × 60 mins · colour

US dates: 5 Feb 1967–8 June 1969

UK dates: 7 Jan–16 June 1968 (12 editions · b/w) BBC1 Sun mostly 7.25pm

MAIN CAST

Tom Smothers
Dick Smothers
Pat Paulsen
Leigh French
Mason Williams
Bob Einstein

CREDITS

writers Tom Smothers, Elaine May, Steve Martin and others · directors various · producers Saul Ilson, Ernest Chambers, Allan Blye

A landmark US television series that caused a furore there and opened up the question of the American networks' susceptibility to self- and outside censorship.

Tom Smothers (born in New York City on 2 February 1937) and his brother Dick (ditto, 20 November 1939) released a number of albums in the early- to mid-1960s, combining comedy with a little music (the older brother played guitar, the younger one bass). Their comedic characters were classic straight-man (Dick, the more handsome one) and thick-head (Tom). After making regular appearances on chat-shows, CBS awarded the pair their own series, hoping that their irreverent, topical humour would go down well with the progressively more liberal 15–30-year-old US audiences. As it transpired, the brothers' comedy was much more topical than CBS had realised. With their overt stance against America's involvement in the Vietnam War, knowing asides about the prevailing drug culture, ready employment of black guests, and a general anti-authoritarian comedic stance, the brothers became folk heroes to the burgeoning counter-culture movement expressing itself in the USA at this time with riots and public protests about the Vietnam War and what was seen as further oppressive behaviour by the US establishment within its own country.

The Smothers' determination to present this type of material infuriated and deeply embarrassed the conservative CBS network, and its in-house censors clashed many times with the brothers, excising not just lines and jokes but whole sketches, segments and songs from their pre-recorded shows. The brothers retaliated by going public with news of the censorship and resiliently fighting many of the decisions. Tom Smothers, who was actively involved in every level of the production, even took the battle to the National Broadcasters Association convention in Washington DC, where he lobbied for support from liberal congressmen and other officials. This move was the last straw for the network, which promptly cancelled the series, despite its high ratings, and refused to rescind its decision in the face of the subsequent public outcry. When screened in the UK (as simply *The Smothers Brothers*) the series produced no such problems, partly because the subject matter was not so close to home and also because, by this time, programmes like **That Was The Week That Was** and **Till Death Us Do Part** had already stretched the boundaries of what was acceptable television fare in Britain. But just two years after the demise of *The Smothers Brothers Comedy Hour*, **All In The Family** – the US version of *Till Death Us Do Part* – succeeded in breaking many of the network taboos and stretched the US TV boundaries as never before.

Other – less controversial – series followed in the 1970s; then, on 3 February 1988, CBS aired *The Smothers Brothers Comedy Hour: The 20th Reunion*, in which the brothers and a guest cast took a look back at their groundbreaking series. This was a prelude to a full new series of *The Smothers Brothers Show* (30 March 1988–23 August 1989) that, unsuccessfully, attempted to place the pairing back in the pantheon of primetime TV.

Snakes And Ladders

UK · C4 (YORKSHIRE) · SITCOM

7 × 30 mins · colour

17 Oct–28 Nov 1989 · Tue 10pm

MAIN CAST

Gavin Sinclair	John Gordon-Sinclair
Giles	Adrian Edmondson
Mr Haverty	Christopher Godwin
Mr Pym	Ron Donachie
Gavin's mum	June Watson
Gavin's dad	Phil McCall
Mr Lambie	Roger Sloman
TV reporter	Elaine Collins
Lord Tewkesbury/ Computer voice	Ed Devereaux
Serena	Lynsey Baxter
Donald	Tony Meyer
Robbie	Steven O'Donnell
Ronald	David Meyer

CREDITS

writers Laurence Marks/Maurice Gran · *executive producer* Vernon Lawrence · *director/producer* Baz Taylor

A satirical Marks and Gran sitcom with Orwellian and Twainian overtones, combining nightmare visions of *1984* with the role-reversal of *The Prince And The Pauper*. The blend was clever, with some delightful touches, but at the end of the day the series generated few laughs.

Snakes And Ladders was set in the Britain of 1999 (ten years beyond at the time of screening), where Thatcherism rules, Lord Branson is revered, television is called Murdochvision, profit is everything, rampant inflation means that the mortgage interest rate *falls* to 37.5 per cent, the Queen has resigned and Charles is king, there are psychiatric 'hospitals' for political detainees, and, most tellingly of all, Britain has a real north/south divide, with security guards manning the border posts and identity papers required to pass from the enslaved north to the idyllic south. In the Northern Sector the weather is perpetually cold and food rationing is *de rigueur*; South Britain enjoys year-round hot weather because of a conveniently-placed hole in the ozone layer.

Into this situation two young men are thrust. Scotsman Gavin (John Gordon-Sinclair) is lucky to get a job as a trainee slave in the Paisley factory of International Entirety, the biggest private company in Britain. It is such a breakthrough that his tenement block throws a communal party to congratulate one of their number being in employment – the first time in seven years; they sing 'We Shall Overcome', albeit half-heartedly, and the Lord Provost comes along to make a speech. Englishman Giles (Adrian Edmondson) is a philandering upper-class oik, relentlessly snotty and stultifyingly snobbish. As the son of the Australian baron Lord Tewkesbury (a title obtained by palm-greasing), the owner of International Entirety, Giles has spent ten years on holiday at Oxford University. To his astonishment, however, Daddy cruelly decides to send him on a company traineeship, to learn every facet of his organisation from the bottom up. To keep his identity a secret Giles is given a pseudonym, Alexander G St Clair, but this is mis-entered into the computer and – enter the role-reversal scenario – Scotsman Gavin suddenly finds himself posted down south, amid extreme wealth, while ghastly Giles experiences life in the northern wastes.

Snug And Cozi

UK · ITV (SCOTTISH) · CHILDREN'S SITCOM

13 × 10 mins · colour

Series One (6) 1 Nov–6 Dec 1996 · Fri 4pm

Series Two (7) 19 Aug–2 Oct 1997 · Tue then Thu mostly 4.05pm

MAIN CAST

Snug	Richard Vobes
Cozi	Nigel Cooper
Emily	Sarah Montgomery

CREDITS

writer Richard Vobes · *executive producer* Elizabeth Partyka · *directors/producers* Martyn Day (series 1), Haldane Duncan (series 2)

Thirteen doses of virtually dialogue-free slapstick comedy for children, depicting the misadventures of two bald aliens, Snug and Cozi, whose home planet, Squadge, is located one hundred million light years distant. Although inexperienced at flying, the pair borrow a rocket and blast off into the blackness, but after encountering a storm of asteroids they crash land on Earth. Here they are befriended by Emily, an 11-year-old schoolgirl, and she introduces them to human customs. In true alien style, of course, Snug and Cozi find it awfully hard to adapt, causing havoc at every turn in an almost identical manner to Laurel and Hardy, the true masters of the genre from 60 years earlier. (Snug is like Laurel; the larger one, Cozi, replicates Hardy's mannerisms.)

Richard Vobes and Nigel Cooper, who played Snug and Cozi, are London-based children's entertainers.

Note. The second series, announced as comprising ten episodes, stopped at seven.

So Haunt Me

UK · BBC (CINEMA VERITY) · SITCOM

19 × 30 mins · colour

Series One (6) 23 Feb–29 Mar 1992 · BBC1 Sun 8.35pm

Special · 20 Dec 1992 · BBC1 Sun 7.45pm

Series Two (6) 10 Jan–14 Feb 1993 · BBC1 Sun 8.20pm

Series Three (6) 2 Jan–6 Feb 1994 · BBC1 Sun 8.25pm

MAIN CAST

Yetta Feldman	Miriam Karlin
Sally Rokeby	Tessa Peake-Jones
Pete Rokeby	George Costigan
Tammy Rokeby	Laura Simmons (Laura Howard)
David Rokeby	Jeremy Green

CREDITS

writer Paul A Mendelson · *directors* John Stroud (13), Sylvie Boden (6) · *producers* Caroline Gold (13), Sharon Bloom (6)

When Pete Rokeby quits his job to concentrate on becoming a writer, he and his family – wife Sally, children Tammy and David – are forced to move into a smaller house in a less pleasant neighbourhood in order to make ends meet. Strangely, their new home is suffused with the whiff of chicken soup, and it soon transpires that they are sharing the house with the ghost of its previous owner, Yetta Feldman. She is the archetypal interfering Jewish mother, and wastes little time in exerting her influence over the (gentile) new occupants. But, for all of her set ways and opinionated views, Yetta has a heart of gold, truly caring for her surrogate family and ending up as their phantomish matriarch.

So Haunt Me provided a welcome return to the TV sitcom for Miriam Karlin – embedded in viewers' hearts and minds as the union shop-steward in **The Rag Trade** – and her support cast, especially George Costigan, fared well too. But the series suffered from a major flaw: while the early scripts constantly alluded to the Rokebys' dishevelled wreck of a new home, the set suggested a thoroughly average terraced house – thus the family's complaints made them come across as terrible whingers, and with homelessness a major concern at this time, their criticisms about the kind of house for which hundreds of thousands of people were desperate, were nothing less than insulting. This was a rare instance of the usually thoroughly efficient set designers working at odds with the script.

So You Think You're Irish

see The Amnesty Galas

So You Think You've Got Troubles

UK · BBC (ALOMO PRODUCTIONS) · SITCOM
6 × 30 mins · colour
17 Oct–28 Nov 1991 · BBC1 Thu 10pm

MAIN CAST
Ivan Fox · · · · · · · · · · · · · · · Warren Mitchell
Charley Adamson · · · · · · · · · · · James Ellis
Anna Adamson · · · · · · · · · · · · · Linda Wray
George Nathan · · · · · · · · · · · · · Harry Towb
Roberta Nathan · · · · · · · · · Stella McCusker
Louise Nathan · · · · · · · · · · · Emer Gillespie
Sean Doherty · · · · · · · · · · · · · John Keegan

CREDITS
writers Laurence Marks/Maurice Gran · directors Mike Holgate (4), Colm Villa (2) · producer Tara Prem

Comedy with a serious edge from **Birds Of A Feather** creators Marks and Gran, starring the man who made Alf Garnett flesh, Warren Mitchell.

Mitchell was cast as a widower, Ivan Fox, the long-serving manager of a London pipe tobacco factory whose job is transferred to Northern Ireland. Fox is a lapsed Jew and feels that, as an agnostic, he'll be mainly left alone by the Protestants and Catholic communities. He is right, but the embattled Belfast Jewish community spies a potential new member and latches on. Soon Fox is having to fend off the question 'Are you a Catholic Jew or a Protestant Jew?' and becoming inexorably embroiled in the 'troubles'. Initially, all he wants is to be left alone – to eat his bacon sandwich in peace, if you like – but the religious passions of those around Fox cause him to re-evaluate his lack of faith. Adding to the turmoil is the personal animosity felt towards Fox by his bigoted Protestant Loyalist factory-hand, Charley Adamson.

These are large themes indeed, so big that the good scripts and fine acting could not cut through the uncomfortable setting: it was

hard to raise laughs in a sitcom when the news bulletins screened an hour before each episode underlined the deadly seriousness of the situation in Ulster. That Marks and Gran were prepared to 'have a go', however, doing so with every attention to detail and no sense of frivolity, speaks volumes for the rapidly growing stature of the writers at this time.

Soap

USA · ABC (WITT-THOMAS-HARRIS PRODUCTIONS) · SITCOM
85 episodes (78 × 30 mins · 7 × 60 mins) · colour
US dates: 13 Sep 1977–20 Apr 1981
UK dates: 15 Sep 1978–5 Feb 1982 (92 × 30 mins) ITV various days and times

MAIN CAST
Jessica Tate · · · · · · · · · Katherine Helmond
Chester Tate · · · · · · · · · · · · Robert Mandan
Eunice Tate · · · · · · · · · · · · · · Jennifer Salt
Corrine Tate · · · · · Diana Canova (1977–80)
Billy Tate · · · · · · · · · · · · · · · · Jimmy Baio
The Major · · · · · · · · · · · · · Arthur Peterson
Mary Campbell · · · · · · · · · · · Cathryn Damon
Burt Campbell · · · · · · · · · · Richard Mulligan
Danny Dallas · · · · · · · · · · · · · · Ted Wass
Jodie Dallas · · · · · · · · · · · · · Billy Crystal
Peter Campbell · · · · · · Robert Urich (1977)
Chuck Campbell · · · · · · · · · · · Jay Johnson
Benson · · · · · · Robert Guillaume (1977–79)
Saunders · · · Roscoe Lee Browne (1980–81)

OTHER APPEARANCES
Dutch · · · · · Donnelly Rhodes (1978–81)
Timothy Flotsky · · · · · Sal Viscuso (1978–79)
Elaine Lefkowitz · · · Dinah Manoff (1978–79)
Sally · · · · · · Caroline McWilliams (1978–79)
Carol David · · · · Rebecca Balding (1978–81)
El Puerco · · · · · Gregory Sierra (1980–81)
Ingrid Svenson · · · Inga Swenson (1978–79)
Detective Donahue · · John Byner (1978–80)

CREDITS
creator Susan Harris · writers Susan Harris (25), Susan Harris/Stu Silver (39), Susan Harris/Stu Silver/Dick Clair/Jenna McMahon (6), Susan Harris/Stu Silver/Dick Clair/Jenna McMahon/Barry Vigon/Danny Jacobson (7), Susan Harris/Jordan Crittenden (4), Susan Harris/Tony Lang (3), Stu Silver/Dick Clair/Jenna McMahon/Barry Vigon/Danny Jacobson (1) · directors Jay Sandrich (51), J D Lobue (33), John Bowab (1) · executive producers Susan Harris, Paul Junger Witt, Tony Thomas · producer Susan Harris

No comedy in the annals of American television has aroused as much advance controversy as *Soap*. On the basis of pre-launch publicity alone there was a concerted effort to have it stopped, with a reputed 32,000 letters arriving at ABC (only nine in favour), sponsors being urged to withdraw advertising revenue and TV stations picketed. (All of which frightened off the BBC in Britain, which passed on the series and allowed ITV to acquire it.) What the US viewers feared was a weekly series that touched heavily upon but made light of homosexuality, organised crime, murder,

male impotence, rampant promiscuity, race, religion and a host of other sensitive issues. The 31,993 complainants were disappointed, however: this most fiery of shows went ahead – and quickly proved itself safe and popular viewing. (Albeit at a late hour: it never went out in the States before 9.30pm and in the UK was usually screened close to midnight.) More than anything else, though, *Soap* was fabulously funny; it successfully put across some wildly creative comedy ideas, was a launching pad to greater success for some of its talented ensemble and, in the manner of the very best US comedy series, packed more laughs per minute than any British rival.

Soap was the creation of Susan Harris, who wanted to lampoon the daytime soap operas that proliferate on American television, not *Dallas* (a primetime series) but the really dross, schlock-operas like *As The World Turns*, *All My Children*, *The Bold And The Beautiful* and others of that woeful ilk. *Soap* employed all the steamy ingredients of these unending serials but hilariously so, and in an ultra-fast paced, half-hour episodic format that usually, like its more serious counterparts, ended in the proverbial cliffhanger. Harris's particular skill, however (elements of **M*A*S*H** here), was to weave genuine, heart-tugging moments of sadness, loss and personal reflection amid the comedy, a theme she would later reprise with equal effect in another of her creations, **The Golden Girls**. The effect was hypnotic, with viewers sent on a dizzying ride that would touch all the emotions and yet never be far from laughter.

To explain in print all that happened in *Soap* would take pages. Safe to say that every character was stretched into every possible situation within his or her orbit. And *what* characters. The series depicted the lives of two families, linked by sisters. First there are the Tates, who live on the better side of Dunns River, Connecticut. Jessica is the ultimate in dizziness – empty-headed, beautifully naïve and, in the end, a coma victim and captive of South American revolutionaries; Chester is her lying, cheating, embezzling, philandering husband who murders and then develops amnesia; Corrine and Eunice are their sex-mad daughters whose choice in men (priests, convicts, murderers, politicians and more) is unusual to say the least; when Corrine has a baby it is possessed by the devil and inflicts great damage until Jessica, unintentionally, performs an exorcism; Billy is their (fairly characterless) younger brother who, as he gets older, is held captive by religious zealots; The Major is Jessica's literally insane father who believes that the Second World War is still in progress; Benson is the family's black butler, who despises all of them except Jessica and treats everyone with contemptuous disdain.

Across the other side of town live the Campbells. Mary is Jessica's sister; her first husband, a mobster, has been murdered by (it turns out) her second husband, Burt. Burt is a loose-limbed jumping-bean of a man who suffers impotence, makes a mess of almost everything he does, gets captured by aliens from a visiting UFO and, eventually, becomes a sheriff. Burt has two sons, one of whom, Peter, has been murdered by Chester for carrying on with both Jessica and Corrine; the second, Chuck, is a psychotic ventriloquist who is never seen without his dummy Bob – man and wooden-man dress alike and carry on all normal (and abnormal) conversations, even though they don't always agree. The first of Mary's two children from her first marriage is Jodie, a homosexual who, to his own surprise, fathers a baby (who is then kidnapped) and then, in an even greater surprise, takes on the personality of a greatly aged East European immigrant Jew; the other son is Danny, a complete numskull who has links with the mob and, unluckily, has two wives murdered. Eventually, Mary gives birth to a new baby but isn't certain if the father is Burt or an alien.

Soap ended on the cliffhanger to end all cliffhangers, with most of the characters put into terrible situations from which there was no chance of escape. This was the only way that such a wild series could have ended, and while millions of viewers mourned its passing, in truth, just about every angle had been wrung out of every situation. Susan Harris's creation – she also had a hand in writing all but one of the episodes and produced the series – was finally over but it was rarely less than wonderful.

Benson was a direct spin-off, Richard Mulligan (who played Burt) went into Harris's *Empty Nest*, Katherine Helmond (Jessica) became a major player in *Who's The Boss?*, Diana Canova (Corrine) starred in *Throb* and Billy Crystal (Jodie), unknown before *Soap*, went on to find great success in the movies.

Note. Following the first complete run of episodes, the entire set of 92 half-hours has twice been screened on British TV, first on C4, from 14 April 1983 to 10 February 1987, and then back on ITV (not all regions, these dates are for London) from 6 November 1988 to 16 August 1992.

Sob Sisters

UK · ITV (CENTRAL) · SITCOM

7 × 30 mins · colour

26 May–7 July 1989 · Fri mostly 8.30pm

MAIN CAST

Liz	Gwen Taylor
Dorothy	Polly Adams
Leo	Freddie Jones
Charlie	Philip Bird
Edna	Beryl Cooke

CREDITS

writer Andrew Marshall · *director* Ray Butt · *executive producer* Mike Holgate · *producer* Christopher Walker

An unimpressive sitcom depicting the adventures of two sisters, Liz and Dorothy, very different from one another but forced to share a run-down flat after the latter's husband suddenly dies.

Hitherto, Dorothy has been accustomed to a comfortable globetrotting existence, being the wife of a successful businessman. Liz has always been single and, working as an assistant to an eccentric vet named Leo, plods along with little more than beans to her name. The seven episodes showed the pair coming to terms with their relationship and trying their best to improve their station.

A Soft Touch

UK · ITV (ATV) · SITCOM

6 × 30 mins · colour

31 July–18 Sep 1978 · Mon 8pm

MAIN CAST

Alison Holmes	Maureen Lipman
Jack Holmes	John Flanagan

CREDITS

writer Connor Fraser · *director/producer* Les Chatfield

Maureen Lipman starred in this single-series sitcom, playing the attractive, talented and industrious Alison Holmes, wife of Jack, an unemployed dreamer whose short-cut-to-success schemes she must thwart. Peter Skellern provided the music, and even turned up in one episode, as did the actor Chris Jagger – brother of Mick.

Making her mark with every successive TV appearance she made at this time, Lipman went on from *A Soft Touch* to *Agony* and fame.

Solo

UK · BBC · SITCOM

13 × 30 mins · colour

Series One (6) 11 Jan–15 Feb 1981 · BBC1 Sun around 9.05pm

Series Two (7) 5 Sep–17 Oct 1982 · BBC1 Sun mostly 8.55pm

MAIN CAST

Gemma Palmer	Felicity Kendal
Mrs Palmer	Elspet Gray
Danny	Stephen Moore

CREDITS

writer Carla Lane · *producer* Gareth Gwenlan

All four stars of *The Good Life* were promoted to their own starring vehicles when that popular series ended; for Felicity Kendal, the move took her away from the role of a devoted wife to that of a woman fed up with being trodden upon.

Butterflies had demonstrated that Carla Lane could take serious subjects and weave humour into them, and she furthered the process with *Solo*, which looked at the life of a 30-year-old woman, Gemma Palmer, coming to terms with – and trying to better – her position in the world. Gemma's life is progressing tolerably well – she has her own flat, a good job and a live-in partner, Danny – when said man has a sexual fling with one of Gemma's friends, the busty Gloria. The incident brings Gemma's life into sharp focus and she realises that she is treated by friends and colleagues as a human doormat. She promptly ejects Danny from the flat – although she remains fond of him and keeps in touch – tells Gloria a few home truths, quits her job and sets about re-creating herself as someone not to be trifled with.

This proves more difficult than she had anticipated, however, for just as Ria in *Butterflies* was prevented from consummating her affair by her conscience and social conditioning, so Gemma is hindered in her quest by her own schooling in life. While she abhors the hypocrisy around her and deplores the double-standards that allow men to get away with more than women, she cannot alter her core beliefs and sensibilities, the traits that make her part of 'the system' and thus its victim.

All this adds up to heavy-sounding material for a sitcom, but it was handled with a light touch and was very much a worthwhile enterprise.

Note. Felicity Kendal reprised her *Solo* role in *The Last Waltz*, a specially scripted production featuring characters from four Carla Lane series (*Bread*, *Butterflies* and *The Liver Birds* were the others) aired by BBC1 on 10 March 1989 as part of **Comic Relief**.

Some Matters Of Little Consequence

UK · BBC · SKETCH

4 × 30 mins · colour

22 Jan–12 Feb 1971 · BBC2 Fri 9.20pm

MAIN CAST

Kenneth Griffith
Frank Thornton
Sheila Steafel

CREDITS

writers David McKellar (4), David Nobbs/Peter Vincent (4), David Climie (3), John Antrobus (2), Raymond Allen (1), Bob Hedley (1), Patricia Newman (1), Fred G Perry (1), Keith Smith (1), Norman Tucker (1) · *script editor* David Nobbs · *producer* Roger Race

A revue-style sketch show encompassing elaborate make-up and costume changes. The assembled team were all established comic actors, eminently experienced in this style of performance, and the writers were out of the top-drawer.

Some Mothers Do 'Ave 'Em

UK · BBC · SITCOM

22 episodes (13 × 30 mins · 6 × 35 mins · 2 × 45 mins · 1 × 50 mins) · colour

Series One (7 × 30 mins) 15 Feb–29 Mar 1973 · BBC1 Thu 8pm

Series Two (6 × 30 mins) 22 Nov–27 Dec 1973 · BBC1 Thu 8.30pm

Special (50 mins) 25 Dec 1974 · BBC1 Wed 7.15pm

Special (45 mins) 25 Dec 1975 · BBC1 Thu 6.55pm

Series Three (6 × 35 mins) 11 Nov–16 Dec 1978 · BBC1 Sat 8.30pm

Special (45 mins) 25 Dec 1978 · BBC1 Mon 7.15pm

MAIN CAST

Frank Spencer · · · · · · · · · Michael Crawford
Betty Spencer · · · · · · · · · · · Michele Dotrice

OTHER APPEARANCES

Mrs Fisher · · · · · · · · · Jane Hylton (series 1)
Mr Lewis · · · · · · · · Glynn Edwards (series 3)

CREDITS

writer Raymond Allen (series 3 storylines by Michael Crawford) · producers Michael Mills (1973–75), Sydney Lotterby (1978)

Basil Fawlty and Frank Spencer are proof-positive that sitcom characters can attain a place in the public psyche immaterial to the few times they were actually seen on television – there were only 12 episodes of *Fawlty Towers* and just 22 of *Some Mothers Do 'Ave 'Em*.

Of course, repeat airings have helped embed Frank Spencer deeply in the collective consciousness, but the fact that he is there at all is down to the startling work of Michael Crawford, whose performances as the well-intentioned but appallingly accident-prone, ineffectual, underachieving wimp, clad in a mac and beret, was one of genius.

Born in Salisbury, Wiltshire, on 19 January 1942, Crawford had been steadily working as an actor since he was a boy, appearing in films, on radio and in dozens of TV roles – usually dramatic – as a youth (in 1959 he was one of the schoolboys in *Billy Bunter Of Greyfriars School*) before rising to starring roles in a number of British black-comedy movies in the 1960s, such as *The Knack* and *How I Won The War* and in the TV series *Not So Much A Programme More A Way Of Life*. But the character of Frank Spencer propelled Crawford from the middle ranks to superstardom.

This was undeniably a worthy success – few people have ever worked harder than Crawford at perfecting their art, and it is arguable that no one else has ever taken so

many personal risks to life and limb while so doing, not even Charlie Drake. Raymond Allen, the writer of *Some Mothers Do 'Ave 'Em*, was generous in his praise of Crawford and the actor's interpretation of the character – indeed, many of Spencer's most effective (and affected) mannerisms and examples of his verbal ineptitude were created by Crawford. His nervous, effete movements and tremulous voice gave Frank Spencer a childlike quality that might have become tedious if it wasn't for the fact that these affectations were combined with some of the most amazing and hilarious physical comedy ever seen on TV. To be truthful, the storylines themselves were never up to much (few viewers can remember them now), but Spencer's penchant for landing himself in spectacular situations caused Crawford to perform some dazzling and downright dangerous stunts in the name of comedy (some of which were unforgettable). From dangling over a cliff-edge from the exhaust pipe of a Morris Minor, to roller-skating underneath a moving articulated lorry, the seemingly fearless Crawford appeared to deem no stunt too risky. It is no exaggeration – and a huge compliment to Crawford, and the production as a whole – to say that these stunts compare with some of the classic work in the field by Buster Keaton.

But it wasn't all carefully contrived stunts. Crawford also invented a panicky, quivering, manic aspect to Spencer's personality, best seen in the episode where his sweet, loving, super-patient and now heavily pregnant wife Betty went into labour and Frank, with the best intentions in the world, created a maelstrom of chaos around her. As Betty, Michele Dotrice provided sympathetic support for Crawford, content to let him explode in all directions while she, the sensible one, concentrated on being the calm eye at the centre of the storm. (Frank duly became father to a daughter, Jessica, at the end of the second series. Naturally, he doted upon her, one child recognising another.)

Crawford went on to massive success in the West End of London and on Broadway, notably in *Barnum* and *Phantom Of The Opera*, but in Frank Spencer he left behind a larger-than-life TV comedy icon who brought pleasure to millions, especially younger viewers, and provided material for a host of TV impressionists many years after he himself had locked the mac and beret in the closet.

Note. On 11 April 1977 (Easter Monday) BBC1 screened *To Be Perfectly Frank*, a behind-the-scenes documentary showing how *Some Mothers Do 'Ave 'Em* was made, with Michael Crawford discussing the character of Frank Spencer and detailing the preparations behind his stunts.

Something For The Weekend

UK · BBC · SKETCH

6 × 30 mins · colour

10 June–15 July 1989 · BBC1 Sat 7.35pm

MAIN CAST

Susie Blake
Mike Doyle
James Gaddas
Mike Hayley
Caroline Leddy

CREDITS

writers Martin Booth (6), Colin Bostock-Smith (6), Paul B Davies (6), Paul Minett/Brian Leveson (6), Stuart Silver (6), Alan Whiting (6), Malcolm Williamson (6), Geoff Atkinson (3), Mike Hayley (3), James Gaddas (2), Bill Naylor (2) · script associates Charlie Adams, Kim Fuller · director/producer Michael Leggo

A sketch show with a risqué title that wasn't borne out by the material, which – owing to the series' early-Saturday-evening scheduling on BBC1 – was family-orientated in nature. A keen cast fared quite well with the skits, musical items and quickies, but, overall, the show lacked cohesion and needed a more rigid format and perhaps a later airtime to succeed. It achieved both when it returned as *Up To Something*.

Something In The City

UK · ITV (JACK HYLTON TV PRODUCTIONS FOR ASSOCIATED-REDIFFUSION) · SITCOM

5 × 30 mins · b/w

6 July–3 Aug 1959 · Mon 8.30pm

MAIN CAST

George Keyes · · · · · · · · · · · · · · · Eric Barker
Betty Keyes · · · · · · · · · · · · · · Joan Benham
Freddie Chiddock · · · · · · · · · · · Deryck Guyler
Phyl Chiddock · · · · · · · · · · · · · Pearl Hackney
Joe Miller · · · · · · · · · · · · · · Peter Hammond
Maisie Miller · · · · · · · · · · · · · · · Diane Hart

CREDITS

writers (see below) · director Kenneth Carter

A star of BBC radio since the Second World War – lending his talents to *Merry-Go-Round* and *Just Fancy* in particular – Eric Barker was the main attraction in this critically slated Jack Hylton production for Associated-Rediffusion.

Barker, Deryck Guyler and Peter Hammond were cast as three commuters who travel by train into the city from the suburbs every morning and return together on the same train in the evenings. The comedy – such as it was – was drawn from the relationships with their left-behind wives (Guyler's wife was played by Barker's real-life partner Pearl Hackney) and the usual array of simple misunderstandings between the sexes – the perennial fallback for a sitcom short on ideas.

The bizarre thing is that somewhere between the USA – where the scripts originated – and the British adaptation, something vital must have gone astray, for in American hands these scripts were extremely popular and well received. Viewers of *Something In The City* were given no clue as to the identity of the writers – quite simply, there was no credit in the titles – because the scripts originated with the American comic Sid Caesar and his writing team, and Hylton's purchase of the UK rights to a great many Caesar scripts remained a secret beyond the corridors of ITV. *The Commuters*, as it was known, ran as a self-contained element within NBC's 1954–57 series *Caesar's Hour* and featured Sid Caesar, Carl Reiner and Howard Morris as the three travellers Bob Victor, George Hansen and Fred Brewster, their wives being Ann, Betty and Alice (various actresses). Whoever adapted the scripts for British TV (it could have been Eric Barker, who was a fine comedy writer) probably wished that they hadn't bothered, though.

See also *The Newcomer*, *The Eric Barker Half-Hour* and *Look At It This Way*.

Something So Right

USA · NBC THEN ABC (BIG PHONE PRODUCTIONS/UNIVERSAL TELEVISION) · SITCOM

24 × 30 mins (to 31/12/97 · continuing into 1998) · colour

US dates: 17 Sep 1996–6 May 1997 (NBC) · ABC from 1998

UK dates: 3 Sep 1997 to date (24 episodes to 31/12/97) C4 weekdays 9am

MAIN CAST

Carly Davis	Mel Harris
Jack Farrell	Jere Burns
Will Pacino	Billy L Sullivan
Nicole Farrell	Marne Patterson
Sarah Kramer	Emily Ann Lloyd
Grace	Carol Ann Susi
Stephanie	Christine Dunford
Sheldon	Barry Jenner
Dante	Michael Milhoan

CREDITS

creators Judd Pillot/John Peaslee · *writers* various · *directors* various · *executive producers* Judd Pillot, John Peaslee, Bob Tischler · *producers* Marica Govons, Jon Spector

A low-key but slick US romantic comedy with its heart in the right place but lacking the edge that distinguishes the merely good sitcoms from the great. The two lead actors were both familiar to US audiences: Mel Harris (Hope in the 1988–91 baby-boomer drama *thirtysomething*) and Jere Burns (the unlikeable Kirk in the US version of *Dear John*).

The female half of *Something So Right* was Carly Davis, a twice-married, twice-divorced mother of two children (Will and Sarah) who have different fathers. The male half was Jack Farrell, also divorced, with a daughter, Nicole. Jack is Will's English teacher, and when he

meets the boy's mother at a parent–teacher evening it is love at first sight. The two then marry and combine their families, forming a mini-*Brady Bunch* for the 1990s. Carly is a professional party-organiser, Jack is a caring new-man and a model father, and episodes revolved around their continuing romance, which develops through their own disbelief that they have found true love at last.

The series was warmly received by US critics but failed to achieve decent enough ratings and so was cancelled by NBC. In re-runs, however, it picked up sizeable audiences; NBC then tried to re-order the programme but the producers had already cut a deal with ABC, hence, as this book went to press, it was set to continue in 1998 on that network.

Something Special

UK · BBC · STANDUP

1 × 30 mins · b/w

27 Apr 1967 · BBC2 Thu 8.05pm

MAIN CAST

Morey Amsterdam

CREDITS

writer Morey Amsterdam · *director/producer* John Street

The standup comedian and writer Morey Amsterdam was a veteran of US TV comedy, guesting in many variety shows and specials. His invitation to come to London to record this BBC special followed his new-found fame as one of the stars of *The Dick Van Dyke Show*. Consequently, Amsterdam had years' worth of gags and one-liners to call upon.

Sometime, Never

UK · ITV (WITZEND PRODUCTIONS FOR MERIDIAN) · SITCOM

8 × 30 mins · colour

Pilot · 17 July 1995 · Mon 8pm

One series (7) 27 Oct–8 Dec 1996 · Sun mostly 10pm

MAIN CAST

Maxine 'Max' Bailey	Sara Crowe
Bernice	Ann Bryson
Harry, school headmaster	Saeed Jaffrey (pilot);
	Paul Chapman (series)
Ian	Harry Burton
Louise Kilgarith	Lucinda Fisher
Jason Williams	Sean Carnegie
Kev	John Hodgkinson (series)

CREDITS

writer Jenny Lecoat · *script editor* Paul Makin (series) · *directors* Baz Taylor (pilot), Sylvie Boden (series) · *executive producers* Allan McKeown (pilot), Tony Charles (series) · *producers* Tony Charles (pilot), Jamie Rix (series)

This second screening in ITV's 1995 *Comedy Firsts* season was the only one to develop into

a full series – no surprise, really: it was the only one with promise. Both pilot and series starred Sara Crowe (the blonde one) and Ann Bryson (the brunette), whose fame had mildly spread as a result of their Philadelphia Cheese TV commercials. In truth this was but one venture for the comedy double-act, who had been playing the pubs and clubs since meeting at drama school.

Crowe was cast as the regretfully still single 'Max' Bailey, an acid-tongued, liberal-minded drama teacher at an inner-city comprehensive school. On the occasion of her 31st birthday she reflects upon her life to date, pondering what has happened to the sophisticated woman she imagined she would become. In despair over her failure to get a promised promotion (instead, the job has gone to a prim 24-year-old graduate, Louise), and furious with her workaholic ex-boyfriend Ian, she turns to best friend Bernice for comfort. But Bernice, who lives in the upstairs flat, has troubles of her own – useless husband Kev and two unruly children being among them – and together they demolish a bottle of cooking sherry. Max vows to be less aggressive first thing the next morning, but the new-leaf turning doesn't last long – a fact witnessed at close hand by pupil Jason Williams.

The writer, standup comedian Jenny Lecoat, created *Sometime, Never* based upon personal experience: like so many children of the 1960s she expected life to be perfect come her thirties, only to find those hopes dashed on the rocks of 1990s reality. Her writing in the pilot episode showed real zip, and the series continued in the same vein. (The opening episode was a essentially a remake of the pilot with a few script variations.) Shown in a later time-slot, the script was more adult than before. Louise's sexual problems, Max's tempestuous on-off relationship with Ian, and her deliberations about whether to follow him to a new job posting, were the subject of more sharply written kitchen chats over the cooking sherry.

Son Of Fred

UK · ITV (ASSOCIATED-REDIFFUSION) · SKETCH

8 × 30 mins · b/w

17 Sep–5 Nov 1956 · Mon 9.30pm

MAIN CAST

Peter Sellers
Valentine Dyall
Kenneth Connor
Graham Stark
Patti Lewis
Max Geldray
Cuthbert Harding
Johnny Vyvyan
Jennifer Lautrec
Mario Fabrizi
The Alberts

CREDITS

writer Spike Milligan · *director/producer* Dick Lester

Following earlier outings with *The Idiot Weekly, Price 2d* and *A Show Called Fred*, Spike Milligan delivered up another batch of scripts, as only he could write them, for the delectation of ITV viewers (by this time not just London but the Midlands and the North too).

Richard (Dick) Lester directed once again and the usual cast of characters helped out, with Peter Sellers as the main man. Interestingly, Milligan restricted himself merely to fleeting walk-on roles. But *Son Of Fred* differed from its predecessors in that Milligan declared himself bored with the usual TV strictures – scenery and the like – and went for between-the-eyes sketch material with simple props, combined with animation sequences. It may have been *Monty Python* 13 years ahead of its time but the powers that went at ITV weren't ready for such anarchy and stopped the run after eight weeks.

Apart from *The Telegoons*, it would be another eight years before *Milligan's Wake* returned Spike to British TV for a full series. An Australian special, *The Gladys Half Hour*, close in style and format to the *Fred* shows, was aired there by ABC on 17 October 1958 but did not show in Britain. For Peter Sellers, meanwhile, there was still *Yes, It's The Cathode-Ray Tube Show!* to come.

Son Of The Bride

UK · BBC · SITCOM

6 × 30 mins · colour

6 June–11 July 1973 · BBC1 Wed 7.30pm

MAIN CAST

Neville Leggit	Terry Scott
Mum	Mollie Sugden
Stan	George A Cooper
Miss McDowdie	Josephine Tewson
Angela	Olivia Hamnett

CREDITS

writer John Kane · *producer* Peter Whitmore

Terry Scott played Neville Leggit, a grown-up man who was still intent on hanging on to his mother's apron strings. When his widowed mother (played by Mollie Sugden) decides to remarry, Neville is devastated and does everything he can to destroy her romance with Stan. When that fails he turns his attention to wrecking their upcoming marriage.

Sonny Hayes & Co

UK · ITV (YORKSHIRE) · SKETCH/STANDUP

1 × 30 mins · colour

1 Jan 1986 · Wed 11.45pm

MAIN CAST

Sonny Hayes
Sally Windross
Andy Petredes
Tony Friel
The Charleys
The West End Boys

CREDITS

writer Sonny Hayes, Sally Windross · *additional material* John Chesterman, Phil Swordlow, Chris Langham · *director/producer* Ian Bolt

A one-off half-hour that combined bizarre sketches with comedy-based magic routines, including a flea circus and a breakdancing Quasimodo.

The Sören Kierkegaard Road Show

see The Montreux Festival

Sorry!

UK · BBC · SITCOM

43 episodes (42 × 30 mins · 1 × short special) · colour

Series One (6) 12 Mar–16 Apr 1981 · BBC1 Thu 8.30pm

Series Two (6) 22 Apr–27 May 1982 · BBC1 Thu 8.30pm

Series Three (6) 28 Oct–2 Dec 1982 · BBC1 Thu 8pm

Short special · part of *The Funny Side Of Christmas* 27 Dec 1982 · BBC1 Mon 8.05pm

Series Four (6) 28 Apr–2 June 1985 · BBC1 Sun 7.15pm

Series Five (6) 10 May–21 June 1986 · BBC1 Sat 6.05pm

Series Six (6) 1 June–6 July 1987 · BBC1 Mon mostly 8.30pm

Series Seven (6) 5 Sep–10 Oct 1988 · BBC1 Mon 8pm

MAIN CAST

Timothy Lumsden	Ronnie Corbett
Phyllis Lumsden	Barbara Lott
Sidney Lumsden	William Moore
Frank	Roy Holder (series 1–3)
Muriel	Marguerite Hardiman
Kevin	Derek Fuke
Jennifer	Wendy Allnutt (series 6)
Pippa	Bridget Brice (series 7)

CREDITS

writers Ian Davidson/Peter Vincent · *director/producer* David Askey

The 'grown-up son living at home with a domineering mum' theme which had formed the basis of the first series of *Now Look Here ...*, was taken to extremes in this long-running vehicle for Ronnie Corbett.

Corbett was cast as Timothy Lumsden, a 41-year-old librarian (ageing, eventually, to 48) still tied to his mother's apron strings. Timothy was a smart enough chap, witty and bright, although his discomfort with women often caused him to blush, stammer and blurt out stupid things in their presence. This awkwardness owed to the overpowering influence of his mother, Phyllis, a scheming, spiteful harridan determined to undermine her son's confidence and to keep him firmly under her thumb. Phyllis Lumsden was truly a monstrous creation, so hideous that it was difficult to feel too much sympathy for anyone prepared to hang around such a Gorgon, especially as Timothy seemed to discount matricide as a suitable solution to his problems. His father, Sidney, suffered similarly and often joined Timothy in silent defiance of Phyllis but she usually managed to crush their resistance as would a steamroller. Timothy's sister, Muriel, who had escaped the family home, was often on hand with sympathetic advice.

It was Timothy's sexual frustration that spurred him to his greatest moments of rebellion and at various times during the run his attraction to a young woman nearly resulted in his leaving home. His sixth series' girlfriend, Jennifer, seemed set to spirit Timothy away but it was not to be. Eventually, the writers took pity on their tragic hero and Timothy was allowed to fly the coop with his latest girlfriend, Pippa, at the end.

Sorry, I'm A Stranger Here Myself

UK · ITV (THAMES) · SITCOM

13 × 30 mins · colour

Series One (7) 15 June–27 July 1981 · Mon 8pm

Series Two (6) 13 Apr–18 May 1982 · Tue 8pm

MAIN CAST

Henry Nunn	Robin Bailey
Tom	David Hargreaves
Mumtaz	Nadim Sawalha
Doreen	Diana Rayworth
Alex	Christopher Fulford

CREDITS

writers David Firth/Peter Tilbury (series 1), David Firth (series 2) · *director/producer* Anthony Parker

Henry Nunn is a plain man at work (he's a librarian by profession) and a hen-pecked husband at home in leafy Datchet. His wife Sybil, it seems, scarcely rouses herself from the television and is seen by viewers only as a waving arm (attached to the actress Pamela Manson), directing Henry hither and thither from an armchair. Suddenly, on his 60th birthday, Henry inherits from his Uncle Crispin a tidy sum of money and, gloriously, ownership of the happy house in which he was born and spent his joyous youth, situated in the (fictitious) Black Country town of Stackley.

Of course, Father Time has his way of screwing up. When Henry quits the library, Sybil and Datchet to return 'home' to Stackley he is immediately at odds with the incumbent neighbours: on one side Tom, a 'red under the bed' union shop-steward, with an interfering wife, Doreen; on the other, Mumtaz, an Asian man who owns the corner shop and likes to cook curries. Worse, there's Alex, a green-haired punk, squatting in his house.

The essence of *Sorry, I'm A Stranger Here Myself* was lack of communication, and the sitcom was serialised, each episode advancing the story from the previous week. The first series was co-written by *Shelley* creator Peter Tilbury with the actor David Firth, the second by Firth alone.

Sorry I'm Single

UK · BBC · SITCOM

9 × 30 mins · b/w

1 Aug–26 Sep 1967 · BBC1 Tue 7.30pm

MAIN CAST

David · · · · · · · · · · · · · · · · Derek Nimmo
Brenda · · · · · · · · · · · · · · Gwendolyn Watts
Karen · · · · · · · · · · · · · · · Elizabeth Knight
Suzy · · · · · · · · · · · · · · · · · · Pik-Sen Lim

CREDITS

writers Ronald Wolfe/Ronald Chesney · producer John Street

Another sitcom for the in-demand Derek Nimmo, who, at this time was not only a TV regular but was also starring on the London stage in *Charlie Girl*. His character here was yet another variation on his 'rather weak, mooning and inadequate young man' that had stood him in great stead in the past and would continue to do so for some years to come. Ronalds Wolfe and Chesney, writers of *The Rag Trade*, provided the scripts.

Nimmo played David, a mature student who (somewhat daringly for the time) shares 'digs' in a converted house in Hampstead, London, with three female tenants – Brenda, a recent divorcee who is looking for her next husband; the mini-skirted Karen, always at loggerheads with David, and whose relationship with David hovers somewhere between platonic and romantic; and Hong Kong-born student Suzy (played by the Malaysian actress Pik-Sen Lim).

The Sound Of Laughter

UK · ITV (ATV) · SITCOMS

6 × 30 mins · colour

A series of one-off sitcom pilots that ATV hoped would develop into series. Only one did – denoted by an asterisk. See individual entries for further details.

28 July 1977	*A Sharp Intake Of Breath
4 Aug 1977	Young At Heart
11 Aug 1977	Bricks Without Straw
18 Aug 1977	What A Performance
25 Aug 1977	After The Boom Was Over
1 Sep 1977	The Best Of Friends

Note. Ten years before this, the title *The Sound Of Laughter* had been used by the ITV

company ABC as the umbrella for nine comedy pilots, screened on Sunday after-noons in the Midlands and the North but not shown in London. None of the nine was elevated into a series.

29 Jan 1967	No Strings (see Arthur Askey's entry for details)
5 Feb 1967	Mister Misfit (see *Join Jim Dale* for details)
12 Feb 1967	That's Show Business (see *Billy Dainty, Esq* for details)
19 Feb 1967	Gentleman Jim (see *Heirs On A Shoestring* for details)
26 Feb 1967	Stiff Upper Lip (see that title)
5 Mar 1967	Around With Allen (see Dave Allen's entry for details)
12 Mar 1967	Hooray For Laughter (see Ted Ray's entry for details)
19 Mar 1967	Did You See Una? (made by Scottish TV; see *Between The Lines* for details)
26 Mar 1967	Hicks And Stokes (see *Spanner In The Works* for details)

Sounding Brass

UK · ITV (ATV) · SITCOM

6 × 60 mins · colour

2 July–6 Aug 1980 · Wed 8pm

MAIN CAST

Horace Gilbert Bestwick · · · · · · · Brian Glover
Leonard Dukes · · · · · · · · · Stephen Hancock
Gerry Thompson · · · · · · · · · · · · · Ray Mort
Mr MacKenzie · · · · · · · · · · · Alex McCrindle
Arthur Mannion · · · · · · · · · · Philip Jackson
Cynthia Wildgoose · · · · · · · · · · Gwen Taylor
Frank Oldfield · · · · · · · · · · · · Teddy Turner
Cyril Bacon · · · · · · · · · · · · · · · Kevin Lloyd

CREDITS

writer Don Shaw · directors John Cooper (3), Don Leaver (3) · executive producer David Reid · producer John Cooper

A six-part series about brass bandsmanship – the Ettaswell Town Band, to be precise, 100 years old, with a glorious past but tarnished present. Its new music director, H G Bestwick, whose father and grandfather had been leaders before him, is a pompous, dictatorial chap – a butcher by trade – determined to put matters to rights and assure the band a glorious future of wealthy sponsors, loyal bandsmen and a place among the exalted bands in the land, like the Black Dyke Mills. But Bestwick's ideas, or rather the manner in which he executes them, find opposition from Mr Dukes, the music master, and from his musicians' love of football, television and drink.

Set and filmed in Etwall, Derbyshire, the author's home village, the series reunited the talents of Brian Glover and Ray Mort, who had appeared together in the excellent trilogy of BBC plays by Peter Terson, *The Fishing Party*, *Shakespeare – Or Bust* and *Three For The Fancy*.

Similar themes were also explored in Yorkshire TV's *Where There's Brass* and the BBC's *Bold As Brass*.

Sounds Like Les Dawson

see DAWSON, Les

South By South-East

UK · ITV (RED ROOSTER FILMS FOR TVS) · CHILDREN'S SITCOM

6 × 30 mins · colour

26 Mar–30 Apr 1991 · Tue mostly 4.40pm

MAIN CAST

Tim Diamond · · · · · · · · · · Dursley McLinden
Nick Diamond · · · · · · · · · · · · · · Colin Dale
Boyle · · · · · · · · · · · · · · · · Gordon Winter
Snape · · · · · · · · · · · · · · · · Michael Feast
Mr Blondini · · · · · · · · · · · Jonathan Coleman

CREDITS

writer/director Anthony Horowitz · executive producers Linda James/Stephen Bayly · producer Richard Turner

A spin-off from the Christmas 1988 British feature film *Just Ask For Diamond* (directed by Stephen Bayly) which had starred Dursley McLinden and Colin Dale with Susannah York, Patricia Hodge, Roy Kinnear and Bill Paterson.

The two male leads reprised their roles in this British–Dutch TV co-production, which once again focused on the activities of perhaps the least successful and most incompetent private eye of all time, a young man named Tim Diamond, operating out of Camden Town in north London. Tim is aided by his 15-year-old brother Nick, the brains of the outfit, as – sparked by a dying man's final words, 'south by south-east' – they investigate a murder case. The man turns out to have been a secret agent, and his words lead the Diamond brothers on a trail across Europe as they seek to preserve the western alliance, no less. There was a strong comedy element, not least in the basic premise of spoofing the films of Alfred Hitchcock, and the title, which parodied his 1959 movie *North By Northwest*. (*Just Ask For Diamond* had certainly spoofed this same thriller genre, although its working title, *The Falcon's Malteser*, which had been used as the name of Anthony Horowitz's original novel, was blocked on legal grounds.)

Also known as *Diamond Brothers – South By South-East*, the TV series attracted a fine supporting cast: among those seen in cameo roles were Jenny Agutter, Monique van der Ven, Anna Massey and Michael Gough.

South Central

USA · FOX (SLICK-MAC/20TH CENTURY-FOX) · SITCOM

13 × 30 mins · colour

US dates: 5 Apr–30 Aug 1994

UK dates: 25 Oct 1994–3 Jan 1995
(10 episodes) C4 Tue around 12 midnight

MAIN CAST

Joan Mosley	Tina Lifford
André Mosley	Larenz Tate
Tasha Mosley	Tasha Scott
Deion Mosley	Keith Mbulo
Bobby Deavers	Clifton Powell
Mayo Bonner	Earl Billings
Lucille	Jennifer Lopez
Rashad	Lamont Bentley
Sweets	Paula Kelly
Dr Raymond McHenry	Ken Page
Nicole	Maia Campbell

CREDITS

creators/executive producers/writers Michael J Weithorn/Ralph R Farquhar · *director* Stan Lathan · *producer* W E Baker

A savagely realistic slice of Los Angeles inner-city life, following a single-parent black family struggling to live in the heart of a dangerous neighbourhood.

Violence hangs in the air all around, with drug dealers, gangsters and street gangs combining to form a ring of terror. Against such almost overwhelming odds, Joan Mosley battles to properly raise her children. Her husband has deserted the family and her eldest son, Marcus, has been murdered by a neighbourhood gang. At the start of the series Joan also loses her well-paid administrative job and is forced to take a poorly paid position in Ujamaa, the community co-operative store where the profit-sharing philosophy inhibits the staff's earning potential. Joan's arrival at the store causes friction between her and a co-worker, Lucille, a fiery Latina. The store is run by the well-intentioned Bobby Deavers, assisted by the sanguine Mayo. Much of the action in *South Central* takes place at Joan's home, however, and centres on her difficult teenager André, a bright and proud lad often led astray by peer pressure. His younger sister Tasha is on the threshold of adulthood but suffers more than the others from the absence of her father, pining for him and periodically attempting to track him down. Completing the household is Joan's third dependant, Deion, an introverted but occasionally mischievous foster-child who never speaks.

South Central was a hard-edged, cleverly written series that pulled no punches in its depiction of the Mosleys' life and benefited enormously from the fine playing of its young cast. Tina Lifford was especially good as Joan, driven by her determination to ensure (sometimes by physical force) that her children are not dragged into the quagmire of drugs and violence that envelops their lives. Strong language, realistic dialogue and an honest and believable family relationship combined to lift *South Central* above the norm. Although the storylines were dramatic there

was snappy dialogue and an added 'laugh-track' highlighted – perhaps needlessly – the comedy elements. It all added up to a classy, stylish series that, although lauded by critics in the US, proved too potent for mainstream audiences and vanished from the schedules after 13 weeks. In the UK, C4 screened ten episodes but, unusually, failed to exploit the series' potential, hiding it away late on Tuesday nights (often after midnight). A pity – *South Central* deserved better treatment.

South Of The Border

UK · ITV (YORKSHIRE) · SITCOM

7 × 30 mins · colour

30 Aug–11 Oct 1985 · Fri 8pm

MAIN CAST

Edgar Rowley	Brian Glover
Ellen Rowley	Belinda Sinclair
Anita Rowley	Mossie Smith
Billy	Robin Parkinson
Nan	Maggie Jones
Warwick	Phil Nice
Finbar	Eugene Geasley
Ashley	Philip Dunbar
Quentin	Christopher Godwin

CREDITS

writer Peter Tinniswood · *director/producer* Derrick Goodwin

Edgar Rowley is a 'Professional Yorkshireman' forced to leave 'the muck of the north' that he loves so much and migrate to suburban London in the hunt for employment and, with utter disdain, to live among southern softies. A beer-swilling, jobless bigot, Rowley never misses an opportunity to ram home his passionate hatred for all that southerners espouse, their lifestyle and values in particular, and despite the presence of his mum and two daughters his chauvinist leanings go unchecked.

A worthwhile sitcom, even though it lasted only one series, *South Of The Border* was distinguished by the presence of the much underrated actor Brian Glover, and the characteristically deft touches of writer Peter Tinniswood.

Spacevets

UK · BBC · CHILDREN'S SITCOM

39 × 15 mins · colour

Series One (13) 29 Sep–22 Dec 1992 · BBC1 Tue 4.05pm

Series Two (13) 28 Sep–7 Dec 1993 · BBC1 Tue 4.20pm

Series Three (13) *Spacevets III* 27 Sep–20 Dec 1994 · BBC1 Tue 4.15pm

MAIN CAST

Captain K (Keith) Pubble	Linden Kirk
	(series 1 & 2)
Captain Skip Chip	Mark Arden (series 3)
Number Two	Bernard Wright
Mona	Ann Bryson
Dogsbody	Robin Kingsland (voice)

CREDITS

creators Stephen Edmondson/Jerome Vincent · *writers* Christopher Middleton, Robin Kingsland, Wayne Jackman · *director* Steven Andrew · *producer* Greg Childs

An above-average entry in the children's sitcom genre, with a witty script and interesting characters and situations. Like a cross between *All Creatures Great And Small* and *Red Dwarf*, *Spacevets* had a classy look and a neat set that belied its relatively small budget.

The series charted the adventures of an Intergalactic Animal Health Service team, travelling the cosmos aboard the craft *Dispensable* in order to tend sick alien animals. The vets are headed by 13-year-old Captain Keith Pubble (played by Linden Kirk – not the first Kirk to boldly go into space), a bright boy, thanks to the computer chip embedded in his forehead. (In the third series Pubble was replaced by Captain Skip Chip, played by Mark Arden, half of the comedy duo Arden and Frost.) The captain's crew, alas, are not so together, and are prone to bickering. Pubble's second officer – Number Two – hails from a planet where numbers are given instead of names (thus his full 'name' is 246390); he is hundreds of years old but, underlining his ineptitude, still hasn't managed to work his way up to captain. The ship's communications officer, Mona, is constantly at loggerheads with Number Two but never happier than when indulging her passion for chocolate. Completing the crew is Dogsbody, the security officer and mechanic first class, a puppet dog voiced by occasional writer Robin Kingsland. (Many of the alien creatures the crew encountered in their adventures were puppets, operated by Richard Robinson.)

Spanner In The Works

UK · BBC · SITCOM

1 × 30 mins · b/w

2 June 1967 · BBC1 Fri 7.30pm

MAIN CAST

Arthur Machin	Norman Rossington
Joe Bamford	Jimmy Jewel
Charlie	Julian Holloway
Alf	Colin Douglas
Peter Mayhew	Arnold Peters

CREDITS

writers Vince Powell/Harry Driver · *producer* Stuart Allen

The first TV role for Jimmy Jewel after the amicable dissolution of his comedy partnership with his cousin Ben Warriss (see **Jewel And Warriss**).

In this *Comedy Playhouse* pilot, Norman Rossington was cast as the owner of a small northern engineering company who believes that his workers are idling; Jewel played his nemesis, the union shop-steward. Cliff Michelmore and Fyfe Robertson, acclaimed BBC-TV reporters (both had been involved in the long-running flagship programme *Tonight*), appeared in *Spanner In The Works* as themselves. Despite the fine cast, no series resulted.

Note. The programme was screened only two months after Rossington, co-starring with Rodney Bewes, had appeared as an idling motor mechanic in *Hicks And Stokes*, an ITV sitcom pilot made by ABC. Written by Ronnie Taylor and produced by Ronnie Baxter, it was shown in the Midlands and the North (but not in London) on 26 March 1967. Rossington was cast as Norman Stokes and Bewes as Billy Hicks, with James Cossins, Barry Halliday and Didi Sullivan playing the minor roles. Again, no series developed.

Spark

UK · BBC · SITCOM

6 × 30 mins · colour

10 Nov–15 Dec 1997 · BBC1 Mon 8.30pm

MAIN CAST

Ashley Parkerwell	James Fleet
Colette Parkerwell	Jan Francis
Mike Parkerwell	Alistair McGowan
Mrs Rudge	Anne Reid
Gillian Wells	Rebecca Raybone
Mrs Wells	Brigit Forsyth
Ursula Craig	Julia Deakin
Beth	Carla Mendonça
Diane	Marianna Reidman

CREDITS

writer Roy Clarke · *director* Angela deChastelai Smith · *executive producer* Mike Stephens

A man in his forties, who has spent the best years of his life under his mother's wing, gets a chance to taste the fruits of life – mostly, the joys of romance – when she dies.

Said man is computer expert Ashley Parkerwell, who already has a girlfriend of sorts, the ghastly Gillian – a grim, dull woman who, urged on by her mother, is determined to marry him. Candidly, she describes their potential love-life thus, 'I've never been keen on sex but I could read or something if you really wanted to do it.' Even the inexperienced Ashley can see the downside of such a relationship although, in Gillian's defence, he notes that she is 'well within reach of the absolute beginner'. Gillian's pursuit of Ashley increases after his mother's death but Ashley's supporters – his stalwart housekeeper Mrs Rudge, and his sympathetic sister-in-law Colette – are firmly of the belief that he can do better, and Ashley is soon set up with a string of dates. His brother Mike, who owns a successful architectural business and cares more for money than anything else, is in despair at his listless brother, but if Colette, bored at home

with nothing to do, wants to interfere, then he has no real objection. First, Ashley pursues Kimberley, a distant cousin he falls for at his mother's funeral, then he has a disastrous encounter with Beth, who works in Mike's office. After that comes a less than fulfilling interlude with Ursula, the wife of a man from whom Mike is hoping to win a business contract, before he becomes wildly attracted to a barmaid, Diane, at his local pub.

James Fleet (*The Vicar Of Dibley*, and the Richard Curtis-written film *Four Weddings And A Funeral*), who was making a habit of playing introverted, unworldly characters, turned in his usual dependable performance, and Jan Francis offered reliable support as Colette. But – belying its title – *Spark* moved with the stately pace of the hearse that took away Ashley's mother in the opening episode. Bittersweet and full of typically colourful Roy Clarke dialogue, it was short on belly laughs and long (overlong, really) on whimsy and artful observation.

Spasms

see *Chalk And Cheese*

Spate Of Speight

UK · ITV (THAMES) · SKETCH

1 × 50 mins · b/w

5 May 1969 · Mon 9.10pm

MAIN CAST

Eric Sykes
Anna Quayle
Joe Baker
Alfred Marks
Miriam Karlin
Kenny Lynch
Cardew Robinson
The Scaffold

CREDITS

writer Johnny Speight · *director/producer* Alan Tarrant

A one-off comedy special that enabled writer Johnny Speight to return to short sketch material and leave behind, temporarily, the half-hour sitcom format of his massively successful BBC series *Till Death Us Do Part*. (Previously, Speight had written radio material for, among others, Frankie Howerd, Cyril Fletcher, Arthur Askey and Vic Oliver, and TV material for Arthur Haynes and Morecambe and Wise.) A number of big names, headed by Eric Sykes, performed in the cleverly titled *Spate Of Speight*.

Spatz

UK · ITV (THAMES/PRODUCERS GROUP INTERNATIONAL) · CHILDREN'S SITCOM

33 × 30 mins · colour

Series One (13) 21 Feb–9 May 1990 · Wed mostly 4.25pm

Series Two (13) 3 Jan–4 Apr 1991 · Thu mostly 4.30pm

Series Three (7) 28 Feb–10 Apr 1992 · Fri mostly 4.40pm

MAIN CAST

Karen Hansson	Jennifer Calvert
T J	Paul Michael
Debbie	Stephanie Charles
Vince Powers	Joe Greco
Dexter	Vas Blackwood
Lily Quang	Ling Tai
Stanley	Jonathan Copestake
Jo	Sue Devaney (series 1)
Freddy	Katy Murphy (series 2 & 3)

CREDITS

creator Andrew Bethell · *writers* Lee Pressman/ Grant Cathro (21), Terry Saltsman (3), David Joss Buckley (3), J D Smith (2), Vito Viscomi (1), Wilson Coneybeare (1), Jim Eldridge (1), David Stafford (1) · *script editors* Terry Saltsman/Lee Pressman/ Grant Cathro (7), Lee Pressman/Grant Cathro (6) · *directors* Stan Swan (18), Neville Green (12), Baz Taylor (3) · *executive producers* Charles Falzon, Alan Horrox · *producers* Alan Horrox/Carol Commisso (series 1), Alan Horrox/Neville Green (series 2), Alan Horrox (series 3)

A children's comedy series, tinged with drama, set in the London branch of Spatz, a (fictional) Canadian-owned hamburger franchise restaurant chain. The first series began as T J, the charming, easy-going Canadian in charge of managing the UK operation, and Karen, the authoritarian Canadian in charge of European co-ordin-ation, were hiring their first Spatz Squad and getting the restaurant open for business. A zany, fast-paced series – it *had* to be, to match the speed of the food – *Spatz* focused on the frantic goings-on among the wacky restaurant/kitchen staff, with romance and intrigue lingering in the air along with the aroma of burgers and fries. Collectively, the Spatz staff were united in their dislike for rival burger chain Blimpy's.

Aimed at 9–15-year-old viewers, the series was an international co-production with Canadian TV and proved a considerable investment for Thames TV. Mirroring its off-the-wall style, guests during the 33 episodes ranged from footballer Gary Lineker to Nicholas Parsons, and ventriloquist Terry Hall with glove puppet Lenny The Lion, stars of 1950s/60s TV but scarcely seen since.

The Spike Jones Show

USA · CBS · SKETCH/MUSICAL HUMOUR

20 × 30 mins · b/w

US dates: 2 Apr–27 Aug 1957

UK dates: 27 Mar–4 Apr 1990 (6 editions) BBC2 various days 4pm

MAIN CAST

Spike Jones and his City Slickers
Helen Grayco

CREDITS

producers Tom Waldman, Dick Darley

Dressed in his trademark loud suits and ever chewing gum, Spike Jones was the maniac-in-chief of the most lunatic bunch of madcap musicians ever assembled – the City Slickers. They were a squad of kamikaze instrumentalists who utilised any objects – spoons, tin baths, duck calls, whoopee cushions, bicycle bells, guns and more – to add to the general cacophony enveloping the particular tune they were intent on murdering.

Jones and his crazy gang first rose to prominence with the 1942 wartime propaganda song 'Der Führer's Face', which became a huge hit. Subsequent successes assured them of lasting fame, and the visual style they invented to mirror the aural debacle led them to make a series of short music films ('soundies') and pursue a career in 'legit' movies. They were also regular TV stars, with hour-long variety series networked first by NBC then CBS from 1954 to 1961. In 1957, by way of a change, CBS mounted a weekly 30-minute run – titled, like the others, *The Spike Jones Show* – that featured short, wacky sketches and cast comedy guest stars amid the musical chaos, and in 1990, BBC2 screened six compilation shows drawn from these programmes, featuring guest stars Zasu Pitts, Jim Backus, and Liberace with his brother George. (Earlier, on 29 December 1986, C4 aired a single hour-length compilation of clips put together by London Films, titled *The Best Of Spike Jones*.)

Born in Long Beach, California, on 14 December 1911, Spike Jones was the major influence upon a line of British musical eccentrics that includes the Temperance Seven, the Alberts, the Bonzo Dog Doo-Dah Band, Bob Kerr's Whoopee Band and Madness. He died on 1 May 1965.

Spike Milligan ... [various shows]

see MILLIGAN, Spike

Spin City

USA · ABC (UBU PRODUCTIONS/LOTTERY HILL ENTERTAINMENT/DREAMWORKS) · SITCOM

36 × 30 mins (to 31/12/97 · continuing into 1998) · colour

US dates: 17 Sep 1996 to date

UK dates: 10 Jan 1997 to date (24 episodes to 31/12/97) C4 Fri 9.30pm

MAIN CAST

Michael Flaherty	Michael J Fox
Ashley Schaeffer	Carla Gugino (1996)
Paul Lassiter	Richard Kind
Mayor Randall Winston	Barry Bostwick
Stuart Bondek	Alan Ruck
James Hobert	Alexander Gaberman
Carter Heywood	Michael Boatman
Nikki Faber	Connie Britton
Janelle	Victoria Dillard
Helen Winston	Deborah Rush

Karen	Taylor Stanley
Stacey Paterno	Jennifer Esposito (from 1997)
Laurie Parres	Paula Marshall (from 1997)
Claudia Sacks	Faith Prince (from 1997)

CREDITS

creators Gary David Goldberg/Bill Lawrence · *writers* Gary David Goldberg, Bill Lawrence and others · *directors* Lee Shallat Chemel and others · *executive producers* Gary David Goldberg, Michael J Fox · *producers* various

Michael J Fox, the diminutive Canadian actor who had first risen to prominence in *Family Ties*, enjoyed mixed fortunes in movies before returning triumphantly to TV in this fast and funny political comedy that made a virtue of the fact that its team of writers were all under 30.

Fox played Mike Flaherty, deputy mayor and spin doctor in chief to Mayor Winston, a hot political figure with presidential looks. Likened by many media pundits to George Stephanopoulos, who had masterminded Bill Clinton's presidential campaign, the cunning and resourceful Flaherty headed a posse of backroom staff who toiled night and day to deflect incoming flak, turn Winston's gaffes into victories, manipulate media stories and generally keep the mayor on track – the crew including gay activist Carter Heywood, who pushed on homosexual issues; and Paul, a press secretary who had the unenviable task of presenting Flaherty's version of events to the media. All of the staff have long decided that the best way to handle Paul is to lie unashamedly to him and keep him in the dark about what is really going on.

In the early episodes Flaherty had a live-in girlfriend, Ashley (played by Carla Gugino), a journalist sometimes hostile to the mayor, but she disappeared before the end of the season, reputedly because Fox's wife, the actress Tracy Pollan, objected to the risqué love scenes between her husband and his co-star. So complete was Ashley's removal from *Spin City* that the character was edited out of repeat airings. Pollan herself turned up in a late-1997 episode as Mike's high-school sweetheart, while Mike's mother, occasionally seen, was played by Meredith Baxter, his ma in *Family Ties*.

Spin Off

UK · ITV (TVS) · CHILDREN'S SITCOM

28 × 10 mins approx · colour

3 Sep 1988–18 Mar 1989 · Sat around 10.55am

MAIN CAST

Hilary Rolls	Roger Sloman
Francesco Fortune	Richard Waites
Lucinda Cartier	Pippa Michaels
Jimmy Lane	Joe Greco
Mazzie	Justine Glenton
Charley Mabey	Wendy Van Der Plank

CREDITS

director/producer David Crozier

A weekly madcap sitcom element within ITV's Saturday-morning children's strand *Motormouth*, with Roger Sloman cast as the general manager of a shop, Richard Waites as his assistant, Pippa Michaels as the manageress and Joe Greco as a bell hop.

Spitting Image

UK · ITV (SPITTING IMAGE PRODUCTIONS FOR CENTRAL · *BBC) · SATIRE

146 editions (137 × 30 mins · 4 × 45 mins · 5 × short specials) · colour

(all programmes are 30 mins unless otherwise stated)

Series One (6) 26 Feb–15 Apr 1984 · Sun 10pm

Series Two (6) 13 May–17 June 1984 · Sun mostly 10pm

Series Three (11) 6 Jan–24 Mar 1985 · Sun mostly 10pm

Series Four (6) 5 Jan–9 Feb 1986 · Sun mostly 10pm

Series Five (6) 30 Mar–4 May 1986 · Sun mostly 10pm

*Short special · part of Comic Relief 25 Apr 1986 · BBC1 Fri after 10.15pm

Special (45 mins) *Down And Out In The White House* 14 Sep 1986 · Sun 9.45pm

Series Six (6) 28 Sep–2 Nov 1986 · Sun 10pm

Special *The Spitting Image 1987 Movie Awards* 4 Apr 1987 · Sat 10.45pm

Special (45 mins) *The Spitting Image Election Special* 11 June 1987 · Thu 10pm

Series Seven (6) 1 Nov–6 Dec 1987 · Sun mostly 10pm

Special · 27 Dec 1987 · Sun 10pm

*Short special *A Question Of Sport Meets Spitting Image* · part of Comic Relief 5 Feb 1988 · BBC1 Fri 8pm

Special *The Ronnie And Nancy Show* 17 Apr 1988 · Sun 9.30pm

Short special · part of *ITV Telethon '88* 29 May 1988 · Sun late-pm

Special (45 mins) *Bumbledown – The Life And Times Of Ronald Reagan* 29 Oct 1988 · Sat 10.15pm

Series Eight (6) 6 Nov–11 Dec 1988 · Sun mostly 10pm

Special (45 mins) *The Sound Of Maggie!* 6 May 1989 · Sat 10.10pm

Series Nine (5) 11 June–9 July 1989 · Sun mostly 9.30pm

Series Ten (6) 12 Nov–17 Dec 1989 · Sun mostly 10.05pm

Series Eleven (6) 13 May–24 June 1990 · Sun mostly 10.05pm

Short special · part of *ITV Telethon '90* 27 May 1990 · Sun late-pm

Series Twelve (6) 11 Nov–16 Dec 1990 · Sun mostly 10.05pm

Series Thirteen (6) 14 Apr–19 May 1991 · Sun mostly 10.05pm

Series Fourteen (6) 10 Nov–15 Dec 1991 · Sun mostly 10.05pm

Special *Election Special* 8 Apr 1992 ·
Wed 10.40pm

Series Fifteen (6) 12 Apr–17 May 1992 ·
Sun mostly 10.05pm

Short special · part of ITV's *Telethon '92*
18 July 1992 · Sat after 9.30pm

Series Sixteen (6) 4 Oct–8 Nov 1992 ·
Sun 10.05pm

Series Seventeen (6) 16 May–20 June 1993 ·
Sun 10.45pm

Series Eighteen (6) 7 Nov–12 Dec 1993 ·
Sun 10pm

Special *Spitting Image Pantomime*
26 Dec 1993 · Sun 10pm

Series Nineteen (6) 1 May–5 June 1994 ·
Sun 10pm

Series Twenty (7) 6 Nov–18 Dec 1994 ·
Sun 10pm

Special *Ye Olde Spittinge Image* 1 Jan 1995 ·
Sun 10.45pm

Series Twenty-One (6) 14 Jan–18 Feb 1996 ·
Sun mostly 11.15pm

MAIN CAST (VOICES ONLY)
Chris Barrie
Rory Bremner
David Coker
Steve Coogan
Hugh Dennis
Harry Enfield
Jon Glover
Alistair McGowan
Jessica Martin
Steve Nallon
Jan Ravens
Enn Reitel
Kate Robbins
John Sessions
Debbie Stephenson
Cliff Taylor

CREDITS
creators Peter Fluck, Roger Law, Martin Lambie-Nairn · *caricaturists* Peter Fluck/Roger Law · *writers* Ian Hislop/Nick Newman, Rob Grant/Doug Naylor, Geoff Atkinson, Richard Curtis, Laurie Rowley, Moray Hunter/Jack Docherty, Andrea Solomons, Guy Jenkin, Tony Sarchet, James Hendrie, Mark Burton, Alistair Beaton, John O'Farrell, Steve Punt, Stuart Silver, Paul Simkin, Pete Sinclair, John Coleman, Roger Blake, John Thomson, Alistair McGowan and others · *script editors* Rob Grant/Doug Naylor, Geoffrey Perkins and others · *directors* Peter Harris (20), Peter Harris/Graham C Williams (1), Graham C Williams (11), Philip Casson (2), Bob Cousins (7), John Stroud (6), Gordon Elsbury (3), Geoffrey Sax (3), John Henderson (10), Steve Bendelack (12), Steve Bendelack/Graham C Williams (6), Steve Bendelack/Andy de Emmony/John Henderson (1), Steve Bendelack/Andy de Emmony (30), Steve Bendelack/Andy de Emmony/Steve Connelly (1), Steve Bendelack/Steve Connelly (5), Steve Bendelack/Andy de Emmony/Beryl Richards (7), Andy de Emmony (1), Sean Hardie (1), Richard Bradley (5), Liddy Oldroyd (6), not known (8) · *producers* Jon Blair/John Lloyd/Tony Hendra (series 1), John Lloyd (series 2–5), Geoffrey Perkins (series 6–8), David Tyler (series 9 & 10), Bill Dare (series 11–18), Giles Pilbrow (series 19–21)

Never in the field of British television endeavour has so much fun been poked with, or wrought from, satire as it was in *Spitting Image*. Unquestionably, the series has been the ultimate in its genre to date, producing four times as many programmes and lasting 11 times longer than the famed *That Was The Week That Was* two decades earlier. While the jokes may not always have hit bullseye, the shots were usually well targeted and the treatment meted out to its subjects deliciously and delightfully vicious, fearing no one and so sacrificing many a previously sacred cow.

In *Spitting Image*, famous characters in British and international life were re-created in the form of latex puppets, which – in the manner of newspaper political cartoons – grossly exaggerated that person's most obvious facial or personality characteristic. Given voices by top-line impressionists and vocal caricaturists, the puppets were manipulated by a team of skilled handlers to act out the quantity of wickedly witty sketches that comprised each edition of the show. Essentially, then, viewing *Spitting Image* was not only like watching your favourite or most despised public figures taking part in topical comedy skits but also seeing and hearing them in a dialogue free of the omnipresent façade of PR gloss and occasional deceit – revealing, perhaps, the true personality underneath, or at the very least, a wicked, exaggerated guess at same. In this fashion, many hundreds – perhaps even a thousand – of people in the news, or faces just plain familiar to TV viewers, spanning the years 1984–96, were lampooned by *Spitting Image*. (To have been a *Spitting Image* target was deemed an honour by many.)

Behind the scenes, the programme was blessed with some brilliant puppeteers, and literally hundreds of people contributed to the scripts over the years. And, of course, *Spitting Image* would have been but naught without its marvellous bands of impressionists. But the most important people behind the series were its three creators, two in particular. The real instigator, although at first he knew not what he was starting, was Martin Lambie-Nairn, who designed graphics for LWT current affairs programmes. Tired of meeting politicians whose first question upon coming off a TV show was always 'How was I?', and keen to see them sent up in some fashion, Lambie-Nairn hit upon the idea of a puppet TV series. He made contact with two genius model-makers, Peter Fluck and Roger Law, whose Plasticine effigies of politicians Lambie-Nairn had seen in magazines. Both men had been around a while – Fluck, indeed, had worked in a minor capacity at *Private Eye* in its formative years, and at *Radio Times* – and were wary of television as a medium. Two further important people, Jon Blair, ex-

Thames TV, and John Lloyd, the co-producer of *Not The Nine O'Clock News*, now freelance having left the BBC, proved valuable allies, however, and within a while Central TV had been hooked as the outlet. After considerable wrangling behind the scenes, the first show went out on 26 February 1984 … and drew an appalling response from the critics.

This remained the way of things for quite some time, until, oddly, a compilation programme of the earliest shows, made for screening at the Montreux TV Festival (where it won a bronze medal) was broadcast in the UK on 29 December 1984 to a great reception, even though it was full of bits that had been previously been afforded harsh criticism. From this point on, *Spitting Image* had many champions among the press and viewing public. Even hurdles like portraying the much revered Queen Mother were overcome, despite such initial shock-horror page-one headlines as the *Daily Mirror*'s 'Spitting Mad! TV's Cruellest Show Takes A Swipe At The Queen Mother' splash. (This was in February 1985.)

Throughout the near 11 years that it was on air, the production schedule of *Spitting Image* was frightening. Each week new moulds were made and faces created in a dedicated *Spitting Image* workshop situated in the Docklands area of London. These were then despatched to Central TV's Birmingham studios for the shooting of the sketches, many utilising scripts still being written at the last possible moment to ensure maximum topicality. (Like perusing an old newspaper, viewing again archive editions of *Spitting Image* is somewhat baffling because one forgets the build-up to a story, remembering only the climax – and sometimes not even that.) As the years passed, though, the show picked up many awards (and the odd lawsuit), enjoyed hit records (with music composed by Philip Pope and Peter Brewis), sold well internationally and was the focus of numerous repeat-compilations and other TV programmes (see footnote). A French adaptation, *Les Guignols*, took to the air, as did a post-Glasnost Russian version, *Kookli*, but attempts to launch *Spitting Image* in the USA proved a little more frustrating, despite the assistance of David Frost as host/co-executive producer, and after three NBC programmes – also seen on British TV – the exercise was abandoned. The first, *Down And Out In The White House* (screened in the USA in two parts, on 30 August and 6 September 1986), portrayed Ronald Reagan as a brainless incompetent and Sylvester Stallone seeking election as the next US president. The second, *The Ronnie And Nancy Show* (4 January 1987), showed Nancy Reagan throwing a surprise party for her and her senile husband's 210th anniversary. The third, *The Spitting Image 1987 Movie*

Awards (26 March 1987), took an irreverent look at Hollywood celebrities, with Leonard Nimoy scheming his way to an Oscar. But while *Spitting Image* failed to take off Stateside, it did inspire the making of a similar series there, **DC Follies**.

It seems a truism that British satire works best when the Conservative Party is in power. *Beyond The Fringe*, *Private Eye*, *TW3* and the Establishment Club were all launched in the Macmillan era, *Spitting Image* was founded under Thatcher. Ironically, her initial portrayal in the series, as more of a man than the men in her Cabinet, may have added to her myth; more biting was the revised portrayal of her as a lunatic, aided by her skinhead henchman Norman Tebbit, and, at the last, as a mad woman with flashing eyes and straitjacket harness. When Thatcher was toppled and John Major became the new PM *Spitting Image* portrayed him as grey through and through, an image that endured.

Although it was often said to be in its final throes (the concluding edition of only the second series was described as 'the last ever', the last show in the sixth series was 'positively the last ever … possibly'), *Spitting Image* flexed its grotesque rubbery muscle for more than a decade. While, late on, there was a general feeling that it was living beyond its 'best by' date, it remained viable, possibly because, for a long time, there was no other outlet for up-to-the-minute satire. However, with Rory Bremner beginning his BBC2 series in 1989, and *Have I Got News For You* arriving on the same channel in 1990, the latter proving an especially good outlet for malice, *Spitting Image* was not essential viewing in the 1990s. New hooks were tried: the 1992 election special was performed for the first time in front of a studio audience, and animation was introduced in 1994, but by 1996 *Spitting Image* had mocked its last and a golden era in British satire was laid to rest.

Note. *Spitting Image* puppets featured in numerous other programmes over the years. Some puppets turned up in the 9 March 1986 episode of the LWT sitcom **Hot Metal**. The scripting of an edition of *Spitting Image* was documented in an ITV schools half-hour first transmitted in *The English Programme* and then first repeated as a stand-alone transmission, *The Writing Of Spitting Image*, on 24 August 1986. Some *Spitting Image* puppets turned up in Central TV's networked one-off hour-length programme *Car Wars – The 1986 Motor Show* on 15 October 1986, in LWT/C4's **Saturday Live** on 14 February 1987, in the **First Aids** charity concert networked by ITV on 27 February 1987 and in *The Secret Policeman's Third Ball*, the film of the March 1987 concerts benefiting Amnesty International, *The Secret Policeman's Biggest Ball*, first screened on TV on 28 October 1989,

and *Amnesty International's Big 30*, networked by Central TV on 28 December 1991 (see **The Amnesty Galas**). The 20 July 1988 edition of the children's ITV series *Kellyvision* (made by Tyne Tees) went behind the scenes at *Spitting Image* to see how the show was put together, as did TVS's *Motormouth* on 26 January 1991. A latex puppet of Bob Hoskins turned up in LWT's *The Trouble With Michael Caine*, screened on 1 January 1989, pointedly asking Caine (the real one) why he accepted every role offered to him. The 11 November 1990 edition of the LWT arts programme *The South Bank Show* featured *Spitting Image*, coinciding with the launch of the twelfth series; some *Spitting Image* puppets turned up in *The Last Cigarette*, a silly celebrity-packed programme put together to promote a forthcoming National No-Smoking Day, screened by ITV on 8 March 1992; and *Spitting Image* representations of the Cabinet were seen in an edition of *The God Tapes*, screened by C4 on Easter Day (3 April) 1994. Spitting Image Productions also made *Thatcherworld*, a special 40-minute show for a BBC2 season about the overthrow of the former Prime Minister, *After Margaret*, screened on 24 October 1993. The programme looked into the future, showing a family (Gary Olsen, Frances Barber and Edna Doré) on a journey around Britain's newest and most exciting theme park devoted to her former Leaderene; numerous *Spitting Image* puppets were seen.

Spitting Image Productions moved into stop-motion animation with *Crapston Villas*, a malevolent soap opera written and directed by Sarah Ann Kennedy. Each ten-minute episode pried into the lives of a bunch of grotesques inhabiting different floors of a single large, ramshackle house. Adult in content and occasionally very funny, the series also sported plenty of the savagery associated with the company's earlier work. *Crapston Villas* first aired on C4 for nine episodes from 27 October 1995; a second series, ten parts, began on 7 November 1997.

See also **The Strip Show**.

Split Ends

UK · ITV (GRANADA) · SITCOM

6 × 30 mins · colour

7 June–12 July 1989 · Wed 8.30pm

MAIN CAST

Cath	Anita Dobson
David	Peter Blake
Clint	Harry Ditson
Ruth Gordon	Barbara New
Aretha	Nimmy March
Herbie	Robin Davies
Lee	Lee Whitlock

CREDITS

creator Len Richmond · writers Len Richmond (5), Jan Etherington/Gavin Petrie (1) · director Alan J W

Bell · *executive producer* David Liddiment · *producer* James Maw

A somewhat wooden and ultimately disappointing series considering the pre-publicity it attracted, built upon the starring role for Anita Dobson, who had shot to fame as Angie Watts in the early years (from 19 February 1985) of the BBC1 soap *EastEnders*.

Dobson was cast here as Cath, the owner of a London hairdressing salon named Teasers (the series' working title). Now in her late thirties, Cath comes under pressure from her overbearing (and possibly Jewish) mother and feels the need to marry. To this end, she agrees to become engaged to Clint, a wealthy, smarmy American stockbroker who likes to talk the language of the office in romantic clinches. But she is also fatally attracted to David, the salon's smoothly flirtatious self-loving senior stylist. Knowing himself too well, and wishing to preserve their friendship, David tries to keep his hands off, but a battle between the men soon ensues, amid which th engagement is called off.

While Cath vacillates between Clint and David, trying to sort out a love life more tangled than her worst clients' hair, the rest of the action is split between the glitzy salon and the drab backroom where the Teasers employees – lovelorn Aretha, gay Herbie and delinquent YTS trainee Lee – drink tea and bicker with one another.

Anita Dobson also sang the theme tune, 'Second Thoughts'. Coincidentally, this was the title of the contemporary BBC Radio 4 sitcom (which later transferred to TV) written by Jan Etherington and Gavin Petrie, and they made their TV debut scripting an episode of *Split Ends*.

Spooner's Patch

UK · ITV (REGENT PRODUCTIONS FOR ATV · *REGENT PRODUCTIONS FOR CENTRAL) · SITCOM

19 × 30 mins · colour

Series One (6) 9 July–6 Aug 1979 · Mon 8pm; 5 Mar–19 Mar 1980 · Wed 11.45pm

Series Two (6) 4 Sep–16 Oct 1980 · Thu 7.30pm

*Series Three (7) 15 Apr–20 May 1982 · Thu 7.30pm; 24 Aug 1982 · Tue 8.30pm

MAIN CAST

Insp Spooner	Ronald Fraser (series 1);
	Donald Churchill (series 2 & 3)
Det Con Bulsover	Peter Cleall
PC Killick	John Lyons
Mrs Cantaford	Patricia Hayes
	(series 2 & 3)
PC Goatman	Norman Rossington (series 1)
Kelly	Dermot Kelly (series 1)

CREDITS

writers Ray Galton/Johnny Speight · director/producer William G Stewart

On paper, this was an arresting prospect: Johnny Speight and Ray Galton, two of the greatest comedy scriptwriters in British TV, teamed for the first time on the small-screen. They had written together in the 1950s, when both were unknown, scripting a stage musical, *Mr Venus* – now, with the retirement of Galton's regular writing partner Alan Simpson, the pair reunited. As it transpired, though, *Spooner's Patch* was a patchy disappointment. Worse, it was dogged by cast changes and ITV industrial action that caused episodes in two of the three series to be rescheduled, destroying continuity.

The series was set in a small Metropolitan Police station, in the fictitious London suburb of Woodley, and centred on the antics of Spooner, a crazed, vain and far from incorruptible Inspector who lives in a flat above the 'cop-shop'. Some of the humour was drawn from dark situations: Spooner has an affair with the wife of a man he has imprisoned for five years, and local shop owners arrive to pay their thanks for the turning of official blind-eyes. Of Spooner's men, PC Goatman is a fascist plain-clothes detective; DC Bulsover likes to think of himself as a Starsky or Hutch-style US TV cop, driving around in a red Ford Anglia with a white flash down the side; and PC Killick reacts to everything with sarcasm. The best support character was the trouble-making traffic warden Mrs Cantaford, played by Patricia Hayes (for whom Johnny Speight had long been a writer), who appeared in the second and third series.

Sports Bloopers

see *Auntie's Sporting Bloomers*

Spotlight

see *The Old Boy Network*

Spring And Autumn

UK · ITV (THAMES) · SITCOM

27 episodes (26 × 30 mins · 1 × short special) · colour

Pilot · 23 Oct 1972 · Mon 8.30pm

Series One (6) 16 July–20 Aug 1973 · Mon 8pm

Short special · part of *All-Star Comedy Carnival* 25 Dec 1973 · Tue 6.30pm

Series Two (6) 24 July–28 Aug 1974 · Wed 8pm

Series Three (6) 20 May–24 June 1976 · Thu 8pm

Series Four (7) 31 Aug–19 Oct 1976 · Tue mostly 8.30pm

MAIN CAST

Tommy Butler · · · · · · · · · · · · · Jimmy Jewel
Charlie Harris (Colin Harris in pilot) · · · · · · ·
 · · · · · · · · · · · · · · · · Gary Williams (pilot);
 · · · · · · · · · · · · · Charlie Hawkins (series)
Vera Reid · · · · · · · · · · · · · June Barry
Brian Reid (Joe Dickinson in pilot) · · · · · · · ·
 · · · · · · · · · · · · · · · · · · Larry Martyn

Betty Harris (Betty Dickinson in pilot) · · · · ·
 · · · · · · · · · · · · · · · Gaye Brown (pilot);
 · · · · · · · · · · · · · · · · Jo Warne (series)

CREDITS

writers Vince Powell/Harry Driver (pilot, series 1 & special), Vince Powell (series 2–4) · *directors/ producers* Stuart Allen (pilot), Ronnie Baxter (series 1 & special), Mike Vardy (series 2), Anthony Parker (series 3 & 4)

Deviating from their usual race/religion topics, writers Powell and Driver created a pleasingly gentle, if predictable, comedy in *Spring And Autumn*. This (and the concurrent *Love Thy Neighbour*) turned out to be their last work together – Driver died in November 1973, between the first and second series.

Spring And Autumn starred Jimmy Jewel (whom the writers had also cast four years earlier in *Nearest And Dearest*) as Tommy Butler, a northerner widower of 70 and former railway employee who leaves behind the crumbling slum that has been his home for 40 years and, gathering up his worldly goods – a chamber-pot and a stuffed parrot named Nelson – takes up residence with his daughter Vera and her husband Brian in their high-rise tower-block flat down south. Butler's son-in-law takes great exception to the old man's intrusive presence because it upsets the balance of routine within his four walls, and also the state of his marriage. He has a point, too: Butler is crabby, clumsy, inflexible and, worse, a hypochondriac. Happily, though, he soon forges a great friendship, not with another pensioner but with a 12-year-old cockney lad, Charlie Harris, who is also new to the area and unwanted by his family: his mum is a busy, hard-up divorcee often out at work, and he hasn't seen his father in years. Despite early attempts by the families to keep them apart, Tommy Butler and Charlie Harris grow inseparable, the older man becoming a father-figure to the boy. As the series progresses so the relationship develops, the boy becoming a teenager and, by the end of the final series, a school leaver.

Note. The pilot edition of *Spring And Autumn* was screened in 1972 and the first full series began ten months later. The first episode of this initial series was a re-make of the pilot, necessary because of cast, relational and character-name changes.

Sprout

UK · ITV (THAMES) · SITCOM

1 × 30 mins · colour

1 July 1974 · Mon 8pm

MAIN CAST

Darwin Sprout · · · · · · · · · · · · John Alderton
John Russell · · · · · · · · · · · · · Julian Holloway
Mr Barker · · · · · · · · · · · · · · Geoffrey Chater

CREDITS

writers Anthony Matheson/Peter Tilbury · *director/producer* Anthony Parker

A single-episode comedy pilot, never developed into a series. John Alderton starred as an oddly named man who, with a mountain of unpaid bills troubling his conscience, is desperate to find a job. After failing at nine successive interviews he asks his flat-mate, John, to help sharpen up his technique.

The co-author of the piece, Peter Tilbury, went on to create a character the mirror image of Darwin Sprout: a man with no conscience who never wanted to work – *Shelley*.

Square Deal

UK · ITV (LWT) · SITCOM

14 × 30 mins · colour

Series One (7) 3 Sep–5 Oct 1988 · Sat mostly 6.45pm

Series Two (7) 1 Sep–13 Oct 1989 · Fri mostly 8.30pm

MAIN CAST

Emma Barrington · · · · · Lise-Ann McLaughlin
Nigel Barrington · · · · · · · · Timothy Bentinck
Sean · · · · · · · · · · · · · · · · · Brett Fancy
Alan · · · · · · · · · · · · · · · Angus Barnett
Max Grout · · · · · · · · · · · · · Jeremy Sinden
Sally · · · · · · · · · · · · · · · · · Jo McEvoy
Hannah · · · · · · · · · · · Beth Porter (series 1)
Brian · · · · · · · · · · · · · Frank Ellis (series 2)
Geraldine Gunter-Forbes · · Georgina Melville
 · · · · · · · · · · · · · · · · · · (series 2)

OTHER APPEARANCES

Julian Pickford · · · · · · · · · · · Anthony Daniels

CREDITS

writer Richard Ommanney · *executive producer* Marcus Plantin · *director/producer* Nic Phillips

A late-1980s sitcom based in a south London square wherein live Nigel and Emma Barrington, a yuppie couple whose apparently comfortable lifestyle is brusquely shaken by the arrival on the scene of Sean, an incurable and impoverished young romantic.

Sean is a determined dreamer who has set himself until his next birthday – eight weeks hence – to make a success of his life; he then bumps into Emma – literally, they have an accident from which he ends up in plaster – and they agree to go into business together, buying a café/sandwich bar. The enterprise will benefit from a perfect blend of their talents: her business knowledge and his acumen as a sandwich-maker – hitherto, he has been selling them to a market stall to support his career as a writer.

With Sean on the scene, Nigel and Emma's relationship rapidly deteriorates, and a love triangle emerges, first in Nigel's mind and then in reality, as Emma realises that, for all his quirks, Sean is more fun to be with than her husband. An estate agent with a cunning mind, Nigel proceeds to wreck his wife's café plans by gazumping her, and talk of a divorce is soon in the air. Later (in the second series) Sean turns his attentions to rock singing, becoming a fledgling star, while Nigel becomes Sean's landlord and develops an interest in his new neighbour, Geraldine.

Modestly successful, if flawed, *Square Deal* starred Lise-Ann McLaughlin (Sally in the light-hearted drama *The Irish RM*; three series for C4, 1983–85) and Timothy Bentinck (David Archer in *The Archers* on BBC Radio 4).

The Square Leopard

UK · ITV (HTV) · CHILDREN'S SITCOM

6 × 30 mins · colour

12 Aug–16 Sep 1980 · Tue 4.45pm

MAIN CAST

Gerald Parish	John Leyton
Mary Lampert	Janet Key
Nesta Wright	Sorcha Cusack
Henry Parish	Raymond Huntley
Adela	Jessica Turner
Joanna	Jayne Tottman
Toby	Toby Waldock
Bill	Marcus D'Amico
Richard	Mark Evans
David	Richard Kellow

CREDITS

writer Peter Miller · *directors* Terry Miller, Jan Darnley-Smith, Ken Price · *executive producer* Patrick Dromgoole · *producer* Peter Miller

A children's series starring John Leyton, the actor with the dashing good looks who, for a while in the early 1960s, flourished as a youthful pop singer ('Johnny Remember Me') resulting from an appearance in the ATV drama serial *Harpers West One*.

Needing a pick-me-up in his career, Leyton agreed to appear in this sitcom, cast as Gerald Parish, a truculent, down-on-his-luck solicitor who, requiring a place to live, rents the ground floor section of a large house. The place is owned by Mary Lampert, a widowed mother of numerous children, and said offspring take an immediate dislike to the law man, a feeling that is mutual. However, when Parish's long-lost father threatens to visit his son, to see how well he has done in life, the solicitor decides to make out that Lampert is his wife and that he is the father of the brats.

Square Pegs

USA · CBS (EMBASSY TELEVISION) SITCOM

20 × 30 mins · colour

US dates: 27 Sep 1982–12 Sep 1983

UK dates: 16 Apr–9 Nov 1983 (20 episodes) C4 Sat 6pm then Wed mostly 6pm

MAIN CAST

Patty Greene	Sarah Jessica Parker
Lauren Hutchinson	Amy Linker
Jennifer DeNuccio	Tracy Nelson
Johnny 'Slash' Ulacewitz	Merritt Butrick
Marshall Blechtman	John Femia
Muffy Tepperman	Jami Gertz
Vinnie Pasetta	Jon Caliri
LaDonna Fredericks	Claudette Wells
Principal Dingleman	Basil Hoffman
Rob Donovan	Steven Peterman
Mr Loomie	Catlin Adams

CREDITS

writers Anne Beatts, Andy Borowitz, Marshall Brickman, Leslie Fuller, Janis E Hirsch, Chris Miller, Rick Mitz, Margaret G Oberman, Rosie Shuster, Susan Silver, David Skinner, Deanne Stillman, Michael D Sutton · *directors* various · *executive producer* Anne Beatts · *producer* Ronald Frazier

Two 14-year-old girls – next-door neighbours and established best friends – arrive new at Weemawee High School, set in Weemawee Heights, somewhere in suburban USA. They're 'freshmen', to use the mixed-sex US vernacular, and try their darnedest to be popular with the fashionable, with-it set. But Patty is gawky, bespectacled and anxiously awaiting frontal development, and Lauren is short, a little overweight and still has brace-capped teeth, so together they're the proverbial square pegs in the title, attempting to get into the round hole represented by some real cool dudes: the vainglorious hunk Vinnie, his snobbish and sickeningly wealthy 'Valley Girl' sweetheart Jennifer, the self-obsessed cheerleader Muffy and the worldly but prejudiced black girl LaDonna Fredericks. The two square pegs mostly fail in their mission but do manage to establish an 'in' with Marshall, the class jester, and Johnny 'Slash' Ulacewitz, a new-wave rocker with a natty line in fashion, to the extent where they begin to feel comfortable at school, at last.

Writer/producer Anne Beatts was one of the principal writers of **Saturday Night Live** in the early 1980s and her involvement in *Square Pegs* ushered in guest appearances by that series' Bill Murray and (in his Father Guido Sarducci guise) Don Novello.

Squawkie Talkie

UK · C4 (ABSOLUTELY PRODUCTIONS) · SKETCH

6 × 30 mins · colour

23 May–27 June 1995 · Tue 8pm

MAIN CAST

John Sparkes
Pete Baikie

CREDITS

writers John Sparkes/Pete Baikie · *director/executive producer* Alan Nixon · *producer* David Housham

An animal-themed sketch show that applied a number of different techniques to stock wild-life film for comic effect. Basic voice-over and re-dubbing of footage raised some chuckles but the best moments were the smarter routines involving the creation of mini-dramas, operas, biographies and mock-adverts.

The Squirrels

UK · ITV (ATV) · SITCOM

28 × 30 mins · colour

Pilot · 8 July 1974 · Mon 8pm

Series One (7) 18 July–29 Aug 1975 · Fri 8.30pm

Series Two (8) 9 July–27 Aug 1976 · Fri 8.30pm

Series Three (12) 25 Nov 1976–10 Feb 1977 · Thu 9pm

MAIN CAST

Mr Fletcher	Bernard Hepton
Rex	Ken Jones
Susan	Patsy Rowlands
Harry	Alan David
Burke	Ellis Jones
Carol	Susan Tracy (pilot);
	Karin MacCarthy (series)

CREDITS

creator Eric Chappell · *writers* Eric Chappell (16), Alan Hackney (3), Brian Finch (3), Richard Harris (2), Kenneth Cope (2), Phil Redmond (2) · *script editor* Colin Shindler · *director/producer* Shaun O'Riordan

Calling upon his observations as a travelling auditor with the East Midlands Electricity Board, Eric Chappell used *The Squirrels* to explore the humorous side of office politicking. The series was set in the accounts department of International Rentals, a (fictitious) television hire company, with six key figures featuring each week – principally, the autocratic boss Mr Fletcher (played by Bernard Hepton, best known as the time as the stern Kommandant in *Colditz*), who fancied himself as a ladies' man; and Rex, a nervous underling (played by the always good value Ken Jones). The majority of the stories centred on office romances, misunderstandings and red-faces at audit time.

Attributing the series' odd title to a line in a BBC Radio 4 play that he had previously written about the same topic (*Poor Glover*, broadcast on 6 March 1974 in the *Thirty-Minute Theatre* slot), Eric Chappell wittily described *The Squirrels* – his first TV sitcom creation, ahead of **Rising Damp** – as being about 'the paranoia and lust for promotion of white-collar workers in confined spaces'. He must had a strong feeling for the idea because 17 years later, in 1991, he revamped it as **Fiddlers Three**.

S-s-s-h! The Wife!

UK · BBC · SKETCH

1 × 10 mins · b/w

6 Apr 1938 · Wed 3pm

MAIN CAST

The husband	Richard Hearne
The wife	Lily Palmer
The friend	George Nelson

CREDITS

writer Richard Hearne

Another one-off comedy sketch, presented under the *Starlight* banner, starring a pre-

Mr Pastry Richard Hearne. As for the storyline – well, the title says it all.

See also *Bath H&C*, *Moving Furniture* and *Take Two Eggs*.

The Staggering Stories Of Ferdinand De Bargos

UK · BBC · SATIRE

24 editions (22 × 20 mins · colour; 1 × 30 mins · colour; 1 × 10 mins · b/w)

Series One (6 × 20 mins) 16 Nov–28 Dec 1989 · BBC2 Thu 10.10pm

Series Two (6 × 20 mins) 4 Apr–9 May 1991 · BBC2 Thu 10.10pm

Special (10 mins · b/w) *The Staggering Story Of Lime Grove* 26 Aug 1991 · BBC2 Mon 6.30pm

Special (30 mins) *The Staggering Year Of Ferdinand De Bargos* 25 Dec 1991 · BBC2 Wed 4.50pm

Series Three (6 × 20 mins) 4 Mar–5 Apr 1993 · BBC2 mostly Thu 10.10pm

Series Four (4 × 20 mins) 30 July–3 Sep 1995 · BBC2 Sun 7.15pm

MAIN CAST (VOICES ONLY)
Enn Reitel
Jon Glover
Jim Broadbent (series 1–3)
Kate Robbins (series 1 & 2)
Susie Blake (series 1)
Caroline Leddy (series 2)
Joanna Brookes (series 3 & 4)
Steve Steen (series 3 & 4)
Ronnie Ancona (series 4)
Alistair McGowan (series 4)
Arabella Weir (short special)

CREDITS
writers Kim Fuller/Geoff Atkinson · *executive producer* Tony Garnett · *producers* Kim Fuller/Geoff Atkinson

A consistently fine series that derived good mileage from its one stock idea: to take archive footage (mostly documentary) and overdub it with comic dialogue performed by gifted voice artists. These short and relatively inexpensive programmes provided many good laughs and were strongly satirical in tone, often commenting on current affairs and royal matters.

The short special *The Staggering Story Of Lime Grove*, utilising footage from the earliest days of British television, was presented as part of a day-long BBC2 tribute to its Lime Grove studios, upon its closure.

See also *The Almost Complete History Of The 20th Century*, *Pallas* and *Klinik!*

Stainless Steel And The Star Spies

UK · ITV (THAMES) · CHILDREN'S SITCOM

1 × 60 mins · colour

1 Jan 1981 · Thu 4.45pm

MAIN CAST
Vicar · · · · · · · · · · · · · · · · · Deryck Guyler
Mum · · · · · · · · · · · · · · · · · Anna Karen
Young girl · · · · · · · · · · Deborah Farrington
Dad · · · · · · · · · · · · · · · · Charles Pemberton
Miss Ruby · · · · · · · · · · · · · · · · · Fabia Drake

CREDITS
writer Gray Jolliffe · *director* Anthony Simmons · *producer* Ray Corbett · *executive producer* Verity Lambert

A New Year's Day comedy special for children written by Gray Jolliffe, a cartoon humorist by profession (he later drew the phenomenally successful Wicked Willie books and merchandising), that combined live-action with puppetry. Executive producer Verity Lambert had been involved in the earliest days of *Doctor Who* and here too the story was science-fictional: the Metaliens, a bunch of alloyed robots – named Stainless Steel, Utensil, the Canz and Gadget – set out to dominate the universe.

Stand Up

UK · ITV (GRANADA) · STANDUP

21 × 30 mins · colour

*Series One (8) 13 Jan–3 Mar 1989 · Fri 10.35pm

*Series Two (7) 14 June–2 Aug 1991 · Fri mostly 11.35pm

*Series Three (6) 25 Sep–30 Oct 1992 · Fri 11.40pm

MAIN CAST
see below

CREDITS
writers cast · *directors* James Wynn (series 1), Spencer Campbell (series 2), Andrew Humphries (series 3) · *executive producer* David Liddiment · *producers* James Maw (series 1 & 2), Andrew Humphries (series 3)

Eighteen years after Granada welcomed through its studio doors the best standup club acts in the north of England, making the remarkably popular and durable series *The Comedians*, it decided to repeat the formula with the younger firebrand comics who were bringing in audiences to the rapidly booming comedy club circuit. In doing so, Granada – always the most prescient of the ITV companies – managed to catch close on 50 of the still nationally unknown young humorists in the act before, in some cases, they went on to bigger and much greater things. In decades to come, when students seek to investigate the 1980s–90s comedy boom, it is to Granada's *Stand Up* they should refer.

The process of making *Stand Up* was similar to that used to present *The Comedians*. Granada invited comics to the studio, recorded their acts and then edited the tapes into half-hour programmes. Initially, material for two shows was taped over a three-day period at the end of 1988, featuring Steve Coogan, Rob Newman, John Hegley, Jim Tavaré, Mike Hayley and Craig Ferguson. Given the green light from this point,

Granada recruited other young comics to flesh out the first series.

These comedians were seen in the first series (numbers in parentheses refer to programme appearances) – Craig Ferguson (6), John Hegley (6), Steve Coogan (4), Michael Redmond (4), Mike Hayley (3), Jim Tavaré (3), Hattie Hayridge (3), Linda Smith (3), Patrick Marber (3), Rob Newman (2), Bert Tyler-Moore (2), Simon Bligh (2), Martha McBriar (2), Boothby Graffoe (1), Bob Mills (1), Tony Morewood (1), Malcolm Hardee (1), Rob Sprackling (1), Bernadine Corrigan (1) and Simon Munnery (1).

Performing in the second series were Jeff Green (4), Hattie Hayridge (3), Kevin Day (3), Rob Newman (3), Frank Skinner (2), Nick Revell (2), John Hegley (2), Sean Hughes (2), Linda Smith (2), Jo Brand (2), Mark Lamarr (2), Steve Coogan (2), Stewart Lee (1), Brenda Gilhooly (1), Felix (1), Malcolm Hardee (1), Niall Macanna (1) and Jack Dee (1).

And in the third series – Lee Evans (3), 'Tommy Cockles' (Simon Day) (3), Alistair McGowan (2), Paul Tonkinson (2), John Hegley (2), Kevin Boyle (2), Sean Lock (2), Dominik Diamond (1), Jo Enright (1), Alan Davies (1), Fred MacAulay (1), Jeff Green (1), Owen O'Neill (1), Michael Redmond (1), Roger D (1), Brendan Riley (1), Mark Lamarr (1), Bob Dillinger (1), Hattie Hayridge (1), Phill Jupitus (1) and Charlie Chuck (1).

*Note. These dates refer to the original Granada screenings in the north-west of England and not to London-ITV transmissions. The first series, eight programmes, was broadcast by London-area ITV some two years after it had been broadcast by Granada, from 30 May to 18 July 1991, at 4am every Thursday night (ie, Friday mornings). The second series, seven programmes, was broadcast in London as *Stand Up II* from 6 November to 18 December 1991, at 3.40am every Wednesday (actually Thursday). Finally, five second-series programmes were repeated by London-area ITV in 1996 (sporadically, 13 August to 29 October, Tuesdays mostly at 11.10pm). The third Granada series has not shown in London. Also never seen in London is a half-hour highlights compilation from all three series, *The Very Best Of Stand Up*, screened locally by Granada on 23 November 1992.

Stand Up Jim Davidson

UK · ITV (THAMES) · STANDUP

6 × 30 mins · colour

5 Mar–9 Apr 1990 · Mon 9.30pm

MAIN CAST
Jim Davidson

CREDITS
script editor Neil Shand · *director/producer* David Clark

An ever more permissive society, coupled with a post-watershed slot, enabled Jim Davidson to deliver an adult standup act in this series, more hard-hitting than the one seen in umpteen editions of *The Jim Davidson Show*. Good fun for those who like their humour a royal shade of blue.

The Stand Up Show

UK · BBC · STANDUP

31 editions (28 × 30 mins · 1 × 40 mins · 1 × 45 mins · 1 × 50 mins) · colour

Pilot · 18 Aug 1994 · BBC1 Thu 11.30pm

Series One (10) 22 Feb–22 Apr 1995 · BBC1 Wed 11.45pm then Sat 11.45pm

Special (40 mins) 23 Sep 1995 · BBC1 Sat 11.50pm

Series Two (9) 28 Oct 1995–6 Jan 1996 · BBC1 Sat mostly 11.50pm

Special (45 mins) 7 Sep 1996 · BBC1 Sat 11.20pm

Series Three (8) 2 Nov–21 Dec 1996 · BBC1 Sat mostly 11.50pm

Special (50 mins) 27 Sep 1997 · BBC1 Sat 12 midnight

MAIN CAST

host · · · · · · · · · · · Barry Cryer (series 1 & 2)
· · · · · · · · · · · · · · · Ardal O'Hanlon (series 3)
and see below

CREDITS

writers various · *linking material* Barry Cryer, Ardal O'Hanlon · *additional material* Iain Pattinson, Robert Fraser Steele · *directors* Peter Howitt (pilot), Mark Mylod (10), Nick Wood (9), Duncan Cooper (8), Geoff Miles (1), Richard Valentine (2) · *producers* Claudia Lloyd (20), Jon Rowlands (7), Geoff Miles (1), Karen Rosie (1)

A straightforward representation of the British standup scene. Refreshingly, in the first two series, it was not a young blade but the comparatively veteran comic/writer Barry Cryer who introduced the acts. In the third, the job was taken over by Ardal O'Hanlon, the standup (he thus appeared in the first two series) who also doubles as a comic actor, playing Dougal McGuire in *Father Ted*. All of the performers worked from the same bare stage, with minimal use of props, and the British comics were sometimes augmented by guests from overseas.

Those seen more than once in *The Stand Up Show* include Al Murray, Rhona Cameron, Phill Jupitus, Scott Capurro, Kevin Day, Jeff Green, Dominic Holland, Lee Hurst, Phil Kay, Sean Lock, John Maloney, Sean Meo, Dylan Moran, Parrot, Simon Pegg and John Thomson. The following also appeared – Bill Bailey, Amanda Bloom, Marcus Brigstocke, Ed Byrne, Otiz Cannelloni, Anthony Clark, Tim Clark, Corky And The Juice Pigs, 'Dame Sybille' (Sean Cullen), Alan Davies, Felix Dexter, Keith Dover, Will Durst, Lynn Ferguson, Kevin Gidea, Rich Hall, Mike Hayley, Hattie Hayridge, Caroline Hook (Caroline Aherne), Mark Hurst, Noel James,

Milton Jones, Patrick Kielty, Mark Lamarr, Simon Lipson, Fred MacAulay, Mark Maier, Alistair McGowan, Donna McPhail, Bob Mills, Richard Morton, Phil Nicol, Graham Norton, Owen O'Neill, Andy Parsons, Michael Redmond, Dave Spikey, Mark Steel, David Strassman, Tommy Tiernan, Paul Tonkinson, the Umbilical Brothers and Tim Vine.

Notes. The 23 September 1995 special featured highlights from the talent-searching 'Open Mic Awards' at the Edinburgh Festival Fringe; the specials of 7 September 1996 and 27 September 1997 featured the highlights of the BBC New Comedy Awards presented from the same event.

Barry Cryer also introduced a six-part radio series of the same format, broadcast on BBC Radio 2 from 10 April 1997 as *Stand Up Two*. Each edition featured four performers – some being established acts, others newly breaking ones. Among those featured were Arj Barker, Geoff Boyz, Jo Enright, Dominic Holland and Will Smith.

Stanelli

UK · BBC · SKETCH

1 × 10 mins · b/w

2 Apr 1937 · Fri 3pm

MAIN CAST

Stanelli

CREDITS

producer Leslie Mitchell

Musical prodigy Stanelli (born Edward Stanley de Groot) was headed for the concert platform as both a conductor and a violinist, and had composed orchestral works including the tone-poem *Atlantis*, when he opted instead for comedy. First he formed a double-act (Stanelli and Edgar) and then, alone, devised *Stanelli's Stag Parties*, a boisterous BBC radio entertainment from 1935 that – in keeping with the BBC's pre-war staid, Reithian era – was later retitled *Stanelli's Bachelor Parties*. A sequel in 1939, *Stanelli's Crazy Cruise*, was set on board a ship. Both series were tremendously popular in their day.

On 2 April 1937 Stanelli made his television debut, introducing viewers to the 'Hornchestra', another device of his own creation – and already well-known to radio listeners – which comprised a weird collection of electric and bulb motor-horns on which he played jazz music. A later TV booking, for 5 November 1937, did not take place although it was announced in *Radio Times*.

See also *Stanelli's Bachelor Party* (next entry).

Stanelli's Bachelor Party

UK · BBC · SKETCH

2 × 30 mins · b/w

8 Sep 1938 · Thu 3pm

24 Nov 1938 · Thu 3pm

MAIN CAST

Stanelli
Norman Long
Russell and Marconi
The Three Musketeers
Jack Wynne
Sydney Jerome
Ernest Shannon

CREDITS

creator/writer Stanelli · *producer* Harry Pringle

A TV version of the popular radio show (see previous entry), first unveiled on 4 July 1935. Most of the supporting crew here were resident in the wireless version, including the comedian Norman Long whose claim to fame was that he was the first entertainer to be 'made' solely by radio.

Stanley Baxter ... [various shows]

see BAXTER, Stanley

Freddie Starr

Born Freddie Fowell (a great name – he surely needn't have changed it) in Liverpool on 9 January 1943, Freddie Starr has been Britain's wildest comedian in the last quarter of the 20th-century, a devastatingly funny man who will go to any length for a laugh. A fine impressionist and physical comic, he slays TV and theatre audiences wherever he plays, but does not suit all tastes – those whose preference is for earthy material find him hilarious from the moment he steps on stage, whereas those who prefer their comedy on the cerebral side rarely consider him amusing. But while audiences have been well entertained by Starr they have also been frustrated by the ups and downs of a career that has mirrored the comic's turbulent and well-publicised private life.

Starr had been in entertainment long before entering TV – working under his real name he appeared as a troubled teenager, Tommy, in Rank's 1957 film about juvenile delinquency, *Violent Playground*, set in his native Liverpool. Rock and roll music was his next outlet – he joined local band Howie Casey And The Seniors and, eventually, fronted Freddie Starr And The Midnighters (at one time represented by the Beatles' manager, Brian Epstein), who released three singles on Decca in 1963–64. Then he moved into impressionism, breaking into TV in *Opportunity Knocks* (he and his musical impressionist group the Delmonts won this three times in the late 1960s) before making a major impact as a solo performer in 1970 *Royal Variety Show* (televised by BBC1 on 15 November). Starr then truly arrived as a major comedy star in the 1972–76 LWT series *Who Do You Do?*, delighting audiences with rubbery body movements, wild antics and off-beam impersonations of such people as Elvis Presley, Mick Jagger, Norman Wisdom, Max Wall and Adolf Hitler. Unpredictability is the essence of the man.

Much of Starr's TV work has been as guest in other people's programmes, and in variety, but listed here, chronologically, are the series with which his name has been uppermost.

Ready Freddie Starr

UK · ITV (LWT) · STANDUP/SKETCH

1 × 45 mins · colour
16 Feb 1974 · Sat 5.15pm

MAIN CAST
Freddie Starr

CREDITS
writer Eric Merriman · *producer* David Bell

Freddie's first own show, recorded in between series of *Who Do You Do?*

The Freddie Starr Show   1

UK · BBC · STANDUP

2 × 45 mins · colour
18 Feb 1976 · BBC2 Wed 9pm
31 Dec 1976 · BBC1 Fri 7.55pm

MAIN CAST
Freddie Starr

CREDITS
writers Freddie Starr (shows 1 & 2), Bryan Blackburn (show 1) · *producer* Terry Hughes

Freddie crossed to the BBC for these two 1976 specials that concentrated on his impressionism skills.

The Freddie Starr Experience

UK · ITV (LWT) · STANDUP/SKETCH

1 × 60 mins · colour
10 Sep 1978 · Sun 8.15pm

MAIN CAST
Freddie Starr

CREDITS
directors Maurice Murphy, David Macmahon

An hour of comedy, song and dance.

Freddie Starr's Variety Madhouse

UK · ITV (LWT) · STANDUP/SKETCH

6 × 45 mins · colour
27 Oct–1 Dec 1979 · Sat 8.15pm

MAIN CAST
Freddie Starr
Russ Abbot

OTHER APPEARANCES
Mike Newman
Toni Palmer
Norman Collier
Bella Emberg

CREDITS
executive producer David Bell · *producer* Ken O'Neill

A very popular weekly series that continued as *Russ Abbot's Madhouse* after Freddie Starr left.

Freddie Starr On The Road

UK · ITV (THAMES) · STANDUP

1 × 80 mins · colour
28 Dec 1981 · Mon 10.15pm

MAIN CAST
Freddie Starr

CREDITS
director/producer Frank Cvitanovich

A specially extended film of Starr on tour, mostly celebratory, part documentary.

From 5 July to 23 August 1983, BBC1 screened *The Freddie Starr Showcase*, eight programmes in which the comedian hosted a talent contest, introducing new variety acts from the stage of the Harrogate Centre, Yorkshire.

Freddie Starr At The Royalty

UK · ITV (THAMES) · STANDUP/SKETCH

1 × 45 mins · colour
31 Dec 1984 · Mon 8pm

MAIN CAST
Freddie Starr

CREDITS
director/producer Keith Beckett

A New Year's Eve special, from Thames TV's own London theatre, the Royalty.

The Freddie Starr Comedy Express

UK · ITV (THAMES) · STANDUP/SKETCH

1 × 60 mins · colour
31 Dec 1985 · Tue 8pm

MAIN CAST
Freddie Starr
Tim Barrett
Vee Brooks
Frank Coda
Anna Dawson
Glynn Edwards
Burt Kwouk
Susan Tagg
Jane West

CREDITS
writers Sid Green, Eric Merriman, Keith Leonard, Len Marten, Freddie Starr · *director/producer* Keith Beckett

Another New Year's Eve special, stuffed with supporting cast members (named

above) and guest stars including Frank Bruno. One highlight was Starr's wonderful spoof of the video made by David Bowie and Mick Jagger for 'Dancing In The Street'.

Freddie Starr

UK · ITV (CENTRAL) · STANDUP/SKETCH

7 editions (2 × 60 mins · 5 × 30 mins) · colour
Special (60 mins) 31 May 1993 · Mon 8pm
Special (60 mins) 22 Sep 1993 · Wed 8pm
One series (5 × 30 mins) 9 May 1984; 8–29 July 1994 · Mon 8pm then Fri 8.30pm

MAIN CAST
Freddie Starr

CREDITS
director/producer Dennis Kirkland

Another 'comeback' for the enigmatic but revelatory Starr. The specials – leading to the series – guest-starred Frank Bruno, Adam Faith, Karl Howman, Les Dennis, Stanley Unwin, Paul Shane and Gerry Marsden, with Derek Deadman and Bob Todd (in one of his last TV appearances before his death) taking part in the Freddie Starr Olympics.

An Audience With Freddie Starr

UK · ITV (LWT) · STANDUP

1 × 60 mins · colour
2 Mar 1996 · Sat 9.05pm

MAIN CAST
Freddie Starr

CREDITS
director David G Hillier · *producer* Mark Linsey

An hour in the company of Starr as he delighted a studio audience full of celebrities and friends. The show was so successful that a second edition was taped in 1997.

The Freddie Starr Show   2

UK · ITV (CARLTON FOR CENTRAL) · STANDUP/SKETCH

7 editions (6 × 30 mins · 1 × 60 mins) · colour
One series (6) 18 July–5 Sep 1996 · Thu 8.30pm
Special (60 mins) 29 Dec 1997 · Mon 8pm

MAIN CAST
Freddie Starr
Derek Deadman

CREDITS
writers Freddie Starr, Sonny Hayes, Wayne Dobson, Richard Lewis, Louis Robinson, Jimmy Marshall, Keith Simmons, Peter Wear and others · *director* David G Hillier · *executive producer* Richard Holloway · *producers* David G Hillier (series), Paula Burdon (special)

A six-part series with new characters, including a Greek waiter, Alexis, and the stuntman Dangerous Dan Magrew. Every edition featured a visiting guest star.

The 1997 Christmas special included a new impression of Hitler, being interviewed by ITV sports presenter Gary Newbon.

In between the series and the special ,Starr played a straight-acting role in the ITV police drama *Supply And Demand*, screened on 5 February 1997.

Another Audience With Freddie Starr

UK · ITV (LWT) · STANDUP

1×60 mins · colour

11 Oct 1997 · Sat 9pm

MAIN CAST

Freddie Starr

CREDITS

director/producer Ian Hamilton · *executive producer* Nigel Lythgoe

A further hour with Starr at his energetic best, entertaining an audience of celebrities.

Starting From Scratch

USA · SYNDICATION (TAFT ENTERTAINMENT/ FLYING UNICORN PRODUCTIONS/MOLSTAR COMMUNICATIONS) · SITCOM

22×30 mins · colour

US dates: October 1988–April 1989

UK dates: 2 May 1992–27 Aug 1994 (22 episodes) ITV Sat around 1pm

MAIN CAST

Dr James Shepherd · · · · · · · · · · · · Bill Daily
Helen Shepherd DeAngelo · · Connie Stevens
Kate Shepherd · · · · · · · · · · · · Heidi Helmer
Robbie Shepherd · · · · · · · · · · · Jason Marin
Rose · · · · · · · · · · · · · · · · · · · Nita Talbot
Frank DeAngelo · · · · · · · · · · Carmine Caridi

CREDITS

creator/writer Brian Cooke · *director* Stan Harris · *executive producers* Perry Rosemond, Victor Solnicki · *producer* Perry Rosemond

Screened in the UK by some ITV companies, including LWT, *Starting From Scratch* is the original US version of the sitcom adapted by LWT for ITV as **Close To Home**, which starred Paul Nicholas as James Shepherd, a divorced vet with a frequently visiting but divorced ex-wife Helen, a smart daughter, an even smarter son, and a witty veterinary assistant who doesn't like animals.

Written by an Englishman in Hollywood, Brian Cooke, *Starting From Scratch* reeked of out-of-place Englishness – mother-in-law jokes, titty jokes, etc – and starred Bill Daily (best known as Captain Roger Healey in **I Dream Of Jeannie**) as the much-put-upon vet working from a home practice. It was awful.

State Of The Union

see DAWSON, Les

The Status Symbol

UK · BBC · SITCOM

1×35 mins · b/w

26 Jan 1962 · Fri 8.40pm

MAIN CAST

Wilfred Swann · · · · · · · · · · · · Alfred Marks
Cyril Bradley · · · · · · · · · · · · · Graham Stark

CREDITS

writers Ray Galton/Alan Simpson · *producer* Graeme Muir

Comic dependables Alfred Marks and Graham Stark starred in this one-off Galton and Simpson sitcom for *Comedy Playhouse*. The status symbol in question was an old Rolls-Royce owned by Wilfred Swann. He wants to get it back on the road but Cyril Bradley's garage is short of customers and he likes the look of it out front …

The Steam Video Company

UK · ITV (THAMES) · FARCES

6×30 mins · colour

19 Jan–23 Feb 1984 · Thu 8pm then 9pm

MAIN CAST

William Franklyn
Barry Cryer
Anna Dawson
Bob Todd
Madeline Smith
Jimmy Mulville

CREDITS

writers Andrew Marshall/David Renwick · *director/producer* David G Hillier · *executive producer* Mark Stuart

An odd series of six individual comedy tales of the macabre – like a cheap, horror version of **Ripping Yarns** – all starring the same repertory cast of established (or new, in the case of Jimmy Mulville) comic actors in a variety of broad roles. Bizarre juxtapositions of plots and characters, old and new, abounded, intermingled with football references. The six editions were 'The Strange Case Of Dr Jekyll', 'Creature From The Black Forest Gateau', 'I Was Hitler's Bookie', 'The Secret Of Plankton Lodge', 'Amityville II – Luton Town 3' and 'The Fall Of The House Of Franklyn'.

Stella Street

UK · BBC (STELLA STREET PRODUCTIONS/TIGER ASPECT) · SITCOM/IMPRESSIONISM

10×10 mins · colour

22 Dec 1997–2 Jan 1998 · BBC2 various days around 11pm

MAIN CAST

Michael Caine/Jack Nicholson/ · · · · · · · · · ·
David Bowie/Mick Jagger/ · · · · · · · · · · · · ·
Jimmy Hill · · · · · · · · · · · · · · · Phil Cornwell
Dirk Bogarde/Keith Richards/ · · · · · · · · · · ·
Joe Pesci/Roger Moore/ · · · · · · · · · · · · · · ·
Mrs Huggett · · · · · · · · · · · · · John Sessions

CREDITS

writers John Sessions, Phil Cornwell, Peter Richardson · *director* Peter Richardson · *executive producer* Charles Brand · *producer* Ben Swaffer

Imagine a run-of-the-mill side-street in Surbiton, Surrey, where Hollywood super-stars Michael Caine, Jack Nicholson and others live cheek by jowl with Jimmy Hill, Mick Jagger, David Bowie and 'ordinary' folk, and you have the premise of *Stella Street* – an odd idea, not entirely successful but with a certain charm, taped inexpensively with hand-held cameras and screened by BBC2 during Christmas 1997.

Promoted as a 'suburban soap', the series constituted ten short sketches in which talented comic actors/impressionists Cornwell and Sessions created an at times brilliant interplay between the celebrity characterisations. Although the superstars were living in reduced circumstances in suburbia they behaved exactly as if they were still in Beverly Hills, Monte Carlo or any other glamorous locale. Ex-Rolling Stones Jagger and Richards, for example, now gathered moss running the neighbourhood store 'Mick And Keith's Corner Shop', selling everything from mops to magazines, but they continued to look and act in their customary profession-ally arrogant, pouting, manner – Richards systematically drinking his way through the shop's entire alcoholic stock. The only non-celebrity in Stella Street to appear before the cameras is 76-year-old Mrs Huggett, who has lived there all of her life and whose job as house cleaner to the stars means she is privy to their many secrets – and also their verbal and physical abuse.

Step By Step

USA · ABC THEN CBS (BICKLEY-WARREN PRODUCTIONS/MILLER-BOYETT PRODUCTIONS/ LORIMAR TELEVISION/WARNER BROS) · SITCOM

151×30 mins (to 31/12/97 · continuing into 1998) · colour

US dates: 20 Sep 1991 to date (ABC to 15 Aug 1997 · CBS from 19 Sep 1997)

UK dates: 28 Mar 1994–13 Apr 1995 (46 episodes) ITV weekdays 10am

MAIN CAST

Frank Lambert · · · · · · · · · · · · · · Patrick Duffy
Carol Foster/Lambert · · · · · Suzanne Somers
Dana Foster · · · · · · · · · · · · · · Staci Keanan
Cody Lambert · · · Sasha Mitchell (1991–96)
John Thomas 'J T' Lambert · · · Brandon Call
Karen Foster · · · · · · · · · · · · Angela Watson
Alicia 'Al' Lambert · · · · · · · · Christine Lakin
Mark Foster · · · · · · · · · Christopher Castile
Brendan Lambert · · · · Josh Byrne (1991–97)
Penny Baker · · · · · Patrika Darbo (1991–93)
Ivy Baker · · · · · · · · · · Penny Rea (1991–93)
Jean-Luc Rieupeyroux · · · · · Bronson Pinchot
· (1997)
Rich Halke · · · · · Jason Marsden (from 1996)
Samantha Milano · · · · · · · · · Alexandra Adi
· (from 1997)

Lilly Foster-Lambert · · · · · · Emily Mae Young
· (from 1997)

CREDITS
creators William Bickley/Michael Warren · *writers* various · *directors* various · *executive producers* William Bickley/Michael Warren, Thomas L Miller/ Robert L Boyett, Alan Eisenstock/Larry Mintz · *producers* John B Collins, Ronny Hallin

Easy and entirely predictable US family sitcom fluff starring Patrick Duffy (Bobby Ewing in *Dallas*) and Suzanne Somers (Chrissy Snow in *Three's Company*).

Frank Lambert (Duffy) is divorced and has three children in his care, Carol Foster (Somers) is a widow with three children in hers, and the pair wed during a holiday in Jamaica. Returning home to Port Washington, Wisconsin, they break the news to their sprogs and unite the families, creating situations 'ripe' for humorous exploitation. The 'three plus three makes comedy' scenario was also the plot of *The Brady Bunch* (1969–1974) but the difference in *Step By Step* was that, here, the two sets of children don't care much for one another – the Lambert kids are rugged and sporty, the Foster kids cerebral (well, kind of) and body-beautiful. Like so many sitcoms of its kind, all the leading characters in *Step By Step* are great-lookers with splendid physiques – cast, obviously, from the Hollywood School Of Truly Beautiful Human Beings.

For the record, Frank is a chaotic individual who owns a construction company; his kids are cool teenager J T (14, athletic but shambolic), Al (12, tomboyish) and Brendan (about 6, smart-ass). Carol is a beautician with an adjoining salon (staffed also by her mother and sister); her kids are, like Carol herself, organised and methodical – Dana (15, impeccable), Karen (14, beautiful) and Mark (about 9, sensitive). Completing the picture is Cody, Frank's utterly stupid young adult nephew, and, right at the very end, a seventh child: Carol and Frank's own baby.

Step Laughing Into The Grave

UK · BBC · STANDUP
1 × 35 mins · colour
30 Mar 1970 · BBC2 Mon 10.25pm
MAIN CAST
John Fortune
John Wells
John Laurie

CREDITS
writers John Fortune/John Wells · *director* Anthony Wheeler · *executive producer* Anthony de Lotbiniere

A one-off special – screened on Easter Monday 1970 – that took the form of a satire on the self-glorifying television autobiography. John Fortune and John Wells wrote and starred, aided by John Laurie and

---

other guests, enthusing over the exhilarating omnipresence of death.

Stephanie Hodge: Straight Up

USA · SHOWTIME (PUCKER PRODUCTIONS/ EASTING DOWN PRODUCTIONS) · STANDUP
1 × 45 mins · colour
US date: 16 Mar 1991
UK date: 6 Feb 1995 · C4 Mon 10.55pm
MAIN CAST
Stephanie Hodge

CREDITS
writer Stephanie Hodge · *director* David Bergman · *executive producers* Stephanie Hodge, Paul Block · *producer* Paul Block

A film of US comedian Stephanie Hodge (Sandy Miller in *Nurses*) in standup mode at the Great American Music Hall in San Francisco in 1991.

Tackling anti-smoking hypocrisy, the body's ageing process, gynaecological indignities, male inadequacies and the joys of good, uncomplicated sex, Hodge strutted across the stage, permanently grinning and barking out lines in a gravel-voice. Strong language peppered the routines but it was used to good effect, and she ended the show with a spectacularly graphic depiction of a wild sexual encounter, a grand climax, if you will.

Steptoe And Son

UK · BBC · SITCOM
59 episodes (55 × 30 mins · 1 × 45 mins · 1 × 40 mins · 2 × short specials) · 29 × b/w · 30 × colour
Pilot (b/w) *The Offer* 5 Jan 1962 · Fri 8.45pm
Series One (5 × b/w) 14 June–12 July 1962 · Thu 8.45pm
Short special (b/w) · part of *Christmas Night With The Stars* 25 Dec 1962 · Tue 7.15pm
Series Two (7 × b/w) 3 Jan–14 Feb 1963 · Thu 7.55pm
Series Three (7 × b/w) 7 Jan–18 Feb 1964 · Tue 8pm
Series Four (7 × b/w) 4 Oct–15 Nov 1965 · BBC1 Mon 7.30pm
Short special (b/w) · part of *Christmas Night With The Stars* 25 Dec 1967 · BBC1 Mon 6.40pm
Series Five (7 × colour) 6 Mar–17 Apr 1970 · BBC1 Fri 7.55pm
Series Six (8 × colour) 2 Nov–21 Dec 1970 · BBC1 Mon 9.20pm
Series Seven (7 × colour) 21 Feb–3 Apr 1972 · BBC1 Mon 9.25pm
Special (45 mins · colour) 24 Dec 1973 · BBC1 Mon 9.30pm
Series Eight (6 × colour) 4 Sep–10 Oct 1974 · BBC1 Wed 9.30pm then Thu 9.35pm
Special (40 mins · colour) 26 Dec 1974 · BBC1 Thu 9.05pm
MAIN CAST
Albert Steptoe · · · · · · · · · Wilfrid Brambell
Harold Steptoe · · · · · · · · · · Harry H Corbett

CREDITS
writers Ray Galton/Alan Simpson · *producers* Duncan Wood (to series 6), John Howard Davies (series 7), Graeme Muir (1973 special), Douglas Argent (series 8 and 1974 special)

A true television classic, charting the love-hate relationship of a widower father and unmarried son who run a decrepit rag-and-bone business in London.

Steptoe And Son was never conceived as a series but was delivered to the BBC as one of a *Comedy Playhouse* season of ten unrelated pieces, a series offered to writers Ray Galton and Alan Simpson after Tony Hancock, whom they had served so marvellously, relinquished their services. The writers relished the opportunity and freedom to explore a world of comedy ideas and were naturally hesitant when the BBC's Light Entertainment chief – noting the hugely positive response to the first of the playlets, *The Offer* – asked them to turn it into a series. They agreed, secretly assuming that the two lead actors would refuse because of other commitments, but both Harry H Corbett and Wilfrid Brambell accepted and a classic was born.

Steptoe And Son was groundbreaking in many ways: it featured established stage/film actors playing humorous characters, not comedians creating extensions of their stage personas which, until this time, was the norm; it dealt with an underclass previously seen on television only in realistic dramas like *Armchair Theatre*; and its underlying theme of the son trying desperately to escape the clutches of his wily father imbued the series with a pathos and poignancy hitherto absent from the sitcom genre. For all these aspects, it was recognised then, and still holds its place now, as a landmark achievement, one of the most important – and, let us not forget, funny – situation comedies of all time.

Originally, the two protagonists had been conceived by the writers as merely partners in a rag-and-bone concern, but when they hit upon the idea of making them father and son, the concept fired the imagination. They decided to keep Harold's age hovering around 40, since they felt that, at this age, there was still a possibility, albeit a slight one, that he might somehow escape. As it was, viewers instantly recognised Harold's dilemma – home was a prison, work was a prison, and not only was escape difficult but to where would he run? Perennially short of money, life was hard, and much as Harold aspired to a greater degree of sophistication (not difficult, considering Albert's truly disgusting personal habits) and a long-term female relationship, he knew that his cunning father would always maintain his grip. As for Albert, he felt that he had done his bit, so was entitled to laze around their ramshackle west London home (Mews Cottage, Oil Drum Lane,

Shepherd's Bush) and expect his son – and horse, Hercules – to cart home the spoils that 'totting' can bring. He also felt entitled to unswerving support from his kith and kin, to look after and provide for him in his dotage.

The series quickly struck a chord with the nation, and the weekly battles between the father and son fast attracted enormous audiences, sometimes in excess of twenty million. (Accurate figures are difficult to assess because ratings at this time were measured in households rather than individual viewers.) Taken to great heights by some truly brilliant Galton and Simpson scripts, and the fine acting of Brambell and Corbett, *Steptoe And Son* was a revelation and loved by virtually everyone – if you enjoyed great, readily funny lines then there were plenty to go around; if you liked your comedy more cerebral, with dark edges, then every episode rewarded. While it would be foolhardy to suggest that anything like *Steptoe And Son*-mania occurred, the series was undoubtedly greatly loved, revered and one of the foremost talking points in Britain in 1962 and 1963. The series garnered the royal seal of approval too, with an appearance of the characters in a specially written segment for the 1963 *Royal Variety Show* (televised by ITV on 10 November). Indeed, *Steptoe And Son* caused such a stir that even American programmers began to take note, and film producer Joseph Levine, in his role as president of Embassy Pictures, acquired the rights to a US adaptation. (His 1965 pilot version for NBC, with the same title, starred heavyweight actor Aldo Rey and Lee Tracy, but although it retained the grittiness of the British original it missed much of the subtlety and was never screened.)

At the end of the fourth series, in 1965, with repeats ensuring it had rarely been off screen since 1962, the *Steptoe And Son* team decided to quit while they were ahead and announced the programme's finish. (They reconvened on TV just twice more in the 1960s, first for a specially written sketch in *The Ken Dodd Show* – BBC1, 24 July 1966 – and then for a short 1967 Christmas special.) But the public didn't forget *Steptoe And Son* and more TV repeats and a BBC radio version (eventually running for 52 episodes: 21 airing between 3 July 1966 and 30 July 1967, and 31 from 21 March 1971 to 25 December 1976) kept it in the nation's collective consciousness to the extent that the programme-makers were always being questioned on the likelihood of its return.

Eventually, in 1970, the show reappeared – now in colour – for a further four series, again blessed with some sublime scripts. Commercially, it enjoyed even greater triumphs second time around, inspiring two feature film spin-offs, *Steptoe And Son* (1972) and *Steptoe And Son Ride Again* (1974), and,

eventually (following a second failed pilot), a successful US version, *Sanford And Son* (1972–77). This was produced by Norman Lear who had scored heavily with **All In The Family**, a US adaptation of **Till Death Us Do Part**. Lear made the junk dealers black, figuring that an oppressed under-class would be more likely running such a downmarket business, and to allow exploration of many of the same racially controversial topics that had made *All In The Family* such a hit. Starring Redd Foxx as Fred Sanford and Demond Wilson as his son Lamont, *Sanford And Son* was an instant ratings smash and remained a popular favourite in the USA for much of its five-year run. (It has never shown on British TV.) Spin-offs included *Grady* (1975–76), *The Sanford Arms* (1977) and *Sanford* (1980–81).

Back in Britain, after the 1974 Christmas special, *Steptoe And Son* finished for the last time, after 12 triumphant years. Brambell and Corbett played the characters just once more after this: in a 1977 Australian touring cabaret show, again scripted for them by Galton and Simpson.

The Steve Allen Show

USA · NBC · SKETCH/STANDUP

approx 156 × 60 mins · b/w

US dates: 24 June 1956–6 June 1960

*UK dates: 5 Oct–7 Dec 1958 (4 editions) BBC irregular Sun 8pm

MAIN CAST
Steve Allen

OTHER APPEARANCES
Dayton Allen
Bill Dana
Gabe Dell
Pat Harrington Jr
Cal Howard
Marilyn Jacobs
Louis Nye
Tom Poston
Don Knotts

CREDITS
writers Leonard Stern, Stan Burns, Herb Sargent, Bill Dana, Marvin Worth, Arne Sultan, Don Hinkley and others · *directors* various · *producer* William O Harbach

The remarkable Steve Allen (born in New York City on 26 December 1921) was one of the dominant figures on American TV in the 1950s and 1960s. He was the originator of NBC's long-running (still-running) late-night entertainment/talk-show *Tonight* in 1954, predating Johnny Carson's involvement by nine years, and had numerous versions of *The Steve Allen Show* on all three major networks between 1950 and 1967 (and in syndication from 1967 to 1969). While he was hosting *Tonight* NBC asked Allen to front a Sunday night show too, a live hour-long programme

to run against CBS's variety flagship *The Ed Sullivan Show*.

Allen was hugely versatile: a comedian, a famous songwriter, a multi-instrumentalist and the author of a number of books on the world of entertainment. He pulled out all the stops in his battle with Sullivan – his shows emphasised cerebral humour and were sometimes satirical, and he managed to secure big-name guest stars including Sammy Davis Jr and young rock and roll singer Elvis Presley. His persistence gathered some reward as *The Ed Sullivan Show* faltered in the ratings, losing the coveted number one slot, although it rallied to survive into the 1970s.

*Note. The BBC aired four editions (re-edited by Philip Barker) of the NBC version of *The Steve Allen Show* in 1958. Thirty-four years later, from 2 September 1992 to 3 June 1993, C4 screened 28 half-hour versions of the series edited from the original kinescopes in Allen's personal collection and fronted by Allen in the early 1990s. One hundred such half-hours were screened in the USA on MTV's Ha! The TV Comedy Network channel from 1 October 1990.

Steve Geray And Magda Kun

UK · BBC · STANDUP

4 editions (2 × 10 mins · 2 × 15 mins) · b/w

23 Mar 1937 · Tue 3.50pm (10 mins)
16 Apr 1937 · Fri 9.45pm (15 mins)
18 May 1937 · Tue 3pm (10 mins)
7 Dec 1937 · Tue 9.15pm (15 mins)

MAIN CAST
Steve Geray
Magda Kun

CREDITS
writers Steve Geray and others · *producers* Dallas Bower (shows 1 & 3), Harry Pringle (show 2), J Royston Morley (show 4)

Four programme for the Hungarian husband-and-wife cabaret stars who appeared in films both separately and together. Here they presented selections of period-costume comedy, sketches and humorous songs, as part of the *Starlight* series.

The Steven Wright Special

USA · HBO · STANDUP

1 × 60 mins · colour

US date: 7 Sep 1985
UK date: 27 Aug 1989 · BBC2 Sun 9.10pm

MAIN CAST
Steven Wright

CREDITS
writer Steven Wright · *director* Walter C Miller · *producer* Peter Lassally

A starring standup show for the brilliant American comic surrealist.

Steven Wright's act almost entirely comprises weird one-line ideas that bring into focus his zany and twisted view of the world. It is a style that is impossible to describe accurately so here are three examples: 'I took out the headlights from my car and put in strobe lights. Now when I'm driving I look like the only one that's moving.' And 'I'm not scared of heights, I'm scared of widths.' And 'A friend of mine had wooden legs, but his feet were real.' Some people just think differently from the rest of us.

See also **The Appointments Of Dennis Jennings**.

Stiff Upper Lip

UK · BBC · SITCOM

1 × 30 mins · b/w

17 May 1968 · BBC1 Fri 8.20pm

MAIN CAST
Sir Reginald Polk-Mowbray
(The Ambassador) · · · · · · · · Richard Vernon
Antrobus (First Secretary) · · · · Michael Bates
Percy (Embassy footman) · · · · · · · · · · · · · ·
· Bernard Bresslaw
Commander Benbow · · · · · · · · · · · · · · · · ·
(Naval Attaché) · · · · · · · · · · · George Baker
Drage (Embassy butler) · · · · John Glyn-Jones
Captain Gore-Strangely · · · · · · · · · · · · · · ·
(Military Attaché) · · · · · · · · · Derek Aylward

CREDITS
creator Lawrence Durrell · adapter/writer Barry Took · producer Michael Mills

The novelist Lawrence Durrell might seem an unlikely source for sitcom material but here he was nonetheless as the author of the short story upon which Barry Took adapted this one-off *Comedy Playhouse* pilot. It was a Cold War comedy, focusing on the bluff and counterbluff strategies of the diplomats in the British Embassy based in the Iron Curtain state of Vulgaria (the exterior scenes were filmed at Althorp, by permission of Earl Spencer). *Stiff Upper Lip* was the title given to Durrell's second collection of short stories about diplomatic incidents, published in 1958; he worked in a number of British embassies from 1939–52.

Note. Michael Mills was certainly familiar with *Stiff Upper Lip* when he came to produce this BBC *Comedy Playhouse*, for he had directed another one-off pilot adaptation of the same piece only the year before on ITV, screened by ABC in the Midlands and the North (but not in London) within the season *The Sound Of Laughter*. The adapter/writer on this occasion was Giles Cooper, with Robert Banks Stewart producing. Robert Coote starred as Sir Claud Polk-Mowbray, Donald Churchill played Dovebasket, James Villiers was Antrobus, David Phethean played Commander Benbow, Edward Caddick was Drage, and there were roles for

David Kernan, Penny Morrell, Michael Trubshawe and others.

Stomping On The Cat

see **The Entertainers**

The Stone Age

UK · BBC (JON BLAIR FILM COMPANY) · SITCOM

1 × 30 mins · colour

2 June 1989 · BBC2 Fri 9pm

MAIN CAST
Dave Stone · · · · · · · · · · · · · · · · Trevor Eve
Clive Anderson · · · · · · · · · · · · · · · · himself
Lizzie Stone · · · · · · · · · · · Carmen du Sautoy
Robert Irving · · · · · · · · · · · · · Jonathan Coy
Herb · · · · · · · · · · · · · · · Roger Lloyd Pack
Pete · Bob Goody

CREDITS
writers Ian Hislop/Nick Newman · director Mandie Fletcher · executive producers John Kilby/Jamie Rix · producer Jon Blair

A *Comic Asides* pilot about a rock superstar worth millions of pounds but who, nonetheless, is profoundly bored with life. Despite the prowess of the writers, Trevor Eve in the lead role and the presence of a strong supporting cast, it was not developed into a series.

Stop That Laughing At The Back

UK · ITV (GRANADA) · CHILDREN'S SKETCH

5 × 30 mins · colour

30 Sep–28 Oct 1987 · Wed 4.45pm

MAIN CAST
Paul Bradley
Nimmy March
Michael Fenton Stevens
Jo Unwin
Hue and Cry

CREDITS
writers various · director Tim Sullivan · executive producer David Liddiment · producer James Maw

A sketch series, aimed fairly and squarely at children, in which the adults never won. Regular skits included the worst parents in history and an advice column, 'Aw, I'm Not Doing That', which showed children how best to escape from parent-given chores.

See also **Bradley**.

The Strange World Of Gurney Slade

UK · ITV (ATV) · SITCOM

6 × 30 mins · b/w

22 Oct–26 Nov 1960 · Sat 8.35pm then 11.10pm

MAIN CAST
Gurney Slade · · · · · · · · · · · Anthony Newley

OTHER APPEARANCES
Bernie Winters

CREDITS
writers Sid Green/Dick Hills · producer Alan Tarrant

A bizarre programme – not such much a sitcom, more a way of life – built around the former East End of London child prodigy Anthony Newley, by this time decidedly an adult star too.

It is difficult to summarise *The Strange World Of Gurney Slade* in a few lines, except to say that it presented a surreal, almost druggy view of life as experienced through the senses of the talented but aloof star. He tripped in and out of reality, *Alice*-like, talked to himself, had two-way conversations with inanimate objects and animals, experienced peculiar relationships with people who stepped out of advertising posters, imagined (and heard) what people were thinking to themselves as they walked along, and conducted conversations with people who couldn't see him because (perhaps) he wasn't really there.

As well as being difficult to summarise, *The Strange World Of Gurney Slade* was scarcely a sitcom as it is usually defined. While it was then – and remains – a fascinating curio piece, it didn't raise many titters, only an appreciation of the fact that this was *weird*, groundbreaking television, years ahead of its time. Even now, though, approaching 40 years on, the episodes seem strange to the point of disturbing. Certainly, back in 1960, viewers were unprepared for their senses to be so assaulted in the name of entertainment, and after four of the six programmes the series was relegated from a peak-time slot to a late-night one.

Sid Green and Dick Hills, whose excellent scripts usually fell into the hands of conventional comics like Dave King and Morecambe and Wise, wrote *The Strange World Of Gurney Slade* so the 'credit' for the series cannot rest entirely with Newley. However, one is tempted to observe that it fits neatly alongside other such avant-garde concepts in which he has been involved, not least his 1969 feature film *Can Heironymus Merkin Ever Forget Mercy Humppe And Find True Happiness?*, a movie best watched under substance influence or when asleep; Newley also named the character Gurney Slade after the Somerset village of the same name, and booked the up-and-coming standup comic Bernie Winters as the only other regular performer in the series – he and Winters had been friends since their teenage years.

To speculate whether *The Strange World Of Gurney Slade* was good or bad, funny or unfunny, is probably missing the point, though, and (more so than any other programme, perhaps) rests entirely in the eyes of the beholder. The series really wasn't made for laughs and the soundtrack does not include audience laughter. It is not impossible to argue, however, that the whole affair may have been one big laugh *on* the audience.

Note. Twenty years on, in 1980, Sid Green wrote a similar series, *Fancy Wanders*, starring Dave King.

Strangers In The Night

see HUMPHRIES, Barry

Streets Apart

UK · BBC · SITCOM

12 × 30 mins · colour

Series One (6) 24 Oct–28 Nov 1988 · BBC1
Mon 8.30pm

Series Two (6) 4 Sep–9 Oct 1989 · BBC1
Mon 8.30pm

MAIN CAST

Sylvia	Amanda Redman
Bernie	James Hazeldine
Jenny	June Barry
Cliff	Desmond McNamara
Tiffany	Julie Saunders
Mandy	Anna Murphy
Paul	Neil Kagan
James	Michael Elwyn (series 1)
Rene	Diane Langton (series 2)

OTHER APPEARANCES

Gran	Edna Doré
Lyn	Lesley Duff
Donna	Annie Bruce (series 2)

CREDITS

writer Adrienne Conway · *director/producer* Sue Bysh

Actress Adrienne Conway wrote this series with a view to appearing in it herself, but by the time she finished the scripts she imagined other people in the roles and couldn't see herself in any of them. A bittersweet love story, it followed the romance of Sylvia and James who had been teenage sweethearts in the East End of London and who now become reacquainted 20 years later. In the interim their lives have taken divergent courses: James is a widower with two children (Paul and Mandy) and drives a London taxi cab for a living; Sylvia is a dedicated career woman (a successful literary agent) with no aspirations to motherhood. But when they meet anew the old spark is still apparent and they embark on a rocky romance made difficult by the fact that they now seem 'streets apart'.

A fine series of gentle humour, the arrival of Rene in the second series, as a competitor for Bernie's affections, added a dash of piquancy to the mix.

Strictly T-T

UK · BBC · SKETCH

6 × 30 mins · b/w

12 Jan–22 Mar 1956 · fortnightly Thu 8pm

MAIN CAST

Terry-Thomas
Kenneth Griffiths
Lorrae Desmond

CREDITS

writers Terry-Thomas, Eric Merriman, Alan Hackney · *producer* Duncan Wood

Following on from Terry-Thomas's highly successful and long-running *How Do You View?*, BBC viewers were invited on fortnightly visits to 'Holdergap-on-Tees', to see the famous comic actor, with a supporting cast, star in these six half-hour shows of 'fun and games'.

One of the writers, Alan Hackney, was the comic novelist who authored the books upon which were based the British comedy films *Private's Progress* (1955) and *I'm Alright Jack* (1959) – both featuring Terry-Thomas.

The series' title was a humorous reference to a phrase in common parlance at the time – 'strictly teetotal' (that is, a non-drinker), which was often abbreviated to 'strictly T-T'.

The Strip Show

UK · C4 (SPITTING IMAGE PRODUCTIONS) · SKETCH

1 × 35 mins · colour

29 Dec 1995 · Fri 10.30pm

MAIN CAST (VOICES)

Ronnie Ancona
Alistair McGowan
Rebecca Front
Enn Reitel

CREDITS

writer/cartoonists Hunt Emerson, Sky Robert-Thompson and others · *producer* Giles Pilbrow

A one-off sketch show that employed different kinds of animation – puppetry, claymation and traditional comic-strip – to create a potpourri of social satire and soap spoofs. The programme was made by Spitting Image Productions, continuing the company's move away from traditional political satires begun some months earlier with *Crapston Villas* (see *Spitting Image*), also screened by C4.

Struck By Lightning

USA · CBS (FELLOWS-KEEGAN COMPANY/ PARAMOUNT) · SITCOM

6 × 30 mins · colour

US dates: 19 Sep–3 Oct 1979 (3 episodes)

UK dates: 9 Apr–14 May 1980 (6 episodes) ITV Wed 5.15pm

MAIN CAST

Frank	Jack Elam
Ted Stein	Jeffrey Kramer
Nora Clavin	Millie Slavin
Brian Clavin	Jeff Cotler
Walt Clavin	Richard Stahl
Glenn	Bill Erwin

CREDITS

writers John Boni, Fred Freeman/Lawrence J Cohen, Bruce Kalish, Bryan K Joseph, Michael A Russnow, Phillip Taylor · *director* Joel Zwick · *executive producers* Arthur Fellows, Terry Keegan · *producers* John Thomas Lenox, Bob Ellison, Steve Pritzker, Marvin Miller

Ted Stein, a young science teacher from Boston, inherits the decrepit Bridgewater Inn, in Massachusetts, and plans to sell it. But then he meets its incredibly ugly caretaker, Frank, who reveals himself to be 231 years old and the creation of Doctor Frankenstein. Frank also declares that said famed doctor is Ted Stein's great-great-great-grandfather. Frank persuades Ted to keep the inn and to set about rediscovering his ancestor's scientific formula, in order that he be given his latest shot and remain alive for another 50 years. Others figuring in the storylines include Nora, the inn's manager; her husband Walt, the local real-estate man; their son Brian; and long-term resident Glenn.

Although the episodes packed some pretty silly ideas – in one, Ted permits a film company to shoot a horror movie at the inn, upsetting Frank – *Struck By Lightning* was not quite as bad as it sounds, some critics admiring its exploration of zany comedic ideas. American audiences thought likewise, however, fleeing from the series as one would a real monster: three episodes were screened in the States before it was cancelled owing to poor ratings. Six had been made by this time, though, and all of them turned up on London-ITV.

Struggle

UK · C4 (LWT) · SITCOM

6 × 35 mins · colour

27 Nov 1983–1 Jan 1984 · Sun mostly 8.45pm

MAIN CAST

Steve Marsh	Tim Pigott-Smith
Sir Bert	Ray Smith
Reg	Paul Rogers
Robin	Peter Machin
Hil	Mary Maddox
Charlie	Trevor Laird
Alan	Terence Budd
Caroline	Clare Clifford
Mayor	Malcolm Russell
Stanley	Ken Jones
Mrs Buggins	Jeanne Doree

CREDITS

writer Peter Jenkins · *script editor* Bernard McKenna · *director/producer* Graham Evans

A not only funny but also thought-provoking sitcom written by the then political columnist of *The Guardian*, Peter Jenkins. The episodes depicted the machinations of two principal protagonists in a borough council: Steve Marsh, the arch-left-wing leader, and his fiercest rival in the chambers, known as Sir Bert. Marsh's attempts to introduce widespread socialism are repeatedly bogged down in Sir Bert's Conservative opposition.

Marsh, the red running the London borough of Southam, is a man who cut his political teeth in the revolutionary cauldron of 1968, when he was still a student at South London Polytechnic. Marsh lives in a council flat and injects tireless devotion into his work to the exclusion of any private life. Such is his belief in equality that he refuses to travel in the chauffeur-driven car to which he is entitled and worries over whether to take his place in the esteemed-people's bunker should the big bomb be dropped. Steve keeps mum about his personal background, however, because it could cause him embarrassment: he is of firmly middle-class stock.

True blue Sir Bert hails from the generation before Steve Marsh – which means that he grew up among post-war austerity and had to complete his national service. He has worked his way up from working-class roots, his employment as a market barrow-boy leading to ownership of a chain of greengrocers' shops in the south and East End of London. These he has now sold, for a whacking profit, capital that he has invested in a variety of businesses – some of doubtful legality – and which permits him to mingle, joyously, in important circles.

Stuck On You

UK · ITV (CENTRAL FOR CARLTON) · SITCOM

1 × 30 mins · colour

16 Mar 1993 · Tue 8.30pm

MAIN CAST

Danny · · · · · · · · · · · · · · · · · Neil Morrissey
Beth · · · · · · · · · · · · · · · · · Amelia Bullmore
Gordon · · · · · · · · · · · · · · · · · Tom Watt
Hazel · · · · · · · · · · · · · · · · · Caroline Milmoe
Mike · · · · · · · · · · · · · · · · · Jeremy Gittins
Cliff · · · · · · · · · · · · · · · · · Anthony Dunn
Policeman · · · · · · · · · · · · · · · · · Roger Frost

CREDITS

writers Mark Bussell/Justin Sbresni · director Nick Hurran · producer Paula Burdon

Although opposites – she is a PR consultant who likes everything clean and tidy, he is a slobbish self-employed sports writer who works from home – Beth and Danny have been lovers for seven years, since their university days. Now they are at loggerheads, their relationship having declined to the point of termination. But the economic recession prevents them from being able to sell the one-bedroom south London flat they bought together, and when Beth starts dating an office colleague, Mike, Danny becomes jealous and competitive, pretending that he too has a new partner, Mini. This turns out to be his car, which he is forced to sleep in … arousing the attention of the police.

A single-episode pilot screened by Carlton as part of its *Comedy Playhouse* season, *Stuck*

On You was peopled by some familiar faces: Neil Morrissey (from *Boon* and **Men Behaving Badly**), two former stars of *Coronation Street* – Amelia Bullmore (who played Steph Barnes) and Caroline Milmoe (Lisa) – and Tom Watt ('Lofty' from *EastEnders*). Despite the cast, however, it was felt that the concept showed insufficient promise to be developed into a series.

Stuff The Week

UK · ITV (LWT) · SKETCH

1 × 30 mins · colour

26 Sep 1997 · Fri 11.30pm

MAIN CAST

Dan Gaster
Will Ing
Paul Powell
Ben Silburn

CREDITS

writers cast · directors Richard Bracewell, Jonathan Glazier · executive producer Humphrey Barclay · producer Gareth Edwards

Four young humour-mongers sit in a room, drink beer and make jokes based on the week's news.

This was the simple premise of *Stuff The Week*, a one-off ITV show that looked like a pilot try-out for a series. Interspersed with the casual studio banter were more formal sketches and location filming, where the cast provided humorous commentary while visiting a place in the news. Flippant and amateurish (possibly intentionally so), there was a germ of an idea here but the material surely would have to be stronger for any full series to succeed.

Style Monsters

UK · BBC (ISLAND VISUAL ARTS) · SITCOM

1 × 30 mins · colour

24 Feb 1989 · BBC2 Fri 9pm

MAIN CAST

Felix · · · · · · · · · · · · · · · · · Grant Russell
Ulla · · · · · · · · · · · · · · · · · Britt Morrow
Sam · · · · · · · · · · · · · · · · · John Markham
Amanda · · · · · · · · · · · · · · · · · Jeanette Driver

CREDITS

writer Matthew Bardsley · director Nick Turvey · producer James Dunford Wood

Felix and Ulla are an ultra-trendy modern coupled obsessed with style and their careers. But their white warehouse home, packed with cult objects, cannot obscure the vacuity of their relationship and lives.

A one-off, pitch-black comedy satirising the yuppie lifestyle prevalent at the time.

Such Is Life

UK · BBC · SKETCH

5 × 30 mins · b/w

24 Apr–19 June 1950 · fortnightly
Mon around 9pm

MAIN CAST

Bobby Howes
Eve Ashley

CREDITS

writers Ted Kavanagh, Carey Edwards, Michael Mills · director/producer Michael Mills

Musical-comedy star Bobby Howes ventured into television playing 'the little man struggling with his conscience' in this themed sketch series. Eve Ashley provided regular support and a cast of rep players filled the remaining roles.

See also *Out Of The World*.

Suddenly Susan

USA · NBC (WARNER BROS) · SITCOM

33 × 30 mins (to 31/12/97 · continuing into 1998) · colour

US dates: 19 Sep 1996 to date

UK dates: 26 Oct 1997 to date (7 episodes to 31/12/97) C4 Sun around 12 midnight

MAIN CAST

Susan Keane · · · · · · · · · · · · · Brooke Shields
Luis Rivera · · · · · · · · · · · · · Nestor Campbell
Vicki Groener · · · · · · · · · · · · · Kathy Griffin
Jack Richmond · · · · · · · · · · · · · Judd Nelson
Todd · · · · · · · · · · · · · · · · · David Strickland
Nana · · · · · · · · · · · · · · · · · Barbara Barrie

CREDITS

creator Clyde Phillips · writers various · directors Steve Zuckerman, Shelley Jensen, Andy Ackerman and others · executive producers Gary Dontzig/Steven Peterman, Dan O'Shannon · producer Frank Pace

About to marry handsome playboy Kip Richmond, Susan Keane experiences an epiphany and, unable to cope with the prospect of spending the rest of her life with him, dashes out of the church and into a new life.

Returning to the offices of *The Street*, a 'What's on in San Francisco'-type magazine, she pleads with the editor, Jack, to be given back her former job as copy-editor. Jack is the brother of the jilted Kip and he answers her request thus: 'You dumped my little brother, you humiliated my father, you put my mother into bed under even more sedation than normal – I can't give you your old job back after that … after *that*, you deserve a promotion!' Clearly, Jack loathes the spoiled, rich lifestyle of his family and, true to his word, offers Susan the chance to write a weekly column for the magazine, figuring that now she is alone and broke she will have a better take of life on the street. Suddenly Susan has her freedom and a raft of new challenges, and a sitcom is born.

Helping Susan out are her fellow office workers, the acid-tongued food and drink critic Vicki Groener; the darkly passionate Hispanic photographer Luis; and office boy

Todd, who is at an awkward stage of his life, torn between his *Star Trek* obsession and his desire to meet women. Back at home, Susan consults with her maternal grandmother, Nana, a free-spirited soul with an exotic past and a liberal outlook on life. She wholeheartedly supports Susan in her quest for a new life and much humour is mined via her use of slang language and advocacy of bad behaviour. But the most rewarding relationship in the series is the one between Susan and Vicki, her spiky colleague (played by standup comedian Kathy Griffin). The couple contrast physically (Griffin is diminutive besides the very tall Shields) and enjoy caustic verbal sparring. Vicki delivers the lion's share of the smart-ass one-liners but Susan's telling ripostes impress her co-worker and a robust friendship develops between them.

In spite of a relatively thin premise and variable quality, *Suddenly Susan* hit its targets well and established Shields as an unlikely, but deserving, sitcom star.

The Suit

UK · ITV (LWT) · SITCOM

1 × 30 mins · b/w

19 Apr 1969 · Sat 7.30pm

MAIN CAST

Howard Butler · · · · · · · · · · · · · Leslie Phillips
Penny Butler · · · · · · · · · · · · · Jennie Linden
Jimmy · · · · · · · · · · · · · · · · · · · Bill Oddie
Burglar · · · · · · · · · · · · · · · · · · Frank Jarvis
Wife · Jan Holden

CREDITS

writers Ray Galton/Alan Simpson · director/producer David Askey

The opening edition in *The Galton & Simpson Comedy*, a weekly showcase of new, one-off G&S ideas screened by ITV in spring 1969. Leslie Phillips starred in this playlet, trying to keep from his wife the details of an awkward burglary at his lover's flat.

The script was re-used in 1997 in *Paul Merton In Galton & Simpson's ...*

The Summer Show

UK · ITV (ATV) · SKETCH/STANDUP

5 × 45 mins · colour

2 Aug–30 Aug 1975 · Sat 5.50pm

MAIN CAST

Marti Caine
Aiden J Harvey
Lenny Henry
Victoria Wood
Trevor Chance

CREDITS

writers Bryan Blackburn, Dick Vosburgh, Tony Hawes · director Peter Harris · producer Colin Clews

Five winning performers in ATV's talent-spotting show *New Faces* combined here in a comedy and music series designed to have a fast-moving style reminiscent of *Rowan And Martin's Laugh-In*. A different theme linked the sketches and songs each week. Established performer Leslie Crowther was on board in the first edition to give the newcomers a guiding hand.

Summer's Here

UK · ITV (JACK HYLTON TV PRODUCTIONS FOR ASSOCIATED-REDIFFUSION) · SKETCH

4 editions (3 × 45 mins · 1 × 60 mins) · b/w

18 July–26 Sep 1957 · occasional
Thu mostly 8.30pm

MAIN CAST

Jill Summers
Michael Bentine

CREDITS

creator Douglas Hurn · writers Dick Vosburgh/Stan Ashton (show 1), Bernard Adler/Ross Parker (shows 2–4) · director Douglas Hurn

Impresario Jack Hylton put comedian Jill Summers at the top of the cast in these four shows that spanned the summer of 1957, recruiting Michael Bentine as her support. (The last of the four was actually titled *Summer's Ending* and ran for an hour instead of 45 minutes.)

The Sun Trap

UK · BBC · SITCOM

6 × 30 mins · colour

25 Apr–30 May 1980 · BBC1 Fri 8.20pm

MAIN CAST

Peter Halliday · · · · · · · · · · · Donald Churchill
Helen Halliday · · · · · · · · · · · · · Zena Walker
Fiona · · · · · · · · · · · · · · · · · · · Joan Benham
Horace · · · · · · · · · · · · · · · Graham Crowden
Harold · · · · · · · · · · · · · · · · · · David Garth
Gloria · · · · · · · · · · · · · · · · · Jo Rowbottom
Ken · · · · · · · · · · · · · · · · · · Peter Schofield
Robert · · · · · · · · · · · · · · · · · Derek Waring

CREDITS

writer David Nobbs · producer Gareth Gwenlan

Great things were expected of this David Nobbs series – following his marvellous *The Fall And Rise Of Reginald Perrin* – but it was something of a disappointment.

The Sun Trap depicted the lives of a group of expatriate Britons on a Mediterranean island, especially newcomers Peter and Helen Halliday. The community seems happy but, inwardly, everyone is dissatisfied; while they all profess to be well rid of Blighty – with its miserable weather and endless strikes – none of the émigrés is really keen to settle into local life, preferring instead to re-create a little piece of England. This isolates them from the local populace and, by same token, throws them uncomfortably close together.

The series mined an area rich in comedy potential but it failed to win over its audience, possibly because, aside from the Hallidays, the remaining characters were genuinely unlikeable.

Sunnyside Farm

UK · BBC (GRANADA) · SITCOM

6 × 30 mins · colour

18 Apr–23 May 1997 · BBC2 Fri 9.30pm

MAIN CAST

Ray Sunnyside · · · · · · · · · · · · · Phil Daniels
Ken Sunnyside · · · · · · · · · · · · · Mark Addy
Ezekial Letchworth · · · · · · · · Michael Kitchen
Mr Mills · · · · · · · · · · · · · · · · · Matt Lucas
Wendy · · · · · · · · · · · · · · · · · Beth Goddard
Justin · · · · · · · · · · · · · · · · · · Tony Gardner

CREDITS

writers Richard Preddy/Gary Howe · director Andy de Emmony · executive producer Justin Judd · producer Spencer Campbell

Brothers Ray and Ken Sunnyside have inherited the ownership of Sunnyside Farm, a dilapidated rural enterprise losing money hand over foot and mouth. Ray wants to sell up and move to the city to enjoy a life of unbridled licentiousness, but the mentally challenged Ken refuses to do so because their late mother insisted the farm be kept in the family.

Ray is an utterly loathsome individual with no saving graces of any kind – he is totally self-centred and, in the opening episode, thinks nothing of trying to get his brother committed to a mental institution so that he can sell the farm without hindrance. Ken is constantly confused and definitely 'two sandwiches short of a picnic', but, in his own ponderous way, is harmless enough. The arrival of new neighbours – middle-class, former city dwellers Wendy and Justin, with their precocious children (Oberon and Titania) – is the catalyst for a change in the Sunnyside lives. Ray is instantly smitten with the pretty and squeaky-clean Wendy, pursuing her with an undisguised lust, oblivious to the feelings of her boring husband. The fact that Ray is the least appealing human on the planet, has no tact and delivers a liberal dose of bullshit (metaphorically *and* literally) doesn't deter him from his hopeless quest. But although Wendy's arrival brings some light into Ray's life, he still faces plenty of misery at the hands of local landowner Ezekial Letchworth, a gentleman thug who has loaned Ray money and will accept his kneecaps as repayment. Also on the scene is Mr Mills, a local character who seems all country warmth and old-fashioned values but, underneath, is a cross-dressing sexual deviant.

A coarse series that revelled in cowpat jokes and invented obscenities ('Chocolate arses!', 'Burt Bacharach!'), what rude energy

Sunnyside Farm possessed was undermined by its charmless characters. Ray was a monster, and actor Phil Daniels' incessant shouting in the role just made him even more irritating. Ken was too loony to attract any sympathy, and the new neighbours lost any appeal they might have mustered by staying put and dealing with Ray when they should have kept as far, far away as possible. Writers Preddy and Howe have some classy sketch-show credits under their belt but *Sunnyside Farm* failed to succeed as a vehicle for translating their edgy talent into situation comedy. All the same, Granada successfully managed to interest CBS in the possibility of an American adaptation, working with the network to produce a pilot episode. It will surely need a lot of changing to succeed.

Superfrank!

see HOWERD, Frankie

Supergran

UK · ITV (TYNE TEES) · CHILDREN'S SITCOM

27 editions (26 × 30 mins · 1 × 60 mins) · colour

Series One (13 × 30 mins) 20 Jan–14 Apr 1985 · Sun mostly 4.30pm

Special (60 mins) 24 Dec 1986 · Wed 4.15pm

Series Two (13 × 30 mins) 8 Mar–31 May 1987 · Sun 4.30pm

MAIN CAST

Supergran	Gudrun Ure
The Scunner Campbell	Iain Cuthbertson
Inventor Black	Bill Shine
Edison	Holly English (series 1); Samantha Duffy (special & series 2)
Willard	Ian Towell (series 1)
Willie	Michael Graham (special & series 2)
Tub	Lee Marshall (series 1); Jason Carrielies (special)
Muscles	Alan Snell
Dustin	Brian Lewis
Reporter	Bill McAllister
Petunia Preston	Gwen Doran
PC Robert Leekie	Terry Joyce
Inspector Muggins	Robert Austin
Postman Pugh	Les Wilde
Ben	Hedley Dodd (series 2)

CREDITS

creator Forrest Wilson · *adapter/writer* Jenny McDade · *directors* Tony Kysh (11), Gerald Blake (5), Roger Cheveley (4), Gerry Mill (3), Anthony Simmons (3), Tim Dowd (1) · *producer* Keith Richardson (series 1), Graham Williams (special & series 2)

Adapting the *Super Gran* series of children's books by Forrest Wilson (first published in 1978, there have been ten, at the last count), Tyne Tees scored great success with two long series of *Supergran* (one word). The stories relate the adventures of a happy and gentle old lady, known as Granny Smith, who, out one day for a stroll in the park, is given great

powers when a magic-ray machine – the brainchild of Inventor Black but stolen by the villainous Scunner Campbell – is accidentally fired at her. Granny's life is never the same again as she metamorphoses into Supergran in order to fight the Scunner Campbell, his assistants Muscles and Dustin and other evil elements, and so protect the good citizens of her home-town Chisleton. (Actual location shooting was done in Tynemouth.) The series made especially good use of the latest available effects, courtesy of which Supergran could be seen to pole-vault herself through very high windows, ride through the air on her tricks-laden, two-wheel, multi-winged Flycycle (actually an adapted butcher's boy's bicycle), and whizz around land and sea in her Skimmer mobile.

Each weekly episode was a self-contained crime-fighting story, made additionally watchable by the remarkable array of guest stars who were happy to take part. These included Billy Connolly (who also co-wrote the series' theme music), Michael Elphick, Roy Kinnear, Sheila Steafel, Irene Handl, Burt Kwouk, Pat Coombs, Spike Milligan, Anna Dawson, Rikki Fulton, Paul Shane, Ken Campbell, Bernard Cribbins, Leslie Phillips, Melvyn Hayes, Anna Karen, Harry Fowler, Michael Medwin, Joan Sims, Patrick Troughton (in his last TV appearance before his death), John Bluthal, Tim Healy, singers Lulu, Gary Glitter and John Otway, sports stars George Best, Geoff Capes, John Conteh, Eric Bristow and Willie Thorne, stuntman Eddie Kidd and two *Carry On* stars, Barbara Windsor and, making his last ever scripted appearance on TV/film, Charles Hawtrey.

Surgical Spirit

UK · ITV (HUMPHREY BARCLAY PRODUCTIONS FOR GRANADA) · SITCOM

50 × 30 mins · colour

Series One (6) 14 Apr–19 May 1989 · Fri 8.30pm

Series Two (7) 27 Apr–8 June 1990 · Fri mostly 8pm

Series Three (7) 4 Jan–15 Feb 1991 · Fri 8.30pm

Series Four (6) 14 Feb–20 Mar 1992 · Fri 8pm

Series Five (7) 19 Feb–2 Apr 1993 · Fri 8.30pm

Series Six (10) 7 Jan–11 Mar 1994 · Fri 8.30pm

Series Seven (7) 26 May–7 July 1995 · Fri 8.30pm

MAIN CAST

Sheila Sabatini	Nichola McAuliffe
Jonathan Haslam	Duncan Preston
Joyce Watson	Marji Campi
George Hope-Wynne	David Conville
Neil Copeland	Emlyn Price
Sister Cheryl Patching	Suzette Llewellyn
Michael Sampson	Beresford Le Roy
Giles Peake	Simon Harrison
Simon Field	Lyndham Gregory (series 1–4)

OTHER APPEARANCES

Daniel Sabatini	Andrew Groves

CREDITS

creator Peter Learmouth · *writers* Peter Learmouth (40), Graeme Garden (5), Raymond Dixon (2), Annie Bruce (1), Annie Wood (1), Paul McKenzie (1) · *directors* John Kaye Cooper (series 1), David Askey (series 2–7) · *executive producers* David Liddiment, Al Mitchell, Andy Harries, Antony Wood · *producer* Humphrey Barclay

A long-running ITV sitcom built around Sheila Sabatini, an esteemed – but feared – senior surgeon at the Gillies Hospital whose verbal strength is such that she has most colleagues quaking in their masks or running elsewhere for cover.

Exercising an ire that was a match for Alf Garnett, Basil Fawlty and Victor Meldrew (but remained rare for a woman in sitcoms), Sabatini cut oral swathes through her fellow surgical staff, dominating the operating theatre with a scalpel-sharp tongue. Combined with her piercing, withering 'don't dare mess with me' gaze, accentuated by the surgical mask covering all but her eyes, and her severely swept-back hairstyle – done not merely for reasons of hygiene, one suspected, but so as to make her appear even more intimidating – few dared stand in Ms Sabatini's way.

Deep down, of course, she turned out to have a soft centre. She was also a major gossip, enjoyed the company of her best friend Joyce Watson – fellow surgeon and surgery administrator – and, slowly but surely, drifted into a relationship with her anaesthetist Jonathan Haslam, a friendship hastened by Watson. Estranged from her first husband, Remo, and bringing up her teenage son Daniel, Sheila Sabatini's affair with Haslam only cemented after she finally obtained a divorce. They eventually married (at the end of the sixth series), by which time she had been promoted to become director of surgery and Daniel, having left school, became a medical student at the Gillies, seconded to his mother. (Much against her very considerable will.)

A cut above the average ITV sitcom fare, *Surgical Spirit* entertained for some six years and remained in better than average health when Granada decided to pull the plug. Certainly, by this time, the series' *raison d'être* seemed to have been blunted – namely, Sheila Sabatini's incessant drive to prove herself just as worthy and just as tough as any of her male colleagues – but Granada's decision suggested an inadvisable exercise in voluntary euthanasia rather than a mercy killing.

Swap You One Of These For One Of Those

UK · ITV (YORKSHIRE) · SITCOM

1 × 30 mins · colour

24 Feb 1977 · Thu 9pm

MAIN CAST

Henry · · · · · · · · · · · · · · · · · Richard Briers
Henry McGee
Jan Waters

CREDITS

writers/associate producers Ray Galton/Alan
Simpson · director/producer Ronnie Baxter ·
executive producer Duncan Wood

Three series into **The Good Life** on BBC1,
Richard Briers jumped channels for this one-
off comedy of the sweet life ... and suburban
wife-swapping parties. It appeared as part of
Yorkshire's *The Galton & Simpson Playhouse*
season.

Sweet Sixteen

UK · BBC · SITCOM

6 × 30 mins · colour

16 Oct–20 Nov 1983 · BBC1 Sun 7.15pm

MAIN CAST

Helen Walker · · · · · · · · · · · · Penelope Keith
Peter Morgan · · · · · · · · · Christopher Villiers
Jane · · · · · · · · · · · · · · · · · · Joan Blackham
Dr Ballantine · · · · · · · · · · · · · · Mike Grady
James Walker · · · · · · · · · · · Matthew Solon
Ken Green · · · · · · · · · · · · · · Victor Spinetti

CREDITS

writer Douglas Watkinson · director/producer
Gareth Gwenlan

Aged 41, Helen Walker is the hard-headed
boss of a building firm. A no-nonsense
woman, used to getting her own way, she
suddenly falls passionately in love with Peter
Morgan, a man 16 years her junior. Luckily,
Morgan also falls for her, so we're off on a
generation-gap romance fraught with all the
problems and misunderstandings suggested
by the scenario.

Writer Douglas Watkinson was known for
heavy dramas like *Maybury* (BBC2, 1981–83)
and this, his first comedy, had dramatic
undercurrents as the key relationship moved
from encounter to courtship to marriage and
pregnancy in just six episodes. The central
dilemma facing Helen was whether she would
be able to retain her status as the big boss
while embarking on a new life as a wife and
mother-to-be. Viewers never discovered the
outcome as the series – of which big things
were hoped – failed to return.

Eric Sykes

Like many of his contemporaries, Eric Sykes
– born in Oldham on 4 May 1923 – discovered a talent to entertain while serving King
and Country during the Second World War.
Afterwards, he set out to carve a career in
comedy by writing scripts: he provided
material for Bill Fraser (whom he had met in

the army) and Frankie Howerd, and then
found his feet with his writing for the BBC
radio phenomena *Educating Archie* and
Variety Bandbox.

Sykes entered TV in 1948, where he
quickly made a name for himself as both a
comedy performer and writer, his credits
appearing in many shows. He made a major
breakthrough with *Pantomania* (BBC, 24
December 1955), a spoof pantomime that
featured many BBC personalities, the credit
for which, impressively, read 'script, special
lyrics and comedy direction by Eric Sykes',
a sign of the versatility that was to come.
(Similar *Pantomania* productions followed
on Christmas Day in 1956 and 1957.) In 1956
Sykes signed a long-term contract as
scriptwriter and variety show presenter for
ATV but it was back at the BBC, with his
1962–65 (and 1972–79) sitcom, *Sykes And A
...*, that he made his biggest impact. (See
information below.)

Eric Sykes developed a hearing problem
in the early 1950s, which has dogged him
ever since – but, although the condition
worsened with time, his near-deafness has
never been apparent from his performances,
which – thanks to his ability to lip-read –
have remained fastidious throughout. Sykes'
screen persona – that of a bumbling,
amateurish soul – belie his dedication to
professionalism and comic perfection, his
major strengths being his ability to weave
complex comedy from single, simple ideas;
his inventiveness at interacting humorously
with inanimate objects; his flawless comic
timing; and the development of his
characteristic theme of an 'ordinary bloke' at
odds with his surroundings and situation.
Allied with his genuine likeability and
refusal to embrace swearing or sex in any of
his work, these strengths have ensured
Sykes an enduring place in the hearts and
minds of generations of British TV viewers
– in short, he is one of all the all-time greats.

See also **Christmas Night With The
Stars** and **The Old Boy Network** (for the
1981 programme *Eric Sykes: One Of The
Great Troupers*), and, for some of Sykes'
writing credits, **Clicquot Et Fils**, **Not
Only ... But Also**, **Spate Of Speight**,
The Terry-Thomas Show, **The Tony
Hancock Show** and **The Idiot Weekly,
Price 2d**.

Dress Rehearsal

UK · BBC · SKETCH

1 × 60 mins · b/w

31 Mar 1956 · Sat 8.30pm

MAIN CAST

Eric Sykes
Lenny The Lion (with Terry Hall)

CREDITS

writer Eric Sykes · producer Ernest Maxin

A comedy-variety show themed around the
concept of a farcical TV dress rehearsal just
prior to transmission. Sykes played the
harassed director, and ventriloquist Terry
Hall added to the mayhem with his famous
furry friend Lenny The Lion. (The
programme was alternatively titled *Eric
Sykes Directs A Dress Rehearsal*.)

Opening Night

UK · BBC · SKETCH

1 × 60 mins · b/w

22 Aug 1956 · Wed 9.15pm

MAIN CAST

Eric Sykes
Kenneth Horne
Irene Handl
Wallace Greenslade
Johnny Vyvyan
Alan Simpson

CREDITS

writer/comedy director Eric Sykes · producer
Ernest Maxin

Another star-studded comedy 'special event'
spoof in the style of *Pantomania* and *Dress
Rehearsal*, once again devised by Sykes.
This time the 'special event' was a real-life
one, the opening of the 1956 National Radio
Show at Earls Court in London. BBC radio
and television were closely connected with
this annual event and this sort of tie-in
programming was very common at the time.

Eric Sykes Presents Peter Sellers

UK · ITV (ATV) · SKETCH/STANDUP

2 × 45 mins · b/w

5 & 12 Jan 1957 · Sat 9pm

MAIN CAST

Peter Sellers
Eric Sykes

CREDITS

writer Eric Sykes · producer Dicky Leeman

A rare combination of two great talents in
their prime, screened under the banner *Val
Parnell's Saturday Spectacular*. (See also
The Peter Sellers Show.)

Closing Night

UK · BBC · SKETCH

1 × 60 mins · b/w

7 Sep 1957 · Sat 8pm

MAIN CAST

Eric Sykes
Alan Simpson
Johnny Speight
Dave Freeman
Dick Vosburgh

CREDITS
writer/director Eric Sykes · *producer* Ernest Maxin

The closing-night extravaganza from the 1957 National Radio Show at Earls Court. (The programme was alternatively titled *National Radio Show: Closing Night.*)

Gala Opening

UK · BBC · SKETCH

1 × 60 mins · b/w
7 Mar 1959 · Sat 7.30pm

MAIN CAST
Eric Sykes
Hattie Jacques
Stanley Unwin

CREDITS
writer/director Eric Sykes · *producer* Ernest Maxin

A characteristic Sykes idea: a spoof 'lavish extravaganza from the Floral Hall, Grapplewick'. The show also featured Hattie Jacques, shortly to become Sykes' long-term sitcom partner.

Sykes And A ...

UK · BBC · SITCOM

60 episodes (35 × 25 mins · 24 × 30 mins · 1 × short special) · b/w
Series One (5 × 30 mins) 29 Jan–26 Feb 1960 · Fri 8.30pm
Series Two (6 × 30 mins) 11 Aug–15 Sep 1960 · Thu 8.30pm
Series Three (6 × 30 mins) 4 Jan–8 Feb 1961 · Wed mostly 8.30pm
Series Four (6 × 25 mins) 14 Apr–19 May 1961 · Fri 8pm
Series Five (8 × 25 mins) 30 Jan–20 Mar 1962 · Tue 8pm
Short special · part of *Christmas Night With The Stars* 25 Dec 1962 · Tue 7.15pm
Series Six (8 × 25 mins) 21 Feb–11 Apr 1963 · Thu 8pm
Series Seven (7 × 25 mins) 25 Feb–7 Apr 1964 · Tue 8pm
Series Eight (6 × 25 mins) 30 Oct–4 Dec 1964 · BBC1 Fri 8pm
Series Nine (7 × 30 mins) 5 Oct–16 Nov 1965 · BBC1 Tue 7.30pm

MAIN CAST
Eric Sykes · himself
Hattie ('Hat') Sykes · Hattie Jacques
Charles Brown · Richard Wattis
· (series 1–3)

CREDITS
writers Eric Sykes, except: Johnny Speight (series 1 & storylines for series 2 & 3), John Antrobus (2 eps in series 2), Spike Milligan (2 eps in series 2) · *directors* Philip Barker (series 1–5, 8 & 9), Sydney Lotterby (1962 special, series 6 & 7) · *producers* Dennis Main Wilson (series 1–5), Sydney Lotterby (1962 special, series 6 & 7), Philip Barker (series 8 & 9)

A really fine comedy series that clicked because of the dream-team combination of Eric Sykes and the comedy-actress Hattie Jacques. The two had occasionally teamed since first working on the radio series *Educating Archie* but here they were forged immutably in the public psyche as a partnership.

In these 60 episodes Eric played 'Eric', a gaunt, accident-prone, eternal child, and Hattie played 'Hattie' (often shortened to 'Hat'), a likeable soul who tended to view the world with wonderment, and put up with Eric's exuberance and erratic behaviour because, improbably, he was her twin brother. Both characters were unmarried (and rarely seemed to work) and the episodes were set in a house they shared at 24 Sebastopol Terrace in East Acton (an area of west London near to the equally fictitious **Steptoe And Son** yard). Initially, Sykes and writer Johnny Speight toyed with the idea of making Eric and Hat a married couple but they then realised the advantage of making them brother and sister – Sykes wisely perceived that it would generate more storylines, with each of them free to pursue romance, and at the same time guarantee the show a different spin from the many other domestic sitcoms of the time. (Johnny Speight wrote the first series, and three writers contributed to the second, but after this Sykes took sole responsibility for the writing.)

The series was titled *Sykes And A ...* so that the given theme of each episode could complete the title. This allowed Sykes to exploit the show's wonderfully simple premise – each programme had a different subject, around which he could create half an hour of comedy, exploring the idea to its comic limits. Although the sheer volume of output led to inevitable inconsistencies in quality, at its best *Sykes* was masterful, several episodes counting among the all-time greats in British TV comedy, among them 'Sykes And A Stranger' (21 April 1961), in which Leo McKern was cast as a rough and ready ex-prisoner who, in pursuance of a schooldays pact, claims Hattie as his fiancée; 'Sykes And A Mouse' (21 March 1963), in which Eric and Hattie try to trap a mouse lodging in their lounge; 'Sykes And A Plank' (3 March 1964), in which Eric tries to transport a piece of timber (see also *The Plank*, below); 'Sykes And A Golfer' (26 October 1965), in which, in a dream, Eric takes on and beats champion golfer Peter Alliss; and, perhaps best of all, 'Sykes And A Haunting' (13 March 1962) in which Eric and Hattie spend the episode accidentally handcuffed together. The series remained popular throughout its life and

royal approval was noted with an appearance of the pair in the 1963 *Royal Variety Show* (televised on 10 November by ITV).

Despite his ever-worsening hearing affliction, in all this time Eric Sykes never lost his innate ability to write fine, inventive comedy or act with immaculate comic timing. Hattie Jacques gave marvellous support throughout as his coy and (comparatively) timid sister – her character was completely opposite to the dragon-like roles normally associated with large women in TV comedy at this time, *à la* Peggy Mount – and Richard Wattis gave sterling support as their snobbish neighbour Mr Brown. (Brown left after the third series – he was said to have emigrated – but he returned for the series' 1972 revival, see below.)

Note. Unrelated to this series, Eric Sykes presented two variety specials for BBC TV in 1963. The first, from Switzerland (17 August), had linking material written by Galton and Simpson; the second, from Sweden (7 September), was linked with material by Terry Nation.

Sykes Versus ITV

UK · ITV (ABC) · SKETCH

1 × 60 mins · b/w
26 Nov 1967 · Sun 8.25pm

MAIN CAST
Eric Sykes
Hattie Jacques
Tommy Cooper
Bernard Bresslaw
Robert Dorning
Irving Davies
Ronnie Brody
Barney Gilbraith

CREDITS
writer Eric Sykes · *producer* Keith Beckett

After two years' absence from a TV starring role, Eric Sykes returned with this one-off special for ITV that took the form of a courtroom trial, in which Eric, in the dock, outlined the reasons why he believed that he *should* do a one-off special for ITV. Aiding his case, as defence, was Hattie Jacques but taking the case against him, as prosecutor, was Tommy Cooper. Other celebrity names also appeared.

The previous year, the BBC had taken cameras to the Shaftesbury Theatre in London to present a 40-minute extract from *Big Bad Mouse* (BBC1, 12 December 1966), the popular stage comedy that starred Sykes and Jimmy Edwards. The play was then given an ITV outing on 26 December 1972 when Thames networked a new 90-minute recording from the Prince Of Wales Theatre, again starring Sykes and Edwards.

Sykes And A Big, Big Show

UK · BBC · SKETCH/SITCOM

6 × 30 mins · colour

26 Feb–2 Apr 1971 · BBC1 Fri 8pm

MAIN CAST

Eric Sykes
Hattie Jacques
Ian Wallace

CREDITS

writer Eric Sykes · *director* Harold Snoad · *producer* Dennis Main Wilson

An ambitious combination of one of Sykes' oldest TV ideas – the staging of a variety show – with various sketches built upon simple premises. The series embraced two types of comedy, physical and situation, and was a genuine attempt (if unsuccessful) to try something new.

Sykes – With The Lid Off

UK · ITV (THAMES) · SKETCH

1 × 60 mins · colour

7 July 1971 · Wed 8pm

MAIN CAST

Eric Sykes
Hattie Jacques
Dilys Watling
Philip Gilbert
Leslie Noyes
Johnny Greenland

CREDITS

writer Eric Sykes · *producer* David Bell

Another ITV comedy special for the man who enjoyed most of his greatest moments with the BBC. Hattie Jacques helped out.

A Policeman's Lot

UK · BBC · SKETCH

1 × short special · colour

part of *Christmas Night With The Stars* 25 Dec 1971 · BBC1 Sat 6.40pm

MAIN CAST

Eric Sykes
Hattie Jacques
Tony Melody
Leslie Noyes

CREDITS

writer Eric Sykes · *producer* Roger Race

An especially-written sketch screened within the BBC's annual comedy jamboree *Christmas Night With The Stars*.

Sykes

UK · BBC · SITCOM

68 × 30 mins · colour

Series One (16) 14 Sep–28 Dec 1972 · BBC1 Thu 8pm
Series Two (15) 10 Sep–17 Dec 1973 · BBC1 Mon mostly 6.40pm
Series Three (8) 17 Oct–5 Dec 1974 · BBC1 Thu 8pm

Series Four (7) 24 Oct–12 Dec 1975 · BBC1 Fri 8pm
Series Five (8) 11 Nov–30 Dec 1976 · BBC1 Thu 7.40pm
Special · 22 Dec 1977 · BBC1 Thu 8.30pm
Series Six (6) 4 Jan–8 Feb 1978 · BBC1 Wed 6.50pm
Series Seven (7) 5 Oct–16 Nov 1979 · BBC1 Fri around 7.35pm

MAIN CAST

Eric Sykes · · · · · · · · · · · · · · · · · · · himself
Hattie ('Hat') Sykes · · · · · · · Hattie Jacques
PC Wilfred 'Corky' Turnbull · · Deryck Guyler
Charles Brown · · · · · · · · · · Richard Wattis
· (series 1–3)
Melanie Rumbelow · · · · · · · · Joy Harington
· (series 5–7)

CREDITS

writer Eric Sykes · *executive producer* Dennis Main Wilson (series 1) · *director/producer* Roger Race

Seven years after the last *Sykes And A …* outing, the series returned for an even longer run, this time in colour. The title now was simply *Sykes* but many of the episodes were straightforward reworkings of the earlier scripts – including, for example, the golfing episode (now with Tony Jacklin instead of Peter Alliss) and 'Stranger' (with Peter Sellers in place of Leo McKern).

The setting was still Sebastopol Terrace (albeit now two doors along, at number 28, in an end-of-terrace house) and Eric and Hattie also remained as they were before: innocents in a scheming world, he the accident-prone, foolish boy who will never grew up, she the wide-eyed, less knowing but remarkably patient sister-cum-mother-figure. (The angriest she ever got was to shout 'Oh, *Eric!*') Returning to provide fine comedic colour was Eric and Hat's irritatingly aloof neighbour Mr Brown (Richard Wattis), joined this time by a local busybody 'PC Plod'-style policeman whom they nicknamed 'Corky' (played by Deryck Guyler). Interestingly, three of these four principal characters – Eric, Hat and Mr Brown – were unmarried and, albeit deep down, somewhat melancholic. (They were joined by a fourth, next-door neighbour Miss Rumbelow, who came to the series after Mr Brown left.) Good fun was enjoyed with a temperamental cuckoo in their cuckoo clock, whom Eric and Hattie named Peter and spoke to as if it was a real bird (in a fine touch typical of Eric Sykes' comedic inventiveness, they did so with such consistency that it became impossible to be sure if they were mad or correct). There were also regular references to a character never seen – Corky's wife, Elsie – and to one very rarely seen, Madge Kettlewell, who ran the baker's shop and was very generous with her doughnuts. (Occasionally played by Joan Sims.)

Like the 1960s series, *Sykes* was good fun – fine, clean, cheaply produced comedy from an age of sitcom innocence. The best years in this revival were the early ones, though; latter episodes were not very good, and the series came to an enforced conclusion after the 1979 run following the death on 6 October 1980 of the marvellous Hattie Jacques, aged a mere 56.

The Eric Sykes Show

UK · ITV (THAMES) · SKETCH

1 × 60 mins · colour

8 June 1977 · Wed 8pm

MAIN CAST

Eric Sykes
Hattie Jacques
Irene Handl
Jimmy Edwards
Peter Cook

CREDITS

writer Eric Sykes · *director/producer* Dennis Kirkland

The first of seven ITV specials screened within a five-year period, with a fine array of guests, including (inevitably) Hattie Jacques, Jimmy Edwards, Irene Handl and, from the next generation, Peter Cook.

Eric Sykes' next ITV outing was screened on 29 December 1977: his 75-minute adaptation of Brandon Thomas's Victorian theatrical comedy *Charley's Aunt*, in which he played the part of Brassett. Jimmy Edwards, Barbara Murray and Gerald Flood were also among the cast.

The Plank

UK · ITV (THAMES) · SKETCH

1 × 30 mins · colour

17 Dec 1979 · Mon 8pm

MAIN CAST

Eric Sykes
Arthur Lowe

OTHER APPEARANCES

Carroll Baker, Lionel Blair, Henry Cooper, Harry H Corbett, Bernard Cribbins, Robert Dorning, Diana Dors, Charlie Drake, Jimmy Edwards, Liza Goddard, Deryck Guyler, Charles Hawtrey, Frankie Howerd, James Hunt, Wilfrid Hyde White, Joanna Lumley, Kenny Lynch, Brian Murphy, Kate O'Mara, Ann Sidney, Reg Varney, Frank Windsor

CREDITS

writer/director Eric Sykes · *producer* Dennis Kirkland

Master of comedy Eric Sykes explored the visual side of humour to great effect in *The Plank*, which he wrote (and also directed) entirely without dialogue: it contained only mime, slapstick, effects and clever ideas. The premise saw Sykes needing one single plank of wood to complete some building work but then – assisted by Arthur Lowe –

getting into scrapes galore when transporting said lumber from timber yard to building site. Along the way a galaxy of TV stars aided or obstructed their cause.

This was Eric Sykes' third realisation of his not-so-wooden idea. 'Sykes And A Plank' was screened as part of his ongoing BBC series, with Hattie Jacques in the main assistant's role. This was followed by a 54-minute film made for the cinema in 1967 (again directed by the author, produced by Jon Penington) which featured an equally all-star cast for the period and Tommy Cooper as the principal support.

The Likes Of Sykes

UK · ITV (THAMES) · SKETCH

1 × 60 mins · colour

1 Jan 1980 · Tue 8pm

MAIN CAST
Eric Sykes
Diana Coupland
John Williams
Debbie Arnold
Hugh Burden
David Battley
Diane Holland
John Comer
Ricardo Montez

CREDITS
writer Eric Sykes · *director/producer* Paul Stewart Laing

A single ITV special in which Sykes dreamed up a Broadway smash musical and then saw his ecstasy turn, scene by scene and number by number, to agony.

Rhubarb Rhubarb!

UK · ITV (THAMES) · SKETCH

1 × 30 mins · colour

15 Dec 1980 · Mon 8pm

MAIN CAST
Eric Sykes
Jimmy Edwards

OTHER APPEARANCES
Bob Todd, Charlie Drake, Hattie Jacques, Roy Kinnear, Bill Fraser, Beryl Reid, Norman Rossington, April Walker, Nicholas Bond-Owen, Robert Carter

CREDITS
writer/director Eric Sykes · *producer* David Clark

Rhubarb Rhubarb! was a 1980 remake for TV of Sykes' dialogue-free film *Rhubarb!*, released to the cinemas in 1970. The word 'rhubarb' – used by actors to feign off-microphone discussion – is the only one uttered, many times over, in this otherwise silent film.

Eric Sykes starred as a police inspector so intent on winning a round of golf that he employs his constable (Jimmy Edwards) to furtively disentangle his ball from the odd spots in which it usually comes to rest. His opponent, however, is the local vicar (played by Bob Todd), who seeks help from an even greater authority to assist his game. A wealth of other TV comedy stars were on the links to get in the way. (Sykes and Edwards had played the same roles in the 1970 film version, in which Harry Secombe was the vicar.)

Hattie Jacques died between the making of *Rhubarb Rhubarb!* and its screening.

If You Go Down In The Woods Today

UK · ITV (THAMES) · SKETCH

1 × 90 mins · colour

29 Apr 1981 · Wed 8.30pm

MAIN CAST
Mr Pangbourne · · · · · · · · · · · · Eric Sykes
Chief Constable · · · · · · · · · · · Robin Bailey
Doctor · · · · · · · · · · · · · · · · · Norman Bird
Ticket collector · · · · · · · · · · · Glyn Houston
Fishfingers · · · · · · · · · · · · · · Roy Kinnear
Colonel Norriss · · · · · · · · · · Fulton Mackay
Guvnor · · · · · · · · · · · · · · Lee Montague
Boozy · · · · · · · · · · · · · · · · · Tony Selby
Knocker · · · · · · · · · · · · · George Sewell
Edison · · · · · · · · · · · · · · · Crispin Dexter

CREDITS
writer/director Eric Sykes · *producer* David Clark · *executive producer* Philip Jones

Another mega-production for Thames TV (the above names constitute only the main players; the full cast numbered dozens). In this, the writer/director/star appeared as Mr Pangbourne, a scoutmaster out with his eight-boy troop in Tangle Woods. Suddenly, Pangbourne and one of the cubs, Edison, become separated from the others and find themselves coming under the surveillance of the MI5, army, navy, air force and criminal elements. (In real life, Sykes had been a keen Boy Scout.)

Sykes described *If You Go Down In The Woods Today* as 'a comedy thriller … an Agatha Christie gone mad', which goes some way to explaining why he had such difficulty in getting his idea off the ground. For fully 20 years he had hawked the 'script' (a one-pager) around British film companies – the closest it reached to fruition during this time being a finished but unreleased 1973 hour-length feature film version entitled (appropriately enough) *You Had Better Go In Disguise*. Hattie Jacques, Arthur Lowe, Simon Oates, Stratford Johns, William Mervyn, Bob Todd, Bill Maynard and Richard Wattis were among the cast.

The Eric Sykes 1990 Show

UK · ITV (THAMES) · SKETCH

1 × 60 mins · colour

14 Apr 1982 · Wed 8pm

MAIN CAST
Eric Sykes
Tommy Cooper
John Williams
Dandy Nichols
Chic Murray
Henry Cooper
Leslie Mitchell

CREDITS
writer Eric Sykes · *director/producer* Dennis Kirkland

Another single special, in which Sykes plotted the near-future of TV, where shows are the items that appear in between the commercials, and have to be paid for accordingly. He himself appeared as the producer, Tommy Cooper as an entertainer, Chic Murray as a TV executive and Dandy Nichols as a wardrobe woman.

It's Your Move

UK · ITV (THAMES) · SKETCH

1 × 30 mins · colour

18 Oct 1982 · Mon 8.30pm

MAIN CAST
Eric Sykes
Tommy Cooper

OTHER APPEARANCES
Richard Briers, Bernard Cribbins, Jimmy Edwards, Irene Handl, Brian Murphy, Andrew Sachs, Sylvia Syms, Bob Todd, Johnny Vyvyan

CREDITS
writer/director Eric Sykes · *producer* Dennis Kirkland

A third dialogue-less film to follow the earlier Thames pieces *The Plank* and *Rhubarb Rhubarb!* Once again, a celebrity-packed cast was on hand with the actions and grunts as a pair of newly weds – and all their neighbours – find that 'Sykes-Cooper & Co' is not exactly the most reliable or careful firm of removal men listed in Yellow Pages.

Mr H Is Late

UK · ITV (THAMES) · SKETCH

1 × 30 mins · colour

15 Feb 1988 · Mon 8pm

MAIN CAST
Eric Sykes
Jimmy Edwards

OTHER APPEARANCES
John Alderton, Bobby Ball, Tommy Cannon, Norman Collier, Charlie Drake, Gabrielle Drake, Linda Hayden, James Hunt, Rula Lenska, Kenny Lynch, Henry McGee, Spike Milligan, Noel Murphy, Richard O'Sullivan, Terry Scott, Paul Shane, Kathy Staff, Sylvia Syms, Freddie Starr, Bob Todd, Dennis Waterman, Eli Woods, Mike Yarwood

CREDITS
writer/director Eric Sykes · *producer* Dennis Kirkland

A fourth dialogue-less film, with undertaker Sykes, traffic warden Edwards and another all-star cast combining to fumble the safe passage of a coffin from the 26th floor of a block of flats to a church in time for a funeral.

The Nineteenth Hole

UK · ITV (REGENT PRODUCTIONS FOR CENTRAL) · SITCOM

7 × 30 mins · colour

5 June–17 July 1989 · Mon 8pm

MAIN CAST

The Secretary	Eric Sykes
George Brady, the Captain	Garfield Morgan
Mr Woodley	John Quayle
Dennis	John Lyons
Mr Bennett	Derek Newark
John, the Steward	Ronnie Brody
Jack	Michael Redfern
Harold, the President	Ivor Roberts
Miranda, the Lady Captain	Charmian May
Sam	John Clegg
Jim Goatman	Norman Rossington

CREDITS

writer Johnny Speight · *directors* William G Stewart (4), Ronnie Baxter (3) · *producer* William G Stewart

Donning flat cap and long-johns, Eric Sykes was cast in this sitcom as the harassed secretary to Prince's Hill Golf Club, located on a private estate, an establishment steeped in chauvinism, ethnic prejudice, homophobia, snobbery and nationalism, and drowning in desperate financial straits. Most of the action took place in the bar (which, in golfing parlance, is the 19th hole), but it wasn't – it has to be said – at all funny, despite the inexplicably generous audience laughter. One of the ITV regions, TSW, actually dropped the series midway through its seven-week run.

Sykes it was who had introduced writer and friend Johnny Speight to the game of golf, both possessing considerable amateur ability at the sport. Speight was a member of Pinner Hill Golf Club, north-west of London, also located on a private estate, but was adamant that the series was a composite of golf club rules and behaviour in general, not his club in particular. If anything, he later reflected, the series made light of some of the more extreme regulations prevalent in such establishments. As if to prove this, Central TV screened *The Nineteenth Hole* to members of a number of golf clubs in the Nottingham area and all present concluded that it had been written about their own.

In 1992, three years after the TV series, Eric Sykes toured with a theatrical production of *The Nineteenth Hole*, co-starring with David Lumsden and Bruce Montague.

The Tab Hunter Show

USA · NBC (FAMOUS ARTISTS/SHUNTO PRODUCTIONS) · SITCOM

32 × 30 mins · b/w

US dates: 18 Sep 1960–10 Sep 1961
UK dates: 5 Jan–26 Sep 1961 (24 episodes)
BBC Thu 7.30pm then Tue around 8pm

MAIN CAST

Paul Morgan	Tab Hunter
Peter Fairfield III	Richard Erdman
John Larsen	Jerome Cowan
Thelma	Reta Shaw

CREDITS

producer Norman Tokar

Born in New York City on 11 July 1931, Andrew Arthur Kelm grew up to become the handsome and athletic Tab Hunter, 1950s American 'beefcake' film actor, pop singer and a dead ringer for Barbie Doll's boyfriend Ken. In this series, designed to cash in on his teen appeal, Tab appeared as cartoonist Paul Morgan, whose *Bachelor-At-Large* comic-strip detailed the woman-friendly adventures of a playboy, and was supposedly based on Paul's own experiences and those of his man-about-town pal Peter. (The town, incidentally, was Malibu Beach, California.) A bevy of beautiful guest stars paraded through the episodes as bait for the rugged hunks, including Tuesday Weld, Elizabeth Montgomery, Mary Tyler Moore, Suzanne Pleshette and, playing identical twins, Gena Rowlands. Despite these attractions, however, the show had a squeaky-clean, innocent atmosphere typical of its era.

Tabitha

USA · ABC (COLUMBIA PICTURES TELEVISION) · SITCOM

12 × 30 mins · colour

US dates: 7 May 1977; 10 Sep 1977–14 Jan 1978
UK dates: 16 June–28 July 1978 & 7 July 1979 (8 episodes) BBC1 Fri 5.05pm

MAIN CAST

Tabitha Stephens	Lisa Hartman
Adam Stephens	David Ankrum
Paul Thurston	Robert Urich
Marvin Decker	Mel Stewart
Aunt Minerva	Karen Morrow

CREDITS

creator Jerry Mayer · writers Barry Blitzer, Bernard M Kahn, Ed Jurist, George Yanok, Martin Donovan, Roland Wolpert · directors Bruce Bilson, Charles S Dubin, Charles Rondeau, Murray Golden, Herb Wallerstein, George Tyne · executive producers Jerry Mayer, George Yanok · producer Robert Stambler

The adventures of Tabitha, first child of Darrin and the good witch Samantha Stephens from **Bewitched**. Although it was only 11 years since she was born in that original series, the magic of television – or, indeed, the magic inherent within her – here transformed Tabitha into a beautiful young woman beginning her career as a television production assistant at station KXLA in California. (Where, coincidentally, her brother Adam – even younger than Tabitha but, clearly, equally as employable – also works.)

Tabitha has, of course, inherited her mother's supernatural powers and is able, with a twitch of her mouth or a touch of the nose, to produce all kinds of magic. Unfortunately, she failed to cast a spell over the show's audience, which proceeded to vanish after just a handful of episodes.

Note. A pilot episode (screened in the USA by ABC on 24 April 1976; not shown in Britain) featured a different cast: Liberty Williams as Tabitha, Bruce Kimmel as Adam) failed to make the grade in that form. In the series, Tabitha was played by Lisa Hartman, who sang the theme song 'It's Magic' and later enjoyed a successful career as a rock singer.

Take A Chance

UK · ITV (THAMES) · CHILDREN'S SITCOM

13 × 25 mins · colour

30 Dec 1980–7 Apr 1981 · Tue 4.20pm

MAIN CAST

Stanley Wates	Stanley Bates
Dawson Chance	himself
various roles	Roy Skelton

CREDITS

writers Lee Pressman (4), Tony Hare (3), Grant Cathro (3), Roy Skelton (2), Geoffrey Armstrong (1) · directors Stan Woodward (9), Daphne Shadwell (4) · executive producer Charles Warren · producer Stan Woodward

A children's sitcom spun-off from the daily weekday pre-school series *Rainbow* and set in the Rose Marie Hotel, a respectable home for resting show-business folk, managed by Stanley Wates. All is quiet until a ventriloquist (Dawson Chance) arrives, with not one but 16 talking dolls.

Take A Letter, Mr Jones ...

UK · ITV (SOUTHERN) · SITCOM

6 × 30 mins · colour

5 Sep–10 Oct 1981 · Sat 7.35pm

MAIN CAST

Graham Jones	John Inman
Joan Warner	Rula Lenska
Brenda	Gina Maher
Ruth	Joan Blackham
Daisy	Christine Ozanne
Maria	Miriam Margolyes
Lucy	Claudine Bowyer
Mr Lewis	Allan Mitchell

CREDITS

writers Ronald Wolfe/Ronald Chesney · director/producer Bryan Izzard

Following the absolutely abysmal **Odd Man Out** – which had 'advanced' John Inman's oh-so-gay screen persona to even greater camp lengths than Mr Humphries' in **Are You Being Served?** – ITV manufactured this vehicle for him, written by the venerable Wolfe and Chesney. Truth be told, Inman was less camp here than before, but only just: he still pouted and distributed quips with a merry twinkle.

Inman was cast as Graham Jones, employed as male secretary/PA to Ms Joan Warner, the business-efficient head of the British arm of Eight Star, an American leisure corporation. Ms Warner was a divorcee, mother of a seven-year-old daughter, Lucy, and owner of a shaggy dog, so – as could be expected – Jones, never short of a stinging word and not one to hold back, felt that his duties should extend beyond the office to embrace Ms Warner's home life too. Without such extension, one suspects, the premise could never have stretched to a full series – one which, remarkably, ITV saw fit to air at peak-time on Saturday evenings. Equally extraordinarily, Miriam Margolyes was among the regular cast, appearing as Ms Warner's 'mad Italian maid' Maria. One would imagine however, that *Take A Letter, Mr Jones* ... no longer features prominently in her otherwise impeccable CV.

Take My Wife

UK · ITV (GRANADA) · SITCOM

6 × 30 mins · colour

17 Jan–7 Mar 1979 · Wed 8.30pm

MAIN CAST

Harvey Hall	Duggie Brown
Maurice Watkins	Victor Spinetti
Josie Hall	Elisabeth Sladen
Mabel Norrington	Joan Benham
Doreen Underhill	Toni Palmer

CREDITS

writer Anthony Couch · director Gordon Flemyng · producer John G Temple

Having made his name in **The Comedians**, Duggie Brown acted out a true-to-life role in this Granada series, appearing as a northern club comedian, Harvey Hall, the type of standup comic wont to cracking spousal jokes beginning with the three lines in the series' title. Said wife, Josie, from elevated stock, understood Harvey but not his choice of profession, while her upper-crust mother (cue mother-in-law jokes by the bucketful) failed to understand anything at all about Harvey. Victor Spinetti played Maurice Watkins, Harvey's London-based booking-agent-cum-fellow-schemer, who was forever promising his comedian that fame was just around the corner.

If nothing else, the series *looked* good: Elisabeth Sladen had latterly been turning heads in time-travelling circles as Sarah Jane Smith in *Doctor Who*, while one episode featured the pin-up model Fiona Richmond as a stripper.

Take Two Eggs

UK · BBC · SKETCH

1 × 15 mins · b/w

16 May 1939 · Tue 3pm

MAIN CAST
Richard Hearne
Lily Palmer
George Nelson

CREDITS
writer Richard Hearne · *producer* Reginald Smith

A 15-minute TV comedy slot for the pre-**Mr Pastry** Richard Hearne, assisted once more by Lily Palmer and George Nelson. (See also **Bath H&C, Moving Furniture** and **S-s-s-h! The Wife!**) The sketch was performed again at 9pm the same day. It had also been presented just over one year previously, during *Half-An-Hour*.

Taking The Floor

UK · BBC (ALOMO PRODUCTIONS) · SITCOM

6 × 30 mins · colour

4 Mar–15 Apr 1991 · BBC1 Mon 8.30pm

MAIN CAST
Brian Wheeler · · · · · · · · · · · Matthew Cottle
Karen Tranter · · · · · · · · · · · Barbara Durkin
Mrs Wheeler · · · · · · · · · · · · · Janet Dale
Mr Wheeler · · · · · · · · · · · Timothy Kightley
Colin Wheeler · · · · · · · · · · · · Dean Gatiss
Mrs Tranter · · · · · · · · · · · · Claire Nielson
Mr Tranter · · · · · · · · · Christopher Godwin

CREDITS
creator Paul Makin · *writers* Paul Makin (3), Geoff Rowley (3) · *executive producers* Allan McKeown, Michael Pilsworth · *director/producer* Derrick Goodwin

The sequinned-and-satin world of ballroom dancing was the setting for this Midlands-based sitcom that followed a talented and ambitious dancer, Brian Wheeler, as he strove to make good as a professional and claw his

way out of mediocrity. The central theme, however, was the mismatching of Brian with the equally talented but insufferably snooty Karen, his dancing partner. Underneath their fixed grins they grimaced at one another, and the cultural clash also spread to the couple's respective parents.

The BBC's enduring ballroom dance series *Come Dancing* (on air since 29 September 1950) had recently enjoyed a surge in popularity owing to the show's modernisation and the dance styles it featured, demonstrating the public's lasting (if peculiar) fascination with the pastime. Lead actors Matthew Cottle and Barbara Durkin made their dance scenes look authentic and were clearly able to put one foot in front of the other without appearing foolish, and the theme of the two opposites having to stay together for the sake of their act was a good one, but the series failed to be renewed for a second season and quickstepped into sitcom history.

The Tale Of Timothy Bagshott

UK · BBC · CHILDREN'S SITCOM

1 × 50 mins · colour

16 Nov 1975 · BBC1 Sun 5.05pm

MAIN CAST
Timothy Bagshott · · · · · · · · · · · Paul Maurel
Auntie Anne · · · · · · · · · Margo Cunningham
Arnold Oates · · · · · · · · · · · · · Harry Jones
Maisie Ooster · · · · · · · · · · · · Fanny Carby
Audrey Bagshott · · · · · · · · · · · Toni Palmer
Jim Bagshott · · · · · · · · · · · · · Bill McGuirk
Mr Korn · · · · · · · · · · · · · · · · · Tim Barrett

CREDITS
writer Fay Weldon · *director* John Bruce · *producer* Frank Hatherley

A one-off children's comedy by Fay Weldon, the novelist and playwright perhaps best known for *The Lives And Loves Of A She Devil* (and, incidentally, from her time as an advertising agency writer, for the slogan 'Go to work on an egg').

When millionaire property developer Jim Bagshott is jailed for fraud his rather posh son Timothy has to go and live with relatives in a council flat on the 21st floor of the decrepit and crumbling Bagshott Towers, a shabby block built by his father's company.

Tales From A Long Room   1

UK · BBC · MONOLOGUE

2 × 15 mins · colour

22 May & 29 May 1980 · BBC2 Thu 10.30pm

MAIN CAST
'The Brigadier' · · · · · · · · · · · · Robin Bailey

CREDITS
writer Peter Tinniswood · *director* Bob Blagden · *producer* Tony Laryea

Peter Tinniswood's best-selling books of marvellous cricketing stories were first

brought to TV with Robin Bailey cast as 'The Brigadier', delivering illustrated lectures with the assistance of a magic lantern.

The two stories here were 'Incident At Frome', dealing with Himmelweit, the only German to play first-class county cricket, and 'The Congo Affair', about the MCC's only tour of the Belgian Congo.

The work has also appeared on BBC Radio 4 – five more stories were read by Robin Bailey from 24 to 28 August 1981, and the series *Tales From The Brigadier* followed a decade later (28 December 1992 to 1 January 1993), read by Richard Wilson. Tinniswood's books on the subject include *The Brigadier In Season, The Brigadier's Brief Lives, The Brigadier's Tour* and *Tales From Witney Scrotum.*

Tales From A Long Room   2

UK · C4 (YORKSHIRE) · MONOLOGUE

13 × 15 mins · colour

Series One (3) 13 Apr–27 Apr 1985 · Sat 8pm
Series Two (10) 8 June–10 Aug 1985 · Sat 8pm

MAIN CAST
'The Brigadier' · · · · · · · · · · · · Robin Bailey

CREDITS
writer Peter Tinniswood · *producer* Vernon Lawrence

Robin Bailey returned as 'The Brigadier' in these 13 instalments made by Yorkshire TV and screened by C4. Bailey was perfectly cast as the hidebound cricketing old boy from the village of Witney Scrotum, and this was, once again, an atmospheric and classy production.

Tales From The Lazy Acre

UK · BBC · SITCOMS

7 × 30 mins · colour

10 Apr–29 May 1972 · BBC1
Mon mostly 10.10pm

MAIN CAST
various roles · · · · · · · · · · · · · Milo O'Shea
Dead Man · · · · · · · · · · · · · · · · David Kelly

CREDITS
writer Hugh Leonard · *producers* James Gilbert (5), James Gilbert/David Croft (2)

More Irish whimsy for comedy actor Milo O'Shea and his **Me Mammy** writer Hugh Leonard. The pair had employed Irish urban myths as the basis for some episodes of that earlier series and here they went one better, depicting separate, unconnected stories each week. David Kelly appeared throughout as Dead Man, the storyteller who introduced each of the tales, and O'Shea took the lead role in each, creating a variety of fascinating characters. The seven programmes were:

The Pick-Pocketer   10 APR

O'Shea as Stevie Fortune.

Judgement Day
17 APR

O'Shea as Judge Devoy. Also featuring Sheila Brennan as Dympna.

Stone Cold Sober
24 APR

O'Shea as Charlie Mahood.

The Bitter Pill
1 MAY

O'Shea again as Stevie Fortune.

The Last Great Pint-Drinking Tournament
8 MAY

O'Shea as Mossy Noonan. Also featuring Liam Redmond and Yootha Joyce.

The Culchie
22 MAY

O'Shea as John Joe Quill.

The Travelling Woman
29 MAY

O'Shea as Mr Rushe. Also featuring Anna Manahan.

Tales From The Poop Deck

UK · ITV (TALKBACK PRODUCTIONS FOR CENTRAL) · CHILDREN'S SITCOM

6 × 25 mins · colour

7 Apr–12 May 1992 · Tue mostly 4.10pm

MAIN CAST

Connie Blackheart · · · · Helen Atkinson Wood
Captain Henry Stallion · · · Nicholas Pritchard
Admiral Dennis De'Ath · · · · · · · Charles Gray
Petty Officer Coleridge · · · · · · · Paul Shearer
Scurvy · · · · · · · · · · · · · · · · Dudley Sutton
Lt Parkinson · · · · · · · · · · · · Colin McFarlane
Honeywell · · · · · · · · · · · · · · · Mike Grady
Albert · · · · · · · · · · · · · · · · · Bunny Reed
narrator · · · · · · · · · · · · · · Griff Rhys Jones

CREDITS

writers Lenny Barker/Vicki Stepney · director John Birkin · executive producers Peter Fincham, Lewis Rudd · producers Adrian Bate/Chris Langham

A sporadically funny children's comedy showcasing the 17th-century treasure-laden adventures of Connie Blackheart, a female pirate. She was the scourge of the King's navy, and especially the mad Admiral De'Ath, as she sailed the seven seas aboard her decrepit *Sea Cow*. Although her boat and crew were run down, she was not – with her flame-red hair, make-up, earrings and finger rings, Blackheart cut a glamorous figure, falling in love with Captain Stallion and marrying him in the final episode.

The series had some novel ideas: De'Ath employed a suave black officer, Parkinson, as his assistant, and episodes were prone to left-field plot diversions, typified when an American cowboy with gun-totin' pantomime

horse suddenly appeared on board the *Sea Cow*. Also, pleasingly, little attempt was made to disguise the fact that the programmes were taped in a studio, and that the galleons were nothing more than model boats sailing on the studio tank.

As well as its fine cast, the series was stamped by the involvement of a high degree of comic talent. TalkBack Productions – Griff Rhys Jones and Mel Smith's company – made it for Central TV; Jones narrated the stories and Smith made a cameo appearance in the last episode; also, their former *Not The Nine O'Clock News* friend Chris Langham appeared, and co-produced the series too. Others seen briefly in *Tales From The Poop Deck* were Ken Campbell and John Wells, while its director – John Birkin – went on to work on such high-flying BBC shows as *Harry Enfield's Television Programme*, *The Thin Blue Line*, *The Fast Show* and *Chef!*

Tales Of Para Handy

see *Para Handy*

Tales Of The Rodent Sherlock Holmes

UK · BBC · CHILDREN'S SITCOM

7 × 25 mins · colour

3 Mar–14 Apr 1990 · BBC1 Sat 8.15am

MAIN CAST

Sherlock Holmes ·
· · · · · · · · · · · · Roland Rat (David Claridge)

CREDITS

writers Dominic MacDonald/David Claridge · producer Steve Haggard

A puppet created and operated by David Claridge, Roland Rat appeared in a great many ITV and BBC children's shows over several years from the mid-1980s, playing host to pop guests, interviewing stars, running game-shows and generally being a wisecracking smartie-pants, usually in the company of his less-sharp sidekick, Kevin the Gerbil. The rodent soared to fame when, given his own morning slot by ITV's ailing breakfast strand TV-am, he was deemed responsible for the sharp rise in ratings that saved the company ship from sinking, albeit temporarily.

Although Roland's hundreds of TV exploits were 'humorous', *Tales Of The Rodent Sherlock Holmes* was an out-and-out comedy series – with dramatic pretensions, no less – hence its inclusion here. The continuing adventure permitted room for guest stars to turn up each week, namely Barbara Windsor, Rodney Bewes, Mollie Sugden, Christopher Ryan, Bernard Bresslaw, Roy Sampson and Liz Smith.

Talk About London

see BENTINE, Michael

Tall, Dark And Handsome

UK · C4 (WINNING FORMAT) · SITCOM

1 × 60 mins · colour

29 Dec 1992 · Tue 11.50pm

MAIN CAST

Blacka and Bello

CREDITS

writers not known · executive producer Malcolm Frederick · producer Phil Bishop

Following their success in the earlier *Blouse And Skirt*, Jamaica's number one comedy double-act Blacka and Bello returned to host their own hour-long show.

Tall Stories

UK · BBC · SKETCH

6 × 20 mins · colour

20 Nov 1971–1 Jan 1972 · BBC2 Sat around 10.30pm

MAIN CAST

Michael Hordern
Richard Briers

CREDITS

writers Lawrence Durrell (2), Robert Graves (2), A D Wintle/Robert Graves (1), A J Alan (2) · director Michael Hart · producer Rosemary Hill

A series of two-hander sketches, with Michael Hordern and Richard Briers acting out humorous episodes from a number of writers. These were simple – usually single-set – interpretations of different 'tall stories', performed with great aplomb.

Tandoori Nights

UK · C4 (PICTURE PALACE/*ANGEL FILMS) · SITCOM

12 × 30 mins · colour

*Series One (6) 4 July–8 Aug 1985 · Thu 9pm
Series Two (6) 9 Oct–13 Nov 1987 · Fri 9pm

MAIN CAST

Jimmy Sharma · · · · · · · · · · · · Saeed Jaffrey
Alaudin · · · · · · · · · · · · · · · · · Tariq Yunus
Asha · Rita Wolf
Delia · · · · · · · · · · · · · · · · Angela Browne
Gran · · · · · · · · · · · · · · · · · · Zohra Segal
Bubbly · · · · · · · · · · · · · · · · · Shelley King
Noor · · · · · · · · · · · · · · · · Andrew Johnson
Fazloo · · · · · · · · · · Topan Ghosh (series 1);
· · · · · · · · · · · · · · Kumall Grewall (series 2)
Gazloo · · · · · · · · · · · · · · · · · · Roly Lamas
Rashid · · · · · · · · · · · · · · · · Badi Uzzaman
Hansa Mia · · · · · · · · · · · Ishaq Bux (series 2)

CREDITS

writers Farrukh Dhondy (6), Meera Syal (2), H O Nazareth (2), Philip Martin (1), Barry Simner (1) · directors Jon Amiel (6), Christopher Menaul (2), Peter Ormrod (2), Pedr James (2) · executive *producer* Peter Ansorge (series 1) · *producer* Malcolm Craddock

One of Farrukh Dhondy's last engagements before being appointed Commissioning Editor of Multicultural Programmes at C4 was to write a new sitcom about a pair of rival Indian restaurants in London. One of the first things he did when he got the job was to axe his current series **No Problem!** so that he wouldn't have two shows running simultaneously. Then, after the first series, to avoid any accusation of self-promotion, Dhondy handed over the writing of his creation to other people.

The new production arrived on screen in July 1985. Dhondy had deliberated over several possible titles, *Tandoori Is The Night*, *Chappati's Over* and *Paperback Raita* all being in the melting pot before *Tandoori Nights* was settled upon. It told the story of Jimmy Sharma, involved the restaurant trade for many a year since opening his first establishment in Brick Lane, in the East End of London. Now he has worked his way up to owning the opulent dining-room the Jewel In The Crown, successful for more than ten years. Then Rashid, a discontented Bengali waiter, leaves his employ and opens a rival restaurant, The Far Pavilions, right across the road, its flock wallpaper proving that his venue is a little less exclusive. (Both *The Jewel In The Crown* and *The Far Pavilions* were titles of Raj stories repopularised on TV, by ITV and C4 respectively, in January 1984.)

Following *No Problem!*, *Tandoori Nights* was only the second Asian sitcom to appear on British TV, but apart from the ethnicity of the characters there was little difference between it and a 'white' series, the comedy situations typically revolving around the in-fighting between the rival restaurants and the problems among the staff and within Jimmy's family.

Jimmy Tarbuck

Born in Liverpool on 6 February 1940, Jimmy Tarbuck rose to fame as the mop-topped, gap-toothed comedian who, famously, had gone to the same school as John Lennon and likewise ascended to the top on the seemingly unstoppable wave of Liverpool talent that swept the UK on the coat-tails of the Beatles in 1963. Tarbuck was one of many TV comics to have served his apprenticeship as a Butlin's Redcoat before embarking upon a successful broadcasting career – this began with his TV debut in **Comedy Bandbox** on 19 October 1963 and then mushroomed following an appearance eight days later on

Val Parnell's Sunday Night At The London Palladium. So great was his success here that he went on to become the resident compere of ATV's famous variety series.

Tarbuck's act consists of a string of short gags, some old, some new, some (depending on the booking) bordering on blue, which he delivers in the chatty style of a drinking acquaintance from the pub. In recent years, though, he has concentrated less on standup comedy and instead utilised his status as a TV personality to host a number of diverse variety shows: *Live From Her Majesty's* (from 16 January 1983) and its successors *Live From The Piccadilly* · (from 28 September 1986) and *Live From The Palladium* (from 5 April 1987). He has also presented quiz-shows, including the long-running *Winner Takes All* (1975–87), hosted LWT's short-lived (one series, from 16 April 1988) Saturday-night entertainment/chat-show *After Ten With Tarbuck*, and a single late-night ITV chat and entertainment show in 1994, *Tarbuck Late*, that led to a series from 11 March 1995.

See also *To Lucifer – A Son*, *Laughs From Her Majesty's* and *Laughs From The Palladium*.

It's Tarbuck!   1

UK · ITV (ATV) · STANDUP/SKETCH

6 × 30 mins · b/w

16 Dec 1964–27 Jan 1965 · Wed 9.10pm

MAIN CAST
Jimmy Tarbuck
Amanda Barrie
Ronnie Corbett
Henry McGee
Bob Todd

CREDITS
writers Austin Steele, George Martin, Ron McDonnell · *producer* Jon Scoffield

Launched little more than a year after his Palladium TV debut, *It's Tarbuck* was the Liverpool comic's first own-series. The title was twice revived, in 1970 and again in 1973, with the same concept: a mixture of standup and sketch material contributed by a team of writers, with a regular supporting cast and guest stars.

Tarbuck At The Prince Of Wales

UK · ITV (ATV) · STANDUP/SKETCH

5 × 60 mins · b/w

24 Apr–5 June 1966 · Sun 8.25pm

MAIN CAST
Jimmy Tarbuck

CREDITS
writer Bryan Blackburn · *producer* Dicky Leeman

Five programmes that ran in off-weeks of the regular *London Palladium Show*, which Tarbuck compered. These new shows were

screened live from the Prince Of Wales Theatre in London, and as well as compering the Liverpool comic performed his own act. Woody Allen appeared as a guest in the 22 May edition.

Tarbuck's Back

UK · ITV (ATV) · STANDUP/SKETCH

6 × 30 mins · b/w

*9 Apr–1 May 1968 · Wed 7pm; 30 Aug 1969 · Sat 7pm

MAIN CAST
Jimmy Tarbuck
Audrey Jeans

CREDITS
writer Bryan Blackburn · *additional material* Ron McDonnell · *producer* Colin Clews

A new series of standup routines, sketches, visiting guest comedians and pop groups, the only regular support coming from comic-actress Audrey Jeans.

*Note. Six programmes were made but only five were screened in the original run; the sixth was transmitted as part of a repeat run a year later.

The Jimmy Tarbuck Show   1

UK · BBC · STANDUP

1 × 45 mins colour

21 July 1968 · BBC2 Sun 8.15pm

MAIN CAST
Jimmy Tarbuck
Ronnie Corbett
Rita Webb
Bryan Blackburn

CREDITS
writer Bryan Blackburn · *additional material* Ron McDonnell · *producer* Kenneth Carter

Presented under BBC2's *Show Of The Week* banner.

The Jimmy Tarbuck Show   2

UK · ITV (ATV) · STANDUP/SKETCH

6 × 30 mins · b/w

7 Nov–12 Dec 1968 · Thu mostly 8pm

MAIN CAST
Jimmy Tarbuck

CREDITS
writer Bryan Blackburn · *additional material* Ron McDonnell · *producer* Colin Clews

Another series, with regular guests.

Tarbuck's Luck

UK · BBC · STANDUP/SKETCH

7 editions (6 × 45 mins · 1 × 50 mins) · colour

Special (50 mins) 29 May 1970 · BBC1 Fri 8pm

One series (6 × 45 mins) 1 Apr–13 May 1972 · BBC1 Sat around 8.45pm

MAIN CAST
Jimmy Tarbuck

CREDITS
writers Mike Craig/Lawrie Kinsley (7), Ron McDonnell (6) · *additional material* Peter Vincent/David Nobbs (3), David Nobbs (1), Austin Steele/Bob Hedley (1) · *producers* Freddie Carpenter/Peter Whitmore (special), Freddie Carpenter/James Moir (series)

The gimmick with this series was to have women as the star's special guests – this being Tarbuck's 'luck'. The female comedic talent that appeared included Joan Sims, June Whitfield, Patricia Hayes, Yootha Joyce, Sheila Steafel, Sheila Bernette, Josephine Tewson and Miriam Karlin.

It's Tarbuck! 2

UK · ITV (ATV) · STANDUP/SKETCH

14 × 30 mins · colour

Series One (7) 12 Dec 1970–23 Jan 1971 · Sat mostly 7.15pm

Series Two (7) 27 Mar–8 May 1973 · Tue mostly 7.05pm

MAIN CAST
Jimmy Tarbuck
Kenny Lynch
Josephine Tewson (series 2)
Frank Williams (series 2)

CREDITS
series 1 writers Ron McDonnell (7), Lawrie Kinsley (7), Mike Craig (6), David McKellar (3), Bryan Blackburn (3); *series 2 writers* Ron McDonnell (7), Lawrie Kinsley (7), Mike Craig (7), Bryan Blackburn (7), Wally Malston (5), Alec Gerrard (2) · *producer* Albert Locke

Reviving the title of his first series, these 14 programmes featured the usual blend of standup routines and sketches.

The Tarbuck Follies

UK · BBC · STANDUP/SKETCH

1 × 45 mins · colour

1 Jan 1973 · BBC1 Mon 8.30pm

MAIN CAST
Jimmy Tarbuck
Clodagh Rodgers
Liz Fraser
Valerie Leon
Daphne Oxenford

CREDITS
writers Eric Davidson, Bryan Blackburn, Bill Solly · *producer* Michael Hurll

Continuing the *Tarbuck's Luck* format of pairing Tarbuck with women, this one-off was set in Tarby's Theatre Club, a modern music-hall, with the comedian as host of a New Year's burlesque show. (Consequently, the humour was broader and more traditional than usual.) The singer Clodagh Rodgers also joined in the comedy routines.

Tell Tarby

UK · ITV (ATV) · STANDUP/SKETCH

6 × 30 mins · colour

29 Oct–3 Dec 1973 · mostly Mon 8.30pm

MAIN CAST
Jimmy Tarbuck
Lynda Bellingham
Kenny Lynch
Hugh Paddick
Josephine Tewson
Stanley Unwin
Frank Williams

CREDITS
writers Dick Hills, Mike Craig, Lawrie Kinsley, Ron McDonnell · *director/producer* Colin Clews

A series in which Tarbuck and his regulars turned the spotlight on to six topics of the day: sex, the NHS, the old days, the weather, TV and hobbies.

The Jimmy Tarbuck Show 3

UK · ITV (ATV) · STANDUP/SKETCH

12 × 30 mins · colour

Series One (6) 27 June–30 July 1974 · mostly Tue 7pm

Series Two (6) 15 Jan–19 Feb 1975 · Wed 9.30pm

MAIN CAST
Jimmy Tarbuck
Hugh Paddick
Norman Chappell
Dilys Watling (series 1)
Lesley Goldie (series 1)
Dilys Laye (series 2)

CREDITS
writers Dick Hills, Mike Craig, Lawrie Kinsley, Ron McDonnell, Roy Tuvey, Maurice Sellar · *director/producer* Alan Tarrant

Jimmy, his series regulars and weekly guests in more themed sketches about life.

Tarbuck – And All That!

UK · ITV (ATV) · STANDUP/SKETCH

5 × 30 mins · colour

26 Apr–24 May 1975 · Sat 10pm

MAIN CAST
Jimmy Tarbuck
Graham Stark
Sheila Steafel
Alison Steadman
Josephine Tewson

CREDITS
writer Eddie Braben · *director/producer* Colin Clews

Five half-hour programmes for Tarbuck scripted by Morecambe and Wise writer Eddie Braben. Young actress Alison Steadman, also born in Liverpool, made one of her first TV appearances here (see also *The Wackers*).

Tarby And Friends

UK · ITV (LWT) · STANDUP/SKETCH

13 editions (11 × 45 mins · 1 × 55 mins · 1 × 60 mins) · colour

Series One (4 × 45 mins · 1 × 55 mins · 1 × 60 mins) 24 Nov–29 Dec 1984 · Sat mostly 7pm

Series Two (7 × 45 mins) 5 Apr–17 May 1986 · Sat 8.30pm

MAIN CAST
Jimmy Tarbuck

CREDITS
writers Wally Malston, Garry Chambers, Colin Edmonds, Alan Wightman, Russel Lane · *director* Alasdair Macmillan · *producer* David Bell

Two series in which the chirpy Scouser entertained at the mike and played host to a succession of humorous and/or melodious 'friends' from 'around the world'. Among the global comics flown into London at great expense by LWT were Russ Abbot, Michael Barrymore, Stan Boardman, Frank Carson, Norman Collier, Jimmy Cricket, Bobby Davro, Les Dennis, Lenny Henry, Chic Murray and Roy Walker.

Note. A few hours before the 10 May 1986 edition of this series, Everton played Liverpool in the FA Cup Final. As a Liverpudlian, Jimmy Tarbuck was a natural host of sections of ITV's coverage of the event, meeting players past and present, as well as other Scouse personalities, in special *Tarby And Friends* sequences. The premise was deemed good enough to be revived a year later, when Coventry played Tottenham on 16 May 1987.

An Audience With Jimmy Tarbuck

UK · ITV (LWT) · STANDUP

1 × 60 mins · colour

22 Oct 1994 · Sat 9pm

MAIN CAST
Jimmy Tarbuck

CREDITS
director Ian Hamilton · *producer* Patricia McGowan

Another of LWT's occasional *An Audience With …* series, Tarbuck entertaining famous friends from the worlds of show business and sport, all of whom featured extensively in camera cutaways.

Taxi

USA · ABC THEN NBC (JOHN CHARLES WALTERS PRODUCTIONS/PARAMOUNT) · SITCOM

113 episodes (112 × 30 mins · 1 × 60 mins) · colour

US dates: 12 Sep 1978–15 June 1983

*UK dates: 17 Apr 1980–23 Dec 1985 (110 × 30 mins) BBC1 Thu 8.05pm then various dates and times

MAIN CAST

Alex Reiger (sometimes Rieger) · · · · · · · · · ·
· Judd Hirsch
Louie De Palma · · · · · · · · · · · · Danny DeVito
Tony Banta · · · · · · · · · · · · · · · · Tony Danza
Elaine O'Connor Nardo · · · · · · Marilu Henner
Latka Gravas · · · · · · · · · · · · · Andy Kaufman
Bobby Wheeler · · · · Jeff Conaway (1978–81)
John Burns · · · · · · Randall Carver (1978–79)
'Reverend' Jim 'Iggy' Ignatowski
(James Caldwell) · · · · · · · · Christopher Lloyd
· (1979–83)
Simka Dahblitz Gravas · · · · · · · · Carol Kane
· (1982–83)

OTHER APPEARANCES

Jeff Bennett · · · · · · · · · · · · · J Alan Thomas
Zena Sherman · · · · · · · · · · · Rhea Perlman

CREDITS

creators James L Brooks, Stan Daniels, David
Davis, Ed Weinberger · writers Glen Charles/Les
Charles (17), Barry Kemp (14), Ken Estin (12),
Ken Estin/Sam Simon (12), Ken Estin/
Sam Simon/Al Aidekman (1), Sam Simon (5),
David Lloyd (12), Ian Praiser/Howard Gewirtz (10),
Earl Pomerantz (9) and others (21) · directors
James Burrows (76), Noam Pitlik (11), Michael
Zinberg (6), Richard Sakai (4), Danny DeVito (3),
Michael Lessac (3), Stan Daniels (3), Harvey Miller
(2), Howard Storm (2), Jeff Chambers (1), Joan
Darling (1), Will MacKenzie (1), Ed Weinberger (1) ·
executive producers James L Brooks, Stan Daniels,
Ed Weinberger (all), David Davis (1978–79) ·
producers Glen Charles/Les Charles (1978–81),
Ken Estin, Howard Gewirtz, Ian Praiser (1981–82),
Ken Estin, Richard Sakai, Sam Simon (1981–82)

When *The Mary Tyler Moore Show*
finished, its principal creative axis –
producers Brooks, Daniels, Davis and
Weinberger – contemplated their next move,
wondering how they could follow such a
fantastic hit. It transpired that they didn't
only follow it, they *topped* it, with *Taxi*, a
series that set a new standard for ensemble
comedy.

It all began when Brooks, still with MTM
Enterprises, began toying with the idea of a
sitcom about cabbies; staff writer Jerry Belson
suggested that the company pay for the TV
option on an article published in the 22
September 1975 issue of *New York Magazine*:
'Night Shifting For The Hip Fleet', by Mark
Jacobson, all about the disparate people who
work for a cab company. (Jacobson later
negotiated a per-episode fee, and co-scripted a
two-parter, 'Shut It Down'.) Belson then left to
pursue a career as a movie writer and Brooks
and some of his colleagues quit MTM to form
their own company. MTM was aghast at
the sudden departure of its major talent but
showed good faith by allowing the team to
buy the rights to the *New York Magazine*
article for the same fee that the company had
paid, about $500. The newly incorporated
John Charles Walters Company then formed a
production unit at Paramount and went about
the creation of *Taxi*.

The series' core character, Alex Reiger, was
written with the actor Judd Hirsch in mind,
but it took the producers' powers of
persuasion to make him accept the role,
following his previous, unsuccessful TV lead
in the 1976–77 police drama *Delvecchio*. The
rest of the cast came from auditions: Marilu
Henner impressed the producers enough to
rewrite her character to specifically suit her
style, and, likewise, Tony Danza's image
forced the writers to rethink the character
of Tony Banta, who had originally been
perceived as older.

The premise of *Taxi*, like all good ideas,
was a simple one: it charted the lives and
relationships of a bunch of New York taxi
drivers, stationed at a depot in Manhattan,
the Sunshine Cab Company. Most of the
cabbies considered themselves to be 'passing
through' the job, treading water while waiting
for their real careers to resume. Alex, the elder
statesman, was the exception. A divorcee,
unlucky in relationships, he was the longest-
serving cabbie; ambition had all but deserted
him and he seemed resigned to his dead-end
job for the rest of his life. Another recent
divorcee was Elaine: she had taken the job as
a cabbie to earn enough money to open her
own art gallery. Elaine and Alex duly formed
the central hub of the show, almost
representing surrogate mother–father figures
for the more unstable other drivers. They
were also attracted to one another and
consummated their relationship in one
episode before returning to the status quo,
fearing the romance would spoil their
friendship.

The others drivers were Tony Banta, an
unsuccessful boxer who still harboured
dreams of being a world champion; Bobby
Wheeler, a struggling actor who aspired to
the big time and who, eventually, was
persuaded by his colleagues to return to
Hollywood. And then there was Latka, a
foreign cabbie who spoke a strangulated form
of English and employed a totally baffling
logic: he and his wife Simka – who both
hailed from a small but unnamed East
European homeland – conversed in a strange,
mythical, guttural gobbledygook. Latka was
not in the writers' original premise: the part
was created after the producers saw the
standup comedian Andy Kaufman perform at
the Comedy Store in New York. His act was to
effect the speech and mannerisms of a baffled
foreigner, a man so hapless that audiences felt
excruciatingly embarrassed for him until, at
the end, he turned the tables and spectators
realised they had been duped. (Space is too
short here to go in to the full, amazing story
of the weird but talented Kaufman, who died
in strange circumstances in 1984.) Another
character added to the original premise was
the Reverend Jim, who made such an impact
when appearing in a first-season episode that

he was brought back as a regular (taking the
place of another character, John Burns, who
wasn't working out). Jim was permanently
spaced-out, owing to his 1960s hippy lifestyle.
The actor Christopher Lloyd was marvellous
as the mad, raving, yet well-meaning Jim and
he soon became an audience favourite.

Working against the camaraderie of the
cab drivers was their awful boss, the mean
and nasty Louie De Palma, brilliantly played
by Danny DeVito. The diminutive Louie, who
ran his charges with the relish of a prison
warder, was originally conceived as a minor
role but DeVito's characterisation took the
part to the heights and the writers responded
by promoting him in the storylines. DeVito
was relentless in his refusal to soften the
character, and even when he started a
romance with Zena (played by the actor's
real-life girlfriend and later wife, Rhea
Perlman) he maintained his trademark
meanness. Despite this, constant exposure to
Louie encouraged audiences to warm to him –
he became the typical character whom people
'love to hate'.

Plots involved the ups and downs of the
cabbies' lives and their constant conflicts with
Louie, and the scripts were of an exceedingly
fine quality – the realistic blend of
conversation and situation, formulated on
The Mary Tyler Moore Show, was again
utilised triumphantly. Once more, most of the
work colleagues came from flawed family
situations but banded together as a surrogate
family. Even Louie fitted into this scenario:
an unpopular person, yes, but still one of
the family. While the series' themes were
traditional – fellowship, colleagues united
against adversity, unfulfilled ambitions
and unrealised romances – its style was
revolutionary. After four wildly successful
seasons, though, ABC considered that the
show had seen better days and decided not
to renew its option. But the new head of
programming at rival network NBC was
Grant Tinker – formerly with MTM
Enterprises – and, in a pleasingly
symmetrical move, he picked up the series
for its last season.

The creative team behind *Taxi* certainly
left a hard act to follow; some commentators
thinking it impossible for them to create such
a winning scenario for a third time. They
were wrong. The year that *Taxi* ended the
team had another series in development, one
destined to become bigger than both *The
Mary Tyler Moore Show* and *Taxi* – **Cheers**.

*Note. Less than two years after BBC1
screened its final *Taxi*, the series switched to
ITV (not all regions). A total of 52 episodes,
beginning with the pilot, were screened in the
London area from 17 August 1987 to 21
September 1988, all in post-midnight slots.

Tea At The Ritz

UK · ITV (GRANADA) · SITCOM

1 × 30 mins · b/w

6 June 1963 · Thu 7.30pm

MAIN CAST

George Podmore ······ Norman Rossington
Arnold Barnes ··········· Ronnie Stevens
Rene Barnes ············· Ann Lancaster
Mrs Gutter ················ Rita Webb

CREDITS

writers Barry Took/Peter Miller/James Kelly ·
director Graeme McDonald · producer Peter Eton

A single-episode comedy, one of four written by **Bootsie And Snudge** authors Took, Miller and Kelly and screened by Granada in a special mid-1963 season titled *Comedy Four*.

Tea At The Ritz starred Norman Rossington as George Podmore, a salesman who takes over the running of a run-down cinema, the Ritz, so old that it still serves tea to its customers in the intermission. Podmore determines to do away with the tradition and, moreover, to begin screening sex films.

Teach Yourself Gibberish

UK · ITV (GRANADA) · CHILDREN'S SKETCH

6 × 30 mins · colour

17 Sep–22 Oct 1982 · Fri 5.15pm

MAIN CAST

Alberto y Los Trios Paranoias (C P Lee, Jimmy Hibbert, Bruce Mitchell, Simon White, Captain Mog, John Peter-Scott)
John Branwell
Annie Hulley

CREDITS

writer C P Lee · director Eugene Ferguson · producer Diana Bramwell

An insane collection of sketches – usually on a given weekly theme – that starred the musical mirth-makers Alberto y Los Trios Paranoias (a very popular gigging band of the time) and was written by one of their number.

Tears Before Bedtime

UK · BBC · SITCOM

7 × 30 mins · colour

29 Mar–10 May 1983 · BBC1 Tue 8.30pm

MAIN CAST

Anne Dickens ·········· Geraldine McEwan
Geoffrey Dickens ········ Francis Matthews

CREDITS

writer Richard Waring · director/producer Harold Snoad

Another variation of domestic disharmony from writer Richard Waring – this time depicting a pair of forty-something parents who decide they can no longer live with the cacophonous pop music, outlandish fashions and 'modern' behaviour of their offspring, aged 18, 19 and 20. They decide to move out, leaving their house to the children, and relocate in a tatty basement flat 70 miles away. But starting over, making new friends and finding new work is not so easy the second time around …

Despite the classy cast and old-firm dependency of writer Waring and producer Snoad, *Tears Before Bedtime* ran for just one series.

Ted On The Spot

UK · ITV (YORKSHIRE) · SKETCH

1 × 60 mins · colour

11 Apr 1979 · Wed 8pm

MAIN CAST

Ted Rogers
Kenneth Connor
Henry McGee
Janet Brown
Chris Emmett
Sydney Arnold
Len Marten
The Barron Knights
Diane Langton

CREDITS

not known

Ted Rogers had been a standup comic on stage and in TV variety for many years when, in 1978, Yorkshire Television invited him to host its game-show series *3-2-1*. National stardom followed, as did this one-hour special in which, with guests, Rogers looked at politics, bureaucracy and British society.

See also *… And So To Ted*.

The Ted Ray Show

see RAY, Ted

The Telegoons

see MILLIGAN, Spike

The Telephone Call

UK · BBC · SITCOM

1 × 30 mins · b/w

19 Jan 1962 · Fri 8.45pm

MAIN CAST

Lionel Baxter ··············· Peter Jones
Sandra Baxter ············· June Whitfield
Mr Croxley ············· Richard Caldicot
Mr Gore-Willoughby MP ······· Derek Bond
BBC producer ·············· Harold Lang

CREDITS

writers Ray Galton/Alan Simpson · producer James Gilbert

Taking time out from **The Rag Trade**, Peter Jones starred in this Galton and Simpson playlet for *Comedy Playhouse*. He was cast as Lionel Baxter, a man who is so worried about the deteriorating world situation that he decides to do something about it with the aid of his telephone.

Telethon Night Out

UK · ITV (LWT) · STANDUP

1 × 30 mins · colour

17 July 1992 · Fri 12.30am

MAIN CAST

Bradley Walsh
Gareth Hale
Norman Pace
Shane Richie
Brian Conley

CREDITS

directors Chris Fox, Simon Cochrane, Steven Wood · producer Ian Cross

A one-off half hour – listed in the press as *Comedy Night Out* – screened to raise the curtain on ITV's *Telethon '92*. The programme was recorded in the LWT staff bar a fortnight before broadcast, at an event staged to raise funds for the upcoming TV event. Chris Tarrant and Jeremy Beadle were on hand to encourage the donations, and musical entertainment was provided by the Nolans, Midge Ure, Status Quo and the comedian Brian Conley.

Television's Christmas Party

UK · BBC · SKETCH/STANDUP

4 editions (2 × 105 mins · 1 × 100 mins · 1 × 90 mins) · b/w

25 Dec 1951 · Tue 7.30pm (90 mins)
Television's Second Christmas Party
25 Dec 1952 · Thu 7.30pm (105 mins)
25 Dec 1953 · Fri 7.30pm (105 mins)
25 Dec 1954 · Fri 7.50pm (100 mins)

MAIN CAST

see below

CREDITS

producers Walton Anderson (show 1), Bryan Sears/Bill Lyon-Shaw (show 2), Bill Lyon-Shaw (shows 3 & 4)

These four entertainment extravaganzas united many of TV's most popular figures for a feast of seasonal fun and games. In this pre-video era, the performers had to forsake their Christmas Day evenings at home and broadcast the show live from the BBC's studio, whereas the advent of pre-recording allowed the show's successor, **Christmas Night With The Stars**, to feature recently made versions of popular series filmed on the series' particular sets.

The comic talent appearing in the four shows were Terry-Thomas (1951 & 53), Jewel and Warriss (1951), Norman Wisdom (1951–53), Ethel Revnell (1951 & 52), Arthur Askey (1952–4), Betty Driver (1952), Tommy Cooper (1952 & 54), John Slater (1952 & 53), Frankie Howerd (1952), Max Bygraves (1953), Fred Emney (1954), Bob Monkhouse and Denis Goodwin (1954), Harry Secombe (1954) and Wilfred Pickles (1954).

Teliffant

UK · BBC · CHILDREN'S SKETCH

16 × 25 mins · colour

2 Feb–6 July 1979 · BBC1 Fri mostly 3.20pm

MAIN CAST
Wynford Ellis Owen
Mici Plwm
Olwen Rees
Myfanwy Talog
Richard Jones

CREDITS
producer Bryn Richards

A Welsh-language children's sketch show originally transmitted only in Wales but then repeated in England for young Welsh speakers (the dates, above, reflect the networked broadcasts). *Teliffant* literally translates to 'a trunkful of fun and laughter'.

Tell It To The Judge

see KING, Dave

Tell It To The Marines

UK · ITV (JACK HYLTON TV PRODUCTIONS FOR ASSOCIATED-REDIFFUSION) · SITCOM

30 × 30 mins · b/w

23 Sep 1959–13 Apr 1960 · Wed mostly 7pm

MAIN CAST
L/S White · · · · · · · · · · · · · Alan White
Marine Cpl Surtees · · · · · · · · Ronald Hines
Dalrymple · · · · · · · · · · · Ian MacNaughton
Major Howard · · · · · · · · · · · · · Jack Allen
Lt Raleigh · · · · · · · · · · · · · Henry McGee
Commander Walters · · · · · · · · · · · Ian Colin
Petty Officer Woodward · · · · John Baskcomb
Whittle · · · · · · · · · · · · · · · Ian Whittaker
Tubby · · · · · · · · · · · · · · Norman Chappell

CREDITS
creator Ted Willis · *writers* Eric Paice/Malcolm A Hulke, Brad Ashton/Dick Vosburgh and others · *directors* Milo Lewis (29), Tig Roe (1)

Keen to repeat the great success that Granada was achieving with *The Army Game*, Jack Hylton – whose exclusive contract to provide A-R's entertainment programmes was soon to end – brought to the screen another 'service' sitcom, this one depicting the rivalry that had long existed between the Marines and the Royal Navy. Despite being created by Ted Willis (of *Dixon Of Dock Green* fame) and boasting a good cast and 'name' writers, with theme music by the then in-vogue jazz player Chris Barber, and a director, Milo Lewis, who had been closely associated with Granada's series, *Tell It To The Marines* was an unmitigated 30-week flop. Lewis's comment before the series began – 'Viewers should find it very amusing' – sounded more like an order than a wish, and audiences everywhere disobeyed, rapidly tiring of the endless squabbles that proliferated from the two sets of top-brass right down through the ranks.

Tell Tarby

see TARBUCK, Jimmy

Ten Minutes

UK · BBC · STANDUP

1 × 10 mins · b/w

19 May 1954 · Wed 5pm

MAIN CAST
Stan Stennett

CREDITS
writer Stan Stennett · *producer* Robert Tronson

An accomplished comic, singer, guitarist and trumpeter, Stan Stennett was born in Cardiff on 30 July 1925 and made his show-business debut in a comedy-harmonica combo, the Harmaniacs. His first big break came when he was appointed resident comic on the BBC Wales radio show *Welsh Rarebit*; he then became the resident comic on the BBC's long-running TV variety series *The Black And White Minstrel Show*.

This 1954 appearance on BBC TV was a solo ten-minute spot for the popular comedian. He later (in 1966) hosted a teenage talent contest series, *Stan At Ease*, for the West of England/Wales ITV franchise TWW, and compered Granada's travelling entertainment series *Road Show* in 1969. Neither series was networked.

See also *The Coal Hole Club* and *What A Performance*.

The 10%ers

UK · ITV (GRANT NAYLOR FOR CARLTON) · SITCOM

15 × 30 mins · colour

Pilot · 23 Feb 1993 · Tue 8.30pm
Series One (7) 18 Apr–6 June 1994 · Mon 9.30pm
Series Two (7) 9 July–3 Sep 1996 · Tue 8.30pm then 10.40pm

MAIN CAST
Dominic Eden · · · · · · · · · · · · · Clive Francis
Atin · · · · · · · · · · · · · · · · · Benedict Taylor
Tony · · · · · · · · · · · · · · · · · Colin Stinton
Joan · · · · · · · · · · · · · · · Elizabeth Bennett
Helen · · · · · Gabrielle Cowburn (not series 2)
Gloria · · · · · · · · · · · · · · Madge Ryan (pilot);
· · · · · · · · · · · · · Irene Sutcliffe (series 1 & 2)
Enid · · · · · · · · · · · Hilda Braid (series 1 & 2)
Vanessa · · · · · · · · · Emma Cunliffe (series 2)

CREDITS
creators Rob Grant/Doug Naylor · *writers* Rob Grant/Doug Naylor (pilot), Doug Naylor (6), Doug Naylor/Mark Herman (1), Doug Naylor/Paul Alexander/John W Reiger (1), Paul Alexander (1), John W Reiger (1), James Hendrie (2), Steve Punt (1), Michael J Prescott (1) · *executive producer* Doug Naylor (series 1 & 2) · *directors/producers* Rob Grant/Doug Naylor (pilot), Marcus Mortimer (series 1), Ed Bye (series 2)

A frantic office-based sitcom revolving around the staff of a top London talent agency, Eden Management. Eden's clients range from theatrical types to sexy TV weather girls via heavy-metal stars, novelists, playwrights, muscle-bound hunks, singers and Hollywood actors – in short, anyone in the entertainment world capable of earning a crust and giving the company one-tenth in commission. Dominic Eden (deliciously played by Clive Francis) is the head of the agency, in turns unctuous and panic-stricken, a man who recognises that while his company creams off its ten per cent, every penny is earned in sweat.

The humour was drawn from the fact that the assorted agents who make up Eden Management are as egotistical and corrupt as their clients. Those reporting to Dominic Eden include Tony, a sleazy and crass American; the self-absorbed Joan; the unscrupulous and insensitive but suave (and oddly named) Atin; and the politically correct Helen, who is keen to invest long-term in people who may not, in the long term, amount to much. (She left after the first series, and was replaced by Vanessa.) The company also employs a pair of elderly secretaries-cum-receptionists, matronly Gloria and dotty Enid. Jonathan Ross, Jim Bowen and Nicholas Parsons appeared as themselves in single episodes.

First seen as a pilot in Carlton's 1993 *Comedy Playhouse* series, *The 10%ers* was created by **Red Dwarf** maestros Grant and Naylor – the latter also wrote and executive-produced – giving the series a somewhat frantic and anarchic frame of reference that suggested an unlikely blend of *Fawlty Towers* and *Executive Stress*. The result was good in parts, with some occasionally excellent ideas, but the episodes quickly became predictable; indeed, the second series lost favour with ITV programming executives and was relegated to a later time slot mid-run.

Terry And Julian

see CLARY, Julian

Terry And June

see *Happy Ever After*

Terry Scott

UK · BBC · STANDUP

1 × 10 mins · b/w

21 Nov 1955 · Mon 5pm

MAIN CAST
Sammy · · · · · · · · · · · · · · · · · · · Terry Scott

CREDITS
writer Terry Scott · *producer* Dennis Robertson

Screened as part of the BBC's *For The Children* strand, this was a ten-minute presentation in which the up-and-coming Terry Scott introduced viewers to his tongue-tied, finger-twisting schoolboy character, Sammy. The comic employed variations of this character throughout his career.

For Scott's main TV work see *Great Scott – It's Maynard!*, *Happy Ever After*/*Terry And June*, *Hugh And I*, *Scott Free* and *Scott On …*

Terry-Thomas

UK · BBC · STANDUP

1 × 30 mins · b/w
20 July 1963 · Sat 9.55pm

MAIN CAST
Terry-Thomas
Sheree Winton
Donald Sutherland

CREDITS
deviser/writer Terry-Thomas · *producer* Johnnie Stewart

A rare early-1960s television appearance for Terry-Thomas who at this time was enjoying international film successes – he made this TV one-off shortly after finishing the Cinerama comedy *It's A Mad, Mad, Mad, Mad World* for director Stanley Kramer. The programme was alternatively titled *Terry-Thomas Says How Do You View?* (echoing the title of his acclaimed 1949–53 series *How Do You View?*) and featured Canadian actor Donald Sutherland, who was working in the UK at the time, as support.

Tribute was paid to Terry-Thomas in another excellent edition of *Heroes Of Comedy*, screened by C4 on 17 November 1995.

The Terry-Thomas Show

UK · ITV (ATV) · SKETCH/STANDUP

1 × 60 mins · b/w
29 Mar 1958 · Sat 10.30pm

MAIN CAST
Terry-Thomas
Eric Sykes
Lorrae Desmond

CREDITS
producer Hugh Rennie

A single special for the likeable gap-toothed 'cad', screened as part of the ITV weekly stage entertainment strand *Val Parnell's Saturday Spectacular*.

Tess And Jim

UK · BBC · STANDUP

3 × 60 mins · b/w
29 Sep–24 Nov 1956 · monthly Sat mostly 9pm

MAIN CAST
Tessie O'Shea
Jimmy Wheeler

Charlie Drake
Charles Hawtrey (show 3)

CREDITS
writers Sid Colin/Talbot Rothwell · *producer* George Inns

A short series – screened under the *Saturday Comedy Hour* banner – starring the musical comedians Tessie O'Shea and Jimmy Wheeler. Both were veterans: the larger-than-life banjo-playing O'Shea, who seemingly delighted in her descriptive nickname 'Two Ton', had been on stage since 1926; the fiddle-playing Wheeler had toured for 20 years with his father in the famous double-act Wheeler And Wilson before becoming a successful solo act. This series was screened soon after his own series, *The Jimmy Wheeler Show*.

See also *Christmas Cracker*.

Thank You Sir, Thank You Madam

UK · BBC · SITCOM

1 × 30 mins · b/w
31 May 1968 · BBC1 Fri 8.20pm

MAIN CAST
Wally	David Lodge
Ralph	Peter Glaze
Flipper	Gordon Rollings
Alec	John Grieve
Barmaid	Veronica Clifford

CREDITS
writers George Evans/Derek Collyer · *producer* James Gilbert

A *Comedy Playhouse* one-off centring on Wally, the leader of a quartet of cockney buskers. After a heated argument, Wally decides to prove his indispensability by leaving the troupe and establishing a rival band of street musicians.

Note. *Thank You Sir, Thank You Madam* – unlisted in the schedules – was screened as a last-minute replacement for the advertised *Comedy Playhouse* episode, *Current Affairs*, written by George Wadmore and Pat Dunlop, and starring Harold Goodwin, Arthur White, Kenneth Fortescue, Ken Parry and Robert Dorning. This was never screened.

That Beryl Marston … !

UK · ITV (SOUTHERN) · SITCOM

6 × 30 mins · colour
24 July–28 Aug 1981 · Fri 8.30pm

MAIN CAST
Georgie Bodley	Julia McKenzie
Gerry Bodley	Gareth Hunt
Harvey	Peter John
Phil	Jonathon Morris
Jane	Jayne Stevens
Alan	Lewis Fiander

CREDITS
writer Jan Butlin · *directors* Douglas Argent (4), Bryan Izzard (2) · *producer* Bryan Izzard

A single-series sitcom, the title of which owed to the existence of Beryl Marston, a notorious (fictional) Sussex sex-pot with whom principal character Gerry Bodley is having an affair. (Beryl herself is never seen in the series.) Gerry is a successful business executive who lives in Brighton with his wife Georgie, who runs a busy curio shop. Both the husband and the wife, in other words, are successful in business and prosperous in life – but not in their rotten marriage. Though they still live together, theirs is a rift so deep that neither their children Jane and Alan nor their friends Harvey and Phil can bridge the gap. And Georgie has especial reason to curse that Beryl Marston …

That Show

UK · ITV (SOUTHERN) · SKETCH

6 × 30 mins · b/w
*1 Oct–5 Nov 1964 · Thu mostly 7.30pm

MAIN CAST
Sid Green
Dick Hills

CREDITS
writers Sid Green/Dick Hills · *director* Terry Yarwood

Writers and performers Sid Green and Dick Hills – best known to viewers from *The Morecambe And Wise Show* – starred in this series, an outlet for their latest sketch material. Six programmes were screened by London-area ITV in early 1965, having aired in the south of England (the series was made by Southern Television) the previous October–November. Sid and Dick returned to front another show (*Those Two Fellers*) for ABC in 1967.

*Note. These dates reflect the Southern TV screenings. The series aired on London-area ITV from 1 January to 5 March 1965 (Fridays at 10.35pm).

That Was The Week That Was

UK · BBC · SATIRE

37 × 50 mins · b/w
Series One (23) 24 Nov 1962–27 Apr 1963 · Sat around 10.40pm
Series Two (14) 28 Sep–28 Dec 1963 · Sat around 10.30pm

MAIN CAST
David Frost
Millicent Martin
Kenneth Cope
David Kernan
Bernard Levin
Lance Percival
William Rushton
Roy Kinnear
Timothy Birdsall (series 1)
Bernard Levin
Al Mancini
Robert Lang (series 2)

CREDITS

writers David Frost/Christopher Booker, Keith Waterhouse/Willis Hall, Peter Lewis/ Peter Dobereiner, David Nathan/Dennis Potter, David Nobbs/Peter Tinniswood, Robert Gillespie/ Charles Lewson, Andrew Roth/Joe Haines, John Cleese, Gerald Kaufman, Herbert Kretzmer, John Albery, John Antrobus, Ned Sherrin/ Caryl Brahms, John Braine, Quentin Crewe, Brian Glanville, Bernard Levin, Leslie Mallory, David Mason, Peter Shaffer, Kenneth Tynan, Peter Veale, Steven Vinaver, Johnny Speight and others · *producer* Ned Sherrin

A biting, live, late-night satire series that broke new ground in television's relationship with politics, redefined the BBC's perceived neutrality and opened up TV comedy to embrace attacks on hitherto sacred cows: politicians, religions and even royalty among them.

That Was The Week That Was – or *TW3* as it was and remains more conveniently known – was an irreverent weekly look at domestic and foreign current-affairs, with a particular emphasis on people in power and their behaviour in and out of office. Stirred by the daring deeds of the quartet performing the landmark satirical stage revue **Beyond The Fringe** – a production so boldly audacious in its attacks on authority that it was the talk of the country in 1961 and 1962 – the incumbent BBC director-general Hugh Carleton Greene (brother of novelist Graham Greene), who had taken up the office in 1960, was determined to steer the Corporation away from the cosiness of the 1950s towards a harder, sharper future. He conceived the idea of a weekly TV programme that would 'prick the pomposity of public figures' and charged Ned Sherrin, the producer of *Tonight*, a lightweight, early-evening current-affairs magazine, to go away and make it happen. (*TW3* was hence the product of the BBC's current-affairs department, not light entertainment, much to the latter's chagrin.)

Sherrin already had experience of the kind of team he wanted to assemble (see **Oxford Accents**) and duly found them performing on the cabaret circuit. After a couple of untransmitted pilots – the first was co-presented by Brian Redhead (then a *Tonight* journalist) and David Frost and included appearances by Eleanor Bron, John Fortune and John Bird before they went off to tour America with their revue *The Establishment*; the second was hosted by Frost alone – Sherrin was confident he had ironed out the wrinkles and the show was unveiled on 24 November 1962.

The format and style of *TW3* was innovative in itself: singer Millicent Martin performed the opening theme song (same melody but different lyrics every week to reflect topical events) and this was then followed by a succession of sketches,

discussions, satirical songs and often searing monologues, all linked by the host of the show, David Frost. (It was this series that made him famous, much to the irritation of many of his contemporaries.) Cameras were positioned at odd angles to deliver bird's-eye views of the set, and the decision to keep such equipment in view greatly added to the 'live' and 'on-the-edge' feel of the show. The satirical humour was sometimes savage (though not always – the memory can sometimes play tricks) and quite unlike anything seen or heard before on the small-screen. The series made stars of virtually all its players, elevating Roy Kinnear, Lance Percival, Willie Rushton, Millie Martin and Kenneth Cope to national figures. Bernard Levin, the newspaper columnist and intelligentsia member, regularly appeared in *TW3* in bitter live discussions and, memorably, was attacked in one edition by a member of the studio audience.

By a stroke of good fortune, *TW3* coincided with the Stephen Ward/Christine Keeler/Profumo affair, which gave the impressive team of writers more than enough material to keep politicians and authority figures squirming for many weeks. Although it did not appeal to all classes of viewer, *TW3* was essential watching and a principal topic of conversation among readers of the quality broadsheet newspapers, and its impact upon the hearts and minds of such viewers – most of whom had never realised that public figures could lead disreputable lives – was such that the BBC was persuaded to keep the series off the air in 1964, the year of a General Election. It never returned, but a slew of successors appeared in its place, none making the same impact. At the very least, though, *TW3* established Saturday-night TV as Satireday-night.

This was not the end of the story, however, for the format of *TW3* was sold to the USA; the American version (under the same title) was piloted by NBC on 10 November 1963, hosted by Henry Fonda, and a resulting series of half-hour programmes ran from 10 January 1964 to 4 May 1965. In this, Elliot Reed was the host (until autumn 1964, when David Frost arrived from England to take over), with Alan Alda, Buck Henry, Phyllis Newman, Henry Morgan and singer Nancy Ames among the regular cast. Three further one-off US specials aired, on 4 January 1973, 26 December 1976 and 22 April 1985. In Australia the series inspired *The Mavis Bramston Show*, a huge hit that ran from 1964 to 1968 and featured a host of established and upcoming humorists, including John Bluthal, Miriam Karlin and Ronnie Stevens.

Notes. Timothy Birdsall – who provided the show's surreal single-frame cartoons, drawn

on the spot – died aged just 26 after the first series, in June 1963; a programme celebrating his work for *TW3* – titled simply and respectfully *Timothy Birdsall* – was aired by the BBC on 23 December 1963. Five days later, the last ever *TW3* was aired, comprising a review of the year that mixed new sketches with repeated highlights and which was actually titled *That Was The Year That Was*.

The edition of 23 November 1963 paid eloquent tribute to President Kennedy, assassinated in Dallas the day before. An audio recording of the show, which included a piece by Dame Sybil Thorndike, was issued in the USA as an album soon afterwards as *That Was The Week That Was – The British Broadcasting Corporation's Tribute To John Fitzgerald Kennedy*, climbing to number five on the chart. (This disc was not issued in the UK, where an Abbey Road studio re-recording of various *TW3* skits and mono-logues, produced by George Martin, was issued by Parlophone in 1963.)

See also ABC Of Britain.

That's Entertainment

see The Montreux Festival

That's Life, Says Max Wall

see WALL, Max

That's Love

UK · ITV (TVS) · SITCOM

26 × 30 mins · colour

Series One (7) 19 Jan–1 Mar 1988 · Tue 9.30pm

Series Two (6) 8 Feb–15 Mar 1989 · Wed 9.30pm

Series Three (6) 24 Sep–29 Oct 1990 · Mon 9.30pm

Series Four (7) 11 Feb–24 Mar 1992 · Tue 9.30pm

MAIN CAST

Donald Redfern	Jimmy Mulville
Patsy Redfern	Diana Hardcastle
Amanda Owen	Lynne Pearson
Gary Owen	Rob Spendlove (series 1);
	Neil Pearson (series 2–4)
Olive	Vivienne McKone (series 1 & 2)
Zoe Redfern	Zoe Hodges
Matthew Redfern	Matthew Cole
Victor	Ralph Nossek
Babs	Phyllida Law
The Owen children	
(series 1–3)	Eleanor Puttock;
	Romy Chasan (series 1 & 2);
	Olivia Silver (series 3);
	Matthew Perry;
	Lloyd Meikle (series 1),
	Alice May Wilkinson (series 2),
	Laura Elliott (series 3)
Laurel Manasotti	Liza Goddard (series 3)
Hank	Nicolas Colicos (series 3 & 4)
Geoffrey	Robin Meredith (series 3)
Tristan Beasley	Tony Slattery (series 4)

CREDITS
writer Terence Frisby · *director* John Stroud · *executive producers* John Kaye Cooper/Sarah Lawson (series 1), Gill Stribling-Wright/Sarah Lawson (series 2–4) · *producer* Humphrey Barclay

Marriage counsellors declare that the best prescription for a happy union is for a couple to talk. Wed for seven years, and nominally content until husband discovers the extent of wife's pre-marital sexual liaisons, Donald and Patsy Redfern talk and talk until long after the cows have come home, a good deal of their conversations being in the form of disputes. Donald is a tax lawyer with a sharp legal brain, but slightly wet with it; Patsy is an interior designer with a sharp, lethal tongue and a liberated personality.

A modern-day sitcom about middle-class wedlock – a 1980s version of the 1960s' *Marriage Lines*, if you like – *That's Love* charted the course of the Redferns' bumpy marital 'bliss', a union blessed with two children, their live-in nanny Olive, and a mother-in-law (Patsy's mother, Babs, who made frequent appearances, together with her husband Victor). Despite their problems, though, Donald and Patsy were viewed as marital role-models by their frequently seen friends the Owens, Amanda Owen being exasperated by her husband Gary's wayward, macho behaviour – he still liked to put it about a bit, even though he was fiercely protective of their four children. In series three, Donald Redfern did some straying of his own, albeit reluctantly, when he worked with a rich, glamorous and widowed client, Laurel Manasotti, and this led him and Patsy to seek marriage guidance in series four. Unexpectedly, the counsellor, Tristan Beasley, proceeded to fall head over heels in love with Patsy in the process.

Tristan was played by Tony Slattery – his first sitcom part – underlining the 'new-comedy' aspect of *That's Love*, with Jimmy Mulville in the lead role (a member of the *Who Dares, Wins* and *Chelmsford 123* teams and writer/producer of so many hit shows in recent years) and Neil Pearson (*Chelmsford 123*, *Drop The Dead Donkey* and DS Tony Clark in the BBC cop series *Between The Lines*) playing Gary Owen from the second series onwards. Diana Hardcastle appeared as Patsy, and her real-life one-year-old daughter, Alice May Wilkinson, was cast in the second series as Joe, youngest of the Owen children. Even the writer, Terence Frisby – he based the sitcom on his stage-play *It's Alright If I Do It* – got in on the act, appearing in one final-series episode.

That's My Boy

UK · ITV (YORKSHIRE) · SITCOM
37 × 30 mins · colour

Series One (6) 23 Oct–27 Nov 1981 · Fri 8.30pm
Series Two (8) 7 Jan–25 Feb 1983 · Fri 8.30pm
Special · 23 Dec 1983 · Fri 7.45pm
Series Three (7) 27 Apr–8 June 1984 · Fri 8.30pm
Special · 28 Dec 1984 · Fri 6.30pm
Series Four (7) 18 Jan–8 Mar 1985 · Fri mostly 9.30pm
Series Five (7) 21 Feb–4 Apr 1986 · Fri 8.30pm

MAIN CAST
Ida Willis · · · · · · · · · · · · · · · Mollie Sugden
Robert Price · · · · · · · · · · · Christopher Blake
Angie Price · · · · · · · · · · · · Jennifer Lonsdale
Wilfred Willis · · · · · · · · · · · · · Harold Goodwin
Mrs Price · · · · · · Clare Richards (series 1–4)
Miss Parfitt · · · Deddie Davies (series 4 & 5)
Mrs Cross · · · · · · Thelma Whiteley (series 5)

CREDITS
writers Pam Valentine/Michael Ashton · *directors* Graeme Muir (22), Don Clayton (8), Graham Wetherell (7) · *producer* Graeme Muir

Ida Willis is a no-nonsense, interfering housekeeper whose temperament is ill-suited to her clients. She finally finds herself in the employ of a doctor, Robert Price, and his pleasant wife Angie, and moves into their luxurious London flat, upon which it occurs to her that Robert is the baby boy she gave up for adoption at birth. Her name for him then was Shane (which she continues to use) and, what with her new-found standing, and her character being what it is, she quickly asserts herself over everybody. In particular, she brushes up against Robert's 'other' mother, the widowed Mrs Price, a snooty social climber whose airs and graces are contemptible to our feet-on-the-ground heroine Ida. The fourth series of *That's My Boy* saw Robert's job relocate to the Yorkshire village of Little Birchmarch; Ida makes the move with Robert and Angie where her pining for London (odd, considering she's clearly a northern character) is partly assuaged by helping his new practice, the finding of a new friend (Miss Parfitt) and occasional visits from her brother Wilfred.

That's My Boy was a starring vehicle for Mollie Sugden, the venerable British sitcom actress enjoying good fortune at this time on the back of her roles in *The Liver Birds* and, most especially, *Are You Being Served?* The Ida Willis character was in keeping with Sugden's perceived TV persona: blowsy, domineering, opinionated, forthright … yet curiously appealing. As soon as *That's My Boy* finished she went straight into another Valentine and Ashton creation, *My Husband And I*.

That's Your Funeral

UK · BBC · SITCOM
7 × 30 mins · colour

Pilot *Last Tribute* 25 Mar 1970 · BBC1 Wed 7.30pm
One series (6) 22 Jan–26 Feb 1971 · BBC1 Fri 8.30pm

MAIN CAST
Basil Bulstrode · · · · · · · · · · · · · Bill Fraser
Emanuel Holroyd · · · · · · · Raymond Huntley
Percy · · · · · · · · · · · · · · · · David Battley
Charlie · · · · · · · · · · · · · · · · David King

CREDITS
writer Peter Lewis · *producers* Michael Mills (pilot), Douglas Argent (series)

The funny side of the funeral industry was explored in this north-of-England sitcom, written by *Daily Mail* theatre critic Peter Lewis.

The series plundered the urban mythologies of the industry for its storylines – wrong body, lost body, not-quite-dead body, and so on – and returned Bill Fraser to the world of sitcom after a rest from the genre following the demise of *Bootsie And Snudge* and *Foreign Affairs*, casting him as the bombastic boss Basil Bulstrode. Despite the dubious taste of the idea, the public sufficiently took to the original *Comedy Playhouse* pilot, titled *Last Tribute*, to ensure a series; this, in turn, spawned a 1972 feature film, also called *That's Your Funeral*, directed by John Robins, written by Lewis and featuring the original TV cast (minus David King) in a story of Bulstrode and a rival undertaking firm that turns out to be a front for a drug-smuggling scheme. The film was pitched somewhat blacker than the series (it even featured a car chase with hearses) and didn't rate very highly with the public.

ITV later made the most of funereal fun with its more successful *In Loving Memory*.

Them

UK · BBC · SITCOM
5 × 30 mins · colour
27 July–24 Aug 1972 · BBC1 Thu 10.15pm

MAIN CAST
Coat Sleeves · · · · · · · · · · · · · · Cyril Cusack
Cockney · · · · · · · · · · · · · · · · James Booth

CREDITS
writer Johnny Speight · *director* Harold Snoad · *producer* Dennis Main Wilson

A Johnny Speight sitcom depicting two vagrants: an Irishman nicknamed 'Coat Sleeves' and his cockney colleague, who team up to tramp the highways and byways of the country, sharing adventures, food and their peculiar philosophies on life. The comedic conflict arose not between the two men but with representatives of the conventional world: policemen, publicans, businessmen and others. In short, *Them* highlighted the clashes between the ordinary man in the street and the extraordinary gentlemen of the road.

Speight saw value in tramp characters: he had achieved much success with Arthur Haynes as a lazy itinerant in a number of memorable sketches for *The Arthur Haynes Show*. In 1983–84 he returned to the theme once more, exploring the distaff side of vagrancy in *The Lady Is A Tramp*.

Then Churchill Said To Me

UK · BBC · SITCOM

6 × 30 mins · colour

*1982 (not screened)

MAIN CAST

Private Potts/General Fearless Freddy
Hollocks · · · · · · · · · · · · · · · Frankie Howerd
Colonel Robin Witherton · · Nicholas Courtney
Petty Officer Joan Bottomley
· Joanna Dunham
Norman · · · · · · · · · · · · · · Michael Attwell
other role · · · · · · · · · · · · · · · Shaun Curry
other role · · · · · · · · · · · · · · James Chase
other role · · · · · · · · · · · Linda Cunningham

CREDITS

writers Maurice Sellar/Lou Jones · *director* Martin Shardlow · *producer* Roger Race

Frankie Howerd in a Second World War romp. The series was set in the British government's secret underground HQ in London in 1941, with Howerd cast as a dithering underling, Private Potts, a general dogsbody who seemed to be a direct descendant of the factotums he had played in the TV series *Up Pompeii!* and *Whoops Baghdad* and feature films *Up The Chastity Belt* and *Up The Front*. To make matters slightly different this time, Howerd's skiving and cowardly Potts happened to be the spitting image of Fearless Freddy Hollocks, a respected general with a will of iron, and he played both roles.

Storylines revolved around Potts' attempts to stay out of trouble while he caused mayhem at every turn. Much of his time was spent looking after Colonel Witherton and avoiding the screeching (but out of view) Sergeant Major McRuckus. Once again, Howerd employed the technique of addressing his TV viewing audience directly, using them as confidants to his story, but by this time – a decade after *Up Pompeii!* – the novelty had worn off and the overriding impression was that everything about *Then Churchill Said To Me* was forced, that it was trying too hard to recapture an earlier style.

*Note. The series was a victim of unfortunate timing: scheduled for broadcast in early 1982, it was cancelled owing to the Falklands War, when any war-related material – even series as silly and as unrelated as *Then Churchill Said To Me* – was deemed unsuitable for general entertainment. (The BBC may also have realised that the series was a duffer, for when the war was over the series was kept

hidden.) But in the same way that Churchill's subterranean wartime HQ was eventually opened to the public, the TV series was finally unveiled too, on the cable/satellite station UK Gold. (The first of several screenings ran from 1 March to 5 April 1993.)

See also Frankie Howerd's combined entry.

There Comes A Time ...

UK · ITV (YORKSHIRE) · SITCOM

7 × 30 mins · colour

20 Feb–3 Apr 1985 · Wed 8.30pm

MAIN CAST

Tony James · · · · · · · · · · · · · · Andrew Sachs
Vanessa James · · · · · · · · · · · Judy Cornwell
Peter James · · · · · · · · · · · · · · Robert Daws
Jane James · · · · · · · · · · · · · Colette Barker
Dr Harry Eaton · · · · · · · · · · · · · Alan David

CREDITS

writer Wally K Daly · *director/producer* Ronnie Baxter

Tony James is a suit-and-tie business executive whose attitude to life is irrevocably altered when he is informed by his doctor that he has a bizarre, ultra-rare and incurable disease, and that his time left alive is severely limited. James sets out to establish the meaning of life, acting most strangely in the process and mystifying his wife and family with his erratic behaviour.

Andrew Sachs starred, still hoping to find a major comedy role that didn't require him to wear a waiter's jacket and speak with a Spanish accent. In his previous ITV sitcom, *Dead Ernest*, he was already deceased – in *There Comes A Time* ... he was still alive, just.

There's A Lot Of It About

see MILLIGAN, Spike

There's Always Hope

see HOPE, Bob

These Are The Days

see Reggie Little

These Are The Shows

UK · BBC · SKETCH/STANDUP

1 × 45 mins · b/w

28 Sep 1957 · Sat 8pm

MAIN CAST

Tony Hancock
Sidney James
Professor Edwards · · · · · · · · Jimmy Edwards
Oliver Pettigrew · · · · · · · · · · · Arthur Howard
Jimmy Wheeler
Dave Morris
Charlie Chester

Hylda Baker
Paul Eddington

CREDITS

writers Frank Muir/Denis Norden, Ray Galton/Alan Simpson · *producer* Francis Essex

A one-off special looking at the forthcoming light entertainment shows for the new (1957) BBC TV season. Tony Hancock and Sid James appeared as the famous *Hancock's Half Hour* characters in a script especially written by Galton and Simpson; Jimmy Edwards and Arthur Howard appeared as their *Whack-O!* characters in a script especially written by Muir and Norden. Also appearing to plug their coming shows were Jimmy Wheeler (*The Jimmy Wheeler Show*), Dave Morris (*Club Night*), Hylda Baker (*Be Soon*), and Charlie Chester (*The Charlie Chester Show* and *Educated Evans*). Non-comedy guests in *These Are The Shows* included Eamonn Andrews, Vera Lynn, Jack Payne, David Nixon, Jack Warner, zither player Shirley Abicair and the Beverley Sisters.

These Friends Of Mine

see *Ellen*

They Came From Somewhere Else

UK · C4 (TVS) · SITCOM

6 × 30 mins · colour

14 July–18 Aug 1984 · Sat 10pm

MAIN CAST

The Stranger · · · · · · · · · · · · · Robin Driscoll
Martin · · · · · · · · · · · · · · · · · · Tony Haase
Colin · · · · · · · · · · · · · · · · · Pete McCarthy
Wendy · · · · · · · · · · · · · · Rebecca Stevens
The 'They're Coming' Man · · · Paddy Fletcher
Shauna · · · · · · · · · · · · · · · Tamsin Heatley
Professor · · · · · · · · · · · · · · · · · Patti Bee
Anthony · · · · · · · · · · · · · · · Peter Leabourne
Sergeant · · · · · · · · · · · · · · · · David Gale
WPC Julie · · · · · · · · · · · · · · · Ella Wilder
Mrs Maynard · · · · · · · · · · · · · · Hilda Braid
First GI · · · · · · · · · · · · · · · · Harry Ditson
Second GI · · · · · · · · · · · · · Tyrone Huggins

CREDITS

writers Robin Driscoll/Tony Haase/Pete McCarthy/Rebecca Stevens · *director* Jim Hill · *producer* John Dale

A curious comedy that blended sci-fi with parodies of soaps and adventure programmes, and with a dash of horror thrown into the mix. The writers and main cast were four people who worked under the collective name Cliff Hanger, and they developed the series from a stage production they had mounted in Brighton.

The humorously exciting – and, frankly, bizarre – episodes were set in the (fictional) new town of Middleford, wherein materialised a curious attaché case and the mysterious Stranger, who might just have been an alien in human form, and where zombies roamed, liver rained down from the sky, twilight zones were entered and, when people weren't suffering from a migraine epidemic, they were liable to explode.

See also *Mornin' Sarge*.

Thick As Thieves

UK · ITV (LWT) · SITCOM

8 × 30 mins · colour

1 June–20 July 1974 · Sat mostly 8.30pm

MAIN CAST

Stan	John Thaw
George Dobbs	Bob Hoskins
Annie	Pat Ashton

OTHER APPEARANCES

Norman	Reg Lye
Spiggy	Johnny Briggs
Tommy Hollister	Trevor Peacock
Sgt Black	Michael Robbins
Daphne	Nell Curran

CREDITS

writers Dick Clement/Ian La Frenais · *directors* Derrick Goodwin (7), Mike Gibbon (1) · *producer* Derrick Goodwin

After serving a three-year sentence, George Dobbs, a small-time house-burglar, is released from prison one day earlier than expected and arrives back at his terraced house in Fulham (south-west London) to find his best friend opening the front-door, topless, his face covered in shaving foam and wearing Dobbs' pyjama bottoms. It is immediately apparent that while Dobbs has been 'doing time', his buddy, Stan, also a crook, has been 'doing his missus'. But said wife, Annie, has affections for both men, and a tricky – though funny – *ménage-à-trois* develops, forming the basis of each episode.

Sharply written, well observed and wonderfully titled, *Thick As Thieves* was in all ways a fine sitcom, albeit a short-lived one: after just one series the writers Dick Clement and Ian La Frenais took their 'two-criminals' idea to the BBC where, seven weeks later, they launched **Porridge**, developed from the Ronnie Barker pilot series **Seven Of One**. The criminals in the two series were very different but shared non-violent temperaments: in *Thick As Thieves* the men attempted to come to terms with the deception and the awkward domestic circumstances, using – at worst – harsh words, and exercising a curious lower-middle-class morality. The men are plainly different: while Dobbs has more nous, more get up and go, Stan is a plain-thinking, artless individual to whom life happens; he's not a million miles, indeed, from the persona of another screen Stan – Mr Laurel.

Clement and La Frenais personally selected the actors whom they wished to fill these two key roles, and their choices were inspired. Stan was played by John Thaw, already well-established but just about to take off as the hardened cop Regan in *The Sweeney*. (Indeed, that series' pilot was aired in the same week as the premiere episode of *Thick As Thieves*.) Playing the part of George, and hiding behind black horn-rimmed glasses, was Bob Hoskins, his first regular TV role after two years of occasional parts as a criminal in cop series like *Softly Softly*. Clearly, at this time, Hoskins was considered only for felon roles, leading up to his starring part in the 1979 film *The Long Good Friday*.

Clement and La Frenais reused elements from these *Thick As Thieves* scripts in their 1993 sitcom **Over The Rainbow**, which was itself based on their screenplay for the hit movie *The Commitments*. In its early stages, indeed, *Over The Rainbow* was modelled particularly closely on *Thick As Thieves* and carried that working title.

Thicker Than Water 1

UK · BBC · SITCOM

7 × 30 mins · b/w

17 Feb–31 Mar 1969 · BBC1 Mon 7.30pm

MAIN CAST

Jim Eccles	Jimmy Jewel
Aggie Plunkett	Jean Kent
Vicki Eccles	Roberta Rex
Janet Eccles	Carolyn Moody
Carol Eccles	Jill Kerman
Albert Pike	Mike Lucas
Robert Bean	Gerald Moon

CREDITS

writer Peter Robinson · producer Douglas Argent

A BBC sitcom in which Jimmy Jewel was cast as a fishmonger, Jim Eccles. He is a man of simple pleasures but circumstances often conspire to threaten his established and beloved routines. The main thorn in his side is a neighbour, Aggie Plunkett, who seems to have more on her mind than just community spirit when she interferes in his life. A widower, Jim has three young adult daughters – Vicki, Janet and Carol – who kept him on the hop.

After his long career as a standup comedian (see **Jewel and Warriss**), Jimmy Jewel was taking to sitcom acting like a duck to water, and was already established as the co-star of a concurrent ITV series, **Nearest And Dearest**. His only problem, he admitted, was that he constantly had to underplay his performances in order to counter the exaggerated style he had developed during his years on stage in the double-act.

Thicker Than Water 2

UK · ITV (YORKSHIRE) · SITCOM

7 × 30 mins · colour

Pilot *Where There's Brass* 16 Mar 1980 · Sun 8.45pm

One series (6) 28 Apr–9 June 1981 · Tue 8.30pm

MAIN CAST

Joseph Lockwood	Derek Smith (pilot);
	Joss Ackland (series)
Alan Lockwood	Colin Farrell
Malcolm (Neil in pilot) Lockwood	
	Michael Tarn (pilot);
	Peter Denyer (series)
Harry Fishwick (Askwith in pilot)	
	Peter Denyer (pilot);
	David Battley (series)
Hilda Bayliss	Ann Penfold (pilot)
Arnold Broadhurst	Timothy Bateson
	(series)
Arthur Boyd	Denis Gilmore (series)

CREDITS

writer Dick Sharples · *director/producer* Ronnie Baxter

Set in 1920s Yorkshire – all cloth-caps, cobblestones, whippets and unemployment – *Thicker Than Water* drew its humour from a widowed father, Joseph Lockwood, and his two unmarried adult sons, Alan and Malcolm. By day, the three are motor mechanics, by night the brothers are tuxedoed dance-band musicians in Al Lockwood's Syncopated Serenaders, the type of band that then proliferated in British ballrooms, dispensing music for fox-trots, waltzes and soft-shoe shuffles. Meanwhile, Joseph is perpetually unlucky in his quest for a good woman to tend his needs.

The series developed from a pilot, *Where There's Brass*, which had a substantially different cast and a slight twist in the storyline: Joe Lockwood was a spare-time conductor of the Brigthorpe Brass Band.

The Thin Blue Line

UK · BBC (TIGER ASPECT) · SITCOM

14 × 30 mins · colour

Series One (6) 13 Nov–18 Dec 1995 · BBC1 Mon 8.30pm

Special · 26 Dec 1995 · BBC1 Tue 8.50pm

Series Two (6) 14 Nov–19 Dec 1996 · BBC1 Thu 9.30pm

Special · 23 Dec 1996 · BBC1 Mon 9.30pm

MAIN CAST

Insp Raymond Fowler	Rowan Atkinson
Sgt Patricia Dawkins	Serena Evans
PC Kevin Goody	James Dreyfus
PC Maggie Habib	Mina Anwar
PC Gladstone	Rudolph Walker
DI Derek Grim	David Haig
DC Kray	Kevin Allen (series 1)
Det Boyle	Mark Addy (series 2)
Mayoress Wickham	Lucy Robinson

CREDITS

writer Ben Elton · director John Birkin · *producers* Geoffrey Perkins, Ben Elton

Blackadder alumni – writer Ben Elton, star Rowan Atkinson – reunited for this sitcom, centred around Gasforth police station. But although Atkinson's character was the focus of attention, this was very much an ensemble piece, with Elton attempting to create a series with the comedic style of **Dad's Army**, a series he greatly admires.

Atkinson was cast as Inspector Raymond Fowler, the head of the station and an old-fashioned, by-the-book policeman, scrupulously honest and totally dedicated both to the job in hand and to his team of uniformed officers. These comprise his desk sergeant, Patricia Dawkins, Fowler's girlfriend of 10 years standing; veteran of the force PC Gladstone, an unexcitable and rather pedestrian officer; the fey and eager PC Goody; and Indian PC Maggie Habib, the level-headed, brightest one of the bunch. These uniformed officers clashed constantly with the other occupants of the station: the plain-clothed detectives, led by DI Grim and DC Kray. Considering themselves a cut above the 'beat' officers, Grim and Kray liked to believe that anything they were working on was more important than routine police duties. This 'enemy-within' scenario echoed the Verger and ARP Warden irritants in *Dad's Army* – and, again in the style of that earlier series, the storylines revolved more around the interplay of the characters than the task they were assigned: here it was catching criminals; in *Dad's Army* it was preparing for war.

This, then, was the set up. Typical of Ben Elton's work, there were plenty of convoluted lines for Atkinson to deliver, which he did with his impeccable style and to great comedic effect. But, on the down side, there were a number of aspects about *The Thin Blue Line* that refused to gel. PC Goody was something of an enigma, coming across as an over-the-top gay (in a manner reminiscent of Mr Humphries of *Are You Being Served?*) whereas he was actually hetero and had a burning desire for PC Habib. Goody was thus presented to viewers as limp and wimpish rather than simply affected, and any sort of liaison with the sharp Habib seemed highly improbable. (To be fair, actor James Dreyfus still managed to attain plenty of laughs with his delicate delivery.) Elsewhere, to qualify the fact that Sergeant Dawkins would put up with the emotionally-cold Fowler, she was presented as a hopeless romantic convinced that he would eventually become the lover she desired, and such obviously blinkered thinking weakened the character and made her merely a cipher. The plain-clothed detectives carried on as if they were in *The Sweeney* and had little going for them beyond this, and the West Indian, Gladstone, was given so little to do that his inclusion almost smacked of tokenism. Despite these reservations, however, *The Thin Blue Line* had some fine moments and improved as the episodes ticked by.

Perhaps the series' biggest problem was in perception, however: *The Thin Blue Line* was so different to Elton and Atkinson's usual hilariously savage wit that the only way to derive any great enjoyment from it was to overlook the identity of these prime movers and simply view the series as one would have done any other sitcom of, say, the early 1970s. This proved impossible for many, who simply could not understand why the ever-radical Elton had so willingly created such a broad, old-fashioned piece of work.

Thingumybob

UK · ITV (LWT) · SITCOM

8 × 45 mins · b/w

2 Aug–20 Sep 1968 · Fri 7.30pm then 8.30pm

MAIN CAST

Bob Bridge	Stanley Holloway
Fay Bridge	Rose Hill
Bert Ryding	John Junkin
Monica Ryding	Kate Williams
Mrs Green	Stella Tanner
George	Bert Palmer
Henry	Wally Patch

CREDITS

writer Kenneth Cope · director/producer David Askey

The inaugural sitcom produced by London's new weekend ITV franchise LWT – the premiere episode went out on the station's opening night – *Thingumybob* provided the first lead role in a British comedy series for Stanley Holloway, a star all-round-entertainer throughout the century on stage, in films, on radio and on record. Aged 78 at the time of its making, Holloway played the part of Bob Bridge, nicknamed 'Thingumybob', a pensioner with too much time on his hands and too little idea of how to fill it, beyond taking Storm, his dog, for walks. As a consequence, he was often getting into light mischief, either inside the terraced house he shared with his wife Fay or with his pal Bert Ryding, the local newsagent.

Although taped in LWT's London studio, *Thingumybob* was set in Liverpool and written by Kenneth Cope, best known on-screen for his participation in *That Was The Week That Was*, as Jed Stone in *Coronation Street* and as the ghostly Marty Hopkirk in *Randall And Hopkirk (Deceased)*, which began in 1969. The *Thingumybob* brass-band theme music was composed and produced by Paul McCartney.

Before *Thingumybob*, the only British TV comedy to have featured Stanley Holloway was the adaptation of P G Wodehouse's **Blandings Castle**, which starred Ralph Richardson. He did, however, star in the *US* sitcom *Our Man Higgins* (ABC, 1962–63), playing the English butler whose name was embodied in the title. The series was imported by some regional ITV stations in 1963 but was not screened in the London area.

See also The Barnstormers.

3rd Rock From The Sun

USA · NBC (THE CARSEY-WERNER COMPANY) · SITCOM

50 episodes (47 × 30 mins · 3 × 60 mins to 31/12/97 · continuing into 1998) · colour

US dates: 9 Jan 1996 to date

UK dates: 24 Oct 1996 to date (44 × 30 mins · 1 × 60 mins to 31/12/97) BBC2 mostly Thu 9pm

MAIN CAST

Dick Solomon	John Lithgow
Sally Solomon	Kristen Johnston
Harry Solomon	French Stewart
Tommy Solomon	Joseph Gordon-Levitt
Dr Mary Albright	Jane Curtin
Nina Campbell	Simbi Khali

OTHER APPEARANCES

August	Shay Astar
Officer Don	Wayne Knight
Leon	Ian Lithgow
Bug	David DeLuise
Pitman	Chris Hogan
Caryn	Danielle Nicolet

CREDITS

creators Bonnie Turner/Terry Turner · writers Bonnie Turner/Terry Turner, Michael Glouberman, Bob Kushell, Bill Martin, Andrew Orenstein, Mike Schiff, Christine Zander and others · directors Robert Berlinger, James Burrows, Terry Hughes and others · executive producers Bonnie Turner, Terry Turner, Marcy Carsey, Tom Werner, Caryn Mandabach · producers Patrick Kienlen, Bob Kushell, Christine Zander and others

US programme makers have often exploited the comic potential of extra-terrestrials trying to blend in with everyday American society – **My Favorite Martian**, **Mork And Mindy**, **ALF** and the Coneheads (within **Saturday Night Live**) had all mined laughs from the situation, but perhaps the finest realisation of the premise has been *3rd Rock From The Sun*.

Created by Bonnie and Terry Turner (co-writers of the *Wayne's World* and *Coneheads* movies), the premise of *3rd Rock From The Sun* was deceptively simple: four aliens arrive on Earth – in a small Ohio town, to be precise – on a short field-trip, their mission being to gather information about the planet and its inhabitants. To expedite this, they assume the guise of an Earth family, the Solomons, comprising Dick, his sister Sally, brother Harry and son Tommy. Dick (played by John Lithgow) is the mission's High Commander and he fulfils a similar role in the family, a sort of father figure to the others. To gain access to the information he requires, he uses his superior intelligence (and forged papers) to become a university lecturer, working in the physics department. Here he meets and is attracted to a colleague, Dr Mary Albright; such are his feelings towards her, and his determination to understand them, that Dick prolongs the mission indefinitely, against the wishes of his team.

His first lieutenant has metamorphosed into Sally (brilliantly played by Kristen Johnston), a tall, attractive woman still retaining all the aggressive traits of her previous non-female being. Her body becomes a battleground for the two identities raging within, as her alien being becomes absorbed – and is virtually swamped – by her Earth character and its needs and desires. Perversely, the oldest member of the team has been incarnated as a teenager, Tommy, but although he too retains traces of his alien identity – wisdom, worldliness, common sense – he also falls victim to the needs of his host body and finds his life increasingly muddled by the onset of puberty. And then there's Harry, who seems to be along just for the ride (perhaps as ballast). He employs a bizarre logic and ceaseless misunderstanding of basic human workings, making him a dangerous liability, especially since the quartet do all they can to keep their extra-terrestrial origins secret. Other recurring characters include Shay Astar as August, Tommy's acerbic girlfriend; and Ian Lithgow (John's real-life son), as Leon, one of Dick Solomon's students.

Although a basic and perhaps unoriginal idea, the execution of *3rd Rock From The Sun* was superb. The battles endured by the strongly drawn alien characters in coming to terms with their environment and Earth bodies added spice to the convoluted plots and witty dialogue, and strong support was provided as Dr Albright by Jane Curtin (who had previously played the Earth-visiting alien Prymaat The Conehead in **Saturday Night Live** and in the subsequent spin-off feature film), and by Simbi Khali as the feisty, perennially mini-skirted assistant Nina. But it was the towering performance of John Lithgow – a revelation as the academically brilliant but socially inept Dick – that gave the series its biggest lift. His comic timing was as impeccable as his handling of the snappy dialogue and physical comedy, and he fully merited the acting Emmy he received after the first season of *3rd Rock From The Sun*.

Note. The final episode of the 1996–97 US season (not screened in Britain to the end of 1997) was a one-hour special with some segments presented in 3D.

Third Time Lucky

UK · ITV (YORKSHIRE) · SITCOM

7 × 30 mins · colour

6 Aug–17 Sep 1982 · Fri 8.30pm

MAIN CAST

George Hutcheson	Derek Nimmo
Beth Jenkins	Nerys Hughes
Clare Hutchenson	Deborah Farrington
Jenny Hutchenson	Lorraine Brunning
Millie King	Angela Douglas
Henry King	Gerald Flood
Bruce Jenkins	Clifford Earl
Sally Jenkins	Angela Piper
Mrs MacTaggart	Josie Kidd
Mr MacTaggart	Robert Fyfe
Mr Ho Moy	Eiji Kusuhara

CREDITS

writer Jan Butlin · *director/producer* Graeme Muir

George, an electrical sales manager and a twit, married Beth 18 years ago. They had two daughters, Jenny and Clare. Eleven years after the wedding came the divorce. George then married Millie. Beth married Bruce Jenkins. Both ended in divorce. Millie has since married Henry King. Millie and Beth are friends. Bruce has since married Sally. Now George and Beth have a chance meeting, take a shine to one another and plan to marry each other all over again. *Third Time Lucky* focused on how they would inform the children, becalm the many ex's and plan the complicated marriage. But they managed to do it all, despite a break-up along the way, and duly wed in the final episode.

The writer, Jan Butlin, admitted to having a wall-chart within her vision while writing the scripts, showing who had been married to whom, and who had brought up whose children. Sadly, the viewers had no such guide and were often flummoxed, and there were precious few laughs along the way to alleviate the puzzlement.

Thirty Minutes Worth

see WORTH, Harry

This Is David Lander / This Is David Harper

UK · C4 (HAT TRICK PRODUCTIONS) · SITCOM

12 × 30 mins · colour

Series One (6) *This Is David Lander* 31 Oct–5 Dec 1988 · Mon 8.30pm
Series Two (6) *This Is David Harper* 2 Nov–7 Dec 1990 · Fri mostly 10.30pm

MAIN CAST

David Lander	Stephen Fry (series 1)
David Harper	Tony Slattery (series 2)

CREDITS

writer Tony Sarchet · *script editor* Paul Mayhew-Archer · *director* Graham Dixon · *executive producer* Denise O'Donoghue · *producers* Paul Mayhew-Archer (series 1), Mary Bell (series 2)

The adventures of a fearless fact-finding journalist whose foot-in-the-door style and determination that right must prevail over wrong-doers usually results in a severe roughing up … for himself. With a hopeless feel for timing, the people's champion walks into bother at every turn, suffering endless indignities as well as bruises and broken bones for his troubles.

Finely spoofing the hard-nosed investigative documentary style of the genre, two TV series were filmed – the first starred Stephen Fry as David Lander, the second Tony Slattery as David Harper, cast in the part after Fry's other commitments prevented him from being available. Fry it was who made the role his own, though, having already appeared as Lander in four BBC Radio 4 series of programmes – all titled *Delve Special* – before the format was adapted for TV. Lampooning as it did the no-nonsense style of such radio journalists as Roger Cook (who reported for a R4 programme called *Checkpoint* before gaining his own ITV show, *The Cook Report*, from 1987) and John Waite (*Face The Facts*), the series was ideally suited for the aural medium, and many of the original R4 scripts were adapted for the TV run.

Apart from Lander/Harper, the TV casts changed each week to suit the storylines, but among those appearing were Mark Arden, Janine Duvitski, Gordon Kennedy, Neil Pearson, Philip Pope, Caroline Quentin, Tony Robinson, David Ryall, Arthur Smith, Juliet Stevenson and Peter Tilbury. The four R4 series, four episodes apiece, also written by Tony Sarchet and produced by Paul Mayhew-Archer, aired 3–24 August 1984, 6–27 September 1985, 5–26 September 1986 and 28 August–18 September 1987. Here there was a rep cast of supporting players, including Peter Acre, Mark Arden, Robert Bathurst, Brenda Blethyn, Harry Enfield, Stephen Frost, Julia Hills, Jack Klaff, Felicity Montagu, Phil Nice, Jan Ravens, Tony Robinson, Andrew Sachs, Arthur Smith and Moray Watson.

Thompson

UK · BBC · SKETCH

6 × 30 mins · colour

10 Nov–15 Dec 1988 · BBC1 Thu 9.30pm

MAIN CAST

Emma Thompson
Phyllida Law
Imelda Staunton

OTHER APPEARANCES

Kenneth Branagh
Stephen Moore
Robbie Coltrane
Joanna David
Charles Kay
Josette Simon
Mark Kingston

CREDITS

writer Emma Thompson · *director* John Stroud · *producer* Humphrey Barclay

Born in London on 15 April 1959, Emma Thompson (daughter of Eric Thompson, whose creative talents brought the French children's animation series *The Magic Roundabout* to English-language viewers, via the BBC) first made her mark in comedy as a leading player in the Cambridge Footlights. The 1981 revue in which she appeared, *The Cellar Tapes*, was particularly successful, winning a Perrier award at the Edinburgh Festival Fringe and being filmed for TV (see **The Cambridge Footlights**). Appearing soon afterwards in Granada TV's *Alfresco*, Thompson quickly became assimilated into the burgeoning 'alternative' comedy scene, rising to prominence at the same time as other women (French and Saunders, Victoria Wood, Ruby Wax and more) were equally making headway in the hitherto male-dominated sphere. In 1988, the BBC gave Thompson her own series, eponymously titled, and she opted for a format that featured short but elaborate sketches designed to capitalise upon her versatility as a comic actress. This style, used before by Diane Rigg for *Diana* and in *The Tracey Ullman Show*, had always proven unpopular with British critics and viewers, and *Thompson* failed to halt the trend, attracting an excessive degree of vitriol. Criticism levelled at the series ranged from 'pretentious' and 'incomprehensible' to the plain 'unfunny'.

As the writer and star, Thompson had nowhere to hide from this flak, which – in hindsight – seems to have been more of a witch-hunt than constructive criticism. The series was certainly flawed, though, with little of the subject matter reaching the collective funny bone; perhaps unwisely, it employed a style that seemed to shun overt comedy and funny lines in favour of ironic caricature and precision performances – fine for a drama, perhaps, OK for revue, but difficult to pull off in the confines of a primetime BBC1 sketch show. Lesser talents may have found it difficult to bounce back from such an experience but Thompson's versatility kept her busy on stage, TV and in movies. Indeed, the failure of *Thompson* did little to restrict her meteoric rise to Oscar-winning international stardom (gained, some have noted, without any reference to her 'alternative' past).

See also *Emma Thompson: Up For Grabs*.

Those Kids

UK · ITV (ABC) · CHILDREN'S SITCOM

17 × 30 mins · b/w

*Series One (8) 9 June–28 July 1956 · Sat mostly 5.30pm

Series Two (7) 15 Sep–27 Oct 1956 · Sat 4.30pm

Specials (2) 15 Dec & 22 Dec 1956 · Sat 5pm

MAIN CAST

Mr Oddy · · · · · · · · · · · · · · Peter Butterworth
Agatha · · · · · · Totti Truman-Taylor (series 2)
Henry · · · · · · · · · · · · · · · · George Howell
Maisie · · · · · · · · · · · · · · · · · · Lynn Grant

Mike · · · · · · · · · · · · · · · · · · David Higson
Robert · · Christopher Sandford (series 1 & 2)
Sally · · · · · · · · · · · · · · · · Shandra Walden
Jackie · · · · · · · · · · · · Terry Cooke (series 1)
Al · · · · · · · · Peter Soule (series 2 & specials)

CREDITS

writer/producer Patricia Latham · *director* Vivian Milroy

A popular series of the time, starring the ubiquitous children's entertainer (and future *Carry On* star) Peter Butterworth. Here he played Mr Oddy, a kindly ex-sailor. In the second series, Agatha (Totti Truman-Taylor) was his imperious elder sister, and so bad was her bossiness that Oddy ran away from his cottage and employed the assistance of his nieces and nephews, who lived in a nearby block of flats, to worry her out of the place, enabling his return. The childrens' scrapes with their aunt, and the problems they unwittingly caused their beloved uncle, formed the basis of the weekly episodes.

*Note. The first series was screened only in the Midlands and the North, not in London.

Those Two Fellers

UK · ITV (ABC) · SKETCH

6 × 30 mins · b/w

5 May–9 June 1967 · Fri 9.10pm then 7pm

MAIN CAST

Sid Green
Dick Hills
Diane Rachelle

CREDITS

writers Sid Green/Dick Hills · *director* Keith Beckett

Through their years on screen, as supporting players to Dave King and Morecambe and Wise, for whom they also wrote, Sid and Dick frequently heard themselves described as 'those two fellers' and decided it would make a good series title. These ABC programmes were an unusual mixture of sketch and chat, with Frankie Howerd, Bob Monkhouse, Morecambe and Wise, Bruce Forsyth, Ted Ray and Arthur Askey appearing, in that order, as guests of the week. Young comic Diane Rachelle assisted.

See also *That Show*.

The Thoughts Of Chairman Alf

see *Till Death Us Do Part*

Three Fights, Two Weddings And A Funeral

see COOGAN, Steve

Three For Two

see BALL, Lucille

Three In A Bed

UK · ITV (THAMES) · SITCOM

1 × 30 mins · colour

22 Feb 1972 · Tue 10.30pm

MAIN CAST

Ernest · · · · · · · · · · · · · · · · Norman Chappell
Syd · Syd Little
Eddie · · · · · · · · · · · · · · · · · · · Eddie Large
Arnold · · · · · · · · · · · · · · · · · · Leslie Noyes
Bert · · · · · · · · · · · · · · · · · Anthony Jackson
Percy · · · · · · · · · · · · · · · · Roy Barraclough
Olive · · · · · · · · · · · · · · · Jacqueline Clarke
Frederick · · · · · · · · · · · · · · · · John Barrard

CREDITS

writers Brian Chasser/Mike Firman · *director/producer* Royston Mayoh

A major breakthrough for the standup comic duo Little and Large, given their first TV outing beyond the talent-spotting show *Opportunity Knocks*. This one-off sitcom was directed and produced by that series' producer, Royston Mayoh, who would continue to promote their cause. The story centred around a darts match between two rival pubs, the Ploughman's Boots and the Lady's Garter.

See **Little And Large** for the pairing's other TV work.

Three Live Wires

UK · ITV (ASSOCIATED-REDIFFUSION) · SITCOM

26 × 30 mins · b/w

15 May–6 Nov 1961 · Mon 8pm

MAIN CAST

Mike · · · · · · · · · · · · · · · · · Michael Medwin
Malcolm · · · · · · · · · · · · · · · · Bernard Fox
George Smithers · · · · · · · · George Roderick
The Manager · · · · · · · · · · · · Deryck Guyler
Higgenbottom · · · · · · · · · · · Derek Benfield

CREDITS

writers James Kelly/Peter Miller (21), James Kelly/Peter Miller/Ray Rigby (2), Ray Rigby (1), Ray Rigby/Bernard Fox (1), Gerald Kelsey/Dick Sharples (1) · *directors* Christopher Hodson (17), John P Hamilton (7), Don Gale (2)

Definitely the golden boy of the moment, following his leap to fame as Springer in *The Army Game*, Michael Medwin was the clear star of this A-R sitcom, cast as the repair foreman of a TV sales and servicing shop. The series was set in London and Medwin's character, Mike, was an unabashed cockney, speaking much of the time in rhyming slang. His two fellow 'live wires', George (another cockney) and Malcolm (a northerner), shared a workbench with him in the repair room and there was also a fourth mechanic, the clumsy clot Higgenbottom. Deryck Guyler was cast as the shop manager, despairing of his work-shy employees with an air of bumbling pomposity that got right up their tubes.

Before this series, the leading trio – Michael Medwin, Bernard Fox and George Roderick –

had all appeared in **The Love Of Mike**, produced by A-R in 1960.

In the style of US sitcoms, *Three Live Wires* enjoyed a long season, 26 episodes, and each one featured a guest star. Among those who appeared were Peter Vaughan, Dudley Moore with his jazz trio, Dickie Henderson, Arthur Lowe, Freddie Mills and Vic Wise, while young comic Ronnie Corbett was among the supporting cast on three occasions.

Three Of A Kind   1

UK · BBC · STANDUP/SKETCH

11 × 30 mins (8 × b/w · 3 × colour)

Series One (6 × b/w) 12 June–17 July 1967 · BBC2 Mon 8.05pm

Series Two (2 × b/w · 3 × colour) 30 Oct–27 Nov 1967 · BBC2 Mon 8.05pm

MAIN CAST
Ray Fell
Mike Yarwood
Lulu

OTHER APPEARANCES
Malcolm Clare (series 2)
Audrey Bayley (series 2)
Alix Kirsta (series 2)
Frances Pidgeon (series 2)
Christine Pockett (series 2)

CREDITS
writers Brad Ashton (11), Austin Steele (7), Julius Emmanuel (6), Barry Knowles/Les Lilley (5), Peter Robinson (3), Dan Douglas (3), Neil Shand (2), Joe Steeples/Peter Tonkinson (1) · *script editor* Austin Steele · *producers* John Ammonds (series 1), Sydney Lotterby (series 2)

Separately, comedian/singer Ray Fell and impressionist Mike Yarwood had been on the verge of breaking into TV for some time, attending auditions, appearing in variety one-offs and unscreened pilots, before this series gave each of them his first big break. Pop singer Lulu completed the trio, providing songs as well as acting alongside Fell and Yarwood in the comedy sketches. Fate being what it is, Fell's TV career soon evaporated while Yarwood became one of the biggest entertainers on British TV in the 1970s (see his own combined entry for coverage of his career). The series' tone was resolutely middle-of-the-road, its intention being to capture both family audiences and more youthful viewers.

Note. BBC2 began broadcasting in colour from 1 July 1967 but the metamorphosis from monochrome was a gradual one, hence the final three episodes of *Three Of A Kind* were taped in colour whereas the previous two in the series were black and white.

Three Of A Kind   2

UK · BBC · SKETCH

18 editions (16 × 30 mins · 1 × 35 mins · 1 × short special) · colour

Series One (4) 1 July–22 July 1981 · BBC1 Wed 8.30pm

Series Two (6) 27 Nov 1982–8 Jan 1983 · BBC1 Sat 8.20pm

Short special · part of *The Funny Side Of Christmas* 27 Dec 1982 · BBC1 Mon 8.05pm

Special (35 mins) 2 May 1983 · BBC1 Mon 8.45pm

Special Three (6) 3 Sep–8 Oct 1983 · BBC1 Sat 8.25pm

MAIN CAST
Lenny Henry
Tracey Ullman
David Copperfield

CREDITS
writers Kim Fuller (11), Mike Radford (9), Bob Sinfield (9), David McKellar (7), Rob Grant/ Doug Naylor (7), Tony Sarchet (7), Helen Murry/ Jamie Rix/Nick Wilton (7), Terry Ravenscroft (5), Andrea Solomons (5), Ian Hislop (4), Nick Revell (4), Chris Miller (3), Gareth Hale/Norman Pace (3), James Hendrie (3), David Copperfield (2), Lenny Henry (2), Graham Dean Buxton (2), Howard Huntridge (2), Barry Bowes (2), Howard Imber (2), James Bibby (1) · *script associate* Kim Fuller · *producers* Paul Jackson (all but short special) · Martin Shardlow (short special)

A funny, fast-moving, non-satirical, mainstream sketch show that made Tracey Ullman a household name and emphasised the burgeoning talent of Lenny Henry. The third member of the team, David Copperfield (real name Stanley Barlow) did not capitalise on the success of the series as much as his two co-stars but was equally important to its balance.

Like most comedy series, *Three Of A Kind* set out to be as funny as it could be; but – unlike most other series – it filled every nanosecond of airtime with gags, wall to wall, top to bottom, in an effort to do so. Apart from its use of video trickery and teletext-style 'Gagfax', which printed jokes on screen in between the sketches, the humour was delivered straight – adopting an 'in-your-face' style without any 'side' or pretensions to grandeur, and, as befitting a pre-watershed BBC1 primetime slot, purposefully lacking the savagery associated with much of the concurrent 'alternative' scene.

Tracey Ullman was particularly impressive, proving funny in a wide variety of character roles and more than capable of holding a tune for the show's music spoofs. (Simultaneous to the series she pursued a successful career as a singer, recording a strong album and enjoying three top ten singles in 1983.) Lenny Henry also fared well, demonstrating his comedic panache; the series caught him in transition from being a *Tiswas* (and *O.T.T.*) funster to mastering his art. David Copperfield was also versatile, and often played foil to the other two.

But whatever the merits of *Three Of A Kind*, and it had plenty, its most important role was as a springboard for its talent – stars

and writers alike. As with **Not The Nine O'Clock News**, the show employed an 'open-door' script policy that attracted many first-time or struggling writers. Consequently, it provided early exposure for the work of such later luminaries as Grant and Naylor, Hale and Pace, Ian Hislop and Nick Revell.

Unfortunately, the series' state-of-the-art (1981–83) presentation makes it seem dated when viewed today, more so than other contemporary series that were not so high-tech. All the same, *Three Of A Kind* was an important series … of a kind.

Three Piece Suite

UK · BBC · SKETCH

6 × 30 mins · colour

8 Mar–12 Apr 1977 · BBC2 Tue 9pm

MAIN CAST
Diana Rigg

CREDITS
writers (see below for explanation) Richard Waring (1a), Roy Clarke (1b), Keith Waterhouse/Willis Hall (1c & 3c), Terence Brady/Charlotte Bingham (2a & 5c), Michael Sadler (2b, 4a & 6a), Dick Clement/ Ian La Frenais (2c), Hugh Leonard (3a), Alexander Woolcot (3b), Neil Shand (4b), John Esmonde/Bob Larbey (4c), Carla Lane (5a), Tina Brown (5b), Jilly Cooper (6b), Alan Coren (6c) · *producer* Michael Mills

Following her unsuccessful US sitcom *Diana*, Ms Rigg made a much better stab at TV comedy with this well-crafted series.

Each edition featured three separate, extended sketches, and top-notch writers were commissioned to provide material written especially for the series. (In the credits above, the number/letter in parentheses refers to the edition number – and position within that edition – of the writer's work; ie, the third sketch in the fourth programme is denoted as 4c.) Each vignette featured a star supporting cast more associated with straight acting than comedy, although Tony Britton, Patsy Rowlands and (in the final programme) John Cleese, were among the contributors.

The sketches tended to be bittersweet rather than broad, and usually carried a serious underlying theme. This has long proven a tricky area for TV comedy and, although such series tend to attract a cult following, they rarely prove attractive to a wider audience, as Eleanor Bron and, later, Emma Thompson, discovered.

Three Rousing Tinkles

UK · BBC · SITCOM

7 × 30 mins · b/w

Series One (3) 7 May–21 May 1966 · BBC2 Sat mostly 9.40pm

Series Two (4) *Four Tall Tinkles* 2 Jan–23 Jan 1967 · BBC2 Mon 8.05pm

MAIN CAST

Middie Paradock · · · · · · · · · Pauline Devaney
Bro Paradock · · · · · · · · · · · · · · Edwin Apps

CREDITS

writer N F Simpson · producer Stuart Allen

The surrealist playwright N F Simpson had already baffled theatre audiences with his *One Way Pendulum* (about the loopy Groomkirkby family) and *A Resounding Tinkle*, before scripting these bizarre series especially for screening on BBC2.

In *Three Rousing Tinkles* – and its sequel, *Four Tall Tinkles* – Simpson presented the further adventures of Middie and Bro Paradock, who had first appeared in the successful 1957 stage comedy *A Resounding Tinkle*. The Paradocks live in a world where logic has gone haywire and the everyday activities of normal life are distorted to the point of insanity, a situation to which the inhabitants of that world seem completely oblivious. On stage, Middie and Bro had been played by Wendy Craig and Nigel Davenport, and on 30 November 1961, on ITV, Granada's *Television Playhouse* had presented a version starring Tenniel Evans and Billie Whitelaw. The lead actors for these new television adventures were real-life husband and wife Edwin Apps and Pauline Devaney. (They were writers too, their clerical sitcom *All Gas And Gaiters* being launched as a *Comedy Playhouse* pilot during the run of *Three Rousing Tinkles*.)

N F Simpson obviously delighted in these opportunities to subvert the TV medium, writing marathon titles for his episodes, including such gems as 'The Father By Adoption Of One Of The Former Marquis Of Rangoon's Natural Grand-Daughters', 'If Those Are Mr Heckmondwick's Own Personal Pipes They've Been Lagged Once Already' and 'The Best I Can Do By Way Of A Gate-Leg Table Is A Hundredweight Of Coal'.

See also World In Ferment.

Three To One On

UK · BBC · SKETCH

1 × 35 mins colour

16 Jan 1969 · BBC2 Mon 10.25pm

MAIN CAST

Ben Aris
John Gould
Joyce Rae
David Wood

CREDITS

writers Terence Brady, John Gould, David Wood, Michael Bogdanov, Michael Palin/Terry Jones · director Michael Mills

A one-off TV version of a revue featuring three men and one woman. Michael Palin and Terry Jones, Pythons before the year was out, were among the writers. On stage, *Three To*

One On was presented at the Playhouse, Salisbury, in July 1968.

Three 'Tough' Guys

UK · ITV (ATV) · SITCOM

6 × 30 mins · b/w

24 June–2 Sep 1957 · fortnightly
Mon mostly 8.30pm

MAIN CAST

Harry Green
Warren Mitchell
Peter Welch

CREDITS

writers John Law/Bill Craig · producers Cecil Petty (4), Hugh Rennie (2)

An early ITV sitcom from Law and Craig, depicting the adventures of three hapless criminals who bungle every caper.

Warren Mitchell was a 31-year-old up-and-coming, RADA-trained British actor, later to achieve lasting flame as comedy icon Alf Garnett; Harry Green was an American comic actor with years of burlesque and film experience who had moved to England.

Three Up Two Down

UK · BBC · SITCOM

25 × 30 mins · colour

Series One (6) 15 Apr–20 May 1985 · BBC1 Mon 8.30pm

Series Two (6) 7 Apr–19 May 1986 · BBC1 Mon 8.30pm

Series Three (7) 6 Sep–18 Oct 1987 · BBC1 Sun 7.15pm

Series Four (6) 14 May–18 June 1989 · BBC1 Sun 7.15pm

MAIN CAST

Sam Tyler · · · · · · · · · · · · · · Michael Elphick
Daphne Trenchard · · · · · · · · · Angela Thorne
Angie Tyler · · · · · · · · · · · · · Lysette Anthony
Nick Tyler · · · · · · · · · · · · · · · · Ray Burdis
Rhonda · · · · · · · · · · · Vicki Woolf (series 4)

CREDITS

writer Richard Ommanney · director Mandie Fletcher (series 1), John B Hobbs (series 2–4) · producer David Askey (series 1), John B Hobbs (series 2–4)

When Angie and Nick Tyler produce a baby they decide to aid their financial predicament by renting out their basement, which is coveted by both Nick's father, Sam, and Angie's, mother, Daphne. Sharing is the only solution, but the Cheltenham-bred Daphne, who has never forgiven her daughter for marrying a 'common' photographer, is even less enamoured with his father, a somewhat coarse cockney. Both of the new grandparents are widowed and both possess a stubborn streak, thus circumstance and bloody-mindedness results in the unlikely co-habitation. Soon enough, as so often happens in sitcom-land, a romance blossoms, coarse Sam taking quite a shine to the snobbish

Daphne, an affection that remains one-way for a while until she, in turn, recognises his appeal. The comedy arose from the clash of his broad cockney brashness and her refined country sensibilities, and it rarely failed to deliver on this front.

Angela Thorne, who had made an impact as Penelope Keith's sidekick in *To The Manor Born*, had demonstrated her star potential with a dazzling performance as Margaret Thatcher in the hit stage-show *Anyone For Denis?*, and *Three Up, Two Down* proved well suited to her style. Her co-star, Michael Elphick, brought a thick-eared delivery and slower-paced acting style that neatly contrasted with Thorne's performance and correctly emphasised the differences between them. However, it was the possibility that Daphne and Sam would link up romantically that kept viewers on tenterhooks, although so unlikely was the prospect that much interest centred on just how it could be plausibly achieved. The writer duly obliged, introducing into the scenario a girlfriend for Sam – next-door neighbour Rhonda – who acted as the catalyst in bringing Sam and Daphne together.

Three Up, Two Down was a massive audience pleaser and a perfect example of an unexceptional though eminently watchable sitcom that exploited a simple premise to its logical extreme and then didn't hang around to outstay its welcome. A US version, *5 Up, 2 Down*, was attempted, with Nick and Angie Tyler (Jeffrey D Sams and Jackie Mari Roberts) giving birth to triplets, thus causing their feuding respective parents Sam Tyler and Daphne Fitzgerald (Cleavon Little and Emily Yancy) to descend upon their offspring, both determined to help the couple tend their newly arrived family. Richard Ommanney and producer Winifred Hervey-Stallworth were credited with the pilot, which aired on the CBS network on 5 June 1991, although no series developed.

Three's A Crowd

USA · ABC (THE NRW COMPANY/BERGMANN-TAFFNER/D L TAFFNER) · SITCOM

22 × 30 mins · colour

US dates: 25 Sep 1984–9 Apr 1985

UK dates: 11 Nov–16 Dec 1992 (6 episodes) ITV Wed 5am

MAIN CAST

Jack Tripper · · · · · · · · · · · · · · · · John Ritter
Vicky Bradford · · · · · · · · · · · Mary Cadorette
James Bradford · · · · · · · · · · · Robert Mandan
E Z Taylor · · · · · · · · · · · · · · · Alan Campbell

CREDITS

creators Johnnie Mortimer/Brian Cooke · writers various · directors Dave Powers and others · executive producers Ted Bergmann, Michael Ross, Bernie West, George Burditt · producers Martin Rips, Joseph Staretski, George Sunga

Three's A Crowd was the US adaptation of the British sitcom **Robin's Nest**, spun-off from **Three's Company**, the US version of **Man About The House**. (The premise was all but identical to the British *Robin's Nest* – see entry for details.) Here, the lead character, Jack Tripper, fell for a sexy flight attendant named Vicky and they lived together, unmarried, above the restaurant, Jack's Bistro, which they jointly owned with Vicky's disapproving father, James (played by Robert Mandan, Chester Tate in **Soap**). The fourth character – a one-armed Irish dishwasher in *Robin's Nest* – was a local surfing dude, E Z (pronounced 'easy' in American), who was Jack's assistant chef. The restaurant was located not in Fulham but in Ocean Vista, California.

Three's A Crowd was much less successful than *Three's Company* and lasted only 22 episodes compared to its parent show's 169. Just six of the 22 were screened by London-area ITV, all deep into the night.

Three's Company

USA · ABC (THE NRW COMPANY/TTC
PRODUCTIONS/D L TAFFNER) · SITCOM

169 episodes (166 × 30 mins · 3 × 60 mins) · colour

US dates: 15 Mar 1977–18 Sep 1984

*UK dates: 12 Feb–14 Dec 1981 (13 × 30 mins)
ITV various weekdays around 12 midnight

MAIN CAST

Jack Tripper	John Ritter
Janet Wood	Joyce DeWitt
Christmas 'Chrissy' Snow	Suzanne Somers (1977–81)
Helen Roper	Audra Lindley (1977–79)
Stanley Roper	Norman Fell (1977–79)
Larry Dallas	Richard Kline (1978–84)
Ralph Furley	Don Knotts (1979–84)
Cindy Snow	Jenilee Harrison (1980–82)
Terri Alden	Priscilla Barnes (1981–84)
Lana Shields	Ann Wedgeworth (1979–80)

CREDITS

creators Johnnie Mortimer/Brian Cooke · *writers* various · *directors* Bill Hobin, Dave Powers · *executive producers* Don Nicholl, Michael Ross, Bernie West, Budd Grossman, George Burditt, Ted Bergmann, Don Taffner · *producers* Bill Richmond, Gene Perrett, George Burditt, George Sunga, Martin Rips, Joseph Staretski, George Sunga, Don Nicholl, Michael Ross, Bernie West

The American adaptation of the popular ITV sitcom **Man About The House** was itself screened in Britain on the commercial channel (albeit not in all regions). The first episode, indeed, was titled 'A Man About The House' and utilised much the same script as the British opening episode, in which trainee chef Jack Tripper (the US Robin Tripp) is found sleeping in the bath by two attractive young women after an all-night party.

The series was extremely popular in the States and ran for 135 episodes more than its British parent. Common to both, talk of sex (distinct from *active* sex, that is) was the basis for most of the storylines, and American religious leaders and other zealots objected loud and long, citing *Three's Company* as the worst example of what then was termed 'jiggle TV'. Jack was a red-blooded heterosexual but Janet (sensible) and Chrissy (dizzy blonde) tried to convince landlords Helen and Stanley Roper that he was gay, so that they might allow him to shack up with them in their Santa Monica apartment. Helen eventually became wise but Stanley continued to believe the ruse. Many of the British scripts were utilised – which goes some way to explaining the shows' frantic pace – and the threesome even socialised in a British-style pub, the Regal Beagle.

When Norman and Stanley left the series to be set up in their own spin-off *The Ropers* (the US version of **George And Mildred**) they were replaced by a middle-aged hipster, Ralph Furley, and life carried on pretty much as before. Chrissy was axed from the show when, reportedly, the producers refused to cave in to Suzanne Somers' contractual demands, being replaced as Janet and Jack's flat-mate first by Janet's bungling cousin Cindy Snow and then by a nurse, Terri Alden.

The final episode of *Three's Company* paved the way for the sequel, **Three's A Crowd**, which was the US adaptation of the British series **Robin's Nest**. This too aired in Britain – see previous entry.

*Note. Commencing six years after it showed these 13 episodes, London-area ITV screened 171 half-hours of *Three's Company*, between 18 August 1987 and 4 November 1992, all deep into the twilight hours, usually at 4am.

Throb

USA · SYNDICATION (SWANY/TAFT
ENTERTAINMENT) · SITCOM

48 × 30 mins · colour

US dates: Sep 1986–1988

UK dates: 8 Jan 1988–11 Feb 1990
(23 episodes) ITV Fri 12.30am then Sat after 12 midnight

MAIN CAST

Sandy Beatty	Diana Canova
Zachary Armstrong	Jonathan Prince
Jeremy Beatty	Paul W Walker (1986–87); Sean de Veritch (1987–88)
Meredith	Maryedith Burrell
'Blue'	Jane Leeves
Phil Gaines	Richard Cummings Jr

CREDITS

creator Fredi Towbin · *writers* George Bloom, Andy Cowan, Jeffrey Duteil, Daniel Finnerman, Ann L Gibbs/Joel Kimmel, Andy Goldberg, Lee Grant, Barbara Herndon, Susan Herring, Sandy Krinski, Michael Lessac, Laura Levine, Richard Marcus, Jerry Rannow, Hollis Rich, Jill Sacco, Michael Short, George Tibbles, Fredi Towbin, Seth A Weisbord, Jay Wolf · *executive producer* Sy Rosen · *directors* various · *producer* Fredi Towbin

A spin on the youth end of the record industry, and how a 33-year-old can feel ancient within the set-up. *Throb* starred Diana Canova (Corrine Tate in **Soap**) as Sandy Beatty, who has moved to New York City from upstate Buffalo and is working as an administrative assistant in the Manhattan office (well, loft space) of an independently owned new-wave record label, Throb. Beatty is divorced, with a 12-year-old son Jeremy, and is easily the most sensible person among the bunch of weirdoes in and visiting the office. These include the short-in-stature Zach Armstrong (the Throb boss who is attracted to Beatty), and Beatty's promiscuous English colleague Prudence Anne Bartlett – nicknamed 'Blue' – who dresses more outrageously than the label's acts and wishes more than anything else to keep her advanced age (27) a secret, for fear that it will vanquish all her talk of being a young hipster. Blue and Sandy share an apartment in later episodes, their lifestyles clashing in every way. A number of music stars passed through *Throb* in cameo roles, including James Brown, Deniece Williams and Donny Osmond.

Supposed to be a broad Londoner, Blue was played by Jane Leeves, later to appear in **Frasier** as a Mancunian, Daphne Moon. In reality, Leeves hails from East Grinstead, East Sussex, and moved to the USA in 1984 in the hopes – spectacularly achieved – of advancing her career. In England, before her departure, she had only managed a few very low-key ITV appearances, turning up in a Bruce Forsyth special, *Nice To See You!* (21 December 1981) and playing a bimbette in **The Benny Hill Show**.

Note. C5 screened six episodes of *Throb* in 1997, usually deep into the night.

Thundercloud

UK · ITV (YORKSHIRE) · SITCOM

13 × 30 mins · colour

*22 May–31 July 1979 · Tue 7.30pm

MAIN CAST

Lt Cmdr 'Monty' Morgan	John Fraser
CPO Hawkins	James Cosmo
Bella Harrington	Sarah Douglas
Cmdr Flint	Derek Waring
Ord-Seaman Collins	Paul Aston
Dr Smith	Frank Gatliff

CREDITS

creator/executive producer Ian Mackintosh · *writers* Ian Mackintosh (5), Gidley Wheeler (4), Philip Broadley (2), Anthony Skene (2) · *directors* David Reynolds (8), Gerald Blake (5) · *producer* Keith Richardson

A light-hearted Second World War romp, filmed without an audience, depicting the activities at a Royal Navy coastal station in Yorkshire.

Because it has the name HMS *Thundercloud*, the Admiralty believes the coastal station to be a ship, sailing the North Sea and busily tracking down and destroying German U-boats. To this end, it continually sends vital equipment, which the crew – Doctor Smith and Chief Petty Officer Hawkins among them – cheerfully sell off on the black market. Commander Flint, meanwhile, prefers to spend his time flexing his green fingers in the garden. Only Lieutenant Commander Morgan remains a stickler for procedure and rules, although he too has a distraction in the shapely form of the vicar's attractive but naïve daughter Bella Harrington, who is sweet on him.

The series was devised, part written and executive-produced by Ian Mackintosh, a former Lieutenant Commander in the Royal Navy who also created the respected *Warship* documentary series for BBC1 (1973–77).

*Note. London-area screenings were curtailed after 11 episodes by the long strike that affected all ITV stations in the late summer of 1979 (in the capital the commercial channel was blank from 6 August to 24 October). The final two episodes were not shown by London-area ITV but were screened elsewhere.

Tickets For The Titanic

UK · C4 (REGENT PRODUCTIONS) · SITCOMS
6 × 60 mins · colour

Six black comedies on the theme of British life in the 1980s. Alistair Beaton wrote two of them, Andy Hamilton likewise, his future **Drop The Dead Donkey** collaborator Guy Jenkin scripted one, as did Barry Pilton. See individual entries for further details.

4 Mar 1987	Keeping Score
11 Mar 1987	The Way, The Truth, The Video
18 Mar 1987	Checkpoint Chiswick
24 Feb 1988	Pastoral Care
2 Mar 1988	Incident On The Line
9 Mar 1988	Everyone A Winner

Till Death Us Do Part

UK · BBC · SITCOM

56 episodes (26 × 30 mins · colour; 24 × 30 mins · b/w; 1 × 45 mins · colour; 1 × 40 mins · b/w; 1 × 25 mins · b/w; 1 × 20 mins · colour; 1 × short special · b/w; 1 × short special · colour)

Pilot (25 mins · b/w) 22 July 1965 · BBC1 Thu 8.50pm

Series One (7 × 30 mins · b/w) 6 June–1 Aug 1966 · BBC1 Mon 7.30pm

Series Two (10 × 30 mins · b/w) 26 Dec 1966–27 Feb 1967 · BBC1 Mon mostly 7.30pm

Special (40 mins · b/w) *Till Closing Time Us Do Part* 27 Mar 1967 · BBC1 Mon 8.20pm

Short special (b/w) · part of *Christmas Night With The Stars* 25 Dec 1967 · BBC1 Mon 6.40pm

Series Three (7 × 30 mins · b/w) 5 Jan–16 Feb 1968 · BBC1 Fri mostly 8.20pm

Special (20 mins · colour) *The Campaign's Over* aka *Up The Polls* 18 June 1970 · BBC1 Thu 10.05pm

Short special (colour) · part of *Christmas Night With The Stars* 25 Dec 1971 · BBC1 Sat 6.40pm

Series Four (6 × 30 mins · colour) 13 Sep–25 Oct 1972 · BBC1 Wed 9.25pm

Special (45 mins · colour) 26 Dec 1972 · BBC1 Tue 9.10pm

Series Five (7 × 30 mins · colour) 2 Jan–28 Feb 1974 · BBC1 Wed 9.25pm

Series Six (7 × 30 mins · colour) 31 Dec 1974–12 Feb 1975 · BBC1 Wed mostly 9.25pm

Series Seven (6 × 30 mins · colour) 5 Nov–17 Dec 1975 · BBC1 Wed 9.25pm

MAIN CAST

Alf Garnett (Alf Ramsey in pilot) ·	Warren Mitchell
Elsie 'Else' Garnett (Else Ramsey in pilot) · · · · · · · · · · · · · · · · · Gretchen Franklin (pilot); · · · · · · · · · · · · Dandy Nichols (series 1–6)	
Rita · · · · · · · · · · · · · · · · · · ·	Una Stubbs
Mike · · · · · · · · · · · · · · · · · · ·	Anthony Booth

OTHER APPEARANCES

Min Reed · · · · · · · · · · · · · · ·	Patricia Hayes
Bert Reed · · · · · · · · · · · · · · · · · · ·	Alfie Bass
Gran ·	Joan Sims
Paki-Paddy · · · · · · · · · · · · · ·	Spike Milligan
Wally · · · · · · · · · · · · · · · · · · ·	John Junkin
Wally Carey · · · · · · · · · · · · · · ·	Hugh Lloyd
Mrs Carey · · · · · · · · · · · · · · ·	Pat Coombs
other role · · · · · · · · · · · · · · · · ·	Roy Kinnear

CREDITS

writer Johnny Speight · director Douglas Argent (not all episodes) · producer Dennis Main Wilson

A seminal sitcom that became a blueprint for the maturation of the genre, on both sides of the Atlantic. Johnny Speight's creation Alf Garnett was a true larger-than-life figure, and one of the few television characters to achieve an almost Dickensian importance in the public psyche, even entering the vocabulary as a descriptive term for similar individuals.

Years earlier, Speight had developed for Arthur Haynes (**The Arthur Haynes Show**) a belligerent socialist character with an aggressive attitude and deep chip on his shoulder; Garnett was a right-wing variation on the theme: an ill-educated, shockingly opinionated, loud-mouthed, appallingly tempered, deeply angry, Tory-voting, prudish, monarchist bigot, a deeply working-class man who nonetheless had no time for his kind and wouldn't hear a bad word said about the rich and the privileged – not an obvious character to become a TV phenomenon, granted, but this he most

certainly became. Called Alf Ramsey in the *Comedy Playhouse* pilot episode, the surname was changed in deference to the England football manager, also Alf Ramsey, who guided England to the World Cup victory a month after the first series began. Speight turned his Alf into Garnett after a road in Wapping called Garnet Street. The series was set in Wapping, in what has since become a gentrified landscape, home to prosperous businesses and City types who dwell in its newly built de luxe homes. In the 1960s, at the time of *Till Death Us Do Part*, it was badly run-down, very poor and still wrecked by Hitler's bombs that had devastated the Docklands area two decades earlier, a part of London never visited by tourists or listed in the guide books.

Till Death Us Do Part depicted a working-class household comprising Alf and his much put-upon wife Elsie ('Else'), with their slightly trendy daughter Rita and her long-haired 'leftie' husband Mike, who had insufficient money for a place of their own and so shared the cramped Wapping house with the Garnetts. In particular, the comedy arose from the polar-opposite opinions held by Alf and Mike – who could and did argue about absolutely everything under the sun. Mike might have been superficially better informed than Alf but he shared the same intransigence of belief which meant that all arguments ended in stalemate, with neither side learning from the other. The only time the two men seemed to reach an accord was when they both fled to the nearby pub, became inebriated and shared the drunkards' skewed vision of the world. The pub, to Alf, was his principal respite, the place to which he would bolt when, at the end of yet another bitter domestic argument, he realised either that he could take it no further or that he had been outsmarted.

Utilising the new-found television freedoms that series such as **That Was The Week That Was**, **Steptoe And Son** and the ITV (ABC) drama series **Armchair Theatre** had pioneered, *Till Death Us Do Part* crackled with a rare energy, employing a style previously unexplored in the sitcom genre: a cross between kitchen-sink drama and observational comedy. Its scripts were peppered with bad language – everything but the strongest of swear words – and its 'colourful' vocabulary, typified by Alf's street-slang description of ethnic minorities ('wog', 'wop', 'blackie', 'coon', 'mick' and others), generated an avalanche of protests. Such language was scarcely ever heard on TV in any form, and had never before been used in a situation comedy series, all of which at this time, bar *Steptoe And Son*, remained twee, insipid and lightweight by comparison. Sadly, the weight of protests over Speight's employment of such vocabulary – honed and shaped by producer Dennis Main Wilson – often obscured the qualities of the episodes, some of which were quite magnificent, like brilliant, compelling half-hour stage dramas. Unlike other sitcoms, *Till Death Us Do Part* gave the viewers cause to think; its arguments were never ratified but both sides of an issue were presented – usually in an intentionally simplistic and heavy-handed way. The *Financial Times* called the series 'The rampaging, howling embodiment of all the most vulgar and odious prejudices that slop about in the bilges of the national mind.'

With his misanthropic outlook, Garnett was an ugly character on paper, but when made flesh by Warren Mitchell he seemed far more human – more to be pitied than hated. (Mitchell was not the first choice for the role: Peter Sellers, Leo McKern and Lionel Jeffries were all previous contenders.) Inevitably, though, Garnett held an appeal for some viewers, who felt that he was expressing their opinions too: a fact that Speight, a hard-line socialist, neither intended nor envisaged. Despite appearances, his series was never a racist comedy, and Alf Garnett, who held such monstrous opinions, was intended to look like a fool, not a hero, for possessing them. *Radio Times* wrote at the time, 'If you laugh with Alf Garnett you have merely been entertained. If you laugh at him you have been entertained and informed – and that's a victory for Johnny Speight.' Still, many viewers took great exception to the programme's content, although, as Warren Mitchell later commented, pithily, 'Johnny Speight is a great satirist, and satire has always gone over the heads of the idiots.'

Opinions as to the advisability of allowing racists like Garnett to air their views in such an environment have differed widely ever since. Certainly, at its worse, the series features some volatile material that is difficult to defend (like the Pakistani-Irish character Paki-Paddy played by a blacked-up Spike Milligan, who later resurfaced in Speight's sitcom **Curry And Chips**), but, at its best, *Till Death Us Do Part* was a hysterically funny, beautifully crafted piece of work, brought to life by four very convincing comic actors.

In addition to Warren Mitchell's virtuoso performance as Alf, Anthony Booth was excellent as Mike, who was as staunchly left-wing, Labour-loving and republicanist as Garnett was the opposite. A layabout who never seemed to work, Mike liked to tend to his appearance (Alf taunted him accordingly, calling him 'Shirley Temple' on account of his flowing hair) while his Liverpool background caused Alf to belittle him as 'you randy Scouse git'. Rita mostly stayed in the background, preferring to ignore her husband and her father's ceaseless arguments, but occasionally she chipped in with her opinion, usually when aghast at one of her father's particularly outlandish statements. Also very much on the receiving end of Alf's ire was Else, who put up with more mental abuse at the hands of her husband than any woman should have to suffer. His favourite phrase for his partner, whose rare statements indicated a below-average intelligence, was 'you silly moo' – meaning, obviously, cow; the animal epithet was promptly returned, *her* favourite retort being the forcefully spat 'pig!'. As Else, Dandy Nichols did not have a great deal to contribute, and the veteran actress, faced with having to stay on set for long periods without dialogue, developed 'bits of business' to keep herself busy (like reading the telephone book), some of which were memorable scene-stealers. Nichols bowed out after the start of the sixth series owing to ill-health (her character was despatched to Australia to look after an invalid relative) and Patricia Hayes, as Min, with Alfie Bass as her husband Bert, stepped into the series as Alf's neighbours, presenting him with new – but just as bewildering – opponents. In later episodes Rita had a baby, making Alf a belligerent grandfather.

Till Death Us Do Part garnered similar bouquets and brickbats when its format was adapted for an American version, **All In The Family**, and two UK feature-film spin-offs *Till Death Us Do Part* (1969) and *The Alf Garnett Saga* (1972, with Adrienne Posta and Paul Angelis as Rita and Mike). The cast also appeared in a specially written piece in the 1972 *Royal Variety Show* (televised by BBC1 on 5 November). In addition to the specials and sequels listed below, Warren Mitchell appeared on TV as Garnett in a number of chat-shows and guest roles, notably in Dusty Springfield's BBC1 show *Dusty* on 15 August 1967, on the same channel's **The Main Attraction** on 16 July 1983 and in **Comic Relief** on 5 February 1988. He also appeared in *Hogan In London*, the Australian comedian Paul Hogan's second TV special, aired in his home country by the Seven Network (but never seen in the UK) on 22 August 1973.

A German version of *Till Death Us Do Part* was less successful, however. In this, the local producers had made the Garnett character resemble Hitler and the series was taken off by public demand. Johnny Speight then received a letter from the head of German TV that explained 'We just haven't got the racial bigotry in Germany that you have in England'.

The Thoughts Of Chairman Alf At Christmas

UK · ITV (ATV) · STANDUP

1 × 30 mins · colour

26 Dec 1980 · Fri 9.30pm

MAIN CAST

Alf Garnett · · · · · · · · · · · · · Warren Mitchell

CREDITS

writer Johnny Speight · *director/producer* William G Stewart

Subtitled 'On Yer Actual Boxing Day', this one-off special showed Alf Garnett, solo, facing a studio audience and railing them with his thoughts about topical matters. The programme was announced as being the first in an occasional series but it was the only one, although a full run of *Till Death ...* developed within months (see below).

Notes. The title *The Thoughts Of Chairman Alf* originated in a 1976 Garnett stage production at Stratford East, London. A 1994 presentation of the production, taped at the Beck Theatre in Hayes, west of London, by Classic Pictures/BMG, was issued on video and subsequently screened by British satellite/cable TV station UK Gold. (The writer, as usual, was Johnny Speight, the director Robert Garofalo.) Slightly reworked, *The Thoughts Of Chairman Alf* was re-presented to a celebrity-packed studio in *An Audience With Alf Garnett*, networked on ITV by LWT on 5 April 1997. (See **An Audience With ...**)

On 25 October 1994, C4's *Without Walls* documentary series presented *The National Alf*, an appraisal of the character of Alf Garnett. Another, similar programme, *The Life And Times Of Alf Garnett*, in which Arthur Smith looked at Johnny Speight's creation, was screened by BBC2 on 5 January 1997.

On 29 December 1996 BBC1 presented *The Spirit Of 66 With Alf Garnett*, a comedic look back on England's 1966 World Cup soccer triumph, hosted by arguably England's loudest supporter. (Garnett always claimed that his beloved West Ham United won the World Cup for England, captained as they were by Bobby Moore, the Hammers' skipper, and with all four goals being scored by West Ham players.)

Till Death ...

UK · ITV (ATV) · SITCOM

6 × 30 mins colour

22 May–3 July 1981 · Fri 10.30pm

MAIN CAST

Alf Garnett	Warren Mitchell
Elsie 'Else' Garnett	Dandy Nichols
Min	Patricia Hayes
Rita	Una Stubbs
Michael Jr	John Fowler

CREDITS

writer Johnny Speight · *director/producer* William G Stewart

The return of Alf Garnett, a little older but no wiser. He and Else have now retired to Eastbourne and are sharing a place with Min, following the death of her husband Bert. The difficulties of surviving as a pensioner and the occasional visits of Rita and his punk grandchild Michael provided the comedy conflict in this mediocre sequel.

In Sickness And In Health

UK · BBC · SITCOM

47 × 30 mins · colour

Series One (6) 1 Sep–13 Oct 1985 · BBC1 Sun 9.30pm

Special (1) 26 Dec 1985 · BBC1 Thu 8.30pm

Series Two (6) 4 Sep–9 Oct 1986 · BBC1 Thu mostly 9.30pm

Special (1) 23 Dec 1986 · BBC1 Tue 9.30pm

Series Three (6) 22 Oct–26 Nov 1987 · BBC1 Thu 8.30pm

Special (1) 25 Dec 1987 · BBC1 Fri 10.05pm

Series Four (7) 7 Sep–19 Oct 1989 · BBC1 Thu 8.30pm

Special (1) 25 Dec 1989 · BBC1 Mon 9.40pm

Series Five (10) 1 Sep–3 Nov 1990 · BBC1 Sat mostly 8.20pm

Special (1) 30 Dec 1990 · BBC1 Sun 10pm

Series Six (7) 21 Feb–3 Apr 1992 · BBC1 Fri 8pm

MAIN CAST

Alf Garnett · · · · · · · · · · · · Warren Mitchell
Elsie 'Else' Garnett · · · · · · · Dandy Nichols
· · · · · · · · · · · · · · · · · · · (series 1 & special 1)
Mrs Hollingbery · · · · · · · · Carmel McSharry
· (1986–92)
Winston · · · · · Eamonn Walker (series 1–3)
Arthur · · · · · · · · · · · · · · · · · Arthur English
Fred Johnson · · · · · · · · · · · · Ken Campbell
Mrs Johnson · · Eileen Kennally (1985–89);
· · · · · · · · · · · · · · · · · Tricia Kelly (1990–92)
Rita · Una Stubbs
Michael · · · · · · · · · · James Ellis (series 6)

OTHER APPEARANCES

Harry the Milkman · · · · · · · · · Harry Fowler
Goldie · · · · · · · · · · · · · · · · Richard Speight
Min Reed · · · · · · · · · · · · · · Patricia Hayes
Pele · · · · · · · · · · · Vas Blackwood (series 4)
Ricky · · · · · · · · · · · · John Bluthal (series 4)
Railene · · · · · · · · · Noeline Brown (series 4)
Mr Carey · · · · · · · · · · Hugh Lloyd (series 5)
Mrs Carey · · · · · · · · Pat Coombs (series 5)

CREDITS

writer Johnny Speight · *producers* Roger Race (1985–89), Richard Boden (1990–92)

Proving the remarkable durability of the character, Alf Garnett returned to the BBC for a new run of episodes and, in so doing, clocked up his fourth decade on the small-screen.

In the first series of *In Sickness And In Health* Alf found plenty to moan about, having to push about the wheelchair-bound Else and being confronted by his new home-help, the black and 'gay' Winston. But his problems increased in the second series following his wife's death (Dandy Nichols passed away in real life on 6 February 1986) and the arrival of a new thorn in his side, widowed landlady Mrs Hollingbery.

Throughout the run, Alf remained his cantankerous self, now even more jaundiced because his beloved Tory Party, in power since 1979, was in the hands of a 'grocer's daughter' and, at their hands, the welfare state that he needed so badly was failing him. The problems of just getting by so dominated Alf's life that he became noticeably more tolerant against situations he would previously have railed against, achieving an uneasy friendship with Winston and eventually courting Mrs Hollingbery, albeit solely for the extra comfort her cooking and life savings might bring. They even became engaged and travelled to Australia to wed, Alf counting on the generosity of her brother Ricky to help buy them a house – but to no avail. Alf and his bride-to-be returned to the discomfort of east London and Alf was jilted at the altar. Nevertheless, he maintained a grudging relationship with Mrs Hollingbery, and, one day, helping her to move some furniture, he uncovered a fortune in bank notes. Alf spent his last few episodes with riches beyond his wildest dreams ... but still with plenty to complain about.

While never catching the robust and rude energy of the original series, *In Sickness And In Health* was nevertheless a polished piece of work with many fine moments.

Note. In 1997, the ITV company Carlton, in conjunction with the cable/satellite channel UK Gold, made a short series of brief programmes – each about seven minutes – in which, with his typical 'wisdom', Alf Garnett debated topical issues, usually in conversation with Mrs Hollingbery (played once again by Carmel McSharry), who lives in the upstairs flat. Titled *A Word With Alf*, the agreement allowed UK Gold the right to show them first (which it did, on occasional dates from 30 November 1997) with network ITV screenings set to follow in 1998. Johnny Speight wrote the scripts, the executive producer was Andrew Keyte and the director/producer Richard Boden.

Tim Allen Rewires America

USA · SHOWTIME (MESSINA BAKER ENTERTAINMENT) · STANDUP

1 × 60 mins · colour

US date: 7 Dec 1991

UK date: 28 Dec 1993 · C4 Tue 10.20pm

MAIN CAST

Tim Allen

CREDITS

director Ellen Brown · *producers* Richard Baker, Rick Messina

Through the phenomenal success of *Home Improvement*, comedian Tim Allen became one of the hottest figures on US TV. In this cable-made special, viewers were treated to his famous standup routine, which had partly inspired the hit series.

Although a 'golden boy' with American audiences, Allen's charms, and those of his sitcom, failed to attract the same degree of interest in the UK – *Tim Allen Rewires America* holds the dubious distinction of attracting the smallest audience (235,000) in a decade for a comedy show on British TV.

The Tim Vine Christmas Present

UK · C5 (GRUNDY) · STANDUP/SKETCH

1 × 60 mins · colour

24 Dec 1997 · Wed 7pm

MAIN CAST

Tim Vine
Steve Brody
Tom Butcher
Sarah Greene
John Archer
Seeta Indrani
Sophie Lawrence
Shaun Williamson

CREDITS

writer Tim Vine · *director* Phil Chilvers · *producers* Robin Greene, Richard Hearsey

A seasonal special for the comedian/presenter best known to C5 viewers as the host of the game-show *Whittle*. In this Christmas special Vine was given more room to indulge his love of excruciating puns, which peppered his lightning-fast spiel. Jokes, sketches and musical comedy numbers on festive activities were also the order of the day, one of the show's highlights being a recurring mime sketch, 'The Silent Man', in which he interpreted a number of fairly silly scenarios such as 'man wakes up thinking it is Christmas, discovers it is August and then develops a toothache'. The good-humoured show traded heavily on Vine's amiability but over-egged the pudding somewhat with a sickly final musical sequence featuring other stars from C5 and ITV shows.

Time After Time

see CONLEY, Brian

The Time And Motion Man

UK · BBC · SITCOM

1 × 30 mins · b/w

29 July 1965 · BBC1 Thu 8.50pm

MAIN CAST
Kingsley Binns · · · · · · · · · · · Leslie Phillips
Lilian French · · · · · · · · · · · · Pauline Delany
Rainbow · · · · · · · · · · · · · · · Richard Moore
Taxi driver · · · · · · · · · · · · · · · · Billy Milton

CREDITS
writers Dick Clement/Ian La Frenais · *producer* Graeme Muir

Cast against his usual type, Leslie Phillips starred in the title role here as an intense, work-obsessed, precise man whose job is to establish ways in which people can be more efficient. This permeates every aspect of his life, causing him to suggest short-cuts not only as part of his job but when he is out and about, in a café and the Post Office, for example.

A *Comedy Playhouse* offering from the famous team of Clement and La Frenais, this is one of their ideas that didn't become a television classic.

Time For Baxter

see BAXTER, Stanley

Time Of My Life

UK · BBC · SITCOM
6 × 30 mins · colour
18 Mar–22 Apr 1980 · BBC1 Tue 8.30pm

MAIN CAST
Ken Archer · · · · · · · · · · · · · · Mark Kingston
Joan Archer · · · · · · · · · · · · · Amanda Barrie

CREDITS
writer Jim Eldridge · *director* Martin Shardlow · *producer* Dennis Main Wilson

The arrival of the 1980s ushered in a spate of comedies taking mid-life crises as their theme. Such series were more obviously moored in reality than normal sitcom fare, their protagonists facing recognisable everyday problems, in contrast to the traditional domestic sitcoms where stories revolved around the husband's boss coming home for dinner and the wife's inability to cook.

A subject once thought taboo for the sitcom, divorce, provided the topic for further seriously themed sitcoms (such as *Roger Doesn't Live Here Anymore* and *Dear John*) but first out of the gate was *Time Of My Life*. In this, Ken Archer's life takes a phenomenal turn for the worse when, in one day, our hero, 49-years-old, is made redundant after 33 years with the same company, and his wife of 23 years leaves him for a man 20 years his junior. Yet this is just the start of a series of disasters that descend upon Ken like a set of plagues, his misfortune being so great that even his repeated attempts at suicide fail through sheer bad luck. He is mugged, taken hostage, his cheques bounce, he is arrested, committed to an asylum, and more.

Unremitting in its ill-treatment of its lead character, the series attracted a degree of controversy, some viewers feeling that such catastrophes were too serious – and too real for many – to be the basis of comedy. But writer Jim Eldridge (this was his first TV series) and producer Dennis Main Wilson insisted that it was about survival against the odds and not about drowning in a sea of troubles. *Time Of My Life* only lasted for one series but its themes of desertion, depression, redundancy and divorce were now seen as fair game for sitcom writers.

Tin Pan Alice

UK · ITV (GRANADA) · SITCOM
1 × 30 mins · b/w
15 Aug 1963 · Thu 7.30pm

MAIN CAST
Athene Seyler
Warren Mitchell
Carole Carr

CREDITS
writer Peter Coke · *script editor* Barry Took · *director* Eric Fawcett · *producer* Peter Eton

Originally scheduled as one of Granada's *Comedy Four* season, but then delayed, this single-episode sitcom starred the marvellous veteran actress Athene Seyler (aged 74 at this time) as an old biddy running an outmoded music shop, who unexpectedly discovers that she has a 'hit' record within her grasp. Warren Mitchell co-starred, and the singer Carole Carr was on hand to sing the song in question.

To Lucifer – A Son

UK · BBC · SITCOM
1 × 25 mins · b/w
29 June 1967 · BBC1 Thu 9.30pm

MAIN CAST
Nick, Son of Lucifer · · · · · · · · Jimmy Tarbuck
Lucifer · · · · · · · · · · · · · · · John Le Mesurier
St Patrick · · · · · · · · · · · · · · · Dermot Kelly
First woman · · · · · · · · · · · · · Pat Coombs
Second woman · · · · · · · · · · · · Rita Webb
Man · · · · · · · · · · · · · · · · · · · Eddie Malin
Man · · · · · · · · · · · · · · · · · · Tommy Godfrey
Old lady · · · · · · · · · · · · · · · Gladys Dawson
German general · · · · · · · · · · · Gabor Baraker
Arthur English (voice only)

CREDITS
writer Johnny Speight · *producer* Dennis Main Wilson

A single-episode *Comedy Playhouse* pilot from Johnny Speight that cast John Le Mesurier as the rather Hell-weary devil, somewhat at odds with his ambitious with-it son (played by the standup comedian Jimmy Tarbuck) who has trendy ideas on how to make Hell more up-to-date. Speight wrote the part especially for Tarbuck, who appeared in the Easter 1967

special edition of *Till Death Us Do Part* (*Till Closing Time Us Do Part*).

To The Manor Born

UK · BBC · SITCOM
21 × 30 mins · colour
Series One (7) 30 Sep–11 Nov 1979 · BBC1 Sun 8.45pm
Special · 25 Dec 1979 · BBC1 Tue 8pm
Series Two (6) 5 Oct–9 Nov 1980 · BBC1 Sun 8.35pm
Series Three (7) 18 Oct–29 Nov 1981 · BBC1 Sun 7.15pm

MAIN CAST
Audrey fforbes-Hamilton · · · · Penelope Keith
Richard DeVere · · · · · · · · · · · Peter Bowles
Marjory Frobisher · · · · · · · · · Angela Thorne
Brabinger · · · · · · · · · · · · · · · John Rudling
Mrs Polouvicka · · · · · · · · · · · Daphne Heard
Ned · · · · · · · · · · · · · · · · · · Michael Bilton
Rector · · · · · · · · · · · · · · · · · Gerald Sim

CREDITS
writers Peter Spence (20), Christopher Bond (1) · *script associate* Christopher Bond · *producer* Gareth Gwenlan

The Good Life elevated Penelope Keith from well-respected minor actress to the status of a fully-fledged star, and her next sitcom, *To The Manor Born*, proved to be equally as popular. She had already proved adept at milking laughs out of snobbery, and so was ideal in the part of Audrey fforbes-Hamilton, a well-to-do, upper-class elitist who falls on hard times following the death of her husband. So desperate are her financial straits that Audrey is forced to sell her husband's huge Grantleigh Estate and thus move out of its stately manor house, the manor to which she has become accustomed, and into the humble coach-house in the grounds. To make matters worse, the new owner of the manor is a nouveau-riche businessman, Richard DeVere, a man of distant Czech ancestry whom Audrey views as rather common and vulgar because he made his millions in the wholesale grocery business.

Accompanying fforbes-Hamilton on her 'downward spiral' is her loyal but decrepit butler Brabinger, and her close friend Marjory Frobisher. Audrey tries to come to terms with her new social standing and the real world of launderettes, buses and supermarkets, but her deeply ingrained feelings of superiority, and her natural tendency to want her own way, cause her many problems. Slowly, however, she mellows and begins to consider that she may have misjudged DeVere, who seems to have hidden depths and, after all, is rather dashing. After the initial love-hate relationship that has developed – the antagonism all coming from her – it eventually, inevitably, becomes love-love. Finally, in the last episode, Audrey and Richard are married, and so she is reinstated as the lady of the manor.

Peter Spence created the idea in 1968, for a projected radio series to feature Penelope Keith and Bernard Braden – in this first version, Braden played an American businessman, not a Czech descendant. But although it was recorded, the show never aired, and it was only after the premise had been novelised that it finally arrived on TV, with the American element dropped and Christopher Bond on board to help translate the idea for the small-screen. (Bond himself wrote the final episode.) Although the TV production came across as twee to some viewers, it struck a chord with a large section of the public, the high-profile casting, allied to the British fascination with class, proving irresistible; the series attracted huge viewing figures, sometimes in excess of 20 million, and the final episode was seen by almost 24 million, easily the biggest-ever audience for a single programme on British TV, beaten only in 1996 by **Only Fools And Horses**. The exterior scenes were filmed on location at the thousand-acre Cricket St Thomas estate in Somerset, with Grantleigh House being, in reality, Cricket House.

Note. *To The Manor Born* finally appeared in its originally intended medium when BBC Radio 2 aired ten especially recorded episodes from 25 January to 29 March 1997, six being adaptations by Peter Spence of his TV scripts, four being written expressly for the purpose. Penelope Keith and Angela Thorne reprised their TV roles but Keith Barron played Richard DeVere in place of Peter Bowles.

Together Again

UK · ITV (JACK HYLTON TV PRODUCTIONS FOR ASSOCIATED-REDIFFUSION) · STANDUP/SKETCH

6 × 30 mins · b/w

5 Apr–14 June 1957 · fortnightly Fri 8.30pm

MAIN CAST
Bud Flanagan
Chesney Allen

CREDITS
writer Bud Flanagan · *director* John Phillips

A meander down memory lane with Flanagan and Allen, appearing together in public, in a full show, for the first time since their partnership split in 1946. In six gentle shows they reworked vintage sketch material and sang old favourites such as 'Underneath The Arches' and 'Run Rabbit Run'. A feast of nostalgia was guaranteed, and the shows – thankfully preserved on film – are a valuable record of the beloved double-act.

See also *The Crazy Gang, Friday Night With ...* and *Bud.*

Tom, Dick And Harriet

UK · ITV (THAMES) · SITCOM

12 × 30 mins · colour

Series One (6) 13 Sep–18 Oct 1982 · Mon 8pm
Series Two (6) 13 Jan–17 Feb 1983 · Thu 7.30pm

MAIN CAST
Thomas Maddison ········· Lionel Jeffries
Richard Maddison ············ Ian Ogilvy
Harriet Maddison ·········· Brigit Forsyth

CREDITS
writers Johnnie Mortimer/Brian Cooke · *director/producer* Michael Mills

Another sitcom from the prodigious Mortimer and Cooke. Thomas Maddison (a second sitcom role for Lionel Jeffries inside seven months – following **Father Charlie**) is newly widowed but far from sad about it. For 40 years he has been hen-pecked in deepest Cornwall, denied the opportunity to smoke, drink or so much as look at another woman. Now his wife has gone and Thomas can't wait to get going – he scoots to London and descends upon his son Richard and his wife Harriet, determined to make up for lost time. His lodging, disgusting habits and womanising lifestyle certainly impinge upon them: they're both busy well-manicured executives – him in advertising, her in magazine publishing – and the apple cart is well and truly capsized. During the second series, Harriet has conceived and (in a speedy nine months) delivers Tom a grandson.

Tom, Dick And Harriet (a great title, this) spawned a US adaptation, *Foot In The Door*, which CBS launched in 1983 and then cancelled after just six episodes. In this, the widow was Jonah Foot (played by the fine comedy actor Harold Gould), who quits his home in rural New Hampshire for the Manhattan apartment of his son Jim (Kenneth Gilman) and his wife Harriet (Diana Canova – Corrine in **Soap** and later to star in **Throb**).

Tom, Dick And Harry

UK · ITV (YORKSHIRE) · CHILDREN'S SITCOM

6 × 10 mins · colour

20 May–24 June 1976 · Thu 12 noon

MAIN CAST
Tom ····················· Jim Bywater
Dick ····················· Ted Richards
Harry ···················· Pete Ivatts

CREDITS
writer Jim Bywater · *director/producer* Lesley Smith

A flat-sharing knockabout sitcom for the under-fives, written by and co-starring Jim Bywater.

Tom, Dick And Mary

USA · NBC (KAYRO-VUE PRODUCTIONS) · SITCOM

12 × 30 mins · colour

US dates: 5 Oct 1964–4 Jan 1965
UK dates: 30 Oct 1964–14 Jan 1965 (12 × b/w) BBC2 Fri 7.35pm then Thu mostly 8.50pm

MAIN CAST
Dr. Tom Gentry ············· Don Galloway
Mary Gentry ··············· Joyce Bulifant
Dr Dick Moran ············· Steve Franken
Dr Krevoy ················· John Hoyt
Horace ··················· J Edward McKinley
Cliff Murdock ·············· Guy Raymond

CREDITS
producer Les Colodny

Strapped for cash and unable to afford their own apartment, newly-weds Dr Tom Gentry and his wife Mary solve their problem by sharing with one of Tom's medical colleagues, fellow intern Dick Moran. The comedy arose as they got in each other's way (similarly to the later UK sitcom **The Cuckoo Waltz**).

In the USA, the series was screened as one of a trio of sitcoms – along with *Karen* and *Harris Against The World* – that aired under the generic title *90 Bristol Court*, the novel idea being that all three series were set in the same Southern California apartment building at this address. They were screened, one after another, in a 90-minute slot, and each programme was introduced by the building superintendent, Cliff Murdock, who eavesdropped on the lives of its occupants.

Don Galloway, the star of *Tom, Dick And Mary*, became better known to British viewers as Ed Brown in the 1967–75 US detective series *Ironside*.

Tom Ewell

UK · BBC · STANDUP

1 × 30 mins · colour

2 Mar 1970 · BBC2 Mon 9.40pm

MAIN CAST
Tom Ewell
Georgia Brown
Lionel Murton

CREDITS
writers James Thurber, William Saroyan, Ogden Nash · *director* Roger Ordish · *producer* James Gilbert

A one-off BBC special, recorded in London, starring the American comic actor Tom Ewell (probably best remembered as the man tempted by sexy neighbour Marilyn Monroe in the 1955 movie *The Seven Year Itch*). The British-born but Canadian-domiciled actor Lionel Murton, and the British singer-actress Georgia Brown, who regularly worked in the States, assisted with the performances of classic American comedy material.

Ewell's US sitcom *The Tom Ewell Show* (CBS, 1960–61) aired in the UK in at least one ITV region from July 1963, but not in the London area. The series cast the star as Tom Potter, a real-estate agent whose domestic life is peopled entirely by women (wife, mother-in-law and daughters). Ewell went on to appear in the detective drama *Baretta* (1975–78) and in the sitcom **Best Of The West**.

Tom O'Connor …
[various shows]

see O'CONNOR, Tom

Tommy Cooper …
[various shows]

see COOPER, Tommy

Tommy Davidson: Illin' In Philly

USA · SHOWTIME (PUCKER PRODUCTIONS) · STANDUP

1 × 45 mins · colour

US date: 5 Oct 1991

UK date: 13 Feb 1995 · C4 Mon 10.55pm

MAIN CAST
Tommy Davidson

CREDITS
director Keith Truesdell · *producer* Paul Block

A recording of a one-man show by the rising black comedy star Tommy Davidson (one of the *In Living Color* team), filmed at the Shubert Theatre in Philadelphia. He combined comedy routines about horror films and commercials with impressions of singers Elton John, Stevie Wonder and Al Green.

Tonight With Dave Allen

see ALLEN, Dave

The Tony Ferrino Phenomenon

see COOGAN, Steve

The Tony Hancock Show

see HANCOCK, Tony

Too Close For Comfort / The Ted Knight Show

USA · ABC (DON-EL PRODUCTIONS) THEN SYNDICATION (D L TAFFNER/METROMEDIA/LBS COMMUNICATIONS) · SITCOM

151 × 30 mins · colour

US dates: 11 Nov 1980–Sep 1985 (*Too Close For Comfort*); Apr–Sep 1986 (*The Ted Knight Show*)

*UK dates: 29 July 1986–15 Nov 1989 (79 episodes of *Too Close For Comfort*) C4/ITV Tue around 11.30pm (C4) then mostly Thu 4am (ITV)

MAIN CAST
Henry Rush · · · · · · · · · · · · · · · · · Ted Knight
Muriel Rush · · · · · · · · · · · Nancy Dussault
Jackie Rush · · · · · Deborah Van Valkenburgh
Sara Rush · · · · · · · · · · · · · · Lydia Cornell
Monroe Fiscus · · · · · · · · · · · J M J Bullock

OTHER APPEARANCES
Iris Martin · · · · · Audrey Meadows (1982–83)

CREDITS
creators Brian Cooke, Arne Sultan, Earl Barrett · *writers* Brian Cooke, Arne Sultan, Earl Barrett, George Yanok and others · *directors* various · *executive producers* Don Taffner, Arne Sultan, Aaron Ruben · *producers* Earl Barrett, Jerry McPhie, Volney Howard, George Yanok

The American adaptation of Brian Cooke's Thames TV sitcom **Keep It In The Family**. In the British original, Dudley Rush drew the newspaper strip-cartoon *Barney – Adventures Of A Bionic Bulldog*. In this US version, Henry Rush was the creator of the *Cosmic Cow* children's comic strip. In *Keep It In The Family*, Dudley lived with his wife Muriel while their curvaceous daughters Susan and Jacqui occupied the downstairs flat in their north London house. In *Too Close For Comfort*, Henry's wife was Muriel and their nubile daughters were Jackie and Sara, and they all lived together in a two-storey San Francisco duplex. Storylines were borrowed from the British version but then extended much further – 129 episodes were wrung from the uncomplicated concept as opposed to the British tally of 31 – by the arrival of the Rushes' third child (with both parents in their forties), baby Andrew, in 1982, whose thoughts were given a voice audible to the audiences, and by visiting guest stars like Audrey Meadows (Alice Kramden in *The Honeymooners*) as Henry's mother-in-law. Throughout the run, however, the undoubted star of the show was Ted Knight (real name Tadewurz Wladzui Konopka), who had shot to fame, after years of obscure parts, as Ted Baxter, the dullard, self-obsessed newsreader in *The Mary Tyler Moore Show*. In truth, Knight played Henry Rush in virtually the same way as he did Baxter, gleaning confirmed laughs vicariously from a character whom American TV viewers had long taken to their hearts.

ABC networked 63 episodes of *Too Close For Comfort*, from 11 November 1980 to 15 September 1983, but then cancelled the show, considering its best days past. (Just before doing so, however, on 5 May 1983, the network aired a pilot for a proposed spin-off series, *Family Business*, with the Rush family guest appearing in this opening episode. It went no further.) Right away, however, *Too Close For Comfort* went back into production for 'first-run syndication', with 66 additional episodes being made for overseas sale and domestic screening from 2 April 1984. Finally, from April 1986, the series was officially retitled *The Ted Knight Show* and the scenario altered from San Francisco to Mill Valley, to where Henry and Muriel had moved home – finally shedding their troublesome children – and where Henry had purchased part-ownership of a local newspaper, *The Marin Bugler*. But with just 22 episodes in the can, everything came to an end when Knight died of cancer that August, aged 62.

*Note. *Too Close For Comfort* was first seen in Britain on C4, which aired 13 episodes from 29 July to 28 October 1986. These were then screened again on London-area ITV from 20 August to 12 November 1987, at the start of a run that led to 66 further, previously unseen, episodes being shown from 19 November 1987 to 15 November 1989.

Too Much Monkey Business

UK · BBC · SITCOM

1 × 30 mins · colour

12 Dec 1974 · BBC1 Thu 8pm

MAIN CAST
Jim · · · · · · · · · · · · · Norman Rossington
Laura · · · · · · · · · · · · · · · · Pat Heywood
Andy · · · · · · · · · · · · · · · George Innes
Mr Barnes · · · · · · · · · · · · John Ringham
Barry · · · · · · · · · · · · · · Harold Goodwin
Brian · · · · · · · · · · · · · Michael O'Hagan

CREDITS
writer Roy Kendall · *producer* Douglas Argent

A sitcom pilot starring Norman Rossington, the reliable comic actor who had shot to fame as 'Cupcake' in **The Army Game** and then gone on to play a number of starring roles on TV and in feature films. Here he was cast as Jim, a man who is made redundant from his job and replaced by a chimpanzee. No series developed.

See also **Spanner In The Works**.

Took And Co

UK · ITV (YORKSHIRE) · SKETCH

7 × 30 mins · colour

7 Aug–18 Sep 1977 · Sun mostly 11pm

MAIN CAST
Barry Took
Robin Bailey
Andrew Sachs
David Battley
Chris Emmett
Gwen Taylor

CREDITS
writers Alan Coren, Chris Miller, Chris Emmett, David Renwick, Tony Bilbow, Miles Kington, A F G Lewis, E S Turner, Melody Sachs, Andrew Sachs · *director/producer* Vernon Lawrence

A good series, with Barry Took introducing sketches contributed by a stellar cast of writers and performed by some fine character actors. As a result of this connection, director/producer Vernon Lawrence later worked with Robin Bailey on **Tales From A Long Room** and with Gwen Taylor in **Duty Free**, while Yorkshire Television employed Chris Emmett as resident comic in the quiz-show *3-2-1*.

See also **N.U.T.S.**

Tooth And Claw

UK · BBC · SITCOM

1 × 30 mins · b/w

28 Apr 1969 · BBC1 Mon 7.30pm

MAIN CAST

Reuben Tooth · · · · · · · · · · · Warren Mitchell
Sydney Claw · · · · · · · · · · · · Marty Feldman
Clanders · · · · · · · · · · · · · Richard Caldicot
Silt · · · · · · · · · · · · · · · · · Anthony Dawes
Waiter · · · · · · · · · · · · · · Norman Chappell
narrator · · · · · · · Ronald Fletcher (voice only)

CREDITS

writers Marty Feldman/Barry Took · director Roger Race · producer Barry Lupino

The script of *Tooth And Claw* (written in 1965) sat on the shelf for four years before being produced as a *Comedy Playhouse* one-off starring Warren Mitchell and the co-writer of the piece, Marty Feldman. This was a typical over-the-top premise from writers Took and Feldman, centring on two Jewish multi-millionaires – bitter rivals whose overriding passion is to out-do each other. No series developed.

The Top Secret Life Of Edgar Briggs

UK · ITV (LWT) · SITCOM

13 × 30 mins · colour

15 Sep–20 Dec 1974 · Sun 7.25pm then Fri 7pm

MAIN CAST

Edgar Briggs · · · · · · · · · · · · · · David Jason
Jennifer Briggs · · · · · · · · · · Barbara Angell
Cathy · · · · · · · · · · · · · · Elizabeth Counsell
The Commander · · · · · · · · · · Noel Coleman
Greville · · · · · · · · · · · · · Gary Waldhorn
Spencer · · · · · · · · · · · · · · · · · Mark Eden
Buxton · · · · · · · · · · · · · Michael Stainton

CREDITS

writers Bernard McKenna/Richard Laing (12), David Jason (1) · directors Bryan Izzard (11), Bruce Gowers (2) · producer Humphrey Barclay

Another rung on the long ladder to super-stardom for the diddy DJ, David Jason, given a further helping hand by producer Humphrey Barclay, who had 'discovered' him performing in a Bournemouth pier theatre and launched him on TV in 1968 in *Do Not Adjust Your Set*.

Barclay remained keen to see his protégé get to the top, placing him in this funny spy spoof (like a Whitehall version of *Get Smart*) written by McKenna and Laing. With his trilby and pipe, Edgar Briggs was a hopeless counter-espionage agent, transferred to the Secret Intelligence Service by dint of an administrative error. Proud to be British and devoted to his wife Jennifer, he would have probably indulged in some extra-maritals provided, first, that his assistant Cathy had invited him, and, second, that he could have overcome his shyness. Although as much a danger to the SIS as to the enemy, Briggs

always managed to turn his ineptitude into dubious successes that were the envy of his associates. Such escapades usually involved much prat-foolishness and pratfalls, with Jason – blessed with a particular talent for falling over in funny ways – performing all his own stunts in the manner that Michael Crawford was doing in the BBC's *Some Mothers Do 'Ave 'Em* at this time.

Topper

USA · CBS (LOVETON-SCHUBERT PRODUCTIONS) · SITCOM

78 × 30 mins · b/w

US dates: 9 Oct 1953–30 Sep 1955

UK dates: 27 Dec 1955–29 Aug 1957 (36 episodes) ITV Tue 7.30pm then various days and times

MAIN CAST

George Kerby · · · · · · · · · · · Robert Sterling
Marion Kerby · · · · · · · · · · · · Anne Jeffreys
Cosmo Topper · · · · · · · · · · · Leo G Carroll
Henrietta Topper · · · · · · · · · · · Lee Patrick
Mr Schuyler · · · · · · · · · · · · Thurston Hall
Katie · · · · · · · Kathleen Freeman (1953–54)
Maggie · · · · · · · · · Edna Skinner (1954–55)

CREDITS

creator Thorne Smith · writers George S Oppenheimer, Philip Rapp · director Philip Rapp · producers John W Loveton, Bernard L Schubert

The first 'fantasy' comedy series on American TV, *Topper* extended the life of a book and a trio of films into a major hit of its time, and a fascinating period piece when re-viewed today.

This is the premise: George and Marion Kerby are a zesty, fun-loving couple enjoying a fifth wedding anniversary skiing holiday in Switzerland when they are killed in an avalanche, along with their potential rescuer, a St Bernard dog. As they pass to 'the other side' their spectral selves return home, to inhabit once again their country house in New York. When they arrive they see that it is being looked over as a potential purchase by an ageing bank executive, Cosmo Topper, and his prim wife Henrietta. All three ghosts – including, that is, the alcohol-tippling St Bernard, who has accompanied them on the ghostly journey, and whom they name Neil – make themselves visible and audible to Mr Topper and they encourage him to buy it.

Although they view him with affection, the ghosts – being the mischievous sort – delight in getting Topper into no end of trouble. His biggest problem is that the spectres are visible only to him – not to Henrietta, nor to his banking boss Mr Schuyler, nor to their maids Katie or Maggie or any of the numerous house visitors – so Topper's sanity is repeatedly called into question by those who find him talking to (apparently) nobody. On the credit side of the balance sheet, though, George ('that most sporting spirit')

and Marion ('the ghostess with the mostess') liberate inside Topper a joyous free-spirit that the hitherto dull banker has keep hidden for far too long, something that comes as an understandable – and unwelcome – shock to Henrietta.

Everybody played their part well. English actor Leo G Carroll (who had appeared as the ghost of Marley in the 1938 film of Dickens' *A Christmas Carol* and would later appear as the urbane Mr Waverly in *The Man From U.N.C.L.E.*) was a fine Topper, and Robert Sterling and Anne Jeffreys, the Kerbys, certainly displayed plenty of zip. They were just married to each other in real life at the time, so perhaps needed little direction to come across on TV as healthy lovers, and, unusually for the period, equals in their partnership. The series also benefited from what, at the time, were effective camera techniques. Trick photography made the ghostly Kerbys and their dog seem trans-parent, and this film was overlaid on top of scenes with mortals so that everyone could be seen together. Household items also seemed to move of their own accord when the Kerbys were at their most playful, propelled by wires that were invisible (mostly) to the cameras.

All of the characters were born in the 1930s novel *The Jovial Ghosts*, written by Thorne Smith. (All but the dog that is: Smith's original story had the Kerbys being killed in a car smash, hence there was no St Bernard on the scene.) The novel was then turned into a movie, *Topper*, in 1937, produced by the Hal Roach studio and starring Cary Grant and Constance Bennett as the Kerbys and Roland Young as Cosmo. This led to two direct movie sequels, *Topper Takes A Trip* (1938) and *Topper Returns* (1941), and a 1945 NBC radio series, *The Adventures Of Topper*. Since the 1950s there have been two failed attempts at reviving the creation on TV: *Topper Returns* (screened in the USA on 19 March 1973) was a half-hour pilot that starred John Fink, Stefanie Powers and Roddy McDowall; *Topper* (9 November 1979) was a two-hour TV special with Andrew Stevens, Kate Jackson and Jack Warden.

Thirty-six episodes, drawn from both US seasons, were screened by London-area ITV in the 1950s, and BBC2 presented *Topper* to a new generation of viewers with 12 episodes from 9 May to 31 August 1983.

Tottering Towers

UK · ITV (THAMES) · CHILDREN'S SITCOM

13 × 30 mins · colour

20 Oct 1971–12 Jan 1972 · Wed 5.20pm

MAIN CAST

43rd Duke of Tottering · · · · · William Mervyn
Daffy · · · · · · · · · · · · · · · · Stacey Gregg
Dick · · · · · · · · · · · · · · · · · · Tom Owen
Mrs Pouncer · · · · · · · · · · · · · Avice Landon

Gabbige	David Stoll
Geko	Leon Lissek
Miss Twitty	Patsy Rowlands
'Fingers' Fish	John Louis Mansi
Benny the Nose	Vic Wise
PC Poppy	David Lodge
Sammy the Fog	Bernard Spear
Boysie	Keith Marsh
Joe the Creep	Robert Gillespie
Prayer-book Perce	Talfryn Thomas
Mimi	Magda Miller
Soapy Cyril	Tim Barrett
Bertie Bogmoss	Sam Kydd
Harry O'Hara	Harry Towb

CREDITS

writers Max Oberman (4), Milo Cortese (3), Meretrix Quill (3), Antiphone Pavo (3) · directors/producers Adrian Cooper (7), Vic Hughes (6)

A fine cast distinguished this wacky children's sitcom, led by the plummy-voiced William Mervyn (the sitcom *All Gas And Gaiters*, the detective series *Mr Rose* and the feature film *The Railway Children* were among his recent credits).

Mervyn played the 43rd Duke of Tottering, who lived at the haunted ancestral stately pile Tottering Towers, situated in the village of Tottering Sideways, near Sumweir-on-Thames. The Duke went around in a deer-stalker hat and leather motoring coat and was a master inventor (his creations included a speaking suit of armour whom he named Gilbert, a fishing bicycle, a flying scooter, and a machine to protect his rhubarb patch) but his gadgets never quite worked out the way he would have wished. Unfortunately, the Duke was also deep in debt and the bailiffs were closing in. So, too, were a pair of burglars, Benny the Nose and 'Fingers' Fish, who planned to rob the fortune they believed was stashed inside the mansion. To the rescue came two teenagers: an American history student girl named Daffy and the nephew of the Duke's housekeeper Mrs Pouncer, Dick. The 13 episodes depicted the youngsters' battle to save the Duke from bankruptcy, the thieves and himself.

Note. Two of the accredited writers appear to be pseudonyms; their true identities remain undisclosed.

A Touch Of Spice

UK · BBC · SITCOM

6 × 30 mins · colour

9 Mar–13 Apr 1989 · BBC1 Thu 8.30pm

MAIN CAST

Victoria Morrison	Julia Watson
Dawn McKenzie	Natalie Ogle
Clive	Martin Jacobs
Helen	Virginia Stride

CREDITS

writer Francis Greig · director/producer Sue Bysh

A simple but refreshingly youthful series that probably needed more time to find its feet but came to a halt after one series.

Victoria and Dawn are close friends who share a flat and work at the same restaurant, Victoria as a commis-chef, Dawn as a waitress. They both loathe their jobs, mostly because of the unwanted attentions of the lecherous chef, Fred Ponsonby. The situation finally becomes intolerable and the young women leave to form their own catering company, aided by their friend Clive and hindered by Victoria's mother, Helen.

A Touch Of The Casanovas

UK · ITV (THAMES) · SITCOM

1 × 45 mins · colour

31 Dec 1975 · Wed 10.15pm

MAIN CAST

Francisco	Frankie Howerd
Casanova	Stuart Damon
Clementina	Patsy Rowlands
Teresa	Madeleine Smith

CREDITS

writers Sid Colin/Hugh Stuckey · director/producer Michael Mills

Keen to repeat the great success of *Up Pompeii!*, and perhaps to improve upon the dire *Whoops Baghdad*, Frankie Howerd came up with the idea for a Casanova series on ITV, in which he would portray the great lover's body-servant, Francisco. Despite the announcement of a full series for 1976, the idea failed to proceed beyond a single pilot episode, screened the previous New Year's Eve.

See also Frankie Howerd's combined entry.

A Touch Of The Norman Vaughans

UK · ITV (ATV) · STANDUP

12 × 30 mins · b/w

3 Jan–27 Mar 1964 · Fri 10.05pm

MAIN CAST

Norman Vaughan

CREDITS

writers Eric Merriman (6), Lew Schwarz (6) · producers Colin Clews, Alan Tarrant, Albert Locke

Following his elevation to stardom as presenter of the weekly variety show *Val Parnell's Sunday Night At The London Palladium*, the Liverpool-born comic Norman Vaughan was given his own networked ITV series, set for six editions but extended to 12. There were guest acts each week and plenty of opportunities for Norman to repeat his 'swinging' and 'dodgy' catchphrases to the studio audience and viewers at home.

See also Scott Free and The Norman Vaughan Show.

A Touch Of The Sun

see EMERY, Dick

Tracey And Me

UK · ITV (ASSOCIATED-REDIFFUSION) · SITCOM

3 × 30 mins · b/w

17 July–31 July 1956 · Tue 10pm

MAIN CAST

Tracey	Joan Heal
Wally	Leslie Phillips
Mr Crudnick	George Benson
Dorothy	Nicolette Roeg
Hyacinth	Sandra Dorne
Miss Peabody	Edna Fryer
Albert	Robert Webber

CREDITS

writer John Crilley · director Peter Croft

One of the many 'husband-and-wife' sitcoms that followed the success of *I Love Lucy*, *Tracey And Me* co-starred former child actor Leslie Phillips, 32 at the time, as a young architect named Wally – the 'Me' in the series' title – and comic actress Joan Heal as the dizzy Tracey, who was perpetually getting into scrapes and trying her husband's patience. Wally preferred to retreat to the office, where he had engaged a beautiful secretary …

Seemingly set for a long run, *Tracey And Me* was retired after three episodes.

The Tracey Ullman Show

USA · FOX (GRACIE FILMS) · SKETCH

82 editions (79 × 30 mins · 2 × 60 mins · 1 × 90 mins) · colour

US dates: 5 Apr 1987–1 Sep 1990

UK dates: 8 Jan 1988–30 Aug 1991 (46 × 30 mins) BBC2 Fri 9pm then Thu 9.30pm then Fri 9.35pm

MAIN CAST

Tracey Ullman
Julie Kavner
Dan Castellaneta
Joe Malone
Sam McMurray

CREDITS

creators Jerry Belson, James L Brooks, Ken Estin, Heide Perlman · writers Jerry Belson, James L Brooks, Allan Burns, Dan Castellaneta, Ken Estin, Kim Fuller, Marc Flanagan, Joe Malone, Heide Perlman, Miriam Trogdon, Ken Levine/David Isaacs · directors various · executive producers Jerry Belson, James L Brooks, Ken Estin, Heide Perlman, Sam Simon · producers James L Brooks, Richard Sakai

Following her rise to fame on *Three Of A Kind* and further successes in *A Kick Up The Eighties* and *Girls On Top*, the British comic actress Tracey Ullman (born in Buckinghamshire on 30 December 1954) stretched her career into new areas, enjoying much success as a pop singer and breaking into feature films with roles in Paul McCartney's *Give My Regards To Broad Street* (1984), *Plenty* (1985) and *Jumpin' Jack Flash* (1986). During this latter period she moved to Hollywood to capitalise on her burgeoning reputation, but found it difficult to kick-start a US TV career. Her breakthrough came when she sent tapes of her work to James L Brooks, the writer/producer of classic sitcoms *Taxi* and *Cheers*. Brooks was impressed and worked with Ullman to find the right vehicle for her varied talents. In 1987 they launched *The Tracey Ullman Show* on the newly formed Fox network, and it was an instant hit.

The format of the show capitalised on Ullman's acting ability and mastery of dialects and characterisation by placing her in different comedy playlets each week, some only a few minutes long, some lasting for more than half the programme. She was also supported by a regular cast and by weekly special guests, and her dancing was choreographed by the then unknown Paula Abdul. This format had been explored before by other headlining female comedy stars (**Beryl Reid**, Diana Rigg in *Diana*, and, later, Emma Thompson in *Thompson*) but none succeeded as well as *The Tracey Ullman Show*, which was nominated for five Emmys during its first year and, indeed, became the first Fox show to win the prestigious award. Adding to the mix were animated sections, usually just a few seconds long, which appeared between the sketches. These were drawn by Matt Groening, whose successful syndicated newspaper comic-strip, *Life In Hell*, had attracted a huge cult following among young people, who identified with its cast of offbeat, somewhat unsettling characters inhabiting an oppressive and depressive version of the world. For TV, rather than just rehash the strip, Groening tried out new ideas and characters, the most appealing ones being the members of a dysfunctional working-class family, the Simpsons. James L Brooks realised the potential of these primitive, jerky cartoons and later developed them into the smash-hit animated sitcom **The Simpsons**.

In the UK, *The Tracey Ullman Show* met with no success at all, many critics and viewers objecting to what they saw as the 'phoney Americanisation of Our Tracey'. Also, the pace of the shows was perhaps too slow for British audiences, and the nature of the sketches – which embraced pathos, desperation and dramatic situations – was not of a style to which British audiences respond well (witness the critical slamming that *Diana* and *Thompson* accrued). The BBC also elected to omit the animated *Simpsons* sequences, perhaps thinking them too weirdly American for British audiences, so viewers had no chance to see this cult in the making.

Ullman must have been disillusioned with her home country's response, although – being British herself – she probably could have predicted the cynical reception that it was bound to receive.

Tracey Ullman: A Class Act

UK · ITV (WITZEND/SELECTV FOR MERIDIAN) · SATIRE

1 × 50 mins · colour

9 Jan 1993 · Sat 10pm

Hethers

CAST

Jackie Pillsworth/	
Janine 'Janey' Pillsworth	Tracey Ullman
Frank Pillsworth	Michael Palin
Mrs Birdsall	Susan Wooldridge

writers Dick Clement/Ian La Frenais

Air Travel

CAST

Clare/Trevor Ayliss	Tracey Ullman
'Nick Watkins'	Timothy Spall
'Nigel Summersby'	Alan Gilchrist
Terri	Susan Wooldridge

writers Gary Howe/Richard Preddy

Thirty-Seven Up

CAST

Kelly/Virginia/Denise	Tracey Ullman
Timothy/Steve	Michael Palin
Peter	Guy Edwards

writer Kim Fuller

CREDITS

additional material Tracey Ullman · *director* Les Blair · *executive producers* Allan McKeown, Tony Charles · *producer* Jo Wright

A 50-minute (US: one-hour) special, comprising three self-contained shorts, which marked a one-off return of Britain's prodigal comedian Tracey Ullman from the USA. Having lived Stateside for nine years to this point, Ullman was aware that the one aspect of British life she did not miss was its all-permeating class system. Supported by a number of top names, principally Michael Palin, she was cast in a variety of roles in the three well-scripted short comedies, each of which took a swipe at the class system. (The programme also had a second purpose: it formed part of Meridian TV's application for the ITV franchise for the south of England, which it duly won.)

Hethers, written by Clement and La Frenais, saw Ullman and Michael Palin play a lower-middle-class couple (bordering on working-class) with upper-middle-class aspirations, denying themselves all luxuries so that they could afford to send their daughter Janine to Hetherington Hall School For Girls, a very expensive boarding establishment for daughters of the elite. They succeed, but she endures a torrid time there amid snooty fellow students until, after five

years, 'Janey' (as she now calls herself) has become so hoity-toity that she completely rejects her parents – a point which, it transpires, they have wished for all along. (A sequel to *Hethers* was included in *Tracey Ullman – Takes On New York*.)

Howe and Preddy's *Air Travel* depicted a Florida-to-London Heathrow flight aboard Class Air, the only airline where seats are allocated according to one's class and where the working-class pilots upwardly change their names and accents to make intercom announcements. Tracey Ullman was most convincing here as Trevor, a singing and dancing gay male air steward with a perfect handle on where his passengers should be seated.

Poking fun at the absurdities of the class system, *Thirty-Seven Up* by Kim Fuller (who also wrote sketches for Ullman's US series **The Tracey Ullman Show**) lampooned a novel, award-winning sequence of Granada TV documentary films, researched and mostly directed by Michael Apted, in which chosen children from various classes and backgrounds were interviewed at the age of seven (in *Seven Up*, the 5 May 1964 edition of *World In Action*) and then revisited every seven years for, successively, *Seven Plus Seven* (15 December 1970), *Twenty-One* (9 May 1977), *28 Up* (20–21 November 1984) and *35 Up* (22 May 1991) in order to trace their development and life stories. Fuller's *Thirty-Seven Up* focused on three children: a working-class tearaway girl named Kelly scrapping her way through the state-school system, the middle-class grammar school boy Peter, and the upper-class prep school toff Timothy, who had his life mapped out in front of him: Charterhouse, Cambridge, barrister, wife, MP, sex scandal and cirrhosis of the liver. Interviewed at succeeding seven-year stages the spoof showed how they grew up (or not, in Peter's case – he stayed young) and followed the paths their class dictated.

In addition to the three main pieces, *Tracey Ullman: A Class Act* also included a very short (two-minute) fourth piece entitled *Powder Room*, set in the ladies' toilet of a large London department store. In this, Ullman appeared in four different guises: a poodle-carrying elderly lady, a makeover artist from the shop floor, a dowdy Scots woman and a cockney taxi driver.

Tracey Ullman: A Class Act was so successful that a second programme, *Tracey Ullman – Takes On New York*, made in and primarily for America, was screened on British TV exactly one year later. This, in turn, led to a major US series, *Tracey Ullman – Takes On*, broadcast in North America by the cable network HBO, but not screened in Britain until C5 announced that it had bought ten editions (the first series) for showing from January 1998.

Tracey Ullman – Takes On New York

USA · HBO (WITZEND PRODUCTIONS/SELECTV) · SATIRE

1 × 60 mins · colour

US date: 9 Oct 1993

UK date: 9 Jan 1994 · ITV Sun 11pm

The Johnsons

CAST

Penny Johnson/	
Linda Granger	Tracey Ullman
Gordon Johnson	Dan Castellaneta

writer Tony Sheehan

Family Reunion

CAST

'Janey' Pillsworth/	
Jackie Pillsworth	Tracey Ullman
Frank Pillsworth	Michael Williams

writers Dick Clement/Ian La Frenais

The Rosenthal Affair

CAST

Fern Rosenthal	Tracey Ullman
Harry Rosenthal	Michael Tucker

writers Stephen Nathan/Marc Flanagan

CREDITS

director Don Scardino · *executive producers* Allan McKeown, Tony Charles · *producer* David Wimbury

Following *Tracey Ullman: A Class Act*, screened first in Britain and then in the USA on the cable channel HBO (23 November 1993), the US-based British comedian compiled another three-in-one special – this time made and set in America. *Tracey Ullman – Takes On New York* chronicled the adventures of three couples visiting the Big Apple for the weekend. As stated in the previous entry, the success of this programme – Ullman won a 1995 CableACE award for her numerous excellent performances – led to a full HBO series entitled *Tracey Ullman – Takes On*, weekly half-hours broadcast by the Fox network from 24 January 1996. This series, in turn, has won Ullman further Emmy, Golden Globe, and CableACE awards.

The Johnsons featured Ullman as the ultra-excitable Penny Johnson, a tourist in New York with her over-anxious husband Gordon (played by Dan Castellaneta, a regular in *The Tracey Ullman Show* and the voice of Homer in *The Simpsons*). Everything goes wrong as they set out to see actress Linda Granger (Ullman again), publicised as being '100-per-cent cancer-free', in her Broadway stage comeback *Finian's Rainbow*.

Written by Dick Clement and Ian La Frenais, *Family Reunion* was a sequel to the *Hethers* segment of *Tracey Ullman: A Class Act* (see that entry for details). It is now nine years since Janey Pillsworth has set eyes upon her parents Jackie and Frank (the latter now played by Michael Williams, replacing

Michael Palin), having brutally turned her back on them as 'common'. Living in New York as the ultra successful editor of the swanky *Manhattan* magazine, Janey is the subject of a TV show for which, planned as a happy reunion surprise, the TV company flies over her parents from England.

In the third film, *The Rosenthal Affair*, Ullman starred as a neurotic Jewess, Fern Rosenthal, whose daughter is about to be married in New York City. Visiting from out of town, Fern and her husband (played by Michael Tucker, Stuart Markowitz in *LA Law*) are determined to show off in front of their future in-laws from Michigan.

The Linda Granger, Janey Pillsworth and Fern and Harry Rosenthal characters, as well as the gay flight attendant Trevor Ayliss from *Tracey Ullman: A Class Act*, went on to feature regularly in the weekly series *Tracey Ullman – Takes On*.

The Train Now Standing

UK · ITV (LWT) · SITCOM

15 × 30 mins · colour

Series One (7) 20 May–1 July 1972 · Sat mostly 5.10pm

Series Two (8) 8 July–2 Sep 1973 · Sun 9.30pm

MAIN CAST

Hedley Green	Bill Fraser
Peter Pringle	Hugh Walters
Rosie	Pamela Cundell (series 1)
George	Norman Mitchell (series 1)
Mr Foskins	Bartlett Mullins (series 1)
Fred	Arthur White (series 1)
Bill	George Waring (series 1)
Charlie	Geoff L'Cise (series 1)
Mr Potts	Denis Lill (series 1)
Mr Pitts	Garfield Morgan (series 2)
Brenda	Brenda Peters (series 2)
Ken	Ken Wynne (series 2)

CREDITS

writers Jon Watkins/John Swallow (series 1), Ian La Frenais (4 eps in series 2), Jon Watkins (3 eps in series 2), Geoff Rowley/Andy Baker (1 ep in series 2) · *director/producer* Derrick Goodwin

Bill Fraser – excellent as Snudge in *The Army Game* and *Bootsie And Snudge* – starred in this railway sitcom, cast as Hedley Green, station master at Burberry Halt, a decrepit, sleepy country spot on the Milchester line. Time has stood still here, and Hedley Green (his name sounding a bit like a station itself) presides over his little bit of Olde Englande, still wearing the uniform of the long-since-demised Great Western Railway and utilising a rule book that came into force in 1933. Visited by three trains a day but never by any inspectors, the war veteran Green and his younger, more impressionable assistant, Peter Pringle, spend their time dealing with life's minor crises, usually caused by the area manager (a Mr Potts in the first series, a Mr Pitts in the second). Comfortable with the past, uneasy

with the present and suspicious of the future, Green usually manages to muddle through, gaining vital and free sustenance from the one-penny Nestlé's chocolate vending machine by applying a swift boot to the appropriate place. Outdoor scenes for the series were filmed on location at a disused station in Bodiam, East Sussex.

The 'forgotten-railway' premise was also the basis for *Oh, Doctor Beeching!*, screened by BBC1 from 1995.

The Trev And Simon Summer Special

UK · BBC · SKETCH

1 × 30 mins · colour

29 July 1995 · BBC1 Sat 5.50pm

MAIN CAST

Trev Neal

Simon Hickson

CREDITS

writers Trev Neal/Simon Hickson · *executive producer* Colin Gilbert · *producers* Dave Behrens, Caroline Roberts

The enthusiastic comic double-act Trev and Simon made their mark with a host of appearances in BBC1 Saturday-morning children's series *Going Live!* (1987–93) and *Live & Kicking* (from 1993). As well as proving adept at quick-witted interplay with guest stars, they created many wacky characters and presented sketches in a knowing style reminiscent of *Tiswas*, the cult children's show popular with adults (1974–82). In recognition of the pair's obvious appeal to older viewers, they were given this one-off comedy special in which to display their talents to a wider audience. (This in turn led to the series *Trev And Simon's Transmission Impossible*.)

They brought with them the best of their established routines, including 'The World Of The Strange' and Russ and Ross from the PVC Car Boot Shopping Channel, and introduced new characters: chefs Jeff and Geoff from *Cook That*, the Petrol Shop Boys, and the Chemists, the latest in their long line of bizarre retailers.

Trev And Simon's Transmission Impossible

UK · BBC · SKETCH

21 × 15 mins · colour

Series One (6) 30 Oct–4 Dec 1996 · BBC2 Wed 6.45pm

Special · 21 Dec 1996 · BBC1 Sat around 10.30am

Series Two (14) 8 Jan–16 Apr 1997 · BBC2 Wed 6.45pm

MAIN CAST

Trev Neal

Simon Hickson

CREDITS

writers Trev Neal/Simon Hickson · *director* Sue Morgan · *executive producer* Chris Bellinger · *producer* David Mercer

Following the *Trev And Simon Summer Special*, the comic duo were given a regular early-evening slot on BBC2 to continue their business. New characters this time included art experts Dominic and Daniel in *Art For 'Em*; Picklin' Jeff, the man who'll pickle just about anything; the Da Silva brothers, examining natural history in *Fortunate To Be Human*; and Lincoln Egg and 'friend', paranormal investigators of *The Eggs Files*.

The 21 December 1996 special was a seasonal one-off presented as part of *Live & Kicking*. Indeed, apart from the series detailed above, the duo regularly presented *Transmission Impossible* segments during the 1997 run of the children's magazine show.

See also *Scrooge*.

Tricky Business

UK · BBC · CHILDREN'S SITCOM

27 × 25 mins · colour

Series One (9) 6 Apr–1 June 1989 · BBC1
Thu 4.35pm

Series Two (9) 5 Apr–31 May 1990 · BBC1
Thu 4.30pm

Series Three (9) 4 Apr–30 May 1991 · BBC1
Thu 4.35pm

MAIN CAST

Crabtree	Marcus Clarke (series 1 & 2)
Mrs Breeze	Una Stubbs (series 1)
Mr Breeze	John Quayle (series 1)
Lucy	Sally Anne Marsh (series 1)
Joe	Jolyon Stephenson (series 1)
Abby	Charlotte Lee (series 1)
Zak	Darren Cudjoe (series 1)
Woody	David Wood (series 2)
Mr Sadd	John Surman (series 2)
Mickie	Paul Zenon (series 2 & 3)
Jeannie	Sonia May (series 2)
Hanna	Prudence Oliver (series 2)
Zoe	Patsy Palmer (series 2)
Norman Grinn	Robin Sneller (series 2)
Daniel	Anthony Davis (series 2)
Matthew	Thomas Duncan (series 2)
Bernie	Bernie Clifton (series 3)
Derek Yates	Leslie Schofield (series 3)
Debbie	Rebecca Front (series 3)
Eddie Farrow	Terry Randall (series 3)

CREDITS

writers David Till (3 eps of series 1), John Walker (3 eps of series 1), Colin Bennett (3 eps of series 1), Jim Bywater (series 2), Tony Hare (series 3) · *directors* David Crichton (series 1), Adrian Mills (series 2), Martin Hughes (series 3) · *producers* Richard Simkin (series 1), Judy Whitfield (series 2), Martin Hughes (series 3)

A children's sitcom with varying set-ups. The first series was set in a magic shop, Tricky Business, run by Mr and Mrs Breeze, who were known professionally as 'Bright And Breezy'. But there was a major upheaval for the second – new cast, writer (Jim Bywater), director and producer – in which the character Crabtree moved centre-stage, sharing the spotlight with newcomers Woody and Mickie. And there was a similar new broom sweeping away in the third and final series – in this, standup comedian Bernie Clifton was the lead, supported by a roster of commendable talent including Rebecca Storm. The premise this time was that Bernie had inherited an old theatre from his Aunt Agnes (Aggie), the bequest carrying the condition that the venue feature magic acts.

Resident conjuror Paul Zenon also doubled as the series' magic adviser, the storylines allowing for the appearance of a guest magician, and often concentrating on a particular trick or style of conjuring.

Trinder Box

UK · BBC · STANDUP

10 editions (9 × 45 mins · 1 × 60 mins) · b/w

20 June–24 Oct 1959 · fortnightly
Sat mostly 7.30pm

MAIN CAST

Tommy Trinder

CREDITS

writer Denis Goodwin · *additional material* David Ellis · *producer* Barry Lupino

Born in Streatham, south London, on 24 March 1909, Tommy Trinder was one of the best-loved comedians in Britain either side of the Second World War, his catchphrase, 'You lucky people!', and trademark pork-pie hat becoming nationally known. Fast-talking and quick-thinking, Trinder had appeared on TV since its earliest days but, never quite trusting the new medium, rationed his appearances. Following this series, however, he became a regular face on the small-screen, eventually committing himself to a long run as compere of the ATV variety series *Val Parnell's Sunday Night At The London Palladium*.

Trinder made his first stage appearance in 1922 and enjoyed minor successes in music-hall, working men's clubs and revue before making many films – he was an adept actor – from 1940. His comedy persona struck a winning balance between apparent aggression and charm – 'If it's laughter you're after, Trinder's the name,' he would announce – and his notorious ad-libbing talent made him a confident all-round performer, able to deal easily with on-stage problems, interruptions or diversions. This assuredness permitted him to be more adventurous than many of his contemporaries, and so *Trinder Box* – his first and only starring TV series – had a much looser format than similar ventures, the style of the show changing from week to week at the whim of the star and the producer. As was traditional, song and dance routines featured throughout, as did guest stars – most notably Phil Silvers, who made his first live British TV appearance in the opening edition. (At one time Trinder was considered for a British version of the comedy stage-musical *Top Banana*, which had made Silvers a star in the USA.)

On 24 July 1967, Trinder looked back on his career for an edition of BBC2's *Suddenly It's … * series. He died on 10 July 1989, aged 80.

See also *Comedy Bandbox, Friday Night With … and The Old Boy Network*.

Tripper's Day

UK · ITV (THAMES) · SITCOM

6 × 30 mins · colour

24 Sep–29 Oct 1984 · Mon 8pm

MAIN CAST

Norman Tripper	Leonard Rossiter
Hilda Rimmer	Pat Ashton
Alf Battle	Gordon Gostelow
Mr Christian	Paul Clarkson
Sylvia	Liz Crowther
Hardie	Philip Bird
Higgins	Andrew Paul
Laurel	David John
Marlene	Charon Bourke
Dottie	Vicky Licorish

CREDITS

creator/writer Brian Cooke · *directors/producers* Michael Mills (5), Anthony Parker (1)

That Leonard Rossiter should have thought *Tripper's Day* worth his trouble is unfathomable. That he should then have the misfortune to die and have it cemented as his final sitcom is little less than tragic.

Rossiter played the title role, Norman Tripper: moustachioed, down from the north to manage a London supermarket, Supafare, and in charge of the biggest bunch of good-for-nothings ever to constitute a shop staff. Tripper's task – trying to keep his charges in line – was a bit like Hedges' in *Please, Sir!*, and about as successful. His staff smoked, insulted customers and skived at every opportunity, and every one of them was a born 'sitcom character': there was the hopeless security manager Alf Battle; the university-keen trainee manager, Mr Christian; the strike-talking union shop-steward, Mr Hardie; the witless, gum-chewing, nail-filing check-out girls; the snidey secretary Sylvia; the blowsy widowed canteen supervisor Hilda Rimmer, at whom Tripper once made a pass. And so on, and on, and on, for six desperate episodes.

With its perky synthesiser music, cheapo looking sets (the inside of a supermarket was constructed at Thames' Teddington studio) and the harsh lighting necessary for video recording, *Tripper's Day* was visibly and audibly a loser before the dialogue even kicked in. And this, surprisingly for a Brian Cooke creation, was devoid of any subtlety, each joke being sticky-labelled in capital letters and about as funny as a wobbly supermarket trolley thrust into your ankles.

Leonard Rossiter died on 5 October 1984, between the screening of the second and third episodes and just short of his 58th birthday. What a sorry exit for such a great comic actor. Thames TV, however, believing there to be life in *Tripper's Day* yet, saw fit to revive it two years later with a new headlining star ...

Slinger's Day

UK · ITV (THAMES) · SITCOM

12 × 30 mins · colour

Series One (6) 3 Sep–8 Oct 1986 · Wed 8.30pm
Series Two (6) 9 Sep–14 Oct 1987 · Wed 8pm

MAIN CAST

Cecil Slinger	Bruce Forsyth
Hardie	Philip Bird
Fred	David Kelly
Mr Christian	Paul Clarkson
Sylvia	Liz Crowther (series 1)
Higgins	Andrew Paul (series 1)
Dottie	Vicky Licorish (series 1)
Colin	Charlie Hawkins (series 2)
Shirley	Jacqueline de Peza (series 2)
Marilyn	Johanna Hargreaves (series 2)
Miss Foster	Suzanne Church (series 2)

CREDITS

creator Brian Cooke · *writers* Vince Powell (6), Brian Cooke (2), Alex Shearer (2), Ian Davidson/Peter Vincent (1), Andrew Marshall/David Renwick (1) · *director/producer* Mark Stuart

Two years after Leonard Rossiter's tragically premature death, Bruce Forsyth stepped into his shoes as the manager of Supafare. Since his character name was Cecil Slinger, the series was retitled *Slinger's Day*. To date, it has proven Brucie's only sitcom role, and it's not difficult to see why: although a very talented entertainer, Forsyth is not quite the world's greatest actor. Perhaps because of this, Thames permitted the star to display his game-show-style patter and characteristic prancing almost as often, it seemed, as he adhered to the scripts. Slinger's job, much like his predecessor's, was to manage a store in the face of every possible kind of adversity, his woeful staff being his biggest problem. Suffice to say that the laughs were obtained more cheaply than his store's bargain-bin items.

The inexplicable ability of this comedy premise to lure top names continued with the North American adaptation of the series, *Check It Out*, imported across the Atlantic – like so many other Thames TV creations – by D L Taffner. Don Adams, the former standup who had excelled in the spy-spoof

sitcom *Get Smart*, was cast as Howard Bannister, the manager of Cobb's Supermarket. Here were all the old characters once again, now played by US/Canadian actors: Mr Christian, Alf, the pop tarts on the check-out et al. Slaughtered by the critics for its sorry scripts, bad acting and cheap sets, *Check It Out* nonetheless extended to 66 episodes between 1985 and 1988, taped in Toronto and first seen on CTV in Canada before being screened in America on USA Cable and then going into first-run syndication.

Tropic

UK · ITV (ATV) · SITCOM

6 × 30 mins · colour

29 July & 5 Aug 1979 · Sun 9pm; 24 Nov–15 Dec 1979 · Sat 12 midnight

MAIN CAST

Andrew Maiby	Ronald Pickup
Audrey Maiby	Hilary Tindall
Polly Blossom-Smith	Hilary Pritchard
Rev Ivor Boon	John Clive
Geoffrey Turvey	Ronald Lacey
Lizzie Maiby	Kate Dorning
Cynthia Turvey	Charlotte Howard
Bessie White	Lynne Morgan
Bert White	John Alderson
Grandad	Tony Sympson
Simon Grant	James Cormack
Ena Grant	Bobbie Brown
Hercules	George Malpas
Primrose	Nichola McAuliffe
Miss Dogfoot	Stephanie Cole

CREDITS

writer Leslie Thomas · *director/producer* Matthew Robinson · *executive producer* Greg Smith

Adapted by Leslie Thomas from his 1974 novel *Tropic Of Ruislip*, this series of six half-hours brought to the small-screen the best-selling and notorious comic account of suburban goings-on, lifting the net-curtain on life in Plummers Park, an estate of flat-roof houses in London's north-western suburbia, full of commuting executives and their lonely, sex-starved wives.

Many domestic situations were spied upon therein but the Maiby household was the principal focus: Andrew is a local journalist whose dreamy attentions are assaulted by a young girl, Bessie White, from the nearby council estate. His wife Audrey is wondering where her life is headed, and their daughter Lizzie is growing up alarmingly fast. Through six episodes – unfortunately interrupted by a long ITV strike – viewers were taken on a giddying, sometimes hilarious tour of the estate, into the houses with rural, pretty names, the pub, the golf club and the commuter trains that the male residents populated.

The series was filmed on location in Carpenders Park, just south of Watford,

which – despite the naming of Ruislip in the title – is the town where Leslie Thomas actually set his delightful, fictional story.

Trouble For Two

UK · BBC · SITCOM

4 × 30 mins · b/w

12 May–2 June 1958 · Mon 7.50pm

MAIN CAST

Jacqueline Mackenzie	herself
Lorrae Desmond	herself
Char	Donald Churchill

CREDITS

writers Johnny Whyte/Jacqueline Mackenzie · *producer* Ronald Marsh

A show-business sitcom combining the London-based, Australian singer Lorrae Desmond with British comic-actress Jacqueline Mackenzie as two bright young things sharing a London flat. Donald Churchill played their char-man.

Desmond was a popular figure with British viewers and was no stranger to the world of TV comedy, having appeared often in Terry-Thomas's · *How Do You View?* (1949–53). Mackenzie's style of mischievous satire relied upon her elastic facial features and talent for vocal mimicry, which, combined, enabled her to enact different personalities. The series didn't click with viewers however, and only ran for four episodes.

Trouble In Mind

UK · ITV (HIGHTIMES PRODUCTIONS FOR LWT) · SITCOM

9 × 30 mins · colour

24 Feb–31 Mar 1991; 30 June–14 July 1991 · Sun mostly 7.15pm

MAIN CAST

Adam Charlesworth	Richard O'Sullivan
Julia Charlesworth	Susan Penhaligon
Dr Malcolm Barclay	Nicholas Day
Stanley Chambers	Jim McManus

CREDITS

creator Greg Brennan · *writers* Colin Bostock-Smith (5), Tony Millan/Mike Walling (2), others (2) · *director* Terry Kinane · *executive producer* Robin Carr · *producer* Al Mitchell

Quietly spoken, middle-aged Adam Charlesworth is a successful psychiatrist, with a home practice, whose two children have flown the coop – son Joe travelling the world and daughter Lucy working for the BBC. With free time on her hands at last, Adam's wife Julia is embarking upon a career of her own too, as a landscape gardener, working in partnership with Stanley Chambers from the garden centre. Adam doesn't take the garden business scheme seriously and doesn't think that Julia is either, but he is wrong, and is also troubled by the fact that he has to have a vasectomy, Julia being of the age where she must be taken off the pill. This latter event brings the Charlesworths into regular contact with the family GP, Malcolm Barclay.

Trouble In Mind was a profoundly weak and lifeless sitcom, relentlessly middle-class and middle of the road. Reacting fast to viewer apathy, ITV relegated the series to a later time slot and then took it off the air mid-run. Three more episodes were screened after a three-month interlude but it went no further.

The Trouble With Harry

see WORTH, Harry

The Trouble With Lilian

UK · ITV (LWT) · SITCOM

6 × 30 mins · b/w

3 July–7 Aug 1971 · Sat mostly 5.40pm

MAIN CAST

Madge · · · · · · · · · · · · · · · · · · Dandy Nichols
Lilian · · · · · · · · · · · · · · · · · · · Patricia Hayes

CREDITS

writer Jennifer Phillips · director Howard Ross

This was the TV version of a BBC Radio 4 comedy series, *The Trouble With You Lillian*, which starred Beryl Reid and Patricia Hayes as two elderly women living in the same space. Despite their friendship they endure something of a fractious relationship, caused in part by the fact that Madge is the tenant and Lilian her lodger, and that Madge bullies Lilian as a result. The series was broadcast in 12 episodes (3 October–7 November 1967 and 6 October–10 November 1969). The TV run had a slightly amended title and Lilian was spelled thus, and some of the scripts were adapted from the radio series.

Around this same period Jennifer Phillips also wrote the TV sitcom *Wink To Me Only* with Beryl Reid in mind, so the actress was replaced by Dandy Nichols in the TV version of *The Trouble With Lilian*. Hayes and Nichols worked very well together and later reunited in *Till Death Us Do Part*.

Troubles & Strife

UK · ITV (CENTRAL) · SITCOM

13 × 30 mins · colour

Series One (6) 11 Nov–16 Dec 1985 · Mon 8pm
Series Two (7) 3 July–14 Aug 1986 · Thu 9pm

MAIN CAST

The Rev Clifford James · · · · · · Steven Pacey
Christine · · · · · · · · · · · · · Annette Badland
Mary · · · · · · · · · · · · · · · · Maureen Beattie
Cherry · · · · · · · · · · · · · · · Patricia Brake
Harry Price · · · · · · · · · · · · · Robert Blythe
Annette · · · · · · · · · · · · · · · · Liz Gebhardt
Rosita Pearman · · · · · · · · · · · Anna Karen
Margaret · · · · · · · · · · · · · · Carol Macready
Fiona · · · · · · · · · · · · · · · · Diana Weston
Sophie · · · · · · · · · · · · · · · Victoria Williams

Tess · · · · · · · · · · · · Julia Binsted (series 1)
Christopher · · · · · · · · Mike Grady (series 2)

CREDITS

writer Joan Greening · director/producer Shaun O'Riordan

The arrival at St Anselm's Church of Clifford James, a dishy and unmarried young reverend, causes a real stir among the parish's Young Wives group, chaired by Margaret. As veritable vicarage groupies, they flutter around him and try to run his life, hindering his own attempts to find a life partner.

Apart from Steven Pacey, who played the vicar, and the scheming church choirmaster Harry Price (played by Robert Blythe), the cast was virtually all-female. The series' author, Joan Greening, had been a member of Young Wives church groups in Windsor and then in Royston, so she knew the characters inside out, honing in on twittery women for the key roles.

Troubles & Strife instigated a return to TV for two former ITV sitcom favourites. Liz Gebhardt – who had played Maureen, ever mooning over Mr Hedges in **Please, Sir!** – was cast as the dowdy Annette, one of the wives, yes, ever mooning over the new vicar. And Anna Karen, who had succumbed to make-up and costume that turned her natural looks into the ultra plain Olive in both **On The Buses** and **The Rag Trade**, once again allowed herself to be portrayed as a character far from her usual self, that of the alcoholic, bad-tempered, foul-mouthed, sex-obsessed and overdressed church-hall caretaker. (Still, at least no one recognises her in the street.)

The True Adventures Of Christopher Columbus

UK · BBC · SATIRE

4 episodes (1 × 30 mins · 1 × 25 mins · 2 × 20 mins) · colour

28 July–31 July 1992 · BBC2 Tue to Fri around 8pm

MAIN CAST

Christopher Columbus · · · · · · Patrick Barlow
King Ferdinand · · · · · · · · · · Tim Pigott-Smith
Queen Isabella · · · · · · · Miranda Richardson
Guacanagari · · · · · · · · · · · Victor Banerjee
Herald · · · · · · · · · · · · · · · Freddie Jones
Old sea dog · · · · · · · · · · · · · Graham Stark

CREDITS

writer Patrick Barlow · directors Patrick Barlow/ Philip Bonham-Carter · producer George Faber

An alternative contribution to the celebrations marking the 500th anniversary of Christopher Columbus's discovery of America. In an anarchic portrayal of the heroic explorer, Patrick Barlow (the misguided light behind **The National Theatre Of Brent**) exploded a few myths

as he set out to spoof and rewrite history in his inimitable fashion. A fine cast supported.

True Love

see *My Wonderful Life*

The Truth About Verity

UK · ITV (ATV) · SITCOM

1 × 30 mins · colour

28 Aug 1975 · Thu 7pm

MAIN CAST

Verity Martin · · · · · · · · · · · · · Sylvia Syms
Mr Frisby · · · · · · · · · · · · · · John Savident
Alison Bentley · · · · · · · · · · · · Jenny Hanley
Hugh · · · · · · · · · · · · · · · · · John Carlin
Roger · · · · · · · · · · · · · · · Ed Devereaux

CREDITS

writer Jon Watkins · director/producer John Scholz-Conway

A single-episode shot in the *Comedy Premiere* season of pilots networked by ATV in summer 1975. Sylvia Syms starred but no series developed.

Trying Times

USA · PBS (KCET/JSD PRODUCTIONS; KCET/ CCC OF AMERICA/JSD ENTERTAINMENT/QUALLI PRODUCTIONS) · SITCOM ANTHOLOGY

12 x 30 mins · colour

US dates: 19 Oct–23 Nov 1987 & 12 Oct 1989–16 Nov 1989
UK dates: 12 Jan–29 Mar 1992 (10 editions) BBC2 Sun mostly 9.05pm

A US comedy anthology series on the theme of modern-day angst, featuring an outstanding array of acting, writing and directorial talent. Each edition mined the same basic formula, the principal character introducing the story as a flashback. Details of the episodes are as follows.

A Family Tree   US 19 OCT 1987/UK 12 JAN 1992

MAIN CAST

Rosanna Arquette, David Byrne

CREDITS

writers Beth Henley/Budge Threlkeld · director Jonathan Demme · producer Jon Denny

A young woman survives a hilariously disastrous encounter with her future in-laws.

Drive, She Said   US 26 OCT 1987/UK 19 JAN 1992

MAIN CAST

Teri Garr, Ron Silver, Catherine Bach

CREDITS

writer Wendy Wasserstein · director Sheldon Larry · producer Jon Denny

A New Yorker who has never needed to drive attends motoring school in order to escape her mid-life crisis.

Get A Job   US 2 NOV 1987/UK 26 JAN 1992

MAIN CAST
Steven Wright

CREDITS
writer Earl Pomerantz · *director* Allan Goldstein · *producer* Jon Denny

A 30-year-old 'professional student' beats the system when his parents kick him off the dole.

Bedtime Story   US 9 NOV 1987/UK 2 FEB 1992

MAIN CAST
Spalding Gray, Jessica Harper

CREDITS
writers Spalding Gray/Renee Shafransky · *director* Michael Lindsay-Hogg · *producer* Jon Denny

A man lies awake at night wondering whether or not to become a father, while his girlfriend's biological clocks ticks away.

The Visit   US 16 NOV 1987/UK 9 FEB 1992

MAIN CAST
Jeff Daniels, Julie Hagerty, Swoosie Kurtz

CREDITS
writer Christopher Durang · *director* Alan Arkin · *producer* Jon Denny

A married couple face pressure when the husband's high school sweetheart passes through town.

Moving Day   US 23 NOV 1987/UK 16 FEB 1992

MAIN CAST
Candice Bergen, Keanu Reeves, Bruno Gerussi

CREDITS
writer Bernard Slade · *director* Sandy Wilson · *producer* Jon Denny

An optimistic divorcee watches with helpless hysteria as moving day reveals more than dust behind the bureau.

Hunger Chic   US 12 OCT 1989/UK 23 FEB 1992

MAIN CAST
Carrie Fisher, Griffin Dunne, Danitra Vance

CREDITS
writer George C Wolfe · *director* Buck Henry · *producer* Jon Denny

A self-absorbed yuppie couple employ a magical housekeeper and have to confront a series of bizarre occurrences.

The Hit List   US 19 OCT 1989/UK 1 MAR 1992

MAIN CAST
Geena Davis, Peter Riegert

CREDITS
writer A R Gurney · *director* Michael Lindsay-Hogg · *producer* Jon Denny

A middle-aged suburban family man comes home to find a beautiful stranger in his house recounting tales of international intrigue.

Death And Taxes   US 26 OCT 1989/UK 8 MAR 1992

MAIN CAST
Sally Kirkland, Peter Scolari

CREDITS
writer Albert Innaurato · *director/producer* Jon Denny

Guilt forces a tax evader to confess after his beautiful tax attorney falls in love with the tax auditor.

The Sad Professor   US 2 NOV 1989/UK 29 MAR 1992

MAIN CAST
Judge Reinhold, Stockard Channing, Linda Purl

CREDITS
writer Richard Greenberg · *director* Christopher Guest · *producer* Jon Denny

In order to overcome his discontent, a young and talented professor embarks upon an extramarital affair with an unlikely colleague.

The Boss   US 9 NOV 1989/NOT SHOWN IN UK

MAIN CAST
Jean Stapleton, Corey Feldman

CREDITS
writer Marilyn Suzanne Miller · *director* Alan Arkin · *producer* Jon Denny

Forced to find work, a recently widowed woman takes a job with a fast-food burger franchise run by a tyrannical 19-year-old.

A Good Life   US 16 NOV 1989/NOT SHOWN IN UK

MAIN CAST
Robert Klein, Sheila McCarthy

CREDITS
writer Terrence McNally · *director* Sheldon Larry · *producer* Jon Denny

Recognising the endless frustrations of his life, a man asserts his independence by resuming smoking, despite the protestations of his wife.

Turn It Up!

see JEWEL, Jimmy and Ben Warriss

Turn Out The Lights

UK · ITV (GRANADA) · SITCOM
6 × 55 mins · b/w
2 Jan–6 Feb 1967 · Mon mostly 8pm

MAIN CAST

Leonard Swindley	Arthur Lowe
Wally Hunt	Robert Dorning

CREDITS
writers Peter Eckersley/Kenneth Cope (2), Peter Eckersley (1), Anthony Skene (1), Stanley Hearn (1), John Finch (1) · *directors* Michael Cox (3), David Boisseau (3) · *producer* Derek Granger

A sequel to *Pardon The Expression*, with Leonard Swindley and Wally Hunt continuing the professional relationship they had formed at Dobson and Hawks. Sacked from the store at the end of that series, they became amateur sleuths in *Turn Out The Lights*, which mixed humour with light-drama in six near-hour-length episodes.

As before, Swindley (Arthur Lowe) had the more dominant character, full of bluster and a misguided sense of self-confidence. In the first episode he and Hunt became absorbed by astrology and were invited to travel around Britain, giving WI lectures. They met the oddest people along the way, developing a Holmes-and-Watson relationship as they investigated beyond the veil, seeking out the truth behind the crystal balls, flickering lanterns, bumps in the night, seances and poltergeists.

Like *Pardon The Expression*, this new series was screened after *Coronation Street* – the series that launched the Swindley character – giving fans of the soap, in this instance, close on 90 minutes of familiar entertainment.

Turnbull's Finest Half-Hour

UK · ITV (YORKSHIRE) · SITCOM
6 × 30 mins · colour
19 Nov–31 Dec 1972 · Sun 12.30pm

MAIN CAST

Major Clifford Turnbull	Michael Bates
Bernard Pratt	Blake Butler
Faye Bush	Liz Fraser
Roddy Cheever-Jones	Jonathan Lynn
Rex Rivoli	Roddy Maude-Roxby
Jellico Withers	Leonard Trolley
Sir Zachary Stein	Raymond Huntley
Charlie	Alan Helm

CREDITS
writers Ken Hoare/Mike Sharland · *director/producer* Bill Hitchcock

A single-series sitcom about a (fictitious) small, new ITV franchise, Pentagon Television. It rapidly enters dire financial straits and the chairman, Sir Zachary Stein, is desperate to find a man fool enough to take it over. There, before his very eyes, is a retired major, Clifford Turnbull, who agrees to get in among the creaky programmes and cranky staff with a determination to boost the flagging ratings and cut costs with military style orderliness and precision.

Three years later, Eric Idle used the same premise – a small, cash-strapped under-staffed TV station – for his sketch series *Rutland Weekend Television*.

Tutti Frutti

UK · BBC · COMEDY SERIAL

6 × 60 mins · colour

3 Mar–7 Apr 1987 · BBC1 Tue 9.30pm

MAIN CAST

Danny McGlone	Robbie Coltrane
Suzi Kettles	Emma Thompson
Vincent Diver	Maurice Roëves
Eddie Clockerty	Richard Wilson
Bomba MacAteer	Stuart McGugan
Fud O'Donnell	Jake D'Arcy
Dennis Sproul	Ron Donachie
Janis Toner	Katy Murphy

CREDITS

writer John Byrne · *director* Tony Smith · *producer* Andy Park

John Byrne's hilarious comic opus charting the fortunes of the Majestics, the Scottish 'Kings Of Rock'. They are about to embark on their silver jubilee tour when lead singer, Big Jazza, drops dead. His younger brother Danny, home from New York for the funeral, reacquaints himself with the band and deputises for his late brother as the tour goes ahead. Also in the picture is Danny's old flame, Suzi Kettles, a sharp cookie happy to pick up the guitar; she too joins the band and from that moment their fortunes take a turn for the better.

This was a corking comedy-drama featuring dazzling dialogue and all-round knock-out performances. Robbie Coltrane was particularly outstanding as the rotund but sexy Danny, and Emma Thompson was appealing as the sharp, strong and independent Suzi. Their romance was played out against a background of funny, dramatic and touching scenes depicting a band, well past its best-by date, suddenly finding a new lease of life. Adding to the heady brew was Richard Wilson as the Majestics' hilariously dour manager Eddie (almost a prototype Victor Meldrew), and Katy Murphy as his lippy secretary Janis Toner. A joy.

TV Offal

UK · C4 (*ASSOCIATED-REDIFFUSION) · SATIRE

1 × 35 mins · colour

31 Oct 1997 · Fri 11.10pm

MAIN CAST

Victor Lewis-Smith

CREDITS

writer Victor Lewis-Smith · *director/producer* John Hayward-Warburton

A pilot for a proposed series in which Victor Lewis-Smith cast a jaundiced eye over the flotsam and jetsam of British TV history. An eclectic miscellany of footage was subjected to his peculiar brand of caustic analysis, resulting in sometimes cruel humour which, in places, was very funny. Different strands included Honest Obituary, in which Lewis-Smith killed off his least favourite TV presenters; Kamikaze Karaoke, in which music performances were overdubbed with different pieces; and The Pilots That Crashed, when terrible moments from failed shows of the past were disinterred.

Savage though he could be, few other presenters tackled this sort of arcane material with such relish and Lewis-Smith's love/hate relationship with the small-screen has consistently produced odd gems such as this. A full series of *TV Offal* was in the pipeline as this book went to press, set to air in spring 1998.

*Note. The programme was made by Associated-Rediffusion, but not the company of this name that served London-area ITV from 1955–68 (actually, just Rediffusion for the last four of those years). Victor Lewis-Smith bought the name for his own TV production company upon discovering that it was dormant.

See also *Credible Credits, Inside Victor Lewis-Smith* and *The Secret Life Of TV*.

TV Squash

UK · ITV (YORKSHIRE) · SKETCH

6 × 30 mins · colour

26 July–30 Aug 1992 · Sun around 11pm

MAIN CAST

Angelo Abela
Gabrielle Cowburn
Andrew Dunn
Treva Etienne
Lucinda Fisher
Caroline Gruber
Geraldine McNulty
Phil Nice

CREDITS

directors Vic Finch (5), Catherine Morshead (1) · *producers* Angelo Abela/Simon Wright

An adult-orientated series that took a swipe at television, spoofing soaps, police dramas, sports programmes, game-shows and much else via some hard-hitting sketches that contained a smattering of bad language. Specific editions were given over to sending up BBCs 1 and 2, C4 and ITV's Saturday schedule.

Each edition of *TV Squash* featured guests familiar to British TV viewers, among them John Altman (Nick Cotton in *EastEnders*), Tony Blackburn, Roy Hattersley MP, Brian Johnston, Patrick Moore, Nick Owen and Anne Diamond, Nicholas Parsons, Cynthia Payne, Eric Sykes and various sporting stars.

The Twenty-First Century Show

UK · BBC · SKETCH

1 × 35 mins · colour

12 Apr 1979 · BBC1 Thu 8.25pm

MAIN CAST

Graeme Garden

Bill Oddie
Ann Hamilton
Henry McGee
Andrew Ray
Judy Loe

CREDITS

writers Graeme Garden/Bill Oddie · *director/producer* Jim Franklin

Two thirds of *The Goodies* were behind this humorous and fantastic look at the world in the year 2001. Elaborate visual effects – and the presence of *The Goodies'* director, Jim Franklin – guaranteed a familiar style.

24 Carrott Gold

see CARROTT, Jasper

Twice A Fortnight

UK · BBC · SKETCH

10 × 30 mins · b/w

21 Oct–23 Dec 1967 · BBC1 Sat around 11pm

MAIN CAST

Bill Oddie
Graeme Garden
Michael Palin
Terry Jones
Jonathan Lynn
Dilys Watling
Tony Buffery
Ronald Fletcher

CREDITS

writers Graeme Garden/Bill Oddie, Michael Palin/Terry Jones · *director/producer* Tony Palmer

A sketch series that borrowed liberally from the brilliant BBC radio show *I'm Sorry, I'll Read That Again* (and featured two of that show's stars, Bill Oddie and Graeme Garden), *Twice A Fortnight* is mostly of interest now for its position in a family tree as much as its content, being one of the several shows that led up to *Monty Python's Flying Circus* and *The Goodies*.

But *Twice A Fortnight* also had a built-in element of self-destruction – creative arguments raged between Oddie and the director/producer Tony Palmer; the studio audience, served with drinks and encouraged to be rowdy, sometimes drowned out the cast; and the intentional mix of a wide range of comedy styles hindered rather than helped the flow, some of the programmes being undisciplined and chaotic. To make matters worse, much of the material, originally written for *I'm Sorry, I'll Read That Again*, failed to work so well on TV.

Michael Palin and Terry Jones fared better than most of the participants; their main contribution was to write and appear in a number of short sketches, more controlled and coherent because they were pre-filmed and not performed in front of the vociferous audience. (These led to the creation of a separate series, *The Complete And Utter History Of Britain*.) Even Oddie, who disagreed with Palmer about most things, was impressed by the director's visual flair; together with Garden, he concentrated on developing a style for filming visual comedy (jump-cuts, speeded-up motion, odd camera angles and so on) that would prove very useful when making *The Goodies*.

Twice A Fortnight deliberately steered clear of satire and most editions bore a humorous, easily understood subtitle – the first, for instance, was 'Match Of The Day, Part 2' because it followed the BBC1 soccer series; others were 'Peter West Lives!', 'Even Before Alan Melville' and 'Suddenly, It's Sooty'. The series also promoted rock music (Tony Palmer was in the process of preparing the first proper documentary about rock, *All My Loving*, screened by BBC1 under the *Omnibus* arts banner on 3 November 1968) – the Who played in the opening and closing programmes, Cat Stevens, Cream and the Small Faces were among the other guests.

Twice Knightly

UK · C4 (BARRON KNIGHTS) · SKETCH

1 × 60 mins · colour
25 Dec 1983 · Sun 6.15pm

MAIN CAST
The Barron Knights (Barron Anthony Osmond, Butch Baker, Dave Ballinger, Duke D'Mond, Peter 'Peanut' Langford)

CREDITS
director Terry Steel · *producer* Butch Baker

A second C4 special featuring the pop pastiche merchants.

See also *Get Knighted* and *The Barron Knights Show*.

Two Ceasefires And A Wedding

UK · BBC · SITCOM

1 × 30 mins · colour
31 Aug 1995 · BBC2 Thu 11.25pm

MAIN CAST
Billy · · · · · · · · · · · · · · · · Michael McDowell
Emer · · · · · · · · · · · · · · · · Nuala McKeever
Cal · · · · · · · · · · · · · · · · · Damon Quinn
Da · · · · · · · · · · · · · · · · · · Tim McGarry
Ma · · · · · · · · · · · · · · · · · · Olivia Nash
Uncle Andy · · · · · · · · · · · · · Martin Reid
Paul · · · · · · · · · · · · · · · · · Peter Omeara

CREDITS
writers cast · *director* Stephen Butcher · *producer* Jackie Hamilton

A Romeo-and-Juliet-like story of lovers from opposing factions in Northern Ireland, presented by the Ulster-based comedy team the Hole In The Wall Gang.

The project developed from a sketch in the gang's award-winning BBC Radio Ulster comedy series *A Perforated Ulster* (10 parts, 17 April–5 June 1993; 10 more, 16 April–4 June 1994), the recurring 'Love Across the Barricades' item that detailed the turbulent love affair between Billy, a member of the Royal Ulster Constabulary, and Emer, the daughter of an IRA commander. In 1994, a 30-minute compilation of these sketches was broadcast across the UK by BBC Radio 4 under the title *Billy And Emer*, prompting this decision to transfer it to television. *Two Ceasefires And A Wedding* duly became BBC Northern Ireland's first sitcom, which, after airing locally, enjoyed a national broadcast on 31 August 1995.

The 'troubles', of course, remain a constantly difficult area for comedy. To accommodate the ever-changing political landscape the script was rewritten several times during production.

See also *The Empire Laughs Back*.

The Two Charleys

UK · BBC · SITCOM

6 × 30 mins · b/w
8 Apr–13 May 1959 · Wed 7.30pm

MAIN CAST
Charlie Charles · · · · · · · · · · · Charlie Chester
Ethel Charles · · · · · · · · Eleanor Summerfield

CREDITS
writers Sheila Hodgson/Allan Prior (5), Sheila Hodgson/Allan Prior/David Whitaker (1) · *producer* Dennis Main Wilson

Following their casting as married performers George and Lily Pepper in *Red Peppers*, Noël Coward's backstage musical comedy playlet (BBC, 19 December 1958), Charlie Chester and Eleanor Summerfield had this sitcom series, loosely based on the Coward piece, written especially for them. In *The Two Charleys* they played Charlie and Ethel Charles, a touring variety act who shared their backstage adventures with the weekly TV audience. It all added up to a rare combination of Coward-like sophisticated wit and the broader humour of the traditional British sitcom, late-1950s style.

Note. Subsequent to the 1958 version, BBC1 has twice re-presented Coward's *Red Peppers* – on 15 December 1969, with Dora Bryan and Bruce Forsyth in the lead roles; and on 21 April 1991, with Joan Collins and Anthony Newley.

Two D's And A Dog

UK · ITV (THAMES) · CHILDREN'S SITCOM

6 × 30 mins · colour
10 July–4 Aug 1970 · Fri 5.20pm

MAIN CAST
Dotty Charles · · · · · · · · · · · · Denise Coffey
Dingle Bell · · · · · · · · · · · · · · David Jason

CREDITS
writer Jan Butlin · *director/producer* Daphne Shadwell

Reuniting the team behind the *Captain Fantastic* serial that had played so successfully as part of *Do Not Adjust Your Set* (and then *Magpie*), Denise Coffey, David Jason and director/producer Daphne Shadwell, with writer Jan Butlin, put together this single-series children's sitcom.

Coffey played the appropriately named Dotty Charles, who finds herself penniless after her father passes away. All she has is a friend – the clumsy Dingle Bell, who (oddly, for a man who cannot drive) was employed as her late father's chauffeur – and a sheepdog, Fido. Provided it will pay, they set out to seek work, any work, and meet an odd bunch of characters along the way, as well as a bizarre assortment of offers. (Which, of course, they accept.)

Special photography and studio effects, and a number of top names – Rupert Davies, Robert Dorning, Gerald Flood, Patricia Hayes, Glyn Houston, Miriam Karlin, Frank Thornton and Norman Vaughan – added to the fun, and Bill Fraser appeared twice as the rather sinister Foggitt. (Blunt character names littered Fraser's CV, Foggitt, Foggen, Claude Snudge, Basil Bulstrode and Bert Baxter being among them.)

Two Fat Rorys

see BREMNER, Rory

Two In Clover

UK · ITV (THAMES) · SITCOM

14 episodes (7 × 30 mins · b/w; 6 × 30 mins · colour; 1 × short special · colour)
Series One (7 × b/w) 18 Feb–1 Apr 1969 · Tue 8.30pm

Short special (colour) · part of *All-Star Comedy Carnival* 25 Dec 1969 · Thu 6pm

Series Two (6 × colour) 12 Feb–19 Mar 1970 · Thu mostly 6.55pm

MAIN CAST
Sid Turner · · · · · · · · · · · · · · Sidney James
Vic Evans · · · · · · · · · · · · · · · Victor Spinetti

OTHER APPEARANCES
Landlord · · · · · · · · · · · · · · · · Victor Platt
Policeman · · · · · · · · · · · · · · · Bill Pertwee

CREDITS
writers Vince Powell/Harry Driver · *director/producer* Alan Tarrant

Preceding *The Good Life* by six years, *Two In Clover* was a 'back-to-the-soil' sitcom in which a pair of stressed-out nine-to-fivers turned their backs on the rat race – in their case, a City insurance firm, where they worked as invoice clerks – and retreated to the country village of Fletchley in their

Morris-Minor, intent on turning over new leaves. They bought a smallholding, Clover Farm, and soon became bogged down in all manner of … strife, finding the lifestyle less glamorous and, with no knowledge of how to manage chickens, pigs, sheep and cows, more mucky than they had imagined. They also found the locals unwelcoming.

Sid James – the perpetual 'Sid', his surname this time being Turner – played his customary crafty-cockney character, with one eye on the birds and the other on the beer, and his jowls bobbing with every dirty chuckle. Co-starring as Welshman Vic Evans was Welsh-born Victor Spinetti, and the two struck up a good comic rapport, with James as the comedic hub and Spinetti his foil. (Although billed, Spinetti was unable to appear in one episode, and his place was taken by Richard Davies – perhaps the producer hoped that viewers would not be able to distinguish one Welshman from another.) *Dad's Army* stars John Le Mesurier, James Beck and Bill Pertwee (the latter on a semi-regular basis) turned up among the episodes, while an unlikely guest star in the final programme was the Yorkshire cricketer 'Fiery' Fred Trueman.

Sid James, writers Powell and Driver and director/producer Alan Tarrant had all worked together previously, on *George And The Dragon*. Within a year of *Two In Clover*, Thames placed James in the much more successful *Bless This House*.

291 Club

UK · ITV (LWT) · STANDUP

7 × 60 mins · colour

Series One (7) 8 Nov–21 Dec 1991 · mostly Fri around 11pm

Series Two (7) 8 May–19 June 1993 · Sat mostly 12.05am

MAIN CAST
various

CREDITS
director Steven Wood · *producers* Charlie Hanson/Paul Lewis (series 1), Beverley Randall (series 2)

A comedy-and-music show, performed by black acts at the rowdy 291 Club at the Hackney Empire in east London, where the audience was encouraged to cheer their support or jeer their dislike for the brave stage acts. Many of the latest and newest standup comedians performed; Miles Crawford was the regular comedy host. Almost as soon as LWT had screened the first series on London-area ITV it was repeated nationally by C4 (8 January to 19 February 1992).

Another, similar series, showing variety acts trying out at the same theatre's Sunday Selection talent night, was screened by C4

from 30 August to 27 September 1997 (four editions) as *Nights Out At The Empire*.

See also *1st Exposure* and *Pyjamarama*.

The Two Of Us   1

USA · CBS (MARBLE ARCH PRODUCTIONS) · SITCOM

19 × 30 mins · colour

US dates: 6 Apr 1981–24 Feb 1982

UK dates: 16 Oct–23 Dec 1983 (8 episodes) ITV mostly Sun 12 midnight

MAIN CAST
Robert Brentwood · · · · · · · · · · · Peter Cook
Nan Gallagher · · · · · · · · · · · · Mimi Kennedy
Cubby Royce · · · · · · · · · · · · · · · Oliver Clark
Gabrielle 'Gabby' Gallagher · · · · · · Dana Hill
Reggie Cavanaugh · · · · · · · · Tim Thomerson

CREDITS
creator Bill MacIlwraith · *writers* Eric Cohen, Katherine D Green, Charlie R Hauck, Arthur Julian, Tom Whedon · *directors* various · *producers* Charlie R Hauck, Martin Starger

The US adaptation of the popular British sitcom *Two's Company*, in which an American author, domiciled in London, engages an awfully British, supercilious butler, champion of disdain and the withering put-down. Here, the butler – formerly a cultural attaché to the UN – was named Robert Brentwood, the setting was East 23rd Street in New York City and the American woman, Nan Gallagher – a divorcee with a toothy smart-ass brat of a teenage daughter (Gabby) and (because Nan's a slob) a domestic life with which she cannot cope – was the host of a TV chat-show, *Mid-Morning Manhattan*.

Of particular interest to British viewers, the role of Robert Brentwood was taken by Peter Cook, the only ever sitcom part for this genius of comedy. Cook was on holiday in the USA in 1981 when CBS invited him to record a pilot for the show. A series soon developed, but it didn't last for long and, to be truthful, it is not difficult to see why: as even his best friends admitted during the eulogies that followed his early death in 1995, Peter Cook, while blessed with an extraordinary comic talent, was never much of an actor.

'Experts' summing up Cook's career claim that, with *The Two Of Us*, he was trying to establish himself in America to match or even emulate his erstwhile partner Dudley Moore, who had emigrated to Hollywood a few years earlier and become a movie star. Whatever the truth, *The Two Of Us* was too wooden and obvious to succeed and Cook swiftly returned to England – to the security of Hampstead, his beloved Spurs and *Private Eye* – remembering this Hollywood episode with disdain.

The Two Of Us   2

UK · ITV (LWT) · SITCOM

32 episodes (30 × 30 mins · 1 × 45 mins · 1 × 60 mins) · colour

Series One (7 × 30 mins) 31 Oct–12 Dec 1986 · Fri 8.30pm

Series Two (6 × 30 mins) 11 Sep–16 Oct 1987 · Fri mostly 8.30pm

Special (60 mins) 23 Dec 1988 · Fri 7.30pm

Series Three (8 × 30 mins) 6 Jan–24 Feb 1989 · Fri 8.30pm

Series Four (9 × 30 mins · 1 × 45 mins) 14 Jan–18 Mar 1990 · Sun 8.15pm then 7.15pm

MAIN CAST
Ashley Phillips · · · · · · · · Nicholas Lyndhurst
Elaine · Janet Dibley
Perce · · · · · · · · Patrick Troughton (series 1);
· · · · · Tenniel Evans (series 2–4 & special)
Colin Phillips · · · · · · · · · · · · Paul McDowell
Lilian Phillips · · · · · · · · · · · Jennifer Piercey
Gordon · · · · · · · · · · · Mark Jax (not series 4)

OTHER APPEARANCES
Karen · · · · · · · · · · · · · · · · · Francesca Hall
Joyce · · · · · · · · · · · · · · · · Elizabeth Morgan

CREDITS
writer Alex Shearer · *directors* Robin Carr (15), Terry Kinane (10), John Gorman (4), Marcus Plantin (3) · *executive producer* Marcus Plantin (series 2 & 3 & special) · *producers* Marcus Plantin (series 1), Robin Carr (series 2–4 & special)

Emerging from the shadow of David Jason and *Only Fools And Horses*, Nicholas Lyndhurst was never less than excellent in this long-running, if mostly slight, ITV sitcom. He played Ashley Phillips, a computer programmer by profession and an average sort of a guy in every way, except – for the laughs have to come from somewhere – that he also possesses a sharp line in repartee. Ashley is in love with Elaine but although they live together, sharing a basement flat, they're not married. Ashley is the marrying kind, Elaine is not, and she has denied his five proposals. He wants to live in semi-detached comfort with a mortgage, a wife and a baby; she, the daughter of a doctor, works in a crèche and wants *life* in her life, not marriage and certainly no babies at this stage – she and Ashley are both in their mid-twenties – because she gets enough of them at work. Although devoted to one another, Ashley and Elaine have little in common and view life from different perspectives.

Ashley often seeks solace in and advice from his free-spirited, widowed grandfather Percival (Perce), and also from his friend Gordon, but reels away from his parents, especially his mother, Lilian, who is interfering, bossy and, above all else, prudish, forbidding he and Elaine from sleeping together when they come to visit on occasional weekends. Ashley and Elaine finally tie the knot midway through the final series, though, and in the last episode she falls pregnant, so Ashley had his way (in both senses of the expression).

Janet Dibley, virtually new to TV when given the co-starring role here (but later given the lead part in another Alex Shearer sitcom, *The Gingerbread Girl*) played Elaine convincingly well and Patrick Troughton was excellent as Perce in the first series. His death on 28 March 1987, while attending a *Doctor Who* convention in the USA, resulted in Tenniel Evans (one of the very few actor/ priests in the business) picking up the part from then on.

2 Point 4 Children

UK · BBC · SITCOM

43 episodes (42 × 30 mins · 1 × 40 mins) · colour

Series One (6) 3 Sep–8 Oct 1991 · BBC1 Tue 8.30pm

Series Two (7) 9 Sep–20 Oct 1992 · BBC1 Tue 8.30pm

Special · 22 Dec 1992 · BBC1 Tue 8pm

Series Three (6) 7 Sep–12 Oct 1993 · BBC1 Tue 8.30pm

Special · 20 Dec 1993 · BBC1 Mon 8.30pm

Series Four (6) 5 Sep–10 Oct 1994 · BBC1 Mon 8.30pm

Special · 26 Dec 1994 · BBC1 Mon 8.40pm

Series Five (6) 2 Oct–6 Nov 1995 · BBC1 Mon 8.30pm

Special · 24 Dec 1995 · BBC1 Sun 8.15pm

Series Six (7) 14 Nov–20 Dec 1996 · BBC1 Thu mostly 8.30pm

Special (40 mins) *2 Point 4 Christmas* 26 Dec 1996 · BBC1 Thu 8.20pm

MAIN CAST

Bill Porter · · · · · · · · · · · · · · · · Belinda Lang
Ben Porter · · · · · · · · · · · · · · · · · Gary Olsen
Jenny Porter · · · · · · · · · · · · Clare Woodgate
· (series 1 & 2);
· · · · · · · · Clare Buckfield (series 3 onwards)
David Porter · · · · · · · · · · · · · · · John Pickard
Rona · Julia Hills
Biker (Angelo Shepherd) · · · · · · · · Ray Polhill
· (series 1 & 2)
Christine · · · Kim Benson (series 2 onwards)

OTHER APPEARANCES

Bette/Belle · · · · · · · · · · · · · · · · · · Liz Smith
Dora Grimes · · · · · · · · · · · · · Annette Kerr
Leonard Grimes · · · · · · · · · · · Stanley Lloyd
Tina · · · · · · · · · · Patricia Brake (series 1);
· · · · · · Sandra Dickinson (series 2 onwards)
Aunty Pearl · · · · · · · · · · · · · · · Barbara Lott
Jake The Klingon · · · · · · · · Roger Lloyd Pack
Tony · · · · · · · · · · · · · · · · · · · Tom Roberts
Laura · · · · · · · · · · · · · · · · · · · Arbel Jones
Clive · · · · · · · · · · · · · · · · Nathan Valante
Maggie Faith · · · · · · · · · · · · Annie Lambert

CREDITS

writer Andrew Marshall · *directors* Richard Boden (35), Nick Wood (8) · *producers* Richard Boden (35), Andrew Marshall (8)

On the surface, the Porters are a normal family – indeed, even the series' title *2 Point 4 Children*, the fabled average family size,

alludes to their normality (as well as the fact that the husband/father is still a bit of a child himself). Yet, though the individual members – central-heating engineer Ben; his wife, catering worker Bill; and their teenage children David and Jenny – are unexceptional, the situations in which the family find themselves are anything but. Bad luck, strange occurrences and poor judgement all conspire to turn the Porters' world topsy-turvy.

Sitcom-wise, the shape of the series itself is also different from the norm, because, from the earliest episodes, it has centred not on the husband, Ben, but on his wife, Bill. (The author, Andrew Marshall, claims that Bill is merely a diminution of his original Wilhelmina, not of his making, but the Bill and Ben scenario is nonetheless neatly suggestive of *The Flowerpot Men*.) Even with the focus on Bill, the series still avoids the traditional woman-as-wife-and-mother theme of other series, instead portraying her as a fully-rounded person in her own right, unconfined by her family.

At the start of the series Bill worked in a bakery with her best friend and neighbour, the man-hungry Rona. By the second she had lost the job and had to cope with a mind-numbing period of unemployment before launching a catering business with Rona. Although competent and level-headed, Bill was aware that she may have missed out on a certain, wilder side of life; in the first series this dissatisfaction was manifested by her crush on a handsome biker, Angelo. His death in a road accident robbed her of the real thing but he continued to haunt her dreams, even appearing as an angel when her son David was seriously ill with tetanus.

Ben is a man of simple tastes and pleasures; besides when he's trying out some childish prank, he seems to desire a simple life and probably has fewer aspirations than his wife, although in later episodes, when suffering a mid-life crisis, he began to question his existence in much the same way that Bill had been doing. Both David and his older sister Jenny are stereotypically drawn teenagers, although they seem even more acutely embarrassed by their parents than is normal – understandable, perhaps, given the situations into which the adults descend.

Another individual quality of the series was the fact that the family relationship was totally believable. Unlike most sitcom families, the Porters didn't have a fixed take on one another – they had wild mood swings and vacillated between love and a grudging tolerance. The production also employed a buccaneering style that allowed it to play with the genre, sometimes spoofing other shows or stretching its own perceived reality – the Christmas specials, for instance, have featured the cast in a glitzy song and dance

number, not the sort of thing one saw in *Not In Front Of The Children*.

The public took to *2 Point 4 Children* immediately and by the third series it was attracting ratings of more than 13 million, the sort of figure also being enjoyed by Andrew Marshall's former writing partner David Renwick with his sitcom *One Foot In The Grave*. There were certain similarities between the two series – both had larger-than-life plots involving seemingly ordinary people, both were unafraid to use pathos or black comedy, and both knew the humour value of outlandish props. Also, both featured an array of memorable second-string characters who could be called upon when the plot demanded. In *2 Point 4 Children* these included Roger Lloyd Pack as Ben's *Star Trek*-fanatic rival-plumber Jake The Klingon, Sandra Dickinson as Ben's rich sister Tina and the wonderful Liz Smith as both Bill's chain-smoking mother Bette and her Aunt Belle (Bette's sister).

There were no new episodes in 1997, but a seventh series was being taped for screening in early 1998.

The Two Ronnies

UK · BBC · SKETCH

*98 editions (72 × 45 mins · 20 × 50 mins · 2 × 60 mins · 2 × short specials · 1 × 30 mins · 1 × 55 mins) · colour

Series One (8 × 45 mins) 10 Apr–29 May 1971 · BBC1 Sat 8.15pm

Short special · part of *Christmas Night With The Stars* 25 Dec 1971 · BBC1 Sat 6.40pm

Series Two (8 × 45 mins) 16 Sep–4 Nov 1972 · BBC1 Sat mostly 7.35pm

Short special · part of *Christmas Night With The Stars* 25 Dec 1972 · BBC1 Mon 6.55pm

Series Three (8 × 45 mins) 27 Sep 1973–3 Jan 1974 · BBC2 fortnightly Thu 9.25pm

Special (60 mins) *The Two Ronnies Old-Fashioned Christmas Mystery* 26 Dec 1973 · BBC1 Wed 9.35pm

Series Four (8 × 45 mins) 2 Jan–20 Feb 1975 · BBC2 Thu 9.30pm

Special (30 mins) *The Picnic* 1 Jan 1976 · BBC2 Thu 9pm

Series Five (8 × 45 mins) 4 Sep–23 Oct 1976 · BBC1 Sat 8.15pm

Series Six (9 × 45 mins) 12 Nov 1977–7 Jan 1978 · BBC1 Sat 8.20pm

Series Seven (8 × 45 mins) 26 Dec 1978–10 Feb 1979 · BBC1 mostly Sat 8.25pm

Series Eight (7 × 45 mins) 1 Nov–13 Dec 1980 · BBC1 Sat mostly 8.10pm

Special (50 mins) 26 Dec 1980 · BBC1 Fri 7.25pm

Series Nine (7 × 45 mins) 5 Dec 1981–23 Jan 1982 · BBC1 Sat mostly 8.05pm

Special (50 mins) 25 Dec 1981 · BBC1 Fri 7.45pm

Special (55 mins) *By The Sea* 12 Apr 1982 · BBC1 Mon 7.40pm

Special (45 mins) 25 Dec 1982 · BBC1
Sat 7.30pm

Series Ten (6 × 50 mins) 10 Dec 1983–14 Jan
1984 · BBC1 Sat 8.10pm

Special (60 mins) *The Ballad Of Snivelling And
Grudge* 25 Dec 1984 · BBC1 Tue 8.55pm

Series Eleven (5 × 50 mins) 13 Feb–20 Mar
1985 · BBC1 mostly Sat 8.10pm

Series Twelve (6 × 50 mins) 25 Dec 1985–1 Feb
1986 · BBC1 mostly Sat 8.10pm

Special (50 mins) 25 Dec 1987 · BBC1
Fri 7.25pm

MAIN CAST
Ronnie Corbett
Ronnie Barker

CREDITS
main writers Gerald Wiley (Ronnie Barker), Peter
Vincent, Spike Mullins, David Nobbs, Barry Cryer,
David Renwick, Dick Vosburgh, David Newman/
Peter Osbourne, (*The Picnic* and *By The Sea*
writers 'Dave Huggett/Larry Keith' – Ronnie
Barker pseudonyms) · *other writers/additional
material* Michael Palin/Terry Jones, John Cleese/
Graham Chapman, Eric Idle, Ian Davidson/
Eric Geen, Bryan Blackburn, Bill Solly,
Mike Radford, John Sullivan/Freddie Usher,
Geoff Atkinson and others · *script associate*
Ian Davidson · *producers* Terry Hughes (42),
Michael Hurll (14), Marcus Plantin (12), Paul
Jackson (9), Peter Whitmore (9), Brian Penders
(8), Bill Wilson (1), Marcus Mortimer (1)

For the tenure of their long BBC run, the two
Ronnies – Messrs Barker and Corbett – were
second only to Morecambe and Wise as the
best-rated comedy double-act on British TV.
Not that they were in any sense competing or
overshadowed – *The Two Ronnies* has long
established its claim as one of the most
successful British comedy series of them all;
safe, yes, but of vast majority appeal.

There were big differences between the
style of the Ronnies and Morecambe and
Wise. Whereas the latter played 'themselves'
in all of their routines, the Ronnies performed
as comedy character actors, slipping into
a huge variety of different guises and
personalities to execute their humour. Also,
the Two Ronnies were not an established
double-act *per se*, thus there was no 'funny-
man/straight-man' aspect to their
relationship, both being capable of filling
either (or neither) role. This versatility
ensured that their material could be drawn
from a vast pool of writers, the high quality
of the work being the only proviso, not
the identity of its author. The series thus
maintained an open-door policy and was able
to select both commissioned and speculative
material. As it transpired, perhaps the most
productive writer of them all was Gerald
Wiley, a man whose first TV credit was a
sketch for *Frost On Sunday*. No one knew
anything about this man except that his
material was of a uniformly high standard,
but, eventually, it transpired that he was

really Ronnie Barker, hiding under one of his
many writing pseudonyms and utilising the
clandestine method to ensure that his work
was considered on merit, not because he was
one of the show's co-stars. Even with his
cover blown, 'Wiley' continued to write,
contributing some of the elaborately filmed
episodic sketches that were serialised
throughout different series.

These adventures usually cast the
recurring private detectives Charley Farley
(Corbett) and Piggy Malone (Barker) – or
variations on the characters – and were
hugely popular, with a number of guest stars
gladly helping out. *The Two Ronnies*, indeed,
gloried in several regular features, spots
which, rather than growing tiresome, became
more and more admired and cherished with
familiarity. Every show had a 'Ronnie-in-the-
chair' solo spot for Corbett, in which he
delivered a rambling comedy monologue
that, while straying wildly from the original
subject, always managed to get back on
course at the finish. (These interludes were
written by Spike Mullins.) Other recurring
ideas were Barker's solo written-and-
performed skits involving elaborate wordplay and tongue-twisting speeches; and party
sketches, where either Barker or Corbett
would turn out to be an extremely irritating
or unusual figure. Unforgettably, every
edition opened with the two Ronnies sitting
behind desks reading terribly corny but
nonetheless very funny spoof news items; the
penultimate item in the show was usually a
richly humorous musical spoof in which
the Ronnies danced, marched, paraded or
pretended to be musicians while delivering a
comedy lyric; and the closing item in every
show was a further selection of spoof news
items, back at the desks, which would end
with Corbett bidding the audience 'goodnight
from me', to which Barker would add 'and it's
goodnight from him'.

Quite apart from the great comedy material
and the expert manner in which it was
delivered, much of the success of *The Two
Ronnies* owed to the chemistry between the
two stars, who, like Morecambe and Wise,
clearly enjoyed one another's company and
were friends off-screen as well as on. They
had first teamed in 1966 on *The Frost
Report* (BBC) and renewed the working
partnership in *Frost On Sunday* (made by
Rediffusion and then LWT), a chat-show
interspersed with brief comedy items.
Recognising the potential of the pairing, BBC
executives lured them back to the Corporation
to star in their own show. After two
introductory specials (see *The Ronnie
Barker Yearbook*) the first series was
unveiled on 10 April 1971, and it became the
backbone of the BBC's comedy output for the
next 15 years, accorded the honour of regular

primetime Christmas and Easter specials.
Two such programmes were the stand-alone
productions *The Picnic* and *By The Sea*,
dialogue-free ventures that embraced a good
deal of seaside-style sauciness – a particular
interest of Ronnie Barker, who wrote the
scripts under pseudonyms – and were
reminiscent of his silent film short *Futtock's
End* (1969, directed by Bob Kellett).

In 1978, a stage version of *The Two
Ronnies* played at the London Palladium and
it proved so successful that the pair went on
to tour Australia with the production; in 1987,
the Ronnies returned Down Under to present
The Two Ronnies In Australia, a series of six
50-minute shows for the 9 Network, produced
by Brian Morelli, which combined new
material with some recycled pieces. (These
have not shown in Britain.)

Another fine aspect of *The Two Ronnies*
is that both stars remained free to pursue
individual ventures in between their collaborative series. Hence both starred in a number
of sitcoms during this period, Corbett most
notably in *Sorry!* and Barker in *Porridge*
and *Open All Hours*. Barker's retirement
in 1988 severed the partnership, however,
although it ensured that *The Two Ronnies*
had the distinction of finishing while still
very popular. Various subsequent series of
compilations have also proven remarkably
successful.

*Note. A compilation of the two specials that
aired as a prelude to *The Two Ronnies* (*The
Ronnie Barker Yearbook* and *Ronnie Corbett
In Bed*) was repeated on 27 May 1972 as a
Two Ronnies special. It has not been counted
in this figure, however.

Two Up, Two Down

UK · BBC · SITCOM

6 × 30 mins · colour
11 May–15 June 1979 · BBC1 Fri 8pm

MAIN CAST

Jimmy	Paul Nicholas
Flo	Su Pollard
Stan	Norman Tipton
Sheila	Claire Faulconbridge

CREDITS
writer Janey Preger · *director* Roger Cheveley ·
producer Tara Prem

A short-lived sitcom that not only had an
unusual premise but also invited viewers to
believe, incredibly, that Paul Nicholas and
Su Pollard were a partnership.

When Stan and Sheila move into their newly built house they find a couple of squatters,
Jimmy and Flo, already installed in their bedroom. With the law seemingly unable to force
their removal – at least not immediately –
they reluctantly decide to share.

Compared to the strait-laced Stan and
Sheila, Jimmy and Flo are wildly

unconventional, so much that the 'straights' become strangely fascinated by their interlopers' lifestyle and philosophy. Although wealthier, respected and more typically accomplished than the squatters, Stan and Sheila begin to realise that their life is missing the laid-back, devil-may-care panache of the other couple and start to change their habits accordingly.

Two's Company · 1

UK · ITV (GRANADA) · SKETCH

23 × 30 mins · b/w

*Series One (8) 9 May–11 July 1956 · Wed 10pm

Series Two (15) 19 Sep–26 Dec 1956 · Wed 10pm

MAIN CAST

Libby Morris (series 1 & first 8 eds of series 2)
Peter Butterworth (first 5 eds of series 1)
Dick Emery (series 2)
Nicolette Roeg (last 5 eds of series 2)
Kenneth Connor (series 2)

CREDITS

writers Len Fincham/Lawrie Wyman, Johnny Speight, Maurice Wiltshire, Dick Barry · *director* Peter Eton

An early Granada sketch series featuring the so-called 'rubber-faced comedienne' Libby Morris, who had arrived in England from her native Canada in June 1955 and scored immediate success in the music-with-humour programme *The Jack Jackson Show*. Young comic Peter Butterworth appeared in the first four editions, and Dick Emery and Kenneth Connor throughout the second series; Nicolette Roeg replaced Morris when she left the second series part way through, at which point Emery was given the top billing.

*Note. The first series was screened only in the North.

See also *Meet Libby Morris*.

Two's Company · 2

UK · ITV (LWT) · SITCOM

29 × 30 mins · colour

Series One (6) 6 Sep–11 Oct 1975 · Sat 10pm

Series Two (8) 24 Oct–25 Dec 1976 · mostly Sun 8.20pm

Series Three (8) 22 Jan–26 Mar 1978 · Sun around 9.30pm

Series Four (7) 14 Jan–4 Mar 1979 · Sun 9.15pm

MAIN CAST

Dorothy McNab · · · · · · · · · · · Elaine Stritch
Robert Hiller · · · · · · · · · · · · Donald Sinden

CREDITS

writer Bill MacIlwraith · *directors* Stuart Allen (series 1), Humphrey Barclay (series 2–4) · *producers* Stuart Allen (series 1), John Reardon (series 2–4)

A cut above the sitcom norm, *Two's Company* depicted the bristling but grudgingly content relationship between a pushy American woman and the old-school-tieish English butler-cook-handyman she employed to run her Chelsea townhouse. Although the odd guest would visit, the episodes were virtually two-handers, crackling with dialogue so good that the players could scarcely suppress smiling as they delivered their lines.

Both the lead characters were well drawn and admirably played by consummate actors. Elaine Stritch, who had not long moved to England, was cast as Dorothy McNab, the abrasive American author of thriller books, thrice married, thrice divorced, always on the attack, smoking cheroots and berating her man-servant with a loud gravelly voice. The theatrically voiced Donald Sinden played bachelor Robert Hiller: suave, self-assured, the essence of British decorum, feeling as negatively about Americans as Dorothy felt about the English. Life became a battle over who would gain the whip hand.

The first series of *Two's Company* was screened only by London-area ITV but the subsequent ones were networked and, deservedly, became very popular. A less good American adaptation, **The Two Of Us**, starred Mimi Kennedy as the American and Peter Cook as her English butler.

TW3

see *That Was The Week That Was*

Tygo Road

UK · BBC (POLA JONES FILMS) · SITCOM

6 × 30 mins · colour

Pilot · 19 May 1989 · BBC2 Fri 9pm

One series (5) 15 May–12 June 1990 · BBC2 Tue 9pm

MAIN CAST

Adam Hartley · · · · · · · · · · · · Kevin McNally
Kate · · · · · · · · · · · · · Isobel Black (not pilot)
Clare · · · · · · · · · · · · · · · · Deborah Norton
Leo · · · · · · · · · · · · · · · · · Steven O'Donnell
Gary · · · · · · · · · · · · · · · · · Vas Blackwood
Lionel · · · · · · · · · · · · · · · Gordon Gostelow
Spinnij · · · · · · · · · · · · · · · · · · Bill Bailey
Val · · · · · · · · · · · · · · · · · · Leila Bertrand
Selina · · · · · · · · · · · · · · · Alisa Bosschaert

CREDITS

writers Richard Cottan/Christopher Douglas · *director* Bob Spiers · *executive producers* John Kilby, Jamie Rix · *producer* Andre Ptaszynski

An acerbic inner-city sitcom set in the Tygo Road Community Centre, a towering edifice dominating the landscape between the Town Hall and the Wat Tyler Infants School, and representing to many of its regulars the last bastion against the seemingly unstoppable onslaught of Thatcherism.

Kevin McNally starred as Adam Hartley, the new administrator of the centre, and among his flock were Spinnij, the clown, and the rough, right-wing tramp Lionel. Later in the series, Lionel surprised them all by dying and bequeathing the centre £5000 – a legacy that would only pass to them if they obeyed certain conditions.

Tygo Road developed from a single-episode pilot screened in the *Comic Asides* season, then repeated on 8 May 1990 as a prelude to the full series.

The UK Show

UK · BBC · STANDUP

2 × 40 mins · colour

19 Aug 1978 · BBC1 Sat 11.35pm
26 Aug 1978 · BBC1 Sat 11pm

MAIN CAST
Peter Moloney
John Laurie (show 1)
Chic Murray (show 1)
Kenny Smiles (show 1)
Barbara Windsor (show 2)
Joe Brown (show 2)
James Ellis (show 2)

CREDITS
producer Barry Bevins

Humour hunter Peter Moloney fronted these two shows, which compared styles of humour in different areas around the UK. In the first, examples of Scottish and Welsh wit were contrasted; in the second, Ulster and cockney comedy were examined. The format permitted Moloney to talk to people in the street, enticing them to tell jokes.

Notes. Another journey into 'people humour' was the 1975 series *A Joke's A Joke*, made by LWT (eight editions, 6 September to 25 October), in which producer David Bell took his camera team around the country, filming factory and office workers in the act of cracking gags.

In 1992 ITV networked *Only Joking*, a series in which members of the public told funny stories while joke-telling families battled against the clock. Bradley Walsh was the host, Dave Lee and Dave Wolfe the resident comics. (Seven editions, 25 April to 13 June.)

Also in 1992, BBC1 presented *Joker In The Pack* – for details see Marti Caine's combined entry.

Ukridge

UK · BBC · SITCOM

7 × 30 mins · b/w

15 July–26 Aug 1968 · BBC1 Mon 7.30pm

MAIN CAST
Stanley Featherstonehaugh Ukridge · · · · · · ·
· Anton Rodgers
Aunt Julia · · · · · · · · · · · · · Marian Spencer
Corky · · · · · · · · · · · · · · · · · Julian Holloway

CREDITS
creator P G Wodehouse · *adapter/writer* Richard Waring · *producer* Joan Kemp-Welch

Another dip into Wodehouse's world of chinless wonders, formidable aunts, brilliant butlers and idle aristocrats. This time Stanley Ukridge, portrayed winningly by Anton Rodgers, took centre-stage for this series which aired under *The World Of Wodehouse* banner.

Ukridge is the black sheep of the Wodehouse menagerie, an indolent rogue with a quick eye for easy money and a character devoid of the moral strictures that keep his literary contemporaries (like Bertie Wooster) on the straight and narrow. Ukridge has a never-ending supply of get-rich-quick schemes, few of which pay any sort of dividend. In this series we found our anti-hero arranging an accident for insurance purposes, becoming mixed up in the murky world of boxing management, trying his hand at turf accountancy and launching a dog-training school.

A BBC Radio 4 adaptation of the stories aired from 21 December 1992 to 25 January 1993, with Griff Rhys Jones in the title role.

See also ***Uncle Fred Flits By, Blandings Castle, The World Of Wooster, Wodehouse Playhouse, Mr Wodehouse Speaking, The Reverent Wooing Of Archibald*** *and* ***Jeeves And Wooster.***

Uncle Fred Flits By

UK · BBC · SITCOM

1 × 25 mins · b/w

16 June 1967 · BBC1 Fri 7.35pm

MAIN CAST
Uncle Fred (Earl of Ickenham) · · · · · · · · · · ·
· · · · · · · · · · · · · · · · Wilfrid Hyde White
Connie Parker · · · · · · · · · · · · Avis Bunnage
Pongo Twistleton · · · · · · · · · · Jonathan Cecil
Julia Parker · · · · · · · · · · · · · · · Janina Faye
Wilberforce Robinson · · · · · · George Pensotti

CREDITS
creator P G Wodehouse · *adapter/writer/producer* Michael Mills

A further attempt to create a series out of the wonderful world of Wodehouse, following the success of *The World Of Wooster* and *Blandings Castle*. Once again, Michael Mills was the brains behind the adaptation, but this *Comedy Playhouse* introduction to the well-meaning but muddle-headed Earl of Ickenham failed to duplicate the success of the earlier outings – even with the great Wilfrid Hyde White in the lead role – and no series followed.

Uncle Jack ...

UK · BBC · CHILDREN'S SITCOMS

24 × 25 mins · colour

Series One (6) *Uncle Jack And Operation Green*
4 Oct–8 Nov 1990 · BBC1 Thu 4.35pm

Series Two (6) *Uncle Jack And The Loch Noch Monster* 3 Oct–7 Nov 1991 · BBC1 Thu 4.35pm

Series Three (6) *Uncle Jack And The Dark Side Of The Moon* 1 Oct–5 Nov 1992 · BBC1 Thu 4.35pm

Series Four (6) *Uncle Jack And Cleopatra's Mummy* 30 Sep–4 Nov 1993 · BBC1 Thu 4.35pm

MAIN CAST
Uncle Jack · · · · · · · · · · · · · · · · Paul Jones
Vixen · · · · · · · · · · · · · · · Fenella Fielding
M · · · · · · · · · · · · · · · · · Roger Hammond
Cynthia Birdwood · · · · · · · · · · · Vivian Pickles
Kate · · · · · · · · Helen Lambert (series 1 & 2);
· · · · · · · · · · · · · · · Sarah Lambert (series 3)
Michael · · · · Guiseppe Peluso (series 1 & 2)
Dorothy · · · · · · · · · · · · · · · · Tricia George

CREDITS
writer Jim Eldridge · *producer* Jeremy Swan

Uncle Jack (Paul Jones) is an eccentric cross between an eco-warrior and a mad scientist. His activities embroil him and members of his family (usually nieces and nephews) in various unlikely adventures and constant danger. Jack has a regular nemesis, the evil Vixen (played by the ever-watchable Fenella Fielding), whose plans invariably spell disaster for the ecology of the planet.

Writer Jim Eldridge invented a children's hero for the 1990s with the swashbuckling Jack, and initially kept the blend of comedy and drama that had proved popular with his earlier series *Bad Boyes*. By the third series, however, *Radio Times* ceased labelling *Uncle Jack* as a 'comedy-drama' and called it simply 'drama', perhaps feeling that the Earth's ecological extermination was no laughing matter.

Uncle Tulip

UK · BBC · SITCOM

1 × 30 mins · colour

8 Apr 1971 · BBC1 Thu 7.45pm

MAIN CAST
Uncle Tulip · · · · · · · · · · · · · · · · Renu Setna
Uncle Ranjit · · · · · · · · · · · · · Frank Olegario
Dr Johnson · · · · · · · · · · · Geoffrey Lumsden
Charlie · · · · · · · · · · · · · · · Madhav Sharma
Anna · Yasmin

CREDITS
writer Rene Basilico · *producer* Douglas Argent

A commendable *Comedy Playhouse* attempt at an ethnic sitcom, a few years ahead of its time. Renu Setna starred as Uncle Tulip, who arrives in England from Kenya to look after his niece, Anna, and nephew, Charlie. He finds the two disturbingly anglicised and sets about the task of reminding them of their heritage. No series developed.

Under And Over

UK · BBC · SITCOM

6 × 30 mins · colour

Pilot · 8 Jan 1971 · BBC1 Fri 8.30pm

One series (5) 24 Sep–22 Oct 1971 · BBC1
Fri 8pm

MAIN CAST

Dec	Dec Cluskey
Con	Con Cluskey
John	John Stokes
Lord Brentwood	Robert Keegan
Landlord	Tommy Godfrey
Hawkins	Jack Smethurst

CREDITS

writers David Climie/Austin Steele · *directors*
Roger Race (5), David Askey (1) · *producer* Austin
Steele

Developed from a *Comedy Playhouse* pilot,
this was a real curio piece: a sitcom series
starring the three members of the popular
Irish vocal trio the Bachelors, Dec, Con and
John. They were cast as Irish navvies
working on the Waterloo Tunnel in London.
Unfortunately the public didn't dig the idea
and only one series was made.

Under The Moon

UK · BBC · SITCOM

1 × 30 mins · colour

18 Sep 1995 · BBC1 Mon 8.30pm

MAIN CAST

Francesca Jensen	Samantha Bond
Donald Thackeray	Mark Aiken
Megan Phillips	Geraldine Fitzgerald
Hugo Tripp	Malcolm Sinclair
Alex	Nicholas Boulton
Sarah	Kacey Ainsworth
Gavin	Peter Moreton
Clifford	Cliff Parisi
Heena	Archie Panabi
Miss Prudhomme	Helen Fraser
Joe	Arthur Nightingale

CREDITS

writer Paul A Mendelson · *director/producer* Paul
Harrison

The sixth and last in a series of unrelated
comedies screened by BBC1 in the late
summer of 1995, *Under The Moon* told the
story of a career-woman, Francesca Jensen,
who has decided to have a baby independently of its father and remains determined that
the new arrival will in no way interrupt her
media job, as assistant marketing director of
E Brock & Sons, chocolate manufacturers.

As the event draws close, though, her
boss, the oily Hugo Tripp, and colleagues –
smoothie Gavin and bitchy Sarah – seem
intent on making capital out of her temporary
absence. Only the wimpish Gavin, and
Francesca's secretary, Heena, seem at all
loyal. Jensen's oldest friend is Megan Phillips,
a hardened features writer, who has published a newspaper article about Francesca and

her plans for single parenthood. But said
piece is read by Donald Thackeray, the 'one-
night stand' who fathered the baby; he
recognises the woman in the article's
accompanying photograph, works out the
date and intercepts Jensen at the hospital,
managing to be present at the baby's birth.
Francesca is anything but pleased to see him
and even more irate when she learns that he
isn't the Oxford Don he pretended to be but
is in fact called Don and lives in Oxford. She
tries to shake him off, even attempting to
buy his non-involvement, but Donald keeps
tracking her, with the help of his taxi-driver
friend, Clifford. At the end of the episode
Francesca thinks that Donald has dropped
out of the picture but he remains determined
to wheedle his way into lives of Francesca
and their baby.

The raison d'être of a pilot, of course, is to
lay the groundwork for a series, and *Under
The Moon* – with its elaborate premise and
full cast – was clearly intended to launch a
hopefully long run of subsequent episodes.
But while there were some good moments, the
pilot did not offer a great deal of promise and
there was no further development.

Underworld Knights

UK · BBC · SITCOM

1 × 30 mins · b/w

5 Oct 1963 · Sat 9pm

MAIN CAST

Vogler	Ron Moody
Froggy	Bryan Pringle
Crook 1	Blake Butler
Crook 2	Trevor Peacock
Café server	Pat Coombs

CREDITS

creator A J Bacon · *writer* Trevor Peacock ·
producer Philip Barker

A *Comedy Playhouse* entry from the talented
actor/writer Trevor Peacock, starring
character actor Ron Moody as a crime writer.
No series developed.

Union Castle

UK · ITV (GRANADA) · SITCOM

7 × 30 mins · colour

19 Apr–7 June 1982 · Mon 8pm

MAIN CAST

Lord Mountainash	Stratford Johns
Wordsworth	Moray Watson
Ursula, Lady Thaxted	Wanda Ventham
Annie	Lyndon Hughes
Elizabeth Steel	Carol Macready

CREDITS

writer Eric Paice · *director* Douglas Argent ·
producer Eric Prytherch

Union Castle starred former TV detective
'heavy' Stratford Johns (*Z Cars, Softly, Softly,
Barlow At Large*) as Lord Mountainash of the

Valleys, a trade-union baron who has
engineered his own peerage – he was once
known as plain Evan Evans.

As the former general secretary and
now president of the Confederation of Shop
Stewards and Allied Workers (COSSAW),
Mountainash purchases Runnymeade Castle,
an ancestral pile set in four thousand acres
of land, and moves in, together with his
daughter Annie. Here he meets Wordsworth,
the resident arch-Tory, union-hating butler,
and – aided (and sometimes embarrassed)
by 'Red Betty', the union's militant general
secretary Elizabeth Steel – fights against
the erosion of union power effected by the
Thatcher government and supported by
the upper-crust Lady Thaxted, who lives
in a cottage in the Runnymeade Castle
grounds.

The series provided a return to sitcom
ways for writer Eric Paice, who scripted
episodes of **Gert And Daisy** and **Tell It
To The Marines** in 1959 before majoring
heavily on BBC dramas, contributing scores
of scripts to *Dixon Of Dock Green, The
Brothers* and *Secret Army*. For *Union Castle*,
Paice wrote late in order to ensure that the
scripts were as topical as possible.

United States

USA · NBC (OTP PRODUCTIONS) · SITCOM

*13 × 30 mins · colour

US dates: 11 Mar–29 Apr 1980 (7 episodes)

UK dates: 27 Apr–13 July 1980 (7 episodes)
BBC1 Sun 9.55pm

MAIN CAST

Richard Chapin	Beau Bridges
Libby Chapin	Helen Shaver
Dylan Chapin	Rossie Harris
Nicky Chapin	Justin Dana

CREDITS

writer Larry Gelbart · *director* Nick Havinga ·
producer Larry Gelbart

Bafflingly retitled *Married* in the UK, *United
States* was an ambitious attempt by
M*A*S*H architect Larry Gelbart to
produce a groundbreaking and thought-
provoking adult sitcom that shirked many of
the genre's traditions, appearing without a
'laugh-track' and theme music and bearing
handwritten credits.

The Chapins – husband Richard, wife
Libby, sons Dylan and Nicky – were a modern-day family and faced realistic, modern-
day dilemmas that, unlike in virtually all
other sitcoms, were never conveniently tied
up at the end of the episodes. The comedy
was entirely verbal, inter-family discussions
providing the nub of each week's story. These
discussions were frank in nature, tackling
subjects – such as death, and infidelity – still
considered unsuitable subjects for mainstream US network sitcoms in 1980. Predictably, the series polarised its audience, albeit

with more detractors than supporters. Conversation-based comedy scored heavily in later years, in particular the hugely successful **Seinfeld**, but *United States* was quickly cancelled.

*Note. Although only seven episodes aired in the original run, 13 were made and all have been screened subsequent to the first run.

The Unrecorded Jasper Carrott

see CARROTT, Jasper

The Up And Down, In And Out, Roundabout Man

UK · ITV (THAMES) · CHILDREN'S SKETCH
13 × 15 mins · colour
21 May–13 Aug 1973 · Mon mostly 12.25pm
MAIN CAST
Ben Benison

CREDITS
creator Rex Bloomstein · *writers* Geoff Rowley/ Andy Baker · *directors* Andrew Holmes (7), Brian Chaston (3), David Gill (2), Rex Bloomstein (1) · *producers* Arthur Solomon, Rafi Rafaeli

A pre-school venture written by Rowley and Baker, best known for their sitcom work, and starring mime artist Ben Benison (later to appear in the BBC1 series *Vision On*) in a series of slapstick adventures of the banana-skin variety.

Up Our Street

UK · BBC · CHILDREN'S SITCOMS
13 × 15 mins · colour
Series One (6) 10 June–15 July 1985 · BBC1 Mon mostly 4.20pm
Series Two (7) 12 Sep–24 Oct 1985 · BBC1 Thu 3.55pm
MAIN CAST
various

CREDITS
writers (see below) · *executive producer* Cynthia Felgate · *producer* Greg Childs

A series of unrelated wacky stories, each with a different cast and writer, linked only by the unnamed 'street' of the title.

Episodes in the first series were: *The Chewing Gum Rescue* (written by Margaret Mahy), *Jelly At The Ritz* (Penny Casdagli), *Molly And The Seaweed Hypermarket* (Victoria Wood), *The Boy Who Hated Shopping* (Eric Church), *Rooms To Let* (Margaret Mahy), *Frying Tonight* (Diane Wilmer).

Series Two: *Simon And The Witch* (Margaret Stuart Barry), *The Birthday Burglar* (Margaret Mahy, adapted by Penny Casdagli), *Jimmy's Story* (Nick Wilton), *The End Of The Line* (Mark Bunyan), *Strange Events In The Life Of The Delmonico Family*

(Margaret Mahy), *Strange Things At Sea* (Penny Casdagli), *Alistair Grittle And The Library Monsters* (Marilyn Sadler/Roger Bollen).

Up Pompeii!

UK · BBC · SITCOM
14 episodes (8 × 35 mins · 6 × 30 mins) · colour
*Pilot (35 mins) 17 Sep 1969 · BBC1 Wed 9.10pm
Series One (7 × 35 mins) 30 Mar–11 May 1970 · BBC1 Mon mostly 9.10pm
Series Two (6 × 30 mins) 14 Sep–26 Oct 1970 · BBC1 Mon 9.20pm

MAIN CAST
Lurcio	Frankie Howerd
Ludicrus Sextus	Max Adrian (pilot & series 1);
	Wallas Eaton (series 2)
Ammonia	Elizabeth Larner
Nausius	Kerry Gardner
Senna	Jeanne Mockford (series 1 & 2)
Erotica	Georgina Moon
Plautus	Walter Horsbrugh (pilot);
	William Rushton (series 1)

CREDITS
writers Talbot Rothwell (pilot & series 1), Talbot Rothwell/Sid Colin (series 2) · *producers* Michael Mills (pilot), David Croft (series 1), Sydney Lotterby (series 2)

Despite his many successes as a standup comic, both in his own series and as a guest in variety shows (see his combined entry for details), it is with this relatively short-running comedy that Frankie Howerd made his greatest impact on the British public, a sitcom in which he was cast as a Roman slave serving in Pompeii.

The series owed a huge debt to the Burt Shevelove/Larry Gelbart and Stephen Sondheim musical *A Funny Thing Happened On The Way To The Forum*, in which Frankie Howerd had played two roles (Prologus and Pseudolus) during its highly successful London stage run from October 1963. *Up Pompeii!* – very loosely based on the 2000-year-old writings of Plautus, and featuring jokes *far* older – was written by Talbot Rothwell, a veteran of the industry who had scripted for Norman Wisdom, Terry-Thomas (**How Do You View?**), Arthur Askey and Ted Ray, but who, more tellingly, was one of the major writers of the *Carry On* film series. *Radio Times*, indeed, correctly labelled the *Up Pompeii!* pilot as 'A sort of "Carry On Up The Forum."'

Lurcio was the slave for Ludicrus, a government senator, and his busty wife Ammonia, and every episode embroiled him as the innocent pawn in a complex plot that threatened his easy-going lifestyle, his job or even his life, although all would be happily resolved at the end of each story, Lurcio

usually escaping his fate by the skin of his teeth. Unlike virtually every other sitcom ever made, however, the storylines were never the essence of this series – *Up Pompeii!* was a purpose-built vehicle for Frankie Howerd's distinctive stage-honed comedic style, giving him every opportunity to share confidences with the audience (both in the studio and at home) via constant asides, usually commenting on the improbability of the plot and the standard of the acting or writing. In so doing, Howerd constantly stepped in and out of both his character and the time-frame; this, of course, made a mockery of the premise, but viewers did not care a jot, since this was what they wanted and expected from him. Similarly, there was no elaborate location filming – the architectural glories of Pompeii were reproduced as a single polystyrene set in the BBC's studio in Shepherd's Bush, a fact that Lurcio was more than happy to point out.

The scripts were laden down with *Carry On*-style double entendres, awful puns and generally broad humour; in addition to the regulars, *Up Pompeii!* gloried in a visiting cast that changed with every episode, and these character names reveal all about the series' level and focus of wit – Ambi Dextrus, Bilius, Bumshus, Caushus, Daili, Felonius, Filfia, Hernia, Hidius, James Bondus, Pussus Galoria, Lecherous, Preshus, Lititia, Lusha, Mucas, Nefarius, Nubian, Nymphia, Odius, Oilus, Pitius, Ponderous, Scrophulus, Soppia, Spurios, Stovus Primus, Tarta, Tittia, Twiggia, Verminus and Virginia. Despite or perhaps because of this 'subtlety', and Howerd's unique style, the series worked a treat and became a huge hit, once again demonstrating Britons' unending love for sexual innuendo and smut.

Following the 1969 pilot episode, both the resulting TV series were made in 1970 (the second was written by Rothwell with his regular collaborator Sid Colin, another *Carry On* alumni), and a feature film version, *Up Pompeii* (written by Sid Colin, directed by Bob Kellett), was released in 1971 with Michael Hordern in the role of Ludicrus and Barbara Murray as Ammonia. Two further movies starring Howerd were inspired by the series but took the format into different periods of history (a similar style was employed years later with the **Blackadder** TV series): *Up The Chastity Belt* (director Bob Kellett, 1971, written by Sid Colin/Ray Galton/Alan Simpson), set during the crusades, with Howerd as the gormless serf Lurkalot; and *Up The Front* (Bob Kellett, 1972, written by Sid Colin/Eddie Braben), based in the First World War, with Howerd as gormless under-footman Lurk.

In 1973, back on the BBC, Howerd appeared in **Whoops Baghdad**, an

Arabian Nights-style variation on *Up Pompeii!*, and – following a one-off *Further Up Pompeii!* special aired in 1975 (see below) – he tried to revive the formula again with the ITV programme **A Touch Of The Casanovas**. The following year a four-part Australian TV series *Up The Convicts* (written by Hugh Stuckey) featured Howerd as ex-convict Jeremiah Shirk, who becomes the household help to Sir Montague and Lady Fitzgibbon in yet another twist on the original theme, and he also starred in a Canadian series, *Oh Canada*.

Notes. As stated above, every episode of *Up Pompeii!* featured guest actors. Those appearing in these 14 BBC episodes included George Baker, Lynda Baron, John Cater, Pat Coombs, Derek Francis, Robert Gillespie, Geoffrey Hughes, John Junkin, Jean Kent, David Kernan, Michael Knowles, Larry Martyn, Bill Maynard, Norman Mitchell, Hugh Paddick, Wendy Richard, John Ringham, Nicholas Smith, Mollie Sugden, Leon Thau, Queenie Watts, Paul Whitsun-Jones, Barbara Windsor (as Nymphia), and, before he was given the fixed role of Ludicrus, Wallas Eaton.

*The pilot was made in colour but first screened by BBC1 when the channel was still monochrome.

Further Up Pompeii!

UK · BBC · SITCOM

1 × 45 mins · colour

31 March 1975 · Mon 9.10pm

MAIN CAST

Lurcio · · · · · · · · · · · · · · · · Frankie Howerd
Ludicrus · · · · · · · · · · · · · · · Mark Dignam
Ammonia · · · · · · · · · · · · · Elizabeth Larner
Nausius · · · · · · · · · · · · · · · Kerry Gardner
Pollux · · · · · · · · · · · · · · · · · · John Cater
Senna · · · · · · · · · · · · · · Jeanne Mockford
Prodigus · · · · · · · · · · · · · · Leon Greene
Hernia · · · · · · · · · · · · · · · Owlen Griffiths
Erotica · · · · · · · · · · · · · Jennifer Lonsdale
Claudius · · · · · · · · · · · · · · Cyril Appleton
Scrubba · · · · · · · · · · · · · Lindsay Duncan

CREDITS

writer Talbot Rothwell · producer David Croft

On Easter Monday 1975, precisely five years after the first series began, the BBC screened a one-off revival of the old warhorse. All the old jokes abounded.

Further Up Pompeii

UK · ITV (LWT) · SITCOM

1 × 45 mins · colour

14 Dec 1991 · Sat 7.55pm

MAIN CAST

Lurcio · · · · · · · · · · · · · · · Frankie Howerd
Colossa · · · · · · · · · · · · · Joanna Dickens
Petunia · · · · · · · · · · · · · · Elizabeth Anson
Villainus Brutus · · · · · · · · · · · John Bardon

Noxius · · · · · · · · · · · · · · · · Russell Gold
Ambiguous · · · · · · · · · · · · · Peter Geeves
Typhus · · · · · · · · · · · · · · · · Roy Evans
Gluteus Maximus · · · · · · · · · · · Tim Killick
Umbilicus · · · · · · · · · · · · · · · Gary Rice
Claudius · · · · · · · · · · · · · · Barry James

CREDITS

writers Paul Minett/Brian Leveson · director Ian Hamilton · producer Paul Lewis

Maximising the resurgence of interest in Howerd that occurred shortly before his death, ITV (which, hitherto, had never been part of the story) revived the *Pompeii* formula for one last time in 1991, fully 16 years after the previous BBC escapade. Scripted by new writers, and with an all-new cast save for Howerd, it was a turgid affair, however – more of an epilogue than a prologue – bringing to mind the old cliché about reheating a soufflé. It was set in the time of Caligula, where Lurcio, now a freeman with slaves of his own, runs a small business, the Bacchus wine bar. As Senna would have said, 'Oh, woe, woe, woe'.

Up Sunday

UK · BBC · SATIRE

55 editions (34 × 25 mins · 21 × 30 mins) · colour

Series One (21 × 30 mins) 6 Feb–16 July 1972 · BBC2 Sun around 11.15pm
Series Two (12 × 25 mins) 5 Nov 1972–28 Jan 1973 · BBC2 Sun around 11pm
Special (25 mins) *Up The Channel* 31 Dec 1972 · BBC2 Sun 10.35pm
Series Three (12 × 25 mins) 1 Apr–17 June 1973 · BBC2 Sun around 11.30pm
Series Four (8 × 25 mins) 28 Oct–16 Dec 1973 · BBC2 Sun around 11.05pm
Special (25 mins) *Up Christmas* 23 Dec 1973 · BBC2 Sun 11.45pm

MAIN CAST

Clive James
John Wells
William Rushton
James Cameron
Kenny Everett (series 1 & 2)
Keith Dewhurst (series 3)

CREDITS

writers cast · producer Ian Keill

A satirical overview of the week's events, initially under the auspices of the production crew from *Line-Up*, BBC's weekday nightly look at the arts and current affairs.

Up Sunday was sometimes quite savage in its humour but it escaped the controversies of earlier, similar series, simply because so few were watching. Guest stars appeared in most editions, with John Fortune, Eric Idle, Ivor Cutler and Vivian Stanshall all turning up more than once. The 31 December 1972 special, *Up The Channel*, took a satirical look at the Common Market.

Up The Elephant And Round The Castle

UK · ITV (THAMES) · SITCOM

23 × 30 mins · colour

Series One (6) 30 Nov 1983–11 Jan 1984 · Wed 8.30pm
Series Two (8) 8 Jan–26 Feb 1985 · Tue 8pm
Series Three (9) 12 Sep–7 Nov 1985 · Thu mostly 8pm

MAIN CAST

Jim London · · · · · · · · · · · · · · · Jim Davidson
Wanda Pickles · · · · · · · · · · · · · Sue Nicholls
Dad London · · · · · · · · · · · · · · John Bardon
Mum London · · · · · · · · · · · Rosalind Knight
· (series 1 & 2)
Councillor Bertram Allnut · · · · Roger Sloman
· (series 1)
Councillor Arnold Moggs · · · · · · Nicholas Day
· (series 2 & 3)
Terence 'Tosh' Carey · · · · · · · · Brian Capron
· (series 1 & 2)
Vera Spiggott · · · · Sara Corper (series 1 & 2)
Brian the barman · · · · · · · · · · · · Brian Hall
Lois Tight · · · · · · · · Anita Dobson (series 1)

CREDITS

writers Spike Mullins (9), Geoff McQueen (6), Jim Eldridge (3), Colin Bostock-Smith (2), Peter Learmouth (1), Tony Hoare (1), Louise Ford (1) · script associate Spike Mullins · director/producer Anthony Parker

Hardly a contender for the sitcom hall of fame, this was a vehicle for the comedian Jim Davidson, hitherto a standup comic. (See **The Jim Davidson Show** for details of the bulk of his TV career). In *Up The Elephant And Round The Castle*, Davidson was a cockney Jim-the-lad bachelor, on the dole, chasing birds, boozing down the Freemasons Arms and getting into all manner of scrapes – and not entirely legal ones at that. (The law enforcers – predictably, remembering his 'nick-nick' catchphrase – were portrayed as dozy coppers.)

Scarcely acting out of character, Davidson was cast as Jim London and he was the inheritor of a terraced Victorian house – 17 Railway Terrace – situated under a bridge in the Elephant and Castle district of south London, bequeathed to him by his Aunt Minnie. Unluckily for Jim, there is a sitting squatter upstairs, Mr Wilkins (who is never seen although his sound is clearly heard through the ceiling). Jim is also saddled with some dodgy neighbours, among them a borough councillor, Bertram Allnut (succeeded, even more unbelievably, in the second and third series by yet another councillor, Arnold Moggs), Vera Spiggott, an unsexy young woman still living at home who fancies Jim like mad, and Wanda Pickles, a larger than life sex-pot whose husband Stan is in maximum-security jail at Parkhurst. Pickles is always barging in with a cheery greeting and pursuing a quickie on the sofa, but London is disparaging and denying of his loins. He is also saddled with a few dodgy mates, the attentions of the DHSS and visits from his Dad, sheltering from the verbal battering he receives from his 'missus'.

Aimed fairly and squarely at his devoted fans (Davidson actually read *The Sun* on camera), *Up The Elephant And Round The Castle* was a curious mixture of sitcom and music-hall-style standup swagger. In what was patently a studio set, some episodes opened with Davidson emerging from his front door in a shortie dressing-gown, socks and shoes, stretching, announcing 'morning, world' and making a straight-to-camera pronouncement, introducing the latest laddish episode in his life by way of a flashback. Seen along the way, in early TV roles, were Anita Dobson (later to star in *EastEnders*), Christopher Ellison (*The Bill*) and Linda Robson (*Birds Of A Feather*).

See also the sequel, *Home James!*

Up The Garden Path

UK · ITV (HUMPHREY BARCLAY PRODUCTIONS FOR GRANADA) · SITCOM

18 × 30 mins · colour

Series One (6) 2 May–6 June 1990 · Wed 8pm

Series Two (6) 29 May–3 July 1991 · Wed 9.30pm

Series Three (6) 27 May–1 July 1993 · Thu 8.30pm

MAIN CAST

Isabelle 'Izzy' Comyn · · · · · · Imelda Staunton
Dick Barnes · · · · · · · · · · · · · · · · Mike Grady
Maria Shadwell · · · · · · · · Tessa Peake-Jones
Gwyn Jenkins · · · · · · · · · · · · · Tom Mannion
Michael Tristram · · · · · · Nicholas Le Prevost
Louise Tristram · · · · · · · · · · · · Susan Kyd
Roger 'Razors' Razebrook · · · · · Rene Zagger
Charles Armstrong · · · David Robb (series 2)
Bill Bailey · · · · · · · Neil McCaul (series 2 & 3)
Linda · · · · · · · Adrienne O'Sullivan (series 3)

CREDITS

writer Sue Limb · *director* David Askey · *executive producers* David Liddiment/Al Mitchell (series 1 & 2), Andy Harries/Al Mitchell (series 3) · *producer* Humphrey Barclay

One of the finest radio-and-TV sitcoms in recent years, Sue Limb's *Up The Garden Path* related the trials of the wonderfully named Izzy Comyn (played by the fast-rising Imelda Staunton), a woman in her thirties who tumbles, always in hope, from one love entanglement to another, her dalliances doomed to fail because of her fatal attraction to inappropriate men and propensity for telling lies in order to extricate herself from given situations. Inevitably, as the fibs pile up, dragging Izzy ever deeper into a hole, she is forced to live them out or admit defeat – such reversals usually leading our heroine to stuff her mouth full of chocolate cakes, gateaux and biscuits, which do few favours for her skin or figure.

Not exactly blessed with attractive personal habits or hygiene, Izzy staggers through a life she herself makes chaotic, with her closest friends playing a major part. Unfairly, for that is the way of things, the pal Izzy appreciates the least is the one she should cherish the most: Dick, the pottery teacher at the same London inner-city school where Izzy teaches English. A gentle, duffel-coated soul from Derbyshire, Dick's devotion to Izzy combines unadulterated idolatry with unrequited love. He would make her a marvellously loyal and supportive partner but Izzy just isn't interested. So Dick has to be satisfied with remaining her marvellously loyal and supportive friend, constantly pushed to one side when a new beau is in the wings, or crassly embroiled in her affairs by some convenient fib she has invented to impress another man. Only after a long time (in the third series) does Dick finally accept Izzy's indifference to him, and while they remain friends and flatmates he finds a partner of his own, the school PE teacher Linda. Izzy's best friend is Maria, the history teacher at the same school, whose marriage to her life-lusting Welsh husband Gwyn is not without crises but survives, just, thanks to Izzy's help. For a brief period Maria declares herself in love with Izzy, but then realises that she is not and falls pregnant with Gwyn's baby, born in time for the final series.

At the beginning of the first series Izzy is having an affair with a married man, Michael (played joyously to the hilt by Nick Le Prevost). Michael is a loveable scoundrel with a boundless enthusiasm for extramarital affairs. His lovely wife Louise, who knows her husband all too well, is remarkably forgiving, seeing the little boy in her partner and recognising that he is beyond change. Louise and Izzy soon forge a great friendship until they both fall in love with Bill, a Cambridge tutor who cannot yield to his feelings for Izzy until he has emotionally recovered from his former marriage. In between times, Izzy falls for an upper-class twit, Charles, cancelling at the eleventh hour what would certainly have been a disastrous union.

Throughout the first two series, one of Izzy's pupils, nicknamed Razors, clearly has a crush on his teacher, and he moves up slowly on the rails. The second series ended after he declared his hand and Izzy agreed to go out on a date. In the final series, after Razors has left school, they are an item, despite the substantial age difference. With her biological time-clock ticking away, Izzy is keen to have a baby, in or out of a relationship, but is nonetheless shocked to discover that she has been made pregnant by Razors ... And all the while she continues to spurn the one man who loves her for what she is, the wimpish Dick. (The radio version finished differently, with Dick offering to be surrogate father to Izzy's

child, living 'as single parents ... together, like'.)

Notwithstanding the convoluted nature of the friendships and relationships, *Up The Garden Path* was a feast from first episode to last. Written with great subtlety by Sue Limb – already the author of the excellent Radio 4 comedy *The Wordsmiths At Gorsemere*, and shortly afterwards to launch the Dulcie Domum newspaper columns/books/radio readings – the comedy came in equal measures from Izzy Comyn's anxiety and embarrassment, and broadly expounded the moral of a young woman muddling her way through self-imposed crises and, though one realised this was not her aim, gaining her feminist stripes in the process. Limb's tactic of having Izzy play out her own life dramas in classroom discussions or role-model situations with her adolescent school pupils, either as a means of showing her what to do next or to focus her thoughts, was one of many brilliant touches on the author's part.

Up The Garden Path was originally published as a novel, Sue Limb's first, in 1984, and the author adapted her own creation into 30-minute scripts for both a BBC Radio 4 version, recorded without an audience, and this Granada TV production, with. (The BBC, incredibly, passed up the opportunity to transfer its radio series to TV.) The radio and TV runs extended to three series each: the first radio series was based on the novel and the second was written fresh for the radio medium (although it then became a sequel book, *Love's Labours*) – both then transferred straight to TV. The third series was written for both TV and radio. The three BBC radio series ran thus: six episodes, 7 November–12 December 1987; eight episodes, 15 October–3 December 1988; six episodes, 17 November–22 December 1993, making 20 episodes in all. The radio cast was largely the same as the TV version except that Maria was played by Marty Cruickshank, Gwyn by Siôn Probert first then Dafydd Hywel then Probert again, and Louise by Phyllida Nash.

Up The Junction

UK · ITV (MENTORN FILMS FOR ANGLIA) · STANDUP

6 × 45 mins · colour

*27 Apr–1 June 1991 · Sat mostly 1.15am

MAIN CAST

host · Will Durst
Les and Robert

CREDITS

writers cast · *producer* Alexandra Jackson

Six programmes of comedy and music recorded at the Junction Club in Cambridge. The American comic Will Durst was the host, Les and Robert were regulars, and Jack Dee, Mark Hurst, Felix, David Baddiel, the

Reduced Shakespeare Company, Jo Brand, Randolf The Remarkable, Bob Mills and Otiz Cannelloni were among the acts seen during the series.

*Note. These dates refer to London-area screenings. The series was shown by its maker, Anglia, on Saturday nights from 19 January to 16 March 1991.

Up The Workers

UK · ITV (ATV) · SITCOM

14 × 30 mins · colour

Pilot · 4 Sep 1973 · Tue 10.30pm

Series One (7) 1 May–12 June 1974 · Wed 8.30pm

Series Two (6) 25 Feb–14 Apr 1976 · Wed 8.30pm

MAIN CAST

Richard (Dicky) Bligh · · · · · · · · Henry McGee
Bernard Peck · · · · · · · · · · · · Lance Percival
Sid Stubbins · · · · · · · · · · · · · Norman Bird
Sir Henry Carmichael · · · · · · · · · · · Ivor Dean
· · · · · · · · · · · · · · · · · · (pilot & series 1)
Sir Charles · · · Charles Lloyd Pack (series 2)
Bert Hamflitt · · · · · · · Gordon Rollings (pilot);
· · · · · · · · · · · · · · · Dudley Sutton (series 1)
Fred Hamflitt · · · · · Victor Maddern (series 2)
Mick Briggs · · · · · · Charles Bolton (series 1)
Deidre Hargreaves · · · · · · Lynn Smith (pilot);
· · · · · · · · · · · · · · Trudi Van Doorn (series 1)
Arthur Henthorne · · · · · · · · Peter Hill (pilot)
Andrea · · · · · · · · · · · · Lesley Duff (series 2)
Mavis · · · · · · · · · Vivienne Martin (series 2)
Fergy · · · · · · · · · · · · · Léon Vitali (series 2)

CREDITS

creator Lance Percival · writers Tom Brennand/Roy Bottomley · directors/producers John Scholz-Conway (pilot & series 1), Alan Tarrant (series 2)

In the strike-strewn 1970s it was inevitable that a sitcom would use industrial relations as its focus. Although written by Brennand and Bottomley, the series' co-star Lance Percival came up with the idea for the punningly titled *Up The Workers*, basing the action at a small Midlands factory, Cockers Components Ltd, and suggesting that worker-management strife should form the hub of the episodes.

Percival played the part of the labour relations officer, Bernard Peck, whose position in the pecking order was uncomfortably between his co-star Henry McGee's role as managing director of the company, Richard (Dicky) Bligh, and that of the shop-steward Sid Stubbins (Norman Bird). A decade after *The Rag Trade* the cry of 'everybody out!' was heard in TV comedy once again as the Cocker workers took umbrage against the arrival of new Japanese machinery, the prospect of too little or too much overtime and many other crises. All concerned would doubtless have been pleased to see, however, that none of the episodes was blighted by the frequent ITV technicians' strikes that marked the decade.

Up To Something

UK · BBC · SKETCH

7 × 30 mins · colour

2 July–13 Aug 1990 · BBC1 Mon 8.30pm

MAIN CAST

Suzy Aitchison
Frances Dodge
Mike Hayley
Lewis MacLeod
Shane Richie
David Schneider

CREDITS

writers Bill Naylor, Stuart Silver, Terry Morrison, Garry Chambers, Shane Richie, Clive Whichelow, Mike Hayley, Charlie Adams, David Schneider, Kim Fuller, Armando Iannucci, Richard Herring, Paul Minett/Brian Leveson, Tim Firth and others · director/producer Michael Leggo

A second stab for the *Something For The Weekend* creative team, this time with a substantially different cast – only Mike Hayley survived from the original series. It was, once again, a worthwhile effort, but the show still lacked the edge necessary to guarantee a long run and a place in the affections of the viewing public.

The Upchat Line

UK · ITV (THAMES) · SITCOM

7 × 30 mins · colour

26 Sep–7 Nov 1977 · Mon 8pm

MAIN CAST

'Mike Upchat' · · · · · · · · · · · John Alderton

CREDITS

writer Keith Waterhouse · director/producer Robert Reed

According to Mike Upchat, there were many ways to bed a bird; here, indeed, was a man always on the lookout for overnight accommodation with a pretty young woman. Mike Upchat was not his real name, of course, and no one ever found out what this was; it was also not the only pseudonym he would employ in his schemes to wile his way into a woman's bed. Nor did Upchat refrain from claiming all manner of vocations – most of the time he said he was a writer but he could also be anything from a psychologist to a piano-tuner, depending on what he considered would impress a woman most. In short, then, Mike Upchat was an incorrigible liar, using his way with words to get his way with women. En route to his many conquests he made a number of enemies, of course, usually jealous boyfriends and husbands or angry parents, but this never stopped him in his desperate desire to find a bed for the night, preferably with someone warm to snuggle up to. It soon became obvious why: quite apart from his carnal lust, Upchat 'lived' in a left-luggage locker at Marylebone Station and had no bed of his own.

John Alderton starred as the oddly loveable rogue Upchat in this unusual Keith Waterhouse creation, and the support cast (women) changed with each episode. There was a sequel, *The Upchat Connection*, a year later – see next entry.

The Upchat Connection

UK · ITV (THAMES) · SITCOM

7 × 30 mins · colour

24 Oct–5 Dec 1978 · Tue 8.30pm

MAIN CAST

'Mike Upchat' · · · · · · · · · · · Robin Nedwell
Maggie · · · · · · · · · · · · · · Susan Jameson
Polly · · · · · · · · · · · · · Bernadette Milnes

CREDITS

writer Keith Waterhouse · director/producer Robert Reed

John Alderton declined to appear in a second series of *The Upchat Line* so Keith Waterhouse came up with a superb ruse to keep his fictional character alive: at the start of the series it was revealed that Mike had gone to Australia but that, before departing, he had raffled the key to his Marylebone left-luggage locker, the winner inheriting his prized cache of pseudonyms, address book and, to start proceedings, a blind date. This brilliant concept thus ensured that all the remaining scripts could remain unaltered for, in a *Doctor Who*-style move, while the actor had gone the character remained the same. Robin Nedwell duly took over the role, carrying on much as before.

The Upper Crusts

UK · ITV (LWT) · SITCOM

6 × 30 mins · colour

25 Feb–1 Apr 1973 · Sun 9.30pm

MAIN CAST

Lady Seacroft · · · · · · · · · Margaret Leighton
Lord Seacroft/ ·
Lord Seacroft Sr · · · · · · · · · · · Charles Gray
Davina Seacroft · · · · · · · · · · · · Lalla Ward
Gareth Seacroft · · · · · · · · · · · · Martin Neil

CREDITS

writers Keith Waterhouse/Willis Hall · director/producer Mark Stuart

Lord and Lady Seacroft have gone both down and up in the world: down because they are forced to live in drastically reduced circumstances, up because their new home is a high-rise council flat. The source of their decline in fortunes is one man: Lord Seacroft Sr, who – in a final, sorry move before being accidentally shot dead – loses the family fortune in a card game. Lord and Lady Seacroft, with their ghastly children Davina and Gareth, are forced to auction the family heirlooms and face up to a new life, having to seek work and mix with the riff-raff.

Two heavyweight actors dominated this Waterhouse and Hall sitcom: Charles Gray (who, in the opening episode, played Seacrofts senior and junior) and Margaret Leighton, both established stars of the cinema. Sadly, they could not prevent this riches-to-rags creation going the way of the Seacrofts' estate. Waterhouse and Hall later based another sitcom in a council flat: *Queenie's Castle*.

The Upper Hand

UK · ITV (COLUMBIA/TRI-STAR FOR CENTRAL) · SITCOM

95 episodes (94 × 30 mins · 1 × 60 mins) · colour

Series One (12) 1 May–14 Aug 1990 · mostly Tue 8.30pm

Special · 27 Dec 1990 · Thu 8.30pm

Series Two (13) 18 Feb–20 May 1991 · Mon 8pm

Series Three (13) 5 Nov 1991–11 Feb 1992 · Tue 8.30pm

Series Four (19) 20 Oct 1992–22 Feb 1993 · Tue 8.30pm then Mon 8pm

Series Five (16) 9 Sep–23 Dec 1993 · Thu 8.30pm

Series Six (13 × 30 mins · 1 × 60 mins) 6 Jan–8 Apr 1995 · mostly Fri 8.30pm

Series Seven (7) 2 Sep–7 Oct 1996 · Mon 8.30pm

MAIN CAST

Charlie Burrows · · · · · · · · · · · · Joe McGann
Caroline Wheatley · · · · · · · · · Diana Weston
Laura West · · · · · · · · · · · · Honor Blackman
Joanna Burrows · · · · · · · · · · · · Kellie Bright
Tom Wheatley · · · · · · · · · · · William Puttock

CREDITS

creators Blake Hunter/Martin Cohan · *writers* same as *Who's The Boss?* and Colin Bostock-Smith (3) · *script associate* Greg Freeman · *directors* Martin Shardlow (49), Martin Dennis (31), Mike Holgate (8), Michael Owen Morris (7) · *executive producer* Paul Spencer · *producer* Christopher Walker

Some months after ITV began screening *Who's The Boss?* it premiered *The Upper Hand*, the British adaptation of that hit US sitcom. (At one point it was going to be called *Man-Maid*.) Though it ran for 101 fewer episodes than its US counterpart, *The Upper Hand* quickly became one of ITV's most popular and durable comedies of the period, enjoying a six-year run and good audience ratings.

Premise details for *The Upper Hand* can be found under the entry for *Who's The Boss?* with these changes: the widowed former St Louis Cardinals baseball star Tony Micelli was now the widowed former Tottenham Hotspur footballer Charlie Burrows; the city he quit was not New York but London; his daughter was not Samantha but Joanna; he

obtained a job in rural Henley-upon-Thames instead of Connecticut, with divorced advertising agency executive Caroline Wheatley instead of divorced advertising agency executive Angela Bower; her son was named Tom instead of Jonathan and her sex-mad mother was Laura, not Mona. Everything else from *Who's The Boss?* came across the Atlantic intact, including the scripts, which were the same as the American originals except for localised changes. Since US sitcoms usually require weekly guest stars *The Upper Hand* had the same, with Anthony Newley (three times), Tim Brooke-Taylor, Millicent Martin and former footballer Kevin Keegan among those who appeared. A virtually identical set was utilised too, the settee facing the audience as it does in so many US sitcoms, and the kitchen/lounge being accessed by a swing door, and US theme music was used – not from *Who's The Boss?* though, but, curiously, from *Knots Landing*.

The three principal stars of *The Upper Hand* played their parts well, with Joe McGann starring as Charlie Burrows (the refined surroundings of Oxfordshire smoothed the rough edges of his London accent as the years passed), Diana Weston cast as the glamorous executive divorcee, and Honor Blackman, a 1960s sex symbol in *The Avengers*, revelling in the part of the sexy gran Laura, although she underplayed the role in comparison with her US counterpart, Katherine Helmond.

In a novel move, Helmond came over to Britain to feature in the last episode of the fourth series of *The Upper Hand*, thus appearing in both US and UK versions of the same programme, albeit in different roles. This was the episode in which, after years of dilly-dallying, Charlie and Caroline finally declared their love for one another. They became engaged at the end of the fifth series and wed in the pouring rain during what was meant to be the last ever episode, an hour-length edition screened on Easter Saturday 1995. This, for the first time, took *The Upper Hand* beyond *Who's The Boss?*, which had concluded with Tony and Angela remaining unwed.

It was something of a surprise, therefore, that *The Upper Hand* returned for one final series in 1996, during which Caroline fell pregnant. American writers continued to supply the dialogue for four of these final seven episodes, the other three being scripted by the British writer Colin Bostock-Smith. This really was the end of the road, though, for the unfulfilled 'will-they-won't-they?' sexual tension between Charlie and Caroline that had given *The Upper Hand* so much of its fizz was no longer present.

Us Girls

UK · BBC · SITCOM

12 × 30 mins · colour

Series One (6) 27 Feb–2 Apr 1992 · BBC1 Thu 8.30pm

Series Two (6) 10 Mar–14 Apr 1993 · BBC1 Wed 8.30pm

MAIN CAST

Bev · · · · · · · · · Joanne Campbell (series 1);
· · · · · · · · · · · · Nicola Blackman (series 2)
Aisha · · · · · · · · · · · · · Marlaine Gordon
Grandma Pinnock · · · · · · · · Mona Hammond
Grandad Pinnock · · · · · · · · · · · Allister Bain
Catherine · · · · · · · · · · · · · · Kerry Potter
Gail · · · · · · · · · · · · · · · · · · Doña Croll

CREDITS

writer Lisselle Kayle · *script consultant* Sharon Foster · *script editor* Anne Pivcevic · *director/producer* David Askey

A sitcom that drew laughter from the cultural clashes across three generations of British-domiciled West Indian women.

Bev was the one in the middle, trying desperately to live an independent life but suffering interference form both her sullen teenage daughter Aisha and her nagging mother (known only as Grandma). The biggest clash occurred over Bev's involvement with a black lifestyle magazine, *Shades*, edited by the sharp-dressing, quick-talking Gail. Initially, Bev works for the local council, writing for the magazine only in her spare time, but by the second series she has quit her day job to work full time for *Shades*, much to the chagrin of both Aisha, who sees the household struggling with the corresponding drop in income, and Grandma, who feels that her daughter is wasting her life. (Until she wins an award, that is, and gets to go on television.) Needless to say, Grandma and granddaughter get on like a house on fire, and Bev's only family ally is her henpecked father (Grandad).

Us Girls was a gentle family comedy that had a universal appeal in its story of conflicting generations. The cast was uniformly good but the best performance was by Mona Hammond, who, as the cranky grand dame of the clan, delighted in squeezing every ounce of humour from the lines with a wonderful use of exaggerated accent and authentic patois.

USA High

USA · USA NETWORK (PETER ENGEL PRODUCTIONS/RHYSHER ENTERTAINMENT/ NBC) · CHILDREN'S SITCOM

75 × 30 mins (to 31/12/97 · continuing into 1998) · colour

US dates: 4 Aug 1997 to date

UK dates: 5 Apr 1997 to date (49 episodes to 31/12/97) C5 Sat and Sun mostly 2pm

MAIN CAST

Jackson Green · · · · · · · · · · · · Josh Holland

Lauren Fontaine	Elena Lyons
Christian Mueller	Thomas Magiar
Winnie Barnes	Marquita Terry
Bobby Lazzarini	James Madio
Ashley Elliot	Kristen Miller
Gabrielle Dupre	Angela Visser
Patrick Elliot	Nicholas Guest

CREDITS

creators/executive producers Peter Engel/Leslie Eberhard · *writers* various · *directors* various · *producer* Sue Feyk

From the **Saved By The Bell** stable, this was yet another series about good-looking teens at high school. The twist in *USA High*, however, was the setting being an American school in Paris, with (mostly) Americans as pupils. The featured regulars were British headmaster Mr Elliot and his daughter Ashley who attended the school (some truly bizarre English accents on these two); handsome chancer Jackson, a surfing dude from San Diego; his German pal, Christian Mueller; pretty but sometimes devious friends Lauren and Winnie; irritating wheeler-dealer Lazzarini and beautiful French administrator Miss Dupre. Their adventures in Paris (all taped in a California studio) and their rites of passage dilemmas formed the basis of what was – like many of its contemporary series – anodyne, unchallenging, superficial and sterile entertainment.

In the UK, the series aired on the brand-new C5, most episodes being screened at weekends within *The Mag*, a wraparound title for various shows made for (and sometimes by) pre-teens and teens. Unusually, the UK transmissions of *USA High* preceded the US launch, which occurred four months later; there, the episodes aired five afternoons a week on the cable channel USA Network.

Valentine Park

UK · ITV (CENTRAL) · SITCOM

12 × 30 mins · colour

Series One (6) 19 June–24 July 1987 ·
Fri 7.30pm

Series Two (6) 22 July–26 Aug 1988 · Fri 5.15pm

MAIN CAST

Tom	Ken Jones
Mrs Giles	Liz Smith
Max	David Thewlis
Claire	Katie Newell
Bodie	Daniel Peacock
Doyle	Bernard Padden (series 1)
Maggie	Penny Morrell
Wendy	Jennifer Guy
Mr Smackley	Ellis Dale (series 2)
Philip	Ken Farrington (series 2)

CREDITS

creators Nicholas Hyde/Glen Cardno · *writers*
Nicholas Hyde/Glen Cardno (series 1), Mike
Walling/Ian Whitham (2 episodes), Niall Clark/
Sandy Wood/Richard Sparks (2 eps), Geoff Rowley
(1 ep), not known (1 ep) · *directors* Nic Phillips
(series 1), John Woods (series 2) · *executive
producer* Jon Scoffield · *producer* Glen Cardno

A rather curious sitcom. There was nothing
wrong with the cast – Ken Jones, Liz Smith
and Danny Peacock were involved – but the
humour was roundly criticised for being
juvenile. Sure enough, when LWT brought
it back for a second series, it went out in a
children's time-slot, Fridays at 5.15pm, albeit
in school-holiday time.

Jones was cast as Tom, the head gardener
in a large public park, proud of his marigolds
but saddened to see that the park has a new
employee, his errant godson Max. Also
working there are two laddish young men,
Bodie and Doyle, who – as their names
suggest – like to think of themselves as
players in *The Professionals*, and, as the
park's security officers, have the licence to
behave accordingly. Max, who boards with
the mad landlady Mrs Giles (Liz Smith),
falls in love with Claire, who lives with her
irrational mother Maggie (played by Penny
Morrell, real-life wife of George Cole).

Valentine Park was co-created and the first
series was co-written by Nicholas Hyde, a

30-year-old public parks gardener from Kent
with no previous writing experience.

Valentine's Night

UK · ITV (ATV) · SKETCH

1 × 60 mins · b/w

6 Sep 1958 · Sat 8pm

MAIN CAST

Dickie Valentine

CREDITS

producer Brian Tesler

A single show starring singer-comedian
Dickie Valentine with 'some of his showbiz
friends', screened within the weekly *Saturday
Spectacular* strand.

See also *Dickie Valentine, The Dickie
Valentine Show* **and** *Free And Easy.*

Valerie / Valerie's Family / The Hogan Family

USA · NBC THEN CBS (TAL PRODUCTIONS/
LORIMAR TELEVISION/MILLER BOYETT
PRODUCTIONS) · SITCOM

110 × 30 mins · colour

US dates: 1 Mar 1986–18 June 1990 (NBC); 15
Sep 1990–20 July 1991 (CBS)

UK dates: 27 Oct 1986–16 June 1992
(75 episodes) (32 episodes of *Valerie* · 27 Oct
1986–10 Nov 1987; 43 episodes of *The Hogan
Family* : 9 Jan 1989–16 June 1992) BBC1
Mon 3.25pm then various days and times

MAIN CAST

Valerie Hogan	Valerie Harper (1986–87)
Sandy Hogan	Sandy Duncan (1987–91)
David Hogan	Jason Bateman
Willie Hogan	Danny Ponce
Mark Hogan	Jeremy Licht
Michael Hogan	Josh Taylor
Lloyd Hogan	John Hillerman (1990–91)
Rich	Tom Hodges (1986–89)

CREDITS

writers Charlie R Hauck, Chip Keyes/Doug Keyes,
Judy Pioli, Rick Mitz and others · *directors* Peter
Baldwin, Jeff Chambers, Howard Storm and
others · *executive producers* Thomas L Miller,
Robert L Boyett, Tony Cacciotti · *producers* Robert
L Boyett, Charlie R Hauck, Chip Keyes, Doug
Keyes, Judy Pioli and others

A run-of-the-mill US sitcom that was more
intriguing off-screen than on. The original
premise was clear-cut: *Rhoda* star Valerie
Harper was cast as Valerie Hogan, a working
mother with three boys – David, Willie and
Mark – and a husband, Michael, who, being
an aeroplane pilot, is away for much of the
time. When the series began, the eldest son,
David, was a girl-crazy teenager and his twin
brothers Mark and Willie were cute pre-teens.

This unremarkable family situation came
to an abrupt end in 1987 when a dispute
between Harper and the series' producers
could not be resolved. Harper was written out
of the series, her character dying in a car

crash, and Michael – needing help to raise the
family – asked Valerie's unmarried sister
Sandy (Sandy Duncan) to move in. The title
changed accordingly, first to *Valerie's Family*
and then *The Hogan Family* and everything
continued much as before, except … well, the
death of the mother cast an understandable
shadow over the antics of the family, and,
despite initial attempts to ignore it, a new
sense of seriousness pervaded the show,
allowing the writers to explore issues that
hitherto might not have been suitable. The
most obvious example of this was the
February 1987 episode in which the children
discovered their pal, Rich, had Aids; other
episodes dealt with pornographic videos,
drink-driving and drugs.

In a final, ironic twist to the saga, Valerie
Harper went on to star in a CBS sitcom, *City*
(not seen on British TV), which was scheduled directly opposite *The Hogan Family* over
on NBC. And, in *City*, her co-star was Lu
Anne Ponce, brother of Danny Ponce from
The Hogan Family.

The Valiant Varneys

see VARNEY, Reg

The Valley Express

UK · BBC · SITCOM

1 × 30 mins · b/w

21 Apr 1969 · BBC1 Mon 7.30pm

MAIN CAST

Stan	David Baxter
Reg	Richard Davies
Jenny	Nerys Hughes
Pet-shop owner	Jessie Evans
TV director	Graeme Garden

CREDITS

writer John Lloyd · *producer* James Gilbert

A *Comedy Playhouse* pilot set in the offices of
The Valley Express, a local Welsh newspaper
wherein work journalists Reg and Stan. Bored
by the stupefyingly dull stories they have to
cover, the men decide to fabricate exciting
news items and sell them on to Fleet Street.
What starts as a prank soon leads to trouble,
though, as predicted by Jenny, Stan's wary
wife. No series developed.

Note. The author, John Lloyd, was the
Braden's Week producer, not the John Lloyd
who produced *Not The Nine O'Clock News.*

Variations On A Theme

UK · ITV (YORKSHIRE) · SITCOM

1 × 30 mins · colour

17 Mar 1977 · Thu 9pm

MAIN CAST

John Bird
Frances de la Tour
Norman Chappell

CREDITS
writers/associate producers Ray Galton/Alan Simpson · *director/producer* Ronnie Baxter · *executive producer* Duncan Wood

A one-off *Galton & Simpson Playhouse* production co-starring Frances de la Tour and John Bird. After years of serious and comical stage work, de la Tour was finally a household name, following her role as Miss Jones in **Rising Damp**.

Reg Varney

Born on 11 July 1922 in West Ham, east London, the comedy actor Reg Varney began his show-business career as a pianist/singer, performing in working men's clubs and then graduating to army shows, variety and revue. Focusing on his talents as a comedian, Varney launched a post-war stage act which, for a time, featured Benny Hill as his straight man; working solo, Varney made his TV debut in the BBC series *Variety* on 9 June 1947 and then became a radio regular throughout the 1950s.

Stardom first beckoned for Varney when he was cast in the hit BBC sitcom **The Rag Trade** (1961–63) and it was consolidated when he was the undoubted star in **On The Buses** (1963–73), ITV's hugely popular comedy about a bus driver. Both were penned by the same writers, Ronnie Wolfe and Ronnie Chesney, and both allowed Varney to be much like his real self: a likeable, cheery, working-class man adept at expressing the range of human emotions.

Varney also appeared in a number of feature films, but he retired in the early 1980s, his last TV series ending in 1976.

See also **Beggar My Neighbour**, **Here Come The Double Deckers**, and **The Plank**.

Reg Varney   1
UK · BBC · STANDUP
1 × 15 mins · b/w
3 Oct 1952 · Fri 9pm
MAIN CAST
Reg Varney
CREDITS
writers Peter Myers/Alec Grahame · *producer* Kenneth Carter

Varney was best known to 1950s TV viewers for his 'naughty-schoolboy' comic persona, and he appeared in the guise in this one-off broadcast, his first starring vehicle, screened within the *Spotlight* strand.

The Valiant Varneys
UK · BBC · CHILDREN'S SITCOMS
15 × 30 mins · b/w

Series One (9) 9 July–3 Sep 1964 · BBC1
Thu 5.10pm
Series Two (6) 2 Apr–7 May 1965 · BBC1
Fri 5.05pm
MAIN CAST
Reg Varney
CREDITS
writer David Cumming · *director* Peter Whitmore · *producers* Johnny Downes (7 eps in series 1), Harry Carlisle (2 eps in series 1), Johnny Downes/Vere Lorrimer (1 ep in series 2), Vere Lorrimer (5 eps in series 2)

Following the demise of *The Rag Trade*, Reg Varney starred in this series for younger viewers that, each week, looked back at the exploits of Varney's fictitious ancestors.

This was a neat idea, affording different situations and period settings each week, from the days of King Arthur to the Victorian world of the British Raj in India. Supported by a different guest cast every episode, Varney tackled the many lead roles with characteristic gusto, and the young audiences at the BBC Television Theatre, from where the shows were broadcast (*à la Crackerjack*) were vocal in their approval.

The Other Reg Varney
UK · ITV (LWT) · STANDUP/SKETCH
1 × 60 mins · colour
9 Aug 1970 · Sun 8.50pm
MAIN CAST
Reg Varney
Peter Jones
Shari Lewis
Frank Thornton
Dilys Watling
Percy Herbert
CREDITS
writers Ronald Wolfe/Ronald Chesney, Peter Dulay, Reg Varney · *director* Howard Ross · *producer* Mark Stuart

An hour-length special featuring the star of LWT's big sitcom *On The Buses* performing standup and sketch material, mostly scripted by his *Buses* writers Wolfe and Chesney. It also allowed him to exhibit his talents as a pianist. Principal support came from Peter Jones, with whom Varney had starred in the BBC series *The Rag Trade* (another two Ronnies job) and *Beggar My Neighbour*.

Note. This programme was repeated on 17 June 1972 under the title *The Reg Varney Comedy Hour*.

The Reg Varney Revue
UK · ITV (LWT) · SKETCH
6 editions (5 × 45 mins · 1 × 60 mins) · colour
18 Nov–23 Dec 1972 · Sat mostly 6.15pm
MAIN CAST
Reg Varney
Pat Coombs
Elizabeth Counsell

David Lodge
Frank Thornton
George Chisholm
CREDITS
writers Dick Vosburgh, Wally Malston, Garry Chambers, David Cumming · *director/producer* Bryan Izzard

A weekly comedy-and-music series for the star of current series *On The Buses*. There were different guests each week as well as a regular team of support players.

Reg Varney   2
UK · ITV (ATV) · SKETCH
14 × 30 mins · colour
Series One (7) 15 Aug–26 Sep 1973 · Wed 8pm
Series Two (7) 11 Feb–30 Mar 1974 · mostly Sat 5.25pm
MAIN CAST
Reg Varney
Henry McGee
Pat Coombs (series 2)
CREDITS
writers Dick Vosburgh, Roy Tuvey/Maurice Sellar, Garry Chambers, Wally Malston · *directors/producers* William G Stewart (series 1), Alan Tarrant (series 2)

Having left the final series of *On The Buses* in April 1973, before its conclusion, Reg Varney was fast off the mark with a new production for ATV. These two series presented new sides of the cockney comic, in which he sang and played the piano to book-end the comedy sketches. Henry McGee (joined in the second series by Pat Coombs, who had also appeared in the very first edition) offered support.

Down The 'Gate
UK · ITV (ATV) · SITCOM
12 × 30 mins · colour
Series One (5) 23 July–20 Aug 1975 · Wed 8pm
Series Two (7) 18 July–29 Aug 1976 · Sun 7.25pm
MAIN CAST

Reg Furnell	Reg Varney
Irene Furnell	Dilys Laye
Old Wol	Reg Lye
Len Peacock	Tony Melody (series 1)
Mr Preston	Percy Herbert (series 2)

CREDITS
creator Reg Varney · *writers* Roy Tuvey/Maurice Sellar · *directors/producers* William G Stewart (series 1), Alan Tarrant (series 2)

Following the two series of sketch shows, Varney came up with an idea for a sitcom in which he starred as a porter at Billingsgate Fish Market in London, providing him with unlimited opportunity to indulge in cockney banter and cod humour. Two series were made but, sadly, outstanding they were not. Dilys Laye played Reg's wife, Irene.

Ver-r-r-ry Interesting

USA · NBC (GEORGE SCHLATTER-ED FRIENDLY PRODUCTIONS) · STANDUP/SKETCH

1 × 60 mins · colour

US date: 18 Mar 1971

UK date: 22 July 1971 · BBC2 Thu 9.20pm

MAIN CAST

Arte Johnson
Bing Crosby
Nancy Kulp
Elke Sommer

CREDITS

writers Ron Friedman, Coslough Johnson, Arte Johnson · *director* Bill Foster · *producers* Saul Ilson, Ernest Chambers

A special show for one of the prime performers in *Rowan And Martin's Laugh-In*, Arte Johnson, appearing here in a number of sketches and skits, including the German-soldier character he created for that series, who famously uttered 'ver-r-r-ry interrresting … but shhtupid'.

The programme aired in the UK as *The Arte Johnson Show*, under the *Show Of The Week* banner.

Very Big Very Soon

UK · ITV (CENTRAL) · SITCOM

6 × 30 mins · colour

19 July–23 Aug 1991 · Fri 7pm

MAIN CAST

Harry James	Paul Shane
Beattie	Kate David
Ernie Chester	Tim Wylton
Avril	Sheila White
Matthew Kite	Andrew Maclean
Vic	Shaun Curry

CREDITS

writer Daniel Peacock · *director* Paul Harrison · *producer* Glen Cardno

Written by actor-writer Daniel Peacock (the son of actor-writer Trevor Peacock), *Very Big Very Soon* depicted the struggles of a dodgy northern variety agent, Harry James, as he used his wiles to find work for his bunch of no-hope clients: a roster of bingo callers, ventriloquists, magicians, memory men and the like.

Paul Shane was cast in the lead role, a part not a million miles from his Ted Bovis character in *Hi-de-Hi!* Kate David played Beattie, Harry James's much put-upon secretary.

Very Important Pennis

see KAYE, Paul

The Very Merry Widow

UK · BBC · SITCOM

19 × 30 mins · b/w

Series One (7) 27 Nov 1967–15 Jan 1968 · BBC1 Mon 7.30pm

Series Two (6) 9 Sep–14 Oct 1968 · BBC1 Mon 7.30pm

Series Three (6) *The Very Merry Widow And How* 23 May–11 July 1969 · BBC1 Fri 8.20pm

MAIN CAST

Jacqueline (Jacqui) Villiers	Moira Lister
Mrs Frayle	Molly Urquhart
Freddie Phillipson	Donald Hewlett
Roger	Jimmy Thompson (series 3)
Francis	Jeffrey Gardiner (1 ep in series 3); Nicholas Parsons (5 eps in series 3)
Jennifer Villiers	Sally Thomsett
Mavis Anstruther	Diana King
François	Georges Lambert (series 2 & 3)

OTHER APPEARANCES

Henrietta Greaves	Margaret Courtenay (series 1 & 2)
Millicent Dickson	Elizabeth Allan (series 1 & 2)
Mr Tiffin	A J Brown (series 1 & 2)
Constance Cartwright	Beryl Mason (series 1)
Lady Phillipson	Cicely Courtneidge (series 2 & 3)
Connie	Beryl Mason (series 3)
Katie	Patricia Hayes (series 3)
Miss Sims	Gilly McIver (series 3)

CREDITS

writer Alan Melville · *producers* Robin Nash (7 eps in series 1 & 2), Graeme Muir (6 eps in series 1 & 2), John Howard Davies (series 3)

A re-teaming of writer Alan Melville and star Moira Lister, following their previous collaboration on *The Whitehall Worrier*. Melville decided to write a starring vehicle for the glamorous, South African-born Ms Lister and he adapted *The Very Merry Widow* from his 1953 stage-play *Dear Charles* (see footnote) to do so.

In the series, Lister was cast as Jacqui Villiers, whose husband Charles has drowned off Cape Finisterre after borrowing the yacht of a friend, Lord Carroway. Equally distressing for Jacqui is the fact that Charles also borrowed Lady Carroway for the trip. To make matters even worse, instead of inheriting a good deal of money, Jacqui has been left only with his debts, some £20,000 worth; in order to pay them she embarks upon a determined quest to raise cash, taking a variety of jobs along the way, such adventures forming the basis of the storylines. To keep the wolf from the door, and stay in her cherished London mews flat, she also takes in a lodger, Freddie Phillipson.

Jacqui is helped in her ventures by her friends Mavis, Millicent and Henrietta, and by her teenage daughter Jennifer (played by Sally Thomsett, later to be one of the two flat-sharing young women enjoying a *Man About The House*), who is still at school. Her late husband's principal creditors, however – the bookmaker, wine merchant and bank manager – are all chasing their money.

In the third series Jacqui finally settles into a permanent job as a market researcher for *How?* magazine (clearly modelled on the consumer publication *Which?*), hence the revised title *The Very Merry Widow And How.* New to the cast in this final series were Francis and Roger, her bosses at the magazine, played by Nicholas Parsons and Jimmy Thompson, respectively. Several of the 19 episodes featured a guest star, these including Norman Bird, Richard Briers, Dandy Nichols, Hugh Paddick, Arnold Ridley, Beryl Reid and Terry Scott.

*Note. The play *Dear Charles*, about a single woman bringing up her three fatherless children in Paris, and reminiscing on past romances, was itself based on an earlier work, *Les Enfants d'Edouard*, by Marc-Gilbert Sauvajon and Frederick Jackson. *Dear Charles* was dramatised by the BBC on 27 April 1961.

Vic Reeves Big Night Out

see Reeves and Mortimer

Vic's Grill

UK · BBC · SKETCH

6 × 30 mins · b/w

18 Apr–27 June 1951 · fortnightly Wed 8.55pm then 8.15pm

MAIN CAST

Vic Wise
Norman Wisdom
Beryl Reid
Ernest Maxin
Eddie Leslie
John Hanson

CREDITS

writer Sid Colin · *producer* Bill Lyon-Shaw

One of a quartet of alternating comedians on the famous BBC radio series *Variety Bandbox*, the diminutive Vic Wise made sufficient impact to be given this successful television series in which he was cast as the friendly Jewish proprietor of a café, a man who constantly gets his 'weeze mixed up with his wubble-ews', calling himself 'Wicky Wise'. Regular visitors, including Norman Wisdom (who perfected his 'Gump' character during the series), Beryl Reid and Ernest Maxin (later to become a top TV comedy producer), provided comedy support and, as usual in these early TV shows, song and dance numbers also featured.

Born David Bloom in Southampton in 1900, Wise was truly multi-talented: he trained as a dancer and was a dance director for Warner Bros in Hollywood (which left him with an American accent), an accomplished magician, a character actor and a comedian. He died in 1976.

The Vicar Of Dibley

UK · BBC · SITCOM

10 episodes (6 × 30 mins · 2 × 40 mins · 1 × 45 mins · 1 × short special) · colour

Series One (6 × 30 mins) 10 Nov–15 Dec 1994 · BBC1 Thu 8.30pm

Special (40 mins) 8 Apr 1996 · BBC1 Mon 8.30pm

Special (45 mins) 25 Dec 1996 · BBC1 Wed 10pm

*Short special · part of Comic Relief 24 Mar 1997 · BBC1 Tue 8.45pm

Special (40 mins) 26 Dec 1997 · BBC1 Fri 9pm

MAIN CAST
Geraldine Granger	Dawn French
David Horton	Gary Waldhorn
Hugo Horton	James Fleet
Alice Tinker	Emma Chambers
Frank Pickle	John Bluthal
Jim Trott	Trevor Peacock
Owen Newitt	Roger Lloyd Pack
Letitia Cropley	Liz Smith
	(to April 1996 special)

CREDITS
creator Richard Curtis · *writers* Richard Curtis (6), Richard Curtis/Paul Mayhew-Archer (3) · *directors* Dewi Humphreys (7), John Howard Davies (1), Gareth Carrivick (1) · *producers* Jon Plowman (6), Jon Plowman/Sue Vertue (3) [no credits available for Comic Relief special]

When their ancient vicar, Pottle, dies during the middle of a service, the villagers of Dibley prepare for a suitable replacement, hoping that the new man is young and enthusiastic enough to stir the locals from their apathy and get a decent-sized congregation packing into the church instead of the recent single-figure attendances. What they get is Geraldine Granger, a chocolate-guzzling, joke-cracking, irreverent reverend who breezes into the place like a breath of fresh air. The parish council is generally bemused by its new spiritual guardian but its head figure, local squire David Horton, is simply outraged by her appointment and takes steps to have her replaced. Geraldine's optimistic outlook and obvious enthusiasm prove popular with the wacky villagers, however, and David is forced reluctantly to accept her appointment, forming a working friendship although often disagreeing fundamentally on policy or method.

Although, on paper, this may seem like yet another entry in the canon of religious-themed sitcoms, *The Vicar Of Dibley*, like **Father Ted**, had a decidedly 1990s feel and approach. The ordination of female vicars was still a controversial and topical issue when the series first aired, and that debate fuelled the comedy for the first few episodes. Later however, when the novelty of a woman vicar wore off, the series relied upon the interplay between the major characters. Although Geraldine (reputedly inspired by real-life Reverend Joy Carroll of Streatham,

south London) was the centrepiece of the series, it was performed as a comedy ensemble, with the inner-sanctum of the church council providing the team support. Apart from the pompous, Conservative, egocentric Horton, the council members comprised his son, the hapless Hugo; the vague parish clerk, Frank; the incomprehensible Jim Trott; the straight-talking land worker Owen; and the elderly flower-arranger Letitia. The other main player was the verger, Alice Tinker, a staggeringly naïve, off-beam young woman with the IQ of a kettle, who went on to become engaged to Hugo, much to the distress of his father. All of these characters were extreme in one way or another, and their particular idiosyncrasies – like Alice's massive lack of reasoning, Hugo's bizarre waffling and Letitia's mind-boggling culinary creations, mixing, for example, anchovies with peanut butter, or ham with lemon curd – all helped bring a greatly pleasing, surreal tone to what was otherwise a relatively straightforward situation. (The Letitia character, portrayed by the great Liz Smith, was killed off in the April 1996 Easter special.)

In the middle of it all, as the fun-loving but comparatively 'normal' Geraldine, was Dawn French, giving yet another spot-on performance that utilised her talent for delivering complicated funny lines. The series' creator and principal writer, Richard Curtis (a guiding light in the **Comic Relief** events) worked on *Not The Nine O'Clock News*, *Blackadder* and *Mr Bean* before this and had touched upon religious themes in sketches for Rowan Atkinson and, of course, in sections of his smash-hit movie *Four Weddings And A Funeral* (1994, director Mike Newell). With Curtis and Dawn French at the helm of the series it was a little surprising that *The Vicar Of Dibley* was not more extreme and hard-edged – initially, in fact, there were criticisms that it was twee and middle-of-the-road – but closer inspection revealed just how clever the series was, the scripts managing to convey subversive ideas in such a subtle and humorous way that they passed by almost unnoticed. The very notion of a woman vicar being sexy and cracking ribald gags was revolutionary in itself; every episode indeed featured a short post-credits sequence in which Geraldine told Alice a bawdy joke, with Alice – being too dense to understand them – reacting in a number of weird ways, all inappropriate.

*Note. The 1997 Comic Relief short special *BallykissDibley* crossed *The Vicar Of Dibley* with the BBC's other hit religion-based series, the light-drama *Ballykissangel*, with Stephen Tompkinson reprising his role of Father Peter Clifford from that series.

Victor Borge In Concert

Victor Borge Presents … Comedy In Music

see BORGE, Victor

Victoria Wood … [various shows]

see WOOD, Victoria

View By Appointment

see *Wink To Me Only*

The Village Store

see *Mr Pastry*

The Virgin Fellas

see *Birds In The Bush*

Visiting Day

UK · BBC · SITCOM

1 × 30 mins · b/w

2 Feb 1962 · Fri 8.45pm

MAIN CAST
Cakebread	Bernard Cribbins
Mother	Betty Marsden
Father	Wilfrid Brambell
First patient	Hugh Lloyd
Nurse Forbes	Molly Weir

CREDITS
writers Ray Galton/Alan Simpson · *producer* Barry Lupino

A Galton and Simpson *Comedy Playhouse* playlet set in a hospital, drawing upon the writers' experiences of the TB sanatorium in which they met. (See *Get Well Soon*.) Here, in a poignant reminder of earlier hospital procedure, the patients prepare for the emotional rollercoaster ride of visiting day – a time anticipated with relish by most of the inmates, but not by all.

The script was reused in 1997 in *Paul Merton In Galton & Simpson's …*

The Vital Spark

see *Para Handy*

!Viva Cabaret!

UK · C4 (TV21 PRODUCTIONS) · STANDUP

13 editions (7 × 50 mins · 6 × 45 mins) · colour

Series One (7 × 50 mins) 14 Apr–26 May 1993 · Wed 10.30pm

Series Two (6 × 45 mins) 20 May–24 June 1994 · Fri 10.30pm

MAIN CAST
see below

CREDITS
writers cast · *directors* David G Hillier (series 1),
Julia Knowles (series 2) · *producers* Dave Morley,
Graham K Smith, Ivan Douglass

A trendy attempt to re-create the mood of a
smoky cabaret club on television. Musical
guests (in particular, recurring appearances
from Tom Jones and Eartha Kitt) provided
tuneful interludes but this was heavily
comedy-led.

Many stars of the comedy circuit guested
but arguably the physical comedian Lee
Evans, who appeared five times in the series,
made the biggest impact. Of the other
contributors, there were four appearances by
the Doug Anthony All-Stars, Mark Thomas
and 'Lily Savage' (Paul O'Grady), three by
Harry Hill, two each by Greg Proops, Bob
Downe and 'Gayle Tuesday' (Brenda
Gilhooly) and one apiece by Sandra Bernhard,
Julian Clary, Rowland Rivron, Mike McShane,
Brad Stine, Raymond Kingsbury, Alan
Davies, Les, the Two Marks, 'Bernard Right-
On' (John Thomson), Trev and Simon, and
Barry Cryer.

The Wackers

UK · ITV (THAMES) · SITCOM

6 × 30 mins · colour

19 Mar–23 Apr 1975 · Wed 9.30pm

MAIN CAST

Billy Clarkson	Ken Jones
Mary Clarkson	Sheila Fay
Bernadette Clarkson	Alison Steadman
Raymond Clarkson	Keith Chegwin
Tony Clarkson	David Casey
Maggie Clarkson	Pearl Hackney
Charlie	Bill Dean
Joe Farrell	Joe Gladwin

CREDITS

writer Vince Powell · *director/producer* Anthony Parker

In his first creation since the death of writing partner Harry Driver, Vince Powell once again tried to draw humour from ethnic differences. *The Wackers* – as the title might suggest – was set in Liverpool, focusing on the Clarkson family, half of whom were Protestant and half Catholic, half of whom supported Liverpool FC and half Everton. They lived in the poor Dingle area of the city, with its streets of back-to-back houses, and the opening episode saw Dad (Ken Jones) return from two years 'at sea' – prison, in other words. Although the series was made by London-ITV company Thames (for whom Powell was employed as a comedy consultant) the writer is a Mancunian and lived in Liverpool for four years, so he has an understanding of the unique local brand of humour.

Ken Jones and Sheila Fay – both native Liverpudlians and married to each other in real life too – were the husband and wife here, and their children were played by David Casey, the future children's television presenter Keith Chegwin and a 28-year-old fast-rising actress (also Liverpool-born), Alison Steadman.

The Wackers was not a success, though, and audiences grew tired of its incontinence jokes.

Waiting

UK · ITV (MENTORN FILMS FOR SCOTTISH) · SITCOM

1 × 30 mins · colour

31 July 1995 · Mon 8pm

MAIN CAST

Beryl Oldham	Brigit Forsyth
Maurice Ribley	Patrick Barlow
Dr Roger Capstick	Peter Jones
Amanda Cookson	Ashley Jensen
Dr Duncan Pettifer	Simon Slater
Dr Anna Chen	Sarah Lam

CREDITS

writer Jim Hitchmough · *executive producer* Tom Gutteridge · *director/producer* Charlie Hanson

A doctor's surgery was the setting for the fourth pilot in ITV's 1995 *Comedy Firsts* season, written by Jim Hitchmough, the author of *Watching*. Now that Hillcroft Medical Centre is an NHS fund-holder, a vacancy has arisen for a practice manager. Beryl, the efficient, long-serving receptionist, is clear favourite for the post but then a pompous ex-army man, Maurice Ribley, arrives for an interview, full of rigid middle-management-speak and military gobbledygook. Ribley is something of a con man, putting other applicants off the job, but doctors Pettifer, Chen and most importantly Capstick – the forgetful, ageing senior partner at Hillcroft – give him the job.

This decision would be inexplicable were it not for the fact that such a move was meant to set up a series, in which the Beryl and her behind-the-counter assistant Amanda would work together snide by snide with Ribley. As no series developed, this stand-alone half-hour was fairly poor stuff, despite the impressive cast.

Waiting For God

UK · BBC · SITCOM

47 episodes (46 × 30 mins · 1 × 45 mins) · colour

Series One (7) 28 June–9 Aug 1990 · BBC1 Thu 8.30pm

Series Two (10) 5 Sep–7 Nov 1991 · BBC1 Thu 8.30pm

Series Three (10) 10 Sep–12 Nov 1992 · BBC1 Thu 8.30pm

Special (45 mins) 23 Dec 1992 · BBC1 Wed 8pm

Series Four (10) 9 Sep–11 Nov 1993 · BBC1 Thu 8pm

Special · 22 Dec 1993 · BBC1 Wed 9.30pm

Series Five (8) 8 Sep–27 Oct 1994 · BBC1 Thu 8.30pm

MAIN CAST

Diana Trent	Stephanie Cole
Tom Ballard	Graham Crowden
Harvey Bains	Daniel Hill
Jane Edwards	Janine Duvitski
Geoffrey Ballard	Andrew Tourell
Marion Ballard	Sandra Payne

OTHER APPEARANCES

Sarah	Lucy Ashton
Jenny	Dawn Hope
Basil	Michael Bilton
Antonio	Chico Andrade
Reverend Dennis Sparrow	Tim Preece
	(from series 3)

CREDITS

writer Michael Aitkens · *directors* Gareth Gwenlan (42), Sue Bysh (5) · *producer* Gareth Gwenlan

The adventures of two geriatric delinquents as they pass their time railing against a world where the young are revered and the elderly are held in contempt.

This OAP onslaught was launched from the Bayview Retirement Village, an old people's estate of luxury bungalows and apartments. In one such dwelling lives the former photo-journalist Diana Trent, a formidable, acid-tongued, bloody-minded, belligerent individual whose motto in life is 'If you're angry you know you're still alive'. And Diana has plenty to be angry about – though in full possession of her faculties and with a razor-sharp mind, people refuse to see beyond the ageing exterior and treat her accordingly. They presume her aggression and stinging ripostes to be the rambling eccentricities of a miserable old biddy unable to fend for herself, not realising that it is born of the frustration at their appalling misconception.

Newly installed in the apartment next to Diana's is Tom Ballard, a gentler, optimistic soul who counters the vagaries of life by living in a fantasy world of his own making. His delusions make him something of a subversive and soon he is spreading unrest in the community hall, the meeting place and dining room for the Bayview residents. Much to the chagrin of Bayview's manager – the morose but ambitious Harvey Bains – Diana views a kindred spirit in her neighbour and soon the two are inseparable, presenting a united front and delivering double jeopardy for all who get in their way. Other regular characters in the series are Tom's weak but well-meaning and terribly boring son Geoffrey with his nymphomaniac, dipso-maniac, harridan of a wife, Marion, and Harvey's doting secretary, Jane.

Finally (in the fourth series), Tom and Diana move in together, delightfully scandalising everyone by 'living in sin' and continuing to wage their war against an uncaring society; the rest of the main players have their own agendas too – Geoffrey tries to leave the awful Marion; Jane spends her years 'trying to fine-tune the less charming sides' of Harvey's character; and Harvey suffers endless frustrations in his attempts to join a local golf club.

Waiting For God certainly had many fine moments, mostly from Stephanie Cole, who spat out Diana's venomous barbs with relish. As Tom, Graham Crowden was a good sidekick and the pair conjured up many a laugh between them. But the rest of the regulars were somewhat two-dimensional and seemed almost to come from another, less classy sitcom. The boring Geoffrey, well, bored; Marion was too hideous to be remotely real; Harvey, likewise, was unbelievably vacuous and self-centred; and poor Jane was far too weak-willed and dim to evoke any sympathy. This last part was played by Janine Duvitski, who also had to deal with Victor Meldrew in **One Foot In The Grave** where she played Pippa, a character similar to Jane on the surface but one much more satisfyingly drawn.

Wake Up! With Libby And Jonathan

UK · ITV (ELEPHANT PRODUCTIONS FOR TYNE TEES) · SITCOM

1 × 30 mins · colour
14 July 1994 · Thu 8.30pm

MAIN CAST
Jonathan Hughes · · · · · · · · · · · Nigel Planer
Libby Hughes · · · · · · · · · · · · · Susie Blake
Jeff Shreeve · · · · · · · · · · · · Stephen Moore
Dennis · · · · · · · · · · · · · · · Paul Humpoletz
Kim · · · · · · · · · · · · · · · · Robert McKewley
Mac · · · · · · · · · · · · · · · · · Clare Cathcart
Ali · · · · · · · · · · · · · · · · · · · Sukie Smith
Grace · · · · · · · · · · · · · · · · Lucinda Fisher
Ned Hawking · · · · · · · · · · · Andrew Dunford

CREDITS
deviser Nigel Planer · writer Andrew Nickolds · executive producer Christine Williams · director/producer Jamie Rix

A one-off comedy pilot spoofing the chatty daytime live TV shows populating morning TV in Britain: at this time BBC1 had Anne and Nick, not married but definitely possessing a mutual chemistry, while ITV had married couple Richard and Judy. *Wake Up!*, the spoof show, was hosted by married couple Jonathan and Libby. But away from the camera, off the comfy sofa and behind the sincere smiles, their marriage is deep in doo-doo. She's a hard bitch with a university education, he's a handsome-ish chap worrying about hair loss. Already sleeping in separate beds, the pair are never less than caustic with one another. Libby also takes to task everyone involved in the programme, including their producer Jeff, who was her first husband; brainless on-screen weather-girl Grace, whom she fires; and researcher Kim. On this particular day everything goes wrong on the show and the pair are left to decide who, upon their divorce, will take custody of the catchphrase 'If, like me …' that Jonathan has so carefully honed and then registered.

Nigel Planer (who also devised the storyline) played Jonathan Hughes and Susie Blake was cast as Libby, the type of character

she had already portrayed in **Victoria Wood's All Day Breakfast** in 1992. Although daytime TV makes for easy spoof material it's something of a surprise that no series evolved from *Wake Up!*, but BBC Radio 4 has successfully developed a sitcom along similar lines, *Life, Death And Sex With Mike And Sue*, aired in 1996 and 1997, and, at the time of writing, comics Lee and Herring (see **Fist Of Fun**) were preparing a new BBC2 series for screening in early 1998, *This Morning With Richard Not Judy*.

Walking The Planks

UK · BBC · SITCOM

1 × 30 mins · colour
2 Aug 1985 · BBC1 Fri 8.30pm

MAIN CAST
Ron Archer · · · · · · · · · · · · · Michael Elphick
Richard Talbot · · · · · · · · · · · Richard Wilson
Miss Baxter · · · · · · · · · · · · Vivienne Martin
Trevor Archer · · · · · · · · · · · Gary Raynsford

CREDITS
writers Harold Snoad/Michael Knowles · director/producer Harold Snoad

A wooden BBC sitcom pilot, set in 1946, that featured Michael Elphick as Ron Archer, a none-too-bright but resourceful individual who buys a seaside pier in the hope of turning it into a commercial success. (At this time there were several instances of piers being sold at token prices, as low as a penny, so long as the buyer was prepared to spend a fortune on renovation.) Exploring a similar theme, *Playland*, another pilot but this one unaired, was taped by the BBC a few years earlier, written by Dick Fiddy and Mark Wallington and produced by Dennis Main Wilson.

Walking The Planks got a second bite at the cherry, however, for after the BBC decided not to commission a full series the co-writer Michael Knowles took the script to Yorkshire TV which duly offered a full complement of seven episodes, networked in 1987 as **High & Dry**.

Max Wall

Max Wall was born Maxwell George Lorimer on 12 March 1908 in Brixton, south London, the latest in a long line of family entertainers – his father, Jack Lorimer, was a well-known comedian from Forfar, Scotland.

Max enjoyed success on stage from the age of 14 with a strange dance routine that he developed, being billed as 'the boy with the educated feet', and then becoming a speciality dancer in *The London Revue* in 1925. His career suffered when he left his first wife and married a beauty queen, considered a shocking move at the time, and

it was only late in life that he came to be regarded as one of the greats of the British stage, his renaissance beginning with a part in the London stage musical *Cockie* in 1974. True to form, the dour and temperamental Wall ascribed this late discovery of his talent to the fact that he lived so long – he was still performing until shortly before his death on 22 May 1990 at the age of 82.

Max Wall had 'funny bones' and made the most of them, developing a strangely exaggerated, hunched, crazy-legged walk (much imitated since by Freddie Starr); combined with his verbal dexterity, he produced a unique blend of spoken and physical comedy, his best-known comic creation being the demonic world-famous concert pianist Professor Wallofski.

See also *Alfred Marks Time, Born And Bred, Comedy Bandbox, Davie, Inside George Webley, Jane, The Main Attraction* and *Will The Real Mike Yarwood Stand Up?*

Meet Max Wall

UK · BBC · STANDUP

1 × 30 mins · b/w
4 Dec 1955 · Sun 7.45pm

MAIN CAST
Max Wall

CREDITS
writer Max Wall · producer George Inns

A chance for viewers to enjoy the antics of Professor Wallofski.

The Max Wall Show

UK · BBC · STANDUP/SKETCH

11 × 30 mins · b/w
5 Feb–24 June 1956 · fortnightly Sun 7.45pm

MAIN CAST
Max Wall

CREDITS
director John Street · producer George Inns

At the time of this BBC series, Wall was enjoying considerable London stage success in the robust musical *The Pyjama Game*, and he brought some of that razzmatazz, song-and-dance style to the TV shows, more often choosing to appear in striped blazer and boater than in the dark attire with which he was most associated.

Wall prepared for the TV series by seeking out new, undiscovered talent and employed these people in the shows to bring an air of freshness. (He also featured guest stars, including Betty Driver and the comedy ventriloquist Terry Hall.) Wall worked terribly hard on the series (which, being 1956, was broadcast live) and had no qualms about chastising the studio audience if they didn't give the full roar of approval to routines that he thought deserved greater acclaim.

That's Life, Says Max Wall

UK · ITV (JACK HYLTON TV PRODUCTIONS FOR ASSOCIATED-REDIFFUSION) · STANDUP/ SKETCH

6 × 30 mins · b/w

16 Sep–25 Nov 1957 · fortnightly Mon 9.30pm

MAIN CAST

Max Wall

CREDITS

writers Johnny Speight/Dick Barry · *additional material* Max Wall · *director* Bimbi Harris

Six live programmes in which Wall took an unusual look at life. The star contributed the odd item but the writing was really done by Johnny Speight and Dick Barry; the former went on to script *Till Death Us Do Part*.

An Evening With Max Wall

UK · C4 (LONDON VIDEO PRODUCTIONS) · STANDUP

1 × 60 mins · colour

6 Nov 1982 · Sat 8.15pm

MAIN CAST

Max Wall
William Blezard
Tony Parkinson

CREDITS

director Philip Casson · *producer* Roger Morris

An hour in the company of the veteran comic and mime artist, recorded on stage at the Garrick Theatre, London, in 1981, with his trademark characteristics of aggression and wit in full flow.

The programme was first repeated by C4 on Christmas Eve 1983, at which point it was followed by *It's Got To Be Funny Hasn't It?*, a further 60 minutes in which Wall reflected on his career in conversation with Peter Williams.

Another programme of note was *Max Wall: A Life Class* (Granada for C4, 25 December 1990), a single half-hour showing Wall being questioned by students from Manchester and Liverpool art colleges who then went away and produced portraits based on the knowledge they had acquired about his life.

Wallace & Gromit

The stars of three half-hour animated adventures, Wallace & Gromit are a delightfully odd couple: the inventor and cheese fanatic Wallace (voiced by actor Peter Sallis) and his clever dog Gromit, a plucky canine with a range of human-like emotions, including 'attitude'.

The films are made by the Claymation process, a painstaking form of three-dimensional animation in which moulded clay models are filmed in a stop-action process, with minute movements given to the models in between each shot. The modern-day master of the art is Nick Park, who – supported by a highly creative team – works for the British company Aardman Animations. The genius of Park's *Wallace & Gromit* productions is their hugely ambitious scope, which takes the characters – based in the north of England, in and around their home at 62 West Wallaby Street – on a whirlwind ride that incorporates cartoon-like pacing with Hollywood blockbuster-like special effects, all played out with glorious and hilarious irony.

Wallace & Gromit first appeared in the 30-minute film *A Grand Day Out* (1990, director Nick Park, first aired by C4 on 24 December 1990). Stuck for ideas about how to enjoy the forthcoming bank holiday, and realising to their horror that they are clean out of Wensleydale cheese, Wallace & Gromit decide to visit the moon, anticipating an abundant and free cheese supply. Remembering, just, to take their crackers, they blast off and duly land on the moon, but run up against a disused vending machine that seems determined to prevent them from slicing up the surface for their snack. Eventually they have to flee, but the machine grabs two sheets of metal off the spacecraft which it happily uses to fulfil its dream of skiing.

A Grand Day Out became a *cause célèbre* on the world's animation circuit and was also nominated for an Oscar. As a result, BBC Enterprises (later BBC Worldwide), the commercial arm of the BBC, agreed to co-finance with Aardman further Wallace & Gromit escapades – from which they could also release videos and licence a massive range of merchandising. The first fruit of the joint venture was *The Wrong Trousers*, unveiled by BBC2 on 26 December 1993. In this, Wallace acquires a pair of 'techno trousers' for Gromit's birthday, which he describes as 'fantastic for walkies and a valuable addition to our modern lifestyle'. Falling on hard times, Wallace advertises for a lodger and thus a small penguin (actually the wanted criminal Feathers McGraw) joins the household. Disguised as a cockerel – by popping a red plastic glove on his head – McGraw uses the techno trousers to steal a priceless diamond from a local museum, but in a thrilling chase finale he is caught and Wallace & Gromit settle down once more after their exhausting escapade.

The Wrong Trousers, too, was a huge success and won the coveted Oscar for best short animation in 1994. It was followed two years later by *A Close Shave* (BBC2, 24 December 1995), wherein Wallace & Gromit operate a successful window-cleaning business, and romance blossoms when Wallace meets Wendolene, the owner of the shop Wendolene's Wools. She and her mean cyber-dog Preston, meanwhile, have been sheep rustling – he wants to turn the animals into dog food, Wendolene wants the wool. When one of the sheep, the plucky Shaun, escapes and settles into 62 West Wallaby Street, Preston frames Gromit for the rustling and the dog is sent to prison. He is sprung from his cell in a daring escape, however, and Wallace and Shaun set out to prove his innocence. *The Wrong Trousers* brought yet another Oscar success to director Nick Park. (He also wrote the *Wallace & Gromit* scripts – *A Grand Day Out* on his own and collaborating with Bob Baker on the two subsequent films.)

Note. Aardman Animations – named after an early character – first came to public notice with its Morph character, invented for the BBC1 art miscellany *Vision On* (1964–76), a programme that was enjoyed by children of all ages but made a particular play for the deaf and hard-of-hearing. On the surface, Morph was a vaguely humanoid Plasticine model, but he had an ability to metamorphose ('morph') into other objects and shapes. In so doing, and by introducing changes in expression, and employing sound effects, the animators were able to suggest a wide range of emotions for the character. Having honed these skills, the creators went on to much more sophisticated productions, including the fine Oscar-winning *Creature Comforts* (1990, director Nick Park, first screened on British TV by C4 on 18 April 1990) in which model animal figures were animated to real-life voices.

The Walrus And The Carpenter

UK · BBC · SITCOM

7 episodes (1 × 35 mins · 6 × 25 mins) · b/w

Pilot (35 mins) 14 Dec 1963 · Sat 9.35pm

One series (6 × 25 mins) 2 Mar–6 Apr 1965 · BBC1 Tue mostly 8pm

MAIN CAST

Gascoigne Quilt · · · · · · · · · · · · · Felix Aylmer
Luther Flannery · · · · · · · · · · · · Hugh Griffith

CREDITS

writers Marty Feldman/Barry Took · *producers* Michael Mills (pilot), James Gilbert (series)

The Walrus And The Carpenter – originally to have been titled *You're Only Old Once* – depicted the lives of ex-schoolteacher Gascoigne Quilt and an illiterate Welsh ex-seaman, Luther Flannery.

Quilt is a literate, mild-mannered soul who has never fully recovered from the one love affair that cost him his career and set his life out of kilter; Flannery, on the other hand, is a bear of a man who has spent his life womanising and drinking hard liquor. Their symbiotic relationship means that Quilt has someone to whom he can pass on his learning while Flannery has a chance to become literate and thus open doors hitherto closed to him. Emboldened by their friendship, the pair embark upon adventures, usually argumentatively and suggested by mere whimsy, in a similar style to that employed by the greying musketeers in **Last Of The Summer Wine** many years later. Guest actors also contributed: Warren Mitchell twice and Doris Hare and Ronnie Barker once apiece.

Note. Barry Took was under contract to Granada when the BBC aired the pilot episode in its *Comedy Playhouse* strand, so Marty Feldman, erroneously but necessarily, was credited as sole writer. Took was freelancing once again by the time the series was made so was able to be credited.

Watch This Space

UK · BBC · SITCOM

6 × 30 mins · colour

17 Jan–21 Feb 1980 · BBC1 Thu 8.30pm

MAIN CAST

Brian Reeves	Christopher Biggins
Bob	Peter Blake
Claire	Liza Goddard
Brenda	Gillian Taylforth
Jonathan	Leo Dolan

CREDITS

writers Ronald Wolfe/Ronald Chesney · *producer* Roger Race

Having created series in a fashion workshop (**The Rag Trade**) and a bus depot (**On The Buses**), writers Wolfe and Chesney set *Watch This Space* in an advertising agency.

The series starred Christopher Biggins as the boss of the agency, with Peter Blake and Liza Goddard as his two main creative staff, whose quality of work was never the same after they married. The storylines exploded many of the industry's secrets – for example, the opening episode showed how the agency employed a model with very small hands for a confectionery advertisement, so as to make the featured chocolate bar seem bigger. Apparently, such revelations didn't please professional advertisers; fortunately for them, however, the show also failed to please many viewers, and failed to return after the first series.

Watching

UK · ITV (GRANADA) · SITCOM

56 episodes (54 × 30 mins · 2 × 60 mins) · colour

Series One (7) 5 July–16 Aug 1987 · Sun 10pm
Special · 27 Dec 1987 · Sun 9.15pm
Series Two (7) 19 Feb–1 Apr 1988 · Fri 8.30pm
Special (60 mins) 24 Dec 1988 · Sat 7.05pm
Series Three (6) 3 Mar–7 Apr 1989 · Fri mostly 8.30pm
Series Four (9) 1 Dec 1989–2 Feb 1990 · Fri 8pm
Series Five (10) 14 Dec 1990–15 Feb 1991 · Fri 8pm
Special (60 mins) 25 Dec 1991 · Wed 6.30pm
Series Six (6) 3 Jan–7 Feb 1992 · Fri 8pm
Special · 1 Jan 1993 · Fri 8pm
Series Seven (7) 21 Feb–4 Apr 1993 · Sun mostly 7.25pm

MAIN CAST

Malcolm Stoneway	Paul Bown
Pamela Wilson/Lynch	Liza Tarbuck
Brenda Wilson	Emma Wray
Mrs Stoneway	Patsy Byrne
Harold	Al T Kossy
Cedric	Bill Moores
Terry Milton	Perry Fenwick (series 1–3 & 7)
Sidney Clough	Philip Fox (series 1 & 1987 special)
David Lynch	John Bowler (series 2–7 & 1988/91/93 specials)
Susan Roberts	Liz Crowther (series 2 & 3)
Oswald	Dave Dutton (series 3–5)
Chris	Russell Boulter (series 4)
Lucinda Davis/Stoneway	Elizabeth Morton (series 5 & 6 & 1991/93 specials)
Joyce Wilson	Noreen Kershaw (series 5–7 & 1991/93 specials)
Gerald Wilson	Andrew Hilton (series 5–7 & 1991/93 specials)
Jonathan MacMillan	Richard Good (series 6 & 1993 special)
Roz	Ally Vuli (series 7)

CREDITS

creator/writer Jim Hitchmough · *director* Les Chatfield · *producers* David Liddiment (series 1 & 2 & 1987 special), Les Chatfield (series 3–7 & 1988/91/93 specials) · *executive producer* David Liddiment (from 1988 special)

Brenda and Pamela Wilson are sisters whose idea of fun is to go out to their local pub, the Grapes, and watch men, trying to guess their backgrounds, how old they are, what religion and what job they have. Into the pub walks Malcolm Stoneway, a watcher of a different kind: he's a keen ornithologist. Unaware of this, Brenda manoeuvres him into asking her out, and for their first date he collects her in his motorcycle sidecar and heads out into the country with his binoculars. She hates every minute of it, thinking of him as 'a 14-carat wimp'. And yet, against all odds, a relationship develops.

Thus was born one of ITV's most durable sitcoms of recent years. Not merely based in but veritably governed by Liverpool, its environs, people, humour and values, *Watching* came over as a cross between **The Liver Birds** and *Letter To Brezhnev*, and writer Jim Hitchmough certainly produced some funny lines and original stories, brimming with Scouse wit and pathos.

A former teacher and merchant seaman on cargo boats out of Liverpool, Hitchmough contributed sketches to **Not The Nine O'Clock News**, one of which clearly had something going for it: it was developed first into a stage-play and then into this six-year sitcom. As the writer of all 56 episodes of *Watching*, Hitchmough was prolific and his scripts were dialogue-rich, perhaps extending to twice the word-count of most half-hour sitcoms.

The Wilsons live in Liverpool. Brenda is a very vocal Scouser, out for a slightly dangerous life. Exuding coarse manners, she's every inch a rough diamond. Pamela drinks ale and is similarly hewn. Their mother, Joyce (seen regularly from the fifth series) wants rid of all her offspring ('I like to think of my children having a good time … somewhere else') because they interfere with her own social life. This extends, even, to Brenda and Pamela's much younger brother, the super-sharp-witted Gerald.

The Stoneways live in the more upmarket Meols (pronounced mells), over on the Wirral. Mrs Stoneway, mother of the slow-witted Malcolm, is more welcoming and accommodating, but would rather her son went around with someone she perceives as having their more refined class and standing. But Brenda and Malcolm fall in love, and while the relationship is fraught with difficulties they end up sharing a flat together. Pamela, too, settles down, marrying David Lynch and giving birth to daughter Zelda, but theirs is an even more tempestuous relationship. Malcolm was also married, at the end of the fifth series – but not to Brenda: their relationship had stuttered to a halt and he was immediately wooed and won by a nursing sister, Lucinda, someone much more suited to his mother's taste. In an episode reminiscent of *The Graduate*, Brenda raced to the church to interrupt the wedding but arrived too late. All was well in the end, though: Malcolm and Lucinda broke up, he reunited with Brenda and they headed for the altar in the final episode.

In addition to its wit and enterprising storylines, *Watching* was blessed with good acting performances, particularly from Liza Tarbuck (Jimmy's daughter) as Pamela, and Emma Wray (real name Jill Wray), who was appearing in her first TV role, cast as Brenda.

Watt On Earth

UK · BBC · CHILDREN'S SITCOM

24 × 15 mins · colour

Series One (12) 11 Nov–17 Dec 1991 · BBC1 Mon/Tue 4.20pm
Series Two (12) 16 Nov–23 Dec 1992 · BBC1 Mon/Wed 4.20pm

MAIN CAST

Watt	Garth Napier Jones

Sean Ruddock · · · · · · · · · · · · · Tom Brodie
Zoë Ruddock · · · · · · · · · · Jessica Simpson
Tom Ruddock · · · · · · · · · · · · · · Simon Cook
Val Ruddock · · · · · · · · · · · · Heather Wright

CREDITS

writers Pip Baker/Jane Baker · *director* Roger
Singleton-Turner · *producer* Angela Beeching

A children's series – written by *Doctor Who*
alumni Pip and Jane Baker – in which young
Sean Ruddock is befriended by an alien
named Watt, a 300-year-old creature whose
human form is that of a man in his early
twenties. Even from the rest of his family,
Sean has to keep Watt's existence secret, and
although the alien's ability to
'transanimateobjectify' into any object helps
with the charade the general denseness of his
extra-terrestrial chum causes Sean untold
problems. Still, his parents, who edit a small
newspaper, remain in the dark, even if they
do think that their son is a bit of an odd fish,
always talking to himself. Adding drama to
the proceedings were other travellers from
Watt's planet who were determined to take
him back.

Ruby Wax

Born in Chicago on 19 April 1953, Ruby
Wax has made her home in the UK and,
following a spell studying at the Royal
Scottish Academy of Music And Drama, and
a five-year stint with the Royal Shakespeare
Company, established herself as one of the
leading comedians of her time. After writing
for *Not The Nine O'Clock News* and
the C4 spoof chat-show *For 4 Tonight*,
making guest appearances on TV and
writing for/acting in *Girls On Top*, Wax
developed an outrageous style in which she
interacts with the public and celebrities in
unscripted encounters, relying upon her
natural wit to create humour in the situation.
Her on-screen persona is that off a fast-
talking, highly demanding, pushy
loudmouth who can move effortlessly
between toadying up to and insulting her
subjects. Somehow she also manages to
make the whole thing palatable to her
victims, deftly keeping the tone teasing
rather than overtly offensive. She has
utilised this approach in a number of series
and specials that combined comedy with
documentary, travelogue and chat-show
formats. These programmes defy easy
categorisation and although not solely
comedy are listed here for reference
purposes. (All programmes colour.)

See also *Mama's Back!*, *Absolutely Fabulous*
and *The Comic Strip Presents ...*

Don't Miss Wax

Two series, extending 25 Apr 1987–1 Mar
1988; 16 × 30 mins; C4 (Noel Gay
Television). A themed chat-show, with
regular assistant Norman Lovett.

Miami Memoirs

6 Jan 1989; 1 × 75 mins; C4 (Aspect Film and
Television Productions). A comedy
travelogue tracing Wax's formative years.

East Meets Wax

13 Jan 1989; 1 × 95 mins; C4 (Aspect Film
and Television Productions). A comedy
travelogue reporting on Russia.

Wax-On-Wheels

12 May–16 June 1989; 6 × 50 mins; C4
(Aspect Film and Television Productions). A
travelogue/chat-show around Britain.

Class Of 69

23 Dec 1989; 1 × 60 mins; C4 (Aspect Film
and Television Productions). Ruby attends
her Chicago high-school reunion.

Hit And Run

2 Jan–30 Jan 1990; 5 × 30 mins; BBC1
(Aspect/Raw Produce). A travelogue/chat-
show.

The Full Wax

Four series, extending 19 Jan 1991–4 Dec
1994; 24 × 30 mins; BBC1. A celebrity chat-
show, with guests coming to Wax.

Ruby Takes A Trip

31 Dec 1991; 1 × 70 mins; BBC2 (Waxing
Lyrical). Ruby attempts to discover the
meaning of life with new-agers in San
Francisco.

Wax Acts

29 Aug 1992; 1 × 60 mins; ITV (Central
Music/Raw Produce). Ruby brings her
touring one-woman show to TV in a
performance taped at the Wimbledon
Theatre in July 1992.

Wax After Birth

27 Feb 1993; 1 × 20 mins; BBC2, as part of
themed *Birthnight* evening. Wax on the
subject of childbirth.

Wax Cracks Hollywood
[aka *Ruby Takes You There*]

17 Oct 1993; 1 × 30 mins; BBC2. Ruby's
satirical look at Hollywood.

Wax Uncut

18 June and 2 July 1994; 2 × 30 mins; BBC1.
Uncut versions of interviews with Billy
Crystal and Shelley Winters from *The Full
Wax*.

Wax Cracks Cannes

17 May 1995; 1 × 30 mins; BBC1. Ruby
reports from the annual Cannes Film
Festival.

Ruby's Health Quest

11 July–22 Aug 1995; 6 × 30 mins; BBC1.
A health series.

Ruby Does The Season

1 Sep–6 Oct 1995; 6 × 30 mins; ITV
(Meridian, but not screened in the London-
area). Ruby examines the English social
season.

Ruby Wax Meets ...

Two series and one special, extending from
28 Jan 1996 to 24 Feb 1997; 8 × 50 and 6 × 30
minutes; BBC1. A celebrity chat-show, with
Wax flying out to meet the guests (Imelda
Marcos, Pamela Anderson, the Duchess Of
York and others) in their own environment.
(This series was exported to the USA, where
Wax was promoted as the outrageous
'American in England ... even more
offensive than Joan Rivers'. The interviews
were re-edited for a weekly half-hour
programmes on the Fox network (9 June–29
July 1997), three per show.

Ruby

12 May–4 June 1997; 12 × 40 mins; BBC2. A
thrice-weekly chat-show with celebrity
guests.

The Way, The Truth, The Video

UK · C4 (REGENT PRODUCTIONS) · SITCOM

1 × 60 mins · colour

11 Mar 1987 · Wed 10pm

MAIN CAST

Michael · Peter Firth
Inspector Crocker · · · · · · · · · · · Ian Bannen
Mrs Pollard · · · · · · · · · · · · · Annette Crosbie
Faith · · · · · · · · · · · · · · · · · Lindsey Readman
Hope · · · · · · · · · · · · · · · · · · · Gregg Butler
Charity · · · · · · · · · · · · · · · · Andrea Wray
The Queen · · · · · · · · · · · · Jeannette Charles

CREDITS

writer Alistair Beaton · *director* Barbara Derkow ·
producer William G Stewart

The second of the six individual comedies
aired under the generic title *Tickets For The
Titanic* concerned a 1980s-style charismatic
TV evangelist, Michael, who informs his
audiences that 'God is an increasingly viable
grass-roots option'. Seeking to revive
Puritanism he enlists the aid of one Mrs
Pollard, a campaigner for decent morals, and
Inspector Crocker, a corrupt law enforcer,
and, seeking a ban on pornography, goes to
the lengths of embarrassing the Queen when
she unveils what she believes to be a portrait
of President Reagan.

Wayne And Shuster

Teamed as teenagers in a Toronto high school, Johnny Wayne and Frank Shuster first found fame in Canada during the Second World War, performing in *The Army Show* on radio. Entertaining servicemen was a key part of their early years as a double-act: they presented the first stage-show in Normandy after the D-Day invasion, and headed their own unit during the Korean War in 1953. The style of their comedy was gentle, literate satire, with neither performer locked into comic or straight-man roles. Their long-running CBC series, *The Wayne And Shuster Hour*, featured a regular supporting cast and a number of recurring character creations, most notably Professor Waynegartner (Wayne), detective Johnny Chan and, in a series of skits about the French Revolution, the Brown Pumpernickel (Wayne) and François Maldette (Shuster).

The duo's fame spread throughout the USA too, chiefly through their record number of appearances, 67, on CBS's top-rated Sunday-night variety series *The Ed Sullivan Show*, and they three times journeyed to Britain to make shows for exclusive screening. They also had a pair of home-made specials exported to Britain before, in 1983, their shows were screened by C4 on a weekly basis.

Wayne And Shuster In London

UK · BBC · SKETCH

1 × 45 mins · b/w

22 Dec 1962 · Sat 8pm

MAIN CAST

Johnny Wayne
Frank Shuster

CREDITS

writer Johnny Wayne · *producer* James Gilbert

Canada's top comedy team had already managed to crack the US market and here tried to woo British audiences with a show made in London for the BBC. Wayne and Shuster ascribed their popularity to the fact that they managed to appeal to a diverse range of audiences and age groups.

The Wayne And Shuster Hour

CANADA · CBC · SKETCH

120 approx × 60 mins · b/w and colour

Canadian dates: 1954–1967

UK dates: 27 Mar 1964 · ITV Fri 9.10pm (b/w) & 17 July 1965 · BBC2 Sat 7.50pm (b/w)

MAIN CAST

Johnny Wayne
Frank Shuster
Joe Austin
Eric Christmas

Don Cullen
Jack Duffy
Paul Kligman
Sylvia Lennick
Ben Lennick
Pegi Loder
Larry Mann
Paul Soles
Marilyn Stuart

CREDITS

writer Johnny Wayne/Frank Shuster · *directors/ producers* Drew Crossan (1954–58), Don Hudson (1958–63), Bill Davis (1963–65), Stan Jacobson (1965–67)

Wayne and Shuster's long-running CBC series. Two editions were networked on British screens, the first by ITV on Good Friday 1964, the second by the BBC after the show had won the Silver Rose Of Montreux in 1965. On both occasions the programmes were retitled *The Wayne And Shuster Show*.

The Wayne And Shuster Show

UK · BBC · SKETCH

2 × 50 mins · b/w

4 Sep 1965 · BBC1 Sat 8.30pm

25 Sep 1965 · BBC1 Sat 8.30pm

MAIN CAST

Johnny Wayne
Frank Shuster
The Dudley Moore Trio
Una Stubbs

CREDITS

writers Johnny Wayne/Frank Shuster · *producer* James Gilbert

Tom Sloan, then Head of BBC-TV Light Entertainment, met Wayne and Shuster in Montreux in 1965 (see above) and invited them to Britain to make two new shows for the BBC that would utilise the same scatter-gun style of comedy that had featured in the earlier award-winning programme. The Dudley Moore Trio provided the music for both the BBC shows and Una Stubbs, who had just displayed her comic talent in the pilot of *Till Death Us Do Part*, appeared as a dancer.

Notes. Wayne and Shuster's next appearance on British TV occurred on 30 December 1965 when London-area ITV screened a one-off documentary, imported from the USA, in which they celebrated the career of Jack Benny. This was one of a series of documentary tributes the pair fronted at this time, screened in the States by CBS as *Wayne And Shuster Take An Affectionate Look At…*

After this, the comics were featured in two 60-minute programmes, *Wayne And Shuster*, made by Granada TV and screened in the north-west of England – they were not networked – on 10 and 17 July 1969. (Gordon Flemyng was the producer.)

Wayne And Shuster

CANADA · CBC · SKETCH

80 × 30 mins · colour

Canadian dates: 1968–81

UK dates: 11 Jan 1983–11 May 1984 (26 editions) C4 mostly Tue 5.30pm

MAIN CAST

Johnny Wayne
Frank Shuster

CREDITS

writers Johnny Wayne/Frank Shuster · *executive producer* Len Starmer · *producers* Norman Campbell, Barry Cranston, Johnny Wayne, Frank Shuster

Shows aired in Canada as *The Wayne And Shuster Comedy Special*, *The Wayne And Shuster Comedy Hour* and *Super Comedy With Wayne And Shuster* were re-edited and packaged by CBC for domestic syndication and overseas sale. C4 bought a batch of 26 programmes and began screening them in the UK soon after it took to the air.

We Got It Made

USA · ABC/SYNDICATION (MGM-UA/INTERMEDIA ENTERTAINMENT/THE FARR ORGANISATION) · SITCOM

48 × 30 mins · colour

US dates: 8 Sep 1983–30 Mar 1984 (24 ABC episodes); 1987–88 (24 syndicated episodes)

UK dates: 27 Jan–21 Nov 1984 (22 ABC episodes) BBC1 Fri 8.25pm then Wed 11.25pm; 27 Apr–14 Dec 1990 (23 syndicated episodes) ITV Fri 12.20am

MAIN CAST

Mickey MacKenzie · · · · · · · · · · · ·	Teri Copley
Jay Bostwick · · · · · · · · · · · · · · ·	Tom Villard
David Tucker · · · · · ·	Matt McCoy (1983–84);
· · · · · · · · · · · · · · · · · ·	John Hillner (1987–88)
Claudia · · · · · ·	Stepfanie Kramer (1983–84)
Beth · · · · · · · · · · ·	Bonnie Urseth (1983–84)
Max Papavasilios Sr · · · · · ·	Ron Karabatsos
· ·	(1987–88)
Max Papavasilios Jr · · · ·	Lance Wilson-White
· ·	(1987–88)

CREDITS

creators Gordon Farr/Lynne Farr Brao · *writers* Gordon Farr/Lynne Farr Brao, Chick Mitchell/ Geoffrey Neigher, Laura Levine, Jeffrey Ferro/ Fredric N Weiss and others · *director* Alan Rafkin · *executive producers* Gordon Farr, Fred Silverman

Among US media watchers, this series vies with *My Mother The Car* for the Worst Ever Sitcom 'honour', no mean feat in a country that has produced hundreds of humour-free comedies over the years. This is not to say that the USA is bad at producing sitcoms – far from it, for since the late 1970s they have proved to be masters of the genre, generating arguably the best examples in the world. The truth, however, is that American TV churns out a huge amount of product, and to counterbalance the diamonds at one end of the scale are shows like *We Got It Made*.

It is said that no one sets out to make a bad sitcom, but people do set out to cash in on an existing trend and often think that mere duplication of a theme will be enough to produce a carbon-copy hit. The role model for *We Got It Made* – a series in all ways as inept as the grammar of its title – was the British hit **Man About The House**, or, to be more accurate, **Three's Company**, the broader US adaptation of that series. *Three's Company* had been a ratings phenomenon in the USA at its height in the late 1970s, and it was an obvious target for cloning. In *We Got It Made*, instead of having one man live with two women, as in the original series, we had one stunning woman (the Marilyn Monroe-like Teri Copley) move in with two full-blooded men. The premise was that sloppy bachelor boys Jay and David – an importer and a lawyer respectively – advertised for a live-in maid, and instead of getting the expected fifty-something Gorgon, got living-doll Mickey. This suited the boys but Beth and Claudia, their respective girlfriends, freaked at the prospect, and confusion, misunderstanding, duplicity and chaos followed. Throughout the series the boys lusted after their busty Mrs Mop, but being a simple 'jiggle' show (US TV industry slang for teasing fare featuring well-developed women bouncing around suggestively) their dreams were never realised.

With all the vulgarity but none of the charm of *Three's Company*, *We Got It Made*, unsurprisingly, was cancelled after one season, but, unexpectedly, reappeared in a revamped version for 24 further episodes in 1987. Teri Copley once again starred as the dream cleaner and Tom Villard appeared as sloppy Jay, but John Hillner was installed as the new David and the girlfriends were absent. This should have meant that the boys had a clear field to dally with the daily, but once again tele-morality prevailed and sex remained a subject heard but never seen. A total of 23 of these latter episodes were screened in Britain by at least one ITV region, the London area, from 27 April 1990.

We Got Problems

UK · BBC · STANDUP

1 × 50 mins · b/w

3 Jan 1967 · BBC2 Tue 9.05pm

MAIN CAST
Dick Gregory

CREDITS
writer Dick Gregory · *producer* Dennis Main Wilson

The black American comedian Dick Gregory in a show specially recorded by the BBC.

Gregory was born in St Louis on 12 October 1932 and grew up in conditions of extreme poverty. These super-tough childhood experiences not only provided him with eye-opening, hardened material for his comedy act but also instilled within him a profound social conscience. But while he earned wide respect from his championing of political and social causes, his charitable work, his commitment to the civil-rights movement, and his sheer determination to use his wealth and celebrity to fight injustices, Gregory's incisive observations and hard-hitting comments on contemporary mores and attitudes were not popular among many members of the establishment. In short, he made a number of enemies and was on the receiving end of a well-publicised bout of police brutality.

In *We Got Problems*, Gregory opened with 20 minutes of material from his stage act and then spent the remainder of the programme answering questions from the audience.

We Have Ways Of Making You Laugh

UK · ITV (LWT) · SKETCH

9 × 30 mins · b/w

*23 Aug–18 Oct 1968 · Fri 7pm

MAIN CAST
Frank Muir
Dick Vosburgh
Gina Warwick
Kenneth Cope
Eric Idle
Trisha Noble

CREDITS
writers cast · *script editor* Dick Vosburgh · *director* Bill Turner · *producer* Humphrey Barclay

We Have Ways Of Making You Laugh, the very first programme intended (see footnote) for screening by LWT, at 7pm on Friday 2 August 1968, was introduced and linked – then and every week – by the company's own Head of Entertainment, Frank Muir. After his friendly 'Good evening, world' greeting, and the Don Partridge theme music, viewers were treated to half an hour of live jokes and sketch material written by the cast. This changed week by week (not all of the names above took part in every show) and included contributions from a pre-**Monty Python** Eric Idle.

We Have Ways Of Making You Laugh, indeed, was instrumental in launching the big-time career of Terry Gilliam – he contributed his first ever animation work on TV when producer Humphrey Barclay invited him to put together a sequence to accompany some recordings of Jimmy Young's BBC radio show. So limited was the budget that Gilliam had to move cut-outs, a method so successful that it remained.

*Note. Although the first programme was performed, it was only when the live show was finished that the cast and crew were informed that it had not been broadcast, the result of a union dispute. The following two editions were then cancelled, and the fourth, on 23 August, became the first to be seen by viewers. This and the remaining eight were screened without any problems.

We Know Where You Live

UK · C5 (WITZEND PRODUCTIONS/PARAMOUNT COMEDY CHANNEL) · SKETCH

12 × 30 mins · colour

6 Apr–23 June 1997 · mostly Mon 11.40pm

MAIN CAST
Simon Pegg
Fiona Allen
Sanjeev Bhaskar
Jeremy Fowlds
Ella Kenion
Amanda Holden

CREDITS
writers Martin Curtis, Mike Haskins, Richard Preddy/Gary Howe, Georgia Pritchett, Brian West, Russell Young and others · *director* Nick Jones · *executive producer* Tony Charles · *producers* Richard Parker, David Tomlinson

A fast-paced sketch show performed by an energetic troupe of young talents. The sketches had no overall theme but were modernistic in nature, spoofing MTV presenters and utilising such contemporary devices as security-camera footage, mobile phones, hidden miniaturised cameras and the like. The cast acquitted themselves well but the uneven quality of the writing and overriding cheap look of the show (it was doubtless made on a tiny budget) worked against them. Still, in a lean period for sketch shows, it was welcoming that the new C5 – unlike ITV – was willing to take a chance on a genre that traditionally has introduced so much comedy talent to British TV.

We'll Think Of Something

UK · ITV (THAMES) · SITCOM

6 × 30 mins · colour

1 Sep–13 Oct 1986 · Mon 8pm

MAIN CAST

Les Brooks	Sam Kelly
Maureen Brooks	Marcia Warren
Dennis	Roger Sloman
Irene	Maggie Jones
Norman	Ray Mort
Eddie	Philip Dunbar
Dave	Jimmy Reddington
Old Mr Brooks	John Barrard
Doctor Khan	Tariq Yunus
Policeman	Ian Bleasdale

CREDITS
writer Geoff Rowley · *director/producer* John Howard Davies

A short-lived sitcom set in Manchester (but made by Thames) starring Sam Kelly as Les Brooks, a middle-aged man, recently made redundant but determined his keep his pecker up and not join the dole queue. Indeed, he is intent on cocking a snook at the system, coming up with a continuous supply of grandiose money-making schemes that, inevitably, fail as he encounters the law of Sod. Together with mates Eddie and Dennis he totally exasperates his wife Maureen, who resorts to working in a pub in order to bring home some cash.

Weekend In Wallop

UK · ITV (LWT) · STANDUP

1 × 120 mins · colour

30 Dec 1984 · Sun 10pm

MAIN CAST

Maria Aitken
Rowan Atkinson
Billy Connolly
Peter Cook
Stephen Fry
Hugh Laurie
Norman Lovett
Rik Mayall (also as 'Kevin Turvey')
Ned Sherrin
Arthur Smith
Mel Smith
John Wells

CREDITS

writers cast · *director* Stephen Pile

A filmed account of a glorious weekend deep in the Hampshire countryside, when a horde of famous names from the realms of British TV, drama, art, writing and poetry descended upon the tiny village of Nether Wallop to take part in its First International Arts Festival, held in a 400-capacity marquee. (Only the names of those performers principally associated with comedy are listed above.)

The event was real tongue-in-cheek stuff, coming about after Stephen Pile, critiquing the Edinburgh Festival for *The Sunday Times*, suggested a new venue. He directed this TV film.

The Weekenders

see Reeves and Mortimer

Welcome Back, Kotter

USA · ABC (THE KOMACK CO/WOLPER PRODUCTIONS/WARNER BROS) · SITCOM

95 × 30 mins · colour

US dates: 9 Sep 1975–3 Aug 1979

UK dates: 8 Dec 1981–11 July 1983
(26 episodes) ITV weekdays 11.05am then Tue 3.45pm

MAIN CAST

Gabe Kotter	· · · · · · · · · · · ·	Gabriel Kaplan
Julie Kotter	· · · · · · · · · · · ·	Marcia Strassman
Mr Woodman	· · · · · · · ·	John Sylvester White
Juan Epstein	· · · · · · · · · · · ·	Robert Hegyes
Freddie 'Boom Boom' Washington	· · · · · · ·	
· · · · · · · · · · · · · · · ·		Lawrence-Hilton Jacobs
Arnold Horshack	· · · · · · · · · · · ·	Ron Palillo
Vinnie Barbarino	· · · · · · · · · · · ·	John Travolta
Judy Borden	· · ·	Helaine Lembeck (1975–77)
Rosalie Totzie	· · ·	Debralee Scott (1975–76)
Verna Jean	· · · ·	Vernee Watson (1975–77)
Todd Ludlow	· · · · ·	Dennis Bowen (1975–77)
Maria	· · · · · · · ·	Catarina Cellino (1975–76)
Angie Globagoski	· · · ·	Melonie Haller (1978)
Beau De Labarre	· · · · · · ·	Stephen Shortridge
· · · · · · · · · · · · · · · · · · · ·		(1978–79)
Carvelli	· · · · · · ·	Charles Fleischer (1978–79)
Murray	· · · · · · · · · · ·	Bob Harcum (1978–79)
Mary Johnson	· · · · ·	Irene Arranga (1978–79)

CREDITS

creators Gabriel Kaplan/Alan Sacks · *writers* various · *directors* Bob LaHendro, Bob Claver and others · *executive producer* James Komack · *producers* Alan Sacks, Eric Cohen, George Yanok, Nick Arnold, Bill Richmond, Gene Perrett, George Bloom

Similar in concept and enactment to ***Please, Sir!*** (but without any acknowledgement), the US sitcom *Welcome Back, Kotter*, was co-created by Gabriel Kaplan, who played its starring role, Gabe Kotter, a teacher employed at the same Brooklyn school, James Buchanan High, that he attended as a child. His task is to educate the 'remedial' class, a bunch of no-hope delinquent teenagers known as 'The Sweathogs', among whom are Vinnie Barbarino (a tough, hip Italian), Juan Epstein (an animal blend of Jew and Puerto Rican), Freddie 'Boom Boom' Washington (a black dude) and Arnold Horshack (a moron among morons). The kids, of course, also had a *marvellous* sense of humour, and the nattiest line in fashion – which, in the mid to late 1970s, meant excessively flared trousers and floppy lapels.

Before the series, Kaplan was a little-known standup comic, his best routine being a drunken impersonation of the venerable American TV variety host Ed Sullivan. Brooklyn-born, he himself had been in a 'remedial' class in a local high school, and *Welcome Back, Kotter* was his autobiographical tip-of-the-hat to a single teacher who had given him hope and an education when everyone else had given up; his fellow classmates were all depicted in the series and he himself played the teacher's role, slightly adapted, one suspects, for Kotter was the hippest teacher in the United States, eager to educate but not necessarily within prescribed rules, and to lend a laugh to every situation.

Virtually from the start, *Welcome Back, Kotter* was a huge hit, displeasing educational authorities but giving kids across America a weekly selection of wisecracks to repeat when next they went into school. The theme song – 'Welcome Back', sung by former Lovin' Spoonful vocalist John Sebastian – made number one on the US singles chart in May 1976; and the role of Barbarino brought stardom to the hitherto little-known John Travolta, who leaped from

Welcome Back, Kotter into *Saturday Night Fever*, *Grease*, and henceforth appeared only infrequently in the series (at which time the Sweathogs gained a new member, Beau De Labarre, a southerner).

As with *Please, Sir!*, these schoolkids were unlike any the viewers might have experienced in their own youth – hardly surprising, considering the actors were in their twenties (*well* into them, in some cases). As the final year of *Welcome Back, Kotter* rolled around so it began to follow them drifting into a working existence: Barbarino, for one, became a hospital orderly. Kaplan himself – as Kotter – appeared only sketchily towards the end (which, by all accounts, would have been welcomed by cast and crew alike, for he seems to have made himself distinctly unpopular during the four years they were all together).

Welcome Back, Kotter was similar to *Please, Sir!* in one other interesting respect too: none of the 'kids' (with the notable exception of Travolta) was seen much again.

Well Anyway

UK · BBC · SITCOM

7 × 30 mins · colour

24 Sep–5 Nov 1976 · BBC2 Fri 9pm

MAIN CAST

John Dally	· · · · · · · · · · · · · · · · · ·	John Bird
John Chance	· · · · · · · · · · · · · ·	John Fortune

CREDITS

writers John Bird/John Fortune · *producer* Dennis Main Wilson

An 'odd-couple' sitcom from the two Johns, Bird and Fortune.

Bird was cast as John Dally, a chap living in a flat in the west London district of Earls Court (reputedly, the set was based on Bird's own Earls Court flat). He has plenty of sidelines – photography; private detective work; model making for the Open University – but no main business, and most of his time is spent idling. One night, Dally answers the front door and there stands John Chance (John Fortune), who claims that they were best friends at Cambridge some 16 years previously and who needs a place to stay for the night while a new bathroom is fitted in his Eaton Square house. Dally is reluctant to allow this, but Chance employs smoothly persuasive tactics and is soon ensconced inside; he then stays indefinitely.

The humour centred on the two characters' different types of seediness, Dally being shiftless, Chance an inefficient conman. But the series was not successful and John Bird admitted that it was sub-standard, although he considered that it improved as it went along. Having written two episodes of a second series, Bird and Fortune were told that the BBC would not bring it back. Deflated by the experience, the former contemplated taking time off from TV writing, but the following year he scripted and appeared in a Cleo Laine and Johnny Dankworth series, *And Now* (four editions, BBC2, 11 August to 1 September 1977), the premise here showing the musical twosome rehearsing for a forthcoming television special but being constantly interrupted by Bird and Willie Rushton.

See also *The Long Johns*.

Welsh Rarebit

UK · BBC · SKETCH

4 editions (1 × 45 mins · 3 × 30 mins) · b/w
Special (45 mins) 26 Aug 1952 · Tue 8.15pm
One series (3) 4 Dec–18 Dec 1957 ·
Wed 7.30pm

MAIN CAST
Tommy Trouble · · · · · · · · · · · · George David
Nebo No-No · · · · · · · · · · · · · · Tudor Walters
Anthony Oliver
Albert Ward and Les Ward

CREDITS
main writer E Eynon Evans · *producers* Mai Jones (special), Mai Jones, Selwyn Roderick (series)

Welsh Rarebit has a special place in the affections of Welsh people. It began in 1941 as a travelling variety show, touring to Second World War troops and expatriates to keep them in touch with events in their Welsh homeland. The producers of the show, Mai Jones and Lyn Joshua, composed a stirring theme tune especially for the production, the epochal 'We'll Keep A Welcome In The Hillside'.

When the show was adapted for BBC radio it became an enormous success, more popular with listeners in Wales than the radio comedy flagship *It's That Man Again*. Shortly afterwards, on 15 August 1952, the BBC's television service was finally extended to Wales and the west of England, a landmark event celebrated 11 days later by a TV adaptation of *Welsh Rarebit*; five years later still, in 1957, there was a short-run series too.

The TV versions included the regular radio-sketch feature 'The Adventures Of Tommy Trouble', zany double-act Albert and Les Ward and the gentle humour of Anthony Oliver in the role of a storyteller. Mai Jones was a rarity of the time, a female variety producer, doubtless given the TV job through her long association with the production.

Weren't You Marcia Honeywell?

UK · BBC · SITCOM

1 × 30 mins · colour
7 Sep 1972 · BBC1 Thu 9.30pm

MAIN CAST
Marcia Honeywell · · · · · · · · · Betty Marsden
Bernard Hooper · · · · · · · · · · · Hugh Paddick
Grahame Toms · · · · · · · · · · · · · Royce Mills
Housekeeper · · · · · · · · · · · Hilda Fenemore
Pearl · · · · · · · · · · · · · · · · · · · Jo Garrity

CREDITS
writer Ken Hoare · *producer* Douglas Argent

The murder of Israeli athletes by Palestinian terrorists at the Munich Olympics shocked the world. It also threw the BBC TV schedules into chaos – with the Games suspended for a day and coverage being redesigned almost hourly, the BBC had to find quick replacement programmes. One consequence was the screening of a pair of *Comedy Playhouse* episodes that were waiting to be shown later in the year – one was *Weren't You Marcia Honeywell?*, the other – which fared considerably better – was ***Are You Being Served?***

In the first of these Betty Marsden played the title character, a woman who lives with Bernard Hooper. In years gone by they had been a successful duo, romantic singers in an age when such acts were much in demand. Marcia still harbours dreams of re-establishing their glory days and when a television producer moves into their village she does her level best to ingratiate herself. It transpires, however, that he is only involved with *Scrutiny*, a dull-current affairs programme. But because of her persistence he passes on her name to a colleague in the drama department. Marcia duly secures a cherished TV role – that of a middle-aged hag.

Weren't You Marcia Honeywell? was not developed into a series.

West End Tales

UK · ITV (ATV) · SITCOM

7 × 30 mins · colour
16 Feb–6 Apr 1981 · Mon 8pm

MAIN CAST
Fiddler · · · · · · · · · · · · · · · · · Robin Nedwell
The Bishop · · · · · · · · · · · · · Garfield Morgan
Checkie · · · · · · · · · · · · · · · · Larry Martyn
Ma · Toni Palmer
Sgt Dobbs · · · · · · · · · · · · · · · Peter Childs
Tina · · · · · · · · · · · · · · · · · · Susan Skipper

CREDITS
writer Keith Waterhouse · *director* James Gatward · *producers* Colin Frewin/Keith Beckett

Written by *Billy Liar* creator Keith Waterhouse, *West End Tales* showed three wideboys from Soho ducking and diving through their daily lives, evading 'real' work and the local henchmen.

The leader of the trio was the appropriately named Fiddler, a likeable scoundrel who made money by gambling on the horses and who lived above a café run by the often exasperated Ma. The Bishop and Checkie were his two cronies.

Whack-O!

UK · BBC · SITCOM

63 episodes (47 × 30 mins · b/w; 13 × 30 mins · colour; 3 × short specials · b/w
Series One (6) 4 Oct–13 Dec 1956 · fortnightly Tue mostly 8pm
Short special · part of *These Are The Shows* 28 Sep 1957 · Sat 8pm
Series Two (10) 1 Oct–3 Dec 1957 · Tue mostly 7.30pm
Series Three (7) 23 Sep–4 Nov 1958 · Tue mostly 7.30pm
Short special · part of *Christmas Night With The Stars* 25 Dec 1958 · Thu 6.25pm
Series Four (6) 12 May–16 June 1959 · Tue 7.30pm
Series Five (6) 10 Nov–15 Dec 1959 · Tue 7.30pm
Short special · part of *Christmas Night With The Stars* 25 Dec 1959 · Fri 6.20pm
Series Six (6) 13 May–17 June 1960 · Fri mostly 8.30pm
Series Seven (6) 22 Nov–27 Dec 1960 · Tue 7.30pm
Series Eight (13 × colour) *Whacko!* 27 Nov 1971–26 Feb 1972 · BBC1 Sat 5.05pm

MAIN CAST

SCHOOL STAFF:
Headmaster, Professor James Edwards · · · *MA (applied for)* · · · · · · · · · · · Jimmy Edwards
Assistant Headmaster Oliver Pettigrew · · · · ·
· · · · · · · · · · · · · Arthur Howard (series 1–7);
· · · · · · · · · · · · · · · Julian Orchard (series 8)
F D Price-Whittaker (English Literature) · · · · ·
· · · · · · · · · · · · · · · Kenneth Cope (series 1)
G D St J Dinwiddie (Latin and Greek) · · · · ·
· · · · · · · · · · · · · · · · John Garside (series 1)
L B Hackett (Higher Mathematics) · · · · · · · ·
· · · · · · · · · · · · · · · · Arthur Bush (series 1)
R D Spelthorne (Lower Mathematics) · · · · · ·
· · · · · · · · · · · · · · · Tony Sympson (series 1)
S A Smallpiece (Geography) · · · Norman Bird
· (series 1)
Matron · · · · · · · · · Barbara Archer (series 1);
· · · · · · · · · · · · · Elisabeth Fraser (series 2);
· · · · · · · · · · · Charlotte Mitchell (series 5)
M Aristide Beaumarie (Modern Languages) ·
· · · · · · · · · · · · · · Victor Baring (series 1 & 2)
L J Halliforth BSc · Edwin Apps (series 3–7);
· · · · · · · · · · · · · · · Peter Greene (series 8)
R Palmer (History) · · · · John Lewis (series 3)
G Perkins (Geography) · · · · Michael Stainton
· (series 3)
R P Trench MA · · · · · · · Peter Glaze (series 3)
Mr Snaith · · · · · Christopher Hodge (series 4)
Mr Tuppington · · · · · · John Forbes-Robertson
· (series 4)
Mr Cope-Willoughby · · · · · · · Frank Raymond
· (series 5–7)
Mr Dinwiddie · · · · · · · · · · · · Gordon Phillott
· · · · · · · · · · · · · · · · · · · (series 6 & 7);
· · · · · · · · · · · · · Harold Bennett (series 8)
Mr Proctor · · · · · · Brian Rawlinson (series 6);
· · · · · · · · · · · · · · · · · · John Legg (series 8)
Mr Forbes · · · · · · · · · · Keith Smith (series 7)
Schoolmaster · · · · · Philip Howard (series 2)
Schoolmaster (Carpentry) · · · · · · · John Scott
· (series 2)

PUPILS:
Lumley · · · · · · · · · · John Stirling (series 1–3)

Taplow · · · · · · · · John Hall (series 1, 2 & 6);
· · · · · · · · · · · · · · · · Gary Warren (series 8)
Phipps · · · · · · · · · · Robert O'Leary (series 4)
Crombie · · · · · · · · Jimmy Ray (series 4 & 5)
Phillpot · · · · · · · · · · Derek Needs (series 4)
Potter · · · · · · · · · · · Paul Norman (series 5)
Hoyle · · · · · · · · · · Stephen Portch (series 6);
· · · · · · · · · · · · · · David Spooner (series 8)
Rawlinson · · · · · · · Geoffrey Paget (series 6)
Parker · · · · · · · · · · · Richard Dean (series 6)

CREDITS

writers Frank Muir/Denis Norden · script adapter Robert Gray (series 8) · producers Douglas Moodie (series 1–6), Eric Fawcett (series 7), Douglas Argent (series 8)

A fondly remembered and long-running sitcom that eavesdropped on the shenanigans at a small, past-its-prime public school, Chiselbury, presided over by the awful Professor James Edwards – alias the dependable Jimmy Edwards.

Most episodes bore the legend 'A Weekly School Report', but the first series of half-dozen episodes was subtitled 'Six Of The Best', this – along with the programme's title – being an allusion to Headmaster Edwards' penchant for solving pupil disciplinary problems by recourse to the cane. Because of the farcical unreality of the situation, and the tradition of such treatment of schoolchildren in British comedy culture – witness *The Beano* comic hero *Dennis The Menace* and the slipperings from his father that concluded most escapades – the antics of Edwards were viewed as harmless and totally acceptable at the time. In later years, such behaviour, even if handled in the same sort of unreal manner, was not met with similar tolerance (see *Hardwicke House*).

Edwards' boisterous, almost fraudulent Professor – an established part of his stage act – became a TV favourite here, a larger-than-life, eye-rolling, loud monstrosity who seemed to exemplify writers Muir and Norden's ultimate revenge on bad teachers everywhere. The character made more than a passing nod to comic actor Will Hay's schoolmaster persona, which he developed on stage (from the sketch 'Bend Down'), in films (*Boys Will Be Boys*, 1935; *Good Morning Boys*, 1938; and *The Ghost Of St Michaels*, 1941) and on BBC radio (*Diary Of A Schoolmaster*). The two characters shared certain traits: greed, shiftiness, duplicity, a tendency to gamble and a lack of academic ability; however, they differed in that Edwards was more of a bully and was quicker to grasp the money-making merits of any situation. Indeed, Edwards' character resembled Ernie Bilko in his desire to fleece his charges of their pocket money and feather his own nest by arranging private enterprise under the guise of traditional school business. The assistant master at Chiselbury was Mr Pettigrew (played by Arthur Howard) and, as

co-author Muir later noted, he and Professor Edwards developed 'a kind of Laurel and Hardy relationship'.

Whack-O! was so successful that a feature film spin-off – *Bottoms Up!* – was released in 1959 (director Mario Zampi), with Edwards, Arthur Howard and Gordon Phillott reprising their Chiselbury TV roles. The film was written by Michael Pertwee, with Muir and Norden getting an 'additional dialogue' credit. Shortly after the end of the seventh and (supposedly) last TV series, a radio production – Muir and Norden's scripts adapted by David Climie – aired on the BBC Light Programme (45 episodes, 23 May 1961–22 July 1963). Then, in 1971, it was decided to bring the TV show out of retirement and a colour series (with the slightly altered title *Whacko!*), aimed at a younger audience, reworked some of the earlier scripts. Julian Orchard replaced Arthur Howard for these 13 episodes.

Note. Jimmy Edwards and Arthur Howard appeared in a sketch screened as part of *Christmas Night With The Stars* in 1960, but – although written by Muir and Norden, and produced by Eric Fawcett – this was a courtroom sketch, not a *Whack-O!* episode. Cyril Fletcher, Pip Hinton, Eric Robinson, Johnny Vyvyan and magicians Chan Canasta and David Nixon also appeared.

What A Performance

UK · ITV (ATV) · SITCOM

1 × 30 mins · colour

18 Aug 1977 · Thu 7pm

MAIN CAST

Vera · Anna Quayle
Arnold Bingham · · · · · · · · · · · Stan Stennett
Brenda · · · · · · · · · · · · · · · · Marjie Lawrence
David · · · · · · · · · · · · · · · · · · · Robin Bailey
Brian Jones · · · · · · · · · · · · · Andrew Sachs
Thomas G Reed · · · · · · · · · · · · · Noel Davis

CREDITS

writer Kenneth Cope · director/producer Shaun O'Riordan

A single comedy screened within ATV's season *The Sound Of Laughter*. It was written by *Randall And Hopkirk (Deceased)* star Kenneth Cope and dwelt upon the workings of an amateur dramatic society, and what happened when the director, Thomas G Reed, walked out, leaving one of the cast, Brian Jones, to take over.

What A Turn Up

UK · ITV (ATV) · SITCOM

1 × 30 mins · colour

7 Aug 1975 · Thu 7pm

MAIN CAST

Wally Warner · · · · · · · · · · · · · · Bernard Lee
George Warner · · · · · · · · · · · Anton Rodgers

Margaret Warner · · · · · · · · · · · Vivian Pickles
Lesley Warner · · · · · · · · · · · · · Nina Thomas
Simon Fennell · · · · · · · · · · · · · David Neville
Mr Fennell · · · · · · · · · · · · Ronald Leigh-Hunt
Justin Warner · · · · · · · · · · · · · · · Martin Neil

CREDITS

writers Brian Clemens/Dennis Spooner · director/producer John Scholz-Conway

This opening edition of *Comedy Premiere*, an ATV season of *Comedy Playhouse*-style single-episode sitcoms, centred on the return to his home in England of Wally Warner (Bernard Lee), on the very day of his granddaughter's wedding. It was written by Clemens and Spooner, best known for their involvement in all the classic ITV (ITC) action-adventure series of the period.

What Are You Doing After The Show?

UK · ITV (LWT) · SKETCH

7 × 45 mins · colour

10 Jan–21 Feb 1971 · Sun mostly 11.15pm

MAIN CAST

Trevor Adams
Pete Atkin
Rob Buckman
Julie Covington
Russell Davies
Maggie Henderson
Hilary Pritchard

CREDITS

script editors Geoff Rowley/Andy Baker · directors David Chapman (5), Mike Newell (1), Alan Wallis (1) · producer Paul Knight

A late-night sketch show screened in the London area and showcasing the talents of some future stars.

What Did You Say This Thing Was Called, Love?

see *Where Was Spring?*

What You Lookin' At?

UK · ITV (HUMPHREY BARCLAY PRODUCTIONS FOR LWT) · SITCOM

7 × 30 mins · colour

17 July–28 Aug 1993 · Sat mostly 6pm

MAIN CAST

Trevor · · · · · · · · · · · · · · · · Robert McKewley
Jane Wainwright · · · · · · · · · Trevyn McDowell
Colin · Bill Moody
Lynford · · · · · · · · · · · · · · · · Gary McDonald
Mrs Williams · · · · · · · · · · · · · Angela Wynter
Vanessa · · · · · · · · · · · · · · · · Marcia Hewitt
Elaine · · · · · · · · · · · · · · · · · · · Kelly Marcel

CREDITS

writer/director Trix Worrell · script editor Christopher Skala · executive producers Al Mitchell, Mark Robson · producer Humphrey Barclay

A lively early-evening ethnic sitcom from the team behind **Desmond's** – creator/writer Trix Worrell and producer Humphrey Barclay – clearly pitched at an adolescent audience.

The series was set in and around a mixed-race but principally black youth club in Battersea, south London, and mostly focused on the relationship between its 'problem' teenager Trevor, also known as Too Bad, and Jane Wainwright – an attached but unmarried white woman from cultured Berkshire – engaged on a probationary basis as the club leader. Blessed with a fast line in repartee, Too Bad is not really the bad lad people make out, but his background bears all the classic problem hallmarks: missing father, mum out at work all day, and forced to look after his much younger brother Darren. When he's not actually in trouble with Jane or the law, Trevor is merely suspected of being behind everything that goes wrong. His friends include Jason and members of the gangs the Faces and the Wicked Sisters. The other main players in the series included Jane's assistant Mrs Williams, the caretaker Colin – labelled 'a human racist' because he hates everyone, except his dog Pumpkin – and the sports teacher Lynford. World-beating British athlete Linford Christie guested, as himself, in the final episode.

Surprisingly risqué for its time-slot, *What You Lookin' At?* was clearly influenced by the raft of black-teen sitcoms proliferating in America in the 1990s, a fact reflected in the set design, editing technique, music, fashion, dialogue-style and the enthusiastic, obviously young studio audience.

What's Going On Here?

USA · WNEW · NEW YORK · SKETCH

1 × 30 mins · b/w

US date: 10 May 1963

UK date: 12 July 1963 · ITV Fri 10.45pm

MAIN CAST
Peter Cook
John Bird
Patrick B McCormick
Roger Bowen
MacIntyre Dixon
Bob Kaliban

CREDITS
writers Peter Cook, John Bird, Bud Trillin · *director* Arthur Forrest · *producers* Jean Vanden Heuvel, Clay Felker · *TV presentation* Jonathan Miller

Subtitled 'A Shrewd And Somewhat Rude Look At The News', this was a humorous, verging on satirical, look at the presentation of American TV news by a team of British and American humorists, including Peter Cook and John Bird. The show was put together by Cook's **Beyond The Fringe** colleague Jonathan Miller, at the request of executives at WNEW-TV (New York's esteemed Channel 5) who wished to stage

there a US version of something equivalent to the British *That Was The Week That Was*. This was not it, but a US version of the BBC series was indeed mounted soon afterwards.

What's On Next?

UK · ITV (THAMES) · SKETCH

23 editions (17 × 30 mins · 6 × 45 mins) · colour

Series One (5 × 45 mins) 16 Aug–20 Sep 1976 · Mon 6.45pm

Special (45 mins) 11 Apr 1977 · Mon 6.45pm

Series Two (4 × 30 mins) 13 June–4 July 1977 · Mon 8pm

Series Three (7 × 30 mins) 6 Apr–18 May 1978 · Thu mostly 9pm

Series Four (5 × 30 mins) 1 Aug–29 Aug 1978 · Tue mostly 8.30pm

Special (30 mins) 25 Oct 1978 · Wed 8pm

MAIN CAST
William Franklyn
Barry Cryer
Jim Davidson
Anna Dawson
Bob Todd
Andonia Katsaros (1976–77)
Pam Ayres (1976–77)
Sandra Dickinson (1976–77)
Hinge and Bracket (series 1 & special 1)
Cheryl Gilham (series 2 & 3)
Linda Lou Allen (1978)
Anne Bruzac (1978)
Steve Veidor (1978)

CREDITS
series 1 writers Barry Cryer, Dave Freeman, Neil Shand, Bernie Sharp, John Junkin · *series 2–4 writers* Barry Cryer, Bernie Sharp, John Junkin, David Renwick, Eddie Braben · *other writers* Andrew Marshall (2 eds), Terry Ravenscroft (1), Len Marten (1) · *directors* Mark Stuart (12), Stuart Hall (7), Ronald Fouracre (3), Dennis Kirkland (1) · *producer* Mark Stuart

A quick-paced sketch show of the kind usually mounted by the BBC but put together here by Thames. The pun-laced scripts were submitted by top writers, the main contributor, Barry Cryer, also appearing on screen. Actor William Franklyn, best known at this time for his 'Sshh … you know who' Schweppes TV commercials, was the straight man linking the items (and suffering as the butt of many jokes), and the series was instrumental in the development of two personalities who had gained early success on ITV talent shows: Jim Davidson (from *New Faces*), still up and coming at 22 and best known at this time for his 'nick-nick' routine, and the yokel-accented poet/humorist Pam Ayres (*Opportunity Knocks*), then aged 28.

What's Up Dockers

UK · C4 (RDF TELEVISION) · STANDUP

1 × 60 mins · colour

2 May 1997 · Fri 11.05pm

MAIN CAST
Julian Clary
Phil Kay
Eddie Izzard
Jo Brand
Jeff Green
Rob Newman
Ronnie Ancona
Neville Raven
Milton Jones
Sean Hughes
Steve Coogan
Alistair McGowan
Alan Davies

CREDITS
writers cast · *director* Hamish Hamilton · *executive producers* David Frank, Martin Durkin · *producer* Lisa Clark

An all-star comedy concert staged on behalf of dismissed Liverpool dockers, who had been fighting for more than a year to be reinstated. On film in the city, Julian Clary provided a brief background to the dispute and interrupted the show with filmed inserts of his discussions with a group of dockers' wives. The concert itself took place at the London Palladium and featured a host of well-known comics, each performing for about five minutes. The result was a high-class selection box of some of the liveliest material on the circuit.

Whatever Happened To The Likely Lads

see *The Likely Lads*

Where Do I Sit?

UK · BBC · STANDUP

3 × 30 mins · colour

19 Feb–5 Mar 1971 · BBC2 Fri 9.20pm

MAIN CAST
Peter Cook

CREDITS
writer Peter Cook · *producers* Ian MacNaughton/Peter Cook

A spectacular disaster for Peter Cook. The format crossed comedy with chat-show (guests included Spike Milligan, S J Perelman, Johnny Speight and Kirk Douglas) to produce a rambling, unscripted, out-of-control programme made all the more dicey by the fact that, apart from some pre-filmed sequences, it was transmitted live and Cook was obviously very nervous indeed, and a little bit the worse for alcohol. (Famously, instead of asking Douglas 'How are you?' he said 'Who are you?'.) The filmed sections were not much better: in one, Cook impersonated Cilla Black and went up to Batley, Yorkshire, so that he could jump out in front of people and ask, as Cilla did for her then current BBC1 series, 'Do you know who I am?'.

Originally planning to screen 13 editions, the BBC pulled the plug after just three – citing, as the main reasons, concerns over the dubious taste of some of the material, and the uneasy mix of genres. Executives must also have been concerned by the reviews, which included such choice terms as 'dismally embarrassing' and 'truly pathetic'. The series also attracted controversy – most of it surrounding a sketch about God and the subsequent brouhaha when a member of the audience criticised the piece only to be verbally roughed up by the unrepentant Cook. Despite, or perhaps because of, such incidents the three transmitted editions did at least achieve healthy viewing figures.

Where The Buffalo Roam

UK · BBC · SITCOM

1 × 30 mins · colour

21 Aug 1995 · BBC1 Mon 8.30pm

MAIN CAST

Jimmy Dunn	Stephen McGann
Glyn Hunter	Ricky Tomlinson
Pam Dunn	Anne Reid
Wayne	Daniel Ryan
Siobhan	Tracy Whitwell

CREDITS

writers Mark Bussell/Justin Sbresni · *director/producer* Mike Stephens

A one-off pilot episode, not developed into a series.

Bored with his job as a security guard, Jimmy Dunn dreams of building up a financial empire; unfortunately, no sooner has he settled upon a scheme than he comes up with another and abandons the first. Jimmy lives at home with his mother Pam, a competition addict, and her live-in boyfriend Glyn, a compulsive gambler. The middle-aged couple whisper sweet nothings to one another and canoodle about the house like a pair of lovesick teenagers, much to Jimmy's embarrassment. He himself is courting, going out with a dental nurse, Siobhan, who loyally supports his various schemes but becomes increasingly aware of his inability to see an idea through to its conclusion. Completing the cast is Jimmy's friend and neighbour Wayne, who is easily swayed and goes to great lengths to avoid confrontation.

Where There's Brass

see *Thicker Than Water* [2]

Where Was Spring?

UK · BBC · SKETCH

13 editions (5 × 30 mins · 7 × 25 mins · 1 × 40 mins) · colour

Special (40 mins) *What Did You Say This Thing Was Called, Love?* 9 June 1968 · BBC2 Sun 9.15pm

Series One (5 × 30 mins) 27 Jan–24 Feb 1969 · BBC2 Mon mostly 10.25pm

Series Two (7 × 25 mins) 12 July–23 Aug 1970 · BBC2 Sun mostly 9.55pm

MAIN CAST

Eleanor Bron

John Fortune

CREDITS

writers John Fortune/Eleanor Bron · *directors* Vere Lorrimer (special), Terry Hughes (series 1 & 2) · *producer* Ned Sherrin

A *Show Of The Week* special and two subsequent series for Fortune and Bron, showcasing their inventively sharp man/woman dialogues that had been so successful in *Not So Much A Programme More A Way Of Life* and *BBC-3*. The 13 programmes embraced sophisticated, witty and surprisingly adult sketch material, covering a multitude of modern-day concerns: angst-ridden relationships, pre-marital affairs, post-marital affairs and family rifts of every man/woman complexion: husband and wife, lover and mistress, ex-husband and ex-wife, and so on. The pair employed some improvisation in the pieces and this, together with their comedic style and the chosen themes, marked them out as British versions of the American improvisational double-act Mike Nichols and Elaine May.

Both series carried a distinctive style, particularly the first, with illustrations drawn by Klaus Voormann, special photography by Clive Arrowsmith and a weekly musical number written by Ray Davies and performed by his band the Kinks.

Which Way To The War

UK · ITV (REG GRUNDY PRODUCTIONS FOR YORKSHIRE) · SITCOM

1 × 30 mins · colour

19 Aug 1994 · Fri 8.30pm

MAIN CAST

Cpl Roy Muller	William Tapley
Pvt Stan Hawke	Simon Baker Denny
Cpl Tony Genaro	Terry John
Pvt Jock Stewart	Robert Hands

CREDITS

writers Jeremy Lloyd/David Croft · *executive producer* Don Reynolds · *producer* David Croft

Never developed into a series, this was a pilot intended to launch a new Lloyd and Croft sitcom. As with their BBC success *'Allo 'Allo!*, the setting was the Second World War, 1942, although here the landscape was the Western Desert in Libya.

A pair of Australian and a pair of British soldiers become detached from their units, set up base in a ruined farmhouse and are joined by an ambulance-full of Italian women who appear to be nurses. They turn out to be prostitutes …

The storyline was similar to Croft's *The Birds In The Bush*, an Australian TV series, screened in 1972, about two English men living among a horde of beautiful women in an outback farmhouse.

The Whitehall Worrier

UK · BBC · SITCOM

7 × 30 mins · b/w

Pilot *The Mallard Imaginaire* 5 July 1966 · BBC1 Tue 7.30pm

One series (6) 13 Jan–17 Feb 1967 · BBC1 Fri 7.30pm

MAIN CAST

The Rt Hon Mervyn Pugh	Robert Coote
Janet Pugh	Moira Lister
David Pugh	Michael Wennick (pilot);
	Karl Lanchbury (series)
Michele Pugh	Celia Hewitt
Roger Deere	Jonathan Cecil
Mrs Nicholson	Daphne Anderson
Miss Dempster	Nan Munro
Mr Harrison	Arthur Howard
Mrs Frome	Barbara Ogilvie

CREDITS

writer Alan Melville · *producer* Graeme Muir

In the pilot episode, aired as part of *Comedy Playhouse*, a mallard waddles on to the in-tray of government minister Mervyn Pugh and lays an egg, bringing the work of his department to a halt for three weeks until said bird has hatched its brood. This was typical of the unlikely situations that dogged the minister during the short run of this satirical series, much to the distress of his whipping-boy … er, assistant, Roger Deere, and civil servants Miss Dempster and Mr Harrison.

Domestically, Mervyn Pugh's life is no simpler: having discovered his affair with Mrs Nicholson, his wife Janet is countering with dalliances of her own. His son, David, has a penchant for unsuitable and potentially embarrassing girlfriends, and his daughter Michele takes her political protests too far, often finding herself in trouble with the police. Even the cook has caught religious mania. No wonder he worried.

Writer Alan Melville adapted the idea from an unproduced full-length film script he had written, but the series was not voted a hit by the viewing electorate. He and his female star Moira Lister fared better with their next collaboration, *The Very Merry Widow*.

Whizzkid's Guide

UK · ITV (SOUTHERN) · CHILDREN'S SKETCH

6 × 25 mins · colour

1 Apr–6 May 1981 · Wed 4.20pm

MAIN CAST

Arthur Mullard

Rita Webb

Patrick Newell

Kenneth Williams

Sheila White

CREDITS
writer Peter Eldin · *director/producer* Michael Grafton-Robinson

A visual guidebook for children, showing them how to handle life at school. The scripts – which were adapted by Peter Eldin, a magician, from his best-selling book *The Whizzkid's Handbook* – focused on such topics as how to cheat at school sports and exams, writing out lines and digesting school dinners. Kenneth Williams was his usual good value, and any series that paired Arthur Mullard and Rita Webb can't – ahem – have been all bad.

Who Dares, Wins …

UK · C4 (HOLMES ASSOCIATES · *WHO DARES WINS PRODUCTIONS) · SKETCH

31 editions (22 × 45 mins · 9 × 60 mins) · colour
Special (60 mins) 4 Nov 1983 · Fri 10.05pm
Series One (8 × 60 mins) 12 May–30 June 1984 · Sat mostly 10.50pm
*Series Two (8 × 45 mins) 2 Nov–21 Dec 1985 · Sat 11pm
*Series Three (8 × 45 mins) 1 Nov–20 Dec 1986 · Sat mostly 11pm
*Series Four (6 × 45 mins) 20 Apr–25 May 1988 · Wed mostly 11pm

MAIN CAST
Rory McGrath
Jimmy Mulville
Philip Pope
Tony Robinson
Julia Hills (all except special)
Brenda Blethyn (special only)
William Hootkins (special only)

CREDITS
writers Colin Bostock-Smith (not series 4), Andy Hamilton, Guy Jenkin, Rory McGrath, Jimmy Mulville, Tony Sarchet; Laurie Rowley (special only) · *directors* Graeme Matthews (special), David MacDonald (4 eds in series 1), John Stroud (series 1–3), Vic Finch (all series 4), Jimmy Mulville (occasional, series 4) · *producers* Andy Hamilton/Denise O'Donoghue

A very successful, winning sketch show for C4 that spanned five years and was popular among viewers and critics alike – while being lambasted by the clean-up TV campaigners. Some of the writers had been involved with the BBC's *Not The Nine O'Clock News* and virtually all of the team were gaining great experience at this time writing for BBC radio-comedy shows. Without doubt, the credentials of all the players and writers were favourably established with *Who Dares, Wins* … (sometimes written as *Who Dares Wins*).

It all began as a single special to celebrate (two days late) C4's first anniversary. The programme was screened live, with new material written right up to the evening of the broadcast (a habit that writers Jenkin and Hamilton continued with *Drop The Dead Donkey*). That opening show and the eight programmes that constituted the first series all had subtitles to follow the *Who Dares, Wins* … tag, such as *A Week In Benidorm, A Camping Holiday In Beirut, Frank Bough's Cardigan, Martina Navratilova's Wristband* and *A Mysterious Rash*. Throughout the four series the material was plentiful, fresh, witty, perhaps provocative, occasionally raunchy and usually spot-on, embracing sex topics and language that might once have been termed 'bad'. Frustratingly, however, religion remained a taboo, and one early show that included a Jesus joke brought a cascade of complaints. A number of running gags more than made up for this, though, including pandas that were hatching a plan to escape from a zoo, Julia Hills appearing as a nervous, clumsy TV interviewer, and Tony Robinson appearing in the nude, his vital blushes spared only by a hand or a stray object.

'Who Dares Wins', incidentally, was originally an SAS slogan, and had been adopted as the title of a 1982 movie. Never before in the history of British TV comedy had the SAS been the cause of so much fun.

Note. In addition to the above listing, the *Who Dares, Wins* … team appeared together in C4's 1986–87 New Year's special *Come Dancing With Jools Holland* and in *Hysteria 2*. Three of the team (Mulville, McGrath and Pope) also appeared in *Chelmsford 123*.

Who Do You Do?

UK · ITV (LWT) · IMPRESSIONISM

57 editions (56 × 30 mins · 1 × 45 mins) · colour
Series One (6) 8 Jan–12 Feb 1972 · Sat 6.05pm
Series Two (10) 9 July–10 Sep 1972 · mostly Sun 9.30pm
Series Three (13) 25 Feb–18 May 1973 · Sun 7.25pm then Fri 8.30pm
Special *Christmas Who Do You Do?* 29 Dec 1974 · Sun 7.25pm
Series Four (12) *New Who Do You Do?* 2 Feb–20 Apr 1975 · Sun 7.25pm
Special (45 mins) *A Special Who Do You Do?* 26 Dec 1975 · Fri 7pm
Series Five (13) *Now Who Do You Do?* 22 Feb–23 May 1976 · Sun 7.25pm
Special *Now Who Do You Do?* 20 Aug 1976 · Fri 7pm

MAIN CAST
Freddie Starr (series 1–4 & 1974 special)
Peter Goodwright (series 1, 2, 5 & 1974–76 specials)
Pat Dailey and Bill Wayne (series 2 & 3)
Roger Kitter (series 3)
Paul Melba (series 3)
Johnny More (series 4)
Faith Brown (1975–76 specials & series 5)
Janet Brown (1975–76 specials & series 5)
Little and Large (series 5)

CREDITS
creator Jon Scoffield · *writers* Dick Vosburgh (all), Barry Cryer (series 1–4 and 1974 special), Wally Malston (series 3), Garry Chambers (specials, series 4 & 5), Peter Vincent (1975–76 specials & series 5) · *producer* Jon Scoffield

Comedy impressionism edited to effect machine-gun rapidity (the average skit, it was reckoned, lasted just over 30 seconds). The series confirmed the arrival of Freddie Starr as a major British entertainer (see his combined entry for career background), and there seemed no limit to which this flexible and quite eccentric comic would not go to raise a laugh, dazzling audiences with his imitations of everyone from Max Wall to Tarzan by way of Mick Jagger, Elvis Presley, Norman Wisdom, the wrestler Adrian Street, Tom Jones and scores of others.

Sterling support was given by the under-appreciated impressionist Peter Goodwright, and literally dozens of others. Among those offering regular/semi-regular assistance were Margo Henderson (series 1), Janet Brown (series 2 & 3), Paul Melba (series 2 & 3) and Johnny More (series 3), and *Who Do You Do?* also provided early TV exposure for Russ Abbot (solo and with his musical group the Black Abbots), Dustin Gee, Jerry Stevens, Little and Large, Aiden J Harvey, Les Dennis and, in the 1976 run, Michael Barrymore.

Note. *Who Do You Do?* was revived by Central TV for a 30-week run from 23 June 1995, screened in the Midlands but not networked. The series was akin to an impressionism showcase, with dozens of little-known acts from around the country trying their hand on television. Establishing a link with the 1970s run, Aiden J Harvey appeared as the principal performing anchor and Jon Scoffield returned as director.

Who Is Secombe?

see SECOMBE, Harry

Who Is Sylvia?

see DRAKE, Charlie

Who's Afraid Of The Big Bad Bear?

UK · ITV (THAMES) · CHILDREN'S SITCOM

1 × 30 mins · colour
14 June 1974 · Fri 4.50pm

MAIN CAST
Kate Carter · · · · · · · · · · · · Barbara Mitchell
Geoff Carter · · · · · · · · · · · · · · · Harry Towb
Tess Carter · · · · · · · · · · · · · · · Lynne Miller
Joe · Peter Daly

CREDITS
writer Adele Rose · *director* Leon Thau · *producer* Ruth Boswell

The fourth edition in Thames' series of *Funny Ha Ha* individual children's comedies conveyed a family dilemma: Tess Carter, a pretty 19-year-old, is hung up about a somewhat feeble young man called Joe. So her mother, brothers and sisters determine to prevent him from becoming one of the family by creating a practical joke about a huge bear. No series developed.

Who's The Boss?

USA · ABC (HUNTER-COHAN PRODUCTIONS/ COLUMBIA PICTURES TV/EMBASSY COMMUNICATIONS) · SITCOM

196 episodes (195 × 30 mins · 1 × 60 mins) · colour

US dates: 20 Sep 1984–25 Apr 1992

UK dates: 8 Jan 1990–18 Dec 1992
(81 × 30 mins) ITV Mon then Thu mostly 5.10pm

MAIN CAST

Tony Micelli	Tony Danza
Angela Bower	Judith Light
Mona Robinson	Katherine Helmond
Samantha Micelli	Alyssa Milano
Jonathan Bower	Danny Pintauro

CREDITS

creators Blake Hunter/Martin Cohan · *writers* Blake Hunter and others · *directors* Tony Singletary, Bill Persky and others · *executive producers* Martin Cohan, Blake Hunter, Danny Kallis, Phil Doran, Bud Wiser · *producers* various

This original version of what, in Britain, was adapted as **The Upper Hand** was an easy, unchallenging role-reversal comedy starring gravel-voiced young beefcake Tony Danza – best known as Tony Banta, the aspiring world champion boxer in **Taxi** – as housekeeper to a beautiful blonde widowed mother. (US TV being what it is, shortly after the launch of *Who's The Boss?* another young hunk, Scott Baio, starred in another sitcom about a another young single male housekeeper, in **Charles In Charge**.)

A baseball star with the St Louis Cardinals until injury forced him into retirement, macho Tony Micelli is a widower with a ten-year-old daughter, Samantha, on his hands. Eager to quit bustling Brooklyn and his job as a fish delivery man they head out to leafy Connecticut, where he intends to find work. Instead he bumps into one Mona Robinson, who considers him suitable for the post of housekeeper to her daughter, Angela Bower, a divorced advertising agency executive who has little time to keep house or raise her brat of a son Jonathan, aged seven. Tony and Samantha move into the Bower household, so that he can be a live-in domestic, running the house and family while Angela is out; his duties are overseen – and interfered with – by the ever-visiting, man-hungry Mona (played sexily by Katherine Helmond).

Although the series never rose above lightweight domestic fun, and the scripts tended towards the lame, *Who's The Boss?* ran for eight long years, during which time

every possible domestic incident occurred and the children proceeded through the school system and into and out of relationships of their own. Tony himself took classes, going on to become a supply teacher. And, surprise, surprise, despite their greatly different backgrounds and interests, Tony and Angela quickly learned to enjoy one another's company to the point where, despite the comings and goings of Angela's dates, a relationship brewed. It was one that they seemed unwilling to ferment, however, and it wasn't until seven years had passed, in 1991, that the inevitable finally occurred and they recognised, after a *lot* of to-ing and fro-ing, that they couldn't live apart. (By this time, Samantha, far from ten, had also wed.) But still Tony and Angela remained single, which is where the series ended.

Two episodes of *Who's The Boss?* served as pilots for potential spin-offs, 'Charmed Lives' and 'Mona' (the latter being an attempt to give Katherine Helmond her own series), but neither developed. However, another episode, titled 'Life's A Ditch', evolved into the US sitcom *Living Dolls* (ABC, 1989).

Meanwhile, the purchase of UK adaptation rights led to a British version of *Who's The Boss?* – the popular *The Upper Hand*, which, with local changes, utilised the same scripts.

Who's Your Friend?

UK · BBC · SITCOM

1 × 30 mins · colour

15 Jan 1970 · BBC1 Thu 7.30pm

MAIN CAST

Jimmy Sampson	Bernard Cribbins
Laura Marshall	Maggie Fitzgibbon
Mr Walters	Frank Thornton

CREDITS

writer Terence Edmond · *producer* Graeme Muir

A *Comedy Playhouse* pilot set in an escort agency, starring talented comedy actor Bernard Cribbins as a professional escort, Jimmy Sampson. The programme had a good cast and a neat title but it failed to graduate into a series.

Whoops Apocalypse

UK · ITV (LWT) · SITCOM

6 × 30 mins · colour

14 Mar–18 Apr 1982 · Sun mostly 10pm

MAIN CAST (EPISODE NUMBERS IN PARENTHESES)

President Johnny Cyclops	Barry Morse (all)
The Deacon	John Barron (all)
Premier Dubienkin	Richard Griffiths (1, 3, 5, 6)
Commissar Solzhenitsyn	Alexei Sayle (1, 3, 4, 6)
Kevin Pork	Peter Jones (2, 3, 5, 6)
Foreign Secretary	Geoffrey Palmer (2, 3, 5, 6)
Chancellor of the Exchequer	Richard Davies (2, 3, 5, 6)
Shah Mashiq Rassim	Bruce Montague (1, 2, 4, 6)
Lacrobat	John Cleese (3, 4, 5, 6)
Jay Garrick	Ed Bishop (1, 4, 5, 6)
Abdab	David Kelly (1, 2, 4, 6)

OTHER APPEARANCES

Lt Botko	Roger Phillips (1 & 3)
Jonathan Hopper	John Barrard (1 & 3)
Martha Hopper	Nellie Hanham (1 & 3)
Secretary	Sarah Whitlock (1 & 3)
Newsreader Jay Garrick	Ed Bishop (2 & 3)
Admiral Blinsky	George Claydon (3 & 6)
Wheelchair	Gabor Vernon (3 & 6)
Dripfeed	Frank Duncan (3 & 6)
Jeb Grodd	Lou Hirsch (3 & 4)
Dr Weinigger	Olivier Pierre (5 & 6)
Chaplain	John Sterland (5 & 6)

CREDITS

writers Andrew Marshall/David Renwick · *director* John Reardon · *producer* Humphrey Barclay

Whoops Apocalypse painted a frightening but fantastic picture of international politics and brinkmanship, as lunatic world leaders made awesome decisions with nary a prior thought but with devastating effect. As such, it was then, and remains, an extraordinary sitcom – topical, anarchic, inspired, alternative – of a kind and style familiar, perhaps, to viewers of BBC2 or the emerging C4, but a real departure for network ITV.

In *Whoops Apocalypse*, as in then 'real' life, the balance of world power is held by the leaders of Russia (the ageing Dubienkin) and the United States. The American president, much despised in his home country and cravenly seeking restoration of his popularity, happens (no coincidence, obviously) to be a former screen actor, the recently lobotomised Johnny Cyclops. Stranded in the middle of the pair is the lame, moronic British PM, Kevin Pork, aided by his Foreign Secretary (Dave) and Chancellor of the Exchequer (Brian). Also queering the picture is the mad master-of-disguise Lacrobat – the world's most hunted international terrorist and nuclear-bomb-stealer – and, perhaps most frighteningly of all, the Deacon, the fanatical, God-fearing American security adviser, a man who believes he has a direct hotline to the deity. (At the time, although *Whoops Apocalypse* authors Marshall and Renwick claimed prior ignorance of the fact, the US security adviser, General Haig, was known within White House circles as the Vicar.) All the while, the Shah of Iran has been deposed and secret Western attempts to restore his brother to power fail to amount to much (at one point, he is stuck on a cross-channel ferry). Disastrously, in the final episode, a Quark nuclear bomb accidentally destroys Israel, sending the planet cascading towards the Third World War and nuclear holocaust.

The casting of *Whoops Apocalypse* was exceptional: the players included John Cleese (as Lacrobat) appearing in his only sitcom outside of his own *Fawlty Towers*, John Barron and Geoffrey Palmer from *The Fall And Rise Of Reginald Perrin*, Richard Griffiths, Peter Jones, David Kelly, Ed Bishop, Bruce Montague, Richard Davies, Barry Morse and, from the new so-called 'alternative comedy' movement, Rik Mayall (who appeared in one episode) and Alexei Sayle. It might just be stretching belief to suggest that every one of these and the remainder of the huge cast understood *all* that was going on in their scripts, for certainly much of the series left viewers baffled, but, then again, since the world has always been governed by decisions of uncomprehending madness then the sitcom was merely an exaggerated but otherwise accurate reflection of the fact.

A less impressive feature film version of *Whoops Apocalypse* was released in 1987 (director Tom Bussmann), again scripted by Marshall and Renwick and featuring a stellar cast, including Loretta Swit, Peter Cook, Michael Richards, Alexei Sayle, Rik Mayall, Ian Richardson, Herbert Lom, Richard Wilson, Graeme Garden, John Sessions and Richard Murdoch.

Whoops Baghdad

UK · BBC · SITCOM
6 × 30 mins · colour
25 Jan–1 Mar 1973 · BBC1 Thu mostly 10.10pm
MAIN CAST
Ali Oopla · · · · · · · · · · · · · · Frankie Howerd
The Wazir · · · · · · · · · · · · · · · Derek Francis
Fatima · · · · · · · · · · · · · · Josephine Tewson
Saccharine · · · · · · · · · · · · · Hilary Pritchard
Boobiana · · · · · · · · · · · · · · · · Anna Brett
various roles · · · · · · · · · · · · · · Alan Curtis
Derti Dhoti · · · · · · · · · · · · · · Larry Martyn
Imshi · · · · · · · · · · · · · · · Norman Chappell
CREDITS
writers Sid Colin/David McKellar/David Nobbs (2), Sid Colin/Roy Tuvey/Maurice Sellar (1), Sid Colin/David McKellar/Roy Tuvey/Maurice Sellar (1), Roy Tuvey/Maurice Sellar (1), Peter Vincent/Bob Hedley (1) · *producer* John Howard Davies

A late slot for the saucy antics of Frankie Howerd as Ali Oopla, bond-servant to the Wazir of Baghdad. And so it came to pass that this was a reworking of the *Up Pompeii!* formula, plain and simple, with Howerd himself commenting that the series featured 'new costumes but the same old jokes'. The prominent cleavages, bejewelled midriffs and naked thighs of Harem girls decorated the set while the usual direct-to-camera double entendres, malapropisms, lame puns, dodgy names (*lots* of people called Mustapha …), · readings and sharing of confidences filled every moment of every episode. For Howerd, this sort of performance was as easy as falling off a magic carpet.

See also Frankie Howerd's combined entry.

Whose Diary Is It Anyway?

UK · BBC · SATIRE
1 × 35 mins · colour
9 Aug 1995 · Wed 11.15pm
MAIN CAST
Bee · Ali Briggs
Georgia · · · · · · · · · · · · · · · Mandy Colleran
Daisy · · · · · · · · · · · Mandy Redvers Higgins
CREDITS
writer Mandy Redvers Higgins · *director/producer* Elspeth Morrison

An accomplished satire from the No Excuses disability cabaret company, set in Liverpool. The trio of Ali Briggs (partially deaf), Mandy Colleran (wheelchair user) and Mandy Redvers Higgins (blind) cast themselves as Bee, Georgia and Daisy as they set out to make 'a week-in-the-life video-diary' programme for a BBC producer. Through a series of short pieces, the three highlight the prejudices and condescension suffered by people who are as able-minded as the next person but physically disabled.

Ironically, though, it is the BBC producer whose attitudes are the most deeply insulting – 'I want to see your pain as you walk into that lamp-post!' he instructs, beseeching that the diary should cover 'all the issues, the *real* issues about disability'. Although its content is all too genuine, marking out the indignities constantly suffered by disabled in everyday life, he then rejects the finished result, considering it 'unreal'.

Like other programmes made the BBC's Disability Programmes Unit – see also *The Alphabet Soup Show* and *In Stitches With Daphne Doesgood* – the net result of *Whose Diary Is It Anyway?*, screened as part of the *Over The Edge* series, was not so much riproaringly funny as deeply ironic and eye-opening.

Wife Begins At 40

UK · BBC · SITCOM
1 × 90 mins · colour
28 Dec 1988 · BBC1 Wed 9.30pm
MAIN CAST
Linda Harper · · · · · · · · · · · · · Liza Goddard
George Harper · · · · · · · · · · · · · Ray Cooney
Roger Dixon · · · · · · · · · · · · · John Quayle
Bernard Harper · · · · · · · · · · · John Horsley
Betty Dixon · · · · · · · · · · · · · Tricia George
Leonard Harper · · · · · · · · · · · · Grant Piro
CREDITS
writers Arne Sultan/Earl Barrett/Ray Cooney · *director/producer* Harold Snoad

A TV-recorded farce, co-written by and co-starring Ray Cooney; he cast himself as George Harper, a man who rediscovers the romantic aspect of his personality after a vasectomy.

Although described as a 'comedy play' this was, in essence, a 90-minute one-off sitcom, performed at the BBC studios in front of an audience and produced and directed by sitcom stalwart Harold Snoad.

The Wild House

UK · BBC CHILDREN'S SITCOM
12 × 25 mins · colour
8 Jan–26 Mar 1997 · BBC1 Wed 4.35pm
MAIN CAST
Natalie Wild · · · · · · · · · · · · · Ellie Beaven
Serena Wild · · · · · · · · · Honeysuckle Weeks
Arthur Wild · · · · · · · · · · · · · · Peter Kelly
Mrs Wild · · · · · · · · · · · · · Annette Ekblom
Mr Wild · · · · · · · · · · · · · · · Philip Bird
CREDITS
writer Jean Buchanan · *additional material* Yvonne Coppard/Mark Haddon · *director* Roger Singleton-Turner · *producer* Marilyn Fox

A smart and cute serialised children's series, set in the home of the crazy Wild family: mum, dad and three precocious children.

Taking centre-stage is Natalie, a clever and articulate 13-year-old making the transition from childish concerns to teenage woes – worrying about clothes, boyfriends and all that. With his obsession about wildlife, Natalie's brother Arthur, 10, seems intent on becoming the next David Attenborough; sister Serena, meanwhile, aged 16, just wants a boyfriend. Mum and Dad have (in the stories) less to do than their offspring but, at various times, all of the Wilds speak directly to the camera commenting upon their lives while random dream-like images are projected behind them.

Wild Oats

UK · ITV (CELADOR PRODUCTIONS FOR CARLTON) · SITCOM
1 × 30 mins · colour
2 Mar 1993 · Tue 8.30pm
MAIN CAST
Roland Jackson · · · · · · · · · Leslie Grantham
David Jackson · · · · · · · · · · Jonathon Morris
Jennifer · · · · · · · · · · · · · · Julie Bramall
Paul · · · · · · · · · · · · · · · · Fraser James
Deidre · · · · · · · · · · · · · · · Eve Ferret
CREDITS
writers Steve Knight/Mike Whitehill · *director/producer* Nic Phillips

A single-episode pilot screened by Carlton as part of its *Comedy Playhouse* season. *Wild Oats* was built around the actor Leslie Grantham, etched into viewers' minds as 'Dirty Den' in the BBC soap *EastEnders* but who, in the 1990s, was trying various roles, starring in drama series *Winners And Losers*, *The Paradise Club* and *99–1*. Co-starring with him here was Jonathon Morris, Adrian Boswell in Carla Lane's sitcom *Bread*.

Grantham was cast as Roland, an advertising executive and ageing pony-tailed Lothario living the London-playboy life of champagne, a leather sofa and no commitments, but who reaps the harvest of his youthful oat-sewing in the shape of his 23-year-old son David, who unexpectedly descends upon him from Oldham, catching him 'in the act'. The north-south cultural divide, and the suddenness of David's arrival, spark a sequence of events, but, ultimately, Roland comes to accept that the time has come for him to be a father.

Despite displaying plenty of promise – even if it did echo the premise of **Home To Roost** and **Relative Strangers** – *Wild Oats* was not developed into a series.

Note. This programme is unrelated to a short-lived US sitcom of the same title that aired in America in September 1994 and was seen in Britain on the cable/satellite channel Sky One.

Wild, Wild Women

UK · BBC · SITCOM

7 × 30 mins · b/w

Pilot · 24 May 1968 · BBC1 Fri 8.20pm

One series (6) 6 Jan–10 Feb 1969 · BBC1 Mon 7.30pm

MAIN CAST

Millie	Barbara Windsor
Mr Harcourt	Derek Francis (pilot);
	Paul Whitsun-Jones (series)
Daisy	Penelope Keith (pilot);
	Pat Coombs (series)
Albert	Ken Platt (series)
Ruby	Sonia Fox (pilot);
	Toni Palmer (series)
Blossom	Jennie Paul (pilot);
	Jessie Robbins (series)
Ginny	Daphne Heard (series)
Flo	Yvonne Paul (series)
Maude	Anna Karen (series)
Mrs Harcourt	Joan Sanderson (series)
Clarence	Ronnie Stevens (pilot)
Lord Hurlingham	David Stoll (pilot)
Lady Hurlingham	Zena Howard (pilot)

CREDITS

writers Ronald Wolfe/Ronald Chesney · *producers* Philip Dale (pilot), Barry Lupino (series)

A period-piece variation on **The Rag Trade** from the same writers, Ronnie Wolfe and Ronnie Chesney, and starring Barbara Windsor (who appeared in that earlier series) as a young and sprightly cockney.

Windsor was cast as Millie, the leader of a group of garment workers in a milliner's shop, catering to the fashion demands of British women in 1902. As with *The Rag Trade*, the comedy developed from the conflict between the workers and the management (Harcourt and his apprentice Albert), but an extra spin was applied to the situation by the atmosphere of female emancipation that was gripping the nation at

the time. Hence, the women assumed a new, feisty spirit as they slowly shrugged off male domination and began to demand equal rights. British 'sauce' was added by way of Harcourt's lecherous leanings and the women's frank discussions on subjects once deemed unladylike.

Although energetic and handsomely mounted, *Wild, Wild Women* failed to attract the same measure of popularity as *The Rag Trade* and, after the initial *Comedy Playhouse* pilot, lasted for just one series. Way down in the regular cast list was Anna Karen (actually Anna Karon in these credits), whom Wolfe and Chesney steered to sitcom stardom soon afterwards as the dowdy Olive in **On The Buses** (and also in the 1977–78 ITV revival of *The Rag Trade*).

Note. Ken Platt, who played Albert, had previously figured in the starring role in a single-episode sitcom screened only in local areas by the Midlands/North ITV weekend franchise ABC. Titled *Daft As A Brush*, it aired late-night on 2 December 1967 within a *Comedy Playhouse*-style strand titled *Comedy Tonight*. Platt was cast as Ken, a painter and decorator who gets into trouble with the daughter of one of his clients, played by the lovely Aimi MacDonald. The idea, which was not developed into a series, was written by Alec Travis and produced for ABC by Pat Johns.

Wilderness Road

UK · BBC · SITCOM

6 × 30 mins · colour

21 July–25 Aug 1986 · BBC1 Mon 8.30pm

MAIN CAST

Moon	Robin Driscoll
Cage	David Sibley
Alan	Peter Jonfield
Keith	Gary Olsen
Arch	Leslie Sands
Nancy	Veronica Quilligan

CREDITS

writers Richard Cottan/Bob Goody · *director* Susan Belbin · *producer* John Kilby

A quirky slice of street life, centring around Cage and Moon, two bantering pals and their unlikely acquaintances, stripper Nancy and dour pub landlord Arch. The series was written by actor-writers Richard Cottan and Bob Goody.

Episodes charted the lads' attempt to make something of themselves. Although often divided in thought, they are united in adversity as they try to avoid the menacing Alan and Keith, two heavies working for a mysterious and dodgy individual who seems intent upon taking over the business in Wilderness Road, including the pub, the Sun, which doubles as Moon and Cage's place of business and home.

Will The Real Mike Yarwood Stand Up?

see YARWOOD, Mike

William

UK · BBC · CHILDREN'S SITCOM

12 × 25 mins · b/w

Series One (6) 26 May–30 June 1962 · Sat 5.25pm

Series Two (6) 30 Mar–4 May 1963 · Sat 5.25pm

MAIN CAST

William Brown	Dennis Waterman
	(series 1);
	Denis Gilmore (series 2)
Ginger	Christopher Witty
Henry	Bobby Bannerman (series 1);
	Kaplan Kaye (series 2)
Douglas	Carlo Cura
Violet Elizabeth Bott	Gillian Gostling
Mrs Brown	Patricia Marmont
Mr Brown	Lockwood West
Ethel Brown	Suzanne Neve
Mrs Bott	Marjorie Gresley

CREDITS

creator Richmal Crompton · *adapter/writer* C E Webber · *producer* Leonard Chase

When she wrote her first *William* story for the women's magazine *Home* in 1917, Richmal Crompton could not have imagined the life that her creation would assume, going on to appear in 38 *William* books, in feature films (*Just William's Luck*, 1947, and, the following year, *William Comes To Town* [aka *William Goes To The Circus*], both directed by Val Guest), in stage-plays, various BBC radio series (most famously the first attempt, which ran from 1945 to 1952), this 1960s television series, the 1970s ITV series **Just William** and a 1990s BBC revival of the same name. The childless Crompton, who died in 1968, claimed to have based the mischief-making, trouble-finding lad partly on a nephew and partly on her brothers. Following an attack of polio in 1924, she gave up schoolteaching and produced the first full-length novel based upon the character whom she had previously written about for magazines. Originally intended for an adult readership, the stories soon accrued great popularity with younger readers and so she concentrated on writing for them.

In 1946 TV viewers saw William Brown in the flesh for the first time when John Clark and Jacqueline Boyer (who played Violet Elizabeth), starring at that time in the radio version, appeared in character in *Just William At The Zoo* (25 August 1946), a special edition of the popular *At The Zoo* series. The following year (23 December 1947) BBC cameras visited the Granville Theatre in Fulham, south-west London, and showed a full *Just William* stage-play in which, once again, John Clark played the title role. Then, on 24 January 1951, the BBC presented *Just William* as a 75-minute television play targeted at family viewing – Robert Sandford took the lead in the production which was written by Alick Hayes and directed by Joy Harington.

For this 1960s television series, child actor Dennis Waterman – later more famous as a TV tough guy in dramas *The Sweeney* and *Minder* – was a particularly good choice, possessing an impish, mischievous demeanour. In the second series Waterman was replaced by 14-year-old Denis Gilmore, who, according to press reports, was turning down an attractive American movie offer (he had worked for Disney in the past) to appear as William. In a *Radio Times* article accompanying the 1994 television series, Gilmore revealed that he still had a book signed by Richmal Crompton indicating how much she had enjoyed his portrayal of the character.

Note. Richmal Crompton herself appeared on TV for the first time in October 1947, when she talked to the BBC's new radio William, Julian Denham.

'Wilton's' – The Handsomest Hall In Town

UK · BBC · STANDUP

1 × 45 mins · colour

26 Dec 1970 · BBC2 Sat 6.30pm

MAIN CAST

John Wilton · · · · · · · · · · · · · · · · Bill Fraser
E W Mackney · · · · · · · · · · · · · Spike Milligan
Gus Elen · · · · · · · · · · · · · · · Warren Mitchell
J W Page · · · · · · · · · · · · · · · · Eric Robinson

WITH

Peter Sellers
Keith Michell
Pat Kirkwood
Ronnie Barker
Billy Russell
Gina Astralita

CREDITS

writer Jimmy Perry · *producer* Michael Mills

A seasonal television tribute to Wilton's Music Hall, a popular London venue situated just off Cable Street in Wapping, by the River Thames. The hall had been built behind a public house, the Prince of Denmark, by the owner of that establishment, John Wilton, and it was open for business from 1857 to 1887, during which time many of the period's top acts performed there.

In this TV production, a top-rank billing of current comedians and entertainers impersonated those stars of yesteryear to re-create the flavour of an 1860 night at Wilton's. Special permission was obtained to reopen the venue for this one night only, and part of the programme's budget was spent in partially restoring the hall to its former

glories. Having survived the ravages of the Second World War and dereliction, Wilton's has continued to be looked after, and, to the pleasure of many, remains intact at the time of writing (1997).

Appropriately, the programme was introduced by Billy Russell, who achieved fame in the 1920s with his character Old Bill, a blustering, wheezy First World War veteran he had based on Bruce Bairnsfather's walrus-moustached cartoon character seen in *Punch* at the time. After enjoying success in his later years as a character actor, Russell died in 1971.

The Wim Sonneveld Show

UK · BBC · STANDUP

1 × 45 mins · b/w

25 Feb 1959 · Wed 8.30pm

MAIN CAST

Wim Sonneveld
Ellen Vogel
Hans Van Manen
Albert Mol
Joop Doderer
Johnny Jordaan

CREDITS

writer Wim Sonneveld · *producer* Dennis Main Wilson

A rare chance for British viewers to see the versatile Dutch comedian Wim Sonneveld, who brought some of his associates over from Holland with him, including dancer and choreographer Hans Van Menan. The studio antics were supplemented by some filmed sketches.

Sonneveld was first seen by British viewers as one of the performers in the all-star television musical *Hit The Headlines* (BBC, 5 April 1957), a 90-minute spectacular that also starred Terry-Thomas and Dickie Valentine and was written by Ray Galton and Alan Simpson for the series *The World Our Stage*.

Wink To Me Only

UK · BBC · SITCOM

7 × 30 mins · b/w

Pilot *View By Appointment* 3 May 1968 · BBC1 Fri 8.20pm

One series (6) 11 June–16 July 1969 · BBC1 Wed 8.20pm

MAIN CAST

Sydney Jelliot · · · · · · · · · · · · · Hugh Paddick
Irene (Rene) Jelliot · · · · · · · · · · · Beryl Reid
Marjorie · · · · · · · · · · · Pauline Collins (pilot)
Jimmy · · · · · · · · · · · · · Derek Fowlds (pilot)

CREDITS

writer Jennifer Phillips · *producers* Robin Nash (pilot), Douglas Argent (series)

In the *Comedy Playhouse* pilot, *View By Appointment*, the Jelliots are a friendless

couple who decide to attract company by putting their house up for sale and treating potential purchasers as guests to be wined and dined. This habit of solving problems in bizarre ways formed the basis of the ensuing series, *Wink To Me Only*. Jennifer Phillips (one of the few women sitcom writers of the time) designed the premise with Beryl Reid and Hugh Paddick in mind for the principal roles.

Winning Widows

UK · ITV (ATV) · SITCOM

13 × 30 mins · b/w

Series One (6) 9 Sep–18 Nov 1961 · fortnightly Sat mostly 9.30pm

Series Two (7) 21 Sep–2 Nov 1962 · Fri 9.15pm

MAIN CAST

Martha · · · · · · · · · · · · · · · · · Peggy Mount
Mildred · · · · · · · · · · · · · · · · · Avice Landon

CREDITS

writers Sid Green/Dick Hills · *directors* Colin Clews/Dicky Leeman (series 1) · *producer* Alan Tarrant

When *The Larkins* appeared to have finished (in fact, it returned in 1963, after three years off screen), ATV teamed Peggy Mount, the raging battleaxe star of that series, with its producer Alan Tarrant, in *Winning Widows*, scripted by Sid Green and Dick Hills.

Here, Mount played … a raging battleaxe, Martha, who, like her sister Mildred, is a widow. Each sister has been married three times and now, approaching the third age, they decide to cut costs and live together, hoping to settle down in their semi-detached villa just outside London and live out the rest of their lives in relative peace. It doesn't work out as well as they intended, of course. Menacing and livid in equal measure, Martha is a ranting, rabble-rousing realist. Mildred, however, is of the childlike, trembling romantic sort, prone to finding herself in embarrassing situations, especially with the male of the species, a position with which Martha – in a most vocal fashion – certainly has no truck.

Men, in one shape or another, formed the basis for the sisters' troubles, and *Winning Widows*, appearing virtually a decade before *The Liver Birds*, was the first sitcom in which two women were the focus. Male guest stars appeared in each second series episode, among them Pete Murray, Hugh Paddick, Davy Kaye, Bernard Cribbins, Ronnie Stevens, David Stoll (who also appeared twice in the first run), Wallas Eaton, Joe Melia and the pop singer Craig Douglas, for whom – in a most unlikely scenario – the sisters decided to run a fan club.

Mike And Bernie Winters

Mike Weinstein (born in Islington, north London, on 15 November 1930) and Bernie Weinstein (ditto, 6 September 1932) were brothers who formed a double-act and became famous, after a change of surname, as Mike and Bernie Winters, one of the foremost such partnerships in Britain in the 1960s. Although rarely able to escape the shadow of Morecambe and Wise, they worked hard throughout the 1950s (mostly on stage) and 1960s–70s (ITV) until splitting the act in 1978.

The Winters filled the customary double-act roles – one (Bernie) was dumb, the soft touch, tall, broad, and goofy in a toothy way; the other (Mike) was shorter, leaner, better looking, cooler and harder, often prompting Bernie, through frustration, to threaten him with what became his catchphrase, 'I'll smash your face in'. As designed, Mike did the feeding and Bernie got most of the laughs. They deliberately played on the fact that they were Jewish, with Bernie pulling Mike's cheeks and squawking 'choochy face' at given opportunities.

Accomplished musicians, Mike and Bernie entered show business in 1945, seriously from 1952, and slowly worked their way up the comedy ladder, their earliest known TV appearance being in the BBC's *Variety Parade* on 25 June 1955. A couple of years later they occupied a comedy slot in British TV's first pop show, *Six-Five Special* (BBC, 1957–58), and then it was a long wait, with ubiquitous appearances in other peoples' shows, until ABC gave them their biggest break: inviting them to host the weekly variety series *Big Night Out* and *Blackpool Night Out* from 1963 to 1965. From there they were on their way.

The act broke up, acrimoniously, in 1978, with Mike going into business in America and Bernie signing a deal with Thames TV that saw him score much success with game- and quiz-shows, and with the sketch series ***Bernie*** in which he found a new partner: a St Bernard dog whom he named Schnorbitz. The brothers made their peace in the 1980s but never worked together again, and Bernie died on 4 May 1991, aged just 58.

Mike And Bernie's Show   1

UK · ITV (ABC) · STANDUP/SKETCH

*10 × 35 mins · b/w

Series One (3) 3 Apr–24 Apr 1966 · Sun around 4.45pm

Series Two (7) 13 Aug–24 Sep 1966 · Sat 8.35pm

MAIN CAST
Mike Winters
Bernie Winters

CREDITS
writers John Warren/John Singer, John Muir/Eric Geen, Brad Ashton · *director* Keith Beckett

Following their considerable weekly exposure as hosts of *Big Night Out* and *Blackpool Night Out*, this was Mike and Bernie Winters' first own series. Lionel Blair, with his troupe of dancers, featured in every edition, as he had also done in those two variety seasons, and there was also a weekly slapstick sketch, with custard pies abounding.

*Note. The ten programmes were made in one stretch, in spring 1966, but they were aired as outlined, with a short run of three followed four months later by the remaining seven. The first three were not screened by London-area ITV.

Mike And Bernie's Music Hall

UK · ITV (ABC) · STANDUP/SKETCH

6 × 45 mins · b/w

18 Mar–22 Apr 1967 · Sat 5.45pm

MAIN CAST
Mike Winters
Bernie Winters

CREDITS
writers Brad Ashton, Steve Hyde, George Evans/Derek Collyer · *producer* Pat Johns

Comedy from the Winters and their guests (who altered from week to week but included Tommy Cooper and Ted Ray), with music.

Mike And Bernie's Show   2

UK · ITV (ABC) · STANDUP/SKETCH

3 × 45 mins · b/w

30 Dec 1967–13 Jan 1968 · Sat 6.15pm

MAIN CAST
Mike Winters
Bernie Winters

CREDITS
writers Brad Ashton, George Evans/Derek Collyer · *director* Tom Clegg · *producer* Pat Johns

Apart from the absence of dancer Lionel Blair these three shows repeated the same formula as the 1966 editions of *Mike And Bernie's Show*, with the Winters' supported by weekly guests (one of whom was the young Les Dawson).

Mike And Bernie's Show   3

UK · ITV (THAMES) · STANDUP/SKETCH

6 × 45 mins · b/w

13 Nov–18 Dec 1968 · Wed 6.45pm

MAIN CAST
Mike Winters
Bernie Winters

CREDITS
writers Brad Ashton, Wally Malston, Geoff Rowley/Andy Baker · *script editors* Jack Douglas, Brad Ashton · *producer* Pat Johns

A weekly series, with guests as usual, including a pastiche of *The Lone Ranger* that opened each edition.

Mike And Bernie's Show   4

UK · ITV (THAMES) · STANDUP/SKETCH

8 × 45 mins · b/w

30 June–1 Sep 1969 · Mon 6.45pm

MAIN CAST
Mike Winters
Bernie Winters

CREDITS
writers Peter Tonkinson and others · *script editor* Brad Ashton · *director/producer* Peter Frazer-Jones

More comedy and music (from guests) in the usual quantities.

Mike And Bernie's Scene

UK · ITV (THAMES) · STANDUP/SKETCH

7 × 45 mins · colour

27 Apr–8 June 1970 · Mon 6.45pm

MAIN CAST
Mike Winters
Bernie Winters

CREDITS
script editor Brad Ashton · *director/producer* Peter Frazer-Jones

Yet more comedy and music.

Mike And Bernie's Special: A Tale Of Two Winters

UK · ITV (THAMES) · STANDUP/SKETCH/ SITCOM

1 × 60 mins · colour

30 Sep 1970 · Wed 8pm

MAIN CAST
Mike Winters
Bernie Winters
Sacha Distel
Joan Collins
Des O'Connor
Peter Jones
Lionel Blair
Julie Ege

CREDITS
writers Vince Powell/Harry Driver · *director/producer* Peter Frazer-Jones

Something of an oddity this: a one-hour 'spectacular' (so-called) that mixed the Winters' usual jokey banter with music and also acting from guests in a situation-comedy setting written by the Powell/Driver partnership. As if all this wasn't unsettling enough, Joan Collins appeared as Des O'Connor's wife.

Mike And Bernie's Show 5

UK · ITV (THAMES) · SITCOM

1 × 60 mins · colour

9 June 1971 · Wed 8pm

MAIN CAST

Mike Winters · · · · · · · · · · · · · · · himself
Bernie Winters · · · · · · · · · · · · · · himself
Major Mills · · · · · · · · · · · · · Peter Jones
Col Muller · · · · · · · · · · · · Garfield Morgan
Gloria · · · · · · · · · · · · · · · · · Lynda Baron
Mrs Bolton · · · · · · · · · · · · · Patsy Smart
Joe Collier · · · · · · · · · · · · · · Bill Pertwee

CREDITS

writers Vince Powell/Harry Driver ·
director/producer Alan Tarrant

Further departing from their standup personae, here the Winters starred in their own epic life story, written for them by Powell and Driver. This was the brothers' first TV outing in which they had to act, and they were supported by other actors playing specified roles. One, Lynda Baron, was marking a TV comeback, having been out of the limelight since appearing as a topical comedy singer in *BBC-3* in 1965–66. Said comeback would lead, eventually, to *Open All Hours*.

Mike And Bernie

UK · ITV (THAMES) · SITCOM

6 × 30 mins · colour

14 Dec 1971–18 Jan 1972 ·
Tue mostly 6.55pm

MAIN CAST

Mike Winters · · · · · · · · · · · · · · himself
Bernie Winters · · · · · · · · · · · · · himself

CREDITS

writers Vince Powell/Harry Driver ·
director/producer Stuart Allen

Their recent TV shows had seen the Winters dipping a collective toe in the water of scripted situation comedy; in this six-part series they jumped right in. One is tempted to continue the metaphor and suggest that they were out of their depth, but perhaps it is safer to say, rather, that the series failed to make much of a splash. The pair were cast as starving, unsuccessful, unemployed music-hall comedians on the lookout for work, and the scrapes they got themselves into were, not to pussyfoot around, absolutely ridiculous.

Familiar faces appearing in one episode apiece included Peter Jones, Bill Pertwee, David Hamilton, Fred Emney, Sam Kydd, Roy Barraclough, Billy Dainty (twice) and, no joking, Chelsea footballers Peter Osgood, Ron Harris and Charlie Cooke.

Mike And Bernie Winters' All-Star Christmas Comedy Carnival

see All-Star Comedy Carnival

The Mike And Bernie Show 1

UK · ITV (THAMES) · STANDUP/SKETCH

1 × 60 mins · colour

21 June 1972 · Wed 8pm

MAIN CAST

Mike Winters
Bernie Winters
Bob Todd
Patrick Cargill
Millicent Martin

CREDITS

writer Eric Merriman · director/producer Keith Beckett

Following their sitcom adventures, Mike and Bernie returned to standup and sketch material with this one-off Thames special, produced for them by Keith Beckett, who had worked with the brothers in the ABC days of 1966.

Mike And Bernie's Show 6

UK · ITV (THAMES) · STANDUP/SKETCH

1 × 60 mins · colour

9 Aug 1972 · Wed 8pm

MAIN CAST

Mike Winters
Bernie Winters
Kenneth Haigh
Barbara Murray

CREDITS

writer Eric Merriman · director/producer Keith Beckett

Guests here were recruited from two of ITV's drama series: Kenneth Haigh (starring at this time as Joe Lampton in *Room At The Top*) and Barbara Murray (Lady Wilder in *The Power Game*).

Mike And Bernie's Show: The Redman And Ross Story

UK · ITV (THAMES) · SITCOM

1 × 60 mins · colour

1 Jan 1973 · Mon 10.30pm

MAIN CAST

Charlie Ross · · · · · · · · · · · · · Mike Winters
Joe Redman · · · · · · · · · · · · Bernie Winters
Willie Topple · · · · · · · · · · · · · Peter Noone
Pauline Ross · · · · · · · · · · · · · Sylvia Syms
Jenny Jones · · · · · · · · · · · · · Sheila White
Barnie Balham · · · · · · · · · · Reginald Marsh
Gerard Prince · · · · · · · · · · · · Derek Francis

CREDITS

writer Ronnie Taylor · director/producer Peter Frazer-Jones

A one-off special that saw Mike and Bernie playing other people for the first time: they appeared as Redman and Ross, a fictional comedy duo touring in revue, living in digs and hating the sight of each other. The programme was scripted for them by Ronnie Taylor but it accurately presaged the

Winters' own acrimonious falling out that occurred a few years later.

The Mike And Bernie Show 2

UK · ITV (ATV) · STANDUP/SKETCH

6 × 60 mins · colour

31 Mar–9 June 1973 · Sat mostly 5.50pm

MAIN CAST

Mike Winters
Bernie Winters

CREDITS

writer Bryan Blackburn · directors Colin Clews, Paul Stewart Laing · producer Colin Clews

Back to basics: comedy, music and Lionel Blair's dancing.

Norman Wisdom

One of the greatest British comics of all time – a legend in his own lifetime, indeed – Norman Wisdom was born in Marylebone, London, on 4 February 1915. He endured a particularly harsh childhood, obtaining only a rudimentary education and having to work from an early age in order to survive – at 14 he was a miner, at 15 a cabin boy on a freighter, and many other such menial jobs followed, each only for a brief period. Before his sixteenth birthday Wisdom was penniless, and sleeping rough on the streets. A kindly coffee-stall owner who provided occasional free drinks then suggested that the youngster enrol as a bandsman in the army. This he did, and his potential as an entertainer became apparent here. Wisdom appeared at concert parties, mixing dancing and comedy, and he also became flyweight boxing champion of his regiment. But instead of choosing the sport for his career he opted for show business – knockabout rather than knockouts – and under the stage name Dizzy Wizzy scored his first success as a physical comedian. He turned professional in 1946, billed as 'Norman Wisdom, The Successful Failure'.

A period of touring followed, and Wisdom made his TV debut on 22 November 1947 in the programme *Variety*, but still his career was hardly in good shape. The next year, however, he struck gold – when deputising for an indisposed entertainer he gained rave word-of-mouth reviews that brought him to the attention of impresario Val Parnell. The big man wanted to employ Wisdom for a show at the London Palladium but the comic was already under contract to Parnell's rival, the Delfont agency; Bernard Delfont decided Wisdom should play at *his* theatre, the London Casino, and he was soon top of the

London Casino, and he was soon top of the bill and on the road to lasting fame.

Wisdom managed to succeed in all mediums: TV, record, stage and, particularly, feature films. Although best remembered for the many movies in which he starred as his famous 'Gump' character – an innocent but game chap, imbued with pathos and dressed in a suit two sizes too small – he became a truly international star, hugely popular not only in Britain and Commonwealth countries but in the most unlikely of places such as Albania and remote areas of the former Soviet Union, where his personal appearances filled stadiums. Fans of great comedy everywhere have warmed to the archetypal little funny man who is a master at all forms of physical comedy and can so expertly turn from tears of joy to tears of sadness within seconds.

Wisdom fulfilled many television engagements – as listed below – but arguably his greatest achievements on the small-screen were his appearances on *Val Parnell's Sunday Night At The London Palladium*, ITV's flagship variety series. He made six, but it was the final two that merit particular mention. On both 29 November 1959 and 3 December 1961, Wisdom and the show's host, Bruce Forsyth, performed the entire hour without support acts, combining inventive performances of song, patter and spectacular slapstick and including (on both occasions) the famous sketch in which the pair played inept decorators. Thankfully, the second show survives on film, a marvellous TV record of Wisdom at his greatest.

Since the mid-1970s, Norman Wisdom's feature appearances (that is, beyond chat-shows) on British television have been confined to tributes and documentaries. The first to be screened was *Just Wisdom* (C4, 27 December 1986) which mixed clips of his best TV, film and stage moments with newly shot stage material. The star also looked back over his life and career in a particularly compelling edition of LWT's arts series *The South Bank Show* (ITV, 22 August 1993).

Wisdom has also scored as a straight actor, demonstrating an unexpected talent for serious drama, especially with his tour de force performance as a man dying from cancer in BBC2's *Playhouse* presentation *Going Gently*, screened on 5 June 1981.

See also *Cuckoo College* and *Vic's Grill*.

Wit And Wisdom

UK · BBC · SKETCH

2 × 45 mins · b/w

18 Oct 1948 · Mon 3pm
30 Aug 1950 · Wed 8.45pm

MAIN CAST
Norman Wisdom

CREDITS
producer Richard Afton

At the time of the first of these shows, in 1948, Wisdom had enjoyed a rapid elevation from middle-of-the-bill comedian to star, thanks to an audience-storming appearance on a London Casino variety bill. The 29-year-old who had billed himself as 'The New British Comedian', was duly – and rightly – hailed as 'the next big thing'.

The first of these two shows was subtitled '45 Minutes Of High Speed Variety' and it starred Wisdom with a number of acts, including international comedians the Arnaut Brothers. As was customary at the time, the entire cast re-assembled for a repeat performance later in the week (20 October, 8.30pm).

The Norman Wisdom Show   1

UK · BBC · SKETCH

1 × 60 mins · b/w

27 Feb 1952 · Sat 8.15pm

MAIN CAST
Norman Wisdom
Eddie Leslie

CREDITS
writer Eddie Leslie · *additional material* Clifford Stanton · *producer* Bill Lyon-Shaw

An hour-long comedy spectacular showcasing the multi-talented Wisdom, with his comic foil Eddie Leslie.

Norman Wisdom

UK · BBC · STANDUP

1 × 20 mins · b/w

27 July 1952 · Sun 8.25pm

MAIN CAST
Norman Wisdom

CREDITS
writer Eddie Leslie · *producer* Bill Lyon-Shaw

A one-off special in which Wisdom reprised some of favourite routines at the request of viewers.

The Norman Wisdom Show   2

UK · BBC · SKETCH

3 × 60 mins · b/w

6 Oct–1 Dec 1956 · monthly Sat 9pm

MAIN CAST
Norman Wisdom
Eddie Leslie

CREDITS
writers Norman Wisdom and others · *producer* Ernest Maxin

Wisdom was a huge star by this time, managing the incredibly difficult achievement of succeeding on stage, in films,

as a singing star and on television. The series was presented under the banner *Saturday Comedy Hour*.

The Norman Wisdom Show   3

UK · ITV (ATV) · SKETCH/STANDUP

1 × 60 mins · b/w

21 Sep 1957 · Sat 8.30pm

MAIN CAST
Norman Wisdom

CREDITS
director/producer Bill Lyon-Shaw

Screened under the banner *Val Parnell's Saturday Spectacular*.

Wisdom made no further regular TV appearances for some 13 years after this – although he continued to appear as a star guest in other shows and in chat-shows – preferring to concentrate on his film and stage work.

Norman

UK · ITV (ATV) · SITCOM

6 × 30 mins · colour

2 Apr–7 May 1970 · Thu 9pm

MAIN CAST
Norman Wilkins · · · · · · · · · Norman Wisdom
Mrs Tate · · · · · · · · · · · · · · · · Sally Bazely
Frank Baker · · · · · · · · · · · · · · David Lodge

CREDITS
writers Ray Cooney/John Chapman · *director/producer* Alan Tarrant

His fine film career winding to a close, this was Norman Wisdom's first starring television sitcom. Alas, it was not a great start. Scripted by farceurs Cooney and Chapman – who had written *Not Now, Darling*, the successful London stage-play and feature film which, with Wisdom new to the starring role, had sadly flopped on Broadway – it tried to straddle the fence between sophistication, slapstick and surrealism, and never quite effected the balance. At the very least, however, it proved that there was more to Our Norman than his legendary 'Gump' character, stumbling around in his too-tight jacket yelling 'Mr Grimsdale'. In *Norman* (Norman *always* seemed to play 'Norman'), Wisdom quit a deathly boring nine-to-five job with the Inland Revenue in dramatic fashion, flinging his in-tray through the window and punching a fist-sized hole in his bowler-hat, and so was free to pursue a talent for music, plunging into one sorry weekly situation after another, heaped with accidents and 'ooh-er'-type misunderstandings.

Note. Wisdom's association with ATV at this time, preceding *Norman*, began with a variety series made in England – and screened by ITV – but aimed primarily at an

American TV sale. (It went out there from 14 May to 13 August 1969 as *Kraft Music Hall Presents Sandler & Young*.) Wisdom was a recurring guest, generating laughter from his tomfoolery, singing and dancing, and playing alongside the main stars – the singers Tony Sandler and Ralph Young – as well as Judy Carne (the English 'sock it to me' comedian from *Rowan And Martin's Laugh-In*) and occasional guests such as Ella Fitzgerald, Lena Horne and, most regularly, the American comic giant Sid Caesar. The scripts were written by Sid Green/Dick Hills and Gordon Farr and the British screenings began on 21 September 1969 and, in a shortened second batch, 2 July 1970.

Nobody Is Norman Wisdom

UK · ITV (ATV) · SITCOM

6 × 30 mins · colour

26 June–7 Aug 1973 · Tue around 7pm

MAIN CAST
Nobody · · · · · · · · · · · · · Norman Wisdom
Mother · · · · · · · · · · · · · · · Natalie Kent
Grace · · · · · · · · · · · · · · Priscilla Morgan

CREDITS
creators Watt Nicholl/John Sichel · *writers* Watt Nicholl/John Sichel/Bob Hedley · *director/producer* John Scholz-Conway

As Norman Wisdom's film career is sprinkled with sparkling gems so his latter-day TV career is littered with single-series flops, the sum total of which robbed the great little man of a rousing end to a memorable career. *Nobody Is Norman Wisdom* – in which Norman was Nobody, in every sense of the word – was a sorry attempt to master the sitcom genre. Not for the first time, Wisdom portrayed the archetypal little man battling against the world, and also here against an domineering mother – a role that another comic to whom the term diminutive could be applied, Ronnie Corbett, also felt obliged to explore in sitcoms.

In *Nobody Is Norman Wisdom*, Nobody has a girlfriend, Grace, who encourages him to expand his horizons and live out his Walter Mitty-like fantasies. Peter Glaze, Windsor Davies, Henry McGee and David Lodge were among the recognisable faces helping out (one episode each) – to no avail. While Wisdom's hope that the series could do without an audience or canned-laughter and would stand or fall on its own merits went sadly awry – it fell.

A Little Bit Of Wisdom

UK · ITV (ATV) · SITCOMS

20 × 30 mins · colour

Series One (7) 9 Apr–21 May 1974 · Tue 7.05pm

Series Two (6) 10 Jan–14 Feb 1975 · Fri 7pm
Series Three (7) 30 Mar–11 May 1976 · Tue 7.05pm

MAIN CAST
Norman · · · · · · · · · · · · · · · Norman Wisdom
Albert Clark · · · · · Robert Keegan (series 3)
Linda Clark · · · · · · Frances White (series 3)
Alec Potter · · · · · · · Neil McCarthy (series 3)

CREDITS (SERIES 1 & 2)
writers Lew Schwarz (4), Dick Sharples (2), John Kane (1), Max Marquis (1), Philip Parsons (1), Jon Watkins (1), not known (3) · *script editor* Dick Sharples · *director/producer* John Scholz-Conway

CREDITS (SERIES 3)
writers John Kane (3), Lew Schwarz (2), Ronnie Taylor (1), Jon Watkins (1) · *directors* Les Chatfield, Keith Farthing · *producer* Les Chatfield

A vehicle for Norman Wisdom that changed its comedic approach: the first two series (13 episodes) were individual comedy plays scripted by an assortment of writers, the only constant being Wisdom's buffoonish 'Norman' character. The third series was a traditional sitcom, with Norman – singularly ineligible – just about holding down a job as clerk in a builder's office run by Robert Keegan. Neil McCarthy was Norman's flatmate, while Frances White, who appeared with Wisdom in the feature film *A Stitch In Time*, playing Keegan's daughter and Norman's obligatory love interest.

It's Norman

UK · ITV (ATV) · SKETCH

1 × 60 mins · colour

28 Dec 1974 · Sat 8.30pm

MAIN CAST
Norman Wisdom
David Nixon
Terry Scott

CREDITS
writers Norman Wisdom, Jon Watkins, Philip Parson · *director/producer* John Scholz-Conway

A one-hour special featuring the little man clowning in the energetic manner that brought him millions of loyal fans.

The Norman Wisdom Show   4

UK · BBC · STANDUP

1 × 35 mins · colour

29 Dec 1976 · BBC2 Wed 8.25pm

MAIN CAST
Norman Wisdom
Rod Hull and Emu
Tony Fayne

CREDITS
writers Austin Steele and others · *director* Alan Boyd · *producer* John Ammonds

Wisdom returned to the BBC for this one-off, which he made on the understanding that a series would follow, although none did.

This was the BBC's entry in the Knokke Television Festival for 1976. Under the rules of the competition the competing TV services had three days in which to rehearse and produce a 30–35 minute comedy show, the winner being awarded the coveted top prize, The Golden Sea-swallow. *The Norman Wisdom Show* ostensibly utilised Wisdom's then stage-show, blending standup knockabout comedy with pathos, songs and general mayhem. The show started out billed as *The Tony Fayne Show* (a comedian in his own right, Fayne was Wisdom's long-time stage foil) but his attempts to open the show with a song were constantly interrupted by Wisdom, who sat in the audience but then climbed the stage to take over. The comic clowning, performed before an international audience, seemed to strike the right chord – Wisdom was a faultless performer of such routines – and the show duly won the top prize.

With Bird Will Travel

UK · ITV (ATV) · SKETCH

6 × 30 mins · b/w

26 June–31 July 1968 · Wed mostly 7pm

MAIN CAST
John Bird
Edward Hardwicke
Carmen Munroe

CREDITS
writer John Bird · *producer* John Sichel

Topical humour and political satire from writer/performer John Bird. He and Carmen Munroe were at the centre of each programme, 'directing' the sketch sequences from a TV control room.

WKRP In Cincinnati

USA · CBS (MTM ENTERPRISES) · SITCOM

90 × 30 mins · colour

US dates: 18 Sep 1978–20 Sep 1982
*UK dates: 3 Sep 1981–26 Dec 1988
(76 episodes) ITV/C4 various days and times

MAIN CAST
Andy Travis · · · · · · · · · · · · · · · · Gary Sandy
Jennifer Marlowe · · · · · · · · · · Loni Anderson
Arthur 'Big Guy' Carlson · · · · · · Gordon Jump
Les Nessman · · · · · · · · · · · Richard Sanders
Gordon 'Venus Flytrap' Sims · · · · · · Tim Reid
Herbert R Tarlek Jr · · · · · · · · · · Frank Bonner
Bailey Quarters · · · · · · · · · · · · Jan Smithers
Johnny 'Dr Johnny Fever' Caravella · · · · · · · ·
· Howard Hesseman
Lillian 'Mama' Carlson · · · · · · Sylvia Sidney
· (pilot);
· · · · · · · · · · · · · · · · · · Carol Bruce (series)
Carmen Carlson · · · · · · · · Allyn Ann McLerie
Lucille Tarlek · · · · · · · · · · · · · Edie McClurg
Hirsch · Ian Wolfe

CREDITS

creator/executive producer Hugh Wilson · *writers* various · *directors* Michael Zinberg, Asaad Kelada, Will MacKenzie, Rod Daniel, Linda Day and others · *producers* Blake Hunter, Bill Dial, Steven Kampmann, Peter Torokvei

One of the better American ensemble-sitcoms, *WKRP In Cincinnati* depicted the daily working lives of the personnel at what, at first, was a tranquil Ohio AM radio station, ineffectively managed by Arthur Carlson and owned by his domineering mother Lillian. WKRP – situated at 1530 on the dial – delivered continually poor ratings until one day (in the premiere episode), newly engaged programme director Andy Travis made a unilateral decision to kick out the jams and turn the station over to solid rock. Most of the staff took the switch well, some immediately developing new rock and roll personas. Mother Lillian, of course, was horrified, and not even the promise of a swing into profit within two years could placate her; however, she was so surprised to see her normally spineless son keenly defend the change that she acquiesced.

As mentioned, the nub of *WKRP In Cincinnati* was its ensemble humour. The lines were great but it was the characters who made the show so compelling and funny. The balding morning jock John Caravella dubbed himself Dr Johnny Fever and became a born-again silver-tongued hipster. A flamboyant black dude DJ, nicknamed Venus Flytrap and the Sultan Of Sound, took over the evening show; Les Nessman was the inflated news-reader and agricultural reporter prone to mispronunciations; wealthy Jennifer Marlowe was WKRP's sexy blonde (and deceptively intelligent) receptionist, disposed to wearing low-cut dresses; the station's only other woman, Bailey Quarters, was the general factotum; and the pressure-cooker sales manager Herb Tarlek wore clothes that were even louder than the rock music broadcast over the airwaves.

The series' four-year run embraced some fabulous comedy moments and running jokes and the series was a consistent ratings winner – most viewer's · favourite episode (aired by London-ITV on 8 October 1981) was the one with the Thanksgiving Giveaway prank, when, failing to realise that the birds could not fly, live turkeys were tossed out of a helicopter on to people in a car park. The final episode was riveting, with Lillian Carlson re-assessing her decision to allow the station to adopt rock and Johnny Fever staunchly defending the move.

Unable to leave a good idea alone, *WKRP In Cincinnati* was unwisely revived in 1991 with a bunch of consistently poor new episodes that went into what the Americans call 'first-run syndication' – that is, they were screened by independent stations, not the network-owned ones. (Some titled the new series *WKRP In Cincinnati*, others *The New WKRP In Cincinnati*.) These episodes – in which only four of the original characters were featured: Arthur Carlson, Les Nessman, Herb Tarlek and Lillian Carlson, flanked by a whole new supporting cast – have been carried on cable/satellite channels receivable in Britain but have not been screened by British terrestrial TV. This is no loss; indeed, those who have seen the 1990s episodes, and not the 1978–82 ones, can surely have no idea why the series is so admired.

*Note. British terrestrial screenings of the original 1978–82 episodes have been complicated. London-area ITV showed 12 episodes, dotted around the schedule, between 3 September 1981 and 3 September 1982. C4 then screened 26 episodes from 8 July 1983 to 24 September 1984 in more regular slots (Fridays 8.30pm, Fridays 5pm, Mondays 5.30pm). Then ITV screened 50 episodes – 38 previously unseen, 12 repeats – from 2 September 1987 to 26 December 1988, deep into Wednesday nights, first at 2.30am then 4am.

Wodehouse Playhouse

UK · BBC · SITCOMS

20 episodes (13 × 35 mins · 7 × 30 mins) · colour

Series One (7 × 30 mins) 23 Apr–4 June 1975 · BBC1 Wed 9.25pm

Series Two (6 × 35 mins) 26 Mar–7 May 1976 · BBC1 Fri 8.25pm

Series Three (7 × 35 mins) 31 Oct–12 Dec 1978 · BBC2 Tue 9.10pm

MAIN CAST

John Alderton
Pauline Collins (series 1 & 2)
P G Wodehouse (series 1)

CREDITS

creator P G Wodehouse · *adapter/writer* David Climie · *producers* David Askey (series 1), Michael Mills (series 2), Gareth Gwenlan (series 3)

Classy TV adaptations of the non-Wooster, non-Blandings Wodehouse short stories. Husband-and-wife team Alderton and Collins shared top billing in the first two series, supported by excellent guest casts, with Alderton and guests soldiering on alone for the final run of seven editions. The stories came from all corners of the Wodehouse world but there was particular emphasis on the extended Mulliner clan, with Alderton portraying various members of the eccentric family. P G Wodehouse was especially fond of these adaptations and appeared in person to introduce the seven first series stories, recorded just prior to his death at the age of 93 on 14 February 1975.

Note. Alderton continued his forays into the world of Wodehouse by reading three of the master's short stories in the five-part series *Welcome To Wodehouse*, a praiseworthy attempt by BBC1 to turn on children to the work of 'Plum', broadcast by BBC1 from 8 January to 5 February 1982. (Paul Eddington read the other two stories.)

See also *The World Of Wooster, Mr Wodehouse Speaking, The Reverent Wooing Of Archibald, Ukridge, Blandings Castle, Uncle Fred Flits By* and *Jeeves And Wooster*.

The Wolvis Family

UK · BBC · SATIRE

6 × 30 mins · colour

4 May–8 June 1991 · BBC2 Sat mostly 9.35pm

MAIN CAST

Dr Graham Wilcockson	Nicholas Woodeson
Herbert Wolvis	John Joyce
Sylvia Wolvis	Janet Dale
Wendy Wolvis	Honey Hazel
Stuart Wolvis	Charlie Condou
Spencer Hogg	Christopher Chescoe

CREDITS

writers Tim Lubbock/Roger Parsons · *director* Roger Parsons · *producer* Kevin Loader

When Stuart Wolvis runs away from home, West Byfleet social services track him down, finding that he is living rough with his friend, Spencer Hogg. Now safely ensconced back in the bosom of his loved ones – parents Herbert and Sylvia and sister Wendy – Stuart has stopped talking altogether. In an attempt to break through to their once-happy son, the Wolvis family (and Spencer) agree to a series of therapy sessions, in front of a television studio audience, with counsellor Dr Graham Wilcockson. The resulting sessions uncover many secrets perhaps best left untold, and peel back the veneer of the Wolvises' apparent normality to reveal a truly bizarre family.

This genuinely radical attempt to achieve something new within the field of TV comedy could easily have been mistaken for the real thing by any unsuspecting viewer accidentally tuning in. The actors played the scripts dead straight, which made the strange situations and bizarre revelations even more shocking, yet still believable. The series' intensity and introverted mood meant that it did not suit all tastes, but it certainly deserves full marks for effort and originality. A forgotten gem.

The Wonder Years

USA · ABC (THE BLACK-MARLENS COMPANY/ NEW WORLD TELEVISION) · SITCOM

114 episodes (113 × 30 mins · 1 × 60 mins) · colour

US dates: 31 Jan 1988–12 May 1993

UK dates: 20 Aug 1989–6 June 1993 (115 × 30 mins) C4 Sun 6.30pm

MAIN CAST

Kevin Arnold	Fred Savage
(adult voice by Daniel Stern)	
Jack Arnold	Dan Lauria
Norma Arnold	Alley Mills
Karen Arnold	Olivia d'Abo
Wayne Arnold	Jason Hervey
Gwendolyn 'Winnie' Cooper	
	Danica McKellar
Paul Pfeiffer	Josh Saviano

OTHER APPEARANCES

Coach Ed Cutlip	Robert Picardo

CREDITS

creators Neal Marlens/Carol Black · writers Mark B Perry (16), Bob Brush (13), Matthew Carlson (10), Mark Levin (10), Todd W Langen (7), Sy Rosen (7), David M Stern (7), Carol Black/Neal Marlens (6), Craig Hoffman (6), Jon Jarmon Feldman (5) and others · directors Michael Dinner (20), Ken Topolsky (13), Steve Miner (10), Daniel Stern (10), Peter Baldwin (9), Nick Marck (6) and others · executive producers Neal Marlens/Carol Black, Bob Brush, Michael Dinner, Sy Rosen · producers David Chambers, Michael Dinner, Ken Topolsky, Denise Moss, Sy Dukane, Mark B Perry, Mark Levin

Episodes in the life of a boy – Kevin Arnold, excellently played by child actor Fred Savage – passing through his early teenage years in the late-1960s and early-1970s. The stories were recounted from the perspective of 20 years hence, Kevin's adult voice narrating his younger self's thoughts and feelings. From this distance, the man is able to see the value in life's rich tapestry of learning, no matter how painful the experiences may have been at the time.

Shot on film, The Wonder Years was essentially a series of very watchable essays about middle-class suburban family life, and although it was set in the epochal late-1960s it could also hold true for any period. Just about classifiable as a sitcom – the term 'dramady' has also been used to describe it – the series was unsurpassed for making people smile, the humour emanating from scenes of poignancy as much as anything else. In essence, then, The Wonder Years was not a million miles from the movie Summer Of '42, generating soul warmth rather than rip-snorting laughs. But perhaps its closest antecedent was Rob Reiner's 1986 movie Stand By Me, which similarly depicted life seen through the eyes of a 12-year-old and likewise employed the device of an off-screen adult narrator (the boy grown up) to put the story in context.

The series ran in 'real time', its storylines spanning the five years that it was on air, beginning in 1968, when Kevin was a 12-year-old just starting out at Robert F Kennedy Junior High School, passing through to McKinley High School and then into young adulthood and summer jobs in 1973. Along the way Kevin matured from skateboarding kid to adolescence, experiencing everything from first dates to first kisses, by way of a broken voice and zits. Kevin's parents, Jack and Norma, were wartime children finding it hard to adjust to 1960s liberalism. Norma tended to over-mother Kevin while Jack, mostly at work, communicated with him in the way that most men communicate: with great difficulty and in awkward emotion-repressed moments. Kevin's elder sister Karen was a flower-child and his elder brother Wayne teased him relentlessly. Kevin's best friend was Paul, a gangly bespectacled individual, and his best girl was the feisty Winnie Cooper, who lived over the road. Kevin and Winnie fashioned a relationship that was more on-off than a light switch, but deep-rooted all the same. By 1990 Karen had moved out of the Arnold house, leaving the series in 1992; she returned in the final episode (screened in America as an hour-length programme but in Britain as two half-hours), heavily pregnant and about to make Kevin an uncle.

That final episode was a humdinger, but it also frustrated the show's producers, who, latterly, had been feeling hampered by the ABC network's prudishness. Naturally, as Kevin matured, so the series needed to broaden its perspective. But ABC insisted that even a tastefully filmed one-second shot of Kevin tenderly placing his hand on a woman's breast for the first time be excised. In the final episode, a pivotal sequence in which Kevin and Winnie faced up to their unbreakable bond was faded out before any indication arrived on screen that, as the producers wished, they make love for the first time. Whatever, at the end of the episode, Kevin's adult voice revealed the events in their lives from this point on: his father died two years later; his mother became a successful businesswoman; Wayne took over Jack's furniture business; Paul went to Harvard to study law and Winnie went to France to study art history. But she and Kevin kept their promise to remain in contact – they wrote to each other weekly for eight years and when she returned to the USA he met her at the airport … with his wife and eight-month-old first son.

Although its theme song was Joe Cocker's hit version of the Beatles' 'With A Little Help From My Friends', and every episode included appropriately selected pop songs of the era, The Wonder Years never traded on nostalgia value alone. Essentially the brainchild of husband-and-wife team Neal Marlens and Carol Black – who created the series, produced it for their own company, sometimes wrote and occasionally directed the episodes – its intention, to quote executive producer Bob Brush, was never to be 'in the business of providing America with a happy half-hour'. But the 114 episodes had just such an effect.

See also **Boy Meets World**.

Victoria Wood

Born on 19 May 1953 in Prestwich, Lancashire (but raised in Bury), Victoria Wood was studying drama and theatre arts at Birmingham University when, in 1974, she auditioned for the talent-spotting ATV series New Faces. Billed as someone who could 'write and sing her own music' she passed the audition, went on the show and won, but her victory amounted to little at this stage beyond slightly improved cabaret bookings and a place in a five-week August 1975 ATV series for New Faces winners, **The Summer Show**. Odd TV spots came and went after this and Wood did not appear regularly in the medium until spring 1976 when the BBC1 consumer programme That's Life engaged her each week to sing a topical song at the piano. Still real success eluded her, and when Wood went out on tour at this time as support to Jasper Carrott few people laughed.

Victoria Wood's breakthrough came with the writing (dialogue and music) of her first play, when aged 24. Titled Talent, it was good enough to be noticed by Granada, which, under the Screenplay banner, put it on television on 5 August 1979, the eve of the long ITV industrial dispute. Set in a northern night-club, Talent depicted two young women: the sexy and ambitious Julie, an aspiring singer in the Shirley Bassey mould, and her more tentative overweight friend Maureen; Julie Walters played Julie and Wood herself was cast as Maureen, the two cementing a recently discovered friendship that went on to bring delight to millions. Talent won Wood three prestigious writing awards, including those given by Plays And Players and Evening Standard, and two more fine plays followed: Nearly A Happy Ending (Granada for ITV, 1 June 1980), again featuring the Julie and Maureen characters; and Happy Since I Met You (Granada for ITV, 9 August 1981), a bittersweet but humorous tale of a relationship between Frances (Julie Walters) and Jim (Duncan Preston), in which Wood did not appear.

Before this third Granada drama, however, Wood and Walters had embarked upon a run of sketch shows with that title, a series that lead to the classic 1985–86 BBC series As Seen On TV, which was so good as to make Victoria Wood a prized national treasure.

A Victoria Wood script will always stand out from the crowd and be distinctively hers. She is a concise writer at once able to make her work meaningful by speaking the language of the viewer or listener. Her vocabulary conjures up real images of everyday life from an acutely British perspective. At the same time, though, her use of surrealistic imagery can send the mind reeling into uncharted waters. Whether or not she sees it this way, Victoria Wood is surely of the same mould as Alan Bennett, possessing an aural vision that can draw the humour out of everyday mundanity. She is a naturally witty woman with a gift for making people see the funny side of life. Moreover, she seems a genuinely pleasant person. Still only in her forties, we will, hopefully, be blessed with the pleasure of Victoria Wood's wit and wisdom for decades to come.

Victoria Wood was the subject of LWT/ITV's arts programme *The South Bank Show* on 15 September 1996.

See also Comic Relief.

Wood And Walters

UK · ITV (GRANADA) · SKETCH

8 × 30 mins · colour

Special *Two Creatures Great And Small* 1 Jan 1981 · Thu 10.20pm

One series (7) 1 Jan–21 Feb 1982 · mostly Sun 10pm

MAIN CAST
Victoria Wood
Julie Walters

CREDITS
writer Victoria Wood · *director* Stuart Orme · *producers* Peter Eckersley (special), Brian Armstrong (series)

A not always brilliant – but not far short of it – sketch series starring two fast-emerging talents. At the very least, *Wood And Walters*, a fine blend of comedy sketches and comedy songs, showed a great promise that would be delivered to perfection in *As Seen On TV*. (The series was given a repeat airing on C4 from 29 May 1983, after Walters had become a film star in *Educating Rita*.)

Wood met the Smethwick-born Walters when aged 17 at Manchester Polytechnic – she was hoping to enrol there but wasn't accepted, whereas Walters, four years older, was coming to the end of her studies – and they didn't see each other again until the summer of 1978 when playing in revue at the Bush Theatre in London.

Another regular engagement for Wood at this time, anachronistic but probably valuable in terms of experience, was as the weekly musical support act in *The Little And Large Party*, a BBC Radio 2 series broadcast from 29 March to 17 May 1981. Among Wood's TV performances in this period, she introduced/narrated/appeared in an Arts Council film, *The Pantomime Dame*, looking at this unusual creation and some of its exponents (Arthur Askey, Billy Dainty, Terry Scott), screened by C4 on

16 December 1982. And she was the subject of a 20-minute BBC schools TV programme, *Scene*, first transmitted by BBC2 on 9 May 1985.

Victoria Wood – As Seen On TV

UK · BBC · SKETCH/STANDUP

13 editions (12 × 35 mins · 1 × 40 mins) · colour

Series One (6 × 35 mins) 11 Jan–15 Feb 1985 · BBC2 Fri 9pm

Series Two (6 × 35 mins) 10 Nov–15 Dec 1986 · BBC2 Mon 9.35pm

Special (40 mins) 18 Dec 1987 · BBC2 Fri 9pm

MAIN CAST
Victoria Wood
Julie Walters
Celia Imrie
Duncan Preston
Susie Blake

CREDITS
writer Victoria Wood · *director/producer* Geoff Posner

A regular company of fine performers, good production values, incisive scripts and a snappy pace added up to a five-star gem in *As Seen On TV*. The series rarely dipped below brilliant and featured numerous delights, such as Wood's hilariously authentic dialogue and her surprisingly stinging satirical characters (Susie Blake as a continuity announcer with 'attitude', incredibly bitchy daytime TV show hosts, venomously cruel gossips, and so on). All this plus the screamingly funny continuing TV soap spoof *Acorn Antiques*, with its wobbly sets, sensationalist plots, appalling acting, crude camerawork and dopey dialogue, uncannily reminiscent of bad soaps in general and *Crossroads* in particular.

Wood was the driving force but she was wonderfully served by a cast that seemed instinctively to understand how to reap maximum effect from already fine lines. *As Seen On TV* firmly established Wood as the leader of a happily increasing group of female comics (French and Saunders, Ruby Wax, Tracey Ullman, Emma Thompson) thriving in what was, hitherto, a virtually exclusively male domain.

Note. Highlights from the series were broadcast by BBC Radio 4 in two half-hour programmes (18 and 25 April 1992), as *Victoria Wood – As Heard On TV*.

An Audience With Victoria Wood

UK · ITV (LWT) · STANDUP

1 × 60 mins · colour

10 Dec 1988 · Sat 9.05pm

MAIN CAST
Victoria Wood

CREDITS
writer Victoria Wood · *executive producer* Nicholas Barrett · *director/producer* David G Hillier

One of the best editions of LWT's long running *An Audience With ...* series, Wood shining from first to last while entertaining an audience of celebrities and friends.

Victoria Wood

UK · BBC · SITCOMS

6 × 30 mins · colour

16 Nov–21 Dec 1989 · BBC1 Thu 8.30pm

As a departure from her sketch shows, Wood next made a series of individual comedy playlets, using some members of her regular troupe as well as guest actors.

Pleasing though it was to find the star unwilling to rest on her laurels, this series, while commendably ambitious, was a mite disappointing. Though filled with cracking dialogue and well-drawn characters, the witty lines seemed contrived in this environment, often at odds with the storyline. For other writers the series might have been considered a triumph; as a follow-on from *As Seen On TV* it was a trifle flat.

Mens Sana In Thingummy Doodah   16 NOV 1989

MAIN CAST

Victoria	Victoria Wood
Nicola	Julie Walters
Lill	Lill Roughley
Dana	Liza Tarbuck
Connie	Meg Johnson
Sallyanne	Georgia Allen

CREDITS
writer Victoria Wood · *director* Kevin Bishop · *producer* Geoff Posner

Attempting to be fit and thin means raw broccoli, saunas and trips to the gym. But Victoria thinks there must be more to life.

The Library   23 NOV 1989

MAIN CAST

Victoria	Victoria Wood
Sheila	Anne Reid
Madge	Carol Macready
John	Richard Kane
Keith	Philip Lowrie
Richard	David Henry
Ted	Danny O'Dea

CREDITS
writer Victoria Wood · *director/producer* Geoff Posner

Sheila comes to the library to play a dating-agency tape on the video machine. Well-meaning Victoria tries to help the path of true love but it all goes badly wrong.

Over To Pam
30 NOV 1989

MAIN CAST

Victoria · · · · · · · · · · · · · · · Victoria Wood
Pam Cunard · · · · · · · · · · · · · Julie Walters
Lorraine · · · · · · · · · · · · · · Kay Adshead
Saundra · · · · · · · · · · · · · · · Meg Johnson
Jim · · · · · · · · · · · · · · · · · · · Hugh Lloyd
Caroline · · · · · · · · · · · · · · · Julia St John
Sue · · · · · · · · · · · · · · · · · · Lill Roughley

CREDITS

writer Victoria Wood · director Kevin Bishop · producer Geoff Posner

Self-centred, snobbish, hypocritical TV host Pam Cunard meets her match when she goes live on the air with a 'common' member of the public.

We'd Quite Like To Apologise
7 DEC 1989

MAIN CAST

Victoria · · · · · · · · · · · · · · · Victoria Wood
Joyanne · · · · · · · · · · · · · · · Julie Walters
Una · · · · · · · · · · · · · · · · · · · Una Stubbs
John · · · · · · · · · · · · · · · · · · Philip Lowrie
Barbara · · · · · · · · · · · · · · · Lill Roughley
Kathy · · · · · · · · · · · · · · · · Jane Horrocks
Carol · · · · · · · · · · · · · · · · · · Celia Imrie
Check-out girl · · · · · · · · · · · · · Susie Blake

CREDITS

writer Victoria Wood · director Kevin Bishop · producer Geoff Posner

While awaiting a delayed take-off, aeroplane passengers sit in the departure lounge and discuss previous holidays and their hopes for this one.

Val De Ree (Ha Ha Ha Ha Ha)
14 DEC 1989

MAIN CAST

Victoria · · · · · · · · · · · · · · · Victoria Wood
Jackie · · · · · · · · · · · · · · · · · Celia Imrie
Susan · · · · · · · · · · · · · · · · · · Joan Sims
Mim · · · · · · · · · · · · · · · · · · · Avril Angers
Jamie · · · · · · · · · · · · · Michael Lumsden

CREDITS

writer Victoria Wood · director Kevin Bishop · producer Geoff Posner

Victoria and Jackie's walking tour of the moors goes less than smoothly, thanks to an un-erectable tent and the hostile woman who runs the Youth Hostel.

Staying In
21 DEC 1989

MAIN CAST

Victoria · · · · · · · · · · · · · · · Victoria Wood
Moira · · · · · · · · · · · · · · · · Patricia Hodge
Hilary · · · · · · · · · · · · · · · · Phyllis Calvert
Gerald · · · · · · · · · · · · · · · Roger Brierley
Dulcie · · · · · · · · · · · · · · · · Lill Roughley
Julia · · · · · · · · · · · · · · · · · · Celia Imrie
Alan · · · · · · · · · · · · · · · · · Jim Broadbent

CREDITS

writer Victoria Wood · director/producer Geoff Posner

Shy, TV-obsessed Victoria finds herself at posh Moira's dinner party. She would have had a better time staying in …

Victoria Wood: Sold Out

UK · ITV (GOOD FUN FOR LWT) · STANDUP

1 × 65 mins · colour

25 Apr 1992 · Sat 9.25pm

MAIN CAST

Victoria Wood

CREDITS

writer Victoria Wood · executive producer Geoffrey Durham · director/producer Marcus Mortimer

A straightforward stage recording of Wood's one-woman show, taped at the Mayflower Theatre in Southampton in 1991.

Victoria Wood's All Day Breakfast

UK · BBC · SKETCH/STANDUP

1 × 50 mins · colour

25 Dec 1992 · BBC1 Fri 9pm

MAIN CAST

Victoria Wood
Julie Walters
Celia Imrie
Susie Blake
Duncan Preston
Lill Roughley

CREDITS

writer Victoria Wood · director/producer Geoff Posner

A Christmas special in which the preponderance of morning-TV magazine shows and other non-peak-time fare came under the satirical gaze of Wood and her regular posse. As with all good teams, the understanding and interplay between the members was natural, incisive and seemed effortless. Granted, these are easy targets for lampooning, but few people are as adept as Wood at observing and sending up all the dimensions, her resulting script cutting to the quick.

Note. Victoria Wood's next major TV work was the TV film *Pat And Margaret*, broadcast under the *Screen One* banner by BBC1 on 11 September 1994. It was a bittersweet tale of two sisters – one dowdy, the other an American soap star – who are reunited after many years on a TV show. Julie Walters and Wood portrayed the sisters, with Celia Imrie and Duncan Preston also among the cast.

Victoria Wood: Live In Your Own Home

UK · BBC · STANDUP/SKETCH

1 × 50 mins · colour

25 Dec 1994 · BBC1 Sun 9.40pm

MAIN CAST

Victoria Wood

CREDITS

writer Victoria Wood · director/producer Geoff Posner

A one-woman Christmas Day special featuring standup routines, monologues and sketches.

Woodcock

UK · BBC · SITCOM

1 × 30 mins · colour

16 Jan 1994 · BBC2 Sun 9pm

MAIN CAST

Captain · · · · · · · · · · · · · · · Prunella Scales
Jasper (ship's parrot) · · · · · · · Frank Skinner
Slyme · · · · · · · · · · · · · · · · Jonathan Hyde
Cyril · · · · · · · · · · · · · · · · Michael Angelis
Woodcock · · · · · · · · · · · Phelim McDermott
Edna · · · · · · · · · · · · · · · · Imelda Staunton
Dr McGregor · · · · · · · · · · · · · · John Bett
Father · · · · · · · · · · · · · · · · · John Rogan
Dai · · · · · · · · · · · · · · · · · · Andy Hockley
Gareth · · · · · · · · · · · · · · · · James Warrior

CREDITS

writer Ian McPherson · director/producer Michael Leggo

A wacky, stage-bound over-the-top nautical romp, with a young cabin boy, Woodcock, press-ganged into joining a clapped-out old tug in Portsmouth harbour in 1793. His preconceptions of an idyllic but exciting life on the ocean waves are dashed on the rocks when he meets the lunatic crew.

This *Comic Asides* one-off was too extreme for many tastes, although **Captain Butler**, a series with a somewhat similar style, set sail on C4 three years later.

Woody Allen

UK · ITV (GRANADA) · STANDUP

1 × 45 mins · b/w

10 Feb 1965 · Wed 9.40pm

MAIN CAST

Woody Allen

CREDITS

writer Woody Allen · director Philip Casson · producer Johnny Hamp

During the second phase of his career, Woody Allen was a standup comic. The first had seen him as a behind-the-scenes writer of jokes for Sid Caesar and Pat Boone's American TV shows. The third, of course – his writing of, direction of and starring roles in a string of wonderful movies – justly elevated Allen to superstardom.

Woody Allen's standup years spanned the 1960s, and it was in 1965 that he came to England, principally to appear in his first-written feature film, *What's New Pussycat*. While he was in the country, Granada TV, easily the most far-sighted of the ITV franchisees at the time, invited Allen to perform his standup act – honed in Greenwich Village clubs – in its Manchester studios. Woody duly delivered, verbalising his New York Jewish neuroses to a receptive local audience and performing his best material, including the famous 'Moose' joke.

When Allen visited England in 1966 (to shoot his part in *Casino Royale*) he appeared as a guest in **Tarbuck At The Prince Of Wales** (ATV/ITV, 22 May) and the 1 September edition of *Dusty*, the singer Dusty Springfield's BBC1 series; and he hosted the 10 October edition of Rediffusion's variety show *Hippodrome*. Allen was also seen on British TV in two editions of the variety series *The Andy Williams Show*, imported from the USA and screened by BBC1 on 19 August 1966 and BBC2 on 5 January 1968.

The Worker

see DRAKE, Charlie

The World According To Smith & Jones

see Smith and Jones

World In Ferment

UK · BBC · SKETCH

6 × 30 mins · colour

23 June–28 July 1969 · BBC2 Mon 8.50pm

MAIN CAST

Nancy Chuff	Angela Thorne
Doug Searchbaker	Jack Shepherd
Chris Champers	Dinsdale Landen
Gerald Pikestaff	John Bird
various folk singers	Eleanor Bron
Madame Astoria	Irene Handl
various roles	Doug Fisher
various roles	Queenie Watts

CREDITS

writer N F Simpson · *producer* Ned Sherrin

A typically surreal enterprise from N F Simpson, taking a topsy-turvy look at modern life by way of a zany spoof of TV current-affairs programmes in general and Granada's *World In Action* in particular. In each edition, the host, Nancy Chuff, introduced reports from her two investigative journalists, Doug Searchbaker and Chris Champers, and invited comments from her studio regulars: 'resident expert' Gerald Pikestaff and 'resident celebrity' Madame Astoria. Eleanor Bron appeared as a number of folk singers (among them Lottie Ilgenfritz, Dolores Stokowski, Hildegarde Schindelstein and Conchita Gonzales) and weekly guest artists were also on hand, including Patsy Rowlands, Arthur

Lowe, Roy Kinnear, Dudley Moore, Fred Emney and Willie Rushton.

See also **Three Rousing Tinkles**.

The World Of Beachcomber

see MILLIGAN, Spike

The World Of Bob Hope

see HOPE, Bob

The World Of Cilla

UK · BBC · SITCOM

1 × 30 mins · colour

3 Feb 1973 · BBC1 Sat 8.45pm

MAIN CAST

Cilla	Cilla Black
Mother	Avis Bunnage
Father	John McKelvey
The fiancé	Sam Kelly
other role	John Clive

CREDITS

writer Ronnie Taylor · *producer* Sydney Lotterby

Cilla Black was one of a number of British pop singers – Dusty Springfield, Sandie Shaw, Cliff Richard, Engelbert Humperdinck and Lulu were others – to be given their own variety series by the BBC in the late 1960s, but few took to TV with the same relish as the lassie from Liverpool; now, indeed, in the late 1990s, her undoubtedly successful singing career has been dwarfed by her considerable TV achievements, hosting popular 'people programmes' for LWT, *Blind Date* and *Surprise, Surprise*.

Before this strand was added to her CV, however, Cilla several times toyed with comedy, presumably with an eye to becoming a light-comic actress once her singing career was in decline. Comedy guest stars featured heavily in the long-running BBC1 series *Cilla* (1968–76) and she regularly appeared with them in sketches and routines. On 3 February 1973 the BBC decided to go the whole hog and present a sitcom built around her talents; *The World Of Cilla* (the last half-hour of her one-hour show) was the star's most serious attempt yet at being a comedy actress – she played a bride-to-be – and it gave her a taste for the genre. In 1975 she continued the initiative, crossing to ITV for two series of individual sitcoms – a sort of Cilla *Comedy Playhouse* – titled **Cilla's Comedy Six** and **Cilla's World Of Comedy**. There, as here, the writer was Ronnie Taylor.

A World Of His Own

UK · BBC · SITCOM

13 × 25 mins · b/w

Series One (7) 31 July–11 Sep 1964 · BBC1
Fri mostly 8pm

Series Two (6) 22 Jan–26 Feb 1965 · BBC1
Fri 8pm

MAIN CAST

Stanley Blake	Roy Kinnear
Helen Blake	Anne Cunningham

CREDITS

writer Dave Freeman · *producers* David Croft, Graeme Muir

A sitcom for Roy Kinnear, in which he was cast as Stanley, a 'super day-dreamer' whose over-worked imagination means that even relatively mundane tasks, like helping his wife buy a pair of shoes, trigger the most fantastic flights of fancy. Stanley is left with a vacant look on his face while his mind drifts far and wide through time and space, from the War Of The Roses to alien planets.

The World Of Lee Evans

UK · C4 (GRANADA) · SITCOMS

4 × 30 mins · colour

2 June–23 June 1995 · Fri 9pm

A series of comedy playlets designed to highlight the physical talents of comedian Lee Evans. Each programme was a self-contained episode (there were two in the first show, making five playlets altogether) and all featured Evans in hapless guises, usually at odds with his environment and the people around him. The storylines all carried an underlying dark edge.

The Late Shift   2 JUNE

MAIN CAST

Lee Evans
John Thomson

CREDITS

writer Lee Evans · *director* Jim Doyle · *executive producer* Andy Harries · *producer* Mathew Leys

On his first shift in a new job at an all-night garage, the speaker system fails and so the sales assistant (Evans) if forced to communicate with a customer (Thomson) by mime.

Meet The Folks   2 JUNE

MAIN CAST

Lee Evans
Caroline Aherne
Prunella Scales
Tony Selby

CREDITS

writer Lee Evans · *director* Andrew Gillman · *executive producer* Andy Harries · *producer* Miles Ross

Evans suffers agonies when he prepares to meet the parents (Scales, Selby) of his girlfriend (Aherne) for the first time.

Off The Rails

9 JUNE

MAIN CAST
Lee Evans
Joanne Unwin

CREDITS
writer Lee Evans · *director* Andrew Gillman · *executive producer* Andy Harries · *producer* Miles Ross

Evans and girlfriend (Unwin) plan a romantic weekend in Scotland travelling up on the overnight sleeper train.

One Late Night

16 JUNE

MAIN CAST
Lee Evans
Phil Daniels

CREDITS
writer Lee Evans · *director* Andrew Gillman · *executive producer* Andy Harries · *producer* Miles Ross

Driving alone on the motorway late one night Evans picks up a hitchhiker, then it is announced on the radio that an axe-wielding murderer is on the loose. But which one of them is it?

Mr Confidence

23 JUNE

MAIN CAST
Lee Evans
Phil Daniels

CREDITS
writer Lee Evans · *director* Jim Doyle · *executive producer* Andy Harries · *producer* Mathew Leys

Evans has fallen in love with the girl next door but is hopelessly tongue-tied. To overcome the problem he enrols in a course run by Mr Confidence (Daniels).

The World Of Wodehouse

see *Blandings Castle* and *Ukridge*

The World Of Wooster

UK · BBC · SITCOM

20 × 30 mins · b/w

Series One (6) 30 May–4 July 1965 · BBC1 Sun mostly 9.40pm
Series Two (7) 4 Jan–15 Feb 1966 · BBC1 Tue 7.30pm
Series Three (7) 6 Oct–17 Nov 1967 · BBC1 Fri 8.20pm

MAIN CAST
Jeeves · · · · · · · · · · · · · · · · · · · Dennis Price
Bertie Wooster · · · · · · · · · · · Ian Carmichael
Aunt Agatha · · · · · · · · · · · · · · · Fabia Drake
Aunt Dahlia · · · · · · · · · Eleanor Summerfield
Roberta 'Bobbie' Wickham · · · · · Tracy Reed
Richard 'Bingo' Little · · · · · · · · Derek Nimmo
Sir Roderick Glossop · · · Paul Whitsun-Jones
Mrs Little · · · · · · · · · · · · · Deborah Stanford

CREDITS
creator P G Wodehouse · *adapters/writers* Richard Waring (10), Michael Mills (9), Michael Pertwee (1) · *producer* Michael Mills

P G Wodehouse's marvellous comic creations – amiable ass Bertie Wooster and his wonder-butler Jeeves – first appeared in the short story *Extricating Young Gussie* in 1915 and they went on to become one of the most beloved double-acts in English literature. Although always a tricky blighter to adapt – much of the flavour of the pieces arises from the jaunty prose style adopted by Wooster, the first-person narrator of most of the stories – this TV series was nonetheless a resounding success, due in no small part to the spot-on casting, not just of the two stars but throughout the casts. Fine comedy character actors Ian Carmichael and Dennis Price may have been somewhat old for the lead roles but their deft, light-comedy touch compensated for that anomaly. (A BBC Radio 4 adaptation, *What Ho, Jeeves!*, which aired from 1973 to 1981, starred Richard Briers as Wooster and Michael Hordern as Jeeves.)

Wooster's world is populated by rich, idle gentleman, dreamy but determined women, irate fathers and fearsome aunts. Plots revolve around star-crossed romances, white lies that grow into complex misunderstandings, assumed identities and the quest for the sort of lazy life a chap born on the right side of the street, with a tidy packet in his pocket, could reasonably expect. Locations for these excitements are Bertie's Central London pad, in Berkeley Street, Mayfair; the country estates of various relatives and friends; and the Drones Club, drinking and dining hole of the upper classes. Dashingly dressed, with a monocle firmly held in the eye, Bertie often turns up at such venues only to discover that he is accidentally engaged to a deb he scarcely knows; he then has to frantically avoid their fathers or homicidal ex-boyfriends; worse still, he has to face his awesome aunts. Jeeves invariably saves the day through a piece of razor-sharp thinking and a dazzlingly intricate scheme, which not only extricates Bertie from the soup but also manages to effect the path of true love for the characters who really should be engaged.

Note. Although Jeeves' first name is never referred to in the series, it is revealed in the 1971 novel *Much Obliged, Jeeves*, wherein Wooster describes the moment thus, "'Hullo Reggie,' he said and I froze in my chair, stunned by the revelation that Jeeves first name was Reginald …'

See also *Blandings Castle*, *Ukridge*, *Mr Wodehouse Speaking*, *Wodehouse Playhouse*, *Uncle Fred Flits By*, *The Reverent Wooing Of Archibald* and, in particular, *Jeeves And Wooster*, the excellent 1990–93 adaptation of Wodehouse's classic stories, starring Stephen Fry and Hugh Laurie.

The Worst Day Of My Life

AUSTRALIA · ABC · CHILDREN'S SITCOMS

6 × 30 mins · colour

Australian dates: Dec 1991–Jan 1992

UK dates: 16 Sep 1992–30 Mar 1993 (6 episodes) BBC1 various days around 4.30pm

CREDITS
writers Harold Dover, Karin Altmann, Barbara Gliddon · *directors* Peter Baroutis, Mandy Smith · *executive producer* David Taft · *producer* Rod Rees

An Australian comedy anthology for younger viewers, looking at the events that combine to create the worst day of the featured child's life, usually starting with a small lie, a twist of the rules or a desire for revenge. All the stories presented happy endings, however.

Up The Creek

UK 16 SEP 1992

A scheme to finance a desperately needed guitar amp lands Paul (played by Garry Perazzo) in hot water.

On The Run

UK 4 NOV 1992

Guy (played by Michael Hammett) is so fed up at being grounded by his mother that he runs away, and into trouble.

Out Of Your Mind

UK 23 DEC 1992

Kerry (played by Erica Kennedy) finds a magic crystal that enables her to read other people's minds, but she soon regrets her eavesdropping.

War And Puss

UK 5 JAN 1993

Tim (played by Jim McKinnon) takes his sister's bike and accidentally runs over a friend's cat.

Normal

UK 23 MAR 1993

Danny (played by Eamon Kelly) tries to hide from his school girlfriend the fact that his parents are hippies.

Mum's Going To Kill You

UK 30 MAR 1993

Lucy (played by Aimee Robertson) disobeys her mother's instruction not to leave the house, beginning a catalogue of extraordinary events.

Harry Worth

Harry Worth was born Harry Illingsworth, in Tankersley, near Barnsley, on 20 November 1917. His father, a miner, died in a pit accident the following year but, as was customary, the young Harry Worth also went down the mines when he was 14. While serving during the Second World War he discovered an ability to entertain, and, after borrowing a book on ventriloquism from the local public library, became intent on pursuing his fame and fortune with such an act.

After making his stage debut at the Bradford Mechanics' Institute in 1946, and his TV debut in the BBC's *New To You* on 2 March 1948, Worth worked the variety theatres and music-halls before abandoning ventriloquism on the advice of Stan Laurel and then Oliver Hardy (he toured Britain on the same variety bill as Laurel and Hardy in 1952 and again in 1953–54), re-inventing himself as a standup comic. In so doing, working without the crutch that the dummies (named Fotheringay and Clarence) represented, Worth was very nervous. The first time he did this, in Newcastle, the theatre audience latched on to his anxiety and Worth realised that he could develop the genuinely apologetic, uncertain, nervous persona as his professional act. This effected a highly successful transformation, and after years of stage work Worth became a long-running star of radio and TV, appearing in numerous sitcoms, sketch shows and variety programmes, always utilising the manner of the bumbling, dithering, bespectacled incompetent. His best period by far was the 1960s, when first runs and repeats meant that he was rarely off the TV or radio, but his 1970s switch from the BBC to ITV precipitated a decline in popularity and his last TV series was screened in 1980 (although he continued to work on radio until 1988). He died on 20 July 1989, aged 71.

See also *Scoop*.

The Trouble With Harry

UK · BBC · SITCOM

6 × 30 mins · b/w

1 Jan–4 Feb 1960 · Fri 7.30pm then Thu 6.20pm

MAIN CAST
Harry Worth · · · · · · · · · · · · · · · · · · · himself
Aunt Victoria · · · · · · · · · · · · · · · Noël Hood
Doris · · · · · · · · · · · · · · · · Paddy Edwards

CREDITS
writers Ronnie Taylor (5), Ronnie Taylor/Frank Roscoe (1) · *producer* John Ammonds

This was Worth's first national TV series, following his appearance in a north-only TV programme in March 1959. (Until 1965, all of Worth's BBC TV programmes were produced in Manchester.)

The title *The Trouble With Harry* recalled Hitchcock's black-comedy film of the same name, released in 1955 but all resemblance ended there. In the series, Harry Worth played a timid, rather ineffectual aspiring author whose formidable aunt (played by Noël Hood) keeps him on the straight and narrow. Paddy Edwards played Doris, the maid.

Here's Harry

UK · BBC · SITCOM

60 editions (59 × 30 mins · 1 × short special) · b/w

Series One (6) 11 Oct–15 Nov 1960 · Tue 7.30pm

Short special · part of *Christmas Night With The Stars* 25 Dec 1960 · Sun 6pm

Series Two (5) 4 May–8 June 1961 · Thu 7.30pm

Series Three (8) 14 Nov 1961–2 Jan 1962 · Tue mostly 8pm

Series Four (12) 8 Oct–24 Dec 1962 · Mon mostly 8pm

Series Five (10) 25 Oct–27 Dec 1963 · Fri 7.45pm

Series Six (8) 13 Oct–1 Dec 1964 · BBC1 Tue 8pm

Series Seven (10) 8 Oct–10 Dec 1965 · BBC1 Fri 7.30pm

MAIN CAST
Harry Worth · · · · · · · · · · · · · · · · · · himself

CREDITS
writers Eddie Maguire, Vince Powell/Harry Driver, Frank Roscoe (series 1–6); Ronnie Taylor (series 7); Lew Schwarz (short special) · *producers* John Ammonds (series 1–6), John Street (series 7), Dennis Main Wilson (short special)

This harmless, slight but friendly series is the best remembered of Worth's sitcoms and it guaranteed him a long-term soft-spot in the hearts of the viewing nation. The programmes were set in the fictional town of Woodbridge, but the storylines, such as they were, were incidental to the performances: viewers simply knew that, whatever the plot, they were in for half an hour of calamity, Worth dropping clangers in every situation into which he was hesitatingly thrust. It is perhaps for this reason that the series is best remembered not for its plots but for its novel opening title sequence, in which the star used his reflection in a Manchester shop window to create an optical illusion with his arms and legs.

There was little in the way of a regular supporting cast because storylines – which usually pitted Harry against officialdom in one form or another – varied from week to week, but an informal rep company of regular faces were often among the cast, including Patrick Newell, Stuart Saunders, Vi Stevens, Deryck Guyler, Ivor Salter, Jack Woolgar and Reginald Marsh.

Harry Worth

UK · BBC · SITCOM

38 episodes (37 × 30 mins · 1 × short special) · b/w

Series One (10) 28 Oct–30 Dec 1966 · BBC1 Fri 7.30pm

Series Two (9) 3 Oct–28 Nov 1967 · BBC1 Tue 7.30pm

Short special · part of *Christmas Night With The Stars* 25 Dec 1967 · BBC1 Mon 6.40pm

Series Three (10) 21 Oct–23 Dec 1968 · BBC1 Mon 7.30pm

Series Four (8) 18 Nov 1969–13 Jan 1970 · BBC1 Tue 7.30pm

MAIN CAST
Harry Worth · · · · · · · · · · · · · · · · · himself

CREDITS
writer Ronnie Taylor · *producers* Graeme Muir (series 1 & 2), Duncan Wood (series 2 & 3), Eric Fawcett (series 2), Douglas Argent (series 4)

A follow-up to the long-running *Here's Harry*. In this new series writer Ronnie Taylor attempted to take the Worth character farther afield than in his previous domestic adventures. The premise was largely the same, however: dressed in his grey suit and trilby hat, he staggered from one misunderstanding to another, exasperating representatives of officialdom and even, in the penultimate episode, a beautiful young French woman (played by Alexandra Bastedo) who, inexplicably, was desperate to marry him.

This type of comedy was fair game earlier in the 1960s, but towards the end of the decade, as British sitcoms were become more sophisticated (albeit slowly), some of these *Harry Worth* half-hours were not always easy to watch: viewers could become angry rather than delighted at the principal character's inability to grasp the nettle, and the sheer frustration of it all.

Thirty Minutes Worth

UK · ITV (THAMES) · SKETCH

23 editions (22 × 30 mins · 1 × short special) · colour

Series One (8) 31 Oct–19 Dec 1972 · Tue around 7pm

Special (colour) · part of *All-Star Comedy Carnival* 25 Dec 1972 · Mon 5.45pm

Series Two (6) 4 July–8 Aug 1973 · Wed 8pm

Series Three (8) 3 Oct–28 Nov 1973 · Wed 8pm

MAIN CAST
Harry Worth · · · · · · · · · · · · · · · · · himself

CREDITS
series 1 writers Mike Craig, Lawrie Kinsley, Ron McDonnell, Frank Roscoe, Roy Tuvey/Maurice

Sellar; *series 2 writers* Mike Craig, Lawrie Kinsley, Ron McDonnell, Roy Tuvey/Maurice Sellar, George Martin; *series 3 writers* Mike Craig, Lawrie Kinsley, Ron McDonnell, Johnnie Mortimer/Brian Cooke, Jim Wilde, Dave Freeman, Ronnie Taylor · *script editor* Vince Powell · *directors/producers* Les Chatfield (series 1 & 3), William G Stewart (series 2)

In what was considered to be a prized coup, ITV lured Harry Worth away from the BBC, with which he had always been associated, and set him up in a sketch series, *Thirty Minutes Worth*. Each edition saw Harry bumbling and dithering as per his BBC sitcom persona, frustrating the hell out of different supporting casts. Thames wrung three series out of the premise in just 13 months but, clearly, there was a limit to just how much of this humour the viewing audiences could take.

Note. The title *Thirty Minutes Worth* was also used for three of Harry's BBC radio exploits: a 1963 series (written by Frank Roscoe/Vince Powell) and series in 1983 and 1988 (Powell only).

My Name Is Harry Worth

UK · ITV (THAMES) · SITCOM

8 × 30 mins · colour

22 Apr–17 June 1974 · Mon 8pm

MAIN CAST
Harry Worth · · · · · · · · · · · · · · · · · himself
Mrs Maybury · · · · · · · · · · · · · Lally Bowers

OTHER APPEARANCES
George Bailey · · · · · · · · · · · Reginald Marsh

CREDITS
writers Ronnie Taylor (4), George Layton/ Jonathan Lynn (3), Spike Mullins/Peter Robinson (1) · *director/producer* William G Stewart

Harry Worth returned to comedy of the domestic variety with this unsuccessful Thames venture. All the usual ingredients were in place: as the perpetual 'Harry', our friend from the north stumbled his way through a litany of misunderstandings that, while amusing, remained as frustrating for the viewers at home as they were for the victim himself. Here he played a man who moves into a boarding house run by the long-widowed Mrs Maybury, and his attempts to do all the right things for all the right reasons were thwarted time and again from his inability to understand the ways of the world. Lally Bowers played Mrs Maybury and Reginald Marsh made a pair of appearances as her defensive brother George.

Harry

UK · BBC · SKETCH

1 × 40 mins · colour

12 Nov 1976 · BBC2 Fri 9.30pm

MAIN CAST
Harry Worth
Josephine Tewson

CREDITS
writer Ronnie Taylor · *producer* James Moir

A one-off BBC special for Harry Worth in the middle of his ITV career. While the star may have hoped that it would lead to a series, nothing materialised.

How's Your Father?

UK · ITV (YORKSHIRE) · SITCOM

13 × 30 mins · colour

Series One (6) 27 Feb–3 Apr 1979 · Tue mostly 8.30pm

Series Two (7) 18 July–29 Aug 1980 · Fri 7.30pm

MAIN CAST
Harry Matthews · · · · · · · · · · · · Harry Worth
Shirley Matthews · · · · · · · · Debby Cumming
Martin Matthews · · · · · · · · · · Giles Watling
Vera Blacker · · · · · · · Fanny Carby (series 1)
Mrs Simkins · · · · · Sonia Graham (series 2)

CREDITS
writers Pam Valentine/Michael Ashton · *directors* Graeme Muir (9), Don Clayton (4) · *producer* Graeme Muir

Away from TV screens on a regular basis for five years, Harry Worth rejected a number of scripts for his 'comeback' before finally settling on *How's Your Father?* All the same, it was not the success he must have hoped it would be.

He was cast as a recently widowed middle-ager, Harry Matthews, left with the problems of raising his two teenage children, Shirley, 16, and Martin, 19 (played by Giles Watling, son of actor Jack). In the style of his long-established TV persona, Harry was something of a personal disaster area, life's little complications striking him more profoundly than they do everyone else. The premise stretched to two series but, perhaps thankfully, no further. Rising comedy actor-writer Nigel Planer, then 27, appeared in one episode.

Oh Happy Band!

UK · BBC · SITCOM

6 × 30 mins · colour

3 Sep–8 Oct 1980 · BBC1 Wed 8.30pm

MAIN CAST
Harry Worth · · · · · · · · · · · · · · · · · himself
Mr Herbert · · · · · · · · · · · · · Jonathan Cecil
Mr Braithwaite · · · · · · · · · · · · · John Horsley
Mr Sowerby · · · · · · · · · · · · · · · Billy Burden
Mr Pilgrim · · · · · · · · · · · · · Tom Mennard
Mr Giles · · · · · · · · · · · · · · · Tony Sympson
Mrs Draper · · · · · · · · · · · · · · · Jan Holden
Vicar · · · · · · · · · · · · · · · · Harold Bennett
Glenda · · · · · · · · · · · · · · · · · Moira Foot
Mrs Tickford · · · · · · · · · · PeggyAnn Clifford
Miss Mayhew · · · · · · · · · · Margaret Clifton
Winnie · · · · · · · · · · · · · Myrtle Devenish

OTHER APPEARANCES
Man from the Ministry · · · · · · Jeffrey Segal
Mr Turtle · · · · · · · · · · · · · · Ronnie Brody
Vicar's wife · · · · · · · · · · · Mollie Maureen

CREDITS
writers Jeremy Lloyd/David Croft · *producer* David Croft

An odd amalgam of ideas from established sitcom creators Lloyd and Croft. Harry Worth, whose character shares his name, starred as the leader of a brass-band in the small town of Nettlebridge. He and, by association, his band find themselves at the forefront of a campaign against the proposed building of a nearby airport.

Each week, Harry and his cohorts thought up schemes to thwart the airport planners, while also managing to indulge in a spot of stirring brass-band music (actually provided by the Aldershot Brass Ensemble). Considering the usual dependability of the major protagonists here, it is fair to say that *Oh Happy Band!* was flat rather than sharp, however.

Worzel Gummidge

UK · ITV (SOUTHERN) · CHILDREN'S SITCOM

31 episodes (30 × 30 mins · 1 × 60 mins) colour

Series One (7 × 30 mins) 25 Feb–8 Apr 1979 · Sun 5.30pm

Series Two (8 × 30 mins) 6 Jan–24 Feb 1980 · Sun 5.30pm

Series Three (8 × 30 mins) 1 Nov–20 Dec 1980 · Sat mostly 5.15pm

Special (60 mins) *Worzel's Christmas Special* 27 Dec 1980 · Sat 5.20pm

Series Four (7 × 30 mins) 31 Oct–12 Dec 1981 · Sat mostly 5.05pm

MAIN CAST
Worzel Gummidge · · · · · · · · · · · Jon Pertwee
John Peters · · · · · · · · · · · · · · Jeremy Austin
Sue Peters · · · · · · · · · · · Charlotte Coleman
Mr Peters · · · · · · · · · · · · · · · · Mike Berry
Mrs Braithwaite · · · · · · · · · · · Megs Jenkins
· · · · · · · · · · · · · · · · (series 1–3 & special)
Mr Braithwaite · · · · · · · · · · · Norman Bird
PC Parsons · · · · · · · · · · · · Norman Mitchell
Aunt Sally · · · · · · · · · · · · · · · Una Stubbs
Mr Shepherd · · · · · · · · · · · Michael Ripper
The Crowman · · · · · · · · · · · Geoffrey Bayldon
Harry · · · · · · · · · Denis Gilmore (series 1–3)
Mrs Bloomsbury-Barton · · · · · · · · Joan Sims
· (series 1–2)
Saucy Nancy · · Barbara Windsor (series 2–3)
Enid Simmons · · Sarah Thomas (series 2–3)

OTHER APPEARANCES
Sgt Beetroot · · · · · · · · · · · · · · Bill Maynard
Dolly Clothespeg · · · · · · · · · · Lorraine Chase

CREDITS
creator Barbara Euphan Todd · *writers* Keith Waterhouse/Willis Hall (1 ep with Jon Pertwee) · *directors* James Hill (30), David Pick (1) · *executive producers* Lewis Rudd (1979–80), Al Burgess (1981) · *producer* James Hill

Created by Barbara Euphan Todd and first unveiled to the public in a 1935 BBC radio *Children's Hour* broadcast, *The Scarecrow Of Scatterbrook*, Worzel Gummidge – a scarecrow who comes to life – has demonstrated a remarkable longevity and multi-generational appeal, appearing in ten books, 1950s radio and TV series (**Worzel Gummidge Turns Detective**), a late 1980s TV series produced in New Zealand (see next entry) and, most successfully of all, this worthy 1979–81 ITV filmed production (repeated by C4 from 19 October 1986 to 17 May 1987).

Here, the rascally but dim scarecrow of Scatterbrook Farm was brilliantly portrayed by the comedy actor Jon Pertwee, who had achieved fame on BBC radio in *The Navy Lark* and then, in a bold move, accepted the role of Doctor Who (1970–74). Pertwee remembered the *Worzel Gummidge* books from his youth and suggested a new small-screen version to Southern TV. Barbara Euphan Todd had died in February 1976, so Keith Waterhouse and Willis Hall were recruited to write the scripts and a host of star names invited to play roles.

Key among these was former dancer Una Stubbs, of *Till Death Us Do Part* fame, who appeared as the bad-tempered, antique-fairground wooden doll Aunt Sally. Despite her mean ways, Worzel dreamed of marrying the selfish and bossy Sally, although he fancied other maidens too, like Saucy Nancy (Barbara Windsor), the figurehead from an old galleon ship. (In the books, however, Worzel was married, to the gentle Earthy Mangold.) Child actress – destined to become an adult star – Charlotte Coleman was cast as Sue Peters. Although initially shocked to discover that the muddied scarecrow can walk and talk, a fact that they keep secret from the adults, Sue and her brother John were Worzel's faithful young friends throughout the entertaining 31 episodes.

Worzel Gummidge Down Under

UK/NEW ZEALAND · C4/TOTI PRODUCTIONS/
CREATIVE ARTS · CHILDREN'S SITCOM

22 × 30 mins · colour

Series One (10) 4 Oct–6 Dec 1987 · C4
Sun 11.30am

Series Two (12) 29 Jan–16 Apr 1989 · C4
Sun 11.30am

MAIN CAST

Worzel Gummidge	Jon Pertwee
Aunt Sally	Una Stubbs
Mickey	Jonathan Marks
Manu	Olivia Ihimaera-Smiler
The Crowman	Bruce Phillips
Professor Pike	Michael Haigh (series 1)
Rooney	Gerald Bryan (series 1)
Mrs Te Wheke	Patupatu Ripley (series 1)
Mrs Peacock	Joy Watson (series 1)
Travelling Scarecrowmaker	Wi Kuki Kaa (series 1)
PC Peacock	Ross Jolly (series 2)

Bulbous Cauliflower	David Weatherley (series 2)
Robert Mahoney	Aaron Taylor (series 2)

CREDITS

creator Barbara Euphan Todd · *series 1 writers* Keith Waterhouse/Willis Hall · *series 2 writers* Frances Walsh, James Hill, Anthony McCarten and others · *director* James Hill · *producer* Grahame J McLean

Six years after the last ITV series, the warty Worzel Gummidge, with his ghastly love-object Aunt Sally, returned to television in an unusual setting: New Zealand. The new location was explained away thus: on display in an antiques shop, Aunt Sally is bought by a folk-museum curator from NZ and is despatched Down Under to appear as an exhibit. Worzel pursues her as an aeroplane stowaway, although he has to avoid the clutches of the evil Travelling Scarecrow-maker, and the pair find themselves enjoying new comic adventures at a location just outside of Wellington. Two series of new programmes materialised – the first scripted, as before, by Waterhouse and Hall – with the cast showing a few more wrinkles but enjoying the same old fun.

Worzel Gummidge Turns Detective

UK · BBC · CHILDREN'S SITCOM

4 × 30 mins · b/w

10 Feb–3 Mar 1953 · Tue 5pm

MAIN CAST

Worzel Gummidge	Frank Atkinson
Earthy Mangold	Mabel Constanduros
Aunt Sally	Totti Truman-Taylor

CREDITS

creator/writer Barbara Euphan Todd · *producer* Pamela Brown

The first TV outing for the scatty scarecrow: a four-parter screened within the BBC's *Children's Television* strand. Frank Atkinson played Worzel and Mabel Constanduros re-created her radio role as Earthy Mangold.

See also the previous two entries.

Wrath

see KAYE, Paul

The Wrong Trousers

see Wallace & Gromit

Wyatt's Watchdog

UK · BBC · SITCOM

6 × 30 mins · colour

17 Oct–21 Nov 1988 · BBC1 Mon 8pm

MAIN CAST

Major Wyatt	Brian Wilde

Peter Pitt	Trevor Bannister
Edwina	Anne Ridler
Virginia	April Walker
Sgt Springer	James Warrior

CREDITS

writer Miles Tredinnick · *director/producer* Alan J W Bell

When his sister Edwina is burgled in broad daylight, retired soldier Major Wyatt is spurred into action, and, without finding out the proper procedures from the police, forms his own Neighbourhood Watch group. The resulting incompetent ensemble are a motley bunch indeed, united by a common cause but divided by personality clashes. The most apparent conflict is between Wyatt and the smarmy womaniser Peter Pitt, a burglar-alarm salesman who sees the group in purely crude terms, as means for selling his product and meeting women.

During his sojourn from *Last Of The Summer Wine*, Brian Wilde played Major Wyatt, a character who, on the surface at least, wasn't a million miles away from Foggy Dewhurst in that earlier series. With the boom in Neighbourhood Watch schemes in this period, the series was timely and the group was a plausible way of achieving an ensemble sitcom situation, bringing together different and conflicting personalities.

WYSIWIG

UK · ITV (YORKSHIRE) · CHILDREN'S SITCOM

5 × 30 mins · colour

29 June–27 July 1992 · Mon 4.15pm

MAIN CAST

Wysiwyg ('Dave')	Nick Wilton
Globyool	Clive Mantle
other role	Julie Dawn Cole
other role	Linda Hartley
other role	Norman Wills

CREDITS

script editor Nick Wilton · *director/producer* Patrick Titley

A children's sci-fi comedy series about Wysiwyg, an alien reporter for InterGalactic Television, who arrives from space on a mission to send back films about life on Earth, its people and their peccadilloes. He is assisted in this task, just, by a technician, Globyool, who has to keep control of the independently minded floating Rovercam camera. InterGalactic TV's transmissions interrupt normal British TV viewing, though, including quiz-shows and the vital World Ludo Championships from Barcelona.

Episodes of *WYSIWYG* – an acronym of What You See Is What You Get, a phrase much used in computer-speak – were funny in places, bizarre and even dark in others, with humour from the **Monty Python** school of comedy.

Xa! Xa!

UK · BBC · STANDUP/SKETCH

1 × 55 mins · b/w

27 Aug 1966 · BBC2 Sat 8.50pm

MAIN CAST

Vaughan James
Malcolm Muggeridge
Michael Glenny
Erik de Mauny
Timothy Bateson
Richard Marner
Carmel Cryan
Alec Bregonzi
Ronald Lacey
Russell Waters

CREDITS

translators Vaughan James, Max Hayward, Harry Shukman, C G Bearne · *producer* Maurice Harvey

Subtitled 'An Inquiry Into Humour, Wit And Satire In The USSR', this one-off programme presented British TV viewers with a chance to experience Russian humour, via translations of classic and contemporary pieces read and performed by six actors.

The show's four presenters all had particular a interest in the field: Vaughan James was fluent in Russian and had a strong affection for the country; Malcolm Muggeridge had ties with the Soviet Union after being sent there as a young journalist in 1932; Michael Glenny was a writer and expert on Soviet theatre; and Erik de Mauny had been the BBC's Moscow correspondent for three years. They purposefully chose text from material readily available in the USSR and attempted to demonstrate their perception of the two types of Russian humour: one being a broad and rollicking sense of fun, the other being strong, biting satire.

See also *Arkady Raikin*.

Xerxes

SWEDEN · SVERIGES TELEVISION · CHILDREN'S SITCOM

6 × 30 mins · colour

Swedish dates: 1988

UK dates: 3 Aug–7 Sep 1989 (6 episodes) C4 Thu 6.30pm

MAIN CAST

Xerxes · · · · · · · · · · · · · · · · · · Benny Haag
Tony · · · · · · · · · · · · · · · · · · Joakim Borjlind
Pekka · · · · · · · · · · · · · · · · Kalle Westerdahl

CREDITS

director Peter Schildt

The only Swedish situation comedy screened on British TV, broadcast in the native tongue with English subtitles. *Xerxes*, so named after the lead character, portrayed the adventures of three young men, friends at school, who leave education and set out to find work and chase women. The series proved very popular with Swedish viewers, especially pubescent girls who considered the boys good pin-up material.

World War, was used for the feature film *Yanks*, directed by John Schlesinger and released in 1979. Written by Colin Welland and Walter Bernstein, this too was set in Lancashire and starred Vanessa Redgrave and Richard Gere.

Yanks Go Home

UK · ITV (GRANADA) · SITCOM

13 × 30 mins · colour

Series One (7) 22 Nov 1976–3 Jan 1977 · Mon 8pm

Series Two (6) 8 Aug–19 Sep 1977 · Mon 8.30pm

MAIN CAST

Cpl Vince Rossi · · · · · · · · · · · Stuart Damon
Cpl Pasquale · · · · · · · · · · · · Freddie Earlle
Col Ralph Kruger · · · · · · · Alan MacNaughton
· (series 1)
Sgt Gus Pulaski · · · · · · · · · · · · · Bruce Boa
Pfc Burford Puckett · · · · · · · · Richard Oldfield
· (series 1)
Leonard Chambers · · Norman Bird (series 1)
Mrs Chambers · · Daphne Oxenford (series 1)
Phoebe Sankey · · · · · · · · · · · Meg Johnson
Doreen Sankey · · · · · · · · Catherine Neilson
Harry Duckworth · · · · · · · · · · · · David Ross
Bert Pickup · · · · · · · · · · · · Harry Markham
Col Irving · · · · · · · · Lionel Murton (series 2)
Randall Todd · · · · · · · Peter Sallis (series 2)
Pvt Floyd Tutt · · · · · · · Jay Benedict (series 2)

CREDITS

writers H V Kershaw (5), John Stevenson (3), Anthony Couch (2), Michael Carter (1), Julian Roach (1), Stuart Damon (1) · *directors* Eric Prytherch (series 1), Roger Cheveley (series 2) · *producer* Eric Prytherch

A comedy series that made light of the curious, often strained relationship that existed between American servicemen and the English townsfolk and villagers around whom they were billeted during the Second World War. The not-so-subtly titled *Yanks Go Home* was set in the north-west town of Warrington, in 1942, where the cigar-chomping US Air Force troops took over the local air base, handing out stockings, chocolate and chewing gum to the lassies from Lancashire and putting themselves about a bit. Local girl Doreen Sankey made particular friendships with the troops, having a relationship with Private Tutt that, in the final episode, led to the altar.

The same theme, of the 'overpaid, overfed, oversexed and over here' Americans making friends with 'our girls' during the Second

Mike Yarwood

Born in Bredbury, Cheshire, on 14 June 1941, Mike Yarwood was one of Britain's best-loved entertainers throughout the 1970s, a comic impressionist par excellence who, for a generation of TV viewers, defined the genre.

After entering show business by performing in a pub talent contest, Yarwood trod the boards for many years, performing in pubs and clubs while working as a travelling salesman, and then, after turning pro, playing in cabaret and summer shows. He made his TV debut on ABC's *Comedy Bandbox* on 21 December 1963 (he was also the studio audience warm-up act), in which he impersonated Harold Wilson, Malcolm Muggeridge and both Albert and Harold Steptoe. It was his remarkably accurate impression of Wilson that cut the mustard, though, and as Wilson became Britain's new Prime Minister in 1964, Yarwood gained a good deal of mileage from it, adding, for good measure, an equally sharp impression of Edward Heath, the leader of the opposition. The following year Yarwood made a successful guest appearance on ATV's *Val Parnell's Sunday Night At The London Palladium* and subsequent TV variety spots led to a short-lived 1965 BBC1 series *Let's Laugh* and his engagement two years later as one of the trio of bright young things in the BBC2 series *Three Of A Kind*. From here, Yarwood gained his own series – detailed below – and became a giant in his field.

As every public figure knows, though, for every peak there is a trough, and Mike Yarwood's descent began as the 1980s dawned. His switch from the BBC to ITV accelerated the decline and Yarwood's crises of confidence led him to seek refuge in alcohol. ITV was never as secure a home for the impressionist as the BBC had been, and the rudeness and toughness that distinguished the emerging new wave of 'alternative' comedians served to underline the lack of bite in Yarwood's material. At the same time, animated impressionism bounced on to TV in the form of *Spitting Image*'s savage, latex caricatures – its breadth of coverage being too great for any one impressionist to cover alone. Yarwood's work now seemed outmoded, and in 1987,

with most of his viewers long tuned-out, he parted ways with ITV and dropped out of sight. Happily, he surfaced again in the mid-1990s, and while he was not given any further starring series he popped up on television on a few occasions at this time, notably on the BBC2 panel-game *Have I Got News For You* (10 November 1995).

Will The Real Mike Yarwood Stand Up?

UK · ITV (ATV) · IMPRESSIONISM

6 editions (5 × 30 mins · 1 × 45 mins) · b/w

31 Dec 1968–4 Feb 1969 · Tue mostly 8.30pm

MAIN CAST

Mike Yarwood
Dilys Watling
Len Lowe

CREDITS

writers Tony Hawes/Eric Davidson · *additional material* Edwin Foxall (1) · *producer* Bill Hitchcock

A first starring show for the young comic impressionist who almost single-handedly moved the genre in Britain away from the standard impersonations (Bud Flanagan, James Cagney, Humphrey Bogart) to contemporary celebrities from the worlds of pop, TV, sport and politics. Yarwood was supported by different guest stars each week, including fellow impressionist Peter Goodwright and comedians Bob Monkhouse and Max Wall.

Shortly before this, in July 1968, Yarwood appeared in another ATV series, confusingly titled *⅝ths To ⅞ths*, screened only in the local Midlands area.

The Real Mike Yarwood?

UK · ITV (ATV) · IMPRESSIONISM/SKETCH

4 editions (3 × 30 mins · 1 × short special) · b/w

One series (3) 14 Apr–28 Apr 1969 · Mon 9.30pm

Short special · part of *All-Star Comedy Carnival* 25 Dec 1969 · Thu 6pm

MAIN CAST

Mike Yarwood
Dilys Watling

CREDITS

writers Eric Davidson/Peter Myers (series), Tony Hawes/Bryan Blackburn (special) · *producers* Barry Langford, Michael Kent (series); Albert Locke (special)

A change of title and format for this second Yarwood series. This time there was a greater emphasis on comedy situations and less reliance upon impersonations as Yarwood tried to move to a broader entertainment base. Dilys Watling was again on hand to provide welcome support. Following this series Yarwood married Sandra Burville, a former member of the pop dance troupe the Gojos, who regularly appeared in his ATV series and had also entertained in the BBC's *Three Of A Kind*.

Look – Mike Yarwood!

UK · BBC · IMPRESSIONISM/SKETCH

50 editions (43 × 30 mins · 4 × 40 mins · 1 × 45 mins · 2 × short specials) · colour

Series One (10) 14 May–23 July 1971 · BBC1 Fri 8.30pm

Short special · part of *Christmas Night With The Stars* 25 Dec 1971 · BBC1 Sat 6.40pm

Series Two (10)19 May–21 July 1972 · BBC1 Fri 8.30pm

Short special · part of *Christmas Night With The Stars* 25 Dec 1972 · BBC1 Mon 6.55pm

Series Three (10) 30 June–1 Sep 1973 · BBC1 Sat mostly 8.40pm

Special *The Mike Yarwood Christmas Show* 25 Dec 1973 · BBC1 Tue 7.05pm

Series Four (4 × 40 mins) 4 May–25 May 1974 · BBC1 Sat mostly 8.20pm

Special (45 mins) *The Mike Yarwood Show* 15 Nov 1974 · BBC1 Fri 8.15pm

Series Five (6) 12 Apr–17 May 1975 · BBC1 Sat 8.30pm

Series Six (6) 3 Jan–7 Feb 1976 · BBC1 Sat 8.35pm

MAIN CAST

Mike Yarwood
Peter Noone (series 1–3)
Adrienne Posta (series 1 & 2)
Cheryl Kennedy (1 special, series 3 & 4)
Larry Martyn (1 special, series 5)

CREDITS

writer Eric Davidson · *additional material* Spike Mullins (6), Mike Craig/Lawrie Kinsley (2) · *producers* James Moir (15), Michael Hurll (12), David O'Clee (11), John Ammonds (5), Colin Chapman (5), not known (2)

With a switch to the BBC, Mike Yarwood became firmly established as the nation's favourite impressionist with these 50 programmes spanning five years, performing standup material (alone on stage at the microphone) and in sketches. His range of impersonations was wide: Prince Charles, politicians such as Wilson, Heath, George Brown, James Callaghan and Denis Healey, union leader Vic Feather, TV rugby league commentator Eddie Waring, football manager Brian Clough, TV personalities Malcolm Muggeridge, Jimmy Savile, Eamonn Andrews, Hughie Green, Bruce Forsyth, Patrick Moore and Magnus Pyke, political interrogator Robin Day, comics Harry Worth, Benny Hill, Tommy Cooper, Eric Morecambe, Ken Dodd and sitcom characters Albert and Harold Steptoe, Frank Spencer from *Some Mothers Do 'Ave 'Em*, Alf Garnett from *Till Death Us Do Part* and Basil Fawlty from *Fawlty Towers*. Yarwood's ability to impersonate was awesome, and he was also blessed with some clever writing, brand new material

being written in the style of the person being lampooned.

Notes. Proving that he was not upset by Yarwood's impersonations, Harold Wilson awarded the comic the OBE in his Resignation Honours List in 1976.

Running concurrent with these TV series was a BBC radio show, *Listen – Mike Yarwood*.

Mike Yarwood

UK · BBC · IMPRESSIONISM/SKETCH

1 × 45 mins · colour

21 Feb 1974 · BBC2 Thu 9pm

MAIN CAST

Mike Yarwood

CREDITS

writer Eric Davidson · *producer* James Moir

A one-off special televised from the Talk Of The Town in London and showing the impressionist in cabaret, performing many of the routines made famous in his BBC1 series *Look – Mike Yarwood*. The programme was screened in the *Show Of The Week* strand on BBC2.

Mike Yarwood In Persons   1

UK · BBC · IMPRESSIONISM/SKETCH

29 editions (22 × 30 mins · 1 × 45 mins · 4 × 40 mins · 2 × 35 mins) · colour

Special (30 mins) 31 May 1976 · BBC1 Mon 8.15pm

Special (40 mins) *The Mike Yarwood Christmas Show* 27 Dec 1976 · BBC1 Mon 7.55pm

Series One (6 × 30 mins) 8 Jan–19 Mar 1977 · BBC1 fortnightly Sat 8.40pm

Special (35 mins) *The Mike Yarwood Christmas Show* 25 Dec 1977 · BBC1 Sun 8.20pm

Series Two (5 × 30 mins) 28 Jan–25 Mar 1978 · BBC1 Sat 8.30pm

Special (35 mins) *The Mike Yarwood Show* 29 May 1978 · BBC1 Mon 8.15pm

Special (45 mins) *The Mike Yarwood Christmas Show* 25 Dec 1978 · BBC1 Mon 8pm

Series Three (6 × 30 mins) 22 Sep–1 Dec 1979 · BBC1 fortnightly Sat around 8.15pm

Special (40 mins) *The Mike Yarwood Christmas Show* 25 Dec 1979 · BBC1 Tue 7.20pm

Series Four (4 × 30 mins) 3 Oct–14 Nov 1981 · BBC1 fortnightly Sat 8pm

Special (40 mins) *The Mike Yarwood Christmas Show* 25 Dec 1980 · BBC1 Thu 8.05pm

Special (40 mins) 26 Dec 1981 · BBC1 Sat 7.35pm

MAIN CAST

Mike Yarwood
Janet Brown (3 specials, series 2 & 3)

CREDITS

writers Eric Davidson (29), Neil Shand (29), David Renwick (7) · *producers* James Moir (10), John Ammonds (8), Alan Boyd (6), Peter Whitmore (5)

Yarwood was still in fine fettle at this time, and his Christmas shows, in particular,

attracted huge audiences. The BBC promoted Yarwood to the prime slot in the entire year's broadcasting when Morecambe and Wise switched channels to ITV. Remarkably, his viewing figures trounced the double-act's ITV rating (a point that he might have done well to remember when he himself made the same move), and it seemed, at this time, that he could do no wrong. With the rise of Margaret Thatcher, Janet Brown was brought into the show and some lively double-acts ensued, especially when Yarwood brought Brown's version of Thatcher up against his own favourite impersonation of the time, Robin Day.

Notes. The second series, five editions from 28 January 1978, was originally intended as six from 14 January 1978, but the first show was cancelled.

A compilation, *The Best Of Yarwood*, was screened by BBC1 on 3 September 1978.

Mike Yarwood In Persons   2

UK · ITV (THAMES) · IMPRESSIONISM/SKETCH

27 editions (15 × 30 mins · 12 × 60 mins) · colour

Special (60 mins) *Yarwood In Town* 8 Sep 1982 · Wed 8pm

Special (60 mins) *The Mike Yarwood Christmas Show* 21 Dec 1982 · Tue 8pm

Series One (6 × 30 mins) 10 Jan–14 Feb 1983 · Mon 8pm

Special (60 mins) *The Mike Yarwood Hour* 27 Dec 1983 · Tue 7.45pm

Special (60 mins) *It's Mike Yarwood* 9 May 1984 · Wed 8pm

Series Two (9 × 30 mins) 17 Oct–12 Dec 1984 · Wed 8.30pm

Special (60 mins) *The Mike Yarwood Show* 26 Dec 1984 · Wed 7.15pm

Special (60 mins) *The Mike Yarwood Special* 19 June 1985 · Wed 8pm

Special (60 mins) *The Mike Yarwood Show* 24 Sep 1985 · Tue 8pm

Special (60 mins) *Mike Yarwood's Christmas Special* 23 Dec 1985 · Mon 8pm

Special (60 mins) 2 July 1986 · Wed 8pm

Special (60 mins) *Yarwood's Royal Variety Show* 30 Sep 1986 · Tue 8pm

Special (60 mins) *The Yarwood Chat Show* 22 Dec 1986 · Mon 8pm

Special (60 mins) *The Mike Yarwood Show* 15 Dec 1987 · Tue 8pm

MAIN CAST

Mike Yarwood
Suzanne Danielle (occasional)
Kate Robbins (occasional)

CREDITS

writers Eric Merriman (15), Eddie Braben (12), Eric Davidson (9), David Renwick (8), Barry Cryer (7), Bill Naylor (3), Charlie Adams (3), John Junkin (3), Bryan Blackburn (2), Colin Edmonds (2), John Palmer (1), Derek Cairns (1), Kim Fuller (1), William Rushton (1), Gavin Osbon (1) · *script associates* Dick Hills (7), John Junkin (1) ·

directors/producers Keith Beckett (14), David G Hillier (10), Philip Casson (2), John Ammonds (1)

Yarwood's switch from the BBC to ITV – which paid him bigger fees and promised a larger production budget – coincided with, and probably hastened, the impressionist's decline. That he was a first-class mimic is beyond doubt, and he had some fine writers providing his material, but Yarwood's work suffered from a self-imposed lack of bite. Hence, although his impersonation of Harold Wilson was technically far superior to the one by satirist John Bird, it was nowhere near as savage and, consequently, less effective. In an era when being cutting meant being credible, Yarwood remained the good guy, refusing to go for the jugular, seeing himself as a popular entertainer and not a political satirist.

The shows had plenty of good moments, however, especially when Yarwood impersonated Prince Charles with Suzanne Danielle portraying Princess Diana, and when he became Prince Andrew to Kate Robbins' terrifying version of Sarah Ferguson. But despite these and other new characters (Ronald Reagan, for one), Mike Yarwood's star was flickering. In a final throw of the dice Thames decided to screen three specials with different formats, the first simply bearing the name *Mike Yarwood In Persons*, the next with a royal theme (*Yarwood's Royal Variety Show*) and the third a chat-show spoof (*The Yarwood Chat Show*) but they were to no avail – the impressionist performed just one starring show in 1987 and that was his last.

Note. Thames produced and networked *Mike Yarwood – This Is Him!* (11 April 1984), an hour-long programme in which the star discussed his work and revealed his technique, and where some of his subjects (among them Eamonn Andrews, Harold Wilson, David Frost and Bruce Forsyth) discussed how it felt to be impersonated.

Yes, But Seriously ...

UK · BBC · SITCOM

1 × 30 mins · b/w

16 Oct 1963 · Wed 6.35pm

MAIN CAST
Tony · Tony Tanner
Barbara · · · · · · · · · · · · · · · · Barbara Young
Mother · · · · · · · · · Rex Robinson (voice only)

CREDITS
writer Ken Hoare · *producer* Lennie Mayne

An odd one-off sitcom starring Tony Tanner and Barbara Young as a pair of screenwriters charged with the task of producing a script for a pair of big-name film stars about to make their TV debut; in so doing, they imagine themselves in those roles, such sequences forming the bulk of the programme. The role of Mother, a voice-only part, was played by a man, Rex Robinson. No series developed.

Yes – Honestly

UK · ITV (LWT) · SITCOM

26 × 30 mins · colour

Series One (13) 9 Jan–2 Apr 1976 · Fri 8.30pm then 7.30pm

Series Two (13) 15 Jan–23 Apr 1977 · Sat mostly 9.45pm

MAIN CAST
Matthew Browne · · · · · · · · · Donal Donnelly
Lily Pond/Browne · · · · · · · · · · Liza Goddard

OTHER APPEARANCES
Mrs Pond · · · · · · · · · · · Eve Pearce (series 1)
Mrs Pond · · · · · · · Irene Hamilton (series 2)
Littlema · · · · · · · Beatrix Lehmann (series 1)
June · · · · · · · · · · Georgina Melville (series 2)
Mr Krocski · · · · · · · · · · · · · · · Dudley Jones

CREDITS
writers Terence Brady/Charlotte Bingham · *directors* John Reardon (19), Les Chatfield (7) · *producer* Humphrey Barclay

Yes – Honestly was an obvious sequel to *No – Honestly*, although the lead names and actors changed and there was no direct storyline continuity. In that original series, John Alderton and Pauline Collins had starred as husband and wife Charles and Clara Danby. Here, Donal Donnelly and Liza Goddard were husband and wife Matthew and Lily Browne.

Again, the episodes followed the course of the relationship, from first meeting – when unsuccessful music composer Matthew (affectionately known as Matt), who has little if any time for women, hires Lily Pond (a beautiful witty woman of Russian ancestry) as his typist – through to marriage. There were two series; Georgie Fame wrote and sang the theme tune for the first, also turning up in two episodes, as pop singer Clive Powell (his real name) and as himself. And, as she had done so successfully for *No – Honestly*, Lynsey de Paul wrote and performed the theme music for the second series.

Yes, It's The Cathode-Ray Tube Show!

UK · ITV (ASSOCIATED-REDIFFUSION) · SKETCH

6 × 30 mins · b/w

11 Feb–18 Mar 1957 · Mon 9.30pm

MAIN CAST
Peter Sellers
Michael Bentine
David Nettheim

CREDITS
creators/writers Michael Bentine, David Nettheim · *director/producer* Kenneth Carter

Although seen in three comedy series in 1956 – *The Idiot Weekly, Price 2d*; *A Show Called Fred* and *Son Of Fred* – Peter Sellers was committed to one more under his contract with Associated-Rediffusion. The staff director/producer behind the three, Richard (Dick) Lester, had moved on by early 1957, and Spike Milligan was busy on other projects, so Sellers suggested that his former fellow Goon Michael Bentine be brought in as the presiding comic genius, writing the scripts and appearing with him in sketches. Bentine, in turn, recruited an Australian writer/actor, David Nettheim, with whom he had worked Down Under on the radio series *Three's A Crowd*, and between them they concocted six bizarre TV programmes of typical Bentinian madness, one surreal idea heaped on top of another. Not even the title was sacred: each week, one word fell off the opening sequence, so that only the word 'Yes' showed at the beginning of the final edition.

Through this series, Bentine and Nettheim came to be acquainted with Dick Lester, and a BBC radio series, *Round The Bend*, soon developed, a single edition airing in 1957 and then two full series in 1959 and 1960. Peter Sellers was not a part of these. Bentine and Lester also worked together again on TV, in 1958–59 in *After Hours*.

Yes Minister

UK · BBC · SITCOM

23 episodes (21 × 30 mins · 1 × 60 mins · 1 × short special)

Series One (7) 25 Feb–7 Apr 1980 · BBC2 Mon mostly 9pm

Series Two (7) 23 Feb–6 Apr 1981 · BBC2 Mon 9pm

Series Three (7) 11 Nov–23 Dec 1982 · BBC2 Thu 9pm

Short special · part of *The Funny Side Of Christmas* 27 Dec 1982 · BBC1 Mon 8.05pm

Special (60 mins) 17 Dec 1984 · BBC2 Mon 8.30pm

MAIN CAST
The Rt Hon James Hacker · · · Paul Eddington
Sir Humphrey Appleby · · · · · Nigel Hawthorne
Bernard Woolley · · · · · · · · · · · Derek Fowlds
Annie Hacker · · · · · · · · · · · Diana Hoddinott
Sir Arnold Robinson · · · · · · · John Nettleton

OTHER APPEARANCES
Sir Frederick ('Jumbo') · · · · · · John Savident
· (series 1)
Frank Weisel · · · · · Neil Fitzwilliam (series 1)
Lucy Hacker · · · · · · · Gerry Cowper (series 1)
Ludovic Kennedy · · · · · · · · · · · · · · · himself

CREDITS
writers Antony Jay/Jonathan Lynn · *directors/ producers* Stuart Allen (first episode), Sydney Lotterby (other 6 eps in series 1), Peter Whitmore (series 2 & 3 & specials)

First-class political satire, admired not only by the public but also by politicians of all persuasions, and reputedly Prime Minister

Thatcher's favourite show. One of the shining lights of the 1980s for the BBC, *Yes Minister* became the first programme to win the BAFTA Best Comedy Series award three years in succession, during which time it became, entirely deservedly, a national institution. Clever and complex plotting, cracking and convoluted dialogue, accurately drawn observations and top-notch acting all combined to create a Rolls-Royce of a series that ran with the smoothness of that engine and the precision of a ministerial cover-up. Co-writer Jonathan Lynn saw the show in simple terms: a Jeeves-and-Wooster concept wherein 'the servant is cleverer than his master'.

Yes Minister depicted the career of a new minister – James Hacker PC, MP, BDc (Econ) – as he negotiates the workings of government office. Hacker represents an unspecified political party but is clearly a moderate, either centre-right (most likely) or centre-left. He enters office as Minister of Administrative Affairs with enthusiasm and ambition, determined to make his mark upon public life, but soon comes to realise that his hands are tied by complex bureaucratic regulations that seem both indecipherable and insurmountable. His Private Secretary, the pedantic Bernard Woolley, does his best to steer Hacker through the minefield, but whatever progress the two of them make is usually revealed as a dead-end. This is because, keeping one or more steps ahead of Hacker, is his Permanent Secretary, Sir Humphrey Appleby KCB, MVO, MA (Oxon), a silky-smooth senior civil servant with a treasure trove of baffling phrases, paradoxical reasoning and enigmatic explanations. In Sir Humphrey's hands, Hacker is merely the ball in a Machiavellian game of political ping-pong.

In every episode, the hapless Hacker, not the most intelligent of men, attempts to carry through what he believes to be a bright, new initiative or policy, intended to cut costs or improve public services (and, at the same time, to promote his name), only to find his plans re-routed or derailed by the usually imperturbable Sir Humphrey. To the civil servant, one minister is just like the next, irrespective of his political persuasion: an unavoidable irritant who most not, at any cost, be allowed to run the country. That is the job of the civil servants, and it is his solemn duty to uphold the status quo and, at the same time, feather the bed of his kind by ensuring that few civil servants, if any, ever lose their jobs as a result of government actions. To Sir Humphrey and his colleagues there is a right way of doing things – their way – and a wrong way, and that is the end of the matter.

But while, in their initial encounters, Sir Humphrey was easily able to outmanoeuvre

Hacker, without ever seeming insubordinate, the writers permitted the minister to becomes more confident as the series progressed, giving him the occasional victory over his adversary … er, colleague. Then (in the December 1984 special), for reasons that he himself was never fully aware, Hacker was elevated to Prime Minister …

Antony Jay, Jonathan Lynn's co-writer, first observed the constricting manner in which civil servants block the work of government when he attended a 1972 lecture given by Barbara Castle to the Civil Service college and became aware that there was something called 'ministry policy' which was distinct from 'minister's policy'. Coupled with his admiration for the relationship dynamic in **Steptoe And Son**, Jay was convinced that a minister and his Whitehall ministry mandarin could form the basis for an effective comedy series. John Cleese, who had attended Cambridge with Lynn and was in partnership with Jay (in the Video Arts training films company) introduced the two men to one another and they agreed to collaborate, Jay bringing to the project his inside knowledge of political wrangling, Lynn his innate comic brain. The result of their partnership was a sublime sitcom, blessed with super-sharp scripts, and, not to be forgotten, truly perfect portrayals of the three main characters – Paul Eddington as the minister, hesitant about the extent of his jurisdiction and usually out-manoeuvred by either Sir Humphrey or his political masters; Derek Fowlds as the keen but slightly naïve Bernard, and, perhaps best of all, Nigel Hawthorne as Sir Humphrey Appleby, giving a faultless performance as the general in command. Just as *Yes Minister* opened viewers' eyes to the machinations behind the power, so 'Sir Humphrey' became the buzz-word for high-ranking civil servants, now an established part of the modern-day vocabulary.

Note. Sixteen episodes of *Yes Minister* were re-recorded for broadcast by BBC Radio 4, with all the principal cast reprising their roles. There were two series of eight episodes apiece, airing 18 October to 7 December 1983 and 8 October to 27 November 1984. In 1997, Derek Fowlds stepped back into the role of Bernard Woolley to read Antony Jay's *How To Beat Sir Humphrey: Every Citizen's Guide To Fighting Officialdom*, broadcast in three daily parts by Radio 4 from 29 September to 1 October.

Yes, Prime Minister
UK · BBC · SITCOM

17 episodes (16 × 30 mins · 1 × short special)

Series One (8) 9 Jan–27 Feb 1986 · BBC2 Thu 9pm

Short special · part of Comic Relief 25 Apr 1986 · BBC1 Fri 10.15pm

Series Two (8) 3 Dec 1987–28 Jan 1988 · BBC2 mostly Thu 9pm

MAIN CAST

The Rt Hon James Hacker · · ·	Paul Eddington
Sir Humphrey Appleby · · · · ·	Nigel Hawthorne
Bernard Woolley · · · · · · · · · · ·	Derek Fowlds
Annie Hacker · · · · · · · · · · · ·	Diana Hoddinott
Dorothy Wainwright · · · · · · ·	Deborah Norton
Sir Arnold Robinson · · · · · · · ·	John Nettleton
Sir Frank · · · · · · · · · · · · · · ·	Peter Cellier

OTHER APPEARANCES

Ludovic Kennedy · · · · · · · · · · · · · · ·	himself

CREDITS

writers Antony Jay/Jonathan Lynn · *director/producer* Sydney Lotterby

With Jim Hacker's elevation to 10 Downing Street the series returned with a new title, *Yes, Prime Minister*.

Hacker was now the top dog although he remained more or less impotent, still tethered to Sir Humphrey's leash. But he was learning, beginning to pull and give the occasional growl, assisted by a new adviser, Dorothy Wainwright, a fiercely intelligent bulldog of a woman who was even a match for Sir Humphrey and his Civil Service colleagues.

While the message of the overall premise remained intact – that power is in the hands of those who run the bank, not those who sign the cheques – *Yes, Prime Minister* was second-rate compared to *Yes Minister*, a disappointing dessert after a sumptuous main course. Although it was possible to believe that Hacker could be a minister – being photographed drunk after a party, making a fool of himself in radio and television interviews with his inability to answer straightforward questions – it was stretching credibility to see the man as Prime Minister and the storylines suffered accordingly. As a standalone series it would have been reasonably well accepted, as a sequel it was a disappointment.

Yonely
UK · BBC · MUSICAL COMEDY

1 × 40 mins · colour

21 Mar 1969 · BBC2 Fri 8.25pm

MAIN CAST

John Yonely

CREDITS

producer Terry Henebery

A single special for the American-based international musical humorist John Yonely, entertaining with his mix of music, comedy and mime. The show was recorded at the Talk Of The Town in London. Sadly, the star himself was not around to see it on TV: on 26 December 1968, four days after the programme was recorded, Yonely and his wife were killed when their private plane crashed en route to Reno.

You ANC Nothing Yet

UK · C4 (HOLMES ASSOCIATES/MICHAEL KUSTOW PRODUCTIONS) · STANDUP

1 × 60 mins · colour
27 Apr 1996 · Sat 12.05am

MAIN CAST
Pieter-Dirk Uys

CREDITS
writer Pieter-Dirk Uys · *director* Lol Lovett · *producers* Michael Kustow, Andrew Holmes

Filmed on stage in his homeland (Manenberg), South African comedian Pieter-Dirk Uys here cast his satirical eye over the new South Africa. The white humorist – who describes himself as a portly, gay, Jewish Afrikaner – delighted a mostly 'coloured' audience with his reminiscences of the dark days of apartheid and his take on the problems and scandals of the new regime. Clever use of costumes, props, facial gestures and the odd dip into Afrikaans enabled Uys to impersonate a number of different characters, including Afrikaner stereotypes and national leaders de Klerk, Botha and Mandela. But the audience responded most warmly to his hilarious impression of Archbishop Desmond Tutu and his extended routine as Winnie Mandela. Uys still courted controversy, unafraid to snipe at what he perceived as the inadequacies of the new black political rulers or the more dubious activities of the ANC. As he pointed out, he's a satirist, that's his job.

See also *Message To Major.*

You Can't Be Serious

UK · ITV (THAMES) · CHILDREN'S SKETCH

6 × 30 mins · colour
1 Aug–5 Sep 1978 · Tue 4.45pm

MAIN CAST
Tommy Pender
Nigel Rhodes
Andre Francois
Debbie Flynn
Ismet Mehmet
Mandy Nunn
Debbie Padbury
Jackie Watkins

CREDITS
writers cast · *director/producer* Roger Price

Another series of sketches written and performed by the young starlets at Anna Scher's Children's Theatre in north London, following *You Must Be Joking!* and *Pauline's Quirkes*, which had featured teenage hopefuls Pauline Quirke and Linda Robson.

Each edition of *You Can't Be Serious* featured an adult guest star: David Hamilton, Dave Prowse, Clive Dunn, Stephen Lewis, Pauline Quirke herself (now 18), and Derek Griffiths.

You Gotta Be Jokin'

UK · BBC · STANDUP/SKETCH

8 × 30 mins · colour
27 Apr–15 June 1991 · BBC1 Sat mostly 6.35pm

MAIN CAST
Shane Richie
George Marshall
Billy Pearce
Maddi Cryer
Annette Law

CREDITS
writers cast and Charlie Adams, Terry Morrison, Kim Fuller, Vicky Pile, Peter Hickey, Clive Whichelow, Richard Parker, Geoff Cole, Ronnie Barbour, Garry Chambers, Alan Wightman, John Langdon, John Lea and others · *script associate* Charlie Adams · *directors* Bill Wilson (4), Tony Newman (4) · *producer* Bill Wilson

'Five young performers, appearing on television for the first time, present half an hour of fast standup comedy, with a generous helping of characters, a large portion of impressions and a double order of talent' said the publicity for this series, neatly overlooking the fact that Shane Richie had been appearing (albeit irregularly) on TV for a number of years and that Maddi Cryer had recently worked with Little and Large.

The young quintet went about their business with energy and enthusiasm, peppering the eight programmes with various styles of comedy. Sketches, spoofs and songs never ran more than two minutes long, and recurring characters included lager lout Tone (Richie), the lisping four-year-old Trudie (Law), and Madeline Leader the dog breeder (Cryer).

You Must Be Joking!

UK · ITV (THAMES) · CHILDREN'S SKETCH

15 × 30 mins · colour
Series One (8) 28 May–16 July 1975 · Wed 4.50pm
Series Two (7) 23 Apr–4 June 1976 · Fri 4.50pm

MAIN CAST
Ray Burdis
John Blundell
Pauline Quirke
Elvis Payne
Jim Bowen
Michael Holloway
Flintlock
Linda Robson (series 1)
Bill Rice (series 1)

CREDITS
series 1 writers Ray Burdis, John Blundell, Jim Bowen, Pauline Quirke, Anna Scher, Charles Verrall · *series 2 writers* Ray Burdis, John Blundell, Roger Price · *directors* Roger Price (series 1), Neville Green (series 2) · *producer* Roger Price

Two series of slapstick, satire and straight gags written and performed by teenagers from the Anna Scher Children's Theatre in Islington, north London, under the guidance

of the only adult on the show, the former star of *The Comedians*, Jim Bowen. One of the three main hosts was 16-year-old schoolgirl Pauline Quirke and occasional first series programmes also featured Linda Robson (they teamed up again 14 years later for *Birds Of A Feather*) while 14-year-old Gary Kemp (later to sing with the rock band Spandau Ballet and act in the feature film *The Krays*) provided some of the music.

See also subsequent series *Pauline's Quirkes* and *You Can't Be Serious*.

You Must Be The Husband

UK · BBC · SITCOM

13 × 30 mins · colour
Series One (7) 8 Sep–20 Oct 1987 · BBC1 Tue 8.30pm
Series Two (6) 29 Feb–4 Apr 1988 · BBC1 Mon mostly 8.30pm

MAIN CAST
Tom Hammond · · · · · · · · · Tim Brooke-Taylor
Alice Hammond · · · · · · · · · · · · · Diane Keen
Miranda · · · · · · · · · · · · · · · · Sheila Steafel
Gerald · · · · · · · · · · · · · · · · Garfield Morgan

CREDITS
writer Colin Bostock-Smith · *directors* John Kilby (series 1), Richard Boden (series 2) · *producer* John Kilby

A BBC sitcom with an intriguing premise, looking at the pressures put upon one spouse by the sudden financial success of the other.

Tim Brooke-Taylor was cast as Tom Hammond, who has motored along nicely for 20 years with his wife Alice. They have twin 18-year-old children and a moderate but comfortable lifestyle. A budding writer, Alice suddenly achieves success when her sexy blockbuster novel becomes a best-seller. In a moment, it seems, the Hammonds are very wealthy, but this financial influx has a pronounced downside. While Tom is thrilled for and proud of his wife and her new-found success, his role in the marriage changes; he is suddenly a bit-part player in her success story, a spectator on the sidelines as she rides the rollercoaster to fame and fortune.

To exacerbate matters, Alice's literary agent, Miranda, is a hard-bitten husband-hater who regards Tom as a millstone around her protégé's neck; she urges Alice to move on to 'better things'. Alice's meteoric rise also pulls Tom's career in bathroom fittings sharply into focus: it seemed fine beforehand but now he realises that it is going nowhere and he is filled with a sense of hopelessness, unassuaged by his boss Gerald. All these factors sit alongside an even greater concern that dogs Tim's consciousness: where did his wife get the inspiration for her steamy sex scenes? Did she do research? And if so, with whom?

You Must Be The Husband was a good idea that didn't quite gel, despite the reliable casting. The basic theme, although sharp, never quite developed over the episodes, with Tom caught in a trap of perpetually fearing that his wife was conducting an affair, despite evidence to the contrary and Alice's attempts to convince him that she still loved him.

You Rang, M'Lord?

UK · BBC · SITCOM

26 episodes (25 × 50 mins · 1 × 60 mins) · colour

Special (60 mins) 29 Dec 1988 · BBC1 Thu 8pm

Series One (5) 14 Jan–11 Feb 1990 · BBC1 Sun 7.15pm

Series Two (7) 11 Nov–23 Dec 1990 · BBC1 Sun 7.15pm

Series Three (7) 10 Nov–22 Dec 1991 · BBC1 Sun 7.15pm

Series Four (6) 20 Mar–24 Apr 1993 · BBC1 Sat 6.10pm

MAIN CAST

SERVING STAFF:

Alf Stokes	Paul Shane
James (Jim) Twelvetrees	Jeffrey Holland
Ivy Teasdale	Su Pollard
Henry	Perry Benson
Mabel	Barbara New
Mrs Lipton	Brenda Cowling
Myrtle	Barbara Windsor (series 3)

GENTRY:

Lord George Meldrum	Donald Hewlett
The Honourable Teddy Meldrum	Michael Knowles
Lady Lavender	Mavis Pugh
Poppy	Susie Brann
Cissy	Catherine Rabett

OTHERS:

Lady Angela Shawcross	Angela Scoular
Sir Ralph Shawcross	John Horsley
PC Wilson	Bill Pertwee

CREDITS

writers Jimmy Perry/David Croft · directors David Croft (13), Roy Gould (13) · producer David Croft

In the trenches during the First World War, two foot-soldiers come upon the unconscious figure of an officer. Assuming him to be dead, one of them, Alf, attempts to rob the man, much to the disgust of his comrade, the steadfast James. When they realise that he is alive they carry him to safety, and the officer, the Honourable Teddy Meldrum, tells them that he is forever in their debt. Nearly ten years later, we find that Meldrum has repaid said debt to James – he is now serving as 'head of the household' to Teddy's brother Lord Meldrum, a factory-owning aristocrat, and his sprawling family. Following the death of a butler, shifty Alf Stokes reappears on the scene too, claiming his side of the deal; he is duly appointed as the new butler, much against the wishes of James, who remembers all too well Alf's criminal tendencies. At the same time, Alf arranges for a new parlour maid, Ivy, to join the staff. Unbeknown to the others, Ivy is really Alf's daughter and is

ensconced in the house to (sometimes unwillingly) help her father swindle the Meldrums out of their money.

All this was portrayed in the premiere episode; subsequent programmes depicted Alf's attempts to fulfil his nefarious dreams, and James's stalwart opposition to this unsavoury character. The battle of wills was played out against a background of heated passion, not all of it unrequited. James was desired both upstairs (by Poppy) and downstairs (by Ivy), while the (not so) Honourable Teddy tried desperately to have his way with Ivy, not necessarily because he fancied her but because it was 'the done thing' to do it with parlour maids. Even Meldrum was parking his boots under the bed of the married but promiscuous Lady Shawcross, while the other young female member of the family, Cissy, dressed like a man, spoke like a man, walked like a man and seemed to have the desires of a man – making Perry and Croft's sitcom an unlikely groundbreaker in the recurring portrayal of a lesbian character.

The writers were determined that *You Rang, M'Lord?* should have a classy air about it, in keeping with its subject and making it look more like the sort of period dramas (especially *Upstairs, Downstairs*) that it was parodying. To that end, the episodes were 'drama-length' (50 minutes) and the sets, lighting and camerawork were of a quality more normally associated with such productions. Unlike the writers' previous works (*Hi-de-Hi!*, *It Ain't Half Hot Mum* etc, featuring many of the cast used here), however, the lead characters were not loveable; in fact, Alf was quite menacing and James was just too snobbish and unbending a character to generate a response from the audience. This combination of production values and darker characterisation seemed to work against the series, and the normally loud and broad humour of such ensemble romps was uncomfortable in the surroundings. While far from a ratings disaster, it nonetheless failed to attract the level of audiences normally reached by Perry and Croft.

You'd Never Believe It

UK · ITV (JACK HYLTON TV PRODUCTIONS FOR ASSOCIATED-REDIFFUSION) · STANDUP/SKETCH

5 × 60 mins · b/w

5 Jan–26 Apr 1956 · monthly Thu 8pm

MAIN CAST

Max Miller
Nat Gonella

CREDITS

directors Kenneth Carter, Douglas Hurn

The only regular TV series for the great Max Miller was this rather run-down affair, produced by the impresario Jack Hylton.

Born Thomas Henry Sargent in Brighton on 21 November 1894, the flamboyant

'Cheekie Chappie' Miller built his top-rated reputation by way of his music-hall and variety work, where – dressed in his trademark gaudy plus-fours, white hat and kipper tie – he managed to hint at blue jokes and risqué patter relatively unhindered. He was never overtly rude and neither a dirty word not a swear word passed his lips professionally; his skill, aided by consummate comic timing, was to leave such thoughts dangling in the minds of his audiences … and then accuse them of being 'filthy'. On TV, of course, Miller was much more restricted in what he could say. Each of these five programmes featured guest acts, with musicians and dancers padding out the bills. At its peak before, during and after the Second World War, Miller's career was in decline by this time, and TV viewers did not see the great man – perhaps the greatest ever British standup comedian – at his best. He died on 7 May 1963, aged 68.

Notes. Sharing top-billing with Tessie O'Shea, Miller also appeared in each of the three editions of a Jack Hylton/A-R variety series, *See You, Soho*, screened on 16 January, 13 February and 13 March 1958.

There have been a number of Miller tributes on TV over the years. Among these are *Applause! Applause!*, made by Thames and screened by ITV on 10 April 1969, and *Here's A Funny Thing* (A Bright Thoughts Company Productions for C4), aired on 20 November 1982, in which John Bardon repeated his brilliant one-man tip-of-the-hat to the great comic, which he had been performing on stage. Two other major salutes to the comic were the BBC2's *40 Minutes: I Like The Girls That Do* (16 February 1989), written and directed by cartoonist Gerald Scarfe, and C4's excellent *Heroes Of Comedy* (27 October 1995).

See also **Around The Town**.

You'll Never Get Rich

see **The Phil Silvers Show**

You'll Never Walk Alone

UK · ITV (YORKSHIRE) · SITCOM

1 × 30 mins · colour

9 Sep 1974 · Mon 8pm

MAIN CAST

Maurice Pouncey	Brian Glover
Marjory Pouncey	Maureen Lipman
Trevor	Gordon Rollings
First man	Peter Jones
Second man	Norman Chappell
Third man	Paul McDowell

CREDITS

writers Ray Galton/Alan Simpson · producer Vernon Lawrence

An immaculately cast single-episode comedy from Galton and Simpson that followed the journey down to London of three fanatical Leeds United football supporters, heading to Wembley to see their team play in the FA Cup Final. Bedecked in rosettes, scarves, badges, hats and with rattles in hand, Maurice, his wife Marjory and their friend Trevor board the train and are staggered to find three other men, sharing the journey, whose lifeblood does not thrill to the scent of soccer. Maurice takes it upon himself to act as lay preacher, converting the non-believers.

You're Invited

UK · ITV (GRANADA) · STANDUP/SKETCH

1 × 30 mins · b/w
9 Sep 1960 · Fri 8.55pm

MAIN CAST
Jonathan Winters
Evelyn Tyner
Sylvia Sands

CREDITS
director David Main

A single programme, made and networked by Granada and featuring the visiting Jonathan Winters. (A week later, in the same slot, Granada broadcast a second starring vehicle for a US comic: *The Carol Burnett Show*.)

One of the most inventive of all American standup comedians, Winters was born in Dayton, Ohio, on 11 November 1925. By 1950 he was working in New York night-clubs and he broke into television around 1955, appearing regularly on *Tonight* and *The Steve Allen Show*. Brilliant at inventing sound effects to embellish his comedy routines, Winters created some memorable comedy characters, including Chester Honeyhugger, the 84-year-old swinger Maudie Frickert, and King Kwasi of Kwasiland. Similar to Spike Milligan, Winters has suffered from mental instability and manic depression, but his humour, treading on or near the line, is suffused with wonderfully inspired ideas that often comes with the territory. His comedy greatly inspired Robin Williams, and the young comic was able to work with his idol when Winters was cast in *Mork And Mindy* in 1981–82.

You're Only Young Twice   1

UK · ITV (ATV) · SITCOM

6 × 30 mins · colour
5 July–9 Aug 1971 · Mon 8.30pm

MAIN CAST
Henry Armitage · · · · · · · · · · Liam Redmond
Matron Lottie Orchard · · · · · · · Adrienne Corri
Peter · · · · · · · · · · · · · · · · · Peter Copley
Mark · · · · · · · · · · · · · · George Woodbridge
Reg · · · · · · · · · · · · · · · · · · Leslie Dwyer
Giulio · · · · · · · · · · · · · · · · · · Vic Wise
Corrinna · · · · · · · · · · · · · Carmen Munroe

Benny · · · · · · · · · · · · · · · Anthony Jackson
Mr Freestone · · · · · · · · · · · · Walter Swash
Ambrose · · · · · · · · · · · · · · · · John Dolan

CREDITS
writer Jack Trevor Story · script editor Philip Hinchcliffe · director David Askey · producer Shaun O'Riordan

A gentle comedy, *You're Only Young Twice* depicted life inside a home for OAPs, Twilight Lodge, where the residents are far from incapable of raising a laugh. The author, Jack Trevor Story, carefully injected a thoughtful side to the humour too, showing how a roomful of people who happen to be ageing but can still enjoy an active, stimulating conversation or activity, can be sent to bed, like children, at one clap of the matron's hands. Adrienne Corri, whose stormy private life tended to attract more press coverage than her acting roles, starred as the bewitching matron, assisted by Carmen Munroe as the nurse.

Hitherto, Jack Trevor Story was best known for his crime writing: *Dixon Of Dock Green*, *Fraud Squad* and more. He returned to the screen in 1979–80 with an unusual series, *Jack On The Box*, in which he looked, in humorous documentary style, at the talking points of the era by way of fictional scripts.

Six years after this ATV series, Yorkshire TV launched a sitcom entitled *You're Only Young Twice* which was set in an old people's home, Paradise Lodge. Despite the obvious similarities, no tie was acknowledged between the two productions.

You're Only Young Twice   2

UK · ITV (YORKSHIRE) · SITCOM

31 × 30 mins · colour
Series One (7) 6 Sep–18 Oct 1977 · Tue 7.30pm
Series Two (8) 5 June–24 July 1978 · Mon 8pm
Series Three (7) 31 May–12 July 1979 · mostly Thu 8pm
Special · 24 Dec 1979 · Mon 6.05pm
Special · 23 Dec 1980 · Tue 8.30pm
Series Four (7) 23 June–11 Aug 1981 · Tue 8.30pm

MAIN CAST
Flora Petty · · · · · · · · · · · · · Peggy Mount
Cissie Lupin · · · · · · · · · · · · · Pat Coombs
Dolly Love · · · · · · · · · · · · · Lally Bowers
Mildred Fanshaw · · · · · · · · · · · Diana King
Miss Milton · · · · · · · · · · · · Charmian May
Miss Finch · · · · · · · · · · · · Georgina Moon
Roger · · · · · · · · · · · · · · · · Johnny Wade

CREDITS
writers Pam Valentine/Michael Ashton · directors Graeme Muir (30), Don Clayton (1) · producer Graeme Muir

An all-too-predictable, easy ITV sitcom, sadly short on genuine laughs, that still managed to run to more than 30 episodes over four years.

The setting was Paradise Lodge – 'superior residence for retired gentlefolk' – a large detached house (proprietress Miss Milton) wherein lived four women of independent means: an ageing film actress, Dolly; the motorbike riding Mildred; the dotty Cissie; and the irascible Flora. This last-named character was the clear star of the show, affording yet one more battleaxe role for the redoubtable Peggy Mount. Always complaining, ever dominant, Flora sported a hairstyle to match her severe character and was more than a match for anyone, most especially Cissie, over whom she lorded life from first episode to last. Mount and Pat Coombs (Cissie) had previously worked together in the ITV comedy series *Lollipop Loves Mr Mole* and, in 1984, after *You're Only Young Twice*, reunited for a single-episode TV sitcom *It's Never Too Late*.

Young And Foolish

UK · ITV (ATV) · SKETCH/STANDUP

4 × 45 mins · b/w
6 Oct–27 Oct 1956 · Sat 9pm

MAIN CAST
Chic Murray
Maidie Murray
Dickie Henderson
Michael Holliday
Jack Parnell

CREDITS
writers Bill Craig/John Law · producer Dicky Leeman

A short series, presented on ITV by impresario Val Parnell, which mixed 'song, fun and dance' but was particularly well represented by humour, with appearances from Dickie Henderson and the Scottish husband-and-wife team Chic and Maidie Murray.

Young At Heart   1

UK · ITV (ATV) · SITCOM

1 × 30 mins · colour
4 Aug 1977 · Thu 7pm

MAIN CAST
Albert Sculley · · · · · · · · · · · Stratford Johns
Leonard Jarvis · · · · · · · · · · Richard Pearson

CREDITS
writer Ronnie Taylor · director/producer Les Chatfield

Two sixty-somethings find that nothing tests their friendship more than the rivalry over their mutual grandson: who cares for him the most and whom the boy prefers. This single-episode comedy was networked by ATV in its *Comedy Playhouse*-style season *The Sound Of Laughter*, but no series developed.

Young At Heart 2

UK · ITV (ATV · *CENTRAL) · SITCOM

19 × 30 mins · colour

Series One (6) 14 Apr–19 May 1980 ·
Mon mostly 8pm

Series Two (7) 14 May–2 July 1981 · Thu 8pm

*Series Three (6) 24 Sep–5 Nov 1982 ·
Fri 8.30pm

MAIN CAST

Albert Collyer · · · · · · · · · · · · · · · John Mills
Ethel Collyer · · · · · · · · · · · · · Megs Jenkins
Barbara Charlton · · · · · · · · · · · Carol Leader
· (series 1 & 2)
Norman Charlton · · · · · · · · · · · David Neilson
· (series 1 & 2)
Barman · · · · · · · · · · · · · James Duggan

CREDITS

writer Vince Powell · director/producer Stuart Allen

Particularly popular among pensioners, for obvious reasons, *Young At Heart* depicted the humorous side of retirement.

Albert Collyer is a strongly principled man forced to retire, much against his wishes, from a job he has held for 50 years, man and boy, at a pottery works in Stoke-on-Trent (where the series is set). He is 65, and the law's the law – he has to quit work. He looks forward to a marvellous future but can't quite reach out and grab it; he's active but doesn't have an interest to pursue beyond football, the pub, the neighbours Barbara and Norman, and occasional sightings of his grandchildren; he's a penny-pincher, moaning about the inadequacies of his pension; he mopes about in his flat cap, smoking his pipe and getting under the feet of his wife Ethel.

Young At Heart was a two-hander for a pair of very familiar faces: Sir John Mills, 72 at the time the series began, and Megs Jenkins. It was something of a reunion for them: they had appeared together in the 1949 film *The History Of Mr Polly*. Mills also sang the series' theme song.

The Young Comedians

USA · HBO · STANDUP

1 × 60 mins · colour

US date: 14 Dec 1991

UK date: 22 Aug 1992 · BBC1 Sat 12.50am

MAIN CAST

Paul Rodriguez
Haywood Banks
Paul Billerey
Cathy Lattmann
Rick Reynolds

CREDITS

not known

A US TV special – HBO's '14th Annual Young Comedians Show' – with host Paul Rodriguez introducing some of the hottest young American comedy stars. The Mexican-American Rodriguez, the son of immigrant farm labourers, was America's most famous Hispanic comedian.

Young, Gifted And Broke

UK · ITV (CENTRAL) · SITCOM

7 × 30 mins · colour

3 June–15 July 1989 · Sat mostly 6.15pm

MAIN CAST

Frank · · · · · · · · · · · · · · · · James Hazeldine
Paul · · · · · · · · · · · · · · · · Simon O'Brien
Linda · · · · · · · · · · · · · · · · Mary Healey
Lucy · · · · · · · · · · · · · · · Kate Emma Davies
Adrian · · · · · · · · · · · · · · · Mark Monero
Tamsin · · · · · · · · · · · · · · · Elena Ferrari
Aysha · · · · · · · · · · · · · · · Cheryl Miller
Greg · · · · · · · · · · · · · · · · Jason Rush
Bolton · · · · · · · · · · · · · Steven O'Donnell
Alan · · · · · · · · · · · · · · · · Bobby Bragg

CREDITS

creators Laurence Marks/Maurice Gran · writers Gary Lawson/John Phelps · directors Glyn Edwards (6), Gerry Mill (1) · executive producer Ray Butt · producer Margaret Bottomley

A sitcom depicting the adventures of five street-sharp teenagers – Paul, Adrian, Tamsin, Aysha and Greg – in the Youth Training Scheme (YTS) who begin working for an electronics company, run by Frank. They swiftly come to the realisation that they have a long way to go before reaching even the bottom of the ladder, but they set out to climb the rungs anyway, by a mixture of means fair and foul.

Simon O'Brien was cast as Paul – he had been Damon Grant in C4's Liverpool soap *Brookside* before asking for his character to be killed off so that he could pursue other acting ventures.

The Young Lady From London

UK · BBC · CHILDREN'S SITCOM

6 × 30 mins · b/w

22 Nov–27 Dec 1959 · Sun mostly 5pm

MAIN CAST

Jane Holland/ ·
Anna Kotzeroth · · · · · · · · · · · Anne Castaldini
Aristide Klipfel · · · · · · · · · · · · · · Hugh David
Otto · · · · · · · · · · · · · · · · · Steve Plytas
Konstantin Jesky · · · · · · · · · · · Oliver Burt
King Klaus · · · · · · · · · · · · · William Mervyn
Prince Laszlo · · · · · · · · · · · · · Sandor Eles
Vera Dean · · · · · · · · · · · · · Hannah Watt
Miss de Marchmont · · · · · · · · · Pauline Letts

CREDITS

writer/producer Rex Tucker

A comedy serial that provided humorous escapism for younger viewers, albeit with a complicated plot. It depicted the adventures of 16-year-old Jane Holland, who wins a trip to Paris in a newspaper's design-a-dress competition. Here she discovers the existence of her exact double, the international concert pianist Anna Kotzeroth, who is in love Prince Laszlo, the son of the exiled King Klaus of Soldania. Jane becomes involved in the lives of Anna and her prince and eventually ends up in Stingerstau, the Soldanian capital, being pursued by two dubious journalists, Aristide and Otto.

The Young Ones

UK · BBC · SITCOM

12 × 35 mins · colour

Series One (6) 9 Nov–14 Dec 1982 · BBC2
Tue 9pm

Series Two (6) 8 May–19 June 1984 · BBC2
Tue 9pm

MAIN CAST

Rik · Rik Mayall
Vyvyan · · · · · · · · · · · · · · Adrian Edmondson
Neil · · · · · · · · · · · · · · · · · Nigel Planer
Mike · · · · · · · · · · · · · · · Christopher Ryan
The Balowski family · · · · · · · · · Alexei Sayle

CREDITS

writers Ben Elton, Rik Mayall/Lise Mayer · additional material Alexei Sayle · producer Paul Jackson

A mad, helter-skelter, rude, awesomely violent, unpredictable, swaggering, staggering, joyously infantile, exhilarating steam-roller of a sitcom, *The Young Ones* provided the breakthrough for the new generation of aggressive and forthright 'alternative' comedians.

By 1981, certain members of the 'alternative comedy' movement were beginning to turn up on television. Rik Mayall had arguably the highest profile and at least a little leverage with television producers. On stage, he had perfected an off-the-wall poet character, Rik, a pompous, radical prat whom he had brought to TV in *Boom Boom … Out Go The Lights*; Mayall and his then-girlfriend Lise Mayer talked about the sort of home life such a bloke might have, and what other characters might live with him. Firstly they thought of 'Adrian Dangerous', the mad, fearless, self-abusing, heavy-metal-loving lunatic punk that Ade Edmondson portrayed opposite Mayall's Richard Dangerous alter ego in the Dangerous Brothers routine that was a popular part of their stage act. Then there was Nigel Planer's brainless, hippy character 'Neil' (who had also appeared in *Boom Boom … Out Go The Lights*). Finally, they envisaged for Peter Richardson a shifty, slightly mysterious and overwhelmingly 'normal' character.

With a quartet formed in his mind, Mayall saw the potential for a sitcom series and took the idea to TV producer Paul Jackson, who thought it was worth a try. But Jackson and Richardson had clashed over *Boom Boom …* so Richardson was dropped (he went off to develop *The Comic Strip Presents …*) and, after casting around for a replacement, Christopher Ryan was found in his stead.

Mayall, Mayer and Ben Elton wrote the scripts, with Mayall and Mayer working as a team and Elton alone; the two elements had to be combined for every script, Elton later saying that this method accounted for the show's lack of discipline which, perversely, greatly added to its appeal. The writers decided to call their series *The Young Ones*.

The premise was simple: the series depicted a flatshare from hell, with four anarchic, lazy, dysfunctional students living on the breadline and hating and abusing one another. But it was the *style* of *The Young Ones* rather than the idea that gave the show its individuality. It gloriously reflected the free-basing, high-octane, in-your-face, unpredictable quality of 'alternative' comedy and turned its back on all of the old, established rules and clichés of television humour to present 35 minutes of rampaging, violent slapstick which had more in common with Warner Bros cartoons than with situation comedy as known to this point. A huge range of bizarre ideas was tethered to the loosest possible storylines and confusion was deliberately added by sudden cutaways to characters and situations not involved in the plot. The show also had musical guests – a first for a sitcom – whose appearances somehow had to be accommodated within the story. Whatever its merits or shortcomings, *The Young Ones* certainly succeeded in *looking* different, and that was half the battle won. The 'establishment', at first, was horrified and reviled in equal measure.

The Young Ones found a cult audience right away – students and young adults in the 16–25-year-old band – but others were slow to catch on and it wasn't until repeat screenings that the series began to amass a sizeable audience. After the first series, the TV cast toured a stage version of *The Young Ones*, which played 23 decent-sized venues around Britain from February to May 1983. The show was introduced by Rik Mayall in his 'Kevin Turvey' persona and, at first, was wildly overlong, but by the end of the tour the players had cut it to a really tight piece and also learned much more about their characters. As a result, the second TV series was more confident and assured than the first and was also treated more seriously, even meriting the honour of a *Radio Times* front cover. As with punk and new wave music a few years earlier, the mainstream had found a way to accommodate the young rebels, and their outlandish ideas and styles were becoming assimilated into the norm.

Though perhaps lacking some of the raw verve of the first series, the second run of *The Young Ones* maintained a very high quality and, at the same time, demonstrated a maturation of the acting and writing talent. In the final episode, 'Summer Holiday', the main characters were killed off when their double-

decker bus exploded after tumbling over a cliff. This intentionally conclusive ending emphasised the players' reluctance to remain overlong in one situation, preferring instead to move on to other ideas – another break with tradition. Despite their untimely end, the team have occasionally reappeared, usually at fund-raising events and most memorably when singing along with Cliff Richard to 'Living Doll', a charity release that became a number-one hit single in April 1986. And in July 1984 Nigel Planer stepped out, solo, as neil (so written) to release a hippy-dippy cover version of Traffic's 'Hole In My Shoe', which peaked at the same number on the singles chart, two, as the original had done 17 years earlier.

The 12 episodes of *The Young Ones* featured many other members of the comedy cabaret circuit in guest roles, many appearing on TV for the first time. These included Mark Arden and Stephen Frost, Keith Allen, Helen Atkinson Wood, Jim Barclay, Chris Barrie, Arnold Brown, Robbie Coltrane, Lee Cornes, Andy de la Tour, the co-writer Ben Elton, Dawn French and Jennifer Saunders, Stephen Fry and Hugh Laurie, Gareth Hale and Norman Pace, Lenny Henry, Helen Lederer, Norman Lovett, Pauline Melville, Paul Merton, Daniel Peacock, David Rappaport, Tony Robinson and Emma Thompson. *Not The Nine O'Clock News* stars Mel Smith and Griff Rhys Jones also appeared, as did, with a nod to the previous generation of young blades, Terry Jones from *Monty Python*. Alexei Sayle appeared in many episodes, principally as Jerzy Balowski, the landlord of their slum, but also as other members of this mad East European family. (He wrote these sections himself.) But, undeniably anarchic though *The Young Ones* was, its main protagonists have realised, in retrospect, that it followed quite a traditional sitcom pattern – the four members were cast as a conventional surrogate family unit, with Mike as the father, Neil in the mother role and Rik and Vivian as the two bickering teenage kids. In the midst of all the mayhem, it was difficult to spot this at the time.

See also *Come Dancing With Jools Holland*, *Comic Relief*, *Bottom* and *Filthy, Rich And Catflap*.

Your Mother Wouldn't Like It

UK · ITV (CENTRAL) · CHILDREN'S SKETCH

21 × 25 mins · colour

Series One (7) 1 Nov–20 Dec 1985 · Fri 4.50pm

Series Two (7) 22 Aug–3 Oct 1986 · Fri mostly 4.50pm

Series Three (7) 18 Nov 1987–13 Jan 1988 · Wed mostly 4.50pm

MAIN CAST

Loaf	Ian Kirkby
Lonnie	Paul Stark
Cans	Tom Anderson (series 1)
Mary Rose	Karen Murden (series 1 & 2)
Pam, the announcer	Christina Norris (series 1 & 2)
The Wimp	Simon Schatzberger (series 1)

Other roles · · · · Richard Allenson (series 2), Julian Aubrey (series 2 & 3), Karl Collins (series 2 & 3), Ashley Cowdrey (series 2 & 3), Richard de Sousa (series 2 & 3), Alison Dury (series 2 & 3), Stacey Green (series 2 & 3), Tessa Harrison (series 2), Oliver Hawker (series 2 & 3), Pui Fan Lee (series 2), Julie Schatzberger (series 2 & 3), Dena Snelgrove (series 2), Tracie Stanley (series 2 & 3), Philip Wombwell (series 2 & 3), Phoebe Wood (series 2), Keeley Coxon (series 3), Mark Dexter (series 3), James Hooton (series 3), Gina Kawecka (series 3), Amanda Loy Ellis (series 3), Katie McReynolds (series 3), Steven Ryde (series 3), Shamaun Rafiq (series 3), Jason Smith (series 3), Shanila Wahid (series 3), Simon Townley (series 3), Debbie Wiseman (series 3), Tony Wharmby (series 3), Sally Johnson (series 3)

CREDITS

writers Bob Hescott (series 1–3), Mike Maynard (series 1 & 3), Peter Corey (series 2 & 3), Hugh Grant (series 2), Bob Hescott (series 2 & 3), Chris Lang (series 2), Andy Taylor (series 2), Gail Renard (series 2 & 3), Rick Vanes (series 3), Nigel Crowle (series 3), Russell Lewis (series 3) · *additional material* Sue Townsend (series 1) · *script editors/associates* Trevor McCallum (series 1 & 2), Peter Corey (series 3) · *directors* Paul Harrison/David Foster (7), Paul Harrison (6), Tony Cox (4), Mike Holgate (4) · *executive producer* Lewis Rudd · *producers* Peter Murphy (series 1 & 2), Paul Harrison/Sue Nott (series 3)

An innovative children's sketch production – winner of a Bafta Award for Best Children's Entertainment Programme – that spoofed and satirised life as experienced by youngsters and teenagers, and created such characters as the Superman-like Tweeman, superhero Street Budgie, Loaf and his tea-lady mother (both played by Ian Kirkby), the Tapeworm Puppet and, in the first series, journalist/reporter the Wimp. This latter part was taken by Simon Schatzberger, who was playing Adrian Mole in the first stage version of Sue Townsend's creation. Completing the connection, Townsend scripted the weekly Wimp sketches. The players were drawn from some of the 140 members of the Central Junior Television Workshop, based in Nottingham and sponsored by Central TV.

Some of the best-received sketches were set in Palace Hill, a *Grange Hill*-like comprehensive school supposedly attended by Princes William and Harry. These led to a spin-off series, *Palace Hill*, networked by Central from November 1988.

Your Show Of Shows

USA · NBC (MAX LIEBMAN PRODUCTIONS) · SKETCH

160 × 90 mins · b/w

US dates: 25 Feb 1950–5 June 1954

UK dates: 3 Oct 1990–13 Sep 1991 (28 × 30 mins) C4 Wed around 12 midnight then Fri around 1.20am

MAIN CAST

Sid Caesar
Imogene Coca
Carl Reiner
Howard Morris (1951–54)
Tom Avera (1950–51)

CREDITS

creators Max Liebman · *writers* Mel Tolkin, Lucille Kallen, Mel Brooks, Larry Gelbart, Bill Persky, Sam Denoff, Neil Simon, Woody Allen and others · *producer* Max Liebman

Your Show Of Shows is a bona fide American TV classic: a splendid 90-minute live comedy-variety series that dominated the genre at the time and indicated just what television comedy could achieve.

At the helm was Sid Caesar, a dour man offstage but, on it, a comedic dynamo of perfectly timed slapstick and outrageous verbal gobbledygook. Born on 8 September 1922 in Yonkers, New York, Caesar later claimed that it was while listening to the immigrant labourers who frequented his father's restaurant that he developed his great skill of imitating vocal inflections, dialects and the cadences of foreign languages. His first successes, on stage, employed routines featuring such verbal gymnastics. Broadway producer Max Liebman worked with Caesar at this time before putting the comic on television in *The Admiral Broadway Revue* (DuMont/NBC, 1949) alongside another of his protégés, Imogene Coca. Liebman was then approached by NBC and invited to create a live revue for the network, and he duly built a show around the *Admiral Broadway Revue* regulars Caesar, Coca and Tom Avera, with writers Mel Tolkin and Lucille Kallen.

Your Show Of Shows was unveiled on 25 February 1950 and benefited from one important lesson that Liebman and his crew had learned on the previous series: the camera was placed on the stage to create a more intimate atmosphere. Also aiding the new show's success, Caesar's growing confidence meant that his delivery, which previously had been marred by coughs and hesitations, improved immeasurably. Soon after, Carl Reiner was added for comic support and, later, so was Howard Morris (also from *The Admiral Broadway Revue*). Initially, Coca and Caesar performed separate routines, but when Coca ran out of solo material Liebman suggested she team up with Caesar. The result was dynamic: Coca and Caesar worked superbly together, a double-act made in heaven. Their slots quickly became the highlight of the show and the entire format was altered to showcase them. They performed many memorable routines over the years, the best being the recurring misadventures of the

ill-matched married couple Charlie and Doris Hickenlooper. Other outstanding moments from *Your Show Of Shows* included the silent-movie and contemporary-movie spoofs starring the main cast, and the array of colourful characters that Caesar invented, especially Italian film expert Guiseppe Marinara and jazz musician Progress Hornsby.

After *Your Show Of Shows*, Caesar, Reiner and Morris appeared together in *Caesar's Hour* (NBC 1954–57) but the absence of Imogene Coca was sorely evident. Then, in 1958, the BBC lured Caesar and his crew, including Coca, to London for **Sid Caesar Invites You**, in which certain skits from *Your Show Of Shows* were re-performed. This bold move gave UK viewers first glimpse of the US dream team, although some of the material may have been familiar – the impresario Jack Hylton had purchased a quantity of sketches and jokes for his Associated-Rediffusion ITV comedy shows.

On 5 April 1967 the four central figures reunited for *The Sid Caesar, Imogene Coca, Carl Reiner, Howard Morris Special* on CBS (not screened in Britain) and in 1973 Liebman gathered together many of the best sketches for a feature film release, *Ten From Your Show Of Shows*. He also repackaged the surviving material for *The Best Of Show Of Shows*, a TV series of 65 half-hours – 28 of these turned up on C4 in the 1990s (under the title *Sid Caesar's Show Of Shows*), each programme featuring a number of sketches and comedy routines but without the variety aspect of the original programmes.

A reunion of Caesar with many of his writers, including Brooks, Reiner and Simon, taped in front of an enthusiastic Los Angeles audience, was screened in Britain on 24 December 1996 as *Caesar's Writers*, a one-hour celebration shown under the BBC2 *Arena* arts-documentary banner.

Yus My Dear

UK · ITV (LWT) · SITCOM

19 × 30 mins · colour

Series One (6) 11 Jan–15 Feb 1976 · Sun 7.25pm

Series Two (13) 3 Sep–4 Dec 1976 · Fri 8.30pm then Sat mostly 7pm

MAIN CAST

Wally Briggs	Arthur Mullard
Lily Briggs	Queenie Watts
Benny Briggs	Mike Reid
Molly	Valerie Walsh

CREDITS

writers Ronald Wolfe/Ronald Chesney · *director/producer* Stuart Allen

In this sequel to **Romany Jones**, Wally and Lily Briggs have gorn up in the world: from a gypsy caravan site to a council house. Wally has also suddenly grown an adult brother,

Benny, whose attributes include staying on the dole and a seemingly pathological urge to sponge off his big bruvver, to the point where he too – much to the chagrin of Lily – moves into the council house.

In the first series, Benny has a girlfriend, the blowsy Molly, to whom he becomes engaged, but the relationship falters in the second. Wally is earning a fair wage from his bricklaying job but he doesn't need much persuading from his sibling to enjoy a flutter on the dogs. (The part of Benny was the first 'acting' role for cockney comic Mike Reid, from **The Comedians**, a career path that would lead to Frank Butcher in *EastEnders*.)

To be blunt, *Yus My Dear* was even worse than *Romany Jones*, and must rank as one of the most excruciating sitcoms of all time, a real black-spot on Wolfe and Chesney's CV. Blessed are those who spent all of 1976 out of the country, though: they missed the whole thing.

Zero Hour

USA · ABC · SKETCH

1 × 60 mins · colour

US date: 1 May 1967

UK date: 3 Sep 1967 · BBC2 Sun 8.55pm

MAIN CAST

Zero Mostel
Joshua Mostel
Sudie Bond
Barney Martin
John Pleshette

CREDITS

writers John Aylesworth, Ian Hunter, Pat McCormick, Jack Burns, Avery Schreiber, Mel Brooks · *director* Dwight Hemion · *producers* Gary Smith, Dwight Hemion

Born in Brooklyn on 28 February 1915, Samuel Joel Mostel – the son of an orthodox rabbi – began performing comedy in 1942 to support his hobby as an artist. He was nicknamed Zero because this, others deemed, was his chance of finding success. But succeed he did, winning Tony awards for his Broadway performances in Ionesco's *Rhinoceros* in 1961, in *A Funny Thing Happened On The Way To The Forum* (1962, in the same two roles that Frankie Howerd performed in the later London version) and in *Fiddler On The Roof* (1964).

Mostel demonstrated his style of zany and frantic slapstick farce in this one-off TV special made by ABC and screened four months later by the BBC. Skits included his impressions of a coffee percolator and a baby discovering hands, and a sketch in which he appeared as a famous tenor being interviewed by a bright female journalist. Among the supporting cast was Zero's son Joshua, nine-years-old at this time but later an adult actor on film and TV.

The following year, 1968, Zero Mostel enjoyed perhaps his greatest moment, appearing as the harassed Broadway producer in the movie *The Producers*, written and directed by *Zero Hour* co-writer Mel Brooks.

Zero Mostel died on 17 September 1977.

Zig And Zag's Dirty Deeds

UK · C4 (PLANET 24/WORKING TITLE TELEVISION/ZIG AND ZAG ENTERPRISES) · CHILDREN'S SITCOM

8 × 30 mins · colour

Special · 25 Dec 1994 · Sun 5.30pm

One series (7) 5 May–16 June 1996 · Sun 5.05pm

MAIN CAST

Zig And Zag

CREDITS

writers Zig And Zag · *director* Angelo Abela · *producer* Simon Wright

Puppets Zig And Zag, a pair of furry, bug-eyed brothers from the planet Zog, made a huge impact as comedy relief on C4's anarchic entertainment miscellany *The Big Breakfast* (1992 to date). The quick-witted, smart-mouthed aliens proved adept at grilling celebrities live on air and soon attracted a cult following. As a result, they were also given their own comedy series, a pastiche of *Challenge Anneka* (the BBC1 series where presenter Anneka Rice performed a difficult good deed) wherein, among other tasks, they helped presenter Chris Evans to mount a *Gingerella* musical, aided *Coronation Street* star Reg Holdsworth to attract show business personalities to the opening of his restaurant Planet Reg, and assisted 'supermodel' Elle MacPherson in her attempts to retrieve some stolen unflattering photos.

Eighteen months before the series, Richard Wilson and Stan Boardman appeared in a one-off Christmas special, alternatively titled *Zig And Zag – Entertainment Cops*, in which the Zogian superstars acted as 'comedy police', booking anyone who wasn't up to scratch comedically.

Notes. The identity of the Zig And Zag writers/puppeteers/voices has not been revealed because they wish to remain anonymous.

A new Zig And Zag series was being planned as this book was being completed, for screening in summer 1998.

Zu Jung Um Blond Zu Sein

see The Montreux Festival

Zzzap!

UK · ITV (THE MEDIA MERCHANTS FOR MERIDIAN) · CHILDREN'S SKETCH

58 editions (32 × 15 mins · 26 × 20 mins) · colour

Series One (10 × 20 mins) 8 Jan–12 Mar 1993 · Fri 3.55pm

Series Two (10 × 20 mins) 7 Jan–11 Mar 1994 · Fri 3.55pm

Series Three (10 × 15 mins) 6 Jan–10 Mar 1995 · Fri 3.55pm

Series Four (10 × 15 mins) 5 Jan–8 Mar 1996 · Fri mostly 3.45pm

Series Five (4 × 15 mins) *Zzzap! Christmas Annuals* 29 Nov–20 Dec 1996 · Fri 3.40pm

Series Six (6 × 20 mins) 10 Jan–14 Feb 1997 · Fri 3.55pm

Series Seven (7 × 15 mins) 14 Oct–2 Dec 1997 · Tue mostly 4pm

Special (15 mins) *Zzzap! Christmas Annual* 16 Dec 1997 · Tue 4pm

MAIN CAST

Cuthbert Lilly · · · · · · · · · · · · Richard Waites
Daisy Dare · · · · · · · · · · · · Deborah McCallum
The Handymen · · · · · · · · · · · · Sarah Pickthall
Smart Arty · · · · · · · · · · · · · · · Neil Buchanan

CREDITS

director Adrian Hedley · *executive producer* Richard Moss · *producers* Tim Edmunds, Neil Buchanan

An award-winning confection aimed at young children, both deaf and hearing, and presented in the form of a comic – something like a cross between *Vision On* and *The Dandy*. The humour is broadly slapstick in nature and performed without dialogue, just grunts and exclamations, with words flashing on the screen in the manner of the 1960s series *Batman*.

The principal features in *Zzzap!* are Cuthbert Lilly (He's Dead Silly), basic slapstick strongly reminiscent of the silent film era; Daisy Dare, who loves to become embroiled in messy challenges; the Handymen, a pair of hands that demonstrate crafts and tricks; and the Gallic painter Smart Arty, whose works of art spring to life. This last character is played by Neil Buchanan, who co-produces the series with Tim Edmunds for their company the Media Merchants; before *Zzzap!*, Buchanan's credentials were already well established with children through his presentation of the acclaimed ITV crafts series *Art Attack*.

Lewisohn's Lists

Programmes listed in these appendices are those detailed in the book.

US series *not* screened on British television are excluded.

Top 20 lists 744

British & American sitcoms combined
British sitcoms
BBC sitcoms
British Commercial TV sitcoms
American sitcoms
British sketch-shows
The worst ever British sitcoms?
The worst ever American sitcoms?

Sitcom series with radio connections 746

British TV sitcoms previously broadcast on radio
British TV sitcom series later re-recorded for radio

Transatlantic sitcom adaptations 747

Britain to America
America to Britain

The most episodes of sitcoms... 748

Britain, 50+ episodes
American, 100+ episodes
100+ screenings on British TV of American series

Familiar sitcom themes 750

Services
Alien/sci-fi
School
Medical
Church
Jewish
Detective/police

Top 20 lists

British & American sitcoms combined

1 *Seinfeld* (USA)
2 *Fawlty Towers* (UK)
3 *The Phil Silvers Show* (USA)
4 *Porridge* (UK)
5 *Yes Minister* (UK)
6 *Frasier* (USA)
7 *M*A*S*H* (USA)
8 *Till Death Us Do Part* (UK)
9 *Hancock* (UK)
10 *Whatever Happened To The Likely Lads* (UK)
11 *The Larry Sanders Show* (USA)
12 *The Mary Tyler Moore Show* (USA)
13 *The Fall And Rise Of Reginald Perrin* (UK)
14 *The Good Life* (UK)
15 *Steptoe And Son* (UK)
16 *Only Fools And Horses* (UK)
17 *Cheers* (USA)
18 *The Dick Van Dyke Show* (USA)
19 *Dad's Army* (UK)
20 *The Honeymooners* (USA)

British sitcoms

1 *Fawlty Towers* (BBC)
2 *Porridge* (BBC)
3 *Yes Minister* (BBC)
4 *Till Death Us Do Part* (BBC)
5 *Hancock* (BBC)
6 *Whatever Happened To The Likely Lads* (BBC)
7 *The Fall And Rise Of Reginald Perrin* (BBC)
8 *The Good Life* (BBC)
9 *Steptoe And Son* (BBC)
10 *Only Fools And Horses* (BBC)
11 *Dad's Army* (BBC)
12 *Rising Damp* (ITV)
13 *Absolutely Fabulous* (BBC)
14 *One Foot In The Grave* (BBC)
15 *Open All Hours* (BBC)
16 *After Henry* (ITV)
17 *Blackadder Goes Forth* (BBC)
18 *Agony* (ITV)
19 *Father Ted* (C4)
20 *The Young Ones* (BBC)

BBC sitcoms

1 *Fawlty Towers*
2 *Porridge*
3 *Yes Minister*
4 *Till Death Us Do Part*
5 *Hancock*
6 *Whatever Happened To The Likely Lads*
7 *The Fall And Rise Of Reginald Perrin*
8 *The Good Life*
9 *Steptoe And Son*
10 *Only Fools And Horses*
11 *Dad's Army*
12 *Absolutely Fabulous*
13 *One Foot In The Grave*
14 *Open All Hours*
15 *Blackadder Goes Forth*
16 *The Young Ones*
17 *The Vicar Of Dibley*
18 *Men Behaving Badly*
19 *I Didn't Know You Cared*
20 *Last Of The Summer Wine*

British Commercial TV sitcoms

1 *Rising Damp*
2 *After Henry*
3 *Agony*
4 *Father Ted*
5 *The New Statesman*
6 *Drop The Dead Donkey*
7 *Girls On Top*
8 *For The Love Of Ada*
9 *Brass*
10 *Bless Me, Father*
11 *Outside Edge*
12 *Up The Garden Path*
13 *The Last Of The Baskets*
14 *Bootsie And Snudge*
15 *A Fine Romance*
16 *Home To Roost*
17 *The Larkins*
18 *Doctor In The House*
19 *Second Thoughts*
20 *Shelley*

American sitcoms

1 *Seinfeld*
2 *The Phil Silvers Show*
3 *Frasier*
4 *M*A*S*H*
5 *The Larry Sanders Show*
6 *The Mary Tyler Moore Show*
7 *Cheers*
8 *The Dick Van Dyke Show*
9 *The Honeymooners*
10 *The Beverly Hillbillies*
11 *Police Squad*
12 *Soap*
13 *Dream On*
14 *Friends*
15 *Roseanne*
16 *Get Smart*
17 *Taxi*
18 *The Addams Family*
19 *Car 54, Where Are You?*
20 *All In The Family*

British sketch-shows

1 *Monty Python's Flying Circus* (BBC)
2 *The Morecambe And Wise Show* (ITV/BBC)
3 *Not Only ... But Also* (BBC)
4 *Not The Nine O'Clock News* (BBC)
5 *The Fast Show* (BBC)
6 *The Two Ronnies* (BBC)
7 *It's Marty* (aka *Marty*) (BBC)
8 *Victoria Wood: As Seen On TV* (BBC)
9 *French And Saunders* (BBC)
10 *Harry Enfield* (*Television Programme* and *Chums*) (BBC)
11 *Q* (BBC)
12 *The Stanley Baxter Show* (BBC/ITV)
13 *The Arthur Haynes Show* (ITV)
14 *At Last The 1948 Show* (ITV)
15 *The Benny Hill Show* (BBC/ITV)
16 *A Bit Of Fry And Laurie* (BBC)
17 *Alexei Sayle's Stuff* (BBC)
18 *Who Dares, Wins ...* (C4)
19 *The Kenny Everett Video Show* (ITV)
20 *Do Not Adjust Your Set* (ITV)

The worst ever British sitcoms?

20 *Sir Yellow* (ITV)
19 *Up The Elephant And Round The Castle* (ITV)
18 *Trouble In Mind* (ITV)
17 *Take A Letter, Mr Jones ...* (ITV)
16 *My Husband And I* [1987–88] (ITV)
15 *Constant Hot Water* (ITV)
14 *High & Dry* (ITV)
13 *Come Back Mrs Noah* (BBC)
12 *Tripper's Day/Slinger's Day* (ITV)
11 *High Street Blues* (ITV)
10 *Room Service* (ITV)
9 *Romany Jones* (ITV)
8 *Rule Britannia* (ITV)
7 *Selwyn* (ITV)
6 *Don't Drink The Water* (ITV)
5 *Odd Man Out* (ITV)
4 *In For A Penny* (ITV)
3 *Plaza Patrol* (ITV)
2 *Yus My Dear* (ITV)
1 *Bottle Boys* (ITV)

The worst ever American sitcoms?

20 *The Flying Nun*
19 *Makin' It*
18 *One Of the Boys*
17 *Gilligan's Island*
16 *Just Our Luck*
15 *Starting From Scratch*
14 *Dusty's Trail*
13 *The Charmings*
12 *Me And The Chimp*
11 *Mr Merlin*
10 *The Munsters Today*
9 *Punky Brewster*
8 *Running The Halls*
7 *Mr Smith*
6 *California Dreams*
5 *Small Wonder*
4 *Saved By The Bell*
3 *We Got It Made*
2 *Saved By The Bell: The College Years*
1 *Saved By The Bell: The New Class*

Sitcom series with radio connections

British TV sitcoms previously broadcast on radio

whether originating on radio or as books, plays, feature films, etc

An Actor's Life For Me
After Henry
Charters And Caldicott
Club Night
The Darling Buds Of May
Doctor In The House
Educating Archie/Here's Archie
Gert And Daisy
The Glums
Hancock's Half-Hour
The Hitch-Hiker's Guide To The Galaxy
Jennings
Just Jimmy
A Life Of Bliss
Life With The Lyons
Living It Up
Marlene Marlowe Investigates
The Preventers
Pull The Other One
Sam And Janet
Second Thoughts
The Secret Diary Of Adrian Mole, Aged 13 $^3/_4$
The Squirrels
This Is David Lander/This Is David Harper
The Trouble With Lilian
Up The Garden Path
William
Worzel Gummidge

British TV sitcom series later re-recorded for radio

either originating on TV or as books, plays, feature films, etc

All Gas And Gaiters
As Time Goes By
Big Jim And The Figaro Club
Blandings Castle
Brothers-In-Law
Dad's Army
Hugh And I
The Likely Lads/Whatever Happened To The Likely Lads
Marriage Lines
Not In Front Of The Children
One Foot In The Grave
Shelley
Steptoe And Son
To The Manor Born
Ukridge
Whack-O!
The World Of Wooster
Yes Minister

Additionally, *The Telegoons* was a variation of *The Goon Show*. Several TV sketch shows have originated on radio, such as *Naked Video* (which began as *Naked Radio*), *The Day Today* (*On The Hour*), *Knowing Me, Knowing You*, *KYTV* (*Radio Active*), *The Jasper Carrott Trial* and *The Mary Whitehouse Experience*. Beyond the scope of this book, TV comedy quiz-shows, panel-games and the like, such as *Whose Line Is It Anyway?*, *Have I Got News For You* (based upon *The News Quiz*), *Just A Minute*, *They Think It's All Over* and *Room 101*, also began on BBC radio.

Transatlantic sitcom adaptations

Britain to America

British	American
Agony	The Lucie Arnaz Show
Are You Being Served?	Beane's Of Boston PB
Astronauts	The Astronauts PB
Billy Liar	Billy
Birds Of A Feather	Stand By Your Man
The Bounder	The Bounder PB
Butterflies	Butterflies PB
Dad's Army	Rear Guard PB
Dear John	Dear John*
The Fall And Rise Of Reginald Perrin	Reggie*
Fawlty Towers	Snavely PB; Amanda's
A Fine Romance	A Fine Romance PB
For The Love Of Ada	A Touch of Grace
Full House	No Place Like Home PB
George And Mildred	The Ropers
Girls On Top	(title not known) PU
Home To Roost	You Again?
Keep It In The Family	Too Close For Comfort* / The Ted Knight Show
The Likely Lads	Stuebenville PU
Love Thy Neighbour	Love Thy Neighbor
Man About The House	Three's Company*
The Many Wives Of Patrick	The Many Wives Of Patrick PU
Men Behaving Badly	Men Behaving Badly
Mind Your Language	What A Country!
Miss Jones And Son	Miss Winslow And Son
My Wife Next Door	My Wife Next Door PB
Nearest And Dearest	Thicker Than Water
News At Twelve	News At Twelve PU
Nightingales	Nightingales PU
No – Honestly	No – Honestly PU
On The Buses	Lotsa Luck
One Foot In The Grave	Cosby
Pig In The Middle	Oh, Madeline*
Porridge	On The Rocks
The Rag Trade	The Rag Business PB
Red Dwarf	Red Dwarf PU
Rising Damp	27 Joy Street PU
Robin's Nest	Three's A Crowd*
Second Time Around	Second Time Around PU
A Sharp Intake Of Breath	Harry's Battles PB
Steptoe And Son	Sanford And Son
Three Up, Two Down	5 Up, 2 Down PB
Till Death Us Do Part	All In The Family*
Tom, Dick And Harriet	Foot In The Door
Tripper's Day/Slinger's Day	Check It Out
Two's Company	The Two Of Us*

America to Britain

American	UK
'The Commuters'	Something In The City (from Caesar's Hour)
Ethel And Albert	Chintz
The Golden Girls	Brighton Belles
Good Times	The Fosters
Mad About You	Loved By You
Married ... With Children	Married For Life
Maude	Nobody's Perfect
Starting From Scratch	Close To Home
Who's The Boss?	The Upper Hand

Notes.

PB indicates that the programme only extended to a pilot, not a full series. PU indicates that said pilot was not broadcast.

* Indicates that the US adaptation has itself aired on UK terrestrial TV.

Note. Six further US adaptations were being planned when this book went to press, of the British series Blind Men, Faith In The Future, Game On, Holding The Baby, Keeping Up Appearances and Sunnyside Farm.

Beyond the sitcom format, other UK comedy shows that have been adapted for the US market include That Was The Week That Was (the US version had the same title), Not The Nine O'Clock News (adapted as Not Necessarily The News) and Spitting Image (which led to DC Follies).

The most episodes of sitcoms...

Britain, 50+ episodes
to 31/12/97

162 *Last Of The Summer Wine*[1] (BBC)
154 *The Army Game* (ITV)
148 The *Doctor* series[2] (ITV/BBC)
138 *Chucklevision* (BBC)
128 *Sykes*[3] (BBC)
116 *The Dickie Henderson Show* (sitcom version) (ITV)
110 *Bodger And Badger* (BBC)
109 *Till Death Us Do Part*[4] (BBC/ITV/BBC)
104 *Bootsie And Snudge*[5] (ITV)
95 *The Upper Hand* (ITV)
93 *Mike & Angelo*[1] (ITV)
89 *Birds Of A Feather*[1] (BBC)
87 *The Liver Birds* § (BBC)
85 *'Allo 'Allo!* (BBC)
83 *Dad's Army* (BBC)
79 *Hugh And I* (BBC)
77 *The Goodies* (BBC/ITV)
76 *On The Buses* (ITV)
74 *Bread* (BBC)
71 *Desmond's* (C4)
71 *Joan And Leslie/Leslie Randall Entertains* (ITV)
71 *Shelley* (ITV)
69 *Are You Being Served?* (BBC)
67 *Never The Twain* (ITV)
65 *Bless This House* (ITV)
65 *Terry And June* (BBC)
64 *Hancock's Half-Hour/Hancock* (BBC)
63 *Only Fools And Horses* (BBC)
63 *Whack-O!*[5] (BBC)
60 *Drop The Dead Donkey* (C4)
60 *Here's Harry* (BBC)
59 *Steptoe And Son* (BBC)
59 *The Rag Trade*[5] (BBC/ITV)
58 *Hi-de-Hi!* (BBC)
58 *Rentaghost* (BBC)
57 *Please, Sir!* (ITV)
56 *It Ain't Half Hot Mum* (BBC)
56 *Love Thy Neighbour* (ITV)
56 *Watching* (ITV)
53 *The Brittas Empire* (BBC)
52 *Beryl's Lot* (ITV)
52 *Me & My Girl* (ITV)
51 *Billy Bunter Of Greyfriars School* (BBC)
50 *Surgical Spirit* (ITV)

1 Further series screened in 1998 will have increased this figure
2 All the UK-made *Doctor* series combined
3 A combination of *Sykes And A ...* and *Sykes*
4 A combination of *Till Death Us Do Part*, *Till Death ...* and *In Sickness And In Health*
5 Original and revival runs combined

American, 100+ episodes
to 31/12/97

380 *My Three Sons*
343 *The Jack Benny Program*
325 *Mary Hartman, Mary Hartman*
291 *The Burns And Allen Show*
274 *The Beverly Hillbillies*
270 *Cheers*
256 *Happy Days*
254 *Bewitched*
251 *M*A*S*H*
251 *Married ... With Children*
238 *The Life Of Riley*
231 *Murphy Brown* *
220 *Roseanne*
212 *Petticoat Junction*
211 *Coach*
202 *Alice*
202 *All In The Family*
197 *The Cosby Show*
196 *Who's The Boss?*
193 *Night Court*
189 *Diff'rent Strokes*
188 *The Simpsons* *
184 *Newhart*
180 *I Love Lucy*
178 *Laverne And Shirley*
178 *The Golden Girls*
173 *The Bob Cummings Show*
170 *Empty Nest*
170 *Green Acres*
169 *Barney Miller*
169 *Three's Company*
168 *Hogan's Heroes*
168 *The Mary Tyler Moore Show*
165 *Family Ties*
161 *Home Improvement* *
160 *Seinfeld* *
158 *Benson*
158 *The Dick Van Dyke Show*
156 *The Lucy Show*
154 *Hazel*
151 *Step By Step* *
151 *Too Close For Comfort/ The Ted Knight Show*
150 *Perfect Strangers*
147 *The Many Loves Of Dobie Gillis*
146 *Dennis The Menace*
144 *Here's Lucy*
144 *Mister Ed*
144 *The Fresh Prince Of Bel Air*
143 *A Different World*
143 *The Phil Silvers Show*

139 *I Dream Of Jeannie*
139 *McHale's Navy*
138 *Get Smart*
130 *Private Secretary*
128 *The Doris Day Show*
126 *Charles In Charge*
122 *Kate & Allie*
119 *Doogie Howser, MD*
118 *9 To 5*
118 *Dream On*
117 *The Brady Bunch*
116 *Silver Spoons*
115 *Brothers*
114 *The Odd Couple*
114 *The Wonder Years*
113 *Head Of The Class*
113 *Taxi*
111 *Blossom*
111 *Saved By The Bell: The New Class* *
110 *Amen*
110 *Valerie* (etc)
108 *Rhoda*
107 *My Favorite Martian*
105 *Frasier* *
105 *Grace Under Fire* *
102 *ALF*

* Further episodes screened in 1998 will have increased this figure

100+ screenings on British TV of American series

to 31/12/97

270 *Cheers*
252 *M*A*S*H*
220 *Roseanne*
199 *The Cosby Show*
188 *Alice*
187 *Happy Days*
178 *The Golden Girls*
173 *I Love Lucy*
157 *The Dick Van Dyke Show*
156 *The Lucy Show*
148 *The Beverly Hillbillies*
146 *Diff'rent Strokes*
143 *A Different World*
132 *The Burns And Allen Show*
130 *The Phil Silvers Show*
121 *Kate & Allie*
115 *The Wonder Years*
114 *The Brady Bunch*
113 *Benson*
111 *Coach* *
110 *Taxi*
108 *Blossom*
108 *Rhoda*
105 *My Three Sons*
103 *Dennis The Menace* (as *Just Dennis*)
100 *Home Improvement* *
100 *I Dream Of Jeannie*

* Further episodes screened in 1998 will have increased this figure

Notes. In some instances, British channels screen more episodes of American sitcoms than are shown on US television, the result of hour-length shows being split into two half-hours.

Repeat runs may have subsequently increased these tallies. These figures refer to *initial-run* broadcasts.

Familiar sitcom themes

Services

The Airbase (UK)
The Army Game (UK)
Blackadder Goes Forth (UK)
Colonel Trumper's Private War (UK)
Dad's Army (UK)
F Troop (USA)
Get Some In! (UK)
HMS Paradise (UK)
Hogan's Heroes (USA)
M*A*S*H (USA)
McHale's Navy (USA)
Merry-Go-Round (UK)
No Time For Sergeants (USA)
The Phil Silvers Show (USA)
Private Benjamin (USA)
The Sky Larks (UK)
Tell It To The Marines (UK)
Thundercloud (UK)
Yanks Go Home (UK)

School

A J Wentworth, BA (UK)
Billy Bunter Of Greyfriars School (UK)
Bonjour La Classe (UK)
The Boot Street Band (UK)
California Dreams (USA)
Chalk (UK)
Chris Cross (UK)
Educating Marmalade (UK)
The Eggheads (UK)
Gruey (UK)
Hang Time (USA)
Hardwicke House (UK)
Head Of The Class (USA)
Jennings At School (UK)
Julia Jekyll And Harriet Hyde (UK)
Knight School (UK)
Mind Your Language (UK)
Palace Hill (UK)
Pinkerton's Progress (UK)
Please, Sir! (UK)
Porterhouse Blue (UK)
Running The Halls (USA)
Saved By The Bell (etc) (USA)
Square Pegs (USA)
USA High (USA)
Welcome Back, Kotter (USA)
Whack-O! (UK)

Alien/sci-fi

ALF (USA)
The Bumblies (UK)
Come Back Mrs Noah (UK)
The Groovy Fellers (UK)
Halfway Across The Galaxy And Turn Left (Australia)
Hard Time On Planet Earth (USA)
The Hitch-Hiker's Guide To The Galaxy (UK)
Kappatoo/Kappatoo II (UK)
Kinvig (UK)
Luna (UK)
Mike & Angelo (UK)
Mork And Mindy (USA)
My Favorite Martian (USA)
Out Of This World (USA)
Red Dwarf (UK)
Snug And Cozi (UK)
Spacevets (UK)
They Came From Somewhere Else (UK)
3rd Rock From The Sun (USA)
Watt On Earth (UK)
WYSIWYG (UK)

Medical

Doctor At Large (UK)
Doctor At Sea (UK)
Doctor At The Top (UK)
Doctor Down Under (Australia)
Doctor In Charge (UK)
Doctor In The House (UK)
Doctor On The Go (UK)
Doctor's Daughters (UK)
Don't Wait Up (UK)
Doogie Howser, MD (USA)
E/R (USA)
Get Well Soon (UK)
Health And Efficiency (UK)
House Calls (USA)
Let The Blood Run Free (Australia)
M*A*S*H (USA)
Never Say Die (UK)
Nurses (USA)
Only When I Laugh (UK)
Rude Health (UK)
Surgical Spirit (UK)
Tom, Dick And Mary (USA)

Church

All Gas And Gaiters (UK)
All In Good Faith (UK)
Amen (USA)
Bless Me, Father (UK)
Father Charlie (UK)
Father Matthew's Daughter (UK)
Father Ted (UK)
Going My Way (USA)
Hell's Bells (UK)
Oh Brother! (UK)
Oh Father! (UK)
Our Man At St Mark's/Our Man From St Mark's (UK)
Out Of Tune (UK)
Troubles & Strife (UK)
The Vicar Of Dibley (UK)

Jewish

Agony (UK)
Alexander The Greatest (UK)
Every Silver Lining (UK)
Fish (USA)
A Little Big Business (UK)
Making Faces (UK)
Never Mind The Quality, Feel The Width (UK)
Private Benjamin (USA)
Rhoda (USA)
Roots (UK)
So You Think You've Got Troubles (UK)
Vic's Grill (UK)

Detective/police

Ace Crawford, Private Eye (USA)
Bakersfield PD (USA)
Barney Miller (USA)
Campus Cops (USA)
Car 54, Where Are You? (USA)
Charters And Caldicott (UK)
Coppers End (UK)
The Detectives (UK)
Emery Presents (UK)
Follow That Dog (UK)
Funky Squad (Australia)
The Fuzz (UK)
Glas Y Dorlan (UK)
The Great Detective (UK)
The Growing Pains Of PC Penrose/Rosie (UK)
Herlock And Sholmes (UK)
Holmes And Yoyo (USA)
It's Murder. But Is It Art? (UK)
John Browne's Body (UK)
Lazarus And Dingwall (UK)
Marlene Marlowe Investigates (UK)
Mornin' Sarge (UK)
Murder Most Horrid (UK)
Nobody's Perfect (shown in UK as *Hart Of The Yard*) (USA)
Operation Good Guys (UK)
Pacific Station (USA)
Police Squad (USA)
Sledge Hammer! (USA)
Spooner's Patch (UK)
The Thin Blue Line (UK)

Chronology of Important Events in British TV

1936

2 November — Launch of the world's first 'high definition' TV service, by the BBC. Receivable only in London.

1937

12 May — The BBC mounts its first 'outside broadcast' to televise the Coronation.

1938

3 April — The BBC's first Sunday TV transmission.

1939

1 September — Television transmission ceases for the duration of the Second World War.

1946

7 June — The BBC resumes TV transmissions, still available only in the London area.

1949

17 December — BBC TV extends to the Midlands, the first area beyond London.

1951

12 October — BBC TV extends to the North of England.

1952

14 March — BBC TV extends to Scotland.
15 August — BBC TV extends to Wales and the West of England.

1953

1 May — BBC TV extends to Northern Ireland.
2 June — The BBC screens the Coronation.

1954

12 November — BBC TV extends to the South of England.
14 December — BBC TV extends to North-East of Scotland.
17 December — BBC TV extends to the South-West of England.

1955

1 February — BBC TV extends to the East of England.
22 September — ITV launches Britain's first commercial television channel, with programmes for the London area. The local providers are Associated-Rediffusion (A-R) on weekdays and – after a name change from Associated Broadcasting Company (ABC) – Associated TeleVision (ATV) at weekends (commencing 24 September).
3 October — BBC TV extends to the Channel Islands.

1956

17 February — ITV extends to the Midlands, the local provider being ATV on weekdays and ABC Television at weekends (commencing 18 February).
3 May — ITV extends to Lancashire and Yorkshire, the local provider being Granada Television on weekdays and ABC at weekends (commencing 5 May).

1957

31 August — ITV extends to Central Scotland, the local provider being Scottish Television.

1958

14 January — ITV extends to South Wales and the West of England, the local provider being TWW.
30 August — ITV extends to Central South and South-East England, the local provider being Southern Television.

1959

15 January — ITV extends to the North-East of England, the local provider being Tyne Tees Television.
27 October — ITV extends to the East of England, the local provider being Anglia Television.
31 October — ITV extends to Northern Ireland, the local provider being Ulster Television.

1961

29 April — ITV extends to the South-West of England, the local provider being Westward Television.
1 September — ITV extends to the border area of England and Scotland, the local provider being Border Television.
30 September — ITV extends to North-East Scotland, the local provider being Grampian Television.

1962

1 September — ITV extends to the Channel Islands, the local provider being Channel Television.
14 September — ITV extends to West and North Wales, the local provider being Wales (West and North) Television. Welsh-language programming is a key part of its brief. (The company merges with TWW in January 1964.)

1964

9 February — BBC Wales is launched, providing Welsh-language TV programming.
6 April — Associated-Rediffusion is renamed Rediffusion.

20 April	Launch of BBC2, the BBC's second channel, available at this point only from the London transmitter. The first channel, hitherto known only as BBC Television, is renamed BBC1.
6 December	BBC2 extends to the Midlands.

1965

12 September	BBC2 extends to Wales and the West of England.
31 October	BBC2 extends to the North of England.

1966

15 January	BBC2 extends to the South of England and further areas of Yorkshire. (The remaining areas are reached soon afterwards.)

1967

1 July	BBC2 broadcasts in colour for the first time. (Only selected programmes at this point; the full output becomes colour on 2 December.)

1968

3 March	TWW transmissions cease. Harlech Television (HTV) begins supplying ITV programming to the West of England and all of Wales from the following day (4 March).
28 July	ABC broadcasts its final programmes. From the following weekend (2 August) ATV becomes a seven-days-a-week company in the Midlands for the first time.
29 July	Yorkshire Television is launched. Granada, which hitherto provided ITV programmes to the North (except the North-East) on weekdays, now broadcasts seven-days-a-week but to the North-West only.
29 July	Rediffusion transmissions cease. The station merges with ABC to become Thames Television, delivering weekday broadcasting to the London area from the following day (30 July).
2 August	London Weekend Television (LWT) commences, delivering ITV programmes to the London area from Friday evening to Sunday night.

1969

15 November	BBC1 and ITV begin colour transmissions. (The service gradually becomes national over the next year.)

1974

23 September	BBC launches its teletext service, Ceefax. (Eventually, all British TV channels, including cable/satellite, carry text services.)

1979

10 August	With some stations having been blank since 6 August, the entire ITV network (except for Channel Television) is forced off air by industrial action. Although far from being the only British TV strike this is certainly the longest, ITV enduring a 75-day break until the resumption of services on 24 October.

1981

11 August	Westward transmissions cease. Television South West (TSW) takes over from the following day (12 August).
31 December	Further ITV franchise changes. ATV transmissions cease and (from 1 January 1982) Central Independent Television takes over programme provision in the Midlands. Southern loses franchise to Television South (TVS).

1982

2 November	The launch of Channel 4, Britain's second commercial and fourth nationally available terrestrial channel (subject, at first, to local reception difficulties). Also launched, in Wales, is a Welsh-language channel, Sianel Pedwar Cymru (S4C).

1983

28 January	The BBC launches its breakfast TV programming.
1 February	ITV launches its breakfast TV programming, TV-am.

1989

5 February	Britain's first four satellite TV channels are launched by Sky.

1992

31 December	ITV franchise changes. A number of providers cease transmissions at midnight, superseded on 1 January 1993 by new companies: Carlton takes over weekday programme provision in the London area, replacing Thames. Meridian takes over from TVS in the South, Westcountry Television takes over from TSW in the West and GMTV takes over from TV-am as ITV's national breakfast-TV provider.

1997

30 March	The launch of Channel 5, Britain's third commercial and fifth nationally available terrestrial channel (subject, at first, to local reception difficulties).

Bibliography

Source materials consulted in the course of researching and writing this book.

Television Programmes/records/Archives

Substantial information in this book has been gleaned from press and publicity materials issued by the BBC, the plethora of ITV companies past and present and American TV networks and distributors. I have also been fortunate in gaining access to internally distributed archive documents and programme production files for a number of ITV companies, including several no longer functioning, the BBC's extensive programme files and, crucially, its programme-index. Cast and production credits have been corroborated by reference to a substantial collection of comedy programmes taped over the past 20 years.

The numerous BBC libraries have yielded valuable information, as have the ITC library, the British Library Newspaper Library at Colindale and the film and TV information database at the BFI.

Publications issued by the non-profit-making TV research organisation Kaleidoscope have been very useful in establishing transmission details and archive holdings of British-made programmes. (For details contact Kaleidoscope Publishing, 47 Ashton Road, Ashton, Bristol BS3 2EQ, England.)

Magazines, Newspapers and Journals

British daily and evening newspapers, national and provincial, 1936 to date.

Radio Times, published by the BBC from September 1923 to date. TV issues began with the launch of the service in November 1936. BBC programme information published exclusively here in magazine form until February 1991, since when *Radio Times* has listed details of all channels.

TV Times, published in London from September 1955 to September 1968.

London ITV programme information. All regional variations also consulted. At this time, certain other ITV regions published their own programme journals; those consulted for this volume include *TV World* (for ATV/ABC areas), *Television Weekly* (for TWW) and *The Viewer* (for Tyne Tees).

TVTimes, published in London from September 1968 to date. ITV (and, from November 1982, C4) programme information published exclusively here in magazine form until February 1991, since when it has listed details of all channels. All regional variations also consulted, principally for Granada, Yorkshire, Central, TVS/Meridian and Scottish TV programming.

Broadcast (incorporating *Television Week*), the British TV industry trade magazine, weekly; currently published.

The Stage (incorporating *Television Today*), the British entertainments newspaper, weekly since 1880; currently published.

TV Mirror, a weekly consumer magazine published in Britain in the 1950s.

TV Guide, the principal weekly TV consumer publication (listings and features) in the USA, April 1953 to date.

The Box, a monthly TV consumer magazine, published in Britain in 1997.

Primetime, an occasional, subscription-only TV fan magazine, published in Britain 1981–91.

Cor!, an occasional, subscription-only TV fan magazine, currently published. (For details contact Robert Ross, 24 Richmond Road, Basingstoke, Hampshire RG21 5NX, England.)

Laugh: The Comedy Magazine, an occasional, subscription-only TV fan magazine, currently published. (For details contact Peter Tatchell, PO Box 394, Caulfield East, Victoria 3145, Australia.)

Books

In addition to the information books listed below, reference has been made to scores of biographies and autobiographies of artists, writers, producers, directors and industry figures pertaining to the field of television and/or radio comedy.

A&E Entertainment Almanac, 1996, 1997, 1998, Rowan, Beth and various eds; Houghton Mifflin Company, Boston.

The Addams Chronicles: Everything You Ever Wanted To Know About The Addams Family, Cox, Steven; HarperPerennial/HarperCollins, New York; 1991.

All Star TV Annual, various up to 1970; various eds; various publishers, London.

America On The Rerun: TV Shows That Never Die, Story, David; Citadel Press/Carol Publishing Group, New York; 1993.

Archie & Edith, Mike & Gloria: The Tumultuous History Of All In The Family, McCrohan, Donna; Workman Publishing, New York; 1987.

A TV Show Book, various up to 1968, various eds, Purnell, London.

A TV Television Star Book/Who's Who In Show Biz, various up to 1964, various eds, Purnell, London.

The Australian Film And Television Companion, Harrison, Tony; Simon & Schuster, Australia; 1994.

BBC Handbook/Yearbook/Annual Report, various 1928–87, various eds, BBC and various publishers, London.

The Beverly Hillbillies, Cox, Stephen; Contemporary Books, Chicago; 1988.

The Bewitched Book, Pilato, Herbie J; Delta/Dell Publishing, New York; 1992.

Beyond The Fringe … And Beyond, Bergan, Ronald; Virgin Books/W H Allen & Co, London; 1989.

Black And White In Colour: Black People In British Television Since 1936, ed Pines, Jim; BFI Publishing, London; 1992.

Box Of Delights: The Golden Years Of Television, Kingsley, Hilary, and Tibballs, Geoff; Macmillan, London; 1989.

Bring Me Laughter: Four Decades Of TV Comedy, Crowther, Bruce, and Pinfold, Mike; Columbus Books, London; 1987.

British Film Institute Film And Television Yearbook/Handbook, 1983–98, various eds, BFI, London.

British Television: Your Guide To Over 1100 Favourite Programmes, comp Vahimagi, Tise; Oxford University Press, Oxford; 1994.

Broadcasting It, Howes, Keith; Cassell, London; 1993.

The Carry On Companion, Ross, Robert; Batsford, London; 1996.

Classic Sitcoms: A Celebration Of The Best In Prime-Time Comedy, Waldron, Vince; Macmillan, New York; 1987.

Comedy Greats: A Celebration Of Comic Genius Past And Present, Took, Barry; Equation/Thorsons Publishing Group, Wellingborough; 1989.

Comics: A Decade Of Comedy At The Assembly Rooms, Connor, John; Papermac/Macmillan, London; 1990.

The Complete Book of M*A*S*H, Kalter, Suzy; Harry N Abrams, New York; 1984.

The Complete Directory To Prime Time Network And Cable TV Shows: 1946–Present, 6th ed, Brooks, Tim, and Marsh, Earle; Ballantine Books, New York; 1995.

The Complete Directory To Prime Time TV Stars 1946–Present, Brooks, Tim; Ballantine Books/Random House, New York; 1987.

The Complete Encyclopedia Of Television Programs 1947–79, 2 vols, Terrace, Vincent; Thomas Yoseloff, London; 1976.

The Critics' Choice: The Best Of TV Sitcoms, Javna, John; Harmony Books/Crown Publishers, New York; 1988.

Cult TV: The Essential Critical Guide, Lewis, Jon E, and Stempel, Penny; Pavilion Books, London; 1993.

Curtain Up: The Story Of The Royal Variety Performance, Delfont, Lord; Robson Books; 1989.

Daily Mail All Channels TV Book; Daily Mail, London; 1958.

The Dick Van Dyke Show, Weissman, Ginny, and Sanders, Coyne Steven; St Martin's Press, New York; 1983.

Didn't You Kill My Mother-In-Law?: The Story Of Alternative Comedy In Britain From The Comedy Store To Saturday Live, Wilmut, Roger, and Rosengard, Peter; Methuen, London; 1989.

The Encyclopedia Of Animated Cartoons, Lenburg, Jeff; Facts On File, Oxford; 1991.

The Encyclopedia Of TV Science Fiction, Fulton, Roger; Boxtree/Macmillan, London; 1990.

Experimental Television, Test Films, Pilots And Trial Series; 1925–95, Terrace, Vincent; McFarland & Co, North Carolina; 1997.

Eye On TV: The First 21 Years Of Independent Television 1955–76, various eds, Independent Television Publications, London; 1976.

Favourite Families Of TV, Denis, Christopher Paul, and Denis, Michael; Citadel Press/Carol Publishing Group, New York; 1992.

The (British) Film & Television Year Book, various from 1946–89, ed Noble, Peter; various publishers, London.

Fifty Years Of Television: A Guide To Series And Pilots 1937–88, Terrace, Vincent; Cornwall Books, New Jersey; 1991.

Footlights: A Hundred Years Of Cambridge Comedy, Hewison, Robert; Methuen, London; 1983.

40 Years Of British Television, Harbord, Jane, and Wright, Jeff; Boxtree, London; 1995.

Frasier, Graham, Jefferson; Pocket Books, New York; 1996.

From Fringe To Flying Circus: Celebrating A Unique Generation Of Comedy 1960–80, Wilmut, Roger; Eyre Methuen, London; 1980.

Funny Business: The Greatest Names In Comedy, Housham, David, and Frank-Keyes, John; Boxtree, London; 1992.

Funny Way To Be A Hero, Fisher, John; Frederick Muller, London; 1973.

Girl Film And Television Annual, 1957–65; Longacre Press, London.

The Golden Age Of Radio, Gifford, Denis; Batsford, London; 1985.

Goodnight Children … Everywhere, Hartley, Ian; Midas Books, Kent; 1983.

The Great TV Sitcom Book, Mitz, Rick; Perigee Books/The Putnam Publishing Group, New York; 1988.

The Green Room Book/Who's Who On The Stage, various eds, T Sealey Clark & Co, London; 1907.

The Guinness Book Of Classic British TV, 1st and 2nd eds, Cornell, Paul, Day, Martin, and Topping, Keith; Guinness Publishing, London; 1993 and 1996.

The Guinness Book Of Sitcoms: Over 1000 Situation Comedies On British TV In The Last 60 Years, Taylor, Rod; Guinness Publishing, London; 1994.

The Guinness Book Of TV Facts And Feats, Passingham, Kenneth; Guinness Superlatives, London; 1984.

The Guinness Television Encyclopedia, Evans, Jeff; Guinness Publishing, London; 1995.

Ha Bloody Ha: Comedians Talking, Cook, William; Fourth Estate, London; 1994.

Hailing Taxi, Lovece, Frank, with Franco, Jules; Prentice Hall Press/Simon & Schuster, New York; 1988.

Halliwell's Film Guide, various eds since 1979, Halliwell, Leslie; Paladin/Grafton Books/Collins Publishing Group, London.

Halliwell's Filmgoer's Companion, various eds since 1965, Halliwell, Leslie; Paladin/Grafton Books/Collins Publishing Group, London.

Halliwell's Television Companion, three eds from 1979, Halliwell, Leslie, with

Purser, Philip; Granada Publishing, London.

Harrap's Book Of 1000 Plays: A Comprehensive Guide To The Most Frequently Performed Plays, Fletcher, Steve, Jopling, Norman, and contributors; Harrap Publishing Group, London; 1989.

Harry And Wally's Favorite TV Shows, Castleman, Harry, and Podrazik, Walter J; Prentice Hall Press, New York; 1989.

Harry Enfield And His Humorous Chums, Enfield, Harry; Penguin Books, London; 1997.

Hello Campers: Celebrating 50 Years Of Butlin's, Read, Sue; Transworld Publishers, London; 1986.

Honey, I'm Home!: Sitcoms Selling The American Dream, Jones, Gerard; St Martin's Press, New York; 1993.

How Sweet It Was – Television: A Pictorial Commentary On Its Golden Age, Shulman, Arthur, and Youman, Roger; Bonanza Books/Crown Publishers, New York; 1966.

Imaginary People: A Who's Who Of Modern Fictional Characters, Pringle, David; Paladin/Grafton Books/Collins Publishing Group, London; 1989.

Independent Television In Britain 1946–80, 4 vols, Sendall, Bernard, and Potter, Jeremy; IBA/ITA, London; 1982–90.

International Television (& Video) Almanac, various eds from 1952, Quigley Publications, New York.

Into The Box Of Delights: A History Of Children's Television, Home, Anna; BBC Books, London; 1993.

The ITV Encyclopedia Of Adventure, Rogers, Dave; Boxtree, London; 1988.

ITV Yearbooks (TV and radio) 1963–88; various eds; IBA, London.

ITV Annual For Boys And Girls, ed Thomas, Huw; TV Publications, London; 1963.

Jack Benny: The Radio And Television Work, The Museum Of Television and Radio; ed O'Neill, Ellen; HarperPerennial/HarperCollins, New York; 1991.

Jack Hylton Presents, Logan, Pamela W; BFI Publishing, London; 1995.

Joe Franklin's Encyclopedia Of Comedians, Franklin, Joe; Citadel Press, New Jersey; 1979.

The Joke's On Us: Women In Comedy From Music Hall To Present, Banks, Morwenna, and Swift, Amanda; Pandora Press/Routledge & Kegan Paul, London; 1987.

Kindly Leave The Stage!, The Story Of Variety 1919–1960, Wilmut, Roger; Methuen, London; 1985.

Laughter In The Air, Took, Barry; Robson Books/BBC, London; 1976.

Les Brown's Encyclopedia Of Television, 3rd ed, Brown, Lester; Visible Ink Press/Gale Research, Detroit; 1992.

The Life And Times Of Maxwell Smart, McCrohan, Donna; St Martin's Press, New York; 1988.

Life Before And After Monty Python: The Solo Flights Of The Flying Circus, Johnson, Kim 'Howard'; St Martin's Press, New York; 1993.

Look-In TV Annual, various eds 1970s and 80s; Independent Television Publications/Reed International, London.

Love Is All Around: The Making Of The Mary Tyler Moore Show, Alley, Robert S, and Tinker, Grant A; Delta/Dell Publishing, New York; 1989.

M*A*S*H: The Exclusive Inside Story, Reiss, David S; Arthur Barker/Weidenfeld, London; 1981.

Monty Python: A Chronological Listing Of The Troupe's Output, And Articles And Reviews About Them 1969–89, McCall, Douglas L; McFarland & Co, North Carolina; 1991.

MTM 'Quality Television', eds Feuer, Jane, Kerr, Paul, and Vahimagi, Tise; BFI Publishing, London; 1984.

The Munsters: Television's First Family Of Fright, Cox, Stephen; Contemporary Books, Chicago; 1989.

Museum Of Broadcast Communications Encyclopedia Of Television, 3 vols, ed Newcomb, Horace; Fitzroy Dearborn Publishers, London and Chicago; 1997.

Nick At Nite's Classic TV Companion, ed Hill, Tom; Fireside/Simon & Schuster, New York; 1996.

The Official Dick Van Dyke Show Book, Waldron, Vince; Hyperion, New York; 1994.

The Official Honeymooners Treasury, Crescenti, Peter, and Columbe, Bob; Galahad Books/Putnam Publishing Group, New York; 1989.

A Pictorial History Of Radio, Settel, Irving; Grosset & Dunlap, New York; 1960.

A Pictorial History Of Television, Settel, Irving, and Laas, William; Grosset & Dunlap, New York; 1969.

Prime Time Network Serials 1964–93, Morris, Bruce B; McFarland & Co, North Carolina; 1997.

Prime-Time Hits: 1950 To The Present, Sackett, Susan; Billboard/Watson-Guptill Publications, New York; 1993.

Quinlan's Illustrated Directory Of Film Comedy Stars, Quinlan, David; Batsford, London; 1992.

Radio & Television Who's Who, 3rd ed, comp Andrews, Cyrus; George Young Publications, London; 1954.

Radio Comedy 1938–68, Foster, Andy, and Furst, Steve; Virgin Publishing, London; 1996.

The Radio Companion: The A–Z Guide To Radio From Inception To The Present Day, Donovan, Paul; Grafton/HarperCollins, London; 1991.

Radio's Golden Years: An Encyclopedia Of Radio Programs 1930–60, Terrace, Vincent; A S Barnes and Co, California; 1981.

Red Dwarf Programme Guide, Howarth, Chris, and Lyons, Steve; Virgin Publishing, London; 1993.

Revolutionary Laughter: The World Of Women Comics, ed Warren, Roz; The Crossing Press, California; 1995.

Roy Hudd's Cavalcade Of Variety Acts: A Who Was Who Of Light Entertainment 1945–60, Hudd, Roy, with Hindin, Philip; Robson Books, London; 1997.

Same Time Same Station: An A–Z Guide To Radio, Lackmann, Ron; Facts On File, New York; 1996.

Saturday Night Live: The First Twenty Years, ed Cader, Michael; Cader Books/Houghton Mifflin, New York; 1994.

Serials On British Television 1950–94, Baskin, Ellen; Scolar Press, Aldershot; 1996.

Slapstick: The Illustrated Story Of Knockabout Comedy, Staveacre, Tony; Angus & Robertson Publishers, London; 1987.

The Stage Year Book, eds throughout 20th-century; various eds; various publishers, London.

Star TV & Film Annual, various eds up to 1968; Odhams, London.

Syndicated Television: The First Forty Years 1947–87, Erickson, Hal; McFarland & Co, North Carolina; 1989.

Television 1970–80, Terrace, Vincent; A S Barnes & Co, California; 1981.

The Television Annual, 1950–61, ed Baily, Kenneth; Odhams Press, London.

Television Character And Story Facts, Terrace, Vincent; McFarland & Co, North Carolina; 1993.

Television Comedy Series: An Episode Guide To 153 Sitcoms In Syndication, Eisner, Joel, and Krinsky, David; McFarland & Co, North Carolina; 1984.

Television Jubilee: The Story Of 25 Years Of BBC Television, Ross, Gordon; W H Allen, London; 1961.

Television Series Revivals: Sequels Or Remakes Of Cancelled Shows, Goldberg, Lee; McFarland & Co, North Carolina; 1993.

Television Specials: 3201 Entertainment Spectaculars 1939–93, Terrace, Vincent; McFarland & Co, North Carolina; 1995.

Television: The First Forty Years, Davis, Anthony; Independent Television Publications, London; 1976.

Television Writers Guide, ed Naylor, Lynne; Lone Eagle Publishing Co, Los Angeles; 1993.

The Television Yearbook, ed Fiddy, Dick; Virgin Books, London; 1985.

The Television Yearbook 1990–91, Lovece, Frank; Perigee Books/The Putnam Publishing Group, New York; 1992.

Television's Greatest Hits, Gambaccini, Paul, and Taylor, Rod; Network/BBC Books, London; 1993.

They Made Us Laugh, Mellor, Geoff J; George Kelsall, Littleborough; 1982.

Tooth & Claw: The Inside Story Of Spitting Image, Chester, Lewis; Faber and Faber, London; 1986.

Total Television: The Comprehensive Guide To Programming From 1948 To The Present, 4th ed, NcNeil, Alex; Penguin Books, New York; 1996.

TV & Radio Year Book, annual 1958–1974, various eds, various publishers, London.

TV Book: The Ultimate Television Book, ed Fireman, Judy; Workman Publishing Co, New York; 1977.

The TV Encyclopedia: The Most Comprehensive Guide To Everybody Who's Anybody In Television, Inman, David; Perigee Books/The Putnam Publishing Group, New York; 1991.

The TV Guide TV Book, Weiner, Ed and various eds; HarperPerennial/HarperCollins, New York; 1992.

The TV Holdings Of The National Film And Television Archive 1936–79, eds Baker, Simon, and Terris, Olwen; BFI Publishing, London; 1994.

TV Laughtermakers: The Story of Comedy, Davis, Anthony; Boxtree, London; 1989.

TV Mirror Annual 1956, Amalgamated Press, London; 1955.

TV Season 1974–75; 1975–76; 1976–77 and 1977–78, comp/ed David, Nina; The Oryx Press, Phoenix.

TV Unforgettables: Over 250 Legends Of The Small Screen, Hayward, Anthony and Deborah; Guinness Publishing, Enfield; 1993.

25 Years Of ITV 1955–80, Independent Television Books/Michael Joseph, London; 1980.

The Ultimate TV Trivia Book, Terrace, Vincent; Faber and Faber, Boston; 1991.

Unsold Television Pilots 1955 Through 1989, Goldberg, Lee; McFarland & Co, North Carolina; 1990.

Variety Movie Guide: Over 5000 Reviews From 1914 To 1991, ed Elley, Derek; Hamlyn, London; 1991.

The Very Best Of The Very Worst Bad TV, Nelson, Craig; Delta/Dell Publishing, New York; 1995.

VideoHound's Golden Movie Retriever 1997: The Complete Guide To Movies On Videocassette, Laserdisc And CD, various eds, Visible Ink Press/Gale Research, Detroit; 1997.

Watching TV: Four Decades Of American Television, Castleman, Harry, and Podrazik, Walter J; McGraw-Hill Book Co, New York; 1982.

What's On The Box?, Lazell, David; Evergreen, Cheltenham; 1991.

What's On The Wireless?, Lazell, David; Evergreen, Cheltenham; 1989.

Who's Who In Broadcasting: A Biographical Record Of The Leading Personalities Of The Microphone, ed Moseley, Sydney A; Sir Isaac Pitman & Sons, London; 1933.

Who's Who In The Theatre, various eds since 1912; Sir Isaac Pitman & Sons, London.

Who's Who In TV, various magazines 1970s to date, Dell Publishing Co, New York.

Who's Who On Television, nine eds; various publishers in association with *TVTimes*, London; 1970–96.

The Wireless Stars, Nobbs, George; Wensum Books, Norwich; 1972.

The World Radio And Television Jubilee Issue Annual, ed Pedrick, Gale; Sampson Low, Marston & Co, London; 1947.

Written Out Of Television: A TV Lover's Guide To Cast Changes 1945–94, Lance, Steve; Madison Books, Maryland; 1996.

Index of Writers, Creators, Devisers, Adapters and providers of Additional Material

This index indicates the number of times, where more than once, that the person named appears in the Credits section on a given page.

Index of Directors, Producers and Executive Producers

This index indicates the number of times, where more than once, that the person named appears in the Credits section on a given page.

Index of Actors and Performers